Mid-Atlantic

Are we meeting your travel needs?

Send written comments to:

AAA Member Comments
1000 AAA Drive, Box 61
Heathrow, FL 32746-5063

Published by:
AAA Publishing
1000 AAA Drive
Heathrow, FL 32746-5063
Copyright AAA 2005

Printed in the USA by
Quebecor World, Buffalo, NY

Photo Credit: (Cover & Title Page)
Blue Ridge Parkway, VA
© Tom Algire/SuperStock

 Printed on recyclable paper.
Please recycle whenever possible.

Stock #4608

Mid-Atlantic

■ *Virginia*

■ *West Virginia*

Featured Information

Want to plan a fun and affordable trip quickly and easily? Visit **aaa.com** to get exclusive travel information, find ways to save money and access easy-to-use travel planning tools.

Searchable TourBook®guides. Find AAA's famous TourBook travel information including: Approved hotels (get Diamond ratings, member discounts on room rates, plus online reservations), Approved restaurants, recommended attractions, local events, and detailed destination descriptions.

AAA TripTiks®. Create your own customized TripTik: get door-to-door driving directions and maps, find AAA Approved hotels and reserve a room, locate AAA recommended restaurants, and discover things to do and see at your destination and along the way.

AAA Drive Trips*. Review AAA recommended drive trips.

Vacation Getaways. Take to the skies, hit the high seas or select a tour and receive exclusive benefits from AAA's Preferred Travel Partners.

Travel Guides. Get a 5% discount on AAA's famed travel guides at aaa.com/barnesandnoble.

Disney® Vacations. Get exclusive benefits and savings on AAA Vacations® Disney vacation packages.

Hertz Rental. Save up to 20% on car rental.

Show Your Card & Save. Search for savings on lodging, travel, entertainment, retail, and e-merchants.

AAA Travel Money. Get no-fee travelers cheques, foreign currency and prepaid cards.

AAA Map Gallery*. Know the best way to go wherever you travel.

Cash Back. Get up to a 5% rebate every time you use your AAA credit card to gas up.

AAA Approved Auto Repair. Find your nearest AAR shop to get your car ready for the road.

Travel to aaa.com to do all your vacation planning!

aaa.com

Travel With Someone You Trust®

How do you define relaxation?

Four Points by Sheraton Denver Southeast

The Four Points® by Sheraton **Four Comfort Bed**™ is redefining relaxation. With a plush top mattress, cozy duvet and mountain of overstuffed pillows, it's exactly what you need for a great night's sleep. For reservations, call **1 (866) 782-7737** or visit **starwood.com/aaa**. Best Rates, Guaranteed.

Show Your Card & Save

MEMBER OF  STARWOOD PREFERRED GUEST

Four Points®
Sheraton

The Four Points by Sheraton Four Comfort Bed is currently rolling out and will be in all Four Points by Sheraton hotels no later than July 1, 2005. Visit fourpoints.com to find out which hotels currently feature the bed and for complete details on Best Rates, Guaranteed. ©2004 Starwood Hotels & Resorts Worldwide, Inc.

Trust
the AAA TourBook® guide for objective travel information. Follow the pages of the TourBook Navigator to thoroughly understand this unique member benefit.

Making Your Way Through the AAA Listings

Attractions, lodgings and restaurants are listed on the basis of merit alone after careful evaluation, approval and rating by one of our full-time, professionally trained Tourism Editors. Annual evaluations are unannounced to ensure that our Tourism Editors see an establishment just as our members would see it.

Those lodgings and restaurants listed with an 〔fyi〕 icon have not gone through the same evaluation process as other rated properties. Individual listings will typically denote the reason why this icon appears. Bulleted recreational activity listings are not inspected but are included for member information.

An establishment's decision to advertise in the TourBook guide has no bearing on its evaluation or rating. Advertising for services or products does not imply AAA endorsement.

How the TourBook is
Organized

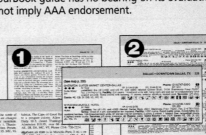

Geographic listing is used for accuracy and consistency. This means attractions, lodgings and restaurants are listed under the city in which they physically are located—or in some cases under the nearest recognized city. The Comprehensive City Index located in the back of the book contains an A-to-Z list of cities. Most listings are alphabetically organized by state, province, region or island; city; and establishment name. A color is assigned to each state or province so that you can match the color bars at the top of the page to switch from ❶ **Points of Interest** to ❷ **Lodgings and Restaurants.**

Destination Cities and Destination Areas

The TourBook guide also groups information by destination city and destination area. If a city is grouped in a destination vicinity section, the city name will appear at its alphabetical location in the book, and a handy cross reference will give the exact page on which listings for that city begin. Maps are placed at the beginning of these sections to orient you to the destinations.

❸ **Destination cities,** established based on government models and local expertise, are comprised of metropolitan areas plus nearby vicinity cities.

Destination areas are regions with broad tourist appeal. Several cities will comprise the area.

All information in this TourBook guide was reviewed for accuracy before publication. However, since changes inevitably occur between annual editions, we suggest you contact establishments directly to confirm prices and schedules.

Points of Interest Section

Orientation maps

near the start of each Attractions section show only those places we call points of interest. Coordinates included with the city listings depict the locations of those cities on the map. A GEM symbol (☟) accents towns with "must see" points of interest which offer a *Great Experience for Members*®. And the black ovals with white numerals (**22** for example) locate items listed in the nearby Recreation Areas chart.

Destination area maps

illustrate key travel areas defined by local travel experts. Communities shown have listings for AAA approved attractions.

National park maps

represent the area in and around the park. Some campground sites and lodges spotted on the maps do not meet AAA/CAA criteria, but are shown for members who nevertheless wish to stay close to the park area.

Walking or self-guiding tour maps

correspond to specific routes described in TourBook guide text.

City maps

show areas where numerous points of interest are concentrated and indicate their location in relation to major roads, parks, airports and other landmarks.

Lodgings & Restaurants Section

Destination area maps
illustrate key travel areas defined by local travel experts. Communities shown have listings for AAA-RATED® lodgings and/or restaurants.

Spotting maps
show the location of lodgings and restaurants. Lodgings are spotted with a black background (**22** for example); restaurants are spotted with a white background (**23** for example). Spotting map indexes have been placed immediately after each map to provide the user with a convenient method to identify what an area has to offer at a glance. The index references the map page number where the property is spotted, indicates if a property is an Official Appointment and contains an advertising reference if applicable. It also lists the property's diamond rating, high season rate range and listing page number.

Downtown/city spotting maps
are provided when spotted facilities are very concentrated. GEM points of interest also appear on these maps.

Vicinity spotting maps
spot those properties that are outside the downtown or city area. Major roads, landmarks, airports and GEM points of interest are shown on vicinity spotting maps as well. The names of suburban communities that have AAA-RATED® accommodations are shown in magenta type.

Featured Information Section

Driving distance maps
are intended to be used only for trip-distance and driving-time planning.

Sample Attraction Listing

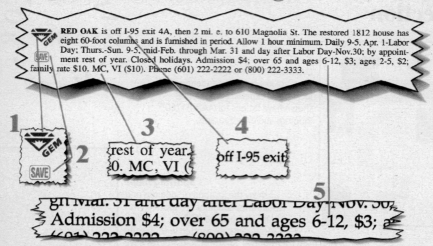

RED OAK is off I-95 exit 4A, then 2 mi. e. to 610 Magnolia St. The restored 1812 house has eight 60-foot columns and is furnished in period. Allow 1 hour minimum. Daily 9-5. Apr. 1-Labor Day; Thurs.-Sun. 9-5, mid-Feb. through Mar. 31 and day after Labor Day-Nov.30; by appointment rest of year. Closed holidays. Admission $4; over 65 and ages 6-12, $3; ages 2-5, $2; family rate $10. MC, VI ($10). Phone (601) 222-2222 or (800) 222-3333.

1   rest of year.
         0. MC, VI (

4   off I-95 exit

5   gh Mar. 31 and day after Labor Day-Nov. 30;
         Admission $4; over 65 and ages 6-12, $3; a

1 This attraction is of exceptional interest and quality and therefore has been designated a AAA GEM—offering a *Great Experience for Members*®.

2 Participating attractions offer AAA/CAA, AAA MasterCard or AAA Visa cardholders a discount off the attraction's standard admission; members should inquire in advance concerning the validity of the discount for special rates. Present your card at the admission desk. A list of participating points of interest appears in the Indexes section of the book. The SAVE discount may not be used in conjunction with other discounts. Attractions that already provide a reduced senior or child rate may not honor the SAVE discount for those age groups. All offers are subject to change and may not apply during special events, particular days or seasons or for the entire validity period of the TourBook. Shopping establishments preceded by a SAVE icon also provide discounts and/or gift with purchase to AAA/CAA members; present your card at the mall's customer service center to receive your benefit.

3 | AX=American Express | DS=Discover | MC=MasterCard |
|---|---|---|
| CB=Carte Blanche | JC=Japan Credit Bureau | VI=VISA |
| DC=Diners Club | | |

4 Unless otherwise specified, directions are given from the center of town, using the following highway designations: I (interstate highway), US (federal highway), Hwy. (Canadian or Caribbean highway), SR (state route), CR (county road), FM (farm to market road), FR (forest road), MM (mile marker), Mex. (Mexican highway).

5 Admission prices are quoted without sales tax. Children under the lowest age specified are admitted free when accompanied by an adult. Days, months and age groups written with a hyphen are inclusive. Prices pertaining to points of interest in the United States are quoted in U.S. dollars; prices for Canadian province and territory points of interest are quoted in Canadian dollars; prices for points of interest in Mexico and the Caribbean are quoted as an approximate U.S. dollar equivalent.

Bulleted Listings: Casino gambling establishments are visited by AAA personnel to ensure safety; casinos within hotels are presented for member information regardless of whether the lodging is AAA approved. Recreational activities of a participatory nature (requiring physical exertion or special skills) are not inspected. Wineries are inspected by AAA Tourism Editors to ensure they meet listing requirements and offer tours. All are presented in a bulleted format for informational purposes.

These Show Your Card & Save® partners provide the listed member benefits. Admission tickets that offer greater discounts may be available for purchase at the local AAA/CAA club. The discount applies to the cardholder; the attraction, at its discretion, may also offer the discount to up to five family members.

Attraction Partners

SeaWorld/Busch Gardens (aaa.com/seaworld)

[SAVE] Save $5 on general admission at the gate at SeaWorld and Busch Gardens

[SAVE] Save $3 on general admission at the gate at Sesame Place, Water Country USA and Adventure Island

[SAVE] Save 10% on select up-close dining. Reservations are required; visit Guest Relations for details

Six Flags Theme Parks

[SAVE] Save $4 on general admission at the gate

[SAVE] Save $12 on general admission at the gate each Wednesday

[SAVE] Save 10% on selected souvenirs and dining (check at main gate for details)

Universal Orlando (aaa.com/universal)

[SAVE] Save $4 on a 2-day/2-park pass or $5 on a 3-day/2-park pass at Universal Orlando's theme parks (savings apply to tickets purchased at the gate)

[SAVE] Save 10% on select dining and souvenirs at both Universal Orlando theme parks and at select Universal CityWalk Orlando restaurants (except Emeril's)

Universal Studios Hollywood (aaa.com/universal)

[SAVE] Save $3 on a 1-day Universal Studios pass (savings applies to tickets purchased at the gate)

[SAVE] Save 10% on select dining and souvenirs at Universal Studios Hollywood and Universal CityWalk

Gray Line (aaa.com/grayline)

[SAVE] Save 10% on sightseeing tours of 1 day or less

Restaurant Partners

Landry's Seafood House, The Crab House, Chart House, Muer Seafood Restaurants, Joe's Crab Shack

[SAVE] Save 10% on food and non-alcoholic beverages at Landry's Seafood House, The Crab House, Chart House, Muer Seafood Restaurants and Joe's Crab Shack and 10% on merchandise at Joe's Crab Shack. Savings applicable to AAA/CAA member and up to five additional people

Hard Rock Cafe

[SAVE] Save 10% on food, non-alcoholic beverages and merchandise at all U.S. and select Canadian and international locations. Savings applicable to AAA/CAA member and up to five additional people.

Visit aaa.com to discover all the great Show Your Card & Save® discounts in your area.

Sample Lodging Listing

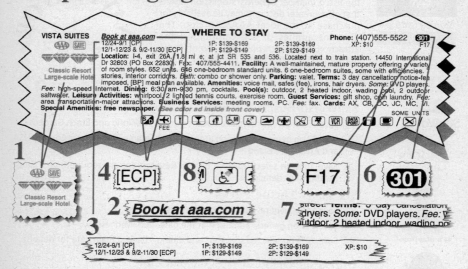

1   AAA or CAA indicates our Official Appointment (OA) lodgings. The OA program permits properties to display and advertise the AAA or CAA emblem. We highlight these properties with red diamonds and classification. Some OA listings include special amenities such as free continental breakfast; expanded continental breakfast or full breakfast; early check-in/late check-out; free room upgrade or preferred room, such as ocean view or poolside (subject to availability); free local phone calls; and free daily newspaper. This does not imply that only these properties offer these amenities. The AAA or CAA sign helps traveling members find accommodations that want member business.

◆◆◆◆◆   or   ◆◆◆◆◆   The number of diamonds—not the color—informs you of the overall level of quality in a lodging's amenities and service. More diamond details appear on page 16.

Classic Resort Large-scale Hotel or Classic Resort Large-scale Hotel: All diamond rated lodgings are classified using three key elements: style of operation, overall concept and service level. See pages 22-23 for details about our Lodging Classifications and Subclassifications.

Member Values

SAVE   Official Appointment properties guarantee members a minimum 10% discount off the standard room rates published in TourBook guides or the lowest public rate available at the time of booking for the dates of stay, for standard rooms.

S/D   Establishments offer a minimum senior discount of 10% off the listed rates. This discount is available to members 60 or older.

ASK   Many properties offer discounts to members even though the lodgings do not participate in a formal discount program. The ASK is another reminder to inquire about available discounts when making your reservations or at check-in.

Discounts normally offered at some lodgings may not apply during special events or holiday periods. Special rates and discounts may not apply to all room types. Some Member Values may not apply in Mexico or the Caribbean.

To obtain published rates or discounts, you must identify yourself as a AAA or CAA member, request AAA rates when making reservations and have written confirmation sent to you. The SAVE or senior discount may not be used in conjunction with other discounts. At registration, show your membership card and verify the room rate.

Discounts normally offered at some lodgings may not apply during special events or holiday periods. Special rates and discounts may not apply to all room types. Some Member Values may not apply in Mexico or the Caribbean.

The rates listed for approved properties are provided to AAA by each lodging and represent the regular (rack) rate for a standard room. Printed rates, based on rack rates and last room availability, are rounded to the nearest dollar. Rates do not include taxes and discounts. U.S., Mexican and Caribbean rates are in U.S. dollars; rates for Canadian lodgings are in Canadian dollars.

2 Book at aaa.com - Internet Reservations
Indicates AAA/CAA members can conveniently check room availability and make reservations in a secure online environment at aaa.com.

3 Rate Lines
Shown from left to right: dates the rates are effective; meal plan provided with rates (see Meal Plan Indicators-if no plan noted, rate includes room only); rates for 1 person or 2 persons; extra person charge (XP); and any applicable family plan indicator.

Rates Guaranteed
AAA/CAA members are guaranteed that they will not be charged more than the maximum regular rate printed in each rate range for a standard room. Rates may vary within the range depending on season and room type. Listed rates are based on last standard room availability. Rates for properties operating as concessionaires for the U.S. National Park Service are not guaranteed due to governing regulations. Rates in the Mexico TourBook are not guaranteed and may fluctuate based on the exchange rate of the peso.

Exceptions
Lodgings may temporarily increase room rates, not recognize discounts or modify pricing policies during special events. Examples of special events range from Mardi Gras and Kentucky Derby (including pre-Derby events) to college football games, holidays, holiday periods and state fairs. Although some special events are listed in AAA/CAA TourBook guides, it is always wise to check, in advance, with AAA travel professionals for specific dates.

Discounts
Member discounts will apply to rates quoted, within the rate range, applicable at the time of booking. Special rates used in advertising, and special short-term, promotional rates lower than the lowest listed rate in the range, are not subject to additional member discounts.

4 Meal Plan Indicators
The following types of meal plans may be available in the listed room rate:
AP = American Plan of three meals daily
BP = Breakfast Plan of full hot breakfast
CP = Continental Plan of pastry, juice and another beverage
ECP = Expanded Continental Plan, which offers a wider variety of breakfast items
MAP = Modified American Plan of two meals daily
See individual listing "Terms" section for additional meal plans that are not included in the room rate.

> Check-in times are shown in the listing only if they are after 3 p.m.; check-out times are shown only if they are before 10 a.m.

5 Family Plan Indicators
F = Children stay free
D = Discounts for children
F17 = Children 17 and under stay free (age displayed will reflect property's policy)
D17 = Discount for children 17 and under

6 Lodging Locators
Black ovals with white numbers are used to locate, or "spot," lodgings on maps we provide for larger cities.

7 Unit Types
Unit types, amenities and room features preceded by the word "Some" indicate the item is available on a limited basis, potentially within only one unit.

8 Lodging Icons
A row of icons is included with each lodging listing. These icons represent the member values, member services, and facilities offered by that lodging. See page 19 for an explanation of each icon.

The Lodging Diamond Ratings

AAA Tourism Editors evaluate and rate each lodging based on the overall quality, the range of facilities and the level of services offered by a property. The size, age and overall appeal of an establishment are considered as well as regional architectural style and design.

While guest services are an important part of all diamond ratings, they are particularly critical at the four and five diamond levels. A property must provide a high level of service, on a consistent basis, to obtain and support the four and five diamond rating.

These establishments typically appeal to the budget-minded traveler. They provide essential, no-frills accommodations. They meet the basic requirements pertaining to comfort, cleanliness, and hospitality.

These establishments appeal to the traveler seeking more than the basic accommodations. There are modest enhancements to the overall physical attributes, design elements, and amenities of the facility typically at a modest price.

These establishments appeal to the traveler with comprehensive needs. Properties are multifaceted with a distinguished style, including marked upgrades in the quality of physical attributes, amenities and level of comfort provided.

These establishments are upscale in all areas. Accommodations are progressively more refined and stylish. The physical attributes reflect an obvious enhanced level of quality throughout. The fundamental hallmarks at this level include an extensive array of amenities combined with a high degree of hospitality, service, and attention to detail.

These establishments reflect the characteristics of the ultimate in luxury and sophistication. Accommodations are first-class. The physical attributes are extraordinary in every manner. The fundamental hallmarks at this level are to meticulously serve and exceed all guest expectations while maintaining an impeccable standard of excellence. Many personalized services and amenities enhance an unmatched level of comfort.

The lodging listings with **fyi** in place of diamonds are included as an "information only" service for members. The icon indicates that a property has not been rated for one or more of the following reasons: too new to rate; under construction; under major renovation; not evaluated; or may not meet all AAA requirements. Those properties not meeting all AAA requirements are included for either their member value or because it may be the only accommodation available in the area. Listing prose will give insight as to why the **fyi** designation was assigned.

Guest Safety

Room Security

In order to be approved for listing in AAA/CAA TourBook guides for the United States and Canada, all lodgings must comply with AAA's guest room security requirements.

In response to AAA/CAA members' concern about their safety at properties, AAA-RATED® accommodations must have dead-bolt locks on all guest room entry doors and connecting room doors.

If the area outside the guest room door is not visible from inside the room through a window or door panel, viewports must be installed on all guest room entry doors. Bed and breakfast properties and country inns are not required to have viewports. Ground floor and easily accessible sliding doors must be equipped with some other type of secondary security locks.

Tourism Editors view a percentage of rooms at each property since it is not feasible to evaluate every room in every lodging establishment. Therefore, AAA cannot guarantee that there are working locks on all doors and windows in all guest rooms.

Fire Safety

Because of the highly specialized skills needed to conduct professional fire safety inspections, AAA/CAA Tourism Editors cannot assess fire safety.

Properties must meet all federal, state and local fire codes. Each guest unit in all U.S. and Canadian lodging properties must be equipped with an operational, single-station smoke detector. A AAA/CAA Tourism Editor has evaluated a sampling of the rooms to verify this equipment is in place.

For additional fire safety information, read the page posted on the back of your guest room door, or write:

**National Fire Protection Association
1 Batterymarch Park
P.O. Box 9101
Quincy, MA 02269-9101**

Requirements for some features, such as door locks and smoke detectors/sprinkler systems, differ in Mexico and the Caribbean. If a property met AAA's security requirements at the time of the evaluation, the phrase "Meets AAA guest room security requirements" appears in the listing.

Access for Mature Travelers and Travelers with Disabilities

Qualified properties listed in this guide are shown with symbols indicating they meet the needs of the hearing-impaired or offer some accessible features for mature travelers or travelers with disabilities.

Hearing Impaired

Indicates a property has the following equipment available for hearing-impaired travelers: TDD at front desk or switchboard; visual notification of fire alarm, incoming telephone calls, door knock or bell; closed caption decoder; text telephone or TDD for guest room use; telephone amplification device, with shelf or electric outlet next to guest room telephone.

Accessible Features

Indicates a property has some accessible features meeting the needs of mature travelers and travelers with disabilities. Lodging establishments will provide at least one guest room meeting the designated criteria as well as accessible restrooms and parking facilities. Restaurants provide accessible parking, dining rooms and restrooms.

> AAA/CAA strongly urges members to call the property directly to fully understand the property's exact accessibility features. Some properties do not fully comply with AAA/CAA's exacting accessibility standards but may offer some design standards that meet the needs of some guests with disabilities.

> AAA/CAA does not evaluate recreational facilities, banquet rooms, or convention or meeting facilities for accessibility.

Service Animals

> No fees or deposits, even those normally charged for pets, may be charged for service animals. Service animals fulfill a critical need for their owners—they are *not* pets.

The Americans With Disabilities Act (ADA) prohibits U.S. businesses that serve the public from discriminating against persons with disabilities. Some businesses have mistakenly denied access to persons who use service animals. ADA, a federal mandate, has priority over all state and local laws, as well as a business owner's standard of business, which might bar animals from the premises. Businesses must permit entry to guests and their service animals, as well as allow service animals to accompany guests to all public areas of a property. A property is permitted to ask whether the animal is a service animal or a pet, and whether the guest has a disability. The property may not, however, ask questions about the nature of the disability, the service provided by the animal or require proof of a disability or certification that the animal is a service animal.

Note: These regulations may not apply in Canada, Mexico or the Caribbean.

What The Lodging Icons Mean

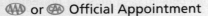

Member Values
(see p. 14)

AAA or **AAA** Official Appointment

SAVE Offers minimum 10% discount or lowest public rate *(see p. 14)*

ASK May offer discount

SD Offers senior discount

fyi Informational listing only

Member Services

✈ Airport transportation

🛏 Pets allowed

🍴 Restaurant on premises

🍴+ Restaurant off premises (walking distance)

24🍴 24-hour room service

🍸 Cocktail lounge

👶 Child care

Accessibility Feature
(see p. 18)

&M Accessible features

♿ Roll-in showers

👂 Hearing impaired

Safety Features
(Mexico and Caribbean only)

S Sprinklers

D Smoke detectors

Leisure Activities

🎲 Full service casino

🏊 Pool

🏋 Health club on premises

🏋+ Health club off premises

✗ Recreational activities

In-Room Amenities

✗ Designated non-smoking rooms

AC No air conditioning

TV No TV

CTV No cable TV

VCR VCR

🎬 Movies

DATA PORT Data port/modem line

☎ No telephones

🗄 Refrigerator

▣ Microwave

▣ Coffee maker

Availability and Additional Fees

If an in-room amenity is available only on a limited basis (in one or more rooms), the term "SOME UNITS" will appear above those icons. Fees may be charged for some of the services represented by the icons listed here. The word "FEE" will appear below each icon when an extra charge applies.

SOME UNITS

&M **👂** **VCR** **🎬** **▣** / **✗** **DATA PORT** **🗄** /
FEE FEE   FEE

Preferred Lodging Partners

Show Your Card & Save
AAA. Every Day.

SAVINGS. SELECTION. SATISFACTION. — When contacting one of the partners listed, you will be given AAA's best rates for your dates of stay. Your valid membership card must be presented at check-in.

SATISFACTION GUARANTEE — If you are not satisfied with any part of your stay, you must provide the property the opportunity to correct the situation during your stay. If the matter cannot be resolved, you will be entitled to recompense for a portion of, or your entire, stay. Satisfaction guarantee varies by chain.

Select the chain you want and have your membership card available when making a reservation and checking in.

Visit Over 1,100 AAA Offices **Click** aaa.com **Call** 866-AAA-SAVE

C H O I C E   H O T E L S   I N T E R N A T I O N A L

Making Reservations

When making reservations, you must identify yourself as a AAA or CAA member. Give all pertinent information about your planned stay. Ask about the lodging's pet policy, or the availability of any other special feature that is important to your stay. Request written confirmation to guarantee: type of room, rate, dates of stay, and cancellation and refund policies. At registration, show your membership card. Note: Age restrictions may apply.

Confirm Deposit, Refund and Cancellation Policies

Most establishments give full deposit refunds if they have been notified at least 48 hours before the normal check-in time. Listing prose will note if more than 48 hours notice is required for cancellation. However, when making reservations, confirm the property's deposit, cancellation and refund policies. Some properties may charge a cancellation or handling fee.

When this applies, "cancellation fee imposed" will appear in the listing. If you cancel too late, you have little recourse if a refund is denied.

When an establishment requires a full or partial payment in advance, and your trip is cut short, a refund may not be given.

When canceling reservations, phone the lodging immediately. Make a note of the date and time you called, the cancellation number if there is one, and the name of the person who handled the cancellation. If your AAA/CAA club made your reservation, allow them to make the cancellation for you as well so you will have proof of cancellation.

Review Charges for Appropriate Rates

When you are charged more than the maximum rate listed in the TourBook guide for a standard room, question the additional charge. If management refuses to adhere to the published rate, pay for the room and submit your receipt and membership number to AAA/CAA within 30 days. Include all pertinent information: dates of stay, rate paid, itemized paid receipts, number of persons in your party, the room number you occupied, and list any extra room equipment used. A refund of the amount paid in excess of the stated maximum will be made if our investigation indicates that unjustified charging has occurred.

Get the Room You Reserved

When you find your room is not as specified, and you have written confirmation of reservations for a certain type of accommodation, you should be given the option of choosing a different room or finding one elsewhere. Should you choose to go elsewhere and a refund is refused or resisted, submit the matter to AAA/CAA within 30 days along with complete documentation, including your reasons for refusing the room and copies of your written confirmation and any receipts or canceled checks associated with this problem.

How to Get the Best Room Rates

You'll find the best room rate if you book your reservation in advance with the help of a travel professional or agent at your local AAA/CAA office.

If you're not yet ready to make firm vacation plans or if you prefer a more spontaneous trip, take advantage of the partnerships that preferred hotel chains have arranged with AAA. Phone the toll-free number 866-AAA-SAVE that has been set up exclusively for members for the purpose of reserving with these Show Your Card & Save® chain partners.

Even if you were unable to make a reservation, be sure to show your membership card at the desk and ask if you're being offered the lowest rate available for that time. Many lodgings offer reduced rates to members.

Lodging Classifications

To ensure that your lodging needs/preferences are met, we recommend that you consider an establishment's classification when making your travel choices.

While the quality and comfort at properties with the same diamond rating should be consistent (regardless of the classification), there are differences in typical décor/theme elements, range of facilities and service levels. Please see the descriptions below.

Hotel Royal Plaza, Lake Buena Vista, FL

Large-scale Hotel

A multistory establishment with interior room entrances. A variety of guest unit styles is offered. Public areas are spacious and include a variety of facilities such as a restaurant, shops, fitness center, spa, business center, or meeting rooms.

Baymont Inn, Dallas/Ft. Worth-Airport North, TX

Small-scale Hotel

A multistory establishment typically with interior room entrances. A variety of guest unit styles is offered. Public areas are limited in size and/or the variety of facilities available.

Best Western Deltona Inn, Deltona, FL

Motel

A one- to three-story establishment typically with exterior room entrances facilitating convenient access to parking. The standard guest units have one bedroom with a bathroom and are typically similar in décor and design throughout. Public areas are limited in size and/or the variety of facilities available.

Country Inn

Similar in definition to a bed and breakfast, but usually larger in scale with spacious public areas and offers a dining facility that serves at least breakfast and dinner.

Greenville Inn, Greenville, ME

1884 Paxton House Inn, Thomasville, GA

Bed & Breakfast

Small-scale properties emphasizing a high degree of personal touches that provide guests an "at home" feeling. Guest units tend to be individually decorated. Rooms may not include some modern amenities such as televisions and telephones, and may have a shared bathroom. Usually owner-operated with a common room or parlor separate from the innkeeper's living quarters, where guests and operators can interact during evening and breakfast hours. Evening office closures are normal. A continental or full, hot breakfast is served and is included in the room rate.

Sands of Kahana, Kahana, Maui, HI

Condominium

Vacation-oriented or extended-stay, apartment-style accommodations that are routinely available for rent through a management company. Units vary in design and décor and often contain one or more bedrooms, living room, full kitchen, and an eating area. Studio-type models combine the sleeping and living areas into one room. Typically, basic cleaning supplies, kitchen utensils and complete bed and bath linens are supplied. The guest registration area may be located off-site.

Cabin/Cottage

Vacation-oriented, small-scale, freestanding houses or cabins. Units vary in design and décor and often contain one or more bedrooms, living room, kitchen, dining area, and bathroom. Studio-type models combine the sleeping and

Desert Rose Inn, Bluff, UT

living areas into one room. Typically, basic cleaning supplies, kitchen utensils, and complete bed and bath linens are supplied. The guest registration area may be located off-site.

Ranch

Typically a working ranch with an obvious rustic, Western theme. In general, equestrian-related activities are featured, but ranches may include other animals and activities as well. A variety of guest unit styles is offered in a family-oriented atmosphere.

Lost Valley Ranch, Deckers, CO

Vacation Home

Vacation-oriented or extended-stay, large-scale, freestanding houses that are routinely available for rent through a management company. Houses vary in design and décor and often contain two or more bedrooms, living room, full kitchen, dining room, and multiple bathrooms. Typically, basic cleaning supplies, kitchen utensils, and complete bed and bath linens are supplied. The guest registration area may be located off-site.

ResortQuest, Hilton Head Island, SC

Lodging Subclassifications

The following are subclassifications that may appear along with the classifications listed above to provide a more specific description of the lodging.

Casino

Extensive gambling facilities are available such as blackjack, craps, keno, and slot machines. **Note:** This subclassification will not appear beneath its diamond rating in the listing. It will be indicated by a dice icon and will be included in the row of icons immediately below the lodging listing.

Classic

Renowned and landmark properties, older than 50 years, well-known for their unique style and ambience.

Historic

These properties are typically over 75 years of age and exhibit many features of a historic nature with respect to architecture, design, furnishings, public record, or acclaim. Properties must meet one of the following criteria:

- Maintained the integrity of the historical nature
- Listed on the U.S. National Register of Historic Places
- Designated a U.S. National Historic Landmark
- Located in a U.S. National Register Historic District

Separate criteria designate historic properties in Canada, Mexico and the Caribbean.

Resort

Recreation-oriented, geared to vacation travelers seeking a specific destination experience. Travel packages, meal plans, theme entertainment, and social and recreational programs are typically available. Recreational facilities are extensive and may include spa treatments, golf, tennis, skiing, fishing, or water sports, etc. Larger resorts may offer a variety of guest accommodations.

Sample Restaurant Listing

WHERE TO DINE

THE SEASONS RESTAURANT   *Menu on aaa.com*   **Dinner:** $16-$36   **Phone:** 336/555-5555   5
Location: On I-459, exit 13 (US 31); 0.3 mi n of jct SR 862. 1000 Ocean Blvd 35244. **Hours:** 6 pm-10 pm. Closed: Mon, also Tues 5/1-11/15. **Reservations:** suggested. **Features:** Guests are in for a treat at this top-notch establishment. Dining is an all-around pleasurable experience—from the wait staff's casually elegant service approach to the tranquil, oceanfront setting to the striking grounds views from the cozy dining area. The chef transforms ingredients, based on what is seasonally and regionally available, into mouthwatering dishes. Decadent desserts put an exclamation mark on the meal. Dressy casual attire; cocktails; entertainment. **Parking:** valet. **Cards:** AX, CB, DC, DS, MC, VI. **Classic**

Regional American

2 Dinner: $16-$36   **5** Classic   **6** 5

1 Regional American   Menu on aaa.com   **3** Cards: AX, DC, DS, MC, VI.   **4** [icons]

1 🔺🔺🔺 or 🔺🔺 indicates our Official Appointment (OA) restaurants. The OA program permits properties to display and advertise the 🔺🔺🔺 or 🔺🔺 emblem. We highlight these properties with red diamonds and cuisine type. The 🔺🔺🔺 or 🔺🔺 sign helps traveling members find restaurants that want member business.

🔻🔻🔻 or 🔻🔻🔻🔻 The number of diamonds—not the color—informs you of the overall level of quality for food and presentation, service and ambience. Menus for red Diamond restaurants can be viewed on aaa.com.

A cuisine type is assigned for each restaurant listing. AAA currently recognizes more than 90 different cuisine types.

2 Prices represent the minimum and maximum entree cost per person. Exceptions may include one-of-a-kind or special market priced items.

3 AX = American Express
CB = Carte Blanche
DC = Diners Club
DS = Discover
JC = Japan Credit Bureau
MC = MasterCard
VI = VISA

4 These three icons are used in restaurant listings. When present, they indicate: the presence of a cocktail lounge, the lack of air conditioning, and/or that the restaurant has a designated non-smoking section or is entirely smoke-free.

5 If applicable, restaurants may be further defined as:

Classic—renowned and landmark restaurant operations in business longer than 25 years, known for unique style and ambience.

Historic—properties must meet one of the following criteria:
- Listed on the U.S. National Register of Historic Places
- Designated a U.S. National Historic Landmark
- Located in a U.S. National Register Historic District

Separate criteria designate historic properties in Canada, Mexico and the Caribbean.

6 These white ovals with black numbers serve as restaurant locators and are used to locate, or "spot," restaurants on maps we provide for larger cities.

The Restaurant Diamond Ratings

AAA Tourism Editors are responsible for determining a restaurant's diamond rating based on established criteria.

These criteria were established with input from AAA trained professionals, members and restaurant industry experts. They are purposely broad to capture what is typically seen throughout the restaurant industry at each diamond rating level.

A one diamond restaurant must meet basic requirements pertaining to management, cleanliness and overall quality. The primary focus is on providing wholesome, straightforward and familiar food at an economical price. Generally, the menu selection is limited to a restaurant's specialty, such as hamburgers, fried chicken, pizza or tacos. Service is limited, in many instances self service, and the surroundings are often utilitarian.

A two diamond restaurant displays noticeable enhancements to food presentation such as the use of common garnishes in combination with the dishware. Typically, the menu offers a wide selection featuring familiar favorites or home-style foods often cooked to order and reasonably priced. The service, while often limited, is plain-speaking and relaxed. The surroundings, while limited in scope, typically reflect a clear theme. All elements combine to provide a familiar, often family-oriented experience.

A three diamond restaurant often employs a professional chef and a supporting staff of highly trained cooks. The menu is skillfully prepared and often reflects interpretations of the latest trends or a mastering of traditional cuisine. Typically, there are expanded offerings of beverages in compliment to the menu such as, international/regional wines, specialty beers, cocktails and soft drinks. The front of the house is headed by a professional dining room manager with a compliment of efficient service staff. The service reflects some degree of refinement such as reservations accepted, personal assistance or the ability to adapt to a guests's specific needs. The decor reflects the use of well-coordinated design mediums that provide a distinct theme and good comfort. Restaurants at this level convey an entry into fine dining and are often positioned as an adult-oriented experience.

A four diamond restaurant is geared to individuals in search of a distinctive fine-dining experience. Often orchestrated by an executive chef and an accomplished staff, menus reflect a high degree of creativity and complexity using imaginative presentations to enhance high quality, market fresh ingredients. The equally proficient service staff demonstrates a strong desire to meet or exceed guest expectations. A wine steward is typically available to provide menu-specific knowledge on wine selection. The ambiance is highly refined, comfortable and well coordinated incorporating quality materials and a variety of upscale design enhancements that give a first-class impression. The overall dining experience is typically expensive.

A five diamond restaurant is renowned and consistently provides a world-class experience. This is *haute cuisine* at its best. Menus are cutting edge, using only the finest ingredients available. Food is prepared in a manner that is highly imaginative and unique. The combination of technique and ingredients is extraordinary reflecting the impeccable artistry and awareness of highly acclaimed chefs. A maitre d' heads an expert service staff that exceeds guest expectations by attending to every detail in an effortless and unobtrusive manner.

The restaurants with [fyi] in place of diamonds are included as an "information only" service for members. These establishments provide additional dining choices but have not yet been evaluated.

YOU'RE READY...

NOW YOU'RE READY FOR ANYTHING.

Travelers Cheques

Available in US Dollars, Canadian Dollars, Euros, and Pounds Sterling; AAA VISA® Travelers Cheques are accepted worldwide.

TravelMoney® Card

Make purchases at millions of Visa debit merchants or withdraw local currency at over 870,000 Visa ATMs in the USA and around the world.

Foreign Currency

We supply over 100 different currencies and can advise which is the best for your destination.

AAA TRAVEL MONEY
Know Before You Go.

Visit Participating AAA offices   **Click** aaa.com/travelmoney   **Call** 866-339-3378

Savings for all Seasons

Hertz rents Fords and other fine cars. ® REG. U.S. PAT. OFF. © HERTZ SYSTEM INC., 1999/2606-99

No matter the season, Hertz offers AAA members exclusive discounts and benefits.

Operating in 150 countries at over 7,000 locations, Hertz makes traveling more convenient and efficient wherever and whenever you go. Hertz offers AAA members discounts up to 20% on car rentals worldwide.

To receive your exclusive AAA member discounts and benefits, mention your AAA membership card at time of reservation and present it at time of rental. **In addition**, to receive a free one car class upgrade, in the United States mention PC# 929714, in Canada mention PC# 929725 and in Puerto Rico mention PC# 929736 at the time of reservation. Offer available through 12/15/05.

For reservations and program details, call your AAA Travel office or the Hertz/AAA Desk at **1-800-654-3080**.

Show Your Card & Save

AAA. Every Day.

exactly.

Everything

Dreams Become Reality With AAA Travel

EXPLORE THE MOUNTAINS, THE DESERTS, AND THE CITIES - ANYWHERE, ANYTIME - WITH AAA, THE MOST TRUSTED NAME IN TRAVEL.®
LET AAA TRAVEL TAKE CARE OF ALL YOUR TRAVEL NEEDS. TO RECEIVE EXCLUSIVE AAA MEMBER BENEFITS, CALL OR VISIT YOUR NEAREST AAA TRAVEL OFFICE, OR CLICK ON www.aaa.com TODAY.

Travel With Someone You Trust.®
www.aaa.com

Delaware

Fort Delaware
The pentagon-shaped building served as a prison during the Civil War

Hagley Museum
Mills along the Brandywine River recall the du Pont family's big boom

The Green
William Penn designed a patch of grass in Dover where history was later made

New Castle
Step back in time to explore restored vintage homes

Longwood Gardens
Fountains and flowers grace this estate near Wilmington

Brandywine River, Wilmington / © Gibson Stock Photography

the
first
state

Delaware is a mecca for history buffs. The first to ratify the Constitution, it boasts significant sites and too many restored buildings to count. From north to south reminders of the past are bound to cross your path.

Gingerbread does not go stale in Laurel; about 800 colorful Victorian houses appear much as they did in the 18th and 19th centuries.

Erected in 1638, the first log cabin sits proudly in Wilmington.

The granite, pentagon-shaped fortress of Fort Delaware looms on Pea Patch Island. Woodburn, the Dover governor's mansion since 1965, was reputed to have been a station on the Underground Railroad. And the Amish way of life is alive and well near Dover—the clop of horses' hooves echoes along modern, blacktop roads.

Ghosts of noteworthy residents are omnipresent. Thomas McKean, a delegate to the Continental Congress of 1774, practiced law in New Castle. John Dickinson, the Penman of the American Revolution who wrote the Articles of Confederation and documents protesting British rule, lived in Dover. And the Robinson House in Wilmington served as a home for George Washington during the Revolutionary War.

The people of Delaware have meticulously preserved their past. Every footstep in Delaware is a tread back in time. So start stepping!

One way to acquaint yourself with Delaware is to rely on its oldest "residents." Restored houses and taverns, abandoned mills, groomed village greens and meticulous gardens sprinkle the state, silently declaring their chapter in history. Evidence of big events that helped shape the area turn up around every bend.

In New Castle, cobblestone roads dating from Colonial days serve as a path to the past. Dwellings that line the streets bear diverse architectural styles, mirroring the melting pot of cultures that has called the town home. Fabrics from Great Britain, the Netherlands, Sweden and the United States flap in the breeze over the Georgian-style courthouse; the flags represent four changes in ownership.

William Penn finally claimed New Castle for Great Britain in 1682, designating it the Colonial capital. And some things have changed little over time, such as the Federal-style white balustrade on the roof of the Read House, or the Victorian gardens, which appear much as they did at first planting in 1847.

If you pressed your nose against the glass of a keystone-topped window on New Castle's Amstel House in the 18th century, you may have caught a glimpse of George Washington; it is rumored that he attended a wedding here. Nearby, the brick Dutch House, with its steeply-pitched gambrel roof, is a memento left by the city's Dutch founders.

Turning the Wheels of Time

A water wheel on the banks of the tree-draped Brandywine River in Wilmington still turns on occasion, reminding passersby of the early importance of water power. The rushing river prompted E.I. du Pont to choose the site for his gunpowder manufacturing mill in the 19th century. A "form follows function" approach was taken during construction; the building consists of three stone walls and a fourth, facing the river, built of wood. In the event of an accident, the wooden wall would be blown toward the water, saving the structure and minimizing deaths.

Patches in the fourth wall grimly recall a day in March 1818 when 40 workers were not so lucky. A witness reported that the bang of the explosion "burst upon the ear like the report of a cannon," and "souls were hurled into an unknown eternity."

Henry Hudson claims the territory for the Dutch; he finds the area inhabited by Lenni Lenape Indians.

1609

Delaware falls under British rule.

1664

Inhabitants of the first European settlement are massacred by Indians.

1631

Proprietor William Penn allows colonists to establish their own legislature.

1704

1638

Swedes establish New Sweden colony at Wilmington, the first permanent settlement under leadership of Dutchman Peter Minuit.

© Corbis

Delaware Historical Timeline

1776

Delaware's Caesar Rodney casts the deciding vote for the Declaration of Independence.

© Bettmann/Corbis

Which George is it?

History oozes out of every blade of grass on The Green in Dover. The square is a spitting image of its original platting in 1722. During the Revolutionary War, the tract served as a meeting place for Delaware's Continental Regiment; they mustered here in 1775 and set out on a march to join Washington's army in the fight for independence. Blue hen chickens, noted for their pugnacious nature, waddled along to fight with the men.

One year later: The Declaration of Independence is read aloud to crowds gathered on The Green. Their enthusiasm shows in the shouts of "Freedom!" and the torching of King George III's portrait. Near The Green, a tavern now known as the Kent County Court House upheld the same independent spirit—locals maintain that it sported a sign showing the shoulders of the "Old George" and a face painted over with the likeness of the "New George."

And overlooking the square was the Golden Fleece Tavern, where, on a chilly December day in 1787, delegates to Delaware's Constitutional Congress took a deep breath and voted to ratify the Constitution, making Delaware the first state to do so. A bronze plaque commemorates the site.

Going Dutch

Coined the "first town in the first state," the harbor port of Lewes was settled by the Dutch in 1631. To commemorate its 300th anniversary, residents erected the Zwaanedael building; the elaborate stonework and ornamental gable are copies of similar features adorning a town hall in Holland.

Among brightly painted Victorian homes in Lewes stands one near-casualty of war, the cedar-shingled Cannonball House. Why the name? You guessed it—during a British bombardment in the War of 1812, a cannonball was fired at the house and lodged into the wall, becoming a permanent part of the structure. Fortunately, the naval attack resulted only in the death of a chicken and the wounding of a pig.

Through careful preservation of original architecture and landscaping, Delaware history and culture remain vital. The physical appearance of many sites, coupled with the tradition they embrace, makes for a fascinating story. And what a tale—how the First State sparked the development of a nation.

John Dickinson, Penman of the American Revolution, drafts the Articles of Confederation.

1777

© Stapleton Collection/Corbis

Salvagers retrieve the hull of the sunken HMS *DeBraak* off the coast of Lewes.

1986

Delaware becomes the first state to ratify the U.S. Constitution.

1787

1838

A railroad connecting Philadelphia and Baltimore is completed, encouraging industrial development of northern Delaware.

Office of Governor Minner

2001

Ruth Ann Minner takes office as Delaware's first female governor.

Recreation

When you're looking for recreation in Delaware, two words suffice: the beach. About 25 miles of coastline nevertheless add up to excitement.

Hang ten! Step into a wet suit and shoot the curl at the designated **surfing** zone just north of Indian River Inlet, home of the state surfing championships. The frothy waters off Rehoboth and Dewey beaches attract surfers as well.

Colorful **windsurfing** sails dot the shallow bays at Delaware Seashore State Park in Rehoboth Beach. Salty breezes cater to **sailing,** and **boaters** can explore numerous coves. Delaware Bay is another great place where first mates can cast off. **Swimmers,** boaters and even beavers feel right at home at Lums Pond State Park in Bear.

Picture yourself casually paddling amid wildflowers, lily pads and stands of bald cypress trees. It isn't paradise, just the designated wilderness **canoe** trail at Trap Pond State Park. If a wilder ride is more your style, look into **tubing** down Brandywine Creek in Wilmington.

Go Fish

The lure of the rod and reel is difficult to resist in Delaware. **Fishing** in Killens Pond State Park hooks bluegill, catfish, carp, crappie, largemouth bass, perch and pickerel. Brandywine Creek and Trap Pond state parks also attract fishing enthusiasts. Two piers make for pleasant casting at Lums Pond, where **ice fishing** is an option in winter. Those 16 years of age and older must have a license to fish freshwater ponds and non-tidal streams.

Bethany Beach, Cape Henlopen State Park, Delaware Seashore State Park and Fenwick Island are all hot spots for **surf fishing.** A permit is required to drive onto the beach; check with the park offices for more information.

Anglers frequent the banks of the Indian River Inlet and Bay, where **deep-sea fishing** charters can be arranged; catches of the day include drum, flounder, rockfish and weakfish. Fisherman's Wharf in Lewes is a starting point for excursions in search of marlin and tuna; phone (302) 645-8862.

Hikers traipse along shaded former logging paths leading to rocky outcrops at White Clay Creek State Park. The Twin Valley Trail climbs to Arc Corner Monument, where you can stand with one foot in Delaware and the other in Pennsylvania; Possum Hill hikers cross the Mason-Dixon Line on their route.

A wildlife observation tower is the terminus of a hiking trail at Fort Delaware State Park. Swamp Forest Trail at Lums Pond State Park circles the sylvan lake. While you stroll, try and catch a glimpse of those beavers!

Take your bike to Bellevue State Park in Wilmington, where you can pedal along roughly 3 miles of paved **biking** trails.

For the Birds

Make some new winged acquaintances while **birdwatching.** Grab your binoculars and climb to the top of the refurbished World War II observation tower at Cape Henlopen State Park in Rehoboth Beach for a bird's-eye view. At Gordon's Pond, toward the south end of the park, bird lovers can see osprey, as well as the endangered piping plover and American bald eagle. The dunes at Fenwick Island State Park also are home to several species of endangered seabirds, including the least tern and black skimmer.

Follow the trails on Burton's Island in Delaware Seashore State Park for a peek at noisy gulls and terns nesting in the salt marshes. Also be sure to check out the Bombay Hook National Wildlife Refuge in Smyrna; it's a habitat for migrating and wintering ducks and northbound migrating geese. The marshes of Fort Delaware State Park provide a summer home for nine species of egrets, herons and ibis.

Feeling Crabby?

Crabbing and **clamming** have long been associated with Delaware beaches, and there's a delicious reason why. The Indian River and Little Assawoman and Rehoboth bays are good places to start digging; you'll have the best luck from April to early fall. **Shellfishing** is popular from May through November.

Recreational Activities

Throughout the TourBook, you may notice a Recreational Activities heading with bulleted listings of recreation-oriented establishments listed underneath. Similar operations also may be mentioned in Destination City recreation sections. Since normal AAA inspection criteria cannot be applied, these establishments are presented only for information. Age, height and weight restrictions may apply. Reservations often are recommended and sometimes are required. Addresses and/or phone numbers are provided so visitors can contact the attraction for additional information.

Fast Facts

POPULATION: 783,600.

AREA: 2,057 square miles; ranks 49th.

CAPITAL: Dover.

HIGHEST POINT: 448 ft., near Ebright Road, Brandywine.

LOWEST POINT: Sea level, Atlantic Ocean.

TIME ZONE(S): Eastern. DST.

MINIMUM AGE FOR UNRE-STRICTED DRIVER'S LICENSE: 16 years, 10 months.

SEAT BELT/CHILD RESTRAINT LAWS: Seat belt required for driver and all passengers 16 and older. Ages 7-16 must use an approved child restraint or seat belt. Child safety seat required for age 7 and under and less than 60 pounds in all seats.

HELMETS FOR MOTORCY-CLISTS: Required.

RADAR DETECTORS: Permitted.

FIREARMS LAWS: Contact the Delaware State Police, Ordnance Section, 391 Clark Farm Rd. Smyrna, DE 19977; phone (302) 659-6020.

HOLIDAYS: Jan. 1; Martin Luther King Jr. Day, Jan. (3rd Mon.); Presidents Day, Feb. (3rd Mon.); Good Friday; Memorial Day, May (last Mon.); July 4; Labor Day, Sept. (1st Mon.); Columbus Day, Oct. (2nd Mon.); Veterans Day, Nov. 11; Election Day; Thanksgiving, Nov. (4th Thurs.); Dec. 25.

TAXES: Delaware does not have a statewide sales tax, but there is an 8 percent hotel occupancy tax.

INFORMATION CENTERS: State welcome centers that provide details about state attractions, accommodations, historic sites, parks and events are on I-95 between exit 1 and exit 3 on the edge of Newark, phone (302) 737-4059; and at the junction of US 13 and SR 1 north of Smyrna, phone (302) 653-8910. The I-95 center is open daily 8-8; closed Dec. 25. The US 13 center is open Mon.-Fri. 7-5, Fri.-Sun. 7-7, Memorial Day-Labor Day; daily 7-5, rest of year.

FURTHER INFORMATION FOR VISITORS:

Delaware Tourism Office
99 Kings Hwy.
Dover, DE 19901
(866) 284-7483 or
TTY (800) 232-5460

RECREATION INFORMATION:

Delaware Division of Parks and Recreation
89 Kings Hwy.
Dover, DE 19901
(302) 739-4702

FISHING AND HUNTING REGULATIONS:
Delaware Division of Fish and Wildlife
89 Kings Hwy.
Dover, DE 19901
(302) 739-5295

	JAN	FEB	MAR	APR	MAY	JUNE	JULY	AUG	SEPT	OCT	NOV	DEC
Delaware Temperature Averages Maximum/Minimum From the records of the National Weather Service												
Wilmington	41 / 26	42 / 25	51 / 32	63 / 42	74 / 52	82 / 61	86 / 66	84 / 64	78 / 57	67 / 46	55 / 36	44 / 27

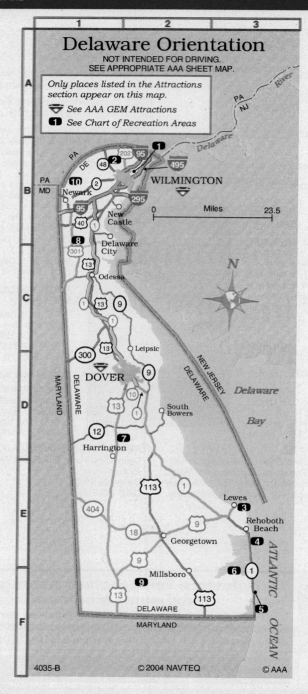

Delaware Orientation

NOT INTENDED FOR DRIVING.
SEE APPROPRIATE AAA SHEET MAP.

Only places listed in the Attractions
section appear on this map.

⏷ See AAA GEM Attractions
❶ See Chart of Recreation Areas

WILMINGTON

PA
DE

PA
MD

Newark

New
Castle

Delaware
City

Odessa

Leipsic

DOVER

South
Bowers

Harrington

Lewes

Rehoboth
Beach

Georgetown

Millsboro

MARYLAND

DELAWARE

NEW JERSEY

DELAWARE

Delaware
Bay

Delaware

River

Delaware

DELAWARE
MARYLAND

ATLANTIC OCEAN

0   Miles   23.5

N

4035-B   © 2004 NAVTEQ   © AAA

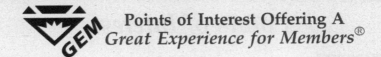

Points of Interest Offering A
Great Experience for Members®

Dover (D-2)

BIGGS MUSEUM OF AMERICAN ART—On display is Sewell C. Biggs' personal art and antiques collection, which spans 200 years and surveys major periods in American art. See p. 39.

Wilmington (B-2)

BRANDYWINE RIVER MUSEUM—A converted 19th-century gristmill displays American art. Of particular interest are works by three generations of the Wyeth family. See p. 45.

HAGLEY MUSEUM—On the site of the original du Pont gunpowder mills and estate, the museum and restored mills show the development of water power on the Brandywine River. See p. 46.

LONGWOOD GARDENS—Superb outdoor gardens feature elaborate fountains, lakes, woodlands, formal gardens and exotic tropical displays. See p. 46.

WINTERTHUR, AN AMERICAN COUNTRY ESTATE—Galleries explore the history and development of American decorative arts, focusing on social customs, techniques, symbolism and style. See p. 47.

RECREATION AREAS

	MAP LOCATION	CAMPING	PICNICKING	HIKING TRAILS	BOATING	BOAT RAMP	BOAT RENTAL	FISHING	SWIMMING	PETS ON LEASH	BICYCLE TRAILS	WINTER SPORTS	VISITOR CENTER	LODGE/CABINS	FOOD SERVICE
STATE															
Bellevue (B-2) 329 acres 4 mi. n.e. of Wilmington off I-95. Historic. Game courts, horse trails.	❶		•	•				•			•	•	•		
Brandywine Creek (B-1) 1,010 acres 9 mi. n.w. of Wilmington at jct. SRs 92 and 100 and Adams Dam Rd. Horse trails.	❷		•	•				•			•	•	•	•	
Cape Henlopen (E-3) 6,000 acres 1 mi. e. of Lewes on SR 9. Historic. Nature trails. *(See Rehoboth Beach p. 43)*	❸	•	•	•				•	•	•	•	•	•		
Delaware Seashore (E-3) 2,799 acres 5 mi. from Dewey Beach to Indian River Inlet off SR 1. Sailing, windsurfing. *(See Rehoboth Beach p. 43)*	❹	•	•	•	•	•		•	•	•		•			•
Fenwick Island (F-3) 442 acres extending from South Bethany Beach to Fenwick Island off SR 1.	❺		•		•	•	•	•	•	•					
Holts Landing (F-3) 203 acres 9 mi. n.e. of Dagsboro off SR 26 on the s. shore of the Indian River. Horse trails, pier, playground.	❻		•	•	•	•		•		•					
Killens Pond (D-2) 1,098 acres 12 mi. s. of Dover off US 13. Historic. Canoeing; nature trails.	❼	•	•	•	•	•	•	•	•	•		•		•	
Lums Pond (B-1) 2,091 acres 10 mi. s. of Newark off SR 71. Historic. Game courts, nature trails.	❽	•	•	•	•	•	•	•	•	•		•			
Trap Pond (F-2) 2,689 acres 6 mi. s.e. of Laurel off SR 24. Horse trails, nature trails.	❾	•	•	•	•	•	•		•	•		•		•	•
White Clay Creek (B-1) 3,214 acres 3 mi. n. of Newark via SR 896. Historic. Horse trails.	❿		•	•				•			•	•			

Points of Interest

DELAWARE CITY (B-1) pop. 1,453, elev. 4'

A river wharf occupied the site of Delaware City for the quarter century following 1800. In 1814 the Department of the Navy allowed the construction of a battery and fortifications on the Delaware River at what was then called Newbold's Point. Around 1825 streets were laid out at the junction of the Delaware River and the Chesapeake and Delaware Canal, which was being dug across the peninsula.

By the time the canal opened in 1829, however, railroads were handling most of the freight the canal had been built to ship. Delaware City's wide streets and grand name thus became reminders of a boom that never came.

The fortifications are gone from Newbold's Point, but Battery Park remains, offering a view of the river, Pea Patch Island and the New Jersey shoreline from the foot of Clinton Street. In the park is a restored Chesapeake and Delaware Canal lock built in 1829.

FORT DELAWARE STATE PARK is on Pea Patch Island. The park is accessible only by a ferry that departs from the dock at the foot of Clinton St. The 288-acre park features an 1859 fort, a museum displaying Civil War memorabilia, nature trails and an observation tower that provides views of nesting spots for egrets, herons and other wading birds.

Private boats are not permitted in the park. Picnicking is permitted. Allow 4 hours minimum. Wed.-Sun. and holidays 10-6, mid-June through Labor Day; Sat.-Sun. and holidays 10-6, last weekend in Apr. to mid-June and weekend after Labor Day-last weekend in Sept. Ferries to the park depart on the hour beginning at 10; the last ferry returns at 5:30. Admission (includes ferry fare) $6; ages 2-12, $4. AX, DS, MC, VI. Phone (302) 834-7941.

DOVER (D-2) pop. 32,135, elev. 37'

Although one early missionary feared the prevalent "bugs and mascatoes," Dover was established in 1683 as the seat of Kent County and adopted as the state capital in 1777 after British forces invaded New Castle, forcing statesmen to flee south. Delaware's deciding vote for independence from British rule had been cast in Philadelphia a year earlier by Continental Congress delegate Caesar Rodney, whose historic 80-mile ride from Dover brought

him to Independence Hall just minutes before the debate closed.

The city grew quickly in the early 18th century, with stately houses built around an attractive green designed by William Penn. It was at the Golden Fleece Tavern on The Green that Delawareans voted in 1787 to ratify the Constitution, making Delaware the first of the 13 states to do so.

Dover residents were divided about the slavery issue, but many prominent families helped runaway slaves escape to the North by means of the Underground Railroad. One such station may have been Woodburn, now the governor's residence, on King's Highway south of Division Street.

Dover claims as its favorite daughter astronomer Annie Jump Cannon, who developed a prismatic technique of telescopic photography that enabled her to classify more than 400,000 stars. Her work at the Harvard Observatory during the first half of the 20th century contributed greatly to the Henry Draper Catalog, which is still used by astronomers.

Although Legislative Hall has been in use only since 1933, its 18th-century style handmade brick exterior and interior woodwork give it the same appearance as much of historic Dover. Visitors may view the governor's reception area and portraits of Delaware's governors and World War II heroes. The building is on Legislative Avenue between Duke of York and William Penn streets. Guided tours through the chambers of the 1910 Delaware Supreme Court Building at 55 The Green are available on request; phone (302) 255-0093.

Fine 18th- and 19th-century houses remain concentrated around The Green and north and south State Street. Many examples of Victorian architecture line S. State and S. Bradford streets, and 19th-century commercial structures still stand along Lockerman Street.

The Old Dover Historic District includes Christ Church, The Green, the Richardson and Robbins Complex, Wesley College and Woodburn, birthplace of Annie Jump Cannon.

Live harness racing takes place at Dover Downs on US 13 November through April; phone (302) 674-4600 or (800) 711-5882.

Note: Policies vary concerning admittance of children to pari-mutuel betting facilities. Phone for information.

Dover International Speedway at Dover Downs hosts two weekends of NASCAR racing in June and September; phone (302) 674-4600.

Central Delaware Chamber of Commerce: 435 N. DuPont Hwy. (US 13), Dover, DE 19901; phone (302) 678-0892.

Self-guiding tours: Brochures outlining tours to many of the city's most interesting buildings and attractions are available at the Delaware State Museums Visitor Center, 406 Federal St.; phone (302) 739-4266.

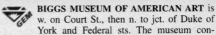 **BIGGS MUSEUM OF AMERICAN ART** is w. on Court St., then n. to jct. of Duke of York and Federal sts. The museum contains Sewell C. Biggs' personal art and antiques collection, which was in the making for more than half a century. It is in the 1858 former Kent County Levy Court House, one of the state's first fireproof buildings.

Works spanning 200 years survey major periods in American art. Exhibits feature the paintings of regional artists and celebrated masters: Albert Bierstadt, William Merritt Chase, Childe Hassam, George Inness, Charles Willson Peale, Frank Schoonover and Gilbert Stuart. The collection also includes pastels, drawings and sculpture.

Biggs' assemblage of fine furniture and silver represents the work of some of the best Delaware and Philadelphia craftsmen of the Colonial and Federal periods. Guided tours are available. Allow 1 hour minimum. Wed.-Fri. 10-4, Sat. 9-5, Sun. 1:30-4:30; closed major holidays. Free. Phone (302) 674-2111.

[SAVE] **DELAWARE AGRICULTURAL MUSEUM AND VILLAGE,** 2 mi. n. to 866 N. DuPont Hwy. (US 13) at jct. US 13 Alt., illustrates agricultural heritage and rural life. The exhibition hall houses tractors, horse-drawn equipment and farming implements dating from 1670 through the 1950s. Buildings dating from the Civil War era to about 1900 include a one-room schoolhouse, sawmill, barbershop, train station, farmhouse, general store, country church and blacksmith and wheelwright shops.

Allow 1 hour, 30 minutes minimum. Tues.-Sat. 10-4, Sun. 1-4, Apr.-Dec.; Tues.-Sat. 10-4, rest of year. Closed holidays. Admission $5; over 59 and ages 6-17, $3. DS, MC, VI. Phone (302) 734-1618.

DELAWARE ARCHAEOLOGY MUSEUM AND MUSEUM OF SMALL TOWN LIFE, 316 S. Governor's Ave., occupies an 18th-century former Presbyterian church and chapel. The Delaware Archaeology Museum displays artifacts dating from North America's most recent ice age to the present, with emphasis on Delaware's American Indian history. The Museum of Small Town Life depicts village commerce through five re-created 19th-century shops. Exhibits chronicling the history of the phonograph are in the Johnson Victrola Museum. Allow 30 minutes minimum. Tues.-Fri. 10-3:30, state holidays 9-5; closed major holidays. Free. Phone (302) 739-4266.

DELAWARE'S STATE HOUSE is on the e. side of The Green at S. State St. The restored 1792 building contains period furnishings, building artifacts and historical photographs and documents. Programs about state history and the Underground Railroad are offered. Guided tours start at the Delaware State Museums Visitor Center behind the statehouse. Allow 30 minutes minimum. Guided 30-minute tours leave Tues.-Fri. 10-3:30, Sat. and state holidays 9-5, Sun. 1:30-4:30; closed major holidays. Free. Phone (302) 739-4266.

DELAWARE STATE POLICE MUSEUM, 1425 N. DuPont Hwy., features uniforms, weapons, vehicles and equipment used in law enforcement. Other exhibits include an interactive mock crime scene and a police memorial. Visitors can sit at an emergency call center console. Allow 30 minutes minimum. Mon.-Fri. 9-3, third Sat. of the month 11-3; closed holidays. Free. Phone (302) 739-7700.

JOHN DICKINSON PLANTATION, 6 mi. s. on US 113, then .1 mi. e. to 340 Kitts Hummock Rd., was the boyhood home of John Dickinson, known as the Penman of the American Revolution and attributed with drafting the Articles of Confederation in 1778. Dickinson's 1740s brick house and reconstructed farm complex exemplify area 18th-century plantation architecture. Allow 1 hour, 30 minutes minimum. Tours are available Tues.-Sat. 10-3:30 (also Sun. 1:30-4:30, Mar.-Dec.); closed holidays. Last tour begins 30 minutes before closing. Donations. Phone (302) 739-3277.

GEORGETOWN (E-2) pop. 4,643

ELSIE WILLIAMS DOLL COLLECTION is w. of SR 113 on SR 18 in the library of the Delaware Technical and Community College. The collection includes a wide variety of dolls by such makers as Bru, Madame Alexander and Peggy Nisbet. Allow 30 minutes minimum. Mon.-Thurs. 8 a.m.-10 p.m., Fri. 8-4:30, Sat. 9-1; closed major holidays and Dec. 20-Jan. 4. Free. Phone (302) 856-9033.

TREASURES OF THE SEA EXHIBIT, on the Delaware Technical and Community College campus w. of SR 113 on SR 18, displays jewels, gold and silver ingots and coins, bronze cannons and gold chains recovered from the ill-fated Spanish galleon *Nuestra Señora de Atocha*. Carrying an estimated $400 million in treasure, the ship sank in a 1622 hurricane. Videotapes chronicle the discovery of the galleon; visitors also may listen to a recording about the finding of the cannons.

Allow 1 hour minimum. Mon.-Tues. 10-4, Fri. noon-4, Sat. 9-1; closed major holidays and school vacations. Admission $2.50; over 65, $2; students with ID $1; under 4 free. For holiday and vacation schedule phone (302) 856-5700.

HARRINGTON (D-1) pop. 3,174, elev. 63'

In central Delaware's agricultural region, Harrington is home to the Delaware State Fair. The fairgrounds complex on US 13 features Quillen Arena and an ice rink for public skating and hockey matches.

Harrington Raceway, at the fairgrounds, offers spring and fall harness racing sessions; phone (302) 398-7223.

Note: Policies vary concerning admittance of children to pari-mutuel betting facilities. Phone for information.

MESSICK AGRICULTURAL MUSEUM, 1.2 mi. w. of jct. US 13 and SR 14W on Walt Messick Rd., houses an extensive collection of early 1900s farm implements. Horse-drawn plows and vehicles, including a covered wagon, represent farm life in the 19th century. An early 20th-century kitchen and smokehouse are furnished in period. The museum has a collection of classic automobiles and trucks spanning several decades. Allow 1 hour minimum. Mon.-Fri. 7:30-5. Free. Phone (302) 398-3729.

LEIPSIC (C-2) pop. 203

Leipsic (LIP-sic) was named after the German fur-shipping city, Leipzig. Between 1836 and the beginning of the railroad era in 1855 the town had a busy port that shipped lumber, grain and oysters to Philadelphia. The port, active until 1940, is now used mainly by pleasure craft and the remaining Delaware oyster dredge boats.

BOMBAY HOOK NATIONAL WILDLIFE REFUGE, 2 mi. n. on SR 9, then about 2.5 mi. e. on Whitehall Neck Rd., is primarily a refuge for migrating ducks, geese and shore birds, but wildlife can be seen year-round. Nature trails and a 12-mile round trip driving route offer opportunities to explore the 15,978-acre refuge, and observation towers provide a panorama of the area. The Allee House, off SR 9, is a 1753 Queen Anne farmhouse furnished with period pieces; guided tours are available.

Refuge open daily dawn-dusk. Visitor center open Mon.-Fri. 8-4 (also Sat.-Sun. 9-5, Mar.-May and Sept. 1 to mid-Dec.). House tours are given Sat.-Sun. 1-4, Mar.-May and Sept. 1 to mid-Dec. Admission $4 per private vehicle, $2 for persons arriving by bicycle or on foot, under 16 and over 61 free. Phone (302) 653-6872.

LEWES (E-3) pop. 2,932, elev. 17'

West of Cape Henlopen, Lewes (LOO-is) was founded in 1631 by a group of settlers from Hoorn, Holland. Originally called *Zwaanendael*, Valley of the Swans, the little colony intended to establish an agricultural and whaling industry, but the Siconese Indians destroyed it within a year. The interruption was brief, however. Promptly rebuilt, the town flourished, surviving pirate attacks, British bombardment in the War of 1812 and the profusion of summer vacationers to its beaches.

The DeVries Monument on Pilottown Road commemorates the early Dutch settlement. Constructed before the exact position of the Dutch fort was determined, the monument later was discovered to be on the site of the fortification's north bastion.

Lewes is the traditional home of the pilots who guide ships up Delaware Bay. This maritime orientation also makes the town a natural site for the Marine College of the University of Delaware; student enrollment is approximately 100.

Ferries connect Lewes with Cape May, N.J., daily. The 17-mile trip takes 70 minutes. For information write Cape May-Lewes Ferry, Lewes Terminal, P.O. Box 517, Lewes, DE 19958; phone (302) 644-6030 or (800) 643-3779. Cape May-Lewes ferry information also is available at AAA Mid-Atlantic, 55 Greentree Dr., in Dover; phone (302) 674-8020.

Lewes Chamber of Commerce and Visitor's Bureau: 120 Kings Hwy., Lewes, DE 19958; phone (302) 645-8073.

Self-guiding tours: Brochures and maps are available from the chamber of commerce and visitor bureau.

FISHERMAN'S WHARF, 3 mi. e. of SR 1 on SR 9 (Anglers Rd.), just across the drawbridge, offers dolphin- and whale-watching cruises. Lighthouse and sunset cruises as well as fishing excursions also are available.

Two-hour dolphin cruises depart daily at 9 and 3, 3-hour dolphin and whale-watching cruises at 11:30, mid-June through Sept. 1 (weather permitting). Dolphin cruise $20; under 13, $10. Dolphin and whale-watching cruise $25; under 13, $15. Hours and fares may vary; phone ahead. MC, VI. Phone (302) 645-8862.

FISHER-MARTIN HOUSE is at Kings Hwy. and Savannah Rd. The restored early 18th-century structure presents changing exhibits and houses the Lewes Chamber of Commerce and Visitor's Bureau. Allow 30 minutes minimum. Mon.-Fri. 10-4 (also Sat. 9-3, Sun. 10-2, Memorial Day weekend-Sept. 30). Free. Phone (302) 645-8073.

LEWES HISTORICAL SOCIETY COMPLEX, at Shipcarpenter and Third sts., encompasses a number of historic structures. Among the buildings are Thompson Country Store, a furnished 19th-century store moved from a site near Milford; Plank House, a tiny one-room log cabin built before 1700; and the 1789 Burton Ingraham House, furnished with Chippendale and Empire antiques. Ryves Holt House, at Second and Mulberry streets, contains a visitor center.

Allow 1 hour, 30 minutes minimum. Guided tours are given Mon.-Fri. 10-4, Sat. 10-1, Memorial Day-Labor Day. Fee $6, under 12 free. Phone (302) 645-7670.

PRIME HOOK NATIONAL WILDLIFE REFUGE is 8 mi. n. via SR 1, then 1 mi. e. on Broadkill Beach Rd. (SR 16). Black and wood ducks, Canada geese, mallards and pintails congregate spring and fall at this 9,000-acre marsh habitat for migratory waterfowl. Indigenous mammals include red and gray foxes, white-tailed deer and the endangered Delmarva fox squirrel. A half-mile boardwalk and more than 7 miles of canoe trails are available.

Allow 1 hour, 30 minutes minimum. Refuge open daily dawn-dusk. Refuge headquarters Mon.-Fri. 7:30-4 (also Sat.-Sun. 9-4, Apr.-Nov.). Free. Boat launch fee $1. Phone (302) 684-8419.

SEASIDE NATURE CENTER, 1 mi. e. on US 9 past Cape May-Lewes Ferry to Cape Henlopen State Park, has a variety of exhibits, including several large fish aquariums, mounted birds, whale and dolphin skulls, and touch tanks. The Seaside Interpretive Trail, a self-guiding tour of the natural and human history of Cape Henlopen, leads from the center to the coast. An observation tower used during World War II is open for tours.

Allow 30 minutes minimum. Daily 9-4. Park entrance fee May-Oct. $5 per private out-of-state vehicle, $2.50 per private in-state vehicle; free to all, rest of year. Center free. Phone (302) 645-6852.

ZWAANENDAEL MUSEUM is at Savannah Rd. and Kings Hwy. This Dutch Renaissance building is an adaptation of the town hall at Hoorn in the Netherlands. Within are exhibits of historic military and maritime artifacts dating from 1631 to the War of 1812, including items from the wreckage of an 18th-century ship, the *DeBraak,* discovered off the Delaware coast in 1986. Allow 30 minutes minimum. Tues.-Sat. 10-4:30, Sun. 1:30-4:30; closed holidays. Free. Phone (302) 645-1148.

WINERIES

- **Nassau Valley Vineyards Winery and Visitors Center,** 2 mi. w. on US 9 to jct. US 404 and SR 1, then .5 mi. n. on SR 1 to overpass, then w. onto CR 14B, following signs to 33 Nassau Commons. Tues.-Sat. 11-5, Sun. noon-5. Phone (302) 645-9463.

MILLSBORO (F-2) pop. 2,360, elev. 26′

NANTICOKE INDIAN MUSEUM, at jct. SRs 24 and 5, is in a restored community schoolhouse. Exhibits interpret the history and development of the Nanticoke Indians, Delaware's first residents and its only remaining American Indian tribe. Highlights include basketwork, ceremonial dress, pottery, arrowheads and stone implements. Belongings of Chief John Big Tree, the model for the Indian Head nickel, also are featured. Allow 30 minutes minimum. Tues.-Sat. 10-4. Admission $2; ages 3-11, $1. Phone (302) 945-7022.

NEWARK (B-1) pop. 28,547, elev. 137′

Newark originated as the crossroads of two Lenni Lenape Indian trails spanning the peninsula between the Chesapeake Bay and the Delaware

---

DID YOU KNOW

Delaware has tax-free shopping.

River. The intersection gradually matured into a village, and brickyards, mills and tanneries developed in the vicinity.

Legend maintains that in 1777 Betsy Ross' flag was flown for the first time at nearby Cooch's Bridge, the site of Delaware's only Revolutionary War battle. The Battle of Cooch's Bridge took place west off SR 896 via Welsh Tract Road or Old Baltimore Pike.

IRON HILL MUSEUM OF NATURAL HISTORY, I-95 to SR 896, then 1 mi. s. to 1355 Old Baltimore Pike, is housed in a former one-room schoolhouse built by the du Pont family in 1923. Collections include rocks, minerals, floral and faunal specimens, archeological and historical displays, mounted birds and iron exhibits. Hiking trails pass old iron ore mining pits and a replica of an early American Indian encampment. Allow 1 hour, 30 minutes minimum. Tues.-Wed. 10-2, Thurs.-Fri. 9-2, Sat. noon-4; closed holidays. Admission $1, under 6 free. Phone (302) 368-5703.

UNIVERSITY OF DELAWARE visitor center is at 196 S. College Ave. The 17,500-student campus is noted for the elm-lined mall (The Green) extending from Old College to Laurel Hall. Allow 2 hours minimum. Guided 90-minute tours are given Mon.-Fri. at 10, noon and 2; Sat. by reservation at 10 and noon. Tours are not available holidays and during final exams. Free. Phone (302) 831-8123.

NEW CASTLE (B-1) pop. 4,862, elev. 17'

William Penn first set foot in North America near what is now the corner of Strand and Delaware streets. The town prospered under Penn's Quaker administration, producing two signers of the Declaration of Independence—George Read and Thomas McKean.

New Castle was a trade center until 1824 when a fire leveled the business district. Although the New Castle-Frenchtown Railroad gave New Castle new life in 1832, in the mid-19th century the main railroad lines were rerouted through Wilmington, isolating the town. New Castle's resulting seclusion has had one desirable effect: Much of its Colonial and Federal architecture remains unaltered.

The Old Library Museum, housed in a restored 1892 Victorian library designed by Philadelphia architect Frank Furness and featuring a cupola, skylight and leaded-glass doors, presents changing historic exhibits; phone (302) 322-2794.

New Castle's inhabitants own a 700-acre tract of land dating from the earliest days of Dutch settlement. Administered by the Trustees of New Castle Common instead of the municipal government, its many uses yield considerable revenue for the common good of the community.

Self-guiding tours: Brochures for the New Castle Heritage Trail walking tour are available at the New Castle Court House (*see attraction listing*) and the city administration building at the corner of Third and Delaware streets across from The Green.

The tour covers historic areas and buildings dating from the mid-17th century.

AMSTEL HOUSE, 2 E. Fourth St., is an example of 18th-century Georgian architecture. The 1730s house, once the home of Governor Nicholas Van Dyke Sr., interprets life in the Colonial period through furnishings, an open-hearth kitchen and household equipment. Allow 30 minutes minimum. Tues.-Sat. 11-4, Sun. 1-4, Mar.-Dec.; by appointment rest of year. Closed holidays. Admission $4. Combination ticket with Dutch House $6. Phone (302) 322-2794.

DUTCH HOUSE, 32 E. Third St., was built in the late 17th century and is one of the oldest brick houses in the state. The structure contains decorative arts and historical artifacts, plus 17th- and 18th-century Colonial Dutch furnishings characteristic of a settler's house. Allow 30 minutes minimum. Tues.-Sat. 11-4, Sun. 1-4, Mar.-Dec.; by appointment rest of year. Closed holidays. Admission $4. Combination ticket with Amstel House $6. Phone (302) 322-2794.

THE GREEN, on Delaware St. between Third and Market sts., was laid out by Peter Stuyvesant in 1655. The Green and adjacent Market Square were the sites of fairs and weekly markets until the early 19th century. An 1809 U.S. arsenal and the 1798 New Castle Academy are on The Green.

NEW CASTLE COURT HOUSE MUSEUM is at 211 Delaware St. between Market and Third sts., Built in 1732, the courthouse was occupied by the Colonial Assembly until 1776, was the site of the adoption of Delaware's first constitution on Sept. 20, 1776, and served as the state's first capitol until 1777. It has been restored to its 1804 appearance and contains portraits, artifacts and furnishings relating to Delaware history. Allow 30 minutes minimum. Tues.-Sat. 10-3:30, Sun. 1:30-4:30; closed state holidays. Free. Phone (302) 323-4453.

OLD PRESBYTERIAN CHURCH, 25 E. Second St., is believed to have been the direct successor of the original Dutch Reformed Church of 1657. Built in 1707, it was one of several churches forming the first presbytery in America. The cemetery contains marked graves dating from the early 1700s. Daily 8-noon. Free. Phone (302) 328-3279.

ORIGINAL TICKET OFFICE, at the Battery on the s. side of Delaware St., was part of the now defunct New Castle and Frenchtown Railway. One of the first in the nation, the 1832 office marked the eastern terminus of the line. It was moved to its present site in the 1950s. Nearby is a section of reconstructed track with wooden rails pegged to stone sleepers, the forerunner of wooden railroad ties. The interior of the building is not accessible. Free.

READ HOUSE AND GARDENS, 42 The Strand, was built in 1801-03 by the son of George Read, one of the signers of the Declaration of Independence. A fine example of Federal architecture, the

22-room mansion is furnished in period and features carved woodwork, relief plasterwork and gilded fanlights. Tours highlight the lifestyles of three resident families. A 1.5-acre formal Victorian garden graces the grounds.

Allow 30 minutes minimum. Tues.-Thurs. and Sun 11-4, Fri.-Sat. 10-4, Mar.-Dec.; Sat. 10-4, Sun. 11-4, by appointment rest of year. Closed holidays. The house is open only by guided 35- to 45-minute tours; departure times vary. Last tour departs at closing. Admission $5; over 64 and ages 13-21, $4; ages 6-12, $2. MC, VI. Phone (302) 322-8411.

THE STRAND, near the river, is a block-long street bordered by shady brick walks and brick gutters. A number of townhouses dating from the 18th century survived the great fire that swept the street in 1824. The law office of Thomas McKean, a delegate to the Continental Congress of 1774, was at 22 The Strand. Packet Alley runs from The Strand to the river.

ODESSA (C-1) pop. 286, elev. 52′

With its emergence in the early 19th century as one of the area's most important grain shipping ports, the name of the town known as Cantwell's Bridge was changed to Odessa, after Russia's seaport. Farmers brought their produce to town, where it was shipped down Appoquinimink Creek to the Delaware River, then to domestic and foreign ports.

The significance of the port was eclipsed in the mid-1800s with the coming of the railroad. The railroad bypassed the city on its way through the Delmarva Peninsula and the Midwest became the nation's major grain producing region. Odessa was a primary station of the Underground Railroad prior to the outbreak of the Civil War. Well-preserved examples of 18th- and 19th-century architecture line Odessa's shaded streets.

REHOBOTH BEACH (E-3) pop. 1,495

Rehoboth is a biblical term meaning "room enough." Its remote location kept the beach area almost untouched until 1872 when the Rehoboth Beach Camp Meeting Association of the Methodist Episcopal Church purchased land along the sea and platted a town. Made accessible by a railroad line extended from Lewes in 1878, the town was the site of revival camp meetings until the 1880s.

When the highway replaced the railroad in the 1920s, Rehoboth Beach was well on its way to becoming a popular resort. The nearest ocean resort to the nation's capital, the town is deluged every summer by humidity-weary Washingtonians. Natives of Delaware seem scarce by comparison in the summer capital.

Clamming, crabbing, nature cruises, deep-sea and freshwater fishing, golfing, birding, sailing and swimming are some of the recreational pursuits available to visitors.

Camping is available at Delaware Seashore State Park *(see Recreation Chart and the AAA Mideastern CampBook)* on a 7-mile strip of land between the Atlantic Ocean and the Rehoboth and Indian River bays. Cape Henlopen State Park *(see Recreation Chart and the AAA Mideastern CampBook)* offers sand dunes, camping, nature trails, bathhouses, surf fishing and swimming areas where Delaware Bay meets the Atlantic Ocean.

Rehoboth Beach-Dewey Beach Chamber of Commerce and Visitor Center: Rehoboth Railroad Station, 501 Rehoboth Ave., P.O. Box 216, Rehoboth Beach, DE 19971; phone (302) 227-2233 or (800) 441-1329. *See color ad.*

Shopping areas: SAVE Rehoboth Outlets on SR 1 has more than 150 outlet stores, including Ann Taylor, Bugle Boy, Izod, L.L. Bean, Oneida, Pierre Cardin, Reebok and Van Heusen.

SOUTH BOWERS (D-2)

The residents of the few dozen cottages that constitute South Bowers are far from being the area's first inhabitants. Excavations at South Bowers revealed remnants of an American Indian culture several thousand years old that inhabited Milford Neck between the Murderkill and Mispillion rivers.

These natives of the Middle Woodland period enjoyed rich hunting and fishing and the yields of the fertile soil. Based on artifacts unearthed in the area, archeologists believe the region was the eastern terminus of an early trade route extending as far west as the Great Lakes.

WILMINGTON (B-2) pop. 72,664, elev. 134′

Wilmington was named by the Quakers who laid out the city in 1731. The settlement grew into an important market and shipping center. Industrial growth followed, stimulated by Wilmington's accessibility to other eastern ports and by the abundant water power in the Brandywine River Valley.

In the early 19th century Wilmington attracted Éleuthère Irénée du Pont and his two sons, who intended to finance a colony based on Utopian ideas. Seeing a need for high-quality gunpowder, however, the du Ponts abandoned their original plan, and in 1803 their new Eleutherian Mills produced the first barrel of Du Pont powder. The du Pont influence was instrumental in shaping Delaware's largest city into an industrial, financial and shipping hub.

A highlight of Wilmington's downtown renewal effort is the 1871 Grand Opera House, with its ornate cast-iron facade. The building, on the Market Street Mall, now serves as the Delaware Center for the Performing Arts. Free tours are available by reservation; phone (302) 658-7897. The Custom House, Sixth and King streets, was Wilmington's first federal building. Built in 1855, it is noted for its simple but bold exterior lines and impressive interior.

The Quaker Hill Historic District, downtown between Jefferson and Tatnall streets and Second and Eighth streets, was Wilmington's first neighborhood. It contains residences built 1745-1890, 19th-century churches and an 1816 Quaker meeting hall with a large cemetery.

A mile-long river walk connects the Brandywine River Museum *(see attraction listing)* with the 18th-century John Chads House, built by a local innkeeper and ferry operator. The house is open for tours, which include a beehive oven baking demonstration.

The Wilmington and Western Railroad offers 1- and 2-hour scenic rides through the Red Clay Valley area on weekends as well as seasonal specialty rides May through December. For schedule and fare information phone (302) 998-1930.

Greater Wilmington Convention and Visitors Bureau: 100 W. 10th St., Suite 20, Wilmington, DE 19801; phone (800) 489-6664 or (800) 422-1181. *See color ad p. 382.*

Self-guiding tours: Maps for a self-guiding walking tour of the Quaker Hill Historic District are available from the Quaker Hill Historic Preservation Foundation at 521 N. West St.; phone (302) 658-9295.

BRANDYWINE PARK AND ZOO is at 1001 N. Park Dr. along the Brandywine River between Augustine and Market sts. The 180-acre park was designed by the creator of New York City's Central Park, Frederick Law Olmstead, and features the Josephine Garden, which has 118 Japanese cherry

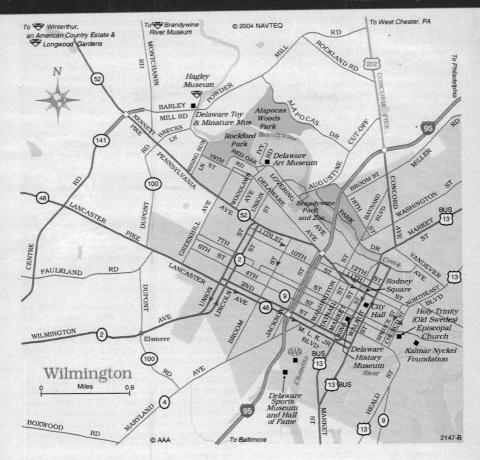

trees. The zoo houses Florida bobcats, Siberian tigers, small mammals and a variety of North and South American reptiles and birds.

Allow 2 hours minimum. Park daily dawn-dusk. Zoo daily 10-4. Park free. Zoo $4; over 62 and ages 3-11, $2. Phone (302) 571-7747.

BRANDYWINE RIVER MUSEUM, in Chadds Ford, Pa., on US 1 just s. of Creek Rd., is a 19th-century gristmill converted into a museum of American art. Works by three generations of the Wyeth family are featured, with one gallery devoted to the paintings of Andrew Wyeth. The galleries in the restored mill have original beams, pine floors and white plaster walls. The museum grounds are landscaped with native plants and wildflowers.

Via a shuttle bus connection, visitors may take a 1-hour guided tour of the nearby N.C. Wyeth house and studio, restored to their 1945 appearance, or Kuerner Farm, the inspiration for more than 1,000 paintings completed during Andrew Wyeth's 70-year friendship with the Kuerner family.

Allow 1 hour, 30 minutes minimum. Museum open daily 9:30-4:30; closed Dec. 25. House and studio tours or Kuerner Farm tours are given Wed.-Sun. 10-3:15, first Wed. in Apr. to mid-Nov. Admission $8, over 64 and students with ID $5, under 6 free. Tours $5. Under 6 are not permitted on tour. Audiotape tour $3. MC, VI. Phone (610) 388-2700.

DELAWARE ART MUSEUM, 2301 Kentmere Pkwy., contains the Bancroft Collection of English pre-Raphaelite art, one of the most important in the country, and paintings by American artists Thomas Eakins, Winslow Homer, Maxfield Parrish, Howard Pyle, John Sloan, and Andrew, Jamie and N.C. Wyeth. A children's gallery uses hands-on activities to stimulate creativity. Changing exhibits and an art research library provide further enrichment.

Allow 1 hour minimum. Tues.-Fri. 10-4, Sat. 10-5, Sun. 1-5. Library available by appointment. Closed Jan. 1, Thanksgiving and Dec. 25. Admission $7; over 59, $5; students with ID $2.50; under 6 free; free to all Sat. 10-1. AX, DS, MC, VI. Phone (302) 571-9590.

DELAWARE HISTORY MUSEUM, 504 N. Market St., features the interactive, multimedia permanent exhibition Distinctively Delaware. Changing exhibits feature art, costumes, toys, antiques, re-created scenes and historic photographs. Grandma's Attic is a learn-and-play discovery center for children. Allow 30 minutes minimum. Mon.-Fri. noon-4, Sat. 10-4; closed holidays. Phone ahead for current exhibit information. Admission $4; over 65 and college students with ID $3; ages 2-17, $2. MC, VI. Phone (302) 656-0637.

SAVE **DELAWARE MUSEUM OF NATURAL HISTORY,** 5 mi. n.w. on SR 52, contains a variety of natural history exhibits in naturalistic settings, from native flora and fauna to specimens representing Africa and the Great Barrier Reef. Noteworthy are an extensive shell collection and mounted African animals and extinct birds. The Discovery Room features hands-on exhibits and activities.

Food is available. Allow 1 hour, 30 minutes minimum. Mon.-Sat. 9:30-4:30, Sun. noon-4:30; closed Jan. 1, Easter, July 4, Thanksgiving and Dec. 25. Admission $6; over 59 and ages 3-17, $4. MC, VI. Phone (302) 658-9111.

DELAWARE SPORTS MUSEUM AND HALL OF FAME is off I-95 exit 6, following signs to Frawley Stadium. The museum chronicles Delaware sports history from 1860 to the present through photographs, artifacts and memorabilia. Among more than 200 sports notables highlighted are Olympic athletes, professional players, coaches, journalists and sportscasters. A 12-minute videotape provides an overview. Allow 30 minutes minimum. Mon.-Sat. noon-5, Apr.-Oct. Admission $4; over 49, $3; ages 13-19, $2. MC, VI. Phone (302) 425-3263.

DELAWARE TOY & MINIATURE MUSEUM is 3 mi. n. on SR 52 and .5 mi. n. to SR 141, then s. following signs to Hagley Museum (see attraction listing). The museum holds a collection of antique and contemporary doll houses, miniatures and sample furniture. Featured are American and European dolls, toy trains, boats and planes from the 18th century to the present. Enameled brass figurines and miniature vases dating from 600 B.C. also are displayed.

Allow 1 hour minimum. Guided 1.5- to 2.5-hour tours are available by reservation. Open Tues.-Sat. 10-4, Sun. noon-4; closed holidays. Admission $6; over 60, $5; ages 2-12, $3. MC, VI. Phone (302) 427-8697.

GEM **HAGLEY MUSEUM,** 3 mi. n. on SR 52 and .5 mi. n. on SR 141, then s. to 6 Old Barley Mill Rd., following signs, occupies 235 landscaped acres on the site of the original du Pont gunpowder mills, estate and gardens. Many restored mills show the development of water power on the Brandywine River.

The Henry Clay Mill is an old stone cotton-spinning shop housing a visitor center and interactive science exhibits tracing DuPont Co. history, from explosives manufacturing to the development of chemical products that changed the world. Highlights include Jeff Gordon's #24 DuPont NASCAR race car and a space suit made of DuPont materials.

Eleutherian Mill, a Georgian house erected by Éleuthère Irénée du Pont in 1803, contains furnishings reflecting the tastes of five generations of du Ponts.

Allow 3 hours minimum. Daily 9:30-4:30, Mar. 15-Dec. 30; Sat.-Sun. 9:30-4:30, rest of year. Closed Thanksgiving and Dec. 25. Guided tours are given daily every 30 minutes 10-3:30, Mar. 15-Dec. 31; Mon.-Fri. at 1:30 and Sat.-Sun. every 30 minutes 10-3:30, Jan. 1-Mar. 14. Admission (includes Henry Clay Mill) $11; over 61 and students with ID $9; ages 6-14, $4; family rate $30. Admission to Henry Clay Mill $5; ages 6-14, $2. AX, MC, VI. Phone (302) 658-2400.

HOLY TRINITY (OLD SWEDES) EPISCOPAL CHURCH, 606 Church St., was built in 1698 and is said to be the oldest active church in North America. Once of Swedish Lutheran affiliation and plain, it is now Episcopal and somewhat ornate. Allow 30 minutes minimum. Wed.-Sat. 10-4. Admission $2. Phone (302) 652-5629.

Hendrickson House is a Swedish stone farmhouse erected in Pennsylvania in 1690. Dismantled and rebuilt on the current site, the structure now houses the library, museum and office of Old Swedes Foundation. Admission included with Holy Trinity Episcopal Church.

***KALMAR NYCKEL* FOUNDATION** is at 1124 E. Seventh St., adjacent to Swedes Landing. The *Kalmar Nyckel* is a re-creation of the ship that brought the first European settlers to the Delaware Valley in 1638. The shipyard contains a small museum with a videotape that documents the ship's construction using Old World techniques. The ship rotates between the shipyard and to two other Wilmington docks: the Port of Wilmington and Bank One Center on the Riverfront.

Allow 30 minutes minimum. Thurs.-Sun. 10-4, Nov.-Apr.; closed holidays. Phone ahead for the ship docking schedule. Admission $5; ages 6-12, $4. AX, DS, MC, VI. Phone (302) 429-7447.

GEM **LONGWOOD GARDENS** is about 12 mi. n. at jct. US 1 and SR 52 near Kennett Square, Pa. Once the country estate of industrialist Pierre S. du Pont, Longwood is famous for its superb grounds that include elaborate fountains, two lakes, woodlands, wildflowers, a formal rose garden, a conservatory and greenhouses.

The Peirce-du Pont House, occupied by du Pont until 1954, contains an exhibit tracing the 300-year historical and horticultural evolution of Longwood Gardens through photographs, artifacts, videotapes and family home movies.

Fountains and more than 11,000 types of plants are the main summer outdoor attractions. Masses of flowering plants adorn the 3.5-acre heated conservatory, which is particularly colorful November through April. Half-hour musical illuminations take place at the main garden fountain on select evenings June through August.

Allow 2 hours minimum. Visitor center and outdoor gardens daily 9-6, Apr.-Oct. (also Tues., Thurs. and Sat. 6 p.m.-1 hour after dusk, June-Aug.); 9-9, Thanksgiving-Jan. 5; 9-5, rest of year. Conservatory opens at 10. Admission Thanksgiving-early Jan. $15; ages 16-20, $6; ages 6-15, $2. Admission Apr. 1-day before Thanksgiving $14 ($10 on Tues.); ages 16-20, $6; ages 6-15, $2. Admission rest of year $12 ($8 on Tues.); ages 16-20, $6; ages 6-15, $2. Hours and prices may vary; phone ahead. AX, DS, MC, VI. Phone (610) 388-1000, or (800) 737-5500 in the mid-Atlantic area.

ROCKWOOD MUSEUM, off I-95 exit 9 (Marsh Rd.) at 610 Shipley Rd., is a rare example of Rural Gothic architecture. The 72-acre estate contains an 1851 manor house furnished as it was in 1895. Also on the grounds are a conservatory, the gardener's cottage, the carriage house, several outbuildings, a lighted walking trail and six acres of gardens that exemplify fine landscape design. Guided tours and food are available. Allow 1 hour minimum. Daily 7-7; closed major holidays. Free. Phone (302) 761-4340.

RODNEY SQUARE, bounded by Market, King, 10th and 11th sts., contains an equestrian statue of Caesar Rodney. This Delaware statesman made a hurried night ride from Dover to Philadelphia on July 2, 1776, to sway a tie vote to the side of independence.

 WINTERTHUR, AN AMERICAN COUNTRY ESTATE is 6 mi. n.w. off I-95 exit 7 (Pennsylvania Ave.) on SR 52. The former home of Henry Francis du Pont was designed in the style of an English country estate and holds one of the richest collections of decorative arts made or used in America 1640-1860. Hands-on exhibits and interactive displays explore the history and development of American decorative arts. The Campbell Collection of Soup Tureens also is displayed.

The 979-acre estate reflects du Pont's interest in horticulture and includes a 60-acre naturalistic garden of native and exotic plants complemented by waterways, meadows and woodlands. Flowering plants bloom successively late January through November. A children's garden, tram rides and guided garden walks are available as are a variety of guided mansion and grounds tours lasting 45 minutes to 2 hours.

Allow 2 hours minimum. Tues.-Sun. 10-5; closed Jan. 1, Thanksgiving and Dec. 25. Last tour ticket sold at 3:45. Admission $15; over 62 and ages 12-18, $13; ages 2-11, $5. Guided tours $5-$15. Reservations are recommended for tours in May and Dec. AX, DS, MC, VI. Phone (302) 888-4600, (800) 448-3883, or TTY (302) 888-4907.

District of Columbia

A Monumental City

The spirit of America iconized in obelisks, domes and colonnaded shrines

Our Nation's Front Yard

Open spaces, parks and grassy malls complement this federal showplace

Art and Culture

The District abounds with venerable museums, theaters and galleries

Cherry Blossoms

Trimming the Tidal Basin, to tout the natural beauty of our capital city

Historic Structures

Celebrated monuments define the history of a world power

U.S. Capitol
©Richard Cummins
SuperStock

the heart of the nation

Constitution Gardens / © SuperStock

The District of Columbia represents America.

Tourists crouch on the ground in an attempt to snap a photo of the Washington Monument, leaving with a 3 x 5 of most of the tower and a lot of sky. Family members search in silence for names of their loved ones at the Vietnam Memorial, taking with them a name etching and a memory.

Artists and history buffs wander the hallowed halls of the Smithsonian, conjuring plans to leave their mark on this world. Parks provide a spot for ordinary people to stroll and, unfortunately, for the underprivileged to sleep. Foreign dignitaries are wined and dined, while residents meander along the streets of Georgetown, popping in and out of boutiques.

Sidewalks feel the hustling feet of VIPs. Blades of grass on the Mall are matted from the heavy footsteps of protesters. Mourners gaze at the sea of white headstones at Arlington National Cemetery. The president holds press conferences for a field of reporters amid flashing bulbs, which are in turn broadcast to a nation of viewers.

Comedians poke fun at the town, while presidents sing its glory—and opinions from citizens and foreigners fall everywhere in between.

All these ideas of what the capital is, should be or should not be help define it. Washington, D.C., is the people it represents, the freedom it stands for, the power it holds, the history it preserves and the future it promises.

From the District of Columbia pulses the heartbeat of the nation. And it pounds quickly: Policies are debated, bills are made laws, protests are staged, heroes are honored, lobbyists "do lunch" and scandals sizzle. Government, economic and social issues in the District all sprout from one seed—politics.

Politics had a hand in determining the location of the "federal city." Thomas Jefferson and Virginians wanted the permanent capital of the new nation to be along the Potomac River; to gain this demand they backed Northerner Alexander Hamilton's Assumption Bill. The final decision was conceded to George Washington, who chose what Jefferson termed "that Indian swamp in the wilderness." It's been a hotbed for debate ever since.

The task of forging a visionary capital of monuments, broad avenues and spacious circles fell upon French-born architect Pierre Charles L'Enfant. His grandiose concept featured 100-foot-wide streets and one avenue a mile long. Some thought his plan foolhardy, but Washington endorsed it.

L'Enfant's vision included two focal points: the Capitol and the President's Mansion. He placed the two structures just far enough from each other to reinforce the separation of powers between the legislative and executive branches of government.

1600 Pennsylvania Avenue

The White House has been the scene of many events in American history, making this address a symbol of the vigor of American democracy. Outside, reporters line the avenue that fronts Lafayette Square, clamoring for the latest scoop. Camera lights shine, illuminating the stately white edifice in the background. It seems that everyone wants a glimpse into the oldest public building in Washington.

And it's no wonder. The business associated with our nation's highest office takes place behind these walls. The president conducts meetings that determine national and international policy, signs new legislation, entertains dignitaries and carries out countless other duties.

Every U.S. president since Washington has called this structure home, leaving his stamp on the nation's history. Throughout the mansion, furnishings, portraits and decor are tangible representations both of alliances with other countries and the personal touches of past residents.

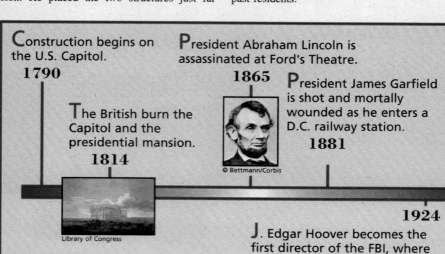

Construction begins on the U.S. Capitol.
1790

The British burn the Capitol and the presidential mansion.
1814

Library of Congress

President Abraham Lincoln is assassinated at Ford's Theatre.
1865

© Bettmann/Corbis

President James Garfield is shot and mortally wounded as he enters a D.C. railway station.
1881

1924

J. Edgar Hoover becomes the first director of the FBI, where he serves for 48 years.

Library of Congress

Washington, D.C. Historical Timeline

The People's House

The nucleus of L'Enfant's design was the U.S. Capitol. Its lofty stature is not only due to its location on Capitol (formerly Jenkins) Hill; governed by tradition, it is here that congressional leaders determine the laws of the land.

Under one of the world's largest domes—the magnificent cast iron Rotunda—members of the House and Senate engage in spirited debates that have caused gavels to split and tempers to flare.

Tradition continues in the number of memorials found in Washington. Monuments and museums honor everyone from war veterans to presidents to postal workers. And among the most impressive is the monument dedicated to Thomas Jefferson.

A Renaissance Man

Architect, diplomat, horticulturist, inventor, musician, political philosopher, scientist, president—Jefferson amassed a long list of achievements during his lifetime. It's fitting that his memorial occupies a prominent site on the southeast bank of the Tidal Basin. The circular domed structure, modeled on the Pantheon in Rome, is an adaptation of the classical style of architecture that Jefferson admired. In spring the memorial is exquisitely framed by clouds of pale pink blossoms adorning the Japanese cherry trees.

A street named for the same man runs the southern length of the National Mall, that swath of green anchored at one end by the U.S. Capitol and at the other by the Washington Monument.

Surrounded by a dizzying assortment of landmarks, the Mall becomes an enormous sardine can during annual Fourth of July festivities. Political demonstrations led by suffragettes and Rev. Dr. Martin Luther King, Jr. also have attracted record crowds. In the 1980s silence fell over the Mall when it was blanketed by the Names Project Quilt, a memorial to those suffering from AIDS.

Whatever the cause, Washington opens its arms. The city that functions as national headquarters for "the land of the free and the home of the brave" honors the worthy, preserves the past, looks to the future and welcomes the visitor.

President John F. Kennedy establishes the Peace Corps.
1961

John F. Kennedy Library

President Bill Clinton faces impeachment hearings by the House of Representatives.
1998

© Dennis Brack/Black Star Publishing/Picture Quest

Martin Luther King Jr. delivers his moving "I Have a Dream" speech on the steps of the Lincoln Memorial.
1963

© The Nobel Foundation

1974
Richard Nixon becomes the first U.S. president to resign from office.

1995
800,000 African-American men gather on the Mall for the Million Man March.

2001
Terrorists hijack American Airlines Flight 77 and crash it into the west face of the Pentagon.

Recreation

While the majority of D.C. visitors focus on sightseeing, an escape from all that concrete and marble offers a welcome respite. Take a break from history and explore the present on one of the area's trails or rivers. After all, you just may find yourself unwinding alongside a local politician.

Plenty of **bicycling** trails wind their way in and around the city. Although bicycles are forbidden on Theodore Roosevelt Island—a memorial and wildlife refuge with about 2 miles of wooded **hiking** trails—the parking lot serves as a starting point for many routes.

For a "moving" monumental view, try the Potomac Tour. Start pedaling at Theodore Roosevelt Island and follow the recreation paths along the shores of the Potomac River, circling East Potomac Park. If they aren't crowded with strollers and joggers, cruise the National Mall's gravel pathways.

The 18-mile Mount Vernon Trail follows the Potomac River's Virginia border from Theodore Roosevelt Island south to Mount Vernon, George Washington's estate. It's rated the most scenic due to sweeping views of the river; quaint houses line the route as you pass through Old Town Alexandria.

Ride the Rail-Trail

Locals refer to abandoned railway paths converted to recreational trails as "rail-trails," and one in particular is not to be missed. Head east on the 4-mile-long Custis Trail to connect with the popular 45-mile Washington & Old Dominion Trail. The WOD, as locals call it, is crowded with bikers, **inline skaters** and **horseback riders.** Shady bridle paths in northern Rock Creek Park also cater to equestrians.

The towpath of the Chesapeake & Ohio (C & O) Canal follows the banks of the Potomac River for 184 miles from Washington, D.C., to Cumberland, Md.; sites along the paved route include Great Falls, the Monocacy River Aqueduct and historic Harpers Ferry. **Campers** also set up tents along the trail.

The Potomac River offers a full range of white water for paddling enthusiasts. **Kayakers** looking for a rush will want to put in just below Great Falls, where there are exciting class II and III runs. On the Maryland side, a hot spot for **canoeists** exists upstream from the Old Anglers Inn. Little Falls, inside the Beltway above Chain Bridge, is a quick but daring class IV rapid.

Leisurely paddling can be found on the Anacostia River, Swains Lock on the C & O Canal and scenic Jug Bay Wetlands Sanctuary on the Patuxent River. The tributaries, harbors and coves of Chesapeake Bay are secluded spots for exploring in a canoe or **sea kayak.** Here **anglers** can cast for bass, flounder and trout.

Boating also is popular on the bay; its largely undeveloped shoreline provides a tranquil view from the deck of a sailboat.

Winter Wonderland

When the snowflakes fall, snap those **ski** racks to the top of your car and head to the slopes. A short drive rewards you with a variety of choices: Some popular resorts are Wisp near McHenry, Md.; Bryce near Basye, Va.; Blue Knob near Claysburg, Pa.; and Timberline near Davis, W.Va.

Twirl a pirouette or take small, wobbly steps with national monuments as a backdrop—**ice skating** is an option at the National Gallery Ice Rink on the Mall, 9th Street and Constitution Avenue.

Fans of almost any professional sport have something to cheer for: In Washington, the Capitals play **hockey;** the Redskins play **football;** the United play **soccer;** and the Wizards play **basketball.** Nearby Baltimore is home to the Orioles, Ravens and Thunder, pros in **baseball, football** and **lacrosse,** respectively.

And collegiate athletics are no less important. The programs of six area universities—American, Georgetown, George Washington and Howard in the District, George Mason University in Virginia and the University of Maryland—rouse fans out of their seats.

Recreational Activities

Throughout the TourBook, you may notice a Recreational Activities heading with bulleted listings of recreation-oriented establishments listed underneath. Similar operations also may be mentioned in Destination City recreation sections. Since normal AAA inspection criteria cannot be applied, these establishments are presented only for information. Age, height and weight restrictions may apply. Reservations often are recommended and sometimes are required. Addresses and/or phone numbers are provided so visitors can contact the attraction for additional information.

Fast Facts

AREA: 67 square miles.

HIGHEST POINT: 410 ft., Tenleytown in N.W. section.

LOWEST POINT: Sea level, Atlantic Ocean.

TIME ZONE(S): Eastern. DST

MINIMUM AGE FOR UNRESTRICTED DRIVER'S LICENSE: 18.

SEAT BELT/CHILD RESTRAINT LAWS: Seat belts required for driver and passengers 16 and older; children ages 8 to 16 must use an approved child restraint or seat belt. Child safety seats are required for children under 8.

HELMETS FOR MOTORCYCLISTS: Required for driver and passenger.

RADAR DETECTORS: Not permitted.

FIREARMS LAWS: Contact the D.C. Gun Control Office, 300 Indiana Ave. N.W., Washington, DC 20001; phone (202) 727-4275.

HOLIDAYS: Jan. 1; Martin Luther King Jr. Day, Jan. (3rd Mon.); Washington's Birthday, Feb. (3rd Mon.); Memorial Day; July 4; Labor Day; Columbus Day, Oct. (2nd Mon.); Veterans Day, Nov. 11; Thanksgiving; Dec. 25.

INFORMATION CENTERS: Kiosks at the Ellipse, Jefferson Memorial, Lafayette Park, Lincoln Memorial, National Gallery of Art, Washington

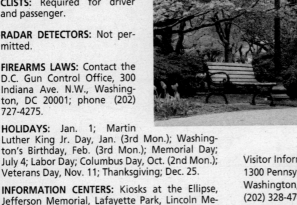

Monument and the Smithsonian Museums of Air and Space, American History and Natural History dispense information about places and events in the city. For information about places to visit, concerts, art shows, recreation and other activities, contact The Washington, D.C., Convention and Visitors Association, (202) 789-7000; the National Capital Park Service, (202) 619-7275; and the Visitor Information Center, (202) 328-4748 or (866) 324-7386.

FURTHER INFORMATION FOR VISITORS:

D.C. Committee to Promote Washington
901 7th St. N.W., 4th floor
Washington, DC 20001
(202) 789-7000

National Park Service
Public Information Office
U.S. Department of the Interior
1100 Ohio Dr. S.W.
Washington, DC 20242
(202) 619-7222

Smithsonian Information Center
Smithsonian Institution
P.O. Box 37012
Washington, DC 20013-7012
(202) 633-1000
or TTY (202) 357-1729

Visitor Information Center
1300 Pennsylvania Ave. N.W.
Washington, DC 20005
(202) 328-4748
(866) 324-7386

District of Columbia Temperature Averages Maximum/Minimum
From the records of the National Weather Service

	JAN	FEB	MAR	APR	MAY	JUNE	JULY	AUG	SEPT	OCT	NOV	DEC
Washington	44/30	46/29	54/36	66/46	76/56	83/65	87/69	85/68	79/61	68/50	57/39	46/31

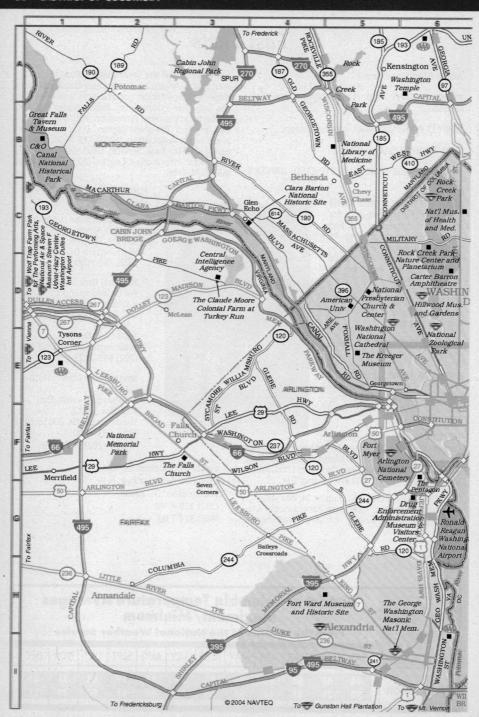

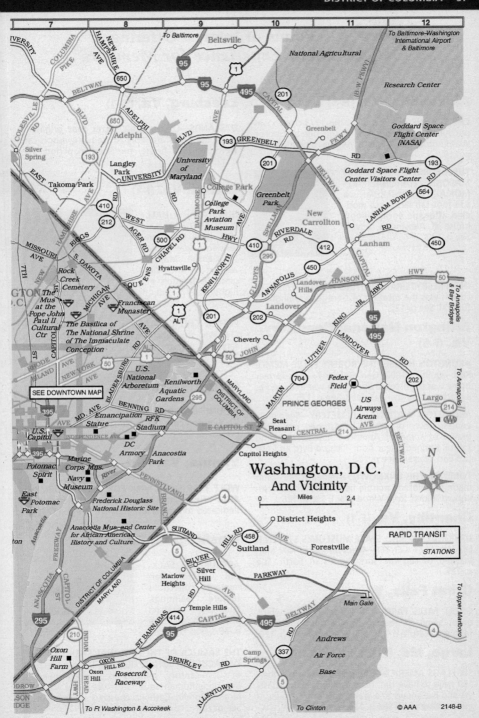

Washington, D.C.
And Vicinity

Points of Interest Offering A
Great Experience for Members®

Alexandria, Va. (H-5)

CHRIST CHURCH—Pew 60 of this 1773 church was purchased for 36 pounds, 10 shillings by George Washington, who was a regular attendee. See p. 119.

THE GEORGE WASHINGTON MASONIC NATIONAL MEMORIAL—The memorial is a 333-foot-tall landmark modeled after the ancient lighthouse at Alexandria, Egypt. See p. 120.

OLD PRESBYTERIAN MEETING HOUSE—This 1774 church was the location of George Washington's funeral. See p. 120.

Arlington National Cemetery, Va. (F-5)

ARLINGTON HOUSE, THE ROBERT E. LEE MEMORIAL—Built in 1802, Gen. Robert E. Lee's former home was confiscated during the war and used as a place to bury the war dead. See p. 125.

ARLINGTON NATIONAL CEMETERY—Seemingly endless rows of white headstones mark the graves of some of America's heroes, including John F. Kennedy, Rear Adm. Richard Byrd and Justice Earl Warren. See p. 125.

TOMB OF THE UNKNOWNS—Beneath the tomb made of Colorado marble lies the body of an unknown soldier from World War I. See p. 126.

Chantilly, Va. (F-1)

NATIONAL AIR AND SPACE MUSEUM'S STEVEN F. UDVAR-HAZY CENTER—Discover here how man learned to slip the surly bonds of Earth. See p. 127.

Great Falls, Va. (C-1)

GREAT FALLS PARK—The Potomac River, which drops some 77 feet in thunderous rapids and falls, is a feature of this 800-acre park. See p. 128.

Largo, Md. (E-12)

SIX FLAGS AMERICA—The park offers more than 100 ways to have fun, from thrilling rolling coasters and live shows to a water park with a million-gallon wave pool. See p. 116.

Leesburg, Va. (D-1)

OATLANDS—Of the 3,400 acres that originally made up this estate, only 261 remain; visitors can view the 1804 house, furnished in period. See p. 129.

Lorton, Va. (I-1)

GUNSTON HALL PLANTATION—This 1755 brick Georgian residence was home to George Mason, author of the Virginia Declaration of Rights of 1776 and one of the framers of the U.S. Constitution. See p. 129.

POHICK CHURCH—Used as a stable during the Civil War, this church, where George Washington served as a vestryman for 23 years, was restored 1902-17. See p. 129.

Mount Vernon, Va. (I-6)

MOUNT VERNON—The final home of George Washington contains personal effects of our first president. See p. 131.

Vienna, Va. (E-1)

WOLF TRAP FARM PARK FOR THE PERFORMING ARTS—This is the country's only national park dedicated to the performing arts. See p. 132.

Washington, D.C.

ARTHUR M. SACKLER GALLERY—Permanent collections feature paintings, sculpture, ceramics and Asian art. See p. 76.

THE BASILICA OF THE NATIONAL SHRINE OF THE IMMACULATE CONCEPTION—A large collection of 20th-century mosaics is housed in this Byzantine-Romanesque structure, one of the largest Roman Catholic churches in the world. See p. 76.

CORCORAN GALLERY OF ART— American paintings, sculpture and drawings from the 18th century are on display. Also featured are pottery and tapestries as well as contemporary art. See p. 77.

DEPARTMENT OF STATE—Part of the Executive Branch, the agency is responsible for formulating and implementing U.S. foreign policy. See p. 78.

EXPLORERS HALL, NATIONAL GEOGRAPHIC SOCIETY—Interactive geographic science exhibits depict expeditions sponsored by National Geographic. See p. 78.

FORD'S THEATRE NATIONAL HISTORIC SITE—Restored to its 1860s appearance, this is where Abraham Lincoln was fatally shot by John Wilkes Booth on April 14, 1865. See p. 79.

FRANCISCAN MONASTERY—Called Mount St. Sepulchre, the monastery features replicas of Holy Land shrines. See p. 79.

FRANKLIN DELANO ROOSEVELT MEMORIAL—Four outdoor rooms depict the 12 years that FDR served as president. See p. 79.

FREER GALLERY OF ART—The Freer features calligraphy and porcelain as well as notable collections of American paintings, Japanese art and Korean ceramics. See p. 80.

HILLWOOD MUSEUM AND GARDENS—Cereal heiress and art connoisseur Marjorie Merriweather Post bought and expanded this mansion to house her extensive collection of decorative and fine art objects, which includes ornate Fabergé Easter eggs. See p. 80.

HIRSHHORN MUSEUM AND SCULPTURE GARDEN—American and European art spanning the 19th century to the present encompasses works by Georgia O'Keeffe, Jackson Pollock and others. See p. 80.

INTERNATIONAL SPY MUSEUM—You won't encounter James Bond or Maxwell Smart here, but you'll see gadgets as fantastic as theirs. See p. 80.

THE JOHN F. KENNEDY CENTER FOR THE PERFORMING ARTS—American and international music, drama, dance and film are presented in the nation's memorial to President Kennedy. See p. 81.

KOREAN WAR VETERANS MEMORIAL—Erected in gratitude to those 1.5 million American personnel who served in Korea 1950-53, the memorial features statues of patrolling soldiers. See p. 81.

LIBRARY OF CONGRESS—Thomas Jefferson's personal collection of 6,000 volumes formed the basis of the national library, founded in 1800. See p. 82.

LINCOLN MEMORIAL—This inspiring marble structure features 36 columns and a colossal seated statue of Abraham Lincoln. See p. 82.

THE MUSEUMS AT THE POPE JOHN PAUL II CULTURAL CENTER—Explore a 2,000-year-old religion in this thoroughly contemporary building. See p. 83.

NATIONAL AIR AND SPACE MUSEUM—The museum is devoted to the history and development of air and space technology. See p. 83.

NATIONAL GALLERY OF ART—The National Gallery's East and West buildings offer an outstanding collection of painting and sculpture, from old masters to contemporary artists. See p. 85.

NATIONAL MUSEUM OF AFRICAN ART—Bronze, wood, ivory and ceramic objects depict the traditional arts of Africa. See p. 86.

NATIONAL MUSEUM OF AMERICAN HISTORY, BEHRING CENTER—Displays at this museum focus on the scientific, cultural, technological and political development of the United States. See p. 86.

NATIONAL MUSEUM OF THE AMERICAN INDIAN—Native American design principles play an integral role in the Smithsonian's newest museum, an exhibition space for Indian arts, history and material culture. See p. 88.

NATIONAL MUSEUM OF NATURAL HISTORY—The multitude of exhibits at this ever-popular museum highlight natural history and human cultures. See p. 88.

NATIONAL PORTRAIT GALLERY—The gallery is devoted to portraiture of Americans who made significant contributions to the nation. See p. 88.

NATIONAL POSTAL MUSEUM—Hands-on exhibits portray the history and development of our nation's mail service. See p. 88.

NATIONAL WORLD WAR II MEMORIAL—This memorial salutes a generation of Americans who fought and helped win the most devastating conflict in world history. See p. 89.

NATIONAL ZOOLOGICAL PARK—Several thousand exotic animals, including Sumatran tigers, lowland gorillas and Komodo dragons, call this 163-acre biological park home. See p. 89.

ORGANIZATION OF AMERICAN STATES BUILDING—The headquarters of the general secretariat of the Organization of American States (OAS) is one of the loveliest buildings in the capital. See p. 90.

POTOMAC PARK—Exceptionally beautiful in spring when the cherry trees are in bloom, this area along the Tidal Basin has facilities for outdoor recreation. See p. 90.

ROCK CREEK PARK—Acres of natural woodland in the middle of the city encompass bridle paths, trails and athletic facilities. See p. 91.

ST. MATTHEW'S CATHEDRAL—Built in 1840 in the Renaissance style, the church features an inscription in marble commemorating the funeral of John F. Kennedy. See p. 91.

CATHEDRAL OF
ST. MATTHEW
THE APOSTLE

SMITHSONIAN AMERICAN ART MUSEUM—Exhibits include the oldest national art collection, paintings, sculptures, portraits and photographs. See p. 92.

THE SMITHSONIAN INSTITUTION—Sixteen Washington museums and galleries comprise this complex, founded for the increase and diffusion of knowledge. See p. 92.

SUPREME COURT BUILDING—The unanimous opinion is that the interior of this 1935 building is stunning. See p. 93.

THOMAS JEFFERSON MEMORIAL—Supported by Ionic columns, this graceful, circular domed structure features panels inscribed with significant Jefferson writings as well as a large statue of the president. See p. 94.

UNITED STATES CAPITOL—One of the nation's most familiar landmarks, this imposing marble building contains about 550 rooms. See p. 94.

UNITED STATES HOLOCAUST MEMORIAL MUSEUM—The tragedy of the Holocaust is depicted through artifacts, photographs, films and oral histories. See p. 94.

U.S. BOTANIC GARDEN—Founded in 1820, this facility is dedicated to showcasing the aesthetic, cultural, economic, therapeutic and ecological importance of plants. See p. 95.

VIETNAM VETERANS MEMORIAL—A life-size statue of three servicemen stands near the V-shaped black granite walls that honor the men and women who served in the U.S. Armed Forces in Vietnam. See p. 96.

VOICE OF AMERICA—Depression-era Ben Shahn murals are featured along with a film and broadcast activities in the newsroom of a worldwide radio and television service that broadcasts in 53 languages. See p. 96.

WASHINGTON MONUMENT—Honoring our first president, this marble obelisk stands 555 feet from base to tip. It rises from the center of a knoll on the National Mall, surrounded by 50 American flags. See p. 96.

WASHINGTON NATIONAL CATHEDRAL—A beautiful example of Gothic architecture, this cathedral was completed in 1990 after 83 years of construction. Statues, stained-glass windows, gardens and a carillon are among its most noteworthy features. See p. 96.

WHITE HOUSE—The executive mansion has been the home of every U.S. president except George Washington. Antiques, presidential portraits and rich decorative accents all contribute to the preservation of American history. See p. 96.

Drive

See

Stay

Play

DO IT ALL WITH AAA!

Vacation planning, travel and destination information, AAA's famous maps and TripTiks®, TourBook® guides, air, cruise, tour, rail, and hotel reservations, attraction tickets and more! It's all part of the service for AAA members! Choose whatever method fits you best — online, in person, or by phone — to enjoy helpful services like these:

- Online TourBook® guide featuring hotel information AAA Diamond ratings.
- Internet TripTik® itinerary planner rated No. 1 by the *Wall Street Journal.*
- Travel accessories such as luggage, travel guides, car games for the kids, and more.

- Ready-to-go, 2- to 5-day AAA Drive Trips vacation* for major U.S. and Canadian travel destinations.
- Flights, cruises and tours and expert advice from AAA Travel professionals.
- AAA Travel money options including no fee Travelers Cheques.
- AAA Credit Cards featuring up to a 5% gas rebate.

With AAA's expert travel information and pricing power behind you, you'll enjoy better quality and value than you'll find anywhere else. And, with AAA's extensive range of products and services, you'll enjoy complete, hassle-free vacation planning from a single source you know and trust.

Before your next vacation, visit aaa.com or your nearest AAA office. Discover the many ways AAA can help you drive more, see more, stay more and play more!

TRAVEL WITH SOMEONE YOU TRUST®

aaa.com

*PRODUCTS AND SERVICES AVAILABLE THROUGH PARTICIPATING AAA AND CAA CLUBS.

Washington

City Population: 572,059   Elevation: 25 ft.

Popular Spots

Library of Congress................(see p. 82)
The Smithsonian Institution.........(see p. 92)
United States Capitol................(see p. 94)

By Car

Although it does not enter Washington itself, the Capital Beltway (I-495) encircles the city and interchanges with all major approach routes. The eastern portion is part of I-95, a major artery linking Baltimore to the north and Richmond, Va., to the south. US 1 and the Gladys Spellman Parkway (also called the Baltimore-Washington Parkway or SR 295) approach Washington from the north; US 50, SR 4 and SR 5 come from eastern and southern Maryland. Leading into the city from the south, via Alexandria and Arlington, Va., are US 1 and I-395.

The remainder of the beltway is intersected by US 29 from the Baltimore area and I-270, which links the metropolitan area with transcontinental I-70 at Frederick, Md. Interchanging with the Virginia part of I-495 are I-66 and US 50, both of which cross the Piedmont from the west and converge at the Theodore Roosevelt Bridge.

Air Travel

Visitors arriving by plane can land at Ronald Reagan Washington National Airport, Washington Dulles International Airport or Baltimore-Washington International Airport (BWI). Frequent transportation services into town are available from all three airports.

Just across the Potomac River from the District is Ronald Reagan Washington National Airport, the most centrally located of the three major facilities serving the Washington area. To get to downtown D.C. from terminal A, B or C, follow the exit signs and take the George Washington Memorial Parkway north to the 14th Street Bridge exit (officially, the Arland D. Williams Jr. Memorial Bridge northbound and the George Mason Bridge southbound). Once across the bridge, you will be on 14th Street going north, which runs just west of the Smithsonian museums on the National Mall. To reach Arlington, Alexandria or other nearby Virginia

Union Station / © R. Krubner / Robertstock

suburbs, take the I-395 South exit off the parkway (just past the 14th Street Bridge exit).

Taxi fare from Ronald Reagan Washington National Airport into Washington averages about $12 but depends on the length of the trip. Metrobus and Metrorail both serve the airport as well. Non-rush hour fares are $1.25 and $1.35, respectively; Metrorail fares are higher during rush hours, depending upon the destination.

Washington Dulles International Airport is about 26 miles west of downtown Washington via I-66 and the Dulles Access Road (SR 267), just west of Herndon, Va. To reach downtown Washington, exit the airport terminal and take the Dulles Access Road east to I-66; continue east on I-66, which enters the District via the Theodore Roosevelt Bridge. Cross the bridge and you will be on Constitution Avenue eastbound. A taxi ride into downtown from Dulles costs about $45.

Washington Flyer offers transportation between Ronald Reagan Washington National Airport, Dulles International Airport and major hotels in downtown D.C. Buses depart National for Dulles on the hour 6 a.m.-11 p.m. Mon.-Fri. The Sat.-Sun. and holiday schedule is every 2 hours 6 a.m.-2 p.m.

Getting There — starting on this page

Getting Around — starting on p. 64

What To See — starting on p. 75

What To Do — starting on p. 97

Where To Stay — starting on p. 419

Where To Dine — starting on p. 455

and on the hour 2-11 p.m. From Dulles to Ronald Reagan Washington National Airport, the schedule is on the hour 5 a.m.-11 p.m. Mon.-Fri.; Sat.-Sun. and holidays, every 2 hours 5 a.m.-1 p.m. and on the hour 1-11 p.m. Inter-airport services is $16 one way, $26 round trip (MC, VI).

Washington Flyer service is available from Dulles to the West Falls Church Metro station. Buses depart every half-hour; one-way fare $8, round trip $14. For additional Washington Flyer schedule and fare information phone (703) 685-1400 or (888) 927-4359.

Baltimore-Washington International Airport is about 30 miles northeast of the city via the Gladys Spellman Parkway (SR 295). From the airport terminal area, follow the exit signs to SR 295, then take the parkway west toward the Washington area. You can either exit east or west onto the Beltway or continue into the city; the parkway ends at New York Avenue just before the District line.

Taxi service from Baltimore-Washington International Airport costs about $45, although fares depend upon the zone serviced. Rail transportation to the airport is available from Union Station in Washington. Super Shuttle provides van service from the Washington metro area to Baltimore-Washington International, Ronald Reagan Washington National and Dulles International airports, with 24-hour advance reservations recommended; phone (800) 258-3826.

Car rental agencies in Washington are numerous; most have conveniently located offices in the city and nearby Maryland and Virginia suburbs. Reservations are recommended and should be made in advance of your arrival; your local AAA/CAA club can provide this assistance or additional information.

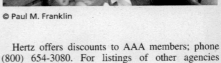

© Paul M. Franklin

Hertz offers discounts to AAA members; phone (800) 654-3080. For listings of other agencies check the telephone directory.

Rail Service

After falling into an advanced state of disrepair in the early 1980s, Union Station was completely renovated (with three levels of upscale shopping added) and reopened in 1988. Trains pull into the Train Concourse at 1st Street and Massachusetts Avenue N.E. at all hours; phone (202) 906-3000. Amtrak's Metroliner travels to New York daily in about 3 hours. Trains depart for Baltimore-Washington International Airport every hour from 7:20 a.m. to 10:10 p.m. For trains that run from Baltimore-Washington International Airport, phone (800) 872-7245 for reservations.

Buses

The Greyhound Lines Inc. bus terminal is at 1st and L streets N.E.; phone (800) 231-2222.

Getting Around

Street System

Pierre L'Enfant's plan for the capital did not take into account the demands of modern traffic. Although streets are laid out in a basic grid pattern divided into four quadrants, there are several confusing traffic circles and a number of one-way streets. An easy-to-read street map will come in handy for those unfamiliar with the city.

In the central part of the District, streets running north-south are numbered; those running east-west are designated by letters (with the exception of J, X, Y and Z). This general pattern is crisscrossed in both directions by diagonal avenues named after states. Where avenues intersect there are traffic circles and rectangular parks or squares.

North, East and South Capitol streets and the National Mall divide the diamond-shaped District of Columbia into quadrants; the Capitol is the central starting point for the street numbering system. The quadrant initials—N.W., N.E., S.W. and S.E.—are an integral part of any Washington address; they determine which of four possible locations is correct. Southwest is by far the smallest, encompassing a few government buildings, the Tidal Basin, the Maine Avenue waterfront along the Washington Channel and Fort Lesley J. McNair, intended by

L'Enfant to be the capital's chief fortification and a major 19th-century U.S. weapons arsenal.

Most of Washington's tourist attractions and its wealthiest neighborhoods are concentrated in the northwest quadrant, along with American, Georgetown, George Washington and Howard universities, the University of the District of Columbia, Rock Creek Park and Walter Reed Army Medical Center. Most of Northeast and Southeast are residential, as is the upper part of Northwest.

North of W Street, east-west streets are assigned two-syllable alphabetical names (Belmont, Quincy, Randolph), then three-syllable names (Buchanan, Hamilton, Underwood). Above Whittier Street in upper Northwest, alphabetical names shift to trees and plants with two- (Aspen), three- (Butternut) or four-syllable (Geranium) names. At this point the District ends and Maryland begins, which no doubt delighted planners.

Some illogical aspects of the city street system confuse even residents. Pennsylvania Avenue, for example, enters southeast Washington from suburban Maryland; is interrupted at Independence Avenue S.E. by the Capitol grounds; picks up again at 1st Street N.W.; is interrupted at 15th Street by the Ellipse; picks up again around the corner at the intersection of 15th Street and New York Avenue N.W.; and continues west past the White House into Georgetown, where it turns into M Street.

Traveling east of the Capitol on Pennsylvania can be equally confusing; once you cross 15th Street, you are on New York Avenue. And 17th

National World War II Memorial / © Paul M. Franklin

The Informed Traveler

Whom To Call

Emergency: 911
Police (non-emergency): (202) 727-1010
Time: (202) 844-2525 or (202) 844-1212
Temperature: (202) 936-1212
Hospitals: George Washington University, (202) 715-4000; Howard University, (202) 865-6100; MedStar-Georgetown Medical Center, (202) 444-3000; Providence, (202) 269-7000; Sibley Memorial, (202) 537-4000; Washington Hospital Center, (202) 877-7000.

Where To Look

Newspapers
The major newspapers, both distributed in the morning, are *The Washington Post* and the *Washington Times.* The weekly *Washington Afro-American* is available at newsstands, as are various smaller dailies and weeklies. Events are listed in the *City Paper,* a free weekly, and the daily *Style* or *Friday Weekend* sections of the *Post.*

Radio
Washington radio station WTOP (1500 AM) is an all-news/weather station; WAMU (88.5 FM) is a member of National Public Radio.

Visitor Information
Visitor Information Center: Ronald Reagan Building, 1300 Pennsylvania Ave. N.W., Washington, DC 20005; phone (202) 328-4748 or (866) 324-7386.
The center has brochures, city guides, interactive computers, an introductory video and staff to answer questions. Those over age 15 must have ID to enter the building. Open Mon.-Fri. 8:30-5:30, Sat. 9-4, Mar. 15-Labor Day; Mon.-Fri. 9-4:30, rest of year.
Washington, D.C. Convention and Visitors Association: 901 7th St. N.W., 4th floor, Washington, DC 20001; phone (202) 789-7000.
The association publishes a quarterly calendar of events and the *African-American Heritage and Multicultural Guide,* a brochure to help visitors explore the city's black heritage. Information is available by mail only.

What To Pack

Summers are warm and humid, and during spells of sweltering weather, high temperatures can hover between 95 and 100, accompanied by steamy humidity. Washingtonians anticipate the occasional brief burst of refreshing weather in July and August—sunny, breezy afternoons around 80 degrees, with low humidity and blue skies.

Washington winters can be raw, with a few nights plunging into the single digits and blustery days when the thermometer fails to rise above freezing. Some winters have

Ronald Reagan Washington National Airport
© J. Neubauer/Robertstock

practically no snow, while others can deal out several snowfalls and the occasional near blizzard. The District also is susceptible to ice storms. For winter driving, make sure your vehicle is equipped with snow tires.

Spring and fall are short but exceedingly pleasant, with daytime highs in the 60s and 70s and nighttime lows in the 40s and 50s. April, May and October are the nicest months of the year, with sunny days and low humidity. *For additional information see temperature chart p. 55.*

Casual clothes are fine for sightseeing. Comfortable walking shoes are essential. Sunglasses and a hat come in handy in summer, a hat and gloves in winter. A jacket and tie may be required or advised at some of the finer restaurants.

Sales Tax: The District of Columbia's sales tax is 5.75 percent. There is a hotel tax of 14.5 percent and a 10 percent food and beverage tax. The sales tax in neighboring Maryland is 5 percent, in Virginia 4.5 percent; lodging taxes vary by county.

Destination Washington, D.C.

A culturally diverse blend of young and old, rich and poor—the District of Columbia is a true representation of the United States.

A merica's past was charted in the hallowed halls of the same buildings that camera-laden tourists spend vacations visiting. Elegant memorials recall the deeds of our nation's founding fathers. And the country's treasures can be seen in museums and galleries lining the expanse of green known as the Mall.

© Ann Purcell/Virginia Tourism Corporation

Marine Corps War Memorial, Arlington National Cemetery, Va.
This 78-foot-high memorial is dedicated to Marines who have given their lives for their country since 1775. (See listing page 125)

© Stephanie Maze
Corbis

National Zoological Park, Washington, D.C.
A toothy Tyrannosaurus rex looms in the background as visitors examine an elephant tusk at this 163-acre park. (See listing page 89)

See
Downtown
map page 68

P laces included in this AAA Destination City:

Thomas Jefferson Memorial, Washington, D.C.
This bronze statue of our third president towers over visitors to his memorial, which is based on the design for his home at Monticello. (See listing page 94)

© James P. Blair / Corbis

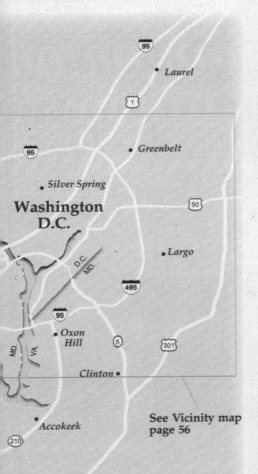

95

Laurel

1

95

Greenbelt

Silver Spring

Washington D.C.

50

D.C.
MD.

Largo

495

95

Oxon Hill

5

301

MD.

VA.

Clinton

Accokeek

210

301

See Vicinity map page 56

National Air and Space Museum, Washington, D.C.
These World War II planes are a small sample of the aircraft displayed in this hangarlike Smithsonian facility. (See listing page 83)

© J. Neubauer / Robertstock

The Smithsonian Institution Castle, Washington, D.C.
The administrative home of 16 museums and galleries, the "Castle" has an information center offering an orientation to D.C. attractions. (See listing page 92)

© T. Dietrich / Robertstock

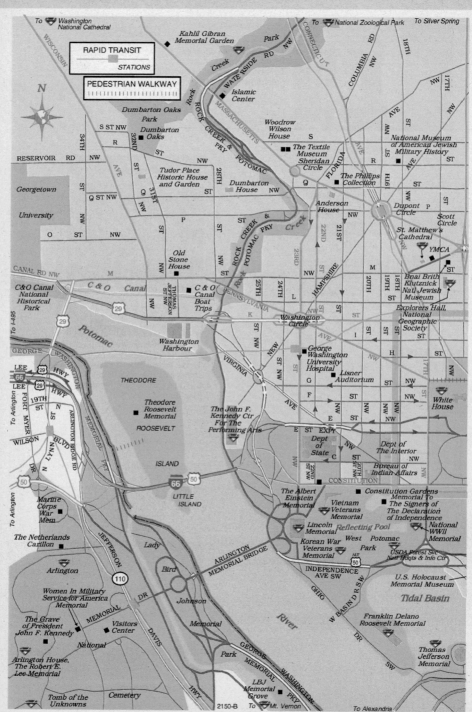

To Washington National Cathedral
To National Zoological Park
To Silver Spring

RAPID TRANSIT
STATIONS
PEDESTRIAN WALKWAY

N

Kahlil Gibran Memorial Garden

Rock Creek Park

WATERSIDE DR NW

CONNECTICUT RD

COLUMBIA RD

18TH
17TH
NW
AVE

Islamic Center

WISCONSIN

MASSACHUSETTS

ROCK CREEK & POTOMAC PKY

Woodrow Wilson House

National Museum of American Jewish Military History

Dumbarton Oaks Park

Dumbarton Oaks

S ST NW

34TH
32ND
R
ST
NW

The Textile Museum
Sheridan Circle

FLORIDA

AVE

R

19TH

RESERVOIR RD NW

Tudor Place Historic House and Garden

28TH

31ST
ST
NW

Q ST NW

Dumbarton House NW

The Phillips Collection

NW
ST

Georgetown University

ST
NW

P

ST

NW

ROCK CREEK & POTOMAC PKY

Creek

Anderson House
NW

22ND

21ST

Dupont Circle

Scott Circle

St. Matthew's Cathedral

YMCA

O ST NW

23RD

NW

M

20TH
19TH
18TH

Bnai Brith Klutznick Natl Jewish Museum

CANAL RD NW

Old Stone House

M

NW

HAMPSHIRE

NW

ST

C&O Canal National Historical Park

C & O Canal

THOMAS JEFFERSON ST NW

C & O Canal Boat Trips

PENNSYLVANIA

25TH
24TH

L

ST

Explorers Hall, National Geographic Society

To I-495

29

29

Potomac

Washington Harbour

VIRGINIA

Washington Circle

NEW YORK ST NW

AVE

K

I

ST

H
ST

White House

GEORGE

LEE HWY

66

29

THEODORE

ROOSEVELT

ISLAND

George Washington University Hospital

Lisner Auditorium

G
ST

F
ST

NW

NW

NW

17TH

NW

ST

LEE HWY

29

FORT MYER

19TH
N
ST

WILSON

ARLINGTON BLVD

MEMORIAL PKY

Theodore Roosevelt Memorial

The John F. Kennedy Ctr For The Performing Arts

E ST EXPY

Dept of State

NW

22ND ST NW

Dept of The Interior

NW

Bureau of Indian Affairs

50

ARLINGTON BRIDGE RD

US 50

66

50

LITTLE ISLAND

CONSTITUTION

20TH ST NW

The Albert Einstein Memorial

Constitution Gardens

Constitution Gardens Memorial To The Signers of The Declaration of Independence

To Arlington

Marine Corps War Mem

JEFFERSON

Lady

Vietnam Veterans Memorial

Lincoln Memorial

Reflecting Pool

West Potomac Park

National WWII Memorial

The Netherlands Carillon

Arlington

MEMORIAL DR

Bird

ARLINGTON MEMORIAL BRIDGE

Korean War Veterans Memorial

INDEPENDENCE AVE SW

ALT 50

USDA Forest Svc Natl Hdqts & Info Ctr

U.S. Holocaust Memorial Museum

Women In Military Service for America Memorial

110

Johnson

OHIO

W BASIN DR SW

Tidal Basin

The Grave of President John F. Kennedy

DAVIS

Memorial

River

Franklin Delano Roosevelt Memorial

Visitors Center

National

Arlington House, The Robert E. Lee Memorial

Park

GEORGE WASHINGTON MEMORIAL PKY

Thomas Jefferson Memorial

Tomb of the Unknowns

Cemetery

2150-B

LBJ Memorial Grove

To Mt. Vernon

To Alexandria

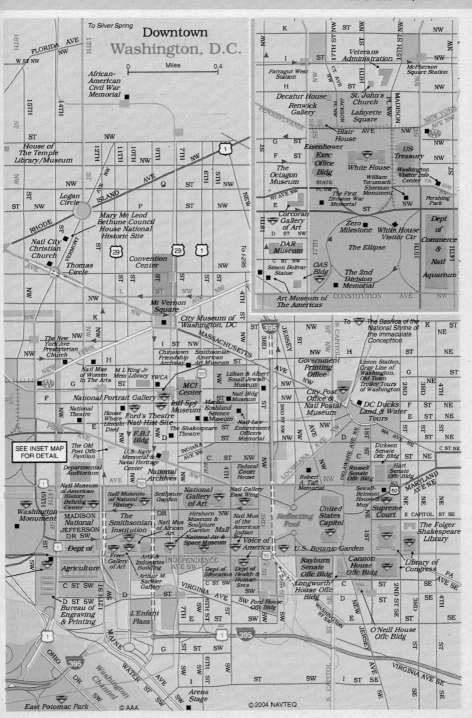

Downtown
Washington, D.C.

To Silver Spring

African-American Civil War Memorial

House of The Temple Library/Museum

Logan Circle

Natl City Christian Church

Thomas Circle

Mary Mc Leod Bethune Council House National Historic Site

Convention Center

Mt Vernon Square

City Museum of Washington, DC

The New York Ave Presbyterian Church

Chinatown Friendship Archway

Smithsonian American Art Museum

Natl Mus of Women In The Arts

M L King Jr Mem Library

YWCA

Lillian & Albert Small Jewish Museum

National Portrait Gallery

MCI Center

Intl Spy Museum

Natl Bldg Museum

National Theatre

House Where Lincoln Died

Ford's Theatre Natl Hist Site

The Shakespeare Theatre

Marian Koshland Science Museum

Natl Law Enforcement Officers Memorial

The Old Post Offc Pavilion

F.B.I. Bldg

Departmental Auditorium

SEE INSET MAP FOR DETAIL

U.S. Navy Memorial & Naval Heritage Center

National Archives

Federal Court House

Robert A. Taft Memorial

Natl Museum of American History, Behring Center

Sculpture Garden

National Gallery of Art

Natl Gallery East Wing

United States Capitol

Washington Monument

MADISON JEFFERSON DR SW

Natl Museum of Natural History

The Smithsonian Institution

Hirshorn Museum & Sculpture Garden

Natl Mus of African Art

Natl Air & Space Museum

Natl Mus of the American Indian

Voice of America

U.S. Botanic Garden

Reflecting Pool

Supreme Court

The Folger Shakespeare Library

Dept of Agriculture

Freer Gallery of Art

Arts & Industries Building

Arthur M. Sackler Gallery

INDEPENDENCE AVE SW

Dept of Education

Dept of Health & Human Svcs

Rayburn Senate Offc Bldg

Cannon House Offc Bldg

Library of Congress

Bureau of Engraving & Printing

L'Enfant Plaza

VIRGINIA AVE

SW Ford House Offc Bldg

Longworth House Offc Bldg

O'Neill House Offc Bldg

East Potomac Park

Washington Channel

Arena Stage

© 2004 NAVTEQ

To I-295

To I-295

Inset: Downtown Washington, D.C.

Veterans Administration

McPherson Square Station

Farragut West Station

Decatur House

Renwick Gallery

St. John's Church

Lafayette Square

Blair House

Eisenhower Exec Office Bldg

White House

Washington Visitor Info Center

The Octagon Museum

STATE

William Tecumseh Sherman Monument

US Treasury

Corcoran Gallery of Art

The First Division War Memorial

Zero Milestone

White House Visitor Ctr

Pershing Park

Dept of Commerce & Natl Aquarium

DAR Museum

The Ellipse

Simon Bolivar Statue

OAS Bldg

The 2nd Division Memorial

Art Museum of The Americas

To The Basilica of the National Shrine of the Immaculate Conception

Government Printing Office

Union Station, Gray Line of Washington, Old Town Trolley Tours of Washington

City Post Office & Natl Postal Museum

DC Ducks Land & Water Tours

Dirksen Senate Offc Bldg

Russell Senate Offc Bldg

Hart Senate Offc Bldg

Sewall-Belmont House & Mus

Metro Stops Closest to Points of Interest

African-American Civil War Museum ...... U St.-Cardozo Station

The Albert Einstein Memorial .... Foggy Bottom-GWU

Anacostia Museum and Center for African American History and Culture .... Anacostia

Anacostia Park .... Anacostia

Anderson House .... Dupont Circle

Arthur M. Sackler Gallery .... Smithsonian

Arts and Industries Building .... Smithsonian

The Basilica of the National Shrine of the Immaculate Conception .... Brookland-CUA

Bureau of Engraving and Printing .... Smithsonian

Chinatown Friendship Archway . Gallery Place-Chinatown

City Museum of Washington, D.C. .... Gallery Place-Chinatown

Constitution Gardens .... Foggy Bottom-GWU

Corcoran Gallery of Art .... Farragut North or West

DAR Museum .... Farragut North or West

Decatur House .... Farragut North or West

Department of Agriculture .... Smithsonian

Department of State .... Foggy Bottom-GWU

Department of the Interior Museum ...... Farragut West

Dumbarton House .... Dupont Circle

Emancipation Statue .... Eastern Market

Explorers Hall, National Geographic Society ..... Farragut North or West

Folger Shakespeare Library .... Capitol South or Union Station

Ford's Theatre .... Metro Center

Franciscan Monastery .... Brookland-CUA

Franklin Delano Roosevelt Memorial .... Smithsonian

Freer Gallery of Art .... Smithsonian

Hillwood Museum and Gardens .... Van Ness-UDC

Hirshhorn Museum and Sculpture Garden .. L'Enfant Plaza

House of the Temple Library/Museum .... Dupont Circle

International Spy Museum ..... Gallery Place-Chinatown

Islamic Center .... Dupont Circle

J. Edgar Hoover F.B.I. Building .... Metro Center

The John F. Kennedy Center for the Performing Arts .... Foggy Bottom-GWU

Kenilworth Aquatic Gardens .... Deanwood

Korean War Veterans Memorial .... Foggy Bottom-GWU

Lafayette Square .... Farragut West

Library of Congress .... Capitol South

Lincoln Memorial .... Foggy Bottom-GWU

Marian Koshland Science Museum ... Judiciary Square or Gallery Place-Chinatown

Marine Corps Museum ..... Navy Yard or Eastern Market

MCI Center .... Gallery Place-Chinatown

The Museums at the Pope John Paul II Cultural Center .... Brookland-CUA

National Air and Space Museum .... L'Enfant Plaza

National Aquarium .... Federal Triangle

National Archives .... Archives-Navy Memorial

National Building Museum .... Judiciary Square

National City Christian Church .... McPherson Square

National Gallery of Art .... Archives-Navy Memorial or Judiciary Square

National Law Enforcement Officers Memorial ... Judiciary Square

The National Mall .Foggy Bottom-GWU, Federal Triangle, Smithsonian, L'Enfant Plaza, Archives-Navy Memorial, Federal Center or Capitol South

National Museum of African Art .... Smithsonian

National Museum of American History, Behring Center .... : .... Federal Triangle or Smithsonian

National Museum of the American Indian . L'Enfant Plaza or Federal Center SW

National Museum of American Jewish Military History .... Dupont Circle

National Museum of Health and Medicine .. Takoma Park or Silver Spring

National Museum of Natural History . Federal Triangle or Smithsonian

National Museum of Women in the Arts ... Metro Center

National Portrait Gallery .... Gallery Place-Chinatown

National Postal Museum .... Union Station

National World War II Memorial .... Smithsonian

National Zoological Park .Woodley Park-Zoo or Cleveland Park

The Navy Museum .... Eastern Market or Navy Yard

The New York Avenue Presbyterian Church Metro Center or McPherson Square

The Octagon .... Farragut North or West

The Old Post Office Pavilion .... Federal Triangle

Old Stone House .... Foggy Bottom-GWU

Organization of American States Building . Farragut West or North

The Phillips Collection .... Dupont Circle

Renwick Gallery .... Farragut West

Rock Creek Cemetery .... Fort Totten

St. John's Church .... McPherson Square

St. Matthew's Cathedral . Dupont Circle or Farragut North

Senate and House Office Buildings ...... Capitol South or Union Station

Sewall-Belmont House and Museum ..... Capitol South or Union Station

The Shakespeare Theatre ...... Archives-Navy Memorial

Smithsonian American Art Museum .... Gallery Place-Chinatown

Smithsonian Institution Building (The Castle) .Smithsonian

Supreme Court Building .. Capitol South or Union Station

The Textile Museum .... Dupont Circle

Tudor Place Historic House and Garden .... Dupont Circle

United States Capitol .... Capitol South or Union Station

United States Holocaust Memorial Museum . .Smithsonian

U.S. Botanic Garden .... Federal Center SW

USDA Forest Service National Headquarters and Information Center .... Smithsonian

U.S. National Arboretum .... Stadium-Armory

U.S. Navy Memorial and Naval Heritage Center .... Archives-Navy Memorial

Vietnam Veterans Memorial .... Foggy Bottom-GWU

Voice of America .... Federal Center SW

Washington Monument .... Smithsonian

White House McPherson Square, Metro Center or Federal Triangle

Woodrow Wilson House .... Dupont Circle

Street N.W. heads north from Constitution Avenue only as far as K Street, where it then links with Connecticut Avenue.

Adding to the frustration level of drivers was the closing in 1995 of Pennsylvania Avenue to automobile traffic in front of the White House. Done for security reasons, it nevertheless created some initial havoc for the thousands of downtown workers and tourists who had daily negotiated the 2-block stretch between 15th and 17th streets N.W. Traffic engineers responded by redirecting traffic on nearby streets and installing new signals, signs and pavement markings, while inline skaters, bicyclists and strollers savored the newfound peace and quiet and the refreshing lack of exhaust fumes.

The speed limit is 25 mph or as posted; on major arteries it is usually 30 mph. A right turn on a red light is permitted unless otherwise posted. High-beam headlights are prohibited at all times.

Business areas, particularly in the downtown core, are congested throughout the day. Avoid rush hours if at all possible. If you are spending the day sightseeing but are staying in nearby Maryland or Virginia—and driving a car—leave in plenty of time to avoid the outbound exodus of city workers. The backup on I-395 southbound begins early (particularly on Fridays and the beginning of holiday weekends), and traffic soon slows to a painful crawl.

Also remember that carpooling regulations (HOV) govern the number of people in vehicles that use certain heavily traveled highways, such as I-66 and I-395 inside the Beltway. Signs denote designated HOV lanes; the restrictions apply during both morning (6:30 to 9 a.m.) and evening (4 to 6:30 p.m.) rush-hour periods.

Parking

Despite luring millions and millions of tourists annually with an abundance of sightseeing attractions, Washington is distinctly less generous in supplying them with parking spaces. On-street parking downtown is limited, particularly near the National Mall and the major museums. Violations are strictly enforced; pay close attention to all signs in the vicinity of any space you are lucky enough to find.

Meters are closely monitored, and as soon as the "expired" flag pops up in the window a vehicle is fair game to be ticketed. Most meters run for only an hour, so visitors taking in the museums along the Mall should designate someone to keep the device supplied with quarters. The problem eases on weekends, when meters are not running.

© 2004 maps.com

BALTIMORE–WASHINGTON INTERNATIONAL AIRPORT

Map labels: Satellite Parking, To I-695, 170, Satellite Parking, Parking, Aviation Blvd, Spring Lane, Elm Rd, Elkridge Landing Rd, To State Rt. 295, COMMUTER TERMINAL, Concourse E, Concourse D, NORTH TERMINAL, Parking, Concourse C, Parking, Parking, Concourse B, Concourse A (under construction), SOUTH TERMINAL, 170, To State Rt. 100, 405

Parking is free on Jefferson and Madison drives north and south of the Mall Mon.-Fri. 10-1, but these spots are invariably filled. If you venture off the Mall looking for a space, watch for signs in residential neighborhoods; often street parking is reserved for residents, and a special zone sticker must be displayed on the front windshield. You can park on the street in such neighborhoods, but usually only for a 2-hour period. In Georgetown parking and standing are banned on M Street between 29th Street and Key Bridge, as well as on Wisconsin Avenue between K and O streets, Friday and Saturday nights from 6:30 p.m. to 4 a.m.

Be sure to park only between the marked lines on the pavement; drivers of small cars are often tempted to squeeze into a space that is not really legal. Parking is prohibited within 10 feet of a fire hydrant, 25 feet of a stop sign and 40 feet of an intersection. Parking statutes are strictly enforced by tickets, but cars are generally towed only when they endanger public safety. If your vehicle is towed Friday after 7 p.m. or anytime on weekends, you must wait until the following Monday after 9 a.m. to retrieve it.

No Standing zones also are enforced; automobiles are not permitted to be in those areas except briefly to pick up or discharge passengers. For additional details, contact the D.C. Department of Public Works; phone (202) 576-7217.

Downtown commercial lots and garages can be expensive, many charging $12 or more per day, with discounts for those arriving early in the morning or late in the afternoon. Some stores may offer shoppers a parking discount; inquire at the individual establishment. Many garages close by about 7 p.m., making them impractical for attending evening events. For a cheaper and frequently more convenient alternative, consider Metro (see Public Transportation).

Taxis & Limousines

Rather than meters, taxicabs in Washington use the zone system to determine fares. The basic zone charge is $6.25 per person, with a $1.50 surcharge for each additional

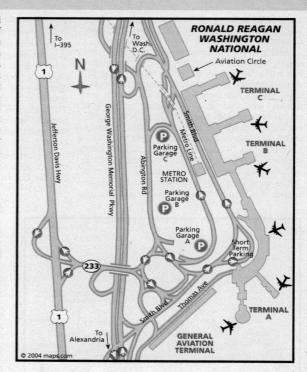

person (an additional $1.50 is charged for travel to another zone). There also is a $1.25 surcharge per person (or group of persons traveling together) for weekday taxi service that commences between 4 and 6:30 p.m. The maximum basic fare for one person within the District is $13.25. Other factors, from the amount of baggage to the time of day, might increase the fare.

The rates quoted above are for cabs hailed on the street; rates increase by about $1.50 when a cab is requested by telephone. Taxi rates for trips into or from nearby points in Maryland and Virginia will vary; make sure you determine the rate with the driver in advance. Cabs with Virginia or Maryland license plates may transport passengers in and out of the District, but not between points within the District. Cab companies include Capitol, (202) 546-2400; Diamond, (202) 387-6200; Liberty, (202) 636-1600; and Yellow, (202) 544-1212. Limousine service in and around Washington averages $50 per hour, excluding tax and tip.

Public Transportation

Washington's heavy traffic congestion and chronic lack of public parking make public transportation an enticing alternative indeed. The red, white and blue buses of the Metro system reach nearly every point in the D.C. area for $1.25; senior citizens and the physically impaired, 60c. Express fare is $3. Up to two children 4 years of age and younger may ride free with each adult paying full fare; over 4 pay the adult fare.

A regional 1-day pass offers unlimited rides on regular Metrobuses and other local buses. The fare is $3; on express buses, the pass covers $1.25 of the $3 fare. A free transfer is valid for unlimited Metrobus connections (including round trips) within a 2-hour period; ask the driver for a transfer. A free Metrorail to Metrobus transfer, available at the entrances to Metro stations, is worth 90c off the bus fare.

Metrobus operates daily 24 hours, but service intervals vary by time of day, during the week and on weekends to best meet demand. Exact fare is required. For information about special and reduced fares phone (202) 637-7000.

Metrorail is a clean, architecturally striking subway that provides access to most of the city's attractions and is an efficient and economical means of getting around. Stations functioning as major transfer points between lines are Metro Center, Gallery Place-Chinatown, L'Enfant Plaza, Pentagon, Rosslyn, Stadium-Armory, King Street and Fort Totten.

The Red Line runs from Glenmont, Md., to Shady Grove, Md., via downtown Washington. The Yellow Line runs from Mt. Vernon Square in Washington to Huntington, south of Alexandria, Va., via Ronald Reagan Washington National Airport. The Blue Line connects Addison Road in Prince Georges County, Md., with the Franconia/Springfield station via Washington; it is in the process of

Passes and Tickets from U.S. Senators and Representatives

Passes for both the House and Senate galleries must be obtained from your senator or representative (see United States Capitol). Although these passes may be available on a walk-in basis, it is suggested that visitors contact their senator or representative several months in advance, because the number of passes is limited. Senator and representative names often can be found in the front matter of your telephone directory.

Digital Archives

Requests for White House tours also must be made through your senator or representative and are accepted up to 6 months in advance; tours are scheduled approximately 1 month before the requested date.

In addition to gallery passes, your legislators can provide tickets for special tours of the F.B.I. Building, Capitol, Supreme Court, Bureau of Engraving and Printing, State Department, Kennedy Center, Treasury Department and National Archives. Tickets should be reserved as early as possible, but some facilities permit tickets to be reserved only 1, 2 or 3 months in advance because of the possibility of ceremonies or other unscheduled closings. Generally, a maximum of five tickets per facility may be issued under one name. Your legislator's office can tell you more.

To contact your legislator, phone the congressional main switchboard at (202) 224-3121, give your legislator's name and ask to be connected to his or her office. The switchboard operator may be able to answer general questions but cannot issue passes or tickets.

being extended to Largo, Md. The Orange Line travels between New Carrollton, Md., and Vienna, Va., via Washington. The Green Line extends from Greenbelt, Md., south to Branch Avenue in Prince George's County, Md., via Washington.

Maps at each station's mezzanine provide route and fare information; station managers also are available on the mezzanine. Route maps are posted near the doors of each train car. Farecard machines at each station dispense the magnetically encoded cards needed by each rider to enter and leave station faregates.

The minimum fare is $1.35; additional charges depend on the distance traveled and whether you enter the system during regular fare hours (Mon.-Fri. 5:30-9:30, 3-7 and 2 a.m.-closing) or reduced fare hours (all other times). **Note:** If using Metro in the evening, check the scheduled departure time for the last train; at many stations it departs before the system closes. Final departure times are posted in each station kiosk.

The maximum one-way fare is $3.90 during peak hours, $2.35 during off-peak hours. Two children under 5 may ride free with each paying passenger. The Metrorail One-Day Pass entitles riders to unlimited rail travel Mon.-Thurs. 9:30 a.m.-midnight, Fri. 9:30 a.m.-3 a.m., Sat. 7 a.m.-3 a.m., Sun. and holidays 7 a.m.-midnight. The fare is $6.50.

Parking lots and garages are available at most of the suburban stations, but they often are full by 8 a.m. on weekdays. Parking at Metro-operated lots is free on weekends and federal holidays. Parking fees must be paid using a SmarTrip card, sold in vending machines at stations where parking is available. These permanent, rechargeable plastic farecards also can be used in Metro stations. For SmarTrip card information phone (888) 762-7874.

Metrorail operates Mon.-Thurs. 5:30 a.m.-midnight, Fri. 5:30 a.m.-3 a.m., Sat. 7 a.m.-3 a.m., Sun. 7 a.m.-midnight. Hours are reduced on the following holidays: Jan. 1, Martin Luther King, Jr. Day, Presidents' Day, Memorial Day, July 4, Labor Day, Columbus Day, Veterans Day, Thanksgiving, and Dec. 25 and 31.

Intervals between trains vary by time and route, but are usually about 5 minutes during rush hour and 12 minutes at other times. For further information about routes and rates phone (202) 637-7000, or TTY (202) 638-3780.

One- or multiday passes and other farecards can be purchased at the Metro sales offices at 600 5th St. N.W. (Mon.-Fri. 10-3) and 12th and F streets N.W. (Mon.-Fri. 7:30-6:30), and at the Pentagon Transit Center in Arlington, Va. (Mon.-Fri. 7-6:30). Metro fare cards, tokens and passes also are available at nearly 400 participating retail outlets and at Commuter Stores in the Crystal City Underground Mall, the Ballston Common Shopping Mall and Rosslyn Center (all in Arlington).

Note: In the *Points of Interest* section attraction listings include the nearest Metrorail (M:) stop if applicable. *Also see page 70.*

Smithsonian Institution Building (The Castle) / © W. Metzen/Robertstock

What To See

AFRICAN-AMERICAN CIVIL WAR MEMORIAL, jct. 10th and U sts. N.W. at 1200 U St. N.W. (M: U St.-Cardozo Station), is a tribute to African-Americans who served in the Union forces during the Civil War. The 10-foot-tall bronze "Spirit of Freedom" sculpture depicts soldiers and sailors from the various armed services. Low semicircular walls bear the names of the 209,145 members of the United States Colored Troops (USCT) as well as those of the 7,000 white officers who led them. Allow 30 minutes minimum. Mon.-Fri. 10-5, Sat. 10-2. Free. Phone (202) 667-2667.

THE ALBERT EINSTEIN MEMORIAL stands in a shady grove of trees at the s.w. corner of the National Academy of Sciences at 2101 Constitution Ave. N.W. (M: Foggy Bottom-GWU). Robert Berks created this 12-foot seated bronze statue of the most widely known modern physicist. Einstein is casually seated on a granite bench, while at his feet much of the known universe is depicted on a 28-foot circular sky map that shows stars to the sixth magnitude. Daily 24 hours. Free. Phone (202) 334-2000.

ANACOSTIA MUSEUM AND CENTER FOR AFRICAN AMERICAN HISTORY AND CULTURE of the Smithsonian Institution is located at 1901 Fort Place S.E. (M: Anacostia) in Fort Stanton Park, approximately 8 mi. from the National Mall. The museum is devoted to exploring and documenting the social experiences and cultural expressions of persons of African descent. Its collection of approximately 6,000 objects dates from the early 1800s and focuses on such key areas as religion and spirituality, dance and contemporary popular culture. The museum also hosts a revolving program of exhibitions and educational activities.

Allow 30 minutes minimum. Daily 10-5; closed Dec. 25 and during exhibition installation. Free. Phone (202) 633-1000 for general information, (202) 357-2020 for recorded information, or TTY (202) 357-1729.

ANACOSTIA PARK lies on both sides of the Anacostia River in the n.e. and s.e. sections of the city (M: Anacostia). In 1608, a year after the founding of Jamestown, Capt. John Smith made his way up the Potomac River and discovered the large Indian village of Nacotchtank, which is believed to have been in the southern end of what is now Anacostia Park.

The 1,271-acre park contains tennis and basketball courts, soccer and baseball fields, a swimming pool, a skating rink and a pavilion. Fishing and bicycling are permitted. Allow 30 minutes minimum. Daily 7:30 a.m.-dusk. Free. Phone (202) 690-5182.

ANDERSON HOUSE, 2118 Massachusetts Ave. N.W. (M: Dupont Circle), is the headquarters, library and museum of The Society of the Cincinnati, which was founded by the officers of the Continental Army and Navy in 1783. Displays pertain to the American Revolution. European and Oriental decorative arts also are exhibited. Allow 1 hour minimum. Museum open Tues.-Sat. 1-4; closed major holidays and during society meetings. Library open by appointment Mon.-Fri. 10-4. Free. Phone (202) 785-2040.

ARMED FORCES MEDICAL MUSEUM—
see National Museum of Health and Medicine p. 88.

ARTHUR M. SACKLER GALLERY of the Smithsonian Institution, 1050 Independence Ave. S.W. (M: Smithsonian), is entered from a pavilion in the Enid A. Haupt Garden behind the Smithsonian Institution Building (the Castle). The gallery is housed in a three-level complex that, except for the entrance pavilion, is entirely underground.

The Sackler Gallery contains a permanent collection of art from the Mediterranean to Japan. Included are objects in bronze, jade, silver, gold, lacquer and ceramics, as well as paintings and sculpture that span ancient times to the present. The gallery also features changing exhibitions of Asian art from museums around the world. Free guided tours are available; phone for schedule. Allow 1 hour minimum. Daily 10-5:30; closed Dec. 25. Free. Phone (202) 633-1000 for general information, (202) 357-2020 for recorded information, or TTY (202) 357-1729.

Enid A. Haupt Garden is above the National Museum of African Art, the Arthur M. Sackler Gallery and the S. Dillon Ripley Center. This is a 4.2-acre rooftop garden with a Victorian parterre bordered by two thematic gardens. Among the plants on display are saucer magnolias, katsura trees and weeping beeches. Collections of 19th-century urns, benches and wickets grace the garden's brick paths.

Daily 6:30 a.m.-dusk. Free guided tours are available spring through fall on selected days (weather permitting); phone for schedule. Free. Phone (202) 633-1000 for general information, (202) 357-2020 for recorded information, or TTY (202) 357-1729.

ARTS AND INDUSTRIES BUILDING of the Smithsonian Institution, 900 Jefferson Dr. S.W. (M: Smithsonian), was built to exhibit materials acquired from the 1876 Philadelphia Centennial Exposition. From the early 1990s through January 2004 the museum featured special changing exhibitions about art, history, science and culture.

Between the building and the Hirshhorn Museum, the Mary Livingston Ripley Garden has a variety of colorful herbaceous and woody perennials, shrubs and trees, augmented by seasonal annuals and tropical plants along a serpentine brick walkway. Along Jefferson Drive between the building and the Smithsonian Castle is the Kathrine Dulin Folger Rose Garden, where roses, annuals, perennials and woody plants are chosen to provide year-round interest.

Note: The Arts and Industries Building is currently closed for renovation. The Discovery Theater, which features performances for children, has been relocated to the S. Dillon Ripley Center (next to the Smithsonian Castle). Free guided tours of the gardens are available spring through fall on selected days (weather permitting); phone for schedule. Gardens free.

Phone (202) 633-1000 for general information, (202) 357-2020 for recorded information, or TTY (202) 357-1729.

THE BASILICA OF THE NATIONAL SHRINE OF THE IMMACULATE CONCEPTION, Michigan Ave. at 4th St. N.E. (M: Brookland-CUA), is said to be the largest Roman Catholic church in America and one of the largest in the world. The Crypt Church has been in use since the late 1920s; the Great Upper Church was dedicated in 1959. The shrine is Byzantine-Romanesque in style and structure. There is no steel skeleton or framework; it is made entirely of stone, brick, tile and concrete.

The shrine houses a large collection of 20th-century mosaics. Artworks include Vatican Studio mosaic reproductions of Bartolomé Esteban Murillo's "Immaculate Conception" and Titian's "Assumption" as well as a large mosaic of "Christ in Majesty" by John de Rosen. Memorial tablets cover the walls and columns of Memorial Hall, where the coronation tiara of Pope Paul VI is displayed.

Food is available. Allow 1 hour minimum. Daily 7-7, Apr.-Oct.; 7-6, rest of year. Guided tours are offered Mon.-Sat. 9-3, Sun. 1:30-4. Guest artists give organ recitals Sun. at 6 p.m., preceded by a carillon recital at 5:30 on the 56-bell carillon in Knights' Tower, June-Aug. Free. Phone (202) 526-8300.

BUREAU OF ENGRAVING AND PRINTING, s. of the Washington Monument grounds at 14th and C sts. S.W. (M: Smithsonian), is the site where the U.S. government designs, engraves and prints currency, bonds and other miscellaneous items. A visitor center contains related exhibits, including various engraved cards and uncut currency sheets that may be purchased. Flash photography is not permitted.

Allow 30 minutes minimum. Tours are given Mon.-Fri. 10-2 and 6-7 p.m., May 6-Aug. 30; Mon.-Fri. 10-2, rest of year. Same-day tickets for tours may be obtained at the booth on Raoul Wallenberg Place beginning at 8 a.m. Tickets are limited, and lines often form an hour or more before ticket booth opens. One person may obtain up to eight tickets. A valid photo ID is required. Note: Bookbags, backpacks and sharp objects are not allowed in the building. Closed federal holidays and Dec. 23-Jan. 2. Free. Phone (202) 874-2330 or (866) 874-2330.

CHINATOWN FRIENDSHIP ARCHWAY, 7th and H sts. N.W. (M: Gallery Place-Chinatown), marks the entrance to the eight-block Chinatown neighborhood, bounded by H, I, 6th and 11th sts. One of the largest single-span archways in the world, the intricate red, green, blue and gold structure is decorated with 7,000 tile and 272 painted dragons in the styles of the Ming and Kuing dynasties.

The Chinese New Year's parade passes under the archway, which was dedicated in 1986 by the mayors of Beijing, China and the District of Columbia. The parade takes place between late January and mid-February, depending on the lunar calendar.

CONSTITUTION GARDENS, on Constitution Ave. between 17th and 23rd sts. near the Reflecting Pool and the Lincoln Memorial (M: Foggy Bottom-GWU), is a 52-acre park containing a 6-acre lake and a 1-acre garden. The Vietnam Veterans Memorial *(see attraction listing p. 96)* is in the park. This tranquil, shady retreat is especially lovely in spring. Daily 24 hours. Free. Phone (202) 426-6841.

Memorial to the Signers of the Declaration of Independence is in the middle of the lake in Constitution Gardens. It consists of large granite blocks carved with replicas of the 56 signatures on the Declaration of Independence. A landscaped garden surrounds the memorial. Daily 24 hours. Phone (202) 426-6841.

National Air and Space Museum
© W. Metzen/Robertstock

CORCORAN GALLERY OF ART, 17th St. between E St. and New York Ave. N.W. (M: Farragut North or Farragut West), has an extensive collection of American paintings, drawings, prints and sculpture from the 18th century to the present.

The Corcoran's permanent collection includes the W.A. Clark Collection of European paintings and sculpture, tapestries and pottery; the Salon Doré, an ornate example of 18th-century interior design; and American painter Albert Bierstadt's panoramic canvas "The Last of the Buffalo." The gallery also presents changing exhibits of contemporary art and works by fine art photographers and local artists. Guided tours are given Wed.-Mon. at noon.

Food is available. Wed.-Mon. 10-5 (also Thurs. 5-9). Admission $6.75, senior citizens $4.75, students with ID $3, under 12 free, family rate $12; free to all Mon. 10-5 and Thurs. 5-9. Phone (202) 639-1700.

DAR MUSEUM is at 1776 D St. N.W. (M: Farragut North or Farragut West). The museum, in Memorial Continental Hall, consists of 33 period rooms displaying such decorative arts as furniture, ceramics, glass, paintings and silver made or used in early America. Changing exhibits are presented in the museum gallery.

Constitution Hall, a 3,702-seat auditorium, was designed by John Russell Pope in monumental neoclassic style. It serves as a venue for special events as well as a variety of popular music concerts.

Museum Mon.-Fri. 8:30-4, Sat. 9-5. Tours Mon.-Fri. 10-2:30, Sat. 9-4:30. Free. Phone (202) 879-3241, or (202) 628-4780 for concert information.

DAR Library, 1776 D St. N.W., was founded in 1896. This genealogical research facility is located in Memorial Continental Hall. The library is open Mon.-Fri. 8:30-4, Sat. 9-5; closed federal holidays and to non-DAR members for 2 weeks in July. Use of library free to DAR members; nonmembers $6. Phone (202) 879-3229.

DECATUR HOUSE, entrance at 1610 H St. N.W. (M: Farragut North or Farragut West), was designed by Benjamin Latrobe for naval hero Stephen Decatur and his wife Susan. Completed in 1818 shortly after the White House and St. John's Church were built, this was the first private residence on Lafayette Square.

Constructed of red brick in the austere Federal style, the three-story town house was the scene of lavish parties given by the Decaturs, who were then one of the capital's most socially prominent couples. After Decatur was killed in a duel in 1820, the house served as the unofficial residence for a string of American and foreign dignitaries while simultaneously being occupied by slaves. It was opened to the public as a museum in the early 1960s.

A guided tour includes the mansion's eight furnished period rooms, which are filled with ceramics, silver, textiles and works of art. Changing exhibits also are presented.

Tours Tues.-Sat. 10-5 (also Thurs. 5-8), Sun. noon-4; closed major holidays. Donations. Phone (202) 842-0920.

DEPARTMENT OF AGRICULTURE occupies the Administration and South Agricultural buildings, extending from 12th to 14th sts. S.W., between C St. and Jefferson Dr. (M: Smithsonian). Department information is available at the Visitors Information Center in room 103A of the Administration Building, between Independence Ave. and Jefferson Dr. Exhibits are frequently displayed on the Jamie L. Whitten Patio. Visitor center open Mon.-Fri. 9-3; closed holidays. Phone (202) 720-4197 for the visitor center.

DEPARTMENT OF STATE, 2201 C St. N.W. (M: Foggy Bottom-GWU), has occupied this building since 1947; an extension was completed in 1961. Part of the Executive Branch, the agency is responsible for formulating and implementing U.S. foreign policy.

Forty-five-minute tours of the eighth-floor diplomatic reception rooms are available. These elaborately decorated rooms, used by the Secretary of State, the Vice President and Cabinet members to entertain dignitaries, contain furnishings from the 1750-1825 period. Publications and travel information are available from the Public Information Service.

Tours are offered Mon.-Fri. at 9:30, 10:30 and 2:45. No strollers, backpacks or packages are permitted, and storage facilities are not available. Free. Tours are not recommended for children under 12. A photo ID is required for admittance. Reservations are required and should be made approximately 4 weeks in advance. Phone (202) 647-3241, TTY (202) 736-4474, or (202) 647-6575 for publications and travel information.

DEPARTMENT OF THE INTERIOR MUSEUM, 1849 C St. N.W., is in the Department of the Interior building, which covers two city blocks from C to E sts. and 18th to 19th sts. N.W. (M: Farragut West). The building contains many New Deal murals that are viewable only appointment; reservations must be made 2 weeks in advance. Museum exhibits illustrate the development, use and conservation of natural resources, the art and architecture of the building, as well as crafts by American Indians and Pacific Islanders.

Allow 30 minutes minimum. Mon.-Fri. 8:30-4:30, third Sat. of the month 1-4; closed federal holidays. Free. A photo ID is required for adult admittance. Reservations are required (2 weeks in advance) for guided tours and viewing of the murals in restricted areas. Phone (202) 208-4743.

DUMBARTON HOUSE is in Georgetown at 2715 Q St. N.W. (M: Dupont Circle). This Federal-period house, built about 1800, was the home of Joseph Nourse, Register of the U.S. Treasury 1781-1829. The building contains fine examples of Federal furniture, paintings, silver and Chinese export porcelain, as well as letters and documents signed by George Washington, Thomas Jefferson and Dolley Madison.

Allow 1 hour minimum. Guided 45-minute tours are given Tues.-Sat. at 10:15, 11:15, 12:15 and 1:15; closed federal holidays and Thanksgiving weekend. Fee $5, students with ID free. Phone (202) 337-2288.

DUMBARTON OAKS garden entrance is at 1703 32nd St. N.W. The 19th-century house contains a research center for Byzantine and medieval civilizations studies, pre-Columbian studies and the history of landscape architecture. Collections include a library of more than 100,000 volumes and an art collection representing the early Christian and Byzantine periods. The 10-acre gardens incorporate traditional French, English, and Italian design elements.

Gardens open daily 2-6, Mar. 15-Oct. 31; 2-5, rest of year. Closed federal holidays, Dec. 24 and in inclement weather. Museum open Tues.-Sun. 2-5; closed federal holidays, Dec. 24 and in inclement weather. Gardens admission Mar. 15-Oct. 31 $5; senior citizens and under 12, $3. Gardens free rest of year. House by donation. Phone (202) 339-6409 for docent tour information, or (202) 339-6401 for recorded information.

DUMBARTON OAKS PARK is entered via Lovers' Ln., off R St. between Avon Pl. and 31st St. N.W. The park occupies 27 acres of the former 50-acre estate of Robert Woods Bliss. Accessible only by foot, this wooded area is most attractive from early April to late June. Allow 30 minutes minimum. Daily 8-dusk. Free. Phone (202) 282-1063.

EMANCIPATION STATUE is at the w. end of Lincoln Park on E. Capitol St. between 11th and 13th sts. N.E. (M: Eastern Market). The sculpture, created by Thomas Ball, depicts a slave being liberated by Abraham Lincoln. It was paid for by donations from emancipated slaves and was dedicated in 1876 with Frederick Douglass in attendance. Also in Lincoln Park is the Mary McLeod Bethune Memorial.

ENID A. HAUPT GARDEN— *see Arthur M. Sackler Gallery p. 76.*

EXPLORERS HALL, NATIONAL GEOGRAPHIC SOCIETY is at 17th and M sts. N.W. (M: Farragut North or Farragut West). This interactive geography science center features exhibits depicting famous National Geographic-sponsored expeditions. Adjoining Explorers Hall is Grosvenor Auditorium, where guest lecturers present programs on a variety of subjects.

Allow 1 hour minimum. Mon.-Sat. and holidays 9-5, Sun. 10-5; closed Dec. 25. Free. Phone (202) 857-7588, or (202) 857-7700 for lecture and film information.

F.B.I. BUILDING— *see J. Edgar Hoover F.B.I. Building p. 81.*

FOLGER SHAKESPEARE LIBRARY is at 2nd and E. Capitol sts. S.E., just e. of the Library of Congress (M: Capitol South or Union Station). This neoclassic building has a Tudor-inspired interior. Changing exhibits featuring Shakespearean and Renaissance items, including paintings and rare books and manuscripts, are displayed in the Folger Great Hall. A permanent multimedia exhibition in the Shakespeare Gallery allows visitors to electronically browse through the library's collection and listen to music performed by the Folger Consort. Lectures, theater programs, concerts, plays and readings of poetry and fiction are presented regularly.

Mon.-Sat. 10-4; closed federal holidays. Tours are given Mon.-Fri. at 11, Sat. at 11 and 1. Exhibits free; admission charged for evening events. Phone (202) 544-7077.

FORD'S THEATRE NATIONAL HISTORIC SITE is at 511 10th St. N.W. (M: Metro Center). This theater, in which President Abraham Lincoln was fatally shot by John Wilkes Booth on Apr. 14, 1865, has been restored to its 1860s appearance. Rangers provide short talks recounting the atmosphere of Washington during the Civil War and the story of the assassination. Musical productions and plays about prominent Americans also are staged.

Allow 1 hour minimum. Theater open daily 9-5. Ranger talks 9:15-noon and 2:15-4:15. Closed Dec. 25. Theater performances are presented Tues.-Sun. at 7:30 p.m.; matinees Thurs. at 1, Sat.-Sun. at 2:30. Phone to confirm times. The theater closes at 12:30 before matinees and sometimes on short notice for rehearsals. Theater free. Ticket prices for performances vary. Phone (202) 426-6924, or (202) 347-4833 for the box office.

Ford's Theatre Museum is in the basement of Ford's Theatre. Exhibits depict the assassination and display the gun that John Wilkes Booth used to kill Lincoln. Daily 9-5; closed Dec. 25.

House Where Lincoln Died (Petersen House) is at 516 10th St. N.W., across from Ford's Theatre. The president was carried to this house after being shot in Ford's Theatre; he died the following morning. Built in 1849 by William Petersen, the house has been restored to its 1860s appearance. Daily 9-5; closed Dec. 25. Free. Phone (202) 426-6924.

FRANCISCAN MONASTERY, 14th and Quincy sts. N.E. (M: Brookland-CUA), is called Mount St. Sepulchre, The Holy Land of America. The monastery features replicas of Holy Land shrines including the Grotto of Bethlehem, Nazareth, the Holy Sepulchre in Jerusalem and the Roman Catacombs. Church and gardens open daily 9-5. Tours are given on the hour Mon.-Sat. 9-11 and 1-4, Sun. 1-4. Free. Phone (202) 526-6800.

FRANKLIN DELANO ROOSEVELT MEMORIAL is in W. Potomac Park along the Tidal Basin between the Jefferson and Lincoln memorials (M: Smithsonian). Four of the five outdoor rooms depict the 12 years (1933-45) FDR served as America's 32nd president. The memorial contains plants, pools, waterfalls, fountains, quiet alcoves, 12 sculptures and 21 Roosevelt quotations carved into the granite walls.

The Prologue Room contains a life-size statue of Roosevelt in a wheelchair. The second room, representing his first term, contains another life-size statue, while the third room focuses on the Great Depression and contains three sculptures that capture the mood of the times: "Despair," a weary rural couple; "Hunger," an urban bread line; and "Hope," a man listening to one of FDR's fireside chats. Dominated by a 9-foot statue of FDR and his dog, Fala, the fourth room depicts World War II. A 30-foot-long bas-relief of Roosevelt's funeral cortege is in the fifth room.

Allow 1 hour minimum. Daily 9:30 a.m.-midnight; closed Dec. 25. Free. Phone (202) 619-7222 or (202) 426-6843.

FREDERICK DOUGLASS NATIONAL HISTORIC SITE (Cedar Hill), 1411 W St. S.E., was the last home of the one-time slave, statesman and human rights activist, who died in 1895. Many of the house's 19th-century Victorian furnishings are original. The visitor center's interpretive exhibits and film document Douglass' life.

Allow 1 hour minimum. Daily 9-5, mid-Apr. to mid-Oct.; 9-4, rest of year. Closed Jan. 1, Thanksgiving and Dec. 25. Free. Phone (202) 426-5961.

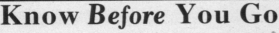

FREER GALLERY OF ART of the Smithsonian Institution is on the National Mall at Jefferson Dr. and 12th St. S.W. (M: Smithsonian). The gallery houses an Asian collection of Japanese art, Korean ceramics, Buddhist art, South Asian art, Islamic art and Chinese art that includes ancient works, porcelains, calligraphy and paintings. An underground exhibition area leads to the Smithsonian's other Asian art museum, the Arthur M. Sackler Gallery *(see attraction listing p. 76).*

A collection of American paintings includes works by Thomas Wilmer Dewing, Abbott Handerson Thayer and Dwight William Tryon. "Harmony in Blue and Gold: The Peacock Room," an elaborate dining room designed and executed by James McNeill Whistler, is his only existing interior scheme. Displayed in this room is Whistler's "The Princess from the Land of Porcelain" and a collection of Chinese blue and white porcelain.

Allow 2 hours minimum. Daily 10-5:30; closed Dec. 25. Free guided tours are available; phone for schedule. Free. Phone (202) 633-1000 for general information, (202) 357-2020 for recorded information, or TTY (202) 357-1729.

HILLWOOD MUSEUM AND GARDENS is at 4155 Linnean Ave. N.W. (M: Van Ness-UDC). This 1926 Georgian-style mansion contains comprehensive collections of 18th- and 19th-century Russian imperial art as well as 18th-century French decorative arts. The Porcelain Room features china services and glassware commissioned by Catherine the Great. The Icon Room exhibits icons, gold and silver chalices and an array of jeweled items by Carl Fabergé. The Drawing Room contains tapestries and 18th-century French furniture.

A one-room *dacha*, or Russian summer house, displays Russian decorative art. Gardens on the 25-acre estate include a formal garden, a French parterre, a Japanese-style garden and a rose garden.

Guided tours and food are available. Allow 2 hours, 30 minutes minimum. Tues.-Sat. 10-5, Feb.-Dec.; closed federal holidays. Admission $12; over 64, $10; students with ID and ages 6-18, $7. Under 6 are not permitted in the museum but may visit the gardens. Reservations are required. AX, MC, VI. Phone (202) 686-8500 or (877) 445-5966.

HIRSHHORN MUSEUM AND SCULPTURE GARDEN of the Smithsonian Institution is on the National Mall on Independence Ave. at 7th St. S.W. (M: L'Enfant Plaza). This museum houses a collection of American and European art spanning the late 19th century to the present. The permanent collection includes works by Jean Dubuffet, Willem de Kooning, Georgia O'Keeffe, Jackson Pollock, Auguste Rodin, Mark Rothko and David Smith and is shown on a rotating basis.

When it opened in 1974, the cylindrical building was as controversial as many of the works it contains. The galleries on the upper two floors follow the circular contours of the walls. The outer loops of galleries generally display paintings and prints; the inner loops display works of sculpture. Across from the museum on the National Mall is a sunken garden, with large works in stone and metal.

Food is available outside on the plaza in season. Allow 1 hour minimum. Daily 10-5:30; closed Dec. 25. Free guided tours of the museum and garden are available; phone for schedule. Free. Phone (202) 633-1000 for general information, (202) 357-2020 for recorded information, or TTY (202) 357-1729.

HOLOCAUST MEMORIAL MUSEUM— *see United States Holocaust Memorial Museum p. 94.*

HOUSE OF THE TEMPLE LIBRARY/MUSEUM is at 1733 16th St. N.W. (M: Dupont Circle). This building, modeled after the tomb of Mausolus at Halicarnassus (now Bodrum) in Asia Minor, displays Masonic memorabilia, works by and about Scottish poet Robert Burns and many of the personal belongings of J. Edgar Hoover. There is an extensive library of Masonic and related subjects.

Allow 2 hours minimum. Guided tours Mon.-Fri. 8-2. Free. Phone (202) 232-3579.

INTERNATIONAL SPY MUSEUM is at 800 F St. N.W. (M: Gallery Place-Chinatown). The museum houses devices related to the history and practice of espionage. Interactive exhibits provide an insider's view into the world of spying and emphasize its importance in recent history.

U.S. Capitol / © Paul M. Franklin

Food is available. Allow 2 hours minimum. Daily 10-8, Apr.-Oct.; 10-6, rest of year. Closed Jan. 1, Thanksgiving and Dec. 25. Admission $13; over 64, $12; ages 5-18, $10. Advance tickets are available at the museum or through Ticketmaster; no service charge applies. AX, DS, MC, VI. Phone (202) 393-7798, or TTY (202) 654-2840.

ISLAMIC CENTER is at 2551 Massachusetts Ave. N.W. (M: Dupont Circle). This Islamic Mosque is an institution of Muslim worship, education and culture, contains a library of works about Islam and presents changing exhibitions. The minaret, about 160 feet high, and the mosaic inscriptions in Arabic of verses from the Holy Koran are noteworthy. Tours that include talks about Islam by an officer of the center are available.

Allow 1 hour minimum. Mon.-Fri. 10-5. Donations. Female visitors must cover themselves except for their hands, face and feet. Phone (202) 332-8343.

J. EDGAR HOOVER F.B.I. BUILDING is on E St. between 9th and 10th sts. N.W. (M: Metro Center). Exhibits explain the history and jurisdiction of the FBI as well as the work of the FBI laboratory. Guided 1-hour tours, which begin at the 9th and E Street entrance, include a firearms demonstration.

Tours are given Mon.-Fri. 8:45-11:45; closed holidays. Hours may vary; phone ahead. **Note:** Tours have been discontinued while parts of the building are being renovated and are scheduled to be reinstated by late 2005 or 2006. Free. Phone (202) 324-3447.

JEFFERSON MEMORIAL— *see Thomas Jefferson Memorial p. 94.*

THE JOHN F. KENNEDY CENTER FOR THE PERFORMING ARTS is on Rock Creek Pkwy. at the end of New Hampshire Ave. N.W., overlooking the Potomac River just n. of the Theodore Roosevelt Bridge (M: Foggy Bottom-GWU).

Opened in 1971, the Kennedy Center is both Washington's showplace for the performing arts and a tribute to President John F. Kennedy. Kennedy was instrumental in raising funds for the National Cultural Center—a facility envisioned by President Dwight D. Eisenhower, who signed legislation to create it in 1958. Congress designated the center a "living memorial" to Kennedy 2 months after his November 1963 assassination.

American and international music, opera, dance, theater and film are presented in seven facilities: the Eisenhower Theater, the Opera House, the Concert Hall, the Terrace Theater, the Theater Lab, Millennium Stage and the Film Theater.

Free performances are given daily at 6 p.m. on the Millennium Stage; no tickets are required, and shows cover a range of art forms. Free guided tours depart from the parking plaza on Level A and feature the Hall of States, the Hall of Nations and the main theaters. Food is available. Tours Mon.-Fri.

10-5, Sat.-Sun. 10-1, except Jan. 1 and Dec. 25. Box office open Mon.-Sat. 10-9, Sun. and holidays noon-9.

Tours free. Ticket prices vary with event. Full-time students, over 64, persons with permanent disabilities and military grades E-1 through E-4 are eligible for a limited number of half-price tickets. There is a charge for parking. AX, DC, MC, VI. For information or to charge tickets phone (202) 467-4600, (800) 444-1324 or TTY (202) 416-8524 daily 10-9. For guided tour information phone (202) 416-8340.

KENILWORTH AQUATIC GARDENS are w. of I-295 (Kenilworth Ave.) between Quarles and Douglas sts., on Anacostia Ave. (M: Deanwood). The gardens occupy 14 acres on the west bank of the Anacostia River. Known for bird-watching opportunities, the marsh contains 44 ponds filled with a large variety of water plants. Water lilies, lotuses, water hyacinths and other flowering plants bloom May through September; the best viewing is before 1 p.m.

Allow 1 hour, 30 minutes minimum. Gardens open daily 7-4, visitor center daily 8-4; closed Jan. 1, Thanksgiving and Dec. 25. Free. Phone (202) 426-6905.

KOREAN WAR VETERANS MEMORIAL is near the Lincoln Memorial between the Reflecting Pool and Independence Ave. (M: Foggy Bottom-GWU). It was erected in gratitude to those 1.5 million American military personnel who served in Korea 1950-53. The statues of 19 poncho-clad soldiers give the impression of moving warily uphill through an unknown terrain of rice paddies, seemingly cautioning visitors who have accidentally encountered the patrol.

From a distance, the etched images on a 164-foot-long polished gray granite wall appear to be of the mountainous and rolling topography of Korea, but up close are actually military archives photographs of support forces. The memorial is in shades of black, gray and white, as are the recorded images of this forgotten war. Daily 8 a.m.-midnight; closed Dec. 25. Free. Phone (202) 426-6841.

THE KREEGER MUSEUM is at 2401 Foxhall Rd. N.W. Designed by Philip Johnson, this impressive postmodern, travertine-faced structure was once the residence of philanthropist David Kreeger and his wife Carmen. The Kreeger collection features 1870s-1970s European and American art as well as African masks and figures.

The museum is open only by reserved guided tour. Allow 1 hour, 30 minutes minimum. Ninety-minute tours are given Tues.-Fri. at 10:30 and 1:30, Sat. at 10:30, noon and 2, Sept.-July; closed Jan. 1, July 4, Thanksgiving, day after Thanksgiving and Dec. 25. Under 12 are not permitted except on Sat. tours. Fee $8, over 64 and students with ID $5. Phone (202) 337-3050 or (202) 338-3552.

LAFAYETTE SQUARE is across Pennsylvania Ave. from the White House and bounded by such historic buildings as Blair House and Decatur House (M: Farragut West). The major monument in Washington's best-known square is an equestrian statue of Andrew Jackson by Clark Mills. Its proximity to the Executive Mansion makes Lafayette Square a favored site for protests and demonstrations.

L'ENFANT PLAZA is bounded by D St. S.W., the 12th St. Expwy. ramp, the 9th St. Expwy. and the Southwest Frwy. (M: L'Enfant Plaza). The design of this plaza, dedicated in 1968, is ornamental as well as functional, blending old and new. The surface structure includes Washington's only paved square—a sweeping area with a central landscaped garden surrounded by modern office buildings. A subterranean complex consists of a shopping mall, movie theater, restaurants and parking lots.

LIBRARY OF CONGRESS, across from the Capitol at 1st St. and Independence Ave. S.E. (M: Capitol South), is a complex of three buildings. The library contains 54 million books and other printed materials, more than 57 million manuscripts and extensive files of maps, prints, photographs, musical scores, recordings, newspapers, reels of microfilm and the papers of 23 U.S. presidents.

Of particular note in the Jefferson Building is the permanent "American Treasures of the Library of Congress" exhibit, consisting of more than 200 items relating to the country's past. Rotating exhibits are arranged in three categories: Memory (history), Reason (philosophy, law, science and geography) and Imagination (fine arts, architecture, music, literature and sports).

Food is available. Jefferson Building open Mon.-Sat. 10-5:30. First-floor exhibition areas in the Madison Building open Mon.-Fri. 8:30-5, Sat. 8:30-6. Other exhibition areas open Mon.-Sat. 8:30-5. Closed holidays. Free. Phone (202) 707-8000 to verify exhibition schedule, or (202) 707-9779 for the visitor information center.

James Madison Memorial Building is across from the Jefferson Building. Opened in 1980, this contemporary structure contains reading rooms and exhibit halls. First-floor exhibition areas open Mon.-Fri. 8:30-5, Sat. 8:30-6; closed holidays. Free.

John Adams Building is behind the Jefferson Building. This 1939 Art Deco edifice offers a general business and science reading room and Near Eastern, African, Asian and Hebraic reading rooms. Mon.-Sat. 8:30-5; closed holidays. Free.

Thomas Jefferson Building is across from the Capitol at 1st St. and Independence Ave. S.E. (M: Capitol South). The first Library of Congress building, constructed in 1897, is distinguished by its richly ornamental Italian Renaissance architecture. The main halls and some of its reading rooms feature elaborately decorated vaulting; intricate sculpture; and fine paintings, murals and mosaics. The

Great Hall rises 75 feet from a marble floor to a stained-glass ceiling.

Building open Mon.-Sat. 10-5:30. Guided tours are given Mon.-Fri. at 10:30, 11:30, 1:30, 2:30 and 3:30, Sat. at 10:30, 11:30, 1:30 and 2:30. "American Treasures" exhibit Mon.-Sat. 10-5. A local history and genealogy reading room is available Mon. and Wed.-Thurs. 8:30 a.m.-9:30 p.m., Tues. and Fri.-Sat. 8:30-5. Free.

LILLIAN AND ALBERT SMALL JEWISH MUSEUM, 701 3rd St. N.W. at G St. N.W. (M: Judiciary Square), is in the original Adas Israel Synagogue, founded in 1876 and reputed to be the District's oldest synagogue. The museum depicts Jewish lifestyles and contributions to the greater Washington, D.C. area. Allow 30 minutes minimum. Open Sun.-Thurs. by appointment only; closed holidays. Admission $3. Phone (202) 789-0900.

LINCOLN MEMORIAL is on the National Mall off 23rd St. N.W., aligned with the Capitol and the Washington Monument (M: Foggy Bottom-GWU). Between the Lincoln Memorial and the Washington Monument lie two reflecting pools with a combined length of 2,292 feet. The stately marble structure, designed by Henry Bacon, stands just before the approach to Arlington Memorial Bridge. Its 36 Doric columns, one for each state in existence at the time of Lincoln's death, symbolize the Union.

Dominating the interior is the colossal seated statue of Lincoln by Daniel Chester French. Two of Lincoln's more famous speeches—the eloquent Gettysburg Address and his Second Inaugural Address—are carved on the north and south walls of the memorial. Murals by Jules Guerin allegorize the themes of emancipation and reunion.

Allow 30 minutes minimum. Daily 8 a.m.-midnight; closed Dec. 25. Interpretive tours are given by request. Free. Phone (202) 426-6895.

MARIAN KOSHLAND SCIENCE MUSEUM is in the Keck Center at 500 5th St. N.W.; the entrance is at 6th and E sts. N.W. (M: Judiciary Square or Gallery Place-Chinatown). On-site parking is not available. The museum contains three major exhibits focusing on such contemporary scientific issues as DNA and gene sequencing and global climate change. The sophisticated interactive displays, which incorporate findings from reports published by the National Academy of Sciences, allow visitors to examine in depth the evidence behind scientific discovery.

Allow 1 hour minimum. Wed.-Mon. 10-6; closed Jan. 1, Thanksgiving and Dec. 25. Last admission 1 hour before closing. Admission $5; over 65, ages 5-18 and students and active duty military with ID, $3. MC, VI. Phone (202) 334-1201 or (888) 567-4526.

MARINE CORPS MUSEUM is in Bldg. 58 in the Washington Navy Yard at 11th and O sts. S.E. (M: Navy Yard or Eastern Market). This museum traces the 200-year history of the U.S. Marine Corps through dioramas, firearms, uniforms and art, including photographs by David Douglass Duncan. The prized exhibit is the flag raised at Iwo Jima on Feb. 23, 1945. Mon.-Fri. 10-4 (also Fri. 4-8, Memorial Day-Labor Day); closed federal holidays. **Note:** Due to security concerns, phone ahead to verify entry information. Free. Phone (202) 433-3401.

MARY McLEOD BETHUNE COUNCIL HOUSE NATIONAL HISTORIC SITE is at 1318 Vermont Ave. N.W. (M: McPherson Square). Former home of Mary McLeod Bethune, the Victorian townhouse contains exhibits, a 20-minute video about her life and the National Archives of Black Women's History. Bethune founded Daytona Educational and Industrial School for Negro Girls in 1904, which became Bethune-Cookman College. In 1935 she became a special advisor to President Franklin D. Roosevelt. Allow 1 hour minimum. Mon.-Sat. 10-4; closed major holidays. Free. Phone (202) 673-2402.

THE MUSEUMS AT THE POPE JOHN PAUL II CULTURAL CENTER is at 3900 Harewood Rd. N.E. (M: Brookland-CUA). This architecturally stunning complex explores faith and cultural diversity through rotating art exhibits, including art from the renowned Vatican Museums, as well as interactive galleries, music, lectures and cultural programs.

The Mountain of the Lord exhibit displays models of Jerusalem's Temple Mount, while the annual international Nativity exhibit attracts visitors from around the world. A scaled-down, interactive Children's Gallery gives young visitors the opportunity to participate in such activities as ringing bells and creating stained-glass windows. The Papal and Polish Heritage Room contains artifacts and memorabilia pertaining to Pope John Paul II, along with such personal items as his rosary and a pair of skis. Within the center's peaceful chapel is an almost life-size portrait of St. Thérèse of Lisieux.

Food is available. Allow 2 hours minimum. Tues.-Sat. 10-5, Sun. noon-5; closed Jan. 1, Memorial Day, July 4, Labor Day, Thanksgiving and Dec. 25. Admission $5, senior citizens and students with ID $4, family rate $15. AX, DS, MC, VI. Phone (202) 635-5400. *See color ad.*

NATIONAL AIR AND SPACE MUSEUM of the Smithsonian Institution is on the National Mall at 7th St. and Independence Ave. S.W. (M: L'Enfant Plaza). It is devoted to presenting the history, science and technology of air and space flight.

In the Milestones of Flight gallery, visitors can touch a moon rock and view such historically important items as Charles Lindbergh's *Spirit of St. Louis*, Chuck Yeager's Bell X-1 *Glamorous Glennis*, John Glenn's spacecraft *Friendship 7*, the

Apollo 11 Command Module *Columbia* and a Viking Mars Lander. The Wright brothers' 1903 Flyer is on display in the exhibition "The Wright Brothers & the Invention of the Aerial Age."

IMAX films are shown on the five-story screen in the Lockheed Martin IMAX Theater, and multimedia shows are presented in the Albert Einstein Planetarium.

A shuttle bus runs every 90 minutes beginning at 9 a.m. between the museum and the Steven F. Udvar-Hazy Center in Chantilly, Va. Food is available. Allow 2 hours minimum. Daily 10-5:30; closed Dec. 25. Free guided tours are offered daily; phone for schedule. Museum free. A fare is charged for the shuttle bus. A fee is charged for IMAX and planetarium shows; phone to verify prices.

Phone (202) 633-1000 for general information, (202) 357-2020 for recorded information, or TTY (202) 357-1729. Phone (877) 932-4629 for IMAX and planetarium information.

 NATIONAL AIR AND SPACE MUSEUM'S STEVEN F. UDVAR-HAZY CENTER— *see Chantilly, Va., p. 127.*

NATIONAL AQUARIUM is on the lower level of the Herbert C. Hoover Building (the Department of Commerce) at 14th St. and Constitution Ave. N.W. (M: Federal Triangle). Constructed in 1931, the aquarium is a direct descendent of the first public aquarium in the United States. It exhibits 1,200 freshwater and saltwater fish and other aquatic creatures. A touch tank for children features horseshoe crabs, hermit crabs and snails.

Allow 30 minutes minimum. Daily 9-5; closed Thanksgiving and Dec. 25. Last admission 30 minutes before closing. Feeding shows are conducted daily at 2. Shark shows Mon., Wed. and Sat. Piranha shows Tues., Thurs. and Sun. Alligator shows Fri. Admission $5; over 59 and military with ID $4; ages 2-10, $2. Phone (202) 482-2825.

NATIONAL ARCHIVES, Constitution Ave. between 7th and 9th sts. N.W. (M: Archives-Navy Memorial), preserves federal government records of enduring value. The Rotunda for the Charters of Freedom displays the Declaration of Independence, the Constitution and the Bill of Rights. The multimedia Public Vaults exhibition allows visitors to eavesdrop on presidential conversations, view newly declassified top-secret documents and investigate the sinking of the *Titanic,* among other experiences.

Documentary film series as well as a film about the National Archives are shown in the William G. McGowan Theater. Allow 1 hour minimum. Exhibit halls open daily 10-9, Memorial Day weekend-Labor Day; 10-7, Apr. 1-Fri. before Memorial Day; 10-5:30, rest of year. Closed Dec. 25. Free. Phone (202) 501-5205, or TTY (202) 501-5404. For program and events information phone (866) 272-6272.

NATIONAL BUILDING MUSEUM occupies the block on F St. between 4th and 5th sts. N.W. (M: Judiciary Square). Housed in a massive brick building completed in 1887, the museum's rotating exhibits trace and interpret the history of American buildings, including architecture, design, engineering, construction and urban planning. The permanent exhibit is Washington: Symbol and City. The dramatic Great Hall, site of 15 presidential inaugural balls, contains 75-foot-tall brick Corinthian columns.

Food is available. Allow 1 hour minimum. Mon.-Sat. 10-5, Sun. 11-5; closed Jan. 1, Thanksgiving and Dec. 25. Guided 1-hour tours are offered Thurs.-Sat. at 11:30, 12:30 and 1:30, Sun. at 12:30 and 1:30, Mon.-Wed. at 12:30. Admission $5. Phone (202) 272-2448.

NATIONAL CITY CHRISTIAN CHURCH, 5 Thomas Cir. at Massachusetts Ave. and 14th St. N.W. (M: McPherson Square), is the national cathedral of the Christian Church (Disciples of Christ). The neoclassic sanctuary was designed by John Russell Pope in 1930. Free half-hour organ recitals are given Thurs. at 12:15, Feb.-July and early Sept.-Dec. 31. A short videotape about the history of the church is available.

Guided tours are available. Mon.-Fri. 9-5, Sun. 8:30-2. Free. Reservations are required for guided tours. Phone (202) 232-0323.

NATIONAL GALLERY OF ART is housed in two buildings along Constitution Ave. between 3rd and 7th sts. N.W. (M: Archives-Navy Memorial or Judiciary Square). The classical West Building, designed by John Russell Pope, and the contemporary East Building, designed by I.M. Pei, are linked by a paved plaza and an underground concourse. The West Building contains one of the world's finest collections of western European paintings and sculpture spanning the 13th century to the present, including Italian, Flemish, British and American art and French Impressionist works. The East Building focuses on contemporary art by European and American artists.

Major traveling exhibitions are mounted regularly. The gallery also offers a concert series, lectures and films. Near the West Building is a 6-acre outdoor sculpture garden featuring works by such artists as Roy Lichtenstein, Tony Smith, Claes Oldenburg and Coosje van Bruggen.

Guided tours and food are available. Gallery open Mon.-Sat. 10-5, Sun. 11-6. Sculpture garden open Mon.-Sat. 10-7 (also Fri. 7-9 p.m.), Sun. 11-7, Memorial Day-Labor Day; Mon.-Sat. 10-5, Sun. 11-6, rest of year. Gallery and garden closed Jan. 1 and Dec. 25. East Building tours Mon.-Fri. at 10:30 and 1:30, Sat.-Sun. at 11:30, 1:30 and 3:30. West Building tours Mon.-Fri. at 11:30, Sat. at 10:30 and 12:30, Sun. at 12:30 and 4:30. Sign language interpretation is offered with 3 weeks' notice. Gallery talks begin in the West Building Rotunda or the East Building Art Information Desk. Lectures given Sun. at 2 in the East Building auditorium. Concerts Sun. at 7 p.m., Oct.-June. Visitors should phone ahead to verify tour location and time.

Gallery free. Self-guiding tour audiotapes of the permanent collection can be rented for $5; special exhibition audiotapes vary in price. Guided tours $6, over 64 and students with ID $5. Phone (202) 737-4215, or TTY (202) 842-6176.

NATIONAL LAW ENFORCEMENT OFFICERS MEMORIAL is at Judiciary Square between E and F sts. and 4th and 5th sts. N.W.; a museum and visitor center is 2 blks. w. at 605 E St. N.W. (M: Judiciary Square). Inscribed on marble walls are the names of the more than 16,000 law enforcement officers who have died in the line of duty since the first known death in 1792. The 3-acre memorial contains landscaped gardens, symbolic bronze statues of lions, tree-lined pathways, an 80-foot reflecting pool and a visitor center. Guided tours are available by appointment.

Allow 30 minutes minimum. Memorial open daily 24 hours. Visitor center open Mon.-Fri. 9-5, Sat. 10-5, Sun. noon-5; closed Jan. 1, Thanksgiving and Dec. 25. Free. Phone (202) 737-3213. *See color ad.*

The National Mall

The National Mall is the focus of many of Washington's events and celebrations, an arrival and departure point for visiting dignitaries and the location of many of the city's most famous landmarks. The Mall's swath of green between the Capitol and the Washington Monument also is a gathering place for cyclists, skaters, strollers and those just wanting to stretch out on the grass. It has become a sort of national common that visitors and locals alike can rightfully regard as their own.

The grounds of the Washington Monument divide the National Mall into two distinct sections. To the east lie the Capitol, the U.S. Botanic Garden, the Department of Agriculture and 10 Smithsonian museums. To the west lie the Korean War Veterans Memorial, the Lincoln Memorial, the National World War II Memorial, the Vietnam Veterans Memorial, Constitution Gardens and the Reflecting Pool, which is almost four-tenths of a mile long. The total distance from the steps of the Lincoln Memorial to the Capitol grounds is about 2 miles. A secondary axis intersects the Mall—also at the Washington Monument grounds—extending from the White House (about a half-mile north of the monument) to the Thomas Jefferson Memorial (about a half-mile south). Nearly half the attractions listed under *Points of Interest* are either on or along this cross of parkland or—like the Franklin Delano Roosevelt Memorial—a short walk from it.

Digital Archives

If such distances seem daunting, Tourmobile shuttles and Old Town Trolley Tours link most of the major sights *(see What To Do, Sightseeing).* Parking in the area is at a premium, but several Metro stations are within a block or two of the National Mall, and the entrance to the Blue/Orange Line's Smithsonian Station is right on the Mall.

THE NATIONAL MALL extends from the Capitol grounds to the Lincoln Memorial (M: Foggy Bottom-GWU, Federal Triangle, Smithsonian, L'Enfant Plaza, Archives-Navy Memorial, Federal Center and Capitol South).

The rectangular area between the Capitol and the Washington Monument is a popular spot for strolling, picnicking or just relaxing on one of the many benches. This section is lined on both sides by stately American elm trees and 10 Smithsonian Institution museums. On the east side of the Capitol Reflecting Pool, at the foot of the Capitol grounds, is the Ulysses S. Grant Memorial, a powerful sculptural group depicting the general on horseback, flanked by Union cavalry and artillery soldiers. *See sidebar.*

NATIONAL MUSEUM OF AFRICAN ART of the Smithsonian Institution, 950 Independence Ave. S.W. (M: Smithsonian), is entered from a pavilion in the Enid A. Haupt Garden behind the Smithsonian Institution Building (the Castle). Except for the entrance pavilion, the museum is housed in a three-level complex that is entirely underground.

The museum focuses on the rich artistic heritage of the African continent, presenting arts from the living traditions of diverse African cultures. Its permanent collection of bronze, wood, ivory, cast metal and ceramic objects is an important resource for the study of African art and culture. Changing exhibitions also are presented.

Daily 10-5:30; closed Dec. 25. Free. Phone (202) 633-1000 for general information, (202) 357-2020 for recorded information, or TTY (202) 357-1729.

NATIONAL MUSEUM OF AMERICAN HISTORY, BEHRING CENTER of the Smithsonian Institution is on Constitution Ave. between 12th and 14th sts. N.W. (M: Federal Triangle or Smithsonian). The museum depicts the scientific, cultural, social, technological and political development of the United States. Venerated objects like the lap desk Thomas Jefferson used to draft the Declaration of Independence share the museum with such notable items as an Edison light bulb. Visitors also can watch conservators at work preserving the Star-Spangled Banner through a 50-foot, floor-to-ceiling window.

AAA is a proud sponsor of the permanent exhibition "America on the Move," which examines how transportation in the United States from 1876 to the present has shaped our identity from a mostly rural nation into a major economic power. Among other recent permanent exhibitions is "The American Presidency: A Glorious Burden," which explores the public, personal, ceremonial and executive boundaries of the nation's highest office.

Note: The museum is undergoing major renovation but remains open; however, many exhibits may be closed. Free guided tours are available; phone for schedule. Food is available. Daily 10-5:30; closed Dec. 25. Free. Phone (202) 633-1000 for

Smithsonian
National Museum of American History
Behring Center

See how we got here.

Immerse yourself in a new museum experience and explore how transportation has changed America. **National Museum of American History**, Washington, D.C. americanhistory.si.edu/onthemove.

AMERICA
ON THE MOVE

general information, (202) 357-2020 for recorded information, or TTY (202) 357-1729.

NATIONAL MUSEUM OF THE AMERICAN INDIAN of the Smithsonian Institution is on the National Mall at 4th St. and Independence Ave. S.W. (M: L'Enfant Plaza or Federal Center SW), between the National Air and Space Museum and the U.S. Capitol. Opened Sept. 21, 2004, this curvilinear structure of Kasota buff-colored limestone—evocative of natural rock sculpted over time by wind and water—reflects Native Americans' close relationship with nature. Wetlands, meadowlands and a hardwood forest surround the building.

The museum is a centerpiece for performances and public and education programs, as well as a primary space for both permanent and temporary exhibitions on Indian arts, history and material culture. Food is available. Daily 10-5:30; closed Dec. 25. Free. Timed passes are required and are available at the museum. Phone (202) 633-1000 for general information, (202) 357-2020 for recorded information, or TTY (202) 357-1729.

NATIONAL MUSEUM OF AMERICAN JEWISH MILITARY HISTORY is at 1811 R St. N.W. (M: Dupont Circle). Exhibits include photographs, bugles, binoculars, stirrups, posters, hand-painted illustrated maps of troop movements, flags and firearms from the Revolutionary War to the present. A permanent exhibition recounts World War II hero Julius Klein's historic life and work, and changing exhibits are regularly presented. Guided 90-minute tours are available. Mon.-Fri. 9-5, Sun. by appointment; closed Jewish and most federal holidays. Donations. Phone (202) 265-6280.

NATIONAL MUSEUM OF HEALTH AND MEDICINE is on the Walter Reed Army Medical campus, 6900 Georgia Ave. at Elder St. N.W. (M: Takoma Park or Silver Spring). A short taxi ride is necessary from the Metro stop to the museum, or visitors can take Metrobuses 52, 53 or 54 from the Takoma Park stop to Butternut Street.

This facility was established during the Civil War as a center for the collection of specimens for research in military medicine and surgery. The museum's exhibits focus on personal and public health and promote an understanding of medicine past, present and future, with special emphasis on American military medicine.

Note: Although there are several gates around the campus, visitors may enter through the Elder Street gate only, and must present a valid photo ID. Allow 1 hour, 30 minutes minimum. Daily 10-5:30; closed Dec. 25. Docent-led tours begin at 1 on the second and fourth Sat. of the month. Free. Phone (202) 782-2200.

NATIONAL MUSEUM OF NATURAL HISTORY of the Smithsonian Institution, 10th St. and Constitution Ave. N.W. (M: Federal Triangle or Smithsonian), is devoted to the study of human cultures and the diversity of nature.

Permanent exhibitions include the Janet Annenberg Hooker Hall of Geology, Gems and Minerals, which showcases a collection of gemstones—including the legendary Hope Diamond—and minerals, as well as a section on mining and plate tectonics.

The Kenneth E. Behring Family Hall of Mammals features more than 270 mammals in lifelike poses that tell the 225 million-year-old story of mammal evolution and adaptation from the Polar regions to the Sahara Desert. Other popular attractions are the dinosaur exhibits and the O. Orkin Insect Zoo, which has tarantula feedings on most days.

The Discovery Center includes the 487-seat Johnson IMAX Theater. Hands-on learning activities are offered in the Discovery Room. Outside, along the sidewalk between the museum and the 9th Street tunnel, is the Butterfly Habitat Garden, a living showcase of plants that support butterflies during their life cycle.

Free guided tours are available Mon.-Fri., Sept.-June; phone for schedule. Food is available. Museum open daily 10-5:30. Discovery Room open most days year-round; phone for schedule. Closed Dec. 25. Museum free. Phone (202) 633-1000 for general information, (202) 357-2020 for recorded information, or TTY (202) 357-1729. Phone (877) 932-4629 for IMAX film schedule and prices.

NATIONAL MUSEUM OF WOMEN IN THE ARTS is in the renovated former Masonic Grand Lodge of the National Capital at 1250 New York Ave. and 13th St. N.W. (M: Metro Center). The museum, housed in a restored 1907 Renaissance Revival structure, is dedicated to the recognition of women artists. The permanent collection includes more than 2,500 works.

Food is available. Mon.-Sat. 10-5, Sun. noon-5; closed Jan. 1, Thanksgiving and Dec. 25. Admission $8, over 59 and college students with ID $6, under 19 free. Phone (202) 783-5000 or (800) 222-7270.

NATIONAL PORTRAIT GALLERY of the Smithsonian Institution is housed in part of the Old Patent Office Building on F St. between 7th and 9th sts. N.W. (M: Gallery Place-Chinatown). The third oldest government building in Washington, the Patent Office Building served as a Civil War hospital and was the scene of Abraham Lincoln's second inaugural ball.

Note: The gallery is undergoing major renovations and is scheduled to reopen July 4, 2006. During this time, many of its exhibitions are traveling; phone for travel schedule. Free. Phone (202) 633-1000 for general information, (202) 357-2020 for recorded information, or TTY (202) 357-1729.

NATIONAL POSTAL MUSEUM of the Smithsonian Institution is at 2 Massachusetts Ave. N.E. (M: Union Station). This museum is housed on the lower level of the Old City Post Office, which was built in 1914. The hands-on museum offers exhibitions portraying the history of the nation's mail service and includes one of the largest collections of stamps and philatelic materials in the world.

Of note are the major galleries Binding the Nation, Customers and Communities, Moving the Mail, The Art of Cards and Letters, and the Philatelic & Rarities Galleries. The museum also houses the Library Research Center, which includes more than 40,000 volumes and manuscripts.

Free guided tours are available by appointment. Sign language interpretation is offered with 3 weeks' notice. Daily 10-5:30; closed Dec. 25. Free. Phone (202) 633-1000 for general information, (202) 357-2020 for recorded information, (202) 633-5535 for guided tours and sign language interpretation, or TTY (202) 357-1729. Phone (202) 633-9370 for the Library Research Center.

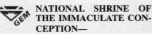

NATIONAL SHRINE OF THE IMMACULATE CONCEPTION—
see The Basilica of the National Shrine of the Immaculate Conception p. 76.

NATIONAL WORLD WAR II MEMORIAL is on the National Mall at the e. end of the Reflecting Pool, between the Lincoln Memorial and the Washington Monument (M: Smithsonian). The 7.4-acre site honors the 16 million men and women who served in the U.S. armed forces during the war, the more than 400,000 who died and the millions who supported the war effort at home.

Two 43-foot arches at the north and south ends of the oval-shaped memorial plaza mark the war's two major theaters, Atlantic and Pacific, while 56 17-foot-tall stone pillars—representing the U.S. states, territories and the District of Columbia at the time of the war—form the memorial's outer boundary. Daily 24 hours. Free. Phone (202) 426-6841.

NATIONAL ZOOLOGICAL PARK of the Smithsonian Institution borders Rock Creek Park, with entrances in the 3000 blk. of Connecticut Ave., on Harvard St. and on Beach Dr. The zoo can be reached via Metrorail's Red Line (M: Woodley Park-Zoo/Adams Morgan or Cleveland Park). Connecticut Ave. bus lines stop at the zoo's main entrance.

The National Zoo is noted for a pair of pandas—Tian Tian and Mei Xiang—as well as Sumatran tigers, Asian rhinoceroses, orangutans, lowland gorillas and Komodo dragons. The indoor and outdoor exhibits together house several thousand animals. Other features include the Invertebrate Exhibit; Pollinarium, a plant reproduction exhibit; Think Tank, an animal thinking exhibit; a cheetah exhibit; Amazonia, a replica of the Amazon rain forest; and American Prairie, a biological, environmental and cultural exhibition. Animal demonstrations are offered daily.

Free guided tours are available by appointment. Food is available. Grounds open daily 6 a.m.-8 p.m., during DST (early Apr.-late Oct.); 6-6, rest of year. Most buildings open daily 10-6, during DST; 10-4:30, rest of year. Closed Dec. 25. Zoo free. Hourly parking rates apply. Phone (202) 673-0127,

Washington National Cathedral / © Paul M. Franklin

(202) 673-4800 for recorded information, TTY (202) 673-7800, or (202) 673-4956 for guided tour information.

THE NAVY MUSEUM, in buildings 70 and 76 at the Washington Navy Yard, 11th and O sts. S.E. (M: Eastern Market or Navy Yard), interprets the history of the U.S. Navy from 1775 to the present. Exhibits depict important battles and early naval heroes, and trace developments in weapons and technology. Highlights include a gun deck section, a fully rigged foremast fighting top from the frigate USS *Constitution* and a submarine room with operating periscopes. Outdoor parks display guns and a cannon.

Allow 1 hour minimum. Mon.-Fri. 9-4, Sat.-Sun. 10-5; closed Jan. 1, Thanksgiving and Dec. 24 and 25. **Note:** Due to security concerns, entry may be restricted; phone ahead. Free. Nonmilitary visitors must make an appointment 24 hours in advance. Phone (202) 433-4882.

USS *Barry* is docked at Pier 2 within the Washington Navy Yard. The destroyer, which saw action during the Cuban missile blockade and in Vietnam, was commissioned in 1956 and was decommissioned in 1982. Visitors can take a self-guiding tour of the ship, which is on permanent display. Allow 1 hour minimum. Daily 10-4; closed Thanksgiving and Dec. 25. Free. Phone (202) 433-3377.

THE NEW YORK AVENUE PRESBYTERIAN CHURCH is at 1313 New York Ave. N.W. (M: Metro Center or McPherson Square). The church was organized 1803; its distinguished members have included John Quincy Adams and Abraham Lincoln. The current Federal-style structure, built in 1951, contains 19 contemporary stained-glass windows. Lincoln's pew, hitching post and the original manuscript of his proposal to abolish slavery can be seen.

Church office open Tues.-Fri. 9-5, Sun. 9-1. Guided tours are offered after Sun. worship services. Phone (202) 393-3700.

THE OCTAGON MUSEUM is at 18th St., New York Ave. and E St. N.W. (M: Farragut North or Farragut West). Built 1799-1801 by architect William Thornton, this Federal-style residence served as the executive mansion for President James Madison in 1814 after the White House was burned by the British during the War of 1812. The Octagon is now a historic house museum owned by the American Architectural Foundation. The second-floor galleries have exhibits about architecture and design.

Allow 1 hour minimum. Guided tours are given Tues.-Sun. 10-4; closed Jan. 1, Thanksgiving and Dec. 25. Admission $5, senior citizens and students with ID $3. Phone (202) 638-3221.

THE OLD POST OFFICE PAVILION is at 12th St. and Pennsylvania Ave. N.W. (M: Federal Triangle). The Romanesque Revival Old Post Office was built in 1899 as the country's postal headquarters. The renovated building now contains shops and eateries. The 315-foot clock tower houses 10 bells given by Great Britain for the U.S. Bicentennial. A glass elevator connects the Pavilion and the bell-ringing chamber; another elevator continues to the 12th-floor observation deck, which offers panoramic views.

Food is available. Building open Mon.-Sat. 10-7, Sun. noon-6, Apr. 1-Labor Day; otherwise varies. Closed Jan. 1, Thanksgiving and Dec. 25. Tower tours Mon.-Sat. 9-5, Sun. 10-6. Tower closes Thurs. at 6:30. Last tour begins 15 minutes before closing. Hours may be extended; phone to confirm schedule. Free. Phone (202) 289-4224, or (202) 606-8691 for clock tower information.

OLD STONE HOUSE is at 3051 M St. N.W. in Georgetown (M: Foggy Bottom-GWU). The oldest building in Washington, it dates from 1765 and is an excellent example of pre-Revolutionary architecture. Restored and furnished in period, it is open for self-guiding tours. Wed.-Sun. noon-5; closed Jan. 1, July 4, Thanksgiving and Dec. 25. Free. Phone (202) 426-6851.

ORGANIZATION OF AMERICAN STATES BUILDING, 17th St. and Constitution Ave. N.W. (M: Farragut West or Farragut North), is headquarters of the general secretariat of the Organization of American States (OAS). The building contains a tropical patio entrance hall, the Hall of Heroes and Flags, the Liberator Simón Bolívar Room, the Hall of the Americas and an Aztec Garden. Guided tours are offered by appointment. Mon.-Fri. 9-5:30; closed

holidays. Free. Phone (202) 458-3000, or (202) 458-3927 for tour appointments.

Art Museum of the Americas, 201 18th St. N.W., directly behind the Organization of American States Building, houses the OAS permanent collection of Latin American and Caribbean art. Guided tours are offered by appointment. Tues.-Sun. 10-5; closed federal holidays and Good Friday. Free. Phone (202) 458-6016.

THE PHILLIPS COLLECTION is at 1600 21st St. N.W., at Q St. (M: Dupont Circle); street parking is limited. The most famous work in this distinguished collection of 19th-century and contemporary American and European paintings is Pierre Auguste Renoir's "Luncheon of the Boating Party." There also are outstanding Impressionist paintings by Paul Cézanne, Edgar Degas, Claude Monet and Vincent van Gogh, as well as works by Paul Klee, Georgia O'Keeffe, Mark Rothko and other artists. The museum regularly presents temporary exhibits in the Goh Annex.

Note: "Luncheon of the Boating Party" is on tour through spring 2005. Guided tours are available. Allow 1 hour minimum. Museum open Tues.-Sat. 10-5 (also Thurs. 5-8:30), Sun. noon-7 (noon-5 in summer); closed federal holidays. Concerts Sun. at 5, Sept.-May. Artful Evenings featuring live music and gallery talks are offered Thurs. 5-8:30. Admission Tues.-Fri. by donation. Admission Sat.-Sun. and to special exhibitions $8, over 61 and students with ID $6, under 19 free. Artful Evenings admission $8. Phone (202) 387-2151.

POTOMAC PARK is divided into West and East Potomac parks. Ohio Drive follows the river, the Washington Channel and the Tidal Basin. This drive is exceptionally beautiful in early April, when 3,000 Japanese cherry trees are in bloom around the Tidal Basin and East Potomac Park. There are facilities for golfing, picnicking, swimming, tennis and ball games; pedal boats can be rented at the Tidal Basin.

RENWICK GALLERY of the Smithsonian American Art Museum is at 17th St. and Pennsylvania Ave. N.W. (M: Farragut West). The gallery focuses on contemporary American crafts and features a permanent collection of works in glass, ceramics, wood, fiber and metal. In keeping with this Second Empire building designed by James Renwick in 1859, the Grand Salon is furnished in the style of the 1860s and 1870s.

Allow 30 minutes minimum. Daily 10-5:30; closed Dec. 25. Free guided tours are available on selected days; phone for schedule. Free. Phone (202) 633-1000 for general information, (202) 357-2020 for recorded information, or TTY (202) 357-1729.

ROBERT A. TAFT MEMORIAL stands 1 blk. n. of the Capitol and 2 blks. w. of the Russell Office Building on Constitution Ave. between New Jersey

Ave. and 1st St. N.W. (M: Union Station). It consists of a 100-foot-tall tower with 27 matched bells and a 10-foot bronze statue. The bells strike the hour and sound the quarter-hour. Taft was senator from Ohio 1938-53, and the son of President William Howard Taft. Selections are played on the electronic keyboard July 4 at 2; other concerts take place on an irregular basis. Free.

ROCK CREEK CEMETERY is at Rock Creek Church Rd. and Webster St. N.W. (M: Fort Totten). Established in 1719, this is Washington's oldest cemetery. St. Paul's Episcopal Church, the District's only Colonial church, is on the grounds. One of the best-known memorials is the Adams Memorial, created by Augustus Saint-Gaudens. Others are the Ffoulke memorial "Rabboni" by Gutzon Borglum and the Boardman memorial "Journey of Life" by James Earle Fraser. Cemetery open daily 7-dusk. Office open for genealogy research Mon.-Fri. 9-5, Sun. 9-1. Phone (202) 829-0585.

ROCK CREEK PARK follows the course of Rock Creek through n.w. Washington. Its 1,754 acres of natural woodland encompass drives, bridle paths, a riding center, tennis courts, two exercise courses, picnic areas, a golf course, athletic fields and many footpaths, bicycle trails and jogging trails.

The remains of Fort De Russy, one of a circle of 68 forts that defended the city during the Civil War, stands near Oregon Avenue and Military Road and can be reached on foot. One-acre Battleground National Cemetery is located at 6625 Georgia Ave. N.W. On Beach Drive north of Military Road is the log studio of eccentric poet Joaquin Miller, who wrote "Song of the Sierras." Concerts take place at Carter Barron Amphitheatre, 16th Street and Colorado Avenue N.W., late June through late August.

Park daily 24 hours. Park free. For park information phone (202) 895-6000 or (202) 895-6239. Phone (202) 426-0486 for concert information.

Kahlil Gibran Memorial Garden is on Massachusetts Ave. N.W. between 30th and 34th sts. N.W., opposite the British Embassy. It is dedicated to early 20th-century Lebanese-American poet and philosopher Kahlil Gibran. Visitors follow a stone walkway across a footbridge that leads to the memorial area. Granite benches engraved with quotations surround a fountain in the center of the garden. Daily 24 hours. Free.

Peirce Mill is at Tilden St. and Beach Dr. N.W. in Rock Creek Park. The Peirce Barn, next to the mill, has exhibits about the history of milling on Rock Creek and about the restoration work being done on the mill. It is a good starting point for a tour of Rock Creek because a park ranger is stationed there and can supply maps and directions to other parts of the park.

Note: The 1820s mill is closed for repairs until at least 2005. Barn open Sat.-Sun. noon-4; closed Jan. 1, July 4 and Dec. 25. Hours may vary; phone ahead. Free. Phone (202) 895-6000.

Rock Creek Park Nature Center and Planetarium, near Military Rd. at 5200 Glover Rd. N.W., offers an observation beehive, exhibits about the park's wildlife and forest, a hands-on nature discovery room, guided nature walks and wildlife displays. Facilities include an auditorium, a planetarium and self-guiding nature trails.

Allow 30 minutes minimum. Wed.-Sun. 9-5; closed Jan. 1, July 4, Thanksgiving and Dec. 25. Planetarium shows Wed. at 4, Sat.-Sun. at 1 and 4. Free. Under 4 are not permitted at planetarium shows, and ages 4-7 must be with an adult. Phone (202) 895-6070 or (202) 895-6239 for recorded event information.

 **SACKLER GALLERY—** see Arthur M. Sackler Gallery p. 76.

ST. JOHN'S CHURCH (Episcopal) is at 16th and H sts. N.W., opposite Lafayette Sq. (M: McPherson Square). This is known as the Church of the Presidents because every president since its establishment in 1815 has attended one or more services. Several of the stained-glass windows are dedicated to famous statesmen. Allow 30 minutes minimum. Daily 9-3; closed federal holidays and during services. Guided tours are offered after services on the first Sun. of each month. Free. Phone (202) 347-8766.

ST. MATTHEW'S CATHEDRAL is at 1725 Rhode Island Ave. N.W. (M: Dupont Circle or Farragut North). Established in 1840, the present Renaissance-style church was completed in 1895. Both the altar and the baptismal font were gifts from India. The altar is made of white marble with colored floral insets reminiscent of decorations in India's Taj Mahal.

The work of French and Italian craftsmen is displayed in the faceted windows, frescoes, marble and mosaics throughout the church. An inscription in marble commemorates the funeral of assassinated President John F. Kennedy. Guided tours are available by appointment. Allow 30 minutes minimum. Sun.-Fri. 6:30-6:30, Sat. 7:30-6:30, holidays 7:30-1. Free. Phone (202) 347-3215.

SENATE AND HOUSE OFFICE BUILDINGS are on opposite sides of Capitol Plaza (M: Capitol South or Union Station). Three of the four House offices face Independence Ave. between 1st St. S.W. and 1st St. S.E.

The Rayburn Building is the westernmost of the four House buildings; the Longworth Building is next door, followed by the O'Neill Building. The Cannon Building is at the junction of 1st Street S.E. and Independence Ave. S.E. The Senate offices—the Russell, Dirksen and Hart buildings—are on Constitution Avenue between Delaware Avenue and 2nd Street N.E.

Senators travel from offices to the Capitol via subways, which visitors also may use. Senate offices open Mon.-Fri. 8-6, Sat. 9-1. House offices

The Smithsonian Institution

Congress puzzled for more than a decade over what to do with James Smithson's strange and unprecedented bequest. A wealthy British scientist, Smithson willed his entire fortune of a half-million dollars to a country he had never visited, "to found at Washington, under the name of the Smithsonian Institution an Establishment for the increase and diffusion of knowledge...." Some congressmen argued against accepting the gift at all; others proposed a university, an observatory, a school for teachers or a library. What they finally settled on in 1846 was a natural history museum and research center of sorts, an institutional seedling that was to grow in size and scope at a remarkable rate.

The Smithsonian's vast collection chronicles nearly every facet of human endeavor, from the masterful to the mundane.

Digital Archives

But the Institution also encompasses research installations, observatories, libraries and facilities for preserving and restoring artifacts as well as offering publications, lectures, classes and other educational programs.

The first-time visitor is often surprised to learn that nearly all of the buildings on the National Mall are Smithsonian museums: the Arthur M. Sackler Gallery; the Arts and Industries Building (currently undergoing renovations); the Freer Gallery of Art; the Hirshhorn Museum and Sculpture Garden; the National Air and Space Museum; the National Museum of African Art; the National Museum of American History, Behring Center; the National Museum of the American Indian; the National Museum of Natural History; and the Smithsonian Institution Building (the Castle), the original building, completed in 1855.

Other facilities include the Anacostia Museum and Center for African American History and Culture; the National Portrait Gallery (under renovation and scheduled to reopen July 4, 2006); the National Postal Museum; the Renwick Gallery of the Smithsonian American Art Museum; the Smithsonian American Art Museum (under renovation and

open Mon.-Fri. 8-6, Sat. 8-1. Visitors arriving after 6 p.m. must register. Phone (202) 224-3121.

SEWALL-BELMONT HOUSE AND MUSEUM, 144 Constitution Ave. N.E. (M: Capitol South or Union Station), has been the headquarters of the National Woman's Party since 1929. The original structure was built in 1750; the main house was added in 1799. It contains antique furniture, party memorabilia and portraits of women important to the women's suffrage campaign. Also presented is a videotape about the suffrage and equal rights movements.

Allow 30 minutes minimum. Tues.-Fri. 11-3, Sat. noon-4; closed federal holidays. Donations. Phone (202) 546-3989.

THE SHAKESPEARE THEATRE, 450 7th St. N.W. in the Lansburgh Building (M: Archives-Navy Memorial), presents Shakespearean and other classical plays, as well as educational programs and special events. One such event is the "Shakespeare Theatre Free For All," a free outdoor production held in June at the Carter Barron Amphitheatre.

Guided tours of the theater are available. Regular performances run year-round. Tickets range from $15-$66. Regular performances sell out quickly, so it is best to reserve tickets early. Reservations are required for guided tours. Phone (202) 547-3230 for guided tour reservations, (202) 547-1122 or (877) 487-8849 for performance information or tickets, or TTY (202) 638-3863.

 SMITHSONIAN AMERICAN ART MUSEUM is housed in part of the Old Patent Office Building on F St. between 7th and 9th sts. N.W. (M: Gallery Place-Chinatown). This monumental Greek Revival structure, the third oldest government building in the city, served as a hospital during the Civil War and was the scene of Abraham Lincoln's second inaugural ball.

Note: The museum is undergoing major renovations and is scheduled to reopen July 4, 2006. During this time, the museum is sponsoring exhibitions at the Renwick Gallery (see attraction listing p. 90) and is touring Highlights from the Smithsonian American Art Museum, composed of five thematic exhibitions. Free. Phone (202) 633-1000 for general information, (202) 357-2020 for recorded information, or TTY (202) 357-1729.

THE SMITHSONIAN INSTITUTION encompasses 18 museums and galleries, including one in Chantilly, Va., and two in New York City. The National Zoo also is part of the Smithsonian. Ten of the museums line the National Mall from 3rd St. to 14th St. N.W.

Nearby are the National Portrait Gallery, the National Postal Museum, the Renwick Gallery and the Smithsonian American Art Museum (see sidebar page 86 and separate attraction listings). Elsewhere in the city is the Anacostia Museum and Center for African American History and Culture, and in Chantilly, Va., the National Air and Space Museum's Steven F. Udvar-Hazy Center.

Most Smithsonian museums are open daily 10-5:30. Extended summer hours are determined annually; phone for times. Closed Dec. 25. Free. Phone (202) 633-1000 for general information, (202) 357-2020 for recorded information, or TTY (202) 357-1729.

S. Dillon Ripley Center is entered through a small glass-enclosed kiosk located above ground on Jefferson Dr. between the Freer Gallery of Art and the Smithsonian Castle (M: Smithsonian). Part of the underground complex that includes the National Museum of African Art and the Arthur M. Sackler Gallery, the center houses the International Gallery, featuring changing exhibitions, and The Smithsonian Associates' Discovery Theater and classrooms.

Daily 10-5:30; closed Dec. 25. Free. Phone for Discovery Theater show times and prices. Phone (202) 633-1000 for general information, (202) 357-2020 for recorded information, TTY (202) 357-1729, or (202) 357-1500 (voice and TTY) for the Discovery Theater.

Smithsonian Institution Building (The Castle) is on the National Mall at 1000 Jefferson Dr. S.W. (M: Smithsonian). The Institution's first building, completed in 1855, houses the administrative headquarters and contains the tomb of James Smithson, the Institution's benefactor. The Smithsonian Information Center has interactive touch-screen programs, two electronic wall maps of the area and an orientation theater.

Free guided tours of The Castle are available on selected days; phone for schedule. Food is available. Allow 1 hour minimum. The Smithsonian Information Center is open daily 9-5:30; closed Dec. 25. Free. Phone (202) 633-1000 for general information, (202) 357-2020 for recorded information, or TTY (202) 357-1729.

SUPREME COURT BUILDING faces the Capitol between Maryland Ave. and E. Capitol St. N.E. (M: Capitol South or Union Station). This white marble edifice is where the country's highest judicial body holds its sessions. Exhibits and a film describing the court are presented on the ground floor. All sessions are open to the public; seating is on a first-come, first-served basis.

The richly ornamented, Corinthian Classical-style building was completed in 1935. The entrance, with the mandate on the architrave of "Equal Justice Under Law," is flanked by the statues "Contemplation of Justice" and "Authority of Law." The panels on the massive bronze doors depict the history of the development of law. The five-story, self-supporting marble and bronze spiral staircases are architectural masterpieces.

Food is available. Allow 1 hour minimum. Building open Mon.-Fri. 9-4:30; closed federal holidays, during inclement weather and occasionally for cleaning. The court often hears arguments Mon.-Wed., Oct. 1-late Apr. When it hands down opinions, these take place Mon. at 10, Oct.-June. Lectures are given in the courtroom every hour on

The Smithsonian Institution
(continued)

scheduled to reopen July 4, 2006); and the National Zoological Park. The National Air and Space Museum's Steven F. Udvar-Hazy Center is located near Washington Dulles International Airport in nearby Chantilly, Va.

Before exploring the museums, visitors are encouraged to first stop by the Information Center in the Castle to plan their visit. While there, be sure to give thanks to James Smithson; his tomb—rescued in 1904 by Alexander Graham Bell from an endangered cemetery in Genoa, Italy—lies in a crypt off the north entrance. It is a resting place he would surely approve of, as he would the multifarious Institution he helped found for "the increase and diffusion of knowledge."

Note: The East and West Buildings of the National Gallery of Art and the John F. Kennedy Center for the Performing Arts are not administered by the Smithsonian Institution.

America on the Move

With AAA as a co-sponsor, the Smithsonian's National Museum of American History opened the largest exhibition in its 40-year history in November 2003. "America on the Move" immerses visitors in the history of transportation in the United States from 1876 to the present. The exhibition showcases the Smithsonian's popular transportation collections in 15 historic settings. Visitors to the exhibition will:

- Celebrate with townspeople in Santa Cruz, Calif., as they welcome a railroad to the isolated town in 1876.
- Come "aboard" the 1920s U.S. Lighthouse Service Ship *Oak* in New York harbor.
- Join the morning commute on the Chicago Elevated.
- Watch as Horatio Nelson Jackson and Sewall K. Crocker pull their 20-horsepower 1903 Winton out of a mud hole during the first transcontinental automobile trip in 1903.
- Walk 40 feet of pavement from Route 66, one of the first great interstate highways.

"America on the Move" thoroughly and entertainingly explores transportation's social and economic effects on our lives, communities and country.

the half-hour 9:30-3:30 when court is not sitting. Free. Phone (202) 479-3211.

THE TEXTILE MUSEUM, 2320 S St. N.W. (M: Dupont Circle), is devoted to the handmade textile arts. Changing exhibits cover both traditional techniques and modern masters. Much of the collection can be viewed on slides in The Arthur D. Jenkins Library, which has more than 20,000 books and periodicals about textiles. The Textile Learning Center shows how textiles are made and highlights their cultural and artistic significance.

Allow 1 hour minimum. Mon.-Sat. 10-5, Sun. 1-5. Library open Wed.-Fri. 10-2, Sat. 10-4. Closed

Lincoln Memorial / © Paul M. Franklin

federal holidays and Dec. 24. Highlight tours are given the first Wed. of the month at 1 and Sat.-Sun. at 1:30, Sept.-May; other tours are by appointment. Admission $5. Phone (202) 667-0441.

THOMAS JEFFERSON MEMORIAL is on the s.e. side of the Tidal Basin. The monument to the author of the Declaration of Independence and the country's third president is a circular Classical dome supported by 54 Ionic columns. The central memorial room contains a 19-foot bronze statue of Jefferson by Rudolph Evans; panels on the surrounding walls are inscribed with the statesman's most significant writings. Allow 30 minutes minimum. Open 8 a.m.-midnight; closed Dec. 25. Guided tours are given by request daily 8 a.m.-11:45 p.m. Free. Phone (202) 426-6821.

[SAVE] **TUDOR PLACE HISTORIC HOUSE AND GARDEN** is in Georgetown at 1644 31st St. N.W. (M: Dupont Circle). The 1816 neoclassic house was built by Thomas Peter and his wife, Martha Custis Peter, granddaughter of Martha Washington. Set in 5.5 acres of gardens, it reflects six generations of family life, illustrated in paintings, furniture and decorative arts, including an important collection of Mount Vernon heirlooms.

Allow 1 hour minimum. Guided 45-minute house tours offered Tues.-Fri. at 10, 11:30, 1 and 2:30, Sat. on the hour 10-3, Sun. on the hour noon-3; closed major holidays. Garden open Tues.-Sat. 10-4, Sun. noon-4. House tour $6; over 64, $5; ages 2-12, $2. Garden only $2. No cameras are permitted inside the house. Reservations are suggested for guided tours. Phone (202) 965-0400, ext. 102.

UNITED STATES CAPITOL is on Capitol Hill in a 59-acre park (M: Capitol South or Union Station). The Capitol, based on Dr. William Thornton's 1792 design, with revisions by subsequent architects over a 200-year period, is 751 feet long and 350 feet wide, and contains about 550 rooms. A 19.5-foot-tall statue of Freedom surmounts the dome.

The two wings, constructed of marble, contain the Senate and House chambers. The central part of the building includes the Rotunda, Statuary Hall and the original Supreme Court and Senate chambers.

Note: The Capitol is open to the public only by guided tours. Obtain House or Senate gallery passes from your senator or representative by phoning his/her office *(see sidebar page 73)*. Visitors from outside the United States can obtain an International Visitor's Pass by presenting a valid passport or other photo ID at the South Visitors Facility, the departure point for tours.

Mon.-Sat. 9-4:30; closed Thanksgiving and Dec. 25. Tickets for tours are required and are available on a first-come, first-served basis (one ticket per person) beginning at 8:15 a.m. at the Capitol Guide Service kiosk near the intersection of 1st St. S.W. and Independence Ave. Free. Phone (202) 225-6827 for recorded information.

UNITED STATES HOLOCAUST MEMORIAL MUSEUM has entrances on 14th St. S.W. and at 100 Raoul Wallenberg Pl. S.W. (M: Smithsonian); there is no parking at the museum and limited parking in the area. The museum presents the history of the 6 million Jews and millions of others who suffered and died at the hands of the Nazis during their rule of Germany 1933-1945. Part of the mission of the museum is to teach the implications of the Holocaust for contemporary life.

The architecture of the limestone and brick building incorporates many references to the Holocaust, including towers like those used to watch over prisoners in the concentration camps. The three-floor permanent exhibition depicts the story of the Holocaust through artifacts, photographs, films and oral histories. To personalize the experience, upon entry each visitor is given an identity card bearing the name and picture of a Holocaust victim.

Note: The permanent exhibition is recommended for visitors age 11 and older. Daniel's Story: Remember the Children is designed for ages 8 and older. Flash photography and video cameras are not permitted in the permanent exhibition. Free timed passes are required for admission to the permanent exhibition, but passes are not needed to enter the museum or for any special exhibitions. A limited number of same-day passes are available daily starting at 10 a.m. at the box office on the 14th St. side of the building. There is a limit of four passes per person and a service charge for advance passes. Food is available. Allow 2 hours minimum.

Daily 10-5 (also Tues. and Thurs. 5:30-8, Apr. 1 to mid-June); closed Yom Kippur and Dec. 25. Last admission to the permanent exhibition is 1 hour before closing. Free. Phone (202) 488-0400, or TTY (202) 448-0406. For advance pass information phone (800) 400-9373.

U.S. BOTANIC GARDEN is on the w. side of the Capitol at 1st St. and Maryland Ave. S.W. (M: Federal Center S.W.). Founded in 1820, the garden is a plant museum. Visitors enter the conservatory through the Garden Court, where there are splashing fountains and colorful, exotic foliage. The 100-foot-tall, glass-enclosed Palm House has a catwalk that allows visitors to view the tree canopy from above. From late May to late September hanging baskets and pots of summer-blooming annuals are displayed on the outdoor terrace.

Bartholdi Park, on Independence Avenue across from the rear entrance to the conservatory, contains the Bartholdi Fountain, a rock garden, a formal parterre, native plants, therapeutic plants, and changing seasonal displays of annuals and perennials.

Flower shows are offered throughout the year; phone for details. Allow 1 hour, 30 minutes minimum. Conservatory open daily 10-5. Free. Phone (202) 225-8333, or (202) 225-7099 for flower show schedules.

USDA FOREST SERVICE NATIONAL HEADQUARTERS AND INFORMATION CENTER is at 1400 Independence Ave. S.W. in the Yates Federal Building (M: Smithsonian). The information center features an animatronic Smokey the Bear that greets visitors, as well as interactive touch-screen exhibits, a log cabin interior with videos and historical items, and an 8-foot by 20-foot photo wall explaining the purpose of the Forest Service. Allow 30 minutes minimum. Daily 8-4, Mar. 15-Sept. 15; Mon.-Fri. 8-4, rest of year. Closed federal holidays Sept. 16-Mar. 14. Free. Phone (202) 205-1680.

U.S. NATIONAL ARBORETUM is just e. of jct. US 50 (New York Ave.) and Bladensburg Rd.; entrances are on New York Ave. and R St. N.E. (M: Stadium-Armory). This 446-acre arboretum contains many introduced and native plants commonly grown in the eastern United States. A network of foot trails and 9.5 miles of roads enables visitors to observe thousands of primarily woody plants. Narrated 40-minute tram tours provide a good introduction to this peaceful refuge from hectic Washington.

Allow 1 hour minimum. Grounds open daily 8-5. Administration Building open Mon.-Fri. 8-4:30

Lafayette Square / © Richard Cummins / SuperStock

(also Sat.-Sun. 8-5, Mar. 1 to mid-Nov.). The National Bonsai and Penjing Museum Collection is open daily 10-3:30. Tram tours Sat.-Sun. and holidays at 10:30 (if not previously booked), 11:30, 1, 2, 3 and 4, mid-Apr. to mid-Oct. Closed Dec. 25. Admission free. Tram tour $4; over 54, $3; ages 4-16, $2; under 4 free on lap. Phone (202) 245-4523.

U.S. NAVY MEMORIAL AND NAVAL HERITAGE CENTER is at Pennsylvania Ave. and 7th St. N.W. (M: Archives-Navy Memorial). The base is a ground-level granite map of the world 100 feet in diameter, illustrating the enormity of Earth's ocean surface compared to land areas. Surrounded by fountains, pools, flag masts and 26 bronze relief sculptures depicting naval history, the map serves as an amphitheater for free outdoor summer concerts as well as traditional Navy ceremonies. The statue of the Lone Sailor is emblematic of the classic U.S. Navy bluejacket.

Allow 1 hour minimum. Memorial open daily 24 hours. Concerts are provided by the U.S. Navy Band and other service bands every Tues. at 8 p.m., Memorial Day-Labor Day. Free. Phone (202) 737-2300, ext. 733, or (800) 821-8892.

Naval Heritage Center is behind the Navy Memorial's n.e. quadrant at Pennsylvania Ave. N.W. and 7th St. (M: Archives-Navy Memorial). Features include videotapes, a sculpture depicting a Navy family homecoming, an electronic Navy Memorial Log listing some 300,000 naval service veterans, rotating exhibits and a reference library. "At Sea" is a

36-minute naval battle operations film shown at noon.

Guided tours are available. Open Mon.-Sat. 9:30-5, Mar.-Oct.; Tues.-Sat. 9:30-5, rest of year. Closed Jan. 1, July 4, Thanksgiving and Dec. 25. Free. Phone (202) 737-2300, ext. 733 or (800) 821-8892.

VIETNAM VETERANS MEMORIAL, near the Lincoln Memorial between the Reflecting Pool and Constitution Ave. (M: Foggy Bottom-GWU), honors the men and women who served in the U.S. Armed Forces in Vietnam. Its polished black granite walls are inscribed with the names of the dead listed chronologically by date of casualty; the names of the missing also are listed.

A life-size statue of three servicemen stands near the V-shaped walls; each one carries a dog tag in a different place. Wreath ceremonies take place on Memorial Day and Veterans Day. The Memorial to Honor Women Who Served in Vietnam honors the more than 265,000 women who served during the Vietnam War with a statue depicting three servicewomen coming to the aid of a wounded soldier.

Allow 30 minutes minimum. Daily 8 a.m.-11:45 p.m.; closed Dec. 25 Free. Phone (202) 619-7222.

VOICE OF AMERICA is at 330 Independence Ave. S.W. (M: Federal Center S.W.). This worldwide service, which supplies broadcasts in more than 50 languages, provides a 45-minute guided tour of its facilities. Included are the radio and television studios and the newsroom. Visitors taking the tour also see the 1940 Ben Shahn mural "The Meaning of Social Security." Tours Mon.-Fri. at 10:30, 1:30 and 2:30; closed holidays. Free. Reservations are required for tours. Phone (202) 619-3919.

WASHINGTON MONUMENT stands at the w. end of the National Mall. The grounds extend from 14th to 17th sts. and from Constitution to Independence aves. N.W. (M: Smithsonian). The cornerstone for a monument to honor the first president was laid July 4, 1848, but was not completed until 1884, when a 3,300-pound marble capstone, topped with a 9-inch pyramid of cast aluminum, was set in place. The marble obelisk rises just over 555 feet from a knoll in the center of the grounds, surrounded by 50 American flags. An elevator runs to the observation room at the 500-foot level.

Allow 1 hour minimum. Daily 9-4:45; closed Dec. 25. Tickets are required and are available on a first-come, first-served basis daily 8-4:30 at the kiosk on 15th Street near Madison Drive. The line for same-day tickets forms at 7:30 or earlier, and all are usually distributed before noon. Tickets also are available from 24 hours to up to 5 months in advance and can be reserved by phoning the monument's toll-free number. Same-day tickets free. Advance ticket reservations $2 per ticket. Phone (202) 426-6841, or (800) 967-2283 daily 10-10 for advance tickets.

WASHINGTON NATIONAL CATHEDRAL (Episcopal) is on Mount St. Alban at Massachusetts and Wisconsin aves. N.W. Officially the Cathedral Church of St. Peter and St. Paul, this impressive example of Gothic architecture is said to be the sixth largest cathedral in the world. It was completed in 1990 after 83 years of construction. The top of the Gloria in Excelsis Central Tower, one of the last towers in the world to contain both a carillon and a 10-bell peal, is the highest point in Washington.

Decorative features include elaborate stone carvings and large stained-glass rose windows, as well as statues of Abraham Lincoln and George Washington. Notable individuals interred in the cathedral are Adm. George Dewey, secretaries of state Cordell Hull and Frank Kellogg, Helen Keller and President Woodrow Wilson.

Various guided tours and a CD-based audio tour are available. Scheduled tours are 30 minutes, unscheduled tours are 15 minutes, mid-Mar. through June 30; all tours are 45 minutes, rest of year. Allow 1 hour minimum. Cathedral open Mon.-Fri. 10-8, late May-Labor Day; Mon.-Fri. 10-5:30, Sat. 10-4:30, Sun. 8-6:30, rest of year. Closed during special services. Guided cathedral tours Mon.-Sat. 10-11:30 and 12:45-3:15, Sun. 12:45-2:30. Cathedral services Mon.-Sat. at 7:30, noon, 2:30 and 5:30 (no 5:30 service Sat.), Sun. at 8, 9, 10, 11, 4 and 6:30 (no 10 a.m. service July-Aug.). Pipe organ demonstrations Wed. at 12:30. Peal bell recitals Sun. at 12:15. Carillon recitals Sat. at 12:30. The cathedral towers are closed during Code Orange Alerts.

Admission $4, senior citizens $3, children $2. Phone (202) 537-6200, or (202) 364-6616 for a weekly listing of special events.

WHITE HOUSE is at 1600 Pennsylvania Ave. N.W. (M: McPherson Square, Metro Center or Federal Triangle for the visitor center); street parking in the vicinity is not available. James Hoban's design was chosen for the presidential mansion in 1792, and the building was completed in 1800. A 1948-52 renovation preserved the exterior walls and rebuilt the interior. The West Wing, location of the President's Oval Office, was constructed in 1902. This has been the home of every president except George Washington.

Within the White House Visitor Center, at the southwest corner of 15th and E sts. N.W., are exhibits and a 30-minute videotape that describe the history and architecture of the Executive Mansion.

Note: Self-guiding public tours of the White House are available Tues.-Sat. 7:30-12:30 (excluding federal holidays) for groups of 10 or more people only. Tour requests must be made through one's member of Congress (senator or representative) and are accepted up to 6 months in advance; tours are scheduled on a first-come, first-served basis approximately 1 month before the scheduled date. Visitors from outside the United States can obtain an International Visitor's Pass by presenting a valid passport or other photo ID. Visitor center open daily 7:30-4. Tours free. Visitor center free. Phone (202) 456-7041 for 24-hour recorded information, or (202) 208-1631 for the visitor center.

WOODROW WILSON HOUSE is at 2340 S St. N.W. (M: Dupont Circle). From 1921 until his death in 1924, former President Woodrow Wilson lived in this 1915 Georgian Revival townhouse on Embassy Row. The house is filled with personal furnishings and mementos of the 28th president's career, and is the only presidential museum in Washington. Allow 1 hour minimum. Guided tours Tues.-Sun. 10-4; closed federal holidays. Admission $5; over 62, $4; students with ID and ages 7-18, $2.50. AX, MC, VI. Phone (202) 387-4062.

What To Do

Sightseeing

Sightseeing tours cover the city and most major suburban points of interest. Your local AAA office can provide information about tours of embassies, houses and gardens that occur periodically *(see Special Events)*. For more information visit one of the AAA Mid-Atlantic offices. Visitors can obtain access to services and tours by contacting their U.S. senators and representatives before leaving home.

Boat Tours

C & O CANAL BOAT TRIPS—
see Chesapeake and Ohio Canal National Historical Park, Md., p. 182.

POTOMAC SPIRIT, departing Pier 4 at 6th and Water sts. S.W. (M: Waterfront), offers a narrated cruise (90 minutes each way) on the Potomac River plus a 3.5-hour stopover at George Washington's Mount Vernon estate. Other sites include Fort Washington, Ronald Reagan Washington National Airport, Old Town Alexandria and the Torpedo Factory Art Center. Food is available.

Allow 5 hours minimum. Ask about refund policies. Trips depart Tues.-Sun. at 8:30 a.m., mid-Mar. through early Oct. (also sails Memorial Day and Labor Day); Sat.-Sun. at 9, mid-Oct. through last weekend in Oct. Fare (includes admission to Mount Vernon) $32; over 59, $31; ages 6-11, $23. Parking $10. Reservations are recommended. AX, MC, VI. Phone (202) 554-8000.

Bus, Limousine or Trolley Tours

Individually operated limousine tours are sold by the drivers near the various information kiosks. Most taxi companies also can provide sightseeing services. Bus tours range in price from about $10 to $65, depending on length of tour and itinerary, and include trips around Washington, Mount Vernon

and all stops between. Tour companies are listed in the telephone directory.

DC DUCKS LAND & WATER TOURS begin and end at Union Station, 50 Massachusetts Ave. N.E. (M: Union Station). These nonstop, 90-minute narrated tours aboard rebuilt World War II amphibious vehicles roll past the monuments and museums along the Mall and splash down into the Potomac River. Tours daily on the hour 10-4, mid-Mar. to Oct. 31 (weather permitting); closed July 4. Hours may vary. Fare $28; ages 4-12, $14. AX, DC, DS, MC, VI. Phone (202) 832-9800.

GRAY LINE OF WASHINGTON tours depart from the Gray Line Terminal, on the first parking level of Union Station, 50 Massachusetts Ave. N.E. Gray Line offers a variety of tour packages, including a multilingual tour available in nine languages. Seasonal tours are available to Colonial Williamsburg, Busch Gardens Williamsburg, Gettysburg and Monticello. Some combination tours are available. Fares include all applicable admission charges. AX, MC, VI. Phone (202) 289-1995.

The Interiors of Public Buildings Tour (Tour BA) is a 9-hour tour that stops at the White House Visitor Center, Ford's Theatre, Petersen House, the National Museum of American History, Behring Center, the National Air & Space Museum and the National World War II Memorial. A stop also is made at the U.S. Capitol (Monday through Saturday). The Supreme Court Building, the Thomas Jefferson Memorial, the Tidal Basin and a number of government buildings can be viewed from the coach.

National Museum of Natural History / © Andre Jenny/Alamy Images

Tours depart Mon.-Sat. at 8:30 a.m.; no tours Jan. 1, Thanksgiving and Dec. 25. Fare $40; ages 3-11, $20.

Lil' Red Trolley All Day Tour (Tour T) passes are available for the 2.25-hour tour or for unlimited hopping on and off all day. Stops include the National World War II Memorial; Washington National Cathedral; the National Zoo; the Lincoln, Vietnam

Veterans and Korean War memorials; the Washington Monument; the United States Holocaust Memorial Museum; Arlington National Cemetery; Embassy Row; the Franklin Delano Roosevelt Memorial; the National Air & Space Museum; and the National Gallery of Art. Daily year-round. Fare $28; ages 3-11, $14.

The Mount Vernon and Alexandria Tour (Tour D) is a 4-hour tour that includes a stop at Christ Church (not available during services), George Washington's place of worship in Alexandria, Va., and then continues to Mount Vernon to visit his home, gardens and farm. Tours depart daily at 8:30 a.m. (also at 2, late June-early Oct.); no tours Jan. 1, Thanksgiving and Dec. 25.

Fare $30; ages 3-11, $15. All-day combination tour (Tour DC) with The Washington, Embassy Row & Arlington National Cemetery Tour $50; ages 3-11, $25.

The Washington After Dark Tour (Tour L) is a 3-hour tour that features Washington's monuments and buildings illuminated by floodlights. Stops include the Kennedy Center (as available) and the Lincoln, Vietnam Veterans, Korean War, Marine Corps and Franklin Delano Roosevelt memorials. The U.S. Capitol, Supreme Court Building, Library of Congress, House and Senate office buildings, White House, Georgetown and the Marine Corps War Memorial are seen en route. Tour departs daily at 7:45 p.m.; no tours Jan. 1, July 4, Thanksgiving, and Dec. 24-25 and 31. Fare $30; ages 3-11, $15.

The Washington, Embassy Row & Arlington National Cemetery Tour (Tour C) is a 4-hour tour that includes stops at the Lincoln, Korean War, Marine Corps and Vietnam Veterans memorials and Arlington National Cemetery for a tram tour to the Changing of the Guard ceremony and the Kennedy gravesites. Many downtown sites as well as the Pentagon, Georgetown and Embassy Row can be seen en route.

Tours depart daily at 2 (also at 8:30 a.m., late June-late Oct.); no tours Jan. 1, Thanksgiving and Dec. 25. Fare $30; ages 3-11, $15. All-day combination tour with The Mount Vernon and Alexandria Tour $50; ages 3-11, $25.

OLD TOWN TROLLEY TOURS OF WASHINGTON depart from any one of 17 stops, including Union Station at 50 Massachusetts Ave. N.E. This 2-hour narrated tour passes most of Washington's major attractions, from Capitol Hill to Washington National Cathedral, and includes the Smithsonian museums, the White House and Arlington National Cemetery. Unlimited free reboarding within one loop is permitted on the trolleys, which pass 17 designated stops at least every 30 minutes.

Daily 9-5:30, during DST; 9-4:30, rest of year. Closed Thanksgiving and Dec. 25. Fare $28; ages 4-12, $14. AX, DC, DS, MC, VI. Phone (202) 832-9800.

TOURMOBILE SIGHTSEEING INC., departing from various locations, offers several narrated sightseeing shuttle tours around Washington landmarks, with stops at up to 21 different sights on or near the National Mall and four sites at Arlington National Cemetery. Two-day combination tickets are available for The Washington/Arlington National Cemetery Tour and either The Mount Vernon or The Frederick Douglass tour.

Tickets can be purchased year-round from Tourmobile drivers, at the Tourmobile Ticket/Information booth at Arlington National Cemetery, or from other ticket kiosks along the National Mall in the summer. Parking is available in the visitor parking lot near the Thomas Jefferson Memorial (free) and in the Arlington National Cemetery visitor parking lot ($1.25 per hour for first 3 hours, then $2 per hour). **Note:** Tour itineraries, times and rates are all subject to change; phone to verify. Tours offered daily, except Dec. 25. Phone (202) 554-5100 or (888) 868-7707. *See ad p. 74.*

The Arlington National Cemetery Tour begins at the cemetery visitor center on Memorial Dr. and includes the Kennedy gravesites; the Tomb of the Unknowns for the Changing of the Guard ceremony; and Arlington House, the Robert E. Lee Memorial. Tickets are available at the Arlington National Cemetery ticket booth. Daily 8:30-6:30, Apr.-Sept.; 8:30-4:30, rest of year. No tours Dec. 25. Last tour begins 30 minutes before closing. Fare $6; ages 3-11, $3.

The Frederick Douglass Tour departs Arlington National Cemetery and the Washington Monument ticket booths. The 2.5-hour tour includes landmarks on Capitol Hill, Cedar Hill (the former home of Frederick Douglass), the Mary McLeod Bethune Memorial and Lincoln Park. Tours daily at noon, June 15-Labor Day. **Note:** Phone to verify schedule; the tour may not be offered in 2005. Fare $7; ages 3-11, $3.50. Reservations in person are required and should be made 30 minutes before departure. Phone to verify prices.

The Mount Vernon Tour leaves from Arlington National Cemetery and the Washington Monument ticket booths. The 4-hour tour includes a scenic 17-mile excursion along the George Washington Parkway via Old Town Alexandria to George Washington's estate and gardens at Mount Vernon. Tours depart daily at 10, noon and 2, Apr.-Oct. **Note:** Phone to verify schedule; the tour may not be offered in 2005. Fare, including admission to home, gardens and exhibits, $25; ages 3-11, $12. Reservations in person are required and should be made 30 minutes before departure. Phone to verify schedule and prices.

The Washington/Arlington National Cemetery Tour begins at sites along and near the Mall marked by Tourmobile stop signs. This tour provides narrated sightseeing shuttle service to 25 historic sites, including the White House; the Washington Monument; the Jefferson, Lincoln,

Vietnam War and Korean War memorials; the United States Holocaust Memorial Museum; the Smithsonian museums; the Kennedy Center; and Arlington National Cemetery.

There is unlimited free reboarding throughout the day. Daily 9-6:30, June 15-Labor Day; 9:30-4:30, rest of year. Closed Jan. 1 and Dec. 25. Fare $20; ages 3-11, $10.

Driving Tours

A 3-hour driving cassette tape tour of the District of Columbia and Mount Vernon is available by mail from CCInc. Auto Tape Tours and at area hotels and gift shops for $12.95 (plus $2 for shipping and handling); phone (201) 236-1666.

Walking Tours

A walk among the monuments and monumental buildings of Washington, D.C. is sure to leave a lasting impression on all but the most jaded traveler. The District's imposing white-columned facades have come to symbolize the United States, its government and its principles. America's founding fathers chose this classical motif as befitting a young republic committed to the ancient Greek ideal of democracy.

The following three tours focus on the U.S. Capitol and vicinity, the museums surrounding the Mall, and the White House and vicinity. Each tour should take 3-4 hours, depending on your pace and the number of listed sites you visit along the way. Those that appear in bold type have detailed listings on the preceding pages. Even if you decide not to visit a site, reading the listing when you reach that point should make the tour more interesting.

Because parking in the District is difficult even on a good day, avoid driving whenever possible. The easiest way to get around is to use Washington Metrorail. Trains run Mon.-Thurs. 5:30 a.m.-midnight, Fri. 5:30 a.m.-3 a.m., Sat. 7 a.m.-3 a.m., Sun. 7 a.m.-midnight; opening and closing times

are scaled back on federal holidays. Fares range between $1.35 and $3.90, depending on distance traveled and whether you travel during regular or off-peak hours.

Dramatic spotlighting illuminates many public buildings after dusk, although most of them aren't open at this time. In good weather, early evening is a pleasant time to stroll around the Capitol, the Mall museums or the White House, when otherwise stark white or gray edifices are bathed in a mellow glow.

Note: Although restrooms can be found within most public buildings around Capitol Hill and on the Mall, they may not always be convenient. It's a good idea to take advantage of the facilities whenever you get a chance.

Walking Tour: The Capitol

See map below. From the Capitol South Metro station at 1st Street S.E. between C and D streets S.E., go north up the hill on 1st Street and cross C Street. The austere marble facade on your right belongs to the James Madison Building of the **Library of Congress,** which comprises three buildings (named for Presidents Adams, Jefferson and Madison).

By far the most elaborate of the three is the Italian Renaissance-style Jefferson Building, which will be on your right after you cross Independence Avenue. Completed in 1897 and renovated for its centennial, the building features an ornate exterior that is but a foretaste of the splendor inside.

The golden Torch of Learning atop a central cupola indicates the building's purpose. A beautiful fountain along 1st Street features the Roman god Neptune and his court. As you approach the main entrance, notice the faces set in the keystones above several first-floor windows. There are 33 in all, and each represents a different ethnic group. A little higher up, framed by circular windows, are the busts of nine important authors: Dante, Demosthenes, Ralph Waldo Emerson, Benjamin Franklin,

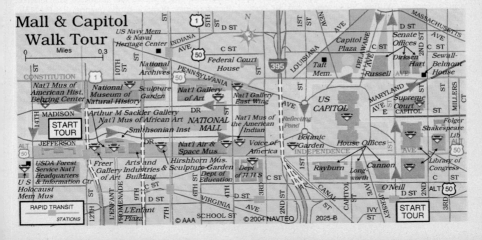

Johann Wolfgang von Goethe, Nathaniel Hawthorne, Washington Irving, Thomas Babington Macaulay and Sir Walter Scott.

Three pairs of decorative bronze doors originally served as the building's main entrance, but now these are opened only for special occasions. Visitors must enter via the ground-floor doorway below, where stairs lead back up to the first floor's Great Hall vestibule. Here you may have to remind yourself that you're standing in a library and not a European-style palace.

Constructed of white Italian marble, this vast room features stained-glass skylights 75 feet above the multihued, brass-inlaid marble floor. The ornamental touches are almost too numerous to take in: stucco ceilings accented with gold leaf, murals, mosaics, Corinthian columns, sweeping arches and classical statues. Don't overlook the Great Hall's East Corridor, which contains two of the library's most precious items: the Giant Bible of Mainz and the Gutenberg Bible, one of only three vellum copies in existence.

Beyond the Great Hall is the Main Reading Room, which is accessible only by way of the library's free public tours during the height of tourist season in spring and early summer. Even then you are limited to seeing the room from behind the Visitors Gallery's transparent, sound-dampening walls. The view, however, is worth it.

From the base of its massive columns to the domed ceiling 160 feet above, the Main Reading Room is richly detailed. Octagonal in shape, it has walls and columns made of brown, red and cream-colored marble from three continents. Semicircular, stained-glass windows bear the seals of the 48 contiguous states. Between these windows stand eight larger than life-size statues of female allegorical figures representing religion, commerce, history, art, philosophy, poetry, law and science.

A few feet below and on either side of the figures stand 16 bronze statues of men who have distinguished themselves in those eight fields, including Moses, Christopher Columbus, Ludwig van Beethoven, William Shakespeare and Sir Isaac Newton. Murals, bas-reliefs, plaster rosettes, balustrades and baroque molding complete this impressive chamber.

If the other two library buildings look newer than the Jefferson Building, that's because they are. The Adams Building was completed in 1939, the Madison Building in 1981. Together the three contain more than 120 million items, making the Library of Congress the world's largest.

From the library's main exit on 1st Street, go right around the corner onto E. Capitol Street and cross 2nd Street S.E. Just south is **The Folger Shakespeare Library,** which houses rare books and manuscripts, paintings, engravings, costumes and musical instruments. Henry Clay Folger, who founded the library with his wife Emily, was a president of Standard Oil Co. and a devotee of all things Shakespearean for most of his life. The neoclassic building was completed in 1932 to house

the Folgers' collection; it is adorned with nine bas-reliefs showing scenes from Shakespeare's plays.

Leaving the library, return to E. Capitol Street and turn left, following it 2 blocks to the entrance of the **United States Capitol.** George Washington laid the cornerstone of this familiar landmark in 1793, but most of what is visible was built in the next century, including the Capitol's north and south wings and the distinctive 287-foot-tall cast-iron dome, all of which were added 1855-70.

Up to 5 million people visit the Capitol every year, and for obvious reasons: Not only is this the hallowed center of representative government and political power in the United States, but it is a splendid building filled with historic and artistic treasures as well.

At the Capitol's heart is the rotunda, a grand circular space 96 feet across beneath the dome that connects the north and south wings. From the statues and large, historically themed paintings on the lower walls look upward to the canopy over the inner dome, 180 feet above, which is adorned with a fresco by Constantino Brumidi titled "The Apotheosis of Washington." Restored in 1988, the 4,664-square-foot fresco depicts George Washington ascending to the heavens flanked by 15 female figures—two symbolizing Liberty and Victory, the others representing the 13 original states. A painted frieze designed to look like a bas-relief forms a band beneath the rotunda's windows and illustrates scenes from American history.

Other sights within the Capitol include the Hall of Columns; National Statuary Hall (formerly the Old Hall of the House of Representatives); the Old Supreme Court Chamber; the Old Senate Chamber; the Crypt, located beneath the rotunda; and the ornate Brumidi Corridors. Tours of the Capitol are given regularly; however, to gain access to the current congressional chambers, you must first obtain a pass from one of your representatives or senators. *See sidebar p. 73.*

Remember that the Capitol is the point from which the city's streets are numbered and lettered; therefore, pay attention to the quadrant (N.E., N.W., S.E. or S.W.) of the streets or addresses you wish to find.

From the Capitol, cross 1st Street N.E. on the north side of E. Capitol Street. The imposing white building in front of you is the **Supreme Court Building,** where the creed "Equal Justice Under Law" is written on the facade. The seated female figure to the left is titled "Contemplation of Justice," while the male counterpart opposite her is called "Guardian of Law."

The third branch of government did not have its own building until 1935. For almost a century and a half of its existence, the court met in various locations, including the Capitol. It was not until 1929 that William H. Taft—who was chief justice at the time and a former U.S. president to boot—was able to convince Congress of the court's need for its own home, authorizing the creation of the current neoclassic building.

Designed to match surrounding structures, the Supreme Court possesses many noteworthy features, including a Great Hall lined with the busts of every chief justice who has presided over the court since it was established. The hall leads to the marble-trimmed Court Chamber, which looks like a theater thanks to the plush red curtain suspended behind the bench. Considering the weighty Constitutional issues that are debated in this room, the theaterlike ambience seems appropriate.

To learn more about the court and what cases are currently being argued, stop by the information desk beneath the statue of Chief Justice John Marshall on the ground floor. Here you'll find exhibits, portraits of justices and a film. You'll also be able to see one of the building's two, five-story-tall marble staircases that creates a striking vista as it spirals upwards without a central column for support.

Turn north after leaving the Supreme Court and follow Maryland Avenue northeast to 2nd Street N.E., where Maryland and Constitution avenues meet, and go north across Constitution. On the corner of 2nd and Constitution is the **Sewall-Belmont House and Museum,** headquarters of the National Woman's Party since 1929. Within the red-brick house, built about 1700, are displays relating to the women's suffrage and equal rights movements.

From there head west on Constitution Avenue and turn right on 1st Street N.E. On either side of you are the Dirksen and Russell **Senate office buildings.** Cross C and D streets N.E. and Massachusetts Avenue. The large, white-granite edifice ahead of you is Union Station. Before it stands a 1912 monument to Christopher Columbus made up of three flagpoles, a semicircular fountain and a 15-foot statue of the explorer facing the Capitol.

Built in 1907 during the heyday of railway travel, Union Station was designed to serve as the gateway to America's capital city and is an important example of the Beaux Arts style. Inspired by ancient Roman baths and triumphal arches, architect Daniel Burnham designed the station's main hall, distinguished by a 96-foot-tall barrel-vaulted ceiling made up of recessed, gilded panels. Statues adorn both the exterior and interior; a few of the 46 Roman legionnaires encircling the main hall had to be redesigned due to concern that their skimpy uniforms would scandalize passengers.

Like many stately train stations built before the advent of air travel, Union Station endured a period of decline and decay until it was abandoned in the 1970s. When renovations began in the 1980s, large portions of ceiling had collapsed and mushrooms were discovered growing on the floor. But the station was returned to its original splendor and also found new life as a retail and entertainment complex boasting numerous restaurants and cafes, more than 100 stores and a multiscreen movie complex. The building also houses a Metrorail station and is Amtrak's hub and headquarters.

From Union Station walk back toward the Capitol via Delaware Avenue N.E. Once you cross D

Street N.E., Capitol Plaza will be on your right. If you're a shutterbug then get your camera ready. This spacious park's reflecting pool and fountain make an especially picturesque foreground for the Capitol. Just west of the plaza across New Jersey Avenue is the **Robert A. Taft Memorial.** This 100-foot bell tower, dedicated in 1959, honors the influential Ohio senator who became known as "Mr. Republican" for his outspoken opposition to President Franklin D. Roosevelt's New Deal policies. Son of President Taft, the senator died of cancer in 1953. His statue stands before the tower.

From the Taft memorial, cross Constitution Avenue and then go immediately right across 1st Street N.W. Continuing south down 1st Street, you'll enter Union Square with its monuments and Reflecting Pool. The first memorial you'll come to is the Peace Monument, at Pennsylvania Avenue and 1st Street N.W. Dedicated to those who served at sea during the Civil War, the memorial depicts two female figures representing Grief weeping on the shoulder of History.

The next memorial honors Ulysses S. Grant, Union general and U.S. president. The 65-foot-tall central figure shows the general on horseback impassively gazing westward. His poise contrasts sharply with the artillery and cavalry statuary groups frozen in action at either side of him. Said to be the largest equestrian statue in America, the memorial was dedicated in 1922, having taken the artist 2 decades to complete.

The James A. Garfield Monument stands at 1st Street and Maryland Avenue S.W. and honors the 20th president, who was assassinated in 1881 after serving only 4 months in office. Garfield was a brigadier general during the Civil War and held public office as both a U.S. senator and representative before being elected president. The monument features a lifelike statue of Garfield atop a cylindrical pedestal. The three figures arranged around the base represent different phases of his career: student, officer and statesman.

Just south of the Garfield Monument across Maryland Avenue S.W. is the **U.S. Botanic Garden.** Established by Congress in 1820 as a research facility to cultivate and distribute plants from around the world to benefit the American people, it has existed at its current location on the Capitol grounds since 1933. The Palm House and Garden Court in the Conservatory feature soaring glass walls. Also part of the Botanic Garden is Bartholdi Park, across Independence Avenue from the Conservatory. The centerpiece of this demonstration garden is a fanciful cast-iron fountain complete with sea nymphs and tritons; it was designed by Frédéric Auguste Bartholdi, sculptor of the Statue of Liberty.

After leaving the Botanic Garden, turn right on 1st Street S.W. to Independence Avenue. Cross Independence and turn left, following it east across 1st Street, S. Capitol Street and New Jersey Avenue S.E. Turn right onto 1st Street S.E.; the Capitol South Metro station is 1 block south across C Street S.E. on the right.

⚠ Walking Tour: The National Mall

See map page 99. From the Smithsonian Metro station, on the Mall opposite where 12th Street S.W. meets Jefferson Drive S.W., follow the short gravel path to the sidewalk, cross Jefferson Drive and turn left. Just ahead on the right is the **Freer Gallery of Art,** which contains Chinese paintings, Islamic metalwork, Indian sculpture, Korean ceramics and Japanese lacquer.

Although primarily dedicated to Asian art, the Freer also exhibits American paintings and prints from the late 19th century and is noted for The Peacock Room. This finely detailed interior space was designed by James McNeill Whistler 1876-77; it served as a dining room in a London mansion before being relocated to the museum's southeast corner.

Leaving the Freer, turn right, still going east on Jefferson Drive. Next door is the administrative building of the **Smithsonian Institution.** Nicknamed The Castle because of its red sandstone walls, towers, mullioned windows and Romanesque details, this 1855 structure is the work of James Renwick Jr., who also designed the Smithsonian's Renwick Gallery near the White House and St. Patrick's Cathedral in New York. The Castle houses an information center and the tomb of James Smithson, the institution's benefactor. A domed entry pavilion between the Castle and the Freer leads to the S. Dillon Ripley Center, a three-level underground structure built in 1987 that includes an International Gallery, offices and classrooms.

The decorative domes and pyramids on either side of the Smithsonian Castle are entrances to the underground **Arthur M. Sackler Gallery** and the **National Museum of African Art.** Connected to the Freer by a skylighted gallery, the Sackler continues the Smithsonian's Asian art collection with a focus on changing exhibitions. Inside the National Museum of African Art you'll find traditional objects from the sub-Saharan continent, including highly wrought sculptures, carvings and masks.

Continue east to the **Arts and Industries Building,** which was built in 1881 to house items from the 1876 Centennial Exhibition in Philadelphia. Above the entrance, a statue grouping portrays Columbia shielding seated figures representing Science and Industry. The museum is currently closed for renovation.

What appears to be an alien spaceship next door is actually the **Hirshhorn Museum and Sculpture Garden.** In sharp contrast to the 19th-century architecture nearby, the cylindrical Hirshhorn building makes a fitting showplace for one of America's best collections of modern art. Glass-walled ambulatories overlook a central courtyard with a fountain, allowing visitors to see art pieces in natural lighting. Name a 20th-century artistic movement and it is likely represented in the collection: Pop Art, Abstract Expressionism, Cubism, Minimalism, Surrealism and several other "isms." Unusual, twisting, curving shapes loom within the museum's sunken outdoor sculpture garden, across the sidewalk on the building's Mall side.

East of the Hirshhorn across 7th Street S.W. is the capital's most visited museum, the **National Air and Space Museum.** Crowds come in droves here to see history-making flying machines dramatically suspended in cavernous exhibit spaces. From the Wright Flyer to rockets and lunar landers, the spectrum of air- and spacecraft on display traces the evolution of flight, delighting busloads of tourists and school children in the process.

The high concentration of large museums will take its toll on even the most energetic of sightseers, one reason the Mall is amply lined with shaded benches for rest stops. Vendor carts also sell a variety of refreshments along the way. If you require assistance or information, visit one of the National Park Service's green and blue kiosks or flag down one of the mounted police officers who patrol the Mall.

From the Air and Space Museum, continue down Jefferson Drive. Across 4th Street N.W. is the **National Museum of the American Indian.** The newest Smithsonian museum is distinguished by undulating walls of buff-colored limestone. Inside this cultural resource center are performance spaces and exhibition areas.

Turn left onto 4th Street S.W. and walk toward the modern glass and concrete structure ahead on the right. This is the **National Gallery of Art's East Building,** which features contemporary art as well as changing exhibits. It is linked with the gallery's main facility by a paved plaza and an underground concourse. Take either one to the West Building's older and more classical collections.

From the West Building's Mall exit go down the large flight of stairs and turn right, going west on Madison Drive. Taking a short detour from the Mall, turn right again at 7th Street N.W. The park on your left is the National Gallery of Art's Sculpture Garden; works by Claes Oldenburg, Joan Miró and Isamu Noguchi are on display here year-round. Cross Constitution Avenue, and between 7th and 9th streets N.W. you'll come to a mammoth neoclassic building, the **National Archives.** It contains the nation's triumvirate of governmental blueprints: the Declaration of Independence, the Constitution and the Bill of Rights. Also between 7th and 9th streets is the **U.S. Navy Memorial and Naval Heritage Center,** behind Exhibition Hall on Pennsylvania Avenue.

From the Archives go back across Constitution Avenue, proceed south 1 block on 7th Street N.W., then turn west onto Madison Drive on the Mall. One block ahead on the right is the **National Museum of Natural History,** with treasures that include natural and cultural specimens ranging from the Hope Diamond to a giant squid. Enter the rotunda and prepare to be greeted by an African elephant showing off its raised trunk and lengthy tusks. Even more intimidating displays await intrepid visitors in the skeleton-crowded Dinosaur Hall.

Another block west along Madison Drive is the **National Museum of American History, Behring Center,** home to such familiar objects of Americana as a covered wagon, steam locomotive and a 19th-century general store. You can see such historic items as Lewis and Clark's compass and even Cold War-era submarines, or if you're more interested in America's popular culture, there's Muhammad Ali's boxing gloves, Evel Knievel's motorcycle and Dorothy's ruby slippers from "The Wizard of Oz." Another museum highlight: a colorful collection of First Ladies' gowns.

From the museum return to Madison Drive N.W. and continue west to 14th Street. Turn left, cross Madison and go south toward Jefferson Drive. Halfway across the walkway, pause to take in the view of the Mall's tallest landmarks, the Capitol and the **Washington Monument.** Turn left at Jefferson Drive; the Smithsonian Metro station, where you began, is on the left.

🚶 Walking Tour: The White House

See map below. Beginning at the McPherson Square Metro station's White House/Vermont Avenue exit at the corner of Vermont Avenue and I Street N.W., go 1 block west on I Street to 16th Street N.W. Turn left and go south on 16th to the end of the block. On your left is **St. John's Church.** Painted yellow and white with a distinctive golden-roofed steeple, St. John's is known as the Church of the Presidents due to the number of commanders-in-chief who have worshiped here over the years.

Cross H Street N.W. to **Lafayette Square,** the park opposite the main entrance to the **White House.** A statue of Andrew Jackson presides over squirrels, chess players and the occasional placards and protestors. Impressive monuments at the park's four corners honor foreign-born Revolutionary War heroes: Baron von Steuben of Prussia, Brig. Gen. Thaddeus Kosciusko of Poland, Maj. Gen. Comte de Rochambeau of France and Maj. Gen. Marquis de Lafayette, the Frenchman for whom the park is named.

Go right and walk west through the park along H Street, crossing Jackson Place N.W. On the corner is **Decatur House,** which was the first private home in this part of the city.

Farther south on Jackson Place and around the corner to the right on Pennsylvania Avenue N.W. is Blair House. It was named for its original owner, Francis Preston Blair, founder of *The Washington Globe* newspaper during President Andrew Jackson's term of office and one of the founders of the Republican Party. It was in Blair House that Robert E. Lee, at President Abraham Lincoln's insistence, was offered the command of the Union army, which he declined. The house later served as a residence for President Harry S. Truman while the White House was being renovated 1948-52.

Next door is the Lee House, the former home of Blair's daughter and son-in-law. The Blair and Lee houses have been combined and serve as guest

quarters for visiting dignitaries; both are closed to the public.

Next to Lee House is the **Renwick Gallery** of the Smithsonian American Art Museum, which displays changing exhibits of American decorative arts, crafts and design. The 1858 building was the first home of the Corcoran Gallery of Art and is such a splendid example of Second Empire style that its name was changed in the 1960s to honor the architect who designed it, James Renwick Jr.

Walk south across Pennsylvania Avenue N.W. and down 17th Street N.W. to the stately Old Executive Office Building, now called the Eisenhower Executive Office Building. Another example of Second Empire architecture, it was built 1871-88 to house the State, War and Navy Departments and is filled with elegant details and furnishings.

Cross 17th Street to the right and proceed down New York Avenue N.W. 1 block to **The Octagon Museum.** This weathered, red-brick house, really more of a hexagon than an octagon, was built 1798-1800 and was the temporary home of President and Mrs. James Madison after the White House was burned during the War of 1812. The marvelous architecture is both practical and decorative and explains why the house is now a museum of The American Institute of Architects, whose headquarters building looms behind it.

White House Walking Tour

RAPID TRANSIT — STATIONS

© AAA   © 2004 NAVTEQ

Head 2 blocks south on 18th Street. Between C and D streets N.W. is Constitution Hall, where concerts are presented throughout the year. On the same block is the **DAR Museum** and the national headquarters of the Daughters of the American Revolution.

One block south of Constitution Hall across C Street at the corner of 18th Street and Virginia Avenue N.W. is the **Art Museum of the Americas.** This small gallery contains a collection of colorful and insightful works by Latin American artists. Across 18th Street stands a regal equestrian statue of South American revolutionary leader Simón Bolívar; the monument was a gift from Venezuela.

The art museum is a part of the **Organization of American States Building** (OAS) complex. The main building is entered around the corner from the museum on 17th Street N.W. Inside is a lush atrium filled with tropical foliage and centered about an Aztec-themed fountain. Busts of Latin American heroes line the walls.

Continue up 17th Street 2 blocks to E Street N.W. and the **Corcoran Gallery of Art.** Its entrance flanked by two lounging lions, this palatial Beaux Arts building has changing exhibits ranging from classic masterpieces to contemporary photography. Named for 19th-century banker and founder

U.S. National Arboretum / © Paul M. Franklin

William Wilson Corcoran, it is one of the nation's oldest museums.

Leaving the Corcoran's main entrance, turn right, cross 17th Street at the corner and go east along E St., which links with West and East Executive avenues beside the White House. Opposite the south lawn of the White House is the Ellipse, where the Zero Milestone marks the original center of the city.

Originally called the President's House, the **White House** got its current name after it was painted white to cover scorch marks left after the British burned it in 1814. The White House Visitor Center on the southwest corner of 15th and E

streets features exhibits and a 30-minute video that describe the history and architecture of the Executive Mansion.

From E Street turn left onto E. Executive Avenue and follow it north. Yet another equestrian statue is on your right; this one honors Civil War Gen. William Tecumseh Sherman, remembered for his march through Georgia and capture of Savannah.

Farther on, the Treasury Building, pictured on the back of the $10 bill, is on the right opposite the White House's East Gate. Construction of this Greek Revival building, the headquarters for the Treasury Department, began in 1836 and was completed 33 years later. Inside, the Andrew Johnson Suite is where President Andrew Johnson conducted business after Lincoln's assassination. Other rooms include the Salmon P. Chase Suite; the Cash Room, where President Ulysses S. Grant's inaugural reception was held; and the 1864 burglar-proof Vault.

Continue north across Pennsylvania Avenue N.W.; note that E. Executive Avenue is now called Madison Place. Follow Madison Place N.W. and cross H Street. Traveling on the left side of the street, continue north up Vermont Avenue; the McPherson Square Metro station entrance is at the end of the block on the left.

Self-guiding Walking Tours

For those exploring the Dupont Circle area, the Dupont-Kalorama Museum Walk brochure outlines a walking tour of historic buildings near the circle. To get a copy, send a self-addressed stamped No. 10 envelope to The Textile Museum, 2320 S Street N.W., Washington, DC 20008, or pick one up at The Textile Museum *(see attraction listing p. 94)* or other sites along the tour; phone (202) 667-0441.

The Washington, D.C. Black History National Recreation Trail consists of various neighborhoods that played an important role in the community from the time of slavery to the mid-20th century. For information phone the National Park Service, (202) 619-7222.

Attraction and tour information highlighting African-American history in Washington, D.C. can be found in the "African-American Heritage and Multicultural Guide," available at the Washington, D.C., Convention and Visitors Association; phone (202) 789-7000.

Spectator Sports

D.C. is not usually thought of as a sports-crazy town in the sense that Chicago or Pittsburgh are. However, the city goes wild for the **Washington Redskins,** who draw strength from an across-the-board contingent of fans.

Major league baseball returns to the District—for the first time since the fondly remembered Washington Senators moved to Texas following the 1971 season—when the Montréal Expos arrive in April 2005. In the meantime, spectators can choose from four additional professional sports teams—basketball's **Washington Wizards**, the WNBA's (Women's National Basketball Association) **Mystics,** hockey's **Washington Capitals** and soccer's **D.C. United.** In addition, six area universities—American, Georgetown, George Washington and Howard in the District, George Mason University in Virginia and the University of Maryland—offer intercollegiate sports action.

Basketball

Legions of local fans head to the **MCI Center**, 7th and F streets N.W. (M: Gallery Place-Chinatown), to take in a Washington Wizards game. The Wizards are thrice Eastern Conference champs and walked away victorious over the Golden State Warriors in the 1977-78 NBA finals. The action takes place from November to April; phone (202) 628-3200. The MCI Center also is home to the WNBA Mystics, who began play in 1998.

Impressive NCAA champions the **Hoyas** hail from Georgetown University and are widely known by hometown rooters as well as by those who follow the Division IA circuit. Basketball fans also should check out the **American University Eagles,** the **George Washington University Colonials,** the **Howard University Bison,** the **University of Maryland Terrapins** (the Terps) and the **George Mason University Patriots.** The **D.C. Armory**, 3rd and M streets N.E., offers exhibition basketball games.

Football

The Washington Redskins—three-time Super Bowl champions in 1983, 1988 and 1992—have an army of followers notorious for their zeal. Hear that whooshing noise? It's the sound of fans sucking up every last home game ticket in town. They are more precious than gold; sports fans interested in seeing the Skins play would be better served trying to track down some preseason tickets instead.

FedEx Field, off I-495/I-95 exit 15A (Central Ave. East) or 17A (Landover Rd. East) in nearby Landover, Md., is packed with fans from September to December; phone (301) 276-6050 for ticket information or (301) 276-6248 for recorded directions. Meanwhile, the University of Maryland's football team, the Terrapins, play their home games at **Byrd Stadium**.

Hockey

The **Washington Capitals** have been around since the 1974-75 season, and waged a division-winning campaign in 1999-2000. The season runs from October through April at the MCI Center; phone (202) 432-7328 for tickets and information.

Horse Racing

Several tracks around the District offer horse racing; **Rosecroft Raceway** in Fort Washington, Md.,

Potomac River / © John Hartman/Alamy Images

(301) 567-4000, and **Laurel Park Race Course**, (301) 725-0400, in Laurel, Md., are the closest. All programs are flat races unless otherwise noted; dark days—days when no live racing is scheduled—are announced during the meets.

Public transportation is available from downtown D.C. to the tracks. For information contact the Maryland Transit Administration (MTA); phone (410) 539-5000 or (866) 743-3682 Mon.-Fri. 6 a.m.-7 p.m.

Track seasons are usually from early October through March at Laurel; mid-January to mid-December (for three nights a week) at Rosecroft; from mid-March to early June at Pimlico, near Baltimore, (410) 542-9400; from late August to early September at Timonium, (301) 725-0400, also near Baltimore; and from early January to mid-December at Charles Town, W.Va.

Note: Policies concerning admittance of children to pari-mutuel betting facilities vary. Phone for information.

Soccer

D.C. also is home to Major League Soccer's D.C. United, a professional team that plays at **RFK Stadium**, 2400 E. Capitol St. S.E. For ticket information contact D.C. United customer service; phone (202) 587-5000.

Recreation

No matter what the season, activities in the Washington metropolitan area are plentiful. And who knows: You may find yourself jogging, bicycling or fishing not only with the locals but with a congressional power broker as well. For information contact the D.C. Department of Parks and Recreation; phone (202) 673-7665.

Bicycling

Bicycling can be enjoyed along the **C & O Canal towpath** and on **Rock Creek Park** trails. The **Washington and Old Dominion Trail** (W & OD or "WOD" to locals) is an excellent 45-mile paved, multi-use path that runs from I-395 at Shirlington near the Potomac River through Leesburg, Va., meandering through the cities of Falls Church, Vienna and Herndon, Va., to Purcellville, Va. Close to the city, the WOD overlooks busy I-66 as it winds through Arlington residential areas; the farther west you go the less crowded the trail becomes. Once past Herndon, the rural landscapes and flat terrain offer great bicycling.

Bicycles can be rented at **Fletcher's Boat House**, at the intersection of Reservoir and Canal roads N.W. It is open from early March through October; phone (202) 244-0461. Another in-town outlet is **Thompson's Boat Center**, Rock Creek Parkway and Virginia Avenue N.W. in Georgetown. Bikes can be rented from March through November; phone (202) 333-9543.

Bike the Sites, in the Old Post Office Pavilion at 1100 Pennsylvania Ave. N.W. (M: Federal Triangle), offers guided bicycle tours as well as mountain bike and stroller rentals. Safety equipment is included. Summer rental hours are Sun.-Thurs. 9-7, Fri.-Sat. 9-8. Phone (202) 842-2453.

Fishing

The area's best fishing is in the **Chesapeake Bay**, the ocean and in Shenandoah mountain streams. Anglers need not be afraid to cast a line along the **Potomac River's** Maryland shore from the Wilson Bridge south to Fort Washington Park; this once-polluted river has made a remarkable comeback. A trip to **Fletcher's Cove** on the Potomac, about a mile above Key Bridge, or to the rocky gorge at **Chain Bridge** might net a catch of white shad or herring.

Golf

Public golf courses can be found at three locations in the District. Tee times are awarded on a first-come, first-served basis. There is Langston Golf Course, 2600 Benning Rd. N.E., (202) 397-8638; and East Potomac Golf Course, 972 Ohio Dr. S.W., (202) 554-7660, which has two nine-hole courses and one 18-hole course. Rock Creek Public Golf Course, 6100 Rittenhouse St. N.W., has one 18-hole course that can be played as two nine-hole courses; phone (202) 882-7332 for greens fees.

Outside the District, public 18-hole golf courses include: Falls Road Golf Course, 10800 Falls Rd., Potomac, Md., (301) 299-5156; Greendale Golf Course, 6700 Telegraph Rd., Alexandria, Va., (703) 971-6170; Herndon Centennial Golf Course, 909 Ferndale Ave., Herndon, Va., (703) 471-5769; Redgate Golf Course, 14500 Avery Rd., Rockville,

Md., (240) 314-8730; Reston National Golf Course, 11875 Sunrise Valley Dr., Reston, Va., (703) 620-2470; and the University of Maryland Golf Course, University Boulevard, College Park, Md., (301) 314-4653.

Horseback Riding

Horseback riding is possible on the shady bridle paths in northern **Rock Creek Park**. Horses can be rented for guided rides at **Rock Creek Park Horse Center**, Military and Glover roads N.W.; phone (202) 362-0117 for fees and schedule. Other nearby stables are listed in the telephone directory.

Jogging and Walking

Using your own two feet in Washington goes beyond just the sightseeing sense; jogging and walking are almost a way of life for residents and workers. The most popular spot by far is the Mall—specifically the rectangle between 3rd and 14th streets and Constitution and Independence avenues N.W.—where you might see senators and other members of Washington's political elite burning off some extra calories and stress on this 4-mile sightseeing route. Joggers also traverse Memorial Bridge between the Lincoln Memorial and Arlington National Cemetery; the visual attraction is the Potomac and its grassy banks.

The **Mount Vernon Trail** provides two running courses. The shorter one begins near the pedestrian walkway leading to Theodore Roosevelt Island and runs south past Ronald Reagan Washington National Airport to Old Town Alexandria (a little over 3 miles). For the truly fit, a delightfully scenic 9-mile path follows the Potomac's banks from Alexandria south to Mount Vernon.

For a breathtaking outing camouflaged by nature, try the 15 miles of trails crisscrossing Rock Creek Park. One of the best runs is a 4-mile stretch paralleling the creek from Georgetown to the National Zoo. The gravel- and dirt-packed towpath alongside the C & O Canal offers a serene, wooded setting for short runs (about 4 miles round trip between Georgetown and Fletcher's Boat House) or really serious training—well into Maryland, if you are so inclined.

Tennis

The city offers a number of public outdoor courts to choose from. Some, however, are in less-than-desirable locations, so check out neighborhoods in advance. National Park Service courts, which do not require permits but charge a fee, are at **Hains Point** in East Potomac Park, 1090 Ohio Dr. S.W., and in Rock Creek Park near 16th and Kennedy streets N.W. Reservations are suggested.

For a complete list of court locations and information about fees and permits, write the D.C. Parks and Recreation, 3149 16th St. N.W., Washington, DC 20010; phone (202) 673-7646.

Water Sports

The Potomac River is good for an invigorating powerboat ride or a soothing sail. Boats and canoes can be rented at Fletcher's and Thompson's, mentioned in the Bicycling section, and at **Jack's Boathouse**, 3500 Water St. (at the end of K Street in Georgetown, beneath the intersection of Key Bridge and the Whitehurst Freeway), (202) 337-9642; rental season is April through October. Paddleboats can be rented on the Tidal Basin's east side in front of the Thomas Jefferson Memorial.

Riding the rapids of **Great Falls** as they course between Virginia and Maryland will appeal to those with an adventurous side. Although no river wild, the Potomac does work up quite a bit of white water nevertheless. The bluffs above the river offer a fine vantage point for those who would rather watch than participate. For information, contact the ranger station at Great Falls, Va.; phone (703) 285-2966.

Swimming is available at the 34 outdoor and six indoor pools of the D.C. Department of Recreation; local YMCA and YWCA branches also have facilities. Swimmers and sunbathers with more time on their hands can try the ocean or bay beaches, a 3- to 4-hour drive.

Georgetown / © Gibson Stock Photography

streets N.E. This restored 1907 train station on Capitol Hill contains not only Amtrak's headquarters and a working train station, but more than 130 shops and restaurants and a multiscreen movie complex. It features barrel-vaulted ceilings, Romanesque columns, spiral staircases, and intricate decorative painting and gold leaf. Greeting visitors who arrive by train is a bronze statue of A. Philip Randolph, founder of the Sleeping Car Porters

Winter Sports

When sightseeing becomes a bone-chilling proposition during Washington's occasional frigid winter days, spend some time ice skating at one of several area rinks. Two of the nicest spots are the **Sculpture Garden Outdoor Rink**, on Constitution Avenue between 7th and 9th streets N.W., and the Pershing Park Ice Rink, (202) 737-6938, on Pennsylvania Avenue between 14th and 15th streets N.W.

Shopping

The Washington metropolitan area is neither a center of manufacturing nor a region known for locally produced items. It is, however, one of the nation's most affluent areas, and as a result, there are more malls and specialized shopping districts than one could imagine. And those searching for just the right memento to commemorate their trip are definitely in luck: Washington offers a mountain of souvenirs of every stripe.

Antiques

An area with a concentration of craft and antique shops is **Howard Avenue** in Kensington, Md. Within a five-block section an array of antique furniture and decorative items is housed in more than 40 Victorian buildings. These buildings also contain numerous art galleries and craft studios.

Malls

One of the city's most elegant settings for mall shopping is at **Union Station** (M: Union Station), along Massachusetts Avenue between 1st and 2nd

Union and orchestrator of the 1963 March on Washington for Jobs and Freedom.

Among the three escalator-connected levels of stores are such retailers as Crabtree & Evelyn and Victoria's Secret. In the East Hall you will find expensive, high-quality items—everything from collector postage stamps to handcrafted kaleidoscopes—in a plush atmosphere accented by potted palms and mahogany kiosks. The enormous food court on the lower level has an around-the-world smorgasbord of interesting choices in addition to the usual pizza and sandwiches. It makes for a colorful scene, particularly at lunchtime when nearby office workers and Hill aides show up in droves.

The Shops at Georgetown Park occupy four stories and an entire block at 3222 M St. N.W., just off the intersection of M Street and Wisconsin Avenue. The brick exterior adheres to the Federal style characteristic of much Georgetown architecture. The interior, however, is elaborately Victorian, with more than 80 shops and restaurants situated amid wrought iron, potted parlor palms and grand chandeliers, all bathed by a huge skylight. Christian Bernard, for jewelry and fine watches, and gourmet food purveyor Dean & DeLuca are among the retailers.

A legion of suburban malls provide shopping opportunities—and crowded parking lots—galore. Just across the Potomac in Arlington, Va., is **Fashion Centre at Pentagon City**, one of the few shopping areas outside the city with its own subway stop (M: Pentagon City). A spectacular glass atrium encloses some 130 stores on four levels, among them Macy's and Nordstrom, plus a food court. Also in Arlington is **Ballston Commons**, 4238 Wilson Blvd. at Glebe Road (M: Ballston), with Hecht's, numerous chain outlets and a fast-food court.

Springfield Mall, just east of I-95 exit 169A (M: Franconia-Springfield), is about 10 miles south of downtown D.C. There are more than 230 stores, including JCPenney and Macy's, as well as 10 movie theaters, several bookstores, restaurants and a food court.

One of the first major malls to open in the suburbs was **Tysons Corner Center**, just off the Beltway on SR 7 (Leesburg Pike). It contains five major department stores—Bloomingdale's, Hecht's, JCPenney, Lord & Taylor and Nordstrom—and more than 250 smaller shops. A slightly more upscale neighbor is **Tysons Galleria**, 2001 International Dr. (across Chain Bridge Road/SR 123 from Tysons Corner Center). Macy's, Neiman Marcus and Saks Fifth Avenue anchor more than 100 specialty boutiques.

Other big centers include **Landmark Mall** and **Fair Oaks Shopping Center** in Virginia and **Iverson Mall**, **Lakeforest Mall**, **Montgomery Mall**, **Westfield Shoppingtown** and **White Flint Mall** in Maryland.

Markets

The **Eastern Market**, 1 block north of Pennsylvania Avenue at 7th Street and North Carolina Avenue S.E. (M: Eastern Market), was established in 1873. This Capitol Hill landmark is one of the city's few remaining public markets. The enclosed South Hall, open Tues.-Sun., houses a variety of food stalls selling produce, meat, poultry, seafood, dairy products, baked goods and flowers. An open-air, seasonal farmers market and neighborhood flea market operate on weekends.

Outlets

Almost everyone, it seems, goes to **Potomac Mills**, just off I-95 (Potomac Mills exit #156), 25 miles south of Washington and about a 45-minute drive (depending on traffic). More than a mile long, it attracts busloads of D.C. area shoppers and regional bargain hunters from as far away as Pennsylvania, a popularity that leads Potomac Mills to bill itself as Virginia's biggest tourist attraction. Among the many outlets are Eddie Bauer, Guess and Saks Fifth Avenue.

Specialty Districts

Shopping in Washington offers as much variety as sightseeing. The downtown shopping area is centered on F Street near 14th Street N.W.; the landscaped section between 12th and 14th is **F Street Plaza**. Hecht's, downtown's only remaining department store, offers fine clothing, linens and gifts. The grand old building at 14th and F streets, formerly occupied by Garfinckel's department store, is now home to a Borders bookstore.

The **Old Post Office Pavilion** (M: Federal Triangle), 12th Street and Pennsylvania Avenue N.W., occupies the Romanesque Revival structure that formerly housed the Old Post Office. Stylishly renovated, it has specialty stores and a food court.

The Shops at National Place (M: Metro Center), along F Street between 13th and 14th streets N.W., is a four-tiered complex of more than 80 restaurants and specialty boutiques. It extends from the National Press Building to the J.W. Marriott (you can enter the shops through the hotel) and is conveniently located near the National Theatre.

For exclusive browsing, try the upper Northwest neighborhood of Chevy Chase. **Mazza Gallerie**, along Wisconsin Avenue at the D.C./Maryland border (M: Friendship Heights), is a four-level complex anchored by fashionable Neiman Marcus and supplemented by such retail outlets as the Saks Fifth Avenue Men's Store and Williams-Sonoma.

Close by at 5255 Western Ave. N.W. (near Jenifer Street) is the D.C. location of Lord & Taylor, which carries fine men's and women's clothing, shoes, linens and other items. Brooks Brothers, Gianni Versace and Saks Fifth Avenue are among the names vying for the attention of your wallet along a stretch of Wisconsin Avenue just above the District line in Montgomery County, Md.

Also in this neighborhood is **Chevy Chase Pavilion**. Situated above the Friendship Heights Metro station, it offers more mall-oriented retailers, from Ann Taylor to Pottery Barn.

Connecticut Connection, 1101 Connecticut Ave. (M: Farragut North), is a centrally located downtown shopping and dining complex. Where Connecticut Avenue intersects Massachusetts Avenue, **Dupont Circle** is an eclectic blend of embassy buildings, art galleries, bookstores and sidewalk cafes.

The **Adams-Morgan** neighborhood, bounded by Columbia Road, 16th Street and Connecticut and Florida avenues N.W., offers specialty stores, second-hand bookshops, and numerous ethnic groceries and restaurants. The shops along 18th Street N.W. from Florida Avenue north to Columbia Road are filled with funky jewelry and furniture, reggae and world music CDs, and Caribbean- and African-inspired clothing. **Note:** Parking is challenging during the day and next to impossible at night. The closest Metro station is Dupont Circle; exit at Q Street and walk up Connecticut Avenue to Columbia Road.

The **Indian Craft Shop**, inside the Department of the Interior along with the Department of the Interior Museum *(see attraction listing p. 78)*, sells exquisite handmade jewelry, pottery, beadwork, weavings, baskets, sand paintings and other crafts created by more than 45 different tribal groups. A photo ID is necessary to enter the building; the C Street entrance is open to the public. The shop is open Mon.-Fri. 8:30-4:30, third Sat. of the month 10-4.

Other treasures can be found at the **Smithsonian Institution**. Individual shops reflect the focus and collections of the world's largest complex of museums, art galleries and research facilities. They feature crafts from around the world, books, recordings, educational toys, jewelry, kites, and Smithsonian reproductions and adaptations. The shops are open daily 10-5:30; some have extended summer hours. Phone (202) 633-1000.

Despite the crowded sidewalks, a serious shortage of parking and the absence of a convenient Metro station, **Georgetown** is many Washingtonians' favorite place to shop. Perhaps the reason is that instead of wandering through the sterile, enclosed corridors of the malls you're in the fresh air, strolling charming streets through a historic neighborhood. Antiques, cookware, contemporary fashions, china and glassware, fabrics and rare books are only a few of the items to be found in the little shops along and just off Wisconsin Avenue and M Street.

As much fun as Georgetown is **Old Town Alexandria**, Va. (M: King Street). The Torpedo Factory Art Center *(see attraction listing p. 121)* offers workshops and sales outlets for local artists. The heart of Old Town is the intersection of King and Washington streets, but the shopping opportunities also include Cameron Street and Tavern Square. From the Metro station, a DASH city bus will take you to any of these areas; the fare is $1.

Performing Arts

Although the opening of **The John F. Kennedy Center for the Performing Arts** *(see attraction listing p. 81)* more than 3 decades ago was a major catalyst in heating up Washington's fine arts scene, the city is home to all sorts of venues. The Kennedy Center is the star, with its seven concert, opera, drama and cinema halls, but there are many other fine facilities.

University groups, dinner theaters and open-air facilities like Virginia's **Wolf Trap Farm Park for the Performing Arts** *(see attraction listing p. 132)* offer live entertainment throughout the year. And a number of performances are free, such as the National Park Service's military band concerts at various monuments during the summer months and the chamber music concerts offered by the Library of Congress.

Weekend magazine, published in the Friday edition of *The Washington Post*, gives complete listings for current and upcoming cultural events in the Washington area. *City Paper*, a free weekly available at local bookstores, newsstands and curbside vending machines, also has detailed listings for theater, music, film, dance, gallery and performance art events.

For bargain hunters, TICKETplace, 407 7th St. N.W., around the corner from the Woolly Mammoth Theatre (M: Archives or Gallery Place), sells half-price (plus a service charge equal to 12 percent of the ticket's face value) advance tickets to a variety of performing arts events in the D.C. area. Full-price, advance-sale tickets to some events are available as well. Only credit cards are accepted. The booth is open Tues.-Fri. 11-6, Sat. 10-5; phone (202) 842-5387.

The John F. Kennedy Center for the Performing Arts
© R. Krubner/Robertstock

Dance

The **Washington Ballet** presents works both classical and contemporary, mostly at the **Kennedy Center Opera House** but also at the center's Eisenhower Theater and other venues. Each December the company stages the holiday classic "The Nutcracker." Such prestigious companies as the Bolshoi Ballet and the American Ballet Theater give frequent Washington performances. The **Howard University Dance Ensemble** and the annual dance series presented by **Mount Vernon College** provide opportunities for visitors to attend a wide variety of modern and ethnic dance performances. The **Smithsonian Institution** frequently presents national and international dance troupes; for information phone (202) 633-1000.

Film

First-run movie theaters are plentiful in the District, although parking is not. The most readily available parking is at theaters on upper Wisconsin and Connecticut avenues. The **Cineplex Odeon Uptown**, 3246 Connecticut Ave. N.W. (M: Cleveland Park), and the **Cineplex Odeon Cinema**, 5100 Wisconsin Ave. N.W. (M: Friendship Heights), are good places to see current hits.

Foreign, arthouse and independent films are often shown at the **Cineplex Odeon Outer Circle**, 4849 Wisconsin Ave. N.W. (M: Tenleytown-AU), and the **Cineplex Odeon Dupont Circle**, 1350 19th St. N.W. (M: Dupont Circle).

The Kennedy Center's **American Film Institute Theater** (M: Foggy Bottom-GWU) is the best of the repertory theaters, often focusing on a particular genre or the works of a single director; documentaries, movie classics and cinematic obscurities also are part of AFI's eclectic programming. Free shuttle buses run from the Metro station to the theater. For schedule information phone (202) 833-2348.

Documentaries and experimental films are often shown at the **Hirshhorn Museum and Sculpture Garden** and the **National Gallery of Art's East Building**; for information about programs, contact the individual museums.

The **AFI Silver Theatre and Cultural Center**, 8633 Colesville Rd. in Silver Spring, Md. (M: Silver Spring), includes a restored 1938 movie house and two contemporary stadium theaters providing state-of-the-art presentation facilities for a variety of screenings, from classics to cult films to new releases. For recorded program information phone (301) 495-6700.

Music

The John F. Kennedy Center for the Performing Arts presents a variety of nationally and internationally acclaimed artists. Under the direction of Leonard Slatkin, the **National Symphony Orchestra** performs in the center's spacious **Concert Hall**. The season runs from September to June. Chamber music societies, choral groups and symphony orchestras from around the world perform here as well; for information phone (202) 467-4600. In the summer months the orchestra performs outdoors at Wolf Trap Farm Park for the Performing Arts.

Constitution Hall, at 18th and D streets N.W., focuses on musical events. **Lisner Auditorium** of George Washington University, 21st and H streets N.W., is the scene of a wider variety of concerts, recitals and sometimes opera and ballet. For information phone (202) 994-6800.

One of Washington's best bargains is the series of free chamber music concerts given by the **Library of Congress** at different theaters and auditoriums. For schedule and ticket information phone (202) 707-5502. The **Juilliard String Quartet** is in residence during October, November and December, performing on the library's rare Stradivarius instruments.

The airy **West Garden Court** in the National Gallery of Art is the scene of free concerts Sunday evenings at 7 from October through June. Programs consist of a variety of guest artists and the **National Gallery Orchestra**. Four concerts in March or April constitute a festival of American music. For program information phone (202) 842-6941.

From September through May, Sunday afternoon chamber concerts take place in the paneled **Music Room** at The Phillips Collection, 1600 21st St. N.W. (at Q Street). They begin promptly at 5 (early arrival is recommended); phone (202) 387-2151. Free lunchtime jazz concerts take place at the **Frances and Armand Hammer Auditorium** in the **Corcoran Gallery of Art** on the first and third Wednesday of the month at 12:30. Tickets are not required; for information phone (202) 639-1770.

From October to May, the **Folger Consort,** the resident Renaissance music ensemble at the Folger Shakespeare Library, presents a series of instrumental and vocal performances in the library's **Elizabethan Theatre**, 201 E. Capitol St. S.E. (M: Capitol South or Union Station); phone (202) 544-7077. Chamber music groups perform on selected Sundays from October through April at the **National Academy of Sciences** auditorium, 2101 Constitution Ave. N.W. (M: Foggy Bottom-GWU), which is celebrated for its fine acoustics. A photo ID is required to enter the building. For schedule information phone (202) 334-2436.

During summer, visitors enjoy outdoor performances at **Carter Barron Amphitheatre**, in upper northwest Washington at 16th Street and Colorado Avenue N.W. in Rock Creek Park (near the Maryland line). Events range from funk, jazz and blues bands, R & B and gospel singers, and oldies groups to performances by dance companies, the National Symphony Orchestra and The Shakespeare Theatre. Some shows are free, but all require tickets; phone (202) 426-0486 for information, or (202) 397-7328 for advance tickets.

Wolf Trap is D.C.'s premier destination for "music under the stars," and is the summer home of the National Symphony Orchestra. From October to mid-May, performances move inside to the **Barns at Wolf Trap** *(see attraction listing p. 132)*, three-quarters of a mile south of the park at 1635 Trap Rd. The 350-seat theater is composed of two barns featuring everything from chamber music and opera to folk, jazz, country and bluegrass. For ticket information phone the box office at (703) 938-2404. About half of the seats in the **Filene Center** is uncovered; the stage and open-sided canopy are built to take advantage of a natural slope. Less expensive and unprotected seating is available on the lawn.

Warm weather also ushers in the National Park Service's free weekly concert series, held by military bands on the steps of the U.S. Capitol and the national monuments. The U.S. Air Force Band presents a free guest artist concert series with nationally known performers at **DAR Constitution Hall**, 18th and D streets N.W., Sunday afternoons during February. Phone (202) 628-4780 for schedule and ticket information.

The U.S. Marines schedule their own free parade, including band, drum and bugle corps and silent drill team, at the **Marine Barracks**, 8th and I streets S.E. (M: Eastern Market), on Fri. at 8:45 p.m. from the first weekend in May through the last weekend in August. Parking is available at Maritime Plaza, 12th and M streets S.E.; a free shuttle bus provides transportation from the plaza to the barracks and back. Reservations should be made at least 3 weeks in advance. For reservations write Protocol Officer, Marine Barracks, 8th and I sts. S.E., Washington, D.C. 20390-5000; phone (202) 433-6060 for recorded information.

For something less formal and with no reservations required, the Marine Drum and Bugle Corps and Silent Drill Team present Sunset Parades every

Tuesday at 7 p.m. from the first Tuesday in May to the third Tuesday in August at the Marine Corps War Memorial. Take a blanket or lawn chair; no seats are provided. Shuttle bus service to this free performance is provided from the parking lot next to the Arlington National Cemetery Visitor Center from 5-7 and 8-9 p.m.; the parking fee is $1.25 per hour for the first 3 hours, then $2 per hour. For information phone (202) 433-4173.

Twilight Tattoo, another sunset parade, is performed by the U.S. Army Band and The 3rd U.S. Infantry most Wednesdays at 7 p.m. (weather permitting) from mid-April through late July on the Ellipse (M: Federal Triangle); phone (202) 685-2888.

Another great deal is the free summer concert series given June through August by military bands of the U.S. armed forces. Many of them take place at the outdoor Sylvan Theatre, just off 15th Street N.W. near the Washington Monument, as well as on the lower West Terrace of the U.S. Capitol. These traditional concerts feature occasional vocalists and include stirring patriotic marches as well as pops and classical selections. For schedule information phone (703) 696-3399 (Army), (202) 433-2525 (Navy), (202) 767-5658 (Air Force) or (202) 433-4011 (Marines).

Opera

The Kennedy Center Opera House has three levels and a stage curtain of gold and red Japanese silk. The plush setting is utilized for seasonal performances by the **Washington Opera** that take place from November to March. Seven productions are performed in their original languages, with English supertitles. Standing-room-only tickets go on sale at the Kennedy Center box office on Saturday beginning at 10 a.m. for performances the following week. For performance and ticket information phone (202) 467-4600 or (800) 444-1324.

Theater

Washington is a theatergoer's delight. Broadway-bound plays often have their last tryouts here, and there are several excellent repertory companies. Among the Kennedy Center's venues is the **Eisenhower Theater**, where smaller-scale dramas are presented, while lavish musicals play the 2,300-seat Opera House. The **Theater Lab** features free children's programs and in the evening the long-running play "Shear Madness," a humorous murder mystery that differs every time it is presented.

The center's intimate **Terrace Theater** has a varied menu of chamber music concerts, opera, choral recitals, comedy revues and theater offerings, along with solo performances from classical violinists to multimedia performance artists. For Kennedy Center show and ticket information phone (202) 467-4600 or (800) 444-1324.

The **Warner Theatre**, 513 13th St. N.W. between E and F streets (M: Metro Center), opened in 1924 as a vaudeville house, was an old-fashioned movie palace during the 1960s and functioned mainly as a rock concert venue in the 1970s and '80s. Shut down and then reopened in 1992 following extensive renovations, it now provides an ornately decorative setting for dance performances, touring Broadway and off-Broadway shows, and popular headlining entertainers and musicians. For general information phone (202) 783-4000 Mon.-Fri. 9-6.

Ford's Theatre *(see attraction listing p. 79)* has a tragic past—it was where President Abraham Lincoln was assassinated in 1865. An October-to-July schedule of contemporary plays and musicals takes place in the theater itself, which has been carefully restored to its former appearance—although the 1860s-style chairs are of questionable comfort. Phone (202) 347-4833.

Razzle-dazzle hits appear at the **National Theater**, 1321 Pennsylvania Ave. (M: Metro Center), which has operated continuously since 1835. It was lavishly renovated in the early 1980s and is managed by New York's Shubert Organization, making the National Washington's closest thing to a big, Broadway-style theater. For ticket information phone (202) 628-6161 or (800) 447-7400.

The **Arena Stage** complex, at 6th and Maine streets S.W. (M: Waterfront-SEU), is home to D.C.'s most lauded ensemble company. Founded by now-retired director Zelda Fichandler in 1950, the Arena over the years has nurtured the stage careers of such luminaries as Jane Alexander and James Earl Jones. New plays and emerging playwrights are emphasized during the September-to-June season. The facility has three stages: the **Arena**, a theater-in-the-round; the **Kreeger**, a proscenium; and the **Old Vat Room**, a cabaret-style space; phone (202) 488-3300.

In the Lansburgh building at 450 7th St. N.W., **The Shakespeare Theatre** *(see attraction listing p. 92)* specializes, naturally, in the Bard's works. The renowned ensemble moved to its present location in 1992 after 2 decades of performances at the Folger Shakespeare Library on Capitol Hill. There are four premium productions during the year—three Shakespearean plays and at least one other classical work. Educational programs and special events are presented as well, including the Shakespeare Theatre Free For All, a free outdoor production held in June. Tickets for regular performances sell out quickly; reserve early.

Smaller professional resident theaters abound. Contemporary plays—including new productions—are presented at **The Studio Theatre**, 1333 P St. N.W. (M: Dupont Circle). For box office information phone (202) 332-3300. The troupe at the tiny **Source Theatre Company**, 1835 14th St. N.W. between S and T streets (M: U Street), actively supports emerging and local playwrights and promotes new plays. For schedule information phone (202) 462-1073.

The **Woolly Mammoth Theatre Company** has a reputation for staging some of the city's most artistically provocative productions. Currently based at the Kennedy Center's AFI Film Theater, the company is scheduled to relocate to a new, state-of-the-art facility at 7th and D streets N.W. in March 2005. For ticket information phone the box office at (202) 393-3939. The **GALA Hispanic Theatre** presents works by classic and contemporary Latin and Latin-American playwrights. Productions are staged at the Warehouse Theater, 1021 7th St. N.W. (M: Mount Vernon Square-UDC); phone (202) 234-7174.

A growing number of small professional resident theaters are developing solid reputations and provide a variety of performances year-round. The **Horizons Theatre**, 3700 South Four Mile Run in Arlington, Va., focuses on plays by and about women and their experiences; phone (703) 578-1100. The **Round House Theatre** has two locations—in Bethesda and Silver Spring, Md.—offering new plays as well as classics. For ticket information phone (240) 644-1100.

Special Events

Washington's events are almost as numerous as its bureaucrats; scarcely a week goes by without some sort of festival, celebration or show. Contact the Washington, D.C., Convention and Visitors Association at (202) 789-7000.

The season begins with the Washington Antique Show at the Omni Shoreham Hotel in early January. In mid-January Martin Luther King Jr. Day is celebrated throughout the metropolitan area. Chinese New Year Festival celebrants parade through the streets of Chinatown and enjoy the holiday menus of the area's restaurants in January and sometimes February. Abraham Lincoln's Birthday on Feb. 12 is commemorated at the Lincoln Memorial with a wreath ceremony and a reading of the Gettysburg Address. In February George Washington's Birthday festivities are held at Mount Vernon in Alexandria, Va.

The St. Patrick's Day Parade marches down Constitution Avenue on the Sunday closest to Mar. 17; the Festival of St. Patrick is celebrated throughout the city for the entire month. The Smithsonian Institution sponsors a Kite Festival on the Washington Monument grounds in late March or early April. Children ages 8 and younger are invited onto the White House lawn the Monday following Easter Sunday for the Easter Egg Roll; a special Easter Egg Hunt for Blind Children on the Washington Monument grounds lets children search for electronic beeping eggs that can be exchanged for prizes.

A burst of pale pink flowers begins one of the city's most cherished events. The National Cherry Blossom Festival in early April starts with a parade and includes music, pageants and a Japanese lantern lighting ceremony. The more than 6,000 cherry trees that line the Tidal Basin near the Thomas Jefferson Memorial are illuminated at night during the approximately weeklong blooming season so their delicate beauty is always visible.

Also in April is the Georgetown House Tour, when one of the city's most fashionable neighborhoods opens its doors to the public. Serving one of the top 10 movie markets in the country, the District's theaters participate in the Washington, D.C. International Film Festival in late April. The White House Spring Garden Tour follows later in the month, and the month ends with the Smithsonian's Washington Craft Show at the National Building Museum, 440 F St. N.W.

Jazz aficionados will not want to miss Duke Ellington's Birthday Celebration. Live performances pay tribute to this musical giant and native Washingtonian in early May.

Also in May is the Georgetown Garden Tour and the Goodwill Embassy Tour, which gives the public a chance to tour various gardens and embassies; proceeds go to Davis Memorial Goodwill Industries. In mid-May you can help Sts. Constantine and Helen Greek Orthodox Church, 4115 16th St. N.W., celebrate Greek Spring Festival; Greek food, music, dance and crafts are featured.

In late June the Festival of American Folklife celebrates different regions and cultural aspects of the nation with music, crafts and food. The capital's biggest party is, of course, July 4th; Independence Day celebrations include a noon parade, symphony concerts and events on the Mall, all followed by a huge fireworks display over the Washington Monument beginning at 9 p.m.

To spice up the end of summer, residents sample the music, cuisine and culture of Washington's Latin community during the Latin-American Festival, held in late July on the Mall. Adams-Morgan Day in mid-September is a colorful mix of ethnic food, music and crafts.

In late October the Washington International Horse Show is held in the MCI Center. Also in late October is the grueling Marine Corps Marathon. The Pageant of Peace/Lighting of the National Christmas Tree in mid-December makes the holiday season official. Kwanzaa, the traditional African-American celebration of the harvest, is commemorated for several days in late December at the Anacostia Museum and Center for African American History and Culture.

Nightlife

While many people associate Washington evenings with the sort of glittering, black-tie social events that frequently are held at the Kennedy Center, collars are loosened in this bureaucratic town as well. Many nightspots are concentrated in a couple of neighborhoods, making it easy to plan an evening out. Just decide what you want to do; whatever it is, there are bound to be options.

A couple of Georgetown establishments are local favorites for a drink, a bite or some casual socializing. Although there are now several area branches, **Clyde's of Georgetown**, 3236 M St. N.W., is the original outpost, first opening its doors in 1963. The upscale tavern fare is solidly reliable; phone

(202) 333-9180. Two blocks away is **J. Paul's,** 3218 M St. N.W., another popular watering hole with good bar food; phone (202) 333-3450.

Weekend magazine, published in the Friday edition of *The Washington Post*, and the *City Paper*, a free weekly, carry complete listings of local nightspots.

Comedy Clubs

The Improv, 1140 Connecticut Ave. N.W. between L and M streets (M: Farragut North), presents local and national comics, many of whom are familiar from network and cable shows. Making dinner reservations will get you a better seat—but then again, you may not want to sit too close and become part of the act; phone (202) 296-7008.

Dance Clubs

Most clubs in D.C. cater to a trend-hopping clientele. **Nation,** 1015 Half St. S.E. (M: Navy Yard), attracts the college crowd with state-of-the-art sound, special dance nights and a busy concert schedule; phone (202) 554-1500. **Rumors,** 1900 M St. N.W. (M: Farragut West or Farragut North), offers Top 40 and popular '80s dance music and is packed with young professionals on Friday and Saturday nights; phone (202) 466-7378.

Folk/Bluegrass

Across the Potomac in Alexandria, Va., is the **Birchmere,** 3701 Mt. Vernon Ave., one of the area's oldest and best-liked clubs. The 500-seat venue focuses on music (although you also can order food and drinks). The Birchmere got its start with country, folk and bluegrass, but rock, alternative, jazz and gospel artists also play here. Patrons are politely but firmly asked to remain quiet during performances. Phone (703) 549-7500.

Jazz & Blues

Blues Alley, 1073 Wisconsin Ave. N.W. (below M Street), is the city's premier spot for jazz. Big-name instrumentalists and singers appear regularly at this intimate Georgetown club. The menu items, named after jazz greats, have a distinct Creole touch. You can see the show without ordering dinner (there is a cover charge), but you may not get the best seats; phone (202) 337-4141.

Just above Dupont Circle at 1517 Connecticut Ave. N.W. (M: Dupont Circle) is **Kramerbooks & afterwords.** Whether for breakfast while perusing *The Washington Post*, an after-work hangout or a place to hear live music, this bookstore and cafe is a D.C. institution. Kramerbooks is open Sun.-Thurs. 7:30 a.m.-1 a.m., Fri.-Sat. 24 hours. Musicians perform Wed.-Sat. evenings; the music ranges from jazz and blues to acoustic guitar.

Rock

RFK Stadium, 2400 E. Capitol St. S.E., hosts occasional big-name concerts and all-day music festivals; phone (202) 547-9077. Pop and hip-hop concerts take place at the **MCI Center,** 601 F St. N.W. at 7th Street; phone (202) 628-3200. Another big arena is the 10,000-seat **Patriot Center,** 4500 Patriot Cir. (just off SR 620/Braddock Road and University Drive) in Fairfax, Va., phone (703) 993-3000.

Two amphitheaters offer summer concerts. **Nissan Pavilion at Stone Ridge** in Bristow, Va., has a covered, open-air pavilion with reserved seating for 10,000, plus an additional 12,000 lawn seats. Two huge video screens enhance the view of the stage. The pavilion is about a 45-minute drive from Washington via I-66; take exit 44 (Route 234 Bypass), continue to the second light and turn right on Wellington Road; then west 3 miles to the entrance. Phone (703) 754-6400 for general information, (800) 551-7328 for ticket information, or (703) 754-1288 for the concert line.

Merriweather Post Pavilion in Columbia, Md. has a similar lineup of pop, rock, hip-hop, country and adult contemporary performers. It is located off US 29 in Columbia, Md. (about halfway between Washington and Baltimore). Take the Beltway (I-495) to I-95 north toward Baltimore, then exit 38B (SR 32 West) to US 29 exit 16A and proceed north toward Columbia. Phone (410) 715-5550 for general information, or (800) 551-7328 to purchase tickets.

A variety of name artists appear at **DAR Constitution Hall,** 18th and D streets N.W. (M: Farragut West); phone (202) 628-4780. **Note:** It is a 10- to 15-minute walk from the Metro station to the hall.

Lisner Auditorium, at 21st and H streets N.W. on the campus of George Washington University (M: Foggy Bottom/GWU), offers a little bit of everything: rock and alternative bands, mainstream headliners, world music groups, dance and symphony performances, comedians, performance artists, special film showings and lectures. The box office is open Tues.-Fri. 11-5 and accepts cash or checks only; phone (202) 994-6800.

The **9:30 Club,** 815 V St. N.W. (M: U Street-Cardozo), moved to its present, larger quarters in 1996 following 15 years as a quintessential punk and alternative music club at its former F Street location. It still books a similar lineup, from the newest buzz names to established acts; phone (202) 265-0930.

The Washington, D.C. Vicinity

Nearby Maryland

ACCOKEEK (I-8) pop. 7,349, elev. 190'

Accokeek occupies the site of the Indian village Moyaone that Capt. John Smith marked on a map. Settlers burned the village in 1622 as a reprisal during American Indian uprisings. Not all the residents were killed; the Piscataways who survived settled along Piscataway Creek. About 1,000 skeletons, some of which date from the early Christian era, as well as pottery and tools from 8000-1000 B.C. have been unearthed.

NATIONAL COLONIAL FARM, 4 mi. w. of jct. SRs 373 and 210, offers exhibits pertaining to historic agriculture in Maryland. The farm is a living-history museum that presents a glimpse of life on an 18th-century tobacco plantation. The area also features the Ecosystem Farm, an organic vegetable farm using sustainable agricultural techniques. Nature trails also are available.

Allow 1 hour minimum. Tues.-Sun. 10-4, mid-Mar. to mid-Dec.; Sat.-Sun. 10-4, rest of year. Closed Jan. 1, Martin Luther King, Jr. Day, Nov. 11, Thanksgiving and Dec. 25. Guided tours of the Ecosystem Farm are given Sat.-Sun. at 11, of the Colonial Farm Sat.-Sun. at 1 and 3. Admission $2; ages 3-12, 50c; family rate $5. Phone (301) 283-2113.

BETHESDA (C-5) pop. 55,277, elev. 303'

Bethesda takes its name from the 1820 Bethesda Presbyterian Church (Bethesda Meeting House) on the Georgetown-Frederick Pike (Old National Road). The city is home to the National Cancer Institute, the National Institutes of Health, the National Naval Medical Center and other research facilities, making it the second largest employment center in the state.

Conference and Visitors Bureau of Montgomery County—Bethesda: 12900 Middlebrook Rd., Germantown, MD 20874; phone (301) 916-0698 or (800) 925-0880.

NATIONAL LIBRARY OF MEDICINE is at 8600 Rockville Pike (M: Red Line to Medical Center Station). Originally established in 1836 as the Library of the Army Surgeon General's Office, the library is a source of biomedical information for health professionals. One-hour guided tours begin in the visitor center, which is located in the lobby of the Lister Hill Center Building 38A. Tours include an 11-minute videotape as well as a tour of the library.

Parking is limited. Allow 1 hour minimum. Library open Mon.-Fri. 8:30-5 (also Thurs. 5-9), Sat. 8:30-12:30, Labor Day-Memorial Day; Mon.-Fri. 8:30-5, Sat. 8:30-12:30, rest of year. Closed federal holidays and the Sat. preceding Mon. holidays. Visitor center open Mon.-Fri. 9-4; closed federal holidays. Guided tours Mon.-Fri. at 1:30. Free. Phone (301) 496-6308.

CHESAPEAKE AND OHIO CANAL NATIONAL HISTORICAL PARK—
see Maryland p. 182.

CLINTON (I-11) pop. 26,064, elev. 248'

Originally named Surrattsville for John Surratt, who was appointed the town's postmaster in 1854, Clinton is off SR 5 (Branch Avenue) southeast of Washington, D.C.

John Wilkes Booth stopped at the Surratt residence after he assassinated President Abraham Lincoln. Accused of involvement in Booth's crime, Mary Surratt was found guilty by the military commission responsible for the alleged conspirators' trial and hanged. The debate over Mary Surratt's connection with Lincoln's assassination still rages.

His Lordship's Kindness, a Georgian mansion built in 1787, is on a 138-acre horse farm at 7606 Woodyard Rd. It has been the home of many dignitaries and is furnished with a variety of antique pieces and replicas; phone (301) 856-0358.

ALL ABOUT TOWN tours depart from most local hotels. Narrated half-day, full-day and 2-day sightseeing excursions are offered. The itineraries include government buildings, the National Air and

DID YOU KNOW

?

Before becoming president of the United States, Harry S Truman worked for AAA.

Space Museum, the National Museum of Natural History, Arlington National Cemetery and Mount Vernon. Washington by Twilight tours provide views of illuminated memorials and the Capitol dome.

Morning tours, lasting a half or a full day, depart at 7:30 a.m. Afternoon tours depart at 1:15 and return at 5. Evening tours depart at 7:30 p.m. and return at 10:45. All-day tours depart at 6:45 a.m. and return at 5. Departure times vary by location of the hotel at which you are picked up. Closed Jan. 1, Thanksgiving and Dec. 25. Fares $26-$78, ages 3-11 half price when accompanied by an adult. Reservations are required. Phone (301) 856-5556.

SAVE **SURRATT HOUSE AND MUSEUM,** 9118 Brandywine Rd., is the restored 1852 home of Mary Surratt. Guides in period dress conduct tours of the house and tavern and explain the house's role as the first stop on John Wilkes Booth's escape route through southern Maryland. Allow 1 hour minimum. Thurs.-Fri. 11-3, Sat.-Sun. noon-4, mid-Jan. through mid-Dec. Last tour begins 30 minutes before closing. Admission $3; over 59, $2; ages 5-18, $1. Phone (301) 868-1121.

COLLEGE PARK (C-9) pop. 24,657, elev. 70′

COLLEGE PARK AVIATION MUSEUM is off I-95/495 exit 23, 1.6 mi. s. on US 1, 1 mi. e. on Paint Branch Pkwy., then just n. to 1985 Corporal Frank Scott Dr. This museum relates the history of the College Park Airport, in continuous use since 1909, using vintage aircraft, hands-on exhibits and film of early flight attempts. An animatronic Wilbur Wright describes the pioneer aviator's adventures as a flight instructor here.

Allow 30 minutes minimum. Daily 10-5; closed major holidays. Admission $4; over 59, $3; ages 3-17, $2. MC, VI. Phone (301) 864-6029.

GLEN ECHO (C-4) pop. 242, elev. 153′

Glen Echo's use as a cultural and educational center by the National Chautauqua Assembly ended when a rumor of malaria began in the fall of 1891. The Washington Railway and Electric Company later purchased the land and developed it into a major amusement park. From 1900 until 1968, Washingtonians rode the streetcar from the city to Glen Echo for a day in the country.

Conference and Visitors Bureau of Montgomery County—Glen Echo: 12900 Middlebrook Rd., Germantown, MD 20874; phone (301) 916-0698 or (800) 925-0880.

CLARA BARTON NATIONAL HISTORIC SITE, 5801 Oxford Rd., was the home of the founder and first president of the American Red Cross from 1897 until her death in 1912, and served as the early headquarters of that organization. Built according to the floor plan of a Red Cross relief structure used after the flood of 1889 at Johnstown, Pa., the 1891 house is furnished with some items that once belonged to Barton.

Allow 1 hour minimum. Guided tours are given daily on the hour 10-4; closed Jan. 1, Thanksgiving and Dec. 25. Last tour begins at 4. Free. Phone (301) 492-6245.

GLEN ECHO PARK is at 7300 MacArthur Blvd. Here the National Park Service administers more than 200 arts classes to the public, and an extensive artists-in-residence program offers performances, demonstrations and workshops. Historic buildings house the working studios of glass, ceramics and metalwork artisans; an art gallery displays some of their creations. Two children's theaters, the Puppet Company and Adventure Theater, present year-round shows. An antique carousel operates May through September.

Picnic facilities are available. Park open 6 a.m.-1 a.m.; closed Thanksgiving and Dec. 25. Social dances take place Fri.-Sun. in the 1933 Spanish Ballroom. Rangers provide tours Sun. at 2. Park may be open additional evening and weekend hours depending on class schedules. Free. Phone (301) 492-6229.

GREENBELT (B-11) pop. 21,456, elev. 180′

Greenbelt was constructed 1935-38 as a planned community and garden city with funds from the New Deal administration of President Franklin Roosevelt. Depression glass and 1937 furnishings designed specifically for the Greenbelt houses are part of the glimpse of the past that can be had at the Greenbelt Museum at 10B Crescent Rd., one of the town's original houses. Guided tours of the museum are offered by reservation. Exhibitions are displayed across the street at the community center gallery; phone (301) 474-1936.

GODDARD SPACE FLIGHT CENTER VISITORS CENTER, off I-95 exit 22A, then 2.2 mi. e. following signs, offers programs, special events and presentations pertaining to the nation's space program. Exhibits in the Earth Science and Space Science galleries are open to the public. Visitor center open Tues.-Fri. 9-5, Sat.-Sun. noon-4; closed Jan. 1, Thanksgiving and Dec. 25. Free. Phone (301) 286-8981.

KENSINGTON (A-5) pop. 1,873, elev. 301′

Kensington is best known for its array of antique shops, housed in more than 40 Victorian buildings within a five-block area along Howard Avenue. Several of the shops also contain art galleries, potters and other artisans. Working demonstrations are sometimes offered in this area, which is known as Antique Row.

Conference and Visitors Bureau of Montgomery County—Kensington: 12900 Middlebrook Rd., Germantown, MD 20874; phone (301) 916-0698 or (800) 925-0880.

WASHINGTON TEMPLE AND VISITOR CENTER OF THE CHURCH OF JESUS CHRIST OF LATTER-DAY SAINTS is off I-495 exit 33 to Beach Dr., 1 mi. e. on Beach Dr., then n. to Stoneybrook

Dr. The visitor center on the grounds of the white marble temple features a copy of Bertel Thorvaldsen's eight-foot statue "Christus," and offers a variety of multimedia presentations, Christmas events and films about the temple.

The temple is closed to the public. Holiday programs include a nativity scene nightly in December. Allow 1 hour minimum. Visitor center daily 10-9. Free. Phone (301) 587-0144.

LARGO (E-12) pop. 8,408, elev. 180′

East of Washington, D.C., this bedroom community is of interest to visitors primarily for its proximity to Six Flags America *(see attraction listing)*.

Prince George's County Conference and Visitors Bureau: 9200 Basil Ct., Suite 101, Largo, MD 20774; phone (301) 925-8300. *See color ad.*

SIX FLAGS AMERICA is about 5 mi. e. of Beltway (I-495/I-95) exit 15A at 13710 Central Ave. This 170-acre theme and water park features more than 100 rides, shows and attractions. Highlights include eight roller coasters, including Batwing, Jokers Jinx, The Wild One and Superman-Ride of Steel.

For non thrill-seekers there are The Penguin's Blizzard River, Looney Tunes Movie Town and a variety of live shows. Paradise Island Water Park features a million-gallon wave pool, Monsoon Lagoon and a variety of slides and other attractions.

Food is available. Allow 5 hours minimum. Park open daily, late May-Labor Day; some Sat.-Sun. in Apr. and Sept.-Oct. Hours vary; phone ahead. Water park open Memorial Day-Labor Day; phone ahead for schedule. Admission (includes water park) $36.99, over 61 and children under 54 inches tall $25.99, under 4 free. Parking $9. AAA members

save 10 percent on select in-park dining and merchandise. Check at the park's Guest Relations window for details. AX, DS, MC, VI. Phone (301) 249-1500.

LAUREL (A-10) pop. 19,960

A suburb northeast of Washington, D.C., Laurel was once a small industrial center. Cotton and grain no longer draw visitors, but horse racing does from early October through March. Laurel Park has been offering Thoroughbred racing since 1911. The track features the International, a race that presents leading horses from around the world. Phone (301) 725-0400.

Note: Policies concerning admittance of children to pari-mutuel betting facilities vary. Phone for information.

Shopping areas: The main shopping complex in the area is Laurel Mall on US 1, which features Hecht's and JCPenney among its 110 stores.

MONTPELIER MANSION AND CULTURAL ARTS CENTER is reached by taking Laurel-Bowie Rd. (SR 197) off Gladys Spellman (Baltimore-Washington) Pkwy., then following signs .2 mi. n. to jct. Muirkirk Rd. The center has three galleries with changing exhibits. Visitors are encouraged to watch artists, whose talents range from painting and sculpting to rug hooking and jewelry making. The Montpelier Mansion, next to the cultural arts center, was built 1774-83 and is a fine example of Georgian architecture, complete with boxwood gardens on the grounds.

Allow 30 minutes minimum. Arts center open daily 10-5. Guided tours of the mansion are given on the hour Sun.-Thurs. noon-3. Arts center free. Guided tours $3; senior citizens $2; ages 5-18, $1.

Phone (301) 953-1993, (410) 792-0664 in Baltimore, (301) 953-1376 for mansion tour information or TTY (301) 490-2329.

NATIONAL WILDLIFE VISITOR CENTER is 2 mi. e. on Powder Mill Rd. off the Baltimore-Washington Pkwy. to 10901 Scarlet Tanager Loop. Within the 12,750-acre Patuxent Research Refuge, the center's interactive exhibits focus on global environmental issues, migratory bird routes, wildlife habitats and endangered species recovery efforts. Surrounding forests, lakes and trails provide opportunities for recreation and educational programs.

Allow 2 hours minimum. Open daily 10-5:30. Tram tours are available spring through mid-June and Sept.-Nov. on weekends, and daily late June through Aug. 31. Admission free. Tram tours $3; over 54, $2; under 13, $1. Phone (301) 497-5760, or TTY (301) 497-5779.

OXON HILL (I-8) elev. 220′

Since the 17th century Oxon Hill has been associated with the estate belonging to the Addison family, long prominent in southern Maryland history. The present manor was built in the late 1920s for Sumner Welles, President Franklin Roosevelt's undersecretary of state; phone (301) 839-7782.

Fort Foote Park, 1.5 miles west off SR 210, contains the crude concrete and stone gun emplacements and earthworks of Fort Foote, built to protect Washington, D.C. during the Civil War.

The thunder of hooves rather than artillery is heard year-round four to five nights a week as harness racing takes place at Rosecroft Raceway, just off the Maryland 4A exit of the Beltway; phone (301) 567-4000.

Note: Policies concerning admittance of children to pari-mutuel betting facilities vary. Phone for information.

FORT WASHINGTON PARK is off I-495/I-95 exit 3A to SR 210S, then 4 mi. s. to Fort Washington Rd., then 3.5 mi. s.w. to the park entrance. This imposing 1824 masonry structure overlooking the Potomac River can be entered by a drawbridge over a dry moat. Two guardrooms provide a glimpse of military life and punishment. The superb view from the front wall takes in both Washington to the north and Mount Vernon to the south.

Picnicking is permitted. Allow 1 hour minimum. Park open daily 8-dusk, visitor center daily 9-5; closed Jan. 1, Thanksgiving and Dec. 25. Admission $5 per private vehicle, $3 per person (walk-in, bicycle or bus). Phone (301) 763-4600.

OXON HILL FARM is off I-495/I-95 exit 3A and Oxon Hill Rd. Comprising 512 acres, this working early 20th-century farm also depicts agricultural practices of the 17th century to the present through displays of livestock and other animals, machinery, barns and gardens. Picnicking is permitted. Allow 1 hour minimum. Daily 8-4:30; closed Jan. 1, Thanksgiving and Dec. 25. Free. Phone (301) 839-1176, or TTY (301) 839-1176.

ROCKVILLE (A-5) pop. 47,388, elev. 432′

Rockville traces its history to 1776, when irate citizens vowed to cut off all trade with England until the tea tax was lifted. A prosperous Washington suburb, Rockville's pockets of Victorian architecture, brick sidewalks and large trees help preserve some of the city's old essence amid the prevailing suburban sprawl.

The Mansion Art Gallery of Rockville, 603 Edmonston Dr., offers free art exhibitions that change monthly. The graves of F. Scott Fitzgerald, his wife and his daughter are in the cemetery of the 1817 St. Mary's Catholic Church, in one of Rockville's seven historic districts.

Conference and Visitors Bureau of Montgomery County—Rockville: 12900 Middlebrook Rd., Germantown, MD 20874; phone (301) 916-0698 or (800) 925-0880. *See color ad p. 71.*

SAVE **BEALL-DAWSON HOUSE** is at 103 W. Montgomery Ave. This restored 1815 house is furnished in period. The Federal exterior complements its interior, which is designed in the neoclassic style of Robert Adam. The small brick building to the rear of the house was the original dairy house. Docents conduct guided tours.

Allow 30 minutes minimum. Tues.-Sun. noon-4; closed major holidays. Admission $3; senior citizens and students over 13, $2. Phone (301) 762-1492.

The Research Library is in the Beall-Dawson complex at 103 W. Montgomery Ave. This library has a collection of books, maps, documents and photographs pertaining to Montgomery County history and genealogy. Tues.-Sat. 10-4, Sun. 1-4. Library admission $5, senior citizens and students with ID $2. Phone (301) 340-2974.

Stonestreet Museum of 19th-Century Medicine is on the grounds of the Beall-Dawson House at 103 W. Montgomery Ave. Included in the Beall-Dawson House tour, this 1850 building exhibits antiquated medical instruments, apothecary accessories and period furniture.

ROCK CREEK REGIONAL PARK is 4 mi. e. on SR 28, then 2 mi. n. on Muncaster Mill Rd. to Avery Rd. Lake Needwood offers canoe, pedal boat and rowboat rentals Memorial Day through Labor Day. The *Needwood Queen* offers 20-minute lake cruises on weekends and holidays, May 1 through Labor Day. Both lakes allow fishing. The park also contains hiking and bicycle trails, an archery range, nine- and 18-hole golf courses, and picnic areas. Meadowside Nature Center has exhibits.

Park open daily dawn-dusk; closed major winter holidays. Nature center open Tues.-Sat. 9-5. Park free. Boat launch $4. Phone (301) 948-5053, (202) 495-2525 for picnic shelter reservations, (202) 924-4141 for the nature center, or (202) 762-1888 for boat information. *See Maryland Recreation Chart.*

SILVER SPRING (B-7) pop. 76,540, elev. 340'

In 1842 *Washington Globe* editor Francis Preston Blair discovered a spring in a heavily wooded area north of Washington, D.C. He later purchased the land around the spring, built a home and named it Silver Spring after the sparkling water. By 1899 the first post office was built, and Blair became the first postmaster for the small farming community.

Conference and Visitors Bureau of Montgomery County—Silver Spring: 12900 Middlebrook Rd., Germantown, MD 20874; phone (301) 916-0698 or (800) 925-0880.

SEVENTH-DAY ADVENTIST CHURCH WORLD HEADQUARTERS is at 12501 Old Columbia Pike. Free guided tours begin in the main lobby. Various facets of the church's history, beliefs and activities are presented. The tour includes a visit to the estate of Ellen G. White, one of the founding members of the church. Food is available. Allow 1 hour minimum. Tours Mon.-Thurs. at 10:30 and 1:30, Fri. at 9 and 10:30; closed major holidays. Free. Phone (301) 680-6310.

WHEATON (A-6) elev. 469'

Wheaton took its name from Union general Frank Wheaton, who helped defend Washington, D.C. from his post at Fort Stevens; the fort still stands on Georgia Avenue. Wheaton also was home to Charles Francis Jenkins, owner of more than 400 patents and perfecter of the home television set; Jenkins delivered the nation's first television broadcast in 1923.

Conference and Visitors Bureau of Montgomery County—Wheaton: 12900 Middlebrook Rd., Germantown, MD 20874; phone (301) 916-0698 or (800) 925-0880.

BROOKSIDE GARDENS is 2 mi. n. of I-495 exit 31A via SR 97 (Georgia Ave.) to Randolph Rd., then 2 blks. e. to Glenallan Ave., then .7 mi. s. to 1800 Glenallan Ave. It features two conservatories and 50 acres of outdoor gardens. Plantings include winter, formal, rose, fragrance and azalea gardens. Tropical plants in the conservatories accent the seasonal flower displays. There also is a horticultural library on the premises.

Guided tours are available. Educational programs are offered. Allow 30 minutes minimum in winter, 1 hour minimum rest of year. Grounds open daily dawn-dusk. Conservatories open daily 10-5. Visitor center daily 9-5. Horticultural reference library schedule varies; phone ahead. Closed Dec. 25. Free. Phone (301) 962-1400.

BROOKSIDE NATURE CENTER is 2 mi. n. of I-495 exit 31A via SR 97 (Georgia Ave.) to Randolph Rd., then 2 blks. e. to Glenallen Ave., then .7 mi. s. to 1400 Glenallan Ave. In addition to hiking trails, this wooded area offers a primitive weather station, a re-created pioneer homestead, animal exhibits and a hands-on learning center for children. Picnic facilities are available. Allow 30 minutes minimum. Tues.-Sat. 9-5, Sun. 1-5. Trails daily dawn-dusk. Closed major holidays. Free. Phone (301) 946-9071.

NATIONAL CAPITAL TROLLEY MUSEUM is 5 mi. n. between New Hampshire Ave. and Layhill Rd. at 1313 Bonifant Rd. Offerings include the permanent exhibit "Streetcar Communities" and a slide presentation about Washington, D.C. trolleys. A 1.7-mile trolley ride also is offered.

Allow 1 hour minimum. Sat.-Sun. noon-5, Jan.-Nov. (also Thurs.-Fri. 11-3, mid-June to mid-Aug., and Thurs.-Fri. 10-2, Mar. 15-May 15 and Oct. 1-Nov. 15); Sat.-Sun. 5-9, rest of year. Closed Jan. 1 and Dec. 24-25 and 31. Last trolley departs 30 minutes before closing. Museum free. Trolley $3; ages 2-17, $2. Phone (301) 384-6088.

Nearby Virginia

ALEXANDRIA (H-5) pop. 128,283, elev. 20′

Although an integral part of the Washington, D.C. metropolitan area, Alexandria is a distinct city in its own right. It was established in 1749 by a group of Scottish merchants and named for John Alexander, who had purchased the land in 1669. During the Revolutionary period Alexandria was a principal Colonial ports as well as a trade, social and political center.

George Washington maintained a town house in Alexandria. During his residence he organized the Friendship Fire Co., was elected vestryman of Christ Church Parish and was a member of the Masonic Lodge, becoming its Charter Master in 1788.

Alexandria also was the home of Revolutionary War general "Light Horse" Harry Lee, and the boyhood home of his son, Robert E. Lee. During the Civil War the city was captured and occupied by Federal forces, who used it as a base of operations for various Union campaigns in Virginia.

Through careful guardianship and planning, parts of Alexandria have managed to retain the appearance of another century. Old Town Alexandria, extending westward from the Potomac River, is the major historical area (see Alexandria Walking Tour p. 121). The city's DASH bus system connects the King Street and Braddock Road Metro stations with various Old Town locations. The fare is $1 (exact change only) and includes a transfer good for 4 hours for the return trip. Phone (703) 370-3274 for route and schedule information.

The cruise ship Dandy, at the foot of Prince Street, is an enclosed ship offering 2-hour luncheon and 3-hour dinner-dance cruises on the Potomac River. Phone (703) 683-6076 for information and reservations.

The Special Events hotline maintained by the Alexandria Department of Recreation, Parks and Cultural Activities provides information about local music events; phone (703) 883-4686.

Alexandria Convention and Visitors Association: 421 King St., Suite 300, Alexandria, VA 22314; phone (703) 838-4200, (800) 388-9119 or TTY (703) 838-6494. See color ad p. 500.

Self-guiding tours: Among the visitors association's offerings are a walking tour brochure, Civil War walking tour and bicycle trail maps, a parking map and a parking pass good for 24 hours of free parking.

Shopping areas: Old Town Alexandria's streets are lined with galleries, antique shops and boutiques. Landmark Mall is on Duke Street; its anchor stores are Hecht's, Lord & Taylor and Sears. The Torpedo Factory Art Center (see attraction listing p. 121) offers specialty items.

ALEXANDRIA BLACK HISTORY MUSEUM, 902 Wythe St., interprets the contributions of African-Americans to Alexandria's history and culture from 1749 to the present. A guided tour is offered. Allow 30 minutes minimum. Tues.-Sat. 10-4; closed Jan. 1, Easter, July 4, Thanksgiving and Dec. 25. Free. Phone (703) 838-4356.

CARLYLE HOUSE is at 121 N. Fairfax St. In 1753 this stone, Georgian-Palladian mansion was the grandest in the new town of Alexandria. The house features rich architectural detail, authentic paint colors and fine furnishings, and the grounds include a garden laid out in 18th-century style, with brick walkways and boxwood parterres. Exhibits interpret the domestic life of a Colonial gentleman, his family and his slaves.

Allow 1 hour minimum. Tours every half-hour Tues.-Sat. 10-4:30, Sun. noon-4:30, Apr.-Oct.; Tues.-Sat. 10-4, Sun. noon-4, rest of year. Closed Jan. 1, Thanksgiving and Dec. 25. Admission $4; ages 11-17, $2. Phone (703) 549-2997.

CHRIST CHURCH (Anglican) is at 118 N. Washington St. near Columbus and Cameron sts. Built 1767-73, this Georgian-style brick church, with a Palladian chancel window unusual for its time, is in nearly original condition. George Washington purchased Pew 60 for 36 pounds and 10 shillings when the church first opened, and he regularly attended services. Robert E. Lee, who also attended services regularly, was confirmed in the church in 1853. The cut-glass chandelier, under the gallery, represents one of the most advanced types of lighting fixtures available in the early 19th century.

Allow 30 minutes minimum. Mon.-Sat. 9-4, Sun. 2-4, except during services; closed holidays and after services Jan. 1, Thanksgiving and Dec. 25. Donations. Phone (703) 549-1450.

COLLINGWOOD LIBRARY AND MUSEUM ON AMERICANISM is on the Potomac River at 8301 E. Boulevard Dr. The oldest part of Collingwood Mansion dates from 1783. The museum presents presidential china, American Indian artifacts and displays about Revolutionary War heroes. Books in the library, devoted exclusively to American history, can be used on the premises. Mon. and Wed.-Sat. 10-4, Sun. 1-4; closed federal holidays, the weekend after Thanksgiving and Dec. 18-Jan. 4. Free. Phone (703) 765-1652.

FORT WARD MUSEUM AND HISTORIC SITE is at 4301 W. Braddock Rd., just e. of I-395 between King St. and Seminary Rd. Fort Ward, on 45 acres, was one of the forts that formed a defensive ring around Washington during the Civil War, and the museum presents changing exhibits pertaining to that conflict. Interpretive programs, an orientation videotape and lectures are offered throughout the year. Free evening concerts are held outdoors Thursdays, July through August.

Picnicking is permitted. Park open daily 9-dusk. Museum open Tues.-Sat. 9-5, Sun. noon-5; closed Jan. 1, Thanksgiving and Dec. 25. Donations. A fee may charged during special events. Phone (703) 838-4848.

FRIENDSHIP FIREHOUSE is at 107 S. Alfred St., between King and Prince sts. Established in 1774 as Alexandria's first volunteer fire company, Friendship Firehouse claims George Washington as a founding member. The current structure dates to 1855. Hand-drawn fire engines and historic firefighting apparatus are displayed, as are Victorian furnishings and ceremonial objects. Allow 30 minutes minimum. Fri.-Sat. 10-4, Sun. 1-4; closed Jan. 1 and Dec. 25. Free. Phone (703) 838-3891.

[SAVE] **GADSBY'S TAVERN MUSEUM,** 134 N. Royal St., comprises the original 1785 Georgian tavern and the 1792 City Tavern and Hotel. The tavern, with its taproom, small dining room and assembly room, and the hotel ballroom were a center for Alexandria's social and political life. Interpretive programs are offered year-round.

Tues.-Sat. 10-5, Sun.-Mon. 1-5, Apr.-Sept.; Wed.-Sat. 11-4, Sun. 1-4, rest of year. Closed Jan. 1, Thanksgiving and Dec. 25. Guided tours are available at a quarter before and a quarter past each hour. Last tour begins 15 minutes before closing. Admission $4; ages 11-17, $2. Phone (703) 838-4242.

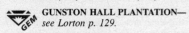

THE GEORGE WASHINGTON MASONIC NATIONAL MEMORIAL surmounts Shooter's Hill at the w. end of King St. The 333-foot-tall landmark is modeled after the ancient lighthouse at Alexandria, Egypt. The Replica Room contains original furnishings of Alexandria Lodge No. 22, the lodge in Alexandria over which Washington was the first Worshipful Master under Virginia charter.

The nine floors of exhibits include a colossal statue of George Washington in Memorial Hall and a museum that features the Washington family Bible among numerous other artifacts. The memorial also houses a research library and is topped by a 360-degree observation deck providing a view of the metropolitan Washington area.

Daily 9-5; closed Jan. 1, Thanksgiving and Dec. 25. Guided tours are given at 9:30, 11, 1, 2:30 and 4. Free. Phone (703) 683-2007.

GEORGE WASHINGTON'S RIVER FARM is off George Washington Memorial Pkwy., 4 mi. s. of Old Town Alexandria, on the Potomac River at 7931 E. Boulevard Dr. George Washington bought this property in 1760, and he may also have planted the two black walnut trees that still stand in the meadow near the main buildings. The manor house was built in the early 20th century. Now headquarters for the American Horticultural Society, the 25-acre site contains display, test and children's

gardens. Classes, lectures and horticultural resources are offered.

Allow 30 minutes minimum. Mon.-Fri. 8:30-5 (also Sat. 9-1, late Apr.-Sept. 30); closed holidays. Free. Phone (703) 768-5700 or (800) 777-7931.

GUNSTON HALL PLANTATION— *see Lorton p. 129.*

LEE-FENDALL HOUSE MUSEUM, 614 Oronoco St., was built in 1785 by Alexandria civic leader Philip Richard Fendall and remained in the family until 1903. It is furnished with period antiques, including many Lee possessions. John L. Lewis, U.S. labor leader, owned the house 1937-69.

Guided tours depart on the hour Tues.-Sat. 10-4, Sun. 1-4; closed holidays. Last tour begins 1 hour before closing. Admission $4; ages 11-17, $2. Phone (703) 548-1789.

THE LYCEUM is at 201 S. Washington St. This museum of Alexandria's history presents changing exhibits, lectures, concerts and educational programs. Built in 1839 as the city's first cultural center, the building was occupied by both Confederate and Union troops during the Civil War. Mon.-Sat. 10-5, Sun. 1-5; closed Jan. 1, Thanksgiving and Dec. 24-25. Free. Phone (703) 838-4994.

MOUNT VERNON— *see Mount Vernon p. 131.*

OLD PRESBYTERIAN MEETING HOUSE is at 316 S. Royal St. between Wolfe and Duke sts. Established in 1774, the meeting house became a gathering place for patriots during the Revolutionary War, and was the site of George Washington's funeral sermons in December 1799. During the Civil War it was used as a hospital.

In the churchyard are the graves of John Carlyle and the Unknown Revolutionary War Soldier. The old-fashioned gate pews of this still-active church have been retained. The keys to the sanctuary are available at the church office. Mon.-Fri. 8:30-4:30. Free. Phone (703) 549-6670.

THE POTOMAC RIVERBOAT CO. vessels dock at the City Marina behind the Torpedo Factory Art Center and at Washington Harbor in Georgetown. Three narrated cruises are offered: the Alexandria by Water Cruise, a 40-minute narrated excursion along the waterfront; the 2-hour, round-trip Washington by Water Monuments Cruise/Water Taxi Service, a trip past Washington landmarks; and George Washington's Mount Vernon Cruise, an excursion to Mount Vernon that includes admission to the estate.

Alexandria by Water Cruise departs on the hour Tues.-Fri. 11-2, Sat. noon-10, Sun. noon-8, May 1-Sept. 6; Sat.-Sun. noon-7, in Apr.; Sat. noon-10, Sun. noon-8, Sept. 7-Oct. 11. Washington by Water Monuments Cruise (Alexandria departures) Thurs.-Sat. 11:30-10:30, Mon.-Wed. 11:30-9:30, Sun. 11:30-8:30, June 14-Sept. 6; Tues.-Sat. 11:30-9:30,

Sun. 11:30-8:30, May 1-June 13; Tues.-Fri. 11:30-9:30, Sat. 11:30-10:30, Sun. 11:30-8:30, Sept. 7-Oct. 11; Sat.-Sun. 11:30-5:30, in Apr. Washington by Water Monuments Cruise (Georgetown departures) Mon.-Wed. 12:30-10:30, Thurs.-Sat. 12:30-11:30, Sun. 12:30-9:30, June 14-Sept. 6; Tues.-Sat. 12:30-10:30, Sun. 12:30-9:30, May 1-June 13; Tues.-Fri. 12:30-10:30, Sat. 12:30-11:30, Sun. 12:30-9:30, Sept. 7-Oct. 11; Sat.-Sun. 12:30-6:30, in Apr. George Washington's Mount Vernon Cruise departs Tues.-Sun. at 11, May 1-Sept. 6; Sat.-Sun. at 11, Apr. and Sept. 7-Oct. 11. Departure times may vary; please phone ahead.

Tickets are sold at the ticket booth located at the marina and visitor center. Alexandria fare $8; over 60, $7; ages 2-12, $5. Washington round-trip fare $16; over 60, $15; ages 2-12, $8. Washington one-way fare $10; ages 2-12, $5. Mount Vernon fare $27; over 60, $26; ages 6-10, $15. Mount Vernon fares include admission to the estate. Phone (703) 548-9000 or (877) 502-2628.

RAMSAY HOUSE VISITORS CENTER is at 221 King St. The original Ramsay House, one of the oldest structures in the city, was moved to this site in 1749 by William Ramsay, a founder and first lord mayor of Alexandria. It burned down in 1949 and was replaced by the current building, which is staffed by Alexandria Convention and Visitors Association employees. Daily 9-5 (9-noon, Dec. 24 and 31); closed Jan. 1, Thanksgiving and Dec. 25. Free. Phone (703) 838-5005.

STABLER-LEADBEATER APOTHECARY MUSEUM has its entrance at 105 S. Fairfax St. Founded in 1792 by Quaker pharmacist Edward Stabler, this is said to be Alexandria's oldest mercantile establishment; George Washington, James Monroe and Robert E. Lee were patrons. Old account books, prescriptions, early medical wares and a collection of period apothecary containers can be seen in their original setting. The shop remained in the family until 1933.

Mon.-Sat. 10-4, Sun. 1-5; closed major holidays. Admission $2.50; ages 11-17, $2. Phone (703) 836-3713.

TORPEDO FACTORY ART CENTER is at 105 N. Union St. between King and Cameron sts. Built for the manufacture of torpedo casings for World War I and World War II, the building now contains 84 studios and six galleries where visitors can watch artists and crafters at work. Works by more than 160 artists are displayed and for sale. The center includes the Art League School. Daily 10-5; closed Jan. 1, Easter, July 4, Thanksgiving and Dec. 25. Free. Phone (703) 838-4565.

Alexandria Archaeology Museum and Laboratory is on the third floor of the Torpedo Factory Art Center. This museum displays and interprets objects from recent excavations in Alexandria. The collection has items dating from 3000 B.C. to the early 20th century. A library also is maintained. Museum open Tues.-Fri. 10-3, Sat. 10-5, Sun. 1-5; closed

Jan. 1, Easter, July 4, Thanksgiving and Dec. 25. Free. Phone (703) 838-4399.

WOODLAWN PLANTATION is 7.5 mi. s. on US 1 at jct. with SR 235. The land, originally part of Mount Vernon, was a gift from George Washington to his nephew, Maj. Lawrence Lewis, and Lewis's wife Eleanor "Nelly" Custis, a granddaughter of Martha Washington. Dr. William Thornton, who designed the 1805 mansion, was the first architect of the Capitol. The 19th-century period rooms and restored formal gardens are open for viewing.

Picnicking is permitted. Allow 1 hour minimum. Daily 10-5, Mar.-Dec. (also Presidents' Day). Admission $7.50; grades K-12, $3. Combination ticket with Frank Lloyd Wright's Pope-Leighey House $13; grades K-12, $5. AX, MC, VI. Phone (703) 780-4000.

Frank Lloyd Wright's Pope-Leighey House is on the Woodlawn Plantation grounds. The Usonian house was designed by Wright and exhibits many of the significant contributions he made to contemporary architecture. The house also contains original furnishings designed by the architect.

Allow 30 minutes minimum. Daily 10-5, Mar.-Dec. (also Presidents' Day). Admission $7.50; grades K-12, $3. Combination ticket with Woodlawn Plantation $13; grades K-12, $5. AX, MC, VI. Phone (703) 780-4000.

⨀ Walking Tour: Alexandria

Refer to the Alexandria Walking Tour map on the next page. This tour of Old Town takes 2-3 hours, depending on your pace and the number of listed sites you visit along the way. Those that appear in bold type have detailed listings on the preceding pages. Even if you decide not to visit a site, reading the listing when you reach that point should make the tour more interesting.

If you drive into Alexandria, you can pick up a free 24-hour parking proclamation from the visitor center at Ramsay House. The passes are valid only when using 2-hour metered spaces; upon arrival, you should insert enough change in the meter to give yourself time to pick up the parking pass and return to your car with it. To receive a pass, you must provide state identification and your license plate number.

Served by both the Blue and Yellow lines, the King Street Metro station is about a mile west of Ramsay House. The city's DASH bus system connects the King Street and Braddock Road Metro stations with various Old Town locations. The fare is $1 (exact change only) and includes a transfer good for 4 hours for the return trip.

If street-side parking is at a premium—and it will be on weekdays—there are several parking garages in the area as well. The most convenient is the City Hall garage (during evenings and weekends only) at the corner of King and Fairfax streets. Other nearby garages are across Union Street from

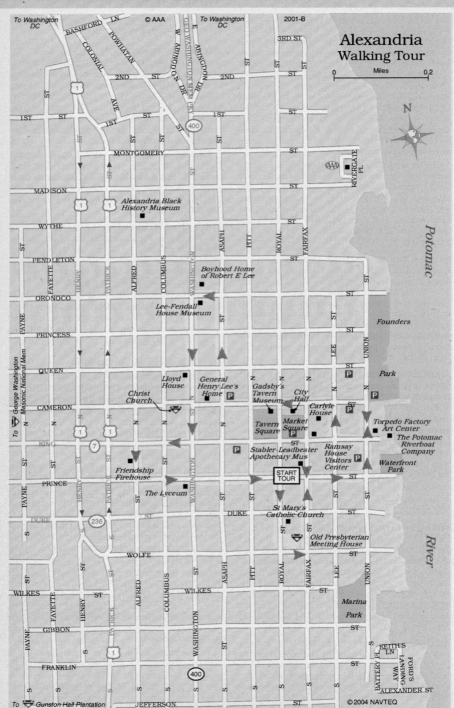

Alexandria
Walking Tour

Miles
0   0.2

N

To Washington
DC

To Washington
DC

© AAA

2001-B

BASHFORD LN

POWHATAN

COLONIAL AVE

2ND   ST

1ST   ST

MONTGOMERY

MADISON

WYTHE

PENDLETON

FAYETTE

ORONOCO

PRINCESS

QUEEN

CAMERON

KING

PRINCE

DUKE

WOLFE

WILKES

GIBBON

FRANKLIN

1ST   ST

3RD ST

2ND

ST

ST

ST

ST

ST

ST

ST

ST

W ABINGDON DR

E ABINGDON DR

GEO WASHINGTON MEM HWY

400

RIVERGATE PL

Potomac

Alexandria Black
History Museum

Boyhood Home
of Robert E Lee

Lee-Fendall
House Museum

Founders

ASAPH

PITT

ROYAL

FAIRFAX

LEE

UNION

Park

Lloyd
House

General
Henry Lee's
Home

Gadsby's
Tavern
Museum

City
Hall

Carlyle
House

Christ
Church

Tavern
Square

Market
Square

Torpedo Factory
Art Center

The Potomac
Riverboat
Company

Stabler-Leadbeater
Apothecary Mus

Ramsay
House
Visitors
Center

Waterfront
Park

Friendship
Firehouse

START
TOUR

The Lyceum

St Mary's
Catholic Church

DUKE

Old Presbyterian
Meeting House

River

WILKES

Marina
Park

KEITH'S
LN

FORD'S
LANDING
WAY

BATTERY PL

ALEXANDER ST

To Gunston Hall Plantation

JEFFERSON

ST

©2004 NAVTEQ

George Washington
Masonic National Mem

PAYNE

FAYETTE

HENRY

PATRICK

ALFRED

COLUMBUS

WASHINGTON

ST MARY

the Torpedo Factory; at 200 Queen St.; at 10 Thompson Alley; at the Courthouse, 111 S. Pitt St.; at 115 S. Union St.; and at 210 N. St. Asaph St.

Note: In keeping with Old Town's quaint ambience, many of its sidewalks are brick-paved. Watch your step or you'll risk tripping over the occasional protruding paver.

Few areas offer a more pleasant stroll into another century than Old Town Alexandria. Here visitors can enjoy shady cobblestone streets closely flanked by 18th- and 19th-century houses with luxuriant courtyards. Newer buildings emulate the prevailing architectural style, helping to preserve this historic district's charm.

Begin your tour at **Ramsay House**—the city's visitor center—at 221 King St., which is on the corner of King and Fairfax streets.

From the Ramsay House, walk east on King Street toward the river. Turn left at Lee Street, and follow Lee to the corner of Cameron Street for a view of Cameron Mews, mews being another word for alley or back street. This Colonial town house development exemplifies Alexandria's approach to new housing in Old Town. Turn left on Cameron Street and walk past the lovely gardens on the southwest corner of Cameron and Lee. These belong to the **Carlyle House.**

John Carlyle, a Scottish merchant and city founder, built this grand Georgian Palladian manor 1751-53. Two years after its completion, Gen. Edward Braddock and five Colonial governors met there to discuss funding a campaign against the French during the French and Indian War. The issue of financing the war later became so contentious that it led to the American Revolution.

Continue west on Cameron, which is one of the city's most interesting shopping streets. The north side of the block between Fairfax and Royal streets has many boutiques and specialty shops. Opposite is the block-long, brick City Hall, and behind it is airy Market Square. The market held here every Saturday morning is reputed to be the nation's oldest.

The neat brick facades facing Cameron Street between Royal and Pitt streets hide Tavern Square, named for historic **Gadsby's Tavern Museum,** which forms its northeast corner. Made up of two buildings—the 1770 City Tavern and 1792 City Hotel—Gadsby's Tavern prospered due to its location along the main stage route between Williamsburg and Boston. For many years it was a center for social and political life in the city.

Proceed 1 block west on Cameron past George Washington's reconstructed town house, which is the clapboard house on the street's south side. Washington stayed here when business or bad weather prevented him from returning to his Mount Vernon estate. Like many historic homes, it is a private residence not open to the public.

Turn right on tree-lined St. Asaph Street, where the town homes are beautified by landscaped courtyards and pocket gardens. As you cross Princess

Street, look left to see a section of restored cobblestone roadway between St. Asaph and Washington streets.

Make a left at Oronoco, and on the right as you approach Washington Street you'll find the boyhood home of Gen. Robert E. Lee, which is a private residence. Lee lived here from age 5 until he left to enroll at West Point when he was 18. Across the street, on the southeast corner of Oronoco and Washington, stands the 1785 **Lee-Fendall House Museum.** Home to generations of Robert E. Lee's relatives, the house contains a variety of items that once belonged to this celebrated Virginia family.

Head south on Washington Street. On the southwest corner of Queen and Washington is the 1797 Lloyd House, one of the city's best examples of late Georgian architecture. Turn left on Cameron; on your left, at 611 Cameron, is a small, red-brick house that once belonged to Revolutionary War hero Gen. Henry "Light Horse Harry" Lee. Due to financial difficulties, Lee was forced to move his family—including young son Robert Edward—to this house from their Stratford Hall Plantation *(see attraction listing p. 294)*. The Lees lived here 1810-12; it is currently a private residence.

The peaceful grounds of **Christ Church** occupy the southwest corner of Washington and Cameron. Completed in 1773, the Georgian-style church remains an active house of worship. George Washington was an early parishioner; his original pew is preserved inside. A silver plaque marks the spot where Robert E. Lee was confirmed in 1853.

The church grounds served as Alexandria's cemetery until 1809; its oldest tombstone is dated Mar. 20, 1791. Just inside the wall on Washington Street, a mass grave holds the remains of 34 Confederate soldiers who were reburied here after the Civil War.

Continue south on Washington Street for a block and turn right on King Street. The tower you see ahead of you, west of the walking tour route, is **The George Washington Masonic National Memorial.** Dedicated in 1932, it stands atop Shooter's Hill, which was the site of a Civil War fort. An observation deck on the ninth level offers a fantastic bird's-eye view of Alexandria and the monuments and government buildings of the nation's capital.

Go 2 blocks west and turn left on Alfred Street. The **Friendship Firehouse,** which by tradition claimed George Washington as a member, is on the west side of Alfred. The Friendship Fire Co. was founded in 1774, and the current building was completed in 1855. Among the historic firefighting equipment inside are leather water buckets, antique fire engines and ceremonial regalia used for parades.

Continue south on Alfred Street, and at the corner turn left onto Prince Street. Walk 2 blocks to the corner of Prince and Washington streets. The bronze Confederate Statue stands within the intersection. Dedicated in 1889, it depicts a Confederate soldier gazing south with head bowed and arms folded across his chest. The memorial, the base of which is inscribed with the names of 100 Confederate dead, marks the spot where more than 700 Alexandrians left the Union-occupied city to fight for the Confederacy.

Adjacent is the two-story, Greek Revival structure known as **The Lyceum** (lie-SEE-um), an interpretive center for the history of Alexandria. Lyceums were early 19th-century organizations that promoted public debates and lectures on a host of topics. Formed in 1834, the Alexandria Lyceum hosted its first programs at a local school. These programs were so popular that the organization was soon able to fund construction of a grand hall to serve as its headquarters and main venue, which is the building (completed in 1839) you see today. Eventually Alexandrians began applying the organization's name to the hall itself, and it remained the center of the city's intellectual life until the Civil War.

Cross Washington Street, continue east to Royal Street and turn right. The neat, well-maintained homes in this block of Royal are typical restored 18th-century houses, many marked with the oval Early Buildings Survey registry plaque.

Across Duke Street on the east side of Royal is St. Mary's Catholic Church; beyond the church, turn left into what appears to be a small grassy play yard. You are actually approaching the **Old Presbyterian Meeting House** through its churchyard, which contains 18th-century grave markers and the Tomb of the Unknown Revolutionary War Soldier.

Upon reaching the front of the meetinghouse, turn left and proceed 2 blocks, crossing Duke and Prince streets. The **Stabler-Leadbeater Apothecary Museum** is at 107 S. Fairfax St.; the entrance is next door. This former pharmacy operated under the same family from 1796 until the Great Depression forced it to close in 1933. At that time the entire contents were bought at auction by a pharmaceutical association for a museum, which opened in 1939. Inside the shop you'll find wooden boxes hand lettered with the names of medicinal herbs, along with a huge collection of drug tins and hand-blown bottles.

Return to Prince Street and make a left. Gentry Row, along the 200 block of Prince Street, boasts the Fairfax House, 207 Prince St., and other homes typical of those built by the city's wealthiest inhabitants during the late 1700s. Number 209 next door belonged at one time to George Washington's longtime physician, Dr. James Craik.

The 1850 Athenaeum (also known as the Old Dominion Bank Building), on the northwest corner of Prince and Lee streets, is an excellent example of Greek Revival architecture. Originally a banking house, the Athenaeum now houses contemporary art shows.

Continue east across Lee Street. You are now walking along Captains' Row, named for sea captain John Harper, who had many of the Federal-style houses built for his numerous children.

Turn left on Union Street and cross King. The **Torpedo Factory Art Center** is on your right. This

waterfront facility, constructed in 1918, produced torpedo casings through World War II. For years afterward it was used for storage until someone hit upon the idea for using it to house art studios.

More than 160 artists working in such media as sculpture, photography, painting, printmaking, jewelry, ceramics and glass are represented, and numerous examples of their work are on display. The center also houses the Alexandria Archaeology Museum and Laboratory, where you can view items recovered from excavations throughout Alexandria. Most of these are from the late 1600s to the early 1900s, but many prehistoric artifacts are on display as well.

From the Torpedo Factory, return to Ramsay House by making a right on King Street. If your feet are willing, a stroll along this main thoroughfare, which is lined with specialty shops, pubs and ethnic restaurants, can be an enjoyable way to conclude your tour.

Two points of interest not included in the perimeter of the walking tour are **The Alexandria Black History Museum,** 638 N. Alfred St., which documents the history of African-Americans in Alexandria and Virginia from 1749 to the present, and the partially restored bastions of **Fort Ward** and its interpretive museum, at 4301 W. Braddock Rd.

ARLINGTON (F-5) pop. 189,453

Arlington, on the southwest bank of the Potomac, is a suburb of Washington, D.C. One of the smallest counties in the United States, it covers 25.7 square miles, of which about 4.6 square miles are federal property. Some of the major centers of development (the county contains no incorporated communities) are Ballston, Clarendon, Columbia Pike, Crystal City, Rosslyn and Shirlington.

Within Arlington is The Pentagon, one of the world's largest office buildings. The five-sided structure, which was completed in 1943 after only 16 months of construction, covers 29 acres and houses branches of the Department of Defense.

Arlington Visitors Center: 735 S. 18th St., Arlington, VA 22202; (703) 228-5720 or (800) 677-6267. *See color ad p. 74.*

Shopping areas: At the Crystal City Metro station there is a collection of underground boutiques, restaurants and clothing stores. Fashion Centre at Pentagon City, at the Pentagon City Metro station, features Macy's, Nordstrom and more than 150 other stores. For above-ground shopping Ballston Common, at Wilson Boulevard and Glebe Road, offers an indoor array of more than 120 stores, including Hecht's and JCPenney.

DRUG ENFORCEMENT ADMINISTRATION MUSEUM & VISITORS CENTER is at 700 Army Navy Dr. (M: Pentagon City). Located on the ground floor of an office building, the DEA Museum presents the history of federal drug law enforcement, from 19th-century opium dens to today's organized drug cartels. Displays include drug paraphernalia and items—such as a helicopter and customized motorcycles—confiscated during drug raids. Allow 30 minutes minimum. Street parking is limited. Tues.-Fri. 10-4; closed federal holidays. Free. Phone (202) 307-8956.

FORT MYER is at 204 Lee Ave. off the I-395 Washington Blvd. exit, near Arlington National Cemetery. A military post since 1863, tenants include the U.S. Army Band Pershing's Own and the 3rd Infantry (The Old Guard), whose duties include conducting ceremonies for visiting dignitaries and military funerals, serving as escort for the president and standing guard at the Tomb of the Unknowns.

Visitors must show two valid forms of ID, and vehicles are subject to search. Arrive early for events. Phone (703) 607-8000 for the changing of the guard schedule, or (703) 696-3944 for information about the fort.

LBJ MEMORIAL GROVE is s. of Memorial Bridge along George Washington Memorial Pkwy. in Lady Bird Johnson Park, a Potomac River island. A granite memorial to President Lyndon B. Johnson on the 15-acre island is surrounded by stones inscribed with quotations from his works. Daily 24 hours. Free.

 ARLINGTON NATIONAL CEMETERY (F-5)

Directly across the Potomac River west of Washington (M: Arlington National Cemetery), Arlington National Cemetery was established in 1864 on the confiscated estate of Robert E. Lee. It is an impressive sight, with seemingly endless rows of simple white headstones. Imposing stones and monuments mark the graves of many individuals and groups.

Among those buried are the original owners of the estate, George Washington Parke Custis and his wife Mary Lee Fitzhugh Custis, in addition to Pierre L'Enfant, President William Howard Taft, Chief Justice Oliver Wendell Holmes Jr., Gen. John J. Pershing, Rear Adm. Robert E. Peary, three-time presidential nominee William Jennings Bryan, Rear Adm. Richard E. Byrd, Lt. Gen. Claire L. Chennault, Gen. Hoyt S. Vandenberg, Secretary of State John Foster Dulles, Gen. George C. Marshall, Chief Justice Earl Warren, President John F. Kennedy, Sen. Robert F. Kennedy, First Lady Jacqueline Kennedy Onassis, Gen. Omar Bradley, Medal of Honor recipient Audie Murphy and heavyweight champion boxer Joe Louis.

The cemetery is open daily 8-7, Apr.-Sept.; 8-5, rest of year. Paid parking is available off of Memorial Drive; people visiting gravesites of relatives can obtain a temporary pass to drive into the cemetery.

For the general public, Tourmobiles that leave from the visitor center provide the only motorized transportation through the cemetery (*see attraction listing p. 98*). A 2-hour narrated tour covers all major points of interest. Parking is $1.25 per hour for the first three hours, $2 per hour thereafter. Tourmobile fare $6; ages 3-11, $3.

Those over 65 and the physically impaired should apply at the information window for a pass that will allow them to drive into the cemetery. Individuals over 65 must present identification that verifies date of birth; the physically impaired must show their handicapped placard. Phone park information at (703) 607-8000, or Tourmobile at (202) 554-5100.

ARLINGTON HOUSE, THE ROBERT E. LEE MEMORIAL is where young Lee courted and married Mary Anna Randolph Custis and where they lived 1831-61. Mrs. Lee inherited the property from her father, George Washington Parke Custis, grandson of Martha Washington. He began building the house in 1802 on land purchased by his father, John Parke Custis. Here in 1861 Lee chose to resign his commission in the U.S. Army to defend his native state.

Administered by the National Park Service, the mansion has been restored to its 1861 appearance and contains some of the original Custis and Lee family furnishings. The grand portico faces the river and affords a splendid view of Washington.

Allow 30 minutes minimum. House open daily 9:30-4:30; museum open daily 8-4:30. Closed Jan. 1 and Dec. 25. Free. Parking is available for a fee at Arlington National Cemetery. Phone (703) 235-1530.

CONFEDERATE MEMORIAL, on the w. side of the cemetery off McPherson Dr., was erected by the United Daughters of the Confederacy in 1914 to honor their dead and to symbolize a reunited North and South. The graves of Confederate soldiers and veterans who died in the Washington, D.C. area are arranged in concentric circles around the monument.

THE GRAVE OF PRESIDENT JOHN F. KENNEDY is on the slope below Arlington House. The site is marked by an eternal flame and excerpts from his inaugural address. Next to it is the grave of his wife Jacqueline, their infant son Patrick and an unnamed stillborn daughter. Near them is the grave of his brother, Sen. Robert F. Kennedy, also the victim of an assassin's bullet.

MARINE CORPS WAR MEMORIAL stands on a promontory at the n. end of the cemetery. The memorial is a 78-foot, 100-ton portrayal of Joseph Rosenthal's photograph of the raising of the flag on Iwo Jima during World War II. The figures were cast in bronze from a model created by Felix de Weldon. The Sunset Parade, also known as the Iwo Jima Memorial Parade, is a color ceremony featuring the Marine Silent Drill Team, Color Guard and Drum and Bugle Corps.

Parade begins Tues. at 7, last Tues. in May-third Tues. in Aug. (Aug. parades begin at 6:30). Free bus service to the ceremony runs from the Arlington National Cemetery visitors' parking area. Phone (202) 433-6060.

MAST OF THE BATTLESHIP USS *MAINE*, which was sunk in Havana Harbor on Feb. 15, 1898, is surrounded by the graves of the 62 known and 167 unknown men who died in the explosion. The explosion that sank the battleship is one of a series of events that led to the beginning of the Spanish-American War.

MEMORIAL AMPHITHEATER, an elliptical, white marble structure, honors those who have defended the nation. It seats approximately 6,000 people.

Unknowns Memorial Display Room, between the amphitheater and the Tomb of the Unknowns, contains tributes to the Unknown Dead of World Wars I and II and the Korean and Vietnam wars. Easter service begins at 6 a.m., Memorial Day and Veterans Day services begin at 11 a.m.

THE NETHERLANDS CARILLON is off US 50 just outside the n. end of the cemetery, next to the Marine Corps War Memorial. This gift from the Netherlands was in gratitude for the United States' aid during and after World War II. Each of the original 49 bells represents a different segment of the Netherlands' population. A 50th bell was added in 1995, on the 50th anniversary of the liberation of the Netherlands.

Allow 30 minutes minimum. Concerts are given Sat. 2-4 in May, on July 4 and in Sept.; Sat. 6-8 p.m., June-Aug. Free. Phone (703) 289-2530.

TOMB OF PIERRE L'ENFANT is in front of Arlington House. French engineer L'Enfant planned the city of Washington; his original plan is on the tomb.

TOMB OF THE UNKNOWN DEAD OF THE CIVIL WAR is a stone and masonry burial vault marking the mass grave of the 2,111 unidentified soldiers who died on nearby Virginia battlefields during the Civil War.

TOMB OF THE UNKNOWNS is striking in its simplicity. The die piece of Colorado marble on which the sculpture is carved is one of the largest blocks ever quarried. Before carving, it weighed 50 tons. Lying in a sarcophagus beneath the tomb is the body of an unknown American soldier brought back from France after World War I. In 1958 the remains of unknown American military personnel from World War II and the Korean War were interred in marked crypts at the head of the tomb.

Specially selected members of the Army's 3rd U.S. Infantry (The Old Guard) guard the tomb 24 hours a day. During the day the guard is changed every half-hour, Apr.-Sept.; every hour, rest of year. It is changed every 2 hours throughout the night, all year.

WOMEN IN MILITARY SERVICE FOR AMERICA MEMORIAL, on Memorial Dr. at the entrance to the cemetery, honors women who have served in the armed forces. The semicircular memorial features an information center, a theater, exhibits and

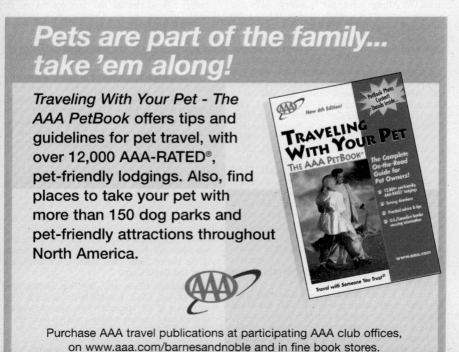

an interactive computer kiosk. Daily 8-7, Apr.-Sept.; 8-5, rest of year. Closed Dec. 25. Free. Phone (703) 533-1155 or (800) 222-2294.

CHANTILLY (F-1) pop. 41,041

NATIONAL AIR AND SPACE MUSEUM'S STEVEN F. UDVAR-HAZY CENTER is at 14390 Air and Space Museum Pkwy., near Washington Dulles International Airport. This facility allows the public to see the 80 percent of the collection that is not on loan or displayed at the museum's flagship building on the National Mall.

More than 200 aircraft and 135 spacecraft ultimately will be displayed, including a Concorde SST and the B-29 Superfortress *Enola Gay*, which dropped the first atomic bomb. Also displayed are 135 rockets, spacecraft and space artifacts, including an Orbiting Solar Observatory prototype, a CRAY-1 Supercomputer and the Space Shuttle *Enterprise*, the first reusable spacecraft. Facilities also include simulators and an IMAX theater.

A shuttle bus runs every 90 minutes beginning at 9 a.m. between the Mall museum and the center; a fare is charged. Food is available. Allow 2 hours minimum. Daily 10-5:30; closed Dec. 25. Free guided tours are offered daily; phone for schedule. Center free. A fee is charged for parking. Admission is charged for simulator rides and the IMAX theater. Phone (202) 633-1000 for general information, (202) 357-2020 for recorded information, or TTY (202) 357-1729. For shuttle fare, fees and IMAX theater schedule phone (877) 932-4629.

[SAVE] **SULLY HISTORIC SITE** is on SR 28 about .7 mi. n. of US 50 and 5 mi. s. of the Dulles Toll Rd. at 3601 Sully Rd. This house was built in 1794 by Richard Bland Lee, uncle of Robert E. Lee and northern Virginia's first congressman. The restored house is furnished with antiques of the Federal period and appears much as it did 1795-1811. Features include the kitchen/laundry, smokehouse, stone dairy, slave quarters, and flower and vegetable gardens.

Allow 2 hours minimum. Guided 45-minute house tour offered on the hour Wed.-Mon. 11-4. Guided outbuildings and grounds tour at 2. Closed Jan. 1, Thanksgiving and Dec. 25, and during part of Jan. for maintenance. House tour $5; students with ID $4; over 60 and ages 5-15, $3. House and outbuildings $7; students with ID $6; over 60 and ages 5-15, $5. Grounds free except during events. Phone (703) 437-1794, or TTY (703) 324-3988.

DUMFRIES (I-2) pop. 4,937

It was from the town of Dumfries in 1800 that the itinerant bookseller and former Anglican priest Parson Mason Locke Weems launched his popular biography "Life of Washington." The highly fictionalized book is best known for its story about young Washington chopping down a cherry tree and confessing to his father, "I cannot tell a lie."

The Weems-Botts Museum, 3914 Cameron St., originally served as Weems' bookshop. The property was later purchased by Benjamin Botts, a prominent defense lawyer who represented Aaron Burr in his 1807 treason trial. Picnic facilities are available. Phone (703) 221-3346.

PRINCE WILLIAM FOREST PARK— *see Triangle p. 132.*

FAIRFAX (F-1) pop. 21,498, elev. 365'

Located in prosperous, populous Fairfax County, Fairfax is the site of the original wills of George and Martha Washington; they are housed in the Judicial Center at 4010 Chain Bridge Rd.

Built in 1800, the original Fairfax County Courthouse at 4000 Chain Bridge Rd. has been used continuously except during the Civil War, when Union troops occupied the town and used it as a stable. A monument to the first Confederate officer killed during the Civil War stands on the courthouse grounds.

Ratcliff-Allison House (Earp's Ordinary), built in the early 1800s, is on Main Street between University Drive and SR 123. In 1820 it began operating as a post office. The original half of the building reflects specifications that were set by the Virginia Assembly for houses built in 1805.

Central Fairfax Chamber of Commerce: 3975 University Dr., Suite 350, Fairfax, VA 22030; phone (703) 591-2450. *See color ad p. 387.*

Self-guiding tours: The Fairfax Museum and Visitors Center publishes and distributes an illustrated brochure about local historic buildings and sites *(see attraction listing).*

Shopping areas: Fair Oaks Shopping Center, I-66 and US 50, has more than 200 stores, including Hecht's, JCPenney, Lord & Taylor, Macy's and Sears.

FAIRFAX MUSEUM AND VISITORS CENTER is at 10209 Main St. Housed in the 1873 Historic Fairfax Elementary School, the museum presents changing exhibits about local history. Allow 30 minutes minimum. Daily 9-5; closed Jan. 1, Easter, Thanksgiving and Dec. 24-25. Free. Phone (703) 385-8414.

NATIONAL FIREARMS MUSEUM is on the main floor of the National Rifle Association's headquarters at 11250 Waples Mill Rd.; take I-66 exit 57A, go .5 mi. e. on US 50, then .3 mi. n. on Waples Mill Rd. Displays include antique firearms from wars significant in America's history, as well as modern engraved handguns. Dioramas, historical replicas and guns previously belonging to celebrities also are exhibited. Daily 10-4; closed major holidays. Free. Phone (703) 267-1600.

FALLS CHURCH (F-3) pop. 10,377, elev. 364'

A Fairfax County suburb, Falls Church dates from the mid-1700s and the formation of Truro Parish, for which George Washington was a vestryman 1762-84.

Greater Falls Church Chamber of Commerce: 417 W. Broad St., Falls Church, VA 22046; phone (703) 532-1050.

Shopping areas: Tysons Galleria, SR 123 and International Drive, includes Macy's, Neiman Marcus and Saks Fifth Avenue as well as some 100 specialty shops. Bloomingdale's, Hecht's, JCPenney, Lord & Taylor and Nordstrom, plus more than 200 other stores, can be found at Tysons Corner Center, off SRs 7 and 123.

THE FALLS CHURCH (Episcopal) is near the intersection of US 29 (Lee Hwy.) and SR 7 (Broad St.) at 115 E. Fairfax St. Founded in 1732, the first church building was erected in 1733 near a road that led to the falls of the Potomac River—hence the name that later was adopted by the town. The present building, completed in 1769, served as a recruiting station during the Revolution, and in the Civil War it was used as a Federal hospital.

Renovations to restore the structure to its 18th-century appearance were completed in 1959. Allow 30 minutes minimum. Mon.-Fri. 9-5. Free. Phone (703) 532-7600.

GREAT FALLS (C-1) pop. 8,549

COLVIN RUN MILL HISTORIC SITE is on SR 7 at Colvin Run Rd., 7 mi. w. of I-495 (Capital Beltway) exit 47A. The restored 19th-century mill still grinds cornmeal and whole wheat flour, and the miller's house and barn contain historical exhibits. A general store also is on the grounds.

Allow 1 hour minimum. Wed.-Mon. 11-5, Mar.-Dec.; 11-4, rest of year. Closed Jan. 1, Thanksgiving and Dec. 25. Mill and house tours are offered. Last tour departs 1 hour before closing. Buildings admission $5; students with ID $4; over 60 and ages 5-15, $3. Grounds free except during events. Phone (703) 759-2771 or TTY (703) 324-3988.

GREAT FALLS PARK is w. on SR 193 to Old Dominion Dr. Here the Potomac River plunges a total of 77 feet in a series of picturesque falls and thundering rapids. One-mile-long Mather Gorge is walled by irregular palisades. Biking, cross-country skiing and white-water rafting are among the possible recreational activities.

Within the 800-acre park are remnants of a skirting canal constructed about 1785 by the Patowmack Co., of which George Washington was founder and president. The canal had a series of locks that enabled boats to re-enter the river after having bypassed the falls. There is no direct access between the Virginia and Maryland sides. The Maryland side is part of Chesapeake and Ohio Canal National Historical Park (*see Chesapeake and Ohio Canal National Historical Park, Md., p. 182*).

Note: Extreme care must be taken when visiting this beautiful but hazardous natural area. Signs indicate treacherous spots. Stay on the trails and observe the signs. Picnicking is permitted, but alcoholic beverages are not. Park grounds open daily 7 a.m.-dusk; closed Dec. 25. Three-day admission pass $5 per private vehicle or $3 per pedestrian, motorcyclist, bicyclist or on horseback.

Visitor Center is within walking distance of the falls overlooks at 9200 Old Dominion Dr. The center has displays, a slide show about park history and changing exhibits. Ranger-led and historical programs vary with the seasons. Picnic facilities are available. Mon.-Fri. 10-5, Sat.-Sun. 10-6, Apr. 15-Oct. 15; daily 10-4, rest of year. Closed Dec. 25. Phone (703) 285-2965.

LEESBURG (D-1) pop. 28,311, elev. 313'

One of the oldest towns in northern Virginia, Leesburg was an outfitting post during the French and Indian War. In 1758 the House of Burgesses passed a bill authorizing the establishment of a town at that site.

During the War of 1812, when the city of Washington was in flames, 22 wagonloads of U.S. documents, including the Declaration of Independence, the Articles of Confederation, the Constitution, much of George Washington's correspondence, and Congressional and State Department records were brought to Leesburg for safekeeping.

The fourth armed engagement of the Civil War took place northeast of Leesburg at Balls Bluff. On Oct. 21, 1861, Confederate forces inflicted devastating losses upon four Union regiments under the command of Col. Edward D. Baker. Among the injured was a 20-year-old lieutenant from Massachusetts, Oliver Wendell Holmes Jr., who later became chief justice of the United States Supreme Court.

The National Cemetery at Balls Bluff is purportedly the smallest in the nation. Surrounding the cemetery is Balls Bluff, a regional park with hiking trails and picnicking; phone (703) 737-7800.

Since 1828 a ferry has carried passengers and freight across the quarter-mile-wide Potomac between a point northeast of Leesburg and Whites Ferry, Md. The *Gen. Jubal Early* still crosses daily dawn to dusk.

Several of Leesburg's older homes are open to the public during Historic Garden Week in late April.

Loudoun Convention Visitors Association: in Historic Market Station at 108-D South St., Leesburg, VA 20175; phone (703) 771-7525 or (800) 752-6118.

Self-guiding tours: A walking-tour booklet of Leesburg's historic district is available from The Loudoun Museum.

LEESBURG ANIMAL PARK is at 19270 James Monroe Hwy. It is home to a variety of animals, including parrots and lemurs. Children can touch and feed domesticated animals in a petting area. Pumpkinville includes a trip to a 3-acre farm play area and pumpkin patch in addition to other park activities. Pony and wagon rides also are available. Allow 1 hour, 30 minutes minimum.

Park open Tues.-Sun. 10-3 (also Fri.-Sun. 3-5), Apr. 1-late Sept. Pumpkinville takes place the last weekend in Sept. through early Nov. Admission $7.95; over 55 and ages 2-12, $5.95. Pumpkinville $9 Sat.-Sun., $6 Mon.-Fri. Pony rides $2.50, wagon rides $1. MC, VI. Phone (703) 433-0002.

THE LOUDOUN MUSEUM is at 16 Loudoun St. S.W. It offers visitors a look into Loudoun County's past through displays of memorabilia. Hands-on exhibits, an audiovisual presentation, lectures and workshops are available. Mon.-Sat. 10-5, Sun. 1-5; closed Jan. 1, Thanksgiving and Dec. 24-25. Phone to verify holiday schedule. Admission $2, over 64 and students with ID $1, under 10 free. Phone (703) 777-7427 or (703) 777-8331.

MORVEN PARK is w. on SR 7 Bus. Rte., then n. on Morven Park Rd. and w. on Old Waterford Rd. The gardens of this 1,200-acre estate surround the Westmoreland Davis Mansion, which has 16 restored rooms containing tapestries, rugs and artifacts from Europe and Asia, and also contains the Museum of Hounds and Hunting. The Winmill Carriage Collection displays more than 70 antique carriages. The Morven Park Steeplechase Races are held in mid-October.

Note: The mansion is undergoing a multiyear preservation effort. Tours continue, although some viewing areas may be affected. Allow 2 hours minimum. Tours depart on the hour Fri.-Mon. noon-4, Apr.-Nov. Admission $7; over 55, $6; ages 6-12, $1. Phone (703) 777-2414.

OATLANDS is about 6 mi. s. on US 15 to 20850 Oatlands Plantation Ln. This stately 22-room, 1804 mansion combines Federal and Greek Revival styles. The house is furnished with French and American art and antiques. Just 261 of the plantation's original 3,400 acres remain. The grounds retain the original basic design, with 4 acres of formal gardens and an 1810 greenhouse. The surrounding fields are the setting for point-to-point races, antiques fairs, dog shows and many other events.

Picnicking is permitted. Allow 1 hour minimum. Open Mon.-Sat. 10-5, Sun. 1-5, Apr. 1-Dec. 30; closed Thanksgiving and Dec. 24-25. Guided 30- to 45-minute tours are given on the hour. Last tour begins 1 hour before closing. Fee $10; over 60 and ages 6-16, $9. Garden tour only $7. MC, VI. Phone (703) 777-3174.

TARARA VINEYARD AND WINERY—
see Lucketts p. 129.

LORTON (I-1) pop. 17,786, elev. 100′

GUNSTON HALL PLANTATION is 4 mi. e. on SR 242 from US 1 to 10709 Gunston Rd. This 1755 brick Georgian residence was designed by William Buckland and built for George Mason, the author of the Virginia Declaration of Rights of 1776 and one of the framers of the U.S. Constitution. The house features woodcarvings in a variety of styles. The English and American furnishings are from the 18th century and earlier. Guided tours are given of the main floor; visitors may take a self-guiding tour of the second-story bedrooms and grounds.

Next to the main house are such reconstructed outbuildings as the kitchen, laundry, dairy, smokehouse and schoolhouse. The formal 18th-century gardens contain an English boxwood allée originally planted by Mason. Deer and eagle sightings are possible from a nature trail leading to the Potomac River.

Allow 1 hour minimum. Daily 9:30-5; closed Jan. 1, Thanksgiving and Dec. 25. House tours are given daily every half-hour. Admission $8; over 59, $7; grades 1-12, $4. Phone (703) 550-9220.

POHICK CHURCH (Episcopal) is 2 mi. s.w. on US 1 at 9301 Richmond Hwy. This was the Colonial parish church of Mount Vernon, Gunston Hall and Belvoir. George Washington chose the site and served as vestryman for 23 years. George Mason, a vestryman for 37 years, served on the building committee.

During the Civil War the original 1774 interior was torn out by Union troops and the building was used as a stable. The building was restored 1902-17. The old stone baptismal font was found many years later serving as a trough in a nearby farmyard. Mon.-Fri. 9-4:30, Sat.-Sun. 10-5. Free. Phone (703) 339-6572.

LUCKETTS (D-1)

WINERIES

• **Tarara Vineyard and Winery**, 3 mi. e. on CR 662 following signs to 13648 Tarara Ln. Daily 11-5, Feb.-Dec.; Sat.-Sun. 11-5, rest of year. Last tasting is at 4:30. Phone (703) 771-7100.

DID YOU KNOW

The Washington Redskins' 72-41 victory over the New York Giants in 1966 was the highest scoring game in NFL history.

MANASSAS (G-1) pop. 35,135, elev. 312'

The juncture of the Manassas Gap and the Orange & Alexandria railroads in the 1850s created the hamlet of Manassas (ma-NAS-sas). During the Civil War this tiny junction became a bloody pawn between two contending armies. Fought over and burned, Manassas was a key to the heart of Virginia and the site for hospitals, fortifications and supply depots for both North and the South.

When the war ended, the railroad became the basis of the town's economy, which was further spurred in the last half of the 20th century by the growth of the Washington, D.C. metropolitan area. The Historic Manassas Visitor Center is at 9431 West St.; phone (703) 361-6599.

Prince William County/Manassas Convention and Visitors Bureau: 8609 Sudley Rd., Suite 105, Manassas, VA 20110; phone (703) 396-7130 or (800) 432-1792.

Self-guiding tours: Brochures outlining driving and walking tours are available from the Historic Manassas Visitor Center and The Manassas Museum *(see attraction listing).*

SAVE **THE MANASSAS MUSEUM** is at 9101 Prince William St. The museum depicts the history and culture of Manassas and the northern Virginia Piedmont region through artifacts, photographs and videotape presentations. Highlights include 19th-century toys, a Confederate regimental flag, weapons and African-American history exhibits. Living-history programs are presented throughout the year.

Tues.-Sun. and Mon. federal holidays 10-5; closed Jan. 1, Thanksgiving and Dec. 24-25. Admission $3; over 59 and ages 6-17, $2. Phone (703) 368-1873.

MANASSAS NATIONAL BATTLEFIELD PARK (G-1)

Manassas National Battlefield Park, on SR 234 between I-66 and US 29, marks the site north of the strategically important railroad junction at Manassas where two great battles of the Civil War—the First and Second Battles of Manassas, or Bull Run—were fought.

On July 21, 1861, picnickers and other sightseers observed a well-equipped but ill-trained Union Army under Gen. Irvin McDowell as it battled the Confederate Army under Gens. Pierre Beauregard and Joseph Johnston. After 10 hours of deadly fighting it became apparent that this conflict was not going to decide the war, as most had expected. The Union army, finally broken by Confederate forces, was forced to retreat toward Washington, D.C. It was at this battle that Gen. Thomas J. Jackson earned the nickname Stonewall.

When the armies returned to the plains of Manassas in August 1862, they were no longer young recruits in colorful new uniforms. A year of war had hardened both armies and brought the Confederacy to the peak of its power, soon to be realized

with the outcome of this battle. The encounter also proved to be a bloody demonstration of Robert E. Lee's genius, as he defeated the larger army of Gen. John Pope in 3 days of fighting.

A walking trail on Henry Hill offers scenic views of the first battlefield. The focal point of the hill is an equestrian statue of Gen. Stonewall Jackson. The Stone House, which served as a field hospital in both battles, is open seasonally. A driving tour of the park encompasses the main points of the second battle as well as areas involved in both engagements. Two 5-mile hikes around the battlefield are detailed in a pamphlet available at the visitor center.

The Second Manassas Expedition Guide tape and CD driving tour by TravelBrains is available at the visitor center and by mail; phone (888) 458-6475.

The Henry Hill Visitor Center has a museum and theater that shows the 45-minute film "Manassas: End of Innocence"; a 3-D map illustrates the strategies of the first battle. Grounds open daily dawn-dusk. Visitor center open daily 8:30-5; closed Thanksgiving and Dec. 25. Stone House open daily 1-4, June-Aug. Park admission $3, under 17 free. Theater admission $3, under 17 free. For information phone the visitor center at (703) 361-1339 or the park headquarters at (703) 754-1861.

McLEAN (D-2) pop. 38,929, elev. 303'

SAVE **THE CLAUDE MOORE COLONIAL FARM AT TURKEY RUN** is 2.5 mi. e. on SR 193 from I-495 exit 44 to 6310 Georgetown Pike. This is a small-scale representation of a low-income homestead during the late Colonial period, with a costumed family performing the farm tasks. In addition to field crops, old breeds of cattle, chickens, turkeys and hogs are on the farm. Re-enactments of Colonial market fairs are held on the third full weekend in May, July and October.

Allow 30 minutes minimum. Wed.-Sun. 10-4:30, Apr. 1 to mid-Dec.; closed Thanksgiving. Admission $3; over 60 and ages 3-12, $2. Events slightly higher. Phone (703) 442-7557.

THEODORE ROOSEVELT ISLAND is accessible by pedestrian bridge from the Virginia shore; a parking lot is off the northbound lane of George Washington Memorial Pkwy. just n. of the Theodore Roosevelt Bridge. The island lies in the Potomac River between Rosslyn, Va., and the John F. Kennedy Center for the Performing Arts (M: Rosslyn).

This 91-acre memorial honors the nation's 26th president. A massive granite monument includes a 17-foot bronze statue of Roosevelt and four towering slabs inscribed with his ideas about nature, youth, manhood and the state. More than 50 species of trees and some 200 varieties of wildflowers flourish. Wayside exhibits are in English and Spanish. Dogs on leash are permitted. Allow 30 minutes minimum. Daily 8-dusk. Free. Phone (703) 289-2530.

MIDDLEBURG (G-1) pop. 632, elev. 492'

WINERIES

- **Piedmont Vineyards**, 3 mi. s. on SR 626. Daily 11-6, Apr.-Oct.; 11-5, rest of year. Closed Jan. 1, Thanksgiving, and Dec. 24-25 and 31. Phone (540) 687-5528.

MOUNT VERNON (I-6) pop. 28,582

MOUNT VERNON is at the s. end of George Washington Memorial Pkwy. overlooking the Potomac River. George Washington's final term of residence at Mount Vernon, from 1783 until his death in 1799, was interrupted by his tenure as president. Both George and Martha Washington are buried here.

The mansion has been restored to appear as it was during the last year of Washington's life and contains much of the original furniture. Displays include the bed in which Washington died, his sword and the key to the Bastille presented to him by Marquis de Lafayette. Visitors can tour Washington's tomb, gardens and 12 outbuildings.

The Pioneer Farmer site offers hands-on activities and contains a reconstruction of Washington's round barn, where horses walk the second floor threshing wheat.

Baby strollers are not permitted inside the mansion. Allow 1 hour minimum. Daily 8-5, Apr.-Aug.; 9-5 in Mar. and Sept.-Oct.; 9-4, rest of year. Grounds are cleared 30 minutes after closing. Admission $11; over 62, $10.50; ages 6-11, $5. AX, DS, MC, VI. Phone (703) 780-2000, or TTY (703) 799-8697.

OCCOQUAN (I-2) pop. 759, elev. 80'

The historic town of Occoquan, its name taken from a Dogue Indian word meaning "at the end of the water," was a recognized community in 1734. By the late 18th century the area was a thriving port and milling town dependent on the waterpower of the Occoquan River.

A brief moment of fame came during the Civil War when Gen. Wade Hampton made his headquarters in the Hammill Hotel, now a collection of shops and offices.

One of Virginia's first cotton mills, built in 1828, hummed with 1,000 spindles before it was silenced by fire during the Civil War. The village flourished until deepening silt in the Occoquan River prevented vessels from reaching the mills.

Prince William County Visitor Information Center: 200 Mill St., Occoquan, VA 22125; phone (703) 491-4045.

Self-guiding tours: A brochure offering a walking tour of the historic district and a list of local artists and galleries is available at the visitor information center.

Shopping areas: There are more than 120 specialty shops in the compact historic district. Many are housed in original historic buildings and offer antiques and crafts. Several miles south via I-95 is Potomac Mills, which has more than 225 factory outlet stores including Benetton, Calvin Klein, IKEA, Laura Ashley, Nordstrom Rack and Sears.

PARIS (G-1)

Settlers of the area around Paris came through the Blue Ridge Mountains by way of Ashby's Gap, north of town. During the Civil War the Confederates and later the Federals used a hill in Paris as a signal station.

SKY MEADOWS STATE PARK is 1 mi. s. on SR 17. This 1,863-acre park has rolling pastures and woodlands, scenic views, access to the Appalachian Trail, picnic facilities, hiking and horseback riding trails and a visitor center in the 1835 Mount Bleak House. The visitor center offers interpretive programs.

Park open daily 8-dusk. Admission $3 per private vehicle Mon.-Fri., $4 Sat.-Sun., Apr.-Oct.; $2 rest of year. Phone (540) 592-3556 or (800) 933-7275. *See the Virginia Recreation Chart.*

QUANTICO (I-1) pop. 561, elev. 35'

Quantico is one of the nation's largest Marine Corps installations and the site of the Marine Corps Combat Development Command. At the entrance is a replica of the Marine Corps War Memorial, a statue depicting the flag raising on Mount Suribachi during the World War II battle for Iwo Jima. The original stands at the north end of Arlington National Cemetery *(see place listing p. 125).*

Quantico National Cemetery is off I-95 on CR 619W. Ceremonies on Memorial Day and Veterans Day feature color guards from area veterans' organizations.

STERLING (C-1) elev. 300'

LOUDOUN HERITAGE FARM MUSEUM is 2 mi. n. on SR 28, then 1 mi. e. on Church Rd. and .4 mi. n. on Cascades Pkwy. to the Claude Moore Park entrance. Some 300 years of agricultural history unfold at this interpretive complex tracing the farming ventures of 10 generations of Loudoun County residents. Kids can dress up and play

---

DID YOU KNOW

President Abraham Lincoln proclaimed the first national Thanksgiving Day in 1863.

farmer for the day in an interactive exhibit area. Allow 1 hour minimum. Tues.-Sat. 10-5. Admission $5; senior citizens and students with ID $4; ages 2-12, $3. DS, MC, VI. Phone (703) 421-5322.

TRIANGLE (I-1) pop. 5,500, elev. 161′

PRINCE WILLIAM FOREST PARK is accessed by taking I-95 s. to exit 150B, then .2 mi. w. to Joplin Rd. (SR 619 w.). Covering more than 17,000 acres, the park offers hikers more than 37 miles of hiking trails and 21 miles of biking trails. Cabins and camping facilities are available. Park rangers offer regularly scheduled interpretive programs. Historic and nature exhibits are displayed at the Pine Grove Visitor Center.

Only campers and cabin occupants are admitted after dark, except when there are evening programs. Park open daily dawn-dusk. Visitor center open daily 9-5. Admission $5 per private vehicle; permits are good for 3 days. Phone (703) 221-7181. *See the Virginia Recreation Chart and the AAA Mideastern CampBook.*

VIENNA (E-1) pop. 14,453, elev. 345′

WOLF TRAP FARM PARK FOR THE PERFORMING ARTS is off I-495 (Capital Beltway) exit 11S, then SR 123 to SR 7, following signs. Wolf Trap is the only national park dedicated to the performing arts. Opera, symphony, jazz, folk, musical, country, dance and popular music productions are presented from late May to early September. The Filene Center, the largest of Wolf Trap's several venues, is an open-air pavilion with a sloping lawn that can accommodate an audience of 7,000; it is situated in a setting of rolling hills and woodland.

Picnicking is permitted. Food is available. Park open daily 7 a.m.-dusk, except 2 hours prior to and 1 hour following park festivals and Filene Center performances. Park free. Lawn seating for Filene Center shows starts at $10; other ticket prices vary by performance. Check local newspapers for schedules and prices. AX, MC, VI. Phone (703) 255-1800 for general information, or (703) 218-6500 or (800) 955-5566 for ticket information.

The Barns at Wolf Trap is .5 mi. s. of Wolf Trap Farm Park at 1635 Trap Rd. This 352-seat facility—Wolf Trap's indoor performance space—has superb acoustics created by the wood interior and enhanced by a state-of-the-art sound system. Bluegrass, chamber music, country, folk, jazz, zydeco and other performances take place October to mid-May.

Phone the Barns box office for information about performance schedules. Shows $10-$15. Reservations are required. MC, VI. Phone (703) 938-2404.

Adams-Morgan / © Paul M. Franklin

This ends listings for the Washington, D.C. Vicinity.

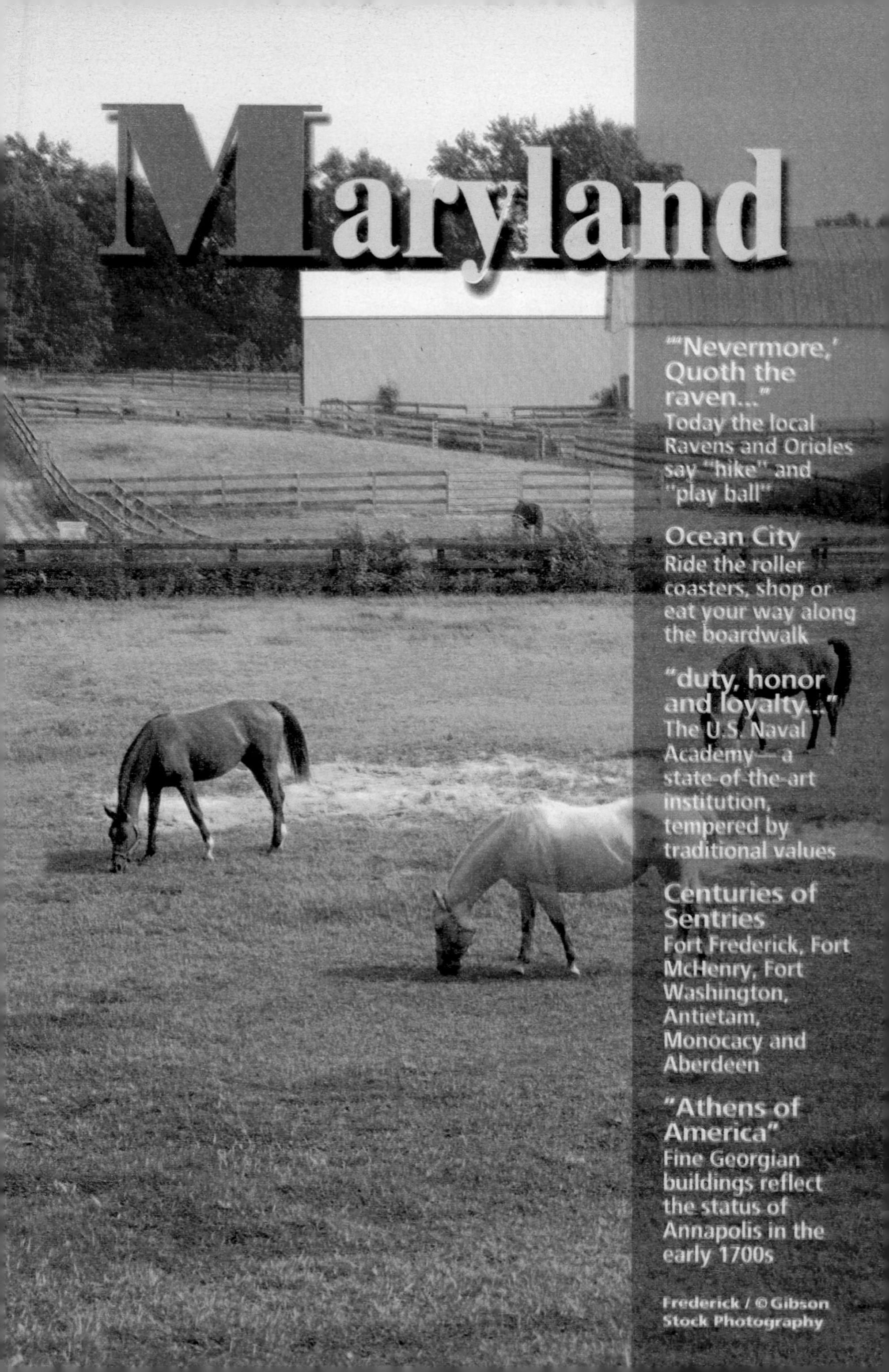

Maryland

"'Nevermore,' Quoth the raven..."
Today the local Ravens and Orioles say "hike" and "play ball"

Ocean City
Ride the roller coasters, shop or eat your way along the boardwalk

"duty, honor and loyalty..."
The U.S. Naval Academy— a state-of-the-art institution, tempered by traditional values

Centuries of Sentries
Fort Frederick, Fort McHenry, Fort Washington, Antietam, Monocacy and Aberdeen

"Athens of America"
Fine Georgian buildings reflect the status of Annapolis in the early 1700s

Frederick / © Gibson Stock Photography

from shore to sparkling shore

Chesapeake Bay / © Roger Miller / Robertstock

Maryland's identity is anchored in the waters that boldly sprawl across its inland mass. How could it not be? There's water all over the place!

Twenty-three principal rivers and numerous other bays infiltrate this gun-shaped state. More than 400 miles of water are tributary to the Chesapeake Bay.

Of Maryland's 23 counties, 16 border the tidal shoreline. So, too, do the state's largest city, Baltimore, and its capital, Annapolis.

It's not just simple ubiquity that makes all this water so vital; it's everything the water sustains.

The harvesting of crabs, clams and oysters provided a livelihood for generations of watermen who plied the

Chesapeake—named for the Native
American word *chesepiook,* meaning
"great shellfish bay" in skipjacks.

The Port of Baltimore is a hub of
international importing and exporting.

Central to the national defense, the
U.S. Naval Academy produces many of
the top officers in the U.S. Navy and
Marine Corps.

And,
of course,
where there's
lots of water, there's
opportunity galore for
recreation.

Labor and leisure exist in harmony on
Maryland's expansive shore.

"Maryland is for crabs."

Or at least that's the tongue-in-cheek slogan a witty T-shirt manufacturer made popular in the 1970s as a parody of the motto coined by the state's southern neighbor, Virginia.

Literally speaking, the state *is* for crabs. Heck, the Maryland blue variety is the state crustacean. And it's for oysters and clams, too. It's a veritable water wonderland.

As if the fact that Maryland has a state crustacean isn't curious enough, its maritime past also is recalled via the similarly unusual claim of a state boat—the skipjack—and a state dog, the Chesapeake Bay retriever, named for a prominent tributary.

Although the Atlantic coastline stretches just 31 miles, that distance multiplies more than a hundredfold—to 3,190 miles—if you factor in the shoreline along the rivers and bays.

Exhibits at the Baltimore, Brannock and Chesapeake Bay maritime museums and the Calvert Marine Museum all recall the importance of water in Maryland's history.

Even the name of one of its counties—Allegany—means "beautiful stream."

In addition to an attractive setting, the state boasts its fair share of human achievers—musicians, actors and writers who together constitute a veritable fountain of creativity.

A Cultured Pool of Talent

A grave in Mount Olivet Cemetery in Frederick serves as a lasting tribute to Francis Scott Key, who was born and buried in the same state where he composed "The Star-Spangled Banner."

Ragtime performer Eubie Blake perfected his talents in the honky-tonks of Baltimore, his hometown. Live performances in the city's Eubie Blake National Jazz Institute carry on his musical tradition. Another Baltimore-born musician, Billie Holiday, gave her beautiful voice to the rich sounds of jazz and the blues.

Acclaimed Shakespearean actor Ira Aldridge, of Bel Air, performed for a U.S. president, Queen Victoria and the archduke of Chambory.

Although he never attended the U.S. Naval Academy in Annapolis, let alone served so much as a day in any branch of the service, Baltimore resident Tom Clancy is a commanding author of military drama.

Baltimore Town is established.
1729

The U.S. Naval Academy is founded at Annapolis.
1845

The Treaty of Paris, ending the Revolutionary War, is ratified at Annapolis.
1784

America's bloodiest battle so far is fought at Antietam during the Civil War.
1862

1814
Francis Scott Key writes the "Star-Spangled Banner" following the bombardment of Fort McHenry.

© David Forbert/SuperStock

Maryland Historical Timeline

1893
The Johns Hopkins School of Medicine opens in Baltimore.

A pair of Baltimore-bred writers, no doubt influenced by the city's decidedly blue-collar roots, shared a penchant for politics. Upton Sinclair espoused the cause of socialism in "The Jungle," while the writings of H.L. Mencken show a libertarian lean.

It was in Baltimore that master of the macabre Edgar Allan Poe fell in love with his cousin, who was 13 when the two exchanged vows. Displays in the Enoch Pratt Free Library explore his mysterious life; Poe's grave lies in the city's Westminster Hall and Burying Ground.

A formidable literary inspiration was born in Charles County. Josiah Henson, who observed the treatment of slaves, was interviewed by Harriet Beecher Stowe and inspired her novel, "Uncle Tom's Cabin."

Making Progressive Strides

Although its links to a creative past are impressive, Maryland's visionaries have had a much more definitive impact on history.

Harriett Tubman, born in Dorchester County, escaped from slavery and returned to the South to help more than 300 other slaves flee via the Underground Railroad. One of the former stops on this route now operates as the Baltimore Civil War Museum.

During a 1909 expedition, Baltimore-born Matthew A. Henson placed the Stars and Stripes at the North Pole.

Despite dropping out of school at age 12, entrepreneur Johns Hopkins amassed a fortune through hard work and wise investments. His legacy lives on in the Baltimore hospital and university that bear his name.

Baltimore native Thurgood Marshall was a highly regarded lawyer and civil rights pioneer before serving as the first African-American justice on the U.S. Supreme Court.

Although he never played for the Orioles, Baltimore native Babe Ruth propelled the game of baseball to a higher level as he unleashed the home run-hitting power that earned him the nickname "Sultan of Swat." Displays in the Babe Ruth Birthplace/Baltimore Orioles Museum pay tribute to him and other Maryland baseball greats, including Cal Ripken Jr.

Maryland's doors have opened wide to a long list of fascinating folks. From its rolling western mountains to its eastern coastal plain, it's ready to welcome you, too.

Maryland becomes the first state in the Union to adopt an income tax.
1938

Middle East peace talks between Israel and the Palestine Liberation Organization take place at Wye River Conference Center, resulting in the signing of the Wye River Memorandum on Oct. 23.
1998

1973
Urban renewal in Baltimore is encouraged through the "homesteading" of abandoned properties.

2000
Maryland is the first state to require built-in locks on all new handguns sold after Jan.1, 2003.

2002
By winning the lieutenant governor post, Michael Steele becomes the first African-American elected to statewide office in Maryland.

Recreation

With the Atlantic Ocean lapping at its eastern shores and the Potomac River and Chesapeake Bay reaching like crooked fingers into the mainland, Maryland is a water lover's dream.

Soak up the sun, relish the scenery or go **swimming** in the breakers at Assateague Island National Seashore, near Berlin.

Once you've received permission to go **scuba diving**, slip into your wet suit and explore the underwater world of the William Houck Area in Cunningham Falls State Park, off SR 77 west of Thurmont. Phone (301) 271-7574 for details about submitting requests.

Wind surfing is good at Chesapeake Beach; Gunpowder Falls State Park, east of Chase; Kentmoor Marina on Kent Island, 5 miles south of US 50 on SR 8; and Sandy Point State Park, east of Cape St. Claire. **Sailing** is huge almost anywhere you find water. Annapolis is especially scenic.

For a rough-and-tumble adventure, check out **white-water rafting** on the Potomac and Youghiogheny (the "Yock") rivers. Runs on the latter have such colorful names as Meatcleaver and Backbender. **Canoeing** and **kayaking** trips are a peaceful diversion in the Patuxent River in Calvert County and the Patapsco River, near Ellicott City. The section of the Potomac River at Great Falls also is popular; portages are necessary at most locks.

Catch of the Day

Greenbrier Lake in Boonsboro is a big **fishing** destination because of its trout, bluegill and bass. The coffee-colored waters of the Pocomoke River near Snow Hill are home to largemouth bass, catfish and crappie. Annapolis, Crisfield, Point Lookout, Solomons and Tilghman Island are favorite starting points for bay fishing, which yields bluefish, channel bass, croakers and trout. Excellent marlin grounds lie off Ocean City.

Assawoman Bay, north of Ocean City, is a **clamming** hot spot. Popular spots for **crabbing** line the rivers and bay in southern Maryland and the eastern shore, particularly at Deal Island and Point Lookout.

Flintstone's Billmeyer/Belle Grove Wildlife Management Area—with its plentiful populations of turkeys, ruffed grouse, woodcocks, deer, squirrels and rabbits—is prime **hunting** territory. Such waterfowl as Canada geese, wigeons, pintails, shovelers and black ducks abound at Deal Island. Contact the Maryland Department of Natural Resources for information about fishing and hunting licenses.

The Chesapeake and Ohio Canal Trail (the C & O)—a 184-mile route between Cumberland and the Georgetown neighborhood of Washington, D.C.—caters to anyone who enjoys **bicycling.** You can take a pleasant, shaded ride at the Georgetown end or, if you're up to it, tackle the entire stretch. The 15 miles of paths in Patuxent River Park, south of Upper Marlboro, challenge off-road cyclists.

Sharing the Trails with Snakes

The **hiking** trails at Cunningham Falls State Park, south of Thurmont, are tough. Although the rocky, wooded terrain makes for an exciting trek, it's also an ideal habitat for copperheads and rattlesnakes.

Stake out a spot on the water's edge and enjoy a secluded **camping** getaway in Janes Island State Park, west of Crisfield. The island is accessible only by boat.

Catch some cold-weather exercise while **cross-country skiing** in New Germany and Herrington Manor state parks, both in Garrett County; or **snowshoeing** through Catoctin Mountain Park in Thurmont. Let the chill nip at your nose as you take on the **downhill skiing** runs at Wisp, in McHenry, or go **snowmobiling** on the ungroomed trails in Potomac State Forest.

If you're up for an unusual pursuit, check out the state sport: **jousting.** Competitors on horseback charge through an arena and catch rings of decreasing size on a lance. Maryland's most renowned tournament is held the last Saturday in August in Port Republic.

Recreational Activities

Throughout the TourBook, you may notice a Recreational Activities heading with bulleted listings of recreation-oriented establishments listed underneath. Similar operations also may be mentioned in Destination City recreation sections. Since normal AAA inspection criteria cannot be applied, these establishments are presented only for information. Age, height and weight restrictions may apply. Reservations often are recommended and sometimes are required. Addresses and/or phone numbers are provided so visitors can contact the attraction for additional information.

Fast Facts

POPULATION: 5,296,486.

AREA: 10,577 square miles; ranks 42nd.

CAPITAL: Annapolis.

HIGHEST POINT: 3,360 ft., Backbone Mountain.

LOWEST POINT: Sea level, Atlantic Ocean.

TIME ZONE(S): Eastern. DST.

MINIMUM AGE FOR UNRESTRICTED DRIVER'S LICENSE: 17 years, 7 months.

SEAT BELT/CHILD RESTRAINT LAWS: Seat belts required for driver and all front-seat passengers over 16; ages 6-16 must use an approved child restraint or seat belt; child safety seat required for under 6 years or under 40 pounds.

HELMETS FOR MOTORCYCLISTS: Required for driver and passenger.

RADAR DETECTORS: Permitted, except in commercial vehicles.

FIREARMS LAWS: Vary by state and/or county. Contact Maryland State Police, Handgun Permits, 1711 Belmont Ave., Baltimore, MD 21244; phone (410) 799-0191.

HOLIDAYS: Jan. 1; Lincoln's Birthday, Feb. 12; Washington's Birthday, Feb. (3rd Mon.); Maryland Day, Mar. 25; Good Friday; Memorial Day, May (last Mon.); July 4; Labor Day, Sept. (1st Mon.); Defenders' Day, Sept. 12; Columbus Day, Oct. (2nd Mon.); Veterans Day, Nov. 11; Thanksgiving; Dec. 25.

TAXES: Maryland's statewide sales tax is 5 percent. A 1 to 13 percent lodging and amusement tax also may be imposed.

INFORMATION CENTERS: State welcome centers are on I-68 eastbound from the West Virginia border near Friendsville; I-68 east- and westbound at Hancock; I-70 east- and westbound near Myersville; US 13 northbound at Pocomoke City near the Virginia border; US 301 north- and southbound near Centreville; US 301 northbound at Newburg; US 15 just south of the Pennsylvania border near Emmitsburg; on I-95 north- and southbound near Savage; on I-95 north- and southbound near Perryville; and at the State House in Annapolis. Centers are open daily 8-6, Memorial Day-Labor Day; 9-5, rest of year. Hours may vary. Centers are closed Jan. 1, Easter, Thanksgiving and Dec. 25.

AREA CODE REQUIRED: Whenever you make a local call within Maryland you must dial the area code as well as the seven-digit telephone number.

FURTHER INFORMATION FOR VISITORS:

Maryland Office of Tourism Development
Redwood Tower, 9th Floor
217 E. Redwood St.
Baltimore, MD 21202
(800) 394-5725

RECREATION INFORMATION:

Maryland Department of Natural Resources
State Forest and Parks Service
580 Taylor Ave.
Annapolis, MD 21401
(410) 260-8186

FISHING AND HUNTING REGULATIONS:

Fishing:

Fisheries Administration
Maryland Department of Natural Resources
580 Taylor Ave.
Annapolis, MD 21401
(800) 688-3467

Hunting:

Wildlife Division
Maryland Department of Natural Resources
Tawes State Office Bldg., Wing E1
Annapolis, MD 21401
(410) 260-8540

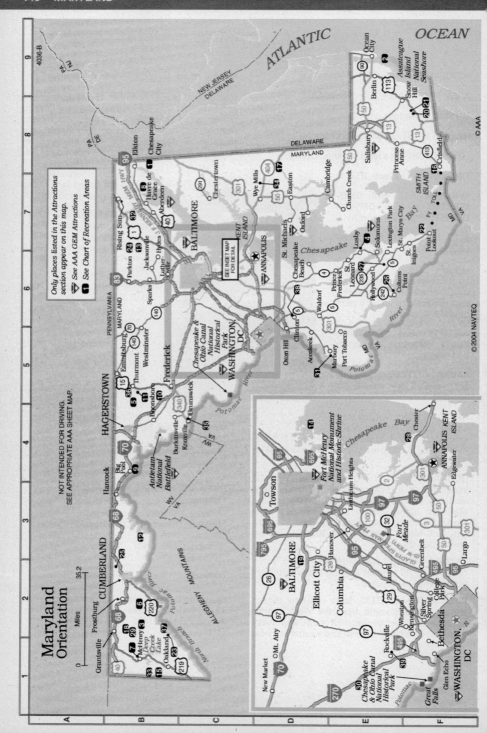

Maryland Orientation

NOT INTENDED FOR DRIVING.
SEE APPROPRIATE AAA SHEET MAP.

Miles 35.2
0

Only places listed in the Attractions section appear on this map.

▽ See AAA GEM Attractions

🅱 See Chart of Recreation Areas

© 2004 NAVTEQ

© AAA

4036-B

Points of Interest Offering A *Great Experience for Members*®

Aberdeen (B-7)

U.S. ARMY ORDNANCE MUSEUM—Trace the development of weaponry through this collection of everything from ammunition to combat vehicles. See p. 173.

Annapolis (F-4)

HAMMOND-HARWOOD HOUSE—This fine example of late American Colonial architecture is furnished with Early American decorative arts pieces. See p. 175.

MARYLAND STATE HOUSE—The Treaty of Paris, which officially ended the Revolutionary War, was ratified here. See p. 175.

U.S. NAVAL ACADEMY—Ogle Hall, completed by 1739, reverberated with the footsteps of George Washington and the Marquis de Lafayette. See p. 176.

WILLIAM PACA HOUSE AND GARDEN—Paved over with asphalt in the mid-20th century, the garden was reconstructed using careful research, aerial photography and the features in the background of Charles Wilson Peale's portrait of William Paca. See p. 176.

Antietam National Battlefield (B-4)

ANTIETAM NATIONAL BATTLEFIELD—On September 17, 1862, tens of thousands of Federal and Confederate troops clashed at this site near Sharpsburg resulting in so many casualties that it has been called the bloodiest day of the Civil War. See p. 158.

Baltimore (C-6)

BALTIMORE & OHIO RAILROAD MUSEUM—Visit the country's oldest railroad station and view the extensive collection of rolling stock in this 40-acre indoor/outdoor museum. See p. 163.

BALTIMORE MUSEUM OF ART—More than 100,000 works of art comprise the BMA's permanent collection, which can take you from ancient Egypt to Oceania, and from Rembrandt to Andy Warhol. See p. 163.

BALTIMORE PASSPORT: VOYAGES OF DISCOVERY—This theater experience transports audiences back through time and under the sea with the help of wide screens, special effects and motion simulators. See p. 167.

BALTIMORE ZOO—On the grounds of one of the country's largest city parks, this 161-acre zoo counts a large colony of African black-footed penguins among its 2,000 animals. See p. 168.

EVERGREEN HOUSE—This elegant mansion displays works of the fine and decorative arts and rare books, prints and manuscripts. See p. 168.

MARYLAND HISTORICAL SOCIETY—The everyday objects in the society's museum help trace the link between the past and the present. See p. 169.

MARYLAND SCIENCE CENTER, IMAX THEATER AND DAVIS PLANETARIUM—Hands-on science exhibits offer educational fun for all ages at this multifaceted attraction overlooking the Inner Harbor. See p. 169.

NATIONAL AQUARIUM IN BALTIMORE—Seven stories house a variety of aquatic exhibits, including a 335,000-gallon coral reef and a 1.2 million-gallon bottlenose dolphin habitat as well as other displays that trace the flow of aquatic life from streams and rivers to seas and oceans. See p. 169.

THE WALTERS ART MUSEUM—Some 30,000 works of the fine and decorative arts span 55 centuries. See p. 171.

Fort McHenry National Monument and Historic Shrine (D-4)

FORT McHENRY NATIONAL MONUMENT AND HISTORIC SHRINE—The American defense of this fort against British attack on the night and early morning of Sept. 13-14, 1814, was the inspiration for the U.S. national anthem. See p. 178.

Largo (F-2)

SIX FLAGS AMERICA—The park offers more than 100 ways to have fun, from thrilling rolling coasters and live shows to a water park with a million-gallon wave pool. See p. 116.

St. Michaels (D-7)

CHESAPEAKE BAY MARITIME MUSEUM—From oyster harvesting aboard skipjacks to steam-powered transportation and the solitary lives of lighthouse keepers, this comprehensive waterfront museum highlights Chesapeake Bay's maritime heritage. See p. 193.

Salisbury (E-8)

WARD MUSEUM OF WILDFOWL ART—You wooden want to get decoyed and miss the ducky hand-carved displays here. See p. 194.

Solomons (E-7)

CALVERT MARINE MUSEUM—This facility interprets the paleontology, estuarine biology and maritime history of the tidewater region. See p. 195.

RECREATION AREAS

	MAP LOCATION	CAMPING	PICNICKING	HIKING TRAILS	BOATING	BOAT RAMP	BOAT RENTAL	FISHING	SWIMMING	PETS ON LEASH	BICYCLE TRAILS	WINTER SPORTS	VISITOR CENTER	LODGE/CABINS	FOOD SERVICE
NATIONAL SEASHORE (See place listing)															
Assateague Island (F-9) 39,500 acres 8 mi. s. of Ocean City via SR 611 on Assateague Island.		•	•	•	•			•	•	•	•		•		
ARMY CORPS OF ENGINEERS															
Chesapeake and Delaware Canal (B-8) 8,000 acres 14 mi. long connecting the Delaware River and upper Chesapeake Bay, starting in Chesapeake City off SR 213.	**1**			•	•			•			•				
STATE															
Assateague (E-9) 756 acres 6 mi. s. of Ocean City via SR 611. Crabbing; interpretive programs.	**2**	•	•		•	•	•	•	•	•	•		•		
Big Run (B-2) 300 acres 11 mi. n.w. of Luke on Savage River Rd.	**3**	•	•	•	•			•		•					
Calvert Cliffs (E-7) 1,313 acres 14 mi. s. of Prince Frederick on SRs 2 and 4. Historic. Hunting.	**4**		•	•				•							
Cunningham Falls (B-5) 4,946 acres off US 15 at Thurmont. Historic. Lake, waterfall.	**5**	•	•	•	•	•	•	•	•	•			•	•	•
Dans Mountain (B-2) 481 acres 9 mi. s. of Frostburg on SR 36. Historic. Playground, pool.	**6**		•	•				•	•	•	•				•

RECREATION AREAS

	MAP LOCATION	CAMPING	PICNICKING	HIKING TRAILS	BOATING	BOAT RAMP	BOAT RENTAL	FISHING	SWIMMING	PETS ON LEASH	BICYCLE TRAILS	WINTER SPORTS	VISITOR CENTER	LODGE/CABINS	FOOD SERVICE
Deep Creek Lake (B-1) 1,818 acres 2 mi. n.e. of Thayerville. Maryland's largest freshwater lake. Cross-country skiing; nature trail, snowmobile trails.	7	•	•	•	•	•	•	•	•	•	•	•			
Elk Neck (B-7) 2,188 acres 9 mi. s. of North East on SR 272. Scenic. Bird watching; nature trail.	8	•	•	•	•	•	•	•	•	•	•	•	•	•	•
Fort Frederick (B-4) 561 acres in Big Pool off SR 56, 1 mi. s.w. of I-70 Big Pool exit. Historic. Nature trail. *(See Big Pool p. 181.)*	9	•	•	•	•	•	•	•		•	•	•			•
Gambrill (B-5) 1,137 acres 6 mi. n.w. of Frederick off I-70. Nature trail.	10	•	•	•				•		•	•	•			
Greenbrier (B-4) 1,288 acres 10 mi. e. of Hagerstown on US 40. Hunting; nature trail.	11	•	•	•	•	•	•	•			•	•			•
Green Ridge State Forest (B-3) 38,811 acres in eastern Allegany County, 22 mi. e. of Cumberland; exit 64 off I-68. Historic.	12	•	•	•				•		•	•	•	•		
Gunpowder Falls (B-7) 13,020 acres along the Little and Big Gunpowder rivers s. of Kingsville.	13		•	•	•	•	•	•	•	•	•	•			•
Hart-Miller Island (D-4) 244 acres on the Chesapeake Bay at the mouth of Middle River.	14	•	•					•	•						
Herrington Manor (B-1) 365 acres 5 mi. n.w. of Oakland on CR 20. Cross-country skiing; nature trail, ski rentals.	15		•	•	•		•	•	•	•	•	•		•	•
Janes Island (F-8) 3,147 acres 1.5 mi. n. of Crisfield off SR 413. Crabbing.	16	•	•	•	•	•	•	•					•	•	•
Martinak (D-8) 105 acres 2 mi. s. of Denton off SR 404.	17	•	•	•	•	•	•	•		•			•	•	•
New Germany (B-2) 455 acres 5 mi. s. of Grantsville off US 40 on New Germany Rd. Cross-country skiing; nature trail.	18	•	•	•	•		•	•	•		•	•	•	•	•
Patapsco Valley (D-3) 12,699 acres along the Patapsco River from Baltimore to Liberty Dam w. of Ellicott City on US 40.	19	•	•	•				•		•	•	•	•		
Pocomoke River															
Milburn Landing (F-8) 370 acres 8 mi. w. of Snow Hill off SR 12.	20	•	•	•	•	•		•		•	•				
Shad Landing (F-8) 544 acres 4 mi. s.w. of Snow Hill off US 113.	21	•	•	•	•	•	•	•		•		•		•	•
Point Lookout (F-7) 528 acres on the southern tip of the western shore on SR 5. Historic. *(See Point Lookout p. 191.)*	22	•	•	•	•	•	•	•	•	•	•		•	•	•
Potomac State Forest (B-1) 10,416 acres in southeastern Garrett County, off SR 135.	23	•	•					•	•	•	•		•		
Rocks (B-6) 855 acres 8 mi. n.w. of Bel Air on SR 24. Historic. Scenic. Canoeing, tubing.	24		•	•				•		•		•			
Rocky Gap (B-3) 3,200 acres 6 mi. e. of Cumberland on I-68. Scenic. Ice skating; nature trails.	25	•	•	•	•	•	•	•	•	•			•		•
St. Clement's Island (E-6) 62 acres in the Potomac River near St. Clement's and Breton bays. Historic. Accessible only by boat.	26		•	•	•			•							
St. Mary's River (E-6) 2,176 acres 3 mi. n. of Great Mills, off SR 5 on Camp Cosoma Rd. Hunting.	27		•	•	•	•		•		•		•			
Sandy Point (E-4) 786 acres 7 mi. e. of Annapolis on US 50, on Chesapeake Bay. Bird watching.	28		•	•	•	•	•	•	•	•		•			•
Savage River State Forest (B-1) 52,819 acres mostly s. of I-68 and US 40 near Grantsville.	29	•	•	•	•	•		•		•	•	•	•		
Seneca Creek (E-1) 6,109 acres 2 mi. w. of Gaithersburg on SR 117.	30		•	•	•		•	•		•	•	•	•		•

RECREATION AREAS

Recreation Area	MAP LOCATION	CAMPING	PICNICKING	HIKING TRAILS	BOATING	BOAT RAMP	BOAT RENTAL	FISHING	SWIMMING	PETS ON LEASH	BICYCLE TRAILS	WINTER SPORTS	VISITOR CENTER	LODGE/CABINS	FOOD SERVICE
Smallwood (D-5) 629 acres in Marbury off SR 224. Historic. Boat rentals, marina, playground. *(See Marbury p. 189.)*	31	•	•	•	•	•	•	•						•	•
Susquehanna (B-7) 2,639 acres 3 mi. n. of Havre de Grace on SR 155. Historic. Scenic.	32	•	•	•	•	•		•		•	•	•			
Swallow Falls (B-1) 257 acres 9 mi. n.w. of Oakland on Herrington Manor-Swallow Falls Rd. Maryland's highest waterfall. Cross-country skiing; nature trails.	33	•	•	•				•		•	•	•			
Tuckahoe (D-7) 3,498 acres 6 mi. n. of Queen Anne off SR 404 via SR 480. Flat-water canoeing. Arboretum, lake.	34		•	•	•	•	•	•				•		•	
OTHER															
Brunswick Campsite (C-4) 24 acres on the C&O Canal towpath in Brunswick.	35	•	•	•	•	•		•			•	•			
Catoctin Mountain (B-5) 5,769 acres 2 mi. w. of Thurmont on SR 77. Cross-country skiing; bridle trail, nature trails. *(See Thurmont p. 196.)*	36	•	•	•				•				•	•	•	
Jennings Randolph Lake (B-2) 952 acres in Garrett County, and Mineral County, W. Va. From Bloomington take US 220 to SR 135, then 9 mi. w. to Lake Access Rd. Playground.	37	•	•	•	•	•		•					•		
Louise F. Cosca (D-6) 500 acres on Thrift Rd. near Clinton.	38	•	•	•				•	•		•		•		•
Rock Creek (E-1) 1,740 acres 4 mi. e. of Rockville on SR 28, then 2 mi. n. on Muncaster Mill Rd. to Avery Rd. Nature center. Archery, golf (18 holes, nine holes); nature trails. *(See Rockville in District of Columbia p. 117.)*	39		•	•	•			•	•		•	•			

Maryland Temperature Averages
Maximum / Minimum
From the records of the National Weather Service

	JAN	FEB	MAR	APR	MAY	JUNE	JULY	AUG	SEPT	OCT	NOV	DEC
Baltimore	44 / 25	46 / 26	54 / 33	66 / 43	76 / 53	84 / 61	87 / 66	85 / 65	79 / 58	68 / 46	57 / 34	46 / 26
Frederick	42 / 24	43 / 24	52 / 31	64 / 40	75 / 51	83 / 60	87 / 65	85 / 63	78 / 55	67 / 44	55 / 34	43 / 25

Exploring Maryland

For descriptions of places in bold type, see individual listings.

Northeast

The primary route through Cecil and Harford counties, constituting Maryland's northeast region, is I-95, which enters the state from the north about 3 miles below Newark, Del. The scant 40 miles of this route, traversing a gently rolling plain, give little hint of the attractions to be found but a short distance to either side of the expressway.

To explore the area leave I-95 at the first Cecil County interchange and take SR 279 south for about 2 miles. At SR 213 head north through Cherry Hill and on to Fair Hill. This small town is on the edge of Maryland's horse country. Fair Hill Races, where steeplechase and cross-country racing can be viewed, is a popular northeast attraction.

SR 273 westward from Fair Hill marks the beginning of a scenic drive through grain and dairy farmlands, rolling hills and ever-increasing horse farms. About a mile west of Calvert, a diverting stop can be made at the Plumpton Park Zoo. Four miles farther along SR 273 is **Rising Sun,** an early 18th-century settlement and now a trading and banking center.

Not far beyond Rising Sun SR 273 terminates at US 1. The scenic drive follows the federal highway south on through Conowingo on the banks of the Susquehanna River. As US 1 crosses the river over the Conowingo Dam the view to the north is of Conowingo Lake, a 14-mile product of the river's damming.

Crossing the Susquehanna brings you into Harford County, a pastoral Piedmont area dotted with farms and small towns. Eight miles beyond the river turn north on SR 136. Just below the Pennsylvania state line this route

Harford County, north of Bel Air / © Andre Jenny/Alamy Images

Down by the Bay in Maryland

swings to the west and terminates at Norrisville in the county's northwest corner.

From here take SR 23 south to Madonna. Turn south onto SR 146 and go just beyond the intersection with SR 152 to reach one of northeast Maryland's outstanding attractions: Ladew Topiary Gardens and Manor House in **Jacksonville.** A tour of the 15 seasonal gardens and the estate house displaying paintings, antiques and equestrian memorabilia should not be missed.

On leaving Ladew Gardens, backtrack briefly on SR 146 to SR 152. Take this south to the intersection with SR 147 where a left turn leads to Bel Air. Tudor Hall Museum—in the house in which actor Edwin Booth and his notorious brother, John Wilkes Booth, were born—and the Hays House Museum will lure American history buffs.

From Bel Air take SR 24 south beyond I-95 to Edgewood to begin a tour of northeast Maryland's more industrial and urban areas. From SR 24 a short drive up US 40 takes you to **Havre de Grace** at the point where the Susquehanna meets the Chesapeake.

You will pass the entrance to the **Aberdeen** Proving Ground en route. Its chief attraction, the U.S. Army Ordnance Museum, does not open until ten but a visit could be planned following a tour of Havre de Grace. Then proceed north again on US 40.

After crossing the Susquehanna and re-entering Cecil County, a side trip into Perryville takes you by both the site of Susquehanna Lower Ferry, a crossing much used by 18th-century travelers, and the now-restored Rodgers Tavern, a favorite stopping place of George Washington. Further up US 40, a turnoff onto SR 7 leads to Charlestown, a quiet waterfront village with another restored tavern reflecting its Colonial history.

From Charlestown, SR 7 leads to North East, also an 18th-century town that early became a

MARYLAND'S GOVERNOR EHRLICH SAYS:

PUT THE HONEY-DO LIST DOWN AND BRING YOUR HONEY TO MARYLAND.

To make the most of your precious time off, call for your free Maryland travel guide. **1-800-394-5725.** Or visit **www.VisitMaryland.org.**

Seize the day off

MARYLAND

WELCOME

small manufacturing center. A basket factory and a museum displaying fishing, hunting and boating artifacts peculiar to the Upper Chesapeake region are among the area attractions.

From North East SR 7 leads to **Elkton,** which grew up in the 18th century as a shipping center. The availability of water-power soon brought in the mills that turned it into a factory town.

North of Baltimore / © Tony Sweet/Imagestate

Despite commercial development a number of pre-Revolutionary homes have survived and, though private, are visible to motorists.

From Elkton proceed south on SR 213 to explore the "Chesapeake Country" section of Cecil County. Cut off on SR 285 and follow signs to the Chesapeake and Delaware Canal linking the two bays that define the Delmarva Peninsula. At the Maryland terminus is **Chesapeake City,** a 19th-century town that grew up with the canal construction industry and continues as the center for maintaining the waterway and servicing vessels using it.

Back on SR 213 proceed to Cecilton and turn west on Main Street. Four miles out is Mount Harmon Plantation. This 18th-century tobacco plantation, on the north bank of the Sassafras River, has a restored house furnished with antiques, boxwood gardens and the original tobacco press house.

From Cecilton, your visit to Maryland's northeast section can terminate with the scenic drive north on SR 213 back to I-95. A turn to the south, however, can lead to another Maryland region with a wealth of touring attractions. As you cross the Sassafras River just beyond Frederickton you leave Cecil County behind and enter into the special charm of the Eastern Shore.

The Eastern Shore

Topography, occupational pursuits and history account for differences between the two distinct sections of the Eastern Shore: the Upper Shore and the Southern Eastern Shore. While both include a lengthy stretch of Chesapeake Bay coastline, with fishing villages and yachting marinas, the Upper Shore is an area of farms and small-town ambience while its neighbor to the south is a flat, sandy region marked by pine forests, wetlands, shipping ports and cosmopolitan beach resorts.

The northern two of the four counties constituting Chesapeake Country, as Marylanders know the Upper Shore, are Kent and Queen Anne's. US 301 is the major route through them, but SR 213 affords a more picturesque drive with easy access to scenic and historical attractions.

Motorists coming in from Cecil County on SR 213 enter Kent County at Georgetown, an early 18th-century town that was almost destroyed by the British during the War of 1812. Drivers who enter Kent from the northeast on US 301 can cut off just beyond Sassafras on SR 290 to connect with SR 213 in Galena, where a turn north will lead to Georgetown. Heading south from Georgetown, SR 213 winds through rolling countryside past Locust Grove and Kennedyville, where those interested in antique farm equipment may wish to stop at the Kent Museum.

Chestertown, on the west bank of the Chester River, includes among its attractions pre-Revolutionary War homes, a restored 19th-century general store, an 18th-century tavern and Washington College. The nation's first president was one of the founders of the college.

From Chestertown, SR 20 leads to the southwestern section of the county, an area punctuated by small inlets of the bay. Turn south at Rock Hall onto SR 445 to go to the southernmost tip of the county. At this point a county road leads over to the Eastern Neck Island National Wildlife Refuge where hundreds of Canada geese migrate each autumn.

From the refuge backtrack to Rock Hall and go north on SR 20. About 4 miles up the road is the entrance to Remington Farms, a 3,000-acre wildlife sanctuary and research area with nature trails. After 2 more miles on SR 20 a side trip on Sandy Bottom Road leads to St. Paul's Episcopal Church, Maryland's oldest continuously used Episcopal church.

Continue on SR 20 to Chestertown and take SR 213 south into Queen Anne's County. Visible on the way to Centreville are 18th-century homes still in use. In the town are several opportunities for browsing among collections of Early American memorabilia.

About 7 miles south of Centreville, SR 213 leads to **Wye Mills.** Wye Oak State Park is south of town on SR 662. Also on SR 662 is Old Wye Church, established in 1721. Back in town, SR 213 east leads past the Wye Grist Mill, where grain was ground for Revolutionary War troops.

East of Wye Mills SR 213 runs into SR 404. Follow this into Caroline County and proceed eastward toward Denton. This small manufacturing town with Colonial roots is a trading center for the surrounding rural areas.

En route to Denton you pass the entrance to Tuckahoe State Park, where an environmental education program is offered at the 500-acre arboretum. Fishing, canoeing, hiking and camping are available. South of town on SR 404 is Martinak State Park, another recreational area offering camping facilities. A museum of American Indian artifacts is among the park's attractions.

Beyond Martinak SR 16 forks off SR 404 to the southwest. This rural route through a farming area leads to Preston, a canning and marketing center, and on south to the county line. Just before leaving Chesapeake Country you pass through Linchester, one of the earliest settlements in Caroline County. A gristmill, established in 1681 and reconstructed in the early 19th century, is still in operation.

Chesapeake Bay Maritime Museum, St. Michaels / © M. Berman/Robertstock

As you enter Dorchester County you begin your tour of the Southern Eastern Shore. Three miles south of the county line SR 331 cuts off to the southeast along an officially designated state scenic route. After a few miles the route switches east on SR 392, then south on SR 313 to the Nanticoke River.

Across the river the scenic route leads to Mardela Springs. At US 50 turn east for a 10-mile drive into **Salisbury,** the largest city on the Eastern Shore and the trade center for the Lower Shore. Although it was established in 1732, Salisbury lacks the Colonial appearance of Eastern Shore neighbors to the north. Because mid- and late-19th-century fires obliterated most pre-Victorian structures, it is decidedly a 20th-century city. A bustling commercial center, it has museums, art galleries, a zoo, fashion outlets and a riverfront park that call for a stop.

From Salisbury proceed toward the Atlantic coast on US 50 for about 20 miles. Turn onto access-controlled SR 90, which leads past Ocean Pines and on over to **Ocean City.** The 10-mile long public beach, the attractions of the 3-mile boardwalk, the sport fishing opportunities and the lures of fine seafood restaurants can make an extended stay in this resort city desirable.

Leaving Ocean City take US 50 for 2 miles and turn left on SR 611 to **Assateague Island National Seashore.** Noted for its herds of free-roaming Chincoteague ponies, the park offers camping facilities, nature trails and naturalist-led demonstrations of crabbing and fishing.

From Assateague begin another of Maryland's scenic drives by backtracking on SR 611 to SR 376. Take this west and at **Berlin** go south on US 113 to **Snow Hill.** One of the Southern Eastern Shore's communities dating from the 17th century, Snow Hill has several attractions of a historical nature. Just north of town a side trip on SR 12 passes Furnace Town, a re-created early industrial village at the site of a bog-ore furnace.

Beyond Snow Hill, US 113 passes through Pocomoke River State Park, which offers a view of the Pocomoke Cypress Swamps. The stand of bald cypress is one of the northernmost in the country. On down at the end of US 113 take US 13 westward through Pocomoke City and into Somerset County.

Turn south at Westover to pick up SR 413 for the drive down to **Crisfield** at Maryland's southern

Annapolis / © SuperStock

tip. The town, which calls itself the "Seafood Capital of the World," has numerous attractions related to the seafood industry and also is the point of departure for ferry trips to Smith and Tangier islands.

Backtracking to US 13, proceed to **Princess Anne,** another pre-Revolutionary town that experienced the destruction of most of its Colonial structures by fire. A few have been preserved and can be seen along with Federal and Victorian homes on a self-guiding walking tour.

From Princess Anne follow US 13 to Salisbury and then US 50 to re-enter Dorchester County at Vienna. Leave US 50 for a leisurely drive on county roads down to the southern Dorchester fishing villages. Follow Crossroads to Henry's Crossroads, go west on Griffith Neck Road, then north on Bestpitch Ferry Road and west on Greenbrier, which curves south to merge with Maple Dam Road. Just past the junction take Key Wallace west to SR 335.

On Key Wallace you will pass the Visitor Center of the Blackwater National Wildlife Refuge, winter haven for thousands of Canada geese as well as ospreys, ducks and swans and a sanctuary for bald eagles. Admission is charged for a 5-mile tour on Wildlife Drive and use of the nature trails and observation tower.

Beyond the refuge go south on SR 335 to SR 536. A left turn on SR 536 will take you down to the far point of the area Marylanders know as the "Cape Cod of the South." Continuing on SR 335 instead, you reach the Narrow Ferry Bridge leading to the fishing villages of Hooper Island on the bay.

Coming back to the junction of SRs 335 and 536, follow 335 north to **Church Creek.** Turn right on SR 16 toward **Cambridge.** Almost immediately you will pass Old Trinity Church, one of the oldest churches in use in America. On into Cambridge look for other 18th- and 19th-century buildings as well as several museums and a gallery of local arts.

Taking US 50 north from Cambridge you resume your tour of Chesapeake Country as you cross the Choptank River. About 10 miles north of the river leave US 50 and head west on Almshouse Road, a county route. This will merge with SR 333, which leads to **Oxford,** on the tip of a peninsula between the Tred Avon and Choptank rivers. This boating, shipbuilding and fishing center is one of Talbot County's principal towns.

The Oxford-Bellevue Ferry, crossing the Tred Avon, provides an attractive shortcut to **St. Michaels,** reached from Bellevue via a county road north to SR 33 and then west. This yachting and sailing center is a popular resort town and might be a spot where you'll want to arrange an extended stay.

From St. Michaels take SR 33 eastward to **Easton.** As you enter town you will pass the Third Haven Friends Meeting House, where William Penn sometimes held meetings. Although Easton was established early in the 18th century, this is the only pre-Revolutionary structure still standing. Federal period houses are much in evidence, however.

From Easton, the drive up US 50 brings the tour of the Eastern Shore to a close. Motorists who recall the old drawbridge linking the Eastern Shore mainland to **Kent Island** will find that the Kent Narrows Bridge, opened in 1990, has eliminated the traffic jams that for years impeded travel to and from the shore. Kent Island is still the Eastern Shore's most-used entry/exit point. Discount outlet centers are the attractions to be visited before the Chesapeake Bay Bridge puts the Eastern Shore behind.

Central Maryland

Annapolis, the center of the state's political life, is a well-situated spot at which to commence a tour of central Maryland. At the point where the Severn River flows into Chesapeake Bay, Maryland's capital city is easily reached from the northeast via US 301 and from the west and south by US 50 coming east from I-95.

The home of the U.S. Naval Academy, Annapolis also is a virtual museum of Colonial and 18th- and 19th-century history. As a lively social and cultural center, a sailor's mecca and an architectural show town, this small city has attractions that can claim a tourist's attention for days.

From the cradle of Maryland history a 25-mile drive across the center of Anne Arundel County and into Howard County leads to a city that has become a monument to late 20th-century urban planning. From Annapolis take I-97 to SR 3; go south 1 mile to SR 175 and follow this west through the Fort George Meade National Wildlife Refuge and on into **Columbia.** This planned community includes a college and a hospital on 15,000 acres of what was under-used farmland in the mid-1960s.

For a step back into Maryland's past, take US 29 through the countryside north of Columbia to the outskirts of **Ellicott City.** Follow Old Columbia Pike into this hilly, historic town overlooking the Patapsco River valley, which was the first terminus of the Baltimore and Ohio Railroad.

Leaving Ellicott City on SR 144 you will enter Baltimore County at Catonsville. Founded early in the 18th century, this neighbor of the city of Baltimore was the scene of historic 20th-century civil rights activity.

Beyond Catonsville continue on SR 144 into **Baltimore,** or at I-695 swing up to US 40 for access to Maryland's largest city. Either route will take you into an area convenient for starting a tour of the glittering downtown business district and the entertainment arenas, architectural showpieces and cultural attractions of the Inner Harbor.

Not all the interesting sights of Baltimore are products of the urban renewal that has revolutionized the harbor area; many historic, scientific and educational sites of note are scattered throughout this, the 13th-largest city of the nation. Allow yourself more than a day or two to see it.

The Pimlico Race Course, on Belvedere Avenue in the northwestern section of the city, is the site of the Preakness as well as a number of other major horse races each year. It is Maryland's oldest racetrack. The Jones Falls Expressway (I-83), a good route to the north, is a short distance from the track.

Heading up I-83 and east on I-695 you see a mixture of suburban and exurban territory. Open land is interspersed with housing developments that increasingly expand from the metropolis. However, a short side trip up SR 45 to the little racetrack at Timonium reminds one that central Maryland is horse country. Worthington Valley, a short drive west of Timonium off I-795, is home to several horse farms. In late April the Maryland Hunt Club race is held. First run in 1894, it is one of the country's most demanding steeplechases.

Heading south on I-795 to I-695 and then east brings you to **Lutherville,** home of the Fire Museum of Maryland. Continue south on SR 45 just beyond I-695 to **Towson.** Once a farm community, the city is now the site of light manufacturing plants, corporate headquarters, some state government offices and several colleges.

From Towson proceed east on I-695 to exit 31 and turn north on SR 147 for less-urban exploring. Fork left on Long Green Pike. Follow this to **Hydes** to visit the Boordy Winery. From this point take Hydes Road west to Manor Road. Go north and then west into horse country

Annapolis / © Michael P. Gadomski

along SR 145. At SR 45 a turn northward leads up to Hereford.

At Hereford pick up the scenic drive that winds westward along the northern sector of the state. SR 137 goes over to White House, where a right turn on SR 25 takes you north to Carroll County and on to Alesia near the Pennsylvania border. The scenic route then veers to the southwest on SR 27 and at the SR 30 intersection goes north again to Melrose.

Beyond Melrose go south on SR 496 to **Westminster.** A number of historical attractions and a couple of wineries are to be found in this agricultural and light-manufacturing community and the neighboring small towns.

From Westminster the scenic route follows SR 140 up to **Emmitsburg.** In this town, 3 miles short of the state line, you can visit historical sites related to Elizabeth Ann Seton, the first American woman canonized by the Roman Catholic Church.

From Emmitsburg a drive down US 15 leads to **Thurmont** on the edge of Catoctin Mountain Park. The nearby attractions bring the tour of central Maryland to an end. From Thurmont either continue south on US 15 to begin exploring the Capital Region or head on through the mountain park to enter western Maryland via SR 77.

Western Maryland

Because **Hagerstown,** 3 miles north of I-70 and traversed by US 40 and I-81, is accessible from all directions, it is a good starting place for a tour of Maryland's western region. After exploring the town proceed west on I-70 or US 40. These roads pass through historic small towns, first in fertile valleys and then up the orchard-covered slopes that mark the early stages of the Allegheny Mountains.

At Clear Spring go south on Big Spring Road to SR 56 and turn west to Fort Frederick State Park. Visit the museum, dealing with the fort's role in the French and Indian War, the American Revolution and the Civil War,

and enjoy the park's picnic facilities.

Continue northwest on SR 56, watching for signs of roadside markets as you pass through this fruit-growing region. At **Big Pool** take I-70 west to Exit 1B and follow SR 522 south to Hancock. The outskirts of this small manufacturing city overlook the northernmost stretch of the Potomac River. Civil War hostilities were centered nearby, and reminders of this phase of the town's history are still to be seen.

From Hancock, I-68 becomes the route to follow. It offers a scenic drive through the northern sector of forested mountains in Maryland's far western segment. At various points beyond Sideling Hill, about 6 miles out of Hancock, I-68 divides with the older, more scenic roadway paralleling the principal highway. At the first exit in Allegany County follow scenic SR 40, which winds through Piney Grove and the Bill Meyer Wildlife Management Area before returning to the through route in the midst of the Green Ridge State Forest.

Continuing west on US 40, watch for the scenic overlook a few miles beyond Flintstone. At this point the road curves down to **Cumberland.** This industrial city on the north branch of the Potomac River wraps around a peninsula-like projection of West Virginia. Because of its strategic importance in area history from days of the French and Indian War and its setting in a river valley surrounded by towering mountains, Cumberland offers numerous scenic and historic attractions, including the Western Maryland Scenic Railroad.

From Cumberland alternate US 40/ Centre Street follows the

route of the Indian footpath that provided the roadbed for a section of the first federally funded highway, the National Road, constructed early in the 19th century. In LaVale, it passes Maryland's first and only remaining tollgate house on the National Road. A plaque lists the original tolls for wagons, animals and pedestrians. Farther on, in Clarysville, is an inn built to serve early National Road travelers.

Another National Road inn, operated by Meshach Frost, was the establishment around which the town of **Frostburg** developed. A center of western Maryland's 19th-century coal mining industry, the picturesque mountain town is now the home of Frostburg State University.

Alternate US 40 then heads west to **Grantsville,** passing the Casselman River Bridge, a single-span stone arch built for the National Road in 1813. The town is largely populated by descendants of Amish and Mennonite farmers who moved into the area in the mid-19th century. Nearby attractions include a still-functioning 1797 gristmill and Penn Alps, a remodeled log stagecoach stop now offering demonstrations of Colonial arts and crafts.

From Grantsville alternate US 40 winds through the northern section of Savage River State Forest and on to Keysers Ridge. This is the point at which to cut

War Memorial, Baltimore
© Richard Cummins / SuperStock

Antietam National Battlefield / © Michael P. Gadomski

From Gorman, SR 560 will take you back toward Oakland. At Loch Lynn Heights turn north on SR 135. Deer Park Hotel Road goes off to the right about 4 miles up SR 135. This will lead to the village of Deer Park, a favored vacation resort of Presidents Grant, Harrison and Cleveland as well as of affluent late 19th-century eastern Marylanders. The spacious house, termed a "cottage," in which Cleveland spent his honeymoon stands.

Leaving Deer Park you have a choice of routes. You can proceed on a precipitous drive on SR 135 through Altamont and the lower portion of Savage River State Forest. Beyond McCoole turn north on US 220 toward Cumberland and US 40. However, SR 135 descends the northeastern face of Backbone Mountain with a long steep pitch and presents some treacherous curves.

An alternate would be to cross SR 135 at Deer Park and return to US 219 before heading north to US 40. This will involve some backtracking, but using principal route US 40 rather than the alternate across the northern tier of the area will cut driving time and may provide views you missed initially.

Back in the Hancock area pick up I-70. At interchange #18 take SR 68 southeast for a scenic drive through Washington County. At Lappans turn south on SR 65 and proceed to the **Antietam National Battlefield** at Sharpsburg. Allow several hours to see this and the other historical sites in the area before taking SR 34 to **Boonsboro.**

Just beyond the Crystal Grottoes Caverns on SR 34 turn east onto alternate US 40. To your left about a mile from Boonsboro is Washington Monument State Park. With the hike to the monument and the museum slide presentation, the tour of western Maryland comes to a close. Beyond the park you can begin exploration of the Greater Washington region.

south down the side of the western Maryland triangle. US 219 runs the length of the north/south plateau near the Allegheny ridges and offers easy access to the various attractions along the way.

About 4 miles south of Keysers Ridge a scenic overlook 2,800 feet above sea level offers a dramatic view of valley farmlands surrounded by mountain peaks. A few miles farther Accident/Bear Creek Road, a county route, leads off to the west. Follow this to Friendsville, south of the dam that creates the Youghiogheny Reservoir. Tours of the dam are available, and the Youghiogheny River itself is one of the protected scenic beauties of western Maryland. Trout and bass fishing opportunities abound.

From Friendsville SR 42 will take you back to US 219 a few miles north of Deep Creek Lake, the largest freshwater lake in Maryland. If downhill skiing is on your agenda, turn right on Sang Run Road in McHenry. This will take you to the ski area on 3,080-foot-high Marsh Mountain. For year-round outdoor activities turn left farther down US 219 on a road marked by a sign to Deep Creek Lake State Park.

About 8 miles beyond the state park US 219 brings you into **Oakland.** High on a plateau, in an area local hotels once described as the "Switzerland of America," Oakland and nearby Mountain Lake Park were popular with late 19th-century vacationers.

From Oakland, CR 20 offers access to Swallows Falls State Park and the largest waterfalls in Maryland. Beyond the park the road leads to the Cranesville Sub-Arctic Swamp on the Maryland-West Virginia border. One of the region's most unusual natural phenomena, this 5,000-acre remnant of an ice age forest produces plant life usually found only in regions close to the Arctic Circle. Unfortunately, the paved road ends before reaching the swamp, and final access is by gravel and dirt roads.

South of Oakland US 219 enters Redhouse, on the incline leading to the highest elevation in Maryland, Backbone Mountain. The 3,360-foot peak dominates the lower tip of the western Maryland triangle. From Redhouse US 50 heading east cuts through Backbone Mountain Pass to the other West Virginia boundary at Gorman.

Oxon Hill / © Gibson Stock Photography

Capital Region

Defining this area poses problems because of the ever-expanding nature of the metropolis it abuts. It enlarges as housing subdivisions proliferate, corporations reach out for business park space, federal agencies seek offices beyond the District of Columbia and transportation systems linking the nation's capital with outlying communities multiply.

These touring suggestions are limited to the irregularly-shaped crescent that encompasses the cities of Frederick and Washington and has its western boundary defined by the Potomac from about 3 miles northwest of Brunswick to a little below Accokeek. Included in this area are the southern half of Frederick County, Montgomery County and almost all of Prince George's County.

The primary routes serving the region are I-270 and I-95. Though they pass through pleasing Piedmont countryside both are heavily traveled, especially during commuter rush hours. To enjoy area attractions avoid these routes when possible.

Frederick is a good base from which to explore the surrounding area as well as to visit local attractions. When you have seen the latter take SR 144 east to **New Market** to browse at the antiques capital of Maryland. Then follow SR 75 north from New Market to Glissans Mill Road and turn east to reach the Linganore Wine Cellars at Berrywine Plantations.

For a scenic drive along the Potomac take US 340 west from Frederick to Exit 1 and follow signs to SR 478 south. From Brunswick follow SR 464 to US 15. Take this south to Point of Rocks and turn east on SR 28. Just beyond Tuscarora turn away from the Potomac and go north on SR 85. At Lilypons Road go east not quite 2 miles and make a stop in Lilypons, Maryland's smallest town.

Lilypons is little more than a post office and the site of the Lilypons Water Gardens and Three Springs Fisheries. Ornamental aquatic plants, flashing goldfish and a variety of waterfowl and migratory birds attract visitors all year.

From Lilypons return to Frederick via SR 85 to the north or head on south into Montgomery County. For the latter, SR 28 offers a scenic alternative to I-270.

Return to it from Lilypons Road; turn east and follow SR 28 into **Rockville.** Make this or any of several neighboring communities your base for exploring the Washington suburban area.

Bethesda, Chevy Chase, Gaithersburg, **Glen Echo, Kensington,** Potomac, **Rockville** and **Wheaton** have historic, scientific, scenic and educational attractions for visitors, and all can be reached easily from any lower Montgomery County AAA accommodation; see District of Columbia (West and North Region) listings. Bethesda, **Silver Spring** and Takoma Park have Metrorail stations offering convenient access to Washington attractions.

Complete your tour of Montgomery County by driving north on US 29 through an area that in the not-distant past was open countryside but now is a rapidly developing corridor of high-tech corporations and luxury condominiums. At SR 198 turn east to head into Prince George's County.

Stop in **Laurel** to see the Montpelier Mansion and the Montpelier Cultural Arts Center. You can check out the Laurel Race Track and the Laurel Raceway before taking the Baltimore-Washington Parkway south toward Beltsville. Exit at Powder Mill Road and proceed to the grounds of the Agricultural Research Center, the largest research center operated by the U.S. Department of Agriculture. Tours of the experimental farm are offered by appointment.

From the farm continue south on the Baltimore-Washington Parkway to **Greenbelt,** then take SR 193 south to SR 214. Going west toward **Largo** you will pass Six Flags America, a family theme park featuring rides, shows, games and water-related activities.

Just beyond Upper Marlboro go east on SR 4 to US 301. Take this south and turn left on SR 382. Proceed to Croom Airport Road and follow signs to Patuxent River Park, a restricted-use recreation and ecology education center where you can enjoy hiking, bird watching, canoeing, pontoon tours and exploring a restored 100-year-old village. Fishing and hunting require special permits.

Farther south on SR 382, a left turn on St. Thomas Church Road leads to the entrance of the Merkle Wildlife Refuge, a haven for a wide variety of migratory birds and waterfowl.

Returning toward Upper Marlboro go 5 miles west on SR 4 and take SR 223 south to

working farm demonstrate methods of the late 19th century. Wagon rides, horseback rides and hands-on activities such as milking are special features.

From Oxon Hill take SR 210 south for about 4 miles. Turn right on Fort Washington Road to visit Fort Washington Park on the east bank of the Potomac. This 341-acre national park is on the site of the first fort built to defend the nation's capital.

Southern Maryland

Starting a tour of southern Maryland on US 301 from the north you enter Charles County, the region's largest in area and population. Initially SR 5 shares the roadway with the federal highway, but as you near **Waldorf** it turns left into the town, which is bypassed by US 301. Follow SR 5 for your first touring stop in the region.

Just beyond Waldorf turn left on SR 382 and proceed to SR 232. Turn right and around the corner on SR 232 you will find The Dr. Samuel A. Mudd House Museum. This is the restored plantation home of the surgeon who, without knowing the identity of his patient, set John Wilkes Booth's broken leg following the assassination of Lincoln. Imprisoned for this act, he was later pardoned and honored for services rendered in prison during a yellow fever epidemic.

Back on SR 5 go south and turn right on SR 488. At SR 6 a right turn will take you into La-Plata, site of several notable Tidewater homes. Farther on SR 6 is **Port Tobacco,** one of the oldest continuously occupied towns in America. Fork to the left on Chapel Point Road to visit the reconstructed 1819 federal courthouse and Charles County Museum of Port Tobacco.

Back on SR 6 go west to Doncaster and turn right on SR 344. When this merges with SR 224 fork to the right and proceed to the Smallwood State Park overlooking Mattawoman Creek. Summer weekends you can stop for a tour of Smallwood's Retreat, the restored plantation home of Revolutionary War Gen. William Smallwood, close friend of George Washington and fourth Maryland governor.

Proceed on SR 224 to **Marbury** and turn right on SR 484. At Pisgah take a right again on SR 425. Follow this to SR 6; continue 1 mile farther to the Old Durham Church, attended by Gen. Smallwood and visited by Washington. Return to SR 6 and go east across the county. For a break from historical exploring you might wish to enjoy activities available at scenic 180-acre Gilbert Run Park in Dentsville.

Great Falls of the Potomac, Chesapeake & Ohio Canal NHP
© Skip Brown/Imagestate

Clinton. In the center of town turn left on Brandywine Road. At 9110 Brandywine stop for a tour of the Surratt House and Tavern, the restored home of the woman convicted of aiding John Wilkes Booth as he attempted to flee following the assassination of President Abraham Lincoln. Surratt was the first woman to be executed in the United States for complicity in a crime.

Your next stop should be **Oxon Hill.** Leaving the Garber Facility take St. Barnabas Road south to Oxon Hill Road just beyond I-95. Turn right and proceed to SR 210. Beyond this turn right at the sign for the Oxon Hill Farm. Costumed staff at this

Back on SR 210 continue south for 5 miles toward **Accokeek.** Turn right at Bryan Point Road, which takes you again to the Potomac shore. The road ends at the National Colonial Farm, where agricultural methods and plantation lifestyles of the mid-18th century are demonstrated.

The view of George Washington's Mount Vernon home across the river from the farm provides a fitting end to the tour of the Capital Region, so steeped in the nation's history. From Accokeek SR 373 will lead to Brandywine; take either US 301 to the northeast or SR 5 north to reach I-95. US 301 south is the turn to make to begin a tour of southern Maryland.

One mile beyond Dentsville take SR 231 south to SR 234. A left turn takes you into St. Mary's County via a scenic route. Continue on SR 234 to Chaptico and turn right on SR 242 leading to **Coltons Point.** A museum in this Potomac coastal town honors the first Marylanders—settlers who landed on nearby St. Clement's Island in 1634.

Leaving Coltons Point on SR 242, turn right on SR 234, which shortly merges with SR 5. Follow this into Leonardtown, where the Old Jail Museum and a county library in a restored early 18th-century house are open to visitors.

From Leonardtown take SR 245 through **Hollywood** and out 3 more miles to Sotterley Plantation on the western shore of the Patuxent River. The restored Colonial mansion, English country gardens, slave cabin, smoke house and other original support buildings make this one of southern Maryland's most distinctive attractions.

Return to Hollywood and take SR 235 south. Pass SR 237 and, as you enter **Lexington Park,** watch for Three Notch Road on your left. This is the entrance to the Naval Air Test and Evaluation Museum. If you come to the entrance on SR 235 you have gone a block too far; there is no access to the museum from the base.

From the museum proceed south on SR 235 to Ridge, where the route merges with SR 5. Follow this to Scotland Beach and **Point Lookout** State Park, at the southernmost tip of Maryland's western shore. On a site where Confederate prisoners were held during the Civil War, the park includes a Confederate cemetery and a museum in addition to recreational facilities.

Return to Ridge and continue on SR 5 to Maryland's first capital, **St. Mary's City.** In town follow signs for Historic St. Mary's City, a complex of exhibits and attractions spread over 800 acres. You can expect to spend a day or two seeing the reconstructed town that was settled in 1634 by Maryland's first colonists.

From St. Mary's City continue on SR 5 to Park Hall and go east on Park Hall Road to SR 235. Take this north for about 8 miles and turn right on SR 4. After passing through Town Creek you will cross the Patuxent River and enter Calvert County, at the lower tip of the peninsula between the Patuxent and the Chesapeake Bay.

The first town you enter in Calvert County is **Solomons,** a quiet waterfront community with one of North America's deepest natural ports. Visit the Calvert Marine Museum, the Drum Point Lighthouse and the nearby oyster-packing house and, if time permits, take the hour-long harbor cruise.

From Solomons follow SRs 2 and 4 north, watching for directional signs on side roads to attractions on the Chesapeake shore. SR 497 leads to Cove Point Lighthouse, the oldest tower light on the Chesapeake; other roads lead to Calvert Cliffs State Park, where fossils can be collected on the beach, and to the Calvert Cliffs Nuclear Power Plant Visitors Center. Near **Lusby,** is the 327-acre Flag Ponds Nature Park, with facilities for hiking, fishing and picnicking.

Near Port Republic do not miss a side trip to the Jefferson Patterson Park and Museum. To reach this archeological and environmental preserve from SRs 2/4 take SR 264 south 2 miles, fork to the left on SR 265 and follow signs. On the way back to SRs 2/4 stop at Christ Church on SR 264 to see the garden of biblical plants.

Farther north on SRs 2/4 take SR 506 west. Turn left on Gray's Road to reach the Battle Creek Cypress Swamp Sanctuary. For information see the Points of Interest entry for **Prince Frederick.** Back on SRs 2/4 swing around Prince Frederick and proceed north to the point where the two routes diverge.

Follow SR 2 to Mount Harmony and take Mount Harmony Road east. When this runs into SR 260 continue to **Chesapeake Beach.** This community on the western shore provides a scenic climax to your tour of southern Maryland. After taking in the exhibits at the Chesapeake Beach Railway Museum you can sit on the pier, gaze across the bay, and delight in the graceful ways of the swans and geese.

When you can no longer resist the prodding to return to the workaday world take SR 260 back to Mount Harmony and then on northwest to SR 4. Follow this north to US 301 or on beyond to I-95 for access to your homeward route.

Cove Point Lighthouse
© Richard Cummins/SuperStock

Planning a trip to Washington D.C.?

Check out this must-have guide created just for Washington, D.C. travelers! *AAA Spiral Guide Washington, D.C.*, with its practical design and convenient size, includes a variety of great features:

- Interesting articles about local culture and history.
- A Don't Miss section helps you see it all.
- Insider tips about how to get there and what you'll need.
- Hotel, restaurant, and attraction listings for easy planning.
- At Your Leisure sections for those with more time.

Points of Interest

ABERDEEN—*see Baltimore p. 173.*

ACCOKEEK—*see District of Columbia p. 114.*

ANNAPOLIS—*see Baltimore p. 174.*

ANTIETAM NATIONAL BATTLEFIELD (B-4)

On SR 34/65 at Sharpsburg, Antietam National Battlefield is a more than 3,000-acre site where the Battle of Antietam, as it was called by the Union, or the Battle of Sharpsburg, as it was referred to by the Confederacy, took place Sept. 17, 1862.

On this bloodiest day of the Civil War, 12,410 Union and 10,700 Confederate soldiers were killed or wounded. Gen. George McClellan's 87,000 men met Gen. Robert E. Lee's 41,000 after decisive victories for the South in Virginia. Lee's objective was to invade northern home territory; this was to be his first invasion of the North. Therefore, his forced withdrawal following a tactical draw resulted in a strategic Union victory.

A Confederate victory at Antietam would have been such a blow to the Union that the momentum would have moved to the Confederacy and it probably would have won the war; thus, this victory at Antietam enabled President Abraham Lincoln to issue the Emancipation Proclamation. William S. McKinley, later president of the United States, fought at the site.

General Information and Activities

Maps, tablets and monuments mark the battlefield, and vertical cannon barrels indicate sites where three Union and three Confederate generals died. An 8.5-mile driving tour highlights historic areas of the battlefield. Allow 2 hours minimum. The battlefield is open daily dawn-dusk; closed Jan. 1, Thanksgiving and Dec. 25.

ADMISSION to the park, visitor center and cemetery is $3, under 17 free, family rate $5.

PETS must be restricted at all times, either in vehicles or by leash, and are not allowed in public buildings.

ADDRESS inquiries to the Superintendent, Antietam National Battlefield, P.O. Box 158, Sharpsburg, MD 21782; phone (301) 432-5124.

Points of Interest

ANTIETAM NATIONAL CEMETERY, 1 mi. from battlefield entrance on SR 34, was established in 1865 and contains the graves of 4,776 Union soldiers and those of 261 men who fought in subsequent wars. "The Private Soldier," a monument dedicated to Civil War dead, is a notable landmark. Allow 30 minutes minimum. Daily dawn-dusk. Combined park, cemetery and visitor center admission $3, under 17 free, family rate $5. Phone (301) 432-5124.

VISITOR CENTER, 1 mi. n. of Sharpsburg on SR 65 at the battlefield entrance, has exhibits pertaining to this significant Civil War conflict. Five oil murals by Capt. James Hope, a battle participant, illustrate various Antietam battle scenes. Interpretive talks, a 26-minute film and a 1-hour documentary about Lee's Maryland campaign are offered. An audiotape describing points of interest can be rented or purchased.

Allow 1 hour minimum. Daily 8:30-6, Memorial Day-Labor Day; 8:30-5, rest of year. Closed Jan. 1, Thanksgiving and Dec. 25. Talks scheduled daily, June 1-Labor Day. The 26-minute film is shown every half hour 8:30-noon and 1-4. Combined park, cemetery and visitor center admission $3, under 17 free, family rate $5. Phone (301) 432-5124.

ASSATEAGUE ISLAND NATIONAL SEASHORE (F-9)

Eight mi. s. of Ocean City via SR 611, Assateague Island National Seashore encompasses 39,500 acres (19,000 of which are land), including Assateague Island and nearby small islands. Paralleling the coast of Maryland and Virginia, Assateague Island is a narrow 37-mile-long barrier island with Maryland's Assateague State Park *(see Recreation Chart and Ocean City in the AAA Mideastern CampBook)* at the northern end and the Chincoteague National Wildlife Refuge *(see Chincoteague, Va., p. 231)* at the southern end.

The island is home to Chincoteague ponies that eat marsh grass and drink from freshwater ponds. The horses reportedly are descendants of a 16th-century herd that swam ashore from a sinking Spanish galleon, although a more likely story is that they descended from local farm horses. The island is also a stop-off point during the migration of the endangered peregrine falcon and several waterfowl, including the greater snow goose.

General Information and Activities

The National Park Service operates a visitor center with exhibits at the bridge approach to the north end of the island. Allow 30 minutes minimum. Both the National Park Service and the wildlife refuge operate information centers at the southern end.

Boating, crabbing, fishing, swimming and camping opportunities are available. Naturalists conduct canoe trips, campfire talks, guided nature walks and clamming and fishing demonstrations daily mid-June through August. Because of the importance of the sand dunes to the preservation of the barrier island, visitors are asked to use the marked passageways across the dunes.

Allow 1 hour minimum to see the island. The seashore is open daily 24 hours. Visitor centers are open daily 9-5. *See Recreation Chart and the AAA Mideastern CampBook.*

ADMISSION to the park (including Chincoteague National Wildlife Refuge) is by a 7-day, $10 permit per private vehicle, or a $20 annual permit.

PETS must be restricted at all times, either in vehicles or by leash, and are not allowed in public buildings or on trails.

ADDRESS inquiries to the Superintendent, Assateague Island National Seashore, 7206 National Seashore Ln., Berlin, MD 21811; phone (410) 641-1441, or (410) 641-3030 for camping information.

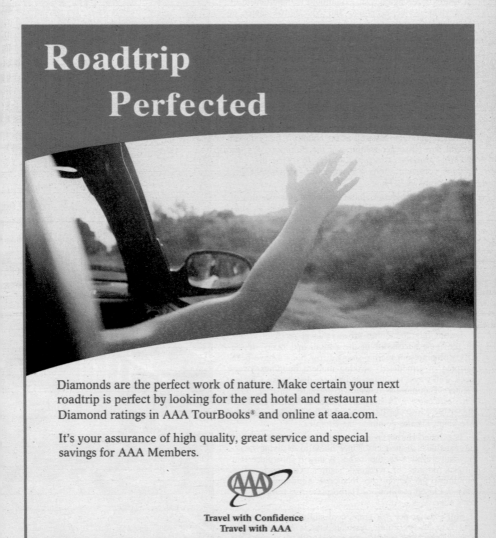

Baltimore

Although its proud natives may sometimes feel over-shadowed by the attention paid to the power and politics of nearby Washington, D.C., Baltimore is important in its own right as the economic and educational center of Maryland.

Founded in 1729 by an act of the Provincial Assembly, the city was incorporated in 1797 with a population of 20,000. During the War of 1812 the British unsuccessfully attacked Baltimore, and Francis Scott Key wrote "The Star-Spangled Banner" while watching the bombardment from a warship anchored in Baltimore Harbor.

Baltimore's history has been a series of firsts. The Mount Clare Station at W. Pratt and Poppleton streets was the starting point for the country's first railroad, the Baltimore and Ohio, as well as the country's first railroad freight and passenger station *(see the Baltimore & Ohio Railroad Museum attraction listing p. 163)*. The first telegraphic communication—"What hath God wrought?"—was received in 1844.

The nation's oldest Catholic cathedral, the Basilica of the Assumption of the Blessed Virgin Mary, is at Mulberry and Cathedral streets; buried in the crypt is John Carroll, the country's first archbishop. Lloyd Street Synagogue, near Lombard, was the first synagogue to be built in Maryland.

Vision and vitality thrive in today's Baltimore. Johns Hopkins University, several medical schools and such colleges as the Peabody Conservatory of Music and the Maryland Institute College of Art are among the institutions that provide the city with a stimulating and innovative learning environment.

Baltimore's continuing urban renewal program is one of the most successful in the nation, and many of the city's omnipresent marble-stooped row houses have been restored or remodeled. Striking modern buildings, overhead walkways, fountains and plazas distinguish Charles Center, Baltimore's downtown business district. One Charles Center, a 24-story skyscraper of bronze glass designed by Mies van der Rohe, and the futuristic-looking Mechanic Theatre dominate the complex.

The Inner Harbor is an example of the pride Baltimoreans take in their city. Once home to decaying factories and warehouses, the harbor is now a showplace that attracts throngs of weekend visitors. Gleaming office buildings, the seven-story National Aquarium and the glass-enclosed pavilions of Harborplace rise from the water's edge.

Still a major port for grain, coal and spices, the harbor also hosts many ethnic festivals and is the permanent home of the last Civil War-era vessel still afloat, the USS *Constellation (see attraction listing p. 170).*

National Aquarium in Baltimore / © Gibson Stock Photography

Downtown / © R. Krubner/Robertstock

Baltimore's ethnic diversity and history are reflected in such venerable neighborhoods as Little Italy, Little Lithuania and H.L. Mencken's beloved Union Square. Offering a fine view of the Inner Harbor is the historic Federal Hill area, the site of a picnic where 4,000 citizens celebrated the ratification of the Constitution in 1788. Fells Point is an old seaport neighborhood with an international flair.

Approaches

By Car

A network of superhighways makes Baltimore easily accessible from all directions. From the south the main approach is I-95, with access to the downtown area via I-395 and the Baltimore-Washington Parkway. Traffic from the west approaches downtown via I-70 and US 40.

Access from the north is via I-83, while traffic from the northeast arrives on I-95. The Baltimore Beltway (I-695); the four-lane Harbor Tunnel Thruway (I-895), a toll road; and the Fort McHenry Tunnel (I-95), also a toll road, combine to provide a complete bypass of the city.

Getting Around

Street System

Charles Street separates east and west Baltimore; Baltimore Street divides the city's north and south sections. Numbered streets run east and west. Except for Eutaw Street, most downtown streets are one way.

The city speed limit for most areas is 30 mph, or as posted. Rush hours are from about 7:30 to 9 a.m. and from about 4 to 6 p.m. Avoid driving during rush hours if possible. A right turn on red is permitted, unless otherwise posted.

Parking

Parking on the street is controlled by meter. Many municipal metered parking lots are in and near downtown. Rates at the numerous commercial lots and garages average about $2.50 an hour.

Public Transportation

Baltimore's public transportation consists of buses, a subway system and light rail. Baltimore's public transportation routes traverse all sections of the city, with most bus routes passing through the downtown area. The fare for bus, Metro and Light Rail is $1.35, with an additional 35c for express routes. Exact fare is required, and the fare box accepts only dollar bills and tokens. Commuter bus service fares vary according to the distance traveled. The bus schedule varies depending upon the route. A $3 unlimited-use day pass is good on the bus, metro and light rail systems.

(continued on p. 163)

The Informed Traveler

City Population: 651,154

Elevation: 445 ft.

Sales Tax: Maryland's statewide sales tax is 5 percent; Baltimore has a 7.5 percent lodging tax; an 11.5 percent tax is levied on automobile rentals.

WHOM TO CALL

Emergency: 911

Police (non-emergency): (410) 396-2525

Time: (410) 844-1212

Temperature: (410) 936-1212

Hospitals: Franklin Square Hospital Center, (443) 777-7000; Greater Baltimore Medical Center, (443) 849-2000; Johns Hopkins Hospital, (410) 955-5000; Maryland General Hospital, (410) 225-8000; Sinai Hospital of Baltimore, (410) 601-9000; University of Maryland Medical Center, (410) 328-8667.

WHERE TO LOOK

Newspapers

The major newspaper is *The Baltimore Sun.*

Radio

Radio station WBAL (1090 AM) is an all-news/weather station; WJHU (88.1 FM) is a member of National Public Radio.

Visitor Information

Baltimore Visitor Center: 401 Light St., Baltimore, MD 21202; phone (410) 837-4636 or (877) 225-8466.

Visitor center hours are daily 9-6. The visitor center offers a combination ticket called the **Harbor Pass,** which provides admission to the Maryland Science Center; National Aquarium in Baltimore; Port Discovery, the Children's Museum in Baltimore; and Top of the World. The pass also includes 1 day of unlimited free rides on the water taxi and numerous discounts in the area. Valid for 3 consecutive days, the Harbor Pass costs $46; ages 3-12, $30.

Monthly *Baltimore* magazine lists dining, entertainment and events information.

TRANSPORTATION

Air Travel

Baltimore-Washington International Airport, about 10 miles south of downtown, is reached via the Baltimore-Washington Parkway and I-195. Limousines operate between principal downtown hotels and the airport. The fare is $28 for one to four persons, $35 for up to six persons, plus a 15 percent tip; phone (410) 519-0000. Taxi service from the airport is $2.30 for the first mile and about $1.40 for each additional mile; phone (410) 859-1100.

Public bus transportation also is available. A shuttle runs every 30 minutes to major downtown hotels; phone (410) 381-2772 or (800) 776-0323. Intercity rail service along Amtrak's northeast corridor is linked with the airport by light rail, as well as by shuttle bus service from the Amtrak station, which is 1 mile away.

Rental Cars

Numerous automobile rental agencies maintain offices at the airport and downtown. Hertz, (410) 850-7400 or (800) 654-3080, offers discounts to AAA members. Check the telephone directory for other car rental agencies.

Rail Service

Pennsylvania Station is at 1515 N. Charles St., between Oliver and Lanvale streets; phone Amtrak, (800) 872-7245.

Buses

The Greyhound Lines Inc. terminals are at 210 W. Fayette St. and Baltimore Travel Plaza, at the intersection of I-95 and O'Donnell Street; phone (800) 231-2222.

Taxis

Taxis are metered. The fare is $1.50 for the first 1/6 mile and 20c for each additional 1/6 mile (30c for county miles), plus 20c for each 30 seconds of waiting time. A $1 charge is added when taxis are ordered by phone. A 50c surcharge is added for trips between 9 p.m. and 5 a.m. Among the larger cab companies are Diamond, (410) 947-3333; Sun, (410) 235-0300; and Yellow Cab, (410) 685-1212. Other companies are listed in the telephone directory.

Public Transport

Baltimore's public transportation consists of buses, a subway system and light rail. *See Public Transportation for details.*

The *Ride Guide* provides information about the MTA bus, metro and light rail systems. For fare and schedule information phone (410) 539-5000 or (866) 743-3682.

The Baltimore Metro subway system runs from downtown at Johns Hopkins Hospital northwest to Owings Mills Station at Painters Mill Road and I-795, with 14 intermediate stations. Free parking is available at Milford Mill, Mondawmin, Reisterstown Plaza, Rogers Avenue, Old Court, Owings Mills and West Cold Spring stations. The system operates Mon.-Fri. 5 a.m.-midnight, Sat.-Sun. 6 a.m.-midnight.

Light Rail service runs between Hunt Valley and Glen Burnie as well as between Baltimore-Washington International Airport and Penn Station. Both lines share 15 stations between Linthicum and University of Maryland/Mount Royal. Trains operate Mon.-Fri. 6 a.m.-midnight, Sat. 8 a.m.-midnight, Sun. 11-7.

What To See

9 FRONT STREET, in Shot Tower Park, was the home of shipping magnate and Baltimore mayor Thorowgood Smith. The Federal-style house was Smith's residence until 1804. Tues.-Thurs. 9-2:30, Fri. 9-2; closed Jan. 1, holidays and week of Dec. 25. Free. Phone (410) 837-5424.

[SAVE] **AMERICAN VISIONARY ART MUSEUM** is at 800 Key Hwy. at jct. Covington St. This museum features the imaginative, creative and intuitive works of self-taught artists. The artists come from diverse work and cultural backgrounds and have created in various conventional and unconventional media. Of interest is the 55-foot high "Whirligig" in the outdoor Central Plaza. Food is available. Allow 1 hour minimum. Tues.-Sun. 10-6; closed Thanksgiving and Dec. 25. Admission $9; over 54 and under 18, $6. Phone (410) 244-1900.

[SAVE] **BABE RUTH BIRTHPLACE/BALTIMORE ORIOLES MUSEUM,** off the 600 block of W. Pratt St. at 216 Emory St., comprises four adjoining row houses, including the birthplace of the "Sultan of Swat." The museum contains numerous photographs, paintings and memorabilia associated with Babe Ruth, Maryland's other baseball greats and the Baltimore Orioles. Film clips of Ruth's life and Orioles' highlights are shown. The furnishings are from the late 1800s.

Allow 1 hour minimum. Daily 10-5, Apr.-Oct. (also 5-7 during Orioles home games); 10-4, rest of year. Closed Jan. 1, Thanksgiving and Dec. 25. Admission $6; over 61, $4; ages 5-16, $3. Phone (410) 727-1539.

BALTIMORE & OHIO RAILROAD MUSEUM is at 901 W. Pratt St. The 40-acre indoor/outdoor museum's extensive collection of locomotives, both originals and replicas, dates from 1829. In addition to examples of many types of engines, the museum contains railroad china and silver, new outdoor train exhibition

platforms, and an exhibit on railroad time and time pieces.

The shops that once surrounded the station built thousands of cars and engines and were known as "The Railroad University." The station's focal point is the roundhouse dome covering a wooden turntable surrounded by 22 stalls that contain cars and locomotives.

Note: Following renovations, the museum was scheduled to reopen in late 2004. Allow 1 hour, 30 minutes minimum. Mon.-Fri. 10-4, Sat. 10-5, Sun. noon-5; closed Jan. 1, Easter, Memorial Day, July 4, Labor Day, Thanksgiving, Dec. 24-25 and Dec. 31. Admission $14; over 59, $10; ages 2-12, $8. Phone (410) 752-2490 to verify schedule and prices.

[SAVE] **THE BALTIMORE CIVIL WAR MUSEUM,** 601 President St., features exhibits, interpretive programs and living history presentations focusing on Baltimore's roles in the Underground Railroad and the Civil War. Allow 1 hour minimum. Daily 10-5; closed Jan. 1, Thanksgiving and Dec. 25. Admission $4; over 59, students with ID and ages 13-17, $3. MC, VI. Phone (410) 385-5188.

BALTIMORE MARITIME MUSEUM, Inner Harbor at Pier 3 on Pratt St., includes the USS *Torsk,* a World War II submarine. Next to the *Torsk* is the *Chesapeake,* a floating lighthouse designed to aid shipping in the bay. Also included is the Coast Guard cutter *Taney,* the last ship afloat to have survived the attack on Pearl Harbor, and the 1856 Seven Foot Knoll Lighthouse, which stood at the entrance to Baltimore Harbor for 133 years before being moved to the Inner Harbor.

Allow 30 minutes minimum. Daily 10-6, July-Aug.; daily 10-5, Mar.-June and Sept.-Dec.; Fri.-Sun. 10-5, rest of year. Admission $7; over 59, $5; ages 6-14, $4. Phone (410) 396-3854.

BALTIMORE MUSEUM OF ART is 3 mi. n. of the Inner Harbor on Art Museum Dr. at N. Charles and 31st sts. Designed by John Russell Pope, architect of the National Gallery of Art in Washington, D.C., the museum houses a permanent collection of more than 100,000 objects, ranging from ancient mosaics to contemporary art. Visitors can see furniture, decorative arts, paintings, miniature and period rooms; art from Africa, the Americas and Oceania; Chinese ceramics; and eight galleries devoted to European old masters. Two sculpture gardens contain 20th-century works by artists from Rodin to Nevelson.

The Cone Collection includes paintings and sculptures by Henri Matisse, Pablo Picasso, Vincent van Gogh and other modern artists. The West Wing for Modern Art houses a large collection of Andy Warhol paintings. Programs, events and special exhibitions are held throughout the year.

Food is available. Wed.-Fri. 11-5 (also Thurs. 5-8 the first Thurs. of the month), Sat.-Sun. 11-6; closed Jan. 1, July 4, Thanksgiving and Dec. 25. Admission $7, over 64 and students with ID $5, under 18 free; free to all first Thurs. of the month. Phone (410) 396-7100.

Destination Baltimore

Clipper City, Baltimore.
Passengers enter the harbor just as sailors did in the original *Clipper City* 150 years ago. (See listing page 171)

Copyright Paul A. Souders Corbis

History buffs will delight in the many sights and sounds of Maryland's largest city.

Relive the battle at Fort McHenry that inspired Francis Scott Key's "The Star-Spangled Banner"; sail away on a restored skipjack oyster boat; or hop aboard a train at the B&O Railroad Museum at Mount Clare Station, starting point of the country's first railroad.

Copyright Gibson Stock Photography

Babe Ruth Birthplace, Baltimore
The Sultan of Swat's birthplace hits a home run with visitors. (See listing page 163)

Places included in this
AAA Destination City:

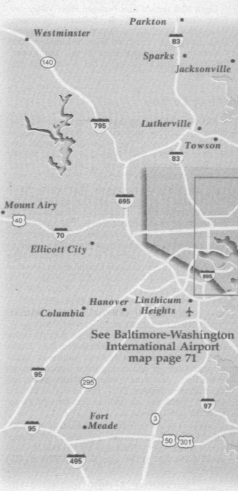

See Baltimore-Washington
International Airport
map page 71

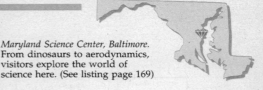

Maryland Science Center, Baltimore. From dinosaurs to aerodynamics, visitors explore the world of science here. (See listing page 169)

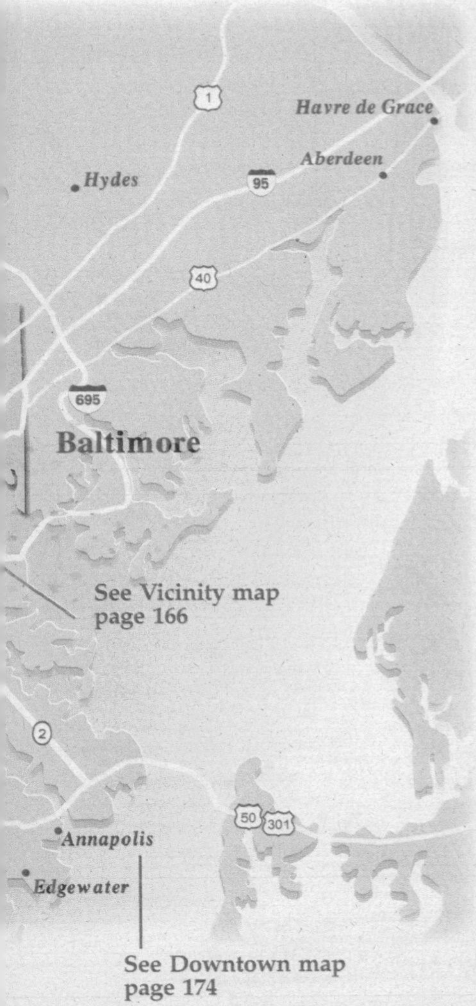

National Aquarium in Baltimore This skeleton of a fin whale hovers in the "Rays: Wings in the Waters" exhibit. (See listing page 169)

See Vicinity map page 166

See Downtown map page 174

Pride of Baltimore Sailing Ship. This replica of an 1812 Baltimore schooner is the city's "Ambassador to the World."

Havre de Grace

Aberdeen

Hydes

Baltimore

Annapolis

Edgewater

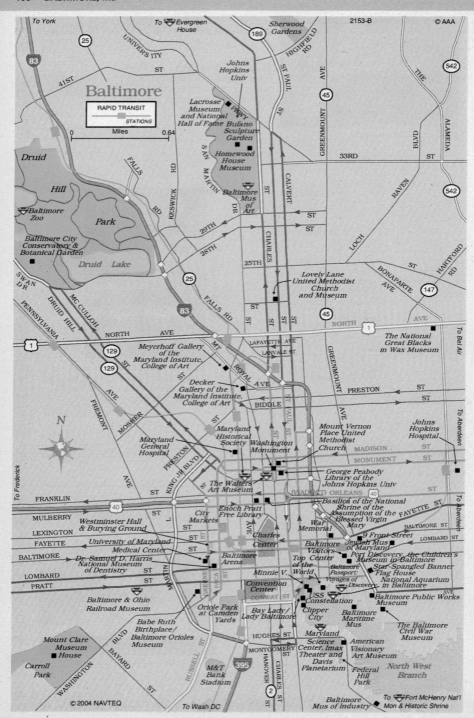

Baltimore

RAPID TRANSIT
STATIONS
Miles
0   0.64

SAVE **BALTIMORE MUSEUM OF INDUSTRY** is at 1415 Key Hwy. Housed in an 1865 oyster cannery, the museum features exhibits about the social and economic history of Baltimore's industries. Re-creations include a print shop, a garment loft, a late 19th-century machine shop and a cannery. Visitors are allowed to operate several machines and can tour the 1906 steam tug *Baltimore*, which was a common sight on the city waterfront for more than 50 years.

Allow 1 hour minimum. Mon.-Sat. 10-4, Sun. 11-4; closed Thanksgiving and Dec. 24-25. Admission $10; over 59 and ages 4-17, $5. Phone (410) 727-4808.

GEM **SAVE** **BALTIMORE PASSPORT: VOYAGES OF DISCOVERY** is in the Pier 4 Bldg. at 621 E. Pratt St. This attraction uses motion simulators, wide projection screens and special effects to create a multi-sensory theater experience that is also educational. Two programs are currently available: Time Elevator America, a trip through history that portrays events during the American Revolution and the Civil War, and The Oceanarium, a deep sea voyage highlighting such sights as sharks, coral reefs and underwater caverns.

Allow 1 hour minimum. Open daily at 10; closing times vary. Closed Thanksgiving and Dec. 25. Admission $13.50; over 59 and military with ID $12.50; ages 3-12, $9.25. Premium seating is available at an additional cost. Under 40 inches tall must use theater's motionless seats. Under age 3 are not permitted. AX, CB, DC, DS, JC, MC, VI. Phone (410) 468-0700.

BALTIMORE PUBLIC WORKS MUSEUM is off E. Falls Ave. at 751 Eastern Ave. Located on the eastern edge of the inner harbor, the museum provides a behind-the-scenes and even under-the-scenes glimpse of how a large city provides necessary utility services to its citizens. Its collection of more than 2,000 items includes photographs, wooden water pipes from the early 19th century and water meters. The museum is in an architecturally striking 1912 sewage pumping station. Tues.-Sun. 10-4; closed major holidays. Admission $2.50; over 54 and ages 6-17, $2. Phone (410) 396-5565.

BALTIMORE ZOO—see Druid Hill Park p. 168.

BASILICA OF THE NATIONAL SHRINE OF THE ASSUMPTION OF THE BLESSED VIRGIN MARY is at Cathedral and Mulberry sts. Planned by Bishop John Carroll and designed by architect Benjamin Henry Latrobe, the basilica was dedicated in 1821, making it the first Roman Catholic Cathedral built in the United States. Among the highlights are the south tower's clock and bells, which sound the "Angelus" daily at 6 a.m., noon and 6 p.m.

Church open daily 7-5. Free guided 1-hour tours. depart Sun. around noon (following the 10:45 service), Mon.-Sat. by appointment. Free. Phone (410) 727-3564.

CHARLES CENTER, comprising several blocks around Charles and Lombard sts., adjoins the Baltimore Arena. Parks and plazas are interspersed with tall office and apartment buildings.

CITY MARKETS are Belair, at Gay and Fayette sts.; Broadway, at Broadway and Fleet sts.; Cross Street, at Charles and Cross sts.; Hollins, at Hollins and Arlington sts.; Lafayette, at Pennsylvania and Laurens sts.; Lexington, at Lexington and Eutaw sts.; and Northeast, at Monument and Chester sts. These large indoor areas are crowded with stalls from which vendors offer a variety of fresh meats, produce, baked goods and seafood.

Lexington and Broadway were founded in the late 18th century; the others began in the mid-19th century. Lexington Market open Mon.-Sat. 8:30-6; Hollins Market open Tues.-Sat. 7-6; all others open Mon.-Sat. 7-6. Free. Phone (410) 685-6169 for Lexington Market, or (410) 276-9498 for all others.

CYLBURN ARBORETUM, 4915 Greenspring Ave., is 207 acres and contains marked trails; a garden of the senses for the physically impaired; an all-American garden; an herb garden; the Heritage Rose Garden, which features species more than 100 years old; and a formal garden. Grounds daily dawn-dusk. Free. Phone (410) 396-0180.

DECKER AND MEYERHOFF GALLERIES OF THE MARYLAND INSTITUTE, COLLEGE OF ART, are in the Fox Building on Mount Royal Ave. and at Mount Royal Station, Cathedral St. and Mount Royal Ave. Rotating exhibits feature works by students, faculty and national and international artists. Mon.-Sat. 10-5, Sun. noon-5. Summer hours may vary; phone ahead. Free. Phone (410) 225-2280.

DR. SAMUEL D. HARRIS NATIONAL MUSEUM OF DENTISTRY, an affiliate of the Smithsonian Institution, is at 31 S. Greene St. on the University of

DID YOU KNOW

Including islands, the shoreline of Maryland is 4,431 miles long.

Maryland Baltimore campus. Visitors can learn about the history of oral health while viewing creatively presented exhibits and artifacts, including George Washington's lower denture and instruments used to treat Queen Victoria. Allow 1 hour minimum. Wed.-Sat. 10-4, Sun. 1-4; closed major holidays. Admission $4.50, over 59 and students with ID $2.50, under 6 free. AX, MC, VI. Phone (410) 706-0600.

DRUID HILL PARK, n.w. section of the city on Druid Park Lake Dr., is reached via Pennsylvania Ave., Eutaw Pl. or Mount Royal Terr. This 744-acre park is one of the country's largest natural city parks and dates from 1688. Daily dawn-dusk. Free. Phone (410) 396-7900.

Baltimore City Conservatory and Botanical Garden, near the entrance of Druid Hill Park, was built in 1888. The conservatory is known locally as "The Palm House" because of its collection of tropical plants. The greenhouses also contain a display of desert plants. A 1-acre garden east of the building has flowering bulbs in April and May and annuals June through October. In addition, chrysanthemums are displayed in November, poinsettias in December and spring flowers at Easter. Thurs.-Sun. 10-3; closed holidays. Free. Phone (410) 396-0180 to confirm schedule.

Baltimore Zoo, within the park, comprises 161 acres, with more than 2,200 birds, mammals and reptiles and a large breeding colony of African black-footed penguins. Highlights include the African Safari Trail and the African Watering Hole with white rhinoceroses and zebras. The Keeper Encounter allows visitors to meet the people who care for the animals. The 8-acre children's zoo features interactive exhibits and a petting farm. The Siberian Summit is a 24-foot climbing wall available for scaling.

Picnicking is permitted. Food is available. Mon.-Fri. 10-4, Sat.-Sun. 10-7, Memorial Day-Labor Day; daily 10-4, rest of year. Closed 1 day in June for a fund-raiser and Dec. 25. Admission $12; over 64, $10; ages 2-11, $8. Reptile House $1. Phone (410) 366-5466.

ENOCH PRATT FREE LIBRARY, 400 Cathedral St. between Franklin and Mulberry sts., is the city's principal public library. Built in a 1930s Art Deco design, the library has permanent displays about Edgar Allan Poe and H.L. Mencken. Guided tours are available by appointment. Mon.-Wed. 10-8, Thurs. 10-5:30, Fri.-Sat. 10-5. Hours may vary; phone ahead. Phone (410) 396-5500.

EVERGREEN HOUSE is at 4545 N. Charles St., 1.5 blks. n. of Cold Spring Ln. This 1850s, 48-room Italianate mansion with classical revival additions and Corinthian columns was home to two generations of discriminating collectors. Among the furnishings are Chinese export porcelains, Tiffany windows and

chandeliers, post-impressionist paintings and sculptures, and 17th-century Belgian tapestries. The libraries contain prints, manuscripts, rare books and other artifacts from around the world. The 1923 theater was created by Leon Bakst, renowned for his sets for Ballet Russes.

Allow 1 hour, 30 minutes minimum. Guided 1-hour tours depart on the hour Mon.-Fri. 10-3, Sat.-Sun. 1-4. Closed Jan. 1, July 4, Memorial Day, Labor Day, Thanksgiving and Dec. 25. Last tour begins at 3. Hours may vary; phone ahead. Fee $6; over 64, $5; students with ID $3. Phone (410) 516-0341.

FEDERAL HILL PARK, Battery St. and Key Hwy., was the site of a Civil War fort. It provides a view of the harbor and city skyline.

 FORT McHENRY NATIONAL MONUMENT AND HISTORIC SHRINE— *see place listing in the Vicinity section p. 178.*

GEORGE PEABODY LIBRARY OF THE JOHNS HOPKINS UNIVERSITY, 17 E. Mount Vernon Pl., has five ornate iron balconies surrounding a marble atrium. Tues.-Fri. 9-5, Sat. 9-1. Free. Phone (410) 659-8179.

HAMPTON NATIONAL HISTORIC SITE— *see Towson in the Vicinity section p. 179.*

[SAVE] **JEWISH MUSEUM OF MARYLAND,** 15 Lloyd St., encompasses the 1845 Lloyd Street Synagogue and the 1876 B'nai Israel Synagogue. The museum displays both permanent and changing exhibits about local and worldwide Jewish art and history. The society maintains a public collection of 150,000 documents, photographs and objects related to the 300-year history of Jewry in Maryland.

Allow 1 hour minimum. Museum open Tues.-Thurs. and Sun. noon-4. Free guided tours are available at 1 and 2:30 and by appointment. Library by appointment. Closed holidays. Admission $8; students with ID $4; under 12, $3. Phone (410) 732-6400 or (877) 376-7190.

JOHNS HOPKINS UNIVERSITY, off N. Charles St., is a small, private liberal arts university founded in 1876 as a graduate research institution. Today the university boasts one of the finest medical schools in the country. The 140-acre campus originally was the estate of Charles Carroll Jr., son of Charles Carroll, one of the signers of the Declaration of Independence. Tours of the campus can be arranged at the Admissions Office, 140 Garland Hall. Tours depart Mon.-Fri. at 10 and 1; a tour occasionally is offered Sat. Hours may vary; phone ahead. Free. Phone (410) 516-8171.

Bufano Sculpture Garden, in Dunning Park behind Mudd Hall, is a wooded area with a paved pathway meandering among 11 sculptures of animals by Beniamino Bufano. Daily 24 hours. Free.

Homewood House Museum, 3400 N. Charles St., was an 1801 wedding gift to Charles Carroll Jr.

from his father. The restored house retains its early 19th-century splendor. Pieces originally owned by the Carroll family are part of the furnishings. Tues.-Sat. 11-4, Sun. noon-4. Last tour begins 30 minutes before closing. Admission $6; over 59, $5; students with ID and ages 6-17, $3. Phone (410) 516-5589.

LACROSSE MUSEUM AND NATIONAL HALL OF FAME, 113 W. University Pkwy., depicts the history of this game through photographs and art, uniforms, equipment, trophies, memorabilia and documentaries that highlight the evolution of the game from the days of the American Indians to the present. Allow 30 minutes minimum. Mon.-Fri. 10-3, June-Jan.; Tues.-Sat. 10-3, rest of year. Closed holidays. Admission $3; ages 5-15, $2. Phone (410) 235-6882.

LOVELY LANE UNITED METHODIST CHURCH AND MUSEUM, 2200 Saint Paul St., was designed by noted architect Stanford White in 1884; White is best known for the design of the Washington Arch in New York City. The museum exhibits Methodist historical materials. Church open Mon.-Fri. 9-3. Museum open Thurs.-Fri. 10-4. Free guided tours of the church are available Sun. at 11, July-Aug.; Sun. at noon, rest of year. Donations. Phone (410) 889-1512 for the church, or (410) 889-4458 for the museum.

MARYLAND HISTORICAL SOCIETY is at 201 W. Monument St. at Park Ave. The society maintains the Museum and Library of Maryland History, which includes the period rooms of the 19th-century Enoch Pratt mansion, and the Darnall Young People's Museum. Housed in the history museum is Francis Scott Key's original manuscript of "The Star-Spangled Banner" and a collection of portraits by American artists, including Benjamin Henry Latrobe, Gilbert Stuart and Thomas Sully. An extensive collection of 19th-century silver pieces includes works by Samuel Kirk.

The museum also exhibits furniture dating 1720-1950 and rare 18th-century costumes and accessories, including Revolutionary War uniforms. In the Darnall Young People's Museum, dioramas trace the history of Maryland, and there is a "touch-table" of Maryland artifacts.

Museums open Wed.-Fri. 10-5, Sat. 9-5, Sun. 11-5. Library open Wed.-Sat. 10-4:30. Museums and library closed holidays. Museum admission $8; over 59 and ages 13-17, $6; ages 3-12, $4. Library admission $6; senior citizens and students with ID $4. Phone (410) 685-3750.

MARYLAND SCIENCE CENTER, IMAX THEATER AND DAVIS PLANETARIUM, 601 Light St. at the Inner Harbor, has live science demonstrations and three floors of hands-on exhibits, including a science arcade and displays related to the Hubble Space Telescope, Earth science, and the human body. The Kids Room is for children under 8.

Permanent exhibits focus on the environment, dinosaurs, and outer space. Multimedia presentations are offered in Davis Planetarium. An IMAX theater with a five-story screen gives visitors a larger-than-life perspective, often in 3-D, on a variety of subjects.

Allow 1 hour, 30 minutes minimum. Sun.-Wed. 10-6, Thurs.-Sat. 10-8, Memorial Day-Labor Day; Tues.-Fri. 10-5, Sat. 10-6, Sun. 11-5, rest of year. The IMAX Theater is open after center hours for evening shows. Closed Thanksgiving and Dec. 25. Admission $14; over 59, $13; under 13, $9.50. IMAX admission $8. Combination admissions also available. AX, MC, VI. Phone (410) 685-5225, or TTY (410) 962-0223.

[SAVE] **MOUNT CLARE MUSEUM HOUSE** is in Carroll Park at 1500 Washington Blvd. at Monroe St. The only pre-Revolutionary mansion within the city limits, this 1760 Georgian-style house was the home of Charles Carroll, barrister and Revolutionary patriot. Originally part of an 800-acre plantation, the estate once contained wheat fields, a gristmill, an ironworks, brick kilns, racing stables, a shipyard and terraced gardens. More than 85 percent of the period furnishings are Carroll family pieces.

Allow 1 hour minimum. Tues.-Sat. 10-4; closed holidays. Guided tours are given on the hour. Last tour begins 1 hour before closing. Admission $6; over 54, $5; ages 5-18, $4. Phone (410) 837-3262.

MOUNT VERNON PLACE UNITED METHODIST CHURCH is at 10 E. Mount Vernon Pl., corner of N. Charles St. This 1874 green serpentine and gray stone church is on the site where Francis Scott Key died in 1843. The ornately carved interior features an organ with 3,827 pipes, and a labyrinth winding two-thirds of a mile. Guided tours are available. Mon.-Thurs. 9-2:30, Fri. 9-noon; closed holidays. Donations. Phone (410) 685-5290.

NATIONAL AQUARIUM IN BALTIMORE, 501 E. Pratt St., is on Piers 3 and 4 in Baltimore's Inner Harbor. This aquarium's seven-story main structure displays a collection of 11,500 aquatic animals representing more than 600 species from around the world.

Other aquatic exhibits include a 335,000-gallon Atlantic Coral Reef featuring hundreds of tropical reef fish; the Open Ocean, home to four species of sharks; a steamy South American rain forest enclosed by a pyramid of glass; and one of the world's largest poison-dart frog collections. The Marine Mammal Pavilion includes an educational arcade and an interactive touch pool called Children's Discovery Cove. The centerpiece of the pavilion, a 1.2 million-gallon Atlantic bottlenose dolphin habitat, offers daily marine mammal presentations.

Note: Lines form early and there often is a long wait outside, so the best time to visit is before 11. Baby strollers must be checked, but backpack baby carriers are provided. Allow 2 hours, 30 minutes minimum. Tickets sold Mon.-Thurs. 9-6, Fri.-Sun.

9-8, July-Aug.; Sat.-Thurs. 9-5, Fri. 9-8, Mar.-June and Sept.-Oct.; Sat.-Thurs. 10-5, Fri. 10-8, rest of year. The aquarium remains open 2 hours after the last ticket is sold. Closed Thanksgiving and Dec. 25. Admission $17.50; over 59, $14.50; ages 3-11, $9.50. AX, DS, MC, VI. Phone (410) 576-3800, or TTY (410) 625-0720.

THE NATIONAL GREAT BLACKS IN WAX MUSEUM, 1601 E. North Ave., is committed to the study and preservation of African-American history. More than 100 life-size wax figures portray people who had significant impact on events in ancient Africa, the Middle Passage, the Civil War, Reconstruction, the Harlem Renaissance and the modern civil rights movement. A 24-foot-by-30-foot replica of a slave ship also is featured.

Guided tours, audiotaped tours, and sign language tours by reservation are available. Allow 30 minutes minimum. Tues.-Sat. 9-6, Sun. noon-6, Jan. 15-Oct. 14 (also Mon. 9-6 in Feb. and July-Aug.); Tues.-Sat. 9-5, Sun. noon-5, rest of year. Closed most federal holidays. Admission $6.80; over 54 and college students with ID $6.30; ages 12-17, $4.80; ages 2-11, $4.55. AX, MC, VI. Phone (410) 563-3404.

PORT DISCOVERY, THE CHILDREN'S MUSEUM IN BALTIMORE is at 35 Market Pl. in Baltimore's Inner Harbor. Educational and interactive exhibits designed for ages 6-12 include time traveling back to ancient Egypt, collecting clues and solving mysteries, climbing around a three-story urban tree house, competing in a television game show and making arts and crafts. *HiFlyer,* a giant helium-filled tethered balloon, takes visitors 450 feet above Baltimore. A library contains resource books.

Food is available. Allow 1 hour, 30 minutes minimum. Mon.-Sat. 10-5 (also Fri. 5-8, July-Aug.), Sun. noon-5, Memorial Day-Labor Day; Tues.-Fri. 9:30-5:30, Sun. noon-5, Oct. 1-day before Memorial Day; Fri. 9:30-4:30, Sat. 10-5, Sun. noon-5, rest of year. Admission $11; ages 3-12, $8.50. AX, MC, VI. Phone (410) 727-8120, or (410) 949-2359 for HiFlyer.

SHERWOOD GARDENS, Stratford Rd. e. of St. Paul St., comprises 6 acres of azaleas, English boxwoods, flowering cherries, dogwoods, magnolias, wisterias and other plants, bordered and interspersed with 80,000 tulips. The peak season is late April to early May. Daily dawn-dusk. Free. Phone (410) 785-0444.

STAR-SPANGLED BANNER FLAG HOUSE, off Albemarle St. at 844 E. Pratt St., was the home of Mary Pickersgill, who made the 15-star and 15-stripe American flag that inspired Francis Scott Key to write "The Star-Spangled Banner." The flag waved above Fort McHenry during its bombardment in 1814.

The 1793 house, which contains Federal-period furniture and a collection of Early American art, may be seen by guided tour. The museum next door commemorates the War of 1812. Guided 40-minute tours Tues.-Sat. 10-3:15. Tour $6; over 64, $5; ages 4-18 and students and military with ID $4. Museum free with house admission. Phone (410) 837-1793.

TOP OF THE WORLD, on the 27th floor of the World Trade Center in Inner Harbor at 401 E. Pratt St., offers a panoramic view of the city and harbor. Exhibits highlight Baltimore's history. Allow 30 minutes minimum. Daily 10-6 (also Sat. 6-8 p.m.), Memorial Day weekend-Labor Day; Wed.-Sun. 10-6, rest of year. Closed Jan. 1, Thanksgiving and Dec. 25. Admission $5; over 59 and military with ID $4; ages 3-12, $3. Phone (410) 837-8439.

USS *CONSTELLATION,* just s. of downtown on Pier 1 at 301 E. Pratt St., is the last all-sail warship built by the U.S. Navy and the only Civil War-era vessel still afloat. Artifacts displayed include a navy cutlass, leg irons and navigation instruments, while hands-on activities include setting sails and turning the capstan. A replica cannon is fired twice daily (weather permitting).

Allow 30 minutes minimum. Daily 10-6, May 1-Oct. 14; 10-4, rest of year. Closed Jan. 1, Thanksgiving and Dec. 25. Hours may vary; phone ahead. Admission $6.50; over 59, $5; ages 6-14, $3.50. Phone (410) 539-1797.

THE WALTERS ART MUSEUM is off Centre St. at 600 N. Charles St. This municipally-owned gallery houses more than 30,000 works of art spanning 55 centuries. Decorative art collections include ceramics, enamels, Fabergé eggs, tapestries and jewelry. Collections include ancient art, medieval art, Renaissance and post-Renaissance sculptures and decorative arts, old masters paintings, 19th-century paintings and sculptures, Asian art, illuminated manuscripts and arms and armor.

Food is available. Wed.-Sun. 10-5 (also first Thurs. of month 5-8); closed Jan. 1, July 4, Thanksgiving and Dec. 24-25. Admission $8; over 64, $6; ages 18-25 and students with ID $5; under 18 free; free to all Sat. 10-1 and all day first Thurs. Phone (410) 547-9000.

WAR MEMORIAL overlooks Memorial Plaza and Gay and E. Fayette sts. This Greek-style memorial honors Maryland citizens killed in World War I. Daily 24 hours. Free.

WASHINGTON MONUMENT, in Mount Vernon Sq. at jct. W. Pratt and N. Charles sts., is dedicated to the nation's first president. A 228-step spiral stairway leads to the top of the monument where four observation windows provide a panorama of the city. A 30-ton statue of George Washington sits atop the monument. No elevators are available. Allow 30 minutes minimum. Tues.-Sun. 10-4; closed holidays. Phone to verify schedule. Admission $1. Phone (410) 396-0929.

WESTMINSTER HALL AND BURYING GROUND, W. Fayette and Greene sts., is the cemetery of the Westminster Presbyterian Church. Buried here are Edgar Allan Poe, James McHenry—U.S. Secretary of War 1797-1800—and a number of other historical figures. Churchyard and catacomb tours are available.

Cemetery open daily 8-dusk; closed holidays. Guided churchyard and catacomb tours Fri. at 6:30 p.m., Sat. at 10 a.m., first and third weekends of each month Apr.-Nov. Church and grounds free. Tours $5; over 59 and under 13, $3. Reservations are required for guided tours. Phone (410) 706-2072.

What To Do

Sightseeing

Several tour companies offer guides who will accompany you on specialized tours focusing on Baltimore historical sites, architecture or art.

Tour companies include Baltimore Shuttle, (410) 254-8687; City Hall Tours, (410) 837-5424; Convention Management Services Ltd., (410) 377-8181; Presenting Baltimore Inc., (410) 539-1344; Rent a Tour, (410) 653-2998; and Short Walk With History, (410) 837-5424.

Boat Tours

Visitors who would rather not walk can travel between attractions at the Inner Harbor aboard water taxis that run approximately every 15 minutes in season, about every 45 minutes the rest of the year. The taxis operate Mon.-Thurs. 10 a.m.-11 p.m., Fri.-Sat. 10 a.m.-midnight and Sun. 10-9, May 1-Labor Day; Mon.-Thurs. 11-9, Fri. 11 a.m.-midnight, Sat. 10 a.m.-midnight and Sun. 10-9 in Apr. and day after Labor day-Oct. 31; daily 11-6, rest of year. Unlimited 1-day pass $6; under 11, $3.

Stops include the Maryland Science Center, IMAX Theater and Davis Planetarium; the National Aquarium in Baltimore *(see attraction listings)*; Harborplace; Little Italy; the Rusty Scupper restaurant; the Pier 6 Concert Pavilion; and piers 5 and 6. Boats also travel to Fells Point and Canton. Phone (410) 563-3901 or (800) 658-8947.

BAY LADY/LADY BALTIMORE, 301 Light St., offers narrated 2-hour lunch tours, 3-hour dinner cruises and a 3-hour Sunday brunch cruise of Baltimore's Inner Harbor and the Chesapeake Bay. Moonlight and theme cruises also are available. Lunch cruise daily at noon. Lunch cruise fare Mon.-Sat. $31.50 (senior citizens $25.50), Sun. $38.95. Reservations are recommended. AX, DS, MC, VI. Phone (410) 727-3113 or (800) 695-2628.

CLIPPER CITY, at the Inner Harbor at the Fingers Piers between the Science Center and Light Street Pavilion, is a replica of an 1854 topsail schooner. Two- and 3-hour trips are offered. Two-hour cruises depart Mon.-Thurs. at 2 and 6, Fri. at 2 and 8, Sat. at noon, 3 and 8, Sun. at 11 (brunch), 3 and 6, mid-Apr. to mid-Oct. Three-hour cruises depart Fri.-Sat. at 8 p.m., and some Sun. at 11 (brunch), mid-Apr. to mid-Oct. Departure times may vary; phone ahead.

Two-hour trip $20; under 10, $5. Three-hour trip $30. Brunch trip $45; under 10, $22.50. Reservations are recommended. AX, MC, VI. Phone (410) 539-6277.

MINNIE V. departs from Harborplace Amphitheatre between the Pratt and Light Street pavilions. This traditional skipjack oyster sailing boat offers 90-minute, history-oriented, narrated tours of Baltimore Harbor, focusing on the history of skipjacks and oystering in the Chesapeake Bay. During the week she is a floating classroom for students.

Cruises depart Sat.-Sun. and holidays at 10:30, 1, 3 and 5, May-Sept. (weather permitting). Fare $15; senior citizens, $12; under 12, $4; under 5 free. Phone (410) 685-0295 to verify schedule.

Walking Tours

Baltimore's old neighborhoods add much to the city's charm. A pleasant day can be spent visiting the historic areas of Federal Hill, Fells Point and Mount Vernon Place, or such ethnic neighborhoods as Little Italy.

"Urban homesteading" got its start in Baltimore's old neighborhoods. Under this program, an old house was purchased for as little as $1 with the understanding that the resident would restore or remodel it within a certain number of years. The eye-catching results can be seen in the Otterbein area on Conway

Street near Sharp Street and in the Stirling Street section off the 1000 block of Monument Street.

Literature, maps and brochures for a walking tour of the city may be obtained from the Baltimore Visitor Information Center, 451 Light St.; phone (410) 837-7026 or (877) 225-8466. In addition, tour information is available at the information kiosks on the west shore promenade of the Inner Harbor and at the Penn Central Railroad Station.

Sports and Recreation

Baseball attracts faithful fans in Baltimore; the Orioles regularly draw big crowds to Oriole Park at Camden Yards; phone (410) 685-9800.

Named for Edgar Allan Poe's "The Raven," National **Football** League Super Bowl XXXV champions Baltimore Ravens compete for gridiron glory at M&T Bank Stadium; phone (410) 261-7283.

The Baltimore Blast, (410) 732-5278, play **indoor soccer** at Baltimore Arena. Some of the nation's top **lacrosse** players make up Baltimore's many NCAA teams, including the Johns Hopkins' Blue Jays, who compete at Homewood Field, Charles Street and University Parkway; phone (410) 235-6882. The Baltimore Bayhawks, one of Major League Lacrosse's newest teams, play outdoor lacrosse at Johnny Unitas Stadium; phone (866) 994-2957.

Horse racing is popular, and Pimlico Race Course has meets September through October; phone (410) 542-9400. The second race of the Triple Crown, The Preakness Stakes, is held at Pimlico the third weekend in May. The racetracks at Laurel and Timonium are an easy drive from the city.

Note: Policies concerning admittance of children to pari-mutuel betting facilities vary. Phone for information.

Golf can be played at Carroll Park, Monroe Street and Washington Boulevard; Clifton Park, Harford Road and St. Lo Drive; Forest Park Golf Course, 2900 Hillsdale at Forest Park Avenue; Mount Pleasant Golf Course, 6001 Hillen Rd.; and Pine Ridge Golf Course, 2001 Dulaney Valley Road in Lutherville.

Tennis players can find public courts at Clifton, Druid Hill and Patterson parks. In the winter **ice-skating** takes place at Patterson Park and at Inner Harbor's Rash Field; phone Baltimore Recreation Department (410) 396-7900.

Boating is enjoyed at the Inner Harbor, Pratt and Light streets, and **fishing** is permitted at Loch Raven Reservoir, the city's principal water source.

Biking enthusiasts have their choice of bicycle trails in Clifton, Herring Run and Patterson parks.

Shopping

In the heart of Baltimore's revitalized financial and office district, Harborplace and The Gallery, at the corner of Light and Pratt streets overlooking the Inner Harbor, features national retailers and a variety of cafes and restaurants divided among three buildings: two glass-enclosed pavilions and, connected via an overhead skywalk, the Gallery, which offers three floors of shopping. A fourth floor consists of restaurants and shops.

A visit to one of the city's indoor food markets can be a fascinating experience. These markets are well-preserved monuments of an older Baltimore and contain aisle after aisle of stalls in which vendors offer wares ranging from meats and produce to fresh seafood from the bay. Some of these markets have served their neighborhoods since the city's earliest days.

Lexington Market, at 400 W. Lexington St., the largest city-operated market since 1782, is open Mon.-Sat. 8:30-6. The Arcade, a contemporary addition, offers everything from fresh produce to local seafood as well as two restaurants and a central stage area for entertainment and community use. **Note:** It is advisable to visit the market only during daylight hours. Leave wallets and handbags in a safe place and travel with a partner. A renovation and revitalization of downtown Baltimore's Westside is currently underway.

Small shops abound in Baltimore. Galleries and restaurants now occupy the elegant houses that long distinguished Charles Street. Lexington Mall, on Lexington Street between Liberty and Howard streets, is a pedestrian mall lined with a variety of establishments.

Those in search of the unusual may want to visit Antique Row in the 700 and 800 blocks of Howard Street. Both blocks have rows of shops and galleries specializing in antiques, art and unusual gifts and collectibles. Mount Washington Village, on Kelly and Sulgrave avenues, encompasses specialty shops and boutiques within a village setting.

Cross Keys Village is a complex of shops and restaurants surrounding a parklike square on Falls Road between Northern Parkway and Cold Spring Lane. The Rotunda, north of downtown at 711 W. 40th St. near Johns Hopkins University, caters to college students and others with its 21 specialty shops.

For something different, the Historic Savage Mill in nearby Savage is an 1820s textile mill turned specialty marketplace where shoppers can find some 50 shops, eateries and art galleries in restored buildings.

Several regional malls are within the metropolitan area. One of the largest, White Marsh Mall, just north of the city off I-95 at exit 67, has a number of major stores, including JCPenney, Macy's and Sears.

Bargain hunters can find plenty of shopping territory at Arundel Mills, 10 miles south of Baltimore off I-95 exit 43 in Hanover via SR 100 E. Included in the complex is Bass Pro Shops Outdoor World, featuring wildlife exhibits and sporting demonstrations.

Other large malls include Eastpoint, I-695 exit 38W; Marley Station, via I-97 exit 14 and SR 100 exit 16 to 7900 Ritchie Hwy. (SR 2); Owings Mills,

I-795 and Owings Mills Boulevard; Security Square, I-695 exit 17 to 6901 Security Blvd.; Towsontown Centre, 825 Dulaney Valley Rd.; and Westview, I-695 exit 15B.

Theater and Concerts

The pleasures of good music can be found in the concerts, ballets and other musical programs presented by the Baltimore Symphony Orchestra. The orchestra performs throughout the season at Joseph Meyerhoff Symphony Hall, 1212 Cathedral St.; phone (410) 783-8100. The home of the Baltimore Opera Company is Lyric Opera House, a replica of Germany's Leipzig Music Hall, 140 W. Mount Royal Ave.; phone (410) 727-6000.

Throughout the summer and early fall, Pier 6 Concert Pavilion in the Inner Harbor presents R&B, rock and country acts featuring numerous individual artists; phone (410) 625-3100.

Hopkins Plaza offers free concerts once a month May through September. Concerts—some of which are free—are regularly scheduled at the acoustically superb Concert Hall of the Peabody Conservatory of Music, 21 E. Mount Vernon Pl.; phone (410) 659-8124. Baltimore Arena is the scene of cultural and sporting events; phone (410) 347-2000.

Baltimore's major regional theater is Center Stage, 700 N. Calvert St., which produces a variety of contemporary and classic plays; phone (410) 332-0033 or TTY (410) 332-4240. Drama devotees can enjoy touring Broadway shows as well as the classics at Morris Mechanic Theatre, Charles and Baltimore streets; phone (410) 625-4200 for schedule information. Other dramatic offerings are staged at the theaters of the Arena Players, 801 McCulloch St., (410) 728-6500, and the Vagabond Players, 806 S. Broadway, (410) 563-9135.

The Theater Project, 45 W. Preston St., is the city's center for avant-garde productions; phone (410) 752-8558. The Cockpit in Court Summer Theatre of Essex Campus of the Community College of Baltimore County presents musicals, dramas and comedies throughout the summer; phone (410) 780-6369.

The Children's Theatre Association, 100 W. 22nd St., offers lighthearted dramas, classic children's literature and fairy tales; phone (410) 366-6403. Several dinner theaters are in and around the city. For schedules of current theatrical and musical offerings check the local newspapers.

Special Events

Baltimore's biggest event, The Preakness Celebration, takes place during May and culminates in the running of The Preakness Stakes at Pimlico Race Course. The celebration includes a parade, hot air balloon race and concerts.

Many of Baltimore's celebrations and festivals take place in the Inner Harbor or in the surrounding parks and plazas. The Inner Harbor also is the site of the Showcase of Nations during which colorful ethnic festivals are held each weekend from June to October; each honors a different group of settlers.

Nearby Timonium hosts the Maryland State Fair in late August. The Fells Point Fun Festival attracts crowds to Baltimore's harbor area in early October. The Baltimore Book Festival is held in mid-September downtown at Mount Vernon Place. The Recreational Vehicle Show, also held in Timonium, is in mid-February.

From late April through mid-May, the Maryland House and Garden Pilgrimage opens homes and gardens in the Baltimore area and around the state for public viewing. Phone (410) 821-6933.

The Baltimore Vicinity

ABERDEEN (B-7) pop. 13,842

Aberdeen is the site of the 75,000-acre Aberdeen Proving Ground, established in 1917 to develop and test ordnance under simulated combat conditions. Outdoor displays about the federal reservation include foreign and U.S. artillery and tanks. Visitor information is available at the main gate on SR 22.

Discover Harford County Tourism Council—Aberdeen: 3 W. Bel Air Ave., Aberdeen, MD 21001; phone (410) 575-7278.

[SAVE] **RIPKEN MUSEUM,** 3 W. Bel Air Ave., displays photographs and memorabilia of baseball idol Cal Ripken Jr. and the Ripken family. **Note:** The museum is temporarily closed pending a move to a new location at Ripken Stadium. Phone ahead to confirm opening date, schedule and admission. Allow 30 minutes minimum. Mon.-Fri. 11-3, Sat. 11-4, Sun.

noon-3:30, June 1-Labor Day; Fri. and Mon. 11-3, Sat. 11-4, Sun. noon-3:30, rest of year. Closed July 4 and Dec. 25. Schedule may vary; phone ahead. Admission $3; over 61, $2; ages 6-18, $1. AX, DS, MC, VI. Phone (410) 273-2525 to verify schedule.

U.S. ARMY ORDNANCE MUSEUM is on Aberdeen Proving Ground 2.7 mi. s. of jct. US 40 and SR 22 on SR 715. The required base day pass is issued only at the Maryland Ave. gate on SR 715. This indoor/outdoor museum contains a collection of small arms, artillery and tanks from most major nations. Displays trace the development of 20th-century weaponry. Many successful and failed prototypes can be seen on the grounds. A driver's license and vehicle registration are required to obtain the base visitor day pass. Daily 9-4:45; closed holidays except Armed Forces Day, Memorial Day, July 4 and Nov. 11. Free. Phone (410) 278-3602 or (410) 278-2396.

ANNAPOLIS (F-4) pop. 35,838, elev. 16'

Annapolis' roots hark back to 1649 when a group of Puritan families from Virginia established the settlement of Providence on the north bank of the Severn River. Within a year a new county was established, named Annarundell after the wife of Cecil Calvert, second Lord Baltimore. By 1684 Anne Arundel Town was laid out on 100 acres across the Severn from Providence. In 1694 the capital was moved to Anne Arundel Town, later renamed Annapolis.

The charter of 1708 makes Annapolis one of the oldest cities in the country. In 1783 and 1784 Congress assembled in Annapolis, making it the first peacetime capital of the United States.

The U.S. Naval Academy was established in Annapolis at the Army's Fort Severn in 1845. Attention focuses on the academy and city in late May during Commissioning Week, when members of the graduating class become naval officers.

In addition to its identity as a Navy center, Annapolis is distinguished by its architecture—the city has the highest concentration of Georgian-style buildings in the nation, including the homes of all four Maryland signers of the declaration of Independence. Altogether, 1,300 buildings from 15 different architectural styles predate 1900, earning Annapolis the title "A museum without walls."

The many public and private Colonial buildings in Annapolis exemplify the life and architecture of the pre-Revolutionary period. An architectural anomaly is the executive residence, Government House, at State Circle and School Street; it was built in the late 1860s in the French Second Empire style, then one side was remodeled in the 1930s in the Georgian revival style. Guided tours of the house are offered by appointment; phone (410) 974-3531.

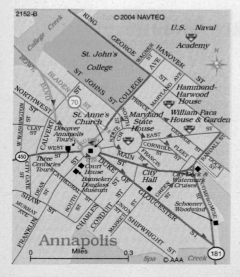

The waterfront, called the City Dock, is one of the best preserved in the country. Historically this is the city's front door, as Annapolis was once an important seaport for trade with Great Britain, the West Indies and West Africa. Today, recreational boaters and sailing schools have made the city a major center for regattas, services and charters.

A variety of tours allows visitors to explore the city and its environs. Tours originate at the Annapolis Visitor Center, 26 West St., and April through September at the information booth at the City Dock; phone (410) 280-0445 or (800) 394-5717.

"Historic Annapolis Walk with Walter Cronkite" is an audio cassette walking tour taking the listener to 18 historic sites. The tour takes about 75 minutes. "Historic Annapolis African-American Heritage Audio Walking Tour" is an audio cassette detailing a 1-hour self-guiding walking tour of historic sites that include houses, museums, cemeteries and the dock where Kunta Kinte landed. At a fee of $5, player and cassette rentals for both tours are available at the Historic Annapolis Foundation Museum store at 77 Main St.; the museum is a collection of historic homes. Phone (410) 268-5576.

Street parking in downtown Annapolis can be difficult, but ample parking is available at the Navy-Marine Corps Stadium. Shuttle trolleys run frequently to and from the downtown area daily. Fare is 75c each way.

Annapolis and Anne Arundel County Conference and Visitors Bureau: 26 West St., Annapolis, MD 21401; phone (410) 280-0445 or (800) 394-5717.

Self-guiding tours: Brochures and maps for self-guiding tours as well as tour and cruise schedules are available year-round at the Annapolis Visitor Center at 26 West St., and April through September at the City Dock information booth.

Shopping areas: Downtown Annapolis has a wealth of specialty shops and boutiques concentrated around Main Street and the city dock area. Other fashionable spots include Maryland Avenue and West Annapolis. Annapolis Mall, at the intersection of SR 450 (Crownsville Road) and US 50, includes Hecht's, JCPenney and Nordstrom. Marley Station, 10 miles north on SR 2/Ritchie Highway near Severna Park, features Hecht's, Macy's and Sears department stores.

BANNEKER-DOUGLASS MUSEUM is in the Old Mount Moriah AME Church at 84 Franklin St. The museum in this 1874-75 brick former church features changing exhibits focusing on prominent Maryland African-Americans. Allow 30 minutes minimum. Tues.-Fri. 10-3, Sat. noon-4. Free. Phone (410) 216-6180.

DISCOVER ANNAPOLIS TOURS departs from the Annapolis Visitor Center at 26 West St. This 1-hour narrated minibus tour introduces passengers to 350 years of local history, architecture, folklore and trivia. The tours pass through residential areas, the waterfront, a section of the Naval Academy, and around the Maryland State House and governor's house.

Departures daily (weather permitting), Apr.-Nov. and during the Christmas-New Year's season; Sat.-Sun. in Mar.; Sat., rest of year. Phone for departure times and to confirm schedule. Closed Jan. 1, Thanksgiving and Dec. 25. Fare $14; ages 11-15, $7; ages 5-10, $3. Fares may vary; phone ahead. Phone (410) 626-6000.

HAMMOND-HARWOOD HOUSE, off King George St. at 19 Maryland Ave., is a preserved Georgian house. Built in 1774 for legislator and planter Matthias Hammond, the Palladian-style building was the last work of renowned architect William Buckland. A museum since 1938, the house features late 18th- and early 19th-century decorative art.

Allow 1 hour minimum. Guided 45-minute tours depart on the hour daily noon-4, Apr.-Oct.; by appointment rest of year. Last tour begins 1 hour before closing. Closed Jan. 1, Thanksgiving and Dec. 25. Admission $6; senior citizens and students with ID $5.50; under 11, $3. MC, VI. Phone (410) 263-4683.

HELEN AVALYNNE TAWES GARDEN is at 580 Taylor Ave. at the Tawes State Office Building across from Navy Stadium. This 5-acre botanical garden features representations of the state's natural environmental communities, from the forested mountains of western Maryland to the sand dunes of the Eastern Shore. Shallow ponds support such wildlife as bullfrogs, ducks, fish, songbirds and turtles. An arc of cultivated plants stands opposite a stately arbor. Guided tours are available by reservation.

Weekdays the garden is entered through Tawes State Office Building; weekend and holiday access is between the Court of Appeals and the Department of Natural Resources buildings. Pets are not permitted. Allow 1 hour minimum. Daily dawn-dusk. Free. Phone (410) 260-8189.

HISTORIC LONDON TOWN GARDENS—
see Edgewater in the Vicinity section p. 177.

MARYLAND STATE HOUSE, on State Cir., is the oldest state capitol in continuous legislative use. It was begun in 1772 and finished 7 years later. Because of its convenient location, the State House served as capitol of the United States from Nov. 26, 1783, to Aug. 13, 1784, until a permanent location was chosen. In the Old Senate Chamber, George Washington resigned his commission as the commander in chief of the Continental Army, and Thomas Jefferson accepted his position as the first United States minister plenipotentiary to foreign governments.

The most significant event, however, took place Jan. 14, 1784, when the Continental Congress ratified the Treaty of Paris, officially ending the American Revolution. Self-guiding tours are available. Allow 1 hour minimum. Building open daily 8:30-5; closed Dec. 25. Guided tours are given

daily at 11 and 3 and by appointment; closed Jan. 1, Easter, Thanksgiving and Dec. 25. Free. Phone (410) 974-3400.

ST. ANNE'S CHURCH (Episcopal), Church Circle, was rebuilt in 1859. It is the third church on this site since the parish was founded in 1692. King William III presented the communion silver in 1695. The St. Anne's Memorial Window, by Tiffany & Co., won first prize for ecclesiastical art at the Chicago World's Fair in 1893. Daily 8-5:30. Free. Phone (410) 267-9333.

ST. JOHN'S COLLEGE is at 60 College Ave. The school received its charter in 1784, succeeding the 1696 King William's School. McDowell Hall was begun in 1742 as the Colonial governor's mansion, but it was never completed as such. The Elizabeth Myers Mitchell Gallery displays changing exhibits during the academic year. Also on the 400-student campus is the 1722 Carroll-Barrister House, which contains administrative offices.

Elizabeth Myers Mitchell Gallery open Tues.-Sun. noon-5 (also Fri. 7-8 p.m.) when exhibits are in place. Phone (410) 263-2371.

SCHOONER WOODWIND departs from Pusser's Landing at the Annapolis Marriott Waterfront Hotel, 80 Compromise St. A replica of classic, early 20th-century yachts, this 48-passenger vessel is outfitted with mahogany woodwork and gleaming chrome. A typical 2-hour cruise includes Annapolis harbor, waterfront views of the U.S. Naval Academy and a trip up the scenic Severn River. Sailors are encouraged to help hoist the four sails or take a turn at the helm. Evening, overnight and charter cruises also are available.

Weekday trips require a minimum of six persons; minimums do not apply weekends. Tues.-Sun. at 11, 1:30, 4 and 6:30, Mon. at 6:30, first week in May-Sept. 30; Tues.-Sun. at 12:30 and 3, Apr. 15-Apr. 30 and in Oct. Weekday daytime sightseeing fare $27; over 60, $25; under 12, $18. Sunset, weekend and holiday cruise fares $32; over 60, $27; under 12, $18. All ticket sales for cruises are not refundable or exchangeable unless the captain cancels the cruise due to unsafe conditions. AX, DS, MC, VI. Phone (410) 263-7837.

THREE CENTURIES TOURS OF ANNAPOLIS conducts tours departing from two locations: the information booth at City Dock and the visitor center at 26 West St. Guides in Colonial attire conduct walking tours of historic Annapolis and the U.S. Naval Academy. Tours include interiors in the academy and the Maryland State House when accessible.

Due to security concerns at sites visited, participants over age 16 must have a photo ID, and no pocket knives may be carried. Allow 2 hours, 15 minutes minimum. Tours depart daily at 10:30 from the visitor center and 1:30 from City Dock, Apr.-Oct.; Sat. at 1:30 from City Dock, rest of year. Fee $11; ages 6-18, $6. Phone (410) 263-5401.

U.S. NAVAL ACADEMY can be accessed via entrance Gate 1 at jct. King George and Randall sts. Covering 338 acres on the south side of the Severn River, the academy is the undergraduate college of the U.S. Navy. It was established in 1845 by Navy Secretary George Bancroft on the site of old Fort Severn. Guided walking tours and information are available at the Armel-Leftwich Visitor Center, which features the film "To Lead and To Serve" and the *Freedom 7* space capsule.

The U.S. Naval Academy Museum in Preble Hall features the exhibit 100 Years & Forward, paintings, flags, medals, historical objects and personal memorabilia. Noteworthy are the Rogers Ship Models Collection and the Beverley R. Robinson Collection of Naval Prints. Noon formation is held before Bancroft Hall, weather permitting, Monday through Friday during the school year.

Note: All visitors over age 15 must be prepared to show a valid photo ID. Only vehicles with Department of Defense stickers or handicapped tags are permitted in the Yard. Grounds open daily 9-5; chapel and crypt of John Paul Jones close at 4. Visitor center open daily 9-5, Mar.-Dec.; 9-4, rest of year. Museum open Mon.-Sat. 9-5, Sun. 11-5. Guided walking tours are offered daily; phone ahead for times. Visitor center and museum closed Jan. 1, Thanksgiving and Dec. 25. Tour $7.50; over 62, $6.50; grades 1-12, $5.50. Phone (410) 263-6933.

WATERMARK CRUISES, departing from the city dock at the foot of Main St., offers a variety of cruises (weather permitting) aboard various vessels. The 90-minute tours include the Severn River, Chesapeake Bay bridges and the Thomas Point Lighthouse. A 3-hour music cruise, a Pirates of the Chesapeake cruise and three lighthouse tours as well as special event cruises also are available. Phone (410) 268-7601 to verify prices.

Annapolis Harbor Tour offers a 40-minute cruise of Annapolis harbor, the Severn River and the banks of the U.S. Naval Academy. Departures on the hour Mon.-Fri. 11-4, Sat.-Sun. 11-7, mid-May through Labor Day; Mon.-Fri. noon-3, Sat.-Sun. 11-6, Apr. 1 to mid-May and day after Labor Day-early Oct. Fare $8; ages 3-11, $4. AX, DS, MC, VI.

Day on the Bay Cruise, a 7.5-hour tour visits one of the following ports of call: Rock Hall or the restored fishing village of St. Michaels. There is a 2.5- to 3-hour stop for lunch.

St. Michaels cruises depart Sat. and Mon. mid-July to late Aug.; on Sat. late May to mid-July and late Aug.-late Sept. Rock Hall cruises depart last Fri. of the month May-Sept. Schedule may vary; phone ahead. Fare for St. Michaels cruise $45-$55; under 12, $22.50-$27.50. Rock Hall cruise $50; under 12, $25. Lunch is not included in the fare. Reservations are recommended. Inquire about refund policies and the minimum number of passengers requirement. AX, DS, MC, VI.

Spa Creek Tour is a 40-minute cruise of Annapolis harbor, including such sights as the U.S. Naval Academy and the residential areas of Spa Creek. Cruises depart on the half-hour Mon.-Fri. 3:30-8:30, a quarter after and a quarter before the hour Sat.-Sun. 1:15-8:15, mid-May through Labor Day; on the half-hour Mon.-Fri. 3:30-6:30, Sat.-Sun. 1:30-6:30, mid-Apr. to mid-May; on the half-hour Mon.-Fri. 3:30-6:30, a quarter after and a quarter before the hour Sat.-Sun. 1:15-7:15, day after Labor Day-early Oct. Fare $8; ages 3-11, $4. AX, DS, MC, VI.

WILLIAM PACA HOUSE AND GARDEN, 186 Prince George St., was the estate of Paca, governor of Maryland and signer of the Declaration of Independence. Built 1763-65, the restored Georgian house, which combines elements of English Georgian style with progressive Maryland additions such as massive end chimneys, contains period furnishings. The garden was originally laid out 1765-72. The restored 2-acre area includes a Chinese Chippendale bridge, a summer house, a fish-shaped pond, formal parterres and a wilderness garden.

Allow 2 hours minimum. Guided 45-minute tours Mon.-Sat. 10-5, Sun. noon-5, Mar. 18-Dec. 31; Thurs.-Sat. 10-5, Sun. noon-4, rest of year. Closed Jan. 1, Thanksgiving and Dec. 24-25. Last tour begins at 3:30, with the gardens closing at 4. Admission $8; senior citizens $7; ages 6-17, $5; family rate (two adults and two children) $25. Phone (410) 267-7619 or (800) 603-4020.

COLUMBIA (D-2) pop. 88,254

Columbia, on US 29 between Washington, D.C., and Baltimore, is a planned community of ten villages designed to improve exurban living and to shape urban growth. It was started in 1966 by visionary developer James Rouse and the first residents arrived in 1967. The town includes residential areas, schools, churches, hospitals, shopping centers, industries and recreation.

The Merriweather Post Pavilion, designed by noted architect Frank Gehry, presents popular music concerts in summer.

Columbia Association Welcome Center: 10221 Wincopin Cir., Columbia, MD 21044; phone (410) 715-3000.

Self-guiding tours: Columbia Lakefront Walking Tour along Lake Kittamaqundi includes such scenery as architecture, fountains, pathways, plazas and public artwork

Shopping areas: The Mall in Columbia, which is reached via the Columbia Town Center exit off US 29, encompasses 200 shops and restaurants including Hecht's, JCPenney, Lord & Taylor, Nordstrom and Sears.

AFRICAN ART MUSEUM OF MARYLAND, off SR 175 .2 mi. s. to 5430 Vantage Point Rd. in historic Oakland Manor, promotes understanding of African art and culture through lectures, exhibits, workshops and tours. Exhibits include sculptured figures, textiles, basketry, jewelry, masks and musical instruments. Allow 30 minutes minimum. Tues.-Fri. 10-4, Sun. noon-4, Oct.-May; Tues.-Fri. and Sun. noon-4, rest of year. Closed holidays. Admission $2; over 54 and ages 2-12, $1. Phone ahead to verify prices. Phone (410) 730-7106.

EDGEWATER (F-3)

HISTORIC LONDON TOWN AND GARDENS, 2 mi. e. via SR 253 and Londontown Rd., depicts accommodations available to the 18th-century traveler. The 1760 tavern is restored and furnished in period. The woodland gardens cover 8 acres; native plants are emphasized throughout. An archeological dig is in progress. Special events and programs are held during the year. Allow 1 hour minimum. Tues.-Sat. 10-4, Sun. noon-4; closed Easter and federal holidays. Admission $7; over 54, $5; ages 7-12, $3. Phone (410) 222-1919.

ELLICOTT CITY (D-2) pop. 56,397, elev. 141'

The site that became Ellicott City was first known as Ellicott Mills, named for three Quaker brothers and the gristmill they established. One of the brothers, Andrew Ellicott, and Benjamin Banneker, a free black born in the area in 1731, were commissioned by George Washington to survey and lay out Washington, D.C. Banneker is said to have successfully reproduced from memory plans originally designed by Pierre L'Enfant, who was dismissed from the project.

Ellicott City became the first terminus outside Baltimore for the Baltimore and Ohio Railroad. Andrew Jackson became the first president to travel by train when he boarded a car here in 1833. Many of the stone buildings that line the narrow, winding streets above the Patapsco River have been preserved.

Another historic site, Patapsco Female Institute Historic Park, at 3691 Sarah's Ln., was one of the first schools in the nation to offer girls an academic education. Now a ruin, the school is the focal point of the park where a variety of recreational activities and special events are offered.

Howard County Visitor Information Center— Ellicott City: 8267 Main St., P.O. Box 9, Ellicott City, MD 21043; phone (410) 313-1900 or (800) 288-8747. *See color ad.*

Self-guiding tours: A brochure outlining a walking tour of the historic district is available at the visitor information center and many area shops.

Shopping areas: The historic district of downtown offers a wealth of restaurants and specialty, antiques and art shops.

B&O RAILROAD STATION MUSEUM, 2711 Maryland Ave. at Main St., is the restored first terminus of the Baltimore & Ohio Railroad and was the destination of America's first steam engine, the "Tom Thumb," in August 1830. Display areas include the stationmaster's quarters, a waiting room, a ticket office and a freight house, which offers a model railroad display of the first 13 miles of the line and a restored 1927 caboose.

Allow 1 hour minimum. Fri.-Sat. 11-4, Sun. noon-5 (also Mon. 11-4, Memorial Day-Labor Day); closed major holidays. Admission $5; over 64, $4; under 13, $3. Phone (410) 461-1944.

◆ FORT McHENRY NATIONAL MONUMENT AND HISTORIC SHRINE (D-4)

To reach Fort McHenry from I-95, take exit 55 (Key Hwy./Fort McHenry Monument) and follow the aqua signs on Key Highway to Lawrence Street. Turn south on Lawrence Street and then go east 1 mile on E. Fort Avenue. It also can be reached by shuttle boat service from Light St. in the Baltimore Inner Harbor.

Guardian of Baltimore's harbor, Fort McHenry was built 1798-1803. During the War of 1812, when the capture of Baltimore was a major British objective, Fort McHenry's resistance to a 25-hour bombardment saved the city from occupation and inspired the writing of the American national anthem.

Francis Scott Key, a young Georgetown lawyer, had sailed from Baltimore to secure the release of Dr. William Beanes, a friend who had earlier been seized by the British. Detained aboard an American truce ship, Key anxiously witnessed the bombardment of Fort McHenry throughout the day and into the night. After dawn on Sept. 14, 1814, the British guns ceased firing, and the sight of the 15-star, 15-stripe flag still defiantly flying over the fort inspired Key to write the poem "The Star-Spangled Banner" which was set to the British tune "Anacreon in Heaven." It was not adopted as the national anthem until Mar. 3, 1931.

The fort never again came under attack. However, it was an active military post periodically over the next 100 years. The fort is restored to its pre-Civil War appearance. Several of the Star Fort buildings contain exhibits of historical and military memorabilia. The replica flagstaff, from which the flag flies 24 hours a day by presidential proclamation, is in the same location as the original.

Park orientation and a 15-minute movie about the Battle of Baltimore and the writing of "The Star-Spangled Banner" are offered in the visitor center. Guided activities, weekend performances by the Fort McHenry Guard (Living History unit) and special programs are given in the summer.

Allow 1 hour minimum. Daily 8-7:45, early June-Labor Day; 8-4:45, rest of year. Closed Jan. 1, Thanksgiving and Dec. 25. Fort admission $5, under 17 free. Additional fee for shuttle boat. Phone (410) 962-4290.

FORT MEADE (E-3)

NATIONAL CRYPTOLOGIC MUSEUM is on Colony 7 Rd. at jct. SRs 32 and 295 near National Security Agency headquarters. The museum recounts the history of encryption and highlights dramatic tales from the secretive world of cryptology. Visitors can see a cipher wheel, a hands-on German enigma machine, an exhibit about the American Indian Code Talkers and slave quilts used to relay information along the Underground Railroad.

A park honors aerial reconnaissance crew members who died in the line of duty. Allow 30 minutes minimum. Mon.-Fri. 9-4 (also first and third Sat. of the month 10–2); closed federal holidays. Free. Phone (301) 688-6524.

HANOVER (E-3) elev. 96'

MEDIEVAL TIMES DINNER AND TOURNAMENT is off I-95 exit 43, 5 mi. e. on SR 100 to exit 10A, then s. to 7000 Arundel Mills Cir. Within a building made to look like an 11th-century European castle, waiters and waitresses dressed in period costumes serve guests a medieval feast. Knights on Andalusian stallions compete in jousting matches and medieval games of skill just a few feet away from dining spectators. A falcon flies throughout the arena during a falconry demonstration.

Allow 2 hours minimum. Wed.-Thurs. at 7, Fri. at 11 and 8, Sat. at 6 and 8:30 and Sun. at 2:30 and 5. Other show times vary. Admission $45.95; under 12, $34.95. Reservations are required. AX, CB, DC, DS, JC, MC, VI. Phone (443) 755-0011 or (888) 935-6878.

HAVRE DE GRACE (B-7)
pop. 11,331, elev. 106'

Havre de Grace rose to prosperity as a mercantile center in the mid-1800s, due in large part to the town's location at the convergence of the Susquehanna River and the Chesapeake Bay. By 1836 a railroad, canal and steamship line served the city. From 1839 to the early 1900s mule-drawn barges carried coal, lumber, grains, ore and iron products between Havre de Grace and Wrightsville, Pa., 45 miles upstream.

Few buildings survived the British torch in the War of 1812. Many examples of the architectural styles favored by wealthy 19th-century merchants have been retained, however, and now serve as offices and homes. The old lock house beside the defunct Susquehanna and Tidewater Canal has been restored as a museum. The Concord Point Lighthouse is among the oldest lighthouses in continuous operation on the East Coast.

Departing the Lighthouse Pier, the skipjack *Martha Lewis* offers 75-minute tours of the Susquehanna Flats and upper Chesapeake Bay. Phone (410) 939-4078.

Havre de Grace Office of Tourism & Visitor Center: 450 Pennington Ave., Havre de Grace, MD 21078; phone (410) 939-2100 or (800) 851-7756.

Self-guiding tours: Maps and literature for a walking tour of the historic district are available Mon.-Fri. 10-2 at the chamber of commerce at 224 N. Washington St.

SAVE **HAVRE DE GRACE DECOY MUSEUM,** off I-95 exit 89 at Market and Giles sts., exhibits displays about the folk art of decoy carving. Included are works that trace the history of the waterfowl hunting decoy and of hunting methods. The Carvers' Workshop displays tools used in the painstaking process of carving and painting, in addition to decoy models in various stages of preparation. Guided tours are available. Allow 30 minutes minimum. Daily 11-4; closed Jan. 1, Easter, Thanksgiving and Dec. 25. Admission $6; over 61, $5; ages 9-18, $2. MC, VI. Phone (410) 939-3739.

HYDES (B-7)

WINERIES

• **Boordy Vineyards**, 12820 Long Green Pike. Mon.-Sat. 10-5, Sun. 1-5; closed Jan. 1, Easter, July 4, Thanksgiving and Dec. 25. Phone (410) 592-5015.

JACKSONVILLE (B-6)

SAVE **LADEW TOPIARY GARDENS AND MANOR HOUSE** is 5 mi. n. on SR 146 to 3535 Jarrettsville Pike. The home belonged to Harvey S. Ladew, artist and foxhunting devotee. Beginning in 1929, Ladew designed the flower gardens, dozens of sculptured animal and geometric topiary figures and the sculptured hedges that grow on 22 acres. The house contains Ladew's collections of English antiques, paintings, and foxhunting and equestrian memorabilia.

Guided tours of the house are available. Garden tours are self-guiding. Allow 1 hour minimum. Grounds open Mon.-Fri. and holidays 10-4, Sat.-Sun. 10:30-5, mid-Apr. through Oct. 31. Guided tours depart on the hour. Last tour 1 hour before closing. House and gardens admission $13; over 61 and students with ID $11; under 12, $5. Gardens admission $10; over 61 and students with ID $8; under 12, $2. MC, VI. Phone (410) 557-9466.

LINTHICUM HEIGHTS (E-3)
pop. 7,500, elev. 171'

Linthicum Heights was named for the Linthicum family, who have been property owners here since 1801. The town borders Baltimore-Washington International Airport, which provides a commercial boost for the area.

HISTORICAL ELECTRONICS MUSEUM, 1 mi. e. of SR 295 off Nursery Rd. exit to 1745 W. Nursery Rd., depicts the history of advanced electronic technology through an extensive display of equipment. Visitors can see the lunar TV camera that transmitted Neil Armstrong's first steps on the moon and the German Enigma machine that encoded messages in World War II. The Fundamentals of Electricity Gallery offers hands-on activities for children. Allow 1 hour minimum. Mon.-Fri. 9-3, Sat. 10-2; closed holidays. Donations. Phone (410) 765-3803.

LUTHERVILLE (B-6)

Named for Reformation leader Martin Luther, the town was founded by Lutheran ministers in 1852 as the location for a seminary for young women. Lutherville developed a reputation as a summer resort and eventually became a suburb of Baltimore.

A historic district preserves 19th-century homes on tree-shaded streets.

Baltimore County Convention and Visitors Bureau: P.O. Box 5426, Lutherville, MD 21094-5426; phone (410) 296-4886.

SAVE **FIRE MUSEUM OF MARYLAND** is at 1301 York Rd., n. on SR 45 from I-695 exit 26B. The main exhibit is 40 fire engines ranging from horse-drawn wagons to contemporary vehicles. Also available are a room explaining how fire alarms once worked and a collection of uniforms. In the Discovery Room children can try on uniforms and climb on a fire engine. Allow 1 hour minimum. Tues.-Sat. 11-4, June-Aug.; Sat. 11-4, rest of year. Closed July 4. Admission $6; over 61, $5; ages 2-12, $4. MC, VI. Phone (410) 321-7500.

MOUNT AIRY (D-1) pop. 6,425

WINERIES

• **Berrywine Plantations Linganore Winecellars** is at 13601 Glissans Mill Rd. Mon.-Fri. 10-5, Sat. 10-6, Sun. noon-6; closed major holidays. Phone (410) 795-6432, (301) 831-5889 in D.C., or (800) 514-8735.

• **Elk Run Vineyards** is at 15113 Liberty Rd. Tues.-Sat. 10-5, Sun. 1-5; closed major holidays. Phone (410) 775-2513.

PARKTON (B-6) elev. 420'

WINERIES

• **Woodhall Wine Cellars** is at 17912 York Rd. Mon.-Sat. 10-5, Sun. noon-5; closed Jan. 1, Easter, Thanksgiving and Dec. 25. Phone (410) 357-8644.

SPARKS (B-6) elev. 420'

WINERIES

• **Basignani Winery** is at 15722 Falls Rd. Wed.-Sat. 11:30-5:30, Sun. noon-6. Phone (410) 472-0703.

TOWSON (D-3) pop. 51,793

Established in 1685 as a stagecoach stop, Towson became a thriving farm community when the fertile soil and abundant game attracted settlers to the area. In the mid-19th century the town became the seat of Baltimore County.

HAMPTON NATIONAL HISTORIC SITE is at 535 Hampton Ln. just off SR 146; from I-695 take exit 27B and turn immediately onto Hampton Ln. A Georgian mansion begun in 1783 by Charles Ridgely, Hampton represents post-Revolutionary War opulence. At its completion in 1790, it was the largest house in the country. The 62-acre site features a formal garden, greenhouses, an ice house, stables, slave quarters and a restored orangery. Guided tours of the mansion are available; guided tours of the farm, garden and outbuildings are available by appointment.

Allow 1 hour, 30 minutes minimum. Mansion and grounds open daily 9-5; closed Jan. 1, Thanksgiving and Dec. 25. Mansion tours begin on the hour. Last house tour begins 1 hour before closing. Free. Phone (410) 823-1309.

WESTMINSTER (B-5) pop. 16,731, elev. 700'

Originally named in 1764 for founder William Winchester, Westminster's name was changed after the beginning of the American Revolution because much of the local mail was being routed to nearby Winchester, Va. During the Civil War the community and its resources were used by both Union and Confederate forces. Westminster's economy is primarily agricultural, with some manufacturing concerns; many residents commute to Baltimore to work.

Carroll County Visitor Center: 210 E. Main St., Westminster, MD 21157; phone (410) 848-1388 or (800) 272-1933.

CARROLL COUNTY FARM MUSEUM, 500 S. Center St., is a 142-acre tract that depicts 19th-century farm life. In addition to a farmhouse furnished in period and a barn containing old farm tools, there are 16 other buildings, nature trails and a pond. Demonstrations of quilting, spinning, weaving, blacksmithing and other crafts take place periodically. Picnicking is permitted. Allow 1 hour minimum. Tues.-Fri. 10-4, Sat.-Sun. and some holidays noon-5, July-Aug.; Sat.-Sun. noon-5, May-June and Sept.-Oct. Admission $3; over 59 and ages 7-18, $2. Phone (410) 876-2667.

UNION MILLS HOMESTEAD AND HOUSE MUSEUM is 7 mi. n. on SR 97 to 3311 Littlestown Pike. This large 1797 clapboard farmhouse was the home of the Shriver families, who operated milling, farming, tannery and canning businesses known collectively as "Union Mills." Furnishings, utensils and other items represent nearly two centuries of American life. Across the lane is the three-story 1797 Union Mills Grist Mill, built with bricks made on the property. Powered by a large waterwheel, the mill still operates.

Tues.-Fri. 10-4, Sat.-Sun. noon-4, June-Aug.; Sat.-Sun. noon-4 in May and in Sept. House or mill admission $2.50; ages 6-12, $1.50. Phone (410) 848-2288.

This ends listings for the Baltimore Vicinity. The following page resumes the alphabetical listings of cities in Maryland.

BERLIN (E-9) pop. 3,491, elev. 45'

CALVIN B. TAYLOR HOUSE MUSEUM, 208 N. Main St., is a restored 1832 Federal-style house furnished in period. One wing features changing exhibits of local memorabilia. Mon., Wed. and Fri.-Sat. 1-4, Memorial Day weekend-Sept. 30. Donations. Phone (410) 641-1019.

FRONTIER TOWN, 4 mi. s. on SR 611 from US 50, depicts the era of the Wild West through staged holdups, street fights, trail rides and cancan shows. Daily 10-6, mid-June through Labor Day. Last admission 1 hour, 30 minutes before closing. Admission $11; ages 4-10, $9. Phone (410) 289-7877 or (800) 228-5590.

BETHESDA — see District of Columbia p. 114.

BIG POOL (B-4)

FORT FREDERICK STATE PARK is off SR 56, 1 mi. s.w. of the I-70 Big Pool exit. The 1756 frontier fort protected Cumberland Valley settlers during the French and Indian War and saw action during the Revolutionary and Civil wars. The visitor center shows a 10-minute orientation film and contains a display of military uniforms. A museum holds material explaining the fort's restoration. Barracks are furnished as they would have been in 1758. Interpreters offer information about the fort's history.

Picnicking is permitted. Food is available. Allow 1 hour minimum. Park and museum open daily 8-dusk, Apr.-Oct.; 10-dusk, rest of year. Visitor center open Mon.-Fri. 8-4, Sat.-Sun. 9-5, May-Sept. Hours may vary; phone ahead. Park closed Thanksgiving and Dec. 24-25. Park free. Museum admission $3; ages 6-12, $2. Phone (301) 842-2155. *See Recreation Chart and the AAA Mideastern CampBook.*

BOONSBORO (B-4) pop. 2,803, elev. 591'

Boonsboro was founded in 1792 by George and William Boone, first cousins of Daniel Boone. The town prospered during the early 1800s thanks to its facilities serving the westward-bound pioneers taking the wagon road through town. The road would later become the National Pike. Stonewall Jackson and J.E.B. Stuart fought Civil War battles in the area.

CRYSTAL GROTTOES CAVERNS is 1.2 mi. s.w. on SR 34. Stalactites, stalagmites and other formations can be seen from illuminated walkways. Thirty-minute guided tours daily every 15 minutes 10-5, Apr.-Oct.; Sat.-Sun. 11-4, rest of year. Last tour begins at closing. Admission $8.50; under 12, $4.50. Phone (301) 432-6336.

WASHINGTON MONUMENT STATE PARK, 147 acres 3 mi. s.e. off US 40A, is along the Appalachian Trail. The restored 34-foot stone monument and observation tower, erected in 1827, commemorates George Washington. Allow 30 minutes minimum. Daily 8-dusk. Admission $2 per vehicle. Phone (301) 791-4767.

BRUNSWICK (C-4) pop. 4,894, elev. 247'

SAVE **BRUNSWICK RAILROAD MUSEUM,** e. of the train station at 40 W. Potomac St., offers hands-on exhibits, an HO scale model railroad replicating stops from Washington's Union Station to Brunswick and railroad memorabilia. Allow 30 minutes minimum. Thurs.-Fri. 10-2, Sat. 10-5, Sun. 1-5, Apr.-Dec.; Fri. 10-2, Sat. 10-4, Sun. 1-4, rest of year. Closed Easter, Thanksgiving and Dec. 25. Admission $5; over 59, $4; ages 6-12, $2.50; ages 3-5, $1.25. MC, VI. Phone (301) 834-7100.

BURKITTSVILLE (B-4) pop. 171

Much of Burkittsville's history is closely tied to that of George Alfred Townsend, a Civil War correspondent and novelist. In tribute to his fellow newspapermen who covered the Civil War, Townsend designed the War Correspondents Memorial. Dedicated in 1896, the memorial is now in Gathland State Park, 1 mile west of town. "The Blair Witch Project" and its sequel "Book of Shadows" were set and filmed in Burkittsville.

CAMBRIDGE (E-7) pop. 10,911, elev. 32'

Cambridge, founded in 1684, was one of a number of towns created in a largely abortive attempt to collect customs fees in Maryland's plantation-based rural economy. Its location on the fertile bank of the Choptank River continues to play a significant role in the local economy. The area's agricultural focus has changed from tobacco to truck farming, however, and a farmers' market takes place every Tuesday and Friday from 8 to noon, July through September; there is no set closing time.

Brannock Maritime Museum, 210 Talbot Ave., depicts the early nautical days of the Chesapeake Bay; phone (410) 228-6938. Christ Episcopal Church stands on the site of the original church; its cemetery contains the graves of local Revolutionary War soldiers and several of Maryland's statesmen; phone (410) 228-3161.

The High Street Historic District, downtown, extends west from the Choptank River. The buildings in this area date from the mid-1700s and exhibit a variety of architectural styles.

In Lloyds, six miles west on SR 343 (Hudson Road), is Spocott Windmill, a reconstruction of the post windmills used to grind grain in 18th- and 19th-century America; the mill generally is not spinning. Also on the grounds are a furnished miller's house built 1775-1840 and an 1870s one-room Victorian schoolhouse. The structures are viewable daily 24 hours. Contact the Windmill Foundation for further information; phone (410) 228-7090.

Dorchester County Tourism: 2 Rose Hill Pl., Cambridge, MD 21613; phone (410) 228-1000 or (800) 522-8687.

Self-guiding tours: Walking tour maps of the historic district and driving tour maps of the county are available at the chamber of commerce or at the

Dorchester County Historical Society at 902 La Grange Ave. The historical society is open Thurs.-Sat. 10-3; otherwise by appointment. Phone (410) 228-7953.

BLACKWATER NATIONAL WILDLIFE REFUGE is 10 mi. s. on SRs 335 and 16 at the confluence of the Blackwater and Little Blackwater rivers. The more than 26,000-acre tract is home to eagles, otters, red foxes and such migratory waterfowl as ducks, geese and swans. The best time to view waterfowl is mid-October to mid-March. Ospreys hatch in early June. A 6.5-mile wildlife drive, two nature trails and a bicycle route offer views. The visitor center has films and exhibits.

Allow 1 hour minimum. Refuge and wildlife drive open daily dawn-dusk. Visitor center open Mon.-Fri. 8-4, Sat.-Sun. 9-5; closed Thanksgiving and Dec. 25. Admission $3 per private vehicle, $1 per pedestrian or bicyclist; under 16 free. Phone (410) 228-2677.

CHESAPEAKE AND OHIO CANAL NATIONAL HISTORICAL PARK (D-1)

The Chesapeake and Ohio Canal National Historical Park follows the Maryland shore of the Potomac River from Georgetown in Washington, D.C., to Cumberland. Begun in 1828, the 184.5-mile canal operated 1850-1924.

Along the canal are 74 lift locks, 11 aqueducts and a number of historic lock houses. About 15 miles northwest of Washington, D.C., the Great Falls of the Potomac makes a thundering descent in a series of picturesque falls and rapids. This portion of the park, accessible via exit 41 off I-495 (Capital Beltway), is at the end of MacArthur Boulevard.

The area is not served by public transportation, and motorized vehicles are not permitted on the towpath. Visitors can view the falls from Amsted Bridge on the Maryland side as well as from scenic overlooks on the Virginia side (*see Great Falls, Va., p. 128*).

General Information and Activities

The Monocacy Aqueduct near Dickerson and the Paw Paw Tunnel near Paw Paw, W.Va., are major attractions. Between Georgetown and Seneca the canal has been refilled with water. A 184-mile towpath runs along the Potomac River; camping and picnic facilities are available. Hikers, bicyclists and canoeists list Great Falls as a favorite spot.

Maps and additional information are available at the park's visitor centers in Cumberland, Great Falls, Hancock and Williamsport, Md., and in the Georgetown section of Washington, D.C. The Hancock center presents an audiovisual history and displays photographs, artifacts and boat replicas.

The Georgetown Visitor Center is open Wed.-Sun. 9-4:30, early Apr.-early Nov.; Sat.-Sun. 9-4:30, rest of year; phone (202) 653-5190. Great Falls Tavern Visitor Center open daily 9-4:45; phone

(301) 299-3613 or (301) 767-3714. Brunswick Visitor Center Thurs.-Fri. 10-2, Sat.-Sun. 10-4, June-Oct.; Fri. 10-2, Sat.-Sun. 10-4, rest of year; phone (301) 834-7100. Williamsport Visitor Center Wed.-Sun. 9-4:30; phone (301) 582-0813. Hancock Visitor Center Fri.-Tues. 9-4:30; phone (301) 678-5463. Western Maryland Station daily 9-5; phone (301) 722-8226. All visitor centers are closed Jan. 1, Thanksgiving and Dec. 25. *See the AAA Mideastern CampBook.*

ADMISSION to the Great Falls area of the park is $5 per private vehicle or $3 per person arriving on foot or by bicycle. Admission charged only at Great Falls.

PETS must be restricted at all times, either in vehicles or by leash, and are not permitted in public buildings.

ADDRESS inquiries to the Superintendent, Chesapeake and Ohio Canal National Historical Park, P.O. Box 4, Sharpsburg, MD 21782; phone (301) 739-4200.

Points of Interest

C & O CANAL BOAT TRIPS depart from 1 blk. s. of M St. between Thomas Jefferson and 30th sts. N.W. in the Georgetown section of Washington, D.C. A mule-drawn replica of a 19th-century canal boat offers 70-minute tours through the historic district. Tickets are sold at the Georgetown Ranger Station, 1057 Thomas Jefferson St. N.W.

Trips depart Thurs.-Sun. at 11, 1:30, 3 and 5, Wed. 11, 1:30 and 3, mid-June to early Sept.; Wed.-Fri. at 11 and 3 and by reservation, Sat.-Sun. at 11, 1:30 and 3, early May to mid-June and early Sept.-early Nov. Fare $8; over 61, $6; ages 4-14, $5. Phone (301) 767-3714 (park) or (202) 653-5190 (Georgetown).

GREAT FALLS TAVERN AND MUSEUM is 3 mi. s. on Falls Rd. then right on MacArthur Blvd., following signs to 11710 MacArthur Blvd. Built 1828-31 as a stop on the canal route, the museum houses exhibits about the history of the canal. Films about the canal are shown continuously. Programs about cultural and natural history also are offered. Allow 1 hour minimum. Daily 9-4:45; closed Jan. 1; Thanksgiving and Dec. 25. Free. Phone (301) 767-3714.

CHESAPEAKE BEACH (D-6) pop. 3,180

CHESAPEAKE BEACH RAILWAY MUSEUM, 2 mi. s. of SR 260 on SR 261, chronicles the history of Chesapeake Beach, once a glittering early 20th-century resort. The museum occupies the railway station, the only surviving building from the town's heyday. Daily 1-4, May-Sept.; Sat.-Sun. 1-4 in Apr. and Oct.; other times by appointment. Free. Phone (410) 257-3892.

CHESAPEAKE CITY (B-8) pop. 787

Chesapeake City came into existence because of the Chesapeake & Delaware Canal, which links Delaware and Chesapeake bays across the Delmarva Peninsula. Work on the canal began in 1803, but the waterway did not open for navigation until 1829. It allows oceangoing vessels serving Baltimore and other northern ports to avoid the 296-mile trip around the peninsula.

The canal proved to be of vital strategic importance during World War II, when ships used it to escape enemy submarines in the Atlantic Ocean. Today, as an avenue for pleasure craft traveling the inland waterway, the canal is the impetus for many of Chesapeake City's businesses.

Cecil County Tourism: 1 Seahawk Dr., Suite 114, North East, MD 21901; phone (410) 996-6290 or (800) 232-4595.

C&D CANAL MUSEUM is off SR 213 at 2nd St. and Bethel Rd. Housed in the original canal pump house complex, the museum includes a working model of a water wheel and lock, paintings, maps, documents and artifacts pertaining to the history of the waterway. Allow 1 hour minimum. Mon.-Fri. 8-4:15; closed holidays. Free. Phone (410) 885-5621 or (410) 885-5622.

CHESTER (F-4) pop. 3,723, elev. 16′

CHESAPEAKE EXPLORATION CENTER is off US 50 exit 41 at Kent Narrows Bridge, then just n. following signs to 425 Piney Narrows Rd. Displays and interactive exhibits tell the history of the Chesapeake Bay area. Visitors can learn how the bay was formed and what life was like for past inhabitants. Fossils and relics of the settlers' existence are included. A brief video explains the construction of the first Bay Bridge. Visitors can learn how to protect the bay. Visitor information about the region also is available.

Allow 30 minutes minimum. Mon.-Fri 8:30-4:30, Sat.-Sun. and national holidays 10-4; closed Easter and Dec. 25. Donations. Phone (410) 604-2100 or (888) 400-7787.

CHESTERTOWN (C-7) pop. 4,746, elev. 36′

A graceful town of 18th-century brick houses facing the Chester River, Chestertown began in 1706 as a port of entry for Cecil, Kent and Queen Anne's counties. During its early years it hosted horse races and traveling theatrical groups. Shipbuilding and trading were economic mainstays.

A spirit of independence prevailed in 1774 when citizens, enraged over England's tea tax, threw overboard tea brought into port by the brigantine *Geddes*. Soon after, Chestertown sent provisions to the similarly inclined town of Boston, which was suffering from the effects of the Boston Port Act.

Washington College was founded in 1782. Named after George Washington, on whom he conferred an honorary degree of doctor of laws, the college was visited by its namesake in 1784.

The Blue Crab

To those who know the Chesapeake Bay, the blue crab symbolizes fine eating and a way of life. Ancestors of the crustacean fed the area's earliest inhabitants more than 10,000 years ago; later, Eastern Archaic and Woodlands Indians left crab shells as testaments to their feasts.

Although blue crabs are found as far north as Cape Cod, as far south as Uruguay and in such exotic places as the lakes of the Nile Delta, they thrive in greatest abundance in the Chesapeake Bay. Scientists credit the bay's varying salinity and the water's shallowness for the large harvests that form the basis of the bay's prosperous crabbing industry.

Digital Archives

Crab harvests vary with changing weather patterns, and some bay experts are concerned about dwindling populations, but the crab still reigns as the king of cuisine in Maryland. Baltimore crab houses fork up spicy renditions of steamed hard-shell crab, which bib-clad patrons consume with the aid of mallets and knives. Succulent crab cakes are considered by many to be the best in the world.

To some, the act of catching these crustaceans is as much fun as eating them. In the bay tributaries, crab fishers use baited trotlines. In the open bay, crab pots are baited and weighted, then cast into the water. Once a crab has entered through the one-way opening, it has no choice but to await its captor. Soft-shell crabs, considered a delicacy, are taken after the molting of one shell and before the hardening of a new one. Both hard-shell and soft-shell crabs are kept alive on ice until they are cooked. Whether served soft or hard or whole or minced, blue crabs are the pride of the Chesapeake.

Kent County Tourism Office: 400 High St., Chestertown, MD 21620; phone (410) 778-0416.

Self-guiding tours: Information about historical driving and walking tours can be obtained from the tourism office.

Shopping areas: The historic downtown area features some 35 shops and eateries.

CHESAPEAKE FARMS, on SR 20, is a 3,300-acre wildlife management demonstration area. Described in the tour brochure are 15 stops, each marked and labeled. The first stop is the main resting area, where as many as 10,000 geese, ducks and other waterfowl can be seen at one time. Many types of plant and animal species—including upland birds, beavers, turtles and nesting wood ducks—are found in the refuge.

Visitors are asked to remain in their vehicles throughout the tour; motorcycles and horses are not permitted. Allow 1 hour minimum. Main resting area open daily dawn-dusk. Habitat tour available Feb. 1-Oct. 10. Schedule may vary; phone ahead. Free. Phone (410) 778-8400.

CHURCH CREEK (E-7) pop. 85, elev. 57′

OLD TRINITY CHURCH is w. of US 50 on SR 16/ Church Creek Rd. The restored church dates prior to 1690 and still is in use. The adjoining cemetery contains graves of the Carroll family, one of whom, Anna Ella Carroll, was such a close advisor to President Lincoln that many consider her an unofficial member of his cabinet. A brilliant military strategist, Carroll devised the Tennessee campaign, credited by some historians with securing the Union's victory in the Civil War.

Church open by appointment. Cemetery open daily 24 hours. Free. Phone (410) 228-2940.

CLINTON— see District of Columbia p. 114.

COLLEGE PARK—
see District of Columbia p. 115.

COLTONS POINT (E-6)

Coltons Point faces St. Clements Island, where the *Ark* and the *Dove,* carrying the first Maryland settlers, dropped anchor on March 25, 1634. On this Potomac River island Gov. Leonard Calvert and Jesuit Father Andrew White erected a large wooden cross and performed the first Roman Catholic Mass in the English-speaking Colonies. A replica of the *Dove* is permanently docked in St. Mary's City *(see attraction listing p. 193).*

ST. CLEMENTS ISLAND-POTOMAC RIVER MUSEUM is at the end of SR 242 on the Potomac River facing St. Clements Island. The museum contains exhibits about Maryland's first settlers and American Indians. Included are a rare gunning skiff and punting gun of the type used for duck hunting in the late 19th and early 20th centuries. Also featured are a replica of the original lighthouse, a waterman's tools and a restored 1820 one-room

school. Water taxi service to St. Clements Island is available seasonally.

Allow 1 hour minimum. Mon.-Fri. 9-5, Sat.-Sun. noon-5, late Mar.-Sept 30.; Wed.-Fri. 9-5, Sat.-Sun. noon-4, rest of year. Closed Mar. 25. Admission $1, under 12 free. Water taxi fare $5; under 13, $3. Phone (301) 769-2222.

COLUMBIA— see Baltimore p. 176.

CRISFIELD (F-8) pop. 2,723, elev. 5′

Crisfield is on an inlet of Tangier Sound, a part of Chesapeake Bay set off and protected by islands. The townspeople lived in relative isolation until 1867, when a railroad was extended to the harbor by John Woodland Crisfield. Said to be built almost entirely on oyster shells, the town has a number of oyster houses at its piers, where visitors can sample the fresh delicacy in season.

Ferries provide daily service to Tangier Island, Va. *(see Tangier, Va., p. 294)* and Smith Island *(see place listing p. 194).*

Somerset County Tourism and Visitor Center Office—Crisfield: 11440 Ocean Hwy., P.O. Box 243, Princess Anne, MD 21853; phone (410) 651-2968 or (800) 521-9189.

SMITH ISLAND SIGHTSEEING CRUISES depart from the Somers Cove Marina on Seventh St. The *Twister,* the *Captain Tyler* and the *Chelsea Lane Tyler* carry passengers to Smith Island daily at 12:30 and return at 5, Memorial Day-Oct. 15. Fare $22; ages 3-11, $11. Reservations are required. Phone (410) 425-2771.

TANGIER ISLAND CRUISES, 1001 W. Main St., offers cruises on the *Steven Thomas* and the *Great Getaway II* to Tangier Island. Cruises depart daily at 12:30 and return at 5:15, May 15 through mid-Oct. Fare $22; ages 6-12, $11. Phone (410) 968-2338 or (800) 863-2338.

CUMBERLAND (B-2) pop. 21,518, elev. 655′

Cumberland took its name in 1787 from Fort Cumberland, the headquarters for Gen. Edward Braddock and Lt. George Washington during the French and Indian War. The one-room headquarters, where 21-year-old Washington assumed his first military command, is the only surviving structure of Fort Cumberland.

Cumberland developed as a transportation center after it was made the western terminus of the Chesapeake & Ohio Canal and the eastern terminus of the National Road—what is now alternate US 40. The first road built with federal funds, the National Road passed through the Cumberland Narrows—a natural gateway through the Appalachian Mountains into the Ohio Valley—and for a time was the main route to the Northwest Territory.

When Cumberland was at its economic peak during the late 19th century, coal and rail barons lived in ornate mansions along Washington Street. Many of these homes, which range in .style from Federal to Georgian Revival, have been restored.

Allegany County Convention and Visitors Bureau—Cumberland: Western Maryland Station Center, 13 Canal St., Cumberland, MD 21502; phone (301) 777-5132 or (800) 508-4748.

Self-guiding tours: Tour brochures of the Fort Cumberland Walking Trail as well as walking and driving tour brochures of the Washington Street Historic District are available at the visitor's bureau.

Shopping areas: Downtown Cumberland, a brick-lined pedestrian mall with fountains and small parks, contains shops in restored early 20th-century buildings.

CHESAPEAKE AND OHIO CANAL NATIONAL HISTORICAL PARK—*see place listing p. 182.*

GORDON ROBERTS HOUSE, 218 Washington St., is headquarters for the Allegany County Historical Society and features 18 rooms furnished with period pieces, antiques and displays depicting life in the mid-1800s. A carriage house also is featured, and a cup of tea is offered as part of a guided tour. Allow 1 hour minimum. Guided tours Tues.-Sat. 10-4; closed Jan. 1, Thanksgiving and Dec. 25. Admission $5, students with ID $3, under 12 free. Phone (301) 777-8678.

WESTERN MARYLAND SCENIC RAILROAD, departing the station center at 13 Canal St., offers 3.5-hour round-trip excursions up 1,300-foot-high Piney Mountain, through Brush Tunnel and into Frostburg aboard a train pulled by either a 1916 Baldwin steam locomotive known as "Mountain Thunder" or a restored diesel engine. Murder mystery and first-class trips also are available.

Steam locomotive excursions depart Fri.-Sun. at 11:30, May-Oct.; Sat.-Sun. at 11:30, Nov. 1 to mid-Dec. Diesel engine trips depart Mon.-Thurs. at 11:30, in Oct.; Thurs. at 11:30, May-Aug. Schedule may vary; phone ahead. Fare $20; over 59, $18; under 13, $10; under age 2 on lap free. Reservations are required. Phone (301) 759-4400 or (800) 872-4650.

EASTON (D-7) pop. 11,708, elev. 38′

Continued use of Colonial architecture is Easton's tribute to its heritage. Settled in the late 17th century, the town was an economic, governmental and cultural center for the Eastern Shore. The 1682 Third Haven Friends Meeting House was built by the Society of Friends and is one of the nation's oldest frame houses of worship. Other notable town landmarks are the 18th-century courthouse and the Tidewater Inn.

Talbot County Office of Tourism—Easton: 11 N. Washington St., Easton, MD 21601; phone (410) 770-8000.

Self-guiding tours: Maps and brochures outlining self-guiding tours can be obtained at the Historical Society of Talbot County *(see attraction listing).*

Shopping areas: Downtown Easton, especially Washington, Harrison, Dover and Goldsborough streets, offers a wide variety of antiques stores, specialty shops and boutiques.

ACADEMY ART MUSEUM, 106 South St. at Harrison St., is housed in two 19th-century structures. Exhibitions of national, regional and local artists change every 6 weeks. The Artists Resource Center is open to the public. Educational programs, including children's programs, are offered throughout the year. A juried craft show is held in mid-October. Mon.-Sat. 10-4, Sept.-July (also Wed. 4-9, Sept.-June). Admission $2; free to all Wed. Phone (410) 822-2787.

HISTORICAL SOCIETY OF TALBOT COUNTY, 25 S. Washington St., features three historic houses, a Federal-style garden and a museum with changing exhibits. Allow 1 hour, 30 minutes minimum. Museum open Mon.-Sat. 10-4; guided tour of the houses at 11:30 and 1:30; closed major holidays. Museum free. Houses tour $5. Phone (410) 822-0773.

EDGEWATER—*see Baltimore p. 177.*

ELKTON (B-8) pop. 11,893, elev. 28′

Originally named Head of Elk by John Smith in 1652 because of its position at the top of the Elk River, Elkton's commercial ties were evident as early as 1683 when a gristmill was built on the Big and Little Elk Creeks. In 1786, shortly after the Revolutionary War, Head of Elk became the county seat of Cecil County, and the following year the town's name was changed to Elkton.

Cecil County Tourism: 1 Seahawk Dr., Suite 114, North East, MD 21901; phone (410) 996-6290 or (800) 232-4595.

THE HISTORICAL SOCIETY OF CECIL COUNTY, 135 E. Main St., is in a building originally constructed as a bank in 1830. In addition to a research library, the historical society features a museum with a country store, a children's room with antique toys, an Early American kitchen and the Sheriff John F. DeWitt Military Museum. Mon. noon-4, Tues. 6-8:30 p.m., Thurs. 10-4, fourth Sat. of the month 10-2; closed holidays. Free. Phone (410) 398-1790.

ELLICOTT CITY—*see Baltimore p. 177.*

EMMITSBURG (B-5) pop. 2,290

Named for a local landowner, Emmitsburg is a few miles northeast of Catoctin Mountain Park *(see Thurmont p. 196),* location of Camp David, the presidential retreat.

NATIONAL FALLEN FIREFIGHTERS MEMO-RIAL, off US 15 S. Seton Ave. exit, then .6 mi. w. following signs to 16825 S. Seton Ave., is on the campus of the U.S. Fire Administration's National Fire Academy and Emergency Management Institute. This 7-foot high stone monument to firefighters who have died in the line of duty is surmounted by a bronze Maltese Cross, a motif on many firefighters' badges. The eternal flame at the base of the monument symbolizes the spirit of firefighters. Allow 30 minutes minimum. Daily 24 hours. Free. Over age 15 must present a photo ID for admission to the campus. Phone (301) 447-1365.

NATIONAL SHRINE GROTTO OF LOURDES, 3 mi. s. on SR 15 to 16300 Old Emmitsburg Rd., overlooks Mount St. Mary's College. The shrine, a replica of the Grotto of Lourdes in France, was established by Father John DuBois in 1805. Paved walkways wind through landscaped gardens containing stone and copper Stations of the Cross, mosaic murals depicting the Mysteries of the Rosary, a bronze statue of Mary and a campanile with 14 bells. Allow 30 minutes minimum. Daily dawn-dusk. Free. Phone (301) 447-5318.

SHRINE OF ST. ELIZABETH ANN SETON, 333 S. Seton Ave., is on the grounds of St. Joseph's Provincial House. In the early 1800s, Mother Seton, founder of the American chapter of the Sisters of Charity, began the country's first parochial school. She was canonized in 1975, the first native-born American woman to be so honored. A visitor center shows a 12-minute film every half-hour, and contains a museum displaying some of Seton's personal effects.

Allow 1 hour, 30 minutes minimum. Visitor center and other buildings open Tues.-Sun. 10-4:30. Basilica open daily 10-4:30. Museum closed major holidays, Easter and the last two weeks of Jan. Hours may vary; phone ahead. Free. Phone (301) 447-6606. *See color ad.*

 FORT McHENRY NATIONAL MONUMENT AND HISTORIC SHRINE—*see Baltimore p. 178.*

FORT MEADE—*see Baltimore p. 178.*

FREDERICK (B-5) pop. 52,767, elev. 271'

Frederick was occupied by both Union and Confederate forces several times. During the Confederate advance toward Sharpsburg and the Battle of Antietam, resident Barbara Fritchie allegedly dared the marching men to shoot her rather than the Union flag she was waving, an act that caused John Greenleaf Whittier to immortalize her in his poem "Barbara Fritchie."

Confederate general Jubal Early occupied the town briefly in 1864 and levied a ransom of $200,000 against its destruction. The town government paid the ransom by borrowing from local banks, which financed the loans with a bond issue. An estimated $600,000 in interest was paid on the bonds before the loans were finally repaid in 1951.

Monocacy National Battlefield, on SR 355, is the site where Union general Lew Wallace's greatly outnumbered troops, many of whom were untried in battle, were defeated by Confederate forces led by Gen. Early on July 9, 1864. The battle, though won by the Confederates, delayed Early's advance on Washington, D.C. With the arrival of Federal reinforcements the next day, the Confederates' hope of taking Washington was thwarted. Their withdrawal into Virginia spared the national capital and marked the Confederacy's last attempt to carry the war into the North.

A visitor center, 4801 Urbana Pike (SR 355), features pamphlets outlining self-guiding tours of the battlefield, as well as an interactive system showing people who fought and lived in Frederick; phone (301) 662-3515.

Tourism Council of Frederick County Visitor Center: 19 E. Church St., Frederick, MD 21701; phone (301) 228-2888. *See color ad.*

Self-guiding tours: The Visitor Center offers a self-guiding driving and walking tour pamphlet of historic Frederick County is 50c.

Shopping areas: Francis Scott Key Mall, 5500 Buckeystown Pike, is anchored by Sears.

Specialty shops selling antiques, crafts, clothing and pottery are plentiful at Shab Row and Everedy

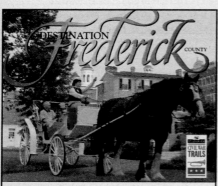

Square on East Street. Nearly 40 antiques shops are scattered around town; a cluster of them can be found on Antique Walk, near South Carroll and East Patrick streets.

SAVE **THE CHILDREN'S MUSEUM OF ROSE HILL MANOR PARK,** 1611 N. Market St., was the home of Thomas Johnson, Maryland's first elected governor. Guided tours of the 1790s house as well as the carriages and garden are available. The museum depicts 19th-century family life; a blacksmith shop and a log cabin are on the grounds. Hands-on displays in quilt-making, carding wool and operating a beaten biscuit machine and cream separator are of special interest.

Mon.-Sat. 10-4, Sun. 1-4, Apr.-Oct.; Sat. 10-4, Sun. 1-4, in Nov. Admission $5; over 54 and ages 3-17, $4. Phone (301) 694-1648.

THE DELAPLAINE VISUAL ARTS CENTER, 40 S. Carroll St., houses works by prominent and local artists, crafts persons and photographers. Traveling exhibits also are featured. Allow 1 hour minimum. Mon.-Sat. 9-5, Sun. 1-4; closed federal holidays. Donations. Phone (301) 698-0656.

SAVE **HISTORICAL SOCIETY OF FREDERICK COUNTY,** 24 E. Church St., features a collection of period furnishings, art and artifacts housed in a restored 1820s Federal-style mansion. A local history and genealogical library also is on the grounds. Allow 1 hour minimum. Mon.-Sat. 10-4, Sun. 1-4. Library Tues.-Sat. 10-4. Closed holidays. Admission $3, under 17 free. Phone (301) 663-1188.

MOUNT OLIVET CEMETERY, s. end of Market St., contains the graves of Francis Scott Key and his wife; at least 408 "Unknown Confederates" from the battles of Antietam and Monocacy; Barbara Fritchie; and Thomas Johnson, Maryland's first elected governor. The Revolutionary War Hessian Barracks are nearby. Daily 8-dusk. Free. Phone (301) 662-1164.

SAVE **NATIONAL MUSEUM OF CIVIL WAR MEDICINE,** just e. of SR 355/Market St. at 48 E. Patrick St., portrays how coping with sickness and death during the Civil War ushered in a new era of medical treatment. Exhibits vividly illustrate different aspects of Civil War medicine and include such re-creations as a field dressing station and field and pavilion hospitals. Other exhibits highlight nursing and embalming. Special events and educational programs are also available.

Guided tours are available. Allow 1 hour minimum. Mon.-Sat. 10-5, Sun. 11-5; closed Jan. 1, Easter, Thanksgiving and Dec. 24-25 and 31. Admission $6.50; over 59 and military with ID $6; ages 10-16, $4.50. AX, MC, VI. Phone (301) 695-1864 or (800) 564-1864. *See color ad p. 186.*

SCHIFFERSTADT ARCHITECTURAL MUSEUM, off US 15 Rosemont Ave. (exit 14) to 1110 Rosemont Ave., is a fine example of German Colonial architecture. Built in 1756, the house reveals early

construction methods and is one of the oldest structures in Frederick. Allow 30 minutes minimum. Wed.-Fri. 10-4, Sat.-Sun. noon-4, Apr. 1 to mid-Dec. Hours may vary; phone ahead. Closed Easter and Thanksgiving. Admission $3, under 12 free. Phone (301) 663-3885.

SUGARLOAF MOUNTAIN is approximately 13 mi. s. via I-270, on SR 109 at the Barnsville-Hyattstown exit. The isolated mountain—a public oasis on a private estate—rises about 1,281 feet above the surrounding countryside. It served as a Union Army signal station during the Civil War. Picnicking and hiking are allowed. No fires are permitted. Daily 8 a.m.-1 hour before dusk. Free. Phone (301) 874-2024.

FROSTBURG (B-2) pop. 7,873, elev. 1,920'

Frostburg owes its founding to the National Road, authorized by an act of Congress in 1806. In 1812 Meshach Frost, son of the first resident, built a log house for his bride. When stagecoach service began in 1818, the house was converted to Highland Hall Inn. Taverns, smithies and houses grew up around the inn, and the cluster of buildings was named Frostburg by the Post Office when mail service began in 1820.

By 1840 the railroad superseded the road, and the town became a commercial center for coal mining. The biggest employer is Frostburg State University, which began as a normal school in 1898; the student enrollment is 5,400. The town has returned to its roots with the restoration of The Old Depot, which dates back to 1891 and is now the destination point for the Western Maryland Scenic Railroad *(see attraction listing in Cumberland p. 185).* The depot center area also includes the Thrasher Carriage Museum *(see attraction listing).*

Allegany County Convention and Visitors Bureau—Frostburg: Western Maryland Station Center, 13 Canal St., Cumberland, MD 21502; phone (301) 777-5132 or (800) 508-4748.

Self-guiding tours: Frostburg's historic district covers 3 blocks along alternate US 40; the oldest structure was built in 1846. Self-guiding tour maps are available Mon.-Fri. 8-4 at City Hall, 37 Broadway; phone (301) 689-6000. Information also is available in nearby Cumberland *(see place listing p. 184)* from the Allegany County Visitors Bureau.

THRASHER CARRIAGE MUSEUM, Depot Center on Depot St., is in a renovated 1800s warehouse. The museum contains 40 late 19th- and early 20th-century horse-drawn vehicles, including formal closed carriages, sleighs, carts and milk wagons. Also displayed are carriage accessories such as hitches, saddles and lap robes. Allow 30 minutes minimum. Wed.-Sat. 10-4, Sun. noon-3, Mar.-Dec.; by appointment rest of year. Last tour begins 1 hour before closing. Admission $4; ages 6-18, $2. Phone (301) 689-3380.

GLEN ECHO — *see District of Columbia p. 115.*

GRANTSVILLE (B-1) pop. 619

Grantsville took its name from Daniel Grant, a Baltimorean who is said to have helped settle the area during the 1790s. The Casselman Hotel, Little Crossings Inn—now the Penn Alps—and Stanton's Mill, all founded 1797-1824, are among the buildings that remain from that era; all still are in use.

About a half-mile east of town is the Casselman Bridge, an 80-foot stone span built in 1813 for the National Road. At the time of its construction it was the country's longest single-span stone arch bridge. Nearby Casselman River Bridge State Park has picnic facilities.

Garrett County Chamber of Commerce—Grantsville: 15 Visitors Center Dr., McHenry, MD 21541; phone (301) 387-4386.

SPRUCE FOREST ARTISAN VILLAGE, .5 mi. e. on alternate US 40, has demonstrations of Colonial and contemporary arts and crafts including bird carving, pottery making, stained-glass working, spinning, weaving and woodcarving. The artisan village is on the grounds of the former Little Crossings Inn, a 19th-century stagecoach stop. The village includes 12 restored log houses and buildings, including a church and mill; two structures date from Revolutionary War days. Allow 1 hour minimum. Mon.-Sat. 10-5, May-Oct.; by appointment rest of year. Donations. Phone (301) 895-3332.

GREAT FALLS—

see Chesapeake and Ohio Canal National Historical Park p. 182.

GREENBELT—*see District of Columbia p. 115.*

HAGERSTOWN (B-4) pop. 36,687, elev. 547′

The Hagerstown area was wilderness when Jonathan Hager settled there in the mid-18th century. In 1762 he laid out a hamlet called Elizabeth Town on part of his land, and settlers of German descent arrived. Although Hager had named the town after his wife, it was known to the others simply as "Hager's Town," a name that was made official in 1813.

One of the first county libraries in the country was founded by local businessmen in 1901. Although residents of the predominantly rural area still considered reading a luxury, the project was an instant success. A few years later, the library began the world's first bookmobile by sending a two-horse wagon equipped with bookshelves to call on isolated farms.

Hagerstown is western Maryland's largest community, noted for a mixture of old and new buildings interspersed with many trees and public parks. Among the city's highlights is the Maryland Theater on Potomac Street, a 1915 vaudeville house designed by Charles Lamb. Home to the Maryland Symphony Orchestra, the restored theater stages regular concerts, symphony productions and shows.

HAGER HOUSE AND MUSEUM, .5 mi. s. on Virginia Ave. in Hagerstown City Park at 110 Key St., offers guided tours of the house built by town-founder Jonathan Hager in 1739. This impregnable building, erected over two springs to assure a protected water supply, served as home, fort and storehouse for its owner. The house is furnished in period; an adjacent museum has artifacts. Allow 30 minutes minimum. Tues.-Sat. 10-4, Sun. 2-5, Apr.-Dec. Admission $4; over 62, $3; ages 6-12, $2. Phone (301) 739-8393.

MILLER HOUSE, 135 W. Washington St., is a Federal-period town house with period furnishings and a replica of an early 19th-century garden. Doll and clock collections, Civil War artifacts, Bell pottery, Chesapeake and Ohio Canal exhibits and the first Hagerstown taxicab—a 1910 Regal—are among the displays. Allow 1 hour minimum. Wed.-Sat. 1-4, Apr.-Nov.; Wed.-Sun. 1-4 in Dec. Admission $5; over 60, $3; under 12 free. Phone (301) 797-8782.

WASHINGTON COUNTY MUSEUM OF FINE ARTS, .5 mi. s. on US 11 in Hagerstown City Park, displays sculptures, paintings, Oriental art objects and changing exhibits. Concerts and lectures are scheduled regularly. Allow 30 minutes minimum. Tues.-Sat. 10-5, Sun. 1-5; closed Jan. 1, Good Friday, July 4, Thanksgiving and Dec. 24-25 and 31. Free. Phone (301) 739-5727.

HANCOCK (B-3) pop. 1,725, elev. 448′

SIDELING HILL EXHIBIT CENTER is on I-68, 6 mi. w. of town; go 2 mi. past exit 77. It is immediately accessible from westbound I-68; eastbound I-68 travelers must stop at the rest stop and cross to it via a pedestrian bridge. The exposure of the surface beneath the crust of the Earth that was created when I-68 was cut through this hill provides the opportunity to examine sedimentary rock types, structural features and relationships of topography.

The center has geologic exhibits including a cross-section of a 350-million-year-old rock formation, displays about indigenous animals and tourist information. Allow 30 minutes minimum. Daily 8:30-5; closed Jan. 1, Easter, Thanksgiving and Dec. 25. Donations. Phone (301) 678-5442.

HANOVER—*see Baltimore p. 178.*

HAVRE DE GRACE—*see Baltimore p. 178.*

HOLLYWOOD (E-6)

SOTTERLEY PLANTATION is 4 mi. n. off of SR 245 at 44300 Sotterley Ln. This 1717 Colonial mansion overlooks woods, pastures and the Patuxent River. Features include a Chippendale stairway, pine paneling with unusual shell alcoves, antique furnishings and English gardens. Original outbuildings, including slave quarters, a "necessary" and a schoolhouse, also are accessible. Guided 45-minute tours of the restored house are available.

Allow 1 hour minimum. Grounds open Tues.-Sat.
10-4, Sun. noon-4, year-round. Guided house tours
on the hour Tues.-Sat. 10-4, Sun. noon-4, May-Oct.
Last tour begins 1 hour before closing. Grounds $2.
Grounds and house tour $7; senior citizens $6; ages
6-16, $5. Phone (301) 373-2280 or (800) 681-0850.

HYDES — see Baltimore p. 179.

JACKSONVILLE — see Baltimore p. 179.

KENSINGTON — see District of Columbia p. 115.

KENT ISLAND (C-7)

Following his exploration of the bay in 1631,
Virginian William Claiborne set up a trading post
on Kent Island, the largest of the Chesapeake Bay
islands. A colony developed and formed the first
Anglican congregation on the Eastern Shore. Although Claiborne fought for possession of the island, England decreed in 1638 that it was part of
Maryland.

The dual William Preston Lane Jr. Memorial
Bridges span the Chesapeake Bay from Kent Island
to Sandy Point, connecting the eastern and western
shores of Maryland.

**Queen Anne's County Department of Business
and Tourism:** 425 Piney Narrows Rd., Chester,
MD 21619; phone (410) 604-2100.

KNOXVILLE (C-4)

RECREATIONAL ACTIVITIES
Recreational Complex
- **River and Trail Outfitters**, 2 mi. w. on US 340,
then n. at blinking lights to 604 Valley Rd.,
Knoxville, MD 21758. Raft trips daily, Apr.
1-Nov. 15 (weather permitting). Hiking and biking tours Mar.-Nov. Cross-country ski trips
Thurs.-Sun., late Dec.-Mar. 31. Canoe and kayak
rentals and lessons; bicycle rentals. Phone (301)
695-5177 or (888) 446-7529.

LARGO — see District of Columbia p. 116.

LAUREL — see District of Columbia p. 116.

LEXINGTON PARK (E-7) pop. 11,021

CECIL'S OLD MILL, 5 mi. n.w. via SR 246W, then
.2 mi. n. on SR 471N (Indian Bridge Rd.), was
built in 1810 as a textile mill. The soil proved unsuitable for growing cotton, so the mill was subse-
quently used as a grist- and sawmill that ceased
operation in 1951. Inside are a grinder, bagger,
wheat cleaning machine and scales. Outside is restored operational sawmill equipment. Today the
mill is the focal point for 50 local craftsmen who
display their works among the mill machinery.

Allow 1 hour minimum. Mon.-Sat. 10-5, Sun.
11-5, Nov. 1-Dec. 23; Thurs.-Sat. 10-5, Sun. 11-5,
mid-Mar. through Oct. 31. Free. Phone (301)
994-1510.

PATUXENT RIVER NAVAL AIR MUSEUM is next
to Gate 1 of Patuxent River Naval Air Station at
22156 Three Notch Rd. (SR 235); the museum is
not on the base. Dedicated to the history of research development and the testing and evaluation
of Navy aircraft, the museum has hands-on displays, a wide-screen videotape presentation, full-
scale aircraft and a flight trainer to educate visitors
about the testing of military flying equipment. Allow 1 hour minimum. Tues.-Sat. 10-5, Sun. 10-4;
closed Jan. 1, Easter, Thanksgiving and Dec. 25.
Free. Phone (301) 863-7418.

LINTHICUM HEIGHTS—
see Baltimore p. 179.

LUSBY (E-7) pop. 1,666

FLAG PONDS NATURE PARK is 10 mi. s. on SR
2/4. The 527-acre park is a shelter for native wildlife, including muskrats, otters, white-tailed deer,
turkeys, foxes and pileated woodpeckers. Plant life
ranges from venerable hardwoods to the blue flag
iris that gives the park its name. Two ponds have
observation platforms. There also are 3 miles of
hiking trails, a wetlands boardwalk, a beach with
fossil formations and a visitor center with wildlife
displays.

Allow 1 hour minimum. Mon.-Fri. 9-6, Sat.-Sun.
9-8, Memorial Day-Labor Day; Sat.-Sun. 9-6, rest
of year. Admission $6 per private vehicle, Apr.-
Sept.; $3 rest of year. Phone (410) 586-1477.

LUTHERVILLE — see Baltimore p. 179.

MARBURY (E-5) elev. 90'

SMALLWOOD STATE PARK, 2750 Sweden Point
Rd., contains the restored home of Gen. William
Smallwood, Revolutionary War commander and
governor of Maryland. The 629-acre park has picnic facilities, four mini-cabins, 16 campsites with
electricity, playgrounds and a marina.

Food is available. Allow 1 hour minimum. Park
open daily 5 a.m.-dusk, May-Sept.; 8-dusk, rest of
year. House open Sun. 1-5, (by appointment mid-
Apr. to mid-Oct.). Admission $2. Boat ramp $5.
Phone (301) 743-7613 or (800) 784-5380. See Recreation Chart and the AAA Mideastern CampBook.

McHENRY (B-1) elev. 2,480'

Covering nearly 3,900 acres, McHenry's Deep
Creek Lake is Maryland's largest freshwater lake
and offers visitors boating, camping, fishing and
swimming opportunities (see Recreation Chart and
Oakland in the AAA Mideastern CampBook). Overlooking Deep Creek Lake is Wisp Ski Resort, featuring 14 miles of downhill ski trails available from
November through March; phone (301) 387-4911.

**Garrett County Chamber of Commerce—
McHenry:** 15 Visitors Center Dr., McHenry, MD
21541; phone (301) 387-4386.

**THE DISCOVERY CENTER AT THE DEEP
CREEK LAKE RECREATION AREA** is 1.5 s. on
US 219 to Glendale Rd., then 1.5 mi. w. to 898

State Park Rd. This interpretive, environmental center on the shore in Deep Creek Lake State Park provides hands-on exhibits about the natural resources of western Maryland. On-site naturalists and rangers lead daily educational programs dealing with the flora, fauna, and cultural and historical heritage of this area. Allow 1 hour minimum. Daily 10-5, Memorial Day weekend-Labor Day; Mon.-Fri. noon-4, Sat.-Sun. 10-4, day after Labor Day-Sept. 30, Sat.-Sun. 10-4, rest of year. Free. Phone (301) 387-7067.

MOUNT AIRY — see Baltimore p. 179.

NEW MARKET (D-1) pop. 427

Founded in 1793 along what would later become the historic National Pike (US 40) between Baltimore and Frederick, New Market was an important stop for early 19th-century travelers. The proximity of the road fostered many travel-related businesses.

Travelers still favor New Market, but today's visitors are searching for bargains in the town's many antiques and craft shops. New Market's historic district includes the original plot laid out by the town's founders.

Shopping areas: Antiques enthusiasts can find more than 35 shops on Main Street.

OAKLAND (B-1) pop. 1,930, elev. 2,385'

Outdoor opportunities abound in Oakland. Herrington Manor State Park, 5 miles north on US 219, offers both summer and winter activities, including cross-county skiing and hiking. Near the confluence of Muddy Creek and the Youghiogheny River, Swallow Falls State Park, 9 miles northwest on CR 20, is home to the state's largest waterfall—Muddy Creek Falls. *See Recreation Chart and the AAA Mideastern CampBook.*

Covering some 600 acres, Cranesville Sub-Arctic Swamp was formed during the ice age. Due to the high elevation and cool climate, the swamp contains vegetation normally found in Arctic regions. The boardwalk through the bog is open during the dry season, in summer and fall.

Garrett County Chamber of Commerce—Oakland: 15 Visitors Center Dr., McHenry, MD 21541; phone (301) 387-4386.

OCEAN CITY (E-9) pop. 7,173

Ocean City is a resort town on a 10-mile barrier island that separates the Atlantic Ocean to the east from a chain of bays—Big Assawoman, Isle of Wight, Montego and Sinepuxent—and the mainland to the west. The Ocean City Inlet, connecting the sea and the bays, offers sport fishing boats and pleasure boats a safe harbor with access to the ocean.

Deep-sea fishing for white and blue marlin, tuna, wahoo and bull dolphin can be arranged through a number of charter boat operators at Bahia Marina, the Dorchester Pier, Shantytown Pier, Talbot Street Pier and West Ocean City Harbor as well as on several large public fishing boats.

Equipment for windsurfing, jet skiing, parasailing and sailing also can be rented at these marinas and at many other locations in Ocean City. The area's natural beauty is highlighted at several golf courses, including some that make the most of seaside locations.

Several scenic evening cruises are available through local restaurants and at the marinas. There also are half-day sailboat cruises.

The 10-mile-long public beach offers a wide sandy expanse for strolling, sunbathing and seaside recreation. Shops, arcades and restaurants line the three-mile boardwalk, which extends from the inlet to 27th Street. A boardwalk train runs about every 20 minutes May through October and on weekends through December. Water parks, miniature golf courses and two full-scale amusement parks with roller coasters—one with a 1902 carousel boasting hand-carved animals—lend a carnival atmosphere.

The Convention Center at 40th and Coastal Highway brings in top entertainers, big band dances, antiques shows and trade shows; phone (800) 626-2326.

Nearby Ocean Downs Racetrack offers harness racing late July through August, and simulcasting year-round; phone (410) 641-0600.

Note: Policies concerning admittance of children to pari-mutuel betting facilities vary. Phone for information.

Ocean City Convention and Visitors Bureau: 4001 Coastal Hwy., P.O. Box 116, Ocean City, MD 21842; phone (410) 289-8181.

Self-guiding tours: Walking, biking, boating and driving tour brochures are available from the Ocean City Hotel, Motel & Restaurant Association, 4001 Coastal Hwy., P.O. Box 340, Ocean City, MD 21842-0340; phone (800) 626-2326. Also offering brochures for a variety of tours as well as sightseeing publications is the Ocean City Chamber of Commerce, 12320 Ocean Gateway, Ocean City, MD 21842; phone (888) 626-3386.

[SAVE] **OCEAN CITY LIFE-SAVING STATION MUSEUM** is at the s. end of the boardwalk on the inlet. Exhibits describe the history of the 1891 station and the many area shipwrecks and rescues. There are displays of early lifesaving equipment and related memorabilia. Models of early hotels, beach fashions and a photographic exhibit of the storms of 1933 and 1962 present Ocean City during different eras. Also displayed are beach sands from around the world, shipwreck artifacts and mermaid-themed objects.

Allow 1 hour minimum. Daily 10-10, June-Sept.; daily 10-4, in May and Oct.; Sat.-Sun. 10-4, rest of year. Admission $3; under 12, $1. Phone (410) 289-4991.

OXFORD (D-7) pop. 771, elev. 9'

Rivaled only by Annapolis among pre-Revolutionary Maryland ports, Oxford was made an official port of entry for the colony in 1683. Prosperous London and Liverpool businesses established branch stores that exchanged goods for tobacco. But with the rise of Baltimore as a commercial port during the Revolutionary War, Oxford lapsed into obscurity.

After the Civil War, shipbuilding, oystering and fish packing revitalized the Eastern Shore town's economy, and they have continued to sustain it. Most of the boats made in Oxford are built for fishing and pleasure.

Local attractions include a replica of the first federal customhouse, built by the collector appointed by George Washington, and the 18th-century home of Robert Morris, whose son, Robert Morris Jr., was a signer of the Declaration of Independence and the finance minister for the Confederation—the initial government of the Continental Congress of the Revolutionary period.

The grave of Lt. Tench Tilghman, who carried the news of Gen. Charles Cornwallis' surrender from Yorktown, Va., to the Continental Congress in Philadelphia, is in the Oxford Cemetery.

Talbot County Office of Tourism—Oxford: 11 N. Washington St., Easton, MD 21601; phone (410) 770-8000.

OXFORD-BELLEVUE FERRY, following signs to the western terminus of SR 333, was established in 1683 and is considered the oldest privately owned ferry in the country. It was propelled by oars until 1886, when powered service began.

The ferry operates every 25 minutes Mon.-Fri. 7 a.m.-9 p.m., Sat.-Sun. 9-9, June 1-Labor Day; Mon.-Fri. 7-dusk, Sat.-Sun. 9-dusk, Mar.-May and day after Labor day-Nov. 30. One-way fare $7 per private vehicle and driver (same day round trip $12), additional vehicle passengers $1 (round trip $2); motorcycles $4 (round trip $7); bicycles $3 (round trip $5); walk-on passengers $2 (round trip $4). Phone (410) 745-9023.

OXON HILL—
see District of Columbia p. 117

PARKTON—*see Baltimore p. 179.*

POINT LOOKOUT (F-7)

POINT LOOKOUT STATE PARK is s. on SR 5. A popular resort before the Civil War, the park is on a peninsula that forms the southern tip of Maryland's western shore. During the war, nearby Fort Lincoln housed more than 20,000 Confederates, almost a fourth of whom died from exposure, starvation and disease. With a beach, fishing pier, picnic area and nature trails, the park is once again a popular recreation site.

Park daily dawn-dusk. Museum daily 10-6, Memorial Day weekend-Labor Day; Sat.-Sun. 10-6, Apr. 1-day before Memorial Day weekend and day after Labor Day-Oct. 31. Day-use fee Mon.-Fri. $4 per private vehicle, Sat.-Sun. and holidays $6 per

person, May-Sept.; daily $4 per private vehicle, rest of year. Phone (301) 872-5688. *See Recreation Chart and the AAA Mideastern CampBook.*

PORT TOBACCO (E-5) elev. 177'

Port Tobacco, originally settled by the English in 1634, became the second largest river port in Maryland. Much of the tobacco sent to England was loaded at the town dock. A severe buildup of silt in the river and the passage of the railroad through nearby La Plata eventually diminished Port Tobacco's importance. Near the end of the 19th century the county seat was moved to La Plata, and the old port languished.

Port Tobacco consists of a village green bordered by a reconstructed Federal-style courthouse, two restored 18th-century houses, one reconstructed 19th-century house and the Salt Box, a restored 1700 house on Cheapside Street. The second floor of the courthouse contains the Charles County Museum of Port Tobacco, which is open Saturday-Monday and has displays and a film about the village; phone (301) 934-4313.

Charles County Office of Tourism: 200 Baltimore St., P.O. Box 2150, LaPlata, MD 20646; phone (800) 766-3386.

PRINCE FREDERICK (E-6) pop. 1,432

Named for a son of King George II, Prince Frederick has served as the seat of Calvert County since 1725. Fire destroyed the town three times: first in the 1740s, then during the War of 1812, and again in 1882.

Department of Economic Development and Tourism: 175 Main St., Prince Frederick, MD 20678; phone (410) 535-4583.

BATTLE CREEK CYPRESS SWAMP SANCTUARY AND NATURE CENTER, 4 mi. s.w. via SR 2/4 and SR 506, then s. on Gray's Rd., contains one of the nation's northernmost stands of bald cypress trees, which range from 75 to more than 500 years old. An elevated quarter-mile boardwalk angles through part of the swamp. A nature center contains natural and cultural history exhibits, including a honeybee hive. Films, demonstrations and programs are scheduled throughout the year.

Picnicking is permitted. Allow 1 hour minimum. Tues.-Sat. 10-5, Sun. 1-5, Apr.-Sept.; Tues.-Sat. 10-4:30, Sun. 1-4:30, rest of year. Trail open daily. Pets are not permitted. Free. Phone (410) 535-5327.

PRINCESS ANNE (E-8) pop. 2,313, elev. 17'

Founded at the headwaters of the Manokin River, Princess Anne is part of Somerset County, which was created by Lord Baltimore's proclamation in 1666. Several Colonial and Federal homes still stand along Mansion Street and US 13S. Of particular interest are Teackle Mansion, which is open for tours some afternoons, and the Washington Hotel.

Somerset County Tourism and Visitor Center Office—Princess Anne: 11440 Ocean Hwy., P.O. Box 243, Princess Anne, MD 21853; phone (410) 651-2968 or (800) 521-9189.

Self-guiding tours: A walking tour brochure detailing many of the town's historic buildings is available at the tourism office.

RISING SUN (B-7) pop. 1,702, elev. 387′

Originally part of Pennsylvania, Rising Sun became part of Maryland when the Mason-Dixon line was established in 1765. In the early 1700s the town was called Summer Hill and had five wagon trails leading into its center and meeting at the Rising Sun tavern; when a post office was established in 1802 the town changed its name to that of this popular meeting spot.

PLUMPTON PARK ZOO, off I-95 exit 100, 5 mi. n. on SR 272, then 1 mi. w. on SR 273 to 1416 Telegraph Rd., features more than 300 species of birds, reptiles and mammals, including North American bison, giraffes, llamas, lynxes, monkeys, water buffaloes, zebras and a tiger. The structures within the park, including a wooden gristmill, date to the 18th century. Allow 1 hour minimum. Daily 10-4, Mar.-Sept.; Thurs.-Mon. 10-4, rest of year. Closed Thanksgiving and Dec. 25. Admission $8; over 59, $7; ages 2-12, $4.50. Phone (410) 658-6850.

ROCKVILLE—*see District of Columbia p. 117.*

ST. INIGOES (F-7)

The town is home to St. Ignatius Church, built in 1785 and named for St. Ignatius Loyola, founder of the Jesuit order. Its cemetery is one of the oldest in America and contains the graves of many Jesuit priests as well as several soldiers of the American Revolution. The key to the church, which is on Villa Road, can be obtained at the Pass and Security Office of the adjacent Naval Electronics Systems Engineering Activities Station.

ST. LEONARD (E-6) pop. 536, elev. 115′

JEFFERSON PATTERSON PARK AND MUSEUM is s. on SR 2/4 to Parron Rd., then left on MacKall Rd. (SR 265), following signs. This 544-acre park on the Patuxent River chronicles the area's long history. The 70 discovered archeological sites range from prehistoric American Indian camps to a Colonial plantation. A self-guiding trail connects the sites and provides a short history of each. Artifacts from various digs, along with local history exhibits, are presented in the visitor center. Nature trails and picnic areas are available. Wed.-Sun. 10-5, Apr. 15-Oct. 15. Free. Phone (410) 586-8500.

ST. MARY'S CITY (F-7)

In March 1634 the *Ark* and the *Dove* sailed up the Potomac River and into the mouth of the St.

Mary's River, carrying the first colonists to arrive in Maryland under the royal charter of Lord Baltimore. A representative government was initiated, and St. Mary's City became the first capital of Maryland. The town prospered on the impetus of government, but farming assumed priority when the capital was moved to Annapolis.

St. Mary's County Department of Economic and Commercial Development: 23115 Leonard Hall Dr., Leonardtown, MD 20650; phone (301) 475-4411. *See color ad.*

HISTORIC ST. MARY'S CITY, on SR 5, is an 800-acre outdoor museum that includes a square-rigged ship, a tobacco plantation, a town center and a Woodland Indian Hamlet. Costumed interpreters in re-created 17th-century settings illustrate life in Colonial Maryland. Maps, brochures and an audiotape tour are available from the museum visitor center.

Wed.-Sun. 10-5, mid-June through mid-Sept.; Tues.-Sat. 10-5, Sun. (town center and visitor center only) 10-5, mid-Mar. through early June and late Sept.-Nov. 30. Complex closed Thanksgiving. Combination ticket for the *Maryland Dove,* State House, tobacco plantation and Woodland Indian Hamlet $7.50; over 59 and students with ID $6; ages 6-12, $3.50. Admission Sun. mid-Mar. through early June and late Sept.-Nov. 30, $5; over 59 and students with ID $4; ages 6-12, $2.50. DS, MC, VI. Phone (240) 895-4990, (240) 895-4960 or (800) 762-1634.

Godiah Spray Tobacco Plantation is a working reconstruction of a 17th-century tobacco plantation. The complex consists of the main dwelling house, a tenant's cottage and tobacco field, two tobacco-drying barns, a kitchen garden and livestock.

The Maryland Dove, on the water behind the State House, is a representation of the small square-rigged ships of the 1630s that brought settlers and cargo to Maryland. Iron murtherers (breech-loading shotguns), compasses, sandglasses and log pumps are among the ship's appointments.

Town Center contains Smith's Ordinary, a reconstructed 17th-century inn; Cordea's Hope, a mercantile; several ghost frames and the State House, a reproduction of the original 1676 building. Work currently is underway on the 1667 Brick Chapel.

Woodland Indian Hamlet is behind the visitors center. Costumed interpreters at this representation of a Yaocomaco Indian settlement demonstrate indigenous ways of life. Visitors to the hamlet can learn how Maryland's native population interacted with the English colonists.

LEONARD CALVERT MONUMENT, next to Historic St. Mary's City, stands on the site where Leonard Calvert signed a treaty with the Yaocomaco Indian king while buying land for the young colony.

TRINITY CHURCH, next to Historic St. Mary's City, dates from 1829 and was built with the bricks of the first state house. Daily 9-5; Sunday services

at 10 June-Aug., at 11 rest of year. Free. Phone (301) 862-4597.

ST. MICHAELS (D-7) pop. 1,193

About the time of the American Revolution St. Michaels began to develop as a noted shipbuilding center. During the War of 1812, St. Michaels' militia successfully repelled two British attacks. Traditional accounts of the attack on Aug. 9, 1813 credit the townspeople with extinguishing all ground lights and hanging lanterns in treetops, causing the British to shoot over the town. Because of the event, St. Michaels earned the nickname "The Town That Fooled The British."

Seafood and agricultural processing industries now sustain the economy, but the town's status as a commercial port seriously declined after the completion of the Chesapeake Bay Bridge in 1951. Visitors are rediscovering the region's unspoiled heritage, preserved by many years of near isolation. One of the better known yachting centers on the East Coast, St. Michaels draws thousands of sailing enthusiasts each summer.

Self-guiding tours: A free brochure describing a historic walking tour down streets lined with 19th-century frame houses is available from a rack outside the town hall at 109 S. Talbot St. and throughout the town; phone (410) 745-9535.

Shopping areas: Downtown St. Michaels, centering on Talbot Street, boasts specialty shops offering antiques, clothing and handmade items.

CHESAPEAKE BAY MARITIME MUSEUM, off SR 33 at Navy Point, is devoted to the history and traditions of the Chesapeake Bay. Skipjacks and other bay craft, waterfowling boats, guns and decoys, paintings and ships models, and the 1879 cottage-style Hooper Strait Lighthouse are among the exhibits in this 18-acre complex. The Steamboat Building deals with the use of the Chesapeake Bay as a highway and the change from sailing to propelled vessels.

Guided tours are available. Picnicking is permitted. Allow 1 hour minimum. Daily 9-6, June-Sept.; 9-5, Mar.-May and Oct.-Nov.; 9-4, rest of year. Closed Jan. 1, Thanksgiving and Dec. 25. Admission $10; over 62, $9; ages 6-17, $5. AX, DS, MC, VI. Phone (410) 745-2916.

DOCKSIDE EXPRESS CRUISES AND TOURS departs from 21604 Chicken Point Rd. on Tilghman Island. A marine biologist/historian conducts 90-minute narrated ecology cruises aboard a 49-passenger vessel. Sights along the cruise path include Colonial manor houses and various animals such as ospreys and blue herons. Also available are a champagne sunset cruise, a 60-minute hisory/nature cruise, and a driving tour and cruise combination. Captains for the cruises are native to the area.

Ecology tour daily at 10 and 2, Memorial Day-Labor Day; Sat.-Sun. at 10 and 2, Mar. 15-day before Memorial Day and day after Labor Day-early Nov. Ecology cruise $30; ages 3-12, $15. Cruises may be preempted by charters, so phone for availability. Reservations are recommended. AX, MC, VI. Phone (410) 886-2643 or (888) 312-7847.

PATRIOT OF ST. MICHAELS (Historic Miles River Cruise) departs from the maritime museum for 60- and 90-minute narrated tours of the Miles River. One-hour tours depart daily at 11, 2:30 and 4, Apr.-Oct. Ninety-minute tour departs daily at 12:30, Apr.-Oct. Fare for 60- or 90-minute tour $14; over 64, $12.50; under 12, $8. Phone (410) 745-3100.

SALISBURY (E-8) pop. 23,743

Originally a settlement at the intersection of American Indian trails and the Wicomico River, Salisbury was chartered in 1732. Beginning as an important stop for freight and passenger coaches, it later became a railroad freight center.

Salisbury is the largest city and second largest port on Maryland's eastern shore as well as the trade and transportation center for the Delmarva Peninsula. Flatboat ferries still operate on the eastern shore. The Upper Ferry at Salisbury is guided by a cable and powered by a small outboard motor as it takes travelers across the Wicomico River.

Newtown Historic District, north of Salisbury Parkway (US 50), covers six blocks. The homes, which reflect several architectural styles, date from the early to late 1800s. Poplar Hill Mansion, (410)

749-1776, and the Art Institute and Gallery, (410) 546-4748, also may be visited.

Wicomico County Convention and Visitors Bureau: Wicomico Youth and Civic Center, 8480 Ocean Hwy., P.O. Box 2333, Delmar, MD 21875; phone (410) 548-4914 or (800) 332-8687.

Self-guiding tours: Information and maps for tours of the historic district are available at the convention and visitors bureau.

SALISBURY ZOOLOGICAL PARK is 1.5 mi. e. on US 50, .5 mi. s. on Civic Ave., w. onto Glen Ave. then s. on Memorial Pl. Nestled on 12 acres, this zoo provides exhibits featuring nearly 400 specimens native to the Americas. Among the major exhibits are jaguars, otters, monkeys and an extensive waterfowl collection. Picnicking is permitted. Allow 1 hour minimum. Daily 8-7, Memorial Day-Labor Day; 8-4:30, rest of year. Closed Thanksgiving and Dec. 25. Donations. Phone (410) 548-3188.

 **WARD MUSEUM OF WILDFOWL ART,** Beaglin Park Dr. at 909 S. Schumaker Dr., displays a comprehensive collection of wildfowl art, including antique decoys, contemporary sculptures and paintings. The museum is named for Lem and Steve Ward of Crisfield, whose works helped promote the art of decoy carving.

After a brief videotape presentation that introduces visitors to the art form, galleries, displays, walk-through exhibits and a theater trace the development of wildfowl art and explore man's impact on the environment. Changing exhibits include works by noted wildfowl and wildlife artists.

Flash photography is prohibited. Allow 1 hour minimum. Mon.-Sat. 10-5, Sun. noon-5; closed major holidays. Admission $7; over 62, $5; college students with ID and grades K-12, $3. Sunday admission $3.50 (except grades K-12), 3 or more persons $8.50. Phone ahead to verify prices. Phone (410) 742-4988.

SILVER SPRING—

see District of Columbia p. 118.

SMITH ISLAND (F-7)

Smith Island was named for Capt. John Smith, who explored the Chesapeake Bay in 1608. The island actually comprises three islands that form an area about 8 miles long and 4 miles wide. Settled in 1657 by English dissenters from Lord Baltimore's colony, Smith Island is populated by descendants of the original Colonists.

Isolation from the mainland has allowed ancient modes of speech and grammatical constructions to survive. For more than three centuries the islanders have derived their livelihoods from the surrounding bay. The three fishing villages on the island are Ewell, Rhodes Point and Tylerton.

Cruises operate to the island from Crisfield, Md., and Reedville, Va. *(see place listings).*

SNOW HILL (F-9) pop. 2,409

Settled as a farming community along the Pocomoke River in 1642, Snow Hill grew into a port town and was made a British royal port in 1694. Warehouses, shipbuilding shops and other businesses sprang up to support the expanding trade, and the town was named the Worcester County seat in 1742. Growth continued despite the decreased national reliance upon water transportation. Snow Hill still is the county seat, but commerce now centers on the agricultural interests that spawned the town.

Worcester County Tourism: 104 W. Market St., Snow Hill, MD 21863; phone (410) 632-3110 or (800) 852-0335. *See color ad.*

Self-guiding tours: A walking tour brochure of the historic area is available from Town Hall, on the corner of Green and Bank streets, or from Purnell Museum at 208 W. Market St.; phone (410) 632-0515.

[SAVE] **FURNACE TOWN LIVING HERITAGE MUSEUM** is 5 mi. n. on SR 12, then 1 mi. w. to 3816 Old Furnace Rd. This re-created 19th-century industrial village features the Nassawango Iron Furnace, Maryland's only bog-ore furnace. A 19th-century garden kitchen, broom house, blacksmith shop, church, print shop, weaver house, woodworkers shop and museum also are on the site. Year-round events include art, music and living-history presentations. A nature trail winds 1 mile into the Pocomoke forest and cypress swamp.

Allow 30 minutes minimum. Daily 10-5, Apr.-Oct. Admission $4; over 60, $3.50; ages 2-18, $2. Phone (410) 632-2032.

SOLOMONS (E-7) pop. 1,536, elev. 20'

The Solomons area includes Solomons Island, near the point where the Patuxent River empties into the Chesapeake Bay. The town's harbor is one of the world's deepest natural ports. Noted as a yacht and boat building center, the resort affords access to fine fishing grounds.

ANNMARIE GARDEN ON ST. JOHN, on Dowell Rd. .5 mi. e. of SR 2/4, features winding paths, sculptures, themed areas and decorated benches within a 30-acre wooded site. The Surveyor's Map is a boardwalk that climbs to 10 feet above the tree canopy. Allow 1 hour minimum. Daily 10-4. Free. Phone (410) 326-4640.

[GEM] **CALVERT MARINE MUSEUM** is s. off SR 2/4 at Solomon's Island Rd. The museum focuses on local maritime history, estuarine biology and marine paleontology. Exhibits include vessels, models, artifacts and displays depicting the maritime history of the Chesapeake Bay and the Patuxent River area. Also featured are fossils collected from the nearby Calvert Cliffs and 17 aquariums with live specimens of various species,

including the river otter. Other offerings include a touch tank and a hands-on Discovery Room.

Also on the grounds is the restored and furnished cottage-type Drum Point Lighthouse, commissioned in 1883 and moved to this site in 1975. The J.C. Lore Oyster House, one-half mile south, has exhibits and films chronicling regional fishing. One-hour harbor tours are available on the historic bugeye *Wm. B. Tennison.*

Allow 1 hour minimum. Museum open daily 10-5; closed Jan. 1, Thanksgiving and Dec. 25. Harbor tours Wed.-Sun. at 2, May-Oct. Museum admission $7; over 54, $6; ages 5-12, $2. Harbor tour $7; ages 5-12, $4. Phone (410) 326-2042.

SPARKS — *see Baltimore p. 179.*

THURMONT (B-5) pop. 5,588

Legend maintains that Jacob Weller and his family, traveling west with a wagon train, stopped at what is now Thurmont in 1751 to nurse a sick child and remained. As a result of the industries introduced by generations of Wellers, the site became a town in which most residents worked as mechanics. By 1811 the hamlet was known as Mechanicstown.

After the railroad made the area readily accessible, the town became a popular resort noted for its mountain scenery. It was renamed Thurmont, "gateway to the mountains."

Catoctin Furnace, 4 miles south via US 15, is a partially restored iron furnace that operated 1777-1903. Visitors may explore the site.

CATOCTIN MOUNTAIN PARK, 2 mi. w. on SR 77, offers self-guiding nature trails, a bridle trail, picnicking, camping, fishing, cross-country skiing and snowshoeing. A visitor center just off SR 77 has information about interpretive programs. The Blue Blazes Still that was in use during Prohibition can be seen. Recreational facilities also are in adjoining Cunningham Falls State Park *(see Recreation Chart and the AAA Mideastern CampBook).*

Park daily dawn-dusk. Visitor center Mon.-Fri. 10-5, Sat.-Sun. 8:30-5; closed federal holidays during the winter. Free. Phone (301) 663-9388. *See Recreation Chart and the AAA Mideastern CampBook.*

TOWSON — *see Baltimore p. 179.*

WALDORF (D-6) pop. 22,312

THE DR. SAMUEL A. MUDD HOUSE MUSEUM is .3 mi. n.e. on Post Office Rd., 1 mi. s.e. on Leonardtown Rd., .5 mi. n.e. on Mattawoman-Beantown Rd., 3 mi. e. on Poplar Hill Rd., then .4 mi. s. to 3725 Dr. Samuel A. Mudd Rd. following signs. The house is where President Abraham Lincoln's assassin, John Wilkes Booth, was treated for a broken leg the morning after the crime. Though unaware of the assassination and the identity of his patient, Dr. Mudd was convicted of complicity and sentenced to life imprisonment. He was pardoned in 1869 by President Andrew Johnson. The house contains family furnishings of the period.

Guided tours are available. Allow 30 minutes minimum. Wed. and Sat.-Sun. 11-4, first weekend in Apr.-late Nov.; closed Easter. Last tour begins 30 minutes before closing. Admission $4; ages 6-16, $1. Phone (301) 274-9358 or (301) 645-6870.

WESTMINSTER — *see Baltimore p. 180.*

WHEATON — *see District of Columbia p. 118.*

WYE MILLS (D-7) elev. 36'

The town of Wye Mills grew up around Old Wye Mill, which produced flour for George Washington's troops at Valley Forge. The restored mill continues to operate and grinds and sells flour the first and third Saturday of the month; phone (410) 827-6909. Wye Church, a quarter-mile south on SR 662, is a restored Colonial structure with a hanging pulpit and box pews. A reconstructed vestry house furnished in period and a parish house built in the 18th-century style are nearby.

It's easy. Just log onto www.mid-atlanticramadas.com or call 1-800-4-Ramada and get our guaranteed best available rate, no questions asked.* However, if for some reason you manage to find a lower public rate on someone else's website, well, then your first night's stay with us, is on us. Proving that there's never been a better time to get your head out of the clouds, and onto one of our pillows.

RAMADA®
A very good place to be.®

MID-ATLANTICRAMADAS.COM or 1.800.4 RAMADA
en español 1.888.709.4021

Virginia

Blue Ridge Splendor

Bursts of yellow, orange and red fill the winding parkway with a mosaic of color as summer turns to autumn

Civil War Battlefields

Once the site of deadly conflict, these now peaceful havens pay homage to those who fought for their beliefs

Jefferson's Virginia

From Monticello to the State Capitol, Jefferson's legacies can be seen throughout his beloved Virginia

Tidewater Delicacies

Save room to sample some of the area's succulent oysters and blue crabs

Chesapeake Bay
© M. Berman
Robertstock

yesterday and today in harmony

Mabry Mill, Blue Ridge Parkway / © J. Irwin/Robertstock

Entrenched in history and entwined with tradition, Virginia not only embraces its past, but thrives on it. Eight presidential homes, two Colonial capitals, more Civil War battlefields than any other state—only Virginia can offer such a historical legacy.

Climb aboard replicas of wooden ships or visit the ruins of Jamestown and witness archeological digs. Stroll along the streets of Colonial Williamsburg and chat with 18th-century merchants. Embrace Richmond's history and discover such treasures as the capitol designed by Thomas Jefferson, and the Museum of the Confederacy, brimming with war memorabilia. Visit Charlottesville, home of Jefferson's Monticello, and have

lunch at Michie Tavern, once
an inn for the wayworn.

Follow in the footsteps of war heroes
as you roam myriad battlefields, walking
where valiant soldiers once fought.
Travel to Manassas, site of the first Civil
War battle; Chancellorsville, where Gen.
Thomas J. "Stonewall" Jackson was
mortally wounded; Petersburg, home of
The Crater, created by a Union explo-
sion that killed 278 Confederate soldiers;
and Appomattox Court House, where
Gen. Robert E. Lee surrendered to Gen.
Ulysses S. Grant.

Step back in time and experience Virginia's flourishing heritage.

A trip through Virginia is a bit of a science-fiction experience. One minute, you're square in the present, sailing on the sparkling waters of Chesapeake Bay. The next, you've stumbled back into the past, amid figures in Colonial attire atop horse-drawn carriages on cobbled streets.

So it is in the Old Dominion, where a quick, 5-mile drive easily can become a journey to a different period in time.

Set the dial in the time capsule to "today," and you're loaded with options.

Hop in the car and head for the mountains. The scenery along Skyline Drive and the Blue Ridge Parkway—both meandering, two-lane roads—is breathtaking. If you prefer to have your breath taken in a more jarring way, buckle yourself into the seat of a theme park roller-coaster.

Start with a lesson about agriculture and finish with a taste test at one of the many wineries that proliferate in northern Virginia.

Experience real-world art. Mother Nature's hands shape limestone like molding clay to create striking natural wonders. The vivid colors of gargantuan formations reflect off the surface of still pools in the chambers of caverns in Front Royal, Luray and New Market.

Natural Bridge, an impressive 215-foot arch, spans Cedar Creek. Its subterranean equivalent, which carves through Powell's Mountain and emerges in a natural amphitheater, is in Natural Tunnel State Park in Duffield.

Succumb to the lure of the sea. Observe the denizens of a wildlife refuge, visit a museum to trace the ocean's impact on the culture or just wade out into the surf, where modest breakers may dampen your swimwear but never your spirits.

If none of that appeals to you, then go take a hike. The Appalachian Trail sets the standard for outdoor adventure.

Through the Pages of History

Turn the time dial backward and explore intriguing eras in history.

Crank it way back and experience what life was like when the first permanent English settlers came to North America. Costumed interpreters at Jamestown Settlement demonstrate how the adventurous colonists coped with the hardships of life in the New World.

To get a little closer to the real thing, cruise to the romantic destination of Tangier

North America's first permanent English colony is founded at Jamestown.

© Andre Jenny/Focus Group /Picture Quest

1607

The seat of government is moved to Williamsburg; Richmond becomes the capital in 1779.

1699

Virginia becomes the 10th state in the Union.

1788

1775
Virginia patriot Patrick Henry makes his famous "Give me liberty or give me death" speech in Richmond.

Library of Congress

1781
British general Charles Cornwallis surrenders to Gen. George Washington at Yorktown, ending the Revolutionary War.

Virginia Historical Timeline

Island. Life on the largely unspoiled island is a radical departure from the hustle and bustle on the mainland. Residents who live and work along the quaint, narrow streets speak in a lingering Elizabethan dialect and adhere to the customs of a bygone era.

Learn something about an American leader by paying a visit to a presidential home. Virginia is the birthplace of eight presidents: George Washington, Thomas Jefferson, James Madison, James Monroe, William Henry Harrison, John Tyler, Zachary Taylor and Woodrow Wilson.

One of Washington's legacies lives on in Winchester. Although his act of leveling a cherry tree often is detailed in lore, lesser known is his requirement that tenants in the Shenandoah Valley plant 4 acres of apple trees. Orchards now envelop the town.

Hub of the Civil War

Bloody battlefields transformed the countryside during the Civil War. Fredericksburg, Manassas, Petersburg, Spotsylvania and Yorktown all suffered the ravages of bitter fighting. Richmond, capital of the Confederacy, was left a smoking ruin.

Born on a Stratford plantation, Robert E. Lee left footprints all over the state as he led the Army of Northern Virginia during the war. He chalked up victories at Richmond and Chancellorsville and tasted defeat at Gettysburg and Appomattox Court House, the site of his surrender to Gen. Ulysses S. Grant. Lee's body is buried beneath a chapel on the campus of Washington and Lee University in Lexington.

Booker T. Washington was among those who laid the framework on which the civil rights movement was built. Born a slave, the Virginia native advised presidents, inspired such philanthropists as Andrew Carnegie and John D. Rockefeller, and founded the Tuskegee Normal and Industrial Institute in Alabama. A national monument southeast of Roanoke pays tribute to his accomplishments.

The state strikes a wide balance between today and yesterday. Whether you're into nature, recreation or exploring the past, you'll have a healthy range of choices here.

If Virginia isn't part of your present, consider it as part of your future.

Confederate general Robert E. Lee surrenders to Union general Ulysses S. Grant at Appomattox Court House.
1865

Library of Congress

L. Douglas Wilder becomes the nation's first elected African-American governor.
1989

© Wally McNamee/Corbis

Archeologists uncover the remains of the original James Fort, abandoned for three centuries.
1996

1941
The War Department begins building the Pentagon in Arlington.

1917
Congress commissions a naval station at Hampton Roads, which will become home to one of the world's largest military installations.

2003
The Lewis and Clark Bicentennial is launched at Monticello, honoring the expedition's Virginian sponsor and leaders.

Recreation

From the sandy shores of Virginia Beach to the hundreds of remote hiking trails in the state's western mountains, Virginia's recreational activities are as varied as its landscape.

Mountain Escapes

The majestic Allegheny, Appalachian, Blue Ridge and Shenandoah mountains, standing like sentinels over western Virginia, offer a wealth of outdoor opportunities. Scenic Skyline Drive, winding along the crest of the Blue Ridge Mountains, runs the length of Shenandoah National Park and provides the perfect backdrop for **bicycling.** Crisp autumn days, with trees ablaze with fiery red and yellow leaves, are ideal for two-wheeling it along the 105 miles of twisting roadway. Frequent overviews allow for breathtaking scenery.

For the more adventurous, **mountain biking** is a popular pastime. Thrillseekers might want to try cruising down the mountain bike trails in Mount Rogers National Recreation Area, home to Virginia's highest elevation.

Grab your **hiking** boots and head to Shenandoah National Park, where more than 500 miles of trails lead trekkers through havens abloom in the spring with azaleas, dogwood and mountain laurel; if you're lucky you might happen upon a chipmunk or deer. Some popular hikes include the Whiteoak Canyon Trail and five nature trails: Fox Hollow, Loft Mountain Deadening, Mathews Arm Traces, Stony Man Mountain and Story of the Forest.

After an action-packed day of romping through the woods, a night of sound slumber beneath the twinkling stars just might be what you need. **Camping** in this pristine wilderness can do wonders for the soul. There are several developed campgrounds available. Some 535 miles of the Appalachian Trail traverses Virginia, offering numerous opportunities for primitive camping. Keep in mind that a back-country permit is required.

Taking to the slopes can be quite rewarding. **Skiing** and **snowboarding** at Virginia's four resorts—Bryce Resort in Basye, The Homestead in Hot Springs, Massanutten near Harrisonburg and Wintergreen Resort near Waynesboro—can be indulged from December to March.

Major **hunting** grounds for deer and turkey are the national forests, game management areas and two military reservations, A.P. Hill and Quantico, which collectively provide more than 2 million acres of public land. Remember that a valid license is required and can be obtained from the Virginia Department of Game and Inland Fisheries, (804) 367-1000.

Coastal Connections

The Tidewater area is a great place for frolicking in the water. Boats can be launched, sails can be hoisted and swimmers can take to the inviting ocean waters. Shipwrecks off the coast entice experienced **scuba divers** to explore the mysterious depths.

Virginia's many rivers, streams and lakes provide countless hours of **swimming, rafting, canoeing** and **kayaking.** For an active outing, canoe down the remote, tree-lined Shenandoah River or take to the rapids on the James River in downtown Richmond, with the city's skyline towering in the background. The Chesapeake Bay is the perfect backdrop for a day of **sailing.**

Mountain streams and inland rivers provide the backdrop for excellent **freshwater fishing.** Several large reservoirs include Lake Anna, Claytor Lake, Smith Mountain Lake, Philpott Reservoir and Kerr Lake. State fish hatcheries help keep the lakes, rivers and streams stocked with trout and bass. Anglers can reel in more than 25 species of fish. Don't forget your valid license.

Saltwater fishing is good at Chincoteague and other barrier islands. The Atlantic Ocean is home to such catches as blue marlin, dolphins, flounder, wahoo, white marlin and yellowfin tuna. The Chesapeake Bay is popular for sport fishing, with some catches weighing in anywhere from 50 to 100 pounds. If the rod and reel are not your style, try scooping up some of the bay's delectable crabs and oysters.

Recreational Activities

Throughout the TourBook, you may notice a Recreational Activities heading with bulleted listings of recreation-oriented establishments listed underneath. Similar operations also may be mentioned in Destination City recreation sections. Since normal AAA inspection criteria cannot be applied, these establishments are presented only for information. Age, height and weight restrictions may apply. Reservations often are recommended and sometimes are required. Addresses and/or phone numbers are provided so visitors can contact the attraction for additional information.

Fast Facts

POPULATION: 7,078,515.

AREA: 40,817 square miles; ranks 36th.

CAPITAL: Richmond.

HIGHEST POINT: 5,729 ft., Mount Rogers.

LOWEST POINT: Sea level, Atlantic Ocean.

TIME ZONE(S): Eastern. DST.

MINIMUM AGE FOR UNRESTRICTED DRIVER'S LICENSE: 18

SEAT BELT/CHILD RESTRAINT LAWS: Seat belts required for driver and front-seat passengers 16 and older. Children 6-16 must be restrained in an approved child restraint or seat belt. Child restraints required under age 6.

HELMETS FOR MOTORCYCLISTS: Required.

RADAR DETECTORS: Not permitted.

FIREARMS LAWS: Vary by state and/or county. Contact Firearms Transactions Office, Virginia State Police, P.O. Box 85608, Richmond, VA 23285-5608; phone (804) 674-2292.

HOLIDAYS: Jan. 1; Lee-Jackson-King Day, Jan. (3rd Mon.); Washington's Birthday, Feb. (3rd Mon.); Memorial Day; July 4; Labor Day; Columbus Day, Oct. (2nd Mon.); Election Day; Veterans Day, Nov. 11; Thanksgiving; Dec. 25.

TAXES: The Virginia statewide sales tax is 4.5 percent, with cities and counties imposing an additional 1 percent increment. Local options also allow admission, lodgings and restaurant taxes of varying increments.

INFORMATION CENTERS: State welcome centers are on US 13S near New Church, just south of the Maryland border; on I-64E southwest of Callaghan, just east of the West Virginia border; on I-66W near Manassas; on I-81S south of the West Virginia border, near Stephenson; on I-81N at the Tennessee border, near Bristol; on I-85N at the North Carolina border, south of Bracey; on I-77 at Lambsburg; on I-77 near Rocky Gap; on I-95N at the North Carolina border, south of Skippers; and on I-95S near Fredericksburg.

FURTHER INFORMATION FOR VISITORS:
Virginia Tourism Corporation
901 E. Byrd St.
Richmond, VA 23219
(800) 847-4822

FISHING AND HUNTING REGULATIONS:
Virginia Department of Game & Inland Fisheries
4010 W. Broad St.
Richmond, VA 23230
(804) 367-1000

NATIONAL FOREST INFORMATION:
Southern Region Information Office
1720 Peachtree Rd. N.W.
Atlanta, GA 30367-9102
(404) 248-9142
(877) 444-6777 (reservations)
National Park Service/D.C. Region
1100 Ohio Dr. S.W.
Washington, DC 20242
(202) 619-7222

RECREATION INFORMATION:
Virginia State Parks
Department of Conservation & Recreation
203 Governor St., Suite 306
Richmond, VA 23219
(804) 786-1712
(800) 933-7275 (reservations)

Virginia Temperature Averages Maximum / Minimum
From the records of the National Weather Service

	JAN	FEB	MAR	APR	MAY	JUNE	JULY	AUG	SEPT	OCT	NOV	DEC
Norfolk	50 / 32	51 / 32	57 / 39	68 / 48	77 / 58	85 / 66	88 / 70	86 / 69	81 / 64	71 / 53	61 / 42	52 / 33
Richmond	48 / 29	51 / 29	58 / 35	69 / 45	78 / 55	86 / 63	88 / 68	87 / 66	81 / 60	71 / 48	60 / 37	50 / 30
Roanoke	47 / 29	49 / 29	56 / 36	68 / 46	78 / 53	85 / 61	88 / 67	87 / 65	81 / 59	70 / 46	57 / 36	48 / 29

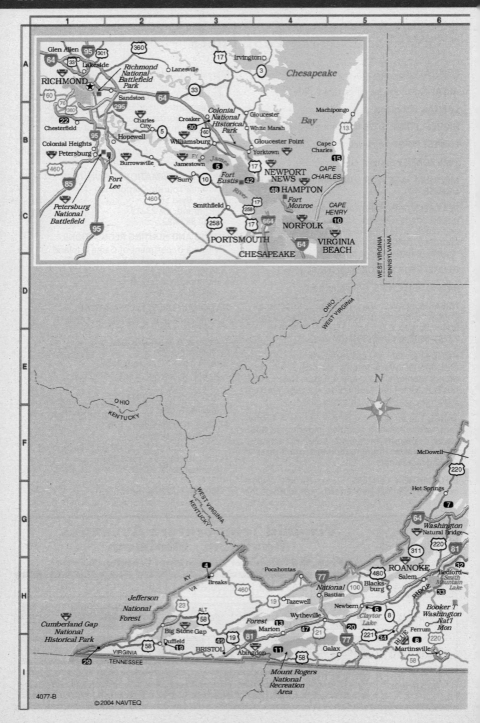

©2004 NAVTEQ

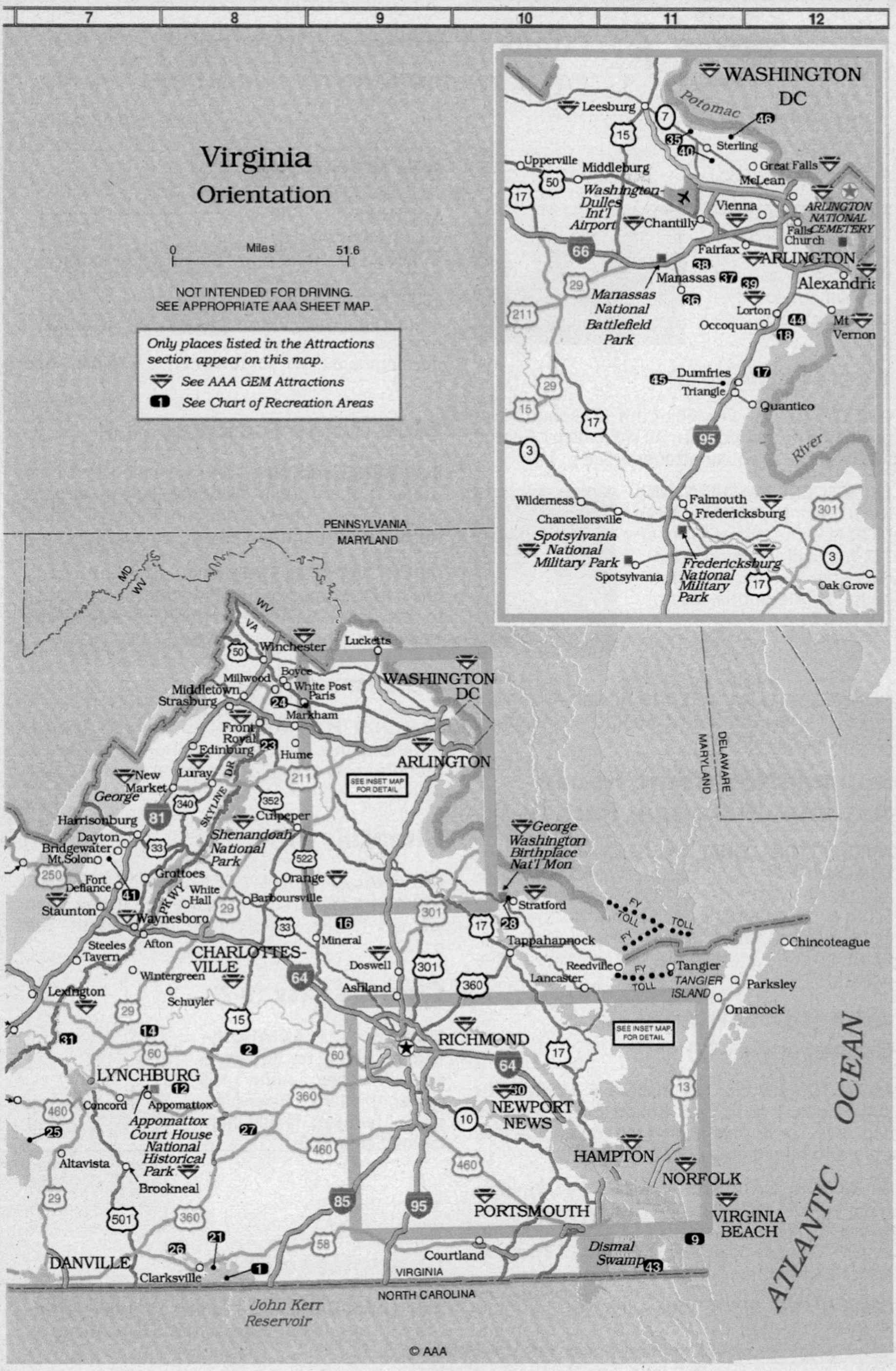

7
8
9
10
11
12
Virginia
Orientation
0 Miles 51.6
NOT INTENDED FOR DRIVING.
SEE APPROPRIATE AAA SHEET MAP.
Only places listed in the Attractions section appear on this map.
See AAA GEM Attractions
See Chart of Recreation Areas
PENNSYLVANIA
MARYLAND
MD
WV
VA
WASHINGTON DC
Potomac
Leesburg
Sterling
Upperville
Middleburg
Great Falls
McLean
Washington-Dulles Int'l Airport
Vienna
ARLINGTON NATIONAL CEMETERY
Chantilly
Falls Church
Fairfax
ARLINGTON
Manassas
Alexandria
Manassas National Battlefield Park
Lorton
Occoquan
Mt Vernon
Dumfries
Triangle
Quantico
River
Wilderness
Falmouth
Chancellorsville
Fredericksburg
Spotsylvania National Military Park
Spotsylvania
Fredericksburg National Military Park
Oak Grove
Winchester
Lucketts
Millwood
Boyce
White Post
Paris
Middletown
Strasburg
Markham
Front Royal
Edinburg
Hume
ARLINGTON
New Market
Luray
George
SKYLINE DR
SEE INSET MAP FOR DETAIL
Harrisonburg
Culpeper
Dayton
Bridgewater
Mt.Solon
Shenandoah National Park
Grottoes
Orange
Fort Defiance
White Hall
Barboursville
Staunton
PKWY
Waynesboro
Mineral
Steeles Tavern
Afton
CHARLOTTES-VILLE
Doswell
Wintergreen
Ashland
Lexington
Schuyler
RICHMOND
LYNCHBURG
Concord
Appomattox
Appomattox Court House National Historical Park
NEWPORT NEWS
Altavista
Brookneal
HAMPTON
NORFOLK
PORTSMOUTH
VIRGINIA BEACH
DANVILLE
Clarksville
Courtland
Dismal Swamp
VIRGINIA
NORTH CAROLINA
John Kerr Reservoir
George Washington Birthplace Nat'l Mon
Stratford
Tappahannock
Reedville
Lancaster
Tangier
TANGIER ISLAND
FY
TOLL
Chincoteague
Parksley
Onancock
MARYLAND
DELAWARE
ATLANTIC OCEAN
© AAA

Points of Interest Offering A
Great Experience for Members®

Abingdon (I-3)

BARTER THEATRE— During the Depression, food, rather than cash, was used as payment for theater tickets. See p. 221.

Alexandria (B-12)

CHRIST CHURCH—Pew 60 of this 1773 church was purchased for 36 pounds, 10 shillings by George Washington, a regular attendee. See p. 119.

THE GEORGE WASHINGTON MASONIC NATIONAL MEMORIAL—The memorial is a 333-foot-tall landmark modeled after the ancient lighthouse at Alexandria, Egypt. See p. 120.

OLD PRESBYTERIAN MEETING HOUSE—This 1774 church was the location of George Washington's funeral. See p. 120.

Appomattox Court House National Historical Park (H-7)

APPOMATTOX COURT HOUSE NATIONAL HISTORICAL PARK—A village of 27 restored buildings represents the day in 1865 when Gen. Robert E. Lee and the Confederate Army of Northern Virginia surrendered to Union general Ulysses S. Grant in the parlor of the McLean House. See p. 222.

Arlington National Cemetery (B-12)

ARLINGTON HOUSE, THE ROBERT E. LEE MEMORIAL—Built in 1802, Gen. Robert E. Lee's former home was confiscated during the war and used as a place to bury the war dead. See p. 125.

ARLINGTON NATIONAL CEMETERY—Seemingly endless rows of white headstones mark the graves of some of America's heroes, including John F. Kennedy, Rear Adm. Richard E. Byrd and Justice Earl Warren. See p. 125.

TOMB OF THE UNKNOWNS—Beneath the tomb made of Colorado marble lies the body of an unknown soldier from World War I. See p. 126.

Big Stone Gap (I-2)

SOUTHWEST VIRGINIA MUSEUM HISTORICAL STATE PARK—Housed in an 1880s home, the museum highlights exploration and development of southwestern Virginia. See p. 223.

Blue Ridge Parkway (H-6)

BLUE RIDGE PARKWAY—This 469-mile scenic road connects Shenandoah National Park in Virginia with the Great Smoky Mountains National Park in North Carolina and Tennessee. See p. 224.

MOUNT MITCHELL STATE PARK—The North Carolina park is named for Dr. Elisha Mitchell, who fell to his death while attempting to ascend the 6,684-foot summit. See p. 226.

Burrowsville (B-2)

BRANDON PLANTATION—Designed by Thomas Jefferson, this Colonial plantation continues to produce beef, corn, soybeans and wheat. See p. 228.

Chantilly (B-11)

NATIONAL AIR AND SPACE MUSEUM'S STEVEN F. UDVAR-HAZY CENTER—Discover here how man learned to slip the surly bonds of Earth. See p. 127.

Charles City (B-2)

SHIRLEY PLANTATION—Former home to Robert E. Lee's mother, Anne Hill Carter, this James River plantation features family heirlooms. See p. 300.

Charlottesville (G-8)

ASH LAWN-HIGHLAND—James Monroe, America's fifth president, lived at this 535-acre estate. See p. 229.

MICHIE TAVERN—Scotsman William Michie built this inn about 1784 as a rest stop for weary travelers. See p. 229.

MONTICELLO— Thomas Jefferson's mountaintop estate reflects his era, accomplishments and diverse interests. See p. 229.

UNIVERSITY OF VIRGINIA—Designed in the neoclassical style by Thomas Jefferson, this university boasts such former students as Edgar Allan Poe and Woodrow Wilson. See p. 230.

Cumberland Gap National Historical Park (I-1)

CUMBERLAND GAP NATIONAL HISTORICAL PARK—The gap, now within a 20,000-acre park, provides a natural passageway through the mountains into Tennessee, western Virginia and Kentucky. See p. 232.

Doswell (G-9)

PARAMOUNT'S KINGS DOMINION— More than 50 rides and shows are presented in eight thematic areas of this 400-acre amusement park. See p. 286.

Fredericksburg (D-11)

JAMES MONROE MUSEUM AND MEMORIAL LIBRARY— This library was owned by James Monroe 1786-92 and today houses one of the largest collections of Monroe memorabilia in the country. See p. 237.

KENMORE PLANTATION & GARDENS—This Tidewater mid-Georgian manor house was the home of George Washington's sister, Betty Washington Lewis. See p. 238.

MARY WASHINGTON HOUSE—The home of George's mother, it was from this house that the newly elected president left for his inauguration after receiving his mother's blessing. See p. 238.

RISING SUN TAVERN—This 1760 house was built for Charles Washington, brother of our first president. See p. 239.

Fredericksburg and Spotsylvania National Military Park (D-11)

FREDERICKSBURG AND SPOTSYLVANIA NATIONAL MILITARY PARK—This 8,400-acre area comprises four great Civil War battlegrounds: Chancellorsville, Fredericksburg, Spotsylvania Courthouse and the Wilderness. See p. 239.

Front Royal (E-8)

SKYLINE CAVERNS— These caves feature rare calcite formations known as anthodites, or cave flowers. See p. 240.

George Washington Birthplace National Monument (F-10)

GEORGE WASHINGTON BIRTHPLACE NATIONAL MONUMENT—On the south side of the Potomac River, the monument contains a replica of a house furnished with antiques from Washington's era. See p. 242.

Great Falls (A-11)

GREAT FALLS PARK—The Potomac River, which drops some 77 feet in thunderous rapids and falls, is a feature of this 800-acre park. See p. 128.

Jamestown (B-3)

JAMESTOWN SETTLEMENT—Built in 1957 to commemorate the 350th anniversary of the founding of Jamestown, this complex features three outdoor living-history areas, an indoor museum and an American Indian village. See p. 302.

Leesburg (A-11)

OATLANDS—Of the 3,400 acres that originally made up this estate, only 261 remain; visitors can view the 1804 house furnished in period. See p. 129.

Lexington (G-7)

LEE CHAPEL & MUSEUM—The 1867 chapel on the campus of Washington and Lee University now is a shrine to Gen. Robert E. Lee. See p. 264.

Lorton (B-11)

GUNSTON HALL PLANTATION—This 1755 brick Georgian residence was home to George Mason, author of the Virginia Declaration of

Rights of 1776 and one of the framers of the U.S. Constitution. See p. 129.

POHICK CHURCH—Used as a stable during the Civil War, this church, where George Washington served as a vestryman for 23 years, was restored 1902-17. See p. 129.

Luray (F-8)

LURAY CAVERNS—The Cathedral Room of these caves features unusually formed stalactites that can produce beautiful music. See p. 265.

Mount Vernon (B-12)

MOUNT VERNON—This final home of George Washington contains personal effects of the first president. See p. 131.

Natural Bridge (G-6)

NATURAL BRIDGE OF VIRGINIA—Supporting US 11, this limestone arch spans Cedar Creek. See p. 268.

New Market (F-7)

ENDLESS CAVERNS—These caves feature stalagmites, stalactites and various other formations. See p. 269.

NEW MARKET BATTLE-FIELD STATE HISTORICAL PARK—A self-guiding tour covers the battlefield where 257 Virginia Military Institute cadets fought in a Union victory on May 15, 1864. See p. 269.

SHENANDOAH CAVERNS—A mile-long guided tour offers spectacular views of cave formations. See p. 270.

Newport News (B-4)

MARINERS' MUSEUM—Situated in a 550-acre park, this museum is dedicated to preserving and interpreting the heritage of the sea. See p. 250.

VIRGINIA LIVING MUSEUM—From the ocean to the mountains this museum explores Virginia's natural heritage, ecosystems, plants and animals. See p. 250.

Norfolk (C-4)

CHRYSLER MUSEUM OF ART—Some 30,000 pieces of art include works by Mary Cassatt, Pablo Picasso and Andy Warhol. See p. 251.

GENERAL DOUGLAS MacARTHUR MEMORIAL—Nine galleries portray the military leader's life and career through various displays. See p. 251.

NAUTICUS, THE NATIONAL MARITIME CENTER—High-tech, interactive exhibits focus on such nautical themes as shipbuilding and navigation. See p. 252.

NORFOLK BOTANICAL GARDEN—Some 155 acres feature various plants; a trackless train and boat provide transportation through the gardens. See p. 252.

Orange (F-8)

MONTPELIER—This former residence of James Madison depicts the lifestyle and history of the Father of the United States Constitution and his family. See p. 270.

Petersburg (B-1)

PAMPLIN HISTORICAL PARK AND THE NATIONAL MUSEUM OF THE CIVIL WAR SOLDIER—Centered on a Civil War battlefield, the museum explores the plight of the common soldier through multimedia exhibits. See p. 271.

Petersburg National Battlefield (C-1)

PETERSBURG NATIONAL BATTLEFIELD—An important holding spot to Richmond, Petersburg saw 10 months of brutal Civil War fighting before falling to the Union army. See p. 272.

Portsmouth (C-3)

CHILDREN'S MUSEUM OF VIRGINIA—More than 90 hands-on exhibits allow children to explore science, nature, art and music. See p. 259.

CHILDREN'S MUSEUM OF VIRGINIA

Richmond (G-9)

AGECROFT HALL—Originally built during the 15th century, this Tudor-style house is surrounded by 23 acres of gardens. See p. 279.

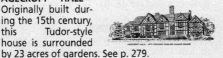

MAYMONT—This 100-acre Victorian country estate features the 1893 Maymont House, formal gardens, an arboretum, a carriage house and a petting zoo. See p. 281.

THE MUSEUM OF THE CONFEDERACY—Founded in 1890, this museum contains one of the largest collections of Civil War artifacts in the country. See p. 281.

VALENTINE RICHMOND HISTORY CENTER—The story of Richmond is told through an extensive collection of artifacts and displays; a tour of the 1812 Wickham House is offered. See p. 282.

VIRGINIA HISTORICAL SOCIETY & MUSEUM—Seven galleries exhibit treasures from Virginia. See p. 282.

VIRGINIA MUSEUM OF FINE ARTS—Fabergé jeweled eggs are just some of the art treasures found in this museum. See p. 282.

VIRGINIA STATE CAPITOL—Designed by Thomas Jefferson, the commonwealth's capitol is modeled after a Roman temple in France. See p. 282.

WHITE HOUSE OF THE CONFEDERACY—This Victorian-style mansion served as home to Confederate President Jefferson Davis during the Civil War. See p. 281.

Roanoke (H-6)

CENTER IN THE SQUARE—Several cultural attractions share this restored 1914 warehouse, including the Art Museum of Western Virginia; the History Museum and Historical Society of Western Virginia; and the Science Museum of Western Virginia and Hopkins Planetarium. See p. 288.

Shenandoah National Park (F-8)

SKYLINE DRIVE—Some 105 miles of scenic highway traverse Shenandoah National Park. See p. 291.

Staunton (F-7)

FRONTIER CULTURE MUSEUM—This living-history farm depicts rural life in Northern Ireland, Germany and England before immigration to North America as well as life on the Appalachian frontier. See p. 292.

Stratford (F-10)

STRATFORD HALL PLANTATION— BIRTHPLACE OF GEN. ROBERT E. LEE—Built in the shape of an H, this Colonial-style estate has been home to four generations of the Lee family. See p. 294.

Surry (B-3)

SURRY NUCLEAR INFORMATION CENTER—Innovative exhibits illuminate the science behind nuclear-generated electricity. See p. 294.

Vienna (B-11)

WOLF TRAP FARM PARK FOR THE PERFORMING ARTS—This is the country's only national park dedicated to the performing arts. See p. 132.

Virginia Beach (C-5)

VIRGINIA AQUARIUM AND MARINE SCIENCE MUSEUM—Hands-on exhibits explore Virginia's marine environment. See p. 254.

Waynesboro (G-7)

P. BUCKLEY MOSS MUSEUM—Amish and Mennonite people are portrayed in the works of this local artist. See p. 295.

Williamsburg (B-3)

BUSCH GARDENS WILLIAMSBURG—More than 100 rides, shows and exhibits portray 17th-century Europe. See p. 304.

COLONIAL WILLIAMSBURG HISTORIC AREA—This expansive living-history site, with restored buildings and costumed interpreters, depicts the 18th-century Colonial capital. See p. 306.

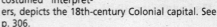

DeWITT WALLACE DECORATIVE ARTS MUSEUM—More than 10,000 decorative items portray area history. See p. 307.

GOVERNOR'S PALACE—The palace is a reconstruction of the 1722 building that served as executive mansion to Virginia's first two governors, Patrick Henry and Thomas Jefferson. See p. 307.

WATER COUNTRY USA—Wave pools, water slides and a high-dive show are just some of the attractions offered at this water park. See p. 308.

Winchester (E-8)

GLEN BURNIE HISTORIC HOUSE AND GARDENS—This opulent 1700s mansion with antiques galore and 6 acres of manicured gardens was built by the son of Winchester's founder. See p. 310.

Yorktown (B-3)

YORKTOWN VICTORY CENTER—Costumed interpreters and exhibits recall the events of the American Revolution. See p. 309.

RECREATION AREAS

	MAP LOCATION	CAMPING	PICNICKING	HIKING TRAILS	BOATING	BOAT RAMP	BOAT RENTAL	FISHING	SWIMMING	PETS ON LEASH	BICYCLE TRAILS	WINTER SPORTS	VISITOR CENTER	LODGE/CABINS	FOOD SERVICE
NATIONAL PARKS *(See place listings)*															
Shenandoah (F-8) 196,149 acres. Western Virginia. Horse rental.		•	•	•				•		•			•	•	•
NATIONAL FORESTS *(See place listings)*															
George Washington and Jefferson 1,800,000 acres. Western Virginia and eastern edge of West Virginia.		•	•	•	•	•	•	•	•	•	•	•	•	•	
NATIONAL RECREATION AREAS *(See place listings)*															
Mount Rogers (I-3) 140,000 acres in southwestern Virginia.		•	•	•				•	•	•	•		•		
ARMY CORPS OF ENGINEERS															
John H. Kerr Reservoir (I-8) 106,860 acres off SR 4 near Boydton. Water skiing.	❶	•	•	•	•	•		•	•	•			•	•	
STATE															
Bear Creek Lake (G-8) 326 acres 5 mi. w. of Cumberland off US 60. Horseback riding trails.	❷	•	•	•	•	•	•	•	•	•					•
Belle Isle (G-10) 733 acres on SR 683 near Litwalton. Saltwater fishing; paddleboats; playground.	❸	•	•	•	•	•	•	•		•	•		•		
Breaks Interstate (H-3) 4,500 acres 7 mi. e. on SR 80. Scenic. Horse rental. *(See Breaks p. 227)*	❹	•	•	•	•	•	•	•	•	•			•	•	•
Chippokes Plantation (B-3) 1,683 acres on the James River 1.5 mi. e. via SR 10, then 3 mi. n. on CR 634. Historic. *(See Surry p. 294)*	❺	•	•	•				•	•	•	•		•	•	•
Claytor Lake (H-5) 472 acres 4 mi. s. of Radford via I-81, then 2 mi. s. on SR 660. Horse rental.	❻	•	•	•	•	•	•	•	•	•			•	•	•
Douthat (G-6) 4,493 acres 6 mi. n. of Clifton Forge on SR 629.	❼	•	•	•	•	•	•	•	•	•			•	•	•
Fairy Stone (I-6) 4,750 acres 8 mi. w. of Bassett on SR 57.	❽	•	•	•	•	•	•	•	•	•			•	•	•
False Cape (I-11) 4,321 acres s.e. of Sandbridge via signs to Little Island Recreation Area. (Accessible only by foot, bicycle or boat.)	❾	•	•	•				•		•	•		•		
First Landing (C-5) 2,888 acres at Cape Henry on US 60.	❿	•	•	•	•			•	•	•	•		•	•	
Grayson Highlands (I-4) 4,754 acres w. of Volney on US 58. Horseback riding trails.	⓫	•	•	•				•		•			•		
Holliday Lake (H-8) 250 acres 6 mi. n.e. of Appomattox on SR 24, then 4 mi. e. via SR 626/629.	⓬	•	•	•	•	•	•	•	•	•			•		•
Hungry Mother (H-4) 2,215 acres 3 mi. n.e. of Marion on SR 16.	⓭	•	•	•	•	•	•	•	•	•			•	•	•
James River (G-7) In Buckingham County on CR 606 near Norwood. Canoeing; horseback riding trails.	⓮	•	•	•		•		•		•	•				
Kiptopeke (B-5) 540 acres 3 mi. n. of the Chesapeake Bay Bridge Tunnel from Virginia Beach on US 13, then w. on SR 704.	⓯	•	•	•	•	•		•		•			•		•
Lake Anna (G-9) 2,304 acres 25 mi. s.w. of Fredericksburg off SR 208.	⓰		•	•	•	•	•	•	•	•			•		•
Leesylvania (C-12) 508 acres 3 mi. e. of Woodbridge off I-95 exit 156.	⓱		•	•	•	•		•		•			•		•
Mason Neck (B-12) 1,814 acres 5 mi. n. of Woodbridge on US 1, then 5.5 mi. e. on SR 242.	⓲		•	•				•		•	•		•		
Natural Tunnel (I-3) 850 acres 3 mi. s. on US 23, then 1 mi. e. on CR 871. *(See Duffield p. 234)*	⓳	•	•	•				•	•	•			•		•
New River Trail/Shot Tower (H-5) 765 acres off I-77 exit 24, then 1.5 mi. n. on US 52. Historic; canoe rental. *(See Wytheville p. 311)*	⓴	•	•	•	•	•	•	•	•	•	•		•		
Occoneechee (I-8) 2,698 acres 1.5 mi. e. of Clarksville on US 58.	㉑	•	•	•	•	•		•		•	•		•		
Pocahontas (B-1) 7,625 acres 4 mi. s.w. of Chesterfield off SR 655.	㉒	•	•	•	•	•	•	•	•	•	•		•		•
Raymond R. "Andy" Guest Jr. Shenandoah River (E-8) 1,604 acres 8 mi. s. of Front Royal off US 340. Horse rental.	㉓	•	•	•		•		•		•			•		
Sky Meadows (E-8) 1,862 acres 1 mi. s. on US 17. Scenic. *(See Paris in the District of Columbia p. 131)*	㉔	•	•	•				•		•			•		

RECREATION AREAS

	MAP LOCATION	CAMPING	PICNICKING	HIKING TRAILS	BOATING	BOAT RAMP	BOAT RENTAL	FISHING	SWIMMING	PETS ON LEASH	BICYCLE TRAILS	WINTER SPORTS	VISITOR CENTER	LODGE/CABINS	FOOD SERVICE
Smith Mountain Lake (H-6) 1,248 acres 26 mi. s. of Bedford via SR 122 to SR 608 to SR 626.	25	•	•	•	•	•	•	•	•	•	•		•	•	•
Staunton River (I-8) 1,597 acres 9 mi. s.e. of Scottsburg on SR 344.	26	•	•	•	•	•		•	•	•					•
Twin Lakes (H-8) 425 acres 3 mi. n.e. of Green Bay off US 360 to SR 613.	27	•	•	•	•	•	•	•	•	•					•
Westmoreland (G-10) 1,299 acres 5 mi. n.w. of Montross on SR 3. Swimming pool.	28	•	•	•	•	•	•	•	•	•				•	•
Wilderness Road (I-1) 200 acres 5 mi. w. of Ewing at US 58 and SR 690. Historic home.	29		•	•						•			•		•
York River (B-3) 2,505 acres 1 mi. n. of Croaker via SR 607, then 2 mi. e. on SR 606. *(See Croaker p. 302)*	30	•	•	•	•	•		•	•	•			•		
BLUE RIDGE PARKWAY															
Otter Creek (G-7) 552 acres at Milepost 61.	31	•	•	•				•		•					
Peaks of Otter (H-6) 4,150 acres at Milepost 86.	32	•	•	•				•		•			•	•	•
Roanoke Mountain (H-6) 65 acres at Milepost 121.	33	•	•	•											
Rocky Knob (I-5) 4,200 acres at Milepost 167.	34	•	•	•				•		•			•	•	•
OTHER															
Algonkian Regional Park (A-11) 500 acres 11 mi. e. of Leesburg and 3 mi. n. of SR 7. Golf, miniature golf; playground.	35		•	•	•	•		•	•	•				•	•
Bull Run Regional Park (B-11) 3 mi. from I-66 Centreville exit, off US 29. Miniature golf, skeet and trap shooting; playground.	36	•	•	•					•	•			•		•
Burke Lake Park (B-11) 888 acres 6 mi. s.w. of I-495 exit 5W via CR 620, CR 645 and CR 123. Golf; carousel, miniature train.	37	•	•	•	•	•	•	•		•	•		•		
Ellanor C. Lawrence Park (B-11) 640 acres .5 mi. n. from I-66 exit 53 via SR 28. Historic.	38		•	•						•			•		
Lake Accotink Park (B-12) 479 acres 3 mi. from I-495 exit 5E via CR 620 and Heming Ave. Canoeing, miniature golf; carousel, playground.	39		•	•	•	•	•	•		•	•				•
Lake Fairfax Park (A-11) 479 acres 7 mi. w. of I-495 exit 10W via SR 7 and CR 606. Cross-country skiing, miniature train; athletic fields, carousel.	40	•	•	•	•			•	•	•		•			•
Natural Chimneys (F-7) 150 acres .5 mi. n.w. on SR 731 following signs. *(See Mount Solon p. 268)*	41	•	•	•				•		•	•		•		
Newport News (B-3) 8,330 acres on SR 143, .5 mi. w. of jct. SR 105 on SR 143. Golf, jogging; archery range. *(See Newport News p. 250)*	42	•	•	•	•	•	•	•		•	•		•		•
Northwest River Park (I-11) 763 acres 15 mi. s. on SR 168, then 3.5 mi. e. on Indian Creek Rd. Miniature golf; playground. *(See Chesapeake p. 256)*	43	•	•	•	•		•	•		•					•
Pohick Bay Regional Park (B-12) I-95S to Lorton exit, s. on US 1 to Gunston Rd., then 3 mi. e. Golf, miniature golf.	44	•	•	•	•	•	•	•	•	•					•
Prince William Forest (C-11) 18,726 acres off I-95 exit 150, then .25 mi. w. on SR 619. *(See Triangle in the District of Columbia p. 132)*	45	•	•	•						•	•		•		•
Riverbend Park (A-12) 409 acres 10 mi. w. of I-495 exit 13 via SR 193, CR 603 and Jeffrey Rd. (CR 1268). Nature center.	46		•	•				•				•	•		
Rural Retreat Lake (I-4) 350 acres 4 mi. s.w. of Rural Retreat off I-81 exit 60, 4 mi. e. on CR 749, then 1 mi. s. on CR 677.	47	•	•	•	•	•	•	•	•	•					•
Sandy Bottom Nature Park (C-4) 456 acres off I-64 at 1255 Big Bethel Rd. in Hampton. Nature center, playground.	48	•	•	•				•		•			•		
Sugar Hollow (I-3) 500 acres in Bristol off Lee Hwy. via I-81 exit 7. Golf; driving range, swimming pool.	49	•	•	•					—	•				•	

Exploring Virginia

For descriptions of places in bold type, see individual listings.

The Eastern Shore

Tales of Blackbeard, herds of wild ponies, secluded fishing villages and unspoiled beaches lend to the romantic atmosphere of Virginia's Eastern Shore.

In 1965 the almost 18-mile Chesapeake Bay Bridge-Tunnel opened, linking mainland Virginia to the southern tip of the Delmarva Peninsula (parts of the peninsula belong to *Dela*ware, *Mary*land and *Virginia*) at Cape Charles. Said to be one of the world's most incredible engineering feats, the bridge-tunnel dips into the water and carries motorists under massive, ocean-bound freighters. The bridge holds a scenic stop, fishing pier and restaurant and connects US 13 from the mainland to the peninsula where it becomes the main run.

Bounded by wetlands, barrier islands and the Atlantic Ocean on the east and the Chesapeake Bay on the west, the 70-mile Delmarva Peninsula and several barrier islands constitute what is called Virginia's Eastern Shore. Capt. John Smith and his exploring party were the first Europeans to visit the area when they mapped the Chesapeake Islands in 1608. In 1614 the Jamestown government purchased the land; 6 years later the English colonized the peninsula.

The grave of John Custis IV lies near **Cape Charles** on the peninsula's bay side. The tomb for this ancestor of the Virginia Custis family bears an epitaph evidently intended to be the last word in a lifelong quarrel with his wife.

Farther north on US 13 is Eastville, a town with a 1644 debtor's prison and the country's

Great Falls Park, Great Falls / © Gibson Stock Photography

Virginia's Past is Ever Present

oldest standing courthouse. The building contains the nation's earliest continuous court records, dating from 1632, including the first account of an American dramatic performance—the 1665 play "The Bear and the Cub"—and the only record of a local court's declaration that the English Parliament's Stamp Act was unconstitutional.

Onancock's deep harbor offers docking for any size craft. Passenger ferries leave Onancock for **Tangier** Island, in the heart of Chesapeake Bay. In 1814 the British established headquarters on Tangier and swayed the young island men into service. But the night before the recruits

were to sail with the British, the Tangier women sank their small boats, and the British had to sail without them.

Tangier Island seems untouched by time. Most of the denizens still speak with Elizabethan idioms and accents, and many customs remain. There is no industry on the island, and its two main roads are 8 to 10 feet wide.

Near the Maryland border, SR 175 branches off US 13 to the east. The NASA Visitor Center is on SR 175, 6 miles east of US 13.

As many remember, Marguerite Henry's famed pony, Misty, was from **Chincoteague.** The ponies are an island trademark; according to local legend they descended from mine horses that swam ashore from a wrecked Spanish galleon centuries ago. Most historians, however, believe the original herd was brought over by the first English colonists who turned them loose on Assateague and Chincoteague in the late 1600s when the ponies began to damage mainland Virginia's crops.

The ponies are rounded up at their home on the southern end of Assateague Island to swim at slack tide (when the tide is changing and there is no movement) across the narrow channel to Chincoteague to be auctioned; the unsold ponies swim back to Assateague. This annual July event draws tens of thousands of spectators.

The Highlands and the Great Valley

Carved by the Shenandoah and James rivers, the Shenandoah Valley is nestled between the Blue Ridge Mountains on the east and the Allegheny Mountains on the west. Conifers and such hardwoods as hickory and walnut dot the valley; copious broomsedge, crabgrass and wire grass that once made this region impassable to frontiersmen blanket the land.

The majestic Blue Ridge, Shenandoah, Allegheny and Cumberland mountains frame Virginia's western border and exhibit some of the most spectacular scenery in the nation. Many of the region's routes are AAA designated scenic byways: the **Blue Ridge Parkway,** Skyline Drive, I-81, I-77 and I-64.

Shawnee Indians lived in villages along the riverbanks of the Shenandoah and the James. In the 1720s the region was settled by people of German, Scottish, Irish and English descent. In 1750 Daniel Boone crossed the valley on his way to find the Cumberland Gap, thereby opening the door to westward expansion beyond the Appalachians into the Mississippi region.

From the southwest corner of the state to the northern border of the mountainous region, I-81 runs parallel to the ranges through the 200-mile patchwork-like Shenandoah Valley. **George Washington and Jefferson National Forests,** with miles of trails and numerous trout streams, stretches through 1.8 million acres of Virginia's Blue Ridge and Allegheny mountains. The forest has deer, turkey, grouse and squirrel hunting, many campgrounds and fishing and swimming lakes.

South of **Marion** on SR 16 is **Mount Rogers National Recreation Area,** containing the highest point in the state at 5,729 feet. I-77 bisects the forest and connects I-81 to the Blue Ridge Parkway and the West Virginia border.

Roanoke, once called Big Lick because of salt marshes that

Grayson Highlands State Park, Mount Rogers National Recreation Area
© Michael P. Gadomski

attracted herds of game, is cradled between the Blue Ridge Mountains to the east and the Allegheny Mountains to the west. I-81 and the Blue Ridge Parkway flank the city. Twenty miles southeast of Roanoke, the **Booker T. Washington National Monument** re-creates the small tobacco plantation where the educator and advisor to presidents was born a slave.

Just south of **Lexington** is one of the seven natural wonders of the world, **Natural Bridge.** The 23-story arch is a product of limestone substratum erosion. The Monocan Indians worshiped "The Bridge of God," and George Washington carved his still-visible initials into the stone. Natural Bridge spans Cedar Creek and supports US 11 but cannot be seen from the highway.

Near Lexington I-81 runs north through the George Washington and Jefferson National

Forests. One of the first national forests established in the East, it includes the largest public hunting ground in the region; the main marks are white-tailed deer, wild turkeys, black bears and some smaller game. Fishing for trout, bass and bluegill is excellent.

The forest's 1 million acres are divided into three chief parts: The largest is in the Allegheny and Shenandoah mountains along the West Virginia border; another is southwest of **Shenandoah National Park,** along the Blue Ridge Parkway and the Appalachian Trail; the third is Massanutten Mountain, between **Front Royal** and **Harrisonburg.**

Scenic I-64 disjoints at I-81 near **Staunton,** resumes farther south near Lexington and continues westward through the Alleghenies and into West Virginia.

Roadside stands with vendors peddling Virginia apples and cider speckle the Shenandoah Valley from Roanoke to **Winchester.** When George Washington owned farmland near Winchester, he required his tenants to plant 4 acres of apple trees in the rich limestone soil, fostering the current production of 5 million bushels of apples a year.

Blue Ridge Parkway and Skyline Drive are actually one road. Skyline Drive runs 105 miles through Shenandoah National Park; at the southern terminus of Skyline Drive the Blue Ridge Parkway begins and heads toward the North Carolina border and on to Great Smoky Mountains National Park. These routes are winding two-lane roads intended for leisurely travel. They do not go to or through any towns, and lodging and food availability are limited. The speed limit on Skyline Drive is always 35 mph.

Skyline Drive runs for 105 miles from Front Royal south to Rockfish Gap, twisting its way through Shenandoah National Park. More than 70 overlooks provide views of the Shenandoah River Valley to the west and the Piedmont to the east. Skyline Drive can be accessed from four points: near **Front Royal** on US 340; at Swift Run Gap, between Stanardsville and Elkton on US 33; at Rockfish Gap, between **Charlottesville** and **Waynesboro** on US 250 near I-64; and at Thornton Gap, between **Luray** and Sperryville on US 211.

Near Thornton Gap Skyline Drive runs through an unusual 610-foot tunnel in the solid granodiorite of Marys Rock. Outside the park underground caverns at Luray are a natural wonder produced when the region's limestone soil eroded. The caverns contain thousands of massive colored formations. Cathedral Room has an unusual "Stalacpipe Organ" using specially tuned stalactites to produce music of almost symphonic quality.

The Blue Ridge Parkway continues Skyline Drive 469 miles from Shenandoah National Park to Great Smoky Mountains National Park in North Carolina. A ride along the parkway reveals weathered farmhouses and barns and miles of split-rail fences. Mountain flowers color the meadows in spring and early summer.

Dogwoods bloom in early May, and in the cool, clear June air mountain laurel, azaleas and rhododendron burgeon. From mid-October through November hickory, maple and sassafras trees burst into fiery flames of gold and red. In winter the parkway offers solitude and crisp beauty.

The parkway ribbons along the natural contours of the southern Appalachian Mountains' crests, granting picturesque overlooks and many natural attractions: Humpback Rocks, Otter Creek, Peaks of Otter (with a 360-degree panorama), Smart View, Roanoke Mountain and Rocky Knob.

The parkway's average elevation is 3,000 feet, and the speed limit is 45 mph with few opportunities to pass, making it truly a scenic route unsuitable for those in a hurry. The parkway is always open, but weather conditions affect the accessibility of certain sections of the road.

Northern Virginia

Northern Virginia, from the Potomac River south to **Fredericksburg** and west to the fall line, is the most diversified region in the state. While much of it borders the District of Columbia—a bustling, cosmopolitan city revolving around the politics and business of the nation's capital—northern Virginia's roots are still deeply planted in the past.

The District's mien spills over into **Arlington** and **Alexandria,** which at one time were part of the capital city. Alexandria, a metropolitan suburb of Washington, is almost wholly contained by I-95/495 (the Capital Beltway) and I-395 (the Shirley Memorial Highway).

Few areas offer a more pleasant trip into an earlier time than

Jamestown Settlement, Jamestown
© SuperStock

Old Town Alexandria, where more than 400 early buildings remain, including the Boyhood Home of Robert E. Lee (a private residence) and Christ Church, where George Washington and Lee worshiped. Lining the cobblestone streets are 18th- and 19th-century town houses, some of which have been converted into Colonial-era shops and restaurants.

Eight miles south of Alexandria at the southern end of the George Washington Memorial Parkway, a AAA designated scenic byway, is the impressive estate and burial place of George Washington— **Mount Vernon**.

Manassas National Battlefield Park / © SuperStock

Arlington is north of Alexandria on the southwest bank of the Potomac via the George Washington Memorial Parkway. One of the smallest counties in the United States, this capital suburb covers only 25.7 square miles, much of it federal property.

Directly across the Potomac from Washington, on the confiscated estate of Robert E. Lee, is **Arlington National Cemetery** with rows of uniform white headstones. At the north end of the cemetery is the Marine Corps War Memorial, an immense bronze depiction of U.S. Marines raising the American flag on Mount Suribachi during the World War II battle for Iwo Jima.

West on I-66 and then west on US 29 is **Falls Church,** named after the 1734 church built near the Little Falls of the Potomac River. George Washington was a vestryman in this Georgian church 1762-84. In a park south of West Street is the original stone marker that was to indicate the western boundary of the District of Columbia, as first conceived in 1791. It marks where Falls Church meets Arlington and Fairfax counties.

North of Falls Church, Old Dominion Drive terminates at

Great Falls Park, which straddles the Potomac with one leg in Maryland and the other in Virginia. Near Washington Dulles International Airport is **Chantilly** and Historic Sully Plantation. This virtually unchanged 1794 home belonged to Richard Bland Lee, who was a member of the first U.S. Congress and instrumental in relocating the nation's capital to Washington in 1800.

West on SR 236 (Little River Turnpike) off I-495 is **Fairfax,** a residential community that holds George and Martha Washington's wills in its Judicial Center on Chain Bridge Road. Fairfax is home to George Mason University.

West on US 50 is historic **Middleburg,** where steeplechase races and fox hunts are still enjoyed. This rural village is in the heart of the John S. Mosby Heritage Area, which lies north and south of US 50 from SR 17 to CR 600; US 50 is a Virginia scenic byway. Three AAA designated scenic byways traverse this region: I-66 from Skyline Drive to its junction with CR 647 near Marshall; SR 7 from its junction with CR 662 west to Berryville; and SR 9 from the West Virginia border to its junction with CR 662. The Appalachian Trail

crosses all three of these scenic routes. Audiotapes of a self-guiding driving tour are available at local visitor centers.

SR 28 from Chantilly leads into SR 29 via I-66 and to **Manassas National Battlefield** where the Civil War battles of the First and Second Manassas, or Bull Run, were fought. Picnickers and other sightseers came out to see this "Sunday afternoon skirmish" that was thought would determine the outcome of the war. "Stonewall" Jackson received his nickname during the first conflict when Confederate general Barnard Bee rallied his men by pointing out, "There is Jackson standing like a stone wall. Let us determine to die here, and we will conquer."

East of the battlefield and 2 miles southwest of **Lorton** stands the 1774 Pohick Church. Gunston Hall, on SR 242, is the home of George Mason, author of the Virginia Declaration of Rights and the Virginia Constitution of 1776. Close by is **Occoquan,** and farther south on I-95 is **Quantico,** one of the largest Marine Corps installations in the nation and home of the Marine Corps Air-Ground Museum.

Farther south is Fredericksburg, which Washington called

"the place of my growing infancy." It also is the place where the cherry tree legend originated. Four major Civil War battles were fought in this area, and Fredericksburg changed hands between Confederate and Union forces seven times. The battlefields are preserved in nearby **Fredericksburg and Spotsylvania National Military Park**.

Other area highlights include the 40-block historic district, one of the country's largest collections of 18th- and 19th-century buildings; James Monroe Museum and Memorial Library; Kenmore Plantation & Gardens, the home of Washington's sister and her family; Mary Washington House, Washington's mother's home; and Rising Sun Tavern, a place where rebel patriots gathered before the Revolutionary War.

In 1777 **Culpeper** citizens responded to Gov. Patrick Henry's call to arms. Almost 100 years later the homes, churches and buildings of Culpeper's residents were used as hospitals during several Civil War battles. And later, Culpeper was the Union Army's headquarters. The town is northwest of Fredericksburg via SR 3.

The Piedmont

From the Blue Ridge Mountains near **Charlottesville** to the fall line near I-95 and south to the North Carolina border is Virginia's heartland. South-central Virginia's serene beauty is manifested in low rolling hills and water rapids, in meadows and pine and hardwood forests, and in clay and limestone covered with broomsedge, crabgrass and wire grass.

The area's scenic routes include I-64 from Charlottesville to Staunton and I-77 in the southwestern corner of the region, extending from I-81 and into North Carolina.

Soon after Tidewater plantations and townsites were developed, Virginia's Colonial population swelled and settlers moved into the Piedmont area. Some people brought Tidewater grace and etiquette; others arrived with only their independent spirit.

Richmond / © Vladpans/eStock Photo

Thomas Jefferson built his grand Monticello near Charlottesville in the foothills of the Blue Ridge Mountains, which Jefferson called "the Eden of the United States." Charlottesville also is home to the University of Virginia, chartered in 1819. The university was a dream of Jefferson, who insisted that religious freedom be an absolute: "The institution will be based on the illimitable freedom of the human mind."

East of Charlottesville via I-64 is historic **Richmond,** once capital of the Confederate States of America and site of Patrick Henry's proclamation, "I know not what course others may take; but as for me, give me liberty or give me death!" The Museum of the Confederacy, next to the White House of the Confederacy at 12th and E. Clay streets, honors the Confederacy.

South of Richmond on I-95 or I-295 and then east on SR 10 is **Hopewell,** an outgrowth of City Point. Flowerdew Hundred, about 10 miles east of Hopewell on SR 10, was founded in 1618 by Sir George Yeardley, governor of the Virginia colony. He purchased 1,000 acres on the south shore of the James River from the Virginia Co., which was attempting to expedite settlement by encouraging private ownership of new plantations known as hundreds. The site is one of the best preserved early 17th-century archeological finds in Virginia. More than 60 sites have been revealed, some dating back to about 9000 B.C.

Farther south on I-95 is **Petersburg.** By 1850 Petersburg was a major tobacco and industrial port where skilled tradesmen were more valuable than slaves. Black workers often earned wages sufficient to purchase their freedom, thus creating the largest free black population in the antebellum South. **Petersburg National Battlefield** is nearby.

US 29 from Charlottesville leads to **Lynchburg,** once a tobacco town that now offers sightseeing tours of its 19th-century historic areas. Thomas Jefferson's personal haven, Poplar Forest, is southwest of Lynchburg, while the last home of his political adversary, Patrick Henry, is a modest frame dwelling called Red Hill at Brookneal approximately 35 miles southeast of Lynchburg on CR 600.

US 460 meets SR 24 at Appomattox, the center of Virginia's heartland. **Appomattox Court House National Historical Park,** 3 miles northeast of Appomattox on SR 24, commemorates the site where Gen. Robert E. Lee's 28,231 remaining Confederate soldiers found themselves surrounded by Bluecoats. Lee surrendered, bringing the Civil War to an end.

The Virginia Civil War Trails are self-guiding automobile tours that allow visitors to retrace the steps taken by both Union and Confederate troops during the Civil War. Red, white and blue interpretive signs throughout the state mark the routes, mostly roads used by the soldiers, and provide historical backgrounds. The "Lee vs. Grant: The 1864 Campaign" route covers some 150 miles and visits more than 30 historical sites starting in Germanna Ford on the Rapidan River and ending in Petersburg. The "Lee's Retreat" trail cover the final days of the Civil War from Petersburg to Appomattox and features 18 historic sites. Other routes include the "1862 Peninsula Campaign," "Shenandoah Valley" and "Northern Virginia." For further information phone (888) 248-4592.

Danville is quartered by north-south US 29 and east-west US 58 near the North Carolina border. The last capital of the Confederacy, it was at Danville that Jefferson Davis received word that Lee had surrendered at Appomattox. The city is still a tobacco town that sells the leaf in loose piles.

Tidewater

Tidewater Virginia, the coastal plain region from the Potomac River south to North Carolina, was the first area on the continent settled by English-speaking people. The Potomac, Rappahannock, James and York rivers cut the northern and central Tidewater into fingers. The Chesapeake Bay and Eastern Shore protect the three narrow peninsulas, or necks. Early settlement naturally took place along these sheltered estuaries, which were means of commerce and transportation. The area's land is flat, but rich in nutrients as well as history.

Colonial Parkway, a AAA designated scenic route, connects **Jamestown, Williamsburg** and **Yorktown** in the southernmost neck of the Tidewater region. **Colonial National Historical Park** includes Jamestown Island, the site of the first permanent English settlement, founded in 1607, and Yorktown Battlefield, where the last important conflict of the Revolutionary War was fought.

At the intersection of US 60 and the parkway is Williamsburg. Originally an outpost of Jamestown called Middle Plantation, Williamsburg was renamed in 1699 and replaced Jamestown as the capital of Virginia. An earlier era is re-created in the nation's largest restored 18th-century town through Colonial shops, artisans demonstrating Colonial crafts, taverns that serve authentic Colonial-era foods and citizens dressed in the attire of the day.

On SR 5 near **Charles City** are several antebellum plantations majestically lining the James River. Among them are Berkeley Plantation, site of the first official Thanksgiving in 1619, and Shirley Plantation, Robert E. Lee's ancestors' home.

Yorktown, at the eastern terminus of Colonial Parkway, is best known as the site of the British surrender that ended the American Revolution. The battlefield surrounds the town.

I-64 intersects the Colonial Parkway, continues east to **Newport News,** on to **Hampton,** **Norfolk** and then around **Portsmouth** to the west. These cities also share the world's largest natural harbor, Hampton Roads.

In the shipbuilding business since 1886, Newport News preserves its maritime heritage through the Mariners' Museum on US 60. Hampton is

Yorktown Victory Center, Yorktown
© Paul M. Franklin

America's oldest continuously English-speaking settlement. Norfolk remains a major shipping port and because of its superior harbor is the headquarters for the U.S. Navy Atlantic Fleet. Nauticus, the National Maritime Center, Norfolk's renovated waterfront and downtown add to the city's nautical charm. Portsmouth is a harbor town across Hampton Roads from Newport News and separated from Norfolk on the east by the Elizabeth River.

The Virginia Beach-Norfolk Expressway extends from the junction of I-264 and I-64 to the coast. **Virginia Beach** has become a family vacation hot spot with 28 miles of golden beaches, excellent fishing, a variety of water sports and local seafood.

Just south of Portsmouth, **Dismal Swamp** stretches over more than 223,000 acres of southeastern Virginia and northeastern North Carolina. Part of the area is a wildlife refuge sheltering black bears, wildcats and thousands of birds in its dense forests, vine and brier thickets and peat bogs.

Points of Interest

ABINGDON (I-3) pop. 7,780, elev. 2,057'

Abingdon was founded in 1778 at the junction of two American Indian foot trails on a site where Daniel Boone had camped some years before. Abingdon is one of the oldest English-speaking towns in the Blue Ridge Mountains.

The Virginia Creeper National Recreation Trail, a 34-mile former railbed of the Virginia-Carolina Railroad, begins in Abingdon. Once an American Indian path, the trail now is popular with hikers, bicyclists, runners and horseback riders. A 15-mile section provides an easy hike on winding trails leading to Damascus.

Abingdon's 20-square-block historic district contains many 19th-century buildings, including museums, craft shops, art studios, galleries and historic lodgings. The area is a thriving arts community with the Arts Depot on Depot Square, offering changing exhibits.

The Virginia Highlands Festival, a showcase of Appalachian culture, takes place over the first 2 weeks of August.

Abingdon Convention and Visitors Bureau: 335 Cummings St., Abingdon, VA 24210; phone (276) 676-2282 or (800) 435-3440.

Self-guiding tours: A walking tour brochure of Abingdon's historic district is available from the visitors bureau.

Shopping areas: Dixie Pottery, off I-81 on SR 11, is home to 100,000 square feet of housewares, including pottery, baskets, arts and craft supplies and kitchenware. The Cave House Craft Shop, 279 E. Main St., offers regionally made wares.

BARTER THEATRE is off I-81 exit 17 at 127 Main St. "The State Theatre of Virginia" was founded in 1933 on the theory that drama could be bartered for food. During the Depression Robert Porterfield convinced 22 Broadway actors that it was better to eat in Virginia than to starve in New York. Though cash is now the accepted medium of payment, Porterfield's original theater offered tickets in exchange for milk, ham, chicken and other edibles.

Barter Theatre is one of the country's oldest professional regional theaters that offers a wide range of productions. Spring, summer and fall repertories allow patrons to see four shows in 2 days.

Performances Wed.-Thurs. at 7:45, Fri.-Sat. at 8:15, Sun. at 7, with matinees Wed.-Thurs. and Sat. at 2 and Sun. at 3, Feb.-Dec. Tickets $19-$38. Reservations are recommended. DS, MC, VI. Phone (276) 619-5400.

FIELDS-PENN 1860 HOUSE MUSEUM is at 208 W. Main St. Guided tours of this historic house museum offer a glimpse of mid- to late-19th-century life. Exhibits include period room settings, decorative arts authentic to the era and a permanent collection of regional pottery, furniture, textiles, metalworks and basketry. Allow 1 hour minimum. Tours depart every 30 minutes Wed. 11-4, Thurs.-Sat. 1-4, Apr.-Dec. Donations. Phone (276) 676-0216 or (800) 435-3440.

WILLIAM KING REGIONAL ARTS CENTER is at 415 Academy Dr. Museum galleries showcase art of the region and the world. On the grounds are resident art studios and an outdoor sculpture garden. Allow 30 minutes minimum. Tues.-Fri. 10-5 (also Tues. 5-9), Sat.-Sun. 1-5; closed major holidays. Free. Phone (276) 628-5005.

AFTON (G-7) elev. 1,360'

WINERIES

- **Afton Mountain Vineyards**, 1.7 mi. w. on SR 6, then 1.2 mi. s. on CR 631 to 234 Vineyard Ln. Wed.-Mon. 10-6, Mar.-Nov.; Wed.-Mon. 10-5, in Dec.; Fri.-Mon. 11-5, rest of year. Closed Jan. 1, Easter, Thanksgiving and Dec. 25. Phone (540) 456-8667.

ALEXANDRIA — see District of Columbia p. 119.

ALTAVISTA (H-7) pop. 3,425, elev. 596'

A relatively young town by Virginia standards, Altavista was founded in 1905 by three Lane brothers who purchased 2,000 acres in Campbell County during construction of the Virginia Railway. In 1912, the Lane family opened a box plant, today known for its cedar chests and furniture.

DID YOU KNOW

The Old Dominion
is home
to more than
70 wineries.

SAVE **AVOCA MUSEUM** is at 1514 Main St. Housed in the 1901 country Victorian home of Revolutionary patriot Col. Charles Lynch, the museum features American Indian artifacts and Civil War items. Thurs.-Sat. 11-3, Sun. 1:30-4:30, mid-Apr. through Oct. 31. Admission $5; over 65, $4; ages 6-18, $2. Phone (434) 369-1076.

APPOMATTOX (H-8) pop. 1,761, elev. 861'

SAVE **FRED'S CAR MUSEUM** is off US 460 bypass to SR 24E. More than 65 classic vehicles manufactured 1906-80 are displayed. Rare models include a 12-cylinder 1939 Lincoln limousine; a 1914 Saxton; a 1936 Packard; a 1946 fire truck; and a 1957 Chevrolet. Allow 30 minutes minimum. Mon.-Sat. 10-5, Sun. 1-5. Admission $5; under 10, $3. Phone (804) 352-0606.

⬇️GEM APPOMATTOX COURT HOUSE NATIONAL HISTORICAL PARK (H-7)

Three miles northeast of Appomattox on SR 24, Appomattox Court House National Historical Park is a 1,744-acre site. On April 9, 1865, Gen. Robert E. Lee's weakened and outnumbered Confederate Army of Northern Virginia was cut off at Appomattox Court House by Gen. Ulysses S. Grant. The two commanders met in the parlor of a house owned by Wilmer McLean, and the Army of Northern Virginia was surrendered to Grant.

Markers designate Grant's and Lee's headquarters, the site of the last shots fired by the Confederate artillery and infantry, and the road where the arms were laid down.

The courthouse building burned in 1892, and a new one was built at the location of the present town of Appomattox. A speculator razed the McLean House in 1893 with the intention of rebuilding it in Washington, D.C. This project failed and the materials, left exposed to the ravages of decay and souvenir hunters, soon were destroyed. The McLean House was reconstructed on the original site by the National Park Service.

A village of 27 structures has been restored to its 1865 appearance. Among the buildings open to visitors are Clover Hill Tavern, county jail, guest house, Jones Law Office, kitchen, McLean House, Meeks General Store and Woodson Law Office.

Exterior restorations include Isbell House, Mariah Wright House and Peers House. The reconstructed courthouse serves as a visitor center and has a museum and an auditorium where audiovisual programs are shown every half-hour.

Living-history programs are presented in summer. Costumed interpreters portraying soldiers from each side answer visitors' questions. Area information is available at the visitor information center in the railroad depot on Main Street in the town of Appomattox.

The park and buildings are open daily 8:30-5; closed Jan. 1, Thanksgiving and Dec. 25. Admission Memorial Day weekend-Labor Day $4 ($10 maximum per private vehicle), under 17 free. Admission rest of year $3 ($5 maximum per private vehicle), under 17 free. Phone (434) 352-8987 for park information, or (434) 352-2621 for area information.

ARLINGTON— *see District of Columbia p. 124.*

⬇️GEM ARLINGTON NATIONAL CEMETERY—
see District of Columbia p. 125.

ASHLAND— *see Richmond p. 285.*

BARBOURSVILLE (F-8) elev. 510'

WINERIES

• **Barboursville Vineyard** is near jct. SR 20/US 33 at 17655 Winery Rd. Tastings Mon.-Sat. 10-5, Sun. 11-5. Tours are offered Sat.-Sun. noon-4. Closed Jan. 1, Thanksgiving and Dec. 25. Phone (540) 832-3824.

BASTIAN (H-4) elev. 2,180'

The Wolf Creek Railroad came to Bastian in 1914 to serve a growing logging industry, and the Virginia Hardwood Lumber Mill opened here in 1927. Thanks to the mill, Bastian was the first town in Bland County to receive electricity. During the Great Depression, thousands of young men worked at a model camp established in Bastian by the Civilian Conservation Corps. The mill and railroad closed after World War II.

WOLF CREEK INDIAN VILLAGE & MUSEUM is off I-77 exit 58, then just n. on US 52. Interpretive guides conduct hands-on tours of the re-created American Indian village, which was constructed near an actual archeological site. Museum displays include excavated artifacts. Nature trails and picnic facilities are on the grounds. Allow 1 hour minimum. Daily 9-5; closed Jan. 1, Thanksgiving and Dec. 24-25. Admission $8; ages 5-16, $5. DS, MC, VI. Phone (276) 688-3438.

BEDFORD (H-7) pop. 6,299

Founded as the town of Liberty in 1782, Bedford soon was renamed after the Fourth Duke of Bedford. The town is home to many historic structures, including Avenel, a former 1838 plantation manor house that once welcomed such visitors as Gen. Robert E. Lee and writer Edgar Allan Poe. Tours are available by appointment; phone (540) 586-1814.

South of town Liberty Lake Park offers some 60 acres for recreational pursuits, including a 2.5-acre stocked lake and hiking trails. East of town is Poplar Park, home to one of the world's largest yellow poplar trees; phone (540) 587-6061.

Bedford Area Welcome Center: 816 Burks Hill Rd., Bedford, VA 24523; phone (540) 587-5681 or (877) 447-3257. *See color ad.*

Shopping areas: The Bedford Farmers Market, downtown on Washington Street, offers fresh fruits and vegetables and homemade wares Tuesday, Friday and Saturday.

BEDFORD CITY/COUNTY MUSEUM is at 201 E. Main St. This former Masonic Lodge built in 1895 houses permanent and changing exhibits related to city and county history, Bedford County Indian artifacts, Civil War relics and local genealogy information. Mon.-Sat. 10-5; closed major holidays. Donations. Phone (540) 586-4520.

THE NATIONAL D-DAY MEMORIAL is at 3 Overlord Cir. A hillside monument pays tribute to the troops that stormed the beach at Normandy on June 6, 1944, fighting for the liberation of Europe. Allow 30 minutes minimum. Daily 10-5; closed Jan. 1, Thanksgiving and Dec. 25. Admission $5; ages 6-16, $3. AX, DS, MC, VI. Phone (540) 586-3329 or (800) 351-3329.

BIG STONE GAP (I-2)
pop. 4,856, elev. 1,334'

Big Stone Gap is at the junction of three forks of the Powell River, which has created a pass through Stone Mountain. This mountain country provided the inspiration and setting for novelist John Fox Jr.'s "The Trail of the Lonesome Pine."

Heart of Appalachia Tourism Authority: 112 Shawnee Ave., P.O. Box 207, Big Stone Gap, VA 24219; phone (276) 523-2005.

THE HARRY W. MEADOR JR. COAL MUSEUM is at jct. E. Third St. and Shawnee Ave. In addition to displays about the coal-mining industry, the museum also features collections of medical and dental equipment, cash registers and antique office machines. Wed.-Sat. 10-5, Sun. 1-5; closed major holidays. Free. Phone (276) 523-9209.

JUNE TOLLIVER HOUSE is at Jerome and Clinton sts. The real-life heroine of the book "The Trail of the Lonesome Pine " lived in this 1896 house while she attended school. It is furnished in period and features school memorabilia. Guided tours are given Tues.-Sat. 10-5, Sun. 2-5, May 1 to mid-Dec. (also Thurs.-Sat. 5-9, July-Aug.). Free. Phone (276) 523-4707.

[SAVE] **John Fox Jr. Museum** is at 117 Shawnee Ave. E. This is the 1888 family home of novelist John Fox Jr. The 22-room house contains original furnishings and memorabilia. It was here that Fox wrote "The Trail of the Lonesome Pine" and other works inspired by life in the Appalachian Mountains. Guided tours are available. Allow 30 minutes minimum. Wed.-Sat. 2-5, Memorial Day-Labor Day; by appointment rest of year. Closed holidays. Admission $3; over 55, $2; under 18, $1. Phone (276) 523-1235.

"Trail of the Lonesome Pine" is performed at the June Tolliver Playhouse on Clinton St. The production is the state's official historical outdoor drama. Inquire about weather policies. Shows are given Thurs.-Sat. at 8 p.m., late June-late Aug. Admission $12; over 55, $10; ages 4-12, $8. Phone (276) 523-1235 or (800) 362-0149.

[GEM] **SOUTHWEST VIRGINIA MUSEUM HISTORICAL STATE PARK** is at 10 W. First St. near Wood Ave. An 1880s house contains exhibits relating to the exploration and development of southwestern Virginia and the lives of the early settlers of that region.

The first floor of the museum features exhibits about the area's coal and iron ore deposits and their

part in the town's "boom and bust" mining past. Second- and third-floor displays offer Victorian and pioneer memorabilia including a quilt exhibit, tools, household furnishings and American Indian artifacts. Guided tours are available by appointment.

Tues.-Thurs. 10-4 (also Mon. 10-4, Memorial Day-Labor Day), Fri. 9-4, Sat. 10-5, Sun. 1-5, Mar.-Dec.; closed Thanksgiving and Dec. 25. Admission $3; ages 6-12, $2. MC, VI. Phone (276) 523-1322.

BLACKSBURG (H-5) pop. 39,573, elev. 2,135′

Blacksburg originally was founded as the Draper's Meadow Settlement in 1748 by a group of German, English and Scot-Irish farmers. The settlement was short-lived, however, when only four people survived a 1755 Shawnee Indian attack in what became known as the Draper's Meadow Massacre. In 1798 the present town was established on land donated by William Black.

Virginia Polytechnic Institute and State University is on US 460, 9 miles from I-81. Founded in 1872, Virginia Tech is the largest university in the state, with more than 25,000 students and some 300 buildings. The 2,600-acre campus blends modern structures with beautiful old stone buildings. Maps and information about tours are available at the visitor center. Museums, art galleries and dining halls are open to the public; phone (540) 231-6000.

Huckleberry Trail, a recreational pathway popular with bicyclists, walkers, runners and inline skaters, connects Blacksburg and Christiansburg, a 6-mile distance. The trail winds along the Huckleberry Rail Line, used by Virginia Tech to transport cadets in the early 1900s.

Montgomery County Chamber of Commerce: 612 New River Rd., Christiansburg, VA 24060; phone (540) 382-4010.

SAVE **HISTORIC SMITHFIELD** is w. off US 460 bypass exit to US 314, on the edge of the Virginia Tech campus at 1000 Smithfield Plantation Rd. Smithfield was built in the 1770s by noted surveyor and patriot Col. William Preston and named for his wife, Susanna Smith. This original frame house was the birthplace of two Virginia governors and the home of a third. The 1,900-acre plantation was one of the earliest and largest estates west of the Blue Ridge Mountains. A demonstration kitchen garden is on the grounds.

Guided tours are available. Thurs.-Sun. 1-5, Apr. 1-first weekend in Dec. Last tour begins 30 minutes before closing. Admission $5; ages 13-17 and students with ID $3; ages 5-12, $2. Phone (540) 231-3947.

GEM BLUE RIDGE PARKWAY

The Blue Ridge Parkway connects Shenandoah National Park in Virginia (see place listing p. 290 and Recreation Chart) and Great Smoky Mountains National Park in North Carolina and Tennessee. The 469-mile scenic road follows the crest of the

Blue Ridge and other ranges at elevations from 649 to 6,047 feet. Only 800 feet wide at certain points, the parkway is constructed free of billboards and with little residential encroachment, allowing for leisurely drives and enjoyment of the surrounding area.

The concept for the construction of the parkway began during Franklin D. Roosevelt's administration in the 1930s. The project, in addition to creating a scenic route linking the two new national parks and spurring tourism, was a way to provide jobs for many of those left unemployed during the peak of the Great Depression. Begun in 1935, the dedication of the completed parkway did not take place until 1987, although sections of the road have been enjoyed by travelers for many years.

The parkway offers panoramas of the Southern Highlands. Among the areas of outstanding scenic interest are Humpback Rocks, Otter Creek, Peaks of Otter, Roanoke Mountain, Rocky Knob and Smart View in Virginia; and Crabtree Meadows, Craggy Gardens, Cumberland Knob, Doughton Park, E.B. Jeffress Park, Julian Price, Linville Falls and Moses H. Cone memorial parks, Mount Pisgah and Waterrock Knob in North Carolina. Wildflowers are in bloom mid-May through August; fall foliage is at its peak in October.

Hiking trails, varying in length from short strolls to the lengthy and strenuous Appalachian Trail, can be reached from many overlooks and parking areas; information can be obtained at parkway visitor centers. During the summer season craft demonstrations and ranger programs at various points along the parkway provide insights into the everyday life and culture of mountain residents.

Concrete mileposts help keep track of mileage along the road, beginning at Milepost 0 at the northern portion and concluding at Milepost 469 at its southern terminus at Great Smoky Mountains National Park. The speed limit of 45 mph is enforced. To drive the entire length, plan on 3 to 5 days at an average speed of 30 mph. For weather and other information contact Blue Ridge Parkway, 199 Hemphill Knob Rd., Asheville, NC 28803.

The Travel Narrator Audio Driving Tour, covering Mileposts 390-469, is available at the Folk Art Center (see attraction listing p. 226). This 90-minute narrated driving tour of the Blue Ridge Parkway from Asheville to Cherokee explores the region's history, people and lore; phone (770) 594-7842.

Food is available at Crabtree Meadows, Doughton Park, Mabry Mill, Mount Pisgah, Otter Creek and Peaks of Otter. There are overnight facilities at Peaks of Otter Lodge, housekeeping cabins at Rocky Knob and lodges at Doughton Park and Mount Pisgah. Other accommodations are nearby but off the parkway.

Pets are permitted if confined or leashed; they are prohibited in overnight facilities. Picnic spots and drinking water are available at intervals along the parkway. Hunting is prohibited.

The parkway is open all year, but sections of the road may be closed during icy or snowy weather. Most park facilities close November through April. Phone (828) 298-0398 for weather or other information, or (800) 727-5928 for emergencies.

Note: *The points of interest below are listed in order, from north to south according to their nearness to the northern terminus of the road at Shenandoah National Park.*

HUMPBACK ROCKS VISITOR CENTER is at Milepost 5.8, 6 mi. s.e. of Afton. The center features an outdoor museum comprised of 1890s farm buildings. Allow 1 hour minimum. Daily 9-5, May-Oct. Schedule may vary; phone ahead. Free. Phone (540) 943-4716.

JAMES RIVER VISITOR CENTER is at Milepost 63.6, 3 mi. n. of Big Island. Exhibits chronicle the story of the James River and the Kanawha Canal. A pedestrian walkway crossing the river leads to a restored canal lock. Daily 9-5, June-Nov.; Sat.-Sun. 9-5, in May. Free. Phone (434) 299-5496.

PEAKS OF OTTER VISITOR CENTER is at Milepost 86, 10 mi. n.w. of Bedford. Exhibits focus on forest ecology and the history of the Peaks of Otter area. Nearby are an 1830s cabin that housed early travelers through the region and a historic farm that offers living-history demonstrations. Daily shuttle-bus trips to the summit of Sharp Top Mountain as well as a walking trail to the summit are available.

Allow 1 hour minimum. Visitor center open daily 9-5, May-Oct. Shuttle bus departs daily on the hour 10-5 (weather permitting), late May-Oct. 31. Farm and trail hours vary. Visitor center free. One-way bus fare $3; under 12, $1.50. Round-trip bus fare $4.50; under 12, $2.25. Phone (540) 586-4496. *See Recreation Chart.*

ROCKY KNOB VISITOR CENTER is at Milepost 169, 8 mi. n.e. of Meadows of Dan. The center provides information about the Rocky Knob recreation area, which covers 4,000 acres. Daily 9-5, May-Oct. Free. Phone (540) 745-9662. *See Recreation Chart and the AAA Mideastern CampBook.*

MABRY MILL is at Milepost 176.1, just n. of jct. US 58, 3 mi. n.w. of Meadows of Dan. A display of pioneer items includes a blacksmith shop, gristmill, sawmill and sorghum press. Allow 1 hour minimum. Daily 8-6, May-Oct. Free. Phone (276) 952-2947.

CUMBERLAND KNOB VISITORS CENTER is at Milepost 217.5 near the state border in N.C. The Civilian Conservation Corps began construction on the parkway here in 1935. Picnic facilities and hiking trails are available. Daily 9-5, May-Oct. Free. Phone (336) 657-8161.

BLUE RIDGE MOUNTAIN FRESCOES are at Milepost 259 in Glendale Springs, N.C., 3 mi. n. of the parkway's jct. with SR 16; and in West Jefferson, N.C., following signs from jct. US 221 Bus. Rte.

and SR 194. North Carolina artist Ben Long painted these religious artworks in two Episcopal churches, Holy Trinity in Glendale Springs and St. Mary's in West Jefferson. Taped narratives describe their history. Allow 1 hour minimum. Daily 24 hours. Donations. Phone (336) 982-3076.

PARKWAY CRAFT CENTER is at Milepost 294, 3 mi. w. of Blowing Rock, N.C. In the former manor house at Moses H. Cone Memorial Park, the center is operated by the Southern Highland Craft Guild. Cone, a wealthy textile manufacturer, built his country estate at the turn of the 20th century. Mountain crafts are demonstrated. Allow 30 minutes minimum. Daily 9-5, Mar. 15-Nov. 30. Free. Phone (828) 295-7938.

LINN COVE VIADUCT AND VISITORS CENTER is at Milepost 304.4, 5 mi. n.e. of Linville, N.C. Of interest in the area is the Linn Cove Viaduct, at Milepost 304. Completed in 1983, the 1,243-foot-long viaduct is one of the most complicated concrete bridges ever built; it skirts the rugged perimeter of Grandfather Mountain. The visitor center has a model of the viaduct. Daily 9-5, May-Oct. Free. Phone (828) 733-1354.

LINVILLE FALLS RECREATION AREA is at Milepost 316.4, 2 mi. n.w. of Linville Falls, N.C. Trails lead to the pedestrian overlooks of Linville Falls and Linville Gorge. Picnicking, fishing and camping are permitted. Allow 3 hours minimum. Park open daily 24 hours. Visitor center open daily 9-5, May-Oct. Free. Phone (828) 765-1045. *See Blue Ridge Parkway in the AAA Southeastern CampBook.*

Linville Gorge is a scenic chasm within Linville Falls Recreation Area at Milepost 316.4 in N.C. Linville Gorge Wilderness, below the falls, is part of Pisgah National Forest and has been set aside for scientific and recreational use. Wiseman's View observation point on the west overlooks the gorge. **Note:** The area is reached only by trail or cross-country travel. A few steep trails are moderately difficult and require some hiking skill. Free. Phone (828) 652-2144.

LINVILLE CAVERNS is at Milepost 317 at Linville Falls, N.C., then 4 mi. s. on US 221. In 1822 the spectacle of trout swimming in and out of the mountainside led settlers on a torch-lit expedition inside the caves. Ever since, their discovery has been a source of fascination and sometimes shelter. During the Civil War, deserting soldiers from both armies sought refuge among the cathedral-like arches, columns and deep passageways. The underground temperature is a constant 52F; a jacket is recommended.

Daily 9-6, June 1-Labor Day; daily 9-5, Apr.-May and day after Labor Day-Oct. 31; daily 9-4:30 in Nov. and Mar.; Sat.-Sun. 9-4:30, rest of year. Guided 30-minute tours are available. Fee for tour $5; over 62, $4; ages 5-12, $3. Phone (828) 756-4171.

MUSEUM OF NORTH CAROLINA MINERALS is at Milepost 331 on SR 226, 5 mi. s. of Spruce Pine, N.C. The museum displays samples of many rocks and minerals found in the area. Cutting, polishing and shaping demonstrations are offered. Allow 30 minutes minimum. Daily 9-5, May-Oct.; 9-noon and 1-5, rest of year. Demonstrations Sun. at 2, June-Oct. Closed Jan. 1 and Dec. 25. Free. Phone (828) 765-2761.

MOUNT MITCHELL STATE PARK is at Milepost 355, 35 mi. n.e. of Asheville, N.C. The park encompasses the 6,684-foot summit of Mount Mitchell, highest peak east of the Mississippi River, and a portion of its slopes. The mountain was named for Dr. Elisha Mitchell, who fell to his death while attempting to prove the mountain's height.

Facilities at this 1,855-acre park include an observation lounge and a tower. A naturalist is on duty in the summer. In spring and winter check road conditions before entering the park. Food is available May-Oct. Parking is available near the summit. Daily 8 a.m.-9 p.m., May-Aug.; 8-8 in Apr. and Sept.; 8-7 in Mar. and Oct.; 8-6, rest of year. Closed Dec. 25. Free. Phone (828) 675-4611.

CRAGGY GARDENS is at Milepost 364.6, 18 mi. n.e. of Asheville, N.C. The Craggy Mountains, at elevations of 5,500-6,000 feet, are a colorful sight when the rhododendrons bloom around mid-June. Trails, picnic facilities and a visitor center are available. Daily 9-5, May-Oct. Schedule may vary; phone ahead. Free. Phone (828) 298-0495.

FOLK ART CENTER is at Milepost 382, 5 mi. n.e. of Asheville, N.C., via I-40 to US 70W exit 55, following signs to the Blue Ridge Pkwy., then .5 mi. n. Operated by the Southern Highland Craft Guild, the center celebrates the tradition of craft work in the southern Appalachian region through demonstrations, special events and changing exhibits of past and present Southern Highlands crafts.

A Blue Ridge Parkway information center is in the facility. Allow 30 minutes minimum. Daily 9-6, Apr.-Dec.; 9-5, rest of year. Closed Jan. 1, Thanksgiving and Dec. 25. Free. Phone (828) 298-7928.

NORTH CAROLINA ARBORETUM is at Milepost 393, 9 mi. s. of Asheville, N.C. Covering 426 acres in the Pisgah National Forest, the arboretum features a visitor education center, bicycle and hiking trails, and five theme gardens reflecting southern Appalachian heritage. Tropical plants, bonsai, and rare and endangered species are cultivated in a state-of-the-art greenhouse, which is open to visitors.

Picnicking is permitted. Allow 30 minutes minimum. Grounds daily 8 a.m.-9 p.m., Apr.-Oct.; 8-7, rest of year. Visitor center Mon.-Sat. 9-5, Sun. noon-5. Greenhouse Mon.-Tues. and Thurs.-Fri. 8-4, Wed. 8-2. Closed Jan. 1, Martin Luther King Jr. Day, Thanksgiving and Dec. 24-25. Free. Parking $6. Phone (828) 665-2492.

MOUNT PISGAH is at Milepost 408.6. Walking trails lead to the 5,721-foot summit. Educational programs are presented in an outdoor amphitheater some evenings June through October. Picnicking is permitted. Food is available. Free. Phone (828) 235-8228.

RICHLAND BALSAM is near Milepost 431, 12 mi. n.e. of Balsam, N.C. A 1.5-mile walking trail winds to the 6,047-foot summit of Richland Balsam Mountain, the highest point on the parkway. Hikers pass through a spruce and fir woodland that is native to northern climates. Trail pamphlets describe this plant community, which is a living relic of the ice age. Free. Phone (828) 298-0398 or (828) 456-9530.

WATERROCK KNOB is at Milepost 451.2, 8 mi. n.w. of Balsam, N.C. The summit commands a 360-degree view of the main ranges of the southern Appalachian Mountains from a 6,000-foot elevation. A visitor information center in the parking area is open daily 10-5, May-Oct. Free. Phone (828) 298-0398 or (828) 456-9530.

WINERIES

- **Château Morrisette Winery** is at Milepost 171.5, exit Black Ridge Rd. (SR 726), then s.w. on SR 777 to 287 Winery Rd. in Meadows of Dan. Wine tastings and tours are offered. Mon.-Thurs. 10-5, Fri.-Sat. 10-6, Sun. 11-5; closed Jan. 1, Thanksgiving and Dec. 25. Phone (540) 593-2865.

BOOKER T. WASHINGTON NATIONAL MONUMENT (H-6)

Booker T. Washington National Monument is 30 miles southeast of Roanoke via US 220 south to Rocky Mount, then north on SR 122. The 223-acre site commemorates Booker T. Washington's first 9 years in slavery by re-creating the environment of his childhood at Burroughs Plantation.

Freed at the end of the Civil War, Booker T. Washington rose from his impoverished childhood to found Tuskegee Normal and Industrial Institute in Alabama and to receive international recognition as an educator, speaker and African-American leader. He graduated from Hampton Institute in 1875 and received honorary degrees from Harvard and Dartmouth.

A visitor center offers exhibits and a 15-minute videotape presentation about Washington's life. Crops and farm animals can be seen from the quarter-mile self-guiding, Plantation Trail. Ancestral sources of food, meat and medicine are marked on the 1.5-mile Jack-O-Lantern Branch Heritage Trail.

Picnic facilities are available. Allow 1 hour minimum. Daily 9-5; closed Jan. 1, Thanksgiving and Dec. 25. Free. Phone (540) 721-2094.

BOYCE (E-8) pop. 426, elev. 572′

THE STATE ARBORETUM OF VIRGINIA is 1.3 mi. e. of US 340 on US 50. Some 170 acres of maintained landscapes and gardens can be explored on foot or by car. More than 1,000 varieties of plants, flowers and trees are on the grounds. A trail winds through an area of native Virginian plants. Picnicking is permitted. Allow 30 minutes minimum. Daily dawn-dusk. Free. Phone (540) 837-1758.

BREAKS (H-3) elev. 1,470'

BREAKS INTERSTATE PARK is off SR 80 on the eastern edge of the Cumberland Mountain Plateau. The park is administered jointly by Kentucky and Virginia. The Russell Fork of the Big Sandy River has cut a "break," a 1,600-foot-deep gorge known as the Grand Canyon of the South, through Pine Mountain. A paved road leads to the canyon rim; overlooks provide excellent views of the gorge, rock formations, caves, springs and vibrant rhododendron. Fishing, boating, pedal-boating, horseback riding, hiking and trail biking are available.

Daily 7 a.m.-11 p.m., Apr. 1-Dec. 21; 7:30-6, rest of year. Overnight facilities, with the exception of vacation cottages, are closed Dec. 24-Mar. 31. Admission $1 per private vehicle. Phone (276) 865-4413 or (800) 982-5122. *See Recreation Chart and the AAA Mideastern CampBook.*

Breaks Interstate Park Visitor Center is off SR 80 on the eastern edge of the Cumberland Mountain Plateau at Breaks Interstate Park. Natural science and historical displays are housed at the center, which provides self-guiding maps of the park's 13 miles of nature and hiking trails. Daily 9-5, May-Oct.; 8-4, in Apr. Free.

BRIDGEWATER (F-7) pop. 5,203, elev. 1,982'

Originally known as Magill's Ford, this crossing place on the North River was later called Bridgeport. By the time a charter was granted in 1835, the town had adopted its present name. Bridgewater College was established in 1880 by Daniel Christian Flory, a young leader of the Church of the Brethren.

REUEL B. PRITCHETT MUSEUM is in Cole Hall on the Bridgewater College campus on E. College St. The Rev. Pritchett, a farmer and minister of the Church of the Brethren, devoted his life to collecting historic articles. Highlights of his 10,000-item collection include a land deed signed by Thomas Jefferson, some 1,000 bottles and glassware, foreign currency and antique weapons. Allow 1 hour minimum. Mon.-Fri. 1-5; closed major holidays. Free. Phone (540) 828-5462.

BRISTOL (I-3) pop. 17,367, elev. 1,680'

State Street, Bristol's main thoroughfare, is bisected by the Tennessee/Virginia border. Brass markers down the street's center denote the dividing line. Although each side has its own government and city services, together they form an important industrial center, which manufactures metal goods, textiles and electronic products.

Evan Shelby, noted American Indian fighter and founder of what became the city of Bristol, built a stockade here in 1776. Daniel Boone and many other distinguished pioneers bartered in Bristol and planned the campaign that defeated the British at the Battle of Kings Mountain in South Carolina.

The city has a theater, an arts center and a ballet company. Recreational activities on the Tennessee side are provided by Steele Creek Park and South Holston Dam and Lake. Sugar Hollow Park is on the Virginia side.

The Bristol Motor Speedway, a half-mile racetrack 5 miles south on US 11E, is on the NASCAR circuit; phone (423) 764-1161. Scenic I-81 passes through Bristol and continues 88 miles south to the I-40 junction.

Bristol Chamber of Commerce and Convention and Visitors Bureau: P.O. Box 519, Bristol, VA 24203; phone (423) 989-4850.

SAVE **BRISTOL CAVERNS** is 5.5 mi. s.e. on US 421, then just e. on Bristol Caverns Hwy. A lighted asphalt trail traverses several levels of the cave, which has many unusual formations. An interesting feature is the walk along the banks of an underground river. Picnicking is permitted. Mon.-Sat. 9-5, Sun. 12:30-5, Mar. 15-Oct. 31; Mon.-Sat. 10-4, Sun. 12:30-4:30, rest of year. Closed Easter, Thanksgiving and Dec. 24-25. Admission $9.50; over 61, $8; ages 5-12, $5. Phone (423) 878-2011.

BROOKNEAL (H-7) pop. 1,259, elev. 537'

One of the smallest incorporated towns in central Virginia, Brookneal was founded in 1802. Patrick Henry, the state's first elected governor, had retired to the area in 1794, spending the last five years of his life at Red Hill plantation. Fire destroyed the manor home in 1919.

RED HILL—PATRICK HENRY NATIONAL MEMORIAL is 5 mi. e. on SR 40, following signs to 1250 Red Hill Rd. The site preserves the last home and burial place of Patrick Henry. The main building has been reconstructed and contains Henry family furnishings. Henry's grave, law office, coachman's cabin, stable, kitchen, and boxwood and herb gardens can be seen. An orientation and introductory videotape begin the tour at the museum and visitor center. Daily 9-5, Mar.-Oct.; 9-4, rest of year. Closed Jan. 1, Thanksgiving and Dec. 25. Admission $6; over 65, $5; ages 5-17, $2. Phone (434) 376-2044.

BULL RUN—

see Manassas National Battlefield Park in the District of Columbia p. 130.

BURROWSVILLE (B-2) elev. 70'

The first land grant in Prince George County was deeded in 1616 to Captain John Martin, one of the founders of Jamestown. A grandson of William Shakespeare was one of several absentee owners before the 7,000-acre property, known as Brandon, passed from Benjamin Harrison III to his sons, Nathanial and William, in 1720. The Brandon Plantation at Burrowsville remains in operation as a working farm, one of the oldest in the country.

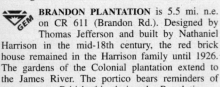 **BRANDON PLANTATION** is 5.5 mi. n.e. on CR 611 (Brandon Rd.). Designed by Thomas Jefferson and built by Nathaniel Harrison in the mid-18th century, the red brick house remained in the Harrison family until 1926. The gardens of the Colonial plantation extend to the James River. The portico bears reminders of two wars—a British ship during the Revolutionary War opened fire from the river, and Union soldiers during the Civil War fired upon and then occupied the house.

The parklike grounds contain old trees and expanses of lawn. The garden is the original plan; plantings include perennials, ornamentals, bulbs and trees native to the area. Brandon Plantation is still a working farm. The principal crops are corn, soybeans and wheat. Beef cattle also are raised on the plantation.

Grounds and gardens open daily 9-5. House open during Garden Week (late Apr.-early May) and by appointment. Grounds and gardens $5; house $5. Phone (757) 866-8486 or (757) 866-8416.

CAPE CHARLES (B-5) pop. 1,134, elev. 7′

This planned community on the Eastern Shore was incorporated in 1886. With its deep harbor, Cape Charles served as a railroad terminus for ferries carrying freight and passengers from Cape Henry at Norfolk. Development slowed after the last ferry terminal closed in 1950. One of the town founders, Alexander Cassatt, was the brother of Impressionist painter Mary Cassatt.

Most of the original town has been preserved as a historic district, with houses reflecting Victorian, Colonial Revival, Craftsman and neo-classic styles.

EASTERN SHORE OF VIRGINIA NATIONAL WILDLIFE REFUGE is at 5003 Hallett Cir. The 745-acre refuge protects four habitats: the Chesapeake Bay, barrier islands, salt marshes and upland forests. Songbirds, raptors and monarch butterflies assemble on the peninsula for the fall migration. Fisherman Island, a military installation during World Wars I and II, is home to brown pelicans and royal terns. A visitor center, wildlife exhibits, trails and an observation deck also are featured.

Allow 1 hour minimum. The refuge is open daily 30 minutes before dawn-30 minutes after dusk. Visitor center daily 9-4, Apr.-Nov.; daily 10-2, Dec. and Mar.; Fri.-Sun. 10-2, rest of year. Closed Jan. 1 and Dec. 25. Peak wildlife viewing time is late Aug.-early Nov. Guided 3-hour tours of Fisherman Island are offered Sat. at 9, Oct.-Mar. Reservations are required for tour. Free. Phone (757) 331-2760.

CAPE HENRY—

see Virginia Beach in the Hampton Roads Area p. 254.

CHANCELLORSVILLE (D-10)

Twelve miles west of Fredericksburg on SR 3, Chancellorsville Battlefield is part of Fredericksburg and Spotsylvania National Military Park *(see place listing p. 239).*

The battles of Chancellorsville and Salem Church, April 27 through May 6, 1863, were among the most important engagements of the Civil War. The Confederate Army of Northern Virginia, under the command of Gen. Robert E. Lee, numbered approximately 60,000. Maj. Gen. Joseph Hooker directed about 134,000 Union troops.

Hooker crossed the Rappahannock River and entrenched his army along a 6-mile line centered at an inn known as Chancellorsville. Lee sent "Stonewall" Jackson to attack the right wing of the Union line, driving it back to Chancellorsville. That evening Jackson's own men accidentally shot him; a week later he died of pneumonia.

The next day Lee attacked, forcing Hooker to withdraw. The result was a brilliant victory for the South that sparked Lee's invasion of Pennsylvania.

The national park visitor center offers exhibits and a 12-minute slide show. A 6-mile, self-guiding driving tour of the battlefield begins near the visitor center parking lot. Another way to tour the battlefield is by following a 3-hour tape tour, available for sale or rent at the visitor center.

Park open daily 8:30-6:30, mid-June through Labor Day; Mon.-Fri. 9-5, Sat.-Sun. 9-6, Apr. 1 to mid-June and day after Labor Day-Oct. 31; daily 9-5, rest of year. Closed Jan. 1 and Dec. 25. Walking tours led by park rangers are conducted in the summer. Phone (540) 786-2880.

CHANTILLY — *see District of Columbia p. 127.*

CHARLES CITY—

see Williamsburg, Jamestown and Yorktown—Virginia's Historic Triangle p. 296.

CHARLOTTESVILLE (G-8)
pop. 45,049, elev. 480′
See map page 229.

Historic Charlottesville, in the foothills of the Blue Ridge Mountains, was the home of Thomas Jefferson and James Monroe. The University of Virginia, founded and designed by Jefferson and first governed by a board whose membership included Jefferson, James Monroe and James Madison, enhances the city.

Meriwether Lewis, who with William Clark was sent on an expedition to explore the Louisiana Purchase, was born near Charlottesville. Frontiersman George Rogers Clark, William Clark's brother, also was born near Charlottesville.

Many old homes and estates in the surrounding countryside reveal Jefferson's architectural influence; the Old Courthouse is a notable example. Albemarle County is known for its horses, dogs and fox hunting as well as its peach and apple orchards.

The Albemarle Pippin apple was developed in the area.

Charlottesville-Albemarle County Convention and Visitors Bureau: Monticello Visitors Center, SR 20S, P.O. Box 178, Charlottesville, VA 22902; phone (434) 977-1783 or (877) 386-1102.

Self-guiding tours: Brochures outlining self-guiding walking tours of Charlotteville's historic downtown and the University of Virginia are available at the convention and visitors bureau, and the downtown visitor center at 108 Second St.; phone (434) 977-6100.

Shopping areas: Charlottesville Fashion Square, jct. US 29 and E. Rio Road, features more than 70 stores, including Belk, Eddie Bauer, JCPenney and Sears. Charlottesville Historic Downtown Pedestrian Mall offers art galleries, restaurants and various specialty shops. Barracks Road Shopping Center, jct. Emmer Street and Barracks Road, features some 80 upscale stores.

ASH LAWN-HIGHLAND is off I-64 exit 121, .5 mi. s. on SR 20, 3 mi. e. on SR 53, then .5 mi. s. on CR 795. The 535-acre estate once was owned by James Monroe, fifth president of the United States. His neighbor Thomas Jefferson personally selected the site and sent his gardeners to plant orchards. Monroe and his wife moved to their tobacco plantation in 1799. Ash Lawn-Highland today retains the feel of an early 1800s working plantation.

Guided tours of the main house, which contains many Monroe possessions, are available daily. Periodic cooking and spinning demonstrations and other activities are offered. The tour also includes the overseer's house and slave quarters. The boxwood gardens feature resident peacocks and a statue of Monroe by Attilio Piccirilli. The Blue Ridge Mountains are visible on the horizon.

Picnicking is permitted. Allow 1 hour minimum. Daily 9-6, Apr.-Oct.; 11-5, rest of year. Closed Jan. 1, Thanksgiving and Dec. 25. Admission $9; over 60, $8; ages 6-11, $5. MC, VI. Phone (434) 293-9539.

LEWIS AND CLARK AND SACAJAWEA MEMORIAL is in Midway Park at Ridge and Main sts. The statue honors Louisiana Purchase explorers Meriwether Lewis and William Clark and their American Indian guide Sacajawea.

MEMORIAL TO GEORGE ROGERS CLARK is on W. Main St., just e. of the University of Virginia. Clark, elder brother of William Clark, is known for his exploration of the Northwest Territory.

MICHIE TAVERN is .5 mi. s. of I-64 on SR 20, then 1 mi. e. on Thomas Jefferson Pkwy. Established by Scotsman William Michie, the 1784 tavern accommodated travelers with food, drink and lodging. In 1927 the inn was moved 17 miles to its present location as part of the 1920s Preservation Movement.

Featured on the tour are a variety of rooms that focus on tavern life and early travel. Included are an Assembly Room, and gentlemen's and ladies' parlors. Living-history programs, offered April through October, let visitors dance a tavern reel and write with a quill pen. Food is available. Daily 9-5; closed Jan. 1 and Dec. 25. Last tour begins 40 minutes before closing. Admission $8; over 65, $7; ages 6-11, $3. AX, MC, VI. Phone (434) 977-1234.

MONTICELLO is off I-64 exit 121, .5 mi. s. on SR 20, then 1.5 mi. e. on SR 53. One of Virginia's most impressive estates, this was Thomas Jefferson's home—when he was not serving in public affairs—from 1770 until his death in 1826. Monticello is truly a reflection of Jefferson's interests and diversity; the domed house contains maps, books, scientific instruments, time-saving inventions and items from Lewis and Clark's journey westward. Guided tours include ten of the main floor's principal rooms, in which the statesman's furniture and personal effects are displayed.

Jefferson died at Monticello July 4, 1826, exactly 50 years after the adoption of the Declaration of Independence. His grave is in the family cemetery on the estate. Also on the grounds are dependencies, a garden terrace, an 8-acre fruit orchard and two vineyards. Tickets are purchased at a ticket office a half-mile from the mansion. Shuttle buses are available for transport to the house.

Backpacks are not permitted. Allow 3 hours minimum. Daily 8-5, Mar.-Oct.; 9-4:30, rest of year. Guided 30-minute tours of the house depart approximately every 5 minutes. Garden tours are offered daily every hour 9:15-4:15, Apr.-Oct. Plantation community tours depart daily every hour 10-3, Apr.-Oct. Children's tours depart daily every

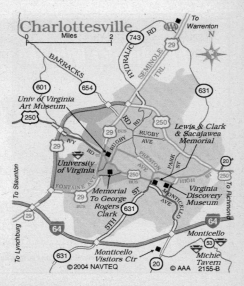

hour 10-3, June 15-Aug. 15. Closed Dec. 25. Admission $13; ages 6-11, $6. AX, MC, VI. Phone (434) 984-9822.

Monticello Visitors Center is off I-64 exit 121, then s. on SR 20. An exhibit, Thomas Jefferson at Monticello, focuses on Jefferson's domestic life and includes about 400 objects and artifacts, many of which were uncovered during archeological excavations at Monticello. The exhibit complements guided tours of the house and grounds; a recorded tour of the exhibit is available for a fee. A 38-minute film, "Thomas Jefferson: The Pursuit of Liberty," is offered.

Visitors center open daily 9-5:30, Mar.-Oct.; 9-5, rest of year. Film shown daily on the hour June 15-Labor Day; at 11 and 2, rest of year. Closed Dec. 25. Visitors center free. The President's Pass, a discounted combination ticket for Monticello, Michie Tavern and Ash Lawn-Highland, can be purchased from the convention and visitors bureau at the visitor center. Phone (434) 977-1783 or (877) 386-1102.

 **MONTPELIER**—*See Orange p. 270.*

UNIVERSITY OF VIRGINIA is in the center of town on US 29 and US 250 Bus. Rtes. Thomas Jefferson founded this "academical village" in 1819 and devoted his final years to its design, construction and curriculum. The state university opened in 1825 with 123 students and a hand-picked faculty of American and European scholars.

Seeking to create an environment in which learning infused daily life, Jefferson planned the school with ten pavilions built around an expansive lawn. Each pavilion contained a professor's home, students' quarters and classrooms. At the heart of the campus was the Rotunda, a domed library modeled after the Pantheon in Rome. The university design is considered an outstanding accomplishment in American architecture. Edgar Allan Poe was among the students who attended dinner at Monticello before Jefferson's death in 1826.

Tours of the Rotunda and lawn are offered daily at 10, 11, 2, 3 and 4, Sept.-Apr. Rotunda tours only are offered daily at 10, 11, 2, 3 and 4, rest of year. No tours are given during exam periods. Free. Parking is available at the Memorial Gym parking lot at Emmet Street and Ivy Road. Phone (434) 924-7969.

Kluge-Ruhe Aboriginal Art Collection is at 400 Peter Jefferson Pl. The gallery features an extensive collection of Australian Aboriginal art. Allow 30 minutes minimum. Tues.-Sat. 9-3. Free. Phone (434) 244-0234.

University of Virginia Art Museum is n. of US 250 (University Ave.) in the Bayly Building at 155 Rugby Rd. First opened in 1935, this fine arts museum contains paintings and sculpture from the 15th through the 20th centuries with an emphasis on American art and art from the Jefferson era. Other highlights include pre-Columbian works and art from the ancient African, American Indian, Asian and Mediterranean cultures. Allow 1 hour minimum. Tues.-Sun. 1-5; closed major holidays. Free. Phone (434) 924-3592.

[SAVE] **VIRGINIA DISCOVERY MUSEUM** is at the e. end of the downtown pedestrian mall. The museum, geared toward children ages 1-10 and their families, invites learning through hands-on activities. Highlights include an art studio; a reconstructed 18th-century pioneer log cabin; a take-apart

table, which enables young visitors to see what makes things work; a working beehive; and a special room for toddlers. Tues.-Sat. 10-5, Sun. 1-5; closed major holidays. Admission $4, under 1 free. Phone (434) 977-1025.

WINERIES

- **First Colony Winery** is off I-64 exit 121A, 11 mi. s. on SR 20, then 1 mi. w. on CR 720 to 1650 Harris Creek Rd. Daily 11-5; closed Jan. 1, Thanksgiving and Dec. 25. Phone (434) 979-7105.

- **Jefferson Vineyards** is off I-64 exit 121A, .7 mi. s. on SR 20, then 2 mi. e. on SR 53 to 1353 Thomas Jefferson Pkwy. Daily 11-5; closed Jan. 1, Thanksgiving and Dec. 25. Phone (434) 977-3042 or (800) 272-3042.

- **Oakencroft Vineyard and Winery** is 3.5 mi. w. of US 29 on Barracks/Garth Rd. Daily 11-5, Apr.-Dec.; Sat.-Sun. 11-5, in Mar.; by appointment rest of year. Closed Jan. 1 and Dec. 25. Phone (434) 296-4188.

CHESAPEAKE—

see Hampton Roads Area p. 256.

CHESTERFIELD—*see Richmond p. 285.*

CHINCOTEAGUE (G-12) pop. 4,317

Local legends say that Chincoteague (SHIN-ko-teeg) ponies, an island trademark, are descendants of mine horses that survived the shipwreck of a 16th-century Spanish galleon. Most historians, however, agree that the first ponies were brought over by the first English colonists, who turned the herds loose on Assateague and Chincoteague in the late 1600s when the horses began to damage their crops.

Off the Eastern Shore in Chincoteague Bay, the 7-mile-long, 1.5-mile-wide island is connected to the mainland by a causeway and bridges. Assateague Island, which includes Assateague Island National Seashore *(see place listing in Md. p. 158)*, shields Chincoteague from the sea. Serpentine waterways, called "guts" by the islanders, punctuate Chincoteague's flat expanses of salt marsh and scrub-pine woods. Duck and goose hunting and deep-sea or channel fishing are excellent.

Chincoteague oysters and clams constitute the island's second-greatest industry, after tourism. The local watermen cultivate oysters and clams on the leased tideflats, or "rocks," surrounding the island and in the inlet. Crabbing is a popular pastime, particularly in the early summer when the blue crabs are out of their hibernation in the Chincoteague Bay mud.

The pony penning, held the last consecutive Wednesday and Thursday in July, probably originated from the colonists' practice of rounding up foals and yearlings to renew their supply of workhorses. On these days the partly wild ponies are rounded up from their home on the southern end of Assateague Island to swim at slack tide (when the tide is changing and there is no movement) across the narrow channel to Chincoteague. Foals are sold at auction; the rest swim back to Assateague. The island's ponies were made famous by Marguerite Henry's book, "Misty of Chincoteague."

Chincoteague Chamber of Commerce: 6733 Maddox Blvd., P.O. Box 258, Chincoteague, VA 23336; phone (757) 336-6161.

CHINCOTEAGUE NATIONAL WILDLIFE REFUGE occupies the Virginia portion of Assateague Island and several barrier islands along the Atlantic coast. Among species of migratory birds within the refuge are snow geese, glossy ibises, great blue herons, sanderlings, peregrine falcons, bald eagles, blue grosbeaks and scarlet tanagers. Several paved trails traverse the refuge. The 3.2-mile wildlife loop is open to walkers and bicyclists all day and to automobiles after 3 until dusk. A visitor center offers educational exhibits.

Daily 5 a.m.-10 p.m., May-Sept.; 6 a.m.-8 p.m. in Apr. and Oct.; 6-6, rest of year. Schedule may vary; phone ahead. Admission $10 per private vehicle (for up to 7 days), physically impaired free. Phone (757) 336-6122.

Tom's Cove Hook Area is at the southern end of Assateague Island. The 5-mile beach offers surf casting, swimming and picnicking. The refuge also maintains the nearby 10-mile Wild Beach, which is a natural wildlife habitat. Chincoteague ponies and other wildlife can be observed throughout the refuge. Pets are not permitted. Daily 5 a.m.-10 p.m., May-Sept.; 6 a.m.-8 p.m. in Apr. and Oct.; 6-6, rest of year. Piping plover nesting areas are closed to public access Mar. 15-Aug. 31. Admission included with Chincoteague National Wildlife Refuge. Phone (757) 336-6577.

NASA WALLOPS FLIGHT FACILITY VISITOR CENTER is off SR 13, then 5 mi. e. on SR 175, next to the main base of the National Aeronautics and Space Administration's Wallops Flight Facility. The center has an exhibit hall focusing on NASA's spaceflight and scientific research programs. Hands-on displays and audiovisual presentations also are offered. Public programs are offered on weekends. Picnicking is permitted. Allow 30 minutes minimum. Daily 10-4, July 4-Labor Day; Thurs.-Mon. 10-4, Mar. 1-July 3 and day after Labor Day-Nov. 30; Mon.-Fri. 10-4, rest of year. Closed federal holidays except Memorial Day, July 4 and Labor Day. Free. Phone (757) 824-2298 or (757) 824-1344.

CLARKSVILLE (I-8) pop. 1,329, elev. 1,468′

Clarksville was established in 1818 at the crossroads of several Occoneechee Indian trading trails. By the mid-19th century, it had become a major tobacco production center. With the damming of the Roanoke River in 1952, Clarkesville became the only town on the newly formed Buggs Island Lake.

PRESTWOULD PLANTATION is 2 mi. n. on US 15, overlooking Buggs Island Lake. Built in 1795 by Sir Peyton Skipwith, the plantation house has original furnishings, rare vintage wallpaper and a library. Guides conduct tours of the house, restored outbuildings and gardens. Allow 1 hour minimum. Tours are offered Mon.-Sat. 12:30-3:30, Sun. 1:30-3:30, Apr. 15-Oct. 31. Admission $8; over 65, $6; ages 6-12, $3. Grounds only $3. Phone (434) 374-8672.

COLONIAL HEIGHTS (B-1) pop. 16,897

Colonial Heights was the site of Gen. Robert E. Lee's headquarters for 5 months in 1864. The falling leaves of autumn exposed his position to the enemy, making it necessary for him to move his encampment elsewhere.

The Violet Bank Civil War Museum occupies the site of Lee's headquarters. Civil War weapons and memorabilia, including small arms bullets, cannon balls and flags, are displayed. On the front lawn of the museum is an enormous "cucumber tree," actually a variety of magnolia, which is claimed to be second in size only to one in India.

Colonial Heights Chamber of Commerce: 201 Temple Ave., Suite E, Colonial Heights, VA 23834; phone (804) 526-5872.

COLONIAL NATIONAL HISTORICAL PARK—

see Williamsburg, Jamestown and Yorktown—Virginia's Historic Triangle p. 300.

CONCORD (H-7) elev. 884′

WINERIES

• **Stonewall Vineyards** is 5 mi. n. of US 460 on SR 608, then w. on SR 721. Daily 11-5; closed Jan. 1, Easter, July 4, Thanksgiving and Dec. 25. Phone (434) 993-2185.

COURTLAND (I-10) pop. 1,270, elev. 32′

Originally named Jerusalem, this settlement was founded in 1791 on 10 acres along the Nottoway River. On Aug. 22, 1831 it experienced one of the nation's bloodiest slave revolts, the Nat Turner Rebellion. When the violent, three-day siege ended more than 150 people were dead. Turner survived the insurrection and escaped, but was captured two months later and quickly convicted. While awaiting execution Turner told his story to attorney Thomas Gray, who later published the account as "The Confessions of Nat Turner." In 1888, the town's name was changed to Courtland, which today serves as the county seat for Southampton County.

SOUTHAMPTON AGRICULTURE & FORESTRY MUSEUM AND HERITAGE VILLAGE is at 26135 Heritage Ln. The village pays tribute to the area's past with antique farming equipment, American Indian artifacts and an old-time country store. Guided tours wind through re-created farm outbuildings, including a smokehouse, a sawmill, a one-room schoolhouse, a country farmhouse, a blacksmith's shop, a doctor's office and an icehouse. Allow 1 hour minimum. Wed. and Sat.-Sun. 1-5, Mar.-Nov.; closed Easter, Mother's Day and Father's Day. Admission $1. Phone (757) 653-9554.

CROAKER—

see Williamsburg, Jamestown and Yorktown—Virginia's Historic Triangle p. 302.

CULPEPER (F-9) pop. 9,664, elev. 423′

George Washington received his surveyor's license, with which he surveyed for proprietor Lord Thomas Fairfax in 1749 at the age of 17, in Culpeper.

As the Revolution became imminent, the Culpeper Minute Men were organized in 1775. Two years later, with volunteers from Fauquier and Orange counties, they marched to Williamsburg in answer to Gov. Patrick Henry's call to arms. Their flag depicted a coiled rattlesnake with the defiant legends "Don't tread on me" and "Liberty or Death." During the Civil War, the wounded from the battles of Cedar Mountain, Kelly's Ford and Brandy Station were treated in makeshift hospitals set up in many Culpeper residences, churches and vacant buildings. The Union Army later established its headquarters at the old Virginia Hotel. The Museum of Culpeper History at 803 S. Main St. houses exhibits recounting the town's vibrant past; phone (540) 829-1749.

Culpeper County Visitor Center: 109 S. Commerce St., Culpeper, VA 22701; phone (540) 825-8628 or (888) 285-7373.

WINERIES

• **Prince Michel Vineyards** is 10 mi. s. on US 29. Daily 10-6; closed Jan. 1, Thanksgiving and Dec. 25. Phone (540) 547-3707 or (800) 800-9463.

 CUMBERLAND GAP NATIONAL HISTORICAL PARK (I-1)

Elevations in the park range from 1,660 ft. at the Cumberland Gap to 3,513 ft. at White Rocks. Refer to AAA maps for additional elevation information.

At the convergence of Kentucky, Tennessee and Virginia, Cumberland Gap National Historical Park covers 20,444 acres of heavily forested, rugged mountains honoring the historic pass.

The gap provides a natural doorway through the mountains. It was first used by migratory animals as a seasonal thoroughfare, then by American Indians, whose footpaths followed the buffalo and deer trails. The westward movement of settlers seemed barred by the Allegheny Ridge until April 1750, when Dr. Thomas Walker discovered the gap while seeking the fabled land to the west, the "Kentucke" of American Indian lore.

Daniel Boone passed through with a hunting party in 1769, and in 1775 he blazed the Wilderness Road. From 1775 to 1796 the gap was only a horse path; although no wagon passed over it during this period, more than 200,000 people made their way through the gap into Kentucky and beyond.

A strategic point during the Civil War, Cumberland Gap changed hands four times without any major battles. Some of the earthwork fortifications remain.

General Information and Activities

With the opening of the Cumberland Gap Highway Tunnel and the rerouting of US 25E through the tunnel, Cumberland Gap and the Wilderness Road have been returned to their late 1700s appearance.

Pinnacle Overlook, providing a view into the gap as well as affording views of the mountain range and parts of three states, is accessible via a 4-mile paved road from the visitor center. No trailers or vehicles more than 20 feet long are allowed.

Still a wild area, the park has almost 70 miles of hiking trails ranging from relatively easy nature trails to those requiring an overnight trek. Many park features, including Sand Cave, a multicolored sandstone overhang, and White Rocks, a prominent sandstone outcropping, can be reached only by trail. Ridge Trail, a 19-mile-long route offering panoramas of the valley, approaches five primitive campsites, all accessible by foot. The park also has 160 developed campsites.

Hensley Settlement can be reached by an all-day hike or, during the summer, by a shuttle. Phone ahead for shuttle service; reservations are recommended. A reconstruction of a community that was occupied 1903-51, the settlement sits atop a mountain in the eastern end of the park. With more than 70 acres of land under cultivation, it has several reconstructed log houses, barns and outbuildings. Reminiscent of a time much earlier than that from which it actually dates, Hensley seems like a community of the late 1700s or early 1800s.

It is not advisable to hike alone; overnight camping requires a permit. Trail guides and other information can be obtained at the visitor center, where a park orientation film is offered. The visitor center also contains a museum with weapons and tools dating from the pioneer and Civil War eras. From Memorial Day through Labor Day ranger-led programs, suitable for the entire family, introduce visitors to the historical, cultural and natural aspects of the park; phone for a schedule of events. *See the AAA Southeastern CampBook.*

The park is open daily 9-dusk. The visitor center at the park entrance is open daily 8-6, June 1-Labor Day; 8-5, rest of year. Closed Dec. 25.

ADMISSION to the park is free.

PETS must be restricted at all times, either in vehicles or by leash, and are not allowed in public buildings.

ADDRESS inquiries to the Superintendent, Cumberland Gap National Historical Park, Box 1848, Middlesboro, KY 40965; phone (606) 248-2817.

Points of Interest

GAP CAVE is .25 mi. s. of Middlesboro on US 25E. Two-hour guided tours of the cave, discovered in 1750, are conducted by lantern light. Rooms and walls are covered with stalactites and stalagmites. Wildlife, including bats and salamanders, can be seen, as can the names of Civil War soldiers carved on the walls.

Note: Full mobility is required. The 1-mile route includes 183 steps. Allow 2 hours minimum. Tours are given daily at 9:30, 12:30 and 3, Memorial Day-Aug. 31; Mon.-Fri. at 10, Sat.-Sun. at 10 and 2, Apr. 1-day before Memorial Day and Sept.-Dec. Tickets must be purchased at the park visitor center 15 minutes in advance of the tour. Fee $8; ages 3-12, $4. Reservations are recommended. Phone (606) 248-2817.

DANVILLE (I-7) pop. 48,411, elev. 565'

The auction method of selling tobacco in piles of loose leaves originated at Neal's Warehouse in Danville in 1858. Large tobacco processing plants such as Dimon Inc. are in the area. Danville also is the home of Dan River Inc., the largest single-unit textile mill in the world; their factory outlet offers bed and bath linens.

Danville was the last capital of the Confederacy; President Jefferson Davis and his cabinet officers moved to the town after the evacuation of Richmond on April 3, 1865. Davis wrote his last proclamation as president in Danville. At the Sutherlin House, 975 Main St., Davis received the news that Gen. Robert E. Lee had surrendered at Appomattox. The Sutherlin House is now Danville Museum of Fine Arts and History *(see attraction listing).*

Lady Astor, the first female member of the British Parliament, was born as Nancy Witcher Langhorne in Danville in 1879. Her cottage birthplace at 117 Broad St. is open by appointment. Information is available at the visitor center; phone (434) 793-5422.

The railroad accident that inspired the popular folk ballad "Wreck of the Old 97" occurred in the town on Sept. 27, 1903, killing nine people. A commemorative marker is on US 58W.

Reflecting Danville's prosperous tobacco and textile heritage, Millionaires Row Historic District along Main Street boasts fine examples of Victorian and Edwardian residential architecture. A few of these private homes are open to the public during the Christmas Walking Tour held the second Sunday in December.

Danville Area Chamber of Commerce and Visitor Center: 635 Main St., Danville, VA 24541; phone (434) 793-5422.

Self-guiding tours: Brochures outlining a walking tour of Millionaires Row and a driving tour of Civil War sites as well as schedules, maps and tours of auction warehouses in the historic district are available from the chamber of commerce and visitor center.

Shopping areas: Piedmont Mall, on Piedmont Drive off the US 29 bypass, has more than 70 stores, including Belk, JCPenney and Sears. The Danville Community Market, at 626 Craghead St., offers fresh produce, baked goods, crafts, artisans and a welcome center on Saturdays, April through December.

DANVILLE MUSEUM OF FINE ARTS AND HISTORY is at 975 Main St. Built in the Italianate style in 1857 by tobacco merchant Maj. William T. Sutherlin, the museum contains original and period furnishings as well as changing art exhibits. Tues.-Fri. 10-5, Sat.-Sun. 2-5; closed major holidays. Free. Phone (434) 793-5644.

[SAVE] **DANVILLE SCIENCE CENTER** is at 677 Craghead St. Housed in an 1899 train station, the science center features hands-on activities, events and touring exhibits. Mon.-Sat. 9:30-5, Sun. 1-5; closed Thanksgiving and Dec. 25. Admission $4, over 54 and ages 4-18, $3. MC, VI. Phone (434) 791-5160.

DAYTON (F-7) pop. 1,344, elev. 1,230′

Daniel Harrison, brother of the founder of the town of Harrisonburg, built his home along Cook's Creek just north of town. The Daniel Harrison House also is known as Fort Harrison due to its solid stone structure with an underground passage to a well and a stockade that once surrounded the home, protecting it from American Indian attacks. Visitors can tour the 18th-century home; phone (540) 879-2280.

SHENANDOAH VALLEY FOLK ART AND HERITAGE CENTER is at 382 High St. Documents and artifacts of the Shenandoah Valley include a permanent exhibit titled Invincible Spirit: History in the Heart of the Shenandoah. The museum also focuses on one of the area's major historical events, Gen. "Stonewall" Jackson's Valley Campaign of 1862. Displays include Civil War artifacts, documents and photographs as well as folk art encompassing works in ceramics, textiles, wood and metals.

Allow 30 minutes minimum. Mon.-Sat. 10-4; closed major holidays and the last week in Dec. Admission $5; ages 5-18, $1. MC, VI. Phone (540) 879-2616.

DISMAL SWAMP (I-11)

In southeastern Virginia and northeastern North Carolina, the Great Dismal Swamp is characterized by forested peat soils and a dense undergrowth of briars and vines. The 223,000-acre area is threaded by canals and ditches, many of which have grown over to resemble green tunnels.

Col. William Byrd of Virginia surveyed the swamp in 1728 and named it Great Dismal. George Washington explored it in 1763, saw its possibilities as a timber producer and commercial canal and formed a company known as The Adventurers for Draining the Great Dismal Swamp. Much of the refuge was once owned by Washington, Patrick Henry and other prominent Virginians. The original swamp area is believed to have covered 2,200 square miles.

Great Dismal Swamp National Wildlife Refuge comprises approximately 107,000 acres of heavily forested land and water. Lake Drummond, a circular lake covering 3,000 acres within the refuge, is in the heart of the swamp. Its average depth is 6 feet, and the unusually pure water is preserved by the tannic acids from the bark of the cypress, juniper and gum trees. Gnarled cypress trees, moss and the dense growth surrounding the lake give it an eerie appearance. The coffee-colored lake has a sandy bottom and is unusual in that it is not formed in a basin, but rather on a gently sloping hillside.

Remnants of an Atlantic white cedar forest can be found in the refuge. Commercially valuable trees include cypress, juniper, red maple and yellow poplar; however, the peat soils make lumbering difficult. Black bears, white-tailed deer, bobcats and otters as well as 203 recorded species of birds inhabit the swamp.

Visitors to the refuge can hike or bicycle the unpaved trails. An interpretive boardwalk is on Washington Ditch Road (vehicles prohibited). The refuge headquarters is at 3216 Desert Road off SR 32S in Suffolk.

Boat access to Lake Drummond is available via a launch on US 17 at the mouth of the feeder ditch, a 3-mile-long shallow waterway connecting the lake with the Dismal Swamp Canal. To enter the lake, boats must be transported across the Corps of Engineers spillway at the head of the feeder ditch via a small motorized tram (1,000 pound weight limit).

The canal, part of the Atlantic Intracoastal Waterway, is the oldest man-made waterway in the country. The Dismal Swamp Canal Welcome Center, 3 miles south of the state line on US 17 on the banks of the canal, attracts visitors from both a major highway and an historic waterway. A North Carolina Wildlife canoe trail provides access to the canal for small, portable boats.

Picnic facilities and viewing areas are available. The refuge is open daily dawn-dusk. Phone (252) 771-8333.

DOSWELL — see Richmond p. 286.

DUFFIELD (I-2) pop. 62

NATURAL TUNNEL STATE PARK is about 5 mi. s. on US 23, then 1 mi. e. on SR 871. An 850-foot natural tunnel was carved through the solid limestone by Stock Creek. The tunnel emerges in a natural amphitheater that measures more than a half-mile around and rises 400 feet above the tunnel entrance. Seven trails, one of which leads to the summit of Lover's Leap, weave through the park. The park has a swimming pool, a chairlift and a visitor center that features interpretive exhibits.

Camping is permitted. Allow 1 hour minimum. Daily 10-6. Chairlift Mon.-Fri. 10-5, Sat.-Sun. and holidays 10-6, Memorial Day-Labor Day. Pool daily 10-6, Memorial Day-Labor Day. Trails open 8 a.m.-dusk. Park free. Chairlift $3, under 6 free. Pool $3; ages 3-12, $2. Parking $2 Mon.-Fri., $3 Sat.-Sun. and holidays. MC, VI. Phone (276) 940-2674, or (800) 933-7275 for camping reservations. *See Recreation Chart.*

DUMFRIES — *see District of Columbia p. 127.*

EDINBURG (E-8) pop. 813

Edinburg was the "Granary of the Confederacy" during the Civil War. Union general Philip Sheridan threatened to leave it "so desolate that a crow flying over would have to carry a knapsack." Edinburg Museum is full of regional curios and artifacts.

Edinburg Area Chamber of Commerce: P.O. Box 85, Edinburg, VA 22824; phone (540) 984-8318.

WINERIES

• **Shenandoah Vineyards** is off I-81 exit 279, w. on Stony Creek Rd., then 1.5 mi. n. on S. Ox Rd. Daily 10-6, Mar.-Nov.; 10-5, rest of year. Closed Jan. 1, Thanksgiving and Dec. 25. Phone (540) 984-8699.

FAIRFAX — *see District of Columbia p. 127.*

FALLS CHURCH —
see District of Columbia p. 127.

FALMOUTH (D-11) pop. 3,624

Chartered in 1720, Falmouth once rivaled Fredericksburg in commercial importance. During the Revolution, James Hunter's ironworks ran full tilt to supply the American Army and Navy with such articles as camp kettles, bayonets and anchors. Tapping into Falmouth's thriving industry, resident Basil Gordon became one of America's first millionaires.

Falmouth is now a subdued but charming relic of its past. George Washington reportedly received his primary education in the town. Noted Falmouth natives include Confederate Secretary of War James Alexander Seddon, and Dr. Kate Waller Barrett, a staunch crusader for social reform. Falmouth served as the headquarters for the Federal Army before and after the Battle of Fredericksburg.

[SAVE] **BELMONT—THE GARI MELCHERS ESTATE AND MEMORIAL GALLERY** is s.w. of jct. US 1 and US 17N at 224 Washington St. (SR 1001). The 18th-century manor house set on 27 acres overlooking the Rappahannock River is preserved as a memorial to its former owner Gari Melchers, the American artist who died in 1932. The house is furnished with antiques and art collected by Melchers and his wife. His studio exhibits more than 75 of his paintings. A visitor center, located in the former carriage house, offers an orientation videotape.

Allow 1 hour minimum. Guided tours Mon.-Sat. 10-5, Sun. 1-5, Mar.-Nov.; Mon.-Sat. 10-4, Sun. 1-4, rest of year. Closed Jan. 1, Thanksgiving and Dec. 24-25 and 31. Admission $7; over 60, $5; ages 6-18, $1. MC, VI. Phone (540) 654-1015.

[SAVE] **WHITE OAK CIVIL WAR MUSEUM** is at 985 White Oak Rd. Located in a renovated 1912 schoolhouse, the museum contains battlefield relics such as buttons, buckles and more than 90,000 bullets. Also displayed are bottles, soldiers' equipment and replicas of campsite huts, which housed soldiers during the winter. Wed.-Sun. 9-5; closed holidays. Admission $3; over 65 and ages 13-17, $1.50; ages 7-12, $1. Phone (540) 371-4234.

FERRUM (I-6) pop. 1,313, elev. 1,300'

Ferrum College was founded in 1913 by the Woman's Missionary Union of the Methodist Church.

BLUE RIDGE INSTITUTE AND MUSEUM is on SR 40W on the campus of Ferrum College. Preserving the heritage of the Blue Ridge region, the museum houses changing exhibits about Blue Ridge folklife. A re-created German-American farm illustrates early 19th-century life complete with period furnishings and costumed interpreters. The Blue Ridge Folklife Festival, the fourth Saturday in October, showcases the region's folk culture.

Allow 2 hours minimum. Museum open Mon.-Sat. 10-4; closed Jan. 1, Thanksgiving and Dec. 25. Farm open Sat. 10-4, Sun. 1-4, mid-May to mid-Aug. Museum free. Farm tours $4; over 60 and ages 6-14, $3. Phone (540) 365-4416.

FORT DEFIANCE (F-7) elev. 1,320'

AUGUSTA MILITARY ACADEMY ALUMNI HOUSE/MUSEUM is off I-81 exit 227, 1 mi. w. to US 11, then 3 mi. n. The museum depicts cadet life and the history of the school that operated 1874-1984. Chronological exhibits are presented in the restored 1870s Roller House, which features Victorian furnishings, a cadet barracks and classroom. Exhibits contain military uniforms, artifacts and memorabilia. Allow 30 minutes minimum. Thurs.-Sun. 10-5, Apr.-Oct.; Wed.-Sun. 10-5, rest of year. Closed Jan. 1, Thanksgiving and Dec. 24-25. Free. Phone (540) 248-3007.

FORT EUSTIS —
see Hampton Roads Area p. 256.

FORT LEE (B-2) elev. 165'

Fort Lee, 2 miles east of Petersburg, is the only U.S. Army quartermaster installation and training center in the nation.

ARMY WOMEN'S MUSEUM is at 2100 Adams Ave. Women's contributions during times of war are depicted through interactive exhibits, artifacts, and a collection of films featuring war recruitment and propaganda. Allow 30 minutes minimum. Tues.-Fri. 10-5, Sat.-Sun. 11-5; closed Jan. 1, Thanksgiving and Dec. 25. Free. Phone (804) 734-4326.

QUARTERMASTER MUSEUM is 1 blk. inside the main gate of Fort Lee. A variety of exhibits portraying the mission of the Quartermaster Corps are featured as well as presidential flags, Civil War memorabilia, Gen. George S. Patton's jeep, Gen. Dwight D. Eisenhower's uniforms and Gen. Ulysses S. Grant's saddle. Tues.-Fri. 10-5, Sat.-Sun. 11-5; closed Jan. 1, Thanksgiving and Dec. 25. Free. Phone (804) 734-4203.

FORT MONROE—
see Hampton Roads Area p. 256.

FREDERICKSBURG (D-11)
pop. 19,279, elev. 69′

Fredericksburg was officially founded and given its present name in 1728, even though settlers had built a fort as early as 1676. Its location in a valley at the head of navigation on the Rappahannock River led to the city's emergence as a prosperous port.

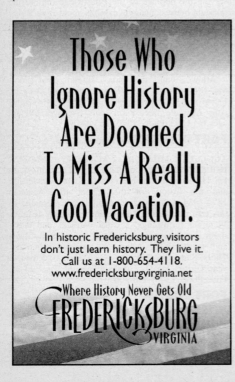

Those Who Ignore History Are Doomed To Miss A Really Cool Vacation.

In historic Fredericksburg, visitors don't just learn history. They live it. Call us at 1-800-654-4118.
www.fredericksburgvirginia.net

Where History Never Gets Old
FREDERICKSBURG VIRGINIA

Fredericksburg was George Washington's boyhood home, his mother's last home and the home of his sister, Betty Washington Lewis. James Monroe set up his first law office in the city in 1786.

Between 1861 and 1865 Fredericksburg was an armed camp and the scene of violent battles. By the end of the Civil War it was desolate, its houses torn by shot and shell and the dead buried in its streets.

The Battle of Fredericksburg was fought on Dec. 13, 1862. The Union Army of 142,551 under Gen. Ambrose Everett Burnside camped on Stafford Heights on the north side of the river. The Confederate force of 91,760 under Gen. Robert E. Lee was entrenched west and south of the town.

The Union troops made repeated unsuccessful attacks on the Confederate fortifications, resulting in Burnside's retreat across the river. On the Union side the dead and wounded numbered 12,653; Confederate casualties totaled 5,309.

After the Battle of Chancellorsville the city served as a hospital for the Confederate wounded; it provided a similar service for the Union forces after the Battle of the Wilderness. The Gothic Revival Fredericksburg Courthouse, erected 1851-52, is still in use today. Its historic documents include the will of Mary Washington. The bell was made by the Paul Revere foundry.

From Fredericksburg SR 3 leads down the historic Northern Neck past such sites as George Washington Birthplace National Monument, Robert E. Lee's birthplace at Stratford and George Washington's mother's birthplace near Lancaster.

Another historic, scenic route is US 17, which follows the Rappahannock River to Tappahannock and Gloucester, crosses the York River to Yorktown and the Colonial Parkway, and continues to Williamsburg.

Fredericksburg Visitor Center: 706 Caroline St., Fredericksburg, VA 22401; phone (540) 373-1776 or (800) 678-4748. *See ad.*

Self-guiding tours: Brochures and maps outlining self-guiding tours of historic Fredericksburg and the area are available from the visitor center. A 14-minute orientation film is shown. Brochures, maps and area information as well as a 10-minute orientation film, also are available at the Spotsylvania Visitor Center, 4704 Southpoint Pkwy.; phone (540) 891-8687 or (800) 654-4118.

Shopping areas: Old Town Fredericksburg boasts an array of boutiques and more than 120 antiques dealers. Spotsylvania Mall, I-95 and SR 3, has more than 120 stores, including five department stores.

BELMONT—THE GARI MELCHERS ESTATE AND MEMORIAL GALLERY—
see Falmouth p. 235.

SAVE **FREDERICKSBURG AREA MUSEUM AND CULTURAL CENTER** is at 907 Princess Anne St. This was once the town hall and market building where locals exchanged political ideas as well as goods and services. It houses a collection of photographs, tools, furniture, paintings, toys, clothing and pottery that traces the history of Fredericksburg and the surrounding area. A Civil War collection is displayed.

Allow 30 minutes minimum. Mon.-Sat. 10-5, Sun. 1-5, Mar.-Nov.; Mon.-Sat. 10-4, Sun. 1-4, rest of year. Closed Jan. 1, Thanksgiving and Dec. 24-25 and 31. Admission $5; ages 6-18, $1. Phone (540) 371-3037.

GEORGE WASHINGTON MASONIC MUSEUM is at 803 Princess Anne St. Masonic artifacts and an original portrait of Washington by Gilbert Stuart are displayed. Allow 30 minutes minimum. Mon.-Sat. 9-4, Sun. 1-4; closed Jan. 1, Thanksgiving and Dec. 25. Admission $2; ages 13-18, $1; ages 6-12, 50c. Phone (540) 373-5885.

GEORGE WASHINGTON'S FERRY FARM is 1.5 mi. e. on SR 3 to 268 Kings Hwy. Though the original dwelling is gone, an archeological excavation marks the site of what is believed to have been Washington's first home. It was here on his father's 600-acre tobacco and corn plantation that Washington purportedly chopped the cherry tree and learned how to survey. Excavations are ongoing. In summer

a demonstration garden features plants typical of those grown on the original plantation. Daily 10-5, Mar.-Dec.; Sat.-Sun. 10-5, rest of year. Closed Jan. 1, Thanksgiving and Dec. 24-25 and 31. Admission $3; ages 6-17, $1.50. Phone (540) 370-0732.

HUGH MERCER APOTHECARY SHOP is at Caroline and Amelia sts. Displays include 18th-century medicinal and surgical supplies, such as leeches, lancets, blisters, purges and herbs. Living-history presentations demonstrate various practices. A physic garden of medicinal herbs adjoins the building where Dr. Hugh Mercer worked prior to joining the Continental Army as a brigadier general in 1776.

Allow 30 minutes minimum. Mon.-Sat. 9-5, Sun. 11-4, Mar.-Nov.; Mon.-Sat. 10-4, Sun. noon-4, rest of year. Closed Jan. 1, Thanksgiving and Dec. 24-25 and 31. Admission $5; ages 6-18, $2. Phone (540) 373-3362.

JAMES MONROE MUSEUM AND MEMORIAL LIBRARY is at 908 Charles St. Monroe owned this property 1786-92 and probably used it while practicing law as a young attorney in Fredericksburg. The museum contains what is said to be the largest collection of

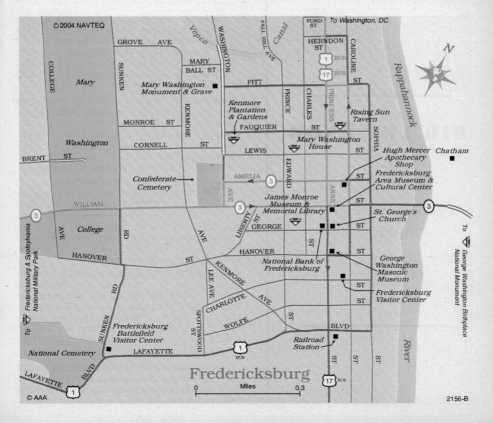

Combination Tickets

Fredericksburg area battlefields, Fredericksburg Area Museum and Cultural Center, George Washington's Ferry Farm, Hugh Mercer Apothecary Shop, James Monroe Museum and Memorial Library, Kenmore Plantation & Gardens, Mary Washington House, Rising Sun Tavern and Belmont (in Falmouth) can be visited by using the Pass to Historic Fredericksburg. The combined admission is $24; ages 6-18, $8.

Another discount option is the Pick Four ticket, which includes any four attractions listed above for a combined admission of $16; ages 6-18, $6.

Passes are available at any of the above attractions and at the Fredericksburg or Spotsylvania Visitor Centers. Phone (800) 654-4118.

Note: It is a good idea to verify hours and admission fees in advance.

DID YOU KNOW

America's first peanuts were grown in Virginia.

Monroe-related material in the country, including belongings of President and Mrs. Monroe and the Louis XVI furniture they bought in Paris when he was minister to France 1794-97.

The collection includes the desk on which Monroe prepared his 1823 address to Congress; a section of this speech became known as the Monroe Doctrine. Also displayed are gems owned by Elizabeth Monroe and gowns she wore at the Court of Napoleon. A library contains historical manuscripts relating to the president and his era. A bronze bust of the fifth president is in the walled garden.

Allow 30 minutes minimum. Mon.-Sat. 10-5, Sun. 1-5, Mar.-Nov.; Mon.-Sat. 10-4, Sun. 1-4, rest of year. Closed Jan. 1, Thanksgiving and Dec. 24-25 and 31. Admission $5; ages 6-18, $1. Phone (540) 654-1043.

KENMORE PLANTATION & GARDENS is at 1201 Washington Ave. Kenmore was the home of Col. Fielding Lewis and his wife, Betty Washington Lewis, sister of George Washington. Built in the early 1770s, this Colonial home is an example of a Tidewater Georgian manor house. The building was used as a hospital during the Civil War. The house is noted for the elaborate, decorative plasterwork on its ceilings and over its fireplaces.

Restoration and archeological research is ongoing; some areas may be closed to visitors. The grounds include a wilderness walking trail. Allow 1 hour minimum. Daily 11-5, Mar.-Dec.; Sat. 11-5, rest of year. Closed Jan. 1, Thanksgiving and Dec. 24-25 and 31. Admission $6; ages 6-18, $3. MC, VI. Phone (540) 373-3381.

Crowninshield Museum is at 1201 Washington Ave. The museum offers an exhibit about Virginia-made furniture, portraits and silver as well as a diorama of Fredericksburg in the late 1700s. Mon.-Fri. 10-5, Sun. noon-5, Presidents Day-Dec. 30; closed Thanksgiving and Dec. 24-25 and 31. Admission included with Kenmore Plantation & Gardens.

MARY WASHINGTON HOUSE is at 1200 Charles St. George Washington bought the house in 1772 for his mother, Mary Ball Washington, who lived here until her death in 1789. It was from this house that Washington left for his inauguration after having received his mother's blessing. The home contains some of Mrs. Washington's favorite possessions.

The old English garden is especially beautiful; some of the first boxwoods Mrs. Washington planted remain, and her sundial still marks the hours. Allow 30 minutes minimum. Mon.-Sat. 9-5, Sun. 11-5, Mar.-Nov.; Mon.-Sat. 10-4, Sun. noon-4, rest of year. Closed Jan. 1, Thanksgiving and Dec. 24-25 and 31. Admission $5; ages 6-18, $1.50. Phone (540) 373-1569.

MARY WASHINGTON MONUMENT AND GRAVE is on Washington Ave. at the end of Pitt St. The first president's mother was buried here in 1789. Andrew Jackson laid the cornerstone for a marble monument to "the Mother of Washington" in 1833. It was never completed, and during the bombardment of Fredericksburg in 1862 it was scarred badly by shellfire. In 1894 President Grover Cleveland dedicated the present marker, a 40-foot granite shaft.

NATIONAL BANK OF FREDERICKSBURG is at 900 Princess Anne St. Built in 1820, the Federal-style Farmers' Bank building contains a restored banking room and local banking artifacts including a scale for weighing gold dust, a counterfeit bank note from the 1800s and bank certificates and correspondence from the 1860s. Allow 30 minutes minimum. Mon.-Fri. 9-2. Free. Phone (540) 899-3243.

RISING SUN TAVERN is at 1306 Caroline St. The house was built about 1760 for Charles Washington, brother of George Washington. It later served as a coach stop. Costumed tavern wenches give living-history tours. Night tours are available through the Fredericksburg Visitor Center. Allow 30 minutes minimum. Daily 9-5, Mar.-Nov.; 10-4, rest of year. Closed Jan. 1, Thanksgiving and Dec. 24-25 and 31. Admission $5; ages 6-18, $1.50. Phone (540) 371-1494, or (800) 678-4748 for night tour information.

ST. GEORGE'S EPISCOPAL CHURCH is at Princess Anne and George sts. The original church was built on this site in 1732; the present structure dates from 1848. It contains a memorial window to Mary Washington and three original Louis Comfort Tiffany windows. In the churchyard are buried William Paul, brother of John Paul Jones, and John Dandridge of New Kent, father of Martha Washington. Daily 9-5. Guided tours Mon.-Fri. 10-3, day after Memorial Day-day before Labor Day. Free. Phone (540) 373-4133.

FREDERICKSBURG AND SPOTSYLVANIA NATIONAL MILITARY PARK (D-11)

In and around Fredericksburg, the park covers about 8,400 acres and includes four great battlefields of the Civil War: Chancellorsville *(see place listing p. 228)*, Fredericksburg, Spotsylvania Court House *(see place listing p. 291)* and the Wilderness *(see place listing p. 295)*.

Due to its strategic location halfway between Richmond and Washington, D.C., Fredericksburg and the surrounding area were of prime military importance to both sides. The intense and continuous fighting resulted in the estimated loss of 65,000 Union soldiers and 40,000 Confederate fighters.

Old Salem Church, which served as a refuge for civilians fleeing the city during the Battle of Fredericksburg, and Fredericksburg National Cemetery are within the park. The church, also the site of a battle during the Chancellorsville campaign, later was used by the Confederates to tend to the wounded of both sides. Also on the grounds is Ellwood, a house standing in the middle of the Wilderness Battlefield that once served as a hospital for Confederates. Near Fredericksburg Battlefield Visitor Center stands a statue of a Confederate sergeant who risked his life to give water to the wounded and dying of the Union Army.

All of the battlefields are in a 17-mile radius of Fredericksburg. Exhibits, paintings, interpretive trails, historic buildings, narrative markers and maps identify Union and Confederate lines and relate the stories of the battles. Roads lead to the battlefields, earthworks and other points of historic interest.

The TravelBrains Fredericksburg Expedition Guide is available at the national park bookstore. This self-guiding walking tour includes an audio CD and a guide book featuring maps of battle sites, photographs and information about armies, monuments, memorials and soldiers. A multimedia CD-ROM also is available.

The park is open daily 8:30-6:30, Memorial Day-Labor Day; 9-5, rest of year. Closed Jan. 1 and Dec. 25. Admission to the park $4, under 16 free. TravelBrains guide book and audio tour CD $19.95; multimedia CD-ROM tour $29.95. Phone (540) 371-0802.

CHATHAM is .5 mi. e. across the Rappahannock River off SR 218. The 18th-century Georgian mansion served as Union headquarters and a field hospital during the Civil War. Clara Barton and Walt Whitman were among those who provided care for the wounded soldiers here. A museum relates the story of Chatham and the role it played in the war. Daily 9-5; closed Jan. 1 and Dec. 25. Admission included in park fee. Phone (540) 371-0802.

"STONEWALL" JACKSON SHRINE is 15 mi. s. of Fredericksburg via I-95, US 1 or SR 2, then by CR 606 to Guinea Station. On the night of May 2, 1863, the Confederate general was mistakenly shot by his own men at Chancellorsville, losing an arm. Jackson was moved by order of Gen. Robert E. Lee to recover at Fairfield Plantation. With the main house already filled with injured soldiers, Jackson's doctors settled him in the plantation office. The room where he died a week later has been preserved.

Daily 9-5, mid-June through Labor Day; Fri.-Tues. 9-5, Apr. 1 to mid-June and day after Labor Day-Oct. 31; Sat.-Mon. 9-5, rest of year. Closed Jan. 1 and Dec. 25. Admission included in park fee. Phone (804) 633-6076.

VISITOR CENTERS are at 1013 Lafayette Blvd. (US 1) and 8 mi. w. of I-95 on SR 3. Both the Fredericksburg and the Chancellorsville visitor centers contain 12-minute slide shows and displays about the battles. Self-guiding walking and driving tours begin at the centers. Tape-recorded, self-guiding driving tours also are offered. Special walking tours of the area are conducted seasonally; phone for schedule.

Allow 1 hour minimum. Daily 8:30-6:30, mid-June through Labor Day; Mon.-Fri. 9-5, Sat.-Sun. 9-6, Apr. 1 to mid-June and day after Labor Day-Oct. 31; daily 9-5, rest of year. Closed Jan. 1 and Dec. 25. Free. A rental fee of $4.95 for self-guiding driving tour includes tape, tape player and map. Phone (540) 373-6122 for the Fredericksburg Visitor Center, or (540) 786-2880 for the Chancellorsville Visitor Center.

FRONT ROYAL (E-8) pop. 13,589, elev. 565'

Front Royal began as Lehew Town, a frontier village on the packhorse road to the east. According to local lore, its current name derives from the command by frustrated military officers for unruly troops to "front the royal oak," which once stood in the public square.

Belle Boyd, the Confederate spy who charmed military secrets out of her Union suitors, used Front Royal as one of her most effective bases. On May 15, 1862, Boyd overheard plans that the Union troops were exiting Front Royal, leaving behind a small force. Boyd relayed this information to Gen. "Stonewall" Jackson, and on May 23, Jackson led his troops into town and the Battle of Front Royal ended with the capture of 750 of the 1,000 Union soldiers. No remains of the battlefield exist.

A popular stopping point for visitors bound for the Skyline Drive (see Shenandoah National Park p. 291), Front Royal has preserved some of its 19th-century atmosphere on Chester Street, in the historic district. The 1787 Balthis House is the oldest building in town. At 101 Chester St. is Ivy Lodge, headquarters of the Warren Heritage Society and home to the Ivy Lodge Museum; phone (540) 636-1446.

Raymond R. "Andy" Guest Jr. Shenandoah River State Park, 8 miles south on US 340, offers a variety of outdoor activities and scenic vistas. See Recreation Chart.

Front Royal Visitor Center: 414 E. Main St., Front Royal, VA 22630; phone (540) 635-5788 or (800) 338-2576.

Self-guiding tours: Brochures describing a walking tour of the historic district are available at the visitor center in the Southern Railway Train Station.

BELLE BOYD COTTAGE is 1 blk. e. of US 340 at 101 Chester St. The 1860s middle-class home was used by the Confederate spy Belle Boyd. Furnished in period, the cottage contains memorabilia depicting the area during the Civil War. Mon.-Fri. 10-4; closed major holidays. Hours may vary; phone ahead. Admission $2; ages 8-16, $1. Phone (540) 636-1446.

 SKYLINE CAVERNS are on US 340, approximately 1 mi. s. of the entrance to Skyline Drive and 1.5 mi. s. of jct. SR 55. The caverns contain calcite formations known as anthodites or cave flowers, found in few caves worldwide. Subterranean streams and cascades are of interest. Indirect illumination is provided. There is a .5-mile tour of the grounds aboard a miniature train (weather permitting).

Guided tours depart every 15-20 minutes daily 9-6:30, June 15-Labor Day; Mon.-Fri. 9-5, Sat.-Sun. 9-6, Mar. 15-June 14 and day after Labor Day-Nov. 14; daily 9-4, rest of year. Admission $14; over 62, $12; ages 7-13, $7. Train fare $3, under 3 free. AX, MC, VI. Phone (540) 635-4545 or (800) 296-4545. See color ad.

[SAVE] **"WARREN RIFLES" CONFEDERATE MUSEUM** is at 95 Chester St. The museum houses documents, guns, pictures, letters from Confederate soldiers and personal items of Belle Boyd and Gens. "Stonewall" Jackson, Robert E. Lee and Turner Ashby. Mon.-Sat. 9-4, Apr. 15-Oct. 31; by appointment Sun. and rest of year. Admission $4, senior citizens $3.60, under 12 free with adult. Phone (540) 636-6982 or (540) 635-2219.

GALAX (I-5) pop. 6,837, elev. 2,382'

Tucked in the Blue Ridge Mountains on the North Carolina state line, Galax is noted for its pristine beauty. The town is named for the leaf of the galax, a plant indigenous to the area. The terrain is popular with mountain bikers, horseback riders and hikers, while placid rivers and streams draw angles, canoeists and kayakers.

Director of Tourism: 111 E. Grayson St., Galax, VA 24333; phone (276) 238-8130.

JEFF MATHEWS MEMORIAL MUSEUM is at 606 W. Stuart Dr. An eclectic collection includes Civil War items, arrowheads, pocketknives, medical and dental equipment and farm machinery. Two restored log cabins and a smithy are on the grounds. Jeff Mathews, one of Galax's first settlers, established the museum with a friend, combining their collections of American Indian artifacts and other memorabilia. Wed.-Sat. 11-4; closed major holidays. Donations. Phone (276) 236-7874.

GEORGE WASHINGTON AND JEFFERSON NATIONAL FORESTS

Elevations in the forests range from 600 ft. near Covington to 5,729 ft. Mount Rogers in the Mount Rogers National Recreation Area. Refer to AAA maps for additional elevation information.

Stretching from Big Stone Gap to Winchester, the George Washington and Jefferson National Forests contain some 1.8 million acres.

The northern end of the forest, known as the George Washington National Forest, extends more than 1 million acres across the Blue Ridge, Massanutten, Shenandoah and Allegheny mountain ranges into West Virginia. Towering over all these ranges is 4,463-foot Elliott Knob, just west of Staunton.

Among the major recreation areas are Brandywine and Todd lakes, respectively west and southwest of Harrisonburg; Elizabeth Furnace, south of Waterlick; Trout Pond, west of Woodstock; Sherando Lake, near Waynesboro; and Lake Moomaw, southwest of Warm Springs.

More than 950 miles of trails wind through the George Washington National Forest leading to scenic views of mountains, valleys and rivers. A portion of the Appalachian Trail traverses the forest, and another trail leads to Crabtree Falls, five cascading waterfalls that are the highest in the Blue Ridge.

A 5-mile loop trail winds gradually to the top of Pompey Mountain and Mount Pleasant. Popular because it is not steep, the trail provides scenic vistas of the Blue Ridge Mountains. Also noteworthy is The Highlands Scenic Tour, a 20-mile scenic drive through the mountains along a steep, twisting road. The Massanutten Gap Visitor Center is on US 211 at New Market Gap, west of Luray.

The southern end of the forest, known as Jefferson National Forest, embraces approximately 710,000 acres in west-central Virginia. A 300-mile portion of the Appalachian Trail runs through the forest; trail shelters are provided.

Jefferson National Forest has more than 1,100 miles of trails, 500 miles of trout streams, 24 developed campgrounds, 25 picnic areas and six fishing and four swimming lakes, some of which have bathhouses. The Cascades National Recreation Trail is a scenic 4-mile hike leading to a 66-foot waterfall. The 4-mile John's Creek Mountain Trail offers panoramic views as it intersects the Appalachian Trail.

Beginning near Wytheville, Big Walker Mountain Scenic Byway winds 16 miles through forested countryside past old farm homesteads, hiking trails, fishing ponds, picnic areas, campgrounds and beautiful mountain vistas. The byway leads up the mountain to Big Walker Lookout, which features a visitor center, swinging bridge and an observation tower, all open daily April through October. Another scenic route, Mount Rogers Scenic Byway, passes through valleys and over mountains rich in the ever-changing colors of leaves and wildflowers.

Nearby are the towns of Abingdon *(see place listing p. 221)*, Big Stone Gap *(see place listing p. 223)*, Blacksburg *(see place listing p. 224)*, Natural Bridge *(see place listing p. 268)*, Roanoke *(see place listing p. 288)*, Winchester *(see place listing p. 310)* and Wytheville *(see place listing p. 311)*.

For information contact the Forest Supervisor, 5162 Valleypointe Pkwy., Roanoke, VA 24019. The main recreation season for George Washington and Jefferson National Forests is April through November. Fees are charged at some sites. Phone (888) 265-0019. *See Recreation Chart and the AAA Mideastern CampBook.*

CAVE MOUNTAIN LAKE RECREATION AREA is 8 mi. s.e. of Natural Bridge. The park contains a 7-acre lake with a beach and bathhouses, hiking trails, picnic facilities, and tent and trailer camping areas. A scenic drive past Cave Mountain Lake climbs Wildcat Mountain, where it forks; the left spur leads to Sunset Field, where it connects with Blue Ridge Parkway. Daily 6 a.m.-11 p.m., May-Oct. Day-use fee $6 per private vehicle. Camping $12. Phone (540) 291-2188.

GEORGE WASHINGTON BIRTHPLACE NATIONAL MONUMENT (F-10)

On the south side of the Potomac River, 38 miles east of Fredericksburg off SR 3 on SR 204, George Washington Birthplace National Monument includes 550 acres and a portion of the old Washington Plantation. John, the first Washington to settle in the area, arrived about 1657. In 1731 his grandson Augustine married Mary Ball of Epping Forest. He brought her to his home on Popes Creek, and there George Washington was born in 1732.

The house, built by Augustine 1722-26, was destroyed by fire on Christmas Day in 1779. Excavations have revealed five original foundations. Since the exact appearance of the original is not known, a memorial house was built to represent an 18th-century plantation home.

Native clay was used to make the bricks for the building, which is furnished with antiques carefully selected to reflect the period of Washington's boyhood. The grounds include a kitchen and garden.

The present Colonial Living Farm re-creates some of the farm scenes of young Washington's environment. The livestock, gardens and crops are historical varieties raised by methods common during the Colonial period.

Also on the grounds is a cemetery containing the graves of 32 members of the family, including George's father, grandfather and great-grandfather. Picnic facilities are available. House and grounds open daily 9-5; closed Jan. 1, Thanksgiving and Dec. 25. Admission $4, under 17 free. Phone (804) 224-1732.

GLEN ALLEN — *see Richmond p. 286.*

GLOUCESTER —
see Hampton Roads Area p. 257.

GLOUCESTER POINT —
see Hampton Roads Area p. 257.

GREAT FALLS — *see District of Columbia p. 128.*

GROTTOES (F-8) pop. 2,114

Known in its early history as Liola and then Shendun, this area was settled around 1735 with a land grant of 60,000 acres on the Shenandoah River. The Grottoes Company was formed in 1889 to develop the local caves and mineral resources; the enterprise folded four years later. The town adopted its present name in 1912.

GRAND CAVERNS REGIONAL PARK is off I-81 exit 235, then 6 mi. e. on SR 256. One of the country's oldest show caverns, the Grottoes cave was discovered in 1804 and opened to the public 2 years later. At different times both Union and "Stonewall" Jackson's Confederate troops visited the Great Cathedral Hall and Grand Ballroom. Signatures of soldiers from both armies are visible on cave walls. Unusual cave formations include calcite shields.

Nature trails, picnicking, tennis, swimming and miniature golf are offered. Guided 1-hour tours daily 9-5, Apr.-Oct. Admission $16; over 60 and military with ID $15; ages 3-12, $9. MC, VI. Phone (540) 249-5705.

HAMPTON — *see Hampton Roads Area p. 257.*

Hampton Roads Area

including Newport News, Norfolk and Virginia Beach

When the *Susan Constant*, the *Godspeed* and the *Discovery* landed at Chesapeake Bay in 1607, our nation's history began. The travelers, led by John Smith, bestowed the name Cape Henry on the site before continuing their journey along the James River and establishing the first permanent English colony in America at Jamestown.

Settlement quickly pushed outward from the James River. The site of present-day Newport News was settled in 1621, with Norfolk following suit in 1682. The Revolutionary War reached the region in 1776 when Norfolk was bombarded by the British; citizens burned the remains of the town to the ground to prevent the enemy's return.

Steeped in the history of the Colonial era, Hampton Roads also holds importance as the site of two key Civil War events. The naval engagement between the CSS *Virginia (Merrimac)* and the USS *Monitor*—the first duel between ironclad warships—was fought in 1862 in the harbor at the mouth of the James River. Three years later Abraham Lincoln and Confederate representatives met aboard the *River Queen*, where unsuccessful negotiations to end the war were conducted.

Virginia Beach was a desolate strip of sand in the 1870s—its only notoriety being that of a graveyard for ships lost along the Atlantic coast—when Congress authorized the construction of four lifesaving stations in the area. Seatack Lifesaving Station developed into the community of Virginia Beach.

The area's ties to the sea were further strengthened when the Newport News Shipbuilding and Dry Dock Company, a leader in the production of ocean liners as well as military vessels, was established in 1886. Soldiers leaving for both world wars embarked from this city; those returning from World War I were honored with the Victory Arch on 25th Street, commemorating all American veterans.

Newport News / © Jeff Greenberg/Alamy Images

Old Towne Historic District, Portsmouth / Portsmouth Convention and Visitors Bureau

Norfolk, with one of the finest harbors in the world, accommodates the largest ships, including supercarriers, merchant ships and U.S. Navy vessels. The Norfolk Naval Shipyard in nearby Portsmouth and the Naval Station and Naval Air Station in Norfolk constitute one of the largest naval facilities in the world.

A merger of Virginia Beach with Princess Anne County created a city with a 29-mile-long coastline. The resort offers an excellent beach and 3 miles of boardwalk. Surf swimming is probably the favorite sport, complemented by aquaplaning, water skiing and boating on inland waters. Fishing also is prime here, and the region is noted for seafood, especially the Lynnhaven oyster.

The term Hampton Roads has come to include the section of southeastern Virginia encompassing Norfolk, Virginia Beach, Newport News, Hampton, Portsmouth and other surrounding towns as well as Williamsburg, Jamestown and Yorktown. Historically the name refers to the place of safe harbor off the Virginia peninsula between the James, Elizabeth and Nansemond rivers and Chesapeake Bay named after the third Earl of Southampton. A "road," in the nautical sense, is a place where ships can safely anchor.

Approaches

By Car

The communities that comprise Hampton Roads Area are accessible from a number of highways. From the north, I-64 approaches Williamsburg, continues through Newport News and Hampton, and tunnels beneath Chesapeake Bay to Norfolk. It then circles west and north, becoming I-664 around Portsmouth, and tunnels through the James River into Hampton again.

From the west, south Hampton Roads is reached via US 13/58/460, which becomes I-264 at its western junction with the I-64 loop. I-264 continues east through Portsmouth and leads into Virginia Beach, at its eastern junction of I-64.

Getting Around

Street System

Hampton Roads' street networks take into account the importance of the area as a seaport. Tunnels cross beneath Chesapeake Bay and the James River, linking North and South Hampton Roads. Myriad bridges span less-accessible tributaries.

Brambleton Avenue and Virginia Beach Boulevard are the major east-west routes through Norfolk; St. Paul's Boulevard is the primary north-south street.

Right turns on red are permitted, unless otherwise posted. As in most large, metropolitan areas, rush hours should be avoided; in Hampton Roads this is 6:30 to 9 a.m. and 3:30 to 6:30 p.m.

(continued on p. 250)

The Informed Traveler

City Population: Newport News 180,150
Elevation: 11 ft.
City Population: Norfolk 234,403
Elevation: 12 ft.
City Population: Virginia Beach 425,257
Elevation: 16 ft.
Sales Tax: Virginia has a 4.5 percent sales tax; cities and counties impose an additional 1 percent. The following towns impose a lodging tax: Newport News, 5.5 percent; Norfolk, 7 percent; and Virginia Beach $1 per night plus 5.5 percent.

WHOM TO CALL

Emergency: 911

Time: *Newport News:* (757) 844-9311; *Norfolk:* (757) 622-9311

Temperature and Weather: *Newport News:* (757) 877-1221; *Norfolk:* (757) 666-1212

Hospitals: *Newport News:* Mary Immaculate, (757) 886-6000; *Norfolk:* Bon Secours-DePaul Medical Center, (757) 889-5000; *Virginia Beach:* Sentara Virginia Beach Hospital, (757) 395-8000.

WHERE TO LOOK

Newspapers

Daily newspapers are *The Virginian-Pilot* and the *Daily Press*.

Radio

Norfolk radio station WNIS (850 AM) is an all news/talk station; WHRV (89.5 FM) is a member of National Public Radio.

Visitor Information

Norfolk Convention & Visitors Bureau: 232 E. Main St., Norfolk, VA 23510; phone (757) 664-6620 or (800) 368-3097.

The Norfolk Convention & Visitors Bureau Visitor Center is off I-64 exit 273, at 9401 4th View St.; phone (757) 441-1852 or (800) 368-3097. *See color ad p. 726.*

Newport News Visitor Center: 13560 Jefferson Ave., Newport News, VA 23603; phone (757) 886-7777 or (888) 493-7386. *See color ad p. 908.*
Virginia Beach Visitor Information Center: 2100 Parks Ave., Virginia Beach, VA 23451; phone (757) 437-4882 or (800) 822-3224. *See color ad p. 753.*

Publications include the weekly *Port Folio* and the bimonthly *Flash Magazine*.

TRANSPORTATION

Air Travel

Norfolk International Airport, served by major airlines, is off I-64 exit 279, then 1 mile east. Newport News/Williamsburg International Airport is off I-64 exit 255B in Newport News.

Rental Cars

Several automobile rental agencies have offices throughout Hampton Roads. Hertz offers discounts to AAA members; phone (757) 855-1961 or (800) 654-3080.

Rail Service

Amtrak train stations in Newport News and Williamsburg provide direct service from Boston, New York, Philadelphia, Baltimore and Washington, D.C.; phone (800) 872-7245. The Newport News station is at 9304 Warwick Blvd.

Buses

Greyhound Lines Inc., (800) 231-2222, is at 11 Dozier Rd. (main gate) at Fort Eustis, (757) 887-2626; 2 W. Pembroke Ave. in Hampton, (757) 722-9861; 701 Monticello Ave. in Norfolk, (757) 625-7500; and 1017 Laskin Rd. in Virginia Beach, (757) 422-2998.

Taxis

Area cab companies include North End Cab Co., (757) 244-4000, in Newport News; Norfolk Checker Taxi, (757) 855-3333; and Yellow Cab Inc., (757) 460-0605, in Virginia Beach. Metered charges are $1.75 to enter and $1.50 per mile in Newport News; $1.75 to enter and $1.40 per mile in Norfolk; and $1.75 to enter and $1.80 per mile in Virginia Beach.

Public Transport

Williamsburg Area Transport (WAT) serves James City County, the city of Williamsburg and the Bruton District of York County. Basic fare is $1; transfers are 25c. Phone (757) 259-4093.

Hampton Roads Transit (HRT) serves the Hampton Roads Area and Newport News. Basic fare is $1.50, transfers are free. Phone (757) 222-6100.

Destination Hampton Roads Area

*L*et the outstanding maritime museums in Norfolk and Newport News set the tone for your visit. But don't be surprised if you find more than nautical landmarks and seafaring lore in the Hampton Roads Area.

*N*orfolk also is home to the Chrysler Museum of Art; nearby Portsmouth boasts the Children's Museum of Virginia; and historic houses and old churches are in almost every community.

Portsmouth CVB

Courthouse Galleries, Portsmouth.
This restored 1846 courthouse features changing art exhibits.
(See listing page 259)

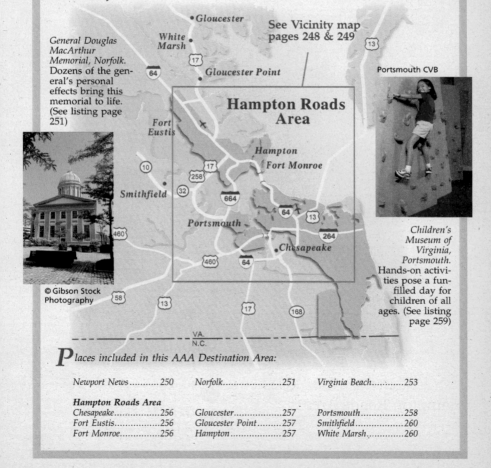

General Douglas MacArthur Memorial, Norfolk. Dozens of the general's personal effects bring this memorial to life. (See listing page 251)

© Gibson Stock Photography

See Vicinity map pages 248 & 249

Portsmouth CVB

Children's Museum of Virginia, Portsmouth. Hands-on activities pose a fun-filled day for children of all ages. (See listing page 259)

*P*laces included in this AAA Destination Area:

Hampton Roads Area

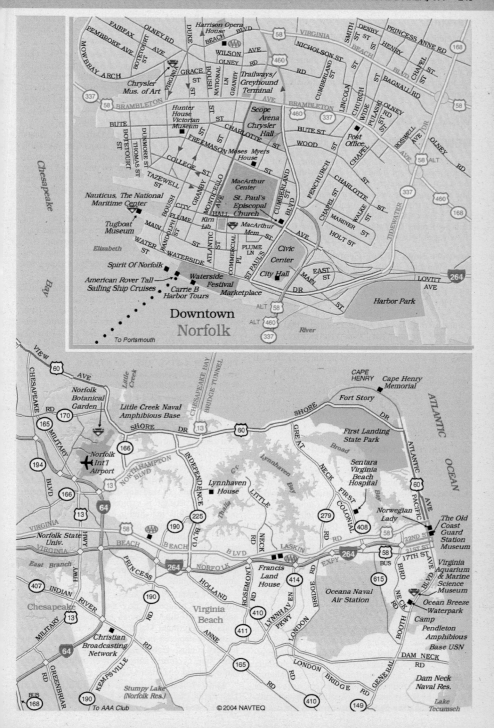

Downtown
Norfolk

Virginia
Beach

Chesapeake

©2004 NAVTEQ

Parking

Metered street parking is available in the downtown areas of Hampton Roads' major cities, and there are numerous public and commercial lots. Rates for public garages vary from 50c an hour to $8 for a full day; commercial lots usually charge slightly more.

What To See

NEWPORT NEWS pop. 180,150

It is said this city gained its name when the Jamestown settlers, ready to abandon their colony, met Capt. Christopher Newport on the James River. The captain's ship was carrying supplies and reinforcements from England, hence "Newport's good news." The captain played a key role in the permanent settlement of Virginia, making five transatlantic voyages between 1607 and 1619.

Newport News Visitor Center: 13560 Jefferson Ave., Newport News, VA 23603; phone (757) 886-7777 or (888) 493-7386. *See color ad p. 908.*

[SAVE] **ENDVIEW PLANTATION** is at 362 Yorktown Rd. Over the span of three wars, the plantation served as a military hospital and training grounds. Water from a spring attracted 3,000 militia during the Revolutionary War. Visitors may explore the cemetery and battlefield on the grounds. Guided tours are available. Allow 30 minutes minimum. Mon. and Wed.-Sat. 10-4, Sun. 1-5, Apr.-Dec.; Mon. and Thurs.-Sat. 1-4, Sun. 1-5, rest of year. Closed Jan. 1, Easter, Thanksgiving and Dec. 25. Admission $6; over 62, $5; ages 7-18, $4. Combination ticket with Lee Hall Mansion and the Virginia War Museum $15; over 62, $12; ages 7-18, $9. Phone (757) 887-1862.

[SAVE] **LEE HALL MANSION** is at 163 Yorktown Rd. The Italianate mansion was built in 1859 by Richard Decauter Lee, a wealthy tobacco planter. Confederate general John Magruder used the house as his headquarters during the Warwick River siege of the 1862 Peninsula Campaign initiated by Union general George McClellan. An exhibit about the campaign is featured. Allow 30 minutes minimum. Tours are offered every half-hour Mon. and Wed.-Sat. 10-4, Sun. 1-5, Apr.-Dec.; Mon. and Thurs.-Sat. 10-4, Sun. 1-5, rest of year. Closed Jan. 1, Easter, Thanksgiving and Dec. 25. Admission $6; over 62, $5; ages 7-18, $4. Combination ticket with Endview Plantation and the Virginia War Museum $15; over 62, $12; ages 7-18, $9. MC, VI. Phone (757) 888-3371.

[GEM] **MARINERS' MUSEUM** is off I-64 exit 258A, following US 17S to 100 Museum Dr. Dedicated to preserving and interpreting the heritage of the sea, the museum [SAVE] features some 35,000 maritime artifacts, including ship models, figureheads, scrimshaw, decorative arts, rare books, maps and navigational instruments. The Defending the Seas gallery explores the history of the U.S. Navy using re-created sections of military ships, including the ready room of an aircraft carrier and the helm section of a submarine.

Other exhibits include the Chesapeake Bay Gallery, the Crabtree Collection of Miniature Ships, the Great Hall of Steam and artifacts from the USS *Monitor,* including the engine register, crew members' silverware and the iconic gun turret. The museum is in a 550-acre park with a picnic area, a 5-mile walking trail and a fishing lake.

Allow 2 hours minimum. Daily 10-5; closed Thanksgiving and Dec. 25. Tours are available Mon.-Fri. at 11 and 1:30; phone ahead to confirm schedule. Admission $8; over 64 and active military with ID $7; ages 6-17, $6. AX, MC, VI. Phone (757) 596-2222 or (800) 581-7245. *See color ad p. 301.*

NEWPORT NEWS CITY PARK is on SR 143 .5 mi. w. of jct. SR 105. The 8,000-acre woodland park includes nature trails and facilities for jogging, fishing, boating, canoeing, paddleboating, bicycling, camping, picnicking, archery, horseback riding and golf.

Confederate gun positions, Union trenches and a dam built to halt Gen. George McClellan's march toward Richmond are visible. The discovery center offers programs and exhibits about the natural features and history of the park. Daily dawn-dusk. Free. Phone (757) 888-3333. *See Recreation Chart.*

PENINSULA FINE ARTS CENTER is at 101 Museum Dr. The center offers changing exhibits from Richmond's Virginia Museum of Fine Arts *(see attraction listing p. 282)* as well as art classes, workshops and special events. Hands-On For Kids, an interactive art gallery, is available. Allow 1 hour minimum. Tues.-Sat. 10-5, Sun. 1-5. Free. Admission may be charged during special events. Phone (757) 596-8175.

[GEM] **VIRGINIA LIVING MUSEUM** is at 524 J. Clyde Morris Blvd., off I-64 exit 258A between SR 143 and US 60. Virginia's natural heritage is explored through indoor and [SAVE] outdoor exhibits that highlight regional geography, geology, ecosystems, plants and animals. An elevated boardwalk winds through a 10-acre nature area, offering views of red wolves, bobcats, eagles, deer and coyotes. Interactive discovery centers invite visitors to handle natural science specimens and live animals.

The Coastal Plain Gallery presents marine life from the Chesapeake Bay estuary. Gems, fossils and cave-dwelling creatures are found in the Virginia Underground Gallery. The James River ecosystem is depicted in the Piedmont and Mountains Gallery. Ghost crabs, sharks, flying squirrels and other live nocturnal animals dwell within the Virginia's World of Darkness Gallery.

Allow 2 hours minimum. Daily 9-6, Memorial Day-Labor Day; Mon.-Sat. 9-5, Sun. noon-5, rest of year. Closed Jan. 1, Thanksgiving and Dec. 24-25.

Museum $11; ages 3-12, $8. Planetarium $3. Combination ticket $13; ages 3-12, $10. Under 3 are not permitted at some planetarium shows. DS, MC, VI. Phone (757) 595-1900. *See color ad.*

SAVE **VIRGINIA WAR MUSEUM** is at 9285 Warwick Blvd. in Huntington Park. More than 60,000 artifacts document U.S. military history from 1775 to the present. Exhibits include propaganda posters, uniforms, vehicles, weapons and accouterments. The museum also has educational programs, a military history film collection and a research library (open by appointment).

Park facilities include a picnic area and tennis courts. Allow 1 hour minimum. Mon.-Sat. 9-5, Sun. 1-5; closed Jan. 1, Thanksgiving and Dec. 24-25. Admission $6; over 62 and military with ID $5; ages 7-18, $4. Combination ticket with Endview Plantation and the Lee Hall Mansion $15; over 62, $12; ages 7-18, $9. Phone (757) 247-8523.

NORFOLK pop. 234,403

In 1680, the General Assembly of Virginia authorized the purchase of a 50-acre tract along the Elizabeth River for "The Towne of Lower Norfolk County." The seller, Nicholas Wise Jr., received 10,000 pounds of tobacco for his land, and the deed was recorded two years later.

GEM **CHRYSLER MUSEUM OF ART** is 3 blks. w. at Olney Rd. and W. Virginia Beach SAVE Blvd. Comprising 30,000 pieces, the museum's diverse collection includes art treasures from ancient Greece, Rome, the Orient and pre-Columbian America; European and American paintings and sculpture; and decorative arts from the 12th century to the present.

Among artists represented are Mary Cassatt, Edgar Degas, Paul Gauguin, Henri Matisse, Pablo Picasso, Jackson Pollock, Pierre Auguste Renoir, Auguste Rodin, Mark Rothko and Andy Warhol. A photography gallery features images of 19th-century pioneers and contemporary artists.

One of the country's most comprehensive glass collections includes more than 8,000 pieces of carved and blown sculptural works. Major pieces by Emile Galle, Rene Lalique and Louis Comfort Tiffany also are on display.

Lectures, films and concerts are scheduled regularly. Food is available. Allow 2 hours minimum. Wed. 10-9, Thurs.-Sat. 10-5, Sun. 1-5; closed Jan. 1, July 4, Thanksgiving and Dec. 25. Admission $7, over 65 and students, teachers and military with ID $5, under 12 free. Admission to all on Wed. by donation. Phone (757) 664-6200.

GEM **GENERAL DOUGLAS MacARTHUR MEMORIAL** is on City Hall Ave. Nine galleries in the former 1847 city hall portray the general's life and military career through displays of gifts, art objects, maps, murals, pictures, models and mementos. MacArthur's trademark military

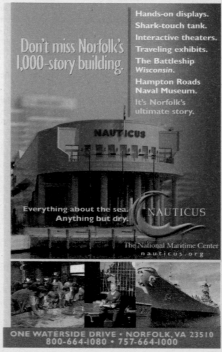

cap, corncob pipe and sunglasses and his 1950 Chrysler Imperial limousine are among the artifacts. The general's books and an extensive collection of correspondence, photographs, scrapbooks and newspapers are housed in a library and archives.

In the main rotunda, the general's tomb is surrounded by inscriptions and flags from his military career. A 24-minute documentary is shown continuously. Mon.-Sat. 10-5, Sun. 11-5; closed Jan. 1, Thanksgiving and Dec. 25. Donations. Phone (757) 441-2965.

SAVE **HERMITAGE FOUNDATION MUSEUM** is at 7637 N. Shore Rd. on the Lafayette River. The Hermitage, a 42-room Tudor-style house built in 1907 by William and Florence Sloane, is noted for its collections of Oriental and Western art and carved wood paneling. The house is open by guided tour; changing exhibitions also are offered. The 12-acre grounds feature gardens and a grotto.

Picnicking is permitted. Allow 1 hour minimum. Tours depart Mon.-Tues. and Thurs.-Sat. at 10:30, noon, 2 and 3:30, Sun. at 1, 2:30 and 4, Feb.-Dec. Changing exhibitions are offered Mon.-Tues. and Thurs.-Sat. 10-5, Sun. 1-5, Feb.-Dec. Grounds open daily dawn-dusk. Closed Thanksgiving and Dec. 25. Admission $5; ages 6-18, $2; military with ID free. Changing exhibitions free. Phone (757) 423-2052.

HUNTER HOUSE VICTORIAN MUSEUM is at 240 W. Freemason St. The 1894 Romanesque mansion was built for merchant and banker James Wilson Hunter. The house displays the family's Victorian furnishings, stained-glass windows and a collection of medical memorabilia, including an early 20th-century electrocardiograph machine. Allow 1 hour minimum. Guided tours are offered Wed.-Sat. 10-3:30, Sun. 12:30-3:30, Apr.-Dec.; closed holidays. Admission $4; over 60, $3; ages 6-18, $1. Phone (757) 623-9814.

SAVE **MOSES MYERS HOUSE** is at Freemason and Bank sts. An example of Federal Period architecture, the 1792 townhouse was built for one of the nation's first millionaires. The restored home contains original furniture as well as artwork by Gilbert Stuart and Thomas Sully. Its furnishings reflect the lifestyle and religious practices of this late 18th-century Jewish merchant family.

Allow 1 hour minimum. Tues. 10-2, Wed.-Sat. 10-4, May-Oct.; Wed.-Sat. 10-4, rest of year. Closed Jan. 1, July 4, Thanksgiving and Dec. 25. Hours may vary; phone ahead. Last tour begins 1 hour before closing. Admission $5; over 64, military with ID and ages 12-18, $3. Phone (757) 441-1526.

NAUTICUS, THE NATIONAL MARITIME CENTER is at One Waterside Dr., downtown on the Elizabeth River. The Norfolk SAVE waterfront complex features more than 150 hands-on exhibits that explore the naval, economic and natural power of the sea. Visitors can feel the texture of a nurse shark's skin, touch a tornado, participate in a naval battle simulation and create a

nightly news-style weather forecast complete with special effects.

On the second floor, the Hampton Roads Naval Museum examines two centuries of naval activity in and around the harbor. The museum manages the day-to-day operations of the Battleship *Wisconsin*, which is berthed at Nauticus. A chronology of the ship's history is presented in "Wisky Walk: Fifty Years of Service."

Food is available. Allow 1 hour minimum. Daily 10-6, Memorial Day-Labor Day; Tues.-Sat. 10-5, Sun. noon-5, rest of year. Closed Jan. 1, Thanksgiving and Dec. 24-25. Admission $9.95; over 55 and military with ID $8.95; ages 4-12, $7.50. AX, MC, VI. Phone (757) 664-1000 or (800) 664-1080. *See color ad p. 251.*

Battleship *Wisconsin* is at Nauticus on Waterside Dr. One of the last and largest battleships built by the U.S. Navy, this vessel was used in World War II, the Korean War and Operation Desert Storm. A self-guiding tour of the main deck includes interactive exhibits depicting the history of the ship and life on board. Allow 1 hour minimum. Daily 10-6, Memorial Day-Labor Day; Tues.-Sat. 10-5, Sun. noon-5, rest of year. Closed Jan. 1, Thanksgiving and Dec. 24-25. Free. Fee for audio tour (available at admission desk) $5, or $3 with Nauticus admission. Phone (757) 664-1000 or (800) 664-1080.

Tugboat Museum is at Nauticus on Waterside Dr. Visitors can explore the deck, wheelhouse, engine room, galley and crew quarters of the 1933 Tug *Huntington*. Exhibits aboard the restored tugboat include historic photographs and videotapes about the marine towing industry. Daily 11-5, Memorial Day-Labor Day; Tues.-Sun. 11-5, Apr. 1-day before Memorial Day and day after Labor Day-Dec. 31. Admission $2; under 12, $1. Phone (757) 627-4884.

NAVAL STATION NORFOLK offers tours that originate at the information center at 9079 Hampton Blvd. The 45-minute bus tours visit sites that include the naval station, piers and the waterfront area. Narrated by U.S. Navy personnel, tours pass by cruisers, destroyers, aircraft carriers and frigates as well as historic homes. The base is home port to more than 100 ships of the Atlantic fleet.

Tours depart daily on the half-hour 10-2:30, late May-early Sept.; on the hour 11-2, early Sept. to mid-Oct. and late Mar.-late May; at noon and 1, mid-Oct. to late Dec. and late Feb.-late Mar.; at 1:30, rest of year. Hours may vary; phone ahead. Guided bus tour $7.50; over 60 and under 12, $5; active military with ID free. Phone (757) 444-7955.

GEM **NORFOLK BOTANICAL GARDEN** is next to Norfolk International Airport. The 155-acre garden includes one of the largest collections of azaleas, camellias, rhododendrons and roses on the East Coast. The climate-controlled Tropical Pavilion houses over 100 varieties of plants from tropical regions around the world. Visitors may tour the gardens by foot on over 12 miles of pathways; guided tours are offered aboard trams and boats.

Food is available. Gardens open daily 9-7, mid-Apr. to mid.-Oct.; 9-5, rest of year. Tram tours depart daily on the hour 10-4, mid-Mar. to mid-Oct. Boat tours daily 10:45-3:45, Apr.-Sept. Gardens $6; over 62, students and military with ID $5; ages 6-16, $4. Boat tour $3; ages 6-16, $2. Tram tour free with admission. Phone (757) 441-5830.

ST. PAUL'S EPISCOPAL CHURCH is at St. Paul's Blvd. and City Hall Ave. Built in 1739 on the site of a 1641 church known as The Chapel of Ease, the present structure was the only building left after the burning of Norfolk in 1776. A cannonball fired from a British ship is embedded in its wall. The church cemetery contains graves dating from the 17th century. Allow 30 minutes minimum. Tues.-Fri. 10-4; closed federal holidays. Donations. Phone (757) 627-4353.

SAVE **VIRGINIA ZOO** is at 3500 Granby St. The zoo is home to more than 300 animals in such exhibits as a farmyard, a waterfowl pond, an environment for large mammals and a building housing small mammals. A botanical conservatory is on the grounds. Daily 10-5; closed Jan. 1, Thanksgiving and Dec. 24-25. Admission $6; over 62, $5; ages 2-11, $3. Phone (757) 624-9937.

VIRGINIA BEACH pop. 425,257

The Jamestown settlers first made landfall on this windswept beach at the mouth of Chesapeake Bay on April 26, 1607. The Old Cape Henry Lighthouse, one of the first public works facilities authorized by Congress, was built here in 1781. Its replacement, the 1881 New Lighthouse, is one of the tallest cast-iron lighthouses in the United States.

Despite beacons and bonfires, hundreds of ships foundered offshore in the 19th century, prompting the construction of four lifesaving stations. In 1891, visitors watched in horror as rescuers struggled to save the crew of the Norwegian bark *Dictator*. The captain's wife and young son were among those who died. The Norwegian Lady, on 25th Street facing the sea, is a 9-foot bronze figurehead commemorating the shipwreck; a twin statue stands in Moss, Norway.

BACK BAY NATIONAL WILDLIFE REFUGE is at 4005 Sandpiper Rd. The 7,000-acre wildlife preserve is bordered by the Atlantic Ocean on one side and by Back Bay on the other. Several trails, some decked, are available for hikers and bicyclists; a tram occasionally runs along the trails. A variety of waterfowl and other wildlife can be seen.

Allow 30 minutes minimum. Trails and refuge open daily dawn-dusk; some trails are closed seasonally. Visitor center open Mon.-Fri. 8-4 (also Sat. 9-4, Apr.-Oct.), Sun. 9-4; closed holidays. Admission Apr.-Oct. $5 per private vehicle; $2 per person on foot or bicycle. Admission free rest of year. Phone (757) 721-2412.

CAPE HENRY MEMORIAL is within the Fort Story Military Reservation. The stone cross commemorates the Jamestown settlers' landfall in the New World. After exploring the cape, christened after Henry, Prince of Wales, the settlers erected a wooden cross and sailed up the James River.

Two other monuments honor the Battle of the Capes, fought offshore between French and British naval forces in 1781. The British defeat played a key role in Washington's victory at Yorktown a month later. Phone (757) 898-2410.

CHESAPEAKE BAY BRIDGE-TUNNEL carries US 13 across the mouth of Chesapeake Bay from Virginia Beach to Virginia's Eastern Shore. Using bridges, tunnels and four man-made islands, the 17.6 mile-long-route offers a panoramic view. Although its individual components are neither the longest nor largest built, the bridge-tunnel is unusual in the number of different types of major structures included in one crossing. The southernmost island has fishing and restaurant facilities. One-way toll $12 for private vehicles. Phone (757) 331-2960.

CHRISTIAN BROADCASTING NETWORK is off I-64 exit 286B, then .5 mi. s.e. on Indian River Rd. to the Studio Headquarters Building. Highlights include tours of the production studios of the Christian Broadcasting Network (CBN) television shows. A collection of paintings and sculptures depicting biblical scenes is displayed. Visitors also can view the taping of the "700 Club" show. Allow 1 hour minimum. Mon.-Fri. 8-5. Tours are given at 10 and 2. Show taping begins at 9 a.m.; seating is at 8:30 a.m. Free. Reservations are required to attend taping. Phone (757) 226-2745.

FRANCIS LAND HOUSE is at 3131 Virginia Beach Blvd. A wealthy planter built the house in the mid-to late 18th century. Guides in period dress tell the story of the Lands and their home. Nature trails are on the grounds. Tues.-Sat. 9-5, Sun. 11-5. Last tour begins 30 minutes before closing. Admission $4; over 60, $3; students with ID and ages 6-12, $2. Phone (757) 431-4000.

LYNNHAVEN HOUSE is n. on Independence Blvd. (SR 225), then e. to 4401 Wishart Rd. The 1725 English-style, brick house is situated on 5 wooded acres that feature a small cemetery, native plant beds and an 18th-century kitchen garden. Guided tours are conducted by interpreters in period dress. Allow 1 hour, 30 minutes minimum. Tues.-Sun. noon-4, May-Oct.; closed holidays. Last tour begins at 3:30. Admission $4; over 60, $3; students with ID and ages 5-16, $2. Phone (757) 460-1688.

SAVE **OCEAN BREEZE WATERPARK** is at 849 General Booth Blvd. This Caribbean-themed park features water slides, the Jungle Falls tube ride, the Runaway Bay Wave Pool, the Buccaneer Bay children's area and the Hurricane thrill ride.

Sun.-Thurs. 10-6, Fri.-Sat. 10-8, Memorial Day weekend-Labor Day. Hours may vary; phone ahead.

Admission $18.95; ages 3-11, $14.95. AX, DS, MC, VI. Phone (757) 422-4444 or (800) 678-9453.

SAVE **THE OLD COAST GUARD STATION MUSEUM** is at 24th St. and Atlantic Ave. Housed in a restored 1903 lifesaving station, the museum traces the history of the U.S. lifesaving and Coast Guard services. Special exhibits chronicle the shipwrecks that occurred off the Virginia coast. An interactive video monitoring system enables visitors to see the ocean and beach from a tower where early lifesavers were stationed. A touch-screen computer system identifies vessels that come into port.

Mon.-Sat. 10-5, Sun. noon-5, day after Memorial Day-Sept. 30; Tues.-Sat. 10-5, Sun. noon-5, rest of year. Closed Jan. 1, Thanksgiving and Dec. 25 and 31. Admission $3; over 60 and military with ID $2.50; ages 6-18, $1. Phone (757) 422-1587.

GEM **VIRGINIA AQUARIUM AND MARINE SCIENCE CENTER** is 1 mi. s. of Rudee Inlet Bridge at 717 General Booth Blvd. SAVE Hands-on exhibits, live animal displays and a multitude of aquariums spotlight Virginia's marine environment. The Norfolk Canyon Aquarium features sharks and other large ocean creatures. Other highlights include a harbor seal habitat, a floor-to-ceiling sea turtle aquarium, a sea turtle hatchling laboratory, an artificial reef touch-tank and an IMAX theater presenting 3-D marine science and nature films.

A nature trail skirts the edge of Owls Creek Salt Marsh and includes a river otter habitat, an aviary and other marsh animal exhibits. Whale-watching, dolphin-watching and salt marsh creek boat trips are available; phone for schedule.

Daily 9-7, Memorial Day-Labor Day; 9-5, rest of year. Closed Thanksgiving and Dec. 25. Museum admission $11.95; over 61, $10.95; ages 3-11, $7.95. IMAX films $7.50; over 61, $6.75; ages 3-11, $6.50. Combination ticket $16.95; over 61, $15.95; ages 3-11, $12.95. MC, VI. Phone (757) 425-3474 for recorded information, (757) 437-2628 for boat trips, or TTY (757) 427-4305. *See color ad p. 253.*

What To Do

Sightseeing

Boat Tours

AMERICAN ROVER TALL SAILING SHIP CRUISES depart from the Waterside in Norfolk. Guests can work the sails, take a turn at the helm or just relax aboard the 135-foot-long, three-mast topsail schooner as it cruises the historic Hampton Roads harbor. The ship is modeled after the cargo schooners that plied the waters of Chesapeake Bay during the 1800s. Narrated 2-hour harbor and 3-hour naval base cruises are offered. Sunset cruises also are available.

Food is available. Cruises depart daily at 3 and 6:30 p.m. (also at 11 Wed.-Sat.), late May to early Sept.; daily at 3 (also at 6 p.m. Fri.-Sun.), mid-Apr.

to late May and early Sept.-late Oct. Hours may vary; phone ahead. Fares $15-$22; under 12, $10-$12. MC, VI. Phone (757) 627-7245.

CARRIE B. HARBOR TOURS leave from the Waterside in Norfolk. Narrated 2.5-hour cruises aboard the *Carrie B,* a replica of a double-decked, 19th-century Mississippi riverboat, pass Navy ships and submarines, commercial freighters and shipyards. Food is available. Cruises depart daily at 11 and 2 (also at 6, June 1-Labor Day), Apr. 1 to mid-Oct. Hours may vary; phone ahead. Fare $16; under 12, $8. AX, MC, VI. Phone (757) 393-4735.

SPIRIT OF NORFOLK departs from the Waterside in Norfolk. Two-hour narrated lunch cruises of the Elizabeth River and the Hampton Roads Harbor include the Norfolk Naval Base and local points of interest. Dinner and moonlight cruises also are available. Lunch cruise departs Mon.-Sat. at noon, Sun. at 1. Boarding is 30 minutes prior to departure. Two-hour lunch cruise $27-$29. Phone to confirm schedules and fares. Reservations are recommended. AX, DS, MC, VI. Phone (866) 211-3803.

Trolley Tours

The 90-minute Norfolk Trolley Tour runs downtown Memorial Day through Labor Day. Trolleys, which depart three times daily from the Waterside, stop at seven attractions; phone (757) 222-6100.

Walking Tours

Virginia Beach's points of interest are designated with roadside markers. Brochures and maps are available from the Visitors Information Center, 2100 Parks Ave., Virginia Beach, VA 23451; phone (757) 491-7866 or (800) 822-3224.

Sports and Recreation

The miles of shoreline and myriad lakes of Hampton Roads provide ample recreational opportunities.

Scuba diving and **snorkeling** entice oceangoers, while the beach is a prime venue for **volleyball.** The area's lakes and waterways are suitable for **water skiing, wind surfing, canoeing** and **kayaking.**

Boating and **fishing** also are popular pursuits. Information about freshwater and saltwater fishing licenses is available through the Virginia Department of Game and Inland Fisheries, (804) 367-1000.

Numerous **golf** courses dot the landscape. Kingsmill Resort in Williamsburg is the site of The Anheuser Busch Golf Classic, a PGA Tour event. Among public courses in *Norfolk* are Lake Wright Golf Course, (757) 459-2255, and Ocean View Golf Course, (757) 480-2094. In *Newport News* is the Golf Club, (757) 886-7925, in Newport News Park.

Some of the public courses in *Virginia Beach* are Bow Creek Municipal Golf Course, (757) 431-3763; Cypress Point Country Club, (757) 490-8822; Family Golf Center at Owl's Creek,

(757) 428-2800; Hell's Point Golf Course, (757) 721-3400; Honey Bee Golf Course, (757) 471-2768; Kempsville Greens, (757) 474-8441; Red Wing Golf Course, (757) 437-4845; and Stumpy Lake Golf Course, (757) 467-6119.

Spectators have several options for sporting entertainment. **Baseball** fans can head to Harbor Park Stadium, 150 Park Ave. in Norfolk, to watch the Tides, a minor-league team; phone (757) 622-2222. The Hampton Roads Admirals play professional **ice hockey** at the Norfolk Scope Convention Center; phone (757) 640-1212.

Shopping

Newport News shoppers head to Patrick Henry Mall, at exit 255A off I-64, which contains Dillard's and Hecht's.

The Waterside Festival Marketplace, 333 Waterside Dr. in *Norfolk,* contains specialty stores offering items such as clothing, toys and gifts; also worth exploring are the waterfront restaurants and nightclubs. Ghent's eclectic boutiques, outdoor cafes and antiques shops draw a colorful mix of people to Colley Avenue and 21st Street. Another shopping option in *Norfolk* is Military Circle Mall, US 13 and US 58, with more than 100 stores, including Hecht's, JCPenney and Sears. MacArthur Center, I-264 City Hall Avenue exit to 300 Monticello Ave., is one of Norfolk's newest shopping malls and offers some 150 stores including Dillard's and Nordstrom.

Lynnhaven Mall, off I-264 and south on Lynnhaven Parkway, and Pembroke Mall, just east of Independence Boulevard on US 58, are both in *Virginia Beach.* The anchor stores at Lynnhaven Mall are Dillard's, Hecht's and JCPenney. Anchor stores at Pembroke Mall are Sears and Stein Mart. Discount shopping is a popular area pursuit.

Theaters and Concerts

With an enduring heritage that includes what is said to be America's first playhouse, built in Williamsburg in 1716, Hampton Roads offers numerous theatrical options.

In *Norfolk* the Virginia Symphony, the resident professional orchestra, performs primarily in Chrysler Hall; phone (757) 892-6366. Performances of the Virginia Opera are staged at Edythe C. and Stanley L. Harrison Opera House; phone (757) 623-1223. The professional Virginia Stage Company stages several major productions as well as second-stage shows and children's theater. Performances are given at Wells Theatre; (757) 627-1234. A variety of performances is offered at Town Point Park, an outdoor theater. Indoor theaters include Little Theatre of Norfolk, (757) 627-8551, Generic Theater, (757) 441-2160, and Hurrah Players Studio, (757) 627-5437.

Peninsula Community Theatre, (757) 595-5728, offers productions in *Newport News*. The Yoder Barn Theatre, (757) 249-4187, housed in a restored 1935 barn at 660 Hamilton Dr., has four stages and presents various shows. Founders Inn, (757) 366-5749, provides theatrical entertainment in *Virginia Beach*. Broadway musical productions are the specialty of the Virginia Musical Theatre troupe, which performs at Virginia Beach Pavilion; phone (757) 340-5446

Special Events

Seldom could it be said that there is nothing to do in Hampton Roads. Festivals, parades and fun abound, whether a holiday is being celebrated or a heritage remembered.

In *Newport News* the heritage of Virginia is celebrated at the Fall Festival in early October; in addition to entertainment and ethnic foods, traditional crafts are displayed, and trades such as woodworking and sheep shearing are demonstrated. The holiday season is acknowledged late November through January 1 during Celebration in Lights, featuring drive-through holiday scenes and multitudes of holiday lights.

Norfolk's International Azalea Festival, held in late April, salutes the NATO Alliance with a parade, air show and other activities.

May ushers in several popular events, including the Virginia Renaissance Faire and Afr'Am Festival. Harborfest, *Norfolk's* waterfront festival in early June, includes fireworks, sailboat races, a parade of boats, water-skiing shows and the arrival of the tall ships. In mid-June the city spices it up with the Bayou Boogaloo & Cajun Food Festival.

Norfolk marks Independence Day with the Town Point Fourth of July Celebration, which features evening fireworks. The Town Point Jazz Festival is an outdoor musical celebration held in late August.

Labor Day weekend is marked by *Norfolk's* American Music Festival, while October kicks off with the Virginia Children's Festival, an all-day program of children's theater, puppet shows, crafts and games. The Chesapeake Bay Maritime Festival & Classic Boat Show in mid-October celebrates the area's maritime heritage.

The yuletide season is celebrated with parades, theater, concerts and numerous events during *Norfolk's* Holidays in the City, beginning in mid-November and continuing through New Year's Eve. The Waterfront New Year's Eve Celebration includes a dropping silver ball and a fireworks display.

Special events in *Virginia Beach* include The Pungo Strawberry Festival in May and the Boardwalk Art Show in mid-June. The Neptune Festival, a 2-week event, begins in mid-September. The festival features a parade, sporting events, food and entertainment.

The Hampton Roads Area

CHESAPEAKE (C-4) pop. 199,184

Chesapeake, in southeastern Virginia, was created in 1963 when Norfolk County and the city of South Norfolk merged. Nine miles of industrial waterfront property line the southern branch of the Elizabeth River.

Though relatively new as a city, Chesapeake was one of the first areas explored by Capt. John Smith and later settled about 1620. In the 1770s American and British forces clashed at this site in the Battle of Great Bridge.

Stretching south from Chesapeake are two separate branches of the Intracoastal Waterway, providing boaters with a choice of two scenic routes to Florida. Next to Great Bridge Locks, through which the waterway passes, is Great Bridge Locks Park, containing an observation deck, boat ramp, nature trail and picnic facilities.

Northwest River Park has a fragrance garden for the blind and facilities for horseback riding and canoeing *(see Recreation Chart and the AAA Mideastern CampBook)*. An untamed wilderness is nearby at the Dismal Swamp *(see place listing p. 234)*.

Hampton Roads Chamber of Commerce—Chesapeake: 400 Volvo Pkwy., Chesapeake, VA 23320; phone (757) 622-2312.

Shopping areas: Area malls include Chesapeake Square Mall, at the corner of Portsmouth Boulevard and Taylor Road, and Greenbrier Mall, off I-64 exit 289B (Greenbrier Parkway South). Chesapeake Square has Dillard's, Hecht's, JCPenney and Sears; Greenbrier Mall features Dillard's, Hecht's and Sears.

FORT EUSTIS (B-3)

During World War I, Camp Eustis was established as a school for Railway Artillery Fire. In World War II it was an anti-aircraft artillery training center. Today Fort Eustis is the home of the U.S. Army Transportation Corps.

U.S. ARMY TRANSPORTATION MUSEUM is s.w. of I-64 exit 250A on the post. Miniature models and dioramas as well as full-size vehicles, helicopters, winged aircraft, trains and marine vessels depict more than 200 years of Army transportation history. Exhibits pertaining to World War II, Korea and Vietnam include a L-19 airplane, a H-19 helicopter and a Huey helicopter. Tues.-Sun. 9-4:30; closed federal holidays. Free. Phone (757) 878-1115.

FORT MONROE (C-4) elev. 7'

Named in honor of President James Monroe, Fort Monroe was one of the few forts in the South not captured by the Confederates at the outbreak of hostilities. The fort was an important base in the

Chesapeake Bay for the Union Army and Navy during the Civil War.

Construction began on the fort in 1819 and ended in 1834. Continuously occupied since 1823, it is shaped like a seven-point star and is surrounded by a water-filled moat, which is 8 feet deep and 60 to 150 feet wide. The supremacy of Fort Monroe was challenged by the Confederate ironclad *Merrimac*, whose mission was to attack the Union Fleet. The Federal ironclad *Monitor* arrived, and a battle with the *Merrimac* ensued.

After the war Confederate President Jefferson Davis was confined at Fort Monroe until 1867. Visitors can view his prison cell at the Casemate Museum, which chronicles Fort Monroe's history. The museum contains exhibits about the battle between the ironclads, other important events of the Civil War and army artillery memorabilia; phone (757) 788-3391. Also nearby is the Chapel of the Centurion.

GLOUCESTER (B-3) elev. 75'

Gloucester (GLOSS-ter), in Tidewater Virginia, is noted for its many historical landmarks that have remained undisturbed. The 1766 Courthouse, on the Court Green, is enclosed by a brick wall. The Old Debtors Prison dates from the mid-18th century. Several old estates are in this region near Gloucester and near White Marsh *(see place listing p. 260)*. Long Bridge Ordinary, a stagecoach tavern built in 1732, is open during Garden Week in late April. Dr. Walter Reed, instrumental in the eradication of yellow fever, was born in nearby Belroi.

Gloucester Chamber of Commerce: P.O. Box 296, Gloucester, VA 23061; phone (804) 693-2425.

GLOUCESTER POINT (B-4) pop. 9,429

Located on the York River, Gloucester Point has been a strategic town throughout its history. The town originally was called Tyndall's Point in honor of an early mapmaker.

VIRGINIA INSTITUTE OF MARINE SCIENCE is off US 17, .8 mi. n. of Coleman Bridge over the York River. This research institute and graduate school of the College of William and Mary maintains eight aquariums containing saltwater fish indigenous to the area. Exhibits include a living oyster reef. Mon.-Fri. 9-4:30 (also Sat. 10-2, day after Memorial Day-Labor Day); closed Jan. 1-2, Memorial Day, Thanksgiving, day after Thanksgiving and Dec. 24-31. Free. Phone (804) 684-7000.

HAMPTON (C-4) pop. 146,437, elev. 3'

Settled in 1610, Hampton is the oldest continuously English-speaking settlement still in existence in the nation. In 1619 it was one of the original boroughs in the Virginia Legislature.

One of the first battles of the Revolutionary War in Virginia was fought in Hampton in October 1775. Hampton again was invaded and partially burned by British forces in 1813. The first planned land battle of the Civil War was fought at Big Bethel in Hampton in 1861. In August 1861 the town was burned again, this time by Confederates to prevent its falling into Union hands.

Fought in Hampton Roads was the world's first conflict between two ironclad vessels, the CSS *Virginia (Merrimac)* and the USS *Monitor.* Each failed to pierce the other's armor, but the *Virginia* destroyed two other ships, the *Congress* and the *Cumberland.*

Fort Monroe *(see place listing p. 256)* and Hampton University, formerly Hampton Institute of which Booker T. Washington was an alumnus, are in the city. North off SR 134 is Langley Air Force Base, headquarters for the 1st Fighter Wing and a number of other units. The nearby NASA Langley Research Center served as the original training site for the nation's first seven astronauts.

Preserving Hampton's aviation legacy is the 15-acre Air Power Park, 413 W. Mercury Blvd., which has a collection of vintage jets and rockets as well as historical exhibits. Hampton Carousel, an antique carousel with hand-carved horses and chariots, operates at 610 Settlers Landing Rd.

The Hampton area is the center of Virginia's fishing industry. Oysters and Chesapeake Bay blue crabs are of particular importance. Fishing piers (fees are charged) include Buckroe Beach, a bayside vacation area reached via Pembroke Avenue, and Grandview, north off Beach Road. Grandview Nature Preserve, an undeveloped area a .5-mile walk from State Park Drive, is open daily.

Hampton Convention & Visitor Bureau Visitor Center: 120 Old Hampton Ln., Hampton, VA 23666; phone (757) 727-1102 or (800) 800-2202.

BLUEBIRD GAP FARM is at 60 Pine Chapel Rd. between I-64 and Queen St. The farm has domestic and wild animals and various fowl as well as a display of farm machines and a barn. Picnic facilities and a play area are on the grounds. Wed.-Sun. 9-5; closed major holidays. Free. Phone (757) 727-6739.

FORT MONROE—*see place listing p. 256.*

HAMPTON HISTORY MUSEUM is downtown in the Hampton Visitor Center building at 120 Old Hampton Ln. Four centuries of regional history are presented, including colonization, the Revolutionary and Civil wars, Reconstruction, the growth of the seafood industry and the early days of NASA's space flight program. Interactive exhibits depict the arrival of Capt. John Smith, the demise of Blackbeard and the 1861 burning of Hampton. Changing exhibits also are presented. Allow 1 hour minimum. Mon.-Sat. 10-5, Sun. 1-5, Memorial Day-Labor Day; Mon.-Sat. 10-5, rest of year. Closed Jan. 1, Thanksgiving and Dec. 25. Admission $5; over 61 and ages 4-12, $4. MC, VI. Phone (757) 727-1610.

THE HAMPTON UNIVERSITY MUSEUM is off I-64 exit 267 then w. on Hampton University's Tyler St., following signs. Founded in 1868, it is one of the oldest museums in Virginia. Displays include a collection of traditional art objects and artifacts from North America and sub-Saharan Africa. Also featured are American Indian art and works by contemporary African-American and African artists. Maps are available for self-guiding walking tours of five national historic sites within the campus. Allow 1 hour minimum. Mon.-Fri. 8-5, Sat. noon-4; closed school holidays. Free. Phone (757) 727-5308.

(SAVE) *MISS HAMPTON II HARBOR CRUISES* depart from Hampton Visitor Center at 120 Old Hampton Ln. The narrated cruise sails into the Hampton Roads harbor past Blackbeard's Point and Old Point Comfort to Fort Wool, where a guided walking tour of the historic fort is provided. The cruise continues on past the aircraft carriers, guided missile cruisers, destroyers and submarines docked at Norfolk Naval Base.

Allow 2 hours, 30 minutes minimum. Departures daily at 10 and 2, Memorial Day weekend-Labor Day; at 10, mid-Apr. to day before Memorial Day weekend and day after Labor Day-Oct. 31. Fare $18; over 60 and military with ID $15; ages 6-12, $9. Reservations are recommended. Phone (757) 722-9102 or (888) 757-2628.

ST. JOHN'S EPISCOPAL CHURCH is at 100 W. Queens Way. Built in 1728, the church houses one of the nation's oldest English-speaking parishes, which was founded in 1610. Its most precious relic is Communion silver that dates from 1618. The stained-glass window depicting the baptism of Pocahontas was donated by American Indian students at Hampton University. The parish museum contains artifacts from previous sites, including a 1599 Bible and a 1632 prayer book. Mon.-Fri. 9-3:30, Sat. 9-noon; closed major holidays. Free. Phone (757) 722-2567.

(SAVE) VIRGINIA AIR AND SPACE CENTER is off I-64 exit 267, then 1 mi. w. to 600 Settlers Landing Rd. The center features aircraft and spacecraft suspended from a 94-foot ceiling. Adventures in Flight presents interactive exhibits about the Wright Brothers and regional contributions to aviation history. A NASA display includes the Apollo 12 command module, a lunar lander, moon rocks and a Mars meteorite. Also featured is an IMAX theater. A seven-story observation deck provides panoramic views.

Daily 10-5 (also Thurs.-Sun. 5-7, Memorial Day-Labor Day); Mon.-Sat. 10-5, Sun. noon-5, rest of year. Closed Thanksgiving and Dec. 25. Space center admission $8.50; over 64 and military with ID $7.50; ages 3-11, $6.50. Space center and one IMAX presentation $12; over 64 and military with ID $11; ages 3-11, $9.50. IMAX only $7.50; over 64 and military with ID $6.50; ages 3-11, $6. MC, VI. Phone (757) 727-0900 or (800) 296-0800.

PORTSMOUTH (C-3) pop. 100,565, elev. 11′

Because of the location's accessibility to water and a ready supply of timber for shipbuilding,

Portsmouth earned a king's grant for settlement in 1620. Ownership alternated between the crown and mariners until it was repatented in 1716 by Col. William Crawford, presiding justice of Norfolk County. Crawford donated the four corners of High and Court streets for a market, a jail, a courthouse and a church. The restored 1762 Trinity Episcopal Church is the town's oldest building.

Portsmouth was a strategic military objective in early U.S. conflicts. During the Revolution, after seven British vessels had bombarded and set fire to Portsmouth and the surrounding Tidewater areas, Benedict Arnold set up headquarters and the British line of defense on Hospital Point, then called Fort Nelson.

During the early months of the Civil War the Virginia Militia wrested control of the naval shipyard from the Union. After the Federal troops burned and abandoned Portsmouth, the Confederates raised the frigate *Merrimac* and turned it into the world's first ironclad battleship, the CSS *Virginia*.

Beginning as a marine yard in 1767, the Norfolk Naval Shipyard is the largest in the world. Besides the CSS *Virginia*, the shipyard produced the *Chesapeake*, the sister of the *Constitution* and one of the Navy's first warships.

Trolley tours highlight the Olde Towne Historic District, which is distinguished by a fine collection of period homes with a rich diversity of architectural styles. One of 45 sites along the tour, the Hill House, 221 North St., is an 1800s English basement dwelling containing its original furnishings; phone (757) 393-5111 or (757) 393-5327.

Ferry service between Norfolk and Portsmouth resumed on the Elizabeth River in the early 1980s; the river was first crossed in 1636 by North America's first pedestrian ferry. The ferry is operated by Hampton Roads Transit; an information station is at North Landing, 6 Crawford Parkway.

Portsmouth Convention and Visitors Bureau: 505 Crawford St., Suite 2, Portsmouth, VA 23704; phone (757) 393-5327 or (800) 767-8782. *See color ad p. 258.*

Self-guiding tours: A brochure describing a walking tour of Olde Towne's historic district is available at the visitor center on the waterfront; phone (757) 393-5111.

Shopping areas: The Olde Towne Historic District offers various small specialty shops including antiques stores.

CHILDREN'S MUSEUM OF VIRGINIA is at 221 High St. More than 90 hands-on displays challenge the imagination of both children and adults. Exhibits focus on science, art, music, communications, cultural diversity and technology.

Among the learning stations are the Bubbles area, where children can study refraction, reflection, geometry and surface tension by using wands to create bubbles; The City, which features role-playing; and Every Body, which teaches about health and physiology.

Kids' artwork is displayed on refrigerator doors in Too Cool Gallery. A 64-seat planetarium presents changing shows. Also featured is the Lancaster Train and Toy Collection.

Allow 1 hour minimum. Mon.-Sat. 9-5, Sun. 11-5, Memorial Day-Labor Day; Tues.-Sat. 9-5, Sun. 11-5, rest of year. Closed Jan. 1, Thanksgiving and Dec. 24-25. Admission $6, under 2 free. A $9 Key Pass also includes admission to the Courthouse Galleries, *Portsmouth* Lightship Museum and Portsmouth Naval Shipyard Museum. Phone (757) 393-5258 or (800) 767-8782. *See color ad p. 258.*

COURTHOUSE GALLERIES is at High and Court sts. Visitors to the restored 1846 courthouse can view modern cultural works and changing exhibits from international and regional artists. Mon.-Sat. 10-5, Sun. noon-5, Memorial Day-Labor Day; Tues.-Sat. 10-5, Sun. 1-5, rest of year. Closed Jan. 1, Thanksgiving and Dec. 25. Admission $3, under 2 free. A $9 Key Pass also includes admission to the Children's Museum of Virginia, *Portsmouth* Lightship Museum and Portsmouth Naval Shipyard Museum. Phone (757) 393-8543.

PORTSMOUTH LIGHTSHIP MUSEUM adjoins the Portsmouth Naval Shipyard Museum. This former Coast Guard lightship was one of many used to assist mariners in navigating dangerous shoals at night. With lights attached to their masts, lightships were anchored in strategic locations off the coast. Museum exhibits include artifacts relating to lightship service, photographs, uniforms and Coast Guard equipment as well as realistically appointed officers' and crews' quarters.

Mon.-Sat. 10-5, Sun. noon-5, Memorial Day-Labor Day; Tues.-Sat. 10-5, Sun. 1-5, rest of year. Closed Jan. 1, Thanksgiving and Dec. 25. Hours may vary; phone ahead. Admission $3. A $9 Key Pass also includes admission to the Courthouse Galleries, Children's Museum of Virginia and Portsmouth Naval Shipyard Museum. Phone (757) 393-8741.

PORTSMOUTH NAVAL SHIPYARD MUSEUM is at the foot of High St. on the Elizabeth River waterfront. Paintings, models and exhibits trace the history of the U.S. Navy, with emphasis on the Portsmouth-Norfolk area's role. Noteworthy are the models of the CSS *Virginia*, the U.S. *Delaware*, and the nation's first dry-docked ship.

Mon.-Sat. 10-5, Sun. noon-5, Memorial Day-Labor Day; Tues.-Sat. 10-5, Sun. 1-5, rest of year. Closed Jan. 1, Thanksgiving and Dec. 25. Admission $3. A $9 Key Pass also includes admission to the Courthouse Galleries, Children's Museum of Virginia and *Portsmouth* Lightship Museum. Phone (757) 393-8591.

VIRGINIA SPORTS HALL OF FAME is at 206 High St. Displays include photographs, plaques, personal equipment and biographical sketches of noted Virginia athletes. Tues.-Sat. 10-5; closed holidays. Hours may vary; phone ahead. Free. Phone (757) 393-8031.

SMITHFIELD (C-3) pop. 6,324

Known internationally for its hams, Smithfield is one of Virginia's best preserved Colonial seaports. The town's Old Courthouse of 1750 *(see attraction listing)*, still stands on Main Street not far from the 1752 Smithfield Inn. The downtown historic district features more than 60 buildings that represent Colonial, Federal and Victorian architectural styles.

Smithfield and Isle of Wight Convention and Visitors Bureau: 335 Main St., P.O. Box 37, Smithfield, VA 23431; phone (757) 357-5182 or (800) 365-9339.

Self-guiding tours: Maps that detail 65 points of interest on the Old Town Walking Tour are available at the visitors bureau.

Shopping areas: The Smithfield Historic District offers antique shops, art galleries and specialty stores.

BOYKINS TAVERN is 7 mi. e. on Main St. to 17130 Monument Cir. Built in 1762 by Maj. Francis Boykin, the tavern served as a gathering spot for travelers and those conducting business at the nearby courthouse and jail. It remained in the Boykin family until 1831. Two downstairs rooms and a basement kitchen re-create the original tavern surroundings. Other rooms feature period antiques and artifacts. Guided tours are available. Allow 30 minutes minimum. Thurs.-Sat. 11-4, Sun. 1-4; closed major holidays. Free. Phone (757) 365-9771 or (800) 365-9339.

FORT BOYKIN HISTORIC PARK is n. on CR 674, then e. on CR 673 to 7410 Fort Boykin Tr. The park preserves the remains of a fort erected in 1623 to protect American colonists. Built in the shape of a seven-pointed star, the fort was used in every major military campaign fought on American soil. "The Castle" was renamed for Gen. Francis Boykin

during the Revolutionary War. On the bluffs above the James River, the park features gardens, views of the Atlantic fleet and a trail with markers. Picnicking is permitted. Daily 8-dusk (weather permitting). Free. Phone (757) 357-2291 or (800) 365-9339.

ISLE OF WIGHT MUSEUM is at 103 Main St. The history of the Smithfield ham is among the local exhibits at the museum, which features Civil War memorabilia, American Indian artifacts and archeological items. Tues.-Sat. 10-4, Sun. 1-5; closed Jan. 1, July 4, Thanksgiving and Dec. 24-25. Free. Phone (757) 357-7459.

OLD COURTHOUSE OF 1750 is downtown at 130 Main St. Designed after the Colonial Capitol in Williamsburg, the original part of this building was constructed in 1750. Legal disputes of the day were settled here until 1800. The three-room building was then renovated and expanded into a 10-room, three-story mansion. The main courtroom has been restored to period. Guided tours are available. Allow 30 minutes minimum. Tues.-Sun. 10-4; closed holidays. Free. Phone (757) 356-9016 or (800) 365-9339.

ST. LUKE'S SHRINE is 2 mi. s.e. on SR 10 at 14477 Benns Church Blvd. The Old Brick Church is said to be among the oldest church of English foundation standing in America. A brick dated 1632 was found in the original walls and is displayed. Artwork and paneling have been restored. The Gothic church's 1630 English chamber organ is purported to be the oldest of its type in the United States. Confederate soldiers camped in the church cemetery during the Civil War. Tues.-Sat. 9:30-4, Sun. 1-4, Feb.-Dec.; closed Dec. 25. Last tour begins at 3:30. Free. Phone (757) 357-3367.

WHITE MARSH (B-3) elev. 55'

Abingdon Episcopal Church is on US 17 near White Marsh. The first house of worship on this site was built about 1655 and attended by Mildred Warner, grandmother of George Washington. The present church dates from 1755; phone (804) 693-3035.

This ends listings for the Hampton Roads Area.
The following page resumes the alphabetical listings
of cities in Virginia.

HARRISONBURG (F-7)
pop. 40,468, elev. 1,338'

Harrisonburg was named after founder Thomas Harrison, who settled at the crossroads of an American Indian path and the Spotswood Trail about 1739. Supplying lands for municipal expansion, Harrison's two sons followed a tradition set by their father when he donated land to Rockingham County for the erection of a courthouse in 1779.

Gen. Turner Ashby, one of the most respected Confederate officers of the Valley Campaign, fell in battle at Harrisonburg on June 6, 1862, while protecting Gen. "Stonewall" Jackson's approach to Port Republic. Of Ashby, Jackson wrote, "As a partisan officer, I never knew his superior. His daring proverbial, his powers of endurance almost incredible..."

Harrisonburg lies in the heart of the Shenandoah Valley noted for its deep agrarian roots, vistas, many caverns and prime fishing waters. The cave nearest town is Endless Caverns in New Market (see place listing p. 269), 11 miles north on US 11. The Shenandoah River, Lake Shenandoah and Silver Lake are known for their trout and bass fishing. Developed recreational areas of the George Washington and Jefferson National Forests (see place listing p. 241) are nearby.

The arts flourish in Harrisonburg. Court Square Theater, on Court Square, opens its doors for various plays, films and concerts; phone (540) 433-9189. The Blue Ridge Theatre Festival is a professional theater company that presents musicals, comedies and dramas at the Court Square Theater; phone (540) 564-1998.

Harrisonburg-Rockingham Convention and Visitors Bureau: 10 E. Gay St., Harrisonburg, VA 22802; phone (540) 434-2319.

Self-guiding tours: Information regarding a walking tour of the historic area is available from the convention and visitors bureau.

Shopping areas: Valley Mall, off US 33, is anchored by Belk, JCPenney and Peebles.

VIRGINIA QUILT MUSEUM is off I-81 exit 245, just w. on Port Republic Rd., then 1 mi. n. to 301 S. Main St. (US 11). Antique and contemporary quilts are displayed in the 1856 Warren-Sipe House. Guided tours are available. Allow 30 minutes minimum. Mon. and Thurs.-Sat. 10-4, Sun. 1-4; closed major holidays. Admission $5; over 59, $4; students with ID $3; ages 6-12, $2. Phone (540) 433-3818.

HOPEWELL (B-2) pop. 22,354, elev. 5'

Hopewell is an outgrowth of old City Point, which was founded in 1613 by Sir Thomas Dale as the second English settlement in America. In 1622 the town was wiped out by an American Indian attack, and not until the Civil War did the community revive. Its deep-water access made City Point a natural supply base, which Gen. Ulysses S. Grant transformed into a vast base of operations for his siege of Petersburg.

At the close of the Civil War, City Point returned to being a hamlet. The modern successor to City Point emerged with the building of a dynamite factory by E.I. du Pont on the site of Hopewell Farms in 1911. World War I sparked a boom that evaporated by 1920, with Hopewell again becoming a quiet village. Diversified industry once more has brought prosperity to this seaport.

Merchant's Hope Church, 6 miles southeast on SR 10, then a half-mile west on SR 641, is an example of 1657 Colonial architecture. Six miles past the church on SR 10 and then 3.5 miles north on Flowerdew Hundred Road is a working farm established in 1619. Flowerdew Hundred resides on one of the earliest original land grants in Virginia. Some 200,000 artifacts have been recovered from the site, many of which are displayed in a museum on the grounds. The farm is open to visitors on weekends and by appointment; phone (804) 541-8897.

Hopewell Visitors Center: 4100 Oaklawn Blvd., Hopewell, VA 23860; phone (804) 541-2461 or (800) 863-8687. See ad.

Self-guiding tours: A brochure detailing a walking tour of the City Point National Historic District is available at the visitor center. A dozen audiovisual exhibits lining the streets depict the 10-month

period General Grant occupied the area. The center also offers walking and driving tour brochures of the Crescent Hills area, where some 42 Sears ready-to-assemble homes built 1926-37 can be seen. *See ad p. 261.*

CITY POINT UNIT is at the end of Cedar Ln. Eight miles behind Union lines, City Point served as Gen. Ulysses S. Grant's headquarters during the siege of Petersburg. The unit is part of Petersburg National Battlefield *(see place listing p. 272).* From June 1864 to April 1865, the busy seaport supplied some 100,000 soldiers and served as the nerve center of the Union war effort. President Abraham Lincoln twice visited Grant's command post. *See ad p. 261.*

Appomattox Manor is at Cedar Ln. and Pecan Ave. The 1763 plantation manor belonged to the Eppes family for 300 years. When Gen. Ulysses S. Grant arrived on June 15, 1864, he set up a tent on the east lawn. A cabin was later built for the general, who directed the Union war effort here until April 2, 1865. Dr. Eppes had to borrow money to buy and dismantle the Union structures when he returned home after the war. Daily 9-5; closed Jan. 1, Thanksgiving and Dec. 25. Free. Phone (804) 458-9504.

City Point Early History Museum is in St. Dennis Chapel at 609 Brown Ave. Artifacts and exhibits depict Colonial, Civil War and early 20th-century history of the town of City Point. An archeological exhibit from Kippax Plantation, the home of Pocahontas' granddaughter, is displayed. Allow 30 minutes minimum. Mon.-Sat. 9-4:30, Sun. 1-4:30, Apr.-Oct. Donations. Phone (804) 458-2564. *See ad p. 261.*

WESTON MANOR is on Weston Ln. and 21st Ave. Overlooking the Appomattox River, this 18th-century home has retained much of its original interior woodwork, and its 12 rooms are furnished with period antiques. Union general Philip Sheridan purportedly occupied the house during the Civil War. The grounds and gardens also are open to the public. Guided tours are available. Allow 1 hour minimum. Mon.-Sat. 10-4:30, Sun. 1-4:30, Apr.-Oct. Admission $4, under 12 free with adult. Phone (804) 458-4682. *See ad p. 261.*

HOT SPRINGS (G-6) elev. 2,195′

Hot Springs is in a scenic valley surrounded by forested mountains. The medicinal springs have made it a health resort for generations. Summer and winter sports facilities are available. *See the AAA Mideastern CampBook.*

Bath County Chamber of Commerce: P.O. Box 718, Hot Springs, VA 24445; phone (540) 839-5409.

RECREATIONAL ACTIVITIES
Skiing

• **The Homestead** is off SR 220. Write P.O. Box 2000, Hot Springs, VA 24445. Mon.-Fri. 9-5,

Sat.-Sun. 8-5, Nov.-Mar. Phone (540) 839-7721 or (800) 838-1766.

HUME (E-8) elev. 80′

WINERIES

• **Oasis Winery** is off I-66 exit 27, 4.8 mi. s.w. on SR 647, then 10.7 mi. w. on SR 635. Daily 10-5. Guided tours are given daily at 1 and 3. Closed Jan. 1, Thanksgiving and Dec. 25. Phone (540) 635-7627 or (800) 304-7656.

IRVINGTON (A-3) pop. 673

At the end of the Northern Neck peninsula between the Rappahannock and Potomac rivers, Irvington long has been associated with Tides Inn, a golf and water sports resort that has been open since 1947. Cruises of the Rappahannock and the coves of Carter's Creek are available.

Irvington Chamber of Commerce: P.O. Box 282, Irvington, VA 22480; phone (804) 438-6230 or (804) 438-5447.

HISTORIC CHRIST CHURCH is 2.5 mi. n. on SR 200, then 1 mi. w. on CR 646 following signs. The ornate tomb of Robert "King" Carter, who financed and built the church in 1735, is on the grounds. The brick church stands as it was built, without heat or electricity. Of interest is a marble baptismal font, a three-decker pulpit, a Queen Anne holy table and original communion silver. Carter Reception Center and Museum offers a videotape presentation and guided tours.

Church open daily 9-5. Center open Mon.-Sat. 10-4, Sun. 2-5, Apr.-Nov. Donations. Guided tour $2. Phone (804) 438-6855.

JAMESTOWN—
see Williamsburg, Jamestown and Yorktown—Virginia's Historic Triangle p. 302.

JAMESTOWN NATIONAL HISTORIC SITE—
see Colonial National Historical Park in Williamsburg, Jamestown and Yorktown—Virginia's Historic Triangle p. 300.

JEFFERSON NATIONAL FOREST—
see George Washington and Jefferson National Forests p. 241.

LAKESIDE—*see Richmond p. 286.*

LANCASTER (G-10) elev. 89′

Lancaster boasts several buildings of historical interest. Lancaster County Courthouse, built in 1860, contains records that are complete to 1652. Mary Ball Washington Museum and Library, a four-building complex on SR 3 at the courthouse, honors George Washington's mother, who was born in Lancaster County.

Lancaster House, built about 1798, contains a museum with Washington family memorabilia and historical items pertaining to the county and the

Northern Neck. The adjacent 1819 Old Jail houses the archives and historical lending library.

A genealogical library is housed in the Stewart-Blakemore Building. The Old Clerk's Office, which dates from 1797, displays county artifacts.

LANESVILLE (A-2) elev. 107′

Archeological evidence of the Pamunkey Indians in the Lanesville area dates back 10,000 years. An English treaty signed by King Charles II in 1677 established articles of peace and a tribal territory that remains in existence today. The Pamunkey Indian Reservation encompasses some 1,200 acres in King William County.

PAMUNKEY INDIAN MUSEUM is on SR 30 past jct. SR 30/SR 633. The museum displays artifacts and exhibits about the Pamunkey Indians, once part of the Powhatan confederacy. Tues.-Sat. 10-4, Sun. 1-4. Admission $2.50; over 54, $1.75; ages 7-15, $1.25. Phone (804) 843-4792.

LEESBURG — *see District of Columbia p. 128.*

LEXINGTON (G-7) pop. 6,867, elev. 1,100′

Four American generals—George Washington, Robert E. Lee, Thomas J. "Stonewall" Jackson and George C. Marshall—have played major roles in historic Lexington. The two Confederate heroes had homes and are buried in the historic town.

Restored downtown includes the Alexander-Withrow House, one of the few buildings that survived the 1796 fire that raged through town. Lawyers' Row and Court House Square were laid out as part of the original town in 1778.

Just beyond Lexington, the Theater at Lime Kiln presents plays and concerts from Memorial Day through Labor Day. The Virginia Horse Center, off SR 39, offers horse shows, workshops and seminars.

Of scenic interest is rugged Goshen Pass Natural Area, 15 miles northwest on SR 39. Here the southwest face of Little North Mountain drops sharply from 3,600 feet to the Maury River, about 1,800 feet below. Rhododendrons, mountain laurels, pines and dogwoods grow profusely along the river and the surrounding mountains. Traversed by stagecoaches in the 19th century, Goshen Pass is enjoyed today for the recreational activities it provides.

A 7-mile stretch of railbed between Lexington and Buena Vista has been developed into the Chessie Nature Trail. The trail is designed for pedestrians who enjoy hiking, bird-watching, running, fishing, cross-country skiing and picnicking. Vehicles, including bicycles, are not allowed on the trail.

Lexington Visitor Center: 106 E. Washington St., Lexington, VA 24450; phone (540) 463-3777 or (877) 453-9822. *See color ad.*

Self-guiding tours: A brochure with information about several walking tours is available at the visitor center.

SAVE "STONEWALL" JACKSON HOUSE is at 8 E. Washington St. This was the home of Gen. Thomas J. Jackson from 1859 until his death in 1863, a result of wounds received at the Battle of Chancellorsville. The house and garden are restored and furnished with many original pieces and personal effects. Changing exhibits and guided tours are offered. Mon.-Sat. 9-5, Sun. 1-5; closed Jan. 1, Easter, Thanksgiving and Dec. 25. Last tour departs 30 minutes before closing. Admission $6; ages 6-17, $3. MC, VI. Phone (540) 463-2552.

VIRGINIA MILITARY INSTITUTE is off Main St. Founded in 1839, this was the nation's first state-supported military college. On the National Register of Historic Districts, VMI is noted for its

military and academic programs; the Barracks is a National Historic Landmark. Alumni include Gen. George C. Marshall and Adm. Richard E. Byrd. **Note:** The VMI Museum and Jackson Memorial Hall are closed for renovation. Some of their exhibits have been temporarily moved to the George C. Marshall Museum and Library. Allow 1 hour minimum. Mon.-Fri. 8-4:30. Tours are given Mon.-Fri. at 11:15 and 3:15 and by appointment during the academic year. Closed Jan. 1-4, week of Thanksgiving and Dec. 20-31. No tours are given during exam periods. Free. Phone (540) 464-7784.

George C. Marshall Museum and Library is at the w. end of the VMI parade ground on Letcher Ave. The building houses the World War II chief of staff's papers and material relating to U.S. military and diplomatic history through much of the 20th century. An electric map with narration traces the developments of World War II. Displayed are the Nobel Peace Prize awarded Marshall in 1953 and the Academy Award presented to Gen. Frank McCarthy, the VMI graduate who produced the movie "Patton."

Daily 9-5; closed Jan. 1, Thanksgiving and Dec. 25. Admission $3; over 62, $2; under 18 free. Phone (540) 463-7103.

WASHINGTON AND LEE UNIVERSITY is off Jefferson St. (US 11). A white colonnaded building houses the college, which dates from the 1749 founding of Augusta Academy. Later known as Liberty Hall, the academy was endowed by George Washington and renamed Washington Academy in 1798. Gen. Robert E. Lee was president of the college from the end of the Civil War until his death in 1870, after which the university took its present name.

Lee Chapel & Museum is on the Washington and Lee University campus. Built in 1867 under Lee's supervision, the Victorian-style chapel now stands as a shrine to the general. It preserves Lee's office just as he left it on Sept. 28, 1870, a few weeks before his death. Edward Valentine's recumbent statue of Lee is at the far end of the chapel. Lee and his family are buried beneath the chapel on the museum level. The museum traces the history of the university, focusing on the heritage of its namesakes. The Washington-Custis-Lee Collection of portraits includes Charles Willson Peale's portrait of Washington.

Allow 1 hour minimum. Mon.-Sat. 9-5, Sun. 1-5, Apr.-Oct.; Mon.-Sat. 9-4, Sun. 1-4, rest of year. Closed Jan. 1, Thanksgiving, day after Thanksgiving and Dec. 24-25 (reduced hours Dec. 26-31). Free. Phone (540) 463-8768.

LORTON — *see District of Columbia p. 129.*

LUCKETTS — *see District of Columbia p. 129.*

LURAY (F-8) pop. 4,871, elev. 819'

Luray was settled by a group of German-Swiss at the base of Massanutten Mountain along the

South Fork of the Shenandoah River. Laid out in 1812, Luray was close enough to Virginia's untamed wilderness that some of its early homes contained thick stone forts within their walls to guard against the constant threat of American Indian attacks. These forts, usually in the basement, were kept supplied with firewood and food and often included a tunnel that connected with a well.

Hiking, fishing and boating can be enjoyed in developed recreational areas of George Washington and Jefferson National Forests *(see place listing p. 241 and the AAA Mideastern CampBook)* and in Shenandoah National Park *(see place listing p. 290)*, to the east.

Page County Chamber of Commerce: 46 E. Main St., Luray, VA 22835; phone (540) 743-3915.

LURAY CAVERNS is 1 mi. w. on US 211 and 340 bypass. The massive chambers, 30 to 140 feet high, contain a variety of formations all in beautiful natural color. In the Cathedral Room is the Stalacpipe Organ, which is purported to be the world's largest musical instrument. It uses specially tuned stalactites to produce music of symphonic quality. Lighted and paved walkways lead visitors past towering stone columns and crystal pools.

Guided 1-hour tours depart every 20 minutes daily 9-7, June 15-Labor Day; daily 9-6, Apr.1-June 14 and day after Labor Day-Oct. 31; Mon.-Fri. 9-4, Sat.-Sun. 9-5, rest of year. Admission (includes Car and Carriage Caravan) $18; over 61, $16; ages 7-13, $8. AX, DS, MC, VI. Phone (540) 743-6551. *See color ad p. 264.*

Car and Carriage Caravan is near the entrance to Luray Caverns. The progress of transportation is depicted through carriage and automobile exhibits. Among the more than 140 items on display are an 1892 Benz, a 1904 Cadillac, a 1935 Hispano-Suiza and many early Ford models. Daily 9-8:30, June 15-Labor Day; daily 9-7:30, Apr. 1-June 14 and day after Labor Day-Oct. 31; Mon.-Fri. 9-5:30, Sat.-Sun. 9-6:30, rest of year. Admission is included with the caverns.

The Garden Maze is at 970 US 211W at Luray Caverns. Visitors must navigate a half-mile path through 8-foot-high arborvitae trees by solving riddles along the way. The 1-acre ornamental garden features misting fog, fountains and a cave. Allow 30 minutes minimum. Daily 9:30-7, June 15-Labor Day; daily 9:30-6, Apr. 1-June 14 and day after Labor Day-Oct. 31; Mon.-Fri. 9:30-4, Sat.-Sun. 9:30-5, rest of year. Admission $5; ages 7-13, $4. AX, DS, MC, VI. Phone (540) 843-0769.

Singing Tower is 1 mi. w. on US 211 at the entrance to Luray Caverns. Situated in a parklike setting, the Belle Brown Northcott Memorial is built of sandstone from Massanutten Mountain. The 117-foot carillon, 25 feet square at the base, contains 47 bells; the largest weighs 7,640 pounds, the smallest 12.5 pounds. Recitals, which last about 45 minutes, are given Tues., Thurs. and Sat.-Sun. at 8 p.m., June-Aug.; Sat.-Sun. at 2, Apr.-May and Sept.-Oct. Free. Phone (540) 743-6551.

RECREATIONAL ACTIVITIES

Canoeing

- **Downriver Canoe Company** is at 884 Indian Hollow Rd., P.O. Box 10, Bentonville, VA 22610. Mon.-Fri. 9-6, Sat.-Sun. 7-7, Apr.-Oct. Phone (540) 635-5526 or (800) 338-1963.

- **Shenandoah River Outfitters Inc.** is at 6502 S. Page Valley Rd., Luray, VA 22835. Daily 8-5, Apr.-Nov. Phone (540) 743-4159 or (800) 622-6632.

LYNCHBURG (H-7) pop. 65,269, elev. 517'

A ferry established by John Lynch in 1757 was the nucleus of the original settlement that became Lynchburg, laid out on 45 acres of Lynch's land. He built the region's first tobacco warehouse in 1785.

During the Civil War the city was a supply base for the Confederate Army. It was for the possession of these stores that the Battle of Lynchburg was fought June 18, 1864, when Union general David Hunter made an unsuccessful attempt to capture the city from Confederates commanded by Gen. Jubal

A. Early. Throughout the Civil War Lynchburg served as a major hospital center.

Within the old city cemetery is the Old Confederate Cemetery, containing 2,201 graves and the Pest House Medical Museum, a restored 1840s medical office and house of quarantine depicting the conditions under which medicine was practiced in the late 1800s; phone (434) 847-1465.

Lynchburg has several 19th- and early 20th-century residential districts. Five hills in the "City of Seven Hills" are National Register Historic Districts. Court House Hill is home of Lynchburg Museum at the Old Courthouse (see attraction listing) and is named after the first courthouse built in 1813. Diamond and Garland hills represent the wealth of the tobacco era with magnificent residences of wealthy citizens. Federal Hill was Lynchburg's first suburb. On Daniel's Hill, Cabell Street is reminiscent of the Victorian elegance in the 1890s.

Lynchburg salutes the James River in mid-June with the Bateau Festival. It kicks off an 8-day trek in which flat-bottomed boats, once used to transport tobacco and other goods, pole their way from Lynchburg to Richmond.

Lynchburg Regional Convention and Visitors Bureau: 216 Twelfth St., Bateau Landing, Lynchburg, VA 24504; phone (434) 847-1811 or (800) 732-5821. See color ad p. 265.

Self-guiding tours: Brochures outlining walking and driving tours of Lynchburg's historic areas are available from the visitors bureau.

AMAZEMENT SQUARE—THE RIGHTMIRE CHILDREN'S MUSEUM is at 27 Ninth St. This dynamic learning environment encourages children to play, learn and solve problems through four floors of hands-on exhibits. Visitors can explore global and regional topics, the arts and humanities, history, culture, science, health and technology. Allow 1 hour minimum. Tues.-Sat. 10-5 (also Mon. 10-5, July-Aug.), Sun. 1-5; closed major holidays. Admission $4.50, under 2 free. MC, VI. Phone (434) 845-1888.

THE LEGACY MUSEUM OF AFRICAN-AMERICAN HERITAGE is at 403 Monroe St. The galleries feature rotating exhibits targeting the history of African-Americans in central Virginia. Guided tours are available. Picnicking is permitted. Allow 30 minutes minimum. Thurs.-Sat. noon-4, Sun. 2-4; closed major holidays. Admission $2; senior citizens and children over 6, $1. Phone (434) 845-3455.

LYNCHBURG MUSEUM AT THE OLD COURTHOUSE is at 901 Court St. Exhibits detail the history of Lynchburg. Built in 1855, the Greek Revival court building houses displays of Monacan Indian artifacts, Quaker relics and Civil War memorabilia. Exhibits also chronicle Lynchburg's transition from a tobacco trading center in the early 1800s to a modern industrial city. Allow 30 minutes minimum.

Daily 10-4; closed Jan. 1, Thanksgiving and Dec. 24-25. Admission $1, under 12 free. Phone (434) 847-1459.

MAIER MUSEUM OF ART is off Rivermont Ave. at 1 Quinlan St. on the campus of Randolph-Macon Woman's College. The museum's permanent collection focuses on American paintings of the 19th and 20th centuries. The galleries display works by such artists as Thomas Hart Benton, Mary Cassatt, Childe Hassam, Georgia O'Keeffe and Jamie Wyeth. Changing exhibits also are displayed. Allow 30 minutes minimum. Tues.-Sun. 1-5, late Aug.-late May; Wed.-Sun. 1-4, rest of year. Closed holidays and mid- to late Dec. Free. Phone (434) 947-8136.

POINT OF HONOR is at 112 Cabell St. The 1815 mansion was the home of one of Lynchburg's most prominent citizens, Dr. George Cabell Sr., physician and friend to Patrick Henry. The distinctive octagon-bay facade overlooks the James River. The dwelling's interior woodwork, furnishings and other appointments have been restored to their Federal period appearance. Re-created kitchen and stable buildings provide glimpses into early 19th-century lifestyles.

Allow 30 minutes minimum. Guided tours of the house and gardens are given daily 10-4; closed Jan. 1, Thanksgiving and Dec. 24-25. Admission $6; over 60, $5; ages 6-16, $2. Phone (434) 847-1459.

SAVE **THOMAS JEFFERSON'S POPLAR FOREST** is off SR 460, n. on SR 811, then e. on SR 661. The brick octagonal villa, one of only two homes that Jefferson designed for himself, was his retreat when he visited his working plantations in Bedford County.

The Palladian-style house is undergoing restoration. Guided tours and displays explain the restoration process as well as plantation life. Guided 40-minute tours are offered Wed.-Mon. 10-4, Apr.-Nov.; closed Thanksgiving. Admission $8; over 60, $6; ages 6-16, $1. Phone (434) 525-1806. See color ad p. 265.

MACHIPONGO (A-5) elev. 40'

This barrier island on the Atlantic Ocean is part of Virginia's Eastern Shore, famed for its natural beauty, abundant wildlife, bountiful fishing and rural charm.

SAVE **EASTERN SHORE OF VIRGINIA BARRIER ISLANDS VISITOR CENTER** is at 7295 Young St. Exhibits and artifacts depict significant events, landmarks and people who played a role in the history of the state's barrier islands. The museum is in a restored 19th-century building on the Historic Almshouse Farm, which was established in 1803 to care for the destitute. Guided tours are available. Allow 30 minutes minimum. Mon.-Sat. 10-4; closed holidays. Admission $4; over 64, $3; students with ID and ages 6-17, $2. Phone (757) 678-5550.

MANASSAS—see District of Columbia p. 130.

MANASSAS NATIONAL BATTLEFIELD PARK—

see District of Columbia p. 130.

MARION (I-4) pop. 6,349

Marion was named for Gen. Francis Marion, known as the "Swamp Fox" during the Revolution because of the guerilla warfare tactics he used against the British in South Carolina. A popular vacation base, Marion is surrounded by the George Washington and Jefferson National Forests *(see place listing p. 241)* and is near Hungry Mother State Park *(see Recreation Chart and the AAA Mideastern CampBook).*

Chamber of Commerce of Smyth County: 214 W. Main St., P.O. Box 924, Marion, VA 24354; phone (276) 783-3161.

STATE TROUT CULTURE STATION is 2 mi. s. on SR 16. Trout hatched and raised in the State Fish Hatchery stock waterways throughout the state. Guided tours are available by appointment. Daily 8-3:30. Free. Phone (276) 782-9314.

MARKHAM (E-8)

WINERIES
- **Naked Mountain Vineyard** is off I-66 exit 18, then 1.5 mi. n. on Leeds Manor Rd. Daily 11-5. Phone (540) 364-1609.

MARTINSVILLE (I-6) pop. 15,416

VIRGINIA MUSEUM OF NATURAL HISTORY is at 1001 Douglas Ave. Exhibits include scale models of dinosaurs as well as casts of actual dinosaur tracks from Virginia and a life-size replica of a ground sloth. Educational activities and other programs are conducted regularly; changing exhibits also are offered. Mon.-Sat. 10-5, Sun. 1-5; closed major holidays. Admission $4; senior citizens $3; ages 12-18, $3; ages 3-11, $2. Phone (276) 666-8600.

McDOWELL (F-7) elev. 2,107'

On the eastern edge of McDowell, on US 250, a sign and monument identify McDowell Battlefield where "Stonewall" Jackson turned back a Federal attack. At Sitlington's Hill the second battle and first victory of Jackson's Valley Campaign took place. Nearby McDowell Presbyterian Church was used as a hospital during the war; soldiers are buried in the cemetery.

Highland County Chamber of Commerce: P.O. Box 223, Monterey, VA 24465; phone (540) 468-2550.

McLEAN — *see District of Columbia p. 130.*

MIDDLEBURG — *see District of Columbia p. 131.*

MIDDLETOWN (E-8) pop. 1,015, elev. 660'

The Battle of Cedar Creek took place October 19, 1864, when Confederate general Jubal Early executed a surprise attack on Gen. Philip Sheridan's army encamped on Cedar Creek, south of Middletown. Sheridan was at Winchester when the firing began, and he raced to the scene of the battle. Meeting the retreating soldiers about a mile north of Middletown, he not only halted the flight of his troops but also galvanized them to attack and defeat Early.

The Cedar Creek Battlefield Visitors Center, 8437 Valley Pike, overlooks the battlefield and offers interpretive displays, battle mementos and a videotape focusing on the battle and the Shenandoah Valley Campaign of 1864. Phone (540) 869-2064.

The Wayside Theater, which gives matinee performances Wednesday and Saturday and evening performances Wednesday through Sunday, is one of the oldest professional theaters in Virginia. The theater is well-known for comedies, musicals and farces, with most of its casting done out of New York; phone (540) 869-1776.

For those interested in one of America's favorite snack foods, visit the Route 11 Potato Chip Factory at 7815 Main St. Purportedly the smallest chip factory in the country, it has a viewing area where visitors can watch production of the hand-made chips; phone (540) 869-0104.

SAVE **BELLE GROVE PLANTATION** is 1 mi. s. on US 11, then .5 mi. w. on Belle Grove Rd. Maj. Isaac Hite Jr. acquired the 483-acre parcel in 1783, the same year he married Nelly Conway Madison, sister of the future president. During the Civil War, Union troops repeatedly occupied the estate, which was the focus of the Battle of Cedar Creek in October 1864. On the grounds of the limestone manor house are gardens, orchards, an overseer's house, a slave cemetery and original outbuildings.

Allow 2 hours minimum. Mon.-Sat. 10-4, Sun. 1-5, Apr.-Oct. Tours also are offered Thanksgiving weekend and during the Christmas season. Last tour departs 45 minutes before closing. Admission $7; over 65, $6; ages 6-12, $3. Special events admission varies. AX, DS, MC, VI. Phone (540) 869-2028.

MILLWOOD (E-8) elev. 520'

Millwood lies near the Shenandoah River. Descendants of Tidewater aristocrat Robert "King" Carter built several large estates in and around Millwood in the late 18th century. One of these wealthy settlers, Nathaniel Burwell, built Carter Hall 1790-98. Among Carter Hall's guests were "Stonewall" Jackson and Edmund Randolph.

Before completing Carter Hall, Burwell had become partners with Gen. Daniel Morgan in building a mill. Morgan, who had been one of the Revolutionary War's most brilliant leaders, supervised the construction of the mill and its first years of operation. Burwell-Morgan Mill remained a vital outlet for its wheat-growing neighbors until 1953, surviving not only the Civil War but also several changes of ownership. Today a miller conducts tours of the restored mill, which again grinds flour and corn-meal; phone (540) 837-1799.

Another site, Historic Long Branch, is an 1811 Greek revival mansion sitting on 400 rolling acres. Situated in the midst of Virginia hunt country, the estate once was owned by Lord Fairfax and Robert "King" Carter. For tour information phone (540) 837-1856 or (888) 558-5567.

MINERAL (G-9) pop. 424, elev. 463′

Originally known as Tolersville, the town of Mineral was renamed in 1890 after deposits of copper, gold, mica and sulphur were discovered in the area.

NORTH ANNA NUCLEAR INFORMATION CENTER is 2.5 mi. e. on CR 618, then 6.3 mi. n. on CR 700. Maintained by Dominion Virginia Power, the center offers displays about the development and operation of nuclear power plants and the generation of electricity. Films, slide shows and lectures complement the displays. Picnicking is permitted. Allow 30 minutes minimum. Guided tours of the center are available Mon.-Fri. 9-4; closed major holidays. Free. Phone (804) 771-3200.

MONTICELLO—
see Charlottesville p. 229.

MOUNT ROGERS NATIONAL RECREATION AREA (I-4)

The visitor center for the Mount Rogers National Recreation Area, in the highlands of southwestern Virginia, is at 3714 SR 16. The 140,000-acre recreation area is part of George Washington and Jefferson National Forests *(see place listing p. 241)*. Mount Rogers is the highest point in the state at 5,729 feet; a trail to the top begins at Grindstone Campground and Grayson Highlands State Park *(see Recreation Chart and the AAA Mideastern CampBook)*.

Broad mountain meadows and forests of spruce, fir and northern hardwood provide settings for seven developed campgrounds, five of which are open May through September while the other two are open all year.

A network of trails includes a 60-mile segment of the Appalachian Trail and others suitable for cross-country skiing. Three primitive horse camps adjoin the Virginia Highlands Horse Trail. The area offers good trout fishing and deer and turkey hunting.

The visitor center is open Mon.-Fri. 8-4:30, Sat. 9-5, Sun. 1-5, Memorial Day to mid-Oct.; Mon.-Fri. 8-4:30, rest of year. Phone (276) 783-5196 or (800) 628-7202. *See Recreation Chart.*

MOUNT SOLON (F-7) elev. 1,322′

NATURAL CHIMNEYS REGIONAL PARK is .5 mi. n.w. on SR 731 via signs. The park comprises seven natural limestone towers. Nature trails, a

swimming pool, campgrounds and picnic areas are available.

Sun.-Wed. 9-5, Thurs. and Sat. 9-6, Fri. 9-8, May 31-Aug. 31; daily 9-5, mid-Apr. through May 30 and Sept.-Oct.; Sat.-Sun. 9-5, Mar. 1 to mid-Apr.; by appointment rest of year. Admission $4 per person or $8 per private vehicle. Pool $3; ages 4-12, $2.50. Phone (540) 350-2510 or (888) 430-2267. *See Recreation Chart.*

MOUNT VERNON—
see District of Columbia p. 131.

NATURAL BRIDGE (G-6) elev. 1,078′

Natural Bridge, known by the Monacan Indians as The Bridge of God, was a site of worship. George Washington surveyed the property and carved his initials, which still are visible, in its stone. In 1774 Thomas Jefferson bought the bridge for 20 shillings from King George III, built a cabin for visitors and installed a caretaker.

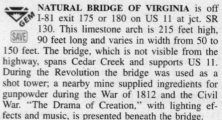

NATURAL BRIDGE OF VIRGINIA is off I-81 exit 175 or 180 on US 11 at jct. SR 130. This limestone arch is 215 feet high, 90 feet long and varies in width from 50 to 150 feet. The bridge, which is not visible from the highway, spans Cedar Creek and supports US 11. During the Revolution the bridge was used as a shot tower; a nearby mine supplied ingredients for gunpowder during the War of 1812 and the Civil War. "The Drama of Creation," with lighting effects and music, is presented beneath the bridge.

Allow 1 hour minimum. Bridge open daily 8-dusk. Drama presentations daily at dusk, Apr.-Oct.; Sat. at dusk, rest of year. Admission $10; over 62, $9; ages 6-15, $5. Combination rate with Natural Bridge Caverns and Natural Bridge Wax Museum $18; ages 6-15, $8.50. AX, DS, MC, VI. Phone (540) 291-2121 or (800) 533-1410.

Monacan Indian Living History Village is on US 11. This re-created village features interpreters in period costume and demonstrations of rope making, weaving, meal preparation, canoe building, hide tanning and other activities. Monacan Indians lived in the area about 300 years ago. Guided tours are available. Picnicking is permitted. Food is available. Allow 1 hour minimum. Daily 9-5, Apr.-Nov.; closed Thanksgiving. Admission included with Natural Bridge of Virginia. Phone (540) 291-2121 or (800) 533-1410.

Natural Bridge Caverns is on US 11. Guided 45-minute tours highlight the cavern stalagmites, stalactites, underground streams and waterfall. The temperature in the caverns is a constant 54 F.

Allow 1 hour minimum. Tours depart every 20 minutes daily 10-5, Mar.-Oct. Admission $8; over 62, $6; ages 6-15, $4.50. AX, DS, MC, VI. Phone (540) 291-2121 or (800) 533-1410.

Natural Bridge Wax Museum is on US 11. More than 150 life-size replicas of historical figures are featured in scenes depicting the history of the Shenandoah Valley, American Indian legends and folklore. Visitors can tour the wax museum factory and see how the figures are made. Daily 9-9, June-Aug.; 10-4, rest of year. Hours may vary; phone ahead. Admission $8; over 62, $6; ages 6-15, $5. Combination rate with the Natural Bridge of Virginia and the Natural Bridge Caverns $18; ages 6-15, $8.50. MC, VI. Phone (540) 291-2426.

NEWBERN (H-5) elev. 2,136′

WILDERNESS ROAD REGIONAL MUSEUM is off I-81 exit 98 following brown signs. The museum preserves several early 19th-century log buildings that were part of a planned community on the Wilderness Road. Exhibits include regional artifacts, photographs and furniture. A brochure detailing a walking tour of Newbern's historic district is available at the museum. Allow 30 minutes minimum. Mon.-Sat. 10:30-4:30, Sun. 1:30-4:30. Admission $2; ages 6-12, $1. Phone (540) 674-4835.

NEW MARKET (F-7) pop. 1,637, elev. 1,060′

One of the more spectacular events of the Civil War occurred during the Battle of New Market on May 15, 1864. Compelled by necessity, Gen. John Breckinridge ordered cadets from Virginia Military Institute to confront the Union forces under Gen. Franz Sigel. The boys, whose average age was 18, were to be kept in reserve until needed to fill a gap in the advancing line, but in the confusion of battle, they were accidentally put on the front line. Five were killed and 15 wounded.

The cadets' heroism in holding the line for 30 minutes helped to defeat Sigel's seasoned troops, who then retreated north.

Shenandoah Valley Travel Association: P.O. Box 1040, New Market, VA 22844; phone (540) 740-3132.

Self-guiding tours: A walking tour brochure is available from the travel association, off I-81 exit 264.

ENDLESS CAVERNS is off I-81 exit 264, then 3 mi. s. on US 11. No end has been discovered to these caverns, which include an impressive array of stalactites, stalagmites, giant columns, flowstone and limestone pendants, and such chambers as Snowdrift, Fairyland and Grand Canyon.

Picnicking is permitted. Allow 1 hour, 30 minutes minimum. Guided tours daily 9-6, June 15-Labor Day; 9-5, Mar. 15-June 14 and day after Labor Day-Nov. 14; 9-4, rest of year. Closed Dec. 25. Admission $14; ages 4-12, $6. MC, VI. Phone (540) 896-2283.

NEW MARKET BATTLEFIELD STATE HISTORICAL PARK is off I-81 exit 264 at 8895 Collins Pkwy. On May 15, 1864, 257 cadets from the Virginia Military Institute aided veteran Confederate troops in victory over Union forces here. On the park grounds is a farm belonging to Jacob and Sarah Bushong dating from the early 1800s; eight re-created dependencies are on the property. A brochure covering a self-guiding walking tour of the battlefield is available at the park visitor center.

Allow 1 hour minimum. Daily 9-5; closed Jan. 1, Thanksgiving and Dec. 24-25. Admission $8; over 59, $6; students with ID $4; under 6 free. Admission includes The Hall of Valor, Bushong Farm complex and the battlefield walking tour. Phone (540) 740-3101 or (866) 515-1864.

The Hall of Valor is off I-81 exit 264 at 8895 Collins Pkwy. The courage of VMI cadets is commemorated with exhibits and a 45-minute film,

"Field of Lost Shoes." A hall with models and dioramas presents a chronological overview of the Civil War. Allow 2 hours minimum. Daily 9-5; closed Jan. 1, Thanksgiving and Dec. 24-25. Admission included with New Market Battlefield State Historical Park.

SHENANDOAH CAVERNS is 2 mi. w. of I-81 exit 269 at 261 Caverns Rd. A guided 1-hour tour begins with an elevator descent to the cave's subterranean entrance hall. Colorful and pure-white formations are visible in 17 rooms, which are connected by a mile of level pathways. Among the highlights are the crystal-laden Diamond Cascade, the Bacon Formations, the Grotto of the Gods and the Oriental Garden. The temperature in the caverns remains a constant 56 F; a jacket and comfortable walking shoes are recommended.

Picnicking is permitted. Food is available June-Aug. Tours depart daily 9-6:15, June 16-Sept. 1; 9-5:15, Apr. 15-June 15 and Sept. 2-Oct. 31; 9-4:15, rest of year. Closed Dec. 25. Admission (includes American Celebration on Parade and Mainstreet of Yesteryear) $17.50; over 62, $15.75; ages 6-14, $7. AX, DS, MC, VI. Phone (540) 477-3115 or (888) 422-8376. *See color ad p. 269.*

American Celebration On Parade is at 397 Caverns Rd. at Shenandoah Caverns. A 40,000-square-foot exhibit hall contains a collection of parade floats, props and stage settings from America's entertainment and political history, including the Rose Parade, presidential inaugurations, the Miss America pageant, Thanksgiving parades and world summit meetings. Guided 30-minute tours are offered daily 9-6:15, June 16-Sept. 1; 9-5:15, Apr. 15-June 15 and Sept. 2-Oct. 31; 9-4:15, rest of year. Closed Dec. 25. Admission included with Shenandoah Caverns. Phone (540) 477-4300. *See color ad p. 269.*

Mainstreet of Yesteryear is at 261 Caverns Rd. at Shenandoah Caverns. Antique, animated window displays that appeared in famous department stores include Cinderella at the ball, a 100-figure circus parade, toy soldiers and a miniature presidential inaugural parade. Daily 9-5; closed Dec. 25. Admission included with Shenandoah Caverns. Phone (540) 477-3115.

NEWPORT NEWS—
see Hampton Roads Area p. 250.

NORFOLK—*see Hampton Roads Area p. 251.*

OAK GROVE (D-12) elev. 69′

WINERIES

• **Ingleside Plantation Vineyards** is off SR 3, then 2.5 mi. s. on CR 638 (Leeds Town Rd.). Mon.-Sat. 10-5, Sun. noon-5. Phone (804) 224-8687.

OCCOQUAN—*see District of Columbia p. 131.*

ONANCOCK (G-11) pop. 1,525, elev. 20′

This waterfront village was established in 1680 on the Chesapeake Bay's eastern shore. The name is said to come from an American Indian word meaning "a foggy place."

KERR PLACE is at 69 Market St. The Federal-style mansion was built in 1799 by merchant John Shepherd Kerr. Visitors can view rooms furnished in period. Allow 30 minutes minimum. Tues.-Sat. 10-4, Mar. 1-Dec. 20. Admission $5; under 18, $2. Phone (757) 787-8012.

TANGIER ISLAND CRUISES departs from 2 Market St. A 1.5-hour trip crosses the Chesapeake Bay to the tiny island of Tangier (*see place listing p. 294*), where visitors can stroll the narrow streets of the quaint town. Cruises depart daily at 10 and return at 3:30, Memorial Day weekend-Oct. 15. Fare $22; ages 6-12, $11. Phone (757) 891-2240.

ORANGE (F-8) pop. 4,123

Settled in 1734, Orange was home to Col. James Taylor II, great-grandfather to two American presidents, James Madison and Zachary Taylor. Robert E. Lee worshipped at St. Thomas Episcopal Church on Caroline Street during the winter of 1863-64; the tree where he tied his horse, Traveler, is marked.

Orange County Visitors Center: 122 E. Main St., Orange, VA 22960; phone (540) 672-1653.

JAMES MADISON MUSEUM is at 129 Caroline St. The museum honors James Madison, the fourth president of the United States and chief architect of the Constitution. Exhibits detail his life and contributions to the American political system and include such items as Madison memorabilia, antique tools and agricultural implements.

Mon.-Fri. 9-5, Sat. 10-5, Sun. 1-5, Mar.-Dec.; Mon.-Fri. 9-5, rest of year. Closed Jan. 1, Easter, Thanksgiving and Dec. 25. Admission $4; over 60, $3; ages 6-16, $1. Phone (540) 672-1776.

MONTPELIER is 4 mi. s.w. on SR 20 (Constitution Hwy.). Owned by the Madison family 1723-1844, the property was called "a squirrel's jump from heaven" by James Madison, fourth president of the United States. The 2,700-acre estate includes more than 130 buildings, extensive gardens and forests, and a steeplechase course.

A visit to Montpelier provides an opportunity to learn about Madison, the Father of the Constitution, and Dolley Madison, America's "first" First Lady. The mansion is undergoing an extensive restoration that will return the home to its original 1820s appearance. Behind-the-scenes tours and special exhibits invite visitors to witness the work in progress. The Montpelier Education Center features historic room re-creations and a collection of Madison furniture.

Note: The mansion will remain open during the restoration, but portions may occasionally close to the public. Guided tours are available. Picnicking is permitted. Daily 9:30-5:30, Apr.-Oct.; 9:30-4:30, rest of year. Closed Thanksgiving and Dec. 25. Admission $11; over 60, $10; ages 6-14, $6. MC, VI. Phone (540) 672-2728.

PARIS—*see District of Columbia p. 131.*

PARKSLEY (G-12) pop. 837, elev. 43'

Henry R. Bennett, a traveling salesman, laid out the town of Parksley in 1884 during construction of the Eastern Shore Railway. In the 160-acre planned community, selling liquor meant the immediate loss of one's property. Benjamin Parks, upon whose farm Parksley was built, soon fled the constraints of town life for a new seaside home.

EASTERN SHORE RAILWAY MUSEUM is at 18468 Dunne Ave. A train depot houses railroad memorabilia and a model train exhibit. Visitors may tour antique railroad cars. Allow 30 minutes minimum. Daily noon-4, June-Sept.; Wed.-Sun. noon-4 and by appointment rest of year. Closed Jan. 1, Thanksgiving and Dec. 25. Admission $2, under 13 free. Phone (757) 665-7245.

PETERSBURG (B-1) pop. 33,740, elev. 100'

Petersburg began in 1645 as Fort Henry, a frontier fort and trading post. In 1781 a British force under generals William Phillips and Benedict Arnold marched on the town, which was inadequately garrisoned by 1,000 men under Gen. Friedrich von Steuben. After a short skirmish to cover his retreat, von Steuben withdrew across Pocahontas Bridge, burning it behind him. Later Marquis de Lafayette bombarded the city. It was in Petersburg that Gen. Charles Cornwallis gathered British troops for the Yorktown campaign.

By the time it was incorporated as a city in 1850, Petersburg had become a thriving industrial and commercial center, with tobacco warehouses, cotton and flour mills and iron foundries. Economic success was followed by a cultural blossoming; schools, colleges, churches and theaters flourished.

Unfortunately, Petersburg's importance as an industrial and transportation center of the Confederacy made it a prime target for Gen. Ulysses S. Grant's armies. In the summer of 1864 the surrounding countryside turned into a battlefield. Stray shells struck 800 homes. For 10 months the city suffered hunger and cannon bombardment before it fell to the Union near the close of the Civil War *(see Petersburg National Battlefield p. 272).*

Not long after the war's end, Mary Logan, wife of Union commander Gen. John A. Logan, witnessed a group of schoolgirls placing flowers on the graves of Petersburg defenders at the Old Blandford Church. Deeply moved when she saw the ritual repeated the next year, she related the story to her husband, who took steps that ultimately led to the observance of Memorial Day as a national holiday.

Petersburg also remembers the favorite pastime of softball. The United States Specialty Sports Association Hall of Fame Museum at 3935 S. Crater Rd. features memorabilia about the history of softball; phone (804) 732-4099.

Petersburg Visitor Center: 425 Cockade Alley, Petersburg, VA 23803; phone (804) 733-2400 or (800) 368-3595.

Self-guiding tours: The visitor center offers a variety of maps outlining tours of Petersburg and its Old Towne historic district as well as Lee's Retreat. This 26-stop driving tour through seven counties connecting Petersburg to Appomattox follows the route of Gen. Robert E. Lee at the end of the Civil War.

Petersburg's African-American heritage is one of the oldest in the country. By the mid-19th century, the area had one of the largest free black populations in the state. A self-guiding tour brochure outlining Petersburg's African-American historic sites is available at the visitor center and at Petersburg museums.

BLANDFORD CHURCH AND RECEPTION CENTER is at 319 S. Crater Rd. Known in Colonial times as the Brick Church on Well's Hill, the church was built 1735-37. Its 15 stained-glass windows by Tiffany Studios are memorials donated by the Confederate States. Blandford Cemetery contains the graves of 30,000 Confederate soldiers and the unmarked grave of British general William Phillips. The reception center, at 111 Rochelle Ln., offers exhibits of artifacts and record books.

Daily 10-5; closed Jan. 1, Thanksgiving and Dec. 24-25. Admission $5, over 59, ages 6-11 and military with ID $4. Phone (804) 733-2396 or (800) 368-3595.

CENTRE HILL MANSION is on Centre Hill Ct. off Franklin St. Extensive renovations to this 1823 Federal-style mansion took place in the 1840s and again in 1901, thereby depicting the architectural evolution that paralleled the Victorian era. Period antiques include a rare 1886 Knabe Art grand piano that is 9 feet long. Daily 10-5; closed Jan. 1, Thanksgiving and Dec. 24-25. Admission $5; over 59, military with ID and ages 6-11, $4. Phone (804) 733-2400 or (800) 368-3595.

PAMPLIN HISTORICAL PARK AND THE NATIONAL MUSEUM OF THE CIVIL WAR SOLDIER is off I-85 exit 63A to 6125 Boydton Plank Rd. Visitors witness Civil War life at this 422-acre park featuring three museums, a Civil War battlefield and four preserved homes, including a restored 1812 plantation. Outdoor, living-history demonstrations are presented daily. At the National Museum of the Civil War Soldier visitors walk through camps and entrenchments, view 3,000 artifacts and trace the careers of common soldiers.

Three miles of marked trails lead through the Civil War battlefield where an 1865 Union victory forced Confederate troops to evacuate Petersburg and Richmond. Reconstructed soldier huts, preserved earthworks and artillery emplacements are seen. The Battlefield Center contains artifacts, uniforms, an electric map and a multimedia battle presentation.

Picnicking is permitted. Food is available. Allow 3 hours minimum. Daily 9-6, mid-June to mid-Aug.; 9-5, rest of year. Closed Jan. 1, Thanksgiving and Dec. 25. Admission $13.50; over 61, $12; ages 6-11, $7.50. AX, DS, MC, VI. Phone (804) 861-2408 or (877) 726-7546.

SIEGE MUSEUM is at 15 W. Bank St. The human side of the Civil War is presented through exhibits depicting the lives of the citizens of Petersburg while under siege. A 20-minute film shows the contrast between the city before the war and as it was during the 10 months preceding Lee's surrender. Daily 10-5; closed Jan. 1, Thanksgiving and Dec. 24-25. Admission $5; over 59, ages 7-12 and military with ID $4. Phone (804) 733-2400 or (800) 368-3595.

PETERSBURG NATIONAL BATTLEFIELD (C-1)

The 2,659-acre Petersburg National Battlefield, 2 miles east of Petersburg via Washington/Oaklawn St. (SR 36), was established to preserve and interpret the battlefields where 10 months of grim

trench warfare sapped the strength of Gen. Robert E. Lee's Confederate army and led to the fall of Richmond.

Petersburg was an important point through which supplies moved to Richmond, as five railroads converged at Petersburg with only one line leading to the capital city.

Despite disastrous losses at Wilderness, Spotsylvania Court House and Cold Harbor, Gen. Ulysses S. Grant moved on from Richmond, intending to cut off its line of communication with the South at Petersburg and compel the evacuation of the Confederate capital. Four days of furious fighting—June 15-18, 1864—forced the Confederate line back about a mile, where the armies entrenched and Grant began his siege.

Between June 25 and July 23, Union volunteers, including many Pennsylvania coal miners, dug a 511-foot-long mine shaft that ended beneath the Confederate line. Quietly carrying out tons of soil in cracker boxes, the Union men packed the shaft with 4 tons of black powder which, when ignited, created a 170- by 60-foot crater 30 feet deep. The blast produced 278 casualties. Only faulty Union plans in the following battle and the prompt action of Confederate troops saved the city. The deep depression created by the explosion is called The Crater.

Confederate lines stretched farther south and west as the soldiers were forced to defend both the

eastern and western sectors against the Union's attempt to take the city. On April 3, 1865, Lee evacuated Petersburg and Richmond, an action that culminated 1 week later in his surrender at Appomattox Court House. About 42,000 Union and 28,000 Confederate soldiers were casualties in the Petersburg Campaign.

The park includes miles of original earthworks. Outstanding features are The Crater; Battery Five, where Grant's army first struck and from which he later shelled Petersburg with a 17,000-pound seacoast mortar known as "The Dictator"; Fort Stedman, where Lee's last grand offensive failed; the site of Fort Morton, near which the concentration of Union artillery used at the Battle of The Crater was stored; City Point, the Union supply center and logistics base where Grant and President Lincoln conferred for 2 weeks near the end of the siege *(see Hopewell p. 262)*; Five Forks Battlefield, about 17 miles southwest of Petersburg, site of the last major battle for the South Side Railroad on April 1, 1865; and Poplar Grove National Cemetery, where 6,000 Union soldiers are buried.

The 4-mile self-guiding Battlefield Tour begins at the Eastern Front Visitor Center; part of the tour road is reserved for hikers and cyclists. From four points on the tour road, walks lead to major battle sites. The 16-mile Siege Line Tour picks up where the Battlefield Tour ends and leads to park areas south and west of Petersburg. Park grounds open daily 8-dusk; closed Jan. 1, Thanksgiving and Dec. 25.

EASTERN FRONT VISITOR CENTER is at the park entrance off Oaklawn St. (SR 36). The Petersburg campaign is depicted through exhibits, battlefield relics, maps and models. Self-guiding tour maps and a recorded narration of the 37-mile driving tour of the battlefield (available in audiotape or CD-ROM) are available. Visitor center open daily 9-5; closed Jan. 1 and Dec. 25. Admission (good for 7 days) $5 per private vehicle or $3 per person arriving by other means. Audiotape $7.50, CD-ROM $12.95. Phone (804) 732-3531.

POCAHONTAS (H-4) pop. 441, elev. 2,300′

In 1873, Maj. Jed Hotchkiss hired a surveyor to explore a 500,000-acre tract along the Bluestone River. The report noted a coal bed used for fuel by a local blacksmith, and Hotchkiss brought the discovery to the attention of investors. A railroad was built to the site, and the first shipment of "smokeless" Pocahontas coal was delivered to Norfolk in 1883. When the original shaft was depleted decades later, the company town turned it into a show mine.

POCAHONTAS EXHIBITION COAL MINE AND MUSEUM is off SR 102 and CR 644, on CR 659. The museum preserves the history of the Pocahontas Coal Mine, which opened in 1882 and operated

for 73 years. Exhibits of mining equipment are displayed. Demonstrations include coal cutting, blasting and loading as well as the old method of hand undercutting. The mine maintains a constant 52 F temperature. Guided tours are available. Allow 30 minutes minimum. Mon.-Sat. 1-6, Sun. noon-5, Apr.-Oct. Admission $7; ages 6-12, $4.50. AX, DS, MC, VI. Phone (276) 945-2134.

PORTSMOUTH—
see Hampton Roads Area p. 258.

QUANTICO—*see District of Columbia p. 131.*

REEDVILLE (G-11) elev. 10′

Reedville's history is intertwined with that of the Potomac River and Chesapeake Bay. On Virginia's Northern Neck, the city was the home of wealthy fishermen and factory owners whose fortunes were made from the menhaden that populated those waters. Their Victorian mansions can be seen along Main Street. Reedville retains its ties to the water, as fishing charters and cruises to nearby Smith and Tangier islands are popular with visitors.

REEDVILLE FISHERMEN'S MUSEUM is on US 360 in the historic district. The museum comprises Walker House, a restored fisherman's home, and Covington Building, which contains two galleries—one with the permanent collection and the other with rotating exhibits. An outside exhibit features traditional boats and equipment. Allow 30 minutes minimum. Daily 10:30-4:30, May-Oct.; Fri.-Mon. 10:30-4:30, Nov. 1 to mid-Jan.; Sat.-Sun. 10:30-4:30, Mar.-Apr. Admission $3, under 12 free. Phone (804) 453-6529.

SMITH ISLAND CRUISE operates from the Chesapeake Bay/Smith Island KOA Campground, 2.5 mi. n.e. of jct. US 360 and CR 652 (Sunnybank Rd.). The narrated 13.5-mile cruise across the Chesapeake Bay to Smith Island, Md. *(see place listing p. 194)*, takes 1.5 hours each way. Upon arrival, visitors embark on a narrated bus tour of remote Ewell Village, the largest of three settlements on the island. Lunch at a restaurant in the village is optional. Cruises depart Tues.-Sun. at 10 (weather permitting) and return at 3:45, May 15-Oct. 15. Fare $24.50; ages 3-12, $13. Reservations are required. Phone (804) 453-3430 or (804) 453-4051.

VIRGINIA CRUISES departs the dock off US 360; following signs. The narrated boat trip to quaint Tangier Island *(see place listing p. 294)* crosses the Chesapeake Bay, taking 1.5 hours each way. Passengers are given 2.5 hours on the island. The ship departs daily at 10 and returns at 3:45, May 1-Oct. 15. Fare $22; ages 4-12, $11. Reservations are required. Phone (804) 453-2628.

Richmond

The capital of Virginia, Richmond combines the atmosphere of a gracious cultural center, the legacy of an absorbing past and the technological drive of a progressive city.

From its founding, Richmond has been linked with the activities of patriots, presidents of both the United and the Confederate States, and several authors. Many historical shrines and reminders of the events Richmond has witnessed are found throughout the city.

In 1609 Capt. John Smith bought from the Indian chief Powhatan a tract of land near the present site of Richmond and founded a settlement he called "None Such." The city was laid out in 1737 by Col. William Byrd and designated the state capital in 1779.

In 1775 the Virginia Convention met at St. John's Church. The roster, a "Who's Who" of Colonial days, contains the names of Benjamin Harrison, Thomas Jefferson, Richard Henry Lee, Edmund Pendleton, Peyton Randolph, George Washington and George Wythe. Patrick Henry made his speech, proclaiming, "I know not what course others may take; but as for me, give me liberty or give me death!"

In 1861 the Ordinance of Secession was passed, and Richmond soon became the capital of the Confederate States of America. Gen. Irvin McDowell, Gen. George McClellan, Gen. Ambrose Everett Burnside, Gen. Joseph Hooker, Gen. George Meade and Gen. Ulysses S. Grant in succession failed to subdue the Southern capital.

Grant finally succeeded, but not by capturing the city itself. In 1864, after the Battle of Cold Harbor near Mechanicsville, Grant abandoned the project of taking Richmond directly and started the siege of Petersburg, which ended in the Confederacy's downfall. When Richmond was evacuated, Confederate troops burned the government warehouse; the spreading flames destroyed most of the city.

The Governor's Mansion on the northeast corner of Capitol Square dates 1811-13. On the site have lived four U.S. presidents; three of them—Thomas Jefferson, James Monroe and John Tyler—also served as governors of Virginia, and William Henry Harrison lived in the mansion while his father was governor.

The renovation of several historic districts has brought new vitality to the downtown area. At Byrd and 12th streets are canal locks built in 1854 as part of a canal system George Washington proposed to complete between the Tidewater region and the Kanawha River. A self-guiding tour and an outdoor museum border the canal; the canal area offers concerts, boat tours and recreational activities.

Shockoe Slip, between the financial district and the James River, was the center for the milling and tobacco

Maymont / © Jeff Greenberg/eStock Photo

Virginia State Capitol / © Andre Jenny/Alamy Images

industries in the 19th century. The warehouses have been restored, the narrow streets have been re-cobbled and the neighborhood is now a high-light of Richmond's dining and night life; boutiques, restaurants, craft shops, office buildings and residences fill the street.

Shockoe Bottom, just past the slip along E. Cary, E. Franklin and E. Main streets between 17th and 25th streets, also has been developed into a lively area of restaurants, nightclubs, art galleries, shops, warehouse apart-ments and a farmers' market. Past flooding of the James River prohibited restoration of the area until a floodwall was built, spurring restoration of the historic neighborhood. The 17th-century Farmer's Market on Main and 17th streets is home to summertime produce and autumn pumpkins. A downtown landmark, Main Street Sta-tion, has been restored and once again welcomes daily train travelers to the city.

Church Hill, on the East End above Shockoe Bot-tom, is poised above the James River. The area is home to tree-lined streets and renovated townhouses.

Named for the layout of streets that fan out toward the west, the Fan District is bordered by Belvidere Street on the east, Boulevard on the west, Monument Avenue on the north and Main Street on the south. Within the Fan's boundaries are late 19th-century town houses with interesting architectural features as well as the academic campus of Virginia Common-wealth University. VCU's Medical College of Vir-ginia campus is 1.5 miles east in the downtown area. Other institutions of higher learning in the Richmond area include Virginia Union University on North Lombardy Street; the University of Richmond in West End; Randolph-Macon College in nearby Ash-land; and Virginia State University in Ettrick.

The statues along Monument Avenue were origi-nally laid out in 1890 with the dedication of the Lee Monument. Graced by a diverse mix of slate-roofed Classical Revival mansions, churches, apartments and stately oak and maple trees, the avenue is considered one of America's most beautiful. It is purported to be the only U.S. street to be designated a historic land-mark. The 7-mile-long stretch begins at Lombardy Street and runs to Horsepen Road/Glenside Drive in Henrico County. Only the easternmost mile contains statues, beginning west to east with the most recent addition, tennis great Arthur Ashe, who was born and raised in the city. Ashe's statue is at Roseneath Av-enue. The statue of Civil War naval officer Matthew Fontaine Maury, inventor of the electronic torpedo, followed by other Civil War heroes including Thomas J. "Stonewall" Jackson, Jefferson Davis, Robert E. Lee and J.E.B. Stuart.

Jackson Ward on the north side of Broad Street is a historic African-American district with Federal and Greek Revival houses; the nation's first

(continued on p. 279)

The Informed Traveler

City Population: 197,790

Elevation: 15 ft.

Sales Tax: Virginia levies a 4.5 percent sales tax with cities and counties imposing an additional 1 percent increment. The Richmond area has a lodging tax of 10.5 percent.

WHOM TO CALL

Emergency: 911

Fire: (804) 780-6663

Police (non-emergency): (804) 646-5100

Time and Temperature: (804) 732-2121

Hospitals: Chippenham Medical Center, (804) 320-3911; Henrico Doctors' Hospital, (804) 289-4500; Retreat Hospital, (804) 254-5100; VCU Health Systems, (804) 828-9000.

WHERE TO LOOK

Newspapers

The daily newspaper is the *Richmond Times-Dispatch*.

Radio

Richmond radio station WRVA (1140 AM) is all news/talk stations; WCVE (88.9 FM) is a member of National Public Radio.

Visitor Information

Richmond Metropolitan Convention & Visitors Bureau: 401 N. Third St., Richmond, VA 23219; phone (804) 783-7450 or (888) 742-4666.

Walk-in visitor centers are off I-95 exit Fifth St. at 405 N. Third St.; on the Canal Walk at 470 Tredegar St.; and at the Richmond International Airport.

TRANSPORTATION

Air Travel

The Richmond International Airport, off I-64 exit 197A, is served by American Airlines, (800) 433-7300; Continental Airlines, (800) 525-0280; Delta Airlines, (800) 221-1212; Northwest Airlines, (800) 225-2525; United Airlines, (800) 241-6522; and USAirways, (800) 245-4882.

Limousine service is available between the greater Richmond area and the airport; phone (804) 222-7226.

Rental Cars

Hertz, at Richmond International Airport, offers discounts to AAA members; phone (804) 222-7228 or (800) 654-3080. For listings of other agencies check the telephone directory.

Rail Service

The Amtrak Train Station is at 7519 Staples Mill Rd.; phone (800) 872-7245.

Buses

The Greyhound Lines Inc. bus terminal is at 2910 N. Boulevard St. across from The Diamond baseball field; phone (804) 254-5938 or (800) 231-2222.

Taxis

Some of the larger cab companies include Acton, (804) 360-7106; Yellow, (804) 222-7300; and Metro (804) 353-5000. Base fare is $2.50 for the first one-fifth mile, $1.50 per each additional mile and 30c for each minute of delay, including traffic. Base fare rises $1 for each additional passenger over age 6 and for rides between 9 p.m. and 6 a.m.

Public Transport

The Greater Richmond Transit Co. (GRTC) operates buses throughout most of the city and parts of Henrico County. The base fare is $1.25; transfers cost 15c. A Super Saver Ticket is $10 per book of 10; senior citizens $5. Phone (804) 358-4782 for information.

Destination Richmond

What has *not* changed in Richmond speaks of its progress. With a reverence for the past and an eye to the future, preservationists have ensured that historic treasures will be enjoyed by generations to come. Here's how to see them:

Gaze out over Capitol Square from the observation deck atop city hall. Take a walking tour of a historic neighborhood. Or cruise up and down the James River.

© Dementi Studio
Richmond Metro CVB

The Edgar Allan Poe Museum, Richmond. A master of macabre literature, Poe resided in Richmond for most of his life. (See listing page 280)

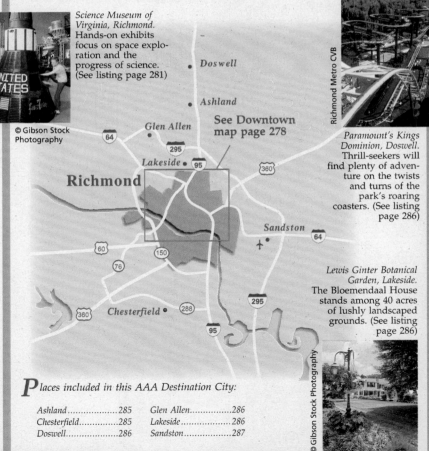

Science Museum of Virginia, Richmond. Hands-on exhibits focus on space exploration and the progress of science. (See listing page 281)

© Gibson Stock Photography

Richmond Metro CVB

Paramount's Kings Dominion, Doswell. Thrill-seekers will find plenty of adventure on the twists and turns of the park's roaring coasters. (See listing page 286)

Lewis Ginter Botanical Garden, Lakeside. The Bloemendaal House stands among 40 acres of lushly landscaped grounds. (See listing page 286)

© Gibson Stock Photography

Places included in this AAA Destination City:

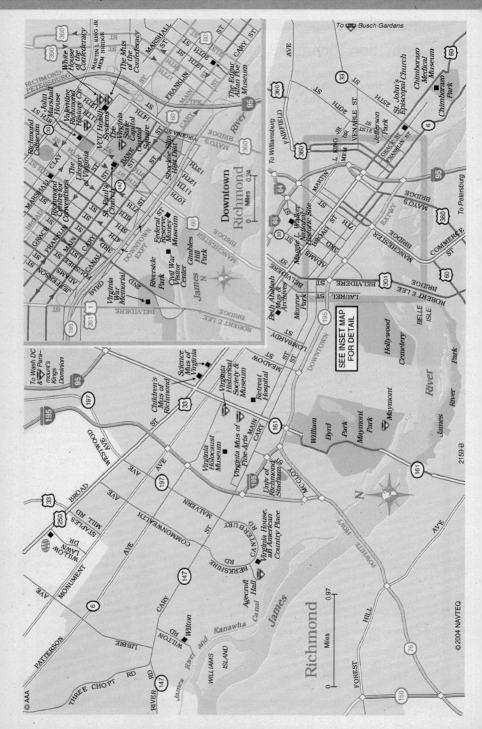

To Busch Gardens

Downtown Richmond

Richmond

© AAA

©2004 NAVTEQ

2159-B

African-American-owned bank and insurance companies were chartered in this area. There also is a monument to Bill "Bojangles" Robinson, who was born in the area. Also in the neighborhood is the Black History Museum and Cultural Center of Virginia at 00 Clay St. Housed in an 1832 Federal and Greek Revival building, the museum is a repository for artifacts detailing the lives of African-Americans in Virginia; phone (804) 780-9093.

Approaches

By Car

Richmond is served by numerous highways, including two major interstates. To the southwest, I-295 misses Richmond by sprouting off I-95 in Petersburg and catches up with I-95 north of Richmond in northern Henrico County; I-295 continues westward until it dead-ends into I-64 near Short Pump. The 3rd Street approach offers access to downtown on I-95 (Richmond-Petersburg Turnpike) from the north; take Broad Street if entering from the south.

East-west I-64 from Williamsburg enters the city from the southeast, joins up with I-95 downtown and then re-emerges south of Dumbarton near Joseph Bryan Park to continue its trek northwest toward Charlottesville. The 3rd Street exit off I-64 provides access to downtown if coming from the west; the 5th Street exit off I-64 takes you downtown from the east.

SR 150 semicircles the western side of the city, coming in from the south as the Chippenham Parkway on the James River in eastern Chesterfield County, crossing the James River to the west of Richmond as Parham Road, crossing I-64 northwest of the city and joining US 301/Chamberlayne Road north of Richmond near I-295.

US 1/301 enters the city from the south as Jefferson Davis Highway, crosses the James River over the Robert E. Lee Bridge, becomes Belvidere Street as it runs through downtown, and splits just north of I-95 (Richmond-Petersburg Parkway) with US 1 heading north as Brook Road and US 301 heading northeast as Chamberlayne Road.

Getting Around

Street System

Downtown Richmond is bounded by the James River to the south and I-95 to the north and east.

Belvidere Street (US 1/301) is roughly the eastern edge of downtown. Broad Street (US 250) bisects the area.

Richmond resembles a grid pattern. Numbered streets 1st through 40th fall either in the East End (in the Church Hill and Shockoe Bottom area) or on the South Side (in the Forest Hill and Brainbridge area). Some streets change names, including Monument Avenue, which becomes W. Franklin Street at Stuart Circle; Malvern becomes Westwood as it crosses Broad Street; and The Boulevard flows into Hermitage Road northbound and Westover Hill Boulevard southbound as it traverses the river (it changes again to Belt Boulevard as it crosses Midlothian Turnpike).

Six bridges cross the James River east to west: I-95/Richmond-Petersburg Turnpike, Mayo's Bridge (US 360), Manchester Bridge (US 60), Robert E. Lee Bridge (US 1/301/Belvidere Street), Boulevard Bridge (SR 161) and Powhite Parkway (SR 76).

Many of the roads throughout Richmond are toll roads, including the Boulevard Bridge (SR 161) over the James River; SR 195/Downtown Expressway from Powhite Parkway to I-95; and the Powhite Parkway Bridge over the James River.

The city speed limit is 30 mph, or as posted. Rush hours are usually 7:30-9 a.m. and 4-6 p.m. Unless otherwise posted, a right turn on red is permitted.

Parking

Like any big city, Richmond has some downtown street parking; metered parking is limited and strictly monitored. If your car is towed from a downtown street, phone police information at (804) 646-5100. Numerous parking lots and garages are available throughout the city. Hourly rates vary from 50c-$2.50.

What To See

AGECROFT HALL is at 4305 Sulgrave Rd. in Windsor Farms. Built in the late 15th century in Lancashire, England, this Tudor manor house was dismantled in the late 1920s and shipped to its present location overlooking the James River.

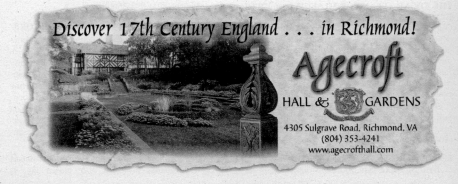

Discover 17th Century England . . . in Richmond!

Agecroft
HALL & GARDENS
4305 Sulgrave Road, Richmond, VA
(804) 353-4241
www.agecrofthall.com

Outstanding features include the original hand-carved oak paneling, leaded-glass windows and furnishings from the Tudor and early Stuart periods (1580-1640). The house is surrounded by 23 acres of lawns, woodlands and several Elizabethan gardens.

Tours begin with a 10-minute film portraying the home in its English location and its shipment to this country. Allow 1 hour minimum. Tues.-Sat. 10-4, Sun. 12:30-5; closed national holidays. Admission $7; over 64, $6; students with ID $4; under 6 free. Phone (804) 353-4241. *See color ad p. 279.*

BETH AHABAH MUSEUM & ARCHIVES is at 1109 W. Franklin St. Virginia's museum of Jewish history and culture features a collection passed down from one of the oldest Jewish congregations in America. The museum houses changing exhibits of documents, historical photographs and religious objects. An archival collection may be used for historical and genealogical research. Allow 30 minutes minimum. Sun.-Thurs. 10-3; closed Jan. 1, Memorial Day, July 4, Labor Day, Thanksgiving and Jewish holidays. Donations. Phone (804) 353-2668.

CAPITOL SQUARE lies between 9th and Governor sts. and Broad and Bank sts. in front of the Virginia State Capitol. At the heart of the square is the Washington Monument, a 60-foot-high equestrian statue surrounded by patriots of the American Revolution. To the east is the Executive Mansion, the official residence of Virginia's governors since 1813. To the north is the 1894 Old City Hall; the new City Hall across the street offers a 19th-floor observation deck. The 1824 Bell Tower houses a visitor center. The Square is open daily 24 hours. Free. Phone (804) 698-1788.

CHILDREN'S MUSEUM OF RICHMOND is at 2626 W. Broad St. Interactive exhibits allow children to explore the human body, learn about the river ecosystems, work in a grocery store, experiment in the Inventor's Laboratory and create artwork. Allow 30 minutes minimum. Tues.-Sat. 9:30-5 (also Mon. 9:30-5, Memorial Day-Labor Day), Sun. noon-5; closed Jan. 1, Thanksgiving and Dec. 24-25. Admission $7, senior citizens $6, under 1 free. Phone (804) 474-2667 or (877) 295-2667.

THE EDGAR ALLAN POE MUSEUM is at 1914-16 E. Main St. Although Poe never resided in the 1737 Old Stone House—Richmond's oldest residence—he lived and worked in the area for much of his life. The museum features Poe's personal memorabilia and rare first editions, a gallery with James Carling illustrations inspired by "The Raven," and a large-scale model of early 19th-century Richmond focusing on Poe's life in the city.

Guided tours depart on the hour Tues.-Sat. 10-4, Sun. 11-4; closed major holidays. Admission $6, over 55 and students with ID $5. MC, VI. Phone (804) 648-5523.

FEDERAL RESERVE MONEY MUSEUM is at 701 E. Byrd St. More than 500 items depict the history of currency and coins. The museum contains such items as compressed tea bricks that could be spent or brewed; and a coin from the Kingdom of Lydia, the birthplace of coinage. Exhibits chronicle Colonial and U.S. monies. Mon.-Fri. 9:30-3:30. Free. Reservations are required. Phone (804) 697-8110.

HOLLYWOOD CEMETERY is at the n. end of Robert E. Lee Bridge at 412 S. Cherry St. and Albemarle St. Several noted Virginians are buried here, including Presidents John Tyler and James Monroe, Confederate President Jefferson Davis, Gen. Fitzhugh Lee, John Randolph, Gen. J.E.B. Stuart, Gov. William Smith and Gen. George E. Pickett. A 90-foot-high granite pyramid honors 18,000 buried Confederate soldiers. The cemetery, which opened in 1849, is named for the holly trees that grow in the area.

Maps and brochures are available for a fee at the cemetery office. Grounds open daily 8-6 during DST; 8-5, rest of year. Office Mon.-Fri. 8:30-4:30. Guided walking tours are offered Mon.-Sat. at 10, Apr.-Oct. Grounds free. Walking tour $7. Phone (804) 648-8501 for the office, or (804) 649-0711 for tour information.

[SAVE] **JOHN MARSHALL HOUSE** is at 818 E. Marshall St. The house was built in 1790 for Chief Justice Marshall, who occupied it until his death in 1835. The residence retains the original woodwork, paneling and many furnishings. Guided tours Tues.-Sat. 10-4:30, Sun. noon-5; closed major holidays. Last tour begins 30 minutes before closing. Admission $6; over 65, $5; ages 7-12, $4. Phone (804) 648-7998.

LEWIS GINTER BOTANICAL GARDEN—
see Lakeside p. 286.

THE LIBRARY OF VIRGINIA is at 800 E. Broad St. Treasures from the library's extensive collection of books, manuscripts, maps and artwork—the commonwealth's records from the colony's founding through the present—are displayed to the public. Research facilities are available. Allow 30 minutes minimum. Tues.-Sat. 9-5; closed holidays. Free. Phone (804) 692-3500.

MAGGIE L. WALKER NATIONAL HISTORIC SITE is at 600 N. 2nd St. The daughter of a former slave, Maggie Lena Walker rose to prominence in Richmond as a businesswoman and community leader in the early 1900s. Among her many accomplishments was the founding of the St. Luke Penny Savings Bank, the first chartered bank in the country started by a woman. Her home in the Jackson Ward district has been restored to its 1930s appearance. A visitor center offers an audiovisual presentation and exhibits.

Allow 30 minutes minimum. House tours depart every 30 minutes Mon.-Sat. 9-5; closed Jan. 1,

Thanksgiving and Dec. 25. Free. Phone (804) 771-2017.

MAYMONT is at 2201 Shields Lake Dr. This 100-acre, late-Victorian country estate typifies Gilded Age opulence. Built in 1893 by Maj. and Mrs. James Dooley, the 33-room mansion overlooks the James River. The estate features the Maymont House Museum, original outbuildings, a carriage collection and gardens. Twelve restored rooms of the mansion, furnished with original pieces, are open to guided tours. The Robbins Nature & Visitor Center includes giant aquariums, interactive exhibits and a 20-foot waterfall. More than 400 animals are presented at the native Virginia wildlife exhibits, the children's farm and the nature center. Tram, carriage and hay wagon rides are offered.

Food is available. Grounds daily 10-7, Apr.-Oct.; 10-5, rest of year. Guided house tours are offered Tues.-Sun. noon-4:30. Closed Jan. 1, Thanksgiving and Dec. 25. Tram rides are offered Tues.-Sun. noon-5. Hay wagon rides Sat.-Sun. 1-4, June-Aug. Carriage rides by appointment. House admission $5. Nature center $4. Children's Farm $2. Tram, carriage and hayrides each $3; under 12, $2. Phone (804) 358-7166.

MEADOW FARM MUSEUM—
see Glen Allen p. 286.

THE MUSEUM OF THE CONFEDERACY is 2 blks. n. of Broad St. at 1201 E. Clay St. Founded in 1890, the museum interprets the Civil War through one of the largest collections of Confederate artifacts, paintings and documents.

Some 15,000 artifacts include military equipment and clothing that belonged to Confederate leaders, among them Jefferson Davis, Robert E. Lee, J.E.B. Stuart and Thomas J. "Stonewall" Jackson; artifacts documenting the lives of free and enslaved African Americans; art illustrating the Confederate experience; and more than 500 flags relating to the Confederate armed forces and government. On display is the 1869 painting "The Last Meeting of Lee and Jackson," a 15-foot painting depicting the moment Jackson went off to Chancellorsville, where he was mortally wounded.

Allow 1 hour minimum. Mon.-Sat. 10-5, Sun. noon-5; closed Jan. 1, Thanksgiving and Dec. 25. Admission $7; over 61 and military with ID $6; ages 7-18, $3. Combined admission for museum and White House of the Confederacy $10; over 61 and military with ID $9; ages 7-18, $5. Free parking is available at the Medical College of Virginia Hospital visitor/patient parking deck on Clay St. (museum will validate parking slip). AX, MC, VI. Phone (804) 649-1861.

White House of the Confederacy is next to the Museum of the Confederacy. This was the executive mansion of President Jefferson Davis and his family during the Civil War. The house was saved from demolition by the Confederate Memorial Literary Society in 1890 and served as the Confederate Museum until the mid-1970s. After 10 years of restoration and the return of many of its original furnishings, the mansion has regained its Victorian opulence. Eleven period rooms are on exhibit. Guided tours start in the basement and explore the first and second floors.

Allow 1 hour minimum. Mon.-Sat. 10-5, Sun. noon-5; closed Jan. 1, Thanksgiving and Dec. 25. Last tour begins 1 hour before closing. Admission $7; over 61 and military with ID $6; ages 7-18, $4.

 PARAMOUNT'S KINGS DOMINION—
see Doswell p. 286.

ST. JOHN'S EPISCOPAL CHURCH is at 2401 E. Broad St. Erected in 1741, the church was the site from which Patrick Henry delivered his "Liberty or Death" speech in favor of independence. The Second Virginia Convention is re-enacted Sunday at 2 p.m., Memorial Day through Labor Day. The surrounding burial ground contains the graves of George Wythe, the first Virginia signer of the Declaration of Independence, and Elizabeth Arnold Poe, mother of Edgar Allan Poe.

Guided tours are offered Mon.-Sat. 10-3:30, Sun. 1-3:30; closed Jan. 1, Easter, Thanksgiving and Dec. 24-25 and 31. Last tour begins at closing. Admission $5; over 64, $4; ages 7-18, $3. Phone (804) 648-5015.

ST. PAUL'S CHURCH is at Grace and 9th sts. President Jefferson Davis and Gen. Robert E. Lee worshiped here. Nearly everything in the church, including the windows commemorating Lee, is a memorial. Mon.-Sat. 10-4, Sun. 8-3; closed holidays. Free. Phone (804) 643-3589.

SCIENCE MUSEUM OF VIRGINIA is off US 95 and US 64, at 2500 W. Broad St. The museum, in a former 1919 train station, offers more than 250 hands-on exhibits as well as demonstrations, displays and touring exhibitions. A planetarium with an IMAX theater features large-format films and multimedia shows.

Mon.-Sat. 9:30-5 (also Fri.-Sat. 5-7, Memorial Day weekend-Labor Day), Sun. 11:30-5; closed Thanksgiving and Dec. 25. Film and show times vary; phone ahead. Museum admission $8; over 60 and ages 4-12, $7.50. Film $8, under 4 free with adult. Museum and film $15; over 60 and ages 4-12, $14.50. MC, VI. Phone (804) 864-1400 or (800) 659-1727.

THREE LAKES NATURE CENTER AND AQUARIUM is off I-95N, 1.7 mi. n.e. on Chamberlayne Ave./US 301, .9 mi. s.e. on Wilkinson Rd., then .1 mi. w. to 400 Sausiluta Dr. The 132-acre park features a 50,000-gallon freshwater aquarium. Exhibits pertain to the park's three lakes, wetlands, forest and animal life. Hands-on activities are offered as well as nature trails and fishing. Picnicking is permitted. Allow 30 minutes minimum. Tues.-Fri. 10-5, Sat.-Sun. noon-5, June-Aug.; Tues.-Sun. noon-5, Mar.-May and Sept.-Nov.; Sat.-Sun. noon-5, rest of year. Free. Phone (804) 261-8230.

VALENTINE RICHMOND HISTORY CENTER is at 1015 E. Clay St. in historic downtown. Changing exhibits from its extensive collections tell the story of Richmond and those who shaped the city. The collections include decorative and industrial arts, paintings and prints. Complementing these artifacts are more than half a million photographs of the city and the surrounding area as well as extensive manuscript and book collections. A gallery is devoted to one of the South's largest costume and textile collection.

Wickham House was built in 1812 by John and Elizabeth Wickham, one of Richmond's wealthiest couples. Guided tours interpret the lives of 31 residents, black and white, including the Wickhams' 17 children. The elegant house, with its magnificent freestanding stairway, rare neo-classical wall paintings and carved ornamentation, typifies late Federal architecture.

Guided tours of the home are offered. Food is available. Tues.-Sat. 10-5, Sun. noon-5; closed Jan. 1, Thanksgiving and Dec. 24-25. Guided house tours depart on the hour Tues.-Sat. 11-4, Sun. 1-4. Admission (including tour) $7; senior citizens and students with ID $6; ages 7-12, $4; ages 3-6, $1. AX, DS, MC, VI. Phone (804) 649-0711.

VIRGINIA AVIATION MUSEUM—
see Sandston p. 287.

VIRGINIA HISTORICAL SOCIETY & MUSEUM is at 428 N. Boulevard. Museum galleries exhibit rare Virginia treasures. The Story of Virginia, an American Experience explores the development of Virginia from the Colonial period and the Civil War through World Wars I and II to the present. Highlights include such early archeological specimens as a 17th-century Virginia dug-out canoe, an 18th-century smokehouse and kitchen, a re-creation of Francis Lightfoot Lee's dining room, a Conestoga wagon and a Richmond streetcar.

A library, Civil War murals and Confederate-made weapons also are featured. Battle Abbey, the original building, is a memorial to the Confederate soldier. Picnicking is permitted. Allow 1 hour minimum. Mon.-Sat. 10-5, Sun. 1-5; closed Jan. 1, Easter, July 4, Thanksgiving and Dec. 24-25 and 31. Admission $5; over 54, $4 ($2 on Tues.); students with ID and children $3; free to all Mon. Phone (804) 358-4901.

VIRGINIA HOLOCAUST MUSEUM is in Shockoe Bottom at 2000 E. Cary St. The museum contains memorabilia, archives, audiovisual presentations and re-creations of scenes related to the Holocaust. A special exhibit is dedicated to the Ipps family, who fled from the Kovno Ghetto in Lithuania and survived in an underground bunker for 9 months. Visitors can climb into a model of the 9-by-12-foot hiding place, which sheltered 13 people. Allow 1 hour minimum. Mon.-Fri. 9-5, Sat.-Sun. 11-5; closed Jan. 1, Thanksgiving, Dec. 25 and Jewish holidays. Donations. Not recommended for children under 9. Phone (804) 257-5400.

VIRGINIA HOUSE, AN AMERICAN COUNTRY PLACE is at 4301 Sulgrave Rd. This American adaptation of an English country estate was home to U.S. ambassador Alexander Weddell and his wife, Virginia. Reconstructed from a centuries-old English manor, the house is furnished with Elizabethan oak furniture, Flemish tapestries and Spanish Colonial art. Landscape architect Charles Gillette designed the gardens.

Picnicking is permitted. Allow 1 hour minimum. Grounds Mon.-Sat. 10-4, Sun. 12:30-5; closed Jan. 1, July 4, Thanksgiving and Dec. 25. Guided house tours are offered on the hour Fri.-Sat. 10-3, Sun. 1-4, and by appointment. Admission $5; over 59, $4; students with ID and ages 6-18, $3. Combination ticket with Virginia Historical Society $6; over 59, $5; students with ID and children $4. Phone (804) 353-4251.

VIRGINIA MUSEUM OF FINE ARTS is at 200 N. Boulevard. Ancient to contemporary art is represented in collections of paintings, prints, jewelry, decorative arts and sculpture at the museum, one of the largest of its kind in the South. Among the highlights are Fabergé jeweled objects, including five Russian Imperial Easter eggs, and a life-size marble statue dating from the first-century reign of the Roman emperor Caligula.

The museum features fine collections of the art of India, Nepal and Tibet; British sporting art; French impressionist and post-impressionist art; art nouveau; art deco; and furniture. Among artists with works on display are Edgar Degas, Francisco Goya, Claude Monet and John Singer Sargent. **Note:** Some galleries will be closed during 2005 due to museum expansion; phone ahead for updates. Food is available. Wed.-Sun. 11-5; closed Jan. 1, July 4, Thanksgiving and Dec. 25. Donations. Fee charged for special exhibits. Phone (804) 340-1400 or TTY (804) 340-1401.

VIRGINIA STATE CAPITOL is on Capitol Sq. The capitol building was designed by Thomas Jefferson after the Maison Carrée, a Roman temple in Nimes, France. The central part was completed in 1788; the wings were added 1904-06. In the rotunda is the statue of George Washington by Jean Antoine Houdon; it is the only statue for which he posed. Also in the rotunda is the hidden interior dome, seen only from inside the building, and busts of seven other Virginia-born presidents.

In the central part of the capitol are the Old Senate Hall and the Old Hall of the House of Delegates, where the General Assembly held its sessions 1788-1904. In the Old Hall, Aaron Burr was tried for treason in 1807 and Robert E. Lee received his commission as commander of the Virginia forces in 1861.

Note: Public tours of the building's interior are suspended for 2005 because of restoration work. Guided outdoor tours of the Capitol Square grounds and public monuments are offered. Tours are offered on the hour.

Mon.-Fri. 9-5, Sat. 10-4, Sun. hours vary; closed Jan. 1, Thanksgiving and Dec. 25. Last tour begins 1 hour before closing. Free. Street parking is nearby. Parking is permitted in the square when the legislature is not in session. Phone (804) 698-1788.

VIRGINIA WAR MEMORIAL is at the n. end of Robert E. Lee Bridge at 621 S. Belvidere St. (US 1). Virginian casualties of World War II and the Korean, Vietnam and Persian Gulf conflicts are honored here. The memorial contains the names of those who were slain; bronze coffers display war artifacts. Daily 8 a.m.-10 p.m. Free. Phone (804) 786-2050.

WILLIAM BYRD PARK is at the s. end of Boulevard at Idlewood Ave. The park contains the Christopher Columbus Monument, the World War I Memorial with its 56-bell carillon, and Dogwood Dell Amphitheatre. The Festival of Arts, featuring ballets, plays and musical performances, takes place at the amphitheater from mid-June to mid-August. Phone (804) 646-3355.

WILTON HOUSE MUSEUM is at 215 S. Wilton Rd. off Cary St. Built in 1753, Wilton was the home of William Randolph III, cousin to Thomas Jefferson. Before the house was moved in 1934, it stood on the banks of the James River about 7 miles east of Richmond, making it Richmond's only James River plantation home. Portraits of members of the Randolph family and period furnishings fill the spacious rooms.

Tours are given Tues.-Fri. 1-4:30, Sat. 10:30-4:30, Sun. 1:30-4:30, Mar.-Jan.; otherwise by appointment. Closed holidays. Last tour begins 45 minutes before closing. Admission $5, over 62 and students with ID $4, under 6 free. Phone (804) 282-5936.

What To Do

Sightseeing

Bus Tours

Historic Richmond Tours offers guided bus tours with pickup available at most downtown hotels and the visitor center on Robin Hood Road; phone (804) 780-0107.

Walking Tours

Historic Richmond Tours offers guided walking tours of the downtown area on Sunday afternoons April through October. The tour covers such historic areas as the Riverfront, Shockoe Bottom, Church Hill, the Court End, Jackson Ward, Monroe Ward and Richmond's Wall Street; phone (804) 780-0107.

Richmond Discoveries offers guided walking tours of Hollywood Cemetery on the last Sunday of each month March through October. Tours are $7; phone (804) 222-8595.

Visitors can view remnants of the James River and Kanawha Canal that once flowed westward 197 miles to the Allegheny Mountains. Highlights along the 1.5-mile walk, which runs between 7th and 12th streets, include views of Belle Isle, Brown's Island, Tredegar Iron Works, and the James River and Kanawha Tidewater Connection Locks.

Belle Isle, once home to a Civil War prison camp, can be reached by the pedestrian bridge under the Lee Bridge at 7th and Tredegar streets. A 1-mile walking trail allows visitors to walk along the falls and view the historic earthworks. Brown's Island is the former site of the Confederate Laboratory that exploded in 1863, killing some 50 workers.

Visitors can view remnants of the buildings of Tredegar Iron Works, the most important iron works in the South during the Civil War. The armor used for the CSS *Virginia*, formerly the USS *Merrimac*, was manufactured at this plant. Historical markers along the river recall the area's history.

Running along the James River, the Richmond Floodwall is a 1-mile-long concrete levee that varies in height from 7 feet to 30 feet. Self-guiding tour brochures are available for 50c from the Richmond Metropolitan Convention & Visitors Bureau Information Center at 405 N. Third St. Highlights of the walk atop the levee include views of the river where walkers can spot various wildlife, including blue herons, Canada geese and turtles.

Sports and Recreation

Centrally located, Richmond offers a wealth of recreational opportunities. To the west are the Blue Ridge and Shenandoah mountains and the chance for such winter sports as **skiing** and **sledding.** To the east are Chesapeake Bay and the Atlantic Ocean where anglers and water sports enthusiasts alike can revel in the miles of shoreline.

The James River is a great place to lure in smallmouth bass; catfish, bream, largemouth bass and muskie also can be caught. Saltwater **fishing** can be found nearby in the Hampton Roads area and in Chesapeake Bay. For information about fishing licenses contact the Virginia Department of Game and Inland Fisheries; phone (804) 367-1000.

White-water **rafting, kayaking, tubing** and **canoeing** also are available on the James River. White-water canoe trips depart from James River Park, 22nd Street and Riverside Drive. The Richmond Raft Co., 4400 E. Main St., offers guided rafting trips on the James; phone (804) 222-7238. Adventure Challenge offers kayaking and tubing trips; phone (804) 276-7600.

Some 60 parks can be found throughout the greater Richmond area. Some of the activities available at the parks include **tennis, bicycling, hiking,** picnicking, **swimming, boating** and **horseback riding.** For information contact the Department of Parks, Recreation and Community Facilities; phone (804) 780-5733 in Richmond, (804) 748-1623 in Chesterfield County, (804) 501-5100 in Henrico County or (804) 365-4695 in Hanover County.

James River Park, at 22nd Street and Riverside Drive, is a good place to fish or hike. As part of the park, Belle Isle is reached via a footbridge on Tredegar Street or from the parking lot on 22nd Street. The island has walking trails with interpretive signs, a floating fishing pier and the opportunity for kayaking, canoeing, bicycling and **rock climbing.**

Pocahontas State Park, in nearby Chesterfield, offers more than 7,000 acres of outdoor opportunities for **camping,** swimming, hiking, boating and fishing.

More than 20 public and private **golf** courses can be found within the Richmond area. Some of the public and semi-private courses are Birkdale, (804) 739-8800, 8511 Royal Birkdale Dr. in Chesterfield; The Crossings, (804) 261-0000, 800 Virginia Center Pkwy. in Glen Allen; Glenwood, (804) 226-1793, 3100 Creighton Rd.; The Hollows, (804) 798-2949, 14501 Greenwood Church Rd. in Montpelier; Mill Quarter Plantation, (804) 598-4221, 1525 Mill Quarter Rd. in Powhatan; River's Bend, (804) 530-1000, 11700 Hogan's Alley Dr.; and Sycamore Creek, (804) 784-3544, 1991 Manakin Rd. in Manakin-Sabot.

Spectator sports abound in Richmond. **Baseball** fans can cheer on the Richmond Braves, a minor league team of the Atlanta Braves. The Braves play ball from April through September at The Diamond on the Boulevard; phone (804) 359-4444 for ticket information.

Ice hockey fans can be found downtown at the Richmond Coliseum where the Richmond River-Dogs play in the United Hockey League; phone (804) 225-7825 for ticket information.

The Richmond Kickers play **soccer** in the United States Interregional Soccer League at the University of Richmond Stadium at Douglas Avenue and McCloy Street; phone (804) 644-5425 for schedule and tickets.

With four major colleges and universities in the area, Richmond is home to many rivalrous collegiate games. **Basketball** and **football** are popular at the University of Richmond where the Spiders play ball in Robins Center and UR Stadium, respectively; phone (804) 289-8363. The Virginia Commonwealth University Rams play baseball and basketball; phone (804) 828-1726. The Panthers at Virginia Union University play football on campus at Hovey Field and basketball at the Arthur Ashe Center near The Diamond; phone (804) 342-1484. A variety of sports is offered at Randolph-Macon College in Ashland, including basketball, football and both men's and women's soccer, baseball, **lacrosse** and **field hockey;** phone (804) 752-7223.

Richmond is home to the Richmond International Raceway (RIR), which hosts several NASCAR **automobile racing** events throughout the year. Located at the Richmond Raceway Complex, the raceway houses some 105,000 reserved seats; phone (804) 345-7223 for tickets and information.

Shopping

From Americana antiques to trendy boutiques, Richmond offers a wealth of shopping experiences.

For those searching for a taste of the past, Shockoe Slip is a three-block area on Cary Street where cobblestone streets and brick buildings house boutiques, shops and eateries in renovated tobacco buildings and warehouses. This area near the river once was the city's commercial center. Just a few blocks east is another rejuvenated area, Shockoe Bottom. Dating to 1737, the 17th Street Farmers' Market at Main Street is one of the oldest public marketplaces in the country. Local produce is offered during the summer months.

West of Shockoe Slip is the Sixth Street Marketplace, stretching from Grace Street to the Richmond Coliseum. This emporium blends historic buildings and modern specialty shops as well as restaurants and food booths. Another noteworthy shopping area is Carytown, a nine-block area of Cary Street between Nansemond and Boulevard known for its eclectic shops and sidewalk cafes.

Some 45 specialty shops are available on Libbie and Grove Avenues in the West End. Sycamore Square, off Midlothian Turnpike in Chesterfield County, offers Colonial-style buildings housing boutiques and galleries. Numerous antiques shops are located throughout the area, including several downtown off Broad Street.

Area malls include Chesterfield Towne Center, US 60 and Huguenot Road; Cloverleaf, Chippenham Parkway and US 60; Regency Square, Parham and Quioccasin roads; Shops at Willow Lawn, Willow Lawn Drive and Broad Street; Stony Point Fashion Park, off I-95 at Chippenham Pkwy.; and Virginia Center Commons, I-95 and I-295 exit 43C (US 1).

Theater and Concerts

Built upon a rich history, Richmond's cultural scene began in 1786 with the opening of the city's first theater. The Landmark Theater, 6 N. Laurel St., was formerly known as the Mosque because of its resemblance to a Moslem Temple. Built in 1926 by the Shriners, the 3,500-seat theater today offers performances by national touring companies; phone (804) 646-4213. The Carpenter Center for the Performing Arts, in restored 1928 Loew's Theatre, houses such productions as Broadway plays and performances by the Richmond Symphony; phone (804) 225-9000 for ticket and event information.

The Theatre IV building at 114 W. Broad St. originally was founded in 1911 as the Empire Theatre and underwent restoration in the early 1990s. It is now home to a children's theater; phone (804) 344-8040. The historic Barksdale Theatre was founded as Richmond's first dinner theater. The theater is now in The Shops at Willow Lawn and presents classical and contemporary performances; phone (804) 282-2620. Another historic theater, the Byrd Theatre, 2908 W. Cary St., was built in 1928 and offers contemporary movies; phone (804) 353-9911.

Offering five major concerts and several smaller venues, the Richmond Symphony is for classical music lovers; phone (804) 788-1212. The Richmond Philharmonic also presents four concerts a year throughout town; phone (804) 673-7400 for information. Concerts by top-name performers regularly take place at the Richmond Coliseum, 601 E. Leigh St.; phone (804) 780-4956 for event information.

Opera buffs can enjoy several works presented by the Virginia Opera October through March at the Carpenter Center for the Performing Arts; phone (804) 673-7282.

The Richmond Ballet, the commonwealth's only professional troupe, performs year-round and travels throughout Virginia presenting its repertoire of both classical and contemporary works; phone (804) 344-0906.

Special Events

February is a busy month in Richmond with the Camping/RV Show early in the month, the Boat Show mid-month and the Home and Garden Show rounding out February; all three events take place at the Richmond Raceway Complex. The Maymont Flower and Garden Show is held in the middle of the month at the Greater Richmond Convention Center.

The Strawberry Hill Races are held in early April and feature a steeplechase race. Historic Garden Week takes place throughout the state at various times in April. During this special event, special homes and gardens are opened up to the public for viewing.

The Virginia State Horse Shows take place in mid-April, late June and August. In early May Byrd Park is home to Arts in the Park, one of the largest outdoor craft shows on the East Coast.

Mid-July brings the Big Gig music festival held at various locations downtown and the World Gardenfest for Children in Lewis Ginter Botanical Garden.

Confederate sailors, and Marine troops portray life at Fort Darling at the height of the Civil War during the Living History Encampment at Drewry's Bluff in mid-October. In November the Richmond Centre presents the Hand Workshop's Craft and Design Show where more than 200 craftspeople display their wares.

The Richmond Vicinity

ASHLAND (G-9) pop. 6,619, elev. 221′

This turn-of-the-20th-century railroad town originally was developed as a resort for Richmond residents. The village grew and later assumed the name of Henry Clay's Kentucky estate. When the railroad company gave land to the Methodist Church in 1866, the church moved its Randolph-Macon College to Ashland. The town has various Victorian houses.

Ashland Visitor Center: 112 N. Railroad Ave., Ashland, VA 23005; phone (804) 752-6766 or (800) 897-1479.

Self-guiding tours: The information center, located in the 1923 train depot on Railroad Avenue, provides information about self-guiding tours; guided walking tours also are offered.

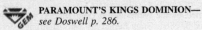 **PARAMOUNT'S KINGS DOMINION—** *see Doswell p. 286.*

SAVE **SCOTCHTOWN** is about 9 mi. n.w. on SR 54, then n. on CR 671 to Scotchtown Rd. Best known as the home of Patrick Henry, Scotchtown was built by Col. Charles Chiswell in 1719 and is one of the state's oldest surviving plantations. The original plan for a grand castle was scaled back after a fever epidemic killed most of the Scottish crew. The manor was the childhood home of Dolley Payne, who married James Madison. Patrick Henry owned the house 1771-78; family belongings are displayed.

Tues.-Sat. 10-4:30, Sun. 1:30-4:30, Apr.-Oct.; Sat. 10-4:30, Sun. 1:30-4:30 in Mar. and Nov. Closed holidays. Admission $7; over 64, $5; ages 6-18, $4. Phone (804) 227-3500.

CHESTERFIELD (F-1) elev. 209′

A number of the earliest land grants to English colonists lay along the south side of the James River and were recorded in Chesterfield's courthouse. During the American Revolution the courthouse served as the headquarters for Baron von Steuben. The importance of this training facility provoked the British—with the aid of Benedict Arnold—to burn the courthouse in 1781.

Nearby off SR 10 (Ironbridge Rd.) is SAVE Henricus Historical Park, the site of the second permanent English settlement in the New World. Built along the James River, Henricus was established by Sir Thomas Dale in 1611 and wiped out by an American Indian attack in 1622. Visitors to the site can view re-enactments of Colonial tasks. A hiking trail with historical markers runs along the river. Phone (804) 706-1340.

SAVE **CHESTERFIELD COUNTY MUSEUM** is on SR 10 in the Courthouse Complex. The history of Chesterfield County is chronicled through a variety of exhibits from prehistoric times into the 20th century. Built as a replica of the 1750 courthouse, the museum displays ancient tools, American Indian artifacts, Civil War items and a 19th-century country store. Next door, visitors can view the original cells of the 1892 Old Jail. Guided tours are available. Allow 30 minutes minimum. Mon.-Fri.

10-4, Sun. 1-4; closed holidays. Combination ticket to the museum and Magnolia Grange $5, senior citizens $3, students with ID $2. Phone (804) 777-9663.

MAGNOLIA GRANGE is on SR 10 across from the Courthouse Complex. The 1822 Federal-style plantation home, furnished in period, boasts distinctive architecture, ornate ceiling medallions and sophisticated carvings on the mantel, doorway and window frames. Guided tours are available. Allow 30 minutes minimum. Mon.-Fri. 10-4, Sun. 1-4; closed holidays. Combination ticket to the grange and Chesterfield County Museum $5, senior citizens $3, students with ID $2. Phone (804) 777-9663.

DOSWELL (G-9) elev. 145′

Originally known as Hanover, the town was the home of James Doswell, a Revolutionary War veteran. His estate, Bullfield, was noted for its winning racehorses. Hanover was renamed in the 1890s in honor of Maj. Thomas Doswell, who returned from the Civil War to open a hotel and continue the family's horse-breeding business.

PARAMOUNT'S KINGS DOMINION is .5 mi. e. off I-95 exit 98 on SR 30. A 300-foot replica of the Eiffel Tower stands at the gates to this 400-acre theme park, which features live shows, thrill and family rides and a water park. KidZville and Nickelodeon Central are areas designed for the younger set. Among a dozen roller-coasters are Shockwave, a stand-up, looping steel coaster; Hypersonic XLC, an air-launched ride that goes from 0 to 80 mph in 1.8 seconds; and Flight of Fear, an indoor coaster that runs in total darkness. Scooby-Doo! and the Haunted Mansion is an interactive, animated ride geared to families. Volcano, The Blast Coaster rockets out of a volcanic crater.

Swimsuits are required at WaterWorks, where the main attractions are Pipeline Peak, purported to be the world's tallest enclosed dark water slide; Big Wave Bay, a 250,000-gallon wave pool; and Surf City Splash House, a family play station.

Park open daily, Memorial Day-Labor Day; Sat.-Sun., late March-day before Memorial Day and first Sat. after Labor Day-late Oct. WaterWorks open early May-Labor Day. Hours of operation vary depending on the season; phone ahead. Admission $44.99; over 54, $38.99; ages 3-6, $29.99. Parking $8. DS, MC, VI. Phone (804) 876-5000.

GLEN ALLEN (A-1) pop. 12,562, elev. 855′

First called Mountain Road Crossing, this settlement on the Chickahominy River became known as Glen Allen for an early resident, Benjamin Allen. In 1713, William Sheppard received a land grant for Meadow Farm, which remained in his family until 1993.

MEADOW FARM MUSEUM is off I-295 Woodman Rd. S. exit 45, then n.w. on Mountain Rd. to Crump Park entrance following signs. In 1860, Dr. and Mrs. John Sheppard and their nine children lived on this farm, now a living-history museum. On some weekends, costumed interpreters demonstrate the family's daily chores in the kitchen, garden, doctor's office, blacksmith forge and barnyard.

An orientation center features exhibits about rural southern life. Nature trails offer a wide variety of activities including bird-watching, fishing and picnicking. Park open daily dawn-dusk. Farmhouse and orientation center open Tues.-Sun. noon-4, Mar.-Nov.; Sat.-Sun. noon-4, rest of year. Closed Thanksgiving and Dec. 22-25. Free. Phone (804) 501-5520.

LAKESIDE (A-1) pop. 11,157, elev. 190′

[SAVE] **LEWIS GINTER BOTANICAL GARDEN** is 1.5 mi. n. of I-95 exit 80 (Lakeside Ave./Hilliard Rd.) at 1800 Lakeside Ave. This 40-acre garden offers year-round beauty with thousands of annuals and perennials. A 63-foot-tall classical domed conservatory houses orchids and changing displays. Outdoor areas include a healing garden, a sunken garden, an Asian garden and an island garden. Children's activities include a hide-and-seek, exploration game.

Historic Bloemendaal House offers displays, hands-on workshops and lectures by gardening experts. Food is available. Daily 9-5; closed Jan. 1, Thanksgiving and Dec. 24-25. Admission $9; over 55, $8; ages 3-12, $5. Phone (804) 262-9887.

RICHMOND NATIONAL BATTLEFIELD PARK (A-2)

Headquartered in Richmond with battlefields in Hanover, Henrico and Chesterfield counties, the park commemorates the struggle for possession of the Confederate capital. Seven Federal attacks on Richmond took place during the Civil War. The park, consisting of 10 units, preserves the sites of the two efforts that came close to success—Gen. George McClellan's Peninsula Campaign of 1862 and Gen. Ulysses S. Grant's Overland Campaign in 1864. Completely touring the park involves a 60-mile drive.

Of McClellan's campaign, the park includes the sites of the important Seven Days' Battles at Beaver Dam Creek, Watt House (Gaines' Mill) and Malvern Hill. Near Glendale National Cemetery is the site of another battle. Grant's campaign is represented by the battlefield at Cold Harbor, where on June 3, 1864, Grant hurled his army at strongly fortified Confederate positions, resulting in nearly 5,000 casualties. That September, Grant also made several more attacks across the James River on Confederates at Fort Harrison and New Market Heights.

Several Confederate strongholds, including Fort Harrison and Drewry's Bluff (Fort Darling), and Union-built Fort Brady are in the park. Living-history programs are presented in summer. The park's units are open daily dawn-dusk; closed Jan. 1, Thanksgiving and Dec. 25. Free. Phone (804) 226-1981.

CHIMBORAZO MEDICAL MUSEUM is at 3215 E. Broad St. The massive Chimborazo Hospital, built in 1861, treated more than 76,000 Confederate patients during the Civil War. The 40-acre hilltop site was said to be named by a Richmond traveler for a volcano in Ecuador. An exhibit and film tell the story of hospital life. Daily 9-5; closed Jan. 1, Thanksgiving and Dec. 25. Phone (804) 226-1981.

CIVIL WAR VISITOR CENTER AT TREDEGAR IRON WORKS is at 470 Tredegar St. The main visitor center to Richmond National Battlefield Park contains three floors of audiovisual presentations and exhibits about Richmond's role in the Civil War. Park maps are offered at the center, which is the beginning point for a self-guiding driving tour of Seven Days' Battles sites. Daily 9-5, closed Jan. 1, Thanksgiving and Dec. 25. Free. Phone (804) 771-2145.

COLD HARBOR BATTLEFIELD VISITOR CENTER is 5 mi. s.e. of Mechanicsville on SR 156. The center has exhibits about the 1864 battle and an electronic battle map. A one-mile trail starts behind the center. Daily 9-5; closed Jan. 1, Thanksgiving and Dec. 25. Phone (804) 730-5025.

FORT HARRISON VISITOR CENTER is off SR 5 on Battlefield Park Rd. Brochures and exhibits are offered. A walking trail leads through the remains of the fort, which was captured by 2,500 union soldiers on Sept. 29, 1864. Daily 9-5, June-Aug. Trail daily dawn-dusk.

GLENDALE/MALVERN HILL BATTLEFIELDS VISITOR CENTER is on SR 156 at the Glendale National Cemetery on Willis Church Rd. This center features exhibits and an electronic battle map about the Glendale and Malvern Hill battles of the 1862 Seven Days Campaign. Wed.-Sun. 9-5. Phone (804) 795-5017.

SANDSTON (A-2) elev. 165'

[SAVE] **VIRGINIA AVIATION MUSEUM** is at Richmond International Airport, off I-64E exit 197, following signs to 5701 Huntsman Rd. The museum offers a tour through aviation history with planes from World War I to World War II. Included are a late 1920s open cockpit mail plane and a plane belonging to Virginia native Adm. Richard E. Byrd. Other displays include aviation artifacts, flying clothes and equipment. Virginia's Aviation Hall of Fame is in the museum.

Allow 1 hour minimum. Mon.-Sat. 9:30-5, Sun. noon-5; closed Thanksgiving and Dec. 25. Admission $5.50; over 59, $4.50; ages 4-12, $3. MC, VI. Phone (804) 236-3622.

This ends listings for the Richmond Vicinity.
The following page resumes the alphabetical listings
of cities in Virginia.

RICHMOND NATIONAL BATTLEFIELD PARK—*see Richmond p. 286.*

ROANOKE (H-6) pop. 94,911, elev. 940′

Roanoke, the commercial and medical center of southwest Virginia, is rich in history and Virginia tradition. Diverse products manufactured include railroad cars, fabricated steel, electronic components, furniture, plastics, textiles and clothing.

Surrounding lakes, state parks and national forests offer recreational opportunities, including hiking, picnicking and camping along the Appalachian Trail and the Blue Ridge Parkway *(see place listing p. 224)*. Fishing and boating are popular activities at nearby Smith Mountain Lake *(see Recreation Chart)*.

Downtown Roanoke boasts many historic landmarks, including a 1907 fire station, a historic farmers' market and the Tudor-style Hotel Roanoke. The city's farmers' market was first opened in 1882; it still operates Monday through Saturday on the same site, downtown on Market Square. A city landmark, the 100-foot-tall Roanoke Star was erected on top of Mill Mountain in 1949; the star is illuminated each night, and the site offers a scenic overlook of the Roanoke Valley.

Photographs and exhibits at the O. Winston Link Museum, in the restored Norfolk & Western Railway station at 101 Shenandoah Ave., chronicle the final years of railroad steam engines; phone (540) 982-5465.

Roanoke Valley Convention & Visitors Bureau: 101 Shenandoah Ave., Roanoke, VA 24016; phone (540) 342-6025 or (800) 635-5535. *See color ad.*

Self-guiding tours: A downtown visitor center on Market Street offers a visitors guide, which includes a walking tour of downtown Roanoke.

Shopping areas: Valley View Mall, I-581 exit 3E, offers more than 100 stores, including Belk, Hecht's, JCPenney and Sears. Tanglewood Mall on Electric Road is anchored by Belk and JCPenney.

CENTER IN THE SQUARE is off I-581 downtown at One Market Sq. This restored 1914 warehouse is adjacent to Roanoke's historic farmers' market. The center houses seven independent cultural organizations, including Mill Mountain Theatre, a professional theater. Musicals, comedies, dramas and family productions are featured in the theater. Phone (540) 342-5700 for the center, or (540) 342-5740 or (800) 317-6455 for theater information.

Art Museum of Western Virginia is off I-581 downtown at One Market Sq. in Center in the Square. The museum houses a permanent collection of American art and decorative arts from the 19th and 20th centuries. Modern, contemporary and

changing exhibitions also are featured. Art Venture, an interactive gallery and art center, offers visitors a hands-on experience. Guided tours are available. Tues.-Sat. 10-5, Sun. 1-5; closed major holidays. Admission $3, under 12 free. Art Venture $3, family rate $7. (540) 342-5760.

History Museum and Historical Society of Western Virginia is off I-581 downtown at One Market Sq. in Center in the Square. Historical collections pertain to the history of western Virginia. Hands-on exhibits and a display titled Crossroads of History help guests learn about Virginia's past. A research library is available. Rotating exhibits are featured. Tues.-Fri. 10-4, Sat. 10-5, Sun. 1-5. Library open by appointment. Closed holidays. Admission $3; over 60 and ages 6-17, $2. Phone (540) 342-5770.

Science Museum of Western Virginia and Hopkins Planetarium is off I-581 downtown at One Market Sq. in Center in the Square. Interactive exhibits explore the wonders of science. Exhibits are devoted to light, sound, geology, the human body, animals, weather and the Internet. Traveling exhibits also are featured. Hopkins Planetarium presents programs related to stars, planets and galaxies. The museum also offers the MegaDome Theatre, featuring large-screen films.

Tues.-Sat. 10-5, Sun. 1-5; closed major holidays. Exhibits only $8; over 59, $7; ages 3-12, $6. Exhibits and planetarium $10; over 59, $9; ages 3-12, $8. Exhibits, planetarium and MegaDome films $13; over 59, $12; ages 3-12, $7. Prices may vary; phone ahead. Phone (540) 342-5726 or (540) 342-5710.

HARRISON MUSEUM OF AFRICAN AMERICAN CULTURE is off I-581 exit 4W, then 5 blks. s. to 523 Harrison Ave. Housed in Harrison School—the first public high school for African-American students in southwestern Virginia—the museum displays artifacts and memorabilia that preserve and interpret African-American heritage. Changing art exhibits feature local, regional and national artists. Thurs.-Fri. 5-9, Sat. 1-5; closed holidays. Free. Phone (540) 345-4818.

[SAVE] **MILL MOUNTAIN** is off Jefferson St. at Walnut Ave., following signs. Rising about 1,000 feet within the city limits, the mountain is topped by a city park and Mill Mountain Zoological Park. At the crest is the 88-foot-high Roanoke Star, which is illuminated at night. City park open daily 6 a.m.-11 p.m. Free.

MILL MOUNTAIN ZOOLOGICAL PARK is on Walnut Ave. at the top of Mill Mountain. More than 55 species of animals include snow leopards, a Siberian tiger, hawks, red pandas, prairie dogs and reptiles. Several vantage points offer views of the city. ZooChoo train rides are available. Allow 30 minutes minimum. Daily 10-4:30; closed Dec. 25. ZooChoo operates daily Apr.-Dec. (weather permitting). Admission $6.75; over 60, $6.07; ages 3-11, $4.50. ZooChoo rides $2. DS, MC, VI. Phone (540) 343-3241. *See color ad p. 288.*

TO THE RESCUE MUSEUM is off I-581 exit Franklin Rd./Salem, then .5 mi. n. on SR 419 to 4428 Electric Rd. in the Tanglewood Mall. The museum offers a look into national emergency services performed by medical technicians and paramedics. Interactive exhibits include the original "jaws of life" and a 911 display with simulated calls and videotapes of actual rescues. An exhibit featuring pieces of the World Trade Center honors the victims of the 2001 attacks.

The National Emergency Medical Services Memorial is dedicated to rescuers who died in the line of duty. Allow 30 minutes minimum. Tues.-Fri. noon-6, Sat. 10-9; closed major holidays. Admission $2; under 11, $1. Phone (540) 776-0364.

[SAVE] **VIRGINIA MUSEUM OF TRANSPORTATION** is at 303 Norfolk Ave. A historic freight station houses steam, electric and diesel locomotives, railcars and cabooses; a large two-tier, O-gauge model train layout; a model circus; antique carriages, automobiles and trucks; and aviation equipment. The museum collection includes more than 50 pieces of rolling stock. Star Station offers interactive exhibits for children, including helicopter and space module simulators. Mon.-Fri. 11-4, Sat. 10-5, Sun. 1-5; closed some holidays. Admission $7; over 60, $6; ages 3-11, $5. MC, VI. Phone (540) 342-5670. *See color ad p. 288.*

[SAVE] **VIRGINIA'S EXPLORE PARK** is off the Blue Ridge Pkwy. at Milepost 115, then 1.5 mi. e. on Roanoke River Pkwy. The 1,100-acre. living-history environmental and recreational park features a 1671 American Indian village, a 1740s frontier life area and an 1850s area with a farmstead, a blacksmith shop, barns and a one-room schoolhouse. Interpreters in period dress staff the facilities.

Hiking trails, 12 miles of mountain bike trails, and fishing, canoeing and kayaking on the Roanoke River appeal to nature enthusiasts. Food is available. Allow 2 hours minimum. Wed.-Sat. 10-5, Sun. noon-5, first Wed. in May through last Sun. in Oct. Admission $8; over 60, $6; ages 3-11, $4.50. MC, VI. Phone (540) 427-1800 or (800) 842-9163. *See color ad p. 288.*

SALEM (H-6) pop. 24,747

Fort Lewis was built near present-day Salem in 1752 to protect area settlers. The town was chartered in 1802 upon land previously owned by the son of Gen. Andrew Lewis, the fort's namesake. Roanoke College, then a Lutheran men's school, moved to Salem in 1847. After the Civil War, the growing town marketed itself as the "Switzerland of the South." A major blizzard devastated the local economy in 1890.

[SAVE] **DIXIE CAVERNS** is off I-81 exit 132 to 5753 W. Main St. Guided 45-minute tours take visitors through still-growing caverns that go up into the mountain instead of down into the earth. Allow 1 hour minimum. Daily 9:30-6, June-Sept.; 9:30-5, rest of year. Closed Dec. 25. Admission $7.50; ages 5-12, $4.50. AX, DS, MC, VI. Phone (540) 380-2085. *See color ad p. 288.*

THE SALEM MUSEUM is off I-81 exit 140, then .5 mi. e. to 801 E. Main St. The restored Williams-Brown House served as a residence, post office and general store during the Civil War. Built in 1845, the house sits on the Great Wagon Road where stage coaches, pioneers on horseback and Confederate soldiers traveled.

Exhibits include a collection of local American Indian artifacts and displays that trace Salem's history from its early settlement to present day. Guided tours are available. Allow 30 minutes minimum. Tues.-Fri. 10-4, Sat. noon-5. Donations. Phone (540) 389-6760.

SANDSTON—*see Richmond p. 287.*

SCHUYLER (G-8) elev. 400′

It was in Schuyler, in the foothills of the Blue Ridge Mountains, that author Earl Hamner Jr. grew up and recorded his childhood memories in journals that were to be the basis for the popular television show "The Waltons."

WALTON'S MOUNTAIN MUSEUM is on SR 617. The museum is in the Schuyler Elementary School, across the street from the boyhood home of Earl Hamner Jr., creator of "The Waltons." Re-creations of sets include John-Boy's bedroom, the family kitchen and living room and Ike Godsey's store. The Baldwin sisters' "recipe" machine is among show memorabilia on display. A 30-minute audio-visual presentation precedes the guided tour.

Allow 1 hour, 30 minutes minimum. Daily 10-4, first Sat. in March-last Sun. in Nov.; closed Easter, last Sat. in Sept. and Thanksgiving. Admission $5; over 60, $4; ages 6-12, $2. Phone (434) 831-2000 or (888) 266-1981.

SHENANDOAH NATIONAL PARK (F-8)

Elevations in the park range from 600 ft. at the north entrance to 4,050 ft. at the summit of Hawksbill Peak. Refer to AAA maps for additional elevation information.

The park extends approximately 70 miles along the crest of the Blue Ridge Mountains, between Front Royal on the north and Waynesboro on the south. In one of the most beautiful and historic regions of the East, Shenandoah National Park embraces one of the highest and most scenic portions of the Blue Ridge. Shenandoah, an American Indian name, is thought to mean "Daughter of the Stars."

Spur ridges from the mountain crest blend into the rolling land of the Shenandoah Valley on the west and the wooded hills, orchards and fields of the Piedmont on the east. Between these ridges are deep, timbered hollows and cascading streams.

The 4,050-foot Hawksbill Peak and the 4,010-foot Stony Man are among the highest points in northern Virginia. Notable among the passes through the Blue Ridge are Thornton, Swift Run and Rockfish gaps, which form three of the four primary entrances into the park.

The park's 196,149 acres contain hundreds of miles of hiking trails and scenic viewpoints and are home to many species of plant and animal life. The park is a wildlife sanctuary harboring about 50 varieties of mammals, from chipmunks and groundhogs to deer and bears. Some 200 kinds of birds and a number of reptiles have been observed. The only poisonous snakes are rattlesnakes and copperheads, neither of which is encountered often. It is illegal to feed or harm wild animals.

There are nearly 100 species of trees. Most common are the hardwoods, which produce the annual blaze of autumn color; their height of brilliance usually occurs from mid- to late October. About 1,100 species of flowering plants have been identified. Wildflowers typically bloom from May through late fall. Azaleas and mountain laurel are strikingly beautiful in late spring; redbud and dogwood trees also flower at lower elevations in early spring.

General Information and Activities

Shenandoah National Park is open all year although facilities close in winter. Permits for back-country camping are required and are available free of charge at the park headquarters, entrance stations and visitor centers.

Free guided hikes and walks, slide shows and campfire programs are available; schedules are posted on park bulletin boards and published in "The Overlook," a park guide.

Information is available on weekdays at park headquarters, approximately 4 miles west of Thornton Gap on US 211.

The Harry F. Byrd Sr. Visitor Center, at Big Meadows (Milepost 51), has rotating exhibits and shows films about the park. Dickey Ridge Visitor Center (Milepost 4.6) offers an orientation program and exhibits. The Loft Mountain Information Center at Milepost 79.5 offers exhibits and information. The Harry F. Byrd Sr. and Dickey Ridge visitor centers are open daily 9-5, early spring through late fall, with extended hours during summer weekends.

Hiking trails within the park cover more than 500 miles, including a 101-mile section of the Appalachian Trail, the mountain footpath from Maine to Georgia. Among the most popular trails are the Whiteoak Canyon Trail and several shorter trails, including Limberlost, Stony Man and Frazier Discovery. Trail maps are available at park entrance stations, visitor centers and concession units.

One- and 2.5-hour guided horseback rides leave May through October from Skyland.

Free picnic grounds with water, fireplaces, tables and restrooms are found at Dickey Ridge, Elkwallow, Pinnacles, Big Meadows, Lewis Mountain, South River and Loft Mountain. *See Recreation Chart and the AAA Mideastern CampBook.*

ADMISSION to the park is $10 per private vehicle or $5 per person arriving by bicycle, bus, motorcycle or on foot. Permits are good for 7 days. An annual pass is $20.

PETS are permitted in the park only if they are leashed, crated or otherwise restricted at all times. Some trails are closed to pets.

ADDRESS inquiries to the Superintendent, Shenandoah National Park, 3655 US 211E, Luray, VA 22835-9036; phone (540) 999-3500.

Points of Interest

SKYLINE DRIVE runs along the ridgecrest the entire length of the park and can be entered at four points: near Front Royal on US 340; at Thornton Gap between Luray and Sperryville on US 211; at Swift Run Gap between Stanardsville and Elkton on US 33; and at Rockfish Gap between Charlottesville and Waynesboro on US 250/I-64. The speed limit is 35 mph.

The 105-mile drive is one of the most spectacular scenic highways in the East. Parking overlooks offer views of the Piedmont to the east and the Shenandoah Valley to the west. Across the Shenandoah Valley rise Massanutten Mountain and, farther away, the Allegheny Mountains.

Not far from Thornton Gap is a 610-foot tunnel through the solid granodiorite of Marys Rock. The highest point on the road is at the north entrance to Skyland, where the elevation is 3,680 feet. Blue Ridge Parkway *(see place listing p. 224)* extends

469 miles from the southern end of Skyline Drive to Great Smoky Mountains National Park in North Carolina and Tennessee.

An audio tour describing the highlights, features and history of the Skyline Drive is available for $10 at the two northernmost entrance stations, Front Royal and Thornton Gap as well as at concessioners and park visitor centers. Phone (540) 999-3582 to order audio tour.

SMITHFIELD—*see Hampton Roads Area p. 260.*

SPOTSYLVANIA (D-11) pop. 3,833

The Battle of Spotsylvania Court House was fought May 8-21, 1864. The site is preserved as part of Fredericksburg and Spotsylvania National Military Park *(see place listing p. 239).*

In spite of losing about 17,000 men in the Battle of the Wilderness, Gen. Ulysses S. Grant pressed on toward Richmond. On May 8, north of Spotsylvania, the Union Army of the Potomac met Lee's Confederate Army of Northern Virginia. Fighting continued for 2 weeks, resulting in approximately 30,000 casualties; among them was Union general John Sedgwick, who was killed by a sharpshooter.

The fighting reached its zenith May 12 when Union and Confederate armies struggled for 20 hours over a turn in the Confederate logworks known as the Bloody Angle. Though neither side could claim victory, Grant continued toward Richmond.

Spotsylvania County Visitor Center: 4704 Southpoint Pkwy., Fredericksburg, VA 22407; phone (540) 891-8687 or (800) 654-4118.

STAUNTON (F-7) pop. 23,853, elev. 1,382′

One of the oldest cities west of the Blue Ridge Mountains, Staunton (STAN-tun) was settled by John Lewis in 1732. It was named for Lady Rebecca Staunton, the wife of Gov. William Gooch. The town was laid out in 1747, and by 1800 its population had reached 1,000. Staunton's growth was aided by the opening of rail service in 1854 and its proximity to extensive mining operations.

Because it remained largely unscathed during the Civil War, Staunton has one of Virginia's finest collections of 19th-century architecture. Trinity Episcopal Church on Beverley Street was built in 1855 on the site of the building in which the Virginia Assembly took refuge in 1781, after escaping the British. Visitors can view 12 Tiffany stained-glass windows in the church.

In the 1840s Staunton became home to the Augusta Female Seminary and the Virginia Female Institute. Today these schools thrive as Mary Baldwin College and Stuart Hall School, a female boarding school.

Staunton also is noted as the early home of Woodrow Wilson, the most recent of the eight Virginia-born presidents. Free guided walking tours of the historic town depart from the presidential library *(see attraction listing)* on Tuesday, Thursday and Saturday at 10, June through October.

Staunton-Augusta Visitor Center: 1290 Richmond Rd., P.O. Box 810, Staunton, VA 24402; phone (540) 332-3972 or (800) 332-5219. *See color ad.*

Self-guiding tours: Staunton features five National Historic Districts packed with more than 1,000 historic buildings. Walking tour maps of historic Staunton are available from the visitor center.

FRONTIER CULTURE MUSEUM is off I-81 exit 222, then .3 mi. w. on US 250.

The living-history facility features reconstructed working farms of the 17th, 18th and 19th centuries. Costumed interpreters depict life in Germany, Northern Ireland and England. Living-history demonstrations at a reconstructed 19th-century American farm show a rich European influence on Appalachian cultural traditions.

Typical farmhouses from Germany, England and Northern Ireland have been moved and re-assembled at the museum. Many of Virginia's early colonists were representative of the farmers who occupied these historic homes. A short film about the development of the museum project is available. Changing exhibits focus on European and American culture. The self-guiding tour covers five-eighths of a mile.

Allow 2 hours minimum. Daily 9-5, mid-Mar. through Nov. 30; 10-4, rest of year. Closed Jan. 1, Thanksgiving and Dec. 25. Admission $10; over 60, $9.50; ages 6-12, $6. AX, DS, MC, VI. Phone (540) 332-7850.

SHENANDOAH SHAKESPEARE—BLACKFRIARS PLAYHOUSE is at 10 S. Market St. The company presents Elizabethan plays and other works at the Blackfriars Playhouse, modeled after Shakespeare's original indoor theater. In 17th-century tradition the audience closely surrounds the stage and often interacts with the performers. Pre-show lectures and educational programs also are offered. Guided theater tours are available. Allow 1 hour minimum for tours. Evening and matinee performances are presented Wed.-Sun., Sept.-May. Show times vary; phone ahead. Tours are offered Mon.-Fri. at 11 and 2, Sat. at 11, year-round. Tickets $26; over 64 and students with ID $22; under 12, $18. Guided tours $5. AX, MC, VI. Phone (540) 851-1733.

SUNSPOTS STUDIOS is downtown at 202 S. Lewis St. Working artisans at this commercial studio demonstrate the technique of blowing molten glass into handcrafted decorative objects. Allow 1 hour minimum. Mon.-Sat. 9:30-5:30, Sun. 11:30-5. Free. Phone (540) 885-0678.

SAVE **WOODROW WILSON PRESIDENTIAL LIBRARY** is at 18-24 N. Coalter and Frederick sts. Exhibit galleries and archives in a restored 1855 mansion interpret Wilson's legacy as a scholar, university president, politician, statesman and 28th President of the United States. Adjacent to the museum is the Greek Revival house where Wilson was born in 1856. The birthplace home is restored to depict the Wilsons' family life in the Shenandoah Valley before the Civil War. A Victorian garden is on the grounds.

Allow 1 hour minimum. Mon.-Sat. 10-5, Sun. noon-5, Mar.-Oct.; Mon.-Sat. 10-4, Sun. noon-4, rest of year. Closed Jan. 1, Thanksgiving and Dec. 25. Admission $8.25; college students with ID and ages 13-18, $5; ages 6-12, $3. MC, VI. Phone (540) 885-0897 or (888) 496-6376.

STEELES TAVERN (G-7) elev. 1,680'

David Steele settled here in 1781, offering lodging to travelers on the road between Staunton and Lexington. The village that grew up around the tavern would be the birthplace of two revolutionary labor-saving devices, the Gibbs sewing machine and the McCormick reaper.

WALNUT GROVE (McCORMICK'S FARM) is off I-81 exit 205, then about 1 mi. e. on SR 606. Cyrus McCormick and his father perfected and marketed the first mechanical grain reaper here in 1831. Cyrus' smithy, now a museum, contains an original reaper. Daily 8-5, Apr.-Dec.; Mon.-Fri. 8-5, rest of year (weather permitting). Free. Phone (540) 377-2255.

STRASBURG (E-8) pop. 4,017, elev. 637'

German settlers were drawn to the Bavarian-like countryside around Strasburg in the late 1700s. Beginning in the 19th century, pottery-making rose to such prominence that the community was dubbed "Pot Town." By 1908, however, its six potteries had closed. Strasburg's economy is based primarily on printing and the manufacture of automotive parts. The city also is a favorite stop for antique hunters.

Strasburg Chamber of Commerce: 132 W. King St., Strasburg, VA 22657; phone (540) 465-3187. *See color ad p. 888.*

Self-guiding tours: A self-guiding walking tour brochure is available from the chamber of commerce.

Shopping areas: Strasburg Antique Emporium, 150 North Massanutten St., features a multitude of vendors specializing in Civil War memorabilia, furniture, vintage clothing, reproductions and art.

SAVE **CRYSTAL CAVERNS AT HUPP'S HILL** is off I-81 exit 298, then .5 mi. s. on Old Valley Pike (US 11). The caverns, once used by both Shawnee Indians and Civil War soldiers, contain formations such as terraced flowstone. Allow 1 hour, 30 minutes minimum. Daily 10-5; closed Jan. 1, Easter, Thanksgiving and Dec. 24-25 and 31. Tours are given at 11, 12:30, 2 and 3:30. Admission $10; over 64 and ages 7-17, $8. MC, VI. Phone (540) 465-5884.

SAVE **Stonewall Jackson Museum** is off I-81 exit 298, then .5 mi. s. on Old Valley Pike (US 11). This 10-acre site played a role in the 1864 Battle of Hupps Hill and other campaigns. A half-mile walking tour highlights lunettes and trenches built by Gen. Philip Sheridan's troops. Exhibits detail "Stonewall" Jackson's campaign with maps, photographs, original artifacts and hands-on reproductions. Children can dress in Civil War garb while playing in a mock encampment. Daily 10-5, Apr.-Oct.; 10-4, rest of year. Closed Jan. 1, Easter, Thanksgiving and Dec. 24-25 and 31. Admission $5; over 55 and ages 7-17, $4. MC, VI. Phone (540) 465-5884.

THE JEANE DIXON MEMORIAL LIBRARY is at 150 N. Massanutten St. A collection of personal possessions, documents and furnishings depict the life of psychic Jeane Dixon, perhaps best known for her prediction of the 1963 Kennedy assassination. Exhibits illustrate her accomplishments and predictions as well as skeptics' attempts to debunk her work. Allow 1 hour minimum. Fri.-Mon. 10-5, May-Oct. and by appointment. Tours are offered at 10 and 2. Admission $5; over 61, students with ID and ages 6-18, $4. MC, VI. Phone (540) 465-5999.

SAVE **THE MUSEUM OF AMERICAN PRESIDENTS** is off I-81 exit 298, then 2 mi. s.e. on US 11 to 130 N. Massanutten St. Highlights include the desk on which James Madison drafted the Federalist Papers, White House doors, a reproduction of Washington's Rising Sun chair, a variety of handwritten letters of the presidents and presidential portraits. A one-room schoolhouse offers hands-on displays for children. Allow 30 minutes minimum. Fri.-Mon. 10-5, May-Oct. and by appointment. Admission $5; over 61, students with ID and ages 6-18, $4. MC, VI. Phone (540) 465-5999.

STRASBURG MUSEUM is 2 blks. e. of jct. US 11 and E. King St. on SR 55. The town's old railroad station houses a pottery collection, toys, apparel, home implements, farm tools and shop machines that date from the mid-1800s. Settings include Colonial and Victorian rooms and cooper's, potter's and blacksmith's shops. Civil War exhibits also are featured. Daily 10-4, May-Oct. Admission $2; ages 13-18, $1; under 13, 50c. Phone (540) 465-3175.

STERLING — *see District of Columbia p. 131.*

STRATFORD (F-10)

The land for Stratford Hall Plantation was purchased in 1717 by Thomas Lee, president of the

Council of Virginia and acting governor 1749-50. The manor he built overlooking the Potomac River would be home to four generations of the Lee family, including Gen. Robert E. Lee, who was born there in 1807. Thomas' sons, Richard Henry and Francis Lightfoot, were the only brothers to sign the Declaration of Independence. "Light Horse" Harry Lee, Robert E. Lee's father, was a Revolutionary War general.

STRATFORD HALL PLANTATION— BIRTHPLACE OF ROBERT E. LEE is off SR 3 to SR 214, then 1 mi. following signs. Owned by the Lee family 1717-1822, the plantation still is operated in the manner of that era. Visitors can wander more than 1,600 acres of woods, meadows, gardens and cultivated fields. The house, built in 1730 in the shape of an H, is among the finest examples of Colonial architecture in the United States. Original Lee family pieces, including Robert E. Lee's crib, are among the period furnishings. The visitor center offers a museum.

Auxiliary buildings include an 18th-century kitchen and a coach house. A reconstructed mill grinds corn, wheat, oats and barley (weather permitting) on Saturdays, March through October. More than two miles of nature trails crisscross the plantation. Food is available. Grounds daily 9:30-5; closed Jan. 1, Thanksgiving and Dec. 24-25 and 31. House tours are offered 10-4. Admission $9; over 60 and military with ID $8; ages 6-11, $5. Phone (804) 493-8371.

SURRY (B-3) pop. 262

Capt. William Powell obtained a land grant along the Chippokes Creek in 1619. The property passed to Col. Henry Bishop, who expanded the plantation to its present 1,400 acres. It is said the Chippokes mansion survived the Civil War because its owner supplied liquor to both sides.

BACON'S CASTLE is 7 mi. e. on SR 10 following signs. The 1665 house is one of few surviving examples of Jacobean architecture in America. Its Flemish curvilinear gables, triple chimney stacks and cruciform design are architectural features that are virtually extinct. A 17th-century garden is next to the castle. A 13-minute videotape explains the history of the house, which is furnished with 17th- and 18th-century antiques. Guided tours are available. Tues.-Sat. 10-4, Sun. noon-4, Apr.-Oct.; Sat. 10-4, Sun. noon-4 in Mar. and Nov. Admission $7; over 65, $5; ages 6-18, $4. Phone (757) 357-5976.

CHIPPOKES PLANTATION STATE PARK is 1.5 mi. e. via SR 10, then 3 mi. n. on CR 634. A working farm since the early 1600s, this estate on the James River retains a plantation atmosphere. Old mulberry trees, remnants of America's attempt to establish a silk industry, grow throughout the park. An interpretive tour road and hiking and bicycle trails explore the grounds. The Farm and Forestry Museum contains antique farm and forestry equipment that help detail the area's history.

Tours of the 1854 mansion are given Fri.-Mon. 1-5, Memorial Day-Labor Day; Sat.-Sun. 1-5, first weekend in Apr.-day before Memorial Day and day after Labor Day-last weekend in Oct. Museum open Wed.-Sun. and holidays 10-5, Memorial Day-Labor Day; Sat.-Sun. 10-5, first weekend in Apr.-day before Memorial Day and day after Labor Day-last weekend in Oct. Combination pass for mansion and museum $6; ages 6-12, $3. Parking $3 Sat.-Sun. and holidays, Apr.-Oct.; $2 other days. Parking fees vary during events. Phone (757) 294-3625. *See Recreation Chart.*

SMITH'S FORT PLANTATION is across the river from Jamestown on SR 31, about 2 mi. from the ferry. Capt. John Smith built a fort on this site in 1609. The house was built in the 18th century on land that Powhatan gave John Rolfe when Rolfe married Pocahontas. A footpath leads to the original fort site. Tues.-Sat. 10-4, Sun. noon-4, Apr.-Oct.; Sat. 10-4, Sun. noon-4 in Mar. and Nov. Admission $7; over 65, $5; college students with ID and ages 6-18, $4. Phone (757) 294-3872.

SURRY NUCLEAR INFORMATION CENTER is 10 mi. e. on SR 10 to SR 650, then 5 mi. n. Innovative displays and hands-on exhibits illuminate the science behind nuclear-generated electricity. Using muscle power, visitors produce electricity with a bicycle generator; measure radioactivity with a Geiger counter; and learn about nuclear power from uranium mining to electricity generation. Environmental exhibits focus on the James River and area wildlife. Film topics include electrical safety, nuclear technology and the safe storage of nuclear fuel.

Mon.-Fri. 9-4; closed holidays. Free. Phone (757) 357-5410.

TANGIER (G-11) pop. 604

Discovered and named in 1608 by Capt. John Smith, Tangier Island was settled in 1686 by John Crockett and his sons' families. In 1814 it was headquarters of a British fleet that ravaged the Chesapeake Bay. Until recently it had few visitors because of its inaccessibility. Many customs and much of the appearance of an earlier era remain. Natives of the island still speak with a trace of an Elizabethan accent.

Since the 1800s Tangier's fishermen have supplied the Eastern Shore of Maryland with crabs and oysters. Crab farms lie along the island's shore and in open tanks perched on pilings in the harbor, which is crowded with fishing craft and sailboats. Duck hunting, fishing and swimming are permitted.

There are only a few cars and trucks on the island; bicycles and motor scooters are popular means of transportation. The island's two streets are only 8 to 10 feet wide.

Boat trips to the island depart from Onancock *(see place listing p. 270)* and Reedville *(see place listing p. 273)* as well as Crisfield, Md. *(see place listing in Maryland p. 184).* Reservations are required.

TAPPAHANNOCK (G-10) pop. 2,068

In 1680 the General Assembly passed an act for "cohabitation," creating Tappahannock and 15 other towns. The act was vetoed by King Charles II, but later revived under William and Mary. Despite these delays in sanctioning its existence, Tappahannock grew into a prosperous Colonial port and county seat.

Tappahannock-Essex County Chamber of Commerce: P.O. Box 481, Tappahannock, VA 22560; phone (804) 443-5241.

TANGIER ISLAND AND RAPPAHANNOCK RIVER CRUISES depart from US 17 and US 360. An all-day cruise travels up the Rappahannock River to Ingleside Plantation Vineyards *(see Oak Grove p. 270)* for tours and tastings. Trips depart Tues.-Sun. at 10 and return at 4:30, May-Oct. Fare $22; ages 4-12, $11. Fare includes buffet. Reservations are required. Phone (804) 453-2628.

TAZEWELL (H-4) pop. 4,206, elev. 2,372'

Settled in 1799, the village was named for Henry Tazewell, a member of the Virginia House of Burgesses and later a state senator.

HISTORIC CRAB ORCHARD MUSEUM AND PIONEER PARK is 4 mi. w. on US 19/460. Exhibits depict the history of Tazewell County and southwestern Virginia from prehistoric times to the present. Displays include fossils, prehistoric artifacts, a diorama of late Woodland Indians, horse-drawn equipment, and 18th- and 19th-century weapons, tools and furnishings. Within the park is a settlement containing log and stone buildings.

Mon.-Sat. 9-5, Sun. 1-5, Memorial Day-Labor Day; Mon.-Sat. 9-5, rest of year. Closed Jan. 1, Thanksgiving and Dec. 25. Admission $8; over 60, $7; ages 6-11, $4; family rate $22.50. MC, VI. Phone (276) 988-6755.

TRIANGLE— *see District of Columbia p. 132.*

UPPERVILLE (A-10) elev. 537'

TRINITY EPISCOPAL CHURCH is downtown on US 50. Architect H. Page Cross adapted the style of 12th- and 13th-century French country churches for his 1955 design. Most of the stone and wood used in the church was fashioned by local men who made their cutting tools in a forge on the grounds. Of interest are the sculptured ornamentations on the pews, pulpit and columns, and the windows of the nave and choir, which were made in Amsterdam. Daily 9-4. Free. Phone (540) 592-3343.

VIENNA— *see District of Columbia p. 132.*

VIRGINIA BEACH—
see Hampton Roads Area p. 253.

WAYNESBORO (G-7) pop. 19,520

Located in the Shenandoah Valley, Waynesboro was the site of the last major Civil War battle in central Virginia. The area offers visitors a variety of historical and natural attractions as well as many recreational opportunities found along Skyline Drive *(see Shenandoah National Park p. 291)* and the Blue Ridge Parkway *(see place listing p. 224).*

 P. BUCKLEY MOSS MUSEUM is off I-64 exit 94, then .25 mi. s. on US 340 to 150 P. Buckley Moss Dr. The works of local artist P. Buckley Moss are housed in a building that resembles a 19th-century valley home. The subjects of Moss' works include Shenandoah Valley scenery and the Amish and Mennonite people of the area. The museum also reflects the artist's devotion to helping those with learning disabilities. Allow 1 hour minimum. Mon.-Sat. 10-6, Sun. 12:30-5:30. Free. Phone (540) 949-6473.

WHITE HALL (F-8) elev. 722'

WINERIES

- **White Hall Vineyards** is 8 mi. w. of US 29 on Barracks/Garth Rd., then 1.5 mi. n. w. to 5282 Sugar Ridge Rd. Wed.-Sun. 11-5, Mar. 2-Dec. 14; closed major holidays. Phone (434) 823-8615.

WHITE MARSH—
see Hampton Roads Area p. 260.

WHITE POST (E-8) elev. 607'

White Post takes its name from the white post erected by surveyor George Washington to mark the route to Lord Thomas Fairfax's wilderness manor, Greenway Court. A white post on SR 277 still points the way to Fairfax's estate, torn down in 1858.

Following his residency at Belvoir with his cousin William Fairfax, Lord Thomas Fairfax moved to White Post in 1748 and built Greenway Court, where he threw lavish parties for his male acquaintances. He lived at Greenway Court until his death at the age of 91. Legend has it that Fairfax, a loyal Tory, took to his bed and died soon after he learned of Gen. Charles Cornwallis' surrender.

WILDERNESS (D-10) elev. 247'

The Wilderness, a region of dense thickets south of the Rapidan River, is where Gen. Ulysses S. Grant opened his 1864 campaign. In the Battle of the Wilderness, beginning on May 5, Grant's troops met Gen. Robert E. Lee's Confederates, and fighting raged for 2 days.

Fierce attacks and counterattacks swept through the Wilderness. The woods caught fire, making an inferno in which many of the wounded perished. By the end of the second day neither side had gained the advantage. On May 7 Grant again started his army toward Richmond, but he met Confederate resistance at Spotsylvania Court House *(see Spotsylvania p. 291).*

The Wilderness is now a part of Fredericksburg and Spotsylvania National Military Park *(see place listing p. 239).*

Williamsburg, Jamestown and Yorktown

Virginia's Historic Triangle

Williamsburg began as Middle Plantation, an outpost of Jamestown, in 1633. It was adjacent to a palisade that the settlers built across the peninsula between the James and York rivers.

Because of its strategic location and the strength of its defenses, Middle Plantation soon became important to the colony. In 1676 rebel Nathaniel Bacon and his followers held a convention here, and a year later the General Assembly met after Bacon burned the statehouse at Jamestown.

When the capital of the colony was removed from Jamestown in 1699, a new planned city was laid out at Middle Plantation named Williamsburg in honor of King William III. For 81 years it was the seat of government and the social and cultural center of Virginia. In 1780 Gov. Thomas Jefferson relocated the capital to Richmond, 50 miles to the west at the fall line of the James River.

CHARLES CITY (B-2) elev. 45′

Charles City County, established in 1616, is wedged in between the James and Chickahominy Rivers. From its very beginning the area has been tied to America's history. Chief Powhatan and his daughter Pocahontas were early residents; they were followed by Benjamin Harrison, presidents William Henry Harrison and John Tyler, and Robert E. Lee. Their tobacco farms and plantations lined the James River, on or just off scenic SR 5, near the Colonial capitals of Williamsburg and Jamestown and convenient to the later capital, Richmond.

Westover, one of the several plantation homes, was built about 1730 by Richmond founder William Byrd II.

Water Country USA / Williamsburg CVB

Colonial National Historical Park / © Jeff Greenberg/Alamy Images

Visitors can view the grounds where tulip poplars and gardens overlook the James River.

SAVE **BERKELEY PLANTATION** is 6.5 mi. w. on SR 5, then 1 mi. s. to 12602 Harrison Landing Rd. The 1726 Georgian mansion is the birthplace of both Benjamin Harrison V, a signer of the Declaration of Independence, and William Henry Harrison, ninth U.S. president. "Taps" was composed here while Gen. George McClellan used Berkeley as a Civil War headquarters. The grounds feature five terraces that contain restored boxwood and flower gardens along the James River. Costumed guides lead tours.

Daily 9-5; closed Thanksgiving and Dec. 25. Admission $10.50; ages 13-16, $7; ages 6-12, $5.50. MC, VI. Phone (804) 829-6018 or (888) 466-6018.

EDGEWOOD PLANTATION is on SR 5 at 4800 John Tyler Memorial Hwy. The restored 7,000-square-foot Gothic mansion, built by Spenser Rowland in 1849, features a freestanding, winding, three-story staircase as well as 10 fireplaces. Guided tours take in 11 rooms containing antique furnishings, Victorian memorabilia and period clothing. Two gazebos, formal gardens, slave quarters and a 1725 gristmill are on the grounds.

Daily 11-3; closed major holidays. Admission $9; ages 7-10, $4. Victorian Christmas (Nov. 10-Dec. 31) $10; ages 7-10, $5. A grounds and gardens combination ticket with North Bend Plantation, Piney Grove at Southall's Plantation and Westover is available. Phone (804) 829-2962.

NORTH BEND PLANTATION is 1 mi. e. on SR 5, then 1 mi. s. on CR 619 to 12200 Weyanoke Rd. The 1819 Greek Revival-style house was built by John Minge for his wife Sarah Harrison, sister of William Henry Harrison. Other original buildings on the grounds include a dairy barn and a smokehouse. House tours are available by appointment. Grounds daily 9-5. Grounds $3; ages 8-18, $1. A grounds and gardens combination ticket with Edgewood, Piney Grove at Southall's Plantation and Westover is available. Phone (804) 829-5176.

SAVE **PINEY GROVE AT SOUTHALL'S PLANTATION** is .1 mi. e. on SR 5, then 6 mi. n. on CR 615 to 16920 Southall Plantation Ln. A collection of buildings that exemplify regional architectural styles includes Piney Grove, a late 18th-century log house built on site by Furneau Southall. Among the structures moved to the grounds are a modest 1835 plantation house and an 1857 post-and-beam residence. Gardens and a nature trail also are on the property. Allow 30 minutes minimum. Grounds are open for self-guiding tours daily 9-5. Admission $3. A combination ticket with Edgewood, North Bend Plantation and Westover is available. Phone (804) 829-2480.

(continued on p. 300)

Destination Williamsburg Jamestown & Yorktown

*V*isiting this historic area is like taking a refresher course in American History 101. Places and faces here have popped right off the pages of textbooks.

*S*tudy the 17th-century site of the first Thanksgiving and see its faithful re-creation, Jamestown Settlement. Talk with colonists in 18th-century Colonial Williamsburg. But don't dwell on the past—20th-century theme parks also are memory makers.

© Gibson Stock Photography

College of William and Mary, Williamsburg. Thomas Jefferson, James Monroe and John Tyler are among the alumni of this second oldest U.S. college. (See listing page 306)

Water Country USA, Williamsburg. Grab an inner tube and get ready to slip and slide your way through the park. (See listing page 308)

Williamsburg Area CVB

Williamsburg Area CVB

Shirley Plantation, Charles City. The original 18th-century architectural features on the main floor include hand-carved woodwork. (See listing page 300)

Williamsburg Area

Croaker

See Area map page 299

17

To Charles City

5

Williamsburg

64

Yorktown

105

Jamestown

17

Virginia Tourism Corporation

Yorktown Battlefield. Visitors can experience a hands-on history lesson on the battlefield grounds. (See listing page 301)

*P*laces included in this AAA Destination Area:

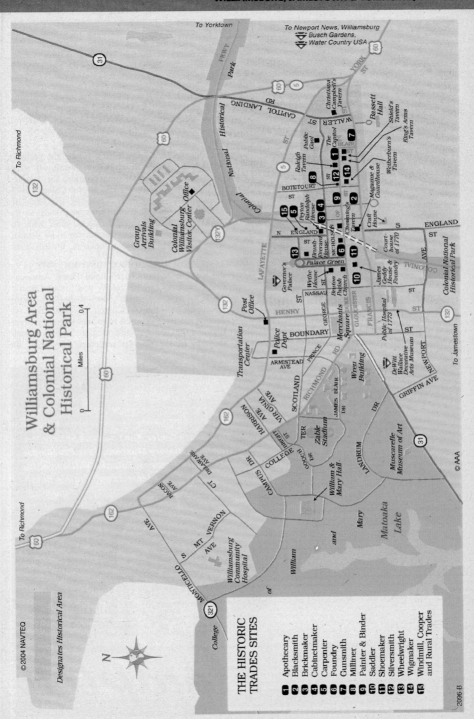

Williamsburg Area & Colonial National Historical Park

© 2004 NAVTEQ

Designates Historical Area

To Richmond

To Richmond

To Yorktown

To Newport News, Williamsburg
Busch Gardens,
Water Country USA

Group Arrivals Building

Colonial Williamsburg Visitor Center

Post Office

Transportation Center

Police Dept

Williamsburg Community Hospital

William and Mary Hall

Zable Stadium

Wren Building

Muscarelle Museum of Art

DeWitt Wallace Decorative Arts Museum

Public Hospital of 1773

Governor's Palace

Palace Green

Wythe House

Bruton Parish Church

Merchants Square

James Geddy House & Foundry

Courthouse of 1770

Magazine & Guardhouse

Craft House

Peyton Randolph House

Raleigh Tavern

Public Gaol

The Capitol

Christiana Campbell's Tavern

Shield's Tavern

King's Arms Tavern

Wetherburn's Tavern

Bassett Hall

Colonial National Historical Park

To Jamestown

Matoaka Lake

THE HISTORIC TRADES SITES

1. Apothecary
2. Blacksmith
3. Brickmaker
4. Cabinetmaker
5. Carpenter
6. Foundry
7. Gunsmith
8. Milliner
9. Painter & Binder
10. Saddler
11. Shoemaker
12. Silversmith
13. Wheelwright
14. Wigmaker
15. Windmill, Cooper and Rural Trades

© AAA

2006-B

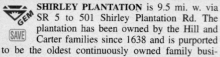

SHIRLEY PLANTATION is 9.5 mi. w. via SR 5 to 501 Shirley Plantation Rd. The plantation has been owned by the Hill and Carter families since 1638 and is purported to be the oldest continuously owned family business in the United States. The present mansion, built in 1723, was the birthplace of Anne Hill Carter and the setting for her marriage to "Light Horse" Harry Lee. In later years their son, Gen. Robert E. Lee, was a frequent visitor.

Family portraits, silver and furniture handed down for 11 generations still grace the mansion, which sits on a bluff of the James River. A carved-walnut staircase rises three stories without visible support and is said to be the only one of its kind in America. The plantation also includes four brick outbuildings set in a Queen Anne-style courtyard. A stable, smokehouse and dovecote are other original structures.

Allow 1 hour minimum. Grounds daily 9-6. House daily 9-5; closed Thanksgiving and Dec. 25. Last tour begins at 4:45. Admission $10.50; over 60, $9.50; ages 6-18, $7; active military with ID free. AX, MC, VI. Phone (804) 829-5121 or (800) 232-1613.

COLONIAL NATIONAL HISTORICAL PARK (B-3)

On the peninsula between the York and James rivers, Colonial National Historical Park covers 9,000 acres. It embraces Jamestown National Historic Site; Yorktown Battlefield; the Colonial Parkway; and the Cape Henry Memorial. Park headquarters is in the Yorktown Visitor Center. Combination Jamestown/Yorktown admission is $10; under 17 free.

COLONIAL PARKWAY links Jamestown, Williamsburg and Yorktown. The speed limit is 45 mph or as posted; there are no service facilities. Yorktown also can be reached from Williamsburg via SR 143 and SR 238.

From the Jamestown Visitor Center the parkway follows the James River before turning inland to Williamsburg, where it tunnels under the restored city. Just beyond the tunnel is the Colonial Williamsburg Visitor Center. Traveling overland, the parkway passes plantation sites and ends at the Yorktown Visitor Center. Turnouts, most with explanatory markers, permit pauses for more detailed observation. The parkway is open at all times. Free.

JAMESTOWN NATIONAL HISTORIC SITE is on the western end of the Colonial Pkwy. America's first permanent English colony was founded here in 1607. Of the settlement's turn-of-the-17th-century structures, only the Old Church Tower survives. Archeologists have exposed ruins and original foundations on the 22.5-acre site, creating an approximate diagram of the original settlement. Some of the

more than 350,000 artifacts excavated are displayed at the 1907 Dale House.

The Jamestown entrance station is open daily 8:30-4:30. Dale House and excavation open site daily 10-4. Closed Jan. 1 and Dec. 25. Admission $8 (good for 7 days), under 16 free. Phone (757) 229-1733.

House of Burgesses Monument is on the western end of the Colonial Pkwy. The names of the members of the first representative legislature in America are listed.

Hunt Shrine is on the western end of the Colonial Pkwy. The Rev. Robert Hunt is credited with celebrating the first recorded Anglican Service in Virginia in 1607.

Jamestown Visitor Center is on the western end of the Colonial Pkwy. An orientation program, models, dioramas, paintings and 17th-century objects portray the story of the Jamestown National Historic Site. Visitors can watch glassblowing demonstrations at the reconstructed glasshouse near the park entrance. Nearby, the original ruins of Jamestown's 1608 glass furnace are all that remain of the colony's dream of a livelihood from glassmaking.

Ranger-led walking tours and an audiotape driving tour are available. Daily 9-5; closed Dec. 25. Admission included with Jamestown National Historic Site. Phone (757) 229-1733.

New Towne is on the western end of the Colonial Pkwy. The site includes numerous 17th-century buildings as well as the ruins of Ambler House and the New Towne section of old James City, which developed during the 1620s. The old streets are open, and sites of former structures are marked along a 1-mile self-guiding walking trail.

Old Church Tower is on the western end of the Colonial Pkwy. at Jamestown National Historic Site. The only surviving ruin of the 17th-century town was the tower of Jamestown's first brick church. Begun in 1639, it was used until about 1750. Memorial tablets mark the foundations of an earlier wooden church, built in 1617, where the first assembly met.

It is estimated that hundreds of burials took place in the church graveyard. A wooden cross was erected in 1957 in memory of those who died during the first years of the settlement.

Statue of John Smith overlooks the James River in Old Towne. Created by William Couper, the statue was erected in 1909.

Statue of Pocahontas is in Old Towne. The work of William Ordway Partridge was erected in 1922 to honor the American Indian princess who befriended the Jamestown settlers.

Tercentenary Monument is on the western end of the Colonial Pkwy. Erected in 1907, the monument commemorated the 300th anniversary of the Jamestown colony's founding.

JAMESTOWN SETTLEMENT—
see Jamestown p. 302.

see Jamestown p. 302.

YORKTOWN BATTLEFIELD is on the eastern end of the Colonial Pkwy. The last major battle of the Revolutionary War was fought here in 1781, when Gen. Charles Cornwallis sought to establish a British naval port at Yorktown with 8,300 soldiers. Gen. George Washington moved his American army into Virginia to reinforce the Marquis de Lafayette's allied forces; the French fleet blockaded Chesapeake Bay. Under siege by 17,600 Continental troops, Cornwallis surrendered.

Two driving tours begin at the visitor center. The tour road is open daily 8-dusk. Admission $5, under 17 free. Phone (757) 898-2410.

The Battlefield Site is on the eastern end of the Colonial Pkwy. Encampment areas and siege works are preserved at the Yorktown site, which includes Moore House, where the terms of surrender were negotiated. Rebuilt fortifications include Fusiliers' Redoubt of the British, Grand French Battery and Redoubt No. 9. British Redoubt No. 10, partially reconstructed, is thought to be where the allied commanders signed the articles of surrender. The positions of the armies during the siege are marked.

Grace Episcopal Church is on the eastern end of the Colonial Pkwy. at Yorktown Battlefield. Built of native marl about 1697, the church was used as a

magazine during the siege of Yorktown. It was burned partially in 1814 but later rebuilt. Communion silver dating from 1649 is still in use. Among the graves in the churchyard is that of Thomas Nelson Jr., a signer of the Declaration of Independence. Daily 9-3. Free. Phone (757) 898-3261.

Moore House is accessible from the Yorktown Battlefield tour route. The commissioners from the combined American and French armies met with British representatives on Oct. 18, 1781, in the house and drafted the terms of Gen. Charles Cornwallis' surrender.

Nelson House is at the s.w. corner of Main and Nelson sts. Built about 1729, the Georgian-style house was owned by Gen. Thomas Nelson Jr., a signer of the Declaration of Independence.

Washington's Headquarters Site is outside town. This stop on the 9-mile Encampment Drive is near other sites including the French Cemetery and the French Artillery Park.

Yorktown Monument To Alliance and Victory is at Main St. The statue commemorates the alliance with France and the victory over the British.

Yorktown Visitor Center is .75 mi. s. of Yorktown on the edge of town, at the e. end of the Colonial Pkwy. The center includes an observation deck, a reconstructed section of a gun deck and a British frigate captain's cabin. A 16-minute film relates the events of the siege. The automobile tours begin at this point; self-guiding tour leaflets and taped tours of the battlefield are available. Audiotape tours are available for purchase. Daily 9-5; closed Dec. 25. Admission included with Yorktown Battlefield. Phone (757) 898-2410.

CROAKER (B-3) elev. 110'

York River State Park *(see Recreation Chart)*, east of Croaker on the York River, is a part of coastal Virginia's system of estuaries. The park's visitor center has displays, videotaped programs and exhibits focusing on the delicate estuarine environment, where freshwater and saltwater meet to create a habitat rich in marine plant and animal life. A parking fee or admission fee is charged. Phone (757) 566-3036.

JAMESTOWN (B-3) elev. 5'

One hundred and four Englishmen endured a 4-month sea passage to reach the shores of Virginia in 1607. Sponsored by the Virginia Co. of London, Jamestown was to be England's first permanent colony in the New World and, it was hoped, a profitable one for its investors. The unfamiliar climate, disease and starvation almost thwarted those plans; less than a third of the settlers survived the first year. When tobacco was introduced as a cash crop around 1613, the colony finally began to prosper.

 JAMESTOWN SETTLEMENT is on SR 31 next to Colonial National Historical Park and Historic Jamestowne. The settlement was established in 1957 to celebrate the 350th anniversary of

Jamestown's founding. A 15-minute introductory film, "Jamestown: The Beginning" is presented in a 250-seat theater. Gallery exhibits trace Jamestown's origins in England and depict the Virginia colony's first century. Also explored is the influence of the European, African and Powhatan Indian cultures that shaped the colony's development.

Three outdoor living history areas—replicas of three ships, a Colonial fort and a Powhatan Indian village—provide a glimpse of life during the early 1600s. A riverfront discovery area explores water transportation and the economic aspects of boat-building, fishing and trading. Special events are celebrated throughout the year, including Thanksgiving weekend's Food and Feasts of Colonial Virginia.

Allow 2 hours minimum. Museum and outdoor exhibits open daily 9-6, June 15-Aug. 15; 9-5, rest of year. Closed Jan. 1 and Dec. 25. Admission $11.75; ages 6-12, $5.75. Combination ticket with Yorktown Victory Center $17; ages 6-12, $8.25. Phone (757) 253-4838 or (888) 593-4682.

Discovery, Godspeed and *Susan Constant* are moored in the James River near the re-created fort. The ships are reproductions of the 17th-century sailing vessels that transported the first settlers to Virginia in 1607. Costumed interpreters discuss the 4-month voyage and 17th-century shipboard life. Admission included with Jamestown Settlement.

James Fort is at Jamestown Settlement. The fort is a re-creation of the three-cornered, palisaded structure that was home to the first Jamestown settlers. Wattle-and-daub structures, including a church, the governor's house, a storehouse and an armory, represent the town's earliest residences and public buildings. Costumed interpreters demonstrate gardening, cooking, carpentry, blacksmithing and military activities. Visitors can try on armor and play games of quoits and ninepins. Admission included with Jamestown Settlement.

Powhatan Indian Village is at Jamestown Settlement. The lifestyle of the 17th-century Powhatan Indians is presented as it was encountered by the English settlers in 1607. The village, which consists of several houses, a garden and a ceremonial dance circle, is based on archeological findings, eyewitness drawings and accounts of the period. Costumed interpreters tend gardens, twist grass into rope, scrape out canoes and make tools. Admission included with Jamestown Settlement.

JAMESTOWN ISLAND EXPLORER departs from 2080 Jamestown Rd. at Jamestown Marina. Narrated, 1-hour nature cruises around Jamestown Island focus on wildlife and history. Sunset cruises lasting 1.5 hours also are offered. Food is available. Nature cruises depart daily at 11, 1, 3 and 5, June 12-Aug. 30; Tues.-Sun. at 11, 1 and 3, Apr.-June and Aug. 31-Oct. 25. Fare $12; over 59, $11; ages 7-15, $6. MC, VI. Phone (757) 259-0400.

WILLIAMSBURG (B-3) pop. 11,998, elev. 78'

"That the future may learn from the past" is the theme for the Colonial Williamsburg Foundation,

FOR AN AUTHENTIC COLONIAL TAVERN EXPERIENCE,

GO TO AN AUTHENTIC COLONIAL WILLIAMSBURG TAVERN.

At these restored taverns, in the heart of the Historic Area, the 18th century is so close you can taste it. Shields Tavern serves up everything from colonial classics to modern favorites, along with healthy doses of wit from Mr. Shields himself. Or choose Christiana Campbell's Tavern, Chowning's Tavern, or King's Arms Tavern. Whether you prefer seafood or steaks, a quiet table or a spirited bar, an authentic colonial experience is always on the menu. Each tavern also offers children's dishes, vegetarian selections and seasonal garden dining. Casual attire is appropriate. All major credit cards are accepted. And dinner reservations are strongly recommended.

Colonial Williamsburg Taverns

WILLIAMSBURG, VIRGINIA   1.800.251.2811   COLONIALWILLIAMSBURG.COM

8/02

Colonial Williamsburg Visitor Center

Northeast of the Governor's Palace, the Colonial Williamsburg Visitor Center is open daily 9-5, mid-June to early Sept.; 9-4, rest of year. Holiday hours may vary. Go to the center first for tickets and information. Streets in the Historic Area are closed to automobiles. Park at the Visitor Center; shuttle buses leave for the historic area every few minutes.

Three general admission passes are available for Colonial Williamsburg. The Colonial Sampler (1-day pass) includes all buildings and museums except Bassett Hall, The Capitol, DeWitt Wallace Museum of Decorative Arts and the Governor's

Digital Archives

Palace. The Key to the City (2-day pass) and Freedom Pass (good for 1 year) include admission to all Colonial Williamsburg exhibition buildings and museums. All passes include the Colonial Williamsburg bus system and an orientation film. The 1-day pass is $33; ages 6-17, $16. The 2-day pass is $45; ages 6-17, $23. The annual pass is $57; ages 6-17, $29.

Note: It is a good idea to verify hours and admission fees in advance.

Further information about Colonial Williamsburg's points of interest can be obtained by writing Colonial Williamsburg Foundation, Fulfillment Department, Box 1776, Williamsburg, VA 23187; phone (800) 447-8679.

which operates this restoration project. Through extensive research, the 301-acre Colonial area of the city has been restored as nearly as possible to its 18th-century appearance.

Within this historic area are 88 buildings that survived from the 1700s. In addition, more than 400 others have been faithfully rebuilt on their original sites.

Stately public buildings and a variety of Colonial homes, shops, taverns and gardens are on or just off historic Duke of Gloucester Street, the main thoroughfare of the city. Busy modern shops are clustered in Merchants Square at the west end, near the College of William and Mary.

Interpreters dressed in 18th-century attire populate the historic area. Fife and drum parades take place April through October.

Williamsburg Area Convention and Visitors Bureau: 421 N. Boundary, P.O. Box 3585, Williamsburg, VA 23187; phone (757) 253-0192 or (800) 368-6511.

Shopping areas: Merchants Square, on Gloucester Street near the College of William and Mary, is a downtown specialty shopping hub. It includes four Colonial Williamsburg stores including Craft House, which features antique-reproduction furniture and decorative accessories.

Bargain hunters find more than 90 upscale retailers, including Coach, Eddie Bauer, Jones New York and Nautica, at the Prime Outlets at Williamsburg on Richmond Road. The Williamsburg Outlet Mall, also on Richmond Road, offers more than 40 discount stores including Bass, Dockers and Farberware.

Some 400 antique vendors display their wares at the Williamsburg Antique Mall on Lightfoot Road. Handcrafted colonial-style candles are available at the Williamsburg Candle Factory on US 60W; and the Williamsburg Pottery Factory, 5 miles west on US 60, offers woven baskets, brass pieces, china and crystal as well as pottery.

BUSCH GARDENS WILLIAMSBURG, 3 mi. e. on US 60 or off I-64 exit 242A, is a European-themed adventure park with a 17th-century flair, more than 40 thrill rides, shows and a children's adventure area. Nine European hamlets celebrate the cultures of England, Scotland, France, Germany, Italy and Ireland.

The pulse-quickening Apollo's Chariot plummets 825 feet, and the inverted coaster Alpengeist takes "skiers" on a chilling ride at speeds up to 67 mph. Loch Ness Monster, a serpentine ride, has double interlocking loops. The Big Bad Wolf, a free-flight coaster, flies through a Bavarian village.

R.L. Stine's Haunted Lighthouse 4-D is an immersive film experience with visual and multisensory effects. Youngsters will enjoy Dumphrey and his dragon friends in a musical adventure area. Other musical shows include American Jukebox.

Roman Rapids is a white-water raft ride, and Escape from Pompeii, with an erupting Mt. Vesuvius,

BUY & BOUNCE.

With a two- or three-day Bounce Ticket; you can visit Busch Gardens Williamsburg in the morning, Water Country USA in the afternoon, or visit one park for the whole day! Plan your time however you want – *it's all up to you.* The Bounce Ticket allows you unlimited admission to both parks and is valid for the entire 2005 season.

Even better, as an AAA member, you receive special pricing.

Purchase tickets at participating AAA offices or online at aaa.com/buschgardens.

AAA MEMBERS:
Save *Even More* with a
2- or 3-Day
Bounce Ticket

WATER COUNTRY USA   *Busch* GARDENS.

The other side is closer than you think.

WILLIAMSBURG, VA

Coming Spring 2005

results in a wet retreat from the volcano. Jack Hanna's Wild Reserve is an up-close visit with wolves. Ireland is celebrated with strolling entertainers; Irish Thunder, a dance and musical show; and the 3-D action journey of Corkscrew Hill.

Park open daily at 10, early May-Labor Day; closing times vary. Park open at 10, late Mar.-early May and day after Labor Day-late Oct.; days and closing times vary. Phone ahead to confirm schedule. Admission $46.99; ages 3-6, $39.99. Multi-day and combination tickets with Water Country USA are available. Rates may vary; phone ahead. Parking $8-$12. AX, DS, MC, VI. Phone (800) 343-7946. *See color ad p. 305.*

COLLEGE OF WILLIAM AND MARY is at the w. end of Duke of Gloucester St. Harvard is the only U.S. college older than William and Mary. Chartered by King William III and Queen Mary II of England in 1693, the state university numbers among its alumni three presidents—Thomas Jefferson, James Monroe and John Tyler.

Muscarelle Museum of Art is on Jamestown Rd. (SR 31) at College of William and Mary. The museum hosts traveling exhibits and contains a permanent collection of some 4,000 paintings, graphics and sculpture. The collection includes work from American artists such as Milton Avery, Paul Cadmus, Jasper Cropsey, Hans Hofmann, Jacob Lawrence, Georgia O'Keeffe, John Frederick Peto and Henry Ossawa Tanner. Wed. and Sat.-Sun. noon-4, Thurs.-Fri. 10-4:45; closed holidays. Galleries free. Special exhibitions $5, under 12 free. Phone (757) 221-2700.

Wren Building is at the w. end of Duke of Gloucester St. at College of William and Mary. The design of the building, which dates from 1695, has been attributed to English architect Sir Christopher Wren. Although damaged by three fires, the outer walls are still largely original. The chapel, great hall, convocation room and a classroom have been furnished to appear as they probably did in the 18th century. This is said to be the oldest academic building still in use in the United States. Mon.-Fri. 10-5, Sat. 9-5, Sun. noon-5. Free. Phone (757) 221-1540.

COLONIAL WILLIAMSBURG HISTORIC AREA is off I-64 exit 238, following signs. This 301-acre, outdoor living-history museum re-creates the spirit and culture of everyday life in the 18th-century capital of Virginia.

After 1780, when Richmond became Virginia's capital, Williamsburg reverted to the status of a quiet college town. Fearing that many of its historic buildings would be lost, a local minister persuaded John D. Rockefeller Jr. to finance the restoration of the Colonial town. In 1926 the two men embarked on an ambitious project with architects, archeologists and historians to preserve some 70 structures.

Colonial Williamsburg is a step back in time to the 18th century, where costumed interpreters—

tradespeople, housewives, slaves, freemen, governmental officials and soldiers—go about their everyday duties. Many of the buildings can be visited on self-guiding tours, while others are open for guided tours only.

Pets on leashes are permitted in some outdoor areas. Various performances depicting aspects of Colonial life take place daily throughout the historic area. Admission tickets, which are required to enter most buildings and to ride the shuttle, are available at the Visitor Center *(see Visitor Center box)*, the Greenhow Lumber House ticket office on Duke of Gloucester Street and at Merchants Square Information Station.

Bassett Hall is at 522 E. Francis St. This was the Williamsburg home of John D. and Abby Aldrich Rockefeller. The 18th-century house is named for Martha Washington's nephew, Burwell Bassett, who owned it 1800-39. It is furnished to reflect the Rockefellers' lifestyle during the 1930s when they were instrumental in restoring Colonial Williamsburg. A 10-minute videotape presentation precedes a tour of the house and grounds.

Allow 30 minutes minimum. Thurs.-Tues. 9-5. Admission included with Colonial Williamsburg multiple admission tickets (not included with 1-day pass). Reservations are required. Phone (757) 220-7645 or (800) 447-8679.

Bruton Parish Church is at the n.w. corner of Duke of Gloucester St. and the Palace Green. Dr. W.A.R. Goodwin, rector of this church in the early 1900s, approached John D. Rockefeller with the idea of preserving Colonial Williamsburg. The church itself was erected 1712-15 to replace an earlier building and has been restored. The bell in the tower, rung for many important events since 1761, still rings for services. Guided tours are conducted Mon.-Sat. 9-5, Sun. 1-5 (also Thurs. at 8 p.m. during the summer). Candlelight recitals are given Tues. and Sat. at 8 p.m. during the summer. Free. Phone (757) 229-2891.

The Capitol is at the e. end of Duke of Gloucester St. Completed in 1705, the Capitol was destroyed by fire in 1747. Reconstruction lasted until 1753, but this second building also burned. The 1705 Capitol has been rebuilt on its original foundation and furnished in period. Daily 9-5, with extended hours during peak seasons. Holiday hours may vary. Dancing, entertainment and other evening programs take place on a varying schedule. Admission included with Colonial Williamsburg multiple-day tickets (not included with 1-day pass).

Courthouse of 1770 is on Duke of Gloucester St., e. of the Palace Green. Costumed interpreters demonstrate the workings of local 18th-century government and justice, culminating in a re-enactment of a typical courtroom proceeding. A brief background of Colonial law and the building's history also is provided. Tues.-Sun. 9-5, with extended hours during peak seasons. Hours may vary. Admission included with all Colonial Williamsburg tickets.

DeWitt Wallace Decorative Arts Museum is entered through the lobby of the Public Hospital. An underground introductory gallery opens into a two-story atrium and the main galleries. On the second-floor balcony are life-size portraits of King George III and George Washington. Although similar in style, these two paintings present dramatic differences in interpretation, a fact shared by many of the museum's collection of more than 10,000 decorative objects dating 1600-1830.

The different regional renditions and techniques in American furniture, ceramics, metalwork, paintings, textiles, maps and prints become evident as many of these objects stand side by side with their English counterparts. The broad scope of the collection gives a detailed picture of the furnishings and lifestyle of 18th-century Williamsburg. Food is available. Daily 11-6, with extended hours during peak seasons. Admission included with Colonial Williamsburg multiple-day tickets (not included with 1-day pass). Phone (757) 220-7645 or (800) 447-8679.

Governor's Palace faces the Palace Green. The palace was completed in 1722 under the supervision of Gov. Alexander Spotswood. He and six other royal governors resided here until 1775, when the last governor, Lord Dunmore, fled in the face of armed resistance to royal authority in the colony. It then served as the executive mansion for the commonwealth's first two governors, Patrick Henry and Thomas Jefferson, until the capital was moved to Richmond in 1780.

The original building was destroyed by fire a year later while being used as a military hospital for soldiers wounded at Yorktown. The palace is reconstructed and furnished with rare period antiques. Its adjoining dependencies, gardens, courtyard and canal are all open to visitors. Daily 9-5, with extended hours during peak seasons. Holiday hours may vary. Admission included with Colonial Williamsburg multiple-day tickets (not included with 1-day pass).

The Historic Trades Sites are throughout Colonial Williamsburg. The arts, trades and crafts of the old town are revived by costumed tradespeople who explain and skillfully demonstrate 200-year-old methods of the apothecary, basketmaker, blacksmith, brickmaker, cabinetmaker, carpenter, cooper, founder, gunsmith, miller, milliner, printer and binder, saddler and harnessmaker, shoemaker, silversmith, weaver, wheelwright and wigmaker.

Hours vary seasonally. Some trades are demonstrated outdoors (weather permitting). Admission is included with all Colonial Williamsburg tickets.

James Geddy House and Foundry is at Duke of Gloucester St. and the Palace Green. The house was built in the 1760s. James Geddy Jr. operated a silversmith business here; a foundry and 18th-century furnishings can be seen. Fri.-Wed. 9-5. Hours may vary.

Magazine and Guardhouse is on Market Square. The storehouse for arms and ammunition was built in 1715. The magazine displays firearms and military artifacts. Daily 9-5. Hours may vary.

Peyton Randolph House faces Market Square. The home of the president of the First and Second Continental Congresses was a gathering place for leaders of the Virginia colony. A bedroom paneled in oak is the only known room of its kind in the area. Thurs.-Mon. 9-5. Hours may vary.

Public Gaol is at Nicholson St., near the Capitol. This 1704 jail with later additions is completely restored and includes an early form of indoor plumbing and cells for criminals. Daily 9-5. Hours may vary.

Public Hospital of 1773 is on the s.e. corner of Francis and Henry sts. This building was reconstructed on the original site of the Public Hospital for Persons of Insane and Disordered Minds. Opened in 1773, it was the first public institution in the English Colonies devoted solely to the treatment of mental illness. An exhibit on the first floor focuses on the history of the hospital. Other subjects addressed are the underlying reasons for the facility's establishment, its doctors, patients and methods of treatment. Daily 11-6. Hours may vary.

Raleigh Tavern is on Duke of Gloucester St. near the Capitol. Erected before 1742, the tavern became a center of social and political life before the Revolution. George Washington, Thomas Jefferson and Patrick Henry are a few of the patriots who helped make history here. It was in the Apollo Room that students at the College of William and Mary are said to have founded the Phi Beta Kappa Society in 1776. The building was reconstructed after a fire destroyed it in 1859. Tues.-Sun. 9-5. Hours may vary.

Wetherburn's Tavern is on the s. side of Duke of Gloucester St. near the Capitol. George Washington frequently visited this tavern, which figured prominently in the commercial life of Williamsburg and has been in continuous use for more than 200 years. Mon.-Thurs 9-5. Hours may vary.

Wythe House faces Palace Green s. of Prince George St. Built in the mid 18th century, the house was occupied from about 1755 to 1791 by George Wythe, one of the period's most prominent lawyers. He was Thomas Jefferson's and John Marshall's teacher, a signer of the Declaration of Independence and the first law professor in an American college. Thurs.-Tues. 9-5. Hours may vary

HISTORIC AIR TOURS depart from Williamsburg-Jamestown Airport at 102 Marclay Rd. An aerial perspective of historic sights is available on a choice of narrated air tours—Historic Triangle, James River and Hampton Roads. All tours include Williamsburg and Jamestown Island.

Flights range from 35 minutes to 1 hour. Departures require a minimum of two passengers. Departures daily 9-dusk. Fares $45-$60. Reservations are recommended. MC, VI. Phone (757) 229-7330.

 **JAMESTOWN SETTLEMENT—** *see Jamestown p. 302.*

THE ORIGINAL GHOSTS OF WILLIAMSBURG CANDLELIGHT TOUR departs from Barnes & Noble on Duke of Gloucester St. Guided tours explore the streets of Williamsburg by lantern. Based on the works of author L.B. Taylor Jr., the narrative incorporates folklore and local history. Allow 1 hour, 30 minutes minimum. Tours depart nightly at 8 (also at 8:45, June-Aug.); closed major holidays. Fee $9, under 7 free. Tickets are sold at the Williamsburg Attraction Center at Prime Outlets Mall on US 60W. Reservations are required. AX, DS, MC, VI. Phone (757) 253-1058 or (877) 624-4678.

PRESIDENTS PARK is off I-64 exit 242B at 211 Water Country Pkwy. This is an outdoor sculpture garden and museum with 16- to 18-foot-tall monuments of the American presidents, each with color-coded signs that contain biographical information, events and accomplishments. Another exhibit chronicles 14 defining moments in American history such as the Revolution, the Civil War, World Wars I and II, the civil rights movement and space exploration. Guided tours are available. Food is available. Allow 1 hour minimum. Daily 9-9, Apr.-Aug.; daily 10-6, rest of year. Closed Jan. 1 and Dec. 25. Admission $9.75; over 54, $8.75; ages 6-17, $6.50. Guided tours $2. AX, DS, MC, VI. Phone (757) 259-1121 or (800) 588-4327. *See color ad.*

WATER COUNTRY USA is 3 mi. w. off I-64 exit 242B on SR 199. This 320-acre water park features more than 35 water rides and slides as well as live entertainment. The park blends high-tech thrills, water elements and an interactive children's play area with a 1950s and 1960s surf theme.

Hubba Hubba Highway is a free-floating interactive river ride where coconuts, cactus and geysers provide a drenching experience. Meltdown provides a high-speed toboggan race down a flume full of twists, turns and banks.

Visitors can dare the darkness at Malibu Pipeline; experience Aquazoid, a special-effect family white-water rafting ride; dive down five stories of white water at Big Daddy Falls; and plunge downward into a hydrochute on Lemon Drop. Peppermint Twist features a tangle of tubes, while Nitro Racer's super-speed slide stirs up the water.

Other rides include Jet Scream; Rampage; Surfer's Bay, a wave pool; H2O UFO; Cow-A-Bunga; and Kids' Kingdom/Adventure Island. Divers, trampolinists and acrobats perform in the gymnastic and dive show Aquallenium. Entertainment is available at United We Soar, a 20-minute show featuring divers, acrobats and trampoline artists.

Food is available. Park open daily at 10, late May-late Aug.; Sat.-Sun. at 10, early May-late May and early Sept. to mid-Sept. Closing times vary. Schedule may vary; phone ahead. Admission $34.99; ages 3-6, $27.99. Multi-day and combination tickets with Busch Gardens Williamsburg are available. Rates may vary; phone ahead. Parking $8-$12. AX, DS, MC, VI. Phone (800) 343-7946. *See color ad p. 305.*

WINERIES

- **Williamsburg Winery** is off I-64 exit 242A (SR 199), .5 mi. n.w. to Brookwood Ln. following signs to 5800 Wessex Hundred. Mon.-Sat. 10-6, Sun. 11-6, Apr.-Oct.; Mon.-Sat. 10-5, Sun. 11-5, rest of year. Closed Jan. 1, Thanksgiving and Dec. 25. Phone (757) 229-0999.

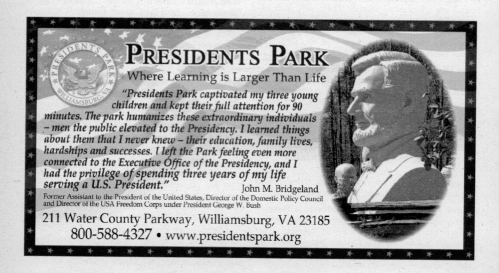

YORKTOWN (B-4) pop. 203, elev. 12'

Yorktown, founded in 1691, was a busy 18th-century tobacco port. The town is best remembered for the Battle of Yorktown, which effectively ended the Revolutionary War. Less than 100 years later, Yorktown was embroiled in another major battle when Union general George McClellan landed his troops at Fort Monroe in 1862 and opened the Peninsular Campaign.

Gen. John Magruder, commanding the Confederate forces, fortified Yorktown and threw a line of trenches from town to the James River. Magruder marched his outnumbered forces back and forth behind the fortifications and convinced McClellan that he was facing a force twice the size of his own.

So convincing was Magruder's charade that the Union forces slowed their advance and began to besiege the town. Rather than having his troops risk being bottled up in Yorktown, Gen. Joseph Johnston, replacing Magruder, moved them toward Williamsburg. The Union forces moved into Yorktown and retained control throughout the rest of the war.

Nine 18th-century buildings survived the 1781 Battle of Yorktown and can still be seen. While most are private, several are open to the public, including Nelson House and Moore House. The restored Somerwell House, at Main and Church streets, was once an 18th-century inn and is now a private residence.

The 1693 Sessions House, the oldest house in Yorktown, was used by Gen. James Negley as headquarters during the Federal occupation. The Sessions and Somerwell houses are closed to the public.

The headquarters and one of the visitor centers for the Colonial National Historical Park (see place listing p. 300) are on the northeast edge of town at the end of the Colonial Parkway. For further information about the park and homes phone (757) 898-3400.

York County Public Information Office: 224 Ballard St., P.O. Box 532, Yorktown, VA 23690-0532; phone (757) 890-3300.

SWAN TAVERN GROUP is at Main and Ballard sts. The original 18th-century buildings—a tavern, kitchen, smokehouse and stable—were destroyed when a Union Army powder magazine in the York County Courthouse across the street exploded in December 1863. These reconstructions are of interest for their exterior appearance.

WATERMEN'S MUSEUM is e. on SR 238 to 309 Water St. Five galleries portray the history of Virginia's watermen, who worked on or with the waters of the Chesapeake Bay and its tributaries. Exhibits include ship models, paintings, dioramas, photographs and tools. Tues.-Sat. 10-4, Sun. 1-4, Apr. 1-Thanksgiving; Sat. 10-4, Sun. 1-4, rest of year. Hours may vary; phone ahead. Admission $4; ages 6-18, $1. Phone (757) 887-2641.

YORK COUNTY COURTHOUSE is at 300 Ballard St. Records date from 1633. Mon.-Fri. 9-5. Free. Phone (757) 890-3350.

YORKTOWN BATTLEFIELD—
see Colonial National Historical Park p. 301.

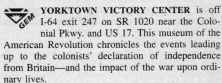 **YORKTOWN VICTORY CENTER** is off I-64 exit 247 on SR 1020 near the Colonial Pkwy. and US 17. This museum of the American Revolution chronicles the events leading up to the colonists' declaration of independence from Britain—and the impact of the war upon ordinary lives.

The Witnesses to Revolution gallery presents the stories of 10 individuals who lived during this turbulent time. Converging on Yorktown describes the multinational nature of forces that met here in 1781. Yorktown's Sunken Fleet reveals the history of the *Betsy* and other British ships scuttled or lost during the siege. Children's Kaleidoscope is a discovery room that provides opportunities for interactive learning and play.

Daily life during the Revolution is re-created in an outdoor Continental Army encampment and a 1780s farm where costumed interpreters fire muskets, tend crops and discuss medical practices of the day.

Allow 2 hours minimum. Daily 9-6, June 15-Aug. 15; 9-5, rest of year. Closed Jan. 1 and Dec. 25. Admission $8.25; ages 6-12, $4. Combination ticket with Jamestown Settlement $17; ages 6-12, $8.25. Phone (757) 253-4838 or (888) 593-4682.

Yorktown Arts Foundation—Galleria on the York is at 7907 George Washington Memorial Hwy. The works of regional artists and craftsmen are featured. Mon.-Sat. 10-5; Sun. noon-4; closed major holidays. Free. Phone (757) 898-3076.

DID YOU KNOW

The Shenandoah Valley town of Winchester changed hands 72 times during the Civil War.

**The previous listings were for Williamsburg, Jamestown and Yorktown.
This page resumes the alphabetical listings of cities in Virginia.**

WINCHESTER (E-8) pop. 23,585, elev. 717'

Established in 1732 by German, Scottish and Irish settlers heading south from Pennsylvania, Winchester played a major part in the French and Indian and Civil wars. It was in Winchester in 1748 that George Washington, in the employ of Lord Thomas Fairfax, began his surveying career. He also built Fort Loudoun and had his headquarters in the town as commander on the Virginia frontier 1755-58. In addition, Washington was elected in Winchester to the Virginia House of Burgesses in 1758 and 1761.

During the Civil War, the town changed hands at least 72 times, including 13 times in a day. The First, Second and Third battles of Winchester occurred in 1862, 1863 and 1864. The Confederate and National cemeteries contain the bodies of 7,500 Union and Confederate soldiers. The 55-acre Mount Hebron Cemetery, E. Boscawen St. in the historic district, includes the Stonewall Confederate Cemetery and two original church cemeteries. Among its monuments is one dedicated to 829 unknown Confederate dead.

An early landlord in the Shenandoah Valley, George Washington required each tenant to plant 4 acres of apples. As a result extensive orchards surround Winchester.

Lower Shenandoah Valley history is preserved in books, manuscripts and archives at the Handley Regional Library, an elaborate 1908 beaux-arts structure at the corner of Braddock and Picadilly streets; phone (540) 662-9041.

Winchester-Frederick County Convention and Visitor Bureau: 1360 S. Pleasant Valley Rd., Winchester, VA 22601; phone (540) 542-1326 or (800) 662-1360.

Self-guiding tours: The visitor bureau, housed in a restored gristmill, has brochures detailing walking and driving tours as well as videotape presentations about the area.

SAVE **ABRAM'S DELIGHT MUSEUM** is 1 blk. n. of US 50 at 1340 S. Pleasant Valley Rd. The oldest house in Winchester, this two-story limestone structure was built in 1754 by an early Quaker, Isaac Hollingsworth. His father, Abraham, had declared the property "a delight to behold." Furnished in period, the house contains a large center hall and an open-hearth kitchen. Furnishings and artwork from the 18th and 19th centuries are exhibited.

Allow 30 minutes minimum. Guided tours Mon.-Sat. 10-4, Sun. noon-4, Apr.-Oct. Admission $5; over 60, $4.50; ages 7-18, $2.50. Combination ticket with George Washington's Office Museum and "Stonewall" Jackson's Headquarters $10; over 60, $9; ages 7-18, $4; family rate $20. Phone (540) 662-6519 or (540) 662-6550.

CHRIST EPISCOPAL CHURCH is at Washington and Boscawen sts. In the courtyard is the tomb of Lord Thomas Fairfax, proprietor of the Northern Neck of Virginia, who lived near Winchester at Greenway Court 1739-82 *(see White Post p. 295)*. The courtyard is open daily 24 hours. Free. Phone (540) 662-5843.

SAVE **GEORGE WASHINGTON'S OFFICE MUSEUM** is s. on US 11 at jct. S. Braddock and W. Cork sts. This small log building served as Washington's office 1755-56 while he built Fort Loudoun. Visitors can see some of Washington's personal effects and related artifacts, including rare surveying instruments.

Mon.-Sat. 10-4, Sun. noon-4, Apr.-Oct. Admission $5; over 60, $4.50; ages 7-18, $2.50; family rate $12. Combination ticket with Abram's Delight Museum and "Stonewall" Jackson's Headquarters $10; over 60, $9; ages 7-18, $4; family rate $20. Phone (540) 662-4412.

GEM SAVE **GLEN BURNIE HISTORIC HOUSE AND GARDENS** is at 801 Amherst St. (SR 50W). The house was built in 1794 by Robert Wood, son of Winchester founder Col. James Wood. It is furnished with 18th- and 19th-century antiques, paintings and decorative objects collected by Julian Wood Glass Jr., the last family descendent to reside at Glen Burnie. The property's 6 acres of manicured grounds include formal Chinese, water, rose, parterre, herb and vegetable gardens with fountains, statues and shady passages made from flowering crab apple trees. A family cemetery also is on the grounds.

Note: In April 2005 the Museum of the Shenandoah will open on the Glen Burnie grounds. Allow 2 hours minimum. Museum Tues.-Sun. 10-4. House and gardens Tues.-Sun. 10-4, Apr.-Oct. Last house tour is 30 minutes before closing. Admission for the house or museum $8; senior citizens and ages 7-18, $6. Combination ticket $12; senior citizens and ages 7-18, $10. Gardens only $6. MC, VI. Phone (540) 662-1473.

SAVE **SHENANDOAH VALLEY DISCOVERY MUSEUM** is at 54 S. Loudon St. Exhibits, which are created for all ages, are based on science, math and art. Highlights include brain teasers, an art room, a take-apart room and a climbing wall. Changing exhibits also are featured. Allow 1 hour minimum. Mon.-Sat. 9-5, Sun. 1-5. Admission $5. Phone (540) 722-2020.

SAVE **"STONEWALL JACKSON'S" HEADQUARTERS** is s. on US 11 at 415 N. Braddock St. The 1854 Gothic Revival house served as Jackson's headquarters from November 1861 to March 1862. The house contains many of Jackson's possessions, prints, pictures and artifacts of the Civil War. Also displayed are items that belonged to topographer Jed Hotchkiss and cavalry general Turner Ashby.

Allow 30 minutes minimum. Mon.-Sat. 10-4, Sun. noon-4, Apr.-Oct.; Fri.-Sat. 10-4, Sun. noon-4, in Mar. and Nov.-Dec. Admission $5; over 60, $4.50; ages 7-18, $2.50. Combination ticket with Abram's Delight Museum and George Washington's Office Museum $10; over 60, $9; ages 7-18, $4; family rate $20. Phone (540) 667-3242.

WINTERGREEN (G-7) elev. 734'

WINERIES

- **Wintergreen Winery** is .5 mi. w. on SR 664 from jct. SR 151. Daily 10-6, Apr.-Oct.; 10-5, rest of year. Closed Jan. 1, Thanksgiving and Dec. 25. Phone (434) 361-2519.

WYTHEVILLE (H-4) pop. 7,804, elev. 2,230'

At the crossroads of early pioneer routes, Wytheville (WITH-vill) was a 19th-century transportation center. The mountain town in the Blue Ridge Highlands later became a summer resort. Wytheville was the site of several Civil War skirmishes, including a July 1863 attack by Union forces under Col. John Toland. The wife of President Woodrow Wilson, Edith Bolling Galt, was born in Wytheville in 1872.

Wytheville Area Convention and Visitors Bureau: 150 E. Monroe St., P.O. Box 533, Wytheville, VA 24382; phone (276) 223-3355.

Self-guiding tours: Pre-Civil War homes and Wytheville's historic district are the highlights of a walking tour brochure available at the visitor center.

NEW RIVER TRAIL/SHOT TOWER STATE PARK is off I-77 exit 24, then 1.5 mi. n. on US 52. A fortress-like tower, built in 1807, was used to make lead shot. The lead was melted and poured through sieves from the top, falling 150 feet into a kettle of water.

Foster Falls, 2 miles from the tower, serves as the headquarters for New River Trail State Park, a 57-mile greenway. The park is popular for hiking, bicycling, fishing, canoeing, picnicking and horseback riding.

State park daily 8 a.m.-10 p.m., Memorial Day-Labor Day; 8-dusk, rest of year. Tower grounds daily 8-dusk, Apr.-Oct. Tower open daily 10-6, May-Sept.; Sat.-Sun. 10-6 in Apr. and Oct. Tower and Foster Falls parking Mon.-Fri. $2, Sat.-Sun. $3. Phone (276) 699-6778. *See Recreation Chart.*

YORKTOWN—*see Williamsburg p. 309.*

Some Things Never Change...
...Some Do

Sweethearts - and licensed drivers - since age 16.

For more than 50 years, Peter and Anna have shared a love for the open road. Now, with more time to travel, they're determined to keep tabs on factors that can affect their driving safety.

Using the easy new *AAA Roadwise Review* program on their home computer, the Johnsons are pairing up to check their skills in areas associated with crash risk in older drivers. Repeating the tests periodically will help pinpoint changes in areas such as visual acuity and flexibility. The self-paced program identifies challenges as well as solutions, making driving safer for everyone.

AAA Roadwise Review is available at local club offices. For more information, visit aaa.com.

LIFELONG
SAFE MOBILITY

West Virginia

Rapidly Flowing Rivers

Rushing waters beckon adventurers to the New, Gauley and Cheat rivers

Pottery, Baskets and Woodcrafts

The arts, crafts and music of the state are synonymous with its mountain culture

Harpers Ferry

Some say the Civil War began here when John Brown made a stand against slavery

The Mountain State

Backpacking, hiking, skiing, biking, fishing—there's plenty to do in West Virginia's mountains

Blazing a Trail

Pioneer forts are testaments to the rigors of frontier life in early settlements

Audra State Park, near Belington
©Michael P. Gadomski

"almost heaven"

Lewisburg / © Andre Jenny/Alamy Images

Rocky peaks receding toward a mist-dimmed horizon. Rivers churned to a froth, rushing through narrow canyons. Waterfalls tumbling down steep hills into secluded alpine valleys. Vast forests ablaze with autumn color. These images only begin to describe West Virginia.

Born during a war that nearly destroyed the nation, the Mountain State has endured a troubled history of Civil War battles, mountaineer feuds and coal mining labor disputes. But thanks to abundant highland beauty, the state has left its past difficulties far behind to become a playground for skiers, whitewater rafters, hikers and anyone else who loves the outdoors.

This is not to say that West Virginians have forgotten their heritage. Descendants

of self-reliant pioneers still craft objects that were once necessities of frontier life. Shops selling quilts, pottery, baskets, woodwork, hand-crafted furniture and other homemade items are easy to find.

What's more, carefully restored sites like Harpers Ferry, Blennerhassett Island and Wheeling's Independence Hall show how seriously the locals take their history. Honoring the past and enjoying the spectacular scenery of the present are clearly a source of mountaineer pride. One visit and you'll understand why.

If you closed your eyes and ran a finger along a 3-D map of West Virginia, one trait would be immediately noticeable: mountains. Like raised bumps in a Braille book, the state's rugged terrain explains a lot about it.

"Mountaineers Are Always Free"

If it weren't for mountains, West Virginia might not exist as a separate state at all. Originally part of Virginia, this remote inland region was settled later and placed very different demands on its inhabitants than the benign coastal plain. This resulted in a rift between the highland pioneers and their wealthier tidewater relatives. By the time the Civil War broke out, the split was so vast that when Virginia seceded from the Union, several western counties seceded from *it*, thus giving birth to West Virginia.

Aptly named, the Mountain State is indeed the most mountainous east of the Mississippi. Blanketed with trees and cut through by swift-flowing streams, the chain of craggy peaks—part of the ancient Appalachians—stretches along West Virginia's entire eastern border. This may once have been the capital of coal country, but today the most used natural resources are above ground. West Virginia's scenic grandeur and recreation

destinations draw hundreds of thousands of tourists each year.

Tops on their list are ski slopes renowned for being some of the best east of the Rockies; names like Timberline, Canaan Valley and Snowshoe come to mind. An ever-growing number of white-water rafters challenge the rapids of the New, Gauley and Cheat rivers.

The thrill of these sports is intensified by the scenery. One sight to behold is the 1,000-foot-deep canyons of the New River Gorge National River, most dazzlingly viewed from the bridge perched above its raging waters. And although no one rafts down the plummeting streams of Blackwater, Hill Creek and Holly River falls, their beauty still draws tourists from all over.

Perhaps the greatest natural assets are stunning mountain vistas like those at Spruce Knob, the highest point in West Virginia. Located in the extensive Monongahela National Forest, this peak is in Spruce Knob-Seneca Rocks National Recreation Area, one of the most popular rock climbing areas in the East.

Scenic Railways and Fall Foliage

Part of a once-extensive railway network for transporting lumber, the Cass Scenic

West Virginia Historical Timeline

Colonial governor William Berkeley sends an expedition to the West Virginia region.
1669

The first permanent settler, Morgan Morgan, moves to Bunker Hill in Berkeley County.
1726

The last battle of the Revolutionary War is fought at Fort Henry in Wheeling.
1782

1742
Coal is discovered in Kanawha County.

© Bettmann/Corbis

1859
John Brown and a small band of abolitionists raid the federal arsenal at Harpers Ferry.

Railroad carries passengers to a viewing area just below lofty Bald Knob for breathtaking views of the surrounding countryside. In fall, the landscape blazes with color as untold millions of leaves change hue. Similarly, West Virginia's many picturesque covered bridges were originally built for practical reasons but are now the focus of the pleasantly impractical endeavor of sightseeing.

Other man-made attractions also are worth seeking out. Victorian historic districts in Parkersburg, Wheeling and Charleston, the state capital, evoke the coal boom era. You'll also want to see the capitol building and its impressive 293-foot-tall golden dome.

And as if West Virginia weren't hilly enough, the Adena culture created artificial hillocks 2,000 years ago near Moundsville as vertical graveyards for the dead. Are you more interested in the future than the past? Tour the National Radio Astronomy Observatory, perched in the mountains near Green Bank. Here astronomers tune in to galactic noise to learn more about the universe.

At the opposite end of the elevation spectrum is West Virginia's lowest point, Harpers Ferry. But the town's biggest claim to fame is abolitionist John Brown's 1859 raid on the federal arsenal. He was defeated after considerable bloodshed and hanged, but the incident inflamed tensions between North and South and brought the nation closer to civil war. Nearby Harpers Ferry National Historical Park preserves the scene of the conflict.

The state's dramatic scenery continues underground thanks to the many caves scattered throughout the highlands. In Greenbrier Valley, Lost World Caverns features huge subterranean rooms and waterfalls up to 235 feet below the surface. And even if you can't tell the difference between a stalagmite and a stalactite you'll still enjoy Smoke Hole Caverns west of Petersburg and Seneca Caverns near Riverton, which have both.

Today bathers in search of therapeutic balm still flock to White Sulphur Springs and Berkeley Springs. The warm, mineral-laden waters bubbling up from these depths were discovered by American colonists more than 200 years ago. You won't want to linger long in the tub, though; a state filled with such spectacular sights just begs to be explored.

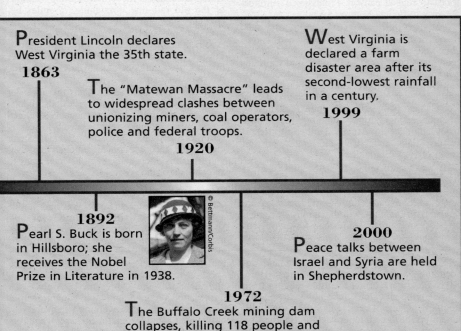

President Lincoln declares West Virginia the 35th state. **1863**

The "Matewan Massacre" leads to widespread clashes between unionizing miners, coal operators, police and federal troops. **1920**

West Virginia is declared a farm disaster area after its second-lowest rainfall in a century. **1999**

1892 Pearl S. Buck is born in Hillsboro; she receives the Nobel Prize in Literature in 1938.

2000 Peace talks between Israel and Syria are held in Shepherdstown.

1972 The Buffalo Creek mining dam collapses, killing 118 people and leaving thousands homeless.

Recreation

Although West Virginia was once isolated from the rest of the country by rugged Appalachians peaks, these same mountains now lure outdoor enthusiasts in droves. For travelers who enjoy alfresco activities—be they with paddles or pedals—the Mountain State is paradise.

Go With the Flow

If **white-water rafting** floats your boat, remember these names: Gauley, Cheat and New. The big three of West Virginia rafting rivers enjoy a world-wide reputation for superior white water. The Gauley River has 100 major rapids on a 28-mile course. Be forewarned: The Upper Gauley is not for the faint of heart. This Class V river challenges even expert river guides. Exciting boulder-strewn rapids also characterize the Cheat River, but because there are no dams controlling its flow, suitable water levels are limited to spring.

Despite its name, the New River is one of the oldest in North America. Here you'll find a full range of white-water rafting options. The Lower New has swirling Class IV and V rapids, while the Upper New features calmer water. Both have plenty of lovely scenery, from lush forest to rugged canyon. Professional outfitters are easy to find at all three rivers.

Another thrilling way to enjoy the outdoors here is **skiing**. The renowned Snowshoe ski area on top of Cheat Mountain features a network of 53 slopes and trails including Cupp Run, with its 1,500-foot vertical drop lasting more than 1.5 miles. On the northern edge of Monongahela National Forest, Canaan Valley Resort State Park has 34 interconnecting slopes running the gamut from beginner to expert. Timberline Resort features Salamander Run, the longest ski trail south of New England.

If you would rather fight the pull of gravity, then **rock climbing** is your sport. Cliffs at New River Gorge near Fayetteville challenge even expert climbers. Those who are unafraid of heights will be amply rewarded after a climb up the sandstone tower of Seneca Rocks; a stunning panorama of North Fork River and its environs awaits.

When you're tired of ascending and descending, **camping** is a great option. Holly River State Park offers facilities ranging from fully equipped cabins to tent sites and RV hookups. Cedar Creek State Park includes amenities designed to appeal to families on vacation. Quaint log cabins and the lovely Glade Creek Grist Mill distinguish Babcock State Park, while Pipestem Resort State Park, located on Bluestone Gorge, attracts campers with its dramatic views.

Avid anglers won't have any trouble finding a spot to cast a lure in West Virginia. Places such as Laura Anderson Lake are stocked with trout and are open for **fishing** year-round. Middle Island Creek, which is more river than creek, teems with large mouth bass and channel catfish. Named after the state's favorite son, Stonewall Jackson Lake occupies the center of the similarly named state park. Catches to brag about here are bass, crappie and walleye.

West Virginians put their lakes to other uses as well. Tygart Lake State Park is great for **boating, swimming** and **water skiing.** The calm waters of Summersville Lake also make it perfect for water skiing.

Happy Trails to You

Many of the railways that carried lumber and coal from West Virginia's highlands have been converted to **hiking, biking** and **horseback riding** trails. The state has more than 300 miles of rails-to-trails paths offering a range of scenic treks. For more information about these, phone (800) 225-5982.

One standout is North Bend Rail Trail, which ascends to the Wolf Summit terminus of the old rail line. Stretching 72 miles between Parkersburg and Wilsonburg, it passes over numerous bridges and through tunnels. Another favorite is scenic Greenbrier River Trail, a narrow strip of state park that passes through two tunnels and follows alongside the river for part of its length.

Hikers can wander along paths that meander past hemlock groves, red spruce woods, moors, bogs and waterfalls in Monongahela National Forest. Trails connect several scenic locales at Camp Creek State Park south of Beckley. Savor the rugged landscape around Smoke Hole Canyon from two loop trails, one of which leads to an overlook of the gorge.

Recreational Activities

Throughout the TourBook, you may notice a Recreational Activities heading with bulleted listings of recreation-oriented establishments listed underneath. Similar operations also may be mentioned in Destination City recreation sections. Since normal AAA inspection criteria cannot be applied, these establishments are presented only for information. Age, height and weight restrictions may apply. Reservations often are recommended and sometimes are required. Addresses and/or phone numbers are provided so visitors can contact the attraction for additional information.

Fast Facts

POPULATION: 1,808,344.

AREA: 24,232 square miles; ranks 41st.

CAPITAL: Charleston.

HIGHEST POINT: 4,861 ft., Spruce Knob.

LOWEST POINT: 240 ft., Potomac River at Harpers Ferry.

TIME ZONE(S): Eastern. DST.

MINIMUM AGE FOR UNRESTRICTED DRIVER'S LICENSE: 17.

SEAT BELT/CHILD RESTRAINT LAWS: Seat belts required for all front-seat occupants and ages 9-18; approved child restraints or seat belt required for ages 4-8; child restraints required for under age 4 or under 40 pounds.

HELMETS FOR MOTORCYCLISTS: Required for driver and passenger.

RADAR DETECTORS: Permitted.

FIREARMS LAWS: Vary by state and/or county. Contact the West Virginia State Police, 725 Jefferson Rd., South Charleston, WV 25309; phone (304) 746-2100.

HOLIDAYS: Jan. 1; Martin Luther King Jr. Day, Jan. (3rd Mon.); Lincoln's Birthday, Feb. 12; Presidents Day, Feb. (3rd Mon.); Memorial Day, May (last Mon.); West Virginia Day, June 20; July 4; Labor Day, Sept. (1st Mon.); Columbus Day, Oct. (2nd Mon.); Veterans Day, Nov. 11; Thanksgiving; Dec. 24-25.

TAXES: West Virginia's statewide sales tax is 6 percent. Cities and counties may impose lodgings taxes of up to 3 percent.

INFORMATION CENTERS: State welcome centers are on US 340 at Harpers Ferry; on I-64 westbound at White Sulphur Springs and eastbound at Huntington; on I-77 north- or southbound at Princeton (exit 9), northbound at Milepost 18 near Princeton, northbound near Mahan, southbound at Beckley and southbound near Mineral Wells; on I-70 westbound near the Pennsylvania state line, close to Valley Grove; on I-79 southbound north of Morgantown; and on I-81 northbound 2 miles north of the Virginia state line near Ridgeway, and southbound 1 mile south of the Maryland state line near Williamsport. Most centers are open daily 9-5, with extended hours during the summer; closed major holidays.

FURTHER INFORMATION FOR VISITORS:

West Virginia Division of Tourism
90 MacCorkle Ave. S.W.
Charleston, WV 25303
(800) 225-5982

RECREATION INFORMATION:

West Virginia Division of Tourism
90 MacCorkle Ave. S.W.
Charleston, WV 25303
(800) 225-5982

FISHING AND HUNTING REGULATIONS:

West Virginia Division of Natural Resources
State Capitol Complex
Charleston, WV 25305
(304) 558-2771

NATIONAL FOREST INFORMATION:

U.S. Forest Service
200 Sycamore St.
Elkins, WV 26241-3962
(304) 636-1800
(877) 444-6777 (reservations)

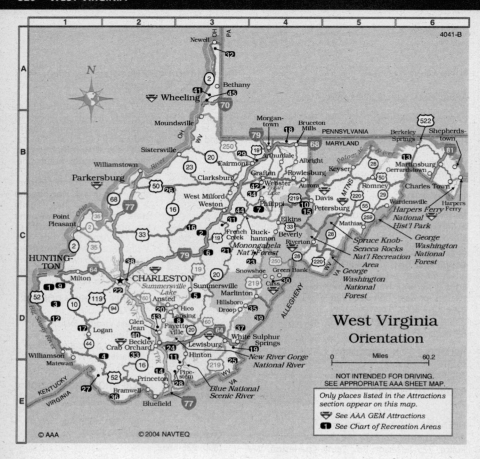

4041-B

West Virginia
Orientation

NOT INTENDED FOR DRIVING.
SEE APPROPRIATE AAA SHEET MAP.

Only places listed in the Attractions
section appear on this map.
See AAA GEM Attractions
See Chart of Recreation Areas

© AAA   © 2004 NAVTEQ

West Virginia Temperature Averages
Maximum / Minimum
From the records of the National Weather Service

	JAN	FEB	MAR	APR	MAY	JUNE	JULY	AUG	SEPT	OCT	NOV	DEC
Charleston	45/28	47/28	55/34	66/44	76/53	82/61	85/64	83/63	79/57	68/46	55/36	46/29
Huntington	47/28	49/29	57/34	69/44	79/53	86/62	88/66	88/65	82/58	71/46	58/36	48/30
Parkersburg	43/26	47/27	53/33	65/43	75/53	83/62	86/65	85/64	79/57	68/46	54/35	44/28

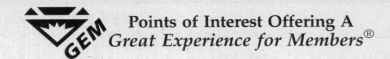

Points of Interest Offering A
Great Experience for Members®

Beckley (D-2)

THEATRE WEST VIR-GINIA—The story of the infamous feud between the Hat-fields and McCoys is the theme of one of the musical produc-  tions presented outdoors in a cliffside amphitheater. See p. 328.

Cass (D-4)

CASS SCENIC RAILROAD—Steam locomotives once used to haul logs now transport passengers past panoramic mountain scenery to the top of 4,800-foot-tall Bald Knob. See p. 332.

Charleston (D-2)

WEST VIRGINIA STATE CAPITOL—A golden dome tops the Mountain State's capitol, designed by renowned architect Cass Gilbert; the building is a landmark along the Kanawha River. See p. 333.

Davis (C-4)

BLACKWATER FALLS STATE PARK—Observation points allow for scenic views of amber water plung-ing 65 feet into a deep gorge; stair-  ways leading to the base of the falls provide a closer look. See p. 333.

Harpers Ferry National Historical Park (C-6)

HARPERS FERRY NATIONAL HISTORICAL PARK—Exhibits and museums in more than two dozen restored 19th-century buildings reflect historical events, including legendary abolitionist John Brown's arsenal raid. See p. 336.

Lewisburg (D-3)

LOST WORLD CAVERNS—Flowstone formations, stalactites and stalagmites are some of the natural wonders to be seen in the cave's 52 F environment. See p. 339.

Parkersburg (C-2)

BLENNERHASSETT ISLAND HISTORICAL STATE PARK—The park is home to a reconstructed Palladian-style mansion originally built in 1798 by aristocrat Harman Blennerhassett, who later fled the island after a treasonous plot with Aaron Burr was revealed. See p. 342.

Petersburg (C-5)

SMOKE HOLE CAVERNS—Legend has it the caverns were formerly used by American Indians to smoke meat and by settlers to make moonshine; today they're explored for their underground beauty. See p. 343.

Riverton (C-5)

SENECA CAVERNS—Cave coral, rimstone and travertine are just a few of the subterranean rock formations in these caverns originally used by the Seneca Indians for ceremonial rituals. See p. 344.

Wheeling (B-3)

OGLEBAY RESORT—Formal gardens, a cascading water fountain, a glass museum and a historic mansion grace the grounds of this 1,650-acre park; golf, tennis, swimming and hiking are among the recreational activities available. See p. 349.

OGLEBAY'S GOOD ZOO—Animals native to North America live in natural habitats at this 30-acre zoo; an 1863 train takes visitors on a 1.5-mile trip through the wildlife park. See p. 349.

RECREATION AREAS

	MAP LOCATION	CAMPING	PICNICKING	HIKING TRAILS	BOATING	BOAT RAMP	BOAT RENTAL	FISHING	SWIMMING	PETS ON LEASH	BICYCLE TRAILS	WINTER SPORTS	VISITOR CENTER	LODGE/CABINS	FOOD SERVICE
NATIONAL FORESTS *(See place listings)*															
Monongahela 909,000 acres in eastern West Virginia.		•	•	•	•	•	•	•	•	•			•	•	
NATIONAL RECREATION AREAS *(See place listings)*															
Spruce Knob-Seneca Rocks (C-4,C-5) Eastern West Virginia.			•	•				•	•	•			•		
NATIONAL RIVERS															
Bluestone National Scenic River (E-3) 4,300 acres on SR 20 s. of Hinton in Bluestone State Park.			•	•	•			•		•	•				
New River Gorge (E-3) 62,000 acres between Fayetteville and Hinton. *(See place listing p. 341)*			•	•				•	•	•			•		
ARMY CORPS OF ENGINEERS															
Beech Fork Lake (D-1) 720 acres about 15 mi. s.e. of Huntington on SR 152.	**1**	•	•	•	•	•	•	•	•	•			•		•
Burnsville Lake (C-3) 970 acres just off I-79 Burnsville exit. Water skiing.	**2**	•	•	•	•	•	•	•	•	•			•		•
East Lynn Lake (D-1) 1,005 acres 10 mi. s. of Wayne on SR 37. Water skiing.	**3**	•	•	•	•	•	•	•	•	•			•		•
R.D. Bailey Lake (E-2) 630 acres 30 mi. e. of Williamson. Water skiing.	**4**	•	•	•	•	•		•	•	•			•		•
Summersville Lake (D-3) 2,798 acres 7 mi. s. of Summersville off US 19 on SR 129. Scuba diving, water skiing.	**5**	•	•		•	•	•	•	•	•			•		•
Sutton Lake (C-3) 1,440 acres 5 mi. n.e. of Sutton. Water skiing.	**6**	•	•	•	•	•	•	•	•	•			•		•
STATE															
Audra (C-4) 355 acres 10 mi. w. of Belington off CR 11. Playground.	**7**	•	•	•					•						•
Babcock (D-3) 4,127 acres 4 mi. s.w. of Clifftop on SR 41. Nature programs. Scenic. Gristmill; horse rental.	**8**	•	•	•				•	•	•		•		•	•
Beech Fork (D-1) 3,981 acres 15 mi. s.e. of Huntington on SR 152. Playground.	**9**	•	•	•	•	•	•	•	•	•			•	•	•
Blackwater Falls (C-4) 1,688 acres about .25 mile s.w. of Davis off SR 32 via signs. Nature programs. Scenic. Cross-country skiing, horse rental. *(See Davis p. 333)*	**10**	•	•	•				•	•	•		•	•	•	•
Bluestone (E-3) 2,155 acres 4 mi. s. of Hinton on SR 20. Water skiing.	**11**	•	•	•	•	•	•	•	•	•				•	•
Cabwaylingo (D-1) 8,123 acres 5 mi. s.e. of Dunlow off SR 152. Hunting.	**12**	•	•	•				•	•					•	
Cacapon Resort (B-6) 6,115 acres 10 mi. s. of Berkeley Springs on US 522. Golf (18-hole); horse rental, playground.	**13**	•	•	•		•	•	•	•			•		•	•
Camp Creek (E-2) 5,897 acres 3 mi. n.w. of Camp Creek.	**14**	•	•	•				•			•				•
Canaan Valley Resort (C-4) 6,015 acres 10 mi. s. of Davis on SR 32. Cross-country and downhill skiing, golf (18-hole); bicycle rental, summer chairlift rides. *(See Davis p. 333)*	**15**	•		•				•	•	•	•	•	•	•	•
Cedar Creek (C-3) 2,443 acres 8 mi. s. of Glenville off US 33.	**16**	•	•	•		•	•	•	•						•
Chief Logan (D-1) 3,303 acres 3 mi. n. of Logan off SR 10. Outdoor drama.	**17**	•	•	•				•	•	•	•				•
Cooper's Rock (B-4) 12,713 acres 8 mi. w. of Bruceton Mills on I-68. *(See Bruceton Mills p. 331)*	**18**	•	•	•				•				•			
Greenbrier (D-4) 5,130 acres 4 mi. s.w. of White Sulphur Springs via US 60 and Harts Run Rd. Nature programs.	**19**	•	•	•					•				•		
Hawks Nest (D-2) 276 acres 1.75 mi. w. on US 60 in Ansted. Historic. Scenic. *(See Ansted p. 326)*	**20**		•	•				•					•	•	•
Holly River (C-3) 8,292 acres 2 mi. n. of Hacker Valley off SR 20.	**21**	•	•	•				•	•					•	•
Kanawha (D-2) 9,302 acres 12 mi. s. of Charleston on Kanawha Forest Dr. Hunting; horse rental.	**22**	•	•	•					•		•				
Kumbrabow (C-4) 9,474 acres 5 mi. w. of Elkwater off US 219. Hunting.	**23**	•	•	•				•						•	

RECREATION AREAS

	MAP LOCATION	CAMPING	PICNICKING	HIKING TRAILS	BOATING	BOAT RAMP	BOAT RENTAL	FISHING	SWIMMING	PETS ON LEASH	BICYCLE TRAILS	WINTER SPORTS	VISITOR CENTER	LODGE/CABINS	FOOD SERVICE
Little Beaver (D-3) 562 acres 10 mi. s.e. of Beckley on I-64 to SR 9, following signs.	24	•	•	•	•			•	•	•					
Moncove Lake (E-3) 896 acres 6 mi. n. of SR 3 on SR 8 near Gap Mills.	25	•	•	•	•			•	•	•					
North Bend (C-2) 1,405 acres 2 mi. e. of Cairo off SR 31. Nature programs. Miniature golf, tennis; bicycle rental.	26	•	•	•	•	•	•	•	•	•	•			•	•
Panther (E-1) 7,810 acres 3 mi. s. of Panther, following signs.	27	•	•	•				•	•						
Pipestem Resort (E-3) 4,023 acres on SR 20. Nature programs. Scenic. Golf (18-hole), tennis; horse rental. *(See Pipestem p. 343)*	28	•	•	•	•		•	•	•			•	•	•	•
Pricketts Fort (B-3) 188 acres about 2.5 mi. w. off I-79 exit 139 n. of Fairmont. *(See Fairmont p. 334)*	29		•	•	•	•		•					•	•	
Seneca (D-4) 11,684 acres 4 mi. s.w. of Dunmore off SR 28.	30	•	•	•	•		•	•			•			•	
Stonewall Jackson Lake (C-3) more than 2,000 acres 2 mi. e. of I-79 near Weston. Golf (18-hole).	31	•	•	•	•	•		•				•	•	•	
Tomlinson Run (A-3) 1,398 acres 2 mi. n. of New Manchester off SR 8. Tent and camping gear rental.	32	•	•	•	•		•	•	•	•					
Twin Falls Resort (E-2) 3,776 acres 8 mi. n.e. of Pineville. Nature programs. Golf (18-hole), tennis.	33	•	•	•				•					•	•	•
Tygart Lake (C-4) 2,134 acres 2 mi. s. of Grafton on CR 44 along e. bank of Tygart River Reservoir. Scuba diving, water skiing.	34	•	•	•	•	•		•	•				•	•	•
Watoga (D-4) 10,100 acres 10 mi. s. of Huntersville (turn at park sign on SR 39, then 10 mi. s.). Nature programs. Horse rental.	35	•	•	•	•		•	•	•			•	•	•	
OTHER															
Berwind Lake (E-2) 18,093 acres 17 mi. s. of Welch off SR 16.	36	•	•	•	•		•	•	•						
Blue Bend (D-3) 4 mi. w. of Alvon off SR 92.	37	•	•	•				•	•	•					
Coonskin Park (D-2) 1,200 acres 5 mi. n. of Charleston on SR 114. Golf, swimming, tennis.	38	•	•	•				•	•	•					
Lake Sherwood (D-4) 11 mi. n.e. of Neola on SR 14.	39	•	•	•	•	•	•	•	•	•					
Lake Stephens (D-2) 2,500 acres 9 mi. w. of Beckley on SR 3.	40	•	•	•				•	•	•					•
Oglebay Resort (A-3) 1,650 acres in Wheeling 5 mi. n.e. on SR 88. Horse rental, zoo. *(See Wheeling p. 349)*	41		•	•	•			•	•	•		•	•	•	•
Pleasants Creek (C-4) 3,373 acres 10 mi. n. of Philippi off US 119/250.	42	•													
Plum Orchard Lake (D-2) 2,953 acres off US 19 between Mount Hope and Oak Hill.	43	•	•	•	•	•	•	•	•						
Pringle Tree (C-4) 4.5 acres 2 mi. n. of Buckhannon off US 119 and SR 20.	44		•		•	•		•		•					
Wheeling Park (B-3) 406 acres in Wheeling 4 mi. e. on US 40 at 1801 National Rd. *(See Wheeling p. 349)*	45		•		•			•	•	•		•	•		•

When You Really Need to Speak Their Language... Let the IDP Speak for You

When traveling overseas, carry an **International Driving Permit...** even if you're not planning to drive. Should you need to communicate with foreign authorities, this recognizable form of identification can help you get on your way more quickly. Valid in over 150 countries, the permit contains information translated into ten languages.

Before you travel the world, travel to any AAA office for your International Driving Permit. Bring your valid U.S. driver's license, $10, and two passport-size photos (also available at AAA offices).

Travel With Someone You Trust®

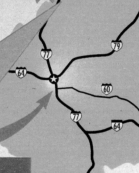

Points of Interest

ALBRIGHT (B-4) pop. 247, elev. 1,291′

RECREATIONAL ACTIVITIES
White-water Rafting

- **Laurel Highlands River Tours** departs from SR 26. Write P.O. Box 107, Ohiopyle, PA 15470. Trips run daily Mar.-June. Phone (724) 329-8531 or (800) 472-3846.

- **Mountain Streams** departs from SR 26. Write 235 Quarry Run Rd., Morgantown, WV 26508. Cheat River trips depart daily, mid-Mar. to mid-June. Cheat Narrows trips depart daily, May-Sept. Big Sandy River and Tygart River trips depart Sat.-Sun., mid-Mar. to mid-May. Phone (304) 594-0333 or (800) 723-8669.

- **White Water Adventures Inc.** departs from SR 26. Write P.O. Box 31, Ohiopyle, PA 15470. Cheat River trips depart daily, mid-Mar. through Oct. 31. Phone (724) 329-8850 or (800) 992-7238.

- **Wilderness Voyageurs Inc.** departs .75 mi. n. on SR 26. Write P.O. Box 97, Ohiopyle, PA 15470. Trips depart daily Mar.-Oct. Phone (304) 329-8336 or (800) 272-4141.

ANSTED (D-2) pop. 1,576, elev. 1,312′

Ansted, originally settled by Baptists in 1790, was named New Haven by a group of New England Spiritualists who came to the town in 1830. The following year it was renamed after British scientist David T. Ansted, who had interested English investors in building coal-mining operations. On a knoll overlooking the town, Westlake Cemetery contains the grave of Julia Neale Jackson, Gen. Thomas "Stonewall" Jackson's mother.

CONTENTMENT is .75 mi. n.w. on US 60. Confederate colonel George Imboden's antebellum home, built in 1830, has been restored. A museum and one-room country schoolhouse are on the grounds. Mon.-Sat. 10-5, Sun. 1-5, June-Sept.; Sun. 1-5:30, in May by appointment. Admission $2; under 12, $1. Phone 304(304) 658-5695.

HAWKS NEST STATE PARK is 1.75 mi. w. on US 60. The 276-acre park is named for a sweeping lookout point above the New River. A rustic museum displays American Indian and pioneer artifacts. Food is available. Park open daily 24 hours. Museum 9-5. Free. Phone (304) 658-5196 or (800) 225-5982. *See Recreation Chart.*

Hawks Nest Canyon Tramway runs from the park lodge to the marina. The aerial tram descends 446 feet to the bottom of the New River Gorge. The tramway operates Tues.-Fri. 11-4:45, Sat.-Sun. 11-6:45, Memorial Day-Labor Day; Sat.-Sun. 11-6:45, May 1-day before Memorial Day and day after Labor Day-Oct. 26. Fare $3; over 59 and ages 5-12, $2. AX, MC, VI.

ARTHURDALE (B-4) elev. 1,780′

The homestead community of Arthurdale was created in 1934 by the federal government. Eleanor Roosevelt guided the New Deal project that helped

displaced coal miners and their families start a new life during the Great Depression. The First Lady was a frequent visitor to the town; her husband made his only presidential graduation address there in 1938.

ARTHURDALE HERITAGE NEW DEAL MUSEUM is at jct. Q and A sts. Unveiled by Eleanor Roosevelt in the 1930s, the 165 buildings of the first New Deal homestead include houses, schools, a health clinic, a community center and a dairy farm. Visitors may tour the administration building museum, a 1935 homestead, a blacksmith's forge, a vintage service station and the historic Center Hall. A self-guiding driving tour brochure is available.

Allow 1 hour minimum. Mon.-Fri. 10-2, Sat. noon-5, Sun. 2-5, May-Oct.; Mon.-Fri. 10-2, rest of year. Guided tours offered daily May-Sept.; by appointment in Oct. Admission $5; over 54, $4; elementary school students $3. AX, DS, MC, VI. Phone (304) 864-3959.

AURORA (C-4) elev. 2,641'

Aurora is in a region where West Virginia's state tree, the sugar maple, is plentiful. American Indians once collected the sap, which runs in early spring, in wooden troughs and heated it with hot stones. The sap, now gathered using metal buckets or networks of plastic tubing that lead to large tanks, is then processed in modern evaporating plants.

Cathedral State Park, 1 mile east on SR 50, comprises 133 acres of virgin timber and offers 5 miles of walking trails, a nature area and picnic facilities. An eastern hemlock tree, more than 500 years old and 121 feet tall, stands in the park. For further information phone (304) 735-3771.

BECKLEY (D-2) pop. 17,254, elev. 2,300'

Beckley is the center of southern West Virginia's smokeless coal region. The bituminous coal mined in this area is a higher grade of coal that produces less smoke when burned.

Beckley is the northern anchor of the Coal Heritage Trail which winds its way past company stores, miners' houses, railroad yards, coal tipples and 500 small company towns on its way south to Bluefield; follow SR 16 southwest to US 52, which heads south and east to Bluefield, the end of the trail. Mile markers along the way indicate points of interest. Another scenic drive runs south along US 19 in Bluestone Canyon.

Southern West Virginia Convention & Visitors Bureau: 200 Main St., Beckley, WV 25801; phone (304) 252-2244 or (800) 847-4898. *See color ad p. 329.*

Shopping areas: Crossroads Mall, at SR 16 and US 19 in north Beckley, houses such stores as Belk, JCPenney and Sears. Raleigh Mall, on SR 16 and US 19, features Elder-Beerman.

BECKLEY EXHIBITION COAL MINE is at 106 Adair St. in New River Park. Veteran miners lead underground tours of a vintage coal mine, providing visitors an opportunity to see how a turn-of-the-20th-century mine operated. A coal mining museum and coal camp homes, schools, a miner's shanty and churches provide a glimpse into life in a typical coal camp. Bring a jacket, as the mine is a constant 58 F.

Picnicking is permitted. Allow 1 hour, 30 minutes minimum. Daily 10-5:30, Apr.-Oct. Admission (includes Youth Museum of Southern West Virginia & Mountain Homestead) $12; over 54, $10.50; ages 4-12, $8.50. MC, VI. Phone (304) 256-1747.

TAMARACK is off I-64/77 exit 45. This showcase for the state's cultural heritage and traditions displays West Virginia-made juried arts, foods and agricultural products. The facility also has nature trails, gardens, a fine arts gallery and a theater. Demonstration areas allow visitors to see artisans at work creating such items as pottery, glass, woodcrafts and quilts. Allow 30 minutes minimum. Daily 8-8, Apr.-Dec.; 8-7, rest of year. Free. Phone (304) 256-6843 or (888) 262-7225. *See color ad p. 329.*

GEM **THEATRE WEST VIRGINIA** is 15 mi. e. on I-64 to exit 129B at Grandview. Out- **SAVE** door dramas are presented at the Cliffside Amphitheatre on the New River Gorge National River. "Hatfields and McCoys" is a musical drama about the infamous feuding families, and "Honey in the Rock" tells the story of the state's Civil War birth. A different Broadway musical is featured each summer.

Inquire about weather policies. Shows are presented Tues.-Sun. at 8:15, mid-June to late Aug. Admission $15; senior citizens $13; under 12, $7. Reservations are recommended. MC, VI. Phone (304) 256-6800 or (800) 666-9142 for reservations.

YOUTH MUSEUM OF SOUTHERN WEST VIRGINIA & MOUNTAIN HOMESTEAD, 106 Adair St. in New River Park, features a planetarium and changing displays about science and the arts, including interactive exhibits about color, electricity and magnetism.

The Mountain Homestead features traditional craft demonstrations in an Appalachian pioneer village complete with a log house and barn, a one-room schoolhouse, a weaver's shed, a blacksmith shop, a moonshine still and a country store.

Allow 1 hour minimum. Mon.-Sat. 10-6, Apr.-Oct.; Tues.-Sat. 10-5, rest of year. Phone for planetarium show schedule. Admission $7. A combination ticket with Beckley Exhibition Coal Mine is available. Phone (304) 252-3730.

BERKELEY SPRINGS (B-6)
pop. 663, elev. 612'

The Berkeley Springs, famous for their supposed curative properties, were a haven for American Indians long before Europeans discovered their soothing waters. A thriving community had been established by the time George Washington arrived in 1748 to survey the area for its owner, Lord Thomas Fairfax. In 1776, Washington assisted in establishing the town as a health resort under the name of Bath, which remains its official name.

More than a dozen members of the Colonial elite were among original lot owners—George and Martha Washington bought property in the area. The springs continue to flow from five main sources at the rate of 1,000-1,500 gallons per minute; the water maintains a uniform temperature of 74 F.

Though known for its spas, Berkeley Springs is also gaining notice as an arts community. The town is home to a growing number of art and craft galleries and shows. Ten miles south, Cacapon Resort State Park *(see Recreation Chart)* offers an 18-hole golf course, a lodge, a lake beach and trails to the top of Cacapon Mountain.

Berkeley Springs-Morgan County Chamber of Commerce: 127 Fairfax St., Berkeley Springs, WV 25411; phone (304) 258-3738 or (800) 447-8797.

BERKELEY SPRINGS STATE PARK is near the center of town at 2 S. Washington St. Several bathhouses offer a variety of baths, massages and other heat treatments. The historic Roman Bath House has been in use since 1815.

Allow 1 hour minimum. Main building open daily 10-6 (also Fri. 6-9 p.m., Apr.-Oct.); closed Jan. 1, Easter, Thanksgiving and Dec. 25. Old Roman Bath House open daily 10-6 (also Fri. 6-8 p.m., Apr.-Oct.). Swimming pool open daily, Memorial Day weekend-Labor Day. Bath and massage Mon.-Thurs. $38; Fri.-Sun. and holidays $43. Bath and shower $25. Bath $20. Pool $3; senior citizens $2.50; under 12, $2. Reservations are recommended 1 month in advance; a deposit is required. AX, DC, DS, MC, VI. Phone (304) 258-2711 or (800) 225-5982.

BETHANY (A-3) pop. 985, elev. 818'

Bethany centers on Bethany College, a liberal arts school chartered in 1840 by Alexander Campbell, a leader of religious and educational reform in the 19th century. The son of a Presbyterian minister, Campbell sailed from Scotland to the United States in 1809. He became the principal founder of one of the largest religious movements in the United States, from which developed the Christian Churches, the Christian Church (Disciples of Christ) and the Churches of Christ.

Self-guiding tours: Tour maps and brochures are available at Historic Bethany Center on the Bethany College campus. Sights include the Campbell Mansion and cemetery, Old Main, Delta Tau Delta Founder's House and Museum, and Old Bethany Meeting House. More extensive tours are available upon request; phone (304) 829-7285.

[SAVE] **CAMPBELL MANSION** is .75 mi. e. on SR 67. Alexander Campbell's 24-room home was host to such noted historic figures as Henry Clay, Jefferson Davis and President James Garfield. Eighteen rooms of the late 1700s homestead are furnished in period and include Campbell's hexagonal brick study and a schoolroom. A smoke house is on the grounds. The Campbell family cemetery is nearby.

Allow 1 hour minimum. Guided tours Mon.-Fri. 10-noon and 1-4, Sat.-Sun. by appointment; closed holidays and commencement day. Last tour begins 1 hour before closing. Admission $4; ages 6-17, $2. AX, DS, MC, VI. Phone (304) 829-4258.

BEVERLY (C-4) pop. 651, elev. 1,946'

Originally christened Edmunton in honor of Virginia governor Edmund Randolph, Beverly was later renamed after the governor's mother. The town was chartered in 1790. During the Civil War, the Battle of Rich Mountain brought the area under Union control, and federal troops occupied the town for two years. Beverly served as the county seat until 1899, when the Western Maryland Railroad established the community of Elkins to the north.

Rich Mountain/Historic Beverly Visitor Center: 4 Court St., P.O. Box 227, Beverly, WV 26253; phone (304) 637-7424.

Self-guiding tours: A self-guiding walking tour brochure of the Beverly historic district and a driving tour of Civil War sites along the Beverly-Fairmont Turnpike are available from the visitor center on the town square.

DAVID GOFF HOUSE is at Main and Court sts. Col. David Goff, a prominent Beverly lawyer, bought the house in 1830 and finished most of the present structure. After he and his family fled south during the Civil War, the house became a U.S. Army hospital. Signatures, unit names and drawings by injured soldiers cover the walls. Letters, newspaper accounts and battle scenes of the Rich Mountain campaign are displayed. Allow 30 minutes minimum. Tues.-Sat. 10-5, Sun. noon-5. Free. Phone (304) 637-0450.

RICH MOUNTAIN BATTLEFIELD is 5 mi. w. on Rich Mountain Rd. On July 11, 1861, General George McClellan's Union troops routed the Confederates who controlled the Staunton-Parkersburg Pike across Rich Mountain. Confederate earthworks, a homestead site and inscriptions carved by soldiers are visible. A visitor center is housed in the Bushrod Crawford Store, which served as McClellan's headquarters.

Guided tours are available by appointment. Allow 30 minutes minimum. Mon.-Sat. 9-4, Sun. noon-4, June-Aug.; Mon.-Fri. 9-4, rest of year.

Closed Memorial Day, July 4 and Labor Day. Donations. Phone (304) 637-7424.

BLUEFIELD (E-2) pop. 11,451, elev. 2,560′

Founded in 1889 as the regional headquarters of the Norfolk & Western Railway, remnants of the natural-gravity switching yards remain in Bluefield. Named for the many chicory flowers growing wild along the hillsides, the town attracted many industries, including coal mining.

South of town, the border between the two Virginias is on the crest of East River Mountain. A sister city, Bluefield, Va., lies to the southwest. The West Virginia city's original municipal building, built in 1924, now houses the Bluefield Area Arts Center, an active center for visual and performing arts.

Pinnacle Rock State Park, 8 miles northwest off US 52, is known for its namesake 3,100-foot sandstone formation. Picnicking, hiking and fishing can be enjoyed at this scenic park.

Bluefield is the southern anchor of the Coal Heritage Trail which winds its way past company stores, miners' houses, railroad yards, coal tipples and 500 small company towns on its way north to Beckley; follow US 52 northwest to SR 16, which meanders north and east to Beckley. Mile markers along the way indicate points of interest.

Baseball comes to Bluefield in mid-June when the minor league Bluefield Orioles, part of the Appalachian League, play ball at Bowen Field in City Park.

Mercer County Convention and Visitors Bureau: 500 Bland St., P.O. Box 4088, Bluefield, WV 24701; phone (304) 325-8438 or (800) 221-3206.

Self-guiding tours: Examples of historic Victorian architecture can be seen on a walking tour of downtown Bluefield. Brochures are available at the chamber of commerce on Bland Street and the convention and visitors bureau office in the Bluefield Area Arts Center on Bland Street.

Shopping areas: Mercer Mall, at US 460 and SR 25, has more than 70 stores, including Belk, JCPenney and Sears.

EASTERN REGIONAL COAL ARCHIVES is at 600 Commerce St. in the Craft Memorial Library. The collection of coal mining memorabilia includes artifacts, diaries, photographs, mining equipment, films and research materials. Allow 30 minutes minimum. Mon.-Fri. 9:30-5; closed major holidays. Free. Phone (304) 325-3943.

BRAMWELL (E-2) pop. 426, elev. 2,253′

Its economy fired by the nearby coal fields, Bramwell was once considered the richest town in the country, having 19 millionaires. The symbol of its wealth, the Bramwell Bank, gained fame when it floated the largest Liberty Bond during World War I, resulting in the commonly used 1920s phrase "solid as the Bank of Bramwell."

The Depression brought an end to prosperity and closed the bank, but many of the structures representative of West Virginia's gilded age have been preserved in the town's historic district.

Self-guiding tours: Walking tour maps are available at city hall and the Coal Heritage Trail Southern Interpretive Center. The sights include several mansions and buildings in the business district. For more information contact the Bramwell Town Hall; phone (304) 248-7114.

BRUCETON MILLS (B-4)
pop. 74, elev. 1,527′

COOPER'S ROCK STATE FOREST is 8 mi. w. on I-68 at exit 15 (CR 73/12). The park comprises 12,713 acres of mountainous woodland. Among the forest's features are miles of nature and cross-country skiing trails and an overlook with a view of the 1,200-foot-deep Cheat River Gorge. Camping, fishing, hunting, mountain bicycling, picnicking and rock climbing are popular activities. Food is available April through November. Park open daily 8-dusk. Free. Phone (304) 594-1561. *See Recreation Chart and the AAA Mideastern CampBook.*

Henry Clay Iron Furnace is accessible from a 1-mi. trail off CR 73/12. One of the few surviving examples of an early 19th-century iron furnace, the 30-foot-high square stack was built from local stone in the 1830s and operated through the 1840s. Except for a small glade, the surrounding forest shows no sign of the community that flourished for 12 years, shipping pig iron as far away as St. Louis.

BUCKHANNON (C-3) pop. 5,725, elev. 1,433′

RECREATIONAL ACTIVITIES
Hot Air Ballooning

- **Mountain Air Balloons** is at 100 Woodall Ln., Buckhannon, WV 26201. Transportation is provided to the departure point. Tours depart daily at 6 a.m. and 4 p.m., May-Nov. (weather permitting). Reservations are required. Phone (304) 472-0792.

CASS (D-4) elev. 2,437′

Once a large lumbering community, Cass retains the history of its greatness at the beginning of the 20th century. The Cass Country Store is in the former West Virginia Pulp and Paper General Store, purported to have been the largest company store in the world.

The Historical Museum houses a collection of wildlife exhibits and relics pertaining to the timber and mining industry, including one of the largest band saws in the world. The Cass Showcase is a historic diorama depicting the Cass Railroad in its lumbering days and includes a reproduction of the town during the lumber boom at the beginning of the 19th century.

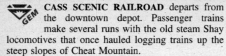

CASS SCENIC RAILROAD departs from the downtown depot. Passenger trains make several runs with the old steam Shay locomotives that once hauled logging trains up the steep slopes of Cheat Mountain.

The rail excursions, which offer scenic mountain vistas, include a 2-hour round-trip to Whittaker Station and a 22-mile, 5-hour round-trip excursion to the top of Bald Knob. Also available is a 5-hour trip to Spruce, an abandoned logging town along Shavers Fork of the Cheat River. Trips are preceded by a slide presentation that relates the town's lumbering history. Other trips also are available.

The 2-hour trip runs daily at noon and 2:30, Memorial Day weekend-Labor Day and Oct. 1 to mid-Oct.; Fri.-Sun. at noon and 2:30, day after Labor Day-Sept. 30 and mid-Oct. through Oct. 31. A 9:30 departure is available on select dates, Memorial Day weekend-Oct. 31. The 5-hour trip departs Tues.-Sun. and holiday Mon. at 10:30, Memorial Day weekend-Labor Day and Oct. 1 to mid-Oct.; Fri.-Sun. at 10:30, day after Labor Day-Sept. 30; Thurs.-Sun. at 10:30, mid-Oct. through Oct. 31.

Fare for 2-hour trip Mon.-Fri. $13; ages 5-12, $8. Sat.-Sun. $15; ages 5-12, $10. Fare for 5-hour trip Tues.-Fri. $17; ages 5-12, $10. Sat.-Sun. $19; ages 5-12, $12. AX, MC, VI. Phone (304) 456-4300 or (800) 225-5982.

CHARLESTON (D-2) pop. 53,421, elev. 601′

Capital of the state, Charleston was founded in 1794. From 1788-95, Daniel Boone lived across the river. He served in the Virginia Assembly in 1791. Remains of an American Indian burial ground are in South Charleston at MacCorkle Avenue and D Street.

Serving as a regional cultural center, Clay Center for the Arts & Sciences houses a performance hall and a black box theater as well as museums and a planetarium. Off I-64 exit 100 (Leon Sullivan Way), the center is home to the West Virginia Symphony Orchestra.

The Midland Trail Scenic Highway/US 60 travels from Charleston to White Sulphur Springs *(see place listing p. 349)* through pastoral scenery and past the rugged New River Gorge. *See color ad p. 329.*

Appalachian music, ethnic and traditional foods, West Virginia arts and crafts, dancing, storytelling and contests are part of the Vandalia Gathering, held on the Capitol lawn and in the Cultural Center on Memorial Day weekend. Vandalia, proposed as the 14th colony during the late 1760s, had many backers, including Benjamin Franklin; the new colony's boundaries would have encompassed most of present-day West Virginia, in addition to much of what is now Kentucky. However, because of the strained relations between the fledgling American colonies and Great Britain, the plan never came to fruition.

For racing fans, Tri-State Racetrack and Gaming Center, 12 miles west of Charleston off I-64 exit 47, offers greyhound racing. The glass-enclosed facility has more than 4,000 seats and a clubhouse. Phone (800) 224-9683.

Note: Policies concerning admittance of children to pari-mutuel betting facilities vary. Phone for information.

Charleston Convention and Visitors Bureau: 200 Civic Center Dr., Charleston, WV 25301; phone (304) 344-5075 or (800) 733-5469.

Shopping areas: Charleston Town Center, downtown between Quarrier and Lee streets, has 135 stores including JCPenney, Kaufmann's, Sears and numerous specialty shops. Capitol Street, the main street of Old Charleston, offers shops and restaurants housed in 19th-century buildings.

Open daily year-round, the Capitol Market at 800 Smith St. offers both indoor and outdoor shopping. The restored former Kanawha and Michigan Railway Depot now houses specialty shops and eateries, and an outdoors farmer's market provides fresh local produce as well as flowers, shrubs and trees.

AVAMPATO DISCOVERY MUSEUM, downtown at 300 Leon Sullivan Way at the Clay Center, has interactive science exhibits, an art gallery, and a theater with a planetarium, large-format films and laser shows. Science galleries include The Gizmo Factory's physical science exhibits; Earth City, which explores the forces that shaped the state; a gallery about health and wellness; and a fanciful space for children under 6. The art museum's primary focus is on 19th- and 20th-century paintings.

Food is available. Allow 1 hour, 30 minutes minimum. Museum open Tues.-Sat. 10-5, Sun. noon-5, July-Aug.; Wed.-Sat. 10-5, Sun. noon-5, rest of year. Planetarium shows and films are offered several times daily. Admission (includes museum, planetarium and film) $12.50; senior citizens and ages 3-18, $10. Admission to individual attractions and other combination admissions also are available. AX, DS, MC, VI. Phone (304) 561-3575.

CRAIK-PATTON HOUSE is at 2809 Kanawha Blvd. E. Built in 1834 by James Craik, the house later was purchased by George Smith Patton, a Confederate colonel and grandfather of World War II Gen. George S. Patton. The restored house, which was moved from its original location on Virginia Street, is furnished true to mid-19th-century style. Landscaped grounds feature herb and boxwood gardens. Allow 1 hour minimum. Wed.-Sat. 10-5, Sun. noon-5. Admission $4, children $2, family rate $10. Phone (304) 925-5341.

CULTURAL CENTER is in the West Virginia State Capitol Complex at Greenbrier and Washington sts. The center houses a 500-seat theater, reference library, archives and art exhibits. A re-creation of a settler's cabin and country store also are on the property. Mon.-Thurs. 9-8, Fri.-Sat. 9-6, Sun. noon-6. Free. Phone (304) 558-0162.

WEST VIRGINIA STATE CAPITOL is on Kanawha Blvd. E., facing the Kanawha River. This masterpiece of architect Cass Gilbert was completed in 1932. The outstanding feature is the rotunda's 23-karat gold-leaf dome, 180 feet above the main floor. From its center hangs a 2-ton rock crystal chandelier, 8 feet in diameter. The second-floor ceiling is decorated with a panel design showing leaves of West Virginia's native trees.

The building's office wings house the state administrative departments, including the Supreme Court and Law Library. Guided tours are available. Mon.-Fri. 9-3:30, Sat. 1-5. The Governor's Mansion, next to the Capitol, is open Thurs.-Fri. 9:30-11:30. Both buildings closed Jan. 1, Thanksgiving and Dec. 25. Reservations are required for the Governor's Mansion and are suggested for other areas. Free. Phone (304) 558-4839.

CHARLES TOWN (C-6) pop. 2,907, elev. 513'

Charles Town was named for George Washington's brother, who laid out the town in 1786. Streets bear the names of Washington's family members. After his raid on Harpers Ferry, John Brown was tried and hanged for treason in Charles Town.

Automobile races take place nearby at Summit Point Raceway, April through October; phone (304) 725-8444. Thoroughbred horse racing has drawn crowds since 1786. Charles Town Races, 1 mile east on US 340, is open all year; phone (304) 725-7001 or (800) 795-7001.

Note: Policies concerning admittance of children to pari-mutuel betting facilities vary. Phone for information.

Charles Town marks the West Virginia terminus of the scenic portion of SR 9, which runs eastward into Virginia. From Charles Town it is 6 miles to the Virginia border.

Jefferson County Chamber of Commerce: 29 Keys Ferry Rd., Suite 200, P.O. Box 426, Charles Town, WV 25414; phone (304) 725-2055 or (800) 624-0577.

JEFFERSON COUNTY COURTHOUSE is at George and Washington sts. The original one-room courthouse, built in 1803 on land donated by Charles Washington, was incorporated into the present building. The room where John Brown was tried is open to the public. Mon.-Fri. 9-5 (also Fri. 5-7). Free. Phone (304) 728-3240.

JEFFERSON COUNTY MUSEUM is at 200 E. Washington St. in the lower level of the Charles Town Library. Displays include memorabilia of the Washington family and John Brown, Jefferson County historical relics and many Civil War items. Tues.-Sat. 11-4, Apr.-Nov. Free. Phone (304) 725-8628.

CLARKSBURG (C-3) pop. 16,743, elev. 1,034'

From 1861 until the first battle of Bull Run, Clarksburg was the headquarters for Gen. George B. McClellan. It also served as a Union depot throughout the war. Gen. William E. Jones' Confederate cavalry passed through in 1863 on the raid that destroyed military points on the B & O Railroad.

Clarksburg was the birthplace in 1824 of Gen. Thomas J. "Stonewall" Jackson, hero of the Confederacy. The site is marked by a bronze plate at 326-328 W. Main St. An equestrian statue of Jackson is on the northeast corner of the Court House Plaza. The military leader spent most of his boyhood 20 miles south at Jackson's Mill *(see Weston p. 346)*.

Greater Bridgeport Conference & Visitors Center: 164 W. Main St., Bridgeport, WV 26330; phone (304) 842-7272 or (800) 368-4324. *See color ads starting on p. 324.*

Shopping areas: Meadowbrook Mall, off I-79 exit 121, has Elder-Beerman, JCPenney and Sears among its stores.

CRAB ORCHARD (D-2)
pop. 2,761, elev. 2,292'

WINERIES

- **Daniel Vineyards** is at 200 Twin Oaks Rd. Tours and tastings Mon.-Sat. 10-6, Sun. 1-6; closed major holidays. Phone (304) 252-9750 or (877) 378-1990.

DAVIS (C-4) pop. 624, elev. 3,200'

Incorporated in 1885, Davis was born of the lumber boom. Today the area is a mecca for mountain bikers and rafters. Ten miles south, Canaan Valley Resort State Park *(see Recreation Chart)* is an all-year resort and conference center. Downhill and cross-country skiing are popular in winter; golf on an 18-hole championship course, hiking, tennis and swimming prevail during the summer. Deer often cross the golf course early and late in the day. Other privately operated resorts and camping facilities also are available in the Canaan (ka-NAIN) valley.

Of historical significance is the Fairfax Stone, 7 miles north of town off US 219, which marked the western boundary of Lord Fairfax's lands. Under the terms of the grant issued by the king of England, Lord Fairfax owned all the lands between the Potomac and the Rappahannock rivers, and this marker served as the base point for the boundary between Maryland and Virginia (now West Virginia).

Tucker County Convention and Visitors Bureau: William Avenue at 4th Street, P.O. Box 565, Davis, WV 26260; phone (304) 259-5315 or (800) 782-2775. *See color ads starting on p. 324.*

BLACKWATER FALLS STATE PARK is about .25 mi. s.w. off SR 32, following signs. The scenic Blackwater Falls are 65 feet high, and the gorge below is more than 525 feet deep. An observation point is on the gorge's rim; stairways descend to the foot of the falls. Recreational activities include cross-country skiing, paddleboating, hiking, horseback riding, picnicking, swimming, tennis, bicycling, sledding, volleyball and nature programs.

Food is available. Park open daily 6 a.m.-10 p.m. Waterfall accessible 6 a.m.-dusk. Campgrounds available last week in Apr.-Oct. 31; cabins and lodge facilities are available all year. Free. Phone (304) 259-5216. *See Recreation Chart.*

DROOP (D-3) elev. 3,000′

Droop is traversed by the scenic portion of SR 55/US 219, which runs 86 miles between Huttonsville to the north and Lewisburg to the south.

DROOP MOUNTAIN BATTLEFIELD STATE PARK is 3 mi. s. on US 219. The 287-acre park was the scene of a Civil War battle that ended the last serious Confederate resistance in the state. Seven different hiking trails, an observation tower, a cemetery and several monuments are on the grounds. A log cabin museum contains Civil War memorabilia. Picnicking is permitted. Allow 30 minutes minimum. Park open daily 6 a.m.-10 p.m. Museum 10-2. Free. Phone (304) 653-4254.

ELKINS (C-4) pop. 7,032, elev. 1,940′

Elkins, on the Tygart Valley River in the Potomac Highlands, is in a region that contains many of West Virginia's highest mountains. Named for Stephen B. Elkins, secretary of war and U.S. senator 1895-1911, the city was a center for railroad, timber and coal operations. The mountains provide a variety of recreational opportunities. Ski areas are nearby in the Monongahela National Forest *(see place listing p. 340)*, which maintains its headquarters in Elkins.

Elkins is at the crossroads of three scenic highways. From Fairmont to the north, the scenic section of US 250 passes through, running south to Huttonsville. US 219 runs south jointly with US 250 to Huttonsville and then continues on to White Sulphur Springs. US 33 crosses them in Elkins, following the Tygart River into town before heading east into some of the region's most spectacular scenery. The Stuart Memorial Drive, which passes Stuart Recreation Area and 4,020-foot Bickles Knob, runs between Elkins and Alpena.

Potomac Travel Council: P.O. Box 1456, Elkins, WV 26241; phone (304) 636-8400.

SAVE **NEW TYGART FLYER** departs from the depot at 12th St. and Davis Ave. A 4-hour, 46-mile round trip takes passengers through the Cheat River Mountain canyons and the Tygart Valley, past waterfalls, through an "S" curve tunnel and across a bridge over the Cheat River. A parlor car, available at an additional cost, includes food. Other excursions also are offered.

Allow 4 hours minimum. Departures Thurs.-Sun. at 11, in Oct.; Fri.-Sun. at 11, late June-late Aug.; select Sat. and Sun. at 11, May 1-late June, late

Aug.-Sept. 30 and in early Nov. Other departures may be available; phone ahead. Coach fare $25; over 59, $29; ages 4-11, $19. Reservations are recommended. AX, DS, MC, VI. Phone (304) 456-4935 or (877) 686-7245.

FAIRMONT (B-3) pop. 19,097, elev. 884′

Fairmont occupies the steep hills surrounding the Monongahela River, which divides the town into east and west sections. Originally two towns, Palatine and Middletown, Fairmont was incorporated in 1843. Ferries shuttled people and supplies across the river until 1852, when a suspension bridge unified the town.

During the 1850s railroad access encouraged the development of coal mines in the area. While coal continues to be a source of employment, today the town is on a high-tech corridor with a NASA software facility and a software consortium. Other Fairmont products include mine machinery and aluminum.

Fifteen miles south off SR 310, Valley Falls State Park features a series of waterfalls generated by the Tygart Valley River. The park's 1,145 acres are popular with anglers, picnickers and hikers. Fairmont is the northern end of the scenic section of US 250, which runs 73 miles to Huttonsville and continues as US 219 to Lewisburg.

Fairmont Convention and Visitors Bureau: 110 Adams St., Fairmont, WV 26554; phone (304) 368-1123.

SAVE **PRICKETTS FORT STATE PARK,** about 2.5 mi. w. off I-79 exit 139, contains a reconstructed log fort similar to one built in 1774 to protect settlers from American Indian attacks. The museum captures West Virginia's 18th-century lifestyle through costumed interpreters and craft demonstrations.

The visitor center offers exhibits about the Monongahela Valley's history. The park also has a nature trail and a hiking trail that follows a converted rail bed to Fairmont.

Picnicking is permitted. Allow 2 hours minimum. Park open daily 6 a.m.-10 p.m. year-round. Historical attractions open daily 10-4:30, mid-Apr. through Oct. 31. Park free. Historical attractions admission $6; over 55, $5; ages 6-12, $3. Phone (304) 363-3030. *See Recreation Chart.*

FAYETTEVILLE (D-2)
pop. 2,754, elev. 1,750′

Settled in 1818, Fayetteville was named for Marquis de Lafayette in 1837. A historical marker on the town lawn identifies Fayetteville as the site where the military tactic of indirect firing—the shooting over friendly troops into enemy positions beyond—was first used during the Civil War.

Fayetteville's proximity to the New and Gauley rivers has made it a center for recreation. Both these rivers are famous for their challenging whitewater rapids, which are considered some of the best in the country.

Northeast of Fayetteville is the New River Gorge Bridge, one of the longest steel-arch span bridges in the world and one of the highest bridges in the nation. The arch spans 1,700 feet, while the bridge itself stretches 3,030 feet across the gorge. At 876 feet, it is 321 feet higher than the Washington Monument.

Fayetteville lies along scenic US 19, which runs 45 miles from the West Virginia Turnpike/I-77 at Bradley to I-79 near Sutton.

RECREATIONAL ACTIVITIES
Horseback Riding

- **Canyon Rim Ranch** is off US 19, s. on Court St. (CR 16) to Gatewood Rd., then 3 mi. on Cunard Rd. Write Box 601B, Fayetteville, WV 25840. Other activities are offered. Daily Apr.-Nov. Phone (304) 574-3111.

White-water Rafting

- SAVE **Appalachian Wildwaters Inc.** is 2.5 mi. s. on US 19 exit Appalachian Dr. to Broadway. Write P.O. Box 100, Rowlesburg, WV 26425. Trips on the New and Gauley rivers depart Apr.-Oct. Phone (304) 454-2475 or (800) 624-8060.

- **Cantrell Ultimate Rafting** is w. on Court St. (CR 16), then .5 mi. s. on Gatewood Rd. following signs. Write Rt. 4, Box 2, Fayetteville, WV 25840. Other activities are offered. Trips on the New and Gauley rivers depart daily Apr.-Oct. Phone (304) 574-2500 or (800) 470-7238.

- **Drift-a-Bit Whitewater Rafting** is 1.7 mi. n. of jct. US 19 and SR 16, following signs. Write P.O. Box 885, Fayetteville, WV 25840. Trips on the New and Gauley rivers depart daily Mar. 16-Oct. 19. Phone (304) 574-3282 or (800) 633-7238.

- **Passages to Adventure** is at US 19 and Maple Ln. Write P.O. Box 71, Fayetteville, WV 25840. Other activities are offered. Trips on the Lower New River run late Mar.-Oct. 31. Phone (304) 574-1037 or (800) 634-3785.

- **Raft West Virginia Inc.** is off US 19 exit Whitewater Ave. Write Rt. 3, Box 459A, Fayetteville, WV 25840. Other activities are offered. New River trips depart daily Mar.-Oct. Gauley River trips depart daily Sept.-Oct. Phone (304) 574-1004 or (800) 782-7238.

- **Rivers Whitewater Rafting** is off US 19 exit Fayette Station Rd., then .5 mi. w. Write P.O. Box 39, Lansing, WV 25862. Other activities are offered. Trips depart Apr.-Oct. Phone (304) 574-3834 or (800) 879-7483.

- SAVE **USA Raft** is at jct. SR 16 and Appalachian Dr. Write P.O. Box 277, Rowlesburg, WV 26425. New and Gauley river trips depart Mar.-Nov. Phone (304) 454-2475 or (800) 872-7238.

FRENCH CREEK (C-3) elev. 1,500′

French Creek was first settled in 1808 by a party from Massachusetts. The name came from a local legend about three Frenchmen who prospected for gold in the area in 1725.

WEST VIRGINIA STATE WILDLIFE CENTER is s. on SR 20 at CR 11. The center exhibits native and introduced animals and birds in natural settings. Among the animals exhibited are bison, elk, mountain lions, snakes, river otters, timber wolves, white-tailed deer and wild turkeys. Food and picnic facilities are available. Allow 2 hours minimum. Daily 9-6, May-Aug.; 9-5, rest of year (weather permitting). Admission $3; ages 3-15, $1.50. Phone (304) 924-6211.

GEORGE WASHINGTON AND JEFFERSON NATIONAL FORESTS—
see place listing in Virginia p. 241.

GERRARDSTOWN (C-6) elev. 676′

Gerrardstown, in the Eastern Panhandle, was first settled in 1742 by 14 Baptist families from New Jersey. In 1787 the town was founded and named for the Rev. David Gerrard, who enlarged the town by platting 100 lots of his own property to be sold to new settlers. The many older buildings in the village have led to its being described as "a 19th-century community restored."

Gerrard House, in the center of the village, is one of the oldest known buildings in West Virginia. Built in 1743 by John Hays, it was later the home of David Gerrard. The two-story stone house, heavily constructed for protection not only from the elements but also from the American Indians, retains much of its original woodwork. The first floor is open to the public on weekends; phone (304) 229-1617.

GLEN JEAN (E-2) elev. 1,600′
RECREATIONAL ACTIVITIES
White-water Rafting

- SAVE **West Virginia Adventures** is off US 19 on Wood Mountain Rd. Write P.O. Box 243, Glen Jean, WV 25846. Rafting trips on the New and Gauley rivers depart daily Apr.-Oct. Phone (304) 465-2025 or (800) 292-0880.

GRAFTON (B-4) pop. 5,489, elev. 1,002′

While still a part of Virginia, Grafton was incorporated in 1856. The town was a key point in the Civil War because of its location on the B&O Railroad. At the beginning of the war, Confederate colonel George A. Porterfield and a small contingent established a base in Grafton. Bailey Brown, who during the Battle of Philippi became the first Union soldier killed by Confederate forces, is buried in Grafton National Cemetery at 431 Walnut St.

Grafton-Taylor County Convention and Visitors Bureau: P.O. Box 513, Grafton, WV 26354; phone (304) 265-1589.

THE INTERNATIONAL MOTHER'S DAY SHRINE is at 11 E. Main St. Andrews Methodist Episcopal Church was the site of the first observance of

Mother's Day, May 10, 1908. Tues.-Fri. 10-4, Sat. by appointment, mid-Apr. to late Oct. Free. Phone (304) 265-1589.

TYGART RIVER DAM AND LAKE is 2 mi. s., following signs from US 50 or US 119. The dam was built to control floods on the Monongahela River and reduce the crest of the Ohio River during flood times. The dam is 207 feet thick at the base, 1,921 feet long and 230 feet high. The reservoir, which covers 3,440 acres and has a 32-mile shoreline, provides opportunities for swimming, fishing and hiking. Phone (304) 265-6148 or (800) 225-5982. *See Recreation Chart and the AAA Mideastern CampBook.*

GREEN BANK (D-4) elev. 2,700'

NATIONAL RADIO ASTRONOMY OBSERVATORY is on SR 92 in Deer Creek Valley. Guided tours of the radio astronomy research center include a 15-minute slide show followed by a narrated bus ride to see the radio telescopes. The science center also includes exhibits and educational demonstrations.

Food is available. Allow 1 hour minimum. Open daily 8:30-7, Memorial Day weekend-Oct 31; Wed.-Sun. 10-5, rest of year. Closed Jan. 1, Easter, Thanksgiving and Dec. 25. Tours are given on the hour 9-6, Memorial Day weekend-Oct. 31; at 11, 1, 3 and 5, rest of year. Free. Phone (304) 456-2011 Mon.-Fri. or (304) 456-2150 Sat.-Sun.

HARPERS FERRY (C-6) pop. 307, elev. 282'

The town of Harpers Ferry is at the confluence of the Potomac and Shenandoah rivers, separating Maryland, Virginia and West Virginia. The federal arsenal and armory built in 1796 manufactured many of the muskets and rifles used in the War of 1812 and the Civil War. These buildings were the targets of abolitionist John Brown's notorious raid.

On the night of Oct. 16, 1859, Brown, accompanied by 18 members of his 21-man "army," surprised and captured the armory and arsenal. His intent was to incite the slaves to insurrection and arm them from the government stores. After considerable bloodshed, the raiders were captured by U.S. Marines under Col. Robert E. Lee. Brown and six of his followers were tried for treason, convicted and hanged at Charles Town.

During the Civil War, Harpers Ferry was regarded by the Union command as a key to the safety of Washington, D.C. In 1861 the small federal garrison abandoned the town before a force of Virginians, but destroyed the arsenal before leaving. It was never rebuilt. The following year Gen. Thomas "Stonewall" Jackson captured the federal garrison after a terrific bombardment, taking 12,500 Union soldiers as prisoners before moving on to join Lee at Antietam.

The Appalachian Trail passes nearby, and the Shenandoah and Potomac rivers offer opportunities for fishing, canoeing and rafting.

JOHN BROWN WAX MUSEUM is at 168 High St. Life-size figures depict the life of John Brown. Daily 9-5, Mar. 15-Dec. 15. Admission $5.50; ages 6-12, $3.50. Phone (304) 535-6342.

RECREATIONAL ACTIVITIES
White-water Rafting

• **Blue Ridge Outfitters** is 4 mi. w. on US 340 at Frontage Rd. Write P.O. Box 750, Harpers Ferry, WV 25425. Other activities are offered. Shenandoah trips depart daily at 9 and 2:15, Apr.-Oct. Phone (304) 725-3444.

• **River Riders Inc.** is s. off US 340 on Millville Rd., following signs to 408 Alstadts Hill Rd. Write P.O. Box 1260, Harpers Ferry, WV 25425. Other activities are offered. Trips depart daily Apr.-Oct. Phone (304) 535-2663 or (800) 326-7238.

▼GEM HARPERS FERRY NATIONAL HISTORICAL PARK (C-6)

Harpers Ferry National Historical Park borders US 340 at the scenic confluence of the Shenandoah and Potomac rivers. The park is comprised of several areas: the Lower Town Historic District, Maryland Heights, Loudon Heights, Bolivar Heights, Cavalier Heights, Short Hill and Virginius Island. Maps and guides are available at the park visitor center on Cavalier Heights, about 1 mile west of the Shenandoah River bridge.

Congress authorized a national monument here in 1944, and the area was declared a National Historical Park in 1963. Shuttle buses connect the visitor center with the Lower Town Historic District, the site where George Washington persuaded the federal government to construct a national armory and arsenal and where John Brown led his famous raid in 1859.

Park exhibits and museums in more than two dozen restored 19th-century buildings, including John Brown's fort, John Brown Museum, the Provost Marshal office, Civil War Museum; Industry Museum and Restoration Museum, reflect the diverse historical events that shaped the region: the first successful application of interchangeable manufacture; the arrival of the first successful American railroad; John Brown's attack on slavery; the largest surrender of Federal troops during the Civil War; and the education of former slaves at Storer College, one of the earliest integrated schools in the United States.

Guided tours are available throughout the summer. Hiking trails lead to Maryland Heights, 1,448 feet above the rivers, where remnants of Civil War fortifications and campsites are visible. A walking tour of Virginius Island on the banks of the Shenandoah River reveals the ruins of a once-thriving industrial community. The foundries, mills and factories that survived the war were leveled by record floods in 1870 and 1889.

The park and visitor center are open daily 8-5; closed Jan. 1, Thanksgiving and Dec. 25. Admission (valid for 3 days) is $6 per private vehicle; $4 for individuals. Phone (304) 535-6298. *See color ads starting on p. 324.*

HARPER HOUSE is accessible via stone steps leading uphill from High St. The lower level of this 1782 home, the oldest surviving structure in Harpers Ferry, exhibits an armory worker's apartment.

JOHN BROWN MONUMENT stands by the B&O Railroad. The granite monument marks the original site of the firehouse where Brown and his men made their stand.

JOHN BROWN'S FORT is on Arsenal Square. The 1848 brick armory firehouse was the scene of Brown's capture. Dismantled and moved to Chicago after the Civil War, the building was later restored to a site 150 feet east of its original location.

HICO (D-3) elev. 2,056′

Hico received its name in 1895 when the postmaster moved the post office from his house to a nearby store. The store sold a brand of tobacco called Hico, and the post office was named for it.

Hico is at the intersection of two scenic highways. US 60 passes Hico on its 71-mile run between White Sulphur Springs and Gauley Bridge, and US 19 passes Hico about halfway along its 45-mile scenic stretch from Bradley to Sutton.

RECREATIONAL ACTIVITIES
White-water Rafting

- SAVE **Adventures Mountain River** departs at US 60 and US 19 on Sunday Rd. Write P.O. Box 88, Hico, WV 25854. Other activities are offered. New River and Gauley River trips run late Mar.-late Oct. Phone (304) 658-5266 or (800) 822-1386. *See color ad p. 329.*

- **North American River Runners** departs .2 mi. w. of US 19 on US 60. Write P.O. Box 81, Hico, WV 25854. Other activities are offered. Trips depart Mar.-Oct. Phone (304) 658-5276 or (800) 950-2585.

HILLSBORO (D-4) pop. 243, elev. 2,303′

As with many frontier towns, Hillsboro was established by a man who was running from his past. In 1765 John McNeil fled into the wilderness believing he had killed a man in a boxing match. Two brothers, Charles and Jacob Kinnison, found him during an expedition and gave McNeil news of his opponent's recovery. McNeil would not be swayed to return with them, but he persuaded the Kinnisons to stay and help build a new settlement.

From Huttonsville to the north, scenic SR 55/US 219 runs 86 miles to Lewisburg, traversing Hillsboro near Watoga State Park *(see Recreation Chart and the AAA Mideastern CampBook).*

PEARL S. BUCK BIRTHPLACE MUSEUM is .5 mi. n. on US 219. The restored 1892 home in which the Nobel Prize-winning author was born is furnished in period and contains some original pieces and memorabilia. On the grounds is the boyhood home of Buck's father, Absalom Sydenstricker. Picnicking is permitted. Guided 45-minute tours are offered Mon.-Sat. and holidays 9-4:30, May-Oct. Admission $6; senior citizens $5; ages 6-18, $1. Phone (304) 653-4430.

HINTON (E-3) pop. 2,880, elev. 1,372′

Hinton, a historic railroad town on the New River, was once the main terminal for the Chesapeake & Ohio Railway. Ten miles north via SR 26 (River Road) is Sandstone Falls, a noted spot among anglers for catfish and bass. West on SR 20, the New River Gorge National River Visitor Center *(see place listing p. 341)* features historic and scenic photographs of the area and is open seasonally.

Bluestone Dam, 1 mile south via SR 20 on the New River, forms 2,040-acre Bluestone Lake, providing recreational options such as boating, fishing and picnicking; phone (304) 466-1234 for information.

Summers County Convention and Visitors Bureau: 206 Temple St., Hinton, WV 25951; phone (304) 466-9230.

Self-guiding tours: Brochures outlining a walking tour of Hinton's historic district, with more than 200 buildings of historic and architectural interest, are available at the convention and visitors bureau.

HINTON RAILROAD MUSEUM is at 206 Temple St. This museum displays artifacts of the Chesapeake & Ohio Railway. The John Henry Woodcarving exhibit features wood sculptures by folk artist Charlie Permelia. In one display 98 figurines represent every railroad job that existed in 1870. Allow 30 minutes minimum. Mon.-Thurs. 9-5, Fri.-Sat. 9-9, Sun. noon-4. Donations. Phone (304) 466-1433.

HUNTINGTON (D-1) pop. 51,475, elev. 565′

Huntington lies in a semicircle between low hills and the Ohio River. Eleven miles of floodwalls protect the city. Founded in 1871 by Collis P. Huntington, who was then president of the Chesapeake & Ohio Railroad, the city has become a busy industrial center and trans-shipping point. Among the products manufactured in the area are chemicals, clothing, glass and steel.

The city's Civic Center, One Civic Center Plaza, draws convention business to Huntington and plays host to entertainment events. Marshall University offers guided campus tours through the Welcome Center; phone (304) 696-6833 or (800) 642-3499.

The rose garden in Ritter Park, on McCoy Road between 8th and 12th streets, displays four species and 87 varieties of roses. Virginia Point, a park at the mouth of the Big Sandy River, has a boat-launching ramp and a camping area. The Ohio River also offers recreational opportunities. Public launching ramps and a marina provide boaters access to the river.

Camden Park, an amusement park just west of the city on US 60, offers 26 rides, including two wooden roller coasters and a 1907 carousel; trips on a replica of a stern-wheeler; and shows by nationally known recording artists. Phone (304) 429-4321 or (866) 822-6336.

Cabell-Huntington Convention and Visitors Bureau: 739 3rd Ave., P.O. Box 347, Huntington, WV 25708; phone (304) 525-7333 or (800) 635-6329.

Shopping areas: Huntington Mall, off I-64 exit 20B, contains JCPenney, Lazarus-Macy's and Sears among its stores. Heritage Village, a restored railway yard at 11th Street and Veterans Memorial Boulevard, offers shops and restaurants housed in old warehouses and boxcars.

HERITAGE FARM MUSEUM AND VILLAGE is off I-64 exit 8 (5th St.), 1 mi. w. on Johnstown Rd., then 1.7 mi. s. to 3300 Harvey Rd. Appalachian heritage is preserved in more than 12 restored buildings, including a sawmill, blacksmith shop, country store, one-room school and log church. A petting zoo, animal barn and nature walk are featured. Museum displays include farm machinery, steam tractors, covered wagons, early automobiles and home technology.

Allow 1 hour minimum. Mon.-Sat. 10-3; closed holidays. Guided 2-hour tours $8; over 64, $7; ages 3-12, $6. Guided 1-hour tour $6; over 64, $5; ages 3-12, $4. Petting zoo/nature walk $3. Phone (304) 522-1244.

HUNTINGTON MUSEUM OF ART is at 2033 McCoy Rd. in Park Hills. Collections include 19th- and 20th-century sculpture, 19th-century French and English paintings, Ohio Valley glass, decorative arts, Georgian silver, plants and firearms. Also available are special exhibits and a children's art museum. Marked nature trails are on the grounds. Food is available. Allow 1 hour minimum. Tues.-Sat. 10-5 (also Tues. 5-9), Sun. noon-5; closed Jan. 1, Thanksgiving and Dec. 25. Free. Phone (304) 529-2701.

KEYSER (B-5) pop. 5,303, elev. 809'

The country around Keyser was a frequent battleground during the Civil War. A supply point for both armies, the community changed hands 14 times during the war. Nancy Hanks, mother of Abraham Lincoln, was born nearby on Doll Farm at Mikes Run.

Fort Ashby, on SR 46 near its intersection with SR 28, was built in 1755 and is the only remaining fort of the 69 that George Washington built to protect western Virginians. The fort is open by appointment. Write Fort Ashby, P.O. Box 97, Fort Ashby, WV 26719; phone (304) 298-3319 or (304) 298-3722.

Mineral County Convention and Visitors Bureau: Grand Central Business Center, Suite 2011, Keyser, WV 26726; phone (304) 788-2513.

LANSING (D-3) elev. 1,864'

Along with nearby Fayetteville and Hico *(see place listings p. 334 and p. 337)*, Lansing serves as a base of operations for outfitters offering trips down the New River. The Canyon Rim Visitor Center *(see attraction listing p. 342)* provides information about the New River Gorge National River.

NEW AND GAULEY RIVER ADVENTURES departs off US 19 exit Lansing Rd. Float trips are offered on the New and Gauley rivers. White-water rafting packages also are available. Inquire about age/weight restrictions, refund and weather policies. Trips depart daily, Mar.-Nov. New River fare $45-$300; Gauley River fare $75-$250. AX, DS, MC, VI. Phone (304) 574-3008 or (800) 759-7238.

RECREATIONAL ACTIVITIES
White-water Rafting

- **Class VI River Runners** is .1 mi. n. of the New River Gorge Bridge exit off US 19, then .5 mi. w. on Ames Heights Rd.; bear left at the fork in the road. Write P.O. Box 78, Lansing, WV 25862. Trips depart daily Apr.-Oct. Phone (304) 574-0704 or (800) 252-7784.

- **Wildwater Expeditions Unlimited** is 1.25 mi. n. of the New River Gorge Bridge at jct. US 19 and Milroy Grose Rd. Write P.O. Box 155, Lansing, WV 25862. Other activities are offered. Trips depart daily Apr.-Oct. Phone (304) 658-4007 or (800) 982-7238.

LEWISBURG (D-3) pop. 3,624, elev. 2,300'

Lewisburg's name was changed from Camp Union to honor Gen. Andrew Lewis, who organized the Virginia militia in 1774 for a campaign against the Shawnee. Lewis led his frontiersmen to victory at the Battle of Point Pleasant, said to be the first battle of the American Revolution. Andrew Lewis Park on N. Jefferson Street was the site where the militia assembled for the historic campaign.

The Civil War made yet another battleground out of Lewisburg. On May 23, 1862, the Confederate forces of Henry Heth clashed with the Union troops of George Crook, who later would win renown as the captor of Apache chief Geronimo. Although the Union force was victorious, Lewisburg remained a Confederate outpost for most of the war.

Some of Lewisburg's old buildings still bear scars of the battle, and a cross-shaped mass grave on McElhenny Road holds the remains of 95 unknown Confederate soldiers killed during the Battle of Lewisburg.

Carnegie Hall, on Church Street, was a 1902 gift from Andrew Carnegie to the Lewisburg Female Institute, later known as Greenbrier College. The building now serves as an arts and education center; phone (304) 645-7917 for information about performances and exhibits.

Professional theatrical productions are staged by Greenbrier Valley Theatre. Musicals, dramas, comedies, children's plays, musical concerts, and literary and poetry readings are offered year-round; phone (304) 645-3838 for information.

The Greenbrier River Trail, a 76-mile trail for hikers and bicyclers, runs along the Greenbrier River from Caldwell to Cass *(see place listing p. 331)*; the entrance to the trail at Caldwell is 3 miles east via US 60. The trail, originally part of the Chesapeake & Ohio rail system, provides access to the river for fishing, canoeing and cross-country skiing.

Greenbrier County Visitors Center—Lewisburg: 540 N. Jefferson St., Lewisburg, WV 24901; phone (304) 645-1000 or (800) 833-2068.

Self-guiding tours: Booklets outlining tours of the Battle of Lewisburg and the 236-acre historic district, containing more than 60 18th- and 19th-century buildings of historic and architectural interest, are available at local motels and at the visitors center. Brochures containing information about self-guided tours of the county's covered bridges, scenic overlooks and historic sites are also available at the visitors center.

LOST WORLD CAVERNS is 1.5 mi. n. via Court St./Fairview Rd. Discovered in 1942 by speleologists from Virginia Polytechnic Institute, the caves contain a number of large rooms with stalactite, stalagmite and flowstone formations as well as impressive displays of pure calcite. One formation is more than 40 feet high and has a circumference of 25 feet. The caverns' temperature is a constant 52 F.

Picnicking is permitted. Warm clothing is recommended. Allow 1 hour minimum. Self-guiding tours daily 9-7, May 15-Labor Day; 9-5, Apr. 1-May 14 and day after Labor Day-Thanksgiving; 10-4, rest of year. Closed Jan.1, Easter, Thanksgiving and Dec. 25. Last admission 45 minutes before closing. Admission $10; ages 6-12, $5. DS, MC, VI. Phone (304) 645-6677 or (866) 228-3778.

NORTH HOUSE HISTORY MUSEUM is .5 mi. w. on US 60 to 301 W. Washington St. The restored 1820 house displays antiques and artifacts dating from the early 1700s to the late 1800s, including Civil and Revolutionary war items and a Conestoga wagon. The library and its archives contain documents and family records from the same period. Allow 30 minutes minimum. Mon.-Sat. 10-4; closed Jan. 1, Memorial Day, July 4, Labor Day, Thanksgiving and Dec. 25. Admission $4; over 55, $3.50; ages 6-17, $2. Phone (304) 645-3398.

OLD STONE CHURCH is 2 blks. s.w. of US 60 and US 219 on Church St. Built to replace a log structure, the church was constructed of native stone by Scottish settlers in 1796. The original slave balcony and hand-hewn woodwork are noteworthy. The church is home to one of the earliest Presbyterian congregations in the state. Daily 9-5. Free. Phone (304) 645-2676.

LOGAN (D-2) pop. 1,630, elev. 671'

The burial site of "Devil Anse" Hatfield, the family leader in the infamous feud with the McCoys, lies south of Logan on SR 44 at Sarah Ann. A life-size statue imported from Italy marks his grave. The grave site is on private property. An outdoor amphitheater at Chief Logan State Park *(see Recreation Chart and the AAA Mideastern CampBook)* presents "The Aracoma Story," a play based on a local American Indian legend, and other dramas.

Logan County Chamber of Commerce: 214 Stratton St., P.O. Box 218, Logan, WV 25601; phone (304) 752-1324.

MARLINTON (D-3) pop. 1,204, elev. 2,127'

Marlinton was named after Jacob Marlin, one of its early settlers. The town is known as "the birthplace of rivers" because eight major rivers—the Cheat, Cranberry, Elk, Greenbrier, Shaver's Fork, Williams, Tygart and the Gauley and its tributaries—have their sources in the area. It also is a noted hunting area: Bears, deer, ruffed grouse and wild turkeys are plentiful in the region.

Marlinton marks an approximate halfway point along the scenic portion of SR 55/US 219, a scenic highway which runs 86 miles. The town also lies midway along the 76-mile Greenbrier River Trail, a hiking, bicycling and cross-country skiing trail that runs between North Caldwell and Cass.

Pocahontas County Tourism Commission Visitor Center: 700 4th Ave., P.O. Box 275, Marlinton, WV 24954; phone (304) 799-4636 or (800) 336-7009.

POCAHONTAS COUNTY HISTORICAL MUSEUM is .25 mi. s. on US 219 from jct. SR 39. A 1904 house contains documents, photographs, implements, clothes and other items depicting county history. Of particular interest is a Swiss music box that plays 36 tunes. Mon.-Sat. 11-5, Sun. 1-5, early June-Labor Day. Admission $2; ages 12-18, $1. Phone (304) 799-6659.

MARTINSBURG (B-6) pop. 14,972, elev. 457'

Founded in the 18th century, Martinsburg developed into an important shipping center with the construction of the Baltimore & Ohio Railroad in the 1850s. During the late 19th century orchards were planted in surrounding areas, and today Martinsburg has become a distribution center for apples and peaches. The preparation of these fruits for shipment can be viewed at Jefferson Orchards on SR 9 in Kearneysville, about 10 miles southeast of town.

Martinsburg was torn apart by the Civil War because of Union and Confederate occupation, internal strife and the proximity of many battles. The town was the home of Belle Boyd, a beautiful 17-year-old Confederate spy who shot a Union soldier in her parents' home after he had made threats against her mother.

Martinsburg-Berkeley County Convention and Visitors Bureau: 208 S. Queen St., Martinsburg, WV 25401; phone (304) 264-8801 or (800) 498-2386.

Shopping areas: Anchor shops at the Martinsburg Mall, between I-81 exits 12 and 13, are The Bon-Ton, JCPenney and Sears.

MATEWAN (E-1) pop. 498, elev. 700′

The infamous Hatfield and McCoy feud started in the Tug River Valley near present-day Matewan on Aug. 7, 1882, when Ellison Hatfield was killed by three McCoy brothers. The argument was said to have originated over a stolen hog, although court records indicate trouble between the families of William Anderson "Devil Anse" Hatfield and Randolph McCoy as early as the Civil War. The violence lasted only 6 years, but the press continued to sensationalize the feud for many years afterward.

The town of Matewan was established in 1895 with the extension of the Norfolk and Western Railway and the opening of the Williamson Coalfield. In 1920, as the United Mine Workers of America attempted to organize miners, a strike led to an armed confrontation in which 10 people died. The Matewan Massacre, as the incident came to be known, led to widespread clashes between miners and coal operators, police and federal troops.

MATEWAN WALKING TOUR begins at the McCoy Building on Mate St. An exhibit features early photographs of the area and its citizens. The self-guiding tour route traces Matewan's history as evidenced by buildings from the late 1800s to early 1900s. Sites include locations immortalized by the Hatfield and McCoy feud and the Matewan Massacre. Brochures are available. Allow 30 minutes minimum. Tues.-Sat. 10-5, Sun. noon-5. Free. Phone (304) 426-4239.

MATHIAS (C-5) elev. 1,531′

LOST RIVER STATE PARK is 4 mi. w. of SR 259 on CR 12, following signs. The park encompasses 3,712 acres of woodlands, part of which is virgin timber. The park was once a portion of the resort known as Lee's Sulphur Springs, which was developed by the Lee family. The springs were a part of the land grant awarded to Henry "Light Horse Harry" Lee, father of Robert E. Lee. Henry Lee's restored summer cabin, now a museum, is on the grounds.

Swimming and horseback riding are available. Allow 1 hour minimum. Park open daily 8-dusk. Museum open by appointment. Free. Phone (304) 897-5372 or (800) 225-5982.

MILTON (D-1) pop. 2,206, elev. 586′

BLENKO GLASS CO., off I-64 exit 28 to US 60, then w. to Fairgrounds Rd., is known for handmade contemporary tableware and stained glass. A visitor center houses displays and a museum containing early glassware, glassmaking equipment, military uniforms and historic documents.

Visitors may view artisans using the earliest-known techniques of glass blowing. A pond-side floral garden contains stained-glass pieces. Allow 30 minutes minimum. Observation area and guided tours Mon.-Fri. 8-3; closed holidays, the first 2 weeks in July and mid-Dec. through Jan. 1. Visitor center Mon.-Fri. 8-4, Sat. 9-4, Sun. noon-4. Free. Phone (304) 743-9081.

MONONGAHELA NATIONAL FOREST

Elevations in the forest range from 900 ft. at Petersburg to 4,861 ft. at Spruce Knob. Refer to AAA maps for additional elevation information.

Monongahela National Forest encompasses ten West Virginia counties in the Allegheny Mountains. Noted for its rugged terrain, highland bogs, blueberry thickets and vistas of exposed rocks, the forest was established in 1911 after widespread cutting of eastern forests. Many of the 909,000-acre forest's natural attractions are visible from the summit of 4,861-foot Spruce Knob (see Spruce Knob-Seneca Rocks National Recreation Area p. 345). The Cranberry Glades, Seneca Rocks (see Spruce Knob-Seneca Rocks National Recreation Area p. 345) and July-blooming rhododendrons are among the region's highlights.

Many good routes traverse the forest; some provide picturesque drives. The 45-mile Highland Scenic Highway between Richwood and Marlinton offers spectacular views of the Allegheny Highlands. US 250 offers some exceptional scenery. Between Huttonsville and the Virginia line the highway crosses 4,353-foot Top of Allegheny. A 60-mile section of US 33 from Elkins east to Franklin also offers splendid vistas.

Bears, deer, grouse, rabbits, squirrels and turkeys can be hunted in season. The forest contains 129 miles of warm-water fishing and 576 miles of trout streams. Gaudineer Scenic Area, off US 250 north of Durbin, protects 140 acres of virgin red spruce. The Dolly Sods Wilderness Area, 10,215 acres west of Hopeville, offers wide views and upland bogs with unusual plants. In the 20,000 acres of Otter Creek Wilderness Area hiking trails thread through mountainous terrain. Fernow Experimental Forest, administered by the U.S. Forest Service, adjoins Otter Creek; hunting is permitted in season.

Other wilderness areas within the forest are Cranberry, Laurel Fork North and Laurel Fork South. The forest is traversed by some 500 miles of hiking trails and an extensive backwoods road and trail system for hiking, mountain biking and horseback riding. An excellent hiking guide to the forest is available for a fee from the West Virginia Conservancy, P.O. Box 306, Charleston, WV 25321.

For further information contact the Forest Supervisor, Monongahela National Forest, 200 Sycamore St., Elkins, WV 26241; phone (304) 636-1800, voice and TTY. *See Recreation Chart and the AAA Mideastern CampBook.*

CRANBERRY MOUNTAIN NATURE CENTER is 23 mi. e. of Richwood on SR 39 at SR 150. Forest ecology, history and wildlife are depicted through exhibits and lectures. A self-guiding nature trail winds through the forest. A boardwalk provides access to the Cranberry Glades Botanical Area, which contains bog vegetation that is far south of its normal range. Daily 9-5, Apr.-Oct. Free. Phone (304) 653-4826.

MORGANTOWN (B-4) pop. 26,809, elev. 869′

Morgantown, on the east bank of the Monongahela River, is the seat of Monongalia County and the home of West Virginia University. Near the Evansdale campus is the WVU Health Sciences Center.

Cooper's Rock State Forest *(see Bruceton Mills p. 331)*, 13 miles east off I-68, offers 12,713 acres of forest, interesting rock formations, hiking trails, cross-country ski trails, camping and picnic areas, a 19th-century iron furnace and a spectacular view of the Cheat River Valley. Swimming and boating are popular activities at Cheat Lake, just east of town on I-68.

A 52-mile section of the West Virginia Rail Trail follows the Monongahela River through Morgantown. Ideal for walking, bicycling, jogging and inline skating, the trail is paved within city limits. Morgantown is at the western end of the scenic portion of I-68, which runs east to Hancock, Md.

Greater Morgantown Convention and Visitors Bureau: 201 High St., Morgantown, WV 26505; phone (304) 292-5081 or (800) 458-7373.

Shopping areas: Morgantown Mall, at the junction of I-79 exit 152 and US 19, features more than 75 specialty shops and four department stores. Seneca Center, in the old Seneca Glass Factory at 709 Beechurst Ave., contains specialty shops.

CORE ARBORETUM is on Monongahela Blvd. just s. of the WVU Coliseum. Some 3 miles of trails wind past hundreds of labeled species of trees, shrubs and native wildflowers in this 50-acre classroom. The arboretum serves as a research facility and outdoor classroom for West Virginia University. Allow 1 hour minimum. Daily dawn-dusk. Free. Phone (304) 293-5201.

PERSONAL RAPID TRANSIT (PRT) connects the Evansdale and downtown WVU campuses with the central business district. This computer-operated transit system, launched in 1975, includes five stations along a 9-mile corridor and carries up to 15,000 riders per day. The automated "people mover" serves as a transportation laboratory for engineering students and urban planners. Guided tours are available by reservation.

Operating Mon.-Fri. 6:30 a.m.-10:15 p.m., Sat. 9:30-5, late Aug.-late May; Mon.-Fri. 6:30 a.m.-6:15 p.m., Sat. 9:30-5, rest of year. Closed university holidays. Fare 50c. Phone (304) 293-5011.

MOUNDSVILLE (B-3) pop. 9,998, elev. 647′

Moundsville, first known as Grave Creek, started as a cabin built in 1771 by Joseph, Samuel and James Tomlinson about 300 yards from the Grave Creek Burial Mound. In 1865 the town consolidated with Mound City and was named after the large prehistoric burial mound from the Adena Indian culture.

Marshall County Chamber of Commerce: 609 Jefferson Ave., Moundsville, WV 26041; phone (304) 845-2773.

GRAVE CREEK MOUND ARCHAEOLOGY COMPLEX is at 801 Jefferson Ave. and 8th St. via SR 2. Considered the largest prehistoric Indian burial mound of its kind, the 69-foot mound was built more than 2,000 years ago and was originally surrounded by a moat. The Delf Norona Museum contains a collection of artifacts of the Adena period (approximately 1000 B.C. to beyond A.D. 1). Allow 1 hour minimum. Mon.-Sat. 10-4:30, Sun. 1-5; closed major holidays. Admission $3; ages 6-16, $2. Phone (304) 843-4128.

[SAVE] **WEST VIRGINIA PENITENTIARY** is at 8th St. and Jefferson Ave. This Gothic-style fortress was built by convict labor in 1867 as the state's first territorial prison. Guided 90-minute tours allow visitors to step inside a 5-foot-by-7-foot cell and see the electric chair, the gallows and North Hall, where inmates were confined 22 hours a day. Hand-painted murals adorn the walls.

Tours depart on the hour Tues.-Sun. 10-4, Apr.-Nov.; by appointment rest of year. Closed Easter, Thanksgiving and Dec. 25. Admission $8; senior citizens $7; ages 6-10, $5. DC, DS, MC, VI. Phone (304) 845-6200.

NEWELL (A-3) pop. 1,602, elev. 691′

THE HOMER LAUGHLIN CHINA CO. is on SR 2, 1 mi. s. of the Newell Bridge at the Ohio River. Said to be the largest American maker of domestic and hotel china, the company claims to have produced one-third of all the china sold in the United States. The company was founded in 1871 and introduced the popular Fiesta line of china in 1936. Guided tours are preceded by a slide presentation.

Allow 1 hour minimum. Open Mon.-Tues. 9:30-7, Wed. and Fri.-Sat. 9:30-5, Sun. noon-5. Tours are given Mon.-Thurs. at 10:30 and 12:30. Closed major holidays. Free. Reservations are required for tours. Phone (304) 387-1300.

NEW RIVER GORGE NATIONAL RIVER (E-3)

The New River Gorge National River encompasses 53 miles of the New River and its narrow gorge that wind through the Appalachian Mountains from Hinton to the New River Gorge Bridge (US 19) near Fayetteville. Contrary to its name, the New is believed to be one of the oldest rivers in North America; it was part of the ancient Teays River system, which originated more than 65 million years ago. Unlike most of the world's rivers, it flows northward.

The river's human history began about 12,000 years ago when prehistoric Indians lived and hunted in the area. The portion of the river within the park, however, was largely unsettled due to the dangerous and often impassable rapids and steep gorge walls. In 1873 the C&O Railroad was completed through the gorge and provided access to the exposed rich seams of coal in the mountains.

For the next 80 years the area was a booming industrial center, whose heart was the 18-odd communities in the lower canyon from Prince to Fayette Station. But as the mines were worked out, people began to leave the gorge's coal towns. Forest has since reclaimed most of the towns and mine sites.

General Information and Activities

The New is regarded as one of the best rivers in the state for small-mouth bass fishing. In addition, muskellunge, walleye, catfish and carp test the skill of anglers. Some of the river's tributaries are stocked with trout. The most popular portion of the New for fishing is the upper section from Hinton to McCreery.

The New River is said to rival the Colorado for its white-water rafting opportunities. The 30 miles of the lower portion from McCreery to the New River Gorge Bridge draw white-water rafting enthusiasts each year from early April to mid-October. Many outfitters with highly skilled guides provide both scenic and white-water trips through the gorge and are primarily located at the northern end of the river.

Other popular recreational activities within the park include picnicking, camping, hiking, mountain biking, canoeing, kayaking, horseback riding, and rock climbing. *See Recreation Chart.*

ADDRESS inquiries to the Superintendent, New River Gorge National River, National Park Service, Box 246, Glen Jean, WV 25846. Phone (304) 465-0508.

VISITOR CENTERS include locations on US 19 n. of Fayetteville, SR 25 in the Thurmond railroad depot, SR 9 in Grandview and SR 20 w. of Hinton (*see place listing p. 337*). Each center offers brochures, maps and historic background on the river and the surrounding area; park rangers provide information and orientation services. Grandview's center is noted for its overlooks, trails and spring display of rhododendrons. The Fayetteville visitor center is open year-round; all others are open seasonally.

Canyon Rim Visitor Center is 2 mi. n. of Fayetteville on US 19. Panoramic views of the gorge and the New River Gorge Bridge are offered at the center, which also features exhibits and a slide presentation. Daily 9-6, Memorial Day-Labor Day; 9-5, rest of year. Closed Jan. 1, Thanksgiving and Dec. 25. Free. Phone (304) 574-2115.

PARKERSBURG (C-2) pop. 33,099, elev. 151'

Parkersburg's strategic location at the confluence of the Little Kanawha and Ohio rivers aided its development as an industrial center. An early visitor was George Washington, who surveyed land above the city on the Ohio River. In 1810 the Virginia legislature passed an act to found the town, known as Neal's Station and Newport prior to being incorporated as Parkersburg. Improved transportation modes and routes to the area soon followed. West Virginia's first oil wells were drilled nearby in 1860, which made Parkersburg the supply and shipping point for the "black gold" fields.

The Oil, Gas and Industrial Historical Museum, 119 Third St., commemorates the historical significance to the area of these industries. The region also was blessed with natural gas fields; gas soon became the major source of fuel for the growing number of industrial plants. More than 100 industries produce chemicals, glass, metals, plastics and other products.

A rails-to-trails conversion, the North Bend Rail Trail extends for 72 miles from its trailhead near Parkersburg to Wolf Summit near Clarksburg. The scenic trail runs through 13 tunnels constructed by the Baltimore and Ohio Railroad 1853-57 and crosses 36 bridges.

Parkersburg/Wood County Convention and Visitors Bureau: 350 Seventh St., Parkersburg, WV 26101; phone (304) 428-1130 or (800) 752-4982. *See color ads starting on p. 324.*

Self-guiding tours: Brochures outlining a walking tour of historic buildings are available at the convention and visitors bureau.

BLENNERHASSETT ISLAND HISTORICAL STATE PARK is in the Ohio River, reached by stern-wheeler from Point Park at Second and Ann sts. Harman Blennerhassett, an exiled Irish aristocrat, built his island mansion in 1798. He became involved with Aaron Burr in an alleged plot to establish an empire in the Southwest and was forced to flee the island with his family in 1806 when the conspiracy came to light. Both men were eventually acquitted of treason, but their lives were ruined.

Fire destroyed the abandoned mansion in 1811. The Palladian-style house has been reconstructed upon its original foundation, and guided tours of the interior are offered. Narrated mule-drawn wagon rides recount the area's history.

Picnic facilities and food are available. Allow 3 hours minimum. Open Tues.-Fri. 10-4:30, Sat. 10-5:30, Sun. noon-5:30, May 1-Labor Day; Thurs.-Sat. 11-4:30, Sun. noon-4:30, day after Labor Day-Oct. 31. Park admission free. Mansion tour $2; ages

3-12, $1. Wagon rides $4.50; ages 3-12, $2.50. Phone (304) 420-4800 or (800) 225-5982.

Blennerhassett Museum is downtown at Second and Juliana sts. Three floors are dedicated to archeological and historical exhibits. A 12-minute videotape reveals the history of the Blennerhassett family and its island. Allow 30 minutes minimum. Tues.-Fri. 10-5, Sat. 10-6, Sun. 11-6, May 1-Labor Day; Tues.-Sat. 10-5, Sun. 11-5, day after Labor Day-Oct. 31; Tues.-Sat. 11-5, Sun. 1-5, Nov.-Dec.; Sat. 11-5, Sun. 1-5, rest of year. Admission $2; ages 3-12, $1. Phone (304) 420-4800 or (800) 225-5982.

Stern-wheelers depart for the island from Point Park at Second and Ann sts. Trips run Tues.-Sun. on the hour 10-4, May 1-Labor Day; Thurs.-Sat. on the hour 10-3, Sun. noon-4:30, day after Labor Day-Oct. 31. To tour the mansion, depart from Point Park no later than 3 p.m.; the last shuttle leaves the island at 5:30 p.m. Fare $8; ages 3-12, $7. AX, CB, DS, MC, VI. Phone (740) 423-7268.

THE PARKERSBURG ART CENTER is at 725 Market St. The center presents changing visual art displays of work by nationally known and local artists as well as traveling exhibitions. Guided tours are available by appointment. Open Tues.-Sat. 10-5, Sun. 1-5; closed major holidays. Admission $2, children free; free to all Wed. Phone (304) 485-3859.

PETERSBURG (C-5) pop. 2,423, elev. 937′

On the south branch of the Potomac River, Petersburg was settled in 1745. It was named after German colonist Jacob Peterson, who established the town's first store. During the Civil War the town served as a Union outpost along the contested border between the North and South. Nearby earthworks were constructed by troops from Illinois and Ohio in 1863.

Because it is near the entrance to Monongahela National Forest and Spruce Knob-Seneca Rocks National Recreation Area *(see place listings p. 340 and p. 345)*, Petersburg is considered a recreation center, and calls itself the "Home of the Golden Trout." Area outfitters provide information, equipment and guides for hunting, fishing and canoeing trips into the surrounding wilderness.

PETERSBURG GAP is e. on US 220 and SR 55. The South Branch of the Potomac River breaks through Orr's Mountain at this point. The cliffs on the south side rise to a height of 800 feet. The "Pictured Rocks" are where figures of a fox and an ox or buffalo appear to have been carved into the cliffs.

SMOKE HOLE CAVERNS is 8 mi. s.w. on SR 28/55. Unusual formations include one of the world's longest ribbon stalactites and an underground lake and stream. The caverns were reportedly used by American Indians to smoke meat and by enterprising settlers to make "moonshine." A 19th-century still is displayed. A wildlife museum is on the grounds. The caverns maintain a constant temperature of 56 F.

Picnic facilities are available. Guided tours every half-hour daily 9-5. Admission $9; senior citizens $8.25; ages 5-12, $5. AX, DC, DS, MC, VI. Phone (304) 257-4442 or (800) 828-8478.

PHILIPPI (C-4) pop. 2,870, elev. 1,247′

The first land battle of the Civil War occurred at Philippi (FIL-uh-pee) on June 3, 1861. Col. B.F. Kelley and a detachment of Federal troops from George McClellan's army surprised and routed the newly recruited Confederates under the command of Col. George Alexander Porterfield.

Spanning the Tygart River is a covered bridge that was originally built in 1852 and was used by both Confederate and Union forces during the battles. The bridge burned in 1989 but has been completely restored and is the only covered bridge still in use as a federal highway. From Fairmont to the north, the scenic portion of US 250 passes through Philippi on its 73-mile journey to Huttonsville.

Barbour County Chamber of Commerce: P.O. Box 5000, Philippi, WV 26416; phone (304) 457-1958.

[SAVE] **ADALAND MANSION** is 4 mi. n. on US 119 to SR 76, then 1 mi. n. to Adaland Rd. This 1870 brick mansion features Neo-Greek architecture, period wallpaper and antique furnishings. Details include woodwork of native hardwood, double porches, an outside walnut stairway, travelers' rooms and a metal roof with handmade brackets. Guided tours are offered. Allow 1 hour minimum. Wed.-Thurs. and Sat. 11-5, Sun 1-5, May-Dec.; closed Easter, Thanksgiving and Dec. 25. Admission $5, under 12 free. AX, DC, DS, MC, VI. Phone (304) 457-1587.

BARBOUR COUNTY HISTORICAL MUSEUM is at 146 N. Main St. Housed in a renovated railroad station, the museum features Civil War memorabilia, antiques, books and two mummies. Mon.-Sat. 11-4, Sun. 1-4, May-Oct.; by appointment rest of year. Museum free. Mummy exhibit $1. Phone (304) 457-4846.

PIPESTEM (E-3) elev. 2,389′

PIPESTEM RESORT STATE PARK is on SR 20. The 4,024-acre park covers a broad plateau overlooking the Bluestone River Gorge. The resort offers camping, canoeing, cross-country skiing, golfing, horseback riding, swimming, tennis and rental paddleboats. Nature programs also are offered. Plays and concerts are presented in the summer. An aerial tram, ascending 3,600 feet, departs from the visitor center.

Food is available. Allow 1 hour minimum for aerial tram. Park open daily 6 a.m.-10 p.m. Tram daily 7 a.m.-midnight (closed Tues. and Thurs. 1-4), May-Oct. Park free. Tram $4; ages 5-12, $3. AX, DC, MC, VI. Phone (304) 466-1800 or (800)

225-5982. *See Recreation Chart and the AAA Mid-eastern CampBook.*

POINT PLEASANT (C-1)
pop. 4,637, elev. 561'

Point Pleasant is in a growing resort area near the confluence of the Kanawha and Ohio rivers. It is said that when George Washington surveyed this area in the 1740s, he referred to it as the Pleasant Point. A reconstruction of Fort Randolph, the best known of the town's forts, is in Krodel Park. A showplace for many of the town's events, the fort is open from mid-April through October. The 44-acre park also contains campsites, paddleboats, a playground and a miniature golf course, and allows fishing; phone (304) 675-2360.

The 11,164-acre Chief Cornstalk Public Hunting and Fishing Area, southeast of town, is accessible via a hard-surfaced road that branches west off SR 35 near Southside.

Mason County Area Chamber of Commerce: 305 Main St., Point Pleasant, WV 25550; phone (304) 675-1050.

C.F. McCLINTIC WILDLIFE MANAGEMENT AREA is 5 mi. n. on SR 62, then 1 mi. e. on Potters Creek Rd. (CR 11). Hunting for deer, grouse, quails, rabbits and waterfowl is popular in the 3,066-acre area. More than 30 impoundments allow for warm-water fishing for a wide variety of species, including bluegill, bass, catfish and northern pike. While there are neither marked hiking trails nor visitor centers, primitive campsites are available. Open daily 24 hours. Office hours Mon.-Fri. 8:30-4:30. Admission free. Camping $5. Phone (304) 675-0871.

TU-ENDIE-WEI STATE PARK is at the southern end of town at 1 Main St. and jct. Ohio and Kanawha rivers. The land was named "tu-endie-wei" or "the point between two waters" by the Wyandotte Indians. At this site on Oct. 10, 1774, Gen. Andrew Lewis and 1,100 Virginia frontiersmen were attacked by Shawnee chief Cornstalk and a like number of American Indians.

The day-long battle at the site is said to have been the opening engagement of the American Revolution. Park open Mon.-Sat. 10-4:30, Sun. 1-4:30, May-Oct. Free. Phone (304) 675-0869.

Mansion House is in the park at 1 Main St. Built by Walter Newman in 1796 as a public inn, the building is the oldest in the Kanawha Valley. Constructed of hewn logs, it has two fireplaces and contains local Colonial furniture and heirlooms as well as relics from the Battle of Point Pleasant. Mon.-Sat. 10-4:30, Sun. 1-4:30, May-Nov. Free.

WEST VIRGINIA STATE FARM MUSEUM is 6 mi. n. on SR 62, then .7 mi. e. to Camp Conley Rd., following signs. This 50-acre museum features log cabins built in the early 1800s, a replica of an old Lutheran church, a one-room schoolhouse built around 1870, a print shop, a chapel, a taxidermic collection, a doctor's office, a country store, farm equipment including a collection of tractors, a working blacksmith shop, an herb garden, railroad cars and a barn. Picnicking is permitted. Allow 1 hour, 30 minutes minimum. Tues.-Sat. 9-5, Sun. 1-5, Apr. 1-Nov. 15. Donations. Phone (304) 675-5737.

PRINCETON (E-2) pop. 6,347, elev. 2,460'

Mercer County, at the southern tip of West Virginia, bears the name of General Hugh Mercer, a Revolutionary War hero who was mortally wounded in 1777 at the Battle of Princeton in New Jersey. The county seat, Princeton, honors the place where he died.

Princeton-Mercer County Chamber of Commerce: 910 Oakvale Rd., Princeton, WV 24740; phone (304) 487-1502. *See color ads starting on p. 324.*

THOSE WHO SERVED WAR MUSEUM is at 1500 W. Main St. This museum houses more than 750 war relics and personal effects, the majority from World War II, with additional displays dating from the Civil War to Desert Storm. Allow 30 minutes minimum. Mon.-Fri. 10-4; closed holidays. Free. Phone (304) 487-8397 or (304) 487-3670.

RIVERTON (C-4) elev. 1,809'

SENECA CAVERNS is 3 mi. e. of US 33 via Seneca Caverns Rd. to German Valley Rd. Visitors travel along a .75-mile passage through the caverns at a depth ranging from 25-165 feet below ground level. Lighted trails provide access to the caverns' unusual mineral formations including cave coral, rimstone, stalactites, stalagmites and travertine.

Other formations include Mirror Lake, a reflective underground pool, and the Grand Ballroom, featuring a natural balcony. The caverns served as a refuge for the Seneca Indians from cold winters and for ceremonial rituals during the 1600s and 1700s. Gemstone mining is avaiable.

Picnicking is permitted. Food is available. Warm clothing and comfortable walking shoes are recommended. Allow 1 hour minimum. Guided 55-minute tours depart every 20 minutes daily 9-6:45, June-Aug.; 10-4:45, Sept.-Oct.; 10-4, rest of year. Admission $9; over 62, $8.25; ages 6-12, $5.50. AX, DS, MC, VI. Phone (304) 567-2691 or (800) 239-7647.

ROMNEY (C-5) pop. 1,940, elev. 820'

Incorporated in 1762, Romney is one of the oldest settlements in West Virginia. During the Civil War, the town is said to have changed hands at least 56 times. The West Virginia State Schools for the Deaf and Blind were established at Romney in 1870.

Departing from the Wappocomo Station, 1.5 miles north on SR 28, the Potomac Eagle Scenic Railroad offers narrated 3-hour excursions through scenic mountain valleys. Bald eagles are often sighted on the trips, which run on Saturday, May through September, and daily in October; phone (304) 424-0736.

Hampshire County Chamber of Commerce: 91 S. High St., Taggart Hall, Romney, WV 26757; phone (304) 822-7221.

TAGGART HALL CIVIL WAR MUSEUM AND VISITOR'S CENTER is .1 mi. s. on US 50 at 91 S. High St. In a clapboard house built 1795-98 by Quaker Francis Taggart, the museum features artifacts from the Civil War and the French and Indian War as well as historical items from Hampshire County. The building also houses the county visitor center. Allow 30 minutes minimum. Mon.-Sat. 9-4, Sun. noon-4; closed Dec. 25. Donations. Phone (304) 822-7221.

ROWLESBURG (B-4) pop. 613, elev. 1,402'

RECREATIONAL ACTIVITIES
White-water Rafting
- SAVE **USA Raft** is 3 mi. n. off US 50 on SR 72 at jct. Buffalo and Catherine sts. Write P.O. Box 277, Rowlesburg, WV 26425. Trips depart daily Mar.-Oct. Phone (304) 454-2475 or (800) 872-7238.

SENECA ROCKS—
see Spruce Knob-Seneca Rocks National Recreation Area p. 345.

SHEPHERDSTOWN (B-6)
pop. 803, elev. 402'

The site of one of the earliest settlements in West Virginia, Shepherdstown was established by English and German farmers who had crossed the river from Pennsylvania into this area before 1730. The legal grant to the land was purchased by Thomas Shepherd in 1732.

Originally named Mecklenburg, the name was changed to Shepherdstown in 1798. While living in Shepherdstown in 1787, James Rumsey gave the first public exhibition of his steamboat. A monument on the banks of the Potomac commemorates this successful demonstration. On German Street are Shepherd College, built in 1871, and the Entler Hotel, built in 1786.

Shepherdstown Visitors Center: 102 E. German St., Shepherdstown, WV 25443; phone (304) 876-2786.

SISTERSVILLE (B-2) pop. 1,588, elev. 590'

Charles Wells settled Sistersville in the early 19th century. In 1839 the town was incorporated and named in honor of his daughters Sarah and Deliah, the 18th and 19th of his 22 children.

Sistersville's relatively quiet posture as a farming and trade community on the Ohio River changed dramatically in 1889 with the discovery of oil on an area farm. Oil barons descended upon the town,

building unsightly rigs as well as many stately homes and a striking business district along Wells Street. The oil boom ended in 1915, returning the town to its earlier lifestyle but leaving a legacy of handsome buildings that represent a variety of architectural styles.

A ferry takes passengers from Sistersville across the Ohio River to Fly, Ohio. The ferry, which can hold up to eight automobiles, operates Mon.-Sat. 6-6, Sun. 9-6.

Self-guiding tours: A brochure outlining a walking tour past many historic buildings is available at The Wells Inn, 316 Charles St., Sistersville, WV 26175; phone (304) 652-1312.

SNOWSHOE (D-4)

RECREATIONAL ACTIVITIES
Skiing
- **Snowshoe Mountain Resort** is off US 219 at SR 66. Write P.O. Box 10, Snowshoe, WV 26209. Other activities are offered. Skiing daily Thanksgiving-early Apr. Phone (304) 572-1000 or (877) 441-4386.

SPRUCE KNOB-SENECA ROCKS NATIONAL RECREATION AREA (C-4, C-5)

The Spruce Knob-Seneca Rocks National Recreation Area is composed of two sections within the Monongahela National Forest *(see place listing p. 340)*. The larger Seneca Rocks unit is especially noted for rugged terrain and white-water boating and rock-climbing opportunities. Camping, fishing and hiking are popular during spring and summer. Hunting is permitted in season. Cross-country skiers prefer the higher elevations in the Spruce Knob unit, where trails are plentiful. For further information, phone (304) 257-4488. *See Recreation Chart.*

SENECA ROCKS is off US 33 and SR 28 at the town of Seneca Rocks. Rising above the North Fork River, this 900-foot-tall mass of intricately eroded quartzite sandstone is one of the most impressive rock formations in the East and is considered to be an excellent rock-climbing area.

The Seneca Rocks Discovery Center in town offers film and slide presentations, hikes and outdoor demonstrations. The adjacent patio contains exhibits about Seneca Rocks. Daily 9-4:30, Apr.-Nov. Free. Phone (304) 567-2827.

SMOKE HOLE lies along Smoke Hole Rd. n. of Upper Tract in the Seneca Rocks unit; take FR 79 s. from jct. SR 28 at Cabins. The half-mile-deep gorge was formed by the south branch of the Potomac River as it ran between North and Cave mountains. A road leads northwest from US 220, traverses a portion of the gorge and ends at the Big Bend Campground. Among Smoke Hole's notable formations is Eagle Rock, which towers upward from the river.

SPRUCE KNOB is w. of US 33 by a forest road about 2.5 mi. s. of Riverton. Spruce Knob is the highest point in West Virginia at 4,861 feet *(see Monongahela National Forest p. 340)*. Numerous overlooks provide scenic views on the road to the summit, which features an observation tower and an interpretive trail.

Nearby Spruce Knob Lake is stocked with trout and offers good fishing, especially during the spring and fall. Since the partially paved road has unprotected shoulders at some points, caution is advised. The road should not be attempted by inexperienced drivers or during hazardous driving conditions. Camping is available.

SUMMERSVILLE (D-3)
pop. 3,294, elev. 1,926′

Nancy Hart, a Confederate spy, led an attack on Summersville in 1861. During the battle a Union force was captured, and the town was burned. Hart escaped to Confederate lines but returned after Gen. Robert E. Lee's surrender. US 19, a 45-mile scenic highway linking I-79 at Sutton and the West Virginia Turnpike at Bradley, passes Summersville near Summersville Lake *(see Recreation Chart and the AAA Mideastern CampBook)*.

The Gauley River National Recreation Area, between Summersville and Swiss, protects 25 miles of the Gauley River and 6 miles of its tributary, the Meadow River. The Gauley is known for its rapids, white-water rafting and fishing opportunities. The recreation area can be reached from Carnifex Ferry Battlefield State Park *(see attraction listing)* or Summersville Dam off SR 129 and from SR 39. Information is available at park headquarters, P.O. Box 246, Glen Jean, WV 25846; phone (304) 465-0508.

Summersville Area Chamber of Commerce: 1 Wilderness Rd., P.O. Box 567, Summersville, WV 26651; phone (304) 872-1588.

CARNIFEX FERRY BATTLEFIELD STATE PARK is 10 mi. s.w. off US 19 at Keslers Cross Lanes. A Civil War engagement was fought on this 156-acre site Sept. 10, 1861. The park museum contains Civil War relics from the battle. A Civil War battle re-enactment weekend takes place in September of odd-numbered years. Park open daily dawn-dusk. Museum open Sat.-Sun. and holidays 10-5, Memorial Day weekend-Sept. 12. Free. Phone (304) 872-0825.

WINERIES
- **Kirkwood Winery and Isaiah Morgan Distillery** is 1 mi. n. on US 19, then .5 mi. e. to 1350 Phillips Run Rd. Tours and tastings Mon.-Sat. 9-5, Sun. 1-5; closed Jan. 1, Thanksgiving and Dec. 25. Phone (304) 872-7332 or (888) 498-9463.

WARDENSVILLE (C-5) pop. 246, elev. 1,011′

The Lost River, west of Wardensville along SR 55/259, vanishes many times during its course, appearing and disappearing close to the highway.

About 4.3 miles southwest of town, the river flows under Sandy Ridge, emerging on the other side to form the Cacapon River. Lost River State Park *(see attraction listing p. 340)* is 23 miles south in Mathias.

WEBSTER (C-4) pop. 9,719, elev. 1,019′

THE ANNA JARVIS BIRTHPLACE MUSEUM is .2 mi. w. on US 119. The 1854 two-story home was the birthplace of Anna Jarvis, the founder of Mother's Day. The establishment of this holiday was a fervent wish of Ms. Jarvis' mother. Gen. George McClellan used the house as his headquarters during the Civil War while planning the war's first land battle. The museum contains more than 5,500 artifacts relating to Ms. Jarvis and the war. Allow 30 minutes minimum. Tues.-Sun. 10-4, Apr.-Dec.; closed Dec. 25. Admission $5. MC, VI. Phone (304) 265-5549.

WEST MILFORD (C-3) pop. 651, elev. 980′

WATTERS SMITH MEMORIAL STATE PARK is 2 mi. s. on Duck Creek Rd., following signs. The park contains a replica of a log cabin built in 1796 by Watters Smith, the first pioneer in this area. The Smith family lived on the site until 1948. The park also includes a museum with historical items and memorabilia of the Smith family, a residence built in 1876, a blacksmith shop and several barns. Hiking trails, a swimming pool and mountain biking are available.

Picnicking is permitted. Park daily 7-dusk, Memorial Day weekend-Labor Day. Museum daily noon-5. Pool Thurs.-Tues. 11-7. Admission $3; ages 4-11, $2. Phone (304) 745-3081.

WESTON (C-3) pop. 4,317, elev. 982′

Weston serves as a commercial center for an agricultural area and supports glass industries. Surveyed by Thomas "Stonewall" Jackson's grandfather, the town contains several rambling Victorian-era homes. The former Weston State Hospital is surrounded by vast landscaped grounds. The main building, begun in 1860 and completed in 1865, has 9 acres of floor space and is said to be the largest hand-cut stone building in the United States.

The Citizens Bank Building at 201 Main Ave. is noted among devotees of classic Art Deco architecture. Built 1928-1930, this 54-foot tall Indiana limestone structure is believed to be the tallest single-story building in the United States; the wrought-iron work is by the noted artist Samuel Yellen. Inside, the woodwork is hand-carved American walnut, and the 45-foot suspended plaster ceiling has a relief of the Great Seal of West Virginia. Also of interest in town is the West Virginia Genealogical and Historical Library and Museum, which is open to the public for research; phone (304) 269-7091.

Nearby Stonewall Jackson Lake State Park surrounds the state's second-largest lake. This park offers many recreational opportunities and facilities.

For more information phone (304) 269-0523. *See Recreation Chart.*

In recent years Weston has gained recognition for its unusual Christmas lights display on Main Street. Called "Dancing Snowflakes," this computerized light show includes 32 snowflakes that dance down the street in more than 15 pattern variations. The snowflakes are accompanied by Santa and his nine reindeer, which prance on the rooftops. The 39-minute show runs continuously daily from dusk to 1 a.m., day after Thanksgiving through January 1.

Lewis County Convention and Visitors Bureau: 345 Center Ave., P.O. Box 379, Weston, WV 26452; phone (304) 269-7328.

WVU JACKSON'S MILL CENTER FOR LIFE-LONG LEARNING is about 4 mi. n. on US 19. In 1921 Jackson's Mill became the first state 4-H camp in the nation. The 523-acre site includes an amphitheater, livestock pavilions, gardens, recreation facilities and hiking trails. During Labor Day weekend the conference center hosts more than 100 artisans for the Stonewall Jackson Heritage Arts and Crafts Jubilee, which includes historic re-enactments and concerts.

Center open Mon.-Fri. 8-4:30. Center free. An admission fee is charged for the jubilee. Phone (304) 269-5100 or (800) 287-8206, or (304) 269-1863 or (800) 296-1863 for jubilee information.

Jackson's Mill Historic Area, at the second gate on the West Fork River, is on the original 5 acres of "Stonewall" Jackson's boyhood home. Gristmill and water-driven sawmill components, farm implements, weaving equipment and blacksmithing and carpentry tools are displayed. A log cabin from the 1700s is furnished in period, and an 1800s cabin serves as a visitor center. A working gristmill also is on the grounds.

Tues.-Sun. 10-5, Memorial Day-Labor Day; Thurs.-Sun. 10-5, day after Labor Day-Oct. 31; Sat.-Sun. 10-5, in May. Admission $5; senior citizens $4; ages 5-12, $2. AX, DS, MC, VI. Phone (800) 287-8206, ext. 158.

WHEELING (B-3) pop. 31,419, elev. 645'

Wheeling lies along the scenic portion of I-70, which continues into Pennsylvania to the east and Ohio to the west. The last battle of the American Revolution was fought in Wheeling Sept. 11-13, 1782, when Fort Henry was attacked by a force of 40 British soldiers and 260 Indians. The news of the peace had not yet reached this outpost. Ebenezer and Silas Zane, who founded the city in 1769, led the defending forces. Their sister, Betty, brought powder from the Zane cabin to the fort; her efforts saved the garrison. The site of the fort is marked by a memorial stone on Main Street.

When Virginia seceded from the Union, delegates from the western counties met at Wheeling and set up the "Restored Government of Virginia," with Wheeling as the capital. After West Virginia was formally admitted to the Union in 1863,

Wheeling was the capital until 1870 and again 1875-85.

The 900-foot-long Wheeling Suspension Bridge, built in 1849, is one of the world's longest. Henry Clay, while visiting Wheeling a year after the bridge opened, described it as "a rainbow to behold." Festooning the bridge are 154 specially designed globe lights.

Wheeling's history as a frontier port where the National Road met the Ohio River is evident in the Old Town section; some of the buildings are open to the public by tour. Victorian Wheeling Homes Tour, which departs from Eckhart House at 823-R Main St., offers tours of the Hazlett-Fields, Hess, Eckhart and John List houses. Tours are conducted Saturday and Sunday at 1; phone (304) 233-1600 or (800) 733-1870.

Near the Dallas Pike exit of I-70, Cabela's Sporting Goods offers outdoor-related items such as hunting and fishing gear. In addition to retail goods, its showroom also features a diorama of animals depicted in their native habitat; a walk-through freshwater aquarium with fish native to the area; a representation of a 30-foot-tall mountain with waterfalls, streams and a trout pond; and a museum with a collection of trophy deer.

On Saturday nights crowds gather at the Capitol Music Hall for "Jamboree USA," which is broadcast throughout the United States and Canada. From June through August the Wheeling Heritage Port hosts Wheeling's Waterfront Wednesdays where free concerts are featured. Greyhound racing takes place daily at Wheeling Downs throughout the year; phone (304) 232-5050 or (877) 946-4373.

Note: Policies concerning admittance of children to pari-mutuel betting facilities vary. Phone for information.

Wheeling Convention and Visitors Bureau: 1401 Main St., Wheeling, WV 26003; phone (304) 233-7709 or (800) 828-3097. *See color ad p. 324 & p. 348.*

Shopping areas: Ten miles west on I-70 is Ohio Valley Mall, whose more than 150 stores include JCPenney, Kaufmans and Sears. North Main Street's Victorian Wheeling (Old Town) has antique and specialty shops; from I-70 exit 1A go north on Main Street. Wheeling's Historic Centre Market, S. Main Street to 21st Street to Market Street, features antique and craft shops in and around the refurbished Centre Market House.

[SAVE] **THE KRUGER STREET TOY & TRAIN MUSEUM** is off I-70 exit 5, .1 mi. w. on US 40, then .2 mi. s. to 144 Kruger St. Housed in a restored 1906 three-story Victorian school building, the museum contains toy trains, trucks, cars, aircraft and boats; toy firearms and military equipment; dolls and doll houses; play sets; household items; riding toys; and photographs and memorabilia relating to toy manufacturing. Many displays are interactive.

Guided tours are available. Daily 9-8, Memorial Day-Dec. 31; Fri.-Mon. 9-5, rest of year. Hours may vary; phone ahead. Closed Jan. 1, Easter, Thanksgiving and Dec. 25. Last tour leaves 1 hour before closing. Admission $8; over 64, $7; ages 10-18, $5. MC, VI. Phone (304) 242-8133 or (877) 242-8133.

OGLEBAY RESORT is off I-70 at US 40, then 5 mi. n. on SR 88. This 1,650-acre resort offers gardens, nature trails, stables, a zoo and two museums. Activities include golf, tennis, swimming, trail rides, pedal-boating and fishing.

Cascading Waters on Schenk Lake are displayed twice nightly during the summer in a computerized light and sound show. In November and December a million holiday lights decorate the park for the Winter Festival of Lights.

Food is available. Park open daily 9-dusk. All-day pass (excluding rental equipment) for zoo, museums, par 3 golf, miniature golf, tennis, fishing, pedal boats, train, trolley, and outdoor pool $12.50, Memorial Day weekend-Labor Day. Festival of Lights $5 per private vehicle, $5 per person for trolley rides. AX, DC, MC, VI. Phone (304) 243-4000 or (800) 624-6988. *See Recreation Chart.*

Bissonnette Gardens covers 16 acres between the park museums. Formal and herb gardens, an arboretum, landscape lighting and water displays are featured in this re-creation of gardens that existed at the turn of the 20th century. Spring arrives with tulips, summer offers displays of annuals, and mums are a fall highlight. Audio tour stations are located along brick paths. Picnicking is permitted. Daily 9-dusk, mid-Apr. to late Oct. Gardens free. Phone (304) 243-4010 or (800) 624-6988.

Carriage House Glass Museum is on a hilltop in the park. The museum houses a large collection of glassware produced 1817-1939. Exhibits include flint glass, lead crystal, cut glass and a 21-gallon Sweeney punch bowl. Also featured are glass-blowing demonstrations and a videotape about the history of glassmaking in the valley.

Food is available. Allow 30 minutes minimum. Museum open Mon.-Sat. 10-5, Sun. noon-5, June-Aug; hours vary rest of year. Admission $5; ages 3-17, $1. AX, MC, VI. Phone (304) 243-4058 or (800) 624-6988.

Henry Stifel Schrader Environmental Education Center offers three nature trails that cover almost 5 miles, featuring overlooks, wildlife observation areas and waterfalls. More than 130 species of butterflies can be found in the flower gardens. Mon.-Sat. 10-5, Sun. noon-5. Free. Phone (304) 242-6855.

Mansion Museum contains historical material and is furnished with items reflecting Ohio Valley life in the early days. The mansion, the former summer home of Col. and Mrs. Earl W. Oglebay, is furnished to represent different eras of Wheeling's past. Changing exhibits are presented. Mon.-Sat. 10-5, Sun. noon-5. Admission $5, under 13 free.

AX, DC, MC, VI. Phone (304) 242-7272 or (800) 624-6988.

Oglebay's Good Zoo provides natural settings for 85 North American species. The Discovery Lab offers hands-on exhibits for children, while a planetarium provides shows for all ages. An 1863 train tours the zoo along a 1.5-mile track. An O-gauge model train is part of an indoor display. A children's farm, deer contact areas and a natural science theater also are available.

Mon.-Fri. 10-5, Sat.-Sun. 10-6, June-Aug.; hours vary rest of year. Admission $6.25; ages 3-12, $5.25. Train ride $1.25. AX, DC, MC, VI. Phone (304) 243-4030 or (800) 624-6988.

WEST VIRGINIA INDEPENDENCE HALL MUSEUM is at 16th and Market sts. This former Custom House is considered to be the Civil War birthplace of West Virginia. Restored rooms and a film interpret the building's history. West Virginia: Born of the Civil War is a permanent exhibit of 3-D maps, artifacts and audiovisual displays depicting the rise to statehood and the war in West Virginia.

Allow 30 minutes minimum. Daily 10-4, Mar.-Dec.; Mon.-Sat. 10-4, rest of year. Closed major holidays. Admission $3, students with ID $2, under 6 free. Phone (304) 238-1300.

WHEELING PARK is 4 mi. e. on US 40 at 1801 National Rd. The 406-acre park contains paddle-boating facilities, a covered ice-skating rink, indoor and outdoor tennis courts, a miniature golf course, a nine-hole golf course, a swimming pool and waterslide. Food is available. Daily 10-7, late May-early Sept. Daily passes start at $6 on Mon., $7.50 Tues.-Sun. and holidays AX, DC, DS, MC, VI. Phone (304) 243-4085. *See Recreation Chart.*

WHITE SULPHUR SPRINGS (D-4)
pop. 2,315, elev. 1,917′

White Sulphur Springs was a fashionable health and pleasure resort as early as 1778. It was named after its mineral springs, which are said to possess curative qualities. The site of the original spring is on the grounds of the Greenbrier Hotel.

From the time America entered World War II until July 1942, Axis diplomats and their dependents who had been stationed in Washington, D.C., were interned in the Greenbrier until they could be exchanged for American diplomats and their dependents who were in the Axis countries. For the duration of the war the hotel was used as a soldiers' hospital. In 1948 the 6,500-acre estate reopened as a luxury hotel.

Nearby are the 5,130-acre Greenbrier State Forest for camping, hiking and swimming *(see Recreation Chart and the AAA Mideastern CampBook)*; Greenbrier River Trail for bicycling, cross-country skiing and hiking; the southern terminus of the 220-mile Allegheny Trail for hikers; and Organ Cave, a Confederate arsenal during the Civil War.

Greenbrier County Visitors Center—White Sulphur Springs: 540 N. Jefferson St., Lewisburg, WV 24901; phone (304) 645-1000 or (800) 833-2068.

WHITE SULPHUR SPRINGS NATIONAL FISH HATCHERY is on US 60. Several thousand rainbow trout are distributed annually from the facility to streams in the Monongahela National Forest *(see place listing p. 340)*. A visitor center houses aquariums and displays describing some of the hatchery's activities. A self-guiding tour of the hatchery begins at the visitor center. Allow 1 hour minimum. Mon.-Fri. 7-3, Feb.-Nov. A guided tour is given Fri. at 2. Free. Phone (304) 536-1361.

WILLIAMSON (D-1) pop. 3,414, elev. 600′

Williamson is the business center for the vast coalfields of the Tug Valley area in West Virginia and Kentucky. Symbolic of coal's importance to the region is the Tug Valley Chamber of Commerce Building at Second Avenue and Court Street. Known as the Coal House, it was built in 1933 from 65 tons of locally mined coal.

Tug Valley Chamber of Commerce: P.O. Box 376, Williamson, WV 25661; phone (304) 235-5240.

WILLIAMSTOWN (B-2) pop. 2,996, elev. 610′

FENTON ART GLASS CO. is just off I-77 exit 185 following signs to 420 Caroline Ave.; it also is reached via SR 2/14/31 or US 50. Guided 40-minute tours cover the entire glass-making process, from the furnace to the finished product, including decorating. All Fenton pressed or blown glass is handmade.

Factory tours are offered Mon.-Fri. 8:15-3; phone for additional times and schedule changes. No tours are given holidays and for 2 weeks late June-early July. Children under 2 are not permitted on tours. Free. Phone (304) 375-7772 or (800) 319-7793.

Fenton Glass Museum exhibits more than 1,500 examples of Fenton glass and glass produced in Ohio Valley plants from 1880 to the present. A 22-minute video about the making of Fenton glass is shown regularly. Mon.-Fri. 8-8, Sat. 8-5, Sun. noon-5, Apr.-Dec.; Mon.-Sat. 8-5, Sun. noon-5, rest of year. Closed Jan. 1, Easter, Thanksgiving and Dec. 25. Free. Phone (304) 375-7772.

Choose Well.
AAA Approved.

Approved

Discover the secret to choosing well, every time ...
AAA Approved.

From simple motels to rustic ranches to luxury resorts, rest assured you've chosen well. **AAA's professional evaluators** have tested the locks and peeked under the beds, checking for qualities like cleanliness, service, and value — assigning a rating from one to five Diamonds.

Choose your Diamond rated accommodations from the AAA TourBook® listings, in print and on aaa.com, and look for the bold red AAA logo on signage and billboards.
Choose AAA Approved.

For more information on **AAA Lodging Diamond Ratings**, turn to page 16.

Show Your Card
Approved Lodging

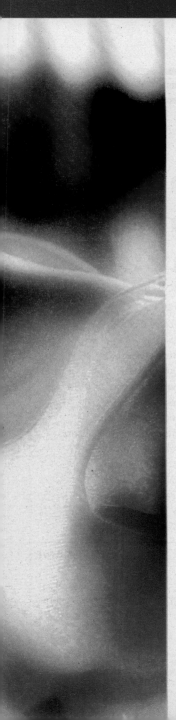

Delaware

Brandywine River,
Wilmington
© Gibson Stock
Photography

BEAR pop. 17,593

——— WHERE TO STAY ———

AMERICINN LODGE & SUITES BEAR/WILMINGTON   *Book at aaa.com*   **Phone:** (302)326-2500
▼▼▼▼   All Year   1P: $69-$199   2P: $69-$199   XP: $10   F14
Location: I-95, exit 4, 3.3 mi se on SR 1, exit 160, then just e on US 40. 875 Pulaski Hwy 19701. **Fax:** 302/326-1050.
Small-scale Hotel   **Facility:** 75 units. 69 one-bedroom standard units, some with whirlpools. 6 one-bedroom suites ($149-$299), some with whirlpools. 3 stories, interior corridors. *Bath:* combo or shower only. **Parking:** on-site.
Terms: package plans. **Amenities:** high-speed Internet (fee), dual phone lines, irons, hair dryers. **Pool(s):** heated indoor. **Leisure Activities:** sauna, whirlpool, exercise room. **Guest Services:** coin laundry. **Business Services:** meeting rooms, fax (fee). **Cards:** AX, CB, DC, DS, MC, VI. *(See color ad p 379)*

SOME UNITS
(ASK) (S/D) (T1+) (&M) (&) (⌐) (⌐) (≥) (✕) (☂) (DATA PORT) (▦) / (✕) (VCR) (🖥) (🖨) /
FEE

BETHANY BEACH pop. 903

——— WHERE TO STAY ———

HOLIDAY INN EXPRESS BETHANY BEACH   *Book at aaa.com*   **Phone:** (302)541-9200
▼▼▼▼   5/28-9/4 [ECP]   1P: $139-$319   2P: $139-$319   XP: $10   F17
    9/5-11/12 [ECP]   1P: $79-$189   2P: $79-$189   XP: $10   F17
    3/1-5/27 [ECP]   1P: $79-$179   2P: $79-$179   XP: $10   F17
Small-scale Hotel   11/13-2/28 [ECP]   1P: $79-$149   2P: $79-$149   XP: $10   F17
Location: On SR 1, 0.5 mi s of jct SR 26. 710 S Coastal Hwy 19930. **Fax:** 302/541-4057. **Facility:** 100 one-bedroom standard units, some with whirlpools. 4 stories, interior corridors. *Bath:* combo or shower only. **Parking:** on-site. **Terms:** 2 night minimum stay - seasonal, 7 day cancellation notice-fee imposed. **Amenities:** dual phone lines, voice mail, irons, hair dryers. **Pool(s):** outdoor. **Leisure Activities:** limited exercise equipment. **Guest Services:** coin laundry. **Business Services:** meeting rooms, fax (fee). **Cards:** AX, CB, DC, DS, MC, VI.

SOME UNITS
(ASK) (S/D) (T1+) (&M) (&) (⌐) (≥) (☂) (DATA PORT) (🖥) (🖨) (▦) / (✕) /

——— The following lodgings were either not evaluated or did not meet AAA rating requirements but are listed for your information only. ———

RESORT QUEST AT BEAR TRAP   **Phone:** 850/337-1684
(fyi)   Not evaluated. **Location:** Off SR 1, near beach. Marketplace at Sea Colony 19930. Facilities, services, and decor characterize a mid-range property.

RESORT QUEST AT SEA COLONY   **Phone:** 850/337-1684
(fyi)   Not evaluated. **Location:** Off SR 1, oceanfront. Marketplace at Sea Colony 19930. Facilities, services, and decor characterize a mid-range property.

——— WHERE TO DINE ———

THE COTTAGE CAFE   **Lunch:** $6-$10   **Dinner:** $10-$20   **Phone:** 302/539-8710
▼▼ ▼▼   **Location:** On SR 1, 0.7 mi s of jct SR 26. Rt 1, Hickmans Beach Plaza 19930. **Hours:** 11 am-9 pm, Fri & Sat 10 am-10 pm; 11 am-10 pm, Fri-11 pm, Sat & Sun 8 am-11 pm 3/30-9/5. **Closed:** 11/24, 12/25.
American   **Reservations:** not accepted. **Features:** Traditional American cuisine served in a casual comfortable dining atmosphere. The staff is friendly and helpful, the atmosphere is suitable for families and the menu ranges from chicken, beef, seafood and pasta. Casual dress; cocktails. **Parking:** on-site. **Cards:** AX, DC, MC, VI.
(🍸) (✕)

REDFIN SEAFOOD GRILL & FISH MARKET   **Dinner:** $16-$38   **Phone:** 302/573-0100
▼▼▼▼   **Location:** On SR 1, 1 mi n of jct SR 26. 1111 Hwy 1 19930. **Hours:** 5 pm-10 pm; to 9 pm 10/1-5/1. Closed major holidays; also Mon & Tues 10/1-5/1. **Reservations:** not accepted. **Features:** Just off Rt 1 on the northern end of Bethany Beach you'll find this delightful little seafood restaurant, overlooking the salt pond. The setting is simple and comfortable and the staff is friendly and helpful. Fresh fish is their speciliity, with dishes
Seafood   as semolina crusted halibut with fried potato sticks and roasted asparagus and a wild mushroom lobster marsala sauce or grilled sea bass over a mushroom risotto. Casual dress; cocktails. **Parking:** on-site. **Cards:** AX, MC, VI.
(✕)

SEDONA   **Dinner:** $24-$31   **Phone:** 302/539-1200
(AAA)   **Location:** Just e of SR 1. 26 Pennsylvania Ave 19930. **Hours:** Open 3/1-10/30 & 2/15-2/28; 5 pm-10 pm. **Closed:**
▼▼▼▼   Mon-Thurs 2/15-5/15 & 9/6-10/30. **Reservations:** suggested. **Features:** Creative American cuisine is offered in this stylish little restaurant. The staff is friendly and helpful. The kitchen displays their talents with
American   each dish served. Casual dress; cocktails. **Parking:** street. **Cards:** AX, DS, MC, VI.
(✕)

CLAYMONT pop. 9,220

——— WHERE TO STAY ———

DARLEY MANOR INN BED & BREAKFAST   *Book at aaa.com*   **Phone:** (302)792-2127
▼▼▼▼   All Year   1P: $95-$129   2P: $99-$149   XP: $10
Location: I-495, exit 5, just s. 3701 Philadelphia Pike 19703. **Fax:** 302/798-6143. **Facility:** Both modern and historic features enhance the individually decorated guest rooms at this 19th-century home; three rooms
Historic Bed   have fireplaces. Designated smoking area. 5 units. 2 one-bedroom standard units. 3 one-bedroom suites
& Breakfast   ($109-$149). 3 stories (no elevator), interior corridors. *Bath:* combo or shower only. **Parking:** on-site.
Terms: office hours 10 am-10 pm, check-in 4 pm, 2 night minimum stay - seasonal and/or weekends, age restrictions may apply, 7 day cancellation notice-fee imposed, [BP] meal plan available. **Amenities:** video library, irons, hair dryers. *Some:* CD players. **Leisure Activities:** limited exercise equipment. **Business Services:** business center. **Cards:** AX, DC, MC, VI.

SOME UNITS
(T1+) (✕) (VCR) (☂) (DATA PORT) / (🖥) (🖨) /

HOLIDAY INN SELECT WILMINGTON

AAA **SAVE** *Book at aaa.com*   **Phone:** (302)792-2700

All Year   1P: $99-$159   2P: $99-$159

Location: I-95, exit 11, just w on SR 92; I-495, exit 6 (Naamans Rd). 630 Naamans Rd 19703. **Fax:** 302/796-6182. **Facility:** 189 units. 186 one-bedroom standard units. 3 one-bedroom suites. 8 stories, interior corridors. *Bath:* combo or shower only. **Parking:** on-site. **Terms:** small pets only ($50 deposit, $10 extra charge).

Large-scale Hotel **Amenities:** dual phone lines, voice mail, irons, hair dryers. **Dining:** 6 am-2 & 5-10 pm, Sat & Sun from 7 am, cocktails. **Pool(s):** outdoor. **Leisure Activities:** limited exercise equipment. **Guest Services:** sundries, valet laundry, area transportation-within 10 mi. **Business Services:** meeting rooms, business center. **Cards:** AX, CB, DC, DS, MC, VI. **Special Amenities:** free local telephone calls and free newspaper. *(See color ad p 381)*

SOME UNITS

DEWEY BEACH pop. 301

—————— **WHERE TO STAY** ——————

ATLANTIC OCEANSIDE MOTEL

Phone: 302/227-8811

AAA **SAVE**

7/5-8/29	1P: $79-$199	2P: $79-$199	XP: $10	F16
6/1-7/4	1P: $49-$149	2P: $49-$149	XP: $10	F16
8/30-11/7	1P: $39-$109	2P: $39-$109	XP: $10	F16
3/17-5/31	1P: $35-$99	2P: $35-$99	XP: $10	F16

Motel   **Location:** Jct SR 1 and McKinley St. 1700 Hwy 1 19971. **Fax:** 302/227-4039. **Facility:** 59 one-bedroom standard units, some with efficiencies. 3 stories (no elevator), exterior corridors. *Bath:* combo or shower only. **Parking:** on-site. **Terms:** open 3/17-11/7, 2 night minimum stay - seasonal and/or weekends, 7 day cancellation notice-fee imposed, pets ($5 extra charge 3/14-5/31 & 9/7-11/10). **Amenities:** hair dryers. **Pool(s):** small heated outdoor. **Leisure Activities:** sun deck. **Business Services:** fax (fee). **Cards:** AX, DC, DS, MC, VI. *(See color ad below)*

SOME UNITS

ATLANTIC VIEW MOTEL

Phone: 302/227-3878

AAA **SAVE**

6/24-8/27	1P: $149-$214	2P: $149-$214	XP: $15	F9
4/1-6/23	1P: $59-$192	2P: $59-$192	XP: $15	F9
8/28-11/6	1P: $49-$164	2P: $49-$164	XP: $15	F9

Motel   **Location:** Jct SR 1 and Clayton St, just s. Located on the beach. 2 Clayton St 19971. **Fax:** 302/227-5372. **Facility:** 35 one-bedroom standard units. 4 stories (no elevator), interior corridors. **Parking:** on-site. **Terms:** open 4/1-11/6, office hours 8 am-11 pm, 2 night minimum stay - seasonal, 7 day cancellation notice-fee imposed. **Amenities:** irons, hair dryers. **Pool(s):** outdoor. **Guest Services:** coin laundry. **Business Services:** fax (fee). **Cards:** AX, DC, MC, VI. **Special Amenities:** free continental breakfast.

SOME UNITS

BAY RESORT MOTEL AND EFFICIENCIES

Phone: 302/227-6400

AAA **SAVE**

6/24-8/27	1P: $129-$259	2P: $129-$259	XP: $20	F11
5/27-6/23	1P: $69-$169	2P: $69-$169	XP: $20	F11
8/28-10/24	1P: $65-$169	2P: $65-$169	XP: $20	F11
4/8-5/26	1P: $59-$129	2P: $59-$129	XP: $20	F11

Motel   **Location:** Jct SR 1 and Bellevue St at Bayard Ave, just s. Located on the bay. 126 Bellevue St 19971 (PO Box 461). **Fax:** 302/227-4377. **Facility:** 68 one-bedroom standard units, some with efficiencies. 3 stories (no elevator), exterior corridors. **Parking:** on-site. **Terms:** open 4/8-10/24, office hours 6 am-midnight, 2 night minimum stay - seasonal, 7 day cancellation notice-fee imposed, weekly rates available, package plans. **Amenities:** irons, hair dryers. **Pool(s):** outdoor. **Leisure Activities:** fishing, crabbing. **Guest Services:** coin laundry. **Business Services:** fax (fee). **Cards:** DC, MC, VI. **Special Amenities:** free local telephone calls.

SOME UNITS

BELLBUOY MOTEL

Phone: 302/227-6000

6/16-8/21	2P: $69-$175	XP: $15	F18
8/22-9/23	2P: $75-$169	XP: $15	F18
4/15-6/15	2P: $50-$89	XP: $15	F18
9/24-11/1	2P: $50-$75	XP: $15	F18

Motel   **Location:** SR 1, on oceanside block of Van Dyke St. 21 Van Dyke St 19971. **Fax:** 302/227-8536. **Facility:** 16 one-bedroom standard units, some with kitchens. 3 stories (no elevator), exterior corridors. **Parking:** on-site. **Terms:** open 4/15-11/1, 2 night minimum stay - seasonal and/or weekends, 7 day cancellation notice-fee imposed, pets ($10 extra charge). **Amenities:** safes. **Cards:** AX, DS, MC, VI.

BEST WESTERN GOLD LEAF
Book at aaa.com Phone: (302)226-1100

AAA (SAVE)

	5/21-9/8	1P: $189-$289	2P: $189-$289	XP: $20	F17
	11/16-2/28	1P: $69-$199	2P: $69-$199	XP: $20	F17
	9/9-11/15	1P: $99-$179	2P: $99-$179	XP: $20	F17
	3/1-5/20	1P: $79-$109	2P: $79-$109	XP: $20	F17

Small-scale Hotel **Location:** On SR 1; center. 1400 Hwy 1 19971. Fax: 302/226-9785. **Facility:** 75 one-bedroom standard units, some with whirlpools. 4 stories, interior corridors. **Parking:** on-site. **Terms:** 2 night minimum stay - seasonal and/or weekends, 3 day cancellation notice-fee imposed, package plans, pets ($20 extra charge 9/15-5/15). **Amenities:** voice mail, safes, irons, hair dryers. **Pool(s):** outdoor. **Guest Services:** coin laundry. **Business Services:** meeting rooms, fax (fee). **Cards:** AX, CB, DC, DS, MC, VI. **Special Amenities:** free continental breakfast and free local telephone calls. *(See color ad p 371)*

SOME UNITS

DEWEY BEACH SUITES & MOTEL
Phone: 302/226-0233

	7/1-9/15	1P: $129-$309	2P: $129-$309	XP: $10	F15
	5/16-6/30	1P: $79-$169	2P: $79-$169	XP: $10	F15
Motel	9/16-11/15	1P: $59-$169	2P: $59-$169	XP: $10	F15
	4/15-5/15	1P: $59-$129	2P: $59-$129	XP: $10	F15

Location: SR 1 at Rodney Ave. 1406 Hwy 1 19971. Fax: 302/226-0233. **Facility:** 24 units. 8 one- and 16 two-bedroom standard units. 3 stories (no elevator), exterior corridors. **Parking:** on-site. **Terms:** open 4/15-11/15, 3 night minimum stay - seasonal and/or weekends, 7 day cancellation notice-fee imposed. **Amenities:** hair dryers. **Pool(s):** outdoor. **Cards:** AX, CB, DC, DS, JC, MC, VI.

SOME UNITS

THE MARINA SUITES
Book at aaa.com Phone: (302)227-1700

AAA (SAVE)

	4/1-9/10	1P: $129-$249	2P: $129-$259	XP: $10	F18
	9/11-10/31	1P: $129-$179	2P: $139-$189	XP: $10	F18
	3/1-3/31 & 11/1-2/28	1P: $59-$99	2P: $59-$99	XP: $10	F18

Small-scale Hotel **Location:** On SR 1. Located at the marina. 1117 Hwy 1 19971. Fax: 302/227-8958. **Facility:** 84 units. 29 one-bedroom standard units, some with whirlpools. 55 one-bedroom suites, some with whirlpools. 4 stories, interior corridors. *Bath:* combo or shower only. **Parking:** on-site. **Terms:** 2 night minimum stay - weekends, 3 day cancellation notice-fee imposed, package plans. **Amenities:** voice mail, irons, hair dryers. **Pool(s):** outdoor. **Guest Services:** coin laundry. **Business Services:** fax (fee). **Cards:** AX, DC, MC, VI.

SOME UNITS

SEA-ESTA MOTEL I
Phone: (302)227-7666

AAA (SAVE)

| | 6/1-10/15 | | 2P: $49-$159 | XP: $12 | F12 |
| | 4/15-5/31 | | 2P: $45-$139 | XP: $12 | F12 |

Location: SR 1 at Houston St. 2306 Hwy 1 19971 (713 Rehoboth Ave, REHOBOTH BEACH). Fax: 302/227-1742. **Facility:** 30 one-bedroom standard units. 3 stories (no elevator), exterior corridors. **Parking:** on-site. **Terms:** open 4/15-10/15, 2-3 night minimum stay - seasonal, 3 day cancellation notice, package plans, pets ($8 extra charge). **Amenities:** hair dryers. **Business Services:** fax (fee). **Cards:** AX, DC, DS, MC, VI. **Special Amenities:** free local telephone calls and free newspaper. *(See color ad below)*

SOME UNITS

SEA-ESTA MOTEL III
Phone: (302)227-4343

AAA (SAVE)

	5/1-9/1		2P: $49-$189	XP: $12	F12
	9/2-2/28		2P: $44-$129	XP: $12	F12
Motel	3/1-4/30		2P: $44-$89	XP: $12	F12

Location: Jct SR 1 and Rodney St. 1409 Hwy 1 19971 (713 Rehoboth Ave, REHOBOTH BEACH). Fax: 302/227-3049. **Facility:** 33 one-bedroom standard units with efficiencies (no utensils). 3 stories, exterior corridors. **Parking:** on-site. **Terms:** 2-3 night minimum stay - seasonal, 3 day cancellation notice, package plans, pets ($6 extra charge). **Amenities:** hair dryers. **Business Services:** fax (fee). **Cards:** AX, DC, DS, MC, VI. **Special Amenities:** free local telephone calls and free newspaper. *(See color ad below)*

SOME UNITS

THE SURF CLUB HOTEL

Phone: 302/227-7059

◆◆◆

Motel

7/1-9/6	1P: $185-$215	2P: $185-$215	XP: $15	F12
4/15-6/30	1P: $70-$180	2P: $70-$180	XP: $15	F12
9/7-2/28	1P: $70-$135	2P: $70-$135	XP: $15	F12
3/1-4/14	1P: $50-$90	2P: $50-$90	XP: $15	F12

Location: Just e of SR 1; center. 1 Read St 19971. Fax: 302/227-3487. **Facility:** Smoke free premises. 49 units. 48 one-bedroom standard units with efficiencies. 1 vacation home. 4 stories (no elevator), exterior corridors. **Parking:** on-site. **Terms:** office hours 8 am-10 pm, 2 night minimum stay - seasonal, 7 day cancellation notice, 3 days 9/15-5/15, weekly rates available. **Amenities:** video library, CD players, voice mail. **Pool(s):** outdoor. **Leisure Activities:** sauna, whirlpool, bicycles. **Guest Services:** coin laundry. **Business Services:** fax (fee). **Cards:** AX, DS, MC, VI.

WHERE TO DINE

CRABBER'S COVE

Dinner: $8-$19

Phone: 302/227-3888

◆◆ ◆◆◆

American

Location: SR 1; center; in Rudder Towne complex. 113 Dickinson St 19971. **Hours:** Open 5/15-9/8; 4 pm-10 pm, Sun from 3 pm. **Reservations:** not accepted. **Features:** All-you-can-eat crabs are the specialty at this family-oriented restaurant, which has a menu that centers on seafood but also includes steak, rib and chicken choices. A lobster tank and picture windows that look out on the bay carry out the nautical feel. Weather permitting, the windows are retracted to allow an open-air ambience. That combined with plastic patio furniture gives diners the feel of participating in a large picnic. Viewing evening sunsets is an added attraction. Casual dress; cocktails. **Parking:** on-site. **Cards:** AX, DC, DS, MC, VI.

RUSTY RUDDER

Lunch: $7-$10   **Dinner:** $14-$27

Phone: 302/227-3888

◆◆ ◆◆

Steak & Seafood

Location: SR 1; center; in Rudder Towne complex. 113 Dickinson St 19971. **Hours:** 11:30 am-10 pm. Closed: 12/25; also Mon-Wed 1/1-3/15. **Features:** On the bay one block from the beach, this casual, nautically themed restaurant builds its menu around prime rib and seafood. An all-you-can-eat land and sea buffet is laid out daily during the summer and on Friday the rest of the year. The lunch menu is served until 4 pm. Casual dress; cocktails; entertainment. **Parking:** on-site. **Cards:** AX, DC, DS, MC, VI.

DOVER pop. 32,135

―――― WHERE TO STAY ――――

COMFORT INN-DOVER *Book at aaa.com* Phone: 302/674-3300

5/1-10/31 [ECP]	1P: $89-$109	2P: $99-$129	XP: $10	F17
3/1-4/30 & 11/1-2/28 [ECP]	1P: $75-$89	2P: $80-$99	XP: $10	F17

Motel

Location: SR 1, exit 95, 2 mi n on US 113, then 0.3 mi n on US 13. Located in a commercial area. 222 S DuPont Hwy 19901. Fax: 302/674-5439. **Facility:** 94 one-bedroom standard units. 2 stories (no elevator), exterior corridors. **Parking:** on-site. **Amenities:** voice mail, safes (fee), irons, hair dryers. **Pool(s):** outdoor. **Leisure Activities:** limited exercise equipment. **Guest Services:** valet and coin laundry. **Business Services:** fax (fee). **Cards:** AX, DC, DS, MC, VI. **Special Amenities:** free expanded continental breakfast and free local telephone calls.

SOME UNITS

COMFORT SUITES-DOVER *Book at aaa.com* Phone: (302)736-1204

5/1-8/31 [ECP]	1P: $90-$200	2P: $90-$200	XP: $10	F18
9/1-11/15 [ECP]	1P: $80-$200	2P: $80-$200	XP: $10	F18
3/1-4/30 & 11/16-2/28 [ECP]	1P: $75-$200	2P: $75-$200	XP: $10	F18

Small-scale Hotel

Location: SR 1, exit 104, 0.3 mi s on US 13. 1654 N DuPont Hwy 19901. Fax: 302/736-1204. **Facility:** 64 units. 58 one-bedroom standard units, some with whirlpools. 6 one-bedroom suites with whirlpools. 3 stories, interior corridors. *Bath:* combo or shower only. **Parking:** on-site. **Amenities:** safes (fee), irons, hair dryers. *Some:* dual phone lines. **Pool(s):** small outdoor. **Guest Services:** valet and coin laundry. **Business Services:** meeting rooms, fax (fee). **Cards:** AX, CB, DC, DS, MC, VI.

SOME UNITS

DAYS INN DOVER *Book at aaa.com* Phone: (302)674-8002

4/1-10/31	1P: $85-$130	2P: $95-$140	XP: $10	F18
3/1-3/31 & 11/1-2/28	1P: $75-$115	2P: $85-$125	XP: $10	F18

Motel

Location: SR 1, exit 104, 2.8 mi s on US 13. Located in a commercial area. 272 N DuPont Hwy 19901. Fax: 302/674-2195. **Facility:** 81 one-bedroom standard units, some with efficiencies (no utensils). 1 story, exterior corridors. **Parking:** on-site. **Terms:** package plans. **Amenities:** voice mail, safes, hair dryers. *Some:* irons. **Guest Services:** coin laundry. **Business Services:** fax (fee). **Cards:** AX, DC, DS, MC, VI. **Special Amenities:** free expanded continental breakfast and free local telephone calls.

SOME UNITS

DOVER DOWNS HOTEL & CONFERENCE CENTER Phone: (302)857-2190

All Year	1P: $145-$215	2P: $145-$215	XP: $25	F18

Large-scale Hotel

Location: SR 1, exit 104, 1.9 mi s on US 13. Located adjacent to Dover Downs Race Track. 1131 N DuPont Hwy 19903 (PO Box 843). Fax: 302/857-2198. **Facility:** A full-service hotel offering handsome, comfortable guest rooms and inviting public spaces, the property is attached to a casino. 232 units. 207 one-bedroom standard units. 25 one-bedroom suites ($275-$675), some with whirlpools. 10 stories, interior corridors. *Bath:* combo or shower only. **Parking:** on-site and valet. **Terms:** check-in 4 pm, 3 day cancellation notice. **Amenities:** video games (fee), dual phone lines, voice mail, safes, irons, hair dryers. *Some:* CD players, fax. **Dining:** 4 restaurants, 7 am-10 & 11-1 am, cocktails, entertainment. **Pool(s):** small heated indoor. **Leisure Activities:** whirlpool, steamrooms, exercise room. **Guest Services:** gift shop, valet laundry. **Business Services:** conference facilities. *Fee:* administrative services, fax. **Cards:** AX, DS, MC, VI. **Special Amenities:** free room upgrade and preferred room (each subject to availability with advance reservations). *(See color ad p 38)*

SOME UNITS

FAIRFIELD INN & SUITES BY MARRIOTT-DOVER *Book at aaa.com* Phone: (302)677-0900

All Year	1P: $109-$139	2P: $109-$139

Small-scale Hotel

Location: SR 1, exit 104, 2.7 mi s on US 13. Locatd in a commercial area. 655 N DuPont Hwy 19901. Fax: 302/677-0907. **Facility:** 77 units. 58 one-bedroom standard units. 19 one-bedroom suites ($119-$159). 4 stories, interior corridors. *Bath:* combo or shower only. **Parking:** on-site. **Terms:** 2 night minimum stay - seasonal and/or weekends, cancellation fee imposed, package plans. **Amenities:** high-speed Internet, dual phone lines, voice mail, irons, hair dryers. *Some:* CD players. **Pool(s):** small heated indoor. **Leisure Activities:** whirlpool, limited exercise equipment. **Guest Services:** valet and coin laundry. **Business Services:** PC, fax (fee). **Cards:** AX, DC, DS, MC, VI.

SOME UNITS

HAMPTON INN-DOVER *Book at aaa.com* Phone: (302)736-3500

All Year [ECP]	1P: $99-$275	2P: $109-$300

Small-scale Hotel

Location: SR 1, exit 104, 1 mi s. Located in a commercial area. 1568 N DuPont Hwy 19901. Fax: 302/736-6402. **Facility:** 81 units. 78 one-bedroom standard units, some with whirlpools. 3 one-bedroom suites with whirlpools. 4 stories, interior corridors. *Bath:* combo or shower only. **Parking:** on-site. **Amenities:** voice mail, irons, hair dryers. **Pool(s):** outdoor. **Leisure Activities:** limited exercise equipment. **Guest Services:** valet laundry. **Business Services:** fax (fee). **Cards:** AX, CB, DC, DS, MC, VI.

SOME UNITS

HOLIDAY INN EXPRESS HOTEL & SUITES DOVER *Book at aaa.com* Phone: (302)678-0600

5/1-11/1	1P: $109-$139	2P: $109-$139	XP: $10	F
3/1-4/30 & 11/2-2/28	1P: $79-$119	2P: $79-$119	XP: $10	F

Small-scale Hotel

Location: SR 1, exit 104, just s on US 13. 1780 N DuPont Hwy 19901. Fax: 302/678-1133. **Facility:** 81 units. 73 one-bedroom standard units, some with whirlpools. 8 one-bedroom suites ($119-$199) with whirlpools. 5 stories, interior corridors. *Bath:* combo or shower only. **Parking:** on-site. **Terms:** cancellation fee imposed, [ECP] meal plan available. **Amenities:** dual phone lines, voice mail, irons, hair dryers. **Pool(s):** outdoor. **Leisure Activities:** limited exercise equipment. **Guest Services:** valet and coin laundry. **Business Services:** meeting rooms, business center. **Cards:** AX, CB, DC, DS, JC, MC.

SOME UNITS

LITTLE CREEK INN
▼▼▼
Historic Bed
& Breakfast

Phone: 302/730-1300

All Year   1P: $100-$125   2P: $150-$195
Location: SR 1, exit 98, 1 mi e on SR 8; 2.2 mi e of jct US 13. 2623 N Little Creek Rd 19901. Fax: 302/730-4070. **Facility:** A farmhouse dating from 1860, Little Creek Inn offers a quiet setting just on the outskirts of Dover; guest rooms are individually decorated. Smoke free premises. 4 units. 3 one- and 1 two-bedroom standard units, some with whirlpools. 3 stories (no elevator), interior corridors. **Parking:** on-site. **Terms:** office hours 9 am-9 pm, age restrictions may apply, pets (dogs only, in designated unit). **Pool(s):** outdoor. **Leisure Activities:** exercise room. **Guest Services:** complimentary laundry. **Business Services:** fax (fee). **Cards:** AX, MC, VI.

RED ROOF INN DOVER   *Book at aaa.com*
▼▼
Small-scale Hotel

(fee).

Phone: 302/730-8009

Property failed to provide current rates
Location: SR 1, exit 104, 2.7 mi s on US 13. 652 N State St 19901. Fax: 302/730-8864. **Facility:** 57 units. 53 one-bedroom standard units. 4 one-bedroom suites. 4 stories, interior corridors. *Bath:* combo or shower only. **Parking:** on-site. **Terms:** small pets only. **Guest Services:** coin laundry. **Business Services:** fax

SOME UNITS

SHERATON DOVER HOTEL   *Book at aaa.com*
▼▼▼
Large-scale Hotel

Phone: (302)678-8500

All Year   1P: $129   XP: $10   F18
Location: SR 1, exit 104, 1 mi s on US 13. Located in a commercial area. 1570 N DuPont Hwy 19901. Fax: 302/678-9073. **Facility:** 156 units. 153 one-bedroom standard units, some with whirlpools. 3 one-bedroom suites ($295) with whirlpools. 7 stories, interior corridors. **Parking:** on-site. **Terms:** 2 night minimum stay - seasonal, cancellation fee imposed, package plans. **Amenities:** video games (fee), dual phone lines, voice mail, irons, hair dryers. *Some:* high-speed Internet, fax. **Dining:** Tango's Bistro, see separate listing. **Pool(s):** heated indoor. **Leisure Activities:** whirlpool, exercise room. **Guest Services:** valet laundry, area transportation. **Business Services:** conference facilities, business center. **Cards:** AX, DC, DS, JC, MC, VI.

SOME UNITS

------- **WHERE TO DINE** -------

ATWOOD'S RESTAURANT   Lunch: $7-$13   Dinner: $14-$25   Phone: 302/674-1776
◆◆ ◆◆
American
Location: 0.5 mi w of US 13 on Alternate US 13. 800 N State St 19901. **Hours:** 11 am-9 pm, Fri & Sat-10 pm, Sun-7 pm; Sunday brunch. Closed: 1/1, 7/4, 12/25; also Mon. **Reservations:** suggested. **Features:** The soothing lakeside setting at the Blue Coat accentuates the appeal of all house specialties: seafood, hand-cut steak, veal and poultry, with an expertly seasoned stuffed flounder proving a popular choice. Entertainment is offered on Saturday. Casual dress; cocktails. **Parking:** on-site. **Cards:** AX, DC, DS, MC, VI.

EIGHT SIXTY FIVE   Lunch: $7-$13   Dinner: $16-$27   Phone: 302/734-9430
◆◆ ◆◆
American
Location: SR 1, exit 104, 2.8 mi s on US 13. 865 N DuPont Hwy 19901. **Hours:** 11 am-3 & 4-10 pm, Sun 4 pm-9 pm. Closed major holidays. **Features:** On a busy highway, near Dover Downs, this intimate restaurant offers a relaxing, upscale atmosphere. The chef/owner prepares a nice selection of meat and fish dishes, such as Grilled Rack of Lamb, Salmon En Croute or Lobster Penne to mention a few. Casual dress; cocktails. **Parking:** on-site. **Cards:** AX, CB, DC, DS, JC, MC, VI.

SHUCKER'S PIER 13   Lunch: $5-$20   Dinner: $10-$30   Phone: 302/674-1190
◆
Seafood
Location: SR 1, exit 104, 2.8 mi s on US 13. 889 N DuPont Hwy 19901. **Hours:** 11 am-10 pm, Fri & Sat-11 pm, Sun 11:30 am-9 pm. Closed: 3/27, 11/24, 12/25. **Reservations:** accepted, Mon-Thurs. **Features:** This casual restaurant is popular with the locals. The menu offers seafood, pasta and meat dishes. Casual dress; cocktails. **Parking:** on-site. **Cards:** AX, DC, DS, MC, VI.

TANGO'S BISTRO   Lunch: $8-$15   Dinner: $15-$27   Phone: 302/678-8500
◆◆ ◆◆
American
Location: SR 1, exit 104, 1 mi s on US 13; in Sheraton Dover Hotel. 1570 N DuPont Hwy 19901. **Hours:** 6:30 am-10:30 pm, Sat from 7 am, Sun 7 am-2 pm. Closed: 12/25. **Reservations:** suggested. **Features:** Serving contemporary American cuisine in a casual, comfortable atmosphere. Chicken Chesapeake — hand-seared chicken breast with jumbo lump crabmeat — is just one of several popular specialties of the house, as well as the French onion soup. Casual dress; cocktails. **Parking:** on-site. **Cards:** AX, CB, DC, DS, MC, VI.

FENWICK ISLAND pop. 342

------- **WHERE TO STAY** -------

ATLANTIC COAST INN
◆◆ ◆◆
Motel

Phone: 302/539-7673

7/1-8/28	1P: $99-$179	2P: $99-$179	XP: $10	F11
6/18-6/30	1P: $79-$179	2P: $79-$179	XP: $10	F11
4/25-6/17 & 8/29-9/30	1P: $59-$159	2P: $59-$159	XP: $10	F11

Location: Jct SR 1 and 54. Lighthouse Rd & Coastal Hwy 19944. Fax: 302/539-8069. **Facility:** 54 units. 52 one-bedroom standard units, some with efficiencies. 2 two-bedroom suites ($99-$298) with kitchens. 2 stories (no elevator), exterior corridors. *Bath:* combo or shower only. **Parking:** on-site. **Terms:** open 4/25-9/30, 3 night minimum stay - seasonal and/or weekends, 5 day cancellation notice-fee imposed, [AP] meal plan available, small pets only ($10 extra charge, off season). **Pool(s):** outdoor. **Guest Services:** coin laundry. **Business Services:** fax (fee). **Cards:** AX, CB, DC, DS, MC, VI.

SOME UNITS
FEE

——— **WHERE TO DINE** ———

HARPOON HANNAS   **Lunch:** $6-$10   **Dinner:** $9-$30   **Phone:** 302/539-3095
▼▼▼ ▼▼   **Location:** SR 54, 0.8 mi w of Coastal Hwy. SR 54 & Bay 19944. **Hours:** 11 am-11 pm, Sun from 10 am.
                 Features: Looking for a fun, energetic come-as-you-are crowd and a nautical view? Hannas menu offers
Seafood   tempting choices such as crab imperial, Maryland style crab cakes, fried or broiled and surf n' turf (lobster
                 and a charbroiled filet mignon). There's even a tiki bar. Casual dress; cocktails. **Parking:** on-site.
Cards: AX, DS, MC, VI.

NANTUCKETS   **Dinner:** $23-$35   **Phone:** 302/539-2607
▼▼▼▼   **Location:** On SR 1, just n of jct W SR 54. Rt 1 & Atlantic Ave 19944. **Hours:** 5 pm-10 pm; to 11 pm 5/29-9/30.
                 Reservations: suggested. **Features:** The restaurant offers a bit of New England on the Eastern shore, with
Seafood   a menu of fresh seafood, crab cakes and black Angus steak. The walls of the charming old beach cottage,
                 which was converted into this fine dining establishment, are adorned with original artwork. Casual dress;
cocktails. **Parking:** on-site. **Cards:** AX, CB, DC, DS, MC, VI.

GEORGETOWN pop. 4,643

——— **WHERE TO STAY** ———

COMFORT INN & SUITES-GEORGETOWN   *Book at aaa.com*   **Phone:** (302)854-9400
(AAA) (SAVE)   All Year   1P: $79-$249   XP: $10   F18
▼▼▼▼   **Location:** On US 113, 0.5 mi n of jct SR 404. 507 N DuPont Hwy 19947. Fax: 302/855-9121. **Facility:** 71 one-
                 bedroom standard units, some with whirlpools. 2 stories (no elevator), interior corridors. **Parking:** on-site.
Small-scale Hotel **Terms:** 3 day cancellation notice, in season, package plans, pets ($15 extra charge). **Amenities:** irons, hair
                 dryers. **Pool(s):** outdoor. **Business Services:** meeting rooms, fax (fee). **Cards:** AX, CB, DC, DS, MC, VI.

HARRINGTON pop. 3,174

——— **WHERE TO STAY** ———

AMERICINN LODGE & SUITES OF HARRINGTON   *Book at aaa.com*   **Phone:** (302)398-3900
▼▼▼▼   5/1-10/1 [ECP]   1P: $92-$102   2P: $100-$110   XP: $8   F12
                 3/1-4/30 & 10/2-2/28 [ECP]   1P: $82-$92   2P: $90-$100   XP: $8   F12
Small-scale Hotel **Location:** On US 13, 0.6 mi s of jct SR 14. 1259 Corn Crib Rd 19952. Fax: 302/398-4300. **Facility:** 70 units. 66
                 one-bedroom standard units, some with whirlpools. 4 one-bedroom suites ($111-$182). 2 stories, interior
corridors. *Bath:* combo or shower only. **Parking:** on-site. **Terms:** package plans, pets ($20 extra charge, small dogs only).
Amenities: irons, hair dryers. **Pool(s):** heated indoor. **Leisure Activities:** sauna, whirlpool, exercise room. **Guest Services:**
coin laundry. **Business Services:** meeting rooms, fax (fee). **Cards:** AX, DC, DS, MC, VI. *(See color ad p 379)*

HOLIDAY INN EXPRESS HOTEL &
SUITES-HARRINGTON   *Book at aaa.com*   **Phone:** 302/398-8800
▼▼▼▼   All Year [CP]   1P: $119-$159   2P: $119-$159   XP: $10   F18
                 Location: Jct SR 14, on US 13. 17271 S DuPont Hwy 19952. Fax: 302/398-8260. **Facility:** 86 one-bedroom
Small-scale Hotel standard units. 3 stories, interior corridors. *Bath:* combo or shower only. **Parking:** on-site. **Amenities:** dual
                 phone lines, voice mail, irons, hair dryers. **Pool(s):** outdoor. **Leisure Activities:** exercise room. **Business**
Services: meeting rooms, fax (fee). **Cards:** AX, CB, DC, DS, MC, VI.

LEWES pop. 2,932

——— **WHERE TO STAY** ———

THE HERITAGE INN AND GOLF CLUB   **Phone:** (302)644-0600
(AAA) (SAVE)   7/1-8/30   1P: $109-$229   2P: $109-$229   XP: $10   F12
                 5/1-6/30   1P: $79-$169   2P: $79-$169   XP: $10   F12
▼▼▼▼   8/31-2/28   1P: $59-$169   2P: $59-$169   XP: $10   F12
                 3/1-4/30   1P: $59-$119   2P: $59-$119   XP: $10   F12
Small-scale Hotel **Location:** 1.5 mi s on SR 1. Located in a commercial area. 2 Postal Ln 19958 (PO Box 699, REHOBOTH BEACH,
                 19971). Fax: 302/644-8522. **Facility:** 86 units. 85 one-bedroom standard units, some with whirlpools. 1 one-
bedroom suite with whirlpool. 4 stories, interior corridors. *Bath:* combo or shower only. **Parking:** on-site. **Terms:** 3 day
cancellation notice, package plans. **Amenities:** voice mail, irons, hair dryers. **Pool(s):** outdoor. **Leisure Activities:** limited
exercise equipment. *Fee:* golf-9 holes. **Business Services:** meeting rooms, fax (fee). **Cards:** AX, DS, MC, VI.
Special Amenities: free continental breakfast and free local telephone calls. *(See color ad p 375)*

THE INN AT CANAL SQUARE   **Phone:** 302/644-3377
(AAA) (SAVE)   5/21-10/1 [ECP]   1P: $205-$265   2P: $205-$265   XP: $20   D12
                 4/10-5/20 [ECP]   1P: $150-$205   2P: $150-$205   XP: $20   D12
▼▼▼▼   10/2-2/28 [ECP]   1P: $105-$205   2P: $105-$205   XP: $20   D12
                 3/1-4/9 [ECP]   1P: $120-$170   2P: $120-$170   XP: $20   D12
Small-scale Hotel **Location:** On the canal. 122 Market St 19958. Fax: 302/644-3565. **Facility:** Smoke free premises. 24 units. 20
                 one-bedroom standard units, some with whirlpools. 2 one- and 2 two-bedroom suites, some with kitchens
and/or whirlpools. 4 stories, interior corridors. *Bath:* combo or shower only. **Parking:** on-site. **Terms:** office hours 7 am-11 pm, 2
night minimum stay - seasonal and/or weekends, 7 day cancellation notice-fee imposed, package plans, 2% service charge,
small pets only ($150 deposit). **Amenities:** dual phone lines, voice mail, irons, hair dryers. *Some:* CD players. **Guest Services:**
valet laundry. **Business Services:** meeting rooms, fax (fee). **Cards:** AX, MC, VI.

SLEEP INN & SUITES   *Book at aaa.com*

Phone: (302)645-6464

6/21-10/31 [ECP]	1P: $99-$209	2P: $99-$209	XP: $10 F18
5/16-6/20 [ECP]	1P: $89-$189	2P: $89-$189	XP: $10 F18
3/1-5/15 [ECP]	1P: $79-$99	2P: $79-$99	XP: $10 F18
11/1-2/28 [ECP]	1P: $49-$99	2P: $49-$99	XP: $10 F18

Small-scale Hotel **Location:** On SR 1, 1.5 mi s. Located in a commercial area. 1595 Hwy 1 19958. Fax: 302/644-8897. **Facility:** 80 one-bedroom standard units, some with whirlpools. 4 stories, interior corridors. *Bath:* combo or shower only. **Parking:** on-site. **Terms:** 2 night minimum stay - seasonal and/or weekends, pets ($15 extra charge). **Amenities:** dual phone lines, voice mail, safes (fee), irons, hair dryers. **Pool(s):** heated outdoor. **Leisure Activities:** limited exercise equipment. **Guest Services:** coin laundry. **Business Services:** meeting rooms, fax (fee). **Cards:** AX, DS, MC, VI. **Special Amenities:** free expanded continental breakfast and preferred room (subject to availability with advance reservations).

VESUVIO MOTEL

Phone: 302/645-2224

5/1-9/30	1P: $75-$105	2P: $95-$135	XP: $5
3/1-4/30	1P: $55-$85	2P: $55-$85	XP: $5
10/1-2/28	1P: $50-$65	2P: $50-$65	XP: $5

Motel **Location:** Just e on US 9 business route. 105 Savannah Rd 19958. **Facility:** 16 one-bedroom standard units. 2 stories (no elevator), exterior corridors. **Parking:** on-site. **Terms:** office hours 9 am-midnight, 2 night minimum stay - weekends, 3 day cancellation notice-fee imposed. **Cards:** AX, MC, VI.

------ WHERE TO DINE ------

THE BUTTERY

Lunch: $7-$15   **Dinner:** $22-$32   **Phone:** 302/645-7755

Location: 2nd and Savannah sts (US 9 business route). 102 2nd St 19958. **Hours:** 11 am-2:30 & 5-9 pm, Fri & Sat-10 pm, Sun 10:30 am-2:30 & 5-9 pm. Closed: 1/1, 12/25. **Reservations:** suggested. **Features:** In the heart of the historic shopping and gallery district, the quaint, converted residence provides a charming setting for casual lunches and more formal dinners. The kitchen is skilled in preparing such dishes as osso buco, grilled duck breast and jumbo lump crab cakes. The staff is friendly and professional. Dressy casual; cocktails. **Parking:** street. **Cards:** DS, MC, VI.

American

LIGHTHOUSE RESTAURANT AT LEWES

Lunch: $4-$14   **Dinner:** $12-$29   **Phone:** 302/645-6271

Location: Just e, n of US 9 business route. Savannah & Anglers Rd 19958. **Hours:** 7 am-9 pm, Fri & Sat-9:30 pm. Closed: 11/24, 12/25. **Features:** A basic, family-style seafood establishment, the canal-front restaurant features such choices as Chesapeake crab soup and a teriyaki-marinated grilled tuna sandwich. The complimentary after-dinner cruises, available during the summer, are a big draw. Casual dress; cocktails. **Parking:** on-site. **Cards:** MC, VI.

Seafood

ROSE & CROWN RESTAURANT & PUB

Lunch: $5-$10   **Dinner:** $12-$20   **Phone:** 302/645-2373

Location: Just n of US 9 business route. 108 2nd St 19958. **Hours:** 11 am-9 pm, Fri & Sat-10 pm. Closed major holidays. **Reservations:** suggested. **Features:** Look for a bit of "jolly old England" in Lewes Historic District at the Rose & Crown. The English pub-style dining features Black Angus beef, seafood pasta dishes, homemade dessert and traditional fish and chips. The service is pleasant and helpful. Casual dress; cocktails. **Parking:** street. **Cards:** AX, DC, MC, VI.

Steak & Seafood

LITTLE CREEK pop. 195

------ WHERE TO DINE ------

VILLAGE INN

Dinner: $15-$27   **Phone:** 302/734-3245

Location: On SR 9, just s. Rt 9, S Little Creek Rd 19961. **Hours:** 4 pm-10 pm. Closed: 11/24, 12/25; also Mon & Tues. **Reservations:** accepted. **Features:** After savoring one of the house specialties, such as crab imperial, guests should save room for homemade strawberry shortcake. The decor is decidedly Early American, with framed pictures depicting Colonial times. The atmosphere is casual and the service friendly. Casual dress; cocktails. **Parking:** on-site. **Cards:** MC, VI.

Steak & Seafood

LONG NECK pop. 1,629

------ WHERE TO STAY ------

SEA ESTA II

Phone: (302)945-5900

5/1-9/10		2P: $49-$139	XP: $15 F12
9/11-10/31		2P: $42-$89	XP: $15 F12
3/1-4/30		2P: $42-$69	XP: $15 F12
11/1-2/28		2P: $42-$55	XP: $15 F12

Motel **Location:** On SR 23, 1.1 mi s of jct SR 24, 5 and 23. A19 Long Neck Rd 19968. Fax: 302/945-6027. **Facility:** 32 one-bedroom standard units. 1 story, exterior corridors. **Parking:** on-site. **Terms:** 2 night minimum stay - seasonal and/or weekends, pets ($8 extra charge). **Amenities:** irons, hair dryers. **Pool(s):** outdoor. **Business Services:** fax (fee). **Cards:** AX, CB, DC, DS, MC, VI. **Special Amenities:** free local telephone calls and free newspaper.

MARSHALLTON

———— **WHERE TO DINE** ————

CAFFE BELLISSIMO SEAFOOD ITALIANO
RISTORANTE — **Lunch:** $5-$13 — **Dinner:** $9-$23 — **Phone:** 302/994-9200
Italian — **Location:** Jct SR 41 and 2. 3421 Kirkwood Hwy 19808. **Hours:** 11 am-9 pm, Fri-10 pm, Sat noon-10 pm, Sun noon-9 pm. Closed: 11/24, 12/25. **Reservations:** accepted. **Features:** Bellissimo justifiably shows off its innovative Italian cuisine with the chicken bella — sauteed chicken breasts with fresh tomato and white wine sauce, topped with lump crabmeat and mozzarella. Generous portions of pasta are served along with daily specials. Casual dress; cocktails. **Parking:** on-site. **Cards:** AX, DC, DS, MC, VI.

MILFORD pop. 6,732

———— **WHERE TO STAY** ————

AMERICINN LODGE & SUITES — **Phone:** 302/839-5000
[fyi] — All Year — 1P: $59-$199 — 2P: $59-$199 — XP: $10 — F12
Small-scale Hotel — Too new to rate, opening scheduled for October 2004. **Location:** SR 1 s to US 113 S. 699 N DuPont Blvd 19963. Fax: 302/839-5050. **Amenities:** 57 units, coffeemakers, microwaves, refrigerators, pool. **Terms:** 2 night minimum stay - seasonal and/or weekends. **Cards:** AX, CB, DC, DS, MC, VI.

———— **WHERE TO DINE** ————

GEYER'S RESTAURANT — **Lunch:** $5-$10 — **Dinner:** $9-$19 — **Phone:** 302/422-5327
American — **Location:** US 113, 0.3 mi n of jct SR 36. 556 S DuPont Blvd 19963. **Hours:** 9 am-8:30 pm, Fri-9 pm, Sat 3:30 pm-9 pm. Closed major holidays; also Sun. **Reservations:** accepted. **Features:** Families, locals and travelers enjoy Geyer's, particularly on the weekend with the well-prepared all-you-can-eat seafood specials. But throughout the week, the emphasis is on Black Angus beef as well as fresh seafood. Dessert is prepared on the premises. Casual dress; cocktails. **Parking:** on-site. **Cards:** DS, MC, VI.

SAIL LOFT RESTAURANT — **Lunch:** $5-$10 — **Dinner:** $14-$31 — **Phone:** 302/422-5858
American — **Location:** US 113, 1.5 mi n of jct SR 1. 1517 Bay Rd 19963. **Hours:** 11:30 am-2:30 & 4:30-9 pm, Sat from 4:30 pm, Sun noon-8 pm. Closed major holidays; also Tues 10/1-11/30 & 1/1-5/30. **Reservations:** suggested, weekends. **Features:** The most popular selections are prime rib and seafood although chicken, veal and beef are also offered. Tempting desserts are homemade. The nautical-style decor and pleasant service complement the casual atmosphere. Casual dress; cocktails. **Parking:** on-site. **Cards:** AX, DS, MC, VI.

MILLSBORO pop. 2,360

———— **WHERE TO STAY** ————

ATLANTIC INN-MILLSBORO — **Phone:** 302/934-6711

	7/1-8/27	1P: $89-$219	2P: $89-$219	XP: $10	F11
Motel	5/20-6/30	1P: $69-$199	2P: $69-$199	XP: $10	F11
	8/28-2/28	1P: $69-$179	2P: $69-$179	XP: $10	F11
	3/1-5/19	1P: $69-$139	2P: $69-$139	XP: $10	F11

Location: US 113, just s of SR 24. 210 E DuPont Hwy 19966. Fax: 302/934-6711. **Facility:** 82 one-bedroom standard units. 2 stories (no elevator), exterior corridors. **Parking:** on-site. **Terms:** 3 night minimum stay - seasonal, cancellation fee imposed, small pets only ($10 fee 10/1-4/30). **Amenities:** *Some:* irons. **Pool(s):** outdoor. **Guest Services:** coin laundry. **Business Services:** meeting rooms, fax (fee). **Cards:** AX, DC, DS, MC, VI.

SOME UNITS

NEWARK pop. 28,547

———— WHERE TO STAY ————

BEST WESTERN DELAWARE INN AND CONFERENCE CENTER-WILMINGTON/NEWARK *Book at aaa.com* Phone: (302)738-3400

(AAA) (SAVE) All Year [ECP]   1P: $89-$169   2P: $89-$169   XP: $10   F12
Location: I-95, exit 3 southbound; exit 3A northbound, 0.3 mi e on SR 273 E, then just n. 260 Chapman Rd 19702.
Fax: 302/738-3414. **Facility:** 95 one-bedroom standard units. 2 stories (no elevator), interior corridors.
Parking: on-site. **Terms:** small pets only ($10 extra charge). **Amenities:** high-speed Internet, voice mail,
Small-scale Hotel irons, hair dryers. **Dining:** 5 pm-10 pm, cocktails. **Pool(s):** outdoor. **Leisure Activities:** volleyball. **Guest Services:** valet and coin laundry. **Business Services:** meeting rooms, fax (fee). **Cards:** AX, DS, MC, VI.
Special Amenities: free expanded continental breakfast and free room upgrade (subject to availability with advance reservations). *(See color ad below)*
SOME UNITS

🄢🄓 🐾 🍴 🍽 🍸 ⬜ 🏊 🛗 🎥 [DATA PORT] ▣ / ✕ 🔲 🖥 /
FEE

COMFORT INN OF NEWARK *Book at aaa.com*   Phone: (302)453-9100

(AAA) (SAVE) 11/1-2/28   1P: $79-$190   2P: $79-$190   XP: $10   F18
3/1-10/31   1P: $74-$185   2P: $74-$185   XP: $10   F18
Location: I-95, exit 3 southbound; exit 3B northbound, 0.4 mi w on SR 273. 100 McIntosh Plaza 19713.
Fax: 302/453-9114. **Facility:** 105 one-bedroom standard units. 2 stories (no elevator), interior/exterior
Motel corridors. *Bath:* combo or shower only. **Parking:** on-site. **Amenities:** irons, hair dryers. **Leisure Activities:** putting green, limited exercise equipment. **Guest Services:** coin laundry. **Business Services:** fax (fee). **Cards:** AX, DC, DS, MC, VI. **Special Amenities:** free continental breakfast and preferred room (subject to availability with advance reservations).
SOME UNITS

🄢🄓 🖐 🏋M 🛗 ⬜ 🎥 [DATA PORT] ▣ / ✕ 🔲 🖥 /

COMFORT SUITES-NEWARK/WILMINGTON *Book at aaa.com*   Phone: (302)266-6600

(AAA) (SAVE) All Year [ECP]   1P: $89-$199   2P: $89-$199   XP: $10   F16
Location: I-95, exit 3A northbound; exit 3 southbound, 0.8 mi e on SR 273 E. 56 S Old Baltimore Pike 19702.
Fax: 302/266-6500. **Facility:** 66 units. 65 one-bedroom standard units, some with whirlpools. 1 one-
bedroom suite ($149-$199) with whirlpool. 3 stories, interior corridors. *Bath:* combo or shower only.
Small-scale Hotel **Parking:** on-site. **Amenities:** high-speed Internet, voice mail, irons, hair dryers. **Pool(s):** small heated
indoor. **Leisure Activities:** limited exercise equipment. **Guest Services:** valet laundry. **Business Services:** meeting rooms, PC, fax (fee). **Cards:** AX, DC, DS, JC, MC, VI. **Special Amenities:** free expanded continental breakfast and free local telephone calls.
SOME UNITS

🄢🄓 🏋M 🛗 🏊 🎥 [DATA PORT] 🔲 🖥 ▣ / ✕ /

COUNTRY INN & SUITES BY CARLSON NEWARK/WILMINGTON *Book at aaa.com*   Phone: (302)266-6400

(AAA) (SAVE) All Year [ECP]   1P: $99-$209   2P: $99-$209   XP: $10   F16
Location: I-95, exit 4B, 0.3 mi n on SR 7, exit 166, then 0.4 mi w on SR 58 (Churchmans Rd). 1024 Old Churchman's
Rd 19713. Fax: 302/266-6300. **Facility:** 55 units. 50 one-bedroom standard units, some with whirlpools. 5
one-bedroom suites ($149-$259), some with efficiencies and/or whirlpools. 3 stories, interior corridors. *Bath:*
Small-scale Hotel combo or shower only. **Parking:** on-site. **Amenities:** high-speed Internet, dual phone lines, voice mail,
irons, hair dryers. **Leisure Activities:** limited exercise equipment. **Guest Services:** valet and coin laundry.
Business Services: meeting rooms, business center. **Cards:** AX, CB, DC, DS, MC, VI. **Special Amenities:** free expanded
continental breakfast and free local telephone calls. *(See color ad p 366)*
SOME UNITS

🄢🄓 🖐 🛗 ✕ 🎥 [DATA PORT] 🖥 / 🔲 🖥 /

COURTYARD BY MARRIOTT-NEWARK AT THE UNIVERSITY OF DELAWARE

Phone: 302/737-0900

Small-scale Hotel

All Year   1P: $109-$229

Too new to rate, opening scheduled for November 2004. **Location:** 0.6 mi n on SR 896, from the University of Delaware campus. 400 Pencader Way 19716. Fax: 302/737-0990. **Amenities:** 126 units, restaurant, coffeemakers, pool. **Cards:** AX, CB, DC, DS, MC, VI.

COURTYARD BY MARRIOTT-NEWARK/CHRISTIANA   *Book at aaa.com*

Phone: 302/456-3800

Small-scale Hotel

All Year   1P: $79-$164

Location: I-95, exit 4B, 0.3 mi n on SR 7, exit 166, then just e on SR 58 (Churchmans Rd). Located adjacent to shopping complex. 48 Geoffrey Dr 19713. Fax: 302/456-3824. **Facility:** 152 units. 140 one-bedroom standard units. 12 one-bedroom suites ($199). 4 stories, interior corridors. *Bath:* combo or shower only. **Parking:** on-site. **Terms:** [BP] meal plan available. **Amenities:** high-speed Internet, dual phone lines, voice mail, irons, hair dryers. **Pool(s):** heated indoor. **Leisure Activities:** whirlpool, exercise room. **Guest Services:** valet and coin laundry. **Business Services:** meeting rooms, fax (fee). **Cards:** AX, CB, DC, DS, JC, MC, VI.

SOME UNITS

(ASK) (S/D) (⬛) (🍴) (⛓M) (⛨) (◿) (⟲) (📷) (DATA PORT) (⬛) / (✕) /

DAYS INN WILMINGTON/NEWARK   *Book at aaa.com*

Phone: (302)368-2400

Motel

All Year   1P: $55-$125   2P: $55-$125

Location: I-95, exit 4B, 0.3 mi n on SR 7, exit 166, then 0.3 mi w on SR 58 (Churchmans Rd). 900 Churchmans Rd 19713. Fax: 302/731-8620. **Facility:** 142 one-bedroom standard units, some with whirlpools. 3 stories, exterior corridors. **Parking:** on-site. **Terms:** pets ($10 extra charge). **Amenities:** voice mail, hair dryers. *Some:* irons. **Pool(s):** outdoor. **Guest Services:** valet laundry. **Business Services:** meeting rooms, fax (fee). **Cards:** AX, DC, DS, MC, VI. **Special Amenities:** free continental breakfast and free local telephone calls.

SOME UNITS

(S/D) (🐾) (🍴) (⟲) (📷) (DATA PORT) (⬛) / (✕) (📱) (⬛)
FEE

EMBASSY SUITES NEWARK/WILMINGTON SOUTH   *Book at aaa.com*

Phone: (302)368-8000

Large-scale Hotel

All Year [BP]   1P: $119-$279   2P: $119-$279   XP: $15   F18

Location: I-95, exit 1B southbound; exit 1 northbound, 0.8 mi n on SR 896. Located opposite the University of Delaware stadium. 654 S College Ave 19713. Fax: 302/368-8975. **Facility:** 154 one-bedroom suites. 6 stories, interior corridors. *Bath:* combo or shower only. **Parking:** on-site. **Terms:** cancellation fee imposed. **Amenities:** dual phone lines, voice mail, safes, irons, hair dryers. *Fee:* video games, high-speed Internet. **Pool(s):** heated indoor. **Leisure Activities:** whirlpool, exercise room. **Guest Services:** gift shop, complimentary evening beverages, valet and coin laundry, area transportation. **Business Services:** conference facilities, business center. **Cards:** AX, DC, DS, JC, MC, VI.

SOME UNITS

(ASK) (S/D) (🍴) (Y) (⛓M) (⛨) (◿) (⟲) (📷) (DATA PORT) (📱) (⬛) (⬛) / (✕) /

FAIRFIELD INN BY MARRIOTT NEWARK/WILMINGTON   *Book at aaa.com*

Phone: (302)292-1500

Motel

All Year   1P: $69-$149   2P: $69-$149

Location: I-95, exit 4B, 0.3 mi n on SR 7, exit 166, then just e on SR 58 (Churchmans Rd). Located in a shopping complex. 65 Geoffrey Dr 19713. Fax: 302/292-8655. **Facility:** 135 one-bedroom standard units. 3 stories, interior/exterior corridors. **Parking:** on-site. **Amenities:** voice mail, irons, hair dryers. **Pool(s):** heated outdoor. **Guest Services:** valet laundry. **Business Services:** fax (fee). **Cards:** AX, CB, DC, DS, JC, MC, VI.

SOME UNITS

(ASK) (S/D) (🍴) (◿) (⟲) (✛) (📷) (DATA PORT) (⬛) / (✕) (📱) /

HAMPTON INN NEWARK/WILMINGTON   *Book at aaa.com*

Phone: (302)737-3900

Small-scale Hotel

All Year   1P: $89-$99   2P: $99-$109

Location: I-95, exit 3 southbound; exit 3B northbound, 0.5 mi w on SR 273. 3 Concord Ln 19713. Fax: 302/737-2630. **Facility:** 121 one-bedroom standard units. 4 stories, interior corridors. **Parking:** on-site. **Terms:** cancellation fee imposed. **Amenities:** video games (fee), voice mail, irons, hair dryers. **Pool(s):** outdoor. **Guest Services:** valet and coin laundry. **Business Services:** meeting rooms, fax (fee). **Cards:** AX, CB, DC, DS, MC, VI.

SOME UNITS

(ASK) (🍴) (⛓M) (◿) (⟲) (✛) (📷) (DATA PORT) (⬛) / (✕) /

HAWTHORN SUITES LTD   *Book at aaa.com*   Phone: (302)369-6212

AAA SAVE

Small-scale Hotel

All Year 1P: $179 2P: $179
Location: I-95, exit 3 southbound; exit 3A northbound, just e. 410 Eagle Run Rd 19702. Fax: 302/369-6205. **Facility:** 76 one-bedroom standard units, some with efficiencies and/or whirlpools. 4 stories, interior corridors. *Bath:* combo or shower only. **Parking:** on-site. **Terms:** cancellation fee imposed. **Amenities:** high-speed Internet (fee), dual phone lines, voice mail, irons, hair dryers. **Pool(s):** small outdoor. **Leisure Activities:** limited exercise equipment. **Guest Services:** valet and coin laundry. **Business Services:** meeting rooms, business center. **Cards:** AX, CB, DC, DS, MC, VI. **Special Amenities:** free full breakfast and early check-in/late check-out.

SOME UNITS

HILTON WILMINGTON/CHRISTIANA   *Book at aaa.com*   Phone: (302)454-1500

AAA SAVE

Large-scale Hotel

All Year 1P: $99-$219 2P: $99-$219 XP: $10 F16
Location: I-95, exit 4B, 0.3 mi n on SR 7, exit 166, then 0.4 mi w on SR 58 (Churchmans Rd). Located in a business park area. 100 Continental Dr 19713. Fax: 302/454-0233. **Facility:** 266 units. 263 one-bedroom standard units. 3 one-bedroom suites. 4 stories, interior corridors. **Parking:** on-site. **Terms:** cancellation fee imposed, package plans, small pets only (with prior approval). **Amenities:** high-speed Internet (fee), dual phone lines, voice mail, irons, hair dryers. **Dining:** 6:30 am-9 pm, Sat & Sun from 7 am, cocktails. **Pool(s):** outdoor. **Leisure Activities:** whirlpool, exercise room. **Guest Services:** valet laundry, airport transportation-New Castle County Airport, area transportation-within 10 mi. **Business Services:** conference facilities, business center. **Cards:** AX, CB, DC, DS, JC, MC, VI. **Special Amenities:** free local telephone calls and free newspaper.

SOME UNITS

FEE

HOLIDAY INN WILMINGTON-NEWARK   *Book at aaa.com*   Phone: (302)737-2700

Small-scale Hotel

All Year 1P: $87-$102 2P: $87-$102
Location: I-95, exit 3 southbound; exit 3B northbound, 0.3 mi w on SR 273. 1203 Christiana Rd 19713. Fax: 302/737-3214. **Facility:** 143 one-bedroom standard units. 2 stories (no elevator), exterior corridors. **Parking:** on-site. **Amenities:** video games (fee), voice mail, irons, hair dryers. **Pool(s):** outdoor. **Leisure Activities:** limited exercise equipment. **Guest Services:** valet and coin laundry. **Business Services:** meeting rooms, fax (fee). **Cards:** AX, CB, DC, DS, JC, MC, VI.

SOME UNITS

FEE FEE

HOMESTEAD STUDIO SUITES
HOTEL-NEWARK/CHRISTIANA   *Book at aaa.com*   Phone: (302)283-0800

Small-scale Hotel

All Year 1P: $79-$99 2P: $84-$104 XP: $5 F17
Location: I-95, exit 4B, 0.3 mi n on SR 7, exit 166, then 0.4 mi w on SR 58 (Churchmans Rd). Located at rear of Christiana Executive Campus. 333 Continental Dr 19713. Fax: 302/283-0804. **Facility:** 141 one-bedroom standard units with efficiencies. 3 stories, interior corridors. *Bath:* combo or shower only. **Parking:** on-site. **Terms:** office hours 6:30 am-11 pm, weekly rates available, pets ($27 extra charge). **Amenities:** voice mail, irons, hair dryers. **Guest Services:** valet and coin laundry. **Business Services:** fax (fee). **Cards:** AX, CB, DC, DS, JC, MC, VI.

SOME UNITS

FEE FEE

HOMEWOOD SUITES BY HILTON
NEWARK/WILMINGTON SOUTH   Phone: 302-453-9700

fyi

Small-scale Hotel

All Year [BP] 1P: $99-$149 2P: $99-$149 XP: $15 F18
Too new to rate, opening scheduled for September 2004. **Location:** I-95, exit 1B southbound; exit 1 northbound, 0.8 mi n on SR 896. Located oppsite the University of Delaware Stadium. 640 S College Ave 19713. Fax: 302/453-9600. **Amenities:** 91 units, pets, coffeemakers, microwaves, refrigerators, pool. **Terms:** cancellation fee imposed. **Cards:** AX, CB, DC, DS, JC, MC, VI.

HOWARD JOHNSON INN & SUITES - WILMINGTON/NEWARK   Book at aaa.com
Phone: (302)368-8521

AAA [SAVE]

All Year [ECP]   1P: $50-$89   2P: $55-$99   XP: $10   F18

◆◆ ◆◆

Location: I-95, exit 1B southbound; exit 1 northbound, 0.3 mi n on SR 896. 1119 S College Ave 19713. Fax: 302/368-9868. **Facility:** 142 one-bedroom standard units, some with whirlpools. 2 stories (no elevator), interior corridors. **Parking:** on-site. **Terms:** cancellation fee imposed, package plans, small pets only ($10

Small-scale Hotel   fee). **Amenities:** voice mail, safes (fee), irons, hair dryers. **Pool(s):** outdoor. **Leisure Activities:** limited exercise equipment. **Guest Services:** valet and coin laundry, airport transportation (fee)-Philadelphia & Baltimore-Washington International airports. **Business Services:** meeting rooms, fax (fee). **Cards:** AX, CB, DC, DS, JC, MC, VI. **Special Amenities: free expanded continental breakfast and free newspaper.** *(See color ad p 367)*

SOME UNITS

[S/D] [icons] FEE FEE [icons] [DATA PORT] [icons] / [X] [icons] VCR [icons] FEE

QUALITY INN BY CHOICE HOTELS-UNIVERSITY   Book at aaa.com
Phone: (302)368-8715

AAA [SAVE]

All Year [ECP]   1P: $54-$89   2P: $59-$99   XP: $5   F18

◆◆ ◆◆

Location: I-95, exit 1B southbound; exit 1 northbound, 0.3 mi n on SR 896. Located in a commercial area. 1120 S College Ave 19713. Fax: 302/368-6454. **Facility:** 102 one-bedroom standard units. 2 stories (no elevator), exterior corridors. **Parking:** on-site. **Terms:** pets ($10 fee, in designated units). **Amenities:** voice mail.

Motel   *Some:* irons, hair dryers. **Pool(s):** outdoor. **Guest Services:** valet laundry. **Business Services:** meeting rooms, fax (fee). **Cards:** AX, CB, DC, DS, JC, MC, VI. *(See color ad below)*

SOME UNITS

[S/D] [icons] FEE [icons] [DATA PORT] / [X] [icons] FEE

RED ROOF INN-WILMINGTON   Book at aaa.com
Phone: (302)292-2870

◆

4/17-11/5   1P: $56-$75   2P: $62-$81   XP: $6   F18

3/1-4/16   1P: $50-$66   2P: $56-$72   XP: $6   F18

11/6-2/28   1P: $50-$63   2P: $56-$69   XP: $6   F18

Motel   **Location:** I-95, exit 4B, 0.5 mi n on SR 7. 415 Stanton Christiana Rd 19713. Fax: 302/292-2879. **Facility:** 119 one-bedroom standard units. 3 stories, exterior corridors. **Parking:** on-site. **Amenities:** video games (fee), voice mail. **Business Services:** fax (fee). **Cards:** AX, CB, DC, DS, MC, VI.

SOME UNITS

[icons] [DATA PORT] / [X] /

RESIDENCE INN BY MARRIOTT   Book at aaa.com
Phone: 302/453-9200

◆◆◆

All Year   1P: $99-$169   2P: $99-$169

Small-scale Hotel   **Location:** I-95, exit 3 southbound; exit 3A northbound, 0.3 mi w on SR 273 E, then 0.5 mi s. 240 Chapman Rd 19702. Fax: 302/453-8122. **Facility:** 120 units. 112 one-bedroom standard units with efficiencies. 8 one-bedroom suites with kitchens. 2 stories (no elevator), exterior corridors. *Bath:* combo or shower only. **Parking:** on-site. **Terms:** pets ($50 extra charge). **Amenities:** voice mail, irons, hair dryers. **Pool(s):** heated outdoor. **Leisure Activities:** whirlpool, sports court. **Guest Services:** complimentary evening beverages: Mon-Thurs, valet and coin laundry, area transportation. **Business Services:** meeting rooms, fax (fee). **Cards:** AX, DC, DS, JC, MC, VI.

SOME UNITS

[icons] FEE [icons] [DATA PORT] [icons] / [X] /

SLEEP INN-NEWARK   Book at aaa.com
Phone: (302)453-1700

AAA [SAVE]

All Year   1P: $89   2P: $89   XP: $10   D18

◆◆ ◆◆

Location: I-95, exit 1B southbound; exit 1 northbound, 0.8 mi n on SR 896. Located opposite the University of Delaware stadium. 630 S College Ave 19713. Fax: 302/453-1710. **Facility:** 96 one-bedroom standard units. 3 stories, interior corridors. *Bath:* combo or shower only. **Parking:** on-site. **Terms:** 30 day cancellation notice-fee

Small-scale Hotel   imposed, weekly rates available. **Amenities:** voice mail, irons, hair dryers. **Leisure Activities:** limited exercise equipment. **Guest Services:** valet and coin laundry. **Business Services:** meeting rooms, fax (fee). **Cards:** AX, DS, JC, MC, VI.

SOME UNITS

[S/D] [icons] [DATA PORT] [icons] / [X] /

——— WHERE TO DINE ———

ALI BABA RESTAURANT
Middle Eastern
Lunch: $4-$13   **Dinner:** $6-$13   **Phone:** 302/738-1111
Location: I-95, exit 1B, 2.5 mi n on SR 896, 0.5 mi e on E Delaware Ave, then just w; downtown. 175 E Main St 19711. **Hours:** 11:30 am-10 pm, Fri-11 pm, Sat 12:30 pm-11 pm, Sun 12:30 pm-10 pm. Closed major holidays. **Reservations:** accepted. **Features:** Patrons can sample Middle Eastern cuisine made from Moroccan and Lebanese recipes. The traditional Moroccan atmosphere incorporates tapestries and sofa seating in the back room and traditional seating in the front. Casual dress. **Parking:** street. **Cards:** AX, MC, VI.

CAFFE GELATO
Mediterranean
Lunch: $6-$16   **Dinner:** $14-$21   **Phone:** 302/738-5811
Location: I-95, exit 1B, 2.5 mi n on SR 896, 0.5 mi e on E Delaware Ave, then just w; downtown. 90 E Main St 19711. **Hours:** 11 am-10 pm, Sun-3 pm. **Closed:** 3/27, 11/24; also 12/23-1/1. **Reservations:** suggested. **Features:** On bustling Main St., near the University of Delaware, this intimate cafe prepares Mediterranean cuisine with a Northern Italian influence. The kitchen creates a wide range of daily specials in addition to the regular menu items. The lunch menu is available till 5pm and offers salads, soups, panini and pasta dishes. Save room for gelato, it's homemade and a rainbow of flavors are offered. In addition to beer and wine, after dinner cordials are available. Casual dress; beer & wine only. **Parking:** on-site. **Cards:** AX, DS, MC, VI.

IRON HILL BREWERY & RESTAURANT
American
Lunch: $7-$11   **Dinner:** $15-$20   **Phone:** 302/266-9000
Location: I-95, exit 1B, 2.5 mi n on SR 896, 0.5 mi e on E Delaware Ave, then just w; downtown. 147 E Main St 19711. **Hours:** 11:30 am-9 pm, Fri & Sat-10 pm. **Closed:** 12/25. **Reservations:** not accepted. **Features:** Handcrafted beers made on the premises match with the innovative American cuisine. The downtown dining room is casual, comfortable and friendly. Light fare is available throughout the day, and the dinner menu begins at 5 pm. Casual dress; cocktails. **Parking:** street. **Cards:** AX, DC, DS, MC, VI.

LA CASA PASTA RESTAURANT
Italian
Lunch: $7-$15   **Dinner:** $10-$32   **Phone:** 302/738-9935
Location: I-95, exit 1A southbound; exit 1 northbound, 1.5 mi s. Rt 896 & Four Seasons Pkwy 19702. **Hours:** 11 am-10 pm, Mon-9 pm, Fri & Sat-midnight, Sun noon-9 pm. **Closed:** 11/24, 12/25. **Reservations:** suggested. **Features:** For more than 20 years, the unpretentious restaurant has served fresh seafood, veal and pasta dishes. Casual dress; cocktails. **Parking:** on-site. **Cards:** AX, DC, DS, MC, VI.

MICHAEL'S FAMILY RESTAURANT & PUB
American
Lunch: $4-$8   **Dinner:** $10-$24   **Phone:** 302/368-4230
Location: I-95, exit 4B, 0.3 mi n on SR 7, exit 166, then 0.4 mi w. 1000 Churchmans Rd 19713. **Hours:** 10 am-10 pm, Fri & Sat-11 pm, Sun 8 am-10 pm. **Closed:** 12/25. **Features:** Buffet choices in the upscale, contemporary restaurant include prime rib, huge mussels and snow crab legs. The regular menu focuses primarily on sandwiches, burgers and seafood. Neon lighting, glass blocks and skylights all lend to the contemporary feel. Casual dress; cocktails. **Parking:** on-site. **Cards:** AX, DS, MC, VI.

NONNA RISTORANTE
Italian
Lunch: $6-$14   **Dinner:** $9-$32   **Phone:** 302/737-9999
Location: I-95, exit 4B, 0.3 mi n on SR 7, exit 166, 0.8 mi w on SR 58 (Churchmans Rd), then 0.7 mi s on SR 4; in The Omega Shop. 4621 Stanton Ogletown Rd 19713. **Hours:** 11 am-10 pm, Sat & Sun from noon; Sat & Sun from 3 pm 5/31-9/6. Closed major holidays. **Reservations:** accepted, Sun-Thurs. **Features:** The small, shopping plaza restaurant prepares consistently good Northern and Southern Italian cooking. Offerings on the varied menu range from veal and seafood to pasta and pizza. The wine list offers a nice selection, including many by-the-glass choices. Casual dress; beer & wine only. **Parking:** on-site. **Cards:** AX, DC, MC, VI.

NEW CASTLE pop. 4,862

——— WHERE TO STAY ———

DUTCH INN
Motel
Phone: (302)328-6246
All Year   **1P:** $55-$60   **2P:** $55-$60   **XP:** $10   **F10**
Location: I-295, exit Dover/Shore Points, 2.5 mi s on US 13, 40 and 301. 111 S DuPont Hwy 19720. Fax: 302/328-9493. **Facility:** 41 one-bedroom standard units. 1 story, exterior corridors. Bath: combo or shower only. **Parking:** on-site. **Terms:** weekly rates available, package plans, pets ($10 extra charge). **Business Services:** fax (fee). **Cards:** AX, DS, MC, VI.

QUALITY INN SKYWAYS   *Book at aaa.com*
Motel
Phone: (302)328-6666
All Year   **1P:** $94-$104   **2P:** $94-$104   **XP:** $10   **F18**
Location: I-95, exit 5A, 0.8 mi s on SR 141, exit 1B, 0.5 mi s on US 13, 40 and 301; I-295, exit New Castle Airport/US 13 S, 1.8 mi s on US 13, 40 and 301. Located in a commercial area next to the airport. 147 N DuPont Hwy 19720. Fax: 302/322-3791. **Facility:** 142 units. 102 one-bedroom standard units, some with kitchens. 40 one-bedroom suites ($159-$169), some with whirlpools. 1-2 stories (no elevator), interior/exterior corridors. Bath: combo or shower only. **Parking:** on-site. **Terms:** weekly rates available, package plans, small pets only ($10 fee, in designated units). **Amenities:** voice mail, irons, hair dryers. Some: high-speed Internet (fee), safes. **Pool(s):** outdoor. **Leisure Activities:** picnic area, barbecue grill. **Guest Services:** sundries, valet and coin laundry, area transportation-within 10 mi. **Business Services:** meeting rooms, PC, fax (fee). **Cards:** AX, CB, DC, DS, JC, MC, VI.

WILLIAM PENN GUEST HOUSE
Historic Bed & Breakfast
Phone: 302/328-7736
All Year [ECP]   **1P:** $75-$95   **2P:** $75-$95
Location: Between Market and Third sts. Located in a historic district, opposite courthouse. 206 Delaware St 19720. **Facility:** This Colonial-style brick home dates from 1682; phone for seasonal closures. Smoke free premises. 4 one-bedroom standard units. 3 stories (no elevator), interior corridors. Bath: some shared or private. **Parking:** on-site. **Terms:** 2 night minimum stay - seasonal, age restrictions may apply, 5 day cancellation notice-fee imposed. **Cards:** DS, MC, VI.

——— WHERE TO DINE ———

AIR TRANSPORT COMMAND RESTAURANT   **Lunch:** $7-$12   **Dinner:** $15-$42   **Phone:** 302/328-3527

American

Location: US 13, 0.3 mi s of Wilmington Airport entrance. 121 N DuPont Hwy 19720. **Hours:** 11 am-10 pm, Fri & Sat-11 pm, Sun 10 am-10 pm. **Reservations:** suggested, weekends. **Features:** Authentic World War II memorabilia decorates the restaurant inside and out. Entree selections include prime rib, steak, filet mignon, barbecue ribs, seafood, veal and chicken. The crisply attired wait staff provides prompt, pleasant service. Casual dress; cocktails. **Parking:** on-site. **Cards:** AX, CB, DC, DS, MC, VI.

THE ARSENAL AT OLD NEW CASTLE   **Lunch:** $7-$14   **Dinner:** $15-$25   **Phone:** 302/328-1290

American

Location: Center of historic district; directly behind courthouse. 30 Market St 19720. **Hours:** 11:30 am-9 pm, Fri & Sat-10 pm, Sun 11 am-8 pm. Closed: 12/24, 12/25; also Mon. **Reservations:** suggested. **Features:** In an 1809 former militia barracks in the heart of the historic district, the restaurant serves traditional American fare. Attired in faux colonial garb, the staff reinforces the history themes employed in the inn's various rooms. The tavern has a Civil War theme, and the upstairs function room is decorated in colonial fashion. The elegant Federal decor of the main dining room conjures visions of the War of 1812 era. Casual dress; cocktails. **Parking:** street. **Cards:** AX, DC, DS, MC, VI.

JESSOP'S TAVERN & COLONIAL RESTAURANT   **Lunch:** $6-$15   **Dinner:** $6-$22   **Phone:** 302/322-6111

American

Location: In downtown historic district. 114 Delaware St 19720. **Hours:** 11 am-3 & 5-10 pm, Sun 10 am-4 pm. Closed: 1/1, 11/24, 12/24, 12/25. **Reservations:** suggested. **Features:** American and English pub fare is served in hearty portions amid the ambience of a 1724 Colonial brick home. The crab chowder, chicken pot pie and fish & chips are popular choices. Both Swedish and Dutch culinary influences also reflect New Castle's early heritage. Casual dress; cocktails. **Parking:** street. **Cards:** AX, CB, DC, DS, MC, VI. **Historic**

POLIDORO ITALIAN GRILL   **Lunch:** $7-$9   **Dinner:** $9-$20   **Phone:** 302/322-1500

Italian

Location: I-95, exit 5A, 0.8 mi on SR 141, exit 1B, then 0.6 mi s on US 13, 40 and 301; I-295, exit New Castle Airport/US 13 S, 1.8 mi s on US 13, 40 and 301. 129 N DuPont Hwy 19720. **Hours:** 11 am-11 pm, Fri-midnight, Sat noon-midnight, Sun noon-10 pm. Closed: 12/25. **Reservations:** suggested, weekends. **Features:** The contemporary decor with the 2-story ceiling, decorative lighting and black and white pictures of Italy set a casual, comfortable atmosphere for any occasion. The staff is friendly and helpful. The menu offers a nice selection of pasta, beef and seafood dishes. Casual dress; cocktails. **Parking:** on-site. **Cards:** AX, DC, DS, MC, VI.

SALTY SAM'S PIER 13   **Lunch:** $5-$9   **Dinner:** $11-$40   **Phone:** 302/323-1408

Seafood

Location: US 13, 40, and 301; 2.8 mi s of jct I-295. 130 S DuPont Hwy 19720. **Hours:** 11 am-10 pm, Sun from 2 pm. Closed major holidays. **Reservations:** suggested, weekends. **Features:** An extensive variety of seafood and steak is served in the lively, family-oriented atmosphere of Salty Sam's. Casual dress; cocktails. **Parking:** on-site. **Cards:** AX, DC, DS, MC, VI.

REHOBOTH BEACH pop. 1,495

——— WHERE TO STAY ———

ADMIRAL HOTEL   **Phone:** 302/227-2103

Motel

7/1-9/30	2P: $209-$369	XP: $10	F12
5/27-6/30	2P: $129-$259	XP: $10	F12
3/1-5/26 & 10/1-2/28	2P: $89-$209	XP: $10	F12

Location: Immediately off the boardwalk. 2 Baltimore Ave 19971. Fax: 302/227-3620. **Facility:** 73 units. 72 one-bedroom standard units. 1 one-bedroom suite. 5 stories, exterior corridors. *Bath:* combo or shower only. **Parking:** on-site. **Terms:** 2 night minimum stay - seasonal, 7 day cancellation notice-fee imposed, package plans. **Amenities:** voice mail, irons, hair dryers. **Pool(s):** heated indoor. **Leisure Activities:** whirlpool. **Business Services:** fax (fee). **Cards:** AX, DS, MC, VI. **Special Amenities:** free local telephone calls and preferred room (subject to availability with advance reservations). *(See color ad below)*

SOME UNITS

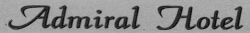

AMERICINN LODGE & SUITES OF REHOBOTH
BEACH · *Book at aaa.com*

Phone: (302)226-0700

5/1-9/30	1P: $119-$199	2P: $119-$199	XP: $10	F
3/1-4/30 & 10/1-2/28	1P: $79-$99	2P: $79-$99	XP: $10	F

Small-scale Hotel **Location:** Just w of SR 1; 1.3 mi n of jct SR 1A. 329Z Airport Rd 19971. Fax: 302/226-1037. **Facility:** 50 units. 46 one-bedroom standard units, some with whirlpools. 4 one-bedroom suites ($139-$269), some with whirlpools. 2 stories (no elevator), interior corridors. *Bath:* combo or shower only. **Parking:** on-site. **Terms:** 2 night minimum stay - seasonal, pets ($20 fee). **Amenities:** irons, hair dryers. **Pool(s):** heated indoor. **Leisure Activities:** sauna, whirlpool. **Guest Services:** coin laundry. **Business Services:** meeting rooms, fax (fee). **Cards:** AX, CB, DC, DS, MC, VI.
(See color ad p 379)

SOME UNITS
[ASK] [S] [🐾] [📺] [&M] [📶] [♨] [🏊] [DATA PORT] [🍴] [📺] / [✕] [VCR] /
FEE   FEE

ATLANTIC INN & SUITES

Phone: (302)227-0401

5/6-9/30	1P: $69-$169	2P: $69-$169	XP: $10	F12
10/1-11/30	1P: $59-$119	2P: $59-$119	XP: $10	F12
4/1-5/5	1P: $59-$89	2P: $59-$89	XP: $10	F12

Motel **Location:** SR 1, 1.3 mi s of jct SR 24. Located in the outlet area. 4353 Hwy 1 19971. Fax: 302/227-0401. **Facility:** 74 units. 39 one- and 27 two-bedroom standard units. 8 one-bedroom suites. 2 stories (no elevator), exterior corridors. **Parking:** on-site. **Terms:** open 4/1-11/30, 2 night minimum stay - seasonal and/or weekends, 7 day cancellation notice-fee imposed. **Pool(s):** outdoor. **Business Services:** fax (fee). **Cards:** AX, DS, MC, VI.

SOME UNITS
[ASK] [S] [🍴] [🏊] [PTV] [📺] [DATA PORT] / [✕] [🍴] [📺] /

THE ATLANTIS INN

Phone: 302/227-9446

6/1-9/6	1P: $89-$209	2P: $89-$209	XP: $10	F11
9/7-11/13	1P: $59-$189	2P: $59-$189	XP: $10	F11
5/2-5/31	1P: $79-$149	2P: $59-$149	XP: $10	F11
3/18-5/1	1P: $59-$109	2P: $59-$109	XP: $10	F11

Motel **Location:** At Rehoboth Ave and 2nd St; downtown. 154 Rehoboth Ave 19971. Fax: 302/227-9446. **Facility:** 97 units. 95 one-bedroom standard units, some with efficiencies. 2 one-bedroom suites ($99-$279) with efficiencies. 4 stories, exterior corridors. *Bath:* combo or shower only. **Parking:** on-site. **Terms:** open 3/18-11/13, 2 night minimum stay - seasonal, 7 day cancellation notice-fee imposed, package plans, small pets only ($10 extra charge 3/15-5/28 & 9/3-11/15). **Pool(s):** outdoor. **Guest Services:** coin laundry. **Business Services:** fax (fee). **Cards:** AX, DS, MC, VI.

SOME UNITS
[ASK] [S] [🛏] [🍴] [🏊] [DATA PORT] / [✕] [🍴] [📺] [📺] /
FEE

BEACH VIEW MOTEL

Phone: 302/227-2999

6/24-9/5 [CP]	1P: $149-$197	2P: $149-$197	XP: $15	F11
5/27-6/23 [CP]	1P: $55-$175	2P: $55-$175	XP: $15	F11
9/6-11/13 [CP]	1P: $48-$155	2P: $48-$155	XP: $15	F11
4/1-5/26 [CP]	1P: $48-$98	2P: $48-$98	XP: $15	F11

Motel **Location:** Just w of boardwalk; downtown. 6 Wilmington Ave 19971. Fax: 302/226-2640. **Facility:** 38 one-bedroom standard units. 4 stories, exterior corridors. **Parking:** on-site. **Terms:** open 4/1-11/13, office hours 7 am-midnight, 7 day cancellation notice-fee imposed. **Amenities:** irons, hair dryers. **Pool(s):** small outdoor. **Guest Services:** coin laundry. **Business Services:** fax (fee). **Cards:** AX, DC, MC, VI.

SOME UNITS
[ASK] [S] [🍴] [🏊] [📺] [DATA PORT] [🍴] [📺] / [✕] /

THE BELLMOOR INN & SPA · *Book at aaa.com*

Phone: 302/227-5800

Property failed to provide current rates

Small-scale Hotel **Location:** 1 blk s of Rehoboth Ave, jct 2nd St. 6 Christian St 19971 (PO Box 1). Fax: 302/227-0323. **Facility:** Smoke free premises. 78 units. 70 one-bedroom standard units, some with efficiencies and/or whirlpools. 5 one- and 2 two-bedroom suites with whirlpools, some with kitchens. 1 cottage. 2-4 stories, interior/exterior corridors. *Bath:* combo or shower only. **Parking:** on-site and valet. **Amenities:** high-speed Internet, dual phone lines, voice mail, irons, hair dryers. *Some:* DVD players, CD players. **Pool(s):** outdoor, small outdoor. **Leisure Activities:** whirlpool, exercise room, spa. **Guest Services:** gift shop, complimentary laundry. **Business Services:** meeting rooms, business center.

SOME UNITS
[🍴] [&] [🏊] [✕] [✕] [📺] [DATA PORT] [🍴] [📺] / [VCR] [📺] /

BOARDWALK PLAZA HOTEL

Phone: (302)227-7169

(AAA) [SAVE]

◊◊◊◊

Small-scale Hotel

6/10-10/9	1P: $224-$489	2P: $224-$489	XP: $25	F6
3/1-6/9	1P: $104-$374	2P: $104-$374	XP: $25	F6
10/10-11/26	1P: $124-$299	2P: $124-$299	XP: $25	F6
11/27-2/28	1P: $89-$249	2P: $89-$249	XP: $25	F6

Location: Just n of Rehoboth Ave; oceanfront at Olive Ave. Located on the boardwalk. Oceanfront at Olive Ave 19971. Fax: 302/227-0561. **Facility:** A Victorian ambience pervades this beachfront hotel set on the boardwalk and offering some guest rooms overlooking the ocean. 84 units. 39 one-bedroom standard units, some with whirlpools. 42 one- and 3 two-bedroom suites ($149-$499), some with efficiencies, kitchens and/or whirlpools. 4 stories, interior corridors. *Bath:* combo or shower only. **Parking:** on-site and valet. **Terms:** 3 night minimum stay - seasonal and/or weekends, 3 day cancellation notice, package plans. **Amenities:** video library (fee), DVD players, CD players, high-speed Internet, voice mail, irons, hair dryers. *Some:* honor bars. **Dining:** Victoria's, see separate listing. **Leisure Activities:** whirlpool, exercise room. **Business Services:** meeting rooms. **Fee:** PC, fax. **Cards:** AX, DC, DS, MC, VI. **Special Amenities:** free local telephone calls and free newspaper. *(See color ad below)*

SOME UNITS

⊗⊗⊗⊗⊗⊗⊗⊗ / ⊗⊗⊗ /
FEE

THE BREAKERS HOTEL & SUITES

Phone: 302/227-6688

(AAA) [SAVE]

◊◊ ◊◊

Motel

7/1-9/1 [CP]	1P: $145-$299	2P: $145-$299	XP: $10	F16
3/1-6/30 [CP]	1P: $55-$250	2P: $55-$250	XP: $10	F16
9/2-1/1 & 2/1-2/28 [CP]	1P: $55-$199	2P: $55-$199	XP: $10	F16

Location: Just n of Rehoboth Ave. 105 2nd St 19971. Fax: 302/227-2013. **Facility:** 98 units. 60 one-bedroom standard units. 36 one- and 2 two-bedroom suites, some with whirlpools. 5 stories, exterior corridors. **Parking:** on-site. **Terms:** open 3/1-1/1 & 2/1-2/28, 2 night minimum stay - seasonal and/or weekends, 3 day cancellation notice-fee imposed, pets ($10 fee 10/1-4/30, in designated units). **Amenities:** safes (fee). **Pool(s):** small heated indoor/outdoor. **Leisure Activities:** limited exercise equipment. **Business Services:** meeting rooms, fax (fee). **Cards:** AX, DS, MC, VI. **Special Amenities:** free continental breakfast and free local telephone calls.

SOME UNITS

⊗⊗⊗⊗⊗⊗⊗⊗ / ⊗ /
FEE

BRIGHTON SUITES HOTEL

Phone: (302)227-5780

(AAA) [SAVE]

◊◊◊

Small-scale Hotel

7/1-9/4	1P: $194-$299	2P: $194-$299	XP: $25	F11
5/27-6/30	1P: $119-$269	2P: $119-$269	XP: $25	F11
9/5-2/28	1P: $89-$199	2P: $89-$199	XP: $10	F11
3/1-5/26	1P: $64-$189	2P: $64-$189	XP: $10	F11

Location: Just s of Rehoboth Ave. 34 Wilmington Ave 19971. Fax: 302/227-6815. **Facility:** Designated smoking area. 66 units. 3 one-bedroom standard units. 63 one-bedroom suites. 4 stories, interior corridors. **Parking:** on-site. **Terms:** 2 night minimum stay - seasonal and/or weekends, 5 day cancellation notice-fee imposed, package plans. **Amenities:** video library, DVD players, dual phone lines, safes, irons, hair dryers. **Dining:** 6 am-2 pm. **Pool(s):** small heated indoor. **Leisure Activities:** limited exercise equipment. **Guest Services:** area transportation-within 5 mi. **Business Services:** meeting rooms, fax (fee). **Cards:** AX, DS, MC, VI. **Special Amenities:** free local telephone calls. *(See color ad p 373)*

SOME UNITS

⊗⊗⊗⊗⊗⊗⊗⊗⊗ / ⊗⊗⊗ /
FEE

COMFORT INN REHOBOTH BEACH   *Book at aaa.com*   Phone: (302)226-1515

All Year   1P: $59-$299   2P: $59-$299   XP: $10   F17
Location: On SR 1, 1.5 mi n. Located in the outlet mall area. 4439 Hwy 1 19971. Fax: 302/226-1550. **Facility:** 97 units. 94 one-bedroom standard units, some with whirlpools. 3 one-bedroom suites with whirlpools. 3 stories, interior corridors. *Bath:* combo or shower only. **Parking:** on-site. **Terms:** check-in 4 pm, 2 night minimum stay - seasonal, 3 day cancellation notice. **Amenities:** irons, hair dryers. **Pool(s):** outdoor. **Guest Services:** coin laundry. **Business Services:** meeting rooms, PC, fax (fee). **Cards:** AX, CB, DC, DS, MC, VI. **Special Amenities:** free expanded continental breakfast and free local telephone calls. *(See color ad below)*

SOME UNITS

DELAWARE INN

Phone: 302/227-6031

AAA SAVE

Bed & Breakfast

5/15-9/15 [ECP]	1P: $130-$230		XP: $25
3/1-5/14 & 9/16-10/31 [ECP]	1P: $80-$180		XP: $25
11/1-2/28 [ECP]	1P: $80-$100		XP: $25

Location: Jct Delaware Ave and 2nd St, just e; downtown. 55 Delaware Ave 19971. Fax: 302/226-1788. **Facility:** Smoke free premises. 7 one-bedroom standard units. 3 stories (no elevator), interior corridors. *Bath:* some shared or private, combo or shower only. **Parking:** on-site. **Terms:** office hours 8 am-10 pm, 2 night minimum stay - weekends, age restrictions may apply, 10 day cancellation notice-fee imposed, package plans, no pets allowed (owner's pets on premises). **Amenities:** hair dryers. **Leisure Activities:** beach chairs, towels & umbrellas, bicycles. **Guest Services:** coin laundry. **Business Services:** fax (fee). **Cards:** DS, MC, VI.

ECONO LODGE

Book at aaa.com

Phone: (302)227-0500

AAA SAVE

Motel

5/16-9/15 [CP]	1P: $99-$199	2P: $99-$199	XP: $10	F16
3/1-5/15 & 9/16-2/28 [CP]	1P: $39-$99	2P: $39-$99	XP: $10	F16

Location: SR 1, 1.3 mi s of jct SR 24. 4361 Hwy 1 19971. Fax: 302/227-2170. **Facility:** 123 units. 98 one- and 2 two-bedroom standard units, some with efficiencies and/or whirlpools. 23 one-bedroom suites ($99-$249). 3-4 stories, interior/exterior corridors. **Parking:** on-site. **Terms:** check-in 4 pm, 2 night minimum stay - weekends, cancellation fee imposed. **Amenities:** *Some:* hair dryers. **Pool(s):** outdoor. **Leisure Activities:** picnic benches. **Guest Services:** coin laundry. **Business Services:** meeting rooms, fax (fee). **Cards:** AX, DC, DS, MC, VI.

SOME UNITS

HAMPTON INN REHOBOTH BEACH/LEWES

Book at aaa.com

Phone: (302)645-8003

Small-scale Hotel

All Year	1P: $59-$219	2P: $69-$229	XP: $10	F18

Location: On SR 1, 2 mi n. Located in the outlet mall area. 4529 Hwy 1 19971. Fax: 302/645-7003. **Facility:** 85 one-bedroom standard units, some with whirlpools. 4 stories, interior corridors. *Bath:* combo or shower only. **Parking:** on-site. **Terms:** 2 night minimum stay - weekends, 3 day cancellation notice-fee imposed, [ECP] meal plan available, package plans. **Amenities:** video games (fee), voice mail, irons, hair dryers. *Some:* dual phone lines. **Pool(s):** heated indoor. **Leisure Activities:** limited exercise equipment. **Guest Services:** coin laundry. **Business Services:** meeting rooms, business center. **Cards:** AX, CB, DC, DS, MC, VI.

SOME UNITS

HENLOPEN HOTEL

Phone: (302)227-2551

AAA SAVE

Small-scale Hotel

7/1-9/4	1P: $220-$400	2P: $220-$400	XP: $10	F17
5/27-6/30	1P: $160-$300	2P: $160-$300	XP: $10	F17
9/5-11/9	1P: $150-$300	2P: $150-$300	XP: $10	F17
4/1-5/26	1P: $90-$250	2P: $90-$250	XP: $10	F17

Location: 0.5 mi n on 1st St from Rehoboth Ave. 511 N Boardwalk 19971. Fax: 302/227-8147. **Facility:** 93 units. 87 one-bedroom standard units. 6 one-bedroom suites, some with efficiencies. 8 stories, exterior corridors. **Parking:** on-site. **Terms:** open 4/1-11/9, 2 night minimum stay - seasonal and/or weekends, 10 day cancellation notice. **Dining:** 5 pm-11 pm; closed Mon 4/1-5/31 & 9/7-11/7, cocktails. **Business Services:** meeting rooms, fax (fee). **Cards:** AX, DS, MC, VI. *(See color ad below)*

HOLIDAY INN EXPRESS-REHOBOTH BEACH

Book at aaa.com

Phone: 302/227-4030

Small-scale Hotel

4/2-9/1 [ECP]	1P: $199-$500	2P: $199-$500	XP: $10	F18
9/2-9/25 [ECP]	1P: $89-$450	2P: $89-$450	XP: $10	F18
9/26-2/28 [ECP]	1P: $89-$299	2P: $89-$299	XP: $10	F18
3/1-4/1 [ECP]	1P: $79-$199	2P: $79-$199	XP: $10	F18

Location: On SR 1, just n. 4289 Hwy 1 19971. Fax: 302/227-9455. **Facility:** 81 one-bedroom standard units. 4 stories, interior corridors. *Bath:* combo or shower only. **Parking:** on-site. **Terms:** 7 day cancellation notice-fee imposed. **Amenities:** voice mail, irons, hair dryers. **Pool(s):** outdoor. **Leisure Activities:** limited exercise equipment. **Guest Services:** coin laundry. **Business Services:** meeting rooms, fax (fee). **Cards:** AX, CB, DC, DS, MC, VI.

SOME UNITS

THE OCEANUS MOTEL

AAA SAVE

Motel

Phone: 302/227-8200

6/26-9/4	1P: $149-$239	2P: $149-$239	XP: $15	F11
5/8-6/25	1P: $69-$189	2P: $69-$189	XP: $15	F11
9/5-11/6	1P: $69-$179	2P: $69-$179	XP: $15	F11
3/18-5/7	1P: $69-$109	2P: $69-$109	XP: $15	F11

Location: Just s of Rehoboth Ave. 6 2nd St 19971 (PO Box 324). Fax: 302/227-0323. **Facility:** 38 one-bedroom standard units. 3 stories (no elevator), exterior corridors. **Parking:** on-site. **Terms:** open 3/18-11/6, 2 night minimum stay - seasonal and/or weekends, 7 day cancellation notice-fee imposed, [CP] meal plan available, package plans. **Pool(s):** outdoor. **Guest Services:** coin laundry. **Cards:** DC, MC, VI. **Special Amenities:** free continental breakfast and free local telephone calls.

QUALITY INN & SUITES OF REHOBOTH   *Book at aaa.com*

AAA SAVE

Small-scale Hotel

Phone: (302)226-2400

7/1-10/14	1P: $159-$309	2P: $159-$309	XP: $10	F
5/15-6/30	1P: $99-$189	2P: $99-$189	XP: $10	F
3/1-5/14 & 10/15-2/28	1P: $79-$169	2P: $79-$169	XP: $10	F

Location: 1 mi s. 3100 Hwy 1 19971. Fax: 302/226-7722. **Facility:** 65 units. 55 one- and 9 two-bedroom standard units. 1 one-bedroom suite. 4 stories, interior corridors. *Bath:* combo or shower only. **Parking:** on-site. **Terms:** check-in 4 pm, 2 night minimum stay - seasonal, 7 day cancellation notice-fee imposed, package plans. **Amenities:** irons, hair dryers. **Pool(s):** heated indoor. **Business Services:** meeting rooms, fax (fee). **Cards:** AX, DC, DS, MC, VI. **Special Amenities:** free continental breakfast and free local telephone calls.

SOME UNITS

SEA-ESTA IV, III & I

AAA SAVE

Motel

Phone: (302)227-5882

5/1-9/1	2P: $49-$169	XP: $12	F12
3/1-4/30	2P: $39-$159	XP: $12	F12
9/2-2/28	2P: $39-$129	XP: $12	F12

Location: 1 mi s. 3101 Hwy 1 19971 (713 Rehoboth Ave). Fax: 302/226-8155. **Facility:** 36 one-bedroom standard units. 3 stories, exterior corridors. **Parking:** on-site. **Terms:** 2-3 night minimum stay - seasonal, 3 day cancellation notice, package plans, pets ($6 fee). **Amenities:** hair dryers. **Pool(s):** small heated outdoor. **Business Services:** fax (fee). **Cards:** AX, DC, DS, MC, VI. **Special Amenities:** free local telephone calls and free newspaper. *(See color ad p 358)*

FEE

SEA WITCH, BEWITCHED & BEDAZZLED

AAA SAVE

Bed & Breakfast

Phone: (302)226-9482

All Year [BP]	1P: $145-$295	2P: $145-$295	XP: $50

Location: Jct Rehoboth Ave, just ne. 71 Lake Ave 19971. **Facility:** Victorian antiques and reproductions add charm to this residential-area B&B just outside of downtown; all guest rooms have remote-control fireplaces. Smoke free premises. 5 one-bedroom standard units, some with whirlpools. 2 stories (no elevator), interior corridors. *Bath:* combo or shower only. **Parking:** on-site. **Terms:** office hours 7 am-9:30 pm, 2 night minimum stay - seasonal, age restrictions may apply, 14 day cancellation notice-fee imposed, weekly rates available, package plans, no pets allowed (owner's pet on premises). **Amenities:** video library, DVD players, high-speed Internet, voice mail, irons, hair dryers. **Leisure Activities:** whirlpool, beach chairs & towels. *Fee:* massage. **Guest Services:** valet laundry. **Business Services:** meeting rooms, PC, fax (fee). **Cards:** AX, DC, DS, MC, VI.

SOME UNITS

--------- **WHERE TO DINE** ---------

1776 EASTERN SHORE STEAKHOUSE

Steak & Seafood

Dressy casual; cocktails.

Dinner: $15-$40

Phone: 302/645-9355

Location: On SR 1, 2.5 mi n; in Midway Shopping Center. 4590 Hwy 1 19971. **Hours:** 5 pm-10 pm. Closed: 3/27, 11/24, 12/25. **Reservations:** suggested. **Features:** Dry-aged steaks are the house specialty, but the extensive seafood offerings shouldn't be overlooked. The shopping plaza restaurant has developed a strong local following. Service is professional and friendly, and the atmosphere is comfortable albeit a little loud. **Parking:** on-site. **Cards:** AX, CB, DC, DS, MC, VI.

ABSTRACTIONS SUSHI BAR AND RESTAURANT

Sushi

Dinner: $24-$44   **Phone:** 302/226-0877

Location: Corner of 2nd St and Rehoboth Ave. 203 Rehoboth Ave 19971. **Hours:** 5 pm-11 pm. Closed: 1/1; also Sun-Tues 1/1-4/1. **Reservations:** suggested. **Features:** Just a few blocks from the boardwalk, the cozy restaurant and sushi bar displays a hip interior. For those who can't decide, there are chef's sampler selections of sushi and sashimi. Anyone with an aversion to raw fish will be more than satisfied with one of the cooked entrees, such as Thai curry, sesame-dusted salmon or filet mignon. Also served are varied creative martinis and decadent desserts. Casual dress; cocktails. **Parking:** on-site (fee). **Cards:** AX, DS, MC, VI.

ADRIATICO RISTORANTE & CAFE

Italian

Lunch: $13-$19   **Dinner:** $25-$30   **Phone:** 302/227-9255

Location: Corner of 1st St and Baltimore; center. 30 Baltimore 19971. **Hours:** 11 am-3 & 4:30-10 pm, Fri & Sat-10:30 pm; 4:30 pm-9 pm 10/31-6/1. Closed: 1/1, 12/25. **Reservations:** suggested. **Features:** In the heart of downtown, the cozy Italian restaurant specializes in veal, seafood, chicken and pasta; seasonal patio dining is available. Casual dress; cocktails. **Parking:** on-site (fee). **Cards:** AX, MC, VI.

ANN MARIE'S SEAFOOD & ITALIAN RESTAURANT

Italian

Dinner: $11-$29   **Phone:** 302/645-6262

Location: On SR 1, just e of jct SR 24. 4537 Hwy 1 19971. **Hours:** 4 pm-10 pm; to 9 pm, Fri & Sat-10 pm 10/1-5/1. Closed: 12/24, 12/25. **Reservations:** accepted. **Features:** Ann Marie's Restaurant has been serving the Rehoboth community since 1977. Now located near the outlet malls, this family restaurant continues to provide good Italian cooking using family recipes, as well as nice selection of seafood dishes. Lobster and crab cakes with jumbo, lump crabmeat are a couple of the menu favorites. The atmosphere is casual and is a great place to bring the family. A childrens menu is available. Casual dress; cocktails. **Parking:** on-site. **Cards:** AX, DC, DS, MC, VI.

BIG FISH GRILL

Seafood

Dinner: $10-$30   **Phone:** 302/227-3474

Location: Just s. 4117 Hwy One 19971. **Hours:** 5 pm-9 pm, Fri 4:30 pm-9:30 pm, Sat 4 pm-9:30 pm, Sun 4 pm-9 pm; 4:30 pm-9:30 pm, Sat & Sun 4 pm-9:30 pm 5/30-9/5. Closed: 3/27, 11/24, 12/25. **Reservations:** not accepted. **Features:** The main attraction is fresh seafood, which is prepared using original recipes and fresh, homemade ingredients. Beef and pasta dishes appeal to those looking for something different. The casual, loud and comfortable restaurant is popular with locals and tourists alike. In summer, don't be surprised by an hour wait for a table. Casual dress; cocktails. **Parking:** on-site. **Cards:** AX, DS, MC, VI.

BLUE MOON RESTAURANT

American

Dinner: $26-$50   **Phone:** 302/227-6515

Location: Between 1st and 2nd sts. 35 Baltimore Ave 19971. **Hours:** Open 3/1-1/6 & 2/1-2/28; 6 pm-10 pm, Sun also 11 am-2. **Reservations:** suggested. **Features:** Less than two blocks from the ocean and inside a striking beach house, this restaurant specializes in modern American cuisine with international influences. The wine selection is impressive. Casual dress; cocktails. **Parking:** street. **Cards:** AX, CB, DC, DS, MC, VI.

THE CAMEL'S HUMP

Mediterranean

Lunch: $6-$9   **Dinner:** $17-$36   **Phone:** 302/227-0947

Location: Center of town. 21 Baltimore Ave 19971. **Hours:** Open 4/1-10/1; 11 am-10 pm. **Features:** Middle Eastern decor and servers in billowy Arabian pants lend to the ethnic dining experience in this quiet restaurant. Such traditional Mediterranean fare as shish kabobs with couscous are menu staples. Servers are knowledgeable and pleasant. Casual dress; cocktails. **Parking:** street. **Cards:** MC, VI.

CELSIUS RESTAURANT & TAPAS BAR

Mediterranean

Dinner: $19-$28   **Phone:** 302/227-5767

Location: Jct 2nd St and Wilmington Ave, just e; downtown. 50-C Wilmington Ave 19971. **Hours:** 5 pm-10 pm. Closed: 12/25; also Thurs 12/1-5/1. **Reservations:** suggested. **Features:** The two chef-owners combine their talents in the delightful Mediterranean restaurant. The fine-dining atmosphere is cozy. A good selection of daily specials complements the seasonally changing menu. The wine list is extensive. Casual dress; cocktails. **Parking:** street. **Cards:** AX, CB, DC, DS, MC, VI.

CHEZ LA MER RESTAURANT   *Menu on aaa.com*

Continental

Dinner: $17-$36   **Phone:** 302/227-6494

Location: Corner 2nd St and Wilmington Ave. 210 2nd St 19971. **Hours:** Open 4/15-10/20; 5:30 pm-10 pm, Fri & Sat-10:30 pm, in season. Closed: Mon-Wed 4/15-5/31 & 10/1-10/20. **Reservations:** suggested. **Features:** Conveniently located just a block from the main street of this beachfront resort community, this charmingly renovated house is marked by a rustic stone fireplace, an open-air rooftop deck, an enclosed sun porch and a country French dining room. Bouillabaisse is one specialty, as are the house pate, mussels and crab imperial. The wine list is extensive. Dressy casual; cocktails. **Parking:** street. **Cards:** AX, DC, DS, MC, VI.

THE CULTURED PEARL

Asian

Japanese, Thai

Lunch: $7-$14   **Dinner:** $14-$29   **Phone:** 302/227-8493

Location: Just w of the boardwalk. 19 Wilmington Ave 19971. **Hours:** 11 am-2:30 & 5-10 pm; 11 am-2:30 & 4:30-11 pm 5/31-9/6. Closed: 11/24, 12/25; also Tues 9/7-5/29; Mon & Wed 10/1-4/31. **Reservations:** suggested. **Features:** Guests can listen to birds chirping as they dine in the Japanese garden setting at a table or the sushi bar. Patio seating under the stars is available, weather permitting. The kitchen is skillful in preparing Japanese, Thai and American dishes. Casual dress; cocktails. **Parking:** street. **Cards:** MC, VI.

ESPUMA

Mediterranean

Dinner: $24-$36   **Phone:** 302/227-4199

Location: At 1st St. 28 Wilmington Ave 19971. **Hours:** 5:30 pm-10 pm. Closed: 12/25. **Reservations:** suggested. **Features:** The chef/owner prepares sophisticated Mediterranean cuisine with a Spanish influence. The Paella, a traditional Spanish entree, is wonderfully prepared, using an abundance of fresh shell fish. The wine selection is well thought out and compliments the cooking very nicely. The dining room offers a fun, colorful atmosphere, with original artwork displayed. Casual dress; cocktails. **Parking:** street. **Cards:** AX, DC, MC, VI.

FUSION

American

Dinner: $25-$34   Phone: 302/226-1940

Location: Jct 2nd St and Wilmington Ave, just e; downtown. 50 Wilmington Ave 19971. **Hours:** 5:30 pm-10 pm. Closed: 1/1, 11/24, 12/25; also Sun-Wed 1/2-4/1. **Reservations:** suggested. **Features:** Artistically presented, innovative American cuisine with Pan-Asian influences served in simple, but elegantly upscale contemporary atmosphere. Casual dress; cocktails. **Parking:** street. **Cards:** AX, DC, DS, MC, VI.

JAKE'S SEAFOOD HOUSE

Seafood

Lunch: $10-$19   **Dinner:** $21-$34   Phone: 302/227-6237

Location: Corner of 1st St and Baltimore; center. 29 Baltimore 19971. **Hours:** Open 4/1-11/1; 11:30 am-9 pm, Fri & Sat-10 pm. Closed: 12/25. **Features:** Located downtown, the casual restaurant offers seafood with an Old Baltimore taste. Casual dress; cocktails. **Parking:** street. **Cards:** AX, DC, DS, MC, VI.

JAKE'S SEAFOOD HOUSE RESTAURANT

American

Lunch: $5-$34   **Dinner:** $5-$34   Phone: 302/644-7711

Location: On SR 1, 1.5 mi n. 4443 Hwy 1 19971. **Hours:** 11:30 am-10 pm, Fri & Sat-11 pm. Closed: 11/24, 12/25. **Features:** Looking for a bite to eat after shopping at the outlet malls or a day at the beach? The lively, fun restaurant offers a nice selection of seafood dishes prepared in an Old Baltimore style. Casual dress; cocktails. **Parking:** on-site. **Cards:** AX, DS, MC, VI.

JUST IN THYME

American

Dinner: $13-$28   Phone: 302/227-3100

Location: 1.1 mi s on SR 1. 31 Robinson Dr & Hwy 1 19971. **Hours:** 5 pm-10 pm; also Sun 11 am-2 pm 5/1-9/30. Closed: 12/25; also Mon 1/1-2/28. **Reservations:** suggested. **Features:** This comfortable, homey atmosphere is suitable for any occasion. Dishes prepared by the chef/owner blend a Continental influence with American style. A notable local favorite is carpetbagger steak, a black Angus filet mignon stuffed with Saga blue cheese and jumbo lump crabmeat. Dressy casual; cocktails. **Parking:** on-site. **Cards:** AX, CB, DC, DS, MC, VI.

LA LA LAND RESTAURANT & BAR

International

Dinner: $20-$32   Phone: 302/227-3887

Location: Just w of boardwalk. 22 Wilmington Ave 19971. **Hours:** Open 4/15-12/31; 6 pm-11 pm. Closed: Mon-Thurs 4/15-4/30 & Mon-Wed 10/1-12/31. **Reservations:** suggested. **Features:** The highest-quality seafood and meats are prepared imaginatively to reflect international influences that draw from Asia, India, France and America. The eclectic, colorfully decorated restaurant is just steps from the boardwalk. Casual dress; cocktails. **Parking:** street. **Cards:** AX, DC, DS, MC, VI.

RAMS HEAD TAVERN

International

Lunch: $14-$18   **Dinner:** $19-$34   Phone: 302/227-0807

Location: Corner of 1st St and Willington Ave just e; just w of the boardwalk. 15 Wilmington Ave 19971. **Hours:** 11 am-1 am. **Reservations:** accepted. **Features:** Less than a block from the boardwalk is the tavern, which dishes up sumptuous fare and frothy beer. This place is part of a collection of eateries and entertainment venues in Maryland and Delaware. For starters, try beer-battered shrimp or steak chili. Entree offerings include something for everyone, including fish tacos, pasta, cioppino, jambalaya, crab cakes, burgers and sandwiches, including one with fried oysters. Casual dress; cocktails. **Parking:** on-site (fee). **Cards:** AX, DS, MC, VI.

RISTORANTE ZEBRA

Northern Italian

Dinner: $16-$36   Phone: 302/226-1160

Location: Jct Rehoboth Ave, just ne. 32 Lake Ave 19971. **Hours:** Open 3/28-1/3; 5:30 pm-10 pm. Closed: 1/1, 12/25; also Mon 4/27-5/28 & 9/3-1/1. **Reservations:** required, weekends in summer. **Features:** The restaurant has a strong local following due to its consistent Italian cooking. The skilled kitchen uses only fresh ingredients in preparing its seasonally changing menu, which lists a nice selection of pasta, veal, beef, chicken and seafood dishes. The setting is casually upscale with exotic decor in the three dining rooms; hand-painted walls and artwork reflect the animals of Africa. Patrons may elect to dine inside or on the open porch. Dressy casual; cocktails. **Parking:** street. **Cards:** AX, MC, VI.

TUTTO BENE RISTORANTE ITALIANO

Northern Italian

Dinner: $13-$26   Phone: 302/644-9005

Location: 2.5 mi n on SR 1; in Midway Shopping Center. 22 Midway Shopping Center 19971. **Hours:** 4 pm-10 pm, Fri & Sat-11 pm. Closed: 11/24, 12/25; also Tues. **Reservations:** suggested. **Features:** Tucked away in this shopping plaza this Italian restaurant offers an upscale, yet relaxed setting, attentive professional service and very good Northern Italian cooking. A couple of Chef DiLeo house specialties include Lobster Fra Diablo and Bone-in Filet Mignon. The menu offers a nice selection of meat, fish and pasta dishes. Limousine service available within 15 miles to/from local hotels. Dressy casual; cocktails. **Parking:** on-site. **Cards:** AX, DC, DS, MC, VI.

VICTORIA'S

Continental

Lunch: $8-$14   **Dinner:** $17-$32   Phone: 302/227-0615

Location: Just n of Rehoboth Ave; oceanfront at Olive Ave; in Boardwalk Plaza Hotel. Olive Ave & Boardwalk 19971. **Hours:** 7 am-10 pm, Fri & Sat-11 pm. **Reservations:** suggested. **Features:** Your dining experience begins with an ocean view amid traditional Victorian decor. Attractive presentations and well-prepared dishes are consistent from appetizer to dessert. The outdoor patio is open seasonally. Sunday brunch is available off season. Dressy casual; cocktails. **Parking:** on-site (fee). **Cards:** AX, CB, DC, DS, MC, VI.

(See color ad p 372)

SEAFORD pop. 6,699

———— WHERE TO STAY ————

BEST WESTERN SEAFORD INN　*Book at aaa.com*　　　　　　　　**Phone:** (302)629-8385

🔺🔺🔺 [SAVE]
♦♦♦ ♦♦♦
Motel

5/26-9/6	1P: $99-$120	2P: $99-$120
3/1-5/25	1P: $65-$75	2P: $65-$75
9/7-2/28	1P: $50-$70	2P: $50-$70

Location: 0.8 mi n on US 13 from SR 20. 225 N Dual Hwy 19973. Fax: 302/629-4961. **Facility:** 93 one-bedroom standard units, some with efficiencies and/or whirlpools. 3 stories, exterior corridors. **Parking:** on-site. **Terms:** package plans. **Amenities:** voice mail, irons, hair dryers. **Pool(s):** heated indoor. **Leisure Activities:** sauna, limited exercise equipment. **Guest Services:** coin laundry. **Business Services:** meeting rooms, fax (fee). **Cards:** AX, DC, DS, MC, VI. **Special Amenities:** free expanded continental breakfast and early check-in/late check-out. *(See ad below)*

SOME UNITS
[🆂ᴅ] [📶] [🛎] [♿] [🏊] [📽] [DATA PORT] [📞] [🍽] [🖥] / [❌]

HAMPTON INN SEAFORD　　*Book at aaa.com*　　　　　　　　　**Phone:** 302/629-4500

♦♦♦
Small-scale Hotel

All Year　　　　　　　1P: $74-$199　　　　2P: $74-$199
Location: 1.5 mi n on US 13 from SR 20. Located adjacent to a shopping plaza. 799 N Dual Hwy 19973. Fax: 302/629-2990. **Facility:** 66 one-bedroom standard units. 3 stories, interior corridors. *Bath:* combo or shower only. **Parking:** on-site. **Amenities:** dual phone lines, voice mail, irons, hair dryers. **Pool(s):** heated indoor. **Leisure Activities:** whirlpool, limited exercise equipment. **Guest Services:** valet and coin laundry. **Business Services:** meeting rooms, business center. **Cards:** AX, CB, DC, DS, JC, MC, VI.

SOME UNITS
[ASK] [🆂ᴅ] [📶] [♿] [🛎] [🏊] [📽] [DATA PORT] [📞] [🍽] [🖥] / [❌]

HOLIDAY INN EXPRESS-SEAFORD　　*Book at aaa.com*　　　　　**Phone:** (302)629-2000

♦♦♦
Small-scale Hotel

All Year　　　　　1P: $71-$250　　　2P: $76-$255　　　XP: $5　　　F18
Location: On US 13, just s of SR 20 W. 210 N Dual Hwy 19973. Fax: 302/629-9898. **Facility:** 81 one-bedroom standard units, some with whirlpools. 4 stories, interior corridors. *Bath:* combo or shower only. **Parking:** on-site. **Amenities:** dual phone lines, voice mail, irons, hair dryers. **Pool(s):** outdoor. **Leisure Activities:** exercise room. **Guest Services:** valet and coin laundry. **Business Services:** meeting rooms, business center. **Cards:** AX, DC, DS.

SOME UNITS
[ASK] [📶] [♿] [🛎] [🏊] [📽] [DATA PORT] [🖥] / [❌] [📞] [🍽] /

———— WHERE TO DINE ————

BON APPETIT RESTAURANT　　　　**Lunch:** $8-$12　　　**Dinner:** $18-$22　　　**Phone:** 302/629-3700

♦♦
French

Location: 1.2 mi w on Middleford Rd from jct US 13; downtown. 312 High St 19973. **Hours:** noon-2:30 & 5-9 pm, Sat from 5 pm. Closed: 1/1, 11/24, 12/24, 12/25; also Sun, Mon & 6/26-7/7. **Reservations:** suggested. **Features:** The chef-owner changes the intimate downtown restaurant's menu monthly. Comfort characterizes the setting, which includes white tablecloths, candlelit tables and fresh flowers at lunch or dinner. A five-course selection is available. Dressy casual; cocktails. **Parking:** street. **Cards:** AX, DS, MC, VI.　　　[❌]

SMYRNA pop. 5,679

———— WHERE TO DINE ————

THE THOMAS ENGLAND HOUSE RESTAURANT　　　**Dinner:** $11-$25　　　**Phone:** 302/653-1420

♦♦♦
Continental

Location: 1 mi s on US 13; just off US 1, exit 114. 1165 S DuPont Hwy 19977. **Hours:** 4 pm-9 pm, Fri & Sat-10 pm. Closed: 5/30, 9/5, 12/25. **Reservations:** suggested. **Features:** Each of the five casually, elegant dining rooms in this 1711 Greek Colonial mansion is expertly staffed with servers displaying a good knowledge of the Continental menu. Seafood, beef, veal and poultry are mainstays, with the crab imperial a most popular choice. Casual dress; cocktails. **Parking:** on-site. **Cards:** AX, DS, MC, VI. **Historic**　　　[🍸] [❌]

WILMINGTON pop. 72,664

─────── **WHERE TO STAY** ───────

BEST WESTERN BRANDYWINE VALLEY INN *Book at aaa.com* Phone: (302)656-9436

AAA SAVE | 5/1-11/12 | 1P: $99-$159 | 2P: $99-$159 | XP: $10 | F17
| 11/13-2/28 | 1P: $99-$149 | 2P: $99-$149 | XP: $10 | F17
| 3/1-4/30 | 1P: $99-$139 | 2P: $99-$139 | XP: $10 | F17

Motel **Location:** I-95, exit 8, 1 mi n on US 202. Located in a commercial area. 1807 Concord Pike 19803. **Fax:** 302/656-8564. **Facility:** 94 units. 93 one-bedroom standard units, some with whirlpools. 1 one-bedroom suite ($150-$250). 2 stories (no elevator), exterior corridors. **Parking:** on-site. **Terms:** [CP] meal plan available, package plans. **Amenities:** video library, voice mail, irons, hair dryers. *Some:* DVD players, high-speed Internet. **Pool(s):** outdoor, wading. **Leisure Activities:** whirlpool, limited exercise equipment. **Guest Services:** valet laundry, area transportation-within 10 mi. **Business Services:** meeting rooms, fax (fee). **Cards:** AX, CB, DC, DS, MC, VI. **Special Amenities:** free continental breakfast and free local telephone calls. *(See color ad p 380)*

SOME UNITS

BRANDYWINE SUITES HOTEL *Book at aaa.com* Phone: (302)656-9300

All Year | 1P: $149-$249 | 2P: $149-$249

Small-scale Hotel **Location:** Between 7th and 8th sts; downtown. 707 N King St 19801. **Fax:** 302/656-2459. **Facility:** 49 units. 6 one-bedroom standard units. 43 one-bedroom suites. 4 stories, interior corridors. *Bath:* combo or shower only. **Parking:** on-site (fee). **Terms:** package plans. **Amenities:** voice mail, irons, hair dryers. **Leisure Activities:** limited exercise equipment. **Guest Services:** valet laundry. **Business Services:** meeting rooms, PC, fax (fee). **Cards:** AX, DC, DS, MC, VI.

SOME UNITS

COURTYARD BY MARRIOTT-DOWNTOWN *Book at aaa.com* Phone: 302/429-7600

All Year | 1P: $79-$159

Small-scale Hotel **Location:** I-95, exit 7, 0.3 mi e; between 11th and 12th sts; downtown. 1102 West St 19801. **Fax:** 302/429-9167. **Facility:** 123 one-bedroom standard units, some with whirlpools. 10 stories, interior corridors. *Bath:* combo or shower only. **Parking:** on-site (fee). **Terms:** cancellation fee imposed. **Amenities:** high-speed Internet, dual phone lines, voice mail, irons, hair dryers. **Leisure Activities:** exercise room. **Guest Services:** valet and coin laundry. **Business Services:** meeting rooms, fax (fee). **Cards:** AX, CB, DC, DS, JC, MC, VI.

SOME UNITS

COURTYARD BY MARRIOTT WILMINGTON/BRANDYWINE *Book at aaa.com* Phone: (302)477-9500

All Year | 1P: $99-$139 | 2P: $99-$139 | XP: $10 | F18

Small-scale Hotel **Location:** I-95, exit 8, 3.8 mi n, just off US 202. Located in a commercial area. 320 Rocky Run Pkwy 19803. **Fax:** 302/477-0929. **Facility:** 78 units. 75 one-bedroom standard units. 3 one-bedroom suites. 3 stories, interior corridors. *Bath:* combo or shower only. **Parking:** on-site. **Amenities:** dual phone lines, voice mail, irons, hair dryers. **Pool(s):** heated indoor. **Leisure Activities:** whirlpool, limited exercise equipment. **Guest Services:** valet and coin laundry. **Business Services:** meeting rooms, fax (fee). **Cards:** AX, CB, DC, DS, MC, VI.

SOME UNITS

DAYS INN WILMINGTON *Book at aaa.com* Phone: (302)478-0300

AAA SAVE | 3/1-10/31 [ECP] | 1P: $89-$129 | 2P: $89-$129 | XP: $10 | F12
| 11/1-2/28 [ECP] | 1P: $75-$129 | 2P: $75-$129 | XP: $10 | F12

Motel **Location:** I-95, exit 8, 4 mi n on US 202; jct SR 92 (Naamans Rd). 5209 Concord Pike 19803. **Fax:** 302/478-2401. **Facility:** 96 one-bedroom standard units. 2 stories (no elevator), exterior corridors. *Bath:* combo or shower only. **Parking:** on-site. **Terms:** package plans, pets ($10 fee, with prior approval). **Amenities:** high-speed Internet, voice mail, safes (fee), irons, hair dryers. **Guest Services:** valet and coin laundry. **Business Services:** administrative services, fax (fee). **Cards:** AX, DC, DS, MC, VI. **Special Amenities:** free expanded continental breakfast and free newspaper. *(See color ad p 381)*

SOME UNITS

DOUBLETREE HOTEL WILMINGTON *Book at aaa.com* Phone: (302)478-6000
All Year 1P: $79-$364 2P: $79-$364 XP: $10 F18
Location: I-95, exit 8, 3.8 mi n on US 202. Located adjacent to Concord Shopping Mall. 4727 Concord Pike, Rt 202
Large-scale Hotel 19803. Fax: 302/477-1492. **Facility:** 244 units. 236 one-bedroom standard units. 8 one-bedroom suites. 5-7
stories, interior corridors. *Bath:* combo or shower only. **Parking:** on-site. **Terms:** package plans.
Amenities: dual phone lines, voice mail, irons, hair dryers. *Fee:* video games, high-speed Internet. **Pool(s):** heated indoor.
Leisure Activities: whirlpool, limited exercise equipment. **Guest Services:** valet and coin laundry, area transportation.
Business Services: conference facilities, business center. **Cards:** AX, DC, DS, JC, MC, VI.

SOME UNITS
FEE

HOLIDAY INN-NORTH *Book at aaa.com* Phone: (302)478-2222
All Year 1P: $70-$105 2P: $75-$110 XP: $10 F16
Location: I-95, exit 8, 3 mi n on US 202. 4000 Concord Pike 19803. Fax: 302/479-0850. **Facility:** 138 one-
bedroom standard units. 2 stories (no elevator), exterior corridors. *Bath:* combo or shower only. **Parking:**
on-site. **Terms:** package plans. **Amenities:** video games (fee), dual phone lines, voice mail, irons, hair
Small-scale Hotel dryers. **Dining:** 6:30 am-10 pm, cocktails. **Pool(s):** outdoor. **Guest Services:** valet and coin laundry.
Business Services: meeting rooms, fax (fee). **Cards:** AX, CB, DC, DS, JC, MC, VI. **Special Amenities:**
free local telephone calls and free newspaper.

SOME UNITS
FEE

HOMEWOOD SUITES BY HILTON BRANDYWINE
VALLEY *Book at aaa.com* Phone: (302)479-2000
All Year 1P: $175-$250 2P: $185-$250
Location: I-95, exit 8, 3.8 mi n, just off US 202. Located in a commercial area. 350 Rocky Run Blvd 19803.
Small-scale Hotel Fax: 302/479-0770. **Facility:** 113 units. 105 one- and 8 two-bedroom suites with efficiencies. 4 stories,
interior corridors. *Bath:* combo or shower only. **Parking:** on-site. **Terms:** cancellation fee imposed.
Amenities: video games (fee), dual phone lines, voice mail, safes, irons, hair dryers. *Some:* DVD players. **Pool(s):** heated
outdoor. **Leisure Activities:** hiking trails, jogging, exercise room. **Guest Services:** sundries, valet and coin laundry, area
transportation. **Business Services:** meeting rooms, business center. **Cards:** AX, CB, DC, DS, JC, MC, VI.

SOME UNITS

HOTEL DU PONT   *Book at aaa.com*   Phone: (302)594-3100
(AAA) (SAVE)   All Year   1P: $179-$399   2P: $179-$399   XP: $25   F12
▼▼▼▼   **Location:** I-95, exit 7, 0.5 mi se; downtown. 11th & Market St 19801. Fax: 302/594-3108. **Facility:** Opened in
              1918, this luxury hotel has ornately decorated public areas and spacious guest units with plush, upholstered
Large-scale Hotel   seating. 217 units. 206 one-bedroom standard units, some with whirlpools. 11 one-bedroom suites ($450-
              $650) with whirlpools. 13 stories, interior corridors. **Parking:** on-site (fee) and valet. **Terms:** cancellation fee
              imposed, package plans. **Amenities:** video games (fee), dual phone lines, voice mail, safes, honor bars,
irons, hair dryers. **Dining:** The Green Room, see separate listing. **Leisure Activities:** sauna, exercise room. *Fee:* massage.
Guest Services: gift shop, valet laundry, area transportation-within city limits, beauty salon. **Business Services:** conference
facilities, business center. **Cards:** AX, CB, DC, DS, MC, VI. Affiliated with A Preferred Hotel.

SOME UNITS
(⊞) (¶) (24) (⌂) (⊞) (⊘) (◿) (⊠) (¶) (DATA PORT) / (⊠) (VCR) (▭)
FEE

MCINTOSH INN OF WILMINGTON   *Book at aaa.com*   Phone: (302)479-7900
▼▼ ▼▼   All Year [ECP]   1P: $65-$89   2P: $65-$89   XP: $10   F18
              Location: I-95, exit 8, 3.8 mi n, just off US 202. Located in a commercial area. 300 Rocky Run Pkwy 19803.
Small-scale Hotel   Fax: 302/479-5098. **Facility:** 71 units. 69 one-bedroom standard units. 2 one-bedroom suites. 4 stories,
              interior corridors. *Bath:* combo or shower only. **Parking:** on-site. **Amenities:** voice mail, irons. **Leisure**
Activities: limited exercise equipment. **Guest Services:** sundries, valet laundry. **Business Services:** fax (fee). **Cards:** AX, CB,
DC, MC, VI.

SOME UNITS
(¶+) (⅚M) (⊠) (◿) (¶) (DATA PORT) / (⊠) (■) (▭) /

SHERATON SUITES WILMINGTON   *Book at aaa.com*   Phone: (302)654-8300
(AAA) (SAVE)   4/4-6/30 & 9/12-2/28   1P: $105-$225   2P: $105-$225   XP: $15   F12
▼▼▼▼   3/1-4/3 & 7/1-9/11   1P: $99-$225   2P: $99-$225   XP: $15   F12
              Location: I-95, exit 7, 0.3 mi e; downtown. 422 Delaware Ave 19801. Fax: 302/654-6036. **Facility:** 223 one-
              bedroom suites. 16 stories, interior corridors. **Parking:** on-site (fee). **Terms:** package plans, pets (small
Large-scale Hotel   dogs only). **Amenities:** voice mail, irons, hair dryers. **Some:** video games, high-speed Internet. *Some:* dual
              phone lines, fax. **Dining:** 6:30 am-10 pm, Sat & Sun from 7 am, cocktails. **Pool(s):** heated indoor. **Leisure**
Activities: sauna, exercise room. **Guest Services:** sundries, valet and coin laundry. **Business Services:** conference facilities,
business center. **Cards:** AX, CB, DC, DS, JC, MC, VI.

SOME UNITS
($⊟) (🐾) (¶) (⊤) (⅚M) (◿) (🛥) (¶) (DATA PORT) (■) (▭) / (⊠) (■)

WYNDHAM WILMINGTON   *Book at aaa.com*   Phone: (302)655-0400
(AAA) (SAVE)   All Year   1P: $99-$149   2P: $99-$149   XP: $10   F18
▼▼▼▼   **Location:** King and 7th sts; downtown. 700 N King St 19801. Fax: 302/655-0430. **Facility:** 219 units. 213 one-
              bedroom standard units. 6 one-bedroom suites ($150-$199). 9 stories, interior corridors. *Bath:* combo or
Large-scale Hotel   shower only. **Parking:** on-site (fee). **Terms:** cancellation fee imposed, small pets only ($75 fee).
              Amenities: high-speed Internet (fee), voice mail, irons, hair dryers. **Dining:** 6:30 am-11 & 5-11 pm, Fri-11
              pm, Sat 7 am-1 & 5-11 pm, Sun 7 am-1 & 5-10 pm, cocktails. **Pool(s):** heated indoor. **Leisure**
Activities: exercise room. **Guest Services:** valet laundry, area transportation-Amtrak & downtown area. **Business Services:**
conference facilities, PC, fax (fee). **Cards:** AX, CB, DC, DS, JC, MC, VI.

SOME UNITS
(⊞) (¶) (⅚M) (⊠) (◿) (🛥) (¶) (DATA PORT) (▭) / (⊠) (■)
FEE   FEE

────── **WHERE TO DINE** ──────

821 MARKET STREET BISTRO   **Lunch:** $10-$15   **Dinner:** $19-$26   Phone: 302/652-8821
▼▼▼▼   **Location:** Between 8th and 9th sts; across from Grand Opera House. 821 N Market St 19801. **Hours:** 5:30 pm-9 pm,
              Wed also 11:30 am-2:30 pm, Fri-10 pm, Sat 5 pm-10:30 pm. Closed major holidays; also Sun.
Mediterranean   **Reservations:** suggested. **Features:** Innovative Mediterranean cuisine reflecting Italian and French
              influences is what diners find at the cozy restaurant. Chef Lawry uses only the freshest, highest-quality
ingredients to prepare his delightful creations. The menu changes monthly. Valet parking is available after 5:45 pm. Dressy
casual; cocktails. **Parking:** no self-parking. **Cards:** AX, CB, DC, DS, MC, VI.
(⅚M) (⊤) (⊠)

CAFE MEZZANOTTE   **Lunch:** $8-$14   **Dinner:** $16-$39   Phone: 302/658-7050
▼▼▼▼   **Location:** Jct 11th and Tatnall sts. 1007 Orange St 19801. **Hours:** 11 am-2:30 & 5-10 pm, Sat & Sun from 5 pm.
              Closed major holidays. **Reservations:** suggested. **Features:** In the heart of the downtown business district,
Italian   this Italian restaurant has an upscale, relaxing atmosphere, as well as a popular Martini bar. The menu
              offers a nice selection of homemade pasta, meat and seafood dishes. Everything is prepared fresh in the
kitchen, sauces, soups, bread and desserts. Dressy casual; cocktails. **Parking:** no self-parking. **Cards:** AX, DS, MC, VI.
(⅚M) (⊤) (⊠)

COLUMBUS INN   **Lunch:** $8-$17   **Dinner:** $17-$29   Phone: 302/571-1492
(AAA)   **Location:** I-95, exit 7, 1 mi nw on SR 52. 2216 Pennsylvania Ave 19806. **Hours:** 11 am-3 & 5-11 pm, Fri-midnight,
▼▼▼   Sat 5 pm-midnight, Sun 10 am-3 & 5-9 pm; Sun-3 pm 1/1-6/30. Closed major holidays; also Sun 7/1-8/31.
American   **Reservations:** suggested. **Features:** The well-established restaurant's American cuisine has pleased locals
              for years. On the periodically changing menu, diners always will find certified Angus beef and fresh seafood
              preparations. Fine selections make up the award-winning wine list. Dressy casual; cocktails; entertainment.
              Parking: valet. **Cards:** AX, DC, DS, MC, VI.
(⊤) (⊠)

DEEP BLUE BAR & GRILL   **Lunch:** $8-$12   **Dinner:** $17-$26   Phone: 302/777-2040
▼▼▼▼   **Location:** Jct of 11th and Tatnall sts. 111 W 11th St 19801. **Hours:** 11:30 am-3 & 5:30-10 pm, Fri-11 pm, Sat 5
              pm-11 pm. Closed major holidays; also Sun. **Reservations:** accepted. **Features:** For diners in the mood for
Seafood   seafood, the contemporary downtown bistro is just the place. The kitchen staff is skilled and innovative,
              which is evident in the taste of such dishes as seared tuna over wasabi mashed potatoes and truffle-crusted
salmon. The raw bar comprises oysters from around the world. Dressy casual; cocktails. **Parking:** on-site (fee). **Cards:** AX, CB,
DC, DS, MC, VI.
(⅚M) (⊤) (⊠)

THE GREEN ROOM

AAA
Continental

Lunch: $12-$19 **Dinner:** $25-$37 **Phone:** 302/594-3155
Location: I-95, exit 7, 0.5 mi se; downtown; in Hotel Du Pont. 11th & Market St 19801. **Hours:** 6:30-11 am, 11:30-2 & 6-10:30 pm, Sun 10 am-2 & 6-10:30 pm. **Reservations:** suggested. **Features:** This formal dining room has large windows with ornate draperies overlooking the bustling downtown Wilmington scene. Its beautiful dark wood wall columns and ceiling beams, masterful gold leaf embellishments, massive chandeliers and mezzanine piano balcony offers up a glorious feast for the eyes to match the elegantly presented Continental dishes including seafood, lamb and filet mignon. Semi-formal attire; cocktails. **Parking:** valet.
Cards: AX, CB, DC, DS, JC, MC, VI.

HARRY'S SAVOY GRILL & BALLROOM

Steak & Seafood

Lunch: $6-$15 **Dinner:** $18-$30 **Phone:** 302/475-3000
Location: I-95, exit 11, 2.5 mi w on SR 92 (Naamans Rd). 2020 Naamans Rd 19810. **Hours:** 11:30 am-10:30 pm, Fri-midnight, Sat 4:30 pm-midnight, Sun noon-9 pm. Closed: 12/25. **Reservations:** suggested. **Features:** Casual and fun, the bustling restaurant boasts a menu of such specialties as prime rib, horseradish-crusted salmon and creme brulee. French posters, a vivid mural and cozy fireplaces add to the comfortable feel. Service is swift and friendly. Dressy casual; cocktails. **Parking:** on-site. **Cards:** AX, DC, DS, MC, VI.

IRON HILL BREWERY & RESTAURANT

American

Lunch: $7-$11 **Dinner:** $15-$20 **Phone:** 302/472-2739
Location: I-95, exit 6, just s on S Madison; at the riverfront area. 710 S Madison St 19810. **Hours:** 11:30 am-1 am, Sun from 11 am. Closed: 11/24, 12/25; also for dinner 12/24, for lunch 1/1. **Reservations:** accepted, for lunch and brunch. **Features:** Hand-crafted beers made on the premises match with the innovative American cuisine. Along the riverfront, the setting is casual and comfortable. Seasonal outdoor seating is an option. Casual dress; cocktails. **Parking:** on-site. **Cards:** AX, DC, DS, MC, VI.

PAN TAI RESTAURANT

Asian

Lunch: $5-$10 **Dinner:** $10-$19 **Phone:** 302/652-6633
Location: I-95, exit 7, 0.8 mi n on SR 52, 0.3 mi w. 837 N Union St 19805. **Hours:** 11:30 am-2:30 & 5-10 pm, Fri-10:30 pm, Sat 5 pm-10:30 pm. Closed major holidays; also Sun. **Reservations:** suggested. **Features:** The menu features selections of Southeast Asian cuisine — Thai, Vietnamese and Indonesian — all served in an intimate atmosphere. A few of the local favorites include hot and sour shrimp soup, pad Thai noodles and the kung pao shrimp. Casual dress; cocktails. **Parking:** street. **Cards:** AX, MC, VI.

TOSCANA

Northern
Italian

Lunch: $8-$15 **Dinner:** $12-$24 **Phone:** 302/654-8001
Location: I-95, exit 7, just s on SR 52 to Delaware Ave, 0.5 mi n on Delaware Ave, then just w. 1412 N DuPont St 19806. **Hours:** 11:30 am-2 & 5-10 pm, Wed-Fri to 11 pm, Sat 5 pm-11 pm, Sun 5 pm-9 pm. Closed major holidays. **Features:** Tuscan cooking is expertly prepared and complemented by an extensive wine selection. The casually upscale cafe is comfortable, and service is friendly and attentive. Patio seating is available when the weather cooperates. Live jazz is featured Wednesday nights. Dressy casual; cocktails. **Parking:** on-site. **Cards:** AX, CB, DC, DS, MC, VI.

WALTER'S STEAKHOUSE

AAA
Steak House

Dinner: $14-$32 **Phone:** 302/652-6780
Location: I-95, exit 7, 0.8 mi n on SR 52, then just w. 802 N Union St 19805. **Hours:** 5 pm-11 pm, Sun 4 pm-10 pm. Closed: 1/1, 11/24, 12/25; also 7/3-7/10. **Reservations:** suggested. **Features:** Aged black Angus beef rules the menu in the cozy atmosphere of the upscale, yet casual, steakhouse. The restaurant also serves veal and lamb, along with two of the most popular seafood-oriented house specials: crab imperial and shrimp scampi. Casual dress; cocktails. **Parking:** on-site. **Cards:** AX, DS, MC, VI.

WATERWORKS CAFE

American

Lunch: $5-$15 **Dinner:** $17-$29 **Phone:** 302/652-6022
Location: On the Brandywine; downtown. 103 E 16th St 19801. **Hours:** 11:30 am-2 & 5:30-9 pm, Fri-10 pm, Sat 5:30 pm-10 pm. Closed major holidays; also Sun & Mon. **Reservations:** suggested, weekends. **Features:** Overlooking Brandywine Creek, the eatery seasonally opens its patio for dining and sports a contemporary decor. The kitchen prepares good American fare with a Continental touch. Dressy casual; cocktails. **Parking:** on-site. **Cards:** AX, DS, MC, VI.

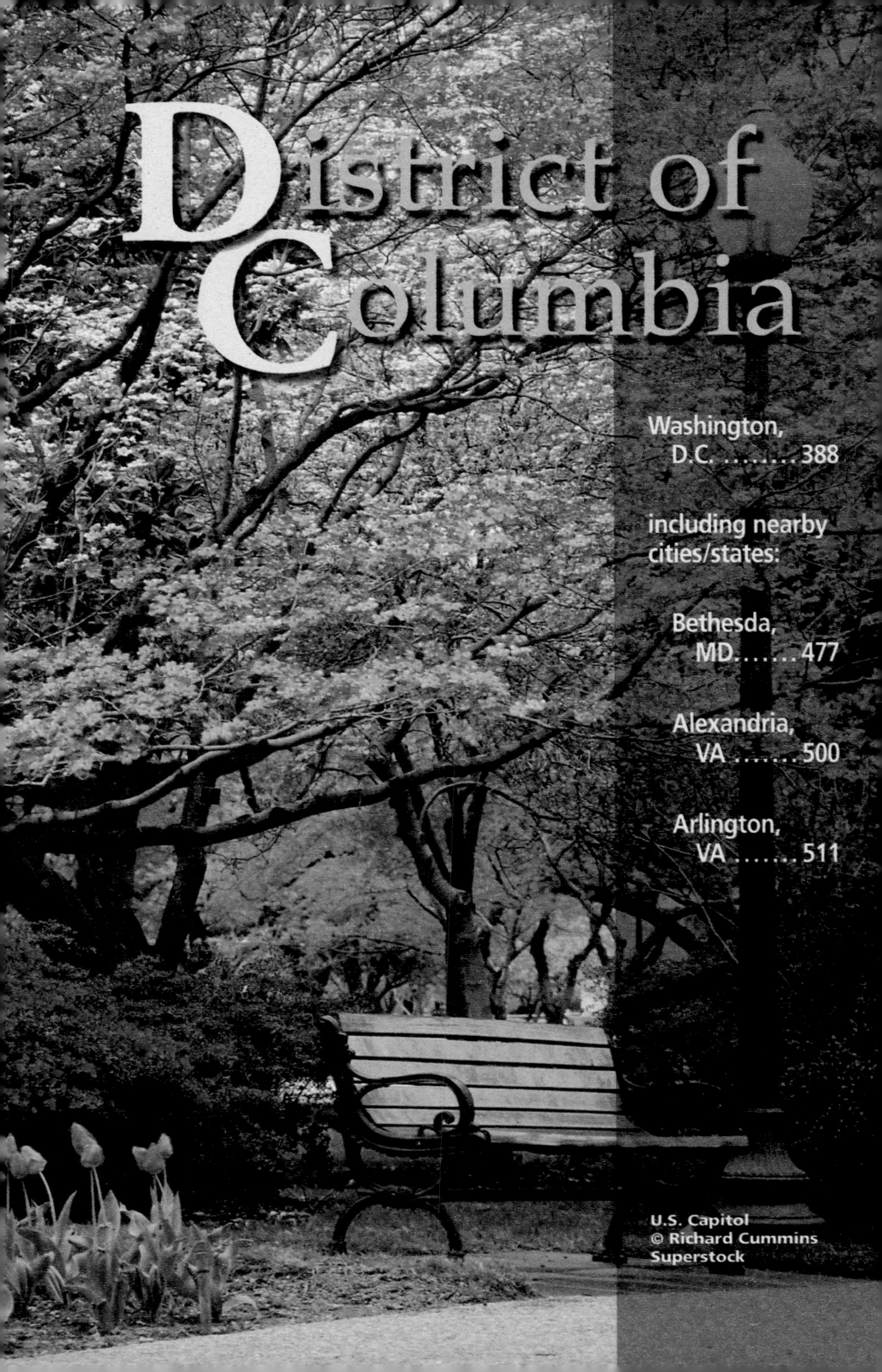

District of Columbia

U.S. Capitol
© Richard Cummins
Superstock

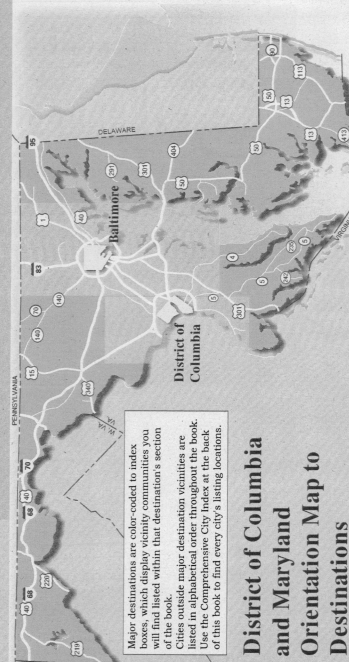

District of Columbia and Maryland Orientation Map to Destinations

Major destinations are color-coded to index boxes, which display vicinity communities you will find listed within that destination's section of the book.

Cities outside major destination vicinities are listed in alphabetical order throughout the book. Use the Comprehensive City Index at the back of this book to find every city's listing locations.

Historic Mount Vernon

Entertainment at Wolf Trap

Tysons Corner Shopping Center

New National Air and Space Museum Steven F. Udvar-Hazy Center

Nearby National Attractions

Fairfax County, where great vacations take flight.

World-class museums. National historic sites. The best in outdoor entertainment. With so much to do, why not take your next vacation to new heights?

Visit
Fairfax
County Virginia

www.visitfairfax.org
1-800-732-4732

"You'll love being in the middle of things"

Destination Washington, D.C.

pop. 572,059

*T*ransformed from a swampy bog along the Potomac River into the capital city of a fledgling nation by Pierre Charles L'Enfant's visionary planning, Washington, D.C., is the seat of federal government and power.

*M*overs and shakers reside here. National policy is determined. History is created. Yet amidst the politics and power struggles, everyday life exists as well. Residents and visitors alike enjoy the culture, recreation and shopping that a world-class city provides.

© Mark Downey Virginia Tourism Corporation

Lincoln Memorial, Washington, D.C. Overlooking the Potomac River, the white, templelike memorial to Abraham Lincoln features 36 columns, one for every state in the Union when he died. (See listing page 82)

See Area map page 404

Bicycling in Potomac Park, Washington, D.C. Cherry blossoms create a beautiful backdrop for bicyclists and joggers along the Tidal Basin in Potomac Park. (See listing page 90)

Washington D.C. CVB

*P*laces included in this AAA Destination City:

© Richard T. Nowitz / Corbis

Dupont Circle, Washington, D.C.
Despite the hum of activity around them at this popular urban gathering place, two chess players remain focused on their game.

See Area map page 399

See Area map page 416

Laurel

Beltsville

Greenbelt

Chevy Chase · Adelphi · College Park · Bowie

Silver Spring · New Carrollton · Lanham

Washington D.C. · Landover Hills · Landover

Largo

DC / MD

495

See Downtown map page 390

Camp Springs

VA / MD

Clinton

See Area map page 414

See Area map page 416

© R. Krubner / Robertstock

The John F. Kennedy Center for the Performing Arts, Washington, D.C.
A bronze bust of President Kennedy presides over the Grand Foyer during a quiet moment before one of the more than 3,000 performances at this cultural center each year. (See listing page 81)

© Joseph Sohm / Corbis

Rowing Team, Potomac River.
A racing crew on the Potomac River takes a break from rowing practice.

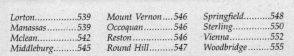

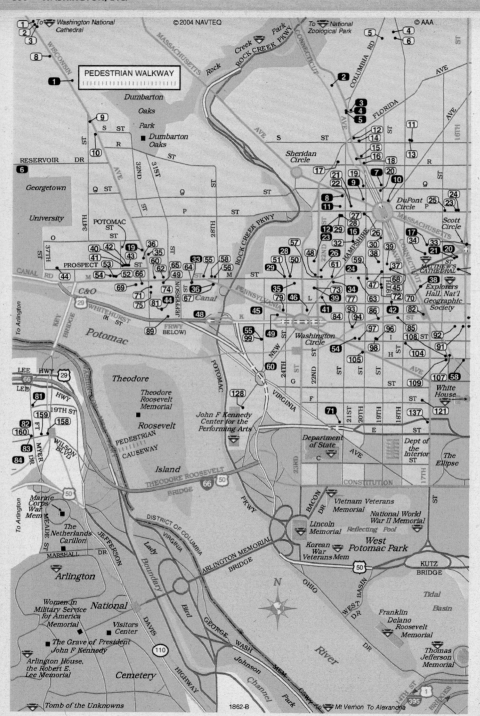

© 2004 NAVTEQ   © AAA

To Washington National Cathedral

To National Zoological Park

PEDESTRIAN WALKWAY

Dumbarton Oaks Park

Dumbarton Oaks

WISCONSIN

MASSACHUSETTS

Rock Creek Park

ROCK CREEK PKWY

CONNECTICUT

COLUMBIA RD

FLORIDA

AVE

16TH

Sheridan Circle

RESERVOIR   DR

Georgetown

Georgetown University

32ND   31ST

POTOMAC ST

PROSPECT   ST

CANAL RD

C&O

DuPont Circle

Scott Circle

ST MATTHEW'S CATHEDRAL

Explorers Hall, Nat'l Geographic Society

Rock Creek Pkwy

Canal

PENNSYLVANIA

WHITEHURST (K) ST

KEY BRIDGE

Potomac

FRWY BELOW)

To Arlington

LEE   HWY

LEE

19TH ST

WILSON   BLVD

FT   MYER

MEADE ST

MARSHALL   DR

Theodore Roosevelt Memorial

Roosevelt

PEDESTRIAN CAUSEWAY

Island

Washington Circle

NEW   ST

VIRGINIA

24TH   22ND   21ST   20TH   19TH   18TH   17TH

White House

John F Kennedy Center for the Performing Arts

Department of State

Dept of the Interior

The Ellipse

THEODORE ROOSEVELT BRIDGE

CONSTITUTION

To Arlington

Marine Corps War Mem

The Netherlands Carillon

Arlington

Women In Military Service for America Memorial

Visitors Center

The Grave of President John F Kennedy

Arlington House, the Robert E. Lee Memorial

Cemetery

National

JEFFERSON   DR

DAVIS

Lady   Boundary

Bird

GEORGE   WASH

Johnson   Channel   Park

DISTRICT OF COLUMBIA

VIRGINIA

ARLINGTON MEMORIAL   BRIDGE

MEM

OHIO   DR

WEST BASIN   DR

River

Vietnam Veterans Memorial

Lincoln Memorial

Reflecting Pool

Korean War Veterans Mem

National World War II Memorial

West Potomac Park

KUTZ BRIDGE

Tidal Basin

Franklin Delano Roosevelt Memorial

Thomas Jefferson Memorial

Tomb of the Unknowns

To Mt Vernon To Alexandria

1862-B

BRIDGES

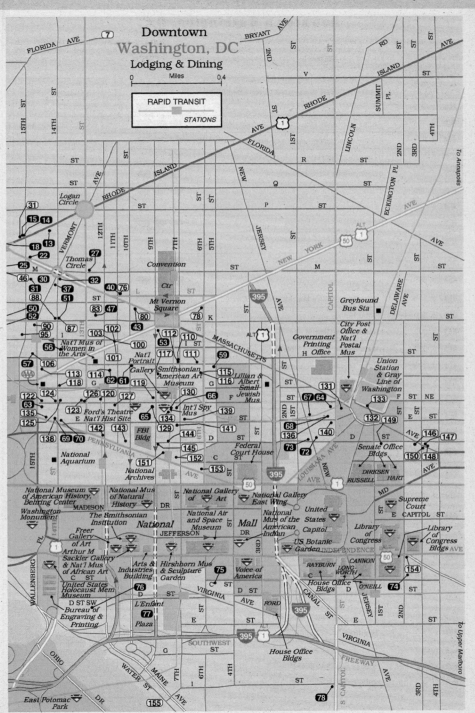

Downtown Washington, DC
Lodging & Dining

RAPID TRANSIT

STATIONS

Miles 0 0.4

Logan Circle

Thomas Circle

Convention Ctr

Mt Vernon Square

Nat'l Mus of Women in the Arts

Nat'l Portrait Gallery

Smithsonian American Art Museum

Lillian & Albert Small Jewish Mus

Int'l Spy Mus

Ford's Theatre Nat'l Hist Site

FBI Bldg

National Aquarium

National Archives

Federal Court House

Greyhound Bus Sta

City Post Office & Nat'l Postal Mus

Government Printing Office

Union Station & Gray Line of Washington

Senate Office Bldgs

DIRKSEN RUSSELL HART

National Museum of American History, Behring Center

Washington Monument

The Smithsonian Institution

Freer Gallery of Art

Arthur M Sackler Gallery & Nat'l Mus of African Art

United States Holocaust Mem Museum

Bureau of Engraving & Printing

L'Enfant Plaza

National Mus of Natural History

Arts & Industries Building

National Gallery of Art

National Air and Space Museum

Hirshhorn Mus & Sculpture Garden

Voice of America

National Gallery East Wing

National Mus of the American Indian

United States Capitol

US Botanic Garden

RAYBURN LONGWORTH House Office Bldgs O'NEILL

House Office Bldgs

Supreme Court

Library of Congress

Library of Congress Bldgs

East Potomac Park

Downtown Washington, D.C.

This index helps you "spot" where approved accommodations and restaurants are located on the corresponding detailed maps. Lodging rate ranges are for comparison only and show the property's high season; rates are per night, unless only weekly (W) rates are available. Restaurant rate range is for dinner, unless only lunch (L) is served. Turn to the listing page for more detailed rate information and consult display ads for special promotions.

Spotter/Map Page Number	OA	**DOWNTOWN WASHINGTON** - Lodgings	Diamond Rating	Rate Range High Season	Listing Page
1 / p. 390		Holiday Inn Georgetown - see color ad p 437	◇◇◇	$99-$199	438
2 / p. 390		Jurys Normandy Inn	◇◇◇	$89-$185	442
3 / p. 390		Hilton Washington - see color ad p 426	◇◇◇	$99-$369	435
4 / p. 390	AAA	**The Churchill Hotel** - see color ad p 427	◇◇◇	$249-$339 SAVE	425
5 / p. 390		Courtyard by Marriott-Northwest	◇◇◇	$89-$279	428
6 / p. 390		Georgetown University Conference Hotel	◇◇◇	$129-$229	431
7 / p. 390	AAA	**The Dupont at the Circle**	◇◇◇	$140-$300 SAVE	429
8 / p. 390		The Westin Embassy Row	◇◇◇	$209-$289	454
9 / p. 390	AAA	**Hilton Washington Embassy Row** - see color ad p 434	◇◇◇	$129-$319 SAVE	435
10 / p. 390		Jurys Washington Hotel	◇◇◇	$99-$305	442
11 / p. 390		Radisson Barcelo Hotel Washington - see color ad p 446	◇◇◇	$159	446
12 / p. 390	AAA	**Residence Inn by Marriott-Dupont Circle**	◇◇◇	$149-$299 SAVE	447
13 / p. 390	AAA	**Hotel Helix** - see color ad p 422	◇◇◇	$139-$309 SAVE	440
14 / p. 390	AAA	**Holiday Inn-Central** - see color ad p 435	◇◇◇	$189-$209 SAVE	438
15 / p. 390	AAA	**Washington Terrace Hotel** - see ad p 453	◇◇◇	$129-$299 SAVE	454
16 / p. 390	AAA	**Hotel Madera** - see color ad p 422	◇◇◇	$149-$349 SAVE	440
17 / p. 390	AAA	**Topaz Hotel** - see color ad p 422	◇◇◇	$149-$339 SAVE	452
18 / p. 390	AAA	**Hotel Rouge** - see color ad p 422	◇◇◇	$139-$309 SAVE	441
19 / p. 390	AAA	**The Georgetown Inn** - see color ad p 431	◇◇◇	$139-$339 SAVE	429
20 / p. 390	AAA	**Courtyard by Marriott-Embassy Row**	◇◇◇	$129-$229 SAVE	427
21 / p. 390	AAA	**Beacon Hotel & Corporate Quarters** - see color ad p 421	◇◇◇	$279-$379 SAVE	419
22 / p. 390		Homewood Suites by Hilton Washington DC/Thomas Circle - see color ad p 438	◇◇◇	$179-$229	438
23 / p. 390		Embassy Suites Hotel-Washington DC-Downtown	◇◇◇	$119-$359	429
24 / p. 390	AAA	**St. Gregory Luxury Hotel & Suites** - see color ad p 421	◇◇◇	$289-$399 SAVE	450
25 / p. 390	AAA	**The Jefferson, A Loews Hotel** - see color ad p 441	◇◇◇◇	$195-$405 SAVE	442
26 / p. 390	AAA	**Washington Marriott Hotel**	◇◇◇	$179-$269 SAVE	452
27 / p. 390		Comfort Inn Convention Center - see color ad p 427	◇◇	$116-$179	427
28 / p. 390	AAA	**Park Hyatt Washington, D.C.** - see color ad p 445	◇◇◇◇	$306-$410 SAVE	446
29 / p. 390		The Fairmont Washington, DC	◇◇◇◇	$169-$529	429
30 / p. 390	AAA	**Wyndham Washington, D.C.**	◇◇◇	$120-$183 SAVE	454
31 / p. 390		The Madison	◇◇◇	$229-$299	444
32 / p. 390	AAA	**Holiday Inn Downtown** - see color ad p 434	◇◇◇	$189-$229 SAVE	438
33 / p. 390	AAA	**Latham Hotel Georgetown** - see color ad p 431	◇◇◇	$139-$339 SAVE	442

Spotter/Map Page Number	OA	DOWNTOWN WASHINGTON - Lodgings (continued)	Diamond Rating	Rate Range High Season	Listing Page
34 / p. 390	AAA	Wyndham City Center	◆◆◆	$119-$229 SAVE	454
35 / p. 390	·	The Westin Grand	◆◆◆	$209-$289	454
36 / p. 390	AAA	Four Seasons Hotel Washington D.C.	◆◆◆◆◆	$595-$1550 SAVE	429
37 / p. 390	AAA	Residence Inn by Marriott-Washington DC-Vermont Ave	◆◆◆	$259 SAVE	447
38 / p. 390	AAA	Renaissance Mayflower Hotel	◆◆◆◆	$159-$409 SAVE	447
39 / p. 390		The Ritz-Carlton, Washington, DC	◆◆◆◆◆	$259-$645	450
40 / p. 390		Morrison-Clark Historic Inn and Restaurant	◆◆◆	$289-$309	444
41 / p. 390	AAA	Best Western-New Hampshire Suites Hotel - see color ad p 423	◆◆	$179-$260 SAVE	419
42 / p. 390	AAA	Lincoln Suites Downtown - see color ad p 443	◆◆	$165-$195 SAVE	444
43 / p. 390		Henley Park Hotel	◆◆◆	$289-$309	432
44 / p. 390		The Ritz-Carlton, Georgetown	◆◆◆◆◆	$260-$550	447
45 / p. 390	AAA	Washington Suites Georgetown - see color ad p 453	◆◆◆	$188-$248 SAVE	453
46 / p. 390	AAA	One Washington Circle Hotel - see color ad p 445	◆◆◆	$129-$429 SAVE	445
47 / p. 390	AAA	Four Points Sheraton Washington DC Downtown - see color ad p 430	◆◆◆	$244-$264 SAVE	429
48 / p. 390		Georgetown Suites-Harbour Building - see color ad p 430	◆◆	$155-$285	431
49 / p. 390		The Melrose Hotel, Washington DC	◆◆◆	$209	444
50 / p. 390		Capital Hilton - see color ad p 426	◆◆◆	$99-$379	419
51 / p. 390		Hamilton Crowne Plaza Hotel Washington - see color ad p 432	◆◆◆	$124-$324	432
52 / p. 390	AAA	The St. Regis	◆◆◆◆	$230-$385 SAVE	452
53 / p. 390	AAA	Renaissance Washington DC Hotel	◆◆◆	$99-$359 SAVE	447
54 / p. 390		Hotel Lombardy	◆◆	Failed to provide	440
55 / p. 390	AAA	The River Inn - see color ad p 450	◆◆◆	$99-$405 SAVE	450
56 / p. 390	AAA	Hilton Garden Inn Washington DC Franklin Square	◆◆◆	$109-$259 SAVE	434
57 / p. 390		Sofitel Lafayette Square Washington DC	◆◆◆◆	$380-$480	452
58 / p. 390		The Hay-Adams	◆◆◆◆	$550-$5500	432
59 / p. 390		Red Roof Inn Downtown Washington, D.C.	◆◆	$120-$150	447
60 / p. 390		Doubletree Guest Suites, Washington DC	◆◆◆	$109-$279	428
61 / p. 390	AAA	Grand Hyatt Washington at Washington Center - see color ad p 433	◆◆◆	$149-$340 SAVE	432
62 / p. 390		Marriott at Metro Center	◆◆◆	$249-$369	444
63 / p. 390	AAA	Hotel Washington - see ad p 441	◆◆	$200-$325 SAVE	442
64 / p. 390	AAA	Phoenix Park Hotel - see color ad p 446	◆◆◆	$169-$299 SAVE	446
65 / p. 390		Courtyard by Marriott-Convention Center	◆◆◆	$144-$244	427
66 / p. 390	AAA	Hotel Monaco Washington DC	◆◆◆◆	$169-$479 SAVE	441
67 / p. 390		The Washington Court Hotel	◆◆◆	$119-$359	452
68 / p. 390	AAA	The Hotel George	◆◆◆	$169-$434 SAVE	440
69 / p. 390		The Willard InterContinental	◆◆◆◆	$209-$610	454
70 / p. 390		J W Marriott Pennsylvania Ave	◆◆◆	$309-$369	442

Spotter/Map Page Number	OA	DOWNTOWN WASHINGTON - Lodgings (continued)	Diamond Rating	Rate Range High Season	Listing Page
71 / p. 390		State Plaza Hotel	◈◈	$119-$225	452
72 / p. 390	AAA	Holiday Inn Washington DC on The Hill - see color ad p 439	◈◈◈	$129-$394 SAVE	438
73 / p. 390	AAA	Hyatt Regency Washington On Capitol Hill - see color ad p 433	◈◈◈	$119-$250 SAVE	442
74 / p. 390	AAA	Capitol Hill Suites - see color ad p 425	◈◈	$139-$219 SAVE	419
75 / p. 390	AAA	Holiday Inn Capitol - see color ad p 436	◈◈◈	$129-$289 SAVE	435
76 / p. 390		Mandarin Oriental, Washington D.C.	◈◈◈◈	$350-$8000	444
77 / p. 390	AAA	Loews L'Enfant Plaza Hotel - see color ad p 443	◈◈◈	$119-$274 SAVE	444
78 / p. 390	AAA	Best Western Capitol Skyline - see color ad p 423	◈◈	$139-$209 SAVE	419
		DOWNTOWN WASHINGTON - Restaurants			
1 / p. 390	AAA	Old Europe	◈◈	$9-$20	466
2 / p. 390		Heritage India	◈◈◈	$8-$23	462
3 / p. 390		Busara	◈◈	$8-$16	457
4 / p. 390		Leftbank	◈◈	$15-$26	463
5 / p. 390		The Grill from Ipanema	◈◈	$13-$22	461
6 / p. 390		Felix Restaurant and The Spy Lounge	◈◈◈	$14-$27	460
7 / p. 390		Florida Avenue Grill	◈	$5-$10	461
8 / p. 390		Saveur	◈◈◈	$9-$23	468
9 / p. 390		Cafe Divan	◈◈	$6-$18	458
10 / p. 390		Bistrot Lepic	◈◈◈	$15-$20	457
11 / p. 390		Lauriol Plaza	◈◈	$7-$18	463
12 / p. 390		Ruth's Chris Steak House	◈◈◈	$17-$32	468
13 / p. 390		Rosemary's Thyme Bistro	◈◈	$8-$18	468
14 / p. 390	AAA	**Thaiphoon**	◈◈	$7-$15	469
15 / p. 390		Anna Maria's Restaurant	◈◈	$9-$25	455
16 / p. 390		Bistrot du Coin	◈◈	$10-$21	456
17 / p. 390		Nora	◈◈◈	$35-$43	466
18 / p. 390		La Tomate	◈◈	$12-$24	463
19 / p. 390		Etrusco	◈◈◈	$14-$23	460
20 / p. 390		Raku-An Asian Diner	◈◈	$9-$14	468
21 / p. 390		Obelisk	◈◈◈	$60-$65	466
22 / p. 390		Pizzeria Paradiso	◈	$8-$16	467
23 / p. 390		Skewer's	◈◈	$6-$18	469
24 / p. 390		BUA	◈	$8-$13	457
25 / p. 390		Sushi Taro	◈◈	$25-$30	469
26 / p. 390		Johnny's Half Shell	◈◈	$12-$22	462
27 / p. 390		Pesce	◈◈	$13-$25	467
28 / p. 390		Be Du Ci	◈◈◈	$12-$24	456
29 / p. 390		Mimi's American Bistro	◈◈	$12-$23	465

Spotter/Map Page Number	OA	DOWNTOWN WASHINGTON - Restaurants (continued)	Diamond Rating	Rate Range High Season	Listing Page
㉚ / p. 390		Levante's	♦♦	$8-$25	463
㉛ / p. 390		15 ria	♦♦♦	$16-$23	455
㉜ / p. 390	AAA	**Firefly**	♦♦♦	$17-$21	461
㉝ / p. 390	AAA	**Bar Rouge**	♦♦	$7-$13	456
㉞ / p. 390		Iron Gate Restaurant	♦♦♦	$19-$25	462
㉟ / p. 390		Paolo's Ristorante	♦♦	$10-$20	467
㊱ / p. 390		Neyla-A Mediterranean Grill	♦♦♦	$15-$32	465
㊲ / p. 390		Bacchus Restaurant	♦♦	$13-$17	456
㊳ / p. 390	AAA	**I Ricchi**	♦♦♦	$15-$31	462
㊴ / p. 390		Palm Restaurant	♦♦♦	$14-$38	467
㊵ / p. 390		Cafe Milano	♦♦	$13-$35	458
㊶ / p. 390		Peacock Cafe	♦♦	$9-$19	467
㊷ / p. 390		Bangkok Bistro	♦♦	$11-$19	456
㊸ / p. 390		Morton's of Chicago	♦♦♦	$25-$42	465
㊹ / p. 390		1789 Restaurant	♦♦♦	$18-$38	455
㊺ / p. 390		Penang	♦♦	$5-$22	467
㊻ / p. 390		The Restaurant at The Jefferson	♦♦♦	$25-$37	468
㊼ / p. 390		Sam & Harry's	♦♦♦	$25-$35	468
㊽ / p. 390		Asia Nora	♦♦♦	$20-$27	456
㊾ / p. 390		Miss Saigon	♦♦	$10-$15	465
㊿ / p. 390	AAA	**Melrose** - see color ad p 445	♦♦♦♦	$25-$45	464
(51) / p. 390		The Bistro	♦♦♦	$14-$28	456
(52) / p. 390		Fettoosh	♦	$12-$19	460
(53) / p. 390		Amma Vegetarian Kitchen	♦	$5-$11	455
(54) / p. 390		Aditi Indian Cuisine	♦♦	$8-$16	455
(55) / p. 390		Mendocino Grille & Wine Bar	♦♦♦	$27-$40	464
(56) / p. 390		Zed's Ethiopian Cuisine	♦♦	$8-$14	470
(57) / p. 390		Blackie's	♦♦♦	$25-$41	457
(58) / p. 390		La Chaumiere	♦♦♦	$15-$30	463
(59) / p. 390		Vidalia	♦♦♦	$23-$30	470
(60) / p. 390		Old Glory, All American Bar-B-Que	♦	$8-$22	466
(61) / p. 390		Meiwah Restaurant	♦♦	$10-$24	464
(62) / p. 390		Mie N Yu	♦♦♦	$14-$29	465
(63) / p. 390		David Greggory Restau Lounge	♦♦♦	$18-$28	459
(64) / p. 390		Michel Richard Citronelle	♦♦♦♦	$75-$115	464
(65) / p. 390	AAA	**Bistro Francais**	♦♦	$8-$25	456
(66) / p. 390		J. Paul's	♦	$12-$23	462
(67) / p. 390	AAA	**Seasons**	♦♦♦♦	$37-$55	469
(68) / p. 390		Famous Luigi's	♦♦	$9-$23	460
(69) / p. 390		Clyde's of Georgetown	♦♦	$11-$23	459

Spotter/Map Page Number	OA	DOWNTOWN WASHINGTON - Restaurants (continued)	Diamond Rating	Rate Range High Season	Listing Page
70 / p. 390		Cafe Promenade	◆◆◆	$17-$30	458
71 / p. 390		Filomena Ristorante	◆◆◆	$15-$30	460
72 / p. 390		Oodles Noodles	◆	$6-$10	466
73 / p. 390		The Grill	◆◆◆◆	$35-$58	461
74 / p. 390	AAA	**Sea Catch Restaurant**	◆◆◆	$18-$32	469
75 / p. 390		Ching Ching Cha	◆	$11	459
76 / p. 390		Morrison-Clark Restaurant	◆◆◆	$14-$25	465
77 / p. 390		Galileo	◆◆◆	$24-$35	461
78 / p. 390		Marrakesh	◆◆	$25	464
79 / p. 390		Marcel's	◆◆◆◆	$26-$42	464
80 / p. 390		Coeur de Lion	◆◆◆	$20-$35	459
81 / p. 390		Fahrenheit	◆◆◆	$25-$51	460
82 / p. 390		Morton's The Steakhouse	◆◆◆	$23-$42	465
83 / p. 390	AAA	**Corduroy**	◆◆◆	$18-$27	459
84 / p. 390		Mr K's	◆◆◆	$16-$38	465
85 / p. 390		Restaurant Kolumbia	◆◆◆	$20-$35	468
86 / p. 390		Teatro Goldoni	◆◆◆	$15-$30	469
87 / p. 390		14K	◆◆	$18-$29	455
88 / p. 390		DC Coast	◆◆◆	$19-$29	459
89 / p. 390		Tony & Joe's Seafood Place	◆◆	$17-$32	470
90 / p. 390		Gerard's Place	◆◆◆◆	$30-$50	461
91 / p. 390		Olives	◆◆◆	$15-$32	466
92 / p. 390		McCormick & Schmick's Seafood Restaurant	◆◆◆	$7-$22	464
93 / p. 390		The Prime Rib	◆◆◆	$18-$39	467
94 / p. 390		Bombay Palace Restaurant	◆◆◆	$16-$25	457
95 / p. 390		Georgia Brown's	◆◆◆	$15-$23	461
96 / p. 390		Kaz Sushi Bistro	◆◆	$12-$23	462
97 / p. 390		Primi Piatti	◆◆	$17-$29	467
98 / p. 390		Aroma Indian Restaurant	◆◆	$10-$16	455
99 / p. 390	AAA	**Dish**	◆◆◆	$17-$25	460
100 / p. 390		Luigino	◆◆	$13-$25	463
101 / p. 390		Capitol City Brewing Company-Downtown	◆◆	$8-$16	459
102 / p. 390		Haad Thai	◆◆	$9-$13	461
103 / p. 390		Sushi Aoi	◆	$9-$25	469
104 / p. 390		Taberna Del Alabardero	◆◆◆	$50-$75	469
105 / p. 390		Kinkead's Restaurant	◆◆◆	$24-$35	462
106 / p. 390		Cafe 15	◆◆◆	$26-$34	458
107 / p. 390		The Bombay Club	◆◆◆	$8-$19	457
108 / p. 390		Equinox	◆◆◆	$22-$32	460
109 / p. 390		The Oval Room	◆◆◆	$16-$25	466

Spotter/Map Page Number	OA	DOWNTOWN WASHINGTON - Restaurants (continued)	Diamond Rating	Rate Range High Season	Listing Page
(110) / p. 390		Fado' Irish Pub	◆◆	$9-$13	460
(111) / p. 390		Lei Garden	◆◆	$8-$25	463
(112) / p. 390		Capital Q	◆	$8-$15	458
(113) / p. 390		Bobby Van's Steakhouse	◆◆◆	$19-$35	457
(114) / p. 390		Regatta Raw Bar	◆◆	$11-$25	468
(115) / p. 390		Burma	◆	$7-$11	457
(116) / p. 390		Kanlaya Thai Cuisine	◆◆	$9-$16	462
(117) / p. 390		Zaytinya	◆◆◆	$15-$20	470
(118) / p. 390		CEIBA	◆◆◆	$18-$27	459
(119) / p. 390		McCormick & Schmick's Seafood Restaurant	◆◆◆	$18-$30	464
(120) / p. 390		The Oceanaire Seafood Room	◆◆◆	$17-$35	466
(121) / p. 390		Maxim	◆◆◆	$21-$32	464
(122) / p. 390		Old Ebbitt Grill	◆◆	$13-$25	466
(123) / p. 390		Finemondo Italian Country Kitchen	◆◆◆	$14-$24	461
(124) / p. 390		Butterfield 9	◆◆◆	$18-$36	457
(125) / p. 390		Red Sage	◆◆◆	$8-$35	468
(126) / p. 390		M & S Grill	◆◆◆	$13-$35	463
(127) / p. 390		Tosca	◆◆◆	$20-$40	470
(128) / p. 390		Roof Terrace Restaurant & Bar at The Kennedy Center	◆◆	$20-$32	468
(129) / p. 390		Gordon Biersch Brewery Restaurant	◆◆	$11-$26	461
(130) / p. 390		Zola	◆◆◆	$16-$25	470
(131) / p. 390		Capitol City Brewing Co Capitol Hill	◆◆	$8-$23	458
(132) / p. 390		America	◆◆	$9-$18	455
(133) / p. 390		B. Smiths Restaurant	◆◆◆	$17-$30	457
(134) / p. 390	AAA	Poste—Modern Brasserie	◆◆◆	$18-$28	467
(135) / p. 390		Occidental Restaurant	◆◆◆	$22-$40	466
(136) / p. 390		Bistro Bis	◆◆◆	$18-$29	456
(137) / p. 390		Cafe Des Artistes	◆	$8-$11	458
(138) / p. 390		The Willard Room	◆◆◆◆	$28-$40	470
(139) / p. 390		District Chophouse & Brewery	◆◆	$19-$28	460
(140) / p. 390		La Colline	◆◆◆	$14-$27	463
(141) / p. 390		Jaleo	◆◆	$11-$20	462
(142) / p. 390		Les Halles	◆◆	$14-$26	463
(143) / p. 390		TenPenh Restaurant	◆◆◆	$19-$36	469
(144) / p. 390		Cafe Atlantico	◆◆◆	$18-$24	458
(145) / p. 390	AAA	The Caucus Room	◆◆◆	$25-$35	459
(146) / p. 390		La Brasserie	◆◆	$9-$27	462
(147) / p. 390		Two Quail	◆◆	$15-$25	470
(148) / p. 390		Cafe Berlin	◆◆	$15-$19	458

Spotter/Map Page Number	OA	DOWNTOWN WASHINGTON - Restaurants (continued)	Diamond Rating	Rate Range High Season	Listing Page
(149) / p. 390	AAA	The Monocle on Capitol Hill	◆◆	$15-$29	465
(150) / p. 390		The White Tiger	◆◆	$10-$25	470
(151) / p. 390		Signatures	◆◆◆◆	$22-$45	469
(152) / p. 390		701 Pennsylvania Avenue	◆◆◆	$15-$25	455
(153) / p. 390		The Capital Grille	◆◆◆	$19-$36	458
(154) / p. 390		Barolo	◆◆◆	$18-$30	456
(155) / p. 390		Phillips Flagship	◆	$14-$27	467
ARLINGTON, VA - Lodgings					
(81) / p. 390		Holiday Inn Rosslyn - see color ad p 440	◆◆◆	$130-$180	516
(82) / p. 390	AAA	Best Western Washington Key Bridge	◆◆	$89-$159 SAVE	511
(83) / p. 390	AAA	Hyatt Arlington at Key Bridge - see color ad p 433	◆◆◆	$119-$250 SAVE	516
(84) / p. 390	AAA	Residence Inn by Marriott Arlington At Rosslyn - see color ad p 501	◆◆◆	$127-$229 SAVE	517
ARLINGTON, VA - Restaurants					
(158) / p. 390	AAA	Tom Sarris' Orleans House	◆	$8-$22	523
(159) / p. 390		Tivoli Restaurant	◆◆◆	$17-$29	523
(160) / p. 390		Mezza 9	◆◆◆	$19-$29	521

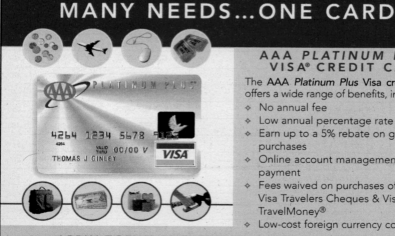

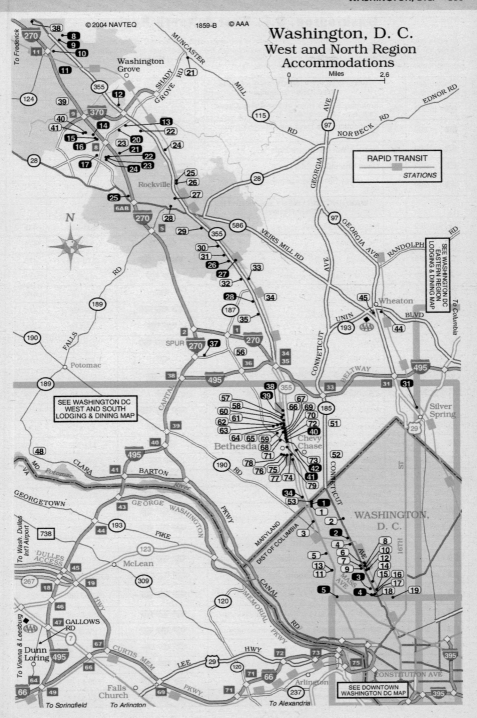

© 2004 NAVTEQ   1859-B   © AAA

Washington, D. C.
West and North Region
Accommodations

Miles
0   2.6

RAPID TRANSIT
STATIONS

To Frederick

Washington Grove

SEE WASHINGTON DC EASTERN REGION LODGING & DINING MAP

To Columbia

Rockville

Wheaton

SEE WASHINGTON DC WEST AND SOUTH LODGING & DINING MAP

Potomac

Silver Spring

SPUR

Bethesda

Chevy Chase

WASHINGTON, D.C.

Georgetown

To Wash. Dulles Int'l Airport

McLean

MARYLAND
DIST OF COLUMBIA

DULLES ACCESS

GALLOWS RD

To Vienna & Leesburg

Dunn Loring

Falls Church

To Springfield   To Arlington

Arlington

To Alexandria

SEE DOWNTOWN WASHINGTON DC MAP

Washington, D.C. West & North Region

This index helps you "spot" where approved accommodations and restaurants are located on the corresponding detailed maps. Lodging rate ranges are for comparison only and show the property's high season; rates are per night, unless only weekly (W) rates are available. Restaurant rate range is for dinner, unless only lunch (L) is served. Turn to the listing page for more detailed rate information and consult display ads for special promotions.

Spotter/Map Page Number	OA	WASHINGTON (WEST AND NORTH REGION) - Lodgings	Diamond Rating	Rate Range High Season	Listing Page
1 / p. 399	AAA	Embassy Suites Hotel at The Chevy Chase Pavilion - see color ad p 473	◇◇◇	$149-$369 SAVE	473
2 / p. 399	AAA	Connecticut Ave Days Inn - see color ad p 472	◇◇	$134-$164 SAVE	472
3 / p. 399	AAA	Marriott Wardman Park Hotel	◇◇◇	$109-$344 SAVE	473
4 / p. 399	AAA	Omni Shoreham Hotel	◇◇◇◇	$349-$389 SAVE	473
5 / p. 399		The Savoy Suites Georgetown - see color ad p 451	◇◇	$99-$239	474
		WASHINGTON (WEST AND NORTH REGION) - Restaurants			
1 / p. 399		Maggiano's Little Italy	◇◇◇	$11-$33	475
2 / p. 399		Thai Room	◇◇	$7-$12	475
3 / p. 399		Matisse	◇◇◇	$18-$26	475
4 / p. 399		Charlie Chiang's Restaurant	◇◇	$8-$20	474
5 / p. 399		Cafe' Ole'	◇	$5-$8	474
6 / p. 399		Palena	◇◇◇	$9-$66	475
7 / p. 399		Yenching Palace	◇◇	$8-$13	476
8 / p. 399		Yanyu	◇◇◇	$15-$38	475
9 / p. 399		Nam-Viet Pho-79	◇	$6-$14	475
10 / p. 399		Lavandou	◇◇	$15-$19	474
11 / p. 399		2 Amy's	◇	$7-$12	474
12 / p. 399		Ardeo Restaurant	◇◇◇	$14-$23	474
13 / p. 399		Cactus Cantina	◇◇	$7-$17	474
14 / p. 399		Pesto Ristorante	◇◇	$11-$20	475
15 / p. 399		Petits Plats	◇◇	$13-$23	475
16 / p. 399		Lebanese Taverna	◇◇	$14-$20	474
17 / p. 399		New Heights	◇◇◇	$17-$28	475
18 / p. 399		Robert's Restaurant	◇◇◇	$11-$28	475
19 / p. 399		Cashion's Eat Place	◇◇◇	$19-$30	474
		GAITHERSBURG, MD - Lodgings			
8 / p. 399		Courtyard by Marriott-Gaithersburg/Lake Forest	◇◇◇	$99-$144	485
9 / p. 399	AAA	Holiday Inn-Gaithersburg	◇◇◇	$79-$129 SAVE	486
10 / p. 399		Hilton Washington DC North/Gaithersburg - see color ad p 486	◇◇◇	$79-$199	486
11 / p. 399		TownePlace Suites by Marriott-Gaithersburg	◇◇◇	$59-$149	487
12 / p. 399		Summerfield Suites by Wyndham-Gaithersburg	◇◇◇	$135-$175	487
13 / p. 399	AAA	Comfort Inn Shady Grove	◇◇◇	$59-$129 SAVE	485
14 / p. 399		Gaithersburg Marriott Washingtonian Center	◇◇◇	$80-$229	486
15 / p. 399		Residence Inn by Marriott-Gaithersburg	◇◇◇	$99-$179	487
16 / p. 399		Gaithersburg SpringHill Suites by Marriott	◇◇◇	$84-$157	486

Spotter/Map Page Number	OA	GAITHERSBURG, MD - Lodgings (continued)	Diamond Rating	Rate Range High Season	Listing Page
17 / p. 399		Homestead Studio Suites Hotel-Gaithersburg/Rockville	▽▽	$85-$110	486
		GAITHERSBURG, MD - Restaurants			
38 / p. 399		Flaming Pit	▽▽	$11-$37	487
39 / p. 399		Il Porto Restaurant	▽▽	$7-$13	487
40 / p. 399		Tara Thai	▽▽	$8-$13	487
41 / p. 399		Rico Y Rico	▽▽▽	$8-$28	487
		ROCKVILLE, MD - Lodgings			
20 / p. 399		Red Roof Inn-Rockville	▽▽	$67-$96	496
21 / p. 399	AAA	**Woodfin Suites Hotel**	▽▽▽	$124 [SAVE]	497
22 / p. 399	AAA	**Quality Suites and Conference Center** - see color ad p 403	▽▽▽	$109-$169 [SAVE]	495
23 / p. 399	AAA	**Sleep Inn-Rockville** - see color ad p 403	▽▽	$89-$129 [SAVE]	496
24 / p. 399		Courtyard by Marriott-Rockville	▽▽▽	$129-$149	495
25 / p. 399	AAA	**Best Western Washington Gateway Hotel** - see color ad p 494	▽▽	$69-$179 [SAVE]	494
26 / p. 399	AAA	**Ramada Inn Rockville** - see color ad p 496	▽▽	$89-$179 [SAVE]	496
27 / p. 399		Doubletree Hotel & Executive Meeting Center Rockville	▽▽▽	$99-$269	495
28 / p. 399		Park Inn Suites-Rockville - see color ad p 495 & p 589	▽▽	$99-$110	495
		ROCKVILLE, MD - Restaurants			
21 / p. 399		Wurzburg-Haus Restaurant	▽▽	$9-$19	498
22 / p. 399		Nick's Chophouse	▽▽▽	$17-$31	498
23 / p. 399		Thai Farm Restaurant	▽▽	$7-$15	498
24 / p. 399		Il Pizzico	▽▽	$10-$16	497
25 / p. 399		Caribbean Feast	▽	$4-$13	497
26 / p. 399		Cuban Corner Restaurant	▽	$10-$15	497
27 / p. 399		Taste of Saigon	▽▽	$7-$15	498
28 / p. 399		Bombay Bistro	▽▽	$9-$13	497
29 / p. 399		Benjarong Thai Restaurant	▽▽	$9-$14	497
30 / p. 399		A & J Restaurant	▽	$1-$6	497
31 / p. 399		Mykonos Grill	▽▽	$10-$22	497
32 / p. 399		Tara Thai	▽▽	$8-$13	498
33 / p. 399		Timpano Italian Chophouse	▽▽	$10-$28	498
34 / p. 399		Il Pinito Trattoria	▽▽	$8-$15	497
35 / p. 399		Addie's	▽▽▽	$18-$27	497
		SILVER SPRING, MD - Lodgings			
31 / p. 399	AAA	**Holiday Inn-Silver Spring**	▽▽▽	$99-$199 [SAVE]	499
		CHEVY CHASE, MD - Lodgings			
34 / p. 399		Holiday Inn-Washington/Chevy Chase	▽▽▽	$139	483
		CHEVY CHASE, MD - Restaurants			
51 / p. 399		Tavira	▽▽▽	$17-$23	483
52 / p. 399	AAA	**La Ferme Restaurant**	▽▽▽	$20-$27	483
53 / p. 399		Ristorante Terrazza	▽▽▽	$14-$25	483

Spotter/Map Page Number	OA	BETHESDA, MD - Lodgings	Diamond Rating	Rate Range High Season	Listing Page
37 / p. 399		Marriott Suites Bethesda	♦♦♦	$119-$269	479
38 / p. 399	AAA	**Four Points by Sheraton Bethesda - see** color ad p 478	♦♦♦	$75-$159 SAVE	477
39 / p. 399		Holiday Inn Select Bethesda	♦♦♦	$160-$186	478
40 / p. 399		Golden Tulip Bethesda Court Hotel - see color ad p 478	♦♦	$135	477
41 / p. 399	AAA	**Hyatt Regency Bethesda - see color ad p** 433	♦♦♦	$99-$275 SAVE	479
42 / p. 399		Residence Inn by Marriott-Bethesda-Downtown	♦♦♦	$239-$279	479
		BETHESDA, MD - Restaurants			
56 / p. 399		Jean-Michel Restaurant	♦♦♦	$18-$26	480
57 / p. 399		Bacchus Restaurant	♦♦	$13-$17	479
58 / p. 399		Grapeseed-American Bistro & Wine Bar	♦♦♦	$20-$29	480
59 / p. 399		Le Vieux Logis	♦♦	$19-$28	480
60 / p. 399		Cesco Trattoria	♦♦♦	$12-$25	479
61 / p. 399		Oodles Noodles	♦♦	$6-$10	480
62 / p. 399		Passage to India	♦♦♦	$9-$23	481
63 / p. 399	AAA	**Tragara**	♦♦♦	$17-$29	481
64 / p. 399		La Miche	♦♦♦	$20-$30	480
65 / p. 399		Matuba Japanese Restaurant	♦	$8-$20	480
66 / p. 399		Napa Thai	♦♦	$8-$16	480
67 / p. 399		Haandi	♦♦	$9-$17	480
68 / p. 399		Rio Grande Cafe	♦♦	$9-$19	481
69 / p. 399		Sweet Basil	♦♦	$9-$21	481
70 / p. 399		Foong Lin Restaurant	♦♦	$7-$16	480
71 / p. 399		Cafe Bethesda	♦♦♦	$23-$29	479
72 / p. 399		Black's Bar & Kitchen	♦♦♦	$18-$26	479
73 / p. 399		The Original Pancake House	♦	$5-$10(L)	480
74 / p. 399		Thyme Square Cafe	♦♦	$10-$20	481
75 / p. 399		Cameron's Seafood Market	♦	$6-$14	479
76 / p. 399		Penang	♦	$7-$20	481
77 / p. 399		Tara Thai	♦♦	$8-$14	481
78 / p. 399		Bethesda Crab House	♦	$20	479
79 / p. 399		Persimmon	♦♦♦	$18-$24	481
		WHEATON, MD - Restaurants			
44 / p. 399		Dusit Thai Cuisine	♦	$7-$11	499
45 / p. 399		Anchor Inn Seafood Restaurant	♦♦	$11-$27	499
		POTOMAC, MD - Restaurant			
48 / p. 399		Old Anglers Inn	♦♦♦	$22-$30	494

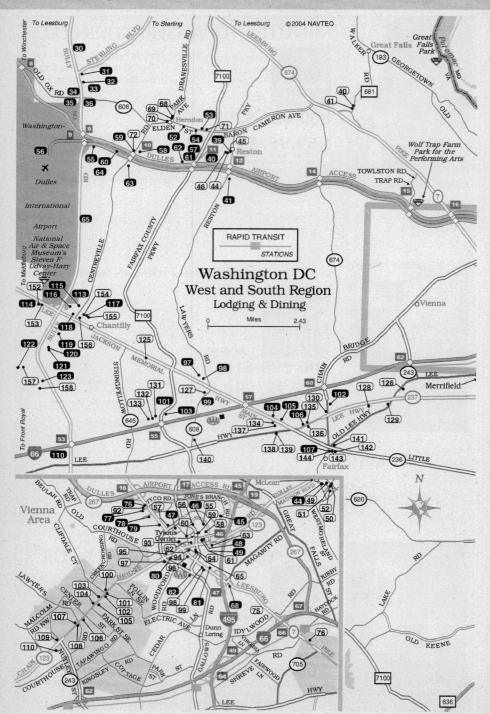

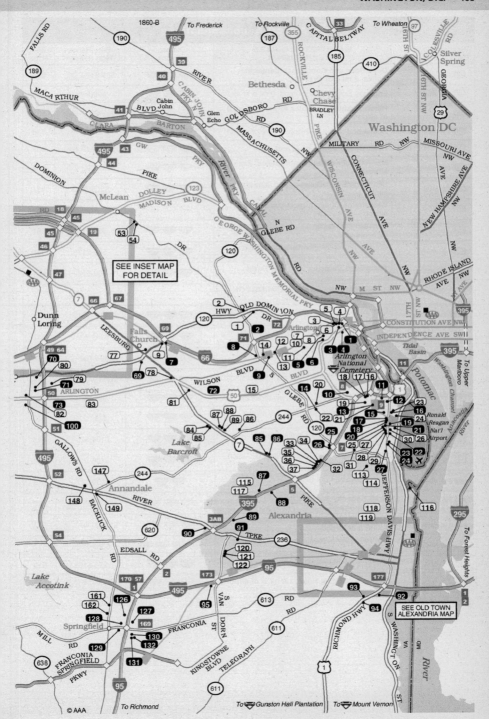

✈ Airport Accommodations

Spotter/Map Page Number	OA	WASHINGTON DULLES INTERNATIONAL	Diamond Rating	Rate Range High Season	Listing Page
59 / p. 404	AAA	**Days Hotel and Conference Center at Dulles, 2 mi e of airport**	◇◇◇	$89-$179 SAVE	535
63 / p. 404		Embassy Suites Dulles Airport, 2 mi e of airport	◇◇◇	$99-$319	535
65 / p. 404	AAA	**Hilton Washington Dulles Airport, 4.5 mi s of airport**	◇◇◇	$67-$307 SAVE	535
60 / p. 404		Homewood Suites by Hilton, 2 mi e of airport	◇◇◇	$109-$219	536
55 / p. 404	AAA	**Hyatt Dulles, 2 mi e of airport**	◇◇◇	$89-$249 SAVE	536
58 / p. 404	AAA	**Marriott Suites Washington-Dulles, 2 mi e of airport**	◇◇◇	$99-$299 SAVE	536
64 / p. 404		Staybridge Suites Dulles Airport, 4 mi e of airport	◇◇◇	$205-$265	537
56 / p. 404	AAA	**Washington Dulles Airport Marriott, at airport**	◇◇◇	$89-$249 SAVE	537
32 / p. 404		Hampton Inn Washington-Dulles Airport, 2.5 mi ne of airport	◇◇◇	$59-$159	551
30 / p. 404		Holiday Inn Washington Dulles International Airport, 2.5 mi ne of airport	◇◇◇	$69-$179	551
31 / p. 404		TownePlace Suites by Marriott at Dulles Airport, 2.5 mi ne of airport	◇◇◇	$69-$179	551
		RONALD REAGAN WASHINGTON NATIONAL			
24 / p. 404		Courtyard by Marriott Crystal City, 0.5 mi nw of airport	◇◇◇	$99-$219	512
16 / p. 404		Crowne Plaza Hotel Washington National Airport, 1.5 mi nw of airport	◇◇◇	$149-$289	512
19 / p. 404	AAA	**Crystal City Marriott at Reagan National Airport, 1 mi nw of airport**	◇◇◇	$289-$700 SAVE	512
17 / p. 404	AAA	**Crystal Gateway Marriott Hotel, 1 mi nw of airport**	◇◇◇	$289-$700 SAVE	512
21 / p. 404		Days Inn Crystal City, 0.8 mi nw of airport	◇◇◇	$89-$219	512
12 / p. 404		Doubletree Hotel-Crystal City, 1.5 mi n of airport	◇◇◇	$79-$219	513
15 / p. 404		Embassy Suites Hotel Crystal City, 1.5 mi nw of airport	◇◇◇	$104-$254	513
22 / p. 404		Hilton Crystal City at Reagan National Airport, 0.7 mi nw of airport	◇◇◇	$108-$179	514
27 / p. 404		Holiday Inn National Airport, 0.5 mi nw of airport	◇◇	$139-$279	515
23 / p. 404	AAA	**Hyatt Regency Crystal City at Reagan National Airport, 0.5 mi n of airport**	◇◇◇	$89-$235 SAVE	516
11 / p. 404	AAA	**Residence Inn by Marriott-Pentagon City, 1.7 mi n of airport**	◇◇	$119-$249 SAVE	517
13 / p. 404		The Ritz-Carlton, Pentagon City, 1.8 mi n of airport	◇◇◇◇	$389-$689	517
18 / p. 404		Sheraton Crystal City Hotel, 1 mi nw of airport	◇◇◇	$85-$165	519
10 / p. 404	AAA	**Sheraton National Hotel, 1.3 mi w of airport**	◇◇◇	$89-$279 SAVE	519

Washington, D.C. West & South Region

This index helps you "spot" where approved accommodations and restaurants are located on the corresponding detailed maps. Lodging rate ranges are for comparison only and show the property's high season; rates are per night, unless only weekly (W) rates are available. Restaurant rate range is for dinner, unless only lunch (L) is served. Turn to the listing page for more detailed rate information and consult display ads for special promotions.

Spotter/Map Page Number	OA	ARLINGTON, VA - Lodgings	Diamond Rating	Rate Range High Season	Listing Page
1 / p. 404		Courtyard by Marriott-Arlington/Rosslyn - see color ad p 501	◆◆◆	$219-$229	512
2 / p. 404	AAA	Comfort Inn Ballston	◆◆	$79-$200 [SAVE]	511
3 / p. 404		Quality Inn-Iwo Jima - see color ad p 517	◆◆	$79-$159	516
4 / p. 404	AAA	The Virginian Suites - see color ad p 518	◆◆	$99-$159 [SAVE]	519
5 / p. 404		Hilton Garden Inn Arlington/Courthouse Plaza	◆◆◆	$71-$189	515
6 / p. 404	AAA	Quality Hotel Courthouse Plaza - see color ad p 420	◆◆	$109-$209 [SAVE]	516
7 / p. 404	AAA	Econo Lodge-Metro Arlington - see color ad p 513	◆◆	$90-$149 [SAVE]	513
8 / p. 404	AAA	Holiday Inn Arlington - see color ad p 515	◆◆◆	$107-$179 [SAVE]	515
9 / p. 404		Hilton Arlington and Towers - see color ad p 514	◆◆◆	$89-$309	513
10 / p. 404	AAA	Sheraton National Hotel - see color ad p 518	◆◆◆	$89-$279 [SAVE]	519
11 / p. 404	AAA	Residence Inn by Marriott-Pentagon City - see color ad p 501	◆◆◆	$119-$249 [SAVE]	517
12 / p. 404		Doubletree Hotel-Crystal City	◆◆◆	$79-$219	513
13 / p. 404		The Ritz-Carlton, Pentagon City	◆◆◆◆	$389-$689	517
14 / p. 404		Days Inn Pentagon	◆◆	$81	512
15 / p. 404		Embassy Suites Hotel Crystal City	◆◆◆	$104-$254	513
16 / p. 404		Crowne Plaza Hotel Washington National Airport	◆◆◆	$149-$289	512
17 / p. 404	AAA	Crystal Gateway Marriott Hotel - see color ad p 501	◆◆◆	$289-$700 [SAVE]	512
18 / p. 404		Sheraton Crystal City Hotel - see color ad p 451	◆◆◆	$85-$165	519
19 / p. 404	AAA	Crystal City Marriott at Reagan National Airport - see color ad p 501	◆◆◆	$289-$700 [SAVE]	512
20 / p. 404		Hampton Inn & Suites Reagan National Airport	◆◆◆	$89-$199	513
21 / p. 404		Days Inn Crystal City	◆◆◆	$89-$219	512
22 / p. 404		Hilton Crystal City at Reagan National Airport - see color ad p 514	◆◆◆	$108-$179	514
23 / p. 404	AAA	Hyatt Regency Crystal City at Reagan National Airport - see color ad p 433	◆◆◆	$89-$235 [SAVE]	516
24 / p. 404		Courtyard by Marriott Crystal City	◆◆◆	$99-$219	512
25 / p. 404	AAA	Best Western-Pentagon/Reagan Airport - see color ad p 424	◆◆	$119-$169 [SAVE]	511
26 / p. 404	AAA	Comfort Inn Pentagon	◆◆◆	$129-$179 [SAVE]	511
27 / p. 404		Holiday Inn National Airport - see color ad p 516	◆◆	$139-$279	515
		ARLINGTON, VA - Restaurants			
1 / p. 404		Cafe Parisien Express	◆	$6-$12	520
2 / p. 404		Metro 29 Diner	◆◆	$5-$20	521
3 / p. 404		Guajillo	◆	$8-$20	520
4 / p. 404		Cafe Asia	◆◆	$7-$12	519
5 / p. 404		Village Bistro	◆◆	$10-$22	523

Spotter/Map Page Number	OA	**ARLINGTON, VA - Restaurants (continued)**	Diamond Rating	Rate Range High Season	Listing Page
6 / p. 404		Red Hot & Blue	▼	$6-$20	522
7 / p. 404		Mexicali Blues	▼	$5-$11	521
8 / p. 404		Harry's Tap Room	▼▼▼	$9-$24	521
9 / p. 404	◬	**La Cote D'Or Cafe**	▼▼▼	$20-$29	521
10 / p. 404		Queen Bee Restaurant	▼▼	$6-$10	522
11 / p. 404		El Pollo Rico	▼	$4-$10	520
12 / p. 404		Tara Thai	▼▼	$8-$13	522
13 / p. 404		Cafe Tirolo	▼▼	$8-$16	520
14 / p. 404		Rio Grande Cafe	▼▼	$10-$20	522
15 / p. 404		Crystal Thai Restaurant	▼▼	$8-$16	520
16 / p. 404		Lebanese Taverna	▼▼	$12-$19	521
17 / p. 404		Thaiphoon	▼▼	$7-$15	522
18 / p. 404		Sin e Irish Pub and Restaurant	▼▼	$7-$16	522
19 / p. 404		Woo Lae Oak	▼▼	$12-$21	523
20 / p. 404		Matuba	▼	$9-$16	521
21 / p. 404		The Grill	▼▼▼▼	$28-$33	520
22 / p. 404		Rincome Thai Cuisine	▼▼	$8-$14	522
23 / p. 404		San Antonio Bar & Grill	▼	$10-$18	522
24 / p. 404		Morton's The Steakhouse	▼▼▼	$32-$59	521
25 / p. 404	◬	**Athena Pallas**	▼▼	$9-$19	519
26 / p. 404		Ruth's Chris Steak House	▼▼▼	$18-$36	522
27 / p. 404		Top Thai Restaurant	▼	$8-$14	523
28 / p. 404		Cafe Italia	▼▼	$9-$17	520
29 / p. 404		The Portofino Restaurant	▼▼	$15-$22	521
30 / p. 404		Legal Sea Foods	▼▼	$12-$30	521
31 / p. 404		El Cuscatleco Restaurant	▼	$7-$20	520
32 / p. 404		Capitol City Brewing Co Shirlington	▼▼	$6-$16	520
33 / p. 404		T.H.A.I. in Shirlington	▼▼	$8-$16	522
34 / p. 404		Bistro Bistro	▼▼	$11-$22	519
35 / p. 404		Carlyle	▼▼▼	$12-$22	520
36 / p. 404		Aroma Indian Cuisine	▼▼	$11-$18	519
37 / p. 404		Aladdin's Eatery	▼▼	$5-$10	519
		STERLING, VA - Lodgings			
30 / p. 404		Holiday Inn Washington Dulles International Airport - see color ad p 536	▼▼▼	$69-$179	551
31 / p. 404		TownePlace Suites by Marriott at Dulles Airport	▼▼▼	$69-$179	551
32 / p. 404		Hampton Inn Washington-Dulles Airport	▼▼▼	$59-$159	551
33 / p. 404	◬	**Country Inn & Suites by Carlson** - see color ad p 847, p 550	▼▼▼	$89-$159 (SAVE)	550
34 / p. 404	◬	**Fairfield Inn by Marriott-Dulles Airport** - see ad p 550 & color ad p 501	▼▼▼	$69-$159 (SAVE)	551
35 / p. 404		Homestead Studio Suites Hotel-Dulles/Sterling	▼▼▼	$91-$106	551
36 / p. 404		Microtel Inn & Suites Dulles International Airport	▼▼	$69-$189	551

Spotter/Map Page Number	OA	RESTON, VA - Lodgings	Diamond Rating	Rate Range High Season	Listing Page
39 / p. 404	AAA	**Hyatt Regency Reston** - see color ad p 433	♦♦♦♦	$109-$319 [SAVE]	547
40 / p. 404		Homestead Studio Suites Hotel-Reston	♦♦♦	$95-$120	546
41 / p. 404		Sheraton Reston Hotel - see ad p 546	♦♦♦	$79-$199	547
		RESTON, VA - Restaurants			
44 / p. 404		Paolo's Ristorante	♦♦	$8-$24	547
45 / p. 404	AAA	**Market Street Bar & Grill**	♦♦♦	$15-$30	547
46 / p. 404		Clyde's of Reston	♦♦	$6-$16	547
		MCLEAN, VA - Lodgings			
44 / p. 404	AAA	**Staybridge Suites by Holiday Inn-McLean/Tysons Corner**	♦♦♦	$170-$230	543
45 / p. 404		Hilton McLean Tysons Corner - see color ad p 426	♦♦♦	$69-$317	543
46 / p. 404	AAA	**The Ritz-Carlton, Tysons Corner**	♦♦♦♦	$429-$599 [SAVE]	543
47 / p. 404	AAA	**Best Western Tysons Westpark Hotel**	♦♦	$79-$159 [SAVE]	542
48 / p. 404	AAA	**Holiday Inn Tysons Corner** - see color ad p 543	♦♦♦	$229-$279 [SAVE]	543
49 / p. 404		Courtyard by Marriott, Tysons Corner	♦♦♦	$69-$259	542
		MCLEAN, VA - Restaurants			
49 / p. 404		Pulcinella The Italian Host	♦♦	$9-$20	545
50 / p. 404		Cafe Taj	♦♦	$8-$21	544
51 / p. 404		The Greek Taverna	♦♦	$14-$18	544
52 / p. 404		Kazan Restaurant	♦♦	$13-$24	544
53 / p. 404		Tachibana	♦♦	$7-$30	545
54 / p. 404		Cafe Oggi	♦♦♦	$13-$28	544
55 / p. 404	AAA	**Maestro**	♦♦♦♦♦	$74-$104	544
56 / p. 404		P.F. Chang's China Bistro	♦♦	$9-$18	545
57 / p. 404		McCormick & Schmick's	♦♦♦	$14-$30	545
58 / p. 404		Palm Restaurant at Tysons II	♦♦♦	$17-$38	545
59 / p. 404		Maggiano's Little Italy	♦♦♦	$12-$30	545
60 / p. 404		Taste of Saigon	♦♦	$8-$15	545
61 / p. 404		Flemming's Prime Steakhouse and Wine Bar	♦♦♦	$19-$35	544
62 / p. 404		Da Domenico	♦♦	$12-$28	544
63 / p. 404		Neisha Thai Cuisine	♦♦	$18-$25	545
64 / p. 404		Busara	♦♦	$20-$26	544
65 / p. 404		J.R.'s Stockyards Inn	♦♦	$17-$25	544
		HERNDON, VA - Lodgings			
52 / p. 404		Holiday Inn Express - Reston/Herndon - see color ad p 536	♦♦♦	$59-$159	536
53 / p. 404	AAA	**Comfort Inn Dulles International Airport** - see color ad p 501	♦♦♦	$69-$119 [SAVE]	534
54 / p. 404		Residence Inn by Marriott-Herndon/Reston	♦♦♦	$229	537
55 / p. 404	AAA	**Hyatt Dulles** - see color ad p 433	♦♦♦	$89-$249 [SAVE]	536
56 / p. 404	AAA	**Washington Dulles Airport Marriott** - see color ad p 501	♦♦♦	$89-$249 [SAVE]	537
57 / p. 404		SpringHill Suites by Marriott - see color ad p 501	♦♦♦	$69-$189	537

Spotter/Map Page Number	OA	HERNDON, VA - Lodgings (continued)	Diamond Rating	Rate Range High Season	Listing Page
58 / p. 404	AAA	**Marriott Suites Washington-Dulles** - see color ad p 501	◇◇◇	$99-$299 SAVE	536
59 / p. 404	AAA	**Days Hotel and Conference Center at Dulles**	◇◇◇	$89-$179 SAVE	535
60 / p. 404		Homewood Suites by Hilton	◇◇◇	$109-$219	536
61 / p. 404		Hawthorn Suites	◇◇◇	$99-$185	535
62 / p. 404		Courtyard by Marriott/Herndon-Reston - see color ad p 501	◇◇◇	$69-$99	535
63 / p. 404		Embassy Suites Dulles Airport	◇◇◇	$99-$319	535
64 / p. 404		Staybridge Suites Dulles Airport	◇◇◇	$205-$265	537
65 / p. 404	AAA	**Hilton Washington Dulles Airport**	◇◇◇	$67-$307 SAVE	535
		HERNDON, VA - Restaurants			
68 / p. 404		Russia House	◇◇◇	$15-$28	537
69 / p. 404	AAA	**Zeffirelli Ristorante Italiano**	◇◇◇	$12-$21	537
70 / p. 404		Ice House Cafe	◇◇	$12-$26	537
71 / p. 404		Cantina D'Italia	◇◇◇	$8-$20	537
72 / p. 404		The Flight Deck Restaurant	◇◇	$7-$18	537
		FALLS CHURCH, VA - Lodgings			
68 / p. 404		Doubletree Hotel and Executive Meeting Center at Tysons Corner	◇◇◇	$74-$259	532
69 / p. 404		TownePlace Suites by Marriott-Falls Church	◇◇◇	$89-$199	532
70 / p. 404		Homewood Suites by Hilton-Falls Church	◇◇◇	$109-$209	532
71 / p. 404		Fairfax-Merrifield Residence Inn by Marriott - see color ad p 501	◇◇◇	$139-$259	532
72 / p. 404	AAA	**Comfort Inn Arlington Boulevard-DC Gateway** - see color ad p 501	◇◇	$71-$129 SAVE	532
73 / p. 404		Fairview Park Marriott - see color ad p 501	◇◇◇	$79-$259	532
		FALLS CHURCH, VA - Restaurants			
75 / p. 404		Tara Thai	◇◇	$9-$14	534
76 / p. 404		Haandi	◇◇	$9-$17	533
77 / p. 404		Argia's	◇◇◇	$8-$22	533
78 / p. 404		Pistone's Italian Inn	◇◇◇	$10-$24	533
79 / p. 404		2941 Restaurant	◇◇◇◇	$23-$28	532
80 / p. 404		Sir Walter Raleigh Inn	◇	$15-$21	534
81 / p. 404		Mark's Duck House	◇◇	$6-$25	533
82 / p. 404		Sweetwater Tavern	◇◇	$12-$25	534
83 / p. 404		Celebrity Delly	◇	$5-$15	533
84 / p. 404		Neisha Thai Cuisine	◇◇	$9-$25	533
85 / p. 404		Peking Gourmet Inn	◇◇	$9-$35	533
86 / p. 404		Flavors Soul Food	◇	$8-$11	533
87 / p. 404		Rabieng	◇	$9-$14	534
88 / p. 404		Duangrat's	◇◇◇	$10-$28	533
89 / p. 404		Raaga	◇◇◇	$9-$18	533
		VIENNA, VA - Lodgings			
76 / p. 404		Sheraton Premiere At Tysons Corner	◇◇◇	$229	552
77 / p. 404		Residence Inn by Marriott-Tysons Corner	◇◇◇	$179-$299	552

Spotter/Map Page Number	OA	VIENNA, VA - Lodgings (continued)	Diamond Rating	Rate Range High Season	Listing Page
78 / p. 404	AAA	Comfort Inn Tysons Corner - see color ad p 403	▽▽	$129-$159 SAVE	552
79 / p. 404		Embassy Suites Hotel Tysons Corner	▽▽▽	$109-$409	552
80 / p. 404		Residence Inn by Marriott Tysons Corner-Mall	▽▽▽	$119-$269	552
81 / p. 404		Tysons Corner Marriott Hotel - see color ad p 501	▽▽▽	$259	552
82 / p. 404		Homestead Studio Suites Hotel-Tysons Corner	▽▽	$110-$135	552
		VIENNA, VA - Restaurants			
92 / p. 404		Bombay Tandoor	▽▽	$9-$17	553
93 / p. 404		Clyde's of Tysons Corner	▽▽	$10-$23	553
94 / p. 404		Sam & Harry's	▽▽	$18-$45	554
95 / p. 404		Hunan Lion	▽▽▽	$8-$25	553
96 / p. 404		Konami	▽▽	$12-$20	553
97 / p. 404		Paya Thai	▽▽	$7-$13	554
98 / p. 404		Morton's - The Steakhouse	▽▽▽	$24-$42	554
99 / p. 404	AAA	**Colvin Run Tavern**	▽▽▽▽	$22-$39	553
100 / p. 404	AAA	**Ristorante Bonaroti**	▽▽▽	$15-$30	554
101 / p. 404		Aarathi	▽▽	$7-$12	553
102 / p. 404		Le Canard	▽▽▽	$17-$30	554
103 / p. 404		Amma Vegetarian Kitchen	▽	$4-$5	553
104 / p. 404	AAA	**Bistro 123**	▽▽▽	$13-$22	553
105 / p. 404	AAA	**Cafe Renaissance**	▽▽▽	$13-$24	553
106 / p. 404		La Provence Restaurant	▽▽▽	$19-$26	553
107 / p. 404		Marco Polo Restaurant & Caterers	▽▽	$10-$27	554
108 / p. 404		Tara Thai	▽▽	$8-$13	554
109 / p. 404		Nizam's Restaurant	▽▽	$13-$22	554
110 / p. 404		Sunflower Vegetarian Restaurant	▽▽	$8-$11	554
		ALEXANDRIA, VA - Lodgings			
85 / p. 404		Homewood Suites by Hilton-Alexandria	▽▽▽	$189-$299	504
86 / p. 404		Hampton Inn-Alexandria	▽▽▽	$139-$149	502
87 / p. 404		Hilton Alexandria Mark Center - see color ad p 426	▽▽▽	$89-$299	502
88 / p. 404		Sheraton Pentagon South Hotel	▽▽▽	$115-$170	505
89 / p. 404		Hawthorn Suites LTD-Alexandria	▽▽	$99-$179	502
90 / p. 404		Comfort Inn-Alexandria Landmark	▽▽	$83-$120	500
91 / p. 404	AAA	**Washington Suites-Alexandria** - see color ad p 506	▽▽▽	$99-$209 SAVE	507
92 / p. 404		Hampton Inn Alexandria/Old Town Area-South	▽▽▽	$134-$159	502
93 / p. 404	AAA	**Travelers Motel**	▽▽	$65-$89 SAVE	505
94 / p. 404		Red Roof Inn-Alexandria	▽▽	$73-$95	504
95 / p. 404	AAA	**Comfort Inn Alexandria** - see color ad p 501	▽▽	$104 SAVE	500
		ALEXANDRIA, VA - Restaurants			
113 / p. 404		RT's Restaurant	▽▽	$13-$25	509
114 / p. 404		Bombay Curry Company	▽▽	$8-$11	507

Spotter/Map Page Number	OA	ALEXANDRIA, VA - Restaurants (continued)	Diamond Rating	Rate Range High Season	Listing Page
(115) / p. 404		Clyde's at Mark Center	▽▽	$13-$23	507
(116) / p. 404	⟨AAA⟩	**Potowmack Landing Restaurant**	▽▽	$13-$29	509
(117) / p. 404		Haad Thai	▽▽	$8-$14	508
(118) / p. 404		Evening Star Cafe'	▽▽	$15-$25	508
(119) / p. 404		Monroe's-An American Trattoria	▽▽	$11-$17	509
(120) / p. 404		Satay Sarinah	▽	$7-$16	509
(121) / p. 404		Akaska	▽	$10-$20	507
(122) / p. 404		Savio's Italain Restaurant and Bar	▽▽	$8-$15	509
		FAIRFAX, VA - Lodgings			
(97) / p. 404	⟨AAA⟩	**Hilton Garden Inn Fairfax** - see color ad p 528	▽▽▽	$79-$249 SAVE	529
(98) / p. 404		Sierra Suites Hotel-Fairfax	▽▽▽	$69-$135	529
(99) / p. 404		Homestead Studio Suites Hotel-Fair Oaks	▽▽	$80-$105	529
(100) / p. 404		Homestead Studio Suites Hotel-Falls Church/Merrifield	▽▽	$95-$120	529
(101) / p. 404		Residence Inn by Marriott-Fair Lakes - see color ad p 501	▽▽▽	$189-$209	529
(102) / p. 404	⟨AAA⟩	**Best Western Fairfax** - see color ad p 424	▽▽	$89-$129 SAVE	527
(103) / p. 404	⟨AAA⟩	**Hyatt Fair Lakes**	▽▽▽	$99-$269 SAVE	529
(104) / p. 404		Courtyard by Marriott-Fair Oaks - see color ad p 501	▽▽▽	$69-$189	528
(105) / p. 404	⟨AAA⟩	**Comfort Inn University Center** - see color ad p 527	▽▽▽	$69-$139 SAVE	528
(106) / p. 404		Hampton Inn-Fairfax	▽▽▽	$125-$145	528
(107) / p. 404		Bailiwick Inn	▽▽▽	$165-$225	527
		FAIRFAX, VA - Restaurants			
(125) / p. 404		Beacon Street Boston Cafe	▽▽	$8-$25	530
(126) / p. 404		Jaipur Royal Indian Cuisine	▽▽▽	$8-$18	531
(127) / p. 404		Chutzpah, A Real New York Deli	▽	$7-$15	530
(128) / p. 404	⟨AAA⟩	**The Espositos Italian Restaurant**	▽	$7-$16	531
(129) / p. 404		Arties	▽▽	$12-$27	530
(130) / p. 404		Bombay Bistro	▽▽	$8-$14	530
(131) / p. 404		Cantina D'Italia	▽▽	$8-$23	530
(132) / p. 404		Arigato Sushi-Fairlakes	▽▽	$10-$35	530
(133) / p. 404	⟨AAA⟩	**Star Thai**	▽▽	$7-$15	531
(134) / p. 404		Bravo's Italian Cafe	▽▽	$8-$26	530
(135) / p. 404		Dolce Vita	▽▽	$8-$20	531
(136) / p. 404		Pars Restaurant	▽▽	$9-$20	531
(137) / p. 404		The Lamplighter Restaurant	▽▽	$15-$26	531
(138) / p. 404		Arigato Sushi-Fairfax	▽▽	$10-$35	529
(139) / p. 404		Pad Thai	▽	$7-$13	531
(140) / p. 404		Sakoontra	▽▽	$7-$12	531
(141) / p. 404		The Connaught Place	▽▽	$9-$18	531
(142) / p. 404		Bellissimo	▽▽▽	$13-$25	530
(143) / p. 404		Saigon Corner	▽	$7-$10	531
(144) / p. 404		Bailiwick Inn Restaurant	▽▽▽	$59-$69	530

Spotter/Map Page Number	OA		Diamond Rating	Rate Range High Season	Listing Page
110 / p. 404		**CENTREVILLE, VA - Lodgings**			
		SpringHill Suites by Marriott Centreville/Chantilly - see color ad p 501	◆◆◆	$94-$129	523
		CHANTILLY, VA - Lodgings			
113 / p. 404		Wingate Inn Dulles Airport-Chantilly	◆◆◆	$140-$169	525
114 / p. 404		Hampton Inn Washington Dulles International Airport South - see color ad p 524	◆◆◆	$69-$129	524
115 / p. 404		TownePlace Suites by Marriott-Chantilly	◆◆◆	$84-$144	525
116 / p. 404		Fairfield Inn by Marriott-Chantilly/Dulles South - see color ad p 501	◆◆◆	$113-$129	524
117 / p. 404		Comfort Suites Chantilly-Dulles Airport	◆◆◆	$69-$199	524
118 / p. 404		Courtyard by Marriott-Dulles Airport - see color ad p 501	◆◆◆	$69-$199	524
119 / p. 404		Holiday Inn Select Chantilly-Dulles Expo Center	◆◆◆	$99-$199	525
120 / p. 404		Homestead Studio Suites Hotel-Dulles/Chantilly	◆◆	$91-$116	525
121 / p. 404		Sierra Suites Hotel-Chantilly	◆◆	$69-$135	525
122 / p. 404	AAA	**Westfields Marriott - see color ad p 501**	◆◆◆◆	$129-$169 [SAVE]	525
123 / p. 404	AAA	**AmeriSuites (Dulles Airport South/Chantilly) - see color ad p 423**	◆◆◆	$159-$179 [SAVE]	524
		CHANTILLY, VA - Restaurants			
152 / p. 404		Thai Basil	◆◆	$9-$14	526
153 / p. 404		Picante! The Real Taco	◆	$8-$15	526
154 / p. 404		Backyard Grill and Bar	◆◆	$10-$20	525
155 / p. 404		Oasis Indian Restaurant	◆	$7-$15	526
156 / p. 404		Otani Japanese Steak House	◆◆	$15-$30	526
157 / p. 404		Palm Court at Westfields Marriott	◆◆◆	$20-$33	526
158 / p. 404		Blue Water Grille	◆◆	$8-$22	526
		SPRINGFIELD, VA - Lodgings			
126 / p. 404		TownePlace Suites by Marriott	◆◆◆	$149-$199	549
127 / p. 404		Courtyard by Marriott - Springfield - see color ad p 501	◆◆◆	$79-$179	548
128 / p. 404		Holiday Inn Express Springfield - see color ad p 548	◆◆	$103-$114	549
129 / p. 404		Red Roof Inn Springfield	◆◆	$75-$90	549
130 / p. 404		Hampton Inn Washington DC/Springfield	◆◆◆	$139-$144	549
131 / p. 404		Comfort Inn Washington DC/Springfield	◆◆◆	$119-$129	548
132 / p. 404	AAA	**Hilton Springfield - see color ad p 548**	◆◆◆	$89-$199 [SAVE]	549
		SPRINGFIELD, VA - Restaurants			
161 / p. 404		Mike's American Grill	◆◆	$10-$21	549
162 / p. 404		Manila Cafe	◆	$8-$12	549
		GREAT FALLS, VA - Restaurants			
40 / p. 404		Serbian Crown Restaurant	◆◆◆	$19-$30	534
41 / p. 404	AAA	**Dante Ristorante**	◆◆◆	$17-$25	534
		ANNANDALE, VA - Restaurants			
147 / p. 404		Silverado	◆◆	$12-$24	511
148 / p. 404		Domani Ristorante	◆◆	$12-$19	511
149 / p. 404		Ribster's	◆◆	$7-$16	511

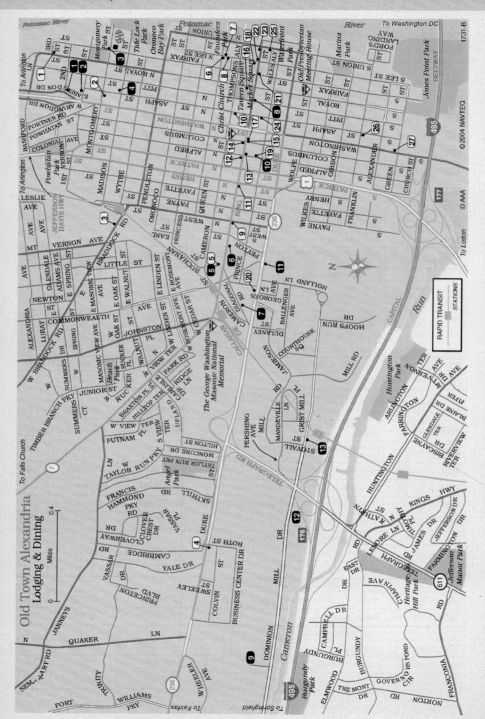

Old Town Alexandria
Lodging & Dining

Old Town Alexandria

This index helps you "spot" where approved accommodations and restaurants are located on the corresponding detailed maps. Lodging rate ranges are for comparison only and show the property's high season; rates are per night, unless only weekly (W) rates are available. Restaurant rate range is for dinner, unless only lunch (L) is served. Turn to the listing page for more detailed rate information and consult display ads for special promotions.

Spotter/Map Page Number	OA	ALEXANDRIA, VA - Lodgings	Diamond Rating	Rate Range High Season	Listing Page
1 / p. 414		Best Western-Old Colony Inn - see color ad p 500	◆◆	$109-$159	500
2 / p. 414	AAA	**Holiday Inn Hotel & Suites-Historic District Alexandria** - see color ad p 503	◆◆◆	$129-$239 SAVE	503
3 / p. 414	AAA	**Radisson Hotel Old Town Alexandria** - see color ad p 932, p 504	◆◆◆	$139-$249 SAVE	504
4 / p. 414	AAA	**Sheraton Suites Alexandria** - see color ad p 505	◆◆◆	$109-$229 SAVE	505
5 / p. 414		Hilton Alexandria Old Town	◆◆◆	$119-$289	503
6 / p. 414		Hampton Inn Old Town King Street Metro	◆◆◆	$99-$209	502
7 / p. 414	AAA	**Embassy Suites-Alexandria-Old Town**	◆◆◆	$139-$289 SAVE	502
8 / p. 414	AAA	**Holiday Inn Select-Old Town** - see color ad p 503	◆◆◆	$229-$249 SAVE	504
9 / p. 414		Homestead Studio Suites Hotel-Alexandria	◆◆	$105-$130	504
10 / p. 414	AAA	**Relais & Chateaux Morrison House**	◆◆◆◆	$299-$399 SAVE	505
11 / p. 414	AAA	**Residence Inn by Marriott Alexandria-Old Town** - see color ad p 501	◆◆◆	$129-$339 SAVE	505
12 / p. 414		Courtyard by Marriott-Alexandria - see color ad p 501	◆◆◆	$189-$199	502
13 / p. 414		Holiday Inn Eisenhower Metro	◆◆◆	$79-$200	503
		ALEXANDRIA, VA - Restaurants			
① / p. 414		Cafe Marianna	◆◆	$17-$22	507
② / p. 414		The Stardust Restaurant & Lounge	◆◆	$15-$22	510
③ / p. 414		La Piazza	◆	$9-$10	509
④ / p. 414		Generous George's Positive Pizza & Pasta Place	◆	$6-$15	508
⑤ / p. 414		Seagar's	◆◆◆	$20-$35	510
⑥ / p. 414		Bilbo Baggins	◆◆	$13-$20	507
⑦ / p. 414	AAA	**La Bergerie**	◆◆◆	$17-$25	508
⑧ / p. 414		Ecco Cafe & Pizzaria	◆◆	$9-$16	507
⑨ / p. 414		Hard Times Cafe	◆	$5-$8	508
⑩ / p. 414		King St. Blues	◆◆	$7-$14	508
⑪ / p. 414		Le Gaulois	◆◆◆	$8-$25	509
⑫ / p. 414		Majestic Cafe	◆◆	$16-$22	509
⑬ / p. 414		Taverna Cretekou	◆◆	$10-$25	510
⑭ / p. 414		South Austin Grill	◆◆	$10-$19	510
⑮ / p. 414	AAA	**Scotland Yard Restaurant**	◆◆	$13-$19	509
⑯ / p. 414		Gadsby's Tavern	◆◆	$17-$26	508
⑰ / p. 414		Geranio Restaurant	◆◆◆	$15-$26	508
⑱ / p. 414		Two Nineteen Restaurant	◆◆	$15-$25	510
⑲ / p. 414		Elysium	◆◆◆◆	$67	507
⑳ / p. 414		Stella's	◆◆	$14-$25	510
㉑ / p. 414		Warehouse Bar & Grill	◆◆◆	$8-$26	510
㉒ / p. 414		Il Porto Ristorante	◆◆	$11-$18	508
㉓ / p. 414		Landini Brothers	◆◆◆	$16-$24	508
㉔ / p. 414		Portner's	◆◆	$8-$22	509
㉕ / p. 414		Union Street Public House	◆◆	$7-$23	510
㉖ / p. 414		Blue Point Grill & Oyster Bar	◆◆	$18-$29	507
㉗ / p. 414		Southside 815	◆◆	$7-$17	510

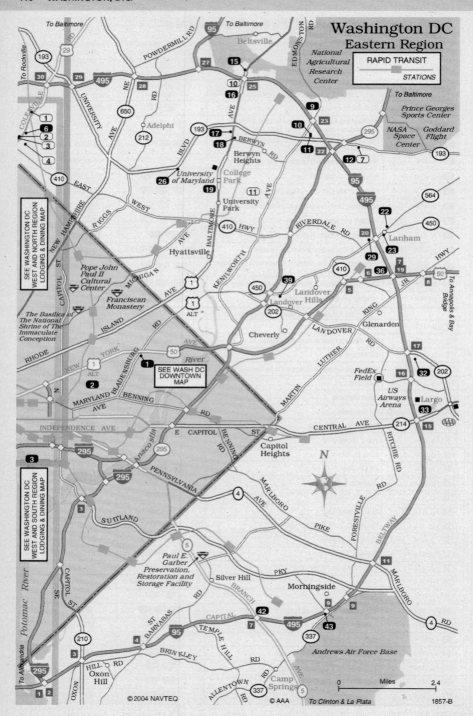

Washington DC
Eastern Region

RAPID TRANSIT
STATIONS

To Baltimore
To Baltimore
To Rockville
To Baltimore

Beltsville

National Agricultural Research Center

Prince Georges Sports Center

NASA Space Center

Goddard Flight

Adelphi

College Park

University of Maryland

University Park

Berwyn Heights

Hyattsville

Pope John Paul II Cultural Center

Franciscan Monastery

The Basilica of The National Shrine of The Immaculate Conception

Lanham

Riverdale Rd

Landover

Landover Hills

Cheverly

Glenarden

FedEx Field

US Airways Arena

Largo

SEE WASH DC DOWNTOWN MAP

SEE WASHINGTON DC WEST AND NORTH REGION LODGING & DINING MAP

SEE WASHINGTON DC WEST AND SOUTH REGION LODGING & DINING MAP

Capitol Heights

Suitland

Paul E. Garber Preservation, Restoration and Storage Facility

Silver Hill

Morningside

Andrews Air Force Base

Oxon Hill

Camp Springs

To Alexandria

To Clinton & La Plata

To Annapolis & Bay Bridge

Potomac River

Anacostia River

©2004 NAVTEQ

© AAA

1857-B

Miles 0   2.4

Washington, D.C. Eastern Region

This index helps you "spot" where approved accommodations and restaurants are located on the corresponding detailed maps. Lodging rate ranges are for comparison only and show the property's high season; rates are per night, unless only weekly (W) rates are available. Restaurant rate range is for dinner, unless only lunch (L) is served. Turn to the listing page for more detailed rate information and consult display ads for special promotions.

Spotter/Map Page Number	OA	WASHINGTON (EASTERN REGION) - Lodgings	Diamond Rating	Rate Range High Season	Listing Page
1 / p. 416	AAA	Travelodge Gateway - see color ad p 420	◆◆	$110 SAVE	476
2 / p. 416		Kellogg Conference Hotel at Gallaudet University	◆◆	$119-$215	476
3 / p. 416		Channel Inn Hotel	◆◆	$155-$175	476
		SILVER SPRING, MD - Lodgings			
6 / p. 416		Hilton Washington DC/Silver Spring	◆◆◆	$129-$219	499
		SILVER SPRING, MD - Restaurants			
1 / p. 416		Mrs. K's Toll House	◆◆	$24-$46	499
2 / p. 416		Crisfield at Lee Plaza	◆◆	$12-$25	499
3 / p. 416		Cubano's	◆◆	$12-$19	499
4 / p. 416		Bombay Gaylord	◆◆	$5-$12	499
		GREENBELT, MD - Lodgings			
9 / p. 416		The Greenbelt Marriott	◆◆◆	$199	489
10 / p. 416		Residence Inn by Marriott-Greenbelt	◆◆◆	$129-$249	489
11 / p. 416		Courtyard by Marriott-Greenbelt	◆◆◆	$149-$159	489
12 / p. 416	AAA	Holiday Inn-Greenbelt-NASA Area - see color ad p 489	◆◆◆	$129-$159 SAVE	489
		GREENBELT, MD - Restaurant			
7 / p. 416	AAA	Royal Jade	◆◆	$7-$20	490
		COLLEGE PARK, MD - Lodgings			
15 / p. 416		Holiday Inn-College Park - see color ad p 484	◆◆◆	$89-$129	485
16 / p. 416		Hampton Inn-College Park	◆◆◆	$95-$199	485
17 / p. 416	AAA	Comfort Inn & Suites University Square - see color ad p 501	◆◆	$109-$129 SAVE	484
18 / p. 416	AAA	Best Western-College Park Inn & Fundome	◆◆	$79-$109 SAVE	484
19 / p. 416		Quality Inn & Suites-College Park	◆◆	$79-$189	485
		COLLEGE PARK, MD - Restaurants			
10 / p. 416		Hard Times Cafe	◆	$7-$10	485
11 / p. 416		94th Aero Squadron	◆◆	$11-$25	485
		LANHAM, MD - Lodgings			
22 / p. 416		Red Roof Inn-Lanham	◆◆	$63-$89	491
23 / p. 416	AAA	Days Inn-Lanham - see color ad p 491	◆◆	$69-$125 SAVE	491
		ADELPHI, MD - Lodgings			
26 / p. 416		University of Maryland University College Inn & Conference Center by Marrio	◆◆◆	$179-$219	477
		NEW CARROLLTON, MD - Lodgings			
29 / p. 416		Ramada Inn New Carrollton	◆◆	$89-$99	494
		LARGO, MD - Lodgings			
32 / p. 416	AAA	Doubletree Club Hotel Washington DC-Largo - see color ad p 428	◆◆	$69-$149 SAVE	492
33 / p. 416	AAA	Hampton Inn-Washington/I-95 - see color ad p 434	◆◆◆	$119 SAVE	492

Spotter/Map Page Number	OA	LANDOVER, MD - Lodgings	Diamond Rating	Rate Range High Season	Listing Page
36 / p. 416		Courtyard by Marriott-New Carrollton	▽▽ ▽▽ ▽▽	$109-$134	490
		LANDOVER HILLS, MD - Lodgings			
39 / p. 416		Comfort Inn-Landover Hills - see color ad p 490	▽▽ ▽▽	$85-$129	490
		CAMP SPRINGS, MD - Lodgings			
42 / p. 416	AAA	Days Inn-Camp Springs/Andrews AFB	▽▽ ▽▽	$59-$99 [SAVE]	483
43 / p. 416	AAA	Holiday Inn Express Camp Springs	▽▽ ▽▽	$99-$119 [SAVE]	483

DOWNTOWN WASHINGTON (See map and index starting on p. 390)

———— WHERE TO STAY ————

BEACON HOTEL & CORPORATE QUARTERS   *Book at aaa.com*   Phone: (202)296-2100   **21**

AAA SAVE	9/7-2/28	1P: $279-$379	2P: $279-$379	XP: $20	F13
▼▼▼	3/1-9/6	1P: $259-$359	2P: $259-$359	XP: $20	F13

Location: 17th St and Rhode Island Ave NW; just w of Scott Circle. 1615 Rhode Island Ave NW 20036. Fax: 202/331-0227. **Facility:** 199 units. 174 one-bedroom standard units, some with efficiencies. 25 one-bedroom suites ($500-$1200) with efficiencies. 9 stories, interior corridors. *Bath:* combo or shower only.
Small-scale Hotel **Parking:** valet. **Terms:** package plans. **Amenities:** CD players, dual phone lines, voice mail, irons, hair dryers. *Fee:* video games, high-speed Internet. *Some:* DVD players (fee). **Dining:** 6:30 am-11 pm, Sat & Sun from 7:30 am, cocktails. **Leisure Activities:** exercise room. **Guest Services:** valet laundry. **Business Services:** meeting rooms, business center. **Cards:** AX, CB, DC, DS, MC, VI. **Special Amenities: free newspaper and free room upgrade (subject to availability with advance reservations).** *(See color ad p 421)*

SOME UNITS

BEST WESTERN CAPITOL SKYLINE   Phone: (202)488-7500   **78**

AAA SAVE	3/1-6/30 & 9/6-11/17	1P: $139-$209	2P: $139-$209	XP: $10	F17
▼▼▼	7/1-9/5 & 11/18-2/28	1P: $79-$189	2P: $79-$189	XP: $10	F17

Location: I-395, exit S Capitol St; S Capitol St and I sts NW. 10 I St SW 20024. Fax: 202/488-0790. **Facility:** 203 units. 197 one-bedroom standard units. 6 one-bedroom suites ($189-$289). 7 stories, interior corridors.
Small-scale Hotel *Bath:* combo or shower only. **Parking:** on-site (fee). **Terms:** [AP], [BP] & [CP] meal plans available, package plans. **Amenities:** voice mail, irons, hair dryers. **Dining:** 6:30 am-10 pm, Sat & Sun from 7 am, cocktails. **Pool(s):** outdoor. **Leisure Activities:** limited exercise equipment. **Guest Services:** gift shop, valet and coin laundry. **Business Services:** meeting rooms. *Fee:* PC, fax. **Cards:** AX, DC, DS, MC, VI. **Special Amenities: free local telephone calls and free newspaper.** *(See color ad p 423)*

SOME UNITS

BEST WESTERN-NEW HAMPSHIRE SUITES HOTEL   *Book at aaa.com*   Phone: (202)457-0565   **41**

AAA SAVE	All Year [ECP]	1P: $179-$260	2P: $179-$260	XP: $10	F17

Location: Just ne of 22nd; between L and M sts NW. 1121 New Hampshire Ave NW 20037. Fax: 202/331-9421. **Facility:** 76 units. 68 one-bedroom standard units. 8 one-bedroom suites. 8 stories, interior corridors. *Bath:* combo or shower only. **Parking:** on-site (fee) and valet. **Terms:** cancellation fee imposed, small pets only
Small-scale Hotel (1st floor units). **Amenities:** voice mail, irons, hair dryers. **Guest Services:** valet and coin laundry. **Business Services:** meeting rooms, fax (fee). **Cards:** AX, DC, DS, MC, VI. **Special Amenities: free expanded continental breakfast and free local telephone calls.** *(See color ad p 423)*

SOME UNITS

CAPITAL HILTON   Phone: (202)393-1000   **50**

▼▼▼▼	All Year	1P: $99-$349	2P: $129-$379	XP: $30	F18

Location: 16th and K sts NW. 1001 16th St NW 20009. Fax: 202/639-5784. **Facility:** 544 units. 531 one-bedroom standard units. 12 one- and 1 two-bedroom suites, some with whirlpools. 12 stories, interior corridors.
Large-scale Hotel **Parking:** valet. **Amenities:** dual phone lines, voice mail, honor bars, irons, hair dryers. *Fee:* video games, high-speed Internet. *Some:* CD players. **Leisure Activities:** steamrooms. *Fee:* massage, aromatherapy, facials, skin care. **Guest Services:** gift shop, valet laundry. **Business Services:** conference facilities, business center. **Cards:** AX, CB, DC, DS, JC, MC, VI. **(See color ad p 426)**

SOME UNITS

CAPITOL HILL SUITES   *Book at aaa.com*   Phone: (202)543-6000   **74**

AAA SAVE	3/1-7/8 & 9/7-12/31 [CP]	1P: $139-$219	2P: $139-$219	XP: $20	F
▼▼▼	7/9-9/6 & 1/1-2/28 [CP]	1P: $125-$185	2P: $125-$185	XP: $20	F

Location: 2 blks from Capitol grounds; at 2nd and C sts SE. Located in a residential area. 200 C St SE 20003. Fax: 202/547-2608. **Facility:** 152 units. 121 one-bedroom standard units. 31 one-bedroom suites. 5 stories,
Small-scale Hotel interior corridors. *Bath:* combo or shower only. **Parking:** valet. **Terms:** cancellation fee imposed. **Amenities:** dual phone lines, voice mail, irons, hair dryers. **Guest Services:** valet and coin laundry. **Business Services:** meeting rooms, fax (fee). **Cards:** AX, CB, DC, DS, JC, MC, VI. *(See color ad p 425)*

SOME UNITS

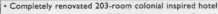

(See map and index starting on p. 390)

THE CHURCHILL HOTEL   *Book at aaa.com*   Phone: (202)797-2000   **4**

AAA SAVE   3/1-7/1 & 9/12-12/31   1P: $249-$339   2P: $249-$339   XP: $20   F16
▽▽▽▽   7/2-9/11 & 1/1-2/28   1P: $199-$259   2P: $199-$259   XP: $20   F16

Small-scale Hotel   **Location:** Just n of Dupont Circle. 1914 Connecticut Ave NW 20009. Fax: 202/328-1984. **Facility:** 144 units. 106 one-bedroom standard units. 38 one-bedroom suites. 9 stories, interior corridors. *Bath:* combo or shower only. **Parking:** valet. **Terms:** cancellation fee imposed. **Amenities:** video games (fee), voice mail, irons, hair dryers. *Some:* dual phone lines. **Dining:** 6:30 am-10:30 pm, cocktails. **Leisure Activities:** limited exercise equipment. **Guest Services:** valet laundry. **Business Services:** meeting rooms, fax. **Cards:** AX, DC, DS, MC, VI.
(See color ad p 427)

SOME UNITS

[⊨] [☼] [📶] [📹] [DATA PORT] / [⊠] [🔒] [🖥] /

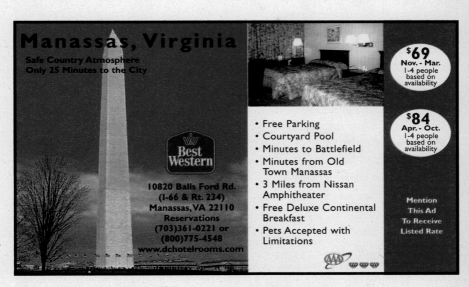

(See map and index starting on p. 390)

COMFORT INN CONVENTION CENTER   *Book at aaa.com*   Phone: (202)682-5300   **27**
All Year   1P: $116-$179   2P: $116-$179   XP: $10   F12
Location: Jct of 13th and M sts NW. 1201 13th St NW 20005. Fax: 202/371-9624. **Facility:** 100 one-bedroom
~Small-scale Hotel   standard units. 9 stories, interior corridors. *Bath:* combo or shower only. **Parking:** valet. **Terms:** 2 night
minimum stay - seasonal, 7 day cancellation notice. **Amenities:** high-speed Internet, voice mail, irons, hair
dryers. **Leisure Activities:** limited exercise equipment. **Guest Services:** valet and coin laundry. **Business Services:** meeting
rooms, PC, fax (fee). **Cards:** AX, CB, DC, DS, JC, MC, VI. *(See color ad below)*

SOME UNITS

COURTYARD BY MARRIOTT-CONVENTION CENTER   *Book at aaa.com*   Phone: 202/638-4600   **65**
All Year   1P: $144-$234   2P: $154-$244   XP: $10   F18
Location: At 9th and F sts NW. Located in Penn Quarter area, near MCI Center. 900 F St NW 20004.
Small-scale Hotel   Fax: 202/638-4601. **Facility:** 188 units. 179 one-bedroom standard units, some with whirlpools. 9 one-
bedroom suites. 10 stories, interior corridors. *Bath:* combo or shower only. **Parking:** valet.
Terms: cancellation fee imposed. **Amenities:** high-speed Internet, dual phone lines, voice mail, irons, hair dryers. **Pool(s):**
small heated indoor. **Leisure Activities:** whirlpool, exercise room. **Guest Services:** valet and coin laundry. **Business Services:**
meeting rooms, fax (fee). **Cards:** AX, DC, DS, MC, VI.

SOME UNITS

COURTYARD BY MARRIOTT-EMBASSY ROW   *Book at aaa.com*   Phone: 202/293-8000   **20**
3/1-6/28 & 9/7-11/22   1P: $129-$229   2P: $129-$229
6/29-9/6 & 11/23-2/28   1P: $109-$179   2P: $109-$179
Location: 16th and Rhode Island Ave NW, at Scott Circle. 1600 Rhode Island Ave NW 20036. Fax: 202/293-0085.
Facility: 156 units., 146 one-bedroom standard units, some with whirlpools. 10 one-bedroom suites. 8
Small-scale Hotel   stories, interior corridors. *Bath:* combo or shower only. **Parking:** valet. **Terms:** 30 day cancellation notice-
fee imposed, package plans. **Amenities:** video games (fee), high-speed Internet, dual phone lines, voice
mail, safes, irons, hair dryers. *Some:* CD players. **Dining:** 6:30 am-10 & 5:30-9:30 pm, Sat & Sun 7 am-11 & 5:30-9:30 pm,
cocktails. **Pool(s):** small heated indoor. **Leisure Activities:** whirlpool, exercise room. **Guest Services:** valet and coin laundry.
Business Services: meeting rooms, fax (fee). **Cards:** AX, DC, DS, MC, VI. **Special Amenities:** free newspaper.

SOME UNITS

(See map and index starting on p. 390)

COURTYARD BY MARRIOTT-NORTHWEST   *Book at aaa.com*   **Phone:** (202)332-9300   **5**
▼▼▼▼ All Year   1P: $89-$279   2P: $89-$279
Location: Just n of Dupont Circle. 1900 Connecticut Ave NW 20009. **Fax:** 202/328-7039. **Facility:** 147 units. 145
Small-scale Hotel   one-bedroom standard units. 2 one-bedroom suites, some with whirlpools. 9 stories, interior corridors. *Bath:*
combo or shower only. **Parking:** on-site (fee) and valet. **Terms:** cancellation fee imposed. **Amenities:** high-
speed Internet, voice mail, safes, irons, hair dryers. **Pool(s):** outdoor. **Leisure Activities:** exercise room. **Guest Services:** valet
and coin laundry. **Business Services:** meeting rooms, business center. **Cards:** AX, CB, DC, JC, MC, VI.   SOME UNITS

DOUBLETREE GUEST SUITES, WASHINGTON DC   *Book at aaa.com*   **Phone:** (202)785-2000   **60**
▼▼▼▼ All Year   1P: $109-$279   2P: $109-$279   XP: $20   F
Location: Just sw at Washington Circle. 801 New Hampshire Ave NW 20037. **Fax:** 202/785-9485. **Facility:** 105
Small-scale Hotel   units. 103 one- and 2 two-bedroom suites with efficiencies. 10 stories, interior corridors. *Bath:* combo or
shower only. **Parking:** valet. **Terms:** cancellation fee imposed, package plans, pets ($20 extra charge, in
designated units). **Amenities:** video games (fee), dual phone lines, voice mail, irons, hair dryers. **Pool(s):** outdoor. **Guest
Services:** valet and coin laundry. **Business Services:** fax (fee). **Cards:** AX, DC, DS, MC, VI.   SOME UNITS

(See map and index starting on p. 390)

THE DUPONT AT THE CIRCLE

Phone: (202)332-5251   **7**

[AAA] [SAVE]

Historic Bed
& Breakfast

All Year [ECP]   1P: $140-$300   2P: $140-$300   XP: $20
Location: Just n of Dupont Circle. 1604 19th St NW 20009. Fax: 202/332-3244. **Facility:** These restored 1885 Victorian town homes are furnished with antiques and reproductions. Smoke free premises. 8 one-bedroom standard units, some with efficiencies and/or whirlpools. 3 stories (no elevator), interior corridors. **Parking:** on-site (fee). **Terms:** office hours 10 am-6 pm, 2 night minimum stay - weekends, age restrictions may apply, 7 day cancellation notice-fee imposed. **Amenities:** video library, voice mail, hair dryers. *Some:* CD players. **Business Services:** fax. **Cards:** AX, CB, DC, DS, MC, VI. **Special Amenities:** free expanded continental breakfast.

SOME UNITS

[S/D] [T↑] [🖤] [✕] [🎞] [DATA PORT] / [TV] [VCR] [▣] [▥] [▣] /

EMBASSY SUITES HOTEL-WASHINGTON
DC-DOWNTOWN   *Book at aaa.com*

Phone: (202)857-3388   **23**

[AAA]

Large-scale Hotel

All Year [BP]   1P: $119-$349   2P: $129-$359   XP: $20   F17
Location: Between M and N sts NW. 1250 22nd St NW 20037. Fax: 202/293-3173. **Facility:** 318 units. 316 one- and 2 two-bedroom suites, some with whirlpools. 9 stories, interior corridors. *Bath:* combo or shower only. **Parking:** on-site (fee). **Terms:** check-in 4 pm, package plans. **Amenities:** video games (fee), dual phone lines, voice mail, irons, hair dryers. *Some:* safes. **Pool(s):** heated indoor. **Leisure Activities:** sauna, whirlpool, exercise room. *Fee:* game room. **Guest Services:** gift shop, complimentary evening beverages, valet and coin laundry. **Business Services:** conference facilities, business center. **Cards:** AX, CB, DC, DS, JC, MC, VI.

SOME UNITS

[ASK] [T↑] [Y] [🐾] [✏] [🏊] [✕] [🎞] [DATA PORT] [▣] [▥] [▣] / [✕] /

THE FAIRMONT WASHINGTON, DC   *Book at aaa.com*

Phone: (202)429-2400   **29**

[AAA]

Large-scale Hotel

11/18-2/28	1P: $169-$529	2P: $169-$529	XP: $30	F17
9/6-11/17	1P: $169-$499	2P: $169-$499	XP: $30	F17
3/1-6/23	1P: $149-$429	2P: $149-$429	XP: $30	F17
6/24-9/5	1P: $149-$379	2P: $149-$379	XP: $30	F17

Location: 24th and M sts NW. Located in the West End. 2401 M St NW 20037. Fax: 202/457-5010. **Facility:** This luxury hotel, in the West End near Georgetown, offers spacious, well-appointed guest rooms and suites with ample work space. 415 units. 396 one-bedroom standard units. 19 one-bedroom suites, some with whirlpools. 10 stories, interior corridors. *Bath:* combo or shower only. **Parking:** valet. **Terms:** check-in 4 pm, 7 day cancellation notice-fee imposed, package plans. **Amenities:** video library, CD players, dual phone lines, voice mail, safes, honor bars, irons, hair dryers. *Fee:* video games, high-speed Internet. *Some:* DVD players. **Dining:** The Bistro, see separate listing. **Pool(s):** lap. **Leisure Activities:** saunas, whirlpool, steamroom. *Fee:* massage. **Guest Services:** gift shop, valet laundry, area transportation (fee). *Fee:* tanning facility. **Business Services:** conference facilities, business center. **Cards:** AX, DC, DS, JC, MC.

SOME UNITS

[ASK] [S/D] [↔] [🛏] [T↑] [24↑] [↑] [🛌M] [✏] [🏊] [🐾] [✕] [🎞] [DATA PORT] [▣] / [✕] [VCR]
      FEE   FEE

FOUR POINTS SHERATON WASHINGTON DC
DOWNTOWN   *Book at aaa.com*

Phone: (202)289-7600   **47**

[AAA] [SAVE]

Large-scale Hotel

11/13-2/28	1P: $244-$264	2P: $244-$264	XP: $20	F
3/1-11/12	1P: $239-$259	2P: $239-$259	XP: $20	F

Location: 12th and K sts NW. Located near the Convention Center. 1201 K St NW 20005. Fax: 202/349-2215. **Facility:** 265 units. 263 one-bedroom standard units. 2 one-bedroom suites ($405-$450) with whirlpools. 11 stories, interior corridors. *Bath:* combo or shower only. **Parking:** valet. **Amenities:** high-speed Internet, dual phone lines, voice mail, safes, honor bars, irons, hair dryers. *Some:* CD players, fax. **Dining:** Corduroy, see separate listing. **Pool(s):** small heated indoor. **Leisure Activities:** exercise room. **Guest Services:** gift shop, valet and coin laundry. **Business Services:** conference facilities, business center. **Cards:** AX, DC, DS, MC, VI. **Special Amenities:** free newspaper and preferred room (subject to availability with advance reservations). *(See color ad p 430)*

SOME UNITS

[S/D] [T↑] [🏊] [🐾] [🎞] [DATA PORT] [▣] / [✕] [▣] [▥] /

FOUR SEASONS HOTEL WASHINGTON D.C.   *Book at aaa.com*

Phone: (202)342-0444   **36**

[AAA] [SAVE]

Large-scale Hotel

3/1-4/30	1P: $595-$1550	2P: $645-$1550	
5/1-2/28	1P: $450-$1550	2P: $500-$1550	

Location: Located in Georgetown. 2800 Pennsylvania Ave NW 20007. Fax: 202/342-1673. **Facility:** This service-oriented hotel in the heart of bustling Georgetown has an ambience of understated elegance. 212 units. 152 one-bedroom standard units. 60 one-bedroom suites ($1550-$5000). 6 stories, interior corridors. *Bath:* combo or shower only. **Parking:** valet. **Terms:** cancellation fee imposed, package plans, small pets only. **Amenities:** CD players, dual phone lines, voice mail, safes, honor bars, irons, hair dryers. *Fee:* video games, high-speed Internet. *Some:* DVD players, fax. **Dining:** 11 am-1 am, cocktails, also, Seasons, see separate listing, entertainment. **Pool(s):** lap. **Leisure Activities:** saunas, whirlpool, steamrooms, aerobic instruction, jogging, spa. **Guest Services:** gift shop, valet laundry, area transportation-limo within the district. *Fee:* personal trainer. **Business Services:** conference facilities, business center. **Cards:** AX, DC, DS, JC, MC, VI. **Special Amenities:** free local telephone calls and free newspaper.

SOME UNITS

[🛏] [T↑] [24↑] [Y] [↑] [✏] [🏊] [🐾] [🛁] [✕] [🎞] [DATA PORT] [▣] / [✕] [VCR] [▣] /

THE GEORGETOWN INN   *Book at aaa.com*

Phone: (202)333-8900   **19**

[AAA] [SAVE]

Small-scale Hotel

All Year   1P: $139-$329   2P: $149-$339   XP: $20   F17
Location: Wisconsin Ave and N St NW, just n of M St NW. Located in Georgetown. 1310 Wisconsin Ave NW 20007. Fax: 202/333-8308. **Facility:** 96 units. 86 one-bedroom standard units. 10 one-bedroom suites. 6 stories, interior corridors. *Bath:* combo or shower only. **Parking:** valet. **Terms:** cancellation fee imposed, package plans. **Amenities:** voice mail, irons, hair dryers. *Fee:* video games, high-speed Internet. **Dining:** 6:30 am-11 pm, Fri & Sat-midnight, Sun-10 pm, cocktails. **Leisure Activities:** exercise room. **Guest Services:** valet laundry. **Business Services:** meeting rooms, business center. **Cards:** AX, DC, DS, MC, VI. **Special Amenities:** free newspaper. *(See color ad p 431)*

SOME UNITS

[T↑] [Y] [✏] [🐾] [🎞] [DATA PORT] [▣] / [✕] [▣] /

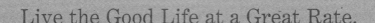

(See map and index starting on p. 390)

GEORGETOWN SUITES-HARBOUR BUILDING   *Book at aaa.com*   Phone: (202)298-1600   **48**
All Year [CP]   1P: $155-$255   2P: $185-$285   XP: $15   F12
Small-scale Hotel   **Location:** Jct K and 29th sts. Located in Georgetown. 1000 29th St NW 20007. Fax: 202/333-2019. **Facility:** 78 units. 42 one-bedroom standard units with efficiencies. 36 one-bedroom suites with kitchens. 6 stories, interior corridors. **Parking:** on-site (fee). **Amenities:** CD players, voice mail, irons, hair dryers. **Leisure Activities:** exercise room. **Guest Services:** valet and coin laundry. **Business Services:** meeting rooms, business center. **Cards:** AX, DC, DS, MC, VI. *(See color ad p 430)*

SOME UNITS

ASK SD TI+ 🅿️ 📷 DATA PORT 🔲 🔲 🔲 / ✕ /

GEORGETOWN UNIVERSITY CONFERENCE HOTEL   *Book at aaa.com*   Phone: (202)687-3200   **6**
All Year   1P: $129-$229
Small-scale Hotel   **Location:** On the campus of Georgetown University; entrance 1, follow signs for the conference center. 3800 Reservoir Rd NW 20057. Fax: 202/687-3297. **Facility:** 146 one-bedroom standard units. 5 stories, interior corridors. **Parking:** on-site (fee). **Terms:** cancellation fee imposed, [AP] & [BP] meal plans available. **Amenities:** high-speed Internet (fee), dual phone lines, voice mail, irons, hair dryers. **Leisure Activities:** limited exercise equipment. **Guest Services:** sundries, valet and coin laundry. **Business Services:** conference facilities, business center. **Cards:** AX, CB, DC, DS, JC, MC, VI. Affiliated with Marriott Hotels, Resorts and Suites.

SOME UNITS

TI 🅿️ 📷 DATA PORT 🔲 / ✕ 🔲 🔲 /

(See map and index starting on p. 390)

GRAND HYATT WASHINGTON AT WASHINGTON CENTER   *Book at aaa.com*

Phone: (202)582-1234   **61**

All Year   1P: $149-$340   2P: $149-$340

Large-scale Hotel   **Location:** Jct 11th and H St NW. 1000 H St NW 20001. Fax: 202/637-4781. **Facility:** 888 units. 844 one-bedroom standard units. 44 one-bedroom suites, some with whirlpools. 13 stories, interior corridors. *Bath:* combo or shower only. **Parking:** on-site (fee) and valet. **Terms:** 3 day cancellation notice-fee imposed, small pets only. **Amenities:** high-speed Internet, voice mail, honor bars, irons, hair dryers. *Some:* DVD players, dual phone lines, fax, safes. **Dining:** 4 restaurants, 6:30 am-10:30 pm, cocktails. **Pool(s):** heated indoor. **Leisure Activities:** steamrooms. *Fee:* saunas, whirlpool, aerobic instruction, massage. **Guest Services:** gift shop, valet laundry. **Business Services:** conference facilities, business center. **Cards:** AX, CB, DC, DS, JC, MC, VI. *(See color ad p 433)*

SOME UNITS

HAMILTON CROWNE PLAZA HOTEL WASHINGTON   *Book at aaa.com*

Phone: (202)682-0111   **51**

9/6-11/18	1P: $124-$324	2P: $124-$324
3/1-6/30	1P: $124-$284	2P: $124-$284
7/1-9/5 & 11/19-2/28	1P: $94-$194	2P: $94-$194

Large-scale Hotel   **Location:** 14th and K sts NW. Located opposite Franklin Park. 1001 14th St NW 20005. Fax: 202/682-9525. **Facility:** 318 units. 301 one-bedroom standard units. 17 one-bedroom suites ($300-$650). 13 stories, interior corridors. *Bath:* combo or shower only. **Parking:** valet. **Terms:** cancellation fee imposed, [AP], [BP], [CP], [ECP] & [MAP] meal plans available, package plans, small pets only. **Amenities:** CD players, voice mail, safes (fee), irons, hair dryers. *Some:* high-speed Internet (fee), fax. **Dining:** 14K, see separate listing. **Leisure Activities:** sauna, exercise room. **Guest Services:** gift shop, valet laundry. **Business Services:** conference facilities, business center. **Cards:** AX, CB, DC, DS, JC, MC, VI. *(See color ad below)*

SOME UNITS

HAMPTON INN WASHINGTON DC CONVENTION CENTER

Phone: 202/842-2500

3/1-6/30 & 9/1-11/18 [ECP]	1P: $169-$199	2P: $179-$209	XP: $10	F18
11/19-2/28 [ECP]	1P: $154-$184	2P: $164-$194	XP: $10	F18
7/1-8/31 [ECP]	1P: $149-$179	2P: $159-$189	XP: $10	F18

Small-scale Hotel   Too new to rate, opening scheduled for January 2005. **Location:** I-395, exit Massachusetts Ave/2nd St, bear right on 2nd St, left on Massachusetts Ave, then right on 6th St. 599 Massachusetts Ave NW 20001. Fax: 202/842-4100. **Amenities:** 228 units, coffeemakers, microwaves, refrigerators, pool. **Terms:** cancellation fee imposed. **Cards:** AX, CB, DC, DS, MC, VI.

THE HAY-ADAMS   *Book at aaa.com*

Phone: (202)638-6600   **58**

All Year   1P: $550-$5500   2P: $550-$5500   XP: $30   F17

Classic Historic Small-scale Hotel   **Location:** 16th and H sts NW, just n of the White House. 16th & H Sts NW 20006. Fax: 202/638-2716. **Facility:** Less than 2 blocks from the McPherson Square Metro Station, this 1927 hotel offers several rooms with a view of the White House. 145 units. 131 one-bedroom standard units. 14 one-bedroom suites ($1300-$5500). 8 stories, interior corridors. *Bath:* combo or shower only. **Parking:** valet. **Terms:** cancellation fee imposed, package plans, small pets only. **Amenities:** CD players, high-speed Internet, dual phone lines, voice mail, safes, honor bars, irons, hair dryers. *Some:* DVD players (fee). **Guest Services:** valet laundry, area transportation. **Business Services:** meeting rooms, business center. **Cards:** AX, CB, DC, DS, JC, MC, VI.

SOME UNITS

HENLEY PARK HOTEL   *Book at aaa.com*

Phone: (202)638-5200   **43**

3/1-6/15 & 9/9-11/22	1P: $289	2P: $309	XP: $20	F17
6/16-9/8 & 11/23-2/28	1P: $239	2P: $259	XP: $20	F17

Historic Small-scale Hotel   **Location:** 10th St and Massachusetts Ave NW. Located near the convention center. 926 Massachusetts Ave NW 20001. Fax: 202/638-6740. **Facility:** This Tudor-style building dating from 1918 offers tastefully furnished accommodations, some compact. 96 units. 91 one-bedroom standard units. 5 one-bedroom suites ($329). 9 stories, interior corridors. **Parking:** valet. **Terms:** cancellation fee imposed. **Amenities:** dual phone lines, voice mail, safes, honor bars, irons, hair dryers. **Dining:** Coeur de Lion, see separate listing. **Guest Services:** valet laundry, area transportation. **Business Services:** meeting rooms, fax (fee). **Cards:** AX, DC, DS, JC, MC, VI.

SOME UNITS

GRAND HYATT WASHINGTON

HYATT ARLINGTON

HYATT REGENCY BETHESDA

HYATT REGENCY CRYSTAL CITY

HYATT DULLES

HYATT REGENCY RESTON

HYATT REGENCY WASHINGTON
ON CAPITOL HILL

We're right where
YOU WANT TO BE.

SAVE IN STYLE.
Enjoy deluxe accommodations in prime
Washington DC area locations with significant
savings exclusively for AAA members. Simply
request the AAA member's rate and present
your card at check-in. For reservations,
call 800 532 1496 or visit hyatt.com.
Feel the Hyatt Touch.

HYATT
HOTELS & RESORTS ®

Preferred rates are valid now through 2/28/06 at participating Hyatt hotels in the U.S. and Canada. AAA members will receive the special AAA rate based on availability. Hyatt Hotels and Resorts encompass hotels and resorts managed, franchised or operated by two separate companies–Hyatt Corporation and its affiliates and affiliates of Hyatt International Corporation. ©2005-06 Hyatt Corp.

(See map and index starting on p. 390)

HILTON GARDEN INN WASHINGTON DC FRANKLIN SQUARE *Book at aaa.com*

Phone: (202)783-7800 **56**

All Year 1P: $109-$259 2P: $109-$259 XP: $20 F
Location: Between H and I sts NW. 815 14th St NW 20005. Fax: 202/783-7801. **Facility:** 300 one-bedroom standard units. 14 stories, interior corridors. *Bath:* combo or shower only. **Parking:** valet. **Terms:** cancellation fee imposed, package plans. **Amenities:** video games (fee), high-speed Internet, dual phone lines, voice mail, irons, hair dryers. **Dining:** 6:30 am-10:30 & 5-10 pm, cocktails. **Pool(s):** small heated indoor. **Leisure Activities:** exercise room. **Guest Services:** sundries, valet and coin laundry. **Business Services:** meeting rooms, business center. **Cards:** AX, CB, DC, DS, JC, MC, VI. **Special Amenities:** free newspaper and preferred room (subject to availability with advance reservations).

Small-scale Hotel

SOME UNITS

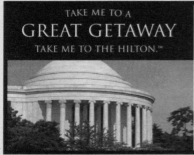

(See map and index starting on p. 390)

HILTON WASHINGTON   *Book at aaa.com*   **Phone:** (202)483-3000   **3**
ᵥᵥᵥᵥ   All Year   1P: $99-$349   2P: $119-$369   XP: $20   F18
Location: Just n of Dupont Circle at T St NW. 1919 Connecticut Ave NW 20009. Fax: 202/232-0438. **Facility:** 1119
Large-scale Hotel   units. 1078 one-bedroom standard units. 41 one-bedroom suites, some with whirlpools. 10 stories, interior
corridors. *Bath:* combo or shower only. **Parking:** on-site (fee). **Terms:** cancellation fee imposed, small pets
only ($10 fee). **Amenities:** dual phone lines, voice mail, irons, hair dryers. **Fee:** video games, high-speed Internet. *Some:* DVD
players. **Pool(s):** heated outdoor, wading. **Leisure Activities:** steamrooms. *Fee:* 3 lighted tennis courts, massage. **Guest
Services:** gift shop, valet laundry. **Business Services:** conference facilities, business center. **Cards:** AX, CB, DC, DS, JC,
MC, VI. *(See color ad p 426)*

SOME UNITS

[icons] FEE FEE [icons] FEE [icons] / [icons] / FEE

HILTON WASHINGTON EMBASSY ROW   *Book at aaa.com*   **Phone:** (202)265-1600   **9**
ᴬᴬᴬ SAVE   3/1-6/30 & 9/11-2/28   1P: $129-$299   2P: $149-$319   XP: $20   F12
7/1-9/10   1P: $109-$279   2P: $129-$299   XP: $20   F12
ᵥᵥᵥᵥ ᵥ   **Location:** Just nw of Dupont Circle. 2015 Massachusetts Ave NW 20036. Fax: 202/328-7526. **Facility:** 193 units.
190 one-bedroom standard units. 3 one-bedroom suites ($179-$349). 9 stories, interior corridors. *Bath:*
Large-scale Hotel   combo or shower only. **Parking:** valet. **Terms:** cancellation fee imposed, [BP] & [CP] meal plans available.
Amenities: high-speed Internet (fee), dual phone lines, voice mail, safes, irons, hair dryers. **Dining:** 6:30-10
am, 11:30-2:30 & 5-11 pm, Sat & Sun 7-11 am, 11:30-2:30 & 5-11 pm, cocktails. **Pool(s):** outdoor. **Leisure Activities:** exercise
room. **Guest Services:** valet laundry. **Business Services:** conference facilities, business center. **Cards:** AX, CB, DC, DS, JC,
MC, VI. **Special Amenities:** free newspaper. *(See color ad p 434)*

SOME UNITS

[icons] / [icons] /

HOLIDAY INN CAPITOL   *Book at aaa.com*   **Phone:** (202)479-4000   **75**
ᴬᴬᴬ SAVE   All Year   1P: $129-$289   2P: $129-$289
Location: Corner of 6th and C sts SW. 550 C St SW 20024. Fax: 202/479-4353. **Facility:** 529 units. 516 one-
ᵥᵥᵥᵥ   bedroom standard units. 13 one-bedroom suites. 9 stories, interior corridors. *Bath:* combo or shower only.
Parking: on-site (fee). **Terms:** 2 night minimum stay - seasonal, cancellation fee imposed.
Large-scale Hotel   **Amenities:** video games (fee), dual phone lines, voice mail, irons, hair dryers. **Dining:** 2 restaurants, 6 am-
10 pm, cocktails. **Pool(s):** outdoor. **Leisure Activities:** exercise room. **Guest Services:** gift shop, valet and
coin laundry. **Business Services:** conference facilities, business center. **Cards:** AX, CB, DC, DS, JC, MC, VI.
(See color ad p 436)

SOME UNITS

[icons] / [icons] /

(See map and index starting on p. 390)

HOLIDAY INN-CENTRAL   *Book at aaa.com*   Phone: (202)483-2000   🔢14

🔺 (SAVE)   3/1-7/3 & 9/5-11/6   1P: $189-$209   2P: $189-$209
             7/4-9/4 & 11/7-2/28   1P: $189-$199   2P: $189-$199
🔻🔻🔻   **Location:** Just e of Scott Circle. 1501 Rhode Island Ave NW 20005. Fax: 202/797-1078. **Facility:** 212 one-
Large-scale Hotel   bedroom standard units. 10 stories, interior corridors. *Bath:* combo or shower only. **Parking:** on-site (fee).
Terms: package plans, small pets only ($100 fee, with prior approval). **Amenities:** video games (fee), dual
phone lines, voice mail, irons, hair dryers. **Dining:** 6:30 am-2 & 5-10 pm, cocktails. **Pool(s):** outdoor.
Leisure Activities: exercise room. *Fee:* game room. **Guest Services:** gift shop, valet and coin laundry. **Business Services:**
meeting rooms. *Fee:* PC, fax. **Cards:** AX, CB, DC, DS, JC, MC, VI. **Special Amenities:** free newspaper and free room
upgrade (subject to availability with advance reservations). *(See color ad p 435)*

SOME UNITS
[S/D] [icons] FEE

HOLIDAY INN DOWNTOWN   *Book at aaa.com*   Phone: (202)737-1200   🔢32

🔺 (SAVE)   3/1-6/30 & 9/1-11/17   1P: $189-$229   2P: $189-$229   XP: $15   F18
             7/1-8/31   1P: $169-$199   2P: $169-$199   XP: $15   F18
🔻🔻🔻   11/18-2/28   1P: $159-$189   2P: $159-$189   XP: $15   F18
             Location: Massachusetts Ave, at Thomas Circle NW. 1155 14th St NW 20005. Fax: 202/783-5733. **Facility:** 212
Large-scale Hotel   units. 211 one-bedroom standard units. 1 one-bedroom suite. 13 stories, interior corridors. *Bath:* combo or
shower only. **Parking:** valet. **Terms:** cancellation fee imposed, small pets only ($45 fee). **Amenities:** dual
phone lines, voice mail, irons, hair dryers. **Dining:** 6:30 am-2 & 5-10 pm, cocktails. **Pool(s):** outdoor. **Leisure
Activities:** exercise room. **Guest Services:** valet and coin laundry. **Business Services:** meeting rooms, business center.
Cards: AX, CB, DC, DS, JC, MC, VI. **Special Amenities:** free newspaper and early check-in/late check-out.
(See color ad p 434)

SOME UNITS
[S/D] [icons] FEE   [icons] FEE FEE

HOLIDAY INN GEORGETOWN   *Book at aaa.com*   Phone: (202)338-4600   🔢1

🔺   All Year   1P: $99-$199   2P: $99-$199   XP: $10   F18
🔻🔻🔻   **Location:** In upper Georgetown area. 2101 Wisconsin Ave NW 20007. Fax: 202/333-6113. **Facility:** 296 units. 292
Large-scale Hotel   one-bedroom standard units. 4 one-bedroom suites. 7 stories, interior corridors. *Bath:* combo or shower
only. **Parking:** on-site (fee). **Amenities:** video games (fee), voice mail, irons, hair dryers. **Pool(s):** outdoor.
Leisure Activities: exercise room. **Guest Services:** gift shop, valet and coin laundry, area transportation. **Business Services:**
meeting rooms, business center. **Cards:** AX, DC, DS, JC, MC, VI. *(See color ad p 437)*

SOME UNITS
(ASK) [S/D] [icons] FEE FEE

HOLIDAY INN WASHINGTON DC ON THE HILL   *Book at aaa.com*   Phone: 202/638-1616   🔢72

🔺 (SAVE)   3/1-5/21 & 11/26-2/28   1P: $139-$229   2P: $139-$229   XP: $20
             9/7-11/25   1P: $129-$219   2P: $129-$219   XP: $20
🔻🔻🔻   5/22-9/6   1P: $109-$189   2P: $109-$189   XP: $20
             Location: On Capitol Hill. 415 New Jersey Ave NW 20001. Fax: 202/638-0707. **Facility:** 343 one-bedroom
Large-scale Hotel   standard units. 10 stories, interior corridors. *Bath:* combo or shower only. **Parking:** on-site (fee). **Terms:** 3
day cancellation notice-fee imposed, package plans. **Amenities:** video games (fee), high-speed Internet,
dual phone lines, voice mail, irons, hair dryers. *Some:* safes. **Dining:** 6 am-11 pm; seasonal sidewalk dining, cocktails. **Pool(s):**
outdoor. **Leisure Activities:** sun deck, exercise room. **Guest Services:** gift shop, valet and coin laundry. **Business Services:**
conference facilities, business center. **Cards:** AX, CB, DC, DS, MC, VI. **Special Amenities:** preferred room (subject to
availability with advance reservations). *(See color ad p 439)*

SOME UNITS
[icons] FEE FEE

**HOMEWOOD SUITES BY HILTON WASHINGTON
DC/THOMAS CIRCLE**   *Book at aaa.com*   Phone: (202)265-8000   🔢22

🔻🔺🔻   All Year   1P: $179-$229   2P: $179-$229   XP: $10   F17
             Location: Just nw of Thomas Circle, on service road. 1475 Massachusetts Ave NW 20005. Fax: 202/265-5810.
Small-scale Hotel   **Facility:** 175 one-bedroom suites with efficiencies. 8 stories, interior corridors. *Bath:* combo or shower only.
Parking: valet. **Terms:** check-in 4 pm, cancellation fee imposed. **Amenities:** video games (fee), high-speed
Internet, dual phone lines, voice mail, irons, hair dryers. **Leisure Activities:** exercise room. **Guest Services:** sundries,
complimentary evening beverages: Mon-Thurs, valet and coin laundry. **Business Services:** meeting rooms, business center.
Cards: AX, CB, DC, DS, MC, VI. *(See color ad below)*

SOME UNITS
(ASK) [S/D] [icons] [VCR] [icons] [DATA PORT] [icons] /[X]/

(See map and index starting on p. 390)

THE HOTEL GEORGE   Book at aaa.com

AAA SAVE

WWWW

Small-scale Hotel

Phone: (202)347-4200   68

3/1-6/23 & 9/6-2/28	1P: $169-$409	2P: $194-$434	XP: $25 F16
6/24-9/5	1P: $149-$409	2P: $174-$434	XP: $25 F16

Location: On Capitol Hill, just n of Capitol grounds. 15 E St NW 20001. Fax: 202/347-4213. **Facility:** 139 units. 138 one-bedroom standard units. 1 one-bedroom suite with whirlpool. 8 stories, interior corridors. *Bath:* combo or shower only. **Parking:** valet. **Terms:** cancellation fee imposed, package plans, pets ($50 deposit). **Amenities:** video games (fee), CD players, high-speed Internet, dual phone lines, voice mail, safes, honor bars, irons, hair dryers. *Some:* DVD players, fax. *Dining:* Bistro Bis, see separate listing. **Leisure Activities:** steamrooms, billiards, exercise room. **Guest Services:** valet laundry. **Business Services:** meeting rooms, fax. **Cards:** AX, CB, DC, DS, MC, VI. **Special Amenities:** free newspaper and early check-in/late check-out.

SOME UNITS

HOTEL HELIX   Book at aaa.com

AAA SAVE

WWWW

Small-scale Hotel

Phone: (202)462-9001   13

3/1-6/29 & 9/6-11/18	1P: $139-$309
6/30-9/5 & 11/19-2/28	1P: $119-$309

Location: Just e of Scott Circle. 1430 Rhode Island Ave NW 20005. Fax: 202/332-3519. **Facility:** 178 units. 160 one-bedroom standard units. 18 one-bedroom suites ($199-$650). 10 stories, interior corridors. *Bath:* combo or shower only. **Parking:** valet. **Terms:** cancellation fee imposed, package plans. **Amenities:** video games (fee), CD players, high-speed Internet, dual phone lines, voice mail, safes, honor bars, irons, hair dryers. *Dining:* 5 pm-10 pm, cocktails. **Leisure Activities:** exercise room. **Guest Services:** valet laundry. **Business Services:** meeting rooms, PC, fax (fee). **Cards:** AX, CB, DC, DS, MC, VI. *(See color ad p 422)*

SOME UNITS

HOTEL LOMBARDY   Book at aaa.com

WWW WWWW

Historic
Small-scale Hotel

Phone: 202/828-2600   54

Property failed to provide current rates

Location: Jct I St and Pennsylvania Ave NW. 2019 Pennsylvania Ave NW 20006. Fax: 202/872-0503. **Facility:** The historic building opened in 1927 as a private residence and was converted to a hotel in 1978. 132 units. 104 one-bedroom standard units. 28 one-bedroom suites. 10 stories, interior corridors. **Parking:** valet. **Amenities:** dual phone lines, voice mail, honor bars, irons, hair dryers. **Leisure Activities:** exercise room. **Guest Services:** valet laundry. **Business Services:** meeting rooms, fax (fee).

SOME UNITS

HOTEL MADERA   Book at aaa.com

AAA SAVE

WWWW

Small-scale Hotel

Phone: (202)296-7600   16

All Year	1P: $149-$349	2P: $149-$349	XP: $20 F16

Location: Between 20th and N sts NW. 1310 New Hampshire Ave NW 20036. Fax: 202/293-2476. **Facility:** 82 one-bedroom standard units. 10 stories, interior corridors. *Bath:* combo or shower only. **Parking:** valet. **Terms:** cancellation fee imposed, package plans, pets (with prior approval). **Amenities:** video games (fee), CD players, high-speed Internet, dual phone lines, voice mail, safes, honor bars, irons, hair dryers. *Some:* DVD players. *Dining:* Firefly, see separate listing. **Guest Services:** valet laundry. **Business Services:** meeting rooms, PC, fax (fee). **Cards:** AX, CB, DC, DS, MC, VI. **Special Amenities:** free newspaper and early check-in/late check-out. *(See color ad p 422)*

SOME UNITS

(See map and index starting on p. 390)

HOTEL MONACO WASHINGTON DC *Book at aaa.com* Phone: (202)628-7177 **66**

(AAA) (SAVE)

| | 3/1-6/29 & 9/6-2/28 | 1P: $169-$479 | 2P: $169-$479 | XP: $20 | F16 |
| | 6/30-9/5 | 1P: $149-$479 | 2P: $149-$479 | XP: $20 | F16 |

Historic
Large-scale Hotel

Location: Between 7th and 8th sts NW. Located opposite the MCI Center, in Penn Quarter area. 700 F St NW 20004. Fax: 202/628-7277. **Facility:** This boutique hotel, in the historic 1839 Tariff Building, has a sophisticated charm; colorful and luxurious rooms range from spacious to cozy. 181 units. 161 one-bedroom standard units, some with whirlpools. 20 one-bedroom suites ($349-$1500) with whirlpools. 4 stories, interior corridors. *Bath:* combo or shower only. **Parking:** valet. **Terms:** cancellation fee imposed, package plans. **Amenities:** video games (fee), CD players, high-speed Internet, dual phone lines, voice mail, safes, honor bars, irons, hair dryers. *Some:* DVD players. **Dining:** Poste—Modern Brasserie, see separate listing. **Leisure Activities:** pool privileges, exercise room. **Guest Services:** complimentary evening beverages, valet laundry. **Business Services:** meeting rooms, business center. **Cards:** AX, CB, DC, DS, MC, VI.

SOME UNITS

 /⊠/

HOTEL ROUGE *Book at aaa.com* Phone: (202)232-8000 **18**

(AAA) (SAVE)

| | 3/1-6/29 & 9/6-11/18 | 1P: $139-$309 | 2P: $139-$309 | XP: $20 | F16 |
| | 6/30-9/5 & 11/19-2/28 | 1P: $129-$309 | 2P: $129-$309 | XP: $20 | F16 |

Small-scale Hotel

Location: Just n of Scott Circle. 1315 16th St NW 20036. Fax: 202/667-9827. **Facility:** 137 one-bedroom standard units. 10 stories, interior corridors. *Bath:* combo or shower only. **Parking:** valet. **Terms:** cancellation fee imposed, package plans, pets (with prior approval). **Amenities:** video games (fee), CD players, high-speed Internet, dual phone lines, voice mail, safes, honor bars, irons, hair dryers. *Some:* DVD players. **Dining:** Bar Rouge, see separate listing. **Leisure Activities:** limited exercise equipment. **Guest Services:** valet laundry. **Business Services:** meeting rooms, PC, fax (fee). **Cards:** AX, CB, DC, DS, MC, VI. *(See color ad p 422)*

SOME UNITS

 /⊠ 🛏 🖼/

(See map and index starting on p. 390)

HOTEL WASHINGTON   *Book at aaa.com*   Phone: (202)638-5900 [63]
AAA SAVE   All Year   1P: $200-$325   2P: $200-$325   XP: $20   F12
             Location: 1 blk e of the White House and 15th St NW; 2 blks from Metro Center. 515 15th St NW
             20004. Fax: 202/638-4275. Facility: The upgraded bathrooms at this hotel dating from 1918 include
Historic   telephones as well as marble finishes. 344 units. 328 one-bedroom standard units. 16 one-bedroom suites.
Large-scale Hotel 10 stories, interior corridors. Bath: combo or shower only. Parking: on-site (fee). Terms: package plans,
small pets only ($25 extra charge). Amenities: video games (fee), voice mail, irons, hair dryers. Dining: 7
am-midnight; rooftop dining 5/1-10/31, cocktails. Leisure Activities: exercise room. Guest Services: gift
shop, valet laundry. Business Services: conference facilities, business center. Cards: AX, CB, DC, MC, VI.
Special Amenities: free newspaper and free room upgrade (subject to availability with advance reservations).
(See ad p 441)

SOME UNITS
[icons] / FEE

HYATT REGENCY WASHINGTON ON CAPITOL HILL   *Book at aaa.com*   Phone: (202)737-1234 [73]
AAA SAVE   All Year   1P: $129-$369   2P: $129-$394   XP: $25   F18
             Location: On Capitol Hill. 400 New Jersey Ave NW 20001. Fax: 202/737-5773. Facility: 834 units. 802 one-
             bedroom standard units. 32 one-bedroom suites. 11 stories, interior corridors. Bath: combo or shower only.
Large-scale Hotel Parking: valet. Terms: 3 day cancellation notice-fee imposed. Amenities: dual phone lines, voice mail,
irons, hair dryers. Some: CD players, safes. Dining: 6:30 am-11 pm, cocktails. Pool(s): heated indoor.
Leisure Activities: Fee: saunas, sun deck, massage. Guest Services: gift shop, valet laundry, airport
transportation (fee)-Baltimore-Washington & Washington Dulles Int'l airports. Business Services: conference facilities,
business center. Cards: AX, CB, DC, DS, JC, MC, VI. *(See color ad p 433)*

SOME UNITS
[icons] FEE [icons] FEE / [icons]

THE JEFFERSON, A LOEWS HOTEL   *Book at aaa.com*   Phone: 202/347-2200 [25]
AAA SAVE   All Year   1P: $195-$405   2P: $195-$405   XP: $35
             Location: 16th and M sts NW. 1200 16th St NW 20036. Fax: 202/331-7982. Facility: Beaux Arts-style
             architecture distinguishes this service-oriented hotel offering concierge and evening housekeeping services.
Small-scale Hotel 100 units. 69 one-bedroom standard units. 31 one-bedroom suites ($689-$3150), some with kitchens (no
utensils) and/or whirlpools. 8 stories, interior corridors. Bath: combo or shower only. Parking: valet.
Terms: 3 day cancellation notice-fee imposed, package plans. Amenities: CD players, dual phone lines,
voice mail, safes, honor bars, irons, hair dryers. Fee: video games, high-speed Internet. Dining: The Restaurant at The
Jefferson, see separate listing. Leisure Activities: exercise room. Guest Services: valet laundry. Business Services: meeting
rooms, fax. Cards: AX, CB, DC, DS, JC, MC, VI. *(See color ad p 441)*

SOME UNITS
[icons] / [icons] /

JURYS NORMANDY INN   *Book at aaa.com*   Phone: (202)483-1350 [2]
             3/1-6/30 & 9/8-11/17   1P: $89-$175   2P: $89-$185   XP: $10   F17
             11/18-2/28   1P: $79-$185   2P: $79-$185   XP: $10   F17
Small-scale Hotel 7/1-9/7   1P: $79-$175   2P: $79-$185   XP: $10   F17
             Location: Just w of Connecticut Ave. 2118 Wyoming Ave NW 20008. .Fax: 202/387-8241. Facility: 75 one-
bedroom standard units. 6 stories, interior corridors. Bath: combo or shower only. Parking: on-site (fee). Amenities: high-speed
Internet, voice mail, safes, irons, hair dryers. Leisure Activities: exercise room privileges. Guest Services: valet and coin
laundry. Business Services: fax (fee). Cards: AX, DC, DS, MC, VI.

SOME UNITS
[icons] / [icons]

JURYS WASHINGTON HOTEL   *Book at aaa.com*   Phone: (202)483-6000 [10]
             11/18-2/28   1P: $99-$290   2P: $99-$305   XP: $15   F17
             3/1-6/30 & 9/8-11/17   1P: $145-$275   2P: $145-$290   XP: $15   F17
Large-scale Hotel 7/1-9/7   1P: $99-$275   2P: $99-$290   XP: $15   F17
             Location: At Dupont Circle, Connecticut and Massachusetts aves NW. 1500 New Hampshire Ave NW 20036.
Fax: 202/328-3265. Facility: 314 units. 308 one-bedroom standard units. 6 one-bedroom suites. 8 stories, interior corridors.
Bath: combo or shower only. Parking: valet. Amenities: high-speed Internet, dual phone lines, voice mail, safes, honor bars,
irons, hair dryers. Leisure Activities: exercise room. Guest Services: valet laundry. Business Services: conference facilities,
business center. Cards: AX, DC, DS, MC, VI.

SOME UNITS
[icons] / [icons] FEE

J W MARRIOTT PENNSYLVANIA AVE   *Book at aaa.com*   Phone: 202/393-2000 [70]
             All Year   2P: $309-$369
             Location: 14th St and Pennsylvania Ave. Connected to a shopping mall. 1331 Pennsylvania Ave NW 20004.
Large-scale Hotel Fax: 202/626-6991. Facility: 772 units. 767 one-bedroom standard units. 5 one-bedroom suites ($359-
             $2500) with whirlpools. 18 stories, interior corridors. Bath: combo or shower only. Parking: on-site (fee) and
valet. Terms: check-in 4 pm, cancellation fee imposed, [AP], [BP] & [CP] meal plans available, package plans.
Amenities: voice mail, safes, honor bars, irons, hair dryers. Fee: video games, high-speed Internet. Some: DVD players.
Pool(s): heated indoor. Leisure Activities: saunas, whirlpool, exercise room. Fee: massage. Guest Services: gift shop, valet
laundry. Business Services: conference facilities, business center. Cards: AX, DC, DS, MC, VI.

SOME UNITS
[icons] / [icons] FEE

LATHAM HOTEL GEORGETOWN   *Book at aaa.com*   Phone: (202)726-5000 [33]
AAA SAVE   All Year   1P: $139-$329   2P: $149-$339   XP: $20   F17
             Location: Between 30th and 31st sts NW. Located in Georgetown. 3000 M St NW 20007-3701. Fax: 202/337-4250.
             Facility: 143 units. 134 one-bedroom standard units. 9 one-bedroom suites. 10 stories, interior corridors.
             Bath: combo or shower only. Parking: valet. Terms: cancellation fee imposed, package plans.
Small-scale Hotel Amenities: voice mail, irons, hair dryers. Fee: video games, high-speed Internet. Some: CD players, dual
phone lines. Dining: Michel Richard Citronelle, see separate listing. Pool(s): outdoor. Leisure
Activities: exercise room. Guest Services: valet laundry. Business Services: meeting rooms, business center. Cards: AX,
DC, DS, MC, VI. Special Amenities: free newspaper. *(See color ad p 431)*

SOME UNITS
[icons] / [icons] /

(See map and index starting on p. 390)

LINCOLN SUITES DOWNTOWN   *Book at aaa.com*   Phone: (202)223-4320   **42**
F17
AAA SAVE
3/1-6/29 & 9/6-10/30 [ECP]   1P: $165-$195   2P: $165-$195   XP: $10   F17
6/30-9/5 & 10/31-2/28 [ECP]   1P: $125-$165   2P: $125-$165   XP: $10   F17
Location: Between 18th and 19th sts NW. 1823 L St NW 20036. Fax: 202/223-8546. **Facility:** 99 one-bedroom
Small-scale Hotel   standard units, some with kitchens. 10 stories, interior corridors. *Bath:* combo or shower only. **Parking:**
valet. **Terms:** package plans, small pets only ($15 extra charge). **Amenities:** video games (fee), voice mail,
irons, hair dryers. **Dining:** 2 restaurants, 8 am-midnight; closed Sun, cocktails. **Guest Services:** valet and
coin laundry. **Business Services:** meeting rooms. *Fee:* PC, fax. **Cards:** AX, CB, DC, DS, MC, VI. **Special Amenities: free
expanded continental breakfast and free newspaper.** *(See color ad p 443)*

SOME UNITS
[icons] / [icons]

LOEWS L'ENFANT PLAZA HOTEL   *Book at aaa.com*   Phone: (202)484-1000   **77**
F17
AAA SAVE
All Year   1P: $119-$249   2P: $144-$274   XP: $25
Location: I-395, exit L'Enfant Plaza/12th St. 480 L'Enfant Plaza SW 20024. Fax: 202/646-4456. **Facility:** 370 one-
bedroom standard units. 15 stories, interior corridors. **Parking:** on-site (fee) and valet. **Amenities:** dual
Large-scale Hotel   phone lines, voice mail, safes, honor bars, irons, hair dryers. **Dining:** 6:30 am-11 pm, cocktails. **Pool(s):**
heated indoor/outdoor. **Leisure Activities:** aerobic instruction. *Fee:* massage. **Guest Services:** gift shop,
valet laundry. **Business Services:** conference facilities, business center. **Cards:** AX, DC, DS, MC, VI.

(See color ad p 443)

SOME UNITS
[icons] / [icons] VCR [icon] /

THE MADISON   *Book at aaa.com*   Phone: (202)862-1600   **31**
3/1-6/30 & 9/6-11/19   1P: $229-$299   2P: $229-$299
7/1-9/5 & 11/20-2/28   1P: $179-$229   2P: $179-$229
Large-scale Hotel   **Location:** 15th and M sts NW. 1177 15th St NW 20005. Fax: 202/785-1255. **Facility:** 353 units. 341 one-
bedroom standard units. 12 one-bedroom suites ($339-$1799), some with whirlpools. 14 stories, interior
corridors. *Bath:* combo or shower only. **Parking:** valet. **Terms:** package plans. **Amenities:** video games (fee), high-speed
Internet, dual phone lines, voice mail, honor bars, irons, hair dryers. **Leisure Activities:** saunas, steamroom, exercise room.
Fee: massage. **Guest Services:** sundries, valet laundry. **Business Services:** conference facilities, business center. **Cards:** AX,
CB, DC, DS, JC, MC, VI.

SOME UNITS
ASK [icons] / [icon] /

MANDARIN ORIENTAL, WASHINGTON D.C.   *Book at aaa.com*   Phone: (202)554-8588   **76**
F11
All Year   1P: $350-$8000   2P: $350-$8000   XP: $30
Location: Jct Independence Ave SW, just s on 12th St SW. 1330 Maryland Ave SW 20024. Fax: 202/554-8588.
Large-scale Hotel   **Facility:** Surroundings at this luxury hotel are sophisticated and elegant, and the staff displays exceptional
attention to detail. 400 units. 347 one-bedroom standard units. 53 one-bedroom suites; some with
whirlpools. 11 stories, interior corridors. *Bath:* combo or shower only. **Parking:** valet. **Terms:** package plans. **Amenities:** video
library, DVD players, CD players, high-speed Internet (fee), dual phone lines, voice mail, safes, honor bars, irons, hair dryers.
Pool(s): heated indoor. **Leisure Activities:** spa. **Guest Services:** gift shop, valet laundry, area transportation. **Business
Services:** conference facilities, business center. **Cards:** AX, CB, DC, DS, JC, MC, VI.

[icons]
FEE

MARRIOTT AT METRO CENTER   *Book at aaa.com*   Phone: (202)737-2200   **62**
F18
All Year   1P: $249-$369   XP: $20
Location: Jct 12th and H sts NW; at Metro Center subway stop. 775 12th St NW 20005. Fax: 202/347-5886.
Large-scale Hotel   **Facility:** 456 units. 453 one-bedroom standard units. 3 one-bedroom suites, some with whirlpools. 14
stories, interior corridors. **Parking:** valet. **Terms:** check-in 4 pm. **Amenities:** voice mail, irons, hair dryers.
Fee: video games, high-speed Internet. **Dining:** Regatta Raw Bar, see separate listing. **Pool(s):** heated indoor. **Leisure
Activities:** sauna, whirlpool. *Fee:* massage. **Guest Services:** gift shop, valet laundry. **Business Services:** conference facilities,
business center. **Cards:** AX, CB, DC, DS, JC, MC, VI.

SOME UNITS
[icons] / [icons] /

THE MELROSE HOTEL, WASHINGTON DC   *Book at aaa.com*   Phone: (202)955-6400   **49**
3/1-6/23 & 9/11-2/28   1P: $209   2P: $209   XP: $20   F17
6/24-9/10   1P: $169   2P: $169   XP: $20   F17
Large-scale Hotel   **Location:** Between 24th and 25th sts NW. 2430 Pennsylvania Ave NW 20037. Fax: 202/955-5765. **Facility:** 240
units. 205 one-bedroom standard units. 35 one-bedroom suites, some with efficiencies (no utensils) and/or
whirlpools. 8 stories, interior corridors. *Bath:* combo or shower only. **Parking:** valet. **Terms:** small pets only ($100 fee).
Amenities: video games (fee), dual phone lines, voice mail, safes, honor bars, irons, hair dryers. *Some:* CD players. **Leisure
Activities:** exercise room. **Guest Services:** valet laundry. **Business Services:** meeting rooms, business center. **Cards:** AX,
CB, DC, DS, MC, VI.

SOME UNITS
ASK [icons] / [icon] /
FEE

**MORRISON-CLARK HISTORIC INN AND
RESTAURANT**   *Book at aaa.com*   Phone: (202)898-1200   **40**
3/1-6/15 & 9/9-11/22 [ECP]   1P: $289   2P: $309   XP: $20   F17
6/16-9/8 [ECP]   1P: $239   2P: $259   XP: $20   F17
11/23-2/28 [ECP]   1P: $239   2P: $239   XP: $20   F17
Historic   **Location:** 11th and L sts NW, just n of Massachusetts Ave. Located near the Convention Center. 1015 L St NW 20001.
Small-scale Hotel   Fax: 202/289-8576. **Facility:** These townhouses dating from 1865 feature varied rooms, some with
balconies overlooking a brick courtyard. 54 units. 41 one-bedroom standard units. 13 one-bedroom suites ($329). 5 stories,
interior/exterior corridors. **Parking:** valet. **Terms:** cancellation fee imposed. **Amenities:** voice mail, honor bars, hair dryers.
Dining: restaurant, see separate listing. **Leisure Activities:** limited exercise equipment. **Guest Services:** valet laundry, area
transportation. **Business Services:** meeting rooms. *Fee:* PC, fax. **Cards:** AX, DC, DS, JC, MC, VI.

SOME UNITS
ASK [icons] / [icon] /

(See map and index starting on p. 390)

ONE WASHINGTON CIRCLE HOTEL   *Book at aaa.com*   Phone: (202)872-1680   46
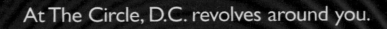
All Year   1P: $129-$429   2P: $129-$429   XP: $20   F17
Location: Between 23rd St and New Hampshire Ave NW. Located opposite George Washington University Hospital. One Washington Circle NW 20037. Fax: 202/887-4989. **Facility:** 151 units. 101 one-bedroom standard units, some with efficiencies. 50 one-bedroom suites with kitchens. 9 stories, interior corridors. *Bath:* combo or shower only. **Parking:** valet. **Terms:** cancellation fee imposed. **Amenities:** video games (fee), CD players, high-speed Internet, dual phone lines, voice mail, irons, hair dryers. **Dining:** 7-10 am, 11:30-2:30 & 5:30-10:30 pm, Fri-midnight, Sat 8-10:30 am, 11:30-2:30 & 5-midnight, Sun 8-10:30 am, 11-2:30 & 5:30-10 pm, cocktails. **Pool(s):** outdoor. **Leisure Activities:** exercise room. **Guest Services:** valet laundry. **Business Services:** meeting rooms, fax (fee). **Cards:** AX, CB, DC, DS, MC, VI. **Special Amenities:** free newspaper and free room upgrade (subject to availability with advance reservations).** *(See color ad below)*

Small-scale Hotel

SOME UNITS

(See map and index starting on p. 390)

PARK HYATT WASHINGTON, D.C.   *Book at aaa.com*   Phone: (202)789-1234   **28**
(AAA) (SAVE)   All Year   1P: $306-$410   2P: $306-$410
▼▼▼ ▼▼▼   **Location:** 24th and M sts NW. Located in the West End. 1201 24th St NW 20037. Fax: 202/419-6795.
Facility: Near Georgetown, this contemporary hotel offers one-bedroom suites and traditional guest rooms,
Large-scale Hotel   all with luxuriously appointed baths. 223 units. 97 one-bedroom standard units. 126 one-bedroom suites,
some with whirlpools. 10 stories, interior corridors. *Bath:* combo or shower only. **Parking:** valet. **Terms:** 3
day cancellation notice-fee imposed, small pets only. **Amenities:** CD players, dual phone lines, voice mail,
safes, honor bars, irons, hair dryers. **Dining:** Melrose, see separate listing. **Pool(s):** heated indoor. **Leisure Activities:** saunas,
whirlpool, steamrooms. *Fee:* massage. **Guest Services:** valet laundry, airport transportation (fee)-Ronald Reagan Washington
National Airport, area transportation-within district, beauty salon. **Business Services:** conference facilities, business center.
Cards: AX, CB, DC, DS, JC, MC, VI. *(See color ad p 445)*

SOME UNITS

[icons] FEE / ⊠ /

PHOENIX PARK HOTEL   *Book at aaa.com*   Phone: (202)638-6900   **64**
(AAA) (SAVE)   3/1-6/30 & 9/6-2/28   1P: $169-$269   2P: $199-$299   XP: $30   F18
7/1-9/5   1P: $119-$209   2P: $149-$239   XP: $30   F18
▼▼▼ ▼▼▼   **Location:** Just n of Capitol grounds. 520 N Capitol St NW 20001. Fax: 202/393-3236. **Facility:** This small,
European-style hotel has a Gaelic-style ambience. 149 units. 143 one-bedroom standard units. 6 one-
Historic   bedroom suites, some with efficiencies or kitchens (no utensils). 9 stories, interior corridors. *Bath:* combo or
Small-scale Hotel   shower only. **Parking:** valet. **Terms:** cancellation fee imposed, [AP] meal plan available, package plans.
Amenities: video games (fee), dual phone lines, voice mail, irons, hair dryers. *Some:* CD players, high-
speed Internet, honor bars. **Dining:** 7 am-10 & 11-1 am, cocktails, entertainment. **Leisure Activities:** exercise room. **Guest
Services:** valet laundry. **Business Services:** meeting rooms, fax. **Cards:** AX, CB, DC, DS, MC, VI. *(See color ad below)*

SOME UNITS

[icons] / ⊠ /

RADISSON BARCELO HOTEL WASHINGTON   *Book at aaa.com*   Phone: 202/293-3100   **11**
▼▼▼▼   All Year   1P: $159   2P: $159   XP: $20   F16
Location: Between 21st and 22nd sts NW; just w of Dupont Circle. 2121 P St NW 20037. Fax: 202/857-0134.
Large-scale Hotel   **Facility:** 301 units. 227 one-bedroom standard units. 73 one- and 1 two-bedroom suites. 10 stories, interior
corridors. **Parking:** valet. **Amenities:** video games (fee), voice mail, safes, irons, hair dryers. **Pool(s):**
outdoor. **Leisure Activities:** exercise room. **Guest Services:** gift shop, valet laundry. **Business Services:** meeting rooms,
business center. **Cards:** AX, CB, DC, DS, JC, MC, VI. *(See color ad below)*

SOME UNITS

[icons] / ⊠ 🕭 /
FEE

(See map and index starting on p. 390)

RED ROOF INN DOWNTOWN WASHINGTON, D.C.   *Book at aaa.com*   **Phone:** (202)289-5959   59

			F18
▼▼▼ ▼▼	4/3-10/29	1P: $120-$140	2P: $130-$150	XP: $10
	10/30-2/28	1P: $90-$110	2P: $100-$120	XP: $10	F18
	3/1-4/2	1P: $90-$105	2P: $100-$115	XP: $10	F18

Small-scale Hotel **Location:** At 5th and H sts NW; in Chinatown. 500 H St NW 20001. **Fax:** 202/682-9152. **Facility:** 195 one-bedroom standard units, some with whirlpools. 10 stories, interior corridors. **Bath:** combo or shower only. **Parking:** on-site (fee). **Amenities:** video games (fee), voice mail, irons, hair dryers. **Leisure Activities:** sauna, limited exercise equipment. **Guest Services:** valet and coin laundry. **Business Services:** fax (fee). **Cards:** AX, CB, DC, DS, MC, VI.

SOME UNITS

RENAISSANCE MAYFLOWER HOTEL   *Book at aaa.com*   **Phone:** (202)347-3000   38

AAA SAVE   3/1-6/21 & 9/6-12/31   1P: $159-$409
   1/1-2/28   1P: $159-$339
▼▼▼ ▼▼▼   6/22-9/5   1P: $149-$309

Classic Historic **Location:** Just n of K St NW; in business district. 1127 Connecticut Ave NW 20036. **Fax:** 202/776-9182.
Large-scale Hotel **Facility:** First opened in 1925, this historic hotel has grand public areas and modern guest rooms and suites which feature marble baths. 657 units. 583 one-bedroom standard units. 74 one-bedroom suites. 10 stories, interior corridors. **Bath:** combo or shower only. **Parking:** valet. **Terms:** cancellation fee imposed, small pets only ($30 fee). **Amenities:** high-speed Internet (fee), dual phone lines, voice mail, honor bars, irons, hair dryers. *Some:* CD players. **Dining:** Cafe Promenade, see separate listing, entertainment. **Leisure Activities:** exercise room. **Guest Services:** gift shop, valet laundry. **Business Services:** conference facilities, business center. **Cards:** AX, CB, DC, DS, MC, VI.

SOME UNITS
FEE

RENAISSANCE WASHINGTON DC HOTEL   *Book at aaa.com*   **Phone:** (202)898-9000   53

AAA SAVE   All Year   1P: $99-$359
   Location: 9th and K sts NW. Located one block from the Washington Convention Center. 999 9th St NW 20001.
▼▼▼ ▼▼▼   **Fax:** 202/289-0947. **Facility:** 807 units. 794 one-bedroom standard units. 13 one-bedroom suites, some with whirlpools. 16 stories, interior corridors. **Bath:** combo or shower only. **Parking:** on-site (fee) and valet.
Large-scale Hotel **Terms:** check-in 4 pm. **Amenities:** video games (fee), voice mail, irons, hair dryers. *Fee:* video games, high-speed Internet. *Some:* dual phone lines. **Dining:** 2 restaurants, 6:30 am-11 pm, cocktails. **Pool(s):** lap. **Leisure Activities:** steamrooms, aerobic instruction. *Fee:* massage. **Guest Services:** gift shop, valet laundry. **Business Services:** conference facilities, business center. **Cards:** AX, CB, DC, DS, JC, MC, VI. **Special Amenities:** free newspaper.

SOME UNITS

RESIDENCE INN BY MARRIOTT CAPITOL   **Phone:** 202/484-8280

[fyi]   All Year [BP]   1P: $229
Small-scale Hotel Too new to rate, opening scheduled for January 2005. **Location:** I-395, exit Maine Ave, left on G St SW, left on 7th St SW, then right. 333 E St SW 20024. **Fax:** 202/484-7320. **Amenities:** 233 units, coffeemakers, microwaves, refrigerators, pool. **Cards:** AX, DC, DS, MC, VI.

RESIDENCE INN BY MARRIOTT-DUPONT CIRCLE   *Book at aaa.com*   **Phone:** 202/466-6800   12

AAA SAVE   All Year   1P: $149-$299
   Location: Between 21st and 22nd sts NW; just w of Dupont Circle. 2120 P St NW 20037. **Fax:** 202/466-9630.
▼▼▼ ▼▼▼   **Facility:** 107 units. 48 one-bedroom standard units with efficiencies. 43 one- and 16 two-bedroom suites, some with efficiencies or kitchens. 10 stories, interior corridors. **Bath:** combo or shower only. **Parking:** on-
Small-scale Hotel site (fee). **Terms:** 2 night minimum stay - seasonal, small pets only ($200 fee, $15 extra charge). **Amenities:** video games (fee), high-speed Internet, dual phone lines, voice mail, irons, hair dryers. **Leisure Activities:** exercise room. **Guest Services:** valet and coin laundry. **Business Services:** meeting rooms, fax (fee). **Cards:** AX, CB, DC, DS, MC. **Special Amenities:** free full breakfast and free newspaper.

SOME UNITS
FEE

RESIDENCE INN BY MARRIOTT-WASHINGTON DC-VERMONT AVE   *Book at aaa.com*   **Phone:** 202/898-1100   37

AAA SAVE   All Year [BP]   1P: $259
   Location: Jct 14th St and Vermont Ave NW, at Thomas Circle. 1199 Vermont Ave NW 20005. **Fax:** 202/898-1110.
▼▼▼ ▼▼▼   **Facility:** 202 units. 182 one-bedroom standard units with efficiencies. 20 one-bedroom suites with kitchens. 12 stories, interior corridors. **Bath:** combo or shower only. **Parking:** valet. **Terms:** check-in 4 pm,
Large-scale Hotel cancellation fee imposed, pets ($150 fee, $8 extra charge). **Amenities:** video games (fee), high-speed Internet, voice mail, irons, hair dryers. **Leisure Activities:** exercise room. **Guest Services:** valet and coin laundry. **Business Services:** meeting rooms, fax (fee). **Cards:** AX, DC, DS, JC, MC, VI. **Special Amenities:** free full breakfast and free newspaper.

SOME UNITS
FEE

THE RITZ-CARLTON, GEORGETOWN   **Phone:** (202)912-4100   44

▼▼▼▼▼ ▼▼▼   All Year   1P: $260-$550
   Location: Just s of jct M St and Wisconsin Ave, off Wisconsin, just e. 3100 South St NW 20007. **Fax:** 202/912-4199.
Small-scale Hotel **Facility:** Elegance, history, and cutting-edge style merge at this intimate hotel in the restored Georgetown incinerator between the river and the canal. 86 units. 52 one-bedroom standard units. 34 one-bedroom suites ($529-$895). 5-6 stories, interior corridors. **Bath:** combo or shower only. **Parking:** on-site (fee) and valet. **Terms:** small pets only ($25 fee). **Amenities:** video library, DVD players, CD players, dual phone lines, voice mail, safes, honor bars, irons, hair dryers. *Fee:* video games, high-speed Internet. *Some:* fax. **Dining:** Fahrenheit, see separate listing. **Leisure Activities:** saunas, steamrooms, spa. **Guest Services:** valet laundry, area transportation. **Business Services:** meeting rooms, business center. **Cards:** AX, CB, DC, DS, JC, MC, VI.

SOME UNITS
FEE   FEE

Smithsonian
National Museum of American History
Behring Center

America on the Move is made possible by generous support from
General Motors Corporation, AAA, State Farm Companies Foundation, The History Channel,
United States Congress, U.S. Department of Transportation, ExxonMobil, American Public
Transportation Association, American Road & Transportation Builders Association,
Association of American Railroads, National Asphalt Pavement Association, The UPS Foundation.

(See map and index starting on p. 390)

THE RITZ-CARLTON, WASHINGTON, DC   *Book at aaa.com*   **Phone:** (202)835-0500   **39**
All Year   1P: $259-$645
Large-scale Hotel   **Location:** At 22nd and M sts NW. 1150 22nd St NW 20037. Fax: 202/835-1588. **Facility:** Luxury, quality and an attentive, service-oriented staff set the tone at this upscale hotel, which features an impressive health club. 300 units. 268 one-bedroom standard units. 32 one-bedroom suites ($459-$900), some with whirlpools. 11 stories, interior corridors. *Bath:* combo or shower only. **Parking:** on-site (fee) and valet. **Terms:** small pets only ($150 deposit). **Amenities:** CD players, dual phone lines, voice mail, safes, honor bars, irons, hair dryers. *Fee:* video games, high-speed Internet. *Some:* DVD players, fax. **Dining:** The Grill, see separate listing. **Pool(s):** heated indoor. **Leisure Activities:** saunas, steamrooms, spa. *Fee:* exercise classes, yoga, spinning. **Guest Services:** gift shop, valet laundry, area transportation, beauty salon. **Business Services:** conference facilities, business center. **Cards:** AX, CB, DC, DS, JC, MC, VI.

SOME UNITS
[icons row]

THE RIVER INN   *Book at aaa.com*   **Phone:** (202)337-7600   **55**
All Year   1P: $99-$385   2P: $99-$405   XP: $20   F12
Small-scale Hotel   **Location:** Between K and I sts NW. Located in the Foggy Bottom area. 924 25th St NW 20037. Fax: 202/337-6520. **Facility:** 126 units. 98 one-bedroom standard units with efficiencies. 28 one-bedroom suites with efficiencies. 9 stories, interior corridors. **Parking:** valet. **Terms:** cancellation fee imposed, package plans, pets ($150 deposit). **Amenities:** DVD players, video games (fee), dual phone lines, voice mail, irons, hair dryers. *Some:* CD players, high-speed Internet. **Dining:** Dish, see separate listing. **Leisure Activities:** limited exercise equipment. **Guest Services:** valet and coin laundry. **Business Services:** meeting rooms, business center. **Cards:** AX, DS, MC, VI. **Special Amenities:** free newspaper and early check-in/late check-out.
(See color ad below)

SOME UNITS
[icons row]

ST. GREGORY LUXURY HOTEL & SUITES   *Book at aaa.com*   **Phone:** 202/530-3600   **24**
9/7-2/28   1P: $289-$399   2P: $289-$399   XP: $20   F13
3/1-9/6   1P: $269-$389   2P: $269-$389   XP: $20   F13
Small-scale Hotel   **Location:** Jct M and 21st sts NW. 2033 M St NW 20036. Fax: 202/466-6770. **Facility:** 154 units. 54 one-bedroom standard units. 100 one-bedroom suites ($599-$1300), some with kitchens. 9 stories, interior corridors. *Bath:* combo or shower only. **Parking:** valet. **Terms:** package plans. **Amenities:** CD players, dual phone lines, voice mail, irons, hair dryers. *Fee:* video games, high-speed Internet. **Dining:** 6:30 am-11 pm, Fri-midnight, Sat 7:30 am-midnight, Sun 7:30 am-11 pm, cocktails. **Leisure Activities:** exercise room. **Guest Services:** valet and coin laundry. **Business Services:** meeting rooms, business center. **Cards:** AX, CB, DC, DS, MC, VI. **Special Amenities:** free newspaper and free room upgrade (subject to availability with advance reservations). *(See color ad p 421)*

SOME UNITS
[icons row]

(See map and index starting on p. 390)

THE ST. REGIS   *Book at aaa.com*   Phone: (202)638-2626   52

AAA SAVE   All Year   1P: $230-$385   2P: $230-$385

WWWW WWWW   **Location:** Just n of the White House, 16th and K sts. 923 16th St NW 20006. Fax: 202/638-4231. **Facility:** Fresh
Historic   flowers, crystal chandeliers and a service-oriented staff create an aura of opulence at this luxury hotel
Large-scale Hotel   dating from 1926. 193 units. 179 one-bedroom standard units. 14 one-bedroom suites ($400-$2500). 8
stories, interior corridors. **Parking:** valet. **Terms:** package plans, small pets only ($35 fee). **Amenities:** high-
speed Internet (fee), dual phone lines, voice mail, fax, safes, honor bars, hair dryers. *Some:* DVD players,
CD players. **Dining:** 7 am-10, noon-2:30 & 6-10 pm, Sat & Sun 7 am-10:30 & noon-2:30 pm, cocktails.
Leisure Activities: exercise room. **Guest Services:** gift shop, valet laundry, area transportation-within 7-10 blks.
Business Services: conference facilities, business center. **Cards:** AX, CB, DC, DS, JC, MC, VI. **Special Amenities:** free newspaper
and preferred room (subject to availability with advance reservations).

SOME UNITS
[icons]

SOFITEL LAFAYETTE SQUARE WASHINGTON DC   *Book at aaa.com*   Phone: (202)730-8800   57

WWWW WWWW   3/1-6/30 & 9/6-2/28   1P: $380-$480   2P: $380-$480   XP: $20   F12
7/1-9/5   1P: $300-$400   2P: $300-$400   XP: $20   F12
Small-scale Hotel   **Location:** Jct 15th and H sts NW. 806 15th St NW 20005. Fax: 202/730-8500. **Facility:** Just blocks away from the
White House this intimate hotel offers richly appointed public areas, contemporary guest rooms and marble
tiled bathrooms. 237 units. 220 one-bedroom standard units. 17 one-bedroom suites ($600-$1200). 12 stories, interior corridors.
Bath: combo or shower only. **Parking:** valet. **Terms:** cancellation fee imposed, package plans, small pets only. **Amenities:** CD
players, high-speed Internet, dual phone lines, voice mail, safes, honor bars, irons, hair dryers. *Some:* DVD players (fee).
Dining: Cafe 15, see separate listing. **Leisure Activities:** exercise room. **Guest Services:** sundries, valet laundry. **Business
Services:** meeting rooms, PC. *Fee:* administrative services, fax. **Cards:** AX, CB, DC, DS, JC, MC, VI.

SOME UNITS
[icons]   FEE

STATE PLAZA HOTEL   *Book at aaa.com*   Phone: (202)861-8200   71

WWW   All Year   1P: $119-$225   2P: $119-$225   XP: $20   F
Location: Between 21st St and Virginia Ave NW. 2117 E St NW 20037. Fax: 202/659-8601. **Facility:** 225 units.
Small-scale Hotel   170 one-bedroom standard units with efficiencies. 55 one-bedroom suites with kitchens. 8 stories, interior
corridors. **Parking:** on-site (fee). **Terms:** cancellation fee imposed. **Amenities:** dual phone lines, voice mail,
safes, honor bars, irons, hair dryers. *Some:* video games, high-speed Internet. **Leisure Activities:** exercise room. **Guest
Services:** valet and coin laundry. **Business Services:** meeting rooms, business center. **Cards:** AX, CB, DC, DS, JC, MC, VI.

SOME UNITS
[icons]

TOPAZ HOTEL   *Book at aaa.com*   Phone: (202)393-3000   17

AAA SAVE   3/1-6/29 & 9/6-11/18   1P: $149-$339   2P: $149-$339   XP: $20   F16
WWW   6/30-9/5 & 11/19-2/28   1P: $139-$339   2P: $139-$339   XP: $20   F16
Location: Just e of Connecticut Ave. 1733 N St NW 20036. Fax: 202/785-9581. **Facility:** 99 one-bedroom
standard units. 10 stories, interior corridors. *Bath:* combo or shower only. **Parking:** valet.
Small-scale Hotel   **Terms:** cancellation fee imposed, package plans. **Amenities:** CD players, high-speed Internet, dual phone
lines, voice mail, safes, honor bars, irons, hair dryers. *Some:* DVD players. *Fee:* high-speed Internet.
Dining: 7 am-10:30 & 5-10:30 pm, cocktails. **Guest Services:** valet laundry. **Business Services:** meeting rooms, PC, fax (fee).
Cards: AX, CB, DC, DS, MC, VI. *(See color ad p 422)*

SOME UNITS
[icons]   FEE

THE WASHINGTON COURT HOTEL   *Book at aaa.com*   Phone: (202)628-2100   67

WWW   All Year   1P: $119-$339   2P: $139-$359   F16
Location: 3 blks from Capitol grounds. 525 New Jersey Ave NW 20001. Fax: 202/879-7918. **Facility:** 264 units.
Large-scale Hotel   260 one-bedroom standard units. 4 one-bedroom suites ($169-$2500), some with whirlpools. 16 stories,
interior corridors. *Bath:* some combo or shower only. **Parking:** valet. **Terms:** check-in 4 pm, 7 day
cancellation notice-fee imposed, small pets only. **Amenities:** dual phone lines, voice mail, irons, hair dryers. *Fee:* video games,
high-speed Internet. *Some:* DVD players, CD players. **Leisure Activities:** exercise room. **Guest Services:** gift shop, valet
laundry. **Business Services:** conference facilities, business center. **Cards:** AX, CB, DC, DS, MC, VI.

SOME UNITS
[icons]   FEE

WASHINGTON MARRIOTT HOTEL   *Book at aaa.com*   Phone: (202)872-1500   26

AAA SAVE   All Year   1P: $179-$269   2P: $179-$269   XP: $10   F
WWW   **Location:** 22nd and M sts NW. 1221 22nd St NW 20037. Fax: 202/872-1424. **Facility:** 418 units. 416 one-
bedroom standard units. 2 one-bedroom suites. 9 stories, interior corridors. *Bath:* combo or shower only.
Parking: on-site (fee). **Terms:** check-in 4 pm, cancellation fee imposed, package plans. **Amenities:** voice
Large-scale Hotel   mail, irons, hair dryers. *Fee:* video games, high-speed Internet. **Dining:** 6:30 am-11 pm, cocktails. **Pool(s):**
heated indoor. **Leisure Activities:** sauna, whirlpool, locker rooms, exercise room. **Guest Services:** gift
shop, complimentary and valet laundry. **Business Services:** conference facilities, business center. **Cards:** AX, CB, DC, DS, JC,
MC, VI. **Special Amenities:** free newspaper and early check-in/late check-out.

SOME UNITS
[icons]

(See map and index starting on p. 390)

WASHINGTON SUITES GEORGETOWN   *Book at aaa.com*   Phone: (202)333-8060   45

3/1-7/31 & 9/6-10/31 [ECP]	1P: $188-$248	2P: $188-$248	XP: $20	F17
8/1-9/5 & 11/1-2/28 [ECP]	1P: $148-$178	2P: $148-$178	XP: $20	F17

Location: Jct 25th St NW and Pennsylvania Ave; 2 blks from Foggy Bottom Metro Station. 2500 Pennsylvania Ave NW 20037. Fax: 202/338-3818. **Facility:** 124 one-bedroom suites with kitchens. 10 stories, interior corridors.

Small-scale Hotel   *Bath:* combo or shower only. **Parking:** valet. **Terms:** pets ($20 extra charge, 1st floor units). **Amenities:** video games (fee), dual phone lines, voice mail, irons, hair dryers. **Leisure Activities:** limited exercise equipment. **Guest Services:** valet and coin laundry. **Business Services:** fax (fee). **Cards:** AX, CB, DC, DS, MC, VI. **Special Amenities:** free expanded continental breakfast and free newspaper. *(See color ad below)*

SOME UNITS

(See map and index starting on p. 390)

WASHINGTON TERRACE HOTEL   *Book at aaa.com*
Phone: (202)232-7000 **15**

(AAA) (SAVE) All Year   1P: $129-$299   2P: $129-$299   XP: $20   F18
Large-scale Hotel **Location:** Off Scott Circle. 1515 Rhode Island Ave NW 20005. Fax: 202/521-7103. **Facility:** 220 units. 211 one-bedroom standard units. 9 one-bedroom suites ($199-$750). 8 stories, interior corridors. *Bath:* combo or shower only. **Parking:** valet. **Terms:** cancellation fee imposed, package plans. **Amenities:** CD players, dual phone lines, voice mail, safes, irons, hair dryers. *Some:* high-speed Internet (fee). **Dining:** 15 ria, see separate listing. **Leisure Activities:** exercise room. **Guest Services:** valet laundry, area transportation-within 10 blks. **Business Services:** meeting rooms, fax (fee). **Cards:** AX, DC, DS, MC, VI. **Special Amenities: free newspaper and free room upgrade (subject to availability with advance reservations).** Affiliated with A Preferred Hotel. *(See ad p 453)*

SOME UNITS

THE WESTIN EMBASSY ROW   *Book at aaa.com*
Phone: (202)293-2100 **8**

All Year   1P: $209-$289   2P: $209-$289   XP: $20   F18
Large-scale Hotel **Location:** Just w of Dupont Circle; at 21st St. 2100 Massachusetts Ave NW 20008. Fax: 202/857-0127. **Facility:** 206 units. 174 one-bedroom standard units. 32 one-bedroom suites ($399-$799), some with whirlpools. 8 stories, interior corridors. **Parking:** valet. **Terms:** package plans, small pets only. **Amenities:** dual phone lines, voice mail, safes, honor bars, irons, hair dryers. *Fee:* video games, high-speed Internet. **Leisure Activities:** saunas, exercise room. *Fee:* massage. **Guest Services:** valet laundry. **Business Services:** conference facilities, business center. **Cards:** AX, MC, VI.

SOME UNITS
FEE

THE WESTIN GRAND   *Book at aaa.com*
Phone: (202)429-0100 **35**

All Year   1P: $209-$289   2P: $209-$289   XP: $20   F18
Large-scale Hotel **Location:** 24th and M sts NW. Located in the West End. 2350 M St NW 20037. Fax: 202/429-9759. **Facility:** 263 units. 258 one-bedroom standard units, some with whirlpools. 5 one-bedroom suites ($399-$799) with whirlpools. 8 stories, interior corridors. *Bath:* combo or shower only. **Parking:** on-site (fee) and valet. **Terms:** package plans. **Amenities:** CD players, high-speed Internet (fee), dual phone lines, voice mail, safes, honor bars, irons, hair dryers. *Some:* fax. **Pool(s):** heated outdoor. **Leisure Activities:** exercise room. **Guest Services:** gift shop, valet laundry. **Business Services:** conference facilities, business center. **Cards:** AX, MC, VI.

SOME UNITS

THE WILLARD INTERCONTINENTAL   *Book at aaa.com*
Phone: (202)628-9100 **69**

All Year   1P: $209-$610   2P: $209-$610   XP: $30   F16
Classic Historic Large-scale Hotel **Location:** Just e of the White House. 1401 Pennsylvania Ave NW 20004. Fax: 202/637-7326. **Facility:** This luxury hotel features an eye-catching architectural design; it is conveniently close to the White House. 341 units. 308 one-bedroom standard units. 33 one-bedroom suites ($500-$4000), some with whirlpools. 12 stories, interior corridors. *Bath:* combo or shower only. **Parking:** valet. **Terms:** cancellation fee imposed, pets (with prior approval). **Amenities:** CD players, high-speed Internet, dual phone lines, voice mail, safes, honor bars, irons, hair dryers. *Fee:* video library, video games. *Some:* DVD players, fax. **Dining:** The Willard Room, see separate listing. **Leisure Activities:** exercise room. **Guest Services:** gift shop, valet laundry. **Business Services:** conference facilities, business center. **Cards:** AX, CB, DC, DS, JC, MC, VI.

SOME UNITS

WYNDHAM CITY CENTER   *Book at aaa.com*
Phone: (202)775-0800 **34**

(AAA) (SAVE) 3/1-6/23 & 9/6-12/15   1P: $119-$209   2P: $119-$229   XP: $20   F17
6/24-9/5 & 12/16-2/28   1P: $99-$179   2P: $99-$199   XP: $20   F17
Large-scale Hotel **Location:** Just e of 22nd and M sts NW. 1143 New Hampshire Ave NW 20037. Fax: 202/331-9491. **Facility:** 352 units. 344 one-bedroom standard units. 8 one-bedroom suites. 9 stories, interior corridors. *Bath:* combo or shower only. **Parking:** valet. **Terms:** cancellation fee imposed. **Amenities:** dual phone lines, voice mail, irons, hair dryers. *Fee:* video games, high-speed Internet. *Some:* CD players. **Dining:** 6:30 am-11 pm, cocktails. **Leisure Activities:** exercise room. **Guest Services:** valet laundry. **Business Services:** conference facilities, business center. **Cards:** AX, DC, DS, JC, MC, VI.

SOME UNITS

WYNDHAM WASHINGTON, D.C.   *Book at aaa.com*
Phone: (202)429-1700 **30**

(AAA) (SAVE) 3/1-6/29   1P: $120-$183   2P: $120-$183   XP: $25   F18
9/6-2/28   1P: $120-$175   2P: $120-$175   XP: $25   F18
6/30-9/5   1P: $99-$140   2P: $99-$140   XP: $25   F18
Large-scale Hotel **Location:** Just w of Thomas Circle. 1400 M St NW 20005. Fax: 202/785-0786. **Facility:** 400 units. 394 one-bedroom standard units. 6 one-bedroom suites with whirlpools. 14 stories, interior corridors. *Bath:* combo or shower only. **Parking:** valet. **Terms:** cancellation fee imposed. **Amenities:** dual phone lines, voice mail, irons, hair dryers. *Fee:* video games, high-speed Internet. *Some:* CD players, fax, honor bars. **Dining:** 2 restaurants, 6:30 am-11 pm, Sat & Sun from 7 am, cocktails. **Leisure Activities:** exercise room. **Guest Services:** gift shop, valet laundry. **Business Services:** conference facilities, business center. **Cards:** AX, DC, DS, MC, VI.

SOME UNITS

(See map and index starting on p. 390)

──────── **WHERE TO DINE** ────────

14K   Lunch: $8-$16   Dinner: $18-$29   Phone: 202/682-0111   **87**
American   **Location:** 14th and K sts NW; in Hamilton Crowne Plaza Hotel Washington. 1001 14th St NW 20005. **Hours:** 6:30 am-10 pm, Fri & Sat-11 pm. **Reservations:** accepted. **Features:** The hotel restaurant sustains a casual, comfortable dining atmosphere. Seasonal sidewalk seating overlooks Franklin Park. The menu centers on well-prepared beef, seafood and pasta dishes. Casual dress; cocktails. **Parking:** valet. **Cards:** AX, DC, DS, JC, MC, VI.

15 RIA   Lunch: $7-$15   Dinner: $16-$23   Phone: 202/521-7101   **31**
American   **Location:** Off Scott Circle; in Washington Terrace Hotel. 1515 Rhode Island Ave NW 20005. **Hours:** 6:30 am-2 & 5:30-11 pm, Sat & Sun from 7 am. **Reservations:** suggested. **Features:** The hotel restaurant has a soothing, stylish dining room and a talented kitchen staff. The chef uses fresh ingredients to prepare contemporary American cuisine and offers daily specials popular with the regulars. The service is professional and efficient. Casual dress; cocktails. **Parking:** valet. **Cards:** AX, CB, DC, DS, MC, VI.

1789 RESTAURANT   Dinner: $18-$38   Phone: 202/965-1789   **44**
American   **Location:** In Georgetown; just e of Georgetown University. 1226 36th St NW 20007. **Hours:** 6 pm-10 pm, Fri & Sat-11 pm. Closed: 7/4, 12/25. **Reservations:** suggested. **Features:** Nestled among narrow streets and busy sidewalks near the university, the restaurant employs a chef who uses fresh local produce to prepare creative American regional dishes with an upscale touch. Prices are reasonable for this level of quality, but diners who find them too steep might opt instead for the prix-fixe selection offered before 6:45 p.m. Waiters aren't the only ones who must dress up, as the formal dress code requires men to don jackets. Semi-formal attire; cocktails. **Parking:** valet. **Cards:** AX, CB, DC, DS, MC, VI.

701 PENNSYLVANIA AVENUE   Lunch: $10-$18   Dinner: $15-$25   Phone: 202/393-0701   **152**
American   **Location:** Market Square; adjacent to the US Navy Memorial, between 7th and 9th sts NW. 701 Pennsylvania Ave NW 20004. **Hours:** 11:30 am-3 & 5:30-10:30 pm, Fri-11:30 pm, Sat 5:30 pm-11:30 pm, Sun 5 pm-9:30 pm. Closed major holidays. **Reservations:** suggested. **Features:** Upscale contempory dining room overlooks the Naval Memorial. Outdoor dining available seasonally. The service is professional and attentive. The menu changes seasonally, however the appetizer of tuna tartar is a tradition. The menu offers a nice variety of contemporary American dishes, ranging from fresh seafood selections to beef and lamb dishes. Dressy casual; cocktails; entertainment. **Parking:** no self-parking. **Cards:** AX, CB, DC, MC, VI.

ADITI INDIAN CUISINE   Lunch: $8-$16   Dinner: $8-$16   Phone: 202/625-6825   **54**
Indian   **Location:** Just e of Key Bridge. 3299 M St NW 20007. **Hours:** 11:30 am-2:30 & 5:30-10 pm, Fri & Sat-10:30 pm, Sun noon-2:30 & 5:30-10 pm. Closed: 1/1, 7/4, 11/24. **Reservations:** suggested, weekends. **Features:** In a two-story townhouse on bustling M Street, the restaurant presents a menu with a wide range of traditional tandoori dishes, as well as a large selection of curries. Choose from lamb, beef, chicken and vegetarian entrees. Casual dress; cocktails. **Parking:** no self-parking. **Cards:** AX, CB, DC, DS, MC, VI.

AMERICA   Lunch: $9-$18   Dinner: $9-$18   Phone: 202/682-9555   **132**
American   **Location:** Just e of N Capitol St; in the west hall of Union Station. 50 Massachusetts Ave NE 20002. **Hours:** 11:30 am-10 pm. Closed: 12/25. **Reservations:** accepted. **Features:** The unusual Union Station setting—with seating in the bi-level dining room, train station lobby or along the outdoor sidewalk—complements the casual atmosphere. The menu lists an extensive selection of items from full dinners to sandwiches, soups and salads. Casual dress; cocktails. **Parking:** on-site (fee). **Cards:** AX, DC, DS, MC, VI.

AMMA VEGETARIAN KITCHEN   Lunch: $5-$11   Dinner: $5-$11   Phone: 202/625-6625   **53**
Indian   **Location:** At 33rd St; in Georgetown. 3291-A M St NW 20007. **Hours:** 11:30 am-2:30 & 5:30-10 pm, Fri & Sat-10:30 pm, Sun noon-3:45 & 5:30-10 pm. Closed major holidays. **Features:** The simple, second-floor spot is not much to look at, but that isn't the case for the view of Virginia's skyline from the window tables. The house's best bets are the two samplers, in which diners can taste Northern or Southern vegetarian curries along with tandoori oven breads. Casual dress; beer & wine only. **Parking:** street. **Cards:** AX.

ANNA MARIA'S RESTAURANT   Lunch: $7-$10   Dinner: $9-$25   Phone: 202/667-1444   **15**
Italian   **Location:** 2 blks from Dupont Circle Metro Station. 1737 Connecticut Ave NW 20009. **Hours:** 11 am-11 pm, Fri-1 am, Sat 5 pm-1 am, Sun 5 pm-11 pm. Closed major holidays. **Reservations:** accepted. **Features:** Established in the late 1950s, this neighborhood restaurant offers dishes from the north and south of Italy. Veal is the house specialty, with a variety of different preparations. The pasta is made fresh daily. Photographs of celebrities who have dined here over the years adorn the dining room walls. Casual dress; cocktails. **Parking:** street. **Cards:** AX, CB, DC, MC, VI.

AROMA INDIAN RESTAURANT   Lunch: $10-$16   Dinner: $10-$16   Phone: 202/833-4700   **98**
Indian   **Location:** Between 19th and 20th sts NW. 1919 I St NW 20006. **Hours:** 11:30 am-2:30 & 5:30-10 pm, Fri-10:30 pm, Sat noon-2:30 & 5:30-10:30 pm. Closed: 12/25; also Sun & for lunch 1/1. **Reservations:** suggested. **Features:** The menu offers authentic, creative tandoori (type of Indian oven) barbecue dishes of lamb, chicken and beef, along with vegetarian selections in an intimate dining atmosphere with banquettes. The portions are manageable and reasonably priced; the service is attentive. Dressy casual; cocktails. **Parking:** no self-parking. **Cards:** AX, CB, DC, DS, MC, VI.

(See map and index starting on p. 390)

ASIA NORA
Dinner: $20-$27 **Phone:** 202/797-4860 (48)
▼▼▼
Asian
Location: Between 22nd and 23rd sts NW. 2213 M St NW 20037. **Hours:** 5:45 pm-10 pm, Fri & Sat 5:30 pm-10:30 pm. Closed major holidays; also Sun & 8/26-9/9. **Reservations:** suggested. **Features:** A soft, subtle ambience pervades the intimate, bi-level dining room. Decorated with Asian artwork. The creatively prepared cuisine, which uses only certified organic meats, fish and vegatables, includes tempting choices blending Asian and American influences. Casual dress; cocktails. **Parking:** on-site (fee) and valet. **Cards:** AX, DS, MC, VI.

BACCHUS RESTAURANT
Lunch: $8-$11 **Dinner:** $13-$17 **Phone:** 202/785-0734 (37)
▼▼ ▼▼
Lebanese
Location: Just w of Connecticut Ave, jct 18th St NW. 1827 Jefferson Pl NW 20036. **Hours:** noon-2:30 & 6-10 pm, Fri-10:30 pm, Sat 6 pm-10:30 pm. Closed major holidays; also Sun. **Reservations:** suggested. **Features:** Authentic Lebanese and Middle-Eastern cuisine is served in intimate surroundings at the Bacchus. Diners choose from a variety of appetizers and several entrees. The lamb and rice with yogurt is tasty. Complimentary valet parking is offered after 6 pm. Casual dress; cocktails. **Parking:** no self-parking. **Cards:** AX, DC, MC, VI.

BANGKOK BISTRO
Lunch: $8-$18 **Dinner:** $11-$19 **Phone:** 202/337-2424 (42)
▼▼ ▼▼
Thai
Location: Between 33rd St and Wisconsin Ave; in Georgetown. 3251 Prospect St 20007. **Hours:** 11:30 am-10:30 pm, Fri & Sat-11:30 pm. Closed: 11/24, 12/25. **Reservations:** suggested, weekends. **Features:** The selections are numerous, ranging from vegetarian dishes to those made with beef, chicken, pork, duck and seafood. Thai fried rice is heaped high on a bisected fresh pineapple. In good weather, outdoor seating is available on the front sidewalk and rear patio. During the week, smoking is allowed in part of the restaurant. The decor is stylish, the servers accommodating and the prices reasonable. Casual dress; cocktails. **Parking:** street. **Cards:** AX, CB, DC, DS, MC, VI.

BAROLO
Lunch: $14-$24 **Dinner:** $18-$30 **Phone:** 202/547-5011 (154)
▼▼▼
Northern Italian
Location: Just e of jct 2nd St SE and Pennsylvania Ave SE. 223 Pennsylvania Ave SE 20003. **Hours:** 11:30 am-2:30 & 5:30-10 pm, Fri-10:30 pm, Sat 5:30 pm-10:30 pm. Closed major holidays; also Sun. **Reservations:** suggested. **Features:** On the second floor of a townhouse across the street from the nation's capitol, the restaurant specializes in preparations from the Piedmont region of Italy. On the menu are some innovative pasta dishes, such as spinach pasta filled with butternut squash and amaretto cookies. Guests linger over dinner as they soak up the warmth of the room's rich, wooden interior and enjoy views of the Capitol. Dressy casual; cocktails. **Parking:** street. **Cards:** AX, DC, DS, MC, VI.

BAR ROUGE
Dinner: $7-$13 **Phone:** 202/232-8000 (33)
AAA
▼▼ ▼▼
American
Location: Just n of Scott Circle; in Hotel Rouge. 1315 16th St NW 20036. **Hours:** 5 pm-11 pm. Closed: 11/24, 12/25. **Features:** The trendy-chic decor invites the young set into an intimate environment of quiet nooks. The eclectic menu may include Maryland crab cakes, carpaccio and innovative salads. Casual dress; cocktails. **Parking:** street. **Cards:** AX, DC, DS, MC, VI.

BE DU CI
Lunch: $8-$29 **Dinner:** $12-$24 **Phone:** 202/223-3824 (28)
▼▼▼
Mediterranean
Location: Jct 21st St, just nw of Dupont Circle. 2100 P St NW 20037. **Hours:** 11:30 am-2:30 & 5:30-10 pm, Sat 5:30 pm-10:30 pm, Sun 5 pm-9 pm. Closed major holidays. **Features:** Savory spices and sun-kissed flavors of many Mediterranean nations meet at this warm spot. The menu is as varied as it is delicious. From branzino to duck to wholesome, freshly made pasta, the dishes are delightful, as is the all-weather sidewalk patio. Dressy casual; cocktails. **Parking:** street. **Cards:** AX, CB, DC, DS, MC, VI.

THE BISTRO
Lunch: $8-$20 **Dinner:** $14-$28 **Phone:** 202/457-5020 (51)
▼▼▼
American
Location: 24th and M sts NW; in The Fairmont Washington, DC. 2401 M St NW 20037. **Hours:** 6:30 am-10:30 pm. Closed major holidays. **Reservations:** suggested. **Features:** The fine-dining establishment lets guests savor a hearty meal while overlooking either the patio or the activity across the street at George Washington University. Dressy casual; cocktails. **Parking:** on-site (fee). **Cards:** AX, CB, DC, DS, MC, VI.

BISTRO BIS
Lunch: $13-$18 **Dinner:** $18-$29 **Phone:** 202/661-2700 (136)
▼▼▼▼
French
Location: On Capitol Hill, just n of Capitol grounds; in The Hotel George. 15 E St NW 20001. **Hours:** 7-10:30 am, 11:30-2:30 & 5:30-10:30 pm. Closed: 12/25. **Reservations:** suggested. **Features:** Just off the lobby of Hotel George, the stylish bistro serves breakfast, lunch and dinner. French fare—such as duck confit with roasted potatoes and seared scallops Provencal with garlic—reflects American influences. Dressy casual; cocktails. **Parking:** on-site (fee) and valet. **Cards:** AX, DC, DS, MC, VI.

BISTRO FRANCAIS
Lunch: $8-$17 **Dinner:** $8-$25 **Phone:** 202/338-3830 (65)
AAA
▼▼ ▼▼
French
Location: In Georgetown. 3128 M St NW 20007. **Hours:** 11 am-3 am, Fri & Sat-4 am. Closed: 12/25; also for dinner 12/24. **Reservations:** accepted. **Features:** A casual, Parisian brassiere atmosphere. The banquette seating is rather intimate. Huge menu offers beef, veal, pate, veal kidneys, mussels and seafood, as well as homemade pastries. A couple of the restaurant signature dishes are the minute steak, steak tartar and rotisserie chicken. Casual dress; cocktails. **Parking:** no self-parking. **Cards:** AX, CB, DC, JC, MC, VI.

BISTROT DU COIN
Lunch: $10-$21 **Dinner:** $10-$21 **Phone:** 202/234-6969 (16)
▼▼ ▼▼
French
Location: Jct Florida Ave NW, 3 blks n of Dupont Circle. 1738 Connecticut Ave NW 20009. **Hours:** 11:30 am-11 pm, Thurs & Fri-1 am, Sat 11 am-1 am, Sun 11 am-11 pm. Closed: 9/5. **Reservations:** suggested. **Features:** The Parisian-style bistro lives up to its "French, fun and friendly" motto. Closely spaced tables contribute to the loud, spirited atmosphere. Guests can sample homemade pates, foie gras and mussels, among other tasty selections. Casual dress; cocktails. **Parking:** no self-parking. **Cards:** AX, DS, MC, VI.

(See map and index starting on p. 390)

BISTROT LEPIC   Lunch: $11-$15   Dinner: $15-$20   Phone: 202/333-0111   ⑩
▼▲▼▲▼
French
Location: In Upper Georgetown. 1736 Wisconsin Ave NW 20007. **Hours:** 11:30 am-2:30 & 5:30-10 pm, Fri & Sat-10:30 pm, Sun-9:30 pm. Closed major holidays; also Mon. **Reservations:** required. **Features:** In Georgetown, there is a French resturant that serves classical and regional cuisine. Menu changes seasonally, but a favorite dish that is on all menus is the La grande salade de Volaille Tiede(organic chicken with poached egg and balsamic vinaigrette). Desserts are made fresh daily. Reservations are required. Dressy casual; wine only. **Parking:** on-site (fee) and street. **Cards:** AX, CB, DS, MC, VI.   ✖

BLACKIE'S   Lunch: $10-$18   Dinner: $25-$41   Phone: 202/333-1100   ㊄
▼▲▼▲▼
Steak & Seafood
Location: 22nd and M sts NW. 1217 22nd St NW 20037. **Hours:** 11:30 am-2 & 5:30-10 pm, Sat & Sun from 5:30 pm. Closed major holidays. **Reservations:** suggested. **Features:** Open since 1946, the restaurant offers some of the most mouthwatering dry-aged grilled beef this side of Texas. A specialty is prime rib of beef roasted over an open fire. The dessert menu is not to be missed. Dressy casual; cocktails. **Parking:** no self-parking. **Cards:** AX, DS, MC, VI.   ▼ ✖

BOBBY VAN'S STEAKHOUSE   Lunch: $11-$35   Dinner: $19-$35   Phone: 202/589-0060   ⑪③
▼▲▼▲▼
Steak House
Location: Between H and I sts NW. 809 15th St NW 20004. **Hours:** 11:30 am-10:30 pm, Sat & Sun from 5 pm. Closed: 1/1, 11/24, 12/25. **Reservations:** suggested. **Features:** The steakhouse prepares one of the best porterhouse steaks in town. Beef is dry-aged on the premises. Seafood lovers will find large lobsters and other seafood dishes. An award-winning wine selection is available. Dressy casual; cocktails. **Parking:** no self-parking. **Cards:** AX, DC, DS, MC, VI.   ▼ ✖

THE BOMBAY CLUB   Lunch: $8-$19   Dinner: $8-$19   Phone: 202/659-3727   ⑩⑦
▼▲▼▲▼
Indian
Location: Between H and I sts; just n of the White House. 815 Connecticut Ave NW 20006. **Hours:** 11:30 am-2:30 & 5:30-10:30 pm, Fri-11 pm, Sat 5:30 pm-11 pm, Sun 11:30 am-2:30 & 5:30-9 pm. Closed: 1/1, 7/4, 12/25. **Reservations:** suggested. **Features:** The decor is tropical and elegant in the theme of the British Officer's clubs of Colonial India. Cuisine represents the regions and cultures of India, such as Moghul, Goa and the Northwest Frontier. Other items are prepared in the tandoor, a clay oven. The sidewalk cafe is a delightful spot on sunny days. Valet parking is available for dinner. Dressy casual; cocktails. **Parking:** no self-parking. **Cards:** AX, DC, MC, VI.   ▼ ✖

BOMBAY PALACE RESTAURANT   Lunch: $13-$18   Dinner: $16-$25   Phone: 202/331-4200   ㊉④
▼▲▼▲▼
Northern Indian
Location: Between 20th and 21st sts NW. 2020 K St NW 20006. **Hours:** 11:30 am-2:30 & 5:30-10 pm, Fri-10:30 pm, Sat noon-2:30 & 5:30-10:30 pm, Sun noon-2:30 & 5:30-10 pm. Closed: 1/1; also for lunch 12/25. **Reservations:** suggested. **Features:** The downtown restaurant, with its stylish dining room, offers tandoori specialties, such as chicken, salmon, lamb chops and jumbo shrimp, all cooked in a charcoal pit oven. The menu does not stop there, as curries, pilafs, biryanis and vindaloos are also available. Semi-formal attire; cocktails. **Parking:** no self-parking. **Cards:** AX, DC, DS, MC, VI.   ✖

B. SMITHS RESTAURANT   Lunch: $10-$18   Dinner: $17-$30   Phone: 202/289-6188   ⑬③
▼▲▼▲▼
Regional American
Location: At N Capitol St; in Union Station. 50 Massachusetts Ave NE 20002. **Hours:** 11:30 am-3 & 5-9 pm, Fri-10 pm, Sat noon-3 & 5-10 pm, Sun 11:30 am-8:45 pm. Closed major holidays. **Reservations:** suggested. **Features:** Guests can experience graceful, Southern-style dining in a beaux arts setting off the lobby of Union Station. The menu centers on Creole recipes and other Southern dishes. Brunch is served on weekends. Dressy casual; cocktails. **Parking:** on-site (fee). **Cards:** AX, DC, DS, MC, VI.   ▼ ✖

BUA   Lunch: $6-$8   Dinner: $8-$13   Phone: 202/265-0828   ㉔
▼▲▼
Thai
Location: Between 16th and 17th sts. 1635 P St NW 20036. **Hours:** 11:30 am-3 & 5-10 pm, Fri-11 pm, Sat noon-4 & 5-11 pm, Sun noon-10:30 pm. Closed major holidays. **Reservations:** suggested. **Features:** The pleasant but simple dining room on the second floor of a restored townhouse is a great spot in which to enjoy a meal of well-prepared dishes of yellow, red and green curries, noodles and tasty appetizers. This is a great place to meet friends after work for a casual but very good meal. Casual dress; cocktails. **Parking:** street. **Cards:** AX, DC, DS, MC, VI.

BURMA   Lunch: $7-$8   Dinner: $7-$11   Phone: 202/638-1280   ⑪⑤
▼▲▼
Burmese
Location: Between H and G sts NW; upstairs; in Chinatown. 740 6th St NW 20001. **Hours:** 11 am-3 & 6-10 pm, Sat & Sun from 6 pm. Closed major holidays. **Reservations:** accepted. **Features:** The Chinatown restaurant prepares Burmese cooking. The menu lists a nice selection of vegetarian, beef, chicken and fish choices, as well as an extensive array of salads and noodle dishes. The simple, second-floor dining rooms are decorated with Burmese and Asian artwork. Casual dress; cocktails. **Parking:** no self-parking. **Cards:** AX, CB, DC, DS, MC, VI.   ✖

BUSARA   Lunch: $6-$9   Dinner: $8-$16   Phone: 202/337-2340   ③
▼▲ ▼▲
Thai
Location: In Upper Georgetown area. 2340 Wisconsin Ave NW 20007. **Hours:** 11:30 am-3 & 5-10:30 pm, Fri-11:30 pm, Sat 11:30 am-4 & 5-11:30 pm, Sun 11:30 am-4 & 5-10:30 pm. Closed: 11/24; also for lunch 7/4 & 12/25. **Reservations:** suggested, weekends. **Features:** Contemporary furnishings and creative lighting give the restaurant a light, fun atmosphere. The menu offers a nice selection of appetizers, soups, salads and entrees. Siamese cooking is creative and consistent. Vegetarian selections are also available. Pad Thai noodles are a popular favorite, and sticky rice and mangos, along with an espresso or cappuccino, is a delightful conclusion to the meal. Casual dress; cocktails. **Parking:** no self-parking. **Cards:** AX, CB, DC, DS, MC, VI.   ▼ ✖

BUTTERFIELD 9   Lunch: $13-$22   Dinner: $18-$36   Phone: 202/289-8810   ⑫④
▼▲▼▲▼
American
Location: Between 6th and F sts NW. 600 14th St NW 20005. **Hours:** 11:30 am-2:30 & 5:30-10 pm, Fri-11 pm, Sat 5:30 pm-11 pm, Sun 5:30 pm-10 pm. Closed major holidays. **Reservations:** suggested. **Features:** The stylish dining room—with high ceilings, soft earth tones, large glass windows, black and white artwork and white tablecloths—sets an upscale air. The seasonally changing menu of Chef Martin Saylor offers contemporary American cuisine. Favorite preparations include golden and red beet Napolean and horseradish-crusted halibut with leek fondue, celeriac mousseline and beet and chive oil. Valet parking is available after 5:30 pm. Dressy casual; cocktails. **Parking:** on-site (fee) and valet. **Cards:** AX, CB, DC, DS, MC, VI.   ▼ ✖

(See map and index starting on p. 390)

CAFE 15   **Lunch:** $17-$26   **Dinner:** $26-$34   **Phone:** 202/730-8700   106
▽▽▽▽   **Location:** Jct 15th and H sts NW; in Sofitel Lafayette Square Washington DC. 806 15th St NW 20005. **Hours:** 6:30-
         10:30 am, 11-2:30 & 6-10:30 pm, Sat & Sun 6:30 am-10:30 & 6-10:30 pm. **Reservations:** suggested.
French   **Features:** Off the lobby of the Sofitel Lafayette Square Hotel is an intimate, upscale dining room offering
         wonderful Contemporay French cuisine. The kitchen displays it's talents with each dish. The prepartion is
simplistic yet sophiscated. The wait staff is professional and attentive and will see to your needs. Dressy casual; cocktails.
Parking: valet. **Cards:** AX, CB, DC, DS, JC, MC, VI.

CAFE ATLANTICO   **Dinner:** $18-$24   **Phone:** 202/393-0812   144
▽▽▽▽   **Location:** Between D and E sts NW. 405 8th St NW 20004. **Hours:** 5 pm-10 pm, Fri & Sat-11 pm. Closed: 11/24,
         12/24, 12/25. **Reservations:** suggested. **Features:** Nuevo Latin American cuisine is rich with Latin
Latino   American and Caribbean spices. The colorful, lively, multilevel dining room is set in the heart of downtown.
         Casual dress; cocktails. **Parking:** no self-parking. **Cards:** AX, DC, DS, MC, VI.

CAFE BERLIN   **Lunch:** $7-$18   **Dinner:** $15-$19   **Phone:** 202/543-7656   148
▽▽▽ ▽▽   **Location:** Between 3rd and 4th sts NE. 322 Massachusetts Ave NE 20002. **Hours:** 11:30 am-10 pm, Fri-11 pm, Sat
          noon-11 pm, Sun 4 pm-10 pm. Closed: 7/4. **Reservations:** suggested. **Features:** New German and
German   continental are Cafe Berlin's hallmark cuisines. Start with a herring appetizer then move on to a sauerbraten
          and red cabbage entree. Top it off with one of a variety of creative and homemade desserts. Outdoor dining
is available in season. Casual dress; cocktails. **Parking:** street. **Cards:** AX, DC, DS, MC, VI.

CAFE DES ARTISTES   **Lunch:** $8-$11   **Dinner:** $8-$11   **Phone:** 202/639-1786   137
▽▽▽   **Location:** 1 blk from the White House on 17th St; in the lobby of the Corcoran Gallery of Art. 500 17th St NW 20006.
       Hours: 11 am-2 pm, Thurs-8 pm, Sun 10:30 am-2 pm. Closed: 1/1, 11/24, 12/25; also Mon & Tues.
American **Features:** Primarily a casual place for soup and sandwiches, the relaxed bistro-style cafe is popular with the
          business lunch crowd. The menu changes periodically depending on events in the art gallery. Choirs and
gospel groups perform at the Sunday brunch. Casual dress; beer & wine only. **Parking:** on-site. **Cards:** AX, CB, DC, DS,
MC, VI.

CAFE DIVAN   **Lunch:** $6-$14   **Dinner:** $6-$18   **Phone:** 202/338-1747   9
▽▽▽ ▽▽   **Location:** Jct 34th St NW; in upper Georgetown. 1834 Wisconsin Ave NW 20007. **Hours:** 11 am-10:30 pm, Fri &
          Sat-11 pm. Closed: 1/1, 12/25. **Reservations:** suggested, weekends. **Features:** Adding to the stylish cafe's
Turkish   visual appeal are Brazilian wood floors, Italian wood furniture and glass windows all around. The menu
          centers on Turkish cooking, including such specialties as doner kebab: thin, marinated lamb and veal strips
served over pita bread with yogurt. The lunch menu is presented until 4 pm. Casual dress; cocktails. **Parking:** no self-parking.
Cards: AX, MC, VI.

CAFE MILANO   **Lunch:** $9-$20   **Dinner:** $13-$35   **Phone:** 202/333-6183   40
▽▽▽ ▽▽   **Location:** Off Wisconsin Ave; just n of M St NW. 3251 Prospect St NW 20007. **Hours:** 11:30 am-1 am, Thurs-Sat to
          2 am. Closed: 11/24, 12/25. **Reservations:** suggested. **Features:** A bright, busy atmosphere punctuates
Italian   this trendy, contemporary cafe, where diners often retreat to the sidewalk to sip an espresso and nibble on
          biscotti. The seasonally changing menu offers a good selection of pasta, pizza, salad and dinners. Lunch
menu served until 4 pm. Dressy casual; cocktails. **Parking:** on-site. **Cards:** AX, CB, DC, DS, MC, VI.

CAFE PROMENADE   **Lunch:** $12-$21   **Dinner:** $17-$30   **Phone:** 202/347-3000   70
▽▽▽▽   **Location:** Just n of K St NW; in business district; in Renaissance Mayflower Hotel. 1127 Conneticut Ave NW 20036.
         Hours: 6:30 am-11 pm. **Reservations:** suggested. **Features:** Taste the flavors of the Mediterranean in the
Mediterranean dining room at the Mayflower Hotel. The service is professional and attentive from the staff in white jackets.
               The spacious dining room is a comfortable setting for any occasion. A Sunday Brunch is offered 11 am-3
pm. Dressy casual; cocktails. **Parking:** valet. **Cards:** AX, CB, DC, DS, JC, MC, VI.

THE CAPITAL GRILLE   **Lunch:** $8-$28   **Dinner:** $19-$36   **Phone:** 202/737-6200   153
▽▽▽   **Location:** Jct 6th St NW. 601 Pennsylvania Ave NW 20004. **Hours:** 11:30 am-3 & 5-10 pm, Thurs-Sat to 11 pm,
       Sun 5 pm-10 pm. Closed major holidays. **Reservations:** suggested. **Features:** Just down the street from
Steak House the Capitol, the high-powered restaurant offers a rich, clubby atmosphere with mahogany-paneled walls and
             leather seating. The house specialty is dry-aged beef, but a nice selection of seafood also is on the menu.
Complimentary valet parking is available for dinner. Dressy casual; cocktails. **Parking:** no self-parking. **Cards:** AX, DS,
MC, VI.

CAPITAL Q   **Lunch:** $8-$15   **Dinner:** $8-$15   **Phone:** 202/347-8396   112
▽▽   **Location:** At 7th and H sts NW. 707 H St NW 20001. **Hours:** 11 am-7 pm, Fri & Sat-8 pm. Closed major
      holidays; also Sun. **Reservations:** accepted. **Features:** The Chinatown restaurant prepares Texas-style
Barbecue barbecue and offers cafeteria-style service. Beef brisket is a specialty, and jalapeno cornbread is popular.
          Casual dress; cocktails. **Parking:** no self-parking. **Cards:** AX, DC, DS, MC, VI.

CAPITOL CITY BREWING CO CAPITOL HILL   **Lunch:** $5-$15   **Dinner:** $8-$23   **Phone:** 202/842-2337   131
▽▽ ▽▽   **Location:** At the Postal Museum, next to Union Station. 2 Massachusetts Ave NE 20002. **Hours:** 11 am-11 pm, Fri &
          Sat-midnight. Closed: 11/24, 12/25. **Reservations:** accepted. **Features:** The fare is simple and wholesome,
American and the surroundings plain and comfortable. You can find good plated full meals, or more basic and quick
          food while on your busy sightseeing schedule. Located just north of the Capitol, this eatery and pub is a
convenient stop. Casual dress; cocktails. **Parking:** no self-parking. **Cards:** AX, DC, DS, MC, VI.

(See map and index starting on p. 390)

CAPITOL CITY BREWING COMPANY-DOWNTOWN   Lunch: $8-$16   Dinner: $8-$16   Phone: 202/628-2222   [101]
American
Location: Between 11th and 12th sts, on the south side of the building; 1 blk n of Metro Center subway stop. 1100 New York Ave NW 20005. **Hours:** 11 am-11 pm, Fri & Sat-midnight. Closed: 11/24, 12/25. **Features:** The fare is simple and wholesome and the surroundings plain and comfortable at the restaurant, also a functioning brewery. Guests can stick to their busy schedules while dropping in for good plated meals or more basic, quick food. The conveniently located eatery and pub is just north of the Metro Center and adjacent to the convention center. Casual dress; cocktails. **Parking:** no self-parking. **Cards:** AX, CB, DC, DS, MC, VI.

THE CAUCUS ROOM   Lunch: $15-$25   Dinner: $25-$35   Phone: 202/393-1300   [145]
American
Location: 9th and D sts NW; in Market Square North. 401 9th St NW 20004. **Hours:** 11:30 am-2:30 & 5:30-10:30 pm, Sat from 5:30 pm. Closed major holidays; also Sun. **Reservations:** suggested. **Features:** Rich cherry wood paneling, polished brass and marble lend to the clubby atmosphere. The kitchen prepares generous portions of prime aged beef and fresh seafood. Don't be surprised to see Democratic and Republican politicians dining at adjacent tables in the bipartisan establishment. The staff is professional and friendly. Valet parking is available during dinner service for a fee. Semi-formal attire; cocktails. **Parking:** no self-parking. **Cards:** AX, DC, DS, MC, VI.

CEIBA   Lunch: $11-$16   Dinner: $18-$27   Phone: 202/393-3983   [118]
Latino
Location: At 14th and G sts NW. 701 14th St NW 20005. **Hours:** 11:30 am-2:30 & 5:30-11 pm, Sat from 5:30 pm. Closed major holidays; also Sun. **Reservations:** suggested. **Features:** Pronounced "SAY-ba," the restaurant carries out a Latin American theme. The dining room is decorated with fabrics, wood and tile from Latin American countries. The menu reflects influences from a variety of regions in Mexico, as well as the Yucatan, Brazil, Argentina and the Caribbean. Dressy casual; cocktails. **Parking:** no self-parking. **Cards:** AX, DC, MC, VI.

CHING CHING CHA   Lunch: $11   Dinner: $11   Phone: 202/333-8288   [75]
Chinese
Location: Between K and M sts; in Georgetown. 1063 Wisconsin Ave NW 20007. **Hours:** 11:30 am-9 pm. Closed: Mon. **Features:** Tea connoisseurs will fall in love with the adorable tea shop and its wide array of Asian infusions. While sipping a soothing brew, patrons can munch on dumplings, curry rolls, a subtle egg flower soup or a bento box of ginger salmon, chicken, beef or tofu. Casual dress. **Parking:** street. **Cards:** AX, DS, MC, VI.

CLYDE'S OF GEORGETOWN   Lunch: $8-$19   Dinner: $11-$23   Phone: 202/333-9180   [69]
American
Location: Just w of jct Wisconsin Ave NW. 3236 M St NW 20007. **Hours:** 11:30 am-midnight, Fri-1 am, Sat 10 am-1 am, Sun 9 am-10:30 pm. Closed: 12/25. **Reservations:** suggested. **Features:** In the heart of Georgetown, the popular saloon has numerous dining rooms in which diners may enjoy a changing selection of consistently good American fare. Casual dress; cocktails. **Parking:** no self-parking. **Cards:** AX, DC, DS, MC, VI.

COEUR DE LION   Lunch: $11-$17   Dinner: $20-$35   Phone: 202/414-0500   [80]
Continental
Location: 10th St and Massachusetts Ave NW; in Henley Park Hotel. 926 Massachusetts Ave NW 20001. **Hours:** 7 am-2 & 5:30-10 pm, Sun-2 pm. **Reservations:** suggested. **Features:** Located in the heart of the capital city inside the historic Henley Park Hotel, the Coeur de Lion offers upscale Continental dining. The dining rooms here are each distinct, but the level of elegance, while understated, never waivers. The atrium roof and creative lighting provides for the most romantic of evenings. Enjoy your dinner while listening to live entertainment, Thursday-Saturday nights. Dressy casual; cocktails; entertainment. **Parking:** valet. **Cards:** AX, CB, DC, DS, MC, VI. **Historic**

CORDUROY   *Menu on aaa.com*   Lunch: $10-$17   Dinner: $18-$27   Phone: 202/589-0699   [83]
American
Location: 12th and K sts NW; in Four Points Sheraton Washington DC Downtown. 1201 K St NW 20005. **Hours:** 6:30 am-10, noon-2:30 & 5:30-10:30 pm, Sat 7 am-11, noon-2:30 & 5-11 pm, Sun 7 am-11, noon-2:30 & 5-10:30 pm. **Reservations:** suggested. **Features:** The New American cuisine of chef Tom Power has brought the hotel dining room to life. The menu changes seasonally using the freshest market ingredients. The wine list offers a nice selection, with a very extensive offering of half bottles. Limited valet parking is available, validated for 2 hours for lunch, 3 hours for dinner. Dressy casual; cocktails. **Parking:** valet. **Cards:** AX, DC, DS, MC, VI.

DAVID GREGGORY RESTAU LOUNGE   Lunch: $12-$18   Dinner: $18-$28   Phone: 202/872-8700   [63]
American
Location: Jct 21st and M sts NW. 2030 M St NW 20036. **Hours:** 11:30 am-2:30 & 5:30-10 pm, Fri-11 pm, Sat 5:30 pm-11 pm, Sun 11 am-2:30 pm. Closed major holidays. **Reservations:** suggested. **Features:** Two chefs share a single vision for creating "American retro forward" cuisine from fresh local and organic ingredients. The light, airy dining atmosphere is enhanced by creative styling and the work of local artists. Sidewalk tables are offered seasonally. Valet parking is available Friday and Saturday nights. Dressy casual; cocktails. **Parking:** no self-parking. **Cards:** AX, DS, MC, VI.

DC COAST   Lunch: $14-$19   Dinner: $19-$29   Phone: 202/216-5988   [88]
American
Location: Jct of 14th and K sts NW; in the Tower Building, ground floor. 1401 K St NW 20005. **Hours:** 11:30 am-2:30 & 5:30-10:30 pm, Fri-11 pm, Sat 5:30 pm-11 pm. Closed major holidays; also Sun. **Reservations:** suggested. **Features:** Casually upscale Beaux Arts styling in the two-story dining room and on the small, glassed-in balcony concentrates on the details. So does Chef Tunks in preparing modern American cuisine. Preparation for the dishes, many of which emphasize seafood, reflects influences from the Southern, Southwestern and Mid-Atlantic areas of the country, as well as the Pacific Rim. Valet parking is available from 5:30 pm for a fee. Dressy casual; cocktails. **Parking:** no self-parking. **Cards:** AX, CB, DC, DS, MC, VI.

(See map and index starting on p. 390)

DISH

American

Lunch: $10-$14   Dinner: $17-$25   Phone: 202/338-8707   **99**
Location: Between K and I sts NW; in The River Inn. 924 25th St NW 20037. **Hours:** 7-10 am, 11:30-2:30 & 5-10:30 pm, Sat & Sun 8 am-10 & 5-10:30 pm. **Closed:** 11/24, 12/24, 12/25. **Reservations:** suggested. **Features:** Off the lobby of The River Inn, the intimate dining room offers a stylish yet simple atmosphere. The kitchen prepares comfort food with a twist. The menu changes seasonally, but a couple signature dishes are standbys. Among them is Mom's meatloaf, a wonderfully prepared blend of veal and beef served with garlic mashed potatoes. Casual dress; cocktails. **Parking:** valet. **Cards:** AX, MC, VI.

DISTRICT CHOPHOUSE & BREWERY   Lunch: $10-$13   Dinner: $19-$28   Phone: 202/347-3434   **139**

American

Location: Between E and F sts NW; just s of MCI center. 509 7th St NW 20004. **Hours:** 11 am-11 pm, Fri-11:30 pm, Sat 2 pm-11:30 pm, Sun 2 pm-10 pm, Mon 11 am-10 pm. **Closed:** 11/24, 12/25. **Reservations:** suggested. **Features:** A half-block from MCI Center, Shakespeare Theater and Gallery Place/Chinatown Metro station, the restored building maintains a nostalgic air. The mezzanine level is a great place to relax at the cigar bar or play billiards. The on-site micro-brew vats produce fine hand-crafted beers. Traditional chophouse fare—juicy, mouthwatering steaks, as well as brick oven pizzas, sandwiches and salads—is at the heart of the menu. Casual dress; cocktails. **Parking:** no self-parking. **Cards:** AX, DC, DS, MC, VI.

EQUINOX   Lunch: $16-$24   Dinner: $22-$32   Phone: 202/331-8118   **108**

American

Location: Between H and I sts NW. 818 Connecticut Ave NW 20006. **Hours:** 11:30 am-2 & 5:30-10 pm, Fri-10:30 pm, Sat 5:30 pm-10:30 pm, Sun 5 pm-9 pm. **Closed** major holidays. **Reservations:** suggested. **Features:** A few blocks from the White House, the restaurant's dining room provides a simple, soothing, upscale ambience. Shaded by umbrellas, the sidewalk terrace is a wonderful spot for lunch. Chef Todd Gray prepares simple, yet sophisticated, contemporary American fare. The seasonally changing menu is driven by the availability of farm-fresh ingredients. Dressy casual; cocktails. **Parking:** no self-parking. **Cards:** AX, CB, DC, DS, MC, VI.

ETRUSCO   Dinner: $14-$23   Phone: 202/667-0047   **19**

Italian

Location: Connecticut Ave NW, just n of Dupont Circle. 1606 20th St NW 20009. **Hours:** 5:30 pm-9:30 pm. Closed major holidays; also Sun. **Reservations:** suggested. **Features:** Just a short walk north of the Dupont Circle Metro Station, you can enjoy traditional Tuscan cuisine while you people-watch from casual sidewalk seating. Or, relax in the bright and lively dining room. Choose from a wide variety of antipasti, pasta, and entrees. The traditional Ribollita is thick and rich, a vegetarian delight! Creative appetizers and a big selection of seafood provide a touch beyond strictly traditional. Dressy casual; cocktails. **Parking:** no self-parking. **Cards:** AX, CB, DC, MC, VI.

FADO' IRISH PUB   Lunch: $9-$13   Dinner: $9-$13   Phone: 202/789-0066   **110**

Irish

Location: Between H and I sts. 808 7th St NW 20001. **Hours:** 11:30 am-10 pm. Closed major holidays. **Features:** Guests can feast on boxty, the traditional Irish potato staple, or kick back with a pint and let the Old World atmosphere take them to a time long ago. Casual dress; cocktails. **Parking:** street. **Cards:** AX, DC, DS, MC, VI.

FAHRENHEIT   Lunch: $15-$31   Dinner: $25-$51   Phone: 202/912-4110   **81**

Nouvelle American

Location: Just s of jct M St and Wisconsin Ave, off Wisconsin, just e; in The Ritz-Carlton, Georgetown. 1010 South St 20007. **Hours:** 6:30 am-10:30, noon-2:30 & 6-10 pm, Fri & Sat-11 pm. Closed: for dinner Sun. **Reservations:** suggested. **Features:** Set in the fascinatingly restored former Georgetown incinerator, the restaurant features decor that is sharp and modern with exposed brick, soaring ceilings, fiery orange glasses and a dominating view of its smokestack. This modern setting contrasts to a menu reminiscent of Old World Italy; the Mediterranean and the clubby dining rooms of the 1950's are recalled with such classic desserts as baked Alaska. Dressy casual; cocktails. **Parking:** on-site and valet. **Cards:** AX, CB, DC, DS, JC, MC, VI.

FAMOUS LUIGI'S   Lunch: $7-$14   Dinner: $9-$23   Phone: 202/331-7574   **68**

Italian

Location: Between M and N sts. 1132 19th St NW 20036. **Hours:** 11 am-midnight, Sun from noon. **Closed:** 11/24, 12/25. **Features:** Operated by the same family since its opening in 1943, the restaurant serves Italian food in a traditional setting with red and white checked tablecloths. Service is friendly. Casual dress; cocktails. **Parking:** street. **Cards:** AX, DC, DS, MC, VI.

FELIX RESTAURANT AND THE SPY LOUNGE   Dinner: $14-$27   Phone: 202/483-3549   **6**

American

Location: Jct 18th St NW and Belmont Rd, just w. 2406 18th St NW 20009. **Hours:** 5:30 pm-10:30 pm, Fri & Sat-11 pm, Sun-10 pm. **Closed:** 12/25. **Reservations:** suggested. **Features:** A decor package that includes faux clouds on the ceiling and a montage cityscape mural that includes prominent landmark buildings from cities around the world define the chic New York-style lounge restaurant. Chef Andrew Chamber blends modern American cuisine with influences from France and Asia when creating its innovative dishes. A kosher dinner with matzo ball soup and beef brisket is a Friday tradition. The lounge features live entertainment six nights weekly. Casual dress; cocktails. **Parking:** street. **Cards:** AX, CB, DC, MC, VI.

FETTOOSH   Lunch: $9-$16   Dinner: $12-$19   Phone: 202/342-1199   **52**

Lebanese

Location: In Georgetown. 3277 M St NW 20007. **Hours:** 11 am-3 am, Fri & Sat-5 am. **Reservations:** suggested, weekends. **Features:** The food is good and the service prompt in the comfortable Lebanese restaurant. Vegetarians will find options galore. Casual dress; cocktails. **Parking:** street. **Cards:** AX, CB, DC, DS, MC, VI.

FILOMENA RISTORANTE   Lunch: $8-$13   Dinner: $15-$30   Phone: 202/338-8800   **71**

Italian

Location: Between K and M sts; in Georgetown. 1063 Wisconsin Ave NW 20027. **Hours:** 11:30 am-11 pm. **Closed:** 1/1, 11/24, 12/25; also evening of 12/24. **Reservations:** suggested. **Features:** This restaurant has a loyal local following, and for good reasons: exceptional food and quality service. The menu features homemade pasta, seafood, meat and poultry, and buffets are laid out Monday through Friday for lunch and on weekends for brunch. The atmosphere blends Old World and garden influences. Dressy casual; cocktails. **Parking:** no self-parking. **Cards:** AX, DC, DS, MC, VI.

(See map and index starting on p. 390)

FINEMONDO ITALIAN COUNTRY KITCHEN   Lunch: $8-$16   Dinner: $14-$24   Phone: 202/737-3100   123
Italian   **Location:** Between 13th and 14th sts NW. 1319 F St NW 20004. **Hours:** 11:30 am-2:30 & 5:30-10 pm, Fri-11 pm, Sat 5:30 pm-11 pm. Closed major holidays; also Sun. **Reservations:** suggested. **Features:** The kitchen prepares good country-style recipes from all regions of Italy. Spit-roasted meats, fish and poultry are seared in their own juices to create a wonderful flavor and are served with traditional sauces and side dishes. The atmosphere is comfortable, and service is professional. Casual dress; cocktails. **Parking:** no self-parking. **Cards:** AX, DC, DS, MC, VI.

FIREFLY   Lunch: $10-$16   Dinner: $17-$21   Phone: 202/861-1310   32
American   **Location:** Between 20th and N sts NW; in Hotel Madera. 1310 New Hampshire Ave NW 20036. **Hours:** 7-10 am, 11:30-2 & 5:30-10 pm. Closed major holidays. **Reservations:** suggested. **Features:** Contemporary American cuisine makes up the seasonally changing menu, which is influenced by both regional and international recipes. The stylish dining room has a floor-to-ceiling firefly tree with candlelit lanterns dangling from the branches. An exhibition kitchen is tucked behind a rustic stone wall. Casual dress; cocktails. **Parking:** valet. **Cards:** AX, DC, DS, MC, VI.

FLORIDA AVENUE GRILL   Lunch: $5-$10   Dinner: $5-$10   Phone: 202/265-1586   7
Soul Food   **Location:** Jct 11th St. 1100 Florida Ave NW 20009. **Hours:** 6 am-9 pm. Closed major holidays; also Sun & Mon. **Features:** Since the 1940s, the famed diner has served delicious soul food and Southern specialties to a host of the famous and infamous whose autographed photographs line the walls. Casual dress. **Parking:** on-site. **Cards:** AX, DC, DS, MC, VI.

GALILEO   Lunch: $13-$19   Dinner: $24-$35   Phone: 202/293-7191   77
Northern Italian   **Location:** Between L and M sts NW. 1110 21st St NW 20036. **Hours:** 11:30 am-2 & 5:30-10 pm, Fri-10:30 pm, Sat 5:30 pm-10:30 pm, Sun 5 pm-10 pm. Closed major holidays. **Reservations:** suggested. **Features:** This simple, yet stylish eatery features artfully prepared dishes using only fresh ingredients. Save room for the highlight of your meal: a simply delicious tiramisu. Some private dining rooms are available. Valet parking is offered during the evening on Monday. Semi-formal attire; cocktails. **Parking:** no self-parking. **Cards:** AX, CB, MC, VI.

GEORGIA BROWN'S   Lunch: $15-$23   Dinner: $15-$23   Phone: 202/393-4499   95
Regional American   **Location:** At McPherson Square; between K and I sts NW. 950 15th St NW 20005. **Hours:** 11:30 am-10:30 pm, Fri-11:30 pm, Sat 5:30 pm-11:30 pm, Sun 10 am-2:30 & 5:30-9 pm. Closed: 5/30, 9/5, 12/25. **Reservations:** suggested. **Features:** The tasty fare at the stylish cafe—a hot spot with the political crowd—reflects the culinary traditions of the South, particularly the Lowcountry of South Carolina. The menu shows flair and inventiveness. Blues and jazz artists perform at Sunday brunch. Dressy casual; cocktails. **Parking:** no self-parking. **Cards:** AX, CB, DC, DS, MC, VI.

GERARD'S PLACE   Lunch: $24-$36   Dinner: $30-$50   Phone: 202/737-4445   90
French   **Location:** At McPherson Square. 915 15th St NW 20005. **Hours:** 11:30 am-2:30 & 5:30-9:30 pm, Sat from 5:30 pm. Closed major holidays; also Sun. **Reservations:** suggested. **Features:** Opposite McPherson Square, the intimate restaurant builds a menu around contemporary French cuisine. Chef/owner Gerard Pangaud uses fresh ingredients in such expertly prepared selections as the signature lobster dish and Chilean sea bass. Desserts are made "a la commande," which requires 25 minutes preparation time. A tasting menu with wine pairings is available. Semi-formal attire; cocktails. **Parking:** no self-parking. **Cards:** AX, DC, MC, VI.

GORDON BIERSCH BREWERY RESTAURANT   Lunch: $7-$15   Dinner: $11-$26   Phone: 202/783-5454   129
American   **Location:** Corner of 9th St. 900 F St NW 20004. **Hours:** 11:30 am-11 pm, Fri & Sat-midnight. Closed: 11/24, 12/25. **Reservations:** suggested. **Features:** Everything about this place is big: tall ceilings with elaborate molding, huge marble pillars and lots of floor space — all remains from a former life as a bank. Added are the towering steel fermentation tanks which are part of the brewery. Some dishes are Asian influenced but there are pastas, roast chickens, grilled steaks, seafood, lamb chops and the like. It's loud, it's fun and the bar is usually crowded. Casual dress; cocktails. **Parking:** street. **Cards:** AX, DC, DS, MC, VI.

THE GRILL   Lunch: $21-$42   Dinner: $35-$58   Phone: 202/974-5566   73
Nouvelle American   **Location:** At 22nd and M sts NW; in The Ritz-Carlton, Washington, DC. 1150 22nd St NW 20037. **Hours:** 6:30-11 am, 11:30-2:30 & 6-10 pm. **Reservations:** suggested. **Features:** Artful and creative dishes reflect regional and global influences. The setting is upscale and stylish, with an open kitchen, silk-draped windows overlooking city sidewalks and excellent place settings. Dressy casual; cocktails. **Parking:** on-site (fee) and valet. **Cards:** AX, CB, DC, DS, JC, MC, VI.

THE GRILL FROM IPANEMA   Lunch: $18   Dinner: $13-$22   Phone: 202/986-0757   5
Brazilian   **Location:** Between 18th St and Belmont Rd. 1858 Columbia Rd NW 20009. **Hours:** 5 pm-11 pm, Fri-11:30 pm, Sat noon-11:30 pm, Sun noon-10 pm. Closed: 7/4, 11/24, 12/25. **Reservations:** accepted. **Features:** You'll enjoy the popular, chic, lively atmosphere with close table spacing. The menu offers an extensive selection of Brazilian dishes and specialties, including moqueca (a seafood stew) and feijoada (a bean pork casserole). Sidewalk dining is seasonal. Casual dress; cocktails. **Parking:** no self-parking. **Cards:** AX, DC, DS, MC, VI.

HAAD THAI   Lunch: $7-$9   Dinner: $9-$13   Phone: 202/682-1111   102
Thai   **Location:** Between 11th and 12th sts on east side of building, 1 blk n of Metro Center subway stop. 1100 New York Ave NW 20005. **Hours:** 11:30 am-2:30 & 5-10:30 pm, Sat noon-10:30 pm, Sun 5 pm-10:30 pm. Closed: 11/24, 12/25. **Reservations:** suggested. **Features:** Just north of Metro Center on the subway and just across the street from the convention center, the eatery is convenient. Although this place bustles at lunch, the atmosphere is more subdued in the evening, when tablecloths are used and some extra tables are removed. Tom kha is nicely spiced, and chicken satay is as good as it looks. Also among the entrees are pad Thai, panang gai and honey roast duck. No monosodium glutamate is used, and dishes can be spiced to taste. Casual dress; cocktails. **Parking:** no self-parking. **Cards:** AX, DC, MC, VI.

(See map and index starting on p. 390)

HERITAGE INDIA **Lunch:** $7-$11 **Dinner:** $8-$23 **Phone:** 202/333-3120 ②

◆◆◆

Indian

Location: In the Glover Park area. 2400 Wisconsin Ave NW 20007. **Hours:** 11:30 am-2:30 & 5:30-10:30 pm, Fri & Sat-11 pm. **Reservations:** suggested. **Features:** The upscale dining room, with Indian photos and artwork, provides a comfortable atmosphere in which patrons can sample superb Indian cooking. The chef blends herbs and spices to create subtle, balanced flavors. Semi-formal attire; cocktails. **Parking:** no self-parking. **Cards:** AX, DC, DS, MC, VI.

⊠

I RICCHI **Lunch:** $12-$31 **Dinner:** $15-$31 **Phone:** 202/835-0459 ㊳

AAA

◆◆◆

Regional Italian

Location: Between M and N sts NW. 1220 19th St NW 20036. **Hours:** 11:30 am-2 & 5:30-10 pm, Fri-10:30 pm, Sat 5:30 pm-10:30 pm. Closed major holidays; also Sun. **Reservations:** suggested. **Features:** The wait staff's inspiring description of the menu is not only informative but also accurate. Tuscan specialties are served in traditional trattoria surroundings. A favorite is the tortellini sage butter. Valet parking is offered after 5:30 pm. Dressy casual; cocktails. **Parking:** on-site (fee). **Cards:** AX, CB, DC, MC, VI.

⊠

IRON GATE RESTAURANT **Lunch:** $11-$14 **Dinner:** $19-$25 **Phone:** 202/737-1370 ㉞

◆◆◆

Mediterranean

Location: Between 17th and 18th sts. 1734 N St NW 20036. **Hours:** 11:30 am-2:15 & 5:30-10 pm, Sat from 5:30 pm. Closed: 9/5; also Sun, week of Thanksgiving & Christmas. **Reservations:** suggested. **Features:** A cozier place can hardly be imagined; the restaurant is comfortably worn and radiates warmth and intimacy, with nooks for couples and booths for friends. Occasionally someone stokes the wood-burning fireplace which continuously crackles. It seems secret and poetic, well away from the modern world. Warmer months find elegant courtyard dining under an arbor of heavy grape vines. Dressy casual; cocktails. **Parking:** street. **Cards:** AX, DC, DS, MC, VI.

⊠

JALEO **Lunch:** $7-$15 **Dinner:** $11-$20 **Phone:** 202/628-7949 (141)

◆◆

Spanish

Location: Jct 7th and E St NW; 3 blks n off Pennsylvania Ave NW; 1 blk s of MCI Center. 480 7th St NW 20004. **Hours:** 11:30 am-10 pm, Tues-Thurs to 11:30 pm, Fri & Sat-midnight. Closed: 11/24, 12/24, 12/25. **Features:** In a popular spot near MCI Center, the bustling Spanish restaurant offers an extensive menu of tapas, as well as full meals. The staff is friendly, and the atmosphere is lively and fun. Casual dress; cocktails. **Parking:** no self-parking. **Cards:** AX, DC, DS, MC, VI.

🍸 ⊠

JOHNNY'S HALF SHELL **Lunch:** $12-$22 **Dinner:** $12-$22 **Phone:** 202/296-2021 ㉖

◆◆

Seafood

Location: W of Dupont Circle. 2002 P St NW 20036. **Hours:** 11:30 am-10:30 pm, Fri & Sat-11 pm. Closed major holidays; also Sun. **Reservations:** suggested. **Features:** Enjoy the casual but upscale atmosphere for lunch or dinner. Crabcakes are their specialty here along with several specialty drinks from the bar. Dressy casual; cocktails. **Parking:** on-site (fee) and street. **Cards:** AX, MC, VI.

🍸 ⊠

J. PAUL'S **Lunch:** $9-$23 **Dinner:** $12-$23 **Phone:** 202/333-3450 (66)

◆

American

Location: Just w of jct Wisconsin Ave NW. 3218 M St NW 20007. **Hours:** 11:30 am-11:30 pm, Fri & Sat-1 am. Closed: 12/25. **Features:** In the heart of Georgetown is the popular dining saloon. It's noisy and the tables are spaced closely, but it's casual, fun and lively. On the menu are traditional dishes, including hickory spare ribs, bayou salmon and Eastern Shore rotisserie chicken. Casual dress; cocktails. **Parking:** no self-parking. **Cards:** AX, DC, DS, MC, VI.

⊠

KANLAYA THAI CUISINE **Lunch:** $8-$11 **Dinner:** $9-$16 **Phone:** 202/393-0088 (116)

◆◆

Thai

Location: Jct H St NW, just s; in Chinatown. 740 6th St NW 20001. **Hours:** 11:30 am-10:30 pm, Fri & Sat-11 pm. **Reservations:** accepted. **Features:** The simple, contemporary dining room provides a nice setting for Thai cuisine. The menu lines up a large selection of vegetarian dishes, as well as traditional recipes. Casual dress; cocktails. **Parking:** no self-parking. **Cards:** AX, DS, MC, VI.

⊠

KAZ SUSHI BISTRO **Lunch:** $6-$13 **Dinner:** $12-$23 **Phone:** 202/530-5500 (96)

◆◆

Japanese

Location: Between 19th and 20th sts. 1915 I St NW 20006. **Hours:** 11:30 am-2 & 6-10 pm, Sat from 6 pm. Closed major holidays; also Sun. **Reservations:** suggested, dinner. **Features:** Chef-owner Kazuhiro Okochi originated a concept he calls "free-style Japanese cuisine," a combination of a relaxed restaurant atmosphere with modern Japanese influences. Employing only the freshest seasonal ingredients, he creates innovative dishes that delight both the eye and palate. Try the tempura bento, grilled baby octopus with seaweed salad. Casual dress; beer & wine only. **Parking:** street. **Cards:** AX, CB, DC, DS, JC, MC, VI.

⊠

KINKEAD'S RESTAURANT **Lunch:** $15-$22 **Dinner:** $24-$35 **Phone:** 202/296-7700 (105)

◆◆◆

American

Location: Between 20th and 21st sts NW. 2000 Pennsylvania Ave NW 20006. **Hours:** 11:30 am-2:30 & 5:30-10 pm, Fri-10:30 pm, Sat 5:30 pm-10:30 pm. Closed major holidays. **Reservations:** suggested. **Features:** The cuisine here is New American with emphasis on seafood. The bi-level restaurant, with a cafe and lounge on the lower level and a pleasant, upscale atmosphere and open kitchen on the top level, is inviting. Valet parking is complimentary during dinner. Dressy casual; cocktails; entertainment. **Parking:** no self-parking. **Cards:** AX, CB, DC, DS, MC, VI.

🍸 ⊠

LA BRASSERIE **Lunch:** $9-$20 **Dinner:** $9-$27 **Phone:** 202/546-9154 (146)

◆◆

French

Location: On Capitol Hill; just ne of the Capitol; jct 3rd St. 239 Massachusetts Ave NE 20002. **Hours:** 10 am-10 pm, Sat from 5 pm. Closed major holidays. **Reservations:** suggested. **Features:** Just blocks from the Capitol, the townhouse restaurant offers cozy dining rooms and a wonderful covered terrace overlooking Massachusetts Avenue. The focus of the seasonally changing menu is on simple, straightforward French food. Casual dress; cocktails. **Parking:** street. **Cards:** AX, MC, VI.

⊠

(See map and index starting on p. 390)

LA CHAUMIERE
French
Lunch: $14-$18   **Dinner:** $15-$30   **Phone:** 202/338-1784   58
Location: In Georgetown; opposite Four Seasons Hotel. 2813 M St NW 20007. **Hours:** 11:30 am-2:30 & 5:30-10:30 pm, Sat from 5:30 pm. Closed major holidays; also Sun. **Reservations:** suggested. **Features:** A consistently popular operation, the established restaurant, with its open-hearth fireplace, exudes the ambience of a secluded country inn. Baked onion soup is subtle and sweet, and pike dumplings in lobster sauce is a local favorite. On Wednesday, the chef prepares wonderful couscous with a spicy combination of boiled beef, lamb, chicken, vegetables and chickpeas with semolina and harissa. Two-hour parking at the Four Seasons Hotel is validated. Dressy casual; cocktails. **Parking:** no self-parking. **Cards:** AX, CB, DC, MC, VI.

LA COLLINE
French
Lunch: $11-$23   **Dinner:** $14-$27   **Phone:** 202/737-0400   140
Location: On Capitol Hill. 400 N Capitol St NW 20001. **Hours:** 7-10 am, 11:30-3 & 6-10 pm, Sat from 6 pm. Closed major holidays; also Sun. **Reservations:** suggested. **Features:** A favorite of many who work on or near Capitol Hill, the handsome, cosmopolitan restaurant has a well-rounded menu. Fresh fish dishes, some smoked, are favorites. Servers are uniformed and professional, and although this place remains busy, staff attentiveness is never flagging. Parking is free after 5 pm. Dressy casual; cocktails. **Parking:** on-site. **Cards:** AX, CB, DC, JC, MC, VI.

LA TOMATE
Italian
Lunch: $11-$14   **Dinner:** $12-$24   **Phone:** 202/667-5505   18
Location: Jct R St NW. 1701 Connecticut Ave NW 20009. **Hours:** 11:30 am-10:30 pm, Thurs-11 pm, Fri & Sat-11:30 pm, Sun-10 pm. Closed: 12/25; also for lunch 1/1. **Reservations:** suggested. **Features:** The bistro's location on a prominent street corner in a popular neighborhood makes it a nice stop for people-watching. Specialties include smoked trout and salmon, plus a wide variety of pasta dishes. The patio is open seasonally. Valet parking is available after 6 pm for a fee. Casual dress; cocktails. **Parking:** no self-parking. **Cards:** AX, DS, MC, VI.

LAURIOL PLAZA
Latino
Lunch: $7-$18   **Dinner:** $7-$18   **Phone:** 202/387-0035   11
Location: Jct 18th and T sts NW. 1835 18th St NW 20009. **Hours:** 11:30 am-11 pm, Fri & Sat-midnight, Sun 11 am-11 pm. Closed: 11/24. **Reservations:** accepted, for lunch. **Features:** The stylish dining room comprises three levels of open, airy ambience. Sidewalk dining is a nice option when the weather cooperates. The menu incorporates a selection of Mexican and Spanish dishes, from tacos and fajitas to seafood, chicken and beef dishes. The kitchen is reliable. Casual dress; cocktails. **Parking:** on-site. **Cards:** AX, DC, DS, MC, VI.

LEFTBANK
International
Lunch: $8-$25   **Dinner:** $15-$26   **Phone:** 202/464-2100   4
Location: In Adams Morgan. 2424 18th St NW 20009. **Hours:** 7 am-2 am, Fri & Sat-3 am. Closed: 11/24, 12/25. **Reservations:** suggested. **Features:** The seasonally changing menu centers on simple, fresh French brasserie fare. The chef also creates weekly specials to complement the menu. Dressy casual; cocktails. **Parking:** valet. **Cards:** AX, DC, DS, MC, VI.

LEI GARDEN
Chinese
Lunch: $8-$25   **Dinner:** $8-$25   **Phone:** 202/216-9696   111
Location: Jct 7th St, just nw. 629-631 H St NW 20001. **Hours:** 11:30 am-11 pm, Fri & Sat-midnight, Sun-10:30 pm. **Reservations:** accepted. **Features:** The Chinatown restaurant offers dining variety, with a traditional menu, a 50- to 60-item lunch buffet and a lunch dim sum parlor in the upstairs banquet room. Live lobster and deep-fried butterfly shrimp served with tangy sauce are just a couple examples from the expansive menu. Casual dress; cocktails. **Parking:** street. **Cards:** AX, DC, DS, MC, VI.

LES HALLES
French
Lunch: $13-$26   **Dinner:** $14-$26   **Phone:** 202/347-6848   142
Location: Between 12th and 13th sts. 1201 Pennsylvania Ave NW 20004. **Hours:** 11:30 am-midnight. **Reservations:** suggested. **Features:** This steakhouse in a brasserie setting offers American beef prepared with a French flair. The seasonal heated sidewalk terrace is a popular spot to dine and people watch. Premium cigars can be purchased in the cigar lounge. Casual dress; cocktails. **Parking:** no self-parking. **Cards:** AX, DC, DS, JC, MC, VI.

LEVANTE'S
Greek
Lunch: $8-$25   **Dinner:** $8-$25   **Phone:** 202/293-3244   30
Location: Just s of Dupont Circle. 1320 19th St NW 20036. **Hours:** 11 am-10 pm, Fri & Sat 11 pm. Closed: 11/24. **Reservations:** accepted. **Features:** Mediterranean coast colors of cobalt blue and yellow project an upbeat mood. Greek- and Turkish-inspired dishes are accented with exotic spices. Casual dress; cocktails. **Parking:** street. **Cards:** AX, MC, VI.

LUIGINO
Italian
Lunch: $9-$16   **Dinner:** $13-$25   **Phone:** 202/371-0595   100
Location: Corner of H and 12th sts NW. 1100 New York Ave NW 20005. **Hours:** 11:30 am-10:30 pm, Fri-11:30 pm, Sat 5:30 pm-11:30 pm, Sun 5:30 pm-10 pm. Closed: 1/1, 12/25. **Reservations:** suggested. **Features:** With all glass walls, the corner location affords a good view of busy sidewalk traffic. Those who are in a hurry can eat at the dining bar with a full view of the kitchen. The selection of well-prepared and flavorful pasta, meat and seafood preparations is good. Service is timely but somewhat impersonal during lunch. Casual dress; cocktails. **Parking:** on-site (fee). **Cards:** AX, DC, DS, MC, VI.

M & S GRILL
Steak House
Lunch: $8-$15   **Dinner:** $13-$35   **Phone:** 202/347-1500   126
Location: At E St NW; metro stop; metro center. 600 13th St NW 20005. **Hours:** 11:30 am-11 pm, Sun & Mon-10 pm. **Reservations:** accepted. **Features:** This place is steeped in the tradition that defines "restaurant." The staff is friendly, and the chefs prepare tasty dishes of beef stroganoff, seafood gumbo and shepherd's pie, as well as homemade desserts. Casual dress; cocktails. **Parking:** street. **Cards:** AX, DC, DS, MC, VI.

(See map and index starting on p. 390)

MARCEL'S
▼▼▼ ▼▼▼
French
Dinner: $26-$42   **Phone:** 202/296-1166   (79)
Location: 1.5 blks nw of Washington Circle. 2401 Pennsylvania Ave NW 20037. **Hours:** 5:30 pm-10:30 pm, Fri & Sat-11 pm, Sun 5 pm-10 pm. Closed: 1/1, 11/24, 12/25. **Reservations:** suggested. **Features:** Chef Robert Wiedmaier and his talented kitchen prepare delicious French food with Belgian influences. The availability of fresh ingredients drives the seasonally changing menu choices. Tuna tartare, a signature dish, is a wonderful starter. A pre-theater menu is presented from 5:30 pm to 7 pm, and valet parking is complimentary. Dressy casual; cocktails; entertainment. **Parking:** no self-parking. **Cards:** AX, CB, DC, DS, MC, VI.

MARRAKESH
▼▼▼ ▼▼
Moroccan
Dinner: $25   **Phone:** 202/393-9393   (78)
Location: Between 6th and 7th sts NW. 617 New York Ave NW 20001. **Hours:** 6 pm-11 pm, Fri & Sat from 5:30 pm, Sun from 5 pm. Closed: 11/24. **Reservations:** required. **Features:** It's well worth taking the time to experience the seven-course Moroccan food and memorable ambience here. Besides the lively belly dancing during dinner, there's also valet parking from 6 pm. No credit cards are accepted. Casual dress; cocktails; entertainment. **Parking:** on-site (fee) and valet.

MAXIM
▼▼▼▼
Russian
MC, VI.
Lunch: $8-$16   **Dinner:** $21-$32   **Phone:** 202/962-0280   (121)
Location: 1 blk w of the old executive office building. 1725 F St NW 20006. **Hours:** 11:30 am-2:30 & 5:30-10:30 pm, Fri-midnight, Sat 5:30 pm-midnight. Closed major holidays; also Sun. **Reservations:** suggested. **Features:** The upscale Russian-Georgian restaurant is just blocks from the White House. Valet parking is available for dinner. Dressy casual; cocktails; entertainment. **Parking:** no self-parking. **Cards:** AX, DS,

MCCORMICK & SCHMICK'S SEAFOOD RESTAURANT
▼▼▼▼
Seafood
Lunch: $7-$22   **Dinner:** $7-$22   **Phone:** 202/861-2233   (92)
Location: Between 16th and 17th sts. 1652 K St NW 20006. **Hours:** 11:30 am-11 pm, Fri-midnight, Sat 2 pm-midnight, Sun 5 pm-10 pm. **Reservations:** suggested. **Features:** A favorite in the Pacific Northwest, the seafood chain has now come to the East Coast. With mahogany-paneled walls, beamed ceilings, stained-glass panels, a lively bar and even a shoe-shine stand, the dining rooms offer a subdued, elegant atmosphere. "Snuggeries," curtained alcoves with tables for six, provide an ideal escape for Washington's power people and families with children. The daily changing menu lists more than 40 varieties of seafood from the Atlantic and Pacific coasts. Casual dress; cocktails. **Parking:** valet and street. **Cards:** AX, CB, DC, DS, JC, MC, VI.

MCCORMICK & SCHMICK'S SEAFOOD RESTAURANT
▼▼▼▼
Seafood
Lunch: $7-$15   **Dinner:** $18-$30   **Phone:** 202/639-9330   (119)
Location: Between 9th and 10th sts NW; metro stop; Gallery Pl/Chinatown. 901 F St NW 20004. **Hours:** 11:30 am-11 pm, Fri-midnight, Sat noon-3 & 4-midnight, Sun 4 pm-10 pm, Mon 11:30 am-10 pm. **Reservations:** accepted. **Features:** A favorite in the Pacific Northwest, the seafood chain has now come to the East Coast. With mahogany paneled walls and a lively bar, the dining rooms offer a subdued, elegant atmosphere. The daily changing menu lists more than 40 varieties of seafood from the Atlantic and Pacific coasts. Dressy casual; cocktails. **Parking:** street. **Cards:** AX, DC, DS, MC, VI.

MEIWAH RESTAURANT
▼▼ ▼▼
Chinese
Lunch: $10-$24   **Dinner:** $10-$24   **Phone:** 202/833-2888   (61)
Location: Jct M St and New Hampshire Ave NW. 1200 New Hampshire Ave NW 20036. **Hours:** 11:30 am-10:30 pm, Fri-11 pm, Sat noon-11 pm, Sun noon-10:30 pm. Closed: 11/24. **Reservations:** accepted. **Features:** The bi-level dining room offers a comfortable, relaxing atmosphere. Photographs of the many politicians who have dined at Meiwah decorate the walls. Sidewalk dining, weather permitting. The food is very well prepared, one of many tasty dishes is the Crispy shredded beef with fried strands of meat and vegetables, the chilies are tamed by caramelized sugar. Casual dress; cocktails. **Parking:** no self-parking. **Cards:** AX, DC, DS, MC, VI.

MELROSE
AAA
▼▼▼ ▼▼▼
American
MC, VI. *(See color ad p 445)*
Lunch: $15-$25   **Dinner:** $25-$45   **Phone:** 202/419-6755   (50)
Location: 24th and M sts NW; in Park Hyatt Washington, D.C. 1201 24th St NW 20037. **Hours:** 6:30 am-2:30 & 5:30-10 pm. **Reservations:** suggested, weekends. **Features:** Windows in the upscale, stylish dining room look out over the terrace fountain and pedestrians on M Street. When the weather cooperates, the terrace is a hot spot. Fresh ingredients are used to prepare creative, seasonally changing dishes. The signature Melrose crab cakes are always on the menu. Desserts are made on the premises. A menu of lighter fare is available from 2:30 pm-10 pm. Semi-formal attire; cocktails. **Parking:** valet. **Cards:** AX, CB, DC, DS, JC,

MENDOCINO GRILLE & WINE BAR
▼▼▼ ▼▼▼
American
Lunch: $19-$28   **Dinner:** $27-$40   **Phone:** 202/333-2912   (55)
Location: Between 29th and 30th sts; in Georgetown. 2917 M St. **Hours:** 11:30 am-3 & 5:30-10 pm, Sat 10 am-3 & 5:30-11 pm, Sun 5:30-10 pm. Closed: 11/24; also 12/24. **Reservations:** suggested. **Features:** A relative newcomer to the Georgetown dining scene, the bistro-style eatery features a wide selection of premium wines by the glass. The weekend a la carte brunch is popular. Among lunch offerings are Thai snapper club, grilled organic Kobe burger and crispy soft-shell crab. Dinner is more formal, with entrees ranging from seared Alaskan halibut to pan-roasted venison to roasted organic chicken. Any of the extensive list of cheese plates, paired with wine, is a great way to end a meal. Dressy casual; cocktails. **Parking:** on-site (fee). **Cards:** AX, DC, DS, MC, VI.

MICHEL RICHARD CITRONELLE
▼▼▼ ▼▼▼
French
Dinner: $75-$115   **Phone:** 202/625-2150   (64)
Location: Between 30th and 31st sts NW; in Latham Hotel Georgetown. 3000 M St NW 20007-3701. **Hours:** 6:30 am-10:30 & 6:30-10 pm, Fri 6:30 am-10:30 & 6-10:30 pm, Sat 7 am-10:30 & 6-10:30 pm, Sun 7 am-10:30 & 6:30-10 pm. Closed: 1/1, 5/30, 9/5; also for lunch 12/25 & Sun 7/1-9/7. **Reservations:** required. **Features:** The stylish restaurant has an open kitchen behind a glass wall, where guests can see the artistry unfold. The skilled chef, Michel Richard, uses quality ingredients to prepare French cuisine with a California influence. Desserts are the chef's signature works. The atmosphere is upscale and relaxing, with a changing-color mood wall, sophisticated table settings and attentive servers. The dinner menu is prix fixe. Sidewalk seating is an option when the weather permits. Jeans are not permitted. Semi-formal attire; cocktails. **Parking:** on-site (fee) and valet. **Cards:** AX, CB, DC, DS, MC, VI.

(See map and index starting on p. 390)

MIE N YU   **Lunch:** $9-$20   **Dinner:** $14-$29   **Phone:** 202/333-6122   62
ᗐᗐᗐ   **Location:** In Georgetown; just w of 31st NW. 3125 M St NW 20007. **Hours:** 11:30 am-11 pm, Fri-midnight, Sat
American   11:30 am-4 & 5-midnight, Sun 11 am-3:45 & 5-11 pm, Mon & Tues 5 pm-11 pm. **Reservations:** suggested.
Features: The small Budha fountain in the window is only a glimpse at the show inside. Glowing lanterns, a
fountain, cushions, draped fabric, dining nooks, and distressed wood not to mention the enormous lively red
Chinese bar hint of Turkey, Morocco, and Tibet. The food follows suit with varied Asian flavors. The menu with many tastings is
packed with creative, very savory dishes like peanut crusted shrimp, mushroom dusted veal chop, Asian BBQ short ribs, 5 spice
ahi tuna, and lemongrass rack of lamb. Dressy casual; cocktails. **Parking:** no self-parking. **Cards:** AX, DC, DS, MC, VI.

MIMI'S AMERICAN BISTRO   **Lunch:** $12-$19   **Dinner:** $12-$23   **Phone:** 202/464-6464   29
ᗐᗐ ᗐᗐ   **Location:** Just w of Dupont Circle. 2120 P St NW 20037. **Hours:** 11:30 am-midnight, Sat & Sun from 11 am.
Closed: 11/24, 12/25. **Reservations:** accepted. **Features:** Singing waiters are on the menu in the theater-
Mediterranean   oriented restaurant. The dining room has an industrial feel with exposed ductwork. Mediterranean cuisine
employs the freshest locally grown produce and organic eggs and meats. Casual dress; cocktails. **Parking:**
street. **Cards:** AX, DC, DS, MC, VI.

MISS SAIGON   **Lunch:** $6-$9   **Dinner:** $10-$15   **Phone:** 202/333-5545   49
ᗐᗐ ᗐᗐ   **Location:** Between 30th and 31st sts. 3057 M St NW 20007. **Hours:** 11:30 am-10:30 pm, Sat noon-11 pm, Sun
noon-10:30 pm. Closed: 7/4, 11/24, 12/25. **Reservations:** accepted. **Features:** The devoted and loyal fan
Vietnamese   base know that this frequently lauded charmer serves fragrant, zesty, well-seasoned dishes. The wonton
soup, rich with tender dumplings, roast pork and onion crisps in a satisfying broth, sauteed steak marinated
in wine butter and garlic, light and crispy golden crepes and hearty caramel shrimp with onion and lemongrass are a sampling.
Palm trees strung with white lights and soft, silky background music create a friendly setting for the meal. Casual dress;
cocktails. **Parking:** street. **Cards:** AX, DC, JC, MC, VI.

THE MONOCLE ON CAPITOL HILL   **Lunch:** $8-$19   **Dinner:** $15-$29   **Phone:** 202/546-4488   149
AAA   **Location:** Just n of the Capitol. 107 D St NE 20002. **Hours:** 11:30 am-10 pm. Closed major holidays; also Sat &
ᗐᗐ   Sun. **Reservations:** suggested. **Features:** The converted Colonial-style townhouse has a casual
American   atmosphere, pictures of the many politicians who have dined here, adorn the walls. Established in the late
1960s, the upbeat, friendly restaurant features selections of aged beef, fresh seafood, pasta and crabcakes.
Dressy casual; cocktails. **Parking:** no self-parking. **Cards:** AX, CB, DC, MC, VI.

MORRISON-CLARK RESTAURANT   **Dinner:** $14-$25   **Phone:** 202/898-1200   76
ᗐᗐᗐ   **Location:** 11th and L sts NW, just n of Massachusetts Ave; in Morrison-Clark Historic Inn and Restaurant. 1015 L St NW
20001. **Hours:** 5:30 pm-9 pm. Closed: Sun & Mon. **Reservations:** suggested. **Features:** Although many
American   publications have bestowed accolades on the upscale restaurant, the food speaks for itself. The kitchen
prepares excellent contemporary American fare in a Victorian setting. Dressy casual; cocktails. **Parking:**
valet. **Cards:** AX, CB, DC, DS, MC, VI. **Historic**

MORTON'S OF CHICAGO   **Dinner:** $25-$42   **Phone:** 202/342-6258   43
ᗐᗐᗐ   **Location:** At Wisconsin and Prospect sts NW. 3251 Prospect St NW 20007. **Hours:** 5:30 pm-11 pm. Closed major
holidays. **Reservations:** accepted. **Features:** This is the place for beef and lots of it. Knowledgeable
Steak House   servers present and fully describe each menu item from a cart. All beef is USDA prime. Portions are
generous in dishes ranging from the 14-ounce filet mignon and 24-ounce porterhouse to farm-raised
salmon, whole Maine lobster and swordfish steaks. Vegetable and potato side dishes are enough to share. An excellent wine
list and tempting desserts complete the experience. The atmosphere is rich without being stuffy. Dressy casual; cocktails.
Parking: valet. **Cards:** AX, DC, MC, VI.

MORTON'S THE STEAKHOUSE   **Lunch:** $13-$20   **Dinner:** $23-$42   **Phone:** 202/955-5997   82
ᗐᗐᗐ   **Location:** Jct L St NW; on Terrace Level of The Washington Square office building. 1050 Connecticut Ave NW.
Hours: 11:30 am-2:30 & 5:30-11 pm, Sat from 5:30 pm, Sun 5 pm-10 pm. Closed major holidays.
Steak & Seafood   **Reservations:** suggested. **Features:** The steakhouse specializes in generous portions of USDA Prime
aged beef, as well as fish, lobster and chicken. This place is known for its animated tableside presentations,
in which servers present and describe the steaks, lobsters and other main courses. Valet parking is available during dinner for a
fee. Dressy casual; cocktails. **Parking:** on-site (fee). **Cards:** AX, DC, MC, VI.

MR K'S   **Lunch:** $8-$15   **Dinner:** $16-$38   **Phone:** 202/331-8868   84
ᗐᗐᗐ   **Location:** Between 21st and 22nd sts. 2121 K St NW 20037. **Hours:** 11:30 am-11 pm, Fri-11:30 pm, Sat noon-
11:30 pm, Sun noon-11 pm. Closed: 11/24, 12/25. **Reservations:** suggested. **Features:** Formally attired
Chinese   service staff deliver a variety of well-prepared dishes, most geared toward American tastes. The elegant
dining room and professional attention make this dining experience memorable. Complimentary valet
parking is offered after 5:30 pm. Semi-formal attire; cocktails. **Parking:** street. **Cards:** AX, CB, DC, MC, VI.

NEYLA-A MEDITERRANEAN GRILL   **Dinner:** $15-$32   **Phone:** 202/333-6353   36
ᗐᗐᗐ   **Location:** Just w of Wisconsin Ave NW; in Georgetown. 3206 N St NW 20007. **Hours:** 5 pm-10:30 pm, Thurs-Sat to
11:30 pm. Closed: 1/1, 12/25. **Reservations:** suggested. **Features:** A Mediterranean grill with much of it's
Mediterranean   heart in the middle east, offering the hip crowds mezze platters of fattoush, hommus, baba ghannoug, grape
leaves, falafel, and the like, and beef or lamb kebabs, shish taouk, and lamb chops while the more
Mediterranean choices are fried calamari with cilantro infused tahini, seafood salad, grilled spiced tuna, porcini scented sea
bass, and other less middle eastern dishes like them. Dressy casual; cocktails. **Cards:** AX, DC, DS,
MC, VI.

(See map and index starting on p. 390)

NORA   **Dinner:** $35-$43   **Phone:** 202/462-5143   ⑰
American
Location: Corner of R St and Florida Ave NW; between 21st St and Florida Ave. 2132 Florida Ave NW 20008. **Hours:** 5:30 pm-10 pm, Fri & Sat-10:30 pm. Closed major holidays; also Sun. **Reservations:** required. **Features:** The tranquil, rustic setting has brick walls, beamed ceilings and hand-crafted quilts displayed. Creative American cuisine is prepared with only organic ingredients—from the flour and sugar to the meats and poultry. Chef Nora Pouillon has received certification from Oregon Tilth, which verifies that 95 percent of ingredients come from certified organic farmers, growers and suppliers. Dressy casual; cocktails. **Parking:** on-site (fee) and valet. **Cards:** AX, MC, VI.

OBELISK   **Dinner:** $60-$65   **Phone:** 202/872-1180   ㉑
Northern Italian
Location: Just w of Dupont Circle. 2029 P St NW 20036. **Hours:** 1st seating 6 pm, 6:30 pm & 7 pm; 2nd seating 8 pm, 8:30 pm & 9 pm. Closed major holidays; also Sun & Mon. **Reservations:** suggested. **Features:** The prix fixe five-course menu at Obelisk changes every day and is driven by the availability of fresh market ingredients. This intimate, well established, chef-owned restaurant employs a knowledgeable, capable and kitchen-smart service staff. Casual dress; cocktails. **Parking:** street. **Cards:** DC, MC, VI.

OCCIDENTAL RESTAURANT   **Lunch:** $10-$25   **Dinner:** $22-$40   **Phone:** 202/783-1475   ⑬⑤
American
Location: 1.5 blks from the White House; adjacent to the Willard Intercontinental. 1475 Pennsylvania Ave NW 20004. **Hours:** 11:30 am-3 & 4:30-10 pm, Fri & Sat-10:30 pm, Sun-9:30 pm. Closed: 1/1, 11/24, 12/24, 12/25. **Reservations:** suggested. **Features:** The fare is contemporary American cuisine with a nice fish selection, as well as grilled meats. The menu offers salad and sandwiches to full meals. The clubby dining atmosphere, displays over 3000 framed black and white pictures of the many political movers and shakers that have dined here over the years. Dressy casual; cocktails. **Parking:** on-site (fee). **Cards:** AX, DC, MC, VI.

THE OCEANAIRE SEAFOOD ROOM   **Lunch:** $12-$20   **Dinner:** $17-$35   **Phone:** 202/347-2277   ⑫⓪
Seafood
Location: Between 12th and 13th sts NW. 1201 F St NW 20004. **Hours:** 11:30 am-10 pm, Fri-11 pm, Sat 5 pm-11 pm, Sun 5 pm-9 pm. Closed major holidays. **Reservations:** suggested. **Features:** Diners in the mood for seafood find that this is the place to come. The menu is printed daily to feature fish flown in daily from around the world. Portions are generous. The stylish, sleek dining room is a comfortable setting in which enjoy a meal, or guests can sit at the oyster bar. Servers are professional and helpful with the menu. Evening valet parking is available for a fee. Dressy casual; cocktails. **Parking:** no self-parking. **Cards:** AX, MC, VI.

OLD EBBITT GRILL   **Lunch:** $9-$25   **Dinner:** $13-$25   **Phone:** 202/347-4800   ⑫⑫
American
Location: 1 blk from the White House, 2 blks from Metro Center, exit 13th St. 675 15th St NW 20005. **Hours:** 7:30 am-midnight, Sat & Sun from 8:30 am. Closed: 12/25. **Reservations:** suggested. **Features:** Around the corner from the White House, the historic downtown eatery is popular with the locals. Uniformed servers are friendly and professional. The menu blends a nice selection of American dishes, raw bar items and creative desserts. Brunch is served on weekends from 8:30 am to 4 pm. Valet parking is available after 5:30 pm. Casual dress; cocktails. **Parking:** no self-parking. **Cards:** AX, DC, DS, MC, VI.

OLD EUROPE   *Menu on aaa.com*   **Lunch:** $5-$10   **Dinner:** $9-$20   **Phone:** 202/333-7600   ①
German
Location: In Upper Georgetown. 2434 Wisconsin Ave NW 20007. **Hours:** 11:30 am-3 & 5-9:30 pm, Fri & Sat-10 pm, Sun 1 pm-9 pm. Closed: 7/4; also 12/24. **Reservations:** suggested, weekends. **Features:** The acclaimed restaurant, which exudes the atmosphere of a German gasthaus, booms with business. Among well-prepared meals is the delicious sauerbraten with red cabbage and dumplings. Veteran servers in Bavarian dress are friendly and thoughtful. Casual dress; cocktails. **Parking:** street. **Cards:** AX, CB, DC, MC, VI.

OLD GLORY, ALL AMERICAN BAR-B-QUE   **Lunch:** $8-$22   **Dinner:** $8-$22   **Phone:** 202/337-3406   ⑥⓪
American
Location: Corner of M St and Wisconsin Ave NW. 3139 M St NW 20007. **Hours:** 11:30 am-10 pm, Fri & Sat-1:30 am, Sun 11 am-10 pm. **Reservations:** accepted, Sun-Thurs. **Features:** The noisy, rustic roadhouse packs them in each night with its well-prepared entrees and frequent live entertainment. The barbecue spare ribs, leg of lamb and Sunday country brunch are among the most popular offerings. Service is friendly and casual. Casual dress; cocktails. **Parking:** no self-parking. **Cards:** AX, CB, DC, DS, MC, VI.

OLIVES   **Lunch:** $12-$19   **Dinner:** $15-$32   **Phone:** 202/452-1866   ⑨①
Italian
Location: At 16th and K sts NW. 1600 K St NW 20006. **Hours:** 11:30 am-2:30 & 5:30-10 pm, Fri-10:30 pm, Sat 5:30 pm-10:30 pm. Closed major holidays; also Sun. **Reservations:** suggested. **Features:** The contemporary Italian cooking uses the freshest ingredients in its seasonally changing menu. The wood-grilled sea bass on horseradish mashed potatoes, has become popular with the locals. The stylish street level dining room offers a casual air, with more formal setting on the lower level. Pay valet parking is available for dinner. Dressy casual; cocktails. **Parking:** no self-parking. **Cards:** AX, DC, MC, VI.

OODLES NOODLES   **Lunch:** $6-$10   **Dinner:** $6-$10   **Phone:** 202/293-3138   ⑦②
Asian
Location: Between L and M sts. 1120 19th St NW 20036. **Hours:** 11:30 am-3 & 5-10 pm, Fri & Sat-10:30 pm. Closed: Sun. **Features:** Guests who can find a spot to squeeze into at lunch are pleased by the steaming bowls of noodle soups, such as roast duck, or steaming plates of noodles topped with grilled meats or seafood. Casual dress; beer only. **Parking:** no self-parking. **Cards:** AX, DS, MC, VI.

THE OVAL ROOM   **Lunch:** $12-$19   **Dinner:** $16-$25   **Phone:** 202/463-8700   ⑩⑨
American
Location: Between H and I sts. 800 Connecticut Ave NW 20006. **Hours:** 11:30 am-3 & 5:30-10 pm, Fri-10:30 pm, Sat 5:30 pm-10:30 pm. Closed: 12/25; also Sun. **Reservations:** suggested. **Features:** A location convenient to the White House and Farragut Square accounts for the elegantly sophisticated restaurant's popularity with politicians, journalists, lobbyists, lawyers and former presidents. Chef Frank Morales prepares seasonal contemporary American cuisine in a chic atmosphere. Favorites include golden cod cakes and hand-harvested sea scallops with caramelized cauliflower and baby bok choy. The flower-bedecked patio offers another seating option. Dressy casual; cocktails. **Parking:** valet and street. **Cards:** AX, DC, MC, VI.

(See map and index starting on p. 390)

PALM RESTAURANT Lunch: $9-$17 Dinner: $14-$38 Phone: 202/293-9091 (39)
American
Location: Between M and N sts NW. 1225 19th St NW 20036. **Hours:** 11:45 am-10:30 pm, Sat from 6 pm, Sun 5:30 pm-9:30 pm. Closed major holidays. **Reservations:** suggested. **Features:** Even if you bring a big appetite you still may leave with a doggy bag. The portions of beef, seafood, pasta and veal are enormous. The dining room walls sport caricatures of the famous and not-so-famous. Complimentary valet parking is offered after 6 pm. Casual dress; cocktails. **Parking:** no self-parking. **Cards:** AX, CB, DC, DS, MC, VI.

PAOLO'S RISTORANTE Lunch: $8-$17 Dinner: $10-$20 Phone: 202/333-7353 (35)
Italian
Location: Just n of M St NW; in Georgetown. 1303 Wisconsin Ave NW 20007. **Hours:** 11:30 am-11:30 pm, Fri & Sat-12:30 am. Closed: 12/25. **Reservations:** suggested, weekends. **Features:** Market-fresh cuisine with a Mediterranean flair is served in a lively, stylish dining room on fashionable Sherbrooke Street. Menu specialties include mussels, bouillabaisse, filet mignon, steak tartare, pan-seared Atlantic salmon, grilled shrimp and rump of lamb. Casual dress; cocktails. **Parking:** no self-parking. **Cards:** AX, CB, DC, DS, MC, VI.

PEACOCK CAFE Lunch: $6-$12 Dinner: $9-$19 Phone: 202/625-2740 (41)
American
Location: Jct Prospect and Wisconsin sts; in Georgetown. 3251 Prospect St NW 20007. **Hours:** 11:30 am-10:30 pm, Fri-11 pm, Sat 10 am-11 pm, Sun 10 am-10:30 pm. Closed: 11/24, 12/25. **Reservations:** suggested. **Features:** In the heart of Georgetown, the hip, trendy cafe is known locally for its full-service fresh fruit and vegetable juice bar, the first of its kind in the city, as well as its weekend brunch. Dressy casual; cocktails. **Parking:** street. **Cards:** AX, DC, DS, MC, VI.

PENANG Lunch: $10 Dinner: $5-$22 Phone: 202/822-8773 (45)
Indonesian
Location: At 19th St. 1837 M St NW 20036. **Hours:** 11:30 am-11 pm, Fri & Sat-1 am, Sun-10 pm. Closed: 11/24, 12/25. **Features:** Malaysian fare with flair is on hand at the upper-level bistro. The menu lists exotic preparations of Indian-style roti canai, satays, noodles, rices and curries. Food is served family-style. Casual dress; cocktails. **Parking:** valet. **Cards:** AX, DC, MC, VI.

PESCE Lunch: $8-$12 Dinner: $13-$25 Phone: 202/466-3474 (27)
Seafood
Location: Between Hopkins and 20th sts, just w of Dupont Circle. 2016 P St NW 20036. **Hours:** 11:30 am-2:30 & 5:30-10 pm, Fri & Sat-10:30 pm, Sun 5 pm-9:30 pm. Closed: 1/1, 11/24, 12/25. **Features:** Fresh seafood, expertly prepared in eye-appealing presentations, is the draw at the compact, popular bistro. Palate-pleasing creations change daily. The no-reservations policy can be challenging. Dressy casual; cocktails. **Parking:** valet and street. **Cards:** AX, MC, VI.

PHILLIPS FLAGSHIP Lunch: $14-$27 Dinner: $14-$27 Phone: 202/488-8515 (155)
Seafood
Location: I-395, exit Maine Ave, just e. 900 Water St SW 20024. **Hours:** 11 am-9 pm, Fri & Sat-10 pm, Sun 10 am-9 pm. Closed: 12/25. **Features:** A large, casual waterfront restaurant overlooking the Washington Channel. They offer an extensive all-you-can-eat buffet, with traditional Maryland seafood, carving table, sushi bar, pasta & salad bar. The house specilty is the crabcakes, using a recipe dating back to 1956. Menu service is also available. Casual dress; cocktails. **Parking:** on-site (fee). **Cards:** AX, CB, DC, DS, MC, VI.

PIZZERIA PARADISO Lunch: $8-$16 Dinner: $8-$16 Phone: 202/223-1245 (22)
Pizza
Location: Just w of Dupont Circle. 2029 P St NW 20036. **Hours:** 11:30 am-11 pm, Fri & Sat-midnight, Sun noon-10 pm. Closed major holidays. **Features:** The dining room is always hopping at the popular pizzeria. The menu is not extensive—listing mainly pizza, salads and panini—but the fresh ingredients are the draw. Sandwiches are made with homemade focaccia rolls, and pizzas are produced in a wood-burning oven. Casual dress; beer & wine only. **Parking:** street. **Cards:** DC, DS, MC, VI.

POSTE—MODERN BRASSERIE Lunch: $12-$21 Dinner: $18-$28 Phone: 202/783-6060 (134)
American
Location: Between 7th and 8th sts NW; in Hotel Monaco Washington DC. 555 8th St NW 20004. **Hours:** 7-10 am, 11:30-2:30 & 5:30-10 pm, Sat & Sun 7 am-10 & 5:30-10 pm. Closed major holidays. **Reservations:** suggested. **Features:** The stylish bistro, in the courtyard at the Hotel Monaco, nurtures a bustling, chic atmosphere. The kitchen skillfully prepares modern American cuisine along the lines of braised short ribs and mushroom risotto. The service staff is friendly and efficient. Dressy casual; cocktails. **Parking:** on-site (fee) and valet. **Cards:** AX, CB, DC, DS, JC, MC, VI.

THE PRIME RIB Lunch: $10-$24 Dinner: $18-$39 Phone: 202/466-8811 (93)
Steak & Seafood
Location: Between 20th and 21st sts NW. 2020 K St NW 20006. **Hours:** 11:30 am-3 & 5-11 pm, Fri-11:30 pm, Sat 5 pm-11:30 pm. Closed: 1/1, 11/24, 12/25; also Sun & for lunch 7/4. **Reservations:** suggested. **Features:** Well-prepared beef and seafood highlight the menu, but as the name suggests, aged, roast prime rib is the specialty. Nicely appointed dining rooms exude a supper club ambience. Good service rounds out the experience. Complimentary valet parking is available for dinner. Formal attire; cocktails; entertainment. **Parking:** no self-parking. **Cards:** AX, CB, DC, MC, VI.

PRIMI PIATTI Lunch: $15-$21 Dinner: $17-$29 Phone: 202/223-3600 (97)
Italian
Location: Off Pennsylvania Ave; between 20th and 21st sts NW. 2013 I St NW 20006. **Hours:** 11:30 am-2:30 & 5:30-10:30 pm, Sat from 5:30 pm. Closed major holidays; also Sun. **Reservations:** suggested. **Features:** The noisy, bustling trattoria offers a fine selection of pasta, seafood and meat dishes as well as a memorable tiramisu. Italian music and European decor characterize the main dining room; a breezy feel envelops the sidewalk dining area. Dressy casual; cocktails. **Parking:** no self-parking. **Cards:** AX, CB, DC, DS, JC, MC, VI.

(See map and index starting on p. 390)

RAKU-AN ASIAN DINER   Lunch: $9-$14   Dinner: $9-$14   Phone: 202/265-7258   (20)
Asian
Location: Jct 19th and Q sts NW. 1900 Q St NW 20009. **Hours:** 11:30 am-10 pm, Fri & Sat-11 pm. Closed: 12/25. **Reservations:** not accepted. **Features:** Just off Dupont Circle you'll find this casual Asian Diner. The menu offers a nice selection of dishes from a variety of Asian countries. Casual dress; cocktails. **Parking:** no self-parking. **Cards:** AX, MC, VI.

RED SAGE   Lunch: $8-$17   Dinner: $8-$35   Phone: 202-638-4444   (125)
Regional American
Location: Jct 14th and F sts NW. 605 14th St NW 20005. **Hours:** 11:30 am-11:30 pm, Sun 4:30 pm-11 pm; downstairs 11:30 am-2 & 5:30-10 pm, Fri-10:30 pm, Sat 5:30 pm-10:30 pm, Sun 5 pm-10 pm. Closed major holidays. **Reservations:** suggested, downstairs. **Features:** The street-level cafe blends casual and fine dining in one location and offers a menu of creative Southwestern and nuevo Latino dishes. Contemporary American dishes with Southwestern influences are the focus of the menu at the downstairs grill. The decor is fun and unusual. Validated garage parking is available after 4:30 pm. Dressy casual; cocktails. **Parking:** street. **Cards:** AX, CB, DC, DS, MC, VI.

REGATTA RAW BAR   Lunch: $11-$25   Dinner: $11-$25   Phone: 202/737-2200   (114)
Seafood
Location: Jct 12th and H sts NW; at Metro Center subway stop; in Marriott at Metro Center. 775 12th St NW 20005. **Hours:** 11:30 am-midnight. **Reservations:** accepted. **Features:** The eatery is a good spot to meet for a quick bite and drinks. Colorful, nautical decor invites happy diners. Casual dress; cocktails. **Parking:** street. **Cards:** AX, DC, DS, MC, VI.

THE RESTAURANT AT THE JEFFERSON   Lunch: $15-$25   Dinner: $25-$37   Phone: 202/833-6206   (46)
American
Location: 16th and M sts NW; in The Jefferson, A Loews Hotel. 1200 16th St NW 20036. **Hours:** 6:30-11 am, 11:30-2:30 & 6-10:30 pm. **Reservations:** suggested. **Features:** In a private hotel near the White House, the elegant, romantic setting is fitting for inspiring fine dining. Delectable sauces—including lobster bearnaise, black peppercorn port sauce and spicy carrot-ginger broth, to name a few—enhance expertly prepared New American cuisine. Dressy casual; cocktails. **Parking:** valet. **Cards:** AX, DS, MC, VI.

RESTAURANT KOLUMBIA   Lunch: $12-$20   Dinner: $20-$35   Phone: 202/331-5551   (85)
American
Location: At 18th St. 1801 K St NW 20006. **Hours:** 11:30 am-10 pm, Sat 5:30 pm-11 pm. Closed major holidays; also Sun, except holidays. **Reservations:** suggested. **Features:** The stylish dining room provides a comfortable setting for any occasion. The menu offers such dishes as roasted chicken Maria stuffed with beet greens or diver scallops with braised veal cheek ravioli, just to mention a few of the tempting selections. Dressy casual; cocktails. **Parking:** street. **Cards:** AX, DC, DS, MC, VI.

ROOF TERRACE RESTAURANT & BAR AT THE KENNEDY CENTER   Dinner: $20-$32   Phone: 202/416-8555   (128)
Regional American
Location: On the roof terrace level at The Kennedy Center. 2700 F St NW 20566. **Hours:** 5 pm-8 pm; open only when there are major performances, Sun-Wed. Closed: for dinner 7/4. **Reservations:** suggested. **Features:** A special-occasion destination, the versatile restaurant looks out over the Potomac River. High ceilings, huge windows and large chandeliers set a romantic tone. Try the sea bass or rack of lamb entrees and the sinful molten chocolate cake for dessert. Dressy casual; cocktails. **Parking:** on-site (fee). **Cards:** AX, CB, DC, DS, MC, VI.

ROSEMARY'S THYME BISTRO   Lunch: $7-$10   Dinner: $8-$18   Phone: 202/332-3200   (13)
Mediterranean
Location: Jct S St NW. 1801 18th St NW 20009. **Hours:** 5 pm-11 pm, Fri & Sat 11 am-midnight, Sun 10 am-10 pm, Mon 5 pm-10 pm. Closed: 11/24, 12/25. **Reservations:** suggested, weekends. **Features:** A neighborhood restaurant serving Mediterranean cuisine using fresh market ingredients. The menu offers a nice selection appetizers, pasta, meat and seafood dishes. Seasonal sidewalk dining available when the weather is appropriate. Casual dress; cocktails. **Parking:** street. **Cards:** AX, DC, DS, MC, VI.

RUTH'S CHRIS STEAK HOUSE   Dinner: $17-$32   Phone: 202/797-0033   (12)
Steak House
Location: At S St NW; metro stop, Dupont Circle. 1801 Connecticut Ave 20009. **Hours:** 5 pm-9:30 pm. Closed: 11/24, 12/25. **Reservations:** accepted. **Features:** Exceptional service, elegant dicor, not to mention their infamous steaks sizzling in butter — make for a memorable dining experience. Dressy casual; cocktails. **Parking:** valet and street. **Cards:** AX, MC, VI.

SAM & HARRY'S   Lunch: $9-$26   Dinner: $25-$35   Phone: 202/296-4333   (47)
Steak House
Location: Between M and N sts NW. 1200 19th St NW 20036. **Hours:** 11:30 am-2:30 & 5:30-10 pm, Sat from 5:30 pm. Closed major holidays; also Sun. **Reservations:** suggested. **Features:** A jazz theme echoes in the restaurant's friendly, clubby atmosphere. The house specialty is prime, aged beef, but the menu also features three- to four-pound lobsters, veal, seafood, chicken, pork and lamb—all in generous portions. Complimentary valet parking is available for dinner. Semi-formal attire; cocktails. **Parking:** no self-parking. **Cards:** AX, CB, DC, DS, MC, VI.

SAVEUR   Lunch: $9-$12   Dinner: $9-$23   Phone: 202/333-5885   (8)
French
Location: In upper Georgetown; Glove Park area. 2218 Wisconsin Ave NW 20007. **Hours:** 11:30 am-2:30 & 5:30-10 pm, Fri-11 pm, Sat 5:30 pm-11 pm, Sun 11 am-2:30 & 5:30-9 pm. Closed major holidays; also Mon. **Reservations:** suggested. **Features:** The setting is casual and comfortable. Tables are spaced well, and the artwork changes periodically. The kitchen is skilled at preparing French cuisine with American influences. Some diners make a meal out of the starters, which are offered in a large selection. Dressy casual; cocktails. **Parking:** no self-parking. **Cards:** AX, DC, DS, MC, VI.

(See map and index starting on p. 390)

SEA CATCH RESTAURANT Lunch: $8-$14 Dinner: $18-$32 Phone: 202/337-8855 (74)
Seafood
Location: Just s of M St; at Canal Square; in Georgetown. 1054 31st St NW 20007. **Hours:** noon-3 & 5:30-10 pm. Closed major holidays; also Sun. **Reservations:** suggested. **Features:** Set along the C&O canal, in the Canal Square complex. The building orginally constructed in 1842, is the birthplace of the first computer. A punched card tabulating machine, designed to be used in the 1890 census. The restaurant specialty is fish. The raw bar offerings are wonderful; enormous, plump and juicy shrimp and at least three types of oysters. The kitchen is very skilled in the preparation of the seafood dishes. Lamb, veal chops, beef and chicken are also available. Dressy casual; cocktails. **Parking:** on-site. **Cards:** AX, CB, DC, DS, MC, VI.

SEASONS *Menu on aaa.com* Lunch: $23-$33 Dinner: $37-$55 Phone: 202/944-2000 (67)
American
Location: Located in Georgetown; in Four Seasons Hotel Washington D.C. 2800 Pennsylvania Ave NW 20007. **Hours:** 6:30-10 am, 11-2 & 6-10 pm, Sat & Sun 7 am-2 & 6-10 pm. **Reservations:** suggested. **Features:** Diners will be pampered in this upscale, relaxing dining room overlooking the trees of Rock Creek Park. Contemporary American cuisine includes a good range of imaginative dishes that change seasonally. A well-chosen wine list is presented. Dressy casual; cocktails. **Parking:** valet. **Cards:** AX, CB, DC, DS, JC, MC, VI.

SIGNATURES Lunch: $12-$24 Dinner: $22-$45 Phone: 202/628-5900 (151)
American
Location: Between 8th and 9th sts. 801 Pennsylvania Ave NW 20004. **Hours:** 11:30 am-3 & 5:30-10 pm, Fri-10:30 pm, Sat 5:30 pm-10:30 pm. Closed major holidays; also Sun. **Reservations:** suggested. **Features:** The restaurant is named for the signed documents and autographed items hanging in lighted shadowboxes on the walls of the classy, columned rooms. The restaurant is beside the Naval Memorial, convenient to the Archives metro stop. A small patio overlooks the memorial's fountain. Entrees range from steaks, tuna and lobster to duck, chicken and sushi. Presentations are as pleasing to the eye as the food is to the palate. Servers are genuine, pleasant and skilled. Dressy casual; cocktails. **Parking:** no self-parking. **Cards:** AX, CB, DC, DS, MC, VI.

SKEWER'S Lunch: $6-$18 Dinner: $6-$18 Phone: 202/387-7400 (23)
Middle Eastern
Location: Between 16th and 17th sts NW. 1633 P St NW 20036. **Hours:** 11:30 am-11 pm. Closed: 11/24, 12/25. **Reservations:** accepted. **Features:** Middle Eastern fare is the cuisine of choice at the casual eatery. Curried dishes, falafel and meze specials all are tasty. Casual dress; cocktails. **Parking:** street. **Cards:** AX, MC, VI.

SUSHI AOI Lunch: $7-$20 Dinner: $9-$25 Phone: 202/408-7770 (103)
Japanese
Location: At 11th St. 1100 New York Ave NW 20005. **Hours:** 11:30 am-2:30 & 5-10:30 pm, Sat from 5 pm. Closed: 7/4, 11/24, 12/25; also Sun. **Reservations:** accepted. **Features:** The cozy restaurant serves well-prepared, familiar Japanese dishes and a number of creative specialties and features contemporary yet casual decor and, of course, a sushi bar. Casual dress; cocktails. **Parking:** no self-parking. **Cards:** AX, DC, MC, VI.

SUSHI TARO Lunch: $10-$15 Dinner: $25-$30 Phone: 202/462-8999 (25)
Japanese
Location: Jct 17th NW and P sts. 1503 17th St NW 20036. **Hours:** 11:30 am-2 & 5:30-10 pm, Fri & Sat-10:30 pm. Closed: 1/1, 11/24, 12/25; also Sun. **Reservations:** suggested. **Features:** Skilled Japanese chefs prepare sushi, sashimi and tempura. Guests may choose seating in a dining room with standard chairs and tables or in a re-created traditional tatami room with the low tables for which Japan is known. Casual dress; beer & wine only. **Parking:** street. **Cards:** AX, CB, DC, DS, JC, MC, VI.

TABERNA DEL ALABARDERO Lunch: $40-$45 Dinner: $50-$75 Phone: 202/429-2200 (104)
Spanish
Location: Entrance on 18th St NW. 1776 I St NW 20006. **Hours:** 11:30 am-2:30 & 5:30-10 pm, Fri & Sat 6 pm-11 pm. Closed major holidays; also Sun. **Reservations:** suggested. **Features:** The menu spotlights cuisine from the Basque region of northern Spain. Beautiful 19th-century Spanish decor lends character to the dining area. Well-prepared entrees of fresh seafood, paella, meat and game are notable. Parking in the adjacent garage is validated. Semi-formal attire; cocktails. **Parking:** no self-parking. **Cards:** AX, DC, DS, MC, VI.

TEATRO GOLDONI Lunch: $13-$22 Dinner: $15-$30 Phone: 202/955-9494 (86)
Italian
Location: Between 19th and 20th sts NW. 1909 K St NW 20006. **Hours:** 11:30 am-2 & 5:30-10 pm, Fri-11 pm, Sat 5 pm-11 pm, Sun 5 pm-9:30 pm. Closed major holidays. **Reservations:** suggested. **Features:** Chef Fabrizio Aielli's kitchen prepares delicious Italian cuisine with a Venetian influence, in a theatrical, contemporary setting. In addition to the ala carte menu, prix-fixed lunch and dinner menu's are available. Extensive selection of wines by the glass. Pay valet parking available for dinner. Dressy casual; cocktails. **Parking:** no self-parking. **Cards:** AX, CB, DC, DS, MC, VI.

TENPENH RESTAURANT Lunch: $13-$18 Dinner: $19-$36 Phone: 202/393-4500 (143)
Pacific Rim
Location: At 10th St and Pennsylvania Ave NW. 1001 Pennsylvania Ave NW 20004. **Hours:** 11:30 am-2:30 & 5:30-10:30 pm, Fri-11 pm, Sat 5:30 pm-11 pm. Closed major holidays; also Sun. **Reservations:** suggested. **Features:** The cuisine of Chef Tunks is Asian-Pacific inspired, with contemporary preparation of indigenous ingredients from the Pacific Rim and Southeast Asia. The striking interior reflects an Asian influence, with statues, teak tables and chairs and fine fabrics. Valet parking is available during dinner. Dressy casual; cocktails. **Parking:** no self-parking. **Cards:** AX, DC, DS, MC, VI.

THAIPHOON Lunch: $6-$8 Dinner: $7-$15 Phone: 202/667-3505 (14)
Thai
Location: 3 blks n of Dupont Circle, just off Connecticut Ave NW. 2011 S St NW 20009. **Hours:** 11:30 am-10:30 pm, Fri & Sat-11 pm. Closed: 11/24, 12/25. **Reservations:** suggested, weekends. **Features:** Good Thai food is served in the intimate, contemporary restaurant just north of Dupont Circle. Listed on the extensive menu are beef, chicken, seafood, noodle and vegetarian dishes. The degree of spiciness is shown on the menu by the number of peppers next to each item. Casual dress; cocktails. **Parking:** no self-parking. **Cards:** AX, DC, DS, MC, VI.

(See map and index starting on p. 390)

TONY & JOE'S SEAFOOD PLACE   Lunch: $8-$15   Dinner: $17-$32   Phone: 202/944-4545   (89)
◆◆ ◆◆◆◆
Seafood
Location: In Georgetown; at Washington Harbour Complex. 3000 K St NW, Suite 10 20007. **Hours:** 11 am-11 pm, Fri & Sat-midnight, Sun-10:30 pm. Closed: 12/25. **Reservations:** suggested. **Features:** Overlooking the scenic Potomac River, the bright, open dining room is the highlight of the casual, bustling restaurant. The outdoor terrace is a great spot to relax and watch boats drive by and crew teams train. The extensive menu offers a wide variety of fresh fish, but beef and chicken selections are also available. Casual dress; cocktails. **Parking:** on-site (fee). **Cards:** AX, CB, DC, DS, MC, VI.

TOSCA   Lunch: $15-$30   Dinner: $20-$40   Phone: 202/367-1990   (127)
◆◆◆ ◆◆◆
Northern
Italian
Location: Just e of the White House; between 11th and 12th sts. 1112 F St NW 20004. **Hours:** 11:30 am-2:30 & 5:30-10:30 pm. Closed major holidays. **Reservations:** suggested, weekends. **Features:** The restaurant has a sophisticated design, formally attired wait staff and a contemporary Northern Italian menu. The staff is knowledgeable about wines and menu items. Casual dress; cocktails. **Parking:** valet and street. **Cards:** AX, CB, DC, DS, JC, MC, VI.

TWO QUAIL   Lunch: $7-$14   Dinner: $15-$25   Phone: 202/543-8030   (147)
◆◆ ◆◆◆
American
Location: Between 3rd and 4th sts NE. 320 Massachusetts Ave NE 20002. **Hours:** 11:30 am-2:30 & 5-10 pm, Fri-11 pm, Sat 5 pm-11 pm, Sun 5 pm-10 pm. Closed: 1/1, 7/4, 12/25; also for lunch on national holidays. **Reservations:** suggested. **Features:** On the outside the restaurant is classic Capitol Hill row house; on the inside it's reminiscent of Grandma's dining room, with Victorian touches, flowery fabrics and knickknacks throughout. The menu features innovative American cuisine. Dressy casual; cocktails. **Parking:** street. **Cards:** AX, DC, DS, MC, VI.

VIDALIA   Lunch: $14-$20   Dinner: $23-$30   Phone: 202/659-1990   (59)
◆◆ ◆◆◆
Regional American
Location: Between 19th and 20th sts. 1990 M St NW 20036. **Hours:** 11:30 am-2:30 & 5:30-10 pm, Fri-10:30 pm, Sat 5:30 pm-10:30 pm, Sun 5 pm-9:30 pm. Closed major holidays. **Reservations:** suggested. **Features:** Diners can step into the basement-level dining room and find a contemporary atmosphere. American cuisine reflects a distinctively Southern accent. Skilled cooks consistently prepare sophisticated, seasonally changing dishes. Among the chef's tempting signature dishes is shrimp and grits. Complimentary valet parking is available during dinner. Dressy casual; cocktails. **Parking:** no self-parking. **Cards:** AX, DC, DS, MC, VI.

THE WHITE TIGER   Lunch: $9-$11   Dinner: $10-$25   Phone: 202/546-5900   (150)
◆◆ ◆◆
Indian
Location: Jct Massachusetts Ave NE and 3rd St. 301 Massachusetts Ave NE 20002. **Hours:** 11:30 am-2:30 & 5-10 pm, Fri-10:30 pm, Sat 5 pm-10:30 pm. Closed: 12/25. **Reservations:** suggested. **Features:** A rare creature in nature, the white tiger was chosen to be emblematic of the restaurant's distinctive position among Indian restaurants. While retaining traditional cuisine, its menu is innovative in appealing to Western palates. Among offerings are such delicacies as Cajun salmon and crabettes—jumbo lump crab cakes done in Indian fashion—and marinated filet mignon, the rare beef dish for an Indian eatery. Hand-carved deities and figurines accent the decor. Dressy casual; cocktails. **Parking:** street. **Cards:** AX, CB, DC, DS, MC, VI.

THE WILLARD ROOM   Lunch: $25-$36   Dinner: $28-$40   Phone: 202/637-7440   (138)
◆◆◆ ◆◆◆
French
Location: Just e of the White House; in The Willard InterContinental. 1401 Pennsylvania Ave NW 20004. **Hours:** 7:30-10 am, 11:30-2 & 6-10 pm, Sat & 8/1-8/31 from 6 pm. Closed: 7/4, 9/5; also Sun. **Reservations:** suggested. **Features:** A stately, elegant dining room with exquisite woodwork. The setting is formal, as jacket and tie are recommended. The contemporary American cuisine is superbly prepared. The chef demonstrates his skills in each dish he creates. The seafood selections are some of his best work. Complimentary valet parking is provided for dinner guests. Semi-formal attire; cocktails. **Parking:** valet. **Cards:** AX, CB, DC, DS, JC, MC, VI. **Historic**

ZAYTINYA   Lunch: $4-$8   Dinner: $15-$20   Phone: 202/638-0800   (117)
◆◆◆
Turkish
Location: Between F St and G Pl NW; Gallery Place/Chinatown Metro stop (exit 9 and G). 701 9th St NW 20001. **Hours:** 11:30 am-11:30 pm, Fri & Sat-midnight, Sun & Mon-10 pm. Closed major holidays. **Features:** The restaurant is a place to see and be seen among the young but not too young. A large, glass-enclosed fish tank of a dining room—with polished gray marble, dark wood accents and upbeat, flattering Euro-music—lends a vibrant mood to an already energetic crowd. The bar is large and just as swank, a great place to meet for drinks. An abundant and varied menu of beautifully presented and flavorful Turkish, Lebanese and Greek meze is full of opportunity. Dressy casual; cocktails. **Parking:** street. **Cards:** AX, CB, DC, DS, MC, VI.

ZED'S ETHIOPIAN CUISINE   Lunch: $7-$11   Dinner: $8-$14   Phone: 202/333-4710   (56)
◆◆ ◆◆
Ethiopian
Location: Jct M and 28th sts; in Georgetown. 1201 28th St NW 20007. **Hours:** 11 am-11 pm. Closed: 11/24, 12/25. **Features:** Zed's has been a Georgetown favorite for over 10 years but has a bright new corner spot offering up two cozy floors with large windows overlooking the street. They serve up authentic cuisine; both meat and Vegetarian dishes stewed with exotic spices. The fun is in the eating; all is served tableside onto large platters and then diners scoop up items with Injera, a spongy flatbread used in place of utensils. Casual dress; cocktails. **Parking:** no self-parking. **Cards:** AX, DC, DS, MC, VI.

ZOLA   Lunch: $10-$23   Dinner: $16-$25   Phone: 202/654-0999   (130)
◆◆◆
American
Location: At 8th and F sts NW. 800 F St NW 20004. **Hours:** 11:30 am-midnight, Sat from 5 pm, Sun 5 pm-10 pm. Closed: 1/1, 11/24, 12/25. **Features:** The influence of the International Spy Museum can be felt in the ambience of its restaurant neighbor. Sleek and sophisticated with a touch of intrigue, this place presents a menu of inventive American cuisine. Valet parking is available in the evening. Dressy casual; cocktails. **Parking:** valet and street. **Cards:** AX, DC, DS, MC, VI.

(See map and index starting on p. 390)

———— *The following restaurants have not been evaluated by AAA* ————
but are listed for your information only.

BRICKSKELLER
Phone: 202/293-1885

[fyi]   Not evaluated. **Location:** Between P and Q sts NW. 1523 22nd St NW 20037. **Features:** Established in 1957, Brickskeller is a tavern with more than 800 brands of American and imported beers. The menu offers traditional American fare, from pizza to South Dakota buffalo steaks and burgers.

CHARLIE PALMER STEAK
Phone: 202/547-8100

[fyi]   Not evaluated. **Location:** Center of downtown. 101 Constitution Ave NW 20001. **Features:** In the Capitol Hill historic site is a fine-dining establishment that prepares bold and progressive American-style cuisine. The menu is lined with game meats, steaks, squab and quail, as well as blue crab and fresh fish.

HARD ROCK CAFE
Phone: 202/737-7625

[fyi]   Not evaluated. **Location:** At 9th and E sts NW. 999 E St NW 20004. **Features:** A popular tourist stop for its bustling atmosphere and collection of Rock n' Roll memorabilia. The menu offers traditional American fare.

PASTA MIA
Phone: 202/328-9114

[fyi]   Not evaluated. **Location:** 1790 Columbia Rd NW 20009. **Features:** Long lines and generous portions are the norm at the small, family-oriented neighborhood restaurant.

SPY CITY CAFE
Phone: 202/654-0999

[fyi]   Not evaluated. **Location:** At F and 8th sts NW. 800 F St NW 20004. **Features:** Museum visitors will appreciate the made-to-order salads, homemade soups and hot and cold offerings in the cafeteria-style eatery.

SUSHI-KO
Phone: 202/333-4187

[fyi]   Not evaluated. **Location:** S of Calvert St. 2309 Wisconsin Ave NW 20007. **Features:** Traditional sushi is the showcase for lunch, but the chef pulls out his inventive Western-influenced Asian dishes, paired with fine French wines, in the evening.

WASHINGTON (WEST AND NORTH REGION) (See map and index starting on p. 399)

———— WHERE TO STAY ————

CONNECTICUT AVE DAYS INN   *Book at aaa.com*   Phone: (202)244-5600 **2**

3/1-6/30 & 9/15-10/31	1P: $134-$154	2P: $144-$164	XP: $10 F17
7/1-9/14 & 11/1-2/28	1P: $104-$124	2P: $114-$144	XP: $10 F17

Location: 1.2 mi n of the National Zoo. 4400 Connecticut Ave NW 20008. Fax: 202/966-9597. **Facility:** 155 one-bedroom standard units. 6 stories, interior corridors. *Bath:* combo or shower only. **Parking:** on-site (fee).
Small-scale Hotel **Amenities:** voice mail, irons, hair dryers. *Fee:* video games, safes. **Dining:** 11 am-10 pm, cocktails. **Guest Services:** gift shop, valet laundry. **Business Services:** meeting rooms. *Fee:* PC, fax. **Cards:** AX, DC, MC, VI. **Special Amenities:** free newspaper. *(See color ad below)*

SOME UNITS

(See map and index starting on p. 399)

EMBASSY SUITES HOTEL AT THE CHEVY CHASE PAVILION

Book at aaa.com   **Phone:** (202)362-9300 ❶

AAA ⟨SAVE⟩   All Year [BP]   1P: $149-$349   2P: $169-$369

Large-scale Hotel   **Location:** SR 355; at Friendship Heights Metro Station. Located opposite the Mazza Gallery Shopping Mall. 4300 Military Rd NW 20015. Fax: 202/686-3405. **Facility:** 198 one-bedroom suites. 9 stories, interior corridors. *Bath:* combo or shower only. **Parking:** on-site (fee). **Terms:** cancellation fee imposed, package plans. **Amenities:** video games (fee), dual phone lines, voice mail, irons, hair dryers. **Pool(s):** heated indoor. **Leisure Activities:** saunas, whirlpool. *Fee:* massage, personal trainers. **Guest Services:** complimentary evening beverages, valet and coin laundry. **Business Services:** meeting rooms, business center. **Cards:** AX, CB, DC, DS, MC, VI. **Special Amenities:** free full breakfast and free newspaper. *(See color ad below)*

SOME UNITS

MARRIOTT WARDMAN PARK HOTEL

Book at aaa.com   **Phone:** (202)328-2000 ❸

AAA ⟨SAVE⟩   All Year   1P: $109-$329   2P: $124-$344   XP: $15   F18

Large-scale Hotel   **Location:** Just w of Connecticut Ave; at Woodley Park/Zoo Metro Station. 2660 Woodley Rd NW 20008. Fax: 202/234-0015. **Facility:** 1334 units. 1247 one-bedroom standard units. 8-10 stories, interior corridors. *Bath:* combo or shower only. **Parking:** on-site (fee) and valet. **Terms:** 7 day cancellation notice, package plans, small pets only (with prior approval). **Amenities:** dual phone lines, voice mail, irons, hair dryers. *Fee:* video games, high-speed Internet. *Some:* fax. **Dining:** 3 restaurants, 6:30 am-11 pm, cocktails. **Pool(s):** outdoor, small outdoor. **Leisure Activities:** steamrooms, exercise room. *Fee:* massage. **Guest Services:** gift shop, valet laundry. **Business Services:** conference facilities, business center. **Cards:** AX, CB, DC, DS, JC, MC, VI. **Special Amenities:** free newspaper.

SOME UNITS

OMNI SHOREHAM HOTEL

Book at aaa.com   **Phone:** (202)234-0700 ❹

AAA ⟨SAVE⟩   All Year   1P: $349-$389   2P: $349-$389   XP: $30   F17

Historic
Large-scale Hotel   **Location:** Just w of Connecticut Ave. Located adjacent to Rock Creek Park. 2500 Calvert St NW 20008. Fax: 202/265-7972. **Facility:** Crystal chandeliers add grandeur to the lobby of this 1930s hotel overlooking Rock Creek Park; guest rooms are well appointed. 836 units. 811 one-bedroom standard units. 24 one- and 1 two-bedroom suites ($389-$2000), some with whirlpools. 5-8 stories, interior corridors. *Bath:* combo or shower only. **Parking:** on-site (fee) and valet. **Terms:** package plans, small pets only ($100 deposit). **Amenities:** video games (fee), dual phone lines, voice mail, honor bars, irons, hair dryers. **Dining:** Robert's Restaurant, see separate listing, entertainment. **Pool(s):** heated outdoor, wading. **Leisure Activities:** whirlpool, jogging, spa. *Fee:* saunas, swimming instruction. **Guest Services:** gift shop, valet laundry. **Business Services:** conference facilities, business center. **Cards:** AX, CB, DC, DS, MC, VI.

SOME UNITS

FEE FEE   FEE   FEE FEE

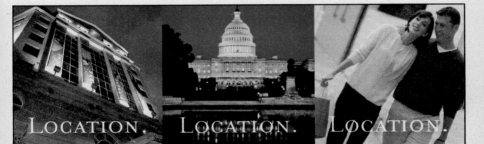

(See map and index starting on p. 399)

THE SAVOY SUITES GEORGETOWN   *Book at aaa.com*   Phone: (202)337-9700   **5**
▼▼▼   All Year   1P: $99-$229   2P: $99-$239   XP: $10   F18
Location: In upper Georgetown area; 0.3 mi s of Massachusetts Ave NW. Located in a residential area. 2505 Wisconsin Ave NW 20007. Fax: 202/337-3644. **Facility:** 152 one-bedroom standard units, some with efficiencies and/or whirlpools. 8 stories, interior corridors. *Bath:* combo or shower only. **Parking:** on-site. **Terms:** package plans. **Amenities:** dual phone lines, voice mail, irons, hair dryers. **Guest Services:** valet and coin laundry, area transportation. **Business Services:** meeting rooms, fax. **Cards:** AX, DC, MC, VI. *(See color ad p 451)*
Small-scale Hotel

SOME UNITS

(ASK) (S/D) (🍴) (&) (🏊) (🐾) (📹) (📠) / (✕) (▣) (💻) /

――――――― **WHERE TO DINE** ―――――――

2 AMY'S   Lunch: $7-$12   Dinner: $7-$12   Phone: 202/885-5700   **11**
▼   **Location:** Cleveland Park. 3715 Macomb St NW 20016. **Hours:** 11 am-11 pm, Sun noon-10 pm. Closed major holidays; also Mon. **Features:** Pizza, Pizza, Pizza, if that is what you are looking for then this is the place to be. A variety of specialty pizzas along with salads, and other dishes makes this a great night for pizza lovers. Casual dress; cocktails. **Parking:** on-site (fee) and street. **Cards:** MC, VI.
Pizza

(✕)

ARDEO RESTAURANT   Dinner: $14-$23   Phone: 202/244-6750   **12**
▼▼▼▼   **Location:** At Macomb St NW; metro stop; Cleveland Park. 3311 Connecticut Ave NW 20008. **Hours:** 5:30 pm-10:30 pm, Sun 11 am-2:30 & 5-10 pm. Closed: 1/1, 12/25. **Reservations:** accepted. **Features:** The trendy bistro offers diners a delectable selection of freshly prepared dishes that may include pan-fried rockfish, crab bisque and wonderful homemade desserts. Dressy casual; cocktails. **Parking:** street. **Cards:** AX, CB, DC, MC, VI.
American

(✕)

CACTUS CANTINA   Lunch: $7-$10   Dinner: $7-$17   Phone: 202/686-7222   **13**
▼▼▼   **Location:** Jct Macomb St. 3300 Wisconsin Ave NW 20016. **Hours:** 11 am-11 pm, Fri & Sat-midnight, Sun 10:30 am-11 pm. Closed: 11/24, 12/25. **Features:** The Tex-Mex cantina is fun, lively and popular with the locals. A great example of the flavorful dishes cooked over a mesquite-wood fire is steak fajitas with fresh vegetables. Crispy chips and salsa are good palate preppers. Outdoor dining is available in season. Casual dress; cocktails. **Parking:** street. **Cards:** AX, CB, DC, DS, MC, VI.
Southwest Mexican

(Y) (✕)

CAFE' OLE'   Lunch: $5-$8   Dinner: $5-$8   Phone: 202/244-1330   **5**
▼   **Location:** Jct Upton St. 4000 Wisconsin Ave NW 20016. **Hours:** 11 am-10 pm, Fri & Sat-11 pm. Closed: 11/24, 12/25. **Features:** The menu outlines an interesting variety of Mediterranean dishes and flavors in appetizer-size servings (meze)—from Moroccan lamb tagine to Tel Aviv nachos to Sicilian tuna kebab. The price range reflects the price of meze, with two or three typically making an entree or meal. Some meze can be served as roll-ups rather than in a dish. The menu also lists panini. Dressy casual; cocktails. **Cards:** AX, DC, DS, MC, VI.
Mediterranean

(✕)

CASHION'S EAT PLACE   Dinner: $19-$30   Phone: 202/797-1819   **19**
▼▼▼   **Location:** Between 18th St and Belmont Rd NW; in the Adams Morgan area. 1819 Columbia Rd NW 20009. **Hours:** 5:30 pm-10 pm, Fri & Sat-11 pm. Closed major holidays; also Mon. **Reservations:** suggested. **Features:** The hand-written menu changes frequently based on the availability of fresh ingredients. The kitchen displays its skill in preparing a variety of dishes with influences from the American South, Italy, France, Spain and Asia. Attentive, helpful staffers will be happy to make recommendations. Dressy casual; cocktails. **Parking:** no self-parking. **Cards:** AX, MC, VI.
American

(✕)

CHARLIE CHIANG'S RESTAURANT   Lunch: $7-$20   Dinner: $8-$20   Phone: 202/966-1916   **4**
▼▼▼   **Location:** Jct Connecticut Ave and Windom Pl. 4250 Connecticut Ave NW 20008. **Hours:** 11 am-10:30 pm. Closed: 11/24. **Reservations:** accepted. **Features:** The popular Chinese restaurant offers Hunan and Szechuan dishes, such as the popular General Tso's chicken and delicious dumplings. The simple, contemporary dining room looks out onto busy Connecticut Avenue. Casual dress; cocktails. **Parking:** on-site. **Cards:** AX, DC, DS, MC, VI.
Chinese

(Y) (✕)

LAVANDOU   Lunch: $10-$14   Dinner: $15-$19   Phone: 202/966-3002   **10**
▼▼▼   **Location:** Jct Macomb St NW; in the Cleveland Park area. 3321 Connecticut Ave NW 20008. **Hours:** 11:30 am-10 pm, Fri-11 pm, Sat 5 pm-11 pm, Sun 5 pm-10 pm. Closed major holidays. **Reservations:** suggested. **Features:** Provencal French fare, extensive menu selections and daily specials make the restaurant popular. The cozy bistro, which exudes a country air, features seafood, chicken and beef. The house specialty is grilled scallops in a red wine sauce. Casual dress; cocktails. **Parking:** on-site (fee) and street. **Cards:** AX, DC, DS, MC, VI.
South French

(✕)

LEBANESE TAVERNA   Lunch: $10-$17   Dinner: $14-$20   Phone: 202/265-8681   **16**
▼▼▼   **Location:** Between Woodley Rd and Calvert St. 2641 Connecticut Ave NW 20008. **Hours:** 11:30 am-2:30 & 5:30-10:30 pm, Fri-11 pm, Sat noon-3 & 5:30-11 pm, Sun 5 pm-10 pm. Closed major holidays. **Reservations:** accepted, prior to 6:30 pm. **Features:** A devoted local following frequents this friendly restaurant. Menu offerings include rotisserie-grilled beef and marinated lamb with potatoes and radishes, as well as a variety of mezza—appetizers hearty enough to serve as a full meal. Casual dress; cocktails. **Parking:** on-site. **Cards:** AX, DC, DS, MC, VI.
Lebanese

(✕)

(See map and index starting on p. 399)

MAGGIANO'S LITTLE ITALY   **Lunch:** $7-$11   **Dinner:** $11-$33   **Phone:** 202/966-5500   ①
Italian
Location: On SR 355; in Chevy Chase area; opposite the Mazza Galleries. 5333 Wisconsin Ave NW 20015. **Hours:** 11:30 am-10 pm, Fri & Sat-11 pm, Sun noon-10 pm. Closed: 11/24, 12/25. **Reservations:** suggested. **Features:** The bustling atmosphere and hearty portions contribute to this eatery's local popularity, but Italian fare prepared with fresh ingredients is the biggest draw. Family-style dining is available for parties of four or more. Valet parking is available in the evenings. Casual dress; cocktails. No self-parking. **Cards:** AX, CB, DC, DS, MC, VI.

MATISSE   **Lunch:** $11-$15   **Dinner:** $18-$26   **Phone:** 202/244-5222   ③
French
Location: Jct Fessenden St NW; 1.8 mi n. 4934 Wisconsin Ave NW 20016. **Hours:** 11:30 am-2:30 & 5:30-10 pm, Fri-10:30 pm, Sat 5:30 pm-11 pm, Sun 11 am-3 & 5-9 pm. Closed major holidays; also Mon. **Reservations:** suggested, weekends. **Features:** The kitchen prepares French and modern American cuisine with Mediterranean influences. Among dishes are duo of duck, which includes a leg confit and a seared breast; rack of lamb crusted with mustard and fresh herbs; and pan-seared tuna steak. The casual yet fine-dining atmosphere offers a comfortable setting for any occasion. Dressy casual; cocktails. **Parking:** on-site. **Cards:** AX, DC, DS, MC, VI.

NAM-VIET PHO-79   **Lunch:** $7-$9   **Dinner:** $6-$14   **Phone:** 202/237-1015   ⑨
Thai
Location: Between Newark and Macomb sts. 3419 Connecticut Ave NW 20008. **Hours:** 11 am-10 pm, Fri & Sat-11 pm. Closed: 11/24, 12/25. **Features:** Overflowing dishes arrive at tables with loyal locals eager to delve into fragrant dishes of fresh flavors. Impressive-looking flash-fried whole fish, noodle soups chock full of goodies, aromatic curries and grilled entrees galore are popular with patrons who know a good thing when they taste it. Perfect for families as there is space, portions are generous, and the digs are casual. Casual dress; cocktails. **Parking:** no self-parking. **Cards:** AX, DC, DS, MC, VI.

NEW HEIGHTS   **Dinner:** $17-$28   **Phone:** 202/234-4110   ⑰
American
Location: Just w of Connecticut Ave NW; opposite Rock Creek Park. 2317 Calvert St NW 20008. **Hours:** 5:30 pm-10 pm, Fri & Sat-11 pm, Sun 11 am-2:30 & 5:30-10 pm. Closed major holidays. **Reservations:** suggested. **Features:** Fresh, flaky grouper served in a sweet corn sauce earns raves. The comfortable, art deco dining room overlooks Rock Creek Park, sidewalk dining is available weather permitting. Seasonal menu changes reflect the availability of fresh local ingredients. Dressy casual; cocktails. **Parking:** valet. **Cards:** AX, DC, DS, MC, VI.

PALENA   **Dinner:** $9-$66   **Phone:** 202/537-9250   ⑥
Northern Italian
Location: 0.5 mi nw of the National Zoo; in Cleveland Park area. 3529 Connecticut Ave NW 20008. **Hours:** 5:30 pm-10 pm. Closed major holidays; also Sun. **Reservations:** suggested. **Features:** Chef Ruta creates wonderful Italian cuisine with French and American influences. The preparation is simple yet sophisticated, and the three-, four- and five-course menu selections change frequently. Service is professional, and the setting is upscale and relaxing. Dressy casual; cocktails. **Parking:** on-site (fee) and valet. **Cards:** AX, DS, MC, VI.

PESTO RISTORANTE   **Dinner:** $11-$20   **Phone:** 202/332-8300   ⑭
Italian
Location: Just s of the National Zoo. 2915 Connecticut Ave NW 20008. **Hours:** 5 pm-10 pm, Fri & Sat-11 pm. Closed major holidays; also Mon. **Reservations:** accepted. **Features:** The intimate cafe has Tuscan yellow walls, white table linens and soft lighting. The chef-owner prepares homemade Northern and Southern Italian dishes. Seasonal patio seating is available. Casual dress; cocktails. **Parking:** no self-parking. **Cards:** AX, DC, DS, MC, VI.

PETITS PLATS   **Lunch:** $7-$15   **Dinner:** $13-$23   **Phone:** 202/518-0018   ⑮
French
Location: At Calvert St. 2653 Connecticut Ave NW 20008. **Hours:** 11:30 am-2:30 & 5:30-10 pm, Fri-11 pm, Sat 11:30 am-4 & 5:30-11 pm, Sun 11:30 am-4 & 5:30-10 pm. Closed major holidays. **Reservations:** accepted. **Features:** Mellow, magnolia-colored walls beckon patrons to relax and enjoy delicious French-inspired cuisine. Seafood is prepared every way imaginable, and rack of lamb, veal, duck and beef dishes also tempt the palate. Sidewalk seating is open seasonally. Casual dress. **Parking:** valet and street. **Cards:** AX, MC, VI.

ROBERT'S RESTAURANT   **Lunch:** $8-$19   **Dinner:** $11-$28   **Phone:** 202/756-5300   ⑱
American
Location: Just w of Connecticut Ave; in Omni Shoreham Hotel. 2500 Calvert St NW 20008. **Hours:** 6:30 am-3 & 5-10:30 pm. **Reservations:** suggested. **Features:** The dining room at the Omni Shoreham Hotel offers upscale setting with a casual air. The outdoor terrace offers a wonderful view of the landscaped grounds and Rock Creek Park. The menu changes with the seasons, though a couple of the chefs signature dishes include the crab cakes and the Vidalia onion soup. Casual dress; cocktails. **Parking:** valet. **Cards:** AX, CB, DC, DS, JC, MC, VI.

THAI ROOM   **Lunch:** $7-$12   **Dinner:** $7-$12   **Phone:** 202/244-5933   ②
Thai
Location: 2 mi n of the National Zoo. 5037 Connecticut Ave NW 20008. **Hours:** 11:30 am-10:30 pm, Sun & Mon-10 pm. Closed: 1/1, 11/24, 12/25. **Reservations:** accepted. **Features:** Patrons can expect spicy food at the well-established neighborhood restaurant, the first Thai restaurant in the Washington area. The modest dining room is comfortable. Parking is available around the back of the building. Casual dress; cocktails. **Parking:** on-site. **Cards:** AX, DC, MC, VI.

YANYU   **Lunch:** $20   **Dinner:** $15-$38   **Phone:** 202/686-6968   ⑧
Asian
Location: At Newark St. 3433 Connecticut Ave NW 20008. **Hours:** noon-2:30 & 5:30-10:30 pm, Sat-2:30 pm. Closed major holidays; also Mon. **Reservations:** suggested. **Features:** Distinctive Asian cuisine with showy, artistic presentations complements the inspiring Far East decor. Those who can't decide on one of the tempting, seafood-focused menu items can try one of four tasting menus, one vegetarian. The staff is polite and accommodating. Dressy casual; cocktails. **Parking:** on-site (fee) and valet. **Cards:** AX, DC, MC, VI.

(See map and index starting on p. 399)

YENCHING PALACE   **Lunch:** $7-$8   **Dinner:** $8-$13   **Phone:** 202/362-8200 ⑦
Chinese
Location: Jct Connecticut Ave NW and Porter St NW; Cleveland Park Metro Stop, west exit. 3524 Connecticut Ave NW 20008. **Hours:** 11:30 am-11 pm, Fri & Sat-11:30 pm, Sun noon-11 pm. **Features:** The current owner's uncle opened here in 1955. In addition to being one of the first restaurants to serve Peking duck without advance notice, this is said to be the place where U.S. and Soviet envoys met to defuse the Cuban missile crisis. The fare is traditional Chinese, heavy on Szechuan and Hunan dishes, but guests just might hear some ask for the menu written for Chinese Embassy regulars. The Sunday buffet is set up from noon to 2:30 pm. Casual dress; cocktails. **Parking:** on-site. **Cards:** AX, DC, DS, MC, VI.
⊠

WASHINGTON (EASTERN REGION)   (See map and index starting on p. 416)
─────────── WHERE TO STAY ───────────

CHANNEL INN HOTEL   _Book at aaa.com_   **Phone:** (202)554-2400 ③
Small-scale Hotel
All Year   1P: $155-$165   2P: $165-$175   XP: $10   F12
Location: I-395, exit Maine Ave, just e. 650 Water St SW 20024. Fax: 202/863-1164. **Facility:** 100 units. 98 one-bedroom standard units. 2 one-bedroom suites ($200-$250). 3 stories, interior corridors. **Parking:** on-site. **Amenities:** voice mail, irons, hair dryers. **Pool(s):** outdoor. **Guest Services:** valet laundry. **Business Services:** meeting rooms, fax (fee). **Cards:** AX, CB, DC, DS, JC, MC, VI.
SOME UNITS
(ASK) (SD) (⊪) (Y) (⊘) (⇌) (⊞) (⊞) (DATA PORT) / (⊠) (⊟)

KELLOGG CONFERENCE HOTEL AT GALLAUDET
   UNIVERSITY   **Phone:** (202)651-6000 ②
Small-scale Hotel
3/1-6/30 & 9/2-11/15   1P: $119-$195   2P: $139-$215   XP: $20   F12
7/1-9/1 & 11/16-2/28   1P: $99-$129   2P: $119-$149   XP: $20   F12
Location: 0.6 mi se from US 50 (New York Ave). 800 Florida Ave NE 20002-3695. Fax: 202/651-6107. **Facility:** 93 units. 87 one-bedroom standard units. 6 one-bedroom suites ($250-$350). 5 stories, interior corridors. _Bath:_ combo or shower only. **Parking:** on-site. **Amenities:** high-speed Internet, irons, hair dryers. **Guest Services:** valet laundry, area transportation. **Business Services:** conference facilities, business center. **Cards:** AX, DC, DS, MC, VI.
SOME UNITS
(ASK) (SD) (⊪) (⌂M) (⊙) (⊘) (⊞) (DATA PORT) (⊡) / (⊠) (VCR) (⊟) (⊞) /
                                      FEE   FEE

TRAVELODGE GATEWAY   _Book at aaa.com_   **Phone:** (202)832-8600 ①
Small-scale Hotel
3/1-10/31 [ECP]   1P: $110   2P: $110   XP: $10   F17
11/1-2/28 [ECP]   1P: $95   2P: $95   XP: $10   F17
Location: US 50 and Alternate Rt 1; just w of entrance to Baltimore-Washington Pkwy, New York Ave. 1917 Bladensburg Rd NE 20002. Fax: 202/529-7546. **Facility:** 150 one-bedroom standard units. 2 stories (no elevator), interior/exterior corridors. _Bath:_ combo or shower only. **Parking:** on-site. **Terms:** pets ($25 deposit). **Amenities:** voice mail, safes (fee), irons, hair dryers. **Dining:** 10 am-11 pm, cocktails. **Pool(s):** outdoor. **Leisure Activities:** limited exercise equipment. **Guest Services:** coin laundry, area transportation-Union Station & Greyhound Bus Terminal. **Business Services:** meeting rooms, fax (fee). **Cards:** AX, CB, DC, DS, MC, VI. **Special Amenities:** free expanded continental breakfast and free room upgrade (subject to availability with advance reservations).
(See color ad p 420)
SOME UNITS
(SD) (🐾) (⊪) (⊙) (⊘) (⇌) (⊞) (DATA PORT) (⊡) / (⊠) (⊟) (⊞) /
     FEE

The Washington, D.C. Vicinity

Nearby Maryland

ADELPHI pop. 14,998 (See map and index starting on p. 416)

─── **WHERE TO STAY** ───

UNIVERSITY OF MARYLAND UNIVERSITY COLLEGE INN & CONFERENCE CENTER BY MARRIOTT *Book at aaa.com*   Phone: 301/985-7300 **26**

1/1-2/28   2P: $179-$219
3/1-12/31   2P: $169-$209

Large-scale Hotel **Location:** I-495, exit 29 eastbound; exit 29B westbound, 3.9 mi e on SR 193; 1.8 mi w on SR 193 from jct US 1. 3501 University Blvd E 20783. Fax: 301/985-7517. **Facility:** 237 units. 231 one-bedroom standard units. 6 one-bedroom suites. 5 stories, interior corridors. *Bath:* combo or shower only. **Parking:** on-site (fee). **Terms:** check-in 4 pm, package plans. **Amenities:** high-speed Internet, voice mail, irons, hair dryers. **Leisure Activities:** exercise room. **Guest Services:** sundries, valet laundry. **Business Services:** conference facilities, business center. **Cards:** AX, DC, DS, MC, VI.

SOME UNITS

BELTSVILLE pop. 15,690

─── **WHERE TO STAY** ───

FAIRFIELD INN BY MARRIOTT - CAPITAL BELTWAY/I-95 *Book at aaa.com*   Phone: (301)572-7100

11/1-2/28 [CP]   1P: $69-$189   2P: $69-$189   XP: $10   F18
3/1-10/31 [CP]   1P: $89-$129   2P: $89-$129   XP: $10   F18

Small-scale Hotel **Location:** I-95, exit 29B, just w on SR 212. Located adjacent to a small shopping plaza. 4050 Powder Mill Rd 20705. Fax: 301/931-6407. **Facility:** 169 units. 168 one-bedroom standard units. 1 one-bedroom suite ($110-$199). 2-4 stories, interior corridors. *Bath:* combo or shower only. **Parking:** on-site. **Terms:** cancellation fee imposed, package plans. **Amenities:** voice mail, irons, hair dryers. *Fee:* video games, high-speed Internet. **Pool(s):** outdoor. **Leisure Activities:** whirlpool, exercise room. *Fee:* game room. **Guest Services:** valet and coin laundry, area transportation-within 5 mi. **Business Services:** meeting rooms, fax (fee). **Cards:** AX, CB, DC, DS, MC, VI. **Special Amenities: free continental breakfast and free local telephone calls.**

SOME UNITS

SHERATON-COLLEGE PARK *Book at aaa.com*   Phone: (301)937-4422

3/1-11/17   1P: $99-$139   2P: $99-$139
11/18-2/28   1P: $89-$129   2P: $89-$129

Small-scale Hotel **Location:** I-95, exit 29B, just w on SR 212; 2 mi n of I-495 (Capital Beltway). 4095 Powder Mill Rd 20705. Fax: 301/937-4455. **Facility:** 205 one-bedroom standard units, some with whirlpools. 9 stories, interior corridors. *Bath:* combo or shower only. **Parking:** on-site. **Terms:** cancellation fee imposed, weekly rates available, [AP], [BP], [CP] & [MAP] meal plans available, package plans. **Amenities:** video games (fee), dual phone lines, voice mail, irons, hair dryers. **Pool(s):** outdoor. **Leisure Activities:** exercise room. **Guest Services:** sundries, valet and coin laundry, area transportation. **Business Services:** meeting rooms, business center. **Cards:** AX, CB, DC, DS, MC, VI. *(See color ad p 451)*

SOME UNITS

BETHESDA pop. 55,277 (See map and index starting on p. 399)

─── **WHERE TO STAY** ───

FOUR POINTS BY SHERATON BETHESDA *Book at aaa.com*   Phone: 301/654-1000 **38**

All Year   1P: $75-$159   2P: $75-$159   XP: $15   F18

Large-scale Hotel **Location:** I-495, exit 34, 1.9 mi s on SR 355. 8400 Wisconsin Ave 20814. Fax: 301/654-0751. **Facility:** 164 one-bedroom standard units. 6 stories, interior corridors. *Bath:* combo or shower only. **Parking:** on-site (fee). **Terms:** cancellation fee imposed, package plans. **Amenities:** high-speed Internet, voice mail, irons, hair dryers. **Dining:** 6:30 am-10:30 pm, cocktails. **Pool(s):** outdoor. **Leisure Activities:** exercise room. **Guest Services:** valet and coin laundry, area transportation-metro, National Institute of Health & downtown. **Business Services:** meeting rooms, PC, fax (fee). **Cards:** AX, DC, DS, MC, VI. **Special Amenities: free local telephone calls and free newspaper.** *(See color ad p 478)*

SOME UNITS
FEE   FEE FEE

GOLDEN TULIP BETHESDA COURT HOTEL *Book at aaa.com*   Phone: 301/656-2100 **40**

3/1-7/31   1P: $135   2P: $135
10/1-10/31   1P: $109   2P: $109
8/1-9/30   1P: $99   2P: $99
11/1-2/28   1P: $89   2P: $89

Small-scale Hotel **Location:** I-495, exit 34, 2.2 mi s on SR 355. 7740 Wisconsin Ave 20814. Fax: 301/986-0375. **Facility:** 74 one-bedroom standard units. 3 stories, interior/exterior corridors. *Bath:* combo or shower only. **Parking:** on-site (fee). **Terms:** weekly rates available. **Amenities:** dual phone lines, voice mail, irons, hair dryers. *Fee:* video games, safes. *Some:* fax. **Leisure Activities:** exercise room. **Guest Services:** valet and coin laundry, area transportation. **Business Services:** fax (fee). **Cards:** AX, DC, DS, MC, VI. *(See color ad p 478)*

SOME UNITS

(See map and index starting on p. 399)

HOLIDAY INN SELECT BETHESDA   *Book at aaa.com*   Phone: (301)652-2000   **39**

	3/1-6/25 & 9/7-12/31	1P: $160-$186	2P: $160-$186	XP: $10	F12
	6/26-9/6 & 1/1-2/28	1P: $150-$167	2P: $150-$167	XP: $10	F12

Large-scale Hotel   **Location:** I-495, exit 34, 2 mi s on SR 355. 8120 Wisconsin Ave 20814. Fax: 301/652-3806. **Facility:** 269 units. 263 one-bedroom standard units. 6 one-bedroom suites ($250-$350), some with whirlpools. 16 stories, interior corridors. *Bath:* combo or shower only. **Parking:** on-site (fee). **Terms:** check-in 4 pm, 3 day cancellation notice-fee imposed, weekly rates available, package plans. **Amenities:** video games (fee), voice mail, safes, irons, hair dryers. **Pool(s):** outdoor. **Leisure Activities:** exercise room. **Guest Services:** gift shop, valet and coin laundry, area transportation. **Business Services:** conference facilities, business center. **Cards:** AX, DC, MC, VI.

SOME UNITS

(ASK) (SD) (✈) (¶) (Y) (&) (⌐) (≥) (📹) (DATA PORT) (💻) / (✕) (🗄) (📺) /
FEE   FEE   FEE

In the Center of Everything. Yet Away From it All.

- Room Service
- High Speed Internet Access
- Fitness Center
- Starwood Preferred Guest

Four Points Sheraton

A relaxing, full service hotel on the outskirts of the Capital.

AAA Rate $85* per night

At Four Points by Sheraton Bethesda, Washington, D.C.'s historical monuments, zoo and other attractions are a short metro ride away, and more than 150 fine restaurants and shops are within walking distance. For reservations, call **1-800-325-3535** and mention code AAA Rate, or visit **fourpoints.com/bethesda** for Best Rates, Guaranteed.

Four Points by Sheraton Bethesda
8400 Wisconsin Avenue, Bethesda, Maryland 20814

MEMBER OF STARWOOD PREFERRED GUEST

WASHINGTON, DC's BOUTIQUE HOTEL

Bethesda Court Hotel

- Special AAA Rates* • Free HBO®, ESPN®, CNN®
- Complimentary Deluxe Continental Breakfast
- European Style Afternoon Tea
- Plush Executive Rooms • In-room safes
- Close to Monuments & Museums
- In the heart of Bethesda's restaurant and exclusive retail district
- Luxury Rooms Collection w/ presidential mattresses w/ pillow tops, goose down comforters & pillows, Egyptian cotton bed linens
- High Speed Wireless Internet Access in Lobby and in Every Room

www.tbchotels.com

BETHESDA
COURT HOTEL

7740 Wisconsin Avenue • Bethesda, MD 20814
800-874-0050 • 301-656-2100

GOLDEN TULIP
BETHESDA COURT HOTEL

*Subject to availability.

(See map and index starting on p. 399)

HYATT REGENCY BETHESDA   *Book at aaa.com*   Phone: (301)657-1234   **41**
(AAA) (SAVE)
Large-scale Hotel
All Year   1P: $99-$275   2P: $99-$275
Location: I-495, exit 34, 2.5 mi s on SR 355; jct of Wisconsin Ave and Old Georgetown Rd. One Bethesda Metro Center 20814. Fax: 301/657-6453. **Facility:** 390 units. 384 one-bedroom standard units. 6 one-bedroom suites, some with whirlpools. 12 stories, interior corridors. *Bath:* combo or shower only. **Parking:** on-site (fee) and valet. **Terms:** 3 day cancellation notice-fee imposed. **Amenities:** dual phone lines, voice mail, irons, hair dryers. *Some:* CD players, high-speed Internet (fee). **Dining:** 6:30 am-10:30 pm, cocktails. **Pool(s):** heated indoor. **Leisure Activities:** saunas, whirlpool, exercise room. **Guest Services:** gift shop, valet laundry. **Business Services:** conference facilities, business center. **Cards:** AX, CB, DC, DS, JC, MC, VI. *(See color ad p 433)*

SOME UNITS

MARRIOTT SUITES BETHESDA   *Book at aaa.com*   Phone: (301)897-5600   **37**
Large-scale Hotel
All Year   1P: $119-$269
Location: I-495, exit 36, 0.6 mi n on SR 187; 0.8 mi e of I-270 spur, exit 1. 6711 Democracy Blvd 20817. Fax: 301/530-1427. **Facility:** 274 one-bedroom suites. 11 stories, interior corridors. **Parking:** on-site (fee). **Terms:** check-in 4 pm. **Amenities:** voice mail, irons, hair dryers. *Fee:* video games, high-speed Internet. **Pool(s):** heated indoor/outdoor. **Leisure Activities:** whirlpool, exercise room. **Guest Services:** sundries, complimentary and valet laundry, area transportation. **Business Services:** meeting rooms, business center. **Cards:** AX, DC, DS, JC, MC, VI.

SOME UNITS

RESIDENCE INN BY MARRIOTT-BETHESDA-DOWNTOWN   *Book at aaa.com*   Phone: (301)718-0200   **42**
Small-scale Hotel
All Year [ECP]   1P: $239-$279   2P: $239-$279
Location: I-495, exit 34, 2.5 mi s on SR 355; entrance on Waverly St. 7335 Wisconsin Ave 20814. Fax: 301/718-0679. **Facility:** 187 units. 177 one- and 10 two-bedroom suites ($239-$279), some with efficiencies or kitchens. 13 stories, interior corridors. *Bath:* combo or shower only. **Parking:** valet. **Terms:** cancellation fee imposed, pets ($200 fee, $10 extra charge). **Amenities:** video games (fee), high-speed Internet, dual phone lines, voice mail, irons, hair dryers. **Pool(s):** outdoor. **Leisure Activities:** saunas, exercise room. **Guest Services:** valet and coin laundry. **Business Services:** meeting rooms, fax (fee). **Cards:** AX, CB, DC, DS, MC, VI.

SOME UNITS
FEE

——— WHERE TO DINE ———

BACCHUS RESTAURANT   Lunch: $8   Dinner: $13-$17   Phone: 301/657-1722   **57**
Lebanese
Location: Just w on Cordell Ave, from jct SR 355, just n. 7945 Norfolk Ave 20814. **Hours:** noon-2 & 6-10 pm, Fri-10:30 pm, Sat 6 pm-10:30 pm, Sun 6 pm-10 pm. Closed: 11/24. **Reservations:** suggested, weekends. **Features:** Lebanese menu selections vary here, from eggplant dip and hummus to "fatte" - a signature casserole made with your choice of lamb, chicken or eggplant and beef. In keeping with the cuisine, the decor is Middle Eastern. Dressy casual; cocktails. **Parking:** valet. **Cards:** AX, DS, MC, VI.

BETHESDA CRAB HOUSE   Lunch: $20   Dinner: $20   Phone: 301/652-3382   **78**
Seafood
Location: Jct Arlington Rd and Bethesda Ave, just w. 4958 Bethesda Ave 20814. **Hours:** 9 am-11 pm, Fri & Sat-midnight, Sun 10 am-11 pm. **Features:** Operating for more than 40 years in the same location, the casual, traditional crab house serves large steamed crabs, jumbo spiced shrimp and jumbo lump crab cakes. Guests can dine in the dining room or, weather permitting, on the canopied patio with picnic tables. Casual dress; beer & wine only. **Parking:** street. **Cards:** MC, VI.

BLACK'S BAR & KITCHEN   Lunch: $7-$12   Dinner: $18-$26   Phone: 301/652-6278   **72**
Seafood
Location: 1 blk w of Wisconsin Ave (SR 355). 7750 Woodmont Ave 20814. **Hours:** 11:30 am-2:30 & 5-10 pm, Fri-11 pm, Sat 5 pm-11 pm, Sun 5 pm-9:30 pm. Closed: 12/25. **Reservations:** suggested. **Features:** The owners of the well-known Addies have a new spot here, where Gulf Coast-style seafood is prepared with just a touch of Asian influences. Prime spots on the patio are much coveted. Casual dress; cocktails. **Parking:** no self-parking. **Cards:** AX, CB, DC, DS, MC, VI.

CAFE BETHESDA   Dinner: $23-$29   Phone: 301/657-3383   **71**
American
Location: Jct Cordell Ave. 5027 Wilson Ln 20814. **Hours:** 5:30 pm-9 pm, Fri & Sat-9:30 pm. Closed major holidays; also Mon. **Reservations:** suggested. **Features:** The modern American menu reflects French influences and includes several complex dishes with ingredients such as Smithfield ham and black or white truffles. While dishes are hearty and appetizing, preparation and presentation of some entrees may only modestly meet expectations raised by the menu price and ingredients. Desserts are made in house; the thin apple tart is excellent. Valet parking is available after 6 pm. Casual dress; beer & wine only. **Parking:** street. **Cards:** AX, CB, DC, MC, VI.

CAMERON'S SEAFOOD MARKET   Lunch: $6-$14   Dinner: $6-$14   Phone: 301/951-1000   **75**
Seafood
Location: I-495, exit 34, 2.5 mi s on Wisconsin Ave. 4831 Bethesda Ave 20814. **Hours:** 9 am-9:30 pm, Fri & Sat-10:30 pm, Sun-9 pm. **Features:** For diners who have a craving for fresh seafood, the small eatery is worth the quick stop. Casual dress; beer & wine only. **Parking:** street. **Cards:** AX, DC, MC, VI.

CESCO TRATTORIA   Lunch: $9-$22   Dinner: $12-$25   Phone: 301/654-8333   **60**
Northern Italian
Location: 0.3 mi w of Wisconsin Ave. 4871 Cordell Ave 20814. **Hours:** 11:30 am-2:30 & 5:30-10 pm, Fri-10:30 pm, Sat 5:30 pm-10:30 pm, Sun 5 pm-10 pm. Closed major holidays; also for lunch Mon. **Reservations:** suggested. **Features:** Simple, comfortable decor suggests an Italian villa, and the covered sidewalk patio is a perfect venue for sipping, dining and people-watching. Award-winning Chef Ricchi prepares traditional Tuscan cuisine, including a wide selection of pasta entrees, as well as veal, beef and seafood dishes. Dressy casual; cocktails. **Parking:** on-site and valet. **Cards:** AX, CB, DC, DS, JC, MC, VI.

(See map and index starting on p. 399)

FOONG LIN RESTAURANT   **Lunch: $5-$8**   **Dinner: $7-$16**   **Phone: 301/656-3427**   70
Chinese
Location: 1 blk w of SR 355, jct Fairmont St. 7710 Norfolk Ave 20814. **Hours:** 11 am-10:30 pm, Fri & Sat-11 pm, Sun noon-10 pm. **Closed:** 11/24. **Reservations:** suggested. **Features:** A favorite of locals, this Chinese restaurant offers an extensive menu featuring regional Hunan, Szechuan and Cantonese cuisine. Casual dress; cocktails. **Parking:** street. **Cards:** AX, MC, VI.

GRAPESEED-AMERICAN BISTRO & WINE BAR   **Dinner: $20-$29**   **Phone: 301/986-9592**   58
American
cocktails.
Location: 0.3 mi w of Wisconsin Ave. 4865 Cordell Ave 20814. **Hours:** 5 pm-10 pm, Fri & Sat-11 pm, Sun-9 pm. **Closed:** 1/1, 11/24, 12/25. **Reservations:** suggested. **Features:** Innovative American cuisine is complemented by an award-winning wine selection. The menu indicates appropriate wine-food matches. Guests can select a half glass, full glass or bottle. A limited selection of cocktails is available. Casual dress; cocktails. **Parking:** street. **Cards:** AX, DC, DS, MC, VI.

HAANDI   **Lunch: $5-$11**   **Dinner: $9-$17**   **Phone: 301/718-0121**   67
Indian
CB, DC, MC, VI.
Location: Just w on Cheltenham Dr, from SR 355, just nw on Norfolk Ave, then just w. 4904 Fairmont Ave 20814. **Hours:** 11:30 am-2:30 & 5-10 pm, Fri & Sat-10:30 pm, Sun noon-2:30 & 5-10 pm. **Closed:** 11/24. **Reservations:** accepted, Sun-Thurs. **Features:** With an upscale, cheerfully bright decor, the storefront eatery has earned the distinction of serving top-notch Indian cuisine and with good reason. The menu lists well-prepared and flavorful chicken, lamb, seafood and vegetarian entrees. Casual dress; cocktails. **Parking:** street. **Cards:** AX, CB, DC, MC, VI.

JEAN-MICHEL RESTAURANT   **Lunch: $11-$15**   **Dinner: $18-$26**   **Phone: 301/564-4910**   56
French
MC, VI.
Location: Jct SR 187 (Old Georgetown Rd) and Democracy Blvd; in Wildwood Shopping Center. 10223 Old Georgetown Rd 20814. **Hours:** 11:30 am-2:30 & 5:30-9:30 pm, Sat from 5:30 pm, Sun 5 pm-9 pm. Closed major holidays; also Sun 7/1-8/31. **Reservations:** suggested. **Features:** This restaurant is well-known for its friendly service and classic French cuisine. Dressy casual; cocktails. **Parking:** on-site. **Cards:** AX, DC, DS, MC, VI.

LA MICHE   **Lunch: $9-$15**   **Dinner: $20-$30**   **Phone: 301/986-0707**   64
French
valet.
Location: 0.5 mi sw on Woodmont Ave, from SR 355, just w on St Elmo Ave. 7905 Norfolk Ave 20814. **Hours:** 11:30 am-2 & 6-9:30 pm, Mon & Sat from 6 pm. **Closed:** 11/24. **Reservations:** suggested. **Features:** Country French cuisine and a decidedly similar decor of earth tones, antiques and hanging baskets add to the dining experience at the comfortably sophisticated restaurant. Popular menu choices include sauteed lobster with pasta and white wine sauce; escargot in garlic and butter; and dessert souffles. Dressy casual; cocktails. **Parking:** on-site and valet. **Cards:** AX, DC, MC, VI.

LE VIEUX LOGIS   **Dinner: $19-$28**   **Phone: 301/652-6816**   59
French
Cards: AX, CB, DC, DS, MC, VI.
Location: 3 blks w of SR 355; I-495, exit 36, 2.2 mi s on SR 187. 7925 Old Georgetown Rd 20814. **Hours:** 5:30 pm-9 pm. **Closed:** 5/30, 7/4, 9/5; also Sun. **Reservations:** suggested. **Features:** The cozy cottage stands out with its hand-painted murals along the outside. The intimate dining room has a country air, with flowers and greenery all around. The kitchen prepares delicious French fare. Casual dress; cocktails. **Parking:** valet.

MATUBA JAPANESE RESTAURANT   **Lunch: $6-$10**   **Dinner: $8-$20**   **Phone: 301/652-7449**   65
Japanese
Casual dress; beer & wine only. **Parking:** street. **Cards:** AX, MC, VI.
Location: 0.3 mi w of SR 355. 4918 Cordell Ave 20814. **Hours:** 11:30 am-2 & 5-10 pm, Fri-10:30 pm, Sat noon-2:30 & 5-10:30 pm, Sun 5 pm-10 pm. **Closed:** 11/24. **Reservations:** suggested. **Features:** Diners can name their favorites from an extensive variety of sushi and rolls: octopus, salmon, sea urchin, crab or numerous other seafood items. The energetic restaurant also provides efficient service although at times there can be a language barrier.

NAPA THAI   **Lunch: $6-$10**   **Dinner: $8-$16**   **Phone: 301/986-8590**   66
Thai
Cards: AX, DC, DS, MC, VI.
Location: 0.3 mi w of SR 355. 4924 St. Elmo Ave 20814. **Hours:** 11:30 am-10 pm, Fri & Sat-11 pm. **Closed:** 11/24; also for lunch 1/1 & 12/25. **Reservations:** accepted. **Features:** An intimate dining room and seasonal outdoor deck area provides a casual, comfortable setting for diners. The menu offers traditional Thai dishes as well as some seasonal inspirations of the kitchen. Casual dress; beer & wine only. **Parking:** street.

OODLES NOODLES   **Lunch: $6-$10**   **Dinner: $6-$10**   **Phone: 301/986-8833**   61
Asian
Location: Between Old Georgetown and Norfolk rds. 4907 Norfolk Ave 20814. **Hours:** 11:30 am-3 & 5-10 pm, Fri & Sat-10:30 pm, Sun 5 pm-10 pm. **Closed:** 7/4, 11/24, 12/25. **Reservations:** suggested, weekends. **Features:** Noodles are the centerpiece of most dishes, with at least 17 offerings featuring them from rice to egg, flat to thin, al dente to crisp. Dishes bring out tasty Asian flavors—some spicy, others mild or plain—in a choice of meats, seafood or strictly vegetarian ingredients. The menu also lists several well-prepared appetizers, soups and salads, as well as plated items without the noodle emphasis. The atmosphere in the storefront restaurant is light and modern. Casual dress; beer & wine only. **Parking:** on-site (fee). **Cards:** AX, DC, MC, VI.

THE ORIGINAL PANCAKE HOUSE   **Lunch: $5-$10**   **Phone: 301/986-0285**   73
American
Parking: on-site. **Cards:** AX, MC, VI.
Location: At Bethesda Place on SR 355; parking entrance on Woodmont Ave. 7700 Wisconsin Ave, Store D 20814. **Hours:** 7 am-3 pm. **Closed:** 11/24, 12/25. **Reservations:** accepted, Mon-Fri. **Features:** A variety of fluffy pancakes, crepes and egg dishes stack the deck in favor of breakfast, but Monday through Friday there is a limited selection of soups, salads and sandwiches. Two-hour validated parking is available. Casual dress.

(See map and index starting on p. 399)

PASSAGE TO INDIA **Lunch:** $7-$12   **Dinner:** $9-$23   **Phone:** 301/656-3373   62
Indian
Location: 3 blks w of SR 355; I-495, exit 36, 2.3 mi s on SR 187. 4931 Cordell Ave 20814. **Hours:** 11:30 am-2:30 & 5:30-10:30 pm. **Closed:** 11/24. **Reservations:** suggested. **Features:** The chef-owner uses fresh ingredients to prepare an array of Indian dishes. The comfortable setting has an upscale air. Efficient, professional servers are helpful with the menu. On Friday and Saturday nights, valet parking is available for a fee. Casual dress; beer & wine only. **Parking:** on-site (fee). **Cards:** AX, DS, MC, VI.

PENANG **Lunch:** $6-$7   **Dinner:** $7-$20   **Phone:** 301/657-2878   76
Asian
Location: Just w of jct Arlington Rd and Bethesda Ave. 4933 Bethesda Ave 20814. **Hours:** 11:30 am-10 pm. **Features:** Malysian cuisine is served in the large converted warehouse setting. Extensive menu that serves vegetarian dishes. Sit and relax by the soothing sound of water flowing down one of the walls. Casual dress; cocktails. **Parking:** street. **Cards:** MC, VI.

PERSIMMON **Lunch:** $8-$12   **Dinner:** $18-$24   **Phone:** 301/654-9860   79
American
Location: I-495, exit 34, 2.8 mi s on SR 355. 7003 Wisconsin Ave 20815. **Hours:** 11:30 am-2 & 5-10 pm, Sat & Sun from 5 pm. **Closed:** 12/25. **Reservations:** suggested. **Features:** A neighborhood restaurant serving contemporary American cuisine. The chef-owner uses fresh ingredients in preparing each dish. The kitchen is creative, the staff is professional and friendly and the setting is colorful and intimate. Casual dress; cocktails. **Parking:** on-site (fee). **Cards:** AX, DC, DS, MC, VI.

RIO GRANDE CAFE **Lunch:** $5-$10   **Dinner:** $9-$19   **Phone:** 301/656-2981   68
Mexican
Location: 2 blks w of SR 355; downtown. 4870 Bethesda Ave 20814. **Hours:** 11 am-10:30 pm, Fri & Sat-11:30 pm. **Closed:** 11/24, 12/25; also for dinner 12/24. **Reservations:** not accepted. **Features:** A loud, energetic cantina design provides a fun and festive dining atmosphere. Mesquite-grilled fajitas and stuffed jumbo shrimp are menu favorites. Casual dress; cocktails. **Parking:** on-site (fee). **Cards:** AX, CB, DC, DS, MC, VI.

SWEET BASIL **Lunch:** $7-$9   **Dinner:** $9-$21   **Phone:** 301/657-7997   69
Thai
Location: I-495, exit 34, 2.3 mi s on SR 187; 2 blks w of SR 355. 4910 Fairmont Ave 20814. **Hours:** 11:30 am-10 pm. **Closed:** 11/24, 12/25. **Reservations:** accepted. **Features:** The kitchen's signature dishes include sweet basil lamb and sweet basil eggplant. Although these selections are distinctive, many other offerings are traditional Thai staples. Patrons' preferences for spiciness are taken into account. Casual dress; cocktails. **Parking:** street. **Cards:** AX, DC, DS, MC, VI.

TARA THAI **Lunch:** $6-$9   **Dinner:** $8-$14   **Phone:** 301/657-0488   77
Thai
Location: 2 blks w of SR 355; downtown. 4828 Bethesda Ave 20814. **Hours:** 11:30 am-10 pm, Fri-11 pm, Sat noon-11 pm, Sun noon-10 pm. **Closed:** 11/24; also for lunch 12/25 & 1/1. **Reservations:** suggested, weekends. **Features:** The underwater wall mural sets the tone at the casual neighborhood restaurant. The kitchen will prepare dishes with extra spices upon request, and monosodium glutamate is not used. Seafood is the specialty, but don't overlook the noodle, beef and chicken dishes. Pad Thai noodles are worth checking out, as is the sticky rice and mango dessert. Casual dress; cocktails. **Parking:** on-site (fee). **Cards:** AX, DC, DS, MC, VI.

THYME SQUARE CAFE **Lunch:** $8-$13   **Dinner:** $10-$20   **Phone:** 301/657-9077   74
American
Location: Corner of Woodmont Ave; downtown. 4735 Bethesda Ave 20814. **Hours:** 11:30 am-9:30 pm, Fri & Sat-10:30 pm. **Closed** major holidays; also 12/24. **Reservations:** suggested, weekends. **Features:** Stylish, imaginative presentation marks the upscale cafe's organic fare, much of which is vegetarian. Artsy touches give the place an upbeat feel. A juice bar is at the center of the dining area. Dressy casual; cocktails. **Parking:** no self-parking. **Cards:** AX, DS, MC, VI.

TRAGARA *Menu on aaa.com*   **Lunch:** $10-$18   **Dinner:** $17-$29   **Phone:** 301/951-4935   63
Northern Italian
Location: 3 blks w of SR 355; I-495, exit 36, 2.3 mi s on SR 187. 4935 Cordell Ave 20814. **Hours:** 11:30 am-2:30 & 5:30-10 pm, Fri-10:30 pm, Sat 5:30 pm-10:30 pm, Sun 5 pm-9 pm. **Closed** major holidays. **Reservations:** suggested. **Features:** Intimate, handsome and elegant, this restaurant is a popular place for romance. Authentic homemade pasta, seafood and meat dishes include such specialties as red snapper with herbs and veal shanks braised in tomato sauce. The homemade ice cream is a treat. Complimentary valet parking for dinner. Dressy casual; cocktails. **Parking:** on-site (fee). **Cards:** AX, CB, DC, MC, VI.

The following restaurants have not been evaluated by AAA but are listed for your information only.

POSITANO RISTORANTE ITALIANO   **Phone:** 301/654-1717
fyi
Not evaluated. **Location:** I-495, exit 36, 2.3 mi w on SR 187; 2 blks of SR 355. 4940-48 Fairmont Ave 20814. **Features:** A local favorite since 1977, the restaurant serves good preparations of seafood, veal, lamb and pasta.

RUTH'S CHRIS STEAK HOUSE   **Phone:** 301/652-7877
fyi
Not evaluated. **Location:** On SR 355. 7315 Wisconsin Ave 20814. **Features:** Exceptional service and elegant decor—not to mention savory steaks sizzling in butter—make for a memorable dining experience.

TAKO GRILL   **Phone:** 301/652-7030
fyi
Not evaluated. **Location:** I-495, exit 34, 2 mi s on SR 355. 7756 Wisconsin Ave 20814. **Features:** The restaurant's most popular entrees include octopus. Among other choices are offerings from the sushi and sake bar.

BOWIE pop. 50,269

———— WHERE TO STAY ————

**COMFORT INN HOTEL & CONFERENCE
CENTER-BOWIE** *Book at aaa.com*   **Phone:** (301)464-0089
▼▼▼▼   3/16-2/28 [ECP]   1P: $106-$147   2P: $106-$147   XP: $10   F18
        3/1-3/15 [ECP]   1P: $102-$144   2P: $102-$144   XP: $10   F18
Small-scale Hotel   **Location:** US 50, exit 13A, jct US 50/301 and SR 3. 4500 NW Crain Hwy 20716 (PO Box 730, 20718). **Fax:** 301/805-5563. **Facility:** 186 units. 166 one-bedroom standard units, some with whirlpools. 20 one-bedroom suites, some with whirlpools. 4-6 stories, interior corridors. *Bath:* combo or shower only. **Parking:** on-site. **Amenities:** voice mail, irons, hair dryers. *Some:* dual phone lines. **Pool(s):** outdoor. **Leisure Activities:** limited exercise equipment. **Guest Services:** valet and coin laundry. **Business Services:** conference facilities, business center. **Cards:** AX, CB, DC, DS, JC, MC, VI.

SOME UNITS
(ASK) (SD) (🍴) (🍽) (⚕M) (👤) (📷) (🏊) (📹) (DATA PORT) (💻) / (✕) (🔒) (📶) /

HAMPTON INN-BOWIE   *Book at aaa.com*   **Phone:** (301)809-1800
▼▼▼▼   3/1-10/31 [ECP]   1P: $99-$139
        11/1-2/28 [ECP]   1P: $89-$129
Small-scale Hotel   **Location:** US 50, exit 11, 0.4 mi s on SR 197. Located next to a movie theater complex. 15202 Major Lansdale Blvd 20716. **Fax:** 301/809-2515. **Facility:** 103 one-bedroom standard units. 3 stories, interior corridors. *Bath:* combo or shower only. **Parking:** on-site. **Terms:** cancellation fee imposed, weekly rates available, package plans, small pets only ($15 fee). **Amenities:** video games (fee), voice mail, irons, hair dryers. **Pool(s):** outdoor. **Leisure Activities:** limited exercise equipment. **Guest Services:** valet and coin laundry. **Business Services:** fax (fee). **Cards:** AX, CB, DC, DS, MC, VI.
(See ad below)

SOME UNITS
(ASK) (SD) (🐾) (🍽+) (⚕M) (👤) (🏊) (📹) (DATA PORT) (🔒) (💻) / (✕) (📶) /
FEE

———— WHERE TO DINE ————

GRACE'S FORTUNE RESTAURANT   **Lunch:** $5-$10   **Dinner:** $8-$24   **Phone:** 301/805-1108
ⓐⓐⓐ   **Location:** US 50, exit 11, 1.4 mi n on SR 197; 1.4 mi e on SR 450; in Free State Mall. 15500 Annapolis Rd 20715.
▼▼▼ ▼▼   **Hours:** 11 am-10 pm, Fri & Sat-10:30 pm, Sun 11:30 am-10 pm. Closed: 11/24. **Features:** Set in a small
         neighborhood shopping plaza, the comfortable restaurant has a koi pond and aquariums that contribute to a
Chinese   soothing atmosphere. The menu offers consistently good selections from various regions of China, all
          served in large portions. Casual dress; cocktails. **Parking:** on-site. **Cards:** AX, DC, MC, VI.   (✕)

MEMPHIS BAR B Q COMPANY   **Lunch:** $6-$18   **Dinner:** $6-$18   **Phone:** 301/809-9441
▼▼▼ ▼▼   **Location:** US 50, exit 13A, jct US 50/301 and SR 3; in Bowie Gateway Center. 4449 Mitcheville Rd 20716. **Hours:** 7
          am-10 pm, Fri & Sat-11 pm. Closed: 11/24, 12/25. **Reservations:** accepted. **Features:** The roadhouse
Barbecue atmosphere, friendly staff and tasty barbecue ribs and sandwiches make this a good stop to grab a bite to
          eat. Ribs, chicken, turkey and beef are hickory-smoked for hours until they are tender. Mild, mustard and
spicy barbecue sauces add to the flavor. Casual dress; cocktails. **Parking:** on-site. **Cards:** AX, DC, MC, VI.   (⚕M) (✕)

STRAWBERRY'S BISTRO   **Lunch:** $9-$18   **Dinner:** $12-$35   **Phone:** 301/262-7300
▼▼▼ ▼▼   **Location:** US 50, exit 11, 0.6 mi s on SR 197; in Bowie Town Center, opposite the food court. 3851 Town Center Blvd
          20716. **Hours:** 11:30 am-3 & 5:30-9 pm, Fri & Sat-11 pm, Sun 11 am-2:30 & 5:30-9 pm; Sunday brunch.
American Closed major holidays; also Mon. **Reservations:** suggested. **Features:** In the heart of Bowie Town Center,
          the little bistro is a great spot for taking a break from shopping. The creative menu lists vegetarian, pasta,
meat and fish dishes. Casual dress; cocktails. **Parking:** on-site. **Cards:** AX, CB, DC, DS, MC, VI.   (⚕M) (✕)

CAMP SPRINGS pop. 17,968   (See map and index starting on p. 416)

———— WHERE TO STAY ————

DAYS INN-CAMP SPRINGS/ANDREWS AFB   *Book at aaa.com*   **Phone:** (301)423-2323   42

AAA SAVE   3/1-10/31   1P: $59-$89   2P: $69-$99   XP: $7   F17
             11/1-2/28   1P: $49-$79   2P: $59-$89   XP: $7   F17
             Location: I-95/495, exit 7B, 0.3 mi n on Auth Rd. 5001 Mercedes Blvd 20746. Fax: 301/702-9420. **Facility:** 125
             one-bedroom standard units. 5 stories, interior corridors. **Parking:** on-site. **Terms:** pets ($10 extra charge).
Small-scale Hotel **Amenities:** voice mail, safes (fee), irons, hair dryers. **Pool(s):** outdoor. **Leisure Activities:** limited exercise
             equipment. **Guest Services:** coin laundry. **Business Services:** meeting rooms, fax (fee). **Cards:** AX, CB,
DC, DS, MC, VI. **Special Amenities: free continental breakfast and free room upgrade (subject to availability with
advance reservations).**

SOME UNITS

HOLIDAY INN EXPRESS CAMP SPRINGS   *Book at aaa.com*   **Phone:** (301)420-2800   43

AAA SAVE   All Year [ECP]   1P: $99-$119   2P: $99-$119
             Location: I-95/495, exit 9. Located across from the Air Force base. 4783 Allentown Rd 20746. Fax: 301/735-5235.
             Facility: 151 one-bedroom standard units. 2-3 stories, interior/exterior corridors. **Bath:** combo or shower
             only. **Parking:** on-site. **Amenities:** video games (fee), dual phone lines, voice mail, irons, hair dryers.
Small-scale Hotel **Leisure Activities:** exercise room. **Guest Services:** valet and coin laundry. **Business Services:** meeting
             rooms, fax (fee). **Cards:** AX, DC, DS, MC, VI. **Special Amenities: free expanded continental breakfast
and free newspaper.**

SOME UNITS

CHEVY CHASE pop. 9,381   (See map and index starting on p. 399)

———— WHERE TO STAY ————

HOLIDAY INN-WASHINGTON/CHEVY CHASE   *Book at aaa.com*   **Phone:** (301)656-1500   34

             All Year   1P: $139   2P: $139
             Location: Jct SR 191, 0.8 mi s on SR 355. 5520 Wisconsin Ave 20815. Fax: 301/656-5045. **Facility:** 214 units.
Large-scale Hotel 203 one-bedroom standard units. 11 one-bedroom suites, some with whirlpools. 12 stories, interior corridors.
             Parking: on-site. **Terms:** check-in 4 pm, cancellation fee imposed. **Amenities:** voice mail, irons, hair dryers.
Some: dual phone lines. **Pool(s):** outdoor. **Leisure Activities:** exercise room. **Guest Services:** gift shop, valet and coin
laundry. **Business Services:** meeting rooms, fax. **Cards:** AX, CB, DC, DS, JC, MC, VI.

SOME UNITS

FEE FEE

———— WHERE TO DINE ————

LA FERME RESTAURANT   **Lunch:** $10-$16   **Dinner:** $20-$27   **Phone:** 301/986-5255   52

AAA   **Location:** Chevy Chase Circle, just e on Western Ave, 1 mi ne. 7101 Brookville Rd 20815. **Hours:** noon-2 & 6-10
             pm, Sat from 6 pm, Sun 11:30 am-2 & 5-9 pm. Closed: 1/1, 7/4, 12/25; also Mon. **Reservations:** suggested.
French   **Features:** The decor in this restored farmhouse is comfortable, romantic country French. Caesar salad,
             soft-shelled crab, filet mignon, fricassee of lobster and Grand Marnier souffle prove to be discerning
             choices. Chateaubriand is a house special. Deck dining is available in season. Dressy casual; cocktails;
             entertainment. **Parking:** on-site. **Cards:** AX, CB, DC, DS, MC, VI.

RISTORANTE TERRAZZA   **Lunch:** $11-$19   **Dinner:** $14-$25   **Phone:** 301/951-9292   53

             Location: I-495, exit 34, 3.9 mi s on SR 355; on terrace level of Chevy Chase Metro Building. 2 Wisconsin Circle
             20815. **Hours:** 11:30 am-2:30 & 5:30-10 pm, Fri-10:30 pm, Sat 5:30 pm-10:30 pm. Closed major holidays;
Northern   also Sun. **Reservations:** suggested. **Features:** In the heart of downtown, the restaurant serves Northern
Italian   Italian cuisine and desserts worth the splurge. Dressy casual; cocktails. **Parking:** on-site. **Cards:** AX, CB,
             DC, DS, MC, VI.

TAVIRA   **Lunch:** $7-$14   **Dinner:** $17-$23   **Phone:** 301/652-8684   51

             Location: I-495, exit 33, 0.7 mi s on SR 185 (Connecticut Ave); in Chevy Chase Bank Building, lower level. 8401
             Connecticut Ave 20815. **Hours:** 11:30 am-2:30 & 5:30-10 pm, Fri-11 pm, Sat 5:30 pm-11 pm, Sun 5 pm-9 pm.
Portuguese   Closed: 1/1, 7/4, 12/25. **Reservations:** suggested. **Features:** The fine-dining restaurant is tucked away on
             the lower level of the Chevy Chase bank building. The kitchen prepares wonderful Portuguese dishes, as
well as other Mediterranean dishes, including Spanish and Italian selections. Complimentary garage parking is available during
dinner. Dressy casual; cocktails. **Parking:** on-site (fee). **Cards:** AX, DC, MC, VI.

CLINTON pop. 26,064

———— WHERE TO STAY ————

COLONY SOUTH HOTEL & CONFERENCE CENTER   *Book at aaa.com*   **Phone:** (301)856-4500

AAA SAVE   All Year   1P: $159-$169   2P: $159-$169   XP: $10   F18
             Location: I-95/495, exit 7A, 5 mi s on SR 5; 1.2 mi s of jct SR 223. Located adjacent to Southern Maryland Hospital
             Center. 7401 Surratts Rd 20735. Fax: 301/868-1439. **Facility:** 195 units. 187 one-bedroom standard units. 8
             one-bedroom suites ($189-$239), some with whirlpools. 3 stories, interior corridors. **Bath:** combo or shower
Large-scale Hotel only. **Parking:** on-site. **Terms:** [AP] & [BP] meal plans available, package plans. **Amenities:** voice mail,
             irons, hair dryers. *Some:* dual phone lines. **Dining:** 7 am-5 pm, Sat-noon; closed Sun, also, The Wayfarer
Restaurant, see separate listing. **Pool(s):** heated indoor. **Leisure Activities:** saunas, whirlpool, water aerobics, 2 lighted tennis
courts, racquetball courts, picnic area, sun deck, jogging. **Fee:** aerobics instruction, massage. **Guest Services:** gift shop, valet
and coin laundry, airport transportation-Ronald Reagan Washington National Airport, area transportation-within 5 mi, Branch Ave
Metro. **Fee:** beauty salon, tanning facility. **Business Services:** conference facilities, fax (fee). **Cards:** AX, CB, DC, DS, MC, VI.

SOME UNITS

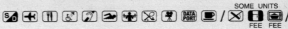

FEE FEE

COMFORT INN-AT ANDREWS AIR FORCE BASE   *Book at aaa.com*   Phone: (301)856-5200

AAA SAVE   All Year [ECP]   1P: $95-$155   2P: $95-$155   XP: $10   F16
Location: I-95/495, exit 7A, 3.2 mi s on SR 5. 7979 Malcolm Rd 20735. Fax: 301/856-7111. **Facility:** 94 one-bedroom standard units. 3 stories, interior corridors. **Parking:** on-site. **Terms:** 3 day cancellation notice. **Amenities:** dual phone lines, voice mail, irons, hair dryers. *Some:* DVD players, safes. **Leisure**
Small-scale Hotel **Activities:** exercise room. **Guest Services:** valet and coin laundry. **Business Services:** meeting rooms, fax (fee). **Cards:** AX, CB, DC, DS, MC, VI. **Special Amenities: free expanded continental breakfast and free local telephone calls.**

SOME UNITS

--------- WHERE TO DINE ---------

THE WAYFARER RESTAURANT   **Lunch:** $9-$15   **Dinner:** $12-$25   Phone: 301/856-3343

AAA   **Location:** I-95/495, exit 7A, 5 mi s on SR 5; 1.2 mi s of jct SR 223; in Colony South Hotel & Conference Center. 7401 Surratts Rd 20735. **Hours:** 6-10 am, 11:30-2:30 & 5:30-10 pm, Sun-9 pm. Closed: 12/25.
Reservations: suggested, weekends. **Features:** The attractive, smoke-free dining room exudes country-style ambience with vaulted beamed ceilings and an inviting fireplace. The menu showcases a nice
Northern   selection of pasta dishes, beef, fresh seafood and poultry. A lunch buffet is available Monday-Friday. Casual
Italian   dress; cocktails. **Parking:** on-site. **Cards:** AX, CB, DC, DS, MC, VI.

COLLEGE PARK pop. 24,657 (See map and index starting on p. 416)

--------- WHERE TO STAY ---------

BEST WESTERN-COLLEGE PARK INN & FUNDOME   *Book at aaa.com*   Phone: (301)474-2800   **18**

AAA SAVE   3/1-11/15 [ECP]   1P: $79-$109   2P: $79-$109   XP: $5   F16
           11/16-2/28 [ECP]   1P: $69-$109   2P: $69-$109   XP: $5   F16
Location: I-95/495, exit 25 northbound; exit 25B southbound, 1.5 mi s on US 1. 8601 Baltimore Ave 20740. Fax: 301/474-0714. **Facility:** 118 one-bedroom standard units. 2 stories (no elevator), interior/exterior
Small-scale Hotel corridors. *Bath:* combo or shower only. **Parking:** on-site. **Amenities:** voice mail, safes (fee), irons, hair dryers. **Dining:** 7 am-11 pm, Fri & Sat-midnight, Sun-10 pm, cocktails. **Pool(s):** heated indoor. **Leisure Activities:** sauna, whirlpool, putting green, enclosed recreation area, limited exercise equipment, shuffleboard. **Guest Services:** valet laundry, area transportation-College Park Metro. **Business Services:** meeting rooms, fax (fee). **Cards:** AX, CB, DC, DS, JC, MC, VI. **Special Amenities: free expanded continental breakfast and free local telephone calls.**

SOME UNITS

FEE   FEE

COMFORT INN & SUITES UNIVERSITY SQUARE   *Book at aaa.com*   Phone: (301)441-8110   **17**

AAA SAVE   3/1-6/15 & 10/1-10/31   1P: $109-$129   2P: $109-$129   XP: $10   F18
           6/16-9/30 & 11/1-2/28   1P: $89-$109   2P: $89-$109   XP: $10   F18
Location: I-95/495, exit 25 northbound; exit 25B southbound, 1.3 mi s on US 1. 9020 Baltimore Ave 20740. Fax: 301/474-7725. **Facility:** 125 units. 92 one-bedroom standard units. 33 one-bedroom suites ($129-
Small-scale Hotel $179). 8 stories, interior corridors. *Bath:* combo or shower only. **Parking:** on-site. **Terms:** 30 day cancellation notice, 2% service charge. **Amenities:** voice mail, irons, hair dryers. *Some:* dual phone lines. **Pool(s):** outdoor. **Leisure Activities:** limited exercise equipment. **Guest Services:** valet and coin laundry, area transportation-within 1 mi. **Business Services:** meeting rooms, fax (fee). **Cards:** AX, CB, DC, DS, MC, VI. *(See color ad p 501)*

SOME UNITS

(See map and index starting on p. 416)

HAMPTON INN-COLLEGE PARK   *Book at aaa.com*   Phone: 301/345-2200   🔟6️⃣
▼▽▽▽ All Year   1P: $95-$199   2P: $95-$199
Small-scale Hotel   **Location:** I-95/495, exit 25 northbound; exit 25B southbound, 0.3 mi s on US 1. 9670 Baltimore Ave 20740. Fax: 301/345-7201. **Facility:** 78 units. 73 one-bedroom standard units, some with whirlpools. 5 one-bedroom suites. 6 stories, interior corridors. *Bath:* combo or shower only. **Parking:** on-site. **Amenities:** dual phone lines, voice mail, irons, hair dryers. **Pool(s):** heated indoor. **Leisure Activities:** limited exercise equipment. **Guest Services:** valet and coin laundry. **Business Services:** meeting rooms, business center. **Cards:** AX, DC, DS, MC, VI.

SOME UNITS
(ASK) (S/D) (🍴✛) (&M) (🛗) (🏊) (📺) (DATA PORT) (💻) (✕) (🛏) (🖥) /

HOLIDAY INN-COLLEGE PARK   *Book at aaa.com*   Phone: 301/345-6700   1️⃣5️⃣
▼▽▽▽ All Year   1P: $89-$129
Small-scale Hotel   **Location:** I-95/495, exit 25 northbound; exit 25A southbound, just n on US 1. 10000 Baltimore Ave 20740. Fax: 301/441-4923. **Facility:** 222 one-bedroom standard units. 4-5 stories, interior corridors. *Bath:* combo or shower only. **Parking:** on-site. **Terms:** cancellation fee imposed, package plans. **Amenities:** voice mail, irons, hair dryers. **Pool(s):** heated indoor. **Leisure Activities:** sauna, whirlpool, exercise room. **Guest Services:** valet and coin laundry, area transportation. **Business Services:** conference facilities, business center. **Cards:** AX, CB, DC, DS, MC, VI.
(See color ad p 484)

SOME UNITS
(ASK) (🍴) (☎) (🛗) (🏊) (✕) (📺) (DATA PORT) (💻) / (✕) (🛏) (🖥) /
FEE FEE

QUALITY INN & SUITES-COLLEGE PARK   *Book at aaa.com*   Phone: (301)276-1000   1️⃣9️⃣
▼▽▽▽ All Year   1P: $79-$189   2P: $79-$189   XP: $5   F18
Motel   **Location:** I-95/495, exit 25 northbound; exit 25B southbound, 2.7 mi s on US 1. 7200 Baltimore Ave 20740. Fax: 301/276-1111. **Facility:** 169 units. 141 one-bedroom standard units, some with efficiencies and/or whirlpools. 28 one-bedroom suites ($109-$309), some with efficiencies. 2-4 stories, exterior corridors. **Parking:** on-site. **Terms:** 14 day cancellation notice. **Amenities:** voice mail, safes (fee), irons, hair dryers. **Pool(s):** outdoor. **Leisure Activities:** limited exercise equipment. **Guest Services:** coin laundry, area transportation. **Business Services:** meeting rooms, fax (fee). **Cards:** AX, CB, DC, DS, MC, VI.

SOME UNITS
(ASK) (S/D) (🍴✛) (🛗) (🏊) (📺) (DATA PORT) (💻) / (✕) (🛏) (🖥) /

——— **WHERE TO DINE** ———

94TH AERO SQUADRON   Lunch: $6-$12   Dinner: $11-$25   Phone: 301/699-9400   1️⃣1️⃣
▽▽▽ **Location:** I-95/495, exit 23, 2.5 mi sw (towards Bladensburg) on SR 201, then 0.3 mi n. 5240 Paint Branch Pkwy 20740. **Hours:** 11 am-10 pm, Fri & Sat-11 pm, Sun 10 am-10 pm. **Reservations:** suggested.
American   **Features:** Overlooking the small airstrip of College Park Airport, the restaurant exudes a casual atmosphere that reflects the mood of an 1800s French farmhouse. World War II memorabilia decorates the inside and out. Prime rib and grilled farmhouse chicken with jack cheese and mushrooms are longtime favorites. Beer cheese soup is a staple. Casual dress; cocktails. **Parking:** on-site. **Cards:** AX, DC, DS, MC, VI.

(🍷) (✕)

HARD TIMES CAFE   Lunch: $7-$10   Dinner: $7-$10   Phone: 301/474-8880   1️⃣0️⃣
▽▽ **Location:** I-95/495, exit 25 northbound; exit 25B southbound, just s on US 1 to Cherry Hill Rd; in The College Park Marketplace. 4738 Cherry Hill Rd 20740. **Hours:** 11:30 am-11 pm, Fri & Sat-midnight, Sun-9 pm. Closed: 11/24,
American   12/25. **Features:** The little shopping plaza cafe is the place to go for patrons in the mood for chili. Varied types—from Texas and Cincinnati to vegetarian and Terkingua Red—are cooked up, along with burgers, hot dogs, chicken sandwiches and salads. Sidewalk seating is open when the weather permits. Beverages include a good selection of beers and margaritas. Casual dress; beer & wine only. **Parking:** on-site. **Cards:** AX, DC, MC, VI.

(✕)

GAITHERSBURG pop. 52,613   (See map and index starting on p. 399)

——— **WHERE TO STAY** ———

COMFORT INN SHADY GROVE   *Book at aaa.com*   Phone: (301)330-0023   1️⃣3️⃣
(AAA) (SAVE)   All Year [BP]   1P: $59-$109   2P: $59-$129   XP: $10   F16
▼▽▽▽   **Location:** I-270, exit 8, 1 mi e on Shady Grove Rd at jct SR 355. 16216 Frederick Rd 20877. Fax: 301/258-1950.
Small-scale Hotel   **Facility:** 127 one-bedroom standard units. 7 stories, interior corridors. **Parking:** on-site. **Terms:** small pets only. **Amenities:** video games (fee), voice mail, irons, hair dryers. **Pool(s):** heated outdoor. **Leisure Activities:** picnic tables, grill, exercise room, horseshoes. **Guest Services:** gift shop, valet and coin laundry, area transportation-Shady Grove Metro & local restaurants. **Business Services:** meeting rooms, fax (fee). **Cards:** AX, CB, DC, DS, JC, MC, VI. **Special Amenities:** free full breakfast and free local telephone calls.

SOME UNITS
(S/D) (🐾) (🍴✛) (🏊) (✕) (📺) (DATA PORT) (🛏) (🖥) (💻) / (✕) /

COURTYARD BY MARRIOTT-GAITHERSBURG/LAKE FOREST   *Book at aaa.com*   Phone: (301)670-0008   8️⃣
▼▽▽▽   All Year   2P: $99-$144
Small-scale Hotel   **Location:** I-270, exit 11, 0.5 mi e. 805 Russell Ave 20879. Fax: 301/948-4538. **Facility:** 203 units. 202 one-bedroom standard units. 1 one-bedroom suite. 7 stories, interior corridors. **Parking:** on-site. **Amenities:** high-speed Internet, voice mail, irons, hair dryers. **Pool(s):** outdoor. **Leisure Activities:** sauna, whirlpool, lighted tennis court, limited exercise equipment. **Guest Services:** valet and coin laundry, area transportation. **Business Services:** meeting rooms, fax (fee). **Cards:** AX, CB, DC, DS, MC, VI.

SOME UNITS
(ASK) (S/D) (✛) (🍴) (☎) (🏊) (✕) (📺) (DATA PORT) (💻) / (✕) (🛏) /
FEE

(See map and index starting on p. 399)

GAITHERSBURG MARRIOTT WASHINGTONIAN CENTER   *Book at aaa.com*

Phone: (301)590-0044   **14**

All Year   1P: $80-$229   2P: $80-$229

Large-scale Hotel

Location: I-270, exit 9B (I-370/Sam Eig Hwy), just w to Fields Rd, 0.8 mi se, then 0.3 mi ne. Located adjacent to restaurant/shopping complex. 9751 Washingtonian Blvd 20878. Fax: 301/212-6155. **Facility:** 284 units. 283 one-bedroom standard units. 1 one-bedroom suite. 11 stories, interior corridors. *Bath:* combo or shower only. **Parking:** on-site. **Terms:** check-in 4 pm, cancellation fee imposed, package plans. **Amenities:** voice mail, irons, hair dryers. *Fee:* video games, high-speed Internet. **Pool(s):** heated indoor. **Leisure Activities:** saunas, whirlpool, jogging, limited exercise equipment. **Guest Services:** sundries, valet laundry, area transportation. **Business Services:** conference facilities, business center. **Cards:** AX, DC, DS, JC, MC, VI.

SOME UNITS

GAITHERSBURG SPRINGHILL SUITES BY MARRIOTT   *Book at aaa.com*

Phone: (301)987-0900   **16**

All Year   1P: $84-$157

Small-scale Hotel

Location: I-270, exit 9B (I-370/Sam Eig Hwy), just w to Fields Rd, 0.8 mi se, then ne. 9715 Washingtonian Blvd 20878. Fax: 301/987-0500. **Facility:** 162 one-bedroom standard units. 6 stories, interior corridors. *Bath:* combo or shower only. **Parking:** on-site. **Terms:** cancellation fee imposed. **Amenities:** high-speed Internet, dual phone lines, voice mail, irons, hair dryers. **Pool(s):** heated indoor. **Leisure Activities:** whirlpool, exercise room. **Guest Services:** valet and coin laundry. **Business Services:** meeting rooms, fax (fee). **Cards:** AX, DC, DS, MC, VI.

SOME UNITS

HILTON WASHINGTON DC NORTH/GAITHERSBURG   *Book at aaa.com*

Phone: (301)977-8900   **10**

All Year   1P: $79-$199   2P: $79-$199   XP: $10   F18

Large-scale Hotel

Location: I-270, exit 11, then e. 620 Perry Pkwy 20877. Fax: 301/977-3450. **Facility:** 301 units. 299 one-bedroom standard units. 2 one-bedroom suites ($199-$399). 3-12 stories, interior corridors. *Bath:* combo or shower only. **Parking:** on-site. **Terms:** cancellation fee imposed, [BP] meal plan available, package plans. **Amenities:** dual phone lines, voice mail, irons, hair dryers. *Some:* high-speed Internet. **Pool(s):** heated indoor/outdoor. **Leisure Activities:** whirlpool, exercise room. **Guest Services:** gift shop, valet and coin laundry, area transportation. **Business Services:** conference facilities, business center. **Cards:** AX, CB, DC, DS, MC, VI. *(See color ad below)*

SOME UNITS

HOLIDAY INN-GAITHERSBURG   *Book at aaa.com*

Phone: (301)948-8900   **9**

All Year   1P: $79-$129   2P: $79-$129

Large-scale Hotel

Location: I-270, exit 11, 0.3 mi e. 2 Montgomery Village Ave 20879. Fax: 301/258-1940. **Facility:** 300 units. 299 one-bedroom standard units. 1 one-bedroom suite ($400-$800). 7-8 stories, interior corridors. *Bath:* combo or shower only. **Parking:** on-site. **Terms:** cancellation fee imposed, small pets only. **Amenities:** voice mail, irons, hair dryers. *Some:* high-speed Internet. **Dining:** 6:30 am-2 & 5:30-10 pm, Sat & Sun from 7 am, cocktails. **Pool(s):** heated indoor. **Leisure Activities:** whirlpool, sun deck, limited exercise equipment. *Fee:* game room. **Guest Services:** gift shop, valet and coin laundry, area transportation-within 5 mi. **Business Services:** meeting rooms, business center. **Cards:** AX, CB, DC, DS, JC, MC, VI. **Special Amenities:** free newspaper and free room upgrade **(subject to availability with advance reservations).**

SOME UNITS

HOMESTEAD STUDIO SUITES HOTEL-GAITHERSBURG/ROCKVILLE   *Book at aaa.com*

Phone: (301)987-9100   **17**

All Year   1P: $85-$105   2P: $90-$110   XP: $5   F17

Small-scale Hotel

Location: I-270, exit 8, just w, then just n. 2621 Research Blvd 20850. Fax: 301/987-9160. **Facility:** 134 one-bedroom standard units with efficiencies. 3 stories, interior corridors. *Bath:* combo or shower only. **Parking:** on-site. **Terms:** weekly rates available, small pets only ($25-$75 fee). **Amenities:** voice mail, irons. *Some:* hair dryers. **Guest Services:** valet and coin laundry. **Business Services:** fax (fee). **Cards:** AX, CB, DC, DS, JC, MC, VI.

SOME UNITS

(See map and index starting on p. 399)

RESIDENCE INN BY MARRIOTT-GAITHERSBURG   *Book at aaa.com*   Phone: (301)590-3003   **15**
All Year   1P: $99-$179   2P: $99-$179
Location: I-270, exit 9B (I-370/Sam Eig Hwy), just w to Fields Rd, 0.8 mi se, then just ne. 9721 Washingtonian Blvd
Small-scale Hotel   20878. Fax: 301/590-2722. **Facility:** 132 units. 57 one-bedroom standard units, some with efficiencies or
kitchens. 51 one- and 24 two-bedroom suites, some with efficiencies or kitchens. 3 stories, interior corridors.
Bath: combo or shower only. **Parking:** on-site. **Terms:** cancellation fee imposed, pets ($100 fee, $6 extra charge).
Amenities: voice mail, irons, hair dryers. **Pool(s):** outdoor. **Leisure Activities:** whirlpool, jogging, exercise room, sports court.
Guest Services: valet and coin laundry. **Business Services:** meeting rooms, fax (fee). **Cards:** AX, CB, DC, DS, JC, MC, VI.

SOME UNITS
(ASK) (S/D) (🛏) (🍴✦) (⊖M) (♿) (🍳) (🏊) (✕) (🐾) (DATA PORT) (🔲) (📶) (💻) /(✕)/
FEE

SUMMERFIELD SUITES BY
WYNDHAM-GAITHERSBURG   *Book at aaa.com*   Phone: (301)527-6000   **12**
All Year [BP]   1P: $135-$175   2P: $135-$175
Location: I-370, exit SR 355, just n to Westland Rd. 200 Skidmore Blvd 20877. Fax: 301/527-1800. **Facility:** 140
Small-scale Hotel   units. 82 one- and 58 two-bedroom suites ($135-$259) with kitchens. 2-3 stories (no elevator), exterior
corridors. *Bath:* combo or shower only. **Parking:** on-site. **Terms:** check-in 4 pm, cancellation fee imposed,
pets ($200 fee, $15 extra charge). **Amenities:** video library, high-speed Internet (fee), dual phone lines, voice mail, irons, hair
dryers. **Pool(s):** outdoor. **Leisure Activities:** whirlpool, limited exercise equipment, sports court. **Guest Services:** sundries,
complimentary evening beverages: Mon-Thurs, valet and coin laundry, area transportation. **Business Services:** meeting rooms,
fax (fee). **Cards:** AX, CB, DC, DS, JC, MC, VI.

SOME UNITS
(ASK) (🛏) (⊖M) (♿) (🍳) (🏊) (✕) (VCR) (🐾) (DATA PORT) (🔲) (📶) (💻) /(✕)/
FEE

TOWNEPLACE SUITES BY
MARRIOTT-GAITHERSBURG   *Book at aaa.com*   Phone: (301)590-2300   **11**
All Year   2P: $59-$149
Location: I-270, exit 11, just e on SR 124 to SR 355, 0.3 mi s, then 0.5 mi sw. Located in a business park. 212 Perry
Small-scale Hotel   Pkwy 20877. Fax: 301/590-0909. **Facility:** 91 units. 60 one-bedroom standard units with efficiencies. 5 one-
and 26 two-bedroom suites with kitchens. 3-4 stories, interior corridors. *Bath:* combo or shower only.
Parking: on-site. **Terms:** [CP] meal plan available, package plans, pets ($75 fee, $5 extra charge). **Amenities:** video games
(fee), high-speed Internet, dual phone lines, voice mail, irons, hair dryers. **Pool(s):** small heated outdoor. **Leisure
Activities:** limited exercise equipment. **Guest Services:** valet and coin laundry. **Business Services:** fax (fee). **Cards:** AX, CB,
DC, DS, MC, VI.

SOME UNITS
(ASK) (S/D) (🛏) (⊖M) (♿) (🍳) (🏊) (🐾) (DATA PORT) (🔲) (📶) (💻) /(✕)/
FEE

——— **WHERE TO DINE** ———

CANTINA D'ITALIA   Lunch: $6-$10   Dinner: $7-$19   Phone: 301/948-8858
Location: Jct SR 124 (Quince Orchard Rd) and Great Seneca Hwy; in Kentlands Shopping Center. 285 Kentlands Blvd
Italian   20878. **Hours:** 11 am-10 pm, Fri & Sat-11 pm, Sun noon-11 pm. Closed: 12/25. **Reservations:** accepted.
Features: Good Italian fare is on the menu at Cantina D' Italia, from veal to pasta and pizza to seafood. The
atmosphere is suitable for any occasion, from family dining to a business meal. Casual dress; cocktails.
Parking: on-site. **Cards:** AX, DC, DS, MC, VI.   (✕)

FLAMING PIT   Lunch: $6-$10   Dinner: $11-$37   Phone: 301/977-0700   **38**
Location: I-270, exit 11, 0.3 mi e, 1 mi n on SR 355. 18701 N Frederick Ave 20879. **Hours:** 11:30 am-10:30 pm, Fri-
11 pm, Sat 4 pm-11 pm, Sun 5 pm-10 pm. Closed major holidays. **Reservations:** suggested. **Features:** The
Steak & Seafood   restaurant's rustic ambience is carried from the stone exterior to the stucco and wood trim dining room. The
menu offers a good selection of meats and seafood, including house specialties prime rib and king crab
legs. The piano lounge offers entertainment nightly and the crowd gets lively as diners are encouraged to join in song. Dressy
casual; cocktails. **Parking:** on-site. **Cards:** AX, CB, DC, DS, MC, VI.   (Y) (✕)

IL PORTO RESTAURANT   Lunch: $5-$13   Dinner: $7-$13   Phone: 301/590-0735   **39**
Location: I-270, exit 9B (I-370/Sam Eig Hwy), 0.8 mi w, 0.3 mi n on Diamondback Dr, then 1.2 mi e; in Festival
Shopping Plaza. 245 Muddy Branch Rd 20878. **Hours:** 11:30 am-10 pm, Sat from noon, Sun noon-9 pm.
Italian   Closed: 11/24, 12/25. **Reservations:** accepted. **Features:** The small shopping-plaza restaurant lets guests
choose from selections of pizza, pasta, veal and seafood. A hand-painted Venetian wall mural sets the
scene in the casual cafe, which is comfortable for families. Casual dress; cocktails. **Parking:** on-site. **Cards:** AX, MC, VI.   (✕)

RICO Y RICO   Lunch: $8-$24   Dinner: $8-$28   Phone: 301/330-6611   **41**
Location: I-270, exit 9B (I-370/Sam Eig Hwy), 0.3 mi w, then s; in Rio Entertainment Center. 9811 Washingtonian Blvd
20878. **Hours:** 11:30 am-2 & 5-9 pm, Fri-10 pm, Sat 5 pm-10 pm, Sun 5 pm-9 pm. Closed: 11/24, 12/25.
International   **Reservations:** suggested. **Features:** The international menu lists a full array of tapas and flavorful entrees.
Dishes such as lomo salteado—a marinated tenderloin sauteed with tomatoes, peppers and onions—and
Caribbean salmon filet make diners want to return for more. The extensive wine selection complements the food well. Dressy
casual; cocktails. **Parking:** on-site. **Cards:** AX, CB, DC, DS, MC, VI.   (Y) (✕)

TARA THAI   Lunch: $6-$10   Dinner: $8-$13   Phone: 301/947-8330   **40**
Location: I-270, exit 9B (I-370/Sam Eig Hwy), 0.3 mi w, then s; in Rio Entertainment Center. 9811 Washingtonian Blvd
20886. **Hours:** 11:30 am-2:30 & 4:30-10 pm, Fri-11 pm, Sat noon-11 pm, Sun noon-10 pm. Closed: 11/24;
Thai   also for lunch 1/1 & 12/25. **Reservations:** accepted. **Features:** An aquatic theme and colorful table tops set
the tone at this casual, stylish restaurant. The kitchen prepares your dish extra spicy if your request it and
MSG is not used. Seafood is their specialty, but don't overlook the noodles, beef, chicken and vegetarian dishes. Casual dress;
cocktails. **Parking:** on-site. **Cards:** AX, DC, DS, MC, VI.   (✕)

(See map and index starting on p. 399)

──────── *The following restaurant has not been evaluated by AAA* ────────
but is listed for your information only.

HUNAN PALACE   **Phone:** 301/977-8600
(fyi)   Not evaluated. **Location:** I-270, exit 8, just e; in Shady Grove Center. 9011 Gaither Rd 20877. **Features:** Locals
               favor this Chinese restaurant, which is known for its Shanghai and Taiwanese dishes.

GERMANTOWN pop. 55,419

──────── **WHERE TO STAY** ────────

FAIRFIELD INN & SUITES BY
MARRIOTT-GERMANTOWN/GAITHERSBURG   **Phone:** 301/916-0750
(fyi)   3/1-11/15   1P: $99-$149   2P: $99-$149
               11/16-2/28   1P: $79-$129   2P: $79-$129
Small-scale Hotel Too new to rate, opening scheduled for October 2004. **Location:** I-270, exit 15B, just w. 20025 Century Blvd
               20874. **Amenities:** 87 units, coffeemakers, microwaves, refrigerators, pool. **Cards:** AX, CB, DC, DS,
MC, VI. *(See color ad below)*

HAMPTON INN GERMANTOWN/GAITHERSBURG   *Book at aaa.com*   **Phone:** (301)428-1300
▼▼▼▼   All Year   1P: $69-$199   2P: $69-$199   XP: $10   F18
               Location: I-270, exit 15A, just e on SR 118. 20260 Goldenrod Ln 20876. Fax: 301/428-9034. **Facility:** 178 units.
Small-scale Hotel 158 one-bedroom standard units, some with whirlpools. 20 one-bedroom suites, some with kitchens and/or
               whirlpools. 6 stories, interior corridors. **Parking:** on-site. **Amenities:** high-speed Internet (fee), voice mail,
irons, hair dryers. **Pool(s):** outdoor. **Leisure Activities:** sauna, exercise room. **Guest Services:** valet and coin laundry, area
transportation. **Business Services:** meeting rooms, fax (fee). **Cards:** AX, CB, DC, DS, JC, MC, VI.

SOME UNITS
(ASK) (SD) (T1) (&M) (📷) (🏊) (💪) (DATA PORT) (🖥) / (✕) (📞) (📠) /

HOMESTEAD STUDIO SUITES
HOTEL-GERMANTOWN   *Book at aaa.com*   **Phone:** (301)515-4500
▼▼▼▼   All Year   1P: $72-$92   2P: $77-$97   XP: $5   F17
               Location: I-270, exit 15B, just w to Aircraft Dr, then just n. 20141 Century Blvd 20874. Fax: 301/515-4565.
Motel   **Facility:** 131 one-bedroom standard units with efficiencies. 2 stories (no elevator), exterior corridors. *Bath:*
               combo or shower only. **Parking:** on-site. **Terms:** office hours 6:30 am-9 pm, weekly rates available, small
pets only ($25-$75 fee). **Amenities:** voice mail, irons. **Leisure Activities:** limited exercise equipment. **Guest Services:** valet
and coin laundry. **Business Services:** fax (fee). **Cards:** AX, CB, DC, DS, JC, MC, VI.

SOME UNITS
(ASK) (SD) (🛏) (T1→) (&M) (♿) (📷) (💪) (DATA PORT) (📞) (📠) (🖥) / (✕) /
        FEE

GREENBELT pop. 21,456   (See map and index starting on p. 416)

──────── WHERE TO STAY ────────

COURTYARD BY MARRIOTT-GREENBELT   *Book at aaa.com*   **Phone:** (301)441-3311   **11**
▼▼◇◇▼
All Year   1P: $149   2P: $159
Location: I-95/495, exit 23, 0.5 mi sw of jct SR 201; off SR 193, just n on Walker Dr. 6301 Golden Triangle Dr 20770.
Small-scale Hotel   Fax: 301/441-4978. **Facility:** 152 units. 140 one-bedroom standard units. 12 one-bedroom suites. 4 stories,
interior corridors. *Bath:* combo or shower only. **Parking:** on-site. **Amenities:** high-speed Internet, voice mail,
irons, hair dryers. **Pool(s):** heated indoor. **Leisure Activities:** whirlpool, limited exercise equipment. **Guest Services:** valet and
coin laundry. **Business Services:** meeting rooms, fax (fee). **Cards:** AX, CB, DC, DS, JC, MC, VI.

SOME UNITS

THE GREENBELT MARRIOTT   *Book at aaa.com*   **Phone:** (301)441-3700   **9**
▼▼◇◇▼
All Year   1P: $199   2P: $199
Location: I-95/495, exit 23, 0.3 mi ne on SR 201. 6400 Ivy Ln 20770. Fax: 301/441-3995. **Facility:** 287 one-
bedroom standard units. 17 stories, interior corridors. *Bath:* combo or shower only. **Parking:** on-site.
Large-scale Hotel   **Terms:** check-in 4 pm, package plans. **Amenities:** dual phone lines, voice mail, irons, hair dryers. *Fee:*
video games, high-speed Internet. **Pool(s):** outdoor, heated indoor. **Leisure Activities:** sauna, whirlpool, 2 lighted tennis courts,
exercise room. **Guest Services:** sundries, valet and coin laundry, area transportation. **Business Services:** conference facilities,
business center. **Cards:** AX, CB, DC, DS, JC, MC, VI.

SOME UNITS

HOLIDAY INN-GREENBELT-NASA AREA   *Book at aaa.com*   **Phone:** (301)982-7000   **12**
ⒶⒶⒶ SAVE
▼▼◇◇▼
All Year   1P: $129-$159   2P: $129-$159
Location: I-95/495, exit 22A, 0.3 mi e; 0.3 mi s of Baltimore-Washington Pkwy and SR 193 (Greenbelt Rd). 7200
Hanover Dr 20770. Fax: 301/345-8271. **Facility:** 205 units. 203 one-bedroom standard units. 2 one-bedroom
suites ($159-$199). 7 stories, interior corridors. **Parking:** on-site. **Amenities:** video games (fee), voice mail,
Large-scale Hotel   irons, hair dryers. **Dining:** 6 am-10 & 11:30-midnight, Sat 8 am-midnight, Sun 8-11 am, cocktails. **Pool(s):**
outdoor. **Leisure Activities:** exercise room, volleyball. **Guest Services:** gift shop, valet and coin laundry,
airport transportation (fee)-Baltimore-Washington International Airport. **Business Services:** meeting rooms, PC (fee), fax.
Cards: AX, CB, DC, DS, JC, MC, VI. **Special Amenities:** free local telephone calls and free newspaper.
(See color ad below)

SOME UNITS
FEE

RESIDENCE INN BY MARRIOTT-GREENBELT   *Book at aaa.com*   **Phone:** (301)982-1600   **10**
▼▼◇◇▼
All Year   1P: $129-$249   2P: $129-$249
Location: I-95/495, exit 23, 0.5 mi sw of jct SR 201; off SR 193, just n on Walker Dr. 6320 Golden Triangle Dr 20770.
Small-scale Hotel   Fax: 301/982-6494. **Facility:** 120 units. 48 one-bedroom standard units with efficiencies. 51 one- and 21
two-bedroom suites, some with efficiencies or kitchens. 4 stories, interior corridors. *Bath:* combo or shower
only. **Parking:** on-site. **Terms:** cancellation fee imposed, package plans, small pets only ($100 fee, $10 extra charge, with prior
approval). **Amenities:** video library (fee), high-speed Internet, dual phone lines, voice mail, irons, hair dryers. **Pool(s):** outdoor.
Leisure Activities: whirlpool, limited exercise equipment, sports court. **Guest Services:** valet and coin laundry, area
transportation. **Business Services:** meeting rooms, business center. **Cards:** AX, DC, DS, MC, VI.

SOME UNITS
FEE

(See map and index starting on p. 416)

──────── **WHERE TO DINE** ────────

ROYAL JADE

Chinese

Lunch: $6-$7   **Dinner:** $7-$20   **Phone:** 301/441-8880

Location: I-95/495, exit 22A, 0.3 mi e, 0.3 mi s of jct Baltimore-Washington Pkwy and SR 193 (Greenbelt Rd). 7701 Greenbelt Rd 20770. **Hours:** 11 am-10 pm, Fri-11 pm, Sat noon-11 pm, Sun noon-10 pm. Closed: 11/24. **Reservations:** accepted. **Features:** On the ground floor of an office building, the popular neighborhood restaurant prepares tasty Szechuan, Hunan, Mandarin and vegetarian dishes—all of which can be eaten in the dining room or taken out. Casual dress; cocktails. **Parking:** on-site. **Cards:** AX, DS, MC, VI.

LANDOVER   (See map and index starting on p. 416)

──────── **WHERE TO STAY** ────────

COURTYARD BY MARRIOTT-NEW CARROLLTON   *Book at aaa.com*   **Phone:** (301)577-3373

Small-scale Hotel

All Year   1P: $109-$134   2P: $109-$134

Location: I-95/495, exit 19B, 0.3 mi w on US 50, follow signs to New Carrollton Train Station, then just e. 8330 Corporate Dr 20785. **Fax:** 301/577-1780. **Facility:** 150 units. 136 one-bedroom standard units. 14 one-bedroom suites. 3-4 stories, interior corridors. *Bath:* combo or shower only. **Parking:** on-site. **Terms:** [MAP] meal plan available, package plans. **Amenities:** high-speed Internet, dual phone lines, voice mail, irons, hair dryers. **Pool(s):** heated indoor. **Leisure Activities:** whirlpool, exercise room. **Guest Services:** valet and coin laundry, area transportation. **Business Services:** meeting rooms, business center. **Cards:** AX, DC, DS, JC, MC, VI.

SOME UNITS

LANDOVER HILLS pop. 1,534   (See map and index starting on p. 416)

──────── **WHERE TO STAY** ────────

COMFORT INN-LANDOVER HILLS   *Book at aaa.com*   **Phone:** (301)322-6000

Small-scale Hotel

3/1-10/31   1P: $85-$129   2P: $85-$129   XP: $10   F
11/1-2/28   1P: $75-$99   2P: $75-$99   XP: $10   F

Location: SR 450, 0.3 mi s of jct Baltimore-Washington Pkwy. 6205 Annapolis Rd 20784. **Fax:** 301/322-2523. **Facility:** 89 one-bedroom standard units, some with whirlpools. 5 stories, interior corridors. **Parking:** on-site. **Terms:** package plans. **Amenities:** irons, hair dryers. **Leisure Activities:** limited exercise equipment. **Business Services:** fax (fee). **Cards:** AX, CB, DC, DS, JC, MC, VI. *(See color ad below)*

SOME UNITS

LANHAM   (See map and index starting on p. 416)

──────── **WHERE TO STAY** ────────

DAYS INN-LANHAM   *Book at aaa.com*   **Phone:** (301)459-6600   **23**

AAA SAVE | 3/1-9/30 | 1P: $69-$125 | 2P: $69-$125 | XP: $8 | F12
| 10/1-2/28 | 1P: $69-$99 | 2P: $69-$99 | XP: $8 | F12

Location: I-95/495, exit 20A, just e on SR 450. Located adjacent to railroad tracks. 9023 Annapolis Rd 20706. Fax: 301/459-6002. **Facility:** 112 one-bedroom standard units, some with whirlpools. 3 stories, interior Small-scale Hotel corridors. **Parking:** on-site. **Amenities:** voice mail, safes, irons, hair dryers. *Some:* DVD players. **Dining:** 7 am-11 pm, cocktails. **Leisure Activities:** limited exercise equipment. **Guest Services:** coin laundry. **Business Services:** meeting rooms, fax (fee). **Cards:** AX, DC, DS, MC, VI. **Special Amenities:** free newspaper. *(See color ad below)*

SOME UNITS
🅂 🍴 🎧 📷 DATA PORT / 🚫 VCR 🔌 📠 /

RED ROOF INN-LANHAM   *Book at aaa.com*   **Phone:** (301)731-8830   **22**

| 4/17-11/1 | 1P: $63-$83 | 2P: $69-$89 | XP: $6 | F18
| 11/2-2/28 | 1P: $56-$76 | 2P: $62-$82 | XP: $6 | F18
Motel | 3/1-4/16 | 1P: $60-$70 | 2P: $66-$76 | XP: $6 | F18

Location: I-95/495, exit 20A, 0.3 mi e on SR 450. 9050 Lanham Severn Rd 20706. Fax: 301/731-4610. **Facility:** 103 one-bedroom standard units. 3 stories, exterior corridors. **Parking:** on-site. **Terms:** small pets only. **Amenities:** video games (fee), voice mail. **Business Services:** fax (fee). **Cards:** AX, CB, DC, DS, MC, VI.

SOME UNITS
🐾 🍴 📷 DATA PORT / 🚫 /

LARGO pop. 8,408   (See map and index starting on p. 416)

——— WHERE TO STAY ———

DOUBLETREE CLUB HOTEL WASHINGTON DC-LARGO   *Book at aaa.com*   Phone: (301)773-0700   **32**
All Year   1P: $69-$149   2P: $69-$149   XP: $10   F18
Location: I-95/495, exit 17A (SR 202); off Capital Beltway. Located in a business park area. 9100 Basil Ct 20774.
Fax: 301/772-2016. **Facility:** 184 units. 182 one-bedroom standard units. 2 one-bedroom suites, some with
whirlpools. 6 stories, interior corridors. *Bath:* combo or shower only. **Parking:** on-site. **Terms:** small pets
Large-scale Hotel   only ($25 fee). **Amenities:** video games (fee), voice mail, irons, hair dryers. **Dining:** 6 am-11 pm, cocktails.
Pool(s): heated indoor. **Leisure Activities:** sauna, limited exercise equipment. **Guest Services:** valet
laundry, area transportation-within 5 mi. **Business Services:** meeting rooms, business center. **Cards:** AX, DC, DS, MC, VI.
Special Amenities: free newspaper. *(See color ad p 428)*

SOME UNITS

FEE

HAMPTON INN-WASHINGTON/I-95   *Book at aaa.com*   Phone: (301)499-4600   **33**
All Year [ECP]   1P: $119   2P: $119
Location: I-95/495, exit 17A, just s on Lottsford Rd, then just e. 9421 W Largo Dr 20774. Fax: 301/350-1561.
Facility: 127 one-bedroom standard units. 6 stories, interior corridors. **Parking:** on-site. **Terms:** cancellation
fee imposed. **Amenities:** video games, voice mail, irons, hair dryers. **Pool(s):** heated indoor. **Leisure**
Small-scale Hotel   **Activities:** exercise room. **Guest Services:** valet laundry, area transportation-Largo Metro Station.
Business Services: meeting rooms, business center. **Cards:** AX, CB, DC, DS, MC, VI. **Special Amenities:**
free expanded continental breakfast and free newspaper. *(See color ad p 434)*

SOME UNITS
FEE FEE

LAUREL pop. 19,960

——— WHERE TO STAY ———

BEST WESTERN MARYLAND INN-LAUREL   *Book at aaa.com*   Phone: (301)776-5300
All Year [ECP]   1P: $79-$119   2P: $84-$124
Location: I-95, exit 33B, just w on SR 198. 15101 Sweitzer Ln 20707. Fax: 301/604-3667. **Facility:** 207 one-
Small-scale Hotel   bedroom standard units. 6 stories, interior/exterior corridors. **Parking:** on-site. **Terms:** 2 night minimum stay
- seasonal. **Amenities:** high-speed Internet, voice mail, irons, hair dryers. *Some:* dual phone lines. **Pool(s):**
heated indoor. **Leisure Activities:** sauna, whirlpool, putting green, exercise room, shuffleboard. *Fee:* game room. **Guest
Services:** gift shop, valet and coin laundry. **Business Services:** meeting rooms, business center. **Cards:** AX, DC, DS, MC, VI.

SOME UNITS

ECONO LODGE LAUREL   *Book at aaa.com*   Phone: (301)776-8008
All Year   1P: $60-$70   2P: $70-$90   XP: $8   F18
Location: Jct SR 198, 1.8 mi n on US 1. Located in a commercial area. 9700 Washington Blvd 20723.
Fax: 301/776-0112. **Facility:** 50 one-bedroom standard units. 2 stories (no elevator), exterior corridors.
Motel   **Parking:** on-site. **Amenities:** hair dryers. **Business Services:** fax (fee). **Cards:** AX, DC, DS, JC, MC, VI.

SOME UNITS

FAIRFIELD INN BY MARRIOTT-LAUREL   *Book at aaa.com*   Phone: (301)498-8900
All Year [ECP]   1P: $89-$109   2P: $89-$109   XP: $10   F18
Location: Jct SR 198, 1.7 mi s on US 1. 13700 Baltimore Ave 20707. Fax: 301/498-5721. **Facility:** 109 one-
Small-scale Hotel   bedroom standard units. 5 stories, interior corridors. *Bath:* combo or shower only. **Parking:** on-site.
Terms: cancellation fee imposed. **Amenities:** video games (fee), voice mail, safes, irons, hair dryers. **Pool(s):** outdoor. **Leisure Activities:** whirlpool, limited exercise equipment. **Guest Services:** valet and coin laundry. **Business Services:** meeting rooms, fax (fee). **Cards:** AX, DC, DS, MC, VI.

SOME UNITS

QUALITY INN & SUITES LAUREL   *Book at aaa.com*   Phone: (301)725-8800

(AAA) (SAVE)   All Year   1P: $95-$249   2P: $95-$249   XP: $5   F
Location: On US 1, 0.5 mi n of jct SR 198. One Second St 20707. Fax: 301/725-7874. **Facility:** 96 units. 86 one-bedroom standard units, some with whirlpools. 10 one-bedroom suites, some with whirlpools. 5 stories, interior/exterior corridors. *Bath:* combo or shower only. **Parking:** on-site. **Terms:** small pets only ($15 extra
Small-scale Hotel   charge, in limited units). **Amenities:** voice mail, irons, hair dryers. *Some:* dual phone lines. **Pool(s):** outdoor. **Leisure Activities:** limited exercise equipment. **Guest Services:** coin laundry. **Business Services:** meeting rooms. *Fee:* PC, fax. **Cards:** AX, CB, DC, DS, JC, MC, VI. **Special Amenities:** free continental breakfast and free local telephone calls. *(See color ad p 492)*

SOME UNITS

RAMADA INN   *Book at aaa.com*   Phone: (301)498-0900

All Year   1P: $59-$139
Location: SR 198, 0.5 mi w of jct Baltimore-Washington Pkwy. 3400 Fort Meade Rd 20724. Fax: 301/498-3203.
Small-scale Hotel   **Facility:** 166 one-bedroom standard units. 2-5 stories, interior/exterior corridors. **Parking:** on-site. **Amenities:** voice mail, irons, hair dryers. *Some:* high-speed Internet (fee), dual phone lines, safes. **Pool(s):** outdoor. **Leisure Activities:** exercise room. **Guest Services:** valet and coin laundry. **Business Services:** meeting rooms, fax (fee). **Cards:** AX, CB, DC, DS, JC, MC, VI.

SOME UNITS

RAMADA LIMITED   *Book at aaa.com*   Phone: 301/498-7750

(AAA) (SAVE)   All Year   1P: $65-$85   2P: $75-$95   XP: $10   F17
Location: Jct SR 198, 1.4 mi n on US 1. 9920 Washington Blvd 20723. Fax: 301/498-7582. **Facility:** 77 one-bedroom standard units, some with whirlpools. 3 stories, exterior corridors. **Terms:** [CP]
Motel   meal plan available. **Amenities:** voice mail. *Some:* irons, hair dryers. **Pool(s):** small outdoor. **Guest Services:** coin laundry. **Business Services:** fax (fee). **Cards:** AX, CB, DC, DS, JC, MC, VI.

SOME UNITS

FEE   FEE

RED ROOF INN-LAUREL   *Book at aaa.com*   Phone: (301)498-8811

4/10-10/29   1P: $58-$78   2P: $64-$84   XP: $6   F18
10/30-2/28   1P: $55-$71   2P: $61-$77   XP: $6   F18
Motel   3/1-4/9   1P: $55-$70   2P: $61-$76   XP: $6   F18
Location: On SR 197, 0.3 mi w of Baltimore-Washington Pkwy. 12525 Laurel Bowie Rd 20708. Fax: 301/498-1490.
Facility: 120 one-bedroom standard units. 3 stories, exterior corridors. *Bath:* combo or shower only. **Parking:** on-site.
Terms: small pets only. **Amenities:** video games (fee), voice mail. **Business Services:** fax (fee). **Cards:** AX, CB, DC, DS, MC, VI.

SOME UNITS

———— WHERE TO DINE ————

BAY 'N SURF SEAFOOD
RESTAURANT   Lunch: $7-$15   Dinner: $14-$40   Phone: 301/776-7021

(AAA)   **Location:** Jct SR 198, 1.4 mi s on US 1. 14411 Baltimore Ave 20707. **Hours:** 11 am-10 pm, Fri-10:30 pm, Sat 3 pm-10:30 pm, Sun 3 pm-9 pm. Closed: 1/1, 9/5, 12/25; also Super Bowl Sun. **Reservations:** suggested, weekends. **Features:** Well-established since its opening in 1965, this rustic, nautical-themed restaurant offers good food presented in old Baltimore style. Featuring traditional jumbo lump crab cakes, crab Imperial
Seafood   and fresh fin fish from around the world. The cream of crab soup is a house favorite. Chicken and beef dishes are also available. Casual dress; cocktails. **Parking:** on-site. **Cards:** AX, CB, DC, DS, MC, VI.

BUDDY'S CRABS & RIBS   Lunch: $15-$30   Dinner: $15-$30   Phone: 301/604-2144

Location: I-95, exit 33A, 1.6 mi e, then 0.6 mi s on US 1. 14707 Baltimore Ave 20707. **Hours:** 11:30 am-10 pm, Fri & Sat-11 pm, Sun 8:30 am-10 pm. Closed: 12/25. **Features:** Nestled in a strip mall of a quaint community,
Steak & Seafood   this eatery features fish and ribs. A very selective and distinctive raw bar is offered. Also many combinations of crab (lump) cake by weight, or try a soft-shell crab all broiled to perfection. For the younger set, there are burgers and sandwich selections. The final act is their rich and delectable dessert. Casual dress; cocktails. **Parking:** on-site. **Cards:** AX, DC, DS, MC, VI.

PASTA PLUS RESTAURANT   Lunch: $5-$12   Dinner: $8-$18   Phone: 301/498-5100

Location: US 1, jct SR 198; in Gorman Plaza Shopping Center. 209 Gorman Ave 20707. **Hours:** 11:30 am-2 & 5-9:30 pm, Fri-10 pm, Sat 5 pm-10 pm, Sun 4 pm-9 pm. Closed major holidays; also Mon. **Features:** A
Italian   nondescript exterior belies the warmth and charm of the small restaurant, a favorite neighborhood haunt for homemade pasta and sauces, veal, fresh seafood and pizza cooked in a wood-burning oven. Service is friendly, efficient and knowledgeable. They operate the carryout market adjacent to the restaurant where diners can take home some real treats. Casual dress; beer & wine only. **Parking:** on-site. **Cards:** AX, CB, DC, DS, MC, VI.

RED HOT & BLUE   Lunch: $6-$15   Dinner: $6-$15   Phone: 301/953-1943

Location: I-95, exit 35A, 1.5 mi e on SR 216; in the historic district, 0.5 mi w of US 1. 677 Main St 20707. **Hours:** 11 am-10 pm, Fri-11 pm, Sat noon-11 pm, Sun noon-9 pm. Closed: 11/24, 12/25. **Features:** The energy and spirit of a roadhouse infuse the fun, festive restaurant. The theme is the Blues. Blues music plays as diners
American   enjoy the Memphis-style pit barbecue. A few of the specialties include pulled-pig sandwiches and wet or dry ribs. The staff is upbeat and attentive. Casual dress; cocktails. **Parking:** on-site. **Cards:** AX, MC, VI.

NEW CARROLLTON pop. 12,589   (See map and index starting on p. 416)

——— WHERE TO STAY ———

RAMADA INN NEW CARROLLTON   *Book at aaa.com*   **Phone:** (301)459-6700   **29**

3/1-6/30	1P: $89-$99	2P: $89-$99
7/1-10/31	1P: $79-$89	2P: $79-$89
11/1-2/28	1P: $69-$79	2P: $69-$79

Large-scale Hotel   **Location:** I-95/495, exit 20B, just w on SR 450. 8500 Annapolis Rd 20784. **Fax:** 301/459-8192. **Facility:** 237 one-bedroom standard units, some with whirlpools. 2-10 stories, interior corridors. *Bath:* combo or shower only. **Parking:** on-site. **Terms:** package plans. **Amenities:** voice mail, irons, hair dryers. **Pool(s):** heated outdoor. **Leisure Activities:** exercise room. *Fee:* game room. **Guest Services:** gift shop, valet and coin laundry, area transportation. **Business Services:** conference facilities, business center. **Cards:** AX, CB, DC, DS, JC, MC, VI.

SOME UNITS
(ASK) (S/D) (🍴) (👤) (📷) (🏊) (🐾) (🎥) (DATA PORT) (🖥) / (✕) (🔒) (🛎) /

POOLESVILLE pop. 5,151

——— WHERE TO DINE ———

MEADOWLARK INN   **Lunch:** $6-$14   **Dinner:** $10-$24   **Phone:** 301/428-8900

Location: SR 107, 0.4 mi e of jct SR 109; next to a small shopping center. 19611 Fisher Ave 20837. **Hours:** 11:30 am-2:30 & 5-9 pm, Fri & Sat-10 pm, Sun noon-8 pm; Sunday brunch 11 am-3:30 pm. Closed: Mon.

American   **Reservations:** suggested. **Features:** Meadowlark Inn is a pleasant, family-owned and operated country restaurant whose menu emphasizes homemade bread, soup, sauces, crabcakes and dessert, all presented in ample portions. The atmosphere is homey and the service staff most friendly and helpful. Casual dress; cocktails. **Parking:** on-site. **Cards:** MC, VI.

(✕)

POTOMAC pop. 44,822   (See map and index starting on p. 399)

——— WHERE TO DINE ———

OLD ANGLERS INN   **Lunch:** $15-$19   **Dinner:** $22-$30   **Phone:** 301/365-2425   **48**

Location: I-495, exit 4, 3 mi w via Clara Barton Pkwy and MacArthur Blvd. 10801 MacArthur Blvd 20854. **Hours:** noon-2:30 & 5:30-10 pm, Sun-9:30 pm. Closed: 1/1; also Mon. **Reservations:** suggested, for dinner.

American   **Features:** Country setting. You enter into the lounge with the ambience of a cozy living room. The stone fireplace roars when the weather is chilly. The dining room, on the second level is accessed by a narrow, spiral staircase. The rustic atmosphere continues in the dining room, with an upscale air. When the weather cooperates, lunch service is offered on the charming slate patio shaded by mature trees and green/white umbrellas around a small fountain. The chef is skilled; dishes are prepared ala-minute. Semi-formal attire; cocktails. **Parking:** on-site. **Cards:** AX, CB, DC, MC, VI.

(🍸) (✕)

ROCKVILLE pop. 47,388   (See map and index starting on p. 399)

——— WHERE TO STAY ———

BEST WESTERN WASHINGTON GATEWAY HOTEL   *Book at aaa.com*   **Phone:** (301)424-4940   **25**
F17

(AAA) (SAVE)   All Year   1P: $69-$169   2P: $79-$179   XP: $10

Location: I-270, exit 6B, just w on SR 28. 1251 W Montgomery Ave 20850. **Fax:** 301/294-6024. **Facility:** 164 units. 158 one-bedroom standard units. 6 one-bedroom suites ($129-$179). 7 stories, interior corridors. *Bath:* combo or shower only. **Parking:** on-site. **Terms:** 2 night minimum stay - seasonal, 3 day cancellation notice, Large-scale Hotel   [BP], [CP] & [MAP] meal plans available, package plans, small pets only ($15 extra charge). **Amenities:** video games (fee), high-speed Internet, dual phone lines, voice mail, irons, hair dryers. **Dining:** 6:30 am-11 & 5-10 pm, Sat 7 am-noon & 5-10 pm, Sun 7-11 am, cocktails. **Pool(s):** outdoor. **Leisure Activities:** limited exercise equipment. *Fee:* game room. **Guest Services:** gift shop, valet and coin laundry, area transportation-Rockville Metro. **Business Services:** meeting rooms, business center. **Cards:** AX, DC, DS, MC, VI. **Special Amenities:** free newspaper. *(See color ad below)*

SOME UNITS
(S/D) (🛏) (🍴) (👤) (📷) (🏊) (🎥) (DATA PORT) (🖥) / (✕) (🔒) (🛎) /
FEE

(See map and index starting on p. 399)

COURTYARD BY MARRIOTT-ROCKVILLE — *Book at aaa.com*
Phone: 301/670-6700 [24]

▼▼▼▼ All Year   1P: $129-$149   2P: $129-$149

Small-scale Hotel **Location:** I-270, exit 8 (Shady Grove Rd), 0.4 mi w. 2500 Research Blvd 20850. Fax: 301/670-9023. **Facility:** 147 units. 134 one-bedroom standard units. 13 one-bedroom suites ($164). 3 stories, interior corridors. *Bath:* combo or shower only. **Parking:** on-site. **Terms:** cancellation fee imposed, package plans. **Amenities:** high-speed Internet (fee), dual phone lines, voice mail, irons, hair dryers. **Pool(s):** heated indoor. **Leisure Activities:** whirlpool, limited exercise equipment. **Guest Services:** valet and coin laundry. **Business Services:** meeting rooms, fax. **Cards:** AX, CB, DC, DS, JC, MC, VI.

SOME UNITS

(ASK) (S/D) (￦) (Y) (🍴M) (🦽) (📶) (➹) (📷) (DATA PORT) (💻) / (✕) (🔋) (📠) /

DOUBLETREE HOTEL & EXECUTIVE MEETING CENTER ROCKVILLE — *Book at aaa.com*
Phone: (301)468-1100 [27]

▼▼▼▼ All Year   1P: $99-$269   2P: $99-$269   XP: $20   F18

Large-scale Hotel **Location:** SR 355, 2 mi s of jct SR 28. Located opposite Twinbrook Metro Stop. 1750 Rockville Pike 20852. Fax: 301/468-0163. **Facility:** 315 units. 298 one-bedroom standard units. 17 one-bedroom suites, some with whirlpools. 8 stories, interior corridors. *Bath:* combo or shower only. **Parking:** on-site (fee). **Terms:** check-in 4 pm. **Amenities:** voice mail, irons, hair dryers. **Pool(s):** heated indoor/outdoor. **Leisure Activities:** sauna, whirlpool, exercise room. **Guest Services:** gift shop, valet laundry, area transportation (fee). **Business Services:** conference facilities, business center. **Cards:** AX, CB, DC, DS, JC, MC, VI.

SOME UNITS

(ASK) (S/D) (🚷) (￦) (Y) (🦽) (➹) (✕) (📷) (DATA PORT) (💻) / (✕) (🔋) (📠) /
FEE

PARK INN SUITES-ROCKVILLE — *Book at aaa.com*
Phone: (301)881-5200 [28]

▼▼ 3/1-6/30   1P: $99-$110   2P: $99-$110   XP: $10   F14
    7/1-10/31   1P: $89-$100   2P: $89-$110   XP: $10   F14
Motel 11/1-2/28   1P: $69-$89   2P: $69-$89   XP: $10   F14

Location: I-270, exit 4A, 2.1 mi e on Montrose Rd, then 0.7 mi s on SR 355. 11410 Rockville Pike 20852. Fax: 301/231-7668. **Facility:** 165 units. 130 one-bedroom standard units. 35 one-bedroom suites ($139-$220) with efficiencies (no utensils). 1-2 stories (no elevator), interior/exterior corridors. *Bath:* combo or shower only. **Parking:** on-site. **Terms:** weekly rates available. **Amenities:** voice mail, hair dryers. *Some:* video games, safes. *Some:* irons. **Pool(s):** outdoor. **Leisure Activities:** exercise room. **Guest Services:** valet and coin laundry, area transportation. **Business Services:** meeting rooms, fax (fee). **Cards:** AX, DC, DS, MC, VI. *(See color ad below & p 589)*

SOME UNITS

(ASK) (S/D) (￦+) (🦽) (➹) (📷) (DATA PORT) (💾) (💻) / (✕) (📠) /

QUALITY SUITES AND CONFERENCE CENTER — *Book at aaa.com*
Phone: (301)840-0200 [22]

(AAA) (SAVE) All Year [BP]   1P: $109-$169   2P: $109-$169   XP: $10   F
▼▼▼▼ **Location:** I-270, exit 8 (Shady Grove Rd), just sw. Located in a business area. 3 Research Ct 20850.

Small-scale Hotel Fax: 301/258-0160. **Facility:** 124 units. 58 one-bedroom standard units. 66 one-bedroom suites. 3 stories, interior corridors. *Bath:* combo or shower only. **Parking:** on-site. **Terms:** package plans, pets ($35 fee). **Amenities:** dual phone lines, voice mail, irons, hair dryers. *Fee:* video games, safes. *Some:* high-speed Internet. **Pool(s):** outdoor. **Leisure Activities:** limited exercise equipment. **Guest Services:** sundries, complimentary evening beverages: Mon-Thurs, valet and coin laundry, area transportation-Shady Grove Metro Station. **Business Services:** conference facilities, business center. **Cards:** AX, CB, DC, DS, JC, MC, VI. **Special Amenities:** free full breakfast and early check-in/late check-out. *(See color ad p 403)*

SOME UNITS

(S/D) (🦽) (➹) (➹) (📷) (DATA PORT) (💾) (📠) (💻) / (✕) (VCR) /
FEE

(See map and index starting on p. 399)

RAMADA INN ROCKVILLE   *Book at aaa.com*   Phone: (301)881-2300   26
All Year   1P: $89-$179   2P: $89-$179   XP: $10   F12
Location: On SR 355, 2 mi s of jct SR 28. Located in a commercial area. 1775 Rockville Pike 20852. Fax: 301/881-9047. **Facility:** 161 one-bedroom standard units. 7 stories, interior corridors. *Bath:* combo or shower only. **Parking:** on-site. **Terms:** package plans. **Amenities:** voice mail, irons, hair dryers. **Dining:** 6 am-9 pm, cocktails. **Leisure Activities:** limited exercise equipment. **Guest Services:** valet laundry, area transportation-within 5 mi. **Business Services:** meeting rooms, fax (fee). **Cards:** AX, CB, DC, DS, JC, MC, VI. **Special Amenities:** free newspaper and early check-in/late check-out. *(See color ad below)*

Small-scale Hotel

SOME UNITS

FEE

RED ROOF INN-ROCKVILLE   *Book at aaa.com*   Phone: (301)987-0965   20
3/17-6/27   1P: $67-$90   2P: $67-$96
6/28-10/29   1P: $67-$88   2P: $72-$94
10/30-2/28   1P: $63-$84   2P: $63-$91
Small-scale Hotel   3/1-3/16   1P: $63-$79   2P: $63-$86
Location: I-270, exit 8 (Shady Grove Rd), 0.5 mi e. 16001 Shady Grove Rd 20850. Fax: 301/527-9581. **Facility:** 188 one-bedroom standard units. 2 stories (no elevator), exterior corridors. *Bath:* combo or shower only. **Parking:** on-site. **Terms:** small pets only. **Amenities:** video games (fee), voice mail. **Guest Services:** area transportation. **Business Services:** fax (fee). **Cards:** AX, CB, DC, DS, MC, VI.

SOME UNITS

SLEEP INN-ROCKVILLE   *Book at aaa.com*   Phone: (301)948-8000   23
All Year   1P: $89-$129   2P: $89-$129   XP: $10   F18
Location: I-270, exit 8 (Shady Grove Rd), just sw. Located in a business area. 2 Research Ct 20850. Fax: 301/948-7406. **Facility:** 107 one-bedroom standard units. 3 stories, interior corridors. *Bath:* combo or shower only. **Parking:** on-site. **Amenities:** video games (fee), voice mail, irons, hair dryers. **Leisure Activities:** pool & exercise room privileges. **Guest Services:** valet and coin laundry, area transportation-Shady Grove Metro Station. **Business Services:** PC, fax (fee). **Cards:** AX, CB, DC, DS, JC, MC, VI. **Special Amenities:** free continental breakfast and early check-in/late check-out. *(See color ad p 403)*

Small-scale Hotel

SOME UNITS

(See map and index starting on p. 399)

WOODFIN SUITES HOTEL   *Book at aaa.com*   Phone: (301)590-9880   **21**
AAA SAVE   All Year [BP]   1P: $124   2P: $124   XP: $15   F13
Location: I-270, exit 8 (Shady Grove Rd), 0.3 mi s; 1 mi w SR 355 via Redland Rd. Located in a business park area.
1380 Piccard Dr 20850. Fax: 301/590-9614. **Facility:** 203 units. 18 one-bedroom standard units. 167 one- and
18 two-bedroom suites, some with efficiencies or kitchens. 3 stories, exterior corridors. *Bath:* combo or
Small-scale Hotel   shower only. **Parking:** on-site. **Terms:** check-in 4 pm, pets ($5 extra charge). **Amenities:** video library, CD
players, voice mail, safes, irons, hair dryers. **Pool(s):** outdoor. **Leisure Activities:** whirlpool, limited exercise
equipment, basketball. **Guest Services:** sundries, complimentary evening beverages: Mon-Thurs, valet and coin laundry, area
transportation-metro & within 5 mi. **Business Services:** meeting rooms, business center. **Cards:** AX, CB, DC, DS, JC, MC, VI.
Special Amenities: free full breakfast.

SOME UNITS

——— WHERE TO DINE ———

A & J RESTAURANT   Lunch: $1-$6   Dinner: $1-$6   Phone: 301/251-7878   **30**
Location: On SR 355, just s of Woodmont Country Club. 1319-C Rockville Pike 20852. **Hours:** 11 am-9 pm, Sat &
Sun from 10 am. Closed: 11/24. **Reservations:** not accepted. **Features:** For those who like dim sum, the
Chinese   Northern Chinese version is worth a try. There are more than 60 items that are spicier and have larger
portions of soups and meats than the Cantonese version. Casual dress. **Parking:** on-site.

ADDIE'S   Lunch: $7-$13   Dinner: $18-$27   Phone: 301/881-0081   **35**
Location: I-270, exit 4A, 1.9 mi e on Montrose Rd, then 1.1 mi s on SR 355. 11120 Rockville Pike 20852. **Hours:** 11
am-2:30 & 5:30-9:30 pm, Fri-10 pm, Sat noon-2:30 & 5:30-10 pm. Closed major holidays; also Sun.
American   **Reservations:** suggested. **Features:** Set back off a busy commercial area, the colorful, fine-dining
establishment is one of the most popular in town. Casual dress; beer & wine only. **Parking:** on-site.
Cards: AX, CB, DC, DS, MC, VI.

BENJARONG THAI RESTAURANT   Lunch: $7-$8   Dinner: $9-$14   Phone: 301/424-5533   **29**
Location: On SR 355; in Wintergreen Plaza. 885 Rockville Pike 20852. **Hours:** 11:30 am-3 & 5-10 pm, Fri & Sat
11:30 am-10:30 pm, Sun 5 pm-10 pm. Closed major holidays. **Reservations:** accepted, Sun-Thurs.
Thai   **Features:** The shopping plaza restaurant offers Thai cuisine in a contemporary atmosphere. Thai artwork
decorates the dining room. Casual dress; cocktails. **Parking:** on-site. **Cards:** AX, DC, DS, MC, VI.

BOMBAY BISTRO   Lunch: $9-$13   Dinner: $9-$13   Phone: 301/762-8798   **28**
Location: 0.5 mi w of SR 355, just n of jct of Washington St; downtown. 98 W Montgomery Ave 20850. **Hours:** 11 am-
2:30 & 5-9:30 pm, Fri-10 pm, Sat noon-3 & 5-10 pm, Sun noon-3 & 5-9:30 pm. Closed: 12/25.
Ethnic   **Reservations:** not accepted. **Features:** Consistently well-prepared cuisine is what the kitchen prepares.
The setting is simple, and service is efficient. Casual dress; beer & wine only. **Parking:** on-site. **Cards:** AX,
DC, DS, MC, VI.

CARIBBEAN FEAST   Lunch: $4-$13   Dinner: $4-$13   Phone: 301/315-2668   **25**
Location: I-270, exit 6A, 1.2 mi e on SR 28, then 1.4 mi n on SR 355; in Saah Plaza. 823 Hungerford Dr 20850.
Hours: 11 am-9 pm, Fri & Sat-9:30 pm. Closed: 1/1, 11/24, 12/25; also Sun. **Features:** Perfect for a quick
Jamaican   bite of the warmth of Jamaica, the restaurant offers a choice of either hot or mild jerk seasoning. Casual
dress. **Parking:** on-site. **Cards:** AX, MC, VI.

CUBAN CORNER RESTAURANT   Lunch: $9-$14   Dinner: $10-$15   Phone: 301/279-0310   **26**
Location: On SR 355; 1 mi n from jct SR 28; in Saah Plaza. 825 Hungerford Dr 20850. **Hours:** 11 am-9 pm, Fri &
Sat-10 pm. Closed major holidays; also Sun. **Features:** Cuban cooking is served in this small, popular
Cuban   restaurant. A local favorite dish is ropa vieja: shredded, stewed flank steak served with rice. Casual dress;
beer & wine only. **Parking:** on-site. **Cards:** AX, MC, VI.

IL PINITO TRATTORIA   Lunch: $7-$12   Dinner: $8-$15   Phone: 301/881-0086   **34**
Location: SR 355 S, 0.5 mi e. 5071 Nicholson Ln 20852. **Hours:** 11 am-2:30 & 5-10 pm, Sun & Mon 5 pm-9 pm.
Closed major holidays. **Reservations:** accepted. **Features:** Traditional dishes are served at the family
Italian   restaurant. The atmosphere is casual and relaxed, allowing for a comfortable family outing. Casual dress;
cocktails. **Parking:** on-site. **Cards:** MC, VI.

IL PIZZICO   Lunch: $8-$13   Dinner: $10-$16   Phone: 301/309-0610   **24**
Location: On SR 355, 2 mi n of jct SR 28. 15209 Frederick Rd 20850. **Hours:** 11 am-2:30 & 5-9:30 pm, Fri-10 pm,
Sat 5 pm-10 pm. Closed major holidays; also Sun. **Reservations:** not accepted. **Features:** This local
Italian   favorite, family-owned restaurant offers consistently good Italian fare. Menu offers a wide variety of pasta
dishes, fresh seafood, veal and prime steak. Service is professional and ambience is comfortable, simple
and tasteful. Dressy casual; beer & wine only. **Parking:** on-site. **Cards:** AX, MC, VI.

MYKONOS GRILL   Lunch: $8-$19   Dinner: $10-$22   Phone: 301/770-5999   **31**
Location: Jct SR 28, 2 mi s on SR 355; in Congressional Shopping Plaza. 121 Congressional Ln 20852. **Hours:** 11:30
am-10:30 pm, Fri & Sat-11 pm. Closed major holidays; also Mon. **Reservations:** suggested, Thurs-Sat.
Greek   **Features:** Slate floors, colorful artwork and white stucco walls with blue trim create a delightful Greek
atmosphere. Dishes are prepared from fresh meats, fish and produce. Dressy casual; cocktails. **Parking:**
on-site. **Cards:** AX, DC, DS, MC, VI.

(See map and index starting on p. 399)

NICK'S CHOPHOUSE   Lunch: $8-$20   Dinner: $17-$31   Phone: 301/926-8869   (22)
▼▼▼   **Location:** I-270, exit 8 (Shady Grove Rd), 0.5 mi e, then 0.6 mi s on Gaither Rd. 700 King Farm Blvd 20850.
Hours: 10:30 am-2:30 & 5:30-10 pm, Fri-11 pm, Sat 5:30 pm-11 pm, Sun 4:30 pm-9 pm; Sunday brunch 11
Steak & Seafood   am-2:30 pm. Closed: 12/25. **Reservations:** suggested. **Features:** The casually upscale steakhouse is on
the ground level of an office building, with patio dining when the weather cooperates. On the menu is a nice
selection of beef and seafood. The staff is professional and provides attentive, friendly service. Dressy casual; cocktails.
Parking: on-site. **Cards:** AX, MC, VI.
☒

TARA THAI   Lunch: $6-$9   Dinner: $8-$13   Phone: 301/231-9899   (32)
▼▼ ▼▼   **Location:** I-270, exit 4A, 2 mi e on Montrose Rd, then just w on SR 355; in Montrose Crossing Shopping Plaza. 12071
Rockville Pike 20852. **Hours:** 11:30 am-3 & 5-10 pm, Fri-11 pm, Sat noon-3:30 & 5-11 pm, Sun noon-3:30 &
Thai   5-10 pm. Closed: 11/24. **Reservations:** suggested. **Features:** The shopping-plaza restaurant has a colorful,
fun dining room with the sea as the motif. Traditional Thai dishes share menu space with vegetarian
selections. The staff is friendly and helpful. Casual dress; cocktails. **Parking:** on-site. **Cards:** AX, DC, DS, MC, VI.
☒

TASTE OF SAIGON   Lunch: $6-$14   Dinner: $7-$15   Phone: 301/424-7222   (27)
▼▼ ▼▼   **Location:** On SR 355, 0.5 mi n of SR 28. 410 Hungerford Dr 20850. **Hours:** 11 am-10 pm, Fri & Sat-11 pm, Sun-
9:30 pm. Closed: 11/24, 12/25. **Reservations:** accepted. **Features:** The kitchen has maintained a
Vietnamese   consistent reputation for its preparations of Vietnamese dishes. Black pepper shrimp, lightly breaded in
black pepper sauce and served with steamed rice, is a local favorite. Casual dress; cocktails. **Parking:** on-
site. **Cards:** AX, CB, DC, DS, MC, VI.
☒

THAI FARM RESTAURANT   Lunch: $6-$9   Dinner: $7-$15   Phone: 301/258-8829   (23)
▼▼ ▼▼   **Location:** I-270, exit 8 (Shady Grove Rd), 0.5 mi e, 0.6 mi s on Gaither Rd, then just w. 800 King Farm Blvd 20850.
Hours: 11:30 am-10 pm, Fri & Sat-10:30 pm, Sun 5 pm-10 pm. Closed: 7/4, 11/24, 12/25. **Features:** The
Thai   colorful, green/yellow dining room, set on the ground floor of an office building, is decorated with muraled
walls and lacquered table tops with rice farmers in the field. The kitchen uses fresh ingredients and does not
use MSG. Menu selections allow diners to mix meats and seafood, as well as offers vegetarian dishes. Casual dress; cocktails.
Parking: on-site. **Cards:** AX, CB, DC, MC, VI.
☒

TIMPANO ITALIAN CHOPHOUSE   Lunch: $10-$15   Dinner: $10-$28   Phone: 301/881-6939   (33)
▼▼ ▼▼   **Location:** I-270, exit 4A, 2 mi e on Montrose Rd, then just n on SR 355; in Montrose Crossing Shopping Plaza. 12021
Rockville Pike 20852. **Hours:** 11:30 am-10 pm, Fri & Sat-11 pm. Closed: 11/24, 12/25.
Italian   **Reservations:** suggested. **Features:** The bi-level dining room is decorated in the theme of a classic, mid-
50s, New York chophouse. Among specialties are one-pound center-cut pork chops and bone-in New York
strip. Pasta, beef and seafood are prepared with an Italian touch. The lunch menu is presented until 4 pm. Dressy casual;
cocktails. **Parking:** on-site. **Cards:** AX, CB, DC, DS, MC, VI.
☒☒

WURZBURG-HAUS RESTAURANT   Lunch: $8-$14   Dinner: $9-$19   Phone: 301/330-0402   (21)
▼▼ ▼▼   **Location:** I-270, exit 8 (Shady Grove Rd), 3.3 mi e to SR 115, then just se; in Red Mill Shopping Center. 7236
Muncaster Mill Rd 20855. **Hours:** 11:30 am-9 pm, Fri & Sat-10 pm, Sun noon-9 pm. Closed: 11/24, 12/25; also
German   for lunch 1/1. **Reservations:** accepted. **Features:** Hearty German and European cuisine—from sauerbraten
to wiener schnitzel—appeals to hearty appetites. Framed prints, knickknacks and music work together to set
a Bavarian mood. A varied selection of wines and imported beers is offered. Casual dress; beer & wine only. **Parking:** on-site.
Cards: AX, DC, DS, MC, VI.
☒

─────────   ***The following restaurants have not been evaluated by AAA***   ─────────
but are listed for your information only.

DAVE AND BUSTERS   **Phone:** 301/230-5151
[fyi]   Not evaluated. **Location:** On SR 355; in White Flint Mall. 11301 Rockville Pike 20852. **Features:** Dave and Busters
comprises 60,000 square feet of high-tech gaming, billiards and shuffleboard. The menu at this busy
establishment offers American fare.

SEVEN SEAS   **Phone:** 301/770-5020
[fyi]   Not evaluated. **Location:** In Federal Plaza, around the back. 1776 E Jefferson St 20852. **Features:** The restaurant
specializes in northern Chinese cuisine with a flair of Taiwanese style. The menu has a variety of seafood,
chicken, beef and noodle dishes to satisfy any appetite.

SILVER SPRING pop. 76,540   (See maps and indexes starting on p. 399, 416)

─────────── **WHERE TO STAY** ───────────

COURTYARD BY MARRIOTT-SILVER SPRING   *Book at aaa.com*   **Phone:** 301/680-8500
▼▼▼   All Year   1P: $144   2P: $154   XP: $10   F
Location: I-95, exit 29B, just e of US 29 off Cherry Hill Rd, 1 mi sw on SR 212, then 1.8 mi w on Cherry Hill; I-495, exit
Small-scale Hotel   30A, 4.3 mi n. 12521 Prosperity Dr 20904. Fax: 301/680-9232. **Facility:** 146 units. 134 one-bedroom standard
units. 12 one-bedroom suites ($174). 3 stories, interior corridors. *Bath:* combo or shower only. **Parking:** on-
site. **Amenities:** high-speed Internet, voice mail, irons, hair dryers. **Pool(s):** heated indoor. **Leisure Activities:** whirlpool,
exercise room. **Guest Services:** valet and coin laundry. **Business Services:** meeting rooms, fax (fee). **Cards:** AX, DC, DS,
MC, VI.
SOME UNITS
⊟ ⬡ ⬯ ⬮ ⬤ ⊡ ⬛ / ☒ ⬛ ⬛ /

(See maps and indexes starting on p. 399, 416)

HILTON WASHINGTON DC/SILVER SPRING   *Book at aaa.com*   **Phone:** (301)589-5200   **6**

1/1-2/28	1P: $129-$209	2P: $139-$219	XP: $10 F18
3/1-12/31	1P: $119-$199	2P: $129-$209	XP: $10 F18

Large-scale Hotel   **Location:** I-495, exit 30B, 1.5 mi s on US 29. 8727 Colesville Rd 20910. Fax: 301/588-6681. **Facility:** 263 units. 224 one-bedroom standard units. 39 one-bedroom suites. 11-13 stories, interior corridors. *Bath:* combo or shower only. **Parking:** on-site (fee) and valet. **Terms:** cancellation fee imposed, package plans. **Amenities:** video games (fee), dual phone lines, voice mail, irons, hair dryers. **Pool(s):** heated indoor. **Leisure Activities:** sauna, exercise room. **Guest Services:** sundries, valet laundry, area transportation. **Business Services:** conference facilities, business center. **Cards:** AX, CB, DC, DS, JC, MC, VI.

SOME UNITS

(ASK) (SD) (🍽) (&M) (&) (ⓓ) (🛥) (🎬) (DATA PORT) (🖥) / (✕) (🛗) (🖨) /
FEE   FEE

HOLIDAY INN-SILVER SPRING   *Book at aaa.com*   **Phone:** (301)589-0800   **31**

All Year	1P: $99-$199	2P: $99-$199	XP: $10 F19

(AAA) (SAVE)   **Location:** I-495, exit 31B, 1 mi s. 8777 Georgia Ave 20910. Fax: 301/587-4791. **Facility:** 231 units. 220 one-bedroom standard units. 11 one-bedroom suites. 16 stories, interior corridors. *Bath:* combo or shower only. **Parking:** on-site (fee). **Amenities:** dual phone lines, voice mail, irons, hair dryers. **Dining:** 6:30 am-10 pm, Large-scale Hotel   cocktails. **Pool(s):** outdoor. **Leisure Activities:** exercise room. **Guest Services:** gift shop, valet and coin laundry, area transportation-Silver Spring Metro & within 3 mi. **Business Services:** conference facilities, business center. **Cards:** AX, CB, DC, DS, JC, MC, VI.

SOME UNITS

(SD) (🍽) (&) (ⓓ) (🛥) (🎬) (DATA PORT) (🖥) / (✕) (🛗) /
FEE

──────── **WHERE TO DINE** ────────

BOMBAY GAYLORD   **Lunch:** $5-$11   **Dinner:** $5-$12   **Phone:** 301/565-2528   **4**

Indian   **Location:** I-495, exit 31, 1.6 mi s on SR 97, just s of jct US 29 (Colesville Rd); downtown. 8401 Georgia Ave 20910. **Hours:** 11:30 am-3 & 5-9:30 pm, Sat & Sun from noon. Closed: 1/1, 11/24, 12/25. **Reservations:** accepted. **Features:** Authentic Indian cuisine is offerd at this downtown Silver Spring restaurant. Tandoori specialties are some of the more popular selections, though the Chicken Tikka Masala and Butter Chicken are worth trying. Casual dress; beer & wine only. **Parking:** no self-parking. **Cards:** AX, MC, VI.

(✕)

CRISFIELD AT LEE PLAZA   **Lunch:** $6-$10   **Dinner:** $12-$25   **Phone:** 301/588-1572   **2**

Seafood   **Location:** I-495, exit 30B, 1.5 mi n of US 29, then just n of jct Georgia Ave; downtown. 8606 Colesville Rd 20910. **Hours:** 11:30 am-10 pm, Fri-11 pm, Sat 4 pm-11 pm, Sun 2 pm-9:30 pm. Closed major holidays. **Reservations:** accepted. **Features:** If your in the mood for seafood this is the right spot. The restaurant has been satisfying the locals since 1988. The kitchen uses jumbo lump crabmeat in preparing it's wonderful crabcakes. The menu offers primarily seafood however a couple beef and chicken dishes are also available. Casual dress; cocktails. **Parking:** no self-parking. **Cards:** AX, CB, DC, DS, MC, VI.

(✕)

CUBANO'S   **Lunch:** $10-$19   **Dinner:** $12-$19   **Phone:** 301/563-4020   **3**

Cuban   **Location:** I-495, exit 31B, 1 mi s on SR 97, then 1 blk w. 1201 Fidler Ln 20910. **Hours:** 11:30 am-10:30 pm, Sat & Sun from 12:30 pm. Closed: 11/24; also 12/31. **Reservations:** suggested. **Features:** The kitchen prepares authentic Cuban fare, with dishes such as the Cuban favorite, Ropa Vieja "Old Clothes" or Filete de Pescado a la Varadero. The setting is comfortable, with sidewalk walk dining available seasonally and the service is professional and efficient. Casual dress; cocktails. **Parking:** on-site. **Cards:** AX, DC, DS, MC, VI.

(✕)

MRS. K'S TOLL HOUSE   **Lunch:** $15-$19   **Dinner:** $24-$46   **Phone:** 301/589-3500   **1**

American   **Location:** I-495, exit 30B, 0.8 mi s on US 29. 9201 Colesville Rd 20910. **Hours:** 11:30 am-2:30 & 5-9 pm, Fri & Sat 4:30 4:30-9:30 pm, Sun 10:30 am-3 & 5-9 pm. Closed: 1/1, 7/4, 12/25; also for lunch 12/24. **Reservations:** suggested. **Features:** Patrons first are struck by the charming atmosphere in the quaint, converted toll house. This well-established spot is attractive to a mixed crowd. The wait staff is efficient and gracious when serving the various prix fixe and a la carte menu selections. Dressy casual; cocktails. **Parking:** on-site. **Cards:** AX, CB, DC, DS, MC, VI. **Historic**

(✕)

──────── *The following restaurant has not been evaluated by AAA* ────────
but is listed for your information only.

EL GAVILAN   **Phone:** 301/587-4197

(fyi)   Not evaluated. **Location:** 8805 Flower Ave 20901. **Features:** A favorite among the Salvadoran folks in town for ceviche and whole crispy fish, as well as a number of interesting combination platters featuring typical dishes as well as grilled shrimp, pork ribs and fajitas.

WHEATON   (See map and index starting on p. 399)

──────── **WHERE TO DINE** ────────

ANCHOR INN SEAFOOD RESTAURANT   **Lunch:** $5-$9   **Dinner:** $11-$27   **Phone:** 301/933-1814   **45**

Seafood   **Location:** I-495, exit 31A, 2 mi n on Georgia Ave. 2509 University Blvd W 20902. **Hours:** 11 am-10 pm, Fri & Sat-11 pm. Closed: 12/25. **Reservations:** suggested, weekends. **Features:** Familiar favorites, such as baked crab imperial, filet mignon in bearnaise sauce and clam chowder, make the casual restaurant popular with families and senior citizens. Casual dress; cocktails. **Parking:** on-site. **Cards:** AX, MC, VI.

(🍸) (✕)

DUSIT THAI CUISINE   **Lunch:** $7-$11   **Dinner:** $7-$11   **Phone:** 301/949-4140   **44**

Thai   **Location:** Just e of jct SR 97 (Georgia Ave), on SR 193. 2404 University Blvd W 20902. **Hours:** 11:30 am-10 pm, Fri & Sat-11 pm. Closed major holidays. **Reservations:** accepted. **Features:** The menu is long and the relative spiciness of each item is indicated. Among offerings are curries with or without coconut milk, fried rice, pad Thai and crispy whole fish. Casual dress; cocktails. **Parking:** on-site (fee). **Cards:** AX, DC, DS, MC, VI.

(✕)

Nearby Virginia

ALEXANDRIA pop. 128,283   (See maps and indexes starting on p. 404, 414)

──── WHERE TO STAY ────

BEST WESTERN-OLD COLONY INN   *Book at aaa.com*   **Phone:** (703)739-2222   **1**
▼▼▼ ▼▼▼   All Year [BP]   1P: $109   2P: $159   XP: $10   F18
Location: George Washington Memorial Pkwy; jct Second and Washington sts. 1101 N Washington St 22314.
Small-scale Hotel   Fax: 703/549-2568. **Facility:** 49 one-bedroom standard units. 2 stories (no elevator), interior corridors.
Parking: on-site. **Amenities:** high-speed Internet, irons, hair dryers. **Leisure Activities:** sauna, whirlpool,
exercise room. **Guest Services:** sundries, valet laundry, area transportation. **Business Services:** meeting rooms, business
center. **Cards:** AX, CB, DC, DS, MC, VI. *(See color ad below)*

SOME UNITS
(ASK) 🛌 ✈ 🕸 ✕ 📷 DATA PORT 💻 / ✕ 🔌 📺 /
FEE FEE

COMFORT INN ALEXANDRIA   *Book at aaa.com*   **Phone:** (703)922-9200   **95**
(AAA) (SAVE)   4/1-6/30 & 7/1-9/30   1P: $104   2P: $104   XP: $5   F18
▼▼▼ ▼▼▼   3/1-3/31 & 10/1-2/28   1P: $86   2P: $86   XP: $5   F18
Location: I-95/495, exit 173, 2 mi e of jct I-395 and 495. 5716 S Van Dorn St 22310. Fax: 703/922-0750.
Small-scale Hotel   **Facility:** 169 units. 151 one-bedroom standard units. 18 one-bedroom suites ($117-$144), some with
whirlpools. 9 stories, interior corridors. **Parking:** on-site. **Amenities:** voice mail, irons, hair dryers. *Some:*
dual phone lines. **Dining:** 4 pm-10 pm, wine/beer only. **Pool(s):** outdoor. **Leisure Activities:** limited
exercise equipment. **Guest Services:** gift shop, valet and coin laundry, area transportation-within 2 mi & Van Dorn St metro.
Business Services: meeting rooms, fax (fee). **Cards:** AX, CB, DC, DS, JC, MC, VI. **Special Amenities:** free local telephone
calls and early check-in/late check-out. *(See color ad p 501)*

SOME UNITS
🛌 🍴 🕸 🐬 📷 DATA PORT 💻 / ✕ 🔌 📺 /

COMFORT INN-ALEXANDRIA LANDMARK   *Book at aaa.com*   **Phone:** (703)642-3422   **90**
▼▼▼ ▼▼▼   3/1-10/31   1P: $83-$114   2P: $89-$120   XP: $6   F18
11/1-2/28   1P: $69-$89   2P: $75-$95   XP: $6   F18
Small-scale Hotel   **Location:** I-395, exit 3B, just w. Located in a commercial and shopping area. 6254 Duke St 22312.
Fax: 703/642-1354. **Facility:** 150 one-bedroom standard units. 6 stories, interior corridors. **Parking:** on-site.
Amenities: dual phone lines, voice mail, safes (fee), hair dryers. *Some:* irons. **Guest Services:** valet laundry, area
transportation. **Business Services:** fax (fee). **Cards:** AX, CB, DC, DS, JC, MC, VI.

SOME UNITS
(ASK) 🛌 🍴 🕸 📷 DATA PORT 💻 / ✕ 🔌 📺 /

(See maps and indexes starting on p. 404, 414)

COURTYARD BY MARRIOTT-ALEXANDRIA   *Book at aaa.com*   Phone: (703)329-2323   [12]
9/12-12/31 & 2/20-2/28   1P: $189-$199
3/1-9/11 & 1/1-2/19   1P: $169-$199
Small-scale Hotel   **Location:** I-95/495, exit 174 (Eisenhower Ave Connector), just n, then 1.7 mi e of Telegraph Rd. 2700 Eisenhower Ave 22314. Fax: 703/329-6853. **Facility:** 176 one-bedroom standard units. 8 stories, interior corridors. *Bath:* combo or shower only. **Parking:** on-site. **Terms:** package plans. **Amenities:** high-speed Internet, voice mail, irons, hair dryers. **Leisure Activities:** exercise room. **Guest Services:** valet and coin laundry, area transportation. **Business Services:** meeting rooms, fax (fee). **Cards:** AX, DC, DS, MC, VI. *(See color ad p 501)*

SOME UNITS
[ASK] [S/D] [🍴] [Y] [&M] [⚙] [⟳] [🎥] [DATA PORT] [▭] / [✕] [🔒] [🖥] /

EMBASSY SUITES-ALEXANDRIA-OLD TOWN   *Book at aaa.com*   Phone: (703)684-5900   [7]
AAA SAVE   All Year [BP]   1P: $139-$289   2P: $139-$289   XP: $20   F18
Location: I-95/495, exit 176, 0.5 mi n on SR 241 N, then 0.5 mi e on SR 236. Located opposite Amtrak and King St Metro Station, in Old Town. 1900 Diagonal Rd 22314. Fax: 703/684-1403. **Facility:** 268 units. 266 one- and 2 two-bedroom suites. 8 stories, interior corridors. *Bath:* combo or shower only. **Parking:** on-site (fee).
Large-scale Hotel   **Terms:** cancellation fee imposed, package plans, small pets only ($20 extra charge, in smoking unts, with prior approval). **Amenities:** video games (fee), dual phone lines, voice mail, irons, hair dryers. *Some:* fax. **Dining:** 11 am-11 pm, cocktails. **Pool(s):** heated indoor. **Leisure Activities:** sauna, whirlpool, sun deck, childrens playroom, exercise room. **Guest Services:** gift shop, complimentary evening beverages, valet and coin laundry, area transportation-within 2 mi. **Business Services:** conference facilities. *Fee:* PC, fax. **Cards:** AX, CB, DC, DS, MC, VI. **Special Amenities: free full breakfast and free newspaper.**

SOME UNITS
[🛏] [🍴] [Y] [&] [⟳] [➤] [✕] [🎥] [DATA PORT] [🔒] [🖥] / [✕] /
FEE

HAMPTON INN-ALEXANDRIA   *Book at aaa.com*   Phone: (703)671-4800   [86]
All Year   1P: $139-$149   2P: $139-$149
Location: I-395, exit 5, 1 mi w on SR 7. 4800 Leesburg Pike 22302. Fax: 703/671-2442. **Facility:** 130 one-bedroom standard units. 4 stories, interior corridors. **Parking:** on-site. **Terms:** [ECP] meal plan available.
Small-scale Hotel   **Amenities:** video games (fee), dual phone lines, voice mail, irons, hair dryers. **Pool(s):** heated outdoor. **Leisure Activities:** exercise room. **Guest Services:** valet laundry. **Business Services:** fax. **Cards:** AX, CB, DC, DS, MC, VI.

SOME UNITS
[ASK] [S/D] [🍴+] [⟳] [➤] [🎥] [DATA PORT] [▭] / [✕] [🔒] /

HAMPTON INN ALEXANDRIA/OLD TOWN   *Book at aaa.com*   Phone: (703)329-1400   [92]
AREA-SOUTH
3/1-6/30 [BP]   1P: $134-$149   2P: $142-$159
7/1-10/31 [BP]   1P: $129-$149   2P: $134-$159
Small-scale Hotel   11/1-2/28 [BP]   1P: $99-$149   2P: $99-$159
Location: I-95/495, exit 177A, just s on US 1. 5821 Richmond Hwy 22303. Fax: 703/329-1424. **Facility:** 156 one-bedroom standard units, some with whirlpools. 7 stories, interior corridors. *Bath:* combo or shower only. **Parking:** on-site. **Terms:** package plans. **Amenities:** dual phone lines, voice mail, irons, hair dryers. **Pool(s):** outdoor. **Leisure Activities:** exercise room. **Guest Services:** gift shop, valet and coin laundry, area transportation. **Business Services:** meeting rooms, business center. **Cards:** AX, DC, DS, MC, VI.

SOME UNITS
[ASK] [S/D] [✈] [🍴+] [&M] [⚙] [⟳] [➤] [🎥] [DATA PORT] [▭] / [✕] [🔒] [🖥] /
FEE FEE

HAMPTON INN OLD TOWN KING STREET METRO   *Book at aaa.com*   Phone: (703)299-9900   [6]
All Year [BP]   1P: $99-$209   XP: $10   F18
Location: I-495, exit 176B, 0.5 mi n on SR 241, 0.5 mi e on SR 236, then just ne on Diagonal Rd. Located in Old Town. 1616 King St 22314. Fax: 703/299-9937. **Facility:** 80 units. 75 one-bedroom standard units. 5 one-bedroom
Small-scale Hotel   suites ($129-$229). 6 stories, interior corridors. *Bath:* combo or shower only. **Parking:** on-site (fee). **Terms:** cancellation fee imposed. **Amenities:** video games (fee), dual phone lines, voice mail, irons, hair dryers. **Pool(s):** outdoor. **Leisure Activities:** limited exercise equipment. **Guest Services:** valet and coin laundry. **Business Services:** meeting rooms, business center. **Cards:** AX, DC, DS, MC, VI.

SOME UNITS
[ASK] [S/D] [🍴+] [&] [⟳] [➤] [🎥] [DATA PORT] [▭] / [✕] [🔒] [🖥] /

HAWTHORN SUITES LTD-ALEXANDRIA   *Book at aaa.com*   Phone: (703)370-1000   [89]
All Year [BP]   1P: $99-$179   2P: $99-$179
Location: I-395, exit 3A, 0.3 mi e on SR 236 to S Van Dorn St, then 0.5 mi n. 420 N Van Dorn St 22304. Fax: 703/751-1467. **Facility:** 185 units. 86 one-bedroom standard units with efficiencies. 91 one- and 8 two-bedroom suites with kitchens. 9 stories, interior corridors. *Bath:* combo or shower only. **Parking:** on-site.
Small-scale Hotel   **Terms:** small pets only ($100 fee). **Amenities:** voice mail, irons, hair dryers. *Some:* high-speed Internet (fee). **Pool(s):** outdoor. **Leisure Activities:** exercise room. **Guest Services:** complimentary evening beverages: Mon-Thurs, valet and coin laundry, area transportation. **Business Services:** meeting rooms, fax (fee). **Cards:** AX, CB, DC, DS, MC, VI.

SOME UNITS
[ASK] [S/D] [🐾] [&] [⟳] [➤] [🎥] [DATA PORT] [🔒] [🖥] [▭] / [✕] /
FEE

HILTON ALEXANDRIA MARK CENTER   *Book at aaa.com*   Phone: (703)845-1010   [87]
All Year   1P: $89-$299   2P: $89-$299   XP: $20   F17
Location: I-395, exit 4, just w. 5000 Seminary Rd 22311. Fax: 703/845-7662. **Facility:** 496 units. 482 one-bedroom standard units, some with whirlpools. 14 one-bedroom suites, some with whirlpools. 5-30 stories, interior corridors. *Bath:* combo or shower only. **Parking:** on-site (fee) and valet. **Amenities:** video games (fee), dual phone lines, voice mail, irons, hair dryers. *Some:* high-speed Internet (fee). **Pool(s):** heated indoor/outdoor. **Leisure Activities:** 2 lighted tennis courts, jogging, exercise room. **Guest Services:** gift shop, valet laundry, area transportation, barber shop. **Business Services:** conference facilities, business center. **Cards:** AX, CB, DC, DS, JC, MC, VI. *(See color ad p 426)*

SOME UNITS
[✈] [🍴] [Y] [&M] [⚙] [⟳] [➤] [✕] [🎥] [DATA PORT] [🔒] [🖥] [▭] / [✕] /

(See maps and indexes starting on p. 404, 414)

HILTON ALEXANDRIA OLD TOWN   *Book at aaa.com*   Phone: (703)837-0440   **5**
All Year   1P: $119-$269   2P: $139-$289   XP: $20   F16
Location: I-95/495, exit 176B, 0.5 mi n on SR 241, 0.5 mi e on SR 236, then just ne on Diagonal Rd. Located adjacent
Large-scale Hotel   to Amtrak and Metro Station, in Old Town. 1767 King St 22314. Fax: 703/837-0454. **Facility:** 241 units. 222 one-
bedroom standard units. 19 one-bedroom suites, some with whirlpools. 7 stories, interior corridors. *Bath:*
combo or shower only. **Parking:** on-site (fee). **Terms:** check-in 4 pm, cancellation fee imposed, package plans, small pets only
($20 fee, in smoking units). **Amenities:** video games (fee), dual phone lines, voice mail, honor bars, irons, hair dryers.
Dining: Seagar's, see separate listing. **Pool(s):** heated indoor. **Leisure Activities:** sauna, exercise room. **Guest Services:**
valet laundry. **Business Services:** conference facilities, business center. **Cards:** AX, CB, DC, DS, MC, VI.

SOME UNITS
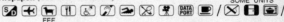

HOLIDAY INN EISENHOWER METRO   *Book at aaa.com*   Phone: (703)960-3400   **13**
All Year   1P: $79-$190   2P: $89-$200   XP: $10   F18
Location: I-95/495, exit 176B, immediate e on Pershing Ave, then s on Stovall Rd; jct Telegraph Rd (SR 214 N) and I-
Large-scale Hotel   95/495. 2460 Eisenhower Ave 22314. Fax: 703/329-0953. **Facility:** 196 one-bedroom standard units. 10 stories,
interior corridors. *Bath:* combo or shower only. **Parking:** on-site. **Terms:** cancellation fee imposed, package
plans. **Amenities:** voice mail, irons, hair dryers. **Pool(s):** heated indoor. **Leisure Activities:** exercise room. **Guest Services:**
gift shop, valet and coin laundry, area transportation. **Business Services:** meeting rooms. **Fee:** PC, fax. **Cards:** AX, CB, DC,
DS, JC, MC, VI.

SOME UNITS
FEE   FEE

HOLIDAY INN HOTEL & SUITES-HISTORIC
DISTRICT ALEXANDRIA   Phone: (703)548-6300   **2**
3/1-6/30 & 9/11-12/31   1P: $129-$239   2P: $129-$239   XP: $20   F12
1/1-2/28   1P: $109-$199   2P: $109-$199   XP: $20   F12
7/1-9/10   1P: $109-$189   2P: $109-$189   XP: $20   F12
Location: George Washington Memorial Pkwy; just e of jct 1st and Washington sts. Located in Old Town. 625 1st St
Large-scale Hotel   22314. Fax: 703/548-8032. **Facility:** 178 units. 161 one-bedroom standard units. 17 one-bedroom suites,
some with whirlpools. 4 stories, interior corridors. *Bath:* combo or shower only. **Parking:** on-site (fee).
Terms: cancellation fee imposed, small pets only ($25 fee). **Amenities:** voice mail, irons, hair dryers. **Fee:** video games, high-
speed Internet. **Dining:** 6:30 am-2 & 5-10 pm, cocktails. **Pool(s):** heated indoor/outdoor. **Leisure Activities:** saunas, whirlpool,
limited exercise equipment. **Guest Services:** valet and coin laundry, airport transportation-Ronald Reagan Washington National
Airport, area transportation-National Airport Metro. **Business Services:** conference facilities, business center. **Cards:** AX, CB,
DC, DS, MC, VI. **Special Amenities:** free newspaper. *(See color ad below)*

SOME UNITS
FEE

(See maps and indexes starting on p. 404, 414)

HOLIDAY INN SELECT-OLD TOWN
Book at aaa.com   Phone: (703)549-6080   **8**

3/1-6/25 & 9/11-11/19	1P: $229-$249	2P: $229-$249	XP: $10 F18
6/26-9/10 & 11/20-2/28	1P: $209-$229	2P: $209-$229	XP: $10 F18

Location: On SR 7; between S Pitt and S Royal sts; just sw of City Hall. Located in Old Town. 480 King St 22314. Fax: 703/684-6508. **Facility:** 227 units. 225 one-bedroom standard units. 2 one-bedroom suites ($450), some with whirlpools. 6 stories, interior corridors. *Bath:* combo or shower only. **Parking:** on-site (fee). **Terms:** cancellation fee imposed, [BP] & [CP] meal plans available, small pets only. **Amenities:** video games (fee), voice mail, safes, irons, hair dryers. *Some:* high-speed Internet. **Dining:** 6:30 am-2 & 5-10:30 pm, cocktails. **Pool(s):** heated indoor. **Leisure Activities:** sauna, bicycles, exercise room. **Guest Services:** valet and coin laundry, airport transportation-Ronald Reagan Washington National Airport, area transportation-King Street Metro. **Business Services:** conference facilities, business center. **Cards:** AX, CB, DC, DS, MC, VI. **Special Amenities: free continental breakfast and free newspaper.** *(See color ad p 503)*

Large-scale Hotel

SOME UNITS

HOMESTEAD STUDIO SUITES HOTEL-ALEXANDRIA
Book at aaa.com   Phone: (703)329-3399   **9**

All Year	1P: $105-$125	2P: $110-$130	XP: $5 F17

Location: I-95/495, exit 174 (Eisenhower Ave Connector), just n to Eisenhower Ave, then 1.2 mi e. 200 Blue Stone Rd 22304. Fax: 703/329-2239. **Facility:** 132 one-bedroom standard units with efficiencies. 3 stories, interior corridors. *Bath:* combo or shower only. **Parking:** on-site. **Terms:** weekly rates available, pets ($25 extra charge). **Amenities:** voice mail, irons, hair dryers. **Guest Services:** sundries, valet and coin laundry. **Business Services:** meeting rooms, fax. **Cards:** AX, CB, DC, DS, JC, MC, VI.

Small-scale Hotel

SOME UNITS

HOMEWOOD SUITES BY HILTON-ALEXANDRIA
Book at aaa.com   Phone: 703/671-6500   **85**

All Year [BP]	1P: $189-$299	2P: $189-$299

Location: I-395, exit 5, 1 mi w on SR 7. 4850 Leesburg Pike 22302. Fax: 703/671-9322. **Facility:** 105 units. 99 one- and 6 two-bedroom suites with efficiencies. 5 stories, interior corridors. *Bath:* combo or shower only. **Parking:** on-site. **Terms:** 3 day cancellation notice. **Amenities:** video games (fee), high-speed Internet, dual phone lines, voice mail, irons, hair dryers. **Pool(s):** outdoor. **Leisure Activities:** whirlpool, exercise room. **Guest Services:** sundries, valet and coin laundry. **Business Services:** meeting rooms, business center. **Cards:** AX, CB, DC, DS, MC, VI.

Small-scale Hotel

SOME UNITS

RADISSON HOTEL OLD TOWN ALEXANDRIA
Book at aaa.com   Phone: (703)683-6000   **3**

3/1-6/30 & 9/11-12/31	1P: $139-$249	2P: $139-$249	XP: $20 F12
1/1-2/28	1P: $119-$209	2P: $119-$209	XP: $20 F12
7/1-9/10	1P: $119-$199	2P: $119-$199	XP: $20 F12

Location: Between 1st St and Montgomery. Located in Old Town. 901 N Fairfax St 22314. Fax: 703/683-7597. **Facility:** 253 units. 249 one-bedroom standard units. 4 one-bedroom suites. 12 stories, interior corridors. *Bath:* combo or shower only. **Parking:** on-site (fee). **Terms:** cancellation fee imposed. **Amenities:** dual phone lines, voice mail, irons, hair dryers. *Fee:* video games, high-speed Internet. **Dining:** 6 am-2 & 4-10 pm, cocktails. **Pool(s):** outdoor. **Leisure Activities:** exercise room. **Guest Services:** valet laundry, airport transportation-Ronald Reagan Washington National Airport. **Business Services:** conference facilities, fax (fee). **Cards:** AX, CB, DC, DS, MC, VI. **Special Amenities: free newspaper.** *(See color ad p 932 & below)*

Large-scale Hotel

SOME UNITS
FEE FEE

RED ROOF INN-ALEXANDRIA
Book at aaa.com   Phone: (703)960-5200   **94**

3/19-11/18	1P: $73-$90	2P: $78-$95	XP: $5 F18
3/1-3/18 & 11/19-2/28	1P: $65-$80	2P: $70-$85	XP: $5 F18

Location: I-95/495, exit 177A, 0.5 mi s on US 1. 5975 Richmond Hwy 22303. Fax: 703/960-5209. **Facility:** 115 one-bedroom standard units. 3 stories, exterior corridors. *Bath:* combo or shower only. **Parking:** on-site. **Terms:** small pets only. **Amenities:** video games (fee), voice mail. **Guest Services:** coin laundry. **Business Services:** fax (fee). **Cards:** AX, CB, DC, DS, MC, VI.

Motel

SOME UNITS

(See maps and indexes starting on p. 404, 414)

RELAIS & CHATEAUX MORRISON HOUSE   *Book at aaa.com*   Phone: (703)838-8000   🔟

(AAA) [SAVE]
♦♦♦♦♦ ♦♦♦♦♦
Small-scale Hotel

4/5-6/30	1P: $299-$399	2P: $299-$399
3/1-4/4 & 7/1-2/28	1P: $249-$399	2P: $249-$399

Location: Jct King and S Alfred sts, just s; in Old Town. 116 S Alfred St 22314. Fax: 703/684-6283. **Facility:** An intimate hotel designed in the Federal style, with an ambience of traditional elegance; afternoon tea service may be arranged. 45 units. 42 one-bedroom standard units. 3 one-bedroom suites. 5 stories, interior corridors. **Parking:** valet. **Terms:** package plans. **Amenities:** safes, hair dryers. *Some:* irons. **Dining:** 5 pm-midnight, cocktails, also, Elysium, see separate listing. **Guest Services:** valet laundry. **Business Services:** meeting rooms, fax (fee). **Cards:** AX, DC, MC, VI.

SOME UNITS
[🍴] [24↑] [↥] [👪] [DATA PORT] / [✕] [VCR] /
　　　　　FEE

RESIDENCE INN BY MARRIOTT ALEXANDRIA-OLD TOWN   *Book at aaa.com*   Phone: (703)548-5474   11️⃣

(AAA) [SAVE]
♦♦♦♦
Large-scale Hotel

All Year [BP]   1P: $129-$339   2P: $129-$339

Location: I-95/495, exit 176, 0.5 mi n on SR 241, then 0.7 mi e on SR 236. 1456 Duke St 22314. Fax: 703/548-5474. **Facility:** 240 units. 114 one-bedroom standard units with efficiencies. 108 one- and 18 two-bedroom suites, some with efficiencies or kitchens. 8 stories, interior corridors. *Bath:* combo or shower only. **Parking:** on-site (fee). **Terms:** cancellation fee imposed, [MAP] meal plan available, package plans, small pets only ($150 fee, $10 extra charge). **Amenities:** video games (fee), high-speed Internet, dual phone lines, voice mail, irons, hair dryers. **Pool(s):** heated indoor. **Leisure Activities:** exercise room. **Guest Services:** complimentary evening beverages: Mon-Thurs, valet and coin laundry. **Business Services:** meeting rooms, fax (fee). **Cards:** AX, DC, MC, VI. **Special Amenities:** free full breakfast and free newspaper. *(See color ad p 501)*

SOME UNITS
[S/D] [🛏] [🍴] [♿M] [↥] [🌀] [🏊] [📹] [DATA PORT] [💾] [📠] [🖨] / [✕] /
　　　　FEE

SHERATON PENTAGON SOUTH HOTEL   Phone: (703)751-4510   88

♦♦♦♦
Large-scale Hotel

3/1-6/30 & 9/6-12/31	1P: $115-$170	2P: $115-$170	XP: $10	F18
1/1-2/28	1P: $105-$155	2P: $105-$155	XP: $10	F18
7/1-9/5	1P: $101-$151	2P: $101-$151	XP: $10	F18

Location: I-395, exit 4, 0.8 mi s of jct SR 7. 4641 Kenmore Ave 22304. Fax: 703/751-9170. **Facility:** 191 units. 184 one-bedroom standard units. 7 one-bedroom suites ($249-$399). 15 stories, interior corridors. *Bath:* combo or shower only. **Parking:** on-site. **Terms:** cancellation fee imposed, pets (dogs only). **Amenities:** dual phone lines, voice mail, irons, hair dryers. *Some:* fax, safes. **Pool(s):** heated indoor. **Leisure Activities:** whirlpool, exercise room. **Guest Services:** sundries, valet laundry, area transportation. **Business Services:** conference facilities, PC (fee). **Cards:** AX, CB, DC, DS, JC, MC, VI.

SOME UNITS
[ASK] [S/D] [✈] [🛏] [🍴] [♿] [🌀] [🏊] [📹] [DATA PORT] [🖨] / [✕] [📠] /
　　　　　　　　　　　　　　　FEE FEE

SHERATON SUITES ALEXANDRIA   *Book at aaa.com*   Phone: (703)836-4700   4️⃣

(AAA) [SAVE]
♦♦♦♦♦
Large-scale Hotel

All Year   1P: $109-$229   2P: $109-$229   XP: $15   F

Location: Just e of Washington St. Located in Old Town. 801 N St Asaph St 22314. Fax: 703/549-8758. **Facility:** 247 one-bedroom suites. 10 stories, interior corridors. *Bath:* combo or shower only. **Parking:** on-site (fee). **Terms:** cancellation fee imposed, package plans, pets (with prior approval, small dogs only). **Amenities:** voice mail, irons, hair dryers. *Fee:* video games, high-speed Internet. *Some:* dual phone lines, fax. **Dining:** 6:30 am-2 & 5-10:30 pm, Sat & Sun from 7 am; hours vary seasonally, cocktails. **Pool(s):** heated indoor. **Leisure Activities:** whirlpool, sun deck, exercise room. **Guest Services:** sundries, valet and coin laundry, airport transportation-Ronald Reagan Washington National Airport, area transportation-Old Town & Metro. **Business Services:** meeting rooms, business center. **Cards:** AX, CB, DC, DS, MC, VI. *(See color ad below)*

SOME UNITS
[S/D] [✈] [🛏] [🍴] [♿] [🌀] [🏊] [✕] [📹] [DATA PORT] [💾] [📠] [🖨] / [✕] /

TRAVELERS MOTEL   Phone: 703/329-1310   93

(AAA) [SAVE]
♦♦♦♦
Motel

All Year   1P: $65-$89   2P: $65-$89   XP: $5   F

Location: I-95/495, exit 177A, just s on US 1. 5916 Richmond Hwy 22303. Fax: 703/960-9211. **Facility:** 29 units. 28 one- and 1 two-bedroom standard units. 1 story, exterior corridors. **Parking:** on-site. **Guest Services:** area transportation-Huntington Metro. **Business Services:** fax (fee). **Cards:** AX, CB, DC, DS, MC, VI. **Special Amenities:** free newspaper.

SOME UNITS
[S/D] [🍴] [📹] [DATA PORT] / [✕] /

(See maps and indexes starting on p. 404, 414)

WASHINGTON SUITES-ALEXANDRIA *Book at aaa.com* **Phone:** (703)370-9600 [91]

AAA SAVE All Year 1P: $99-$159 2P: $99-$209 XP: $10 F17
Location: I-395, exit 3A, 0.8 mi e on SR 236 E (Duke St), then just s. 100 S Reynolds St 22304. Fax: 703/370-0467.
Small-scale Hotel **Facility:** 224 units. 68 one-bedroom standard units with kitchens. 124 one- and 32 two-bedroom suites with kitchens. 9 stories, interior corridors. *Bath:* combo or shower only. **Parking:** on-site. **Terms:** weekly rates available, package plans, pets ($10 extra charge). **Amenities:** video games (fee), dual phone lines, voice mail, irons, hair dryers. **Dining:** 11 am-11 pm, cocktails. **Pool(s):** outdoor. **Leisure Activities:** putting green, sun deck, exercise room. **Guest Services:** valet and coin laundry, area transportation-Van Dorn Metro, within 1 mi; Old Town Alexandria. **Business Services:** meeting rooms, business center. **Cards:** AX, DC, MC, VI. **Special Amenities:** free expanded continental breakfast and free newspaper. *(See color ad p 506)*

SOME UNITS

——— WHERE TO DINE ———

AKASKA **Lunch:** $8-$11 **Dinner:** $10-$20 **Phone:** 703/751-3133 [121]
Location: In S Van Dorn St Station Shopping Center. 514-C S Van Dorn St 22304. **Hours:** 11:30 am-2:30 & 5-10
Sushi pm. Closed major holidays. **Reservations:** accepted. **Features:** Tucked in the South Van Dorn Street Station shopping plaza, the little Japanese gem specializes in sushi prepared from fresh fish, with selections varying based on availability. Crisply fried tempura, buckwheat noodles and teriyaki dishes are other options. Casual dress; beer & wine only. **Parking:** on-site. **Cards:** AX, MC, VI.

BILBO BAGGINS **Lunch:** $8-$12 **Dinner:** $13-$20 **Phone:** 703/683-0300 [6]
Location: Between Fairfax and Lee sts; in Old Town. 208 Queen St 22314. **Hours:** 11:30 am-2:30 & 5:30-10:30
American pm, Fri-Sun 11 am-midnight. Closed: 7/4, 11/24, 12/25. **Features:** The menu features a nice selection of salad, pasta, full meals and homemade dessert, in addition to a variety of wines and micro-brewed beers. The casual and cozy dining rooms occupy three row houses and portray a rustic, intimate atmosphere inside. Casual dress; cocktails. **Parking:** street. **Cards:** AX, CB, DC, DS, MC, VI.

BLUE POINT GRILL & OYSTER BAR **Lunch:** $10-$15 **Dinner:** $18-$29 **Phone:** 703/739-0404 [26]
Location: Jct Franklin and S Washington sts. 600 Franklin St 22314. **Hours:** 11:30 am-3 & 5:30-10 pm, Sun &
Seafood Mon-9:30 pm. Closed: 7/4, 11/24, 12/25. **Reservations:** suggested. **Features:** Creative seafood dishes made with fresh ingredients are on the pleasant cafe's seasonally changing menu. The wine selection complements the food well. Patio seating is an option in the warmer months. Casual dress; cocktails.
Parking: on-site. **Cards:** AX, DS, MC, VI.

BOMBAY CURRY COMPANY **Lunch:** $5-$7 **Dinner:** $8-$11 **Phone:** 703/836-6363 [114]
Location: Jct W Glebe Rd and Mt Vernon Ave; at Calvert Apartment Building. 3110 Mt Vernon Ave 22305.
Indian **Hours:** 11:30 am-2:30 & 5:30-9:30 pm, Fri-10 pm, Sat 5:30 pm-10 pm, Sun 11:30 am-2:30 & 5:30-9:30 pm. Closed: 11/24, 12/25. **Reservations:** accepted. **Features:** The neighborhood restaurant is simple in appearance but rich in menu complexity. Piquant flavors tinge the well-prepared dishes, ranging from curries to kabobs. The fresh-baked bread is worth the extra cost. A lunch buffet is served on Sunday. Casual dress; beer & wine only. **Parking:** on-site. **Cards:** AX, CB, DC, DS, MC, VI.

CAFE MARIANNA **Lunch:** $8-$22 **Dinner:** $17-$22 **Phone:** 703/519-3776 [1]
Location: Jct N Royal and 1st sts. 1201 N Royal St 22314. **Hours:** 11 am-3 & 5-9 pm, Fri & Sat-10 pm, Sun 10
International am-3 pm, Mon 11 am-3 pm. **Reservations:** accepted. **Features:** North of the center of Old Town, the cafe has a casual, neighborhood ambience and clientele. Its menu reflects a variety of international influences, including Italian, Middle Eastern, Creole, Cajun and Asian. Fresh, high-quality ingredients include this place's own home-grown herbs. Desserts in a pastry case at the far end of the dining room are made on the premises. Casual dress. **Parking:** on-site. **Cards:** AX, MC, VI.

CLYDE'S AT MARK CENTER **Lunch:** $8-$16 **Dinner:** $13-$23 **Phone:** 703/820-8300 [115]
Location: I-395, exit 4, 0.3 mi w on Seminary Rd, then 0.3 mi s. 1700 N Beauregard St 22311. **Hours:** 11 am-10 pm,
American Thurs-Sat to 11 pm, Sun 10 am-10 pm. Closed: 12/25. **Reservations:** suggested. **Features:** Ideal for any occasion, Clyde's at Mark Center offers three different settings, as well as outdoor dining, weather permitting. The menu ranges from soups and salads to sandwiches and full meals. Casual dress; cocktails.
Parking: on-site. **Cards:** AX, DS, MC, VI.

ECCO CAFE & PIZZARIA **Lunch:** $8-$15 **Dinner:** $9-$16 **Phone:** 703/684-0321 [8]
Location: Just n of King St (SR 7); in Old Town. 220 N Lee St 22314. **Hours:** 11 am-10 pm, Fri-11 pm, Sat 10 am-
Italian 11 pm, Sun 10 am-10 pm. Closed: 11/24, 12/25. **Reservations:** accepted, Sun-Thurs. **Features:** Steamed mussels fettuccine is served with your choice of white or red sauce and is a popular choice at this local neighborhood restaurant. The innovative menu also showcases fresh seafood and pizza. Live jazz entertainment accompanies Sunday brunch fare. Casual dress; cocktails. **Parking:** street. **Cards:** AX, DC, DS, MC, VI.

ELYSIUM **Dinner:** $67 **Phone:** 703/838-8000 [19]
Location: Jct King and S Alfred sts, just s; in Relais & Chateaux Morrison House. 116 S Alfred St 22314. **Hours:** 7
American am-10 & 5-10 pm, Fri & Sat-10:30 pm, Sun 8-10 am. Closed: for dinner Mon. **Reservations:** suggested.
Features: Inside the elegant 18th-century-style Morrison House, the restaurant no longer presents a traditional written menu. Instead, guests can expect a tableside visit from the chef, who will collaborate with them to create a meal that suits their taste preferences. Each meal is distinctive, even for people who choose the same primary ingredients in the same courses and at the same table. A flight of wine can be paired for each individualized menu. Dressy casual; cocktails. **Parking:** valet. **Cards:** AX, CB, DC, MC, VI.

(See maps and indexes starting on p. 404, 414)

EVENING STAR CAFE'   Lunch: $7-$10   Dinner: $15-$25   Phone: 703/549-5051   118
▼▼▼ **Location:** Just n of jct Monroe Ave; in the Del Ray area. 2000 Mt. Vernon Ave 22301. **Hours:** 11:30 am-2:30 & 5:30-10 pm, Fri & Sat-11 pm, Sun 11:30 am-3 & 5:30-10 pm. Closed major holidays; also for lunch Mon.
American **Reservations:** not accepted. **Features:** A neighborhood restaurant with a counry air, with red laminated table tops, black and white checkered floor tile and exposed ceiling ducts. The kitchen prepares Modern American dishes, such as Grilled Sea Scallops with Roasted Corn Succotash, Grilled Leg of Lamb with Feta Potato Gratin and Blackened Rib-Eye with Roasted Garlic Whipped Potatoes. Casual dress; cocktails. **Parking:** street. **Cards:** AX, DC, DS, MC, VI.

GADSBY'S TAVERN   Lunch: $7-$15   Dinner: $17-$26   Phone: 703/548-1288   16
▼▼▼ **Location:** Just n of King St; in Old Town. 138 N Royal St 22314. **Hours:** 11:30 am-3 & 5:30-10 pm, Sun from 11 am. Closed: 1/1, 12/25. **Reservations:** suggested. **Features:** Experience Colonial dining in an 18th-century tavern at this quaint restaurant. A strolling minstrel performs on the lute or violin as servers in period attire
American cater attentively to diners' needs. The George Washington duck and prime rib are exquisite. Dressy casual;
cocktails. **Parking:** street. **Cards:** AX, DC, DS, MC, VI. **Historic**

GENEROUS GEORGE'S POSITIVE PIZZA & PASTA
   PLACE   Lunch: $6-$15   Dinner: $6-$15   Phone: 703/370-4303   4
▼ **Location:** I-95/495, exit 176, 0.7 mi n on SR 241 (Telegraph Rd), then 0.4 mi w on SR 236. 3006 Duke St 22314.
Hours: 11 am-10 pm, Fri & Sat-midnight. Closed: 11/24, 12/25. **Features:** Bring the family and a smile to
Italian this bright, eclectic and lively eatery boasting 1970s kitchen tables with mismatched chairs. The pizza overflows with your choice of toppings and the pasta is notable. The service staff is young, efficient and friendly. Casual dress; cocktails. **Parking:** on-site. **Cards:** AX, DS, MC, VI.

GERANIO RESTAURANT   Lunch: $8-$18   Dinner: $15-$26   Phone: 703/548-0088   17
▼▼▼ **Location:** Just w of Washington St; in Old Town. 722 King St 22314. **Hours:** 11:30 am-2:30 & 6-10:30 pm, Sat from 6 pm, Sun 5:30 pm-9:30 pm. Closed: 11/24, 12/25; also for lunch 1/1 & 7/4. **Reservations:** suggested.
Features: Freshly cut roses, fireside tables and candlelight dining all contribute to a romantic and beautiful
Italian fine-dining atmosphere. The menu is varied and the servers knowledgeable. Dressy casual; cocktails.
Parking: street. **Cards:** AX, DC, DS, MC, VI.

HAAD THAI   Lunch: $6-$8   Dinner: $8-$14   Phone: 703/575-1999   117
▼▼▼ **Location:** Jct Reading Ave; in a strip mall. 1472 Beauregard St 22311. **Hours:** 11:30 am-3 & 5-10 pm, Fri-11 pm, Sat noon-11 pm, Sun noon-10 pm. Closed: 11/24, 12/25. **Reservations:** suggested. **Features:** Service is
Thai friendly and attentive. The menu lists varied dishes but is shy in the "spicy" categories. Traditional spring rolls are excellent. Decor is reminiscent of a '70s disco but quietly so, with a geometric ceiling and purple lighting. Casual dress; cocktails. **Parking:** on-site. **Cards:** AX, DC, MC, VI.

HARD TIMES CAFE   Lunch: $5-$8   Dinner: $5-$8   Phone: 703/837-0050   9
▼ **Location:** 2 blks w of US 1; in Old Town. 1404 King St 22314. **Hours:** 11 am-midnight. Closed major holidays.
Features: The hot and spicy, down-home operation knocks your socks off with an impressive variety of
American chilies, cooked in styles ranging from Cincinnati to Texas to vegetarian. Country-Western tunes twang from the jukebox as diners sample from many microbrewed beers. Casual dress; cocktails. **Parking:** street.
Cards: AX, MC, VI.

IL PORTO RISTORANTE   Lunch: $7-$9   Dinner: $11-$18   Phone: 703/836-8833   22
▼▼ **Location:** At N Lee St; in Old Town. 121 King St 22314. **Hours:** 11:15 am-midnight, Sun from 4 pm. Closed: 11/24. **Reservations:** suggested. **Features:** Serving traditional Italian dishes for more than 20 years, the
Northern local favorite offers pasta, veal and seafood selections in a rustic cafe setting. Casual dress; cocktails.
Italian **Parking:** street. **Cards:** AX, DS, MC, VI.

KING ST. BLUES   Lunch: $7-$14   Dinner: $7-$14   Phone: 703/836-8800   10
▼▼▼ **Location:** Just n of King St; in Old Town. 112 N St. Asaph St 22314. **Hours:** 11:30 am-10 pm, Fri & Sat-11 pm. Closed: 11/24, 12/25. **Reservations:** accepted. **Features:** Tasty Southern cooking is the specialty at the bi-level townhouse, which has a fun, roadhouse-style atmosphere. The Elwood, with smoked shredded pork
American barbecue, is a favorite. Casual dress; cocktails. **Parking:** street. **Cards:** AX, DC, DS, MC, VI.

LA BERGERIE   Lunch: $10-$16   Dinner: $17-$25   Phone: 703/683-1007   7
ⒶⒶⒶ **Location:** 2 blks n of King St; in Old Town. 218 N Lee St 22314. **Hours:** 11:30 am-2:30 & 5:30-10 pm, Fri & Sat-10:30 pm, Sun 5 pm-9 pm. Closed major holidays. **Reservations:** suggested. **Features:** The well-
▼▼▼ established French restaurant is on the second floor of a historic brick warehouse in Old Town. The dining room, with its brick walls and fresh flowers, sustains an intimate atmosphere. Among specialties are lobster
French bisque, veal chops and Maryland wild rockfish. Dessert souffles are worth saving room for. Semi-formal attire; cocktails. **Parking:** street. **Cards:** AX, CB, DC, DS, MC, VI.

LANDINI BROTHERS   Dinner: $16-$24   Phone: 703/836-8404   23
▼▼▼ **Location:** In Old Town. 115 King St 22314. **Hours:** 5 pm-11 pm. Closed major holidays. **Features:** Family owned and operated, this restaurant has been a fixture of Old Alexandria for years. Make sure you have an
Italian appeite, since all the courses are large in size. Save room for dessert too. Dressy casual; cocktails.
Parking: street. **Cards:** AX, MC, VI.

(See maps and indexes starting on p. 404, 414)

LA PIAZZA
▼▼▼
Italian

Lunch: $5-$7	**Dinner:** $9-$10	**Phone:** 703/519-7711 ③

Location: At West St. 535 E Braddock Rd 22314. **Hours:** 11:30 am-3 & 5-10 pm, Sun 11:30 am-3 pm. Closed: 11/24; also 12/25-1/2. **Features:** Generous portions of home-style Southern Italian cooking is available to locals and commuters for dine-in or take-out. Light and fluffy involtini, with delicately balanced marinara and fried stuffed olives, are favorites. Add a crisp, fresh salad and oven-baked garlic bread for a casual, simply delicious meal. Casual dress. **Parking:** on-site. **Cards:** AX, DS, MC, VI.

╳

LE GAULOIS
▼▼▼
French

Lunch: $8-$14	**Dinner:** $8-$25	**Phone:** 703/739-9494 ⑪

Location: Just w of US 1 S; in Old Town. 1106 King St 22314. **Hours:** 11:30 am-10:30 pm, Fri & Sat-11 pm, Sun-9:30 pm. Closed major holidays. **Reservations:** suggested, weekends. **Features:** The intimate restaurant nurtures the mood of a French country cafe with its cozy fireplace and many plants. Set between two row houses, the outdoor garden area evokes a European air. The menu lists an extensive selection of hearty dishes. The lunch menu is presented until 4 pm. Dressy casual; cocktails. **Parking:** street. **Cards:** AX, CB, DC, DS, MC, VI.

╳

MAJESTIC CAFE
▼▼▼
American

Lunch: $9-$12	**Dinner:** $16-$22	**Phone:** 703/837-9117 ⑫

Location: Between Alfred and Patrick sts; in Old Town. 911 King St 22314. **Hours:** 11:30 am-2:30 & 5:30-10 pm, Fri & Sat-11 pm, Sun 11 am-2:30 & 5:30-10 pm. Closed major holidays; also Mon. **Reservations:** suggested, weekends. **Features:** Chef Susan McCreight Lindeborg brought the retired Majestic Cafe back to life with flashy neon lighting on the original Art Deco facade, a stylish diner atmosphere and flavorful, Southern-influenced American cuisine. The often-changing menu is driven by the availability of fresh market ingredients. Casual dress; cocktails. **Parking:** no self-parking. **Cards:** AX, DC, DS, MC, VI.

╳

MONROE'S-AN AMERICAN TRATTORIA
▼▼
Italian

Dinner: $11-$17	**Phone:** 703/548-5792 ⑪⑨

Location: 0.6 mi e of US 1; 1 mi n of King St Metro Station; in Del Ray area. 1603 Commonwealth Ave 22301. **Hours:** 5 pm-9:30 pm, Fri & Sat-10:30 pm, Sun 9:30 am-2 & 5-9 pm. Closed: 1/1, 7/4, 12/24, 12/25; also for dinner Super Bowl Sun. **Reservations:** accepted. **Features:** This neighborhood restaurant is a favorite of the locals. The menu offers a nice selection of pizzas & pastas, as well as seafood, lamb, veal and chicken dishes. In addition the kitchen prepares a extensive selection of daily specials. Wines selections are extensives and many kind be ordered by the glass. Casual dress; cocktails. **Parking:** on-site. **Cards:** AX, DS, MC, VI.

╳

PORTNER'S
▼▼
American

Lunch: $8-$11	**Dinner:** $8-$22	**Phone:** 703/683-1776 ㉔

Location: Just e of Washington St; between King and Prince sts; in Old Town area. 109 S St. Asaph St 22314. **Hours:** 11 am-10 pm, Fri & Sat-11 pm, Sun 10 am-10 pm. Closed: 12/25. **Reservations:** accepted. **Features:** In a restored 1883 firehouse, the intimate restaurant has a dark wood panel bar that leads to the glass atrium dining room. The eclectic menu incorporates traditional American and Cajun selections. Brunswick stew and pecan-crusted chicken with mustard sauce are local favorites. Casual dress; cocktails. **Parking:** street. **Cards:** AX, CB, DC, DS, MC, VI. **Historic**

☊ ╳

POTOWMACK LANDING
RESTAURANT
ⓂⓂⓂ
▼▼
Seafood

Lunch: $6-$16	**Dinner:** $13-$29	**Phone:** 703/548-0001 ⑪⑥

Location: On George Washington Memorial Pkwy, at Washington Sailing Marina; 1 mi n of Old Town; 3.8 mi s of 14th Street Bridge. 1 Marina Dr 22314. **Hours:** 11:30 am-10 pm, Sun from 10:30 am. Closed: 1/1, 12/25; also for dinner 12/24. **Reservations:** suggested. **Features:** Watch the jets take off and land at Ronald Reagan Washington National Airport, or gaze out at the Potomac River as you dine. The menu offers a nice selection of fresh seafood, pasta and beef dishes. Outdoor deck dining is seasonal. Dressy casual; cocktails. **Parking:** on-site. **Cards:** AX, DC, DS, MC, VI.

☊ ╳

RT'S RESTAURANT
▼▼
Regional American

Lunch: $9-$17	**Dinner:** $13-$25	**Phone:** 703/684-6010 ⑪③

Location: 0.3 mi s of Glebe Rd. 3804 Mt Vernon Ave 22305. **Hours:** 11 am-10:30 pm, Fri & Sat-11 pm, Sun 4 pm-9 pm. Closed major holidays. **Reservations:** suggested. **Features:** The friendly, casual neighborhood restaurant prepares many Creole and Cajun specialties, including Jack Daniels shrimp, spicy she-crab soup, Cajun veal Oscar and the popular crawfish etouffee. Casual dress; cocktails. **Parking:** street. **Cards:** AX, CB, DC, DS, MC, VI.

☊ ╳

SATAY SARINAH
▼
Indonesian

Lunch: $6	**Dinner:** $7-$16	**Phone:** 703/370-4313 ⑫⓪

Location: I-95/495, exit 173, 1 mi n on SR 613; in Van Dorn Station Shopping Plaza. 512-A S Van Dorn St 22304. **Hours:** 11:30 am-3 & 5-10 pm, Fri & Sat-11 pm, Sun-9 pm. Closed: 11/24. **Reservations:** accepted. **Features:** In the Van Dorn Station shopping center, the small, unassuming restaurant specializes in satay offerings. Also on the extensive menu are other preparations of meat, chicken, seafood, rice and noodles, as well as vegetarian dishes. Casual dress; beer & wine only. **Parking:** on-site. **Cards:** DS, MC, VI.

╳

SAVIO'S ITALAIN RESTAURANT AND BAR
▼▼
Italian

Lunch: $7-$11	**Dinner:** $8-$15	**Phone:** 703/212-9651 ⑫②

Location: I-95/495, exit 173, 1 mi n on SR 613; in Van Dorn station. 516 S Van Dorn St 22304. **Hours:** 11 am-10 pm, Fri-Sun to 11 pm. Closed major holidays. **Reservations:** accepted. **Features:** In a shopping plaza, the restaurant builds its menu on both Northern and Southern Italian cooking. In addition to pasta and pizza, selections center on fish or meat. Desserts are homemade. Casual dress; cocktails. **Parking:** on-site. **Cards:** AX, MC, VI.

╳

SCOTLAND YARD RESTAURANT
ⓂⓂⓂ
▼▼▼
Specialty

Dinner: $13-$19	**Phone:** 703/683-1742 ⑮

Location: In Old Town. 728 King St 22314. **Hours:** 6 pm-8 pm. Closed: Mon. **Reservations:** accepted. **Features:** Served in an Old World atmosphere, such dishes as beef Wellington and Scotch eggs—boiled eggs sliced and surrounded by sausage—are flavorful and authentic. One of the owners/waiters dresses in a traditional kilt and speaks with a charming, lilting brogue. The other owner is back in the kitchen skillfully preparing the evening's Scottish fare. Casual dress; cocktails. **Parking:** on-site. **Cards:** AX, MC, VI.

╳

(See maps and indexes starting on p. 404, 414)

SEAGAR'S **Lunch:** $10-$17 **Dinner:** $20-$35 **Phone:** 703/837-7030 (5)
▼▼▼
American   **Location:** I-95/495, exit 176B, 0.5 mi n on SR 241, 0.5 mi e on SR 236, then just ne on Diagonal Rd; in Hilton Alexandria Old Town. 1767 King St 22314. **Hours:** 6 am-3 & 5:30-10 pm, Fri-11 pm, Sat 6:30 am-3 & 5-11 pm, Sun 6:30 am-3 & 5-10 pm. **Reservations:** accepted. **Features:** Just off the lobby of the Hilton Hotel, in Old Town you'll find the hotels dining room. The atmosphere is suitable for any occasion with an upscale yet casual air. The menu offers quality beef and seafood dishes, prepared in the exhibition kitchen. Casual dress; cocktails. **Parking:** on-site. **Cards:** AX, CB, DC, DS, MC, VI.

SOUTH AUSTIN GRILL **Lunch:** $7-$17 **Dinner:** $10-$19 **Phone:** 703/684-8969 (14)
▼▼
Regional Mexican   **Location:** Just w of Washington St; in Old Town. 801 King St 22314. **Hours:** 11:30 am-10 pm, Fri-midnight, Sat 10:30 am-midnight, Sun 10:30 am-10 pm. Closed: 11/24, 12/25; also 12/24 for dinner. **Features:** This Old Town restaurant prepares its many Tex-Mex selections from scratch, such as delicious enchiladas, burritos and fajitas. The fun and lively atmosphere starts in the lounge and at times spills over into the dining room. Casual dress; cocktails. **Parking:** street. **Cards:** AX, DC, DS, MC, VI.

SOUTHSIDE 815 **Lunch:** $6-$11 **Dinner:** $7-$17 **Phone:** 703/836-6222 (27)
▼▼
Southern   **Location:** 0.6 mi s of jct King St. 815 S Washington St 22314. **Hours:** 11:30 am-10:30 pm, Fri & Sat-11 pm. Closed: 11/24, 12/25. **Features:** Great Southern cooking ranges from Lowcountry shrimp and sausage served over creamy grits to jambalaya pasta, gumbo and po'boys. The atmosphere is casual and lively. Casual dress; cocktails. **Parking:** street. **Cards:** AX, CB, DC, DS, MC, VI.

THE STARDUST RESTAURANT & LOUNGE **Lunch:** $7-$11 **Dinner:** $15-$22 **Phone:** 703/548-9864 (2)
▼▼
American   **Location:** Between Washington and St Asaph sts. 608 Montgomery St 22314. **Hours:** 11:30 am-10:30 pm, Fri-11 pm, Sat 5 pm-11 pm, Sun 4:30 pm-9 pm. Closed major holidays. **Reservations:** suggested. **Features:** The neighborhood favorite dining choice features eclectic choices. European/Asian influences lend to food that is as tasty as it is interesting. Casual dress; cocktails. **Parking:** street. **Cards:** AX, DC, DS, MC, VI.

STELLA'S **Lunch:** $7-$14 **Dinner:** $14-$25 **Phone:** 703/519-1946 (20)
▼▼
American   **Location:** On SR 236, in King Street Station, opposite the King Street Metro; in Old Town area. 1725 Duke St 22314. **Hours:** 11:30 am-10 pm, Sun 10 am-9:30 pm. Closed: 1/1, 11/24, 12/25. **Reservations:** suggested. **Features:** The post-war atmosphere is brought to life via framed posters and Stella, a suspended World War II model plane. Anchoring the seasonally changing menu are dishes prepared with fresh local seafood and produce. Patio dining is available during nice weather, and fireside dining is offered in winter. Casual dress; cocktails. **Parking:** street. **Cards:** AX, CB, DC, DS, MC, VI.

TAVERNA CRETEKOU **Lunch:** $8-$13 **Dinner:** $10-$25 **Phone:** 703/548-8688 (13)
▼▼
Greek   **Location:** On SR 7, just e of US 1; in Old Town. 818 King St 22314. **Hours:** 11:30 am-2:30 & 5-10:30 pm, Sat noon-11 pm, Sun 11 am-3 & 5-9:30 pm. Closed: 1/1, 11/24, 12/25; also Mon. **Reservations:** suggested, for dinner. **Features:** The restaurant offers a wide assortment of appetizers—as well as lamb, chicken and seafood dishes—in a Greek tavern setting. The Tuesday-Friday lunch buffet, at which diners can sample two or three Greek entrees with salad and soup, is a popular draw. The courtyard terrace is open seasonally, and live music is offered Thursday nights. Dressy casual; cocktails. **Parking:** street. **Cards:** AX, MC, VI.

TWO NINETEEN RESTAURANT **Lunch:** $7-$15 **Dinner:** $15-$25 **Phone:** 703/549-1141 (18)
▼▼
Regional American   **Location:** In Old Town. 219 King St 22314. **Hours:** 11 am-10:30 pm, Fri & Sat-11 pm, Sun 10 am-4 & 5-10 pm. Closed: for dinner Super Bowl Sun. **Reservations:** suggested. **Features:** Fine New Orleans Creole cuisine is served in three formal Victorian-style dining rooms, on the heated terrace or in the casual Bayou Room on the basement level. Evenings from Tuesday through Saturday, patrons are treated to professional jazz entertainment in the upstairs lounge. The menu lists seafood, beef, chicken and vegetarian dishes. The house specialty Cajun she-crab soup is delicious, as are New Orleans barbecued shrimp. Semi-formal attire; cocktails; entertainment. **Parking:** street. **Cards:** AX, CB, DC, DS, MC, VI.

UNION STREET PUBLIC HOUSE **Lunch:** $7-$23 **Dinner:** $7-$23 **Phone:** 703/548-1785 (25)
▼▼
American   **Location:** Just s of jct King and Union sts; in Old Town. 121 S Union St 22314. **Hours:** 11:30 am-10:30 pm, Fri & Sat-11:30 pm, Sun 11 am-10:30 pm. Closed: 11/24, 12/25. **Features:** Consistently well-prepared food and good service make the restaurant a popular operation for families and social gatherings. The atmosphere is pub-like, and the fare mainly Southern regional with an emphasis on New Orleans. Offerings range from soup, salad and sandwiches to full meals. Casual dress; cocktails. **Parking:** street. **Cards:** AX, CB, DC, DS, MC, VI.

WAREHOUSE BAR & GRILL **Lunch:** $7-$17 **Dinner:** $8-$26 **Phone:** 703/683-6868 (21)
▼▼
Regional American   **Location:** Between Fairfax and Lee sts; in Old Town. 214 King St 22314. **Hours:** 11 am-4 & 5-10:30 pm, Fri-11 pm, Sat 8:30-10:30 am, 11-4 & 5-11 pm, Sun 10 am-4 & 5-9:30 pm. Closed: 1/1, 11/24, 12/25. **Reservations:** suggested. **Features:** How can you resist this authentic New Orleans style Cajun/Creole cuisine — light, flaky rockfish breaded with diced pecans and served with a flavorful, mildly spicy white sauce? About as well as you might resist the warm bread pudding and whipped cream. Dressy casual; cocktails. **Parking:** street. **Cards:** AX, CB, DC, DS, MC, VI.

The following restaurant has not been evaluated by AAA but is listed for your information only.

AL'S STEAK HOUSE **Phone:** 703/836-9443
(fyi)   Not evaluated. **Location:** 0.5 mi e of US 1; in Del Ray area. 1504 Mt. Vernon Ave 22301. **Features:** In the mood for a great Steak & Cheese? This is the place. Plan to carryout out as there is no seating.

ANNANDALE pop. 54,994   (See map and index starting on p. 404)

──────── **WHERE TO DINE** ────────

DOMANI RISTORANTE **Lunch:** $5-$10 **Dinner:** $12-$19 **Phone:** 703/354-9772 148
▼▼▼ ▼▼▼ **Location:** I-495, exit 52B, 0.9 mi e on SR 236. 7410-B Little River Tpke 22003. **Hours:** 10:30 am-10:30 pm, Sun 11
Italian am-10 pm. Closed: 1/1, 11/24, 12/25. **Reservations:** accepted. **Features:** A storefront restaurant, set in a
shopping plaza, offers a comfortable neighborhood ambiance. The menu offers a nice selection of lite fare
and full meals, with subs, pita sandwiches, calzones, pizza and pasta, as well as, chicken, beef and shrimp
dishes. Casual dress; cocktails. **Parking:** on-site. **Cards:** AX, DC, DS, MC, VI.
[X]

RIBSTER'S **Lunch:** $7-$10 **Dinner:** $7-$16 **Phone:** 703/750-2751 149
▼▼▼ ▼▼▼ **Location:** I-495, exit 52B, 1.1 mi e on SR 236. 7243 Little River Tpke 22003. **Hours:** 11 am-11 pm, Sat noon-
Barbecue midnight, Sun noon-10 pm. Closed: 11/24, 12/25. **Reservations:** accepted. **Features:** On a commercial
strip, the neighborhood restaurant offers a relaxed atmosphere. This place is known for its nice selection of
ribs, including baby back, beef or spare ribs, as well as barbecue sandwiches and traditional chicken and
beef dishes. Casual dress; cocktails. **Parking:** on-site. **Cards:** AX, DC, DS, MC, VI.
[X]

SILVERADO **Lunch:** $8-$18 **Dinner:** $12-$24 **Phone:** 703/354-4560 147
▼▼▼ ▼▼▼ **Location:** I-495, exit 52B, 1.6 mi e on SR 236, then 0.3 mi n on John Marr Dr; from Baily's Crossroads, 3.4 mi w on SR
American 244 from jct of SR 7; in Annandale Shopping Center. 7052 Columbia Pike 22003. **Hours:** 11:30 am-11 pm, Fri &
Sat-midnight, Sun-10 pm. Closed: 11/24, 12/25. **Features:** This popular neighborhood restaurant provides a
taste of the American Southwest. The atmosphere if fun, lively and friendly with the Southwest and cowboy
nikniks decorating the restaurant and friendly, upbeat staff always visable and helpful. Casual dress; cocktails. **Parking:** on-
site. **Cards:** AX, DS, MC, VI.
[Y] [X]

ARLINGTON pop. 189,453   (See maps and indexes starting on p. 390, 404)

──────── **WHERE TO STAY** ────────

BEST WESTERN-PENTAGON/REAGAN AIRPORT *Book at aaa.com* **Phone:** (703)979-4400 25
(AAA) (SAVE) 3/1-6/30 & 9/11-10/31 1P: $119-$129 2P: $129-$169 XP: $10 F18
7/1-9/10 & 11/1-2/28 1P: $99-$109 2P: $119-$129 XP: $10 F18
▼▼▼ ▼▼▼ **Location:** I-395, exit 7B northbound; exit 7 southbound, 3.2 mi s of 14th St Bridge. 2480 S Glebe Rd 22206.
Motel Fax: 703/685-0051. **Facility:** 206 one-bedroom standard units. 2 stories (no elevator), exterior corridors.
Bath: combo or shower only. **Parking:** on-site. **Terms:** package plans, small pets only ($10 fee).
Amenities: voice mail, irons, hair dryers. *Fee:* video games, safes. **Pool(s):** outdoor. **Leisure
Activities:** exercise room. **Guest Services:** gift shop, valet and coin laundry, airport transportation-Ronald Reagan Washington
National Airport, area transportation-metro. **Business Services:** meeting rooms, fax (fee). **Cards:** AX, CB, DC, DS, MC, VI.
Special Amenities: free continental breakfast and free room upgrade (subject to availability with advance
reservations). *(See color ad p 424)*
SOME UNITS
[SD] [icons] FEE / [X] [icons] FEE FEE

BEST WESTERN WASHINGTON KEY BRIDGE *Book at aaa.com* **Phone:** (703)522-0400 82
(AAA) (SAVE) All Year 1P: $89-$159 2P: $89-$159
▼▼▼ ▼▼▼ **Location:** I-66, exit 73, just sw of Key Bridge. Located in the Rosslyn area. 1850 N Fort Myer Dr 22209.
Fax: 703/524-5275. **Facility:** 178 units. 164 one-bedroom standard units. 14 one-bedroom suites ($109-
$189). 11 stories, interior corridors. **Parking:** on-site. **Terms:** [ECP] meal plan available, pets ($25 extra
Small-scale Hotel charge). **Amenities:** voice mail, irons, hair dryers. **Pool(s):** outdoor. **Leisure Activities:** exercise room.
Fee: game room. **Guest Services:** gift shop, valet laundry. **Business Services:** meeting rooms. *Fee:* PC,
fax. **Cards:** AX, CB, DC, DS, MC, VI.
SOME UNITS
[icons] FEE / [X] [icons] /

COMFORT INN BALLSTON *Book at aaa.com* **Phone:** (703)247-3399 2
(AAA) (SAVE) All Year 1P: $79-$180 2P: $89-$200 XP: $10 F13
▼▼▼ ▼▼▼ **Location:** I-66, exit 71, jct SR 120. 1211 N Glebe Rd 22201. Fax: 703/524-8739. **Facility:** 126 units. 124 one-
bedroom standard units. 2 one-bedroom suites. 3 stories, interior corridors. **Parking:** on-site.
Terms: cancellation fee imposed, weekly rates available. **Amenities:** voice mail, irons, hair dryers.
Small-scale Hotel **Dining:** 11:30 am-2:30 & 5:30-10:30 pm, cocktails. **Guest Services:** gift shop, valet laundry. **Business
Services:** meeting rooms, fax (fee). **Cards:** AX, DC, DS, MC, VI.
SOME UNITS
[SD] [icons] FEE / [X] [icons] /

COMFORT INN PENTAGON **Phone:** (703)682-5500 26
(AAA) (SAVE) 9/11-10/31 1P: $129-$139 2P: $139-$179 XP: $10 F18
3/1-6/30 1P: $119-$129 2P: $139-$179 XP: $10 F18
▼▼▼ ▼▼▼ 11/1-2/28 1P: $119-$129 2P: $139-$159 XP: $10 F18
7/1-9/10 1P: $109-$119 2P: $129-$139 XP: $10 F18
Small-scale Hotel **Location:** I-395, exit 7B northbound; exit 7 southbound, 3.2 mi s of 14th St Bridge, on SR 120. 2480 S Glebe Rd 22206.
Fax: 703/682-5505. **Facility:** 120 one-bedroom standard units, some with whirlpools. 7 stories, interior
corridors. *Bath:* combo or shower only. **Parking:** on-site. **Terms:** [CP] meal plan available, package plans. **Amenities:** dual
phone lines, voice mail, irons, hair dryers. *Fee:* video games, safes. **Dining:** 6:30 am-11 & 5-10 pm, cocktails. **Leisure
Activities:** pool privileges, limited exercise equipment. **Guest Services:** valet and coin laundry, airport transportation-Ronald
Reagan Washington National Airport, area transportation-Pentagon City Metro. **Business Services:** meeting rooms, PC, fax
(fee). **Cards:** AX, CB, DC, DS, MC, VI. **Special Amenities:** free continental breakfast and free newspaper.
SOME UNITS
[SD] [icons] / [X] [icons] /

(See maps and indexes starting on p. 390, 404)

COURTYARD BY MARRIOTT-ARLINGTON/ROSSLYN   *Book at aaa.com*   Phone: (703)528-2222   **1**

▼▼ ▼▼▼▼

All Year   1P: $219   2P: $229

Small-scale Hotel

Location: I-66, exit 73, 0.3 mi s on Fort Myer Dr, 0.3 mi w on Wilson Blvd, just s on N Pierce St, then just e. Located in Rosslyn area. 1533 Clarendon Blvd 22209. Fax: 703/528-1027. **Facility:** 162 units. 144 one-bedroom standard units. 18 one-bedroom suites. 10 stories, interior corridors. *Bath:* combo or shower only. **Parking:** on-site (fee). **Amenities:** high-speed Internet, dual phone lines, voice mail, irons, hair dryers. **Pool(s):** heated indoor. **Leisure Activities:** whirlpool, exercise room. **Guest Services:** valet and coin laundry, area transportation. **Business Services:** meeting rooms, fax (fee). **Cards:** AX, DC, DS, MC, VI. **(See color ad p 501)**

SOME UNITS

〼 &M 🅴 🖵 ⟳ 🎥 DATA PORT ▦ / ✕ 🗋 ▦ /

COURTYARD BY MARRIOTT CRYSTAL CITY   *Book at aaa.com*   Phone: 703/549-3434   **24**

▼▼ ▼▼▼▼

3/1-7/2 & 9/12-12/31	1P: $99-$219	2P: $99-$219
1/1-2/28	1P: $99-$199	2P: $99-$199
7/3-9/11	1P: $99-$189	2P: $99-$189

Large-scale Hotel

Location: 2 mi s of 14th St Bridge on US 1, just s of jct SR 233. Located in the Crystal City area. 2899 Jefferson Davis Hwy 22202. Fax: 703/549-7440. **Facility:** 272 units. 271 one-bedroom standard units. 1 one-bedroom suite. 14 stories, interior corridors. *Bath:* combo or shower only. **Parking:** on-site (fee). **Terms:** cancellation fee imposed. **Amenities:** video games (fee), voice mail, irons, hair dryers. **Pool(s):** heated indoor. **Leisure Activities:** whirlpool, exercise room. **Guest Services:** valet and coin laundry, area transportation. **Business Services:** meeting rooms, fax (fee). **Cards:** AX, CB, DC, DS, MC, VI.

SOME UNITS

⑤D 🔑 〼 &M 🅴 🖵 ⟳ 🎥 DATA PORT ▦ / ✕ 🗋 ▦ /

CROWNE PLAZA HOTEL WASHINGTON NATIONAL AIRPORT   *Book at aaa.com*   Phone: (703)416-1600   **16**

▼▼ ▼▼▼▼

3/1-6/30	1P: $149-$279	2P: $159-$289
9/9-12/31	1P: $149-$269	2P: $159-$279
1/1-2/28	1P: $139-$199	2P: $149-$209
7/1-9/8	1P: $139-$189	2P: $149-$199

Large-scale Hotel

Location: I-395, exit 8C, 1 mi s of 14th St Bridge off US 1, exit 15th St, then n. Located in Crystal City area. 1489 Jefferson Davis Hwy 22202. Fax: 703/416-1615. **Facility:** 308 units. 296 one-bedroom standard units. 12 one-bedroom suites. 12 stories, interior corridors. *Bath:* combo or shower only. **Parking:** on-site (fee). **Terms:** package plans. **Amenities:** CD players, dual phone lines, voice mail, irons, hair dryers. **Fee:** video games, high-speed Internet. **Pool(s):** outdoor. **Leisure Activities:** exercise room. **Guest Services:** valet laundry, area transportation. **Business Services:** conference facilities, business center. **Cards:** AX, DC, DS, MC, VI.

SOME UNITS

(ASK) ⑤D ✈ 〼 🍸 ⟳ ⛱ 🎥 DATA PORT ▦ / ✕ 🗋 /

CRYSTAL CITY MARRIOTT AT REAGAN NATIONAL AIRPORT   *Book at aaa.com*   Phone: (703)413-5500   **19**

(AAA) (SAVE)

▼▼ ▼▼▼▼

All Year   1P: $289-$700

Large-scale Hotel

Location: US 1, 1.2 mi s of 14th St Bridge; entrance on Eads St. Located in the Crystal City area. 1999 Jefferson Davis Hwy 22202. Fax: 703/413-0192. **Facility:** 343 units. 333 one-bedroom standard units. 10 one-bedroom suites. 11 stories, interior corridors. *Bath:* combo or shower only. **Parking:** on-site (fee). **Terms:** check-in 4 pm. **Amenities:** voice mail, irons, hair dryers. **Fee:** video games, high-speed Internet. **Dining:** 6:30 am-10 pm, cocktails. **Pool(s):** heated indoor. **Leisure Activities:** sauna, whirlpool, sun deck, exercise room. **Guest Services:** sundries, valet and coin laundry, airport transportation-Ronald Reagan Washington National Airport. **Business Services:** conference facilities, business center. **Cards:** AX, CB, DC, MC, VI. *(See color ad p 501)*

SOME UNITS

⑤D 🔑 〼 🍸 &M 🅴 🖵 ⟳ ✕ 🎥 DATA PORT ▦ / ✕ 🗋 /

CRYSTAL GATEWAY MARRIOTT HOTEL   *Book at aaa.com*   Phone: (703)920-3230   **17**

(AAA) (SAVE)

▼▼ ▼▼▼▼

9/12-12/31	1P: $289-$700	2P: $299-$700	XP: $10 F
3/1-7/2	1P: $279-$700	2P: $289-$700	XP: $10 F
1/1-2/28	1P: $249-$700	2P: $269-$700	XP: $10 F
7/3-9/11	1P: $239-$700	2P: $249-$700	XP: $10 F

Large-scale Hotel

Location: 1.3 mi s of 14th St Bridge on US 1; entrance just w on S Eads St. Located in the Crystal City area. 1700 Jefferson Davis Hwy 22202. Fax: 703/271-5212. **Facility:** 697 units. 630 one-bedroom standard units. 67 one-bedroom suites. 18 stories, interior corridors. *Bath:* combo or shower only. **Parking:** on-site (fee). **Terms:** check-in 4 pm. **Amenities:** dual phone lines, voice mail, irons, hair dryers. **Fee:** video games, high-speed Internet. **Dining:** 2 restaurants, 6:30 am-10 pm, cocktails. **Pool(s):** heated indoor/outdoor. **Leisure Activities:** whirlpool, exercise room. **Guest Services:** gift shop, valet and coin laundry, airport transportation-Ronald Reagan Washington National Airport. **Business Services:** conference facilities, business center. **Cards:** AX, DC, DS, JC, MC, VI. *(See color ad p 501)*

SOME UNITS

✈ 〼 🍸 🅴 🖵 ⟳ ⛱ 🎥 DATA PORT ▦ / ✕ 🗋 /

DAYS INN CRYSTAL CITY   *Book at aaa.com*   Phone: (703)920-8600   **21**

▼▼ ▼▼▼▼

All Year   1P: $89-$219   2P: $89-$219   XP: $10   F

Small-scale Hotel

Location: I-395, exit 8C, 1.5 mi s of 14th St Bridge on US 1. Located in the Crystal City area. 2020 Jefferson Davis Hwy 22202. Fax: 703/920-2840. **Facility:** 247 one-bedroom standard units. 8 stories, interior corridors. *Bath:* combo or shower only. **Parking:** on-site (fee). **Amenities:** dual phone lines, voice mail, irons, hair dryers. **Pool(s):** outdoor. **Leisure Activities:** exercise room. **Guest Services:** gift shop, valet and coin laundry, area transportation. **Business Services:** meeting rooms, business center. **Cards:** AX, CB, DC, DS, JC, MC, VI.

SOME UNITS

(ASK) ⑤D 🔑 〼 🍸 🅴 🖵 ⟳ ⛱ 🎥 DATA PORT ▦ / ✕ 🗋 ▦ /

DAYS INN PENTAGON   *Book at aaa.com*   Phone: (703)521-5570   **14**

▼▼▼ ▼▼

4/1-8/31	1P: $81	2P: $81	XP: $7 F
3/1-3/31 & 9/1-2/28	1P: $70	2P: $70	XP: $7 F

Motel

Location: SR 244, just e of jct SR 120. Located in a commercial area. 3030 Columbia Pike 22204. Fax: 703/979-9127. **Facility:** 76 one-bedroom standard units, some with efficiencies. 3 stories, interior/exterior corridors. **Parking:** on-site. **Amenities:** voice mail, irons, hair dryers. **Leisure Activities:** exercise room. **Guest Services:** coin laundry. **Business Services:** fax (fee). **Cards:** AX, CB, DC, DS, MC, VI.

SOME UNITS

(ASK) ⑤D 〼 ⟳ 🎥 DATA PORT 🗋 ▦ / ✕ 🗋 /

(See maps and indexes starting on p. 390, 404)

DOUBLETREE HOTEL-CRYSTAL CITY *Book at aaa.com* **Phone:** (703)416-4100 [12]
All Year 1P: $79-$209 2P: $79-$219. XP: $10 F17
Location: I-395, exit 8C, 0.8 mi s of 14th St Bridge, jct I-395 and US 1. Located in Crystal City area. 300 Army Navy Dr
Large-scale Hotel 22202. **Fax:** 703/416-4126. **Facility:** 631 units. 619 one-bedroom standard units. 12 one-bedroom suites ($99-$299) with whirlpools. 15 stories, interior corridors. *Bath:* combo or shower only. **Parking:** on-site (fee).
Amenities: video games (fee), voice mail, irons, hair dryers. *Some:* high-speed Internet (fee), dual phone lines. **Pool(s):** heated indoor. **Leisure Activities:** exercise room. **Guest Services:** gift shop, valet laundry, area transportation. **Business Services:** conference facilities, business center. **Cards:** AX, CB, DC, DS, JC, MC, VI.

SOME UNITS

(ASK) SD (+) (Y1) (Y) (&M) (&) (D) (≈) (⊛) (DATA PORT) (□) / (X) (🖥) (🖨) /

ECONO LODGE-METRO ARLINGTON *Book at aaa.com* **Phone:** (703)538-5300 [7]
(AAA) (SAVE) 3/1-6/30 [CP] 1P: $90 2P: $149 XP: $10 F18
7/1-10/31 [CP] 1P: $80 2P: $149 XP: $10 F18
11/1-2/28 [CP] 1P: $70 2P: $139 XP: $10 F18
Location: I-66, exit 69, jct US 29 and SR 237, Washington Blvd and Lee Hwy. 6800 Lee Hwy 22213.
Small-scale Hotel **Fax:** 703/538-2110. **Facility:** 47 one-bedroom standard units, some with kitchens and/or whirlpools. 3 stories (no elevator), interior corridors. **Parking:** on-site. **Guest Services:** coin laundry. **Business Services:** fax (fee). **Cards:** AX, CB, DC, DS, JC, MC, VI. **Special Amenities:** free continental breakfast and preferred room (subject to availability with advance reservations). *(See color ad below)*

SOME UNITS

SD (Y1+) (⊛) (DATA PORT) / (X) (VCR) (🖥) (□) /
FEE FEE FEE

EMBASSY SUITES HOTEL CRYSTAL CITY *Book at aaa.com* **Phone:** 703/979-9799 [15]
All Year [BP] 1P: $104-$254 2P: $104-$254 XP: $15 F16
Location: I-395, exit 8C, just s on Eads St, entrance on Eads St; 1 mi s of 14th St Bridge. Located in Crystal City area.
Large-scale Hotel 1300 Jefferson Davis Hwy 22202. **Fax:** 703/920-5947. **Facility:** 267 units. 265 one- and 2 two-bedroom suites. 11 stories, interior corridors. *Bath:* combo or shower only. **Parking:** on-site (fee). **Amenities:** video games (fee), dual phone lines, voice mail, irons, hair dryers. *Some:* high-speed Internet (fee). **Pool(s):** heated indoor. **Leisure Activities:** sauna, whirlpool, exercise room. **Guest Services:** gift shop, complimentary evening beverages, valet and coin laundry, area transportation. **Business Services:** meeting rooms. *Fee:* PC, fax. **Cards:** AX, CB, DC, DS, MC, VI.

SOME UNITS

(ASK) (+) (Y1) (Y) (&M) (D) (≈) (X) (⊛) (DATA PORT) (🖥) (🖨) (□) / (X) (VCR) /

HAMPTON INN & SUITES REAGAN NATIONAL
AIRPORT *Book at aaa.com* **Phone:** (703)418-8181 [20]
All Year [ECP] 1P: $89-$199 2P: $89-$199
Location: I-395, exit 8C, 1.5 mi s of 14th St Bridge on US 1. Located in the Crystal City area. 2000 Jefferson Davis Hwy
Small-scale Hotel 22202. **Fax:** 703/418-4666. **Facility:** 171 units. 157 one-bedroom standard units. 14 one-bedroom suites. 10 stories, interior corridors. *Bath:* combo or shower only. **Parking:** on-site (fee). **Terms:** 3 night minimum stay - seasonal. **Amenities:** *Some:* video games (fee), high-speed Internet, dual phone lines, voice mail, irons, hair dryers. **Pool(s):** heated indoor. **Leisure Activities:** exercise room. **Guest Services:** sundries, valet and coin laundry, area transportation. **Business Services:** meeting rooms, business center. **Cards:** AX, CB, DC, DS, MC, VI.

SOME UNITS

(ASK) (+) (Y1+) (&M) (&) (D) (≈) (⊛) / (X) (K) (TV) (DATA PORT) (🖨) (🖥) (🖨) (□) /

HILTON ARLINGTON AND TOWERS *Book at aaa.com* **Phone:** (703)528-6000 [9]
All Year 1P: $89-$309 2P: $89-$309 XP: $20 F17
Location: I-66, exit 71 (Glebe Rd/SR 120), 0.3 mi e of jct SR 120 and 237 (Glebe Rd and Fairfax Dr). Connected to
Large-scale Hotel Ballston Commons Mall via a skywalk. 950 N Stafford St 22203. **Fax:** 703/528-4386. **Facility:** 209 units. 204 one-bedroom standard units. 5 one-bedroom suites, some with whirlpools. 7 stories, interior corridors. *Bath:* combo or shower only. **Parking:** on-site (fee). **Terms:** cancellation fee imposed, package plans. **Amenities:** high-speed Internet (fee), dual phone lines, voice mail, irons, hair dryers. **Guest Services:** gift shop, valet laundry. **Business Services:** conference facilities, business center. **Cards:** AX, DC, DS, JC, MC, VI. *(See color ad p 514)*

SOME UNITS

(ASK) (Y1) (Y) (&) (D) (⊛+) (⊛) (DATA PORT) (□) / (X) (🖥) /
FEE

(See maps and indexes starting on p. 390, 404)

HILTON CRYSTAL CITY AT REAGAN NATIONAL
AIRPORT *Book at aaa.com*   Phone: (703)418-6800   22

3/1-6/25 & 9/6-12/10	1P: $108-$179	2P: $108-$179	XP: $20 F12
12/11-2/28	1P: $98-$179	2P: $98-$179	XP: $20 F12
6/26-9/5	1P: $98-$149	2P: $98-$149	XP: $20 F12

Large-scale Hotel **Location:** 1.8 mi s of 14th St Bridge on US 1. Located in the Crystal City area. 2399 Jefferson Davis Hwy 22202. Fax: 703/418-3763. **Facility:** 386 units. 379 one-bedroom standard units. 7 one-bedroom suites. 14 stories, interior corridors. *Bath:* combo or shower only. **Parking:** on-site (fee). **Terms:** cancellation fee imposed, package plans. **Amenities:** dual phone lines, voice mail, irons, hair dryers. *Fee:* video games, high-speed Internet. **Pool(s):** heated indoor. **Leisure Activities:** saunas, exercise room. **Guest Services:** gift shop, valet laundry, area transportation. **Business Services:** conference facilities, business center. **Cards:** AX, DC, DS, MC, VI. *(See color ad below)*

SOME UNITS

ASK   S D   ⊁   ┆┆   24   ▼   ⏃   ⊘   ⇒   ⚒   DATA PORT   ▭   /   ✕   ▯   ▭   /
                                                        FEE   FEE

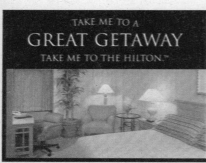

(See maps and indexes starting on p. 390, 404)

HILTON GARDEN INN ARLINGTON/COURTHOUSE
PLAZA   *Book at aaa.com*   Phone: (703)528-4444   **5**

All Year	1P: $71-$189	2P: $71-$189	XP: $20	F

Location: 1.5 mi sw of Theodore Roosevelt Bridge, off US 50, then n. 1333 N Courthouse Rd 22201. Fax: 703/528-4933. **Facility:** 189 units. 182 one-bedroom standard units. 7 one-bedroom suites ($189-$256). 8 stories, interior corridors. *Bath:* combo or shower only. **Parking:** on-site (fee). **Terms:** cancellation fee imposed, [AP], [BP] & [CP] meal plans available. **Amenities:** video games (fee), high-speed Internet, dual phone lines, voice mail, irons, hair dryers. **Leisure Activities:** exercise room. **Guest Services:** sundries, valet and coin laundry, area transportation. **Business Services:** meeting rooms, business center. **Cards:** AX, CB, DC, DS, JC, MC, VI.

SOME UNITS

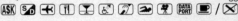

HOLIDAY INN ARLINGTON   *Book at aaa.com*   Phone: (703)243-9800   **8**

3/1-6/16 & 9/6-11/17	1P: $107-$179	XP: $10	F18
11/18-2/28	1P: $98-$179	XP: $10	F18
6/17-9/5	1P: $98-$152	XP: $10	F18

Location: I-66, exit 71 (Glebe Rd/SR 120). 4610 N Fairfax Dr 22203. Fax: 703/527-2677. **Facility:** 221 units. 219 one-bedroom standard units. 2 one-bedroom suites. 9 stories, interior corridors. *Bath:* combo or shower only. **Parking:** on-site (fee). **Terms:** cancellation fee imposed. **Amenities:** video games (fee), voice mail, irons, hair dryers. **Dining:** 6 am-2 & 5-10 pm, Sat & Sun from 7 am, cocktails. **Pool(s):** outdoor. **Leisure Activities:** sauna, limited exercise equipment. **Guest Services:** gift shop, valet and coin laundry, area transportation-within 1 mi & Metro. **Business Services:** conference facilities, fax (fee). **Cards:** AX, DC, DS, JC, MC, VI. **Special Amenities:** free newspaper. *(See color ad below)*

SOME UNITS
FEE FEE

HOLIDAY INN NATIONAL AIRPORT   *Book at aaa.com*   Phone: (703)684-7200   **27**

3/1-6/30	1P: $139-$269	2P: $149-$279
9/9-12/31	1P: $139-$259	2P: $149-$269
1/1-2/28	1P: $129-$189	2P: $139-$199
7/1-9/8	1P: $129-$179	2P: $139-$189

Location: 2 mi s of 14th St Bridge on US 1, jct SR 233. Located in the Crystal City area. 2650 Jefferson Davis Hwy 22202. Fax: 703/684-3217. **Facility:** 280 units. 279 one-bedroom standard units. 1 one-bedroom suite. 17 stories, interior corridors. *Bath:* combo or shower only. **Parking:** on-site (fee). **Terms:** check-in 4 pm, package plans. **Amenities:** video games (fee), high-speed Internet, dual phone lines, voice mail, irons, hair dryers. **Pool(s):** outdoor. **Leisure Activities:** exercise room. **Guest Services:** gift shop, valet and coin laundry, area transportation. **Business Services:** conference facilities, business center. **Cards:** AX, DC, DS, MC, VI. *(See color ad p 516)*

SOME UNITS
FEE FEE

(See maps and indexes starting on p. 390, 404)

HOLIDAY INN ROSSLYN   *Book at aaa.com*   Phone: (703)807-2000   **81**
▼▼▼▼ All Year   1P: $130-$180   2P: $130-$180
Large-scale Hotel   **Location:** I-66, exit 73, just sw of Key Bridge. Located in the Rosslyn area. 1900 N Fort Myer Dr 22209. Fax: 703/522-8864. **Facility:** 307 units. 279 one-bedroom standard units. 28 one-bedroom suites. 19 stories, interior corridors. *Bath:* combo or shower only. **Parking:** on-site. **Terms:** cancellation fee imposed, package plans. **Amenities:** high-speed Internet, dual phone lines, voice mail, safes, irons, hair dryers. *Some:* honor bars. **Pool(s):** heated indoor. **Leisure Activities:** exercise room. **Guest Services:** gift shop, valet and coin laundry. **Business Services:** conference facilities, fax (fee). **Cards:** AX, CB, DC, DS, JC, MC, VI. *(See color ad p 440)*

SOME UNITS
(ASK)(SD)(▥)(Y)(⅙M)(📷)(⊘)(🚭)(≈)(DATA PORT)(🖳)/(⊠)(🔒)/ FEE

HYATT ARLINGTON AT KEY BRIDGE   *Book at aaa.com*   Phone: (703)525-1234   **83**
(AAA) (SAVE)   All Year   1P: $119-$250   2P: $119-$250
▼▼▼▼   **Location:** I-66, exit 73, just sw of Key Bridge. Located in the Rosslyn area across from the Metro. 1325 Wilson Blvd 22209. Fax: 703/908-4790. **Facility:** 304 units. 293 one-bedroom standard units. 11 one-bedroom suites, some with whirlpools. 15 stories, interior corridors. *Bath:* some combo or shower only. **Parking:** on-site (fee) Large-scale Hotel and valet. **Terms:** 3 day cancellation notice-fee imposed. **Amenities:** high-speed Internet, dual phone lines, voice mail, irons, hair dryers. *Some:* safes. **Dining:** Mezza 9, see separate listing. **Leisure Activities:** limited exercise equipment. **Guest Services:** sundries, complimentary and valet laundry. **Business Services:** conference facilities, business center. **Cards:** AX, CB, DC, DS, JC, MC, VI. *(See color ad p 433)*

SOME UNITS
(▥)(Y)(⅙M)(📷)(⊘)(🚭)(DATA PORT)(🖳)/(⊠)(🔒)/ FEE

HYATT REGENCY CRYSTAL CITY AT REAGAN NATIONAL AIRPORT   *Book at aaa.com*   Phone: (703)418-1234   **23**
(AAA) (SAVE)   All Year   1P: $89-$235   2P: $89-$235
▼▼▼▼   **Location:** 2 mi s of 14th St Bridge on US 1, jct SR 233; entrance just e of US 1 on Clark St. Located in the Crystal City area. 2799 Jefferson Davis Hwy 22202. Fax: 703/418-1289. **Facility:** 685 units. 670 one-bedroom standard units. 15 one-bedroom suites, some with whirlpools. 19 stories, interior corridors. *Bath:* combo or shower Large-scale Hotel only. **Parking:** valet. **Terms:** 3 day cancellation notice-fee imposed. **Amenities:** dual phone lines, voice mail, irons, hair dryers. *Some: Fee:* high-speed Internet. **Dining:** 2 restaurants, 6 am-midnight, cocktails. **Pool(s):** heated outdoor. **Leisure Activities:** whirlpool, exercise room. **Guest Services:** gift shop, valet laundry, airport transportation-Ronald Reagan Washington National Airport, area transportation-Crystal City Metro. **Business Services:** conference facilities, business center. **Cards:** AX, CB, DC, DS, JC, MC, VI. *(See color ad p 433)*

SOME UNITS
(✈)(Y)(✈)(🏋)(📷)(⊘)(≈)(📹)(DATA PORT)(🖳)/(⊠)(🔒)/ FEE

QUALITY HOTEL COURTHOUSE PLAZA   *Book at aaa.com*   Phone: (703)524-4000   **6**
(AAA) (SAVE)   3/1-6/13 & 9/13-12/31   1P: $109-$189   2P: $119-$209
▼▼▼▼ ▼▼   6/14-9/12 & 1/1-2/28   1P: $99-$179   2P: $109-$189
Location: 1.5 mi sw of Theodore Roosevelt Bridge on US 50. 1200 N Courthouse Rd 22201. Fax: 703/522-6814. **Facility:** 392 units. 357 one-bedroom standard units, some with whirlpools. 30 one- and 5 two-bedroom Large-scale Hotel suites with kitchens. 3-10 stories, interior/exterior corridors. *Bath:* combo or shower only. **Parking:** on-site. **Terms:** cancellation fee imposed, small pets only ($10 fee, $25 extra charge). **Amenities:** voice mail, irons, hair dryers. *Fee:* video games, safes. **Dining:** 6:30 am-9:30 pm, Sat & Sun from 7 am; closed 12/24-1/1, cocktails. **Pool(s):** outdoor. **Leisure Activities:** saunas, exercise room. **Guest Services:** gift shop, valet and coin laundry, area transportation-courthouse metro. **Business Services:** meeting rooms, business center. **Cards:** AX, CB, DC, DS, JC, MC, VI. **Special Amenities:** early check-in/late check-out. *(See color ad p 420)*

SOME UNITS
(SD)(🛏)(▥)(Y)(⅙)(📷)(⊘)(🚭)(📹)(DATA PORT)(🖳)/(⊠)(🔒)(🖼)/ FEE

QUALITY INN-IWO JIMA   *Book at aaa.com*   Phone: (703)524-5000   **3**
▼▼▼ ▼▼▼   All Year   1P: $79-$159   XP: $10   F17
Small-scale Hotel   **Location:** 1 mi w of Theodore Roosevelt Bridge on US 50. 1501 Arlington Blvd 22209. Fax: 703/522-5484. **Facility:** 141 one-bedroom standard units. 2-3 stories, interior/exterior corridors. **Parking:** on-site. **Terms:** cancellation fee imposed, [AP], [BP] & [CP] meal plans available, package plans, pets ($10 fee, $50 deposit). **Amenities:** voice mail, irons, hair dryers. *Some:* high-speed Internet. **Pool(s):** heated indoor. **Leisure Activities:** limited exercise equipment. **Guest Services:** valet and coin laundry. **Business Services:** meeting rooms, fax. **Cards:** AX, CB, DC, DS, JC, MC, VI. *(See color ad p 517)*

SOME UNITS
(ASK)(SD)(🐾)(🛏)(▥)(≈)(📹)(DATA PORT)(🖳)/(⊠)(🔒)(🖼)/ FEE

(See maps and indexes starting on p. 390, 404)

RESIDENCE INN BY MARRIOTT ARLINGTON AT
ROSSLYN   *Book at aaa.com*   Phone: (703)812-8400   84
All Year   1P: $127-$229
Location: I-66, exit 73, 0.3 mi s on Fort Myer Dr, 0.3 mi w on Wilson Blvd to N Pierce St, then 2 blks e on Clarendon Blvd. Located in the Rosslyn area. 1651 N Oak St 22209. Fax: 703/812-8516. **Facility:** 176 units. 69 one-bedroom standard units with efficiencies. 96 one- and 11 two-bedroom suites, some with efficiencies or
Small-scale Hotel   kitchens. 12 stories, interior corridors. *Bath:* combo or shower only. **Parking:** on-site (fee). **Terms:** weekly rates available. **Amenities:** video games (fee), high-speed Internet, dual phone lines, voice mail, safes, irons, hair dryers. **Leisure Activities:** limited exercise equipment. **Guest Services:** valet and coin laundry. **Business Services:** meeting rooms, fax (fee). **Cards:** AX, CB, DC, DS, JC, MC, VI. **Special Amenities: free expanded continental breakfast and free newspaper.** *(See color ad p 501)*

SOME UNITS

RESIDENCE INN BY MARRIOTT-PENTAGON CITY   *Book at aaa.com*   Phone: (703)413-6630   11
9/12-2/28   1P: $119-$249   2P: $119-$249
3/1-9/11   1P: $119-$239   2P: $119-$239
Location: I-395, exit 8C, just 1 mi s of 14th St Bridge. Located near Fashion Centre Shopping Complex. 550 Army Navy Dr 22202. Fax: 703/418-1751. **Facility:** 299 units. 271 one-bedroom standard units with efficiencies. 28 two-
Large-scale Hotel   bedroom suites with kitchens. 17 stories, interior corridors. *Bath:* combo or shower only. **Parking:** on-site (fee). **Terms:** pets ($200 fee, $8 extra charge). **Amenities:** high-speed Internet, voice mail, irons, hair dryers. **Pool(s):** heated indoor. **Leisure Activities:** whirlpool, sun deck, exercise room. **Guest Services:** complimentary evening beverages: Mon-Wed, valet and coin laundry, airport transportation-Ronald Reagan Washington National Airport, area transportation-within 1 mi. **Business Services:** meeting rooms. *Fee:* PC, fax. **Cards:** AX, CB, DC, DS, JC, MC, VI. **Special Amenities: free full breakfast and free newspaper.** *(See color ad p 501)*

SOME UNITS

FEE

THE RITZ-CARLTON, PENTAGON CITY   *Book at aaa.com*   Phone: (703)415-5000   13
9/6-12/31   1P: $389-$689   2P: $389-$689   XP: $30   F18
1/1-2/28   1P: $369-$669   2P: $369-$669   XP: $30   F18
7/2-9/5   1P: $309-$609   2P: $309-$609   XP: $30   F18
                  1P: $299-$599   2P: $299-$599   XP: $30   F18
Large-scale Hotel
Location: 1 mi s of 14th St Bridge. Located adjacent to the Fashion Centre Shopping Complex. 1250 S Hayes St 22202. Fax: 703/415-5061. **Facility:** At the Pentagon City Metro Station, the service-oriented hotel has richly traditional public areas and handsome guest rooms. 366 units. 345 one-bedroom standard units. 21 one-bedroom suites. 18 stories, interior corridors. *Bath:* combo or shower only. **Parking:** on-site (fee) and valet. **Terms:** cancellation fee imposed, package plans, small pets only. **Amenities:** CD players, dual phone lines, voice mail, safes, honor bars, irons, hair dryers. *Fee:* video games, high-speed Internet. **Dining:** The Grill, see separate listing. **Pool(s):** heated indoor. **Leisure Activities:** saunas, whirlpool, steamrooms. *Fee:* massage, personal trainer. **Guest Services:** gift shop, valet laundry, area transportation (fee), personal trainer. **Business Services:** conference facilities, business center. **Cards:** AX, CB, DC, DS, JC, MC, VI.

SOME UNITS

FEE   FEE FEE FEE

(See maps and indexes starting on p. 390, 404)

SHERATON CRYSTAL CITY HOTEL *Book at aaa.com* **Phone:** (703)486-1111 ☐18
All Year 1P: $85-$165 2P: $85-$165 XP: $20 F12
Location: I-395, exit 8C, 1.4 mi s of 14th St Bridge on US 1; hotel entrance corner of Eads St. Located in the Crystal
Large-scale Hotel City area. 1800 Jefferson Davis Hwy 22202. Fax: 703/769-3970. **Facility:** 210 units. 205 one-bedroom standard units. 5 one-bedroom suites. 15 stories, interior corridors. *Bath:* combo or shower only. **Parking:** on-site
(fee). **Terms:** cancellation fee imposed, pets (dogs only). **Amenities:** voice mail, irons, hair dryers. *Fee:* video games, high-speed Internet. *Some:* dual phone lines, fax. **Pool(s):** outdoor. **Leisure Activities:** sauna, exercise room. **Guest Services:** gift shop, valet laundry, area transportation. **Business Services:** conference facilities, business center. **Cards:** AX, DC, DS, MC, VI. *(See color ad p 451)*

SOME UNITS

SHERATON NATIONAL HOTEL *Book at aaa.com* **Phone:** (703)521-1900 ☐10
All Year 1P: $89-$279 2P: $89-$279 XP: $20 F16
Location: I-395, exit 8A; jct SR 27 and 244, 1.3 mi s of 14th St Bridge. 900 S Orme St 22204. Fax: 703/271-6626.
Facility: 408 units. 391 one-bedroom standard units. 17 one-bedroom suites. 5-17 stories, interior corridors.
Bath: combo or shower only. **Parking:** on-site (fee). **Terms:** [AP] & [MAP] meal plans available, pets (small
Large-scale Hotel dogs only, with prior approval). **Amenities:** video games (fee), dual phone lines, voice mail, irons, hair dryers. *Some:* high-speed Internet (fee). **Dining:** 6:30 am-10:30 pm, cocktails. **Pool(s):** heated indoor.
Leisure Activities: sun deck, exercise room. **Guest Services:** gift shop, valet laundry, airport transportation-Ronald Reagan Washington National Airport, area transportation-Pentagon City Metro, Pentagon. **Business Services:** conference facilities, business center. **Cards:** AX, CB, DC, DS, JC, MC, VI. **Special Amenities:** free local telephone calls and free newspaper.
(See color ad p 518)

SOME UNITS

THE VIRGINIAN SUITES *Book at aaa.com* **Phone:** (703)522-9600 ☐4
3/1-6/30 & 9/1-10/31 1P: $99-$159 2P: $99-$159 XP: $15 F15
7/1-8/31 & 11/1-2/28 1P: $89-$139 2P: $89-$139 XP: $15 F15
Location: 1 mi w of Theodore Roosevelt Bridge, on US 50. 1500 Arlington Blvd 22209. Fax: 703/525-4462.
Facility: 261 units. 165 one-bedroom standard units with efficiencies. 87 one- and 9 two-bedroom suites
Small-scale Hotel ($119-$169) with kitchens. 10 stories, interior corridors. **Parking:** on-site (fee). **Terms:** package plans, pets ($150 extra charge). **Amenities:** video games (fee), voice mail, irons, hair dryers. **Pool(s):** outdoor. **Leisure Activities:** saunas, limited exercise equipment. **Guest Services:** valet and coin laundry, area transportation-metro stop. **Business Services:** meeting rooms. *Fee:* PC, fax. **Cards:** AX, DC, DS, MC, VI. **Special Amenities:** free local telephone calls and free newspaper. *(See color ad p 518)*

SOME UNITS
FEE

—— WHERE TO DINE ——

ALADDIN'S EATERY **Lunch:** $5-$10 **Dinner:** $5-$10 **Phone:** 703/894-4401 ☐37
Location: I-395, exit 6 northbound; exit 7, southbound, just w; at the Village at Shirlington. 4044 S 28th St 22206.
Hours: 11 am-10 pm, Fri & Sat-10:30 pm. Closed: 11/24, 12/25. **Reservations:** accepted. **Features:** The
Lebanese Lebanese restaurant features an extensive selection of vegetarian dishes, but a few chicken, lamb and ground beef dishes also are available. The atmosphere is casual and comfortable, and the seasonal sidewalk tables are popular. Casual dress; beer & wine only. **Parking:** on-site. **Cards:** AX, DS, MC, VI.

AROMA INDIAN CUISINE **Lunch:** $8-$18 **Dinner:** $11-$18 **Phone:** 703/575-8800 ☐36
Location: I-395, exit 6 northbound; exit 7 southbound, then just w; in the Village at Shirlington. 4052 S 28th St 22206.
Hours: 11:30 am-2:30 & 5:30-10 pm, Sat noon-2:30 & 5:30-10 pm; Saturday brunch. Closed: Sun.
Indian **Reservations:** accepted. **Features:** The menu offers an extensive selection of authentic Indian cooking with Tandoori and curry dishes. The dining room is attractive with Indian artwork and tables with pink tablecloths.
Dressy casual; cocktails. **Parking:** on-site. **Cards:** AX, CB, DC, DS, MC, VI.

ATHENA PALLAS **Lunch:** $5-$10 **Dinner:** $9-$19 **Phone:** 703/521-3870 ☐25
Location: Just s of jct S Eads St; in Crystal City area. 556 22nd St S 22202. **Hours:** 11 am-10 pm, Sat from 5 pm.
Closed major holidays; also Sun. **Reservations:** suggested. **Features:** Tucked in the back of the
Restaurant Row area on 23rd St. is a casual, family owned and operated Greek restaurant. The kitchen
Greek prepares a nice selection of traditional and regional Greek foods. When the weather cooperates an outdoor deck is available for seating. Casual dress; cocktails. **Parking:** on-site. **Cards:** AX, CB, DC, DS, JC, MC, VI.

BISTRO BISTRO **Lunch:** $5-$14 **Dinner:** $11-$22 **Phone:** 703/379-0300 ☐34
Location: I-395, exit 6 northbound; exit 7 southbound, just w; at the Village at Shirlington. 4021 S 28th St 22206.
Hours: 11:30 am-10 pm, Fri & Sat-11 pm, Sun 10:30 am-10 pm. Closed: 12/25. **Reservations:** suggested,
weekends. **Features:** The lively cafe, which has seasonal sidewalk seating, boasts a changing menu of
American innovative cuisine, ranging from salad and sandwiches to complete dinners. Servers are friendly and knowledgeable. The Sunday brunch is popular. Casual dress; cocktails. **Parking:** on-site. **Cards:** AX, DC, DS, MC, VI.

CAFE ASIA **Lunch:** $7-$12 **Dinner:** $7-$12 **Phone:** 703/741-0870 ☐4
Location: Jct Pierce St and Wilson Blvd; on ground floor of office building; in Rosslyn area. 1550 Wilson Blvd 22209.
Hours: 11:30 am-11 pm, Fri-midnight, Sat noon-midnight, Sun noon-11 pm. **Reservations:** suggested,
weekends. **Features:** At Cafe Asia you'll find a wide variety of Asian dishes. The menu reflects recipes from
Asian Thailand, Vietnam, Indonesia, China and Japan. The casual dining room with high ceilings, floor to ceiling windows and blonde wood tables and chairs has become a popular spot with the locals. The sushi bar is available for those in the mood for sushi. Casual dress; cocktails. **Parking:** no self-parking. **Cards:** AX, DC, DS, MC, VI.

(See maps and indexes starting on p. 390, 404)

CAFE ITALIA
Italian

Lunch: $6-$9   **Dinner:** $9-$17   **Phone:** 703/521-2565   [28]

Location: 1.5 blks w of US 1; in Crystal City area. 519 S 23rd St 22202. **Hours:** 11 am-10 pm, Fri-11 pm, Sat 5 pm-11 pm, Sun 5 pm-10 pm. Closed major holidays. **Reservations:** accepted, to 8 pm. **Features:** The neighborhood Italian restaurant has been family owned and operated for years. Red checkered tablecloths and oversized kitchen utensils hanging from the beamed ceiling lend to the quaint, casual atmosphere. A covered sidewalk dining section is available. The menu is oriented toward Southern Italian cooking, with an extensive selection of pasta, veal and chicken dishes. Casual dress; cocktails. **Parking:** street. **Cards:** AX, DC, DS, MC, VI.

CAFE PARISIEN EXPRESS
French

Lunch: $3-$9   **Dinner:** $6-$12   **Phone:** 703/525-3332   [1]

Location: At Old Dominion. 4520 Lee Hwy 22207. **Hours:** 8 am-9:30 pm, Sun 9 am-3 pm. Closed major holidays. **Features:** A little slice of Paris is set amid a block of specialty shops. The casually refined eatery treats diners to house-prepared breakfast, lunch and dinner entrees of traditional French fare, including omelets, onion soup and quiches, as well as wonderfully fresh croissants, crepes and brioche, all baked on site. Casual dress; beer & wine only. **Parking:** street.

CAFE TIROLO
Italian

Lunch: $6-$9   **Dinner:** $8-$16   **Phone:** 703/528-7809   [13]

Location: Corner of N Fairfax Dr and Quincy St; behind Tara Thai. 4001 N Fairfax Dr 22203. **Hours:** 11 am-2:30 & 5-9 pm. Closed major holidays; also Sat & Sun. **Features:** In a tidy, little corner of a Ballston office building, behind Tara Thai, the chef, formerly of Tiberio, turns out tasty Italian and Austrian offerings, including his notable, in-house-prepared pastas. The tiny restaurant's tables are at a premium at the noon hour, when the business-lunch crowd is known to frequent, but it's well worth waiting for. Casual dress; beer & wine only. **Parking:** street. **Cards:** AX, MC, VI.

CAPITOL CITY BREWING CO SHIRLINGTON
American

Lunch: $6-$16   **Dinner:** $6-$16   **Phone:** 703/578-3888   [32]

Location: I-395, exit 6 northbound; exit 7 southbound, just w; at Village at Shirlington. 2700 S Quincy St 22206. **Hours:** 11 am-11 pm, Fri & Sat-midnight. Closed: 11/24, 12/25. **Reservations:** accepted. **Features:** Hearty American pub cuisine is served at this bright, trendy spot in a modern "Main Street" re-creation. Enjoy large burgers, overstuffed sandwiches, a German wurst platter, succulent meatloaf and all kinds of finger foods-all of which are well-complemented by the range of freshly brewed beers, ales and ciders. Casual dress; cocktails. **Parking:** on-site. **Cards:** AX, DC, DS, MC, VI.

CARLYLE
American

Lunch: $8-$18   **Dinner:** $12-$22   **Phone:** 703/931-0777   [35]

Location: I-395, exit 6 northbound; exit 7 southbound, just w; at the Village at Shirlington. 4000 S 28th St 22206. **Hours:** 11:30 am-11 pm, Fri & Sat-midnight, Sun 10:30 am-11 pm. Closed: 11/24, 12/25. **Features:** Innovative American cuisine is why this bustling bistro attracts the locals. Menu offerings change seasonally. The staff is friendly and efficient, and the atmosphere casual and fun. Casual dress; cocktails. **Parking:** on-site. **Cards:** AX, DS, MC, VI.

CRYSTAL THAI RESTAURANT
Thai

Lunch: $7-$16   **Dinner:** $8-$16   **Phone:** 703/522-1311   [15]

Location: 1 mi w of jct SR 120, off US 50 at Park Dr; in Arlington Forest Shopping Center. 4819 1st St N 22203. **Hours:** 11:30 am-10 pm, Fri-10:30 pm, Sat noon-10:30 pm, Sun noon-10 pm. Closed: 7/4, 11/24, 12/25; also for lunch 1/1. **Reservations:** accepted. **Features:** Seasonal soft-shell crab, prepared a variety of ways, is the draw at the elegant Thai restaurant. Casual dress; cocktails. **Parking:** on-site. **Cards:** AX, DC, DS, MC, VI.

EL CUSCATLECO RESTAURANT
Spanish

Lunch: $5-$18   **Dinner:** $7-$20   **Phone:** 703/519-8875   [31]

Location: I-395, exit 7B northbound; exit 7 southbound, 3.2 mi s of 14th St bridge, 1 mi s. 2927 S Glebe Rd 22206. **Hours:** 11 am-10 pm. **Features:** The restaurant couples wonderful background music and ambience with a huge and varied menu of Spanish cuisine. Casual dress; cocktails. **Parking:** on-site. **Cards:** AX, CB, DC, DS, JC, MC, VI.

EL POLLO RICO
Peruvian

Lunch: $4-$10   **Dinner:** $4-$10   **Phone:** 703/522-3220   [11]

Location: Between Wilson Blvd and Fairfax Dr. 932 N Kenmore St 22201. **Hours:** 11 am-10 pm. Closed major holidays. **Features:** The first signs guests are in for a great meal are the overflowing parking lot and the great aromas emanating from the tiny spot. Selections are limited to succulent Peruvian roast chicken with mild or spicy dipping sauces, but there are a few choices among the desserts, such as cookies or flan. Casual dress. **Parking:** on-site.

THE GRILL
Continental

Lunch: $12-$25   **Dinner:** $28-$33   **Phone:** 703/412-2760   [21]

Location: 1 mi s of 14th St Bridge; in The Ritz-Carlton, Pentagon City. 1250 S Hayes St 22202. **Hours:** 6:30 am-10:30 pm. **Reservations:** suggested. **Features:** The elegantly traditional restaurant, which sustains a quiet, refined ambience, presents an appetizing menu of sophisticated American and northern European fare. The presentation displays a high degree of imagination, and preparation reveals a trained palate for complementary flavors. The professional and attentive service staff sees to patrons' needs. Semi-formal attire; cocktails. **Parking:** on-site (fee) and valet. **Cards:** AX, CB, DC, DS, JC, MC, VI.

GUAJILLO
Mexican

Lunch: $6-$18   **Dinner:** $8-$20   **Phone:** 703/807-0840   [3]

Location: I-66, exit 73, just s on Ft Meyer, then just w. 1727 Wilson Blvd 22201. **Hours:** 11 am-10 pm. Closed: 12/25. **Features:** Hot tamales and a spicy and fun atmosphere merge at the restaurant. Guests can nibble on chips and black bean salsa while appreciating the friendly service. Casual dress; cocktails. **Parking:** on-site. **Cards:** AX, DS, MC, VI.

(See maps and indexes starting on p. 390, 404)

HARRY'S TAP ROOM   Lunch: $9-$22   Dinner: $9-$24   Phone: 703/778-7788   ⑧
American
Location: 0.4 mi n of N Courthouse Rd. 2800 Clarendon Blvd 22201. **Hours:** 11:30 am-3 & 5:30-11 pm, Sat from 10 am, Sun 10 am-3 & 5:30-10 pm. Closed: 12/25. **Reservations:** suggested. **Features:** Fresh, high quality food sets the tone here at Harry's Tap Room. The bi-level dining room offers an upscale, relaxed atmoshpere suitable for any occasion, it's even kid friendly. The servers are friendly and helpful and will see to your needs. Dressy casual; cocktails. **Parking:** on-site (fee). **Cards:** AX, DC, DS, MC, VI.

LA COTE D'OR CAFE   Lunch: $7-$13   Dinner: $20-$29   Phone: 703/538-3033   ⑨

French
Location: I-66, exit 69, just s on US 29. 6876 Lee Hwy 22213. **Hours:** 11:30 am-3 & 5-10 pm, Fri & Sat 11:30 am-3 & 5:30-11 pm, Sun 11 am-3 & 5:30-9 pm. Closed: 1/1, 5/30, 12/25. **Reservations:** suggested. **Features:** Diners enjoy intimate dining in a country atmosphere. The skilled kitchen prepares dishes from all regions of France, and the chef makes seasonal changes to the menu. Specialty desserts—such as luscious tarte tatin (apple tart) and raspberries baked with hot caramel sauce—are a delicious way to complete a meal. Dressy casual; cocktails. **Parking:** street. **Cards:** AX, DC, MC, VI.

LEBANESE TAVERNA   Lunch: $7-$11   Dinner: $12-$19   Phone: 703/415-8681   ⑯
Lebanese
Location: I-395, exit 8C, just s off Army Navy Dr; in Pentagon Row. 1101 S Joyce St, Suite B30 22202. **Hours:** 11:30 am-3 & 5-10 pm, Fri-10:30 pm, Sat 11:30 am-10:30 pm, Sun noon-9 pm. Closed major holidays. **Reservations:** accepted, until 6:30 pm & 6 pm on Sat. **Features:** Seating can be requested in the charming dining room or on the al fresco patio when the weather cooperates. The kitchen uses traditional Middle Eastern ingredients in preparing Lebanese fare. Casual dress; cocktails. **Parking:** on-site (fee). **Cards:** AX, DC, DS, MC, VI.

LEGAL SEA FOODS   Lunch: $8-$15   Dinner: $12-$30   Phone: 703/415-1200   ㉚
Seafood
Location: At 23rd St S and Jefferson Davis Hwy. 2301 Jefferson Davis Hwy 22202. **Hours:** 11 am-10 pm, Fri & Sat-11 pm, Sun noon-9 pm. Closed: 11/24, 12/25. **Features:** The restaurant prides itself on its reputation for freshness and consistency. More than 40 fresh varieties of seafood can be grilled, broiled, fried or prepared Cajun-style. The clam chowder has been served at every presidential inauguration since 1981. Casual dress; cocktails. **Parking:** street. **Cards:** AX, CB, DC, DS, MC, VI.

MATUBA   Lunch: $6-$13   Dinner: $9-$16   Phone: 703/521-2811   ⑳
Japanese
Location: Just e of jct Columbia Pike and S Walter Reed Dr. 2915 Columbia Pike 22204. **Hours:** 11:30 am-2 & 5:30-10 pm, Fri-10:30 pm, Sat 5:30 pm-10:30 pm, Sun 5:30 pm-10 pm. Closed: 11/24. **Features:** The small store front looks like less than it is but people crowd the small unassuming dining room for well-prepared typical dishes of tempura, teriyaki, sushi, sashimi and the assorted bento box lunches. A small salad bar is a pleasant surprise. Casual dress; beer & wine only. **Parking:** street. **Cards:** AX, MC, VI.

METRO 29 DINER   Lunch: $5-$20   Dinner: $5-$20   Phone: 703/528-2464   ②
American
Location: I-66, exit 71, 0.5 mi n on Glebe Rd (SR 120) at US 20. 4711 Lee Hwy 22207. **Hours:** 6 am-1 am, Fri & Sat-3 am. Closed: 12/25. **Features:** The shiny chrome diner is just what guests might expect. Extensive menu offerings include breakfast items served all day, as well as salads, sandwiches, full meals and a seemingly endless selection of desserts, including cakes and pies made here in the kitchen. Casual dress; cocktails. **Parking:** on-site. **Cards:** AX, CB, DC, DS, MC, VI.

MEXICALI BLUES   Lunch: $5-$11   Dinner: $5-$11   Phone: 703/812-9352   ⑦
Mexican
Location: Jct N Garfield St. 2933 Wilson Blvd 22201. **Hours:** 11 am-10 pm, Fri & Sat-4 am. Closed major holidays. **Features:** The small corner restaurant prepares some solid Mexican, and a few El Salvadoran, dishes at a good value. It's nothing fancy inside, but the service is friendly and attentive. Casual dress; cocktails. **Parking:** street. **Cards:** MC, VI.

MEZZA 9   Lunch: $9-$20   Dinner: $19-$29   Phone: 703/276-8999   ⑯⓪
Mediterranean
Location: I-66, exit 73, just sw of Key Bridge; in Hyatt Arlington at Key Bridge. 1325 Wilson Blvd 22209. **Hours:** 6:30-11 am, 11:30-2 & 5:30-10:30 pm, Sat & Sun 7 am-noon & 5:30-10 pm. **Reservations:** suggested. **Features:** This delightful Mediterranean restaurant nurtures a comfortable, relaxed air in its stylish setting. In addition to a fine selection of entrees, guests can order from a grazing menu. Service is professional and attentive. Casual dress; cocktails. **Parking:** on-site. **Cards:** AX, CB, DC, DS, MC, VI.

MORTON'S THE STEAKHOUSE   Dinner: $32-$59   Phone: 703/418-1444   ㉔
Steak House
Location: 1.2 mi s of 14th St Bridge; in the underground of Crystal City Shopping Complex. 1631 Crystal Square Arcade, Suite 54 22202. **Hours:** 5:30 pm-11 pm, Sun 5 pm-10 pm. Closed major holidays. **Reservations:** suggested. **Features:** Dressy casual; cocktails. **Parking:** on-site (fee) and valet. **Cards:** AX, CB, DC, DS, JC, MC, VI.

THE PORTOFINO RESTAURANT   Lunch: $9-$14   Dinner: $15-$22   Phone: 703/979-8200   ㉙
Northern Italian
Location: 1.5 blks w of US 1; in Crystal City area. 526 S 23rd St 22202. **Hours:** 11 am-2 & 5-10 pm, Sat & Sun from 5 pm. Closed major holidays. **Reservations:** suggested. **Features:** Established in 1970 this family owned and operated Northern Italian restaurant serves a fine selection of veal, seafood, chicken, beef and pasta dishes. Service is professional with waiters attired in tuxedos. Dressy casual; cocktails. **Parking:** on-site. **Cards:** AX, CB, DC, DS, MC, VI.

(See maps and indexes starting on p. 390, 404)

QUEEN BEE RESTAURANT   **Lunch:** $4-$9   **Dinner:** $6-$10   **Phone:** 703/527-3444   ⑩
Vietnamese
Location: Jct Washington and Wilson blvds; opposite Clarendon Metro Station. 3181 Wilson Blvd 22201. **Hours:** 11 am-10 pm. Closed: 7/4, 11/24, 12/25. **Reservations:** accepted. **Features:** A dependable kitchen as the popular, neighborhood restaurant delivers with such dishes as Hanoi-grilled pork, soft-shell crabs and grilled fish. Vietnamese paintings and silk flowers create a comfortable, relaxing atmosphere. Casual dress; beer & wine only. **Parking:** street. **Cards:** AX, DC, MC, VI.   ✕

RED HOT & BLUE   **Lunch:** $6-$20   **Dinner:** $6-$20   **Phone:** 703/276-7427   ⑥
American
Location: Jct Pierce St and Wilson Blvd; on ground floor of office building; in Rosslyn area. 1600 Wilson Blvd 22209. **Hours:** 11 am-10 pm, Fri & Sat-11 pm. Closed: 11/24, 12/25. **Features:** The energy and spirit of a roadhouse infuse the fun, festive restaurant. Memphis-style pit barbecue, with such specialties as pulled-pig sandwiches and wet or dry ribs, is the menu's primary focus. Uniformed servers are upbeat and attentive. Casual dress; cocktails. **Parking:** on-site (fee). **Cards:** AX, DC, DS, MC, VI.   ✕

RINCOME THAI CUISINE   **Lunch:** $8-$14   **Dinner:** $8-$14   **Phone:** 703/979-0144   ㉒
Thai
Location: SR 244, just e of jct SR 120. 3030 Columbia Pike 22204. **Hours:** 11 am-11 pm, Sat & Sun from noon. Closed: 12/25. **Reservations:** accepted. **Features:** The menu compiles an extensive selection of Thai dishes. Framed posters and artwork decorate the simple, comfortable dining room. Casual dress; cocktails. **Parking:** on-site. **Cards:** AX, DC, MC, VI.   ✕

RIO GRANDE CAFE   **Lunch:** $6-$15   **Dinner:** $10-$20   **Phone:** 703/528-3131   ⑭
Mexican
Location: I-66, exit 71, 0.3 mi e of jct SR 120 and 237 (Glebe Rd and Fairfax Dr); in the Ballston area. 4301 N Fairfax Dr 22203. **Hours:** 11 am-10:30 pm, Fri & Sat-11:30 pm. Closed: 11/24, 12/25; also for dinner 12/24. **Features:** A loud, energetic cantina atmosphere—characterized by a warehouse look with raw floors and Mexican music gives this fun and festive restaurant its heart. The mesquite-grilled fajitas and stuffed jumbo shrimp are menu favorites. Sidewalk patio dining when the weather cooperates. Casual dress; cocktails. **Parking:** street. **Cards:** AX, DC, DS, MC, VI.   ✕

RUTH'S CHRIS STEAK HOUSE   **Lunch:** $16-$28   **Dinner:** $18-$36   **Phone:** 703/979-7275   ㉖
Steak House
Location: 1.6 mi s of 14th St Bridge, just e of US 1; in Crystal Park building 3, on the 11th floor; in Crystal City. 2231 Crystal Dr 22202. **Hours:** 11:30 am-10 pm, Sat 5 pm-10:30 pm, Sun 4 pm-9 pm. Closed: 11/24, 12/25. **Reservations:** suggested. **Features:** On the top floor of an office building, the pleasant dining room affords a wonderful view of the Potomac River and Reagan National Airport. USDA Prime beef is the house specialty, but the menu also includes fresh seafood, veal and chicken. Portions are large, and side dishes are served family-style. Valet parking is available for dinner and validated parking for lunch. Dressy casual; cocktails. **Parking:** on-site (fee). **Cards:** AX, DC, DS, MC, VI.   Ⓨ ✕

SAN ANTONIO BAR & GRILL   **Lunch:** $7-$11   **Dinner:** $10-$18   **Phone:** 703/415-0126   ㉓
Tex-Mex
Location: In the mall at the Crystal City Metro entrance. 1664A Crystal Square Arcade 22202. **Hours:** 11 am-10 pm, Sat from noon. Closed: Sun. **Features:** Convenient for travelers on the Metro Blue Line, the restaurant presents a menu of standard, reasonably priced Tex-Mex dishes. The dessert menu is limited. Casual dress; cocktails. **Parking:** no self-parking. **Cards:** AX, CB, DC, DS, JC, MC, VI.   Ⓨ

SIN E IRISH PUB AND RESTAURANT   **Lunch:** $6-$10   **Dinner:** $7-$16   **Phone:** 703/415-4420   ⑱
Irish
Location: Just n of 15th St; behind Fashion Centre at Pentagon City Mall; in Pentagon Row. 1301 S Joyce St 22202. **Hours:** 11 am-2 am. Closed: 11/24, 12/25. **Features:** Representative of typical fare are shepherd's pie, corned beef and cabbage and Irish lamb stew, as well as seafood pasta, pecan-encrusted chicken and Gaelic steak. The decor is authentic, with all but the flooring coming from Ireland. "Snugs," Irish for booths, are private, and one room has a large fireplace. Access to the Pentagon City metro stop is directly through the mall. Casual dress; cocktails. **Parking:** no self-parking. **Cards:** AX, DC, DS, MC, VI.   Ⓜ Ⓨ ✕

TARA THAI   **Lunch:** $6-$8   **Dinner:** $8-$13   **Phone:** 703/908-4999   ⑫
Thai
Location: I-66, exit 71, 0.4 mi e of jct SR 120 (Glebe Rd) and 237 (Fairfax Dr). 4001 N Fairfax Dr 22203. **Hours:** 11:30 am-3 & 5-10 pm, Fri-11 pm, Sat noon-3:30 & 5-11 pm, Sun noon-3:30 & 5-10 pm. Closed: 11/24; also 12/31 & for lunch 1/1. **Reservations:** suggested. **Features:** An aquatic theme and colorful table tops set the tone at this casual, stylish restaurant. The kitchen prepares your dish extra spicy if your request it and MSG is not used. Seafood is their specialty, but don't overlook the noodles, beef, chicken and vegetarian dishes. Casual dress; cocktails. **Parking:** street. **Cards:** AX, MC, VI.   ✕

T.H.A.I. IN SHIRLINGTON   **Lunch:** $6-$16   **Dinner:** $8-$16   **Phone:** 703/931-3203   ㉝
Thai
Location: I-395, exit 6 northbound; exit 7 southbound, just w; in the Village of Shirlington. 4029 S 28th St 22206. **Hours:** 11:30 am-10 pm, Fri & Sat-11 pm. Closed: 11/24; also 9/6 & for lunch 12/25. **Reservations:** accepted. **Features:** Part of a main street setting in the Shirlington area, the stylish Thai restaurant offers tasty authentic dishes and seasonal menu additions. Casual dress; cocktails. **Parking:** on-site. **Cards:** AX, DC, DS, MC, VI.   ✕

THAIPHOON   **Lunch:** $6-$15   **Dinner:** $7-$15   **Phone:** 703/413-8200   ⑰
Thai
Location: I-395, exit 8C, just s on Army/Navy Dr; in Penagon Row. 1301 S Joyce St 22202. **Hours:** 11:30 am-10:30 pm, Fri & Sat-11 pm. Closed: 11/24, 12/25. **Reservations:** accepted. **Features:** Set off the plaza at Pentagon Row, the colorful, trendy Thai cafe prepares food ranging from mild to spicy. Beef "kapow" leaves mouths tingling. Mango and sticky rice is a popular dessert. Casual dress; cocktails. **Parking:** on-site (fee). **Cards:** AX, DC, DS, MC, VI.   ✕

(See maps and indexes starting on p. 390, 404)

TIVOLI RESTAURANT **Lunch:** $10-$13 **Dinner:** $17-$29 **Phone:** 703/524-8900 [159]
▼▼▼▼ **Location:** At Rosslyn Metro Station. 1700 N Moore St 22209. **Hours:** 11:30 am-2:30 & 5:30-10 pm, Sat from 5:30
Northern pm. Closed major holidays; also Sun. **Reservations:** suggested. **Features:** An upscale ambience pervades
Italian the contemporary dining room, where patrons order from a seasonally changing menu of fresh pasta dishes
and tempting homemade pastries. The large wine selection is housed in a glass cellar in the middle of the
dining area. Complimentary garage parking is available after 5 pm. Parking is validated for one hour at
lunch. Dressy casual; cocktails. **Parking:** on-site (fee). **Cards:** AX, CB, DC, DS, MC, VI.

TOM SARRIS' ORLEANS HOUSE **Lunch:** $7-$16 **Dinner:** $8-$22 **Phone:** 703/524-2929 [158]
ⒶⒶⒶ **Location:** I-66, exit 73, 2 blks sw of Key Bridge; in Rosslyn area. 1213 Wilson Blvd 22209. **Hours:** 11 am-10 pm, Fri-
▼▼▼ 11 pm, Sat 4 pm-11 pm, Sun 4 pm-10 pm. Closed: 11/24, 12/25. **Features:** An old New Orleans
American atmosphere—with quaint balconies and Tiffany lamps—pervades the low-key restaurant. Prime rib is the
primary specialty, but the sinful desserts, such as chocolate pie and chocolate bourbon pecan pie, have a
fan base all their own. Casual dress; cocktails. **Parking:** on-site. **Cards:** AX, CB, DC, DS, MC, VI.

TOP THAI RESTAURANT **Lunch:** $7-$10 **Dinner:** $8-$14 **Phone:** 703/521-1305 [27]
▼▼▼ **Location:** 1.5 blks w of US 1; in Crystal City area. 523 23rd St S 22202. **Hours:** 11 am-3 & 5-10 pm, Sat & Sun
Thai from noon. Closed: 1/1, 11/24, 12/25. **Reservations:** accepted. **Features:** The Crystal City restaurant
prepares Thai cuisine in modest surroundings. On the menu is a wide variety, including curry, meat and
seafood dishes, along with noodle and vegetarian selections. The sidewalk deck is popular when the
weather cooperates. Casual dress; beer & wine only. **Parking:** street. **Cards:** AX, DS, MC, VI.

VILLAGE BISTRO **Lunch:** $8-$14 **Dinner:** $10-$22 **Phone:** 703/522-0284 [5]
▼▼▼ ▼▼▼ **Location:** Colonial Village. 1723 Wilson Blvd 22209. **Hours:** 11:30 am-2:30 & 5-10 pm, Fri & Sat-11 pm, Sun 5
French pm-10 pm. Closed major holidays. **Reservations:** suggested. **Features:** Gourmet French food with a touch
of Italian gives this restaurant a busy night. Casual atmosphere draws in people walking by or the shopping
plaza. Pasta, fish, and meat dishes are on the menu. Save room for dessert or an after dinner beverage.
Casual dress; cocktails. **Parking:** on-site (fee) and street. **Cards:** AX, DS, MC, VI.

WOO LAE OAK **Lunch:** $9-$11 **Dinner:** $12-$21 **Phone:** 703/521-3706 [19]
▼▼▼ ▼▼▼ **Location:** Jct 15th St S. 1500 S Joyce St 22202. **Hours:** 11:30 am-10:30 pm. Closed: 1/1.
Korean **Reservations:** suggested. **Features:** The menu lists a wide selection of expertly prepared Korean dishes.
Korean barbecue—ribs, pork or chicken—is prepared on in-table grills. Servers are attentive, knowledgeable
and helpful in recommending dishes such as the tasty and attractive pa jun appetizer, a "pancake" with
scallions, seafood, shredded pork and green pepper. Try the non-alcoholic and traditional dessert drinks for a refreshing and
interesting conclusion to the meal. Dressy casual; cocktails. **Parking:** on-site. **Cards:** AX, DS, MC, VI.

ASHBURN

————— **WHERE TO STAY** —————

EMBASSY SUITES HOTEL DULLES-NORTH **Phone:** 703/723-5300
[fyi] All Year [BP] 1P: $89-$279 2P: $89-$279 XP: $20 F18
Small-scale Hotel Too new to rate, opening scheduled for December 2004. **Location:** SR 28, to Waxpool Rd, on right side. 44610
Waxpool Rd 20147 (44610 Waxpool Rd, DULLES, VA). Fax: 703/723-3318. **Amenities:** 15 units, coffeemakers,
microwaves, refrigerators, pool. **Cards:** AX, DC, DS, MC, VI.

HOMEWOOD SUITES BY HILTON-DULLES NORTH **Phone:** 703/726-1626
[fyi] All Year [BP] 1P: $99-$189 2P: $99-$189 XP: $20 F18
Small-scale Hotel Too new to rate, opening scheduled for December 2004. **Location:** SR 28, to Waxpool Rd, on right side. 44612
Waxpool Rd 20147 (44610 Waxpool Rd, DULLES, VA). Fax: 703/723-3318. **Amenities:** 90 units, coffeemakers,
microwaves, refrigerators, pool. **Cards:** AX, DC, DS, MC, VI.

CENTREVILLE pop. 48,661 (See map and index starting on p. 404)

————— **WHERE TO STAY** —————

SPRINGHILL SUITES BY MARRIOTT
CENTREVILLE/CHANTILLY *Book at aaa.com* **Phone:** (703)815-7800 [110]
▼▼▼▼ All Year 1P: $94-$129
Small-scale Hotel **Location:** I-66, exit 52, n on US 29, 2nd left. 5920 Trinity Pkwy 20120. Fax: 703/815-4100. **Facility:** 136 one-
bedroom standard units. 4 stories, interior corridors. *Bath:* combo or shower only. **Parking:** on-site.
Terms: weekly rates available. **Amenities:** high-speed Internet, voice mail, irons, hair dryers. **Pool(s):**
heated indoor. **Leisure Activities:** whirlpool, exercise room. **Guest Services:** coin laundry. **Business Services:** meeting
rooms, business center. **Cards:** AX, DC, DS, MC, VI. *(See color ad p 501)*

SOME UNITS
ⒶSK ⓈⓄ ♿ 🛏 🎣 📠 🛗 🍽 💻 /✕/

CHANTILLY pop. 41,041 (See map and index starting on p. 404)

———— WHERE TO STAY ————

AMERISUITES (DULLES AIRPORT SOUTH/CHANTILLY)

Phone: (703)961-8160 **123**

(AAA) (SAVE)

▽▽▽▽

Small-scale Hotel

All Year   1P: $159-$179   2P: $159-$179
Location: I-66, exit 53, 2 mi n on SR 28, just w on Westfields Blvd; 1.7 mi s of jct SR 28 and US 50. 4994 Westone Plaza Dr 20151. Fax: 703/961-8163. **Facility:** 124 one-bedroom standard units. 6 stories, interior corridors. *Bath:* combo or shower only. **Parking:** on-site. **Terms:** cancellation fee imposed, pets (in 2nd floor non-smoking units). **Amenities:** voice mail, irons, hair dryers. *Some:* dual phone lines. **Pool(s):** outdoor. **Leisure Activities:** limited exercise equipment. **Guest Services:** valet and coin laundry, airport transportation-Washington Dulles International Airport. **Business Services:** meeting rooms, fax. **Cards:** AX, DC, DS, JC, MC, VI. **Special Amenities:** free expanded continental breakfast and free newspaper. *(See color ad p 423)*

SOME UNITS

[S▲/D] [✦] [🐾] [†Ⅰ┼] [&'] [🍳] [⇌] [☆] [DATA PORT] [🗐] [🖪] [▭] / [✕] /

COMFORT SUITES CHANTILLY-DULLES AIRPORT   *Book at aaa.com*

Phone: (703)263-2007 **117**

▽▽▽▽

Small-scale Hotel

All Year   1P: $69-$199   2P: $69-$199
Location: Jct SR 28, 0.5 mi e on US 50. Located behind the Sully Plaza Shopping complex. 13980 Metrotech Dr 20151. Fax: 703/263-2231. **Facility:** 89 one-bedroom standard units, some with whirlpools. 4 stories, interior corridors. *Bath:* combo or shower only. **Parking:** on-site. **Amenities:** high-speed Internet, dual phone lines, voice mail, irons, hair dryers. **Pool(s):** heated indoor. **Leisure Activities:** sauna, limited exercise equipment. **Guest Services:** valet and coin laundry, area transportation. **Business Services:** meeting rooms, business center. **Cards:** AX, CB, DC, DS, JC, MC, VI.

SOME UNITS

[ASK] [S▲/D] [✦] [†Ⅰ┼] [&M] [🍳] [⇌] [☆] [DATA PORT] [🗐] [🖪] [▭] / [✕] [VCR] /

COURTYARD BY MARRIOTT-DULLES AIRPORT   *Book at aaa.com*

Phone: (703)709-7100 **118**

▽▽▽▽

Small-scale Hotel

All Year   1P: $69-$199   2P: $69-$199
Location: Jct SR 28, just e on US 50. 3935 Centerview Dr 20151. Fax: 703/709-8672. **Facility:** 149 units. 137 one-bedroom standard units. 12 one-bedroom suites ($99-$249). 3 stories, interior corridors. *Bath:* combo or shower only. **Parking:** on-site. **Terms:** weekly rates available, package plans. **Amenities:** high-speed Internet, dual phone lines, voice mail, irons, hair dryers. **Pool(s):** heated indoor. **Leisure Activities:** whirlpool, exercise room. **Guest Services:** valet and coin laundry. **Business Services:** meeting rooms, business center. **Cards:** AX, DC, DS, MC, VI. *(See color ad p 501)*

SOME UNITS

[ASK] [S▲/D] [✦] [†Ⅰ] [&M] [🍳] [⇌] [☆] [DATA PORT] [▭] / [✕] [🖪] [🖪] /

FAIRFIELD INN BY MARRIOTT-CHANTILLY/DULLES SOUTH   *Book at aaa.com*

Phone: (703)435-1111 **116**

▽▽▽▽

Small-scale Hotel

All Year   1P: $113-$129
Location: Jct SR 28, just e on US 50. 3960 Corsair Ct 20151. Fax: 703/435-3163. **Facility:** 85 one-bedroom standard units, some with whirlpools. 3 stories, interior corridors. *Bath:* combo or shower only. **Parking:** on-site. **Terms:** 3 night minimum stay - seasonal, cancellation fee imposed. **Amenities:** dual phone lines, voice mail, irons, hair dryers. **Pool(s):** heated indoor. **Leisure Activities:** whirlpool, limited exercise equipment. **Guest Services:** valet and coin laundry, area transportation. **Business Services:** meeting rooms, fax (fee). **Cards:** AX, DC, DS, JC, MC, VI. *(See color ad p 501)*

SOME UNITS

[ASK] [S▲/D] [✦] [†Ⅰ┼] [&M] [🍳] [⇌] [☆] [DATA PORT] [▭] / [✕] [🖪] [🖪] /

HAMPTON INN WASHINGTON DULLES INTERNATIONAL AIRPORT SOUTH   *Book at aaa.com*

Phone: (703)818-8200 **114**

▽▽▽▽

Small-scale Hotel

All Year [ECP]   1P: $69-$129
Location: Jct SR 28, 1 mi w on US 50. 4050 Westfax Dr 20151. Fax: 703/968-6871. **Facility:** 137 one-bedroom standard units. 7 stories, interior corridors. *Bath:* combo or shower only. **Parking:** on-site. **Terms:** package plans. **Amenities:** video games (fee), voice mail, irons, hair dryers. **Pool(s):** small heated indoor. **Leisure Activities:** whirlpool, limited exercise equipment. **Guest Services:** sundries, valet and coin laundry, area transportation. **Business Services:** meeting rooms, PC, fax (fee). **Cards:** AX, CB, DC, DS, MC, VI. *(See color ad below)*

SOME UNITS

[ASK] [S▲/D] [✦] [†Ⅰ┼] [&M] [🍳] [⇌] [☆] [DATA PORT] [▭] / [✕] [🖪] /
FEE

(See map and index starting on p. 404)

HOLIDAY INN SELECT CHANTILLY-DULLES EXPO CENTER   *Book at aaa.com*   Phone: (703)815-6060   119
All Year   1P: $99-$199   2P: $99-$199
Location: I-66, exit 53, 3 mi n on SR 28, 1 mi s of jct US 50 and SR 28. 4335 Chantilly Shopping Center 20151.
Large-scale Hotel   Fax: 703/815-2388. Facility: 232 units. 220 one-bedroom standard units. 12 one-bedroom suites ($225-$300). 6 stories, interior corridors. Bath: combo or shower only. Parking: on-site. Terms: package plans, small pets only ($20 fee). Amenities: dual phone lines, voice mail, safes, irons, hair dryers. Fee: video games, high-speed Internet. Pool(s): outdoor. Leisure Activities: whirlpool, exercise room. Guest Services: sundries, valet and coin laundry. Business Services: meeting rooms, business center. Cards: AX, DC, DS, MC, VI.
SOME UNITS

HOMESTEAD STUDIO SUITES HOTEL-DULLES/CHANTILLY   *Book at aaa.com*   Phone: (703)263-3361   120
All Year   1P: $91-$111   2P: $96-$116   XP: $5   F17
Location: I-66, exit 53, 3 mi n on SR 28; jct SR 28 and 50, 1 mi s. 4504 Brookfield Corporate Dr 20151.
Motel   Fax: 703/263-0971. Facility: 116 one-bedroom standard units with efficiencies. 2 stories (no elevator), exterior corridors. Bath: combo or shower only. Parking: on-site. Terms: weekly rates available, pets ($75 fee). Amenities: voice mail, irons. Guest Services: valet and coin laundry. Business Services: fax (fee). Cards: AX, CB, DC, DS, JC, MC, VI.
SOME UNITS

SIERRA SUITES HOTEL-CHANTILLY   *Book at aaa.com*   Phone: (703)263-7200   121
All Year [ECP]   1P: $69-$135   2P: $69-$135
Location: I-66, exit 53, 3 mi n on SR 28; jct SR 28 and US 50. 4506 Brookfield Corporate Dr 20151.
Small-scale Hotel   Fax: 703/263-7213. Facility: 88 one-bedroom standard units with efficiencies. 3 stories, interior corridors. Bath: combo or shower only. Parking: on-site. Amenities: high-speed Internet (fee), dual phone lines, voice mail, irons, hair dryers. Pool(s): outdoor. Leisure Activities: limited exercise equipment. Guest Services: valet and coin laundry. Business Services: fax (fee). Cards: AX, CB, DC, DS, JC, MC, VI.
SOME UNITS

TOWNEPLACE SUITES BY MARRIOTT-CHANTILLY   *Book at aaa.com*   Phone: (703)709-0453   115
All Year   1P: $84-$144
Location: Jct SR 28, just e on US 50. 14036 Thunderbolt Pl 20151. Fax: 703/709-0869. Facility: 94 units. 68 one-bedroom standard units with kitchens. 4 one- and 22 two-bedroom suites with kitchens. 3 stories, interior corridors. Bath: combo or shower only. Parking: on-site. Terms: cancellation fee imposed, pets ($100 fee, $5 extra charge). Amenities: high-speed Internet, dual phone lines, voice mail, irons, hair dryers. Pool(s): outdoor. Leisure Activities: limited exercise equipment. Guest Services: valet and coin laundry. Business Services: fax (fee). Cards: AX, DC, DS, MC, VI.
SOME UNITS

WESTFIELDS MARRIOTT   *Book at aaa.com*   Phone: 703/818-0300   122
All Year [BP]   1P: $129-$169   2P: $129-$169
Location: I-66, exit 53, 2 mi n on SR 28, just w on Westfields Blvd, then 0.5 mi n on Stonecraft Blvd; 1.7 mi s of jct SR 28 and US 50. 14750 Conference Center Dr 20151. Fax: 703/818-3655. Facility: The service-oriented hotel offers impressive public areas and comfortable guest rooms designed with the business traveler or conference guest in mind. 335 units. 331 one-bedroom standard units. 4 one-bedroom suites ($279-$695). 4 stories, interior corridors. Parking: on-site and valet. Terms: cancellation fee imposed, package plans. Amenities: high-speed Internet (fee), dual phone lines, voice mail, honor bars, irons, hair dryers. Some: DVD players, CD players. Dining: 6:30 am-midnight, cocktails, also, Palm Court at Westfields Marriott, see separate listing. Pool(s): heated outdoor, heated indoor. Leisure Activities: saunas, whirlpools, steamroom, 8 lighted tennis courts, jogging, spa, basketball, volleyball. Fee: golf-18 holes, bicycles. Guest Services: gift shop, valet laundry, airport transportation-Washington Dulles International Airport, area transportation-Westfields Business Park & golf course. Business Services: conference facilities, business center. Cards: AX, CB, DC, DS, JC, MC, VI. Special Amenities: free newspaper and preferred room (subject to availability with advance reservations). (See color ad p 501)
SOME UNITS

WINGATE INN DULLES AIRPORT-CHANTILLY   *Book at aaa.com*   Phone: (571)203-0999   113
9/16-11/15 [BP]   1P: $140-$169   2P: $140-$169   XP: $10   F18
3/1-6/15 [BP]   1P: $99-$169   2P: $99-$169   XP: $10   F18
6/16-9/15 & 11/16-2/28 [BP]   1P: $79-$152   2P: $79-$152   XP: $10   F18
Small-scale Hotel   Location: Jct SR 28, just e on US 50. 3940 Centerview Dr 20151. Fax: 571/203-0998. Facility: 131 one-bedroom standard units, some with whirlpools. 4 stories, interior corridors. Bath: combo or shower only. Parking: on-site. Amenities: video games (fee), high-speed Internet, dual phone lines, voice mail, safes, irons, hair dryers. Pool(s): heated indoor. Leisure Activities: whirlpool, limited exercise equipment. Guest Services: valet and coin laundry. Business Services: meeting rooms, business center. Cards: AX, CB, DC, DS, MC, VI.
SOME UNITS

―――――― WHERE TO DINE ――――――

BACKYARD GRILL AND BAR   Lunch: $4-$19   Dinner: $10-$20   Phone: 703/802-6400   154
Location: Jct SR 28, 0.5 mi e on US 50; in Sully Plaza. 13999 Metrotech Dr 20151. Hours: 11 am-11 pm, Fri & Sat-midnight, Sun-10 pm. Closed: 12/25. Reservations: accepted. Features: Selections on the restaurant's menu range from salads and sandwiches to steaks and pasta. Casual dress; cocktails. Parking: on-site.
American   Cards: AX, CB, DC, DS, MC, VI.

(See map and index starting on p. 404)

BLUE WATER GRILLE   **Lunch:** $7-$11   **Dinner:** $8-$22   **Phone:** 703/803-1040   (158)
American   **Location:** I-66, exit 53, 2 mi n on SR 28, just w on Westfield Blvd; 1.7 mi s of jct SR 28 and US 50; in Sully Station Shopping Center. 5127 Westfields Blvd 20120. **Hours:** 11 am-11 pm. Closed: 1/1, 12/25. **Reservations:** accepted. **Features:** The casual eatery's American cuisine shows a Cajun and Caribbean twist. Jerk marinated pork loin chops and Cajun-style bone-in beef rib chops are just a couple items on the eclectic menu. A large deck is open during the warmer months, and a roaring fireplace blazes in the dining room when it's cold. Casual dress; cocktails. **Parking:** on-site. **Cards:** AX, CB, DC, DS, MC, VI.

OASIS INDIAN RESTAURANT   **Lunch:** $5-$15   **Dinner:** $7-$15   **Phone:** 703/222-9544   (155)
Indian   **Location:** Jct SR 28, 0.5 mi e on US 50, just n on SR 657 (Centerville Rd); in Sully Plaza. 13971 Metrotech Dr 20151. **Hours:** 11:30 am-2:30 & 5-9:30 pm, Fri-10:30 pm, Sun noon-9:30 pm. Closed: 12/25. **Reservations:** suggested. **Features:** The "Oasis platter" features an assortment of flavorful grilled chicken and lamb kabobs and is one of the authentic Indian house specialties here. Some American fare is available as well as lowfat vegetarian plates. A lunch buffet is served Monday-Friday. Casual dress; beer & wine only. **Parking:** on-site. **Cards:** AX, CB, DC, DS, MC, VI.

OTANI JAPANESE STEAK HOUSE   **Lunch:** $7-$12   **Dinner:** $15-$30   **Phone:** 703/802-3400   (156)
Japanese   **Location:** Jct SR 28, 0.5 mi e on US 50; in Sully Plaza. 13952 Lee Jackson Memorial Hwy 20151. **Hours:** 11:30 am-2 & 5-9:30 pm, Fri-10:30 pm, Sat 5 pm-10:30 pm, Sun 4 pm-9 pm. Closed: 7/4, 11/24, 12/25; also Super Bowl Sun. **Reservations:** accepted. **Features:** Hibachi cooking makes for a delicious and entertaining meal. The chef prepares food with a showy display of his skill with knives. A sushi buffet is available for lunch. The shopping plaza setting allows for ample parking. Casual dress; cocktails. **Parking:** on-site. **Cards:** AX, CB, DC, DS, MC, VI.

PALM COURT AT WESTFIELDS MARRIOTT   **Lunch:** $8-$18   **Dinner:** $20-$33   **Phone:** 703/818-3522   (157)
American   **Location:** I-66, exit 53, 2 mi n on SR 28, just w on Westfields Blvd, then 0.5 mi n on Stonecraft Blvd; 1.7 mi s of jct SR 28 and US 50; in Westfields Marriott. 14750 Conference Center Dr 20151. **Hours:** 6:30 am-2 & 6-10 pm. Closed: Sun. **Reservations:** suggested. **Features:** The full-service dining room offers an elegant setting for any occasion. Among dishes are seared buffalo filet, ahi tuna and Atlantic salmon, seared veal chops and roasted mustard-crusted lamb chops. The staff is professional and attentive. Dressy casual; cocktails. **Parking:** valet. **Cards:** AX, CB, DC; DS, MC, VI.

PICANTE! THE REAL TACO   **Lunch:** $8-$15   **Dinner:** $8-$15   **Phone:** 703/222-2323   (153)
Mexican   **Location:** US 50, 0.6 mi w of jct SR 28; in Chantilly Park Shopping Center. 14511B-C Lee Jackson Hwy 20151. **Hours:** 11 am-10 pm, Fri & Sat-10:30 pm, Sun-9 pm. Closed major holidays. **Features:** Traditional Mexican cooking is offered at this casual family oriented restaurant. The menu offers a nice selection of tacos, enchiladas, burritos and full dinners. Casual dress; cocktails. **Parking:** on-site. **Cards:** AX, DC, DS, MC, VI.

THAI BASIL   **Lunch:** $5-$8   **Dinner:** $9-$14   **Phone:** 703/631-8277   (152)
Thai   **Location:** US 50, 0.6 mi w of jct SR 28. 14511-P Lee Jackson Hwy 20151. **Hours:** 11 am-3 & 5-10 pm. Closed major holidays. **Features:** Tucked in a little shopping plaza, the quaint restaurant presents a menu of skillfully prepared cuisine that is flavored to the guest's preference for spiciness. Pad Thai noodles are a signature dish. Casual dress; beer & wine only. **Parking:** on-site. **Cards:** AX, CB, DC, MC, VI.

CLIFTON pop. 185

——— **WHERE TO DINE** ———

HEART IN HAND   **Lunch:** $7-$12   **Dinner:** $15-$23   **Phone:** 703/830-4111
American   **Location:** US 29 and 211, 4.5 mi s on CR 645 (Clifton Rd). 7145 Main St 20124. **Hours:** 11 am-2 & 5-9 pm, Fri & Sat-9:30 pm, Sun 11 am-3 & 5-8 pm. Closed: 7/4, 12/25. **Reservations:** suggested. **Features:** On the National Register of Historic Places, the restaurant sits in a rural setting and exudes a country atmosphere. Southern touches are evident in much of the cuisine, such as Tennessee ham and bean soup. Taste the homemade raspberry ice cream. Casual dress; cocktails. **Parking:** on-site. **Cards:** AX, CB, DC, DS, MC, VI. **Historic**

THE HERMITAGE INN RESTAURANT   **Dinner:** $30-$50   **Phone:** 703/266-1623
Continental   **Location:** US 29, 211 and CR 645 (Clifton Rd), 4.5 mi s on CR 645 (Clifton Rd). 7134 Main St 20124. **Hours:** 5:30 pm-close, Sun also 11 am-2:30 pm. Closed: 1/1, 7/4, 9/5; also Mon, Tues & Super Bowl Sun. **Reservations:** suggested. **Features:** Delicious French/Mediterranean cuisine is showcased in a restored historic hostelry. The rural setting is tranquil. Three-course prix fixe meals include soup, salad or appetizer, entree and dessert. Dressy casual; cocktails. **Parking:** on-site. **Cards:** AX, DC, DS, MC, VI. **Historic**

DUMFRIES pop. 4,937

——— **WHERE TO STAY** ———

HAMPTON INN-DUMFRIES   *Book at aaa.com*   **Phone:** (703)441-9900
Small-scale Hotel   All Year [BP]   1P: $99-$115   2P: $104-$121 **Location:** I-95, exit 152B, 0.4 mi w on SR 234. 16959 Old Stage Rd 22026. Fax: 703/441-6800. **Facility:** 78 units. 73 one-bedroom standard units. 5 one-bedroom suites ($116-$160) with whirlpools. 4 stories, interior corridors. *Bath:* combo or shower only. **Parking:** on-site. **Amenities:** dual phone lines, voice mail, irons, hair dryers. **Pool(s):** heated indoor. **Leisure Activities:** whirlpool, limited exercise equipment. **Guest Services:** valet laundry. **Business Services:** meeting rooms, business center. **Cards:** AX, CB, DC, DS, MC, VI.

SOME UNITS

QUALITY INN

AAA SAVE

◆◆◆ ◆◆

Small-scale Hotel

All Year [ECP]   1P: $69-$109   2P: $69-$109   XP: $10   **Phone:** (703)221-1141   F18
Location: I-95, exit 152B, just w on SR 234 N. 17133 Dumfries Rd 22026. Fax: 703/221-2010. **Facility:** 187 one-bedroom standard units. 2 stories (no elevator), interior/exterior corridors. **Parking:** on-site. **Terms:** small pets only (in smoking units). **Amenities:** irons, hair dryers. **Pool(s):** outdoor, wading. **Leisure Activities:** limited exercise equipment. *Fee:* game room. **Guest Services:** valet and coin laundry. **Business Services:** meeting rooms, fax (fee). **Cards:** AX, CB, DC, DS, JC, MC, VI. **Special Amenities:** free expanded continental breakfast and free local telephone calls.

SOME UNITS
🅂🄳 🛏 🍽 ⊘ 🏊 📷 DATA PORT 💻 / ✕ 🍴 🖥 /

SLEEP INN QUANTICO   *Book at aaa.com*

AAA SAVE

◆◆◆ ◆◆

Small-scale Hotel

All Year   1P: $69-$109   2P: $69-$109   XP: $6   **Phone:** (703)445-0900   F18
Location: I-95, exit 152A, 0.5 mi e on SR 234, then just s on US 1. 17470 Jefferson Davis Hwy 22026. Fax: 703/221-8897. **Facility:** 56 one-bedroom standard units. 3 stories, interior corridors. *Bath:* combo or shower only. **Parking:** on-site. **Amenities:** voice mail, irons, hair dryers. **Leisure Activities:** sauna, limited exercise equipment. **Business Services:** fax (fee). **Cards:** AX, DC, DS, MC, VI. **Special Amenities:** free continental breakfast and free local telephone calls.

SOME UNITS
🅂🄳 🛁M 🕹 📷 DATA PORT / ✕ 🍴 🖥 💻 /

SUPER 8 MOTEL-DUMFRIES

◆

Small-scale Hotel

All Year   1P: $49-$69   2P: $49-$69   XP: $5   **Phone:** (703)221-8838   F12
Location: I-95, exit 152A, 0.5 mi e on SR 234, then just s on US 1. 17416 Jefferson Davis Hwy 22026. Fax: 703/221-0275. **Facility:** 81 one-bedroom standard units. 3 stories, interior corridors. **Parking:** on-site. **Business Services:** fax (fee). **Cards:** AX, CB, DC, DS, JC, MC, VI.

SOME UNITS
ASK 🅂🄳 🍽 📷 DATA PORT / ✕ 🍴 🖥 /

FAIRFAX pop. 21,498   (See map and index starting on p. 404)

———— WHERE TO STAY ————

BAILIWICK INN   *Book at aaa.com*

◆◆◆◆◆

Historic
Country Inn

All Year [BP]   1P: $165-$225   2P: $165-$225   XP: $25   **Phone:** (703)691-2266   〔107〕
Location: I-66, exit 60, 1.5 mi s; SR 123, just s of jct SR 236. Located in Fairfax City, opposite the old courthouse. 4023 Chain Bridge Rd 22030. Fax: 703/934-2112. **Facility:** Once a private home, this pre-1812 inn offers rooms decorated to reflect the style of historic Virginia personages such as Thomas Jefferson. Designated smoking area. 14 units. 13 one-bedroom standard units, some with whirlpools. 1 one-bedroom suite ($300-$350) with whirlpool. 4 stories (no elevator), interior corridors. *Bath:* combo, shower or tub only. **Parking:** on-site. **Terms:** office hours 7 am-10 pm, 2 night minimum stay - seasonal and/or weekends, age restrictions may apply, 14 day cancellation notice-fee imposed, weekly rates available, package plans. **Amenities:** CD players, honor bars, hair dryers. **Dining:** Bailiwick Inn Restaurant, see separate listing. **Business Services:** fax (fee). **Cards:** AX, MC, VI.

SOME UNITS
ASK 🅂🄳 🍴 ♿ ✕ 📷 DATA PORT 💻 / VCR /
FEE

BEST WESTERN FAIRFAX   *Book at aaa.com*

AAA SAVE

◆◆◆ ◆◆

Small-scale Hotel

3/1-10/31   1P: $89-$129   2P: $89-$129   **Phone:** (703)591-5500   〔102〕
11/1-2/28   1P: $79-$129   2P: $79-$129
Location: I-66, exit 60, 0.5 mi s on SR 123; jct US 29/50. 3535 Chain Bridge Rd 22030. Fax: 703/591-7483. **Facility:** 127 units. 125 one-bedroom standard units. 2 one-bedroom suites. 2-3 stories (no elevator), exterior corridors. **Parking:** on-site. **Terms:** package plans. **Amenities:** video games (fee), voice mail, irons, hair dryers. **Pool(s):** outdoor. **Leisure Activities:** limited exercise equipment. **Guest Services:** valet and coin laundry. **Business Services:** meeting rooms, PC, fax (fee). **Cards:** AX, CB, DC, DS, MC, VI. **Special Amenities:** free full breakfast and free local telephone calls. *(See color ad p 424)*

SOME UNITS
🅂🄳 🍽 ⊘ 🏊 📷 DATA PORT 💻 / ✕ 🍴 🖥 /
FEE FEE

(See map and index starting on p. 404)

COMFORT INN UNIVERSITY CENTER   *Book at aaa.com*   Phone: (703)591-5900   `105`

AAA SAVE   All Year   1P: $69-$139   2P: $69-$139

Location: I-66, exit 57A, 0.8 mi se on US 50, 0.5 mi nw of jct US 29. 11180 Main St 22030. Fax: 703/273-7915. **Facility:** 204 one-bedroom standard units, some with efficiencies and/or whirlpools. 6 stories, interior corridors. **Parking:** on-site. **Terms:** [ECP] meal plan available, small pets only. **Amenities:** video games Small-scale Hotel (fee), voice mail, irons, hair dryers. **Dining:** 11 am-10:30 pm, Fri & Sat-11 pm, cocktails. **Pool(s):** heated indoor. **Leisure Activities:** sun deck, exercise room. *Fee:* game room. **Guest Services:** gift shop, valet and coin laundry, area transportation-Metro & shopping mall, beauty salon. **Business Services:** meeting rooms, PC, fax (fee). **Cards:** AX, CB, DC, DS, MC, VI. **Special Amenities: free expanded continental breakfast and free local telephone calls.** *(See color ad p 527)*

SOME UNITS

COURTYARD BY MARRIOTT-FAIR OAKS   *Book at aaa.com*   Phone: (703)273-6161   `104`

All Year   1P: $69-$189

Location: I-66, exit 57A, 0.5 mi se on US 50; 0.8 mi nw of jct US 29. 11220 Lee Jackson Hwy 22030. Small-scale Hotel Fax: 703/273-3505. **Facility:** 144 units. 132 one-bedroom standard units. 12 one-bedroom suites. 3 stories, interior corridors. *Bath:* combo or shower only. **Parking:** on-site. **Amenities:** high-speed Internet, dual phone lines, voice mail, irons, hair dryers. **Pool(s):** heated indoor. **Leisure Activities:** whirlpool, exercise room. **Guest Services:** valet and coin laundry. **Business Services:** meeting rooms, fax (fee). **Cards:** AX, CB, DC, DS, JC, MC, VI. *(See color ad p 501)*

SOME UNITS

HAMPTON INN-FAIRFAX   *Book at aaa.com*   Phone: (703)385-2600   `106`

All Year [ECP]   1P: $125-$135   2P: $135-$145   XP: $10   F17

Location: I-66, exit 60, 0.7 mi s on SR 123, then 0.7 mi w on US 50/29. Located in a commercial area. 10860 Lee Hwy Small-scale Hotel 22030. Fax: 703/385-2742. **Facility:** 86 one-bedroom standard units. 5 stories, interior corridors. **Parking:** on-site. **Amenities:** video games (fee), dual phone lines, voice mail, irons, hair dryers. **Leisure Activities:** limited exercise equipment. **Guest Services:** valet laundry. **Business Services:** meeting rooms, fax (fee). **Cards:** AX, DC, DS, MC, VI.

SOME UNITS

Expect more at the Hilton Garden Inn® Fairfax.

Located just 20 minutes from Washington DC's monuments and attractions in the upscale suburbs of Northern Virginia. We offer complimentary shuttle transportation to Fair Oaks Mall & the Vienna Metro subway station, an indoor pool & whirlpool, a full-service restaurant and a Pavilion lounge. Just make advance reservations with a call to Hilton's dedicated AAA number, **1-800-916-2221**, or your local AAA travel office. Visit us online at **hiltongardeninn.com**.

3950 Fair Ridge Drive
Fairfax, VA 22033
703-385-7774

Valid AAA membership card required for reservation and at check-in. Hilton HHonors membership, earning of Points & Miles,® and redemption of points are subject to HHonors Terms and Conditions. ©2005 Hilton Hospitality, Inc.

(See map and index starting on p. 404)

HILTON GARDEN INN FAIRFAX   *Book at aaa.com*   Phone: (703)385-7774   **97**
AAA SAVE   All Year   1P: $79-$249   2P: $79-$249   XP: $10   F18
Location: I-66, exit 57B, 1 mi w on US 50. 3950 Fair Ridge Dr 22033. Fax: 703/359-2932. **Facility:** 149 one-bedroom standard units. 5 stories, interior corridors. *Bath:* combo or shower only. **Parking:** on-site.
Small-scale Hotel   **Amenities:** video games (fee), high-speed Internet, dual phone lines, voice mail, irons, hair dryers. **Dining:** 6:30 am-2 & 5-10 pm, Sat & Sun 7 am-noon & 5-10 pm, cocktails. **Pool(s):** small heated indoor. **Leisure Activities:** whirlpool, exercise room. **Guest Services:** sundries, valet and coin laundry, area transportation-within 3 mi. **Business Services:** meeting rooms, business center. **Cards:** AX, CB, DC, DS, JC, MC, VI.
(See color ad p 528)   SOME UNITS
[icons]

HOMESTEAD STUDIO SUITES HOTEL-FAIR OAKS   *Book at aaa.com*   Phone: (703)273-3444   **99**
All Year   1P: $80-$100   2P: $85-$105   XP: $5   F17
Location: I-66, exit 57B, 0.8 mi w on US 50, 0.3 mi s on SR 620 (West Ox Rd), then just se. Located adjacent to Fair Oaks Mall. 12104 Monument Dr 22033. Fax: 703/273-8559. **Facility:** 134 one-bedroom standard units with
Small-scale Hotel   efficiencies. 2 stories (no elevator), exterior corridors. *Bath:* combo or shower only. **Parking:** on-site. **Terms:** office hours 6:30 am-4 am, weekly rates available, pets ($25 extra charge). **Amenities:** voice mail, irons. **Guest Services:** valet and coin laundry. **Business Services:** fax (fee). **Cards:** AX, CB, DC, DS, JC, MC, VI.
SOME UNITS
[icons] FEE   FEE   FEE

HOMESTEAD STUDIO SUITES HOTEL-FALLS CHURCH/MERRIFIELD   *Book at aaa.com*   Phone: (703)204-0088   **100**
All Year   1P: $95-$115   2P: $100-$120   XP: $5   F17
Location: I-495, exit 50A, just w on US 50 to Gallows Rd, then just s. 8281 Willow Oaks Corporate Dr 22031. Fax: 703/204-2741. **Facility:** 128 one-bedroom standard units with efficiencies. 2 stories (no elevator),
Small-scale Hotel   exterior corridors. *Bath:* combo or shower only. **Parking:** on-site. **Terms:** office hours 6:30 am-3 am, weekly rates available, small pets only ($25 extra charge). **Amenities:** high-speed Internet (fee), voice mail, irons. **Guest Services:** valet and coin laundry. **Business Services:** meeting rooms, fax (fee). **Cards:** AX, CB, DC, DS, JC, MC, VI.
SOME UNITS
[icons] FEE   FEE   FEE

HYATT FAIR LAKES   *Book at aaa.com*   Phone: (703)818-1234   **103**
AAA SAVE   All Year   1P: $99-$269   2P: $99-$269
Location: I-66, exit 55 (Fairfax County Pkwy N); in Fair Lakes Shopping Center. 12777 Fair Lakes Cir 22033. Fax: 703/653-6190. **Facility:** 316 units. 315 one-bedroom standard units. 1 one-bedroom suite. 13 stories, interior corridors. *Bath:* combo or shower only. **Parking:** on-site. **Terms:** 3 day cancellation notice-fee
Large-scale Hotel   imposed. **Amenities:** dual phone lines, voice mail, irons, hair dryers. *Some:* video games, CD players, high-speed Internet (fee), fax. **Dining:** 6:30 am-2:30 & 5-10 pm, Sat 7 am-3 & 5-11 pm, Sun 7-9:30 am, 10-2 & 5-10 pm, cocktails. **Pool(s):** heated indoor. **Leisure Activities:** sauna, whirlpool, men & women's locker room, billiards, jogging, exercise room, basketball. **Guest Services:** sundries, valet laundry, area transportation-Metro & Fair Oaks Mall, within 3 mi. **Business Services:** conference facilities, business center. **Cards:** AX, CB, DC, DS, JC, MC, VI.
SOME UNITS
[icons]

RESIDENCE INN BY MARRIOTT-FAIR LAKES   *Book at aaa.com*   Phone: (703)266-4900   **101**
4/1-12/31   1P: $189-$209   2P: $189-$209
3/1-3/31 & 1/1-2/28   1P: $170-$188   2P: $170-$188
Location: I-66, exit 55 (Fairfax County Pkwy N), just w. 12815 Fair Lakes Pkwy 22033. Fax: 703/266-8600.
Small-scale Hotel   **Facility:** 114 units. 30 one-bedroom standard units with efficiencies. 63 one- and 21 two-bedroom suites, some with efficiencies or kitchens. 3 stories, interior corridors. *Bath:* combo or shower only. **Parking:** on-site. **Terms:** pets ($150 fee). **Amenities:** video games (fee), high-speed Internet, voice mail, irons, hair dryers. **Pool(s):** outdoor. **Leisure Activities:** whirlpool, exercise room, sports court. **Guest Services:** valet and coin laundry. **Business Services:** meeting rooms, fax (fee). **Cards:** AX, CB, DC, DS, JC, MC, VI. *(See color ad p 501)*
SOME UNITS
[icons] FEE

SIERRA SUITES HOTEL-FAIRFAX   *Book at aaa.com*   Phone: (703)359-5000   **98**
All Year [ECP]   1P: $69-$135   2P: $69-$135
Location: I-66, exit 57B, 1.2 mi w on US 50. 3997 Fair Ridge Dr 22033. Fax: 703/359-5524. **Facility:** 94 one-bedroom standard units with efficiencies. 3 stories, interior corridors. *Bath:* combo or shower only. **Parking:**
Small-scale Hotel   on-site. **Amenities:** high-speed Internet (fee), dual phone lines, voice mail, irons, hair dryers. **Pool(s):** heated outdoor. **Leisure Activities:** limited exercise equipment. **Guest Services:** valet and coin laundry. **Business Services:** fax (fee). **Cards:** AX, CB, DC, DS, JC, MC, VI.
SOME UNITS
[icons]

-------- **WHERE TO DINE** --------

ARIGATO SUSHI-FAIRFAX   Lunch: $8-$13   Dinner: $10-$35   Phone: 703/352-9338   **138**
Location: Jct US 50, 29 and SR 236, 0.6 mi sw on US 29. 11199-A Lee Hwy 22030. **Hours:** 11:30 am-2:30 & 5-10 pm, Fri-10:30 pm, Sat noon-3 & 5-10:30 pm, Sun 4:30 pm-9:30 pm. Closed major holidays.
Japanese   **Reservations:** accepted. **Features:** The Japanese restaurant sustains a simple yet stylish atmosphere. In addition to sushi, the menu lists a nice selection of beef, chicken and seafood dishes prepared using teriyaki, tempura or simple grilling. An all-you-can-eat sushi lunch is offered weekdays. Casual dress; beer & wine only.
Parking: on-site. **Cards:** AX, DC, MC, VI.
[icon]

(See map and index starting on p. 404)

ARIGATO SUSHI-FAIRLAKES   **Lunch:** $8-$13   **Dinner:** $10-$35   **Phone:** 703/449-8404   `132`
▼▼▼ **Location:** I-66, exit 55 (Fairfax County Pkwy N), 0.3 mi n, then 0.5 mi w on Fair Lakes Pkwy; in Fair Lake Shopping
Japanese   Center. 13039 Fair Lakes Center 22033. **Hours:** 11:30 am-2:30 & 5-10 pm, Fri-10:30 pm, Sat noon-3 & 5-10:30
pm, Sun 4:30 pm-9:30 pm. Closed major holidays. **Reservations:** accepted. **Features:** In the Fairlakes
shopping complex, the Japanese restaurant sustains a simple yet stylish atmosphere. In addition to sushi,
the menu lists a nice selection of beef, chicken and seafood dishes prepared using teriyaki, tempura or simple grilling. An all-
you-can-eat sushi lunch is offered on weekdays. Casual dress; beer & wine only. **Parking:** on-site. **Cards:** AX, DC, MC, VI.

ARTIES   **Lunch:** $9-$17   **Dinner:** $12-$27   **Phone:** 703/273-7600   `129`
▼▼ ▼▼ **Location:** US 50, at Fairfax Circle Centre. 3260 Old Lee Hwy 22030. **Hours:** 11:30 am-10 pm, Tues-Thurs to 11
American   pm, Fri & Sat-midnight. Closed: 11/24, 12/25. **Features:** A lively and energetic atmosphere is what patrons
find at the popular restaurant, which attracts families and the young professional crowd. Fresh fish, filet
mignon, smoked baby back ribs and jambalaya are among favorite dishes. Casual dress; cocktails.
Parking: on-site. **Cards:** AX, DS, MC, VI.

BAILIWICK INN RESTAURANT   **Lunch:** $8-$38   **Dinner:** $59-$69   **Phone:** 703/691-2266   `144`
▼◆▼◆▼ **Location:** I-66, exit 60, 1.5 mi s; SR 123, just s of jct SR 236; in Bailiwick Inn. 4023 Chain Bridge Rd 22030. **Hours:** 7-
American   9 am, Sat & Sun 8:30-10 am, Wed-Fri also noon & 1 pm seatings, Tues-Fri & Sun also 6:30 pm & 8 pm
seatings, Sat also 6 pm & 8:30 pm seatings. Closed: 1/1; also Mon. **Reservations:** suggested.
Features: Your dining adventure at this restored pre-1812 inn starts with a personal greeting at the front
door, followed by appetizers and drinks in the warmly decorated parlor. Seatings for dinner are scheduled; you and other small
parties are ushered to your tables for a romantic dining experience. Menus change every two weeks and reflect new American
cuisine prepared with a classical French twist. Also, enjoy high tea, including sherries, on Thursday and Sunday afternoons.
Dressy casual; cocktails. **Parking:** on-site. **Cards:** AX, MC, VI. **Country inn**

BEACON STREET BOSTON CAFE   **Lunch:** $6-$15   **Dinner:** $8-$25   **Phone:** 703/803-8110   `125`
▼▼ ▼▼ **Location:** Jct SR 7100 (Fairfax County Pkwy), 0.8 mi w on US 50; in Greenbriar Town Center. 13041 Lee Jackson
American   Memorial Hwy 22033. **Hours:** 11 am-10 pm, Fri & Sat-midnight. Closed: 12/25. **Reservations:** accepted.
Features: Locals love the relaxed dining and Boston-themed, publike setting inside the eatery. The menu is
appropriately varied, and staff members are young, capable and efficient. The salad bar is available during
lunch, and a Sunday buffet brunch lures guests from 11 am to 3 pm. Casual dress; cocktails. **Parking:** on-site. **Cards:** AX, CB,
DC, DS, MC, VI.

BELLISSIMO   **Lunch:** $9-$11   **Dinner:** $13-$25   **Phone:** 703/293-2368   `142`
▼▼▼ **Location:** On SR 236, just e of jct SR 123. 10403 Main St 22030. **Hours:** 11:30 am-2 & 5-10:30 pm, Sat 5 pm-10
Northern   pm. Closed major holidays; also Sun. **Reservations:** suggested. **Features:** In the heart of Fairfax City the
Italian   chef/owner of this intimate Northern Italian restaurant prepares mouth watering dishes, using veal, seafood,
chicken, beef and pasta. Dressy casual; cocktails. **Parking:** no self-parking. **Cards:** AX, DC, MC, VI.

BOMBAY BISTRO   **Lunch:** $8-$14   **Dinner:** $8-$14   **Phone:** 703/359-5810   `130`
▼▼ ▼▼ **Location:** I-66, exit 60, 0.3 mi s on SR 123; just n of jct SR 123 and US 50. 3570 Chain Bridge Rd 22030.
Indian   **Hours:** 11:30 am-2:30 & 5-10 pm, Fri-10:30 pm, Sat noon-3 & 5-10:30 pm, Sun noon-3 & 5-10 pm. Closed:
for lunch 12/25. **Features:** The quaint, little restaurant prepares Indian cuisine in serene surroundings.
Lamb vindaloo is a good choice to wake up the taste buds. Casual dress; cocktails. **Parking:** on-site.
Cards: AX, CB, DC, DS, MC, VI.

BRAVO'S ITALIAN CAFE   **Lunch:** $6-$15   **Dinner:** $8-$26   **Phone:** 703/352-0260   `134`
▼▼ ▼▼ **Location:** I-66, exit 57A, 0.5 mi se on US 50, then 0.5 mi nw of jct US 50, 29 and SR 236; in Fairfax Court Shopping
Italian   Plaza. 11250 James Swart Cr 22030. **Hours:** 11:30 am-10 pm, Sat from noon, Sun from 10:30 am. Closed:
11/24, 12/25. **Reservations:** accepted. **Features:** The atmosphere is casual and comfortable, suitable for
social, family or business meals. The menu features homemade pasta, fresh seafood, wood-fire pizza and
the kitchens creations of chicken, veal and beef dishes. Casual dress; cocktails. **Parking:** on-site. **Cards:** AX, DC, DS, MC, VI.

CANTINA D'ITALIA   **Lunch:** $5-$11   **Dinner:** $8-$23   **Phone:** 703/631-2752   `131`
▼▼ ▼▼ **Location:** I-66, exit 55 (Fairfax County Pkwy N), 0.3 mi n on SR 7100, then 0.5 mi w on Fair Lakes Pkwy; in Fair Lakes
Italian   Shopping Center. 13015 Fair Lakes Shopping Center 22033. **Hours:** 11 am-10 pm, Fri & Sat-11 pm. Closed:
11/24, 12/25. **Reservations:** suggested, weekends. **Features:** Good Italian fare is on the menu at Cantina
D' Italia, from veal to pasta and pizza to seafood. The atmosphere is suitable for any occasion, from family
dining to a business meal. Casual dress; cocktails. **Parking:** on-site. **Cards:** AX, CB, DC, DS, MC, VI.

CHUTZPAH, A REAL NEW YORK DELI   **Lunch:** $7-$15   **Dinner:** $7-$15   **Phone:** 703/385-8883   `127`
▼▼ **Location:** I-66, exit 57B, 0.7 mi w on US 50; in Fairfax Towne Center. 12214 Fairfax Towne Center 22033. **Hours:** 7
Deli/Subs   am-9 pm, Sat from 8 am, Sun 9 am-3 pm. Closed: 11/24, 12/25; also Yom Kippur. **Reservations:** not
Sandwiches   accepted. **Features:** The popular delicatessen fits all the requirements of a traditional New York deli. It
offers freshly prepared corned beef, chopped liver, brisket and salads, just to mention a few items.
Sandwiches are overstuffed, and soups are delicious. Casual dress; beer only. **Parking:** on-site. **Cards:** AX,
DS, MC, VI.

(See map and index starting on p. 404)

THE CONNAUGHT PLACE   **Lunch:** $9-$10   **Dinner:** $9-$18   **Phone:** 703/352-5959   [141]
Location: Just e of SR 123; in Fairfax City. 10425 North St 22030. **Hours:** 11:30 am-2:30 & 5-10 pm, Sat noon-3
& 5-10 pm, Sun noon-3 & 5-9:30 pm. Closed: 7/4, 11/24, 12/25. **Reservations:** suggested. **Features:** A
graceful, subtly elegant dining room awaits diners. The menu lists traditional Indian preparations of chicken,
Indian   lamb and seafood, as well as vegetarian dishes. A lunch buffet is laid out every day. Dressy casual;
cocktails. **Parking:** on-site. **Cards:** AX, DC, DS, MC, VI.

DOLCE VITA   **Lunch:** $6-$7   **Dinner:** $8-$20   **Phone:** 703/385-1530   [135]
Location: I-66, exit 60, 0.7 mi s on SR 123, 0.7 mi w on US 50/29. 10824 Lee Hwy 22030. **Hours:** 11:30 am-2:30 &
5-9:30 pm, Fri-10:30 pm, Sat noon-2:30 & 5-10:30 pm, Sun 5 pm-9:30 pm. Closed major holidays.
Italian   **Features:** The small neighborhood restaurant is popular with locals for its reliably good food. Lining the
menu is a nice selection of pizza cooked in a wood-burning brick oven, pasta selections and veal, chicken
and seafood dishes. Casual dress; beer & wine only. **Parking:** on-site. **Cards:** CB, DC, DS, MC, VI.

THE ESPOSITOS ITALIAN
RESTAURANT   **Lunch:** $5-$10   **Dinner:** $7-$16   **Phone:** 703/385-5912   [128]
Location: On US 50 and 20, 0.7 mi w of Fairfax Circle. 9917 Lee Hwy 22030. **Hours:** 11:30 am-2:30 & 5-9:30 pm,
Fri & Sat-10:30 pm. Closed: 1/1, 11/24, 12/25. **Reservations:** accepted. **Features:** Good food is prepared
in a casual setting that's comfortable for families. Menu choices range from pizza and pasta to veal and
Italian   chicken dishes. Casual dress; beer & wine only. **Parking:** on-site. **Cards:** AX, CB, DC, DS, MC, VI.

JAIPUR ROYAL INDIAN CUISINE   **Lunch:** $8-$18   **Dinner:** $8-$18   **Phone:** 703/766-1111   [126]
Location: I-66, exit 62 (Nutley St), 0.5 mi s on SR 243 (Nutley St), 0.5 mi s on US 29; 0.5 mi n on US 29, jct US 50
from Fairfax Circle; at Circle Towers Apartment/Office Building. 9401 Lee Hwy, Unit 105 22031. **Hours:** 11:30 am-2:30
Indian   & 5:30-10 pm. Closed: for dinner 11/25, for lunch 12/25 & 1/1. **Reservations:** suggested. **Features:** The
dining room adorned in colorful window treatments, wood panel and Indian artwork creates a relaxing dining
atmosphere. The menu offers a large selection of Northern Indian dishes, with a variety of preparations of lamb, chicken,
seafood and vegetarian dishes. Lunch buffet is available daily. Dressy casual; cocktails. **Parking:** on-site. **Cards:** AX, DC, DS,
MC, VI.

THE LAMPLIGHTER RESTAURANT   **Lunch:** $8-$12   **Dinner:** $15-$26   **Phone:** 703/273-9300   [137]
Location: I-66, exit 57A, 0.5 mi se on US 50; 0.8 mi nw of jct US 29; in Fairfax Court Shopping Plaza. 4068
Jermantown Rd 22030. **Hours:** 11:30 am-2:30 & 5-10 pm, Sun 11 am-2:30 & 5-9 pm, Mon 5 pm-9 pm. Closed:
Continental   1/1; also Sun 6/1-8/31. **Reservations:** suggested, weekends. **Features:** This Continental restaurant has a
menu that blends Greek, French, Italian and American selections. The setting is comfortable and slightly
upscale. Piano entertainment is provided every night except Sunday. Dressy casual; cocktails; entertainment. **Parking:** on-site.
Cards: AX, DC, MC, VI.

PAD THAI   **Lunch:** $6-$10   **Dinner:** $7-$13   **Phone:** 703/591-2525   [139]
Location: On US 29; 0.6 mi sw from jct US 50/29 and SR 236. 11199-E Lee Hwy 22030. **Hours:** 11 am-10 pm, Sat
noon-10:30 pm, Sun 4:30 pm-9:30 pm. Closed: 1/1, 11/24, 12/25. **Reservations:** accepted. **Features:** The
Thai   small, storefront restaurant serves traditional dishes in a simple, comfortable dining room. Casual dress;
beer & wine only. **Parking:** on-site. **Cards:** AX, MC, VI.

PARS RESTAURANT   **Lunch:** $8-$15   **Dinner:** $9-$20   **Phone:** 703/273-3508   [136]
Location: I-66, exit 60, 0.7 mi s on SR 123, then 0.6 mi w on US 50/129. 10801 Lee Hwy 22030. **Hours:** 11:30 am-
9:30 pm, Fri & Sat-11 pm, Sun 11 am-9:30 pm. Closed: 11/24. **Reservations:** accepted. **Features:** The
Persian   menu lists a good selection of Persian dishes and kebabs; lamb, beef, chicken and seafood preparations;
and a couple American selections. The adventurous should try the lamb tongue appetizer. Lunch and
Sunday brunch are exclusively buffet. Belly dancers perform on Friday and Saturday. Casual dress; cocktails. **Parking:** on-site.
Cards: AX, DS, MC, VI.

SAIGON CORNER   **Lunch:** $4-$7   **Dinner:** $7-$10   **Phone:** 703/691-1928   [143]
Location: Jct SR 236, just e. 4008 University Dr 22030. **Hours:** 11 am-9 pm. Closed major holidays; also Sun.
Reservations: not accepted. **Features:** In the heart of the city, the casual eatery prepares a nice selection
Vietnamese   of noodle soup dishes, rice dishes and chicken and shrimp meals. Casual dress. **Parking:** no self-parking.
Cards: MC, VI.

SAKOONTRA   **Lunch:** $6-$9   **Dinner:** $7-$12   **Phone:** 703/818-8886   [140]
Location: Just n on SR 608 from US 29; 1.9 mi s on SR 608 from jct US 50; in shopping plaza. 12300-C Price Club
Plaza 22030. **Hours:** 11:30 am-10 pm, Fri & Sat-10:30 pm. Closed major holidays. **Reservations:** accepted.
Thai   **Features:** The shopping plaza restaurant has a colorful, casual atmosphere and serves traditional Thai
dishes. The menu blends a nice selection of curries, vegetarian, beef, chicken and seafood dishes. Casual
dress; cocktails. **Parking:** on-site. **Cards:** AX, DC, MC, VI.

STAR THAI   **Lunch:** $6-$10   **Dinner:** $7-$15   **Phone:** 703/222-5452   [133]
Location: I-66, exit 55 (Fairfax County Pkwy N), 0.3 mi n, then 0.5 mi w on Fair Lakes Pkwy; in Fair Lakes Shopping
Center. 13046 Fair Lakes Shopping Ctr 22033. **Hours:** 11:30 am-3 & 4:30-10 pm, Fri-10:30 pm, Sat noon-10:30
pm, Sun noon-10 pm. Closed: 11/24, 12/25. **Reservations:** accepted. **Features:** The shopping plaza
Thai   restaurant has developed a strong local following for its reliable kitchen and intimate atmosphere. A
simplistic, contemporary design characterizes the dining room. Service is friendly and efficient. Casual
dress; cocktails. **Parking:** on-site. **Cards:** AX, MC, VI.

FALLS CHURCH pop. 10,377 (See map and index starting on p. 404)

——— WHERE TO STAY ———

COMFORT INN ARLINGTON BOULEVARD-DC GATEWAY *Book at aaa.com*
Phone: (703)534-9100 **72**
(AAA) (SAVE)
All Year [CP]   1P: $71-$129   2P: $71-$129   XP: $10   F
Location: 5.5 mi w of Theodore Roosevelt Bridge on US 50, 0.5 mi e of jct SR 7. 6111 Arlington Blvd 22044.
Fax: 703/534-5589. **Facility:** 111 units. 110 one-bedroom standard units. 1 one-bedroom suite. 3 stories,
interior corridors. *Bath:* combo or shower only. **Parking:** on-site. **Amenities:** voice mail, irons, hair dryers.
Small-scale Hotel *Some:* dual phone lines. **Pool(s):** outdoor. **Leisure Activities:** limited exercise equipment. **Guest Services:**
valet laundry, area transportation-Ballston Metro. **Business Services:** meeting rooms, PC, fax (fee).
Cards: AX, CB, DC, DS, MC, VI. *(See color ad p 501)*

SOME UNITS

DOUBLETREE HOTEL AND EXECUTIVE MEETING CENTER AT TYSONS CORNER *Book at aaa.com*
Phone: (703)893-1340 **68**
All Year   1P: $74-$259   2P: $74-$259   XP: $10   F18
Location: I-495, exit 47B, just e on SR 7. 7801 Leesburg Pike 22043. Fax: 703/893-0215. **Facility:** 398 units. 387
Large-scale Hotel one-bedroom standard units. 11 one-bedroom suites. 9-11 stories, interior corridors. *Bath:* combo or shower
only. **Parking:** on-site. **Terms:** cancellation fee imposed. **Amenities:** voice mail, irons, hair dryers. *Some:*
high-speed Internet. **Pool(s):** heated indoor. **Leisure Activities:** saunas, whirlpool, exercise room. **Guest Services:** gift shop,
valet laundry, area transportation. **Business Services:** conference facilities, business center. **Cards:** AX, DC, DS, MC, VI.

SOME UNITS
FEE   FEE

FAIRFAX-MERRIFIELD RESIDENCE INN BY MARRIOTT *Book at aaa.com*
Phone: 703/573-5200 **71**
All Year   1P: $139-$249   2P: $149-$259
Location: I-495, exit 50A, just w to SR 650. 8125 Gatehouse Rd 22042. Fax: 703/573-8100. **Facility:** 159 units.
Small-scale Hotel 80 one-bedroom standard units with efficiencies. 48 one- and 31 two-bedroom suites, some with efficiencies
or kitchens. 4 stories, interior corridors. *Bath:* combo or shower only. **Parking:** on-site. **Terms:** weekly rates
available, pets ($150 fee). **Amenities:** voice mail, irons, hair dryers. **Pool(s):** outdoor. **Leisure Activities:** whirlpool, limited
exercise equipment, sports court. **Guest Services:** valet and coin laundry. **Business Services:** meeting rooms, fax (fee).
Cards: AX, CB, DC, DS, MC, VI. *(See color ad p 501)*

SOME UNITS
FEE

FAIRVIEW PARK MARRIOTT *Book at aaa.com*
Phone: (703)849-9400 **73**
1/1-2/28   1P: $79-$259   2P: $79-$259
9/12-12/31   1P: $79-$249   2P: $79-$249
3/1-9/11   1P: $79-$239   2P: $79-$239
Large-scale Hotel **Location:** I-495, exit 50B, just se of US 50 via Fairview Park Dr S. 3111 Fairview Park Dr 22042. Fax: 703/849-8692.
Facility: 395 units. 390 one-bedroom standard units. 5 one-bedroom suites. 15 stories, interior corridors. *Bath:* combo or
shower only. **Parking:** on-site. **Terms:** check-in 4 pm, package plans. **Amenities:** high-speed Internet (fee), voice mail, irons,
hair dryers. **Pool(s):** heated indoor/outdoor. **Leisure Activities:** saunas, whirlpool, jogging, exercise room. **Guest Services:** gift
shop, complimentary and valet laundry, area transportation. **Business Services:** conference facilities, business center.
Cards: AX, CB, DC, DS, MC, VI. *(See color ad p 501)*

SOME UNITS
FEE

HOMEWOOD SUITES BY HILTON-FALLS CHURCH *Book at aaa.com*
Phone: (703)560-6644 **70**
All Year   1P: $109-$209   2P: $109-$209
Location: I-495, exit 50A, just w to SR 650; 0.4 mi n of SR 650. Located in a commercial area. 8130 Porter Rd 22042.
Large-scale Hotel Fax: 703/560-2121. **Facility:** 107 units. 103 one- & 4 two-bedroom suites, some with efficiencies or
kitchens. 7 stories, interior corridors. *Bath:* combo or shower only. **Parking:** on-site. **Terms:** cancellation fee
imposed, small pets only ($100 fee). **Amenities:** video games (fee), high-speed Internet, dual phone lines, voice mail, irons,
hair dryers. **Pool(s):** heated indoor. **Leisure Activities:** whirlpool, limited exercise equipment. **Guest Services:** sundries,
complimentary evening beverages: Mon-Thurs, valet and coin laundry, area transportation. **Business Services:** meeting rooms,
business center. **Cards:** AX, DC, DS, MC, VI.

SOME UNITS
FEE

TOWNEPLACE SUITES BY MARRIOTT-FALLS CHURCH *Book at aaa.com*
Phone: (703)237-6172 **69**
All Year   1P: $89-$199
Location: I-495, exit 50B, 2.5 mi e on US 50, 0.6 mi n on Annandale Rd, then e. 205 Hillwood Ave 22046.
Small-scale Hotel Fax: 703/237-6173. **Facility:** 127 units. 91 one-bedroom standard units with kitchens. 6 one- and 30 two-
bedroom suites with kitchens. 4 stories, interior corridors. *Bath:* combo or shower only. **Parking:** on-site.
Terms: cancellation fee imposed, [CP] meal plan available, pets ($100 fee). **Amenities:** voice mail, irons, hair dryers. **Pool(s):**
small outdoor. **Leisure Activities:** limited exercise equipment. **Guest Services:** valet and coin laundry. **Business Services:** fax
(fee). **Cards:** AX, DC, DS, MC, VI.

SOME UNITS
FEE

——— WHERE TO DINE ———

2941 RESTAURANT   Lunch: $11-$28   Dinner: $23-$28   Phone: 703/270-1500 **79**
Location: I-495, exit 50B to Fairview Park Dr, 0.3 mi n. 2941 Fairview Park Dr 22042. **Hours:** 11:30 am-2 & 5:30-10
pm, Sat from 5:30 pm, Sun 11 am-2:30 & 5-9 pm. Closed: 1/1, 12/25. **Reservations:** suggested.
American **Features:** The stylish, upscale dining room, with floor to ceiling windows reaching up 30 feet, looks out over
a man-made lake. The chef/owner creates wonderful French and American dishes using the freshiest
ingredients available on the seasonally changing menu. The professional and attentive wait staff will see to your needs while
you relax and enjoy your dining expereince. Semi-formal attire; cocktails. **Parking:** valet. **Cards:** AX, DC, MC, VI.

(See map and index starting on p. 404)

ARGIA'S
Italian
Lunch: $8-$20   **Dinner:** $8-$22   **Phone:** 703/534-1033   [77]
Location: I-66, exit 69, 1.5 mi s. 124 N Washington St 22046. **Hours:** 11:30 am-9:30 pm, Fri-10:30 pm, Sat 5 pm-10:30 pm, Sun-9 pm. Closed: 12/25. **Reservations:** suggested, weekends. **Features:** Family portraits adorn the walls of the family-friendly restaurant. Large portions and knowledgeable service prevail. Casual dress; cocktails. **Parking:** on-site and street. **Cards:** AX, DC, DS, MC, VI.

CELEBRITY DELLY
Deli/Subs
Sandwiches
Lunch: $5-$15   **Dinner:** $5-$15   **Phone:** 703/573-9002   [83]
Location: I-495, exit 50B, 1.3 mi e on US 50; in Loehmann's Plaza Shopping Center. 7263-A Arlington Blvd 22042. **Hours:** 9 am-9 pm, Sun-4 pm. Closed: 12/25. **Reservations:** not accepted. **Features:** This New York style deli, has been a favorite of locals since 1975. Serving over-stuffed sandwiches, salads and breakfast all day. Casual dress. **Parking:** on-site. **Cards:** AX, CB, DC, DS, MC, VI.

DUANGRAT'S
Thai
Lunch: $8-$12   **Dinner:** $10-$28   **Phone:** 703/820-5775   [88]
Location: I-395, exit 5, 2.5 mi w on SR 7; in Bailey's Crossroads area. 5878 Leesburg Pike 22041. **Hours:** 11:30 am-2:30 & 5-10:30 pm, Fri-11 pm, Sat 11 am-11 pm, Sun 11 am-10:30 pm. Closed: 11/24. **Reservations:** suggested, weekends. **Features:** The casually elegant restaurant does a booming business, in part because it serves ample portions of well-seasoned food. The professional, thoughtful service staff doesn't hurt, either. Thai artwork and headdresses decorate the dining room. Dressy casual; cocktails. **Parking:** on-site. **Cards:** AX, CB, DC, DS, MC, VI.

FLAVORS SOUL FOOD
Soul Food
Lunch: $8-$11   **Dinner:** $8-$11   **Phone:** 703/379-4411   [86]
Location: Off SR 244, just n of jct SR 7; at Bailys Crossroads area. 3420 Carlyn Hill Dr 22041. **Hours:** 11:30 am-2:30 & 5:30-9 pm, Sat 2 pm-9 pm, Sun 1 pm-7 pm. Closed major holidays; also Mon, Mothers Day & Fathers Day. **Reservations:** not accepted. **Features:** The restaurant is a favorite stop of those in the mood for soul food. Presentations are simple and the atmosphere modest; it's the food that's the focus. Fried chicken and fish, as well as the meaty ribs, keep people coming back. Casual dress; cocktails. **Parking:** on-site. **Cards:** AX, DC, DS, MC, VI.

HAANDI
Indian
Lunch: $5-$13   **Dinner:** $9-$17   **Phone:** 703/533-3501   [76]
Location: I-66, exit 66A westbound; exit 66 eastbound, 2.5 mi w on SR 7 from jct US 50. 1222 W Broad St 22046. **Hours:** 11:30 am-2:30 & 5-10 pm, Fri & Sat-10:30 pm. Closed: 12/25. **Features:** Soft pastels, cut-glass chandeliers and window boxes with Indian paintings create a comfortable dining atmosphere that complements a varied menu of vegetarian, seafood, chicken and lamb selections. Notable is the south Indian specialty vindaloo, chunks of lamb and potato in a spicy curry sauce. Casual dress; cocktails. **Parking:** on-site. **Cards:** AX, DC, DS, MC, VI.

MARK'S DUCK HOUSE
Chinese
Lunch: $6-$25   **Dinner:** $6-$25   **Phone:** 703/532-2125   [81]
Location: 5.7 mi w of Theodore Roosevelt Bridge on US 50, 0.4 mi e of jct SR 7. 6184-A Arlington Blvd 22044. **Hours:** 10 am-11 pm, Fri & Sat-midnight. **Reservations:** accepted. **Features:** The well-established, Hong Kong-style restaurant has an overwhelming menu, with an extensive selection of seafood, some rare and exotic dishes, and delightful Peking duck. Dim sum is served daily from 10 am to 3 pm. Casual dress; beer & wine only. **Parking:** on-site. **Cards:** MC, VI.

NEISHA THAI CUISINE
Thai
Lunch: $5-$11   **Dinner:** $9-$25   **Phone:** 703/933-3788   [84]
Location: SR 7, jct Glen Carlyn Rd; in Culmore Shopping Center. 6037 Leesburg Pike 22041. **Hours:** 11:30 am-3:30 & 5-10 pm, Fri-11 pm, Sat noon-3:30 & 5-11 pm, Sun noon-3:30 & 5-10 pm. Closed: 11/24; also for lunch 12/25 & 1/1. **Reservations:** accepted. **Features:** The small restaurant has a style all its own. In a contemporary, colorful, cavelike setting, the distinctive atmosphere is inviting. Thai cooking is consistent, as the kitchen uses fresh ingredients and makes its own sauces. Casual dress; cocktails. **Parking:** on-site. **Cards:** AX, DC, DS, JC, MC, VI.

PEKING GOURMET INN
Chinese
Lunch: $7-$10   **Dinner:** $9-$35   **Phone:** 703/671-8088   [85]
Location: SR 7, at jct Glen Carlyn Rd; in Culmore Shopping Center. 6029 Leesburg Pike 22041. **Hours:** 11 am-10:30 pm, Fri & Sat-midnight. Closed: 11/24. **Reservations:** suggested, weekends. **Features:** Decorated with a traditional Oriental flair, the busy family eatery is known for its pan-fried dumplings, tableside-carved Peking duck and Szechuan beef proper, which is "surf fried" until golden brown then sprinkled with toasted sesame seeds. Casual dress; cocktails. **Parking:** on-site. **Cards:** AX, MC, VI.

PISTONE'S ITALIAN INN
Italian
Lunch: $7-$18   **Dinner:** $10-$24   **Phone:** 703/533-1885   [78]
Location: I-395, exit 5, 3 mi e on SR 7, then just n. 6320 Arlington Blvd 22044. **Hours:** 11 am-11 pm, Fri & Sat-11:30 pm, Sun noon-10 pm. Closed major holidays. **Features:** The restaurant has a wonderful family atmosphere, great food on a diverse menu and friendly service. Casual dress; cocktails. **Parking:** on-site. **Cards:** AX, CB, DC, MC, VI.

RAAGA
Indian
Lunch: $8-$13   **Dinner:** $9-$18   **Phone:** 703/998-7000   [89]
Location: I-395, exit 5, 2.5 mi w on SR 7; in Bailey's Crossroads area. 5872 Leesburg Pike 22041. **Hours:** 11:30 am-2:30 & 5-10 pm, Fri-10 pm, Sat noon-3 & 5-10:30 pm, Sun noon-3 & 5-10 pm. Closed: 11/24, 12/25. **Reservations:** suggested. **Features:** Butter yellow walls, Indian artwork and cloth tablecloths set a comfortable dining atmosphere that's suitable for any occasion. Lining the menu is a nice selection of Northern Indian dishes and tandoori cooking. Dressy casual; cocktails. **Parking:** on-site. **Cards:** AX, DC, DS, MC, VI.

(See map and index starting on p. 404)

RABIENG
Thai
Lunch: $7-$9   **Dinner:** $9-$14   **Phone:** 703/671-4222   **87**
Location: I-395, exit 5, 2.5 mi e on SR 7; in Baileys Crossroads area. 5892 Leesburg Pike 22041. **Hours:** 11:30 am-10 pm. Closed: 11/24. **Features:** Excellent reputations are hard to live up to but they do a fine job pleasing and surprising guests with dishes that light up diners' palates. Chicken in a coconut peanut curry sauce with basil, delectable crisp-fried catfish with basil and Japanese eggplant and chili peppers are fragrant with fresh herbs and spices, flavors married so well you may smile. The sticky rice with coconut milk and mango is a special, perfect conclusion to a wonderful meal. Casual and no-nonsense with sumptuous food. Casual dress; cocktails. **Parking:** on-site. **Cards:** AX, DC, DS, MC, VI.

SIR WALTER RALEIGH INN
American
Lunch: $8-$11   **Dinner:** $15-$21   **Phone:** 703/560-6768   **80**
Location: I-495, exit 50A, just w on US 50, just n on Gallows Rd, then just e. 8120 Gatehouse Rd 22042. **Hours:** 11:30 am-2 & 5-9 pm, Fri-10 pm, Sat 5 pm-10 pm, Sun 4 pm-8:30 pm. Closed: 12/25. **Features:** Tasty menu choices include steak, prime rib, chicken and seafood dishes served with the well-stocked salad bar. Colonial Williamsburg decor punctuates the dining room. Portions are large. Of note is the flavorful French onion soup. Casual dress; cocktails. **Parking:** on-site. **Cards:** AX, DC, DS, MC, VI.   🍽❌

SWEETWATER TAVERN
American
Lunch: $8-$20   **Dinner:** $12-$25   **Phone:** 703/645-8100   **82**
Location: I-495, exit 50B, jct US 50 and Gallows Rd. 3066 Gatehouse Plaza 22042. **Hours:** 11 am-11 pm, Fri-midnight, Sat 11:30 am-midnight, Sun 11:30 am-11 pm. Closed: 11/24, 12/25. **Features:** The restaurant/brew pub's Western atmosphere is lively and fun. American fare exhibits Southwestern touches. Beers are brewed on the premises. Casual dress; cocktails. **Parking:** on-site. **Cards:** AX, DS, MC, VI.   ♿🍽❌

TARA THAI
Thai
Lunch: $6-$9   **Dinner:** $9-$14   **Phone:** 703/506-9788   **75**
Location: I-495, exit 47B, 0.9 mi e on SR 7; in Idylwood Plaza. 7501-E Leesburg Pike 22043. **Hours:** 11:30 am-3 & 5-10 pm, Fri-11 pm, Sat noon-3:30 & 5-11 pm, Sun noon-3:30 & 5-10 pm. **Reservations:** suggested. **Features:** The aquatic wall murals and colorful table tops set the tone at this casual neighborhood restaurant. The kitchen will prepare your dish extra spicy if your request it and MSG is not used. Seafood is their specility, but don't overlook the noodles, beef and chicken dishes. Casual dress; cocktails. **Parking:** on-site. **Cards:** AX, DC, DS, MC, VI.   ❌

GREAT FALLS pop. 8,549   (See map and index starting on p. 404)

──────── WHERE TO DINE ────────

DANTE RISTORANTE
Northern Italian
Lunch: $8-$14   **Dinner:** $17-$25   **Phone:** 703/759-3131   **41**
Location: SR 743, 0.5 mi n of jct SR 7; 2 mi s of jct SR 193 and 743. 1148 Walker Rd 22066. **Hours:** 11:30 am-2:30 & 5:30-10:30 pm, Sat from 5:30 pm, Sun 4 pm-9 pm. Closed major holidays. **Reservations:** suggested. **Features:** Fine northern Italian cuisine is prepared in the intimate setting of a Victorian-era building. A typical dining experience might include a prosciutto and honeydew appetizer, then veal shank with a lovely, memorable sauce. Dressy casual; cocktails. **Parking:** on-site. **Cards:** AX, CB, DC, DS, MC, VI.   🍽❌

L'AUBERGE CHEZ FRANCOIS
French
Dinner: $52-$61   **Phone:** 703/759-3800
Location: 2 mi n of SR 193. 332 Springvale Rd 22066. **Hours:** 5:30 pm-9:30 pm, Sun 1:30 pm-8 pm. Closed: 1/1, 7/4, 12/25; also Mon. **Reservations:** required. **Features:** Narrow, rolling roads lead to the charming restaurant, which serves country French cuisine. Alsatian specialties and wonderful classics line the menu. The terrace opens when the weather cooperates. Background music adds to the sophistication, as do knowledgeable, trained staff members who can ably assist with wine and entree selections. Jackets or ties are appreciated. Semi-formal attire; cocktails. **Parking:** on-site. **Cards:** AX, CB, DC, DS, MC, VI.   ♿❌

SERBIAN CROWN RESTAURANT
International
Lunch: $8-$22   **Dinner:** $19-$30   **Phone:** 703/759-4150   **40**
Location: SR 743, 0.5 mi n of jct SR 7; 2 mi s of jct SR 193 and 743. 1141 Walker Rd 22066. **Hours:** 11:30 am-3 & 5:30-10 pm, Sat from 5 pm, Sun 4 pm-9 pm, Mon 5:30 pm-10 pm. Closed major holidays. **Reservations:** suggested. **Features:** In the heart of Great Falls is this fabulous place serving Serbian, Russian and French cuisine. The Russian appetizer affords several types of smoked fish, and Charlotte russe is wonderful. Exotic game dishes, such as preparations of lion or bear, are available seasonally. The vodka menu incorporates a wide selection of imported and flavored varieties. Semi-formal attire; cocktails. **Parking:** on-site. **Cards:** AX, CB, DC, DS, MC, VI.   ❌

HERNDON pop. 21,655   (See map and index starting on p. 404)

──────── WHERE TO STAY ────────

COMFORT INN DULLES INTERNATIONAL AIRPORT   *Book at aaa.com*   **Phone:** (703)437-7555   **53**
Small-scale Hotel
| All Year | 1P: $69-$119 | 2P: $79-$119 | XP: $10 | F17 |

Location: SR 267 (Dulles Toll Rd), exit 12, 1.5 mi n, then left on Baron Cameron Ave. 200 Elden St 20170. Fax: 703/437-7572. **Facility:** 104 one-bedroom standard units. 3 stories, interior corridors. *Bath:* combo or shower only. **Parking:** on-site. **Terms:** package plans. **Amenities:** high-speed Internet, voice mail, irons, hair dryers. **Leisure Activities:** exercise room. **Guest Services:** valet laundry, airport transportation-Washington Dulles International Airport. **Cards:** AX, DC, DS, MC, VI. *(See color ad p 501)*

SOME UNITS
🆂🎚 ➡ 🛗 🐾 DATAPORT 🛏 ▦ /❌ 🖨/

(See map and index starting on p. 404)

COURTYARD BY MARRIOTT/HERNDON-RESTON   *Book at aaa.com*   **Phone:** (703)478-9400   [62]
All Year   1P: $69-$89   2P: $79-$99
Small-scale Hotel   **Location:** SR 228 and 606 (truck route), 1 mi w of Elden St; SR 267 (Dulles Toll Rd), exit 10, 0.8 mi n on Centreville Rd, then 1.3 mi ne. Located in a business park. 533 Herndon Pkwy 20170. Fax: 703/478-3628. **Facility:** 146 one-bedroom standard units. 3 stories, interior corridors. *Bath:* combo or shower only. **Parking:** on-site.
Amenities: high-speed Internet, voice mail, irons, hair dryers. **Pool(s):** heated indoor. **Leisure Activities:** whirlpool, exercise room. **Guest Services:** coin laundry. **Business Services:** conference facilities. **Cards:** AX, DC, DS, MC, VI.
(See color ad p 501)

SOME UNITS
[icons]

DAYS HOTEL AND CONFERENCE CENTER AT DULLES   *Book at aaa.com*   **Phone:** (703)471-6700   [59]
All Year   1P: $89-$179   XP: $10   F17
Location: Jct SR 267 (Dulles Toll Rd), exit 10. 2200 Centreville Rd 20170. Fax: 703/742-8965. **Facility:** 326 one-bedroom standard units, some with whirlpools. 7 stories, interior corridors. *Bath:* combo or shower only. **Parking:** on-site. **Terms:** package plans. **Amenities:** voice mail, irons, hair dryers. **Dining:** 6 am-10:30 pm, Large-scale Hotel   Sat & Sun from 7 am, cocktails. **Pool(s):** indoor. **Leisure Activities:** whirlpool, exercise room. **Guest Services:** gift shop, valet laundry, airport transportation-Washington Dulles International Airport. **Business Services:** conference facilities, business center. **Cards:** AX, DC, DS, MC, VI. **Special Amenities:** free room upgrade and preferred room (each subject to availability with advance reservations).

SOME UNITS
[icons]

EMBASSY SUITES DULLES AIRPORT   *Book at aaa.com*   **Phone:** (703)464-0200   [63]
All Year   1P: $99-$319   2P: $99-$319   XP: $10   F18
Small-scale Hotel   **Location:** SR 267 (Dulles Toll Rd), exit 10, just s. 13341 Woodland Park Rd 20171. Fax: 703/464-4699. **Facility:** 150 one-bedroom standard units. 6 stories, interior corridors. *Bath:* combo or shower only. **Parking:** on-site. **Terms:** package plans. **Amenities:** high-speed Internet, voice mail, irons, hair dryers. **Pool(s):** indoor. **Leisure Activities:** whirlpool, exercise room. **Guest Services:** gift shop, complimentary evening beverages, valet laundry, area transportation. **Business Services:** meeting rooms, business center. **Cards:** AX, CB, DC, DS, JC, MC, VI.

SOME UNITS
[icons]

HAWTHORN SUITES   *Book at aaa.com*   **Phone:** (703)437-5000   [61]
All Year   1P: $99-$185   2P: $99-$185
Small-scale Hotel   **Location:** SR 267 (Dulles Toll Rd), exit 11 (Fairfax County Pkwy). 467 Herndon Pkwy 20170. Fax: 703/464-5808. **Facility:** 104 one-bedroom standard units. 4 stories, interior corridors. **Parking:** on-site. **Terms:** cancellation fee imposed, weekly rates available, package plans, small pets only ($250 fee). **Amenities:** high-speed Internet, voice mail, irons, hair dryers. **Pool(s):** outdoor. **Leisure Activities:** whirlpool, exercise room, sports court. **Guest Services:** gift shop, coin laundry. **Business Services:** meeting rooms. **Cards:** AX, DC, DS, MC, VI.

SOME UNITS
[icons]
FEE

HILTON WASHINGTON DULLES AIRPORT   *Book at aaa.com*   **Phone:** (703)478-2900   [65]
All Year   1P: $67-$307   2P: $67-$307   XP: $10   F18
Location: SR 267 (Dulles Toll Rd), exit 9, 3 mi s on SR 28; in a business park. 13869 Park Center Rd 20171. Fax: 703/834-1996. **Facility:** 294 one-bedroom standard units, some with whirlpools. 5 stories, interior corridors. *Bath:* combo or shower only. **Parking:** on-site. **Terms:** package plans, small pets only. **Dining:** 6 am-2 & 5-11 pm, Sat & Sun from Large-scale Hotel   6:30 am, cocktails. **Pool(s):** outdoor, indoor. **Leisure Activities:** saunas, whirlpool, 2 tennis courts. *Fee:* racquetball courts, racquetball instruction, massage. **Guest Services:** gift shop, valet laundry, airport transportation-Washington Dulles International Airport, area transportation-within 5 mi, tanning facility. **Business Services:** conference facilities, business center. **Cards:** AX, CB, DC, DS, JC, MC, VI.

SOME UNITS
[icons]

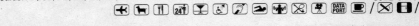

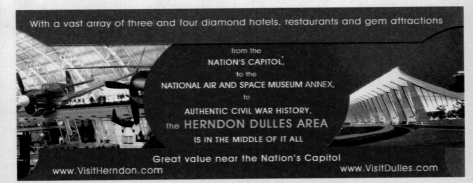

(See map and index starting on p. 404)

HOLIDAY INN EXPRESS - RESTON/HERNDON   *Book at aaa.com*   **Phone:** (703)478-9777   52
All Year   2P: $59-$159
Small-scale Hotel   **Location:** 0.3 mi e on SR 606. 485 Elden St 20170. Fax: 703/471-4624. **Facility:** 116 one-bedroom standard units. 4 stories, interior corridors. *Bath:* combo or shower only. **Parking:** on-site. **Terms:** [ECP] meal plan available, package plans, small pets only ($25 fee). **Amenities:** irons, hair dryers. **Leisure Activities:** exercise room. **Guest Services:** valet laundry, area transportation. **Business Services:** business center. **Cards:** AX, CB, DC, DS, MC, VI. *(See color ad below)*

SOME UNITS

(ASK) (S/D) (✈) (🛏) (¶↑) (&M) (⌗) (☎) (DATA PORT) (🖥) / (✕) (📷) (🖨) /
FEE

HOMEWOOD SUITES BY HILTON   *Book at aaa.com*   **Phone:** 703/793-1700   60
All Year [BP]   1P: $109-$219
Small-scale Hotel   **Location:** SR 267 (Dulles Toll Rd), exit 10, 0.5 mi s on SR 657, then just w. 13460 Sunrise Valley Dr 20171. Fax: 703/793-1899. **Facility:** 109 units. 104 one- and 5 two-bedroom standard units. 7 stories, interior corridors. *Bath:* combo or shower only. **Parking:** on-site. **Terms:** small pets only ($75 deposit, $5 extra charge). **Amenities:** video games, high-speed Internet, voice mail, irons, hair dryers. **Pool(s):** heated indoor. **Leisure Activities:** whirlpool, exercise room. **Guest Services:** complimentary evening beverages: Mon-Thurs, coin laundry, area transportation. **Business Services:** meeting rooms, business center. **Cards:** AX, DC, DS, MC, VI.

SOME UNITS

(ASK) (S/D) (✈) (🛏) (&M) (📠) (☎) (🏊) (VCR) (📷) (DATA PORT) (🖨) (🖥) (🖥) / (✕) /
FEE

HYATT DULLES   *Book at aaa.com*   **Phone:** (703)713-1234   55
(AAA) (SAVE)   All Year   1P: $89-$249   2P: $89-$249
Location: Jct SR 657 and 267 (Dulles Toll Rd), exit 10, 0.5 mi s on Centreville Rd (SR 657), then 1 mi w on Fox Mill Rd. 2300 Dulles Corner Blvd 20171. Fax: 703/713-3410. **Facility:** 317 one-bedroom standard units. 13 stories, interior corridors. *Bath:* combo or shower only. **Parking:** on-site. **Terms:** 3 day cancellation notice-fee imposed. **Amenities:** high-speed Internet, voice mail, irons, hair dryers. *Some:* CD players, fax, safes.
Large-scale Hotel   **Dining:** 6:30 am-2 & 5:30-10:30 pm, cocktails, entertainment. **Pool(s):** indoor. **Leisure Activities:** sauna, whirlpool, sun deck, putting green, billiards, exercise room. **Guest Services:** gift shop, valet laundry. **Business Services:** conference facilities, business center. **Cards:** AX, CB, DC, DS, JC, MC, VI. *(See color ad p 433)*

SOME UNITS

(✈) (¶↑) (☎) (🍴) (&M) (🏊) (☎) (🏊) (✕) (📷) (DATA PORT) (🖥) / (✕) (VCR) (🖨) /

MARRIOTT SUITES WASHINGTON-DULLES   **Phone:** (703)709-0400   58
(AAA) (SAVE)   12/12-2/28   1P: $99-$299   2P: $99-$299
3/1-12/11   1P: $99-$279   2P: $99-$279
Location: Jct SR 657 and 267 (Dulles Toll Rd), exit 10. 13101 Worldgate Dr 20170. Fax: 703/709-0426. **Facility:** 253 one-bedroom standard units. 11 stories, interior corridors. **Parking:** on-site. **Terms:** check-in 4
Large-scale Hotel   pm, cancellation fee imposed, package plans. **Amenities:** high-speed Internet, voice mail, irons, hair dryers. **Dining:** 6:30-10 am, 11:30-2 & 5:30-10 pm, Sat & Sun 7 am-noon & 5:30-10 pm, Sun 7 am-1 & 5:30-10 pm, cocktails. **Pool(s):** outdoor, indoor. **Leisure Activities:** saunas, whirlpool, exercise room. **Guest Services:** gift shop, complimentary laundry, airport transportation-Washington Dulles International Airport. **Business Services:** meeting rooms. **Cards:** AX, CB, DC, DS, JC, MC, VI. *(See color ad p 501)*

SOME UNITS

(S/D) (✈) (¶↑) (🍴) (&M) (🏊) (☎) (✕) (📷) (DATA PORT) (🖥) (🖥) / (✕) (🖨) /

(See map and index starting on p. 404)

RESIDENCE INN BY MARRIOTT-HERNDON/RESTON *Book at aaa.com* Phone: (703)435-0044 **54**

▼▼▼ 4/17-11/19   1P: $229
3/1-4/16 & 11/20-2/28   1P: $209
Small-scale Hotel **Location:** 0.5 mi e on SR 606. 315 Elden St 20170. Fax: 703/437-4007. **Facility:** 168 one-bedroom standard units. 2 stories (no elevator); interior corridors. *Bath:* combo or shower only. **Parking:** on-site. **Terms:** pets ($100 fee, $6 extra charge). **Amenities:** high-speed Internet, voice mail, irons, hair dryers. **Pool(s):** outdoor. **Leisure Activities:** whirlpool, playground, sports court. **Guest Services:** complimentary evening beverages: Mon-Thurs, coin laundry. **Business Services:** meeting rooms. **Cards:** AX, DC, DS, MC, VI.

SOME UNITS

[icons] /✕/

SPRINGHILL SUITES BY MARRIOTT *Book at aaa.com* Phone: (703)435-3100 **57**

▼▼▼ All Year   1P: $69-$189   2P: $69-$189
Location: SR 267 (Dulles Toll Rd), exit 11 (Fairfax County Pkwy). 138 Spring St 20170. Fax: 703/435-5100.
Small-scale Hotel **Facility:** 136 one-bedroom standard units. 4 stories, interior corridors. *Bath:* combo or shower only. **Parking:** on-site. **Terms:** [ECP] meal plan available, package plans. **Amenities:** high-speed Internet, voice mail, irons, hair dryers. **Pool(s):** indoor. **Leisure Activities:** whirlpool, exercise room. **Guest Services:** coin laundry. **Cards:** AX, CB, DC, DS, JC, MC, VI. *(See color ad p 501)*

SOME UNITS

[icons] /✕/

STAYBRIDGE SUITES DULLES AIRPORT *Book at aaa.com* Phone: 703/713-6800 **64**

▼▼▼ All Year   1P: $205-$265   2P: $205-$265
Location: SR 267 (Dulles Toll Rd), exit 10, 0.7 mi s on Centreville Rd (SR 657), then 0.4 mi w. Located in a rural area.
Small-scale Hotel 13700 Coppermine Rd 20171. Fax: 703/713-6824. **Facility:** 112 units. 47 one- and 65 two-bedroom standard units. 2 stories (no elevator); exterior corridors. **Parking:** on-site. **Terms:** package plans, pets ($250 fee). **Amenities:** CD players, high-speed Internet, voice mail, irons, hair dryers. **Pool(s):** outdoor. **Leisure Activities:** whirlpool, exercise room, sports court. **Guest Services:** complimentary evening beverages: Tues-Thurs, complimentary and valet laundry, area transportation. **Business Services:** meeting rooms. **Cards:** AX, DC, DS, JC, MC, VI.

SOME UNITS

[icons] /✕/

WASHINGTON DULLES AIRPORT MARRIOTT *Book at aaa.com* Phone: (703)471-9500 **56**

(AAA) (SAVE) 12/12-2/28   1P: $89-$249   2P: $89-$249
▼▼▼ 3/1-12/11   1P: $89-$239   2P: $89-$239
Location: At Washington Dulles International Airport. 45020 Aviation Dr 20166. Fax: 703/661-8714. **Facility:** 368 one-bedroom standard units. 3 stories, interior corridors. *Bath:* combo or shower only. **Parking:** on-site.
Large-scale Hotel **Terms:** cancellation fee imposed, package plans. **Amenities:** high-speed Internet, voice mail, irons, hair dryers. **Dining:** 2 restaurants, 6 am-2 & 5-midnight, Sat & Sun from 6 am, cocktails. **Pool(s):** outdoor, heated indoor. **Leisure Activities:** whirlpool, 2 lighted tennis courts, softball, picnic pavillion, exercise room, basketball, horseshoes, volleyball. **Guest Services:** gift shop, coin laundry, area transportation-Worldgate Shopping Center. **Business Services:** conference facilities, business center. **Cards:** AX, CB, DC, DS, JC, MC, VI. *(See color ad p 501)*

SOME UNITS

[icons] /✕ ▪ ▪/

——— **WHERE TO DINE** ———

CANTINA D'ITALIA **Lunch:** $6-$10   **Dinner:** $8-$20   Phone: 703/318-7171 **71**
▼▼▼ **Location:** SR 267 (Dulles Toll Rd), exit 12, 1.6 mi n. 150 Elden St 20170. **Hours:** 11 am-10 pm, Fri & Sat-11 pm, Sun noon-10 pm. **Closed:** 1/1, 12/25. **Reservations:** suggested, weekends. **Features:** The knowledgeable,
Italian formally attired wait staff serves classic dishes in an atmosphere enhanced by nice background music. Casual dress; cocktails. **Parking:** on-site. **Cards:** AX, CB, DC, DS, JC, MC, VI. [icons]

THE FLIGHT DECK RESTAURANT **Lunch:** $7-$14   **Dinner:** $7-$18   Phone: 703/834-7202 **72**
▼▼▼ **Location:** SR 657, jct SR 267 (Dulles Toll Rd), exit 10. 2200 Centreville Rd 20170. **Hours:** 7 am-10:30 pm.
Features: Patrons can jet away to the restaurant for friendly service and a wide variety of classic American
American favorites. Casual dress; cocktails. **Parking:** on-site. **Cards:** AX, CB, DC, DS, JC, MC, VI. [icons]

ICE HOUSE CAFE **Lunch:** $6-$12   **Dinner:** $12-$26   Phone: 703/437-4500 **70**
▼▼▼ **Location:** Center. 760 Elden St 20170. **Hours:** 11:30 am-2:20 & 5-10 pm, Fri 11:30 am-2:20 & 4:30-10:30 pm, Sat 4:30 pm-10:30 pm. Closed major holidays; also Sun. **Reservations:** suggested, for dinner.
American **Features:** The focal point of the rustic, lively cafe is an oyster bar that resembles a turn-of-the-20th-century saloon. Signature crab cakes are mixed with scallions and peppers. The chocolate Sheba dessert is decadent. Jazz entertainers perform on weekends. Casual dress; cocktails. **Parking:** on-site. **Cards:** AX, DC, DS, MC, VI.

[icon ✕]

RUSSIA HOUSE **Lunch:** $12-$19   **Dinner:** $15-$28   Phone: 703/787-8880 **68**
▼▼▼ **Location:** Center. 790 Station St 20170. **Hours:** 11:30 am-2:30 & 5:30-10 pm, Sat 5:30 pm-10:30 pm, Sun 5 pm-9 pm, Mon 5:30 pm-10 pm. Closed major holidays. **Reservations:** suggested.
Russian **Features:** Traditional cuisine—such as beef stroganoff, steak Nicolai flambeau and veal Orloff—is well-prepared and flavorful. Colorful Russian artwork decorates the attractive, elegant dining room, where strolling musicians perform on weekends. Nightly specials are well-thought-out. Dressy casual; cocktails. **Parking:** street. **Cards:** AX, DC, MC, VI.

[icon ✕]

ZEFFIRELLI RISTORANTE ITALIANO **Lunch:** $10-$14   **Dinner:** $12-$21   Phone: 703/318-7000 **69**
(AAA) **Location:** Center. 728 Pine St 20170. **Hours:** 11:30 am-2:30 & 5-10 pm. Closed major holidays. **Features:** A friendly atmosphere and knowledgeable staff are two of the restaurant's strong points. Another is the award-
▼▼ winning veal chop entree, a favorite on the hugely varied menu. Casual dress; cocktails. **Parking:** on-site.
Italian **Cards:** AX, CB, DC, DS, MC, VI. [icons]

LEESBURG pop. 28,311

———— WHERE TO STAY ————

BEST WESTERN LEESBURG HOTEL &
CONFERENCE CENTER   *Book at aaa.com*   **Phone: (703)777-9400**

(AAA) (SAVE)   All Year [BP]   1P: $79-$129   2P: $79-$129   XP: $10   F18
▽▽▽▽▽   **Location:** 0.5 mi e on SR 7 business route. 726 E Market St 20176. Fax: 703/777-5537. **Facility:** 99 one-bedroom
standard units. 2 stories, interior corridors. **Parking:** on-site. **Amenities:** high-speed Internet, voice mail,
irons, hair dryers. **Pool(s):** heated outdoor. **Leisure Activities:** exercise room. **Guest Services:** coin
Small-scale Hotel laundry, area transportation-within 10 mi. **Business Services:** meeting rooms, business center. **Cards:** AX,
CB, DC, DS, JC, MC, VI. **Special Amenities:** free full breakfast and free newspaper.

SOME UNITS
[S▾] [✈] [⇆] [✦] [DATA PORT] [🗎] [🍽] [▭] / [✕] /

COMFORT SUITES LEESBURG   *Book at aaa.com*   **Phone: (703)669-1650**

▽▽▽▽▽   4/2-11/1   1P: $109-$125   2P: $114-$129   XP: $5   F18
3/1-4/1 & 11/2-2/28   1P: $99-$119   2P: $104-$124   XP: $5   F18
Small-scale Hotel **Location:** Jct SR 7 and US 15. 80 Prosperity Ave SE 20175. Fax: 703/669-0687. **Facility:** 80 one-bedroom
standard units, some with whirlpools. 4 stories, interior corridors. **Parking:** on-site. **Terms:** check-in 4 pm,
cancellation fee imposed, package plans. **Amenities:** high-speed Internet, voice mail, safes, irons, hair dryers. *Some:* DVD
players, CD players. **Pool(s):** heated indoor. **Leisure Activities:** whirlpool, exercise room. **Guest Services:** coin laundry.
Business Services: meeting rooms, business center. **Cards:** AX, DC, DS, MC, VI.

(ASK) [S▾] [⇆] [✕] [✦] [DATA PORT] [🗎] [🍽] [▭]

HOLIDAY INN AT CARRADOC HALL   *Book at aaa.com*   **Phone: (703)771-9200**

▽▽▽▽▽   All Year   1P: $79-$99   2P: $79-$99
Small-scale Hotel **Location:** 2 mi e on SR 7. 1500 E Market St 20176. Fax: 703/771-1575. **Facility:** 126 one-bedroom standard
units. 2 stories (no elevator), interior corridors. *Bath:* combo or shower only. **Parking:** on-site.
Terms: package plans. **Amenities:** video games, voice mail, irons, hair dryers. **Pool(s):** outdoor. **Leisure
Activities:** exercise room. **Guest Services:** coin laundry. **Business Services:** meeting rooms. **Cards:** AX, CB, DC, DS, JC,
MC, VI.

SOME UNITS
(ASK) [S▾] [✈] [🛏] [¶¶] [Y] [&M] [♿] [⇆] [✦] [DATA PORT] [▭] / [✕] [🗎] [🍽] /
FEE FEE

LANSDOWNE RESORT   *Book at aaa.com*   **Phone: (703)729-8400**

(AAA) (SAVE)   4/3-11/10   1P: $219-$319   2P: $219-$319   XP: $20   F16
11/11-2/28   1P: $209-$309   2P: $209-$309   XP: $20   F16
▽▽▽▽▽   3/1-4/2   1P: $199-$259   2P: $199-$259   XP: $20   F16
Resort   **Location:** SR 7, 3.6 mi w of jct SR 28. 4.4 mi e of jct US 15. 44050 Woodridge Pkwy 20176. Fax: 703/729-4096.
Large-scale Hotel **Facility:** Along the Potomac River, the resort is styled in a Frank Lloyd Wright theme and affords views of
the river and a nearby golf course. 296 one-bedroom standard units. 9 stories, interior corridors. *Bath:*
combo or shower only. **Parking:** on-site and valet. **Terms:** check-in 4 pm, 3 day cancellation notice-fee
imposed, [BP] & [CP] meal plans available, package plans. **Amenities:** high-speed Internet, voice mail, irons, hair dryers.
Some: CD players. **Dining:** Lansdowne Grille, Riverside Hearth, see separate listings. **Pool(s):** outdoor, heated indoor. **Leisure
Activities:** sauna, whirlpools, steamroom, jogging. *Fee:* golf-18 holes, driving range, 3 lighted tennis courts, racquetball court,
children's program weekends, culinary school, bicycles, massage. **Guest Services:** gift shop, valet laundry, airport
transportation (fee)-Washington Dulles International Airport, beauty salon. **Business Services:** conference facilities, business
center. **Cards:** AX, DC, DS, MC, VI. **Special Amenities:** free newspaper.

SOME UNITS
[S▾] [✈] [¶¶] [Y] [🎿] [⇆] [✚] [✕] [✦] [DATA PORT] [▭] / [✕] [VCR] [🗎] /
FEE   FEE

THE NORRIS HOUSE INN   **Phone: 703/777-1806**

▽▽▽   All Year   1P: $85-$115   2P: $110-$150
Bed & Breakfast   **Location:** Just s of SR 7; between Wirt and Liberty sts; center; in historic district. 108 Loudoun St SW 20175-2909.
Fax: 703/771-8051. **Facility:** Smoke free premises. 6 one-bedroom standard units. 3 stories (no elevator),
interior corridors. *Bath:* shared. **Parking:** street. **Terms:** check-in 4 pm, age restrictions may apply, 3 day
cancellation notice, weekly rates available. **Amenities:** hair dryers. **Business Services:** meeting rooms. **Cards:** AX, DS,
MC, VI.

(ASK) [¶¶] [✕] [🅦] [🚭]

———— WHERE TO DINE ————

EIFFEL TOWER CAFE   **Lunch:** $10-$20   **Dinner:** $14-$25   **Phone:** 703/777-5142

▽▽▽   **Location:** Just s of SR 7; between Wirt and Liberty sts; center. 107 Loudoun St SW 20175. **Hours:** 11:30 am-2:30 &
5:30-9:30 pm. Closed major holidays; also Mon & for dinner Sun. **Reservations:** suggested, weekends.
French   **Features:** The Eiffel Tower Cafe combines a wonderful mix of French and American cuisine as well as
offering a soothing, relaxing atmosphere in which to dine. Casual dress; cocktails. **Parking:** street.
Cards: AX, CB, DC, DS, JC, MC, VI.

[Y] [✕]

G G CAFE   **Lunch:** $10-$17   **Dinner:** $10-$24   **Phone:** 703/669-8600

▽▽▽▽   **Location:** Just s of SR 7; between Wirt and Market sts; center. Two W Market St 20176. **Hours:** 11 am-10 pm.
Closed: 12/25. **Reservations:** suggested, weekends. **Features:** The cafe prepares Southern Italian cuisine
South Italian   in a quaint setting with murals. Staff members are friendly. Casual dress; cocktails. **Parking:** street.
Cards: AX, CB, DC, DS, JC, MC, VI.

[Y] [✕]

LANSDOWNE GRILLE   *Menu on aaa.com*   **Lunch:** $9-$16   **Dinner:** $19-$30   **Phone:** 703/729-4073

(AAA)   **Location:** SR 7, 3.6 mi w of jct SR 28; 4.4 mi e of jct US 15; in Lansdowne Resort. 44050 Woodridge Pkwy 20176.
▽▽▽▽   **Hours:** 11 am-10 pm. Closed: Sun. **Reservations:** suggested. **Features:** Overlooking the 18th hole of
Lansdowne Resort's golf course, the comfortably elegant restaurant is best known for its quality steaks. This
American   spot is great for either a quick lunch or leisurely meal. Couples and resort guests are the standard clientele.
Dressy casual; cocktails. **Parking:** on-site. **Cards:** AX, CB, DC, DS, JC, MC, VI.

[Y] [✕]

LIGHTFOOT
▼▼▼▼
American
Lunch: $7-$15   **Dinner:** $8-$33   **Phone:** 703/771-2233
Location: SR 7 business route, just n on US 15; center. 11 N King St 20176. **Hours:** 11:30 am-11 pm, Fri & Sat-midnight, Sun-10 pm. Closed major holidays. **Reservations:** accepted. **Features:** For a satisfying lunch, taste the trademark tomato soup and grilled salmon garnished artfully with fresh vegetables. The chic, colorful bistro is best known for preparing and serving imaginative seasonal fare, including many specialty items. Style and ambience are big assets. Smoking is permitted in the lounge. Casual dress; cocktails. **Parking:** on-site.
Cards: AX, MC, VI.
⊠

RIVERSIDE HEARTH
▼▼▼▼
American
Lunch: $18   **Dinner:** $33   **Phone:** 703/729-4105
Location: SR 7, 3.6 mi w of jct SR 28; 4.4 mi e of jct US 15; in Lansdowne Resort. 44050 Woodbridge Pkwy 20176. **Hours:** 6:30-10:30 am, 11-2 & 6-10 pm. **Reservations:** suggested. **Features:** Patrons can enjoy "upscale" buffet dining, or a la carte selections, for both lunch and dinner. Add in a panoramic view of Sugarloaf and the Potomac countryside for a nice experience in fine dining. Dressy casual; cocktails. **Parking:** on-site.
Cards: AX, CB, DC, DS, JC, MC, VI.
🍷 ⊠

TUSCARORA MILL RESTAURANT
(AAA)
▼▼▼▼
American
Lunch: $7-$25   **Dinner:** $14-$31   **Phone:** 703/771-9300
Location: Just s of SR 7; corner of Loudoun and Harrison sts; center; in Market Station. 203 Harrison St SE 20175. **Hours:** 11:30 am-9:30 pm, Fri & Sat-10 pm, Sun-9 pm. Closed major holidays. **Reservations:** suggested. **Features:** Diversity, atmosphere and polished service await diners at the downtown restaurant. The converted working mill from before the turn of the 20th century has hardwood floors and a deep wooden texture to the walls and tables. Classic American cuisine has wide appeal. Casual dress; cocktails. **Parking:** on-site. **Cards:** AX, DC, DS, MC, VI. **Historic**
⊠

LORTON pop. 17,786

——— WHERE TO STAY ———

COMFORT INN GUNSTON CORNER
▼▼▼▼
Small-scale Hotel
Book at aaa.com
All Year   1P: $89-$139   2P: $89-$139   XP: $10   F16
Phone: (703)643-3100
Location: I-95, exit 163, just w. 8180 Silverbrook Rd 22079. Fax: 703/643-3175. **Facility:** 129 one-bedroom standard units. 4 stories, interior corridors. *Bath:* combo or shower only. **Parking:** on-site. **Terms:** [ECP] meal plan available, package plans, small pets only ($25 extra charge, in smoking units). **Amenities:** video games (fee), voice mail, irons, hair dryers. **Pool(s):** heated outdoor. **Leisure Activities:** limited exercise equipment. *Fee:* game room. **Guest Services:** sundries, valet and coin laundry, area transportation. **Business Services:** meeting rooms, fax (fee).
Cards: AX, DC, DS, JC, MC, VI.
SOME UNITS
(ASK) 🆒 🐾 🍽 🚐 📶 🏊 🎥 📠 ☕ / ⊠ 📱 🖥 /
FEE

——— WHERE TO DINE ———

POLO GRILL
▼▼
American
Lunch: $6-$10   **Dinner:** $10-$20   **Phone:** 703/550-0002
Location: I-95, exit 163, 0.7 mi e on SR 642, just s on Armistead Rd, then just e on Richmond Hwy; in Gunston Plaza Shopping Center. 7784 Gunston Plaza Dr 22079. **Hours:** 11 am-10:30 pm, Fri & Sat-11 pm, Sun 10 am-9:30 pm. Closed major holidays. **Reservations:** accepted. **Features:** The Polo Grill is a popular sports bar and a casual family spot offering tasty pasta, seafood and burgers as well as a handful of items sporting a Cajun/Creole accent. The friendly service won't disappoint and neither will the varied wine list. Casual dress; cocktails. **Parking:** on-site. **Cards:** AX, CB, DC, DS, MC, VI.
🍷 ⊠

MANASSAS pop. 35,135

——— WHERE TO STAY ———

BEST WESTERN BATTLEFIELD INN
(AAA) (SAVE)
▼▼▼▼
Small-scale Hotel
Book at aaa.com
4/2-10/31   1P: $109-$175   2P: $109-$175
3/1-4/1 & 11/1-2/28   1P: $89-$109   2P: $89-$109
Phone: (703)361-8000
Location: I-66, exit 47A westbound; exit 47 eastbound, just s on SR 234, then just w. 10820 Balls Ford Rd 20109. Fax: 703/361-8000. **Facility:** 125 one-bedroom standard units. 2 stories (no elevator), exterior corridors. *Bath:* combo or shower only. **Parking:** on-site. **Terms:** pets ($10 extra charge). **Amenities:** voice mail, safes, irons, hair dryers. **Dining:** 5 pm-11 pm; closed Sun, cocktails. **Pool(s):** outdoor. **Guest Services:** coin laundry. **Business Services:** conference facilities. **Cards:** AX, CB, DC, DS, MC, VI. **Special Amenities:** free continental breakfast and free newspaper.** *(See color ad p 425)*
SOME UNITS
🆒 🐾 🍽 🍷 🎥 🚐 📶 🎥 📠 ☕ / ⊠ 🖥 🖥 /
FEE   FEE   FEE

BEST WESTERN MANASSAS
(AAA) (SAVE)
▼▼
Small-scale Hotel
Book at aaa.com
All Year   1P: $59-$119   2P: $59-$119
Phone: (703)368-7070
Location: I-66, exit 53 (SR 28 S), 5 mi s to Manassas Dr, then just e. 8640 Mathis Ave 20110. Fax: 703/368-7292. **Facility:** 60 one-bedroom standard units, some with whirlpools. 2 stories (no elevator), interior corridors. **Parking:** on-site. **Amenities:** high-speed Internet, voice mail, irons, hair dryers. **Leisure Activities:** sauna, whirlpool, exercise bicycle. **Guest Services:** coin laundry. **Cards:** AX, CB, DC, DS, MC, VI. **Special Amenities:** free expanded continental breakfast and free newspaper. *(See color ad p 424)*
SOME UNITS
🆒 🍽 ⊠ 🎥 📠 🖥 🖥 ☕ / ⊠ /

COMFORT SUITES MANASSAS *Book at aaa.com* Phone: (703)686-1100

	3/1-11/17 [ECP]	1P: $119-$169	2P: $119-$169	XP: $10	F17
	1/1-2/28 [ECP]	1P: $104-$149	2P: $104-$149	XP: $10	F17
	11/18-12/31 [ECP]	1P: $99-$149	2P: $99-$149	XP: $10	F17

Small-scale Hotel **Location:** I-66, exit 47A, just s. 7350 Williamson Blvd 20109. Fax: 703/686-1128. **Facility:** 138 one-bedroom standard units. 4 stories, interior corridors. *Bath:* combo or shower only. **Parking:** on-site. **Terms:** package plans. **Amenities:** high-speed Internet, voice mail, irons, hair dryers. **Pool(s):** heated indoor. **Leisure Activities:** whirlpool, exercise room, game room. **Guest Services:** gift shop, coin laundry. **Business Services:** meeting rooms, business center. **Cards:** AX, CB, DC, DS, JC, MC, VI.

SOME UNITS

COUNTRY INN & SUITES BY CARLSON *Book at aaa.com* Phone: 703/393-9797

| | All Year | 1P: $109-$185 | 2P: $109-$185 |

Small-scale Hotel **Location:** I-66, exit 47B, just n. 10810 Battleview Pkwy 20109. Fax: 703/393-9898. **Facility:** 75 one-bedroom standard units, some with whirlpools. 3 stories, interior corridors. *Bath:* combo or shower only. **Parking:** on-site. **Terms:** cancellation fee imposed. **Amenities:** video games, high-speed Internet, voice mail, irons, hair dryers. **Pool(s):** heated indoor. **Leisure Activities:** whirlpool. **Fee:** game room. **Guest Services:** coin laundry. **Business Services:** meeting rooms. **Cards:** AX, DC, DS, MC, VI. *(See color ad p 847 & below)*

SOME UNITS

COURTYARD BY MARRIOTT
MANASSAS-BATTLEFIELD PARK *Book at aaa.com* Phone: (703)335-1300

| | 3/1-11/15 | 1P: $79-$139 |
| | 11/16-2/28 | 1P: $59-$139 |

Small-scale Hotel **Location:** I-66, exit 47 eastbound; exit 47B westbound, just n on SR 234, then just e. 10701 Battleview Pkwy 20109. Fax: 703/335-9442. **Facility:** 149 one-bedroom standard units. 3 stories, interior corridors. *Bath:* combo or shower only. **Parking:** on-site. **Terms:** 4 night minimum stay - seasonal and/or weekends. **Amenities:** high-speed Internet, voice mail, irons, hair dryers. **Pool(s):** indoor. **Leisure Activities:** whirlpool, exercise room. **Guest Services:** coin laundry. **Business Services:** meeting rooms. **Cards:** AX, DC, DS, JC, MC, VI.

SOME UNITS

DAYS INN

Small-scale Hotel

Phone: (703)368-2800
All Year [ECP] 1P: $69-$119 2P: $75-$119 XP: $6 F18
Location: I-66, exit 47A westbound; exit 47 eastbound, just s on SR 234, then just e. 10653 Balls Ford Rd 20109.
Fax: 703/368-0083. **Facility:** 120 one-bedroom standard units. 2 stories (no elevator), exterior corridors.
Bath: combo or shower only. **Parking:** on-site. **Amenities:** voice mail, hair dryers. *Some:* irons. **Pool(s):** outdoor. **Guest Services:** coin laundry. **Cards:** AX, CB, DC, DS, MC, VI. **Special Amenities: free expanded continental breakfast and free local telephone calls.** *(See ad p 540)*

SOME UNITS

FAIRFIELD INN

Book at aaa.com

Small-scale Hotel

Phone: (703)393-9966
All Year 1P: $109 2P: $109 XP: $10 F18
Location: I-66, exit 47 eastbound; exit 47A westbound, just n on SR 234, then just e. 6950 Nova Way 20109.
Fax: 703/393-9967. **Facility:** 80 one-bedroom standard units. 3 stories, interior corridors. *Bath:* combo or shower only. **Parking:** on-site. **Terms:** cancellation fee imposed, [AP], [BP], [CP] & [ECP] meal plans available. **Amenities:** high-speed Internet, voice mail, irons, hair dryers. **Pool(s):** heated indoor. **Leisure Activities:** whirlpool, exercise room. **Guest Services:** coin laundry. **Cards:** AX, DC, DS, JC, MC, VI. *(See color ad below)*

SOME UNITS

HAMPTON INN

Book at aaa.com

Small-scale Hotel

Phone: (703)369-1100
All Year 1P: $85-$89 2P: $92-$96
Location: I-66, exit 47A westbound; exit 47 eastbound, 0.5 mi s on SR 234. 7295 Williamson Blvd 20109.
Fax: 703/369-4079. **Facility:** 125 one-bedroom standard units. 6 stories, interior corridors. *Bath:* combo or shower only. **Parking:** on-site. **Terms:** [ECP] meal plan available. **Amenities:** high-speed Internet, voice mail, irons, hair dryers. **Pool(s):** outdoor. **Leisure Activities:** exercise room. **Guest Services:** coin laundry. **Business Services:** meeting rooms. **Cards:** AX, DC, DS, MC, VI. **Special Amenities: free continental breakfast and free local telephone calls.**

SOME UNITS

HOLIDAY INN MANASSAS *Book at aaa.com*   Phone: (703)335-0000

AAA SAVE
3/1-12/15 [BP]   1P: $75-$99   2P: $75-$99
12/16-2/28 [BP]   1P: $59-$89   2P: $59-$89
WWWW
Fax: 703/361-8440. **Location:** I-66, exit 47 eastbound; exit 47B westbound, just n on SR 234, then just e. 10800 Vandor Ln 20109.
Small-scale Hotel **Terms:** cancellation fee imposed, package plans, pets ($10 extra charge). **Amenities:** video games, high-speed Internet, voice mail, irons, hair dryers. **Dining:** 6:30 am-10 & 4-10 pm, Sat from 4 pm; closed Sun, cocktails. **Pool(s):** outdoor, heated indoor. **Leisure Activities:** exercise room. **Guest Services:** valet laundry. **Business Services:** meeting rooms. **Cards:** AX, CB, DC, MC, VI. **Special Amenities: free full breakfast and free local telephone calls.** *(See color ad p 541)*

SOME UNITS
(icons) FEE / ✕ ▤ ▣ /

RED ROOF INN-MANASSAS *Book at aaa.com*   Phone: (703)335-9333

WWW
3/30-2/28   1P: $65-$85   2P: $70-$90
3/1-3/29   1P: $60-$85   2P: $65-$90
Motel **Location:** I-66, exit 47 eastbound; exit 47A westbound, just s on SR 234, then just e on Balls Ford Rd. 10610 Automotive Dr 20109. Fax: 703/335-9342. **Facility:** 119 one-bedroom standard units. 3 stories, exterior corridors. *Bath:* combo or shower only. **Parking:** on-site. **Terms:** small pets only. **Amenities:** video games, voice mail. **Cards:** AX, CB, DC, DS, MC, VI.

SOME UNITS
(icons) / ✕ ▤ ▣ /

──── WHERE TO DINE ────

CARMELLO'S & LITTLE PORTUGAL   Lunch: $7-$13   Dinner: $12-$26   Phone: 703/368-5522

AAA
WWW
Northern
Italian
Location: At Center and Battle sts; in Historic Old Town. 9108 Center St 20110. **Hours:** 11:30 am-2:30 & 5-10 pm, Sat from 5 pm, Sun 4 pm-9 pm. Closed major holidays. **Reservations:** suggested. **Features:** Lunch and dinner menus feature pasta, veal, chicken, beef and seafood dishes. Knowledgeable, professional servers circulate in the cozy dining room. Some desserts and breads are prepared on the premises. Angel hair pasta with shrimp is simply wonderful. Casual dress; cocktails. **Parking:** street. **Cards:** AX, DC, DS, MC, VI.

(icons)

CASA CHIMAYO   Lunch: $6-$12   Dinner: $8-$18   Phone: 703/369-2523

WW
Mexican
Location: I-66, exit 47A, just s. 8209 Sudley Rd 20109. **Hours:** 11 am-10 pm, Fri & Sat-11 pm, Sun noon-10 pm. Closed: 12/25. **Features:** The restaurant takes diners back to old Mexico via a wonderful setting. Fresh chips and salsa complement a wide variety of traditional dishes. The staff is exceptionally friendly. Casual dress; cocktails. **Parking:** on-site. **Cards:** AX, CB, DC, DS, JC, MC, VI.

(icons)

CITY SQUARE CAFE   Lunch: $7-$14   Dinner: $9-$22   Phone: 703/369-6022

WWW
Mediterranean
Location: I-66, exit 47, 4.9 mi s on SR 234. 9428 Battle St 20110. **Hours:** 11 am-9 pm, Fri-10 pm, Sat 7:30 am-10 pm, Sun 7:30 am-3 pm. Closed: 12/25. **Features:** City Square Cafe is a family operated restaurant that serves a variety of Inetrnational and American cuisines. A Euro-styles sidewalk cafe when weather permits. Casual dress; cocktails. **Parking:** street. **Cards:** AX, CB, DC, DS, JC, MC, VI.

(icons)

FOSTER'S GRILLE   Lunch: $6-$11   Dinner: $6-$15   Phone: 703/393-2427

W
American
Location: I-66, exit 47A, just s. 7817 Sudley Rd 20109. **Hours:** 11 am-9 pm. Closed: 12/25. **Features:** The eatery is home to the charburger and freshly cut fries. Although the menu may be limited, the staff's enthusiasm is far from it. Casual dress; beer only. **Parking:** on-site.

(icon)

MIKE'S DINER   Lunch: $6-$8   Dinner: $8-$10   Phone: 703/361-5248

W
American
Location: I-66, exit 47A, just s. 8401 Digges Rd 20110. **Hours:** 24 hours. Closed: 12/24. **Features:** Always open, the relaxed diner prepares classic American favorites for all meals. Casual dress; cocktails. **Parking:** on-site. **Cards:** AX, DC, MC, VI.

(icons)

MCLEAN pop. 38,929   (See map and index starting on p. 404)

──── WHERE TO STAY ────

BEST WESTERN TYSONS WESTPARK HOTEL *Book at aaa.com*   Phone: (703)734-2800   47

AAA SAVE
All Year   1P: $79-$159   2P: $79-$159
WWW
Location: I-495, exit 47A, 1.3 mi w on SR 7. 8401 Westpark Dr 22102. Fax: 703/821-8872. **Facility:** 301 units. 287 one-bedroom standard units. 14 one-bedroom suites. 8 stories, interior corridors. *Bath:* combo or shower
Large-scale Hotel only. **Parking:** on-site. **Amenities:** video games (fee), voice mail, irons, hair dryers. *Some:* high-speed Internet (fee). **Dining:** 6:30 am-2 & 5-10 pm, cocktails. **Pool(s):** heated indoor. **Leisure Activities:** sauna, whirlpool, limited exercise equipment. *Fee:* game room. **Guest Services:** gift shop, valet and coin laundry, area transportation-within 5 mi & Metro. **Business Services:** conference facilities, business center. **Cards:** AX, CB, DC, DS, JC, MC, VI. **Special Amenities: early check-in/late check-out and free room upgrade (subject to availability with advance reservations).**

SOME UNITS
(icons) / ✕ ▤ ▣ /

COURTYARD BY MARRIOTT, TYSONS CORNER *Book at aaa.com*   Phone: (703)790-0207   49

WWW
All Year   2P: $69-$259
Small-scale Hotel **Location:** I-495, exit 46A, 0.5 mi s on SR 123, just nw on International Dr, then just se on Greensboro Dr. Located across from two shopping malls. 1960A Chain Bridge Rd 22102. Fax: 703/790-0308. **Facility:** 229 units. 213 one-bedroom standard units, some with whirlpools. 16 one-bedroom suites. 11 stories, interior corridors. *Bath:* combo or shower only. **Parking:** on-site. **Terms:** [AP] meal plan available, package plans. **Amenities:** high-speed Internet, dual phone lines, voice mail, irons, hair dryers. **Pool(s):** heated indoor. **Leisure Activities:** whirlpool, limited exercise equipment. **Guest Services:** sundries, valet and coin laundry, area transportation. **Business Services:** meeting rooms, business center. **Cards:** AX, CB, DC, DS, MC, VI.

SOME UNITS
(icons) / ✕ ▤ ▣ /

Travel the USA.

Active participation required.

Whether you're traveling to the next town or across the country, there's always a Choice hotel nearby that fits your travel plans and budget. Book in advance and as a AAA/CAA member you'll always save at Choice hotels.* Plus, it's easy to earn nights or flights with our reward programs at any of our over 3,000 locations across the U.S. Just visit your local AAA/CAA office, call **800.228.1AAA** or visit choicehotels.com to book your next stay.

CHOICE HOTELS
INTERNATIONAL®

**choicehotels.com
800.228.1AAA**

We'll see you there.

We'll see you there.℠

CHOICE HOTELS INTERNATIONAL

TourBookMark

Lodging Listing Symbols

Member Values
(see pg. 14)

- <AAA> Official Appointment
- [SAVE] Offers minimum 10% discount or lowest public rate
- [ASK] May offer discount
- [S₀] Offers senior discount
- [fyi] Informational listing only

Member Services

- Airport transportation
- Pets allowed
- Restaurant on premises
- Restaurant off premises (walking distance)
- [24] 24-hour room service
- Cocktail lounge
- Child care

Accessibility Features
(see pg. 18)

- [&M] Accessibility features
- Roll-in showers
- Hearing impaired

Leisure Activities

- Full Service Casino
- Pool
- Health Club on premises
- Health Club off premises
- Recreational activities

In-Room Amenities

- Non-smoking rooms
- No air conditioning
- No TV
- No Cable TV
- [VCR] VCR
- Movies
- [DATA PORT] Data port/modem line
- No telephones
- Refrigerator
- Microwave
- Coffee maker

Call property for detailed information about fees & restrictions relating to the lodging listing symbols.

CHOICE HOTELS
INTERNATIONAL.

Your trip across America starts here.

Econo Lodge®

CHOICE HOTELS
INTERNATIONAL.

choicehotels.com
800.228.1AAA

We'll see you there.

(See map and index starting on p. 404)

HILTON MCLEAN TYSONS CORNER   *Book at aaa.com*   Phone: (703)847-5000   **45**
All Year   1P: $69-$317   2P: $69-$317   XP: $25   F18
Large-scale Hotel   **Location:** I-495, exit 46A, 0.3 mi sw on SR 123, just nw on Tysons Blvd, 0.4 mi ne on Galleria/Westpark Dr, then just s. Located in a business park, convenient to shopping malls. 7920 Jones Branch Dr 22102. Fax: 703/761-5100. **Facility:** 458 units. 452 one-bedroom standard units. 6 one-bedroom suites ($299-$1500). 9 stories, interior corridors. *Bath:* combo or shower only. **Parking:** on-site. **Terms:** package plans. **Amenities:** video games (fee), dual phone lines, voice mail, honor bars, irons, hair dryers. *Some:* high-speed Internet (fee). **Pool(s):** heated indoor. **Leisure Activities:** sauna, bicycles, exercise room. **Guest Services:** gift shop, valet laundry, area transportation. **Business Services:** conference facilities, business center. **Cards:** AX, CB, DC, DS, JC, MC, VI. *(See color ad p 426)*   SOME UNITS

HOLIDAY INN TYSONS CORNER   *Book at aaa.com*   Phone: (703)893-2100   **48**
1/1-2/28   1P: $229-$269   2P: $239-$279   XP: $10   F18
3/1-12/31   1P: $219-$259   2P: $229-$269   XP: $10   F18
Large-scale Hotel   **Location:** I-495, exit 46A, 0.5 mi s on SR 123, just nw on International Dr, then just sw on Greensboro Dr. Located in business and shopping area. 1960 Chain Bridge Rd 22102. Fax: 703/893-2062. **Facility:** 316 units. 314 one-bedroom standard units. 2 one-bedroom suites. 3-9 stories, interior corridors. *Bath:* combo or shower only. **Parking:** on-site. **Terms:** cancellation fee imposed, package plans, small pets only ($25 fee). **Amenities:** high-speed Internet, voice mail, irons, hair dryers. *Some:* dual phone lines. **Dining:** 6:30 am-1 am, Sat & Sun from 7 am, cocktails. **Pool(s):** heated indoor. **Leisure Activities:** whirlpool, sun deck, limited exercise equipment. **Guest Services:** gift shop, valet and coin laundry, area transportation-within 1 mi & metro. **Business Services:** conference facilities, business center. **Cards:** AX, DC, DS, MC, VI. *(See color ad below)*   SOME UNITS
FEE   FEE FEE

THE RITZ-CARLTON, TYSONS CORNER   *Book at aaa.com*   Phone: (703)506-4300   **46**
9/11-12/31   1P: $429-$599   XP: $30   F18
3/1-6/25   1P: $430-$570   XP: $30   F18
6/26-9/10   1P: $410-$570   XP: $30   F18
1/1-2/28   1P: $409-$570   XP: $30   F18
Large-scale Hotel   **Location:** I-495, exit 46A, 0.3 mi sw on SR 123, then just nw. Connected to The Galleria at Tysons II. 1700 Tysons Blvd 22102. Fax: 703/506-2694. **Facility:** Warm wood accents, polished marble, quality artwork and abundant fresh flowers lend an air of opulence to this renowned hotel's public areas. 398 units. 365 one-bedroom standard units. 33 one-bedroom suites ($450-$3800), some with whirlpools. 24 stories, interior corridors. *Bath:* combo or shower only. **Parking:** on-site (fee) and valet. **Terms:** [AP], [BP], [CP] & [ECP] meal plans available, package plans, small pets only ($40 extra charge). **Amenities:** video library, CD players, dual phone lines, voice mail, safes, honor bars, irons, hair dryers. *Fee:* video games, high-speed Internet. *Some:* DVD players, fax. **Dining:** 6 am-midnight, Sat from 7 am, Sun from 7 am, cocktails, also, Maestro, see separate listing, entertainment. **Pool(s):** heated indoor. **Leisure Activities:** saunas, whirlpool, steamrooms, jogging, spa. *Fee:* personal trainer. **Guest Services:** sundries, valet laundry, area transportation-within 3 mi & Metro, beauty salon. **Business Services:** conference facilities, business center. **Cards:** AX, DC, DS, JC, MC, VI.   SOME UNITS
FEE

STAYBRIDGE SUITES BY HOLIDAY INN-MCLEAN/TYSONS CORNER   *Book at aaa.com*   Phone: (703)448-5400   **44**
All Year   1P: $170-$230   2P: $170-$230
Small-scale Hotel   **Location:** I-495, exit 46B, 2 mi n on SR 123, then 0.3 mi e on SR 309. Located in a commercial area. 6845 Old Dominion Dr 22101. Fax: 703/506-0001. **Facility:** 143 units. 34 one-bedroom standard units with efficiencies. 86 one- and 23 two-bedroom suites ($170-$230) with efficiencies. 5 stories, interior corridors. *Bath:* combo or shower only. **Parking:** on-site. **Terms:** weekly rates available, package plans, 2% service charge, pets ($75 fee). **Amenities:** video library (fee), high-speed Internet, dual phone lines, voice mail, irons, hair dryers. **Pool(s):** outdoor. **Leisure Activities:** gas grill, limited exercise equipment. **Guest Services:** sundries, complimentary evening beverages: Tues-Thurs, complimentary and valet laundry. **Business Services:** meeting rooms, business center. **Cards:** AX, DC, DS, MC, VI. **Special Amenities:** free expanded continental breakfast and free local telephone calls.   SOME UNITS
FEE

(See map and index starting on p. 404)

─────── WHERE TO DINE ───────

BUSARA

Thai

Lunch: $10-$12   **Dinner:** $20-$26   **Phone:** 703/356-2288   64

Location: I-495, exit 47A, 0.6 mi s on SR 123 to International Dr, then just sw. 8142 Watson St 22102. **Hours:** 11:30 am-3 & 5-10:30 pm, Fri-11 pm, Sat 11:30 am-4 & 5-11 pm, Sun 11:30 am-4 & 5-10:30 pm. Closed: 11/24; also for lunch 12/25 & 1/1. **Reservations:** accepted. **Features:** Diners can enjoy the "zest" of expertly prepared Thai dishes at this restaurant, which offers noodle, vegetarian, seafood and meat dishes. A great start is kanon jeeb—delicious pork and crabmeat dumplings served with soy sauce. Sticky rice and mangoes or Thai custard are mouthwatering endings. Casual dress; cocktails. **Parking:** on-site. **Cards:** AX, DC, DS, MC, VI.

CAFE OGGI

Italian

Lunch: $13-$16   **Dinner:** $28   **Phone:** 703/442-7360   54

Location: Jct SR 123, 0.6 mi e on SR 309. 6671 Old Dominion Dr 22101. **Hours:** 11:30 am-2:30 & 6-10 pm, Sun from 5 pm. Closed major holidays. **Reservations:** suggested. **Features:** The kitchen prepares good Italian cooking. On the menu is a selection of pasta dishes, as well as meats and fish. The comfortable dining room carries out an upscale, contemporary, art-deco look, with mirrored walls and glass blocks. Dressy casual; cocktails. **Parking:** on-site. **Cards:** AX, DC, DS, MC, VI.

CAFE TAJ

Indian

Lunch: $8-$18   **Dinner:** $21   **Phone:** 703/827-0444   50

Location: I-495, exit 46B, 2 mi n on SR 123, then 0.3 mi e on SR 309; in Market Place Complex. 1379 Beverly Rd 22101. **Hours:** 11:30 am-2:30 & 5:30-10 pm, Fri & Sat-10:30 pm. Closed: 7/4, 11/24, 12/25; also for lunch 1/1. **Reservations:** accepted. **Features:** Locals have frequented the small, attractive Indian restaurant for more than a dozen years. The lunch buffet offers a variety of choices. The menu lists tandoori barbecue and kebabs, lamb, chicken, fish and vegetarian selections. Casual dress; cocktails. **Parking:** on-site. **Cards:** AX, DC, DS, MC, VI.

DA DOMENICO

Italian

Lunch: $6-$12   **Dinner:** $12-$28   **Phone:** 703/790-9000   62

Location: I-495, exit 46A, 0.7 mi s on SR 123; jct SR 123 and 7. 1992 Chain Bridge Rd 22102. **Hours:** 11:30 am-11 pm, Sat from 5 pm. Closed major holidays; also Sun. **Reservations:** suggested. **Features:** This family-run restaurant serves homemade pasta, fresh seafood and succulent marinated veal chops. The professional staff makes diners feel welcomed and sees to their needs. Casual dress; cocktails. **Parking:** on-site. **Cards:** AX, CB, DC, DS, MC, VI.

FLEMMING'S PRIME STEAKHOUSE AND WINE BAR   **Dinner:** $19-$35   **Phone:** 703/442-8384   61

Steak House

Location: I-495, exit 46A, 0.5 mi s on SR 123, just nw on International Dr, then se on Greensboro Dr; adjacent to Courtyard by Marriott-Tysons Corner. 1960A Chainbridge Rd 22102. **Hours:** 5 pm-10 pm, Fri & Sat-10:30 pm, Sun 5 pm-9 pm. Closed major holidays. **Reservations:** suggested. **Features:** Just across from the Tysons Corner shopping malls is the contemporary, upscale steakhouse with a casual, friendly air. The main main feature is prime beef, but fresh seafood, chicken and pork are available. What sets this steakhouse apart from others is its selection of more than 100 wines by the glass and its smoke-free dining room and lounge. Dressy casual; cocktails. **Parking:** valet. **Cards:** AX, CB, DC, DS, MC, VI.

THE GREEK TAVERNA

Greek

Lunch: $8-$12   **Dinner:** $14-$18   **Phone:** 703/556-0788   51

Location: I-495, exit 46B, 2 mi n on SR 123, then 0.3 mi e on SR 309; in Market Place Complex. 6828-C Old Dominion Dr 22101. **Hours:** 11:30 am-2:30 & 5-10 pm, Fri-10:30 pm, Sat 5 pm-10:30 pm, Sun 5 pm-9:30 pm. Closed major holidays. **Reservations:** accepted. **Features:** Traditional Greek cooking served in a comfortable setting with slate floor, white washed walls and Greek artwork, recreating a Taverna atmosphere. Casual dress; cocktails. **Parking:** on-site. **Cards:** AX, MC, VI.

J.R.'S STOCKYARDS INN

Steak & Seafood

Lunch: $8-$14   **Dinner:** $17-$25   **Phone:** 703/893-3390   65

Location: I-495, exit 47A, 0.6 mi s on SR 123, to Internatonal Dr, then just sw. 8130 Watson St 22102. **Hours:** 11:30 am-2 & 5-10 pm, Sat from 5 pm, Sun 5-9:30 pm. Closed: 7/4, 11/24, 12/25. **Reservations:** suggested. **Features:** Rustic wood paneling, wagon wheels with lanterns and white tablecloths set the atmosphere in this steakhouse, which has been in operation since 1975. House specialties include aged and marinated beef, prime rib and lobster tail. Dressy casual; cocktails. **Parking:** on-site. **Cards:** AX, DC, DS, MC, VI.

KAZAN RESTAURANT

Turkish

Lunch: $8-$18   **Dinner:** $13-$24   **Phone:** 703/734-1960   52

Location: 0.5 mi e of jct SR 123 and 309; in McLean Shopping Center. 6813 Redmond Dr 22101. **Hours:** 11:30 am-2:30 & 5:30-10 pm, Sat from 5:30 pm. Closed: Sun. **Reservations:** suggested, weekends. **Features:** This Turkish restaurant offers a light, airy dining atmosphere with seasonal sidewalk dining. The house specialty is the lamb kabob; however, do not overlook the rest of the menu with fresh seafood, chicken and vegetarian selections. Doner Kebab, a rare treat, is offered only on Wednesday, Friday and Saturday. Casual dress; cocktails. **Parking:** on-site. **Cards:** AX, DC, MC, VI.

MAESTRO

Italian

Dinner: $74-$104   **Phone:** 703/821-1515   55

Location: I-495, exit 46A, 0.3 mi sw on SR 123, then just nw; in The Ritz-Carlton, Tysons Corner. 1700 Tysons Blvd 22102. **Hours:** 6 pm-10 pm, Sat 5:30 pm-11 pm. Closed: 5/30, 7/4, 9/5; also Sun & Mon. **Reservations:** suggested. **Features:** Chef Fabio Trabocchi orchestrates wonders in the open kitchen, the centerpiece of the elegant dining room. Traditional dishes on his creative menu use similar ingredients to the original recipes, and contemporary recipes reflect his personal style. A seasonal menu showcasing one dominant ingredient also is offered. The sommelier can be helpful in selecting a wine to complement any dish. Dressy casual; cocktails. **Parking:** valet. **Cards:** AX, CB, DC, DS, JC, MC, VI.

(See map and index starting on p. 404)

MAGGIANO'S LITTLE ITALY   Lunch: $7-$18   Dinner: $12-$30   Phone: 703/356-9000   59
▼▼▼▼
Italian
Location: I-495, exit 46A, 0.3 mi sw on SR 123; in The Galleria at Tysons II. 2001 International Dr 22102. **Hours:** 11:15 am-10 pm, Fri & Sat-11 pm, Sun-9 pm. **Closed:** 11/24, 12/25. **Reservations:** suggested. **Features:** This popular restaurant sustains a bustling atmosphere that exudes a pre-World War II feel. On the menu is an extensive selection of Italian dishes, ranging from pasta to veal. A family-style dining option is open to parties of four or more. The weekday lunch menu is offered until 3 pm. Valet parking is complimentary for dinner. Casual dress; cocktails. **Parking:** on-site. **Cards:** AX, CB, DC, DS, MC, VI.

MCCORMICK & SCHMICK'S   Lunch: $7-$14   Dinner: $14-$30   Phone: 703/848-8000   57
▼▼▼▼
Seafood
Location: I-495, exit 47A, 1.3 mi w on SR 7; in Ernst & Young building. 8484 Westpark Dr 22102. **Hours:** 11 am-11 pm, Sun-10 pm. **Reservations:** suggested. **Features:** Guests can choose from some of the freshest seafood from around the world. Dishes are presented in an artistic and creative fashion. Dressy casual; cocktails. **Parking:** on-site (fee). **Cards:** AX, CB, DC, DS, MC, VI.

NEISHA THAI CUISINE   Lunch: $10-$15   Dinner: $18-$25   Phone: 703/883-3588   63
▼▼
Thai
Location: I-495, exit 46A; at Tysons Corner Shopping Mall, outside entrance, opposite Circuit City. 7924 LB Tysons Corner Center 22102. **Hours:** 11 am-10 pm, Fri & Sat-11 pm. **Closed:** 11/24. **Reservations:** suggested. **Features:** Glittering, cavelike walls, a small pond with a footbridge and an open kitchen set the tone for the stylish Thai restaurant. The kitchen prepares many wonderful dishes, such as passion beef with fresh ginger. Casual dress; cocktails. **Parking:** on-site. **Cards:** AX, DC, DS, MC, VI.

PALM RESTAURANT AT TYSONS II   Lunch: $9-$19   Dinner: $17-$38   Phone: 703/917-0200   58
▼▼▼
Steak House
Location: I-495, exit 46A, 0.3 mi sw on SR 123, then just nw. 1750 Tysons Blvd 22102. **Hours:** 11:30 am-11 pm, Sat from 5 pm, Sun 5 pm-10 pm. Closed major holidays. **Reservations:** suggested. **Features:** The atmosphere is fun and lively. Walls are covered with caricatures of loyal locals, national celebrities and politicians. The beef is prime, portions are large, and service is attentive and friendly. Dressy casual; cocktails. **Parking:** valet. **Cards:** AX, CB, DC, DS, MC, VI.

P.F. CHANG'S CHINA BISTRO   Lunch: $7-$16   Dinner: $9-$18   Phone: 703/734-8996   56
▼▼
Chinese
Location: I-495, exit 46A, 0.3 mi sw on SR 123; in The Galleria at Tysons II. 1716-M International Dr 22102. **Hours:** 11 am-10:30 pm, Fri & Sat-11:30 pm. **Closed:** 11/24, 12/25. **Reservations:** not accepted. **Features:** Need a break from shopping? The bustling, contemporary bistro provides hearty portions of well-prepared Chinese food. Choices range from beef and seafood to vegetarian dishes and noodles. The friendly, attentive staff is helpful with the menu. Casual dress; cocktails. **Parking:** on-site. **Cards:** AX, DC, DS, MC, VI.

PULCINELLA THE ITALIAN HOST   Lunch: $7-$15   Dinner: $9-$20   Phone: 703/893-7777   49
▼▼   ▼▼
Regional
Italian
Location: On SR 309, just e of jct SR 123. 6852 Old Dominion Dr 22101. **Hours:** 11:30 am-10:45 pm, Fri-11:15 pm, Sat noon-10:45 pm, Sun noon-9:30 pm. **Closed:** 11/24, 12/25. **Features:** The popular, neighborhood restaurant serves southern Italian dishes—primarily fresh, homemade pasta and pizza made in a wood-burning oven—in ample portions. Dessert consists of traditional offerings. The staff is menu-smart and capable. Casual dress; cocktails. **Parking:** on-site. **Cards:** AX, CB, DC, MC, VI.

TACHIBANA   Lunch: $7-$15   Dinner: $7-$30   Phone: 703/847-1771   53
▼▼   ▼▼
Japanese
Location: Jct SR 123, 0.6 mi e on SR 309, just s. 6715 Lowell Ave 22101. **Hours:** 11:30 am-2 & 5-10 pm, Fri-10:30 pm, Sat noon-2:30 & 5-10:30 pm, Sun 12:30 pm-3 & 5-9:30 pm. Closed major holidays. **Reservations:** not accepted, weekends. **Features:** Looking for the some of the best sushi in the area, then Tachibana is the place. The menu also offers tempura, teriyaki and noodle dishes. Casual dress; cocktails. **Parking:** on-site. **Cards:** AX, DC, DS, MC, VI.

TASTE OF SAIGON   Lunch: $6-$12   Dinner: $8-$15   Phone: 703/790-0700   60
▼▼   ▼▼
Vietnamese
Location: I-495, exit 46A, 0.5 mi s on SR 123, just nw on International Dr, then just sw. 8201 Greensboro Dr 22102. **Hours:** 11 am-10 pm, Fri & Sat-11 pm, Sun-9:30 pm. **Closed:** 11/24, 12/25. **Reservations:** accepted. **Features:** The kitchen has established a consistent reputation for its Vietnamese cooking. The wide-ranging menu lists seafood, chicken, noodle, rice and vegetarian dishes. The setting is contemporary and the staff efficient. Casual dress; cocktails. **Parking:** on-site. **Cards:** AX, DC, DS, MC, VI.

MIDDLEBURG pop. 632

―――――― WHERE TO STAY ――――――

MIDDLEBURG COUNTRY INN   Phone: (540)687-6082
▼▼▼▼
Bed & Breakfast
3/1-12/1 [BP]   1P: $120-$300   2P: $120-$300   XP: $30   F
Location: Just e on US 50. 209 E Washington St 20118 (Box 2065). Fax: 540/687-5603. **Facility:** Canopy beds and fireplaces are featured in every room of this former Episcopal rectory, built sometime between 1820 and 1850. 8 one-bedroom standard units, some with whirlpools. 3 stories (no elevator), interior corridors. **Parking:** on-site. **Terms:** open 3/1-12/1, 7 day cancellation notice-fee imposed. **Amenities:** video library, voice mail, irons, hair dryers. **Leisure Activities:** Fee: horseback riding. **Business Services:** meeting rooms. **Cards:** AX, DS, MC, VI.

SOME UNITS

——— WHERE TO DINE ———

HIDDEN HORSE TAVERN   **Lunch:** $7-$15   **Dinner:** $16-$35   **Phone:** 540/687-3828
American
Location: On US 50; center. 7 W Washington St 20118. **Hours:** 11 am-2:30 & 5:30-9:30 pm, Sun 11 am-2:30 & 5-8 pm, Mon-2:30 pm. Closed: 11/24, 12/25. **Reservations:** suggested, weekends. **Features:** Seafood specialties are served in the pleasant, informal atmosphere of a 200-year-old building. Spicy Mexican potato soup and a tasty crab cake sandwich make a good lunch. Casual to dressy-casual attire is the norm. Patio seating is available. Casual dress; cocktails. **Parking:** on-site. **Cards:** MC, VI. **Historic**

RED FOX INN AND TAVERN   **Lunch:** $8-$13   **Dinner:** $19-$30   **Phone:** 540/687-6301
American
Location: On US 50; center. 2 E Washington St 20117. **Hours:** 11 am-9 pm, Fri & Sat-9:30 pm, Sun-8 pm. **Reservations:** suggested. **Features:** In the center of hunt country, the historic building now houses an attractive bistro that affords good views of the mountains and downtown. Deep wood-grain textures add to the sophisticated feel of the dining room. Uniformed servers are pleasant and offer many suggestions. Peanut soup is among the well-prepared and presented food. Casual dress; cocktails. **Parking:** on-site. **Cards:** AX, DC, DS, MC, VI. **Country Inn**

MOUNT VERNON pop. 28,582

——— WHERE TO DINE ———

THE MOUNT VERNON INN   **Lunch:** $6-$10   **Dinner:** $16-$25   **Phone:** 703/780-0011
American
Location: SR 235 and George Washington Memorial Pkwy; at George Washington's Mount Vernon Estate. George Washington Estate 22121. **Hours:** 11 am-3:30 & 5-9 pm, Sun-4 pm. Closed: 12/25; also for dinner 7/4 & 12/24. **Reservations:** suggested, for dinner. **Features:** Roaring fireplaces, attractive murals and servers dressed in Colonial-era attire set a quaint mood in this charming restaurant. Regional and game specialties, such as venison with peppercorn sauce and peanut-chestnut soup, make up the varied menu. Casual dress; cocktails. **Parking:** on-site. **Cards:** AX, DS, MC, VI.

OCCOQUAN pop. 759

——— WHERE TO DINE ———

SEA SEA & CO   **Lunch:** $7-$11   **Dinner:** $15-$23   **Phone:** 703/690-2004
American
Location: I-95, exit 160B northbound; exit 160 southbound, 0.9 mi n on SR 123; in historic Occoquan. 201 Mill St 22125. **Hours:** 11:30 am-9 pm, Fri-10 pm, Sat 11:30 am-3:30 & 4-10 pm, Sun 11:30 am-3:30 & 4-9 pm. Closed: 11/24, 12/25; also for dinner 7/4. **Features:** The waterfront location, rustic atmosphere and seasonal outdoor seating area make this a popular spot. On the menu is a nice selection of seafood, meats and vegetarian dishes. Casual dress; cocktails. **Parking:** on-site. **Cards:** AX, CB, DC, DS, MC, VI.

RESTON pop. 56,407   (See map and index starting on p. 404)

——— WHERE TO STAY ———

HOMESTEAD STUDIO SUITES HOTEL-RESTON   *Book at aaa.com*   **Phone:** (703)707-9700   **40**
Small-scale Hotel
All Year   1P: $95-$115   2P: $100-$120   XP: $5   F17
Location: SR 267 (Dulles Toll Rd), exit 12 (Reston Pkwy), just n, then just w. 12190 Sunset Hills Rd 20190. Fax: 703/707-9786. **Facility:** 149 one-bedroom standard units. 2 stories (no elevator), exterior corridors. *Bath:* combo or shower only. **Parking:** on-site. **Terms:** weekly rates available, pets ($75 extra charge). **Amenities:** high-speed Internet, voice mail, irons, hair dryers. **Guest Services:** coin laundry. **Cards:** AX, CB, DC, DS, JC, MC, VI.
SOME UNITS

(See map and index starting on p. 404)

HYATT REGENCY RESTON *Book at aaa.com* Phone: (703)709-1234 **39**
AAA SAVE All Year 1P: $109-$319 2P: $109-$319
Location: SR 267 (Dulles Toll Rd), exit 12 (Reston Pkwy); center. 1800 Presidents St 20190. Fax: 703/925-8295.
Facility: This hotel is part of a main-street concept that incorporates numerous shops, restaurants and movie theaters. 518 one-bedroom standard units. 15 stories, interior corridors. *Bath:* combo or shower only.
Large-scale Hotel Parking: on-site and valet. Terms: 3 day cancellation notice-fee imposed. Amenities: CD players, high-speed Internet, voice mail, safes, irons, hair dryers. *Some:* DVD players. Dining: Market Street Bar & Grill,
see separate listing. Pool(s): heated indoor, lap. Leisure Activities: sun deck. *Fee:* saunas, whirlpool, jogging, massage.
Guest Services: gift shop, valet laundry, airport transportation-Washington Dulles International Airport. Business Services:
conference facilities, business center. Cards: AX, CB, DC, DS, JC, MC, VI. *(See color ad p 433)*
SOME UNITS

SHERATON RESTON HOTEL *Book at aaa.com* Phone: (703)620-9000 **41**
All Year 1P: $79-$179 2P: $99-$199 XP: $20 F18
Location: SR 267 (Dulles Toll Rd), exit 12 (Reston Pkwy), just s. 11810 Sunrise Valley Dr 20191. Fax: 703/620-0024.
Facility: 301 one-bedroom standard units. 6 stories, interior corridors. *Bath:* combo or shower only.
Small-scale Hotel Parking: on-site. Terms: cancellation fee imposed. Amenities: video games, high-speed Internet, voice mail, irons, hair dryers. Pool(s): outdoor. Leisure Activities: 2 tennis courts, exercise room, basketball. Guest Services: gift shop, complimentary and valet laundry, area transportation. Business Services: conference facilities, business center.
Cards: AX, DC, DS, MC, VI. *(See ad p 546)*
SOME UNITS

——— **WHERE TO DINE** ———

CLYDE'S OF RESTON Lunch: $6-$11 Dinner: $6-$16 Phone: 703/787-6601 **46**
Location: SR 267 (Dulles Toll Rd), exit 12 (Reston Pkwy); in Reston Town Center. 11905 Market St 20190.
Hours: 11 am-10 pm, Fri & Sat-midnight, Sun 10 am-9 pm. Closed: 12/25. Features: A varied menu of
American sandwiches, salads and full meals is served in the comfortable dining room, which sustains a clubby atmosphere. Parmesan-crusted trout, crab cakes and cannelloni are house specialties at the busy eatery,
which also prepares some lighter fare. Sidewalk seating can be requested seasonally. Casual dress; cocktails. Parking: on-site.
Cards: AX, DC, DS, MC, VI.

MARKET STREET BAR & GRILL Lunch: $8-$16 Dinner: $15-$30 Phone: 703/709-6262 **45**
AAA Location: SR 267 (Dulles Toll Rd), exit 12 (Reston Pkwy); center; in Hyatt Regency Reston. Corner President & Market
sts 20190. Hours: 6:30 am-2:30 & 5:30-10 pm, Fri & Sat-10:30 pm, Sun-9:30 pm. Reservations: suggested.
Features: Seared black sea bass in mango, plantain and Macadamia crust is the house specialty in the
lively, informal grill room. The eclectic menu lines up a nice, varied offering, including house-cured and
American smoked salmon. Live jazz adds to the mood Thursday through Saturday night. Casual dress; cocktails.
Parking: street. Cards: AX, CB, DC, DS, JC, MC, VI.

PAOLO'S RISTORANTE Lunch: $8-$24 Dinner: $8-$24 Phone: 703/318-8920 **44**
Location: SR 267 (Dulles Toll Rd), exit 12 (Reston Pkwy), 0.3 mi n; in Reston Town Center. 11898 Market St 20190.
Hours: 11:30 am-11 pm, Fri & Sat-midnight, Sun-10 pm. Closed: 11/24, 12/25. Features: This busy
Italian restaurant presents a menu of pasta, seafood, veal and pizza. The wood-burning pizza oven and open
kitchen add an informal feel to the setting. The place is fun and energetic and the service staff pleasant and
prompt. Casual dress; cocktails. Parking: on-site. Cards: AX, CB, DC, DS, MC, VI.

ROUND HILL pop. 500

——— **WHERE TO STAY** ———

WEONA VILLA MOTEL Phone: 540/338-7000
AAA SAVE 4/1-12/31 1P: $50 2P: $60 XP: $10 F
Location: 1 mi e on SR 7 business route. 36147 E Loudoun St 20142 (PO Box 141). Facility: 8 one-bedroom
standard units. 1 story, exterior corridors. *Bath:* combo or shower only. Parking: on-site. Terms: open 4/1-
Motel 12/31. Cards: MC, VI.
SOME UNITS

SPRINGFIELD pop. 14,100   (See map and index starting on p. 404)

———— WHERE TO STAY ————

COMFORT INN WASHINGTON DC/SPRINGFIELD   *Book at aaa.com*   Phone: 703/922-9000   **131**

3/15-10/31   1P: $119   2P: $129
3/1-3/14 & 11/1-2/28   1P: $109   2P: $119

Small-scale Hotel   **Location:** I-95, exit 169A, just e on SR 644 E; jct I-395 and 495, 0.8 mi s. Located adjacent to Springfield Mall. 6560 Loisdale Ct 22150. Fax: 703/971-6944. **Facility:** 112 one-bedroom standard units. 5 stories, interior corridors. *Bath:* combo or shower only. **Parking:** on-site. **Amenities:** video games (fee), high-speed Internet, dual phone lines, voice mail, irons, hair dryers. **Guest Services:** complimentary evening beverages: Mon-Thurs, valet and coin laundry, area transportation. **Business Services:** meeting rooms, PC, fax (fee). **Cards:** AX, DC, DS, MC, VI.

SOME UNITS

(ASK) (S&) (🛏) (🍴↺) (🏃) (🅿) (💪) (🐾) (DATA PORT) (🔧) (📺) (💻) / (✕) /

COURTYARD BY MARRIOTT - SPRINGFIELD   *Book at aaa.com*   Phone: (703)924-7200   **127**

All Year   1P: $79-$179   2P: $79-$179   XP: $10   F18

Small-scale Hotel   **Location:** I-95, exit 169A, just e on SR 644 E, then n; jct I-395 and 495, 0.7 mi s. 6710 Commerce St 22150. Fax: 703/924-0505. **Facility:** 191 units. 184 one-bedroom standard units. 7 one-bedroom suites ($119-$209). 4 stories, interior corridors. *Bath:* combo or shower only. **Parking:** on-site. **Amenities:** high-speed Internet, dual phone lines, voice mail, irons, hair dryers. **Pool(s):** heated indoor. **Leisure Activities:** whirlpool, exercise room. **Guest Services:** sundries, valet and coin laundry. **Business Services:** meeting rooms, fax (fee). **Cards:** AX, DC, DS, MC, VI. *(See color ad p 501)*

SOME UNITS

(ASK) (🍴) (&M) (🏃) (🅿) (🏊) (📺) (DATA PORT) (💻) / (✕) (🔧) (📺) /

(See map and index starting on p. 404)

HAMPTON INN WASHINGTON DC/SPRINGFIELD *Book at aaa.com* Phone: (703)924-9444 130

3/15-10/31	1P: $139	2P: $144
3/1-3/14 & 11/1-2/28	1P: $129	2P: $134

Small-scale Hotel **Location:** I-95, exit 169A, just e on SR 644 E; jct I-395 and 495, 0.8 mi s. Located adjacent to Springfield Mall. 6550 Loisdale Ct 22150. Fax: 703/924-0324. **Facility:** 153 one-bedroom standard units. 7 stories, interior corridors. *Bath:* combo or shower only. **Parking:** on-site. **Amenities:** video games (fee), high-speed Internet, dual phone lines, voice mail, irons, hair dryers. **Pool(s):** outdoor. **Guest Services:** valet laundry, area transportation. **Business Services:** fax (fee). **Cards:** AX, DC, DS, MC, VI.

SOME UNITS

HILTON SPRINGFIELD *Book at aaa.com* Phone: (703)971-8900 132

All Year 1P: $89-$199 2P: $89-$199 XP: $10 F

Location: I-95, exit 169A, just e on SR 644 E; jct I-395 and 495, 0.7 mi s. Located adjacent to Springfield Mall. 6550 Loisdale Rd 22150. Fax: 703/971-8527. **Facility:** 244 one-bedroom standard units. 12 stories, interior corridors. *Bath:* combo or shower only. **Parking:** on-site. **Terms:** package plans. **Amenities:** video games Large-scale Hotel (fee), dual phone lines, voice mail, irons, hair dryers. **Dining:** 6 am-2 & 5-10 pm, Sat & Sun from 7 am, cocktails. **Pool(s):** heated indoor. **Leisure Activities:** exercise room. **Guest Services:** gift shop, valet and coin laundry, area transportation-Springfield Metro. **Business Services:** conference facilities, business center. **Cards:** AX, DC, DS, MC, VI. **Special Amenities:** free newspaper and free room upgrade (subject to availability with advance reservations). *(See color ad p 548)*

SOME UNITS

FEE

HOLIDAY INN EXPRESS SPRINGFIELD *Book at aaa.com* Phone: (703)644-5555 128

3/1-6/30 [CP]	1P: $103-$114	2P: $103-$114
9/17-11/16 [CP]	1P: $103-$109	2P: $103-$109
7/1-9/16 [CP]	1P: $95-$103	2P: $95-$103
11/17-2/28 [CP]	1P: $95-$99	2P: $95-$99

Small-scale Hotel **Location:** I-95, exit 169B southbound, just nw of SR 644; exit 169A northbound, just e to Commerce St, 0.5 w, then s; jct I-395 and 495, 0.8 mi s. Located in a commercial and shopping area. 6401 Brandon Ave 22150. Fax: 703/866-4557. **Facility:** 194 one-bedroom standard units. 10 stories, interior corridors. **Parking:** on-site. **Terms:** cancellation fee imposed, package plans. **Amenities:** dual phone lines, voice mail, irons, hair dryers. **Pool(s):** outdoor. **Guest Services:** valet laundry, area transportation. **Business Services:** meeting rooms. **Fee:** PC, fax. **Cards:** AX, CB, DC, DS, JC, MC, VI. *(See color ad p 548)*

SOME UNITS

FEE FEE

RED ROOF INN SPRINGFIELD *Book at aaa.com* Phone: (703)644-5311 129

3/1-6/13	1P: $75-$85	2P: $80-$90	XP: $5	F18
6/14-2/28	1P: $70-$80	2P: $75-$85	XP: $5	F18

Small-scale Hotel **Location:** I-95, exit 169B, just sw of SR 644; jct I-395 and 495, 0.8 mi s. 6868 Springfield Blvd 22150. Fax: 703/644-1077. **Facility:** 190 one-bedroom standard units. 4 stories, interior corridors. *Bath:* combo or shower only. **Parking:** on-site. **Amenities:** video games (fee), voice mail. **Guest Services:** coin laundry. **Business Services:** meeting rooms, fax (fee). **Cards:** AX, CB, DC, DS, MC, VI.

SOME UNITS

TOWNEPLACE SUITES BY MARRIOTT *Book at aaa.com* Phone: (703)569-8060 126

All Year 1P: $149-$199 2P: $149-$199

Location: I-95, exit 169B, just nw of SR 644; jct I-395 and 495, 0.8 mi s. Located in a commercial and shopping area. 6245 Brandon Ave 22150. Fax: 703/569-8061. **Facility:** 148 units. 104 one-bedroom standard units with Small-scale Hotel kitchens. 14 one- and 30 two-bedroom suites with kitchens. 4 stories, interior corridors. *Bath:* combo or shower only. **Parking:** on-site. **Terms:** cancellation fee imposed, pets ($250 fee). **Amenities:** high-speed Internet, voice mail, irons, hair dryers. *Some:* dual phone lines. **Pool(s):** small heated outdoor. **Leisure Activities:** exercise room. **Guest Services:** valet and coin laundry. **Business Services:** meeting rooms, fax (fee). **Cards:** AX, DC, DS, MC, VI.

SOME UNITS

FEE

------- **WHERE TO DINE** -------

MANILA CAFE Lunch: $7-$10 Dinner: $8-$12 Phone: 703/644-5825 162

Location: I-95, exit 169B southbound just w; exit 169A northbound, just w on SR 644; jct of Amherst and Commerce sts; in Commerce Plaza. 7020 Commerce St 22150. **Hours:** 11 am-8 pm, Fri & Sat-9 pm. Closed: 1/1, 11/24, Philippine 12/25. **Reservations:** accepted. **Features:** Located in a busy shopping area, this modest little restaurant offers authentic Philippine cooking. Saturday & Sunday they have an all you can eat buffet. The lunch menu served until 3pm. Casual dress; beer & wine only. **Parking:** on-site. **Cards:** AX, MC, VI.

MIKE'S AMERICAN GRILL Lunch: $8-$18 Dinner: $10-$21 Phone: 703/644-7100 161

Location: I-95, exit 169B southbound; exit 169A northbound, just w on SR 644, then just n on SR 617. 6210 Backlick Rd 22150. **Hours:** 11:30 am-11 pm, Fri & Sat-midnight, Sun-10:30 pm. Closed: 11/24, 12/25. **Features:** The American restaurant has casual yet stylish atmosphere, with brick walls, decorative lighting and numerous private booths. The staff is friendly, energetic and efficient. The menu features certified Angus beef, fresh seafood, pasta and chicken. This restaurant is very popular with the locals. They do not take reservations, but you may call ahead to get on the list. Casual dress; cocktails. **Parking:** on-site. **Cards:** AX, DS, MC, VI.

STERLING   (See map and index starting on p. 404)

──── WHERE TO STAY ────

AMERISUITES (DULLES AIRPORT NORTH/STERLING)   *Book at aaa.com*

Phone: (703)444-3909

All Year   1P: $79-$169   2P: $79-$169   XP: $10   F17
Location: 1.8 mi e on SR 7 from jct SR 28. 21481 Ridgetop Cir 20166. Fax: 703/444-3910. **Facility:** 135 one-bedroom standard units. 6 stories, interior corridors. **Parking:** on-site. **Terms:** package plans, pets ($50 fee). **Amenities:** video games, high-speed Internet, voice mail, irons, hair dryers. **Pool(s):** outdoor. **Leisure Activities:** exercise room. **Guest Services:** coin laundry, area transportation-within 5 mi. **Business Services:** meeting rooms. **Cards:** AX, CB, DC, DS, JC, MC, VI. **Special Amenities:** free expanded continental breakfast and free newspaper. *(See color ad p 423)*

Small-scale Hotel

SOME UNITS

COUNTRY INN & SUITES BY CARLSON   *Book at aaa.com*

Phone: (703)435-2700   **33**

All Year [ECP]   1P: $89-$159   2P: $89-$159   XP: $10   F18
Location: 2 mi n on SR 28, then just s on SR 606. 45620 Falke Plaza 20166. Fax: 703/435-6456. **Facility:** 59 one-bedroom standard units. 3 stories, interior corridors. *Bath:* combo or shower only. **Parking:** on-site. **Terms:** package plans. **Amenities:** high-speed Internet, voice mail, irons, hair dryers. **Leisure Activities:** exercise room. **Guest Services:** coin laundry, airport transportation-Washington Dulles International Airport. **Business Services:** business center. **Cards:** AX, DC, DS, MC, VI. **Special Amenities:** free expanded continental breakfast and free local telephone calls. *(See color ad p 847 & below)*

Small-scale Hotel

SOME UNITS

COURTYARD BY MARRIOTT DULLES TOWN CENTER   *Book at aaa.com*

Phone: (571)434-6400

All Year   1P: $69-$179
Location: 4 mi n on SR 28, then just s on Nokes Rd. 45500 Majestic Dr 20166. Fax: 571/434-6401. **Facility:** 157 one-bedroom standard units, some with whirlpools. 4 stories, interior corridors. *Bath:* combo or shower only. **Parking:** on-site. **Terms:** package plans. **Amenities:** high-speed Internet, voice mail, irons, hair dryers. **Pool(s):** heated indoor. **Leisure Activities:** whirlpool, exercise room. **Guest Services:** coin laundry. **Business Services:** meeting rooms. **Cards:** AX, CB, DC, DS, JC, MC, VI. *(See color ad p 501)*

Small-scale Hotel

SOME UNITS

(See map and index starting on p. 404)

FAIRFIELD INN BY MARRIOTT-DULLES AIRPORT · *Book at aaa.com* · Phone: 703/435-5300 · 34

All Year [ECP] 1P: $69-$159 2P: $69-$159
Location: 1 mi n on SR 28; jct SR 267 (Dulles Toll Rd), exit 9B, just w on CR 606, then just n on Pacific Blvd. 23000 Indian Creek Dr 20166. Fax: 703/435-6699. **Facility:** 106 one-bedroom standard units, some with whirlpools. 3 stories, interior corridors. *Bath:* combo or shower only. **Parking:** on-site. **Terms:** package plans. **Amenities:** high-speed Internet, voice mail, irons, hair dryers. **Pool(s):** heated indoor. **Leisure Activities:** sun deck, exercise room. **Guest Services:** valet laundry, airport transportation-Washington Dulles International Airport, area transportation-within 3 mi. **Business Services:** meeting rooms, business center. **Cards:** AX, CB, DC, DS. **Special Amenities:** free expanded continental breakfast and free local telephone calls.
Small-scale Hotel
(See ad p 550 & color ad p 501)

SOME UNITS

HAMPTON INN-DULLES/CASCADES · *Book at aaa.com* · Phone: (703)450-9595

All Year 2P: $69-$179
Location: SR 28 N, 5 mi to exit 7E; SR 7 to Cascade Pkwy. 46331 McClellan Way 20165 (8401 Connecticut Ave, CHEVY CHASE, MD, 20815). Fax: 703/450-9490. **Facility:** 152 one-bedroom standard units, some with kitchens and/or whirlpools. 6 stories, interior corridors. *Bath:* combo or shower only. **Parking:** on-site. **Terms:** [ECP] meal plan available, package plans, pets ($25 fee). **Amenities:** high-speed Internet, voice mail, irons, hair dryers. **Pool(s):** indoor. **Leisure Activities:** whirlpool, exercise room, sports court. **Guest Services:** gift shop, coin laundry. **Business Services:** meeting rooms, business center. **Cards:** AX, CB, DC, DS, MC, VI.
Small-scale Hotel

SOME UNITS

HAMPTON INN WASHINGTON-DULLES AIRPORT · *Book at aaa.com* · Phone: (703)471-8300 · 32

All Year 2P: $59-$159
Location: SR 267 (Dulles Toll Rd), exit 9B, 1.8 mi n on SR 28, then just ne. 45440 Holiday Dr 20166. Fax: 703/471-8382. **Facility:** 124 one-bedroom standard units. 2 stories (no elevator), exterior corridors. *Bath:* combo or shower only. **Parking:** on-site. **Terms:** [ECP] meal plan available, package plans, small pets only ($10 extra charge). **Amenities:** high-speed Internet, voice mail, irons, hair dryers. **Leisure Activities:** exercise room. **Guest Services:** coin laundry. **Business Services:** meeting rooms, business center. **Cards:** AX, CB, DC, DS, MC, VI.
Small-scale Hotel

SOME UNITS

HOLIDAY INN WASHINGTON DULLES INTERNATIONAL AIRPORT · *Book at aaa.com* · Phone: (703)471-7411 · 30

All Year 2P: $69-$179
Location: SR 267 (Dulles Toll Rd), exit 9B, 1.8 mi n on SR 28. 1000 Sully Rd 20166. Fax: 703/709-0785. **Facility:** 297 one-bedroom standard units, some with whirlpools. 2 stories (no elevator), interior/exterior corridors. *Bath:* combo or shower only. **Parking:** on-site. **Terms:** [AP] meal plan available, package plans, small pets only. **Amenities:** high-speed Internet, voice mail, irons, hair dryers. **Pool(s):** heated indoor. **Leisure Activities:** sauna, whirlpool. *Fee:* game room. **Guest Services:** gift shop, coin laundry. **Business Services:** conference facilities, business center. **Cards:** AX, CB, DC, DS, MC, VI. *(See color ad p 536)*
Small-scale Hotel

SOME UNITS

HOMESTEAD STUDIO SUITES HOTEL-DULLES/STERLING · *Book at aaa.com* · Phone: (703)904-7575 · 35

All Year 1P: $91-$101 2P: $96-$106 XP: $5 · F17
Location: SR 267 (Dulles Toll Rd), exit 9B, 0.8 mi n on SR 28, then just w on SR 606. 45350 Catalina Ct 20166. Fax: 703/904-7629. **Facility:** 134 one-bedroom standard units. 2 stories (no elevator), exterior corridors. *Bath:* combo or shower only. **Parking:** on-site. **Terms:** weekly rates available, pets ($75 extra charge). **Amenities:** voice mail, irons. **Leisure Activities:** basketball, horseshoes, volleyball. **Guest Services:** gift shop, coin laundry. **Cards:** AX, CB, DC, DS, JC, MC, VI.
Small-scale Hotel

SOME UNITS

MICROTEL INN & SUITES DULLES INTERNATIONAL AIRPORT · *Book at aaa.com* · Phone: (703)471-5005 · 36

4/2-11/1 1P: $69-$189 2P: $69-$189
3/1-4/1 1P: $59-$169 2P: $59-$169
11/2-2/28 1P: $59-$129 2P: $59-$129
Location: SR 68, 2 mi n, then just s on SR 606. 45515 Dulles Plaza 20166. Fax: 703/471-5001. **Facility:** 101 one-bedroom standard units. 3 stories, interior corridors. *Bath:* combo or shower only. **Parking:** on-site. **Amenities:** high-speed Internet, voice mail. **Guest Services:** coin laundry. **Cards:** AX, DC, DS, MC, VI.
Small-scale Hotel

SOME UNITS

TOWNEPLACE SUITES BY MARRIOTT AT DULLES AIRPORT · *Book at aaa.com* · Phone: (703)707-2017 · 31

All Year 2P: $69-$179
Location: SR 267 (Dulles Toll Rd), exit 9B, 1.8 mi n on SR 28, then just ne. 22744 Holiday Park Dr 20166. Fax: 703/707-9676. **Facility:** 95 one-bedroom standard units. 3 stories, interior corridors. *Bath:* combo or shower only. **Parking:** on-site. **Terms:** [CP] meal plan available, package plans, pets ($100 fee, $10 extra charge). **Amenities:** video games, high-speed Internet, irons, hair dryers. **Pool(s):** heated outdoor. **Leisure Activities:** exercise room. **Guest Services:** coin laundry. **Cards:** AX, CB, DC, DS, MC, VI.
Small-scale Hotel

SOME UNITS

TOWNEPLACE SUITES BY MARRIOTT STERLING · *Book at aaa.com* · Phone: (703)421-1090

All Year 1P: $59-$199 2P: $59-$199
Location: US 7 to Cascades Pkwy, 0.5 mi n to Palisades Pkwy, just e, then just s. 21123 Whitfield Pl 20165. Fax: 703/421-1091. **Facility:** 95 one-bedroom standard units with kitchens. 3 stories, interior corridors. *Bath:* combo or shower only. **Parking:** on-site. **Terms:** pets ($100 fee, $10 extra charge). **Amenities:** high-speed Internet, voice mail, irons, hair dryers. **Pool(s):** outdoor. **Leisure Activities:** exercise room. **Guest Services:** coin laundry. **Business Services:** business center. **Cards:** AX, DC, DS, MC, VI.
Small-scale Hotel

SOME UNITS

VIENNA pop. 14,453   (See map and index starting on p. 404)

──────── WHERE TO STAY ────────

COMFORT INN TYSONS CORNER   *Book at aaa.com*   Phone: (703)448-8020   **78**
AAA (SAVE)   All Year [CP]   1P: $129-$159   2P: $129-$159   XP: $10   F18
▼▼ ▼▼   **Location:** I-495, exit 47A, 1.8 mi w on SR 7, then just s on Spring Hill Rd; just e of jct SR 267 (Dulles Toll Rd). 1587
Motel   Spring Hill Rd 22182. Fax: 703/448-0343. **Facility:** 250 units. 247 one-bedroom standard units. 3 one-bedroom suites. 3 stories, exterior corridors. **Parking:** on-site. **Terms:** small pets only ($25 fee, $10 extra charge). **Amenities:** voice mail, irons, hair dryers. **Fee:** video games, safes. **Pool(s):** outdoor. **Guest Services:** complimentary evening beverages: Mon-Thurs, valet and coin laundry, airport transportation-Washington Dulles International Airport, area transportation-within 3 mi & Metro. **Business Services:** meeting rooms, business center. **Cards:** AX, CB, DC, DS, JC, MC, VI. **Special Amenities: free continental breakfast and early check-in/late check-out.** *(See color ad p 403)*

SOME UNITS
[S/D] [✈] [🐕] [🍴+] [🏊] [FEE] [🛁+ FEE] [📷] [DATA PORT] [🖥] / [✕] [♿] [📠] /

EMBASSY SUITES HOTEL TYSONS CORNER   *Book at aaa.com*   Phone: (703)883-0707   **79**
▼▼ ▼▼ ▼   All Year [BP]   1P: $109-$399   2P: $119-$409   XP: $10   F
Large-scale Hotel   **Location:** I-495, exit 47A, 1.7 mi w on SR 7; 0.3 mi e of jct SR 267 (Dulles Toll Rd). Located in a commercial and corporate area. 8517 Leesburg Pike 22182. Fax: 703/883-0694. **Facility:** 234 units. 16 one-bedroom standard units. 218 one-bedroom suites ($109-$399). 8 stories, interior corridors. *Bath:* combo or shower only. **Parking:** on-site. **Terms:** 30 day cancellation notice-fee imposed, package plans. **Amenities:** video games (fee), dual phone lines, voice mail, safes, irons, hair dryers. *Some:* high-speed Internet (fee). **Pool(s):** heated indoor. **Leisure Activities:** sauna, whirlpool, exercise room. **Guest Services:** gift shop, complimentary evening beverages, valet and coin laundry, area transportation. **Business Services:** conference facilities, business center. **Cards:** AX, DC, DS, MC, VI.

SOME UNITS
[ASK] [🍴] [📺] [♿] [📷] [🏊] [✕] [📷] [🖥] [🖥] / [✕] [VCR]
FEE

HOMESTEAD STUDIO SUITES HOTEL-TYSONS CORNER   *Book at aaa.com*   Phone: (703)356-6300   **82**
▼▼ ▼▼   All Year   1P: $110-$130   2P: $115-$135   XP: $5   F17
Small-scale Hotel   **Location:** I-495, exit 47A, 0.6 mi w on SR 7, then just s on Gallows Rd. Located in a commercial business/shopping area. 8201 Old Courthouse Rd 22182. Fax: 703/356-6353. **Facility:** 106 one-bedroom standard units with efficiencies. 3 stories, interior corridors. *Bath:* combo or shower only. **Parking:** on-site. **Terms:** weekly rates available, pets ($75 fee, limit 1). **Amenities:** voice mail, irons, hair dryers. **Guest Services:** valet and coin laundry. **Business Services:** meeting rooms, fax (fee). **Cards:** AX, CB, DC, DS, JC, MC, VI.

SOME UNITS
[ASK] [S/D] [🐕] [🍴+] [&M] [♿] [🛁+ FEE] [📷] [DATA PORT] [🖥] [🖥] / [✕] [VCR]
FEE   FEE   FEE

RESIDENCE INN BY MARRIOTT-TYSONS CORNER   *Book at aaa.com*   Phone: (703)893-0120   **77**
▼▼ ▼▼ ▼   All Year   1P: $179-$299   2P: $179-$299   XP: $10   F18
Small-scale Hotel   **Location:** I-495, exit 47A, 1.9 mi w on SR 7, then just s. 8616 Westwood Center Dr 22182. Fax: 703/790-8896. **Facility:** 96 one-bedroom standard units with kitchens. 2 stories (no elevator), exterior corridors. **Parking:** on-site. **Terms:** small pets only ($150 fee, $5 extra charge). **Amenities:** voice mail, irons, hair dryers. **Pool(s):** outdoor. **Leisure Activities:** whirlpool, exercise room, sports court. **Guest Services:** valet and coin laundry. **Business Services:** fax (fee). **Cards:** AX, CB, DC, DS, JC, MC, VI.

SOME UNITS
[ASK] [S/D] [🐕] [🍴+] [🏊] [✕] [📷] [DATA PORT] [🖥] [🖥] [🖥] / [✕]
FEE

RESIDENCE INN BY MARRIOTT TYSONS CORNER-MALL   *Book at aaa.com*   Phone: (703)917-0800   **80**
▼▼ ▼▼ ▼   All Year   1P: $119-$269
Small-scale Hotel   **Location:** I-495, exit 46A, 1.1 mi s on SR 123; 0.3 mi s of jct SR 7 and 123. Located in a commercial business/shopping area. 8400 Old Courthouse Rd 22182. Fax: 703/917-6262. **Facility:** 121 units. 118 one-bedroom suites with efficiencies. 1 one- and 2 two-bedroom suites with kitchens. 6 stories, interior corridors. *Bath:* combo or shower only. **Parking:** on-site. **Terms:** pets ($100 fee). **Amenities:** video games (fee), CD players, high-speed Internet, dual phone lines, voice mail, irons, hair dryers. **Pool(s):** outdoor. **Leisure Activities:** exercise room. **Guest Services:** valet and coin laundry, area transportation. **Business Services:** meeting rooms, fax (fee). **Cards:** AX, CB, DC, DS, JC, MC, VI.

SOME UNITS
[ASK] [S/D] [🐕] [🍴+] [&M] [♿] [📷] [🏊] [📷] [DATA PORT] [🖥] [🖥] [🖥] / [✕] /
FEE

SHERATON PREMIERE AT TYSONS CORNER   *Book at aaa.com*   Phone: (703)448-1234   **76**
▼▼ ▼▼ ▼   3/1-6/30 & 9/6-12/31   1P: $229   2P: $229   XP: $20   F18
7/1-9/5 & 1/1-2/28   1P: $219   2P: $219   XP: $20   F18
Large-scale Hotel   **Location:** SR 7, just e of jct SR 267 (Dulles Toll Rd). Located in a commerical area. 8661 Leesburg Pike 22182. Fax: 703/610-8293. **Facility:** 437 units. 435 one-bedroom standard units. 2 one-bedroom suites with whirlpools. 3-24 stories, interior corridors. *Bath:* combo or shower only. **Parking:** on-site. **Terms:** cancellation fee imposed. **Amenities:** video games (fee), dual phone lines, voice mail, irons, hair dryers. *Some:* high-speed Internet (fee). **Pool(s):** outdoor, heated indoor. **Leisure Activities:** saunas, whirlpool, racquetball courts, exercise room. *Fee:* massage. **Guest Services:** gift shop, valet laundry, area transportation. **Business Services:** conference facilities, business center. **Cards:** AX, DC, DS, MC, VI.

SOME UNITS
[ASK] [🐕] [🍴] [📺] [♿] [📷] [🏊] [✕] [📷] [DATA PORT] [🖥] / [✕] [♿] /

TYSONS CORNER MARRIOTT HOTEL   *Book at aaa.com*   Phone: (703)734-3200   **81**
▼▼ ▼▼ ▼   All Year   1P: $259   2P: $259
Large-scale Hotel   **Location:** I-495, exit 47B, just w on SR 7. Located adjacent to Tysons Corner Shopping Mall. 8028 Leesburg Pike 22182. Fax: 703/734-5763. **Facility:** 390 units. 388 one-bedroom standard units. 2 one-bedroom suites ($299). 15 stories, interior corridors. *Bath:* combo or shower only. **Parking:** on-site. **Terms:** check-in 4 pm. **Amenities:** dual phone lines, voice mail, irons, hair dryers. *Fee:* video games, high-speed Internet. **Pool(s):** heated indoor. **Leisure Activities:** sauna, whirlpool, exercise room. **Guest Services:** gift shop, valet and coin laundry, area transportation. **Business Services:** conference facilities, business center. **Cards:** AX, DC, DS, JC, MC. *(See color ad p 501)*

SOME UNITS
[ASK] [S/D] [🍴] [📺] [♿] [📷] [🏊] [✕] [📷] [DATA PORT] [🖥] / [✕] [♿] /

(See map and index starting on p. 404)

─────── **WHERE TO DINE** ───────

AARATHI   Lunch: $7-$12   Dinner: $7-$12   Phone: 703/938-0100   [101]
▿▿▿ ▿▿▿
　　　　　Location: SR 123, 1.7 mi s of jct SR 7. 409 Maple Ave E 22180. **Hours:** 11:30 am-2:30 & 5:30-10 pm, Fri-10:30
Indian　　pm, Sat noon-3 & 5:30-10:30 pm, Sun noon-3 & 5:30-10 pm. Closed: 11/24, 12/25; also for lunch 1/1.
　　　　　Reservations: accepted. **Features:** The kitchen in the little shopping plaza restaurant has a consistent
tasteful Indian artwork decorates the dining room. Casual dress; cocktails. **Parking:** on-site. **Cards:** AX, DC, DS, MC, VI.   ✕
reputation for preparing good Indian dishes. The lunch buffet is a big draw and a good value. Colorful,

AMMA VEGETARIAN KITCHEN   Lunch: $4-$5   Dinner: $4-$5   Phone: 703/938-5328   [103]
▿▿▿
　　　　　Location: SR 123, 1.8 mi s of jct SR 7. 344-A Maple Ave E 22180. **Hours:** 11:30 am-2:30 & 5:30-9:30 pm, Sat &
Vegetarian　Sun 11:30 am-10 pm. Closed: 12/25. **Reservations:** not accepted. **Features:** A modest little restaurant
　　　　　offering Indian vegetarian selections. It's self-service, it's simple but the food is good. Casual dress.
　　　　　Parking: on-site. **Cards:** AX, DC, DS, MC, VI.   ✕

BISTRO 123   Lunch: $9-$16   Dinner: $13-$22   Phone: 703/938-4379   [104]
ⒶⒶⒶ
　　　　　Location: I-495, exit 47A, 1 mi w on SR 7, then 2 mi s on SR 123. 246 Maple Ave E 22180. **Hours:** 11:30 am-2 &
▿▿▿ ▿▿▿ ▿▿▿　5:30-9 pm, Fri & Sat-10 pm, Mon 5:30 pm-9 pm. Closed: 1/1, 9/5; also Sun. **Reservations:** suggested.
French　　**Features:** Chef-owned and operated, the restaurant lets patrons sample French cooking prepared with flair.
　　　　　Dressy casual; cocktails. **Parking:** on-site. **Cards:** AX, MC, VI.   ✕

BOMBAY TANDOOR   Lunch: $9-$10   Dinner: $9-$17   Phone: 703/734-2202   [92]
▿▿▿ ▿▿▿
　　　　　Location: 0.3 mi s of jct SR 7 and 123; in Westwood 1 Complex. 8603 Westwood Center Dr 22182. **Hours:** 11:30 am-
　　　　　2:30 & 5:30-10 pm, Sat & Sun noon-3 & 5:30-10 pm. Closed: 11/24. **Reservations:** accepted.
Indian　　**Features:** Lamb Chops Masala is one of the chef's recommendations, have it mild or spicy. The kitchen
cocktails. **Parking:** on-site. **Cards:** AX, CB, DC, DS, MC, VI.   ✕
prepares a wide selection of authentic Indian recipes from vegetarian to lamb dishes. Casual dress;

CAFE RENAISSANCE   Lunch: $11-$19   Dinner: $13-$24   Phone: 703/938-3311   [105]
ⒶⒶⒶ
　　　　　Location: SR 123, 2 mi s of jct SR 7; in Glyndon Plaza. 163 Glyndon St 22180. **Hours:** 11:30 am-2:30 & 5:30-10
▿▿▿ ▿▿▿ ▿▿▿　pm, Fri-11 pm, Sat 5:30 pm-11 pm, Sun 5 pm-9 pm. Closed: 1/1. **Reservations:** suggested.
　　　　　Features: Tucked away to the side in this shopping plaza is a delightful little dining room serving both
Continental　French and Italian food. The setting is casual yet has a formality to it with white table linen, shaded candles,
　　　　　flowers at each table and large oil paintings adorning the walls. The staff is professional and friendly. The
　　　　　kitchen is consistent and has pleased locals for over 10 years. Dressy casual; cocktails. **Parking:** on-site.
Cards: AX, DC, DS, MC, VI.   ✕

CLYDE'S OF TYSONS CORNER   Lunch: $7-$15   Dinner: $10-$23   Phone: 703/734-1901   [93]
▿▿▿ ▿▿▿
　　　　　Location: SR 7, just w of SR 123. 8332 Leesburg Pike 22182. **Hours:** 11 am-11:30 pm, Wed-Sat to midnight, Sun
　　　　　10 am-11:30 pm. Closed: 7/4, 12/25. **Reservations:** suggested. **Features:** This casual restaurant is a
American　popular gathering spot for trendy professionals. Sandwiches, pizza, pasta, steak and seafood are among
　　　　　choices that make up the often-changing menu. Service is efficient and professional. Casual dress;
cocktails. **Parking:** on-site and valet. **Cards:** AX, CB, DC, DS, MC, VI.   ⵣ ✕

COLVIN RUN TAVERN   Lunch: $12-$18   Dinner: $22-$39   Phone: 703/356-9500   [99]
ⒶⒶⒶ
　　　　　Location: I-495, exit 47A, 0.4 mi w on SR 7; opposite Tysons Corner Shopping Mall; in Fairfax Square. 8045 Leesburg
▿▿▿ ▿▿▿ ▿▿▿　Pike 22182. **Hours:** 11:30 am-2:30 & 5:30-10 pm, Sat 5:30 pm-10:30 pm, Sun 5 pm-9 pm. Closed major
　　　　　holidays. **Reservations:** suggested. **Features:** Expertly prepared modern American cuisine awaits diners at
American　the stylish restaurant. Among the chef's signature dishes are whole wood-roasted bass and the carving cart,
　　　　　a roast rack of pork with Virginia ham spoon bread. Dressy casual; cocktails. **Parking:** valet. **Cards:** AX,
　　　　　DC, DS, MC, VI.   ⒼⓂ ⵣ ✕

HUNAN LION   Lunch: $5-$8   Dinner: $8-$25   Phone: 703/734-9828   [95]
▿▿▿ ▿▿▿ ▿▿▿
　　　　　Location: I-495, exit 46A on SR 123, 0.3 mi s of jct SR 7. 2070 Chain Bridge Rd 22182. **Hours:** 11:30 am-10:30 pm,
　　　　　Fri & Sat-11 pm. Closed: 11/24; also for lunch 12/25 & 1/1. **Reservations:** suggested. **Features:** Shoppers
Chinese　　ready to take a break from trolling the nearby malls often stop in for Hunan specialties that include General
　　　　　Tso's chicken, orange beef and Peking duck. Lunch service continues until 4 pm but is not offered on
Sunday. Casual dress; cocktails. **Parking:** on-site. **Cards:** AX, CB, DC, DS, MC, VI.   ✕

KONAMI   Lunch: $8-$15   Dinner: $12-$20   Phone: 703/821-3400   [96]
▿▿▿ ▿▿▿
　　　　　Location: I-495, exit 47A, 0.8 mi w on SR 7. 8221 Leesburg Pike 22182. **Hours:** 11:30 am-2:30 & 5-10:30 pm, Sat
　　　　　& Sun noon-3 pm. **Reservations:** accepted. **Features:** The local favorite has an intimate interior and
Japanese　delicious Japanese fare that leave diners full but wanting more. Casual dress; cocktails. **Parking:** on-site.
　　　　　Cards: AX, DS, MC, VI.   ⒼⓂ ✕

LA PROVENCE RESTAURANT   Lunch: $10-$14   Dinner: $19-$26   Phone: 703/242-9110   [106]
▿▿▿ ▿▿▿ ▿▿▿
　　　　　Location: Jct SR 243, 0.4 mi ne on SR 123; in Vienna Shopping Center. 144 W Maple Ave 22180. **Hours:** 11:30 am-
　　　　　2:30 & 5:30-9:30 pm. Closed major holidays; also Sun. **Reservations:** suggested, weekends.
French　　**Features:** This is small French restaurant in a neighborhood shopping plaza, yet the kitchen offers very
　　　　　well-prepared Southern French cooking. Chef specialties lean toward seafood, with a popular salmon dish
and monkfish. Additional selections are available. Dressy casual; cocktails. **Parking:** on-site. **Cards:** AX, DC, MC, VI.   ✕

(See map and index starting on p. 404)

LE CANARD
▼▼▼▼
French
Cards: AX, DC, DS, MC, VI.

Lunch: $8-$15 **Dinner:** $17-$30 **Phone:** 703/281-0070 [102]
Location: Off SR 123, 1.7 mi s of jct SR 7; in shopping plaza. 132 Branch Ave 22180. **Hours:** 11:30 am-2:30 & 5:30-10:30 pm, Sat from 5:30 pm, Sun 5 pm-9 pm. **Reservations:** suggested. **Features:** Tucked in the corner of a little shopping plaza, the quaint and romantic French restaurant presents a menu of duck, veal and fresh seafood. The staff is professional and helpful with the menu. Dressy casual; cocktails. **Parking:** on-site.

MARCO POLO RESTAURANT & CATERERS
▼▼ ▼▼
Italian

Lunch: $9-$13 **Dinner:** $10-$27 **Phone:** 703/281-3922 [107]
Location: SR 123, 0.3 mi e of jct SR 243. 245 Maple Ave W 22180. **Hours:** 11:30 am-10:30 pm, Fri & Sat-11 pm; Sunday brunch 10:30 am-2:30 pm. **Closed:** 1/1, 9/5, 12/25; also Mon. **Reservations:** suggested, weekends. **Features:** This is a family run operation that has been in business for more than 25 years. You will find plenty of continental and Italian selections on the menu. The pasta and sauce are made fresh on the premises. A lunch buffet is available Tuesday-Friday. Dressy casual; cocktails. **Parking:** on-site. **Cards:** AX, CB, DC, MC, VI.

MORTON'S - THE STEAKHOUSE
▼▼▼▼
Steak House

Lunch: $13-$27 **Dinner:** $24-$42 **Phone:** 703/883-0800 [98]
Location: I-495, exit 47A, 0.4 mi w on SR 7; opposite Tysons Corner Shopping Mall; in Fairfax Square. 8075 Leesburg Pike 22182. **Hours:** 11:30 am-2:30 & 5:30-11 pm, Sat from 5:30 pm, Sun 5 pm-10 pm. **Closed:** 1/1, 7/4, 12/25. **Reservations:** suggested. **Features:** Morton's specializes in generous potions of USDA prime aged beef, as well as fish, lobster and chicken. The restaurant is famous for its animated tableside menu presentation, where server's present and describe the steaks, lobsters and other main courses. Complimentary valet parking is available for dinner; luncheon patrons can park for free in the adjacent parking garage. Dressy casual; cocktails. **Parking:** on-site. **Cards:** AX, DC, MC, VI.

NIZAM'S RESTAURANT
▼▼ ▼▼
Turkish

Lunch: $8-$13 **Dinner:** $13-$22 **Phone:** 703/938-8948 [109]
Location: SR 123, 0.3 mi s of jct SR 243. 523 Maple Ave W 22180. **Hours:** 11 am-3 & 5:30-10 pm, Fri-11 pm, Sat 5 pm-11 pm, Sun 4 pm-9 pm. **Closed:** 1/1, 11/24, 12/25; also Mon. **Reservations:** suggested, weekends. **Features:** Servers in vests and bow ties and a crisp dining room give the established restaurant a graceful air. The menu specializes in lamb with an extensive selection of kebabs, including the house specialty doner kebab, available only Tuesday, Friday, Saturday and Sunday. Fresh fish selections are also available. Casual dress; cocktails. **Parking:** on-site. **Cards:** AX, DS, MC, VI.

PAYA THAI
▼▼ ▼▼
Thai

Lunch: $7-$10 **Dinner:** $7-$13 **Phone:** 703/883-3881 [97]
Location: I-495, exit 46A, 1.1 mi s on SR 123; 0.3 mi s of jct SR 123 and 7. 8417 Old Courthouse Rd 22182. **Hours:** 11:30 am-3 & 5-10 pm, Fri-10:30 pm, Sat noon-10:30 pm, Sun noon-10 pm. **Closed:** 11/24. **Reservations:** accepted. **Features:** The small restaurant boasts an award-winning wine selection to go with its beef, chicken, noodle, seafood and vegetarian selections. The kitchen respects guests' desired degree of spiciness. Casual dress; cocktails. **Parking:** on-site. **Cards:** AX, CB, DC, DS, JC, MC, VI.

RISTORANTE BONAROTI
ⒶⒶⒶ
▼▼▼▼
Northern
Italian

Lunch: $9-$18 **Dinner:** $15-$30 **Phone:** 703/281-7550 [100]
Location: SR 123, 1.5 mi s of jct SR 7. 428 E Maple Ave 22180. **Hours:** 11:30 am-2:30 & 5:30-10:30 pm, Sat from 5 pm. **Closed** major holidays; also Sun. **Reservations:** suggested. **Features:** Servers display an excellent knowledge of the menu, which includes offerings such as fried calamari, tender veal and scampi stuffed with crab over risotto in a light creamy sauce. Tastefully decorated in muted tones, the intimate dining room is a perfect setting for a cozy, relaxed experience. Dressy casual; cocktails. **Parking:** on-site. **Cards:** AX, CB, DC, MC, VI.

SAM & HARRY'S
▼▼▼▼
Steak House

Dinner: $18-$45 **Phone:** 703/448-0088 [94]
Location: I-495, exit 47A, 0.9 mi w on SR 7; jct SR 7 and 123. 8240 Leesburg Pike 22182. **Hours:** 5:30 pm-10:30 pm. **Closed:** 1/1, 11/24, 12/25; also Sun. **Reservations:** suggested. **Features:** No need to wonder why this eatery is so popular. It could be the thick steaks or generous portions of chicken, seafood, veal and lamb. Maybe it's the upscale, lively dining room and the knowledgeable, professional service staff. Enjoy deciding! Semi-formal attire; cocktails. **Parking:** on-site and valet. **Cards:** AX, CB, DC, DS, MC, VI.

SUNFLOWER VEGETARIAN RESTAURANT
▼▼ ▼▼
Vegetarian
Cards: AX, CB, DC, DS, MC, VI.

Lunch: $6 **Dinner:** $8-$11 **Phone:** 703/319-3888 [110]
Location: On SR 123, just s of jct SR 243. 2531 Chain Bridge Rd 22181. **Hours:** 11:30 am-9:30 pm, Sun from noon. **Closed:** 11/24, 12/24, 12/25. **Reservations:** not accepted. **Features:** The vegetarian menu blends Japanese, Chinese and Continental dishes. The kitchen uses only fresh ingredients and organic flavor enhancers—never monosodium glutamate—to prepare each item. Casual dress. **Parking:** on-site.

TARA THAI
▼▼ ▼▼
Thai

Lunch: $6-$8 **Dinner:** $8-$13 **Phone:** 703/255-2467 [108]
Location: SR 123, 0.3 mi ne of jct SR 243. 226 Maple Ave W 22180. **Hours:** 11:30 am-3 & 5-10 pm, Fri-11 pm, Sat noon-3:30 & 5-11 pm, Sun noon-3:30 & 5-10 pm. **Closed:** 11/24; also for lunch 12/25 & 1/1. **Reservations:** suggested, weekends. **Features:** The stylish cafe has a contemporary atmosphere with a sea motif. Specialties include whole fresh rockfish and skewered chicken, just to mention a few. Most notable is the nicely presented wild lamb and Pad Thai noodles. Portion sizes are ample. Casual dress; cocktails. **Parking:** on-site. **Cards:** AX, DC, DS, MC, VI.

The following restaurant has not been evaluated by AAA
but is listed for your information only.

THE CAPITAL GRILLE
[fyi]

Phone: 703/448-3900
Not evaluated. **Location:** I-495, exit 47A, 0.5 mi w on SR 7; on ground floor of office building. 1861 International Dr 22102. **Features:** Lending to the clubby atmosphere are mahogany-paneled walls and leather seating. The house specialty is dry-aged beef, but a nice selection of seafood also is available.

WOODBRIDGE pop. 31,941

———— WHERE TO STAY ————

BEST WESTERN POTOMAC MILLS *Book at aaa.com* Phone: (703)494-4433
(AAA) (SAVE) All Year [ECP] 1P: $79-$199 2P: $79-$199 XP: $10 F17
Location: I-95, exit 156, 0.5 mi w. 14619 Potomac Mills Rd 22192. Fax: 703/385-2627. **Facility:** 172 units. 152 one-bedroom standard units. 20 one-bedroom suites. 9 stories, interior corridors. **Parking:** on-site. **Terms:** 30 day cancellation notice-fee imposed. **Amenities:** voice mail, irons, hair dryers. **Pool(s):** outdoor.
Small-scale Hotel **Leisure Activities:** exercise room. **Guest Services:** valet and coin laundry. **Business Services:** meeting rooms, PC, fax (fee). **Cards:** AX, DC, DS, MC, VI. **Special Amenities:** free expanded continental breakfast and free newspaper. *(See color ad p 424)*
SOME UNITS
⬛ 🍽️➕ 🏊 📶 📠 💻 / ✕ 📞 🖨️ /

FAIRFIELD INN BY MARRIOTT POTOMAC MILLS *Book at aaa.com* Phone: (703)497-4000
3/1-11/1 [ECP] 1P: $99-$135 2P: $99-$135
11/2-2/28 [ECP] 1P: $85-$119 2P: $85-$119
Small-scale Hotel **Location:** I-95, exit 158B, 0.8 mi w. Located in a commercial area. 2610 Prince William Pkwy 22192. Fax: 703/497-4009. **Facility:** 85 one-bedroom standard units, some with whirlpools. 3 stories, interior corridors. *Bath:* combo or shower only. **Parking:** on-site. **Amenities:** irons, hair dryers. **Pool(s):** small heated indoor. **Leisure Activities:** limited exercise equipment. **Guest Services:** valet and coin laundry. **Business Services:** meeting rooms, fax (fee). **Cards:** AX, CB, DC, DS, MC, VI.
SOME UNITS
(ASK) 🍽️➕ 🔊M 📶 📠 🏊 📶 💻 / ✕ 📞 🖨️ /

HAMPTON INN-POTOMAC MILLS/WOODBRIDGE *Book at aaa.com* Phone: (703)490-2300
All Year [ECP] 1P: $94-$103 2P: $94-$103
Location: I-95, exit 161 southbound, 1.2 mi sw on US 1, then 0.3 mi n on SR 123; exit 160A northbound. 1240 Annapolis Way 22191. Fax: 703/497-8915. **Facility:** 87 one-bedroom standard units. 4 stories, interior
Small-scale Hotel corridors. *Bath:* combo or shower only. **Parking:** on-site. **Amenities:** dual phone lines, voice mail, irons, hair dryers. **Pool(s):** heated indoor. **Leisure Activities:** whirlpool, limited exercise equipment. **Guest Services:** valet and coin laundry. **Business Services:** fax (fee). **Cards:** AX, DC, DS, MC, VI.
SOME UNITS
(ASK) ⬛ 🔊M 📶 📶 🏊 📶 📠 💻 / ✕ 📞 🖨️ /

HOLIDAY INN EXPRESS HOTEL & SUITES-WOODBRIDGE Phone: 703/576-1600
(fyi) All Year 1P: $119-$169 2P: $119-$169 XP: $10 F18
Too new to rate. Location: I-95, exit 158 to 158B (Manassas). 14030 Telegraph Rd 22192. Fax: 703/576-1605.
Small-scale Hotel **Amenities:** 84 units, coffeemakers, microwaves, refrigerators, pool. **Cards:** AX, DC, DS, JC, MC, VI.

INNS OF VIRGINIA *Book at aaa.com* Phone: (703)490-3400
All Year 1P: $69-$89 2P: $79-$89 XP: $10 F17
Location: I-95, exit 161 southbound, 1 mi sw; exit 160A northbound, 0.5 mi s to US 1, then just e. Located in an industrial area, across from railroad tracks. 951 Annapolis Way 22191. Fax: 703/490-3400. **Facility:** 59 units. 51
Small-scale Hotel one- and 8 two-bedroom standard units. 3 stories (no elevator), interior corridors. **Parking:** on-site.
Business Services: fax (fee). **Cards:** AX, CB, DC, DS, JC, MC, VI.
SOME UNITS
(ASK) ⬛ 📶 📠 / ✕ 📞 🖨️ 💻 /
FEE FEE

POTOMAC MILLS RESIDENCE INN Phone: 703/490-4020
(fyi) All Year 1P: $129-$189 2P: $129-$189
Too new to rate. Location: I-95, exit 158B. 14301 Crossing Pl 22192. Fax: 703/490-4021. **Amenities:** 106 units,
Small-scale Hotel pets, coffeemakers, microwaves, refrigerators, pool. **Terms:** 5 night minimum stay - seasonal, **Cards:** AX, CB, DC, DS, JC, MC, VI.

QUALITY INN AT POTOMAC MILLS   *Book at aaa.com*

Phone: (703)494-0300

(AAA) (SAVE)   All Year [ECP]   1P: $50-$110   2P: $60-$120   XP: $5   F18

◆◆ ◆◆   **Location:** I-95, exit 161 southbound, 1.5 mi s on US 1, just n on SR 123, then just s; exit 160A northbound, 0.5 mi s on SR 123, then just s. Located in a commercial area, truck parking on premises. 1109 Horner Rd 22191. Fax: 703/494-5644. **Facility:** 93 one-bedroom standard units, some with whirlpools. 2 stories (no elevator),

Small-scale Hotel interior corridors. **Parking:** on-site. **Terms:** small pets only ($15 extra charge). **Amenities:** safes (fee). *Some:* irons, hair dryers. **Pool(s):** outdoor. **Leisure Activities:** health club privileges. *Fee:* game room. **Guest Services:** coin laundry. **Business Services:** meeting rooms, fax (fee). **Cards:** AX, DC, DS, MC, VI. **Special Amenities: free expanded continental breakfast and free newspaper.**

SOME UNITS

[icons] SD / FEE [icons]

SLEEP INN WOODBRIDGE   *Book at aaa.com*

Phone: (703)580-9200

(AAA) (SAVE)   All Year [ECP]   1P: $59-$109   2P: $59-$109   F18

◆◆ ◆◆   **Location:** I-95, exit 158B, 1.2 mi w. 14080 Shoppers Best Way 22192. Fax: 703/670-0870. **Facility:** 61 one-bedroom standard units, some with whirlpools. 2 stories, interior corridors. *Bath:* combo or shower only.

Small-scale Hotel **Parking:** on-site. **Terms:** cancellation fee imposed. **Amenities:** voice mail, irons, hair dryers. **Business Services:** fax (fee). **Cards:** AX, DC, DS, JC, MC, VI. **Special Amenities: free expanded continental breakfast and free local telephone calls.**

SOME UNITS

[icons]

WYTESTONE SUITES OF POTOMAC MILLS

Phone: (703)490-4100

(AAA) (SAVE)   3/1-10/31 [BP]   1P: $101-$121   2P: $101-$121   XP: $7   F18

◆◆◆ ◆◆   11/1-2/28 [BP]   1P: $95-$105   2P: $95-$105   XP: $7   F18

Location: I-95, exit 156, 0.5 mi w. 14525 Gideon Dr 22192. Fax: 703/497-8877. **Facility:** 85 one-bedroom suites.

Small-scale Hotel 5 stories, interior corridors. *Bath:* combo or shower only. **Parking:** on-site. **Amenities:** high-speed Internet, dual phone lines, voice mail, irons, hair dryers. **Guest Services:** valet and coin laundry. **Business Services:** meeting rooms, fax (fee). **Cards:** AX, CB, DC, DS, MC, VI. **Special Amenities: free full breakfast and free local telephone calls.**

(See color ad p 555)

SOME UNITS

[icons]

─── **WHERE TO DINE** ───

TIGER THAI RESTAURANT   Lunch: $7-$13   Dinner: $8-$13   Phone: 703/499-8424

◆◆ ◆◆   **Location:** I-95, exit 156, 0.5 mi w; in Potomac Festival Shopping Center. 14443 Potomac Mills Rd 22192.

Thai   **Hours:** 11:30 am-3 & 5-10 pm, Fri-10:30 pm, Sat noon-10:30 pm, Sun noon-10 pm. Closed: 11/24, 12/25; also for lunch 1/1. **Reservations:** accepted. **Features:** The shopping plaza restaurant offers good Thai cooking. The menu is extensive, with beef, seafood, vegetarian, noodle and curry dishes. One of the staff suggestions is Tiger Thai Beef. Casual dress; cocktails. **Parking:** on-site. **Cards:** CB, DC, DS, MC, VI.

[icon]

Adams-Morgan / © Paul M. Franklin

This ends listings for the Washington, D.C. Vicinity.

Maryland

Frederick
©Gibson Stock
Photography

ABERDEEN —*See Baltimore p. 586.*

ACCIDENT pop. 353

——— **WHERE TO DINE** ———

BUMBLE Q'S RESTAURANT	**Lunch:** $5-$15	**Dinner:** $5-$18	**Phone:** 301/387-7667

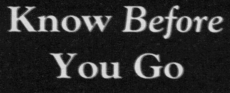

Location: 2 mi s on SR 219, then 3 mi e. 145 Bumble Bee Rd 21520. **Hours:** 11 am-9 pm. Closed: 3/27, 11/24, 12/24, 12/25. **Features:** A local favorite, the restaurant pleases diners with a widely varied menu and American friendly service. Don't pass on the ribs. Casual dress; cocktails. **Parking:** on-site.

ADELPHI —*See District Of Columbia p. 477.*

ANNAPOLIS —*See Baltimore p. 588.*

ANNAPOLIS JUNCTION —*See Baltimore p. 594.*

Know *Before* You Go

Travel plans become crystal clear in the pages of AAA TourBooks® or online at **aaa.com**.

Each of the advertisers makes your travel choices easier by featuring photographs, detailed descriptions, toll-free numbers and Web addresses for their hotels, restaurants or attractions.

Travel with Confidence.
Travel with AAA.

The Symbols of Quality

*D*iamond ratings provide you with an easy way to select quality lodgings and restaurants with the amenities and degree of sophistication you desire. Each property receiving a Diamond rating is thoroughly evaluated and rated using consistent, objective criteria and professional expertise.

One Diamond–This means an establishment meets the basic requirements of comfort, cleanliness, and hospitality. Lodgings are basic, no-frills accommodations appealing to the budget-minded. Restaurants offer simple, wholesome, affordable dining in a casual or self-service style.

Two Diamond–These establishments meet all of the One Diamond standards. Lodgings show modest enhancements in décor and amenities. Restaurants are informal yet rise above the ordinary, often well-suited to family dining.

Three Diamond–They feature a degree of sophistication. Lodgings offer a higher level of physical appeal, comfort and amenities, while restaurants provide a more creative, upscale, adult-oriented experience.

Four Diamond–These establishments create a memorable experience for guests. Lodgings feature a high level of service amid upscale surroundings. Restaurants are geared toward a luxurious, fine dining experience with complex menu offerings and a highly skilled staff.

Five Diamond–AAA's highest award is given to those establishments offering the ultimate in service, quality, refinement, and attention to detail. Both restaurants and lodgings at this level are a first-class, unforgettable experience.

Trust AAA to provide you with objective and accurate ratings of thousands of lodgings and restaurants throughout North America. Know before you go what to expect when you get there.

Destination Baltimore
pop. 651,154

*F*rom spectacular sports to classical culture, Baltimore has something for everyone.

*C*heer on baseball's Orioles in Oriole Park at Camden Yards. Place your bets on your favorite Thoroughbred in May's Preakness at Pimlico Race Course. Or sit back and enjoy the sounds of the Baltimore Symphony Orchestra's summer series at the Inner Harbor.

© Richard Nowitz
Baltimore Area CVB

Baltimore Inner Harbor Skyline. Small pleasure craft float against a backdrop of glass and steel.

© Paul A. Souders / Corbis

U.S. Naval Academy, Annapolis. Midshipmen commemorated the academy's 150th anniversary during ceremonies in 1995. (See listing page 176)

*P*laces included in this AAA Destination City:

See Downtown map page 562

Oriole Park at Camden Yards, Baltimore.
Almost 48,000 fans cheer the hometown team on a sun-drenched day. (See mention page 172)

Shopping in Fells Point in Baltimore.
Copper pots sparkle in this old seaport neighborhood with an international flair. (See mention 161)

See Vicinity map page 566

Maryland State Fair in nearby Timonium.
Visitors have enjoyed this late-August event since 1880. (See mention page 173)

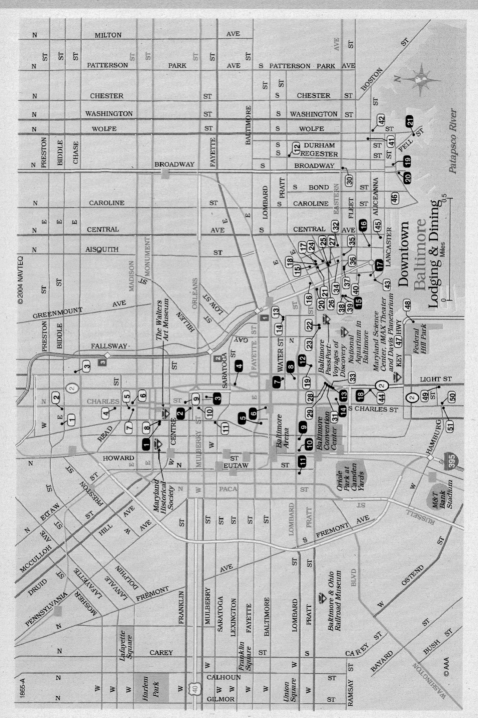

Downtown
Baltimore
Lodging & Dining

Downtown Baltimore

This index helps you "spot" where approved accommodations and restaurants are located on the corresponding detailed maps. Lodging rate ranges are for comparison only and show the property's high season; rates are per night, unless only weekly (W) rates are available. Restaurant rate range is for dinner, unless only lunch (L) is served. Turn to the listing page for more detailed rate information and consult display ads for special promotions.

Spotter/Map Page Number	OA	DOWNTOWN BALTIMORE - Lodgings	Diamond Rating	Rate Range High Season	Listing Page
1 / p. 562	AAA	Peabody Court-A Clarion Hotel - see color ad p 571	◇◇◇	$179-$350 SAVE	576
2 / p. 562	AAA	Mount Vernon Hotel	◇◇	$99-$129 SAVE	576
3 / p. 562		Baltimore's Tremont Park Hotel - see color ad p 572	◇◇◇	$139-$219	572
4 / p. 562		Baltimore's Tremont Plaza Hotel - see color ad p 572	◇◇◇	$139-$219	572
5 / p. 562	AAA	Wyndham Baltimore-Inner Harbor	◇◇◇	$169-$209 SAVE	578
6 / p. 562	AAA	Radisson Plaza Lord Baltimore - see color ad p 589, p 576	◇◇◇	$129 SAVE	577
7 / p. 562		Hampton Inn & Suites-Inner Harbor - see color ad p 574	◆◆◆	$168-$199	574
8 / p. 562		Brookshire Suites	◇◇◇	$179-$209	572
9 / p. 562	AAA	Days Inn Inner Harbor Baltimore - see color ad p 573	◇◇◇	$119-$189 SAVE	574
10 / p. 562	AAA	Holiday Inn-Inner Harbor	◇◇◇	$98-$249 SAVE	575
11 / p. 562	AAA	Baltimore Marriott Inner Harbor	◇◇◇	$299-$399 SAVE	571
12 / p. 562	AAA	Renaissance Harborplace Hotel - see color ad p 577	◇◇◇◇	$269-$279 SAVE	577
13 / p. 562	AAA	Hyatt Regency Baltimore - see ad p 575	◇◇◇◇	$145-$289 SAVE	575
14 / p. 562		Sheraton Inner Harbor Hotel	◆◆◆	$309-$339	577
15 / p. 562		Pier 5 Hotel	◇◇◇	$239-$349	576
16 / p. 562	AAA	Courtyard by Marriott Downtown Inner Harbor	◇◇◇	$174-$219 SAVE	573
17 / p. 562	AAA	Baltimore Marriott Waterfront Hotel	◇◇◇◇	$279-$399 SAVE	571
18 / p. 562	AAA	Harbor Court Hotel - see color ad p 574	◇◇◇◇	$190-$390 SAVE	574
19 / p. 562		Celie's Waterfront Inn	◇◇◇	$109-$239	572
20 / p. 562		Admiral Fell Inn	◇◇◇	$199-$239	571
21 / p. 562		The Inn at Henderson's Wharf - see color ad p 576	◇◇◇	$169-$259	575
		DOWNTOWN BALTIMORE - Restaurants			
1 / p. 562		Abacrombie Fine Food & Accommodations	◇◇◇	$17-$26	578
2 / p. 562		Tampico Mexican Grill	◇◇	$7-$13	582
3 / p. 562		The Prime Rib	◇◇◇	$21-$41	581
4 / p. 562		Brass Elephant	◇◇◇	$20-$30	579
5 / p. 562		The Helmand Restaurant	◇◇	$10-$20	580
6 / p. 562		Akbar Restaurant	◇◇	$10-$17	578
7 / p. 562		Saffron	◇◇◇	$12-$28	582
8 / p. 562	AAA	George's on Mt. Vernon Square	◇◇	$15-$28	580
9 / p. 562		Tio Pepe Restaurant	◇◇◇	$17-$26	582
10 / p. 562		Sotto Sopra	◇◇◇	$15-$30	582
11 / p. 562	AAA	Marconi's	◇◇◇	$10-$30	580
12 / p. 562		Obrycki's Crab House and Seafood Restaurant	◇◇	$16-$30	581

Spotter/Map Page Number	OA	DOWNTOWN BALTIMORE - Restaurants (continued)	Diamond Rating	Rate Range High Season	Listing Page
⑬ / p. 562		Mondo Bondo Italian Bistro	▼▼	$7-$15	581
⑭ / p. 562		Babalu Grill	▼▼▼	$14-$31	578
⑮ / p. 562		Da Mimmo	▼▼	$12-$28	579
⑯ / p. 562		Velleggia's	▼▼	$12-$22	582
⑰ / p. 562		Amicci's	▼▼	$9-$20	578
⑱ / p. 562		Chiapparelli's	▼▼	$12-$28	579
⑲ / p. 562		Windows	▼▼▼	$14-$32	583
⑳ / p. 562		Purple Orchid	▼▼▼	$17-$32	581
㉑ / p. 562		Ciao Bella Restaurant	▼▼▼	$10-$25	579
㉒ / p. 562		Pier 4 Kitchen & Bar	▼▼	$12-$25	581
㉓ / p. 562		ESPN Zone	▼▼	$8-$18	580
㉔ / p. 562		Sabatino's	▼▼	$10-$35	582
㉕ / p. 562		Germano's Trattoria	▼▼	$13-$25	580
㉖ / p. 562		Rocco's Capriccio	▼▼	$15-$32	582
㉗ / p. 562		Aldo's Ristorante	▼▼▼	$16-$45	578
㉘ / p. 562		Paolo's Ristorante	▼▼	$10-$25	581
㉙ / p. 562		Phillips Harborplace	▼▼	$11-$25	581
㉚ / p. 562		Cafe Madrid	▼▼▼	$16-$27	579
㉛ / p. 562		Capitol City Brewing Co-Baltimore	▼▼	$7-$24	579
㉜ / p. 562		La Scala Ristorante Italiano	▼▼▼	$12-$29	580
㉝ / p. 562		Pisces	▼▼▼	$35-$40	581
㉞ / p. 562		Mo's Crab and Pasta Factory	▼▼	$11-$28	581
㉟ / p. 562		Boccaccio Restaurant	▼▼▼	$16-$35	579
㊱ / p. 562		Dalesio's Restaurant of Little Italy	▼▼▼	$9-$24	579
㊲ / p. 562	ⒶⒶⒶ	**Della Notte Ristorante**	▼▼▼	$18-$38	579
㊳ / p. 562		Eurasian Harbor	▼▼▼	$12-$26	580
㊴ / p. 562		Peacock Cafe at Pier 5	▼▼	$9-$20	581
㊵ / p. 562		James Joyce Irish Pub & Restaurant	▼▼	$8-$22	580
㊶ / p. 562		Pierpoint Restaurant & Bar	▼▼	$16-$25	581
㊷ / p. 562		Dueisole Ristorante Italiano	▼▼	$10-$27	580
㊸ / p. 562		Victor's Italian Cafe	▼▼▼	$12-$26	582
㊹ / p. 562		Hampton's	▼▼▼▼	$25-$50	580
㊺ / p. 562		Charleston	▼▼▼▼	$38-$78	579
㊻ / p. 562		The Black Olive	▼▼▼	$20-$32	578
㊼ / p. 562		The Rusty Scupper Resturant	▼▼	$10-$27	582
㊽ / p. 562		Joy America Cafe	▼▼▼	$17-$30	580
㊾ / p. 562		Ten-O-Six Restaurant	▼▼	$13-$23	582
㊿ / p. 562		Banjara Restaurant	▼▼	$10-$19	578
51 / p. 562		Bandaloops	▼▼	$6-$18	578

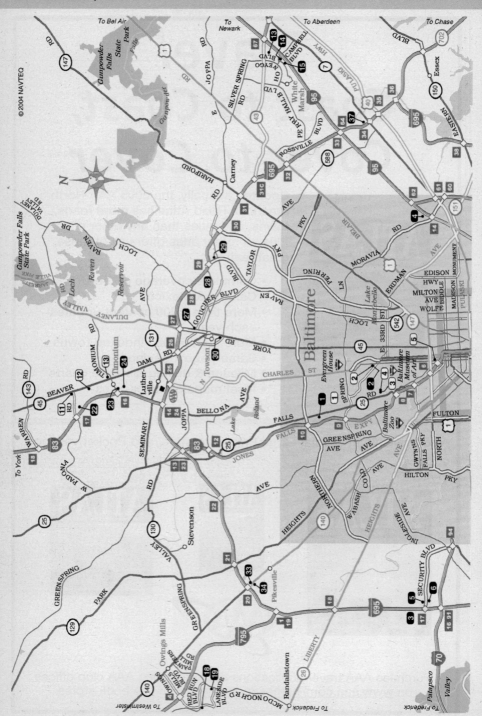

©2004 NAVTEQ

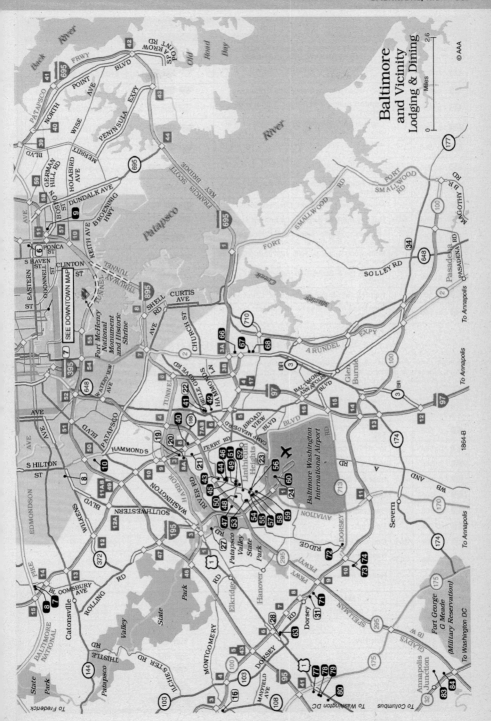

Baltimore
and Vicinity
Lodging & Dining

© AAA

✈ Airport Accommodations

Spotter/Map Page Number	OA	BALTIMORE-WASHINGTON INTERNATIONAL AIRPORT	Diamond Rating	Rate Range High Season	Listing Page
45 / p. 566	AAA	**AmeriSuites (Baltimore/BWI Airport), 2.5 mi n of airport**	◈◈◈	$109-$209 SAVE	604
56 / p. 566		BWI Airport Marriott Hotel, 2 mi n of airport	◈◈◈	$249-$279	604
59 / p. 566	AAA	**Comfort Suites-BWI Airport, 1.8 mi w of airport**	◈◈◈	$79-$249 SAVE	605
52 / p. 566		Courtyard by Marriott-BWI Airport, 2.3 mi n of airport	◈◈◈	$179	606
47 / p. 566		Embassy Suites Hotel Baltimore at BWI, 2.8 mi n of airport	◈◈◈	$119-$299	606
55 / p. 566		Fairfield Inn by Marriott-BWI Airport, 2 mi n of airport	◈◈◈	$69-$159	606
60 / p. 566	AAA	**Four Points by Sheraton BWI Airport, at the airport**	◈◈◈	$89-$239 SAVE	607
57 / p. 566		Hampton Inn BWI Airport, 2 mi n of airport	◈◈◈	$89-$179	607
54 / p. 566	AAA	**Holiday Inn-BWI Airport, 2.4 mi n of airport**	◈◈◈	$98-$199 SAVE	607
46 / p. 566		Homestead Studio Suites Hotel-Baltimore Washington Int'l Airport, 2.5 mi n of airport	◈◈	$91-$106	607
50 / p. 566		Homewood Suites by Hilton-BWI Airport, 2.4 mi n of airport	◈◈◈	$119-$189	607
49 / p. 566		Microtel Inn & Suites-BWI Airport, 2.4 mi n of airport	◈◈	$89-$139	607
58 / p. 566		Red Roof Inn-BWI Airport, 1.8 mi n of airport	◈◈	$73-$99	608
51 / p. 566		Residence Inn by Marriott-BWI Airport, 2.4 mi n of airport	◈◈◈	$119-$199	608

Baltimore and Vicinity

This index helps you "spot" where approved accommodations and restaurants are located on the corresponding detailed maps. Lodging rate ranges are for comparison only and show the property's high season; rates are per night, unless only weekly (W) rates are available. Restaurant rate range is for dinner, unless only lunch (L) is served. Turn to the listing page for more detailed rate information and consult display ads for special promotions.

Spotter/Map Page Number	OA	BALTIMORE - Lodgings	Diamond Rating	Rate Range High Season	Listing Page
1 / p. 566		Radisson Hotel at Cross Keys - see color ad p 589	◈◈◈	$139-$309	585
2 / p. 566		Inn At The Colonnade	◈◈◈	$89-$229	585
3 / p. 566		Holiday Inn Baltimore West	◈◈	$119	585
4 / p. 566	AAA	**Best Inn Moravia**	◈◈	$62-$72 SAVE	584
5 / p. 566		Quality Inn West	◈◈	$70-$115	585
6 / p. 566		Days Inn West/Security Blvd	◈◈	$65-$129	584
7 / p. 566		Days Inn	◈	$109-$129	584
8 / p. 566	AAA	**Comfort Inn Baltimore West**	◈◈	$69-$89 SAVE	584
9 / p. 566	AAA	**Best Western Hotel & Conference Center - see ad p 584**	◈◈◈	$99-$139 SAVE	584
10 / p. 566	AAA	**Holiday Inn Express-Baltimore - see color ad p 575**	◈◈◈	$99-$139 SAVE	585
		BALTIMORE - Restaurants			
1 / p. 566		Petit Louis Bistro	◈◈◈	$14-$35	586
2 / p. 566		Four West	◈◈◈	$14-$44	585
3 / p. 566		Cafe Hon	◈◈	$6-$15	585
4 / p. 566		Mamie's Cafe	◈◈	$6-$25	586
5 / p. 566		Tapas Teatro	◈◈	$6-$16	586
6 / p. 566		Ikaros Restaurant	◈◈	$8-$18	586
7 / p. 566		The Bicycle	◈◈◈	$15-$30	585

Spotter/Map Page Number	OA	BALTIMORE - Restaurants (continued)	Diamond Rating	Rate Range High Season	Listing Page
8 / p. 566		Kibby's Restaurant	◈	$10-$27	586
		WHITE MARSH - Lodgings			
13 / p. 566		Residence Inn by Marriott Baltimore/White Marsh	◈◈◈	$119-$199	615
14 / p. 566		Hilton Garden Inn-White Marsh	◈◈◈	$119-$139	615
15 / p. 566		Hampton Inn at White Marsh	◈◈◈	$119-$139	615
		OWINGS MILLS - Lodgings			
18 / p. 566		Hilton Garden Inn-Owings Mills	◈◈◈	$99-$184	610
19 / p. 566	AAA	**AmeriSuites (Baltimore/Owings Mills) - see color ad p 571**	◈◈◈	$134-$199 [SAVE]	610
		TIMONIUM - Lodgings			
22 / p. 566		Days Hotel & Conference Center Baltimore North	◈◈	$79-$134	612
23 / p. 566		Red Roof Inn-Timonium	◈◈	$65-$96	612
24 / p. 566		Holiday Inn Select Baltimore North	◈◈◈	$129	612
		TIMONIUM - Restaurants			
11 / p. 566		Gibby's Seafood Restaurant	◈◈	$15-$43	612
12 / p. 566		An Poitin Stil	◈◈	$9-$20	612
13 / p. 566		Michael's Cafe	◈◈	$9-$28	612
		TOWSON - Lodgings			
27 / p. 566		Sheraton Baltimore North	◈◈◈	$139-$179	613
28 / p. 566	AAA	**Holiday Inn-Cromwell Bridge**	◈◈◈	$107-$134 [SAVE]	613
29 / p. 566	AAA	**Comfort Inn Towson - see color ad p 613**	◈◈	$99-$179 [SAVE]	613
30 / p. 566		Burkshire Marriott Conference Hotel	◈◈◈	$159-$189	612
		PIKESVILLE - Lodgings			
33 / p. 566		Ramada Inn Baltimore West	◈◈	$73-$89	611
34 / p. 566		Hilton Pikesville	◈◈◈	$108-$178	611
		ROSEDALE - Lodgings			
37 / p. 566		Fairfield Inn by Marriott Baltimore North	◈◈◈	$104-$119	611
		LINTHICUM HEIGHTS - Lodgings			
40 / p. 566		Motel 6 Baltimore-Linthicum Heights #1201	◈	$57-$73	608
41 / p. 566	AAA	**Sleep Inn & Suites Airport - see color ad p 605**	◈◈	$119-$129 [SAVE]	609
42 / p. 566	AAA	**Comfort Inn Airport - see color ad p 605**	◈◈◈	$119-$139 [SAVE]	605
43 / p. 566		Wingate Inn at BWI Airport - see color ad p 608	◈◈◈	$159-$189	609
44 / p. 566		Hilton Garden Inn-BWI	◈◈◈	$129-$199	607
45 / p. 566	AAA	**AmeriSuites (Baltimore/BWI Airport) - see color ad p 571**	◈◈◈	$109-$209 [SAVE]	604
46 / p. 566		Homestead Studio Suites Hotel-Baltimore Washington Int'l Airport	◈◈	$91-$106	607
47 / p. 566		Embassy Suites Hotel Baltimore at BWI	◈◈◈	$119-$299	606
48 / p. 566		Candlewood Suites-BWI	◈◈	$99-$159	605
49 / p. 566		Microtel Inn & Suites-BWI Airport - see color ad p 608	◈◈	$89-$139	607
50 / p. 566		Homewood Suites by Hilton-BWI Airport	◈◈◈	$119-$189	607
51 / p. 566		Residence Inn by Marriott-BWI Airport	◈◈◈	$119-$199	608
52 / p. 566		Courtyard by Marriott-BWI Airport	◈◈◈	$179	606
53 / p. 566		SpringHill Suites by Marriott	◈◈◈	$99-$169	609

Spotter/Map Page Number	OA	LINTHICUM HEIGHTS - Lodgings (continued)	Diamond Rating	Rate Range High Season	Listing Page
54 / p. 566	AAA	Holiday Inn-BWI Airport	◈◈◈	$98-$199 SAVE	607
55 / p. 566		Fairfield Inn by Marriott-BWI Airport	◈◈◈	$69-$159	606
56 / p. 566		BWI Airport Marriott Hotel	◈◈◈	$249-$279	604
57 / p. 566		Hampton Inn BWI Airport	◈◈◈	$89-$179	607
58 / p. 566		Red Roof Inn-BWI Airport	◈◈	$73-$99	608
59 / p. 566	AAA	Comfort Suites-BWI Airport - see color ad p 606	◈◈◈	$79-$249 SAVE	605
60 / p. 566	AAA	Four Points by Sheraton BWI Airport - see color ad p 606	◈◈◈	$89-$239 SAVE	607
		LINTHICUM HEIGHTS - Restaurants			
19 / p. 566		Snyder's Willow Grove	◈◈◈	$10-$25	609
20 / p. 566		G & M Restaurant	◈◈	$8-$25	609
21 / p. 566	AAA	The Olive Grove Restaurant	◈◈◈	$9-$25	609
22 / p. 566	AAA	The Rose Restaurant	◈◈◈	$11-$25	609
23 / p. 566		Moniker's Grille	◈◈◈	$9-$29	609
24 / p. 566		Michener's	◈◈◈	$12-$28	609
		ELKRIDGE - Lodgings			
63 / p. 566	AAA	Best Western Baltimore Washington Airport/I-95	◈◈◈	$90-$110 SAVE	599
		ELKRIDGE - Restaurants			
27 / p. 566	AAA	The Elkridge Furnace Inn	◈◈◈	$18-$30	599
28 / p. 566		Joe Theismann's Restaurant	◈◈	$12-$25	599
		GLEN BURNIE - Lodgings			
66 / p. 566	AAA	Holiday Inn-Baltimore South	◈◈◈	$107-$125 SAVE	601
67 / p. 566	AAA	Days Inn-Glen Burnie	◈◈	$99-$124 SAVE	601
68 / p. 566	AAA	Hampton Inn Glen Burnie - see color ad p 601	◈◈◈	$89-$129 SAVE	601
		HANOVER - Lodgings			
71 / p. 566		Red Roof Inn-BWI Parkway	◈◈	$68-$93	602
72 / p. 566		Holiday Inn Express-BWI Airport	◈◈◈	$135	601
73 / p. 566		Residence Inn by Marriott-Arundel Mills/BWI	◈◈◈	$95-$219	602
74 / p. 566		Hampton Inn & Suites-Arundel Mills/BWI	◈◈◈	$109-$179	601
		HANOVER - Restaurant			
31 / p. 566		Gunning's Seafood Restaurant	◈◈	$7-$22	602
		JESSUP - Lodgings			
77 / p. 566		Holiday Inn Columbia	◈◈◈	$119-$169	604
78 / p. 566		Fairfield Inn by Marriott-Columbia/Jessup	◈◈	$69-$149	604
79 / p. 566		Red Roof Inn-Columbia/Jessup	◈◈	$73-$96	604
80 / p. 566	AAA	Super 8 Motel	◈	$70-$90 SAVE	604
		ANNAPOLIS JUNCTION - Lodgings			
83 / p. 566		TownePlace Suites by Marriott-Baltimore/Ft. Meade	◈◈◈	$59-$139	595
84 / p. 566	AAA	Courtyard by Marriott Ft. Meade @ National Business Park	◈◈◈	$99-$159 SAVE	594
		ELLICOTT CITY - Restaurant			
16 / p. 566		Eggspectation	◈◈	$9-$20	600
		PASADENA - Restaurant			
34 / p. 566		Bella Napoli Italian Restaurant	◈◈◈	$10-$20	611

DOWNTOWN BALTIMORE   (See map and index starting on p. 562)

──── WHERE TO STAY ────

ADMIRAL FELL INN   *Book at aaa.com*   Phone: 410/522-7377   **20**
All Year   1P: $199-$239   2P: $199-$239

Historic
Small-scale Hotel

Location: Corner of Broadway and Thames sts; facing the waterfront. Located in historic Fells Point. 888 S Broadway St 21231. Fax: 410/522-0707. **Facility:** Period pieces, including several canopy beds, decorate some guest rooms in this 1790s inn, which is made up of eight buildings. 80 one-bedroom standard units, some with whirlpools. 5 stories, interior corridors. *Bath:* combo or shower only. **Parking:** on-site (fee) and valet. **Terms:** check-in 4 pm, package plans, $4 service charge, pets ($25 extra charge, with prior approval). **Amenities:** high-speed Internet, voice mail, irons, hair dryers. *Some:* honor bars. **Guest Services:** valet laundry, area transportation. **Business Services:** meeting rooms, fax. **Cards:** AX, DC, DS, MC, VI.

SOME UNITS

(ASK) (S⒟) 🛏 Ⓨ ⒮ 📶 📺 (DATA PORT) 🖥 / ✕ (VCR) 🔲 /
FEE   FEE   FEE FEE

BALTIMORE MARRIOTT INNER HARBOR   *Book at aaa.com*   Phone: (410)962-0202   **11**
(AAA) (SAVE)   3/1-11/19   1P: $299-$399   2P: $299-$399   XP: $20   F17
11/20-2/28   1P: $249-$379   2P: $249-$379   XP: $20   F17

Large-scale Hotel

Location: Pratt and Eutaw sts. Located across from Orioles Park at Camden Yards. 110 S Eutaw St 21201. Fax: 410/625-7892. **Facility:** 524 one-bedroom standard units. 10 stories, interior corridors. *Bath:* combo or shower only. **Parking:** on-site (fee). **Terms:** check-in 4 pm, package plans. **Amenities:** dual phone lines, voice mail, honor bars, irons, hair dryers. *Fee:* video games, high-speed Internet, safes. **Dining:** 6:30 am-2 & 5-10 pm, cocktails. **Pool(s):** heated indoor. **Leisure Activities:** whirlpool, exercise room. **Guest Services:** gift shop, valet and coin laundry. **Business Services:** conference facilities, business center. **Cards:** AX, CB, DC, DS, MC, VI. **Special Amenities:** free newspaper.

SOME UNITS

🍴 Ⓨ ⒮ 🐾 🏊 📺 (DATA PORT) 🖥 / ✕ 🔲 /

BALTIMORE MARRIOTT WATERFRONT HOTEL   *Book at aaa.com*   Phone: (410)385-3000   **17**
(AAA) (SAVE)   All Year   1P: $279-$399   2P: $279-$399

Large-scale Hotel

Location: Center. 700 Aliceanna St 21202. Fax: 410/895-1900. **Facility:** The Baltimore Marriott Waterfront Hotel, right on the Inner Harbor, offers sweeping views; fresh floral arrangements add an aura of elegance. 750 one-bedroom standard units, some with whirlpools. 32 stories, interior corridors. *Bath:* combo or shower only. **Parking:** on-site (fee). **Terms:** check-in 4 pm, cancellation fee imposed. **Amenities:** high-speed Internet, voice mail, safes, irons, hair dryers. *Some:* CD players. **Dining:** 2 restaurants, 6:30 am-2 & 3-11 pm, cocktails. **Pool(s):** indoor. **Leisure Activities:** exercise room. *Fee:* massage. **Guest Services:** gift shop, valet laundry. **Business Services:** conference facilities, business center. **Cards:** AX, DC, DS, JC, MC, VI. **Special Amenities:** free newspaper and preferred room (subject to availability with advance reservations).

SOME UNITS

🍴 (24) Ⓨ ⒧M ⒮ 🏊 📺 (DATA PORT) 🖥 / ✕ (VCR) 🔲 /

(See map and index starting on p. 562)

BALTIMORE'S TREMONT PARK HOTEL   *Book at aaa.com*   Phone: (410)576-1200   **3**
3/1-6/30 & 9/1-10/31   1P: $139-$199   2P: $159-$219   XP: $20   F16
7/1-8/31 & 11/1-2/28   1P: $129-$189   2P: $149-$209   XP: $20   F16
Small-scale Hotel   **Location:** Just s of US 40 E, off Charles St. 8 E Pleasant St 21202. Fax: 410/244-1154. **Facility:** 58 one-bedroom standard units with kitchens. 13 stories, interior corridors. *Bath:* combo or shower only. **Parking:** on-site (fee) and valet. **Terms:** 3 day cancellation notice-fee imposed, package plans. **Amenities:** high-speed Internet, dual phone lines, voice mail, irons, hair dryers. **Guest Services:** valet laundry, area transportation. **Business Services:** meeting rooms. **Cards:** AX, CB, DC, DS, MC, VI. *(See color ad below)*

SOME UNITS
(ASK) (T1) (Y) (&) (@) (+) (%) (DATA PORT) (B) (@) (@) /(X)/

BALTIMORE'S TREMONT PLAZA HOTEL   *Book at aaa.com*   Phone: (410)727-2222   **4**
3/1-6/30 & 9/1-10/31   1P: $139-$199   2P: $159-$219   XP: $20   F16
7/1-8/31 & 11/1-2/28   1P: $129-$189   2P: $149-$209   XP: $20   F16
Large-scale Hotel   **Location:** At St Paul Pl and Saratoga St. 222 St Paul Pl 21202. Fax: 410/685-4215. **Facility:** 303 units. 291 one- and 12 two-bedroom standard units. 37 stories, interior corridors. *Bath:* combo or shower only. **Parking:** valet and street. **Terms:** 3 day cancellation notice-fee imposed, package plans. **Amenities:** high-speed Internet, dual phone lines, voice mail, irons, hair dryers. **Pool(s):** outdoor. **Leisure Activities:** saunas, exercise room. **Guest Services:** coin laundry, area transportation. **Business Services:** meeting rooms. **Cards:** AX, CB, DC, DS, MC, VI. *(See color ad below)*

SOME UNITS
(ASK) (T1) (&) (@) (=) (%) (DATA PORT) (B) (@) (@) /(X)(VCR)/
FEE

BROOKSHIRE SUITES   *Book at aaa.com*   Phone: 410/625-1300   **8**
All Year   1P: $179-$209   2P: $179-$209
Location: Corner of Calvert and Lombard sts. 120 E Lombard St 21202. Fax: 410/625-0912. **Facility:** 97 one-bedroom standard units. 14 stories, interior corridors. *Bath:* combo or shower only. **Parking:** on-site (fee). Small-scale Hotel   **Terms:** package plans, $4 service charge. **Amenities:** video games, high-speed Internet, dual phone lines, voice mail, honor bars, irons, hair dryers. **Leisure Activities:** exercise room. **Guest Services:** valet laundry, area transportation. **Business Services:** meeting rooms, business center. **Cards:** AX, DC, DS, MC, VI.

SOME UNITS
(ASK) (S) (@) (@) (%) (DATA PORT) (@) /(X)(@)/

CELIE'S WATERFRONT INN   Phone: 410/522-2323   **19**
All Year   1P: $109-$209   2P: $129-$239
Location: In historic Fells Point area. 1714 Thames St 21231. Fax: 410/432-3397. **Facility:** This downtown B&B, which includes an answering machine in each room, is walking distance to many shops and restaurants; Bed & Breakfast   check-in must be pre-arranged. Smoke free premises. 9 one-bedroom standard units, some with whirlpools. 3 stories (no elevator), interior corridors. *Bath:* combo or shower only. **Parking:** street. **Terms:** 2 night minimum stay - weekends, age restrictions may apply, 10 day cancellation notice-fee imposed, package plans. **Amenities:** voice mail, irons, hair dryers. *Some:* CD players. **Business Services:** fax. **Cards:** AX, DS, MC, VI.

SOME UNITS
(ASK) (S) (T1+) (X) (VCR) (%) (DATA PORT) (B) (@) /(@)/

(See map and index starting on p. 562)

COURTYARD BY MARRIOTT DOWNTOWN INNER HARBOR   *Book at aaa.com*

Phone: (443)923-4000   **16**

3/1-11/18	1P: $174-$219	2P: $174-$219	XP: $10 F13
11/19-2/28	1P: $129-$159	2P: $129-$159	XP: $10 F13

Small-scale Hotel

Location: On east side of Inner Harbor. 1000 Aliceanna St 21202. Fax: 443/923-9970. **Facility:** 205 one-bedroom standard units, some with whirlpools. 14 stories, interior corridors. *Bath:* combo or shower only. **Parking:** on-site (fee). **Terms:** [BP] meal plan available. **Amenities:** video games (fee), dual phone lines, voice mail, irons, hair dryers. **Dining:** 6:30-10:30 am, Sat & Sun 7-11:30 am. **Pool(s):** heated indoor. **Leisure Activities:** whirlpool, exercise room. **Guest Services:** sundries, valet and coin laundry. **Business Services:** meeting rooms, PC (fee). **Cards:** AX, DC, DS, JC, MC, VI. **Special Amenities:** free newspaper.

SOME UNITS

Exceed your expectations.

In the heart of Baltimore's exciting Inner Harbor District at 10% off for AAA guests (off published rates, subject to availability). An easy stroll to the National Aquarium or the Orioles/Ravens stadium complex. *Not your budget.*

(See map and index starting on p. 562)

DAYS INN INNER HARBOR BALTIMORE   *Book at aaa.com*   Phone: (410)576-1000   9

(AAA) [SAVE]   4/1-11/15   1P: $119-$179   2P: $129-$189   XP: $10   F16
▽▽▽▽▽   3/1-3/31 & 11/16-2/28   1P: $99-$129   2P: $109-$139   XP: $10   F16
Location: Opposite Baltimore Arena. 100 Hopkins Pl 21201. Fax: 410/576-9437. **Facility:** 250 one-bedroom
Small-scale Hotel   standard units. 9 stories, interior corridors. *Bath:* combo or shower only. **Parking:** on-site (fee).
Terms: cancellation fee imposed, package plans. **Amenities:** video games, high-speed Internet, voice mail,
safes (fee), irons, hair dryers. **Dining:** 6:30 am-2 & 5-11 pm, Sat & Sun 6:30 am-noon & 5-11 pm, cocktails.
Pool(s): outdoor. **Leisure Activities:** exercise room. **Guest Services:** valet and coin laundry. **Business Services:** meeting
rooms, business center. **Cards:** AX, DC, DS, JC, MC, VI. *(See color ad p 573)*

SOME UNITS

FEE

HAMPTON INN & SUITES-INNER HARBOR   *Book at aaa.com*   Phone: (410)539-7888   7

▽▽▽▽▽   3/1-11/14 [ECP]   1P: $168-$189   2P: $179-$199
11/15-2/28 [ECP]   1P: $129-$149
Small-scale Hotel   **Location:** Between Lombard and Baltimore sts; corner of Calvert and E Redwood sts. 131 E Redwood St 21202 (5625
O'Donnell St, BALTIMORE, 21224). Fax: 410/539-3345. **Facility:** 116 one-bedroom standard units, some with
whirlpools. 7 stories, interior corridors. *Bath:* combo or shower only. **Parking:** on-site (fee) and valet. **Terms:** cancellation fee
imposed, [ECP] meal plan available. **Amenities:** high-speed Internet, voice mail, irons, hair dryers. **Pool(s):** heated indoor.
Leisure Activities: exercise room. **Guest Services:** sundries, valet and coin laundry. **Business Services:** conference facilities,
business center. **Cards:** AX, CB, DC, DS, MC, VI. *(See color ad below)*

SOME UNITS

HARBOR COURT HOTEL   *Book at aaa.com*   Phone: (410)234-0550   18

(AAA) [SAVE]   11/20-2/28   1P: $190-$390   2P: $190-$390   XP: $15   F18
▽▽▽▽ ▽▽▽▽   3/1-11/19   1P: $220-$380   2P: $220-$380   XP: $15   F18
Location: Facing Inner Harbor. 550 Light St 21202. Fax: 410/659-5925. **Facility:** A spiral staircase in the lobby of
the Harbor Court Hotel leads to two restaurants; a fitness center is available. 195 units. 187 one-bedroom
Large-scale Hotel   standard units. 8 one-bedroom suites ($385-$3500). 8 stories, interior corridors. **Parking:** on-site (fee) and
valet. **Terms:** cancellation fee imposed, package plans. **Amenities:** CD players, dual phone lines, voice
mail, honor bars, irons, hair dryers. *Fee:* video games, high-speed Internet. *Some:* fax. **Dining:** 7 am-10 pm, cocktails, also,
Hampton's, see separate listing, entertainment. **Pool(s):** heated indoor. **Leisure Activities:** saunas, whirlpool. *Fee:* tennis court,
racquetball court, aerobics, yoga, massage. **Guest Services:** gift shop, valet laundry, area transportation (fee). *Fee:* tanning
facility, personal trainer. **Business Services:** conference facilities, business center. **Cards:** AX, DC, DS, MC, VI. Affiliated with A
Preferred Hotel. *(See color ad below)*

SOME UNITS

FEE   FEE

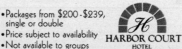

(See map and index starting on p. 562)

HOLIDAY INN-INNER HARBOR   *Book at aaa.com*   Phone: (410)685-3500   **10**

AAA SAVE   All Year   1P: $98-$249   2P: $98-$249
Location: Adjacent to Camden Yards. 301 W Lombard St 21201. Fax: 410/727-6169. **Facility:** 375 one-bedroom
standard units, some with whirlpools. 10-13 stories, interior corridors. *Bath:* combo or shower only. **Parking:**
on-site (fee). **Amenities:** video games (fee), dual phone lines, voice mail, irons, hair dryers. **Dining:** 6:30
Large-scale Hotel   am-10:30 pm, Sat & Sun from 7 am, cocktails. **Pool(s):** indoor. **Leisure Activities:** sauna, exercise room.
Guest Services: gift shop, valet and coin laundry. **Business Services:** conference facilities, PC, fax.
Cards: AX, CB, DC, DS, JC, MC, VI.

SOME UNITS

FEE FEE

HYATT REGENCY BALTIMORE   *Book at aaa.com*   Phone: (410)528-1234   **13**

AAA SAVE   All Year   1P: $145-$289   2P: $145-$289
Location: Facing Harbor Place. 300 Light St 21202. Fax: 410/685-3362. **Facility:** Copiers, fax machines and
printers are available in this hotel's business-class units; some rooms overlook the Inner Harbor. 486 one-
Large-scale Hotel   bedroom standard units. 15 stories, interior corridors. *Bath:* combo or shower only. **Parking:** on-site (fee).
Terms: 3 day cancellation notice-fee imposed. **Amenities:** high-speed Internet, voice mail, safes, honor
bars, irons, hair dryers. *Some:* CD players, fax. **Dining:** 6:30 am-11 pm, cocktails, also, Pisces, see
separate listing. **Pool(s):** outdoor. **Leisure Activities:** sauna, whirlpool, putting green, 2 tennis courts, jogging, basketball. *Fee:*
aerobics, massage. **Guest Services:** gift shop, valet laundry, tanning facility. **Business Services:** conference facilities,
business center. **Cards:** AX, CB, DC, DS, JC, MC, VI. *(See ad below)*

SOME UNITS

THE INN AT HENDERSON'S WHARF   *Book at aaa.com*   Phone: (410)522-7777   **21**

All Year   1P: $169-$259   2P: $169-$259
Location: On waterfront. Located in historic Fells Point area. 1000 Fell St 21231. Fax: 410/522-7087.
Historic   **Facility:** Formerly a tobacco warehouse, this hotel offers tastefully appointed rooms, some with water views
Small-scale Hotel   and a warm ambience. 38 one-bedroom standard units. 6 stories, interior corridors. **Parking:** on-site.
Terms: 2 night minimum stay - seasonal and/or weekends, cancellation fee imposed, [ECP] meal plan
available. **Amenities:** high-speed Internet, voice mail, irons, hair dryers. **Leisure Activities:** exercise room. *Fee:* marina. **Guest
Services:** valet laundry. **Business Services:** meeting rooms, business center. **Cards:** AX, DC, DS, MC, VI.
(See color ad p 576)

SOME UNITS

(See map and index starting on p. 562)

MOUNT VERNON HOTEL *Book at aaa.com*   Phone: (410)727-2000 **2**
All Year [CP] 1P: $99-$109 2P: $109-$129 XP: $10 F
Location: At Franklin St and Saratoga. 24 W Franklin St 21201. Fax: 410/576-9300. **Facility:** 133 one-bedroom standard units, some with whirlpools. 9 stories, interior corridors. **Parking:** on-site (fee). **Amenities:** voice mail, irons, hair dryers. **Leisure Activities:** exercise room. **Guest Services:** valet and coin laundry.
Small-scale Hotel **Business Services:** meeting rooms, business center. **Cards:** AX, DC, DS, MC, VI. **Special Amenities:** early check-in/late check-out and free room upgrade (subject to availability with advance reservations).

SOME UNITS

PEABODY COURT-A CLARION HOTEL *Book at aaa.com*   Phone: (410)727-7101 **1**
3/1-11/1 1P: $179-$350 2P: $179-$350
11/2-2/28 1P: $149-$300 2P: $149-$300
Location: Cathedral St and Mount Vernon Square. 612 Cathedral St 21201. Fax: 410/789-3312. **Facility:** This
Historic vintage hotel dates from 1924; its public spaces are limited. 104 one-bedroom standard units, some with
Small-scale Hotel whirlpools. 13 stories, interior corridors. **Parking:** on-site (fee) and valet. **Terms:** 2 night minimum stay -
seasonal and/or weekends, small pets only ($35 fee, $15 extra charge). **Amenities:** video games, dual
phone lines, voice mail, safes (fee), irons, hair dryers. **Dining:** 6:30 am-10 pm, cocktails, also, George's on
Mt. Vernon Square, see separate listing. **Leisure Activities:** exercise room. **Guest Services:** valet laundry, area transportation-
within 2 mi. **Business Services:** meeting rooms, business center. **Cards:** AX, CB, DC, DS, JC, MC, VI. *(See color ad p 571)*

SOME UNITS

FEE

PIER 5 HOTEL *Book at aaa.com*   Phone: 410/539-2000 **15**
All Year 1P: $239-$349 2P: $239-$349 XP: $20 F17
Location: On the Inner Harbor, at Pier 5. 711 Eastern Ave 21202. Fax: 410/783-1469. **Facility:** Smoke free
Small-scale Hotel premises. 65 one-bedroom standard units, some with whirlpools. 3 stories, interior corridors. *Bath:* combo or
shower only. **Parking:** on-site (fee). **Terms:** package plans, $4 service charge. **Amenities:** high-speed
Internet, dual phone lines, voice mail, safes, irons, hair dryers. **Guest Services:** valet laundry. **Business Services:** meeting
rooms. **Cards:** AX, DC, DS, MC, VI.

SOME UNITS

(See map and index starting on p. 562)

RADISSON PLAZA LORD BALTIMORE   *Book at aaa.com*   Phone: (410)539-8400   **6**
AAA SAVE   3/1-11/17 [CP]   1P: $129   2P: $129   XP: $15   F12
WWW   11/18-2/28 [CP]   1P: $99   2P: $99   XP: $15   F12
Location: At Baltimore and Hanover sts. 20 W Baltimore St 21201. Fax: 410/625-1060. **Facility:** 424 one-bedroom standard units. 23 stories, interior corridors. *Bath:* combo or shower only. **Parking:** on-site (fee) and valet.
Large-scale Hotel **Terms:** cancellation fee imposed, weekly rates available, [AP], [BP], [ECP] & [MAP] meal plans available, package plans. **Amenities:** dual phone lines, voice mail, irons, hair dryers. *Some:* high-speed Internet (fee). **Dining:** 2 restaurants, 6 am-11 pm, cocktails. **Leisure Activities:** saunas, whirlpool, exercise room. **Guest Services:** gift shop, valet laundry. **Business Services:** conference facilities, fax (fee). **Cards:** AX, DC, DS, MC, VI. **Special Amenities: free newspaper and preferred room (subject to availability with advance reservations).** *(See color ad p 589 & p 576)*

SOME UNITS

RENAISSANCE HARBORPLACE HOTEL   *Book at aaa.com*   Phone: (410)547-1200   **12**
AAA SAVE   3/1-11/19   1P: $269   2P: $279   XP: $10   F12
WWWW   11/20-2/28   1P: $209   2P: $219   XP: $10   F12
Location: Opposite Inner Harbor. Located adjacent to a multi-level shopping mall. 202 E Pratt St 21202. Fax: 410/539-5780. **Facility:** Views of the Inner Harbor are featured from some units of the hotel; gallery
Large-scale Hotel shopping is available adjacent to the lobby. 622 one-bedroom standard units, some with whirlpools. 12 stories, interior corridors. *Bath:* combo or shower only. **Parking:** on-site (fee) and valet. **Terms:** check-in 4 pm, cancellation fee imposed. **Amenities:** high-speed Internet (fee), dual phone lines, voice mail, honor bars, irons, hair dryers. *Some:* CD players. **Dining:** Windows, see separate listing. **Pool(s):** heated indoor. **Leisure Activities:** sauna, whirlpool, sun deck, exercise room. *Fee:* massage. **Guest Services:** gift shop, valet laundry. **Business Services:** conference facilities, business center. **Cards:** AX, CB, DC, DS, JC, MC, VI. *(See color ad below)*

SOME UNITS

SHERATON INNER HARBOR HOTEL   *Book at aaa.com*   Phone: (410)962-8300   **14**
WWW   3/1-11/20   1P: $309-$339   2P: $309-$339   XP: $20   F
WWW   11/21-2/28   1P: $279-$309   2P: $279-$309   XP: $20   F
Location: On S Charles St at Conway St. 300 S Charles St 21201. Fax: 410/962-8211. **Facility:** 337 units. 336
Large-scale Hotel one-bedroom standard units. 1 one-bedroom suite. 14 stories, interior corridors. *Bath:* combo or shower only. **Parking:** on-site (fee) and valet. **Terms:** cancellation fee imposed, package plans, pets (with prior approval). **Amenities:** video games (fee), dual phone lines, voice mail, irons, hair dryers. *Some:* CD players. **Pool(s):** heated indoor. **Leisure Activities:** saunas, exercise room. **Guest Services:** gift shop, valet laundry. **Business Services:** conference facilities, business center. **Cards:** AX, CB, DC, DS, MC, VI.

SOME UNITS

(See map and index starting on p. 562)

WYNDHAM BALTIMORE-INNER HARBOR   *Book at aaa.com*   Phone: (410)752-1100   **5**

4/1-11/17	1P: $169-$209	2P: $169-$209	XP: $20	F17
3/1-3/31 & 11/18-2/28	1P: $159-$189	2P: $159-$189	XP: $20	F17

AAA **SAVE**
Location: Between Charles and Liberty sts. 101 W Fayette St 21201. Fax: 410/752-0832. **Facility:** 707 one-bedroom standard units, some with whirlpools. 23-27 stories, interior corridors. *Bath:* combo or shower only.
Large-scale Hotel **Parking:** on-site and valet. **Terms:** check-in 4 pm, cancellation fee imposed. **Amenities:** video games (fee), high-speed Internet, voice mail, irons, hair dryers. *Some:* honor bars. **Dining:** 2 restaurants, 6:30 am-midnight, cocktails. **Pool(s):** outdoor. **Leisure Activities:** exercise room. **Guest Services:** gift shop, valet laundry. **Business Services:** conference facilities, business center. **Cards:** AX, CB, DC, DS, JC, MC, VI.

SOME UNITS

———— WHERE TO DINE ————

ABACROMBIE FINE FOOD & ACCOMMODATIONS   Dinner: $17-$26   Phone: 410/244-7227   **1**
Location: Jct Martin Luther King Jr Blvd and W Biddle St. 58 W Biddle St 21201. **Hours:** 5 pm-10:30 pm, Fri & Sat-11 pm, Sun noon-8 pm. Closed: 12/25; also Mon & Tues. **Reservations:** suggested. **Features:** An elegant
American   dining room with upscale plate presentations and the finest fresh foods with a Regional incorporation of ingredients. Dressy casual; cocktails. **Parking:** no self-parking. **Cards:** AX, DC, DS, MC, VI.

AKBAR RESTAURANT   Lunch: $10-$17   Dinner: $10-$17   Phone: 410/539-0944   **6**
Location: Between Reed and Madison sts. 823 N Charles St 21201. **Hours:** 11:30 am-2:30 & 5-11 pm, Fri-11:30 pm, Sat noon-3 & 5-11:30 pm, Sun noon-3 & 5-11 pm. Closed: 11/24. **Reservations:** accepted. **Features:** A
Indian   local favorite since 1986, the restaurant uses authentic Indian spices and cooking techniques to prepare the lamb, chicken, seafood and vegetarian dishes. The basement level dining room provides an intimate and comfortable setting to enjoy lunch or dinner. A lunch buffet is available every day. Casual dress; cocktails. **Parking:** no self-parking. **Cards:** AX, DC, DS, MC, VI.

ALDO'S RISTORANTE   Dinner: $16-$45   Phone: 410/727-0700   **27**
Location: In Little Italy area. 306 S High St 21202. **Hours:** 5 pm-11 pm, Fri & Sat-midnight, Sun-10 pm. Closed: 1/1, 11/24, 12/25. **Reservations:** suggested. **Features:** A true complement to Baltimore's Little Italy, the
Italian   eatery definitely is worth a visit. Superb food served with expertise and personality in elegant surroundings captures the dining experience in a nutshell. To avoid a parking nightmare, use valet service. Dressy casual; cocktails. **Parking:** valet and street. **Cards:** AX, CB, DC, DS, JC, MC, VI.

AMICCI'S   Lunch: $7-$12   Dinner: $9-$20   Phone: 410/528-1096   **17**
Location: In Little Italy area. 231 S High St 21202. **Hours:** 11 am-10 pm. Closed: 12/25. **Features:** Amicci's is a very casual eatery located in the heart of the Little Italy section of Baltimore. All the classic Italian favorites
Italian   along with friendly service. Do not miss the chance to order the signature Penne Amicci. Casual dress; cocktails. **Parking:** street. **Cards:** AX, CB, DC, DS, JC, MC, VI.

BABALU GRILL   Dinner: $14-$31   Phone: 410/234-9898   **14**
Location: 2 blks w of Pratt St; at Powerplant Live Complex. 32 Market Pl 21202. **Hours:** 5 pm-10 pm, Fri & Sat-11 pm, Sun 4 pm-9 pm. Closed: 1/1, 11/24, 12/25; also Mon. **Reservations:** suggested. **Features:** Just a
Cuban   couple blocks from the Inner Harbor is a lively, fun Cuban restaurant. The menu offers both Cuban and Latin American dishes prepared from family recipes. They have sidewalk dining seasonally and valet parking is available Sunday through Thursday. Casual dress; cocktails. **Parking:** no self-parking. **Cards:** AX, DC, DS, MC, VI.

BANDALOOPS   Lunch: $6-$18   Dinner: $6-$18   Phone: 410/727-1355   **51**
Location: Between W Cross and W Hamburg sts; in Federal Hill. 1024 S Charles St 21230. **Hours:** 11:30 am-10 pm, Fri & Sat-11 pm. Closed major holidays; also Sun. **Reservations:** suggested. **Features:** You'll find a
American   modern dining room lit by skylights once you walk through the narrow turn-of-the-century bar. The modern menu mixes traditional bar food like burgers and crab dip with healthy items such as tuna BLT, unique salads, and daily changing ravioli specials. The lobster ravioli is house specialty which never leaves the menu. Casual dress; cocktails. **Parking:** street. **Cards:** AX, DC, DS, MC, VI.

BANJARA RESTAURANT   Lunch: $8-$19   Dinner: $10-$19   Phone: 410/962-1554   **50**
Location: Between W Cross and W Hamburg sts. 1017 S Charles St 21230. **Hours:** 11:30 am-2:30 & 5-10:30 pm, Fri-11:30 pm, Sat noon-3 & 5-11:30 pm, Sun noon-3 & 4-10 pm. Closed: 11/24. **Reservations:** suggested,
Indian   weekends. **Features:** Very well prepared Northern Indian cuisine is served in this family-owned and -operated restaurant. A lunch buffet is available daily. Casual dress; cocktails. **Parking:** street. **Cards:** AX, DC, MC, VI.

THE BLACK OLIVE   Lunch: $7-$30   Dinner: $20-$32   Phone: 410/276-7141   **46**
Location: In Fells Point area. 814 S Bond St 21231. **Hours:** noon-2 & 5-10 pm, Fri & Sat-10:30 pm, Sun-9 pm. Closed: 12/25. **Reservations:** suggested. **Features:** The family-owned restaurant serves exotic fresh fish,
Greek   including numerous varieties from around the world. Choices are filleted at tableside. Also on the menu are beef and vegetarian dishes. The friendly staff is professional. Casual dress; cocktails. **Parking:** on-site.
Cards: AX, CB, DC, DS, JC, MC, VI.

(See map and index starting on p. 562)

BOCCACCIO RESTAURANT
Lunch: $12-$19   Dinner: $16-$35   Phone: 410/234-1322   35

▼▼▼
Northern Italian
DC, MC, VI.

Location: Between Exeter and Albemarle sts; in Little Italy area. 925 Eastern Ave 21202. **Hours:** 11:30 am-2:30 & 5-11 pm, Sat from 5 pm, Sun 4 pm-10 pm. Closed: 11/24, 12/25. **Reservations:** suggested. **Features:** A subtle formality marks the tastefully decorated dining rooms, while the clublike lounge shows a different face. The beef carpaccio appetizer is flavorful, as is the veal chops entree. Servers in tuxedos are knowledgeable, attentive and prompt. Semi-formal attire; cocktails. **Parking:** valet and street. **Cards:** AX,

BRASS ELEPHANT
Lunch: $9-$17   Dinner: $20-$30   Phone: 410/547-8480   4

▼▼▼
American

Location: Between E Eager and E Read sts. 924 N Charles St 21201. **Hours:** 5:30 pm-9:30 pm, Fri & Sat-11 pm, Sun 4:30 pm-8 pm; 11:30 am-2:30 & 5:30-9:30 pm, Fri & Sat-11 pm 12/1-12/31. Closed major holidays; also Super Bowl Sun. **Reservations:** suggested. **Features:** Exceptionally well-prepared and creatively presented New American cuisine is served in the richly decorated, 18th-century townhouse. Flaky and flavorful, the salmon served over vodka beet sauce is a work of art. An extensive wine list is provided. Semi-formal attire; cocktails. **Parking:** valet. **Cards:** AX, DC, DS, MC, VI.

CAFE MADRID
Dinner: $16-$27   Phone: 410/276-7700   30

▼▼▼
Spanish

Location: Between Eastern Ave and Fleet St; in Fells Point area. 505 S Broadway 21231. **Hours:** 5 pm-10 pm, Fri & Sat-11 pm, Sun 4 pm-9 pm. Closed: 11/24, 12/25; also Mon. **Reservations:** suggested. **Features:** The chef prepares authentic Spanish dishes as well as Continental selections using fresh ingredients, served in an intimate setting. Dishes such as Zarzuela a la Placido Domingo, Mollejas Adobadas Toledana and Fillet Mignon a-la Antonio are a few of the chef's suggestions. Casual dress; cocktails. **Parking:** street. **Cards:** AX, DS, MC, VI.

CAPITOL CITY BREWING CO-BALTIMORE
Lunch: $7-$24   Dinner: $7-$24   Phone: 410/539-7468   31

▼▼
American

Location: I-95, exit 53, 1.6 mi se; Inner Harbor. 301 S Light St 21202. **Hours:** 11 am-11 pm, Fri & Sat-midnight. Closed: 11/24, 12/25. **Features:** Above the foot traffic with views of the harbor, the waterfront restaurant has a rustic interior with exposed ironwork and bags of ingredients used in the microbrewery brews. Al fresco seating under a canopy is another option. Amply portioned sandwiches and entrees cater for fans of surf or turf. A favorite is the "best of the Wurst" platter, which is paired with brew suggestions. Bustling servers keep the environment boisterous. Casual dress; cocktails. **Parking:** on-site (fee). **Cards:** AX, DC, DS, MC, VI.

CHARLESTON
Dinner: $38-$78   Phone: 410/332-7373   45

▼▼▼ ▼▼▼
Regional American

Location: Inner Harbor E; on ground floor of Sylvan Building. 1000 Lancaster St 21202. **Hours:** 5:30 pm-10 pm, Fri & Sat-11 pm, Sun-9 pm. Closed major holidays. **Reservations:** suggested. **Features:** American cuisine prepared from modern and traditional Southern Lowcountry recipes forges an exciting and creative menu. Guests can relax in the comfortably stylish dining room while a professional, attentive and knowledgeable service staff caters to their needs. Dressy casual; cocktails. **Parking:** street. **Cards:** AX, CB, DC, DS, MC, VI.

CHIAPPARELLI'S
Lunch: $8-$15   Dinner: $12-$28   Phone: 410/837-0309   18

▼▼
South Italian

Location: In Little Italy area. 237 S High St 21202. **Hours:** 11 am-10 pm, Fri & Sat-midnight. Closed: 11/24, 12/25. **Reservations:** suggested, weekends. **Features:** Established in the 1940s, the Little Italy restaurant is a longtime favorite of the local crowd. Examples of house specials include wedding soup, Momma Chiapparelli's ravioli, veal cacciatore and homemade tiramisu. The comfortable dining room, with brick walls and soft lighting, is perfect for families or business and social events. Casual dress; cocktails. **Parking:** street. **Cards:** AX, CB, DC, DS, MC, VI.

CIAO BELLA RESTAURANT
Lunch: $7-$14   Dinner: $10-$25   Phone: 410/685-7733   21

▼▼▼
Italian

Location: In Little Italy area. 236 S High St 21202. **Hours:** 11:30 am-10 pm, Sat from 2 pm, Sun 3 pm-9 pm. Closed: 1/1, 12/25. **Reservations:** suggested. **Features:** Northern and Southern Italian cuisine in the serene setting of Ciao Bella Restaurant. Many wine selections and homemade desserts. Ciao Bella means hello beautiful, and that is what you'll say when you see the food. Casual dress; cocktails. **Parking:** valet and street. **Cards:** AX, CB, DC, DS, JC, MC, VI.

DALESIO'S RESTAURANT OF LITTLE ITALY
Lunch: $7-$18   Dinner: $9-$24   Phone: 410/539-1965   36

▼▼▼
Italian

Location: Between Exeter and Albermatte sts; in Little Italy area. 829 Eastern Ave 21202. **Hours:** 11:30 am-3 & 5-10 pm, Fri & Sat-11 pm, Sun 4 pm-9 pm. Closed: 1/1, 11/24. **Reservations:** suggested, weekends. **Features:** Friendly servers display excellent knowledge of the hugely varied menu. Many types of pasta and sauce are combined in delicious dishes. The atmosphere is cozy. Casual dress; cocktails. **Parking:** on-site. **Cards:** AX, CB, DC, DS, MC, VI.

DA MIMMO
Lunch: $7-$14   Dinner: $12-$28   Phone: 410/727-6876   15

▼▼ ▼▼▼
Italian

Location: In Little Italy area. 217 S High St 21202. **Hours:** 11:30 am-11:30 pm, Fri & Sat-1 am. Closed: 11/24, 12/25. **Reservations:** suggested. **Features:** In business since the early 1980s, the cozy restaurant invites guests to an intimate, candlelight experience. On the menu is an extensive selection of homemade pasta, fresh seafood and veal preparations, including the house specialty veal chop. Among other favorites are lobster Tetrazzini and tortellini Pavarotti. Dressy casual; cocktails. **Parking:** on-site. **Cards:** AX, DC, MC, VI.

DELLA NOTTE RISTORANTE
Lunch: $7-$16   Dinner: $18-$38   Phone: 410/837-5500   37

AAA
▼▼▼
Italian

Location: Jct President and Eastern aves; in Little Italy area. 801 Eastern Ave 21202. **Hours:** 11 am-10 pm, Fri & Sat-midnight. Closed: 11/24, 12/25. **Reservations:** accepted. **Features:** Close to downtown on the border of Little Italy, the restaurant presents a menu of veal, chicken and pasta dishes. Patrons savor the in-house-baked breads and pastries. A good wine list and both booth and table seating in the round section of the dining room complement the experience. Dressy casual; cocktails; entertainment. **Parking:** on-site. **Cards:** AX, DC, DS, MC, VI.

(See map and index starting on p. 562)

DUEISOLE RISTORANTE ITALIANO **Dinner:** $10-$27 **Phone:** 410/522-4466 42
Italian
Location: In Fells Point. 1911 Aliceanna St 21231. **Hours:** 5 pm-10 pm, Fri & Sat-11 pm. Closed major holidays; also Mon. **Reservations:** accepted. **Features:** Service is friendly, and generous portions are a hallmark. Fresh fish, veal, chicken, pork and salads large enough to serve two are popular features. Seating is close, and at times the atmosphere is bustling. Casual dress; cocktails. **Parking:** street. **Cards:** AX, DC, DS, MC, VI.

ESPN ZONE **Lunch:** $8-$18 **Dinner:** $8-$18 **Phone:** 410/685-3776 23
American
Location: At the Inner Harbor. 601 E Pratt St 21202. **Hours:** 11:30 am-11 pm, Fri & Sat 11 am-midnight, Sun 11 am-11 pm; 11 am-midnight, Fri & Sat-1 am in summer. Closed: 12/25. **Features:** This lively and popular tourist spot at Inner Harbor serves traditional American fare. The decor is accented with sports memorabilia. Casual dress; cocktails. **Parking:** on-site. **Cards:** AX, DS, MC, VI.

EURASIAN HARBOR **Dinner:** $12-$26 **Phone:** 410/230-9992 38
Asian
Location: In Inner Harbor; at Pier 5. 711 Eastern Ave 21202. **Hours:** 5 pm-10 pm, Fri & Sat-11 pm, Sun 4 pm-9 pm. Closed: 12/25; also Mon. **Reservations:** suggested, weekends. **Features:** Eurasian Harbor offers large and generous portions and wants to keep the asian custom of sharing alive-so pass the plates. Casual dress; cocktails. **Parking:** on-site (fee) and valet. **Cards:** AX, CB, DC, DS, JC, MC, VI.

GEORGE'S ON MT. VERNON SQUARE **Lunch:** $11-$17 **Dinner:** $15-$28 **Phone:** 410/727-7101 8
American
Location: Cathedral St and Mount Vernon Square; in Peabody Court-A Clarion Hotel. 612 Cathedral St 21201. **Hours:** 6:30-10 am, 11-2 & 5-10 pm, Sat & Sun 7 am-10 & 5-10 pm. **Reservations:** accepted. **Features:** Historic Mount Vernon Square is the backdrop for casual dining. This place has a full bar area and many dessert and appetizer choices. Casual dress; cocktails. **Parking:** on-site (fee) and valet. **Cards:** AX, DS, MC, VI.

GERMANO'S TRATTORIA **Lunch:** $7-$14 **Dinner:** $13-$25 **Phone:** 410/752-4515 25
Regional Italian
Location: At S High and Fawn sts; in Little Italy area. 300 S High St 21202. **Hours:** 11:30 am-10 pm, Fri & Sat-11 pm. Closed: 11/24, 12/25. **Reservations:** suggested. **Features:** Family owned since the 1970s, the relaxed, two-story restaurant has three dining areas decorated with turn-of-the-20th-century posters. Excellent entrees are topped by such decadent, made-on-the-premises desserts as tiramisu and Tuscan Napoleon. Casual dress; cocktails. **Parking:** on-site (fee). **Cards:** AX, CB, DC, MC, VI.

HAMPTON'S **Dinner:** $25-$50 **Phone:** 410/234-0550 44
American
Location: Facing Inner Harbor; in Harbor Court Hotel. 550 Light St 21202. **Hours:** 5:30 pm-10 pm, Fri & Sat-11 pm, Sun 10:30 am-2:30 & 5:30-10 pm. Closed: Mon. **Reservations:** suggested. **Features:** This formal dining room provides a refined setting overlooking the Inner Harbor. The chef re-creates the menu seasonally to offer innovative American selections that illustrate a high degree of complexity and polish. Patrons can opt for the chef's prix fixe menu. International and domestic wines are well chosen. Formal attire; cocktails. **Parking:** on-site (fee) and valet. **Cards:** AX, CB, DC, DS, JC, MC, VI.

THE HELMAND RESTAURANT **Dinner:** $10-$20 **Phone:** 410/752-0311 5
Afghan
Location: Between Madison and Read sts; in the Mount Vernon area. 806 N Charles St 21201. **Hours:** 5 pm-10 pm, Fri & Sat-11 pm. Closed: 11/24, 12/25. **Reservations:** suggested, weekends. **Features:** Well-prepared Afghan cuisine is served in an intimate and tasteful setting. The menu lists beef, lamb, chicken and seafood dishes, as well as extensive vegetarian selections. Succulent rack of lamb is offered Friday and Saturday evenings. Casual dress; cocktails. **Parking:** on-site. **Cards:** AX, DC, MC, VI.

JAMES JOYCE IRISH PUB & RESTAURANT **Lunch:** $8-$18 **Dinner:** $8-$22 **Phone:** 410/727-5107 40
Irish
Location: Jct President St and Eastern Ave; in Inner Harbor area. 616 President St 21202. **Hours:** 11 am-2 am. Closed: 12/25. **Features:** The home of Irish hospitality in Baltimore is the James Joyce Irish Pub & Restaurant. No need to be a writer to get great service. Casual dress; cocktails. **Parking:** street. **Cards:** AX, CB, DC, DS, JC, MC, VI.

JOY AMERICA CAFE **Lunch:** $14-$25 **Dinner:** $17-$30 **Phone:** 410/244-6500 48
American
Location: In the Inner Harbor area; Covington St, on 3rd floor of American Visionary Art Museum. 800 Key Hwy 21230. **Hours:** 11:30 am-3 & 5:30-10 pm, Sun-9 pm; Sunday brunch 11 am-3 pm. Closed: 11/24, 12/25; also Mon & Super Bowl Sun. **Reservations:** suggested, weekends. **Features:** The colorful, spicy aura of Latin America and the Caribbean infuses life into the fun, lively restaurant, a great special-occasion spot. Creative cuisine—such as mesquite-grilled fish with a lime drizzle—makes up the seasonally changing menu. Dressy casual; cocktails. **Parking:** on-site (fee). **Cards:** AX, CB, DC, MC, VI.

LA SCALA RISTORANTE ITALIANO **Dinner:** $12-$29 **Phone:** 410/783-9209 32
Italian
Location: Between Exeter and Albemarle sts; in Little Italy area. 1012 Eastern Ave 21202. **Hours:** 4:30 pm-10 pm, Fri & Sat-11 pm, Sun 2 pm-10 pm. Closed: 12/25. **Reservations:** suggested. **Features:** Innovative specials, daily seafood specials and Italian cooking at it's finest will be found at la Scala Ristorante Italiano. Do not miss the cannoli at the end of the meal. Casual dress; cocktails. **Parking:** street. **Cards:** AX, CB, DC, DS, JC, MC, VI.

MARCONI'S **Lunch:** $10-$20 **Dinner:** $10-$30 **Phone:** 410/727-9522 11
American
Location: Center. 106 W Saratoga St 21201. **Hours:** 11:30 am-8:30 pm, Fri & Sat-9 pm. Closed: Sun & Mon. **Features:** A favorite with locals, the restaurant serves traditional American cuisine in a neighborhood townhouse dining room. Casual dress; cocktails. **Parking:** on-site. **Cards:** AX, DC, DS, MC, VI.

(See map and index starting on p. 562)

MONDO BONDO ITALIAN BISTRO   **Lunch:** $7-$15   **Dinner:** $7-$15   **Phone:** 410/244-8080   [13]
Italian
Location: 2 blks w of Pratt St; at Powerplant Live Complex. 34 Market Pl 21202. **Hours:** 11 am-10 pm, Fri & Sat-1 am; closing hours may vary in winter. Closed major holidays. **Reservations:** suggested, weekends. **Features:** The intimate Italian bistro offers salads, pizza, pasta and sandwiches; sidewalk dining is available seasonally. Casual dress; cocktails. **Parking:** no self-parking. **Cards:** AX, MC, VI.

MO'S CRAB AND PASTA FACTORY   **Lunch:** $6-$12   **Dinner:** $11-$28   **Phone:** 410/837-1600   [34]
Seafood
Location: Just s of corner of Albemarle St and Eastern Ave. 502 Albemarle St 21202. **Hours:** 11 am-1 am. Closed: 11/24, 12/25. **Reservations:** suggested. **Features:** Mama mia! Portions of the yummy lasagna are enormous, and the same goes for other pasta, beef and chicken selections. A perfect accompaniment to any dish is the fresh salad with tasty Parmesan dressing. Casual dress; cocktails. **Parking:** street. **Cards:** AX, CB, DC, DS, MC, VI.

OBRYCKI'S CRAB HOUSE AND SEAFOOD RESTAURANT   **Lunch:** $7-$25   **Dinner:** $16-$30   **Phone:** 410/732-6399   [12]
Seafood
Location: Just e of S Broadway. 1727 E Pratt St 21231. **Hours:** Open 3/15-11/15; 11:30 am-11 pm, Sun-9:30 pm. Closed major holidays. **Features:** A warm, inviting atmosphere pervades the energetic restaurant, decorated with brick floors and pillars. The specialty and main attraction is steamed crabs, served on the brown-paper-covered tabletop. Casual dress; cocktails. **Parking:** no self-parking. **Cards:** AX, CB, DC, DS, MC, VI.

PAOLO'S RISTORANTE   **Lunch:** $8-$17   **Dinner:** $10-$25   **Phone:** 410/539-7060   [28]
Italian
Location: At Harbor Place. 301 Light St 21202. **Hours:** 11 am-midnight. Closed: 11/24, 12/25. **Features:** The energetic waterfront restaurant is beside a water taxi landing and close to shopping and attractions. On the menu are pasta, seafood and chicken dishes, as well as pizza made in a wood-burning oven. Daily chef specials are worth trying. Casual dress; cocktails. **Parking:** on-site (fee). **Cards:** AX, CB, DC, DS, MC, VI.

PEACOCK CAFE AT PIER 5   **Lunch:** $6-$14   **Dinner:** $9-$20   **Phone:** 410/547-1333   [39]
American
Location: In Inner Harbor; at Pier 5. 711 Eastern Ave 21202. **Hours:** 7 am-10 pm. Closed: 12/25. **Features:** Peacock Cafe at Pier 5 offers contemporary American cuisine with views of the famed Inner Harbor. Outdoor water view dining in season is available. Casual dress; cocktails. **Parking:** on-site (fee) and valet. **Cards:** AX, CB, DC, DS, JC, MC, VI.

PHILLIPS HARBORPLACE   **Lunch:** $7-$20   **Dinner:** $11-$25   **Phone:** 410/685-6600   [29]
Seafood
Location: At the Inner Harbor. 301 Light St 21202. **Hours:** 11 am-10 pm, Fri & Sat-11 pm. Closed: 12/25. **Features:** In the hub of the Inner Harbor area, the busy restaurant serves an extensive selection of fresh seafood and treats diners to great harbor views. The atmosphere is festive and inviting thanks to the piano bar. A terrace opens seasonally. Casual dress; cocktails; entertainment. **Parking:** on-site (fee). **Cards:** AX, DC, DS, MC, VI.

PIER 4 KITCHEN & BAR   **Lunch:** $9-$18   **Dinner:** $12-$25   **Phone:** 410/659-1200   [22]
American
Location: On the Inner Harbor; at Pier 4. 621 E Pratt 21202. **Hours:** 11 am-11 pm. Closed: 12/25. **Features:** Pier 4 Kitchen & Bar offers specialty drinks, great views of the Inner Harbor, fresh seafood and friendly service. Casual dress; cocktails. **Parking:** street. **Cards:** AX, CB, DC, DS, JC, MC, VI.

PIERPOINT RESTAURANT & BAR   **Lunch:** $6-$10   **Dinner:** $16-$25   **Phone:** 410/675-2080   [41]
Regional American
Location: In Fells Point area. 1822 Aliceanna St 21231. **Hours:** 11:30 am-2:30 & 5-9:30 pm, Fri 11:30 am-2:30 & 5:30-10:30 pm, Sat 5:30 pm-10:30 pm, Sun 10:30 am-1:30 & 4-9 pm; Sunday brunch. Closed: 1/1, 11/24, 12/25; also Mon & Super Bowl Sun. **Reservations:** suggested, lunch. **Features:** Local ingredients are what make the restaurant's creative, contemporary dishes noteworthy. The owner/chef prepares excellent smoked crab cakes and smoked corn chowder. The small neighborhood eatery buzzes with a busy cafe atmosphere. Casual dress; cocktails. **Parking:** street. **Cards:** AX, CB, DC, DS, JC, MC, VI.

PISCES   **Dinner:** $35-$40   **Phone:** 410/605-2835   [33]
Seafood
Location: Facing Harbor Place; in Hyatt Regency Baltimore. 300 Light St 21202. **Hours:** 6 pm-10 pm; Sunday brunch 10 am-2 pm. Closed: 1/1, 12/25; also Mon. **Reservations:** suggested. **Features:** The big draw in the intimate rooftop restaurant is the dramatic panoramic view of the Inner Harbor. Servers are smartly attired, knowledgeable and professional. Dressy casual; cocktails. **Parking:** on-site (fee) and valet. **Cards:** AX, CB, DC, DS, MC, VI.

THE PRIME RIB   **Dinner:** $21-$41   **Phone:** 410/539-1804   [3]
Steak & Seafood
Location: Jct of Calvert and Chase sts; in the Horizon Hotel Building. 1101 N Calvert St 21202. **Hours:** 5 pm-midnight, Sun 4 pm-11 pm. Closed: 11/24. **Reservations:** suggested. **Features:** Generous portions of Chicago aged beef and Chesapeake Bay seafood are professionally and expertly served in an upscale and formal setting. Valet parking is complimentary on Friday and Saturday. Smoking is permitted in the lounge. Jackets are required. Formal attire; cocktails; entertainment. **Parking:** valet. **Cards:** AX, CB, DC, MC, VI.

PURPLE ORCHID   **Lunch:** $7-$11   **Dinner:** $17-$32   **Phone:** 410/837-0080   [20]
French
Location: In the Mount Vernon area. 729 E Platt St 21212. **Hours:** 11:30 am-2:30 & 5-10:30 pm, Fri-11 pm, Sat 5 pm-11 pm, Sun 4 pm-9:30 pm. Closed: 12/25; also Mon. **Reservations:** suggested, weekends. **Features:** The chef/owner and attentive servers appropriately cultivate the menu, which combines French and Asian culinary influences. The surroundings have a well-used, lived-in feel, a testimony to the restaurant's longevity and strong local following. Dressy casual; cocktails. **Parking:** street. **Cards:** AX, DC, DS, MC, VI.

(See map and index starting on p. 562)

ROCCO'S CAPRICCIO   Lunch: $9-$15   Dinner: $15-$32   Phone: 410/685-2710   26
Location: In Little Italy area. 846 Fawn St 21202. **Hours:** 11:30 am-11:30 pm, Fri & Sat-12:30 am. Closed:
Northern Italian — 11/24, 12/25. **Reservations:** suggested, weekends. **Features:** Soft lighting, hand-painted walls and a professionally attired staff set the tone at this intimate restaurant. The staff is versed in the preparation of such menu selections as the house specialty veal chop, which is marinated with fresh herbs, broiled and served in its natural juices. A flavorful tomato and meat sauce tops the tortellini. Dressy casual; cocktails.
Parking: street. **Cards:** AX, CB, DC, DS, MC, VI.

THE RUSTY SCUPPER RESTURANT   Lunch: $8-$18   Dinner: $10-$27   Phone: 410/727-3678   47
Location: In Inner Harbor. 402 Key Hwy 21230. **Hours:** 11:30 am-10 pm; Sunday brunch 11 am-2 pm. Closed:
American — 12/25. **Features:** Guests enjoy incredible Inner Harbor views from the dining area. This place is known for seafood, particularly the not-to-be-missed crab cakes. Casual dress; cocktails. **Parking:** on-site (fee).
Cards: AX, CB, DC, DS, JC, MC, VI.

SABATINO'S   Lunch: $10-$35   Dinner: $10-$35   Phone: 410/727-2667   24
Location: Fawn and S High sts; in Little Italy. 901 Fawn St 21202. **Hours:** 11:30 am-midnight, Fri & Sat-3 am.
Italian — Closed: 11/24, 12/25. **Reservations:** suggested, weekends. **Features:** Excellent wine, rich desserts and flavorful veal are among offerings at the cozy, warm restaurant. Attentive, friendly staff members are familiar both with the menu and the locals who frequent the place. Those with lighter appetites may request half-
orders at lunch. Casual dress; cocktails. **Parking:** on-site (fee) and street. **Cards:** AX, CB, DC, DS, MC, VI.

SAFFRON   Dinner: $12-$28   Phone: 410/528-1616   7
Location: Just n of E Madison St. 802 N Charles St 21201. **Hours:** 5 pm-10 pm, Fri & Sat-11 pm. Closed major
Indian — holidays; also Mon. **Reservations:** suggested. **Features:** The setting is sultry and exotic with walls draped in rich reds and ceilings of flying carpets; the cuisine is equally imaginative as the chef fuses classic Indian influences with modern American and French flavors and techniques. Dressy casual; cocktails. **Parking:**
street. **Cards:** AX, DC, DS, MC, VI.

SOTTO SOPRA   Lunch: $10-$18   Dinner: $15-$30   Phone: 410/625-0534   10
Location: In the Mount Vernon area. 405 N Charles St 21201. **Hours:** 11:30 am-2:30 & 5:30-10:30 pm, Mon-9:30
Italian — pm, Fri & Sat-11:30 pm, Sun 11 am-2:30 & 5:30-9:30 pm. Closed major holidays. **Reservations:** suggested.
Features: Striking features of the stylish, Renaissance-style dining room include full-wall murals and framed mirrors. The owner/chef's imagination is evident in well-prepared dishes, such as poppy/sesame seed-crusted tuna. Save room for one of the wonderful desserts. Dressy casual; cocktails. **Parking:** no self-parking. **Cards:** AX, DC, DS, MC, VI.

TAMPICO MEXICAN GRILL   Lunch: $7-$13   Dinner: $7-$13   Phone: 410/837-9999   2
Location: Jct W Biddle St. 1200 N Charles St 21201. **Hours:** 11 am-3 & 5-11 pm, Fri-midnight, Sat 5 pm-
Mexican — midnight, Sun 4 pm-10 pm. Closed major holidays. **Features:** This colorful spot, outfitted with Mexican tiles, pottery and a long granite bar, serves up authentic Mexican fare with focus on the Yucatan region. Casual dress; cocktails. **Parking:** street. **Cards:** AX, MC, VI.

TEN-O-SIX RESTAURANT   Dinner: $13-$23   Phone: 410/528-2146   49
Location: Between E Hamburg and Poultney sts: 1006 Light St 21230. **Hours:** 5 pm-10 pm, Sun 4 pm-9 pm.
Thai — Closed: 11/24; also Mon. **Reservations:** suggested, weekends. **Features:** Since 1999 this chef-owned Thai restaurant has attracted the locals. The kitchen staff is skilled in both Thai and American cooking, offering
dishes such as drunken noodles, Thai orange chicken, wild Alaskan king salmon and rack of wild boar, to mention a few. Diners may request the degree of spiciness from a range of 1-6, with 6 being Native Thai. Casual dress; beer & wine only. **Parking:** street. **Cards:** AX, MC, VI.

TIO PEPE RESTAURANT   Lunch: $10-$17   Dinner: $17-$26   Phone: 410/539-4675   9
Location: Just e of N Charles St. 10 E Franklin St 21202. **Hours:** 11:30 am-2:30 & 5-10 pm, Fri-11:30 pm, Sat 5
Spanish — pm-11:30 pm, Sun 4 pm-10 pm. Closed major holidays. **Reservations:** required, for dinner. **Features:** Locals are attracted to the Spanish cuisine, which is served in basement-level dining rooms of the row house Tio Pepe calls home. The house specialty is suckling pig, but almost any of the menu choices is well worth a try. Service is attentive. Formal attire; cocktails. **Parking:** street. **Cards:** AX, CB, DC, DS, MC, VI.

VELLEGGIA'S   Lunch: $12-$22   Dinner: $12-$22   Phone: 410/685-2620   16
Location: Corner of E Pratt and Albemarle sts; in Little Italy area. 829 E Pratt St 21202. **Hours:** 11 am-10:30 pm, Fri
Italian — & Sat-midnight. Closed: 12/24, 12/25; also Mon. **Reservations:** suggested, weekends. **Features:** In business since the mid-1930s, the simple, comfortable restaurant mixes a contemporary feel with Old World charm. Pasta dishes, homemade from family recipes, are at the heart of the traditional menu. The wait staff
is knowledgeable and friendly. The parking lot is small. Casual dress; cocktails. **Parking:** street. **Cards:** AX, DC, MC, VI.

VICTOR'S ITALIAN CAFE   Lunch: $10-$15   Dinner: $12-$26   Phone: 410/244-1722   43
Location: In Inner Harbor. 801 Lancaster St 21202. **Hours:** 11 am-10 pm. Closed: 12/25.
Italian — **Reservations:** suggested, weekends. **Features:** The cafe affords great views of the Inner Harbor. Menu selections are wonderfully diverse. Casual dress; cocktails. **Parking:** on-site and street. **Cards:** AX, CB, DC, DS, JC, MC, VI.

(See map and index starting on p. 562)

WINDOWS **Lunch:** $13-$19 **Dinner:** $14-$32 **Phone:** 410/685-8439 ⑲
▼▼◆▼▼ **Location:** Opposite Inner Harbor; in Renaissance Harborplace Hotel. 202 E Pratt St, Fl 5 21202. **Hours:** 6:30 am-10
American pm. **Reservations:** suggested. **Features:** The contemporary, smoke-free dining room affords a spectacular
view of the Inner Harbor. Although crab dishes are the specialty, the menu also lists chicken, beef, pasta
entertainment. **Parking:** on-site. **Cards:** AX, CB, DC, DS, JC, MC, VI. and fresh fish preparations. There's also a breakfast and lunch buffet. Dressy casual; cocktails; ⧖ ✕

---

*The following restaurants have not been evaluated by AAA
but are listed for your information only.*

CAESAR'S DEN **Phone:** 410/547-0820
[fyi] Not evaluated. **Location:** In Little Italy area. 223 S High St 21202. **Features:** A wide selection of wines,
homemade salads and desserts, Caesar's Den offers first rate Italian Cuisine. Located in the heart of the
Little Italy section.

MATSURI **Phone:** 410/752-8561
[fyi] Not evaluated. **Location:** Center. 1105 S Charles St 21230. **Features:** Matsuri offers traditional Japanese
Cuisine featuring sushi and sashimi. Friendly atmosphere and wait staff.

Drive America With AAA

See America
from s e a t o s h i n i n g s e a and everything in between.

Let AAA help you plan your next drive vacation. Whether you're taking
a weekend trip close to home or visiting one of North America's major
travel destinations, *AAA Drive Trips* provide all the information you
need to keep your vacation on course.

Each *AAA Drive Trip* includes a route map, estimated driving time,
mileage, and details about what to see and do along the way.

So, on your next drive vacation, take along AAA —your trusted
provider of quality travel information, including TourBooks® and other
travel guides, TripTiks®, discounted lodging, theme park tickets,
exclusive member discounts, and much more.

Visit us online at *aaa.com* or stop by your local AAA office.

www.aaa.com

Travel With Someone You Trust.®

BALTIMORE pop. 651,154   (See map and index starting on p. 566)

——— **WHERE TO STAY** ———

BEST INN MORAVIA   *Book at aaa.com*
Phone: (410)485-7900   **4**

AAA SAVE
WWWW
Small-scale Hotel

All Year   1P: $62-$72   2P: $62-$72   XP: $5   F14
Location: I-95, exit 60, just w on Moravia Rd, 0.3 mi ne on Moravia Park Dr, then just s; I-895, exit 14. 6510 Frankford Ave 21206. Fax: 410/325-4660. **Facility:** 139 one-bedroom standard units. 6 stories, interior corridors. *Bath:* combo or shower only. **Parking:** on-site. **Terms:** cancellation fee imposed. **Amenities:** voice mail, hair dryers. *Some:* irons. **Dining:** 11:30 am-2 & 5:30-11 pm. **Guest Services:** valet and coin laundry. **Business Services:** conference facilities, fax (fee). **Cards:** AX, DC, DS, MC, VI. **Special Amenities:** free continental breakfast.

SOME UNITS
[icons]

BEST WESTERN HOTEL & CONFERENCE CENTER   *Book at aaa.com*
Phone: (410)633-9500   **9**

AAA SAVE
WWWW
Small-scale Hotel

All Year   1P: $99-$139
Location: I-95, exit 57, just e. Located in a travel plaza. 5625 O'Donnell St 21224. Fax: 410/633-4314. **Facility:** 175 units. 172 one-bedroom standard units, some with kitchens. 3 one-bedroom suites with whirlpools. 12 stories, interior corridors. **Terms:** 2 night minimum stay - seasonal and/or weekends. **Amenities:** voice mail, irons, hair dryers. **Dining:** 6:30 am-10 pm, cocktails. **Pool(s):** heated indoor. **Leisure Activities:** sauna, whirlpool, limited exercise equipment. **Guest Services:** gift shop, valet and coin laundry, area transportation-Inner Harbor. **Business Services:** conference facilities, fax. **Cards:** AX, DC, DS, MC, VI. **Special Amenities:** free continental breakfast. *(See ad below)*

SOME UNITS
[icons]
FEE FEE

COMFORT INN BALTIMORE WEST   *Book at aaa.com*
Phone: (410)744-5000   **8**

AAA SAVE
WWWW
Motel

4/1-9/30   1P: $69-$89   2P: $69-$89
3/1-3/31 & 10/1-2/28   1P: $59-$79   2P: $59-$79
Location: I-695, exit 15A, just e on US 40. 5801 Baltimore National Pike 21228. Fax: 410/788-5197. **Facility:** 94 one-bedroom standard units, some with whirlpools. 3 stories (no elevator), interior/exterior corridors. **Parking:** on-site. **Terms:** [ECP] meal plan available. **Amenities:** high-speed Internet, voice mail, safes, irons, hair dryers. **Leisure Activities:** exercise room. **Guest Services:** coin laundry. **Cards:** AX, DC, DS, MC, VI. **Special Amenities:** free continental breakfast and free local telephone calls.

SOME UNITS
[icons]

DAYS INN   *Book at aaa.com*
Phone: 410/747-8900   **7**

WW
Small-scale Hotel

6/1-9/15   1P: $109-$129   2P: $109-$129   XP: $5   F12
9/16-10/31   1P: $99-$109   2P: $99-$109   XP: $5   F12
3/1-5/31 & 11/1-2/28   1P: $79-$89   2P: $79-$89   XP: $5   F12
Location: I-695, exit 15A, just e. 5701 Baltimore National Pike 21228. Fax: 410/744-3522. **Facility:** 125 one-bedroom standard units, some with whirlpools. 8 stories, interior corridors. **Parking:** on-site. **Terms:** small pets only. **Amenities:** irons, hair dryers. **Pool(s):** outdoor. **Leisure Activities:** exercise room. **Guest Services:** coin laundry. **Business Services:** meeting rooms. **Cards:** AX, DC, MC, VI.

SOME UNITS
[icons]

DAYS INN WEST/SECURITY BLVD   *Book at aaa.com*
Phone: (410)944-7400   **6**

WWWW
Small-scale Hotel

5/1-10/31 [CP]   1P: $65-$129   2P: $70-$129   XP: $5   F12
11/1-2/28 [CP]   1P: $60-$109   2P: $65-$119   XP: $5   F12
3/1-4/30 [CP]   1P: $59-$89   2P: $64-$99   XP: $5   F12
Location: I-695, exit 17, just e. 1660 Whitehead Ct 21207. Fax: 410/944-7905. **Facility:** 100 one-bedroom standard units, some with whirlpools. 2 stories (no elevator), exterior corridors. **Parking:** on-site. **Pool(s):** outdoor. **Guest Services:** coin laundry. **Business Services:** meeting rooms, fax (fee). **Cards:** AX, CB, DC, DS, JC, MC, VI.

SOME UNITS
[icons]

(See map and index starting on p. 566)

HOLIDAY INN BALTIMORE WEST — *Book at aaa.com*
Phone: 410/265-1400 [3]

All Year   1P: $119   2P: $119

Small-scale Hotel **Location:** I-695, exit 17, 0.3 mi nw. 1800 Belmont Ave 21244. **Fax:** 410/281-9569. **Facility:** 133 one-bedroom standard units. 2 stories (no elevator), exterior corridors. *Bath:* combo or shower only. **Parking:** on-site. **Terms:** 2 night minimum stay - seasonal, 3 day cancellation notice-fee imposed, weekly rates available, package plans. **Amenities:** voice mail, irons, hair dryers. **Pool(s):** outdoor. **Leisure Activities:** limited exercise equipment. **Guest Services:** valet and coin laundry, area transportation. **Business Services:** meeting rooms, fax (fee). **Cards:** AX, DC, DS, MC, VI.

SOME UNITS

HOLIDAY INN EXPRESS-BALTIMORE — *Book at aaa.com*
Phone: (410)646-1700 [10]

3/1-10/31 [ECP]	1P: $99-$139	2P: $99-$139	XP: $10	F18
11/1-2/28 [ECP]	1P: $89-$129	2P: $89-$129	XP: $10	F18

Small-scale Hotel **Location:** I-95, exit 50A, just e. 1401 Bloomfield Ave 21227. **Fax:** 410/368-1341. **Facility:** 177 one-bedroom standard units. 4 stories, exterior corridors. **Parking:** on-site. **Terms:** cancellation fee imposed. **Pool(s):** outdoor. **Leisure Activities:** exercise room. **Guest Services:** valet laundry. **Business Services:** meeting rooms, fax (fee). **Cards:** AX, DS, MC, VI. **Special Amenities:** free expanded continental breakfast and free local telephone calls. *(See color ad p 575)*

SOME UNITS

INN AT THE COLONNADE — *Book at aaa.com*
Phone: (410)235-5400 [2]

All Year   1P: $89-$229   2P: $89-$229   XP: $15   F18

Small-scale Hotel **Location:** I-83, exit 9A, 0.5 mi e on Cold Springs Ln to Roland Ave/University Pkwy, then 1 mi s. 4 W University Pkwy 21218. **Fax:** 410/235-5572. **Facility:** 125 units. 123 one- and 2-bedroom standard units. 11 stories, interior corridors. *Bath:* combo or shower only. **Parking:** on-site (fee) and valet. **Terms:** cancellation fee imposed. **Amenities:** high-speed Internet, dual phone lines, voice mail, irons, hair dryers. **Dining:** Four West, see separate listing. **Pool(s):** heated indoor. **Leisure Activities:** whirlpools, exercise room. **Guest Services:** valet laundry, area transportation. **Business Services:** conference facilities, fax. **Cards:** AX, CB, DC, DS, MC, VI. Affiliated with Doubletree Hotels.

SOME UNITS

QUALITY INN WEST — *Book at aaa.com*
Phone: (410)281-1800 [5]

All Year   1P: $70-$110   2P: $75-$115   XP: $5   F

Small-scale Hotel **Location:** I-695, exit 17, just e. 6700 Security Blvd 21207. **Fax:** 410/281-9148. **Facility:** 165 units. 162 one-bedroom standard units, some with whirlpools. 3 one-bedroom suites, some with whirlpools. 3 stories, exterior corridors. **Parking:** on-site. **Terms:** 2 night minimum stay - seasonal and/or weekends. **Amenities:** safes, irons, hair dryers. **Pool(s):** outdoor. **Leisure Activities:** exercise room. **Guest Services:** valet and coin laundry, area transportation. **Business Services:** meeting rooms, fax (fee). **Cards:** AX, CB, DC, DS, MC, VI.

SOME UNITS

RADISSON HOTEL AT CROSS KEYS
Phone: (410)532-6900 [1]

All Year   1P: $139-$229   2P: $159-$309   XP: $20   F16

Small-scale Hotel **Location:** I-83, exit 10A, 0.5 mi s on Falls Rd. 100 Village Sq 21210. **Fax:** 410/532-2403. **Facility:** 147 one-bedroom standard units. 4 stories, interior corridors. *Bath:* combo or shower only. **Parking:** on-site. **Terms:** 2 night minimum stay - seasonal and/or weekends, 3 day cancellation notice-fee imposed, package plans. **Amenities:** video games, high-speed Internet, voice mail, irons, hair dryers. **Pool(s):** outdoor. **Leisure Activities:** jogging, exercise room. **Guest Services:** valet laundry, area transportation. **Business Services:** conference facilities. **Cards:** AX, CB, DC, DS, JC, MC, VI. *(See color ad p 589)*

SOME UNITS

——— WHERE TO DINE ———

THE BICYCLE
Dinner: $15-$30   **Phone: 410/234-1900** [7]

American · **Location:** Jct Fort Ave; in Federal Hill. 1444 Light St 21230. **Hours:** 5:30 pm-10 pm, Fri & Sat-11 pm. Closed major holidays; also Sun. **Reservations:** suggested. **Features:** This modern spot creatively fuses influences from Asia to Europe with American fresh market ingredients for a cuisine style that is uniquely their own. Try to secure a table in the cozy rear dining room that overlooks a walled garden romantically lit with twinkling lights. Dressy-casual; beer & wine only. **Parking:** street. **Cards:** AX, DC, MC, VI.

CAFE HON
Lunch: $6-$15   **Dinner:** $6-$15   **Phone: 410/243-1230** [3]

American **Location:** Just e of jct Roland Ave; in Hampden. 1002 W 36th St 21211. **Hours:** 7 am-9 pm, Fri-10 pm, Sat 9 am-10 pm, Sun 9 am-8 pm. Closed major holidays. **Features:** Nostalgia and kitsch intermingle in this neighborhood spot which celebrates the women of the city, the "hons." Sample fresh-cut fries in gravy, "better than Mom's" meatloaf and fresh-baked desserts including coconut cake and fruit crumble pies. Casual dress; cocktails. **Parking:** street. **Cards:** AX, DC, DS, MC, VI.

FOUR WEST
Lunch: $10-$25   **Dinner:** $14-$44   **Phone: 410/235-8200** [2]

American **Location:** I-83, exit 9A, 0.5 mi e on Cold Springs Ln to Roland Ave/University Pkwy, then 1 mi s; in Inn At The Colonnade. 4 W University Pkwy 21218. **Hours:** 6:30-10 am, 11:30-3:30 & 5:30-10 pm, Fri & Sat-midnight, Sun 7-10:30 am, 11-2:30 & 5:30-10 pm. **Reservations:** suggested. **Features:** A rich, clublike appearance characterizes the handsome, upscale dining room. Creatively prepared dishes use only fresh, high-quality ingredients. Fried lobster tail and Oriental-style barbecued salmon are favorites. Semi-formal attire; cocktails. **Parking:** on-site (fee) and valet. **Cards:** AX, CB, DC, DS, MC, VI.

(See map and index starting on p. 566)

IKAROS RESTAURANT **Lunch:** $6-$11   **Dinner:** $8-$18   **Phone:** 410/633-3750   6
Greek
Location: I-95, exit 59, 1.3 mi w. 4805 Eastern Ave 21224. **Hours:** 11 am-10 pm, Fri & Sat-11 pm. Closed: 11/24, 12/25; also Tues. **Features:** The well-established, urban, neighborhood restaurant offers a number of beef and seafood selections, along with homemade Greek pastry. Guests can't go wrong when ordering the Greek salad, an enormous helping traditionally prepared with feta and olives. Casual dress; cocktails. **Parking:** street. **Cards:** AX, DS, MC, VI.

KIBBY'S RESTAURANT **Lunch:** $6-$15   **Dinner:** $10-$27   **Phone:** 410/644-8716   8
American
Location: I-695, exit 12B (Wilkens Ave), 1.5 mi e; I-95, exit 50B (Caton Ave), 0.3 mi n to Wilkens, then w. 3450 Wilkens Ave 21229. **Hours:** 11 am-9 pm, Fri & Sat-11 pm. Closed: 5/30, 11/24, 12/25. **Reservations:** accepted. **Features:** A simple, pleasant experience awaits diners at the casual, comfortable restaurant. French onion soup is loaded with onions and smothered in cheese, and the tasty sour beef is served with a dumpling. Servers are friendly and knowledgeable. Casual dress; cocktails. **Parking:** on-site. **Cards:** AX, CB, DC, MC, VI.

MAMIE'S CAFE **Lunch:** $4-$8   **Dinner:** $6-$25   **Phone:** 410/366-2996   4
American
Location: Just w of jct Roland Ave; in Hampden. 911 W 36th St 21211. **Hours:** 9 am-10 pm, Sun-9 pm, Mon-5 pm. **Features:** A mix and match of vintage furniture and collectibles decorate the dining rooms in this homey family-run spot. Maryland crab soup, crumb-topped cream cake and sandwich topped with both a crab cake and shrimp salad are local favorites. Casual dress. **Parking:** street.

PETIT LOUIS BISTRO **Lunch:** $14-$28   **Dinner:** $14-$35   **Phone:** 410/366-9393   1
French
Location: I-83, exit 9, 1.2 mi e on Cold Spring Ln, then 1 mi n. 4800 Roland Ave 21210. **Hours:** 11:30 am-2 & 5-9 pm, Sat & Mon from 5 pm, Sun 5 pm-10 pm. Closed: 12/25. **Reservations:** suggested, weekends. **Features:** Petit Louis is a fine French Bistro with an amazing menu and wine selections. Order more Bread when you go. Casual dress; cocktails. **Parking:** on-site. **Cards:** AX, CB, DC, DS, JC, MC, VI.

TAPAS TEATRO **Dinner:** $6-$16   **Phone:** 410/332-0110   5
Spanish
Location: Jct E Lanvale St. 1711 N Charles St 21201. **Hours:** 5 pm-11 pm, Sat 4 pm-midnight, Sun 4 pm-11 pm. Closed major holidays; also Mon. **Features:** With its location adjacent to the Charles Theater, this is a popular pre and post movie spot for locals. The smell of popcorn from next door competes with attention for the scents from the open kitchen. The menu here is all appetizer-sized portions, so get set to sample. Many dishes are authentic Spanish, but flavors from Mediterranean and Asian cuisines show up also. Casual dress; cocktails. **Parking:** street. **Cards:** AX, DC, DS, MC, VI.

The Baltimore Vicinity

ABERDEEN pop. 13,842

──── **WHERE TO STAY** ────

FOUR POINTS BY SHERATON ABERDEEN *Book at aaa.com*   **Phone:** (410)273-6300
Small-scale Hotel

3/1-10/31 [BP]	1P: $94-$109	2P: $99-$114	XP: $5	F10
11/1-2/28 [BP]	1P: $84-$99	2P: $89-$104	XP: $5	F10

Location: I-95, exit 85, just e on SR 22. Located in a commercial area. 980 Hospitality Way 21001. Fax: 410/575-7195. **Facility:** 134 units. 131 one-bedroom standard units. 3 one-bedroom suites ($149). 4 stories, interior corridors. **Parking:** on-site. **Terms:** cancellation fee imposed. **Amenities:** video games (fee), high-speed Internet, dual phone lines, voice mail, irons, hair dryers. **Pool(s):** outdoor. **Leisure Activities:** exercise room. **Guest Services:** valet and coin laundry. **Business Services:** conference facilities, business center. **Cards:** AX, DC, DS, MC, VI.

SOME UNITS

HOLIDAY INN CHESAPEAKE HOUSE   *Book at aaa.com*

Phone: (410)272-8100

All Year	1P: $104-$130	2P: $104-$130

XP: $10   F19

AAA [SAVE]

▽▽▽

Small-scale Hotel

Location: I-95, exit 85, just e on SR 22. 1007 Beards Hill Rd 21001. Fax: 410/272-1714. **Facility:** 122 one-bedroom standard units. 5 stories, interior corridors. **Parking:** on-site. **Terms:** package plans, small pets only. **Amenities:** high-speed Internet, voice mail, irons, hair dryers. **Dining:** 6 am-11 & 5-10 pm, Sat & Sun 7 am-noon & 5-10 pm, cocktails. **Pool(s):** heated indoor. **Leisure Activities:** whirlpool, sun deck, exercise room. **Guest Services:** valet and coin laundry. **Business Services:** conference facilities, business center. **Cards:** AX, CB, DC, DS, JC, MC, VI. **Special Amenities:** free newspaper.

SOME UNITS

[S/D] [🐾] [🍴] [▽] [⌖] [🏊] [✕] [🐕] [DATA PORT] [💻] / [✕] [VCR FEE] [🔲] [🖥] /

QUALITY INN & SUITES

Phone: (410)272-6000

3/1-10/31	1P: $59-$99	2P: $59-$99
11/1-2/28	1P: $54-$89	2P: $54-$89

XP: $8   F12
XP: $8   F12

AAA [SAVE]

▽▽ ▽▽

Small-scale Hotel

Location: I-95, exit 85, just e. 793 W Bel Air Ave 21001. Fax: 410/272-2287. **Facility:** 110 one-bedroom standard units, some with whirlpools. 2 stories (no elevator), interior corridors. **Parking:** on-site. **Amenities:** high-speed Internet, voice mail, irons, hair dryers. **Pool(s):** outdoor. **Guest Services:** coin laundry. **Business Services:** meeting rooms. **Cards:** AX, DC, DS, MC, VI.

SOME UNITS

[S/D] [🍴] [▽] [⌖] [🏊] [🐕] [DATA PORT] [💻] / [✕] [🔲] [🖥] /

RED ROOF INN   *Book at aaa.com*

Phone: (410)273-7800

All Year	1P: $48-$65	2P: $54-$71

▽▽ ▽▽

Small-scale Hotel

Location: I-95, exit 85, just e on SR 22. 988 Hospitality Way 21001. Fax: 410/273-1370. **Facility:** 109 one-bedroom standard units. 2 stories (no elevator), exterior corridors. **Parking:** on-site. **Amenities:** video games (fee), voice mail. **Business Services:** fax (fee). **Cards:** AX, CB, DC, DS, MC, VI.

SOME UNITS

[🐾] [🍴] [⌖] [🐕] [DATA PORT] / [✕] /

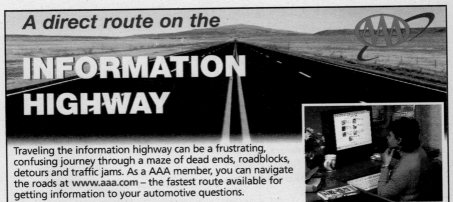

──────── WHERE TO DINE ────────

MAMMA LUCIA'S
♦♦♦ ♦♦♦
Italian

Lunch: $8-$18   **Dinner:** $8-$20   **Phone:** 410/272-0017
Location: I-95, exit 85, just e. 939D Beards Hill Rd 21001. **Hours:** 11 am-9 pm. Closed: 12/25.
Features: Friendly staffers serve eclectic Italian food in a wonderful setting with murals and background music. Casual dress; beer & wine only. **Parking:** on-site. **Cards:** AX, CB, DC, DS, JC, MC, VI.

THE OLIVE TREE RESTAURANT
♦♦♦ ♦♦♦
Italian

Lunch: $5-$9   **Dinner:** $8-$20   **Phone:** 410/272-6217
Location: I-95, exit 85, just e on SR 22. 1005 Beards Hill Rd 21001. **Hours:** 11 am-11 pm. Closed: 12/25.
Reservations: accepted. **Features:** Convenient to the interstate, the casual restaurant maintains the air of Italy. The bountiful offerings the kitchen concocts range from homemade pasta to veal, seafood and poultry selections. Save room for the tempting homemade desserts. Casual dress; cocktails. **Parking:** on-site.
Cards: AX, DC, DS, MC, VI.

ANNAPOLIS pop. 35,838

──────── WHERE TO STAY ────────

ANNAPOLIS COMFORT INN   *Book at aaa.com*
♦♦♦ ♦♦♦
Small-scale Hotel

All Year [CP]   1P: $90-$160   2P: $95-$165   XP: $7   **Phone:** 410/757-8500
F18
Location: 4 mi e on US 50 and 301, exit 28, 0.3 mi n to Old Mill Bottom Rd N, then just e; 3 mi w of Bay Bridge. Located in a semi-rural area. 76 Old Mill Bottom Rd N 21401. Fax: 410/757-4409. **Facility:** 59 one-bedroom standard units, some with whirlpools. 2 stories (no elevator), interior corridors. **Parking:** on-site. **Terms:** 2 night minimum stay - seasonal and/or weekends. **Amenities:** irons, hair dryers. **Leisure Activities:** limited exercise equipment. **Guest Services:** coin laundry. **Business Services:** fax (fee). **Cards:** AX, CB, DC, DS, JC, MC, VI.

SOME UNITS
ASK SD 🐾 📶 💻 / 🖂 DATA PORT /

ANNAPOLIS MARRIOTT WATERFRONT HOTEL   *Book at aaa.com*
AAA SAVE
♦♦♦ ♦♦♦
Large-scale Hotel

4/3-11/11   1P: $279-$550   **Phone:** (410)268-7555
11/12-2/28   1P: $199-$500
3/1-4/2   1P: $189-$500
Location: At the city dock. 80 Compromise St 21401. Fax: 410/269-5864. **Facility:** 150 one-bedroom standard units, some with whirlpools. 6 stories, interior corridors. **Bath:** combo or shower only. **Parking:** valet. **Terms:** check-in 4 pm, 21 day cancellation notice-fee imposed. **Amenities:** CD players, high-speed Internet (fee), voice mail, irons, hair dryers. **Dining:** Pusser's Landing, see separate listing. **Leisure Activities:** exercise room. **Fee:** marina, charter fishing. **Guest Services:** gift shop, valet laundry, airport transportation (fee)-Baltimore-Washington International Airport. **Business Services:** conference facilities, business center. **Cards:** AX, CB, DC, MC, VI.

SOME UNITS
SD 🚷 🍴 📶 🖂 📷 DATA PORT 💻 / 🖂 VCR 🔌 🖥 /
FEE   FEE

BEST WESTERN ANNAPOLIS   *Book at aaa.com*
♦♦♦ ♦♦♦
Motel

6/1-10/31 [ECP]   1P: $72-$139   2P: $72-$139   XP: $10   **Phone:** (410)224-2800
3/1-5/31 & 11/1-2/28 [ECP]   1P: $62-$139   2P: $62-$139   XP: $10   F17
F17
Location: 2.3 mi sw on US 50 and 301, exit 22, just e. 2520 Riva Rd 21401. Fax: 410/266-5539. **Facility:** 142 one-bedroom standard units, some with efficiencies. 2 stories (no elevator), interior/exterior corridors. **Bath:** combo or shower only. **Parking:** on-site. **Amenities:** voice mail, irons, hair dryers. **Fee:** video games, safes. **Pool(s):** outdoor. **Leisure Activities:** limited exercise equipment. **Guest Services:** coin laundry. **Business Services:** meeting rooms, fax (fee). **Cards:** AX, CB, DC, DS, MC, VI. *(See color ad below)*

SOME UNITS
ASK SD 📶 🚷 📶 🌊 📷 DATA PORT 💻 / 🖂 🔌 🖥 /

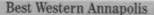

COUNTRY INN & SUITES BY CARLSON-ANNAPOLIS   *Book at aaa.com*   **Phone:** (410)571-6700

  All Year [ECP]   1P: $118-$212   2P: $118-$212

Small-scale Hotel   **Location:** US 50 and 301, exit 23 eastbound; exit 23B westbound, 1 mi w on SR 450. 2600 Housley Rd 21401. **Fax:** 410/571-6777. **Facility:** 100 units. 46 one-bedroom standard units, some with whirlpools. 54 one-bedroom suites. 4 stories, interior corridors. *Bath:* combo or shower only. **Parking:** on-site. **Terms:** 2 night minimum stay - seasonal and/or weekends, cancellation fee imposed, package plans. **Amenities:** voice mail, irons, hair dryers. *Some:* high-speed Internet. **Pool(s):** heated indoor. **Leisure Activities:** whirlpool, exercise room. **Guest Services:** valet and coin laundry, area transportation. **Business Services:** meeting rooms, fax (fee). **Cards:** AX, CB, DC, DS, MC, VI.
(See color ad below)

SOME UNITS
[ASK] [SD] [↑↑+] [icon] [icon] [icon] [icon] [DATA PORT] [icon] / [⊠] [VCR FEE] [icon] [icon] /

COURTYARD BY MARRIOTT   *Book at aaa.com*   Phone: (410)266-1555

(AAA) (SAVE)   3/31-11/14   1P: $109-$179   2P: $119-$189
               11/15-2/28   1P: $84-$144   2P: $94-$159
▽▽▽▽   3/1-3/30   1P: $94-$134   2P: $104-$144
Small-scale Hotel **Location:** 2.3 mi sw on US 50 and 301, exit 22, 0.3 mi s. 2559 Riva Rd 21401. Fax: 410/266-6376. **Facility:** 149 units. 137 one-bedroom standard units. 12 one-bedroom suites ($109-$200). 3 stories, interior corridors. *Bath:* combo or shower only. **Parking:** on-site. **Terms:** [MAP] meal plan available. **Amenities:** high-speed Internet, voice mail, irons, hair dryers. **Dining:** 6:30 am-11 & 5-10 pm, Sat 7 am-noon & 5-10 pm, Sun 7 am-noon, cocktails. **Pool(s):** heated indoor. **Leisure Activities:** whirlpool, sun deck, limited exercise equipment. **Guest Services:** valet and coin laundry. **Business Services:** meeting rooms, fax (fee). **Cards:** AX, CB, DC, DS, JC, MC, VI. **Special Amenities:** free newspaper and early check-in/late check-out.

SOME UNITS

[🍴] [🍸] [🛋M] [♿] [⊘] [🏊] [✕] [📶] [DATA PORT] [💻] [/✕] [🛄] [📷] /

DAYS INN & SUITES HISTORIC ANNAPOLIS   *Book at aaa.com*   Phone: (410)224-4317

▽▽▽ ▽▽▽   3/1-9/30   1P: $99-$196   2P: $99-$196   XP: $10   F18
          10/1-10/31   1P: $99-$189   2P: $99-$189   XP: $10   F18
Small-scale Hotel   11/1-2/28   1P: $79-$109   2P: $79-$109   XP: $10   F18
Location: 2.3 mi sw on US 50 and 301, exit 22 to Riva Rd, then 0.5 mi n. 2451 Riva Rd 21401. Fax: 410/224-6010. **Facility:** 79 one-bedroom standard units, some with whirlpools. 2 stories, interior corridors. **Parking:** on-site. **Terms:** 2 night minimum stay - seasonal, cancellation fee imposed, weekly rates available. **Amenities:** high-speed Internet, voice mail, safes (fee), irons, hair dryers. **Leisure Activities:** limited exercise equipment. **Business Services:** business center. **Cards:** AX, DC, DS, MC, VI. *(See color ad below)*

SOME UNITS

[A$K] [S/D] [🍴] [⊘] [📶] [DATA PORT] [💻] [/✕] [🛄] [📷] /

HAMPTON INN & SUITES-ANNAPOLIS   *Book at aaa.com*   Phone: (410)571-0200

(AAA) (SAVE)   6/1-11/17 [ECP]   1P: $98-$140   2P: $108-$150
               3/1-5/31 [ECP]   .1P: $86-$123   2P: $96-$133
▽▽▽ ▽▽▽   11/18-2/28 [ECP]   1P: $89-$98   2P: $99-$98
               Location: 2.3 mi sw on US 50 and 301, exit 22, just s, then just e on Admiral Cochrane Dr, just n on Spruill Rd, then
Small-scale Hotel just w. 124 Womack Dr 21401. Fax: 410/571-0333. **Facility:** 117 units. 86 one-bedroom standard units. 31 one-bedroom suites ($129-$179) with efficiencies. 5 stories, interior corridors. *Bath:* combo or shower only. **Parking:** on-site. **Terms:** cancellation fee imposed, package plans. **Amenities:** dual phone lines, voice mail, irons, hair dryers. *Fee:* video games, safes. **Pool(s):** heated outdoor. **Leisure Activities:** gas grill, pool table, exercise room. **Guest Services:** sundries, valet and coin laundry. **Business Services:** meeting rooms, business center. **Cards:** AX, CB, DC, DS, MC, VI. **Special Amenities:** free expanded continental breakfast and free local telephone calls.

SOME UNITS

[S/D] [🛋M] [♿] [⊘] [🏊] [📶] [DATA PORT] [💻] [/✕] [VCR] [🛄] [📷] /

HISTORIC INNS OF ANNAPOLIS   *Book at aaa.com*   Phone: (410)263-2641
▽▽▽ ▽▽   All Year   1P: $149   2P: $149   XP: $10   F18
          Location: Facing the State Capitol; in historic district. 58 State Circle 21401. Fax: 410/268-3613. **Facility:** A variety
Historic   of units furnished with antiques is available in this restored 18th-century residence. 127 units. 119 one-
Small-scale Hotel bedroom standard units. 8 one-bedroom suites, some with whirlpools. 3-4 stories, interior corridors. *Bath:* combo or shower only. **Parking:** valet. **Terms:** cancellation fee imposed. **Amenities:** voice mail, irons, hair dryers. **Dining:** The Treaty of Paris, see separate listing. **Guest Services:** valet laundry, area transportation. **Business Services:** meeting rooms, fax (fee). **Cards:** AX, DC, DS, MC, VI.

SOME UNITS

[A$K] [S/D] [🍴] [🍸] [⊘] [🛗] [📶] [DATA PORT] [💻] [/✕] [🛄] [📷] /

HOMESTEAD STUDIO SUITES HOTEL-ANNAPOLIS   *Book at aaa.com*   Phone: (410)571-6600
▽▽▽ ▽▽▽   All Year   1P: $81-$101   2P: $86-$106   XP: $5   F17
          Location: 2.3 mi sw on US 50 and 301, exit 22, just s, then just e. Located in business park area. 120 Admiral
Small-scale Hotel Cochrane Dr 21401. Fax: 410/571-6113. **Facility:** 97 units. 80 one-bedroom standard units with efficiencies. 17 one-bedroom suites with efficiencies. 3 stories, interior corridors. *Bath:* combo or shower only. **Parking:** on-site. **Terms:** weekly rates available, small pets only ($75 fee, limit 1). **Amenities:** dual phone lines, voice mail, irons, hair dryers. *Fee:* video games, safes. **Leisure Activities:** limited exercise equipment. **Guest Services:** valet and coin laundry. **Business Services:** meeting rooms, fax (fee). **Cards:** AX, CB, DC, DS, JC, MC, VI.

SOME UNITS

[A$K] [S/D] [🛏] [🛋M] [♿] [⊘] [📶] [DATA PORT] [🛄] [📷] [💻] [/✕] /
       FEE

LOEWS ANNAPOLIS HOTEL   *Book at aaa.com*   **Phone:** (410)263-7777

  All Year   1P: $99-$259   2P: $99-$259   XP: $30   F18

Location: US 50 and 301, exit 24 eastbound; exit 24A westbound, 1.4 mi s on SR 70, just sw on Calvert St, then just w. 126 West St 21401. Fax: 410/263-0084. **Facility:** 217 units. 211 one-bedroom standard units. 6 one-bedroom suites ($169-$329). 6 stories, interior corridors. *Bath:* combo or shower only. **Parking:** on-site (fee) and valet. **Terms:** 2 night minimum stay - seasonal and/or weekends, cancellation fee imposed, package plans.
Large-scale Hotel   **Amenities:** dual phone lines, voice mail, irons, hair dryers. *Fee:* video games, high-speed Internet.
Dining: Breeze, see separate listing. **Leisure Activities:** exercise room. **Guest Services:** gift shop, valet laundry, area transportation-within 5 mi. **Business Services:** conference facilities, business center. **Cards:** AX, CB, DC, DS, JC, MC, VI.
Special Amenities: free newspaper. *(See color ad below)*

SOME UNITS

🅢🅓 🐕 🛏 🍽 🍸 📷 🚭 📹 | DATA PORT 💻 / ✉ VCR🔲 🔌 /

FEE

THE O'CALLAGHAN HOTEL ANNAPOLIS   *Book at aaa.com*   **Phone:** (410)263-7700

 All Year   1P: $129-$300   2P: $129-$300   XP: $30   F12

Location: US 50 and 301, exit 22 eastbound; exit 24 westbound, 1.4 mi s on SR 70, just sw on Calvert St, then 0.3 mi w. 174 West St 21401. Fax: 410/990-1400. **Facility:** 120 units. 118 one-bedroom standard units. 2 one-bedroom suites ($250-$500). 5 stories, interior corridors. *Bath:* combo or shower only. **Parking:** valet.
Large-scale Hotel   **Terms:** cancellation fee imposed, [AP] meal plan available, package plans. **Amenities:** video games (fee), high-speed Internet, voice mail, safes, irons, hair dryers. **Dining:** 6:30 am-10:30 pm, cocktails. **Leisure**
Activities: limited exercise equipment. **Guest Services:** valet laundry, area transportation-within 4 mi. **Business Services:** meeting rooms, business center. **Cards:** AX, DC, DS, MC, VI. **Special Amenities:** free room upgrade and preferred room (each subject to availability with advance reservations). *(See color ad below)*

SOME UNITS

🅢🅓 🍽 24🛏 🄼 🚹 📷 | DATA PORT 💻 / ✉ 🔌 /

RADISSON HOTEL ANNAPOLIS   *Book at aaa.com*   **Phone:** (410)224-3150

(AAA) [SAVE]

Small-scale Hotel

5/1-10/31	1P: $99-$125	2P: $99-$125	XP: $15	F18
3/1-4/30 & 11/1-2/28	1P: $89-$99	2P: $89-$99	XP: $15	F18

Location: 2.3 mi sw on US 50 and 301, exit 22 to Riva Rd, then 0.3 mi n on Riva Rd. 210 Holiday Ct 21401. Fax: 410/224-3413. **Facility:** 219 one-bedroom standard units. 3-6 stories, interior corridors. *Bath:* combo or shower only. **Parking:** on-site. **Terms:** check-in 4 pm, cancellation fee imposed, pets ($25 fee, $100 deposit). **Amenities:** video games (fee), voice mail, irons, hair dryers. **Dining:** 6:30 am-10 pm, Sat & Sun from 7 am, cocktails. **Pool(s):** outdoor. **Leisure Activities:** exercise room. **Guest Services:** valet laundry, area transportation-within 5 mi. **Business Services:** conference facilities, fax (fee). **Cards:** AX, CB, DC, DS, MC, VI. **Special Amenities: free newspaper.** *(See color ad below & p 589)*

SOME UNITS

[S⌀] [✈ FEE] [🐾 FEE] [🍴] [▽] [ᰧ] [✎] [⇌] [📷] [DATA PORT] [💻] / [✕] [🔒] [🛄] /

RESIDENCE INN BY MARRIOTT-ANNAPOLIS   *Book at aaa.com*   **Phone:** (410)573-0300

Small-scale Hotel

All Year   1P: $99-$289   2P: $99-$289

Location: 2.3 mi sw on US 50 and 301, exit 22 to Riva Rd, then just e. 170 Admiral Cochrane Dr 21401. Fax: 410/573-0316. **Facility:** 102 units. 78 one-bedroom standard units. 24 two-bedroom suites. 2 stories (no elevator), exterior corridors. *Bath:* combo or shower only. **Parking:** on-site. **Terms:** cancellation fee imposed, weekly rates available, pets ($150 fee). **Amenities:** high-speed Internet, voice mail, irons, hair dryers. **Pool(s):** outdoor. **Leisure Activities:** whirlpool, exercise room, sports court. **Guest Services:** valet and coin laundry. **Business Services:** meeting rooms, fax (fee). **Cards:** AX, CB, DC, MC, VI.

SOME UNITS

[ASK] [S⌀] [🐾 FEE] [🔸M] [✎] [ᰧ] [⇌] [✕] [📷] [DATA PORT] [🔒] [🛄] [💻] / [✕] [VCR] /

SHERATON BARCELO HOTEL ANNAPOLIS   *Book at aaa.com*   **Phone:** (410)266-3131

Large-scale Hotel

8/28-11/17	1P: $99-$249	2P: $109-$259	XP: $10	F12
3/1-8/27 & 11/18-2/28	1P: $89-$179	2P: $99-$189	XP: $10	F12

Location: North side of US 50 and 301, exit 23B westbound; exit 23 eastbound. Located opposite Annapolis Westfield Shopping Town. 173 Jennifer Rd 21401. Fax: 410/266-6247. **Facility:** 196 units. 189 one-bedroom standard units. 7 one-bedroom suites. 6 stories, interior corridors. *Bath:* combo or shower only. **Parking:** on-site. **Terms:** cancellation fee imposed, package plans, pets ($50 fee, small dogs only). **Amenities:** dual phone lines, voice mail, irons, hair dryers. *Some:* high-speed Internet (fee), fax. **Pool(s):** heated indoor. **Leisure Activities:** whirlpool, exercise room. **Guest Services:** gift shop, valet laundry, area transportation. **Business Services:** conference facilities, business center. **Cards:** AX, CB, DC, DS, MC, VI. *(See color ad below)*

SOME UNITS

[ASK] [🐾 FEE] [🍴] [▽] [🔸M] [✎] [ᰧ] [⇌] [📷] [DATA PORT] [💻] / [✕] [🔒] [🛄] /

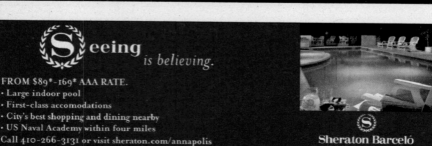

SUPER 8 MOTEL ANNAPOLIS   *Book at aaa.com*   **Phone:** 410/757-2222
      All Year   1P: $65-$120   2P: $75-$120   XP: $5
      Location: 4 mi e on US 50 and 301, exit 28, 0.3 mi n to Old Mill Bottom Rd N, then just e; 3 mi w of Bay Bridge.
Motel   Located in semi-rural area. 74 Old Mill Bottom Rd N 21401. Fax: 410/757-6920. **Facility:** 39 one-bedroom
     standard units. 2 stories (no elevator), exterior corridors. *Bath:* combo or shower only. **Parking:** on-site.
Terms: 2 night minimum stay - weekends, cancellation fee imposed. **Amenities:** irons. **Business Services:** fax (fee).
Cards: AX, CB, DC, DS, MC, VI.

SOME UNITS

WILLIAM PAGE INN   **Phone:** 410/626-1506
      3/16-11/30 [BP]   1P: $140-$250   2P: $140-$250
      3/1-3/15 & 12/1-2/28 [BP]   1P: $120-$205   2P: $120-$205
Historic Bed   **Location:** 3 blks se of State Circle; corner of East and Martin sts. Located in historic Annapolis. 8 Martin St 21401-1716.
& Breakfast   Fax: 410/263-4841. **Facility:** A porch provides a place to catch the breeze at this in-town 1908 home.
     Smoke free premises. 5 one-bedroom standard units, some with whirlpools. 3 stories (no elevator), interior
corridors. *Bath:* some shared or private, combo or shower only. **Parking:** on-site. **Terms:** check-in 4 pm, 2 night minimum stay -
weekends, age restrictions may apply, 10 day cancellation notice, package plans. **Amenities:** CD players. *Some:* DVD players,
hair dryers. **Business Services:** fax (fee). **Cards:** MC, VI.

SOME UNITS

——— **WHERE TO DINE** ———

AQUA TERRA OF ANNAPOLIS   **Dinner:** $23-$29   **Phone:** 410/263-1985
      Location: In Historic Annapolis; just nw of Church Circle. 164 Main St 21401. **Hours:** 5:30 pm-9 pm, Tues-Thurs to
      10 pm, Fri & Sat-11 pm, Sun 5 pm-9 pm. Closed major holidays. **Reservations:** suggested.
American   **Features:** Talented husband-and-wife chef-owners operate the stylish little restaurant in the heart of historic
     Annapolis. Creative cooking reflects influences from both Europe and Asia and fresh ingredients from both
the land and sea. Casual dress; cocktails. **Parking:** street. **Cards:** AX, MC, VI.

BREEZE   **Lunch:** $8-$12   **Dinner:** $15-$31   **Phone:** 410/295-3232
      Location: US 50 and 301, exit 24 eastbound; exit 24A westbound, 1.4 mi s on SR 70, just sw on Calvert St, then just w;
      in Loews Annapolis Hotel. 126 West St 21401. **Hours:** 6:30 am-2 & 5-10 pm. **Reservations:** suggested, for
      dinner. **Features:** Off the lobby of Loews Annapolis Hotel, the dining room sustains a casually upscale
American   atmosphere. The kitchen prepares some distinctive Chesapeake Bay specialties. Casual dress; cocktails.
     Parking: valet. **Cards:** AX, CB, DC, DS, MC, VI.

BUDDY'S CRABS & RIBS   **Lunch:** $6-$12   **Dinner:** $10-$22   **Phone:** 410/626-1100
      Location: Just nw of State Circle. 100 Main St 21401. **Hours:** 11 am-10 pm, Fri & Sat-11 pm, Sun 8:30 am-10
      pm. **Reservations:** not accepted. **Features:** Nestled in the heart of this naval community, this second floor
      restaurant overlooks merchant activity from above. Enjoy either the raw bar choices of clams, mussels,
Seafood   crawfish and more or the cooked variety featuring crab. An eager staff at your beck and call to please you
while you enjoy good food and conversation. Casual dress; cocktails. **Parking:** on-site (fee). **Cards:** AX, DC, DS, MC, VI.

CARROL'S CREEK CAFE   **Lunch:** $5-$15   **Dinner:** $13-$30   **Phone:** 410/263-8102
      Location: 0.3 mi e on 6th St crossing Eastport Bridge, just n; in Eastport. 410 Severn Ave 21403. **Hours:** 11:30 am-4
      & 5-10 pm, Sun 10 am-1:30 & 3-10 pm. **Reservations:** accepted, weekdays. **Features:** Sailing aficionados
      favor the lively restaurant, which overlooks the historic area, harbor and marina. The onion soup—a beef
Seafood   broth with red wine and three cheeses—is delicious. Be prepared for a wait in the summer. Casual dress;
cocktails. **Parking:** on-site. **Cards:** AX, DC, DS, MC, VI.

HARRY BROWNE'S   **Lunch:** $6-$14   **Dinner:** $23-$29   **Phone:** 410/263-4332
      Location: In historic district facing the State Capitol. 66 State Circle 21401. **Hours:** 11 am-3 & 5:30-10 pm, Fri &
      Sat-11 pm, Sun 4:30 pm-9 pm; Sunday brunch 10 am-3 pm. Closed major holidays.
      Reservations: suggested. **Features:** Harry Browne's has been a favorite of locals and statesmen since
Continental   1979. The Continental fare offers such dishes as, Maryland Crab Cakes- served with sauteed spinach,
roasted red pepper coulis and sweet onion marmalade and Rack of Lamb-Served with Potatoes Dauphinoise, Caponata and
Rosemary Demi- Glace. The service is professional and friendly. Valet parking is available Friday & Saturday from 6pm. Dressy
casual; cocktails. **Parking:** street. **Cards:** AX, DC, DS, MC, VI.

INDIA'S RESTAURANT   **Lunch:** $8-$23   **Dinner:** $11-$23   **Phone:** 410/263-7900
      Location: 0.5 mi w of Church Circle. 257 West St 21401. **Hours:** 11:30 am-2:30 & 5-10 pm, Fri & Sat-10:30 pm.
      Reservations: suggested, weekends. **Features:** Representative of the Indian cuisine is a nice selection of
      chicken, lamb and vegetarian dishes. The setting is simple yet comfortable. A $7.95 lunch buffet is available
Indian   on weekdays. Casual dress; cocktails. **Parking:** on-site. **Cards:** AX, DS, MC, VI.

LES FOLIES   **Lunch:** $7-$14   **Dinner:** $13-$24   **Phone:** 410/573-0970
      Location: 2.3 mi sw on US 50 and 301, exit 22. 2552 Riva Rd 21401. **Hours:** 11:30 am-2:30 & 5:30-10:30 pm, Sat
      from 5:30 pm, Sun 5 pm-9 pm. Closed major holidays. **Reservations:** suggested. **Features:** The restaurant
      has a brasserie atmosphere. The kitchen is skillful in French cooking. An extensive raw bar selection is
French   available, as are souffles. Dressy casual; cocktails. **Parking:** on-site. **Cards:** AX, CB, DC, DS, MC, VI.

LEWNES' STEAK HOUSE
Steak & Seafood
Dinner: $17-$32   **Phone:** 410/263-1617
Location: At 4th and Severn sts; in the Eastport section. 401 Fourth St 21403. **Hours:** 5 pm-10 pm, Fri & Sat-10:30 pm, Sun 4 pm-10 pm. **Closed:** 1/1, 11/24, 12/25. **Reservations:** suggested. **Features:** Prime beef is served in generous portions, crab cakes are made with jumbo lump crab meat, and whole Maine lobsters weigh at least three pounds. The neighborhood restaurant has a bar at the entrance and its main dining room upstairs. Casual dress; cocktails. **Parking:** street. **Cards:** AX, DC, MC, VI.

MARIA'S SICILIAN RESTORANTE & CAFE
Italian
Lunch: $7-$16   **Dinner:** $9-$28   **Phone:** 410/268-2112
Location: In the historic district at city dock. 12 Market Space 21401. **Hours:** 11 am-10 pm, Fri & Sat-11 pm. **Closed:** 11/24, 12/25. **Reservations:** suggested. **Features:** At the city dock in historic Annapolis, the family-run restaurant provides an intimate setting for a relaxing meal. The kitchen prepares Sicilian cuisine from family recipes. Casual dress; cocktails. **Parking:** on-site (fee). **Cards:** AX, DC, MC, VI.

MIDDLETON TAVERN
American
Lunch: $8-$35   **Dinner:** $8-$35   **Phone:** 410/263-3323
Location: In the historic district at city dock. 2 Market Space 21401. **Hours:** 11:30 am-midnight, Sat & Sun from 10 am. **Features:** Classic American cuisine exudes a Maryland flavor at the rustic, nautically themed, historic tavern. Diners can treat themselves to a great view of the harbor, either from the second floor or from the seasonal deck. The raw bar offers an array of fresh shellfish. Casual dress; cocktails; entertainment.
Parking: street. **Cards:** AX, DC, DS, MC, VI. **Historic**

NORTHWOODS
Continental
Dinner: $20-$26   **Phone:** 410/268-2609
Location: Just e of SR 70 (Rowe Blvd); 0.8 mi se of US 50, exit 24A. 609 Melvin Ave 21401. **Hours:** 5:30 pm-10 pm, Sun 5 pm-9 pm. Closed major holidays. **Reservations:** suggested. **Features:** A soft, comfortable ambience envelops the restaurant, where cozy couples often visit for upscale, candlelight dining. The complete dinner, which includes appetizer or soup, house salad, entree and a selection from the extensive dessert cart, is available everyday, except Saturday. Dressy casual; cocktails. **Parking:** on-site. **Cards:** AX, CB, DC, DS, MC, VI.

PHILLIPS ANNAPOLIS HARBOR
Seafood
Lunch: $6-$14   **Dinner:** $16-$30   **Phone:** 410/990-9888
Location: At the city dock. 12 Dock St 21401. **Hours:** 11 am-10 pm, Fri & Sat-11 pm. **Closed:** 12/25. **Reservations:** suggested. **Features:** A popular seafood restaurant with a casual atmosphere overlooking the many boats at the City Dock. The menu features fresh seafood as well as beef and chicken dishes. Valet parking is available on weekends in the summer months. Casual dress; cocktails. **Parking:** on-site (fee). **Cards:** AX, DC, DS, MC, VI.

PUSSER'S LANDING
Steak & Seafood
Lunch: $10-$16   **Dinner:** $15-$25   **Phone:** 410/626-0004
Location: At the city dock; in Annapolis Marriott Waterfront Hotel. 80 Compromise St 21401. **Hours:** 6:30 am-10 pm, Fri & Sat-midnight. **Reservations:** suggested. **Features:** The cuisine is eclectic: Maryland seafood specialties, English pub fare and West Indian favorites. Large, fresh oysters with a zesty sauce and an entree of Creole crawfish pasta are excellent choices. There's also outdoor dining (seasonal). Casual dress; cocktails. **Parking:** street. **Cards:** AX, CB, DC, DS, MC, VI.

RAMS HEAD TAVERN
American
Lunch: $8-$12   **Dinner:** $14-$31   **Phone:** 410/268-4545
Location: Just off Church Circle. 33 West St 21401. **Hours:** 11 am-11 pm, Sun from 10 am. **Reservations:** accepted. **Features:** In the historic area, the brew-pub serves good American fare in a friendly, lively setting. An extensive selection of beers, including the ones brewed here, is available. The concert hall offers nationally known entertainment. Casual dress; cocktails. **Parking:** street. **Cards:** AX, DS, MC, VI.

THE TREATY OF PARIS
Continental
Lunch: $8-$14   **Dinner:** $18-$25   **Phone:** 410/216-6340
Location: Facing the State Capitol; in historic district; at Historic Inns of Annapolis. 16 Church Circle 21401. **Hours:** 7-10:30 am, 11:30-2:30 & 5:30-9:30 pm, Fri-10 pm, Sat 8-10:30 am, 11:30-2:30 & 5:30-10 pm, Sun 10 am-2 & 5:30-9:30 pm. **Reservations:** suggested. **Features:** The very good, distinctive nouveau French cuisine is paramount here and served in an elegant, restored 18th century inn. Notable menu selections include a tasty rack of lamb. A lunch buffet is available Monday-Friday. Dressy casual; cocktails. **Parking:** street. **Cards:** AX, CB, DC, DS, MC, VI. **Historic**

ANNAPOLIS JUNCTION   (See map and index starting on p. 566)

———— WHERE TO STAY ————

COURTYARD BY MARRIOTT FT. MEADE NATIONAL BUSINESS PARK   *Book at aaa.com*
Small-scale Hotel
All Year   1P: $99-$159   2P: $99-$159   XP: $10   **Phone:** (301)498-8400
Location: Off SR 32, just w of jct SR 295 (Baltimore-Washington Pkwy). 2700 Hercules Rd 20701. Fax: 301/498-8485. **Facility:** 140 units. 136 one-bedroom standard units. 4 one-bedroom suites ($169-$199). 5 stories, interior corridors. *Bath:* combo or shower only. **Parking:** on-site. **Amenities:** video games (fee), high-speed Internet, dual phone lines, voice mail, irons, hair dryers. **Dining:** 6:30-10 am, 11:30-2 & 4:30-10 pm, Sat & Sun 7 am-11, noon-2 & 4:30-10 pm, cocktails. **Pool(s):** small indoor. **Leisure Activities:** whirlpool, exercise room. **Guest Services:** valet and coin laundry. **Business Services:** meeting rooms, business center. **Cards:** AX, CB, DC, DS, MC, VI. **Special Amenities:** free newspaper.

(See map and index starting on p. 566)

TOWNEPLACE SUITES BY MARRIOTT-BALTIMORE/FT. MEADE   *Book at aaa.com*   Phone: (301)498-7477   83
All Year   1P: $59-$139
Small-scale Hotel   Location: I-95, exit 38A, 2 mi e on SR 32 to exit 11 (Dorsey Run Rd), then just nw. 120 National Business Pkwy 20701. Fax: 301/498-4764. **Facility:** 95 one-bedroom standard units with kitchens. 3 stories, interior corridors. *Bath:* combo or shower only. **Parking:** on-site. **Terms:** cancellation fee imposed, small pets only ($75 fee). **Amenities:** high-speed Internet, voice mail, irons, hair dryers. **Pool(s):** outdoor. **Leisure Activities:** exercise room. **Guest Services:** coin laundry. **Business Services:** business center. **Cards:** AX, DC, DS, MC, VI.
SOME UNITS
ASK SD [icons] FEE [icons] DATA PORT [icons] / [icons] /

BELCAMP

─────── **WHERE TO STAY** ───────

COUNTRY INN & SUITES BY CARLSON   *Book at aaa.com*   Phone: (410)297-9444
3/1-10/31 [ECP]   1P: $79-$165   2P: $79-$165   XP: $10   F13
11/1-2/28 [ECP]   1P: $72-$165   2P: $72-$165   XP: $10   F13
Small-scale Hotel   Location: I-95, exit 80 (SR 543), just e. 1435 Handlir Dr 21015. Fax: 410/297-8866. **Facility:** 81 one-bedroom standard units, some with whirlpools. 3 stories, interior corridors. *Bath:* combo or shower only. **Parking:** on-site. **Terms:** weekly rates available, package plans. **Amenities:** high-speed Internet, voice mail, irons, hair dryers. **Pool(s):** outdoor. **Leisure Activities:** exercise room. **Guest Services:** valet and coin laundry. **Business Services:** meeting rooms, business center. **Cards:** AX, DC, DS, MC, VI. **Special Amenities:** free expanded continental breakfast and free local telephone calls. *(See color ad p 589)*
SOME UNITS
SD [icons] DATA PORT [icons] / [icons] /

SPRINGHILL SUITES BY MARRIOTT   *Book at aaa.com*   Phone: (410)297-4970
All Year [ECP]   1P: $94-$119   2P: $94-$119
Location: I-95, exit 80 (SR 543), just e to SR 7/Philadelphia Rd N. 1420 Handlir Dr 21015. Fax: 410/297-4980. **Facility:** 119 one-bedroom standard units, some with whirlpools. 3 stories, interior corridors. *Bath:* combo or shower only. **Parking:** on-site. **Amenities:** video games, high-speed Internet, dual phone lines, voice mail, irons, hair dryers. **Pool(s):** small heated indoor. **Leisure Activities:** whirlpool, limited exercise equipment.
Small-scale Hotel   **Guest Services:** valet and coin laundry. **Business Services:** meeting rooms, business center. **Cards:** AX, CB, DC, DS, JC, MC, VI.
SOME UNITS
SD [icons] DATA PORT [icons] / [icons] /

WINGATE INN ABERDEEN   *Book at aaa.com*   Phone: (410)272-2929
3/1-12/31 [ECP]   1P: $99-$124   2P: $104-$129   XP: $10   F18
1/1-2/28 [ECP]   1P: $79-$104   2P: $84-$109   XP: $10   F18
Small-scale Hotel   Location: I-95, exit 80 (SR 543), 0.3 mi s on SR 543 to Policy Dr. 1326 Policy Dr 21017. Fax: 410/272-1806. **Facility:** 107 one-bedroom standard units, some with whirlpools. 3 stories, interior corridors. *Bath:* combo or shower only. **Parking:** on-site. **Amenities:** high-speed Internet, dual phone lines, voice mail, safes, irons, hair dryers. **Pool(s):** heated indoor. **Leisure Activities:** whirlpool, exercise room. **Guest Services:** coin laundry. **Business Services:** meeting rooms, business center. **Cards:** AX, CB, DC, DS, JC, MC, VI. *(See color ad p 587)*
SOME UNITS
ASK SD [icons] DATA PORT [icons] / [icons] /

COLUMBIA pop. 88,254

─────── **WHERE TO STAY** ───────

COURTYARD BY MARRIOTT-COLUMBIA   *Book at aaa.com*   Phone: (410)290-0002
All Year   1P: $89-$179   2P: $99-$189   XP: $10   F18
Small-scale Hotel   Location: I-95, exit 41B, 1.3 mi w on SR 175 (Little Patuxent Pkwy), 0.5 mi s on Snowden River Pkwy, just w on McGaw Rd, then 0.4 mi nw. 8910 Stanford Blvd 21045. Fax: 410/290-1663. **Facility:** 152 units. 140 one-bedroom standard units. 12 one-bedroom suites ($169-$239). 4 stories, interior corridors. *Bath:* combo or shower only. **Parking:** on-site. **Terms:** cancellation fee imposed, [BP] meal plan available. **Amenities:** high-speed Internet, voice mail, irons, hair dryers. **Pool(s):** heated indoor. **Leisure Activities:** whirlpool, limited exercise equipment. **Guest Services:** valet and coin laundry. **Business Services:** meeting rooms, fax (fee). **Cards:** AX, CB, DC, DS, JC, MC, VI.
SOME UNITS
ASK SD [icons] DATA PORT [icons] / [icons] /

HAMPTON INN COLUMBIA   *Book at aaa.com*   Phone: (410)997-8555

All Year   1P: $129-$169   2P: $134-$174   XP: $10   F18
Small-scale Hotel   **Location:** I-95, exit 43B, 4 mi w on SR 100, exit 1B. 8880 Columbia 100 Pkwy 21045. Fax: 410/997-8477. **Facility:** 83 one-bedroom standard units, some with whirlpools. 4 stories, interior corridors. *Bath:* combo or shower only. **Parking:** on-site. **Terms:** 3 day cancellation notice. **Amenities:** high-speed Internet, dual phone lines, voice mail, irons, hair dryers. **Pool(s):** heated indoor. **Leisure Activities:** whirlpool, exercise room. **Guest Services:** valet laundry. **Business Services:** meeting rooms, business center. **Cards:** AX, CB, DC, DS, MC, VI. *(See color ad below)*

SOME UNITS

HILTON COLUMBIA   *Book at aaa.com*   Phone: (410)997-1060

All Year   1P: $89-$199   XP: $10   F18
Small-scale Hotel   **Location:** Just e on SR 175 (Little Patuxent Pkwy) from jct US 29, just s on Thunder Hill Rd, then 0.3 mi w on Twin Knolls Rd, 5th entrance. 5485 Twin Knolls Rd 21045. Fax: 410/997-0169. **Facility:** 152 units. 146 one-bedroom standard units. 6 one-bedroom suites. 4 stories, interior corridors. **Parking:** on-site. **Terms:** cancellation fee imposed, package plans. **Amenities:** dual phone lines, voice mail, irons, hair dryers. **Dining:** 6:30 am-10 pm, cocktails. **Pool(s):** heated indoor. **Leisure Activities:** saunas, whirlpool, limited exercise equipment. **Guest Services:** sundries, valet laundry, area transportation-within 5 mi. **Business Services:** conference facilities, business center. **Cards:** AX, CB, DC, DS, JC, MC, VI.

SOME UNITS
FEE   FEE

HILTON GARDEN INN   *Book at aaa.com*   Phone: (410)750-3700

All Year   1P: $89-$199   2P: $89-$199   XP: $10   F18
Small-scale Hotel   **Location:** I-95, exit 43, 2 mi w on SR 100 to exit 3, then just s. 8241 Snowden River Pkwy 21045. Fax: 410/750-8809. **Facility:** 98 one-bedroom standard units. 4 stories, interior corridors. *Bath:* combo or shower only. **Parking:** on-site. **Terms:** package plans. **Amenities:** high-speed Internet, dual phone lines, voice mail, irons, hair dryers. **Pool(s):** heated indoor. **Leisure Activities:** whirlpool, exercise room. **Guest Services:** valet and coin laundry. **Business Services:** meeting rooms, business center. **Cards:** AX, DC, DS, MC, VI.

SOME UNITS

HOMEWOOD SUITES BY HILTON   *Book at aaa.com*   Phone: (410)872-9200

All Year   1P: $99-$199   2P: $99-$199
Small-scale Hotel   **Location:** I-95, exit 41B (Little Patuxent Pkwy), w on SR 175, then right on SR 108, left on Lark Brown, continue on Benson Dr. 8320 Benson Dr 21045. Fax: 410/872-9235. **Facility:** 150 one-bedroom standard units with kitchens. 4 stories, interior corridors. *Bath:* combo or shower only. **Parking:** on-site. **Terms:** check-in 4 pm, cancellation fee imposed, pets ($75 fee). **Amenities:** high-speed Internet, dual phone lines, voice mail, irons, hair dryers. **Pool(s):** outdoor. **Leisure Activities:** whirlpool, exercise room, sports court. **Guest Services:** sundries, valet and coin laundry. **Business Services:** conference facilities, business center. **Cards:** AX, DC, DS, MC, VI.

SOME UNITS
FEE

SHERATON COLUMBIA HOTEL — *Book at aaa.com* Phone: (410)730-3900

(AAA) (SAVE) All Year 1P: $99-$225 2P: $109-$235 XP: $10 F
Location: 1.2 mi w on SR 175 (Little Patuxent Pkwy) from jct US 29, then just s; center. 10207 Wincopin Cir 21044.
Fax: 410/730-1290. **Facility:** 288 units. 286 one-bedroom standard units. 2 one-bedroom suites. 3-10
stories, interior corridors. *Bath:* combo or shower only. **Parking:** on-site. **Terms:** package plans, pets (small
Large-scale Hotel dogs only, in designated units). **Amenities:** voice mail, irons, hair dryers. *Fee:* video games, high-speed
Internet. *Some:* dual phone lines. **Dining:** Waterside Restaurant, see separate listing. **Pool(s):** outdoor.
Leisure Activities: jogging, exercise room. **Guest Services:** gift shop, valet and coin laundry, area transportation-within 5 mi.
Business Services: conference facilities, business center. **Cards:** AX, DC, DS, MC, VI. **Special Amenities:** free newspaper.
(See ad p 596)

SOME UNITS

STAYBRIDGE SUITES BY HOLIDAY INN
BALTIMORE-COLUMBIA — *Book at aaa.com* Phone: (410)964-9494

All Year [BP] 1P: $79-$159 2P: $89-$209
Location: I-95, exit 43B, 4 mi w on SR 100, exit 1B. 8844 Columbia 100 Pkwy 21045. Fax: 410/964-9249.
Small-scale Hotel **Facility:** 118 units. 66 one-bedroom standard units with efficiencies. 29 one- and 23 two-bedroom suites
with kitchens. 3 stories, interior corridors. *Bath:* combo or shower only. **Parking:** on-site. **Terms:** check-in 4
pm, cancellation fee imposed, package plans, pets ($75 fee). **Amenities:** high-speed Internet (fee), dual phone lines, voice
mail, irons, hair dryers. **Pool(s):** outdoor. **Leisure Activities:** exercise room, sports court. **Guest Services:** sundries,
complimentary and valet laundry, area transportation. **Business Services:** meeting rooms, business center. **Cards:** AX, DC,
DS, MC, VI.

SOME UNITS

FEE

WELLESLEY INN & SUITES (COLUMBIA) — *Book at aaa.com* Phone: (410)872-2994

(AAA) (SAVE) All Year 1P: $129-$159 2P: $129-$159
Location: I-95, exit 41B, 1.3 mi w on SR 175 (Little Patuxent Pkwy), 0.5 mi s on Snowden River Pkwy, just w on
McGaw Rd, then 0.3 mi nw. 8890 Stanford Blvd 21045. Fax: 410/872-2995. **Facility:** 137 units. 131 one-bedroom
standard units with efficiencies. 6 one-bedroom suites with kitchens. 3 stories, interior corridors. *Bath:*
Small-scale Hotel combo or shower only. **Parking:** on-site. **Amenities:** dual phone lines, voice mail, irons, hair dryers. *Fee:*
video games, high-speed Internet. **Pool(s):** heated outdoor. **Leisure Activities:** limited exercise equipment.
Guest Services: valet and coin laundry. **Business Services:** fax (fee). **Cards:** AX, CB, DC, DS, MC, VI. **Special Amenities:**
free expanded continental breakfast and free newspaper. *(See color ad p 423)*

SOME UNITS

───── **WHERE TO DINE** ─────

BOMBAY PEACOCK GRILL Lunch: $6-$18 Dinner: $8-$20 Phone: 410/381-7111
Location: I-95, exit 38B, 2 mi w on SR 32 to Shaker Dr/Eden Brook exit, just s, then just e. 10005 Old Columbia Rd
21046. **Hours:** 11:30 am-10 pm, Fri & Sat-11 pm. Closed: 12/25. **Reservations:** accepted.
Indian **Features:** Peacock feathers and exotic statues are among features that give the restaurant its Indian feel.
Fresh vegetable samosa, a deep-fried pastry filled with spiced potatoes and peas, is flavorful and filling. The
lunch buffet is a popular choice. Dressy casual; cocktails. **Parking:** on-site. **Cards:** AX, CB, DC, DS, MC, VI.

CLYDE'S OF COLUMBIA Lunch: $7-$17 Dinner: $11-$20 Phone: 410/730-2829
Location: 1.2 mi w on SR 175 (Little Patuxent Pkwy) from jct US 29, then just s; center. 10221 Wincopin Cir 21044.
Hours: 11:30 am-11 pm, Fri & Sat-midnight, Sun 10 am-11 pm. Closed: 12/25. **Reservations:** accepted.
American **Features:** The popular tavern—with red- and white-checkered tablecloths, a vintage Victorian bar and a
view of the lake—is a great place to grab a bite. The staff is friendly, and the food is good. Classic American
fare ranges from burgers, sandwiches and salad to full dinners. Save room because the desserts are worth it. Casual dress;
cocktails. **Parking:** on-site. **Cards:** AX, DC, DS, MC, VI.

THE KINGS CONTRIVANCE Lunch: $10-$19 Dinner: $14-$32 Phone: 410/995-0500
Location: E of jct US 29 and 32; Shaker Dr exit off SR 32; I-95, exit 38B, 2 mi w on SR 32. 10150 Shaker Dr 21046.
Hours: 11:30 am-2 & 5:30-9 pm, Sat from 5:30 pm, Sun 4 pm-8 pm. Closed major holidays; also Super
American Bowl Sun. **Reservations:** suggested. **Features:** A favorite for special occasions, the restored 19th-century
mansion is attractively decorated and decidedly suburban. Representative of the cuisine, American with a
Continental flair, are such dishes as grilled venison and duck. Bread and pastries are baked on the premises. The early-bird
menu is not offered in December. Semi-formal attire; cocktails. **Parking:** on-site. **Cards:** AX, DC, DS, MC, VI.

THE TOMATO PALACE Lunch: $7-$13 Dinner: $7-$13 Phone: 410/715-0211
Location: Off SR 175 (Little Patuxent Pkwy), 1.5 mi w of jct US 29; center. 10221 Wincopin Cir 21044. **Hours:** 11:30
am-10 pm, Fri & Sat-10:30 pm. Closed: 11/24, 12/25. **Reservations:** accepted. **Features:** The popular,
Italian casual cafe is ideal for family dining. The kitchen prepares 11 varieties of pizza and 15 pasta dishes, as well
as sandwiches, salads and daily specials. Tasty meal toppers include traditional tiramisu and chocolate
bread pudding. Casual dress; cocktails. **Parking:** on-site. **Cards:** AX, DC, DS, MC, VI.

WATERSIDE RESTAURANT Lunch: $8-$13 Dinner: $15-$25 Phone: 410/730-3900
(AAA) **Location:** 1.2 mi w on SR 175 (Little Patuxent Pkwy) from jct US 29, then just s; center; in Sheraton Columbia Hotel. 10207
Wincopin Cir 21044. **Hours:** 6:30 am-2:30 & 5:30-10:30 pm, Sun 6:30-10 am, 10:30-2:30 & 5:30-10 pm.
Reservations: accepted. **Features:** Overlooking Lake Kittamaqundi, the restaurant offers both indoor and
American outdoor dining in a tranquil, intimate setting. Crab cakes served with a remoulade sauce are a favorite.
Casual dress; cocktails. **Parking:** on-site. **Cards:** AX, CB, DC, DS, MC, VI.

EDGEWOOD pop. 23,378

─── **WHERE TO STAY** ───

BEST WESTERN INVITATION INN *Book at aaa.com*
Phone: (410)679-9700

AAA SAVE

4/1-10/31 [ECP]	1P: $69-$99	2P: $69-$99	XP: $10	F18
3/1-3/31 & 11/1-2/28 [ECP]	1P: $59-$79	2P: $69-$89	XP: $10	F18

Location: I-95, exit 77A, just e on SR 24. 1709 Edgewood Rd 21040. Fax: 410/538-3763. **Facility:** 158 one-bedroom standard units. 2 stories (no elevator), exterior corridors. *Bath:* combo or shower only. **Parking:**
Small-scale Hotel on-site. **Terms:** cancellation fee imposed, package plans, small pets only ($50 deposit). **Amenities:** video games (fee), voice mail, safes, irons, hair dryers. **Pool(s):** outdoor. **Leisure Activities:** limited exercise equipment. *Fee:* game room. **Guest Services:** valet and coin laundry. **Business Services:** meeting rooms, fax (fee). **Cards:** AX, CB, DC, DS, JC, MC, VI. **Special Amenities:** free expanded continental breakfast and free local telephone calls. *(See color ad below)*

COMFORT INN-EDGEWOOD CONFERENCE CENTER *Book at aaa.com*
Phone: (410)679-0770

AAA SAVE

4/1-10/31 [ECP]	1P: $69-$99	2P: $69-$99	XP: $10	F18
3/1-3/31 & 11/1-2/28 [ECP]	1P: $59-$99	2P: $59-$99	XP: $10	F18

Location: I-95, exit 77A, just e on SR 24. 1700 Van Bibber Rd 21040. Fax: 410/676-1535. **Facility:** 153 units. 151 one-bedroom standard units. 2 one-bedroom suites ($99-$189). 2 stories (no elevator), exterior corridors.
Small-scale Hotel *Bath:* combo or shower only. **Parking:** on-site. **Terms:** cancellation fee imposed, package plans. **Amenities:** voice mail, safes, irons, hair dryers. **Pool(s):** outdoor. **Leisure Activities:** exercise room. **Guest Services:** valet and coin laundry. **Business Services:** conference facilities, fax (fee). **Cards:** AX, CB, DC, DS, JC, MC, VI. **Special Amenities:** free expanded continental breakfast and free local telephone calls.

DAYS INN-EDGEWOOD *Book at aaa.com*
Phone: (410)671-9990

AAA SAVE

All Year	1P: $62-$90	2P: $62-$90	XP: $5	F17

Location: I-95, exit 77A, just e on SR 24. 2116 Emmorton Park Rd 21040. Fax: 410/671-7802. **Facility:** 73 one-bedroom standard units. 2 stories (no elevator), exterior corridors. *Bath:* combo or shower only. **Parking:**
Small-scale Hotel on-site. **Amenities:** high-speed Internet, voice mail, hair dryers. *Some:* irons. **Guest Services:** coin laundry. **Cards:** AX, CB, DC, DS, JC, MC, VI. **Special Amenities:** free continental breakfast and free newspaper.

HOLIDAY INN EXPRESS   *Book at aaa.com*   **Phone: 410/612-1200**
▼▼▼▼▼   Property failed to provide current rates
          Location: I-95, exit 77A, just e on SR 24. 2118 Emmorton Park Rd 21040. Fax: 410/612-1400. **Facility:** 92 one-
Small-scale Hotel bedroom standard units, some with whirlpools. 3 stories, interior corridors. *Bath:* combo or shower only.
          Parking: on-site. **Amenities:** dual phone lines, voice mail, irons, hair dryers. **Pool(s):** heated indoor.
Leisure Activities: whirlpool, limited exercise equipment. **Guest Services:** valet and coin laundry. **Business Services:**
meeting rooms, business center.

SOME UNITS

⎡🍴⎤ ⎡♿M⎤ ⎡⛱⎤ ⎡🏊⎤ ⎡🎥⎤ ⎡DATA PORT⎤ 🖥 ⎡🖨⎤ 🖥 / ⎡✕⎤ /

SLEEP INN & SUITES   *Book at aaa.com*   **Phone: (410)679-4700**

AAA SAVE   4/1-10/31 [ECP]   1P: $89-$119   2P: $89-$129   XP: $10   F18
▼▼▼▼▼   3/1-3/31 [ECP]   1P: $89-$99   2P: $89-$109   XP: $10   F18
            11/1-2/28 [ECP]   1P: $89-$99   2P: $89-$99   XP: $10   F18
          Location: I-95, exit 77A, just e on SR 24. 1807 Edgewood Rd 21040. Fax: 410/671-6459. **Facility:** 84 units. 68
Small-scale Hotel one-bedroom standard units, some with whirlpools. 16 one-bedroom suites ($99-$169), some with
          whirlpools. 3 stories, interior corridors. *Bath:* combo or shower only. **Parking:** on-site. **Terms:** cancellation
fee imposed, package plans. **Amenities:** high-speed Internet, voice mail, safes, irons, hair dryers. **Pool(s):** small heated indoor.
Leisure Activities: limited exercise equipment. **Guest Services:** coin laundry. **Business Services:** meeting rooms, fax (fee).
Cards: AX, CB, DC, DS, JC, MC, VI. **Special Amenities: free expanded continental breakfast and free local telephone
calls.** *(See color ad p 598)*

SOME UNITS

⎡S🅓⎤ ⎡🍴⎤ ⎡⛱⎤ ⎡🚫⎤ ⎡🏊⎤ ⎡🎥⎤ ⎡DATA PORT⎤ 🖥 / 🖥 ⎡🖨⎤ /

——— WHERE TO DINE ———

VENETIAN PALACE   **Lunch: $5-$12**   **Dinner: $9-$20**   **Phone: 410/679-2330**
▼▼ ▼▼   **Location:** I-95, exit 74, 1 mi s on SR 152, then just e on US 40. 1901 Treetop Dr 21040. **Hours:** 7 am-11 pm.
          Closed: 12/25. **Features:** Treat the family to great food at the Venetian Palace. Italian cuisine and more with
Italian   friendly service. Casual dress; cocktails. **Parking:** on-site. **Cards:** AX, CB, DC, DS, JC, MC, VI.   ⎡🍷⎤ ⎡✕⎤

VITALI'S   **Lunch: $5-$21**   **Dinner: $10-$21**   **Phone: 410/671-9800**
AAA   **Location:** I-95, exit 77A, just e on SR 24. 1709 Edgewood Rd 21040. **Hours:** 7 am-10 & 11:30-10 pm, Sun 7 am-
          10 pm. Closed: 1/1, 11/24, 12/25; also for dinner 12/24. **Features:** The restaurant is convenient to the
▼▼ ▼▼   interstate and numerous motels. The simple dining room has a casual atmosphere, and the staff makes
          patrons feel comfortable with its friendly, efficient service. On the menu is a nice selection of Italian dishes,
Italian   as well as Maryland crab cakes, certified Angus steaks and nightly specials. House specialties are
          highlighted on the menu. Casual dress; cocktails. **Parking:** on-site. **Cards:** AX, CB, DC, DS, MC, VI.
(See color ad p 598)   ⎡🍷⎤ ⎡✕⎤

ELKRIDGE pop. 22,042   (See map and index starting on p. 566)

——— WHERE TO STAY ———

BEST WESTERN BALTIMORE WASHINGTON   **Phone: (410)796-3300**   [63]
AIRPORT/I-95   *Book at aaa.com*
AAA SAVE   All Year   1P: $90-$110   2P: $90-$110   XP: $10   F17
▼▼▼▼▼   **Location:** I-95, exit 43A, 1 mi e, 0.5 mi s of SR 100, exit 6A (SR 103); just e of jct US 1. 6755 Dorsey Rd 21075.
          Fax: 410/379-0471. **Facility:** 133 one-bedroom standard units. 4 stories, interior corridors. *Bath:* combo or
Small-scale Hotel shower only. **Parking:** on-site. **Terms:** package plans. **Amenities:** voice mail, irons, hair dryers. **Dining:** 11
          am-11 pm, Sat-midnight, Sun 9 am-10 pm, cocktails. **Pool(s):** heated indoor. **Leisure Activities:** sauna,
whirlpool, sun deck, exercise room. **Guest Services:** valet laundry, airport transportation-Baltimore-
Washington International Airport. **Business Services:** meeting rooms, fax (fee). **Cards:** AX, CB, DC, DS, JC, MC, VI.
Special Amenities: free expanded continental breakfast.

SOME UNITS

⎡S🅓⎤ ⎡✈⎤ ⎡🍴⎤ ⎡🍷⎤ ⎡⛱⎤ ⎡🚫⎤ ⎡🏊⎤ ⎡✕⎤ ⎡🎥⎤ ⎡DATA PORT⎤ 🖥 / ⎡✕⎤ 🖥 ⎡🖨⎤ /

——— WHERE TO DINE ———

THE ELKRIDGE FURNACE INN   **Lunch: $9-$15**   **Dinner: $18-$30**   **Phone: 410/379-9336**   [27]
AAA   **Location:** Jct Main St and Furnace Ave, 0.5 mi s. 5745 Furnace Ave 21075. **Hours:** 11:30 am-2 & 5-9 pm, Sat 5
          pm-10 pm, Sun 10 am-2 & 4-8 pm. Closed: 3/27, 11/24, 12/25; also Mon & for dinner 12/24.
▼▼▼▼   **Reservations:** suggested. **Features:** On 16 acres of land, the restored circa 1744 tavern retains many
          original features of the Federal/Greek Revival building. The dining room is cozy. On the eclectic menu are
Continental smoked duck and preparations of beef and fish. Dressy casual; cocktails. **Parking:** on-site. **Cards:** AX,
          MC, VI. **Historic**   ⎡✕⎤

JOE THEISMANN'S RESTAURANT   **Lunch: $8-$18**   **Dinner: $12-$25**   **Phone: 410/796-7775**   [28]
▼▼ ▼▼   **Location:** I-95, exit 43A, 1 mi e, then 0.5 mi e on SR 100, exit 6A (SR 103); just e of jct US 1. 6751 Dorsey Rd 21075.
          Hours: 11 am-11 pm. Closed: 12/25. **Features:** Patrons can nosh on a wide variety of menu selections in a
American   casual, sports-themed atmosphere. Casual dress; cocktails. **Parking:** on-site. **Cards:** AX, CB, DC, DS, JC,
          MC, VI.   ⎡🍷⎤ ⎡✕⎤

ELLICOTT CITY pop. 56,397   (See map and index starting on p. 566)

──────── WHERE TO STAY ────────

RESIDENCE INN BY MARRIOTT COLUMBIA   **Phone:** (410)997-7200
▼▼▼▼   All Year   1P: $79-$159
Small-scale Hotel   **Location:** I-95, exit 43B, 4 mi w on SR 100, exit 1B (Executive Park Dr). 4950 Beaver Run Way 21043. Fax: 410/997-7201. **Facility:** 108 units. 45 one-bedroom standard units with efficiencies. 42 one- and 21 two-bedroom suites with kitchens. 3 stories, interior corridors. *Bath:* combo or shower only. **Parking:** on-site. **Terms:** weekly rates available, small pets only ($100 fee, $10 extra charge). **Amenities:** video games (fee), high-speed Internet, voice mail, irons, hair dryers. **Pool(s):** outdoor. **Leisure Activities:** whirlpool, limited exercise equipment, sports court. **Guest Services:** valet and coin laundry. **Business Services:** meeting rooms, fax (fee). **Cards:** AX, CB, DC, DS, JC, MC, VI.

SOME UNITS

(ASK) (SD) (FEE) (†l†) (&M) (&) (⌖) (⤳) (✕) (☆) (DATA PORT) (☐) (⎙) (▣) / (✕) /

TURF VALLEY RESORT & CONFERENCE CENTER   *Book at aaa.com*   **Phone:** (410)465-1500
(AAA) (SAVE)   All Year   1P: $98-$645   2P: $113-$658   XP: $15   F
▼▼▼▼   **Location:** I-70, exit 82 eastbound, 1.5 mi e on US 40; exit 83 westbound, 0.6 mi s on Marriottsville Rd, then 0.8 mi e on Resort   US 40. 2700 Turf Valley Rd 21042. Fax: 410/465-8280. **Facility:** In addition to its impressive meeting facilities, Large-scale Hotel   the resort offers many recreation options including a fine golf course. 220 units. 219 one- and 1 two-bedroom standard units, some with whirlpools. 7 stories, interior corridors. *Bath:* combo or shower only. **Parking:** on-site. **Terms:** check-in 4 pm, cancellation fee imposed, package plans. **Amenities:** high-speed indoor. **Leisure Activities:** saunas, whirlpool, 3 tennis courts, jogging, spa, basketball, volleyball. *Fee:* golf-36 holes, driving range. **Guest Services:** gift shop, valet laundry. **Business Services:** conference facilities. **Cards:** AX, CB, DC, DS, MC, VI.

SOME UNITS

(SD) (†l†) (Y) (&) (⌖) (⤳) (ŧ) (✕) (DATA PORT) (⎙) / (✕) (☐) (▣) /

──────── WHERE TO DINE ────────

THE CRAB SHANTY   Lunch: $7-$14   Dinner: $10-$45   **Phone:** 410/465-9660
▼▼▼ ▼▼   **Location:** US 40, 1 mi w of jct SR 29. 3410 Plumtree Dr 21042. **Hours:** 11:30 am-2:30 & 5-9 pm, Wed & Thurs-10 Seafood   pm, Sat 5 pm-10 pm, Sun 11 am-9 pm. Closed: 1/1, 11/24, 12/25. **Reservations:** accepted. **Features:** Guests can savor good-quality, simply prepared dishes served in ample portions. The interesting decor includes lots of wood and antiques. Some alternatives to seafood are offered. Booth or table seating can be requested, and the lounge is separate from the dining room. Casual dress; cocktails. **Parking:** on-site. **Cards:** AX, CB, DC, DS, MC, VI.

(Y) (✕)

EGGSPECTATION   Lunch: $7-$14   Dinner: $9-$20   **Phone:** 410/750-3115   16
▼▼▼ ▼▼   **Location:** 3 mi w on SR 100, exit 3. 6010 University Blvd 21043. **Hours:** 7 am-8:30 pm, Fri & Sat-10 pm. Closed: American   11/24, 12/25. **Features:** You'll arrive with great eggspectations and depart with your appetite fufilled. Eggspectations is a new concept that serves breakfast, lunch and dinner anytime all day. Casual dress; cocktails. **Parking:** on-site. **Cards:** AX, CB, DC, DS, JC, MC, VI.

(Y) (✕)

KELSEY'S RESTAURANT & SPIRITS   Lunch: $6-$15   Dinner: $8-$20   **Phone:** 410/418-9076
▼▼▼   **Location:** I-70, exit 82 eastbound, 2.5 mi e on US 40; exit 83 westbound, 0.6 mi s on Marriottsville Rd, then 2.9 mi e on American   US 40. 8480 Baltimore National Pike 21042. **Hours:** 11 am-11 pm. Closed: 1/1, 12/25. **Features:** All the finest traditions of an Irish Pub can be found at Kelsey's Restaurant & Sprits. Great food and a family atmosphere. Casual dress; cocktails. **Parking:** on-site. **Cards:** AX, CB, DC, DS, JC, MC, VI.

(Y) (✕)

FALLSTON pop. 8,427

──────── WHERE TO DINE ────────

JOSEF'S COUNTRY INN   Lunch: $8-$12   Dinner: $14-$28   **Phone:** 410/877-7800
▼▼▼▼   **Location:** Just w of SR 152; 3.7 mi n of jct SR 147 and 152. 2410 Pleasantville Rd 21047. **Hours:** 11:30 am-2:30 & Continental   5-10 pm, Fri-11 pm, Sat 5 pm-11 pm, Sun noon-9 pm. Closed: 1/1, 12/25. **Reservations:** suggested. **Features:** The restaurant's Continental menu emphasizes seafood. Among other favorites are the German dishes, such as sauerbraten and Wiener schnitzel, served in generous portions with spaetzle. The staff is friendly and helpful. Dressy casual; cocktails. **Parking:** on-site. **Cards:** AX, DC, DS, MC, VI.

(Y) (✕)

FINKSBURG

──────── WHERE TO DINE ────────

RUDYS' 2900   Lunch: $7-$12   Dinner: $18-$28   **Phone:** 410/833-5777
▼▼▼ ▼▼   **Location:** SR 140, 3 mi nw of I-795; just w of jct SR 91. 2900 Baltimore Blvd 21048. **Hours:** 11:30 am-2:30 & 5:30-Continental   11 pm, Sat from 5:30 pm, Sun 4 pm-9 pm. Closed major holidays; also Mon. **Reservations:** suggested. **Features:** Tasteful surroundings, a relaxing atmosphere and a capable and knowledgeable service staff heighten the positive dining experience. The chef-owner displays his skills in creating contemporary American and regional European dishes. The fall ushers in some tempting game dishes. Dressy casual; cocktails. **Parking:** on-site. **Cards:** AX, DS, MC, VI.

(Y) (✕)

GLEN BURNIE pop. 38,922 (See map and index starting on p. 566)

——— WHERE TO STAY ———

DAYS INN-GLEN BURNIE   *Book at aaa.com*   **Phone:** (410)761-8300   **67**

(AAA) (SAVE)   All Year   1P: $99-$114   2P: $109-$124
⬥⬥⬥   **Location:** I-695, exit 3B eastbound; exit 2 westbound, 0.5 mi s on SR 2. 6600 Ritchie Hwy 21061.
Fax: 410/760-4966. **Facility:** 100 one-bedroom standard units. 3 stories, exterior corridors. *Bath:* combo or
shower only. **Parking:** on-site. **Terms:** cancellation fee imposed, $1 service charge, small pets only ($20
Small-scale Hotel fee). **Amenities:** voice mail, safes (fee), irons, hair dryers. **Pool(s):** outdoor. **Leisure Activities:** exercise
room. **Guest Services:** valet laundry. **Business Services:** meeting rooms, business center. **Cards:** AX,
DC, DS, MC, VI. **Special Amenities: free continental breakfast and free newspaper.**   SOME UNITS

⬛⬛⬛⬛⬛⬛⬛⬛ / ⬛⬛⬛⬛ /
FEE

HAMPTON INN GLEN BURNIE   *Book at aaa.com*   **Phone:** (410)761-7666   **68**

(AAA) (SAVE)   All Year [ECP]   1P: $89-$129
⬥⬥⬥   **Location:** I-695, exit 3B eastbound; exit 2 westbound, 0.5 mi s on SR 2. Located adjacent to Governor Plaza Shopping
Center. 6617 Ritchie Hwy 21061. **Fax:** 410/761-0253. **Facility:** 115 units. 107 one-bedroom standard units. 8
one-bedroom suites ($119-$149). 5 stories, interior corridors. **Parking:** on-site. **Terms:** package plans.
Small-scale Hotel **Amenities:** high-speed Internet, voice mail, irons, hair dryers. **Guest Services:** valet laundry. **Business
Services:** meeting rooms, fax (fee). **Cards:** AX, CB, DC, DS, JC, MC, VI. **Special Amenities: free
expanded continental breakfast and free local telephone calls.** *(See color ad below)*   SOME UNITS

⬛⬛⬛⬛⬛⬛⬛⬛ / ⬛⬛⬛ /
FEE FEE

HOLIDAY INN-BALTIMORE SOUTH   *Book at aaa.com*   **Phone:** (410)636-4300   **66**

(AAA) (SAVE)   3/1-11/15   1P: $107-$125
⬥⬥⬥   11/16-2/28   1P: $97-$107
Location: I-695, exit 3A eastbound; exit 2 westbound, jct SR 2. 6323 Ritchie Hwy 21061. **Fax:** 410/636-2630.
Facility: 127 one-bedroom standard units. 4 stories, interior corridors. *Bath:* combo or shower only.
Small-scale Hotel **Parking:** on-site. **Amenities:** voice mail, irons, hair dryers. **Dining:** 6 am-11 & 5-10 pm, Sat & Sun from 7
am, cocktails. **Pool(s):** outdoor. **Leisure Activities:** exercise room. **Guest Services:** valet and coin laundry.
Business Services: meeting rooms, fax (fee). **Cards:** AX, CB, DC, DS, JC, MC, VI.   SOME UNITS

⬛⬛⬛⬛⬛⬛⬛⬛ / ⬛⬛⬛⬛ /

HANOVER (See map and index starting on p. 566)

——— WHERE TO STAY ———

HAMPTON INN & SUITES-ARUNDEL MILLS/BWI   *Book at aaa.com*   **Phone:** (410)540-9225   **74**

⬥⬥⬥   All Year   1P: $109-$179   2P: $109-$179
Location: I-95, exit 43 (SR 100 eastbound); exit 10A (Arudel Mills Blvd). 7027 Arundel Mills Cir 21076.
Small-scale Hotel **Fax:** 410/540-9224. **Facility:** 131 one-bedroom standard units. 5 stories, interior corridors. *Bath:* combo or
shower only. **Parking:** on-site. **Terms:** cancellation fee imposed. **Amenities:** high-speed Internet, voice
mail, irons, hair dryers. **Pool(s):** outdoor. **Leisure Activities:** exercise room. **Guest Services:** valet and coin laundry, area
transportation. **Business Services:** meeting rooms, business center. **Cards:** AX, DC, DS, MC, VI.   SOME UNITS

(ASK) ⬛⬛⬛⬛⬛⬛⬛⬛ / ⬛ /

HOLIDAY INN EXPRESS-BWI AIRPORT   **Phone:** 410/684-3388   **72**

⬥⬥⬥   All Year   1P: $135   2P: $135
Location: 1 mi e of SR 295, exit SR 100 E to exit 10B; just e of jct SR 176 and 713. 7481 Ridge Rd 21076.
Small-scale Hotel **Fax:** 410/684-3919. **Facility:** 159 one-bedroom standard units. 5 stories, interior corridors. *Bath:* combo or
shower only. **Parking:** on-site. **Terms:** cancellation fee imposed, [ECP] meal plan available.
Amenities: high-speed Internet, voice mail, irons, hair dryers. **Pool(s):** heated outdoor. **Leisure Activities:** exercise room.
Guest Services: valet and coin laundry, area transportation. **Business Services:** meeting rooms, fax (fee). **Cards:** AX, CB,
DC, DS, MC, VI.   SOME UNITS

(ASK) ⬛⬛⬛⬛⬛⬛⬛⬛ / ⬛⬛⬛ /

(See map and index starting on p. 566)

RED ROOF INN-BWI PARKWAY   *Book at aaa.com*   Phone: (410)712-4070   **71**

▼▼ ▼▼	4/14-10/31	1P: $68-$88	2P: $73-$93	XP: $5 F18
	11/1-2/28	1P: $58-$78	2P: $63-$83	XP: $5 F18
Motel	3/1-4/13	1P: $55-$75	2P: $60-$80	XP: $5 F18

Location: 0.7 mi w of SR 295, exit 100, w to exit 8, 0.5 mi se. Located in office park setting. 7306 Parkway Dr S 21076. Fax: 410/712-4078. **Facility:** 108 one-bedroom standard units. 2 stories (no elevator), exterior corridors. **Parking:** on-site. **Terms:** small pets only. **Amenities:** video games, voice mail. **Business Services:** fax (fee). **Cards:** AX, CB, DC, DS, MC, VI.

SOME UNITS
🐕 📶 🅿 🎦 📠 / ✕ 🛢 🖥 /

RESIDENCE INN BY MARRIOTT-ARUNDEL MILLS/BWI   *Book at aaa.com*   Phone: (410)799-7332   **73**

▼▼ ▼▼   All Year [BP]   1P: $95-$219   2P: $95-$219
Location: I-95, exit 43A, 5 mi e on SR 100 to exit 10A, then just n. 7035 Arundel Mills Cir 21076. Fax: 410/799-7356. **Facility:** 131 one-bedroom standard units. 4 stories, interior corridors. *Bath:* combo or shower only. Small-scale Hotel   **Parking:** on-site. **Amenities:** high-speed Internet, dual phone lines, voice mail, irons, hair dryers. **Pool(s):** outdoor. **Leisure Activities:** whirlpool, exercise room, sports court, volleyball. **Guest Services:** complimentary evening beverages: Mon-Thurs, valet and coin laundry, area transportation. **Business Services:** meeting rooms, business center. **Cards:** AX, DC, DS, JC, MC, VI.

SOME UNITS
(ASK) 🆂🅳 ➕ 🐕 ♿ 🏊 ✕ 🎦 📠 🛢 🖥 🖨 / ✕ /

--------- **WHERE TO DINE** ---------

GUNNING'S SEAFOOD RESTAURANT   Lunch: $7-$14   Dinner: $7-$22   Phone: 410/712-9404   **31**
▼▼ ▼▼   **Location:** 0.7 mi w of SR 295, exit 100, w to exit 8, then 0.5 mi e. 7304 Parkway Dr 21076. **Hours:** 11 am-11 pm, Sun noon-10 pm. Closed: 12/25. **Features:** Gunning's Seafood Restaurant boasts of Baltimore's Best American   Crabs, well they are right up there. A fun and casual setting with great seafood and other menu choices. Casual dress; cocktails. **Parking:** on-site. **Cards:** AX, CB, DC, DS, JC, MC, VI.

🍸 ✕

HAVRE DE GRACE pop. 11,331

--------- **WHERE TO STAY** ---------

VANDIVER INN, KENT & MURPHY GUEST SUITES   Phone: (410)939-5200
(AAA) (SAVE)   All Year [BP]   1P: $99-$149   2P: $99-$149   XP: $10   F8
Location: I-95, exit 89, 2.5 mi e on SR 155 to Otsego St, 3 blks e to Union Ave, then s to jct S Union Ave and Fountain ▼▼ ▼▼ ▼▼   St. 301 S Union Ave 21078. Fax: 410/939-5202. **Facility:** The inn is made up of three houses dating from 1886, each offering individually decorated rooms with private baths. Smoke free premises. 17 one-bedroom Historic Bed   standard units, some with whirlpools. 3 stories (no elevator), interior/exterior corridors. *Bath:* combo or & Breakfast   shower only. **Parking:** on-site. **Terms:** 10 day cancellation notice-fee imposed, weekly rates available. **Amenities:** voice mail, irons, hair dryers. *Some:* CD players. **Leisure Activities:** croquet, parlor games. **Business Services:** meeting rooms. **Cards:** AX, DS, MC, VI.

SOME UNITS
🆂🅳 ✕ 🎦 📠 / (VCR) 🛢 🖥 /

--------- **WHERE TO DINE** ---------

THE BAYOU RESTAURANT   Lunch: $6-$13   Dinner: $8-$25   Phone: 410/939-3565
▼▼ ▼▼   **Location:** I-95, exit 89, 2 mi e on SR 155, 0.3 mi w on US 40. 927 Pulaski Hwy 21078. **Hours:** 11:30 am-10 pm. Closed: 12/24-12/26; also Mon. **Reservations:** suggested, weekends. **Features:** Family-oriented and American   popular with local residents, the restaurant features seafood and veal specialties, as well as homemade bread and pie. All-you-can-eat buffets are served Thursday evenings and for weekday lunches. Service is friendly and attentive. Casual dress; cocktails. **Parking:** on-site. **Cards:** AX, CB, DC, DS, MC, VI.

✕

MACGREGOR'S   Lunch: $6-$12   Dinner: $15-$23   Phone: 410/939-3003
(AAA)   **Location:** I-95, exit 89, 2.5 mi e on SR 155, 0.5 mi e on SR 7 (which is Otsego St and becomes Union Ave), bear left on St. John St at Statue of Lafayette. 331 St. John St 21078. **Hours:** 11 am-10 pm, Fri & Sat-11 pm, Sun 10 am-10 ▼▼ ▼▼   pm. **Reservations:** suggested, weekends. **Features:** Seafood is the specialty at the casually elegant restaurant, which has a two-tiered, glass dining room that overlooks the Susquehanna River. A collection of American   decoys—fitting for a town that proclaims itself the "decoy capital of the world"—is one facet of the eclectic decor. A covered deck opens seasonally. Leave room for one of the tempting desserts. Casual dress; cocktails. **Parking:** on-site. **Cards:** AX, DC, DS, MC, VI.

🍸 ✕

TIDEWATER GRILLE   Lunch: $7-$15   Dinner: $15-$30   Phone: 410/939-3313
▼▼ ▼▼   **Location:** I-95, exit 89, 2.5 mi e on SR 155, then 0.5 mi on SR 7 (which is Otsego St and becomes Union Ave). 300 Foot of Franklin St 21078. **Hours:** 11 am-9 pm, Sat-10 pm. Closed: 11/24, 12/25. **Features:** Location, location, American   location. That's just what the restaurant can brag about deservedly from its prime perch on the banks of the Susquehanna River. Guests can take a seat in the casual, comfortable dining room or enjoy outdoor dining on open or covered decks. Casual dress; cocktails. **Parking:** on-site. **Cards:** AX, DC, MC, VI.

🍸 ✕

HUNT VALLEY

———— WHERE TO STAY ————

EMBASSY SUITES BALTIMORE-NORTH   *Book at aaa.com*   Phone: (410)584-1400

(AAA) (SAVE)   All Year [BP]   1P: $179   2P: $179   XP: $15   F18
▼▼▼   **Location:** I-83, exit 20A (Shawan Rd), just e. 213 International Cir 21030. Fax: 410/584-7306. **Facility:** 223 one-
Large-scale Hotel bedroom suites. 8 stories, interior corridors. *Bath:* combo or shower only. **Parking:** on-site. **Terms:** check-in
4 pm, cancellation fee imposed, weekly rates available, package plans. **Amenities:** video games (fee), high-
speed Internet, dual phone lines, voice mail, irons, hair dryers. **Dining:** 11 am-11 pm, cocktails. **Pool(s):**
heated indoor. **Leisure Activities:** sauna, whirlpool, exercise room. **Guest Services:** sundries,
complimentary evening beverages, valet and coin laundry, area transportation-within 5 mi. **Business Services:** conference
facilities, business center. **Cards:** AX, CB, DC, DS, MC, VI. **Special Amenities:** free full breakfast and free newspaper.
(See color ad p 573)   SOME UNITS

[icons] FEE / ⊗ /

HAMPTON INN HUNT VALLEY   *Book at aaa.com*   Phone: (410)527-1500

   All Year [BP]   1P: $76-$116   2P: $86-$126
▼▼▼   **Location:** I-83, exit 20A (Shawan Rd), 2 mi se to SR 45, then just s. Located in a commercial area. 11200 York Rd
Small-scale Hotel 21030. Fax: 410/771-0819. **Facility:** 125 one-bedroom standard units. 7 stories, interior corridors. **Parking:**
on-site. **Terms:** package plans. **Amenities:** high-speed Internet, voice mail, irons, hair dryers. **Leisure**
Activities: limited exercise equipment. **Guest Services:** valet laundry. **Business Services:** meeting rooms, fax (fee).
Cards: AX, CB, DC, DS, JC, MC, VI.
SOME UNITS

[icons] / ⊗ ⊟ ⊟ /

HUNT VALLEY COURTYARD BY MARRIOTT   *Book at aaa.com*   Phone: (410)584-7070

(AAA) (SAVE)   2/9-2/28   1P: $134   XP: $10   F16
     5/1-10/29   1P: $129   XP: $10   F16
▼▼▼   10/30-2/8   1P: $124   XP: $10   F16
     3/1-4/30   1P: $119   XP: $10   F16
Small-scale Hotel **Location:** I-83, exit 20A (Shawan Rd), just ne. 221 International Cir 21030. Fax: 410/584-8151. **Facility:** 146 units.
134 one-bedroom standard units. 12 one-bedroom suites ($124-$174). 3 stories, interior corridors. *Bath:*
combo or shower only. **Parking:** on-site. **Amenities:** high-speed Internet, dual phone lines, voice mail, irons, hair dryers.
Dining: 6:30 am-10 & 5-9:30 pm, Sat & Sun 7-11 am, cocktails. **Pool(s):** heated indoor. **Leisure Activities:** whirlpool, sun
deck, exercise room. **Guest Services:** valet and coin laundry. **Business Services:** meeting rooms, fax (fee). **Cards:** AX, DC,
DS, JC, MC, VI.
SOME UNITS

[icons] / ⊗ ⊟ ⊟ /

MARRIOTT'S HUNT VALLEY INN   *Book at aaa.com*   Phone: (410)785-7000

▼▼▼   All Year   1P: $99-$179   2P: $99-$179
   Location: I-83, exit 20A (Shawan Rd), just e. 245 Shawan Rd 21031-1099. Fax: 410/785-0341. **Facility:** 390 units.
Large-scale Hotel 388 one-bedroom standard units. 2 one-bedroom suites. 4 stories, interior corridors. *Bath:* combo or shower
only. **Parking:** on-site. **Terms:** check-in 4 pm, package plans. **Amenities:** high-speed Internet, voice mail,
irons, hair dryers. **Pool(s):** heated indoor/outdoor. **Leisure Activities:** saunas, whirlpool, 3 tennis courts, exercise room. *Fee:*
massage. **Guest Services:** gift shop, valet laundry, area transportation. **Business Services:** conference facilities, business
center. **Cards:** AX, DC, DS, MC, VI.
SOME UNITS

[icons] FEE / ⊗ ⊟ /

———— WHERE TO DINE ————

THE OREGON GRILLE   **Lunch:** $8-$18   **Dinner:** $19-$34   Phone: 410/771-0505
▼▼▼   **Location:** I-83, exit 20B, 1 mi w. 1201 Shawan Rd 21030. **Hours:** 11:30 am-4 & 5-11 pm, Sun 11 am-3 & 4-10
American   pm. Closed: 12/25; also for lunch 1/1. **Reservations:** suggested. **Features:** Decorated with horse-racing
pictures, dark-wood paneling and candlelit tables, the upscale restaurant is known for the innovative
dishes—such as lobster corn cakes and pan-fried rockfish—its talented chef creates. Beef is another
strength. The staff is professional and attentive. Jackets are required after 5 pm. Monday through Saturday and after 4 pm on
Sunday. Semi-formal attire; cocktails. **Parking:** on-site. **Cards:** AX, DC, DS, MC, VI.

[icons] Y ⊗

JESSUP pop. 7,865   (See map and index starting on p. 566)

———— WHERE TO STAY ————

COMFORT SUITES-COLUMBIA GATEWAY   Phone: 410/799-3779
(fyi)   3/1-11/15   1P: $99-$149   2P: $99-$149
     11/16-2/28   1P: $89-$139   2P: $89-$139
Small-scale Hotel Too new to rate, opening scheduled for September 2004. **Location:** I-95, exit 175 (Jessup). 7164 Waterloo Rd
20794. **Amenities:** 83 units, coffeemakers, microwaves, refrigerators, pool. **Cards:** AX, CB, DC, DS,
MC, VI. *(See color ad p 595)*

COMMODORE JOSHUA BARNEY HOUSE B & B   Phone: 301/362-1900
▼▼▼   All Year [ECP]   1P: $175-$225   2P: $175-$225
   Location: I-95, exit 38A, 1.5 mi e on SR 32, just s on US 1, 0.5 mi w on Howard St, then 1.1 mi n. 7912 Savage Gilford
Historic Bed Rd 20763 (PO Box 429, SAVAGE). Fax: 301/362-6853. **Facility:** A building of historic significance, the
& Breakfast Commodore House is a cozy B&B on six landscaped acres in a residential setting. Smoke free premises. 4
one-bedroom standard units. 3 stories (no elevator), interior corridors. *Bath:* combo or shower only.
Parking: on-site. **Terms:** office hours 9 am-9 pm, check-in 4 pm, 2 night minimum stay - weekends, age restrictions may apply,
30 day cancellation notice-fee imposed. **Amenities:** video library, high-speed Internet, hair dryers. **Business Services:** meeting
rooms, fax. **Cards:** AX, MC, VI.
SOME UNITS

[icons] FEE ⊗ / VCR /

(See map and index starting on p. 566)

FAIRFIELD INN BY MARRIOTT-COLUMBIA/JESSUP   *Book at aaa.com*   Phone: (410)799-1500   **78**
◇◇ ◇◇◇   All Year   1P: $69-$139   2P: $69-$149   XP: $10   F17
Small-scale Hotel   **Location:** I-95, exit 41A; just s of jct US 1 and SR 175. 7300 Crestmount Rd 20794. Fax: 410/799-2716.
Facility: 105 one-bedroom standard units. 4 stories, interior corridors. *Bath:* combo or shower only.
Parking: on-site. **Terms:** package plans. **Amenities:** video games (fee), voice mail, irons, hair dryers.
Leisure Activities: limited exercise equipment. **Guest Services:** valet and coin laundry. **Business Services:** fax (fee).
Cards: AX, CB, DC, DS, JC, MC, VI.

SOME UNITS
(ASK) (S☐) (¶↑) (&M) (&) (🐾) (DATA PORT) / ✕ 🖥 ▤ /

HOLIDAY INN COLUMBIA   *Book at aaa.com*   Phone: (410)799-7500   **77**
◇◇◇◇◇   All Year   1P: $119-$159   2P: $129-$169
Small-scale Hotel   **Location:** I-95, exit 41A; jct US 1 and SR 175. 7900 Washington Blvd 20794. Fax: 410/799-1824. **Facility:** 175
one-bedroom standard units. 4 stories, interior corridors. **Parking:** on-site. **Amenities:** video games (fee),
dual phone lines, voice mail, irons, hair dryers. **Pool(s):** outdoor. **Leisure Activities:** exercise room. **Guest
Services:** valet and coin laundry. **Business Services:** meeting rooms, business center. **Cards:** AX, CB, DC, DS, JC, MC, VI.

SOME UNITS
(ASK) (S☐) (¶↑) (Y) (🏊) (🐾) (DATA PORT) ▤ / ✕ 🖥 ▤ /
FEE

RED ROOF INN-COLUMBIA/JESSUP   *Book at aaa.com*   Phone: (410)796-0380   **79**
◇◇◇ ◇◇◇   3/1-11/12   1P: $73-$90   2P: $79-$96
        11/13-2/28   1P: $68-$83   2P: $74-$89
Motel   **Facility:** 108 one-bedroom standard units. 3 stories, exterior corridors. *Bath:* combo or shower only.
Location: I-95, exit 41A; 0.3 mi s of jct US 1 and SR 175. 8000 Washington Blvd 20794. Fax: 410/796-0389.
Parking: on-site. **Terms:** small pets only (with prior approval, limit 1). **Amenities:** video games (fee), voice mail. **Guest
Services:** coin laundry. **Business Services:** fax (fee). **Cards:** AX, CB, DC, DS, MC, VI.

SOME UNITS
(🛏) (¶↑) (&M) (&) (🐾) (🐾) (DATA PORT) / ✕ 🖥 ▤ /

SUPER 8 MOTEL   Phone: (410)796-0400   **80**
(AAA) (SAVE)   3/1-10/31   1P: $70-$80   2P: $80-$90   XP: $6
        11/1-2/28   1P: $60-$70   2P: $70-$80   XP: $6
◇◇◇   **Location:** I-95, exit 41A; 0.5 mi s of jct US 1 and SR 175. 8094 Washington Blvd 20794. Fax: 410/796-5407.
Motel   **Facility:** 35 one-bedroom standard units, some with whirlpools. 2 stories (no elevator), exterior corridors.
Parking: on-site. **Business Services:** fax (fee). **Cards:** AX, DS, MC, VI.

SOME UNITS
(S☐) (¶↑) (🐾) (🐾) (DATA PORT) / ✕ 🖥 ▤ /

JOPPA

─────── **WHERE TO STAY** ───────

SUPER 8 JOPPA MOTEL   *Book at aaa.com*   Phone: 410/676-2700
(AAA) (SAVE)   All Year   1P: $63   2P: $67
◇◇◇   **Location:** I-95, exit 74, 1 mi s on SR 152, then just w on US 40. 1015 Pulaski Hwy 21085. Fax: 410/676-8202.
Facility: 55 one-bedroom standard units. 2 stories (no elevator), interior/exterior corridors. **Parking:** on-site.
Amenities: hair dryers. **Business Services:** fax (fee). **Cards:** AX, DC, MC, VI. **Special Amenities:** free
Small-scale Hotel   **continental breakfast and free local telephone calls.**

SOME UNITS
(S☐) (&M) (🐾) (DATA PORT) / ✕ 🖥 ▤ /

LINTHICUM HEIGHTS   (See map and index starting on p. 566)

─────── **WHERE TO STAY** ───────

AMERISUITES (BALTIMORE/BWI AIRPORT)   *Book at aaa.com*   Phone: (410)859-3366   **45**
(AAA) (SAVE)   All Year   1P: $109-$199   2P: $170-$209   XP: $10   F21
◇◇ ◇◇ ◇◇   **Location:** I-695, exit 7A, 1 mi s on SR 295, just e on W Nursery Rd. 940 International Dr 21090. Fax: 410/859-3331.
Facility: 128 one-bedroom standard units. 6 stories, interior corridors. *Bath:* combo or shower only.
Parking: on-site. **Terms:** cancellation fee imposed, package plans, small pets only. **Amenities:** voice mail,
Small-scale Hotel   safes, irons, hair dryers. *Some:* dual phone lines. **Pool(s):** heated indoor. **Leisure Activities:** exercise
room. **Guest Services:** valet and coin laundry, airport transportation-Baltimore-Washington International
Airport, area transportation-within 5 mi. **Business Services:** meeting rooms. **Cards:** AX, CB, DC, DS, JC, MC, VI.
Special Amenities: free expanded continental breakfast and free newspaper. *(See color ad p 571)*

SOME UNITS
(S☐) (✈) (🛏) (&M) (&) (🐾) (🐾) (🐾) (DATA PORT) 🖥 ▤ ▤ / ✕ /

BWI AIRPORT MARRIOTT HOTEL   *Book at aaa.com*   Phone: 410/859-8300   **56**
◇◇ ◇◇◇   1/1-2/28   1P: $249-$279   2P: $249-$279
        3/1-12/31   1P: $249-$269   2P: $249-$269
Large-scale Hotel   **Location:** I-695, exit 7A, 1 mi s on SR 295, then 1.2 mi e. 1743 W Nursery Rd 21240. Fax: 410/691-4555.
Facility: 310 one-bedroom standard units, some with whirlpools. 10 stories, interior corridors. *Bath:* combo
or shower only. **Parking:** on-site. **Terms:** cancellation fee imposed, package plans. **Amenities:** video games (fee), high-speed
Internet (fee), voice mail, irons, hair dryers. **Pool(s):** heated indoor. **Leisure Activities:** whirlpool, limited exercise equipment.
Guest Services: gift shop, valet and coin laundry, area transportation. **Business Services:** conference facilities, business
center. **Cards:** AX, CB, DC, DS, JC, MC, VI.

SOME UNITS
(✈) (¶↑) (Y) (&) (🐾) (🐾) (🐾) (DATA PORT) 🖥 / ✕ 🖥 /
FEE

(See map and index starting on p. 566)

CANDLEWOOD SUITES-BWI   *Book at aaa.com*   Phone: (410)850-9214   **48**
All Year   1P: $99-$159   2P: $99-$159   XP: $20   F16
Location: I-695, exit 7A, 1 mi s on SR 295, 1.3 mi e on W Nursery Rd, then 0.3 mi w. 1247 Winterson Rd 21090.
Small-scale Hotel   Fax: 410/850-9215. **Facility:** 125 units. 25 one- and 100 two-bedroom standard units with kitchens. 4 stories, interior corridors. *Bath:* combo or shower only. **Parking:** on-site. **Terms:** cancellation fee imposed, weekly rates available, pets ($150 fee). **Amenities:** CD players, irons, hair dryers. **Leisure Activities:** exercise room. **Guest Services:** valet and coin laundry. **Cards:** AX, DC, DS, JC, MC, VI.

SOME UNITS
(ASK) (SD) (✈) (🛏) (🖥) (VCR) (⚡) (🅿) (🍽) (💻) / (⊗) /

COMFORT INN AIRPORT   *Book at aaa.com*   Phone: (410)789-9100   **42**
(AAA) (SAVE)   All Year [BP]   1P: $119-$139   2P: $119-$139   XP: $8   F18
Location: I-695, exit 6A eastbound; exit 5 westbound, at jct SR 170 and 648. 6921 Baltimore Annapolis Blvd 21225.
Small-scale Hotel   Fax: 410/355-2854. **Facility:** 188 one-bedroom standard units, some with whirlpools. 6 stories, interior corridors. *Bath:* combo or shower only. **Parking:** on-site. **Terms:** package plans. **Amenities:** high-speed Internet, voice mail, safes, irons, hair dryers. *Dining:* The Rose Restaurant, see separate listing. **Leisure Activities:** sauna, whirlpool, exercise room. **Guest Services:** valet and coin laundry, airport transportation-Baltimore-Washington International Airport, area transportation-Amtrak station & light rail. **Business Services:** meeting rooms, business center. **Cards:** AX, CB, DC, DS, JC, MC, VI. **Special Amenities:** free full breakfast and free local telephone calls. *(See color ad below)*

SOME UNITS
(SD) (✈) (🐾) (🍴) (🔥M) (🖥) (🌀) (⊗) (⚡) (DATA PORT) (💻) / (⊗) (VCR) (🅿) (🍽) /
FEE   FEE   FEE

COMFORT SUITES-BWI AIRPORT   *Book at aaa.com*   Phone: (410)691-1000   **59**
(AAA) (SAVE)   All Year [ECP]   1P: $79-$249   2P: $79-$249
Location: I-695, exit 7A, 1 mi s on SR 295, then 1.3 mi e on W Nursery Rd. 815 Elkridge Landing Rd 21090.
Small-scale Hotel   Fax: 410/691-1275. **Facility:** 137 units. 136 one-bedroom standard units. 1 one-bedroom suite with whirlpool. 5 stories, interior corridors. *Bath:* combo or shower only. **Parking:** on-site. **Terms:** cancellation fee imposed, small pets only ($25 extra charge). **Amenities:** video games (fee), high-speed Internet, dual phone lines, voice mail, safes, irons, hair dryers. **Leisure Activities:** limited exercise equipment. *Fee:* pool privileges. **Guest Services:** sundries, valet and coin laundry, airport transportation-Baltimore-Washington International Airport, area transportation-Amtrak station, light rail & local restaurants. **Business Services:** meeting rooms, business center. **Cards:** AX, CB, DC, DS, MC, VI. **Special Amenities:** free expanded continental breakfast and free local telephone calls. *(See color ad p 606)*

SOME UNITS
(SD) (✈) (🛏) (🔥M) (🖥) (⚡) (DATA PORT) (🅿) (💻) / (⊗) (🍽) /
FEE

(See map and index starting on p. 566)

COURTYARD BY MARRIOTT-BWI AIRPORT   *Book at aaa.com*   Phone: (410)859-8855   52
▼▼▼   All Year   1P: $179
Small-scale Hotel   **Location:** I-695, exit 7A, 1 mi s on SR 295, then 0.8 mi e. 1671 W Nursery Rd 21090. Fax: 410/859-5068.
                     Facility: 149 one-bedroom standard units. 3 stories, interior corridors. *Bath:* combo or shower only.
                     Parking: on-site. **Terms:** cancellation fee imposed, package plans. **Amenities:** high-speed Internet, voice
mail, irons, hair dryers. **Pool(s):** heated indoor. **Leisure Activities:** whirlpool, exercise room. **Guest Services:** coin laundry,
area transportation. **Business Services:** meeting rooms. **Cards:** AX, DC, DS, JC, MC, VI.
                                                                                                            SOME UNITS
(ASK) (S/D) (✈) (¶¶) (ℤ) (⛑) (M) (ⅇ) (∅) (⇌) (❄) (DATA PORT) (▦) / (✕) (▯) (▤) /

EMBASSY SUITES HOTEL BALTIMORE AT BWI   *Book at aaa.com*   Phone: 410/850-0747   47
▼▼▼   All Year   1P: $119-$299   2P: $119-$299   XP: $20   F16
Large-scale Hotel   **Location:** I-695, exit 7A, 1 mi s on SR 295, 0.7 mi e on W Nursery Rd, then 0.5 mi w on Winterson. 1300 Concourse Dr
                     21090. Fax: 410/859-0816. **Facility:** 251 units. 250 one- and 1 two-bedroom suites, some with whirlpools. 8
                     stories, interior corridors. **Parking:** on-site. **Terms:** package plans. **Amenities:** high-speed Internet, dual
phone lines, voice mail, irons, hair dryers. **Pool(s):** heated indoor. **Leisure Activities:** saunas, whirlpool, jogging, limited
exercise equipment. **Guest Services:** gift shop, complimentary evening beverages, valet laundry, area transportation.
Business Services: conference facilities, business center. **Cards:** AX, DC, DS, MC, VI.
                                                                                                            SOME UNITS
(✈) (¶¶) (ℤ) (∅) (⇌) (✕) (❄) (DATA PORT) (▯) (▤) (▦) / (✕) /

FAIRFIELD INN BY MARRIOTT-BWI AIRPORT   *Book at aaa.com*   Phone: (410)859-2333   55
▼▼▼   All Year   1P: $69-$149   2P: $69-$159   XP: $10   F17
Small-scale Hotel   **Location:** SR 295, exit Nursery Rd, 1.2 mi e. 1734 W Nursery Rd 21090. Fax: 410/859-2357. **Facility:** 130 one-
                     bedroom standard units. 5 stories, interior corridors. *Bath:* combo or shower only. **Parking:** on-site.
                     Terms: package plans. **Amenities:** high-speed Internet, voice mail, irons, hair dryers. **Pool(s):** outdoor.
Leisure Activities: exercise room. **Guest Services:** coin laundry. **Cards:** AX, CB, DC, DS, JC, MC, VI.
                                                                                                            SOME UNITS
(ASK) (S/D) (✈) (⛑) (⇌) (❄) (DATA PORT) (▦) / (✕) (▯) (▤) /

(See map and index starting on p. 566)

FOUR POINTS BY SHERATON BWI AIRPORT   *Book at aaa.com*   Phone: (410)859-3300   60

AAA SAVE   All Year   1P: $89-$239   2P: $89-$239   XP: $20   F18
Location: I-195, exit 1A, 0.5 mi n on SR 170, just e. 7032 Elm Rd 21240 (PO Box 8741, BALTIMORE).
Fax: 410/859-0565. **Facility:** 201 units. 200 one-bedroom standard units. 1 one-bedroom suite. 2 stories,
interior corridors. *Bath:* combo or shower only. **Parking:** on-site. **Terms:** cancellation fee imposed, package
Small-scale Hotel   plans, small pets only ($25 extra charge, with prior approval). **Amenities:** high-speed Internet, dual phone
lines, voice mail, irons, hair dryers. **Dining:** Michener's, see separate listing. **Pool(s):** outdoor. **Leisure**
Activities: exercise room. **Guest Services:** gift shop, valet laundry, airport transportation-Baltimore-Washington International
Airport, area transportation-Amtrak & light rail. **Business Services:** conference facilities, business center. **Cards:** AX, CB, DC,
DS, JC, MC, VI. **Special Amenities:** free newspaper. *(See color ad p 606)*

SOME UNITS

HAMPTON INN BWI AIRPORT   *Book at aaa.com*   Phone: (410)850-0600   57

All Year   1P: $89-$179
Location: I-695, exit 7A, 1 mi s on SR 295, 1.3 mi e on W Nursery Rd, then just w. 829 Elkridge Landing Rd 21090.
Small-scale Hotel   Fax: 410/691-2119. **Facility:** 182 one-bedroom standard units. 5 stories, interior corridors. *Bath:* combo or
shower only. **Parking:** on-site. **Terms:** package plans, small pets only. **Amenities:** high-speed Internet,
voice mail, irons, hair dryers. **Leisure Activities:** exercise room. **Guest Services:** valet laundry, area transportation. **Business**
Services: meeting rooms, fax (fee). **Cards:** AX, DC, DS, MC, VI.

SOME UNITS

HILTON GARDEN INN-BWI   *Book at aaa.com*   Phone: (410)691-0500   44

All Year   1P: $129-$199   2P: $129-$199   XP: $10   F18
Location: I-695, exit 7A, 1 mi s on SR 295, 0.6 mi e on W Nursery Rd, then just n. 1516 Areo Dr 21090.
Small-scale Hotel   Fax: 410/691-0501. **Facility:** 158 one-bedroom standard units, some with whirlpools. 5 stories, interior
corridors. *Bath:* combo or shower only. **Parking:** on-site. **Amenities:** video games, high-speed Internet,
voice mail, irons, hair dryers. **Pool(s):** heated indoor. **Leisure Activities:** whirlpool, exercise room. **Guest Services:** coin
laundry, area transportation. **Business Services:** meeting rooms, business center. **Cards:** AX, DS, MC, VI.

SOME UNITS

HOLIDAY INN-BWI AIRPORT   *Book at aaa.com*   Phone: (410)859-8400   54

AAA SAVE   3/1-11/14   1P: $98-$199   2P: $98-$199
▼▼▼   11/15-2/28   1P: $98-$184   2P: $98-$184
Location: I-695, exit 7A, 1 mi s on SR 295, 1.3 mi e on W Nursery Rd, then 0.5 mi w. 890 Elkridge Landing Rd 21090.
Fax: 410/684-6778. **Facility:** 260 one-bedroom standard units. 7 stories, interior corridors. *Bath:* combo or
Large-scale Hotel   shower only. **Parking:** on-site. **Terms:** package plans, small pets only ($20 extra charge). **Amenities:** dual
phone lines, voice mail, irons, hair dryers. **Dining:** 6 am-2 & 5-10 pm, Sat & Sun from 6:30 am, cocktails.
Pool(s): outdoor. **Leisure Activities:** exercise room, sports court. **Guest Services:** gift shop, valet and coin laundry, airport
transportation-Baltimore-Washington International Airport, area transportation-Amtrak & light rail. **Business Services:**
conference facilities, business center. **Cards:** AX, CB, DC, DS, MC, VI.

SOME UNITS

HOMESTEAD STUDIO SUITES HOTEL-BALTIMORE
WASHINGTON INT'L AIRPORT   *Book at aaa.com*   Phone: (410)691-2500   46

All Year   1P: $91-$101   2P: $96-$106   XP: $5   F17
Location: I-695, exit 7A, 1 mi s on SR 295, then just e on W Nursery Rd. 939 International Dr 21090.
Fax: 410/691-2972. **Facility:** 137 one-bedroom standard units with efficiencies. 2 stories (no elevator),
Motel   exterior corridors. *Bath:* combo or shower only. **Parking:** on-site. **Terms:** weekly rates available, pets ($75
fee). **Amenities:** voice mail, irons, hair dryers. **Guest Services:** valet and coin laundry. **Business Services:** fax (fee).
Cards: AX, CB, DC, DS, JC, MC, VI.

SOME UNITS

HOMEWOOD SUITES BY HILTON-BWI AIRPORT   *Book at aaa.com*   Phone: (410)684-6100   50

1/1-2/28   1P: $119-$189
3/1-12/31   1P: $109-$179
Location: I-695, exit 7A, 1 mi s on SR 295, 0.7 mi e on W Nursery Rd, then just n. 1181 Winterson Rd 21090.
Small-scale Hotel   Fax: 410/684-6810. **Facility:** 147 units. 140 one- and 7 two-bedroom suites with kitchens. 4 stories, interior
corridors. *Bath:* combo or shower only. **Parking:** on-site. **Terms:** 2 night minimum stay - seasonal and/or weekends,
cancellation fee imposed, [BP] & [MAP] meal plans available, pets ($150 fee, with prior approval). **Amenities:** video games
(fee), dual phone lines, voice mail, irons, hair dryers. **Pool(s):** heated indoor. **Leisure Activities:** whirlpool, limited exercise
equipment. **Guest Services:** sundries, valet and coin laundry, area transportation. **Business Services:** meeting rooms,
business center. **Cards:** AX, DC, DS, MC, VI.

SOME UNITS

MICROTEL INN & SUITES-BWI AIRPORT   *Book at aaa.com*   Phone: (410)865-7500   49

All Year [ECP]   1P: $89-$139   2P: $89-$139   XP: $10   F16
Location: I-695, exit 7A, 1 mi s on SR 295, 0.7 mi e on W Nursery Rd, then just n. 1170 Winterson Rd 21090.
Small-scale Hotel   Fax: 410/865-7510. **Facility:** 110 one-bedroom standard units. 3 stories, interior corridors. *Bath:* combo or
shower only. **Parking:** on-site. **Terms:** cancellation fee imposed. **Amenities:** video games, voice mail, irons,
hair dryers. **Leisure Activities:** exercise room. **Guest Services:** coin laundry, area transportation. **Cards:** AX, CB, DC, DS,
MC, VI. *(See color ad p 608)*

SOME UNITS

(See map and index starting on p. 566)

MOTEL 6 BALTIMORE-LINTHICUM HEIGHTS #1201　　*Book at aaa.com*　　　　　Phone: 410/636-9070　**40**

◆◆ Motel

6/16-9/4	1P: $57-$67	2P: $63-$73	XP: $3	F17
5/27-6/15	1P: $53-$63	2P: $59-$69	XP: $3	F17
3/1-5/26 & 9/5-2/28	1P: $51-$61	2P: $57-$67	XP: $3	F17

Location: I-695, exit 8, just s. 5179 Raynor Ave. 21090. Fax: 410/789-0669. **Facility:** 136 one-bedroom standard units. 3 stories, exterior corridors. *Bath:* shower only. **Parking:** on-site. **Pool(s):** outdoor. **Cards:** AX, CB, DC, DS, MC, VI.

SOME UNITS

RED ROOF INN-BWI AIRPORT　　*Book at aaa.com*　　　　　　　Phone: (410)850-7600　**58**

◆◆ ◆◆ Small-scale Hotel

4/14-11/26	1P: $73-$93	2P: $79-$99	XP: $5	F18
3/1-4/13	1P: $65-$85	2P: $71-$92	XP: $5	F18
11/27-2/28	1P: $70-$80	2P: $76-$86	XP: $5	F18

Location: I-695, exit 7A, 1 mi s on SR 295, 1.3 mi e on W Elkridge Landing Rd, then just w. 827 Elkridge Landing Rd 21090. Fax: 410/850-7611. **Facility:** 131 one-bedroom standard units. 3 stories, exterior corridors. **Parking:** on-site. **Terms:** small pets only. **Amenities:** video games (fee), voice mail. **Guest Services:** coin laundry, area transportation. **Business Services:** meeting rooms, fax (fee). **Cards:** AX, CB, DC, DS, MC, VI.

SOME UNITS

RESIDENCE INN BY MARRIOTT-BWI AIRPORT　　*Book at aaa.com*　　　　Phone: (410)691-0255　**51**

◆◆◆ Small-scale Hotel

All Year　　1P: $119-$199

Location: I-695, exit 7A, 1 mi s on SR 295, 0.7 mi e on W Nursery Rd, then just n. 1160 Winterson Rd 21090. Fax: 410/691-0254. **Facility:** 120 units. 44 one-bedroom standard units with efficiencies. 52 one- and 24 two-bedroom suites with kitchens. 3 stories, interior corridors. *Bath:* combo or shower only. **Parking:** on-site. **Terms:** cancellation fee imposed, pets ($200 fee, $10 extra charge). **Amenities:** video games (fee), high-speed Internet, voice mail, irons, hair dryers. *Some:* dual phone lines. **Pool(s):** outdoor. **Leisure Activities:** whirlpool, exercise room, sports court. **Guest Services:** valet and coin laundry, area transportation. **Business Services:** meeting rooms, fax (fee). **Cards:** AX, CB, DC, DS, JC, MC, VI.

SOME UNITS

(See map and index starting on p. 566)

SLEEP INN & SUITES AIRPORT   *Book at aaa.com*   Phone: (410)789-7223   **41**

(AAA) (SAVE)   All Year [ECP]   1P: $119-$129   2P: $119-$129   XP: $8   F18
Location: I-695, exit 6A eastbound; exit 5 westbound, 0.3 mi n to jct SR 170/648. 6055 Belle Grove Rd 21225.
Fax: 410/789-9501. **Facility:** 145 one-bedroom standard units, some with whirlpools. 7 stories, interior
corridors. *Bath:* combo or shower only. **Parking:** on-site. **Terms:** package plans. **Amenities:** high-speed
Small-scale Hotel Internet, dual phone lines, voice mail, safes, irons, hair dryers. **Leisure Activities:** exercise room. **Guest
Services:** valet and coin laundry, airport transportation-Baltimore-Washington International Airport, area
transportation-Amtrak station & light rail. **Business Services:** meeting rooms, business center. **Cards:** AX, CB, DC, DS, JC,
MC, VI. **Special Amenities: free expanded continental breakfast and free local telephone calls.** *(See color ad p 605)*

SOME UNITS

SPRINGHILL SUITES BY MARRIOTT   *Book at aaa.com*   Phone: (410)694-0555   **53**

All Year [ECP]   1P: $99-$169   2P: $99-$169
Location: I-95 to I-195, e to exit 1A, s on Elm Rd, then sw. 899 Elkridge Landing Rd 21090. Fax: 410/694-0575.
Small-scale Hotel **Facility:** 133 one-bedroom standard units. 4 stories, interior corridors. *Bath:* combo or shower only.
Parking: on-site. **Terms:** package plans. **Amenities:** video games, high-speed Internet, voice mail, irons,
hair dryers. **Pool(s):** indoor. **Leisure Activities:** whirlpool, exercise room. **Guest Services:** coin laundry. **Cards:** AX, DC, DS,
JC, MC, VI.

SOME UNITS

WINGATE INN AT BWI AIRPORT   *Book at aaa.com*   Phone: (410)859-0003   **43**

All Year [CP]   1P: $159-$189   2P: $159-$189   XP: $10   F12
Location: 1 mi s on SR 295, 0.6 mi e on W Nursery Rd, then just n. 1510 Aero Dr 21090. Fax: 410/859-5533.
Small-scale Hotel **Facility:** 129 one-bedroom standard units. 5 stories, interior corridors. *Bath:* combo or shower only.
Parking: on-site. **Terms:** cancellation fee imposed. **Amenities:** high-speed Internet, voice mail, safes, irons,
hair dryers. **Pool(s):** indoor. **Leisure Activities:** whirlpool, exercise room. **Guest Services:** coin laundry, area transportation.
Business Services: meeting rooms, business center. **Cards:** AX, DC, DS, JC, MC, VI. *(See color ad p 608)*

SOME UNITS

——— WHERE TO DINE ———

G & M RESTAURANT   Lunch: $6-$15   Dinner: $8-$25   Phone: 410/636-1777   **20**
Location: I-695, exit 8, just w. 804 N Hammonds Ferry Rd 21090. **Hours:** 11 am-11 pm. **Closed:** 1/1, 12/25.
Features: If you like crab cakes, you'll love G & M Restaurant. Family oriented atmosphere and they will
American ship crab cakes nationwide. Casual dress; cocktails. **Parking:** on-site. **Cards:** AX, CB, DC, DS, JC,
MC, VI.

MICHENER'S   Lunch: $9-$19   Dinner: $12-$28   Phone: 410/859-3300   **24**
Location: I-195, exit 1A, 0.5 mi n on SR 170, just e; in Four Points by Sheraton BWI Airport. 7032 Elm Rd 21240.
Hours: 11 am-10 pm. **Features:** The restaurant combines a classic setting and an intricate menu of beef
Continental and seafood. The formally attired wait staff will help with wine selections. Casual dress; cocktails. **Parking:**
on-site. **Cards:** AX, CB, DC, DS, JC, MC, VI.

MONIKER'S GRILLE   Lunch: $9-$19   Dinner: $9-$29   Phone: 410/859-8300   **23**
Location: I-695, exit 7A, 1 mi s on SR 295, then 1.2 mi e. 1743 W Nursery Rd 21240. **Hours:** 11 am-10 pm.
Features: Moniker's Grille is a fun and casual eatery with a menu that includes many seafood choices- do
Continental not miss the Crab Cakes. Casual dress; cocktails. **Parking:** on-site. **Cards:** AX, CB, DC, DS, JC, MC, VI.

THE OLIVE GROVE RESTAURANT   Lunch: $7-$15   Dinner: $9-$25   Phone: 410/636-1385   **21**
Location: I-695, exit 8, just s. 705 N Hammonds Ferry Rd 21090. **Hours:** 11 am-11 pm. **Closed:** 7/4, 11/24, 12/25.
Reservations: suggested. **Features:** The restaurant combines a wonderful atmosphere with great pasta
and seafood dishes. Service is friendly and thoughtful. Casual dress; cocktails. **Parking:** on-site. **Cards:** AX,
Italian CB, DC, DS, MC, VI.

THE ROSE RESTAURANT   Lunch: $5-$12   Dinner: $11-$25   Phone: 410/636-0300   **22**
Location: I-695, exit 6A eastbound; exit 5 westbound, at jct SR 170 and 648; in Comfort Inn Airport. 6075 Belle Grove
Rd 21225. **Hours:** 6:30 am-10 pm, Sat & Sun-midnight. **Reservations:** suggested. **Features:** Patrons can
relax in the comfortable, quiet atmosphere while perusing a menu of freshly made Continental cuisine. The
Continental piano bar offers entertainment Fridays and Saturdays. Service in the pub is available from 11 am to
midnight. Casual dress; cocktails. **Parking:** on-site. **Cards:** AX, CB, DC, DS, MC, VI.

SNYDER'S WILLOW GROVE   Lunch: $8-$14   Dinner: $10-$25   Phone: 410/789-1149   **19**
Location: I-695, exit 8, just sw. 841 N Hammonds Ferry Rd 21090. **Hours:** 9 am-10 pm. **Closed:** 12/25.
Reservations: suggested, weekends. **Features:** Snyder's Willow Grove is a family run restaurant that long
has been a favorite in the area. Steaks, chops and all sorts of seafood selections. Casual dress; cocktails.
American **Parking:** on-site. **Cards:** AX, CB, DC, DS, JC, MC, VI.

LINWOOD

———— WHERE TO STAY ————

WOOD'S GAIN BED & BREAKFAST
▼▼▼▼
Bed & Breakfast

All Year [BP]   2P: $95-$155   **Phone:** (410)775-0308   **XP:** $30
Location: Just e on SR 75, then just s. 421 McKinstry's Mill Rd 21791. Fax: 410/775-2767. **Facility:** A B&B nestled in the historic village of Linwood, Wood's Gain entices guests with pleasant parlor rooms and a scenic garden. 4 one-bedroom standard units, some with whirlpools. 2 stories (no elevator), interior/exterior corridors. *Bath:* shower or tub only. **Parking:** on-site. **Terms:** check-in 4 pm, 2 night minimum stay - seasonal and/or weekends, 7 day cancellation notice. **Amenities:** hair dryers. **Leisure Activities:** whirlpool, exercise room. **Guest Services:** complimentary evening beverages. **Cards:** MC, VI.

SOME UNITS

(ASK) (&M) (🛏) (✕) (📺) (☎) / (🖥) (💻) /

MOUNT AIRY pop. 6,425

———— WHERE TO DINE ————

BRICK RIDGE RESTAURANT
▼▼▼▼
American

Dinner: $12-$21   **Phone:** 301/829-8191
Location: I-70, exit 68, 3.5 mi n on SR 27. 6212 Ridge Rd 21771. **Hours:** 5 pm-9 pm, Fri & Sat-10 pm, Sun 11 am-2 & 4-9 pm. Closed: 12/25; also Mon. **Features:** The old-time house has brick walls and lovely hardwood floors. On the menu are many classic American beef and seafood favorites. Casual dress; cocktails. **Parking:** on-site. **Cards:** AX, DC, DS, MC, VI.

(✕)

FOUR SEASONS RESTAURANT
▼▼▼ ▼▼▼
American

Lunch: $5-$6   **Dinner:** $9-$11   **Phone:** 301/829-2320
Location: I-70, exit 68, just s. 4506 Old National Pike 21771. **Hours:** 6 am-9 pm. Closed major holidays. **Features:** The Four Seasons Restaurant is a family-run business with a huge local following; it is well worth a quick stop off the interstate. Casual dress. **Parking:** on-site. **Cards:** AX, DS, MC, VI.

(✕)

OWINGS MILLS pop. 20,193   (See map and index starting on p. 566)

———— WHERE TO STAY ————

AMERISUITES (BALTIMORE/OWINGS MILLS)   *Book at aaa.com*
(AAA) (SAVE)
▼▼▼▼▼
Small-scale Hotel

All Year   1P: $134-$199   2P: $134-$199   **Phone:** (410)998-3630   **19**   F18
Location: I-795, exit 4 (Owings Mills Blvd), 0.5 mi s, 0.7 mi e on Red Run Blvd. 4730 Painters Mill Rd 21117. Fax: 410/998-3631. **Facility:** 124 one-bedroom standard units. 7 stories, interior corridors. *Bath:* combo or shower only. **Parking:** on-site. **Terms:** small pets only ($50 fee). **Amenities:** video library, high-speed Internet (fee), voice mail, safes, irons, hair dryers. *Some:* dual phone lines. **Pool(s):** heated indoor. **Leisure Activities:** limited exercise equipment. **Guest Services:** valet and coin laundry, area transportation-within 5 mi. **Business Services:** meeting rooms, fax (fee). **Cards:** AX, CB, DC, DS, JC, MC, VI. **Special Amenities:** free expanded continental breakfast and free newspaper. *(See color ad p 571)*

SOME UNITS

(S/D) (🛏) (&M) (🛎) (🏊) (VCR) (📹) (DATA PORT) (📞) (🖥) (💻) / (✕) /
FEE

HILTON GARDEN INN-OWINGS MILLS   *Book at aaa.com*
▼▼▼▼
Small-scale Hotel

All Year   1P: $99-$184   2P: $99-$184   **Phone:** (410)654-0030   **18**   F
Location: I-795, exit 4 (Owings Mills Blvd), 0.7 mi s. 4770 Owings Mills Blvd 21117. Fax: 410/654-0269. **Facility:** 160 one-bedroom standard units. 6 stories, interior corridors. *Bath:* combo or shower only. **Parking:** on-site. **Terms:** cancellation fee imposed, package plans. **Amenities:** video games (fee), high-speed Internet, dual phone lines, voice mail, irons, hair dryers. **Pool(s):** heated indoor. **Leisure Activities:** whirlpool, exercise room. **Guest Services:** valet and coin laundry. **Business Services:** meeting rooms, business center. **Cards:** AX, CB, DC, DS, MC, VI.

SOME UNITS

(ASK) (S/D) (🍴) (&M) (🛎) (🏊) (📹) (DATA PORT) (📞) (🖥) (💻) / (✕) /

PASADENA pop. 12,093   (See map and index starting on p. 566)

———— **WHERE TO DINE** ————

BELLA NAPOLI ITALIAN RESTAURANT   **Lunch:** $8-$18   **Dinner:** $10-$20   **Phone:** 410/255-9400   **34**
▼▼▼▼ **Location:** 1 mi n on SR 2, 2 mi e. 350 Mountain Road St G 21122. **Hours:** 11 am-10 pm, Fri & Sat-11 pm, Sun-
Italian 8:30 pm. Closed: 12/25. **Features:** Dishes are based on classic Italian recipes. Great murals and background music contribute to the setting. Casual dress; cocktails. **Parking:** on-site. **Cards:** AX, CB, DC, DS, JC, MC, VI.

PIKESVILLE pop. 29,123   (See map and index starting on p. 566)

———— **WHERE TO STAY** ————

HILTON PIKESVILLE   *Book at aaa.com*   **Phone:** (410)653-1100   **34**
▼▼▼▼ All Year   1P: $108-$178   2P: $108-$178   XP: $15   F18
Small-scale Hotel **Location:** I-695, exit 20, just s. 1726 Reisterstown Rd 21208-2984. **Fax:** 410/415-6232. **Facility:** 171 one-bedroom standard units. 5 stories, interior corridors. *Bath:* combo or shower only. **Parking:** on-site. **Terms:** cancellation fee imposed. **Amenities:** video games (fee), dual phone lines, voice mail, irons, hair dryers. **Pool(s):** outdoor. **Leisure Activities:** saunas. *Fee:* 6 lighted indoor tennis courts, massage. **Guest Services:** gift shop, valet laundry. **Business Services:** conference facilities, business center. **Cards:** AX, CB, DC, DS, MC, VI.

SOME UNITS
ASK SO 🍴 📺 🖥 🏊 🛜 📶 ✕ 📽 DATA PORT 💻 / ✕ 🛏 📠 /   FEE FEE

RAMADA INN BALTIMORE WEST   *Book at aaa.com*   **Phone:** (410)486-5600   **33**
▼▼▼ ▼ 7/1-10/31 [CP]   1P: $73-$89   2P: $73-$89
4/1-6/30 [CP]   1P: $73-$84   2P: $73-$84
Small-scale Hotel 11/1-2/28 [CP]   1P: $70-$79   2P: $70-$79
3/1-3/31 [CP]   1P: $70-$74   2P: $70-$74
Location: I-695, exit 20, just e on US 140. 1721 Reisterstown Rd 21208. **Fax:** 410/484-9377. **Facility:** 105 one-bedroom standard units, some with whirlpools. 2 stories (no elevator), exterior corridors. *Bath:* combo or shower only. **Parking:** on-site. **Terms:** 30 day cancellation notice-fee imposed. **Amenities:** voice mail, safes, irons, hair dryers. **Pool(s):** outdoor. **Leisure Activities:** exercise room. **Guest Services:** coin laundry. **Business Services:** meeting rooms, fax (fee). **Cards:** AX, DC, DS, JC, MC, VI.

SOME UNITS
ASK SO 🍴 📺 🖥 🛜 📶 📽 DATA PORT 🛏 📠 💻 / ✕ /

ROSEDALE pop. 19,199   (See map and index starting on p. 566)

———— **WHERE TO STAY** ————

FAIRFIELD INN BY MARRIOTT BALTIMORE NORTH   *Book at aaa.com*   **Phone:** (410)574-8100   **37**
▼▼▼ ▼ All Year [ECP]   1P: $104-$119   2P: $104-$119
Small-scale Hotel **Location:** I-695, exit 34, just n. 4 Philadelphia Ct 21237. **Fax:** 410/574-8204. **Facility:** 131 one-bedroom standard units. 5 stories, interior corridors. *Bath:* combo or shower only. **Parking:** on-site. **Amenities:** voice mail, irons, hair dryers. **Pool(s):** outdoor. **Leisure Activities:** exercise room. **Guest Services:** coin laundry. **Business Services:** meeting rooms. **Cards:** AX, DS, MC, VI.

SOME UNITS
ASK 🖥 🛜 📽 DATA PORT / ✕ 🛏 📠 💻 /

SYKESVILLE pop. 4,197

———— **WHERE TO STAY** ————

INN AT NORWOOD   **Phone:** 410/549-7868
▼▼▼▼ All Year [BP]   1P: $90-$190   2P: $90-$190   XP: $20
Bed & Breakfast **Location:** I-70, exit 80 (SR 32), 8 mi n, just w on Main St, then just w on Church St. 7514 Norwood Ave 21784. **Fax:** 410/716-3778. **Facility:** Featuring a porch and garden, this appealing B&B is located in the historic area close to many shops. 5 one-bedroom standard units, some with whirlpools. 3 stories (no elevator), interior corridors. **Parking:** on-site. **Terms:** age restrictions may apply, 7 day cancellation notice. **Amenities:** hair dryers. *Some:* CD players, irons. **Cards:** AX, MC, VI.

ASK SO ✕ VCR 📽 Z

———— **WHERE TO DINE** ————

BALDWIN'S STATION   **Lunch:** $9-$18   **Dinner:** $11-$25   **Phone:** 410/795-1041
▼▼▼▼ **Location:** I-70, exit 80, 7.6 mi n on SR 32. 7618 Main St 21784. **Hours:** 11 am-9:30 pm, Sun-8:30 pm. Closed: 12/25; also Mon. **Features:** The converted train station still sits yards away from working trains. Yesteryear ambience and wide menu variety await. Casual dress; cocktails. **Parking:** on-site. **Cards:** AX, CB, DC, DS, JC, MC, VI.
American
🍽 ✕

E. W. BECK'S   **Lunch:** $6-$12   **Dinner:** $8-$18   **Phone:** 410/552-4070
▼▼▼ **Location:** I-70, exit 80, 7.7 mi n on SR 32. 7565 Main St 21784. **Hours:** 10 am-10 pm, Sun 4 pm-9 pm. Closed: 12/25. **Features:** A Sykesville tradition, the restaurant serves homespun charm with its ice cream and varied dishes. Casual dress; cocktails. **Parking:** on-site and street. **Cards:** AX, CB, DC, DS, JC, MC, VI.
American
🍽 ✕

TIMONIUM   (See map and index starting on p. 566)

———— WHERE TO STAY ————

DAYS HOTEL & CONFERENCE CENTER
BALTIMORE NORTH   *Book at aaa.com*   Phone: (410)560-1000   **22**

5/1-10/31 [ECP]	1P: $79-$129	2P: $84-$134	XP: $5	F18
3/1-4/30 & 11/1-2/28 [ECP]	1P: $59-$94	2P: $64-$99	XP: $5	F18

Small-scale Hotel   **Location:** I-83, exit 17, just e. 9615 Deereco Rd 21093. **Fax:** 410/561-3918. **Facility:** 145 units. 141 one-bedroom standard units, some with efficiencies. 4 one-bedroom suites ($69-$140), some with efficiencies. 7 stories, interior corridors. **Parking:** on-site. **Amenities:** video games (fee), voice mail, hair dryers. *Some:* irons. **Pool(s):** outdoor. **Leisure Activities:** exercise room. **Guest Services:** valet and coin laundry. **Business Services:** meeting rooms. **Cards:** AX, DC, DS, MC, VI.

SOME UNITS
(ASK) (S/D) (⊪) (Y) (⊘) (⊇) (✦) (DATA PORT) (🖥) (☕) / (✕) (VCR) (📷) /

HOLIDAY INN SELECT BALTIMORE NORTH   *Book at aaa.com*   Phone: (410)252-7373   **24**

All Year	1P: $129	2P: $129	F19

Small-scale Hotel   **Location:** I-83, exit 16A northbound; exit 16 southbound, 0.3 mi se. 2004 Greenspring Dr 21093. **Fax:** 410/561-0182. **Facility:** 246 units. 244 one-bedroom standard units. 2 one-bedroom suites. 5 stories, interior corridors. **Parking:** on-site. **Terms:** cancellation fee imposed, package plans. **Amenities:** high-speed Internet, voice mail, irons, hair dryers. *Some:* fax. **Pool(s):** heated indoor/outdoor. **Leisure Activities:** whirlpool, exercise room. *Fee:* game room. **Guest Services:** valet and coin laundry, area transportation. **Business Services:** conference facilities, business center. **Cards:** AX, CB, DC, DS, JC, MC, VI.

SOME UNITS
(ASK) (S/D) (✦)FEE (⊪) (Y) (⊘) (⊇) (✕) (✦) (DATA PORT) (🖥) / (✕) (🖥)FEE (📷)FEE /

RED ROOF INN-TIMONIUM   *Book at aaa.com*   Phone: (410)666-0380   **23**

4/3-10/29	1P: $65-$90	2P: $71-$96	XP: $6	F18
3/1-4/2	1P: $55-$90	2P: $61-$96	XP: $6	F18
10/30-2/28	1P: $58-$73	2P: $64-$79	XP: $6	F18

Motel   **Location:** I-83, exit 16A northbound; exit 16 southbound, just e. 111 W Timonium Rd 21093. **Fax:** 410/666-1509. **Facility:** 137 one-bedroom standard units. 3 stories, exterior corridors. **Parking:** on-site. **Terms:** small pets only. **Amenities:** video games (fee), voice mail. **Business Services:** fax (fee). **Cards:** AX, CB, DC, DS, MC, VI.

SOME UNITS
(🛏) (⊪+) (✦) (DATA PORT) / (✕) (🖥) (📷) /

———— WHERE TO DINE ————

AN POITIN STIL   **Lunch:** $5-$10   **Dinner:** $9-$20   Phone: 410/560-7900   **12**

Irish   **Location:** I-83, exit 16A northbound; exit 16 southbound, 0.6 mi e on Timonium Rd, then 0.7 mi n on SR 45. 2323 York Rd 21093. **Hours:** 11 am-1 am, Sun-midnight. Closed: 11/24, 12/24, 12/25. **Features:** The bustling Irish pub sticks with the tried and true, including corned beef and cabbage, Irish stew and fish and chips. Plenty of American selections also are available. The atmosphere is lively and fun. Casual dress; cocktails. **Parking:** on-site. **Cards:** AX, DS, MC, VI.

(Y) (✕)

GIBBY'S SEAFOOD RESTAURANT   **Lunch:** $6-$13   **Dinner:** $15-$43   Phone: 410/560-0703   **11**

Seafood   **Location:** I-83, exit 17, 0.6 mi e. 22 W Padonia Rd 21093. **Hours:** 11 am-10 pm, Fri & Sat-11 pm, Sun noon-10 pm. Closed: 11/24, 12/25. **Features:** A casual air sets the tone in the popular, lively restaurant. Locals are frequent diners, and at times waits can be fairly long. The seafood is fresh, with at least 10 specials every week. Although crab is the big draw, the menu lists much more. Casual dress; cocktails. **Parking:** on-site. **Cards:** AX, CB, DC, DS, MC, VI.

(Y) (✕)

MICHAEL'S CAFE   **Lunch:** $7-$11   **Dinner:** $9-$28   Phone: 410/252-2022   **13**

American   **Location:** I-83, exit 16A northbound; exit 16 southbound, 0.6 mi e on Timonium Rd, just n on SR 45. 2119 York Rd 21093. **Hours:** 10:30 am-12:30 am, Fri & Sat-1 am. Closed: 12/25. **Features:** Paraphernalia of sports heroes and movie stars hangs on the walls of the popular restaurant. Maryland jumbo lump crab cakes are the top seller on a menu that also lists chicken, veal, steak and pasta selections. Don't overlook the raw bar. Lighter fare appeals to diners with smaller appetites. Casual dress; cocktails. **Parking:** on-site. **Cards:** AX, DC, DS, MC, VI.

(Y) (✕)

TOWSON pop. 51,793   (See map and index starting on p. 566)

———— WHERE TO STAY ————

BURKSHIRE MARRIOTT CONFERENCE HOTEL   *Book at aaa.com*   Phone: (410)324-8100   **30**

All Year	1P: $159	2P: $189

Small-scale Hotel   **Location:** I-695, exit 27A (Dulaney Valley Rd), 0.8 mi s SR 146 (Dulaney Valley Rd), then 0.5 mi s on SR 45 (York Rd). Located on the campus of Towson University. 10 W Burke Ave 21204. **Fax:** 410/616-3749. **Facility:** 137 units. 72 one-, 59 two- and 6 three-bedroom suites with kitchens. 17 stories, interior corridors. **Bath:** combo or shower only. **Parking:** on-site. **Terms:** check-in 4 pm. **Amenities:** high-speed Internet, voice mail, irons, hair dryers. **Leisure Activities:** exercise room. **Guest Services:** valet laundry. **Business Services:** conference facilities, business center. **Cards:** AX, CB, DC, DS, MC, VI.

SOME UNITS
(⊪) (Y) (♿) (⊘) (✦) (DATA PORT) (🖥) (☕) (🖥) / (✕) /

(See map and index starting on p. 566)

COMFORT INN TOWSON — *Book at aaa.com* Phone: (410)882-0900 [29]
AAA SAVE
All Year 1P: $99-$179 2P: $99-$179 XP: $10 F
Location: I-695, exit 29B, just e. 8801 Loch Raven Blvd 21286. Fax: 410/882-4176. **Facility:** 185 one-bedroom
standard units, some with whirlpools. 5 stories, interior corridors. **Parking:** on-site. **Terms:** cancellation fee
imposed, pets ($15 extra charge). **Amenities:** voice mail, safes (fee), irons, hair dryers. **Dining:** 6:30 am-11
Small-scale Hotel pm, cocktails. **Pool(s):** outdoor. **Leisure Activities:** limited exercise equipment. **Guest Services:** coin
laundry. **Business Services:** meeting rooms, fax (fee). **Cards:** AX, DC, DS, JC, MC, VI.
(See color ad below)

SOME UNITS

HOLIDAY INN-CROMWELL BRIDGE — *Book at aaa.com* Phone: (410)823-4410 [28]
AAA SAVE
3/1-10/31 1P: $107-$134
11/1-2/28 1P: $80-$107
Location: I-695, exit 29A, just s. 1100 Cromwell Bridge Rd 21286. Fax: 410/296-6618. **Facility:** 139 one-bedroom
standard units. 6 stories, interior corridors. *Bath:* combo or shower only. **Parking:** on-site. **Terms:** pets ($25-
Small-scale Hotel $50 deposit). **Amenities:** dual phone lines, voice mail, irons, hair dryers. **Dining:** 6 am-11 & 5-10 pm, Sat &
Sun from 7 am, cocktails. **Pool(s):** outdoor. **Leisure Activities:** exercise room. **Guest Services:** valet and
coin laundry. **Business Services:** meeting rooms, fax (fee). **Cards:** AX, CB, DC, DS, JC, MC, VI.

SOME UNITS

SHERATON BALTIMORE NORTH — *Book at aaa.com* Phone: (410)321-7400 [27]
3/1-7/4 & 9/1-11/20 1P: $139-$179
7/5-8/31 1P: $129-$169
Large-scale Hotel 11/21-2/28 1P: $119-$159
Location: I-695, exit 27A, 0.3 mi s. Connected to Towson Town Center Mall via skywalk. 903 Dulaney Valley Rd 21204.
Fax: 410/296-9534. **Facility:** 284 one-bedroom standard units. 12 stories, interior corridors. **Parking:** on-site (fee) and valet.
Terms: cancellation fee imposed. **Amenities:** high-speed Internet, voice mail, irons, hair dryers. **Pool(s):** heated indoor.
Leisure Activities: saunas, whirlpool, exercise room. **Guest Services:** gift shop, valet laundry, area transportation. **Business
Services:** conference facilities, business center. **Cards:** AX, DC, DS, MC, VI.

SOME UNITS

WESTMINSTER pop. 16,731

──── WHERE TO STAY ────

BEST WESTERN WESTMINSTER CATERING AND CONFERENCE CENTER *Book at aaa.com*

Phone: (410)857-1900

All Year [ECP] 1P: $55-$89 2P: $55-$95 XP: $6 F12

Small-scale Hotel

Location: 1.7 mi w on SR 140 from jct SR 27. 451 WMC Dr 21158. Fax: 410/857-9584. **Facility:** 101 one-bedroom standard units, some with whirlpools. 2 stories (no elevator); interior corridors. **Parking:** on-site. **Amenities:** high-speed Internet, voice mail, irons, hair dryers. **Pool(s):** outdoor. **Guest Services:** valet and coin laundry. **Business Services:** meeting rooms, fax (fee). **Cards:** AX, CB, DC, DS, JC, MC, VI. *(See color ad below)*

SOME UNITS

(ASK) 🖳 🐾 🛟 🏊 🏋 [DATA PORT] 🛏 🖥 ▭ / ✕ /
FEE

THE BOSTON INN

Phone: 410-848-9095

3/1-10/1 1P: $42-$58 2P: $46-$62 XP: $4 F
10/2-2/28 1P: $42-$50 2P: $46-$52 XP: $4 F

Motel

Location: 0.9 mi se on SR 97/140 from jct SR 27. 533 Baltimore Blvd 21157. Fax: 410/848-9326. **Facility:** 118 one-bedroom standard units, some with whirlpools. 1-2 stories (no elevator); exterior corridors. **Parking:** on-site. **Terms:** weekly rates available, pets ($50 deposit, dogs only). **Pool(s):** outdoor. **Guest Services:** coin laundry. **Business Services:** fax (fee). **Cards:** AX, DC, MC, VI.

SOME UNITS

(ASK) 🐾 🍴 🛟 🏋 [DATA PORT] 🛏 🖥 / ✕ (VCR) /
FEE

DAYS INN-WESTMINSTER *Book at aaa.com*

Phone: (410)857-0500

6/1-8/31 1P: $72-$94 2P: $72-$99 XP: $5 F17
3/1-5/31 1P: $63-$94 2P: $66-$98 XP: $5 F17
9/1-11/30 1P: $59-$89 2P: $64-$94 XP: $5 F17
12/1-2/28 1P: $49-$79 2P: $49-$89 XP: $5 F17

Small-scale Hotel

Location: 0.4 mi se on SR 97/140 from jct SR 27, just n. 25 S Cranberry Rd 21157. Fax: 410/857-1407. **Facility:** 97 one-bedroom standard units. 3 stories, interior corridors. **Parking:** on-site. **Terms:** [ECP] meal plan available, package plans. **Amenities:** voice mail, irons, hair dryers. **Pool(s):** outdoor. **Leisure Activities:** exercise room. **Guest Services:** valet and coin laundry. **Business Services:** meeting rooms, fax (fee). **Cards:** AX, CB, DC, DS, MC, VI.

SOME UNITS

(ASK) 🖳 🍴 🚭 🏊 🏋 [DATA PORT] / ✕ 🛏 🖥 ▭ /

WESTMINSTER INN

Phone: 410/876-2893

Property failed to provide current rates

Historic Country Inn

Location: 0.5 mi s of SR 97/140; downtown. 5 S Center St 21157. Fax: 410/876-2893. **Facility:** The inn offers rooms in a main building built as a schoolhouse in 1899 and in a restored row house across from the main building. 24 one-bedroom standard units with whirlpools. 2 stories (no elevator); interior/exterior corridors. **Parking:** on-site. **Terms:** age restrictions may apply. **Amenities:** *Some:* hair dryers. **Pool(s):** heated indoor. **Leisure Activities:** sauna, whirlpool, steamroom, racquetball courts, basketball. **Guest Services:** valet laundry. *Fee:* tanning facility. **Business Services:** meeting rooms, fax (fee).

SOME UNITS

🏊 🛟 ✕ 🏋 [DATA PORT] / ✕ 🛏 🖥 /

──── WHERE TO DINE ────

BAUGHER'S RESTAURANT Lunch: $3-$7 Dinner: $5-$13 Phone: 410/848-7413

American

Location: Jct SR 31 and 32. 289 W Main St 21158. **Hours:** 7:30 am-9 pm. Closed major holidays. **Features:** The well-established, family-owned restaurant has offered traditional country foods since 1948. The ice cream and pies are homemade. An adjacent farm market sells fruit and vegetables from the family orchards and gardens. Casual dress. **Parking:** on-site. **Cards:** DC, MC, VI.

✕

JOHANSSONS DINING HOUSE Lunch: $8-$18 Dinner: $8-$25 Phone: 410/876-0101

American

Location: Just w; center. 4 W Main St 21157. **Hours:** 11 am-1 am. Closed major holidays. **Features:** Fine and casual dining are offered along with Westminster's original brewing company. Casual dress; cocktails. **Parking:** street. **Cards:** AX, CB, DC, DS, JC, MC, VI.

🍽 ✕

WHITE MARSH pop. 8,485   (See map and index starting on p. 566)

———— WHERE TO STAY ————

HAMPTON INN AT WHITE MARSH   *Book at aaa.com*   Phone: (410)931-2200   **15**
All Year   1P: $119-$139   2P: $119-$139
Small-scale Hotel   **Location:** I-95, exit 67B, 0.5 mi w on SR 43 (White Marsh Blvd), then 0.5 mi s on Honeygo Blvd. 8225 Town Center Dr 21236. Fax: 410/931-2215. **Facility:** 127 units. 121 one-bedroom standard units. 6 one-bedroom suites ($139-$169). 4 stories, interior corridors. *Bath:* combo or shower only. **Parking:** on-site. **Amenities:** video games (fee), high-speed Internet, dual phone lines, voice mail, irons, hair dryers. **Pool(s):** outdoor. **Leisure Activities:** limited exercise equipment. **Guest Services:** valet and coin laundry, area transportation. **Business Services:** meeting rooms, business center. **Cards:** AX, CB, DC, DS, JC, MC, VI.

SOME UNITS
(ASK) (TI+) (&M) (&) (🌐) (≈) (🎥) (DATA PORT) (📟) / (X) (🛗) (🖥) /
                                                                                    FEE   FEE

HILTON GARDEN INN-WHITE MARSH   *Book at aaa.com*   Phone: (410)427-0600   **14**
All Year   1P: $119-$139   2P: $119-$139   XP: $10   F18
Small-scale Hotel   **Location:** I-95, exit 67B, 0.5 mi w on SR 43 (White Marsh Blvd), then 0.5 mi s on Honeygo Blvd. 5015 Campbell Blvd 21236 (5015 Campbell Blvd, BALTIMORE). Fax: 410/427-0800. **Facility:** 155 units. 145 one-bedroom standard units. 10 one-bedroom suites ($149-$179). 6 stories, interior corridors. *Bath:* combo or shower only. **Parking:** on-site. **Terms:** [BP] meal plan available. **Amenities:** video games (fee), high-speed Internet, dual phone lines, voice mail, irons, hair dryers. **Pool(s):** heated indoor. **Leisure Activities:** whirlpool, limited exercise equipment. **Guest Services:** valet and coin laundry, area transportation. **Business Services:** meeting rooms, business center. **Cards:** AX, DC, DS, MC, VI.

SOME UNITS
(ASK) (TI) (Y) (&M) (&) (≈) (🎥) (DATA PORT) (📟) (🖥) (🖥) / (X) /

RESIDENCE INN BY MARRIOTT BALTIMORE/WHITE
MARSH   *Book at aaa.com*   Phone: (410)933-9554   **13**
All Year   1P: $119-$199   2P: $119-$199
Small-scale Hotel   **Location:** I-95, exit 67B, just w. 4980 Mercantile Rd 21236 (4980 Mercantile Rd, BALTIMORE). Fax: 410/933-9556. **Facility:** 131 one-bedroom standard units with kitchens. 4 stories, interior corridors. *Bath:* combo or shower only. **Parking:** on-site. **Terms:** cancellation fee imposed, [ECP] meal plan available. **Amenities:** high-speed Internet, voice mail, irons, hair dryers. **Pool(s):** heated indoor. **Leisure Activities:** whirlpool, exercise room, sports court. **Guest Services:** valet and coin laundry. **Business Services:** meeting rooms, business center. **Cards:** AX, CB, DC, DS, JC, MC, VI.

SOME UNITS
(ASK) (🛏) (&) (≈) (X) (🎥) (DATA PORT) (📟) (🖥) (🖥) / (X) /

WOODSTOCK

———— WHERE TO DINE ————

MANGIA ITALIAN GRILL   **Lunch:** $7-$12   **Dinner:** $9-$20   Phone: 410/461-2900
Italian   **Location:** I-70, exit 83, just n. 10795 Birmingham Way 21042. **Hours:** 11 am-11 pm. Closed: 12/25. **Features:** Mangia Italian Grill has huge selection of pasta and sauce that are lovingly prepared and served by an excellent staff. Casual dress; cocktails. **Parking:** on-site. **Cards:** AX, CB, DC, DS, JC, MC, VI.

(Y) (X)

This ends listings for the Baltimore Vicinity.
The following page resumes the alphabetical listings of
cities in Maryland.

BELCAMP —*See Baltimore p. 595.*

BELTSVILLE —*See District Of Columbia p. 477.*

BERLIN pop. 3,491

——— **WHERE TO DINE** ———

ASSATEAGUE CRAB HOUSE & CARRYOUT

Seafood

Lunch: $9-$20   **Dinner:** $9-$20   **Phone:** 410/641-4330
Location: 2 mi s on SR 611 from jct SR 376. 7635 Stephen Decatur Rd 21811. **Hours:** Open 5/15-10/15; noon-9 pm; Mon-Fri from 4 pm 5/15-6/15 & 9/6-10/15. **Features:** It's back to the basics at this informal crab house with painted cement floors, paneled walls and nautical decor. What's important though is the size of the appetite you bring to the all-you-can-eat crab special, which includes corn on the cob and more. Casual dress; beer & wine only. **Parking:** on-site. **Cards:** AX, DS, MC, VI. ✕

BETHESDA —*See District Of Columbia p. 477.*

BOONSBORO pop. 2,803

——— **WHERE TO DINE** ———

HEATHER B'S

American

Lunch: $6-$12   **Dinner:** $6-$20   **Phone:** 301/432-5100
Location: Just s; center. 1 S Main St 21713. **Hours:** 11 am-10 pm, Sun 4 pm-9 pm. Closed: 12/25. **Features:** Heather B's combines a small town flair with a big time cuisine. Knowledgeable and friendly service staff. Casual dress; cocktails. **Parking:** street. **Cards:** AX, CB, DC, DS, JC, MC, VI. 🍸 ✕

OLD SOUTH MOUNTAIN INN

American

Lunch: $7-$12   **Dinner:** $14-$30   **Phone:** 301/432-6155
Location: US 40 Alternate Rt, 1.8 mi e of jct SR 67. 6132 Old National Pike 21713. **Hours:** 5 pm-9 pm, Sat 11:30 am-2:30 & 4-10 pm, Sun 10:30 am-8 pm. Closed: 12/25; also Mon. **Reservations:** suggested. **Features:** Civil War buffs up to see Antietam will revel in the Early American atmosphere, circa 1732, and the popular Victorian-style addition. However, it's the strikingly fine food that put the restaurant on the epicurean's map. Terrace seating is a summer option. Dressy-casual; cocktails. **Parking:** on-site. **Cards:** AX, DC, MC, VI. **Historic** 🍸 ✕

BOWIE —*See District Of Columbia p. 482.*

CAMBRIDGE pop. 10,911

WHERE TO STAY

COMMODORE'S COTTAGE BED AND BREAKFAST

Cottage

Phone: (410)228-6938

All Year [ECP]   1P: $85-$100   2P: $85-$100   XP: $15   F6
Location: US 50, 0.7 mi s on Maryland Ave, just w on Academy and Spring sts, just s on High St, 0.5 mi w on Locust St, then just n. Located in a residential area. 215 Glenburn Ave 21613. Fax: 410/228-6938. **Facility:** 2 cottages. 1 story, exterior corridors. *Bath:* shower only. **Parking:** street. **Terms:** 2 night minimum stay - seasonal and/or weekends, 7 day cancellation notice-fee imposed, weekly rates available, package plans, pets (dogs only, with prior approval). **Amenities:** irons, hair dryers. **Business Services:** fax (fee). **Cards:** MC, VI.

DAYS INN & SUITES CAMBRIDGE

Small-scale Hotel

Book at aaa.com

Phone: (410)228-4444

All Year   1P: $79-$299   2P: $79-$299   XP: $10   F12
Location: On US 50, 0.5 mi e of jct SR 16. 2917 Ocean Gateway 21613. Fax: 410/228-4472. **Facility:** 50 one-bedroom standard units, some with whirlpools. 2 stories, interior corridors. **Parking:** on-site. **Terms:** cancellation fee imposed. **Amenities:** irons, hair dryers. *Some:* high-speed Internet. **Pool(s):** heated outdoor. **Guest Services:** coin laundry. **Business Services:** meeting rooms, fax (fee). **Cards:** AX, DC, DS, MC, VI. **Special Amenities:** free continental breakfast and free newspaper.

SOME UNITS

HYATT REGENCY CHESAPEAKE BAY GOLF RESORT, SPA AND MARINA

Resort
Large-scale Hotel

Book at aaa.com

Phone: (410)901-1234

All Year   1P: $130-$215   2P: $130-$215
Location: US 50 E, 1.2 mi e of Frederick C Malkus Jr Bridge. 100 Heron Blvd 21613. Fax: 410/901-6301. **Facility:** Sprawling golf resort set on the banks of the Choptank River. Luxurious public spaces and guest units. 400 units. 380 one-bedroom standard units. 20 one-bedroom suites, some with whirlpools. 6 stories, interior corridors. *Bath:* combo or shower only. **Parking:** on-site and valet. **Terms:** check-in 4 pm, 3 day cancellation notice-fee imposed, small pets only ($25 extra charge). **Amenities:** video games (fee), dual phone lines, voice mail, safes, irons, hair dryers. **Dining:** 4 restaurants, 6 am-10 pm, cocktails, also, The Water's Edge Grill, see separate listing. **Pool(s):** 2 heated outdoor, heated indoor, wading. **Leisure Activities:** saunas, whirlpool, steamrooms, waterslide, lifeguard on duty, 6 lighted tennis courts, natural wildlife preserve, hiking trails, jogging, playground, spa, shuffleboard, volleyball. *Fee:* paddleboats, sailboats, marina, charter fishing, boat tours, crabbing, kayaks, fly fishing instructions, golf-18 holes, driving range, game room. **Guest Services:** gift shop, valet and coin laundry. **Business Services:** conference facilities, business center. **Cards:** AX, CB, DC, DS, JC, MC, VI. *(See color ad below)*

SOME UNITS

FEE   FEE

HOLIDAY INN EXPRESS-CAMBRIDGE *Book at aaa.com* Phone: (410)221-9900

	6/2-11/29 [ECP]	1P: $99-$159	2P: $99-$159	XP: $15	F18
	4/30-6/1 [ECP]	1P: $89-$109	2P: $89-$109	XP: $15	F18
Small-scale Hotel	3/1-4/29 & 11/30-2/28 [ECP]	1P: $79-$99	2P: $79-$99	XP: $15	F18

Location: US 50, 1.2 mi e of Frederick C Malkus Jr Bridge. 2715 Ocean Gateway 21613. Fax: 410/221-9969. **Facility:** 86 one-bedroom standard units, some with whirlpools. 4 stories, interior corridors. *Bath:* combo or shower only. **Parking:** on-site. **Amenities:** dual phone lines, voice mail, irons, hair dryers. **Pool(s):** heated indoor. **Leisure Activities:** whirlpool. **Guest Services:** valet laundry. **Business Services:** meeting rooms, fax (fee). **Cards:** AX, DC, DS, MC, VI.

SOME UNITS
(ASK) (SD) (TI→) (&M) (&) (⌀) (⌘) (※) (DATA PORT) (⌨) / (✕) (🛏) (🍽) /
FEE FEE

---------- **WHERE TO DINE** ----------

THE WATER'S EDGE GRILL **Lunch:** $8-$12 **Dinner:** $14-$28 Phone: 410/901-1234

American

Location: US 50 E, 1.2 mi e of Frederick C Malkus Jr Bridge; in Hyatt Regency Chesapeake Bay Golf Resort, Spa and Marina. 100 Heron Blvd 21613. **Hours:** 6:30-11 am, 11:30-3 & 5-10 pm; seasonal hours may vary. **Reservations:** suggested. **Features:** This full-service restaurant serves creative American cuisine that emphasizes fresh Eastern Shore ingredients. The staff is friendly and attentive. Views from the floor-to-ceiling windows skim over the pools and the Choptank River. Dressy casual; cocktails. **Parking:** on-site. **Cards:** AX, CB, DC, DS, JC, MC, VI.

(&M) (✕)

CAMP SPRINGS —*See District Of Columbia p. 483.*

CHESAPEAKE BEACH pop. 3,180

---------- **WHERE TO STAY** ----------

CHESAPEAKE BEACH HOTEL AND SPA *Book at aaa.com* Phone: (410)257-5596

| | 4/1-9/30 | 1P: $119-$189 | 2P: $119-$189 | XP: $10 | F18 |
| | 3/1-3/31 & 10/1-2/28 | 1P: $99-$189 | 2P: $99-$189 | XP: $10 | F18 |

Location: Jct SR 261 and Means Ave. Located on the Chesapeake Bay. 4165 Mears Ave 20732. Fax: 301/855-1119. **Facility:** 72 one-bedroom standard units, some with whirlpools. 4 stories, interior corridors. *Bath:* combo or shower only. **Parking:** on-site and valet. **Terms:** 2 night minimum stay - seasonal and/or weekends, cancellation fee imposed, weekly rates available, package plans. **Amenities:** high-speed Internet, dual phone lines, voice mail, irons, hair dryers. *Some:* honor bars. **Pool(s):** heated indoor. **Leisure Activities:** saunas, exercise room, spa. *Fee:* game room. **Guest Services:** sundries, coin laundry. **Business Services:** meeting rooms, business center. **Cards:** AX, DS, MC, VI. **Special Amenities:** free expanded continental breakfast and free newspaper. *(See color ad below)*

SOME UNITS
(SD) (TI→) (&M) (&) (⌀) (✕) (※) (DATA PORT) (⌨) / (✕) /

---------- **WHERE TO DINE** ----------

ROD 'N' REEL RESTAURANT **Lunch:** $6-$16 **Dinner:** $13-$35 Phone: 301/855-8351

Seafood

Location: Jct SR 261 and Mears Ave. Rt 261 & Mears Ave 20732. **Hours:** 11 am-10 pm, Sat 8 am-11 pm, Sun 8 am-10 pm. Closed: 12/25. **Reservations:** suggested, weekends. **Features:** Specializing in seafood since 1946, this waterfront eatery always has a supply of fresh fish on hand. Crabcakes are a local favorite, but much can also be said of the flavorful blackened rockfish supplied in generous portions. Ample parking is available. Casual dress; cocktails. **Parking:** on-site. **Cards:** AX, DS, MC, VI.

(Y) (✕)

CHESAPEAKE CITY pop. 787

------- WHERE TO STAY -------

INN AT THE CANAL
Phone: (410)885-5995
All Year [BP]   1P: $95-$145   2P: $95-$145   XP: $25
Historic Bed & Breakfast
Location: Bohemia Ave and 2nd St. Located in historic village. 104 Bohemia Ave 21915-0187 (PO Box 187). **Fax:** 410/885-3585. **Facility:** This 1870 inn features individually decorated guest rooms with private baths. Smoke free premises. 7 units. 6 one-bedroom standard units. 1 one-bedroom suite ($170-$205). 3 stories (no elevator), interior corridors. *Bath:* combo or shower only. **Parking:** on-site. **Terms:** 2 night minimum stay - seasonal and/or weekends, age restrictions may apply, 10 day cancellation notice-fee imposed, package plans. **Amenities:** voice mail, hair dryers. *Some:* irons. **Guest Services:** gift shop. **Business Services:** meeting rooms, fax (fee). **Cards:** AX, CB, DC, DS, MC, VI.

SOME UNITS
(ASK) (†↓) (✕) (DATA PORT) / (□) /

------- WHERE TO DINE -------

BAYARD HOUSE RESTAURANT
Lunch: $10-$17   **Dinner:** $17-$30   **Phone:** 410/885-5040
American
Location: Alongside Chesapeake and Delaware Canal; in historic district. 11 Bohemia Ave 21915. **Hours:** 11:30 am-3 & 5-9 pm, Fri & Sat-10 pm. Closed: 1/1, 12/24, 12/25. **Reservations:** suggested, weekends. **Features:** Along the banks of the Chesapeake and Delaware Canal, the gracious inn has a colorful history dating back to the 1870s. Guests in the dining rooms and on the popular enclosed porch enjoy great views of the canal and passing boats. The accomplished kitchen prepares a wide range of dishes, from spicy stuffed Anaheim peppers to traditional Maryland crab cakes. Maryland crab soup has become a local favorite. Casual dress; cocktails. **Parking:** street. **Cards:** AX, CB, DC, DS, JC, MC, VI. **Historic**

(Y) (✕)

CHESAPEAKE INN RESTAURANT & MARINA
Lunch: $6-$15   **Dinner:** $10-$29   **Phone:** 410/885-2040
American
MC, VI.
Location: Along side Chesapeake and Delaware Canal; in historic district. 605 Second St 21915. **Hours:** 11 am-10 pm. **Reservations:** suggested, weekends. **Features:** Along the waterfront, the restaurant affords spectacular marina views. Guests can unwind in a relaxing atmosphere with great food, live entertainment and dancing. Casual dress; cocktails; entertainment. **Parking:** on-site. **Cards:** AX, CB, DC, DS, JC,

(Y) (✕)

THE YACHT CLUB RESTAURANT
Dinner: $15-$25   **Phone:** 410/885-2267
American
Parking: on-site. Cards: MC, VI.
Location: Along side Chesapeake and Delaware Canal; in historic district. 225 Bohemia Ave 21915. **Hours:** 3 pm-9 pm, Fri & Sat-10 pm. Closed: 11/24, 12/25; also 12/31. **Reservations:** suggested, weekends. **Features:** Open lunch and dinner hours, the restaurant presents a complete menu of seafood and beef options. Friendly service is a staple, and a warm atmosphere is omnipresent. Casual dress; cocktails.

(Y) (✕)

CHESTERTOWN pop. 4,746

------- WHERE TO STAY -------

BRAMPTON BED & BREAKFAST INN
Phone: 410/778-1860
All Year [BP]   1P: $150-$250   2P: $155-$255   XP: $35
Historic Bed & Breakfast
Location: SR 213 to 291, 0.5 mi w to SR 20, 1 mi s. 25227 Chestertown Rd 21620. **Facility:** This 1860 Greek Revival plantation house has nine rooms that offer either fireplaces or wood stoves. Smoke free premises. 10 one-bedroom standard units, some with whirlpools. 1-3 stories (no elevator), interior/exterior corridors. *Bath:* combo or shower only. **Parking:** on-site. **Terms:** office hours 7 am-9 pm, 2 night minimum stay - weekends, 10 day cancellation notice-fee imposed. **Amenities:** video library, irons, hair dryers. *Some:* DVD players, CD players. **Leisure Activities:** fishing. **Business Services:** meeting rooms, fax (fee). **Cards:** DS, MC, VI.

SOME UNITS
(✕) (CTV) (☎) / (VCR) (□) /

COMFORT SUITES-CHESTERTOWN   *Book at aaa.com*   Phone: (410)810-0555

Small-scale Hotel

All Year   1P: $105-$155   2P: $105-$155

Location: 0.4 mi ne of jct SR 213 and 291. 160 Scheeler Rd 21620. **Fax:** 410/810-0286. **Facility:** 53 one-bedroom standard units, some with whirlpools. 3 stories, interior corridors. *Bath:* combo or shower only. **Parking:** on-site. **Terms:** 2 night minimum stay - seasonal and/or weekends, cancellation fee imposed. **Amenities:** voice mail, safes (fee), irons, hair dryers. **Pool(s):** heated indoor. **Guest Services:** coin laundry. **Business Services:** meeting rooms, fax (fee). **Cards:** AX, DC, DS, MC, VI. **Special Amenities: free expanded continental breakfast and free newspaper.** *(See color ad p 619)*

SOME UNITS

WHERE TO DINE

THE RESTAURANT AT THE IMPERIAL HOTEL   **Lunch:** $10-$18   **Dinner:** $16-$30   **Phone:** 410/778-5000

American

Location: Cross St, just w to High St, then just s, SR 213 to SR 289; in the historic district. 208 High St 21620. **Hours:** 5:30 pm-9 pm, Sun noon-3 pm. Closed: 12/25; also Mon, Tues & 2/26-3/16. **Reservations:** suggested. **Features:** The historic hotel dining room offers a seasonally changing menu of innovative American cuisine that emphasizes fresh, local ingredients. The crab cake is popular, and lamb chops are the house specialty. Dressy casual; cocktails. **Parking:** street. **Cards:** AX, MC, VI.

CHEVY CHASE —*See District Of Columbia p. 483.*

CLINTON —*See District Of Columbia p. 483.*

COLLEGE PARK —*See District Of Columbia p. 484.*

COLUMBIA —*See Baltimore p. 595.*

CRISFIELD pop. 2,723

WHERE TO STAY

PINES MOTEL   Phone: 410/968-0900

Motel

6/1-9/30	1P: $60-$80	2P: $60-$100	XP: $15	F3
3/1-5/31	1P: $40-$60	2P: $45-$65	XP: $10	F3
10/1-2/28	1P: $40-$50	2P: $40-$50	XP: $10	F3

Location: 0.4 mi e of SR 413. Located in a quiet, residential area. 127A N Somerset Ave 21817-1525. **Fax:** 707/356-4950. **Facility:** 40 one-bedroom standard units, some with efficiencies. 1-2 stories (no elevator), exterior corridors. **Parking:** on-site. **Terms:** 7 day cancellation notice. **Amenities:** *Some:* irons, hair dryers. **Pool(s):** outdoor. **Leisure Activities:** picnic facilities. **Business Services:** fax (fee). **Cards:** MC, VI. **Special Amenities: early check-in/late check-out and preferred room (subject to availability with advance reservations).**

SOME UNITS

WHERE TO DINE

THE ORIGNAL CAPTAIN'S GALLEY RESTAURANT   **Lunch:** $5-$10   **Dinner:** $9-$28   **Phone:** 410/968-3313

Seafood

Location: Harborfront. 1021 W Main St 21817. **Hours:** 11 am-9 pm, Fri & Sat-10 pm; to 8 pm, Fri & Sat-9 pm 9/15-5/15. Closed: 11/24, 12/25. **Reservations:** accepted, 10/1-5/30. **Features:** Crab is the house specialty at this family owned and operated waterfront restaurant. Watch the boats coming in with their daily catch from the casual dining room or seasonal open deck. The menu offers a good selection of seafood dishes, as well as "Landlubbers" selections, but crab is king. Casual dress; cocktails. **Parking:** on-site. **Cards:** AX, MC, VI.

WATERMEN'S INN   **Lunch:** $4-$8   **Dinner:** $8-$20   **Phone:** 410/968-2119

Steak & Seafood

Location: Center. 901 W Main St 21817. **Hours:** 11 am-9 pm, Sat from 8 am; hours may vary in winter. Closed: 11/24; also Mon, Tues & 12/24-12/30. **Reservations:** suggested, weekends. **Features:** The atmosphere of the cozy bistro is enhanced by light music and fresh flowers. The menu comprises crabmeat dishes, regional cuisine and seasonal specials such as soft-shell crabs with artichokes and the hand cut grilled rib eye is a local favorite. Casual dress; cocktails. **Parking:** street. **Cards:** AX, DS, MC, VI.

CUMBERLAND pop. 21,518

——— WHERE TO STAY ———

HOLIDAY INN ▼▼▼
Book at aaa.com
Phone: (301)724-8800

| | 5/1-2/28 | 1P: $79-$109 | 2P: $79-$109 |
| | 3/1-4/30 | 1P: $79-$99 | 2P: $79-$99 |

Small-scale Hotel **Location:** I-68, exit 43C, just n; downtown. 100 S George St 21502. Fax: 301/724-4001. **Facility:** 130 one-bedroom standard units. 6 stories, interior corridors. *Bath:* combo or shower only. **Parking:** on-site. **Terms:** 3 day cancellation notice-fee imposed, package plans, small pets only ($10 fee). **Amenities:** dual phone lines, voice mail, irons, hair dryers. **Pool(s):** outdoor. **Guest Services:** valet and coin laundry. **Business Services:** meeting rooms. **Cards:** AX, CB, DC, DS, MC, VI.

SOME UNITS
[ASK] [SD] [🛏] [🍴] FEE [🍸] [🛋] [🏊] [🛁] FEE [🎥] [DATA PORT] [💻] / [✕] [🔌] FEE /

INN AT WALNUT BOTTOM ▼▼▼
Phone: (301)777-0003

	10/1-10/31 [BP]	1P: $103-$157	2P: $103-$157	XP: $15	F12
	3/1-9/30, 11/1-12/23 & 12/26-2/28				
	[BP]	1P: $93-$147	2P: $93-$147	XP: $15	F12

Bed & Breakfast **Location:** I-68, exit 43A, follow signs, between Winton Pl and Smallwood St, guest parking via Winton Pl. 120 Greene St 21502. Fax: 301/777-8288. **Facility:** This B&B is made up of two adjacent townhouses dating from 1820 and 1890; both are furnished with antiques and period reproductions. Smoke free premises. 12 units. 10 one- and 2 two-bedroom standard units, some with kitchens. 2-3 stories (no elevator), interior corridors. *Bath:* some shared or private, combo or shower only. **Parking:** on-site. **Terms:** open 3/1-12/23 & 12/26-2/28, 2 night minimum stay - seasonal, 12 day cancellation notice. **Amenities:** hair dryers. **Leisure Activities:** bicycles. *Fee:* massage. **Cards:** AX, DS, MC, VI.

[ASK] [SD] [🍴] [✕] [🔌]

ROCKY GAP LODGE & GOLF RESORT (AAA) [SAVE] ▼▼▼
Book at aaa.com
Phone: (301)784-8400

	11/1-2/28	1P: $89-$195	2P: $89-$195	XP: $15	F18
	5/29-10/31	1P: $129-$175	2P: $129-$175	XP: $15	F18
	3/1-5/28	1P: $89-$175	2P: $89-$175	XP: $15	F18

Resort Large-scale Hotel **Location:** I-68, exit 50, just n. Located in a quiet area. 16701 Lakeview Rd NE 21530 (PO Box 1199). Fax: 301/784-8408. **Facility:** In the mountains along a scenic lake, this stylish modern resort is an updated version of the classic rustic lodge. 217 one-bedroom standard units, some with whirlpools. 6 stories, interior corridors. *Bath:* combo or shower only. **Parking:** on-site and valet. **Terms:** 3 day cancellation notice-fee imposed, package plans, small pets only ($50 fee). **Amenities:** video games, high-speed Internet, voice mail, safes, honor bars, irons, hair dryers. **Dining:** 2 restaurants, 6:30 am-10 pm, cocktails, also, Lakeside Restaurant, see separate listing. **Pool(s):** indoor/outdoor. **Leisure Activities:** whirlpool, boating, canoeing, paddleboats, 2 lighted tennis courts, recreation programs, hiking trails, jogging, playground, exercise room, basketball, horseshoes, volleyball. *Fee:* golf-40 holes, driving range, massage. **Guest Services:** gift shop, valet laundry. **Business Services:** conference facilities. **Cards:** AX, DC, DS, MC, VI.
(See color ad below)

SOME UNITS
[SD] [🛏] [🍴] FEE [🍸] [GM] [♿] [🛋] [🏊] [✕] [🎥] [DATA PORT] [💻] / [✕] [🔌] [☕] /

——— WHERE TO DINE ———

LAKESIDE RESTAURANT ▼▼▼
Lunch: $7-$14 **Dinner:** $13-$29 **Phone:** 301/784-8400

American **Location:** I-68, exit 50, just n; in Rocky Gap Lodge & Golf Resort. 16701 Lakeview Rd NE 21530. **Hours:** 11:30 am-2 & 5-11 pm. **Features:** In Rocky Gap Lodge, the restaurant affords incredible lake views. Friendly, fast service is a staple. Casual dress; cocktails. **Parking:** on-site. **Cards:** AX, CB, DC, DS, JC, MC, VI.

[🍸] [✕]

DENTON pop. 2,960

——— WHERE TO STAY ———

BEST WESTERN DENTON INN   *Book at aaa.com*   **Phone:** (410)479-8400
AAA SAVE   All Year   1P: $50-$90   2P: $70-$90   XP: $10   F12
▼▼▼ ▼▼▼   **Location:** Jct SR 404 and 313. 521 Fleetwood Rd 21629. Fax: 410/479-8410. **Facility:** 60 one-bedroom standard
Small-scale Hotel   units, some with whirlpools. 2 stories, interior corridors. *Bath:* combo or shower only. **Parking:** on-site.
Amenities: high-speed Internet, voice mail, irons, hair dryers. **Pool(s):** outdoor. **Guest Services:** coin
laundry. **Business Services:** PC, fax (fee). **Cards:** AX, DS, MC, VI. **Special Amenities:** free continental
breakfast and free local telephone calls.

SOME UNITS

[S][D] [M] [&] [≈] [▦] [DATA PORT] [📶] [🛋] [💻] / [✕] /

EASTON pop. 11,708

——— WHERE TO STAY ———

COMFORT INN EASTON   *Book at aaa.com*   **Phone:** 410/820-8333
▼▼▼ ▼▼▼   5/1-10/31 [CP]   1P: $99-$109   2P: $99-$109
           3/1-4/30 [CP]   1P: $89-$109   2P: $89-$109
Motel   11/1-2/28 [CP]   1P: $89   2P: $89
Location: US 50, 0.7 mi n of jct SR 331. 8523 Ocean Gateway 21601. Fax: 410/820-8436. **Facility:** 84 one-
bedroom standard units. 2 stories (no elevator), exterior corridors. **Parking:** on-site. **Amenities:** irons, hair dryers. **Pool(s):**
outdoor. **Leisure Activities:** whirlpool. **Guest Services:** valet laundry. **Business Services:** meeting rooms, fax (fee).
Cards: AX, DC, DS, MC, VI.

SOME UNITS

[ASK] [S][D] [Ⅱ↑] [≈] [▦] [DATA PORT] [💻] / [✕] /

HOLIDAY INN EXPRESS-EASTON   *Book at aaa.com*   **Phone:** (410)819-6500
▼▼▼ ▼▼▼   3/1-9/30   2P: $114-$135   XP: $10   F18
           10/1-11/30   2P: $94-$104   XP: $10   F18
Small-scale Hotel   12/1-2/28   2P: $84-$104   XP: $10   F18
Location: US 50, 0.7 mi n of jct SR 331. 8561 Ocean Gateway 21601. Fax: 410/819-6505. **Facility:** 73 one-
bedroom standard units. 4 stories, interior corridors. *Bath:* combo or shower only. **Parking:** on-site. **Terms:** cancellation fee
imposed. **Amenities:** dual phone lines, voice mail, irons, hair dryers. **Pool(s):** heated indoor. **Leisure Activities:** whirlpool.
Guest Services: valet laundry. **Business Services:** meeting rooms, PC, fax (fee). **Cards:** AX, DC, DS, MC, VI.

SOME UNITS

[ASK] [S][D] [Ⅱ↑] [&] [📷] [≈] [▦] [DATA PORT] [💻] / [✕] /

——— WHERE TO DINE ———

MARTINIS RESTAURANT   **Lunch:** $7-$15   **Dinner:** $17-$25   **Phone:** 410/820-4100
▼▼▼ ▼▼▼   **Location:** SR 333, just w of jct SR 322; at the Easton Club. 28449 Clubhouse Dr 21601. **Hours:** 11 am-9 pm, Sun-8
American   pm; Sun-4 pm 10/1-5/1. Closed: 1/1, 12/25. **Reservations:** suggested. **Features:** The handsome dining
room of this plush, but casual, restaurant overlooks the golf course. Creative selections include Chesapeake
salad, crab cakes and deep-fried crab balls with balsamic vinegar over fresh greens. Casual dress;
cocktails. **Parking:** on-site. **Cards:** AX, DS, MC, VI.

[🍽] [✕]

OUT OF THE FIRE   **Lunch:** $6-$12   **Dinner:** $13-$25   **Phone:** 410/770-4777
▼▼▼ ▼▼▼   **Location:** Between Harrison and Washington sts. 22 Goldsbrough St 21601. **Hours:** 11:30 am-2:30 & 5-9 pm, Fri-
10 pm, Sat 5 pm-10 pm. Closed major holidays; also 12/24 & Sun. **Reservations:** suggested.
Mediterranean   **Features:** The small cafe and wine bar is in the city's historic district. The stone-hearth oven is the focal
point of the dining room and open kitchen. On the menu are stone-hearth pizzas, homemade desserts and
entrees that reflect global influences. Guests may dine at the open-kitchen counter or at the wine bar or may enjoy a glass of
wine and dessert in the lounge. The cafe occasionally features live entertainment on the weekends. Casual dress; cocktails.
Parking: street. **Cards:** AX, DC, DS, MC, VI.

[🍽] [✕]

PLAZA TAPATIA   **Lunch:** $5-$8   **Dinner:** $8-$14   **Phone:** 410/770-8550
▼▼▼ ▼▼▼   **Location:** US 50, 0.5 mi s of jct Dover St. 7813 Ocean Gateway 21601. **Hours:** 11 am-2:30 & 5-10 pm, Sat noon-
10 pm, Sun noon-9 pm. Closed major holidays. **Features:** If your tastebuds are looking for something with a
Mexican   South of the Border flavor, then this is the place. The casual atmosphere with Mexican decorations is
comfortable for any occasion. The food is prepared using authentic Mexican recipes. Casual dress;
cocktails. **Parking:** on-site. **Cards:** AX, MC, VI.

[✕]

RUSTIC INN RESTAURANT   **Lunch:** $5-$14   **Dinner:** $14-$29   **Phone:** 410/820-8212
▼▼▼ ▼▼▼   **Location:** In Talbottown Shopping Center. Harrison St 21601. **Hours:** 11:30 am-2 & 5-10 pm, Sat from 5 pm, Sun
4 pm-9 pm. Closed: 7/4, 11/24, 12/24, 12/25; also for lunch Mon & Wed, Super Bowl Sun.
American   **Reservations:** suggested, weekends. **Features:** Freshly prepared dishes—such as veal, blackened prime
rib and crab cakes—make up the menu in the friendly, neighborhood restaurant. A hand-painted mural of
waterfront life on the Eastern Shore decorates the dining room. Casual dress; cocktails. **Parking:** on-site. **Cards:** AX, MC, VI.

[🍽] [✕]

EDGEWOOD —*See Baltimore p. 598.*

ELK MILLS

———— WHERE TO STAY ————

ELK FORGE BED & BREAKFAST INN, RETREAT
AND SPA   *Book at aaa.com*   Phone: (410)392-9007

▼▼▼   All Year   1P: $97-$210   2P: $97-$210   XP: $18
Bed & Breakfast   **Location:** I-95, exit 109B, 1 mi w on SR 279 to Fletchwood Rd, then 2 mi s on Fletchwood Rd. 807 Elk Mills Rd 21920 (PO Box 107). Fax: 410/392-2954. **Facility:** Nestled on five acres of woods and gardens, Elk Forge Bed & Breakfast Inn, Retreat and Spa offers a gentle oasis to relax and re-energize. 12 units. 8 one-bedroom standard units, some with whirlpools. 4 two-bedroom suites with whirlpools. 3 stories (no elevator), interior/exterior corridors. *Bath:* combo or shower only. **Parking:** on-site. **Terms:** 14 day cancellation notice-fee imposed, [BP] meal plan available, package plans. **Amenities:** video library, CD players, high-speed Internet, voice mail, irons, hair dryers. **Leisure Activities:** whirlpool, putting green, hiking trails, jogging, exercise room, spa, horseshoes, volleyball. **Guest Services:** gift shop, complimentary evening beverages, valet laundry. **Business Services:** meeting rooms, fax (fee). **Cards:** AX, DC, DS, MC, VI.
SOME UNITS
(ASK) (SD) (⊠) (✕) (VCR) (※) (DATA PORT) (▣) / (🛏) (🖨) /

ELKRIDGE —*See Baltimore p. 599.*

ELKTON pop. 11,893

———— WHERE TO STAY ————

ECONO LODGE   *Book at aaa.com*   Phone: (410)392-5010

(AAA) (SAVE)   3/1-10/31   1P: $66-$86   2P: $66-$86   XP: $10   F12
▼▼▼   11/1-2/28   1P: $60-$80   2P: $60-$80   XP: $10   F12
Motel   **Location:** I-95, exit 109A, just e. 311 Belle Hill Rd 21921. Fax: 410/392-5516. **Facility:** 59 one-bedroom standard units. 2 stories (no elevator), exterior corridors. **Parking:** on-site. **Amenities:** irons, hair dryers. **Guest Services:** coin laundry. **Cards:** AX, DS, MC, VI. **Special Amenities:** free continental breakfast and free newspaper.
SOME UNITS
(SD) (※) (DATA PORT) / (✕) (🛏) (🖨) (▣) /

MOTEL 6 ELKTON #768   *Book at aaa.com*   Phone: 410/392-5020

▼   6/2-9/4   1P: $39-$49   2P: $45-$55   XP: $3   F17
Motel   3/1-6/1 & 9/5-2/28 1P: $37-$47   2P: $43-$53   XP: $3   F17
Location: I-95, exit 109A, just e. 223 Belle Hill Rd. 21921. Fax: 410/398-1143. **Facility:** 127 one-bedroom standard units. 2 stories (no elevator), exterior corridors. *Bath:* shower only. **Parking:** on-site. **Cards:** AX, CB, DC, DS, MC, VI.
SOME UNITS
(SD) (♿) (※) (DATA PORT) / (✕) /

SUTTON MOTEL   Phone: 410/398-3830

▼   All Year   1P: $45   2P: $50
Motel   **Location:** US 40, 0.8 mi e of jct SR 213. 405 E Pulaski Hwy 21921. **Facility:** Smoke free premises. 11 one-bedroom standard units. 1 story, exterior corridors. *Bath:* shower only. **Parking:** on-site. **Amenities:** *Some:* irons.
SOME UNITS
(✕) (※) (☎) / (🛏) /

ELLICOTT CITY —*See Baltimore p. 600.*

EMMITSBURG pop. 2,290

———— WHERE TO STAY ————

SLEEP INN & SUITES IN EMMITSBURG   *Book at aaa.com*   Phone: (301)447-0044

(AAA) (SAVE)   4/1-10/31 [ECP]   1P: $89-$129   2P: $89-$129   XP: $10   F18
▼▼ ▼▼   3/1-3/31 & 11/1-2/28 [ECP] 1P: $69-$99   2P: $69-$99   XP: $10   F18
Small-scale Hotel   **Location:** US 15. 501 Silo Hill Pkwy 21727. Fax: 301/447-3144. **Facility:** 79 one-bedroom standard units, some with whirlpools. 3 stories, interior corridors. *Bath:* combo or shower only. **Parking:** on-site. **Terms:** cancellation fee imposed, package plans, pets ($25 fee). **Amenities:** video games, high-speed Internet, voice mail, safes, irons, hair dryers. **Pool(s):** heated indoor. **Leisure Activities:** exercise room. **Guest Services:** coin laundry. **Business Services:** meeting rooms. **Cards:** AX, CB, DC, DS, JC, MC, VI. **Special Amenities:** free expanded continental breakfast and free local telephone calls.
SOME UNITS
(SD) (🍴) (♿) (🐾) (※) (DATA PORT) (🛏) (▣) / (✕) (🖨) /
FEE

———— WHERE TO DINE ————

CARRIAGE HOUSE INN   Lunch: $6-$12   Dinner: $15-$25   Phone: 301/447-2366
(AAA)   **Location:** 1 mi w of US 15. 200 S Seton Ave 21727. **Hours:** 11 am-9 pm, Fri & Sat-10 pm. Closed: 12/25.
▼▼▼   **Reservations:** suggested, weekends. **Features:** For a tasty treat, try seafood scampi—shrimp, scallops and crab arranged on angel hair pasta. At lunch, there's a wide variety of sandwiches and always a tempting tableside dessert display. Dining in the 1857 building is comfortable and relaxed. Casual dress; cocktails. **Parking:** on-site. **Cards:** AX, DS, MC, VI. **Historic**
American
(✕)

FALLSTON —*See Baltimore p. 600.*

FINKSBURG —*See Baltimore p. 600.*

FREDERICK pop. 52,767

——— **WHERE TO STAY** ———

COMFORT INN
Book at aaa.com
Phone: (301)668-7272

All Year [ECP]   1P: $69-$109   2P: $69-$109   XP: $10   F18
Location: I-270, exit 31B, 0.9 mi sw on SR 85. 7300 Executive Way 21704. Fax: 301/668-8383. **Facility:** 73 one-bedroom standard units, some with whirlpools. 3 stories, interior corridors. *Bath:* combo or shower only.
Small-scale Hotel   **Parking:** on-site. **Amenities:** high-speed Internet, dual phone lines, voice mail, irons, hair dryers. **Leisure Activities:** exercise room. **Guest Services:** valet and coin laundry. **Business Services:** meeting rooms. **Cards:** AX, CB, DC, DS, JC, MC, VI. *(See color ad p 626)*

SOME UNITS
(ASK) (S/D) (&M) (&) (⚟) (DATA PORT) (▣) / (✕) /

COMFORT INN RED HORSE FREDERICK   *Book at aaa.com*
Phone: (301)662-0281

5/1-10/31   1P: $99-$159   2P: $99-$159   XP: $10   F17
11/1-2/28   1P: $79-$109   2P: $79-$109   XP: $10   F17
3/1-4/30   1P: $79-$99   2P: $79-$99   XP: $10   F17
Small-scale Hotel   **Location:** Jct US 15, just w on US 40. 998 W Patrick St 21703. Fax: 301/694-7263. **Facility:** 69 one-bedroom standard units, some with whirlpools. 2-4 stories, interior corridors. *Bath:* combo or shower only. **Parking:** on-site. **Terms:** 3 day cancellation notice. **Amenities:** high-speed Internet, voice mail, irons, hair dryers. **Dining:** Red Horse Steak House, see separate listing. **Leisure Activities:** exercise room. **Business Services:** meeting rooms. **Cards:** AX, CB, DC, DS, JC, MC, VI. *(See color ad below)*

SOME UNITS
(ASK) (S/D) (⊘) (&) (⚟) (DATA PORT) (⊟) (▣) (▣) / (✕) /

DAYS INN   *Book at aaa.com*
Phone: (301)694-6600

(AAA) (SAVE)   All Year   1P: $71-$81   2P: $76-$86   XP: $5   F16
Location: I-270, exit 31A, 0.5 mi e on SR 85; I-70, exit 54, 0.5 mi w. 5646 Buckeystown Pike 21704. Fax: 301/831-4242. **Facility:** 119 one-bedroom standard units. 2 stories (no elevator), exterior corridors. **Parking:** on-site. **Terms:** 3 day cancellation notice. **Amenities:** hair dryers. *Some:* irons. **Pool(s):** outdoor. Small-scale Hotel   **Leisure Activities:** playground. **Cards:** AX, CB, DC, DS, MC, VI. **Special Amenities:** free continental breakfast and free local telephone calls.

SOME UNITS
(S/D) (🕯) (🏊) (⚟) (DATA PORT) / (✕) (▣) (▣) /
      FEE   FEE

ECONO LODGE   *Book at aaa.com*
Phone: 301/698-0555

(AAA) (SAVE)   5/1-10/31   1P: $65-$79   2P: $70-$99   XP: $7   F17
3/1-4/30 & 11/1-2/28   1P: $55-$65   2P: $60-$70   XP: $7   F17
Location: Jct SR 85 and 355. Located behind the Exxon station. 6005 Urbana Pike 21704. Fax: 301/620-7453. **Facility:** 108 one-bedroom standard units. 1 story, exterior corridors. **Parking:** on-site. **Terms:** 3 day Small-scale Hotel   cancellation notice. **Amenities:** *Some:* hair dryers. **Business Services:** meeting rooms. **Cards:** AX, DC, DS, MC, VI. **Special Amenities:** free local telephone calls and preferred room (subject to availability with advance reservations).

SOME UNITS
(S/D) (⚟) (DATA PORT) / (✕) (▣) /

FAIRFIELD INN BY MARRIOTT   *Book at aaa.com*
Phone: (301)631-2000

(AAA) (SAVE)   7/3-2/28   1P: $99
3/1-7/2   1P: $94
Location: I-270, exit 31B, 0.5 mi sw on SR 85, then 0.3 mi n on Crestwood Blvd. 5220 Westview Dr 21703. Fax: 301/631-2100. **Facility:** 105 one-bedroom standard units. 3 stories, interior corridors. *Bath:* combo or Small-scale Hotel   shower only. **Parking:** on-site. **Terms:** cancellation fee imposed, [CP] meal plan available. **Amenities:** high-speed Internet, irons, hair dryers. **Pool(s):** indoor. **Leisure Activities:** whirlpool, exercise room. **Guest Services:** valet laundry. **Cards:** AX, DC, DS, MC, VI.

SOME UNITS
(&) (⊘) (🏊) (⚟) (DATA PORT) (▣) / (✕) (▣) (▣) /
      FEE   FEE

FREDERICK COURTYARD BY MARRIOTT *Book at aaa.com*   **Phone:** (301)631-9030

▼▼▼▼ All Year   1P: $94-$134   2P: $94-$134

Small-scale Hotel **Location:** I-270, exit 31B, 0.5 mi sw on SR 85, then 0.3 mi n on Crestwood Blvd. 5225 Westview Dr 21703. Fax: 301/631-9060. **Facility:** 90 one-bedroom standard units, some with whirlpools. 3 stories, interior corridors. *Bath:* combo or shower only. **Parking:** on-site. **Terms:** package plans. **Amenities:** voice mail, irons, hair dryers. **Pool(s):** heated indoor. **Leisure Activities:** whirlpool, exercise room. **Guest Services:** coin laundry. **Business Services:** meeting rooms. **Cards:** AX, DC, DS, MC, VI.

SOME UNITS

FREDERICK RESIDENCE INN BY MARRIOTT   *Book at aaa.com*   **Phone:** 301/360-0010

▼▼▼▼ All Year [BP]   1P: $99-$134

Small-scale Hotel **Location:** I-270, exit 31B, 0.5 mi sw on SR 85, 0.3 mi n on Crestwood Blvd. 5230 Westview Dr 21703. Fax: 301/360-0024. **Facility:** 90 one-bedroom standard units with kitchens. 4 stories, interior corridors. *Bath:* combo or shower only. **Parking:** on-site. **Terms:** cancellation fee imposed, pets ($100 fee, $6 extra charge). **Amenities:** high-speed Internet, dual phone lines, voice mail, irons, hair dryers. **Pool(s):** heated indoor. **Leisure Activities:** whirlpool, exercise room, sports court, basketball, game room. **Guest Services:** complimentary evening beverages: Mon-Thurs, coin laundry. **Business Services:** meeting rooms, fax (fee). **Cards:** AX, DC, DS, JC, MC, VI.

SOME UNITS

HAMPTON INN   **Phone:** (301)698-2500

AAA [SAVE] 4/1-10/31   1P: $104-$110   2P: $104-$110
3/1-3/31 & 11/1-2/28   1P: $99-$104   2P: $99-$104
▼▼▼▼ **Location:** I-270, exit 31B, 0.6 mi w. 5311 Buckeystown Pike (SR 85) 21704. Fax: 301/695-8735. **Facility:** 161 one-

Small-scale Hotel bedroom standard units. 6 stories, interior corridors. **Parking:** on-site. **Terms:** 21 day cancellation notice-fee imposed, package plans, small pets only ($10 extra charge). **Amenities:** video games, high-speed Internet, voice mail, irons, hair dryers. **Dining:** 5 pm-midnight; closed Sun, cocktails. **Pool(s):** outdoor. **Leisure Activities:** exercise room. **Guest Services:** coin laundry. **Business Services:** meeting rooms, business center. **Cards:** AX, DC, DS, MC, VI. **Special Amenities:** free local telephone calls and free newspaper. *(See color ad below)*

SOME UNITS

HAMPTON INN & SUITES-FREDERICK   **Phone:** 301/696-1565

[fyi] Under construction, scheduled to open March 2005. **Location:** I-70, exit 52B (US 15 N); exit 18 (Opossumtown Pike), 0.3 mi on left. 1565 Opossumtown Pike 21702. **Planned Amenities:** coffeemakers, microwaves, Small-scale Hotel refrigerators, pool. *(See color ad below)*

HOLIDAY INN EXPRESS-FSK MALL *Book at aaa.com*   Phone: (301)695-2881

▽▽▽   3/1-10/31   1P: $79-$94   2P: $79-$94   XP: $10   F19
    11/1-2/28   1P: $74-$89   2P: $74-$89   XP: $10   F19

Small-scale Hotel   **Location:** I-270, exit 31A, just e on SR 85. Located in Francis Scott Key Mall. 5579 Spectrum Dr 21703. Fax: 301/695-7639. **Facility:** 100 one-bedroom standard units. 2 stories (no elevator), interior corridors. *Bath:* combo or shower only. **Parking:** on-site. **Terms:** cancellation fee imposed, package plans, small pets only ($25 deposit). **Amenities:** voice mail, irons, hair dryers. **Guest Services:** coin laundry. **Business Services:** meeting rooms. **Cards:** AX, CB, DC, DS, JC, MC, VI.

SOME UNITS
(ASK) (S/D) (🛏FEE) (🍽) (&) (🅿) (🏋FEE) (🎥) (DATA PORT) (📺) / (✕) (📞) (📠) /

HOLIDAY INN-FRANCIS SCOTT KEY MALL *Book at aaa.com*   Phone: (301)694-7500

▽▽▽   All Year   1P: $99-$114   2P: $99-$114
    Location: I-270, exit 31A, just se of SR 85. Located adjacent to shopping mall. 5400 Holiday Dr 21703.

Small-scale Hotel   Fax: 301/694-0589. **Facility:** 155 one-bedroom standard units. 2 stories (no elevator), interior corridors. *Bath:* combo or shower only. **Parking:** on-site. **Terms:** package plans, small pets only. **Amenities:** dual phone lines, voice mail, irons, hair dryers. **Pool(s):** heated indoor. **Leisure Activities:** saunas, whirlpool, miniature golf, exercise room. **Guest Services:** coin laundry. **Business Services:** conference facilities. **Cards:** AX, CB, DC, DS, MC, VI.

SOME UNITS
(ASK) (S/D) (🛏) (🍽) (🍸) (🅿) (🏊) (🎥) (DATA PORT) (📺) / (✕) (📞) (📠) /
FEE FEE

HOLIDAY INN-FREDERICK/FT DETRICK *Book at aaa.com*   Phone: (301)662-5141

(AAA) (SAVE)   4/1-10/30   1P: $75-$98   2P: $75-$98
    3/1-3/31   1P: $67-$98   2P: $67-$98
▽▽▽   10/31-2/28   1P: $67-$89   2P: $67-$89
    Location: Just w on US 40 from jct US 15. 999 W Patrick St 21702. Fax: 301/663-5290. **Facility:** 158 one-

Small-scale Hotel   bedroom standard units. 3 stories, exterior corridors. *Bath:* combo or shower only. **Parking:** on-site. **Terms:** package plans, pets (in designated units). **Amenities:** high-speed Internet, voice mail, irons, hair dryers. **Dining:** 6 am-11 & 5-9 pm, Sat & Sun from 7 am, cocktails. **Pool(s):** outdoor. **Leisure Activities:** exercise room, basketball. **Guest Services:** coin laundry. **Business Services:** meeting rooms. **Cards:** AX, CB, DC, DS, JC, MC, VI.

SOME UNITS
(S/D) (🛏) (🍽) (🍸) (🅿) (🏊) (🎥) (DATA PORT) (📞) (📠) (📺) / (✕) /

MAINSTAY SUITES *Book at aaa.com*   Phone: (301)668-4600

▽▽▽   All Year   1P: $129-$149   2P: $129-$149
    Location: I-270, exit 31B. 7310 Executive Way 21704. Fax: 301/668-4622. **Facility:** 72 one-bedroom standard

Small-scale Hotel   units. 3 stories, interior corridors. *Bath:* combo or shower only. **Parking:** on-site. **Terms:** cancellation fee imposed, pets ($150 deposit, $10 extra charge). **Amenities:** high-speed Internet, voice mail, irons, hair dryers. **Pool(s):** heated indoor. **Leisure Activities:** whirlpool, exercise room. **Guest Services:** coin laundry. **Cards:** AX, CB, DC, DS, MC, VI. *(See color ad below)*

SOME UNITS
(ASK) (S/D) (🛏FEE) (&) (🏊) (🎥) (DATA PORT) (📞) (📠) (📺) / (✕) /

QUALITY INN HISTORIC FREDERICK *Book at aaa.com*   Phone: (301)695-6200

(AAA) (SAVE)   4/1-10/31   1P: $79-$99   2P: $79-$99   XP: $5   F18
    11/1-2/28   1P: $69-$89   2P: $69-$89   XP: $5   F18
▽▽   3/1-3/31   1P: $69-$84   2P: $69-$84   XP: $5   F18
    Location: US 15, exit Jefferson St, just se. 420 Prospect Blvd 21701. Fax: 301/695-7895. **Facility:** 119 one-

Small-scale Hotel   bedroom standard units. 2 stories (no elevator), interior corridors. **Parking:** on-site. **Terms:** small pets only. **Amenities:** voice mail, irons, hair dryers. **Pool(s):** outdoor. **Leisure Activities:** barbecue grills, picnic tables, playground, exercise room. **Guest Services:** coin laundry. **Business Services:** meeting rooms. **Cards:** AX, CB, DC, DS, JC, MC, VI. **Special Amenities:** free continental breakfast and free local telephone calls.

SOME UNITS
(S/D) (🛏) (🅿) (🏊) (✕) (🎥) (DATA PORT) (📞) / (✕) (📞) (📠) /
FEE FEE

SLEEP INN *Book at aaa.com*   Phone: (301)668-2003

▽▽   All Year [CP]   1P: $69-$119   2P: $69-$119   XP: $5   F18
    Location: I-270, exit 31A, just se of SR 85. 5361 Spectrum Dr 21703. Fax: 301/668-3514. **Facility:** 85 one-

Small-scale Hotel   bedroom standard units. 4 stories, interior corridors. *Bath:* combo or shower only. **Parking:** on-site. **Amenities:** video games, voice mail, irons, hair dryers. **Leisure Activities:** exercise room. **Guest Services:** valet laundry. **Business Services:** meeting rooms. **Cards:** AX, DC, DS, MC, VI.

SOME UNITS
(ASK) (S/D) (🎥) (DATA PORT) (📺) / (✕) (📞) (📠) /

TRAVELODGE FREDERICK   *Book at aaa.com*   Phone: 301/663-0500

(AAA) (SAVE)

7/1-10/31 [CP]	1P: $72-$78	2P: $78-$84	XP: $6 F16
3/1-6/30 [CP]	1P: $68-$74	2P: $74-$80	XP: $6 F16
11/1-12/31 [CP]	1P: $64-$70	2P: $70-$76	XP: $6 F16
1/1-2/28 [CP]	1P: $58-$64	2P: $64-$70	XP: $6 F16

Small-scale Hotel **Location:** I-70, exit 54, just n. 200 E Walser Dr 21704. **Fax:** 301/662-6017. **Facility:** 122 one-bedroom standard units, some with whirlpools. 4 stories, interior corridors. **Parking:** on-site. **Amenities:** hair dryers. **Guest Services:** coin laundry. **Business Services:** meeting rooms. **Cards:** AX, DS, MC, VI. **Special Amenities:** free continental breakfast and free newspaper.

SOME UNITS

──────── **WHERE TO DINE** ────────

BARBARA FRITCHIE CANDYSTICK RESTAURANT   Lunch: $4-$10   Dinner: $4-$14   Phone: 301/662-2500
American   **Location:** I-70, exit 48, just n. 1513 W Patrick St 21702. **Hours:** 7 am-10 pm. **Closed:** 12/25. **Features:** Named after a Civil War heroine, the restaurant has been a local favorite since 1910. Guests can expect good food fast. Casual dress. **Parking:** on-site. **Cards:** MC, VI.

BUSH WALLER'S   Lunch: $6-$12   Dinner: $6-$20   Phone: 301/695-6988
American   **Location:** 0.3 mi n; center. 209 N Market St 21701. **Hours:** 3 pm-2 am, Sat & Sun from 11 am. **Closed:** 12/25. **Features:** Bushwaller's is an American Irish Pub with a huge selection of beers and a wide ranging menu. Casual dress; cocktails. **Parking:** street. **Cards:** AX, CB, DC, DS, JC, MC, VI.

DOUBLE TT DINER   Lunch: $5-$12   Dinner: $7-$20   Phone: 301/620-8797
American   **Location:** I-270, exit 31A, just se of SR 85. 5617 Spectrum Dr 21703. **Hours:** 6 am-10 pm. **Closed:** 12/25. **Features:** Step back in time at the Double T T Diner. Nostalgic atmosphere, home-made desserts and a family run caring. Casual dress; beer & wine only. **Parking:** on-site. **Cards:** AX, CB, DC, DS, JC, MC, VI.

DUTCH'S DAUGHTER   Lunch: $7-$18   Dinner: $7-$25   Phone: 301/668-9500
American   **Location:** Jct US 15, just w on US 40. 581 Himes Ave 21703. **Hours:** 11:30 am-3 & 3:30-9:30 pm, Sat & Sun from 3:30 pm; Sunday brunch 10 am-2 pm. **Closed:** 12/25. **Reservations:** suggested. **Features:** The casually formal restaurant prepares many beef and seafood favorites. Private rooms can accommodate up to 300. Casual dress; cocktails. **Parking:** on-site. **Cards:** AX, CB, DC, DS, MC, VI.

MAY'S RESTAURANT   Lunch: $7-$14   Dinner: $7-$22   Phone: 301/662-4233
American   **Location:** I-270, exit 31A, 1 mi e on SR 85, 1 mi n on Grand Rd, then just w on SR 355. 5640 Urbana Pike (Rt 355) 21704. **Hours:** 11:30 am-9:30 pm, Fri & Sat-10 pm, Sun-9 pm. **Closed:** 12/25. **Features:** The family-run restaurant has long been known for fresh seafood and a nice atmosphere. Casual dress; cocktails. **Parking:** on-site. **Cards:** MC, VI.

MOUNTAIN VIEW DINER RESTAURANT   Lunch: $6-$12   Dinner: $6-$16   Phone: 301/696-1300
American   **Location:** 1.2 mi w of US 40 from jct US 15. 1300 W Patrick St 21703. **Hours:** 6 am-midnight. **Closed:** 12/25. **Features:** Mountain View Diner Restaurant offers a huge variety for breakfast, lunch and dinner. The service and decor will remind you of simplier and friendlier days gone by. Casual dress. **Parking:** on-site. **Cards:** MC, VI.

PARGO'S   Lunch: $8-$12   Dinner: $10-$17   Phone: 301/698-1800
American   **Location:** I-270, exit 31A, just e on SR 85; in Francis Scott Key Mall. 5597 Spectrum Dr. **Hours:** 11 am-11 pm, Fri & Sat-midnight, Sun-10 pm. **Closed:** 11/24, 12/25. **Features:** Businesspeople, mall employees and shoppers love the bustling eatery, as evidenced by the long lines that often wait for seating. The menu offers standard favorites, such as pasta and steak, in plentiful portions. Casual dress; cocktails. **Parking:** on-site.
Cards: AX, DC, DS, MC, VI.

RED HORSE STEAK HOUSE   Lunch: $8-$12   Dinner: $17-$30   Phone: 301/663-3030
Steak & Seafood   **Location:** Jct US 15, just w on US 40; in Comfort Inn Red Horse Frederick. 996 W Patrick St 21703. **Hours:** 11:30 am-3 & 4:30-10:30 pm, Sat from 4:30 pm, Sun 4 pm-9 pm. Closed major holidays. **Reservations:** suggested, weekends. **Features:** A big, red horse out front welcomes diners to stop in for traditional surf-and-turf fare. Piping hot French onion soup is delicious. Western touches include stone fireplaces, open beams and lots of rich wood. Casual dress; cocktails. **Parking:** on-site. **Cards:** AX, CB, DC, DS, MC, VI.

FROSTBURG pop. 7,873

──────── **WHERE TO STAY** ────────

DAYS INN & SUITES   *Book at aaa.com*   Phone: (301)689-2050

(AAA) (SAVE)

6/1-10/31 [CP]	1P: $64-$74	2P: $69-$89	XP: $6 F12
5/1-5/31 [CP]	1P: $64-$69	2P: $69-$79	XP: $6 F12
3/1-4/30 [CP]	1P: $59-$69	2P: $59-$69	XP: $6 F12
11/1-2/28 [CP]	1P: $52-$62	2P: $59-$69	XP: $6 F12

Small-scale Hotel **Location:** I-68, exit 34, 1 mi n on SR 36. 11100 New Georges Creek Rd 21532. **Fax:** 301/689-5933. **Facility:** 91 one-bedroom standard units, some with whirlpools. 2 stories (no elevator), interior corridors. **Parking:** on-site. **Terms:** cancellation fee imposed. **Amenities:** irons, hair dryers. **Leisure Activities:** saunas, exercise room. **Guest Services:** coin laundry. **Business Services:** meeting rooms. **Cards:** AX, DC, DS, MC, VI. **Special Amenities:** free continental breakfast and free local telephone calls. *(See color ad p 635)*

SOME UNITS

HAMPTON INN   *Book at aaa.com*   Phone: (301)689-1998
▽▼△▽▼   All Year [ECP]   1P: $74-$89   2P: $84-$99
   Location: I-68, exit 34, 1 mi n on SR 36. 11200 New Georges Creek Rd 21532. Fax: 301/689-2920. **Facility:** 72
Small-scale Hotel   one-bedroom standard units, some with whirlpools. 3 stories, interior corridors. *Bath:* combo or shower only.
   Parking: on-site. **Amenities:** video games, high-speed Internet, dual phone lines, voice mail, irons, hair
dryers. **Pool(s):** indoor. **Leisure Activities:** whirlpool, exercise room. **Guest Services:** coin laundry. **Cards:** AX, DC, DS,
MC, VI.

SOME UNITS
[ASK] [SD] [♿] [🏊] [🎦] [DATA PORT] [🖥] [🛏] [📺] / [✕] /

──────── **WHERE TO DINE** ────────

ACROPOLIS RESTAURANT & LOUNGE   **Dinner:** $12-$25   Phone: 301/689-8277
▽▼△▽▼   **Location:** I-68, exit 34, 1.5 mi n on SR 36, then 0.9 mi w on US 40 Alternate Rt and SR 36; center. 45 E Main St 21532.
Greek   **Hours:** 4 pm-10 pm. Closed: 12/25; also Sun & Mon. **Features:** Acropolis Restaurant & Lounge combines
   Greek and American cuisine in an elegant setting, offering knowledgeable wait staff and wonderful
   background music. Casual dress; cocktails. **Parking:** street. **Cards:** AX, CB, DC, DS, JC, MC, VI.

[Y] [✕]

AU PETIT PARIS   **Dinner:** $12-$30   Phone: 301/689-8946
△△△   **Location:** I-68, exit 34, 1.5 mi n on SR 36, then 1 mi w on US 40 Alternate Rt and SR 36; center. 86 E Main St 21532.
   Hours: 6 pm-9:30 pm. Closed: 1/1, 11/24, 12/25; also Sun & Mon. **Reservations:** suggested.
▽▼△▽▼   **Features:** Family owned and operated since 1960, the small, cozy restaurant is known for expert
French   preparations of such seafood as fresh salmon, as well as beef, veal, lamb, venison and duck. The
   knowledgeable, experienced wait staff gives personalized attention. Dressy casual; cocktails. **Parking:**
   street. **Cards:** AX, CB, DC, DS, MC, VI.

[M] [Y] [✕]

GIUSEPPE'S ITALIAN RESTAURANT   **Dinner:** $11-$20   Phone: 301/689-2220
▽▼△▽▼   **Location:** I-68, exit 34, 1.5 mi n on SR 36, 1 mi w on US 40 Alternate Rt and SR 36; center. 11 Bowery St 21532.
Italian   **Hours:** 4:30 pm-11 pm, Fri & Sat from 3 pm. Closed: 12/25. **Features:** Giuseppe's Italian Restaurant
   combines a bi-level dining room with knowledgeable service and wonderful cuisine. Casual dress; cocktails.
   Parking: on-site and street. **Cards:** AX, CB, DC, DS, JC, MC, VI.

[Y] [✕]

GAITHERSBURG *—See District Of Columbia p. 485.*

GERMANTOWN *—See District Of Columbia p. 488.*

GLEN BURNIE *—See Baltimore p. 601.*

GRANTSVILLE pop. 619

──────── **WHERE TO STAY** ────────

ELLIOTT HOUSE VICTORIAN INN   Phone: (301)895-4250
▽▼△▽▼   All Year [BP]   1P: $85-$150   2P: $85-$150   XP: $25
   Location: I-68, exit 22 westbound, 0.5 mi n on US 219, then 2.1 mi w on US 40; exit 19 eastbound, just n, then 0.9 mi e
Bed & Breakfast   on US 40; behind Penn Alps Restaurant. Located in a quiet area. 146 Casselman Rd 21536. Fax: 301/895-4603.
   Facility: This 1870 Victorian mountain inn on seven acres along the Casselman River features gardens as
well as a deck overlooking the river. Smoke free premises. 9 one-bedroom standard units. 1-2 stories (no elevator),
interior/exterior corridors. *Bath:* combo or shower only. **Parking:** on-site. **Terms:** check-in 4 pm, 2 night minimum stay -
weekends, age restrictions may apply, 7 day cancellation notice-fee imposed, weekly rates available, package plans.
Amenities: video library, hair dryers. *Some:* CD players. **Leisure Activities:** sauna, fishing, bicycles, exercise room. *Fee:*
massage. **Guest Services:** gift shop, complimentary evening beverages. **Cards:** AX, MC, VI.

SOME UNITS
[ASK] [SD] [🍴] [✕] [✕] [VCR] [DATA PORT] [🖥] [📺] / [🖨] /

GRANTSVILLE INN   Phone: (301)895-5993
▽▼△▽   All Year   1P: $59-$102   2P: $64-$109   XP: $5   F
   Location: I-68, exit 22, just s on US 219. Located on south side of interstate exit. 2541 Chestnut Ridge Rd 21536.
Small-scale Hotel   Fax: 301/895-3410. **Facility:** 96 one-bedroom standard units. 4 stories, interior corridors. **Parking:** on-site.
   Terms: package plans, $1 service charge. **Amenities:** irons, hair dryers. **Pool(s):** heated indoor. **Leisure
Activities:** sauna, whirlpool, exercise room. *Fee:* game room. **Guest Services:** coin laundry. **Business Services:** meeting
rooms. **Cards:** AX, DC, DS, MC, VI.

SOME UNITS
[ASK] [SD] [🐕] [🍴] [Y] [🏊] [✕] [🎦] [DATA PORT] [📺] / [✕] [🖥] [🖨] /

──────── **WHERE TO DINE** ────────

PENN ALPS RESTAURANT   **Lunch:** $4-$8   **Dinner:** $7-$16   Phone: 301/895-5985
△△△   **Location:** I-68, exit 22 westbound, 1 mi on Chestnut Ridge Rd, 2 mi w on US 40 Alternate Rt; exit 19 eastbound, 0.3 mi
   n on CR 495, 1 mi e on US 40 Alternate Rt. 125 Casselman Rd 21536. **Hours:** 7 am-8 pm; to 7 pm, Sun-3 pm
▽▼△▽▼   11/1-5/27. Closed: 1/1, 12/24, 12/25. **Features:** The family-oriented restaurant offers traditionally prepared
American   meals, including a nice prime rib and steamed shrimp buffet Friday and Saturday. In keeping with the chalet-
   like structure, the establishment is conveniently located at Artisan Village. Casual dress. **Parking:** on-site.
   Cards: DS, MC, VI.

[✕]

GRASONVILLE pop. 2,193

———— WHERE TO STAY ————

COMFORT INN KENT NARROWS   *Book at aaa.com*   Phone: (410)827-6767
(AAA) (SAVE)   All Year [ECP]   1P: $79-$179   2P: $79-$179   XP: $8   F18
◇◇◇   **Location:** US 50 and 301, exit 42; at Kent Narrows Bridge. 3101 Main St 21638. Fax: 410/827-8626. **Facility:** 92
Motel   one-bedroom standard units, some with kitchens (no utensils) and/or whirlpools. 4 stories, exterior corridors.
Parking: on-site. **Terms:** pets ($25 extra charge 11/1-3/31). **Amenities:** voice mail, irons, hair dryers.
Pool(s): heated indoor. **Leisure Activities:** sauna, whirlpool, sun deck, limited exercise equipment. **Guest
Services:** coin laundry. **Business Services:** meeting rooms, fax (fee). **Cards:** AX, CB, DC, DS, MC, VI.
Special Amenities: free expanded continental breakfast and free newspaper. *(See color ad below)*

SOME UNITS

FEE

HOLIDAY INN EXPRESS-ANNAPOLIS/KENT ISLAND   *Book at aaa.com*   Phone: (410)827-4454
◇◇◇◇   5/1-10/31   1P: $129-$169   2P: $129-$169   XP: $8   F21
3/1-4/30   1P: $109-$119   2P: $109-$119   XP: $8   F21
11/1-2/28   1P: $99   2P: $99   XP: $8   F21
Small-scale Hotel   **Location:** US 50 and 301, exit 42; at Kent Narrows Bridge. 1020 Kent Narrows Rd 21638. Fax: 410/827-0710.
Facility: 76 one-bedroom standard units, some with whirlpools. 3 stories, interior corridors. *Bath:* combo or shower only.
Parking: on-site. **Amenities:** dual phone lines, voice mail, irons, hair dryers. **Pool(s):** outdoor. **Guest Services:** coin laundry.
Business Services: meeting rooms, fax (fee). **Cards:** AX, DC, DS, MC, VI.

SOME UNITS

FEE

SLEEP INN   *Book at aaa.com*   Phone: (410)827-5555
(AAA) (SAVE)   All Year [ECP]   1P: $69-$149   2P: $69-$149   XP: $10   F
◇◇◇◇   **Location:** US 50 and 301, exit 44A westbound; exit 43B eastbound, 0.7 mi ne. 101 VFW Ave 21638.
Fax: 410/827-8801. **Facility:** 59 one-bedroom standard units, some with whirlpools. 2 stories (no elevator),
Small-scale Hotel   interior corridors. *Bath:* combo or shower only. **Parking:** on-site. **Terms:** package plans. **Amenities:** voice
mail, irons, hair dryers. **Pool(s):** outdoor. **Business Services:** meeting rooms, fax (fee). **Cards:** AX, CB,
DC, DS, JC, MC, VI. **Special Amenities:** free expanded continental breakfast and free newspaper.
(See color ad below)

SOME UNITS

——— **WHERE TO DINE** ———

ANNIE'S PARAMOUNT STEAK & SEAFOOD HOUSE   Lunch: $7-$15   Dinner: $12-$30   Phone: 410/827-7103
▼▼▼◆   **Location:** US 50 and 301, exit 42 (Kent Narrows), just n, follow signs. 500 Kent Narrows Way N 21638. **Hours:** 11
Steak & Seafood   am-10 pm, Fri & Sat-11 pm, Sun 9 am-10 pm. Closed: 12/25. **Reservations:** suggested. **Features:** Since
1992, this family owned and operated restaurant has pleased the locals. The menu features Certified Angus
Beef, Seafood and Mediterranean dishes. The staff is professional, friendly and eager to please. Casual
dress; cocktails. **Parking:** on-site. **Cards:** AX, CB, DC, DS, MC, VI.
🍸❌

THE NARROWS   Lunch: $7-$14   Dinner: $12-$29   Phone: 410/827-8113
▼▼ ◆◆   **Location:** US 50 and 301, exit 42 (Kent Narrows), 0.3 mi s. 3023 Kent Narrows Way S 21638. **Hours:** 11 am-9 pm,
Seafood   Fri & Sat-10 pm. Closed: 12/24, 12/25. **Reservations:** suggested, weekends. **Features:** Windows wraparound three sides of the tastefully decorated dining area, which looks out on the harbor. The screened
porch is popular during mild weather. The cream of crab soup is a favorite on a diverse menu of seafood,
beef, lamb, pork and chicken. Lunch menu available to 4 pm. Casual dress; cocktails. **Parking:** on-site. **Cards:** AX, CB, DC,
DS, MC, VI.
🍸❌

GREENBELT —*See District Of Columbia p. 489.*

HAGERSTOWN pop. 36,687

——— **WHERE TO STAY** ———

CLARION HOTEL & CONFERENCE CENTER
ANTIETAM CREEK   *Book at aaa.com*   Phone: (301)733-5100
AAA SAVE   All Year   1P: $69-$99   2P: $69-$99   XP: $10   F17
▼▼ ▼▼   **Location:** I-70, exit 32B, 2.3 mi w on US 40. 901 Dual Hwy 21740. Fax: 301/733-9192. **Facility:** 210 one-bedroom
standard units, some with whirlpools. 2-5 stories, interior corridors. **Parking:** on-site. **Terms:** package plans,
Small-scale Hotel   pets ($10 extra charge). **Amenities:** video games, voice mail, irons, hair dryers. **Dining:** 6:30 am-10 pm,
cocktails. **Pool(s):** heated indoor. **Guest Services:** gift shop, coin laundry, airport transportation-
Hagerstown Airport. **Business Services:** conference facilities. **Cards:** AX, CB, DC, DS, JC, MC, VI.
Special Amenities: free continental breakfast and free newspaper.
SOME UNITS
🅂📞 ✈ 🍴 🍸 ⊘ 🏊 🆓 📷 DATA PORT 🛄 💻 / ❌ VCR 🖥 /
FEE

COMFORT SUITES   *Book at aaa.com*   Phone: (301)791-8100
AAA SAVE   All Year [ECP]   1P: $70-$90   2P: $80-$100   XP: $10   F18
▼▼▼▼   **Location:** I-70, exit 32B, 0.8 mi w on US 40. 1801 Dual Hwy 21740. Fax: 301/766-2079. **Facility:** 75 one-bedroom
standard units, some with whirlpools. 3 stories, interior corridors. **Bath:** combo or shower only. **Parking:** on-
Small-scale Hotel   site. **Amenities:** high-speed Internet, dual phone lines, voice mail, safes, irons, hair dryers. **Pool(s):** heated
indoor. **Leisure Activities:** whirlpool, exercise room. **Guest Services:** coin laundry. **Business Services:**
meeting rooms, business center. **Cards:** AX, DC, DS, JC, MC, VI. **Special Amenities:** free expanded
continental breakfast and free local telephone calls.
SOME UNITS
🅂 📞 🏊 📷 DATA PORT 🛄 🖥 💻 / ❌ /

DAYS INN   *Book at aaa.com*   Phone: (301)739-9050
AAA SAVE   All Year [CP]   1P: $45-$64   2P: $49-$74   XP: $5   F17
▼▼ ▼▼   **Location:** I-70, exit 32, 2 mi n. 900 Dual Hwy 21740. Fax: 301/739-8347. **Facility:** 134 one-bedroom standard
units. 2 stories (no elevator), interior corridors. **Parking:** on-site. **Pool(s):** outdoor. **Leisure**
Small-scale Hotel   **Activities:** playground, exercise room. **Guest Services:** coin laundry. **Business Services:** meeting rooms.
Cards: AX, CB, DC, DS, JC, MC, VI. **Special Amenities:** free continental breakfast and free local
telephone calls.
SOME UNITS
🅂 🏊 📷 DATA PORT / ❌ 🛄 🖥 /

FOUR POINTS BY SHERATON HAGERSTOWN
Book at aaa.com
Phone: (301)790-3010
AAA SAVE
All Year [CP] 1P: $79-$109   2P: $79-$109
Location: I-70, exit 32B, 0.5 mi n. 1910 Dual Hwy 21740. Fax: 301/733-4559. **Facility:** 108 one-bedroom standard units, some with whirlpools. 2 stories (no elevator), interior corridors. **Parking:** on-site. **Terms:** weekly rates available, package plans, pets ($25 deposit). **Amenities:** high-speed Internet, voice mail, irons, hair dryers. **Dining:** Nicholas, see separate listing. **Pool(s):** outdoor. **Leisure Activities:** exercise room. **Business Services:** meeting rooms. **Cards:** AX, CB, DC, DS, JC, MC, VI.
Small-scale Hotel
Special Amenities: free continental breakfast and free local telephone calls. *(See color ad p 630)*

SOME UNITS

HALFWAY HAGERSTOWN SUPER 8
Book at aaa.com
Phone: (301)582-1992
5/1-9/30   1P: $53-$63   2P: $59-$69   XP: $6   F
3/1-4/30 & 10/1-2/28   1P: $47-$57   2P: $53-$63   XP: $6   F
Motel
Location: I-81, exit 5B, just w. 16805 Blake Rd 21740. Fax: 301/582-3488. **Facility:** 62 one-bedroom standard units, some with whirlpools. 2 stories (no elevator), interior corridors. *Bath:* combo or shower only. **Parking:** on-site. **Terms:** pets ($25 deposit). **Amenities:** hair dryers. **Guest Services:** coin laundry. **Cards:** AX, CB, DC, DS, JC, MC, VI.

SOME UNITS

HAMPTON INN HAGERSTOWN
Book at aaa.com
Phone: (301)739-6100
AAA SAVE
3/31-10/31 [ECP]   1P: $89-$99   2P: $89-$99
11/1-2/28 [ECP]   1P: $84-$99   2P: $84-$99
3/1-3/30 [ECP]   1P: $84-$97   2P: $84-$97
Motel
Location: I-70, exit 32B, 1 mi w on US 40. 1716 Dual Hwy 21740. Fax: 301/791-7885. **Facility:** 118 one-bedroom standard units. 4 stories, interior corridors. *Bath:* combo or shower only. **Parking:** on-site. **Amenities:** high-speed Internet, voice mail, irons, hair dryers. **Pool(s):** heated outdoor. **Leisure Activities:** exercise room. **Guest Services:** valet laundry. **Business Services:** meeting rooms. **Cards:** AX, CB, DC, DS, MC, VI. **Special Amenities:** free expanded continental breakfast and free local telephone calls.

SOME UNITS

HAMPTON INN HAGERSTOWN/MAUGANSVILLE
Book at aaa.com
Phone: (240)420-1970
AAA SAVE
All Year   1P: $79-$99   2P: $79-$99
Location: I-81, exit 9, just e. 18300 Peak Cir 21742 (PO Box 2161). Fax: 240/420-1971. **Facility:** 77 one-bedroom standard units, some with whirlpools. 3 stories, interior corridors. *Bath:* combo or shower only. **Parking:** on-site. **Terms:** cancellation fee imposed. **Amenities:** high-speed Internet, voice mail, irons, hair dryers. **Pool(s):** indoor. **Leisure Activities:** exercise room. **Guest Services:** valet laundry, area transportation-within 10 mi. **Business Services:** meeting rooms. **Cards:** AX, DC, DS, MC, VI. **Special Amenities:** free expanded continental breakfast.
Small-scale Hotel

SOME UNITS

HOLIDAY INN EXPRESS HOTEL & SUITES
Book at aaa.com
Phone: (301)745-5644
AAA SAVE
All Year   1P: $83-$159   XP: $7   F18
Location: I-81, exit 5A. 241 Railway Ln 21740 (10228 Governor Land Blvd, Suite 3002, WILLIAMSPORT, 21795). Fax: 301/745-3991. **Facility:** 84 one-bedroom standard units, some with whirlpools. 3 stories, interior corridors. *Bath:* combo or shower only. **Parking:** on-site. **Terms:** [ECP] meal plan available. **Amenities:** high-speed Internet, voice mail, irons, hair dryers. **Pool(s):** heated indoor. **Leisure Activities:** whirlpool, exercise room. **Guest Services:** coin laundry. **Business Services:** meeting rooms, business center. **Cards:** AX, CB, DC, DS, JC, MC, VI. **Special Amenities:** free continental breakfast and free local telephone calls. *(See color ad below)*
Small-scale Hotel

SOME UNITS

MICROTEL INN & SUITES-HAGERSTOWN MD
Book at aaa.com
Phone: (240)527-2700
5/1-10/31 [CP]   1P: $49-$59   2P: $51-$61   XP: $5   F16
3/1-4/30 [CP]   1P: $40-$49   2P: $49-$55   XP: $5   F16
11/1-2/28 [CP]   1P: $40-$49   2P: $45-$50   XP: $5   F16
Small-scale Hotel
Location: I-81, exit 9, just w. 13726 Oliver Dr 21740. Fax: 240/527-2701. **Facility:** 53 one-bedroom standard units, some with whirlpools. 3 stories, interior corridors. **Parking:** on-site. **Terms:** package plans. **Guest Services:** coin laundry. **Cards:** AX, DS, MC, VI.

SOME UNITS

MOTEL 6 - 1259
Motel

Book at aaa.com
All Year
Location: I-81, exit 5, 0.5 mi e, 0.5 mi n of jct I-81 and 70. Located adjacent to shopping mall. 11321 Massey Blvd 21740. Fax: 301/582-0942. **Facility:** 103 one-bedroom standard units. 1 story, exterior corridors. *Bath:* combo or shower only. **Parking:** on-site. **Terms:** small pets only. **Pool(s):** small outdoor. **Guest Services:** coin laundry. **Cards:** AX, CB, DC, DS, MC, VI.

1P: $41-$51   2P: $47-$57   XP: $3

Phone: 301/582-4445
F17

SOME UNITS

PLAZA HOTEL
Small-scale Hotel

Book at aaa.com
All Year
Location: I-81, exit 5, 0.3 mi e, 0.5 mi n of jct I-81 and 70. 1718 Underpass Way 21740. Fax: 301/797-6209. **Facility:** 163 one-bedroom standard units, some with whirlpools. 6 stories, interior corridors. **Parking:** on-site. **Amenities:** high-speed Internet, voice mail, irons, hair dryers. *Some:* CD players. **Dining:** 6:30-10:30 am, 11-1 & 5-8 pm, Fri-9 pm, Sat 7-10:30 am, 11-1 & 5-9 pm, Sun 7-10:30 am, 11-1:30 & 5-8 pm, cocktails. **Pool(s):** heated indoor. **Leisure Activities:** sauna, whirlpool, exercise room. **Guest Services:** valet laundry, airport transportation-Hagerstown Airport. **Business Services:** meeting rooms. **Cards:** AX, CB, DC, DS, MC, VI. **Special Amenities:** free local telephone calls and free newspaper. *(See color ad below)*

1P: $71   2P: $80   XP: $8

Phone: (301)797-2500
F12

SOME UNITS

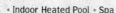

SLEEP INN & SUITES *Book at aaa.com* Phone: (301)766-9449

AAA SAVE All Year 1P: $70-$130 2P: $70-$130 XP: $10 F18
Location: I-70, exit 29, just s. 18216 Col Henry K Douglas Dr 21740. Fax: 301/766-9469. **Facility:** 96 one-bedroom standard units, some with whirlpools. 4 stories, interior corridors. **Bath:** combo or shower only. **Parking:** on-site. **Terms:** small pets only ($10 fee). **Amenities:** safes, irons, hair dryers. **Pool(s):** heated
Small-scale Hotel indoor. **Leisure Activities:** whirlpool, exercise room. **Guest Services:** coin laundry. **Business Services:** meeting rooms. **Cards:** AX, CB, DC, DS, JC, MC, VI. **Special Amenities:** free expanded continental breakfast and free room upgrade (subject to availability with advance reservations). *(See color ad p 632)*

SOME UNITS

[icons] FEE / [icons] /

SUPER 8 MOTEL HAGERSTOWN *Book at aaa.com* Phone: (301)739-5800

5/1-9/30 1P: $45-$54 2P: $50-$63 XP: $5 F17
3/1-4/30 & 10/1-2/28 1P: $39-$48 2P: $45-$56 XP: $5 F17
Motel **Location:** I-70, exit 32B, 2.1 mi nw on US 40. 1220 Dual Hwy 21740. Fax: 301/739-5800. **Facility:** 61 one-bedroom standard units. 3 stories (no elevator), interior corridors. **Parking:** on-site. **Cards:** AX, CB, DC, DS,
MC, VI. *(See color ad p 632)*

SOME UNITS

[ASK] [icons] / [icons]

——— WHERE TO DINE ———

AL POMODORO RISTORANTE Lunch: $8-$12 Dinner: $11-$22 Phone: 301/739-0440
Location: I-70, exit 32B, 2.3 mi w on US 40, then 0.3 mi e on Eastern Blvd. 1101 Opal Ct 21740. **Hours:** 11 am-10 pm, Sat from 4 pm. Closed: 12/25; also Sun. **Features:** The flavors of Southern Italy come alive in
South Italian Neapolitan dishes. Casual dress; cocktails. **Parking:** on-site. **Cards:** AX, CB, DC, DS, JC, MC, VI.

[icons]

BLACK STEER STEAKHOUSE Lunch: $7-$16 Dinner: $7-$16 Phone: 301/790-1070
Location: I-80, exit 1 (in Pennsylvania), just sw on SR 163 at Maryland-Pennsylvania state line. 18203 Mason Dixon Rd 21740. **Hours:** 11 am-9 pm, Fri & Sat-10 pm, Sun-8 pm. Closed: 12/25; also Mon. **Features:** Reasonable prices, an extensive buffet of comfort foods and hearty portions of such staple fare as beef tips make this
Steak House a popular stop for families. The dessert bar includes ice cream, soft brownies and other tempting treats.
Casual dress; beer & wine only. **Parking:** on-site. **Cards:** AX, DC, DS, MC, VI.

[icon]

BURHANS STATION Lunch: $6-$12 Dinner: $8-$20 Phone: 301/790-3000
Location: I-81, exit 5, 0.3 mi e, 2.5 mi n on Wessel, then 0.5 mi w. 301 S Burhans Blvd 21740. **Hours:** 11 am-10 pm. Closed: 12/25. **Features:** At the converted train station, guests can step back into yesteryear and savor
American classic American favorites. Casual dress; cocktails. **Parking:** on-site. **Cards:** AX, MC, VI.

[icons]

FIRESIDE RESTAURANT & LOUNGE Lunch: $6-$12 Dinner: $16-$22 Phone: 301/733-4800
AAA **Location:** I-81, exit 5, 0.3 mi e, 0.5 mi n of jct I-81 and I-70. 1716 Underpass Way 21740. **Hours:** 11 am-1 & 5-10 pm. Closed major holidays. **Features:** A huge fireplace, from which the restaurant derives its name, is the center of attention in the dining room. Service is friendly, and portions are large. Casual dress; cocktails.
American **Parking:** on-site. **Cards:** AX, CB, DC, DS, JC, MC, VI.

[icons]

THE GRILL AT PARK CIRCLE Lunch: $7-$12 Dinner: $10-$25 Phone: 301/797-9100
Location: I-81, exit 5, 2.9 mi e. 325 Virginia Ave 21740. **Hours:** 11:30 am-10 pm, Sat from 4:30 pm. Closed: Sun & Mon. **Reservations:** suggested, weekends. **Features:** A Hagerstown tradition for many years. The Grill at
American Park Circle combines elegantly prepared food with a casual fun atmosphere. Casual dress; cocktails. **Parking:** on-site. **Cards:** AX, CB, DC, DS, JC, MC, VI.

[icons]

NICHOLAS Lunch: $6-$10 Dinner: $11-$18 Phone: 301/790-3640
Location: I-70, exit 32B, 0.5 mi n; in Four Points by Sheraton Hagerstown. 1910 Dual Hwy 21740. **Hours:** 6:30 am-2 & 5-10 pm, Sun 7 am-2 & 5-9 pm. Closed: 12/25. **Reservations:** suggested. **Features:** The good variety of well-prepared food is certainly commendable, namely offerings on the Tuesday-Friday lunch buffet. Pasta,
American seafood, meat, poultry and Greek specialties are foremost on the menu. Service is prompt, knowledgeable and friendly. Casual dress; cocktails. **Parking:** on-site. **Cards:** AX, DC, DS, MC, VI.

[icons]

RED HORSE STEAK HOUSE Dinner: $15-$20 Phone: 301/733-3788
Location: I-70, exit 32B, 1 mi nw on US 40. 1800 Dual Hwy 21740. **Hours:** 4 pm-10 pm, Sun-9 pm. Closed major holidays. **Reservations:** suggested, weekends. **Features:** Businesspeople and families favor this
Steak & Seafood steakhouse, which prepares some daily seafood specials that typically aren't seen at such establishments. Exposed beams and wagon wheels contribute to the country decor. Prime rib is a favorite choice. Casual dress; cocktails. **Parking:** on-site. **Cards:** AX, CB, DC, MC, VI.

[icons]

RICHARDSON'S RESTAURANT Lunch: $5-$12 Dinner: $7-$18 Phone: 301/733-3660
Location: I-70, exit 32B, 2.3 mi w on US 40. 710 Dual Hwy 21740. **Hours:** 11 am-9 pm. Closed: 1/1, 11/24, 12/25. **Features:** Richardson's Restaurant is a culinary landmark in Hagerstown. Family oriented and run for three
American generations. Value priced with friendly service. Casual dress; cocktails. **Parking:** on-site. **Cards:** DS, MC, VI.

[icons]

HANCOCK pop. 1,725

———— **WHERE TO STAY** ————

SUPER 8 MOTEL   *Book at aaa.com*   **Phone:** (301)678-6101
(AAA) (SAVE)   All Year [CP]   1P: $48-$150   2P: $48-$150   XP: $5   F17
◆◆◆ ◆◆   **Location:** I-70, exit 1B, just s. 118 Limestone Rd 21750. **Fax:** 301/678-5376. **Facility:** 50 one-bedroom standard
            units, some with whirlpools. 2 stories (no elevator), interior/exterior corridors. **Parking:** on-site.
            Amenities: irons. **Guest Services:** valet laundry. **Business Services:** meeting rooms. **Cards:** AX, DC, DS,
Small-scale Hotel MC, VI. **Special Amenities:** free continental breakfast and free local telephone calls.

SOME UNITS
[S/D] [🐾] [DATA PORT] / [✕] [🛏] /

———— **WHERE TO DINE** ————

WEAVER'S RESTAURANT & BAKERY   **Lunch:** $5-$12   **Dinner:** $8-$14   **Phone:** 301/678-6346
◆◆◆ ◆◆   **Location:** I-70, exit 1B, just s. 77 W Main St 21750. **Hours:** 11 am-8 pm, Fri-Sun from 7 am. **Closed:** 11/24,
            12/25. **Features:** At Weaver's you'll find homemade soups, sandwiches and desserts. Home town American
American   pride translates to very friendly service. Casual dress. **Parking:** street. **Cards:** MC, VI.
[✕]

HANOVER —See Baltimore p. 601.

HAVRE DE GRACE —See Baltimore p. 602.

HUNT VALLEY —See Baltimore p. 603.

INDIAN HEAD pop. 3,422

———— **WHERE TO STAY** ————

SUPER 8 MOTEL   *Book at aaa.com*   **Phone:** (301)753-8100
(AAA) (SAVE)   All Year   1P: $50-$65   2P: $58-$78   XP: $6   F12
◆◆◆   **Location:** SR 210, 0.6 mi s of jct SR 225. 4694 Indian Head Hwy 20640. **Fax:** 301/753-6247. **Facility:** 44 one-
            bedroom standard units. 3 stories, interior corridors. **Parking:** on-site. **Terms:** cancellation fee imposed,
            weekly rates available, small pets only ($5 fee). **Amenities:** irons. **Guest Services:** coin laundry. **Business**
Small-scale Hotel **Services:** fax (fee). **Cards:** AX, CB, DC, DS, MC, VI. **Special Amenities:** free continental breakfast and
            free local telephone calls.

SOME UNITS
[S/D] [🐾] [&M] [🐾] [DATA PORT] [🛏] [🖨] / [✕] /
FEE

JESSUP —See Baltimore p. 603.

JOPPA —See Baltimore p. 604.

LANDOVER —See District Of Columbia p. 490.

LANDOVER HILLS —See District Of Columbia p. 490.

LANHAM —See District Of Columbia p. 491.

LA PLATA pop. 6,551

———— **WHERE TO STAY** ————

BEST WESTERN LA PLATA INN   *Book at aaa.com*   **Phone:** (301)934-4900
(AAA) (SAVE)   3/1-10/31 [ECP]   1P: $99-$119   2P: $99-$119   XP: $10   F16
            11/1-2/28 [ECP]   1P: $69-$99   2P: $69-$99   XP: $10   F16
◆◆◆ ◆◆   **Location:** Jct SR 6, 0.4 mi s on US 301. 6900 Crain Hwy 20646. **Fax:** 301/934-5389. **Facility:** 73 units. 65 one-
            bedroom standard units. 8 one-bedroom suites ($130-$150). 2 stories (no elevator), interior corridors.
Small-scale Hotel **Parking:** on-site. **Terms:** 3 day cancellation notice, small pets only ($25 fee). **Amenities:** dual phone lines,
            voice mail, irons, hair dryers. **Pool(s):** outdoor. **Leisure Activities:** exercise room. **Guest Services:** coin
laundry. **Business Services:** meeting rooms, fax (fee). **Cards:** AX, CB, DC, DS, MC, VI. **Special Amenities:** free expanded
continental breakfast.

SOME UNITS
[S/D] [🐾] [▢▢] [&M] [🍴] [🏊] [🐾] [DATA PORT] [🛏] [🖨] [☕] / [✕] [VCR] /
FEE

———— **WHERE TO DINE** ————

THE CROSSING AT CASEY JONES   **Lunch:** $6-$19   **Dinner:** $16-$29   **Phone:** 301/932-6226
◆◆◆◆   **Location:** Just e of US 301. 417 E Charles St 20646. **Hours:** 11 am-2:30 & 5-9:30 pm, Fri-10 pm, Sat 5 pm-10
            pm. **Closed:** 1/1, 9/5, 12/25; also Sun. **Reservations:** suggested. **Features:** The dining room of the well-
American   established, family-run restaurant has a casual, comfortable feel. The exhibition kitchen enables diners to
            watch as dishes from the seasonally changing menu are prepared. A nice wine selection is available.
Dressy casual; cocktails. **Parking:** on-site. **Cards:** AX, DC, DS, MC, VI.
[Y] [✕]

GUSTAVO'S RISTORANTE ITALIANO   **Lunch:** $7-$15   **Dinner:** $11-$48   **Phone:** 301/934-6200

Italian

Location: Jct SR 6, just s on US 301. 6810 Crain Hwy 20646. **Hours:** 11 am-10 pm, Fri & Sat to midnight, Sun 10 am-9 pm. Closed: 12/25. **Reservations:** suggested. **Features:** Suitable for any occasion, the restaurant prepares innovative Italian cuisine from fresh ingredients. The menu lists a good selection of fresh seafood, veal and pasta dishes. Dressy casual; cocktails. **Parking:** on-site. **Cards:** AX, CB, DC, DS, JC, MC, VI.

LARGO —*See District Of Columbia p. 492.*

LAUREL —*See District Of Columbia p. 492.*

LA VALE pop. 4,613

———— **WHERE TO STAY** ————

BEST WESTERN BRADDOCK MOTOR INN   *Book at aaa.com*   **Phone:** (301)729-3300

	All Year [CP]	1P: $79-$99	2P: $89-$109	XP: $5	F17

Small-scale Hotel

Location: On US 40, jct SR 53, adjacent to I-68, exit 39W/40E. 1268 National Hwy 21502. Fax: 301/729-3300. **Facility:** 104 one-bedroom standard units, some with whirlpools. 3 stories (no elevator), interior corridors. *Bath:* combo or shower only. **Parking:** on-site. **Amenities:** voice mail, irons, hair dryers. **Pool(s):** indoor. **Leisure Activities:** whirlpool, exercise room. **Guest Services:** valet laundry, area transportation. **Business Services:** meeting rooms. **Cards:** AX, CB, DC, DS, MC, VI.

SOME UNITS

COMFORT INN & SUITES   *Book at aaa.com*   **Phone:** (301)729-6400

	7/2-10/31 [ECP]	1P: $90-$100	2P: $100-$110	XP: $5	F
	5/1-7/1 [ECP]	1P: $80-$90	2P: $90-$100	XP: $5	F
Motel	3/1-4/30 & 11/1-2/28 [ECP]	1P: $72-$77	2P: $82-$87	XP: $5	F

Location: I-68, exit 40 eastbound, 0.4 mi n; exit 39 westbound, 1 mi n. 1216 National Hwy 21502. Fax: 301/729-9472. **Facility:** 67 one-bedroom standard units, some with whirlpools. 3 stories, interior corridors. *Bath:* combo or shower only. **Parking:** on-site. **Amenities:** high-speed Internet, voice mail, irons, hair dryers. **Pool(s):** heated indoor. **Leisure Activities:** whirlpool, exercise room. **Guest Services:** valet and coin laundry. **Business Services:** meeting rooms. **Cards:** AX, DC, DS, MC, VI.

SOME UNITS

OAK TREE INN

Book at aaa.com

(AAA) (SAVE)

Small-scale Hotel

Phone: 301/729-6700

All Year   1P: $69-$79

Location: I-68, exit 40, 0.6 mi s. 12310 Winchester Rd SW 21502. Fax: 301/729-6706. **Facility:** 82 one-bedroom standard units. 3 stories, interior/exterior corridors. *Bath:* combo or shower only. **Parking:** on-site. **Terms:** cancellation fee imposed, weekly rates available, pets ($5 extra charge). **Amenities:** hair dryers. *Some:* irons. **Leisure Activities:** exercise room. **Guest Services:** coin laundry. **Business Services:** meeting rooms. **Cards:** AX, CB, DC, DS, MC, VI. **Special Amenities:** free local telephone calls and early check-in/late check-out. *(See color ad p 635)*

SOME UNITS

SUPER 8 MOTEL

Book at aaa.com

(AAA) (SAVE)

Motel

Phone: (301)729-6265

All Year   1P: $46   2P: $54   XP: $5   F12

Location: I-68, exit 40, 0.4 mi n. 1301 National Hwy 21502. Fax: 301/729-6265. **Facility:** 63 one-bedroom standard units. 3 stories, interior corridors. **Parking:** on-site. **Terms:** small pets only (with prior approval). **Amenities:** safes. *Some:* irons. **Cards:** AX, DC, DS, MC, VI. **Special Amenities:** free continental breakfast and free local telephone calls.

SOME UNITS

------ **WHERE TO DINE** ------

PENNY'S DINER

American

Lunch: $5-$15   **Dinner:** $5-$15   **Phone:** 301/729-6700

Location: I-68, exit 40, 0.6 mi s. 12310 Winchester Rd 21502. **Hours:** 24 hours. **Features:** The diner is a reminder of a memorable era in American history. Appointed in a '50s theme, the restaurant has many wonderful, tempting items, along with genuinely friendly service. Casual dress. **Parking:** on-site. **Cards:** AX, DS, MC, VI.

LEXINGTON PARK pop. 11,021

------ **WHERE TO STAY** ------

BEST WESTERN LEXINGTON PARK

(AAA) (SAVE)

Small-scale Hotel

Phone: (301)862-4100

All Year   1P: $69-$87   2P: $74-$92   XP: $5   F14

Location: 3.2 mi n. Rt 235 20653 (22769 Three Notch Rd, CALIFORNIA, 20619). Fax: 301/862-4673. **Facility:** 120 one-bedroom standard units, some with efficiencies. 3 stories, interior corridors. **Parking:** on-site. **Terms:** [ECP] meal plan available, small pets only. **Amenities:** video games (fee), irons, hair dryers. **Pool(s):** small outdoor. **Leisure Activities:** 2 lighted tennis courts, picnic area with grill, jogging, exercise room, horseshoes, volleyball. **Guest Services:** coin laundry. **Business Services:** business center. **Cards:** AX, CB, DC, DS, JC, MC, VI. **Special Amenities:** free continental breakfast and free local telephone calls.

SOME UNITS

DAYS INN LEXINGTON PARK

Book at aaa.com

(AAA) (SAVE)

Motel

Phone: (301)863-6666

All Year   1P: $84-$89   2P: $84-$89   XP: $10   F18

Location: On SR 235. Located opposite the Patuxent Naval Station. 21847 Three Notch Rd 20653. Fax: 301/863-4691. **Facility:** 165 one-bedroom standard units, some with efficiencies (no utensils). 1-2 stories, exterior corridors. **Parking:** on-site. **Terms:** cancellation fee imposed. **Amenities:** voice mail, irons, hair dryers. *Some:* high-speed Internet. **Dining:** 10:30 am-10 pm, cocktails. **Pool(s):** outdoor. **Guest Services:** coin laundry. **Business Services:** fax (fee). **Cards:** AX, DC, DS, MC, VI. **Special Amenities:** free full breakfast and free local telephone calls.

SOME UNITS

FAIRFIELD INN BY MARRIOTT LEXINGTON PARK

Book at aaa.com

(AAA) (SAVE)

Small-scale Hotel

Phone: (301)863-0203

All Year [ECP]   1P: $95   2P: $95

Location: SR 235, just s to Lexington Park. Located opposite Patuxent Naval Station, Gate 1. 22119 Three Notch Rd 20653. Fax: 301/863-2113. **Facility:** 78 one-bedroom standard units, some with whirlpools. 4 stories, interior corridors. *Bath:* combo or shower only. **Parking:** on-site. **Terms:** 7 day cancellation notice. **Amenities:** high-speed Internet, voice mail, irons, hair dryers. **Pool(s):** small heated indoor. **Leisure Activities:** whirlpool, sun deck, limited exercise equipment. **Guest Services:** valet and coin laundry. **Business Services:** fax (fee). **Cards:** AX, DC, DS, MC, VI. **Special Amenities:** free expanded continental breakfast and free newspaper.

SOME UNITS

HAMPTON INN LEXINGTON PARK

Book at aaa.com

Small-scale Hotel

Phone: (301)863-3200

All Year [ECP]   1P: $95-$99   2P: $95-$99

Location: SR 235, s to Lexington Park. Located opposite Patuxent Naval Station, Gate 1. 22211 Three Notch Rd 20653. Fax: 301/863-7865. **Facility:** 111 units. 101 one-bedroom standard units. 10 one-bedroom suites ($105-$109). 5 stories, interior corridors. *Bath:* combo or shower only. **Parking:** on-site. **Amenities:** voice mail, irons, hair dryers. **Pool(s):** outdoor. **Leisure Activities:** exercise room. **Guest Services:** valet and coin laundry. **Business Services:** meeting rooms, business center. **Cards:** AX, CB, DC, DS, MC, VI.

SOME UNITS

SLEEP INN & SUITES LEXINGTON PARK/SOLOMONS

Book at aaa.com

(AAA) (SAVE)

Small-scale Hotel

Phone: (301)737-0000

All Year [ECP]   1P: $89-$150   2P: $89-$150   XP: $10   F18

Location: SR 235, 0.5 mi n of jct SR 4. 23428 Three Notch Rd 20619 (23428 Three Notch Rd, CALIFORNIA). Fax: 301/737-4426. **Facility:** 81 one-bedroom standard units, some with whirlpools. 3 stories, interior corridors. *Bath:* combo or shower only. **Parking:** on-site. **Terms:** cancellation fee imposed, package plans. **Amenities:** high-speed Internet (fee), dual phone lines, voice mail, irons, hair dryers. **Pool(s):** heated indoor. **Leisure Activities:** whirlpool, exercise room. **Guest Services:** valet and coin laundry. **Business Services:** PC, fax (fee). **Cards:** AX, CB, DC, DS, JC, MC, VI. **Special Amenities:** free expanded continental breakfast and free local telephone calls.

SOME UNITS

LINTHICUM HEIGHTS —See Baltimore p. 604.

LINWOOD —See Baltimore p. 610.

MCHENRY

——— WHERE TO STAY ———

COMFORT INN AT DEEP CREEK   *Book at aaa.com*   Phone: (301)387-4200

5/20-10/29	1P: $79-$129	2P: $79-$129	XP: $6 D18
3/1-4/2	1P: $79-$119	2P: $79-$119	XP: $6 D18
10/30-2/28	1P: $69-$119	2P: $69-$119	XP: $6 D18
4/3-5/19	1P: $69-$89	2P: $69-$89	XP: $6 D18

Small-scale Hotel

Location: 1 mi s on US 219 from jct SR 42. 2704 Deep Creek Dr 21541. **Fax:** 301/387-4204. **Facility:** 75 one-bedroom standard units, some with whirlpools. 4 stories (no elevator), interior corridors. **Parking:** on-site. **Terms:** cancellation fee imposed, small pets only ($15 extra charge). **Amenities:** video library, high-speed Internet, irons, hair dryers. **Pool(s):** outdoor. **Leisure Activities:** exercise room. **Guest Services:** coin laundry. **Business Services:** business center. **Cards:** AX, CB, DC, DS, MC, VI.

SOME UNITS

WISP MOUNTAIN RESORT/HOTEL & CONFERENCE
CENTER   *Book at aaa.com*   Phone: (301)387-5581

12/20-2/28	1P: $109-$199	2P: $109-$199
3/1-12/19	1P: $89-$199	2P: $89-$199

Resort
Small-scale Hotel   **Location:** 1 mi s on US 219 from jct SR 42, just w on Sang Run Rd, 0.3 mi s. 290 Marsh Hill Rd 21541. **Fax:** 301/542-0041. **Facility:** This is a resort for all seasons, with recreational opportunities — especially skiing and golf — for all ages. 169 one-bedroom standard units. 3-7 stories, interior corridors. *Bath:* combo or shower only. **Parking:** on-site. **Terms:** check-in 5 pm, 2 night minimum stay - seasonal and/or weekends, 7 day cancellation notice-fee imposed, weekly rates available, package plans, $4 service charge, pets ($100 deposit). **Amenities:** dual phone lines, voice mail, irons, hair dryers. **Pool(s):** indoor. **Leisure Activities:** whirlpool, 2 lighted tennis courts, racquetball courts, hiking trails, playground, exercise room, basketball, volleyball. *Fee:* golf-18 holes, downhill skiing. **Guest Services:** gift shop, coin laundry. **Business Services:** conference facilities. **Cards:** AX, CB, DC, DS, MC, VI.

SOME UNITS

MOUNT AIRY —See Baltimore p. 610.

NEW CARROLLTON —See District Of Columbia p. 494.

NEW MARKET pop. 427

——— WHERE TO DINE ———

MEALEY'S RESTAURANT   **Lunch:** $8-$18   **Dinner:** $12-$26   **Phone:** 301/865-5488

American   **Location:** I-70, exit 62, 0.3 mi n on SR 75, then 0.7 mi w on SR 144; in historic district. 8 Main St 21774. **Hours:** 3 pm-9 pm, Fri & Sat 11:30-2 & 3-9 pm, Sun noon-8 pm; Sunday brunch 10 am-2 pm. Closed: 7/4, 12/24, 12/25; also Mon. **Reservations:** suggested. **Features:** Prime rib is the specialty, but the menu also lists many fish entrees and homemade soup and dessert. The cozy setting, with areas of the building dating back to 1793, also is the site of a Sunday brunch featuring grilled trout and pork tenderloin. Casual dress; cocktails. **Parking:** on-site. **Cards:** AX, DS, MC, VI. **Historic**

MORGAN'S AMERICAN GRILL   **Lunch:** $7-$16   **Dinner:** $10-$25   **Phone:** 301/865-8100

American   **Location:** I-70, exit 62, just n. 11717 Old National Pike 21774. **Hours:** 11 am-10 pm. Closed: 12/25. **Features:** The grill combines a sleek, contemporary dining environment with a well-balanced menu of seafood, beef, chicken and pork. Casual dress; cocktails. **Parking:** on-site. **Cards:** AX, CB, DC, DS, JC, MC, VI.

NORTH EAST pop. 2,733

-------- WHERE TO STAY --------

CRYSTAL INN

Small-scale Hotel

Book at aaa.com

	1P: $79-$109	2P: $79-$109	XP: $10	F18
5/1-10/31 [ECP]	1P: $79-$109	2P: $79-$109	XP: $10	F18
3/1-4/30 & 11/1-2/28 [ECP]	1P: $69-$99	2P: $69-$99	XP: $10	F18

Phone: (410)287-7100

Location: I-95, exit 100, 0.3 mi se on SR 272. 1 Center Dr 21901. Fax: 410/287-7109. **Facility:** 92 units. 91 one-bedroom standard units, some with whirlpools. 1 one-bedroom suite ($159-$199). 2 stories, interior corridors. **Bath:** combo or shower only. **Parking:** on-site. **Terms:** package plans. **Amenities:** video library, voice mail, irons, hair dryers. **Pool(s):** small heated indoor. **Leisure Activities:** whirlpool, limited exercise equipment. **Guest Services:** coin laundry. **Business Services:** meeting rooms, fax (fee). **Cards:** AX, DC, DS, MC, VI. *(See color ad below)*

SOME UNITS
(ASK) (S) (11+) (&) (⊘) (≈) (VCR) (DATA PORT) (🛏) (🖥) (🗄) / (✕) /

HOLIDAY INN EXPRESS HOTEL & SUITES

Small-scale Hotel

Book at aaa.com

| 3/1-9/30 [ECP] | 1P: $110-$130 |
| 10/1-2/28 [ECP] | 1P: $99-$130 |

Phone: 410/287-0008

Location: I-95, exit 100 southbound, right on SR 272; exit 100A northbound, just e on SR 272. 101 Hotel Plaza 21901. Fax: 410/287-7722. **Facility:** 71 one-bedroom standard units, some with whirlpools. 4 stories, interior corridors. **Bath:** combo or shower only. **Parking:** on-site. **Terms:** package plans. **Amenities:** high-speed Internet, voice mail, irons, hair dryers. **Pool(s):** outdoor. **Leisure Activities:** whirlpool, exercise room. **Guest Services:** valet laundry. **Business Services:** meeting rooms, business center. **Cards:** AX, DC, DS, MC, VI.

SOME UNITS
(ASK) (S) (&) (≈) (🎥) (DATA PORT) (🖥) / (✕) (🛏) (🗄) /

-------- WHERE TO DINE --------

WOODY'S CRAB HOUSE

Seafood
MC, VI.

Lunch: $5-$10   **Dinner:** $12-$30   **Phone:** 410/287-3541

Location: I-95, exit 100, 2 mi e on SR 272. 29 S Main St 21901. **Hours:** 11:30 am-9 pm, Fri & Sat-10 pm, Sun-8 pm; closing hours vary seasonally. Closed major holidays. **Features:** The laid-back restaurant is on Main St. in the historic downtown of North East. The dining room has all the accouterments of a traditional crab house: brown paper covers the tables, a roll of paper towels serves as a centerpiece and servings of peanuts ready to have their shells tossed on the floor. Besides crab, the restaurants offers shrimp, Alaskan snow crab, and chicken and beef dishes. Casual dress; cocktails. **Parking:** street. **Cards:** AX, CB, DC, DS,

(🍽) (✕)

OAKLAND pop. 2,000

-------- WHERE TO STAY --------

HALEY FARM B & B SPA AND RETREAT CENTER

Bed & Breakfast

All Year   2P: $160-$225

Phone: 301/387-9050

Location: 4 mi n on SR 219. 16766 Garrett Hwy 21550. Fax: 301/387-9050. **Facility:** This rural B&B offers manicured gardens, a tranquil setting and good views of the surrounding Maryland hills. 10 one-bedroom standard units, some with kitchens and/or whirlpools. 1 story, interior/exterior corridors. **Parking:** on-site. **Terms:** 2 night minimum stay - weekends, age restrictions may apply, 7 day cancellation notice-fee imposed, weekly rates available, package plans. **Amenities:** CD players, irons, hair dryers. *Some:* DVD players. **Leisure Activities:** fishing. *Fee:* massage. **Cards:** AX, DS, MC, VI. **Special Amenities:** free full breakfast and free local telephone calls.

SOME UNITS
(S) (✕) (VCR) (🎥) / (🛏) (🗄) (🖥) /

OCEAN CITY pop. 7,173

―――― **WHERE TO STAY** ――――

ATLANTIC HOUSE BED AND BREAKFAST
Phone: 410/289-2333

▼▼▼ ▼▼▼	7/1-8/15 [BP]	1P: $125-$185	2P: $125-$185	XP: $20
	8/16-11/28 [BP]	1P: $80-$175	2P: $80-$175	XP: $20
Bed & Breakfast	5/27-6/30 [BP]	1P: $110-$155	2P: $110-$155	XP: $20
	3/31-5/26 [BP]	1P: $80-$125	2P: $80-$125	XP: $20

Location: 5th St and Baltimore Ave. 501 N Baltimore Ave 21842. Fax: 410/289-3133. **Facility:** Smoke free premises. 11 units. 10 one-bedroom standard units. 1 two-bedroom suite ($135-$225) with kitchen. 4 stories (no elevator), interior corridors. *Bath:* some shared or private, combo or shower only. **Parking:** on-site. **Terms:** open 3/31-11/28, office hours 8 am-7 pm, 2 night minimum stay - weekends, age restrictions may apply, 30 day cancellation notice-fee imposed, weekly rates available, package plans. **Leisure Activities:** whirlpool. **Business Services:** fax (fee). **Cards:** DS, MC, VI.

SOME UNITS

[ⓘ⁺] [✕] [☎] [🖪] / [🖨] /

ATLANTIC OCEANFRONT INN
Phone: (410)289-6424

(AAA) (SAVE)
▼▼▼

3/11-10/15 | 1P: $39-$273 | 2P: $39-$273 | XP: $12 | F12

Location: 45th St and oceanfront. 4501 Atlantic Ave 21842 (PO Box 519, 21843). Fax: 410/289-8729. **Facility:** 60 units. 51 one- and 9 two-bedroom standard units with efficiencies. 3-5 stories, interior corridors. **Parking:** on-site. **Terms:** open 3/11-10/15, 7 day cancellation notice-fee imposed. **Amenities:** voice mail, safes (fee).

Small-scale Hotel **Pool(s):** outdoor. **Business Services:** fax (fee). **Cards:** AX, DS, MC, VI.

SOME UNITS

[ⓘ⁺] [🏊] [🎣] [DATA PORT] [🖪] [🖨] [🖥] / [✕] /

BAY SAILS INN
Phone: 410/524-5634

(AAA) (SAVE)
▼▼▼ ▼▼▼

7/1-8/28 | 1P: $109-$179 | 2P: $109-$179 | XP: $10 | F16
4/1-6/30 & 8/29-10/24 | 1P: $34-$159 | 2P: $34-$159 | XP: $10 | F16

Location: At 60th St and Coastal Hwy. 102 60th St 21842 (PO Box 3729, 21843). Fax: 410/723-5123. **Facility:** 64 one-bedroom standard units. 5 stories, interior corridors. **Parking:** on-site. **Terms:** open 4/1-10/24, 2 night

Small-scale Hotel minimum stay - seasonal and/or weekends, 3 day cancellation notice, package plans. **Amenities:** voice mail. **Pool(s):** small outdoor. **Business Services:** fax (fee). **Cards:** AX, DS, MC, VI. **Special Amenities:** free local telephone calls. *(See color ad below)*

[ⓘ⁺] [🏊] [✕] [🎣] [DATA PORT] [🖪] [🖨]

BEST WESTERN OCEAN CITY HOTEL & SUITES
Phone: 410/524-3839

(fyi)

5/6-9/4 | 1P: $149-$399 | 2P: $149-$399 | XP: $10 | F
3/1-5/5 & 9/5-11/5 | 1P: $34-$199 | 2P: $34-$199 | XP: $10 | F

Small-scale Hotel Too new to rate, opening scheduled for September 2004. **Location:** 55th St and Coast Hwy. 5501 Coastal Hwy 21842. Fax: 410/524-1619. **Amenities:** 72 units, coffeemakers, microwaves, refrigerators, pool. **Terms:** open 3/1-11/5, 3 day cancellation notice-fee imposed. **Cards:** AX, CB, DC, DS, JC, MC, VI.

BEST WESTERN SEA BAY INN   *Book at aaa.com*
Phone: (410)524-6100

(AAA) (SAVE)
▼▼▼ ▼▼▼

5/20-9/4 | 1P: $129-$429 | 2P: $134-$429 | XP: $15 | F17
3/1-5/19 & 9/5-10/29 | 1P: $29-$189 | 2P: $34-$189 | XP: $10 | F17
10/30-2/28 | 1P: $29-$99 | 2P: $34-$99 | XP: $10 | F17

Location: Jct 60th St and Coastal Hwy. 6007 Coastal Hwy 21842. Fax: 410/524-1619. **Facility:** 92 one-bedroom

Small-scale Hotel standard units. 5 stories, interior corridors. **Parking:** on-site. **Terms:** 2 night minimum stay - seasonal, 3 day cancellation notice-fee imposed, package plans, pets ($50 deposit, $15 extra charge, no pets 4/1-10/31). **Amenities:** voice mail, irons, hair dryers. **Dining:** 6:30 am-2:30 pm, wine/beer only. **Pool(s):** outdoor. **Leisure Activities:** limited exercise equipment. *Fee:* game room. **Guest Services:** valet and coin laundry. **Business Services:** meeting rooms, fax (fee). **Cards:** AX, DC, DS, MC, VI.

SOME UNITS

[S D] [🛏] [ⓘ⁺] [🏊] [🎣] [DATA PORT] [🖪] [🖨] [🖥] / [✕] /
FEE

CAROUSEL RESORT HOTEL & CONDOMINIUMS   *Book at aaa.com*   Phone: 410/524-1000

 All Year   1P: $59-$309
Location: At 117th St and oceanfront. 11700 Coastal Hwy 21842. Fax: 410/524-7766. **Facility:** 336 units. 225 one-bedroom standard units, some with whirlpools. 15 one-, 72 two- and 24 three-bedroom suites, some with kitchens. 22 stories, interior corridors. **Parking:** on-site. **Terms:** check-in 4 pm, 2 night minimum stay - seasonal and/or weekends, 3 day cancellation notice, package plans. **Amenities:** dual phone lines, voice mail, irons, hair dryers. **Dining:** 7 am-10 pm, cocktails. **Pool(s):** heated indoor. **Leisure Activities:** saunas, whirlpool, lighted tennis court, pool table, exercise room. *Fee:* ice skating, ice skates, game room. **Guest Services:** gift shop. **Business Services:** conference facilities, fax (fee). **Cards:** AX, DS, MC, VI. **Special Amenities:** free newspaper.
(See color ad below)

Large-scale Hotel

SOME UNITS

CASTLE IN THE SAND HOTEL   Phone: 410/289-6846

 6/24-8/27   2P: $156-$310   XP: $8   F11
6/4-6/23   2P: $99-$245   XP: $8   F11
8/28-11/15   2P: $49-$245   XP: $8   F11
3/1-6/3   2P: $49-$175   XP: $8   F11
Small-scale Hotel **Location:** 37th and oceanfront. 3701 Atlantic Ave 21842. Fax: 410/289-9446. **Facility:** 180 units. 98 one-bedroom standard units, some with efficiencies. 46 one- and 7 two-bedroom suites with kitchens. 29 cottages. 2-5 stories, interior/exterior corridors. *Bath:* combo or shower only. **Parking:** on-site. **Terms:** open 3/1-11/15, 3 night minimum stay - seasonal, 14 day cancellation notice, weekly rates available. **Amenities:** video library, irons. *Some:* CD players, safes, hair dryers. **Dining:** 7 am-10 pm; to 2 pm 4/1-5/25 & 9/4-10/31, cocktails. **Pool(s):** outdoor. **Leisure Activities:** Fee: game room. **Guest Services:** coin laundry. **Business Services:** meeting rooms, fax (fee). **Cards:** AX, DC, DS, MC, VI.

SOME UNITS

CLARION RESORT FONTAINEBLEAU HOTEL   *Book at aaa.com*   Phone: (410)524-3535

6/3-8/27   1P: $249-$369   2P: $249-$369   XP: $15   F17
8/28-10/22   1P: $219-$249   2P: $219-$249   XP: $15   F17
3/1-6/2   1P: $129-$239   2P: $129-$239   XP: $15   F17
10/23-2/28   1P: $139-$169   2P: $139-$169   XP: $15   F17
Large-scale Hotel **Location:** 101st St and the ocean. 10100 Coastal Hwy 21842. Fax: 410/524-3834. **Facility:** 250 one-bedroom standard units. 15 stories, interior corridors. *Bath:* combo or shower only. **Parking:** on-site. **Terms:** check-in 4 pm, 3 night minimum stay - seasonal, 3 day cancellation notice, weekly rates available, package plans. **Amenities:** dual phone lines, voice mail, safes, irons, hair dryers. **Dining:** Horizons Restaurant & Nightclub, see separate listing, entertainment. **Pool(s):** heated indoor. **Leisure Activities:** steamroom. *Fee:* sauna, whirlpool, beach concessions, eucalyptus room, massage. **Guest Services:** gift shop, valet laundry, area transportation (fee)-within town. *Fee:* tanning facility. **Business Services:** conference facilities, business center. **Cards:** AX, CB, DC, DS, JC, MC, VI. **Special Amenities:** free local telephone calls and free newspaper. *(See color ad p 641)*

SOME UNITS

THE COCONUT MALORIE RESORT
Phone: 410/723-6100

AAA SAVE

	6/20-10/16	2P: $200-$315
	5/16-6/19	2P: $155-$230
	10/17-2/28	2P: $95-$210
	3/1-5/15	2P: $95-$180

Condominium **Location:** 59th St in-the-Bay. 200 59th St 21842. Fax: 410/524-9327. **Facility:** Overlooking the bay, these luxuriously appointed studios and one-bedroom suites feature Caribbean-style decor. 85 units. 33 one-bedroom standard units with efficiencies and whirlpools. 52 one-bedroom suites ($245-$450) with efficiencies and whirlpools. 5 stories, interior corridors. **Parking:** on-site. **Terms:** check-in 4 pm, 2 night minimum stay - seasonal and/or weekends, 3 day cancellation notice-fee imposed, package plans. **Amenities:** voice mail, irons, hair dryers. *Some:* DVD players. **Pool(s):** outdoor. **Leisure Activities:** limited exercise equipment. **Guest Services:** coin laundry. **Business Services:** meeting rooms, fax. **Cards:** AX, DC, MC, VI. **Special Amenities:** free local telephone calls.

SOME UNITS
[icons] / VCR / FEE

COMFORT INN BOARDWALK *Book at aaa.com*
Phone: (410)289-5155

	5/27-9/4	1P: $129-$329	2P: $129-$329	XP: $10	F12
	9/5-11/26	1P: $39-$234	2P: $39-$234	XP: $10	F12
	3/1-5/26	1P: $39-$189	2P: $39-$189	XP: $10	F12
Small-scale Hotel	2/3-2/28	1P: $39-$109	2P: $39-$109	XP: $10	F12

Location: 5th St and The Boardwalk. 507 Atlantic Ave 21842. Fax: 410/289-6547. **Facility:** 84 one-bedroom standard units, some with efficiencies. 5 stories, interior corridors. **Parking:** on-site. **Terms:** open 3/1-11/26 & 2/3-2/28, 3 night minimum stay - seasonal and/or weekends, 7 day cancellation notice. **Amenities:** voice mail, safes (fee). **Pool(s):** small outdoor, small heated indoor. **Business Services:** fax. **Cards:** AX, CB, DC, DS, MC, VI.

SOME UNITS
[icons] ASK SD / [icons]

COMFORT INN GOLD COAST *Book at aaa.com*
Phone: (410)524-3000

AAA SAVE

	5/27-9/4	1P: $74-$295	2P: $74-$295	XP: $10	F
	9/5-11/6	1P: $85-$185	2P: $85-$185	XP: $10	F
	11/7-2/28	1P: $39-$178	2P: $39-$178	XP: $10	F
	3/1-5/15	1P: $45-$159	2P: $45-$159	XP: $10	F

Small-scale Hotel **Location:** 112th St and Coastal Hwy; bayside. Located adjacent to movie theaters and shopping plaza. 11201 Coastal Hwy 21842. Fax: 410/524-8255. **Facility:** 201 one-bedroom standard units, some with whirlpools. 5 stories, interior corridors. **Parking:** on-site. **Terms:** check-in 4 pm, 2 night minimum stay - seasonal and/or weekends, 3 day cancellation notice, package plans. **Amenities:** voice mail, irons, hair dryers. **Pool(s):** heated indoor. **Leisure Activities:** whirlpool, sun deck, playground, exercise room. **Guest Services:** sundries, coin laundry. **Business Services:** meeting rooms, fax (fee). **Cards:** AX, CB, DC, DS, JC, MC, VI. **Special Amenities:** free local telephone calls and free newspaper.

SOME UNITS
[icons] / [icon]

COMFORT SUITES OCEAN CITY *Book at aaa.com* Phone: (410)213-7171

▽▽▽▽
7/1-9/30	1P: $200-$300	XP: $10 · F18
3/1-6/30 & 10/1-2/28	1P: $100-$200	XP: $10 · F18

Small-scale Hotel **Location:** US 50; 0.7 mi w of Ocean City Bridge. 12718 Ocean Gateway 21842. Fax: 410/213-9898. **Facility:** 84 one-bedroom standard units, some with whirlpools. 3 stories, interior corridors. *Bath:* combo or shower only. **Parking:** on-site. **Terms:** 2 night minimum stay - seasonal, cancellation fee imposed, package plans. **Amenities:** high-speed Internet, dual phone lines, voice mail, safes (fee), irons, hair dryers. **Pool(s):** outdoor. **Leisure Activities:** exercise room. *Fee:* game room. **Guest Services:** coin laundry. **Business Services:** *Fee:* PC, fax. **Cards:** AX, CB, DC, DS, JC, MC, VI.

(ASK) (S/D) (↑↓) (&M) (&) (≈) (♥) (DATA PORT) (🖨) (🖥) (💻)

DAYS INN OCEANFRONT *Book at aaa.com* Phone: (410)289-7161

(AAA) (SAVE)
▽▽▽▽ ▽▽
6/24-9/4	1P: $149-$499	2P: $149-$499	XP: $10 · F17
5/21-6/23	1P: $69-$289	2P: $69-$289	XP: $10 · F17
9/5-10/15	1P: $49-$289	2P: $49-$289	XP: $10 · F17
3/1-5/20	1P: $49-$199	2P: $49-$199	XP: $10 · F17

Small-scale Hotel **Location:** 23rd St and oceanfront. 2210 Baltimore Ave 21842. Fax: 410/289-6525. **Facility:** 138 units. 123 one-bedroom standard units, some with efficiencies. 12 one- and 3 three-bedroom suites ($99-$499) with kitchens. 2-3 stories, exterior corridors. *Bath:* combo or shower only. **Parking:** on-site. **Terms:** open 3/1-10/15, 3 night minimum stay - seasonal, 3 day cancellation notice, package plans. **Amenities:** voice mail, irons, hair dryers. *Fee:* video games, safes. **Dining:** 7 am-9 pm; closed 11/2-3/31, cocktails. **Pool(s):** 2 heated outdoor, wading. **Business Services:** meeting rooms, fax. **Cards:** AX, DS, MC, VI. **Special Amenities:** free continental breakfast and free newspaper. *(See color ad p 645)*

SOME UNITS

(S/D) (↑↓) (Y) (≈) (♥) (DATA PORT) (🖨) (🖥) (💻) / (✕) (VCR) /

DUNES MANOR HOTEL Phone: (410)289-1100

(AAA) (SAVE)
▽▽▽▽
5/27-8/27	1P: $129-$279	2P: $129-$279	XP: $10 · F17
8/28-10/22	1P: $69-$259	2P: $69-$259	XP: $10 · F17
3/1-5/26	1P: $49-$180	2P: $49-$180	XP: $10 · F17
10/23-2/28	1P: $45-$119	2P: $45-$119	XP: $10 · F17

Large-scale Hotel **Location:** 28th St and oceanfront. 2800 Baltimore Ave 21842. Fax: 410/289-4905. **Facility:** 170 units. 164 one-bedroom standard units, some with efficiencies. 6 one-bedroom suites ($99-$385) with efficiencies. 11 stories, interior corridors. **Parking:** on-site. **Terms:** 2 night minimum stay - seasonal and/or weekends, 3 day cancellation notice, package plans. **Amenities:** voice mail, irons, hair dryers. **Dining:** 7:30 am-9 pm, Fri & Sat-10 pm; to 10 pm 5/28-10/15, cocktails. **Pool(s):** heated indoor/outdoor. **Leisure Activities:** whirlpool, limited exercise equipment. **Guest Services:** gift shop. **Business Services:** meeting rooms, fax (fee). **Cards:** AX, DS, MC, VI. *(See color ad below)*

SOME UNITS

(↑↓) (Y) (≈) (♥) (DATA PORT) (🖨) (🖥) (💻) / (✕) /

THE DUNES MOTEL Phone: 410/289-4414

(AAA) (SAVE)
▽▽ ▽▽
6/17-8/27	1P: $99-$279	2P: $99-$279	XP: $10 · F17
3/1-6/16	1P: $39-$199	2P: $39-$199	XP: $10 · F17
8/28-10/8	1P: $29-$179	2P: $29-$179	XP: $10 · F17
2/17-2/28	1P: $39-$79	2P: $39-$79	XP: $10 · F17

Motel **Location:** 27th St and oceanfront. 2700 Baltimore Ave 21842 (2800 Baltimore Ave). Fax: 410/289-0891. **Facility:** 111 units. 109 one-bedroom standard units, some with efficiencies. 2 two-bedroom suites ($59-$309) with kitchens. 3-5 stories, exterior corridors. *Bath:* combo or shower only. **Parking:** on-site. **Terms:** open 3/1-10/8 & 2/17-2/28, 2 night minimum stay - seasonal and/or weekends, 3 day cancellation notice. **Amenities:** voice mail. **Pool(s):** outdoor, wading. **Business Services:** fax (fee). **Cards:** AX, DC, DS, MC, VI.

SOME UNITS

(↑↓) (≈) (🖨) / (✕) (🖥) (💻)

ECONO LODGE OCEANBLOCK *Book at aaa.com* Phone: (410)250-1155

(AAA) (SAVE)
▽▽▽ ▽▽
3/18-10/22	1P: $36-$190 2P: $36-$190	XP: $12

Small-scale Hotel **Location:** 145th St and Coastal Hwy. 14502 Coastal Hwy 21842. Fax: 410/250-0012. **Facility:** 88 one-bedroom standard units with efficiencies. 4 stories, interior corridors. **Parking:** on-site. **Terms:** open 3/18-10/22, 7 day cancellation notice. **Amenities:** safes (fee). **Dining:** 7:30 am-2 pm; closed 10/16-4/20, cocktails. **Pool(s):** heated outdoor. **Business Services:** fax (fee). **Cards:** AX, DS, MC, VI.

SOME UNITS

(S/D) (↑↓) (≈) (♥) (🖨) (🖥) (💻) / (✕) (DATA PORT) /

FENWICK INN

AAA SAVE
▽▽▽▽
Small-scale Hotel

All Year
Location: 138th St and Coastal Hwy. 13801 Coastal Hwy 21842. Fax: 410/250-0087. **Facility:** 201 units. 200 one-bedroom standard units. 1 one-bedroom suite ($99-$250). 8 stories, interior corridors. **Parking:** on-site. **Terms:** check-in 4 pm, 2 night minimum stay - weekends, 3 day cancellation notice-fee imposed, weekly rates available, package plans, small pets only ($10 fee 10/1-3/31). **Dining:** 7 am-11 pm; 8 am-10 pm 11/1-3/31, cocktails. **Pool(s):** heated indoor. **Leisure Activities:** whirlpool. *Fee:* game room. **Business Services:** meeting rooms, fax (fee). **Cards:** AX, CB, DC, DS, JC, MC, VI. **Special Amenities:** early check-in/late check-out and free room upgrade (subject to availability with advance reservations).

| | 1P: $49-$229 | 2P: $49-$229 | XP: $10 | F18 |

Phone: 410/250-1100

SOME UNITS

FLAMINGO MOTEL   *Book at aaa.com*

AAA SAVE
▽▽▽▽
Small-scale Hotel

7/1-8/27	1P: $129-$229	2P: $129-$229	XP: $10	F16
8/28-10/17	1P: $39-$219	2P: $39-$219	XP: $10	F16
3/1-6/30	1P: $39-$209	2P: $39-$209	XP: $10	F16

Location: Oceanside at 31st St. 3100 Baltimore Ave 21842. Fax: 410/289-4472. **Facility:** 112 units. 104 one-bedroom standard units, some with efficiencies. 8 one-bedroom suites. 3-5 stories, interior/exterior corridors. **Parking:** on-site. **Terms:** open 3/1-10/17, 3 night minimum stay - seasonal, 3 day cancellation notice, package plans. **Pool(s):** outdoor, heated indoor. **Business Services:** fax (fee). **Cards:** AX, DS, MC, VI. **Special Amenities:** free local telephone calls. *(See color ad below)*

Phone: 410/289-6464

SOME UNITS

HOLIDAY INN EXPRESS HOTEL & SUITES   *Book at aaa.com*

AAA SAVE
▽▽▽▽
Small-scale Hotel

6/3-9/4 [ECP]	1P: $180-$325	2P: $180-$325	XP: $15	F18
9/5-11/3 [ECP]	1P: $70-$190	2P: $70-$190	XP: $15	F18
3/1-6/2 [ECP]	1P: $70-$180	2P: $70-$180	XP: $15	F18
11/4-2/28 [ECP]	1P: $60-$145	2P: $60-$145	XP: $15	F18

Location: Bayside at 127th St. 12601 Coastal Hwy 21842. Fax: 410/250-8900. **Facility:** 122 units. 118 one-bedroom standard units. 4 one-bedroom suites. 5 stories, interior corridors. *Bath:* combo or shower only. **Parking:** on-site. **Terms:** check-in 4 pm, 3 day cancellation notice-fee imposed, package plans. **Amenities:** dual phone lines, voice mail, irons, hair dryers. **Pool(s):** outdoor, small heated indoor. **Leisure Activities:** whirlpool. **Guest Services:** sundries, coin laundry. **Business Services:** fax (fee). **Cards:** AX, CB, DC, DS, JC, MC, VI. **Special Amenities:** free expanded continental breakfast and free local telephone calls.

Phone: (410)250-7800

SOME UNITS

HOLIDAY INN HOTEL & SUITES OCEAN CITY   *Book at aaa.com*

AAA SAVE
▽▽▽▽
Large-scale Hotel

6/2-9/1		2P: $239-$389	XP: $10	F19
9/2-12/1		2P: $109-$349	XP: $10	F19
3/1-6/1		2P: $139-$319	XP: $10	F19
12/2-2/28		2P: $109-$189	XP: $10	F19

Location: 17th St and The Boardwalk. 1701 Atlantic Ave 21842. Fax: 410/289-3381. **Facility:** 210 units. 209 one- and 1 two-bedroom suites with kitchens, some with whirlpools. 13 stories, interior corridors. *Bath:* combo or shower only. **Parking:** on-site. **Terms:** 3 night minimum stay - seasonal and/or weekends, 3 day cancellation notice-fee imposed, weekly rates available. **Amenities:** dual phone lines, voice mail, irons, hair dryers. *Some:* DVD players. **Dining:** The Coral Reef Restaurant, see separate listing. **Pool(s):** outdoor, heated outdoor, heated indoor. **Leisure Activities:** whirlpool, exercise room. *Fee:* game room. **Guest Services:** gift shop, complimentary laundry. **Business Services:** meeting rooms, fax (fee). **Cards:** AX, DS, MC, VI. **Special Amenities:** free newspaper. *(See color ad p 644)*

Phone: 410/289-7263

SOME UNITS

HOLIDAY INN OCEANFRONT

Phone: (410)524-1600

6/11-9/26	1P: $89-$309	2P: $89-$309	XP: $10 F19
4/9-6/10	1P: $84-$239	2P: $84-$239	XP: $10 F19
9/27-2/28	1P: $54-$174	2P: $54-$174	XP: $10 F19
3/1-4/8	1P: $54-$169	2P: $54-$169	XP: $10 F19

Large-scale Hotel Location: 67th St and oceanfront. 6600 Coastal Hwy 21842. Fax: 410/524-1135. **Facility:** 216 one-bedroom standard units with efficiencies. 8 stories, interior corridors. *Bath:* combo or shower only. **Parking:** on-site. **Terms:** 2 night minimum stay - seasonal and/or weekends, 3 day cancellation notice, weekly rates available, package plans. **Amenities:** irons, hair dryers. **Dining:** Reflections, see separate listing. **Pool(s):** outdoor, heated indoor, 2 wading. **Leisure Activities:** saunas, whirlpools, tennis court, recreation programs, pool table, exercise room, shuffleboard. *Fee:* game room. **Guest Services:** complimentary laundry, tanning facility. **Business Services:** conference facilities, fax (fee). **Cards:** AX, DC, DS, MC, VI. **Special Amenities:** free newspaper. *(See color ad below)*

SOME UNITS

OCEANFRONT ON THE BOARDWALK AT 17TH STREET

A beautiful & spacious all-suite oceanfront resort hotel awaits guests with impeccable service and a Key West soul.

CALL TOLL-FREE **866.OC.SUITE**
866.627.8483 410.289.SAND ONLINE RESERVATIONS www.ocsuites.com

OCEAN CITY, MD

OCEANFRONT RESORT

Your place in the sun!

Located Directly on the Ocean

216 Spacious Efficiency Units with Kitchenettes

Private Oceanview Balconies

Gourmet Restaurant

HBO & Disney Channel

Indoor & Outdoor Pools

Poolside Bar & Grill

Sauna, Hot Tub & Jacuzzi

Tanning Bed & Game Room

Tennis Court & Exercise Room

Complimentary Coffee, Tea, Fresh Fruit & Morning Newspaper

Supervised Children's Activities during Summer Months

Oceanfront & 67th Street, Ocean City, MD • 410-524-1600 • 800-837-3588
ONLINE RESERVATIONS www.holidayinnoceanfront.com
FAMILY MEMBERS AGES 19 & UNDER STAY FREE WHEN SHARING ROOM WITH ADULT.

HOWARD JOHNSON OCEANFRONT INN   *Book at aaa.com*   Phone: (410)289-6401

6/24-9/4	1P: $149-$239	2P: $149-$239	XP: $10 F17
5/21-6/23	1P: $79-$179	2P: $79-$179	XP: $10 F17
9/5-10/15	1P: $44-$149	2P: $44-$149	XP: $10 F17
3/1-5/20	1P: $35-$99	2P: $35-$99	XP: $10 F17

(AAA) (SAVE)
◇◇◇ ◇◇◇
Motel

Location: 24th St and The Boardwalk. 2401 Baltimore Ave 21842. Fax: 410/289-2365. **Facility:** 85 units. 84 one-bedroom standard units, some with whirlpools. 1 one-bedroom suite ($99-$279) with whirlpool. 5 stories, exterior corridors. **Parking:** on-site. **Terms:** open 3/1-10/15, 3 night minimum stay - seasonal, 3 day cancellation notice, package plans. **Amenities:** voice mail, safes (fee), irons, hair dryers. **Dining:** 7 am-3 pm; closed 10/2-4/30. **Pool(s):** outdoor. **Leisure Activities:** whirlpool. **Business Services:** meeting rooms, fax (fee). **Cards:** AX, DS, MC, VI. **Special Amenities:** free newspaper. *(See color ad below)*   SOME UNITS

HOWARD JOHNSON OCEANFRONT PLAZA HOTEL   *Book at aaa.com*   Phone: (410)289-7251

6/24-9/4	1P: $199-$299	2P: $199-$299	XP: $10 F17
5/21-6/23	1P: $99-$229	2P: $99-$229	XP: $10 F17
9/5-2/28	1P: $44-$199	2P: $44-$199	XP: $10 F17
3/1-5/20	1P: $44-$159	2P: $44-$159	XP: $10 F17

(AAA) (SAVE)
◇◇◇ ◇◇◇
Small-scale Hotel

Location: 12th St and The Boardwalk. 1109 Atlantic Ave 21842. Fax: 410/289-4901. **Facility:** 90 one-bedroom standard units. 8 stories, interior corridors. *Bath:* combo or shower only. **Parking:** on-site. **Terms:** 3 night minimum stay - seasonal, 3 day cancellation notice, package plans. **Amenities:** voice mail, safes (fee), irons, hair dryers. **Dining:** 7 am-10 pm, cocktails. **Pool(s):** outdoor, heated indoor. **Leisure Activities:** saunas, whirlpool, limited exercise equipment. *Fee:* beach chairs, beach umbrella, boogie boards, bicycles. **Guest Services:** gift shop, valet laundry. **Business Services:** meeting rooms, fax. **Cards:** AX, DS, MC, VI. **Special Amenities:** free continental breakfast and free newspaper. *(See color ad below)*   SOME UNITS

THE LIGHTHOUSE CLUB HOTEL & THE EDGE AT FAGER'S ISLAND   Phone: (410)524-5400

6/10-9/29	1P: $184-$375	2P: $184-$375	XP: $15 F6
9/30-11/10	1P: $144-$375	2P: $144-$375	XP: $15 F6
3/1-6/9 & 11/11-2/28	1P: $79-$359	2P: $79-$359	XP: $15 F6

(AAA) (SAVE)
◇◇◇◇ ◇◇◇◇
Small-scale Hotel

Location: Bayfront. 56th St in-the-Bay 21842 (201 60th St). Fax: 410/524-3928. **Facility:** 35 units. 33 one- and 2 two-bedroom standard units with whirlpools. 3-4 stories (no elevator), interior corridors. **Parking:** on-site. **Terms:** office hours 7 am-11 pm, check-in 4 pm, 2 night minimum stay - seasonal and/or weekends, age restrictions may apply, 3 day cancellation notice, weekly rates available, package plans. **Amenities:** voice mail, irons, hair dryers. *Some:* DVD players, CD players, safes. **Dining:** Fager's Island, see separate listing. **Business Services:** fax (fee). **Cards:** AX, CB, DC, DS, MC, VI. **Special Amenities:** free continental breakfast and free newspaper.   SOME UNITS

MARIGOT BEACH CONDOMINIUMS　　　　　　　　　　　　　　　　　　　Phone: (410)524-3535

6/3-8/27 Wkly	1P: $1400-$3400	2P: $1400-$3400
8/28-10/22 Dly	1P: $219-$349	2P: $219-$349
3/1-6/2 Dly	1P: $159-$309	2P: $159-$309
10/23-2/28 Dly	1P: $169-$289	2P: $169-$289

Condominium　**Location:** 101st St and the ocean. 10100 Coastal Hwy 21842. Fax: 410/524-4907. **Facility:** These one-, two- and three-bedroom oceanfront condominiums all have balconies and washer/dryer units. 71 units. 16 one-, 42 two- and 13 three-bedroom suites with kitchens. 12 stories, interior corridors. **Parking:** on-site. **Terms:** check-in 4 pm, 7 night minimum stay - seasonal, 30 day cancellation notice, weekly rates available, package plans. **Amenities:** dual phone lines, voice mail, safes, irons, hair dryers. **Pool(s):** heated indoor. **Leisure Activities:** whirlpool, steamrooms. *Fee:* game room. **Guest Services:** valet laundry, area transportation (fee)-within town. **Business Services:** fax (fee). **Cards:** AX, CB, DC, DS, JC, MC, VI. *(See color ad below)*

SOME UNITS

PARADISE PLAZA INN　　*Book at aaa.com*　　　　　　　　　　　　　Phone: (410)289-6381

All Year	1P: $39-$329	2P: $39-$329	XP: $10

F18

Small-scale Hotel　**Location:** 9th St and The Boardwalk. Located on oceanfront, in a commercial area. 3 9th St 21842. Fax: 410/289-1303. **Facility:** 88 units. 80 one- and 4 two-bedroom standard units, some with whirlpools. 4 one-bedroom suites ($59-$399), some with whirlpools. 8 stories, interior corridors. *Bath:* combo or shower only. **Parking:** on-site. **Terms:** check-in 4 pm, 2 night minimum stay - seasonal and/or weekends, 3 day cancellation notice. **Amenities:** dual phone lines, voice mail, irons, hair dryers. *Fee:* video games, safes. **Dining:** 8 am-1 & 5-9 pm; closed Mon & Tues 10/1-4/30, cocktails. **Pool(s):** outdoor. **Guest Services:** gift shop, coin laundry. **Business Services:** meeting rooms, fax (fee). **Cards:** AX, DS, MC, VI. **Special Amenities:** free newspaper and free room upgrade (subject to availability with advance reservations).

SOME UNITS

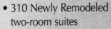

PARK PLACE HOTEL

Phone: 410/289-6440

7/1-9/1	1P: $215-$265	2P: $215-$265	XP: $10 F12
3/1-6/30	1P: $49-$229	2P: $49-$229	XP: $10 F12
9/2-11/27	1P: $49-$189	2P: $49-$189	XP: $10 F12
2/10-2/28	1P: $49-$129	2P: $49-$129	XP: $10 F12

Small-scale Hotel

Location: Between 2nd and 3rd sts. Located on The Boardwalk. 208 N Baltimore Ave 21842 (PO Box 370, 21843). Fax: 410/289-3389. **Facility:** 89 one-bedroom standard units, some with whirlpools. 6 stories, interior corridors. *Bath:* combo or shower only. **Parking:** on-site. **Terms:** open 3/1-11/27 & 2/10-2/28, 3 night minimum stay - seasonal, 5 day cancellation notice-fee imposed. **Amenities:** high-speed Internet (fee), voice mail, safes, irons, hair dryers. *Some:* DVD players (fee). **Pool(s):** heated outdoor. **Leisure Activities:** Fee: game room. **Business Services:** meeting rooms, fax (fee). **Cards:** AX, DC, DS, MC, VI. *(See color ad p 646)*

SOME UNITS

PRINCESS BAYSIDE BEACH HOTEL GOLF CENTER

Phone: 410/723-2900

6/10-9/4	1P: $149-$289	2P: $149-$289	XP: $15 F12
3/1-6/9	1P: $59-$189	2P: $59-$189	XP: $15 F12
9/5-10/28	1P: $59-$179	2P: $59-$179	XP: $15 F12
10/29-2/28	1P: $49-$89	2P: $49-$89	XP: $15 F12

Small-scale Hotel

Location: 48th St and Coastal Hwy. 4801 Coastal Hwy 21842. Fax: 410/723-0207. **Facility:** 194 one-bedroom standard units, some with efficiencies and/or whirlpools. 5 stories, interior corridors. **Parking:** on-site. **Terms:** check-in 4 pm, 7 day cancellation notice, package plans. **Amenities:** safes (fee), hair dryers. **Pool(s):** heated outdoor, heated indoor. **Leisure Activities:** Fee: windsurfing. **Guest Services:** coin laundry. **Business Services:** meeting rooms, fax (fee). **Cards:** AX, CB, DC, DS, MC, VI.

SOME UNITS

PRINCESS ROYALE OCEANFRONT HOTEL & CONFERENCE CENTER

Book at aaa.com

Phone: 410/524-7777

6/10-9/4	1P: $139-$319	2P: $139-$319	XP: $15 F12
3/1-6/9 & 9/5-10/28	1P: $79-$199	2P: $79-$199	XP: $15 F12
10/29-2/28	1P: $49-$149	2P: $49-$149	XP: $15 F12

Large-scale Hotel

Location: 91st St and oceanfront. 9100 Coastal Hwy 21842. Fax: 410/524-7787. **Facility:** 336 units. 309 one-, 23 two- and 4 three-bedroom suites ($139-$309) with kitchens, some with whirlpools. 5-10 stories, interior corridors. **Parking:** on-site. **Terms:** check-in 4 pm, 7 day cancellation notice, package plans. **Amenities:** irons, hair dryers. *Fee:* high-speed Internet, safes. **Dining:** 7 am-11 pm, cocktails. **Pool(s):** heated indoor. **Leisure Activities:** saunas, whirlpools, 2 lighted tennis courts, exercise room, volleyball. *Fee:* miniature golf, tennis equipment, massage, game room. **Guest Services:** gift shop, coin laundry. *Fee:* beauty salon. **Business Services:** conference facilities, fax (fee). **Cards:** AX, CB, DC, DS, MC, VI. *(See color ad p 647)*

SOME UNITS

QUALITY INN BEACHFRONT

Book at aaa.com

Phone: (410)289-1234

6/10-9/5	1P: $160-$280	2P: $160-$280	XP: $5
5/20-6/9	1P: $85-$240	2P: $85-$240	XP: $5
9/6-2/28	1P: $49-$237	2P: $49-$239	XP: $5
3/1-5/19	1P: $49-$185	2P: $49-$185	XP: $5

Small-scale Hotel **Location:** 33rd St and oceanfront. 3301 Atlantic Ave 21842 (PO Box 910, 21843). Fax: 410/289-0123. **Facility:** 109 units. 99 one-bedroom standard units, some with efficiencies and/or whirlpools. 10 one-bedroom suites ($99-$405) with efficiencies, some with whirlpools. 8 stories, interior/exterior corridors. **Parking:** on-site. **Terms:** 3 night minimum stay - seasonal and/or weekends, 14 day cancellation notice, weekly rates available, package plans. **Amenities:** video library (fee), irons, hair dryers. **Dining:** 7 am-1 pm. **Pool(s):** 2 heated outdoor, heated indoor. **Leisure Activities:** sauna, whirlpool, exercise room. *Fee:* game room. **Guest Services:** gift shop, coin laundry, tanning facility. **Business Services:** fax (fee). **Cards:** AX, DC, DS, MC, VI. *(See color ad p 649)*

SOME UNITS

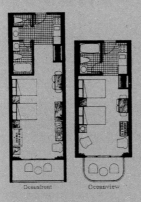

Oceanfront   Oceanview

- 2 Person Whirlpools In Tower Oceanfront Rooms
- New Oceanfront Pool
- Restaurant
- Parking Garage
- Heated Indoor Pool
- Outdoor Pool and Wading Pool For Children
- Fountain and Gift Shop
- Game Room
- Exercise Room
- Surf Fishing
- All Efficiencies Have Ice Maker, Microwave, Apt. Size Range and Large Refrigerators
- Most Rooms with Dividers
- Separate Bedroom Suites w/Sleeping For Up To Six Persons
- Private Whirlpool In Most Rooms

- Oceanview Units
- Color Remote TV
- Wide Guarded Beach
- Reduced Off-Season Rates
- 16 Championship Golf Courses Nearby
- Guest Laundry

One Bedroom Suite

All New Suites Include Two Person Hot Tubs

OPEN YEAR ROUND

Quality Inn Beachfront Hotel

Oceanfront at 33rd St. • P.O. Box 910 • Ocean City, MD 21843

www.qualityinnbeachfront.com • quality@beachin.net

For Reservations Call (410) 289-1234

QUALITY INN-OCEANFRONT 54TH STREET

Book at aaa.com

AAA SAVE ◈◈ ◈◈   Small-scale Hotel

Phone: (410)524-7200

5/20-8/29	1P: $119-$274	2P: $119-$274	XP: $7	F12
8/30-10/4	1P: $84-$209	2P: $84-$209	XP: $7	F12
3/1-5/19	1P: $65-$184	2P: $65-$184	XP: $7	F12
10/5-2/28	1P: $49-$129	2P: $49-$129	XP: $7	F12

Location: At 54th St. 5400 Coastal Hwy 21842. Fax: 410/723-0018. **Facility:** 130 one-bedroom standard units, some with efficiencies. 3-5 stories, interior/exterior corridors. *Bath:* combo or shower only. **Parking:** on-site. **Terms:** 3 night minimum stay - seasonal and/or weekends, 3 day cancellation notice-fee imposed, weekly rates available, package plans. **Amenities:** hair dryers. *Some:* irons. **Dining:** 8 am-9:30 pm; to 11 pm 5/25-9/30, cocktails. **Pool(s):** outdoor, heated indoor, 2 wading. **Leisure Activities:** saunas, whirlpools, tennis court, children's play area, playground, limited exercise equipment. *Fee:* game room. **Amenities:** complimentary laundry, tanning facility. **Business Services:** fax (fee). **Cards:** AX, CB, DC, DS, JC, MC, VI. **Special Amenities:** free local telephone calls and free newspaper.
(See color ad below)

SOME UNITS

RAMADA LIMITED CONVENTION CENTER

Book at aaa.com

◈◈ ◈◈ ◈◈   Small-scale Hotel

Phone: (410)289-6488

5/20-9/3	1P: $79-$229	2P: $79-$229	XP: $15	F17
3/1-5/19	1P: $49-$135	2P: $49-$135	XP: $15	F17
9/4-2/28	1P: $39-$135	2P: $39-$135	XP: $15	F17

Location: 42nd and Coastal Hwy. 4201 Coastal Hwy 21842. Fax: 410/289-1617. **Facility:** 167 units. 160 one-bedroom standard units, some with whirlpools. 7 one-bedroom suites ($69-$229). 7 stories, interior corridors. *Bath:* combo or shower only. **Parking:** on-site. **Terms:** check-in 4 pm, 2 night minimum stay - seasonal and/or weekends, 3 day cancellation notice-fee imposed. **Amenities:** voice mail, irons, hair dryers. *Fee:* video games, safes. **Pool(s):** heated indoor. **Leisure Activities:** *Fee:* game room. **Guest Services:** sundries, coin laundry. **Business Services:** meeting rooms, fax (fee). **Cards:** AX, DC, DS, MC, VI.

SOME UNITS
FEE

STOWAWAY GRAND HOTEL

Book at aaa.com

AAA SAVE ◈◈ ◈◈   Large-scale Hotel

Phone: (410)289-6191

6/10-9/4	1P: $229-$319	2P: $229-$319	XP: $10	F16
4/22-6/9	1P: $109-$199	2P: $109-$199	XP: $10	F16
9/5-2/28	1P: $49-$139	2P: $49-$139	XP: $10	F16
3/1-4/21	1P: $29-$139	2P: $29-$139	XP: $10	F16

Location: 21st St and The Boardwalk. 2100 Baltimore Ave 21842. Fax: 410/289-7591. **Facility:** 251 units. 249 one- and 2 two-bedroom standard units, some with whirlpools. 12 stories, interior corridors. *Bath:* combo or shower only. **Parking:** on-site. **Terms:** check-in 4 pm, 2 night minimum stay - seasonal and/or weekends, 3 day cancellation notice, package plans. **Amenities:** voice mail, irons, hair dryers. **Dining:** 2 restaurants, 7 am-10 pm, cocktails. **Pool(s):** outdoor, heated indoor. **Leisure Activities:** saunas, pool table, exercise room. *Fee:* massage, game room. **Guest Services:** gift shop, coin laundry, beauty salon. **Business Services:** meeting rooms, fax (fee). **Cards:** AX, DC, DS, MC, VI. **Special Amenities:** free newspaper and free room upgrade (subject to availability with advance reservations).

SOME UNITS

──────── **WHERE TO DINE** ────────

ADOLFO'S

◈◈ ◈◈   Italian

Dinner: $7-$24   **Phone:** 410/289-4001

Location: 0.5 mi s of US 50; at the inlet. 806 S Baltimore Ave 21842. **Hours:** 5 pm-close. Closed: 12/15-12/30 & Sun-Tues 10/1-5/1. **Reservations:** suggested. **Features:** The intimate dining room and enclosed porch provide a comfortable setting to dine on the plentiful Italian fare. The menu offers a nice selection of pasta, meat, seafood and chicken dishes. Casual dress; cocktails. **Parking:** on-site. **Cards:** DS, MC, VI.

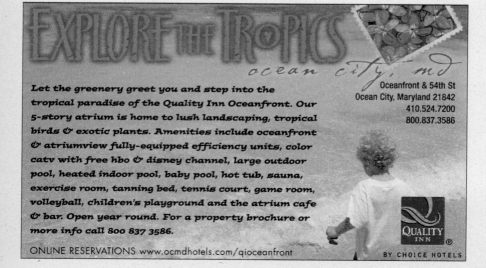

BJ'S ON THE WATER
◆◆◆ ◆◆◆
American

Lunch: $5-$12   **Dinner:** $15-$21   **Phone:** 410/524-7575
Location: 75th St and the Bay. 115 75th St 21842. **Hours:** 11 am-2 am. Closed: 12/24, 12/25. **Reservations:** not accepted. **Features:** Located on the bay, the restaurant has been in operation for more than 20 years. The atmosphere is casual and lively, with a saloon-like bar and an enclosed porch with hanging plants and a bay view. The food ranges from soups and salads to overstuffed sandwiches and complete entrees. The 1 pm duck feeding attracts an abundance of wild ducks. Casual dress; cocktails. **Parking:** on-site. **Cards:** AX, CB, DC, DS, MC, VI.

CAPTAIN'S GALLEY II
◆◆◆ ◆◆◆
Seafood

Lunch: $5-$10   **Dinner:** $12-$26   **Phone:** 410/213-2525
Location: In West Ocean City; 0.7 mi s on Golf Course Rd from jct US 50. 12817 Harbor Rd 21842. **Hours:** Open 3/15-1/2; 11:30 am-10 pm. Closed: 11/24, 12/25. **Reservations:** not accepted. **Features:** Set on the harbor, this casual restaurant has been a favorite of locals for years. They are known for their fresh seafood. The crab cakes, one of the house specialties, is all lump crabmeat, definitely worth checking out. A comfortable atmosphere for families. Casual dress; cocktails. **Parking:** on-site. **Cards:** AX, DC, DS, MC, VI.

COINS PUB & RESTAURANT
◆
American

Lunch: $4-$12   **Dinner:** $10-$24   **Phone:** 410/289-3100
Location: In 28th St Plaza. 2820 Coastal Hwy 21842. **Hours:** 11 am-11 pm. Closed: 12/25. **Features:** Popular with the locals, the little, pub-like restaurant serves consistent American fare. The house specialty is the crab cake. Casual dress; cocktails. **Parking:** on-site. **Cards:** DS, MC, VI.

THE CORAL REEF RESTAURANT
AAA
◆◆◆◆
American

    Dinner: $17-$29   **Phone:** 410/289-6388
Location: 17th St and The Boardwalk; in Holiday Inn Hotel & Suites Ocean City. 1701 Atlantic Ave 21842. **Hours:** 5 pm-9 pm, Fri-10 pm, Sat 7 am-11 & 5-10 pm, Sun 7 am-11 & 5-9 pm. **Reservations:** accepted. **Features:** Off the lobby, just beyond the indoor pool and cafe, you'll find an intimate, upscale dining room with an island plantation ambiance. The menu tempts you with a variety of flavors. Carribbean dishes, such as Island Barbecued Pork Chops, Citrus Chicken Penne and Jamaican Grouper, treat you to the spices of the islands. Chicken Chesapeake, Soft Shell Crabs and Fried Chesapeake Oysters give you the flavor of the Eastern Shore. They use only Certified Angus Beef and Certified Blue Crab. Casual dress; cocktails. **Parking:** on-site. **Cards:** AX, DC, DS, MC, VI.

FAGER'S ISLAND
AAA
◆◆◆
American

Lunch: $7-$13   **Dinner:** $18-$29   **Phone:** 410/524-5500
Location: Bayfront; at The Lighthouse Club Hotel & The Edge at Fager's Island. 60th St in-the-Bay 21842. **Hours:** 11 am-2 am. Closed: 12/25; also for dinner 12/24. **Reservations:** suggested, for dinner. **Features:** As the sun sets, the strains of Tchaikovsky's 1812 Overture rise, just as they have every night since the mid-1970s. The busy, bayfront restaurant serves casual meals all day and shifts to a more fine-dining mode from 5 pm to 10 pm. An award-winning wine selection and exotic microbrewed beers enhance creative menu selections. Entertainment is nightly in season and on weekends in the off-season. Casual dress; cocktails; entertainment. **Parking:** on-site. **Cards:** AX, CB, DC, DS, MC, VI.

FRESCO'S
◆◆◆
American
MC, VI.

    Dinner: $15-$30   **Phone:** 410/524-8202
Location: Jct 83rd St and Coastal Hwy. 8203 Coastal Hwy 21842. **Hours:** 4:30 pm-10 pm, Fri & Sat-11 pm. Closed: 12/24, 12/25. **Reservations:** suggested. **Features:** The casually upscale dining room overlooks the bay. Chef Pino Tomasello's American cuisine is prepared with Mediterranean influences. Selections range from pasta and seafood to beef and chicken. Casual dress; cocktails. **Parking:** on-site. **Cards:** AX, DC, DS,

GALAXY BAR & GRILLE
◆◆◆
American
cocktails.

Lunch: $7-$12   **Dinner:** $16-$36   **Phone:** 410/723-6762
Location: 66th St and Coastal Hwy. 6601 Coastal Hwy 21842. **Hours:** 11:30 am-10 pm. Closed: 11/24, 12/24-12/26; also Super Bowl Sun. **Reservations:** suggested. **Features:** Diners will discover a seasonally changing menu of contemporary American cuisine, creatively prepared using fresh ingredients. The atmosphere is modern and stylish with an open kitchen. Service is professional and attentive. Casual dress; cocktails. **Parking:** on-site. **Cards:** AX, DC, DS, MC, VI.

HARRISON'S HARBOR WATCH
AAA
◆◆◆ ◆◆
Seafood

    Dinner: $12-$27   **Phone:** 410/289-5121
Location: At Inlet Village; south end of boardwalk; 0.5 mi s of US 50 bridge. 806 S Boardwalk & The Inlet 21842. **Hours:** 5 pm-10 pm; from 4:30 pm 7/1-9/3. Closed: Sun-Thurs 11/23-4/15. **Reservations:** suggested. **Features:** Seafood rules at the laid-back restaurant, which affords a great view of the inlet. Not only are there daily specials and an extensive selection of fresh fish, but the menu also includes steak and pasta offerings to appeal to landlubbers. The raw bar is open from 11:30 am to 10 pm. An elevator provides access to the second floor. Casual dress; cocktails. **Parking:** on-site (fee). **Cards:** AX, DS, MC, VI.

THE HOBBIT RESTAURANT
◆◆◆
Continental

Lunch: $9-$14   **Dinner:** $19-$30   **Phone:** 410/524-8100
Location: On the bay. 101 81st St 21842. **Hours:** 11 am-midnight. Closed: 12/23-12/26. **Reservations:** suggested. **Features:** The bayside favorite offers casual dining for lunch and dinner, as well as fine dining in a traditional, elegant dining room overlooking the bay. The decor, including hand-carved lamps on each table, reflects J.R.R. Tolkien novels. Food is consistently good, and reliable servers are friendly and professional. Casual dress; cocktails. **Parking:** on-site. **Cards:** AX, DS, MC, VI.

HORIZONS RESTAURANT & NIGHTCLUB *Menu on aaa.com*
AAA
◆◆◆
American

Lunch: $7-$11   **Dinner:** $16-$35   **Phone:** 410/524-3535
Location: 101st St and the ocean; in Clarion Resort Fontainebleau Hotel. 10100 Coastal Hwy 21842. **Hours:** 6:30 am-2 am, 5-10 pm. **Reservations:** suggested, in season. **Features:** This oceanfront restaurant offers a nice selection of seafood, meats and pasta dishes. An award winning wine list is provided to compliment your meal. After dinner service is completed live entertainment enjoy live entertainment. Casual dress; cocktails; entertainment. **Parking:** on-site. **Cards:** AX, DS, MC, VI.

J/R'S THE PLACE FOR RIBS

American

Dinner: $11-$23   **Phone:** 410/250-3100

Location: 131st St and Coastal Hwy. 13101 Coastal Hwy 21842. **Hours:** Open 3/1-12/31 & 2/14-2/28; 4 pm-10:30 pm, Sun from 3 pm; Thurs-Sun to 9:30 pm 2/14-3/30. Closed: 11/24, 12/25; also Mon-Wed 2/14-3/30. **Reservations:** not accepted. **Features:** Be sure to try the excellent onion loaf with any one of the featured menu items, including barbecue baby back ribs, chicken, prime rib, steak and fresh seafood. The atmosphere is casual and family-oriented with a Western decor; the service is attentive. Casual dress; cocktails. **Parking:** on-site. **Cards:** AX, DS, MC, VI.

J/R'S THE PLACE FOR RIBS

American

Dinner: $11-$23   **Phone:** 410/524-7427

Location: 62nd St and Coastal Hwy. 6104 Coastal Hwy 21842. **Hours:** Open 3/1-1/15 & 1/31-2/28; 4 pm-10:30 pm, Sun from 3 pm. Closed: 11/24, 12/25; also Mon-Thurs 1/14-2/28; Mon-Wed 2/28-3/31 & 10/16-11/30. **Features:** A favorite choice at the popular, energetic eatery is the barbecue baby back ribs. Also on the menu are chicken, prime rib, steak and seafood dishes and an excellent onion loaf. The atmosphere is family-oriented. Smoking is permitted in the lounge. Casual dress; cocktails. **Parking:** on-site. **Cards:** AX, DS, MC, VI.

LA HACIENDA

 Menu on aaa.com

Mexican

Dinner: $7-$17   **Phone:** 410/524-8080

Location: At 81st St. 8003 Coastal Hwy 21842. **Hours:** 5 pm-9:30 pm. Closed: 11/24, 12/25; also Mon & Tues 12/1-2/28. **Reservations:** not accepted. **Features:** In the mood for something from south of the border. This casual Mexican restaurant is popular with locals and tourists alike. The food is good and the service is friendly and efficient. Casual dress; cocktails. **Parking:** on-site. **Cards:** AX, MC, VI.

LIGHTHOUSE SOUND RESTAURANT

American

Lunch: $7-$14   **Dinner:** $9-$29   **Phone:** 410/352-5250

Location: Just across SR 90 bridge from Ocean City; 1.3 mi n of jct SR 90; at Lighthouse Sound Clubhouse. 12723 St. Martin's Neck Rd 21813. **Hours:** 7 am-9 pm, Fri & Sat-10 pm; to 10 pm, Fri & Sat-11 pm 5/31-9/6. Closed: 12/25. **Reservations:** suggested. **Features:** The dining room at The Links at Lighthouse Sound overlooks Assawoman Bay and off in the distance is the skyline of Ocean City. Suitable for any occasion, the dining room is comfortable and casual. The menu offers creatively prepared American dishes using fresh ingredients. Casual dress; cocktails. **Parking:** on-site. **Cards:** AX, DC, DS, MC, VI.

LITTLE ITALY ON THE SHORE

Italian

Dinner: $9-$25   **Phone:** 410/289-0505

Location: 2 blks s of jct US 50. 215 S Baltimore Ave 21842. **Hours:** Open 5/1-12/15; 5 pm-close. Closed: 11/24. **Reservations:** suggested. **Features:** At the southern end of the city, the chef-owned Italian restaurant presents a menu that includes pasta, meat and seafood dishes. The atmosphere is casual and comfortable. Casual dress; cocktails. **Parking:** street. **Cards:** AX, CB, DC, DS, MC, VI.

MARINA DECK RESTAURANT

Steak House

Lunch: $5-$12   **Dinner:** $10-$30   **Phone:** 410/289-4411

Location: Just s of US 50. 306 Dorchester St 21842. **Hours:** Open 4/1-11/15; 7:30 am-1 am. **Reservations:** accepted. **Features:** Established in the late 1970s, the relaxed bayfront restaurant treats guests to beautiful views of the sunset from the dining room and the enclosed terrace. Casual dress; cocktails. **Parking:** on-site. **Cards:** AX, MC, VI.

MARIO'S

American

Dinner: $9-$30   **Phone:** 410/289-9445

Location: 22nd St and Philadelphia Ave. 2204 Philadelphia Ave 21842. **Hours:** Open 4/1-12/4; 5 pm-10 pm. Closed: 11/24, 12/25; also Mon-Wed 4/1-5/28 & 10/1-12/4. **Reservations:** accepted. **Features:** Established in the mid-1950s, the relaxed restaurant is known for Certified Angus beef and seafood, as well as an extensive selection of Italian dishes. Hand-painted wall murals and soft music set a relaxed atmosphere. Casual dress; cocktails. **Parking:** on-site. **Cards:** AX, MC, VI.

MARLIN MOON GRILLE

American

Dinner: $17-$30   **Phone:** 410/213-1618

Location: On US 50, 0.5 mi w of the US 50 Bridge; in West Ocean City; in Francis Scott Key Hotel. 12806 Ocean Gateway 21842. **Hours:** 5 pm-10 pm; hours may vary seasonally. Closed: 1/9-2/2, Mon & Tues. **Reservations:** not accepted. **Features:** Off the lobby of a hotel, the dining room carries off a nautical atmosphere in a comfortable, casual fine-dining setting. The menu lists a nice selection of meat and fish dishes. Casual dress; cocktails. **Parking:** on-site. **Cards:** AX, DS, MC, VI.

NEBULA

American

Dinner: $60-$100   **Phone:** 410/524-8090

Location: 94th St and Coastal Hwy; in shopping strip. 9213 Coastal Hwy 21842. **Hours:** 5 pm-10 pm. Closed: 11/24, 12/25. **Features:** The restaurant offers something other than the traditional Ocean City dining experience. The setting is edgy, yet simplistic, intimate and chic. Guests can choose from a three-course meal or five- or seven-course tasting menus. A la carte items can be ordered from the bar. The seasonally changing menu is driven by the availability of the freshest ingredients. Dressy casual; cocktails. **Parking:** on-site. **Cards:** AX, DC, DS, MC, VI.

OCEAN CLUB RESTAURANT & LOUNGE

American

Lunch: $5-$10   **Dinner:** $15-$25   **Phone:** 410/524-7500

Location: 49th St and oceanfront; in Gateway Resort. 49th St and Coastal Hwy 21842. **Hours:** Open 3/1-1/3 & 1/29-2/28; 11 am-11 pm. Closed: 12/25; also Mon & Tues 11/1-1/3, Tues & Wed 1/29-4/1, for lunch Mon-Thurs 11/1-4/1. **Reservations:** suggested. **Features:** Consistently good food and friendly service are trademarks of this casual, oceanfront restaurant. Outdoor deck seating is popular when the weather is nice. Live entertainment—in the afternoons and nightly in season, and Thursday through Sunday in the off season—encourages diners to dance. Casual dress; cocktails. **Parking:** on-site. **Cards:** AX, DS, MC, VI.

PHILLIPS BY THE SEA
Seafood

Lunch: $4-$10   **Dinner:** $11-$35   **Phone:** 410/289-9121
Location: 13th St and The Boardwalk. 1301 Atlantic Ave 21842. **Hours:** Open 3/1-12/21; 8 am-11 & 5-10 pm, Sat & Sun 8 am-1 & 5-10 pm. **Reservations:** accepted. **Features:** The boardwalk restaurant's Old World atmosphere is evidenced by the semiformal Victorian dining room and charming piano bar. The evening menu features fresh seafood specials, including stuffed flounder. For breakfast, try the flavorful malt waffles.
Casual dress; cocktails; entertainment. **Parking:** on-site. **Cards:** AX, CB, DC, DS, MC, VI.

PHILLIPS CRAB HOUSE
Seafood

Lunch: $6-$12   **Dinner:** $9-$30   **Phone:** 410/289-6821
Location: 21st and Philadelphia Ave. 2004 Philadelphia Ave 21842. **Hours:** Open 4/11-10/31; noon-11 pm; Fri 4 pm-9 pm, Sat & Sun from noon 4/11-5/12; closing hours may vary. Closed: Mon-Thurs 4/11-5/12. **Reservations:** not accepted. **Features:** The crab imperial—jumbo lump crabmeat mixed with mayonnaise and seafood seasoning, baked, then topped with cheddar cheese—is the hands-down favorite at this loud, busy restaurant. A local hot spot since 1957. A seafood buffet is offered nightly, in season. Casual dress; cocktails. **Parking:** on-site. **Cards:** AX, DC, DS, MC, VI.

PHILLIPS SEAFOOD HOUSE
Seafood

Dinner: $10-$29   **Phone:** 410/250-1200
Location: 141st St and Coastal Hwy. 14101 Coastal Hwy 21842. **Hours:** Open 3/1-11/30 & 2/18-2/28; 4 pm-10 pm; closing hours may vary. Closed: Mon & Tues 2/18-5/31, also Wed & Thurs 2/18-4/15. **Features:** Popular with diners of all ages, you'll love the Eastern-shore ambience created by the rustic wood paneling and brick walls, carousel horses, stained-glass panels and Tiffany-style lights. Both a seafood buffet and a la carte menu are offered. Casual dress; cocktails; entertainment. **Parking:** on-site. **Cards:** AX, DC, DS, MC, VI.

REFLECTIONS
American

Dinner: $16-$30   **Phone:** 410/524-5252
Location: 67th St and oceanfront; in Holiday Inn Oceanfront. 6600 Coastal Hwy 21842. **Hours:** 7 am-11:30 & 5-10 pm. **Reservations:** suggested, for dinner. **Features:** Although its location may seem ordinary, there's little typical about the experience here. Noteworthy features include an attractive, bi-level dining room attended by crisp, attentive servers. Representative of the flavorful, creative dishes are Thai curry shrimp and steak Diane prepared tableside. Casual dress; cocktails. **Parking:** on-site. **Cards:** AX, CB, DC, DS, JC, MC, VI.

RISTORANTE ANTIPASTI
Italian

Dinner: $17-$32   **Phone:** 410/289-4588
Location: 33rd St and Coastal Hwy. 3303 Coastal Hwy 21842. **Hours:** 5 pm-10:30 pm; to 11 pm 6/1-9/30. Closed: 1/1, 11/24, 12/25; also Sun & Mon 10/1-5/30. **Reservations:** suggested, in season. **Features:** Chef/owner DiCarlo has developed a strong local following for such preparations as striped bass baked in kosher rock salt, garlic steak and homemade pasta. The staff is efficient and friendly. Dressy casual; cocktails. **Parking:** on-site. **Cards:** AX, DC, DS, MC, VI.

TEQUILA MOCKINGBIRD MEXICAN BAR & GRILL
Mexican

Lunch: $7-$16   **Dinner:** $7-$16   **Phone:** 410/250-4424
Location: At 130th St. 12919 Coastal Hwy 21842. **Hours:** noon-midnight. Closed: 11/24, 12/25; also Wed & Thurs 11/1-3/31. **Features:** This casual shopping plaza restaurant offers a lively, fun atmosphere. The menu offers traditional Mexican fare with tacos, burritos, enchilada and some specility items. Casual dress; cocktails. **Parking:** on-site. **Cards:** AX, MC, VI.

TUTTI GUSTI
Northern Italian

Dinner: $11-$28   **Phone:** 410/289-3318
Location: 33rd St and Coastal Hwy. 3322 Coastal Hwy 21842. **Hours:** 5 pm-10:30 pm; Fri-Sun only 2/14-5/31; call ahead-hours may vary. **Reservations:** suggested. **Features:** Salmon-painted walls, white tablecloths and candlelit tables set a sophisticated atmosphere in the charming, little restaurant. The menu comprises specialties of the northern region, mostly veal, chicken, seafood and pasta. Pasta is made fresh daily. Saturday night osso buco served over risotto is a favorite choice. Dressy casual; cocktails. **Parking:** on-site. **Cards:** AX, DS, MC, VI.

WINDOWS ON THE BAY
Continental

Dinner: $9-$25   **Phone:** 410/723-3463
Location: 61st St and the Bay. 6103 Seabay Dr 21842. **Hours:** 5 pm-9 pm. Closed: 12/24, 12/25. **Reservations:** suggested. **Features:** Striking sunsets over the bay complement the intimate, comfortable dining experience and contemporary ambience. The menu features seafood, beef, veal, pasta, duck and chicken dishes. Casual dress; cocktails; entertainment. **Parking:** on-site. **Cards:** AX, DC, DS, MC, VI.

The following restaurant has not been evaluated by AAA but is listed for your information only.

SEACRETS BAR & GRILL
[fyi]

Phone: 410/524-4900
Not evaluated. **Location:** 49th St and the Bay. 117 W 49th St 21842. **Features:** The tropical atmosphere, outside dining and bayside location will remind you of a Jamaican beach party. Full lunch and dinner menus are available off season, while only light fare is served in season. A cover charge is in effect after 4 pm in season.

OWINGS MILLS —See Baltimore p. 610.

PASADENA —See Baltimore p. 611.

PERRYVILLE pop. 3,672

-------- WHERE TO STAY --------

RAMADA INN PERRYVILLE   *Book at aaa.com*   **Phone:** (410)642-2866

4/1-2/28 [ECP]	1P: $69-$99	2P: $69-$99	XP: $10	F18
3/1-3/31 [ECP]	1P: $59-$99	2P: $69-$99	XP: $10	F18

Small-scale Hotel **Location:** I-95, exit 93, just e. 61 Heather Ln 21903. Fax: 410/575-6954. **Facility:** 104 one-bedroom standard units. 2 stories (no elevator), exterior corridors. **Parking:** on-site. **Terms:** cancellation fee imposed, [CP] meal plan available, small pets only ($5 extra charge, in smoking units). **Amenities:** voice mail, safes, irons, hair dryers. **Leisure Activities:** limited exercise equipment. **Guest Services:** coin laundry. **Business Services:** meeting rooms, fax (fee). **Cards:** AX, CB, DC, DS, JC, MC, VI. *(See color ad below)*

PIKESVILLE —*See Baltimore p. 611.*

POCOMOKE CITY pop. 4,098

-------- WHERE TO STAY --------

HOLIDAY INN EXPRESS-POCOMOKE   *Book at aaa.com*   **Phone:** 410/957-6444

All Year	1P: $109-$149	2P: $109-$149	XP: $10	F16

Small-scale Hotel **Location:** On SR 756 at jct US 13, 0.8 mi nw on US 13 from jct US 113. 125 Newtowne Blvd 21851. Fax: 410/957-2825. **Facility:** 66 one-bedroom standard units, some with whirlpools. 3 stories, interior corridors. *Bath:* combo or shower only. **Parking:** on-site. **Amenities:** dual phone lines, voice mail, irons, hair dryers. **Pool(s):** heated indoor. **Leisure Activities:** limited exercise equipment. **Guest Services:** coin laundry. **Business Services:** meeting rooms, business center. **Cards:** AX, DC, DS, MC, VI.

POOLESVILLE —*See District Of Columbia p. 494.*

POTOMAC —*See District Of Columbia p. 494.*

PRINCE FREDERICK pop. 1,432

-------- WHERE TO STAY --------

HOLIDAY INN EXPRESS PRINCE FREDERICK   *Book at aaa.com*   **Phone:** (410)535-6800

All Year	1P: $114	2P: $114	XP: $10	F18

Small-scale Hotel **Location:** SR 2/4; center. 355 Merrimac Ct 20678 (PO Box 2669). Fax: 410/535-9668. **Facility:** 70 one-bedroom standard units, some with whirlpools. 3 stories, interior corridors. *Bath:* combo or shower only. **Parking:** on-site. **Amenities:** dual phone lines, voice mail, irons, hair dryers. *Some:* CD players. **Guest Services:** valet and coin laundry. **Business Services:** meeting rooms, fax (fee). **Cards:** AX, CB, DC, DS, MC, VI.

-------- WHERE TO DINE --------

OLD FIELD INN   **Dinner:** $16-$30   **Phone:** 410/535-1054

American **Location:** On SR 765; center. 485 Main St 20678. **Hours:** 5 pm-9 pm, Fri & Sat-9:30 pm, Sun-8 pm. Closed major holidays. **Reservations:** accepted. **Features:** Upon entering the drive that winds between large, manicured lawns to this restored residence, diners are transported to a bygone era. Hand-cut steaks, fresh seafood and juicy prime rib are prepared in a relaxed, comfortable atmosphere. Casual dress; cocktails. **Parking:** on-site. **Cards:** AX, DS, MC, VI.

PRINCESS ANNE pop. 2,313

—— WHERE TO STAY ——

WATERLOO COUNTRY INN   **Phone:** (410)651-0883

Historic Country Inn

5/1-10/31 [BP]	1P: $125-$210	2P: $145-$255	XP: $40 F5
3/1-4/30 & 11/1-11/30 [BP]	1P: $110-$190	2P: $125-$235	XP: $40 F5

Location: 3.3 mi w on SR 362 from jct US 13. Located in a rural area. 28822 Mt. Vernon Rd 21853. **Fax:** 410/651-5592. **Facility:** In a picturesque setting overlooking a tidal pond, this restored 1750 residence has individually decorated guest rooms, four with fireplaces. Smoke free premises. 6 units. 5 one-bedroom standard units, some with whirlpools. 1 one-bedroom suite with whirlpool. 3 stories (no elevator), interior corridors. *Bath:* combo or shower only. **Parking:** on-site. **Terms:** open 3/1-11/30, 2 night minimum stay - seasonal and/or weekends, 7 day cancellation notice-fee imposed, package plans, small pets only (in outside building unit). **Amenities:** hair dryers. **Pool(s):** outdoor. **Leisure Activities:** canoeing, fishing, bicycles. **Business Services:** fax (fee). **Cards:** AX, DS, MC, VI.

SOME UNITS

ROCK HALL pop. 1,396

—— WHERE TO STAY ——

INN AT HUNTINGFIELD CREEK   **Phone:** 410/639-7779

Bed & Breakfast

All Year [BP]	2P: $130-$225	XP: $35 F3

Location: 1.8 mi s on SR 445 from jct SR 20. Located in a quiet rural area. 4928 Eastern Neck Rd 21661. **Fax:** 410/639-2924. **Facility:** Attractively decorated guest rooms and a cottage unit with a gas fireplace make up the converted farmhouse, part of a 70-acre working farm. Smoke free premises. 6 one-bedroom standard units. 2 stories (no elevator), interior/exterior corridors. *Bath:* combo, shower or tub only. **Parking:** on-site. **Terms:** office hours 7 am-9 pm, 2 night minimum stay - seasonal and/or weekends, 5 day cancellation notice, pets (in cottage). **Amenities:** *Some:* irons. **Pool(s):** outdoor. **Leisure Activities:** fishing, bicycles, hiking trails. **Business Services:** meeting rooms. **Cards:** AX, MC, VI.

SOME UNITS

MARINERS MOTEL   **Phone:** 410/639-2291

Motel

All Year	1P: $70-$85	2P: $70-$85 XP: $10 F

Location: 0.3 mi e of SR 20. 5681 S Hawthorne Ave 21661. **Fax:** 410/639-2081. **Facility:** 12 one-bedroom standard units. 1 story, exterior corridors. **Parking:** on-site. **Terms:** office hours 9 am-11 pm, weekly rates available, small pets only (with prior approval). **Pool(s):** outdoor. **Leisure Activities:** playground, horseshoes. **Guest Services:** coin laundry. **Business Services:** fax (fee). **Cards:** AX, DS, MC, VI.

SOME UNITS

ROCKVILLE —See District Of Columbia p. 494.

ROSEDALE —See Baltimore p. 611.

ST. MICHAELS pop. 1,193

—— WHERE TO STAY ——

BEST WESTERN ST MICHAELS MOTOR INN   *Book at aaa.com*   **Phone:** (410)745-3333

Motel

4/1-11/15 [CP]	1P: $98-$150	2P: $98-$150	XP: $8 F17
3/1-3/31 & 11/16-2/28 [CP]	1P: $79-$85	2P: $79-$85	XP: $8 F17

Location: 1 mi e on SR 33. 1228 S Talbot St 21663. **Fax:** 410/745-2906. **Facility:** 93 one-bedroom standard units. 2 stories (no elevator), interior/exterior corridors. **Parking:** on-site. **Amenities:** irons, hair dryers. **Pool(s):** 2 outdoor. **Business Services:** meeting rooms, fax (fee). **Cards:** AX, CB, DC, DS, MC, VI. **Special Amenities:** free continental breakfast and free local telephone calls.

SOME UNITS

THE PARSONAGE INN   **Phone:** 410/745-5519

Historic Bed & Breakfast

4/1-10/31 [BP]	2P: $145-$195	XP: $20 F10
3/1-3/31 & 11/1-2/28 [BP]	2P: $125-$165	XP: $20 F10

Location: 0.3 mi w on SR 33. 210 N Talbot St 21663. **Facility:** Brass beds, floral linens, antique furnishings and fireplaces add to the romantic ambience of the lodgings in this 1883 Victorian house. Smoke free premises. 8 units. 7 one-bedroom standard units. 1 one-bedroom suite. 1-2 stories (no elevator), interior/exterior corridors. *Bath:* combo or shower only. **Parking:** on-site. **Terms:** office hours 10 am-8 pm, 2 night minimum stay - weekends, 10 day cancellation notice-fee imposed, small pets only ($25 deposit, in designated unit, with prior approval). **Leisure Activities:** pool & whirlpool privileges, picnic area, bicycles. **Business Services:** fax (fee). **Cards:** MC, VI. **Special Amenities:** free full breakfast and free local telephone calls.

SOME UNITS

FEE

ST. MICHAELS HARBOUR INN, MARINA & SPA   *Book at aaa.com*   **Phone:** (410)745-9001

Small-scale Hotel

5/21-11/30	1P: $189-$525	2P: $189-$525	XP: $15 F18
3/1-5/20	1P: $115-$419	2P: $115-$419	XP: $15 F18
12/1-2/28	1P: $115-$299	2P: $115-$299	XP: $15 F18

Location: 0.3 mi e on SR 33, just n on Seymour Ave, then just w on Meadow St. 101 N Harbor Rd 21663. **Fax:** 410/745-9150. **Facility:** 46 units. 8 one-bedroom standard units, some with whirlpools. 38 one-bedroom suites, some with whirlpools. 3 stories, interior corridors. **Parking:** on-site. **Terms:** check-in 4 pm, 10 day cancellation notice-fee imposed, package plans, 5% service charge. **Amenities:** voice mail, irons, hair dryers. **Dining:** 7 am-10 pm, Sat & Sun from 11 am; seasonal outside dining, cocktails, also, Harbour Lights, see separate listing. **Pool(s):** small heated outdoor. **Leisure Activities:** whirlpool, rental canoes, bicycles, exercise room, spa. *Fee:* paddleboats, marina, aqua bikes, kayaks, water taxi. **Guest Services:** gift shop, valet and coin laundry, airport transportation-Easton Airport, area transportation-within St. Michaels. **Business Services:** meeting rooms, PC, fax (fee). **Cards:** AX, DC, DS, MC, VI. **Special Amenities:** free newspaper.

SOME UNITS

─────── *The following lodging was either not evaluated or did not* ───────
meet AAA rating requirements but is listed for your information only.

THE INN AT PERRY CABIN   Phone: 410/745-2200
[fyi]   Did not meet all AAA rating requirements for locking devices in some guest rooms at time of last evaluation
          on 05/14/2004. **Location:** 0.5 mi w on SR 33. 308 Watkins Ln 21663. Facilities, services, and decor characterize an
Small-scale Hotel upscale property.

─────── **WHERE TO DINE** ───────

208 TALBOT RESTAURANT   Dinner: $23-$32   Phone: 410/745-3838
▽▼▽▼▽   **Location:** 0.3 mi w on SR 33. 208 N Talbot St 21663. **Hours:** Open 3/20-2/18; 5 pm-9 pm, Fri & Sat-10 pm.
          Closed: 12/24, 12/25; also Mon & Tues. **Reservations:** suggested. **Features:** Little pieces of heaven are
American the appetizer of oysters in champagne sauce, and an entree of scallops with wild mushrooms and risotto.
          The full menu features fresh seafood, local products and homemade dessert. Prix fixe menu available only
on Saturday. Dressy casual; cocktails. **Parking:** on-site. **Cards:** DS, MC, VI.
                                                                          [image: Y] [image: X]

CARPENTER STREET SALOON   Lunch: $6-9   Dinner: $9-$17   Phone: 410/745-5111
▽▼▽ ▽▼▽   **Location:** on SR 33; center. 113/115 S Talbot St 21663. **Hours:** 8-11 am, 11:30-3:30 & 4-9:30 pm. Closed: for
          breakfast & lunch 12/25. **Reservations:** accepted. **Features:** Nestled among unique downtown shops is
American this old-time eatery. An eclectic interior of overhead circling train, light shaft with small balloonists, decoys
          and interesting artwork. Order through a pass through window. Fresh local seafood choices, of crab
combinations and more. Try the seaskin cheese and crab on potato skins. Attentive staff with good follow up. A small salad bar
as a side item. Relax, enjoy the street foot traffic, great seafood, and a staff there for you...Bon appetit. Casual dress; cocktails.
Parking: on-site (fee). **Cards:** DS, MC, VI.
                                                                          [image: Y] [image: X]

THE CRAB CLAW   Lunch: $10-$23   Dinner: $14-$23   Phone: 410/745-2900
▽▼▽   **Location:** On the harbor; adjacent to the Chesapeake Bay Maritime Museum. 304 Mill St 21663. **Hours:** Open 3/4-
          12/15; 11 am-9 pm. **Reservations:** suggested, in season. **Features:** A popular choice for crabs, this
Seafood   restaurant overlooks the harbor and specializes in Chesapeake Bay seafood. Casual dress; cocktails.
          Parking: on-site.
                                                                          [image: X]

HARBOUR LIGHTS   Lunch: $7-$15   Dinner: $21-$31   Phone: 410/745-5102
[AAA]   **Location:** 0.3 mi e on SR 33, just n on Seymour Ave, then just w on Meadow St; in St. Michaels Harbour Inn, Marina &
          Spa. 101 N Harbor Rd 21663. **Hours:** 5:30 pm-10 pm, Sat & Sun also 7 am-3 pm. **Reservations:** suggested.
▽▼▽▽▼▽   **Features:** The casually elegant dining room overlooks the harbor, making the view here almost as good as
          the food. The menu offers a nice selection of fresh seafood, including the notable crab soup, and beef.
American Dressy casual; cocktails. **Parking:** on-site. **Cards:** AX, CB, DC, DS, MC, VI.
                                                                          [image: X]

**MICHAEL RORK'S TOWN DOCK
RESTAURANT**   Lunch: $7-$15   Dinner: $17-$26   Phone: 410/745-5577
[AAA]   **Location:** Just n off SR 33; dockside. 125 Mulberry St 21663. **Hours:** 11:30 am-9 pm, Fri & Sat-10 pm; Fri & Sat-
          9 pm 9/4-5/26. Closed: 12/24, 12/25. **Reservations:** suggested. **Features:** Fresh, Eastern-shore seafood is
▽▼▽▽▼▽   the centerpiece of the creative menu. Every seat on the enclosed terrace and on the seasonal open deck
          looks out on the scenic harbor. Casual dress; cocktails. **Parking:** on-site. **Cards:** AX, DC, DS, MC, VI.
American
                                                                          [image: Y] [image: X]

SHERWOOD'S LANDING   Lunch: $17-$24   Dinner: $27-$38   Phone: 410/745-2200
▽▼▽ ▽▼▽   **Location:** 0.5 mi w on SR 33. 308 Watkins Ln 21663. **Hours:** 7 am-10, noon-2:30 & 6-10 pm.
          Reservations: suggested, weekend nights. **Features:** In the Inn at Perry Cabin, the elegant dining room
Continental overlooks the Miles River and is perfect for any occasion: a business meeting, romantic getaway or family
          gathering. The professional, attentive staff displays excellent knowledge of the menu and wine selections.
Creative and artfully prepared dishes use only the freshest local and international ingredients. Dressy casual; cocktails.
Parking: valet. **Cards:** AX, CB, DC, DS, MC, VI.
                                                                          [image: X]

─────── *The following restaurant has not been evaluated by AAA* ───────
but is listed for your information only.

BISTRO ST. MICHAELS   Phone: 410/745-9111
[fyi]   Not evaluated. **Location:** On SR 33; center. 403 S Talbot St 21663. **Features:** The food at this bistro is prepared
          with finesse and the setting is comfortable. Don't miss the wonderful soft-shell crab sandwich.

SALISBURY pop. 23,743

─────── **WHERE TO STAY** ───────

BEST VALUE INN SALISBURY   *Book at aaa.com*   Phone: (410)742-7194
[AAA] [SAVE]   5/27-10/8 [CP]   1P: $69-$149   2P: $69-$149   XP: $10   F14
               3/1-5/26 & 10/9-2/28 [CP]   1P: $49-$89   2P: $49-$89   XP: $10   F14
▽▼▽▽▼▽   **Location:** US 13, 1 mi n of jct US 50 Bypass. Located in a commercial area. 2625 N Salisbury Blvd 21801.
          Fax: 410/742-5194. **Facility:** 115 one-bedroom standard units. 2 stories (no elevator), exterior corridors.
Small-scale Hotel **Parking:** on-site. **Terms:** check-in 4 pm, 2 night minimum stay - seasonal, 3 day cancellation notice-fee
          imposed, pets ($10 fee). **Amenities:** voice mail, safes (fee). **Dining:** 11 am-midnight, cocktails. **Pool(s):**
outdoor. **Guest Services:** coin laundry. **Business Services:** meeting rooms, PC (fee). **Cards:** AX, CB, DC, DS, MC, VI.
Special Amenities: free continental breakfast.

                                                                     SOME UNITS

BEST WESTERN SALISBURY PLAZA *Book at aaa.com* Phone: (410)546-1300

AAA SAVE

	6/1-9/30	1P: $89-$135	2P: $99-$145	XP: $10	F17
	4/1-5/31	1P: $55-$110	2P: $65-$120	XP: $10	F17
	3/1-3/31 & 10/1-2/28	1P: $49-$79	2P: $59-$89	XP: $10	F17

Motel

Location: US 13 business route, 0.5 mi s of US 50 Bypass. Located in a commercial area. 1735 N Salisbury Blvd 21801. Fax: 410/546-0370. **Facility:** 101 one-bedroom standard units. 2 stories (no elevator), exterior corridors. **Parking:** on-site. **Terms:** 2 night minimum stay - seasonal, pets ($10 extra charge). **Amenities:** irons, hair dryers. **Pool(s):** small outdoor. **Leisure Activities:** limited exercise equipment. **Guest Services:** coin laundry. **Business Services:** meeting rooms, business center. **Cards:** AX, CB, DC, DS, JC, MC, VI. **Special Amenities:** free continental breakfast and free local telephone calls. *(See color ad below)*

SOME UNITS

⬛ 🛏️ 📶 🍽️ ➡️ 📺 DATA PORT 💻 / ❌ 🔌 🖥️ /
FEE

COMFORT INN SALISBURY *Book at aaa.com* Phone: (410)543-4666

| | 5/28-10/10 [ECP] | 1P: $89-$139 | 2P: $99-$149 | XP: $10 | F18 |
| | 3/1-5/27 & 10/11-2/28 [ECP] | 1P: $69-$99 | 2P: $79-$109 | XP: $10 | F18 |

Small-scale Hotel

Location: US 13, 0.5 mi n of jct US 13 business route and Bypass. 2701 N Salisbury Blvd 21801. Fax: 410/749-2639. **Facility:** 96 units. 93 one-bedroom standard units, some with whirlpools. 3 one-bedroom suites with whirlpools. 2 stories (no elevator), interior corridors. **Parking:** on-site. **Terms:** 2 night minimum stay - seasonal, package plans, small pets only. **Amenities:** irons, hair dryers. *Fee:* high-speed Internet, safes. **Leisure Activities:** horseshoes, volleyball. **Guest Services:** valet and coin laundry. **Business Services:** meeting rooms, fax (fee). **Cards:** AX, DS, MC, VI.

SOME UNITS

ASK ⬛ 🐕 📶 📷 📺 DATA PORT 🔌 🖥️ 💻 / ❌ /

HAMPTON INN-SALISBURY *Book at aaa.com* Phone: (410)334-3080

AAA SAVE

	5/16-9/24 [ECP]	1P: $84-$170	2P: $94-$180	
	9/25-10/31 [ECP]	1P: $68-$149	2P: $78-$159	
	3/1-5/15 & 11/1-2/28 [ECP]	1P: $68-$99	2P: $78-$109	

Small-scale Hotel

Location: US 13, 0.5 mi n of jct US 50 Bypass. 121 E Naylor Mill Rd 21804. Fax: 410/334-3095. **Facility:** 150 one-bedroom standard units. 5 stories, interior corridors. *Bath:* combo or shower only. **Parking:** on-site. **Terms:** 2 night minimum stay - seasonal. **Amenities:** video games (fee), voice mail, irons, hair dryers. **Pool(s):** heated indoor. **Leisure Activities:** sauna, whirlpool, exercise room. *Fee:* game room. **Guest Services:** valet and coin laundry. **Business Services:** meeting rooms, fax (fee). **Cards:** AX, CB, DC, DS, JC, MC, VI. **Special Amenities:** free expanded continental breakfast and free local telephone calls.

SOME UNITS

⬛ 📶 ♿ 🅼 🛏️ 📷 🏊 ❌ 📺 DATA PORT 💻 / ❌ 🔌 🖥️ /
FEE FEE

MICROTEL INN & SUITES SALISBURY/OCEAN CITY *Book at aaa.com* Phone: (410)742-2626

| | 5/1-9/30 | 1P: $89-$109 | 2P: $89-$109 | XP: $10 | F12 |
| | 3/1-4/30 & 10/1-2/28 | 1P: $49-$55 | 2P: $49-$55 | XP: $10 | F12 |

Small-scale Hotel

Location: Off US 50 business route, just w of jct US 13. 3050 Merritt Mill Rd 21804. Fax: 410/742-9922. **Facility:** 59 one-bedroom standard units. 3 stories, interior corridors. *Bath:* combo or shower only. **Parking:** on-site. **Terms:** package plans. **Amenities:** hair dryers. *Some:* irons. **Guest Services:** coin laundry. **Business Services:** fax (fee). **Cards:** AX, DC, DS, MC, VI.

SOME UNITS

ASK ⬛ 📶 🅼 🛏️ 📷 📺 DATA PORT / ❌ 🔌 🖥️ 💻 /

RAMADA INN AND CONFERENCE CENTER *Book at aaa.com* Phone: (410)546-4400

	5/13-9/4	1P: $80-$139	2P: $80-$139	XP: $10	F18
	3/1-5/12	1P: $75-$99	2P: $75-$99	XP: $10	F18
	9/5-2/28	1P: $65-$99	2P: $65-$99	XP: $10	F18

Large-scale Hotel

Location: US 13 business route, 0.4 mi s of jct Business US 50. 300 S Salisbury Blvd 21801. Fax: 410/546-2528. **Facility:** 156 units. 155 one-bedroom standard units. 1 one-bedroom suite. 5 stories, interior corridors. **Parking:** on-site. **Terms:** [AP] & [BP] meal plans available, small pets only ($25 fee). **Amenities:** video games (fee), voice mail, irons, hair dryers. **Pool(s):** heated indoor. **Leisure Activities:** limited exercise equipment. **Guest Services:** valet laundry. **Business Services:** conference facilities, PC, fax (fee). **Cards:** AX, DC, DS, MC, VI.

SOME UNITS

ASK ⬛ ✈️ 🛏️ 🍽️ 🍷 ➡️ 📺 DATA PORT 💻 / ❌ 🔌 🖥️ /
FEE

SLEEP INN-SALISBURY *Book at aaa.com* Phone: (410)572-5516

| | 5/27-9/15 [ECP] | 1P: $89-$119 | 2P: $99-$129 | XP: $10 | F18 |
| | 3/1-5/26 & 9/16-2/28 [ECP] | 1P: $65-$79 | 2P: $65-$79 | XP: $10 | F18 |

Location: US 50 Business route, just w of jct US 13. 406 Punkin Ct 21804. **Fax:** 410/677-4713. **Facility:** 79 one-bedroom standard units, some with whirlpools. 3 stories, interior corridors. *Bath:* combo or shower only.
Small-scale Hotel **Parking:** on-site. **Amenities:** voice mail. *Some:* high-speed Internet (fee), irons, hair dryers. **Pool(s):** outdoor. **Business Services:** fax (fee). **Cards:** AX, CB, DC, DS, MC, VI. **Special Amenities:** free expanded continental breakfast and free local telephone calls.

SOME UNITS

------ **WHERE TO DINE** ------

BREW RIVER RESTAURANT & BAR **Lunch:** $7-$15 **Dinner:** $9-$29 Phone: 410/677-6757

Location: US 50, 1 blk s; on Wicomico River. 502 W Main St 21801. **Hours:** 11 am-11 pm. Closed: 12/25. **Reservations:** accepted. **Features:** In the heart of town, the casual restaurant appeals to all age groups.
American The menu leans to seafood but doesn't stop there, as beef, chicken and pasta dishes also are available. Casual dress; cocktails. **Parking:** on-site. **Cards:** AX, DS, MC, VI.

CACTUS TAVERNA **Dinner:** $6-$20 Phone: 410/548-1254

Location: On US 13, just n of jct US 50 Bypass. 2420 N Salisbury Blvd 21801. **Hours:** 4 pm-10 pm, Fri & Sat-11 pm. Closed: 11/24, 12/25. **Reservations:** suggested, weekends. **Features:** On a busy highway, opposite
International the Salisbury Mall, this shopping plaza restaurant offers a casual comfortable atmosphere with a Mexican ambiance. The kitchen prepares a wide of array of dishes, from to traditional Mexican selections to South American, Spanish and Mediterranean dishes. Casual dress; beer & wine only. **Parking:** on-site. **Cards:** AX, DS, MC, VI.

GOIN' NUTS CAFE **Lunch:** $5-$7 **Dinner:** $11-$18 Phone: 410/860-1164

Location: Just se of jct US 50 and E Main St, on SR 350; in Market Place East Professional. 947 Mount Hermon Rd 21804. **Hours:** 11 am-11 pm, Sun-10 pm. Closed: 1/1, 11/24, 12/25. **Reservations:** suggested.
International **Features:** The casual restaurant serves international samplings of cuisine from Jamaica, Mexico, Italy, France and the good ol' USA. Servers are friendly and attentive. During warm weather, the patio is a nice spot to relax. Casual dress; cocktails. **Parking:** on-site. **Cards:** AX, MC, VI.

SILVER SPRING —*See District Of Columbia p. 498.*

SNOW HILL pop. 2,409

------ **WHERE TO STAY** ------

RIVER HOUSE INN Phone: (410)632-2722

| | 3/1-11/30 [BP] | 1P: $99-$230 | 2P: $125-$250 | XP: $20 | D13 |

Location: 1 mi w on SR 394 from jct SR 113. 201 E Market St 21863. **Fax:** 410/632-2866. **Facility:** The B&B rises
Historic Bed tastefully decorated cottages set on landscaped grounds that slope down to the Pocomoke River. Smoke
& Breakfast free premises. 4 units. 3 one-bedroom standard units with whirlpools. 1 one-bedroom suite with kitchen and whirlpool. 1-2 stories (no elevator), interior/exterior corridors. **Parking:** on-site. **Terms:** open 3/1-11/30, office hours 7 am-9 pm, 2 night minimum stay - seasonal and/or weekends, 7 day cancellation notice-fee imposed, weekly rates available, package plans, pets ($10 extra charge, small dogs only). **Amenities:** video library, irons, hair dryers. **Business Services:** fax (fee). **Cards:** AX, DS, MC, VI.

FEE

SOLOMONS pop. 1,536

------ **WHERE TO STAY** ------

COMFORT INN BEACON MARINA *Book at aaa.com* Phone: (410)326-6303

	3/1-4/30 [ECP]	1P: $85-$165	2P: $85-$165	XP: $10	F18
	5/1-8/31 [ECP]	1P: $90-$150	2P: $90-$150	XP: $10	F18
	9/1-2/28 [ECP]	1P: $85-$140	2P: $85-$140	XP: $10	F18

Small-scale Hotel **Location:** Off SR 2/4. 255 Lore Rd 20688 (PO Box 869). **Fax:** 410/326-6303. **Facility:** 60 one-bedroom standard units, some with whirlpools. 2 stories (no elevator), interior corridors. **Parking:** on-site. **Amenities:** irons, hair dryers. **Pool(s):** outdoor. **Leisure Activities:** Fee: marina. **Guest Services:** valet laundry. **Business Services:** fax (fee). **Cards:** AX, CB, DC, DS, MC, VI.

SOME UNITS

HOLIDAY INN SELECT SOLOMONS HOTEL *Book at aaa.com* Phone: (410)326-6311

| | All Year | 1P: $109-$159 | 2P: $119-$169 | XP: $10 | F19 |

Location: SR 2/4; center. 155 Holiday Dr 20688 (PO Box 1099). **Fax:** 410/326-1069. **Facility:** 326 units. 319 one-bedroom standard units, some with efficiencies. 7 one-bedroom suites ($159-$229) with efficiencies. 4-5 stories, interior corridors. **Parking:** on-site. **Terms:** package plans. **Amenities:** voice mail, irons, hair dryers.
Large-scale Hotel **Dining:** 6:30 am-10 pm; 5:30 am-11 pm 5/27-9/3, cocktails. **Pool(s):** outdoor. **Leisure Activities:** sauna, 2 tennis courts, tennis equipment, exercise room. *Fee:* marina. **Guest Services:** gift shop, valet and coin laundry. **Business Services:** conference facilities, business center. **Cards:** AX, DC, DS, MC, VI. **Special Amenities:** free local telephone calls and free newspaper.

SOME UNITS

WHERE TO DINE

THE C D CAFE
American

Lunch: $6-$15 **Dinner:** $9-$24 **Phone:** 410/326-3877
Location: 0.5 mi s on SR 2 from Solomons Bridge. 14350 Solomons Island Rd 20688. **Hours:** 11:30 am-2:30 & 5:30-9:30 pm. Closed major holidays. **Features:** The simple cafe has great food and a casual atmosphere. The chef/owners prepare an eclectic selection of American dishes, from seafood to vegetarian. Creme brulee has become the chef's signature dessert. Casual dress; cocktails. **Parking:** on-site. **Cards:** MC, VI.

THE DRY DOCK RESTAURANT
American

Dinner: $17-$30 **Phone:** 410/326-4817
Location: 0.3 mi s on SR 2 from Solomons Bridge, then just e on C St; at Zahnisers Marina. C St 20688. **Hours:** 5 pm-9 pm, Fri & Sat-9:30 pm, Sun 10 am-2 & 5-9 pm. Closed: 1/1, 11/24, 12/25. **Reservations:** required, in summer. **Features:** The menu changes daily at the marina-front restaurant. The kitchen's creativity is reflected in such dishes as crab-stuffed lobster drizzled with lemon dill hollandaise and ginger-seared scallops with spicy Oriental sauce. The second-level dining room, as well as the popular seasonal balcony, provides a great view of the marina. Casual dress; cocktails. **Parking:** on-site. **Cards:** AX, MC, VI.

LIGHTHOUSE INN
Seafood

Dinner: $12-$29 **Phone:** 410/326-2444
Location: 1 mi s on SR 2 from Solomons Bridge. 14636 Solomons Island Rd S 20688. **Hours:** 5 pm-9 pm, Sun 4 pm-8 pm; Fri & Sat-10 pm 4/1-10/30. Closed: 11/24, 12/25; also Super Bowl Sun. **Reservations:** suggested. **Features:** Seafood—most notably crabcakes—is the specialty at the two-story restaurant that looks out on Solomons Harbor and the Patuxent River. A skipjack boat replica serves as the bar. Depending on the night, the mood can range from romantic to buzzing. Casual dress; cocktails. **Parking:** on-site. **Cards:** DC, DS, MC, VI.

STEVENSVILLE pop. 5,880

WHERE TO STAY

KENT MANOR INN *Book at aaa.com*
Country Inn

			Phone: (410)643-5757	
3/1-11/1 [ECP]	1P: $170-$235	2P: $170-$235	XP: $15	F12
11/2-2/28 [ECP]	1P: $99-$190	2P: $99-$190	XP: $15	F12

Location: US 50/301, exit 37, just s on SR 8; 0.5 mi e of Bay Bridge. 500 Kent Manor Dr 21666. Fax: 410/643-8315. **Facility:** Victorian reproductions furnish the individually decorated guest rooms in this 1820 inn set well back from the road. Designated smoking area. 24 units. 23 one- and 1 two-bedroom standard rooms. 3 stories (no elevator), interior corridors. **Parking:** on-site. **Terms:** office hours 7:30 am-8 pm, 2 night minimum stay - weekends, 3 day cancellation notice, package plans, 8% service charge. **Amenities:** hair dryers. **Pool(s):** outdoor. **Leisure Activities:** paddleboats, boat dock, fishing, bicycles, horseshoes, volleyball. **Business Services:** meeting rooms, fax (fee). **Cards:** AX, DC, DS, MC, VI.

SOME UNITS

WHERE TO DINE

KENTMORR RESTAURANT & CRAB HOUSE *Menu on aaa.com*
Seafood

Lunch: $7-$23 **Dinner:** $9-$23 **Phone:** 410/643-2263
Location: 5 mi s on SR 8; jct US 50/301, exit 37, 0.6 mi w. 910 Kentmorr Rd 21666. **Hours:** 11:30 am-9 pm, Fri & Sat-10 pm. Closed: 11/24, 12/25. **Reservations:** suggested. **Features:** The atmosphere is casual and family-oriented at the restaurant, where steamed crabs, fried oysters and a great view of the bay are featured presentations. Pasta and beef dishes also are available. An outdoor dining area provides seasonal seating. Casual dress; cocktails. **Parking:** on-site. **Cards:** DS, MC, VI.

SWANTON

WHERE TO STAY

CARMEL COVE INN
Bed & Breakfast

Phone: (301)387-0067
All Year [BP] 1P: $135-$195 2P: $135-$195
Location: 2.5 mi e on Glendale Rd from US 219. Located on Deep Creek Lake. 105 Monastery Way 21561 (PO Box 644, OAKLAND, 21550). Fax: 301/387-2394. **Facility:** This B&B, originally constructed as a retreat for Carmelite Order priests, includes sections built in 1945 and 1960. Smoke free premises. 10 one-bedroom standard units, some with whirlpools. 2 stories (no elevator), interior corridors. **Bath:** combo or shower only. **Parking:** on-site. **Terms:** check-in 4 pm, 2 night minimum stay - weekends, age restrictions may apply, 5 day cancellation notice-fee imposed. **Amenities:** DVD players, CD players, hair dryers. **Leisure Activities:** canoeing, paddleboats, fishing, tennis court, bicycles. **Guest Services:** gift shop, complimentary evening beverages. **Business Services:** meeting rooms. **Cards:** DS, MC, VI.

SYKESVILLE —See Baltimore p. 611.

THURMONT pop. 5,588

WHERE TO STAY

COZY COUNTRY INN
Country Inn

			Phone: 301/271-4301	
3/1-4/30	1P: $50-$160	2P: $50-$160	XP: $5	F13
5/1-2/28	1P: $50-$150	2P: $50-$150	XP: $5	F13

Location: US 15, just e to SR 806, then 0.4 mi n. 103 Frederick Rd 21788. Fax: 301/271-3107. **Facility:** Family owned since 1929, the inn themes its rooms after former presidents and other dignitaries who have visited nearby Camp David. 21 one-bedroom standard units, some with whirlpools. 1-2 stories (no elevator), exterior corridors. **Bath:** combo or shower only. **Parking:** on-site. **Terms:** cancellation fee imposed. **Amenities:** voice mail, hair dryers. **Dining:** Cozy Restaurant, see separate listing. **Leisure Activities:** sports equipment on loan. **Guest Services:** gift shop. **Business Services:** meeting rooms. **Cards:** AX, DC, MC, VI. **Special Amenities:** free continental breakfast and free local telephone calls.

SOME UNITS

RAMBLER INN

Motel

Phone: 301/271-2424

All Year   1P: $38-$72   2P: $44-$92   XP: $5   F5
Location: US 15 at SR 550. (426 N Church St). **Facility:** 30 one-bedroom standard units. 1 story, interior/exterior corridors. **Parking:** on-site. **Terms:** weekly rates available, package plans, small pets only ($6 extra charge). **Guest Services:** coin laundry. **Business Services:** fax. **Cards:** AX, DC, DS, MC, VI.

SOME UNITS

WHERE TO DINE

COZY RESTAURANT

American

Lunch: $6-$14   Dinner: $10-$20   Phone: 301/271-7373
Location: US 15, just e to SR 806, then 0.4 mi n; in Cozy Country Inn. 105 Frederick Rd 21788. **Hours:** 11 am-9 pm, Sat & Sun from 8 am. Closed: 12/24, 12/25. **Features:** As the name implies, the restaurant is cozy. Guests can choose from a huge selection of entrees and salads, as well as desserts from the buffet. Casual dress; cocktails. **Parking:** on-site. **Cards:** AX, MC, VI.

MOUNTAIN GATE FAMILY RESTAURANT

American

Lunch: $5-$12   Dinner: $5-$12   Phone: 301/271-4373
Location: 1.5 mi s on SR 806; just n on SR 806 (Thurmont exit) off US 15. 133 Frederick Rd 21788. **Hours:** 5 am-11 pm, Fri & Sat-midnight. Closed: 12/25; also for dinner 12/24. **Features:** Families and seniors keep the popular restaurant bustling. Extensive buffets line up such tantalizing fare as ham and cabbage, lasagna and slippery chicken pot pie. Breakfast from the menu can be ordered all day. Casual dress. **Parking:** on-site. **Cards:** DS, MC, VI.

SHAMROCK RESTAURANT   *Menu on aaa.com*

Steak & Seafood

Lunch: $6-$18   Dinner: $13-$21   Phone: 301/271-2912
Location: 1 mi n on US 15 from jct SR 550. 7701 Fitzgerald Rd 21788. **Hours:** 11 am-10 pm, Sun noon-9 pm. Closed: 1/1, 12/25. **Reservations:** suggested, weekends. **Features:** Appealing to locals and travelers on their way to and from Gettysburg, the restaurant has a definite Irish theme. The food is a mixture of salads, mostly seafood appetizers, and steak, seafood and some poultry dishes. Casual dress; cocktails. **Parking:** on-site. **Cards:** MC, VI.

TILGHMAN ISLAND

WHERE TO STAY

CHESAPEAKE WOOD DUCK INN

Historic Bed & Breakfast

Phone: (410)886-2070

4/2-11/25 [BP]   1P: $149-$229   2P: $149-$229
3/1-4/1 & 11/26-2/28 [BP]   1P: $119-$189   2P: $119-$199
Location: SR 33, 0.4 mi w of Knapps Narrows Drawbridge, just s on Gibsontown Rd. 21490 Dogwood Harbor Rd 21671 (PO Box 202). Fax: 413/677-7256. **Facility:** The guest rooms are individually decorated in this 1890 historic house, which affords nice views of sunsets on the water. Smoke free premises. 7 one-bedroom standard units. 3 stories (no elevator), interior corridors. *Bath:* combo or shower only. **Parking:** on-site. **Terms:** office hours 8 am-9 pm, check-in 4 pm, 2 night minimum stay - weekends, age restrictions may apply, 7 day cancellation notice-fee imposed. **Leisure Activities:** rental bicycles. **Business Services:** fax (fee). **Cards:** MC, VI. **Special Amenities:** free full breakfast and free newspaper.

SOME UNITS

THE INN AT KNAPPS NARROW MARINA

Small-scale Hotel

Phone: 410/886-2720

3/1-11/1   2P: $120-$160   XP: $25   F18
11/2-2/28   2P: $80-$120   XP: $25   F18
Location: On SR 33, east side of the bridge. 6176 Tilghman Island Rd 21671 (PO Box 277, TILGHMAN). Fax: 410/886-2716. **Facility:** 20 units. 19 one-bedroom standard units. 1 one-bedroom suite. 3 stories, exterior corridors. **Parking:** on-site. **Terms:** office hours 8 am-9 pm, 2 night minimum stay - seasonal and/or weekends, weekly rates available. **Amenities:** voice mail. **Pool(s):** outdoor. **Guest Services:** coin laundry. **Business Services:** meeting rooms, fax (fee). **Cards:** DS, MC, VI.

SOME UNITS

WHERE TO DINE

THE TILGHMAN ISLAND INN

American

Lunch: $6-$13   Dinner: $19-$33   Phone: 410/886-2141
Location: Just n of Knapps Narrows Drawbridge. 21384 Coopertown Rd 21671. **Hours:** Open 3/1-12/31 & 2/13-2/28; noon-3 & 6-9:30 pm, Fri & Sat-10 pm, Sun noon-3 & 5-9:30 pm. Closed: Wed, also Tues 12/1-3/31. **Reservations:** suggested, weekends. **Features:** This restaurant is located on an isolated island separated only by a drawbridge from the mainland. Dine inside or out; either formal dining areas with tablecloth or casual dining tables with logo umbrellas viewing the passing boats. Enjoy creative selections of seafood with some twists and some land animal choices. Lunch has some classic options of Rueben, soft-shell crab in season, and other creative options. Dressy casual; cocktails. **Parking:** on-site. **Cards:** DS, MC, VI.

TIMONIUM —*See Baltimore p. 612.*

TOWSON —*See Baltimore p. 612.*

WALDORF pop. 22,312

------ WHERE TO STAY ------

COMFORT SUITES WALDORF
Book at aaa.com

AAA SAVE

Small-scale Hotel

Phone: (301)932-4400

All Year · 1P: $99-$149 · 2P: $99-$169 · XP: $10 · F16
Location: Just off US 301, 1 mi n of jct SR 5 business route. 11765 Business Park Dr 20601. Fax: 301/932-7566. **Facility:** 69 one-bedroom standard units, some with whirlpools. 2 stories, interior corridors. *Bath:* combo or shower only. **Parking:** on-site. **Terms:** cancellation fee imposed. **Amenities:** high-speed Internet, dual phone lines, voice mail, safes (fee), irons, hair dryers. **Pool(s):** heated indoor. **Guest Services:** coin laundry. **Business Services:** meeting rooms, fax. **Cards:** AX, CB, DC, DS, MC, VI. **Special Amenities:** free expanded continental breakfast and free local telephone calls.

SOME UNITS

[icons] / ✕ /

ECONO LODGE WALDORF
Book at aaa.com

AAA SAVE

Small-scale Hotel

Phone: (301)645-0022

All Year · 1P: $69-$109 · 2P: $79-$129 · F16
Location: 1 mi n on US 301 from jct SR 228. 11770 Business Park Dr 20601. Fax: 301/645-0058. **Facility:** 87 units. 85 one-bedroom standard units. 2 one-bedroom suites with whirlpools. 2 stories (no elevator), interior corridors. *Bath:* combo or shower only. **Parking:** on-site. **Terms:** cancellation fee imposed. **Amenities:** voice mail, hair dryers. **Guest Services:** coin laundry. **Business Services:** fax (fee). **Cards:** AX, CB, DC, DS, MC, VI.

SOME UNITS

[icons] / ✕ /

HAMPTON INN WALDORF

Small-scale Hotel

Phone: (301)632-9600

All Year · 1P: $96-$129
Location: On US 301; opposite St Charles Towne Plaza. 3750 Crain Hwy 20603. Fax: 301/632-6209. **Facility:** 100 one-bedroom standard units, some with whirlpools. 3 stories, interior corridors. *Bath:* combo or shower only. **Parking:** on-site. **Terms:** cancellation fee imposed, small pets only. **Amenities:** dual phone lines, voice mail, irons, hair dryers. **Pool(s):** outdoor. **Leisure Activities:** limited exercise equipment. **Guest Services:** valet and coin laundry. **Business Services:** meeting rooms, fax (fee). **Cards:** AX, DC, DS, MC, VI.

SOME UNITS

[icons] / ✕ /

HOLIDAY INN WALDORF
Book at aaa.com

Small-scale Hotel

Phone: (301)645-8200

All Year · 1P: $82-$117 · XP: $6 · F19
Location: 0.7 mi s on US 301, from jct SR 228. Located adjacent to shopping mall. 45 St Patrick's Dr 20603. Fax: 301/843-7945. **Facility:** 191 one-bedroom standard units, some with efficiencies. 3 stories, interior corridors. **Parking:** on-site. **Terms:** cancellation fee imposed. **Amenities:** video games (fee), voice mail, irons, hair dryers. **Pool(s):** outdoor. **Leisure Activities:** limited exercise equipment. **Guest Services:** valet and coin laundry. **Business Services:** meeting rooms, fax (fee). **Cards:** AX, CB, DC, DS, JC, MC, VI.

SOME UNITS

[icons] / ✕ /

—————— WHERE TO DINE ——————

SILVER SKEWERS RESTAURANT

Persian
Lunch: $8-$17   Dinner: $8-$17   Phone: 301/396-5758
Location: Just e of US 301, jct Central Ave. 2788 Old Washington Rd 20601. **Hours:** 11:30 am-9 pm, Fri & Sat-10 pm. Closed major holidays. **Reservations:** accepted. **Features:** Set back off the main road, the small, casual restaurant prepares a variety of delicious kebabs: beef, lamb, chicken, shrimp and salmon in combination or alone. Casual dress. **Parking:** on-site. **Cards:** MC, VI.

WESTMINSTER —See Baltimore p. 614.

WHEATON —See District Of Columbia p. 499.

WHITEHAVEN

—————— WHERE TO STAY ——————

WHITEHAVEN BED & BREAKFAST
Historic Bed & Breakfast

			Phone: (410)873-3294
3/1-3/31 & 1/1-2/28 [BP]	1P: $70-$80	2P: $90-$100	XP: $20 F12
4/1-12/31 [BP]	1P: $75	2P: $85	XP: $20 F12

Location: SR 352 to Whitehaven Rd, then w. Located opposite the Whitehaven Ferry Landing. 23844 River St 21856. Fax: 410/873-2162. **Facility:** This B&B across from the river is in two houses, one dating from 1850 and the other from 1886. Smoke free premises. 4 one-bedroom standard units. 2 stories (no elevator), interior corridors. *Bath:* combo or shower only. **Parking:** on-site. **Terms:** office hours 8 am-9 pm, 7 day cancellation notice, package plans, pets (in designated unit, with prior approval). **Leisure Activities:** fishing. **Business Services:** fax (fee). **Cards:** AX, DS, MC, VI.

—————— WHERE TO DINE ——————

THE RED ROOST
Steak & Seafood
Dinner: $12-$18   Phone: 410/546-5443
Location: From SR 352, follow signs. 2670 Clara Rd 21856. **Hours:** Open 3/16-11/6; 5:30 pm-10 pm, Sat from 3 pm, Sun 3 pm-9 pm. **Features:** An eastern shore tradition for 30 years, dining is truly an adventure here! Tucked away off a gravel country road, it's anything but quiet. Be prepared to swing a mallet when ordering the all-you-can-eat crab dinner. The heaping helpings of food and fun are what make this a most popular eatery. Casual dress; cocktails. **Parking:** on-site. **Cards:** AX, DC, MC, VI.

WHITE MARSH —See Baltimore p. 615.

WILLIAMSPORT pop. 1,868

—————— WHERE TO STAY ——————

RED ROOF INN   Book at aaa.com
Small-scale Hotel

			Phone: (301)582-3500
3/1-10/31 [CP]	1P: $49-$64	2P: $54-$69	XP: $5 F17
11/1-2/28 [CP]	1P: $44-$54	2P: $49-$59	XP: $5 F17

Location: I-81, exit 2, 0.3 mi sw on US 11. 310 E Potomac St 21795. Fax: 301/223-8491. **Facility:** 116 one-bedroom standard units. 2 stories (no elevator), exterior corridors. **Parking:** on-site. **Terms:** pets ($5 extra charge, in designated units). **Leisure Activities:** picnic tables. **Cards:** AX, CB, DC, DS, MC, VI. **Special Amenities:** free continental breakfast and free newspaper.

SOME UNITS
FEE

WOODSTOCK —See Baltimore p. 615.

Virginia

Chesapeake Bay
© M. Berman
Robertstock

Virginia Orientation Map
To Destinations

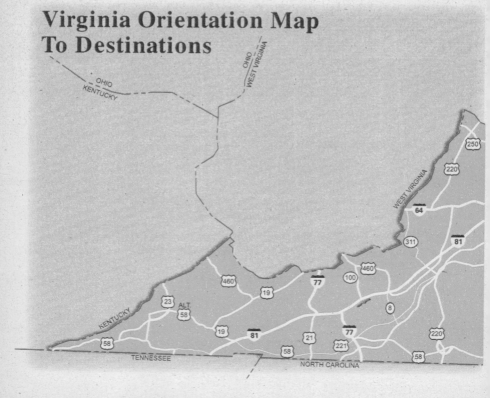

Major destinations are color-coded to index boxes, which display vicinity communities you will find listed within that destination's section of the book.

Cities outside major destination vicinities are listed in alphabetical order throughout this book.

Use the *Comprehensive City Index* at the back of this book to find every city's listing location.

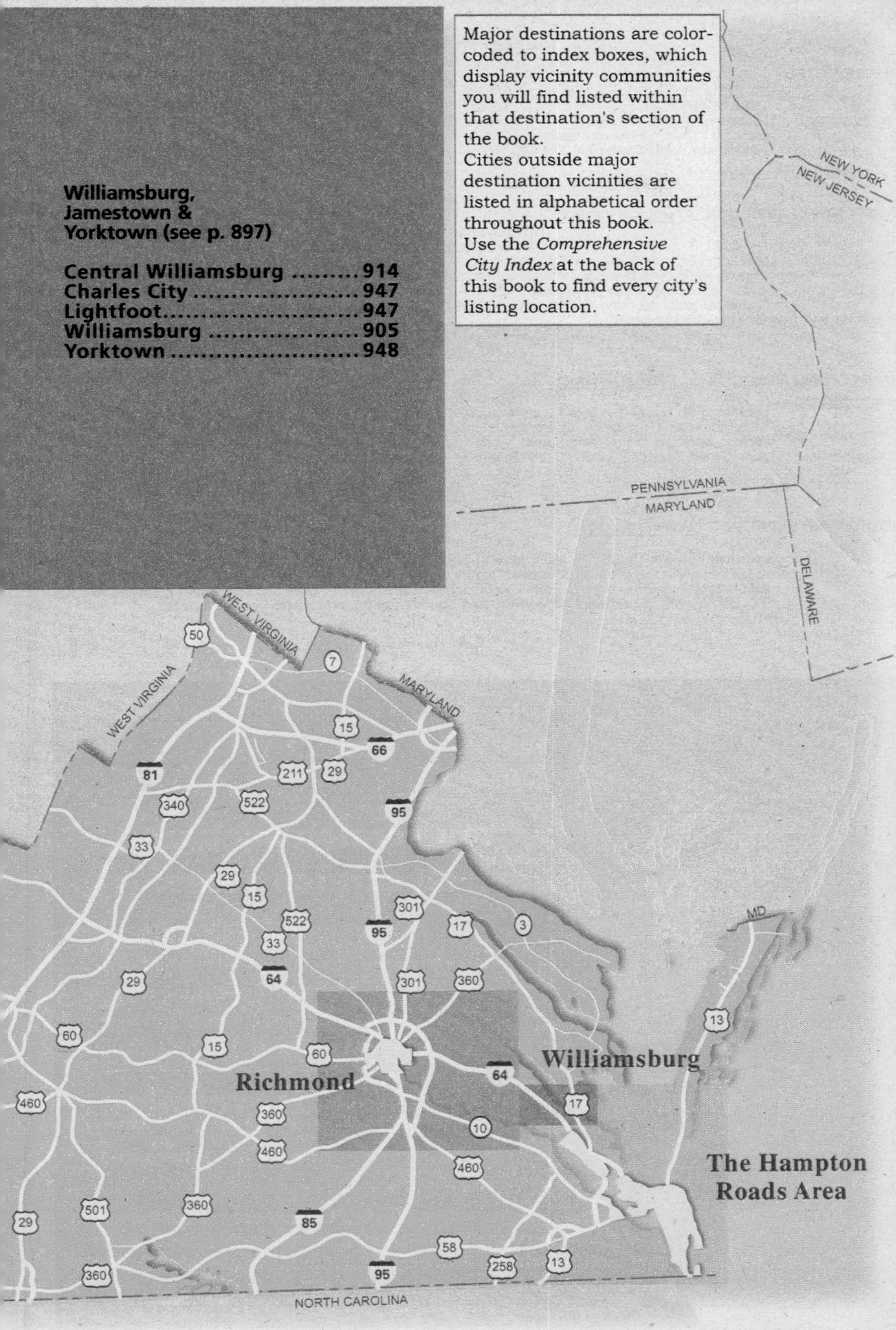

NEW YORK
NEW JERSEY

PENNSYLVANIA
MARYLAND

DELAWARE

WEST VIRGINIA

MARYLAND

WEST VIRGINIA

MD

50

7

15

66

81

211 29

95

340

522

33

29

15

522

95

33

301

17

3

29

64

301

360

60

15

60

13

Richmond

360

Williamsburg

64

17

460

10

460

The Hampton Roads Area

29

501

360

85

460

58

13

29

501

95

258

360

NORTH CAROLINA

ABINGDON pop. 7,780

---------- WHERE TO STAY ----------

ALPINE MOTEL

Phone: (276)628-3178

3/1-10/31 [CP]	1P: $49-$59	2P: $69-$79	XP: $6 F12
11/1-2/28 [CP]	1P: $39-$49	2P: $49-$59	XP: $6 F12

Location: I-81, exit 19 (US 11), 0.5 mi w. 882 E Main St 24210. **Fax:** 276/628-3179. **Facility:** 19 one-bedroom standard units. 1 story, exterior corridors. **Parking:** on-site. **Terms:** cancellation fee imposed. **Amenities:** irons. **Cards:** AX, DS, MC, VI.

Motel

SOME UNITS

COMFORT INN ABINGDON *Book at aaa.com*

Phone: (276)676-2222

3/1-10/31	1P: $66-$200	2P: $73-$200	XP: $10 F18
11/1-2/28	1P: $60-$200	2P: $66-$200	XP: $10 F18

Location: I-81, exit 14, just n. 170 Jonesboro Rd 24210. **Fax:** 276/676-2222. **Facility:** 80 one-bedroom standard units. 2 stories (no elevator), interior corridors. **Parking:** on-site. **Terms:** 2 night minimum stay - seasonal and/or weekends, 3 day cancellation notice. **Amenities:** irons, hair dryers. **Pool(s):** heated outdoor. **Guest Services:** valet laundry. **Cards:** AX, CB, DC, DS, JC, MC, VI. **Special Amenities: free continental breakfast and free local telephone calls.**

Small-scale Hotel

SOME UNITS

HAMPTON INN ABINGDON *Book at aaa.com*

Phone: (276)619-4600

All Year	1P: $85-$105	2P: $90-$110

Location: I-81, exit 17, just e. 340 Commerce Dr 24211. **Fax:** 276/619-4605. **Facility:** 68 one-bedroom standard units, some with whirlpools. 3 stories, interior corridors. **Bath:** combo or shower only. **Parking:** on-site. **Terms:** package plans. **Amenities:** video games, high-speed Internet, voice mail, irons, hair dryers. **Pool(s):** heated outdoor. **Guest Services:** valet laundry. **Business Services:** meeting rooms. **Cards:** AX, DC, DS, MC, VI.

Small-scale Hotel

SOME UNITS

HOLIDAY INN EXPRESS *Book at aaa.com*

Phone: 276/676-2829

All Year	1P: $79-$140	2P: $79-$140	XP: $5 F13

Location: I-81, exit 19 (US 11). 940 E Main St 24210. **Fax:** 276/676-2605. **Facility:** 81 one-bedroom standard units, some with whirlpools. 3 stories, interior corridors. **Bath:** combo or shower only. **Parking:** on-site. **Amenities:** irons, hair dryers. **Pool(s):** outdoor. **Guest Services:** valet and coin laundry. **Cards:** AX, CB, DC, DS, JC, MC, VI. **Special Amenities: free continental breakfast and free newspaper.**
(See color ad p 667)

Small-scale Hotel

SOME UNITS

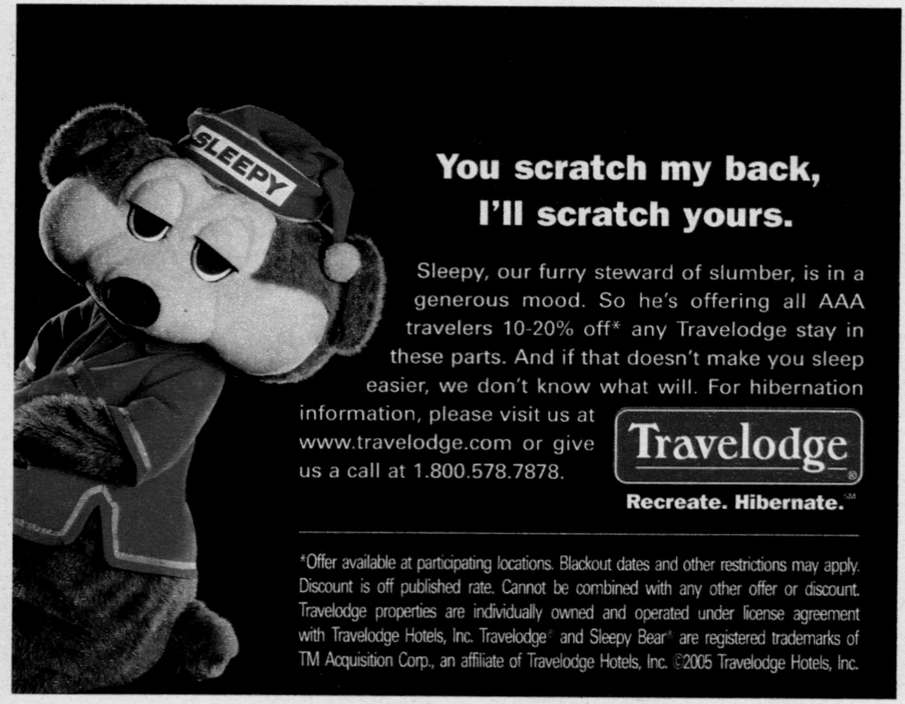

INN ON TOWN CREEK

Bed & Breakfast

Phone: (276)628-4560
All Year 1P: $135 2P: $135 XP: $25 F
Location: I-81, exit 17, 0.8 mi w on Cummings St, then 0.8 mi n. 445 E Valley St 24210 (PO Box 1745, 24212). Fax: 276/628-9611. **Facility:** On four acres of manicured grounds, this brick home with a slate roof offers a solarium as well as rooms furnished with antiques and reproductions. Smoke free premises. 5 one-bedroom standard units. 3 stories (no elevator), interior corridors. *Bath:* some shared or private. **Parking:** on-site. **Terms:** 3 night minimum stay - seasonal, age restrictions may apply, 7 day cancellation notice, package plans. **Amenities:** hair dryers. **Leisure Activities:** whirlpool. **Cards:** AX, DS, MC, VI.

SOME UNITS
(ASK) (X) (VCR) / (🛏) (📷) (📺) /

THE MARTHA WASHINGTON INN, A CAMBERLEY HOTEL   *Book at aaa.com*

(AAA) (SAVE)

Classic Historic
Small-scale Hotel

Phone: (276)628-3161
All Year 1P: $149-$375 2P: $149-$375 XP: $20 F18
Location: I-81, exit 17, 0.7 mi n on Cummings St, then just e. 150 W Main St 24210. Fax: 276/628-8885. **Facility:** Built in 1832 as a private home which later served as a women's college, this red-brick Federalist mansion is set amid landscaped grounds. 62 one-bedroom standard units, some with whirlpools. 3 stories, interior corridors. *Bath:* combo or shower only. **Parking:** on-site. **Terms:** cancellation fee imposed, package plans. **Amenities:** video games, high-speed Internet, voice mail, irons, hair dryers. **Dining:** The Dining Room, see separate listing. **Guest Services:** gift shop, valet laundry, area transportation-within 5 mi. **Business Services:** meeting rooms, PC, fax. **Cards:** AX, CB, DC, DS, MC, VI. **Special Amenities:** free newspaper.

SOME UNITS
(S/D) (✠) (🍴) (⎘) (⌨) (👥) (🐾) (DATA PORT) / (X) (VCR) (🛏) /
FEE

QUALITY INN & SUITES OF ABINGDON   *Book at aaa.com*

Small-scale Hotel

Phone: (276)676-9090
All Year [ECP] 1P: $99-$129 2P: $99-$129
Location: I-81, exit 19 (US 11), just w. 930 E Main St 24210. Fax: 276/676-9091. **Facility:** 75 one-bedroom standard units, some with whirlpools. 4 stories, interior corridors. *Bath:* combo or shower only. **Parking:** on-site. **Terms:** small pets only ($30 fee). **Amenities:** voice mail, irons, hair dryers. **Pool(s):** outdoor. **Leisure Activities:** exercise room. **Guest Services:** valet laundry. **Business Services:** meeting rooms, business center. **Cards:** AX, DS, MC, VI.

SOME UNITS
(ASK) (S/D) (🐾) (⌨) (⇌) (👥) (DATA PORT) (🛏) (📷) (📺) / (X) /
FEE

SUMMERFIELD INN BED AND BREAKFAST

Bed & Breakfast

Phone: (276)628-5905
All Year [BP] 1P: $145-$185 2P: $145-$185 XP: $40
Location: I-81, exit 17, 0.8 mi w on Cummings St, then just n. 101 W Valley St 24210. Fax: 276/628-7515. **Facility:** Spacious public areas, a huge front porch and contemporary rooms in the carriage house enhance this 1920s Colonial Revival home. Smoke free premises. 7 one-bedroom standard units, some with whirlpools. 1-2 stories (no elevator), interior corridors. *Bath:* combo or shower only. **Parking:** on-site. **Terms:** check-in 4 pm, 2 night minimum stay - weekends, age restrictions may apply, 10 day cancellation notice, package plans. **Amenities:** hair dryers. **Guest Services:** complimentary evening beverages. **Cards:** AX, MC, VI.

(🔒M) (X) (DATA PORT)

VICTORIA & ALBERT INN

(AAA) (SAVE)

Historic Bed
& Breakfast

Phone: 276/623-1281
All Year 2P: $125-$165
Location: I-81, exit 17, 0.8 mi w on Cummings St, 0.3 mi e on Valley St, then just n. Located in a quiet residential area. 224 Oak Hill St 24210. Fax: 276/676-0780. **Facility:** Every room in this 1892 Victorian has a fireplace; the property, which is in a neighborhood setting, features a pretty porch and garden areas. Smoke free premises. 5 one-bedroom standard units, some with whirlpools. 3 stories (no elevator), interior corridors. **Parking:** on-site. **Terms:** check-in 3:30 pm, 2 night minimum stay - seasonal and/or weekends, age restrictions may apply, 3 day cancellation notice-fee imposed, package plans. **Amenities:** CD players, hair dryers. *Some:* irons. **Guest Services:** complimentary evening beverages. **Business Services:** fax. **Cards:** AX, CB, DC, DC, MC.

SOME UNITS
(X) (VCR) (📺) (DATA PORT) / (🛏) /

WHITE BIRCHES INN
▼▼▼▼
Historic Bed
& Breakfast

All Year | 1P: $139-$169 | 2P: $139-$169 | XP: $35 | D
Location: I-81, exit 17, 0.8 mi w on Cummings St, 0.7 mi n on Valley St, then just n. 268 Whites Mill Rd 24210. Fax: 276/676-2146. **Facility:** Icon art is placed throughout this 1901 Cape Cod-style house; rooms feature antique four-poster beds and gas fireplaces. Designated smoking area. 5 one-bedroom standard units, some with whirlpools. 2 stories (no elevator), interior corridors. *Bath:* combo or shower only. **Parking:** on-site. **Terms:** 2 night minimum stay - weekends, age restrictions may apply, 10 day cancellation notice-fee imposed, [BP] meal plan available, package plans, no pets allowed (owner's dog on premises). **Amenities:** video library, irons, hair dryers. **Guest Services:** complimentary evening beverages. **Cards:** MC, VI.

Phone: 276/247-2437

[ASK] [S/D] [X] [VCR] [🐾] [DATA PORT]

─────── **WHERE TO DINE** ───────

ALISON'S RESTAURANT
▼▼▼ ▼▼▼
American

Lunch: $6-$10 | Dinner: $6-$18 | Phone: 276/628-8002
Location: I-81, exit 14, just w. 1220 W Main St 24210. **Hours:** 11 am-9 pm. Closed: 12/25. **Features:** The restaurant blends hometown cooking with friendly, delightful service. The menu selection is huge. Casual dress. **Parking:** on-site. **Cards:** MC, VI.

[X]

BELLA'S
▼
American

Lunch: $6-$11 | Dinner: $7-$19 | Phone: 276/628-8101
Location: I-81, exit 19, just w. 872 E Main St 24210. **Hours:** 11 am-11 pm. **Features:** Patrons can look forward to a fun dining experience. Western New York recipes resurface here in the lower .Shenandoah Valley. Quality and consistency are hallmarks. Casual dress; beer only. **Parking:** on-site. **Cards:** MC, VI.

[X]

THE DINING ROOM
ⓐⓐⓐ
▼▼ ▼▼▼
Regional
American

Lunch: $7-$14 | Dinner: $16-$30 | Phone: 276/628-9151
Location: I-81, exit 17, 0.7 mi n on Cummings St, then just e; in The Martha Washington Inn, A Camberley Hotel. 150 W Main 24210. **Hours:** 7-10 am, 11:30-2 & 5-9 pm. Closed: 12/25. **Reservations:** suggested. **Features:** In a pre-Civil War mansion that later served as a girl's college, the moderately upscale restaurant serves fine cuisine with elements of Southern tradition. Those who visit on Friday might opt for the seafood buffet. Dressy casual; cocktails. **Parking:** on-site. **Cards:** AX, DC, DS, MC, VI. **Historic**

[Y] [X]

THE STARVING ARTIST CAFE
▼
American

Lunch: $5-$7 | Dinner: $13-$21 | Phone: 276/628-8445
Location: Just e at 5th traffic light; downtown. 134 Wall St 24210. **Hours:** 11 am-3 & 5-9 pm, Mon-2 pm. Closed major holidays; also Sun. **Features:** Creativity flows here, from the cozy brick building on a side street to the food. Posted on a chalkboard at the entrance, daily specials consist of pasta, sandwiches and salads. Inside are a few tables and a display of local art. Casual dress; beer & wine only. **Parking:** street.
Cards: AX, MC, VI.

THE TAVERN
▼▼▼ ▼▼▼
American

Dinner: $16-$32 | Phone: 276/628-1118
Location: I-81, exit 17, 0.7 mi n on Cummings St, then 0.5 mi e. 222 E Main St 24210. **Hours:** 5 pm-10 pm. Closed major holidays; also Sun. **Reservations:** suggested. **Features:** A restored 1779 stagecoach stop, the dark tavern has brick floors and historic decor. Much of the seating is in the enclosed rear patio or on the second-floor porch. An eclectic selection of beers complements a mix of American and German dishes. Casual dress; cocktails. **Parking:** street. **Cards:** AX, DS, MC, VI. **Historic**

[X]

WITHERS HARDWARE RESTAURANT
ⓐⓐⓐ
▼▼▼ ▼▼▼
American

Lunch: $4-$9 | Dinner: $9-$24 | Phone: 276/628-1111
Location: I-81, exit 17, 1.2 mi n on US 11; center. 260 W Main St 24210. **Hours:** 11 am-10 pm. Closed: 12/25. **Features:** The restored 1895 hardware store features turn-of-the-20th-century, Victorian-style decor and lots of brass, greenery and dark wood. The restaurant is known for prime rib, fresh seafood and attentive servers. The atmosphere is quiet, relaxed and cozy. Casual dress; cocktails. **Parking:** street. **Cards:** AX, CB, DC, DS, JC, MC, VI. **Historic**

[Y] [X]

ALEXANDRIA —*See District Of Columbia p. 500.*

ALTAVISTA pop. 3,425

─────── **WHERE TO STAY** ───────

COMFORT SUITES HOTEL *Book at aaa.com*
▼▼▼ ▼▼▼
Small-scale Hotel

All Year | 1P: $74-$148 | 2P: $81-$158 | XP: $7 | F18
Location: US 29 business route, at jct US 29. 1558 Main St 24517. Fax: 434/369-4007. **Facility:** 65 one-bedroom standard units, some with whirlpools. 2 stories (no elevator), interior corridors. **Parking:** on-site. **Terms:** 2 night minimum stay - seasonal, 7 day cancellation notice, pets ($10 fee). **Amenities:** dual phone lines. *Some:* irons, hair dryers. **Pool(s):** outdoor. **Leisure Activities:** miniature golf. **Guest Services:** gift shop, complimentary evening beverages, valet and coin laundry. **Business Services:** fax. **Cards:** AX, CB, DC, DS, JC, MC, VI.

Phone: (434)369-4000

SOME UNITS
[ASK] [S/D] [🛏] [🍽FEE] [Y] [🏊] [♿] [🐾] [DATA PORT] [🔌] [🍴] / [X] [VCR FEE]

HOLIDAY INN EXPRESS *Book at aaa.com*
▼▼▼ ▼▼▼
Small-scale Hotel

All Year | 1P: $70-$150 | 2P: $75-$155 | XP: $5 | F17
Location: US 29 business route, at jct US 29. 1557 Main St 24517. Fax: 434/369-4985. **Facility:** 66 one-bedroom standard units, some with whirlpools. 2 stories (no elevator), interior corridors. *Bath:* combo or shower only. **Parking:** on-site. **Amenities:** dual phone lines, voice mail, irons, hair dryers. **Leisure Activities:** exercise room. **Guest Services:** valet and coin laundry. **Business Services:** meeting rooms, business center. **Cards:** AX, CB, DC, DS, MC, VI.

Phone: 434/369-4070

SOME UNITS
[ASK] [S/D] [🔒M] [🍳] [🐾] [DATA PORT] [🔌] / [X] [🍴 FEE] [🔌 FEE] /

——— **WHERE TO DINE** ———

BETTY'S KITCHEN
◊ (symbol)
Regional American

Lunch: $5-$7   **Dinner:** $5-$10   **Phone:** 434/369-5363
Location: Center. 534 Main St 24517. **Hours:** 6 am-8 pm, Fri & Sat-8:30 pm. Closed: 11/24, 12/25.
Features: At Betty's Kitchen you'll find the true Southern homestyle dining experience with such favorites as country fried steak, cornbread, and on Mondays chicken and dumplings along with a fine assortment of pies. Casual dress. **Parking:** on-site. **Cards:** AX, DS, MC, VI.

⊠

AMELIA

——— **WHERE TO STAY** ———

WINTERHAM PLANTATION
◊◊◊ (symbols)
Historic Bed
& Breakfast

Phone: (804)561-4519
3/1-1/5 & 1/26-2/28   1P: $100-$250   2P: $100-$250   XP: $25   F12
Location: 1 mi n on SR 609 from US 360. 11441 Grub Hill Church Rd 23002. **Facility:** This historic farmhouse, circa 1840 sits amid rolling hills Gen. Lee's retreat route; it features Civil War relics and large guest rooms and suites. Smoke free premises. 4 units. 2 one- and 1 two-bedroom standard units, some with whirlpools. 1 two-bedroom suite. 2 stories, interior corridors. *Bath:* combo or shower only. **Parking:** on-site. **Terms:** open 3/1-1/5 & 1/26-2/28, 10 day cancellation notice, package plans, no pets allowed (owner's pet on premises). **Leisure Activities:** fishing. **Cards:** AX, DS, MC, VI.

SOME UNITS
(ASK) ⊠ DATA PORT ☎ / VCR 🛏 📷 🖥 /

ANNANDALE —See District Of Columbia p. 511.

APPOMATTOX pop. 1,761

——— **WHERE TO STAY** ———

THE BABCOCK HOUSE
◊◊◊ (symbols)
Historic Bed
& Breakfast

Phone: (434)352-7532
All Year   1P: $95
Location: US 460 business route, just s. 250 Oakleigh Ave 24522. Fax: 434/352-9743. **Facility:** Featuring a grand second-floor veranda, this restored turn-of-the-20th-century inn offers spacious lodgings with fine antiques and wide-plank floors. Smoke free premises. 6 units. 5 one-bedroom standard units. 1 one-bedroom suite ($120). 2 stories (no elevator), interior corridors. *Bath:* combo or shower only. **Parking:** on-site. **Terms:** 3 day cancellation notice. **Amenities:** hair dryers. **Dining:** restaurant, see separate listing. **Cards:** AX, DS, MC, VI.

SOME UNITS
🅂🄳 🍴 ⊠ 🖥 / VCR /

SUPER 8 MOTEL   **Book at aaa.com**
◊ (symbol)
Motel

Phone: (434)352-2339
All Year   1P: $52-$62   2P: $56-$66   XP: $6   F16
Location: US 460, just w of jct US 26. Rt 4, Box 100 24522. Fax: 434/352-2339. **Facility:** 45 one-bedroom standard units. 2 stories (no elevator), interior corridors. **Parking:** on-site. **Terms:** pets ($60 fee, limit 1). **Amenities:** safes. **Business Services:** meeting rooms. **Cards:** AX, DS, MC, VI.

SOME UNITS
(ASK) 🅂🄳 🐾 🍴 📶 DATA PORT / ⊠ 🛏 📷 🖥 /
FEE   FEE

——— **WHERE TO DINE** ———

THE BABCOCK HOUSE
◊◊ (symbols)
Regional American

Lunch: $5-$6   **Dinner:** $16-$19   **Phone:** 434/352-7532
Location: US 460 business route, just s; in The Babcock House. 106 Oakleigh Ave 24522. **Hours:** 11 am-1:30 pm, Sun-2 pm; Tues-Sat dinner by reservation. Closed: Mon & for lunch Sat. **Reservations:** required, for dinner. **Features:** The charming historic inn prepares such lunch choices as fresh salads, sandwiches and daily soups. Desserts, especially hummingbird cake, are a highlight not to be missed. Finer entrees and a more romantic mood appear for evening meals. Casual dress; beer & wine only. **Parking:** on-site. **Cards:** AX, DS, MC, VI.

🄺 ⊠

ARLINGTON —See District Of Columbia p. 511.

ARRINGTON

——— **WHERE TO STAY** ———

HARMONY HILL BED & BREAKFAST
◊◊ (symbols)
Bed & Breakfast

Phone: (434)263-7750
All Year [BP]   1P: $85-$115   2P: $85-$115   XP: $20   D12
Location: 0.9 mi e on SR 665 from US 29. Located in a rural area. 929 Wilson Hill Rd 22922. Fax: 434/263-4457. **Facility:** Smoke free premises. 5 one-bedroom standard units, some with whirlpools. 2 stories (no elevator), interior corridors. *Bath:* combo or shower only. **Parking:** on-site. **Terms:** check-in 4 pm, 2 night minimum stay - seasonal, age restrictions may apply, 14 day cancellation notice, weekly rates available, package plans. **Amenities:** hair dryers. **Leisure Activities:** hiking trails. **Guest Services:** complimentary laundry. **Cards:** DS, MC, VI.

(ASK) 🅂🄳 ⊠ 🄺 ☎

ASHBURN —See District Of Columbia p. 523.

ASHLAND —See Richmond p. 854.

ATKINS pop. 1,138

------ WHERE TO STAY ------

COMFORT INN
AAA SAVE
Small-scale Hotel

Book at aaa.com
3/1-10/31 [ECP]	1P: $59-$175	2P: $65-$179	XP: $10 F16
11/1-2/28 [ECP]	1P: $55-$85	2P: $60-$90	XP: $10 F16

Phone: (276)783-2144

Location: I-81, exit 50, just w, then just n on US 11. 5558 Lee Hwy 24311 (4331 S Lee Hwy, NATURAL BRIDGE, 24578). Fax: 276/782-9668. **Facility:** 50 one-bedroom standard units. 2 stories (no elevator), interior corridors. **Parking:** on-site. **Amenities:** irons, hair dryers. **Cards:** AX, CB, DC, DS, MC, VI. **Special Amenities:** free expanded continental breakfast and free local telephone calls.

SOME UNITS
[S D] [iron] [data port] / [X] /

ATLANTIC

------ WHERE TO DINE ------

------ *The following restaurant has not been evaluated by AAA but is listed for your information only.* ------

BLUE MOON GOURMET CARRYOUT
[fyi]
Phone: 757/824-3995
Not evaluated. **Location:** SR 175, 2.3 mi e of jct US 13. 33032 Chincoteague Rd 23415. **Features:** On the way to the beach, this is the place to stop for organic and healthy fare like fresh-baked breads and smoked fish, including a divine smoked salmon salad.

BARBOURSVILLE

------ WHERE TO DINE ------

BLACKHAWK GRILL
WWW
American

Dinner: $10-$22

Phone: 304/736-9494

Location: I-64, exit 18, just n. 646 Central Ave 25504. **Hours:** 5 pm-10 pm. Closed: 3/27; also Sun & Mon. **Reservations:** suggested. **Features:** Appointed in an English style, the restaurant's dining room is bathed in light that streams in through stained-glass windows. Creativity marks the entrees, as well as the gourmet desserts. Casual dress; cocktails. **Parking:** on-site. **Cards:** AX, MC, VI.

[dine] [X]

BEDFORD pop. 6,299

------ WHERE TO STAY ------

DAYS INN
WWW
Small-scale Hotel

Book at aaa.com
5/1-10/31	1P: $54-$68	2P: $58-$68	
3/1-4/30 & 11/1-2/28	1P: $51-$60	2P: $51-$66	

Phone: (540)586-8286

Location: Jct US 221, 1.5 mi w, on US 460. 921 Blue Ridge Ave 24523. Fax: 540/586-4435. **Facility:** 75 one-bedroom standard units. 2 stories (no elevator), exterior corridors. *Bath:* combo or shower only. **Parking:** on-site, winter plug-ins. **Terms:** small pets only. **Amenities:** hair dryers. *Some:* irons. **Pool(s):** outdoor. **Guest Services:** coin laundry. **Business Services:** fax. **Cards:** AX, DS, MC, VI.

SOME UNITS
[ASK] [S D] [pet] [iron] [outdoor pool] [data port] [box] [box] [box] / [X] /
FEE

SUPER 8 MOTEL
WW
Small-scale Hotel

Book at aaa.com
All Year	1P: $57-$65	2P: $62-$70	XP: $5 F18

Phone: (540)587-0100

Location: 1.5 mi w on US 221 and 460. 842 Sword Beach Ln 24523. Fax: 540/587-0808. **Facility:** 58 one-bedroom standard units, some with whirlpools. 2 stories (no elevator), interior corridors. *Bath:* combo or shower only. **Parking:** on-site. **Business Services:** meeting rooms. **Cards:** AX, CB, DC, DS, MC, VI.

SOME UNITS
[ASK] [S D] [iron] [M] [data port] / [X] [box] [box] [box] /
FEE FEE FEE

BIG STONE GAP pop. 4,856

------ WHERE TO STAY ------

COMFORT INN
WWW
Small-scale Hotel

Book at aaa.com
3/1-8/31 [ECP]	1P: $75-$175	2P: $75-$175	XP: $5 F17
9/1-2/28 [ECP]	1P: $70-$140	2P: $75-$150	XP: $5 F17

Phone: (276)523-5911

Location: US 23, just n. 1928B Wildcat Rd 24219. Fax: 276/523-0726. **Facility:** 61 one-bedroom standard units, some with whirlpools. 3 stories, interior corridors. *Bath:* combo or shower only. **Parking:** on-site. **Amenities:** irons, hair dryers. **Pool(s):** heated indoor. **Leisure Activities:** whirlpool, exercise room. **Guest Services:** coin laundry. **Business Services:** meeting rooms. **Cards:** AX, CB, DC, DS, MC, VI.

SOME UNITS
[ASK] [S D] [iron] [indoor pool] [data port] [box] / [X] [VCR] [box] [box] /

COUNTRY INN MOTEL
AAA SAVE
WW
Motel

All Year	1P: $45	2P: $50	XP: $5 D12

Phone: (276)523-0374

Location: US 23, 1 mi w on US 23 business route and 58A. 627 Gilley Ave 24219. Fax: 276/523-5043. **Facility:** 42 one-bedroom standard units. 2 stories (no elevator), exterior corridors. **Parking:** on-site. **Terms:** package plans, small pets only ($2 extra charge). **Leisure Activities:** basketball, horseshoes. **Cards:** AX, CB, DC, DS, MC, VI.

SOME UNITS

FEE
[box] [box] / [X] /

BLACKSBURG pop. 39,573

------ **WHERE TO STAY** ------

AMERISUITES (BLACKSBURG/UNIVERSITY)   *Book at aaa.com*   **Phone:** (540)552-5636
All Year   1P: $79-$170   2P: $79-$170
Location: I-81, exit 118 (US 460 Bypass), follow signs for Virginia Tech, pass main entrance, right on Prices Fork Rd (SR 412). 1020 Plantation Rd 24060. Fax: 540/552-5138. **Facility:** 94 one-bedroom standard units. 5 stories, interior corridors. *Bath:* combo or shower only. **Parking:** on-site. **Terms:** check-in 4 pm, 2 night minimum
Small-scale Hotel stay - seasonal. **Amenities:** high-speed Internet, voice mail, irons, hair dryers. **Pool(s):** indoor. **Leisure Activities:** exercise room. **Guest Services:** valet and coin laundry. **Business Services:** meeting rooms.
Cards: AX, CB, DC, DS, MC, VI. **Special Amenities:** free expanded continental breakfast and free newspaper.
(See color ad p 870)
SOME UNITS
⬛⬛⬛⬛⬛⬛ / ⬛ /

BEST WESTERN RED LION INN   *Book at aaa.com*   **Phone:** 540/552-7770
Property failed to provide current rates
Location: 1.7 mi w on SR 685; jct US 460 Bypass and Prices Fork Rd. 900 Plantation Rd 24060. Fax: 540/552-6346.
Small-scale Hotel **Facility:** 100 one-bedroom standard units. 2 stories (no elevator), exterior corridors. **Parking:** on-site.
Terms: small pets only. **Amenities:** irons, hair dryers. **Pool(s):** outdoor. **Leisure Activities:** horseshoes,
volleyball. **Guest Services:** valet laundry. **Business Services:** meeting rooms.
SOME UNITS
⬛⬛⬛⬛⬛ / ⬛ ⬛ /
FEE

COMFORT INN   *Book at aaa.com*   **Phone:** (540)951-1500
8/2-2/28 [ECP]   1P: $55-$135   2P: $60-$135   XP: $5   F18
5/13-8/1 [ECP]   1P: $55-$100   2P: $60-$100   XP: $5   F18
3/1-5/12 [ECP]   1P: $55-$88   2P: $60-$88   XP: $5   F18
Location: 3.5 mi s on US 460, jct US 460 Bypass. 3705 S Main St 24060. Fax: 540/951-1530. **Facility:** 80 one-
Small-scale Hotel bedroom standard units, some with whirlpools. 4 stories, interior corridors. **Parking:** on-site. **Terms:** 2 night
minimum stay - seasonal and/or weekends, 7 day cancellation notice-fee imposed, small pets only.
Amenities: high-speed Internet, voice mail, safes, irons, hair dryers. **Pool(s):** heated outdoor. **Leisure Activities:** exercise
room. **Guest Services:** valet laundry. **Business Services:** meeting rooms. **Cards:** AX, CB, DC, DS, JC, MC, VI.
Special Amenities: free local telephone calls and free room upgrade (subject to availability with advance
reservations).
SOME UNITS
⬛⬛⬛⬛⬛⬛⬛ / ⬛⬛⬛ /

HOLIDAY INN BLACKSBURG   *Book at aaa.com*   **Phone:** (540)552-7001
All Year   1P: $79-$149   2P: $79-$149   XP: $10   F17
Location: 0.7 mi e on Prices Fork Rd (SR 412) from jct US 460 Bypass. Located adjacent to Virginia Tech campus. 900
Prices Fork Rd 24060. Fax: 540/552-0827. **Facility:** 148 one-bedroom standard units. 2 stories (no elevator),
Small-scale Hotel interior corridors. *Bath:* combo or shower only. **Parking:** on-site. **Amenities:** video games, high-speed
Internet, dual phone lines, voice mail, safes (fee), irons, hair dryers. **Pool(s):** heated indoor/outdoor. **Leisure Activities:** tennis
court, exercise room, volleyball. **Guest Services:** valet and coin laundry. **Business Services:** meeting rooms. **Cards:** AX, CB,
DC, DS, JC, MC, VI.
SOME UNITS
[ASK] ⬛⬛⬛⬛⬛⬛⬛⬛⬛ / ⬛⬛⬛ /

------ **WHERE TO DINE** ------

BACKSTREETS RESTAURANT   **Lunch:** $7-$15   **Dinner:** $10-$20   **Phone:** 540/552-6712
Location: Center. 207 S Main St 24060. **Hours:** 11 am-11 pm, Fri & Sat-midnight. Closed major holidays.
Features: Specialties at the neighborhood restaurant include Tuscan shrimp, chicken Marsala, pizza and
American tiramisu. Casual dress; beer only. **Parking:** on-site. **Cards:** AX, DS, MC, VI.   ⬛

BOUDREAUX'S CAJUN RESTAURANT   **Lunch:** $5-$16   **Dinner:** $8-$18   **Phone:** 540/961-2330
Location: Center. 205 N Main St 24060. **Hours:** 11 am-11 pm. Closed major holidays. **Features:** Cajun dishes
are the rage in the simple setting. The kitchen accommodates requests for extra-hot food. Casual dress;
Cajun beer only. **Parking:** on-site. **Cards:** AX, DC, DS, MC, VI.   ⬛

CINCO DE MAYO MEXICAN RESTAURANT   **Lunch:** $7-$10   **Dinner:** $7-$17   **Phone:** 540/951-7300
Location: 3.6 mi s on US 460, jct US 460 Bypass. 3703 S Main St 24060. **Hours:** 11 am-11 pm. Closed: 12/25.
Features: Cinco de Mayo Mexican Restaurant is a fun casual dining establishment you will enjoy every
Mexican visit, not just on May 5. Wide variety on the menu and friendly service. Casual dress; cocktails. **Parking:** on-
site. **Cards:** AX, CB, DC, DS, JC, MC, VI.   ⬛⬛

MAXWELL'S   **Lunch:** $10-$20   **Dinner:** $10-$26   **Phone:** 540/552-3300
Location: 0.5 mi n; center. 1204 N Main St 24060. **Hours:** 11:30 am-10 pm, Sat from 5 pm. Closed: 12/25; also
Sun. **Reservations:** suggested, weekends. **Features:** Maxwell's offers a handsome, relaxed and cozy
American atmosphere. Modern plate presentations, taste and an award winning chef. Casual dress; cocktails.
Parking: on-site. **Cards:** AX, CB, DC, DS, JC, MC, VI.   ⬛⬛

NERV RESTAURANT & LOUNGE   **Lunch:** $7-$15   **Dinner:** $10-$25   **Phone:** 540/961-3004
Location: Center. 221 Progress St 24060. **Hours:** 11 am-2 am. Closed: 12/25. **Reservations:** suggested,
weekends. **Features:** The modern, sophisticated restaurant and lounge nurtures an upscale atmosphere.
American Eclectic menu choices are moderately priced. Casual dress; cocktails. **Parking:** on-site. **Cards:** AX, CB,
DC, DS, JC, MC, VI.   ⬛⬛

VINCENT'S RISTORANTE
Italian
MC, VI.

Dinner: $10-$22   **Phone:** 540/552-9000
Location: Jct US 460 and 460 business route, 2.1 mi w on US 460 business route. 1200 S Main St 24060. **Hours:** 4:30 pm-10 pm, Sun 4 pm-9 pm. Closed: 1/1, 11/24, 12/25; also Mon. **Features:** The family-operated Italian eatery prepares many pasta selections, fresh salads, bread and desserts in a setting that emanates Old World charm. Casual dress; beer & wine only. **Parking:** on-site. **Cards:** AX, CB, DC, DS, JC,

ZEPPOLI'S ITALIAN RESTAURANT
Italian

Lunch: $6-$15   **Dinner:** $8-$18   **Phone:** 540/953-2000
Location: 0.6 mi e on Prices Fork Rd (SR 412) from jct US 460 Bypass. 810 University City Blvd 24060. **Hours:** 11 am-10 pm. Closed: 12/24, 12/25. **Features:** The sauces, the bread, the pasta and the sausage are all made on the premises to ensure absolute freshness. Casual dress; cocktails. **Parking:** on-site. **Cards:** AX, CB, DC, DS, JC, MC, VI.

BLUEFIELD pop. 5,078

-------- WHERE TO STAY --------

COMFORT INN-BLUEFIELD   *Book at aaa.com*
Small-scale Hotel

    Phone: (276)326-3688

	1P:	2P:	XP:	
5/8-10/31 [ECP]	1P: $64-$100	2P: $70-$100	XP: $6	F18
3/1-5/7 & 11/1-2/28 [ECP]	1P: $59-$100	2P: $59-$100	XP: $6	F18

Location: I-77, exit 1, 2.7 mi nw on SR 52, then 9.7 mi w on US 460. Rt 19 & 460 W 24605 (Rt 2, Box 222A). **Fax:** 276/326-3688. **Facility:** 61 one-bedroom standard units. 2 stories (no elevator), interior corridors. **Parking:** on-site. **Amenities:** irons, hair dryers. **Pool(s):** heated outdoor. **Leisure Activities:** picnic tables, basketball. *Fee:* golf privileges. **Cards:** AX, DC, DS, MC, VI. **Special Amenities:** free expanded continental breakfast and free local telephone calls.

SOME UNITS

BRIDGEWATER pop. 5,203

-------- WHERE TO DINE --------

BOB-A-REA'S
Italian

Lunch: $6-$12   **Dinner:** $8-$18   **Phone:** 540/828-3433
Location: Just n. 305 N Main St 22812. **Hours:** 6 am-10 pm, Sun from 1 pm. Closed: 12/25; also Mon. **Features:** The family-operated hometown pasta place offers a fun, casual setting ideal for families. Homemade specials make menu appearances daily. Casual dress; beer only. **Parking:** on-site. **Cards:** AX, CB, DC, DS, JC, MC, VI.

NORTH RIVER GRILL
American

Lunch: $6-$14   **Dinner:** $10-$19   **Phone:** 540/828-0700
Location: Center. 101 N Main St 22812. **Hours:** 11 am-10 pm. Closed: 1/1, 11/24, 12/25; also Mon. **Features:** North River Grill features favorites from the Shenandoah Valley like Fried Chicken and Peanut Soup. Casual dress; cocktails. **Parking:** street. **Cards:** AX, CB, DC, DS, JC, MC, VI.

BRISTOL pop. 17,367

-------- WHERE TO STAY --------

BUDGET HOST INN
Motel

    Phone: 276/669-5187

	1P:	2P:	XP:	
All Year	1P: $34-$158	2P: $49-$178	XP: $6	

Location: I-81, exit 1, 2 mi s on SR 421. 1209 W State St 24201. **Fax:** 276/466-5848. **Facility:** 23 one-bedroom standard units, some with whirlpools. 1 story, exterior corridors. **Parking:** on-site. **Terms:** 3 day cancellation notice-fee imposed. **Cards:** AX, DC, MC, VI. **Special Amenities:** free local telephone calls.

SOME UNITS

ECONO LODGE   *Book at aaa.com*
Motel

    Phone: (276)466-2112

	1P:	2P:	XP:	
All Year	1P: $34-$350	2P: $44-$350	XP: $5	F18

Location: I-81, exit 3. 1.5 mi e. Located in a commercial area. 912 Commonwealth Ave 24201. **Fax:** 276/466-0045. **Facility:** 48 one-bedroom standard units. 2 stories (no elevator), exterior corridors. **Parking:** on-site. **Terms:** small pets only ($10 fee). **Amenities:** safes. *Some:* hair dryers. **Cards:** AX, DC, DS, MC, VI.

SOME UNITS

HOLIDAY INN HOTEL & SUITES   *Book at aaa.com*
Large-scale Hotel

    Phone: 276/466-4100

	1P:	2P:	XP:	
All Year	1P: $99	2P: $99	XP: $7	F12

Location: I-81, exit 7, just w. 3005 Linden Dr 24202. **Fax:** 276/466-4103. **Facility:** 226 one-bedroom standard units, some with whirlpools. 10 stories, interior corridors. *Bath:* combo or shower only. **Parking:** on-site. **Terms:** [BP] meal plan available, package plans, small pets only ($10 extra charge). **Amenities:** video games, voice mail, irons, hair dryers. **Pool(s):** heated outdoor. **Leisure Activities:** whirlpool, exercise room. **Guest Services:** valet and coin laundry. **Business Services:** conference facilities. **Cards:** AX, CB, DC, DS, MC, VI.

SOME UNITS

LA QUINTA INN BRISTOL   *Book at aaa.com*

AAA SAVE
Small-scale Hotel

			Phone: (276)669-9353
11/1-2/28	1P: $65-$89	2P: $71-$95	XP: $6 F18
5/16-10/31	1P: $65-$85	2P: $71-$91	XP: $6 F18
3/1-5/15	1P: $62-$72	2P: $68-$78	XP: $6 F18

Location: I-81, exit 7. 1014 Old Airport Rd 24201. Fax: 276/669-6974. **Facility:** 123 one-bedroom standard units. 4 stories, exterior corridors. *Bath:* combo or shower only. **Parking:** on-site. **Terms:** [ECP] meal plan available, small pets only. **Amenities:** video games, high-speed Internet, voice mail, irons, hair dryers. **Pool(s):** outdoor. **Guest Services:** valet laundry. **Business Services:** meeting rooms. **Cards:** AX, DC, DS, MC, VI. **Special Amenities:** free expanded continental breakfast and free local telephone calls.

SOME UNITS

MICROTEL INN & SUITES   *Book at aaa.com*

Small-scale Hotel

			Phone: (276)669-8164
All Year [CP]	1P: $54-$59	2P: $59-$64	XP: $5 F17

Location: I-81, exit 7 northbound, just w; exit southbound, just e. 131 Bristol Rd E 24201. Fax: 276/669-2805. **Facility:** 65 one-bedroom standard units, some with whirlpools. 3 stories, interior corridors. **Parking:** on-site. **Terms:** 5 day cancellation notice, small pets only ($10 extra charge). **Pool(s):** heated indoor. **Leisure Activities:** whirlpool. **Cards:** AX, CB, DC, DS, MC, VI.

SOME UNITS

FEE

MOTEL 6   *Book at aaa.com*

Small-scale Hotel

			Phone: 276/466-6060
All Year	1P: $45-$58	2P: $52-$64	XP: $6 F17

Location: I-81, exit 7, 0.3 mi w. 21561 Clear Creek Rd 24202. Fax: 276/466-0755. **Facility:** 53 one-bedroom standard units. 3 stories, interior corridors. *Bath:* combo or tub only. **Parking:** on-site. **Terms:** cancellation fee imposed, pets ($10 extra charge). **Guest Services:** coin laundry. **Cards:** AX, DS, MC, VI.

SOME UNITS

FEE

SUPER 8 MOTEL   *Book at aaa.com*

Small-scale Hotel

			Phone: (276)466-8800
All Year	1P: $44-$275	2P: $44-$275	XP: $7 F16

Location: I-81, exit 5, just s. 2139 Lee Hwy 24201. Fax: 276/466-6255. **Facility:** 62 one-bedroom standard units. 3 stories (no elevator), interior corridors. **Parking:** on-site. **Terms:** 3 night minimum stay - seasonal, pets ($10 extra charge). **Cards:** AX, DC, DS, MC, VI.

SOME UNITS

FEE

———— WHERE TO DINE ————

ATHEN'S STEAK HOUSE

Steak House

Dinner: $8-$19   **Phone:** 276/466-8271

Location: I-81, exit 3, 2.6 mi s to State St, 0.6 mi e, then just n. 105 Goodson St 24201. **Hours:** 4 pm-10 pm. Closed: 1/1, 11/24, 12/25; also Sun. **Reservations:** accepted. **Features:** The flavors of America and Greece mingle in selections on the restaurant's tempting menu. Most popular are the steaks and homemade desserts, such as baklava and apple pie. Parquet and carpet floors, along with candles and light music, create ambience. Casual dress; cocktails. **Parking:** on-site. **Cards:** AX, MC, VI.

THE VINYARD RESTAURANT

Italian

Dinner: $9-$30   **Phone:** 276/466-4244

Location: I-81, exit 1, 0.5 mi s on US 421. 603 Gate City Hwy 24201. **Hours:** 4 pm-10 pm, Fri & Sat-11 pm. Closed: 7/4, 12/25. **Reservations:** suggested, weekends. **Features:** Patrons can choose from a wide selection of traditional Southern Italian dishes, as well as steak and fish. Lasagna is made from scratch, and prime rib is hand-cut. Meatballs make for a delicious meal addition. Portions are ample. Casual dress; cocktails. **Parking:** on-site. **Cards:** AX, DC, DS, MC, VI.

BUCHANAN pop. 1,233

———— WHERE TO STAY ————

WATTSTULL INN

AAA SAVE
Small-scale Hotel

			Phone: 540/254-1551
All Year		2P: $50-$65	XP: $5 F10

Location: I-81, exit 168, just e on SR 614. Located in a quiet, rural area. 130 Arcadia Rd 24066. Fax: 540/254-9888. **Facility:** 26 one-bedroom standard units. 1 story, exterior corridors. **Parking:** on-site. **Terms:** 7 day cancellation notice-fee imposed. **Dining:** 7 am-9 pm, wine/beer only. **Pool(s):** outdoor, wading. **Cards:** DS, MC, VI.

SOME UNITS

BUENA VISTA pop. 6,349

———— WHERE TO STAY ————

BUENA VISTA MOTEL

AAA SAVE
Motel

			Phone: 540/261-2138
All Year	1P: $35-$65	2P: $40-$70	XP: $5 F12

Location: I-81, exit 188A, 4.3 mi e on US 60, 0.4 mi w of Blue Ridge Pkwy. 447 E 29th St 24416. Fax: 540/261-4430. **Facility:** 19 one-bedroom standard units. 1 story, exterior corridors. **Parking:** on-site. **Terms:** pets ($5 extra charge, in smoking units). **Amenities:** irons, hair dryers. **Cards:** AX, DS, MC, VI.

SOME UNITS

FEE

BURKEVILLE pop. 489

―――― WHERE TO STAY ――――

COMFORT INN BURKEVILLE [CP]   *Book at aaa.com*   Phone: (434)767-3750
(AAA) (SAVE)   All Year [CP]   1P: $75-$145   2P: $75-$145   XP: $6   F17
▽▽▽▽   **Location:** On US 460, just e of jct US 360. 419 N Agnew St 23922. Fax: 434/767-3767. **Facility:** 60 one-bedroom
Small-scale Hotel   standard units, some with whirlpools. 2 stories, interior corridors. *Bath:* combo or shower only. **Parking:** on-
site. **Terms:** cancellation fee imposed, small pets only ($20 fee). **Amenities:** high-speed Internet, dual
phone lines, voice mail, irons, hair dryers. **Dining:** 24 hours. **Pool(s):** heated indoor. **Leisure**
Activities: exercise room. *Fee:* game room. **Guest Services:** coin laundry. **Business Services:** meeting
rooms, fax. **Cards:** AX, CB, DC, DS, JC, MC, VI. **Special Amenities:** free continental breakfast and free newspaper.

SOME UNITS
[icons] FEE / FEE

CALLAGHAN

―――― WHERE TO STAY ――――

MILTON HALL BED AND BREAKFAST   Phone: (540)965-0196
▽▽▽▽   All Year [BP]   1P: $90-$175   2P: $90-$175   XP: $25   D12
Historic Bed   **Location:** I-64, exit 10, just s of US 60/SR 159, 0.5 mi w on Rt 600 (Indian Draft Rd), then just n. 207 Thorny Ln 24426
& Breakfast   (207 Thorny Ln, COVINGTON). Fax: 540/962-8232. **Facility:** Milton Hall is an English Gothic manor house and
a Virginia historic landmark. 5 one-bedroom standard units. 2 stories (no elevator), interior corridors. *Bath:*
combo or shower only. **Parking:** on-site. **Terms:** 2 night minimum stay - seasonal and/or weekends,
cancellation fee imposed, weekly rates available, package plans. **Amenities:** hair dryers. *Some:* irons. **Guest Services:** gift
shop, complimentary evening beverages. **Cards:** MC, VI.

SOME UNITS
[ASK] [icons] / [icons] /

CAPE CHARLES pop. 1,134

―――― WHERE TO STAY ――――

BEST WESTERN SUNSET BEACH RESORT   *Book at aaa.com*   Phone: (757)331-1776
(AAA) (SAVE)   5/27-9/4   1P: $104-$129   2P: $104-$129   XP: $10   F18
▽▽▽▽   9/5-10/10   1P: $76-$113   2P: $76-$113   XP: $10   F18
3/1-5/26   1P: $64-$109   2P: $64-$109   XP: $10   F18
Small-scale Hotel   10/11-2/28   1P: $64-$101   2P: $64-$101   XP: $10   F18
Location: US 13, just n of the Chesapeake Bay Bridge Tunnel. 32246 Lankford Hwy 23310. Fax: 757/331-3744.
Facility: 73 units. 65 one-bedroom standard units. 8 one-bedroom suites ($89-$129). 2 stories (no
elevator), exterior corridors. *Bath:* combo or shower only. **Parking:** on-site. **Terms:** cancellation fee imposed, pets ($10 extra
charge). **Amenities:** irons, hair dryers. **Dining:** 7 am-2 & 5-9 pm, cocktails. **Pool(s):** outdoor. **Leisure Activities:** fishing, sea
kayak, playground, horseshoes, volleyball. **Guest Services:** coin laundry. **Business Services:** meeting rooms, fax. **Cards:** AX,
DC, DS, MC, VI. **Special Amenities:** early check-in/late check-out and free room upgrade (subject to availability with
advance reservations).

SOME UNITS
[icons] FEE / [icons] FEE FEE FEE /

―――― WHERE TO DINE ――――

HARBOR GRILLE & TAKE-OUT MARKET   **Lunch:** $5-$10   **Dinner:** $5-$10   Phone: 757/331-3005
▽▽▽▽   **Location:** Downtown; on the waterfront. 203/205 Mason Ave 23310. **Hours:** 11 am-3:30 pm, Thurs-Sat 5:30 pm-10
American   pm. **Reservations:** suggested. **Features:** The casual spot presents a tasty menu that mixes gourmet with
down-home favorites. Patrons can sit in the friendly bar, the sidewalk cafe or the tiny tapas lounge to enjoy
such favorites as bronzed tuna carpaccio, blackened crab cake, jumbo shrimp salad, coconut cream pie and
treats from the raw bar. Casual dress; cocktails. **Parking:** street. **Cards:** AX, MC, VI.

[icons]

MARIAH'S AT TOWER HILL BED &
BREAKFAST INN   **Dinner:** $18-$28   Phone: 757/331-1700
(AAA)   **Location:** US 13, just w on SR 184 to Parsons Circle, just n; in Tower Hill Bed
▽▽▽▽   Breafast & Inn. 3018 Bowden Landing 23310. **Hours:** 5 pm-10 pm. Closed: 12/24, 12/25; also Mon & Tues.
American   **Reservations:** suggested. **Features:** Guests can dine in Colonial elegance in the main dining room or in
the romantic wine cellar at the elegant inn. The chef masterfully combines his fine training with fresh local
Country Inn   produce and Chesapeake Bay seafood. Casual dress; cocktails. **Parking:** on-site. **Cards:** AX, MC, VI.

[icons]

STINGRAY'S RESTAURANT   **Lunch:** $4-$8   **Dinner:** $8-$20   Phone: 757/331-2505
▽▽▽   **Location:** US 13. 26507 Lankford Hwy 23310. **Hours:** 6 am-9 pm, Fri & Sat 5:30 am-9:30 pm. Closed: 11/24,
Seafood   12/24, 12/25. **Features:** Guests can fill up the car at the gas station, then come inside to fill up themselves.
MC, VI.   Locals and travelers alike flock to the crowded spot for local seafood and Southern favorites cooked the old-
fashioned way. Prices are reasonable. Casual dress; beer & wine only. **Parking:** on-site. **Cards:** DS,

[icons]

CARMEL CHURCH —See *Richmond p. 856.*

CENTRAL WILLIAMSBURG —See *Williamsburg, Jamestown & Yorktown p. 914.*

CENTREVILLE —See *District Of Columbia p. 523.*

CHANTILLY —See *District Of Columbia p. 524.*

CHARLES CITY — *See Williamsburg, Jamestown & Yorktown p. 947.*

CHARLOTTESVILLE pop. 45,049

────── **WHERE TO STAY** ──────

BEST WESTERN-CAVALIER INN   *Book at aaa.com*   Phone: (434)296-8111
(AAA) (SAVE)   All Year [ECP]   1P: $77-$109   2P: $77-$109   XP: $10   F18
▼▼▼   **Location:** Jct US 29 and 250 Bypass, 1.3 mi s on US 29 business route. 105 N Emmet St 22903. Fax: 434/296-3523.
Facility: 118 one-bedroom standard units. 5 stories, interior/exterior corridors. **Parking:** on-site.
Terms: package plans. **Amenities:** voice mail, irons, hair dryers. **Pool(s):** outdoor. **Guest Services:** gift
Small-scale Hotel   shop, valet laundry, area transportation-University of Virginia Hospital. **Business Services:** meeting rooms,
business center. **Cards:** AX, CB, DC, DS, JC, MC, VI. **Special Amenities:** free expanded continental
breakfast. *(See color ad below)*

SOME UNITS
(icons)

BOAR'S HEAD INN   *Book at aaa.com*   Phone: (434)296-2181
(AAA) (SAVE)   4/1-11/27   1P: $175-$304   2P: $175-$304   XP: $15   F17
▼▼▼ ▼▼▼   3/1-3/31 & 11/28-2/28   1P: $165-$297   2P: $165-$297   XP: $15   F17
Resort   **Location:** Jct US 29 Bypass, 1 mi w on US 250. Located in a quiet area. Rt 250 W 22903 (PO Box 5307, 22905).
Large-scale Hotel   Fax: 434/972-6024. **Facility:** On 53 acres in the Blue Ridge foothills, this country-style resort offers
comfortably traditional guest rooms with a historic ambience. 171 one-bedroom standard units, some with
whirlpools. 3 stories, interior/exterior corridors. *Bath:* combo or shower only. **Parking:** on-site.
Terms: check-in 4 pm, 2 night minimum stay - seasonal and/or weekends, 7 day cancellation notice-fee
imposed, package plans, $8 service charge. **Amenities:** video games, high-speed Internet, voice mail, safes, irons, hair dryers.
Dining: 2 restaurants, 7:30 am-10 & 11:45-9:30 pm, cocktails, also, The Old Mill Room, see separate listing. **Pool(s):** 2 outdoor,
wading. **Leisure Activities:** saunas, whirlpool, fishing, driving range, bicycles, playground, spa, sports court. *Fee:* golf-18 holes,
20 tennis courts (6 indoor, 6 lighted), 2 squash courts, aerobics. **Guest Services:** gift shop, valet laundry, area transportation-
University of Virginia. **Business Services:** conference facilities, business center. **Cards:** AX, DC, DS, MC, VI.
Special Amenities: free local telephone calls and free newspaper.

SOME UNITS
(icons)

BUDGET INN   Phone: (434)293-5141
(AAA) (SAVE)   3/1-11/30   1P: $49-$79   2P: $49-$79   XP: $10   D12
▼▼▼   12/1-2/28   1P: $44-$74   2P: $44-$74   XP: $10   D12
Location: Jct US 29 and 250 Bypass, 1.3 mi s on US 29 business route. 140 Emmet St 22903. Fax: 434/979-4529.
Motel   **Facility:** 37 one-bedroom standard units. 2 stories (no elevator), exterior corridors. *Bath:* combo or shower
only. **Parking:** on-site. **Terms:** 7 day cancellation notice-fee imposed. **Cards:** AX, DS, MC, VI.

SOME UNITS
(icons)

COMFORT INN   *Book at aaa.com*   Phone: (434)293-6188
(AAA) (SAVE)   All Year [ECP]   1P: $65-$99,   2P: $65-$99   XP: $8   F18
▼▼▼   **Location:** Jct US 250 Bypass, just n on US 29. 1807 Emmet St 22901. Fax: 434/293-6718. **Facility:** 64 one-
bedroom standard units. 4 stories, interior corridors. *Bath:* combo or shower only. **Parking:** on-site.
Terms: small pets only ($10 extra charge, in smoking units). **Amenities:** voice mail, safes, irons, hair
Small-scale Hotel   dryers. **Pool(s):** outdoor. **Guest Services:** valet laundry. **Cards:** AX, CB, DC, DS, JC, MC, VI.
Special Amenities: free expanded continental breakfast and free newspaper.

SOME UNITS
(icons)   FEE

COURTYARD BY MARRIOTT   *Book at aaa.com*   Phone: 434/973-7100
(AAA) (SAVE)   All Year   1P: $89   2P: $89
▼▼▼   **Location:** US 29, 1.4 mi n of US 250 Bypass. 638 Hillsdale Dr 22901. Fax: 434/973-7128. **Facility:** 150 one-
bedroom standard units. 2-3 stories, interior corridors. *Bath:* combo or shower only. **Parking:** on-site.
Terms: 5 day cancellation notice. **Amenities:** high-speed Internet, dual phone lines, voice mail, irons, hair
Small-scale Hotel   dryers. **Dining:** 6:30-10 am, Sat & Sun 7-11 am, cocktails. **Pool(s):** heated indoor. **Leisure
Activities:** whirlpool, exercise room. **Guest Services:** coin laundry. **Business Services:** meeting rooms.
Cards: AX, DC, DS, MC, VI.

SOME UNITS
(icons)

COURTYARD BY MARRIOT UNIVERSITY MEDICAL CENTER *Book at aaa.com*

Phone: 434/977-1700

All Year   1P: $99-$159   2P: $99-$159

Location: I-64, exit 120, 2 mi n on 5th St, then left. 1201 W Main St 22903. Fax: 434/977-2600. **Facility:** 137 one-bedroom standard units, some with whirlpools. 4 stories, interior corridors. *Bath:* combo or shower only. **Parking:** on-site. **Terms:** 3 day cancellation notice-fee imposed. **Amenities:** high-speed Internet, voice mail, irons, hair dryers. **Pool(s):** indoor. **Leisure Activities:** whirlpool, exercise room. **Guest Services:** gift shop, valet and coin laundry. **Business Services:** meeting rooms, business center. **Cards:** AX, DC, MC, VI.

Small-scale Hotel

SOME UNITS

DAYS INN UNIVERSITY AREA   *Book at aaa.com*

Phone: (434)293-9111

4/1-11/30   1P: $69-$89   2P: $79-$99   XP: $10   F18
3/1-3/31 & 12/1-2/28   1P: $55-$60   2P: $65-$70   XP: $10   F18

Location: I-64, exit 118B (US 29), just n of jct US 250 Bypass. 1600 Emmet St 22901. Fax: 434/977-2780. **Facility:** 129 one-bedroom standard units. 2-3 stories (no elevator), exterior corridors. **Parking:** on-site. **Terms:** [AP] meal plan available, pets ($10 extra charge). **Amenities:** voice mail, safes, irons, hair dryers. **Pool(s):** outdoor, wading. **Leisure Activities:** exercise room. **Guest Services:** coin laundry, area transportation. **Business Services:** meeting rooms. **Cards:** AX, CB, DC, DS, JC, MC, VI.

Small-scale Hotel

SOME UNITS

FEE

DOUBLETREE HOTEL CHARLOTTESVILLE   *Book at aaa.com*

Phone: (434)973-2121

All Year   1P: $79-$136   2P: $79-$136   XP: $10   F18

Location: I-64, exit 118B (US 29), 4 mi n of jct US 250 Bypass. 990 Hilton Heights Rd 22901. Fax: 434/978-7735. **Facility:** 240 one-bedroom standard units, some with whirlpools. 9 stories, interior corridors. *Bath:* combo or shower only. **Parking:** on-site. **Terms:** 2 night minimum stay - seasonal, cancellation fee imposed, package plans, small pets only ($25 extra charge). **Amenities:** voice mail, irons, hair dryers. **Pool(s):** heated outdoor, heated indoor. **Leisure Activities:** whirlpools, 2 tennis courts, exercise room. **Guest Services:** valet laundry. **Business Services:** conference facilities, business center. **Cards:** AX, DC, DS, MC, VI.

Small-scale Hotel

SOME UNITS

FEE   FEE FEE

ECONO LODGE-NORTH   *Book at aaa.com*

Phone: (434)295-3185

All Year   1P: $36-$95   2P: $38-$95   XP: $10   F18

(AAA) (SAVE)   **Location:** US 29, just n of jct US 250 Bypass, just e. 2014 Holiday Dr 22901. Fax: 434/293-7924. **Facility:** 47 one-bedroom standard units. 2 stories (no elevator), exterior corridors. **Parking:** on-site. **Cards:** AX, CB, DC, DS, JC, MC, VI. **Special Amenities:** free local telephone calls and early check-in/late check-out.

Small-scale Hotel

SOME UNITS

FEE FEE

ECONO LODGE-UNIVERSITY   *Book at aaa.com*

Phone: (434)296-2104

All Year [CP]   1P: $39-$140   2P: $46-$160   XP: $5   F18

(AAA) (SAVE)   **Location:** Jct US 250 Bypass, 1 mi s on US 29 business route. Located opposite the University of Virginia. 400 Emmet St 22903. Fax: 434/977-5591. **Facility:** 60 one-bedroom standard units. 2 stories (no elevator), exterior corridors. **Parking:** on-site. **Terms:** small pets only ($10 fee). **Amenities:** safes. **Pool(s):** small outdoor. **Cards:** AX, DC, DS, MC, VI. **Special Amenities:** free continental breakfast.

Motel

SOME UNITS

FEE

ENGLISH INN OF CHARLOTTESVILLE

Phone: (434)971-9900

3/1-10/31 [BP]   1P: $73-$78   2P: $73-$78   XP: $6   F18
11/1-2/28 [BP]   1P: $64-$71   2P: $64-$71   XP: $6   F18

(AAA) (SAVE)   **Location:** US 29 business route, just s of jct US 29 and 250 Bypass. 2000 Morton Dr 22903. Fax: 434/977-8008. **Facility:** 88 one-bedroom standard units. 3 stories, interior corridors. **Parking:** on-site. **Terms:** package plans. **Amenities:** high-speed Internet, voice mail, irons, hair dryers. **Pool(s):** heated indoor. **Leisure Activities:** sauna, exercise room. **Guest Services:** valet laundry, area transportation-Amtrak & bus station. **Business Services:** meeting rooms. **Cards:** AX, DC, DS, MC, VI. **Special Amenities:** free full breakfast and free local telephone calls.** *(See ad below)*

Small-scale Hotel

SOME UNITS

FAIRFIELD INN BY MARRIOTT — *Book at aaa.com* — **Phone: (434)964-9411**

▼▼▼ All Year [CP] 1P: $74-$141 2P: $74-$141 XP: $6 F18
Location: US 29 (Emmet St), 1.3 mi n of US 250 Bypass. 577 Branchlands Blvd 22901. Fax: 434/964-9422.
Small-scale Hotel **Facility:** 121 one-bedroom standard units. 3 stories, interior corridors. *Bath:* combo or shower only.
Parking: on-site. **Terms:** 3 day cancellation notice. **Amenities:** high-speed Internet, irons, hair dryers.
Pool(s): outdoor. **Leisure Activities:** whirlpool. **Guest Services:** valet laundry. **Cards:** AX, CB, DC, DS, MC, VI.

SOME UNITS

(ASK) (SO) (T+) (&) (≈) (⚗) (DATA PORT) (⬛) / (✕) (🛏) (🖨) /

THE FOXFIELD INN — **Phone: 434/923-8892**

(AAA) (SAVE) All Year [BP] 2P: $150-$230 XP: $30
▼▼▼ **Location:** US 250 Bypass, 5.4 mi nw on Barracks Rd (becomes Garth Rd). Located in a rural area. 2280 Garth Rd
22901. Fax: 434/923-0963. **Facility:** Hand-crafted furnishings made by the owner decorate the spacious
Bed & Breakfast units of this welcoming inn; on the grounds are flower beds, a pond and hammocks. Smoke free premises.
5 one-bedroom standard units, some with whirlpools. 1 story, interior corridors. **Parking:** on-site.
Terms: check-in 4 pm, 2 night minimum stay, age restrictions may apply, 10 day cancellation
notice-fee imposed, package plans. **Amenities:** CD players, irons, hair dryers. **Leisure Activities:** whirlpool, bocci, croquet.
Business Services: meeting rooms. **Cards:** MC, VI. **Special Amenities:** free full breakfast and free newspaper.

(✕) (W) (Z)

**HAMPTON INN & SUITES-CHARLOTTESVILLE AT
THE UNIVERSITY MEDICAL CENTER** — *Book at aaa.com* — **Phone: (434)923-8600**

▼▼▼ All Year 1P: $85-$112 2P: $92-$117
Location: US 29 (Emmet St), 1.4 mi e on US 250 (University Ave). 900 W Main St 22903. Fax: 434/923-8601.
Small-scale Hotel **Facility:** 100 one-bedroom standard units, some with kitchens. 5 stories, interior corridors. *Bath:* combo or
shower only. **Parking:** on-site. **Terms:** 3 day cancellation notice, [CP] meal plan available. **Amenities:** high-
speed Internet, voice mail, irons, hair dryers. **Leisure Activities:** exercise room. **Guest Services:** valet and coin laundry.
Business Services: meeting rooms, business center. **Cards:** AX, CB, DC, DS, MC, VI.

SOME UNITS

(ASK) (SO) (⚗) (DATA PORT) (⬛) / (✕) (VCR) (🛏) (🖨) /

HAMPTON INN OF CHARLOTTESVILLE — *Book at aaa.com* — **Phone: (434)978-7888**

▼▼▼ All Year 1P: $79-$87 2P: $88-$95
Location: I-64, exit 118B (US 29), 4 mi on US 29 N/250 Bypass to Washington exit, then 0.5 mi on US 29 N. Located at
Small-scale Hotel Seminole Square Shopping Center. 2035 India Rd 22901. Fax: 434/973-0436. **Facility:** 123 one-bedroom
standard units. 5 stories, interior corridors. **Parking:** on-site. **Amenities:** high-speed Internet, voice mail,
irons, hair dryers. **Pool(s):** outdoor. **Guest Services:** valet laundry, area transportation. **Business Services:** meeting rooms.
Cards: AX, CB, DC, DS, MC, VI.

SOME UNITS

(ASK) (SO) (+) (T+) (🍴) (≈) (🏋) (⚗) (DATA PORT) (⬛) / (✕) /

HOLIDAY INN-MONTICELLO/CHARLOTTESVILLE — *Book at aaa.com* — **Phone: (434)977-5100**

▼▼▼ 3/1-11/30 1P: $85-$90
12/1-2/28 1P: $70-$80
Large-scale Hotel **Location:** I-64, exit 120, just n on SR 631. 1200 5th St SW 22902. Fax: 434/293-5228. **Facility:** 131 one-bedroom
standard units. 6 stories, interior corridors. **Parking:** on-site. **Terms:** pets ($10 extra charge).
Amenities: video games, irons, hair dryers. **Pool(s):** outdoor, wading. **Leisure Activities:** exercise room. **Guest Services:** coin
laundry. **Business Services:** meeting rooms, business center. **Cards:** AX, DC, DS, MC, VI.

SOME UNITS

(ASK) (SO) (🐾) (🍴) (🍷) (�🍸) (≈) (DATA PORT) (⬛) / (✕) (🛏) (🖨) /
FEE

**HOLIDAY INN UNIVERSITY AREA & CONFERENCE
CENTER** — *Book at aaa.com* — **Phone: (434)977-7700**

(AAA) (SAVE) 4/1-11/20 1P: $74-$80 2P: $74-$80 XP: $10 F18
3/1-3/31 & 11/21-2/28 1P: $68-$74 2P: $68-$74 XP: $10 F18
▼▼▼ **Location:** Jct US 250 Bypass, 0.3 mi n on US 29. 1901 Emmet St 22901. Fax: 434/296-8213. **Facility:** 170 one-
bedroom standard units. 7 stories, interior corridors. *Bath:* combo or shower only. **Parking:** on-site.
Small-scale Hotel **Terms:** package plans. **Amenities:** video games, high-speed Internet, voice mail, irons, hair dryers.
Dining: 7 am-11 pm, cocktails. **Pool(s):** heated indoor. **Leisure Activities:** exercise room. **Guest Services:**
coin laundry, area transportation-Amtrak & bus station. **Business Services:** conference facilities. **Cards:** AX, CB, DC, DS, JC,
MC, VI. **Special Amenities:** free local telephone calls and free newspaper.

SOME UNITS

(SO) (+) (🍴) (🍷) (&) (🍸) (≈) (⚗) (DATA PORT) (⬛) / (✕) (🛏) (🖨) /

THE INN AT MONTICELLO — **Phone: 434/979-3593**

(AAA) (SAVE) 3/1-11/15 [BP] 1P: $125-$145 2P: $165-$195 XP: $25
11/16-2/28 [BP] 1P: $125-$140 2P: $135-$165 XP: $25
▼▼▼ **Location:** I-64, exit 121, 0.8 mi s on SR 20. Located in a quiet area. 1188 Scottsville Rd (Rt 20) 22902.
Fax: 434/296-1344. **Facility:** In a hilly area near Monticello, this home dating from the mid-1800s offers
Bed & Breakfast grounds with a hammock for relaxing, as well as lots of roaming room. Smoke free premises. 5 one-
bedroom standard units. 2 stories (no elevator), interior corridors. **Parking:** on-site. **Terms:** check-in 4 pm, 2
night minimum stay - weekends, age restrictions may apply, 14 day cancellation notice-fee imposed, package plans.
Amenities: irons, hair dryers. **Guest Services:** complimentary evening beverages. **Business Services:** meeting rooms.
Cards: AX, MC, VI. **Special Amenities:** free full breakfast and preferred room (subject to availability with advance
reservations).

(✕) (W) (Z)

OMNI CHARLOTTESVILLE HOTEL · *Book at aaa.com* Phone: (434)971-5500

[AAA] [SAVE] ▼▼▼▼ Large-scale Hotel

All Year · Location: I-64, exit 120, 2.3 mi n on SR 631; downtown. Located in historic area. 235 W Main St 22902. Fax: 434/979-4456. Facility: Good views of downtown are offered from this hotel, which is adjacent to a pedestrian mall in the historic area. 208 one-bedroom standard units. 7 stories, interior corridors. Parking: on-site. Terms: cancellation fee imposed, [BP] meal plan available, package plans, small pets only ($50 fee). Amenities: video games, high-speed Internet, voice mail, honor bars, irons, hair dryers. Dining: The Pointe Restaurant and Lounge, see separate listing. Pool(s): outdoor, heated indoor. Leisure Activities: saunas, whirlpool, exercise room. Guest Services: valet laundry. Business Services: conference facilities, business center. Cards: AX, DC, DS, MC, VI. *(See color ad below)*

1P: $119-$179 2P: $119-$179 XP: $15 F17

SOME UNITS
[S/D] [🛏] FEE [🍴] [Y] [🏊] [✕] [🐾] [DATA PORT] [▯] / [✕] [📱] [🖨] FEE /

QUALITY INN-UNIVERSITY AREA · *Book at aaa.com* Phone: (434)971-3746

▼▼▼ Small-scale Hotel

4/1-11/30 · 1P: $69-$89 2P: $79-$99 XP: $10 F18
3/1-3/31 & 12/1-2/28 · 1P: $55-$60 2P: $65-$70 XP: $10 F18
Location: US 29, just n of jct US 250 Bypass, just e on Holiday Dr. 1600 Emmet St 22901. Fax: 434/977-7847. Facility: 69 one-bedroom standard units. 3 stories, exterior corridors. Parking: on-site. Terms: pets ($10 extra charge). Amenities: irons, hair dryers. Guest Services: valet laundry. Cards: AX, CB, DC, DS, JC, MC, VI.

SOME UNITS
[ASK] [S/D] [🛏] FEE [🍴] [🐾] [DATA PORT] [▯] / [✕] [📱] [🖨] /

RAMADA LIMITED-MONTICELLO · *Book at aaa.com* Phone: (434)977-3300

[AAA] [SAVE] ▼▼▼ Small-scale Hotel

All Year [ECP] · 1P: $59-$159 2P: $59-$159 XP: $10 F18
Location: I-64, exit 124 (US 250 E). 2097 Inn Dr 22911. Fax: 434/977-8558. Facility: 99 one-bedroom standard units, some with whirlpools. 2 stories (no elevator), interior corridors. Parking: on-site. Amenities: high-speed Internet, voice mail, safes, irons, hair dryers. Pool(s): outdoor. Leisure Activities: miniature golf, exercise room. Guest Services: coin laundry. Business Services: meeting rooms, business center. Cards: AX, DC, DS, MC, VI. Special Amenities: free expanded continental breakfast and free local telephone calls.

SOME UNITS
[S/D] [🏊] [🐾] [DATA PORT] [▯] / [✕] /

RED ROOF INN OF CHARLOTTESVILLE · *Book at aaa.com* Phone: (434)295-4333

▼▼▼ Small-scale Hotel

3/18-11/14 · 1P: $74-$95 2P: $79-$100 XP: $5 F18
11/15-2/28 · 1P: $69-$79 2P: $74-$84 XP: $5 F18
3/1-3/17 · 1P: $69-$74 2P: $74-$79 XP: $5 F18
Location: US 29 (Emmet St), 1 mi e on US 250 (University Ave). 1309 W Main St 22903. Fax: 434/295-2021. Facility: 135 one-bedroom standard units. 8 stories, interior corridors. Bath: combo or shower only. Parking: on-site. Terms: small pets only. Amenities: video games, irons, hair dryers. Guest Services: coin laundry. Business Services: meeting rooms. Cards: AX, CB, DC, DS, MC, VI.

SOME UNITS
[🛏] [🍴] [🐾] [🖥] [🐾] [📷] [DATA PORT] / [✕] [📱] [🖨] /

RESIDENCE INN BY MARRIOTT · *Book at aaa.com* Phone: (434)923-0300

[AAA] [SAVE] ▼▼▼ Small-scale Hotel

All Year [BP] · 1P: $119-$159
Location: I-64, exit 118B (US 29), 2.5 mi n US 29/250 E, just s on Barracks Rd, then just se. 1111 Millmont St 22903. Fax: 434/923-0318. Facility: 108 one-bedroom standard units. 3 stories, interior corridors. Bath: combo or shower only. Parking: on-site. Terms: cancellation fee imposed, small pets only ($200 fee). Pool(s): heated outdoor. Leisure Activities: whirlpool, playground, exercise room, basketball, volleyball. Guest Services: complimentary evening beverages: Mon-Thurs, valet and coin laundry. Cards: AX, CB, DC, DS, JC, MC, VI. Special Amenities: free full breakfast and preferred room (subject to availability with advance reservations).

SOME UNITS
[S/D] [🛏] FEE [🍴] [🖥] [🏊] [✕] [📷] [DATA PORT] [📱] [🖨] [▯] / [✕] /

SILVER THATCH INN

Phone: 434/978-4686

AAA SAVE

Historic
Country Inn

4/1-11/30 [BP]	1P: $150-$195	2P: $150-$195	XP: $35
3/1-3/31 & 12/1-2/28 [BP]	1P: $150-$185	2P: $150-$185	XP: $35

Location: 5 mi n on US 29, then 0.5 mi e on SR 1520. 3001 Hollymead Dr 22911-7422. **Fax:** 434/973-6156. **Facility:** Dating from 1780, this clapboard inn includes a modern section decorated with furnishings that complement the design of the original. Smoke free premises. 7 one-bedroom standard units. 2 stories (no elevator), interior corridors. *Bath:* combo or shower only. **Parking:** on-site. **Terms:** 2 night minimum stay - seasonal and/or weekends, age restrictions may apply, 7 day cancellation notice, package plans. **Amenities:** CD players, irons, hair dryers. **Dining:** dining room, see separate listing. **Pool(s):** outdoor. **Leisure Activities:** board games. **Business Services:** meeting rooms. **Cards:** AX, CB, DC, MC, VI. **Special Amenities:** free full breakfast and free local telephone calls.

SOME UNITS

SLEEP INN & SUITES MONTICELLO

Book at aaa.com

Phone: (434)244-9969

AAA SAVE

Small-scale Hotel

All Year	1P: $62-$98	2P: $62-$98	XP: $10	F18

Location: I-64, exit 120, just n. 1185 5th St 22902. **Fax:** 434/244-9968. **Facility:** 75 one-bedroom standard units. 3 stories, interior corridors. *Bath:* combo or shower only. **Parking:** on-site. **Terms:** 30 day cancellation notice, package plans, pets ($10 fee). **Amenities:** video games, high-speed Internet, voice mail, safes, irons, hair dryers. **Pool(s):** indoor. **Leisure Activities:** whirlpool, exercise room. **Guest Services:** valet and coin laundry. **Business Services:** meeting rooms. **Cards:** AX, CB, DC, DS, JC, MC, VI. **Special Amenities: free expanded continental breakfast and free local telephone calls.**

SOME UNITS

FEE

SUPER 8 MOTEL/CHARLOTTESVILLE

Book at aaa.com

Phone: 434/973-0888

AAA SAVE

Small-scale Hotel

All Year	1P: $40-$99	2P: $49-$99	XP: $10

Location: US 29, 1 mi n of US 250 Bypass. 390 Greenbrier Dr 22901. **Fax:** 434/973-0888. **Facility:** 65 one-bedroom standard units. 3 stories, interior corridors. **Parking:** on-site. **Terms:** small pets only ($10 extra charge). **Amenities:** safes (fee). **Cards:** AX, DC, DS, MC, VI. **Special Amenities: free local telephone calls and free room upgrade (subject to availability with advance reservations).**

SOME UNITS

FEE

─── WHERE TO DINE ───

ABERDEEN BARN

Dinner: $17-$42

Phone: 434/296-4630

AAA

Steak & Seafood

Location: I-64, exit 118B (US 29), just n of jct US 250 Drive, then just e. 2018 Holiday Dr 22901. **Hours:** 5 pm-11 pm, Sun-10 pm. Closed: 11/24, 12/25. **Reservations:** suggested, Fri & Sat. **Features:** Founded in 1965, the local favorite serves huge portions of quality steaks, prime rib and seafood in a comfortable, clublike atmosphere. Fresh salad, dressing and bread accompany the meals. The restaurant employs a friendly, attentive wait staff. Dressy casual; cocktails; entertainment. **Parking:** on-site. **Cards:** AX, CB, DC, MC, VI.

CARMELLO'S RISTORANTE ITALIANO

Lunch: $7-$11   **Dinner: $20-$30**   **Phone: 434/977-5200**

AAA

Northern
Italian

Location: I-64, exit 118B (US 29 S). 400 Emmet St 22901. **Hours:** 11:30 am-2 & 5-10 pm, Sat 11:30 am-3 & 5-10 pm, Sun 11:30 am-2 & 5-9 pm. Closed: 12/25. **Reservations:** suggested. **Features:** The classic, family-run restaurant emphasizes great food and fine service. Background music contributes to the wonderful setting. Casual dress; cocktails. **Parking:** on-site. **Cards:** AX, CB, DC, DS, MC, VI.

COPACABANA BRAZILIAN INTERNATIONAL

Lunch: $7-$10   **Dinner: $10-$21**   **Phone: 434/973-1177**

Brazilian

Location: US 29, 1.6 mi n of jct US 250 Bypass; in Shopper's World Shopping Center. 400 Shoppers World Ct 22901. **Hours:** 11 am-2:30 & 5-11 pm, Sun from 5 pm. Closed: 11/24, 12/25. **Reservations:** suggested, for dinner. **Features:** Unusual sauces flavor excellent preparations of Brazilian cuisine, including fabulous veal medallions in lemon sauce. The atmosphere is informal. The restaurant is a great alternative for diners who can't get to Rio de Janeiro. Casual dress; cocktails. **Parking:** on-site. **Cards:** AX, DC, MC, VI.

ESCAFE

Lunch: $7-$17   **Dinner: $10-$20**   **Phone: 434/295-8668**

American

Location: I-64, exit 120, 2.4 mi n on SR 361; in downtown mall area. 227 W Main St 22902. **Hours:** 2:30 pm-2 am, Sun 4:30 pm-midnight. Closed: Mon. **Features:** Escafe has a wonderful setting with outdoor dining when weather permits and a whimsical atmosphere. The varied menu is complemented well by the knowledgeable servers. Casual dress; cocktails. **Parking:** street. **Cards:** AX, CB, DC, DS, JC, MC, VI.

FLAMING WOK

Menu on aaa.com   **Lunch: $7-$10**   **Dinner: $7-$16**   **Phone: 434/974-6555**

AAA

Chinese

Location: US 29, 1 mi n of jct US 250 Bypass. 1305 Seminole Tr 22901. **Hours:** 11:30 am-10 pm, Fri & Sat-11 pm. Closed: 11/24. **Features:** Experience the ancient method of cooking on a stone over hot coals while enjoying good Chinese, Japanese and Korean cuisine. A daily lunch buffet (also featuring the stone grill) is laden with a plentiful variety of standard favorites, including sushi. Background music makes guests feel as though they are in the Orient. Casual dress; cocktails. **Parking:** on-site. **Cards:** AX, DC, DS, MC, VI.

THE IVY INN RESTAURANT

Dinner: $18-$30

Phone: 434/977-1222

American

Location: 0.5 mi w on Ivy Rd from US 29 business route, then just n on SR 601. 2244 Old Ivy Rd 22903. **Hours:** 5 pm-9:30 pm. Closed: 1/1, 12/24, 12/25; also Sun. **Reservations:** required. **Features:** In a converted 1816 inn-like residence, the restaurant provides a richly historical and elegant atmosphere for fine dining. Fresh, local ingredients and a great wine list enhance the epicurean aspect, while hardwood floors, wine racks and wonderful paintings add to the ambience. The daily changing menu focuses on extraordinary American cuisine. Dressy casual; cocktails. **Parking:** on-site. **Cards:** AX, DC, MC, VI. **Historic**

L'AVVENTURA

Northern Italian

Dinner: $12-$21 **Phone:** 434/977-1912
Location: I-64, exit 120, 2.5 mi n, then just e; just w of downtown mall. 220 W Market St 22902. **Hours:** 5:30 pm-10 pm. Closed major holidays; also Sun-Tues. **Reservations:** suggested. **Features:** A large, varied wine list and a short, changing menu of sophisticated fare are what the romantic, classy restaurant offers. Homemade sourdough bread is delicious, and chocolate bread pudding with sour cherries is well worth saving room for. Patio seating is available. Dressy casual; cocktails. **Parking:** on-site. **Cards:** AX, MC, VI.

LORD HARDWICK'S

British

Lunch: $6-$12 **Dinner:** $6-$21 **Phone:** 434/295-6668
Location: US 29 business route, just s of jct US 29 and 250 Bypass. 1248 Emmet St 22901. **Hours:** 11 am-10 pm. Closed: 12/25. **Reservations:** suggested, weekends. **Features:** Lord Hardwick's is a classic British style pub with Fish and Chips and lots of British ambience. Casual dress; cocktails. **Parking:** on-site. **Cards:** AX, CB, DC, DS, JC, MC, VI.

LUDWIG'S SCHNITZELHOUSE RESTAURANT

German

Dinner: $15-$24 **Phone:** 434/293-7185
Location: 0.5 mi s on US 29 business route; just s of University of Virginia. 2208 Fontaine Ave 22903. **Hours:** 5 pm-10 pm. Closed: 11/24, 12/25; also Sun & Mon. **Reservations:** suggested, weekends. **Features:** The owner/chef here has created varied menu selections specializing in tasty, traditional favorites, especially veal dishes, homemade salad dressing and dessert. Swiss cuisine is also featured. Many half-portion and light fare items also are available. Quaint setting, very relaxed atmosphere. Very friendly management and service staff. Soothing background music. Casual dress; cocktails. **Parking:** on-site. **Cards:** AX, DC, MC, VI.

MICHIE TAVERN CA 1784

American

Lunch: $15 **Phone:** 434/977-1234
Location: I-64, exit 121A, just s on SR 20, then 1 mi e on SR 53. 683 Thomas Jefferson Pkwy 22902. **Hours:** 11:30 am-3 pm. Closed: 1/1, 12/25. **Features:** Diners are hard-pressed to find a better Colonial-style lunch buffet served in the true Southern tradition. Fried chicken can be savored with a rich array of traditional sides, including stewed tomatoes, black-eyed peas and cornbread. The atmosphere takes its cue from the 200-year-old log cabin setting. Don't miss the walk alongside the mill. The tavern evokes the feel of yesteryear. Casual dress; beer & wine only. **Parking:** on-site. **Cards:** AX, MC, VI. **Historic**

THE OLD MILL ROOM *Menu on aaa.com*

Regional American

Lunch: $9-$14 **Dinner:** $23-$39 **Phone:** 434/972-2230
Location: Jct US 29 Bypass, 1 mi w on US 250; in Boar's Head Inn. Rt 250 W 22903. **Hours:** 7 am-10:30, noon-2 & 6-9:30 pm, Fri-9:30 pm, Sat 7 am-10:30 & 6-9:30 pm, Sun 7 am-10:30 & 6-9 pm. **Reservations:** suggested. **Features:** An Early American atmosphere pervades the restored grist mill, a city fixture since 1834. Gentle rolling hills surround the restaurant. The menu, which changes slightly each night, showcases local ingredients blended in imaginative ways and with a hint of traditional Southern influence. The staff is pleasant and attentive. Top off the meal with the chocolate shining star. Semi-formal attire; cocktails; entertainment. **Parking:** on-site. **Cards:** AX, CB, DC, DS, MC, VI. **Historic**

THE POINTE RESTAURANT AND LOUNGE

Regional American

Lunch: $8-$25 **Dinner:** $8-$25 **Phone:** 434/971-5500
Location: I-64, exit 120, 2.3 mi n on SR 631; downtown; in Omni Charlottesville Hotel. 235 W Main St 22902. **Hours:** 6:30 am-9:30 pm, Fri & Sat-10 pm. **Reservations:** accepted. **Features:** Patrons might start a meal with an appetizer of eggplant Napoleon, then savor grilled salmon with steamed vegetables and couscous. Virginia wine is featured. The decor is airy and light. Casual dress; cocktails. **Parking:** on-site. **Cards:** AX, CB, DC, DS, JC, MC, VI.

RAGAZZI'S

Italian

Lunch: $5-$9 **Dinner:** $8-$13 **Phone:** 434/973-5940
Location: US 29, 1.5 mi n of US 250 Bypass. 900 Shoppers World Ct 22901. **Hours:** 11 am-10 pm, Sun-9 pm. Closed major holidays. **Features:** Contemporary cuisine brings together many Italian and American classics, including many types of pasta. A popular choice is the longtime favorite lasagna. Casual dress; cocktails. **Parking:** on-site. **Cards:** AX, MC, VI.

RHETT'S RIVER GRILL AND RAW BAR

American

Lunch: $6-$15 **Dinner:** $8-$18 **Phone:** 434/974-7818
Location: I-64, exit 118B (US 29), 3.9 mi n of jct US 250 Bypass. 2335 Seminole Tr, Suite 100 22901. **Hours:** 11:30 am-2 & 5:30-10 pm, Fri & Sat-10:30 pm, Sun 10 am-2 pm. Closed major holidays. **Features:** This restaurant is pure fun in a casual place combining great food and personable staff for a fun dining experience. Casual dress; cocktails. **Parking:** on-site. **Cards:** AX, MC, VI.

RISTORANTE AL DENTE

Italian

Dinner: $12-$26 **Phone:** 434/295-9922
Location: I-64, exit 120, 2.4 mi n on SR 631; in downtown mall area. 225 W Main St 22903. **Hours:** 5 pm-10 pm. Closed: 12/25. **Features:** Ristorante al Dente offers an elegant dining haven with amazing Italian cuisine, large wine list and homemade desserts. Casual dress; cocktails. **Parking:** street. **Cards:** AX, CB, DC, DS, JC, MC, VI.

ROCOCO'S

Italian

Lunch: $6-$8 **Dinner:** $9-$17 **Phone:** 434/971-7371
Location: I-64, exit 118 (US 29), 0.3 mi n from jct US 250 Bypass, 0.4 mi w on Hydraulic Rd; in Village Green Shopping Center. 2001 Commonwealth Dr 22901. **Hours:** 11 am-10 pm, Sat from 5 pm, Sun 11 am-3 & 5-10 pm. Closed: 12/25. **Features:** The high-energy restaurant is known for chic and sophisticated food, such as rich, homemade pasta, excellent pizza and decadent dessert made on the premises. The sauteed escarole appetizer, house salad and chicken lasagna entree are flavorful. Casual dress; cocktails. **Parking:** on-site. **Cards:** AX, DS, MC, VI.

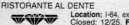

ST. MAARTEN CAFE

American

Lunch: $6-$12 **Dinner:** $8-$18 **Phone:** 434/293-2233
Location: US 29, 1.5 mi e on US 250. 1400 Wertland Ave 22903. **Hours:** 11 am-11 pm. Closed: 12/25. **Features:** St. Maarten Cafe offers eclectic Americn Cuisine in a fun Caribbean atmosphere close to the University of Virginia campus. Casual dress; cocktails. **Parking:** street. **Cards:** AX, CB, DC, DS, JC, MC, VI.

SAM'S KITCHEN

American

Lunch: $5-$10   **Dinner:** $5-$12   **Phone:** 434/977-1619

Location: Just s of US 250 Bypass. 1403 Emmett St 22903. **Hours:** 11 am-3 & 5-midnight. Closed: 1/1, 11/24, 12/25. **Features:** A fun atmosphere prevails in the friendly restaurant. Good food is prepared with a home-style influence. Casual dress. **Parking:** on-site. **Cards:** AX, DS, MC, VI.

**THE SILVER THATCH INN DINING
   ROOM**
American

Dinner: $18-$30   **Phone:** 434/978-4686

Location: 5 mi n on US 29, 0.5 mi e on SR 1520; in Silver Thatch Inn. 3001 Hollymead Dr 22911-7422. **Hours:** 5:30 pm-9 pm. Closed: Sun & Mon. **Reservations:** suggested. **Features:** Contemporary cuisine shows the kitchen's flair for creative sauces and stylish presentation. Patrons visit the historic inn for a distinctive fine-dining experience. The excellent wine list incorporates a good selection of Virginia vintages. Dressy casual; cocktails. **Parking:** on-site. **Cards:** AX, CB, DC, MC, VI.

TIFFANY'S SEAFOOD RESTAURANT
American

Lunch: $5-$11   **Dinner:** $8-$18   **Phone:** 434/293-5000

Location: 0.3 mi e on Ivy Rd from US 29 business route. 2171 Ivy Rd 22903. **Hours:** 11:30 am-10:30 pm, Sun 5 pm-10 pm. Closed major holidays. **Features:** The seafood restaurant specializes in steamed and spiced shrimp. In addition to selections such as seafood with pasta, the menu lists beef dishes. Casual dress; cocktails. **Parking:** on-site. **Cards:** AX, DS, MC, VI.

WILD GREENS
American

Lunch: $7-$11   **Dinner:** $7-$17   **Phone:** 434/296-9453

Location: 0.5 mi w on Barracks Rd from US 29. 2162 Barracks Rd 22903. **Hours:** 11:30 am-9:30 pm, Fri & Sat-10 pm, Sun 11 am-9 pm. Closed major holidays. **Features:** Wonderful murals, beautiful background music and stylish dish presentation are hallmarks of the fine-dining establishment. Each entree includes the signature wild greens salad, a treat not to be missed. Fresh ingredients and a nice wine list are other pluses. Casual dress; cocktails. **Parking:** on-site. **Cards:** AX, MC, VI. **Historic**

CHESAPEAKE —See Hampton Roads Area p. 780.

CHESTER —See Richmond p. 856.

CHESTERFIELD —See Richmond p. 859.

CHILHOWIE pop. 1,827

——— **WHERE TO DINE** ———

TOWN HOUSE GRILL
American

Lunch: $9-$14   **Dinner:** $12-$24   **Phone:** 276/646-8787

Location: I-81, exit 35, just w. 132 E Main St 24319. **Hours:** 11 am-2 & 5-9 pm. Closed: 12/25; also Sun & Mon. **Features:** Guests experience fine dining in a relaxed atmosphere. An expanded wine list is presented, and friendly staffers are a staple. Casual dress; cocktails. **Parking:** on-site. **Cards:** AX, CB, DC, DS, JC, MC, VI.

CHINCOTEAGUE pop. 4,317

—— WHERE TO STAY ——

ASSATEAGUE INN
Phone: 757/336-3738

AAA (SAVE) ◇◇ ◇◇ Motel

6/11-9/5	1P: $102-$150	2P: $102-$150	XP: $5 F12
4/1-6/10	1P: $65-$110	2P: $65-$110	XP: $5 F12
9/6-2/28	1P: $60-$110	2P: $60-$110	XP: $5 F12
3/1-3/31	1P: $60-$90	2P: $60-$90	XP: $5 F12

Location: 0.5 mi n on Main St, 0.8 mi e on Maddox Blvd, then just s on CR 2102 to Chicken City Rd, follow signs. Located in a rustic area. 6570 Coachs Ln 23336 (PO Box 1038). Fax: 757/336-1179. **Facility:** 24 units. 6 one-bedroom standard units. 18 one-bedroom suites with kitchens. 2 stories (no elevator), exterior corridors. **Parking:** on-site. **Terms:** office hours 8 am-9 pm, 2 night minimum stay - seasonal and/or weekends, 6 day cancellation notice. **Amenities:** video library (fee), irons, hair dryers. *Some:* DVD players. **Pool(s):** outdoor. **Leisure Activities:** crabbing dock, exercise room. *Fee:* bicycles. **Business Services:** fax. **Cards:** AX, DC, DS, MC, VI. **Special Amenities: free local telephone calls.**

SOME UNITS

BEST VALUE INN & SUITES   *Book at aaa.com*
Phone: (757)336-6562

AAA (SAVE) ◇◇◇ ◇◇◇ Motel

5/27-9/5 [ECP]	1P: $89-$140	2P: $89-$140	XP: $6 F16
3/1-5/26 & 9/6-2/28 [ECP]	1P: $58-$104	2P: $58-$104	XP: $6 F16

Location: 0.5 mi n on N Main St, just e. 6151 Maddox Blvd 23336. Fax: 757/336-1839. **Facility:** 19 units. 17 one-bedroom standard units. 2 cottages. 1 story, exterior corridors. **Parking:** on-site. **Terms:** office hours 8 am-midnight, 3 day cancellation notice. **Amenities:** hair dryers. *Some:* irons. **Pool(s):** outdoor. **Leisure Activities:** barbecue grill, picnic area. **Guest Services:** gift shop. **Business Services:** fax. **Cards:** AX, DS, MC, VI. **Special Amenities: early check-in/late check-out and preferred room (subject to availability with advance reservations).**

SOME UNITS

FEE

BIRCHWOOD MOTEL
Phone: 757/336-6133

◇◇ ◇◇ Motel

5/21-9/7	1P: $73-$245	2P: $73-$245	XP: $7 F6
4/1-5/20 & 9/8-10/27	1P: $57-$180	2P: $57-$180	XP: $7 F6

Location: 0.8 mi s. 3650 Main St 23336. Fax: 757/336-6535. **Facility:** 32 one-bedroom standard units, some with efficiencies. 1 story, exterior corridors. **Parking:** on-site. **Terms:** open 4/1-10/27, office hours 8 am-11 pm, 2 night minimum stay - seasonal and/or weekends, 3 day cancellation notice-fee imposed. **Amenities:** voice mail. **Pool(s):** outdoor. **Leisure Activities:** bicycles. **Guest Services:** coin laundry. **Business Services:** meeting rooms, fax. **Cards:** AX, DS, MC, VI.

SOME UNITS

CHINCOTEAGUE LODGE   *Book at aaa.com*
Phone: (757)336-6415

AAA (SAVE) ◇ Motel

6/17-9/6	1P: $84-$138	2P: $84-$138	XP: $5 F15
4/1-6/16 & 9/7-10/31	1P: $59-$89	2P: $59-$89	XP: $5 F15

Location: Jct Maddox Blvd, just n. 4417 Deep Hole Rd 23336. Fax: 757/336-3244. **Facility:** 70 one-bedroom standard units. 3 stories (no elevator), exterior corridors. **Parking:** on-site. **Terms:** open 4/1-10/31, office hours 8 am-11 pm, 2 night minimum stay - seasonal, 3 day cancellation notice, package plans. **Amenities:** voice mail. **Pool(s):** outdoor. **Leisure Activities:** screen pavilion, horseshoes, volleyball. **Cards:** AX, DS, MC, VI. **Special Amenities: free local telephone calls and free newspaper.**

SOME UNITS

COMFORT SUITES   *Book at aaa.com*
Phone: (757)336-3700

AAA (SAVE) ◇◇◇ Small-scale Hotel

5/27-9/4 [ECP]	1P: $159-$219	2P: $159-$219	
9/5-10/29 [ECP]	1P: $109-$149	2P: $109-$149	
3/1-5/26 [ECP]	1P: $89-$149	2P: $89-$149	
10/30-2/28 [ECP]	1P: $89-$109	2P: $89-$109	

Location: Just n. 4195 N Main St 23336. Fax: 757/336-5452. **Facility:** 87 one-bedroom standard units, some with whirlpools. 3 stories, interior corridors. *Bath:* combo or shower only. **Parking:** on-site. **Amenities:** high-speed Internet, voice mail, safes (fee), irons, hair dryers. *Some:* DVD players, dual phone lines. **Pool(s):** outdoor, heated indoor. **Leisure Activities:** whirlpool, exercise room. *Fee:* game room. **Guest Services:** sundries, coin laundry. **Business Services:** meeting rooms. **Cards:** AX, CB, DC, DS, MC, VI. **Special Amenities: free expanded continental breakfast and free newspaper.** *(See color ad below)*

SOME UNITS

DRIFTWOOD LODGE

Phone: (757)336-6557

	1P:	2P:	XP:	
6/10-9/5 [ECP]	1P: $79-$120	2P: $79-$120	XP: $9	F16
3/1-6/9 & 9/6-11/28 [ECP]	1P: $77-$97	2P: $77-$97	XP: $9	F16
11/29-2/28 [ECP]	1P: $57-$87	2P: $57-$87	XP: $9	F16

Small-scale Hotel **Location:** 0.5 mi n on N Main St, 1.5 mi e on Maddox Blvd/Beach Rd; at entrance to Assateague National Seashore. 7105 Maddox Blvd 23336 (PO Box 575). Fax: 757/336-6558. **Facility:** 53 units. 51 one- and 2 two-bedroom standard units, some with whirlpools. 3 stories, interior/exterior corridors. **Parking:** on-site. **Terms:** office hours 7 am-10 pm, 2 night minimum stay - seasonal and/or weekends, 3 day cancellation notice. **Amenities:** hair dryers. *Some:* irons. **Pool(s):** heated outdoor. **Guest Services:** coin laundry. **Business Services:** fax. **Cards:** CB, DC, DS, JC, MC, VI. *(See color ad below)*

SOME UNITS

HAMPTON INN & SUITES   *Book at aaa.com*

Phone: (757)336-1616

5/27-9/4	1P: $149-$219	2P: $149-$219
3/1-5/26 & 9/5-10/29	1P: $89-$159	2P: $89-$159
10/30-2/28	1P: $79-$129	2P: $79-$129

Small-scale Hotel **Location:** Just n of downtown. 4179 Main St 23336. Fax: 757/336-1617. **Facility:** 59 one-bedroom standard units, some with whirlpools. 3 stories, interior corridors. *Bath:* combo or shower only. **Parking:** on-site. **Terms:** 2 night minimum stay - seasonal and/or weekends, 3 day cancellation notice. **Amenities:** high-speed Internet, voice mail, irons, hair dryers. **Pool(s):** heated indoor. **Leisure Activities:** whirlpool, exercise room. *Fee:* game room. **Guest Services:** sundries, coin laundry. **Business Services:** meeting rooms, business center. **Cards:** AX, CB, DC, DS, MC, VI.

SOME UNITS

THE INN AT POPLAR CORNER

Phone: 757/336-6115

	1P:	2P:	XP:
5/27-9/4 [BP]	1P: $149-$169	2P: $159-$179	XP: $15
3/20-5/26 & 9/5-11/30 [BP]	1P: $119-$139	2P: $129-$149	XP: $15

Bed & Breakfast **Location:** Just n of downtown. 4248 Main St 23336 (PO Box 905). Fax: 757/336-5776. **Facility:** Guests gain a vantage point on the surrounding town from this elegant inn's wraparound porch; rooms feature whirlpool baths and other luxuries. Smoke free premises. 4 one-bedroom standard units with whirlpools. 3 stories (no elevator), interior corridors. **Parking:** on-site. **Terms:** open 3/20-11/30, 2 night minimum stay - seasonal and/or weekends, age restrictions may apply, 10 day cancellation notice, package plans. **Leisure Activities:** bicycles. **Cards:** MC, VI.

ISLAND MOTOR INN RESORT

Phone: 757/336-3141

	1P:	2P:	XP:	
5/21-9/5	1P: $105-$175	2P: $105-$175	XP: $10	F16
3/1-5/20 & 9/6-11/30	1P: $82-$150	2P: $82-$150	XP: $10	F16
12/1-2/28	1P: $68-$140	2P: $68-$140	XP: $10	F16

Small-scale Hotel **Location:** 0.8 mi n. 4391 Main St 23336. Fax: 757/336-1483. **Facility:** 60 one-bedroom standard units. 3 stories, interior/exterior corridors. **Parking:** on-site. **Terms:** office hours 6 am-1 am, check-in 4 pm, 2 night minimum stay - seasonal, 7 day cancellation notice. **Amenities:** *Some:* hair dryers. **Pool(s):** outdoor, heated indoor. **Leisure Activities:** whirlpool, boat dock, fishing. **Guest Services:** complimentary laundry, tanning facility. **Business Services:** meeting rooms. **Cards:** AX, DC, MC, VI. *(See color ad p 684)*

SOME UNITS

REFUGE INN   *Book at aaa.com*

Phone: 757/336-5511

6/17-9/4	2P: $98-$290	XP: $10	F12
9/5-11/26	2P: $70-$245	XP: $10	F12
3/1-6/16	2P: $70-$235	XP: $10	F12
11/27-2/28	2P: $68-$215	XP: $10	F12

Small-scale Hotel **Location:** 0.5 mi n on N Main St, 1.5 mi e on Maddox Blvd/Beach Rd. 7058 Maddox Blvd 23336 (PO Box 378). Fax: 757/336-6134. **Facility:** 72 units. 70 one-bedroom standard units. 2 one-bedroom suites ($170-$290) with whirlpools. 2 stories (no elevator), interior corridors. **Parking:** on-site. **Terms:** office hours 8 am-10 pm, check-in 4 pm, 2 night minimum stay - seasonal and/or weekends, 3 day cancellation notice. **Amenities:** dual phone lines, voice mail. *Some:* high-speed Internet (fee). **Pool(s):** heated indoor/outdoor. **Leisure Activities:** sauna, whirlpool, hiking trails, playground, exercise room. *Fee:* bicycles. **Guest Services:** gift shop, coin laundry. **Business Services:** meeting rooms, PC (fee), fax. **Cards:** AX, DC, DS, MC, VI. *(See color ad p 684)*

SOME UNITS

SEA SHELL MOTEL

Motel

Phone: 757/336-6589

	1P: $79-$150	2P: $79-$150	XP: $5
6/17-9/6			
5/27-6/16	1P: $58-$150	2P: $58-$150	XP: $5
3/21-5/26 & 9/7-10/9	1P: $49-$150	2P: $49-$150	XP: $5

Location: Just s on S Main St, e on Cleveland Ave. 3720 Willow St 23336. Fax: 757/336-0641. **Facility:** 40 units. 36 one-bedroom standard units, some with efficiencies. 4 one-bedroom suites ($68-$150) with kitchens. 2 stories (no elevator), exterior corridors. *Bath:* combo or shower only. **Parking:** on-site. **Terms:** open 3/21-10/9, office hours 9 am-9 pm, 2 night minimum stay - weekends, 3 day cancellation notice, weekly rates available. **Pool(s):** outdoor. **Business Services:** fax. **Cards:** AX, DS, MC, VI.

SOME UNITS

SUNRISE MOTOR INN

Motel

Phone: 757/336-6671

6/10-9/5	1P: $71	2P: $75	XP: $5	F12
3/14-6/9 & 9/6-12/1	1P: $39-$51	2P: $43-$55	XP: $5	F12

Location: 0.5 mi n on N Main St, 0.8 mi e on Maddox Blvd, then just s on CR 2102. 4491 Chicken City Rd 23336 (PO Box 185). Fax: 757/336-3752. **Facility:** 24 units. 22 one-bedroom standard units. 1 one- and 1 two-bedroom suites ($375-$600) with kitchens. 1 story, exterior corridors. **Parking:** on-site. **Terms:** open 3/14-12/1, office hours 7 am-10 pm, 2 night minimum stay - seasonal and/or weekends. **Pool(s):** outdoor. **Business Services:** fax. **Cards:** AX, DC, DS, MC, VI.

SOME UNITS

WATERSIDE MOTOR INN

Small-scale Hotel

Phone: (757)336-3434

6/10-9/5	1P: $105-$170	XP: $6	F12
3/1-6/9 & 9/6-10/10	1P: $85-$125	XP: $6	F12
10/11-2/28	1P: $76-$112	XP: $6	F12

Location: 0.5 mi s. 3761 S Main St 23336 (PO Box 347). Fax: 757/336-1878. **Facility:** 49 units. 45 one-bedroom standard units. 4 two-bedroom suites ($100-$170) with kitchens. 3 stories, exterior corridors. **Parking:** on-site. **Terms:** office hours 7 am-10 pm, 2 night minimum stay - seasonal, 3 day cancellation notice-fee imposed. **Amenities:** irons, hair dryers. **Pool(s):** heated outdoor. **Leisure Activities:** whirlpool, marina, fishing, tennis court, exercise room. **Guest Services:** coin laundry. **Business Services:** meeting rooms. **Cards:** AX, CB, DC, DS, MC, VI.

SOME UNITS

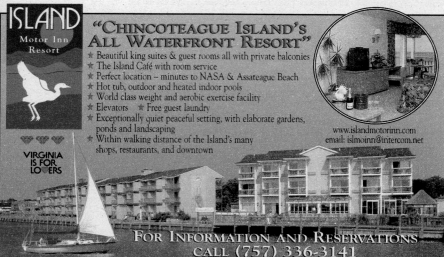

THE WATSON HOUSE

WWW
Historic Bed
& Breakfast

All Year [BP]   1P: $89-$139   2P: $99-$149   XP: $15

Phone: 757/336-1564

Location: Just n of downtown. 4240 Main St 23336 (PO Box 1). Fax: 757/336-5959. **Facility:** This restored 1898 Victorian with the look of a dollhouse offers service-oriented lodgings complemented by authentic period details. Smoke free premises. 5 one-bedroom standard units. 2 stories (no elevator), interior corridors. *Bath:* combo or shower only. **Parking:** on-site. **Terms:** age restrictions may apply, 10 day cancellation notice. **Leisure Activities:** bicycles. **Business Services:** fax. **Cards:** MC, VI.

—— WHERE TO DINE ——

AJ'S...ON THE CREEK

WWW
American

Lunch: $3-$12   **Dinner: $12-$30**   **Phone: 757/336-1539**

Location: 0.5 mi n on Main St, 1 mi e. 6585 Maddox Blvd 23336. **Hours:** Open 3/1-1/21 & 2/14-2/28; 11:30 am-9 pm; to 10 pm in season. Closed: 3/27, 12/25; also Sun. **Reservations:** accepted. **Features:** Dine on sauteed flounder, smothered with scallops, shrimp and crab, amid an intimate, romantically lit setting. Along with fresh grilled fish and seafood, steak, veal and pasta also grace the extensive menu. Screened porch dining is available in summer. Casual dress; cocktails. **Parking:** on-site. **Cards:** AX, DC, DS, MC, VI.

BILL'S SEAFOOD RESTAURANT

AAA
WWW WWW
Seafood

Lunch: $4-$16   **Dinner: $8-$25**   **Phone: 757/336-5831**

Location: 0.5 mi s. 4040 Main St 23336. **Hours:** 5 am-9 pm. Closed: 12/25. **Reservations:** suggested, weekends. **Features:** The fact that the owner also owns a bakery is evident in the exceptional bread found at the casual restaurant. The focus is basic, regional seafood—served grilled, fried or broiled—although a sprinkling of beef and poultry dishes also dots the menu. Casual dress; cocktails. **Parking:** on-site. **Cards:** AX, DC, DS, MC, VI.

CAPT FISH'S STEAMING WHARF

WWW
Seafood

Lunch: $5-$27   **Dinner: $5-$27**   **Phone: 757/336-5528**

Location: Just s on Main St. 3855 Main St 23336. **Hours:** 11 am-10 pm; hours vary seasonally. **Features:** This casual, waterfront, tropical-themed eatery, complete with open-air deck, offers traditionally prepared dishes using the freshest regional seafood. The shrimp are large and spicy, and the flounder light and crispy. Weekend entertainment is featured. Casual dress; cocktails. **Parking:** on-site. **Cards:** MC, VI.

LANDMARK CRAB HOUSE

WWW WWW
Seafood

Dinner: $13-$25   **Phone: 757/336-5552**

Location: Just n to Landmark Plaza. 6172 N Main St 23336. **Hours:** Open 4/1-10/31; 5 pm-10 pm. Closed: Mon 4/1-5/31 & 9/1-10/31. **Features:** Overlooking the Intracoastal Waterway, the restaurant's large, turn-of-the-20th-century themed dining room is a prime setting in which to sample the waters' bounty. Tasty blue crab dishes, flounder and shrimp are served in large portions and complemented by a lengthy salad bar and corn bread. Casual dress; cocktails. **Parking:** on-site. **Cards:** AX, DS, MC, VI.

SHUCKING HOUSE CAFE

WWW WWW
Seafood

Lunch: $6-$15   **Phone: 757/336-5145**

Location: Downtown; in Landmark Plaza. 6162 Main St 23336. **Hours:** Open 4/15-10/31; 8 am-3 pm. Closed: Mon in season. **Reservations:** accepted. **Features:** The glassed-in dining room sits on a pier overlooking the intracoastal waterway. The setting is casual and the menu mostly seafood-oriented, with specialties such as crab cakes and a spicy-sweet tomato-based clam chowder. Casual dress; beer & wine only. **Parking:** on-site. **Cards:** AX, MC, VI.

STEAMERS

AAA
WWW
Seafood

Dinner: $10-$28   **Phone: 757/336-5478**

Location: 0.5 mi n from stop light, 0.3 mi e. 6251 Maddox Blvd 23336. **Hours:** Open 3/1-11/30; 4:30 pm-9 pm. **Reservations:** accepted. **Features:** A favorite of locals, Steamers is always packed in season. No one can deny the more than hearty portions and a casual atmosphere for you to enjoy it in. Fresh seafood from local waters, much of it served in all-you-can-eat platters like crabs and steamed shrimp make this spot a must. Casual dress; cocktails. **Parking:** on-site. **Cards:** AX, DS, MC, VI.

THE VILLAGE RESTAURANT

WWW WWW
Steak & Seafood

Dinner: $10-$22   **Phone: 757/336-5120**

Location: 0.5 mi n on Main St, 1 mi e. 6576 Maddox Blvd 23336. **Hours:** 5 pm-9 pm. Closed: 1/1, 12/24-12/26. **Reservations:** suggested, in season. **Features:** Overlooking the wetlands, the relaxed setting is built to resemble a small village from the outside and cozy and romantic once inside. The menu takes advantage of the freshest local Chesapeake Bay and Atlantic Ocean seafood such as crab, shrimp, flounder, and shellfish. Excellent Crab Imperial. Casual dress; cocktails. **Parking:** on-site. **Cards:** AX, DS, MC, VI.

---

*The following restaurants have not been evaluated by AAA
but are listed for your information only.*

SEA STAR CAFE

[fyi]

Phone: 757/336-5442

Not evaluated. **Location:** Center. 4121 Main St 23336. **Features:** Set downtown in a former mobile ice cream stand, Sea Star Cafe is the spot where locals love to pick up fresh salads and gourmet sandwiches when on the run.

SUGARBAKER'S

[fyi]

Phone: 757/336-3712

Not evaluated. **Location:** Downtown. 4095 Main St. **Features:** Sugarbaker's is a charming bakery in the center of town. Stop at breakfast for donuts, bagels and pastry or at lunch for large salad and overstuffed sandwiches on a variety of fresh-baked bread such as eight-grain or French baguette.

CHRISTIANSBURG pop. 16,947

———— **WHERE TO STAY** ————

ECONO LODGE　　*Book at aaa.com*　　　　　　　　　　　　　　　　　Phone: (540)382-6161

(AAA) (SAVE)
　　　　　3/1-6/30　　　　　1P: $43-$169　　　2P: $48-$169　　　XP: $5　　　F16
　　　　　7/1-10/31　　　　1P: $48-$129　　　2P: $53-$139　　　XP: $10　　F16
　　　　　11/1-2/28　　　　1P: $40-$129　　　2P: $45-$139　　　XP: $5　　　F16
Motel　　**Location:** I-81, exit 118, just w on US 11/460. 2430 Roanoke St 24073. Fax: 540/382-6161. **Facility:** 72 one-bedroom standard units. 2 stories (no elevator), exterior corridors. **Parking:** on-site. **Terms:** package plans, small pets only ($10 extra charge). **Pool(s):** small outdoor. **Cards:** AX, CB, DC, DS, MC, VI.
Special Amenities: free continental breakfast and free local telephone calls.

SOME UNITS

HAMPTON INN CHRISTIANSBURG/BLACKSBURG　　*Book at aaa.com*　　　Phone: (540)381-5874

　　　　　All Year　　　　　1P: $89-$189　　　2P: $99-$189　　　XP: $10　　F18
　　　　　Location: I-81, exit 118, 3 mi w, then just e. 380 Arbor Dr 24073. Fax: 540/381-2723. **Facility:** 119 one-bedroom
Small-scale Hotel　standard units, some with whirlpools. 5 stories, interior corridors. *Bath:* combo or shower only. **Parking:** on-site. **Terms:** 2 night minimum stay - seasonal, 30 day cancellation notice-fee imposed. **Amenities:** voice mail, irons, hair dryers. *Some:* CD players. **Pool(s):** outdoor. **Leisure Activities:** exercise room. **Guest Services:** coin laundry. **Business Services:** meeting rooms. **Cards:** AX, DC, DS, MC, VI.

SOME UNITS

HOLIDAY INN EXPRESS HOTEL & SUITES
CHRISTIANSBURG/BLACKSBURG　　*Book at aaa.com*　　　　　　　Phone: (540)382-6500

　　　　　6/1-7/31　　　　　1P: $92-$139　　　2P: $92-$139
　　　　　3/1-5/31 & 8/1-2/28　1P: $89-$129　　　2P: $89-$129
Small-scale Hotel　**Location:** I-81, exit 118C, just e. 2725 Roanoke St 24073. Fax: 540/381-9220. **Facility:** 74 one-bedroom standard units, some with whirlpools. 4 stories, interior corridors. *Bath:* combo or shower only. **Parking:** on-site. **Terms:** cancellation fee imposed. **Amenities:** high-speed Internet, voice mail, irons, hair dryers. **Pool(s):** heated indoor. **Leisure Activities:** exercise room. **Guest Services:** coin laundry. **Business Services:** meeting rooms, business center. **Cards:** AX, DC, DS, MC, VI.

SOME UNITS

MICROTEL INN & SUITES　　*Book at aaa.com*　　　　　　　　　　Phone: (540)381-0500

　　　　　All Year　　　　　1P: $40-$70　　　2P: $40-$70　　　XP: $5　　　F16
　　　　　Location: I-81, exit 118B, 3 mi w on US 460, then just n; off Arbor Rd. Located in the New River Valley Mall. 135
Small-scale Hotel　Ponderosa Dr 24073 (PO Box 150, 24068). Fax: 540/381-7525. **Facility:** 86 one-bedroom standard units. 3 stories, interior corridors. *Bath:* combo or shower only. **Parking:** on-site. **Amenities:** voice mail. **Leisure Activities:** exercise room. **Guest Services:** coin laundry. **Business Services:** meeting rooms. **Cards:** AX, DC, DS, MC, VI.

SOME UNITS

THE OAKS VICTORIAN INN　　　　　　　　　　　　　　　　　　　Phone: (540)381-1500

(AAA) (SAVE)
　　　　　All Year [BP]　　　　1P: $90-$125　　　2P: $150-$185　　　XP: $25
　　　　　Location: I-81, exit 114, 2 mi w. 311 E Main St 24073. Fax: 540/381-3036. **Facility:** The large guest rooms reflect
Historic Bed　a period ambience but offer modern conveniences in this 1893 Queen Anne Victorian inn. Smoke free
& Breakfast　premises. 8 one-bedroom standard units, some with whirlpools. 3 stories (no elevator), interior corridors. *Bath:* combo or shower only. **Parking:** on-site. **Terms:** check-in 4 pm, age restrictions may apply, 7 day cancellation notice. **Amenities:** video library, hair dryers. **Leisure Activities:** whirlpool. *Fee:* bicycles. **Guest Services:** complimentary evening beverages. **Business Services:** meeting rooms. **Cards:** AX, DS,
MC, VI.

FEE

SUPER 8 MOTEL - CHRISTIANSBURG EAST   *Book at aaa.com*   Phone: (540)382-7421

AAA SAVE
Motel

3/1-11/30	1P: $45-$95	2P: $50-$99	XP: $7 F12
12/1-2/28	1P: $39-$69	2P: $43-$79	XP: $5 F12

Location: I-81, exit 118C. 2780 Roanoke Rd 24073. Fax: 540/381-4149. **Facility:** 63 one-bedroom standard units. 1 story, exterior corridors. **Parking:** on-site. **Terms:** 3 day cancellation notice-fee imposed. **Pool(s):** small outdoor. **Cards:** AX, CB, DC, DS, JC, MC, VI. **Special Amenities:** free continental breakfast and free newspaper. *(See color ad p 686)*

SOME UNITS

SUPER 8 MOTEL-CHRISTIANSBURG WEST   *Book at aaa.com*   Phone: (540)382-5813

Small-scale Hotel

All Year [CP]   1P: $52-$56   2P: $57-$62   XP: $6   F

Location: I-81, exit 118, 1 mi w on US 11/460, then 3.5 mi nw on US 460 Bypass; jct SR 114. 55 Laurel St NE 24073. Fax: 540/382-5813. **Facility:** 50 one-bedroom standard units. 2 stories (no elevator), interior corridors. **Parking:** on-site. **Terms:** 14 day cancellation notice, small pets only ($20 extra charge). **Amenities:** safes. **Cards:** AX, DC, MC, VI.

SOME UNITS
FEE   FEE FEE

——— WHERE TO DINE ———

THE FARMHOUSE   **Dinner:** $15-$22   Phone: 540/382-4253

American
cocktails.

Location: 2 mi w on US 460, 0.3 mi s on Cambria St. 285 Ridinger St 24073. **Hours:** 5 pm-9:45 pm, Sun noon-8:45 pm. Closed: 1/1, 12/24, 12/25. **Features:** Meals are served in a 19th-century farmhouse attractively styled with cozy and private high-backed wood booths. Since 1963, the restaurant has been known for its prime rib, steak, seafood, pasta and chicken dishes, as well as pleasant, dependable service. Casual dress; cocktails. **Parking:** on-site. **Cards:** AX, DC, DS, MC, VI.

THE HUCKLEBERRY RESTAURANT   **Dinner:** $10-$20   Phone: 540/381-2382

American

Location: I-81, exit 118, 0.3 mi e on US 11/460. 2790 Roanoke St 24073. **Hours:** 5 pm-10 pm. Closed: 1/1, 12/25; also Sun. **Reservations:** suggested. **Features:** Decorated in a railroad theme, the rustic log cabin is a cozy place to enjoy foods from a well-balanced menu that includes prime rib, shrimp scampi, baby back ribs and other traditional favorites. Service is friendly and thoughtful. Casual dress; cocktails. **Parking:** on-site. **Cards:** AX, CB, DC, DS, MC, VI.

CLARKSVILLE pop. 1,329

——— WHERE TO STAY ———

BEST WESTERN ON THE LAKE   *Book at aaa.com*   Phone: (434)374-5023

Small-scale Hotel

11/1-2/28	1P: $74-$114	2P: $74-$114	XP: $5 F17
3/1-10/31	1P: $69-$99	2P: $69-$99	XP: $5 F17

Location: Just n of US 58. Located on the lake. 103 Second St 23927. Fax: 434/374-0900. **Facility:** 70 units. 66 one-bedroom standard units. 4 one-bedroom suites ($99-$121). 2 stories (no elevator), interior corridors. **Parking:** on-site, winter plug-ins. **Terms:** 2 night minimum stay - seasonal and/or weekends, 3 day cancellation notice, pets ($10-$20 extra charge). **Amenities:** voice mail, irons, hair dryers. *Some:* dual phone lines. **Pool(s):** outdoor. **Leisure Activities:** boat dock. **Business Services:** meeting rooms, business center. **Cards:** AX, CB, DC, DS, JC, MC, VI.

SOME UNITS
FEE

——— WHERE TO DINE ———

——— The following restaurant has not been evaluated by AAA
but is listed for your information only. ———

MARIPOSA CAFE   Phone: 434/374-4646

fyi

Not evaluated. **Location:** Center; just w of lake. 335 Virginia Ave 23927. **Features:** In the small downtown area of this lake town, the quaint spot offers patrons a wide selection of delicious sandwiches, quiches, pastries and even gourmet groceries.

CLIFTON —See *District Of Columbia p. 526.*

COLLINSVILLE pop. 7,777

——— WHERE TO STAY ———

KNIGHTS INN   *Book at aaa.com*   Phone: (276)647-3716

AAA SAVE
Motel

All Year   1P: $55-$60   2P: $60-$65   XP: $5   F18

Location: Jct US 58, 3 mi n on US 220 business route. 2357 Virginia Ave 24078. Fax: 276/647-1178. **Facility:** 40 one-bedroom standard units. 1-2 stories (no elevator), exterior corridors. **Parking:** on-site. **Terms:** weekly rates available, package plans, pets (in designated units). **Pool(s):** outdoor, wading. **Cards:** AX, DC, DS, MC, VI.

SOME UNITS

QUALITY INN-DUTCH INN HOTEL AND
CONVENTION CENTER *Book at aaa.com*
Phone: (276)647-3721

All Year | 1P: $75-$85 | 2P: $75-$85 | XP: $10 | F18

Small-scale Hotel **Location:** Jct US 58, 3 mi n on US 220 business route. 2360 Virginia Ave 24078. **Fax:** 276/647-4857. **Facility:** 148 one-bedroom standard units. 2 stories (no elevator), exterior corridors. **Parking:** on-site. **Terms:** weekly rates available, package plans, pets ($5 extra charge). **Amenities:** high-speed Internet, voice mail, irons, hair dryers. **Pool(s):** outdoor. **Leisure Activities:** whirlpool, exercise room. **Guest Services:** coin laundry. **Business Services:** meeting rooms. **Cards:** AX, CB, DC, DS, JC, MC, VI.

SOME UNITS

COLONIAL HEIGHTS —See Richmond p. 859.

COVINGTON pop. 6,303

——— **WHERE TO STAY** ———

BEST WESTERN MOUNTAIN VIEW *Book at aaa.com*
Phone: (540)962-4951

5/1-2/28 [BP] | 1P: $82-$102 | 2P: $94-$115 | XP: $12 | F17
3/1-4/30 [BP] | 1P: $77-$97 | 2P: $88-$100 | XP: $11 | F17

Small-scale Hotel **Location:** I-64, exit 16, just n. 820 E Madison St 24426. **Fax:** 540/965-5714. **Facility:** 76 one-bedroom standard units. 2 stories (no elevator), exterior corridors. **Parking:** on-site. **Terms:** pets ($12 extra charge). **Amenities:** irons, hair dryers. **Pool(s):** outdoor, wading. **Leisure Activities:** exercise room. **Guest Services:** coin laundry. **Business Services:** meeting rooms. **Cards:** AX, CB, DC, DS, JC, MC, VI.

SOME UNITS

COMFORT INN *Book at aaa.com*
Phone: (540)962-2141

5/1-2/28 [BP] | 1P: $82-$89 | 2P: $93-$101 | XP: $12 | F18
3/1-4/30 [BP] | 1P: $77-$84 | 2P: $88-$95 | XP: $12 | F18

Motel **Location:** I-64, exit 16, just sw. 203 Interstate Dr 24426. **Fax:** 540/965-0964. **Facility:** 98 one-bedroom standard units. 2 stories (no elevator), interior corridors. **Parking:** on-site. **Terms:** pets ($10 extra charge). **Amenities:** high-speed Internet, irons, hair dryers. **Pool(s):** outdoor. **Leisure Activities:** whirlpool. **Guest Services:** valet laundry. **Business Services:** meeting rooms. **Cards:** AX, CB, DC, DS, JC, MC, VI.

SOME UNITS

HOLIDAY INN EXPRESS *Book at aaa.com*
Phone: 540/962-1200

All Year | 1P: $99-$109

Small-scale Hotel **Location:** I-64, exit 16, just n, then 0.3 mi w. 701 Carlyle St 24426. **Fax:** 540/962-1245. **Facility:** 63 one-bedroom standard units, some with whirlpools. 4 stories, interior corridors. *Bath:* combo or shower only. **Parking:** on-site. **Terms:** cancellation fee imposed. **Amenities:** voice mail, irons, hair dryers. **Pool(s):** heated indoor. **Leisure Activities:** whirlpool, exercise room. **Guest Services:** coin laundry. **Business Services:** meeting rooms, business center. **Cards:** AX, CB, DC, DS, MC, VI.

SOME UNITS

——— **WHERE TO DINE** ———

THE BRASS LANTERN
Dinner: $8-$15
Phone: 540/962-4951

American **Location:** I-64, exit 16, 0.3 mi n. 820 E Madison St 24426. **Hours:** 6 am-10 & 5-9 pm, Fri-9:30 pm, Sat 7 am-10 & 5-9:30 pm, Sun 7 am-10 & 5-9 pm. **Features:** Preset and ready for patrons, the elegant dining room affords wonderful scenic views of the mountains. The focus of the menu is on classic American cuisine. A local favorite for lunch or dinner, this place is well worth the stop off the interstate. Casual dress; cocktails. **Parking:** on-site. **Cards:** AX, DC, DS, MC, VI.

CUCCI'S
Lunch: $6-$12
Dinner: $6-$15
Phone: 540/962-3964

Italian **Location:** I-64, exit 16, just n. 566 E Madison Ave 24426. **Hours:** 11 am-11 pm, Sat-midnight. Closed major holidays; also Sun. **Features:** Cucci's is a family friendly restaurant with many pasta and pizza chocies. Try the famous turnovers. Casual dress; beer & wine only. **Parking:** on-site. **Cards:** AX, MC, VI.

CULPEPER pop. 9,664

——— **WHERE TO STAY** ———

COMFORT INN-CULPEPER *Book at aaa.com*
Phone: (540)825-4900

All Year [ECP] | 1P: $79-$129 | 2P: $79-$129 | XP: $8 | F17

Small-scale Hotel **Location:** 2 mi s on US 29 business route; jct US 29, then just e. 890 Willis Ln 22701. **Fax:** 540/825-4904. **Facility:** 49 one-bedroom standard units. 2 stories (no elevator), exterior corridors. *Bath:* combo or shower only. **Parking:** on-site. **Terms:** small pets only ($15 extra charge). **Amenities:** safes, irons, hair dryers. **Pool(s):** outdoor. **Guest Services:** valet laundry. **Cards:** AX, CB, DC, DS, MC, VI.

SOME UNITS

FOUNTAIN HALL
Phone: (540)825-8200

All Year | 1P: $105-$145 | 2P: $105-$145 | XP: $20

Historic Bed & Breakfast **Location:** Just e of S Main St (US 29 business route) via Chandler St, then just s at Asher St; center. 609 S East St 22701. **Fax:** 540/825-7716. **Facility:** This 1859 Colonial Revival mansion offers three units with private balconies; breakfast is prepared on site. Smoke free premises. 6 one-bedroom standard units, some with whirlpools. 2 stories (no elevator), interior corridors. *Bath:* combo or shower only. **Parking:** on-site. **Terms:** 2 night minimum stay - seasonal and/or weekends, 7 day cancellation notice-fee imposed, package plans. **Amenities:** hair dryers. *Some:* CD players, irons. **Guest Services:** complimentary evening beverages, valet laundry. **Business Services:** meeting rooms. **Cards:** AX, CB, DC, DS, MC, VI.

SOME UNITS

HOLIDAY INN
Book at aaa.com
All Year   1P: $85-$99   **Phone: (540)825-1253**
▼▼▼▼▼
Small-scale Hotel
Location: Jct US 29, 2 mi s on US 29 business route. 791 Madison Rd 22701 (PO Box 1206). **Fax:** 540/825-7134. **Facility:** 158 one-bedroom standard units. 2 stories (no elevator); exterior corridors. *Bath:* combo or shower only. **Parking:** on-site. **Terms:** cancellation fee imposed. **Amenities:** voice mail, irons, hair dryers. **Pool(s):** outdoor, wading. **Leisure Activities:** exercise room. **Guest Services:** coin laundry. **Business Services:** meeting rooms. **Cards:** AX, CB, DC, DS, JC, MC, VI.

SOME UNITS

—— WHERE TO DINE ——

HAZEL RIVER INN RESTAURANT
Lunch: $6-$15   **Dinner: $14-$30**   **Phone: 540/825-7148**
▼▼▼▼▼
American
Location: Just e; center. 195 E Davis St 22701. **Hours:** 11:30 am-9 pm. **Closed:** 12/25. **Reservations:** suggested, weekends. **Features:** Guests can enjoy a fine-dining experience in elegant surroundings. The menu lists a wonderful blend of choices. Casual dress; cocktails. **Parking:** on-site and street. **Cards:** AX, CB, DC, DS, JC, MC, VI.

IT'S ABOUT THYME
Lunch: $5-$15   **Dinner: $8-$28**   **Phone: 540/825-4264**
▼▼ ▼▼
American
Location: Just e on Davis St; center. 128 E Davis St 22701. **Hours:** 11 am-3 & 5:30-10 pm. Closed major holidays; also Sun & Mon. **Features:** The fun and casual downtown restaurant has beautiful murals, friendly people and a dash of European country cuisine. Casual dress; cocktails. **Parking:** street. **Cards:** AX, CB, DC, DS, JC, MC, VI.

KIRSTEN'S OF CULPEPER
Lunch: $5-$11   **Dinner: $9-$26**   **Phone: 540/829-8400**
▼▼▼▼▼
American
Location: Center of downtown. 219 E Davis St, Suite 110 22701. **Hours:** 11:30 am-3 & 5:30-9 pm, Fri & Sat-10 pm, Sun-3 pm. Closed: Mon. **Features:** On the menu is comfort food prepared with a flair. The dining area displays Roman columns and an extensive use of plants. Knowledgeable servers are friendly. Casual dress; cocktails. **Parking:** street. **Cards:** AX, MC, VI.

DAHLGREN pop. 997

—— WHERE TO STAY ——

COMFORT INN-DAHLGREN
Book at aaa.com
All Year [ECP]   1P: $55-$82   2P: $55-$82   XP: $6   F18   **Phone: (540)663-3060**
▼▼▼ ▼▼
Small-scale Hotel
Location: US 301; 2 mi s of entrance to US Navy Surface Weapons Center; 4 mi s of Potomac River Bridge. 4661 James Madison Pkwy 22485 (PO Box 1810, 22448). **Fax:** 540/663-3060. **Facility:** 59 one-bedroom standard units, some with whirlpools. 2 stories (no elevator); interior corridors. *Bath:* combo or shower only. **Parking:** on-site. **Amenities:** irons, hair dryers. *Some:* dual phone lines. **Pool(s):** outdoor. **Leisure Activities:** whirlpool, limited exercise equipment. **Business Services:** fax. **Cards:** AX, CB, DC, DS, MC, VI.

SOME UNITS

HOLIDAY INN EXPRESS
Book at aaa.com
All Year   1P: $68-$80   2P: $68-$80   F   **Phone: (540)644-1500**
▼▼▼ ▼▼
Small-scale Hotel
Location: US 301, 4.2 mi s of Potomac River Bridge, 2 mi s of entrance to US Navy Surface Weapons Center. 4755 James Madison Pkwy 22485. **Fax:** 540/644-9027. **Facility:** 60 one-bedroom standard units, some with whirlpools. 2 stories (no elevator); interior corridors. *Bath:* combo or shower only. **Parking:** on-site. **Terms:** 2 night minimum stay - seasonal, [ECP] meal plan available. **Amenities:** dual phone lines, voice mail, irons, hair dryers. **Pool(s):** outdoor. **Business Services:** meeting rooms, fax. **Cards:** AX, DC, DS, MC, VI.

SOME UNITS
FEE

DALEVILLE pop. 1,454

—— WHERE TO STAY ——

ECONO LODGE-ROANOKE/DALEVILLE
Book at aaa.com
     4/1-10/31   1P: $52-$80   2P: $52-$80   XP: $5   F18   **Phone: 540/992-3000**
▲▲▲ [SAVE]   3/1-3/31 & 11/1-2/28   1P: $45-$68   2P: $45-$68   XP: $5   F18
▼▼ ▼▼
Motel
Location: I-81, exit 150B, just nw on US 220. 446 Roanoke Rd 24083. **Fax:** 540/992-3000. **Facility:** 66 one-bedroom standard units. 2 stories (no elevator); interior corridors. **Parking:** on-site. **Pool(s):** outdoor, wading. **Leisure Activities:** basketball. **Guest Services:** coin laundry. **Cards:** AX, CB, DC, DS, MC, VI. **Special Amenities:** free continental breakfast and free local telephone calls.

SOME UNITS

HOWARD JOHNSON EXPRESS INN
Book at aaa.com
All Year   1P: $65   2P: $72   XP: $6   F   **Phone: (540)992-1234**
▼▼▼ ▼▼
Small-scale Hotel
Location: I-81, exit 150B, just nw on US 220. 437 Roanoke Rd 24083. **Fax:** 540/992-2227. **Facility:** 98 one-bedroom standard units. 1-2 stories (no elevator); exterior corridors. **Parking:** on-site. **Terms:** package plans, small pets only ($15 extra charge, in smoking units). **Amenities:** irons, hair dryers. **Pool(s):** outdoor, wading. **Leisure Activities:** horseshoes, volleyball. **Guest Services:** coin laundry. **Business Services:** meeting rooms. **Cards:** AX, DC, DS, MC, VI.

SOME UNITS
FEE

——— WHERE TO DINE ———

THREE LI'L PIGS BARBEQUE
▼▼▼ ▼▼▼
Barbecue
Lunch: $5-$11   **Dinner:** $6-$14   **Phone:** 540/966-0165
Location: I-81, exit 150, just w on US 220. 120 Kingston Dr 24083. **Hours:** 11 am-10 pm. Closed: 12/25; also Sun.
Features: This restaurant has a catchy name and fresh quality barbeque. Three Li'l Pigs Barbeque hickory smokes it's pork and then slow cooks it for fine flavor. Casual dress; beer & wine only. **Parking:** on-site.
Cards: DS, MC, VI.

☒

DAMASCUS pop. 981

——— WHERE TO STAY ———

APPLE TREE B & B
▼▼▼ ◆◆▼▼
Bed & Breakfast
Phone: (276)475-5261
All Year [BP]   1P: $60-$85   2P: $60-$85   XP: $15   D10
Location: Town center. 115 E Laurel Ave 24236 (PO Box 878). **Facility:** Located on the Appalachian Trail, this B&B offers antique-furnished rooms, some of which are compact. Smoke free premises. 5 units. 3 one-bedroom standard units. 2 one-bedroom suites. 1-2 stories (no elevator), interior corridors. *Bath:* combo or shower only. **Parking:** on-site. **Terms:** 2 night minimum stay - seasonal and/or weekends, 3 day cancellation notice-fee imposed, small pets only (owner's cat on premises). **Amenities:** video library, hair dryers. *Some:* DVD players. **Guest Services:** complimentary evening beverages. **Cards:** MC, VI.

SOME UNITS
(ASK) [S/D] [🐾] [🍴] ☒ [VCR] / [🕿] [📶] [📺] [💻] /

DANVILLE pop. 48,411

——— WHERE TO STAY ———

COMFORT INN & SUITES   *Book at aaa.com*
▼▼▼▼▼▼
Small-scale Hotel
Phone: (434)793-2000
All Year   1P: $69-$124   2P: $74-$129   XP: $5   F17
Location: US 58, just w of jct US 29 business route. Located adjacent to the mall. 100 Tower Dr 24540. Fax: 434/792-4621. **Facility:** 118 one-bedroom standard units, some with whirlpools. 6 stories, interior corridors. **Parking:** on-site. **Terms:** package plans, pets ($10 extra charge). **Amenities:** high-speed Internet, irons, hair dryers. **Pool(s):** outdoor. **Guest Services:** valet and coin laundry. **Business Services:** meeting rooms, business center. **Cards:** AX, CB, DC, DS, JC, MC, VI.

SOME UNITS
(ASK) [S/D] [🐾] [🍴] [🍸] [🏊] [🐾] [📹] [DATA PORT] [💻] / ☒ [📶] [📺]
FEE   FEE FEE

COURTYARD BY MARRIOTT   *Book at aaa.com*
▼▼▼ ◆◆▼▼
Small-scale Hotel
Phone: (434)791-2661
All Year   1P: $86-$96   2P: $86-$96
Location: On US 58, just w of jct US 29 business route. 2136 Riverside Dr 24540. Fax: 434/791-2073. **Facility:** 92 units. 89 one-bedroom standard units. 3 one-bedroom suites ($101-$151). 3 stories, interior corridors. *Bath:* combo or shower only. **Parking:** on-site. **Terms:** 3 day cancellation notice. **Amenities:** high-speed Internet, dual phone lines, voice mail, irons, hair dryers. **Pool(s):** heated outdoor. **Leisure Activities:** whirlpool, exercise room. **Guest Services:** sundries, valet and coin laundry. **Business Services:** meeting rooms, business center. **Cards:** AX, CB, DC, DS, MC, VI.

SOME UNITS
(ASK) [S/D] [🍴] [&M] [♿] [🏊] [📹] [DATA PORT] [💻] / ☒ [📶] [📺] /

HAMPTON INN RIVERSIDE   *Book at aaa.com*
▼▼▼ ◆◆▼▼
Small-scale Hotel
Phone: (434)793-1111
3/1-10/31   1P: $79-$109   2P: $89-$109
11/1-2/28   1P: $70-$99   2P: $70-$99
Location: US 58, 0.5 mi e of jct US 86 and 29. 2130 Riverside Dr 24540. Fax: 434/791-1181. **Facility:** 59 one-bedroom standard units, some with whirlpools. 3 stories, interior corridors. *Bath:* combo or shower only. **Parking:** on-site. **Terms:** 2 night minimum stay - seasonal. **Amenities:** high-speed Internet, voice mail, irons, hair dryers. **Pool(s):** outdoor. **Leisure Activities:** exercise room. **Guest Services:** valet and coin laundry. **Business Services:** meeting rooms, fax. **Cards:** AX, CB, DC, DS, MC, VI.

SOME UNITS
(ASK) [S/D] [🍴] [&M] [♿] [🏊] [📹] [DATA PORT] [📶] [📺] [💻] / ☒

HOLIDAY INN EXPRESS DANVILLE   *Book at aaa.com*
▼▼▼ ◆◆▼▼
Small-scale Hotel
Phone: (434)793-4000
All Year [CP]   1P: $81-$91   2P: $81-$91   XP: $5   F18
Location: US 58, 0.5 mi e of jct US 86 and 29. 2121 Riverside Dr 24540. Fax: 434/799-5516. **Facility:** 98 one-bedroom standard units, some with whirlpools. 3 stories, interior/exterior corridors. **Parking:** on-site. **Terms:** 3 day cancellation notice. **Amenities:** high-speed Internet, voice mail, irons, hair dryers. **Pool(s):** outdoor. **Leisure Activities:** fishing. **Guest Services:** valet laundry. **Business Services:** meeting rooms, PC, fax. **Cards:** AX, CB, DC, DS, MC, VI.

SOME UNITS
(ASK) [S/D] [🍴] [🏊] [🐾] [📹] [DATA PORT] [💻] / ☒ [📶] [📺] /
FEE FEE

INNKEEPER DANVILLE NORTH   *Book at aaa.com*
▼▼▼ ▼▼▼
Motel
Phone: (434)836-1700
All Year [CP]   1P: $52-$62   2P: $52-$62   XP: $5   F18
Location: US 29 N, 2.4 mi n of US 58. 1030 Piney Forest Rd 24540. Fax: 434/836-1700. **Facility:** 52 one-bedroom standard units. 2 stories (no elevator), exterior corridors. **Parking:** on-site. **Terms:** 3 day cancellation notice, small pets only. **Pool(s):** outdoor. **Guest Services:** valet laundry. **Business Services:** fax. **Cards:** AX, CB, DC, DS, MC, VI.

SOME UNITS
(ASK) [S/D] [🐾] [🏊] [🐾] [📹] [DATA PORT] [📶] [📺] / ☒ /

INNKEEPER DANVILLE WEST   *Book at aaa.com*
▼▼▼ ▼▼
Small-scale Hotel
Phone: (434)799-1202
All Year [CP]   1P: $52-$62   2P: $52-$62   XP: $5   F18
Location: US 58 W, just w of jct US 29. 3020 Riverside Dr 24541. Fax: 434/799-9672. **Facility:** 117 units. 114 one-bedroom standard units, some with whirlpools. 3 one-bedroom suites: 2 stories (no elevator), interior/exterior corridors. **Parking:** on-site. **Terms:** 3 day cancellation notice. **Pool(s):** outdoor. **Leisure Activities:** whirlpool. **Guest Services:** valet laundry. **Business Services:** fax. **Cards:** AX, CB, DC, DS, MC, VI.

SOME UNITS
(ASK) [S/D] [🍴] [🏊] [🐾] [📹] [DATA PORT] / ☒ [📶] [📺] [💻] /
FEE FEE

RAMADA INN STRATFORD   *Book at aaa.com*   Phone: (434)793-2500

AAA SAVE

◆◆◆ ◆◆◆

Small-scale Hotel

All Year   1P: $55-$109   2P: $65-$116   XP: $7   F14
Location: US 58, just e of jct US 29 business route. 2500 Riverside Dr 24540. **Fax:** 434/793-6960. **Facility:** 148 units. 140 one-bedroom standard units. 8 one-bedroom suites, some with whirlpools. 2 stories (no elevator), exterior corridors. *Bath:* combo or shower only. **Parking:** on-site. **Terms:** package plans, pets ($25 extra charge). **Amenities:** high-speed Internet, voice mail, irons, hair dryers. *Some:* dual phone lines, safes (fee). **Dining:** Stratford Inn Dining Room, see separate listing. **Pool(s):** heated outdoor, wading. **Leisure Activities:** whirlpool. **Guest Services:** area transportation-within 5 mi. **Business Services:** conference facilities, fax. **Cards:** AX, CB, DC, DS, MC, VI. **Special Amenities:** free full breakfast and free newspaper.

SOME UNITS

[S/D] [✈] [🛏] [🍴] [&M] [&] [≈] [♨] [🐾] [DATA PORT] [☕] / [✕] [VCR] [🔲] [🖥] /
FEE

SLEEP INN & SUITES   *Book at aaa.com*   Phone: (434)793-6090

◆◆◆ ◆◆◆

Small-scale Hotel

All Year [ECP]   1P: $90-$100   2P: $90-$100   XP: $5   F18
Location: On US 58, 1.3 mi e of jct US 29. Located across from Danville Regional Airport. 1483 S Boston Rd 24540. **Fax:** 434/793-6088. **Facility:** 73 units. 67 one-bedroom standard units. 6 one-bedroom suites ($110-$130). 3 stories, interior corridors. *Bath:* combo or shower only. **Parking:** on-site. **Amenities:** high-speed Internet, dual phone lines, voice mail, irons, hair dryers. **Pool(s):** heated outdoor. **Leisure Activities:** whirlpool, exercise room. **Guest Services:** valet and coin laundry. **Business Services:** meeting rooms. **Cards:** AX, CB, DC, DS, MC, VI.

SOME UNITS

[ASK] [S/D] [🍴] [▼] [&M] [&] [≈] [♨] [DATA PORT] [☕] / [✕] [🔲] [🖥] /
FEE FEE

SUPER 8 MOTEL   *Book at aaa.com*   Phone: (434)799-5845

◆◆◆

Motel

MC, VI.

All Year   1P: $49-$59   2P: $55-$65   XP: $6   F3
Location: On US 58, just e of jct US 29 business route. 2385 Riverside Dr 24541. **Fax:** 434/799-5845. **Facility:** 57 one-bedroom standard units. 3 stories, interior corridors. **Parking:** on-site. **Terms:** 2 night minimum stay - seasonal, cancellation fee imposed, pets ($20 deposit). **Amenities:** safes (fee). **Cards:** AX, CB, DC, DS,

SOME UNITS

[ASK] [S/D] [🛏] [🍴] [♨] / [✕] [VCR] [🔲] [🖥] /
FEE

------ **WHERE TO DINE** ------

EL VALLARTA RESTAURANTE MEXICANO   Lunch: $4-$12   Dinner: $6-$12   Phone: 434/799-0506

◆◆◆

Mexican

Location: 1 mi n of US 58 via Piedmont Dr. 418 Westover Pl 24541. **Hours:** 11 am-9 pm, Sat & Sun from noon. **Closed:** 11/24, 12/25. **Features:** With TVs tuned to sports in every corner, the large, friendly spot serves such favorites as fajitas, burritos, tacos with a twist and, for the truly adventurous, menudo. Casual dress; cocktails. **Parking:** on-site. **Cards:** AX, DS, MC, VI.

[&M] [✕]

JOE & MIMMA'S ITALIAN RESTAURANT   Lunch: $4-$9   Dinner: $6-$14   Phone: 434/799-5763

◆◆◆ ◆◆◆

Italian

MC, VI.

Location: On US 58; just w of jct W US 29 business route; in Riverside Shopping Center, rear corner. 3336 Riverside Dr 24541. **Hours:** 11 am-9:30 pm, Fri & Sat-10 pm. **Closed:** Sun & Mon. **Reservations:** suggested, weekends. **Features:** This is a casual dining spot, offering traditional and "new" Italian pasta, veal and seafood dishes as well as calzone and pizza. Of note is a flavorful "penne rustica" in a creamy tomato sauce with a blend of mushrooms, spinach, and sun-dried tomatoes. Casual dress; cocktails. **Parking:** on-site. **Cards:** DC,

[&M] [✕]

MARY'S DINER   Lunch: $5-$10   Dinner: $5-$10   Phone: 434/836-0132

◆◆◆

Southern

Location: US 29 N, 2.7 mi n of US 58. 1201 Piney Forest Rd 24540. **Hours:** 11 am-9 pm. **Features:** The Southern cafeteria is a favorite for locals who rave that its fried chicken is the best. Other specialties include collard greens, cornbread and chicken livers. Folks on the run can take advantage of the drive-through menu. Casual dress. **Parking:** on-site. **Cards:** MC, VI.

[✕]

STRATFORD INN DINING ROOM   Lunch: $6-$9   Dinner: $12-$20   Phone: 434/793-2500

AAA

◆◆◆ ◆◆◆

American

Location: US 58, just e of jct US 29 business route; in Ramada Inn Stratford. 2500 Riverside Dr 24540. **Hours:** 6 am-2 & 5-10 pm, Sat 6 am-11 & 5-10 pm, Sun 6 am-2 pm. **Closed:** 12/25. **Reservations:** suggested, in summer. **Features:** With cozy booths, Early American decor accents and a pianist in the clubby lounge, the dining room strikes a more formal atmosphere than other spots in town. Built on seafood, steaks and some Italian offerings, the traditional menu has changed little in years. Casual dress; cocktails. **Parking:** on-site. **Cards:** AX, CB, DC, DS, MC, VI.

[▼] [✕]

DAYTON pop. 1,344

------ **WHERE TO DINE** ------

THOMAS HOUSE RESTAURANT   Lunch: $5-$12   Dinner: $6-$14   Phone: 540/879-2181

◆◆◆ ◆◆◆

American

Location: Center. 222 Main St 22821. **Hours:** 6 am-8 pm. **Closed:** 1/1, 11/24, 12/25; also Sun. **Features:** Thomas House Restaurant offers home-spun charm and elegance as well as country home cooked favoraites. Casual dress. **Parking:** on-site.

[✕]

DINWIDDIE (See map and index starting on p. 835)

——— **WHERE TO STAY** ———

HOLIDAY INN EXPRESS HOTEL & SUITES *Book at aaa.com*   Phone: (804)518-1515   **21**

AAA SAVE   All Year   1P: $90-$110   2P: $90-$110

Small-scale Hotel   **Location:** I-85, exit 63A, just s. 5679 Boydton Plank Rd 23803. **Fax:** 804/518-1516. **Facility:** 67 one-bedroom standard units, some with whirlpools. 3 stories, interior corridors. *Bath:* combo or shower only. **Parking:** on-site. **Amenities:** high-speed Internet (fee), dual phone lines, voice mail, irons, hair dryers. *Some:* DVD players (fee). **Pool(s):** outdoor. **Leisure Activities:** exercise room. **Guest Services:** valet laundry. **Business Services:** meeting rooms, business center. **Cards:** AX, DC, DS, MC, VI. **Special Amenities:** free continental breakfast and free local telephone calls. *(See color ad p 819)*

SOME UNITS

——— **WHERE TO DINE** ———

THE HOME PLACE RESTAURANT   **Lunch:** $4-$13   **Dinner:** $7-$13   Phone: 804/469-9596

AAA

Southern   **Location:** I-85, exit 53, 1 mi w on SR 703, 1 mi s on US 1, then e. 14712 Spring Creek Rd 23841. **Hours:** 7 am-8 pm, Fri & Sat-9 pm. **Closed:** 12/25. **Reservations:** suggested, Fri & Sat. **Features:** Nestled on 76 acres of beautiful, rustic surroundings and renowned as the birthplace of General Winfield Scott, the name says it all: Southern-style food and friendly service in a converted barn. A great place to have a good meal in a scenic spot. Casual dress; beer & wine only. **Parking:** on-site. **Cards:** MC, VI.

DOSWELL —*See Richmond p. 859.*

DUBLIN pop. 2,228

——— **WHERE TO STAY** ———

COMFORT INN-DUBLIN   *Book at aaa.com*   Phone: (540)674-1100

3/1-9/30 [ECP]   1P: $68-$75   2P: $68-$75   XP: $6   F18
10/1-2/28 [ECP]   1P: $52-$65   2P: $52-$65   XP: $6   F18

Small-scale Hotel   **Location:** I-81, exit 98, just e. 4424 Cleburne Blvd 24084. **Fax:** 540/674-2644. **Facility:** 99 one-bedroom standard units, some with whirlpools. 2 stories (no elevator), interior corridors. **Parking:** on-site. **Terms:** check-in 4 pm, small pets only ($10 extra charge). **Amenities:** safes, irons, hair dryers. **Pool(s):** outdoor. **Leisure Activities:** exercise room. **Guest Services:** valet and coin laundry. **Business Services:** meeting rooms. **Cards:** AX, CB, DC, DS, MC, VI.

SOME UNITS
FEE

HAMPTON INN   *Book at aaa.com*   Phone: (540)674-5700

AAA SAVE   All Year   1P: $74-$94   2P: $79-$99

Small-scale Hotel   **Location:** I-81, exit 98, just s. 4420 Cleburne Blvd 24084. **Fax:** 540/674-5800. **Facility:** 63 one-bedroom standard units. 3 stories, interior corridors. *Bath:* combo or shower only. **Parking:** on-site. **Amenities:** high-speed Internet, voice mail, irons, hair dryers. **Pool(s):** heated indoor. **Leisure Activities:** exercise room. **Guest Services:** coin laundry. **Business Services:** meeting rooms, business center. **Cards:** AX, CB, DC, DS, JC, MC, VI. **Special Amenities:** free expanded continental breakfast and free newspaper.

SOME UNITS

HOLIDAY INN EXPRESS   *Book at aaa.com*   Phone: (540)674-1600

AAA SAVE   All Year   1P: $84-$150   2P: $84-$150   XP: $5   F18

Small-scale Hotel   **Location:** I-81, exit 98, just e. 4428 Cleburne Blvd 24084. **Fax:** 540/674-2600. **Facility:** 62 one-bedroom standard units, some with whirlpools. 3 stories, interior corridors. *Bath:* combo or shower only. **Parking:** on-site. **Terms:** 2 night minimum stay - seasonal and/or weekends, 90 day cancellation notice-fee imposed. **Amenities:** high-speed Internet, voice mail, irons, hair dryers. **Pool(s):** heated indoor. **Leisure Activities:** whirlpool, exercise room. **Guest Services:** valet and coin laundry. **Cards:** AX, CB, DC, DS, JC, MC, VI. **Special Amenities:** free expanded continental breakfast and free local telephone calls.

SOME UNITS

SLEEP INN & SUITES   *Book at aaa.com*   Phone: (540)674-4099

AAA SAVE   3/1-10/31   1P: $69-$89   2P: $69-$89   XP: $5   F12
11/1-2/28   1P: $59-$79   2P: $59-$79   XP: $5   F12

Small-scale Hotel   **Location:** I-81, exit 101, just e. 5094 State Park Rd 24084. **Fax:** 540/674-2874. **Facility:** 67 one-bedroom standard units, some with whirlpools. 3 stories, interior corridors. *Bath:* combo or shower only. **Parking:** on-site. **Amenities:** voice mail, irons, hair dryers. **Pool(s):** heated indoor. **Leisure Activities:** whirlpool, exercise room. **Guest Services:** coin laundry. **Business Services:** meeting rooms, business center. **Cards:** AX, CB, DC, DS, MC, VI. **Special Amenities:** free continental breakfast and free local telephone calls.

SOME UNITS

DUMFRIES —*See District Of Columbia p. 526.*

EMPORIA pop. 5,665

WHERE TO STAY

BEST WESTERN EMPORIA   *Book at aaa.com*

Phone: (434)634-3200

SOME UNITS

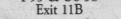

COMFORT INN
AAA SAVE
Book at aaa.com
Small-scale Hotel
All Year   1P: $52-$70   2P: $52-$70   XP: $4   F18
Phone: (434)348-3282
Location: I-95, exit 8, just e on US 301. 1411 Skippers Rd 23847. Fax: 434/348-3282. **Facility:** 96 one-bedroom standard units, some with whirlpools. 2 stories, exterior corridors. **Parking:** on-site. **Amenities:** irons, hair dryers. **Pool(s):** outdoor. **Leisure Activities:** playground. **Business Services:** fax. **Cards:** AX, DC, DS, MC, VI. *(See color ad p 693)*

SOME UNITS

DAYS INN-EMPORIA   *Book at aaa.com*
AAA SAVE
Small-scale Hotel
All Year   1P: $60-$75   2P: $65-$85   XP: $5   F16
Phone: (434)634-9481
Location: I-95, exit 11B, just w on US 58. 921 W Atlantic St 23847. Fax: 434/348-0746. **Facility:** 118 one-bedroom standard units. 2 stories (no elevator), exterior corridors. **Parking:** on-site. **Terms:** small pets only ($8 extra charge). **Amenities:** safes (fee), hair dryers. **Pool(s):** outdoor. **Leisure Activities:** playground. **Guest Services:** coin laundry. **Business Services:** fax. **Cards:** AX, CB, DC, DS, JC, MC, VI. **Special Amenities:** free full breakfast and free local telephone calls.

SOME UNITS
FEE

FAIRFIELD INN & SUITES EMPORIA/I-95   *Book at aaa.com*
Small-scale Hotel
4/1-10/31 [ECP]   1P: $69-$99   2P: $69-$99   XP: $10   F18
11/1-2/28 [ECP]   1P: $67-$89   2P: $67-$89   XP: $10   F18
3/1-3/31 [ECP]   1P: $64-$89   2P: $64-$89   XP: $10   F18
Phone: (434)348-3800
Location: I-95, exit 11A, just e. 104 Cloverleaf Dr 23847. Fax: 434/348-3700. **Facility:** 82 one-bedroom standard units. 3 stories, interior corridors. *Bath:* combo or shower only. **Parking:** on-site. **Terms:** cancellation fee imposed. **Amenities:** high-speed Internet, dual phone lines, voice mail, irons, hair dryers. *Some:* CD players. **Pool(s):** small heated indoor. **Leisure Activities:** whirlpool, exercise room. **Guest Services:** valet and coin laundry. **Business Services:** meeting rooms, business center. **Cards:** AX, CB, DC, DS, MC, VI.

SOME UNITS
FEE FEE

HAMPTON INN   *Book at aaa.com*
AAA SAVE
Small-scale Hotel
4/1-10/31   1P: $64-$70   2P: $70-$76
11/1-2/28   1P: $62-$69   2P: $69-$70
3/1-3/31   1P: $60-$64   2P: $64-$70
Phone: (434)634-9200
Location: I-95, exit 11B, just w on US 58. 1207 W Atlantic St 23847. Fax: 434/348-0071. **Facility:** 115 one-bedroom standard units. 2 stories (no elevator), interior corridors. **Parking:** on-site. **Amenities:** dual phone lines, voice mail, irons, hair dryers. **Pool(s):** outdoor. **Guest Services:** valet laundry. **Business Services:** meeting rooms, fax. **Cards:** AX, CB, DC, DS, MC, VI. **Special Amenities:** free expanded continental breakfast and free newspaper. *(See color ad below)*

SOME UNITS

HOLIDAY INN EXPRESS HOTEL & SUITES   *Book at aaa.com*
AAA SAVE
Small-scale Hotel
All Year   1P: $65-$119   2P: $65-$119
Phone: (434)336-9999
Location: I-95, exit 11B, just w on US 58. 1350 W Atlantic St 23847. Fax: 434/634-2975. **Facility:** 78 one-bedroom standard units. 3 stories, interior corridors. *Bath:* combo or shower only. **Parking:** on-site. **Terms:** 14 day cancellation notice-fee imposed, [ECP] meal plan available. **Amenities:** high-speed Internet, dual phone lines, voice mail, irons, hair dryers. **Pool(s):** small heated indoor. **Leisure Activities:** whirlpool, exercise room. **Guest Services:** coin laundry. **Business Services:** meeting rooms, business center. **Cards:** AX, DC, DS, MC, VI. **Special Amenities:** free expanded continental breakfast and free local telephone calls. *(See color ad p 693)*

SOME UNITS

KNIGHTS INN   *Book at aaa.com*
AAA SAVE
Motel
3/1-8/31   1P: $40-$50   2P: $50-$60   XP: $5   F12
9/1-2/28   1P: $30-$40   2P: $40-$50   XP: $5   F12
Phone: 434/535-8535
Location: I-95, exit 17, 0.5 mi s on US 301. 3173 Sussex Dr 23847. Fax: 434/535-8023. **Facility:** 64 one-bedroom standard units. 1 story, exterior corridors. **Parking:** on-site. **Terms:** package plans, small pets only ($5 extra charge). **Pool(s):** outdoor. **Business Services:** fax. **Cards:** AX, CB, DC, DS, MC, VI.

SOME UNITS
FEE

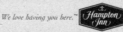

------- WHERE TO DINE -------

PUEBLO VIEJO MEXICAN RESTAURANT   **Lunch:** $3-$10   **Dinner:** $7-$12   **Phone:** 434/348-0362

♦

Mexican

Location: I-95, exit 11B, just w on US 58. 931 W Atlantic St 23847. **Hours:** 11 am-10 pm, Sat & Sun from noon. Closed major holidays. **Features:** Interstate travelers have found a welcome refuge from fast food at this bright new spot. On the menu are tasty dishes served in combination plates, as well as such specialties as marinated shrimp cocktail, chile poblanos and carne asada. Casual dress; cocktails. **Parking:** on-site.

Cards: AX, DS, MC, VI.

[&M] [Y]

EXMORE pop. 1,136

------- WHERE TO STAY -------

BEST WESTERN EASTERN SHORE INN   *Book at aaa.com*   **Phone:** (757)442-7378

(AAA) [SAVE]	5/27-9/4 [ECP]	1P: $85-$103	2P: $85-$103	XP: $8	F
	9/5-12/31 [ECP]	1P: $74-$83	2P: $74-$83	XP: $8	F
♦♦♦	3/1-5/26 [ECP]	1P: $64-$83	2P: $64-$83	XP: $8	F
	1/1-2/28 [ECP]	1P: $64-$71	2P: $64-$71	XP: $8	F

Small-scale Hotel **Location:** US 13, just n of SR 178. 2543 Lankford Hwy 23350 (PO Box 1327). Fax: 757/442-7379. **Facility:** 52 one-bedroom standard units, some with whirlpools. 2 stories (no elevator), interior/exterior corridors. *Bath:* combo or shower only. **Parking:** on-site. **Amenities:** irons, hair dryers. **Pool(s):** heated outdoor. **Guest Services:** coin laundry. **Business Services:** PC, fax. **Cards:** AX, DC, DS, MC, VI. **Special Amenities:** free expanded continental breakfast and free newspaper.

SOME UNITS
[S☐] [📶] [&M] [&] [≈] [🎦] [DATA PORT] [💻] / [✕] [🔒] [🍳] /
FEE   FEE

GLADSTONE HOUSE   **Phone:** (757)442-4614

♦♦♦

Historic Bed & Breakfast

All Year   1P: $125-$175   2P: $125-$175   XP: $15   F5
Location: Business Rt US 13 and SR 178. 12108 Lincoln Ave 23350-0296 (PO Box 296). Fax: 757/442-4546. **Facility:** Originally home to the town doctor, this impressive brick Georgian house has a striking entry punctuated by a grand, wooden spiral staircase. Smoke free premises. 3 one-bedroom standard units. 2 stories, interior corridors. **Parking:** on-site. **Terms:** 14 day cancellation notice. **Amenities:** video library, hair dryers. **Business Services:** fax. **Cards:** AX, DC, MC, VI.

[ASK] [✕] [VCR] [🎦] [☎]

------- WHERE TO DINE -------

THE TRAWLER SEAFOOD
RESTAURANT   **Lunch:** $5-$25   **Dinner:** $5-$25   **Phone:** 757/442-2092

(AAA)

♦♦ ♦♦

Seafood

Location: Just n on US 13. 2555 Lankford Hwy 23350. **Hours:** 11 am-9 pm. Closed: 11/24, 12/25. **Reservations:** suggested, weekends. **Features:** Dark woods, decoys and ocean pictures contribute to the nautical mood in the simple seafood restaurant. All the basics are here: broiled, fried, steamed and blackened. Fresh ingredients make the difference for selections such as the homemade clam chowder. Casual dress; cocktails; entertainment. **Parking:** on-site. **Cards:** AX, DS, MC, VI.

[✕]

FAIRFAX —See District Of Columbia p. 527.

FAIRFIELD

------- WHERE TO DINE -------

WHISTLE STOP CAFE   **Lunch:** $5-$12   **Dinner:** $5-$18   **Phone:** 540/377-9492

♦♦ ♦♦

American

Location: I-81, exit 200, just e. 33 Soapy Pl 24435. **Hours:** 9 am-9 pm. Closed: 12/25; also Mon. **Features:** Shenandoah hospitality at it's finest. This quaint and cozy little cafe offers all the classic American Cuisine favorites as well as a mini-train running overhead. Casual dress; beer & wine only. **Parking:** on-site. **Cards:** DS, MC, VI.

[✕]

FALLS CHURCH —See District Of Columbia p. 532.

FANCY GAP pop. 260

------- WHERE TO STAY -------

DAYS INN   *Book at aaa.com*   **Phone:** (276)728-5101

♦♦ ♦♦	10/1-10/30 [CP]	1P: $50-$80	2P: $55-$85	XP: $5	F13
	4/1-9/30 [CP]	1P: $50-$70	2P: $55-$75	XP: $5	F13
Small-scale Hotel	3/1-3/31 & 10/31-2/28 [CP]	1P: $40-$50	2P: $45-$55	XP: $5	F13

Location: I-77, exit 8, 0.3 mi w; on top of the hill. Located behind Exxon. 142 Kelly Rd 24328. Fax: 276/728-4092. **Facility:** 60 one-bedroom standard units. 2 stories (no elevator), interior/exterior corridors. **Parking:** on-site. **Guest Services:** valet laundry. **Cards:** AX, CB, DC, DS, MC, VI.

SOME UNITS
[ASK] [S☐] [📶] [🎦] / [✕] [🔒] /

DOE RUN LODGE   **Phone:** 276/398-2212

(AAA) [SAVE]

♦♦ ♦♦

Small-scale Hotel

3/1-12/31   1P: $99-$234   2P: $99-$234   XP: $18   F15
Location: MM 189.2 on Blue Ridge Pkwy; 10 mi n from US 52 (parkway entrance). Located in a serene mountain area. (PO Box 280). Fax: 276/398-2833. **Facility:** 27 one-bedroom standard units, some with whirlpools. 2 stories (no elevator), exterior corridors. **Parking:** on-site. **Terms:** open 3/1-12/31, 2 night minimum stay - weekends, 7 day cancellation notice, weekly rates available, package plans, pets ($25 weekly). **Amenities:** video library (fee), hair dryers. *Some:* irons. **Dining:** 5:30 pm-10 pm, weather permitting; closed Mon-Thurs, cocktails. **Pool(s):** outdoor. **Leisure Activities:** saunas, golf privileges, hiking trails. *Fee:* sporting clay & hunting privileges, massage. **Guest Services:** gift shop. **Business Services:** meeting rooms. **Cards:** AX, MC, VI.

SOME UNITS
[🛏] [🍴] [Y] [≈] [✕] [VCR] [🔒] [💻] / [✕] [🍳] /
FEE   FEE

FARMVILLE pop. 6,845

———— WHERE TO STAY ————

COMFORT INN-FARMVILLE *Book at aaa.com*
▼▼▼▼
Small-scale Hotel
DC, DS, MC, VI.

All Year [ECP]   1P: $61-$85   2P: $61-$85   XP: $6
Phone: (434)392-8163   F18
Location: Jct US 460 Bypass and US 15, exit Keysville. 2108 S Main St 23901. Fax: 434/392-3691. **Facility:** 51 one-bedroom standard units, some with whirlpools. 2 stories (no elevator), interior corridors. **Parking:** on-site. **Amenities:** safes (fee), irons, hair dryers. **Pool(s):** outdoor. **Business Services:** fax. **Cards:** AX, CB,

SOME UNITS
[ASK] [S/D] [T|+] [🛏] [▦] [DATA PORT] [▭] / [✕] [▯] [▦] /
FEE FEE

SUPER 8 MOTEL *Book at aaa.com*
▼
Motel

All Year   1P: $45-$105   2P: $51-$105   XP: $6
Phone: (434)392-8196   F16
Location: On US 15, just n of jct US 460. 2012 S Main St 23901. Fax: 434/392-8196. **Facility:** 42 one-bedroom standard units. 2 stories (no elevator), interior corridors. **Terms:** 5 day cancellation notice, pets (in smoking units). **Amenities:** safes (fee). **Cards:** AX, DC, DS, MC, VI.

SOME UNITS
[ASK] [S/D] [🛏] [T|+] [▦] / [✕] [DATA PORT] [▯] /

———— WHERE TO DINE ————

CHARLEY'S WATERFRONT CAFE
▼▼ ▼▼
American

Lunch: $6-$8   **Dinner:** $7-$18   **Phone:** 434/392-1566
Location: Just n on Mill St/US 15 N; downtown. 201 B Mill St 23901. **Hours:** 11 am-10 pm, Fri & Sat-11 pm. Closed: 11/24, 12/25. **Reservations:** suggested, weekends. **Features:** Overlooking a river, the former tobacco warehouse is rustic in appearance, with the centerpiece being a huge scale once used for tobacco. The diverse menu comprises potato skins, spiced wings, blackened tuna Caesar, a great sandwich selection, pasta dishes and perhaps a stir-fry option. Dessert is made from scratch. The casual experience is great for families. Casual dress; cocktails. **Parking:** on-site. **Cards:** AX, DS, MC, VI.
[Y] [✕]

MACADO'S
▼
American

Lunch: $6-$8   **Dinner:** $6-$8   **Phone:** 434/392-8077
Location: Just e of Main St. 200 Third St 23901. **Hours:** 8 am-1 am, Fri & Sat-2 am. Closed: 12/25. **Features:** The lively student hangout is well-loved for its lengthy list of imaginative overstuffed sandwiches and wraps. Macaroni and cheese, chili and oversized ice cream desserts also are popular. Casual dress. **Parking:** on-site. **Cards:** AX, CB, DC, DS, JC, MC, VI.

FINCASTLE pop. 359

———— WHERE TO DINE ————

CAPTAIN'S TAVERN SEAFOOD RESTAURANT & LOUNGE
▼▼▼
Seafood

Lunch: $4-$10   **Dinner:** $9-$25   **Phone:** 540/473-2299
Location: On US 220 N, 1 mi n. US 220 N 24090. **Hours:** 11:30 am-2:30 & 4-9:30 pm, Sat & Sun 11:30 am-9:30 pm. Closed major holidays; also Mon. **Features:** To ensure freshness, seafood is prepared after guests order. The menu comprises a wide variety of dishes. Service is friendly. Casual dress; cocktails. **Parking:** on-site. **Cards:** MC, VI.
[✕]

FISHERSVILLE pop. 4,998

———— WHERE TO STAY ————

HAMPTON INN WAYNESBORO/STUARTS DRAFT *Book at aaa.com*
(AAA) [SAVE]
▼▼▼▼
Small-scale Hotel

All Year [ECP]   1P: $79-$140   2P: $84-$145   XP: $5
Phone: (540)213-9500   F17
Location: I-64, exit 91, just n. 15 Four Square Ln 22939. Fax: 540/213-9501. **Facility:** 66 one-bedroom standard units. 4 stories, interior corridors. *Bath:* combo or shower only. **Parking:** on-site. **Amenities:** high-speed Internet, voice mail, irons, hair dryers. **Pool(s):** heated indoor. **Leisure Activities:** exercise room. **Guest Services:** valet laundry. **Business Services:** meeting rooms. **Cards:** AX, DC, DS, MC, VI. **Special Amenities:** free expanded continental breakfast and free local telephone calls.

SOME UNITS
[S/D] [&] [🛏] [▦] [DATA PORT] [▯] [▦] [▭] / [✕] /

FLINT HILL

———— WHERE TO DINE ————

FOUR AND TWENTY BLACKBIRDS
▼▼▼▼
American

Lunch: $8-$22   **Dinner:** $20-$30   **Phone:** 540/675-1111
Location: Center. 650 Zachary Taylor Hwy 22627. **Hours:** 5:30 pm-9 pm; Sunday brunch 10 am-2 pm. Closed: 7/4, 12/25; also Mon, Tues, 8/3-8/20 & 12/31-1/14. **Reservations:** suggested, weekends. **Features:** Not only is its name distinctive, but the restaurant blends unusual ingredients into memorably good appetizers and entrees. Servers are outgoing. Casual dress; cocktails. **Parking:** on-site. **Cards:** MC, VI.
[✕]

GRIFFIN TAVERN & RESTAURANT
(AAA)
▼▼ ▼▼
American

Lunch: $6-$15   **Dinner:** $9-$21   **Phone:** 540/675-3227
Location: Center. 659 Zachary Taylor Hwy 22627. **Hours:** 11 am-10 pm. Closed: 12/25. **Features:** The new establishment gives patrons a choice of outdoor seating (weather permitting) or cozy, wood-grained surroundings. A griffin collection is on display. Casual dress; cocktails. **Parking:** on-site. **Cards:** AX, CB, DC, DS, JC, MC, VI.
[Y] [✕]

FRANKLIN pop. 8,346

——— WHERE TO STAY ———

COMFORT INN   *Book at aaa.com*   **Phone:** 757/569-0018

Small-scale Hotel

All Year   1P: $63-$79   2P: $65-$84   XP: $9 .   F16
Location: Jct US 58 Bypass and SR 671. 1620 Armory Dr 23851. Fax: 757/569-0018. **Facility:** 77 units. 75 one-bedroom standard units, some with whirlpools. 2 one-bedroom suites ($115-$145) with whirlpools. 2 stories (no elevator), exterior corridors. *Bath:* combo or shower only. **Parking:** on-site. **Terms:** cancellation fee imposed. **Amenities:** video library, irons, hair dryers. **Pool(s):** outdoor. **Leisure Activities:** limited exercise equipment. **Guest Services:** coin laundry. **Business Services:** meeting rooms. **Cards:** AX, CB, DC, DS, MC, VI.

SOME UNITS

ASK SD 📶 🏊 📹 DATA PORT 🖥 📺 🖥 / ✕ VCR /

SUPER 8 MOTEL   *Book at aaa.com*   **Phone:** (757)562-2888
Motel

All Year   1P: $50-$100   2P: $60-$100   XP: $6   F12
Location: Jct US 58 Bypass and SR 671. 1599 Armory Dr 23851. Fax: 757/562-2888. **Facility:** 52 one-bedroom standard units. 2 stories, interior corridors. **Parking:** on-site. **Amenities:** safes (fee). **Guest Services:** coin laundry. **Business Services:** fax. **Cards:** AX, CB, DC, DS, JC, MC, VI.

SOME UNITS

ASK SD 🍴 ♿ &M 📹 DATA PORT / ✕ 🖥 /

FREDERICKSBURG pop. 19,279

——— WHERE TO STAY ———

BEST WESTERN CENTRAL PLAZA   *Book at aaa.com*   **Phone:** (540)786-7404

Motel

3/1-10/31   1P: $57-$67   2P: $72-$77   XP: $5   F12
11/1-2/28   1P: $58-$63   2P: $63-$72   XP: $5   F12
Location: I-95, exit 130B on SR 3. Located adjacent to Spotsylvania Mall. 3000 Plank Rd 22401. Fax: 540/785-7415. **Facility:** 76 one-bedroom standard units. 3 stories (no elevator), exterior corridors. **Parking:** on-site. **Terms:** small pets only ($20 deposit). **Amenities:** voice mail, irons, hair dryers. **Guest Services:** valet and coin laundry. **Business Services:** fax. **Cards:** AX, CB, DC, DS, JC, MC, VI. **Special Amenities:** free continental breakfast and early check-in/late check-out. *(See color ad below)*

SOME UNITS

SD 🐾 🍴 &M 🛏 📹 DATA PORT 🖥 📺 🖥 / ✕ /
FEE   FEE

BEST WESTERN FREDERICKSBURG   *Book at aaa.com*   Phone: (540)371-5050

(AAA) (SAVE)
♦♦♦

Small-scale Hotel

3/1-10/31 [ECP]	1P: $72-$82	2P: $79-$89	XP: $10	F12
11/1-2/28 [ECP]	1P: $57-$62	2P: $67-$72	XP: $10	F12

Location: I-95, exit 130A, 0.3 mi e on SR 3. 2205 William St 22401. Fax: 540/373-3496. **Facility:** 108 one-bedroom standard units. 2 stories (no elevator), exterior corridors. **Parking:** on-site. **Terms:** 15 day cancellation notice, small pets only ($20 deposit, in designated units). **Amenities:** irons, hair dryers. **Pool(s):** outdoor. **Guest Services:** valet and coin laundry. **Business Services:** meeting rooms, fax.
Cards: AX, DC, DS, MC, VI. **Special Amenities:** free expanded continental breakfast and early check-in/late check-out.
(See color ad p 697)

SOME UNITS

[icons]

COMFORT INN FREDERICKSBURG SOUTHPOINT   *Book at aaa.com*   Phone: (540)898-5550

(AAA) (SAVE)
♦♦♦

Small-scale Hotel

4/1-10/31 [ECP]	1P: $79-$89	2P: $79-$89	XP: $6	F18
3/1-3/31 & 11/1-2/28 [ECP]	1P: $69-$79	2P: $69-$79	XP: $6	F18

Location: I-95, exit 126, just s on US 1. Located next to Massaponax Outlet Center. 5422 Jefferson Davis Hwy 22407. Fax: 540/891-2861. **Facility:** 125 one-bedroom standard units. 5 stories, interior corridors. **Parking:** on-site. **Amenities:** voice mail, irons, hair dryers. **Pool(s):** heated indoor. **Leisure Activities:** sauna, exercise room. **Guest Services:** valet laundry. **Business Services:** meeting rooms, fax. **Cards:** AX, DC, DS, MC, VI.
Special Amenities: free expanded continental breakfast and free local telephone calls. *(See ad below)*

SOME UNITS

[icons]

DUNNING MILLS INN ALL SUITES HOTEL   Phone: 540-373-1256

(AAA) (SAVE)
♦♦

Small-scale Hotel

All Year	1P: $69-$89	2P: $69-$89	XP: $10	F12

Location: I-95, exit 126, 3 mi n on US 1. 2305 C Jefferson Davis Hwy 22401. Fax: 540/899-9041. **Facility:** 54 one-bedroom standard units with kitchens. 2 stories (no elevator), exterior corridors. **Parking:** on-site. **Terms:** cancellation fee imposed, weekly rates available, [CP] meal plan available, pets ($200 deposit, $5 extra charge). **Amenities:** high-speed Internet, irons, hair dryers. **Pool(s):** outdoor. **Guest Services:** coin laundry. **Business Services:** fax. **Cards:** AX, DC, DS, MC, VI. **Special Amenities:** free continental breakfast and free local telephone calls.

SOME UNITS

[icons]

FAIRFIELD INN OF FREDERICKBURG   *Book at aaa.com*   Phone: (540)891-9100

♦♦♦

Small-scale Hotel

7/20-8/6 [CP]	1P: $104-$129	2P: $104-$139
8/7-10/30 [CP]	1P: $94-$114	2P: $94-$114
3/1-7/19 [CP]	1P: $87-$114	2P: $87-$114
10/31-2/28 [CP]	1P: $87-$104	2P: $87-$104

Location: I-95, exit 126 southbound; exit 126A northbound, just n on US 1, just e to Market St, then just s. 10330 Spotsylvania Ave 22408. Fax: 540/898-6311. **Facility:** 74 one-bedroom standard units. 3 stories, interior corridors. *Bath:* combo or shower only. **Parking:** on-site. **Terms:** 3 day cancellation notice. **Amenities:** irons, hair dryers. **Pool(s):** heated indoor. **Leisure Activities:** exercise room. **Guest Services:** valet laundry. **Business Services:** meeting rooms, fax (fee). **Cards:** AX, DC, DS, MC, VI.

SOME UNITS

[icons]

HAMPTON INN   *Book at aaa.com*   Phone: (540)371-0330

(AAA) (SAVE)
♦♦♦

Small-scale Hotel

All Year [ECP]	1P: $77-$109	2P: $77-$109	XP: $7	F18

Location: I-95, exit 130A on SR 3 E. 2310 William St 22401. Fax: 540/371-1753. **Facility:** 166 one-bedroom standard units. 2 stories (no elevator), exterior corridors. **Parking:** on-site. **Terms:** small pets only ($10 extra charge, in smoking units). **Amenities:** voice mail, irons, hair dryers. **Pool(s):** outdoor. **Guest Services:** valet and coin laundry. **Business Services:** meeting rooms, fax. **Cards:** AX, CB, DC, DS, MC, VI. **Special Amenities:** free expanded continental breakfast and free newspaper.

SOME UNITS

[icons]

HOLIDAY INN-FREDERICKSBURG NORTH   *Book at aaa.com*   Phone: (540)371-5550

 [AAA] [SAVE]

| 3/1-10/31 | 1P: $90-$95 | 2P: $90-$95 |
| 11/1-2/28 | 1P: $80-$85 | 2P: $80-$85 |

Small-scale Hotel

Location: I-95, exit 133, just nw on US 17. 564 Warrenton Rd 22405. Fax: 540/373-3641. **Facility:** 149 one-bedroom standard units. 2 stories (no elevator), exterior corridors. *Bath:* combo or shower only. **Parking:** on-site. **Terms:** weekly rates available, package plans. **Amenities:** dual phone lines, voice mail, irons, hair dryers. **Dining:** 6:30 am-9:30 pm, cocktails. **Pool(s):** outdoor, heated indoor. **Leisure Activities:** whirlpool, exercise room. *Fee:* game room. **Guest Services:** valet and coin laundry. **Business Services:** meeting rooms, PC, fax. **Cards:** AX, CB, DC, DS, JC, MC, VI. **Special Amenities:** free local telephone calls and free newspaper. *(See color ad below)*

SOME UNITS

[S] [D] [🛏] [🍴] [🍸] [🛶] [❌] [🎮] [DATA PORT] [🔧] [🖥] [💻] / [❌] /

HOLIDAY INN SELECT FREDERICKSBURG   *Book at aaa.com*   Phone: (540)786-8321

[AAA]

| 3/1-7/2 & 9/4-11/5 | 1P: $109-$135 | 2P: $109-$135 | XP: $10 | F |
| 7/3-9/3 & 11/6-2/28 | 1P: $99-$119 | 2P: $99-$119 | XP: $10 | F |

Large-scale Hotel

Location: I-95, exit 130B on SR 3. Located in Central Park, a shopping complex. 2801 Plank Rd 22401. Fax: 540/786-0397. **Facility:** 194 units. 188 one- and 1 two-bedroom standard units, some with whirlpools. 5 one-bedroom suites ($225-$250). 3 stories, interior corridors. *Bath:* combo or shower only. **Parking:** on-site. **Terms:** small pets only ($35 fee). **Amenities:** video games, dual phone lines, voice mail, irons, hair dryers. **Pool(s):** outdoor, wading. **Leisure Activities:** exercise room. **Guest Services:** valet and coin laundry. **Business Services:** conference facilities, business center. **Cards:** AX, DC, DS, MC, VI.

SOME UNITS

[ASK] [S] [D] [🛏] [🍴] [🍸] [&M] [♿] [🏊] [🛶] [🎮] [DATA PORT] [💻] / [❌] [🖥] [🖨] /
   FEE   FEE   FEE

HOWARD JOHNSON HOTEL   *Book at aaa.com*   Phone: (540)898-1800

[AAA] [SAVE]

| 3/1-10/15 | 1P: $69-$99 | 2P: $79-$109 | XP: $5 | F17 |
| 10/16-2/28 | 1P: $59-$89 | 2P: $69-$99 | XP: $5 | F17 |

Small-scale Hotel

Location: I-95, exit 126. 5327 Jefferson Davis Hwy 22408. Fax: 540/898-7354. **Facility:** 131 one-bedroom standard units. 4 stories, interior corridors. *Bath:* combo or shower only. **Parking:** on-site. **Terms:** 3 day cancellation notice, package plans, small pets only ($10 extra charge). **Amenities:** *Some:* high-speed Internet, dual phone lines, irons, hair dryers. **Pool(s):** outdoor. **Leisure Activities:** exercise room. **Guest Services:** coin laundry. **Business Services:** meeting rooms, fax (fee). **Cards:** AX, CB, DC, DS, MC, VI. **Special Amenities:** free expanded continental breakfast. *(See color ad below)*

SOME UNITS

[S] [D] [🛏] [🍴] [♿] [🛶] [🎮] [DATA PORT] [💻] / [❌] [🖥] [🖨] /
       FEE   FEE   FEE

MARRIOTT TOWNE PLACE SUITES   Phone: 540/891-0775

[fyi]

| All Year | 1P: $89-$129 | | XP: $10 | F17 |

Small-scale Hotel

Too new to rate, opening scheduled for September 2004. **Location:** I-95, exit 126. 4700 Market St 22407 (PO Box 1642, SPOTSYLVANIA, 22553). **Amenities:** 93 units. **Terms:** cancellation fee imposed. **Cards:** AX, CB, DC, DS, JC, MC, VI.

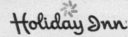

QUALITY INN FREDERICKSBURG *Book at aaa.com* Phone: (540)373-0000

AAA SAVE

3/1-10/31 [CP] 1P: $57-$70	2P: $66-$80	XP: $8 F18
11/1-2/28 [CP] 1P: $49-$60	2P: $57-$70	XP: $8 F18

Small-scale Hotel

Location: I-95, exit 133, just n on US 17. 543 Warrenton Rd 22406. Fax: 540/373-5676. **Facility:** 79 one-bedroom standard units. 2 stories (no elevator), exterior corridors. **Parking:** on-site. **Terms:** pets ($8 extra charge). **Amenities:** irons, hair dryers. **Dining:** 6:30 am-10 pm, cocktails. **Pool(s):** outdoor. **Guest Services:** coin laundry. **Business Services:** meeting rooms, fax. **Cards:** AX, DC, DS, MC, VI. **Special Amenities:** free continental breakfast and free local telephone calls.

SOME UNITS

FEE

RAMADA INN SOUTH *Book at aaa.com* Phone: (540)898-1102

AAA SAVE

5/2-8/13 1P: $59-$109	2P: $59-$109	
3/1-5/1 & 8/14-12/3 1P: $49-$86	2P: $49-$86	
12/4-2/28 1P: $39-$78	2P: $39-$78	

Small-scale Hotel

Location: I-95, exit 126, just n on US 1. 5324 Jefferson Davis Hwy 22408. Fax: 540/898-2017. **Facility:** 198 one-bedroom standard units. 2 stories (no elevator), interior/exterior corridors. **Parking:** on-site. **Terms:** [BP] meal plan available, package plans, small pets only. **Amenities:** high-speed Internet, voice mail, irons, hair dryers. *Fee:* video games, safes. **Dining:** 6:30 am-11 & 5-9:30 pm, cocktails, entertainment. **Pool(s):** heated indoor. **Leisure Activities:** sauna, whirlpool, exercise room. *Fee:* game room. **Guest Services:** valet and coin laundry. **Business Services:** meeting rooms, fax. **Cards:** AX, CB, DC, DS, MC, VI. **Special Amenities:** free newspaper and free room upgrade (subject to availability with advance reservations).

SOME UNITS
/ FEE FEE

ROYAL INN MOTEL Phone: (540)891-2700

AAA SAVE

3/1-8/31 1P: $45-$55	2P: $45-$59	XP: $5 F18
9/1-2/28 1P: $35-$45	2P: $40-$55	XP: $5 F18

Motel

Location: I-95, exit 126, 0.5 mi ne on US 1. Located in a commercial area. 5309 Jefferson Davis Hwy 22408. Fax: 540/891-2700. **Facility:** 27 one-bedroom standard units. 2 stories (no elevator), exterior corridors. **Parking:** on-site. **Terms:** 15 day cancellation notice. **Business Services:** fax. **Cards:** AX, MC, VI.

SOME UNITS

SLEEP INN *Book at aaa.com*
(AAA) (SAVE)
▽▽▽▽
Small-scale Hotel

			Phone: (540)372-6868
4/1-1/31	1P: $70-$95	2P: $80-$105	XP: $10	F18
3/1-3/31 & 2/1-2/28	1P: $60-$75	2P: $70-$95	XP: $10	F18

Location: I-95, exit 133, just w. 595 Warrenton Rd 22406. Fax: 540/899-9193. **Facility:** 68 one-bedroom standard units. 2 stories (no elevator), interior corridors. *Bath:* combo or shower only. **Parking:** on-site. **Terms:** cancellation fee imposed, [CP] meal plan available. **Amenities:** hair dryers. *Some:* irons. **Leisure Activities:** limited exercise equipment. **Guest Services:** coin laundry. **Business Services:** fax (fee). **Cards:** AX, CB, DC, DS, JC, MC, VI. **Special Amenities: free continental breakfast and free local telephone calls.**

SOME UNITS
[S D] [T↑] [✦] [DATA PORT] [▣] / [✕] [▤] [▧] /

SLEEP INN SOUTHPOINT *Book at aaa.com*
(AAA) (SAVE)
▽▽▽▽
Small-scale Hotel

			Phone: (540)710-5500
All Year [CP]	1P: $62-$96	2P: $62-$96	XP: $7	F17

Location: I-95, exit 126 southbound; exit 126B northbound, US 1 S. 5400 Southpoint Blvd 22407. Fax: 540/710-1572. **Facility:** 67 one-bedroom standard units. 3 stories, interior corridors. *Bath:* combo or shower only. **Parking:** on-site. **Amenities:** high-speed Internet, dual phone lines, voice mail, irons, hair dryers. **Pool(s):** outdoor. **Leisure Activities:** exercise room. **Guest Services:** valet and coin laundry. **Business Services:** meeting rooms. **Cards:** AX, DC, DS, MC, VI. **Special Amenities: free continental breakfast and free local telephone calls.** *(See color ad p 700)*

SOME UNITS
[S D] [T↑] [&M] [&] [🖉] [🛥] [✦] [DATA PORT] [▤] [▣] / [✕] [▧] /

WINGATE INN *Book at aaa.com*
▽▽▽▽
Small-scale Hotel

		Phone: (540)368-8000
All Year	1P: $95	2P: $95	XP: $10

Location: I-95, exit 133, just s. 20 Sanford Dr 22406. Fax: 540/368-9252. **Facility:** 93 one-bedroom standard units. 4 stories, interior corridors. *Bath:* combo or shower only. **Parking:** on-site. **Amenities:** video games, high-speed Internet, dual phone lines, voice mail, safes, irons, hair dryers. **Pool(s):** heated indoor. **Leisure Activities:** whirlpool, exercise room. **Guest Services:** valet and coin laundry. **Business Services:** conference facilities, business center. **Cards:** AX, CB, DC, MC, VI.

SOME UNITS
[ASK] [S D] [T↑] [&M] [&] [🛥] [✦] [DATA PORT] [▤] [▧] [▣] / [✕] /

WYTESTONE SUITES HOTEL
(AAA) (SAVE)
▽▽▽▽
Small-scale Hotel

			Phone: (540)891-1112
3/1-10/31 [BP]	1P: $99	2P: $99	XP: $7	F18
11/1-2/28 [BP]	1P: $89	2P: $89	XP: $7	F18

Location: I-95, exit 126, just s on US 1. Located next to Massaponax Outlet Center. 4615 Southpoint Pkwy 22407. Fax: 540/891-5465. **Facility:** 85 one-bedroom suites. 5 stories, interior corridors. *Bath:* combo or shower only. **Parking:** on-site. **Amenities:** high-speed Internet, dual phone lines, voice mail, irons, hair dryers. **Pool(s):** heated indoor. **Leisure Activities:** exercise room. **Guest Services:** valet and coin laundry. **Business Services:** meeting rooms, fax. **Cards:** AX, CB, DC, DS, MC, VI. **Special Amenities: free full breakfast and free newspaper.** *(See color ad p 700)*

SOME UNITS
[S D] [T↑] [&M] [&] [🖉] [🛥] [✦] [DATA PORT] [▤] [▧] [▣] / [✕] /

──── WHERE TO DINE ────

ALLMAN'S BARBECUE
▽
Barbecue

		Phone: 540/373-9881
Lunch: $5-$11	Dinner: $5-$11	

Location: On US 1 (Jefferson Davis Hwy), just n of jct SR 3. 1299 Jefferson Davis Hwy 22401. **Hours:** 11 am-8 pm. Closed major holidays; also Sun. **Features:** For more than 40 years, the same cook has prepared pork barbecue with a sweet peppery sauce at this local institution. The cole slaw recipe is a family secret that dates back 100 years. Casual dress. **Parking:** on-site.

[✕] [✕]

ANDREW'S MEDITERRENEAN BOUNTY
▽▽▽
Mediterranean

		Phone: 540/370-0909
Lunch: $5-$8	Dinner: $7-$17	

Location: Jct Liberty St; in Olde Towne. 600 William St 22401. **Hours:** 11:30 am-2 & 5-9 pm, Sat from 5 pm, Sun 11 am-2 pm. Closed: 1/1, 11/24, 12/25; also Mon. **Reservations:** suggested. **Features:** The aptly named spot shows off the bounty of the Mediterranean Sea and its surrounding regions. Among thoughtful, richly flavored dishes are scungilli and shark. Also on the menu are pasta, lamb and beef selections. Murals of the Greek Isles decorate the dining room. Guests can select from a long list of out-of-the-ordinary international wines and microbrews. Casual dress; cocktails. **Parking:** street. **Cards:** AX, DS, MC, VI.

[✕]

AUGUSTINE'S AT FREDERICKSBURG SQUARE
(AAA)
▽▽▽
Continental

	Phone: 540/310-0063
Dinner: $21-$40	

Location: Just w of Amtrak station; in Olde Towne. 525 Caroline St 22401. **Hours:** 5 pm-9 pm. Closed: 7/4, 11/24, 12/25; also Sun-Tues. **Reservations:** suggested. **Features:** Richly romantic and superbly sophisticated, the restaurant occupies the lower level of an Olde Towne landmark. The monthly changing menu highlights seasonal availability and Continental sophistication. A young staff mixes formal training with genuine warmth and hospitality. Dressy casual; cocktails. **Parking:** street. **Cards:** AX, DC, MC, VI.

[Ψ] [✕]

BANGKOK CAFE
▽▽▽▽
Thai

		Phone: 540/373-0745
Lunch: $6-$14	Dinner: $6-$14	

Location: Just n of Visitor's Center; in Olde Towne. 825 Caroline St 22401. **Hours:** 11:30 am-9 pm, Wed from 4 pm, Fri & Sat 11:30 am-9:30 pm. Closed: Tues & for lunch Wed. **Features:** This casual spot offers authentic Thai cuisine, such as crispy whole fish with basil, pad Thai noodles, four curry varieties, and vegetarian stir fry. The desserts are unusual, using tropical fruits and sweet rice. Thai tea and coffee also are available. Casual dress; beer & wine only. **Parking:** street. **Cards:** CB, DC, DS, MC, VI.

[✕]

BISTRO BETHEM
▽▽▽
American

		Phone: 540/371-9999
Lunch: $5-$10	Dinner: $16-$29	

Location: Jct with Caroline St; in Olde Towne. 309 William St 22401. **Hours:** 11:30 am-2:30 & 5-10 pm. Closed: 1/1, 12/25; also Sun & Mon. **Features:** In a sleek and modern setting with walls that serve as a showcase for rotating displays of artwork, a talented young chef creates a seasonally changing menu of exciting modern American dishes with a Southern flair. Try such specialties as asparagus soup with stilton, chile-roasted salmon and grilled romaine salad. Wine selections are intelligent and thoughtful. Casual dress; cocktails. **Parking:** street. **Cards:** AX, CB, DC, DS, JC, MC, VI.

[✕]

BURGER & KABAB PLACE
Pakistani

Lunch: $5-$11   **Dinner:** $5-$11   **Phone:** 540/370-1878
Location: I-95, exit 133, just e; in Olde Forge Plaza. 367 Warrenton Rd 22405. **Hours:** 11 am-9 pm, Fri-10 pm, Sat noon-10 pm, Sun noon-8 pm. Closed major holidays. **Features:** The menu at this brightly painted casual spot offers purely American burgers and cheesesteaks alongside authentic Pakistani kebabs made with lamb, chicken, or beef. Savory rice pilaf or puffy pita bread is offered alongside. Casual dress. **Parking:** on-site. **Cards:** AX, MC, VI.

CAFE DAVANZO
Italian

Lunch: $5-$8   **Dinner:** $6-$13   **Phone:** 540/372-3335
Location: I-95, exit 130A, jct SR 3. 2312 Plank Rd 22401. **Hours:** 11 am-10 pm, Fri & Sat-11 pm. Closed: 11/24, 12/25. **Features:** This modern, Americanized Italian menu features traditional choices of fresh pasta, including chicken parmigiana and fettuccine with spinach, pine nuts and chicken. The atmosphere here is casual, and the service is well timed and friendly. Casual dress; cocktails. **Parking:** on-site. **Cards:** AX, DS, MC, VI.

CASTIGLIA'S ITALIAN RESTAURANT & PIZZERIA
Italian

Lunch: $8-$14   **Dinner:** $7-$14   **Phone:** 540/373-6650
Location: Jct Charles St; in Olde Towne. 324 William St 22401. **Hours:** 11 am-11 pm, Sun noon-10 pm. **Features:** Watch the streetscape from the small, unassuming spot, which has booths near to large picture windows. The menu of mostly Italian dishes lists varied pasta dishes, seafood and some good veal preparations. Also offered are a few Latino appetizers. The far-from-pretentious setting is comfortably accommodating. Casual dress; cocktails. **Parking:** street. **Cards:** AX, DC, MC, VI.

CLAIBORNE'S
Steak House

Lunch: $4-$14   **Dinner:** $15-$30   **Phone:** 540/371-7080
Location: In Olde Towne; at the train station. 200 Lafayette Blvd 22401. **Hours:** 11:30 am-2 & 5-9 pm, Fri-10 pm, Sat 5 pm-10 pm; Sunday brunch. Closed major holidays. **Reservations:** suggested. **Features:** Sleek sophistication marks the early 1900s train station, decorated with rich wood, historic prints, candlelight and a glowing fireplace. The menu is a showcase for fine steak and low-country specialties, such as shrimp and grits. An extensive list of wines and liquors is offered. The atmosphere is city chic and romantic. Dressy casual; cocktails. **Parking:** on-site. **Cards:** AX, DS, MC, VI.

GOOLRICK'S
American

Lunch: $3-$7   **Phone:** 540/373-9878
Location: Jct George St; in Olde Towne. 901 Caroline St 22401. **Hours:** 9 am-6 pm, Sat-5 pm. Closed major holidays; also Sun. **Features:** Nostalgic pharmacy lunch counter with the oldest operating soda fountain in the country serving up traditional egg creams, milkshakes, and ice cream sodas. Lunch offerings include sandwiches, daily soups, and chili on Saturday. Casual dress. **Parking:** street. **Cards:** MC, VI.

GURU INDIAN CUISINE
Indian

Lunch: $8-$15   **Dinner:** $8-$15   **Phone:** 540/548-1011
Location: I-95, exit 130B, just w on SR 3, then just n; in Uptown Central Park. 1320 Central Park Blvd 22401. **Hours:** 11:30 am-2:30 & 5-9:30 pm, Fri-10 pm, Sat 11:30 am-3 & 5-10 pm, Sun 11:30 am-3 & 5-9:30 pm. **Features:** Once inside guests are lulled into a sense of calm by the cool sounds of the rock waterfall and the rich colors and gold. The menu offers specialties from the tandoor oven including a variety of great breads, curries, and vegetarian offerings. Casual dress; cocktails. **Parking:** on-site. **Cards:** AX, DC, DS, MC, VI.

JAKE & MIKE'S
Menu on aaa.com
American

Lunch: $5-$15   **Dinner:** $16-$27   **Phone:** 540/370-4590
Location: Just w of Olde Towne. 806 William St 22401. **Hours:** 11 am-3 & 6-9 pm, Fri & Sat-10 pm, Sun-3 pm. Closed major holidays; also Mon. **Reservations:** suggested. **Features:** The eclectic Olde Towne spot is a casual place in which to peruse a daily changing menu of sophisticated dishes. Fine, fresh ingredients go into preparations of seafood and beef as well as distinctive salads and luscious desserts. Locals know to call ahead to determine whether their favorites are on the menu that day. Casual dress; beer & wine only. **Parking:** street. **Cards:** AX, DS, MC, VI.

LA PETITE AUBERGE
French

Lunch: $6-$15   **Dinner:** $10-$26   **Phone:** 540/371-2727
Location: Just e of corner of Williams and Charles sts; downtown. 311 William St 22401. **Hours:** 11:30 am-2:30 & 5:30-10 pm, Sat 11:30 am-2:15 & 5:30-10 pm. Closed: 3/27, 11/24, 12/25; also Sun. **Reservations:** required. **Features:** This charming restaurant with a cafe setting offers traditional French dishes, all excellent (most notably the vegetarian plate with rice, red and black beans and ratatouille). The lunch menu also features sandwiches, soup and salad and other treats. Dressy casual; cocktails. **Parking:** street. **Cards:** AX, MC, VI.

MERRIMAN'S
American

Lunch: $7-$10   **Dinner:** $8-$25   **Phone:** 540/371-7723
Location: Across from Visitor's Center; downtown. 715 Caroline St 22401. **Hours:** 11 am-3 & 5-9:30 pm, Sun 10:30 am-4 pm. Closed: 1/1, 11/24, 12/25. **Reservations:** suggested, weekends. **Features:** The exceptional dishes are testimony to the importance of using fresh ingredients and a creative mind. Charming place settings include nice linens, candles and flowers. Friendly servers show an impressive knowledge of the menu and wine list. Casual dress; cocktails. **Parking:** street. **Cards:** CB, DC, DS, MC, VI.

OLDE TOWNE STEAK AND SEAFOOD
Steak & Seafood

Dinner: $22-$35   **Phone:** 540/371-8020
Location: 0.5 mi n of jct William St; in Olde Towne. 1612 Caroline St 22401. **Hours:** 4 pm-10 pm. Closed major holidays; also Sun & Mon. **Reservations:** suggested. **Features:** The setting is warm with wood paneling and roaring fireplaces crowned with stag's heads. The large steaks arrive on sizzling platters and the shrimp are amply stuffed with crabmeat. Casual dress; cocktails. **Parking:** on-site. **Cards:** AX, DC, MC, VI.

OLDE TOWNE WINE & CHEESE DELI
Deli/Subs Sandwiches

Lunch: $5-$10   **Phone:** 540/373-7877
Location: Between Hanover and Charlotte sts; in Olde Towne. 707 Caroline St 22401. **Hours:** 11 am-4 pm. Closed: 3/27, 11/24, 12/25; also Sun. **Features:** The popular lunch spot is known for specialty sandwiches, daily soup and local micro-brews. Casual dress; beer & wine only. **Parking:** street. **Cards:** AX, DS, MC, VI.

OLD TOWN GRILL & CAFE   **Lunch:** $5-$10   **Dinner:** $5-$10   **Phone:** 540/899-9199

American

Location: S of jct William St; in Olde Towne. 722 Caroline St 22401. **Hours:** 8 am-5 pm. Closed major holidays; also Sun. **Features:** Reminiscent of lunch counters of days gone by this small spot serves gourmet updates of old favorites such as burgers with roasted garlic spread, grilled tuna salad, corn fries, salads, and more. Casual dress; beer & wine only. **Parking:** street. **Cards:** AX, DS, MC, VI.

PANCHO VILLA MEXICAN RESTAURANT   **Lunch:** $5-$11   **Dinner:** $5-$11   **Phone:** 540/710-9999

Mexican

Location: Just n on US 1; in Lee's Hill Shopping Center. 10500 Spotsylvania Ave 22408. **Hours:** 11 am-10 pm, Sun-9 pm. Closed major holidays. **Features:** In a festive spot adorned with colorful murals, the restaurant lets guests sample standard favorites, from fajitas to burritos, with frosty margaritas. Casual dress; cocktails. **Parking:** on-site. **Cards:** AX, CB, DC, DS, MC, VI.

PARADISE DINER   **Lunch:** $7-$16   **Dinner:** $7-$16   **Phone:** 540/372-2013

Greek

Location: I-95, exit Falmouth, just e. 268 Warrenton Rd 22406. **Hours:** 7 am-10 pm. Closed major holidays; also Mon. **Features:** Traditional Greek dishes such as souvlaki and gyros along with standard blue plate specials are served up in a warm setting bedecked with strings of white lights and Grecian statues. Casual dress; cocktails. **Parking:** on-site. **Cards:** AX, DS, MC, VI.

PHO SAIGON   **Lunch:** $7-$12   **Dinner:** $7-$12   **Phone:** 540/891-2400

Vietnamese

Location: I-95, exit 126B, 1 mi on US 1, then 0.9 mi w; in Breezewood Station. 10705 Courthouse Rd, Suite 102 22407. **Hours:** 10 am-9 pm, Fri & Sat-10 pm, Sun 11 am-8 pm. Closed: 12/25. **Features:** Sample the light and fresh flavors of Vietnam at this cozy family spot named for a favored noodle soup of the country. Other specialties include garden rolls, a un-fried version of spring rolls, braised quail, and rice vermicelli noodles with grilled meats or seafood. Casual dress; beer & wine only. **Parking:** on-site. **Cards:** MC, VI.

RISTORANTE RENATO   **Lunch:** $5-$9   **Dinner:** $9-$22   **Phone:** 540/371-8228

Italian

Location: I-95, exit 130A, 2 mi e on SR 3 business route; corner of Williams and Prince Edward sts; downtown. 422 William St 22401. **Hours:** 11:30 am-2 & 4:30-10 pm, Sat from 4:30 pm. Closed: 1/1, 11/24, 12/25; also Sun. **Reservations:** suggested, weekends. **Features:** The menu showcases authentic Northern Italian cuisine such as fresh pasta, beef and seafood specialties. Dessert selections — cannoli, stromboli, cheesecake and spumoni — are all homemade. Classical guitar entertainment is offered Friday and Saturday. Dressy casual; cocktails. **Parking:** on-site. **Cards:** AX, MC, VI.

SAMMY T'S   **Lunch:** $3-$18   **Dinner:** $3-$18   **Phone:** 540/371-2008

American

Location: Jct Hanover St, just n of Visitor's Center; in Olde Towne. 801 Caroline St 22401. **Hours:** 11 am-10 pm, Sun-9 pm. Closed major holidays. **Features:** The specialties are freshly made soup, salad, plus a wide variety of vegan, vegetarian entrees, pasta and excellent burgers. A tasty choice is the black bean soup and vegan wrap with spinach and hummus. Try apple crisp, a homemade dessert. Sidewalk dining is available. Casual dress; beer & wine only. **Parking:** street. **Cards:** AX, DS, MC, VI.

———— *The following restaurant has not been evaluated by AAA* ————
but is listed for your information only.

FEAST-O-RAMA   **Phone:** 540/373-9040

[fyi]

Not evaluated. **Location:** Just n of Olde Towne. 1008 Sophia St 22401. **Features:** This small gourmet grocer on the edge of Olde Towne offers all manner of provisions and fine wines as well as a daily assortment of prepared meals on the go.

FRONT ROYAL pop. 13,589

———— **WHERE TO STAY** ————

BLUEMONT INN   **Phone:** (540)635-9447

Motel

All Year   1P: $47-$195   2P: $47-$195

Location: I-66, exit 6, 1.8 mi s on US 340/522. 1525 N Shenandoah Ave 22630. Fax: 540/635-9447. **Facility:** 28 one-bedroom standard units, some with whirlpools. 2 stories (no elevator), exterior corridors. **Parking:** on-site. **Amenities:** *Some:* irons. **Leisure Activities:** barbecue deck. **Cards:** AX, CB, DC, DS, MC, VI. **Special Amenities:** free continental breakfast and free room upgrade (subject to availability with advance reservations).

SOME UNITS

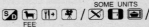

BUDGET INN   **Phone:** (540)635-2196

Motel

All Year   1P: $39-$69   2P: $42-$75   XP: $5   F12

Location: I-66, exit 6, 2.2 mi s on US 340/522 and SR 55. 1122 N Royal Ave 22630. Fax: 540/635-6986. **Facility:** 21 one-bedroom standard units. 1 story, exterior corridors. **Parking:** on-site. **Terms:** weekly rates available, small pets only ($5 extra charge). **Cards:** AX, DC, DS, MC, VI. **Special Amenities:** free local telephone calls and preferred room (subject to availability with advance reservations).

SOME UNITS

FEE

CENTER CITY MOTEL

Phone: (540)635-4050

AAA SAVE

Motel

All Year   1P: $35-$65   2P: $35-$65   XP: $6   F5
Location: I-66, exit 6, 3.5 mi s on US 340. Located in historic Front Royal. 416 S Royal Ave 22630. **Facility:** 14 one-bedroom standard units. 1 story, exterior corridors. **Parking:** on-site. **Cards:** AX, DC, MC, VI.
Special Amenities: free local telephone calls and preferred room (subject to availability with advance reservations).

SOME UNITS

HAMPTON INN/FRONT ROYAL   *Book at aaa.com*

Phone: 540/635-1882

Small-scale Hotel

All Year [BP]   1P: $79-$125   2P: $79-$125
Location: I-66, exit 6, just s. 9800 Winchester Rd 22630. Fax: 540/635-9779. **Facility:** 70 one-bedroom standard units, some with whirlpools. 4 stories, interior corridors. *Bath:* combo or shower only. **Parking:** on-site. **Amenities:** high-speed Internet, dual phone lines, voice mail, irons, hair dryers. **Pool(s):** outdoor. **Leisure Activities:** exercise room. **Guest Services:** valet and coin laundry. **Business Services:** meeting rooms, business center. **Cards:** AX, DC, DS, MC, VI.

SOME UNITS

QUALITY INN-SKYLINE DRIVE   *Book at aaa.com*

Phone: (540)635-3161

AAA SAVE

Small-scale Hotel

All Year   1P: $64-$85   2P: $67-$85   XP: $10   F18
Location: I-66, exit 6, 3.2 mi s on US 522. 10 Commerce Ave 22630. Fax: 540/635-6624. **Facility:** 108 one-bedroom standard units. 3 stories, exterior corridors. **Parking:** on-site. **Amenities:** safes, irons, hair dryers. **Dining:** 7 am-10 pm, beer only. **Pool(s):** outdoor. **Leisure Activities:** picnic area, horseshoes, volleyball. **Guest Services:** coin laundry. **Business Services:** meeting rooms. **Cards:** AX, CB, DC, DS, JC, MC, VI. **Special Amenities:** free local telephone calls and preferred room (subject to availability with advance reservations).

SOME UNITS

RELAX INN

Phone: (540)635-4101

AAA SAVE

Motel

8/1-11/15   1P: $55-$65   2P: $65-$75   XP: $8   F9
3/1-7/31   1P: $50-$60   2P: $60-$70   XP: $8   F9
11/16-2/28   1P: $40-$49   2P: $50-$59   XP: $5   F9
Location: I-66, exit 6, 1.5 mi s on US 340/522. Located in historic Front Royal. 1801 Shenandoah Ave 22630. Fax: 540/635-5765. **Facility:** 20 one-bedroom standard units. 1 story, exterior corridors. **Parking:** on-site. **Terms:** pets ($5 extra charge). **Pool(s):** outdoor. **Leisure Activities:** picnic area, playground. **Cards:** AX, DS, MC, VI. **Special Amenities:** free continental breakfast and early check-in/late check-out.

SOME UNITS
FEE

SCOTTISH INN   *Book at aaa.com*

Phone: 540/636-6168

AAA SAVE

Motel

All Year   1P: $44-$75   2P: $49-$79   XP: $6   F12
Location: I-66, exit 6, 3.8 mi s on US 340, jct SR 55. Located in historic Front Royal. 533 S Royal Ave 22630. Fax: 540/636-3120. **Facility:** 20 one-bedroom standard units. 2 stories (no elevator), exterior corridors. **Parking:** on-site. **Terms:** pets (extra charge). **Cards:** AX, DC, MC, VI. **Special Amenities:** free local telephone calls and early check-in/late check-out.

SOME UNITS
FEE   FEE

TWI-LITE MOTEL

Phone: 540/635-4148

AAA SAVE

Motel

8/1-10/31   1P: $49-$65   2P: $60-$89   XP: $6   F12
5/1-7/31   1P: $45-$55   2P: $55-$65   XP: $6   F12
3/1-4/30   1P: $39-$49   2P: $49-$55   XP: $6   F12
11/1-2/28   1P: $35-$45   2P: $45-$49   XP: $6   F12
Location: I-66, exit 6, 2.3 mi s on US 340/522. 53 W 14th St 22630. Fax: 540/635-6130. **Facility:** 19 one-bedroom standard units, some with whirlpools. 1 story, exterior corridors. **Parking:** on-site. **Terms:** 3 day cancellation notice-fee imposed, weekly rates available, small pets only ($4 extra charge). **Pool(s):** outdoor. **Cards:** AX, CB, DC, DS, JC, MC, VI. **Special Amenities:** free continental breakfast and free local telephone calls.

SOME UNITS
FEE

-------- WHERE TO DINE --------

DEAN'S STEAKHOUSE

Lunch: $6-$14   **Dinner:** $10-$22   Phone: 540/635-1780

Steak House

Location: I-66, exit 6, 3.9 mi s on US 340. 708 S Royal Ave 22630. **Hours:** 10:30 am-10 pm. Closed: 12/25. **Reservations:** suggested, weekends. **Features:** Great steaks, great atmosphere and a friendly wait staff are what is offered at Dean's Steakhouse. A Front Royal tradition. Casual dress; cocktails. **Parking:** on-site. **Cards:** AX, CB, DC, DS, JC, MC, VI.

ROYAL OAK TAVERN

Lunch: $5-$15   **Dinner:** $8-$20   Phone: 540/551-9953

American

Location: I-66, exit 6, 2.2 mi s on US 340/522. 101 W 14th St 22630. **Hours:** 11 am-midnight, Sun noon-10 pm. **Reservations:** suggested. **Features:** The atmosphere is fun and light at the laid-back restaurant. On the menu are classic American favorites and a wide variety of dessert choices. Casual dress; cocktails. **Parking:** on-site. **Cards:** AX, CB, DC, DS, JC, MC, VI.

SOUTH STREET GRILLE

Lunch: $4-$8   **Dinner:** $6-$15   Phone: 540/636-6654

American

Location: I-66, exit 6, 3.3 mi s on US 522. 424A South St 22630. **Hours:** 7 am-9 pm. Closed: 12/25. **Features:** South Street Grille is a trip back in time with a 50's nostalgia decor theme, real hamburgers and shakes, and friendly service. Casual dress. **Parking:** on-site. **Cards:** MC, VI.

GLADE SPRING pop. 1,374

──────── WHERE TO STAY ────────

SWISS INN MOTEL & SUITES   Phone: (276)429-5191
(AAA) (SAVE)   All Year   1P: $39-$59   2P: $45-$65   XP: $5   F12
♦♦ ♦♦   **Location:** I-81, exit 29, just e. 33361 Lee Hwy 24340. **Fax:** 276/429-2233. **Facility:** 32 one-bedroom standard
Motel   units, some with whirlpools. 2 stories (no elevator), exterior corridors. **Parking:** on-site. **Terms:** small pets
only ($7 extra charge). **Amenities:** hair dryers. **Guest Services:** valet laundry. **Cards:** AX, DC, MC, VI.
Special Amenities: free continental breakfast and free local telephone calls.

SOME UNITS

TRAVELODGE   ***Book at aaa.com***   Phone: 276/429-5131
♦   All Year   1P: $45-$259   2P: $49-$265   XP: $8   F12
Motel   **Location:** I-81, exit 29, just e. 12412 Maple St 24340. **Fax:** 276/429-5132. **Facility:** 50 one-bedroom standard
units. 2 stories (no elevator), exterior corridors. **Parking:** on-site, winter plug-ins. **Amenities:** hair dryers.
Cards: AX, DC, DS, MC, VI.

SOME UNITS

GLEN ALLEN —*See Richmond p. 860.*

GLOUCESTER —*See Hampton Roads Area p. 784.*

GLOUCESTER POINT —*See Hampton Roads Area p. 784.*

GOOCHLAND —*See Richmond p. 863.*

GREAT FALLS —*See District Of Columbia p. 534.*

GREENVILLE pop. 886

──────── WHERE TO STAY ────────

BUDGET HOST-HISTORIC HESSIAN HOUSE   Phone: (540)337-1231
(AAA) (SAVE)   3/1-11/15   1P: $40-$65   2P: $45-$75   XP: $6   F12
♦♦ ♦♦   11/16-2/28   1P: $35-$55   2P: $40-$55   XP: $6   F12
Small-scale Hotel   **Location:** I-81, exit 213, 0.3 mi e. Located in a quiet area. 3554 Lee Jackson Hwy 24401-6915 (3554 Lee Jackson Hwy,
STAUNTON, 24401). **Fax:** 540/337-0821. **Facility:** 32 one-bedroom standard units. 2 stories (no elevator),
exterior corridors. **Parking:** on-site. **Terms:** 3 day cancellation notice, package plans, pets ($6 extra charge,
in designated units). **Leisure Activities:** picnic area, playground, basketball. **Cards:** AX, DC, DS, MC, VI.
Special Amenities: free continental breakfast and free local telephone calls.

SOME UNITS

──────── WHERE TO DINE ────────

EDELWEISS RESTAURANT   **Lunch:** $7-$14   **Dinner:** $11-$18   Phone: 540/337-1203
♦♦ ♦♦   **Location:** I-81, exit 213 northbound; 213A southbound, just e on US 11, then just n on US 340. **Hours:** 11:30 am-9
German   pm, Sun-8 pm. **Closed:** 11/24, 12/25; also Mon. **Reservations:** suggested, weekends. **Features:** On the
menu are tasty traditional favorites, from schnitzels and spaetzle to Black Forest cake. The unusual pine log
cabin setting is cozy and relaxed. A nice wine list includes a sampling of German selections. Casual dress;
beer & wine only. **Parking:** on-site. **Cards:** AX, DC, DS, MC, VI.

GRUNDY pop. 1,105

──────── WHERE TO STAY ────────

COMFORT INN   ***Book at aaa.com***   Phone: (276)935-5050
♦♦♦   All Year [ECP]   1P: $54-$130   2P: $59-$135   XP: $10   F15
Small-scale Hotel   **Location:** On US 460, 0.5 mi e. US 460 Main St 24614 (Rt 5, Box 590). **Fax:** 276/935-5050. **Facility:** 70 units. 68
one-bedroom standard units. 2 one-bedroom suites. 4 stories, interior corridors. *Bath:* combo or shower
only. **Parking:** on-site. **Terms:** small pets only ($20 fee). **Amenities:** voice mail, irons, hair dryers. **Leisure
Activities:** exercise room. **Guest Services:** coin laundry. **Business Services:** meeting rooms. **Cards:** AX, CB, DC, DS, JC,
MC, VI.

SOME UNITS

HAMPTON —*See Hampton Roads Area p. 784.*

Destination Hampton Roads Area

*H*ampton Roads, the passage between Chesapeake Bay and the James River, has drawn maritime adventurers from the 1607 arrival of the English colonists to the 20th-century installation of U.S. naval facilities.

*F*ind your own excitement in or near the waters of this "safe harbor." There are rivers to cruise, beaches to ramble, bases to tour and a very unusual bridge-tunnel to cross.

Virginia Beach CVB

Virginia Beach Oceanfront. Catch a glimpse of visitors floating the days away along this sandy coast.

Bicycling, Virginia Beach. Spend the day riding along a shore lined with crashing waves.

© Gibson Stock Photography

© Mark E. Gibson Photophile

Hampton Roads Area

Gloucester

See Area map page 707

Gloucester Point

Hampton

Smithfield

See Area map page 710

Portsmouth

Chesapeake

Suffolk
See Area map page 715

VA.
N.C.

Sculpture, Norfolk. Modern architecture blends well in a city known for its Colonial history.

Waterside Festival Marketplace, Norfolk. Entertainment, restaurants and shopping draw visitors to the waterfront. (See mention page 255)

*P*laces included in this AAA Destination Area:

Norfolk CVB / Virginia Tourism Corporation

Hampton Roads Area
(Newport News)
Lodging & Dining

Hampton Roads Area (Newport News)

This index helps you "spot" where approved accommodations and restaurants are located on the corresponding detailed maps. Lodging rate ranges are for comparison only and show the property's high season; rates are per night, unless only weekly (W) rates are available. Restaurant rate range is for dinner, unless only lunch (L) is served. Turn to the listing page for more detailed rate information and consult display ads for special promotions.

Spotter/Map Page Number	OA	NEWPORT NEWS - Lodgings	Diamond Rating	Rate Range High Season	Listing Page
1 / p. 707	AAA	**Howard Johnson Express**	◆◆	$79-$109 SAVE	723
2 / p. 707	AAA	**Days Inn**	◆◆	$70-$85 SAVE	722
3 / p. 707	AAA	**Travelodge**	◆	$55-$95 SAVE	724
4 / p. 707		Comfort Inn	◆◆◆	$129-$139	722
5 / p. 707		Hampton Inn	◆◆◆	$94-$119	722
6 / p. 707	AAA	**Hampton Inn & Suites**	◆◆◆	$89-$149 SAVE	722
7 / p. 707		Hilton Garden Inn	◆◆◆	$99-$159	722
8 / p. 707	AAA	**Microtel Inn**	◆◆	$60-$99 SAVE	723
9 / p. 707	AAA	**Host Inn**	◆◆	$45-$90 SAVE	723
10 / p. 707	AAA	**Holiday Inn Hotel & Suites**	◆◆◆	$99-$139 SAVE	723
11 / p. 707	AAA	**Point Plaza - Suites & Conference Hotel - see color ad p 933**	◆◆◆	$69-$129 SAVE	723
12 / p. 707	AAA	**Budget Lodge**	◆	$60-$120 SAVE	722
13 / p. 707	AAA	**Days Inn-Oyster Point**	◆◆	$109-$119 SAVE	722
14 / p. 707		Ramada Inn-Newport News/Hampton	◆◆◆	$69-$129	724
		NEWPORT NEWS - Restaurants			
1 / p. 707		Kyung Sung Korean Restaurant	◆	$8-$16	724
2 / p. 707		Samurai Sushi & Hibachi Restaurant	◆◆	$15-$28	725
3 / p. 707		Kappo Nara Seafood & Sushi Restaurant	◆◆	$10-$20	724
4 / p. 707		Plaza Azteca	◆	$6-$13	725
5 / p. 707		Cowboy Syd's	◆◆	$18-$30	724
6 / p. 707		Schlesinger's Chophouse	◆◆◆	$17-$39	725
7 / p. 707		The Tapas Lounge	◆◆◆	$5-$12	725
8 / p. 707		Cities Grill	◆◆	$13-$20	724
9 / p. 707		Al Fresco Ristorante	◆◆	$7-$18	724
10 / p. 707		Nawab Indian Cuisine	◆◆	$7-$12	725
11 / p. 707		El Mariachi Restaurant & Cantina	◆	$5-$10	724
12 / p. 707		Mike's Place	◆	$9-$16	725
13 / p. 707		Rocky Mount Barbecue	◆	$5-$9	725
14 / p. 707		99 Main	◆◆◆	$14-$28	724
15 / p. 707		The Crab Shack	◆◆	$6-$20	724
		YORKTOWN - Lodgings			
17 / p. 707	AAA	**TownePlace Suites by Marriott**	◆◆◆	$125-$139 SAVE	948
18 / p. 707		Courtyard by Marriott	◆◆◆	$129	948
19 / p. 707		Candlewood Suites-Yorktown	◆◆◆	$99-$109	948
		YORKTOWN - Restaurants			
18 / p. 707		Spring Garden	◆	$6-$13	949

Spotter/Map Page Number	OA	YORKTOWN - Restaurants (continued)	Diamond Rating	Rate Range High Season	Listing Page
19 / p. 707		The Glass Pheasant English Tea Room	▼▼ ▼▼	$5-$9(L)	949
20 / p. 707		Empress Restaurant	▼▼	$6-$11	949
		HAMPTON - Lodgings			
22 / p. 707		Candlewood Suites	▼▼ ▼▼ ▼▼	$99-$189	784
23 / p. 707	AAA	**Quality Inn & Suites Conference Center -** see color ad p 707	▼▼ ▼▼ ▼▼	$110-$180 SAVE	786
24 / p. 707		Holiday Inn Hampton Hotel & Conference Center	▼▼ ▼▼ ▼▼	$59-$169	785
25 / p. 707		Hampton Inn	▼▼ ▼▼ ▼▼	$99-$129	785
26 / p. 707	AAA	Comfort Inn	▼▼ ▼▼	$85-$165 SAVE	785
27 / p. 707	AAA	**La Quinta Inn Norfolk (Hampton) -** see color ad p 730	▼▼ ▼▼ ▼▼	$69-$144 SAVE	785
28 / p. 707		Courtyard By Marriott	▼▼ ▼▼ ▼▼	$109-$139	785
29 / p. 707		Ramada Inn	▼▼ ▼▼	$69-$109	786
30 / p. 707		Super 8 Motel	▼▼	$48-$85	786
31 / p. 707		Victoria House Bed & Breakfast	▼▼ ▼▼ ▼▼	$105-$150	786
		HAMPTON - Restaurants			
23 / p. 707		Soya Sushi Bar & Grill	▼▼ ▼▼	$8-$14	787
24 / p. 707		Harpoon Larry's Oyster Bar	▼▼	$7-$20	786
25 / p. 707		Medik's Cafe & Market	▼▼	$6-$10	787
26 / p. 707		The Grate Steak	▼▼ ▼▼	$14-$38	786
27 / p. 707		Delargy's Bistro	▼▼ ▼▼	$7-$20	786
28 / p. 707		Captain George's Seafood Restaurant	▼▼ ▼▼	$17-$23	786
29 / p. 707	AAA	**Sammy & Nicks Family Restaurant**	▼▼	$4-$19	787
30 / p. 707		Tommy's Restaurant	▼▼	$3-$9(L)	787
31 / p. 707		The Pottery Wine & Cheese Shop	▼▼	$6-$10(L)	787
32 / p. 707		Musasi Japanese Restaurant	▼▼ ▼▼	$9-$16	787
33 / p. 707		The Grey Goose	▼▼ ▼▼	$5-$9(L)	786
34 / p. 707		Surfrider Bluewater	▼▼ ▼▼	$6-$20	787

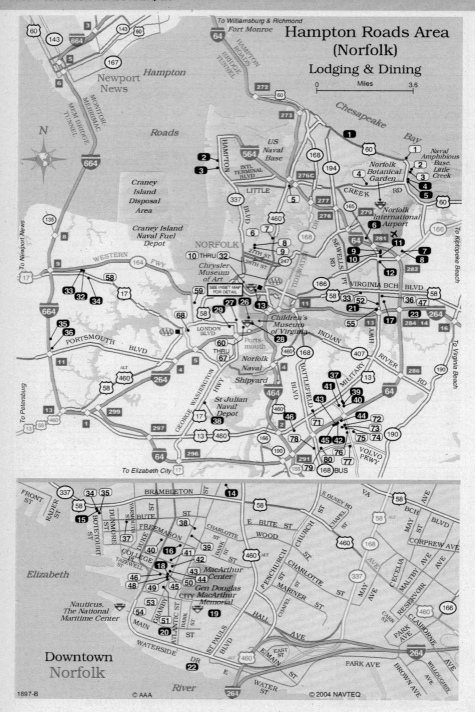

Hampton Roads Area
(Norfolk)
Lodging & Dining

Miles
0   3.6

Downtown Norfolk

1897-B   © AAA   © 2004 NAVTEQ

✈ Airport Accommodations

Spotter/Map Page Number	OA	NORFOLK INTERNATIONAL	Diamond Rating	Rate Range High Season	Listing Page
21 / p. 710	AAA	Best Western-Center Inn, 4.5 mi s of airport	▽▽▽	$89-$149 SAVE	726
17 / p. 710		Doubletree Hotel-Norfolk, 2.5 mi s of airport	▽▽▽	$109-$229	728
6 / p. 710		Econo Lodge Airport, 1 mi s of airport	▽	$60-$150	728
12 / p. 710		Howard Johnson Norfolk Airport, 2 mi s of airport	▽▽▽	$79-$139	730
11 / p. 710	AAA	Hilton Norfolk Airport, 2 mi s of airport	▽▽▽	$199-$229 SAVE	728
10 / p. 710		Holiday Inn Select, 2 mi s of airport	▽▽▽	$79-$159	730
3 / p. 715	AAA	Best Western Inn, 2.5 n of airport	▽▽▽	$75-$155 SAVE	741
4 / p. 715	AAA	Red Roof Inn VA Beach (Norfolk Airport), 2.5 mi n of airport	▽▽	$60-$176 SAVE	762
6 / p. 715		Wingate Inn-Norfolk Airport, 3 mi from airport	▽▽▽	$115-$130	770

Hampton Roads Area (Norfolk)

This index helps you "spot" where approved accommodations and restaurants are located on the corresponding detailed maps. Lodging rate ranges are for comparison only and show the property's high season; rates are per night, unless only weekly (W) rates are available. Restaurant rate range is for dinner, unless only lunch (L) is served. Turn to the listing page for more detailed rate information and consult display ads for special promotions.

Spotter/Map Page Number	OA	NORFOLK - Lodgings	Diamond Rating	Rate Range High Season	Listing Page
1 / p. 710	AAA	Best Western Holiday Sands Inn & Suites - see color ad p 727	▽▽	$99-$159 SAVE	727
2 / p. 710	AAA	Hampton Inn Norfolk Naval Base - see color ad p 729	▽▽▽	$115-$139 SAVE	728
3 / p. 710		Comfort Inn-Naval Base	▽▽▽	$89-$119	727
4 / p. 710	AAA	Tides Inn - see color ad p 769	▽▽	$65-$95 SAVE	732
5 / p. 710		Super 8 Motel	▽	$69-$99	732
6 / p. 710		Econo Lodge Airport	▽	$60-$150	728
7 / p. 710	AAA	Sleep Inn Lake Wright - see color ad p 731	▽▽	$99-$139 SAVE	732
8 / p. 710	AAA	Quality Suites Lake Wright - see color ad p 731	▽▽▽	$119-$159 SAVE	731
9 / p. 710		Residence Inn by Marriott Norfolk Airport	▽▽▽	$79-$159	732
10 / p. 710		Holiday Inn Select	▽▽▽	$79-$159	730
11 / p. 710	AAA	Hilton Norfolk Airport - see color ad p 729	▽▽▽	$199-$229 SAVE	728
12 / p. 710		Hampton Inn Norfolk Airport - see color ad p 729	▽▽▽	$79-$139	730
13 / p. 710	AAA	Bed & Breakfast @ the Historic Page House Inn	▽▽▽▽	$140-$225 SAVE	726
14 / p. 710	AAA	Radisson Hotel Norfolk - see color ad p 932, p 731	▽▽▽	$144-$166 SAVE	731
15 / p. 710	AAA	Freemason Inn	▽▽▽	$145-$245 SAVE	728
16 / p. 710	AAA	Clarion Hotel James Madison	▽▽	$89-$139 SAVE	727
17 / p. 710		Doubletree Hotel-Norfolk - see color ad p 728	▽▽▽	$109-$229	728
18 / p. 710	AAA	Tazewell Hotel and Suites	▽▽▽	$109-$189 SAVE	732
19 / p. 710		Courtyard by Marriott	▽▽▽	$159-$189	727
20 / p. 710		Norfolk Waterside Marriott Hotel - see color ad p 730	▽▽▽	$99-$179	730
21 / p. 710	AAA	Best Western-Center Inn	▽▽▽	$89-$149 SAVE	726

Spotter/Map Page Number	OA	NORFOLK - Lodgings (continued)	Diamond Rating	Rate Range High Season	Listing Page
22 / p. 710		Sheraton Norfolk Waterside Hotel - see color ad p 726	◈◈◈	$79-$179	732
23 / p. 710		SpringHill Suites by Marriott Norfolk/VA Beach	◈◈◈	$109-$169	732
		NORFOLK - Restaurants			
1 / p. 710		Ship's Cabin Bar & Grill	◈◈	$12-$25	737
2 / p. 710		Blue Crab Restaurant	◈◈	$6-$20	733
3 / p. 710		SurfRider-Taylor's Landing	◈◈	$6-$18	737
4 / p. 710		The Azalea Inn	◈	$6-$12	733
5 / p. 710		Uncle Louie's Restaurant	◈◈	$7-$17	737
6 / p. 710		Tanner's Creek Seafood Restaurant & Raw Bar	◈◈	$6-$20	737
7 / p. 710		Mi Hogar Mexican Restaurant	◈	$6-$11	736
8 / p. 710		Enrico's Ristorante	◈◈	$9-$17	735
9 / p. 710		Fellini's	◈◈	$8-$20	735
10 / p. 710		Velvet 25 Bistro	◈◈◈	$16-$27	738
11 / p. 710		The Kosher Place	◈	$5-$16	735
12 / p. 710		Cracker's Little Bar & Bistro	◈◈	$5-$18	734
13 / p. 710		Rajput Indian Cuisine	◈◈	$7-$19	737
14 / p. 710		Siam 21	◈◈	$8-$20	737
15 / p. 710		Amalfi	◈◈◈	$10-$23	733
16 / p. 710		Azar's Natural Foods	◈	$6-$10	733
17 / p. 710		Cora	◈◈	$10-$20	734
18 / p. 710		Kotobuki	◈◈	$9-$18	735
19 / p. 710		Dog N' Burger Grille	◈	$5-$15	734
20 / p. 710		New Belmont	◈◈◈	$12-$21	736
21 / p. 710		Wild Monkey	◈◈	$8-$15	738
22 / p. 710		No Frill Bar & Grill	◈◈	$5-$17	736
23 / p. 710		Baker's Crust Bread Market	◈◈	$5-$20	733
24 / p. 710		Luna Maya Cantina	◈◈	$8-$14	736
25 / p. 710		Bangkok Garden	◈◈	$8-$17	733
26 / p. 710		The Ten Top	◈	$6-$11	737
27 / p. 710		D. C. Chase's	◈◈	$7-$18	734
28 / p. 710		Cogan's	◈	$5-$15	734
29 / p. 710		Cafe Rosso	◈◈◈	$7-$14	734
30 / p. 710		Doumar's Cones & Barbecue	◈	$2-$4	734
31 / p. 710	▲▲▲	**Magnolia Steak**	◈◈	$16-$25	736
32 / p. 710		The Painted Lady	◈◈◈	$13-$26	737
33 / p. 710		The Germany Pantry	◈◈	$9-$17	735
34 / p. 710		Machismo Burrito Bar	◈	$5-$8	736
35 / p. 710		Voila Cuisine International	◈◈◈	$14-$27	738
36 / p. 710		Nawab Restaurant	◈◈	$7-$12	736
37 / p. 710	▲▲▲	**Omar's Carriage House**	◈◈◈	$14-$22	736

Spotter/Map Page Number	OA	**NORFOLK** - Restaurants (continued)	Diamond Rating	Rate Range High Season	Listing Page
38 / p. 710		456 Fish	▽▽▽	$15-$29	733
39 / p. 710		Bodega	▽▽	$6-$10	733
40 / p. 710		Freemason Abbey	▽▽	$6-$18	735
41 / p. 710		La Galleria	▽▽▽	$13-$44	736
42 / p. 710		Domo	▽▽	$8-$18	734
43 / p. 710		Kincaid's Fish, Chop and Steakhouse	▽▽▽	$14-$28	735
44 / p. 710		Havana	▽▽	$13-$20	735
45 / p. 710		Empire Little Bar & Bistro	▽▽	$5-$18	735
46 / p. 710		Cobia Grill	▽▽▽	$11-$24	734
47 / p. 710		Surf Rider West	▽▽	$7-$15	737
48 / p. 710		Jack Quinn's Restaurant & Irish Pub	▽▽	$9-$21	735
49 / p. 710		Club Soda	▽▽▽	$16-$26	734
50 / p. 710		Castaldi's Market & Grill	▽▽	$8-$19	734
51 / p. 710		The 219	▽▽▽	$11-$23	733
52 / p. 710		Mi Hogar Mexican Restaurant	▽	$6-$11	736
53 / p. 710		The Blue Hippo	▽▽▽	$19-$29	733
54 / p. 710	AAA	**Todd Jurich's Bistro!**	▽▽▽▽	$18-$26	737
55 / p. 710		The Grate Steak	▽▽	$8-$33	735
		PORTSMOUTH - Lodgings			
26 / p. 710	AAA	**Holiday Inn-Olde Towne Portsmouth**	▽▽	$116-$135 SAVE	788
27 / p. 710	AAA	**Comfort Inn-Olde Towne**	▽▽▽	$95-$125 SAVE	787
28 / p. 710		Renaissance Portsmouth Hotel and Waterfront Conference Center	▽▽▽	$269-$369	788
29 / p. 710	AAA	**Days Inn Portsmouth/Norfolk**	▽▽	$50-$90 SAVE	787
		PORTSMOUTH - Restaurants			
58 / p. 710		Cafe Mundo	▽	$5-$7	788
59 / p. 710		Market Fare	▽▽▽	$12-$20	789
60 / p. 710		Fusion 440	▽▽▽	$18-$30	789
61 / p. 710		Roger Brown's Restaurant & Sports Bar	▽▽	$6-$17	789
62 / p. 710		Brutti's Cafe	▽▽	$9-$27	788
63 / p. 710		The Bier Garden	▽▽	$6-$14	788
64 / p. 710		Eaton Gogh Cafe	▽	$5-$12	788
65 / p. 710		Sassafras	▽▽▽	$14-$25	789
66 / p. 710	AAA	**Commodore Theatre**	▽	$5-$11	788
67 / p. 710		Cafe Europa	▽▽▽	$12-$15	788
68 / p. 710		Mario's Italian Restaurant	▽▽	$6-$18	789
		CHESAPEAKE - Lodgings			
32 / p. 710		Super 8 Motel	▽	$55-$77	782
33 / p. 710	AAA	**Sleep Inn**	▽▽	$89-$109 SAVE	782
34 / p. 710		Hampton Inn	▽▽▽	$109-$114	781
35 / p. 710	AAA	**Holiday Inn Express Hotel & Suites**	▽▽▽	$119-$159 SAVE	781

Spotter/Map Page Number	OA	CHESAPEAKE - Lodgings (continued)	Diamond Rating	Rate Range High Season	Listing Page
36 / p. 710		SpringHill Suites by Marriott	◇◇◇	$69-$129	782
37 / p. 710		TownePlace Suites By Marriott	◇◇◇	$69-$139	782
38 / p. 710	AAA	**Days Inn-Chesapeake**	◇◇	$75-$100 [SAVE]	780
39 / p. 710		Red Roof Inn	◇◇	$48-$74	782
40 / p. 710		Holiday Inn Chesapeake	◇◇◇	$129-$139	781
41 / p. 710		Hampton Inn Chesapeake	◇◇◇	$79-$139	781
42 / p. 710		Courtyard By Marriott	◇◇◇	$79-$139	780
43 / p. 710		Fairfield Inn by Marriott	◇◇◇	$59-$129	781
44 / p. 710		Hilton Garden Inn-Chesapeake/Greenbriar	◇◇◇	$139-$149	781
45 / p. 710		Comfort Suites	◇◇◇	$69-$129	780
46 / p. 710	AAA	**Econo Lodge Chesapeake**	◇	$59-$99 [SAVE]	781
		CHESAPEAKE - Restaurants			
71 / p. 710		Tida Thai Cuisine	◇	$7-$9	783
72 / p. 710		Taste Unlimited	◇	$4-$10	783
73 / p. 710		Vivo, Your Italian Kitchen	◇◇	$7-$20	783
74 / p. 710		Atlas Grill & Bar	◇◇	$6-$14	782
75 / p. 710		The Grate Steak	◇◇	$12-$32	783
76 / p. 710		The Angry Chef	◇	$7-$11	782
77 / p. 710		El Loro Mexican Restaurante	◇	$6-$10	783
78 / p. 710		Daikichi Sushi Japanese Bistro	◇◇	$12-$19	783
79 / p. 710		Warrior's Mongolian Grill	◇	$10	783
80 / p. 710		Ms Marian's Restaurant	◇	$5-$11	783

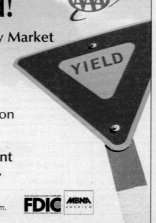

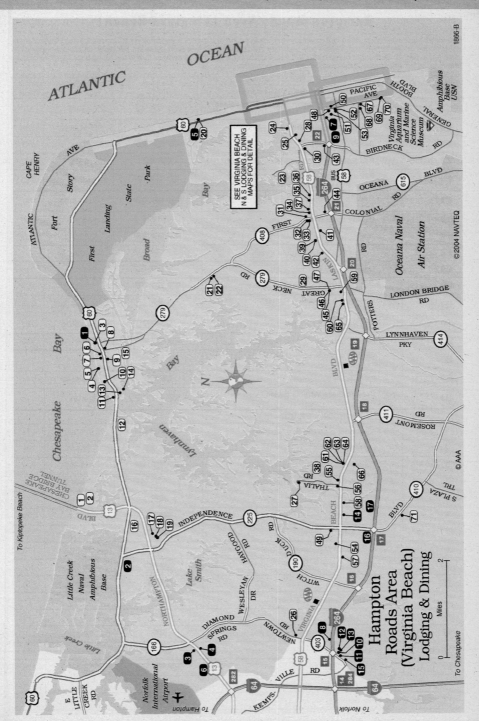

Hampton Roads Area (Virginia Beach) Lodging & Dining

Hampton Roads Area (Virginia Beach)

This index helps you "spot" where approved accommodations and restaurants are located on the corresponding detailed maps. Lodging rate ranges are for comparison only and show the property's high season; rates are per night, unless only weekly (W) rates are available. Restaurant rate range is for dinner, unless only lunch (L) is served. Turn to the listing page for more detailed rate information and consult display ads for special promotions.

Spotter/Map Page Number	OA	VIRGINIA BEACH - Lodgings	Diamond Rating	Rate Range High Season	Listing Page
1 / p. 715	AAA	**Virginia Beach Resort Hotel & Conference Center** - see color ad p 769	◇◇◇	$189-$389 SAVE	770
2 / p. 715	AAA	**Comfort Inn Little Creek**	◇◇	$95-$125 SAVE	746
3 / p. 715	AAA	**Best Western Inn**	◇◇	$75-$155 SAVE	741
4 / p. 715	AAA	**Red Roof Inn VA Beach (Norfolk Airport)**	◇◇	$60-$176 SAVE	762
5 / p. 715	AAA	**Ramada Plaza Resort Oceanfront** - see color ad p 762	◇◇◇	$180-$260 SAVE	762
6 / p. 715		Wingate Inn-Norfolk Airport - see color ad p 770	◇◇◇	$115-$130	770
7 / p. 715	AAA	**Quality Inn Pavilion**	◇◇	$119-$299 SAVE	759
8 / p. 715		TownePlace Suites By Marriott	◇◇◇	$135-$180	767
9 / p. 715	AAA	**DoubleTree Hotel Virginia Beach**	◇◇◇	$99-$229 SAVE	751
10 / p. 715	AAA	**Courtyard By Marriott**	◇◇◇	$154-$169 SAVE	746
11 / p. 715		Hampton Inn Virginia Beach	◇◇	$65-$149	754
12 / p. 715	AAA	**Holiday Inn-Executive Center** - see color ad p 756	◇◇◇	$99-$169 SAVE	756
13 / p. 715		Red Roof Inn-Virginia Beach	◇◇	$73-$105	762
14 / p. 715		Hilton Garden Inn Virginia Beach, Town Center	◇◇◇	$89-$179	754
15 / p. 715	AAA	**La Quinta Inn Norfolk (Virginia Beach)** - see color ad p 730	◇◇◇	$99-$145 SAVE	758
16 / p. 715		Fairfield Inn by Marriott	◇◇	$89-$149	754
17 / p. 715	AAA	**Crowne Plaza Virginia Beach** - see color ad p 748	◇◇◇	$139-$189 SAVE	748
		VIRGINIA BEACH - Restaurants			
① / p. 715	AAA	**Alexander's on the Bay Restaurant**	◇◇◇	$17-$30	771
② / p. 715		Zia Marie	◇◇	$8-$17	780
③ / p. 715		Tradewinds	◇◇◇	$13-$27	779
④ / p. 715	AAA	**Lynnhaven Fish House Restaurant**	◇◇◇	$16-$26	775
⑤ / p. 715		Pier Cafe	◇	$6-$14	777
⑥ / p. 715		Beale St.	◇◇	$7-$20	772
⑦ / p. 715		Cabo Cafe	◇◇	$6-$16	772
⑧ / p. 715		Guadalajara Mexican Bar & Grill	◇	$7-$12	774
⑨ / p. 715		Smokehouse & Cooler	◇◇	$8-$20	778
⑩ / p. 715		H2O	◇◇	$10-$21	774
⑪ / p. 715	AAA	**Duck-In Restaurant & Gazebo**	◇◇	$8-$22	774
⑫ / p. 715		Croakers	◇◇	$10-$20	773
⑬ / p. 715		Bubba's Crabhouse & Seafood Restaurant	◇	$6-$18	772
⑭ / p. 715		Chick's Oyster Bar	◇◇	$8-$20	773
⑮ / p. 715		One Fish Two Fish	◇◇◇	$17-$23	776
⑯ / p. 715		Jenna's Mediteranean Cafe	◇	$5-$8	775
⑰ / p. 715		Bay Gourmet	◇	$6-$10(L)	771

Spotter/Map Page Number	OA	VIRGINIA BEACH - Restaurants (continued)	Diamond Rating	Rate Range High Season	Listing Page
(18) / p. 715		Wisteria	◆◆◆	$15-$20	780
(19) / p. 715		The Lucky Star	◆◆◆	$20-$25	775
(20) / p. 715	▲▲▲	Gus's Mariner Restaurant - see color ad p 762	◆◆◆	$14-$29	774
(21) / p. 715		Coastal Grill	◆◆◆	$13-$20	773
(22) / p. 715		Havana	◆◆	$10-$20	775
(23) / p. 715		The Purple Cow	◆	$5-$8	777
(24) / p. 715		Coyote Cafe & Cantina	◆◆◆	$10-$23	773
(25) / p. 715		Beach Pub	◆	$8-$14	772
(26) / p. 715		Saigon 1 Restaurant	◆	$6-$10	778
(27) / p. 715		Steinhilber's Thalia Acres Inn	◆◆◆	$18-$40	778
(28) / p. 715		La Bella Italia Trattoria	◆◆	$7-$16	775
(29) / p. 715		Atlas Grill & Bar	◆◆	$6-$14	771
(30) / p. 715		Bella Monte	◆◆	$6-$16	772
(31) / p. 715		Nawab Indian Restaurant	◆◆	$9-$15	776
(32) / p. 715		Vivo Cucina	◆◆	$8-$16	779
(33) / p. 715		Bangkok Garden	◆◆	$8-$17	771
(34) / p. 715		Cobalt Grille	◆◆◆	$15-$25	773
(35) / p. 715		The Melting Pot	◆◆◆	$18-$50	776
(36) / p. 715		Otani Japanese Steak House	◆◆	$11-$35	777
(37) / p. 715		Baker's Crust Bread Market	◆◆	$7-$16	771
(38) / p. 715		The Boulevard Cafe	◆	$6-$15	772
(39) / p. 715		Aldo's Ristorante	◆◆◆	$15-$25	771
(40) / p. 715		Mizuno Japanese Restaurant	◆◆◆	$9-$18	776
(41) / p. 715		Terra Nova Natural Foods Grocer & Cafe	◆	$5-$9	779
(42) / p. 715		Captain George's Seafood Restaurant	◆◆	$19-$31	773
(43) / p. 715		Five 0 1 City Grill	◆◆	$7-$21	774
(44) / p. 715		Shogun Japanese Steak House & Seafood	◆◆	$11-$28	778
(45) / p. 715		Sushi & West	◆◆◆	$12-$20	778
(46) / p. 715		Central 111	◆◆	$4-$15	773
(47) / p. 715		Warrior's Grill	◆	$10	779
(48) / p. 715		Beach Bully	◆	$3-$15	771
(49) / p. 715		Federico's	◆◆	$9-$25	774
(50) / p. 715		Osaka Japanese Restaurant	◆◆	$9-$20	777
(51) / p. 715		Fresh Fare Cafe	◆	$4-$8	774
(52) / p. 715		Twysted Fish	◆◆	$5-$23	779
(53) / p. 715		Mary's Restaurant	◆	$3-$6(L)	776
(54) / p. 715		Pho 79	◆	$5-$6	777
(55) / p. 715		Brennan's of Wayside	◆◆◆	$13-$20	772
(56) / p. 715		Shiki Japanese Restaurant	◆	$8-$16	778

Spotter/Map Page Number	OA	VIRGINIA BEACH - Restaurants (continued)	Diamond Rating	Rate Range High Season	Listing Page
57 / p. 715		Napoleon's	▽▽▽	$15-$25	776
58 / p. 715		Silver Diner	▽▽	$6-$15	778
59 / p. 715		Pollard's Chicken	▽	$5-$7	777
60 / p. 715		Scotty Quixx Cafe & Carryout	▽	$5-$9	778
61 / p. 715		Eurasia Restaurant	▽▽▽	$10-$23	774
62 / p. 715	AAA	**Reginella's Italian Ristorante & Pizzeria**	▽	$5-$15	777
63 / p. 715		Misako Sushi Bar & Grille	▽▽	$5-$18	776
64 / p. 715		Bangkok Garden	▽▽	$8-$17	771
65 / p. 715		Vietnam Garden	▽▽	$6-$19	779
66 / p. 715		Azar's Natural Foods	▽	$6-$15	771
67 / p. 715		Tad's Deli	▽	$6-$10	779
68 / p. 715		Shadowlawn Grill	▽▽	$12-$24	778
69 / p. 715		Rockafeller's	▽▽	$8-$23	777
70 / p. 715	AAA	**Rudee's on the Inlet**	▽▽	$9-$20	778
71 / p. 715		Elia's Mediterranean Cuisine	▽	$5-$15	774

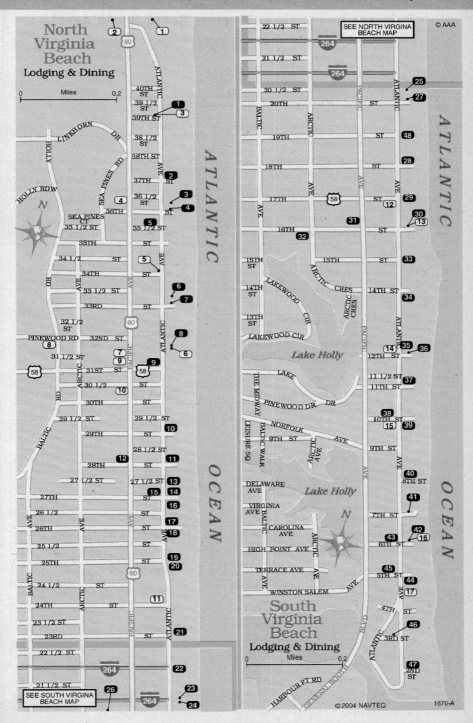

Hampton Roads Area (Virginia Beach-Beach Area)

This index helps you "spot" where approved accommodations and restaurants are located on the corresponding detailed maps. Lodging rate ranges are for comparison only and show the property's high season; rates are per night, unless only weekly (W) rates are available. Restaurant rate range is for dinner, unless only lunch (L) is served. Turn to the listing page for more detailed rate information and consult display ads for special promotions.

Spotter/Map Page Number	OA	**VIRGINIA BEACH** - Lodgings	Diamond Rating	Rate Range High Season	Listing Page
1 / p. 719	AAA	**Holiday Inn SunSpree Resort** - see color ad p 757	◇◇◇	$189-$289 SAVE	756
2 / p. 719		Courtyard by Marriott-Oceanfront North	◇◇◇	$159-$299	748
3 / p. 719	AAA	**The Belvedere Motel**	◇◇	$124-$134 SAVE	739
4 / p. 719		Sheraton Oceanfront Hotel	◇◇◇	$129-$179	766
5 / p. 719	AAA	**Royal Clipper Inn & Suites** - see color ad p 763	◇◇	$99-$169 SAVE	763
6 / p. 719	AAA	**Diplomat Inn Oceanfront** - see color ad p 750	◇◇	$95-$195 SAVE	750
7 / p. 719	AAA	**Four Sails Resort Hotel** - see color ad p 754	◇◇◇	$199-$249 SAVE	754
8 / p. 719	AAA	**Days Inn Oceanfront** - see color ad p 749	◇◇◇	$155-$250 SAVE	749
9 / p. 719		Ramada Limited Atlantic Avenue - see color ad p 761	◇◇	$59-$165	761
10 / p. 719	AAA	**The Oceanfront Inn** - see color ad p 745	◇◇	$134-$241 SAVE	759
11 / p. 719	AAA	**Colonial Inn** - see color ad p 742, p 745	◇◇	$85-$225 SAVE	743
12 / p. 719	AAA	**Comfort Inn** - see color ad p 747	◇◇◇	$104-$229 SAVE	746
13 / p. 719	AAA	**Econo Lodge on the Ocean** - see color ad p 747	◇◇	$104-$259 SAVE	751
14 / p. 719	AAA	**Seaside Motel** - see color ad p 766	◇	$90-$115 SAVE	765
15 / p. 719	AAA	**The Viking Motel** - see color ad p 769	◇◇	$64-$174 SAVE	770
16 / p. 719	AAA	**Sea Gull Motel** - see color ad p 765	◇◇	$90-$190 SAVE	765
17 / p. 719		Holiday Inn Surfside Hotel & Suites	◇◇◇	$109-$299	756
18 / p. 719	AAA	**Seahawk Motel** - see color ad p 766	◇◇	$95-$189 SAVE	765
19 / p. 719		Courtyard by Marriott-Oceanfront South	◇◇◇	$209-$239	748
20 / p. 719	AAA	**Ocean Holiday Hotel** - see color ad p 759	◇◇	$95-$195 SAVE	759
21 / p. 719		The Ambassador Suites - see color ad p 740	◇	$69-$239	739
22 / p. 719		The Marjac Suites - see color ad p 740	◇◇	$69-$239	758
23 / p. 719	AAA	**Econo Lodge Oceanfront** - see color ad p 747	◇◇◇	$104-$269 SAVE	751
24 / p. 719		Holiday Inn Oceanside	◇◇◇	$149-$279	756
25 / p. 719		Comfort Inn-Oceanfront - see color ad p 746	◇◇◇	$119-$399	746
26 / p. 719	AAA	**Sundial Motel & Efficiencies** - see color ad p 767	◇◇	$69-$189 SAVE	766
27 / p. 719		The Capes Ocean Resort - see color ad p 744	◇◇◇	$99-$250	743
28 / p. 719		Howard Johnson Oceanfront Hotel - see color ad p 742, p 757	◇◇	$129-$199	756
29 / p. 719		The Dolphin Inn - see color ad p 742, p 750	◇◇◇	$209-$329	751
30 / p. 719		Boardwalk Resort Hotel and Villas - see color ad p 742, p 741	◇◇◇	$129-$399	741
31 / p. 719	AAA	**Alamar Resort Inn** - see color ad p 738	◇◇◇	$104-$190 SAVE	738
32 / p. 719	AAA	**Barclay Cottage Bed & Breakfast**	◇◇◇	$123-$169 SAVE	739
33 / p. 719	AAA	**The Breakers Resort Inn** - see color ad p 743	◇◇◇	$160-$275 SAVE	743

Spotter/Map Page Number	OA	VIRGINIA BEACH - Lodgings (continued)	Diamond Rating	Rate Range High Season	Listing Page
34 / p. 719	AAA	Sandcastle Oceanfront Resort Hotel - see color ad p 764	◆◆	$99-$259 SAVE	763
35 / p. 719	AAA	Surfside Oceanfront Inn & Suites - see color ad p 768	◆◆	$99-$249 SAVE	767
36 / p. 719		New Castle Hotel - see color ad p 758	◆◆	$99-$229	758
37 / p. 719	AAA	Best Western Oceanfront	◆◆	$129-$219 SAVE	741
38 / p. 719	AAA	Days Inn at the Beach - see color ad p 749	◆◆	$79-$169 SAVE	748
39 / p. 719	AAA	The Dunes Oceanfront - see color ad p 752	◆◆◆	$189-$239 SAVE	751
40 / p. 719		Barclay Towers - see color ad p 740	◆◆◆	$109-$249	739
41 / p. 719		Quality Inn & Suites - see color ad p 740	◆◆◆	$139-$249	759
42 / p. 719		Ramada Inn On the Beach - see color ad p 742, p 761	◆◆◆	$159-$229	761
43 / p. 719		Turtle Cay Resort - see color ad p 742, p 768	◆◆◆	$129-$399	767
44 / p. 719		Clarion Resort - see color ad p 742, p 744	◆◆◆	$129-$399	743
45 / p. 719	AAA	Flagship Inn & Efficiencies	◆	$89-$155 SAVE	754
46 / p. 719		Best Western Beach Quarters Inn - see color ad p 742, p 739	◆◆	$119-$254	741
47 / p. 719		Schooner Inn - see color ad p 740	◆◆	$59-$209	763
48 / p. 719		Fairfield Inn & Suites Virginia Beach Oceanfront	◆◆◆	$179-$239	751
		VIRGINIA BEACH - Restaurants			
1 / p. 719		Orion's	◆◆◆	$19-$30	776
2 / p. 719		The Hunt Room Grill	◆◆◆	$20-$30	775
3 / p. 719		Isle of Capri	◆◆◆	$15-$25	775
4 / p. 719		Taste Unlimited	◆	$4-$7	779
5 / p. 719		Mayflower Cafe	◆◆	$10-$21	776
6 / p. 719	AAA	Timbuktu	◆◆◆	$13-$22	779
7 / p. 719		The Jewish Mother	◆	$5-$10	775
8 / p. 719		Blue Moon Cafe	◆◆	$10-$22	772
9 / p. 719		The Heritage Health Food Cafe & Deli	◆	$4-$9	775
10 / p. 719		Cuisine & Company	◆◆	$5-$10	773
11 / p. 719		Dough Boys California Pizza	◆	$7-$12	773
12 / p. 719		Doughboy's California Pizza	◆	$7-$12	774
13 / p. 719		Rockfish Boardwalk Bar & Sea Grill	◆◆	$6-$22	777
14 / p. 719		The Raven	◆	$6-$20	777
15 / p. 719		IL Giardino	◆◆◆	$12-$32	775
16 / p. 719		Mahi Mah's Seafood Restaurant & Sushi Saloon	◆◆	$8-$21	776
17 / p. 719	AAA	Waterman's Beach Wood Grill	◆◆	$9-$23	779

NEWPORT NEWS pop. 180,150 (See map and index starting on p. 707)

———— WHERE TO STAY ————

BUDGET LODGE
Phone: 757/599-5647 [12]

Motel

All Year   1P: $60-$120   2P: $80-$120   XP: $10   F10
Location: I-64, exit 258B, 0.3 mi n on US 17. 930 J Clyde Morris Blvd 23601. Fax: 757/595-0500. **Facility:** 48 one-bedroom standard units. 2 stories (no elevator), exterior corridors. **Parking:** on-site. **Cards:** AX, DC, MC, VI.

SOME UNITS

COMFORT INN   *Book at aaa.com*
Phone: (757)249-0200 [4]

Small-scale Hotel

5/1-10/31 [ECP]   1P: $129-$139   2P: $129-$139
3/1-4/30 & 11/1-2/28 [ECP]   1P: $109-$119   2P: $109-$119
Location: I-64, exit 255A, just s on Clarie Ln (mall parking lot). Located adjacent to Patrick Henry Mall. 12330 Jefferson Ave 23602. Fax: 757/249-4736. **Facility:** 124 one-bedroom standard units. 3 stories, interior corridors. *Bath:* combo or shower only. **Parking:** on-site. **Terms:** pets ($10 extra charge). **Amenities:** voice mail, irons, hair dryers. **Pool(s):** outdoor. **Guest Services:** valet and coin laundry, area transportation. **Business Services:** meeting rooms, business center. **Cards:** AX, DC, DS, MC, VI.

SOME UNITS
FEE

DAYS INN   *Book at aaa.com*
Phone: (757)874-0201 [2]

Small-scale Hotel

5/1-9/15   1P: $70-$85   2P: $85   XP: $10   F18
3/1-4/30 & 9/16-2/28   1P: $55-$65   2P: $65   XP: $10   F18
Location: I-64, exit 250A (SR 105/Ft Eustis Blvd S), 2.5 mi to US 60 E (Warwick Blvd). 14747 Warwick Blvd 23608. Fax: 757/874-0201. **Facility:** 112 one-bedroom standard units, some with efficiencies (no utensils). 2 stories (no elevator), exterior corridors. **Parking:** on-site. **Terms:** weekly rates available, [CP] meal plan available, pets ($5 extra charge). **Amenities:** safes (fee), hair dryers. *Some:* irons. **Pool(s):** outdoor. **Leisure Activities:** playground. **Guest Services:** coin laundry. **Business Services:** fax. **Cards:** AX, CB, DC, DS, MC, VI. **Special Amenities:** free continental breakfast and free newspaper.

SOME UNITS
FEE

DAYS INN-OYSTER POINT   *Book at aaa.com*
Phone: (757)873-6700 [13]

Small-scale Hotel

5/1-8/31 [ECP]   1P: $109-$119   2P: $109-$119
9/1-10/31 [ECP]   1P: $90-$109   2P: $90-$109
3/1-4/30 [ECP]   1P: $89-$99   2P: $89-$99
11/1-2/28 [ECP]   1P: $85-$95   2P: $85-$95
Location: I-64, exit 255A, 2.5 mi s to Thimble Shoals Dr E, 1 blk to property. 11829 Fishing Point Dr 23606. Fax: 757/873-3755. **Facility:** 125 one-bedroom standard units. 3 stories, interior corridors. **Parking:** on-site. **Terms:** 3 day cancellation notice, weekly rates available, package plans, pets ($10 extra charge). **Amenities:** high-speed Internet, voice mail, irons, hair dryers. *Some:* dual phone lines. **Pool(s):** outdoor. **Leisure Activities:** limited exercise equipment. **Guest Services:** valet laundry, area transportation-within 5 mi. **Business Services:** meeting rooms, fax. **Cards:** AX, CB, DC, DS, MC, VI. **Special Amenities:** free expanded continental breakfast and free local telephone calls.

SOME UNITS
FEE

HAMPTON INN   *Book at aaa.com*
Phone: (757)989-8977 [5]

Small-scale Hotel

All Year   1P: $94-$119
Location: I-64, exit 256B, just e on Victory Blvd (US 17). Located in the Kiln Creek Shopping Center. 151 Ottis St 23602. Fax: 757/989-5882. **Facility:** 80 one-bedroom standard units. 5 stories, interior corridors. *Bath:* combo or shower only. **Parking:** on-site. **Amenities:** dual phone lines, voice mail, irons, hair dryers. **Pool(s):** heated indoor. **Leisure Activities:** whirlpool, exercise room. **Guest Services:** valet and coin laundry, area transportation. **Business Services:** meeting rooms, business center. **Cards:** AX, DC, DS, MC, VI.

SOME UNITS

HAMPTON INN & SUITES   *Book at aaa.com*
Phone: (757)249-0001 [6]

Small-scale Hotel

All Year   1P: $89-$149   2P: $89-$149
Location: I-64, exit 255A, just s. Located across from Patrick Henry Mall. 12251 Jefferson Ave 23602. Fax: 757/249-3911. **Facility:** 120 units. 90 one-bedroom standard units. 30 one-bedroom suites ($109-$159) with kitchens. 4 stories, interior corridors. *Bath:* combo or shower only. **Parking:** on-site. **Amenities:** high-speed Internet, dual phone lines, voice mail, irons, hair dryers. *Some:* CD players. **Pool(s):** outdoor. **Leisure Activities:** exercise room. **Guest Services:** sundries, valet and coin laundry, area transportation-within 3 mi. **Business Services:** meeting rooms, business center. **Cards:** AX, DC, DS, MC, VI. **Special Amenities:** free expanded continental breakfast and free newspaper.

SOME UNITS
FEE FEE

HILTON GARDEN INN   *Book at aaa.com*
Phone: (757)947-1080 [7]

Small-scale Hotel

All Year   1P: $99-$159   2P: $99-$159
Location: I-64, exit 256B, just right. 180 Regal Way 23602. Fax: b57/947-1081. **Facility:** 122 one-bedroom standard units. 3 stories, interior corridors. *Bath:* combo or shower only. **Parking:** on-site. **Terms:** cancellation fee imposed, package plans. **Amenities:** high-speed Internet, dual phone lines, voice mail, irons, hair dryers. **Pool(s):** heated indoor. **Leisure Activities:** whirlpool, exercise room. **Guest Services:** sundries, valet and coin laundry. **Business Services:** meeting rooms, business center. **Cards:** AX, CB, DC, DS, MC, VI.

SOME UNITS

(See map and index starting on p. 707)

HOLIDAY INN-EXPRESS — *Book at aaa.com*
Phone: (757)887-3300

(AAA) (SAVE)

3/1-9/4 [ECP]	1P: $79-$129	2P: $79-$129	XP: $10	F18
9/5-2/28 [ECP]	1P: $59-$99	2P: $59-$99	XP: $10	F18

Location: I-64, exit 250A (SR 105/Ft Eustis Blvd S) to US 60, then 0.3 mi w. 16890 Warwick Blvd 23603. Fax: 757/887-0300. **Facility:** 57 one-bedroom standard units, some with efficiencies. 5 stories, interior Small-scale Hotel corridors. *Bath:* combo or shower only. **Parking:** on-site. **Terms:** cancellation fee imposed. **Amenities:** dual phone lines, voice mail, irons, hair dryers. **Pool(s):** outdoor. **Leisure Activities:** exercise room. **Guest Services:** valet and coin laundry, airport transportation-Newport News/Williamsburg Airport. **Business Services:** meeting rooms, business center. **Cards:** AX, DC, DS, MC, VI. **Special Amenities:** free expanded continental breakfast and free local telephone calls.

SOME UNITS
(S) (D) ✈ (&M) (&) ≋ (※) (DATA PORT) (▣) / (✕) (VCR) (▤) (▦) /

HOLIDAY INN HOTEL & SUITES — *Book at aaa.com*
Phone: (757)596-6417 **10**

(AAA) (SAVE)

All Year | 1P: $99-$139 | 2P: $99-$139 | XP: $10 | F18

Location: I-64, exit 258B. 943 J Clyde Morris Blvd 23601. Fax: 757/596-6199. **Facility:** 122 units. 103 one-bedroom standard units. 19 one-bedroom suites ($139-$189). 5 stories, interior corridors. *Bath:* combo or shower only. **Parking:** on-site. **Terms:** cancellation fee imposed, package plans. **Amenities:** video games, Small-scale Hotel high-speed Internet, dual phone lines, voice mail, safes, irons, hair dryers. *Some:* DVD players, fax. **Dining:** 6-10 am, 11-2 & 5-9 pm, cocktails. **Pool(s):** heated indoor. **Leisure Activities:** exercise room. **Business Services:** meeting rooms. **Guest Services:** sundries, valet and coin laundry, area transportation-within 5 mi. **Business Services:** meeting rooms. **Cards:** AX, CB, DC, DS, MC, VI. **Special Amenities:** free continental breakfast and free newspaper.

SOME UNITS
(S) (D) ✈ (¶↑) (&M) (&) (∅) ≋ (VCR) (※) (DATA PORT) (▣) / (✕) (▤) (▦) /

HOST INN
Phone: 757-599-3303 **9**

(AAA) (SAVE)

All Year | 1P: $45-$80 | 2P: $50-$90 | XP: $8 | D6

Location: I-64, exit 258B, 0.8 mi n. 985 J Clyde Morris Blvd 23601. Fax: 757/591-0405. **Facility:** 50 one-bedroom standard units. 2 stories (no elevator), exterior corridors. **Parking:** on-site. **Terms:** pets ($15 deposit, $8 extra charge). **Pool(s):** outdoor. **Business Services:** fax. **Cards:** AX, DC, DS, MC, VI.

Motel

SOME UNITS
(▱) (¶↑) ≋ (※) (DATA PORT) (▤) (▦) / (✕) (VCR) /
FEE

HOWARD JOHNSON EXPRESS — *Book at aaa.com*
Phone: (757)877-7000 **1**

(AAA) (SAVE)

6/1-9/1 [ECP]	1P: $79-$109	2P: $79-$109	XP: $10	F16
3/1-5/31 [ECP]	1P: $69-$89	2P: $69-$89	XP: $10	F16
9/2-2/28 [ECP]	1P: $49-$69	2P: $59-$69	XP: $10	F16

Location: I-64, exit 255, 2.3 mi e on US 143 (Jefferson Ave). 12880 Jefferson Ave 23608. Fax: 757/872-7303. Motel **Facility:** 40 one-bedroom standard units, some with whirlpools. 2 stories (no elevator), exterior corridors. **Parking:** on-site. **Terms:** cancellation fee imposed. **Amenities:** safes (fee), irons, hair dryers. **Pool(s):** outdoor. **Leisure Activities:** sauna, whirlpool, picnic & grill area, exercise room. **Guest Services:** coin laundry. **Business Services:** meeting rooms. **Cards:** AX, DS, MC, VI. **Special Amenities:** free expanded continental breakfast and free local telephone calls.

SOME UNITS
(S) (D) ≋ (✕) (▤) (▦) (▣) / (✕) (DATA PORT) /

MICROTEL INN — *Book at aaa.com*
Phone: (757)249-8355 **8**

(AAA) (SAVE)

4/1-9/30	1P: $60-$99	2P: $70-$99
3/1-3/31	1P: $60-$70	2P: $70-$80
10/1-2/28	1P: $50-$60	2P: $70-$80

Location: I-64, exit 255A, 0.5 mi s to Operations Dr, then just w. 501 Operations Dr 23602. Fax: 757/249-8874. Small-scale Hotel **Facility:** 89 one-bedroom standard units. 3 stories, interior corridors. *Bath:* combo or shower only. **Parking:** on-site. **Terms:** weekly rates available, package plans. **Amenities:** voice mail, irons. **Guest Services:** valet laundry. **Business Services:** fax. **Cards:** AX, DC, DS, MC, VI. **Special Amenities:** free expanded continental breakfast and free local telephone calls.

SOME UNITS
(S) (D) (¶↑) (&M) (&) (∅) (※) (DATA PORT) / (✕) (▤) (▦) /
FEE FEE

MULBERRY INN — *Book at aaa.com*
Phone: (757)887-3000

(AAA) (SAVE)

3/1-9/4 [ECP]	1P: $79-$129	2P: $79-$129	XP: $10	F18
9/5-2/28 [ECP]	1P: $59-$99	2P: $59-$99	XP: $10	F18

Location: I-64, exit 250A (SR 105/Ft Eustis Blvd S) s to US 60, then 0.3 mi w. Located in a quiet area. 16890 Warwick Blvd 23603. Fax: 757/887-3665. **Facility:** 101 one-bedroom standard units, some with efficiencies. 2 stories Small-scale Hotel (no elevator), interior/exterior corridors. **Parking:** on-site, winter plug-ins. **Terms:** package plans. **Amenities:** voice mail, irons, hair dryers. **Pool(s):** outdoor. **Leisure Activities:** exercise room. **Guest Services:** valet and coin laundry, airport transportation-Newport News/Williamsburg Airport. **Business Services:** meeting rooms, business center. **Cards:** AX, DC, DS, MC, VI. **Special Amenities:** free expanded continental breakfast and free local telephone calls. *(See color ad p 933)*

SOME UNITS
(S) (D) ✈ ≋ (※) (DATA PORT) (▤) (▦) (▣) / (✕) (▦) /

POINT PLAZA - SUITES & CONFERENCE HOTEL — *Book at aaa.com*
Phone: (757)599-4460 **11**

(AAA) (SAVE)

All Year | 1P: $69-$129 | | XP: $10 | F18

Location: I-64, exit 258B, just n on US 17. 950 J Clyde Morris Blvd 23601. Fax: 757/599-4336. **Facility:** 150 units. 80 one-bedroom standard units. 70 one-bedroom suites ($139-$189) with kitchens, some with whirlpools. 2-4 stories, interior/exterior corridors. **Parking:** on-site. **Terms:** cancellation fee imposed, package plans. Small-scale Hotel **Amenities:** dual phone lines, voice mail, safes, irons, hair dryers. **Dining:** 6 am-9 pm, cocktails. **Pool(s):** heated indoor/outdoor. **Leisure Activities:** pool games, barbecue pavilion, exercise room. **Guest Services:** valet and coin laundry, area transportation-Amtrak. **Business Services:** conference facilities, fax. **Cards:** AX, CB, DC, DS, MC, VI. **Special Amenities:** free local telephone calls. *(See color ad p 933)*

SOME UNITS
(S) (D) ✈ (¶↑) (Y) (∅) ≋ (✕) (※) (DATA PORT) (▣) / (✕) (VCR) (▤) (▦) /
FEE FEE FEE

(See map and index starting on p. 707)

RAMADA INN-NEWPORT NEWS/HAMPTON   *Book at aaa.com*   **Phone:** (757)826-4500   **14**

3/16-9/15	1P: $69-$129	2P: $69-$129	XP: $10	F12
3/1-3/15 & 9/16-2/28	1P: $59-$79	2P: $59-$79	XP: $10	F12

Small-scale Hotel   **Location:** On US 17, just nw of jct Mercury Blvd (US 258). 6128 Jefferson Ave 23605. Fax: 757/826-2831. **Facility:** 159 one-bedroom standard units, some with efficiencies (no utensils). 5 stories, interior corridors. **Parking:** on-site. **Terms:** weekly rates available. **Amenities:** voice mail, irons, hair dryers. **Pool(s):** outdoor. **Leisure Activities:** exercise room. **Guest Services:** valet and coin laundry. **Business Services:** conference facilities, business center. **Cards:** AX, DC, DS, MC, VI.

SOME UNITS
(ASK) (S/D) ✈ 🍴 🍸 (&M) 🛥 📷 DATA PORT 💻 / ✕ 🍽 📷 / FEE FEE

TRAVELODGE   *Book at aaa.com*   **Phone:** (757)874-4100   **3**

AAA (SAVE)

All Year   1P: $55-$85   2P: $65-$95   XP: $5   F12

Motel   **Location:** I-64, exit 255B, 1 mi w to Bland Blvd, 1 mi s to Warwick Blvd, then just n. Located in a commercial area. 13700 Warwick Blvd 23602. Fax: 757/898-4765. **Facility:** 48 one-bedroom standard units, some with efficiencies (no utensils). 2 stories (no elevator), exterior corridors. **Parking:** on-site. **Terms:** weekly rates available, $1 service charge. **Business Services:** fax. **Cards:** AX, DS, MC, VI. **Special Amenities:** free local telephone calls and free newspaper.

SOME UNITS
(S/D) 🍴 (&M) 📷 DATA PORT 💻 / ✕ 🍽 📷 /

------- **WHERE TO DINE** -------

99 MAIN   **Dinner:** $14-$28   **Phone:** 757/599-9885   **14**

American   **Location:** Jct Warwick Blvd; in Hilton Village. 99 Main St 23601. **Hours:** 5 pm-9:30 pm, Fri & Sat-10:30 pm. Closed major holidays; also Sun & Mon. **Reservations:** suggested, weekends. **Features:** In the heart of historic Hilton Village, the stylish, sophisticated spot seats diners in cool, paneled booths in the bar or banquettes in the upscale dining room. Fantastic seasonal dishes reflect a decidedly European bistro flair. Dressy casual; cocktails. **Parking:** street. **Cards:** AX, MC, VI.

🍸 ✕

AL FRESCO RISTORANTE   **Lunch:** $7-$11   **Dinner:** $7-$18   **Phone:** 757/873-0644   **9**

Italian   **Location:** I-64, exit 255A, 2 mi s; in Oyster Point Square. 11710 Jefferson Ave 23606. **Hours:** 11 am-3 & 5-10 pm, Sat from 5 pm. Closed major holidays; also Sun. **Features:** Decorated in soothing shades of pink with a Mediterranean mural lining one wall, the casual and charming spot offers a satisfying menu of Italian favorites. Casual dress; cocktails. **Parking:** on-site. **Cards:** AX, DS, MC, VI.

CITIES GRILL   **Lunch:** $6-$10   **Dinner:** $13-$20   **Phone:** 757/595-6085   **8**

American   **Location:** I-64, exit 255A, 3 mi s on Jefferson Ave; in Commerce Plaza; Shops at Barnard Village. 605 Pilot House Dr 23606. **Hours:** 11 am-3 & 5-10 pm, Thurs & Fri-11 pm, Sat noon-3 & 5-11 pm. Closed major holidays. **Reservations:** suggested, weekends. **Features:** The modern American bistro changes its menu seasonally to spotlight the specialties of three or four American cities and their distinctive cuisines. Steak, seafood and pasta serve as a foundation for many creative dishes. Casual dress; cocktails. **Parking:** on-site. **Cards:** AX, DS, MC, VI.

🍸 ✕

COWBOY SYD'S   **Lunch:** $8-$13   **Dinner:** $18-$30   **Phone:** 757/599-5800   **5**

American   **Location:** I-64, exit 255A, 2.3 mi s on Jefferson Ave, just w on Loftis Blvd; in Port Warwick. 3150 William Styron Sq N 23606. **Hours:** 11 am-3 & 5-10 pm, Fri-11 pm, Sat 5 pm-11 pm, Sun 5 pm-10 pm. Closed major holidays. **Reservations:** required. **Features:** A beloved local chef mixes his quirky down-South sensibilities with his sophisticated modern cuisine and love of fine wine. The setting is modern and sleek, and includes sidewalk dining weather permitting. Dressy casual; cocktails. **Parking:** on-site. **Cards:** AX, MC, VI.

(&M) 🍸 ✕

THE CRAB SHACK   **Lunch:** $6-$20   **Dinner:** $6-$20   **Phone:** 757/245-2722   **15**

Seafood   **Location:** I-64, exit Mercury Blvd, 3.7 mi s, at foot of James River Bridge at Huntington Park. 7601 River Rd 23607. **Hours:** 11 am-11:30 pm. Closed: 11/24, 12/25. **Features:** On the shores of the James River, the restaurant offers prime spots on the deck from which to view sunsets and the parade of fishermen. Representative of local seafood are shrimp and crab cakes. Casual dress; cocktails. **Parking:** on-site. **Cards:** AX, DC, DS, MC, VI.

(&M) ✕

EL MARIACHI RESTAURANT & CANTINA   **Lunch:** $4-$10   **Dinner:** $5-$10   **Phone:** 757/596-4933   **11**

Mexican   **Location:** I-64, exit 258A, 1 mi s. 660 J Clyde Morris Blvd 23601. **Hours:** 11 am-10 pm, Fri-11 pm, Sat noon-11 pm, Sun noon-10 pm. Closed major holidays. **Features:** Complete with a sunny deck out front, the restaurant has created a cozy spot from a former burger joint. Traditional favorites line the menu on their own or on combination platters. Casual dress; beer & wine only. **Parking:** on-site. **Cards:** AX, DC, DS, MC, VI.

✕

KAPPO NARA SEAFOOD & SUSHI RESTAURANT   **Lunch:** $5-$10   **Dinner:** $10-$20   **Phone:** 757/249-5395   **3**

Ethnic   **Location:** I-64, exit 255A, 1 mi s on Jefferson Ave, then just w. 550 Oyster Point Rd 23602. **Hours:** 11 am-2 & 5-10 pm, Sat 5 pm-11 pm, Sun 5 pm-10 pm. Closed: 7/4, 11/24, 12/25. **Features:** Excellent, thick pieces of sushi, as well as teriyaki, tempura and other dishes, make up the menu at the quiet, restful restaurant. The professional wait staff in black and white attire provides prompt, friendly service and excellent follow-up. Casual dress; cocktails. **Parking:** on-site. **Cards:** AX, MC, VI.

✕

KYUNG SUNG KOREAN RESTAURANT   **Lunch:** $6-$16   **Dinner:** $8-$16   **Phone:** 757/877-2797   **1**

Korean   **Location:** I-64, exit 255B, 1 mi w to Bland Blvd, 1 mi s to Warwick Blvd, then just n. 13748 Warwick Blvd 23602. **Hours:** 11 am-10 pm. Closed major holidays. **Features:** The setting is simple, but diners are floored by the amount of spicy vegetable sides that come with dishes such as grilled short ribs, chicken bulgogi and kimchee soup. Casual dress. **Parking:** on-site. **Cards:** MC, VI.

✕

(See map and index starting on p. 707)

MIKE'S PLACE
American
Lunch: $5-$9   **Dinner:** $9-$16   **Phone:** 757/599-5500   ⑫
Location: I-64, exit 258A, 2.5 mi s on J Clyde Morris Blvd, then 1.5 mi e; in Warwick Village Shopping Center. 11006 Warwick Blvd, Unit 458 23601. **Hours:** 11 am-10 pm, Fri & Sat-11 pm. Closed: 11/24, 12/25; also Sun 5/31-9/6. **Features:** The laid-back eatery is serious about satisfying hunger and offering comfort. Customers unwind in leather armchairs in the lounge while noshing on such temptations as juicy one-pound burgers, crab dip, prime rib and local seafood. Casual dress; cocktails. **Parking:** on-site. **Cards:** AX, DC, DS, MC, VI.

NAWAB INDIAN CUISINE
Indian
Lunch: $5-$7   **Dinner:** $7-$12   **Phone:** 757/591-9200   ⑩
Location: I-64, exit 255A, 2 mi s; in Oyster Point Square. 11712-K Jefferson Ave 23606. **Hours:** 11:30 am-2:30 & 5-10 pm, Fri & Sat-10:30 pm, Sun noon-3 pm. Closed major holidays. **Features:** Tandoor specialties and bread baked in a clay oven are at the centerpiece of a traditional menu of curried, lamb and vegetarian dishes. The soothing environment features instrumental music and Eastern art. A weekday buffet draws a devoted lunch clientele. Casual dress; cocktails. **Parking:** on-site. **Cards:** AX, DC, DS, MC, VI.

PLAZA AZTECA
Mexican
Lunch: $6-$13   **Dinner:** $6-$13   **Phone:** 757/249-5299   ④
Location: I-64, exit 255, 1.1 mi se. 12099 Jefferson Ave 23606. **Hours:** 11:30 am-10 pm. Closed major holidays. **Features:** The festive Mexican decor includes serapes and a chandelier crafted from Corona bottles. Choose from among the many combination platters prepared with traditional and unusual Mexican specialties. The atmosphere is welcoming to families. Casual dress. **Parking:** on-site. **Cards:** AX, MC, VI.

ROCKY MOUNT BARBECUE
Barbecue
Lunch: $5-$9   **Dinner:** $5-$9   **Phone:** 757/596-0243   ⑬
Location: I-64, exit 255A, 5.6 mi s. 10113 Jefferson Ave 23605. **Hours:** 11 am-8:30 pm, Fri-9 pm. Closed major holidays; also Sat & Sun. **Features:** Down-home favorites, such as meatloaf and Brunswick stew, complement North Carolina-style barbecue pork sandwiches. Casual dress. **Parking:** on-site. **Cards:** AX, DC, DS, MC, VI.

SAMURAI SUSHI & HIBACHI RESTAURANT
Japanese
Lunch: $8-$15   **Dinner:** $15-$28   **Phone:** 757/249-4400   ②
Location: I-64, exit 255A, just s; in Jefferson Green Shopping Center. 12233 Jefferson Ave 23602. **Hours:** 11:30 am-2 & 4-10 pm, Fri & Sat-11 pm. **Reservations:** accepted. **Features:** Patrons can choose from seats at the sushi bar or the teppanyaki tables, where chefs entertain with knife tricks while cooking up delicious shrimp, steak and chicken specialties. Casual dress; cocktails. **Parking:** on-site. **Cards:** AX, DS, MC, VI.

SCHLESINGER'S CHOPHOUSE
Steak House
Lunch: $7-$20   **Dinner:** $17-$39   **Phone:** 757/599-4700   ⑥
Location: I-64, exit 255A, 2.4 mi s on Jefferson Ave to Port Warwick. 1106 William Styron Sq 23606. **Hours:** 11 am-2:30 & 4:30-10 pm, Fri & Sat-11 pm, Sun-9 pm. Closed: 1/1, 12/25. **Reservations:** suggested. **Features:** The decor is sleek and sophisticated at the new steakhouse, which carries out a literary twist. Juicy prime steaks, which are at the heart of the menu, are accented by excellent au gratin potatoes, great breads and distinctive salads. A lengthy wine list, skillful staff and cigar lounge round out the offerings. Dressy casual; cocktails. **Parking:** on-site. **Cards:** AX, DC, DS, MC, VI.

THE TAPAS LOUNGE
American
Lunch: $5-$12   **Dinner:** $5-$12   **Phone:** 757/594-9484   ⑦
Location: I-64, exit 255A, 2.3 mi s on Jefferson Ave, just w on Loftis Blvd; in Port Warwick. 141 Herman Melville Ave 23606. **Hours:** 11 am-2 & 4:30-10 pm, Fri-midnight, Sat 4:30 pm-midnight, Sun 4:30 pm-10 pm. Closed: Mon. **Reservations:** accepted. **Features:** Patrons can sip a custom champagne cocktail while sampling the wide variety of internationally influenced tapas specialties. The chic lounge and sidewalk cafe overlooks the square. Casual dress; cocktails. **Parking:** on-site. **Cards:** DS, MC, VI.

───────── ***The following restaurant has not been evaluated by AAA*** ─────────
but is listed for your information only.

BOXWOOD INN
[fyi]
Phone: 757/888-8854
Not evaluated. **Location:** I-64, exit 247 (Lee Hall) to Yorktown Rd. 10 Elmhurst 23603. **Features:** The laid-back comfort of this historic inn makes it a charming place to stop for lunch.

NORFOLK pop. 234,403   (See map and index starting on p. 710)

─── **WHERE TO STAY** ───

BED & BREAKFAST THE HISTORIC PAGE HOUSE INN

Phone: (757)625-5033   🔳13

AAA SAVE

▽▽▽ ▽▽▽

Bed & Breakfast

All Year [BP]   1P: $140-$225   2P: $140-$225   XP: $30

Location: I-264, exit 9, 1.4 mi n on Waterside Dr to Olney Rd, just w to Mowbray Arch, then just s; in the Ghent historic district. Located adjacent to the Chrysler Museum. 323 Fairfax Ave 23507. Fax: 757/623-9451. **Facility:** Once on the verge of condemnation, this Georgian Revival mansion was restored in 1990 and now shines with detailed woodwork and antique appointments. Smoke free premises. 7 units. 5 one-bedroom standard units, some with whirlpools. 2 one-bedroom suites ($165-$225) with whirlpools. 3 stories (no elevator), interior corridors. **Bath:** combo or shower only. **Parking:** on-site. **Terms:** 2 night minimum stay - seasonal, age restrictions may apply, 7 day cancellation notice, small pets only ($25 extra charge, owner's pets on premises). **Amenities:** video library, high-speed Internet, irons, hair dryers. *Some:* CD players. **Leisure Activities:** bicycles, limited exercise equipment. *Fee:* massage. **Guest Services:** valet laundry. **Business Services:** meeting rooms, fax. **Cards:** AX, MC, VI. **Special Amenities:** free full breakfast and free newspaper.

SOME UNITS

[S/D] 🛏 ✕ ✕ ✕ 📷 [DATA PORT] / [VCR] 🔋 /
      FEE

BEST WESTERN-CENTER INN   *Book at aaa.com*

Phone: (757)461-6600   🔳21

AAA SAVE

▽▽▽ ▽▽▽

Small-scale Hotel

4/1-10/31 [ECP]   1P: $89-$149   2P: $89-$149   XP: $10   F12
3/1-3/31 & 11/1-2/28 [ECP]   1P: $69-$99   2P: $69-$99   XP: $10   F12

Location: I-264, exit 13B, on US 13. 235 N Military Hwy 23502. Fax: 757/466-9093. **Facility:** 152 units. 150 one-bedroom standard units. 2 one-bedroom suites. 2 stories (no elevator), interior/exterior corridors. **Bath:** combo or shower only. **Parking:** on-site. **Terms:** 3 day cancellation notice-fee imposed. **Amenities:** video library (fee), voice mail, irons, hair dryers. *Some:* dual phone lines. **Dining:** The Grate Steak, see separate listing. **Pool(s):** outdoor, heated indoor. **Leisure Activities:** sauna, whirlpool, exercise room. **Guest Services:** valet and coin laundry. **Business Services:** conference facilities, business center. **Cards:** AX, DC, DS, MC, VI. **Special Amenities:** free expanded continental breakfast and free local telephone calls.

SOME UNITS

[S/D] ✈ 🍴 🄳 📶 🏊 ✕ 📷 [DATA PORT] 💻 / ✕ [VCR] 🔋 🖨 /
                                                        FEE

(See map and index starting on p. 710)

BEST WESTERN HOLIDAY SANDS INN & SUITES · *Book at aaa.com* · Phone: (757)583-2621 · **1**

| | 5/27-9/30 | 1P: $99-$159 | 2P: $99-$159 | XP: $10 | F17 |
| | 3/1-5/26 & 10/1-2/28 | 1P: $49-$89 | 2P: $49-$89 | XP: $10 | F17 |

AAA SAVE ◇◇◇◇

Small-scale Hotel

Location: US 60, 4 mi e of Hampton Roads Bridge-Tunnel. 1330 E Ocean View Ave 23503. Fax: 757/587-7540. **Facility:** 86 units. 63 one-bedroom standard units, some with efficiencies. 23 one-bedroom suites with kitchens. 2-5 stories, exterior corridors. *Bath:* combo or shower only. **Parking:** on-site. **Terms:** 2 night minimum stay - seasonal and/or weekends, 3 day cancellation notice, package plans. **Amenities:** voice mail, irons, hair dryers. *Some:* dual phone lines. **Pool(s):** heated outdoor. **Leisure Activities:** exercise room. **Guest Services:** valet and coin laundry. **Business Services:** meeting rooms, fax. **Cards:** AX, CB, DC, DS, MC, VI. **Special Amenities:** free expanded continental breakfast and free newspaper. *(See color ad below)*

SOME UNITS

CLARION HOTEL JAMES MADISON · *Book at aaa.com* · Phone: (757)622-6682 · **16**

| | 5/1-10/31 | 1P: $89-$129 | 2P: $99-$139 | XP: $10 | F |
| | 3/1-4/30 & 11/1-2/28 | 1P: $79-$119 | 2P: $89-$129 | XP: $10 | F |

AAA SAVE ◇◇◇◇

Historic
Small-scale Hotel

Location: Jct Freemason St; downtown. 345 Granby St 23510. Fax: 757/623-5949. **Facility:** Some bathrooms and guest rooms are compact at this landmark hotel dating from 1907. 125 units. 117 one-bedroom standard units. 8 one-bedroom suites. 8 stories, interior corridors. *Bath:* combo or shower only. **Parking:** on-site (fee). **Terms:** package plans, pets ($25 fee). **Amenities:** video games, voice mail, irons, hair dryers. **Dining:** 6:30 am-10 pm, cocktails. **Leisure Activities:** exercise room. **Guest Services:** valet and coin laundry. **Business Services:** conference facilities, business center. **Cards:** AX, DC, DS, MC, VI.

SOME UNITS

COMFORT INN-NAVAL BASE · *Book at aaa.com* · Phone: (757)451-0000 · **3**

◇◇◇◇

	4/1-8/31 [ECP]	1P: $89-$119	2P: $89-$119	
	9/1-1/31 [ECP]	1P: $79-$99	2P: $79-$99	
	3/1-3/31 & 2/1-2/28 [ECP]	1P: $69-$99	2P: $79-$99	XP: $10	F13

Small-scale Hotel

Location: I-64, exit 276 (I-564/Terminal Blvd), 2.5 mi w to Hampton Blvd, then 0.5 mi n. 8051 Hampton Blvd 23505. Fax: 757/451-8394. **Facility:** 120 one-bedroom standard units. 2 stories (no elevator), exterior corridors. **Parking:** on-site. **Terms:** cancellation fee imposed. **Amenities:** video games, irons, hair dryers. **Pool(s):** heated indoor. **Leisure Activities:** whirlpool. **Guest Services:** valet and coin laundry. **Business Services:** fax. **Cards:** AX, DC, DS, MC, VI.

SOME UNITS

COURTYARD BY MARRIOTT · *Book at aaa.com* · Phone: (757)963-6000 · **19**

◇◇◇

| | 6/1-10/31 | 1P: $159-$189 | 2P: $159-$189 | |
| | 3/1-5/31 & 11/1-2/28 | 1P: $149-$179 | 2P: $149-$179 | |

Small-scale Hotel

Location: Between Paul Blvd and Bank St; downtown. 520 Plume St 23510. Fax: 757/963-6001. **Facility:** 140 units. 137 one-bedroom standard units, some with whirlpools. 3 one-bedroom suites ($189-$199). 8 stories, interior corridors. *Bath:* combo or shower only. **Parking:** on-site (fee) and valet. **Amenities:** high-speed Internet, dual phone lines, voice mail, irons, hair dryers. **Pool(s):** heated indoor. **Leisure Activities:** whirlpool, exercise room. **Guest Services:** sundries, valet and coin laundry. **Business Services:** meeting rooms, PC. **Cards:** AX, CB, DC, DS, JC, MC, VI.

SOME UNITS

(See map and index starting on p. 710)

DOUBLETREE HOTEL-NORFOLK   *Book at aaa.com*   **Phone: (757)461-9192**   **17**
　　　　　　　　6/1-8/31　　　　　　1P: $109-$229　　　　　　　　XP: $10　　　　　F17
　　　　　　　　9/1-10/31　　　　　　1P: $99-$179　　　　　　　　XP: $10　　　　　F17
Small-scale Hotel 3/1-5/31 & 11/1-2/28 1P: $89-$139　　　　　　　　XP: $10　　　　　F17
Location: I-264, exit 13B (Military Hwy). Located in Military Circle Mall. 880 N Military Hwy, Suite 35 23502. **Fax:** 757/461-8290. **Facility:** 208 units. 200 one-bedroom standard units. 8 one-bedroom suites ($199-$329). 14 stories, interior corridors. **Bath:** combo or shower only. **Parking:** on-site. **Terms:** 3 day cancellation notice-fee imposed, package plans. **Amenities:** video games, high-speed Internet, voice mail, irons, hair dryers. *Some:* dual phone lines. **Pool(s):** outdoor. **Leisure Activities:** exercise room. **Guest Services:** sundries, valet and coin laundry. **Business Services:** conference facilities. **Cards:** AX, CB, DC, DS, MC, VI. *(See color ad below)*

SOME UNITS
[ASK] [SD] [✈] [🍴] [Y] [⟲M] [♿] [🎣] [➲] [🐾] [DATA PORT] [🖥] / [✕] [🔒] [🖨] /

ECONO LODGE AIRPORT   *Book at aaa.com*   **Phone: (757)855-3116**   **6**
　　　　　　　　5/1-9/10　　　　　　1P: $60-$150　　2P: $60-$150　　XP: $5　　　　　F18
　　　　　　　　3/1-4/30 & 9/11-2/28 1P: $50-$75　　2P: $50-$75　　XP: $5　　　　　F18
Motel
Location: I-64, exit 281 (Military Hwy) westbound, just n: exit 281B (Robin Hood Rd) eastbound, just n to Military Hwy, then just ne. 3343 N Military Hwy 23518. **Fax:** 757/857-6413. **Facility:** 48 one-bedroom standard units. 2 stories (no elevator), exterior corridors. **Parking:** on-site. **Terms:** cancellation fee imposed, small pets only ($25 fee). **Amenities:** *Some:* hair dryers. **Guest Services:** coin laundry. **Business Services:** fax. **Cards:** AX, CB, DC, DS, MC, VI.

SOME UNITS
[ASK] [SD] [✈] [🐾] [🎣] [🔒] [🖨] / [✕] [DATA PORT] [🖥] /
　　　　　　　FEE

FREEMASON INN   [AAA] [SAVE]   **Phone: 757/963-7000**   **15**
　　　　　　　All Year　　　　　　　1P: $145-$245　　2P: $145-$245
Location: Jct of W Brambleton Ave and Botetourt St. Located in West Freemason Historic District. 411 W York St
Historic Bed 23510. **Fax:** 757/233-1897. **Facility:** Set in the historic district, this elegant inn is known for its fine artwork,
& Breakfast   an English courtyard garden and sumptuous five-course breakfasts. Smoke free premises. 4 one-bedroom standard units, some with whirlpools. 3 stories (no elevator), interior corridors. **Parking:** street. **Terms:** 2 night minimum stay - seasonal, age restrictions may apply, 14 day cancellation notice. **Amenities:** high-speed Internet, irons, hair dryers. *Some:* DVD players, CD players. **Business Services:** fax. **Cards:** AX, MC, VI. **Special Amenities:** free full breakfast and preferred room (subject to availability with advance reservations).

[♿+] [✕] [DATA PORT]

HAMPTON INN NORFOLK NAVAL BASE   *Book at aaa.com*   **Phone: (757)489-1000**   **2**
[AAA] [SAVE] 4/1-10/31　　　　　　1P: $115-$129　　2P: $125-$139
　　　　　　　3/1-3/31 & 11/1-2/28 1P: $79-$109　　2P: $89-$119
Small-scale Hotel **Location:** I-64, exit 276 (I-564/Terminal Blvd), 2.5 mi w to Hampton Blvd, then 0.5 mi n. 8501 Hampton Blvd 23505. **Fax:** 757/489-4509. **Facility:** 117 one-bedroom standard units, some with efficiencies (no utensils). 4 stories, interior corridors. **Parking:** on-site. **Terms:** cancellation fee imposed. **Amenities:** voice mail, irons, hair dryers. **Pool(s):** heated indoor. **Leisure Activities:** whirlpool. **Guest Services:** valet laundry. **Business Services:** fax. **Cards:** AX, DS, MC. **Special Amenities:** free expanded continental breakfast and free local telephone calls. *(See color ad p 729)*

SOME UNITS
[SD] [🍴] [⟲M] [➲] [🐾] [♿+] [🎣] [DATA PORT] [🖥] / [✕] [VCR] [🔒] [🖨] /
　　　　　　　FEE　　　　　　　　　　　　　　　　　　　　　　　FEE   FEE

HILTON NORFOLK AIRPORT   *Book at aaa.com*   **Phone: (757)466-8000**   **11**
[AAA] [SAVE] 11/1-2/28　　　　　　1P: $199-$229　　2P: $199-$229　　XP: $15　　F18
　　　　　　　3/1-10/31　　　　　　1P: $179-$209　　2P: $179-$209　　XP: $15　　F18
Small-scale Hotel **Location:** I-64, exit 281 (Military Hwy), just s at jct US 13 and SR 165. 1500 N Military Hwy 23502. **Fax:** 757/466-8802. **Facility:** 249 units. 247 one-bedroom standard units, some with whirlpools. 2 two-bedroom suites. 6 stories, interior corridors. **Bath:** combo or shower only. **Parking:** on-site. **Amenities:** high-speed Internet (fee), dual phone lines, voice mail, honor bars, irons, hair dryers. **Dining:** 3 restaurants, 6 am-11 pm, cocktails, entertainment. **Pool(s):** outdoor. **Leisure Activities:** saunas, whirlpool, 2 lighted tennis courts, exercise room. **Guest Services:** gift shop, valet laundry, area transportation, beauty salon. **Business Services:** conference facilities, business center. **Cards:** AX, CB, DC, DS, JC, MC, VI. **Special Amenities:** free newspaper. *(See color ad p 729)*

SOME UNITS
[✈] [🍴] [24] [Y] [⟲M] [♿] [➲] [✕] [🎣] [DATA PORT] [🖥] / [✕] [🔒] [🖨] /
　　　　　　　　　　　　　　　　　　　　　　　　　　　　　　　　FEE   FEE

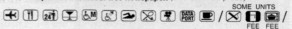

(See map and index starting on p. 710)

HOLIDAY INN SELECT   *Book at aaa.com*   Phone: (757)213-2231   🔟
▽▽▽▽ All Year   1P: $79-$159
Small-scale Hotel   **Location:** I-64 E, exit 281 (Military Hwy). 1570 N Military Hwy 23502. Fax: 757/213-2232. **Facility:** 147 units. 129 one-bedroom standard units, some with whirlpools. 18 one-bedroom suites. 5 stories, interior corridors. *Bath:* combo or shower only. **Parking:** on-site. **Terms:** 3 night minimum stay - seasonal. **Amenities:** video games, high-speed Internet, dual phone lines, voice mail, irons, hair dryers. *Some:* DVD players. **Pool(s):** heated indoor. **Leisure Activities:** whirlpool, exercise room. **Guest Services:** sundries, valet and coin laundry, area transportation. **Business Services:** conference facilities, business center. **Cards:** AX, CB, DC, DS, JC, MC, VI.

SOME UNITS
ASK 🛇 ✈ 🍽 🍸 ⚙ 🛋 ⚙ 🌊 ⚙ DATAPORT 📱 🖥 / ✕ VCR /

HOWARD JOHNSON NORFOLK AIRPORT   *Book at aaa.com*   Phone: (757)466-7474   ⑫
▽▽▽▽ 3/1-11/1   1P: $79-$139   2P: $79-$139   XP: $10   F
        11/2-2/28   1P: $59-$109   2P: $59-$109   XP: $10   F
Small-scale Hotel   **Location:** I-64, exit 281 (Military Hwy S), jct Princess Anne Rd. 1450 N Military Hwy 23502. Fax: 757/466-0117. **Facility:** 130 one-bedroom standard units. 2 stories (no elevator), exterior corridors. *Bath:* combo or shower only. **Parking:** on-site. **Amenities:** video games, voice mail, irons, hair dryers. **Pool(s):** outdoor. **Guest Services:** valet laundry. **Business Services:** fax. **Cards:** AX, CB, DC, DS, MC, VI. *(See color ad p 729)*

SOME UNITS
ASK 🛇 ✈ ⚙ 🌊 ⚙ DATAPORT 📱 / ✕ 🖥 🖥
                                                                                                FEE FEE

NORFOLK WATERSIDE MARRIOTT HOTEL   *Book at aaa.com*   Phone: (757)627-4200   ⑳
▽▽▽▽ All Year   1P: $99-$179   2P: $99-$179   XP: $20   F18
Large-scale Hotel   **Location:** Corner of Main and Atlantic sts; center of downtown. 235 E Main St 23510. Fax: 757/628-6452. **Facility:** 405 units. 404 one-bedroom standard units. 1 one-bedroom suite ($300-$900) with whirlpool. 23 stories, interior corridors. **Parking:** on-site (fee) and valet. **Terms:** check-in 4 pm, cancellation fee imposed. [AP], [BP], [CP], [ECP] & [MAP] meal plans available, package plans. **Amenities:** high-speed Internet (fee), voice mail, irons, hair dryers. *Some:* dual phone lines. **Pool(s):** heated indoor. **Leisure Activities:** saunas, whirlpools, exercise room. **Guest Services:** gift shop, valet and coin laundry. **Business Services:** conference facilities, business center. **Cards:** AX, DC, DS, MC, VI. *(See color ad below)*

SOME UNITS
ASK 🛇 🍽 🍸 ⚙ 🌊 ✕ ⚙ DATAPORT 📱 / ✕ 🖥 /

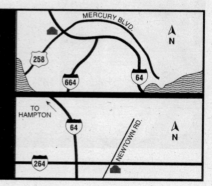

(See map and index starting on p. 710)

QUALITY SUITES LAKE WRIGHT   *Book at aaa.com*   Phone: (757)461-6251   **8**

4/1-9/15 [BP]	1P: $119-$159	2P: $119-$159	XP: $10	F18
9/16-2/28 [BP]	1P: $109-$149	2P: $109-$149	XP: $10	F18
3/1-3/31 [BP]	1P: $109-$139	2P: $109-$139	XP: $10	F18

Small-scale Hotel   **Location:** I-64, exit 282, just w on US 13. 6280 Northampton Blvd 23502. Fax: 757/461-5925. **Facility:** 127 one-bedroom suites, some with whirlpools. 5 stories, interior corridors. *Bath:* combo, shower or tub only. **Parking:** on-site. **Terms:** 3 day cancellation notice, pets ($35 fee). **Amenities:** high-speed Internet, dual phone lines, voice mail, safes (fee), irons, hair dryers. **Dining:** 5 pm-9 pm. **Pool(s):** heated indoor. **Leisure Activities:** exercise room. *Fee:* golf-18 holes. **Guest Services:** gift shop, valet and coin laundry, area transportation-shopping center. **Business Services:** meeting rooms, business center. **Cards:** AX, CB, DC, DS, JC, MC, VI. **Special Amenities:** free full breakfast and free local telephone calls. *(See color ad below)*

SOME UNITS

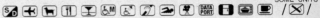
FEE

RADISSON HOTEL NORFOLK   *Book at aaa.com*   Phone: (757)627-5555   **14**

4/1-10/31	1P: $144-$166	2P: $144-$166	XP: $10	F17
3/1-3/31 & 11/1-2/28	1P: $129-$151	2P: $129-$151	XP: $10	F17

Small-scale Hotel   **Location:** Jct Brambleton Ave and St. Pauls Blvd; downtown. Located across from Scope Arena. 700 Monticello Ave 23510. Fax: 757/533-9651. **Facility:** 339 units. 332 one-bedroom standard units. 7 one-bedroom suites ($210-$250). 12 stories, interior corridors. *Bath:* combo or shower only. **Parking:** on-site. **Terms:** cancellation fee imposed, package plans, small pets only ($25 deposit). **Amenities:** video games, voice mail, irons, hair dryers. *Some:* high-speed Internet (fee). **Dining:** 6:30 am-10 pm, cocktails. **Pool(s):** outdoor. **Leisure Activities:** exercise room. **Guest Services:** gift shop, valet and coin laundry, area transportation-downtown, barber shop. **Business Services:** conference facilities, business center. **Cards:** AX, DC, DS, MC, VI. *(See color ad p 932 & below)*

SOME UNITS

FEE

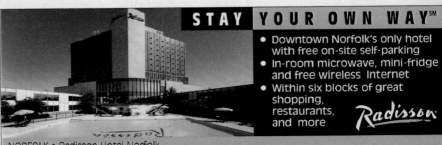

(See map and index starting on p. 710)

RESIDENCE INN BY MARRIOTT NORFOLK AIRPORT   *Book at aaa.com*
Phone: (757)333-3000   **9**

All Year   1P: $79-$159

Small-scale Hotel
Location: I-64, exit 281B (Military Hwy). 1590 N Military Hwy 23502. Fax: 757/333-3001. **Facility:** 130 units. 25 one-bedroom standard units with kitchens. 95 one- and 10 two-bedroom suites with kitchens. 5 stories, interior corridors. *Bath:* combo or shower only. **Parking:** on-site. **Terms:** 3 night minimum stay - seasonal, pets ($75 extra charge). **Amenities:** video games, high-speed Internet, dual phone lines, voice mail, irons, hair dryers. **Pool(s):** heated indoor. **Leisure Activities:** whirlpool, tennis court, exercise room, sports court. **Guest Services:** sundries, complimentary evening beverages: Mon-Fri, valet and coin laundry. **Business Services:** meeting rooms, business center. **Cards:** AX, CB, DC, DS, JC, MC, VI.

SOME UNITS

SHERATON NORFOLK WATERSIDE HOTEL   *Book at aaa.com*
Phone: (757)622-6664   **22**

All Year   1P: $79-$179   2P: $79-$179   XP: $15   F18

Large-scale Hotel
Location: I-264 to Waterside Dr; downtown. Located adjacent to Waterside Festival Marketplace. 777 Waterside Dr 23510. Fax: 757/625-8271. **Facility:** 445 units. 424 one-bedroom standard units. 21 one-bedroom suites ($179-$800). 10 stories, interior corridors. *Bath:* combo or shower only. **Parking:** on-site and valet. **Terms:** 3 day cancellation notice-fee imposed, package plans. **Amenities:** high-speed Internet (fee), dual phone lines, voice mail, irons, hair dryers. *Some:* fax. **Pool(s):** outdoor. **Leisure Activities:** exercise room. **Guest Services:** gift shop, valet laundry, area transportation. **Business Services:** conference facilities, business center. **Cards:** AX, DC, DS, JC, MC, VI.
(See color ad p 726)

SOME UNITS
FEE   FEE   FEE

SLEEP INN LAKE WRIGHT   *Book at aaa.com*
Phone: (757)461-1133   **7**

(AAA) (SAVE)
4/1-9/15 [CP]	1P: $99-$139	2P: $99-$139	XP: $10 F18
9/16-2/28 [CP]	1P: $89-$115	2P: $89-$115	XP: $10 F18
3/1-3/31 [CP]	1P: $89-$109	2P: $89-$109	XP: $10 F18

Small-scale Hotel
Location: I-64, exit 282, just w on US 13. 6280 Northampton Blvd 23502. Fax: 757/461-5925. **Facility:** 107 one-bedroom standard units. 3 stories, interior corridors. *Bath:* combo or shower only. **Parking:** on-site. **Terms:** 3 day cancellation notice, pets ($25 fee). **Amenities:** high-speed Internet, dual phone lines, voice mail, safes (fee), irons, hair dryers. **Dining:** 5 pm-9 pm. **Pool(s):** heated indoor. **Leisure Activities:** exercise room. *Fee:* golf-18 holes. **Guest Services:** gift shop, valet and coin laundry, area transportation-shopping. **Business Services:** meeting rooms, business center. **Cards:** AX, CB, DC, DS, JC, MC, VI. **Special Amenities: free continental breakfast and free local telephone calls.** *(See color ad p 731)*

SOME UNITS
FEE

SPRINGHILL SUITES BY MARRIOTT NORFOLK/VA BEACH   *Book at aaa.com*
Phone: (757)333-3100   **23**

3/1-12/31 [BP]	1P: $109-$169	2P: $109-$169
1/1-2/28 [BP]	1P: $99-$129	2P: $99-$129

Small-scale Hotel
Location: I-64, exit 284B (I-264 E), Newtown Rd S exit. 6350 Newtown Rd 23502. Fax: 757/333-3101. **Facility:** 131 one-bedroom standard units. 6 stories, interior corridors. *Bath:* combo or shower only. **Parking:** on-site. **Amenities:** high-speed Internet, dual phone lines, voice mail, irons, hair dryers. **Pool(s):** heated indoor. **Leisure Activities:** whirlpool, exercise room. **Guest Services:** sundries, valet and coin laundry. **Business Services:** meeting rooms, business center. **Cards:** AX, DC, DS, JC, MC, VI.

SOME UNITS

SUPER 8 MOTEL   *Book at aaa.com*
Phone: (757)588-7888   **5**

5/1-9/15	1P: $69-$89	2P: $79-$99
3/1-4/30 & 9/16-2/28	1P: $49-$69	2P: $59-$79

Motel
Location: US 60/Shore Dr, just n of jct Little Creek Rd. Located adjacent to Little Creek Naval Base, in Ocean View. 7940 Shore Dr 23518. Fax: 757/588-6783. **Facility:** 74 one-bedroom standard units. 3 stories, interior corridors. **Parking:** on-site. **Business Services:** fax. **Cards:** AX, CB, DC, DS, MC, VI.

SOME UNITS

TAZEWELL HOTEL AND SUITES   *Book at aaa.com*
Phone: (757)623-6200   **18**

(AAA) (SAVE)
3/31-9/30	1P: $109-$189	2P: $109-$189	XP: $10 F
3/1-3/30 & 10/1-2/28	1P: $89-$139	2P: $89-$139	XP: $10 F

Historic
Small-scale Hotel
Location: Jct Tazewell St; downtown. 245 Granby St 23510. Fax: 757/457-1516. **Facility:** This hotel dating from 1906 mixes historic architecture with updated neoclassic features. 57 units. 50 one-bedroom standard units. 7 one-bedroom suites ($149-$189). 7 stories, interior corridors. *Bath:* combo or shower only. **Parking:** on-site (fee). **Terms:** cancellation fee imposed. **Amenities:** video library, dual phone lines, voice mail, safes (fee), irons, hair dryers. **Dining:** Empire Little Bar & Bistro, see separate listing. **Leisure Activities:** exercise room. **Guest Services:** valet laundry. **Business Services:** meeting rooms, business center. **Cards:** AX, CB, DC, DS, MC, VI. **Special Amenities: free continental breakfast and free newspaper.**

SOME UNITS
FEE

TIDES INN   *Book at aaa.com*
Phone: (757)587-8781   **4**

(AAA) (SAVE)
6/17-9/5 [ECP]	1P: $65-$90	2P: $65-$95
5/1-6/16 [ECP]	1P: $55-$80	2P: $60-$80
3/1-4/30 & 9/6-2/28 [ECP]	1P: $50-$60	2P: $50-$60

Motel
Location: On US 60/Shore Dr, just n of jct Little Creek Rd and Little Creek Naval Base, Gate 1; in Ocean View. 7950 Shore Dr 23518. Fax: 757/480-6071. **Facility:** 100 one-bedroom standard units, some with efficiencies (no utensils). 2 stories, exterior corridors. **Parking:** on-site. **Terms:** cancellation fee imposed. **Amenities:** hair dryers. **Pool(s):** outdoor. **Leisure Activities:** exercise room. **Guest Services:** valet and coin laundry. **Business Services:** meeting rooms. **Cards:** AX, DC, MC, VI. *(See color ad p 769)*

SOME UNITS

(See map and index starting on p. 710)

———— **WHERE TO DINE** ————

THE 219
American

Lunch: $4-$7   **Dinner:** $11-$23   **Phone:** 757/627-2896   **51**
Location: At Granby and Brook sts; downtown. 219 Granby St 23510. **Hours:** 11:30 am-2:30 & 5-10 pm, Fri-11 pm, Sat 5 pm-11 pm, Sun 5 pm-9 pm. Closed major holidays. **Reservations:** suggested. **Features:** Contemporary, upbeat and located on a rejuvenated city block where diners enjoy modern dishes brushed by Asian, Cajun and other regional and international influences. The renowned banana white chocolate macadamia bread pudding is a must! Casual dress; cocktails. **Parking:** street. **Cards:** AX, DC, MC, VI.

456 FISH
Seafood

Lunch: $6-$11   **Dinner:** $15-$29   **Phone:** 757/625-4444   **38**
Location: Jct Bute St; downtown. 456 Granby St 23510. **Hours:** 11:30 am-2:30 & 5-10 pm, Fri-11 pm, Sat from 5 pm, Sun 5 pm-10 pm. Closed major holidays. **Reservations:** suggested, weekends. **Features:** The high-energy spot sits downtown at the junction of nostalgia and modern. Black-and-white photographs of Norfolk's past line the walls while a wall of water separates the space. Seafood is the specialty, and the menu lines up such favorites as the chefs' Bahamian grouper fingers and pan-seared tuna. Rack of lamb is another good choice. Casual dress; cocktails. **Parking:** on-site. **Cards:** AX, MC, VI.

AMALFI
Italian

Lunch: $6-$15   **Dinner:** $10-$23   **Phone:** 757/625-1262   **15**
Location: Jct 21st St; in Ghent. 2010 Colley Ave 23517. **Hours:** 10:30 am-midnight, Fri & Sat-2 am. Closed: 11/24, 12/25. **Reservations:** suggested. **Features:** This stylish new Italian cafe offers many options for guests. From a full service sit down meal of fresh pasta such as crab ravioli, veal, or other delights to an espresso bar, a market area, and gelato. Casual dress; cocktails. **Parking:** on-site. **Cards:** AX, DC, DS, MC, VI.

THE AZALEA INN
Greek

Lunch: $6-$12   **Dinner:** $6-$12   **Phone:** 757/587-4649   **4**
Location: Jct Shore Dr, 1.4 mi w; in Roosevelt Shopping Center. 2344 E Little Creek Rd 23518. **Hours:** 10 am-2 am. Closed: 11/24, 12/25. **Features:** The well-established, family-friendly spot has been offering Greek and American specialties and tasty pizza for as long as anyone in town can remember. Casual dress; cocktails. **Parking:** on-site. **Cards:** AX, MC, VI.

AZAR'S NATURAL FOODS
Mediterranean

Lunch: $6-$10   **Dinner:** $6-$10   **Phone:** 757/664-7955   **16**
Location: Jct 20th St; in Ghent. 2000 Colley Ave 23517. **Hours:** 10:30 am-9:30 pm, Fri & Sat 10 am-10 pm, Sun noon-8 pm. Closed major holidays. **Features:** A loyal and growing clientele in search of healthful, well-prepared Middle Eastern fare calls the restaurant home. Roll sandwiches, delicatessen staples and many vegetarian items (although meat is available) are specialties. Try the lentil, orzo and vegetable soup or grab items to go from the market. Casual dress; beer & wine only. **Parking:** on-site. **Cards:** AX, DS, MC, VI.

BAKER'S CRUST BREAD MARKET
American

Lunch: $5-$7   **Dinner:** $5-$20   **Phone:** 757/625-3600   **23**
Location: Jct Colley Ave and W 21st St, just e; in The Palace Shops. 330 W 21st St 23517. **Hours:** 8 am-10 pm, Fri & Sat-11 pm. Closed: 1/1, 11/24, 12/25. **Features:** Baker's offers sandwiches, soup and salad (served in a hollowed-out loaf of bread), or rotisserie-grilled items, supplemented by a short list of appetizers and entrees. In keeping with the bistro ambience, there's a crepe bar in the back. Expect a wait. Casual dress; beer & wine only. **Parking:** on-site. **Cards:** AX, DS, MC, VI.

BANGKOK GARDEN
Thai

Lunch: $5-$7   **Dinner:** $8-$17   **Phone:** 757/622-5047   **25**
Location: Jct Colley Ave, just e; in Ghent Palace Shops. 339 W 21st St 23517. **Hours:** 11 am-10 pm, Fri & Sat-10:30 pm, Sun noon-9 pm. Closed major holidays. **Features:** Stylish interior decorated with Thai artwork. Menu offers fresh, healthy authentic fare highlighting fresh seafood, chili peppers, curries, coconuts, tropical fruit and vegetarian dishes. Casual dress; beer & wine only. **Parking:** street. **Cards:** AX, DC, DS, MC, VI.

BLUE CRAB RESTAURANT
Seafood

Lunch: $6-$20   **Dinner:** $6-$20   **Phone:** 757/362-3133   **2**
Location: Jct Little Creek Rd, just n; in East Beach Marina. 4521 Pretty Lake Ave 23518. **Hours:** 4 pm-10 pm, Fri-11 pm, Sat 11 am-11 pm, Sun 11 am-10 pm. Closed major holidays. **Features:** From the verandah of the Florida-inspired restaurant, patrons can watch luxury yachts dock. Fresh Atlantic Ocean seafood is prepared in both traditional and modern ways. Fresh fish stuffed with blue crab dressing is a specialty. Casual dress; cocktails. **Parking:** on-site. **Cards:** AX, DS, MC, VI.

THE BLUE HIPPO
Pacific Rim

Dinner: $19-$29   **Phone:** 757/533-9664   **53**
Location: Between Plume St and City Hall; downtown. 147 Granby St 23510. **Hours:** 5:30 pm-10 pm, Fri & Sat-11 pm, Sun 5 pm-9 pm. Closed: 11/24, 12/25. **Reservations:** suggested. **Features:** Muted primary colors contribute to the striking art deco setting. The chef's creative cosmopolitan fare fuses ideas from Pacific Rim and the Caribbean with French influences. The menu changes every few months to highlight seasonal selections, but keep an eye out for exotic offerings, such as antelope or mako shark. The martini selection is extensive. Casual dress; cocktails. **Parking:** street. **Cards:** AX, DS, MC, VI.

BODEGA
Spanish

Dinner: $6-$10   **Phone:** 757/622-8527   **39**
Location: Jct W Charlotte St; downtown. 442 Granby St 23510. **Hours:** 5 pm-11 pm, Fri & Sat-2 am. Closed: 3/27, 11/24, 12/25. **Features:** A new addition to "restaurant row," Bodega is a fun place that's great for socializing. The tapas menu lays out an intriguing array of appetizer choices, enabling diners to share and sample many tastes. The hearty flavors of Spanish and Mediterranean cuisine punctuate delicious dishes. Casual dress; cocktails. **Parking:** on-site. **Cards:** AX, MC, VI.

(See map and index starting on p. 710)

CAFE ROSSO
▼▼▼
Regional
Italian

Lunch: $5-$9   **Dinner:** $7-$14   **Phone:** 757/627-2078   (29)
Location: Jct Colley Ave and W 21st St, just e. 123 W 21st St 23517. **Hours:** 11:30 am-2:30 & 5-9:30 pm, Fri-10 pm, Sat 5 pm-10 pm, Sun 5 pm-9 pm. Closed major holidays. **Reservations:** suggested, weekends. **Features:** This restaurant sports a European flair and an open kitchen which turn out specialty wood over pizza, unique pasta, and focaccia. Smoky pizza bears such toppers as the house's flavorful lamb sausage, or feta with artichokes, olives and garlic. There's also an array of inspired pasta dishes. Casual dress; cocktails. **Parking:** on-site. **Cards:** AX, MC, VI.

CASTALDI'S MARKET & GRILL
▼▼ ▼▼
Italian

Lunch: $7-$10   **Dinner:** $8-$19   **Phone:** 757/627-8700   (50)
Location: Downtown; in MacArthur Center. 300 Monticello Ave 23510. **Hours:** 11 am-10 pm, Fri & Sat-11 pm, Sun-9 pm. Closed: 11/24, 12/25. **Features:** Patrons can sample pizzas, pasta, veal and more, along with fresh Italian bread and roasted garlic. The talented staff are adept at serenades. Casual dress; cocktails; entertainment. **Parking:** on-site (fee). **Cards:** AX, DC, DS, MC, VI.

CLUB SODA
▼▼▼▼
International

Dinner: $16-$26   **Phone:** 757/200-7632   (49)
Location: Jct Granby St; downtown. 111 Tazewell St 23510. **Hours:** 5 pm-10 pm, Fri & Sat-11 pm. Closed major holidays. **Reservations:** suggested. **Features:** The sleek, super-cool restaurant brings metropolitan style to the city with its suede banquettes and lighted lounge floor. As modern as the decor is the fare, including such dishes as chilled tuna poke, foie gras stuffed dumplings and lobster pasta. Dressy casual; cocktails. **Parking:** street. **Cards:** AX, DS, MC, VI.

COBIA GRILL
▼▼▼
Seafood

Dinner: $11-$24   **Phone:** 757/640-8000   (46)
Location: Between Granby and Boush sts; downtown. 117 W Tazewell St 23510. **Hours:** 4 pm-11 pm. Closed: 11/24, 12/25; also Sun. **Reservations:** accepted. **Features:** The cozy spot uses nautical elements to set the tone for a menu that relies on the fruits of the sea. Specialties include crab cakes and at least two fresh catches of the day, but steak and any of the fresh salads are good choices, too. Casual dress; cocktails. **Parking:** street. **Cards:** AX, DS, MC, VI.

COGAN'S
▼▼▼
Pizza

Lunch: $5-$15   **Dinner:** $5-$15   **Phone:** 757/627-6428   (28)
Location: Jct Washington Pack; in Ghent. 1901 Colonial Ave 23517. **Hours:** 11 am-1:30 am. Closed major holidays. **Features:** The music may be loud and the styles alternative, but the pizza, buffalo shrimp and affordable pasta bowls can't be beat. Local bands often play at the small spot. Casual dress; cocktails. **Parking:** street. **Cards:** DS, MC, VI.

CORA
▼▼▼
Regional American

Lunch: $8-$16   **Dinner:** $10-$20   **Phone:** 757/625-6100   (17)
Location: Jct Colley Ave and W 21st St, just e; in Ghent. 723 W 21st St 23517. **Hours:** 11:30 am-2:30 & 5-10 pm, Sat & Sun-2:30 pm. Closed: 11/24, 12/25. **Reservations:** accepted. **Features:** "Uptown Southern chow" is how the restaurant describes its fare, which comprises such specialties as buttermilk fried chicken, buttermilk fried tomatoes, crab cakes and peach-bourbon pork. Casual dress; cocktails; entertainment. **Parking:** street. **Cards:** AX, DC, DS, MC, VI.

CRACKER'S LITTLE BAR & BISTRO
▼▼ ▼▼
American

Dinner: $5-$18   **Phone:** 757/640-0200   (12)
Location: Just w of jct Colley Ave; in Ghent. 821 W 21st St 23505. **Hours:** 5 pm-2 am. Closed: 11/24, 12/24, 12/25; also 12/31 & Super Bowl Sun. **Features:** The small spot serves numerous tasty dishes in equally small, appetizer-style portions designed for those who like to sample many tastes. Casual dress; cocktails. **Parking:** on-site. **Cards:** AX, DS, MC, VI.

D. C. CHASE'S
▼▼▼
American

Dinner: $7-$18   **Phone:** 757/622-7779   (27)
Location: Jct DeBree St; in Ghent. 328 W 20th St 23517. **Hours:** 5 pm-1:30 am. Closed major holidays. **Features:** In the heart of Ghent, the welcoming bar and live music spot offers seating on a heated patio, as well as in booths inside. The wide-ranging menu encompasses such offerings as burgers, lamb chops, ahi tuna and crab cakes. Casual dress; cocktails. **Parking:** on-site. **Cards:** AX, DC, DS, MC, VI.

DOG N' BURGER GRILLE
▼▼
American

Lunch: $5-$15   **Dinner:** $5-$15   **Phone:** 757/623-1667   (19)
Location: Jct with 20th St; in Ghent. 2001 Manteo St 23517. **Hours:** 11 am-9 pm. Closed major holidays; also Sun. **Features:** Although renovated, the vintage diner retains its nostalgic character, right down to the shiny chrome. Menu choices include delicious barbecue platters, succulent ribs, chili, pitas and, of course, the dogs and burgers that gave this place its name. **Parking:** street. **Cards:** MC, VI.

DOMO
▼▼ ▼▼
Japanese

Lunch: $8-$18   **Dinner:** $8-$18   **Phone:** 757/628-8282   (42)
Location: Jct College Pl; downtown. 273 Granby St 23510. **Hours:** 11:30 am-3 & 5-10 pm, Fri-11 pm, Sat 5 pm-11 pm. Closed: 11/24; also Sun. **Features:** Sparse and neat is this quintessential sushi bar, a popular spot for downtown workers searching for fresh seafood. Besides great sushi, try dishes such as tuna tataki and tasty noodle soup. Casual dress; cocktails. **Parking:** street. **Cards:** AX, DC, DS, MC, VI.

DOUMAR'S CONES & BARBECUE
▼▼▼
Barbecue

Lunch: $2-$4   **Dinner:** $2-$4   **Phone:** 757/627-4163   (30)
Location: Just n of downtown; in Ghent. 20th St and Monticello Ave 23517. **Hours:** 8 am-11 pm, Fri & Sat-12:30 am. Closed major holidays; also Sun. **Features:** Diners can revisit the nostalgic 1950s at this great drive-in, which still offers carhops, tasty barbecue sandwiches and old-fashioned soda fountain favorites. A flash of the headlights prompts a carhop into action. Casual dress. **Parking:** on-site.

(See map and index starting on p. 710)

EMPIRE LITTLE BAR & BISTRO **Dinner:** $5-$18 **Phone:** 757/626-3100 (45)

American

Location: Jct Tazewell St; downtown; in Tazewell Hotel and Suites. 245A Granby St 23501. **Hours:** 5 pm-1:30 am. Closed major holidays. **Features:** In the heart of the revitalized downtown district, this small, trendy haunt prepares tasty dishes from pasta to filet. This place is a great spot for nibblers who love to sample many items at once. Casual dress; cocktails. **Parking:** street. **Cards:** AX, DS, MC, VI.

ENRICO'S RISTORANTE **Lunch:** $5-$11 **Dinner:** $9-$17 **Phone:** 757/423-2700 (8)

Italian

Location: 3 mi n of downtown. 4012 Colley Ave 23508. **Hours:** 11 am-10 pm, Fri-11 pm, Sat 5 pm-11 pm. Closed major holidays; also Sun. **Features:** The spicy flavors of Greece and Italy mix on the neighborhood cafe's menu. Regulars return for baked pasta, veal parmigiana, hearty Greek salads and daily specials, including seafood offerings. Casual dress; cocktails. **Parking:** on-site. **Cards:** AX, MC, VI.

FELLINI'S **Lunch:** $5-$12 **Dinner:** $8-$20 **Phone:** 757/625-3000 (9)

Italian

Location: 3 mi n of downtown. 3910 Colley Ave 23508. **Hours:** 11 am-10 pm, Fri & Sat-11 pm, Sun 4 pm-9:30 pm. Closed: 11/24, 12/25. **Features:** The fun and funky spot has an open, tiled kitchen and intimate booths with chandeliers and draped fabric overhead. The house specialty is individual gourmet pizza, in such varieties as Thai chicken and "killer pie." Also on the menu are homemade pasta dishes, black Angus steak, hearty sandwiches and delicious Greek and Caesar salad. Casual dress; cocktails. **Parking:** on-site. **Cards:** AX, DS, MC, VI.

FREEMASON ABBEY **Lunch:** $6-$18 **Dinner:** $6-$18 **Phone:** 757/622-3966 (40)

American

Location: Jct Freemason and Boush sts; downtown. 209 W Freemason St 23510. **Hours:** 11:30 am-10 pm, Fri & Sat-11 pm, Sun 9:30 am-11 pm. Closed major holidays. **Reservations:** suggested. **Features:** Steak, prime rib, seafood and sandwiches are served in this lofty, restored abbey, complete with an impressive brick and stone exterior. Wooden booths and tables make the atmosphere cozy. Friendly staff members always seem to be wearing smiles. Casual dress; cocktails. **Parking:** on-site. **Cards:** AX, DC, DS, MC, VI.

THE GERMANY PANTRY **Lunch:** $9-$17 **Dinner:** $9-$17 **Phone:** 757/461-5100 (33)

German

Location: Just w from jct Military Hwy. 5329 E Virginia Beach Blvd 23502. **Hours:** 10 am-10 pm, Sun 2 pm-8 pm. Closed: 11/24, 12/25; also Mon. **Reservations:** accepted. **Features:** The restaurant is one of the most warm and welcoming spots around. Among German dishes are sauerbraten, knackwurst, apple strudel and Wiener schnitzel. Also offered are delicatessen fare and German market items. Casual dress; beer & wine only. **Parking:** on-site. **Cards:** AX, DS, MC, VI.

THE GRATE STEAK **Lunch:** $5-$33 **Dinner:** $8-$33 **Phone:** 757/461-5501 (55)

Steak House

Location: I-264, exit 13B, on US 13; in Best Western-Center Inn. 235 N Military Hwy 23502. **Hours:** 11:30 am-2 & 5-10 pm, Sat from 2 pm, Sun noon-9 pm. Closed: 11/24, 12/24, 12/25. **Features:** Locals flock here for prime cuts of Western aged beef that they grill themselves over hot charcoal on the large indoor grill. Casual dress; cocktails. **Parking:** on-site. **Cards:** AX, DC, DS, MC, VI.

HAVANA **Lunch:** $6-$12 **Dinner:** $13-$20 **Phone:** 757/627-5800 (44)

American

Location: Just n; between College and Tazewell sts. 255 Granby St 23510. **Hours:** 11:30 am-2 & 5-10 pm, Fri-11 pm. Closed: 5/30, 11/24, 12/25; also Sun & for lunch Sat. **Reservations:** accepted. **Features:** This successful beach eatery opens a new spot with a more urban flair. Expect the same great innovative cuisine with a Cuban accent such as glazed pork loin, Cubano sandwich and grilled seafood. Locals love the communal dining bar as a place to meet new people. Casual dress; cocktails. **Parking:** street. **Cards:** AX, DS, MC, VI.

JACK QUINN'S RESTAURANT & IRISH PUB **Lunch:** $7-$19 **Dinner:** $9-$21 **Phone:** 757/274-0024 (48)

Irish

Location: Jct Tazewell St; downtown. 241 Granby St 23510. **Hours:** 11:30 am-1 am, Sat & Sun noon-2 am. Closed: 11/24, 12/25. **Features:** Decorated in rich woods imported directly from Ireland, the pub has hand-stenciled walls that enhance the ambience. The wonderful menu comprises hearty stews, fish and chips and lots of lean corned beef. The handsome wood bar, with its privacy screen and coat hooks, offers an array of Irish draft beers and single malts. Casual dress; cocktails; entertainment. **Parking:** street. **Cards:** AX, DS, MC, VI.

KINCAID'S FISH, CHOP AND STEAKHOUSE **Lunch:** $7-$15 **Dinner:** $14-$28 **Phone:** 757/622-8000 (43)

Steak & Seafood

Location: Jct College St; downtown; in MacArthur Center. 300 Monticello Ave #147 23510. **Hours:** 11 am-10 pm, Fri & Sat-11 pm. Closed: 12/25. **Reservations:** suggested. **Features:** Styled with rich woods and fine art, the sophisticated spot serves fine steak, chops and Northwest salmon. The restaurant doesn't skimp on the finer things, such as a rich crab dip, thick filet mignon, choice wines and creme brulee. Casual dress; cocktails. **Parking:** on-site. **Cards:** AX, CB, DC, DS, MC, VI.

THE KOSHER PLACE **Lunch:** $5-$10 **Dinner:** $5-$16 **Phone:** 757/623-1770 (11)

Kosher

Location: Just e of Colley Ave; in Ghent. 738 W 22nd St 23517. **Hours:** 9 am-7 pm. Closed major holidays; also Sat. **Features:** The tiny market and cafe serves tasty delicatessen sandwiches and matzo ball soup all day. In the evening, daily entree specials—ranging from grilled tuna to steak to pastas—join the mix. Casual dress; beer & wine only. **Parking:** on-site. **Cards:** AX, MC, VI.

KOTOBUKI **Lunch:** $9-$18 **Dinner:** $9-$18 **Phone:** 757/628-1025 (18)

Japanese

Location: Jct Colley Ave, just e; in Ghent. 721 W 21st St 23517. **Hours:** 11:30 am-2:30 & 5-10 pm, Fri & Sat-11 pm, Sun 4:30 pm-9:30 pm. Closed: 11/24, 12/25; also Tues. **Reservations:** accepted. **Features:** Crisp lines, an open sushi bar and semi-enclosed tatami tables mark the traditional decor. On the menu are such dishes as maki rolls, nigiri sushi, noodle soups and salmon teriyaki. Casual dress; cocktails. **Parking:** street. **Cards:** AX, DS, MC, VI.

(See map and index starting on p. 710)

LA GALLERIA
♦♦♦♦
Northern
Italian

Dinner: $13-$44   **Phone:** 757/623-3939   ④①
Location: Between Granby and Boush sts; downtown. 120 College Pl 23510. **Hours:** 5:30 pm-11 pm, Fri & Sat-midnight. Closed: 11/24, 12/25; also Sun. **Reservations:** suggested. **Features:** In a renovated warehouse, the restaurant mixes a sleek, modern decor accented by Roman columns with traditional Northern Italian cuisine. Favorites include salmon la Galleria and anything from the brick oven, including pizza and focaccia bread. Casual dress; cocktails. **Parking:** valet. **Cards:** AX, DC, MC, VI.

LUNA MAYA CANTINA
♦♦♦
Latino

Dinner: $8-$14   **Phone:** 757/622-6986   ②④
Location: Jct 21st St and Princess Anne Rd; in Corner Shoppes; in Ghent. 2000 Colonial Ave 23462. **Hours:** 5:30 pm-10 pm, Fri & Sat-10:30 pm. Closed major holidays; also Sun & Mon. **Features:** Fresh ingredients and great tasting food prevail on the limited menu in this small hip eatery run by Bolivian sisters. Burritos, quesadillas, and unusual tamales are accented by a wide variety of salsa and peppers. Great guacamole made fresh to order. All meals start with chipotle salsa and fresh chips. Casual dress; cocktails. **Parking:** on-site. **Cards:** AX, MC, VI.

MACHISMO BURRITO BAR
♦♦
Mexican

Lunch: $5-$8   **Dinner:** $5-$8   **Phone:** 757/624-2424   ③④
Location: Jct W Brambleton Ave and Botetourt St; downtown. 409 W York St 23517. **Hours:** 11 am-9 pm. Closed: 11/24, 12/25. **Features:** The simple spot's excellent burritos are custom-made to diners' specifications. Guests can choose their favorite meat or meat alternative, vegetables and even flavored wraps. Casual dress. **Parking:** street. **Cards:** MC, VI.

MAGNOLIA STEAK
AAA
♦♦♦♦
Regional
American

Lunch: $7-$15   **Dinner:** $16-$25   **Phone:** 757/625-0400   ③①
Location: Jct Colley Ave and W Princess Anne Rd; 1 mi n. 749 W Princess Anne Rd 23517. **Hours:** 11:30 am-10:30 pm, Sat & Sun 5 pm-11 pm. Closed: 11/24, 12/25; also Super Bowl Sun. **Reservations:** suggested, weekends. **Features:** Southern and international influences support featured menu selections of certified Angus beef, fresh seasonal seafood, vegetables, chicken, pasta, ribs and house-smoked barbecue. Outside dining available, weather permitting. Located in the heart of historic Ghent. Decor is hip and elegant. Casual dress; cocktails. **Parking:** on-site and street. **Cards:** AX, MC, VI.

MI HOGAR MEXICAN RESTAURANT
♦♦♦
Mexican

Lunch: $4-$11   **Dinner:** $6-$11   **Phone:** 757/455-5509   ⑤②
Location: I-264, exit 13B, just n on US 13. 471 N Military Hwy 23502. **Hours:** 11 am-10 pm, Fri & Sat-11 pm, Sun noon-9:30 pm. Closed major holidays. **Features:** The bright, friendly spot offers the combination plates most Americans favor, as well as more authentic dishes, such as chicken mole. Casual dress; cocktails. **Parking:** on-site. **Cards:** AX, DS, MC, VI.

MI HOGAR MEXICAN RESTAURANT
♦♦
Mexican

Lunch: $4-$6   **Dinner:** $6-$11   **Phone:** 757/640-7705   ⑦
Location: At foot of Granby St Bridge. 4201 Granby St 23504. **Hours:** 11 am-10 pm, Fri & Sat-11 pm, Sun noon-9:30 pm. Closed: 7/4, 11/24, 12/25. **Features:** This bright friendly spot offers Americans' favorites combination plates as well as more authentic Mexican dishes such as chicken mole. Casual dress; cocktails. **Parking:** on-site. **Cards:** AX, DS, MC, VI.

NAWAB RESTAURANT
♦♦♦
Indian

Lunch: $5-$7   **Dinner:** $7-$12   **Phone:** 757/455-8080   ③⑥
Location: I-264, exit 13B, 0.5 mi n at jct Virginia Beach Blvd. 888 N Military Hwy 23502. **Hours:** 11:30 am-3 & 5-10 pm, Fri & Sat-10:30 pm, Sun noon-3 pm. **Features:** Tandoor specialties and bread baked in a clay oven are at the centerpiece of the traditional menu of curried, lamb and vegetarian dishes. The exotic atmosphere features artwork and instrumental music. A weekday buffet draws an large lunch clientele. Casual dress; cocktails. **Parking:** on-site. **Cards:** AX, DS, MC, VI.

NEW BELMONT
♦♦♦♦
American

Dinner: $12-$21   **Phone:** 757/623-4477   ②⓪
Location: Jct 21st St, just n; in Ghent. 2117 Colonial Ave 23517. **Hours:** 5 pm-2 am, Sun also 11 am-3 pm. Closed major holidays. **Reservations:** suggested. **Features:** With exposed brick and contemporary artwork, the restaurant exudes a modern style. Creativity marks the seasonally changing menu. An upstairs lounge offers live music on weekends and billiards always. Dressy casual; cocktails; entertainment. **Parking:** on-site. **Cards:** AX, DS, MC, VI.

NO FRILL BAR & GRILL
♦♦♦
American

Lunch: $5-$17   **Dinner:** $5-$17   **Phone:** 757/627-4262   ②②
Location: Jct Colley Ave, just e; in Ghent. 806 Spotswood Ave 23517. **Hours:** 11 am-10 pm, Fri & Sat-11 pm. Closed major holidays. **Features:** This small, brightly decorated spot has a cozy neighborhood feel, particularly on its heated patio. The daily menu lists sandwiches, salad, burgers and house specialties, including award-winning ribs, famous chili and other barbecue dishes. Chalkboard specials shine with creativity and fresh seasonal influences. Casual dress; cocktails. **Parking:** on-site. **Cards:** AX, MC, VI.

OMAR'S CARRIAGE HOUSE
AAA
♦♦♦
International

Menu on aaa.com   **Lunch:** $5-$9   **Dinner:** $14-$22   **Phone:** 757/622-4990   ③⑦
Location: Just w of Boush St; in the Freemason District; downtown. 313 W Bute St 23510. **Hours:** 11 am-3 & 5-10 pm, Fri-11 pm, Sat & Sun 5 pm-11 pm. Closed major holidays. **Reservations:** suggested. **Features:** The eclectically decorated former carriage house recalls the ambience of an artist's studio. The menu displays an equally eclectic mix of international influences, with the owner's Moroccan heritage showing strongly on Monday evenings. Casual dress; cocktails. **Parking:** on-site. **Cards:** AX, MC, VI.

(See map and index starting on p. 710)

THE PAINTED LADY Lunch: $6-$9 Dinner: $13-$26 Phone: 757/623-8872 ③②
▼▼▼ **Location:** 1 mi n of downtown on Monticello to 17th St. 112 E 17th St 23517. **Hours:** 11 am-2 & 5-9 pm, Fri & Sat-11 pm, Sun-9 pm. Closed: 7/4, 11/24, 12/25; also Mon. **Reservations:** suggested. **Features:** Housed in two
Continental colorfully restored Victorian homes, this spot sports an unusual decor of antiques and bric-a-brac. Continental cuisine with a Southern accent is served. Afternoon tea from 2:30 pm-5 pm. Dessert and caesar salad are prepared tableside. Children love the "Teddy Bear Tea.". Casual dress; cocktails. **Parking:** on-site. **Cards:** AX, DS, MC, VI.
✕

RAJPUT INDIAN CUISINE Lunch: $5-$19 Dinner: $7-$19 Phone: 757/625-4634 ⑬
▼▼▼ **Location:** Jct Colley Ave, just e; in Ghent; in Center Shops. 742 W 21st St 23517. **Hours:** 11:30 am-2:30 & 5-10 pm, Fri & Sat-11 pm, Sun noon-9:30 pm. **Features:** Sample many Indian specialties off the buffet for lunch
Indian or go straight to the menu for more spicy and unique offerings such as lamb and vegetarian dishes as well as Tandoori-fired bread and meat dishes. Casual dress; cocktails. **Parking:** on-site. **Cards:** AX, DS, MC, VI.
♿M

SHIP'S CABIN BAR & GRILL Lunch: $5-$13 Dinner: $12-$25 Phone: 757/362-4659 ①
▼▼ **Location:** US 60 at jct Shore Dr and E Ocean View Ave. 4110 E Ocean View Ave 23518. **Hours:** 11 am-10 pm. Closed: 11/24, 12/25. **Reservations:** suggested. **Features:** This longtime local landmark now has a fresh
Seafood outlook and new owners. Set on the dunes overlooking the Chesapeake Bay, with a beachside patio and a piano bar inside. The new chefs have brought in their own tastes but also borrow inspiration from its past. Fresh local seafood takes center stage here in dishes such as fresh tuna, crabcakes, and oysters. Casual dress; cocktails. **Parking:** on-site. **Cards:** AX, DS, MC, VI.
🍸 ✕

SIAM 21 Lunch: $6-$9 Dinner: $8-$20 Phone: 757/624-2455 ⑭
▼▼ **Location:** Jct Colley Ave, just e; in Ghent; in the Center Shops. 742G W 21st St 23517. **Hours:** 11:30 am-3 & 5-10 pm, Sun noon-3 & 5-9 pm. Closed: Mon. **Reservations:** suggested. **Features:** The classically French-
Thai trained owner-chef returns to his Thai roots with a menu of authentic specialties. The best seats are at tables beside the hearth. Casual dress; cocktails. **Parking:** on-site. **Cards:** MC, VI.
✕

SURFRIDER-TAYLOR'S LANDING Lunch: $4-$6 Dinner: $6-$18 Phone: 757/480-5000 ③
▼▼ **Location:** Just n of jct Little Creek; under Pretty Lake bridge at Taylor's Landing. 8180 Shore Dr 23518. **Hours:** 11 am-9 pm, Fri & Sat-9:30 pm. Closed major holidays. **Features:** Fresh, simply prepared seafood is the draw
Seafood at the casual restaurant overlooking a marina in the newly revived East Beach neighborhood.. Local boaters and fishermen can't get enough of the daily catch, fresh crab cakes and spears of broccoli topped with fresh hollandaise. Casual dress; cocktails. **Parking:** on-site. **Cards:** AX, DS, MC, VI.
♿M 🍸 ✕

SURF RIDER WEST Lunch: $4-$6 Dinner: $7-$15 Phone: 757/461-6488 ㊼
▼▼ **Location:** I-64, exit 284B (Newtown Rd N); in Stoney Point Center. 700 Newtown Rd 23502. **Hours:** 11 am-10 pm. Closed major holidays; also Sun. **Features:** Simply prepared, fresh seafood is the key at this casual
Seafood restaurant. Locals love the reasonably priced crab cakes, fried flounder and fresh broccoli with hollandaise, as well as the daily assortment of homemade pies. Casual dress; cocktails. **Parking:** on-site. **Cards:** AX, DS, MC, VI.
✕

TANNER'S CREEK SEAFOOD RESTAURANT & RAW
BAR Lunch: $6-$20 Dinner: $6-$20 Phone: 757/423-2430 ⑥
▼▼ **Location:** 1.5 mi nw of jct W 21st St. 5103 Colley Ave 23505. **Hours:** 11 am-10 pm. Closed major holidays. **Reservations:** accepted. **Features:** The casual family spot serves fresh local seafood specialties, such as
Seafood crab cakes, fried shrimp and flounder, as well as such land delicacies as prime rib. Patio seating is a seasonal option. Casual dress; cocktails. **Parking:** on-site. **Cards:** DS, MC, VI.
🍸 ✕

THE TEN TOP Lunch: $6-$8 Dinner: $6-$11 Phone: 757/622-5422 ㉖
▼ **Location:** Jct Colley Ave; in Ghent. 748 Shirley Ave 23517. **Hours:** 11 am-9 pm. Closed major holidays; also Sun. **Features:** In the heart of the Ghent area, the small, funky spot is popular among locals for great take-home
American meals, such as flatbread pizza, Thai noodles, meaty sandwiches and wraps. Pan-roasted salmon is an excellent dinner choice. Casual dress. **Parking:** on-site. **Cards:** AX, MC, VI.
✕

TODD JURICH'S BISTRO! Lunch: $8-$10 Dinner: $18-$26 Phone: 757/622-3210 �554
ⒶⒶⒶ **Location:** Across from Nauticus; downtown. 150 W Main St, Suite 100 23510. **Hours:** 11:30 am-2:30 & 5-11 pm, Sat from 5:30 pm. Closed major holidays; also Sun. **Reservations:** suggested. **Features:** Wonderfully
▼▼▼ ▼▼▼ flavored creations abound at the upscale restaurant, a picture of restrained, urban elegance. Startling
Regional combinations employ fresh local products and evoke influences ranging from Tuscany to Thailand. The wait
American staff is knowledgeable and smooth. Dressy casual; cocktails. **Parking:** on-site (fee) and valet. **Cards:** AX, DS, MC, VI.
🍸 ✕

UNCLE LOUIE'S RESTAURANT Lunch: $6-$10 Dinner: $7-$17 Phone: 757/480-1225 ⑤
▼▼ **Location:** I-64, exit 276C, just sw; in Ward's Corner. 132 E Little Creek Rd 23505. **Hours:** 8 am-11 pm, Fri & Sat-midnight, Sun-10 pm. Closed: 11/24, 12/25. **Reservations:** suggested. **Features:** Listed on the
American contemporary American menu are sandwiches, pasta and homemade baked items. Portions are large and tasty. A gourmet shop and delicatessen occupies the front, while full-service dining is available in the back. Entertainers perform Saturday nights in the adjacent bar. Casual dress; cocktails. **Parking:** on-site. **Cards:** AX, CB, DC, DS, MC, VI.
🍸 ✕

(See map and index starting on p. 710)

VELVET 25 BISTRO   **Dinner:** $16-$27   **Phone:** 757/625-5525   ⑩

American

Location: 3 mi n, jct 25th St; in Ghent. 2502 Colley Ave 23517. **Hours:** 5 pm-10 pm, Fri & Sat-11 pm, Sun-9 pm. Closed: 1/1, 11/24, 12/25. **Reservations:** suggested. **Features:** Sleek, sensual and hip are words that could describe both the mood and the cuisine at the hot spot. The ever-changing menu highlights exotic gourmet elements with style and creativity. Dressy casual; cocktails. **Parking:** on-site. **Cards:** AX, DC, DS, MC, VI.

VOILA CUISINE INTERNATIONAL   **Lunch:** $5-$12   **Dinner:** $14-$27   **Phone:** 757/640-0343   ㉟

Continental

Cards: AX, MC, VI.

Location: Jct Brambleton Ave; downtown. 509 Botetourt St 23510. **Hours:** 11 am-2:30 & 5-10 pm, Sat & Sat from 5 pm, Mon 11 am-2:30 pm. Closed major holidays. **Reservations:** suggested. **Features:** Sultry and elegant this tiny spot is the ultimate spot for romance. Dine on luscious European influenced dishes, sample fine wines, and be served by a warm and professional staff. Dressy casual; cocktails. **Parking:** on-site.

WILD MONKEY   **Dinner:** $8-$15   **Phone:** 757/627-6462   ㉑

American

cocktails. **Parking:** street. **Cards:** AX, DC, MC, VI.

Location: 1 mi n; between Spottswood and Brandon; in Ghent. 1603 Colley Ave 23517. **Hours:** 5 pm-10 pm; Sunday brunch 11 am-2:30 pm. **Features:** The quirky bistro uses a chalkboard menu and wine list to tout its "gourmet diner" cuisine with a highly evident sense of humor. Culinary offerings include $10 meatloaf, bronzed salmon and Norfolk lo mein. Pasta dishes can be topped with salmon or tofu. Casual dress;

VIRGINIA BEACH pop. 425,257   (See maps and indexes starting on p. 715, 719)

——— **WHERE TO STAY** ———

ALAMAR RESORT INN   **Phone:** (757)428-7582   ㉛

6/21-9/3	2P: $104-$190	XP: $10	F18
5/1-6/20	2P: $58-$159	XP: $10	F18
9/4-2/28	2P: $52-$134	XP: $10	F18
3/1-4/30	2P: $36-$110	XP: $10	F18

Motel

Location: I-264, terminus to Pacific Ave, just s. 311 16th St 23451. Fax: 757/428-7587. **Facility:** Smoke free premises. 22 units. 11 one-bedroom standard units. 11 one-bedroom suites with kitchens. 3 stories (no elevator), exterior corridors. **Parking:** on-site. **Terms:** office hours 7 am-2 am, 21 day cancellation notice-fee imposed, weekly rates available, [BP] meal plan available, package plans. **Amenities:** irons, hair dryers. **Pool(s):** heated outdoor. **Leisure Activities:** Fee: game room. **Guest Services:** coin laundry. **Business Services:** fax. **Cards:** AX, DC, MC, VI. **Special Amenities:** free newspaper and early check-in/late check-out. *(See color ad below)*

(See maps and indexes starting on p. 715, 719)

THE AMBASSADOR SUITES

	5/27-9/4	1P: $69-$239	2P: $69-$239	XP: $10	F18
	9/5-10/8	1P: $69-$199	2P: $69-$199	XP: $10	F18
	10/9-2/28	1P: $49-$189	2P: $49-$189	XP: $10	F18
Motel	3/1-5/26	1P: $49-$139	2P: $49-$139	XP: $10	F18

Phone: (757)428-1111 [21]

Location: I-264, just n of terminus. 2315 Atlantic Ave 23451. Fax: 757/437-1854. **Facility:** 54 one-bedroom suites with kitchens. 8 stories, interior/exterior corridors. **Parking:** on-site. **Terms:** check-in 4 pm, 3 night minimum stay - seasonal and/or weekends, 3 day cancellation notice, package plans. **Amenities:** safes (fee). **Pool(s):** heated outdoor. **Guest Services:** coin laundry. **Cards:** AX, DC, DS, MC, VI. **(See color ad p 740)**

BARCLAY COTTAGE BED & BREAKFAST

	5/20-9/11 [BP]	1P: $123-$169	2P: $123-$169
	3/1-5/19 & 9/12-10/31 [BP]	1P: $93-$127	2P: $93-$127
	11/1-2/28 [BP]	1P: $74-$102	2P: $74-$102

Phone: 757/422-1956 [32]

Bed & Breakfast **Location:** I-264, just s of terminus to Artic Ave and 16th St. Located in a residential area. 400 16th St 23451. Fax: 757/422-5449. **Facility:** Double-decker wraparound verandas add visual appeal to this turn-of-the-20th-century beach cottage, which once functioned as a schoolhouse. Smoke free premises. 5 one-bedroom standard units. 2 stories (no elevator), interior corridors. *Bath:* some shared or private, combo or shower only. **Parking:** on-site. **Terms:** 2 night minimum stay - seasonal and/or weekends, age restrictions may apply, 14 day cancellation notice-fee imposed, package plans, no pets allowed (owner's dogs on premises). **Amenities:** CD players, hair dryers. **Cards:** AX, DS, MC, VI. **Special Amenities:** free full breakfast and free local telephone calls.

BARCLAY TOWERS

	5/27-9/4 [ECP]	1P: $109-$249	2P: $109-$249	XP: $10	F18
	9/5-10/22 [ECP]	1P: $69-$199	2P: $69-$199	XP: $10	F18
	3/1-5/26 [ECP]	1P: $65-$149	2P: $65-$149	XP: $10	F18
Small-scale Hotel	10/23-2/28 [ECP]	1P: $59-$99	2P: $59-$99	XP: $10	F18

Phone: (757)491-2700 [40]

Location: I-264, 0.8 mi s of terminus; Atlantic Ave and Ninth St. 809 Atlantic Ave 23451. Fax: 757/428-3790. **Facility:** 84 one-bedroom suites with kitchens. 8 stories, interior corridors. **Parking:** on-site. **Terms:** 3 day cancellation notice, package plans. **Amenities:** voice mail, safes, irons, hair dryers. **Pool(s):** heated indoor. **Leisure Activities:** sauna, whirlpool, exercise room. *Fee:* game room. **Guest Services:** coin laundry. **Business Services:** meeting rooms, fax. **Cards:** AX, CB, DC, DS, MC, VI. **(See color ad p 740)**

SOME UNITS

 / FEE

THE BELVEDERE MOTEL

	5/27-9/4	1P: $124-$134	2P: $124-$134	XP: $8
	9/5-10/2	1P: $84-$94	2P: $84-$94	XP: $8
	3/24-5/26	1P: $54-$78	2P: $54-$78	XP: $8
Motel	10/3-10/23	1P: $54-$64	2P: $54-$64	XP: $8

Phone: 757/425-0612 [3]

Location: I-264, 1 mi n of terminus; Atlantic Ave and 36th St. 3603 Atlantic Ave 23451 (PO Box 451, 23458). Fax: 757/425-1397. **Facility:** 47 one-bedroom standard units, some with efficiencies. 5 stories, exterior corridors. **Parking:** on-site. **Terms:** open 3/24-10/23, 3-5 night minimum stay, 3 day cancellation notice. **Dining:** 7 am-3 pm, wine/beer only. **Pool(s):** heated outdoor. **Leisure Activities:** bicycles. **Business Services:** fax. **Cards:** AX, MC, VI. **Special Amenities:** free local telephone calls.

SOME UNITS

/

(See maps and indexes starting on p. 715, 719)

BEST WESTERN BEACH QUARTERS INN   *Book at aaa.com*   Phone: (757)437-1200   46

▽▽ ▽▽   7/1-9/4 [CP]   1P: $119-$239   2P: $134-$254   XP: $15   F
              5/27-6/30 [CP]   1P: $89-$209   2P: $104-$224   XP: $15   F
Motel   9/5-2/28 [CP]   1P: $39-$149   2P: $54-$164   XP: $15   F
              3/1-5/26 [CP]   1P: $39-$109   2P: $54-$124   XP: $15   F

Location: I-264, 1.2 mi s of terminus at Rudee Inlet. 300 Atlantic Ave 23451. **Fax:** 757/437-1981. **Facility:** 52 one-bedroom standard units, some with efficiencies. 6 stories, exterior corridors. **Parking:** on-site. **Terms:** 3 night minimum stay - seasonal and/or weekends, 3 day cancellation notice-fee imposed, package plans. **Amenities:** voice mail, safes (fee), irons, hair dryers. **Pool(s):** outdoor. **Guest Services:** coin laundry. **Business Services:** fax. **Cards:** AX, CB, DC, DS, MC, VI.
(See color ad p 742 & p 739)

SOME UNITS
(ASK) (S/D) (TI+) (⊘) (➤) (✲) (DATA PORT) (□) / (✕) (🗄) (🖼) /

BEST WESTERN INN   *Book at aaa.com*   Phone: (757)363-2500   3

(AAA) (SAVE)   5/1-9/5   1P: $75-$155   2P: $75-$155
                   3/1-5/20 & 9/6-10/31 1P: $60-$90   2P: $60-$90
▽▽▽▽   11/1-2/28   1P: $50-$70   2P: $50-$70
Motel   **Location:** I-64, exit 282, 1 mi n on US 13. 5718 Northampton Blvd 23455. **Fax:** 757/460-3770. **Facility:** 60 one-bedroom standard units. 2 stories (no elevator), exterior corridors. **Parking:** on-site. **Terms:** 2 night minimum stay - seasonal, package plans. **Amenities:** irons, hair dryers. **Pool(s):** outdoor. **Business Services:** fax. **Cards:** AX, CB, DC, DS, MC, VI. **Special Amenities:** free continental breakfast and free local telephone calls.

SOME UNITS
(S/D) (TI+) (&M) (⊘) (➤) (✲) (DATA PORT) (□) (🖼) (□) / (✕) /

BEST WESTERN OCEANFRONT   *Book at aaa.com*   Phone: (757)422-5000   37

(AAA) (SAVE)   5/1-9/7   1P: $129-$219   2P: $129-$219   XP: $10   F11
                   9/8-9/30   1P: $109-$139   2P: $109-$139   XP: $10   F11
▽▽ ▽▽   3/1-4/30   1P: $59-$129   2P: $59-$129   XP: $10   F11
                   10/1-2/28   1P: $59-$89   2P: $59-$89   XP: $10   F11
Small-scale Hotel **Location:** I-264, 0.6 mi s of terminus, at 11th St. 1101 Atlantic Ave 23451. **Fax:** 757/425-2356. **Facility:** 110 one-bedroom standard units, some with whirlpools. 8 stories, interior corridors. **Parking:** valet. **Terms:** package plans. **Amenities:** voice mail, irons, hair dryers. **Dining:** 7 am-11:30 pm; hours vary off season, cocktails. **Pool(s):** outdoor. **Leisure Activities:** rental bicycles. **Guest Services:** coin laundry. **Business Services:** meeting rooms, fax. **Cards:** AX, CB, DC, DS, MC, VI. **Special Amenities:** free local telephone calls and free newspaper.

SOME UNITS
(S/D) (TI) (Y) (⊘) (➤) (✲) (DATA PORT) (□) (🖼) (□) / (✕) /

BOARDWALK RESORT HOTEL AND VILLAS   *Book at aaa.com*   Phone: (757)213-3099   30

▽▽ ▽▽   6/16-9/5   1P: $129-$399   2P: $129-$399   XP: $15   F12
              3/1-6/15 & 9/6-10/31 1P: $69-$299   2P: $69-$299   XP: $15   F12
Small-scale Hotel 11/1-2/28   1P: $59-$189   2P: $59-$189   XP: $15   F12
Location: I-264, terminus, just s to 16th St. 1601 Atlantic Ave 23451. **Fax:** 757/213-3098. **Facility:** 106 units. 19 one-bedroom standard units. 87 one-bedroom suites with kitchens. 10 stories, interior corridors. **Bath:** combo or shower only. **Parking:** on-site. **Terms:** check-in 4 pm, 3 day cancellation notice-fee imposed. **Amenities:** voice mail, safes (fee), irons, hair dryers. *Some:* high-speed Internet (fee). **Dining:** Rockfish Boardwalk Bar & Sea Grill, see separate listing. **Pool(s):** heated indoor. **Leisure Activities:** whirlpool, exercise room. **Guest Services:** valet and coin laundry. **Cards:** AX, CB, DC, DS, JC, MC, VI. *(See color ad p 742 & below)*   (ASK) (S/D) (TI) (Y) (&M) (&) (⊘) (➤) (VCR) (✲) (DATA PORT) (□) (🖼) (□)

(See maps and indexes starting on p. 715, 719)

THE BREAKERS RESORT INN

(AAA) **[SAVE]** Phone: (757)428-1821 **33**

	5/27-9/5	1P: $160-$275	2P: $160-$275	XP: $10	F16
	9/6-9/28	1P: $100-$275	2P: $100-$275	XP: $10	F16
	3/1-5/26 & 9/29-2/28	1P: $70-$275	2P: $70-$275	XP: $10	F16

Location: I-264, 0.5 mi s of terminus. 1503 Atlantic Ave 23451. Fax: 757/422-9602. **Facility:** 56 units. 40 one-bedroom standard units, some with whirlpools. 15 one- and 1 two-bedroom suites ($80-$275). 9 stories, interior corridors. *Bath:* combo or shower only. **Parking:** on-site. **Terms:** 3 night minimum stay - seasonal, 3 day cancellation notice-fee imposed, package plans. **Amenities:** high-speed Internet, voice mail, irons, hair dryers. **Dining:** 7:30 am-2:30 pm, wine/beer only. **Pool(s):** heated outdoor. **Leisure Activities:** bicycles. **Guest Services:** coin laundry. **Business Services:** fax. **Cards:** AX, DC, DS, MC, VI. *(See color ad below)*

Small-scale Hotel

SOME UNITS

THE CAPES OCEAN RESORT

Phone: (757)428-5421 **27**

	5/27-9/5		2P: $99-$250	XP: $10	D17
	9/6-10/10		2P: $89-$180	XP: $10	D17
	3/1-5/26		2P: $50-$165	XP: $10	D17
Small-scale Hotel	10/11-2/28		2P: $45-$150	XP: $10	D17

Location: s of terminus; jct 20th St and Atlantic Ave. 2001 Atlantic Ave 23451. Fax: 757/422-9213. **Facility:** 59 units. 44 one-bedroom standard units, some with whirlpools. 15 one-bedroom suites, some with whirlpools. 8 stories, interior corridors. **Parking:** on-site. **Terms:** 2 night minimum stay - seasonal and/or weekends, 3 day cancellation notice-fee imposed, package plans. **Amenities:** voice mail, irons, hair dryers. **Pool(s):** heated indoor. **Guest Services:** coin laundry. **Business Services:** meeting rooms. **Cards:** AX, DS, MC, VI. *(See color ad p 744)*

SOME UNITS

[ASK] ... / [VCR] FEE

CLARION RESORT *Book at aaa.com*

Phone: (757)422-3186 **44**

	6/16-9/5	1P: $129-$399	2P: $129-$399	XP: $15	F12
	3/1-6/15 & 9/6-10/31	1P: $69-$299	2P: $69-$299	XP: $15	F12
	11/1-2/28	1P: $59-$189	2P: $59-$189	XP: $15	F12

Small-scale Hotel **Location:** I-264, 1 mi s of terminus; Atlantic Ave and 5th St. 501 Atlantic Ave 23451. Fax: 757/491-3379. **Facility:** 168 units. 48 one-bedroom standard units, some with whirlpools. 120 one-bedroom suites with kitchens. 12 stories, exterior corridors. *Bath:* combo or shower only. **Parking:** on-site. **Terms:** check-in 4 pm, 3 day cancellation notice-fee imposed. **Amenities:** video games, voice mail, safes (fee), irons, hair dryers. **Pool(s):** heated outdoor, heated indoor, wading. **Leisure Activities:** sauna, whirlpools, lighted tennis court, recreation programs in summer. *Fee:* massage, game room. **Guest Services:** valet and coin laundry, tanning facility. **Cards:** AX, CB, DC, DS, JC, MC, VI. *(See color ad p 742 & p 744)*

ASK [SD] ... FEE

COLONIAL INN *Book at aaa.com*

(AAA) **[SAVE]** Phone: (757)428-5370 **11**

	5/1-9/5	1P: $85-$225	2P: $85-$225	XP: $10	F18
	9/6-10/31	1P: $65-$125	2P: $65-$125	XP: $10	F18
	3/1-4/30 & 11/1-2/28	1P: $40-$115	2P: $40-$115	XP: $10	F18

Location: I-264, 0.5 mi n of terminus; jct 28th St. 2809 Atlantic Ave 23451. Fax: 757/422-5902. **Facility:** 222 one-bedroom standard units. 2-8 stories, interior/exterior corridors. *Bath:* combo or shower only. **Parking:** on-site. **Terms:** check-in 4 pm, 3 night minimum stay - seasonal and/or weekends, cancellation fee imposed, package plans. **Amenities:** voice mail, safes (fee). *Some:* irons, hair dryers. **Dining:** 7 am-10 pm; hours vary off season, cocktails. **Pool(s):** outdoor, heated indoor. **Guest Services:** gift shop, coin laundry. **Business Services:** meeting rooms, fax. **Cards:** AX, DS, MC, VI. *(See color ad p 742 & p 745)*

Small-scale Hotel

SOME UNITS

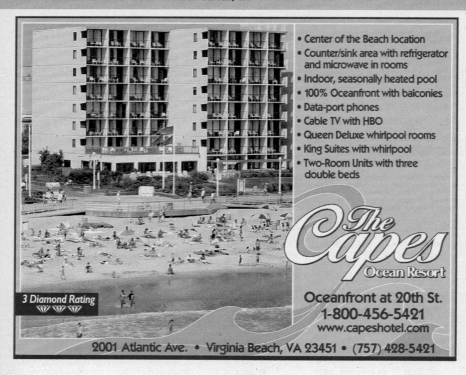

(See maps and indexes starting on p. 715, 719)

COMFORT INN   *Book at aaa.com*   Phone: (757)428-2203   🔟2
AAA SAVE   5/20-9/4 [BP]   1P: $104-$229   2P: $104-$229   XP: $10   F18
▼▼▼   9/5-10/8 [BP]   1P: $69-$149   2P: $69-$149   XP: $10   F18
           3/1-5/19 [BP]   1P: $59-$139   2P: $59-$139   XP: $10   F18
           10/9-2/28 [BP]   1P: $59-$99   2P: $59-$99   XP: $10   F18
Small-scale Hotel **Location:** I-264, 0.5 mi n of terminus. 2800 Pacific Ave 23451. **Fax:** 757/422-6043. **Facility:** 136 units. 135 one-bedroom standard units, some with whirlpools. 1 one-bedroom suite ($99-$259). 7 stories, interior corridors. **Parking:** on-site. **Terms:** 3 night minimum stay - seasonal, 3 day cancellation notice. **Amenities:** high-speed Internet, safes (fee), irons, hair dryers. **Pool(s):** heated outdoor, small heated indoor. **Leisure Activities:** whirlpool, bicycles, exercise room. *Fee:* game room. **Guest Services:** valet and coin laundry. **Business Services:** meeting rooms, fax. **Cards:** AX, CB, DC, DS, MC, VI. **Special Amenities:** free full breakfast and free local telephone calls. *(See color ad p 747)*
SOME UNITS
🅢🅓 🍴 🛶 ⊠ 🎥 DATAPORT 🔲 🖥 🖨 /⊠/

COMFORT INN LITTLE CREEK   *Book at aaa.com*   Phone: (757)460-5566   2
AAA SAVE   5/1-9/30 [ECP]   1P: $95-$125   2P: $95-$125   XP: $10   F16
▼▼▼   3/1-4/30 [ECP]   1P: $69-$89   2P: $75-$95   XP: $10   F16
           10/1-10/31 [ECP]   1P: $79-$89   2P: $79-$89   XP: $10   F16
           11/1-2/28 [ECP]   1P: $59-$79   2P: $65-$85   XP: $10   F16
Motel   **Location:** Just w of Independence Blvd (SR 225). 5189 Shore Dr 23455. **Fax:** 757/460-5571. **Facility:** 59 one-bedroom standard units, some with efficiencies. 2 stories (no elevator), exterior corridors. **Parking:** on-site. **Amenities:** safes (fee), irons, hair dryers. **Pool(s):** outdoor. **Business Services:** fax. **Cards:** AX, DC, DS, MC, VI. **Special Amenities:** free expanded continental breakfast and free local telephone calls.
SOME UNITS
🅢🅓 🍴 🛶 🎥 DATAPORT 🔲 🖥 /⊠ 🖨/

COMFORT INN-OCEANFRONT   *Book at aaa.com*   Phone: (757)425-8200   25
▼▼▼   5/21-9/5   1P: $119-$399   2P: $119-$399   XP: $15   F18
           9/6-10/31   1P: $169-$299   2P: $169-$299   XP: $15   F18
Small-scale Hotel 3/1-5/20   1P: $59-$189   2P: $59-$189   XP: $15   F18
           11/1-2/28   1P: $69-$179   2P: $69-$179   XP: $10   F18
Location: I-264, just s of terminus. 2015 Atlantic Ave 23451. **Fax:** 757/425-6521. **Facility:** 83 one-bedroom suites, some with whirlpools. 10 stories, interior corridors. *Bath:* combo or shower only. **Parking:** on-site. **Terms:** check-in 4 pm, 4 night minimum stay - seasonal and/or weekends, 3 day cancellation notice-fee imposed, package plans. **Amenities:** video games, voice mail, safes (fee), irons, hair dryers. **Pool(s):** heated indoor. **Leisure Activities:** whirlpool, bicycles, exercise room. **Guest Services:** valet laundry. **Business Services:** meeting rooms, business center. **Cards:** AX, DC, DS, MC, VI. *(See color ad below)*
SOME UNITS
ASK 🅢🅓 🍴 🚳 🛶 🎥 ⊠ 🔄 DATAPORT 🔲 🖥 🖨 /⊠/

COURTYARD BY MARRIOTT   *Book at aaa.com*   Phone: (757)490-2002   🔟
AAA SAVE   4/1-8/31   2P: $154-$169
▼▼▼   9/1-10/31   2P: $119-$129
           11/1-2/28   2P: $79-$109
           3/1-3/31   2P: $79-$99
Small-scale Hotel **Location:** I-64, exit 284B (Newton Rd S), 0.5 mi e. 5700 Greenwich Rd 23462. **Fax:** 757/490-0169. **Facility:** 146 units. 134 one-bedroom standard units. 12 one-bedroom suites ($99-$189). 3 stories, interior corridors. *Bath:* combo or shower only. **Parking:** on-site. **Terms:** cancellation fee imposed, [BP] meal plan available. **Amenities:** dual phone lines, voice mail, irons, hair dryers. *Some:* DVD players (fee). **Dining:** 6-10 am, Sat & Sun 7-11 am. **Pool(s):** heated outdoor. **Leisure Activities:** whirlpool, exercise room. **Guest Services:** valet and coin laundry. **Business Services:** meeting rooms, fax. **Cards:** AX, DC, DS, MC, VI.
SOME UNITS
🅢🅓 🍴 🍽 🔄M 🚳 🛶 🎥 DATAPORT 🖥 /⊠ VCR 🔲 🖥
                                                                                    FEE

(See maps and indexes starting on p. 715, 719)

COURTYARD BY MARRIOTT-OCEANFRONT NORTH   Book at aaa.com

Phone: (757)437-0098   **2**

Small-scale Hotel

5/27-9/5	1P: $159-$299	2P: $159-$299
9/6-11/26	1P: $129-$194	2P: $129-$194
3/1-5/26	1P: $109-$159	2P: $109-$159
11/27-2/28	1P: $99-$149	2P: $99-$149

Location: I-264, at terminus; 1 mi n, jct 37th St. 3737 Atlantic Ave 23451. Fax: 757/437-4272. **Facility:** 160 units. 100 one-bedroom standard units, some with whirlpools. 60 one-bedroom suites ($134-$299). 10 stories, interior corridors. *Bath:* combo or shower only. **Parking:** on-site. **Terms:** check-in 4 pm, 3 day cancellation notice-fee imposed. **Amenities:** video games, high-speed Internet, dual phone lines, voice mail, irons, hair dryers. **Pool(s):** heated outdoor, heated indoor. **Leisure Activities:** exercise room. **Guest Services:** sundries, valet and coin laundry. **Business Services:** meeting rooms. **Cards:** AX, CB, DC, DS, JC, MC, VI.

SOME UNITS
(ASK) (SD) (⑪) (☗) (ᕑM) (ᕍ) (⌾) (≈) (🎬) (DATA PORT) (📶) (💻) / (✕) (📷) / FEE

COURTYARD BY MARRIOTT-OCEANFRONT SOUTH   Book at aaa.com

Phone: (757)491-6222   **19**

Small-scale Hotel

7/1-9/7	1P: $209-$239	2P: $209-$239
5/27-6/30	1P: $149-$219	2P: $149-$219
3/1-5/26	1P: $99-$119	2P: $99-$119
9/8-2/28	1P: $89-$119	2P: $89-$119

Location: I-264, n of terminus; at 25th St and Atlantic Ave. Located adjacent to Norwegian Lady Park. 2501 Atlantic Ave 23451. Fax: 757/491-7774. **Facility:** 141 units. 113 one-bedroom standard units, some with whirlpools. 28 one-bedroom suites. 11 stories, interior corridors. *Bath:* combo or shower only. **Parking:** on-site. **Terms:** check-in 4 pm, cancellation fee imposed, package plans. **Amenities:** video games, dual phone lines, voice mail, irons, hair dryers. *Some: Fee:* safes. **Pool(s):** small heated indoor. **Leisure Activities:** exercise room. **Guest Services:** sundries, valet and coin laundry. **Business Services:** meeting rooms, fax. **Cards:** AX, CB, DC, DS, JC, MC, VI.

SOME UNITS
(ASK) (SD) (⑪) (ᕑM) (ᕍ) (⌾) (≈) (🎬) (DATA PORT) (📶) (💻) / (✕) (📷) / FEE

CROWNE PLAZA VIRGINIA BEACH   Book at aaa.com

Phone: (757)473-1700   **17**

(AAA) (SAVE)

Small-scale Hotel

6/17-9/3	1P: $139-$179	2P: $149-$189	XP: $10	F17
3/1-6/16 & 9/4-2/28	1P: $119-$159	2P: $129-$169	XP: $10	F17

Location: I-264, exit 17B (Independence Blvd), 0.5 mi se. 4453 Bonney Rd 23462. Fax: 757/552-0477. **Facility:** 149 one-bedroom standard units, some with whirlpools. 8 stories, interior corridors. *Bath:* combo or shower only. **Parking:** on-site. **Terms:** 2 night minimum stay - seasonal, cancellation fee imposed, [BP] & [MAP] meal plans available. **Amenities:** video games, high-speed Internet, voice mail, safes (fee), irons, hair dryers. **Dining:** 6:30 am-10 pm, cocktails. **Pool(s):** heated indoor. **Leisure Activities:** saunas, whirlpool, exercise room. **Guest Services:** sundries, valet and coin laundry. **Business Services:** conference facilities, business center. **Cards:** AX, CB, DC, DS, JC, MC, VI. **Special Amenities:** free newspaper. *(See color ad below)*

SOME UNITS
(SD) (⑪) (☗) (ᕍ) (≈) (✕) (🎬) (DATA PORT) (💻) / (✕) (📶) (📷) / FEE FEE

DAYS INN AT THE BEACH   Book at aaa.com

Phone: (757)428-6141   **38**

(AAA) (SAVE)

Small-scale Hotel

5/27-9/4	1P: $79-$169	2P: $79-$169	XP: $10	F15
3/1-5/26 & 9/5-2/28	1P: $39-$99	2P: $39-$99	XP: $10	F15

Location: I-264, 0.5 mi s of terminus to 10th St. 1000 Atlantic Ave 23451. Fax: 757/425-1069. **Facility:** 115 one-bedroom standard units, some with efficiencies and/or whirlpools. 6 stories, exterior corridors. **Parking:** on-site. **Terms:** 3 day cancellation notice, [ECP] meal plan available. **Amenities:** safes (fee), irons, hair dryers. **Pool(s):** heated outdoor. **Leisure Activities:** whirlpool. *Fee:* game room. **Guest Services:** gift shop, coin laundry. **Business Services:** meeting rooms, fax. **Special Amenities:** free expanded continental breakfast and free newspaper. *(See color ad p 749)*

SOME UNITS
(SD) (⑪) (≈) (🎬) (📶) (💻) (📷) / (✕) (DATA PORT) /

(See maps and indexes starting on p. 715, 719)

DAYS INN OCEANFRONT   *Book at aaa.com*   Phone: (757)428-7233   **8**

AAA SAVE

5/27-9/5	1P: $155-$250	2P: $155-$250	XP: $10	F12
3/1-5/26	1P: $99-$155	2P: $99-$155	XP: $10	F12
9/6-10/29	1P: $85-$150	2P: $85-$150	XP: $10	F12
10/30-2/28	1P: $55-$105	2P: $55-$105	XP: $10	F12

Small-scale Hotel **Location:** I-264, 0.8 mi n of terminus, just n of jct Laskin Rd (SR 58) at 32nd St. 3107 Atlantic Ave 23451. Fax: 757/491-1936. **Facility:** 120 one-bedroom standard units, some with whirlpools. 8 stories, interior corridors. **Parking:** on-site. **Terms:** 3 day cancellation notice, [AP] meal plan available. **Amenities:** voice mail, safes (fee), hair dryers. *Some:* irons. **Dining:** Timbuktu, see separate listing. **Pool(s):** heated indoor. **Leisure Activities:** whirlpool. **Guest Services:** coin laundry. **Business Services:** meeting rooms, PC, fax. **Cards:** AX, CB, DC, DS, MC, VI. **Special Amenities:** free newspaper. *(See color ad below)*

(See maps and indexes starting on p. 715, 719)

DIPLOMAT INN OCEANFRONT   Phone: (757)428-8811   **6**

6/9-9/5	2P: $95-$195	XP: $5 F11
5/26-6/8	2P: $65-$155	XP: $5 F11
9/6-10/31	2P: $49-$149	XP: $5 F11
3/18-5/25	2P: $45-$135	XP: $5 F11

Motel   **Location:** I-264, 1.5 mi n of terminus; Atlantic Ave and 33rd St. 3305 Atlantic Ave 23451 (PO Box 1030). Fax: 757/422-0972. **Facility:** 35 one-bedroom standard units, some with efficiencies. 5 stories, interior corridors. **Parking:** on-site. **Terms:** open 3/18-10/31, 2 night minimum stay - seasonal, 3 day cancellation notice-fee imposed, $1 service charge. **Pool(s):** outdoor. **Business Services:** fax. **Cards:** AX, DC, DS, MC, VI. **Special Amenities: free newspaper.** *(See color ad below)*

SOME UNITS

(See maps and indexes starting on p. 715, 719)

THE DOLPHIN INN   *Book at aaa.com*   Phone: (757)491-1420   🔢 29

▼▼▼▼	6/17-9/4	1P: $209-$329	2P: $209-$329	XP: $15	F12
	4/1-6/16	1P: $99-$229	2P: $99-$229	XP: $15	F12
Small-scale Hotel	9/5-2/28	1P: $59-$229	2P: $59-$229	XP: $15	F12
	3/1-3/31	1P: $59-$159	2P: $59-$159	XP: $15	F12

Location: I-264, just s of terminus. 1705 Atlantic Ave 23451. **Fax:** 757/425-8390. **Facility:** 54 one-bedroom suites with kitchens and whirlpools. 11 stories, exterior corridors. **Parking:** on-site. **Terms:** 3 night minimum stay - seasonal, 3 day cancellation notice-fee imposed, package plans. **Amenities:** voice mail, safes (fee), irons, hair dryers. **Pool(s):** heated indoor. **Guest Services:** coin laundry. **Business Services:** fax. **Cards:** AX, DC, DS, MC, VI. *(See color ad p 742 & p 750)*

SOME UNITS

ASK SD 🍴 🏊 🎥 DATA PORT 🖥 📷 💻 / ✕ /

DOUBLETREE HOTEL VIRGINIA BEACH   *Book at aaa.com*   Phone: (757)422-8900   🔢 9

| ▲▲▲ SAVE | 5/28-9/5 | 1P: $99-$219 | 2P: $109-$229 | XP: $10 | F18 |
| ▼▼▼▼ | 3/1-5/27 & 9/6-2/28 | 1P: $59-$159 | 2P: $59-$159 | XP: $10 | F18 |

Small-scale Hotel

Location: I-264, exit 22 (Birdneck Rd). Located adjacent to Virginia Beach Pavilion Conference Center. 1900 Pavilion Dr 23451. **Fax:** 757/425-8460. **Facility:** 292 units. 286 one-bedroom standard units. 6 one-bedroom suites. 12 stories, interior corridors. *Bath:* combo or shower only. **Parking:** on-site. **Terms:** check-in 4 pm, 3 day cancellation notice, [AP] meal plan available, package plans, small pets only ($25 fee, in designated units). **Amenities:** voice mail, irons, hair dryers. **Dining:** 6:30 am-10 pm, cocktails. **Pool(s):** heated indoor. **Leisure Activities:** 3 tennis courts, exercise room. **Guest Services:** gift shop, valet laundry, area transportation-beach. **Business Services:** conference facilities, business center. **Cards:** AX, CB, DC, DS, JC, MC, VI. **Special Amenities:** early check-in/late check-out and free room upgrade (subject to availability with advance reservations).

SOME UNITS

SD 🛏 🍴 🍸 📞 🏊 🎥 DATA PORT 💻 / ✕ 📷 / FEE   FEE FEE

THE DUNES OCEANFRONT   *Book at aaa.com*   Phone: 757/428-7731   🔢 39

▲▲▲ SAVE	7/1-9/5	1P: $189-$239	2P: $189-$239	XP: $10	F18
▼▼▼▼	5/27-6/30	1P: $109-$199	2P: $109-$199	XP: $10	F18
Motel	9/6-10/16	1P: $69-$189	2P: $69-$189	XP: $10	F18
	3/18-5/26	1P: $69-$129	2P: $69-$129	XP: $10	F18

Location: I-264, 0.8 mi s of terminus; Atlantic Ave and 10th St. 921 Atlantic Ave 23451. **Fax:** 757/428-7242. **Facility:** 107 one-bedroom standard units, some with whirlpools. 6 stories, interior/exterior corridors. **Parking:** on-site. **Terms:** open 3/18-10/16, 2 night minimum stay - weekends, 3 day cancellation notice, package plans. **Amenities:** irons, hair dryers. **Pool(s):** heated outdoor. **Leisure Activities:** whirlpools, exercise room. *Fee:* bicycles, game room. **Guest Services:** coin laundry. **Business Services:** meeting rooms, fax. **Cards:** AX, DC, DS, MC, VI. **Special Amenities:** free local telephone calls and free newspaper. *(See color ad p 752)*

SOME UNITS

SD 🏊 ✕ 🎥 DATA PORT 🖥 📷 💻 / ✕ /

ECONO LODGE OCEANFRONT   *Book at aaa.com*   Phone: (757)428-2403   🔢 23

▲▲▲ SAVE	5/20-9/4 [ECP]	1P: $104-$269	2P: $104-$269	XP: $10	F18
▼▼▼▼	9/5-10/8 [ECP]	1P: $79-$179	2P: $79-$179	XP: $10	F18
	3/1-5/19 [ECP]	1P: $69-$169	2P: $69-$169	XP: $10	F18
	10/9-2/28 [ECP]	1P: $59-$159	2P: $59-$159	XP: $10	F18

Small-scale Hotel **Location:** I-264, just n of terminus; Atlantic Ave and 21st St. 2109 Atlantic Ave 23451. **Fax:** 757/422-2530. **Facility:** 55 units. 54 one-bedroom standard units, some with efficiencies. 1 one-bedroom suite ($99-$299). 10 stories, interior corridors. *Bath:* combo or shower only. **Parking:** on-site. **Terms:** 3 night minimum stay - seasonal, 3 day cancellation notice, package plans. **Amenities:** safes (fee), irons, hair dryers. **Pool(s):** small heated indoor. **Business Services:** fax. **Cards:** AX, CB, DC, DS, MC, VI. **Special Amenities:** free expanded continental breakfast and free local telephone calls. *(See color ad p 747)*

SOME UNITS

SD 🍴 ♿ 🏊 🎥 DATA PORT 🖥 📷 💻 / ✕ /

ECONO LODGE ON THE OCEAN   *Book at aaa.com*   Phone: (757)428-3970   🔢 13

▲▲▲ SAVE	5/20-9/4 [CP]	1P: $104-$259	2P: $119-$259	XP: $10	F18
▼▼▼▼	9/5-10/8 [CP]	1P: $79-$179	2P: $79-$179	XP: $10	F18
	3/1-5/19 [CP]	1P: $69-$169	2P: $69-$169	XP: $10	F18
	10/9-2/28 [CP]	1P: $59-$159	2P: $59-$159	XP: $10	F18

Motel **Location:** I-264, just n of terminus. 2707 Atlantic Ave 23451. **Fax:** 757/422-1851. **Facility:** 38 units. 36 one-bedroom standard units. 2 one-bedroom suites with kitchens. 3 stories (no elevator), exterior corridors. *Bath:* combo or shower only. **Parking:** on-site. **Terms:** 3 night minimum stay - seasonal, 3 day cancellation notice. **Amenities:** safes (fee), irons, hair dryers. **Pool(s):** heated outdoor. **Leisure Activities:** bicycles. **Cards:** AX, CB, DC, DS, MC, VI. **Special Amenities:** free continental breakfast and free local telephone calls. *(See color ad p 747)*

SOME UNITS

SD 🍴 🏊 🎥 DATA PORT 🖥 📷 💻 / ✕ /

FAIRFIELD INN & SUITES VIRGINIA BEACH
OCEANFRONT   *Book at aaa.com*   Phone: (757)422-4885   🔢 48

▼▼▼▼	5/27-9/29	1P: $179-$239	2P: $179-$239		
	3/1-5/26	1P: $69-$179	2P: $69-$179		
Small-scale Hotel	9/30-10/29	1P: $89-$149	2P: $89-$149		
	10/30-2/28	1P: $69-$109	2P: $69-$109		

Location: I-264, terminus, just s. 1901 Atlantic Ave 23451. **Fax:** 757/422-4886. **Facility:** 114 units. 90 one-bedroom standard units, some with whirlpools. 24 one-bedroom suites. 9 stories, interior corridors. *Bath:* combo or shower only. **Parking:** on-site. **Terms:** check-in 4 pm, 3 day cancellation notice-fee imposed. **Amenities:** video games (fee), dual phone lines, voice mail, irons, hair dryers. *Some:* CD players. **Pool(s):** heated indoor. **Leisure Activities:** exercise room. **Guest Services:** sundries, valet and coin laundry. **Business Services:** business center. **Cards:** AX, DS, MC, VI.

SOME UNITS

ASK 🍴 ♿M 🚗 📞 🏊 🎥 DATA PORT 🖥 📷 💻 / ✕ 📷 / FEE

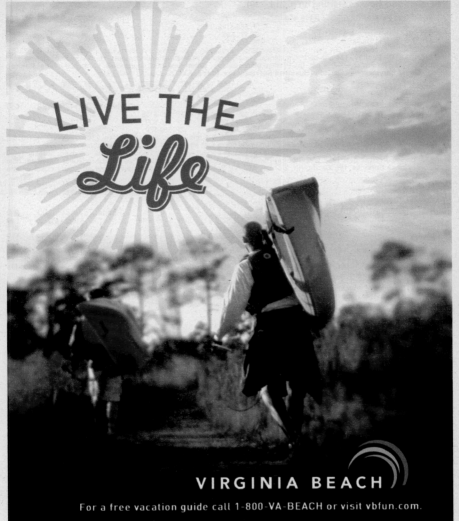

(See maps and indexes starting on p. 715, 719)

FAIRFIELD INN BY MARRIOTT   *Book at aaa.com*   Phone: (757)499-1935   **16**

▼▼ ▼▼	5/1-9/15	1P: $89-$149
	3/1-4/30 & 9/16-11/30	1P: $79-$99
Small-scale Hotel	12/1-2/28	1P: $59-$89

Location: I-264, exit 17B (Independence Blvd), just n to Euclid Rd, then just w. 4760 Euclid Rd 23462. Fax: 757/473-8197. **Facility:** 134 one-bedroom standard units. 3 stories, interior/exterior corridors. *Bath:* combo or shower only. **Parking:** on-site. **Terms:** check-in 4 pm, [ECP] meal plan available. **Amenities:** dual phone lines, irons, hair dryers. **Pool(s):** outdoor. **Guest Services:** valet laundry. **Business Services:** fax. **Cards:** AX, DC, DS, JC, MC, VI.

SOME UNITS
(ASK) (S/D) (YI→) (&M) 🛏 🛌 (+) (🐕) (DATA PORT) / (✕) (🛏) /

FLAGSHIP INN & EFFICIENCIES   Phone: (757)425-6422   **45**

(AAA) (SAVE)	6/1-9/15	1P: $89-$155	2P: $89-$155	XP: $10 F
	5/1-5/31	1P: $69-$99	2P: $69-$99	XP: $10 F
▼▼	3/1-4/30 & 9/16-2/28	1P: $59-$79	2P: $59-$79	XP: $10 F
Motel				

Location: I-264, 1 mi s of terminus; at Atlantic Ave and 6th St. 512 Atlantic Ave 23451. Fax: 757/491-6152. **Facility:** 55 one-bedroom standard units, some with kitchens. 6 stories, exterior corridors. **Parking:** on-site. **Terms:** 2 night minimum stay - seasonal and/or weekends, cancellation fee imposed, weekly rates available, package plans, pets ($30 fee). **Pool(s):** heated outdoor. **Leisure Activities:** Fee: bicycles. **Guest Services:** coin laundry. **Business Services:** fax. **Cards:** AX, DC, DS, MC, VI. **Special Amenities:** free newspaper and early check-in/late check-out.

SOME UNITS
🛏 (YI→) 🛌 (🛏) (🖥) / (✕) 💻 /
FEE

FOUR SAILS RESORT HOTEL   Phone: 757/491-8100   **7**

(AAA) (SAVE)	6/10-8/27	1P: $199-$249	2P: $199-$249	XP: $10 F17
	8/28-10/29	1P: $129-$159	2P: $129-$159	XP: $10 F17
▼▼▼▼	3/1-6/9	1P: $79-$159	2P: $79-$159	XP: $10 F17
	10/30-2/28	1P: $69-$89	2P: $69-$89	XP: $10 F17

Small-scale Hotel **Location:** I-264, 1.5 mi n of terminus, Atlantic Ave and 33rd. 3301 Atlantic Ave 23451 (PO Box 1239). Fax: 757/491-0573. **Facility:** 55 units. 49 one- and 6 two-bedroom suites with kitchens and whirlpools. 13 stories, interior/exterior corridors. **Parking:** on-site. **Terms:** 2 night minimum stay - weekends, 3 day cancellation notice-fee imposed, weekly rates available. **Amenities:** video library (fee), CD players, safes, irons, hair dryers. **Dining:** 7:30 am-9 pm; hours vary off season, cocktails. **Pool(s):** heated indoor. **Leisure Activities:** sauna, bicycles, exercise room. **Guest Services:** coin laundry. **Business Services:** fax. **Cards:** AX, CB, DC, DS, MC, VI. **Special Amenities:** free newspaper. *(See color ad below)*

(S/D) (YI) 🛌 (✕) (VCR) (🐕) (DATA PORT) (🛏) (🖥) 💻

HAMPTON INN VIRGINIA BEACH   *Book at aaa.com*   Phone: (757)490-9800   **11**

▼▼▼▼	All Year	1P: $65-$149	2P: $65-$149

Small-scale Hotel **Location:** I-64, exit 284B to I-264 (Virginia Beach-Norfolk Expwy), then exit Newtown Rd S. 5793 Greenwich Rd 23462. Fax: 757/490-3573. **Facility:** 122 one-bedroom standard units. 4 stories, interior corridors. **Parking:** on-site. **Terms:** cancellation fee imposed. **Amenities:** video games, voice mail, irons, hair dryers. **Pool(s):** outdoor. **Leisure Activities:** exercise room. **Guest Services:** valet laundry. **Business Services:** meeting rooms, fax. **Cards:** AX, CB, DC, DS, MC, VI.

SOME UNITS
(ASK) (S/D) (YI→) (&M) 🛌 🛌 (🐕) (DATA PORT) 💻 / (✕) (🛏) (🖥) /

HILTON GARDEN INN VIRGINIA BEACH, TOWN CENTER   *Book at aaa.com*   Phone: (757)326-6200   **14**

▼▼▼	5/1-9/5	1P: $89-$179	2P: $89-$179	XP: $10 F
	9/6-12/31	1P: $69-$109	2P: $69-$109	XP: $10 F
Small-scale Hotel	3/1-4/30 & 1/1-2/28	1P: $59-$109	2P: $59-$109	XP: $10 F

Location: I-264, exit 17B (Independence Blvd), just n to Virginia Beach Blvd, then just e. 252 Town Center Dr 23462. Fax: 757/326-6222. **Facility:** 176 units. 172 one-bedroom standard units, some with whirlpools. 4 one-bedroom suites ($199-$239) with whirlpools. 7 stories, interior corridors. *Bath:* combo or shower only. **Parking:** on-site. **Terms:** 2 night minimum stay - seasonal, cancellation fee imposed. **Amenities:** video games, high-speed Internet, dual phone lines, voice mail, irons, hair dryers. *Some:* DVD players (fee). **Pool(s):** heated indoor. **Leisure Activities:** whirlpool, exercise room. **Guest Services:** sundries, valet and coin laundry. **Business Services:** meeting rooms, business center. **Cards:** AX, CB, DC, DS, JC, MC, VI.

SOME UNITS
(ASK) (YI) (Y) (&M) (🖥) 🛌 🛌 (🐕) (DATA PORT) (🛏) (🖥) 💻 / (✕) (VCR) /
FEE

(See maps and indexes starting on p. 715, 719)

HILTON VIRGINIA BEACH OCEANFRONT   **Phone:** 757/213-3000

fyi	5/22-9/6	1P: $169-$269	2P: $169-$269	XP: $25	F18
	3/1-5/21	1P: $99-$219	2P: $99-$219	XP: $25	F18
Large-scale Hotel	9/7-2/28	1P: $89-$139	2P: $89-$139	XP: $25	F18

Too new to rate, opening scheduled for March 2005. **Location:** I-264, 0.5 mi n of terminus. 3001 Atlantic Ave 23451. **Amenities:** 295 units, restaurant, pool. **Terms:** 2 night minimum stay - seasonal and/or weekends, 3 day cancellation notice-fee imposed. **Cards:** AX, CB, DC, DS, MC, VI. *(See color ad p 742 & below)*

(See maps and indexes starting on p. 715, 719)

HOLIDAY INN-EXECUTIVE CENTER

AAA SAVE ♦♦♦♦♦♦

Book at aaa.com

Phone: (757)499-4400   **12**

	1P: $99-$169	2P: $99-$169	XP: $10	F19
5/2-9/15				
3/1-5/1 & 9/16-2/28	1P: $89-$139	2P: $89-$139	XP: $10	F19

Location: I-64, exit 284B (Newtown Rd); jct I-64 and 264. 5655 Greenwich Rd 23462. Fax: 757/473-0517. **Facility:** 331 units. 327 one-bedroom standard units. 4 one-bedroom suites ($199-$259). 6 stories, interior Large-scale Hotel corridors. *Bath:* combo or shower only. **Parking:** on-site. **Amenities:** video games, voice mail, irons, hair dryers. **Dining:** 6 am-10 pm, cocktails. **Pool(s):** outdoor, heated indoor. **Leisure Activities:** sauna, whirlpool, exercise room. **Guest Services:** valet laundry. **Business Services:** conference facilities, business center. **Cards:** AX, CB, DC, DS, JC, MC, VI. **Special Amenities:** free full breakfast and free newspaper. *(See color ad below)*

SOME UNITS / FEE FEE

HOLIDAY INN OCEANSIDE

♦♦♦♦♦

Book at aaa.com

Phone: (757)491-1500   **24**

5/16-9/30	1P: $149-$279	2P: $149-$279	XP: $10	F18
5/15 & 10/1-2/28	1P: $79-$199	2P: $79-$199	XP: $10	F18

Small-scale Hotel **Location:** I-264, at terminus; 21st St and Atlantic Ave. 2101 Atlantic Ave 23451. Fax: 757/491-1945. **Facility:** 150 one-bedroom standard units. 12 stories, interior corridors. **Parking:** on-site. **Terms:** 3 night minimum stay - seasonal and/or weekends, 3 day cancellation notice-fee imposed. **Amenities:** video games, voice mail, irons, hair dryers. **Pool(s):** heated indoor. **Leisure Activities:** whirlpool, exercise room. **Guest Services:** valet laundry. **Business Services:** meeting rooms, fax. **Cards:** AX, DC, DS, MC, VI.

SOME UNITS

HOLIDAY INN SUNSPREE RESORT

AAA SAVE ♦♦♦♦♦

Book at aaa.com

Phone: (757)428-1711   **1**

5/27-9/5	1P: $189-$289
9/6-10/31	1P: $84-$199
3/1-5/26	1P: $69-$199
11/1-2/28	1P: $69-$139

Small-scale Hotel **Location:** I-264, 1.4 mi n from terminus; at Atlantic Ave and 39th St. 3900 Atlantic Ave 23451. Fax: 757/425-5742. **Facility:** 266 units. 211 one-bedroom standard units, some with whirlpools. 55 one-bedroom suites. 7 stories, interior corridors. **Parking:** on-site. **Terms:** check-in 4 pm, 3 day cancellation notice-fee imposed. **Amenities:** video games, dual phone lines, voice mail, irons, hair dryers. **Dining:** 2 restaurants, 6:30 am-2 & 5-10 pm, cocktails, also, Isle of Capri, see separate listing. **Pool(s):** outdoor, 2 heated indoor. **Leisure Activities:** whirlpools, kids club in season, exercise room, volleyball. *Fee:* bicycles, game room. **Guest Services:** gift shop, valet and coin laundry. **Business Services:** conference facilities, fax. **Cards:** AX, DC, DS, MC, VI. *(See color ad p 757)*

SOME UNITS

HOLIDAY INN SURFSIDE HOTEL & SUITES

♦♦♦♦

Book at aaa.com

Phone: (757)491-6900   **17**

5/21-9/30	1P: $109-$299	2P: $109-$299
3/1-5/20	1P: $89-$229	2P: $89-$229
10/1-2/28	1P: $69-$199	2P: $69-$199

Small-scale Hotel **Location:** I-264, n of terminus; at Atlantic Ave and 26th St. 2607 Atlantic Ave 23451. Fax: 757/491-2125. **Facility:** 143 units. 125 one-bedroom standard units, some with whirlpools. 18 one-bedroom suites ($99-$299). 10 stories, interior corridors. **Parking:** on-site. **Terms:** check-in 4 pm, 3 night minimum stay - seasonal and/or weekends, 3 day cancellation notice-fee imposed. **Amenities:** video games, high-speed Internet (fee), dual phone lines, voice mail, irons, hair dryers. **Pool(s):** small heated indoor. **Leisure Activities:** whirlpool, exercise room. *Fee:* massage. **Guest Services:** valet and coin laundry. **Business Services:** meeting rooms, fax. **Cards:** AX, DC, DS, MC, VI.

SOME UNITS

HOWARD JOHNSON OCEANFRONT HOTEL

♦♦♦♦

Book at aaa.com

Phone: (757)437-9100   **28**

5/25-9/30	1P: $129-$199	2P: $129-$199	XP: $10	F18
4/1-5/24	1P: $89-$129	2P: $89-$129	XP: $10	F18
3/1-3/31 & 10/1-2/28	1P: $49-$89	2P: $49-$89	XP: $10	F18

Small-scale Hotel **Location:** I-264, just s of terminus; jct 18th and Atlantic Ave. 1801 Atlantic Ave 23451. Fax: 757/428-0827. **Facility:** 107 units. 106 one-bedroom standard units, some with whirlpools. 1 one-bedroom suite ($159-$259). 8 stories, interior corridors. *Bath:* combo or shower only. **Parking:** on-site. **Terms:** check-in 4 pm, 3 day cancellation notice-fee imposed. **Amenities:** voice mail, safes (fee), irons, hair dryers. **Pool(s):** heated indoor. **Leisure Activities:** Fee: bicycles, game room. **Guest Services:** gift shop, coin laundry. **Business Services:** meeting rooms, fax. **Cards:** AX, CB, DC, DS, MC, VI. *(See color ad p 742 & p 757)*

SOME UNITS

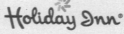

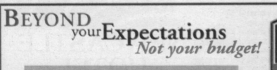

(See maps and indexes starting on p. 715, 719)

LA QUINTA INN NORFOLK (VIRGINIA BEACH)   *Book at aaa.com*   Phone: (757)497-6620   **15**

(AAA) (SAVE)	5/21-9/7	1P: $99-$139	2P: $105-$145	XP: $6	F18
	9/8-10/31	1P: $79-$105	2P: $85-$111	XP: $6	F18
▽▽▽▽	3/1-5/20 & 11/1-2/28	1P: $69-$89	2P: $75-$95	XP: $6	F18

Location: I-64, exit 284B to I-264 (Virginia Beach-Norfolk Expwy), exit Newtown Rd S. 192 Newtown Rd 23462.
Small-scale Hotel Fax: 757/456-9780. **Facility:** 129 units. 126 one-bedroom standard units. 3 one-bedroom suites. 3 stories, interior corridors. **Parking:** on-site. **Terms:** [ECP] meal plan available, small pets only. **Amenities:** video games, voice mail, irons, hair dryers. **Pool(s):** outdoor. **Guest Services:** valet laundry. **Business Services:** fax. **Cards:** AX, DC, DS, MC, VI. **Special Amenities:** free expanded continental breakfast and free local telephone calls.
(See color ad p 730)

SOME UNITS

FEE   FEE

THE MARJAC SUITES   Phone: (757)425-0100   **22**

▽▽▽ ▽▽▽	5/27-9/4	1P: $69-$239	2P: $69-$239	XP: $10	F18
	9/5-10/8	1P: $69-$199	2P: $69-$199	XP: $10	F18
Motel	10/9-2/28	1P: $49-$189	2P: $49-$189	XP: $10	F18
	3/1-5/26	1P: $49-$139	2P: $49-$139	XP: $10	F18

Location: I-264, n of terminus; at 22nd St. 2201 Atlantic Ave 23451. Fax: 757/491-0846. **Facility:** 60 one-bedroom suites with kitchens. 7 stories, exterior corridors. **Parking:** on-site. **Terms:** check-in 4 pm, 3 night minimum stay - seasonal and/or weekends, 3 day cancellation notice, package plans. **Amenities:** safes (fee). **Pool(s):** outdoor. **Leisure Activities:** Fee: bicycles. **Guest Services:** coin laundry. **Business Services:** fax. **Cards:** AX, DC, DS, MC, VI. *(See color ad p 740)*

SOME UNITS

NEW CASTLE HOTEL   Phone: (757)428-3981   **36**

▽▽ ▽▽	5/27-9/4	1P: $99-$229	2P: $99-$229	XP: $15	F18
	3/1-5/26	1P: $49-$169	2P: $49-$169	XP: $15	F18
Small-scale Hotel	9/5-10/8	1P: $79-$149	2P: $79-$149	XP: $15	F18
	10/9-2/28	1P: $49-$119	2P: $49-$119	XP: $15	F18

Location: I-264, 0.6 mi s of terminus. 1203 Atlantic Ave 23451. Fax: 757/491-4394. **Facility:** 83 one-bedroom standard units with whirlpools, some with efficiencies. 10 stories, interior/exterior corridors. **Parking:** on-site. **Terms:** 3 night minimum stay - seasonal and/or weekends, 3 day cancellation notice. **Amenities:** safes (fee), irons, hair dryers. **Pool(s):** heated indoor. **Leisure Activities:** exercise room. **Guest Services:** coin laundry. **Cards:** AX, DC, DS, MC, VI. *(See color ad below)*

SOME UNITS

(See maps and indexes starting on p. 715, 719)

THE OCEANFRONT INN

			Phone: (757)422-0445	**10**
5/13-9/5	1P: $134-$241	2P: $134-$241	XP: $20	F13
9/6-10/16	1P: $58-$174	2P: $58-$174	XP: $20	F13
3/1-5/12	1P: $54-$134	2P: $54-$134	XP: $20	F13
10/17-2/28	1P: $54-$114	2P: $54-$114	XP: $20	F13

Small-scale Hotel **Location:** I-264, n of terminus; at Atlantic Ave and 29th St. 2901 Atlantic Ave 23451. Fax: 757/491-6276. **Facility:** 147 one-bedroom standard units. 7 stories, interior corridors. **Parking:** on-site. **Terms:** check-in 4 pm, 2 night minimum stay - weekends, package plans. **Amenities:** high-speed Internet, irons, hair dryers. **Dining:** 7 am-10 pm, cocktails. **Pool(s):** heated indoor. **Guest Services:** gift shop, valet laundry. **Business Services:** meeting rooms. **Cards:** AX, CB, DC, DS, MC, VI. **Special Amenities:** free newspaper. *(See color ad p 745)*

SOME UNITS

OCEAN HOLIDAY HOTEL

		Phone: (757)425-6920	**20**
6/9-9/5	2P: $95-$195	XP: $6	F12
9/6-2/28	2P: $45-$165	XP: $6	F12
5/26-6/8	2P: $45-$145	XP: $6	F12
3/1-5/25	2P: $45-$135	XP: $6	F12

Small-scale Hotel **Location:** I-264, n of terminus; at Atlantic Ave and 25th St. 2417 Atlantic Ave 23451. Fax: 757/425-7264. **Facility:** 105 one-bedroom standard units, some with whirlpools. 7 stories, interior corridors. **Parking:** on-site. **Terms:** 2 night minimum stay - seasonal, 3 day cancellation notice-fee imposed, $1 service charge. **Dining:** 7 am-11 pm; hours vary off season, cocktails. **Pool(s):** heated indoor. **Leisure Activities:** sun deck. **Business Services:** meeting rooms, fax. **Cards:** AX, DS, MC, VI. **Special Amenities:** free local telephone calls and free newspaper. *(See color ad below)*

SOME UNITS

FEE FEE

QUALITY INN & SUITES   *Book at aaa.com*

			Phone: (757)428-8935	**41**
5/27-9/4	1P: $139-$249	2P: $139-$249	XP: $15	F18
3/1-5/26 & 9/5-10/15	1P: $59-$149	2P: $59-$149	XP: $15	F18
10/16-2/28	1P: $59-$109	2P: $59-$109	XP: $15	F18

Small-scale Hotel **Location:** I-264, 1 mi s of terminus; at Atlantic Ave and 8th St. 705 Atlantic Ave 23451. Fax: 757/425-2769. **Facility:** 124 one-bedroom standard units. 6 stories, interior corridors. **Parking:** on-site. **Terms:** 3 day cancellation notice, package plans. **Amenities:** voice mail, safes (fee), irons, hair dryers. **Pool(s):** outdoor, heated indoor. **Leisure Activities:** Fee: bicycles. **Guest Services:** valet laundry. **Business Services:** conference facilities, fax. **Cards:** AX, CB, DC, DS, JC, MC. *(See color ad p 740)*

SOME UNITS

QUALITY INN PAVILION   *Book at aaa.com*

			Phone: (757)422-3617	**7**
6/16-9/15	1P: $119-$299	2P: $199-$299	XP: $10	F18
3/1-6/15 & 9/16-2/28	1P: $49-$199	2P: $49-$199	XP: $10	F18

Small-scale Hotel **Location:** I-264, at terminus; jct 21st St and Park Ave. Located adjacent to the Pavilion Conference Center. 716 21st St 23451. Fax: 757/428-7434. **Facility:** 109 units. 103 one-bedroom standard units. 6 one-bedroom suites, some with kitchens. 2-4 stories, exterior corridors. **Parking:** on-site. **Terms:** 2 night minimum stay - weekends, 3 day cancellation notice. **Amenities:** irons. *Some:* hair dryers. **Dining:** 7 am-2 & 5-10 pm; hours may vary seasonally, cocktails. **Pool(s):** outdoor. **Guest Services:** complimentary laundry, area transportation. **Business Services:** fax. **Cards:** AX, CB, DC, DS, JC, MC, VI. **Special Amenities:** free local telephone calls and free newspaper.

SOME UNITS

If it's possible for one incredible luxury resort to change your impression of an entire oceanfront, Ocean Beach Club will do it. When completed in Spring 2005, Ocean Beach Club will become the shining star at the north end of the Virginia Beach oceanfront. This gorgeous, top-class vacation resort will afford beautiful beach vistas wrapped in a Key West feel, with a range of stunning accommodations and wonderful amenities inside and out. 1-800-293-8145

WWW.OCEANBEACHCLUBAAA.COM

(See maps and indexes starting on p. 715, 719)

RAMADA INN ON THE BEACH   *Book at aaa.com*   **Phone: (757)425-7800**   42

6/17-9/1	1P: $159-$229	2P: $159-$229
3/1-6/16	1P: $69-$229	2P: $69-$229
9/2-10/31	1P: $69-$169	2P: $69-$169
11/1-2/28	1P: $59-$129	2P: $59-$129

Small-scale Hotel

Location: I-264, 1 mi s of terminus; at Atlantic Ave and 6th St. 615 Atlantic Ave 23451. Fax: 757/437-0470. **Facility:** 167 one-bedroom standard units, some with whirlpools. 8 stories, interior corridors. *Bath:* combo or shower only. **Parking:** valet. **Terms:** check-in 4 pm, 2-5 night minimum stay - seasonal and/or weekends, 3 day cancellation notice, package plans. **Amenities:** video games, voice mail, safes (fee), irons, hair dryers. **Dining:** Mahi Mah's Seafood Restaurant & Sushi Saloon, see separate listing. **Pool(s):** heated indoor. **Leisure Activities:** whirlpool, rental bicycles, exercise room. **Guest Services:** coin laundry. **Business Services:** conference facilities, fax. **Cards:** AX, CB, DC, DS, MC, VI. *(See color ad p 742 & below)*

SOME UNITS   (ASK) (S⬦) (🍴) (🍷) (🎦) (🐕) (🏊) (✕) (🏋) (DATA PORT) (📺) / (✕) (🔵 FEE) (📷 FEE) /

RAMADA LIMITED ATLANTIC AVENUE   *Book at aaa.com*   **Phone: (757)425-7730**   9

6/2-10/27	1P: $59-$165	2P: $59-$165	XP: $8	F18
5/1-6/1	1P: $75-$95	2P: $75-$95	XP: $8	F18
4/1-4/30	1P: $65-$85	2P: $65-$85	XP: $8	F18

Small-scale Hotel

Location: I-264, 0.6 mi n of terminus; at Atlantic Ave and 31st St. 3108 Atlantic Ave 23451. Fax: 757/425-7524. **Facility:** 94 one-bedroom standard units. 5 stories, exterior corridors. *Bath:* combo or shower only. **Parking:** on-site. **Terms:** open 4/1-10/27, check-in 4 pm, 2 night minimum stay - weekends, 3 day cancellation notice, [CP] meal plan available, package plans. **Amenities:** voice mail, safes (fee), irons, hair dryers. **Pool(s):** outdoor, wading. **Business Services:** meeting rooms, fax. **Cards:** AX, DS, MC, VI. *(See color ad below)*

SOME UNITS   (ASK) (S⬦) (🎦) (🏊) (🐕) (DATA PORT) (📺) / (✕) (🔵 FEE) (📷 FEE) /

(See maps and indexes starting on p. 715, 719)

RAMADA PLAZA RESORT OCEANFRONT

Book at aaa.com   Phone: (757)428-7025   **5**

(AAA) (SAVE)	5/27-9/4	1P: $180-$260	2P: $180-$260	XP: $10	F18
	9/5-2/28	1P: $80-$175	2P: $80-$175	XP: $10	F18
◇◇◇◇	4/1-5/26	1P: $105-$155	2P: $105-$155	XP: $10	F18
	3/1-3/31	1P: $85-$105	2P: $85-$105	XP: $10	F18

Large-scale Hotel **Location:** I-264, 2.2 mi n of terminus. Located in a residential area. Atlantic Ave and 57th St 23451 (5700 Atlantic Ave). Fax: 757/428-2921. **Facility:** 245 units. 221 one-bedroom standard units, some with whirlpools. 20 one- and 4 two-bedroom suites ($145-$460). 5-17 stories, interior corridors. *Bath:* combo or shower only. **Parking:** on-site. **Terms:** check-in 4 pm, 2-3 night minimum stay - seasonal and/or weekends, 3 day cancellation notice-fee imposed, package plans, pets ($5 extra charge, in designated units). **Amenities:** video games, voice mail, safes (fee), irons, hair dryers. *Some:* dual phone lines. **Dining:** 2 restaurants, 7 am-10 pm, Fri & Sat-midnight, also, Gus's Mariner Restaurant, see separate listing. **Pool(s):** heated outdoor, heated indoor. **Leisure Activities:** sauna, whirlpool, recreation programs in summer, exercise room, volleyball. *Fee:* kayaks, bicycles. **Guest Services:** gift shop, valet laundry, area transportation-resort area. **Business Services:** conference facilities, business center. **Cards:** AX, DC, DS, MC, VI. **Special Amenities:** free newspaper and preferred room (subject to availability with advance reservations). *(See color ad below)*

SOME UNITS

RED ROOF INN VA BEACH (NORFOLK AIRPORT)

Book at aaa.com   Phone: (757)460-6700   **4**

(AAA) (SAVE)	5/1-9/15	1P: $60-$171	2P: $70-$176	XP: $6	F17
	3/1-4/30 & 9/16-2/28	1P: $50-$100	2P: $56-$100	XP: $6	F17

Motel **Location:** I-64, exit 282, 1 mi n on US 13 (Northampton Blvd). 5745 Northampton Blvd 23455. Fax: 757/460-1262. **Facility:** 148 one-bedroom standard units. 2 stories (no elevator), exterior corridors. **Parking:** on-site. **Terms:** 3 day cancellation notice-fee imposed, package plans, pets ($10 fee). **Amenities:** *Some:* dual phone lines. **Pool(s):** outdoor. **Guest Services:** coin laundry. **Business Services:** fax. **Cards:** AX, CB, DC, DS, MC, VI. **Special Amenities:** free local telephone calls and free newspaper.

SOME UNITS

RED ROOF INN-VIRGINIA BEACH

Book at aaa.com   Phone: (757)490-0225   **13**

◇◇	5/23-8/28	1P: $73-$100	2P: $78-$105	XP: $5	F18
	4/10-5/22	1P: $51-$74	2P: $56-$79	XP: $5	F18
Motel	8/29-2/28	1P: $51-$66	2P: $56-$72	XP: $5	F18
	3/1-4/9	1P: $42-$59	2P: $46-$65	XP: $5	F18

Location: I-64/264, exit 284B (Newtown Rd). 196 Ballard Ct 23462. Fax: 757/490-8220. **Facility:** 108 one-bedroom standard units. 2 stories (no elevator), exterior corridors. **Parking:** on-site. **Terms:** small pets only. **Amenities:** video games, voice mail. **Pool(s):** outdoor. **Business Services:** fax. **Cards:** AX, CB, DC, DS, MC, VI.

SOME UNITS

(See maps and indexes starting on p. 715, 719)

ROYAL CLIPPER INN & SUITES

Phone: (757)428-8992 **5**

6/17-8/27	1P: $99-$169	2P: $99-$169	XP: $10 F12
5/1-6/16	1P: $59-$169	2P: $59-$169	XP: $10 F12
8/28-10/31	1P: $39-$119	2P: $39-$119	XP: $10 F12
3/1-4/30	1P: $39-$109	2P: $39-$109	XP: $10 F12

AAA (SAVE) ◊◊◊ Motel

Location: I-264, exit terminus, 1 mi n. 3508 Atlantic Ave 23451. Fax: 757/491-9302. **Facility:** 87 one-bedroom standard units, some with efficiencies. 5 stories, exterior corridors. **Parking:** on-site. **Terms:** open 3/1-10/31, 3 night minimum stay - seasonal and/or weekends, 3 day cancellation notice-fee imposed, $2 service charge. **Amenities:** high-speed Internet, voice mail, safes (fee), irons, hair dryers. **Pool(s):** small outdoor. **Guest Services:** coin laundry. **Business Services:** fax. **Cards:** AX, DS, MC, VI. **Special Amenities:** free local telephone calls and free newspaper.
(See color ad below)

SOME UNITS

SANDCASTLE OCEANFRONT RESORT HOTEL

Phone: 757/428-2828 **34**

5/27-9/5 [ECP]	1P: $99-$259	2P: $99-$259	XP: $10 F12
9/6-10/31 [ECP]	1P: $49-$149	2P: $49-$149	XP: $10 F12
3/1-5/26 & 11/1-2/28 [ECP]	1P: $49-$109	2P: $49-$109	XP: $10 F12

AAA (SAVE) ◊◊◊ Small-scale Hotel

Location: I-264, terminus, 0.5 mi s at 14th St. Located adjacent to Lynnhaven Fishing Pier. 1307 Atlantic Ave 23451. Fax: 757/422-3184. **Facility:** 150 units. 148 one-bedroom standard units. 2 one-bedroom suites. 9 stories, interior corridors. *Bath:* combo or shower only. **Parking:** on-site. **Terms:** 3 night minimum stay - seasonal and/or weekends, 3 day cancellation notice-fee imposed, package plans. **Amenities:** voice mail, safes (fee), irons, hair dryers. **Dining:** 2 restaurants, 7 am-11 pm; hours vary off season, cocktails. **Pool(s):** heated indoor, wading. **Leisure Activities:** exercise room. *Fee:* bicycles, game room. **Guest Services:** gift shop, coin laundry. **Business Services:** meeting rooms, PC. **Cards:** AX, DC, DS, MC, VI. **Special Amenities:** free expanded continental breakfast and free newspaper.
(See color ad p 764)

SOME UNITS

SCHOONER INN

Phone: (757)425-5222 **47**

5/27-9/4	1P: $59-$209	2P: $59-$209	XP: $10 F18
3/1-5/26	1P: $39-$139	2P: $39-$139	XP: $10 F18
9/5-10/8	1P: $59-$129	2P: $59-$129	XP: $10 F18
10/9-2/28	1P: $39-$99	2P: $39-$99	XP: $10 F18

◊◊ Motel

Location: I-264, 1.4 mi s of terminus. 215 Atlantic Ave 23451. Fax: 757/491-2759. **Facility:** 89 units. 83 one-bedroom standard units, some with efficiencies and/or whirlpools. 6 one-bedroom suites ($69-$259) with kitchens. 6 stories, exterior corridors. *Bath:* combo or shower only. **Parking:** on-site. **Terms:** check-in 4 pm, 3 night minimum stay - seasonal and/or weekends, 3 day cancellation notice, package plans. **Amenities:** safes (fee). *Some:* hair dryers. **Pool(s):** heated outdoor. **Guest Services:** coin laundry. **Business Services:** fax. **Cards:** AX, DC, DS, MC, VI. *(See color ad p 740)*

SOME UNITS

(See maps and indexes starting on p. 715, 719)

SEA GULL MOTEL

Phone: 757/425-5711   **16**

5/27-9/4	1P: $90-$190	2P: $90-$190	XP: $10 F12
9/5-10/29	1P: $45-$145	2P: $45-$145	XP: $10 F12
3/1-5/26	1P: $40-$125	2P: $40-$125	XP: $10 F12
10/30-2/28	1P: $35-$70	2P: $35-$70	XP: $5 F12

Small-scale Hotel **Location:** I-264, 0.5 mi n of terminus; at Atlantic Ave and 27th St. 2613 Atlantic Ave 23451. Fax: 757/425-5710. **Facility:** 51 one-bedroom standard units, some with efficiencies. 4 stories, interior/exterior corridors. **Parking:** on-site. **Terms:** check-in 4 pm, 3 night minimum stay - seasonal, 3 day cancellation notice-fee imposed, [BP] & [MAP] meal plans available, package plans. **Amenities:** irons. **Dining:** 7 am-10 pm; hours vary seasonally, cocktails. **Pool(s):** heated indoor. **Leisure Activities:** whirlpool, sun deck. *Fee:* bicycles. **Business Services:** fax. **Cards:** AX, CB, DC, DS, MC, VI. **Special Amenities:** early check-in/late check-out and preferred room (subject to availability with advance reservations).** *(See color ad below)*

SOME UNITS

SEAHAWK MOTEL

Phone: (757)428-1296   **18**

6/9-9/5	2P: $95-$189	XP: $7 F11
5/26-6/8	2P: $65-$149	XP: $7 F11
3/1-5/25	2P: $45-$139	XP: $7 F11
9/6-10/31	2P: $49-$129	XP: $7 F11

Motel **Location:** I-264, n of terminus; at Atlantic Ave and 26th St. 2525 Atlantic Ave 23451 (PO Box 449, 23458). Fax: 757/491-3265. **Facility:** 48 one-bedroom standard units, some with efficiencies. 6 stories, interior corridors. **Parking:** on-site. **Terms:** open 3/1-10/31, 2 night minimum stay - seasonal, 3 day cancellation notice-fee imposed, $1 service charge. **Pool(s):** heated indoor. **Leisure Activities:** whirlpool. **Guest Services:** coin laundry. **Business Services:** fax. **Cards:** AX, DS, MC, VI. **Special Amenities:** free newspaper. *(See color ad p 766)*

SOME UNITS

SEASIDE MOTEL

Phone: 757/428-9341   **14**

6/10-8/27	2P: $90-$115	XP: $6
8/28-10/1	2P: $60-$90	XP: $6
3/1-6/9	2P: $40-$80	XP: $6
10/2-2/28	2P: $40-$50	XP: $6

Motel **Location:** I-264, n of terminus; at Atlantic Ave and 27th St. 2705 Atlantic Ave 23451. Fax: 757/425-5355. **Facility:** 46 one-bedroom standard units, some with efficiencies. 4 stories, interior/exterior corridors. **Parking:** on-site. **Terms:** 3 night minimum stay - seasonal, 3 day cancellation notice-fee imposed. **Pool(s):** heated indoor. **Leisure Activities:** sun deck. **Business Services:** fax. **Cards:** MC, VI. *(See color ad p 766)*

(See maps and indexes starting on p. 715, 719)

SHERATON OCEANFRONT HOTEL   *Book at aaa.com*   Phone: (757)425-9000   **4**

5/1-8/17	1P: $129-$179	2P: $129-$179
8/18-9/30	1P: $99-$129	2P: $99-$129
3/1-4/30	1P: $59-$129	2P: $59-$129
10/1-2/28	1P: $69-$99	2P: $69-$99

Small-scale Hotel

Location: I-264, 1 mi n of terminus; jct 36th St. 3501 Atlantic Ave 23451. Fax: 757/428-5352. **Facility:** 198 units. 194 one-bedroom standard units, some with whirlpools. 4 one-bedroom suites ($139-$219). 11 stories, interior corridors. *Bath:* combo or shower only. **Parking:** on-site. **Terms:** check-in 4 pm, 3 night minimum stay - seasonal, 3 day cancellation notice-fee imposed, [AP] meal plan available, package plans, pets (small dogs only). **Amenities:** video games, high-speed Internet, dual phone lines, voice mail, irons, hair dryers. **Pool(s):** outdoor, heated indoor. **Leisure Activities:** whirlpools, exercise room. *Fee:* bicycles. **Guest Services:** gift shop, valet laundry. **Business Services:** conference facilities, fax. **Cards:** AX, DC, DS, MC, VI.

SOME UNITS

SUNDIAL MOTEL & EFFICIENCIES   *Book at aaa.com*   Phone: (757)428-2922   **26**

5/16-9/10	1P: $69-$189	2P: $69-$189	XP: $7	F12
3/1-5/15 & 9/11-2/28	1P: $39-$99	2P: $39-$99	XP: $7	F12

Motel

Location: I-264, at terminus; jct 21st St and Pacific Ave. 308 21st St 23451. Fax: 757/491-8218. **Facility:** 67 one-bedroom standard units, some with efficiencies. 3-4 stories (no elevator), exterior corridors. **Parking:** on-site. **Terms:** cancellation fee imposed. **Amenities:** safes (fee), irons, hair dryers. **Pool(s):** outdoor. **Business Services:** fax. **Cards:** AX, DC, DS, MC, VI. **Special Amenities:** free local telephone calls and free newspaper. *(See color ad p 767)*

SOME UNITS

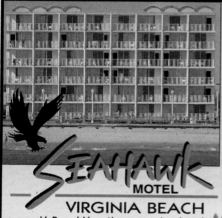

(See maps and indexes starting on p. 715, 719)

SURFSIDE OCEANFRONT INN & SUITES — *Book at aaa.com* — Phone: 757/428-1183 — 35

(AAA) (SAVE)
▽▽▽ ▽▽▽

	5/23-9/4	1P: $99-$249	2P: $99-$249	XP: $10	F
	9/5-10/31	1P: $49-$149	2P: $49-$149	XP: $10	F
	3/1-5/22 & 11/1-2/28	1P: $49-$109	2P: $49-$109	XP: $10	F

Small-scale Hotel **Location:** I-264, 0.5 mi s of terminus; at Atlantic Ave and 12th St. 1211 Atlantic Ave 23451. Fax: 757/428-2243. **Facility:** 99 units. 89 one-bedroom standard units. 10 one-bedroom suites ($109-$299) with whirlpools. 9 stories, interior corridors. **Parking:** on-site. **Terms:** 3 night minimum stay - seasonal and/or weekends, 3 day cancellation notice-fee imposed, package plans. **Amenities:** safes, irons, hair dryers. **Dining:** 6:30 am-1 am; hours vary off season, cocktails. **Pool(s):** heated indoor. **Leisure Activities:** Fee: rollerblade, bicycles. **Guest Services:** gift shop, coin laundry. **Business Services:** meeting rooms, fax. **Cards:** AX, DC, DS, MC, VI. *(See color ad p 768)*

SOME UNITS
(S_D) (❚¶) (➤) (▥) (❙) (▤) / (✕) (▭) /

TOWNEPLACE SUITES BY MARRIOTT — *Book at aaa.com* — Phone: (757)490-9367 — 8

▽▽▽

	5/26-9/30	1P: $135-$180	2P: $135-$180	
	4/1-5/25	1P: $104-$180	2P: $104-$180	
	3/1-3/31 & 10/1-2/28	1P: $94-$180	2P: $94-$180	

Small-scale Hotel **Location:** I-64, exit 284B to I-264 (Virginia Beach-Norfolk Expwy), exit Newtown Rd N. 5757 Cleveland St 23462. Fax: 757/490-9448. **Facility:** 95 units. 69 one-bedroom standard units with kitchens. 4 one- and 22 two-bedroom suites with kitchens. 3 stories, interior corridors. **Bath:** combo or shower only. **Parking:** on-site. **Terms:** cancellation fee imposed, pets ($125 fee). **Amenities:** voice mail, irons, hair dryers. **Pool(s):** outdoor. **Leisure Activities:** exercise room. **Guest Services:** valet and coin laundry. **Business Services:** fax. **Cards:** AX, DC, DS, JC, MC, VI.

SOME UNITS
(ASK) (🛏) (⌖M) (♿) (➤) (▥) (DATA PORT) (❙) (▤) (▭) / (✕) (VCR) /
FEE   FEE

TURTLE CAY RESORT — *Book at aaa.com* — Phone: (757)437-5565 — 43

▽▽▽

	6/16-9/5	1P: $129-$399	2P: $129-$399	XP: $15	F12
	3/1-6/15 & 9/6-10/31	1P: $69-$299	2P: $69-$299	XP: $15	F12
Condominium	11/1-2/28	1P: $59-$189	2P: $59-$189	XP: $15	F12

Location: I-264, 1 mi s of terminus; jct 6th St and Atlantic Ave. 600 Atlantic Ave 23451. Fax: 757/437-9104. **Facility:** Wraparound verandas and green shingled roofs recall Carolina beach cottages. Efficiencies, one- or two- bedroom suites offer comforts of home with gas-lit fireplaces and pine furniture. 121 units. 33 one-bedroom standard units. 86 one- and 2 two-bedroom suites, some with kitchens and/or whirlpools. 3 stories, exterior corridors. **Parking:** on-site. **Terms:** check-in 4 pm, 3 day cancellation notice-fee imposed. **Amenities:** voice mail, safes (fee), irons, hair dryers. **Pool(s):** 2 heated outdoor. **Leisure Activities:** whirlpools. **Guest Services:** valet and coin laundry. **Business Services:** fax. **Cards:** AX, CB, DC, DS, JC, MC, VI. *(See color ad p 742 & p 768)*

SOME UNITS
(ASK) (S_D) (❚¶) (➤) (▥) (▥) (DATA PORT) (❙) (▤) (▭) / (VCR) /
FEE

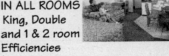

(See maps and indexes starting on p. 715, 719)

THE VIKING MOTEL

Phone: (757)428-7116 **15**

6/9-9/5	2P: $64-$174	XP: $5	F11
5/26-6/8	2P: $49-$159	XP: $5	F11
9/6-10/31	2P: $39-$119	XP: $5	F11
3/1-5/25	2P: $39-$109	XP: $5	F11

Motel **Location:** I-264, 0.5 mi n of terminus; at Atlantic Ave and 27th St. 2700 Atlantic Ave 23451 (PO Box 1030). Fax: 757/491-2767. **Facility:** 81 units. 61 one- and 20 two-bedroom standard units, some with efficiencies. 2-3 stories, interior/exterior corridors. **Parking:** on-site. **Terms:** open 3/1-10/31, 2 night minimum stay - seasonal, 3 day cancellation notice-fee imposed, $1 service charge. **Pool(s):** outdoor. **Business Services:** fax. **Cards:** AX, DC, DS, MC, VI. **Special Amenities:** free local telephone calls and free newspaper. *(See color ad p 769)*

SOME UNITS

VIRGINIA BEACH RESORT HOTEL & CONFERENCE
CENTER   *Book at aaa.com*

Phone: (757)481-9000 **1**

5/27-9/5	1P: $189-$379	2P: $199-$389	XP: $10	F18
3/1-5/26 & 9/6-10/30	1P: $119-$299	2P: $129-$309	XP: $10	F18
10/31-2/28	1P: $99-$229	2P: $109-$239	XP: $10	F18

Large-scale Hotel **Location:** US 60, 3.5 mi e of US 13. 2800 Shore Dr 23451. Fax: 757/496-7429. **Facility:** 295 units. 282 one- and 13 two-bedroom suites. 9 stories, interior corridors. *Bath:* combo or shower only. **Parking:** on-site. **Terms:** check-in 4 pm, 3 day cancellation notice-fee imposed, package plans. **Amenities:** high-speed Internet (fee), dual phone lines, voice mail, irons, hair dryers. **Dining:** 2 restaurants, 7 am-midnight, cocktails, also, Tradewinds, see separate listing. **Pool(s):** outdoor, heated indoor. **Leisure Activities:** sauna, whirlpool, tennis club & golf privileges, recreation programs, bicycles. *Fee:* aqua cycles, waverunners, massage. **Guest Services:** gift shop, valet and coin laundry, area transportation (fee)-oceanfront resort area. **Business Services:** conference facilities, business center. **Cards:** AX, CB, DC, DS, JC, MC, VI. **Special Amenities:** free newspaper and free room upgrade (subject to availability with advance reservations).** *(See color ad p 769)*

SOME UNITS

FEE

WINGATE INN-NORFOLK AIRPORT   *Book at aaa.com*

Phone: (757)363-2901 **6**

7/1-9/30	1P: $115-$130	2P: $115-$130	XP: $10	F17
4/1-6/30	1P: $109-$119	2P: $109-$119	XP: $10	F17
3/1-3/31 & 10/1-2/28	1P: $99-$109	2P: $99-$109	XP: $10	F17

Small-scale Hotel **Location:** I-64, exit 282, just ne on US 13 (Northampton Blvd). 5800 Burton Station Rd 23455. Fax: 757/363-2909. **Facility:** 100 units. 94 one-bedroom standard units. 6 one-bedroom suites ($130-$170) with whirlpools. 4 stories, interior corridors. *Bath:* combo or shower only. **Parking:** on-site. **Amenities:** video games, high-speed Internet, dual phone lines, voice mail, safes, irons, hair dryers. **Pool(s):** heated indoor. **Leisure Activities:** whirlpool, exercise room. **Guest Services:** valet laundry. **Business Services:** meeting rooms, business center. **Cards:** AX, CB, DC, DS, JC, MC, VI. *(See color ad below)*

SOME UNITS

(See maps and indexes starting on p. 715, 719)

——————— *The following lodging was either not evaluated or did not* ———————
meet AAA rating requirements but is listed for your information only.

THE FOUNDERS INN   Phone: 757/424-5511
[fyi]   Not evaluated. **Location:** I-64, exit 286B, just e; located on the campus of the Christian Broadcasting Network & Regent Unversity. 5641 Indian River Rd 23464. Facilities, services, and decor characterize a mid-range property.

——————— **WHERE TO DINE** ———————

ALDO'S RISTORANTE   Lunch: $8-$10   Dinner: $15-$25   Phone: 757/491-1111   39
▼▼▼   **Location:** I-264, exit Laskin Rd (SR 58), 0.3 mi e; in La Promenade Shops. 1860 Laskin Rd 23454. **Hours:** 11 am-11
Italian   pm, Fri & Sat-11:30 pm, Sun 4 pm-11 pm. Closed: 11/24, 12/25. **Reservations:** suggested. **Features:** A hip, local crowd comes for the stylish contemporary decor and the homemade Italian cuisine, prepared fresh daily. Brick-oven pizza, creative and traditional pasta and entrees are dependably well prepared. A pianist entertains Tuesday-Saturday evenings. Casual dress; cocktails; entertainment. **Parking:** on-site. **Cards:** AX, DC, MC, VI.

ALEXANDER'S ON THE BAY   Dinner: $17-$30   Phone: 757/464-4999   1
RESTAURANT
(AAA)   **Location:** Jct US 60 and 13, 0.3 mi w to Pleasure House Rd, 1 mi n to Lookout Rd, then 0.3 mi e to Fentress Rd to
▼▼▼▼   end. 4536 Ocean View Ave 23455. **Hours:** 5 pm-10 pm, Sat-11 pm, Sun-9 pm. Closed: 1/1, 12/25.
Reservations: suggested. **Features:** The romantic setting on the shore of Chesapeake Bay is noted for
Steak & Seafood   beautiful night views of the illuminated bridge. A breezy deck encourages leisurely dining. Creative preparations of seafood, as well as tender steak and veal, mark an impressive menu. Valet parking weekend and seasonally. Dressy casual; cocktails. **Parking:** on-site. **Cards:** AX, DC, DS, MC, VI.

ATLAS GRILL & BAR   Lunch: $6-$10   Dinner: $6-$14   Phone: 757/496-3839   29
▼▼▼   **Location:** On Great Neck Rd at jct First Colonial Rd. 2158 Great Neck Square Shopping Center 23454. **Hours:** 11
American   am-10 pm, Fri & Sat-11 pm. Closed: 12/25. **Features:** Hungry diners munch on heaping portions of comfort food that shows heavy Southern and diner-style influences. Topping the menu are great stick-to-the-ribs dishes, such as meatloaf, chicken pot pie and pork chops, as well as burgers and salads. Casual dress;
cocktails. **Parking:** on-site. **Cards:** AX, DC, MC, VI.

AZAR'S NATURAL FOODS   Lunch: $5-$11   Dinner: $6-$15   Phone: 757/486-7778   66
▼▼▼   **Location:** I-264, exit 17B (Independence Blvd), just e on Bonney Rd. 108 Prescott Ave 23452. **Hours:** 11:30 am-8:30
pm, Fri-9:30 pm. Closed major holidays; also Sun. **Features:** A loyal, growing clientele in search of
Middle Eastern   healthful, well-prepared Middle Eastern fare calls the eatery home. Roll sandwiches, delicatessen offerings and many vegetarian items are specialties, although meat is available. Try the lentil, orzo and vegetable soup, or grab items to go from the market section. Casual dress; beer & wine only. **Parking:** on-site. **Cards:** AX, DS, MC, VI.

BAKER'S CRUST BREAD MARKET   Lunch: $5-$8   Dinner: $7-$16   Phone: 757/422-6703   37
▼▼ ▼▼   **Location:** I-264, exit 21, just n to Hilltop North; 3 mi w of oceanfront on Laskin Rd. 704 Hilltop North Shopping Center
23451. **Hours:** 8 am-9 pm, Fri & Sat-10 pm, Sun-8 pm. Closed: 11/24, 12/25. **Features:** First and foremost,
American   this place is the home of crusty bread loaves and sweet bakery treats. Lunch favorites include interesting sandwiches and daily soup in edible bread bowl, while dinner offerings lean to more sophisticated fare, such as steak, seafood and rotisserie fowl. Seating at the crepe bar in the rear is a special treat. Casual dress; cocktails. **Parking:**
on-site. **Cards:** AX, MC, VI.

BANGKOK GARDEN   Lunch: $6-$9   Dinner: $8-$17   Phone: 757/425-4909   33
▼▼ ▼▼   **Location:** Jct Laskin Rd; in Hilltop Market Plaza. 737 First Colonial Rd 23451. **Hours:** 11 am-10 pm, Fri-10:30 pm,
Sat noon-10:30 pm, Sun noon-9 pm. Closed major holidays. **Features:** Thai artwork decorates the stylish
Thai   interior of this cozy restaurant. On the menu is fresh, healthy fare prepared with fresh seafood, chili peppers, curries, coconuts, tropical fruit and vegetables. Casual dress. **Parking:** on-site. **Cards:** DS,
MC, VI.

BANGKOK GARDEN   Lunch: $5-$7   Dinner: $8-$17   Phone: 757/498-5009   64
▼▼ ▼▼   **Location:** I-264, exit Independence Blvd/Pembroke, just n to US 58, then just e; in Loehmann's Plaza. 4000 Virginia
Beach Blvd 23452. **Hours:** 11 am-10 pm, Fri & Sat-10:30 pm, Sun noon-9 pm. Closed major holidays.
Thai   **Features:** Thai artwork decorates the stylish interior of this cozy restaurant. On the menu is fresh, healthy fare prepared with fresh seafood, chili peppers, curries, coconuts, tropical fruit and vegetables. Casual
dress; cocktails. **Parking:** on-site. **Cards:** AX, DC, DS, MC, VI.

BAY GOURMET   Lunch: $6-$10   Phone: 757/460-3500   17
▼▼   **Location:** Just se of jct Northampton Blvd; in Church Point Commons. 1716 Pleasure House Rd 23455. **Hours:** 10
am-3 pm. Closed major holidays; also Sun. **Features:** The cozy delicatessen and wine shop serves great
Deli/Subs   lunch specialties, including such sandwiches as Brazilian chicken wrap and Mama's meatball sub. Among
Sandwiches   other offerings are daily fresh soups, large salads and delightful desserts. Casual dress; beer & wine only. **Parking:** on-site. **Cards:** AX, DS, MC, VI.

BEACH BULLY   Lunch: $3-$15   Dinner: $3-$15   Phone: 757/422-4222   48
▼▼   **Location:** Jct Mediterrenean St; just w of oceanfront. 601 19th St 23451. **Hours:** 10:30 am-8 pm, Fri & Sat-9 pm;
to 9 pm, Fri & Sat-10 pm 4/3-9/5. Closed: 11/24, 12/25. **Features:** Locals and tourists alike love the laid-
Barbecue   back restaurant for its tangy North Carolina-style barbecue. The establishment is just a few blocks from the oceanfront strip. Casual dress; beer & wine only. **Parking:** on-site. **Cards:** AX, DC, DS, MC, VI.

(See maps and indexes starting on p. 715, 719)

BEACH PUB　　　　**Lunch:** $5-$6　　　**Dinner:** $8-$14　　　**Phone:** 757/422-8817　　㉕
Seafood
Location: 1 mi w of oceanfront. 1001 Laskin Rd 23451. **Hours:** 6:30 am-11 pm. Closed: 11/24, 12/24, 12/25. **Features:** This is an easy-to-locate eatery near the beach, specializing in ample portions of fresh seafood and American dishes for a good price. Side dishes include steak fries, coleslaw, prepared salad, and vegetables. The family atmosphere is casual. Casual dress; cocktails. **Parking:** on-site. **Cards:** AX, DC, DS, MC, VI.

BEALE ST.　　　　**Lunch:** $7-$9　　　**Dinner:** $7-$20　　　**Phone:** 757/481-2000　　⑥
Barbecue
Location: Jct W Great Neck Rd. 2916 Shore Dr 23451. **Hours:** 10 am-10 pm. Closed: 11/24, 12/25. **Features:** Tennessee style barbecue in all forms appear here-chicken, ribs, pork, shrimp, and even nachos at this warm and friendly spot where the menu also includes fried catfish and chili. Casual dress; cocktails. **Parking:** on-site. **Cards:** AX, DS, MC, VI.

BELLA MONTE　　　　**Lunch:** $4-$7　　　**Dinner:** $6-$16　　　**Phone:** 757/425-6290　　㉚
Italian
Location: 1.5 mi w on US 58 from ocean; in Birdneck Point Commons. 1201 Laskin Rd, Suite 100 23451. **Hours:** 11 am-9 pm, Fri & Sat-10 pm. Closed: 1/1, 11/24, 12/25; also Sun. **Reservations:** suggested, Fri & Sat. **Features:** Superlatives abound: "excellent" pasta and salad "marvelous" pastry and "great" gourmet pizza. The gourmet cafe and market offers updated Italian cuisine, including rotisserie, in an artistically stylish dining room. Patio dining is available in season. Casual dress; cocktails. **Parking:** on-site. **Cards:** DC, DS, MC, VI.

BLUE MOON CAFE　　　　**Dinner:** $10-$22　　　**Phone:** 757/437-8230　　⑧
American
Location: Just w of Pacific Ave. 32nd St & Holly Rd 23451. **Hours:** 4:30 pm-midnight. **Features:** The casual and stylish restaurant is the current home of Willie Moats, a favorite local chef. Regulars favor such specialties as potato chip-crusted crab and shrimp cakes, as well as the other creative dishes he turns out. Casual dress; cocktails. **Parking:** on-site. **Cards:** AX, MC, VI.

BLUE PETE'S　　　　**Dinner:** $11-$30　　　**Phone:** 757/426-2005
Steak & Seafood
Location: Pacific Ave S to Rudee Inlet Bridge, to General Booth Blvd, 6 mi to Princess Anne Rd, 3 mi e to Pungo, left on Indian River to end, then left. 1400 N Muddy Creek Rd 23456. **Hours:** 5 pm-10 pm, Fri & Sun from 4 pm; to 9 pm in winter. **Reservations:** suggested. **Features:** A laid-back country ambience pervades this charming restaurant, which sits by a creek with its own paths, island and lighted waterfront decks. Dining rooms are surrounded by nature and offer a peaceful setting. Fresh local seafood is drenched in intriguing sauces and toppings. The signature sweet potato biscuits have been a longtime favorite. Casual dress; cocktails. **Parking:** on-site. **Cards:** AX, MC, VI.

THE BOARDWOK RESTAURANT　　　　**Lunch:** $6-$13　　　**Dinner:** $6-$13　　　**Phone:** 757/426-1700
Chinese
Location: Jct Princess Anne and Sandbridge rds. 1993 Sandbridge Rd 23456. **Hours:** 11:30 am-close. Closed major holidays; also Sun. **Features:** Part tropical bar and part Chinese restaurant, the eatery is the spot for everything from Hunan chicken and wonton soup to grilled fish, island-style. Casual dress; cocktails. **Parking:** on-site. **Cards:** AX, MC, VI.

THE BOULEVARD CAFE　　　　**Lunch:** $6-$11　　　**Dinner:** $6-$15　　　**Phone:** 757/463-1311　　㊳
Greek
Location: I-264, exit Lynnhaven Pkwy, just n to Virginia Beach Blvd, then just n; in Pinewood Shoppes. 2935 Virginia Beach Blvd 23452. **Hours:** 11 am-9 pm. Closed major holidays; also Sun. **Features:** Step inside this small neighborhood spot to feel right at home with the locals. The Greek owners serve great daily specials and Greek and Italian specialties, particularly local seafood and yummy pizza. The dining room is casually comfy. Casual dress; beer & wine only. **Parking:** on-site. **Cards:** MC, VI.

BRENNAN'S OF WAYSIDE　　　　**Lunch:** $6-$8　　　**Dinner:** $13-$20　　　**Phone:** 757/486-0035　　㊵
American
Location: I-264, exit 17B (Independence Blvd), just n to Virginia Beach Blvd, just e to the Shops at Willis Wayside. 4216 Virginia Beach Blvd 23452. **Hours:** 11 am-9 pm, Fri & Sat-10 pm. Closed: 1/1, 11/24, 12/25; also Sun. **Reservations:** suggested. **Features:** You'll find Brennan's tucked away in a small shopping center and once diners are delighted by delicious creations such as soy-maple salmon, pistachio-crusted lamb, and pepper seared tenderloin. Casual dress; cocktails. **Parking:** on-site. **Cards:** AX, DC, DS, MC, VI.

BUBBA'S CRABHOUSE & SEAFOOD RESTAURANT　　　**Lunch:** $6-$18　　　**Dinner:** $6-$18　　　**Phone:** 757/481-3513　　⑬
Seafood
Location: US 60, 2.5 mi e of jct US 13, at east end of the Lynnhaven Inlet Bridge. 3323 Shore Dr 23451. **Hours:** 11 am-10 pm, Fri & Sat-11 pm. Closed: 11/24, 12/25. **Reservations:** accepted. **Features:** This waterfront spot offers prime view of the Lynn haven Inlet's waters and features the freshest catch from its waters such as crab cakes, shrimp, and even a fresh tuna salad and softshell crabs in season. Casual dress; cocktails. **Parking:** on-site. **Cards:** AX, DC, MC, VI.

CABO CAFE　　　　**Dinner:** $6-$16　　　**Phone:** 757/216-2095　　⑦
American
Location: On Shore Dr, just w of jct N Great Neck Rd. 2301 Red Tide Rd 23451. **Hours:** 5 pm-2 am. **Reservations:** accepted. **Features:** The chic lounge gets a crowd of partygoers but also serves great food. All dishes are served tapas style, in appetizer sizes portioned for sharing. Among house specialties are Spanish meatballs, churrasco beef, seviche-style seafood and fried tomatoes with mozzarella. Casual dress; cocktails. **Parking:** on-site. **Cards:** AX, DC, DS, MC, VI.

(See maps and indexes starting on p. 715, 719)

CAPTAIN GEORGE'S SEAFOOD RESTAURANT   Dinner: $17-$31   Phone: 757/721-3463
Seafood
Location: Pacific Ave S to Rudee Inlet Bridge, to General Booth Blvd, 6 mi to Princess Anne Rd, 10.7 mi e to Old Pungo Ferry Rd, then 0.5 mi s. 2272 Old Pungo Ferry Rd 23457. **Hours:** 5 pm-9 pm, Sat from 4:30 pm, Sun from noon. Closed: 12/25; also Mon-Thurs 1/1-4/10. **Features:** The huge all-you-can-eat seafood buffet is taste tempting and the riverfront view relaxing. Alaskan snow crab legs and shrimp are popular with diners as are the oysters, barbecue ribs, salad, cornbread and hush puppies. The service is friendly. Casual dress; cocktails. **Parking:** on-site. **Cards:** AX, MC, VI.

CAPTAIN GEORGE'S SEAFOOD RESTAURANT   Dinner: $19-$31   Phone: 757/428-3494   42
Seafood
Location: I-264, exit Laskin Rd (SR 58), 3.5 mi w of oceanfront. 1956 Laskin Rd 23454. **Hours:** 4:30 pm-10 pm, Sat from 3:30 pm, Sun from noon. Closed: 12/25. **Features:** Get lost in this extensive seafood buffet, featuring Alaskan snow crab legs, shrimp, salmon, stuffed clams, prime rib, manicotti and a huge salad section. And for dessert? Baklava, mousse, banana pudding, pie, cobbler and more are there for the asking. Casual dress; cocktails. **Parking:** on-site. **Cards:** AX, MC, VI.

CENTRAL 111   Lunch: $5-$15   Dinner: $4-$15   Phone: 757/222-1022   46
American
Location: Just n of jct US 58/Virginia Beach Blvd; in Renaissance Place. 401 N Great Neck Rd, Suite 111 23454. **Hours:** 11:30 am-10:30 pm. **Reservations:** accepted. **Features:** The hip new tapas bar presents an all-appetizer menu. A stylish scene of singles sips custom martinis and samples such offerings as baby lamb chops and seared tuna. Casual dress; cocktails. **Parking:** on-site. **Cards:** AX, MC, VI.

CHICK'S OYSTER BAR   Lunch: $8-$20   Dinner: $8-$20   Phone: 757/481-5757   14
Seafood
Location: US 60, 2.5 mi w of jct US 13; at east end of the Lynnhaven Inlet Bridge, then just s. 2143 Vista Cir 23451. **Hours:** 11 am-11 pm, Fri & Sat-midnight, Sun 10 am-11 pm; to 10 pm, Fri & Sat-11 pm, Sun 10 am-9 pm 10/1-3/31; Sunday brunch. Closed: 11/24, 12/25. **Features:** Some come by land, while others just tie their boats at one of the restaurant's waterfront decks. Among specialties are fried shrimp, local shellfish and fresh crabs. Not only are the water views spectacular, but the people-watching also is good. Casual dress; cocktails. **Parking:** on-site. **Cards:** AX, DS, MC, VI.

COASTAL GRILL   Dinner: $13-$20   Phone: 757/496-3348   21
American
Location: 3 mi n of jct Laskin Rd and US 58; 3 mi s of jct Shore Dr; in Mill Dam Crossing. 1427 N Great Neck Rd 23454. **Hours:** 5:30 pm-11 pm, Sat 5 pm-midnight, Sun 5 pm-9:45 pm. Closed major holidays. **Features:** Such highlights as lamb with eggplant puree, spinach salad with chicken livers, pepper-crusted tuna and soft-shell crab are served in an understated bistro punctuated by white tablecloths and handsome artwork. Reservations are not accepted, but neighborhood regulars don't seem to mind the wait. Casual dress; cocktails. **Parking:** on-site. **Cards:** AX, MC, VI.

COBALT GRILLE   Lunch: $6-$9   Dinner: $15-$25   Phone: 757/333-3334   34
American
Location: 3 mi w of oceanfront on Laskin Rd. 762 Hilltop North Shopping Center 23451. **Hours:** 11:30 am-2:30 & 5-10 pm. Closed: 1/1, 12/25; also Sun. **Features:** The stylish and contemporary bistro has quickly become a trendy haunt. From the curved bar up front to the open chrome kitchen, the style is hip and modern. The cuisine also is cutting edge, with global and regional influences. Casual dress; cocktails. **Parking:** on-site. **Cards:** AX, CB, DC, DS, MC, VI.

COYOTE CAFE & CANTINA   Lunch: $5-$9   Dinner: $10-$23   Phone: 757/425-8705   24
Southwest American
Location: 1 mi w of oceanfront on 31st/Laskin Rd; in Linkhorn Shoppes. 972-A Laskin Rd 23451. **Hours:** 11:30 am-2:30 & 5-10:30 pm, Fri & Sat-midnight, Sun 5 pm-10:30 pm. Closed: 11/24, 12/24, 12/25. **Reservations:** suggested. **Features:** Unusually modern Southwestern cuisine, often using the region's fresh local seafood, takes the spotlight. Light fare such as quesadillas is offered as well as many tasty, creative entrees. The atmosphere is lively, bustling and fun, with friendly service. Casual dress; cocktails. **Parking:** on-site. **Cards:** AX, CB, DC, DS, MC, VI.

CROAKERS   Dinner: $10-$20   Phone: 757/363-2490   12
Seafood
Location: US 60, 2 mi e of jct US 13. 3629 Shore Dr 23455. **Hours:** 5 pm-10 pm. Closed: 1/1, 11/24, 12/24, 12/25; also Super Bowl Sun. **Reservations:** suggested. **Features:** In the heart of the local-favorite beach, the casual restaurant naturally serves the freshest local seafood. Specialties include a seafood roll-up, blackened tuna and fish St. Charles. Casual dress; cocktails. **Parking:** on-site. **Cards:** AX, DC, DS, MC, VI.

CUISINE & COMPANY   Lunch: $5-$10   Dinner: $5-$10   Phone: 757/428-6700   10
American
Location: Just w of jct 31st St (Laskin Rd). 3004 Pacific Ave 23451. **Hours:** 9 am-8 pm, Sun-6 pm; to 7 pm 10/1-4/30. Closed: 1/1, 11/24, 12/25. **Features:** Known locally for its elegant catered affairs, the cafe offers similar gourmet delights in a casual setting. Chose from inventive gourmet sandwiches, zesty prepared salad and sinful dessert. Casual dress; beer & wine only. **Parking:** on-site. **Cards:** AX, DS, MC, VI.

DOUGH BOYS CALIFORNIA PIZZA   Lunch: $3-$8   Dinner: $7-$12   Phone: 757/425-7108   11
Pizza
Location: I-264, just n of terminus. 2410 Atlantic Ave 23451. **Hours:** 11 am-1 am; to 10 pm off season. Closed: 1/1, 11/24, 12/25. **Features:** Part of the fun, tropical atmosphere is the sidewalk patio, which overlooks the activity of Atlantic Avenue. Specialty pizzas come with a variety of creative toppings, from Thai-flavored shrimp to Santa Fe chicken. Start with Mom's large Greek salad or cheesy breadsticks. Casual dress; cocktails. **Parking:** no self-parking. **Cards:** AX, DC, DS, MC, VI.

(See maps and indexes starting on p. 715, 719)

DOUGHBOY'S CALIFORNIA PIZZA **Lunch:** $3-$8 **Dinner:** $7-$12 **Phone:** 757/422-6111 ⑫

♦

Pizza

Location: I-264, just n of terminus. 1700 Atlantic Ave 23451. **Hours:** 11 am-1 am; to 10 pm off season. Closed: 1/1, 11/24, 12/25. **Features:** Part of the fun, tropical atmosphere is the sidewalk patio, which overlooks the activity of Atlantic Avenue. Specialty pizzas come with a variety of creative toppings, from Thai-flavored shrimp to Santa Fe chicken. Start with Mom's large Greek salad or cheesy breadsticks. Casual dress; cocktails. **Parking:** no self-parking. **Cards:** AX, DC, DS, MC, VI.

🚭

DUCK-IN RESTAURANT & GAZEBO *Menu on aaa.com* **Lunch:** $4-$18 **Dinner:** $8-$22 **Phone:** 757/481-0201 ⑪

AAA

♦♦

Seafood

Location: US 60, 2.5 mi e of jct US 13 at end of the Lynnhaven Inlet Bridge. 3324 Shore Dr 23451. **Hours:** 11 am-10 pm, Fri & Sat-11 pm, Sun 9 am-10 pm. Closed: 12/25. **Features:** Fresh local seafood is prepared traditionally at the beachside restaurant, which affords wonderful views of Chesapeake Bay and the rolling dunes. Deck seating is available, weather permitting. There's a buffet every night during the summer and on Friday and Saturday nights during the off season. Casual dress; cocktails. **Parking:** on-site. **Cards:** AX, DS, MC, VI.

♿ 🍸 🚭

ELIA'S MEDITERRANEAN CUISINE **Lunch:** $5-$15 **Dinner:** $5-$15 **Phone:** 757/518-2600 (71)

♦

Greek

Location: I-264, exit 17B (Independence Blvd), just s. 485 S Independence Blvd 23452. **Hours:** 11 am-10 pm. Closed: Sun. **Features:** Little thought goes into the decor at the simple spot, as the focus is on the food. The menu is full of affordable dishes, such as moussaka, spanakopita and tasty gyros. Casual dress; beer & wine only. **Parking:** on-site. **Cards:** AX, DS, MC, VI.

EURASIA RESTAURANT **Lunch:** $5-$11 **Dinner:** $10-$23 **Phone:** 757/463-7146 (61)

♦♦♦

Continental

Location: I-264, exit 17B (Independence Blvd), just n to Virginia Beach Blvd (US 58), 0.5 mi e; in Loehmann's Plaza. 4000 Virginia Beach Blvd 23452. **Hours:** 11:30 am-3 & 5:30-9 pm, Fri-10 pm, Sat 5:30 pm-10 pm. Closed: 1/1, 11/24, 12/24, 12/25; also Sun. **Reservations:** suggested. **Features:** Fresh regional ingredients give exceptional flavor to dishes that fuse Thai and European influences, such as roast chicken and Cajun pasta and Shrimp Amarin, and Thai Chicken. Simple, but stylish, decor sets a sophisticated mood in the dining room. Servers are casual and competent. Casual dress; cocktails. **Parking:** on-site. **Cards:** AX, DS, MC, VI.

🚭

FEDERICO'S **Lunch:** $8-$12 **Dinner:** $9-$25 **Phone:** 757/497-1445 ㊾

♦♦

Italian

Location: I-264, exit 17B (Independence Blvd), just n; in Pembroke Plaza. 357 Independence Blvd 23462. **Hours:** 11 am-10 pm, Fri-11 pm, Sat noon-11 pm, Sun 4 pm-9 pm. Closed major holidays; also Mon. **Reservations:** suggested, weekends. **Features:** The casually elegant restaurant's menu centers on dependable favorites, such as veal parmigiana and pasta al vodka. Piano music adds to the weekend atmosphere. Casual dress; cocktails. **Parking:** on-site. **Cards:** DS, MC, VI.

🚭

FIVE 0 1 CITY GRILL **Dinner:** $7-$21 **Phone:** 757/425-7195 ㊸

♦♦

American

Location: I-264, exit exit 22 (Birdneck Rd), n to Birdneck Shoppes. 501 N Birdneck Rd 23451. **Hours:** 4 pm-10 pm. Closed: 1/1, 11/24, 12/24, 12/25; also Super Bowl Sun. **Reservations:** suggested, weekends. **Features:** Enjoy a regularly revised menu of contemporary food, typified by such specialties as Michelob shrimp and baked goat cheese with roasted garlic & prosciutto-wrapped lamb chops. The New York-style restaurant, a hot spot with the trendy beach crowd, lists an impressive inventory of wine. Casual dress; cocktails. **Parking:** on-site. **Cards:** AX, MC, VI.

♿ 🍸 🚭

FRESH FARE CAFE **Lunch:** $4-$8 **Dinner:** $4-$8 **Phone:** 757/491-5383 (51)

♦

Vegetarian

Location: Just n of jct W Cypress St. 700 19th St 23451. **Hours:** 7 am-9 pm, Sat 8 am-6 pm. Closed major holidays; also Sun. **Features:** The simple, mostly vegetarian cafe gets a tanned, buff cast of regulars from both the beach and the neighboring gym. On the menu are tasty health shakes, stuffed pitas and more nutritional treats. Casual dress. **Parking:** on-site. **Cards:** MC, VI.

🚭

GUADALAJARA MEXICAN BAR & GRILL **Lunch:** $5-$12 **Dinner:** $7-$12 **Phone:** 757/481-5511 ⑧

♦

Mexican

Location: Jct Shore Dr/US 60. 2272 W Great Neck Rd 23451. **Hours:** 11 am-10 pm, Fri & Sat-midnight. Closed: 11/24, 12/25. **Features:** A bustling nightlife atmosphere prevails on the neon-lit patio. The menu lists not only traditional Mexican specialties but also coastal dishes, such as grilled fish tacos. Casual dress; cocktails. **Parking:** on-site. **Cards:** DS, MC, VI.

♿ 🍸 🚭

GUS'S MARINER RESTAURANT **Lunch:** $6-$10 **Dinner:** $14-$29 **Phone:** 757/425-5699 ⑳

AAA

♦♦♦

Seafood

Location: I-264, 2.2 mi n of terminus; in Ramada Plaza Resort Oceanfront. 57th St & Atlantic Ave 23451. **Hours:** 7 am-9 pm; to 10 pm in summer. **Reservations:** suggested. **Features:** The upscale dining room overlooks the ocean and offers nightly fresh catches draped in exquisite sauces. Neatly attired servers in colorful vests and bowties show excellent knowledge of the menu and wine list. Save room for sinful dessert. 100% non-smoking on weekends. Dressy casual; cocktails. **Parking:** on-site. **Cards:** AX, DC, DS, MC, VI.
(See color ad p 762)

♿ 🍸 🚭

H2O **Dinner:** $10-$21 **Phone:** 757/496-2528 ⑩

♦♦

American

Location: US 60, 2.8 mi e of jct US 13. 3152 Shore Dr 23454. **Hours:** 5 pm-10 pm, Fri & Sat-midnight. Closed major holidays. **Reservations:** suggested. **Features:** The style is modern and bright and the food creative. Global influences show up even in the crab cakes. An attractive crowd frequents the hip new beach spot. Casual dress; cocktails. **Parking:** on-site. **Cards:** AX, DC, DS, MC, VI.

🚭

(See maps and indexes starting on p. 715, 719)

HAVANA   Lunch: $5-$9   Dinner: $10-$20   Phone: 757-496-3333   ⟨22⟩
▼▼ ▼▼   **Location:** 3 mi s of Shore Dr; in Mill Dam Crossing. 1423 Great Neck Rd 23454. **Hours:** 11:30 am-2 & 5-10 pm, Fri
American   & Sat-11 pm. Closed: 12/25. **Reservations:** suggested, weekends. **Features:** The hip, innovative menu
                takes much inspiration from Cuban cuisine but is not centered on traditional fare. Of note is pork tenderloin
                with soy/citrus glaze and the tropical flavors of the salade de casa. Cigars are welcomed, and a nightly
tapas happy hour from 5 pm-7 pm offers a wide range of appetizers. Casual dress; cocktails. **Parking:** on-site. **Cards:** AX, CB,
DS, MC, VI.

THE HERITAGE HEALTH FOOD CAFE & DELI   Lunch: $4-$9   Dinner: $4-$9   Phone: 757-428-0500   ⟨9⟩
▼▼   **Location:** Jct 31st St/Laskin Rd and Pacific Ave. 314 Laskin Rd 23451. **Hours:** 10 am-6:40 pm, Fri-8:40 pm, Sun
Vegetarian   noon-6:40 pm. Closed: 1/1, 11/24, 12/25. **Features:** Beachgoers and locals know the grocery and
                delicatessen is the spot to find many vegetarian and organic favorites, including sandwiches, smoothies and
                fresh-squeezed juices. A few poultry and seafood offerings are available. Casual dress. **Parking:** on-site.
Cards: DS, MC, VI.

THE HUNT ROOM GRILL   Dinner: $20-$30   Phone: 757-425-8555   ⟨2⟩
▼▼▼▼   **Location:** Pacific Ave and 42nd St; in The Cavalier. 42nd and Pacific 23451. **Hours:** Open 3/1-3/31 & 1/3-2/28; 6
Regional American pm-10 pm, Fri & Sat-11 pm. Closed: Sun-Tues. **Reservations:** suggested. **Features:** In the early days of
                this historic hotel, male guests would retire here after hunting to gather around the enormous hearth, drink
                brandy and roast game. The roaring fire is still the main draw since the dining room is open only in winter
months. The menu centers on hearty fare, such as lamb, duck, steak and, of course, the region's famed seafood. Dressy
casual; cocktails; entertainment. **Parking:** on-site. **Cards:** AX, DC, DS, MC, VI.

IL GIARDINO   Dinner: $12-$32   Phone: 757-422-6464   ⟨15⟩
▼▼▼▼   **Location:** Atlantic Ave and 10th St. 910 Atlantic Ave, Suite 200 23451. **Hours:** 5 pm-11 pm. Closed: 11/24, 12/25.
Italian   **Reservations:** suggested, weekends. **Features:** A loyal following frequents the exciting, upscale restaurant.
                An excellent selection of pasta, veal, seafood, chicken and brick-oven pizza appeals to many tastes. The
                freshly made tiramisu is a rich, decadent delight. A pianist plays on Saturday night. Casual dress; cocktails.
Parking: valet. **Cards:** AX, DC, DS, MC, VI.

ISLE OF CAPRI   Dinner: $15-$25   Phone: 757-428-2411   ⟨3⟩
▼▼▼▼   **Location:** I-264, 1.4 mi n from terminus; at Atlantic Ave and 39th St; in Holiday Inn SunSpree Resort. 39th & Atlantic
Italian   23451. **Hours:** 5 pm-10 pm. Closed: 11/24, 12/24, 12/25. **Reservations:** suggested. **Features:** Perched six
                floors up, the upscale, attractive restaurant boasts gorgeous views of the ocean below. Chef Pasqual has
                been serving his Mediterranean specialities since 1952, but now in a new home. Menu highlights include
Spagetti alla Sangiovannio, Calamerdti di Napoli and Veal Sicilian. Dressy casual; cocktails. **Parking:** on-site. **Cards:** AX, DC,
DS, MC, VI.

JENNA'S MEDITERANEAN CAFE   Lunch: $5-$8   Dinner: $5-$8   Phone: 757-460-0973   ⟨16⟩
▼▼▼   **Location:** Jct Shore Dr, just s. 2104-I Pleasure House Rd 23455. **Hours:** 10:30 am-9 pm. Closed major holidays;
Mediterranean   also Sun. **Features:** The decor is decidedly humble, but guests shouldn't let that steer them away. The
                menu offers excellent Greek dishes from hummus and gyros to baba ghanoush and pita bread. Regulars
                often buy extra to take home. Casual dress; beer only. **Parking:** on-site. **Cards:** CB, DS, MC, VI.

THE JEWISH MOTHER   Lunch: $5-$10   Dinner: $5-$10   Phone: 757-422-5430   ⟨7⟩
▼▼▼   **Location:** I-264, 1 mi n at Pacific Ave, jct 31st St. 3108 Pacific Ave 23451. **Hours:** 8 am-2 am. **Features:** The
Deli/Subs   oceanfront mainstay has been serving great delicatessen sandwiches, noshes, smoked fish and thick
Sandwiches   milkshakes to local teens and music lovers for years. Adding to the lively atmosphere are walls decorated in
                crayon scribbles and a coloring book menu. Casual dress; cocktails; entertainment. **Parking:** on-site.
                Cards: AX, DS, MC, VI.

LA BELLA ITALIA TRATTORIA   Lunch: $7-$16   Dinner: $7-$16   Phone: 757-422-8536   ⟨28⟩
▼▼ ▼▼   **Location:** 1.2 mi w on US 58 (31st St) from oceanfront; in Laskin Center. 1065 Laskin Rd 23451. **Hours:** 11:30 am-
Italian   2:30 & 5-10 pm, Fri & Sat-11 pm. Closed major holidays; also Sun. **Reservations:** suggested.
                Features: Patrons who make it past the delightful bakery and deli-case offerings up front will find a peaceful
                dining room. Traditional flavors punctuate such dishes as black pepper linguine with clams, brick-oven
pizzas and veal saltimbocca. Casual dress; cocktails. **Parking:** on-site. **Cards:** AX, DS, MC, VI.

THE LUCKY STAR   Dinner: $20-$25   Phone: 757-363-8410   ⟨19⟩
▼▼▼▼   **Location:** Jct Northampton Blvd, just sw; in Thoroughgood Center. 1608 Pleasure House Rd 23455. **Hours:** 5:30 pm-
American   10 pm. Closed: 1/1, 11/24, 12/25; also Sun. **Reservations:** suggested. **Features:** The dining room is casual
                and coolly elegant, an intimate setting in which to savor seasonally changing dishes, such as mustard-
                grilled lamb chops and bundled leeks with roast duck and goat cheese. Also delightful are the exciting
appetizers and enticing desserts. Casual dress; cocktails. **Parking:** on-site. **Cards:** AX, MC, VI.

LYNNHAVEN FISH HOUSE
RESTAURANT   Lunch: $8-$15   Dinner: $16-$26   Phone: 757-481-0003   ⟨4⟩
ⓐⓐⓐ   **Location:** Just n of US 60, 2.8 mi e of jct US 13. 2350 Starfish Rd 23451. **Hours:** 11:30 am-10:30 pm. Closed:
▼▼▼▼   11/24, 12/25. **Features:** Perched on the rolling dunes of Chesapeake Bay, the cozy restaurant, a longtime
Seafood   popular spot, has big picture windows that overlook the beach. Fresh, high-quality seafood—much of which
                is presented in more creative preparations—rarely disappoints. Excellent she crab soup served traditionally
                with a hint of sherry. Dressy casual; cocktails. **Parking:** on-site. **Cards:** AX, CB, DC, DS, MC, VI.

(See maps and indexes starting on p. 715, 719)

MAHI MAH'S SEAFOOD RESTAURANT & SUSHI SALOON   Lunch: $5-$11   Dinner: $8-$21   Phone: 757/437-8030   [16]
Seafood
Location: I-264, 1 mi s of terminus; at Atlantic Ave and 6th St; in Ramada Inn On the Beach. 615 Atlantic Ave 23451. **Hours:** 7 am-11 pm. **Closed:** 12/25. **Reservations:** suggested. **Features:** Loud, hip crowds gather at the oceanfront eatery, which offers traditional and innovative sushi as well as fresh, grilled seafood, pasta, and raw-bar items. Open-air patio seating is in high demand in pleasant weather. Late night menu until 12:30 am. Entertainers perform seasonally. Casual dress; cocktails. **Parking:** valet. **Cards:** AX, DC, DS, MC, VI.

MARY'S RESTAURANT   Lunch: $3-$6   Phone: 757/428-1355   [53]
American
Location: W of Atlantic Ave, on 17th St. 616 Virginia Beach Blvd 23451. **Hours:** 6 am-3 pm. **Closed:** 11/24, 12/25. **Features:** A local favorite for more than 40 years, the cozy spot offers such down-home favorites as country-fried steak, barbecue and homemade soup. Desserts include a mouthwatering array of cakes and pies. On the all-day breakfast menu are the Old Virginia, homemade biscuits, omelets and pancakes. Casual dress. **Parking:** on-site. **Cards:** MC, VI.

MAYFLOWER CAFE   Lunch: $7-$16   Dinner: $10-$21   Phone: 757/417-0117   [5]
Mediterranean
Location: I-264, to Pacific Ave, then 1.5 mi n; in Mayflower Apartments. 209 34th St 23451. **Hours:** 11 am-9 pm. **Closed:** 11/24, 12/25; also Sun. **Reservations:** accepted. **Features:** The dining room is small and the kitchen even tinier, but that doesn't stop the chef from turning out great Turkish-Mediterranean fare. Pita bread is fluffy, light and always warm; the gyros savory; and the daily specials always fresh and delicious. Casual dress. **Parking:** street.

THE MELTING POT   Dinner: $18-$50   Phone: 757/425-3463   [35]
Fondue
Location: 1.8 mi w of oceanfront on 31st St/Laskin Rd; in Hilltop East Shopping Center. 1564 Laskin Rd, Suite 182 23451. **Hours:** 5 pm-11 pm, Fri & Sat-midnight. **Reservations:** suggested. **Features:** Fondue goes upscale at the intimate spot, which is well suited for romance. The choicest seafood, steak and pork tenderloin taste even better when cooked tableside in succulent pot sauces. Cheese and chocolate fondues are sure to please, as well. Dressy casual; cocktails. **Parking:** on-site. **Cards:** AX, DS, MC, VI.

MISAKO SUSHI BAR & GRILLE   Lunch: $5-$18   Dinner: $5-$18   Phone: 757/631-6831   [63]
Japanese
Location: I-264, exit 17B (Independence Blvd), just n to Virginia Beach Blvd (US 58), 0.5 mi e; in Loehmann's Plaza. 4000 Virginia Beach Blvd, Suite 176 23452. **Hours:** 11:30 am-2:30 & 4:30-9:30 pm, Fri & Sat-10:30 pm. **Features:** Locals love the weekday lunch buffet of sushi specialties and other Japanese favorites at this stylish spot; dinner offer table service and an even wider array of delicacies. Casual dress; cocktails. **Parking:** on-site. **Cards:** MC, VI.

MIZUNO JAPANESE RESTAURANT   Lunch: $7-$13   Dinner: $9-$18   Phone: 757/422-1200   [40]
Japanese
Location: I-264, exit Laskin Rd (SR 58), 0.3 mi e; in La Promenade Shops. 1860 Laskin Rd, Suite 120 23454. **Hours:** 11:30 am-2 & 5:30-9:30 pm, Fri & Sat-10 pm. **Closed:** major holidays; also Sun & Mon. **Reservations:** suggested, weekends. **Features:** Elegantly prepared Japanese cuisine is sophisticated but sometimes unfamiliar, as in the case of the seaweed salad. The sparse decor in the front dining room is soothing, and private seating is offered in the back. Sushi lovers flock to the bar to watch the chefs in action. Casual dress; beer & wine only. **Parking:** on-site. **Cards:** AX, MC, VI.

NAPOLEON'S   Lunch: $6-$10   Dinner: $15-$25   Phone: 757/497-3400   [57]
French
Location: I-264, exit Witchduck Rd, just n on Virginia Beach Blvd, 0.5 mi e. 4933 Virginia Beach Blvd 23462. **Hours:** 11:30 am-2:30 & 5:30-10 pm. **Closed:** 11/24, 12/24, 12/25; also Sun & Mon. **Reservations:** suggested. **Features:** Parisian-style French cuisine is served in a small house with several intimate dining rooms. Appetizer choices range from baked brie to escargot and entrees from roast duckling to trout amandine. Creme brulee and crepes round out a memorable experience. Casual dress; cocktails. **Parking:** on-site. **Cards:** AX, DS, MC, VI.

NAWAB INDIAN RESTAURANT   Lunch: $7-$10   Dinner: $9-$15   Phone: 757/491-8600   [31]
Indian
Location: Jct US 58/Laskin Rd. 756 First Colonial Rd 23451. **Hours:** 11:30 am-3 & 5-10 pm, Sat & Sun from noon. **Features:** Tandoor specialties and bread baked in a clay oven are at the centerpiece of a traditional menu of curried, lamb and vegetarian dishes. The upscale atmosphere features artwork and instrumental music. A weekday buffet draws a devoted lunch clientele. Casual dress; cocktails. **Parking:** on-site. **Cards:** AX, DC, DS, MC, VI.

ONE FISH TWO FISH   Dinner: $17-$23   Phone: 757/496-4350   [15]
Seafood
Location: Jct US 60 and Shore Dr, just e; in Long Bay Pointe Boating Resort. 2109 W Great Neck Rd 23454. **Hours:** 5 pm-10 pm. **Closed:** major holidays. **Reservations:** suggested. **Features:** Trendy and bright with a distinct Californian feel. Walls of windows showcase excellent views of the Lynnhaven River and passing boats, or sit on the covered open-air patio and enjoy the gentle breezes and lovely sunsets. A shiny chrome exhibition kitchen on the other side of the curved bar turns out market-inspired regional seafood with a creative and modern flair. Dressy casual; cocktails. **Parking:** on-site. **Cards:** AX, MC, VI.

ORION'S   Dinner: $19-$30   Phone: 757/425-8555   [1]
Regional American
Location: Atlantic Ave and 42nd St; on 11th floor of The Cavalier. 42nd & Atlantic Ave 23451. **Hours:** One 5/12-9/5; 6 pm-10 pm, Fri & Sat-11 pm. **Closed:** Sun. **Reservations:** suggested. **Features:** This large dining room atop the hotel affords panoramic oceanfront views from both sides, and makes your meal particularly elegant during sunsets. Cuisine is strongly influenced by the local seafood market and is served amid an elegant art deco/celestial decor with live piano music. Casual dress; cocktails; entertainment. **Parking:** on-site. **Cards:** AX, DC, DS, MC, VI.

(See maps and indexes starting on p. 715, 719)

OSAKA JAPANESE RESTAURANT   Lunch: $6-$11   Dinner: $9-$20   Phone: 757/428-8609   50
Japanese
Location: Jct 19th St. 1807 Mediterranean Ave 23451. **Hours:** 11:30 am-2:30 & 4:30-10 pm, Fri & Sat-11 pm, Sun 4:30 pm-10 pm. **Features:** This small sushi bar is conveneintly located blocks from the beach and the convention center. Traditional and creative rolls, noodle soups, and tempura items are favorites of regulars. Casual dress; cocktails. **Parking:** on-site. **Cards:** AX, DS, MC, VI.

OTANI JAPANESE STEAK HOUSE   Lunch: $7-$14   Dinner: $11-$35   Phone: 757/425-0404   36
Japanese
Location: 3 mi w of oceanfront. 1532 Laskin Rd 23451. **Hours:** 11:30 am-2 & 5-10 pm, Fri-11 pm, Sat 5 pm-11 pm, Sun noon-3 & 5-10 pm. Closed major holidays. **Features:** Watching Japanese chefs in action at the lively spot is as good as eating the food. Guests can sample stir-fried shrimp, steak and more that's even better when paired with delicacies from the sushi bar. Casual dress; cocktails. **Parking:** on-site. **Cards:** AX, CB, DC, DS, MC, VI.

PHO 79   Lunch: $5-$6   Dinner: $5-$6   Phone: 757/687-7844   54
Vietnamese
Location: I-264, exit 17B (Independence Blvd), just w. 4816 Virginia Beach Blvd 23462. **Hours:** 10 am-9 pm, Sun-8 pm. Closed: 11/24, 12/25. **Features:** At the heart of the menu is pho, a traditional noodle soup sometimes called the national dish of Vietnam. Large bowls of steaming soup, each accented with beef or other meats and seasoned with herbs and sauces, are satisfying and healthy. Several generations of the family are warm and hospitable. Spring rolls, interesting desserts and drinks are also noteworthy. Casual dress; beer only. **Parking:** on-site. **Cards:** MC, VI.

PIER CAFE   Lunch: $6-$9   Dinner: $6-$14   Phone: 757/481-5950   5
Seafood
Location: Just n on US 60, 2.8 mi e of jct US 13; on the Lynnhaven fishing pier. 2350 Starfish Rd 23451. **Hours:** Open 4/15-10/15; 11:30 am-midnight; hours vary seasonally. **Features:** The most popular seats in the fun and frivolous eatery on the pier are in the open-air area that sits right over the water. Although brief, the menu's good, with raw-bar items, a cheese board for two, fantastic she crab soup and grilled yellowfin tuna. Casual dress; cocktails; entertainment. **Parking:** on-site. **Cards:** AX, CB, DC, DS, MC, VI.

POLLARD'S CHICKEN   Lunch: $5-$7   Dinner: $5-$7   Phone: 757/340-2565   59
American
Location: 4 mi w of Ocean via US 58/Virginia Beach Blvd at N Great Neck Rd; in London Bridge Shopping Center. 100 London Bridge Ctr 23454. **Hours:** 10 am-9 pm. Closed: 11/24, 12/25. **Features:** There's nothing fancy about the fried chicken, barbecue and seafood on the down-to-earth restaurant's menu, but they sure are good. Inexpensive, casual and enjoyable, the experience here is a great one for families. The honey puffs shouldn't be missed. Casual dress. **Parking:** on-site. **Cards:** AX, MC, VI.

THE PURPLE COW   Lunch: $5-$8   Dinner: $5-$8   Phone: 757/233-7269   23
American
Location: Just w of Oceanfront/Atlantic Ave on 31st St. 981 Laskin Rd 23451. **Hours:** 11 am-9 pm, Fri-10 pm, Sat & Sun 10 am-10 pm. Closed: 11/24, 12/25. **Features:** The 1950s-themed rock 'n' roll diner features favorites from the grill—including burgers and wraps—as well as soda fountain standbys. The setting welcomes families. Casual dress; cocktails. **Parking:** on-site. **Cards:** AX, DS, MC, VI.

THE RAVEN   Lunch: $6-$20   Dinner: $6-$20   Phone: 757/425-1200   14
American
Location: 12th and Atlantic Ave. 1200 Atlantic Ave 23451. **Hours:** 11:30 am-1 am. **Features:** This long-established "locals" spot offers steak, local seafood, sandwiches and burgers. The patio dining area overlooking "the strip" is great for people watching and makes the lively atmosphere and internationally seen T-shirts a special treat. Casual dress; cocktails. **Parking:** on-site. **Cards:** AX, CB, DC, DS, MC, VI.

REGINELLA'S ITALIAN RISTORANTE & PIZZERIA   *Menu on aaa.com*   Lunch: $5-$15   Dinner: $5-$15   Phone: 757/498-9770   62
Italian
Location: I-264, exit 17B (Independence Blvd) to SR 58, 0.5 mi e to Loehmann's Plaza. 4000 Virginia Beach Blvd 23452. **Hours:** 11 am-10 pm, Sun noon-9 pm. Closed major holidays. **Features:** Authentic Italian specialties are the offerings at this cozy family spot, which is owned and operated by natives of Napoli. Try excellent pasta, Napoletana or Sicilian pizza and stromboli. Bookend your entree with tempting antipasto and mouthwatering tiramisu. Casual dress; beer & wine only. **Parking:** on-site. **Cards:** AX, DS, MC, VI.

ROCKAFELLER'S   Lunch: $6-$11   Dinner: $8-$23   Phone: 757/422-5654   69
Seafood
Location: I-264, terminus, 1.3 mi s to Rudee Inlet. 308 Mediterranean Ave 23451. **Hours:** 11 am-11 pm; to 10 pm off season. Closed: 11/24, 11/24, 12/25. **Features:** Overlooking the sparkling waters and marinas of Rudee Inlet, this restaurant is a beautiful spot in which to enjoy local seafood such as crabcakes, flounder, and more. Casual dress; cocktails. **Parking:** on-site. **Cards:** AX, DC, DS, MC, VI.

ROCKFISH BOARDWALK BAR & SEA GRILL   Lunch: $6-$11   Dinner: $6-$22   Phone: 757/213-7625   13
American
Location: I-264, terminus, just s to 16th St; in Boardwalk Resort Hotel and Villas. 1601 Atlantic Ave 23451. **Hours:** 8 am-1 am; hours vary off season. Closed: 12/25. **Reservations:** suggested. **Features:** A rock 'n' roll attitude reigns at the colorful beachside spot, made a fast local favorite for its patio and private "dining pods." Guests can sample any of the three varieties of crab cakes, hushpuppies, burgers and grilled seafood, which are served in mammoth portions, while watching the action both inside and out. Casual dress; cocktails. **Parking:** no self-parking. **Cards:** AX, DC, DS, MC, VI.

(See maps and indexes starting on p. 715, 719)

RUDEE'S ON THE INLET   Lunch: $6-$20   Dinner: $9-$20   Phone: 757/425-1777   (70)
AAA
Seafood   **Location:** I-264, terminus, 1.3 mi s. 227 Mediterranean Ave 23451. **Hours:** 11 am-midnight, Sun 10 am-11 pm. Closed: 11/24, 12/25. **Features:** The open, airy, nautical-themed decor goes well with the menu: fried or broiled fresh seafood served inside or on the outdoor deck overlooking the inlet and marina. The marinated tuna steak and sweet potato chips are delicious at this popular eatery. Casual dress; cocktails. **Parking:** on-site. **Cards:** AX, DC, DS, MC, VI.

SAIGON 1 RESTAURANT   Lunch: $6-$10   Dinner: $6-$10   Phone: 757/518-0307   (26)
Vietnamese   **Location:** I-264 at jct Virginia Beach Blvd. 448 Newtown Rd 23462. **Hours:** 11 am-10 pm. **Features:** The setting couldn't be more simple at the humble spot, which serves a wide variety of fresh and healthy Vietnamese fare. Among specialties are pho noodle soups, rice paper rolls and grilled meats, including quail. Wash down the food with a trendy bubble tea. Casual dress; beer & wine only. **Parking:** on-site. **Cards:** DS, MC, VI.

SCOTTY QUIXX CAFE & CARRYOUT   Lunch: $5-$9   Dinner: $5-$9   Phone: 757/463-7900   (60)
Deli/Subs
Sandwiches   **Location:** In London Bridge Shoppes. 2404 Virginia Beach Blvd 23452. **Hours:** 11 am-10 pm. Closed major holidays; also Sun. **Features:** This tiny spot luckily has a large patio to house all the hungry diners that flock here for their fresh and delicious favorites such as tuna tacos or burritos, cheese steaks, pizza, and gourmet ice cream and milkshakes in ever-rotating specialty flavors. Casual dress. **Parking:** on-site. **Cards:** AX, DS, MC, VI.

SHADOWLAWN GRILL   Dinner: $12-$24   Phone: 757/216-5993   (68)
American   **Location:** 1 mi w from Atlantic Ave on 11th St. 612 Norfolk Ave 23451. **Hours:** 6 pm-11 pm. Closed major holidays; also Mon. **Reservations:** suggested. **Features:** This small eclectic eatery is a popular neighborhood spot with only 20 seats so you might have to wait for the chef's tasty specialties such as New Orleans fish in a bag and the pate of the day or cozy up to the food bar to watch the chef in action, rumor has it he might slide you free tastings. Casual dress; beer & wine only. **Parking:** on-site.

SHIKI JAPANESE RESTAURANT   Lunch: $6-$11   Dinner: $8-$16   Phone: 757/498-4842   (56)
Japanese   **Location:** I-264, exit 17B (Independence Blvd), just n to Virginia Beach Blvd, then 1.2 mi e. 4316B Virginia Beach Blvd 23452. **Hours:** 11:30 am-2:30 & 5-9:30 pm, Fri-10:30 pm, Sat 5 pm-10:30 pm. Closed major holidays; also Sun. **Features:** The tiny, centrally located spot is the prime place for a healthy quick lunch. From fresh sushi to noodle soups to teriyakis, this is how the Japanese eat on the run. Casual dress; beer & wine only. **Parking:** on-site. **Cards:** MC, VI.

SHOGUN JAPANESE STEAK HOUSE & SEAFOOD   Dinner: $11-$28   Phone: 757/422-5150   (44)
Japanese   **Location:** I-264, exit First Colonial Rd, just n to K-Mart Plaza. 550 First Colonial Rd 23451. **Hours:** 5 pm-10 pm, Fri & Sat-11 pm. Closed: 11/24, 12/25. **Reservations:** suggested, Fri & Sat. **Features:** Teppanyaki chefs entertain patrons tableside at the Shogun and cook up quite a good meal. Steak and seafood are the specialties and each entree is accompanied by a shrimp appetizer, salad with ginger dressing, and soup. There's also a sushi bar. Casual dress; cocktails. **Parking:** on-site. **Cards:** AX, CB, DC, DS, MC, VI.

SILVER DINER   Lunch: $6-$15   Dinner: $6-$15   Phone: 757/499-3600   (58)
American   **Location:** I-264, exit 17B (Independence Blvd) eastbound to US 58, just n. 4401 Virginia Beach Blvd 23452. **Hours:** 7 am-midnight. Closed: 12/25. **Features:** The eatery mixes the modern with the retro to create the ultimate American diner bathed in the glow of neon and chrome. Specialties include bite-size hamburgers, meatloaf, hot open-faced sandwiches and more American favorites, all the better when washed down with milkshakes from the soda fountain. Casual dress; cocktails. **Parking:** on-site. **Cards:** AX, DS, MC, VI.

SMOKEHOUSE & COOLER   Dinner: $8-$20   Phone: 757/481-9737   (9)
American   **Location:** Jct Great Neck Rd, just w. 2957 Shore Dr 23451. **Hours:** 5 pm-midnight, Fri & Sat-1 am. **Features:** Although the decor says "casual sports bar," the menu shows a creativity not found elsewhere. Excellent smoked meats—such as chicken and grilled seafood—abound, and even a smoked beef egg roll is a delicious choice. Steak with homemade barbecue sauce is an excellent selection. Casual dress; cocktails. **Parking:** on-site. **Cards:** AX, DS, MC, VI.

STEINHILBER'S THALIA ACRES INN   Dinner: $18-$40   Phone: 757/340-1156   (27)
Seafood   **Location:** I-264, exit Rosemont westbound; exit 17B (Independence Blvd) eastbound to US 58, 1 mi n. 653 Thalia Rd 23452. **Hours:** 5 pm-10 pm. Closed: 11/24, 12/24, 12/25; also Sun. **Features:** Family-owned and operated since 1939, the former country club is charming for its mahogany paneling, vaulted ceiling and riverfront location. The signature dish is fried fantail jumbo shrimp, but the fabulous she crab soup and grilled fresh fish are other good choices. Attentive servers show obvious signs of formal training. Patio dining by the water is available in season. Dressy casual; cocktails. **Parking:** on-site. **Cards:** AX, CB, DC, DS, MC, VI.

SUSHI & WEST   Lunch: $5-$12   Dinner: $12-$20   Phone: 757/631-1004   (45)
Japanese   **Location:** 4 mi w of oceanfront via US 58/Virginia Beach Blvd, just n. 410 N Great Neck Rd 23454. **Hours:** 11:30 am-2:30 & 5:30-10 pm, Sun from 5 pm. Closed major holidays. **Features:** Patrons can be tame and stick to the traditional sushi rolls, but the real fun here is in being adventurous and sampling the creative dishes chef Kim invents daily. Among the innovations are seafood noodle cocktail, panko-crusted sashimi tuna and tuna dome. Casual dress; cocktails. **Parking:** on-site. **Cards:** AX, DS, MC, VI.

(See maps and indexes starting on p. 715, 719)

TAD'S DELI

Deli/Subs
Sandwiches

Lunch: $6-$10   Dinner: $6-$10   Phone: 757/422-3577   67
Location: 0.5 mi w of Atlantic Ave, jct Mediterranean Ave. 600 Norfolk Ave 23451. **Hours:** 7 am-8 pm; hours vary off sesson. Closed: 12/25. **Features:** The smoker is the star of this small delicatessen, which turns out its own smoked tuna, mahi mahi, roast beef, chicken and pork. Guests can order their favorites in an overstuffed sandwich or straight with sides such as macaroni and cheese, potato salad or baked beans. Casual dress. **Parking:** on-site. **Cards:** MC, VI.

TASTE UNLIMITED

Gourmet Grocery

Lunch: $4-$7   Dinner: $4-$7   Phone: 757/422-3399   4
Location: 1 blk w of Atlantic Ave. 3603 Pacific Ave 23451. **Hours:** 10 am-7 pm, Sun-6 pm; to 8 pm 5/31-9/5. Closed: 1/1, 11/24, 12/25. **Features:** A local favorite, the gourmet grocery prepares super sandwiches with a saucy house dressing, as well as savory salads and sides. Such choices can be combined with one of a great selection of international wines for a memorable picnic lunch. Patio tables are available. Casual dress. **Parking:** on-site. **Cards:** AX, MC, VI.

TERRA NOVA NATURAL FOODS GROCER & CAFE

American

Lunch: $5-$9   Dinner: $5-$9   Phone: 757/425-5383   41
Location: Just w of jct First Colonial Rd; in Conte's Bikes Shop. 1805 Laskin Rd 23454. **Hours:** 10 am-6 pm. Closed major holidays; also Sun. **Features:** In a sunny corner of the organic grocery store, you'll find this bright cafe that serves up a delicious list of specialty sandwiches, soups, tostadas, salads, smoothies, and more. Casual dress. **Parking:** on-site. **Cards:** MC, VI.

TIMBUKTU
AAA

American

Lunch: $6-$10   Dinner: $13-$22   Phone: 757/491-1800   6
Location: I-264, 0.8 mi n of terminus, just n of jct Laskin Rd (SR 58) at 32nd St; in Days Inn Oceanfront. Oceanfront at 32nd St 23451. **Hours:** 7-10:30 am, 11:30-3 & 5-9 pm, Fri & Sat-10 pm. Closed: 12/25; also Mon 11/1-3/1. **Reservations:** suggested, weekends. **Features:** Swift service and incredible food, such as sea creatures and assorted veggies circling a bed of garlic mashed potatoes daubed with basil and chive pesto and tomato vinaigrette. Tempting desserts is an understatement. Valet parking is available in season. Casual dress; cocktails. **Parking:** on-site. **Cards:** AX, DC, DS, MC, VI.

TRADEWINDS

Continental

Lunch: $7-$15   Dinner: $13-$27   Phone: 757/481-9000   3
Location: US 60, 3.5 mi e of US 13; jct Shore Dr and N Great Neck Rd; in Virginia Beach Resort Hotel & Conference Center. 2800 Shore Dr 23451. **Hours:** 11 am-3 & 5-10 pm, Sun 8 am-11, noon-3 & 5-10 pm, Sun 10 am-2 & 5-10 pm. **Reservations:** suggested, Fri-Sun. **Features:** A panorama of Chesapeake Bay is available from the dining room of the intimate restaurant. Splendid dishes include lump crab cakes, shrimp and scallop provencal, poached salmon, & seafood Caesar salad. Mouthwatering pastry, bread and dessert are baked on the premises. Dressy casual; cocktails. **Parking:** on-site. **Cards:** AX, DC, DS, MC, VI.

TWYSTED FISH

Steak & Seafood

Lunch: $5-$23   Dinner: $5-$23   Phone: 757/422-3721   52
Location: I-264, 1 mi w of oceanfront. 605 Virginia Beach Blvd 23451. **Hours:** 11 am-10 pm, Sat 5 pm-10 pm. Closed major holidays; also Sun. **Reservations:** required. **Features:** The inside is splashed in color and lively tropical artwork that reflects the fun, casual attitude of the staff. House specialties on a menu of seafood, steak, pasta and vegetarian dishes include hoppin' oysters, overstuffed sandwiches and large salad topped with grilled fish or shrimp. Casual dress; cocktails. **Parking:** on-site. **Cards:** AX, DS, MC, VI.

VIETNAM GARDEN

Vietnamese

Lunch: $6-$19   Dinner: $6-$19   Phone: 757/631-8048   65
Location: SR 58, just w of jct W Great Neck Rd; in London. 2404 Virginia Beach Blvd, Suite 114 23454. **Hours:** 11 am-3 & 5-10 pm, Sat from noon, Sun noon-3 & 5-9 pm. Closed: 11/24, 12/25; also Mon. **Features:** With a light decor highlighted by bamboo and rice paper lanterns, this small spot serves up some of the freshest and healthiest fare around. Start with sesame pancakes and move on to grilled shrimp over noodles or barbecue pork. Casual dress; beer & wine only. **Parking:** on-site. **Cards:** AX, DS, MC, VI.

VIVO CUCINA

Italian

Lunch: $6-$16   Dinner: $8-$16   Phone: 757/422-8999   32
Location: Jct Laskin Rd; in the Marketplace at Hilltop. 741 First Colonial Rd, Suite 107 23454. **Hours:** 11 am-10 pm, Fri & Sat-11 pm. Closed major holidays. **Features:** Rich velvet drapes and black and white prints line the walls. The stylish who want to be seen line the bar at the chic eatery, where the look is modern but the menu is traditional. Casual dress; cocktails. **Parking:** on-site. **Cards:** AX, DS, MC, VI.

WARRIOR'S GRILL

Asian

Lunch: $6-$8   Dinner: $10   Phone: 757/498-0323   47
Location: 3 mi w of oceanfront, just n of Laskin Rd (SR 58); in Renaissance Place. 401 N Great Neck Rd 23454. **Hours:** 11:30 am-10 pm. **Features:** Mongolian barbecue is a great alternative to the traditional all-you-can-eat Asian buffet. Diners choose raw vegetables, meats and sauces, then hand them over to the chefs, who grill the tasty fare. Casual dress; cocktails. **Parking:** on-site. **Cards:** AX, DS, MC, VI.

WATERMAN'S BEACH WOOD GRILL
AAA

Seafood

Lunch: $5-$10   Dinner: $9-$23   Phone: 757/428-3644   17
Location: I-264, 1 mi s of terminus, jct 5th St. 415 Atlantic Ave 23451. **Hours:** 11:30 am-11 pm, Sat-midnight; to 10 pm in winter. Closed: 11/24, 12/24, 12/25. **Reservations:** suggested, in season. **Features:** Specializing in appetizers, dips, raw-bar specialties and lighter versions of seafood dishes, this eatery sports a casual atmosphere in an oceanfront setting. Great views of the boardwalk can be enjoyed from the patio in season. Sunday brunch is offered from October through May. Casual dress; cocktails. **Parking:** on-site. **Cards:** AX, DC, DS, MC, VI.

(See maps and indexes starting on p. 715, 719)

WISTERIA
▼▽▽▽
American

Lunch: $6-$11   **Dinner:** $15-$20   **Phone:** 757/216-2900   18

Location: Jct Northampton Blvd, just sw; in Thoroughgood Commons. 1658 Pleasure House Rd 23455. **Hours:** 11:30 am-2 & 5-9 pm, Fri & Sat-10 pm. Closed: 1/1, 11/24, 12/25. **Reservations:** suggested. **Features:** Patrons can dine by the fireside or on the more intimate second level at the elegant yet relaxing dining room. Sophisticated fare is served in a warm, welcoming atmosphere. Fresh seafood, such as lump crab, is always a favorite, but this place also excels at duck and rack of lamb. Dressy casual; cocktails. **Parking:** on-site. **Cards:** AX, MC, VI.

🅰M 🗙

ZIA MARIE
▽▽▽▽ ▽▽▽▽
Italian

Dinner: $8-$17   **Phone:** 757/460-0715   2

Location: Jct US 60 and 13, 0.3 mi w to Pleasure House Rd, 1 mi n to Lookout Rd, then just e. 4497 Lookout Rd 23455. **Hours:** 5 pm-10 pm. Closed major holidays. **Features:** Part trattoria and part barefoot beach cafe, Zia Marie draws a devoted local clientele. House specialties include heaping bowls of pasta, stuffed eggplant and veal saltimbocca. Casual dress; cocktails. **Parking:** on-site. **Cards:** AX, DC, DS, MC, VI.

🍷 🗙

The following restaurants have not been evaluated by AAA but are listed for your information only.

CHICHO'S
fyi

                                                                 Phone: 757/422-6011

Not evaluated. **Location:** I-264, just n from terminus; between 21st and 22nd sts. 2112 Atlantic Ave 23451. **Features:** Spicy pizza sauce flavors offerings at this local spot, which is open late.

THE PIE PEDDLER
fyi

                                                                 Phone: 757/428-8381

Not evaluated. **Location:** I-264, exit Lasking Rd, 0.3 mi e; in Le Promenade Shops. 1860 Laskin Rd, Suite 109 23454. **Features:** The cozy shop offers a Victorian-style tea room and a wide assortment of traditional and gourmet pies. Tasty lunches such as chicken pot pie with a relish tray on the side can be found during the Christmas shopping season.

TASTE UNLIMITED-BAYVILLE
fyi

                                                                 Phone: 757/464-1566

Not evaluated. **Location:** Jct US 13, 1 mi e. 4097 Shore Dr 23455. **Features:** Part of a local chain, the gourmet food shop offers sandwiches and specialty foods.

The Hampton Roads Area Vicinity

CHESAPEAKE pop. 199,184   (See map and index starting on p. 710)

——— WHERE TO STAY ———

COMFORT SUITES   *Book at aaa.com*

▽▽▽▽
Small-scale Hotel

All Year   1P: $69-$129   **Phone:** (757)420-1600   45

Location: I-64, exit 289B, 0.3 mi s to Greenbrier Mall, just w on Jarman Rd (at Crossways Center) to Crossways Blvd, then 0.3 mi n. 1550 Crossways Blvd 23320. Fax: 757/420-0099. **Facility:** 124 units. 123 one-bedroom standard units. 1 two-bedroom suite with kitchen. 3 stories, interior corridors. **Parking:** on-site. **Terms:** 3 night minimum stay - seasonal. **Amenities:** high-speed Internet, dual phone lines, voice mail, irons, hair dryers. **Pool(s):** outdoor. **Leisure Activities:** sauna, whirlpool, steamroom, exercise room. **Guest Services:** valet and coin laundry. **Business Services:** meeting rooms, fax. **Cards:** AX, CB, DC, DS, JC, MC, VI.

SOME UNITS
(ASK) S🅳 🍽➔ 🅰M ⌕ 🗙 📷 [DATA PORT] 🛏 🍴 ⬜ / 🗙 VCR /

COURTYARD BY MARRIOTT   *Book at aaa.com*
▽▽▽▽
Small-scale Hotel

All Year   1P: $79-$139   **Phone:** (757)420-1700   42

Location: I-64, exit 289B, just s to Jarman Rd, then w. 1562 Crossways Blvd 23320. Fax: 757/420-1939. **Facility:** 90 units. 87 one-bedroom standard units, some with whirlpools. 3 one-bedroom suites. 3 stories, interior corridors. *Bath:* combo or shower only. **Parking:** on-site. **Terms:** 3 night minimum stay - seasonal. **Amenities:** high-speed Internet, dual phone lines, voice mail, irons, hair dryers. **Pool(s):** heated indoor. **Leisure Activities:** whirlpool, exercise room. **Guest Services:** sundries, valet and coin laundry. **Business Services:** meeting rooms, fax. **Cards:** AX, CB, DC, DS, JC, MC, VI.

SOME UNITS
(ASK) S🅳 🍴 🅰M ⌕ ⌨ ⌕ 📷 [DATA PORT] ⬜ / 🗙 🛏 🍴 /

DAYS INN-CHESAPEAKE   *Book at aaa.com*
🅐🅐🅐 SAVE
▽▽▽▽
Motel

5/1-9/8   1P: $75-$100   2P: $75-$100   XP: $5   F17
3/1-4/30 & 9/9-2/28   1P: $40-$75   2P: $45-$80   XP: $5   F17   **Phone:** (757)487-8861   38

Location: I-64, exit 296, 2.5 mi n on US 17. 1439 George Washington Hwy 23323. Fax: 757/485-1549. **Facility:** 53 one-bedroom standard units. 2 stories (no elevator), interior/exterior corridors. **Parking:** on-site. **Terms:** 7 night minimum stay - seasonal, 7 day cancellation notice, weekly rates available, package plans, small pets only ($10 extra charge). **Amenities:** hair dryers. *Some:* irons. **Guest Services:** valet laundry. **Business Services:** fax. **Cards:** AX, DC, DS, MC, VI. **Special Amenities:** free continental breakfast and free newspaper.

SOME UNITS
S🅳 🛏 🍽➔ 📷 [DATA PORT] 🛏 🍴 / 🗙 ⬜ /
FEE

(See map and index starting on p. 710)

ECONO LODGE CHESAPEAKE *Book at aaa.com*　　　　　　　　　Phone: (757)543-2200　**46**

AAA SAVE
　　　　5/16-9/15　　　　　　　　1P: $59-$99　　　　　　2P: $59-$99　　　　XP: $5　　　F13
　　　　3/1-5/15 & 9/16-2/28　　　1P: $49-$69　　　　　　2P: $49-$69　　　　XP: $5　　　F13
Motel　**Location:** I-64, exit 290A, 0.5 mi to S Military Hwy, then 0.5 mi s. 2222 S Military Hwy 23320. Fax: 757/543-0572.
　　　　Facility: 55 one-bedroom standard units, some with efficiencies (no utensils). 2 stories (no elevator),
　　　　exterior corridors. **Parking:** on-site. **Terms:** package plans. **Business Services:** meeting rooms, fax.
　　　　Cards: AX, CB, DC, DS, JC, MC, VI. **Special Amenities: free continental breakfast and free local
telephone calls.**

SOME UNITS
[S/D] [✦] [DATA PORT] [▯] / [✕] [▭] [▱] /

FAIRFIELD INN BY MARRIOTT *Book at aaa.com*　　　　　　　　Phone: (757)420-1300　**43**

　　　　All Year　　　　　　　　　1P: $59-$129
Small-scale Hotel　**Location:** I-64, exit 289B, just s to Greenbrier Mall, then just w on Jarman Rd to Crossways Blvd. 1560 Crossways Blvd
23320. Fax: 757/366-0608. **Facility:** 105 one-bedroom standard units. 3 stories, interior corridors. *Bath:*
combo or shower only. **Parking:** on-site. **Terms:** 3 night minimum stay - seasonal. **Amenities:** high-speed
Internet, dual phone lines, irons, hair dryers. **Pool(s):** outdoor. **Leisure Activities:** exercise room. **Guest Services:** valet and
coin laundry. **Business Services:** meeting rooms, business center. **Cards:** AX, CB, DC, DS, JC, MC, VI.

SOME UNITS
[ASK] [S/D] [¶↑] [&] [&M] [&] [⊇] [✦] [DATA PORT] [▱] / [✕] [▯] [▭] /

HAMPTON INN *Book at aaa.com*　　　　　　　　　　　　　Phone: 757/484-5800　**34**

　　　　6/1-8/31　　　　　　　　　1P: $109-$114　　　　2P: $109-$114　　　XP: $10　　F18
　　　　3/1-5/31　　　　　　　　　1P: $79-$99　　　　　2P: $79-$99　　　　XP: $10　　F18
　　　　9/1-10/31　　　　　　　　1P: $99　　　　　　　2P: $99　　　　　　XP: $10　　F18
Small-scale Hotel　11/1-2/28　　　　　　　　　1P: $79　　　　　　　2P: $79　　　　　　XP: $10　　F18
Location: I-664, exit 9B northbound; exit 8B southbound, 1 mi s on US 17. 3235 Western Branch Blvd 23321. Fax: 757/484-9539.
Facility: 90 one-bedroom standard units. 4 stories, interior corridors. **Parking:** on-site. **Terms:** check-in 4 pm, 2 night minimum
stay - seasonal. **Amenities:** high-speed Internet, voice mail, irons, hair dryers. **Leisure Activities:** sauna, exercise room.
Guest Services: valet and coin laundry. **Business Services:** meeting rooms, fax. **Cards:** AX, DC, DS, MC, VI.

SOME UNITS
[ASK] [S/D] [¶↑] [VCR] [✦] [DATA PORT] [▯] [▭] [▱] / [✕] /

HAMPTON INN CHESAPEAKE *Book at aaa.com*　　　　　　　Phone: (757)420-1550　**41**

　　　　All Year　　　　　　　　　1P: $79-$139
Small-scale Hotel　**Location:** I-64, exit 289A, 2 blks n to Woodlake Dr, then 2 blks e. 701A Woodlake Dr 23320. Fax: 757/424-7414.
Facility: 119 one-bedroom standard units. 4 stories, interior corridors. **Parking:** on-site. **Terms:** 3 day
cancellation notice-fee imposed. **Amenities:** video games, voice mail, irons, hair dryers. **Pool(s):** outdoor.
Guest Services: valet laundry. **Business Services:** meeting rooms, fax. **Cards:** AX, DC, DS, MC, VI.

SOME UNITS
[ASK] [S/D] [¶↑] [⌀] [⊇] [✦✦] [✦] [DATA PORT] [▱] / [✕] [▯] [▭] /

HILTON GARDEN INN-CHESAPEAKE/GREENBRIAR *Book at aaa.com*　　Phone: (757)420-1212　**44**

　　　　5/27-8/31　　　　　　　　1P: $139-$149
　　　　9/1-11/15　　　　　　　　1P: $109-$129
　　　　3/1-5/26　　　　　　　　　1P: $109-$119
Small-scale Hotel　11/16-2/28　　　　　　　1P: $99-$109
Location: I-64, exit 289B, 0.3 mi s on Greenbriar Pkwy, then just w on Jarman Rd (at Crossways Center) to Crossways Blvd. 1565 Crossways
Blvd 23320. Fax: 757/420-7006. **Facility:** 92 one-bedroom standard units, some with whirlpools. 4 stories, interior corridors.
Bath: combo or shower only. **Parking:** on-site. **Terms:** cancellation fee imposed, package plans. **Amenities:** video games,
high-speed Internet, dual phone lines, voice mail, irons, hair dryers. **Pool(s):** heated indoor. **Leisure Activities:** whirlpool,
exercise room. **Guest Services:** sundries, valet and coin laundry, area transportation. **Business Services:** meeting rooms,
business center. **Cards:** AX, DC, DS, MC, VI.

SOME UNITS
[ASK] [S/D] [✦] [¶] [&] [⊇] [✦] [DATA PORT] [▯] [▭] [▱] / [✕] /

HOLIDAY INN CHESAPEAKE *Book at aaa.com*　　　　　　　Phone: 757/523-1500　**40**

　　　　5/1-9/30　　　　　　　　　1P: $129-$139　　　　2P: $129-$139
　　　　3/1-4/30 & 10/1-10/31　　1P: $119-$129　　　　2P: $119-$129
　　　　11/1-2/28　　　　　　　　1P: $99-$109　　　　2P: $99-$109
Small-scale Hotel　**Location:** I-64, exit 289A, n to Woodlake Dr, then just e. Located adjacent to the Chesapeake Conference Center. 725
Woodlake Dr 23320. Fax: 757/523-0683. **Facility:** 229 units. 217 one-bedroom standard units. 12 one-bedroom suites ($109-
$229). 7 stories, interior corridors. **Parking:** on-site. **Terms:** 3 day cancellation notice-fee imposed, [ECP] meal plan available.
Amenities: video games, high-speed Internet (fee), dual phone lines, voice mail, irons, hair dryers. **Pool(s):** heated indoor.
Leisure Activities: sauna, whirlpool, exercise room. **Guest Services:** valet and coin laundry, area transportation. **Business
Services:** conference facilities, administrative services, fax. **Cards:** AX, CB, DC, DS, JC, MC, VI.

SOME UNITS
[ASK] [✦] [¶] [Y] [&M] [⌀] [⊇] [✕] [✦] [DATA PORT] [▱] / [✕] [▯] [▭] /
　　　　　　　　　　　　　　　　　　　　　　　　　　　　　FEE　FEE

HOLIDAY INN EXPRESS HOTEL & SUITES *Book at aaa.com*　　　Phone: (757)465-2222　**35**

AAA SAVE
　　　　3/1-8/31　　　　　　　　　1P: $119-$159　　　2P: $119-$159　　　XP: $5　　　F18
　　　　9/1-2/28　　　　　　　　　1P: $89-$140　　　　2P: $89-$140　　　　XP: $5　　　F18
Small-scale Hotel　**Location:** I-664, exit 11B. 2436 Gum Rd 23321. Fax: 757/465-3222. **Facility:** 90 one-bedroom standard units,
some with whirlpools. 5 stories, interior corridors. *Bath:* combo or shower only. **Parking:** on-site.
Amenities: high-speed Internet, voice mail, irons, hair dryers. **Pool(s):** heated indoor. **Leisure
Activities:** whirlpool, exercise room. **Guest Services:** valet and coin laundry. **Business Services:** meeting
rooms, fax. **Cards:** AX, CB, DC, DS, JC, MC, VI. **Special Amenities: free expanded continental breakfast and free
newspaper.**

SOME UNITS
[S/D] [¶↑] [&M] [&] [⊇] [✦] [DATA PORT] [▯] [▭] [▱] / [✕] /

(See map and index starting on p. 710)

RED ROOF INN   *Book at aaa.com*   Phone: (757)523-0123   **39**

5/27-9/17	1P: $48-$69	2P: $53-$74	XP: $5 F18
3/1-3/27	1P: $45-$60	2P: $50-$65	XP: $5 F18
3/28-5/26	1P: $43-$60	2P: $48-$65	XP: $5 F18
9/18-2/28	1P: $42-$52	2P: $47-$57	XP: $5 F18

Motel

Location: I-64, exit 289A, just n to Woodlake Dr, then just e. 724 Woodlake Dr 23320. **Fax:** 757/523-4763. **Facility:** 108 one-bedroom standard units. 2 stories (no elevator), exterior corridors. **Parking:** on-site. **Terms:** small pets only. **Amenities:** video games, voice mail. **Business Services:** fax. **Cards:** AX, CB, DC, DS, MC, VI.

SOME UNITS / FEE / FEE

SLEEP INN   *Book at aaa.com*   Phone: (757)638-5000   **33**

6/1-8/31	1P: $89-$109	2P: $89-$109	XP: $5 F18
3/1-5/31 & 9/1-11/30	1P: $79-$89	2P: $79-$89	XP: $5 F18
12/1-2/28	1P: $59-$79	2P: $59-$79	XP: $5 F18

Small-scale Hotel

Location: I-664, exit 9B, 1 mi s on SR 17. 3280 Western Branch Blvd 23321. **Fax:** 757/638-5007. **Facility:** 62 one-bedroom standard units. 2 stories, interior corridors. *Bath:* combo or shower only. **Parking:** on-site. **Amenities:** video library, dual phone lines, voice mail, irons, hair dryers. **Leisure Activities:** sauna, exercise room. **Guest Services:** valet laundry. **Business Services:** meeting rooms, fax. **Cards:** AX, DC, DS, JC, MC, VI. **Special Amenities:** free continental breakfast and free local telephone calls.

SOME UNITS

SPRINGHILL SUITES BY MARRIOTT   *Book at aaa.com*   Phone: (757)405-3100   **36**

All Year   1P: $69-$129

Small-scale Hotel

Location: I-664, exit 11B (Portsmouth Blvd E). 2424 Gum Rd 23321. **Fax:** 757/405-3576. **Facility:** 93 one-bedroom standard units. 3 stories, interior corridors. *Bath:* combo or shower only. **Parking:** on-site. **Terms:** 3 night minimum stay - seasonal. **Amenities:** high-speed Internet, dual phone lines, voice mail, irons, hair dryers. **Pool(s):** small heated indoor. **Leisure Activities:** whirlpool, exercise room. **Guest Services:** valet and coin laundry. **Business Services:** meeting rooms, fax. **Cards:** AX, CB, DC, DS, JC, MC, VI.

SOME UNITS

SUPER 8 MOTEL   *Book at aaa.com*   Phone: (757)686-8888   **32**

4/1-10/31	1P: $55-$71	2P: $59-$77	XP: $6 F18
3/1-3/31 & 11/1-2/28	1P: $48-$66	2P: $52-$72	XP: $6 F18

Motel

Location: I-664, exit 9B, 1 mi s on SR 17. 3216 Churchland Blvd 23321. **Fax:** 757/686-8888. **Facility:** 58 one-bedroom standard units. 3 stories, interior corridors. **Parking:** on-site. **Terms:** 3 day cancellation notice, small pets only. **Amenities:** safes (fee). **Guest Services:** coin laundry. **Business Services:** meeting rooms, fax. **Cards:** AX, DC, DS, MC, VI.

SOME UNITS / FEE

TOWNEPLACE SUITES BY MARRIOTT   Phone: (757)523-5004   **37**

All Year   1P: $69-$139

Small-scale Hotel

Location: I-64, exit 289A, just n on Greenbrier Pkwy. 2000 Old Greenbrier Rd 23320. **Fax:** 757/413-5600. **Facility:** 119 units. 93 one-bedroom standard units with kitchens. 4 one- and 22 two-bedroom suites with kitchens. 3 stories, interior corridors. *Bath:* combo or shower only. **Parking:** on-site. **Terms:** 3 night minimum stay - seasonal, pets ($10 extra charge). **Amenities:** high-speed Internet, voice mail, irons, hair dryers. **Pool(s):** heated outdoor. **Leisure Activities:** exercise room. **Guest Services:** valet and coin laundry. **Business Services:** fax. **Cards:** AX, CB, DC, DS, JC, MC, VI.

SOME UNITS / FEE

————— **WHERE TO DINE** —————

3 AMIGOS RESTAURANTE MEXICANO   **Lunch:** $6-$12   **Dinner:** $6-$12   Phone: 757/548-4105

Mexican

Location: I-64, exit 290B, 3.3 mi s. 200 N Battlefield Blvd 23320. **Hours:** 11 am-10 pm, Fri-11 pm, Sun-9 pm. Closed major holidays. **Features:** Overlooking the Intracoastal Waterway, the eatery is a pleasant spot for sampling such dishes as huevos rancheros and chicken with a savory red mole sauce that derives its richness from cocoa beans. The house specialty is a tasty mix of beef and chicken slices covered in cactus, onions and tomatoes. Casual dress; cocktails. **Parking:** on-site. **Cards:** MC, VI.

THE ANGRY CHEF   **Lunch:** $7-$11   **Dinner:** $7-$11   Phone: 757/963-7534   **76**

American

Location: I-64, exit 289B, just w; across from Greenbrier Mall. 1412 Greenbrier Pkwy, Suite 140 23320. **Hours:** 7 am-7 pm, Sat from 8 am, Mon 7 am-3 pm. Closed major holidays; also Sun. **Features:** He might be angry, but he knows how to cook. Locals drop in to the bright and casual spot for a break from the ordinary such as roasted garlic salad, the drunk burger which is marinated in whiskey, seared crab cakes, fresh soups, and daily changing desserts. Casual dress. **Parking:** on-site. **Cards:** DS, MC, VI.

ATLAS GRILL & BAR   **Lunch:** $6-$14   **Dinner:** $6-$14   Phone: 757/420-6222   **74**

American

Location: I-64, exit 289B, just s; across from Greenbrier Mall. 1432 Greenbrier Pkwy 23320. **Hours:** 11 am-10 pm, Fri & Sat-11 pm. Closed major holidays. **Features:** Atlas stakes its claim on "chain row" offering hungry diners heaping portions of comfort food with heavy influences from the South and from traditional diner fare. Great "stick to your ribs" dishes such as meatloaf, chicken pot pie and pork chops, as well as burgers and salad. Casual dress; cocktails. **Parking:** on-site. **Cards:** AX, DS, MC, VI.

(See map and index starting on p. 710)

COURTHOUSE CAFE Lunch: $7-$20   Dinner: $7-$20   Phone: 757/482-7077
♦♦♦ ♦♦♦ **Location:** I-64, exit 290B, 4 mi s on Battlefield Blvd, jct Johnstown Rd; in Wilson Village Shopping Center. 350 S Battlefield Blvd 23322. **Hours:** 11 am-10 pm, Fri & Sat-10:30 pm. Closed major holidays; also Sun.
Regional American **Features:** Reminiscent of the days when the city was more country than suburbia, the cozy, little spot prepares regional seafood specialties, such as stuffed flounder, she crab soup and Hatteras-style clam chowder. Other favorites include prime rib, burgers and sandwiches. Casual dress; cocktails. **Parking:** on-site. **Cards:** DS, MC, VI.
[X]

DAIKICHI SUSHI JAPANESE BISTRO Lunch: $7-$14   Dinner: $12-$19   Phone: 757/549-0200   (78)
♦♦♦ ♦♦♦ **Location:** I-64, exit 290B, just s; in Battlefield Marketplace. 1400 N Battlefield Blvd 23320. **Hours:** 11:30 am-2 & 5:30-9:30 pm, Fri-10 pm, Sat 5:30 pm-10 pm. Closed major holidays; also Sun. **Features:** A sleek, modern
Japanese setting in the heart of suburbia offers stylish preparations of fresh sushi—both traditional and the chef's modern additions. Udon noodles and pork katsu are other tasty plates. Rarely seen in America, pure fresh wasabi accompanies sushi plates. Casual dress; beer & wine only. **Parking:** on-site. **Cards:** MC, VI.
[&M] [X]

EL LORO MEXICAN RESTAURANTE Lunch: $4-$10   Dinner: $6-$10   Phone: 757/436-3415   (77)
♦♦♦ **Location:** I-64, exit 289B, 0.9 mi s. 801 Volvo Pkwy, Suites 114-115 23320. **Hours:** 10 am-10 pm, Fri-11 pm, Sat noon-10 pm, Sun noon-9 pm. Closed major holidays. **Features:** Pinatas and colorful paintings add to the
Mexican festive atmosphere of the traditional Mexican restaurant. The menu is laden with the classics: combination and vegetarian plates, fajitas, tacos, chalupas and, of course, margaritas-in jumbo and Texas-style varieties.
Casual dress; cocktails. **Parking:** on-site. **Cards:** AX, MC, VI.
[X]

THE GRATE STEAK Dinner: $12-$32   Phone: 757/366-5677   (75)
♦♦♦ ♦♦♦ **Location:** I-64, exit 289B, just s to Greenbrier Mall, then just n. 1020 Eden Way N 23320. **Hours:** 5 pm-10 pm, Sat from 2 pm, Sun noon-9 pm. Closed: 11/24, 12/24, 12/25. **Features:** The Grate Steak is known for USDA
Steak & Seafood choice beef, hand-selected and trimmed. One can choose their own cut from the refrigerator case and grill it themselves over live charcoal or let the work be done for them while helping themselves to the salad and potato bar. Casual dress; cocktails. **Parking:** on-site. **Cards:** AX, DC, DS, MC, VI.
[Y] [X]

THE LOCKS POINTE Lunch: $6-$9   Dinner: $13-$24   Phone: 757/547-9618
♦♦♦ ♦♦♦ **Location:** I-64, exit 290B, 3.5 mi s. 136 Battlefield Blvd N 23320. **Hours:** 11:30 am-3 & 5-9 pm, Fri-10 pm, Sat 4 pm-10 pm, Sun 10:30 am-3 & 4-9 pm. Closed: 12/24, 12/25; also Mon. **Features:** Rooms decorated in rich
Seafood wood and lots of glass look out onto the Intracoastal Waterway. Traditional, contemporary preparation of predominantly seafood specials, such as tasty scallops with angel hair pasta, make the restaurant popular.
Casual dress; cocktails. **Parking:** on-site. **Cards:** AX, MC, VI.
[Y] [X]

MS MARIAN'S RESTAURANT Lunch: $5-$11   Dinner: $5-$11   Phone: 757/547-5556   (80)
♦♦♦ **Location:** I-64, exit 290B; adjacent to Sam's Club. 1437 Sam's Dr 23320. **Hours:** 11 am-9 pm. Closed: Sun.
Southern **Features:** All your down-home Southern favorites can be found at Ms. Marian's including fried chicken, barbecue, cornbread, mac n' cheese and even collard greens. Casual dress. **Parking:** on-site. **Cards:** MC, VI.
[&M] [X]

TASTE UNLIMITED Lunch: $4-$10   Dinner: $4-$10   Phone: 757/424-4583   (72)
♦♦♦ **Location:** I-64, exit 289B, just s. 1580 Crossways Blvd 23320. **Hours:** 10 am-7 pm. Closed: Sun. **Features:** A
Deli/Subs local favorite, the gourmet grocery prepares super sandwiches with a saucy house dressing, as well as
Sandwiches savory salads and sides. Such choices can be combined with a bottle from the great selection of international wines for a memorable picnic lunch. Patio tables are available. Casual dress. **Parking:** on-site. **Cards:** AX, MC, VI.

TIDA THAI CUISINE Lunch: $4-$6   Dinner: $7-$9   Phone: 757/543-9116   (71)
♦♦♦ **Location:** I-64, exit 290A, 0.5 mi to Military Hwy, then just n to Chesapeake Crossing Shopping Center. 1937 S Military
Thai Hwy 23320. **Hours:** 11 am-3 & 5-9:30 pm, Fri & Sat-10 pm. Closed: 11/24, 12/25; also 12/31. **Features:** Traditional dishes are presented in the popular eatery's cozy dining room. Many spicy and exotic flavors await diners in such favorites as crab dumplings and coconut soup. Both the food and friendly, attentive service contribute to this place's regular following. Casual dress; beer & wine only. **Parking:** on-site. **Cards:** AX, DS, MC, VI.
[X]

VIVO, YOUR ITALIAN KITCHEN Lunch: $7-$20   Dinner: $7-$20   Phone: 757/361-9444   (73)
♦♦♦ ♦♦♦ **Location:** I-64, exit 289B, just s; across from Greenbrier Mall. 628 Jarman Rd 23320. **Hours:** 11 am-10 pm, Fri &
Italian Sat-11 pm. Closed: 11/24, 12/25. **Features:** All the traditional Italian-American favorites line this menu alongside a few strictly American dishes such as great fried shrimp at this casual spot where black & white prints line the walls and Sinatra croons in the background. Casual dress; cocktails. **Parking:** on-site.
Cards: AX, MC, VI.
[&M] [Y] [X]

WARRIOR'S MONGOLIAN GRILL Lunch: $6-$8   Dinner: $10   Phone: 757/382-7007   (79)
♦♦♦ **Location:** I-64, exit 291 (S Battlefield Blvd), just e to Wal-Mart Way Crossing. 1437 Sam's Dr #113 23320.
Asian **Hours:** 11:30 am-9 pm, Fri & Sat-10 pm. Closed major holidays. **Features:** Mongolian barbecue is a great alternative to the traditional all-you-can-eat Asian buffet. Diners choose raw vegetables, meats and sauces, then hand them over to the chefs, who grill the tasty fare. Casual dress; cocktails. **Parking:** on-site.
Cards: AX, DS, MC, VI.
[X]

GLOUCESTER

——— WHERE TO STAY ———

COMFORT INN GLOUCESTER   *Book at aaa.com*   Phone: (804)695-1900

5/27-9/3 [ECP]	1P: $84-$109	2P: $84-$109	XP: $5	F18
3/1-5/26 & 9/4-11/5 [ECP]	1P: $79-$99	2P: $79-$99	XP: $5	F18
11/6-2/28 [ECP]	1P: $79-$94	2P: $79-$94	XP: $5	F18

Small-scale Hotel   **Location:** US 17, just s. 6639 Forest Hill Ave 23061. **Fax:** 804/695-1901. **Facility:** 79 one-bedroom standard units, some with whirlpools. 3 stories, interior corridors. *Bath:* combo or shower only. **Parking:** on-site. **Terms:** 2 night minimum stay - seasonal and/or weekends, small pets only ($10 extra charge). **Amenities:** voice mail, irons, hair dryers. **Pool(s):** outdoor. **Guest Services:** sundries, valet and coin laundry. **Business Services:** meeting rooms, fax. **Cards:** AX, CB, DC, DS, JC, MC, VI.

——— WHERE TO DINE ———

KELSICK GARDENS   **Lunch:** $5-$10   Phone: 804/693-6500

Gourmet Grocery   **Location:** Downtown. 6604 Main St 23061. **Hours:** 10 am-5:30 pm, Sat-4:30 pm. Closed major holidays; also Sun. **Features:** The well-stocked gourmet grocer and wine shop prepares tasty lunch specials from soups to sandwiches. Daily fresh cakes, crab cake sandwiches and take-home meals are local favorites. Casual dress; beer & wine only. **Parking:** on-site. **Cards:** MC, VI.

STILLWATER'S ON MAIN   **Lunch:** $6-$15   **Dinner:** $10-$24   Phone: 804/694-5618

American   **Location:** Jct Martin St; downtown. 6553 Main St 23061. **Hours:** 11 am-2:30 & 5-9 pm, Mon-2:30 pm. Closed major holidays; also Sun. **Features:** The bright storefront overlooks the center of town. The kitchen prepares a delicious array of specialties, such as Urbanna hot smoked salmon, buffalo steak and local seafood, in preparations with Mediterranean influences. Casual dress; cocktails. **Parking:** on-site. **Cards:** CB, DS, MC, VI.

——— *The following restaurant has not been evaluated by AAA* ———
but is listed for your information only.

LEIGH AND NARDOZZI BAKERY   Phone: 804/693-3854

[fyi]   Not evaluated. **Location:** Downtown. 6672 Main St. **Features:** In the heart of the quaint town is this small bakery, which turns out artisan breads and a short lunch menu of chowders, sandwiches and salads.

GLOUCESTER POINT pop. 9,429

——— WHERE TO DINE ———

RIVER'S INN RESTAURANT & CRAB DECK   **Lunch:** $5-$9   **Dinner:** $17-$22   Phone: 804/642-9942

Seafood   **Location:** From the Coleman Bridge/US 17 N, e on CR 1206/Lafayette Heights Dr to Great Rd N, 0.5 mi e on Terrapin Cove Rd. 8109 Yacht Haven Dr 23062. **Hours:** 11:30 am-3 & 5-9 pm; to 10 pm in season. Closed: Mon 11/1-3/31. **Reservations:** suggested. **Features:** Relax in the scenic waterfront setting and crisp indoor decor while sampling a variety of classic regional seafood specialties. Casual, outdoor deck dining focuses on sandwiches, steamed seafood and raw bar offerings. Service is pleasant and well timed. Casual dress; cocktails. **Parking:** on-site. **Cards:** AX, MC, VI.

——— *The following restaurant has not been evaluated by AAA* ———
but is listed for your information only.

SWEET MADELEINE'S CAFE   Phone: 804/642-1780

[fyi]   Not evaluated. **Location:** On US 17, 1.5 mi n of Coleman Bridge. 2091 George Washington Memorial Hwy. **Features:** Homemade soups, gourmet sandwiches and freshly baked desserts fill the bill at the garden-themed cafe.

HAMPTON pop. 146,437   (See map and index starting on p. 707)

——— WHERE TO STAY ———

CANDLEWOOD SUITES   *Book at aaa.com*   Phone: (757)766-8976   **22**

4/1-10/31	1P: $99-$189
3/1-3/31 & 11/1-2/28	1P: $59-$189

Small-scale Hotel   **Location:** I-64, exit 261B (Hampton Roads Center Pkwy) eastbound; exit 262B (Magruder Blvd) westbound, then n. 401 Butler Farm Rd 23666. **Fax:** 757/766-9553. **Facility:** 98 units. 74 one-bedroom standard units with kitchens. 24 one-bedroom suites with kitchens. 3 stories, interior corridors. *Bath:* combo or shower only. **Parking:** on-site. **Terms:** weekly rates available, pets ($75-$150 extra charge). **Amenities:** video library, video games, CD players, dual phone lines, voice mail, irons, hair dryers. **Leisure Activities:** exercise room. **Guest Services:** sundries, complimentary laundry. **Business Services:** fax. **Cards:** AX, DC, DS, MC, VI.

(See map and index starting on p. 707)

COMFORT INN   *Book at aaa.com*   Phone: (757)827-5052   **26**
⬥⬥⬥ SAVE   6/1-9/10   1P: $85-$160   2P: $90-$165   XP: $10   F18
                9/11-2/28   1P: $65-$120   2P: $70-$125   XP: $5   F18
▽▽▽ ▽▽▽   3/1-5/31   1P: $65-$115   2P: $70-$120   XP: $5   F18
Small-scale Hotel **Location:** I-64, exit 263B (Mercury Blvd). 1916 Coliseum Dr 23666. Fax: 757/827-0666. **Facility:** 66 one-bedroom standard units. 5 stories, interior corridors. **Parking:** on-site. **Terms:** package plans. **Amenities:** high-speed Internet, voice mail, irons, hair dryers. **Pool(s):** outdoor. **Guest Services:** valet and coin laundry. **Business Services:** PC, fax. **Cards:** AX, CB, DC, DS, JC, MC, VI.
SOME UNITS

COURTYARD BY MARRIOTT   *Book at aaa.com*   Phone: 757-838-3300   **28**
▽▽▽ ▽▽▽   1/1-2/28   1P: $109-$139   2P: $109-$139
                3/1-12/31   1P: $99-$129   2P: $99-$129
Small-scale Hotel **Location:** I-64, exit 263B (Mercury Dr), just n to Coliseum Dr, then just w. Located adjacent to Hampton Coliseum. 1917 Coliseum Dr 23666. Fax: 757/838-6387. **Facility:** 146 units. 134 one-bedroom standard units. 12 one-bedroom suites. 3 stories, interior corridors. **Bath:** combo or shower only. **Parking:** on-site. **Terms:** cancellation fee imposed. **Amenities:** dual phone lines, voice mail, irons, hair dryers. **Pool(s):** heated outdoor. **Leisure Activities:** whirlpool, exercise room. **Guest Services:** valet and coin laundry. **Business Services:** meeting rooms, fax. **Cards:** AX, CB, DC, DS, JC, MC, VI.
SOME UNITS

EMBASSY SUITES AT HAMPTON ROADS
CONVENTION CENTER   Phone: 757-827-8200
[fyi]   Under construction, scheduled to open June 2005. **Location:** Jct I-64 and 664. 1700 Coliseum Dr 23666. Fax: 757/827-8010. **Planned Amenities:** coffeemakers, microwaves, refrigerators, pool.
Small-scale Hotel *(See color ad below)*

HAMPTON INN   *Book at aaa.com*   Phone: (757)838-8484   **25**
▽▽▽ ▽▽▽   5/1-9/30 [CP]   1P: $99-$129   2P: $99-$129
                10/1-2/28 [CP]   1P: $94-$114   2P: $94-$114
                3/1-4/30 [CP]   1P: $89-$109   2P: $89-$109
Small-scale Hotel **Location:** I-64, exit 263B (Mercury Blvd), jct SR 58. 1813 W Mercury Blvd 23666. Fax: 757/826-0725. **Facility:** 131 one-bedroom standard units. 6 stories, interior corridors. **Parking:** on-site. **Terms:** 2-3 night minimum stay - seasonal and/or weekends, 3 day cancellation notice. **Amenities:** video games, voice mail, irons, hair dryers. **Leisure Activities:** exercise room. **Guest Services:** valet laundry. **Business Services:** fax. **Cards:** AX, CB, DC, DS, MC, VI.
SOME UNITS
FEE FEE

HOLIDAY INN HAMPTON HOTEL & CONFERENCE
CENTER   *Book at aaa.com*   Phone: (757)838-0200   **24**
▽▽▽ ▽▽▽   All Year   1P: $59-$169   2P: $59-$169
                Location: I-64, exit 263B (Mercury Blvd) westbound; exit 263 eastbound. 1815 W Mercury Blvd 23666.
Large-scale Hotel Fax: 757/838-4964. **Facility:** 320 units. 318 one-bedroom standard units. 2 one-bedroom suites ($180-$375) with whirlpools. 2-4 stories, interior/exterior corridors. **Bath:** combo or shower only. **Parking:** on-site. **Terms:** check-in 4 pm, cancellation fee imposed, small pets only ($25-$50 deposit). **Amenities:** video games, high-speed Internet (fee), voice mail, irons, hair dryers. *Some:* dual phone lines. **Pool(s):** outdoor, heated indoor. **Leisure Activities:** sauna, whirlpool, exercise room. **Guest Services:** gift shop, valet and coin laundry, area transportation. **Business Services:** conference facilities, business center. **Cards:** AX, DC, DS, MC, VI.
SOME UNITS
FEE   FEE

LA QUINTA INN NORFOLK (HAMPTON)   *Book at aaa.com*   Phone: (757)827-8680   **27**
⬥⬥⬥ SAVE   4/29-9/7   1P: $69-$139   2P: $74-$144   XP: $5   F18
                3/1-4/28 & 9/8-2/28   1P: $65-$85   2P: $70-$90   XP: $5   F18
▽▽▽ ▽▽▽   **Location:** I-64, exit 263 (Mercury Blvd), just s. 2138 W Mercury Blvd 23666. Fax: 757/827-5906. **Facility:** 129
Small-scale Hotel units. 126 one-bedroom standard units. 3 one-bedroom suites. 3 stories, interior/exterior corridors. **Bath:** combo or shower only. **Parking:** on-site. **Terms:** [ECP] meal plan available. **Amenities:** video games, voice mail, irons, hair dryers. **Pool(s):** outdoor. **Guest Services:** coin laundry. **Business Services:** fax.
Cards: AX, DC, DS, MC, VI. **Special Amenities:** free expanded continental breakfast and free local telephone calls.
(See color ad p 730)
SOME UNITS
FEE FEE

(See map and index starting on p. 707)

QUALITY INN & SUITES CONFERENCE CENTER *Book at aaa.com*   Phone: (757)838-5011   **23**

AAA SAVE

| | 6/1-8/31 | 1P: $110-$180 | 2P: $111-$180 | XP: $10 | F18 |
| | 3/1-5/31 & 9/1-2/28 | 1P: $90-$150 | 2P: $90-$150 | XP: $10 | F18 |

Small-scale Hotel

Location: I-64, exit 263B (Mercury Blvd), jct SR 58. 1809 W Mercury Blvd 23666. Fax: 757/838-7349. **Facility:** 189 units. 187 one-bedroom standard units. 2 one-bedroom suites. 8 stories, interior corridors. *Bath:* combo or shower only. **Parking:** on-site. **Terms:** check-in 4 pm, cancellation fee imposed, pets ($25 extra charge). **Amenities:** video games, voice mail, safes (fee), irons, hair dryers. **Dining:** 2 restaurants, 6:30 am-10 pm, Fri-11 pm, Sat 7 am-11 pm, Sun 7 am-9 pm, cocktails. **Pool(s):** heated indoor. **Leisure Activities:** exercise room, game room. **Guest Services:** gift shop, valet and coin laundry. **Business Services:** conference facilities, fax. **Cards:** AX, CB, DC, DS, JC, MC, VI. **Special Amenities:** early check-in/late check-out. *(See color ad p 707)*

SOME UNITS

🏷️🐾🍴🍸🏋️M 🛁 📷 🏊 📺 DATA PORT 💻 / ✕ 🛗 🖨️ /
FEE

RAMADA INN   *Book at aaa.com*   Phone: (757)827-7400   **29**

	5/1-8/31	1P: $69-$109
	3/1-4/30	1P: $69-$89
Small-scale Hotel	9/1-12/31	1P: $59-$89
	1/1-2/28	1P: $59-$79

Location: I-64, 263 (Mercury Blvd) eastbound, just n on Mercury Blvd, then just e towards Hampton Coliseum; exit 263B westbound. 1905 Coliseum Dr 23666. Fax: 757/827-4178. **Facility:** 134 one-bedroom standard units. 3 stories, interior/exterior corridors. *Bath:* combo or shower only. **Parking:** on-site. **Amenities:** irons. **Pool(s):** outdoor. **Guest Services:** valet laundry. **Business Services:** fax. **Cards:** AX, DS, MC, VI.

SOME UNITS

ASK 🏷️ 🍴 📷 🏊 📺 DATA PORT / ✕ 🛗 /

SUPER 8 MOTEL   *Book at aaa.com*   Phone: (757)723-2888   **30**

| | All Year | 1P: $48-$85 | 2P: $48-$85 | XP: $6 | F18 |

Motel

Location: I-64, 265B westbound; exit 265C eastbound. 1330 Thomas St 23669. Fax: 757/723-2888. **Facility:** 66 one-bedroom standard units. 2 stories (no elevator), interior corridors. **Parking:** on-site. **Terms:** small pets only ($6 extra charge). **Guest Services:** coin laundry. **Cards:** AX, CB, DC, DS, MC, VI.

SOME UNITS

ASK 🏷️ 🐾 📺 💻 / ✕ DATA PORT 🛗 🖨️ /
FEE   FEE

VICTORIA HOUSE BED & BREAKFAST   Phone: 757/722-2658   **31**

| | All Year [BP] | 1P: $105-$150 | 2P: $105-$150 | XP: $50 |

Historic Bed & Breakfast

Location: I-64, exit 267, 1 mi w to Bridge St, just s to Victoria Blvd, then just w. 4501 Victoria Blvd 23669-4137. Fax: 757/723-5282. **Facility:** This B&B's richly decorated guest rooms offer poster beds, vintage armoires and bathrooms that mix modern amenities with antiques. Smoke free premises. 4 one-bedroom standard units, some with whirlpools. 2 stories, interior corridors. **Parking:** street. **Terms:** age restrictions may apply, 5 day cancellation notice, weekly rates available. **Amenities:** video library, hair dryers. **Leisure Activities:** whirlpool. **Business Services:** fax. **Cards:** AX, MC, VI.

✕ VCR 📺 DATA PORT 🛗

——— **WHERE TO DINE** ———

CAPTAIN GEORGE'S SEAFOOD RESTAURANT   Dinner: $17-$23   Phone: 757/826-1435   **28**

Seafood

Location: I-64, exit 263A (Mercury Blvd), 0.5 mi s. 2710 W Mercury Blvd 23666. **Hours:** 4:30 pm-9:30 pm, Sat from 4 pm, Sun from noon. Closed: 12/25. **Features:** An extensive, all-you-can-eat seafood buffet—which includes everything from Alaskan crab legs and shrimp to prime rib and dessert—satisfies even the heartiest of appetites. Nautical accents such as ropes and fish nets convey the oceanic feel. Casual dress; cocktails. **Parking:** on-site. **Cards:** AX, MC, VI.

✕

DELARGY'S BISTRO   Lunch: $7-$20   Dinner: $7-$20   Phone: 757/825-1450   **27**

Italian

Location: I-64, exit 263 (Mercury Blvd S), just s to Todd's Ln, just s to Todd's Center. 1814A Todds Ln 23666. **Hours:** 11 am-3 & 5-9 pm, Fri-10 pm, Sat 4 pm-10 pm. Closed: Sun. **Reservations:** suggested. **Features:** The casual Italian-American bistro offers up such tasty dishes as shrimp and gorgonzola, steamed mussels and a savory cioppino, which is the house specialty. Casual dress; cocktails. **Parking:** on-site. **Cards:** AX, MC, VI.

🏋️M

THE GRATE STEAK   Dinner: $14-$38   Phone: 757/827-1886   **26**

Steak House

Location: I-64, exit 263B (Mercury Blvd), just n, then just e. 1934 Coliseum Dr 23666. **Hours:** 5 pm-10 pm, Sat from 2 pm, Sun noon-9 pm. Closed: 11/24, 12/24, 12/25. **Features:** Choose your cut of steak, then cook it on an open grill. The quality of beef is excellent, but it's up to you to choose your seasonings. Included with your entree is a baked potato and all the fixings, plus whatever suits your taste buds at the salad bar. Casual dress; cocktails. **Parking:** on-site. **Cards:** AX, CB, DC, DS, MC, VI.

✕

THE GREY GOOSE   Lunch: $5-$9   Phone: 757/723-7978   **33**

American

Location: Olde Merchants Lane in Queens Way Shoppes; downtown. 101-A W Queens Way 23669. **Hours:** 11 am-3 pm. Closed major holidays; also Sun. **Features:** The charming tea room is a quaint spot in which to savor tasty Southern favorites, such as country ham biscuits, Brunswick stew and blue crab soup. Tasty pie and cake selections change daily. Casual dress. **Parking:** street. **Cards:** AX, DS, MC, VI.

🎵 ✕

HARPOON LARRY'S OYSTER BAR   Lunch: $7-$20   Dinner: $7-$20   Phone: 757/827-0600   **24**

Seafood

Location: I-64, exit 263A (Mercury Blvd), 1 mi ne at Armistead Ave. 2000 N Armistead Ave 23666. **Hours:** 11 am-1:30 am. **Features:** Local fliers from Langley make the bar a regular lunch spot. Fresh local seafood is served in enormous portions. Favorites include Hatteras-style clam chowder, a spicy crab cake and excellent Key lime pie, which is the only dessert offered. Casual dress; cocktails. **Parking:** on-site. **Cards:** AX, DC, DS, MC, VI.

✕

(See map and index starting on p. 707)

MEDIK'S CAFE & MARKET — Lunch: $6-$10 — Dinner: $6-$10 — Phone: 757/262-0711 — 25
◇◇
Gourmet Grocery
Location: I-64, exit 263B (Mercury Blvd), just n on W Mercury Blvd to Riverdale Plaza. 1078 W Mercury Blvd 23666. **Hours:** 10 am-7 pm. Closed major holidays; also Sun. **Features:** The market and cafe specializes in natural, organic and healthy meals. Overflowing salads, homemade soups and gourmet sandwiches, some of which are grilled, satisfy a hunger, while the luscious desserts tame a sweet tooth. Among specialties are cusabi tuna salad, Greek grilled cheese and the vegetarian d'lite. Casual dress. **Parking:** on-site. **Cards:** AX, DS, MC, VI.

MUSASI JAPANESE RESTAURANT — Lunch: $7-$11 — Dinner: $9-$16 — Phone: 757/728-0298 — 32
◇◇◇◇
Japanese
Location: I-64, exit 267, 1 mi w to Eaton St, then just n; downtown. 49 W Queens Way 23669. **Hours:** 11 am-2:30 & 5-10:30 pm, Fri-11 pm, Sat 11:30 am-11 pm. Closed major holidays; also Sun. **Features:** The spot—which offers two distinct rooms: the open sushi bar and the other divided into semi-private booths—is usually packed with office workers at lunch but is more peaceful in the evenings. An enormous array of fresh sushi and sashimi is offered, as well as Japanese hot pots and even a few Korean specialties. Casual dress; cocktails. **Parking:** street. **Cards:** AX, CB, DC, DS, MC, VI.

THE POTTERY WINE & CHEESE SHOP — Lunch: $6-$10 — Phone: 757/722-8466 — 31
◇◇
Gourmet Grocery
Location: I-64, exit 267, 1 mi w, then just n; downtown. 22 Wine St 23669. **Hours:** 7:30 am-6 pm, Sat 9 am-5 pm. Closed major holidays; also Sun. **Features:** Hearty sandwiches, daily soups, and gourmet desserts are tasty treats to enjoy either inside or at the sidewalk tables on a sunny day. Casual dress; beer & wine only. **Parking:** on-site. **Cards:** AX, DS, MC, VI.

SAMMY & NICKS FAMILY RESTAURANT — Lunch: $4-$19 — Dinner: $4-$19 — Phone: 757/838-9100 — 29
AAA
◇◇
Steak House
Location: I-64, exit 263A (Mercury Blvd), 1.5 mi s via service road. 2718 W Mercury Blvd 23666. **Hours:** 7 am-10 pm. Closed: 11/24, 12/25. **Features:** Diners who visit the family-friendly restaurant should bring a hearty appetite. Ample portions are the norm, and steak, burgers and Greek dishes the specialties. Save room for a slice of creamy cheesecake or tasty chocolate pie. The friendly staff hustles during the busy lunch period. Casual dress; cocktails. **Parking:** on-site. **Cards:** AX, DS, MC, VI.

SOYA SUSHI BAR & GRILL — Lunch: $6-$9 — Dinner: $8-$14 — Phone: 757/896-8807 — 23
◇◇ ◇◇
Japanese
Location: Just nw of Coliseum Mall; in Coliseum Crossing. 10 Coliseum Crossing 23666. **Hours:** 11:30 am-2 & 5-9 pm, Sun from 5 pm. Closed major holidays. **Features:** The small restaurant displays a crisp, simple decor. Sit at the sushi bar to watch the chefs in action, or select a more quiet table. The menu, heavy on sushi selections, also includes such tempting specialties as teriyaki, udon noodles and soya bento. Casual dress; cocktails. **Parking:** on-site. **Cards:** AX, DS, MC, VI.

SURFRIDER BLUEWATER — Lunch: $6-$20 — Dinner: $6-$20 — Phone: 757/723-9366 — 34
◇◇◇◇
Seafood
Location: I-64, exit 265A, 1.7 mi e on La Salle Ave, 0.5 mi e on Kecoughton Rd, then just se on Ivy Home, follow signs to marina. 1 Marina Rd 23669. **Hours:** 11 am-9 pm, Fri & Sat-10 pm. Closed major holidays. **Features:** Fresh, simply prepared seafood is the draw at the casual restaurant, which affords fabulous riverfront views. Local yachters can't get enough of the daily catch, fresh crab cakes and spears of broccoli topped with fresh hollandaise. Casual dress; cocktails. **Parking:** on-site. **Cards:** AX, DS, MC, VI.

TOMMY'S RESTAURANT — Lunch: $3-$9 — Phone: 757/825-1644 — 30
◇◇
Regional American
Location: Just s of jct Big Bethal Rd. 3406 W Mercury Blvd 23666. **Hours:** 6 am-3 pm. Closed: 1/1, 11/24, 12/25. **Features:** Patrons should be prepared to wait, as regulars pack this spot daily for its satisfying all-day breakfast fare and Southern dishes, such as crab cakes, liver and onions, fried chicken and fried catfish. **Parking:** on-site.

PORTSMOUTH pop. 100,565 (See map and index starting on p. 710)

——— WHERE TO STAY ———

COMFORT INN-OLDE TOWNE — *Book at aaa.com* — Phone: (757)397-7788 — 27
AAA SAVE
◇◇◇◇
Small-scale Hotel

5/1-9/30 [ECP]	1P: $95-$125	2P: $95-$125	XP: $10	F16
10/1-10/31 [ECP]	1P: $79-$89	2P: $89-$99	XP: $10	F16
3/1-4/30 [ECP]	1P: $69-$99	2P: $79-$99	XP: $10	F16
11/1-2/28 [ECP]	1P: $59-$79	2P: $65-$85	XP: $10	F16

Location: 1 mi w on High St, then just n. 347 Effingham St 23704. Fax: 757/397-7873. **Facility:** 62 one-bedroom standard units, some with efficiencies and/or whirlpools. 3 stories, interior corridors. **Bath:** combo or shower only. **Parking:** on-site. **Amenities:** high-speed Internet, safes (fee), irons, hair dryers. **Pool(s):** outdoor. **Leisure Activities:** exercise room. **Guest Services:** valet and coin laundry. **Business Services:** meeting rooms, fax. **Cards:** AX, DC, DS, MC, VI.

SOME UNITS

DAYS INN PORTSMOUTH/NORFOLK — *Book at aaa.com* — Phone: (757)399-4414 — 29
AAA SAVE
◇◇
Motel

All Year	1P: $50-$80	2P: $60-$90	XP: $5	F12

Location: SR 141, 2 blks w of Effingham St. 1031 London Blvd 23704. Fax: 757/399-7066. **Facility:** 61 one-bedroom standard units, some with efficiencies (no utensils). 2 stories, exterior corridors. **Parking:** on-site. **Terms:** package plans. **Amenities:** *Some:* hair dryers. **Leisure Activities:** limited exercise equipment. **Business Services:** fax. **Cards:** AX, DC, DS, MC, VI. **Special Amenities:** free continental breakfast and free newspaper.

SOME UNITS

(See map and index starting on p. 710)

HOLIDAY INN-OLDE TOWNE PORTSMOUTH   *Book at aaa.com*   Phone: (757)393-2573   26

(AAA) (SAVE)
	5/16-9/4	1P: $116-$135	2P: $116-$135	XP: $10	F18
	3/28-5/15	1P: $111-$121	2P: $111-$121	XP: $10	F18
	9/5-2/28	1P: $99-$114	2P: $99-$114	XP: $10	F18
	3/1-3/27	1P: $99-$109	2P: $99-$109	XP: $10	F18

Small-scale Hotel **Location:** Just nw from High St. Located adjacent to the marina. 8 Crawford Pkwy 23704. Fax: 757/399-1248. **Facility:** 219 units. 217 one-bedroom standard units. 2 one-bedroom suites. 4 stories, interior corridors. *Bath:* combo or shower only. **Parking:** on-site. **Terms:** check-in 4 pm. **Amenities:** video games, voice mail, irons, hair dryers. *Some:* high-speed Internet. **Dining:** 6:30 am-2 & 5:30-10 pm, cocktails, entertainment. **Pool(s):** outdoor. **Leisure Activities:** exercise room. **Guest Services:** valet and coin laundry. **Business Services:** conference facilities, fax. **Cards:** AX, CB, DC, DS, JC, MC, VI. **Special Amenities:** free newspaper.

SOME UNITS

⎾S/D⎿ 🛏 🍴 🍸 ♿ 🏊 🏋 [DATA PORT] 💻 / ✕ 🔌 🖼 /
                                                        FEE FEE

**RENAISSANCE PORTSMOUTH HOTEL AND
   WATERFRONT CONFERENCE CENTER**   *Book at aaa.com*   Phone: (757)673-3000   28

All Year   1P: $269-$369   2P: $269-$369

Large-scale Hotel **Location:** Jct Crawford St, just n; downtown. 425 Water St 23704. Fax: 757/673-3030. **Facility:** 249 units. 244 one-bedroom standard units. 5 one-bedroom suites. 13 stories, interior corridors. *Bath:* combo or shower only. **Parking:** on-site (fee). **Terms:** check-in 4 pm, package plans. **Amenities:** video games, high-speed Internet (fee), dual phone lines, voice mail, irons, hair dryers. **Pool(s):** heated indoor. **Leisure Activities:** whirlpool, exercise room. **Guest Services:** sundries, valet laundry. **Business Services:** conference facilities, business center. **Cards:** AX, CB, DC, DS, JC, MC, VI.

SOME UNITS

(ASK) ⎾S/D⎿ 🍴 🍸 ♿M ♿ 🏋 🏊 🏋 [DATA PORT] 💻 / ✕ 🔌 /
                                                            FEE

─────────── **WHERE TO DINE** ───────────

THE BIER GARDEN   Lunch: $3-$8   Dinner: $6-$14   Phone: 757/393-6022   63

German **Location:** Jct Dinwiddie St; center; in Olde Towne. 434 High St 23704. **Hours:** 11 am-9 pm, Fri & Sat-10 pm, Sun noon-9 pm. Closed major holidays; also Mon. **Reservations:** suggested, weekends. **Features:** On the menu are German dishes—sauerbraten, spaetzle, bratwurst and hot potato salad—and an extensive list of European brews. The back room with exposed brick walls is cozy and quiet, and the garden patio overlooks the sidewalk, and the friendly bar lets guests elbow up among neighbors for hot pretzels and potato soup. Casual dress; beer & wine only. **Parking:** on-site. **Cards:** AX, DS, MC, VI.

✕

BRUTTI'S CAFE   Lunch: $5-$10   Dinner: $9-$27   Phone: 757/393-1923   62

American **Location:** Jct High St; in Olde Towne. 467 Court St 23704. **Hours:** 7:30 am-2:30 & 5:30-9:30 pm, Mon-2:30 pm, Fri-10:30 pm, Sat 8:30 am-2:30 & 5:30-10:30 pm, Sun 8:30 am-2 & 5-9 pm. Closed major holidays. **Reservations:** suggested. **Features:** Set in a stylishly restored historic building, the cafe serves its own style of "Ameripean" cuisine in large portions. Specialties include lemon pepper seared tuna, classic steak au poivre, Cajun grilled mahi mahi and wood-fired pizza. Casual dress; cocktails; entertainment. **Parking:** street. **Cards:** AX, DS, MC, VI.

🍸

CAFE EUROPA   Lunch: $5-$11   Dinner: $12-$15   Phone: 757/399-6652   67

Continental **Location:** Just s of Crawford Pkwy; center. 319 High St 23704. **Hours:** 11 am-2 & 5-10 pm, Sat from 5 pm. Closed: 11/24, 12/24, 12/25; also Sun & Mon. **Reservations:** suggested. **Features:** The small, intimate dining room has the feel of romantic French bistro, with a rich wood bar, frosted-glass partitions and exposed brick walls. The menu boasts an impressive mix of European dishes, heaviest on French specialties but incorporating many others. Semi-formal attire; cocktails; entertainment. **Parking:** on-site. **Cards:** MC, VI.

🍸 ✕

CAFE MUNDO   Lunch: $5-$7   Dinner: $5-$7   Phone: 757/483-1483   58

Coffee/Espresso **Location:** I-664, exit 11B, 2 mi w on High St; in the Churchland Shopping Center. 5700 Churchland Blvd, Suite 39 23703. **Hours:** 7 am-8 pm, Fri-10 pm, Sat 9 am-10 pm. Closed major holidays; also Sun. **Features:** The cozy coffee shop presents a menu of gourmet sandwiches, paninis, rich desserts as well as chili and daily soups in bread bowls. A late-afternoon, English-style tea, including scones and cream, also is served. Casual dress. **Parking:** on-site. **Cards:** AX, MC, VI.

✕

COMMODORE THEATRE   *Menu on aaa.com*   Lunch: $5-$11   Dinner: $5-$11   Phone: 757/393-6962   66

American **Location:** Jct Dinwiddie St; in Olde Towne. 421 High St 23704. **Hours:** Hours vary with show times. **Features:** In the restored 1930s movie house, guests can sit in comfortable armchairs and sample such specialties as delicatessen sandwiches, pizza and cinnamon rolls. Orders are placed via tabletop telephones. Of course, there is popcorn, which is topped with 100 percent pure butter. Casual dress; cocktails. **Parking:** street. **Cards:** AX, DS, MC, VI.

♿M ✕

EATON GOGH CAFE   Lunch: $5-$10   Dinner: $5-$12   Phone: 757/397-3752   64

American **Location:** Jct Dinwiddie St; in Olde Towne. 400 High St 23704. **Hours:** 8 am-4 pm, Thurs-Sat to 10 pm. Closed major holidays. **Features:** The fun corner spot is small, but seating is doubled when the large sidewalk patio is used during nice weather. Some of the area's best she crab soup is served alongside gourmet sandwiches, wraps and healthy salads. Leave room for the fabulous cookies and desserts. Casual dress; cocktails. **Parking:** street. **Cards:** AX, MC, VI.

✕

(See map and index starting on p. 710)

FUSION 440   **Dinner:** $18-$30   **Phone:** 757/398-0888   60
▼▼▼▼   **Location:** Jct High St; in Olde Towne. 467 Dinwiddie St 23704. **Hours:** 5 pm-10 pm, Fri & Sat-11 pm, Sun-9 pm; Sunday brunch 10 am-2 pm. **Reservations:** suggested. **Features:** Patrons should prepare to be spoiled by
Continental   culinary indulgence at the chic spot, where even familiar dishes are created in new and imaginative ways. Examples of dishes on the seasonal menu are green tomatoes encrusted with biscotti, chateaubriand with white truffle butter and Caesar salad wrapped in oversized baguette crouton. Dressy casual; cocktails. **Parking:** street.
Cards: AX, DC, DS, MC, VI.   ✕

MARIO'S ITALIAN RESTAURANT   **Lunch:** $6-$18   **Dinner:** $6-$18   **Phone:** 757/399-8970   68
▼▼▼   **Location:** Jct High St and London Blvd, just w. 611 Airline Blvd 23707. **Hours:** 11 am-2 am, Sat & Sun 5 pm-2 am. Closed major holidays. **Features:** Since 1952, the homey restaurant has served up hearty Italian-American
Italian   fare, such as steak pizzaiola, veal Madeira and a fiery shrimp fra diavolo. Casual dress; cocktails. **Parking:** on-site. **Cards:** AX, MC, VI.   ⅂

MARKET FARE   **Dinner:** $12-$20   **Phone:** 757/397-0900   59
▼▼▼▼   **Location:** Jct Broad St; in Port Norfolk. 2622 Detroit St 23707. **Hours:** 5 pm-10 pm, Fri & Sat-11 pm. Closed major holidays; also Sun & Mon. **Features:** In the heart of a revitalized neighborhood near the Midtown
Continental   tunnel lies the tiny bistro with a decidedly European flavor. Continental-inspired offerings include grilled duck sausage, a sophisticated cheese course, paella and pork Wellington. Diners also will find some Southern-influenced choices, such as pan-fried chicken livers and grilled romaine salad. Dressy casual; cocktails. **Parking:** street.
Cards: AX, MC, VI.   ✕

ROGER BROWN'S RESTAURANT & SPORTS BAR   **Lunch:** $6-$17   **Dinner:** $6-$17   **Phone:** 757/399-5377   61
▼▼▼   **Location:** Between Court and Crawford sts; in Olde Towne. 316 High St 23704. **Hours:** 11 am-1 am, Fri & Sat-2 am. Closed: 12/25. **Features:** A famed member of the Los Angeles Rams' "fearsome foursome," local hero
American   Roger Brown turns his attention to delicious dishes from burgers to ribs to seafood. Even non-sports fans can enjoy the fun, multimedia setting. Casual dress; cocktails. **Parking:** street. **Cards:** AX, MC, VI.   ✕

SASSAFRAS   **Lunch:** $6-$11   **Dinner:** $14-$25   **Phone:** 757/399-4480   65
▼▼▼   **Location:** Between Washington and Green sts; in Olde Towne. 606 High St 23704. **Hours:** 11 am-3 & 5:30-10 pm, Fri & Sat-11 pm, Sun 10:30 am-2 & 5:30-9 pm. Closed major holidays; also Mon. **Reservations:** suggested.
Regional American   **Features:** Chic and casual, Sassafras specializes Southern eclectic cuisine on an ever-changing menu of delicious options that may include frazzled onion crusted crab cakes, bourbon-molasses glazed pork tenderloin, or chile-rubbed tuna. Dressy casual; cocktails. **Parking:** on-site. **Cards:** AX, MC, VI.   ⅂ ✕

SMITHFIELD pop. 6,324

——— **WHERE TO STAY** ———

CHURCH STREET INN   **Phone:** (757)357-3176
▼▼▼   All Year [ECP]   1P: $99-$139   2P: $99-$139   XP: $15   F11
   Location: 1 mi e on SR 10 business route. 1607 S Church St 23430. Fax: 757/357-2337. **Facility:** 12 one-
Bed & Breakfast   bedroom standard units, some with whirlpools. 2 stories (no elevator); interior/exterior corridors. **Parking:** on-site. **Terms:** office hours 8 am-8 pm, 3 day cancellation notice. **Amenities:** DVD players, CD players, high-speed Internet. **Guest Services:** valet laundry. **Cards:** AX, DS, MC, VI.   SOME UNITS
(ASK) (S⊡) (¶↑) (✕) (DATA PORT) (▭) / (🛏) (▭) /

ECONO LODGE-BENN'S CHURCH   *Book at aaa.com*   **Phone:** (757)357-9057
(AAA) (SAVE)   All Year   1P: $50-$85   2P: $50-$85   XP: $4   F18
▼▼   **Location:** 3.8 mi s on SR 10, just n on US 258 and SR 32. 20080 Brewers Neck Blvd 23314 (20080 Brewers Neck
Motel   Blvd, CARROLLTON). Fax: 757/365-4108. **Facility:** 72 one-bedroom standard units, some with whirlpools. 2 stories (no elevator); interior corridors. *Bath:* combo or shower only. **Parking:** on-site. **Leisure Activities:** exercise room. **Guest Services:** coin laundry. **Business Services:** fax. **Cards:** AX, CB, DC, DS, JC, MC, VI. **Special Amenities:** free local telephone calls.   SOME UNITS
(S⊡) (&.) (📹) (DATA PORT) (🛏) (▭) / (✕) (▭)

SMITHFIELD INN   **Phone:** 757/357-1752
(AAA) (SAVE)   All Year [BP]   1P: $85-$145   2P: $85-$145   XP: $15   D
▼▼▼   **Location:** Center. 112 Main St 23430. Fax: 757/365-4425. **Facility:** Fronted by a wide veranda, this historic inn
Historic   in the center of town offers elegant suites furnished with fine antiques and rich fabrics. Smoke free
Country Inn   premises. 8 units. 4 one- and 1 two-bedroom standard units. 3 one-bedroom suites. 2 stories, interior corridors. *Bath:* combo or shower only. **Parking:** on-site. **Terms:** cancellation fee imposed, package plans. **Amenities:** video library, high-speed Internet, voice mail, hair dryers. **Dining:** restaurant, see separate listing. **Guest Services:** valet laundry. **Cards:** AX, DC, MC, VI. **Special Amenities:** free full breakfast and free local telephone calls.
(S⊡) (¶↑) (⅂) (♦↑) (✕) (VCR) (📹) (DATA PORT) (🛏)
FEE

SMITHFIELD STATION   **Phone:** (757)357-7700
▼▼▼▼   All Year   1P: $79-$225   2P: $79-$225
   Location: 0.5 mi s on SR 10. 415 S Church St 23430 (PO Box 486, 23431). Fax: 757/357-7638. **Facility:** 22 one-
Small-scale Hotel   bedroom standard units, some with whirlpools. 3 stories (no elevator); interior/exterior corridors. **Parking:** on-site. **Amenities:** dual phone lines, irons, hair dryers. *Some:* DVD players. **Dining:** restaurant, see separate listing. **Pool(s):** small outdoor. **Leisure Activities:** Fee: marina. **Business Services:** meeting rooms, fax. **Cards:** AX, DC, DS, MC, VI.   SOME UNITS
(ASK) (S⊡) (¶↑) (🛶) (📹) (DATA PORT) (▭) / (VCR) (🛏) (▭) /
FEE   FEE

—————— **WHERE TO DINE** ——————

SMITHFIELD GOURMET BAKERY AND CAFE   **Lunch:** $4-$8   **Phone:** 757/357-0045
Location: Center. 218 Main St 23430. **Hours:** 8 am-4 pm, Sun from 10 am. Closed major holidays.
Features: The lunch spot offers sandwiches, pasta salad, dessert and gourmet coffee. Casual dress.
Bakery/Desserts   **Parking:** street. **Cards:** AX, MC, VI.

SMITHFIELD INN   **Lunch:** $7-$9   **Dinner:** $14-$22   **Phone:** 757/357-1752
Location: Center; in Smithfield Inn. 112 Main St 23430. **Hours:** 11:30 am-3 & 5:30-9 pm, Tues & Sun-3 pm.
Closed major holidays; also Mon. **Reservations:** suggested, weekends. **Features:** The elegant dining
Regional American rooms are decorated in period, and complement the menu highlights — modern twists on Southern
favorites, many with a New Orleans flair. Seafood is their specialty and is well-prepared. Garden seating is
available, weather permitting. Dressy casual; cocktails. **Parking:** on-site. **Cards:** AX, DC, DS, MC, VI. **Country Inn**

SMITHFIELD STATION RESTAURANT   **Lunch:** $5-$13   **Dinner:** $17-$33   **Phone:** 757/357-7700
Location: 0.5 mi s on SR 10; in Smithfield Station. 415 S Church St 23430. **Hours:** 11 am-9:30 pm, Fri-10 pm, Sat
8 am-10 pm, Sun 8 am-9:30 pm. Closed: 12/25. **Reservations:** suggested, weekends. **Features:** Designed
Regional American to resemble an old Coast Guard station, the restaurant sits on the Pagan River. The menu emphasizes pork
and seafood, such as the signature crabmeat Smithfield, sauteed lump crabmeat and ham chunks dripping
with melted Monterey Jack cheese. Casual dress; cocktails. **Parking:** on-site. **Cards:** AX, CB, DC, DS, MC, VI.

TWINS OLDE TOWNE INN   **Lunch:** $5-$9   **Phone:** 757/357-3031
Location: Center. 220 Main St 23430. **Hours:** 6 am-5 pm, Wed-3 pm, Sat-11 am. Closed major holidays.
Features: This tiny spot offers up hearty Southern style breakfasts and lunches with specialties such as
Southern   ham, barbecue, chicken and dumplings and country-style sides. Casual dress. **Parking:** street.

SUFFOLK pop. 63,677

—————— **WHERE TO STAY** ——————

HOLIDAY INN-SUFFOLK   *Book at aaa.com*   **Phone:** (757)934-2311
All Year   1P: $80   XP: $10   F18
Location: US 460 at jct US 58 Bypass. 2864 Pruden Blvd 23434. **Fax:** 757/539-5846. **Facility:** 99 one-bedroom
Small-scale Hotel standard units. 2 stories (no elevator), exterior corridors. *Bath:* combo or shower only. **Parking:** on-site.
Terms: cancellation fee imposed, package plans, pets ($100 extra charge). **Amenities:** dual phone lines,
voice mail, irons, hair dryers. **Pool(s):** outdoor. **Leisure Activities:** exercise room. **Guest Services:** valet laundry. **Business
Services:** meeting rooms, fax. **Cards:** AX, DC, DS, MC, VI.

SOME UNITS

This ends listings for the Hampton Roads Area Vicinity.
The following page resumes the alphabetical listings of
cities in Virginia.

HANOVER —*See Richmond p. 863.*

HARRISONBURG pop. 40,468

——— **WHERE TO STAY** ———

BELLE MEADE RED CARPET INN   *Book at aaa.com*   Phone: 540/434-6704
▽▽▽   All Year   1P: $40-$60   2P: $50-$70
Motel   **Location:** I-81, exit 243, just nw. 3210 S Main St 22801. Fax: 540/434-9610. **Facility:** 141 one-bedroom standard units, some with whirlpools. 1 story, exterior corridors. **Parking:** on-site. **Terms:** 4 day cancellation notice-fee imposed, weekly rates available, package plans, small pets only ($5 extra charge). **Amenities:** *Some:* irons. **Pool(s):** outdoor. **Cards:** AX, DC, MC, VI.
SOME UNITS
(ASK) (SD) (🛏) (🛆) (🐾) (📷) (DATA PORT) / (✕) (🔌) (📧) /
FEE

BEST WESTERN HARRISONBURG INN   *Book at aaa.com*   Phone: (540)433-6089
▽▽▽ ▽▽▽   5/1-10/31   1P: $74-$79   2P: $79-$84
    11/1-2/28   1P: $64-$69   2P: $69-$74
Small-scale Hotel   3/1-4/30   1P: $59-$69   2P: $64-$69
Location: I-81, exit 247A, just e on US 33. 45 Burgess Rd 22801. Fax: 540/433-6485. **Facility:** 98 one-bedroom standard units. 3 stories, exterior corridors. *Bath:* combo or shower only. **Parking:** on-site. **Amenities:** irons, hair dryers. **Pool(s):** heated indoor. **Leisure Activities:** sauna, whirlpool, exercise room. **Guest Services:** valet and coin laundry. **Business Services:** meeting rooms. **Cards:** AX, DC, MC, VI.
SOME UNITS
(ASK) (SD) (🍴) (🛆) (🐾) (✕) (📷) (DATA PORT) (🔌) (📧) (📺) / (✕) /

COMFORT INN   *Book at aaa.com*   Phone: (540)433-6066
(AAA) (SAVE)   All Year [ECP]   1P: $75-$95   2P: $79-$99   XP: $10   F19
▽▽▽ ▽▽▽   **Location:** I-81, exit 247A, just e. 1440 E Market St 22801. Fax: 540/433-0793. **Facility:** 102 one-bedroom standard units, some with whirlpools. 2 stories (no elevator), interior corridors. *Bath:* combo or shower only.
Small-scale Hotel   **Parking:** on-site. **Amenities:** video games, irons, hair dryers. **Pool(s):** outdoor. **Leisure Activities:** exercise room. **Guest Services:** valet laundry. **Cards:** AX, CB, DC, DS, JC, MC, VI.
Special Amenities: free expanded continental breakfast and free local telephone calls.
SOME UNITS
(SD) (🛏) (🍴) (🛆) (🐾) (📷) (DATA PORT) (📺) / (✕) (🔌) (📧) /

COURTYARD BY MARRIOTT-HARRISONBURG   *Book at aaa.com*   Phone: (540)432-3031
▽▽▽ ▽▽▽   All Year   1P: $69-$109
Small-scale Hotel   **Location:** I-81, exit 247A, 0.6 mi e on US 33 to University Blvd, then just w. 1890 Evelyn Byrd Dr 22801. Fax: 540/432-3032. **Facility:** 125 one-bedroom standard units. 4 stories, interior corridors. *Bath:* combo or shower only. **Parking:** on-site. **Terms:** 3 night minimum stay - seasonal. **Amenities:** high-speed Internet, voice mail, irons, hair dryers. **Pool(s):** heated indoor. **Leisure Activities:** whirlpool, exercise room. **Guest Services:** valet laundry. **Business Services:** meeting rooms. **Cards:** AX, CB, DC, DS, JC, MC, VI.
SOME UNITS
(ASK) (SD) (🍴) (🛆) (🐾) (📷) (DATA PORT) (📺) / (✕) (🔌) (📧) /

DAYS INN HARRISONBURG   *Book at aaa.com*   Phone: (540)433-9353
(AAA) (SAVE)   All Year [CP]   1P: $45-$150   2P: $55-$170   XP: $7   F18
▽▽▽ ▽▽▽   **Location:** I-81, exit 245, just e. Truck parking on premises. 1131 Forest Hill Rd 22801. Fax: 540/433-5809.
Small-scale Hotel   **Facility:** 89 one-bedroom standard units. 4 stories, interior corridors. **Parking:** on-site. **Terms:** package plans, small pets only ($10 fee). **Amenities:** safes, hair dryers. *Some:* irons. **Pool(s):** indoor. **Leisure Activities:** whirlpool, university jogging trail adjacent. **Guest Services:** coin laundry. **Business Services:** meeting rooms. **Cards:** AX, DC, DS, MC, VI. **Special Amenities:** free continental breakfast and free newspaper.
SOME UNITS
(SD) (🛏) (🛆) (🐾) (🛗) (📷) (DATA PORT) / (✕) (🔌) (📧) (📺) /
FEE

FOUR POINTS BY SHERATON   *Book at aaa.com*   Phone: (540)433-2521
(AAA) (SAVE)   5/1-10/31   1P: $109-$139   2P: $109-$139   XP: $10   F17
▽▽▽ ▽▽▽   3/1-4/30   1P: $99-$109   2P: $99-$109   XP: $10   F17
Small-scale Hotel   11/1-2/28   1P: $89-$109   2P: $89-$109   XP: $10   F17
Location: I-81, exit 247A, just e on US 33. 1400 E Market St 22801. Fax: 540/434-0253. **Facility:** 140 one-bedroom standard units. 4-5 stories, interior corridors. *Bath:* combo or shower only. **Parking:** on-site. **Terms:** 2 night minimum stay - seasonal, package plans. **Amenities:** video games, high-speed Internet, dual phone lines, voice mail, irons, hair dryers. **Dining:** 2 restaurants, 6:30 am-10:30 pm. **Pool(s):** heated indoor, wading. **Leisure Activities:** whirlpool, exercise room. **Guest Services:** valet laundry. **Business Services:** conference facilities. **Cards:** AX, CB, DC, DS, JC, MC, VI. **Special Amenities:** free newspaper.
SOME UNITS
(SD) (🛏) (🍴) (🍸) (🛆) (🐾) (📷) (DATA PORT) (📺) / (✕) (🔌) (📧) /

HAMPTON INN   *Book at aaa.com*   Phone: (540)432-1111
(AAA) (SAVE)   All Year [BP]   1P: $84-$180   2P: $91-$180
▽▽▽ ▽▽▽   **Location:** I-81, exit 247A, 0.5 mi e on US 33 to University Blvd, then just s. 85 University Blvd 22801.
Small-scale Hotel   Fax: 540/432-0748. **Facility:** 163 one-bedroom standard units. 4 stories, interior corridors. **Parking:** on-site. **Terms:** 3 day cancellation notice, package plans. **Amenities:** high-speed Internet, voice mail, irons, hair dryers. *Some:* fax. **Pool(s):** outdoor. **Guest Services:** valet laundry. **Business Services:** meeting rooms, business center. **Cards:** AX, CB, DC, DS, MC, VI. **Special Amenities:** free full breakfast and free newspaper.
SOME UNITS
(SD) (🛆) (🐾) (🛗) (📷) (DATA PORT) (📺) / (✕) (🔌) (📧) /

HARRISONBURG ECONO LODGE

Motel

Book at aaa.com

| All Year [ECP] | 1P: $60-$150 | 2P: $60-$150 | XP: $10 | F18 |

Phone: (540)433-2576
Location: I-81, exit 247A, 0.5 mi e on US 33. 1703 E Market St 22801. Fax: 540/433-2576. **Facility:** 88 one-bedroom standard units, some with whirlpools. 2 stories (no elevator), interior/exterior corridors. **Parking:** on-site. **Terms:** cancellation fee imposed, package plans, small pets only. **Amenities:** hair dryers. **Pool(s):** outdoor. **Guest Services:** coin laundry. **Business Services:** meeting rooms. **Cards:** AX, CB, DC, DS, JC, MC, VI. **Special Amenities:** free expanded continental breakfast and free local telephone calls.

SOME UNITS

HOLIDAY INN EXPRESS

Small-scale Hotel

5/6-10/31	1P: $82-$119
3/1-5/5	1P: $79-$89
11/1-2/28	1P: $75-$86

Phone: (540)433-9999
Location: I-81, exit 243, just w. 3325 S Main St 22801. Fax: 540/433-9494. **Facility:** 72 one-bedroom standard units, some with whirlpools. 3 stories, interior corridors. *Bath:* combo or shower only. **Parking:** on-site. **Terms:** [CP] meal plan available, package plans. **Amenities:** high-speed Internet, voice mail, irons, hair dryers. **Pool(s):** heated indoor. **Leisure Activities:** whirlpool, exercise room. **Business Services:** meeting rooms, business center. **Cards:** AX, CB, DC, DS, JC, MC, VI. **Special Amenities:** free expanded continental breakfast and free local telephone calls.

SOME UNITS

JAMESON INN

Small-scale Hotel

Book at aaa.com

| All Year [ECP] | 1P: $49-$104 |

Phone: (540)442-1515
Location: I-81, exit 247A, just e. 1881 Evelyn Byrd Ave 22801. Fax: 540/442-6655. **Facility:** 67 one-bedroom standard units. 3 stories, interior corridors. *Bath:* combo or shower only. **Parking:** on-site. **Terms:** cancellation fee imposed. **Amenities:** high-speed Internet, voice mail, irons, hair dryers. **Pool(s):** outdoor. **Leisure Activities:** exercise room. **Business Services:** meeting rooms. **Cards:** AX, CB, DC, DS, MC, VI.

SOME UNITS

MOTEL 6 HARRISONBURG #1211

Motel

Book at aaa.com

3/1-5/7	1P: $41-$51	2P: $47-$57	XP: $3	F17
5/8-9/4	1P: $39-$49	2P: $45-$55	XP: $3	F17
9/5-2/28	1P: $37-$47	2P: $43-$53	XP: $3	F17

Phone: 540/433-6939
Location: I-81, exit 247A, just e on US 33. 10 Linda Ln 22801. Fax: 540/564-0289. **Facility:** 113 one-bedroom standard units. 1 story, exterior corridors. *Bath:* combo or shower only. **Parking:** on-site. **Pool(s):** outdoor. **Guest Services:** coin laundry. **Cards:** AX, CB, DC, DS, MC, VI.

SOME UNITS

RAMADA INN
AAA SAVE

Small-scale Hotel

Book at aaa.com

			Phone: (540)434-9981
3/1-10/31	1P: $60-$90	2P: $70-$95	XP: $6 F
11/1-2/28	1P: $50-$70	2P: $55-$75	XP: $6 F

Location: I-81, exit 243, just w, then just n on US 11. 1 Pleasant Valley Rd 22801. Fax: 540/434-7088. **Facility:** 130 one-bedroom standard units. 2 stories (no elevator), exterior corridors. **Parking:** on-site. **Terms:** pets ($10 extra charge). **Amenities:** irons, hair dryers. **Pool(s):** outdoor. **Guest Services:** valet laundry. **Business Services:** meeting rooms. **Cards:** AX, CB, DC, DS, JC, MC, VI. **Special Amenities:** free expanded continental breakfast and free local telephone calls.

SOME UNITS

SLEEP INN

Small-scale Hotel

Book at aaa.com

Phone: (540)433-7100

4/1-10/31 [CP]	1P: $72-$199	2P: $72-$199
3/1-3/31 & 11/1-2/28 [CP]	1P: $62-$89	2P: $62-$89

Location: I-81, exit 247A, 0.5 mi e on US 33 to University Blvd, 0.3 mi s to Evelyn Byrd Ave, then just w. 1891 Evelyn Byrd Ave 22801. Fax: 540/437-2144. **Facility:** 81 one-bedroom standard units. 4 stories, interior corridors. *Bath:* combo or shower only. **Parking:** on-site. **Terms:** check-in 4 pm. **Amenities:** high-speed Internet, voice mail, irons, hair dryers. **Leisure Activities:** exercise room. **Guest Services:** coin laundry. **Cards:** AX, DC, DS, MC, VI.

SOME UNITS

STONEWALL JACKSON INN BED & BREAKFAST

Bed & Breakfast

Phone: 540/433-8233

All Year	2P: $99-$199	XP: $25

Location: I-81, exit 247, 0.8 mi w on US 33. 547 E Market St 22801. Fax: 540/564-1517. **Facility:** This inn is centered in the Shenandoah Valley and offers porches, gardens and pleasant parlor rooms. 10 one-bedroom standard units. 2 stories (no elevator), interior corridors. *Bath:* shower only. **Parking:** on-site. **Terms:** 4 day cancellation notice-fee imposed, [BP] meal plan available, package plans. **Amenities:** hair dryers. *Some:* irons. **Leisure Activities:** whirlpool. **Guest Services:** complimentary evening beverages. **Business Services:** meeting rooms. **Cards:** AX, DS, MC, VI.

SOME UNITS

SUPER 8 MOTEL
AAA SAVE

Motel

(See color ad p 792)

Book at aaa.com

			Phone: (540)433-8888
3/1-10/31	1P: $49-$200	2P: $49-$200	XP: $5 F12
11/1-2/28	1P: $35-$65	2P: $39-$70	XP: $5 F12

Location: I-81, exit 243, just e, then just s on US 11. Located across from truck stop and bus station. 3330 S Main St 22801. Fax: 540/433-8888. **Facility:** 50 one-bedroom standard units. 3 stories (no elevator), interior corridors. **Parking:** on-site. **Terms:** small pets only ($10 extra charge, in designated units). **Cards:** AX, DC, DS, MC, VI. **Special Amenities:** free expanded continental breakfast and free local telephone calls.

SOME UNITS

THE VILLAGE INN
AAA SAVE

Small-scale Hotel

Book at aaa.com

			Phone: (540)434-7355
All Year	1P: $60-$67	2P: $67-$74	XP: $7 F12

Location: I-81, exit 240 southbound, 0.6 mi w on SR 257, then 1.5 mi n on US 11; exit 243 northbound, just w to US 11, then 1.7 mi s. 4979 S Valley Pike 22801. Fax: 540/434-7356. **Facility:** 37 units. 36 one- and 1 two-bedroom standard units, some with whirlpools. 1 story, exterior corridors. **Parking:** on-site. **Terms:** pets ($6 extra charge). **Amenities:** voice mail, irons, hair dryers. **Pool(s):** outdoor. **Leisure Activities:** walking trail, playground, shuffleboard. **Guest Services:** coin laundry. **Business Services:** meeting rooms. **Cards:** AX, CB, DC, DS, MC, VI. *(See color ad p 792)*

SOME UNITS

──────── *The following lodging was either not evaluated or did not* ────────
meet AAA rating requirements but is listed for your information only.

MASSANUTTEN RESORT HOTEL
fyi

Phone: 540/289-4914

Not evaluated. **Location:** I-81, exit 247A, 10 mi e on US 33, 2 mi n on SR 644, 2.5 mi beyond the gatehouse. (PO Box 1227). Facilities, services, and decor characterize a mid-range property.

──────── **WHERE TO DINE** ────────

ASIA INN

Chinese

Lunch: $6-$12	Dinner: $7-$14	Phone: 540/438-8500

Location: 1.7 mi s on SR 42. 2184 John Wayland Hwy 22801. **Hours:** 11:30 am-10:30 pm, Sun noon-4 pm. **Features:** The Asia Inn offers Chinese cuisine with a flair. A huge selection on the menu and a very friendly staff along with a quiet and serene atmosphere. Casual dress; beer & wine only. **Parking:** on-site. **Cards:** AX, CB, DC, DS, JC, MC, VI.

CALHOUN'S

American

Lunch: $6-$12	Dinner: $6-$22	Phone: 540/434-8777

Location: I-81, exit 247, 2.9 mi w on US 33. 41 Court Square 22801. **Hours:** 11 am-10 pm. Closed: 12/25. **Features:** Calhoun's has a large selection of beers, some made on the property, classic American cuisine and a smartly attired wait staff. Casual dress; cocktails. **Parking:** on-site. **Cards:** AX, CB, DC, DS, JC, MC, VI.

DINNER BELL CAFE AT SHENANDOAH HERITAGE MARKET

American

Lunch: $4-$8	Dinner: $5-$12	Phone: 540/437-1901

Location: I-81, exit 243, just s. 121 Carpenter Ln 22801. **Hours:** 10 am-6 pm, Sat from 9 am. Closed: 1/1, 11/24, 12/25; also Sun. **Features:** Hit the bell and head for a good meal at the Dinner Bell Cafe at Shenandoah Heritage Market. Country cooking and friendly surroundings abound. Casual dress. **Parking:** on-site.

FINNIGAN'S CAFE
American

Lunch: $5-$12   **Dinner:** $7-$18   **Phone:** 540/433-9874
Location: Just w; center. 30 W Water St 22801. **Hours:** 11 am-2 am. **Features:** Finnigan's Cove is fun Brew Pub that specializes in fresh seafood and a lively atmosphere. Casual dress; cocktails. **Parking:** street. **Cards:** AX, CB, DC, DS, JC, MC, VI.

JESS' LUNCH #2
American

Lunch: $4-$8   **Dinner:** $4-$10   **Phone:** 540/434-8280
Location: I-81, exit 247A, 0.4 mi e on US 33. 1746 E Market St 22801. **Hours:** 10 am-midnight. **Features:** Tastes of the Shenandoah Valley make up the menu at the casual hometown eatery. Casual dress. **Parking:** on-site.

L'ITALIA RESTAURANT
Italian

Lunch: $5-$10   **Dinner:** $9-$15   **Phone:** 540/433-0961
Location: I-81, exit 247, 0.8 mi w on US 33. 815 E Market St 22801. **Hours:** 11 am-10 pm, Fri & Sat-11 pm. Closed: 12/25. **Features:** Wonderful background music, candles on the tables and attractive murals on the walls make for a cozy, romantic atmosphere. The restaurant enjoys a strong local following. Among favorites is ham- and cheese-stuffed chicken breast sauteed with mushrooms and wine. Fresh bread is served with the salad and meal. Casual dress; cocktails. **Parking:** on-site. **Cards:** AX, CB, DC, DS, MC, VI.

MACONDO'S CARIBBEAN RESTAURANT
Caribbean

Lunch: $7-$14   **Dinner:** $8-$21   **Phone:** 540/432-0851
Location: I-81, exit 247A, just e on US 33. 43 Linda Ln 22802. **Hours:** 11 am-10 pm, Fri & Sat-11 pm. Closed: 12/25. **Features:** A taste of the Caribbean in the Shenandoah Valley. Jerk Chicken, mojo sauces, and Paella along with many other Caribbean cuisine choices. Casual dress; cocktails. **Parking:** on-site. **Cards:** AX, CB, DC, DS, JC, MC, VI.

THE OLYMPIC ROOM
American

Lunch: $6-$12   **Dinner:** $9-$22   **Phone:** 540/433-2521
Location: I-81, exit 247A, just e on US 33. 1400 E Market St 22801. **Hours:** 6:30 am-10:30 pm. **Features:** You do not have to be an Olympic athlete to enjoy the classic American cuisine offered at The Olympic Room. Big selections to choose from and huge portions to relish. Casual dress; cocktails. **Parking:** on-site. **Cards:** AX, CB, DC, DS, JC, MC, VI.

RT'S CHICKEN & GRILLE
American

Lunch: $4-$10   **Dinner:** $4-$15   **Phone:** 540/438-0080
Location: I-81, exit 247, just e. 120 University Blvd 22801. **Hours:** 11 am-8 pm. Closed: 11/24, 12/25; also Sun. **Features:** The restaurant employs a friendly wait staff and presents a varied menu. Barbecue chicken is a flavorful choice. Casual dress. **Parking:** on-site. **Cards:** MC, VI.

HERNDON —See District Of Columbia p. 534.

HILLSVILLE pop. 2,607

———— WHERE TO STAY ————

BEST WESTERN FOUR SEASONS SOUTH   *Book at aaa.com*

3/1-10/31	1P: $65-$89	2P: $70-$99	XP: $10	F18
11/1-2/28	1P: $55-$79	2P: $60-$89	XP: $10	F18

Phone: (276)728-4136

Small-scale Hotel

Location: I-77, exit 14, just w on US 58 and 221. 57 Airport Rd 24343. **Fax:** 276/728-9066. **Facility:** 48 one-bedroom standard units. 1-2 stories (no elevator), exterior corridors. **Parking:** on-site. **Amenities:** irons, hair dryers. **Pool(s):** outdoor. **Cards:** AX, DC, DS, MC, VI. **Special Amenities:** free continental breakfast and free local telephone calls.

SOME UNITS

COMFORT INN & SUITES   *Book at aaa.com*

3/1-10/31 [ECP]	1P: $74-$180	2P: $74-$180	XP: $6	F18
11/1-2/28 [ECP]	1P: $72-$80	2P: $72-$80	XP: $6	F18

Phone: (276)728-9100

Small-scale Hotel

Location: I-77, exit 14, just w. 1994 Carrolton Pike Rd 24343. **Fax:** 276/728-9191. **Facility:** 54 one-bedroom standard units, some with whirlpools. 4 stories, interior corridors. *Bath:* combo or shower only. **Parking:** on-site. **Terms:** 7 day cancellation notice-fee imposed. **Amenities:** dual phone lines, voice mail, irons, hair dryers. **Pool(s):** heated indoor. **Leisure Activities:** whirlpool, exercise room. **Guest Services:** coin laundry. **Business Services:** meeting rooms. **Cards:** AX, CB, DC, DS, JC, MC, VI. **Special Amenities:** free expanded continental breakfast and free local telephone calls.

SOME UNITS

FAIRFIELD INN-HILLSVILLE   *Book at aaa.com*

5/26-10/31	1P: $59-$69	2P: $59-$69	
3/1-5/25 & 11/1-2/28	1P: $59	2P: $59	

Phone: (276)730-9999

Small-scale Hotel

Location: I-77, exit 14, just sw on US 58, then just s. 151 Farmers Market Rd 24343. **Fax:** 276/730-9920. **Facility:** 74 one-bedroom standard units, some with whirlpools. 3 stories, interior corridors. *Bath:* combo or shower only. **Parking:** on-site. **Terms:** cancellation fee imposed. **Amenities:** dual phone lines, irons, hair dryers. **Pool(s):** small heated indoor. **Leisure Activities:** whirlpool, exercise room. **Guest Services:** valet laundry. **Business Services:** meeting rooms. **Cards:** AX, CB, DC, DS, JC, MC, VI. **Special Amenities:** free expanded continental breakfast and free newspaper.

SOME UNITS

HAMPTON INN   *Book at aaa.com*   Phone: 276/728-2345
▼▼▼▼   All Year   2P: $59-$84
Small-scale Hotel   Location: I-77, exit 14, just w on US 58. 90 Farmers Market Rd 24343. Fax: 276/728-7133. Facility: 86 units. 81 one-bedroom standard units. 5 one-bedroom suites ($95-$125) with whirlpools. 4 stories, interior corridors. Bath: shower or tub only. Parking: on-site. Terms: 7 day cancellation notice, [ECP] meal plan available.
Amenities: high-speed Internet, dual phone lines, voice mail, irons, hair dryers. Pool(s): heated indoor. Leisure Activities: whirlpool, exercise room. Guest Services: valet laundry. Business Services: meeting rooms, business center. Cards: AX, DC, DS, JC, MC, VI.

SOME UNITS
(ASK) (S♦) (♦♦♦) (♦M) (♦) (∅) (➤) (♦) (DATA PORT) (⬛) / (🛏) (⬛) /

HOLIDAY INN EXPRESS   *Book at aaa.com*   Phone: (276)728-2120
AAA SAVE   3/1-10/31 [ECP]   1P: $74-$180   2P: $79-$185   XP: $5   F18
          11/1-2/28 [ECP]   1P: $72-$80   2P: $72-$80   XP: $5   F18
▼▼▼▼   Location: I-77, exit 14, just w on US 58 and 221. 85 Airport Rd 24343. Fax: 276/728-0752. Facility: 81 one-bedroom standard units, some with whirlpools. 1-2 stories (no elevator), exterior corridors. Bath: combo or shower only. Parking: on-site. Terms: 7 day cancellation notice-fee imposed, small pets only ($10 extra charge). Amenities: voice mail, irons, hair dryers. Pool(s): small outdoor. Leisure Activities: limited exercise equipment. Guest Services: valet laundry. Business Services: meeting rooms. Cards: AX, CB, DC, DS, JC, MC, VI.
Special Amenities: free expanded continental breakfast and free local telephone calls.

SOME UNITS
(S♦) (♦♦) (♦♦♦) (♦M) (♦) (➤) (♦) (DATA PORT) (🛏) (⬛) (⬛) / (✕) /
FEE

KNOB HILL MOTOR LODGE   Phone: 276/728-2131
AAA SAVE   All Year   XP: $5   F10
          Location: I-77, exit 14, 2.5 mi e on US 58 and 221. 305 E Stuart Dr 24343. Facility: 19 one-bedroom standard
▼▼ ▼▼   units. 1 story, exterior corridors. Bath: combo or shower only. Parking: on-site. Terms: cancellation fee
Motel   imposed. Amenities: hair dryers. Cards: AX, DC, DS, MC, VI.

SOME UNITS
(♦♦♦) (🛏) (⬛) (⬛) / (✕) /

RED CARPET INN   *Book at aaa.com*   Phone: 276/728-9118
▼▼   8/21-9/9 [ECP]   1P: $121-$131   2P: $121-$131   XP: $10   F16
Motel   3/1-8/20 & 9/10-10/30 [ECP]   1P: $38-$68   2P: $43-$68   XP: $5   F16
        10/31-2/28 [ECP]   1P: $38-$50   2P: $43-$50   XP: $5   F16
        Location: I-77, exit 14, just n. 2666 Old Galax Pike 24343 (PO Box 1148). Fax: 276/728-2978. Facility: 41 one-bedroom standard units, some with whirlpools. 2 stories (no elevator), interior corridors. Parking: on-site. Terms: weekly rates available, small pets only ($5 extra charge). Cards: AX, DS, MC, VI.

SOME UNITS
(ASK) (S♦) (♦♦♦) (♦) / (✕) (🛏) (⬛) (⬛) /
FEE

SUPER 8 OF HILLSVILLE   *Book at aaa.com*   Phone: (276)728-4125
AAA SAVE   All Year [ECP]   1P: $59-$150   2P: $59-$150   XP: $6   F15
▼▼ ▼▼   Location: I-77, exit 14, just w on US 58 and 221. 99 Farmers Market Rd 24343. Fax: 276/728-4192. Facility: 65 one-bedroom standard units. 2 stories (no elevator), interior/exterior corridors. Parking: on-site.
Motel   Amenities: Some: irons, hair dryers. Leisure Activities: exercise room. Cards: AX, DC, DS, MC, VI.

SOME UNITS
(S♦) (♦♦♦) (∅) (♦) (DATA PORT) (⬛) / (✕) /

──────── **WHERE TO DINE** ────────

HILLSVILLE FAMILY FISH HOUSE   Lunch: $6-$15   Dinner: $8-$24   Phone: 276/728-7803
▼▼ ▼▼   Location: I-77, exit 14, just e. 867 W Stuart Dr 24343. Hours: 3 pm-9 pm, Fri & Sat-10 pm, Sun 11:30 am-9 pm.
American   Closed: 1/1, 12/25; also Mon & Tues. Features: Hillsville Family Fish House has a huge selection of fish and seafood and a whole lot more. A family atmosphere and friendly service. Casual dress. Parking: on-site. Cards: MC, VI.

(🍽) (✕)

HOPEWELL pop. 22,354   (See map and index starting on p. 835)

──────── **WHERE TO STAY** ────────

CANDLEWOOD SUITES   *Book at aaa.com*   Phone: (804)541-0200   ⬛15
AAA SAVE   All Year   1P: $69-$79   2P: $69-$79
▼▼ ▼▼   Location: I-295, exit 9B (SR 36), just w; adjacent to Oak Lawn Plaza. 5113 Plaza Dr 23860. Fax: 804/541-6622. Facility: 60 units. 48 one-bedroom standard units with kitchens. 12 one-bedroom suites ($87-$100) with kitchens. 3 stories, interior corridors. Bath: combo or shower only. Parking: on-site, winter plug-ins.
Small-scale Hotel   Terms: office hours 7 am-11 pm, pets ($75 extra charge). Amenities: video library, CD players, high-speed Internet, dual phone lines, voice mail, irons, hair dryers. Leisure Activities: exercise room. Guest Services: sundries, valet and coin laundry. Business Services: fax. Cards: AX, CB, DC, DS, JC, MC, VI. Special Amenities: free local telephone calls and preferred room (subject to availability with advance reservations).

SOME UNITS
(S♦) (♦) (♦♦♦) (♦) (VCR) (♦) (DATA PORT) (🛏) (⬛) (⬛) / (✕) /
FEE

ECONO LODGE   *Book at aaa.com*   Phone: (804)541-4849   ⬛12
AAA SAVE   All Year   1P: $69   2P: $69
▼▼ ▼▼   Location: I-295, exit 9A, just e. 4096 Oaklawn Blvd 23860. Fax: 804/415-2016. Facility: 50 one-bedroom standard units, some with efficiencies and/or whirlpools. 3 stories, interior corridors. Bath: combo or shower only. Parking: on-site. Amenities: voice mail, irons. Some: hair dryers. Guest Services: coin laundry.
Small-scale Hotel   Business Services: fax. Cards: AX, DC, DS, MC, VI. Special Amenities: free continental breakfast and free newspaper.

SOME UNITS
(S♦) (♦) (♦♦♦) (♦M) (♦) (VCR) (♦) (DATA PORT) (🛏) (⬛) (⬛) / (✕) /

(See map and index starting on p. 835)

HAMPTON INN-FT LEE   *Book at aaa.com*
Phone: (804)452-1000   **14**

▼▼▼▼▼
Small-scale Hotel

All Year [ECP]   1P: $59-$89   2P: $89

Location: I-295, exit 9B (SR 36), just n. 5103 Plaza Dr 23860. Fax: 804/541-8584. **Facility:** 74 one-bedroom standard units, some with whirlpools. 3 stories, interior corridors. **Parking:** on-site. **Terms:** cancellation fee imposed. **Amenities:** voice mail, irons, hair dryers. **Pool(s):** outdoor. **Leisure Activities:** sauna, exercise room. **Guest Services:** valet and coin laundry. **Business Services:** meeting rooms, fax. **Cards:** AX, CB, DC, DS, MC, VI.

SOME UNITS

(ASK) (S📶) (T🍴) (🖥M) (🏊) (VCR) (🐾) (DATA PORT) (🔌) (📷) (📺) / (✖) /

QUALITY INN
Phone: (804)458-1500   **13**

▼▼▼
Small-scale Hotel

All Year [BP]   1P: $59-$79   2P: $59-$79

Location: I-295, exit 9B (SR 36), just w. 4911 Oaklawn Blvd 23860. Fax: 804/458-9151. **Facility:** 115 one-bedroom standard units, some with efficiencies (no utensils) and/or whirlpools. 2 stories (no elevator), exterior corridors. **Parking:** on-site. **Amenities:** voice mail, irons, hair dryers. **Pool(s):** outdoor. **Leisure Activities:** sauna, whirlpool, exercise room. **Guest Services:** valet and coin laundry, area transportation. **Business Services:** fax. **Cards:** AX, CB, DC, DS, MC, VI.

SOME UNITS

(ASK) (S📶) (T🍴) (🍽) (🏊) (✖) (🐾) (DATA PORT) (🔌) (📷) / (✖) (📺) /

--------- WHERE TO DINE ---------

DOCKSIDE RESTAURANT
Lunch: $5-$9   Dinner: $8-$18   Phone: 804/541-2600

▼▼▼
Seafood

Location: SR 156, just n of jct SR 10; at south end of Benjamin Harrison Bridge. 700 Jordan Point Rd 23860. **Hours:** 11:30 am-10 pm, Fri & Sat-11 pm. Closed: 1/1, 12/25. **Reservations:** suggested. **Features:** The menu showcases fresh local seafood, such as flounder, swordfish and blackened tuna, pasta, steak and salad. Enjoy a panoramic view through the picture windows that overlook the water. The decor is decidedly nautical, with lots of rich wood. Casual dress; cocktails; entertainment. **Parking:** on-site. **Cards:** AX, DS, MC, VI.

(🍽) (✖)

HOT SPRINGS

--------- WHERE TO STAY ---------

THE HOMESTEAD   *Book at aaa.com*
Phone: (540)839-1766

▼▼▼▼ ▼▼▼▼
Resort
Large-scale Hotel

10/28-12/21 [MAP]	1P: $232-$392	2P: $302-$784	XP: $112 F4
12/22-2/28 [MAP]	1P: $484-$684	2P: $554-$684	XP: $157 F4
5/8-10/27 [MAP]	1P: $392-$552	2P: $462-$622	XP: $112 F4
3/1-5/7 [MAP]	1P: $240-$390	2P: $310-$470	XP: $112 F4

Location: Center. Located in a rural area. US 220 24445 (PO Box 2000, Main St). Fax: 540/839-7656. **Facility:** Established in 1766, the mountain resort offers recreation options ranging from golf to horseback riding. 506 one-bedroom standard units. 7 stories, interior corridors. *Bath:* combo or shower only. **Parking:** on-site and valet. **Terms:** check-in 4 pm, 14-day cancellation notice, package plans, 15% service charge. **Amenities:** video games, high-speed Internet, voice mail, safes, honor bars, irons, hair dryers. **Pool(s):** heated outdoor, heated indoor, wading. **Leisure Activities:** sauna, whirlpool, steamroom, canoeing, fishing, recreation programs, hiking trails, jogging, playground, spa. *Fee:* golf-54 holes, 12 tennis courts, downhill & cross country skiing, ice skating, bicycles, horseback riding. **Guest Services:** gift shop, valet laundry. **Business Services:** conference facilities, fax. **Cards:** AX, DC, DS, MC, VI.

SOME UNITS

(🔌) (🍴) (🍽) (🖥) (🐾) (🏊) (🚲) (✖) (📷) (DATA PORT) / (✖) /
FEE   FEE

ROSELOE MOTEL
Phone: 540/839-5373

▼▼
Motel

All Year   1P: $60-$80   2P: $60-$80

Location: 3 mi n. 590 US 220 N 24445 (Rt 1, Box 590). **Facility:** 14 one-bedroom standard units. 1 story, exterior corridors. **Parking:** on-site. **Terms:** pets ($10 extra charge). **Leisure Activities:** horseshoes. **Cards:** AX, CB, DC, DS, MC, VI.

SOME UNITS

(🐎) (📷) (🔌) (📷) (📺) / (✖) /
FEE

--------- WHERE TO DINE ---------

ELLIOTT'S
Lunch: $6-$12   Dinner: $10-$25   Phone: 540/839-3663

▼▼
American

Location: On Main St, just w; center. 3 Main St 24445. **Hours:** 11:30 am-2 & 5:30-9:30 pm. Closed major holidays; also Sun & Mon. **Features:** This restaurant has a small cozy atmosphere with a wonderfully diverse menu and friendly service. Casual dress; cocktails. **Parking:** street. **Cards:** MC, VI.

(🍽) (✖)

IRVINGTON pop. 673

———— WHERE TO STAY ————

THE HOPE AND GLORY INN   Phone: 804/438-6053

▽▽▽▽

Historic Bed & Breakfast

All Year   2P: $190-$350
Location: Just w of CR 200 on King Carter Dr. 65 Tavern Rd 22480 (PO Box 425). Fax: 804/438-5362. **Facility:** The theme is bright and whimsical at the this circa 1890 former schoolhouse and attached cottages with "distressed" antiques and overflowing gardens. Smoke free premises. 13 units. 6 one-bedroom standard units. 1 one-bedroom suite. 6 cottages. 3 stories (no elevator), interior/exterior corridors. *Bath:* combo, shower or tub only. **Parking:** on-site. **Terms:** 2 night minimum stay - weekends, 14 day cancellation notice-fee imposed, weekly rates available, pets ($35 extra charge, in cottages only). **Amenities:** *Some:* CD players. **Dining:** Trick Dog Cafe, see separate listing. **Leisure Activities:** bicycles. *Fee:* boats, charter fishing. **Business Services:** meeting rooms. **Cards:** AX, MC, VI.

SOME UNITS

(A$K) (S🄳) (🛏) (🍴) (🗙) (🗙) (🅦) / (🖂) /
                              FEE

THE TIDES INN   *Book at aaa.com*   Phone: (804)438-5000

🅐🅐🅐 (SAVE)

▽▽▽▽ ▽▽▽▽

Small-scale Hotel

3/1-1/1   1P: $199-$375   2P: $199-$375
Location: 0.3 mi w of CR 200. 480 King Carter Dr 22480. Fax: 804/438-5222. **Facility:** Gracious riverfront resort with a Scottish theme. 106 one-bedroom standard units. 4 stories, interior/exterior corridors. *Bath:* combo or shower only. **Parking:** on-site. **Terms:** open 3/1-1/1, check-in 4 pm, 2 night minimum stay - weekends, 2 day cancellation notice, package plans, $10 service charge, pets ($35 fee, in designated units). **Amenities:** video library, DVD players, CD players, high-speed Internet, dual phone lines, voice mail, safes, honor bars, irons, hair dryers. **Dining:** 4 restaurants, 7 am-11 pm, cocktails, also, The Dining Room at the Tides Inn, see separate listing, entertainment. **Pool(s):** 3 heated outdoor, saltwater. **Leisure Activities:** canoeing, paddleboats, marina, 4 tennis courts, recreation programs, croquet, bicycles, playground, exercise room, spa, sports court, shuffleboard. *Fee:* boats, sailboats, fishing, charter fishing, golf-27 holes. **Guest Services:** gift shop, valet laundry, area transportation. **Business Services:** conference facilities, fax. **Cards:** AX, DC, DS, MC, VI. **Special Amenities:** free newspaper. *(See color ad below)*

SOME UNITS

(🛏) (🍴) (24🏧) (🍽) (🔒) (🛗M) (🐕) (🏊) (🗙) (🗙) (DATA PORT) (💻) / (🗙) (VCR) (📠) (📠) /
  FEE   FEE   FEE

———— WHERE TO DINE ————

THE DINING ROOM AT THE TIDES INN   Dinner: $23-$34   Phone: 804/438-5000

▽▽▽▽

Regional American

Location: 0.3 mi w of CR 200; in The Tides Inn. 480 King Carter Dr 22480. **Hours:** 7 am-11 & 5-10 pm. **Reservations:** required. **Features:** Overlooking Carter's Creek and the marina, the dining room enables guests to sample sophisticated fare prepared with both international and regional Mid-Atlantic influences. Semi-formal attire; cocktails. **Parking:** on-site. **Cards:** AX, MC, VI.

(🛗M) (🍽) (🗙)

TRICK DOG CAFE   Dinner: $17-$28   Phone: 804/438-1055

▽▽▽▽

American

Location: Just w of CR 200 on King Carter Dr; in The Hope and Glory Inn. 4357 Irvington Rd 22480. **Hours:** 5 pm-10 pm, Fri & Sat-11 pm, Sun 11 am-2 & 5-9 pm. Closed: 12/24, 12/25. **Reservations:** suggested. **Features:** The spot is so stylish and hip that guests might forget they're still in the Northern Neck. Lending to the setting's appeal are oversized lampshades, swaths of velvet and crystal chandeliers on the sidewalk patio. The ever-changing menu lines up seasonal selections in modern dishes. Dressy casual; cocktails. **Parking:** on-site. **Cards:** AX, MC, VI.

(🗙)

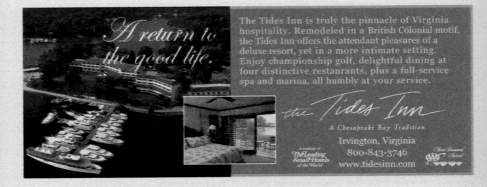

KESWICK

——— WHERE TO STAY ———

KESWICK HALL AT MONTICELLO *Book at aaa.com*
Phone: (434)979-3440

(AAA) [SAVE] All Year   1P: $295-$795   2P: $295-$795   XP: $25   F12
▽▽▽▽ ▽▽▽▽
Location: I-64, exit 129, just n. 701 Club Dr 22947. Fax: 434/977-4171. **Facility:** A service-oriented, upscale
Resort resort offering fine views and luxury appointments. 48 one-bedroom standard units, some with whirlpools. 3
Small-scale Hotel stories, interior corridors. **Parking:** on-site and valet. **Terms:** 3 day cancellation notice-fee imposed,
package plans, small pets only ($75 extra charge). **Amenities:** video library, CD players, high-speed
Internet, voice mail, safes, honor bars, irons, hair dryers. **Dining:** 2 restaurants, 7 am-10 pm, cocktails, also,
Fossett's Restaurant, see separate listing. **Pool(s):** outdoor, heated indoor, heated indoor/outdoor, wading.
Leisure Activities: whirlpools, fishing, 5 lighted tennis courts, recreation programs, archery, billards, croquet, bicycles, exercise
room, volleyball. **Fee:** golf-54 holes, massage. **Guest Services:** gift shop, complimentary evening beverages, valet laundry.
Business Services: conference facilities, business center. **Cards:** AX, DC, DS, MC, VI.

SOME UNITS
🐾 🍴 🍸 🛎M 📼 🏊 ✕ ✕ VCR 🐕 DATA PORT / 🛏 🖥 /
FEE

——— WHERE TO DINE ———

FOSSETT'S RESTAURANT   **Dinner:** $29-$38   **Phone:** 434/979-3440
▽▽▽▽ ▽▽▽▽
Location: I-64, exit 129, just n; in Keswick Hall at Monticello. 701 Club Dr 22947. **Hours:** 6 pm-9 pm.
Reservations: suggested, weekends. **Features:** Named after Thomas Jefferson's chief chef at Monticello,
American the restaurant offers seating in a amazingly elegant dining room that affords estate and golf views.
Wonderful plate presentations accentuate many local gourmet ingredients, which are harvested at the peak
of flavor. Dressy casual; cocktails. **Parking:** on-site and valet. **Cards:** AX, CB, DC, DS, JC, MC, VI.

🍸 ✕

KEYSVILLE pop. 817

——— WHERE TO STAY ———

SHELDON'S MOTEL   **Phone:** (434)736-8434

(AAA) [SAVE] All Year   1P: $41-$70   2P: $49-$75   XP: $8   F12
▽ ▽▽
Location: 1.3 mi n on US 15 and 360 business route. Located in a rural area. 1450 Four Locust Hwy 23947.
Fax: 434/736-9402. **Facility:** 40 one-bedroom standard units. 1-2 stories (no elevator), exterior corridors.
Parking: on-site. **Terms:** check-in 4 pm. **Amenities:** hair dryers. **Dining:** 6:30 am-9:30 pm, wine/beer only.
Small-scale Hotel **Leisure Activities:** exercise room. **Guest Services:** gift shop. **Business Services:** meeting rooms.
Cards: AX, DS, MC, VI. **Special Amenities:** free local telephone calls and early check-in/late check-
out.

SOME UNITS
SD 🐾 🍴 📼 DATA PORT / ✕ 🛏 🖥 /
FEE FEE

KILMARNOCK pop. 1,244

——— WHERE TO STAY ———

HOLIDAY INN EXPRESS *Book at aaa.com*
Phone: 804-436-1500

(AAA) [SAVE] 3/1-9/6   1P: $79-$109   2P: $79-$109   XP: $10   F18
▽▽▽▽ 9/7-2/28   1P: $69-$99   2P: $69-$99   XP: $10   F18
Location: Just n on SR 17. 599 N Main St 22482. Fax: 804/436-9337. **Facility:** 68 one-bedroom standard units.
Small-scale Hotel 2 stories, interior corridors. *Bath:* combo or shower only. **Parking:** on-site. **Terms:** 2 night minimum stay -
seasonal and/or weekends. **Amenities:** dual phone lines, voice mail, irons, hair dryers. **Pool(s):** outdoor.
Business Services: meeting rooms, fax. **Cards:** AX, DC, DS, MC, VI. **Special Amenities:** free
continental breakfast and free local telephone calls.

SOME UNITS
SD 🍴 🛎M 📼 🏊 🐕 DATA PORT / ✕ 🛏 🖥 🖥 /
FEE FEE

——— WHERE TO DINE ———

LEE'S RESTAURANT   **Lunch:** $6-$11   **Dinner:** $6-$11   **Phone:** 804/435-1255
▽
Location: Center. 30 Main St 22482. **Hours:** 7 am-8 pm. Closed: Sun. **Features:** Southern hospitality and
delicious bay country cuisine please patrons of this small Main Street spot. On the menu are many
Regional American preparations of local seafood, homemade pies and daily soups. Casual dress. **Parking:** street.
Cards: MC, VI.

✕

LAWRENCEVILLE pop. 1,275

——— WHERE TO STAY ———

BRUNSWICK MINERAL SPRINGS B & B CIRCA 1785
Phone: (434)848-4010

▽▽▽ All Year   1P: $85-$125   2P: $85-$155   XP: $15
Location: 5 mi e on US 58, 1 mi s on SR 712, then just e. Located in a quiet, rural area. 14910 Western Mill Rd 23868.
Historic Bed Fax: 434/848-9110. **Facility:** Towering oaks shade this Colonial-style plantation home, which has seen
& Breakfast many incarnations since its late-1700s inception as a mineral springs resort. Smoke free premises. 4 units.
2 one-bedroom standard units. 1 two-bedroom suite. 1 cottage ($85). 3 stories (no elevator), interior
corridors. *Bath:* combo or shower only. **Parking:** on-site. **Terms:** check-in 4 pm, 2 night minimum stay - seasonal, age
restrictions may apply, 5 day cancellation notice-fee imposed, package plans, pets (in cottage, owner's dogs on premises).
Amenities: hair dryers. *Some:* irons. **Leisure Activities:** hiking trails. **Business Services:** fax. **Cards:** MC, VI.

SOME UNITS
(ASK) SD 🐾 ✕ 🐕 DATA PORT / 📺 VCR 🕸 🛏 🖥 🖥 /

THREE ANGELS INN AT SHERWOOD
▼▼▼▼▼ All Year [BP]   1P: $95-$110   2P: $95-$110   XP: $20   D12
Phone: 434/848-0830
Historic Bed **Location:** 1.5 mi w on US 58 to jct SR 681. Located in a quiet rural area. 236 Pleasant Grove Rd (SR 681) 23920 (PO & Breakfast Box 883, 23868). **Fax:** 434/848-9696. **Facility:** Built in 1883 as a hospital, the inn is surrounded by shady oak and cedar trees best appreciated from the rocking chairs and swings on its porches. Smoke free premises. 4 one-bedroom standard units. 2 stories (no elevator), interior corridors. **Parking:** on-site. **Terms:** age restrictions may apply, 3 day cancellation notice-fee imposed, [MAP] meal plan available, package plans. **Amenities:** hair dryers. **Business Services:** fax. **Cards:** MC, VI.

SOME UNITS
(ASK) (S/D) (X) (TV) (DATA PORT) / (Z)

LEBANON pop. 3,273

———— WHERE TO STAY ————

LEBANON SUPER 8 MOTEL   *Book at aaa.com*   Phone: (276)889-1800
▼▼▼ ▼▼▼ All Year   1P: $60-$103   2P: $66-$109   XP: $6   F17
Small-scale Hotel **Location:** Just e on SR 654 from US 19 Bypass. 711 Townview Dr 24266. **Fax:** 276/889-1800. **Facility:** 47 one-bedroom standard units, some with whirlpools. 2 stories (no elevator), interior corridors. **Parking:** on-site. **Amenities:** Fee: safes. **Guest Services:** coin laundry. **Cards:** AX, CB, DC, DS, JC, MC, VI.

SOME UNITS
(ASK) (S/D) (&/M) (TV) (DATA PORT) (fee) / (X) /
FEE

LEESBURG —See District Of Columbia p. 538.

LEON

———— WHERE TO STAY ————

THE SUITES AT PRINCE MICHEL   Phone: 540/547-9720
▼▼▼▼ ▼▼▼▼ All Year   1P: $149-$299   2P: $149-$299
Country Inn **Location:** On US 29; center. Located in a quiet area, at Prince Michel Vineyards. 154 Winery Ln 22725. **Fax:** 540/547-3088. **Facility:** A sound system, porch and lavish appointments enhance these accommodations overlooking a mountainous area. 4 one-bedroom suites with whirlpools. 1 story, exterior corridors. **Parking:** on-site. **Amenities:** CD players, voice mail, honor bars, hair dryers. **Dining:** restaurant, see separate listing. **Guest Services:** gift shop, valet laundry, area transportation (fee). **Business Services:** meeting rooms. **Cards:** AX, DC, MC, VI.

(+) (YI) (X) (VCR) (TV) (DATA PORT) (fee) (H) (🖼) (🖳)
FEE

———— WHERE TO DINE ————

THE GRILLE AT PRINCE MICHEL   *Menu on aaa.com*   **Lunch:** $9-$12   **Dinner:** $15-$24   Phone: 540/547-3707
(AAA) **Location:** On US 29; center; in The Suites at Prince Michel. 154 Winery Ln 22725. **Hours:** 11:30 am-2 & 5:30-9 pm; ▼▼▼▼ Sunday brunch 11 am-2 pm. **Closed:** 1/1, 12/25; also Mon-Wed. **Reservations:** required. **Features:** Fresh American local produce and imported ingredients combine in updated versions of classic French recipes. The bistro ambience belies the fabulous food that lines a seasonally changing menu. Variety is the key. Casual dress; cocktails. **Parking:** on-site. **Cards:** AX, DC, DS, MC, VI.

(X)

LEXINGTON pop. 6,867

———— WHERE TO STAY ————

A B&B AT LLEWELLYN LODGE   Phone: (540)463-3235
▼▼▼▼ 3/1-12/31 [BP]   1P: $65-$150   2P: $70-$165   XP: $20
1/1-2/28 [BP]   1P: $60-$139   2P: $65-$149   XP: $20
Bed & Breakfast **Location:** 0.5 mi s on US 11. 603 S Main St 24450. **Fax:** 540/463-3235. **Facility:** This cozy family home is close to many shops as well as to the famed Virginia Military Institute. Smoke free premises. 6 one-bedroom standard units. 2 stories (no elevator), interior corridors. **Bath:** combo or shower only. **Parking:** on-site. **Terms:** age restrictions may apply, cancellation fee imposed, weekly rates available, package plans. **Amenities:** hair dryers. Some: irons. **Guest Services:** complimentary laundry. **Cards:** AX, DS, MC, VI.

SOME UNITS
(X) / (TV) (VCR) (Z) (H) /

BEST WESTERN INN AT HUNT RIDGE   *Book at aaa.com*   Phone: (540)464-1500
(AAA) (SAVE) 4/1-10/31 [ECP]   1P: $74-$145   2P: $79-$150   XP: $10   F15
3/1-3/31 & 11/1-2/28 [ECP]   1P: $64-$84   2P: $69-$89   XP: $10   F15
▼▼▼ ▼▼▼ **Location:** I-64, exit 55, just n on US 11 to SR 39; I-81, exit 191, 0.6 mi w. 25 Willow Spring Rd 24450. Small-scale Hotel **Fax:** 540/463-5345. **Facility:** 100 one-bedroom standard units. 3 stories, interior corridors. **Bath:** combo or shower only. **Parking:** on-site. **Terms:** pets ($25 extra charge, in designated units). **Amenities:** irons, hair dryers. **Dining:** G Willaker's, see separate listing. **Pool(s):** heated indoor/outdoor. **Guest Services:** coin laundry. **Business Services:** conference facilities. **Cards:** AX, CB, DC, DS, JC, MC, VI. **Special Amenities:** free newspaper and preferred room (subject to availability with advance reservations).** *(See color ad p 800)*

SOME UNITS
(S/D) (🛏) (YI) (Y) (&/M) (&) (⌗) (≥) (TV) (DATA PORT) (🖳) / (X) (H) (🖼) /
FEE   FEE   FEE

COMFORT INN-VIRGINIA HORSE CENTER   *Book at aaa.com*   Phone: (540)463-7311
▼▼▼ ▼▼▼ All Year [ECP]   1P: $54-$145   2P: $59-$150   XP: $10   F15
Location: I-64, exit 55, just s on US 11; I-81, exit 191, 0.6 mi w. 62 Comfort Way 24450. **Fax:** 540/463-4590. Small-scale Hotel **Facility:** 80 one-bedroom standard units. 4 stories, interior corridors. **Parking:** on-site. **Terms:** small pets only ($25 extra charge). **Amenities:** irons, hair dryers. **Pool(s):** small heated indoor. **Guest Services:** coin laundry. **Cards:** AX, CB, DC, DS, JC, MC, VI. *(See color ad p 800)*

SOME UNITS
(ASK) (S/D) (🛏) (YI+) (≥) (TV) (DATA PORT) (🖳) / (X) (H) (🖼) /
FEE

COUNTRY INN & SUITES *Book at aaa.com*
Phone: (540)464-9000

(AAA) (SAVE)
3/1-11/15 [ECP]   1P: $98-$170   2P: $110-$180   XP: $10   F18
11/16-2/28 [ECP]   1P: $69-$110   2P: $79-$120   XP: $10   F18
Location: I-81, exit 191, just s on US 11. 875 N Lee Hwy 24450 (PO Box 1105). Fax: 540/464-9016. **Facility:** 66 one-bedroom standard units, some with whirlpools. 4 stories, interior corridors. *Bath:* combo or shower only.

Small-scale Hotel   **Parking:** on-site. **Amenities:** voice mail, irons, hair dryers. **Pool(s):** heated indoor. **Leisure Activities:** whirlpool, exercise room. **Guest Services:** coin laundry. **Cards:** AX, CB, DC, DS, MC, VI.
Special Amenities: free continental breakfast and free local telephone calls. *(See color ad p 847)*

SOME UNITS

DAYS INN KEYDET GENERAL *Book at aaa.com*
Phone: (540)463-2143

(AAA) (SAVE)
3/1-11/15   1P: $60-$75   2P: $65-$85   XP: $5   F12
11/16-2/28   1P: $42-$55   2P: $55-$65   XP: $5   F12
Location: I-81, exit 188B, 4.5 mi on US 60 W; I-64, exit 50, 5 mi on US 60. Located in a quiet area. 325 W Midland Tr 24450. Fax: 540/463-2143. **Facility:** 53 one-bedroom standard units. 1 story, interior/exterior corridors.

Small-scale Hotel   **Parking:** on-site. **Terms:** 3 day cancellation notice, package plans, pets ($5 extra charge). **Amenities:** hair dryers. **Cards:** AX, DC, DS, MC, VI. **Special Amenities:** free continental breakfast and free local telephone calls.

SOME UNITS
FEE

ECONO LODGE *Book at aaa.com*
Phone: (540)463-7371

(AAA) (SAVE)
All Year   1P: $50-$150   2P: $50-$150   XP: $10   F18
Location: I-81, exit 191, just s on US 11. 65 Econo Ln 24450. Fax: 540/463-6095. **Facility:** 48 one-bedroom standard units. 2 stories (no elevator), exterior corridors. **Parking:** on-site. **Terms:** 2 night minimum stay - seasonal and/or weekends, weekly rates available, pets ($10.85 extra charge). **Guest Services:** coin laundry. **Cards:** AX, DS, MC, VI. **Special Amenities:** free continental breakfast and free local telephone calls.

Motel

SOME UNITS
FEE

HAMPTON INN-COL ALTO *Book at aaa.com*
Phone: (540)463-2223

All Year   1P: $83-$220   2P: $93-$255
Location: I-81, exit 188B, 2.5 mi w on US 60. 401 E Nelson St 24450. Fax: 540/463-9707. **Facility:** 86 one-bedroom standard units, some with whirlpools. 3 stories, interior/exterior corridors. *Bath:* combo or shower only. **Parking:** on-site. **Amenities:** voice mail, irons, hair dryers. **Pool(s):** outdoor. **Leisure Activities:** whirlpool, exercise room. **Guest Services:** valet laundry. **Business Services:** meeting rooms. **Cards:** AX, CB, DC, DS, MC, VI.

Small-scale Hotel

SOME UNITS

HISTORIC COUNTRY INNS OF LEXINGTON
Phone: (540)463-2044

All Year [ECP]   1P: $90-$125   2P: $105-$140   XP: $15   D17
Location: Between Washington and Henry sts; center of downtown. 11 N Main St 24450. Fax: 540/463-7262. **Facility:** This property features rooms and suites in two historic townhouses, one dating from 1789 and the other from 1809. 23 one-bedroom standard units, some with whirlpools. 3-4 stories (no elevator), interior/exterior corridors. *Bath:* combo or shower only. **Parking:** on-site. **Terms:** 10 day cancellation notice, package plans. **Amenities:** voice mail. **Business Services:** meeting rooms. **Cards:** DS, MC, VI.

Historic Bed & Breakfast

SOME UNITS

HOLIDAY INN EXPRESS *Book at aaa.com*
Phone: (540)463-7351

(AAA) (SAVE)
4/1-10/31   1P: $60-$125   2P: $65-$130   XP: $10   F18
3/1-3/31 & 11/1-2/28   1P: $50-$80   2P: $55-$85   XP: $10   F18
Location: I-64, exit 55, just s on US 11; I-81, exit 191, 1.6 mi w. 850 N Lee Hwy 24450. Fax: 540/463-5464. **Facility:** 72 one-bedroom standard units. 2 stories (no elevator), exterior corridors. **Parking:** on-site.

Small-scale Hotel   **Terms:** small pets only ($25 extra charge, in smoking units). **Amenities:** voice mail, irons, hair dryers. **Leisure Activities:** picnic tables. **Guest Services:** valet laundry. **Business Services:** meeting rooms.
Cards: AX, DC, DS, MC, VI. **Special Amenities:** free continental breakfast and free room upgrade (subject to availability with advance reservations).

SOME UNITS
FEE

HOWARD JOHNSON INN   *Book at aaa.com*

Phone: (540)463-9181

4/1-11/20	1P: $75-$130	2P: $80-$135	XP: $5	F18
3/1-3/31 & 11/21-2/28	1P: $60-$80	2P: $65-$85	XP: $5	F18

Location: I-81, exit 195, just s on US 11. 2836 N Lee Hwy 24450. Fax: 540/464-3448. **Facility:** 100 one-bedroom standard units. 5 stories, interior corridors. **Parking:** on-site. **Terms:** pets ($5 extra charge). **Amenities:** irons, hair dryers. **Dining:** 6 am-8 pm, Fri & Sat-8:30 pm, cocktails. **Pool(s):** outdoor. **Leisure Activities:** picnic tables. **Guest Services:** coin laundry. **Business Services:** meeting rooms. **Cards:** AX, DC, DS, MC, VI. **Special Amenities:** free local telephone calls and free newspaper.

Small-scale Hotel

SOME UNITS

MAPLE HALL COUNTRY INN

Phone: (540)463-6693

All Year [ECP]	1P: $90-$125	2P: $105-$140	XP: $15	D17

Location: I-81, exit 195, just ne on US 11. 3111 N Lee Hwy 24450. Fax: 540/463-2114. **Facility:** Some units overlook a fishing pond and others have fireplaces in this Greek Revival plantation home, which also has two outbuildings. 21 one-bedroom standard units. 3 stories (no elevator), interior corridors. *Bath:* combo or shower only. **Parking:** on-site. **Terms:** 10 day cancellation notice. **Dining:** Maple Hall Dining Room, see separate listing. **Pool(s):** small outdoor. **Leisure Activities:** fishing, tennis court, hiking trails. **Business Services:** meeting rooms. **Cards:** DS, MC, VI.

Historic
Country Inn

SOME UNITS

RAMADA INN LEXINGTON

Phone: 540/463-6400

All Year	1P: $45	2P: $90	XP: $6	F18

Location: I-81, exit 195, just sw on US 11. 2814 N Lee Hwy 24450. Fax: 540/464-3639. **Facility:** 80 one-bedroom standard units. 4 stories, interior corridors. *Bath:* combo or shower only. **Parking:** on-site. **Terms:** pets ($8 extra charge). **Amenities:** irons, hair dryers. **Pool(s):** heated indoor. **Guest Services:** valet laundry. **Cards:** AX, CB, DC, DS, MC, VI.

Small-scale Hotel

SOME UNITS

RED OAK INNS

Phone: (540)463-9131

5/1-11/30	1P: $65-$95	2P: $70-$105	XP: $10	F16
3/1-4/30 & 12/1-2/28	1P: $55-$70	2P: $60-$75	XP: $8	F16

Location: I-81, exit 195, just sw on US 11. 2809 N Lee Hwy 24450. Fax: 540/463-7448. **Facility:** 149 one-bedroom standard units. 2-3 stories, exterior corridors. **Parking:** on-site. **Terms:** cancellation fee imposed. **Amenities:** *Some:* irons, hair dryers. **Dining:** 6 am-8 pm. **Pool(s):** outdoor. **Leisure Activities:** playground. **Cards:** AX, DC, DS, MC, VI. **Special Amenities:** free local telephone calls and free room upgrade (subject to availability with advance reservations).

Small-scale Hotel

SOME UNITS

SLEEP INN & SUITES

Phone: 540/463-6000

(fyi)

Under construction, scheduled to open September 2005. **Location:** I-64, exit 55, just n. 95 Maury River Rd 24450. Fax: 540/463-6002. **Planned Amenities:** coffeemakers, microwaves, refrigerators, pool. **Terms:** 7 day cancellation notice.

Small-scale Hotel

WINGATE INN   *Book at aaa.com*

Phone: 540/464-8100

All Year	1P: $89-$169	2P: $89-$169	XP: $10	F17

Location: I-64, exit 55, just n. 1100 N Lee Hwy 24450. Fax: 540/464-8105. **Facility:** 86 one-bedroom standard units, some with whirlpools. 4 stories, interior corridors. *Bath:* combo or shower only. **Parking:** on-site. **Terms:** 2 night minimum stay - seasonal and/or weekends, 30 day cancellation notice. **Amenities:** video games, high-speed Internet, voice mail, safes, irons, hair dryers. **Pool(s):** heated indoor. **Leisure Activities:** whirlpool, exercise room. **Guest Services:** coin laundry. **Business Services:** meeting rooms, business center. **Cards:** AX, CB, DC, DS, MC, VI. **Special Amenities:** free continental breakfast and free local telephone calls.

Small-scale Hotel

SOME UNITS

------- **WHERE TO DINE** -------

G WILLAKER'S

Lunch: $5-$12   **Dinner:** $10-$17   **Phone:** 540/464-9499

Location: I-64, exit 55, just n on US 11 to SR 39; I-81, exit 191, 0.6 mi w; in Best Western Inn at Hunt Ridge. 25 Willow Spring Rd 24450. **Hours:** 11 am-10 pm, Fri & Sat-10:30 pm. **Features:** G. Willaker's offers a tremendous place to unwind and enjoy great American classic cuisine. Located close to the Virginia Horse Center. Casual dress. **Parking:** on-site. **Cards:** AX, DS, MC, VI.

American

IL PALAZZO

Lunch: $7-$15   **Dinner:** $10-$22   **Phone:** 540/464-5800

Location: Between Washington and Henry sts; center of downtown. 24 N Main St 24450. **Hours:** 11 am-10 pm. Closed: 12/25; also Mon. **Features:** Fine Italian cuisine is served in a wonderful setting. Standouts include the valued menu, formally attired wait staff and first-class wine list. Casual dress; cocktails. **Parking:** street. **Cards:** AX, CB, DC, DS, JC, MC, VI.

Italian

MAPLE HALL DINING ROOM

Dinner: $12-$30   **Phone:** 540/463-4666

Location: I-81, exit 195, just ne on US 11; in Maple Hall Country Inn. 3111 N Lee Hwy 24450. **Hours:** 5:30 pm-9 pm. Closed: 12/24, 12/25; also 1/1-1/7. **Reservations:** suggested. **Features:** Dining rooms in the 1850s plantation home are decorated in period. A glass-enclosed patio overlooks the garden. Although the menu is limited, the ingredients are upscale in such rich, flavorful dishes as lobster bisque. Friendly servers are trained in fine dining. Home-baked bread adds to the salad and meal. Don't miss the weekly changing dessert menu. Casual dress; cocktails. **Parking:** on-site. **Cards:** DS, MC, VI. **Country Inn**

American

THE PALMS

▼▼ ▼▼
American

Lunch: $6-$12   **Dinner:** $6-$18   **Phone:** 540/463-7911
Location: Between Washington and Henry sts; center of downtown. 101 W Nelson 24450. **Hours:** 11 am-10 pm. Closed: 12/25. **Features:** A touch of the Caribbean in Lexington, VA. The Palms has a wide ranging menu and friendly service. Casual dress; cocktails. **Parking:** street. **Cards:** AX, CB, DC, DS, JC, MC, VI.

REDWOOD FAMILY RESTAURANT

▼▼ ▼▼
American

Lunch: $4-$9   **Dinner:** $6-$12   **Phone:** 540/463-2168
Location: I-64, exit 55, just s on US 11. 898 N Lee Hwy 24450. **Hours:** 7 am-10 pm. Closed: 12/25. **Features:** Popular with locals for its home-style country cooking, the restaurant serves affordable family favorites, such as Virginia ham, fried chicken and rib-eye steak. Try tasty broiled catfish with mixed vegetables or one of the many daily specials. Casual dress. **Parking:** on-site.

SHERIDAN LIVERY INN RESTAURANT

▼▼ ▼▼
American

Lunch: $9-$12   **Dinner:** $18-$29   **Phone:** 540/464-1887
Location: Between Washington and Henry sts; center of downtown. 35 N Main St 24450. **Hours:** 11 am-8 pm, Fri & Sat-9:30 pm. Closed: 1/1, 12/25. **Features:** Nestled in the heart of downtown Lexington, the Sheridan Livery Inn Restaurant is a converted turn of the century stagecoach service stable with an extensive menu. Casual dress; cocktails. **Parking:** street. **Cards:** AX, CB, MC, VI.

THE SOUTHERN INN RESTAURANT

▼▼ ▼▼
American

Lunch: $5-$16   **Dinner:** $7-$22   **Phone:** 540/463-3612
Location: Between Washington and Henry sts; center. 37 S Main St 24450. **Hours:** 11:30 am-10 pm, Sun-9 pm. **Features:** This restaurant offers southern hospitality and great food in a wonderfully cozy atmosphere. The people will make you feel welcome and ensure that you will want to come back again and again. Casual dress; cocktails. **Parking:** on-site. **Cards:** AX, DS, MC, VI.

THE WILLSON-WALKER HOUSE RESTAURANT

▼▼ ▼▼ ▼▼
American

Lunch: $5-$10   **Dinner:** $11-$23   **Phone:** 540/463-3020
Location: In downtown historic district. 30 N Main St 24450. **Hours:** 11:30 am-2:30 & 5:30-9 pm; Sat from 5:30 pm 1/1-3/31. Closed: Sun & Mon. **Reservations:** suggested. **Features:** Crisp linens and candlelight contribute to the elegant but relaxed dining atmosphere at the 1820 Greek Revival town home. Imaginative dishes make good use of regional products, including Virginia wine and cider. Patio seating is an option from May through October. The welcoming veranda adds to the restaurant's charm. Casual dress; cocktails. **Parking:** street. **Cards:** AX, DS, MC, VI. **Historic**

LIGHTFOOT —*See Williamsburg, Jamestown & Yorktown p. 947.*

LORTON —*See District Of Columbia p. 539.*

LOW MOOR pop. 367

——— **WHERE TO DINE** ———

THE CAT AND OWL

▼▼ ▼▼
Steak & Seafood

Dinner: $13-$21   **Phone:** 540/862-5808
Location: I-64, exit 21, just s, then just w, follow signs. 110 Karnes Rd 24457. **Hours:** 5 pm-9 pm. Closed major holidays; also Sun. **Reservations:** suggested. **Features:** Choice rib eye, filet mignon and fresh seafood are served in the family-owned, rich-looking, Victorian-style restaurant. The rural location is worth the drive. The selection of Virginia wines is good. Casual dress; cocktails. **Parking:** on-site. **Cards:** AX, DS, MC, VI.

LURAY pop. 4,871

——— **WHERE TO STAY** ———

BEST VALUE THE CARDINAL INN   *Book at aaa.com*   **Phone:** (540)743-5010

(AAA) SAVE
▼▼
Motel

10/1-11/1	1P: $59-$80	2P: $59-$80	XP: $10
3/1-9/30	1P: $49-$70	2P: $49-$70	XP: $10
11/2-2/28	1P: $39-$59	2P: $39-$59	XP: $10

Location: 1 mi e on US 211 business route. 1005 E Main St 22835. Fax: 540/743-3407. **Facility:** 27 one-bedroom standard units, some with whirlpools. 1 story, exterior corridors. **Bath:** combo or shower only. **Parking:** on-site. **Terms:** weekly rates available, package plans. **Cards:** AX, DC, DS, MC, VI. **Special Amenities:** free continental breakfast and early check-in/late check-out.

SOME UNITS

BEST WESTERN INTOWN OF LURAY   *Book at aaa.com*   **Phone:** (540)743-6511

(AAA) SAVE
▼▼ ▼▼
Small-scale Hotel

5/6-10/29	1P: $75-$110	2P: $80-$110	XP: $10	F12
10/30-11/26	1P: $65-$80	2P: $70-$80	XP: $10	F12
3/1-5/5	1P: $59-$80	2P: $65-$80	XP: $10	F12
11/27-2/28	1P: $59-$65	2P: $65	XP: $10	F12

Location: 0.3 mi w on US 211 business route. 410 W Main St 22835. Fax: 540/743-2917. **Facility:** 40 one-bedroom standard units. 2 stories (no elevator), exterior corridors. **Parking:** on-site. **Terms:** cancellation fee imposed, pets ($20 extra charge). **Amenities:** irons, hair dryers. **Dining:** 6 am-2 & 5-9 pm, wine/beer only. **Pool(s):** outdoor. **Leisure Activities:** playground, horseshoes. **Business Services:** meeting rooms. **Cards:** AX, CB, DC, DS, JC, MC, VI. **Special Amenities:** free local telephone calls and early check-in/late check-out.

SOME UNITS

THE CABINS AT BROOKSIDE

Phone: (540)743-5698

All Year 1P: $85-$195 2P: $85-$195 XP: $10

Cabin

Location: On US 211 Bypass, 4.8 mi e. Located in a quiet rural area. 2978 US Hwy 211 E 22835. Fax: 540/743-1326. **Facility:** A mountain stream runs next to this property, which offers varied log cabins, some with front porches. 9 cabins, some with whirlpools. 1 story, exterior corridors. **Bath:** combo or shower only. **Parking:** on-site. **Terms:** check-in 4 pm, 5 day cancellation notice-fee imposed, package plans. **Amenities:** CD players. **Dining:** Brookside Restaurant, see separate listing. **Leisure Activities:** fishing. **Guest Services:** gift shop. **Business Services:** meeting rooms. **Cards:** AX, CB, DC, DS, MC, VI.

SOME UNITS

DAYS INN-LURAY   *Book at aaa.com*

Phone: (540)743-4521

10/1-11/5	1P: $69-$109	2P: $69-$109	XP: $10	F17
4/1-9/30	1P: $59-$99	2P: $59-$99	XP: $10	F17
3/1-3/31 & 11/6-2/28	1P: $49-$99	2P: $49-$99	XP: $10	F17

Small-scale Hotel

Location: US 211 Bypass, 1.7 mi e of jct US 340. 138 Whispering Hill Rd 22835. Fax: 540/743-6863. **Facility:** 101 one-bedroom standard units, some with whirlpools. 2 stories (no elevator), exterior corridors. **Parking:** on-site. **Terms:** cancellation fee imposed, small pets only ($10 extra charge). **Amenities:** voice mail, hair dryers. **Pool(s):** outdoor, wading. **Leisure Activities:** horseshoes. **Fee:** miniature golf. **Guest Services:** coin laundry. **Business Services:** meeting rooms. **Cards:** AX, CB, DC, DS, MC, VI.

SOME UNITS
FEE

LURAY CAVERNS MOTEL EAST

Phone: (540)743-4531

3/1-11/30 [CP]	1P: $68-$90	2P: $68-$90	XP: $8	F15
12/1-2/28 [CP]	1P: $52-$84	2P: $52-$84	XP: $8	F15

Motel

Location: 1 mi w on US 211 business route. Located across from Luray Caverns. 831 W Main St 22835 (PO Box 748). **Facility:** 44 units. 39 one- and 5 two-bedroom standard units, some with efficiencies (no utensils). 1-2 stories (no elevator), exterior corridors. **Bath:** combo or shower only. **Parking:** on-site. **Terms:** package plans. **Amenities:** hair dryers. **Pool(s):** small outdoor, wading. **Cards:** AX, DS, MC, VI. **Special Amenities:** free continental breakfast and free local telephone calls.

SOME UNITS

LURAY CAVERNS MOTEL WEST

Phone: (540)743-4536

3/21-11/7 [CP] 1P: $68-$90 2P: $68-$90 XP: $8 F15

Motel

Location: 1.5 mi w on US 211 Bypass; w of jct US 211 business route. 1001 US Hwy 211 W Bypass 22835 (PO Box 748). **Facility:** 19 one-bedroom standard units, some with efficiencies (no utensils). 1 story, exterior corridors. **Bath:** combo or shower only. **Parking:** on-site. **Terms:** open 3/21-11/7, package plans. **Amenities:** hair dryers. **Pool(s):** small outdoor, wading. **Cards:** AX, DS, MC, VI. **Special Amenities:** free continental breakfast and free local telephone calls.

SOME UNITS

THE MAYNEVIEW BED & BREAKFAST

Phone: (540)743-7921

All Year [BP] 2P: $110-$150 XP: $25 D12

Historic Bed
& Breakfast

Location: 0.3 mi w on US 211 business route, just n on Lee St, then just w. 439 Mechanic St 22835. Fax: 540/743-7921. **Facility:** This 1865 Victorian home featuring whirlpool and grape arbor is on a hilltop affording good views of the town and the Blue Ridge Mountains. Designated smoking area. 5 one-bedroom standard units. 1-2 stories (no elevator), interior corridors. **Bath:** combo or shower only. **Parking:** on-site. **Terms:** 5 day cancellation notice-fee imposed, package plans, pets ($20 fee, owner's pets on premises). **Amenities:** video library. *Some:* DVD players. **Leisure Activities:** whirlpool. **Guest Services:** TV in common area. **Cards:** DC, MC, VI.

SOME UNITS
FEE

VILLA BELLA VISTA INN

Phone: (540)843-4800

All Year [BP] 1P: $275-$1600 2P: $275-$1600 XP: $75

Bed & Breakfast

Location: US 211 Bypass, 1 mi e from Luray Caverns. 50 Cottage Dr 22835. Fax: 540/843-4802. **Facility:** This newer property offers spacious rooms and pampering amenities such as whirlpools and fireplaces. 6 one-bedroom standard units, some with whirlpools. 2 stories (no elevator), interior/exterior corridors. **Bath:** combo or shower only. **Parking:** on-site. **Terms:** age restrictions may apply, package plans. **Amenities:** CD players, high-speed Internet, hair dryers. **Guest Services:** valet laundry. **Business Services:** meeting rooms. **Cards:** DS, MC, VI.

SOME UNITS

WOODRUFF INNS

Phone: (540)743-1494

9/2-2/28 [BP]	1P: $139-$269	2P: $169-$299	XP: $25	
3/1-9/1 [BP]	1P: $99-$229	2P: $129-$259	XP: $25	

Historic Bed
& Breakfast

Location: 0.3 mi w on US 211 business route. 138 E Main St 22835 (330 Mechanic St). Fax: 540/743-1722. **Facility:** Chandeliers and collectibles decorate these three stately Victorian homes; elegant meals are served in the property's dining room. Designated smoking area. 9 one-bedroom standard units, some with whirlpools. 2-3 stories (no elevator), interior corridors. **Parking:** on-site. **Terms:** 2 night minimum stay - seasonal and/or weekends, age restrictions may apply, 7 day cancellation notice, weekly rates available, package plans. **Amenities:** CD players, hair dryers. *Some:* DVD players, irons. **Dining:** The Restaurant at The Victorian Inn, see separate listing. **Leisure Activities:** whirlpools, 4 garden hot tubs. **Fee:** massage. **Guest Services:** complimentary evening beverages. **Business Services:** meeting rooms. **Cards:** AX, DS, MC, VI. **Special Amenities:** free full breakfast and free local telephone calls.

SOME UNITS

—— WHERE TO DINE ——

ALEXANDER'S

American

Lunch: $4-$13 **Dinner:** $6-$19 **Phone:** 540/743-6511

Location: 0.3 mi w on US 211 business route. 410 W Main St 22835. **Hours:** 6 am-2 & 5-9 pm. Closed: 12/25. **Features:** Alexander's is family oriented eatery with a wide variety on the menu and friendly wait staff. Don't miss the bread pudding. Casual dress. **Parking:** on-site. **Cards:** AX, CB, DC, DS, JC, MC, VI.

BROOKSIDE RESTAURANT **Lunch:** $5-$10 **Dinner:** $7-$17 **Phone:** 540/743-5698

AAA
◆◆ ◆◆
American

Location: On US 211 Bypass, 4.8 mi e; in The Cabins at Brookside. 2978 US Hwy 211 E 22835. **Hours:** Open 3/1-12/10 & 1/18-2/28; 7 am-8:30 pm. **Features:** Diners in the mood for homemade soup or tasty, well-prepared salmon cakes won't be disappointed. The basic eatery prepares a good variety of standard favorites and spreads out a tempting salad bar. Homespun decor and wonderful service are other strengths. Don't miss seeing the brook running beside the restaurant. Casual dress; beer & wine only. **Parking:** on-site. **Cards:** AX, CB, DC, DS, MC, VI.

⊠

DAN'S STEAK HOUSE **Dinner:** $10-$22 **Phone:** 540/743-6285

◆◆ ◆◆
American

Location: I-81, exit 264, 9 mi e. 8512 US 211 W 22835. **Hours:** 5 pm-9 pm, Fri & Sat 4 pm-9:30 pm, Sun noon-9 pm. Closed: 11/24, 12/25. **Features:** A Shenandoah Valley tradition, the steakhouse presents a menu that centers on fine-cut steaks. In addition to a friendly atmosphere, the dining room offers great views of the mountains. Casual dress; cocktails. **Parking:** on-site. **Cards:** DS, MC, VI.

🍴 ⊠

MOM'S COUNTRY KITCHEN **Lunch:** $5-$10 **Dinner:** $6-$15 **Phone:** 540/743-1304

◆◆ ◆◆
American

Location: 0.9 mi w on US 211 business route. 42 E Main St 22835. **Hours:** 7 am-7 pm. Closed: 1/1, 12/25; also Sun. **Features:** Make yourself at home at Mom's Country Kitchen. Good food and happy times abound. Enjoy the wide variety menu and don't miss the hot fudge shortcake. Casual dress. **Parking:** on-site. **Cards:** MC, VI.

⊠

THE PARKHURST RESTAURANT ON RAINBOW HILL **Lunch:** $4-$10 **Dinner:** $6-$14 **Phone:** 540/743-6009

◆◆
American

Location: US 211, 1.7 mi w of Luray Caverns. 2547 US 211 W 22835. **Hours:** 11:30 am-9 pm, Fri & Sat-10 pm. **Features:** The well-established, casual restaurant prepares a variety of soups, salads and entrees, including vegetarian dishes. The list of wines and beers is extensive. Casual dress; beer & wine only. **Parking:** on-site. **Cards:** AX, CB, DC, DS, MC, VI.

🍴 ⊠

THE RESTAURANT AT THE VICTORIAN INN **Lunch:** $12-$30 **Dinner:** $17-$30 **Phone:** 540/743-1494

◆◆◆◆
American

Location: 0.3 mi w on US 211 business route; in Woodruff Inns. 138 E Main St 22835. **Hours:** noon-9 pm. Closed: 12/25. **Features:** In a Victorian inn, the fine-dining establishment presents an excellent wine list to accompany classic American dishes. Background music enhances the relaxed ambience. Service is friendly. Casual dress; cocktails. **Parking:** on-site. **Cards:** AX, DC, DS, MC, VI.

🍴 ⊠

LYNCHBURG pop. 65,269

─── **WHERE TO STAY** ───

BEST WESTERN LYNCHBURG *Book at aaa.com* **Phone:** (434)237-2986

AAA SAVE
◆◆ ◆◆
Motel

5/1-10/31 [ECP]	1P: $74-$150	2P: $74-$150	XP: $5	F17
3/1-4/30 [ECP]	1P: $74-$99	2P: $74-$99	XP: $5	F17
11/1-2/28 [ECP]	1P: $69-$84	2P: $69-$84	XP: $5	F17

Location: Jct US 29 and 460. 2815 Candlers Mountain Rd 24502. Fax: 434/237-3171. **Facility:** 87 one-bedroom standard units. 2 stories (no elevator), exterior corridors. **Parking:** on-site. **Terms:** pets ($25 fee, in designated units). **Amenities:** irons, hair dryers. **Pool(s):** outdoor. **Guest Services:** valet laundry. **Business Services:** meeting rooms. **Cards:** AX, CB, DC, DS, MC, VI. **Special Amenities:** free local telephone calls and free newspaper.

SOME UNITS

[S/D] [🐕] [🍴] [🔲] [🏊] [📷] [DATA PORT] [💻] / [⊠] [📶] [📷] /
FEE

COMFORT INN *Book at aaa.com* **Phone:** (434)847-9041

AAA SAVE
◆◆◆◆
Small-scale Hotel

4/1-10/31 [ECP]	1P: $70	2P: $80	XP: $8	F18
11/1-2/28 [ECP]	1P: $68	2P: $78	XP: $8	F18
3/1-3/31 [ECP]	1P: $67	2P: $77	XP: $8	F18

Location: US 29, exit 7, 2.5 mi s. 3125 Albert Lankford Dr 24501. Fax: 434/847-8513. **Facility:** 120 one-bedroom standard units, some with whirlpools. 5 stories, interior corridors. **Parking:** on-site. **Terms:** package plans, small pets only ($15 extra charge). **Amenities:** voice mail, irons, hair dryers. **Pool(s):** outdoor. **Leisure Activities:** exercise room. **Guest Services:** valet and coin laundry. **Business Services:** meeting rooms, business center. **Cards:** AX, CB, DC, DS, JC, MC, VI. **Special Amenities:** free expanded continental breakfast.

SOME UNITS

[S/D] [🐕] [🍴] [🏊] [📷] [DATA PORT] [💻] / [⊠] [📶] [📷] /
FEE

COURTYARD BY MARRIOTT *Book at aaa.com* **Phone:** (434)846-7900

◆◆◆◆
Small-scale Hotel

All Year 1P: $92-$96

Location: US 29, exit US 501, just e of SR 29, off Candlers Mountain Rd. Located opposite River Ridge Mall. 4640 Murray Pl 24502. Fax: 434/846-7109. **Facility:** 90 units. 87 one-bedroom standard units. 3 one-bedroom suites. 3 stories, interior corridors. **Bath:** combo or shower only. **Parking:** on-site. **Amenities:** high-speed Internet, dual phone lines, voice mail, irons, hair dryers. **Pool(s):** heated indoor. **Leisure Activities:** whirlpool, exercise room. **Guest Services:** valet and coin laundry. **Business Services:** meeting rooms, fax. **Cards:** AX, CB, DC, DS, MC, VI.

SOME UNITS

[ASK] [🍴] [🔲] [🛎] [🏊] [📷] [DATA PORT] [💻] / [⊠] [📶] [📷] /

DAYS INN *Book at aaa.com* **Phone:** (434)847-8655

◆◆◆◆
Small-scale Hotel

All Year [BP] 1P: $69-$89 2P: $69-$89 XP: $8 F17

Location: US 29, exit US 501, just e. Located opposite River Ridge Mall. 3320 Candlers Mountain Rd 24502. Fax: 434/846-3297. **Facility:** 131 one-bedroom standard units. 5 stories, interior corridors. **Parking:** on-site. **Terms:** package plans, small pets only ($10 fee, $40 deposit). **Amenities:** voice mail, hair dryers. *Some:* safes, irons. **Pool(s):** outdoor. **Leisure Activities:** playground, exercise room. **Guest Services:** valet and coin laundry, area transportation. **Business Services:** fax. **Cards:** AX, CB, DC, DS, JC, MC, VI.

SOME UNITS

[ASK] [S/D] [🔲] [🐕] [🍴] [🏊] [📷] [DATA PORT] [💻] / [⊠] [VCR] [📶] [📷] /
FEE   FEE FEE

ECONO LODGE   *Book at aaa.com*

AAA (SAVE) ◇ Motel

Phone: (434)847-1045

5/1-10/31 [CP]	1P: $70-$80	2P: $80-$90	XP: $10	F14
3/1-4/30 [CP]	1P: $60-$65	2P: $65-$70	XP: $10	F14
11/1-2/28 [CP]	1P: $55-$60	2P: $60-$65	XP: $10	F14

Location: US 29, exit 4 southbound; exit 6 northbound, just w. 2400 Stadium Rd 24501. Fax: 434/846-0086. **Facility:** 47 one-bedroom standard units, some with whirlpools. 2 stories (no elevator), exterior corridors. **Parking:** on-site. **Terms:** 3 day cancellation notice, package plans, small pets only ($50 deposit). **Amenities:** hair dryers. *Some:* irons. **Cards:** AX, DC, DS, MC, VI. **Special Amenities:** free continental breakfast and free local telephone calls.

SOME UNITS

(SD) 🛏 📶 FEE 📠 📥 DATA PORT 🖥 / ⊠ 📺 /

FEDERAL CREST INN B&B

AAA (SAVE) ◇◇◇ Historic Bed & Breakfast

Phone: (434)845-6155

| All Year [BP] | 1P: $135-$175 | 2P: $135-$175 | XP: $20 |

Location: US 29, exit 1A (Main St), just w to 11th St, then 0.5 mi s. 1101 Federal St 24504. Fax: 434/845-1445. **Facility:** This Georgian Revival mansion, surrounded by mature magnolia trees, features intricate woodwork and a central staircase beneath a leaded-glass window. Smoke free premises. 4 units. 1 one- and 1 two-bedroom standard units. 2 one-bedroom suites, some with whirlpools. 2 stories (no elevator), interior corridors. *Bath:* combo or shower only. **Parking:** on-site. **Terms:** 2 night minimum stay - seasonal, age restrictions may apply, 10 day cancellation notice-fee imposed, weekly rates available. **Amenities:** video library, hair dryers. **Leisure Activities:** limited exercise equipment. **Business Services:** meeting rooms, fax. **Cards:** AX, DS, MC, VI.

SOME UNITS

(SD) ⊠ VCR DATA PORT / 📠 📥 🖥 /

HAMPTON INN   *Book at aaa.com*

◇◇◇ Small-scale Hotel

Phone: (434)237-2704

| All Year [CP] | 1P: $81-$87 | 2P: $81-$87 |

Location: US 460, exit Candlers Mountain Rd, 0.3 mi w; US 29, exit Candlers Mountain Rd. 5604 Seminole Ave 24502. Fax: 434/239-9183. **Facility:** 65 one-bedroom standard units. 2 stories (no elevator), interior/exterior corridors. *Bath:* combo or shower only. **Parking:** on-site. **Terms:** 3 day cancellation notice. **Amenities:** high-speed Internet, voice mail, irons, hair dryers. **Pool(s):** outdoor. **Guest Services:** valet laundry. **Business Services:** PC, fax. **Cards:** AX, CB, DC, DS, MC, VI.

SOME UNITS

(ASK) (SD) 🍴 &M ⚷ 🍷 🏊 🏌 📷 DATA PORT 🖥 / ⊠ 📠 📥 /

HOLIDAY INN EXPRESS   *Book at aaa.com*

◇◇◇ Small-scale Hotel

Phone: 434/237-7771

| All Year [CP] | 1P: $89 | 2P: $89 |

Location: US 460, exit Candlers Mountain Rd, 0.3 mi w; US 29, exit Candlers Mountain Rd. 5600 Seminole Ave 24502. Fax: 434/239-0659. **Facility:** 102 one-bedroom standard units, some with whirlpools. 3 stories, interior corridors. **Parking:** on-site. **Terms:** 3 day cancellation notice. **Amenities:** high-speed Internet, dual phone lines, voice mail, irons, hair dryers. **Pool(s):** outdoor. **Guest Services:** valet laundry. **Business Services:** meeting rooms, PC, fax. **Cards:** AX, CB, DC, DS, MC, VI.

SOME UNITS

🍴 🏊 🏌 📷 DATA PORT 🖥 / ⊠ 📠 📥 /

HOLIDAY INN SELECT   *Book at aaa.com*

AAA (SAVE) ◇◇◇ Small-scale Hotel

Phone: (434)528-2500

| All Year | 1P: $89 | 2P: $89 | XP: $10 | F18 |

Location: US 29 Expwy, exit 1 (Main St), just w; downtown. 601 Main St 24504. Fax: 434/528-0062. **Facility:** 241 one-bedroom standard units, some with whirlpools. 8 stories, interior corridors. *Bath:* combo or shower only. **Parking:** on-site. **Terms:** cancellation fee imposed, pets ($25 fee). **Amenities:** video games, high-speed Internet, dual phone lines, voice mail, irons, hair dryers. **Dining:** 6:30 am-10:30 pm, cocktails. **Pool(s):** outdoor. **Leisure Activities:** exercise room. **Guest Services:** valet laundry, area transportation-colleges & downtown. **Business Services:** conference facilities, business center. **Cards:** AX, CB, DC, DS, JC, MC, VI. **Special Amenities:** free local telephone calls and free newspaper. *(See color ad below)*

SOME UNITS

(SD) 🔜 🛏 🍴 🍷 &M 🏊 🏌 🖥 / ⊠ FEE 📠 📥 FEE /

LYNCHBURG SUPER 8 MOTEL   *Book at aaa.com*

◇◇ Small-scale Hotel

Phone: (434)846-1668

| All Year [ECP] | 1P: $67-$72 | 2P: $75-$81 | XP: $6 | F12 |

Location: US 29, exit 8B, just e. 3736 Candlers Mountain Rd 24502. Fax: 434/846-1668. **Facility:** 59 one-bedroom standard units, some with whirlpools. 3 stories, interior corridors. *Bath:* combo or shower only. **Parking:** on-site. **Leisure Activities:** exercise room. **Guest Services:** coin laundry. **Business Services:** fax. **Cards:** AX, DC, DS, MC, VI.

SOME UNITS

(ASK) (SD) &M 🏌 📷 DATA PORT / ⊠ 📠 FEE /

RADISSON HOTEL LYNCHBURG *Book at aaa.com*

Phone: 434/237-6333

All Year   1P: $89-$169   2P: $89-$169   XP: $10   F18
Location: US 29 Expwy, exit 8A, just w. 2900 Candlers Mountain Rd 24502. Fax: 434/237-4277. **Facility:** 167 units. 163 one-bedroom standard units. 2 one- and 2 two-bedroom suites. 5 stories, interior corridors. **Parking:** on-site. **Amenities:** high-speed Internet, dual phone lines, voice mail, irons, hair dryers. **Pool(s):** heated indoor. **Leisure Activities:** saunas, whirlpool, exercise room. **Guest Services:** gift shop, valet laundry, area transportation. **Business Services:** conference facilities, business center. **Cards:** AX, CB, DC, DS, JC, MC, VI.

Small-scale Hotel

(See color ad p 932)

SOME UNITS

THE RESIDENCE BED & BREAKFAST

Phone: 434/845-6565

All Year [BP]   1P: $110-$125   2P: $115-$180
Location: US 29, 2 mi w on Main St (becomes Rivermont Ave). Located in the Rivermont Historic District. 2460 Rivermont Ave 24503. Fax: 434/845-6565. **Facility:** This grand Spanish Colonial home is on Rivermont Avenue, which is within walking distance of Randolph-Macon College. Smoke free premises. 4 units. 3 one- and 1 two-bedroom standard units. 2 stories (no elevator), interior corridors. *Bath:* some shared or private. **Parking:** on-site. **Terms:** 2 night minimum stay - seasonal, 10 day cancellation notice-fee imposed, weekly rates available, package plans. **Amenities:** video library. *Some:* hair dryers. **Leisure Activities:** bicycles. **Business Services:** fax. **Cards:** MC, VI.

Historic Bed & Breakfast

SOME UNITS

SLEEP INN LYNCHBURG *Book at aaa.com*

Phone: (434)846-6900

All Year [ECP]   1P: $64-$175   2P: $64-$175   XP: $10   F18
Location: US 29, exit 8B. 3620 Candlers Mountain Rd 24502. Fax: 434/846-6989. **Facility:** 74 one-bedroom standard units. 4 stories, interior corridors. *Bath:* combo or shower only. **Parking:** on-site. **Amenities:** dual phone lines, voice mail, irons, hair dryers. **Leisure Activities:** exercise room. **Guest Services:** valet and coin laundry. **Business Services:** meeting rooms, fax. **Cards:** AX, CB, DC, DS, MC, VI.

Small-scale Hotel

SOME UNITS

WINGATE INN LYNCHBURG *Book at aaa.com*

Phone: (434)845-1700

All Year [ECP]   1P: $89-$179   2P: $97-$189   XP: $10   F17
Location: Just se of US 460. 3777 Candlers Mountain Rd 24502. Fax: 434/845-1800. **Facility:** 131 one-bedroom standard units, some with whirlpools. 5 stories, interior corridors. *Bath:* combo or shower only. **Parking:** on-site. **Terms:** package plans. **Amenities:** video games, high-speed Internet, dual phone lines, voice mail, safes, irons, hair dryers. **Pool(s):** heated indoor. **Leisure Activities:** whirlpool, exercise room. **Guest Services:** valet laundry, area transportation. **Business Services:** meeting rooms, business center. **Cards:** AX, CB, DC, DS, JC, MC, VI.

Small-scale Hotel

SOME UNITS

FEE FEE

─────── **WHERE TO DINE** ───────

THE BISTRO AT 12TH & MAIN

Lunch: $5-$10   **Dinner:** $12-$20   **Phone:** 434/528-0801
Location: Just w of US 29 Expwy. 1208 Main St 24504. **Hours:** 11 am-9 pm, Fri & Sat 8 am-9 pm. Closed major holidays; also Sun. **Reservations:** accepted. **Features:** The owners of the renovated downtown storefront strive to serve "comfort food with a flair." Sandwiches, pizza, steaks, and crab cakes all have spots on the menu. A rear patio opens in warmer months. Casual dress; beer & wine only. **Parking:** street. **Cards:** AX, MC, VI.

American

BULL BRANCH

Dinner: $11-$16   **Phone:** 434/847-8477
Location: Just ne of jct Main St. 109 11th St 24505. **Hours:** 6 pm-9:30 pm, Fri & Sat-10:30 pm. Closed: 1/1, 11/24, 12/25; also Sun & Mon. **Reservations:** accepted. **Features:** In a half basement dimly lit with candles, the dining room makes guests feel as though they've stepped into a 1930s speakeasy, where Humphrey Bogart himself might emerge to take their order. The distinctive menu, printed on translucent rice paper, lists dishes with a touch of an Eastern influence. Food is accented with tangy curries, chutneys and spices. Among more traditional offerings are smashed potatoes and creamed spinach. Casual dress; cocktails. **Parking:** street. **Cards:** AX, MC, VI.

American

BULL'S STEAKHOUSE

Lunch: $5-$8   **Dinner:** $10-$15   **Phone:** 434/385-7581
Location: US 501 N, exit Graves Mill Rd, 2 mi w; in Graves Mill Shopping Center. 1887 Graves Mill Rd 24551. **Hours:** 11 am-10 pm, Fri-10:30 pm, Sat 4:30 pm-10 pm. Closed major holidays; also Sun. **Features:** Steak, prime rib, fajitas and Mexican specialties are menu mainstays at the steakhouse, a warm spot that welcomes guests to get comfortable. Dishes are hearty and satisfying. Casual dress; cocktails. **Parking:** on-site. **Cards:** AX, DC, DS, MC, VI.

Steak House

CHARLEY'S

Lunch: $6-$15   **Dinner:** $6-$15   **Phone:** 434/237-5988
Location: US 29, exit 11. 707 Graves Mill Rd 24502. **Hours:** 11 am-10 pm, Fri & Sat-midnight. Closed: 11/24, 12/25. **Features:** Charley's fits into the traditional mold of American bar and grill so expect to find a friendly casual spot and the standard menu of favorites such as burgers, ribs, fajitas and more. Casual dress; cocktails. **Parking:** on-site. **Cards:** AX, DS, MC, VI.

American

CROWN STERLING

Dinner: $13-$27   **Phone:** 434/239-7744
Location: US 501 N, exit 10A, just e. 6120 Fort Ave 24502. **Hours:** 5:30 pm-9:30 pm, Sat from 5 pm. Closed major holidays; also Sun. **Reservations:** accepted. **Features:** Locally owned and operated for more than 30 years, the restaurant provides ample parking and a cozy interior of fireplaces and wood-paneled walls. Diners get an open view of the cooking area. The aroma of charcoal-grilled steaks wafts through the dining area. Other entrees include preparations of lobster, shrimp, tuna and chicken. Formally attired servers are attentive. Dressy casual; cocktails. **Parking:** on-site. **Cards:** AX, CB, DC, DS, MC, VI.

Steak House

THE DROWSY POET COFFEEHOUSE   Lunch: $5-$8   Dinner: $5-$8   Phone: 434/846-6604
Coffee/Espresso
Location: US 29, exit 8B, just e; in Candlers Station. 3700 Candlers Mountain Rd 24502. **Hours:** 7 am-11 pm, Fri-midnight, Sat 9 am-midnight. Closed: 11/24, 12/25; also Sun. **Features:** Patrons can sip espresso, Italian soda or even a milkshake inside the cozy coffee shop or at iron tables on the patio. Among food offerings are distinctive sandwiches, salads, daily soups and even spicy bean dip. Casual dress. **Parking:** on-site.
Cards: AX, DS, MC, VI.

THE FARM BASKET   Lunch: $4-$7   Phone: 434/528-1107
Deli/Subs
Sandwiches
Location: Jct US 29 business route, 2 mi w. 2008 Langhorne Rd 24501. **Hours:** 10 am-3 pm. Closed major holidays; also Sun. **Features:** This place's box lunches grace many a local's picnic or office desk. Delicious sandwiches, Southern specialties and gourmet desserts are the draw. Among favorites are country ham biscuits, apple dapple cake and traditional side salads, such as tomato aspic and marinated coleslaw. Casual dress. **Parking:** on-site. **Cards:** AX, DC, DS, MC, VI.

GAETANO'S ITALIAN CAFE   Lunch: $4-$9   Dinner: $5-$11   Phone: 434/237-5500
Italian
Location: Across from Lynchburg Regional Airport. 19191 Wards Rd 24502. **Hours:** 11 am-9 pm, Fri & Sat-10 pm, Sun noon-4 pm. Closed: 12/25. **Features:** The humble spot offers a simple setting for freshly prepared Italian meals. Favorites include homemade sausage, pizza, calzones and, for dinner, a selection of pastas. Casual dress. **Parking:** on-site. **Cards:** AX, CB, DC, DS, MC, VI.

ISABELLA'S ITALIAN TRATTORIA   Lunch: $5-$10   Dinner: $9-$20   Phone: 434/385-1660
Northern
Italian
Location: 1 mi n from US 501; in Forest Plaza West Shopping Center. 3225 Old Forest Rd 24501. **Hours:** 11:30 am-2 & 5-9 pm, Fri-10 pm, Sat 5 pm-10 pm. Closed major holidays; also Sun. **Reservations:** suggested. **Features:** Part warm Italian trattoria and part stylish bistro Isabella's brings Northern Italian fare and stone oven cooking to Southwest Virginia with a daily changing menu of rustic pasta, chops, and seafood that utilizes the freshest local produce and imported specialties. Casual dress; cocktails. **Parking:** on-site.
Cards: AX, DS, MC, VI.

JAZZ STREET GRILL   Lunch: $7-$12   Dinner: $12-$17   Phone: 434/385-0100
Regional American
Location: 1 mi n from US 501; in Forest Plaza West Shopping Center. 3225 Old Forest Rd 24501. **Hours:** 11:30 am-10 pm, Fri & Sat-midnight, Sun 11 am-3 pm. Closed major holidays. **Features:** As the name implies, the Jazz Street Grill specializes in New Orleans Creole-style cuisine such as plump crawfish etouffee, shrimp po'boys, blackened dishes, andouille and gumbo. Live entertainment jazzes up the place on Friday and Saturday nights. Casual dress; cocktails. **Parking:** on-site. **Cards:** AX, DS, MC, VI.

LA PLAZA ALEGRE   Lunch: $2-$12   Dinner: $2-$15   Phone: 434/846-0303
Latino
Location: At 12th and Main sts; downtown. 1125 Main St 24504. **Hours:** 11 am-3 & 5-10 pm, Sun 10 am-9 pm. Closed major holidays. **Reservations:** accepted. **Features:** Don't let the diner fool you. Inside, authentic Mexican, Spanish and Latin fare awaits. You can't go wrong with the hearty tortilla soup, the fragrant paellas or the popular fajitas. Freshness abounds, and the black beans and rice are pure comfort. Lynchburg's Main St. never had it so good. Casual dress; cocktails. **Parking:** on-site. **Cards:** AX, DS, MC, VI.

MACADO'S   Lunch: $5-$10   Dinner: $5-$10   Phone: 434/845-6464
Deli/Subs
Sandwiches
Location: US 29, exit 8B, just e. 3744 Candlers Mountain Rd 24502. **Hours:** 8 am-midnight. Closed: 11/24, 12/25. **Features:** The lively student hangout is well-loved for its lengthy list of imaginative overstuffed sandwiches and wraps. Macaroni and cheese, chili and oversized ice cream desserts also are popular. Casual dress; cocktails. **Parking:** on-site. **Cards:** AX, MC, VI.

MAGNOLIA FOODS   Lunch: $4-$8   Dinner: $4-$8   Phone: 434/528-5442
Gourmet Grocery
Location: Adjacent to Randolph Macon Women's College. 2476 Rivermont Ave 24503. **Hours:** 9 am-7 pm, Sat 11 am-5 pm. Closed: Sun. **Features:** A good spot for picking up picnic fixings, the gourmet market and bakery prepares specialty sandwiches, salads and limited entrees. Casual dress; beer & wine only. **Parking:** on-site. **Cards:** AX, MC, VI.

MAIN ST EATERY & CATERING   Lunch: $5-$8   Dinner: $7-$21   Phone: 434/847-2526
Continental
Location: US 29, exit Main St; downtown; center. 907 Main St 24504. **Hours:** 11 am-9 pm, Fri-10 pm, Sat 5 pm-10 pm. Closed major holidays; also Sun. **Features:** A lively, bustling atmosphere fills the restored historic building. The chef/owner's Swiss lineage is reflected in the interesting, eclectic menu. Among dishes are German rahmschnitzel with spaetzle, almond-crusted scallops and pork loin with chipotle sauce. Casual dress; cocktails. **Parking:** street. **Cards:** AX, DC, DS, MC, VI.

MERIWETHER'S MARKET RESTAURANT   Lunch: $6-$9   Dinner: $11-$21   Phone: 434/384-3311
American
Location: US 29, exit Main St, 5.7 mi n and w on Main St, Rivermont and Boonsboro Rd; in Boonsboro Shopping Center. 4925 Boonsboro Rd 24503. **Hours:** 11:30 am-2:30 & 5:30-10 pm, Fri & Sat-11 pm. Closed major holidays; also Sun. **Reservations:** suggested, weekends. **Features:** The contemporary "city-style" dining area and bar is a showcase for the talents of local artists. A seasonally changing menu appeals to the casual gourmet with a contemporary interpretation of Southern cuisine. Among selections are preparations of fresh seafood, such as shrimp and grits, gourmet pizza and innovative salads. Live jazz drifts in the air on Wednesday evenings. Casual dress; cocktails. **Parking:** on-site. **Cards:** AX, MC, VI.

MILAN INDIAN CUISINE   Lunch: $6-$8   Dinner: $8-$16   Phone: 434/237-7990
Indian
Location: Just n of jct Candlers Mountain Rd; in strip mall. 2124 Wards Rd 24502. **Hours:** 11:30 am-2:30 & 5-10 pm, Fri-10:30 pm, Sat noon-3 & 5-10:30 pm, Sun noon-3 & 5-10 pm. **Features:** Tandoori specialties and bread baked in a clay oven are at the centerpiece of the traditional menu of curried, lamb and vegetarian dishes. The exotic atmosphere features artwork and instrumental music. The weekday buffet draws a large lunch clientele. Casual dress; cocktails. **Parking:** on-site. **Cards:** AX, DC, DS, MC, VI.

MILANO'S ITALIAN RESTAURANT   Lunch: $6-$15   Dinner: $7-$15   Phone: 434/384-3400

♦♦ ♦♦♦
Location: Just e of jct US 501; in Oakwood Square. 5006 Boonsboro Rd 24503. **Hours:** 11:30 am-9:30 pm, Fri-10:30 pm, Sat 4 pm-10:30 pm, Sun noon-9:30 pm. Closed: 1/1, 12/25. **Features:** In a small strip mall on the outskirts of the city, this restaurant sports a semi-formal atmosphere, with a fountain as a centerpiece. Traditional Italian Representative of the fare are specialty pizzas, pasta dishes and some classic entrees, including chicken Marsala and veal selections. Casual dress; cocktails. **Parking:** on-site. **Cards:** AX, MC, VI.

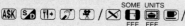

SHADS - UPSTAIRS AT TROTTERS   Lunch: $7-$10   Dinner: $8-$19   Phone: 434/846-3545

♦♦ ♦♦♦
Location: US 29, 2 mi w on Main St/Rivermont Ave; adjacent to Randolph Macon Women's College. 2496 Rivermont Ave 24503. **Hours:** 11:30 am-9:30 pm, Fri & Sat-10 pm, Sun-9 pm. Closed: 12/24, 12/25; also Mon. American **Features:** You'll like the casual, neighborhood setting, including patio seating when weather permits. American specialties range from sandwiches, wraps, and steak to shrimp and grits with a spicy Cajun sauce. Be sure to try the house salad with mandarin oranges. Casual dress; cocktails. **Parking:** street. **Cards:** AX, DS, MC, VI.

SPRING HOUSE DINING ROOM & RECEPTION HALL   Lunch: $12   Dinner: $14-$16   Phone: 434/993-2475

♦♦♦
Location: 10 mi e on US 460. 9789 Richmond Hwy 24504. **Hours:** 4:30 pm-9 pm, Sun noon-8 pm. Closed major holidays; also Mon-Wed. **Features:** Composed entirely of plate-glass windows, the dining room's rear wall affords an expansive view of the lake and woods. The gracious owner embraces Southern-style hospitality, Southern stopping at each table to chat with diners who are treated more like family than customers. Casual dress; cocktails. **Parking:** on-site. **Cards:** MC, VI.

MACHIPONGO

———— WHERE TO DINE ————

———— *The following restaurant has not been evaluated by AAA* ————
but is listed for your information only.

THE GREAT MACHIPONGO CLAM SHACK   Phone: 757/678-5759

[fyi]
Not evaluated. **Location:** On US 13. **Features:** The "Eat & Drive" sign lures many a traveler into the small fish shop for fresh lunch entrees to go. Among choices are steamed clams or shrimp, seafood cake sandwich and stuffed clams.

MADISON pop. 210

———— WHERE TO DINE ————

THE BAVARIAN CHEF   Dinner: $16-$21   Phone: 540/948-6505

♦♦ ♦♦♦
Location: 4 mi s on US 29; 2.2 mi s of jct SR 230. US 29 S 22727. **Hours:** 4:30 pm-9 pm, Sun from 11:30 am. Closed: 1/1, 12/24, 12/25; also Mon & Tues. **Reservations:** suggested. **Features:** You can't go wrong when ordering the Wiener schnitzel, and it arrives at your table fast and hot. The authentic German atmosphere German enhances both the food and the experience. Table spacing can be tight. Costumed staff service is attentive and capable. Casual dress; cocktails. **Parking:** on-site. **Cards:** AX, MC, VI.

BERTINE'S NORTH   Dinner: $12-$25   Phone: 540/948-3463

♦♦ ♦♦♦
Location: US 29 business route; center. 206 S Main St 22727. **Hours:** 6 pm-9 pm. Closed major holidays; also Sun & Mon. **Reservations:** required, Tues-Thurs. **Features:** The menu comprises international and Caribbean Caribbean cuisine, including steak cooked on lava rocks. When the weather is nice, diners often opt for outdoor seating. Casual dress; beer & wine only. **Parking:** street. **Cards:** DC, DS, MC, VI.

MANAKIN —See Richmond p. 863.

MANASSAS —See District Of Columbia p. 539.

MARION pop. 6,349

———— WHERE TO STAY ————

BEST WESTERN-MARION   *Book at aaa.com*   Phone: (276)783-3193

(AAA) (SAVE)
All Year   2P: $50-$75   XP: $5   F16
♦♦ ♦♦
Location: I-81, exit 47, 0.3 mi s on US 11. 1424 N Main St 24354. **Fax:** 276/783-3193. **Facility:** 80 one-bedroom standard units. 2-3 stories (no elevator), exterior corridors. **Parking:** on-site. **Terms:** 30 day cancellation notice-fee imposed, weekly rates available, pets ($7 extra charge). **Amenities:** irons, hair dryers. Small-scale Hotel **Dining:** 4:30 pm-9 pm, cocktails. **Pool(s):** outdoor. **Business Services:** meeting rooms. **Cards:** AX, DC, DS, MC, VI. **Special Amenities:** free continental breakfast and early check-in/late check-out.

SOME UNITS
[icons] FEE   FEE FEE

ECONO LODGE   *Book at aaa.com*   Phone: (276)783-6031

♦♦ ♦♦♦
All Year   2P: $49-$69   XP: $5   F
Location: I-81, exit 47, 0.3 mi s on US 11. 1424 N Main St 24354. **Fax:** 276/782-9990. **Facility:** 40 one-bedroom standard units. 2 stories (no elevator), exterior corridors. **Parking:** on-site. **Terms:** 30 day cancellation Small-scale Hotel notice-fee imposed. **Amenities:** *Some:* irons, hair dryers. **Cards:** AX, DC, DS, MC, VI.

SOME UNITS
[icons] FEE FEE

MARTINSVILLE pop. 15,416

------ WHERE TO STAY ------

BEST LODGE

◈◈ ◈◈

Motel

3/1-10/31	1P: $35-$45	2P: $42-$58	XP: $7 D18
11/1-2/28	1P: $25-$32	2P: $38-$45	XP: $7 D18

Phone: (276)647-3941

Location: Jct US 58, 2.5 mi n on US 220 business route. 1985 Virginia Ave 24112. **Fax:** 276/647-1106. **Facility:** 47 one-bedroom standard units. 2 stories (no elevator), exterior corridors. **Parking:** on-site. **Terms:** 30 day cancellation notice-fee imposed, weekly rates available, package plans, small pets only ($7 extra charge). **Guest Services:** coin laundry. **Cards:** AX, DC, DS, MC, VI.

SOME UNITS

(A$K) (S/D) (🛏) (📶) (🏃) / (✕) (🖥) (📠) (💻) /
FEE

BEST WESTERN MARTINSVILLE INN   *Book at aaa.com*

(AAA) (SAVE)

◈◈◈◈

Small-scale Hotel

All Year [BP]   1P: $79-$109   2P: $89-$119   XP: $10   F18

Phone: (276)632-5611

Location: Jct US 58, 2.3 mi n. US 220 Business Route S 24112 (1755 Virginia Ave). **Fax:** 276/632-1168. **Facility:** 97 one-bedroom standard units. 2 stories (no elevator), exterior corridors. **Parking:** on-site. **Terms:** 3 day cancellation notice. **Amenities:** high-speed Internet, voice mail, irons, hair dryers. **Dining:** 5:30 pm-10 pm, cocktails. **Pool(s):** outdoor, wading. **Guest Services:** coin laundry. **Business Services:** meeting rooms, business center. **Cards:** AX, DC, DS, MC, VI. **Special Amenities:** free full breakfast and free newspaper.

SOME UNITS

(S/D) (🛏) (📶) (🍽) (🍷) (🏊) (♿) (📽) (DATA PORT) (🖥) (📠) (💻) / (✕) /

HAMPTON INN   *Book at aaa.com*

◈◈◈

Small-scale Hotel

All Year   1P: $81-$91   2P: $88-$98

Phone: (276)647-4700

Location: Jct US 58, 2.5 mi n on US 220 business route. 50 Hampton Dr 24112. **Fax:** 276/647-4119. **Facility:** 68 one-bedroom standard units, some with whirlpools. 4 stories, interior corridors. *Bath:* combo or shower only. **Parking:** on-site. **Amenities:** high-speed Internet, dual phone lines, voice mail, irons, hair dryers. **Pool(s):** outdoor. **Leisure Activities:** whirlpool, exercise room. **Guest Services:** coin laundry. **Business Services:** meeting rooms. **Cards:** AX, DC, DS, MC, VI.

SOME UNITS

(A$K) (S/D) (♿) (🏊) (📽) (DATA PORT) (💻) / (✕) (📠) (📠) /

HOLIDAY INN EXPRESS   *Book at aaa.com*

◈◈◈

Small-scale Hotel

All Year [CP]   1P: $78-$85   2P: $78-$85   XP: $5   F18

Phone: (276)666-6835

Location: Jct US 58, 2.4 mi n on US 220 business route. 1895 Virgina Ave 24112. **Fax:** 276/666-0156. **Facility:** 70 one-bedroom standard units, some with whirlpools. 2 stories (no elevator), interior corridors. *Bath:* combo or shower only. **Parking:** on-site. **Terms:** 3 day cancellation notice. **Amenities:** high-speed Internet, voice mail, irons, hair dryers. **Pool(s):** outdoor. **Guest Services:** valet laundry. **Business Services:** meeting rooms. **Cards:** AX, CB, DC, DS, MC, VI.

SOME UNITS

(A$K) (S/D) (♿) (🏊) (🏃) (📽) (DATA PORT) (💻) / (✕) (📠) (📠) /
FEE   FEE

SUPER 8 MOTEL   *Book at aaa.com*

◈◈ ◈◈

Motel

All Year   1P: $49-$59   2P: $55-$65   XP: $6   F14

Phone: 276/666-8888

Location: Jct US 58, 1.5 mi n on US 220 business route. 1044 N Memorial Blvd 24112. **Fax:** 276/666-8888. **Facility:** 54 one-bedroom standard units. 3 stories (no elevator), interior corridors. **Parking:** on-site. **Terms:** 30 day cancellation notice, weekly rates available, small pets only. **Amenities:** safes. **Guest Services:** coin laundry. **Cards:** AX, DC, MC, VI.

SOME UNITS

(A$K) (S/D) (🛏) (📶) (📽) (DATA PORT) / (✕) (📠) (📠) /
FEE   FEE

------ WHERE TO DINE ------

CHINA BUFFET

◈◈

Chinese

Lunch: $4-$11   **Dinner:** $6-$11   **Phone:** 276/632-8689

Location: Jct US 58, 1.5 mi n on US 220 business route. 970 Memorial Blvd 24112. **Hours:** 11 am-10 pm, Fri & Sat-11 pm, Sun noon-10 pm. **Closed:** 11/24, 12/25. **Features:** The star attraction is the 60-item buffet bar, which is loaded with such popular favorites as General Tso chicken, spareribs and sweet and sour pork. The better-than-average family restaurant offers fresh food and prompt, attentive service. Casual dress; beer only. **Parking:** on-site. **Cards:** MC, VI.

(✕)

PIGS-R-US BAR-B-QUE

◈◈

Barbecue

Lunch: $4-$10   **Dinner:** $4-$15   **Phone:** 276/632-1161

Location: Jct US 58, 1.6 mi n US 220 business route, 1 mi e on Commonweath Blvd, then 1.2 mi n. 1014 Liberty St 24112. **Hours:** 11 am-9 pm. **Closed:** 12/25; also Sun. **Features:** Real pit cooked barbeque is offered at this restaurant. Friendly service, racing themed decor and some of the best hushpuppies you'll ever taste. Casual dress; beer only. **Parking:** on-site. **Cards:** MC, VI.

(✕)

MAX MEADOWS pop. 512

------ WHERE TO STAY ------

COMFORT INN   *Book at aaa.com*

(AAA) (SAVE)

◈◈◈

Small-scale Hotel

All Year   1P: $59-$79   ·   2P: $59-$79   XP: $6   F

Phone: (276)637-4281

Location: I-77/81, exit 80, just w. 2594 E Lee Hwy 24382 (2594 N Lee Hwy, WYTHEVILLE). **Fax:** 276/637-4079. **Facility:** 60 one-bedroom standard units, some with whirlpools. 3 stories, interior corridors. **Parking:** on-site. **Terms:** cancellation fee imposed, pets ($10 extra charge). **Amenities:** irons, hair dryers. **Pool(s):** small indoor. **Leisure Activities:** exercise room. **Guest Services:** coin laundry. **Business Services:** meeting rooms. **Cards:** AX, DC, DS, MC, VI. **Special Amenities:** free continental breakfast and free room upgrade (subject to availability with advance reservations).

SOME UNITS

(S/D) (🛏) (📶) (⚿) (♿) (🅿) (🏊) (📽) (DATA PORT) (💻) / (✕) (📠) (📠) /
FEE

GATEWAY MOTEL #2   **Phone:** 276/637-3119

▽▽▽   All Year   1P: $40-$110   XP: $6   D13
Motel   **Location:** I-81, exit 86, just w, then 0.5 mi s on service road. 5465 E Lee Hwy 24360. Fax: 276/637-4428. **Facility:** 10 one-bedroom standard units. 1 story, exterior corridors. **Parking:** on-site. **Terms:** cancellation fee imposed. **Cards:** DS, MC, VI.

SOME UNITS

A$K S/D ▣ ▤ / ✕

HAMPTON INN OF FT. CHISWELL   *Book at aaa.com*   **Phone:** 276/637-4027

◬◬ SAVE   3/1-10/31 [BP]   1P: $70-$160   2P: $75-$160
           11/1-2/28 [BP]   1P: $70-$90   2P: $75-$90
▽▽▽▽   **Location:** I-77/81, exit 80, just w. 199 Ft Chiswell Rd 24360. Fax: 276/637-3551. **Facility:** 63 one-bedroom
Small-scale Hotel   standard units, some with whirlpools. 4 stories, interior corridors. *Bath:* combo or shower only. **Parking:** on-site. **Terms:** 30 day cancellation notice. **Amenities:** high-speed Internet, voice mail, irons, hair dryers. **Pool(s):** outdoor. **Leisure Activities:** limited exercise equipment. **Business Services:** meeting rooms. **Cards:** AX, CB, DC, DS, JC, MC, VI. **Special Amenities:** free full breakfast and free local telephone calls.

SOME UNITS

S/D ▦ ⎈M ⚗ ⇔ ⚐ DATA/PORT ▣ / ✕ ▤ ▥ /

SUPER 8 MOTEL   *Book at aaa.com*   **Phone:** (276)637-4141

◬◬ SAVE   5/31-8/31   1P: $65-$70   2P: $65-$70   XP: $5   F
           3/1-5/30   1P: $60-$65   2P: $60-$65   XP: $5   F
▽▽▽▽   9/1-11/30   1P: $55-$60   2P: $55-$60   XP: $5   F
           12/1-2/28   1P: $50-$55   2P: $50-$55   XP: $5   F
Small-scale Hotel   **Location:** I-77/81, exit 80, just e. 194 Ft Chiswell Rd 24360. Fax: 276/637-3855. **Facility:** 60 one-bedroom
standard units, some with whirlpools. 2 stories (no elevator), exterior corridors. **Parking:** on-site. **Terms:** [CP] meal plan available, pets ($11 fee). **Amenities:** *Some:* irons, hair dryers. **Cards:** AX, DC, DS, MC, VI. **Special Amenities:** free continental breakfast and free local telephone calls.

SOME UNITS

▦ ▦ ⊘ ⚐ DATA/PORT / ✕ ▤ ▥ ▣
FEE

MCGAHEYSVILLE

———— **WHERE TO DINE** ————

HANK'S SMOKEHOUSE AND DELI   **Lunch:** $8-$18   **Dinner:** $10-$21   **Phone:** 540/289-7667

▽▽ ▽▽   **Location:** I-81, exit 247, 6 mi e on US 33. 49 Bloomer Springs Rd 22840. **Hours:** 11 am-3 & 5-9 pm. Closed major
Barbecue   holidays. **Features:** The Southern grill centers its menu on numerous choices of barbecue. A delicatessen and wine shop are adjacent to the dining area. Casual dress; beer only. **Parking:** on-site. **Cards:** MC, VI.

✕

MCLEAN —*See District Of Columbia p. 542.*

MEADOWS OF DAN

———— **WHERE TO DINE** ————

THE RESTAURANT AT CHATEAU MORRISETTE   **Lunch:** $8-$14   **Dinner:** $19-$30   **Phone:** 540/593-2865

▽▽▽▽   **Location:** Blue Ridge Pkwy, between mileposts 171 and 172, exit w on Black Ridge Rd, immediate s on CR 777
Continental   (Winery Rd), 0.3 mi; at the winery. 287 Winery Rd SW 24120. **Hours:** 11 am-2 pm, also Fri & Sat 6 pm-9 pm, Sun 11 am-3 pm. Closed: 1/1, 11/24, 12/24, 12/25; also Mon & Tues. **Reservations:** required, for dinner. **Features:** Guests can experience elegant dining in a romantic French country atmosphere. The hillside location is scenic and charming. Nicely presented farm-raised catfish, game and seafood dishes grace the menu, as do some heavenly desserts. Patio seating is an option in nice weather. Casual dress; beer & wine only. **Parking:** on-site. **Cards:** AX, MC, VI.

A/C ✕

MECHANICSVILLE —*See Richmond p. 863.*

MIDDLEBURG —*See District Of Columbia p. 545.*

MIDDLETOWN pop. 1,015

———— **WHERE TO STAY** ————

SUPER 8 MOTEL   *Book at aaa.com*   **Phone:** (540)868-1800

◬◬ SAVE   All Year   1P: $55-$125   2P: $55-$165   XP: $5   F18
▽▽ ▽▽   **Location:** I-81, exit 302. 2120 Relaince Rd 22645. Fax: 540/868-0094. **Facility:** 49 one-bedroom standard units.
Motel   3 stories, interior corridors. **Parking:** on-site. **Terms:** package plans, small pets only ($10 extra charge). **Pool(s):** heated indoor. **Guest Services:** coin laundry. **Cards:** AX, DC, DS, MC, VI. **Special Amenities:** free continental breakfast and free local telephone calls.

SOME UNITS

S/D ▦ ⇔ ⚐ DATA/PORT / ✕ ▤ /
FEE

WAYSIDE INN SINCE 1797   *Book at aaa.com*   **Phone:** (540)869-1797

▽▽▽▽   All Year   1P: $99-$159   2P: $99-$159
Historic   **Location:** I-81, exit 302, just w to US 11, then 0.4 mi s. 7783 Main St 22645. Fax: 540/869-6038. **Facility:** Said to
Country Inn   have been in continuous operation since 1797, the inn offers lodgings decorated with antiques. Designated smoking area. 22 one-bedroom standard units. 3 stories (no elevator), interior corridors. *Bath:* combo or shower only. **Parking:** on-site. **Terms:** 2 night minimum stay - weekends, cancellation fee imposed, weekly rates available, [CP] meal plan available, package plans. **Dining:** restaurant, see separate listing. **Business Services:** meeting rooms. **Cards:** AX, CB, DC, DS, JC, MC, VI.

A$K S/D ▦ ✕

———— **WHERE TO DINE** ————

WAYSIDE INN SINCE 1797   **Lunch:** $7-$12   **Dinner:** $11-$23   **Phone:** 540/869-1797

▼▼▼ **Location:** I-81, exit 302, just w to US 11, then 0.4 mi s; in Wayside Inn Since 1797. 7783 Main St 22645. **Hours:** 11:30
Regional American am-2:30 & 5-9 pm, Fri & Sat-10 pm. **Reservations:** suggested. **Features:** Rich, creamy peanut soup is a Virginia favorite and a house specialty, along with spoon bread and country ham. The historic inn exudes Colonial ambience. Shenandoah Valley products factor heavily on the menu, which lists a wide variety of classic American cuisine. Casual dress; cocktails. **Parking:** on-site. **Cards:** AX, CB, DC, MC, VI. **Historic**

MIDLOTHIAN —*See Richmond p. 864.*

MINT SPRING

———— **WHERE TO STAY** ————

DAYS INN-STAUNTON   *Book at aaa.com*   **Phone:** (540)337-3031

▼▼ ▼▼   3/1-11/15   1P: $59-$109   2P: $69-$129   XP: $10   F12
              11/16-2/28   1P: $49-$69   2P: $49-$69   XP: $10   F12
Motel   **Location:** I-81, exit 217, just e on SR 654. 372 White Hill Rd 24401. **Fax:** 540/337-3274. **Facility:** 118 one-bedroom standard units. 2 stories (no elevator), exterior corridors. *Bath:* combo or shower only. **Parking:** on-site. **Amenities:** hair dryers. **Pool(s):** outdoor. **Cards:** AX, CB, DC, DS, MC, VI.

SOME UNITS

RED CARPET INN   **Phone:** 540/337-2611

▼▼   Property failed to provide current rates
Location: I-81, exit 217, just w on SR 654. 210 White Hill Rd 24401. **Facility:** 27 one-bedroom standard units. 1-2 stories (no elevator), exterior corridors. **Parking:** on-site. **Terms:** small pets only. **Pool(s):** small heated outdoor. **Business Services:** meeting rooms.
Motel

SOME UNITS

MONTEREY pop. 158

———— **WHERE TO STAY** ————

MOUNTAIN LAUREL INN   **Phone:** 540/468-3401

▼▼▼ All Year [BP]   1P: $75-$115   2P: $85-$125   XP: $15   D10
Historic Bed **Location:** Just w on US 250. Main St 24465 (Box 27). **Facility:** Several shops and restaurants are within walking
& Breakfast distance of the inn, which is set in the mountains and affords scenic views in all directions. Smoke free premises. 4 one-bedroom standard units. 2 stories (no elevator), interior corridors. *Bath:* combo or shower only. **Parking:** on-site. **Terms:** 2 night minimum stay - seasonal and/or weekends, age restrictions may apply, 7 day cancellation notice-fee imposed. **Amenities:** hair dryers. **Guest Services:** complimentary laundry. **Cards:** AX, DS, MC, VI.

SOME UNITS

MOUNTAIN LAKE

———— **WHERE TO STAY** ————

MOUNTAIN LAKE HOTEL   **Phone:** (540)626-7121

AAA SAVE   5/6-11/26 [MAP]   1P: $160-$300   2P: $190-$300   XP: $40   D11
▼▼▼ **Location:** Jct US 460, 6.6 mi n on SR 700; caution steep, narrow paved mountain road. Located in remote area. 115
Resort   Hotel Cir 24136. **Fax:** 540/626-7172. **Facility:** In a remote mountaintop location that was the setting for the
Small-scale Hotel movie "Dirty Dancing," the hotel offers rustic to deluxe lodge and cottage units. 101 units. 81 one-bedroom standard units, some with whirlpools. 20 cottages ($250-$800). 1-2 stories (no elevator), interior/exterior corridors. **Parking:** on-site. **Terms:** open 5/6-11/26, check-in 5 pm, 2 night minimum stay - weekends, 21 day cancellation notice-fee imposed, package plans. **Dining:** 7:30-10 am, 11:30-2 & 5:30-8:30 pm, cocktails. **Pool(s):** outdoor. **Leisure Activities:** sauna, whirlpool, boating, canoeing, paddleboats, boat dock, fishing, kayaks, tennis court, recreation programs in summer, bocci, croquet, carriage rides, mountain bike, hiking trails, playground, horseshoes, shuffleboard, volleyball. **Fee:** massage, game room. **Guest Services:** gift shop, coin laundry. **Business Services:** meeting rooms. **Cards:** AX, CB, DC, DS, MC, VI. **Special Amenities:** free room upgrade and preferred room (each subject to availability with advance reservations).

SOME UNITS

MOUNT CRAWFORD pop. 254

———— **WHERE TO DINE** ————

EVERS FAMILY RESTAURANT   **Lunch:** $6   **Dinner:** $8   **Phone:** 540/433-0993

AAA **Location:** I-81, exit 240, 0.6 mi w on SR 257, then 0.3 mi n. Rt 11 22801. **Hours:** 11 am-8 pm, Fri & Sat-9 pm,
▼ Sun-6 pm. Closed major holidays. **Features:** Value-oriented buffet dining is what the laid-back restaurant is
American all about. Home-style fare includes ham, chicken and lots of country vegetables, such as hominy. The Friday night buffet is stocked with seafood. Servers are prompt and pleasant. Casual dress. **Parking:** on-site. **Cards:** MC, VI.

MOUNT JACKSON pop. 1,664

——— WHERE TO STAY ———

BEST WESTERN-SHENANDOAH VALLEY   *Book at aaa.com*   Phone: (540)477-2911

(AAA) (SAVE)	7/1-10/31	1P: $75-$110	2P: $85-$110	XP: $10	F15
▽▽▽▽▽	4/1-6/30	1P: $65-$110	2P: $85-$110	XP: $10	F15
	11/1-2/28	1P: $65-$75	2P: $75-$85	XP: $10	F15
	3/1-3/31	1P: $58-$62	2P: $69-$72	XP: $10	F15

Small-scale Hotel **Location:** I-81, exit 273, just e. 250 Conickville Rd 22842 (PO Box 799). Fax: 540/477-2392. **Facility:** 92 one-bedroom standard units. 2 stories (no elevator), exterior corridors. **Parking:** on-site. **Terms:** 4 day cancellation notice, pets ($10 extra charge). **Amenities:** irons, hair dryers. **Dining:** 24 hours, cocktails. **Pool(s):** outdoor. **Leisure Activities:** tennis court, basketball. **Guest Services:** gift shop. **Business Services:** meeting rooms. **Cards:** AX, DC, DS, MC, VI. **Special Amenities:** free room upgrade and preferred room (each subject to availability with advance reservations).

SOME UNITS

THE WIDOW KIP'S   Phone: (540)477-2400

▽▽▽▽	All Year	1P: $90-$95	XP: $15	D

Bed & Breakfast **Location:** I-81, exit 273, 1.5 mi s on US 11, just w on SR 263, then just sw on SR 698. Located in a quiet, country setting. 355 Orchard Dr 22842-9753. Fax: 540/477-2409. **Facility:** A library of books and videotapes, sprawling grounds with gardens and two cottages enhance the atmosphere of this restored 1830 Colonial homestead. Smoke free premises. 7 units. 6 one- and 1 two-bedroom standard units. 2 stories (no elevator), interior corridors. *Bath:* combo or shower only. **Parking:** on-site. **Terms:** age restrictions may apply, 7 day cancellation notice, pets (in cottages only). **Amenities:** video library. **Pool(s):** outdoor. **Leisure Activities:** bicycles. **Business Services:** meeting rooms. **Cards:** MC, VI.

SOME UNITS

MOUNT VERNON —*See District Of Columbia p. 546.*

NASSAWADOX pop. 572

——— WHERE TO DINE ———

LITTLE ITALY   Lunch: $6-$16   Dinner: $6-$16   Phone: 757/442-7831

▽▽▽

Italian **Location:** On US 13; center. 10227 Rogers Dr 23413. **Hours:** 11 am-8 pm, Fri & Sat-9 pm. Closed: 11/24, 12/25; also Sun & Mon. **Features:** Those who tire of Eastern Shore seafood houses can stop here for favorite Italian specialties, including baked pasta, pizza and hearty, filling subs. Casual dress. **Parking:** on-site. **Cards:** AX, DS, MC, VI.

NATURAL BRIDGE

——— WHERE TO STAY ———

BUDGET INN   Phone: (540)291-2896

(AAA) (SAVE)	3/1-11/30	1P: $49-$99	2P: $49-$99	XP: $10	F14
▽▽ ▽▽	12/1-2/28	1P: $39-$59	2P: $39-$59	XP: $5	F14

Motel **Location:** I-81, exit 180 northbound, 1 mi nw on US 11; exit 180B southbound, just w. Located in a rural area. 4331 S Lee Hwy 24578. **Facility:** 21 one-bedroom standard units. 1 story, exterior corridors. *Bath:* combo or shower only. **Parking:** on-site. **Terms:** 3 day cancellation notice-fee imposed. **Cards:** AX, CB, DC, DS, MC, VI. **Special Amenities:** free local telephone calls and early check-in/late check-out.

(See color ad p 814)

SOME UNITS

NATURAL BRIDGE INN & CONFERENCE CENTER   *Book at aaa.com*   Phone: (540)291-2121

(AAA) (SAVE)	5/27-11/12	1P: $70-$136	2P: $70-$136	XP: $10	F18
▽▽ ▽▽	3/18-5/26	1P: $60-$120	2P: $60-$120	XP: $10	F18
	3/1-3/17 & 11/13-2/28	1P: $48-$90	2P: $48-$90	XP: $10	F18

Small-scale Hotel **Location:** I-81, exit 175, 1.7 mi n on US 11. 15 Appledore Ln 24578 (PO Box 57). Fax: 540/291-1896. **Facility:** 158 units. 122 one-bedroom standard units. 36 cottages. 2 stories, interior/exterior corridors. *Bath:* combo or shower only. **Parking:** on-site. **Terms:** check-in 4 pm, 3 day cancellation notice-fee imposed, package plans. **Amenities:** voice mail, irons. **Dining:** Colonial Dining Room, see separate listing. **Pool(s):** heated indoor. **Leisure Activities:** tennis court, playground. *Fee:* miniature golf. **Guest Services:** gift shop. **Business Services:** conference facilities, fax (fee). **Cards:** AX, CB, DC, DS, MC, VI. **Special Amenities:** early check-in/late check-out and free room upgrade (subject to availability with advance reservations).

SOME UNITS

RELAX INN   Phone: (540)291-2143

▽▽▽	3/1-11/30	1P: $49-$99	2P: $49-$99	XP: $10	F14
	12/1-2/28	1P: $39-$59	2P: $39-$59	XP: $5	F14

Motel **Location:** I-81, exit 180A, just se. 4852 S Lee Hwy 24578. Fax: 540/291-2143. **Facility:** 15 one-bedroom standard units. 1 story, exterior corridors. *Bath:* combo or shower only. **Parking:** on-site. **Terms:** 3 day cancellation notice-fee imposed. **Cards:** AX, CB, DC, DS, MC, VI.

SOME UNITS

——— **WHERE TO DINE** ———

COLONIAL DINING ROOM

American
Dinner: $13-$28   **Phone:** 540/291-2121
Location: I-81, exit 175, 1.7 mi n on US 11; in Natural Bridge Inn & Conference Center. 15 Appledoor Ln 24578. **Hours:** 7 am-10 & 5:30-9 pm, also Sunday buffet noon-3 pm. Closed: 12/25. **Reservations:** suggested. **Features:** The large, elegant dining room is enhanced with brass chandeliers, opulent window treatments and striking red walls. The charming veranda offers spectacular mountain views. The menu favors Southern entrees, accompanied by traditional spoon bread. Classic American cuisine. Do not miss the opportunity to sample the shrimp and grits appetizer. Casual dress; cocktails. **Parking:** on-site. **Cards:** AX, DC, DS, MC, VI.

FANCY HILL RESTAURANT
American
Lunch: $5-$12   **Dinner:** $7-$14   **Phone:** 540/291-2860
Location: I-81, exit 180A, just e, jct US 11. 4832 S Lee Hwy 24578. **Hours:** 7 am-9 pm, Fri & Sat-9:30 pm; to 8 pm in winter. Closed major holidays; also Wed. **Features:** The casual, informal restaurant, a favorite of families, serves excellent homemade bread and soup and such tasty, traditional fare as grilled chicken. The cheerful, bright dining room is well attended by a friendly staff of thoughtful servers. License plates from most all 50 states adorn the walls. Wonderful scenic mountain views. Casual dress; beer & wine only. **Parking:** on-site. **Cards:** CB, DC, DS, MC, VI.

PINK CADILLAC DINER
American
Lunch: $5-$8   **Dinner:** $5-$13   **Phone:** 540/291-2378
Location: I-81, exit 180, just n on US 11. 4347 S Lee Hwy 24578. **Hours:** 7 am-9 pm. Closed major holidays. **Features:** The '50s come alive again at this restaurant. From Elvis to Marilyn, nostalgia flows from every corner. And the food-classic American fare-is just as great as the atmosphere. Set aside some room to enjoy selections from the ice cream parlor. Casual dress. **Parking:** on-site. **Cards:** AX, DS, MC, VI.

NELLYSFORD

——— **WHERE TO STAY** ———

THE MEANDER INN

Historic Bed
& Breakfast
All Year [BP]   **Phone:** (434)361-1121
2P: $105-$125   XP: $15   F5
Location: 2 mi n on SR 151, 0.5 mi e on SR 612. Located in a quiet area. 3100 Berry Hill Rd 22958. Fax: 434/361-1380. **Facility:** Guests who take to the front porch of this Victorian-era farmhouse are afforded picturesque views of mountains and horse pastures. Smoke free premises. 5 one-bedroom standard units. 2 stories (no elevator), interior corridors. *Bath:* combo or shower only. **Parking:** on-site. **Terms:** 2 night minimum stay - weekends, 14 day cancellation notice, package plans. **Amenities:** hair dryers. **Leisure Activities:** whirlpool, fishing, hiking trails. **Cards:** AX, CB, DC, JC, MC, VI.

NEW CHURCH

——— **WHERE TO STAY** ———

THE GARDEN & THE SEA INN
Historic Country Inn
4/1-11/30 [BP]   **Phone:** 757/824-0672
1P: $75-$205   2P: $75-$205   XP: $15   F12
Location: US 13, 0.3 mi n, just w on CR 710 (Nelson Rd). 4188 Nelson Rd 23415 (PO Box 275). **Facility:** Wraparound porches accent this Victorian home, which offers spacious guest rooms and baths decorated in pastel shades. Smoke free premises. 8 units. 7 one-bedroom standard units, some with whirlpools. 1 one-bedroom suite ($95-$205) with whirlpool. 2 stories (no elevator), interior corridors. **Parking:** on-site. **Terms:** open 4/1-11/30, 2 night minimum stay - weekends, 10 day cancellation notice-fee imposed. **Amenities:** hair dryers. **Dining:** dining room, see separate listing. **Pool(s):** heated outdoor. **Leisure Activities:** exercise room. **Cards:** AX, DC, MC, VI.

SOME UNITS

——— **WHERE TO DINE** ———

The following restaurant has not been evaluated by AAA but is listed for your information only.

THE GARDEN & THE SEA INN
[fyi]
Phone: 757/824-0672
Not evaluated. **Location:** US 13, 0.3 mi n, just w on CR 710 (Nelson Rd); in The Garden & The Sea Inn. 4188 Nelson Rd, PO Box 275 23415. **Features:** The romantic restaurant offers a seasonally changing menu of fresh regional delicacies prepared with a French influence.

NEW MARKET pop. 1,637

———— WHERE TO STAY ————

BLUE RIDGE INN

AAA SAVE

Motel

Phone: (540)740-4136

3/1-11/30	1P: $45-$60	2P: $50-$85	XP: $5 F10
12/1-2/28	1P: $35-$45	2P: $40-$55	XP: $5 F10

Location: I-81, exit 264, 1 mi n on US 11. Located in a quiet rural area. 2251 Old Valley Pike 22844. **Fax:** 540/740-3148. **Facility:** 18 one-bedroom standard units. 1 story, exterior corridors. *Bath:* shower only. **Parking:** on-site. **Terms:** 7 day cancellation notice-fee imposed. **Leisure Activities:** barbecue grill, playground. **Cards:** DS, MC, VI. **Special Amenities:** free local telephone calls and preferred room (subject to availability with advance reservations).

BUDGET INN

AAA SAVE

Motel

Phone: (540)740-3105

3/1-11/15	1P: $29-$55	2P: $35-$79	XP: $7 F10
11/16-2/28	1P: $29-$45	2P: $29-$49	XP: $5 F10

Location: I-81, exit 264, 1 mi n on US 11. Located in a quiet rural area. 2192 Old Valley Pike 22844. **Fax:** 540/740-3108. **Facility:** 14 one-bedroom standard units. 1 story, exterior corridors. *Bath:* combo or shower only. **Parking:** on-site. **Terms:** 3 day cancellation notice-fee imposed, pets ($5 extra charge). **Leisure Activities:** playground, basketball. **Cards:** AX, CB, DC, DS, JC, MC, VI. **Special Amenities:** free local telephone calls and early check-in/late check-out. *(See color ad below)*

SOME UNITS

CROSS ROADS INN B&B

Bed & Breakfast

Phone: 540/740-4157

All Year		2P: $75-$135	XP: $10 F5

Location: I-81, exit 264, 0.6 mi e on US 211. Located in a quiet area. 9222 John Sevier Rd 22844. **Fax:** 540/740-4255. **Facility:** Made-to-order breakfasts can be requested in advance at this small-town inn offering large lodgings and grounds colored by flower gardens. Smoke free premises. 6 one-bedroom standard units, some with whirlpools. 2 stories (no elevator), interior corridors. *Bath:* combo or shower only. **Parking:** on-site. **Terms:** check-in 4 pm, 7 day cancellation notice, package plans. **Amenities:** hair dryers. **Leisure Activities:** whirlpool, playground. **Business Services:** meeting rooms. **Cards:** MC, VI.

SOME UNITS

DAYS INN Book at aaa.com

All Year — 1P: $40-$150 — 2P: $45-$150

Phone: (540)740-4100

XP: $6 — F17

Location: I-81, exit 264, just w on US 211. 9360 George Collins Pkwy 22844. Fax: 540/740-8478. **Facility:** 85 one-bedroom standard units, some with whirlpools. 2 stories (no elevator), exterior corridors. **Parking:** on-site. **Terms:** package plans, small pets only ($5 extra charge). **Amenities:** hair dryers. **Pool(s):** outdoor. Small-scale Hotel **Cards:** AX, CB, DC, DS, JC, MC, VI. **Special Amenities:** free expanded continental breakfast and free newspaper. (See color ad p 814)

SOME UNITS

 FEE

QUALITY INN SHENANDOAH VALLEY — Book at aaa.com

4/29-10/31 — 1P: $59-$109 — 2P: $59-$109

3/1-4/28 & 11/1-2/28 — 1P: $49-$85 — 2P: $49-$85

Phone: (540)740-3141

XP: $6 — F18

XP: $6 — F18

Location: I-81, exit 264, just e on US 11/211, then just n. 162 W Old Cross Rd 22844 (PO Box 100). Fax: 540/740-3250. **Facility:** 100 one-bedroom standard units. 2 stories (no elevator), interior/exterior Small-scale Hotel corridors. **Parking:** on-site. **Amenities:** irons, hair dryers. **Dining:** 6:30 am-9 pm; to 10 pm 5/1-10/31, cocktails. **Pool(s):** outdoor. **Leisure Activities:** playground, exercise room. Fee: miniature golf. **Guest Services:** gift shop, coin laundry. **Business Services:** meeting rooms. **Cards:** AX, CB, DC, DS, MC, VI. **Special Amenities:** free local telephone calls and free newspaper. (See color ad below)

SOME UNITS

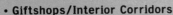

NEWPORT NEWS —See Hampton Roads Area p. 722.

NORFOLK —See Hampton Roads Area p. 726.

NORTON pop. 3,904

──────── WHERE TO STAY ────────

DAYS INN   *Book at aaa.com*   Phone: (276)679-5340
◆◆◆ ◆◆◆   All Year [CP]   1P: $49-$69   2P: $56-$76   XP: $7   F18
Small-scale Hotel   **Location:** Jct US 58 and 23. 375 Wharton Ln 24273. Fax: 276/679-5341. **Facility:** 58 one-bedroom standard units, some with whirlpools. 3 stories, interior corridors. *Bath:* combo or shower only. **Parking:** on-site. **Terms:** pets ($25 fee). **Amenities:** dual phone lines, voice mail, irons, hair dryers. **Leisure Activities:** exercise room. **Guest Services:** coin laundry. **Business Services:** meeting rooms, business center. **Cards:** AX, CB, DC, DS, JC, MC, VI.

SOME UNITS
(ASK) (S/D) [🛏] [🐕] [🚫] [📷] [DATA PORT] [☕] / [✕] [VCR] [🛏] [🖨] /
FEE

NORTON SUPER 8 MOTEL   Phone: (276)679-0893
◆◆◆   All Year [CP]   1P: $51-$61   2P: $57-$67   XP: $6   F12
Small-scale Hotel   **Location:** Jct US 58 and 23. 425 Wharton Ln 24293. Fax: 276/679-0893. **Facility:** 56 one-bedroom standard units. 2 stories (no elevator), interior corridors. **Parking:** on-site. **Amenities:** safes. **Guest Services:** coin laundry. **Business Services:** meeting rooms. **Cards:** AX, DC, DS, MC, VI.

SOME UNITS
(ASK) (S/D) [📷] [DATA PORT] [🛏] / [✕] [🖨] /

OCCOQUAN —See District Of Columbia p. 546.

ONANCOCK pop. 1,525

──────── WHERE TO STAY ────────

CHARLOTTE HOTEL   Phone: (757)787-7400
◆◆◆ ◆◆◆   All Year   2P: $120-$190   XP: $20   F13
Country Inn   **Location:** Just n of jct Market (SR 179) and North sts; downtown. 7 North St 23417 (PO Box 259). Fax: 757/787-9443. **Facility:** Set in the middle of this quaint harbor town, the Charlotte Hotel offers charming rooms equipped with excellent modern amenities. Smoke free premises. 8 one-bedroom standard units. 3 stories (no elevator), interior corridors. *Bath:* shower only. **Parking:** street. **Terms:** office hours 8 am-11 pm, 2 night minimum stay - weekends, age restrictions may apply, 3 day cancellation notice, no pets allowed (owner's dog on premises). **Amenities:** video library, DVD players, video games, hair dryers. **Dining:** Charlotte Restaurant, see separate listing. **Cards:** AX, CB, DC, DS, MC, VI.

(ASK) [🍴] [&M] [✕] [📷] [DATA PORT]

SPINNING WHEEL BED & BREAKFAST   Phone: (757)787-7311
◆◆◆ ◆◆◆   All Year [BP]   1P: $75-$110   2P: $75-$120
Historic Bed   **Location:** Just n of jct Market (SR 179) and North sts. Located in a quiet area. 31 North St 23417 (PO Box 60).
& Breakfast   Fax: 757/787-8555. **Facility:** This 1890s home decorated in a folk-Victorian style mixes sophisticated and primitive antiques. Smoke free premises. 4 one-bedroom standard units. 3 stories (no elevator), interior corridors. *Bath:* shower only. **Parking:** on-site. **Terms:** age restrictions may apply, 3 day cancellation notice, package plans, no pets allowed (owner's pet on premises). **Leisure Activities:** bicycles. **Business Services:** fax. **Cards:** MC, VI.

[🍴+] [✕] [W] [✉]

──────── WHERE TO DINE ────────

ARMANDO'S   Dinner: $8-$30   Phone: 757/787-8044
◆◆◆ ◆◆◆   **Location:** Just n of jct Market (SR 179) and North sts. 10 North St 23417. **Hours:** 5 pm-9 pm, Fri & Sat-10 pm; 5 pm-10 pm, Sun-9 pm in winter. Closed: 3/27, 11/24, 12/25; also Mon & Tues; Mon-Wed in winter.
Mediterranean   **Features:** The Mediterranean menu, kissed by the Argentinian influences of its chef, showcases excellent, innovative seafood, pasta, veal dishes and great house-baked bread. Armando's is a hip spot in this small town. Patio seating is available, weather permitting. Casual dress; cocktails. **Parking:** street. **Cards:** AX, MC, VI.

BIZZOTTO'S GALLERY-CAFFE   Lunch: $6-$10   Dinner: $18-$25   Phone: 757/787-3103
◆◆◆ ◆◆◆   **Location:** 1 mi w of US 13; center. 41 Market St 23417. **Hours:** 11 am-9 pm; Sun from 5 pm in summer. Closed: 12/25; also Sun off season. **Reservations:** suggested. **Features:** The owner is both a chef and an artist, so
Continental   this combination gallery and cafe proves ideal to display his creations on the walls and the plates. Local seafood flavors meet European influences in dishes such as shrimp and spinach bisque, crab cakes on focaccia bread and cod meuniere. Casual dress; cocktails. **Parking:** street. **Cards:** AX, MC, VI.

[✕]

CHARLOTTE RESTAURANT   Dinner: $18-$25   Phone: 757/787-7400
◆◆◆ ◆◆◆   **Location:** Just n of jct Market (SR 179) and North sts; downtown; in Charlotte Hotel. 7 North St 23417. **Hours:** 5:30 pm-9 pm. Closed: 1/1, 11/24, 12/25; also Mon & Tues. **Reservations:** suggested. **Features:** French
American   elegance meets coastal casual at the intimate inn. The chef skillfully integrates Continental and Southern traditions with fresh local ingredients, including the region's great seafood. Homemade ice creams are a specialty. Casual dress; cocktails. **Parking:** street. **Cards:** AX, DC, DS, MC, VI.

[&M] [✕]

STELLA'S   Lunch: $5-$13   Dinner: $5-$13   Phone: 757/789-5045
AAA   **Location:** Jct North St; downtown. 57 Market St 23417. **Hours:** 11 am-10 pm, Fri & Sat-11 pm. Closed major
◆◆◆ ◆◆◆   holidays. **Reservations:** accepted. **Features:** This festive downtown spot offers a family friendly atmosphere downstairs and a more adult-oriented atmosphere upstairs. Italian-American favorites mingle
Italian   with great local seafood in dishes such as spicy shrimp pasta, crab-stuffed pretzels, fried seafood baskets, and linguine with clam sauce. Casual dress; cocktails. **Parking:** street. **Cards:** AX, DC, DS, MC, VI.

ORANGE pop. 4,123

———— WHERE TO STAY ————

GREENOCK HOUSE INN
Phone: 540/672-3625

Historic Bed & Breakfast

All Year [BP]   1P: $105-$170   2P: $125-$190   XP: $20
Location: US 15, just s of jct SR 20. 249 Caroline St 22960. Fax: 540/672-5029. **Facility:** Two of the guest rooms in this 1890 country Victorian farmhouse include working fireplaces. Smoke free premises. 5 one-bedroom standard units, some with whirlpools. 2 stories (no elevator), interior corridors. *Bath:* combo or shower only. **Parking:** on-site. **Terms:** check-in 4:30 pm, 2 night minimum stay - seasonal and/or weekends, cancellation fee imposed, package plans. **Amenities:** hair dryers. *Some:* CD players. **Business Services:** meeting rooms. **Cards:** AX, CB, DC, DS, MC, VI.

SOME UNITS
(ASK) ⊠ 🍴 🕿 🛢 🖵 / �W /

HOLIDAY INN EXPRESS   *Book at aaa.com*
Phone: (540)672-6691

(AAA) (SAVE)
Small-scale Hotel

All Year   1P: $85-$125   2P: $85-$125   XP: $10   F18
Location: US 15, 2.1 mi n of jct SR 20. 750 Round Hill Dr 22960 (PO Box 131). Fax: 540/672-6690. **Facility:** 65 one-bedroom standard units, some with kitchens and/or whirlpools. 2 stories, interior corridors. *Bath:* combo or shower only. **Parking:** on-site. **Terms:** [ECP] meal plan available, package plans. **Amenities:** high-speed Internet, voice mail, irons, hair dryers. **Pool(s):** outdoor. **Leisure Activities:** exercise room. **Guest Services:** coin laundry. **Business Services:** meeting rooms. **Cards:** AX, CB, DC, DS, JC, MC, VI.
Special Amenities: free expanded continental breakfast and free local telephone calls.

SOME UNITS
(S/D) (&) 🏊 🍴 (DATA PORT) 🖵 / ⊠ 🛢 🖵 /

MAYHURST INN
Phone: (540)672-5597

Bed & Breakfast

All Year [BP]   1P: $140-$230   2P: $140-$230   XP: $30   F6
Location: On US 15, 0.5 mi s of town from SR 20 at the divided highway. 12460 Mayhurst Ln 22960. Fax: 540/672-7447. **Facility:** A Virginia landmark, the 1859 Italianate plantation mansion sits amid 200-year-old ash trees; lodgings feature fireplaces with antique marble mantels. Smoke free premises. 7 one-bedroom standard units, some with whirlpools. 4 stories (no elevator), interior corridors. *Bath:* combo or shower only. **Parking:** on-site. **Terms:** check-in 4 pm, 2 night minimum stay - weekends, 10 day cancellation notice-fee imposed, weekly rates available, package plans, no pets allowed (owner's cats on premises). **Amenities:** hair dryers. *Some:* DVD players, CD players. **Leisure Activities:** fishing, jogging. **Guest Services:** complimentary evening beverages. **Cards:** AX, MC, VI.

SOME UNITS
(ASK) (S/D) ⊠ 🕿 / �W (VCR) /

———— WHERE TO DINE ————

CAPE PORPOISE LOBSTER HOUSE   **Lunch:** $5-$11   **Dinner:** $13-$20   Phone: 540/672-0800

American

Location: 0.2 mi n on Business SR 20/Byrd St. 182 Byrd St 22960. **Hours:** 11:30 am-9 pm, Sat-10 pm, Sun 10:30 am-9 pm; Sunday brunch 10:30 am-2:30 pm. Closed: 12/25. **Features:** The fun, casual eatery has an unusual name, but the seafood is fresh, and the staff is friendly. Casual dress; cocktails. **Parking:** on-site. **Cards:** AX, DS, MC, VI.

🍸 ⊠

SILK MILL GRILLE   **Lunch:** $7-$15   **Dinner:** $10-$20   Phone: 540/672-4010

American

Location: US 15, 2 mi n of jct SR 20, just e. 101-A Woodmark St 22960. **Hours:** 11 am-9 pm, Fri & Sat-10 pm, Sun noon-8 pm. Closed: 1/1, 12/25; also Mon. **Reservations:** suggested, weekends. **Features:** A city tradition, the restaurant prepares steaks, sandwiches and seafood. In the historic area, this place is near many attractions. Casual dress; cocktails. **Parking:** on-site. **Cards:** AX, MC, VI.

🍸 ⊠

PETERSBURG pop. 33,740   (See map and index starting on p. 835)

———— WHERE TO STAY ————

BEST WESTERN-STEVEN KENT   *Book at aaa.com*
Phone: (804)733-0600   **8**

(AAA) (SAVE)
Small-scale Hotel

All Year   1P: $49-$80   2P: $49-$80   XP: $5   F18
Location: I-95, exit 45, jct US 301. 12205 S Crater Rd 23805 (PO Box 1910). Fax: 804/862-4549. **Facility:** 135 units. 130 one-bedroom standard units. 5 one-bedroom suites. 2 stories (no elevator), interior/exterior corridors. **Parking:** on-site. **Terms:** [AP] meal plan available, pets ($10 extra charge, in designated units). **Amenities:** voice mail, irons, hair dryers. **Dining:** restaurant, see separate listing. **Pool(s):** outdoor, wading. **Leisure Activities:** putting green, 2 lighted tennis courts, playground, sports court. **Guest Services:** gift shop, coin laundry. **Business Services:** meeting rooms, fax. **Cards:** AX, CB, DC, DS, MC, VI. **Special Amenities:** free local telephone calls and free newspaper. *(See color ad p 818)*

SOME UNITS
(S/D) 🛒 🍴 🌀 🏊 ⊠ 🍴 (DATA PORT) 🖵 / ⊠ 🛢 🖵 /
FEE

COMFORT INN   *Book at aaa.com*
Phone: (804)732-2900   **6**

Small-scale Hotel

All Year   1P: $55-$120   2P: $55-$120   XP: $5   F17
Location: I-95, exit 45, n on US 301. 11974 S Crater Rd 23805. Fax: 804/732-2900. **Facility:** 96 one-bedroom standard units, some with efficiencies (no utensils). 2 stories (no elevator), exterior corridors. **Parking:** on-site. **Terms:** pets ($5 extra charge, in designated units). **Amenities:** hair dryers. **Pool(s):** outdoor. **Guest Services:** coin laundry. **Business Services:** fax. **Cards:** AX, CB, DC, DS, MC, VI. *(See color ad p 818)*

SOME UNITS
(ASK) (S/D) 🍴 🏊 🍴 (DATA PORT) 🛢 🖵 / ⊠ 🖵 /
FEE

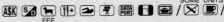

(See map and index starting on p. 835)

DAYS INN   *Book at aaa.com*   Phone: (804)733-4400   **9**
AAA SAVE
5/2-9/1 [ECP]   1P: $60-$100   2P: $60-$100   XP: $7   F16
3/1-5/1 & 9/2-2/28 [ECP]   1P: $50-$80   2P: $50-$80   XP: $7   F16
Location: I-95, exit 45, jct US 301. 12208 S Crater Rd 23805. Fax: 804/861-9559. **Facility:** 155 one-bedroom standard units, some with efficiencies. 2 stories (no elevator), exterior corridors. **Parking:** on-site.
Small-scale Hotel **Terms:** pets ($10 extra charge). **Amenities:** voice mail, irons, hair dryers. **Pool(s):** outdoor. **Leisure Activities:** playground, exercise room. **Guest Services:** coin laundry. **Business Services:** fax. **Cards:** AX, DC, DS, JC, MC, VI. **Special Amenities:** free expanded continental breakfast and free local telephone calls.
(See color ad p 818)

SOME UNITS

⟨SD⟩ ⟨⟩ ⟨⟩ ⟨⟩ ⟨⟩ ⟨DATA PORT⟩ ⟨⟩ ⟨⟩ ⟨⟩ /⟨X⟩/
FEE

ECONO LODGE-SOUTH   *Book at aaa.com*   Phone: (804)862-2717
AAA SAVE
All Year [CP]   1P: $50-$100   2P: $50-$100   F18
Location: I-95, exit 41, just e. 16905 Parkdale Rd 23805. Fax: 804/732-3479. **Facility:** 90 one-bedroom standard units, some with whirlpools. 2 stories, exterior corridors. *Bath:* combo or shower only. **Parking:** on-site.
Terms: cancellation fee imposed, weekly rates available, pets ($10 extra charge). **Pool(s):** outdoor. **Guest**
Small-scale Hotel **Services:** coin laundry. **Business Services:** meeting rooms, fax. **Cards:** AX, DS, MC, VI.
Special Amenities: free continental breakfast and free local telephone calls. *(See color ad below)*

SOME UNITS

⟨SD⟩ ⟨⟩ ⟨⟩ ⟨⟩ ⟨DATA PORT⟩ /⟨X⟩ ⟨⟩ ⟨⟩ ⟨⟩ /
FEE

HAMPTON INN   *Book at aaa.com*   Phone: (804)732-1400   **5**
AAA SAVE
All Year [ECP]   1P: $75-$119   2P: $79-$129   XP: $10   F18
Location: I-95, exit 45, jct US 301. 11909 S Crater Rd 23805. Fax: 804/732-7495. **Facility:** 77 one-bedroom standard units, some with whirlpools. 4 stories, interior corridors. *Bath:* combo or shower only. **Parking:** on-site. **Amenities:** high-speed Internet, dual phone lines, voice mail, irons, hair dryers. **Pool(s):** outdoor.
Small-scale Hotel **Guest Services:** valet and coin laundry. **Business Services:** meeting rooms, fax. **Cards:** AX, CB, DC, DS, JC, MC, VI. **Special Amenities:** free expanded continental breakfast and free newspaper.

SOME UNITS

⟨SD⟩ ⟨⟩ ⟨M⟩ ⟨⟩ ⟨⟩ ⟨⟩ ⟨⟩ ⟨DATA PORT⟩ ⟨⟩ ⟨⟩ ⟨⟩ /⟨X⟩/

(See map and index starting on p. 835)

HOLIDAY INN EXPRESS-PETERSBURG SOUTH
Book at aaa.com   Phone: (804)732-2000   **7**

(AAA) (SAVE)

3/1-9/30 [CP]	1P: $69-$99	2P: $69-$99	XP: $10	F10
10/1-2/28 [CP]	1P: $69-$89	2P: $69-$89	XP: $10	F10

Location: I-95, exit 45, jct US 301. 12001 S Crater Rd 23805. Fax: 804/732-2315. **Facility:** 98 one-bedroom standard units, some with whirlpools. 2 stories (no elevator), interior corridors. **Parking:** on-site. **Small-scale Hotel** **Terms:** cancellation fee imposed. **Amenities:** voice mail, irons, hair dryers. **Pool(s):** outdoor. **Leisure Activities:** playground, limited exercise equipment. **Guest Services:** coin laundry. **Business Services:** meeting rooms, fax. **Cards:** AX, CB, DC, DS, MC, VI. **Special Amenities:** free continental breakfast and free newspaper.

SOME UNITS

MAYFIELD INN
Phone: (804)733-0866   **3**

Historic Bed & Breakfast

All Year   1P: $85-$115   2P: $89-$120   XP: $15   D12

Location: I-85, exit 63B, 1.2 mi ne on US 1/460 business route. 3348 W Washington St 23804 (PO Box 2265). Fax: 804/863-1971. **Facility:** Noted as one of few area structures to survive both the Revolutionary and Civil wars, this Colonial home has pine floors and manicured grounds. Smoke free premises. 4 units. 2 one-bedroom standard units. 2 one-bedroom suites. 3 stories (no elevator), interior corridors. **Bath:** combo or shower only. **Parking:** on-site. **Terms:** 3 day cancellation notice, no pets allowed (owner's cat on premises). **Pool(s):** outdoor. **Business Services:** fax. **Cards:** AX, MC, VI.

SOME UNITS

QUALITY INN
Book at aaa.com   Phone: (804)733-1776   **1**

(AAA) (SAVE)

All Year   1P: $60-$105   2P: $60-$105   XP: $5   F18

Location: I-95, exit 52 southbound; exit 50D northbound; I-85, exit 69; downtown. 405 E Washington St 23803. Fax: 804/861-6339. **Facility:** 120 one-bedroom standard units, some with whirlpools. 3 stories (no elevator), **Small-scale Hotel** exterior corridors. **Parking:** on-site. **Terms:** weekly rates available, package plans, small pets only ($5 extra charge). **Amenities:** voice mail, irons, hair dryers. **Pool(s):** outdoor. **Guest Services:** valet and coin laundry. **Business Services:** meeting rooms, fax. **Cards:** AX, DC, DS, MC, VI. **Special Amenities:** free expanded continental breakfast and free local telephone calls.

SOME UNITS

FEE

RAMADA PLAZA HOTEL PETERSBURG
Book at aaa.com   Phone: (804)733-0000   **2**

3/1-11/1	1P: $89-$169	2P: $89-$169	XP: $15	F17
11/2-2/28	1P: $69-$89	2P: $69-$89	XP: $15	F17

Small-scale Hotel **Location:** I-95, exit 52 southbound; exit 50D northbound; I-85, exit 69; downtown. Located in historic Olde Towne. 380 E Washington St 23803. Fax: 804/733-7085. **Facility:** 192 one-bedroom standard units. 9 stories, interior corridors. **Parking:** on-site. **Amenities:** dual phone lines, voice mail, irons, hair dryers. **Pool(s):** outdoor. **Leisure Activities:** exercise room. **Guest Services:** valet and coin laundry, area transportation. **Business Services:** conference facilities, fax. **Cards:** AX, CB, DC, DS, MC, VI.

SOME UNITS

SUPER 8 MOTEL
Book at aaa.com   Phone: (804)732-6020   **4**

(AAA) (SAVE)

All Year   1P: $55-$95   2P: $65-$95   XP: $10   F18

Location: I-95, exit 48B (Wagner Rd), 0.7 mi w. 3138 S Crater Rd 23805. Fax: 804/732-6637. **Facility:** 32 one-bedroom standard units, some with whirlpools. 2 stories (no elevator), exterior corridors. **Parking:** on-site. **Amenities:** hair dryers. **Cards:** AX, DC, MC, VI. **Special Amenities:** free local telephone calls and **Small-scale Hotel** preferred room (subject to availability with advance reservations).

SOME UNITS

─────── **WHERE TO DINE** ───────

ALEXANDER'S FINE FOOD
Lunch: $5-$8   **Dinner:** $8-$14   Phone: 804/733-7134   **3**

Greek

Location: Just e of Sycamore St; center; in Olde Towne Historic District. 101 W Bank St 23803. **Hours:** 11 am-9 pm, Mon & Tues-3 pm. Closed major holidays; also Sun. **Features:** A simple, little Greek spot, the restaurant serves pasta, subs, salad and assorted entrees. The white walls of the front of the dining room boast an attractive decorative border. Nothing here's too fancy, but everything's plentiful and tasty. Casual dress; beer & wine only. **Parking:** street.

BEST WESTERN-STEVEN KENT RESTAURANT
Lunch: $3-$6   **Dinner:** $6-$16   Phone: 804/733-0500   **8**

American

Location: I-95, exit 45, jct US 301; in Best Western-Steven Kent. 12205 S Crater Rd 23805. **Hours:** 5:30 am-10 pm. **Features:** This quiet, family-oriented restaurant sits amid comfortable, quaint surroundings. Paintings by local artists decorate the walls. The menu focuses on Southern favorites—liver and pork chops among them. Servers are quick and "country friendly.". Casual dress; cocktails. **Parking:** on-site. **Cards:** AX, CB, DC, DS, MC, VI.

THE BRICKHOUSE RUN
Dinner: $10-$19   Phone: 804/862-1815   **1**

American

Location: Between Olde St and Bollingbrook; in Olde Towne; adjacent to visitor's center. 407-409 Cockade Alley 23803. **Hours:** 5 pm-9 pm, Fri & Sat-10 pm. Closed major holidays; also Sun & Mon. **Features:** Traditional British and regional specialties are served in the appropriately decorated English-style pub on a cobblestone lane in Olde Towne. Casual dress; cocktails. **Parking:** street. **Cards:** AX, MC, VI.

KING'S BARBECUE
Lunch: $2-$10   **Dinner:** $2-$10   Phone: 804/732-5861   **5**

American

Location: I-95, exit 52 southbound; exit 50 northbound, 3 mi w. 3221 W Washington St 23803. **Hours:** 11 am-9 pm. Closed: 7/4, 11/24, 12/25; also Mon. **Features:** Don't let the simple setting fool you; you'll discover great pork, barbecue sandwiches and platters, chicken, burgers and fish. And there are a number of side dishes to complement your meal — coleslaw, country vegetables, biscuits and more. Casual dress. **Parking:** on-site. **Cards:** AX, DS, MC, VI.

(See map and index starting on p. 835)

KINGS BARBEQUE NO. 2   Lunch: $5-$9   Dinner: $5-$9   Phone: 804/732-0975   ⑥
Location: I-95, exit 50, 2 mi s. 2910 S Crater Rd 23805. **Hours:** 11 am-8:45 pm. Closed: 11/24, 12/24, 12/25; also Mon. **Features:** Think "Southern country diner circa 1965" and you've captured the personality of the cozy, familiar restaurant. Great vinegar-based barbecue, most notably pork, is the highlight of the menu
Regional American   although burgers and sandwiches also are offered. End with their homemade apple pie just like Grandma made. Casual dress. **Parking:** on-site. **Cards:** AX, DS, MC, VI.

LEONARDO'S RESTAURANT   Dinner: $6-$18   Phone: 804/863-4830   ②
Location: Jct Sycamore St; downtown. 7 Bollingbrook St 23803. **Hours:** 5 pm-9 pm, Fri & Sat-10 pm. Closed major holidays; also Sun & Mon. **Reservations:** suggested, Fri evening. **Features:** Gourmet sandwiches and wraps, salad, soup and light entrees draw diners at lunchtime, while dinner crowds go for more formal
American   fare like filet mignon, tuna, prime rib and pasta. Homemade bread and dessert are excellent. Jazz musicians play on Saturdays. Casual dress; cocktails. **Parking:** on-site. **Cards:** AX, DS, MC, VI.

LONGSTREET'S DELICATESSEN   Lunch: $5-$8   Dinner: $5-$8   Phone: 804/722-4372   ④
Location: I-95, exit 22, just w to Sycamore St. 302 N Sycamore St 23803. **Hours:** 11 am-9 pm. Closed major holidays; also Sun. **Features:** Decorated with American and Oriental antiques, the eatery is a charming mix
Deli/Subs   of gourmet delicatessens, soda fountain and coffee bar. A player piano and a waitress on wheels set the
Sandwiches   mood. Casual dress; beer & wine only. **Parking:** street. **Cards:** MC, VI.

NANNY'S FAMILY RESTAURANT   Lunch: $4-$10   Dinner: $4-$10   Phone: 804/733-6619   ⑦
Location: I-95, exit 45, just n on US 301. 11900 S Crater Rd 23805. **Hours:** 11 am-2:30 pm, Fri-9 pm, Sat 4 pm-9 pm. Closed: Sun & Mon. **Features:** The simple spot in the country has become a local favorite for its
Southern   plentiful buffet of Southern favorites, such as pork barbecue, fried chicken, collard greens, cornbread and fruit cobblers. Casual dress. **Parking:** on-site. **Cards:** MC, VI.

PORTSMOUTH —*See Hampton Roads Area p. 787.*

POUNDING MILL

——— WHERE TO STAY ———

CLAYPOOL HILL SUPER 8 MOTEL *Book at aaa.com*   **Phone:** (276)964-9888
All Year   1P: $49-$79   2P: $54-$79   XP: $6   F12
Location: 0.3 mi w on US 19 and 460. 12367 Gov GC Peery Hwy 24637. Fax: 276/964-9888. **Facility:** 46 one-bedroom standard units, some with whirlpools. 2 stories (no elevator), interior corridors. **Parking:** on-site.
Small-scale Hotel   **Amenities:** safes. **Business Services:** meeting rooms. **Cards:** AX, CB, DC, DS, MC, VI.

SOME UNITS
(ASK) (S⊗) (⏰) (DATA PORT) (🛢) / (✕) (📶) /

PROVIDENCE FORGE —*See Richmond p. 865.*

PULASKI pop. 9,473

——— WHERE TO STAY ———

DAYS INN *Book at aaa.com*   **Phone:** 540/980-2230
6/1-8/31   1P: $50-$125   2P: $50-$125   XP: $10   D17
3/1-5/31 & 9/1-9/30   1P: $50-$90   2P: $50-$125   XP: $10   D17
10/1-2/28   1P: $40-$90   2P: $50-$125   XP: $10   D17
Small-scale Hotel   **Location:** I-81, exit 94, just e. 3063 Old Rt 100 Rd 24301 (PO Box 1266). Fax: 540/980-0297. **Facility:** 60 one-bedroom standard units. 2 stories (no elevator), interior/exterior corridors. **Parking:** on-site. **Terms:** pets ($10 extra charge). **Amenities:** hair dryers. *Some:* irons. **Cards:** AX, DC, DS, MC, VI.

SOME UNITS
(ASK) (S⊗) (🐾) (⏰) (DATA PORT) / (✕) (🛢) (📶) /
FEE

QUICKSBURG

——— WHERE TO STAY ———

STRATHMORE HOUSE BED & BREAKFAST   **Phone:** 540/477-4141
All Year [BP]   1P: $125-$140   2P: $125-$140
Location: I-81, exit 269, just e to SR 11, 1.1 mi n to Wissler Rd, then just w over covered bridge. 658 Wissler Rd 22847. Fax: 540/477-2278. **Facility:** This property is nestled near a covered bridge and offers a retreatlike setting along with attractive rooms and gardens. 4 one-bedroom standard units. 2 stories (no elevator), interior
Bed & Breakfast   corridors. *Bath:* combo or shower only. **Parking:** on-site. **Terms:** 2 night minimum stay - seasonal and/or weekends, age restrictions may apply, 7 day cancellation notice-fee imposed. **Amenities:** irons, hair dryers.
Leisure Activities: badminton, croquet. **Special Amenities:** free full breakfast and free local telephone calls.

(✕) (🅗) (☎)

RADFORD pop. 15,859

—— WHERE TO STAY ——

BEST WESTERN RADFORD INN *Book at aaa.com*
Phone: (540)639-3000
AAA SAVE
All Year [ECP]   1P: $71-$99   2P: $71-$99   XP: $5   F18
Location: I-81, exit 109, 2.7 mi nw on SR 177. 1501 Tyler Ave 24141. Fax: 540/633-0251. **Facility:** 104 one-bedroom standard units, some with whirlpools. 2 stories, interior corridors. **Parking:** on-site. **Terms:** pets
Small-scale Hotel ($10 deposit, $10 extra charge, in smoking units). **Amenities:** voice mail, irons, hair dryers. **Dining:** 6:30-10 am, Sat & Sun 7 am-10 & 11-10 pm, cocktails. **Pool(s):** heated indoor, wading. **Leisure Activities:** saunas, whirlpool, exercise room. **Guest Services:** valet laundry. **Business Services:** meeting rooms, business center. **Cards:** AX, CB, DC, DS, JC, MC, VI. **Special Amenities:** free expanded continental breakfast and free newspaper.
(See color ad below)
SOME UNITS
(icons)

COMFORT INN & SUITES *Book at aaa.com*
Phone: (540)639-3333
AAA SAVE
All Year   1P: $72-$122   2P: $72-$122   XP: $5   F18
Location: I-81, exit 109, just w. 2331 Tyler Rd 24143 (PO Box 1008). Fax: 540/639-6609. **Facility:** 72 one-bedroom standard units, some with whirlpools. 3 stories, interior corridors. *Bath:* combo or shower only.
Parking: on-site. **Amenities:** high-speed Internet, voice mail, safes, irons, hair dryers. **Pool(s):** heated
Small-scale Hotel indoor. **Leisure Activities:** whirlpool, exercise room. **Guest Services:** coin laundry. **Business Services:** conference facilities, business center. **Cards:** AX, DC, DS, MC, VI. **Special Amenities:** free continental breakfast and free room upgrade (subject to availability with advance reservations).
SOME UNITS
(icons)

SUPER 8 MOTEL-RADFORD *Book at aaa.com*
Phone: (540)731-9355
All Year   1P: $51-$56   2P: $57-$65   XP: $6   F17
Location: I-81, exit 109, just w. 1600 Tyler Ave 24141. Fax: 540/731-9555. **Facility:** 58 one-bedroom standard
Motel units. 2 stories (no elevator), interior corridors. **Parking:** on-site. **Terms:** 30 day cancellation notice.
Amenities: safes. **Cards:** AX, DC, MC, VI.
SOME UNITS
(icons)

—— WHERE TO DINE ——

SAL'S RISTORANTE ITALIANO   **Lunch:** $6-$12   **Dinner:** $6-$22   **Phone:** 540/639-9669
Location: I-81, exit 105, just w. 709 W Main St 24141. **Hours:** 11 am-11 pm, Sun noon-10 pm. Closed: 12/25;
Italian also Mon. **Features:** Sal's Ristorante Italiano is a family operated eatery that has been serving quality Italian cuisine over 25 years in the Radford area. Casual dress; cocktails. **Parking:** on-site. **Cards:** AX, CB, DC, DS, JC, MC, VI.
(icons)

RAPHINE

—— WHERE TO STAY ——

DAYS INN-SHENANDOAH VALLEY *Book at aaa.com*
Phone: (540)377-2604
4/22-11/13   1P: $64-$89   2P: $69-$94   XP: $5   F18
3/1-4/21 & 11/14-2/28   1P: $49-$69   2P: $54-$74   XP: $5   F18
Motel **Location:** I-81, exit 205, just sw. Located in a commercial area. 584 Oakland Cr 24472. Fax: 540/377-2430. **Facility:** 86 one-bedroom standard units. 3 stories, interior corridors. **Parking:** on-site. **Terms:** pets ($5 extra charge). **Amenities:** hair dryers. *Some:* irons. **Pool(s):** outdoor. **Guest Services:** coin laundry. **Business Services:** meeting rooms. **Cards:** AX, CB, DC, DS, MC, VI.
SOME UNITS
(icons)

RESTON —*See District Of Columbia p. 546.*

Precautions Can Save A Vacation!

*T*ravelers are faced with the task of protecting themselves while in a strange environment. Although there is no way to guarantee absolute protection from crime, the experts–law enforcement officials–advise travelers to take a proactive approach to securing their property and ensuring their safety.

- Make sure the hotel desk clerk does not announce your room number; if he/she does, quietly request a new room assignment.

- Ask front desk personnel which areas of town to avoid and what, if any, special precautions should be taken when driving a rental car (some criminals target tourists driving rental cars).

- Never open the door to a stranger; use the peephole and request identification. If you are still unsure, call the front desk to verify the identity of the person and the purpose of his/her visit.

- Carry money separately from credit cards or use a "fanny pack." Carry your purse close to your body and your wallet in an inside coat or front trouser pocket. Never leave luggage unattended, and use your business address, if possible, on luggage tags.

- Beware of distractions staged by would-be scam artists, especially groups of children that surround you, or a stranger who accidentally spills something on you. They may be lifting your wallet.

- If using an automatic teller machine (ATM), choose one in a well-lit area with plenty of foot traffic, such as one at a grocery store. Law enforcement officials suggest that machines inside establishments are generally safer to use.

- Use room safes or safety deposit boxes provided by the hotel. Store all valuables out of sight, even when you are in the room.

- Law enforcement agencies consider card-key (electronic) door locks the most secure.

Destination Richmond
pop. 197,790

*A*t the falls of the James River, Richmond was a destination for the purposeful. Traders built warehouses in the Shockoe Slip district; farmers hawked goods on 17th Street; and statesmen convened at the capitol to shape a nation.

*M*ake it your destination for a good time. The Farmer's Market still thrives on 17th Street. Revitalized Shockoe Bottom is where nightlife is the liveliest. And museums of art, history and culture dot downtown Richmond.

Buddy Mays / Virginia Tourism Corporation

Richmond Skyline. Modern towers cast shadows over the Victorian Gothic and neoclassical architecture below.

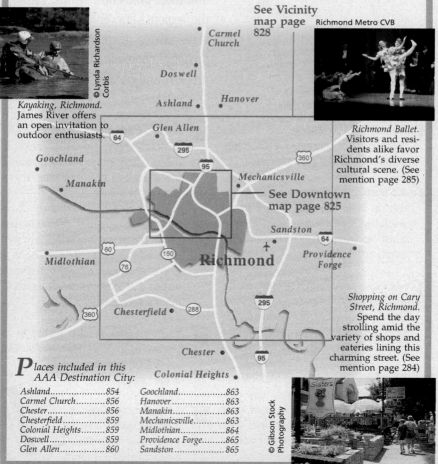

© Lynda Richardson Corbis

Kayaking, Richmond. James River offers an open invitation to outdoor enthusiasts.

See Vicinity map page 828

Richmond Metro CVB

Richmond Ballet. Visitors and residents alike favor Richmond's diverse cultural scene. (See mention page 285)

See Downtown map page 825

Shopping on Cary Street, Richmond. Spend the day strolling amid the variety of shops and eateries lining this charming street. (See mention page 284)

© Gibson Stock Photography

*P*laces included in this AAA Destination City:

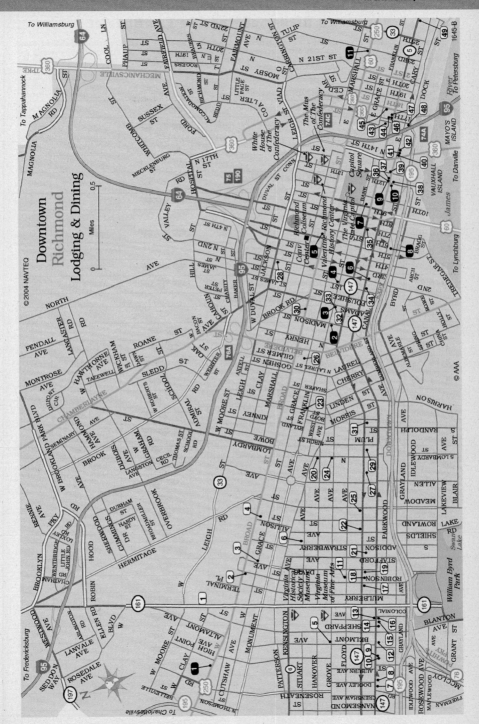

Downtown
Richmond
Lodging & Dining

©2004 NAVTEQ

Downtown Richmond And The Fan District

This index helps you "spot" where approved accommodations and restaurants are located on the corresponding detailed maps. Lodging rate ranges are for comparison only and show the property's high season; rates are per night, unless only weekly (W) rates are available. Restaurant rate range is for dinner, unless only lunch (L) is served. Turn to the listing page for more detailed rate information and consult display ads for special promotions.

Spotter/Map Page Number	OA	DOWNTOWN RICHMOND - Lodgings	Diamond Rating	Rate Range High Season	Listing Page
❶ / p. 825		Comfort Inn & Conference Center-Midtown	◇◇◇	$79-$99	838
❷ / p. 825		Radisson Hotel Historic Richmond - see color ad p 932	◇◇◇	$89-$109	840
❸ / p. 825	AAA	**The Jefferson Hotel** - see color ad p 838	◇◇◇◇◇	$265-$335 SAVE	838
❹ / p. 825	AAA	**Linden Row Inn**	◇◇◇	$95-$155 SAVE	839
❺ / p. 825	AAA	**Richmond Marriott Hotel** - see color ad p 839	◇◇◇	$94-$199 SAVE	840
❻ / p. 825		Quality Inn & Suites	◇◇◇	$79-$179	839
❼ / p. 825	AAA	**Commonwealth Park Suites**	◇◇◇	$93-$123 SAVE	838
❽ / p. 825		Crowne Plaza Richmond	◇◇◇	$139-$159	838
❾ / p. 825	AAA	**The Berkeley Hotel** - see color ad p 837	◇◇◇◇	$190-$250 SAVE	837
❿ / p. 825		Omni Richmond Hotel	◇◇◇	$225-$240	839
⓫ / p. 825		The William Catlin House	◇◇◇	$95-$103	840
		DOWNTOWN RICHMOND - Restaurants			
① / p. 825		Buz and Neds Real Barbecue	◇	$4-$20	841
② / p. 825		Julian's Restaurant	◇◇	$9-$20	843
③ / p. 825		Avenue 805	◇◇	$10-$20	840
④ / p. 825		Cabo's Corner Bistro	◇◇	$15-$30	841
⑤ / p. 825		Zeus Gallery Cafe	◇◇	$20-$30	845
⑥ / p. 825		Strawberry Street Cafe	◇◇	$6-$15	844
⑦ / p. 825		Amici Ristorante	◇◇◇	$14-$25	840
⑧ / p. 825		Acacia	◇◇◇	$13-$23	840
⑨ / p. 825		Chopstix	◇◇	$8-$20	841
⑩ / p. 825		Limani Fish Grill	◇◇◇	$18-$30	844
⑪ / p. 825		Konsta's	◇◇	$7-$22	843
⑫ / p. 825		Farouk's House of India	◇	$7-$12	842
⑬ / p. 825		Coppola's	◇	$5-$10	842
⑭ / p. 825		Indochine	◇◇◇	$10-$24	843
⑮ / p. 825		The Track	◇◇◇	$15-$24	845
⑯ / p. 825		Double T's Red Smoked Barbecue	◇	$6-$18	842
⑰ / p. 825	AAA	**Avalon**	◇◇	$6-$19	840
⑱ / p. 825		Helen's	◇◇◇	$17-$25	843
⑲ / p. 825		Davis & Main	◇◇	$12-$20	842
⑳ / p. 825		Kuba Kuba	◇◇	$6-$16	843
㉑ / p. 825		Southern Culture	◇◇	$7-$17	844
㉒ / p. 825		Stella's	◇◇	$10-$22	844
㉓ / p. 825		Edo's Squid	◇◇	$8-$18	842
㉔ / p. 825		Caffe di Pagliacci	◇◇	$9-$20	841

Spotter/Map Page Number	OA	**DOWNTOWN RICHMOND - Restaurants (continued)**	Diamond Rating	Rate Range High Season	Listing Page
㉕ / p. 825		Bacchus	▽▽▽	$12-$26	840
㉖ / p. 825		Sally Bell's Kitchen	▽	$5-$7(L)	844
㉗ / p. 825		Dogwoods Grille & Spirits	▽▽▽	$19-$31	842
㉘ / p. 825		Croaker's Spot	▽	$9-$33	842
㉙ / p. 825		Border Chophouse & Bar	▽▽	$6-$25	841
㉚ / p. 825	AAA	**Comfort**	▽▽	$10-$18	841
㉛ / p. 825		Cafe Mandolin	▽▽▽	$12-$25	841
㉜ / p. 825	AAA	**Lemaire** - see color ad p 838	▽▽▽▽▽	$21-$36	843
㉝ / p. 825		T. J.'s Restaurant	▽▽▽	$15-$30	845
㉞ / p. 825		The Thai Room at Beauregard's	▽▽	$10-$14	845
㉟ / p. 825		Capital Ale House	▽▽	$7-$20	841
㊱ / p. 825	AAA	**The Dining Room at the Berkeley Hotel**	▽▽▽▽	$22-$32	842
㊲ / p. 825		La Grotta	▽▽▽	$13-$28	843
㊳ / p. 825	AAA	**Pomegranate Euro Bistro**	▽▽▽	$17-$25	844
㊴ / p. 825		Peking Pavilion	▽▽	$8-$14	844
㊵ / p. 825		Europa Mediterranean Cafe and Tapas Bar	▽▽	$10-$23	842
㊶ / p. 825		The Hard Shell	▽▽▽	$12-$24	842
㊷ / p. 825		Rivah Bistro	▽▽▽	$12-$22	844
㊸ / p. 825		Havana '59	▽▽	$12-$28	843
㊹ / p. 825		The Kitchen Table	▽▽▽	$16-$26	843
㊺ / p. 825		Julep's, New Southern Cuisine	▽▽▽	$16-$24	843
㊻ / p. 825		Cafe' Gutenberg	▽▽	$3-$15	841
㊼ / p. 825		River City Diner	▽	$3-$10	844
㊽ / p. 825		Bottoms Up Pizza	▽▽	$4-$10	841
㊾ / p. 825		Millie's Diner	▽▽	$15-$28	844

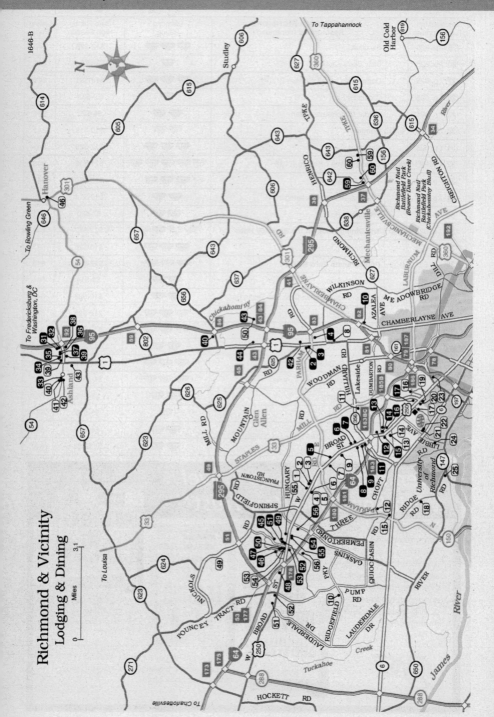

Richmond & Vicinity
Lodging & Dining

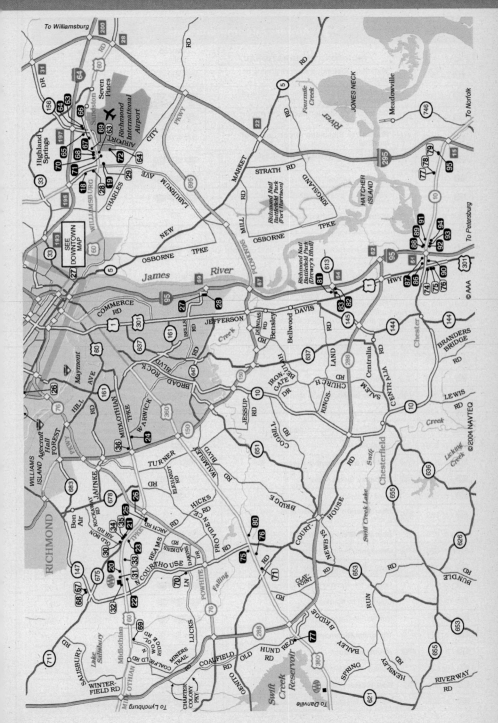

✈ Airport Accommodations

Spotter/Map Page Number	OA	**RICHMOND INTERNATIONAL**	Diamond Rating	Rate Range High Season	Listing Page
18 / p. 828	AAA	**Wyndham Richmond Airport, 1 mi w of airport**	◇◇◇	$99-$119 SAVE	850
68 / p. 828		Comfort Inn Richmond Airport, 0.3 mi w of airport	◇◇◇	$69-$79	865
69 / p. 828	AAA	**Courtyard by Marriott-Richmond Airport, 0.3 mi w of airport**	◇◇◇	$109-$199 SAVE	865
72 / p. 828	AAA	**DoubleTree Richmond Airport, just n of terminal**	◇◇◇	$69-$209 SAVE	865
67 / p. 828		Hampton Inn-Richmond Airport, 0.3 mi w of airport	◇◇◇	$89-$169	865
71 / p. 828		Holiday Inn-Airport, 0.3 mi w of airport	◇◇◇	$79-$169	865
64 / p. 828		Homewood Suites Richmond Airport, 1 mi n of airport	◇◇◇	$89-$129	865
63 / p. 828	AAA	**Microtel Inn & Suites, 0.5 mi n of airport**	◇	$59-$79 SAVE	866
66 / p. 828		Motel 6-Richmond Airport #435, just n of airport	◇	$37-$53	866
65 / p. 828		Wingate Inn Richmond Airport, 1 mi n of airport	◇◇◇	$89	866

Richmond & Vicinity

This index helps you "spot" where approved accommodations and restaurants are located on the corresponding detailed maps. Lodging rate ranges are for comparison only and show the property's high season; rates are per night, unless only weekly (W) rates are available. Restaurant rate range is for dinner, unless only lunch (L) is served. Turn to the listing page for more detailed rate information and consult display ads for special promotions.

Spotter/Map Page Number	OA	**RICHMOND - Lodgings**	Diamond Rating	Rate Range High Season	Listing Page
2 / p. 828		Econo Lodge North-Parham Rd	◇◇	$45-$95	847
3 / p. 828	AAA	**Sleep Inn**	◇◇	$57-$134 SAVE	850
4 / p. 828	AAA	**Holiday Inn-Richmond North**	◇◇◇	$79-$139 SAVE	848
5 / p. 828	AAA	**Quality Inn West End - see color ad p 849**	◇◇◇	$70-$99 SAVE	849
6 / p. 828		Econo Lodge-Richmond West	◇◇◇	$50-$100	847
7 / p. 828		Super 8 Motel	◇	Failed to provide	850
8 / p. 828	AAA	**Comfort Inn Executive Center**	◇◇	$65-$70 SAVE	847
9 / p. 828	AAA	**Embassy Suites Hotel**	◇◇◇	$99-$299 SAVE	848
10 / p. 828		Super 8 Motel	◇	$52-$57	850
11 / p. 828	AAA	**Best Western Executive Hotel - see color ad p 846**	◇◇	$69-$119 SAVE	846
12 / p. 828	AAA	**Sheraton Richmond West**	◇◇◇	$81-$109 SAVE	849
13 / p. 828	AAA	**Residence Inn by Marriott**	◇◇◇	$101-$129 SAVE	849
14 / p. 828		Days Inn-Richmond West	◇◇	$79-$139	847
15 / p. 828		Holiday Inn-Richmond I-64 & West Broad	◇◇◇	$59-$99	848
16 / p. 828		Courtyard by Marriott	◇◇◇	$79-$189	847
17 / p. 828		Holiday Inn-Crossroads	◇◇◇	$78-$104	848
18 / p. 828	AAA	**Wyndham Richmond Airport**	◇◇◇	$99-$119 SAVE	850
19 / p. 828	AAA	**Airport Inn Motel**	◇◇	$54-$84 SAVE	846
20 / p. 828		Holiday Inn Select-Koger South	◇◇◇	$99-$109	848
21 / p. 828	AAA	**Best Western Governor's Inn**	◇◇◇	$81-$135 SAVE	846
22 / p. 828		Hampton Inn-Midlothian Turnpike	◇◇◇	$69-$99	848

Spotter/Map Page Number	OA	**RICHMOND** - Lodgings (continued)	Diamond Rating	Rate Range High Season	Listing Page
23 / p. 828		Sheraton Park South Hotel	◆◆◆	$138	849
24 / p. 828	AAA	**Travel Inn**	◆◆	$45-$65 [SAVE]	850
25 / p. 828	AAA	**AmeriSuites (Richmond/Arboretum)** - see color ad p 837	◆◆◆	$104-$139 [SAVE]	846
26 / p. 828		Homestead Studio Suites Hotel-Richmond/Midlothian	◆◆◆	$58-$83	848
27 / p. 828		Candlewood Suites	◆◆◆	$84-$109	846
28 / p. 828		Ramada Inn Southeast	◆◆◆	$89-$189	849
		RICHMOND - Restaurants			
1 / p. 828		Zorba's	◆◆	$9-$14	854
2 / p. 828		Peking Restaurant	◆◆	$10-$14	853
3 / p. 828		Pasta Luna	◆◆	$10-$20	853
4 / p. 828		Manila! Manila! Cafe & Grille	◆	$8-$19	852
5 / p. 828		Franco's Ristorante	◆◆◆	$18-$26	851
6 / p. 828		Akida Japanese Restaurant	◆◆	$9-$18	850
7 / p. 828		Thai Diner	◆	$7-$10	853
8 / p. 828		Binigi's Cafe & Deli	◆	$4-$10	851
9 / p. 828	AAA	**Tandoor Indian Restaurant**	◆◆	$8-$16	853
10 / p. 828		Shackleford's Restaurant	◆◆	$14-$25	853
11 / p. 828		Vietnam Garden	◆◆	$6-$13	853
12 / p. 828		Melito's	◆◆	$10-$18	852
13 / p. 828		Full Kee Restaurant	◆	$5-$14	851
14 / p. 828		Mexico Restaurant	◆	$4-$12	852
15 / p. 828		Buckhead's	◆◆◆	$22-$41	851
16 / p. 828	AAA	**La Petite France**	◆◆◆	$19-$33	852
17 / p. 828		Graywolf Grill	◆	$8-$13	852
18 / p. 828		Grafiti Grille	◆◆	$7-$20	851
19 / p. 828		The Crazy Greek	◆	$5-$12	851
20 / p. 828		Sal Federico's Italian Restaurant	◆◆◆	$12-$25	853
21 / p. 828		Super Stars Gourmet Pizza	◆	$4-$10	853
22 / p. 828		Yum Yum Good	◆	$5-$13	853
23 / p. 828		India House	◆	$9-$13	852
24 / p. 828		DuJour	◆◆◆	$14-$21	851
25 / p. 828		Azzurro	◆◆◆	$9-$28	850
26 / p. 828		Baker's Crust Bread Market	◆◆	$7-$18	850
27 / p. 828		The Hill Cafe	◆◆	$6-$20	852
28 / p. 828		Grand Dynasty Restaurant	◆	$6-$14	852
29 / p. 828		Cactus Cafe	◆	$7-$13	851
30 / p. 828		Little Saigon	◆◆	$6-$15	852
31 / p. 828		Filiberti's	◆◆	$13-$27	851
32 / p. 828		Dena's Grecian Restaurant	◆	$8-$12	851

Spotter/Map Page Number	OA	RICHMOND - Restaurants (continued)	Diamond Rating	Rate Range High Season	Listing Page
㉝ / p. 828		Bangkok Cafe	◈	$8-$15	850
㉞ / p. 828		Ruchee Indian Restaurant	◈◈	$10-$14	853
㉟ / p. 828		La Siesta Mexican Restaurant	◈◈	$5-$12	852
㊱ / p. 828		Passage to India	◈	$13-$15	852
		ASHLAND - Lodgings			
㉛ / p. 828		Microtel Inn & Suites	◈◈	$69-$109	855
㉜ / p. 828	AAA	**Econo Lodge**	◈	$49-$110 SAVE	855
㉝ / p. 828		The Henry Clay Inn	◈◈◈	$90	855
㉞ / p. 828	AAA	**Sleep Inn & Suites**	◈◈◈	$64-$139 SAVE	855
㉟ / p. 828		Ashland Inn	◈◈	$85-$160	854
㊱ / p. 828	AAA	**Quality Inn & Suites**	◈◈	$50-$100 SAVE	855
㊲ / p. 828		Days Inn Ashland	◈◈	$70-$90	854
㊳ / p. 828		Holiday Inn Express Hotel & Suites	◈◈◈	$79-$129	855
㊴ / p. 828		Hampton Inn	◈◈◈	$89-$129	855
㊵ / p. 828		Hanover House Motor Lodge	◈◈	$79	855
		ASHLAND - Restaurants			
㊴ / p. 828		El Azteca	◈	$6-$17	856
㊵ / p. 828		Ashland Coffee & Tea	◈	$5-$12	856
㊶ / p. 828		Homemades by Suzanne	◈	$5-$8(L)	856
㊷ / p. 828		The Ironhorse Restaurant	◈◈	$8-$30	856
㊸ / p. 828		The Smokey Pig	◈	$4-$19	856
		GLEN ALLEN - Lodgings			
㊷ / p. 828		Howard Johnson Express Inn	◈◈	$65-$150	861
㊸ / p. 828	AAA	**Virginia Crossings Resort -** see color ad p 839	◈◈◈	$119-$179 SAVE	862
㊹ / p. 828	AAA	**Springhill Suites by Marriott**	◈◈◈	$105-$115 SAVE	861
㊺ / p. 828		TownePlace Suites by Marriott	◈◈◈	$59-$89	861
㊻ / p. 828		Richmond Marriott West	◈◈◈	$89-$300	861
㊼ / p. 828	AAA	**AmeriSuites (Richmond/Innsbrook) -** see color ad p 837	◈◈◈	$99-$159 SAVE	860
㊽ / p. 828		Candlewood Suites Richmond-West	◈◈◈	$89-$109	860
㊾ / p. 828		Homewood Suites by Hilton Richmond West End-Innsbrook	◈◈◈	$109-$159	861
㊿ / p. 828		Hilton Garden Inn Richmond Innsbrook	◈◈◈	$79-$159	860
51 / p. 828		Comfort Suites-Innsbrook	◈◈◈	$69-$109	860
52 / p. 828		Hampton Inn-Richmond West	◈◈◈	$86-$112	860
53 / p. 828		Homestead Studio Suites Hotel-Richmond/Innsbrook	◈◈	$54-$79	861
54 / p. 828		Courtyard by Marriott Richmond Northwest	◈◈◈	$129-$139	860
55 / p. 828		Residence Inn by Marriott	◈◈◈	$129-$169	861
56 / p. 828		Holiday Inn Express	◈◈◈	$101	860
		GLEN ALLEN - Restaurants			
㊾ / p. 828		Garland's Way	◈◈	$11-$20	862

Spotter/Map Page Number	OA	**GLEN ALLEN - Restaurants (continued)**	Diamond Rating	Rate Range High Season	Listing Page
⑤⓪ / p. 828		The Glen Restaurant	◆◆◆	$16-$28	862
⑤① / p. 828		Osaka Sushi & Steak	◆◆	$12-$20	862
⑤② / p. 828		Short Pump Grill	◆◆	$11-$27	862
⑤③ / p. 828		Mama Cucina	◆◆◆	$13-$17	862
⑤④ / p. 828		Mexico Restaurant	◆	$7-$11	862
⑤⑤ / p. 828		Bistro R	◆◆◆	$20-$26	862
⑤⑥ / p. 828		The Grapevine II	◆◆◆	$9-$18	862
		MECHANICSVILLE - Lodgings			
⑤⑨ / p. 828		Holiday Inn Express-Richmond-Mechanicsville	◆◆◆	$59-$129	863
⑥⓪ / p. 828		Hampton Inn	◆◆◆	$89-$99	863
		MECHANICSVILLE - Restaurants			
⑤⑨ / p. 828		Peking Restaurant	◆◆	$9-$16	863
⑥⓪ / p. 828		Mexico Restaurant	◆	$6-$13	863
		SANDSTON - Lodgings			
⑥③ / p. 828	AAA	**Microtel Inn & Suites**	◆	$59-$79 SAVE	866
⑥④ / p. 828		Homewood Suites Richmond Airport	◆◆◆	$89-$129	865
⑥⑤ / p. 828		Wingate Inn Richmond Airport	◆◆◆	$89	866
⑥⑥ / p. 828		Motel 6-Richmond Airport #435	◆	$37-$53	866
⑥⑦ / p. 828		Hampton Inn-Richmond Airport	◆◆◆	$89-$169	865
⑥⑧ / p. 828		Comfort Inn Richmond Airport	◆◆◆	$69-$79	865
⑥⑨ / p. 828	AAA	**Courtyard by Marriott-Richmond Airport**	◆◆◆	$109-$199 SAVE	865
⑦⓪ / p. 828		Super 8 Motel	◆	$52-$68	866
⑦① / p. 828		Holiday Inn-Airport	◆◆◆	$79-$169	865
⑦② / p. 828	AAA	**DoubleTree Richmond Airport**	◆◆◆	$69-$209 SAVE	865
		SANDSTON - Restaurants			
⑥③ / p. 828		Mexico Restaurant	◆	$4-$7	866
⑥④ / p. 828	AAA	**Wings**	◆◆	$5-$24	866
		MIDLOTHIAN - Lodgings			
⑦⑤ / p. 828	AAA	**Super 8 Motel**	◆◆◆	$49-$150 SAVE	864
⑦⑥ / p. 828		Hampton Inn-Richmond-South West-Hull Street	◆◆◆	$69-$89	864
⑦⑦ / p. 828		Holiday Inn Express Hotel & Suites-Brandermill	◆◆◆	$59-$89	864
		MIDLOTHIAN - Restaurants			
⑥⑦ / p. 828		Bottega Bistro	◆◆◆	$9-$20	864
⑥⑧ / p. 828		Ruth's Chris Steak House	◆◆◆	$20-$34	864
⑥⑨ / p. 828		Al Dente's Restaurant	◆◆◆	$9-$20	864
⑦⓪ / p. 828		Nuccio's Trattoria & Pizza	◆◆	$5-$16	864
⑦① / p. 828		Saigon Gourmet	◆	$6-$14	864
		CHESTERFIELD - Lodgings			
⑧⓪ / p. 828	AAA	**Royal Inn Motel**	◆	$45-$55 SAVE	859
⑧① / p. 828		Super 8 Motel	◆◆◆	$59-$69	859
⑧② / p. 828	AAA	**Country Inn & Suites, Richmond I-95S** - see color ad p 847	◆◆◆	$59-$99 SAVE	859

Spotter/Map Page Number	OA	CHESTERFIELD - Lodgings (continued)	Diamond Rating	Rate Range High Season	Listing Page
83 / p. 828	AAA	Sleep Inn	◈◈	$59-$99 SAVE	859
		CHESTER - Lodgings			
86 / p. 828		Super 8 Motel	◈	$54-$99	858
87 / p. 828		Fairfield Inn By Marriott	◈◈◈	$59-$149	857
88 / p. 828	AAA	Hampton Inn /	◈◈◈	$79-$129 SAVE	857
89 / p. 828	AAA	Comfort Inn-Richmond/Chester - see color ad p 857	◈◈◈	$59-$119 SAVE	857
90 / p. 828	AAA	Clarion Hotel	◈◈◈	$59-$99 SAVE	857
91 / p. 828	AAA	Quality Inn & Suites	◈◈	$79-$99 SAVE	858
92 / p. 828		Courtyard by Marriott	◈◈◈	$85-$94	857
93 / p. 828		Holiday Inn Express	◈◈◈	$59-$79	857
94 / p. 828		Homewood Suites Richmond/Chester	◈◈◈	$89-$189	858
95 / p. 828	AAA	AmeriSuites (Chester/River's Bend)	◈◈◈	$129-$159 SAVE	856
		CHESTER - Restaurants			
74 / p. 828		Peking Restaurant	◈◈	$7-$12	858
75 / p. 828		Central Park Deli	◈	$5-$7	858
76 / p. 828		Don Papa Grande Mexican Restaurant	◈	$6-$13	858
77 / p. 828		Cesare's Restaurant & Pizzeria	◈	$6-$14	858
78 / p. 828		Narita Japanese Restaurant	◈◈	$7-$50	858
79 / p. 828		Jalapenos	◈◈	$7-$14	858
		HANOVER - Restaurant			
46 / p. 828		Houndstooth Cafe	◈	$4-$22	863

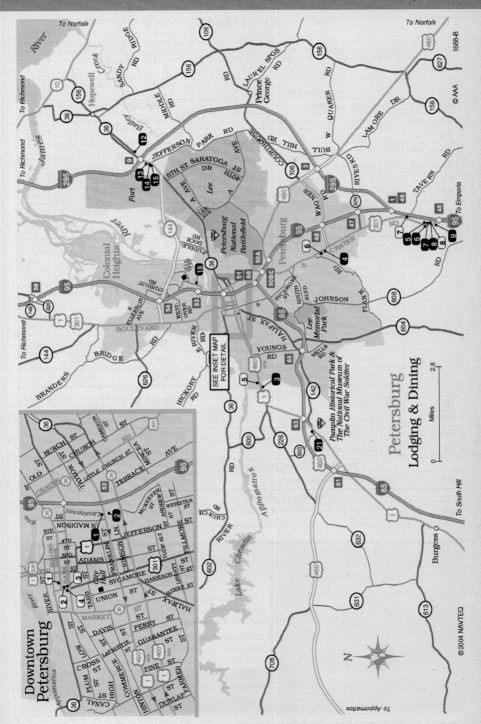

Petersburg

This index helps you "spot" where approved accommodations and restaurants are located on the corresponding detailed maps. Lodging rate ranges are for comparison only and show the property's high season; rates are per night, unless only weekly (W) rates are available. Restaurant rate range is for dinner, unless only lunch (L) is served. Turn to the listing page for more detailed rate information and consult display ads for special promotions.

Spotter/Map Page Number	OA	PETERSBURG - Lodgings	Diamond Rating	Rate Range High Season	Listing Page
❶ / p. 835	AAA	Quality Inn	◈◈	$60-$105 SAVE	820
❷ / p. 835		Ramada Plaza Hotel Petersburg	◈◈◈	$89-$169	820
❸ / p. 835		Mayfield Inn	◈◈◈	$85-$120	820
❹ / p. 835	AAA	Super 8 Motel	◈◈	$55-$95 SAVE	820
❺ / p. 835	AAA	Hampton Inn	◈◈◈	$75-$129 SAVE	819
❻ / p. 835		Comfort Inn - see color ad p 818	◈◈	$55-$120	817
❼ / p. 835	AAA	Holiday Inn Express-Petersburg South	◈◈	$69-$99 SAVE	820
❽ / p. 835	AAA	Best Western-Steven Kent - see color ad p 818	◈◈◈	$49-$80 SAVE	817
❾ / p. 835	AAA	Days Inn - see color ad p 818	◈◈◈	$60-$100 SAVE	819
		PETERSBURG - Restaurants			
① / p. 835		The Brickhouse Run	◈◈◈	$10-$19	820
② / p. 835		Leonardo's Restaurant	◈◈	$6-$18	821
③ / p. 835		Alexander's Fine Food	◈	$8-$14	820
④ / p. 835		Longstreet's Delicatessen	◈	$5-$8	821
⑤ / p. 835		King's Barbecue	◈	$2-$10	820
⑥ / p. 835		Kings Barbeque No. 2	◈	$5-$9	821
⑦ / p. 835		Nanny's Family Restaurant	◈	$4-$10	821
⑧ / p. 835		Best Western-Steven Kent Restaurant	◈◈	$6-$16	820
		HOPEWELL - Lodgings			
⓬ / p. 835	AAA	Econo Lodge	◈◈	$69 SAVE	795
⓭ / p. 835		Quality Inn	◈◈	$59-$79	796
⓮ / p. 835		Hampton Inn-Ft Lee	◈◈◈	$59-$89	796
⓯ / p. 835	AAA	Candlewood Suites	◈◈	$69-$79 SAVE	795
		COLONIAL HEIGHTS - Lodgings			
⓲ / p. 835	AAA	Comfort Suites Southpark	◈◈◈	$95-$149 SAVE	859
		DINWIDDIE - Lodgings			
㉑ / p. 835	AAA	Holiday Inn Express Hotel & Suites - see color ad p 819	◈◈◈	$90-$110 SAVE	692

DOWNTOWN RICHMOND   (See map and index starting on p. 825)

———— WHERE TO STAY ————

THE BERKELEY HOTEL   *Book at aaa.com*   **Phone:** (804)780-1300   **9**

(AAA) (SAVE)   All Year   1P: $190-$235   2P: $205-$250   XP: $15   F
◈◈◈ ◈◈◈   **Location:** Just w of state capitol. Located in Historic Shockoe Slip District. 1200 E Cary St 23219. Fax: 804/648-4728.
Small-scale Hotel   **Facility:** In the tradition of the boutique hotel, the petite Berkeley offers guests highly personalized service and elegant suites in the heart of Shockoe Slip. 55 units. 54 one-bedroom standard units. 1 one-bedroom suite ($675). 6 stories, interior corridors. *Bath:* combo or shower only. **Parking:** on-site (fee) and valet.
Terms: cancellation fee imposed. **Amenities:** high-speed Internet, voice mail, safes, irons, hair dryers.
Dining: dining room, see separate listing. **Guest Services:** valet laundry, area transportation-downtown. **Business Services:** meeting rooms, business center. **Cards:** AX, DC, DS, MC, VI. **Special Amenities:** free newspaper and free room upgrade (subject to availability with advance reservations). *(See color ad below)*

SOME UNITS

🆂🅳 🍴 🏋 ♿ 📶 🎥 🖥️ 💻 / ⊠ 📼 🔌 /
FEE

*T*he Berkeley's European charm and gracious hospitality preserve innkeeping as an art. Its 55 traditionally furnished guest rooms offer a refreshing change from ordinary accommodations. Located in Historic Shockoe Slip, center of unique shops and entertaining night life. Just two blocks from the State Capital.

The **Berkeley** *Hotel*

(AAA)   ◈◈◈

1200 E. CARY STREET • RICHMOND, VA 23219
(804) 780-1300 • 1-888-780-4422
www.berkeleyhotel.com

(See map and index starting on p. 825)

COMFORT INN & CONFERENCE CENTER-MIDTOWN *Book at aaa.com*

Phone: (804)359-4061 **1**

All Year 1P: $79-$99 XP: $10 F18
Location: Jct Broad St and I-95, just e. 3200 W Broad St 23230. Fax: 804/359-3189. **Facility:** 189 units. 187 one-bedroom standard units. 2 one-bedroom suites ($100-$139). 6 stories, interior corridors. *Bath:* combo or shower only. **Parking:** on-site. **Terms:** package plans. **Amenities:** voice mail, irons, hair dryers. **Pool(s):** outdoor. **Guest Services:** valet and coin laundry, area transportation. **Business Services:** meeting rooms, fax. **Cards:** AX, DC, DS, MC, VI.

Small-scale Hotel

SOME UNITS
(ASK) (SD) (fork) (wheelchair) (shuttle) (FEE) (pet) (film) (DATA PORT) (coffee) / (X) (FEE) (fridge FEE) /

COMMONWEALTH PARK SUITES

Phone: (804)343-7300 **7**

(AAA) (SAVE)

1P: $93-$123 2P: $93-$123 XP: $15 F16
Location: Jct 9th and Bank sts; across the green from the state capitol. 901 Bank St 23219. Fax: 804/343-1025. **Facility:** 59 units. 10 one-bedroom standard units. 49 one-bedroom suites. 11 stories, interior corridors. *Bath:* combo or shower only. **Parking:** on-site (fee) and valet. **Terms:** cancellation fee imposed, small pets only ($25 fee). **Amenities:** voice mail, honor bars, irons, hair dryers. *Some:* CD players. **Leisure Activities:** sauna, exercise room. **Guest Services:** valet and coin laundry. **Business Services:** meeting rooms, business center. **Cards:** AX, CB, DC, DS, MC, VI.

Small-scale Hotel

SOME UNITS
(SD) (pet) (Y) (wheelchair) (FEE) (film) (DATA PORT) (coffee) / (X) (VCR) (fridge) /

CROWNE PLAZA RICHMOND *Book at aaa.com*

Phone: (804)788-0900 **8**

1/1-2/28 1P: $139-$159 2P: $139-$159
3/1-12/31 1P: $129-$149 2P: $129-$149
Location: I-95, exit 74A (downtown expwy I-195), exit Canal St. 555 E Canal St 23219. Fax: 804/788-7087. **Facility:** 300 one-bedroom standard units. 16 stories, interior corridors. **Parking:** on-site (fee). **Terms:** [AP], [BP] & [CP] meal plans available. **Amenities:** CD players, dual phone lines, voice mail, irons, hair dryers. *Some:* high-speed Internet. **Pool(s):** heated indoor. **Leisure Activities:** saunas, whirlpool, exercise room. **Guest Services:** gift shop, valet laundry, area transportation. **Business Services:** conference facilities, business center. **Cards:** AX, DC, DS, MC, VI.

Large-scale Hotel

SOME UNITS
(ASK) (fork) (Y) (gym) (shuttle) (X) (film) (DATA PORT) (coffee) / (X) (fridge) (screen) /

THE JEFFERSON HOTEL *Book at aaa.com*

Phone: (804)788-8000 **3**

(AAA) (SAVE)

All Year 1P: $265-$315 2P: $285-$335 XP: $20 F17
Location: Franklin and Adams sts; center. 101 W Franklin St 23220. Fax: 804/225-0334. **Facility:** This ornate 1895 Beaux Arts hotel is a historic landmark with a wealth of striking architectural details including a Tiffany stained-glass rotunda. 264 units. 224 one-bedroom standard units. 40 one-bedroom suites, some with whirlpools. 5-6 stories, interior corridors. **Parking:** on-site (fee) and valet. **Terms:** package plans, pets ($35 extra charge, in designated units). **Amenities:** video library, video games, CD players, dual phone lines, voice mail, safes, honor bars, irons, hair dryers. *Some:* DVD players, fax. **Dining:** 2 restaurants, 6:30 am-midnight, cocktails, also, Lemaire, T. J.'s Restaurant, see separate listings, entertainment. **Pool(s):** heated indoor. **Leisure Activities:** *Fee:* massage. **Guest Services:** gift shop, valet laundry, area transportation-within 3 mi. **Business Services:** conference facilities, business center. **Cards:** AX, DC, DS, MC, VI. **Special Amenities:** free local telephone calls and free newspaper. *(See color ad below)*

Classic Historic
Large-scale Hotel

SOME UNITS
(SD) (pet) (FEE) (fork) (24) (Y) (wheelchair) (shuttle) (pet) (film) (DATA PORT) / (X) (VCR) (fridge) (screen) /

(See map and index starting on p. 825)

LINDEN ROW INN — *Book at aaa.com*   Phone: (804)783-7000 [4]
(AAA) (SAVE)   All Year [CP]   1P: $95-$105   2P: $105-$155   XP: $10   F17
   Location: At 1st and Franklin sts. 100 E Franklin St 23219. Fax: 804/648-7504. **Facility:** The property includes a
   series of Greek Revival townhouses plus carriage houses in a walled garden. 68 units. 62 one-bedroom
   standard units. 6 one-bedroom suites ($145-$195). 4 stories, interior/exterior corridors. *Bath:* combo or
Historic   shower only. **Parking:** on-site (fee) and valet. **Terms:** package plans. **Amenities:** high-speed Internet, voice
Small-scale Hotel   mail, safes (fee), irons, hair dryers. **Dining:** 7 am-10 pm, Sat & Sun from 7:30 am, cocktails. **Guest**
   Services: valet laundry, area transportation-within 3 mi. **Business Services:** meeting rooms, fax.
Cards: AX, CB, DC, DS, MC, VI. **Special Amenities: free continental breakfast and free newspaper.**

SOME UNITS
[SD] [YI] [Y] [handicap] [X] [camera] [DATA PORT] [monitor] / [X] [VCR] [fridge] [microwave] /
FEE   FEE   FEE   FEE

OMNI RICHMOND HOTEL — *Book at aaa.com*   Phone: (804)344-7000 [10]
          1/1-2/28   1P: $225-$240   XP: $20   F18
          3/1-12/31   1P: $220-$235   XP: $20   F18
Large-scale Hotel   **Location:** I-95, exit 74A; I-195, exit Canal St. Located near the historic Shockoe Slip District. 100 S 12th St 23219.
   Fax: 804/648-6704. **Facility:** 361 units. 355 one-bedroom standard units. 6 one-bedroom suites. 19 stories,
interior corridors. **Parking:** on-site (fee) and valet. **Terms:** cancellation fee imposed, package plans, small pets only ($50 fee).
Amenities: video games, high-speed Internet, voice mail, honor bars, irons, hair dryers. *Some:* CD players, dual phone lines.
Pool(s): heated indoor. **Guest Services:** gift shop, valet laundry, area transportation. **Business Services:** conference facilities,
business center. **Cards:** AX, DC, DS, MC, VI.

SOME UNITS
(ASK) [pig] [YI] [Y] [workout] [data] [boat] [handicap] [X] [DATA PORT] [monitor] / [X] [fridge] /
FEE   FEE   FEE

QUALITY INN & SUITES — *Book at aaa.com*   Phone: (804)788-1600 [6]
          All Year   1P: $79-$169   2P: $89-$179   XP: $10   F12
   Location: Jct 2nd St. 201 E Cary St 23219. Fax: 804/788-1661. **Facility:** 100 units. 80 one-bedroom standard
Small-scale Hotel   units, some with whirlpools. 20 one-bedroom suites ($99-$179), some with whirlpools. 6 stories, interior
   corridors. *Bath:* combo or shower only. **Parking:** on-site. **Terms:** cancellation fee imposed. **Amenities:** dual
phone lines, voice mail, safes, irons, hair dryers. **Leisure Activities:** exercise room. **Guest Services:** valet laundry, area
transportation. **Business Services:** meeting rooms, business center. **Cards:** AX, DC, DS, MC, VI.

SOME UNITS
(ASK) [SD] [YI] [workout] [data] [camera] [DATA PORT] [fridge] [microwave] [monitor] / [X] /

(See map and index starting on p. 825)

RADISSON HOTEL HISTORIC RICHMOND   *Book at aaa.com*   **Phone: (804)644-9871**   ②
All Year   1P: $89-$109   2P: $89-$109
Location: Franklin St at Madison. 301 W Franklin St 23220. Fax: 804/344-4380. **Facility:** 230 units. 228 one-
Small-scale Hotel   bedroom standard units. 2 one-bedroom suites. 16 stories, interior corridors. *Bath:* combo or shower only.
Parking: on-site. **Terms:** 3 day cancellation notice, pets ($25 fee). **Amenities:** dual phone lines, voice mail,
irons, hair dryers. *Some: Fee:* video games. **Pool(s):** outdoor. **Leisure Activities:** exercise room. **Guest Services:** valet
laundry, area transportation. **Business Services:** meeting rooms, business center. **Cards:** AX, DC, DS, MC, VI.
(See color ad p 932)

SOME UNITS

(ASK) (S̄D̄) 🛏 🍴 (Ⓣ) 🖼 🐎 🎬 (DATA PORT) 🖥 / ✕ (VCR) 🛁 🖨 /
          FEE   FEE FEE FEE

RICHMOND MARRIOTT HOTEL   *Book at aaa.com*   **Phone: (804)643-3400**   ⑤
(AAA) (SAVE)   All Year   1P: $94-$199   2P: $94-$199
Location: I-95, exit 74C, at 5th and E Broad sts. Located adjacent to the Richmond Coliseum and Richmond Centre.
500 E Broad St 23219. Fax: 804/649-3725. **Facility:** 401 units. 391 one-bedroom standard units. 10 one-
bedroom suites. 18 stories, interior corridors. *Bath:* combo or shower only. **Parking:** on-site (fee).
Large-scale Hotel   **Terms:** check-in 4 pm, cancellation fee imposed, package plans. **Amenities:** high-speed Internet (fee), dual
phone lines, voice mail, irons, hair dryers. **Dining:** 6:30 am-2 & 5-10 pm, cocktails. **Pool(s):** heated indoor.
Leisure Activities: saunas, whirlpool, sun deck, exercise room. **Guest Services:** gift shop, valet and coin laundry, area
transportation-within 3 mi. **Business Services:** conference facilities, business center. **Cards:** AX, CB, DC, DS, MC, VI.
**Special Amenities: early check-in/late check-out and free room upgrade (subject to availability with advance
reservations).** *(See color ad p 839)*

SOME UNITS

(S̄D̄) 🍴 (Ⓣ) 🏊 🐎 ✕ 🎬 (DATA PORT) 🖥 / ✕ 🛁 /

THE WILLIAM CATLIN HOUSE   **Phone: (804)780-3746**   ⑪
All Year [BP]   1P: $95   2P: $103
Location: Between 22nd and 23rd sts; in the Church Hill Historic District. 2304 E Broad St 23223. **Facility:** This richly
appointed house in a historic district features Civil War history books, family heirlooms and period furniture
Historic Bed   including canopy beds. Smoke free premises. 4 units. 2 one- and 2 two-bedroom standard units. 3 stories
& Breakfast   (no elevator), interior/exterior corridors. *Bath:* some shared or private, combo or shower only. **Parking:**
street. **Terms:** 2 night minimum stay - seasonal, age restrictions may apply, 3 day cancellation notice. **Cards:** DS, MC, VI.

SOME UNITS

✕ (CTV) (Z̄) / (PW̄) /

──────── **WHERE TO DINE** ────────

ACACIA   **Lunch:** $5-$9   **Dinner:** $13-$23   **Phone:** 804/354-6060   ⑧
Location: I-195, exit W Cary St, just e; in Carytown. 3325 W Cary St 23221. **Hours:** 11:30 am-2:30 & 5:30-9:30
pm. Closed: 11/24, 12/25; also Sun. **Reservations:** suggested. **Features:** Acacia was first noticed for their
Regional American   unique setting in the nave of a restored church but recently it's the culinary skills of the chef, Dale Reitzer,
which has garnered national acclaim. The menu changes seasonally taking advantage of the freshest
regional fare in creative and light combinations. Tables on the raised patio above the street are a nice spot to enjoy the
streetscape. Dressy casual; cocktails. **Parking:** street. **Cards:** AX, DC, DS, MC, VI.

✕

AMICI RISTORANTE   **Lunch:** $7-$12   **Dinner:** $14-$25   **Phone:** 804/353-4700   ⑦
Location: I-195, exit W Cary St, just e; in Carytown. 3343 W Cary St 23221. **Hours:** 11:30 am-2:30 & 5:30-10 pm,
Fri & Sat 11:30 am-4 & 5:30-11 pm, Sun 5:30 pm-10 pm. Closed major holidays. **Reservations:** suggested.
Northern   **Features:** In a converted turn-of-the-20th-century townhouse, the intimate restaurant has preferred tables
Italian   set amid the twinkling lights of the sidewalk patio. Although the upscale Italian cuisine changes seasonally,
some constant specialties include fresh fennel salad, agnolotti pasta stuffed with spinach and ricotta, and
baby rack of lamb with rosemary and garlic. Service is smooth and professional, and wine choices are excellent. Dressy casual;
cocktails. **Parking:** street. **Cards:** AX, DS, MC, VI.

✕

AVALON   *Menu on aaa.com*   **Dinner:** $6-$19   **Phone:** 804/353-9709   ⑰
(AAA)   **Location:** Just e of Boulevard (SR 161) on W Main St (SR 147); in Historic Fan District. 2619 W Main St 23220.
Hours: 5 pm-2 am. Closed: 11/24, 12/24, 12/25. **Reservations:** suggested. **Features:** The seasonally
changing menu shows a real flair, taking advantage of the freshest ingredients in imaginative ways. Out-of-
Regional   the-ordinary dishes incorporate plenty of fruit, cheese and veggies. Photographs from the '40s and '50s
American   capture notables of the time. Noisy bar crowd later in the evenings. Casual dress; cocktails. **Parking:** street.
Cards: AX, MC, VI.

(Ⓣ) ✕

AVENUE 805   **Lunch:** $5-$12   **Dinner:** $10-$20   **Phone:** 804/353-2505   ③
Location: Just s of jct W Broad St; in Historic Fan District. 805 N Davis Ave 23220. **Hours:** 11:30 am-2 & 5:30-11
pm, Mon & Sat from 5:30 pm, Sun 11 am-3 pm. **Features:** A light-hearted attitude prevails at the fun little
Continental   spot. The constantly changing list of creative specials might include potato-crusted rockfish, seared duck or
what the owner dubs the "menu du always" of "inspired" Italian dishes, such as veal or chicken scaloppine,
varied pasta dishes and delightful shrimp, scallop and crab cakes. Casual dress; cocktails. **Parking:** street. **Cards:** AX, DS,
MC, VI.

✕

BACCHUS   **Dinner:** $12-$26   **Phone:** 804/355-9919   ㉕
Location: Jct W Main St; in Historic Fan District. 2 N Meadow St 23220. **Hours:** 5 pm-11 pm. Closed major
holidays; also Sun. **Reservations:** suggested. **Features:** The charming bistro is tucked in a narrow spot
Continental   with an elaborately carved bar and Roman-themed mural. Modern, creative dishes reflect Mediterranean
influences. Start with classic antipasto or carpaccio, then choose from such well-prepared options as
roasted duck, seared tuna or bouillabaisse. Parking is available across the street after 6 pm. Casual dress; cocktails. **Parking:**
street. **Cards:** AX, MC, VI.

(See map and index starting on p. 825)

BORDER CHOPHOUSE & BAR   **Lunch:** $5-$8   **Dinner:** $6-$25   **Phone:** 804/355-2907   ㉙
Location: Just w of Virginia Commonwealth University. 1501 W Main St 23220. **Hours:** 11 am-2 am. Closed: 11/24,
12/25. **Reservations:** accepted. **Features:** If you crave red meat in a casual fun neighborhood bar setting,
this is your spot. The menu centers on all varieties of steak cuts, plus barbecue ribs with some creative
American   sauces. Most influences are Western, but a few Asian influences surprisingly show up. Try the great
cornbread, fried pickles appetizer or Southern-influenced sides. Casual dress; cocktails. **Parking:** street. **Cards:** AX, DC, DS,
MC, VI.

BOTTOMS UP PIZZA   **Lunch:** $4-$10   **Dinner:** $4-$10   **Phone:** 804/644-4400   ㊽
Location: Jct 17th and Dock sts, just s of E Main St; in the Shockoe Bottom District. 1700 Dock St 23223. **Hours:** 11
am-10 pm, Fri & Sat-2 am. Closed: 11/24, 12/25. **Features:** Diners can choose from such creative toppings
as seafood and vegetables when ordering thick-crust pizza either whole or by the slice. An ideal place to
American   wait while the pizza is baking is in the lively bar, which caters to a young crowd. Popular starters include
wings and fried mozzarella. Casual dress; cocktails. **Parking:** street. **Cards:** AX, DC, DS, MC, VI.

BUZ AND NEDS REAL BARBECUE   **Lunch:** $4-$20   **Dinner:** $4-$20   **Phone:** 804/355-6055   ①
Location: Just n of W Broad St. 1119 N Boulevard 23230. **Hours:** 11 am-8 pm. Closed major holidays; also Sun.
Features: After traveling the country researching the world of barbecue, Buz and Ned have perfected their
spicy-sweet version. Guests can sample brisket, pork, chicken and even buffalo ribs with such traditional
Barbecue   Southern sides as baked beans, macaroni and cheese and jalapeno corn fries. Casual dress; beer & wine
only. **Parking:** no self-parking. **Cards:** AX, MC, VI.

CABO'S CORNER BISTRO   **Dinner:** $15-$30   **Phone:** 804/355-1144   ④
Location: Just e of Science Museum of Virginia. 2053 W Broad St 23220. **Hours:** 5 pm-10:30 pm. Closed major
holidays; also Sun & Mon. **Reservations:** accepted. **Features:** Stylish art deco interior with dining in the
more social lounge as well. Eclectic cuisine mixing European traditions with Southern influences.
Continental   Entertainment nightly specializing in swing jazz and blues. Casual dress; cocktails. **Parking:** on-site.
Cards: AX, CB, DC, MC, VI.

CAFE' GUTENBERG   **Lunch:** $3-$15   **Dinner:** $3-$15   **Phone:** 804/497-5000   ㊻
Location: Jct 17th St; across from the Farmer's Market; in Shockoe Bottom. 1700 E Main St 23223. **Hours:** 8 am-8
pm, Thurs-Sun to midnight. Closed: 1/1, 11/24, 12/25; also Mon. **Reservations:** accepted. **Features:** If
sitting down with a great cup of joe and a good book is your thing, then you'll like this bohemian cafe, which
Coffee/Espresso   houses an eclectic selection of books and magazines for your reading pleasure. But this is no ordinary
coffee joint. There's also beer and wine, as well as soups, salads, tapas, panini sandwiches and dessert. And if you're an early
riser, there's breakfast, and the morning paper, too. Casual dress; beer & wine only. **Parking:** street. **Cards:** DS, MC, VI.

CAFE MANDOLIN   **Lunch:** $5-$9   **Dinner:** $12-$25   **Phone:** 804/355-8558   ㉛
Location: Between Randolph and Brunswick sts; just w of Virginia Commonwealth University; in Historic Fan District.
1309 W Main St 23220. **Hours:** 11:30 am-9 pm, Fri & Sat-9:30 pm. Closed: Sun & Mon.
Reservations: suggested, weekends. **Features:** Quiet and stylish, the smoke-free spot has an open
American   kitchen in the rear and comfy bar seating. The seasonal menu offers an array of ever-changing eclectic
offerings that blend international flavors. Casual dress; cocktails. **Parking:** on-site. **Cards:** AX, CB, DC, MC, VI.

CAFFE DI PAGLIACCI   **Dinner:** $9-$20   **Phone:** 804/353-3040   ㉔
Location: Jct W Broad and N Lombardy St, 0.5 mi s; in Historic Fan District. 214 N Lombardy St 23220. **Hours:** 5 pm-
10 pm, Fri & Sat-11 pm. Closed major holidays; also Sun & Mon. **Reservations:** suggested, weekends.
Features: Tucked on a side street in the historic area, the warm, cozy spot has a whimsical feel enhanced
Italian   by clown artwork, including Red Skelton prints, on the walls. Anchoring the menu are meat dishes, such as
veal stuffed with homemade sausage in a demi-glace, as well as such hearty pasta preparations as seafood linguine. Casual
dress; cocktails. **Parking:** street. **Cards:** AX, DS, MC, VI.

CAPITAL ALE HOUSE   **Lunch:** $7-$20   **Dinner:** $7-$20   **Phone:** 804/643-2537   ㉟
Location: Between 6th and 7th sts. 623 E Main St 23219. **Hours:** 11 am-midnight, Fri-1:30 am, Sat 10 am-1:30
am, Sun 10 am-midnight. Closed: 1/1, 11/24, 12/25. **Features:** Ice troughs shaped to fit drink glasses at the
bar show where the priorities lie. However, the food isn't taken for granted either. Menu selections range
American   from sandwiches to snack-size appetizers to sophisticated entrees. Casual dress; cocktails. **Parking:** street.
Cards: AX, DC, DS, MC, VI.

CHOPSTIX   **Lunch:** $8-$20   **Dinner:** $8-$20   **Phone:** 804/358-7027   ⑨
Location: I-195, exit W Cary St, just e; in Carytown. 3129 W Cary St 23231. **Hours:** 11:30 am-10 pm. Closed: Sun.
Features: Fresh and healthful Vietnamese fare is the specialty at the casual Carytown spot. Favorites
include shrimp on sugar cane, salmon one of four ways, hot pots and green papaya salad. Casual dress;
Vietnamese   cocktails. **Parking:** street. **Cards:** AX, DS, MC, VI.

COMFORT   **Lunch:** $6-$8   **Dinner:** $10-$18   **Phone:** 804/780-0004   ㉚
Location: Jct Jefferson St. 200 W Broad St 23220. **Hours:** 11:30 am-2:30 & 5:30-10:30 pm, Fri & Sat-11 pm.
Closed major holidays; also Sun. **Features:** As the name implies, this spot specializes in comfort foods of
the Southern variety. Among specialties are fried catfish, braised short ribs and roasted duck, which are
Regional   served with plentiful country sides, such as fried green tomatoes, creamed spinach and cheese grits.
American   Casual dress; cocktails. **Parking:** street. **Cards:** AX, MC, VI.

(See map and index starting on p. 825)

COPPOLA'S

*Deli/Subs
Sandwiches*

Cards: MC, VI.

Lunch: $5-$7   **Dinner:** $5-$10   **Phone:** 804/359-6969   ⑬
Location: I-95, exit W Cary St, 1 mi e, then just w of jct Boulevard; in Carytown. 2900 W Cary St 23221. **Hours:** 10 am-8 pm, Thurs-Sat to 9 pm, Sun 11 am-4 pm. Closed major holidays. **Features:** Self described as a "taste of lil' Italy" this cozy New York-style delicatessen is on a busy corner complete with sidewalk tables. Awesome overstuffed sandwiches such as the Industrial Hero, the Mediterranean Magic, or the South Bronx Club. All lunches end well with the NY cannoli. Casual dress; beer & wine only. **Parking:** street.

CROAKER'S SPOT

Soul Food

Lunch: $9-$33   **Dinner:** $9-$33   **Phone:** 804/421-0560   ㉘
Location: Jct 2nd St; in Jackson Ward. 119 E Leigh St 23219. **Hours:** 11 am-9 pm, Thurs-10 pm, Fri-11 pm, Sat noon-11 pm, Sun 11 am-7 pm. Closed major holidays. **Features:** Tucked on a busy corner in historic Jackson Ward, the restaurant serves some of the city's best and most affordable seafood dishes, such as shrimp and grits, shrimp curry and an overflowing seafood platter. Delicious cornbread is a side for all dishes. Casual dress; cocktails. **Parking:** street. **Cards:** AX, CB, DC, DS, JC, MC, VI.

DAVIS & MAIN

American

Dinner: $12-$20   **Phone:** 804/353-6641   ⑲
Location: Jct Davis and W Main sts; in Historic Fan District. 2501 W Main St 23220. **Hours:** 4 pm-midnight. Closed major holidays. **Features:** Termed "American Grill Cuisine" which means using the grill to enhance the freshest ingredients and natural flavors including chicken, seafood and beef choices. Known for their grilled pork tenderloin with Southern chutney, smoked trout appetizer, or spinach and sweet potato salad, as well as nightly blackboard specials. Charming atmosphere in historic district; dark woods, cozy high-backed booths, long friendly bar. Casual dress; cocktails. **Parking:** street. **Cards:** AX, DC, MC, VI.

**THE DINING ROOM AT THE
BERKELEY HOTEL**   *Menu on aaa.com*

Continental

Lunch: $8-$20   **Dinner:** $22-$32   **Phone:** 804/225-5105   ㊱
Location: Just w of state capitol; in The Berkeley Hotel; in Historic Shockoe Slip District. 1200 E Cary St 23219. **Hours:** 7-10:30 am, 11:30-2 & 6-10 pm, Sun 7:30-10:30 am, 11:30-2 & 6-9 pm. Closed: 12/25. **Reservations:** suggested. **Features:** Wonderful menu choices of regional fare are both visually impressive and delicious tasting at this richly appointed downtown dining room. Diners at many tables enjoy a sidewalk view of the cobblestone streets of Shockoe Slip. Dressy casual; cocktails. **Parking:** valet. **Cards:** AX, CB, DC, DS, MC, VI.

DOGWOODS GRILLE & SPIRITS

American

Dinner: $19-$31   **Phone:** 804/340-1984   ㉗
Location: Jct S Allen St; in the Fan Historic District. 1731 W Main St 23220. **Hours:** 5 pm-10:30 pm. Closed major holidays; also Sun & Mon. **Reservations:** suggested. **Features:** Underneath a casual neighborhood ambience lies a sophisticated urban menu. The highest-quality ingredients combine in a fusion of Continental and Southern accents, with a touch of Asian flavor thrown in for exotic measure. Casual dress; cocktails. **Parking:** street. **Cards:** AX, DC, DS, MC, VI.

DOUBLE T'S RED SMOKED BARBECUE

Barbecue

Lunch: $6-$18   **Dinner:** $6-$18   **Phone:** 804/353-9861   ⑯
Location: I-195, exit W Cary St, 1 mi e, then just w of jct Boulevard; in Carytown. 2907 W Cary St 23221. **Hours:** 11 am-10 pm, Fri & Sat-11 pm. Closed major holidays. **Features:** This casual rough-hewn spot with an inviting sidewalk patio features all manner of barbecue specialties from chicken to ribs and 4 different sauces to top it with. Casual dress; cocktails. **Parking:** street. **Cards:** AX, DS, MC, VI.

EDO'S SQUID

Italian

Lunch: $7-$20   **Dinner:** $8-$18   **Phone:** 804/864-5488   ㉓
Location: Between W Grace and Franklin sts; adjacent to the Virginia Commonwealth University campus; 2nd floor. 411 N Harrison St 23220. **Hours:** 11 am-11 pm, Fri & Sat-midnight, Sun 5:30 pm-11 pm. Closed major holidays. **Features:** Locals have long loved the pastas—such as rich, savory carbonara—as well as the fresh fish and osso buco. The cozy, second-floor, brick-walled retreat above the Virginia Commonwealth University campus is a fresh spot in which to savor the food. Casual dress; cocktails. **Parking:** street. **Cards:** AX, MC, VI.

**EUROPA MEDITERRANEAN CAFE AND
TAPAS BAR**

Ethnic

Lunch: $4-$10   **Dinner:** $10-$23   **Phone:** 804/643-0911   ㊵
Location: Just e of jct 14th St; in Shockoe Bottom District. 1409 E Cary St 23219. **Hours:** 11:30 am-2:30 & 5:30-10 pm, Fri & Sat-11 pm, Sun 5:30 pm-10 pm. **Reservations:** accepted. **Features:** The lively downtown spot specializes in tapas, a fun and social Spanish tradition that features multiple plates of savory appetizers. Hot and cold dishes reflect multicultural influences. Among full entrees are several varieties of paella. Casual dress; cocktails. **Parking:** street. **Cards:** AX, DC, DS, MC, VI.

FAROUK'S HOUSE OF INDIA

Ethnic

Lunch: $5-$8   **Dinner:** $7-$12   **Phone:** 804/355-0378   ⑫
Location: I-195, exit Cary St (SR 147), 0.5 mi e; in Carytown Shopping District. 3033 W Cary St 23221. **Hours:** 11:30 am-3 & 5-10:30 pm. **Features:** Indian cuisine, traditional vindaloos and biryanis and a large selection of curry dishes makes this restaurant a crowd pleaser. The all-you-can-eat lunch buffet offers a good variety of fresh, hot dishes, bread, vegetables, salad and rice pudding. Casual dress; beer & wine only. **Parking:** street. **Cards:** AX, DS, MC, VI.

THE HARD SHELL

Seafood

Lunch: $7-$9   **Dinner:** $12-$24   **Phone:** 804/643-2333   ㊶
Location: Just e of jct 14th St; downtown; in Shockoe Bottom District. 1411 E Cary St 23219. **Hours:** 11:30 am-2:30 & 5-10 pm, Fri & Sat-11 pm, Sun 10:30 am-2:30 & 5-9 pm. Closed major holidays. **Reservations:** suggested. **Features:** Exposed brick walls and frequent live jazz performances add to the casual ambience. Patrons are drawn by sophisticated preparations of fresh local and international seafood, as well as raw bar items. Oysters Michelle are a signature dish. The courtyard patio is inviting. Casual dress; cocktails; entertainment. **Parking:** on-site (fee). **Cards:** AX, DC, DS, MC, VI.

(See map and index starting on p. 825)

HAVANA '59
Cuban

Dinner: $12-$28   **Phone: 804/649-2822**   43
Location: Just n of jct 17th and Main sts, across from the Farmer's Market; in Shockoe Bottom District. 16 N 17th St 23219. **Hours:** 5:30 pm-10 pm, Fri & Sat-11 pm. Closed: Sun. **Features:** A lively, rustic, and theatrical atmosphere greets diners, including cards for gin rummy at each table. Served are excellent salad and appetizers, all with nice creative Island and Spanish touches, including coconut shrimp and roast pork tenderloin. Casual dress; cocktails. **Parking:** on-site. **Cards:** AX, CB, DC, DS, MC, VI.

HELEN'S
American

Dinner: $17-$25   **Phone: 804/358-4370**   18
Location: Jct Robinson St; in Fan Historic District. 2527 W Main St 23221. **Hours:** 5:30 pm-10:30 pm, Sun-9:30 pm. Closed major holidays; also Mon. **Reservations:** suggested. **Features:** The casual atmosphere is set by the nostalgic surroundings of this former lunch counter complete with swivel seats at the counter and pressed tin ceilings. The menu sets a decidedly more sophisticated tone with seasonally changing gourmet offerings. Casual dress; cocktails. **Parking:** street. **Cards:** AX, DC, DS, MC, VI.

INDOCHINE
Ethnic

Lunch: $7-$12   **Dinner: $10-$24**   **Phone: 804/353-5799**   14
Location: I-195, exit Cary St Rd, just e; in Carytown Shopping District. 2923 W Cary St 23221. **Hours:** 11:30 am-10 pm. Closed major holidays; also Sun. **Reservations:** accepted. **Features:** Healthy menu items highlight the use of fresh vegetables, seafood, meat, interesting appetizers, and mild and spicy tastes. It's French-influenced Vietnamese cuisine in a cozy, inviting atmosphere with friendly, attentive and prompt service. Casual dress; cocktails. **Parking:** street. **Cards:** AX, DS, MC, VI.

JULEP'S, NEW SOUTHERN CUISINE
Regional American

Lunch: $7-$10   **Dinner: $16-$24**   **Phone: 804/377-3968**   45
Location: Jct 18th St; in Shockoe Bottom. 1719-21 E Franklin St 23219. **Hours:** 11 am-2:30 & 5:30-10 pm, Sat from 5:30 pm, Mon-2:30 pm. Closed major holidays; also Sun. **Reservations:** suggested. **Features:** Housed in one of Richmond's oldest commercial buildings in Shockoe Slip, Julep's, with its spiral staircase and open attic with exposed beams, is a true Southern belle. But her beauty goes way beyond the surface. The tart and oh-so-good fried green tomatoes only add to her charm, as does the hearty blackened bouillabaisse, and the super creamy cheese grits. The regional menu changes seasonally, but its delightful Southern fare will never go out of style. Dressy casual; cocktails. **Parking:** street. **Cards:** AX, MC, VI.

JULIAN'S RESTAURANT
Italian

Lunch: $6-$10   **Dinner: $9-$20**   **Phone: 804/359-0605**   2
Location: Jct N Blvd and Robinson St, just e. 2617 W Broad St 23220. **Hours:** 11 am-10 pm, Fri & Sat-11 pm. Closed: 11/24, 12/25. **Features:** For more than 50 years, the restaurant has fed families bountiful portions of hearty Italian-American fare. Savory baked pastas, cool subs and saucy pizzas are some favorites. Casual dress; cocktails. **Parking:** on-site. **Cards:** AX, DC, DS, MC, VI.

THE KITCHEN TABLE
American

Dinner: $16-$26   **Phone: 804/782-9200**   44
Location: Just n of Main St; across from Farmer's Market; in Shockoe Bottom District. 3 N 17th St 23219. **Hours:** 5 pm-9:30 pm, Fri & Sat-10 pm. Closed: 1/1, 11/24, 12/25. **Reservations:** suggested. **Features:** Located across from the centuries-old farmers market, this art-nouveau storefront features organic produce and hormone-free meats and poultry. The modern American seasonal menu, with its Asian, Latin and Mediterranean influences, includes scampi-style shrimp Diane, with braised collards, caramelized onions and Havarti grits. You'll dine in fine style too; crimson walls, Venetian mirrors and handcrafted woodwork gives the dining room a warm glow, and the overall effect is positively delicious. Casual dress; cocktails. **Parking:** street. **Cards:** MC, VI.

KONSTA'S
Continental

Lunch: $6-$10   **Dinner: $7-$22**   **Phone: 804/359-3122**   11
Location: Jct Robinson St and Floyd Ave; in Historic Fan District. 2526 Floyd Ave 23221. **Hours:** 11:30 am-2:30 & 5-10 pm, Fri-11 pm, Sat 5 pm-11 pm. Closed major holidays; also Sun. **Reservations:** suggested. **Features:** The setting inside is cool with murals, rich woods and lots of stained glass. The menu offers traditional Greek and Italian dishes as well as inspired seafood, pasta and nightly specials. The service is professional. Casual dress; cocktails. **Parking:** on-site. **Cards:** AX, MC, VI.

KUBA KUBA
Cuban

Lunch: $6-$16   **Dinner: $6-$16**   **Phone: 804/355-8817**   20
Location: Jct Park Ave and Lombardy St, 0.5 mi s of W Broad St; in Historic Fan District. 1601 Park Ave 23220. **Hours:** 9 am-9:30 pm, Fri & Sat to 10 pm, Sun 9 am-3 & 5-9:30 pm. Closed major holidays. **Features:** You'll delight in the coziness of this Cuban diner/bodega, located in a small, restored pharmacy/lunch counter. Authentic Cuban roast pork, three paellas and Cuban sandwiches, rich coffee and dessert are menu highlights. There's a market on the premises. Casual dress; beer & wine only. **Parking:** street. **Cards:** AX, MC, VI.

LA GROTTA
Italian

Lunch: $7-$13   **Dinner: $13-$28**   **Phone: 804/644-2466**   37
Location: Jct 13th and E Cary sts; in Historic Shockoe Slip District. 1218 E Cary St 23219. **Hours:** 11:30 am-2:30 & 5:30-10 pm, Fri-11 pm, Sat 5:30 pm-11 pm, Sun 5 pm-9 pm. Closed major holidays. **Reservations:** suggested. **Features:** The quaint restaurant has the feel of entering a cozy wine cellar. Start off with homemade bread with crushed olives and sun-dried tomatoes or fresh pesto. Caesar salad served tableside, roasted quail, excellent carpaccio and rich tiramisu are examples of the savory Italian cucina-style cuisine. Casual dress; cocktails. **Parking:** street. **Cards:** AX, DC, DS, MC, VI.

LEMAIRE

Regional American

Lunch: $10-$19   **Dinner: $21-$36**   **Phone: 804/649-4644**   32
Location: Franklin and Adams sts; center; in The Jefferson Hotel. 101 W Franklin St 23220. **Hours:** 6:30 am-10, noon-2 & 6-9 pm, Fri-10 pm, Sat 6:30 am-11 & 5:30-10 pm, Sun 6:30 am-1 pm. Closed major holidays. **Reservations:** suggested. **Features:** The restaurant delivers a magnificent experience in a spectacular setting. The historic hotel invites formal dining. Innovation takes on traditional Virginia fare in such preparations as barbecue bison, rich veal and spoon bread. All is presented by a polished staff in a series of elegant dining rooms accented by high ceilings, fine art and detailed wood and plaster carvings. Dressy casual; cocktails. **Parking:** on-site and valet. **Cards:** AX, CB, DC, DS, MC, VI. *(See color ad p 838)*

(See map and index starting on p. 825)

LIMANI FISH GRILL Lunch: $6-$20 Dinner: $18-$30 Phone: 804/353-7117 ⑩
Mediterranean **Location:** I-195, exit W Cary St, just e; in Carytown. 3123 W Cary St 23221. **Hours:** 11:30 am-2:30 & 6-10 pm, Sat 11:30 am-3 & 6-10 pm. Closed major holidays; also Sun. **Reservations:** suggested. **Features:** The interior is sleek and modern accented by shades of gray and cobalt; the cuisine earthy and decidedly un-fussy. Chose from a selection of daily catches of the freshest seafood perfectly grilled over aromatic fruitwoods. Casual dress; cocktails. **Parking:** street. **Cards:** AX, MC, VI. ✕

MILLIE'S DINER Lunch: $6-$12 Dinner: $15-$28 Phone: 804/643-5512 ㊾
American **Location:** Jct 26th and E Main sts; in the Shockoe Bottom District. 2603 E Main St 23223. **Hours:** 11 am-2:30 & 5:30-10:30 pm, Sat 10 am-3 & 5:30-10:30 pm, Sun 9 am-3 & 5:30-9:30 pm. Closed: 12/24, 12/25; also Mon. **Features:** Once a lunch spot for tobacco plant workers, the restaurant is now a retro '50s diner, with individual jukeboxes that play vintage music. An often changing, eclectic menu includes dishes made with only fresh ingredients. The wine and beer list is lengthy. Popular brunch spot for the "Devil's Mess". Casual dress; cocktails. **Parking:** street. **Cards:** AX, DS, MC, VI.

PEKING PAVILION Lunch: $6-$10 Dinner: $8-$14 Phone: 804/649-8888 ㊴
Chinese **Location:** Corner of E Cary and Shockoe Slip; in the Historic Shockoe Slip District. 1302 E Cary 23219. **Hours:** 11:30 am-2 & 5-9:30 pm, Fri-10:30 pm, Sat 5 pm-10:30 pm. Closed major holidays. **Reservations:** accepted. **Features:** Traditional dishes—General Tso's chicken, crispy duck and shrimp velvet among them—make up the menu at the quiet, laid-back restaurant. Wood carvings, art and music all show Oriental influences. The place does a hopping business at lunchtime. Casual dress; cocktails. **Parking:** on-site (fee). **Cards:** AX, MC, VI. ⓨ ✕

POMEGRANATE EURO BISTRO Lunch: $5-$12 Dinner: $17-$25 Phone: 804/643-9354 ㊳
Mediterranean **Location:** Just e of jct 12th St; in Shockoe Slip District. 1209 E Cary St 23219. **Hours:** 11:30 am-2 & 5:30-10 pm, Sat from 5:30 pm, Mon-2 pm. Closed major holidays; also Sun. **Reservations:** suggested. **Features:** The pomegranate has long been revered as a powerful aphrodisiac, and at Pomegranate Euro Bistro, the ancient fruit takes center stage, showing up in vinaigrettes, sauces and marinades, and making a stellar appearance in the pomegranate-glazed salmon over Mascarpone polenta and fresh spinach. But could this fruit really have love potion power, or is it the restaurant's intimate setting, replete with dimmed lights and Italian arias, that's casting a spell over the local clientele? Casual dress; cocktails. **Parking:** street. **Cards:** AX, DS, MC, VI.

RIVAH BISTRO Lunch: $6-$12 Dinner: $12-$22 Phone: 804/344-8222 ㊷
French **Location:** Just e of jct 14th St; in Shockoe Bottom District. 1417 E Cary St 23219. **Hours:** 11:30 am-10 pm, Fri & Sat-11 pm, Sun 10:30 am-9 pm. Closed: 1/1, 11/24. **Reservations:** suggested. **Features:** Housed in a restored tobacco warehouse, the stylish Parisian bistro serves delicate French fare and fine wine with a Southern accent. The brick patio is a nice seating alternative during pleasant weather. Dressy casual; cocktails. **Parking:** on-site (fee). **Cards:** AX, DC, MC, VI. ⓨ ✕

RIVER CITY DINER Lunch: $3-$10 Dinner: $3-$10 Phone: 804/644-9418 ㊼
American **Location:** Just e of 17th St; in Shockoe Bottom District. 1712 E Main St 23223. **Hours:** 8 am-10 pm, Fri & Sat-3 am, Sun & Mon-3 pm. Closed: 11/24, 12/25. **Features:** The lively diner is likely to make you nostalgic for poodle skirts and sock hops. Kitschy decor and shiny chrome enliven the dining room. Order from the all-day breakfast menu or enjoy old favorites such as burgers, sandwiches and soda fountain treats. Casual dress; cocktails. **Parking:** street. **Cards:** AX, MC, VI.

SALLY BELL'S KITCHEN Lunch: $5-$7 Phone: 804/644-2838 ㉖
Bakery/Desserts **Location:** Just w of jct Belvidere; adjacent to Virginia Commonwealth University. 708 W Grace St 23220. **Hours:** 8:30 am-4 pm. Closed: Sat & Sun. **Features:** Since 1924, the local landmark has been serving boxed lunches full of old-fashioned homemade specialties. Not only does this place bake its own breads, but it also makes its own mayonnaise. Offerings are purely Southern: deviled eggs, cheese wafers, upside-down cupcakes and potato, macaroni and chicken salads. Casual dress. **Parking:** on-site. **Cards:** MC, VI. ✕

SOUTHERN CULTURE Dinner: $7-$17 Phone: 804/355-6939 ㉑
Regional American **Location:** Jct W Main and Stafford sts; in Historic Fan District. 2229 W Main St 23220. **Hours:** 5 pm-11:30 pm, Sun also 11 am-2:30 pm. Closed major holidays; also Mon. **Features:** A funky, retro feel characterizes the personality of this unique upscale diner that celebrates the Southern Culture with influences of Cajun, Caribbean, and Southwest regions. Expect dishes such as Zydeco Chicken, Tropical Crabcakes, Crawfish Quesdillas and PoBoy sandwiches. Lively atmosphere on weekend evenings, live "Big Band" style jazz on Thursdays. Casual dress; cocktails. **Parking:** on-site. **Cards:** AX, MC, VI.

STELLA'S Lunch: $6-$8 Dinner: $10-$22 Phone: 804/257-9885 ㉒
Greek **Location:** Jct W Main and Shields sts; in Historic Fan District. 2132 W Main St 23220. **Hours:** 11 am-10 pm, Fri & Sat-11 pm. Closed: 11/24, 12/25; also Sun. **Features:** A Mediterranean flair punctuates traditional Greek specialties and preparations of fresh seafood and lamb, while the chalkboard highlights creative specials. The atmosphere bustles, and often there's a wait to be seated. Casual dress; beer & wine only. **Parking:** street. **Cards:** AX, MC, VI. ✕

STRAWBERRY STREET CAFE Lunch: $5-$7 Dinner: $6-$15 Phone: 804/353-6860 ⑥
American **Location:** Jct W Monument Ave, 2 blks s; in Historic Fan District. 421 N Strawberry St 23220. **Hours:** 11 am-2:30 & 5-10:30 pm, Fri-midnight, Sat 11 am-midnight, Sun 10 am-10:30 pm. Closed: 11/24, 12/24, 12/25. **Features:** This long-standing neighborhood favorite boasts a "famous bathtub salad bar" and its large variety of choices. The menu ranges from sandwiches and salad to steak and pasta. Specialties include sun-dried tomato bisque and eggs a la Richmond for brunch. Casual dress; cocktails. **Parking:** street. **Cards:** AX, MC, VI. ✕

(See map and index starting on p. 825)

THE THAI ROOM AT BEAUREGARD'S   Lunch: $4-$10   Dinner: $10-$14   Phone: 804/644-2328   34
Ethnic
Location: At 1st and E Cary sts. 103 E Cary St 23219. **Hours:** 11 am-2:30 & 4:30-10 pm, Fri & Sat-11 pm. Closed: Sun. **Reservations:** suggested. **Features:** Fresh, traditional Thai cuisine is served in this 19th-century townhouse's upscale dining room, graced by lovely artwork. Try the spicy shrimp soup and Pad Thai. The menu also features luscious homemade ice cream, such as chocolate Kevorkian. Casual dress; cocktails. **Parking:** on-site. **Cards:** AX, DS, MC, VI.

T. J.'S RESTAURANT   Lunch: $10-$20   Dinner: $15-$30   Phone: 804/649-4672   33
American
Location: Franklin and Adams sts; center; in The Jefferson Hotel. 101 W Franklin St 23220. **Hours:** 11 am-2 & 5-10 pm. **Reservations:** accepted. **Features:** Guests can dine in the garden-themed dining room or choose a barside table overlooking the glorious lower lobby of the grand hotel. Menu offerings range from sandwiches and Angus burgers to peanut soup and crab cakes. Servers are gracious. Semi-formal attire; cocktails. **Parking:** on-site (fee) and valet. **Cards:** AX, CB, DC, DS, MC, VI.

THE TRACK   Dinner: $15-$24   Phone: 804/359-4781   15
Regional American
Location: I-195, exit W Cary St, just e; in Carytown. 2915 W Cary St 23221. **Hours:** 5 pm-9:30 pm, Fri & Sat-10:30 pm. Closed major holidays; also Sun & Mon. **Reservations:** suggested. **Features:** A Richmond mainstay for 20 years, The Track still impresses regulars with their creative fare served in an intimate setting. The Bounty from local waters' is a specialty served up in new ways alongside lamb, beef, and more. Casual dress; cocktails. **Parking:** street. **Cards:** AX, DS, MC, VI.

ZEUS GALLERY CAFE   Dinner: $20-$30   Phone: 804/359-3219   5
Nouvelle American
Location: Jct Grove Ave, just n; in Historic Fan District. 201 N Belmont Ave 23221. **Hours:** 5 pm-10 pm, Fri & Sat-11 pm, Sun 9 am-2 & 5-9 pm. Closed: 1/1, 11/24, 12/24, 12/25. **Features:** Near the Virginia Museum, the charming, intimate cafe displays the work of local artists. Dishes on the often-changing menu use the freshest seasonal ingredients. Interesting, creative presentation marks the mostly pasta, fish, chicken and beef entrees. Casual dress; cocktails. **Parking:** street. **Cards:** AX, CB, DS, MC, VI.

RICHMOND pop. 197,790   (See map and index starting on p. 828)

———— WHERE TO STAY ————

AIRPORT INN MOTEL
AAA SAVE
◆◆◆
Motel

Phone: (804)222-4200   **19**
F18

All Year   1P: $54-$79   2P: $59-$84   XP: $5
Location: I-64, exit 195, 1.4 mi s. 5121 S Laburnum Ave 23231. Fax: 804/222-2828. **Facility:** 17 one-bedroom standard units, some with whirlpools. 1 story, exterior corridors. **Parking:** on-site. **Terms:** 7 day cancellation notice. **Amenities:** irons, hair dryers. **Business Services:** fax. **Cards:** AX, CB, DC, DS, MC, VI.

SOME UNITS
[icons]

AMERISUITES (RICHMOND/ARBORETUM)   *Book at aaa.com*
AAA SAVE
◆◆◆◆
Small-scale Hotel

Phone: (804)560-1566   **25**
F18

All Year   1P: $104-$139   2P: $104-$139   XP: $10
Location: Jct Powhite Pkwy (US 76) and Midlothian Tpke (US 60), just w. 201 Arboretum Pl 23236. Fax: 804/560-1703. **Facility:** 128 one-bedroom standard units. 6 stories, interior corridors. *Bath:* combo or shower only. **Parking:** on-site. **Terms:** small pets only. **Amenities:** voice mail, irons, hair dryers. *Some:* dual phone lines. **Pool(s):** heated outdoor. **Leisure Activities:** exercise room. **Guest Services:** valet and coin laundry, area transportation-within 5 mi. **Business Services:** meeting rooms, fax. **Cards:** AX, CB, DC, DS, MC, VI. **Special Amenities:** free expanded continental breakfast and free newspaper. *(See color ad p 837)*

SOME UNITS
[icons]

BEST WESTERN EXECUTIVE HOTEL   *Book at aaa.com*
AAA SAVE
◆◆◆
Small-scale Hotel

Phone: (804)672-7007   **11**
F18

All Year   1P: $69-$119   2P: $69-$119   XP: $10
Location: I-64, exit 183C (US 250 W), jct Glenside Dr. 7007 W Broad St 23294. Fax: 804/672-3251. **Facility:** 117 one-bedroom standard units. 4 stories, interior corridors. *Bath:* combo or shower only. **Parking:** on-site. **Amenities:** high-speed Internet (fee), voice mail, irons, hair dryers. **Pool(s):** outdoor. **Leisure Activities:** exercise room. **Guest Services:** coin laundry. **Business Services:** meeting rooms, fax. **Cards:** AX, DC, DS, MC, VI. **Special Amenities:** free expanded continental breakfast and free local telephone calls. *(See color ad below)*

SOME UNITS
[icons]

BEST WESTERN GOVERNOR'S INN   *Book at aaa.com*
AAA SAVE
◆◆◆
Small-scale Hotel

Phone: (804)323-0007   **21**
F17

All Year [ECP]   1P: $81-$135   2P: $81-$135   XP: $5
Location: US 60, 1.5 mi w of jct Powhite Pkwy. 9826 Midlothian Tpke 23235. Fax: 804/272-0759. **Facility:** 80 units. 77 one-bedroom standard units, some with whirlpools. 3 one-bedroom suites. 3 stories, interior corridors. **Parking:** on-site. **Terms:** cancellation fee imposed, package plans. **Amenities:** dual phone lines, voice mail, safes (fee), irons, hair dryers. **Dining:** 5:30 pm-10 pm; closed Sun & Mon, cocktails. **Pool(s):** outdoor. **Leisure Activities:** exercise room. **Business Services:** meeting rooms, fax. **Cards:** AX, CB, DC, DS, JC, MC, VI. **Special Amenities:** free expanded continental breakfast and preferred room (subject to availability with advance reservations).

SOME UNITS
[icons]

CANDLEWOOD SUITES   *Book at aaa.com*
◆◆◆
Small-scale Hotel

Phone: (804)271-0016   **27**

All Year   1P: $84-$109
Location: I-95, exit 69, just n. 4301 Commerce Rd 23234. Fax: 804/271-0024. **Facility:** 104 units. 92 one-bedroom standard units with kitchens. 12 one-bedroom suites with kitchens. 3 stories, interior corridors. *Bath:* combo or shower only. **Parking:** on-site. **Terms:** office hours 7 am-11 pm, cancellation fee imposed, pets ($75 fee). **Amenities:** video library, CD players, dual phone lines, voice mail, irons, hair dryers. **Leisure Activities:** exercise room. **Guest Services:** sundries, complimentary laundry. **Business Services:** fax. **Cards:** AX, DC, DS, MC, VI.

SOME UNITS
[icons]
FEE

(See map and index starting on p. 828)

COMFORT INN EXECUTIVE CENTER   *Book at aaa.com*   Phone: (804)672-1108   **8**
AAA SAVE   All Year   1P: $65-$70   2P: $69-$70   XP: $5   F18
Location: I-64, exit 183C westbound; exit 183 eastbound. 7201 W Broad St 23294. Fax: 804/755-1625.
Small-scale Hotel   **Facility:** 123 units. 122 one-bedroom standard units, some with whirlpools. 1 one-bedroom suite. 2 stories
(no elevator), interior corridors. **Parking:** on-site. **Terms:** package plans. **Amenities:** voice mail, safes (fee),
irons, hair dryers. **Pool(s):** outdoor. **Leisure Activities:** exercise room. **Guest Services:** valet and coin
laundry. **Business Services:** PC. **Cards:** AX, CB, DC, DS, MC, VI. **Special Amenities:** free continental
breakfast and free local telephone calls.
SOME UNITS
[S/D] [†↑] [⊅] [☆] [DATA PORT] [▭] / [✕] [▤] [▱] /

COURTYARD BY MARRIOTT   *Book at aaa.com*   Phone: (804)282-1881   **16**
▽▽▽▽   All Year   1P: $79-$189
Location: I-64, exit 183B westbound; exit 183 eastbound; jct US 250, 0.5 mi e. 6400 W Broad St 23230.
Small-scale Hotel   Fax: 804/288-2934. **Facility:** 145 units. 132 one-bedroom standard units. 13 one-bedroom suites. 2-3
stories, interior corridors. *Bath:* combo or shower only. **Parking:** on-site. **Amenities:** high-speed Internet,
dual phone lines, voice mail, irons, hair dryers. **Pool(s):** outdoor. **Leisure Activities:** whirlpool, exercise room. **Guest Services:**
valet and coin laundry. **Business Services:** meeting rooms, fax. **Cards:** AX, CB, DC, DS, MC, VI.
SOME UNITS
[A$K] [S/D] [†↑] [&M] [⌀] [⊅] [☆] [DATA PORT] [▭] / [✕] [▤] [▱] /

DAYS INN-RICHMOND WEST   *Book at aaa.com*   Phone: (804)282-3300   **14**
▽▽▽▽   5/12-9/18   1P: $79-$139   2P: $79-$139   XP: $10   F17
9/19-10/30   1P: $79-$99   2P: $79-$99   XP: $10   F17
3/1-5/11 & 10/31-2/28   1P: $49-$79   2P: $49-$79   XP: $10   F17
Small-scale Hotel   **Location:** I-64, exit 183B westbound; exit 183 eastbound, 0.3 mi e on W Broad St, just n. 2100 Dickens Rd 23230.
Fax: 804/288-2145. **Facility:** 179 one-bedroom standard units. 7 stories, interior corridors. **Parking:** on-site. **Terms:** small pets
only ($10 extra charge). **Amenities:** voice mail, safes (fee), hair dryers. *Some:* irons. **Pool(s):** outdoor. **Leisure
Activities:** exercise room. **Guest Services:** valet laundry. **Business Services:** meeting rooms, business center. **Cards:** AX,
CB, DC, DS, MC, VI.
SOME UNITS
[A$K] [S/D] [🐾] [†↑] [⌀] [⊅] [☆] [DATA PORT] [▭] / [✕] [▤] [▱] /
FEE

ECONO LODGE NORTH-PARHAM RD   *Book at aaa.com*   Phone: (804)262-7070   **2**
▽▽ ▽▽   5/1-10/31   1P: $45-$90   2P: $45-$95   XP: $6   F
11/1-2/28   1P: $45-$80   2P: $45-$85   XP: $6   F
Motel   3/1-4/30   1P: $45-$80   2P: $45-$80   XP: $6   F
Location: I-95, exit 83B, 0.5 mi w. Located adjacent to Hungary Brook Shopping Center. 8350 Brook Rd 23227.
Fax: 804/262-5180. **Facility:** 31 one-bedroom standard units. 2 stories (no elevator), exterior corridors. **Parking:** on-site.
Business Services: fax. **Cards:** AX, CB, DC, DS, JC, MC, VI.
SOME UNITS
[A$K] [S/D] [†↑] [&M] [☆] [DATA PORT] / [✕] [VCR] [▤] [▱] [▭] /

ECONO LODGE-RICHMOND WEST   *Book at aaa.com*   Phone: (804)672-8621   **6**
▽▽▽▽   All Year [CP]   1P: $50-$85   2P: $55-$100   XP: $10   F17
Location: I-64, exit 183C, 1 mi w. 7300 W Broad St 23294. Fax: 804/755-7155. **Facility:** 124 one-bedroom
standard units. 2 stories (no elevator), exterior corridors. **Parking:** on-site. **Terms:** 15 day cancellation
Small-scale Hotel   notice-fee imposed. **Amenities:** video games, dual phone lines, voice mail, irons, hair dryers. **Pool(s):**
outdoor. **Guest Services:** valet laundry. **Business Services:** meeting rooms, fax. **Cards:** AX, CB, DC, DS, JC, MC, VI.
SOME UNITS
[A$K] [S/D] [†↑] [&M] [⌀] [⊅] [⊞] [☆] [DATA PORT] [▭] / [✕] [▤] [▱] /
FEE   FEE FEE

(See map and index starting on p. 828)

EMBASSY SUITES HOTEL   *Book at aaa.com*

AAA SAVE

Large-scale Hotel

Phone: (804)672-8585   **9**   F18

All Year   1P: $99-$299   XP: $20

Location: I-64, exit 183C. 2925 Emerywood Pkwy 23294. Fax: 804/672-3749. **Facility:** 226 one-bedroom suites. 8 stories, interior corridors. **Parking:** on-site. **Amenities:** video games, high-speed Internet (fee), voice mail, irons, hair dryers. **Dining:** 6:30 am-9:30 & 11-10 pm, Sat & Sun 7 am-10:30 & 11-10 pm, cocktails. **Pool(s):** heated indoor. **Leisure Activities:** whirlpool, exercise room. **Guest Services:** gift shop, complimentary evening beverages, valet and coin laundry, area transportation-within 5 mi. **Business Services:** conference facilities, business center. **Cards:** AX, CB, DC, DS, MC, VI.

SOME UNITS

HAMPTON INN-MIDLOTHIAN TURNPIKE   *Book at aaa.com*

Small-scale Hotel

Phone: (804)897-2800   **22**

3/1-10/31 [ECP]   1P: $69-$99   2P: $69-$99
11/1-2/28 [ECP]   1P: $59-$79   2P: $59-$79

Location: 1.5 mi w of jct Powhite Pkwy (US 76) and Midlothian Tpke (US 60). Located across from Chesterfield Towne Center. 800 Research Rd 23236. Fax: 804/897-5770. **Facility:** 80 one-bedroom standard units. 3 stories, interior corridors. *Bath:* combo or shower only. **Parking:** on-site. **Terms:** 2 night minimum stay. **Amenities:** high-speed Internet, dual phone lines, voice mail, irons, hair dryers. **Pool(s):** heated indoor. **Leisure Activities:** exercise room. **Guest Services:** valet laundry. **Business Services:** meeting rooms, fax. **Cards:** AX, DC, DS, MC, VI.

SOME UNITS

HOLIDAY INN-CROSSROADS   *Book at aaa.com*

Small-scale Hotel

Phone: (804)359-6061   **17**

All Year   1P: $78-$104   2P: $78-$104

Location: I-64, exit 185, 0.8 mi e. 2000 Staples Mill Rd 23230. Fax: 804/359-3177. **Facility:** 144 one-bedroom standard units. 8 stories, interior corridors. *Bath:* combo or shower only. **Parking:** on-site. **Terms:** cancellation fee imposed. **Amenities:** dual phone lines, voice mail, irons, hair dryers. **Pool(s):** outdoor. **Leisure Activities:** exercise room. **Guest Services:** valet and coin laundry. **Business Services:** meeting rooms, fax. **Cards:** AX, CB, DC, DS, JC, MC, VI.

SOME UNITS

HOLIDAY INN-RICHMOND I-64 & WEST BROAD   *Book at aaa.com*

Small-scale Hotel

Phone: 804/285-9951   **15**

All Year   1P: $59-$99   2P: $59-$99

Location: I-64, exit 83B, just e; jct Glenside Dr, just e. 6531 W Broad St 23230. Fax: 804/673-9632. **Facility:** 282 one-bedroom standard units. 7 stories, interior corridors. *Bath:* some combo or shower only. **Parking:** on-site. **Terms:** 7 day cancellation notice-fee imposed, package plans. **Amenities:** video games, dual phone lines, voice mail, irons, hair dryers. **Pool(s):** heated indoor. **Leisure Activities:** whirlpool, exercise room. **Guest Services:** valet and coin laundry. **Business Services:** conference facilities, fax. **Cards:** AX, CB, DC, DS, JC, MC, VI.

SOME UNITS

HOLIDAY INN-RICHMOND NORTH   *Book at aaa.com*

AAA SAVE

Small-scale Hotel

Phone: (804)266-8753   **4**   F17

All Year   1P: $79-$139   2P: $79-$139   XP: $10

Location: I-95, exit 83B. 801 E Parham Rd 23227. Fax: 804/261-1096. **Facility:** 82 one-bedroom standard units. 2 stories (no elevator), interior corridors. *Bath:* combo or shower only. **Parking:** on-site. **Terms:** small pets only ($25 fee). **Amenities:** dual phone lines, voice mail, irons, hair dryers. **Dining:** 7 am-11 pm, cocktails. **Pool(s):** outdoor. **Leisure Activities:** exercise room. **Guest Services:** valet laundry. **Business Services:** meeting rooms, fax. **Cards:** AX, CB, DC, DS, JC, MC, VI. **Special Amenities:** free newspaper and early check-in/late check-out.

SOME UNITS
FEE   FEE

HOLIDAY INN SELECT-KOGER SOUTH   *Book at aaa.com*

Small-scale Hotel

Phone: (804)379-3800   **20**

All Year   1P: $99-$109

Location: Jct Powhite Pkwy (US 76) and Midlothian Tpke (US 60), 1 mi w. Located adjacent to Johnston Willis Hospital. 1021 Koger Center Blvd 23235. Fax: 804/379-2763. **Facility:** 237 units. 231 one-bedroom standard units. 6 one-bedroom suites ($160-$275) with whirlpools. 8 stories, interior corridors. **Parking:** on-site. **Terms:** package plans. **Amenities:** video games, high-speed Internet, voice mail, irons, hair dryers. **Pool(s):** heated indoor/outdoor. **Leisure Activities:** exercise room. **Guest Services:** valet and coin laundry, area transportation. **Business Services:** conference facilities, business center. **Cards:** AX, CB, DC, DS, MC, VI.

SOME UNITS

HOMESTEAD STUDIO SUITES HOTEL-RICHMOND/MIDLOTHIAN   *Book at aaa.com*

Small-scale Hotel

Phone: (804)272-1800   **26**   F17

All Year   1P: $58-$78   2P: $63-$83   XP: $5

Location: Jct Powhite Pkwy (US 76) and Midlothian Tpke (US 60), just w. 241 Arboretum. Pl 23236. Fax: 804/272-6108. **Facility:** 123 units. 113 one-bedroom standard units with kitchens. 10 one-bedroom suites with kitchens. 3 stories, interior corridors. *Bath:* combo or shower only. **Parking:** on-site. **Terms:** office hours 6:30 am-11 pm, weekly rates available, small pets only ($75 fee). **Amenities:** voice mail, irons, hair dryers. *Some:* dual phone lines. **Guest Services:** sundries, valet and coin laundry. **Business Services:** meeting rooms, fax. **Cards:** AX, CB, DC, DS, MC, VI.

SOME UNITS
FEE   FEE   FEE

(See map and index starting on p. 828)

QUALITY INN WEST END   *Book at aaa.com*   Phone: (804)346-0000   **5**
AAA SAVE   All Year [ECP]   1P: $70-$95   2P: $75-$99   XP: $10   F18
WWW   **Location:** I-64, exit 183C westbound; exit 183 eastbound, 1.5 mi w. 8008 W Broad St 23294. Fax: 804/346-4547.
Facility: 191 one-bedroom standard units. 6 stories, interior corridors. *Bath:* combo or shower only.
Parking: on-site. **Terms:** small pets only ($35 fee, $10 extra charge). **Amenities:** video games, voice mail,
Small-scale Hotel   safes (fee), irons, hair dryers. **Pool(s):** outdoor. **Leisure Activities:** limited exercise equipment. **Guest
Services:** coin laundry. **Business Services:** meeting rooms, fax. **Cards:** AX, CB, DC, DS, JC, MC, VI.
Special Amenities: free expanded continental breakfast and early check-in/late check-out. *(See color ad below)*

SOME UNITS
(icons) FEE   /   FEE FEE

RAMADA INN SOUTHEAST   *Book at aaa.com*   Phone: (804)275-7891   **28**
WWW   All Year   1P: $89-$179   2P: $99-$189   XP: $10   F18
Location: I-95, exit 69, just n. Located adjacent to Philip Morris. 4303 Commerce Rd 23234. Fax: 804/377-8490.
Small-scale Hotel   **Facility:** 167 one-bedroom standard units. 4 stories, interior corridors. **Parking:** on-site. **Amenities:** voice
mail, irons, hair dryers. **Pool(s):** outdoor, wading. **Leisure Activities:** exercise room. **Guest Services:** coin
laundry. **Business Services:** meeting rooms. **Cards:** AX, CB, DC, DS, JC, MC, VI.

SOME UNITS
(icons) / (icon)

RESIDENCE INN BY MARRIOTT   *Book at aaa.com*   Phone: 804/285-8200   **13**
AAA SAVE   All Year   1P: $101-$129   2P: $101-$129
WWW   **Location:** I-64, exit 183B, 0.3 mi e, then just n of US 60 (Broad St). 2121 Dickens Rd 23230. Fax: 804/285-2530.
Facility: 80 units. 60 one-bedroom standard units with kitchens. 15 one- and 5 two-bedroom suites with
Small-scale Hotel   kitchens. 2 stories (no elevator), exterior corridors. *Bath:* combo or shower only. **Parking:** on-site.
Terms: cancellation fee imposed, pets ($125 fee). **Amenities:** voice mail, irons, hair dryers. **Pool(s):**
outdoor. **Leisure Activities:** whirlpool, sports court. **Guest Services:** complimentary evening beverages:
Mon-Thurs, valet and coin laundry. **Business Services:** meeting rooms, PC (fee), fax. **Cards:** AX, CB, DC, DS, JC, MC, VI.

SOME UNITS
(icons) FEE   /   (icon) VCR
FEE

SHERATON PARK SOUTH HOTEL   *Book at aaa.com*   Phone: (804)323-1144   **23**
WWW   All Year   1P: $138   2P: $138   XP: $10   F17
Location: US 60, 1 mi w of Powhite Pkwy (US 76). 9901 Midlothian Tpke 23235. Fax: 804/320-5255. **Facility:** 194
Small-scale Hotel   units. 193 one-bedroom standard units. 1 one-bedroom suite. 7 stories, interior corridors. *Bath:* combo or
shower only. **Parking:** on-site. **Terms:** cancellation fee imposed, package plans. **Amenities:** dual phone
lines, voice mail, irons, hair dryers. *Some:* high-speed Internet (fee). **Pool(s):** heated indoor/outdoor. **Leisure
Activities:** whirlpool, jogging, exercise room. **Guest Services:** gift shop, valet laundry, area transportation. **Business Services:**
conference facilities, business center. **Cards:** AX, DC, DS, MC, VI.

SOME UNITS
(icons) /

SHERATON RICHMOND WEST   *Book at aaa.com*   Phone: (804)285-2000   **12**
AAA SAVE   All Year   1P: $81-$109   2P: $81-$109   XP: $10   F18
WWW   **Location:** I-64, exit 183 eastbound; exit 183B westbound. 6624 W Broad St 23230. Fax: 804/288-3961.
Facility: 372 units. 365 one-bedroom standard units. 7 one-bedroom suites. 8 stories, interior corridors.
Bath: combo or shower only. **Parking:** on-site. **Terms:** package plans. **Amenities:** high-speed Internet (fee),
Large-scale Hotel   dual phone lines, voice mail, irons, hair dryers. **Dining:** 6 am-10 pm, cocktails, entertainment. **Pool(s):**
outdoor, heated indoor. **Leisure Activities:** 2 lighted tennis courts, jogging, exercise room. **Guest Services:**
gift shop, valet laundry, area transportation-within 5 mi. **Business Services:** conference facilities, business center. **Cards:** AX,
DC, DS, MC, VI. **Special Amenities:** free newspaper.

SOME UNITS
(icons) /   FEE FEE

(See map and index starting on p. 828)

SLEEP INN   *Book at aaa.com*   Phone: (804)515-7800   **3**
AAA SAVE   All Year   1P: $57-$134   2P: $64-$134   XP: $5   F18
🔷🔷 🔷🔷   Location: I-95, exit 83B, 0.5 mi; adjacent to Hungary Brook Shopping Center. 950 E Parham Rd 23228.
Small-scale Hotel   Fax: 804/515-7700. **Facility:** 71 one-bedroom standard units. 4 stories, interior corridors. *Bath:* combo or
shower only. **Parking:** on-site. **Amenities:** dual phone lines, voice mail, irons, hair dryers. **Guest Services:**
valet and coin laundry. **Business Services:** meeting rooms, fax. **Cards:** AX, DC, DS, MC, VI.
Special Amenities: free continental breakfast and free local telephone calls.

SOME UNITS

【SD】【🍴】【🚹M】【♿】【🏃】【DATA PORT】【💻】/【✕】【🍽️】
                                                        FEE   FEE

SUPER 8 MOTEL   *Book at aaa.com*   Phone: 804/672-8128   **7**
🔷   Property failed to provide current rates
Motel   Location: I-64, exit 183C, just w of jct Glenside Dr. 7200 W Broad St 23294. Fax: 804/672-8128. **Facility:** 49 one-
bedroom standard units. 3 stories (no elevator), interior corridors. **Parking:** on-site. **Amenities:** safes (fee).

SOME UNITS

【🍴】【🚹M】【🏃】【DATA PORT】/【✕】【🍽️】

SUPER 8 MOTEL   *Book at aaa.com*   Phone: 804/262-8880   **10**
🔷   All Year   1P: $52-$57   2P: $52-$57   XP: $6   F12
Motel   Location: I-95, exit 82. 5615 Chamberlayne Rd 23227. Fax: 804/262-8880. **Facility:** 58 one-bedroom standard
units. 3 stories, interior corridors. **Parking:** on-site. **Terms:** 2 night minimum stay - seasonal, cancellation
fee imposed, package plans. **Cards:** AX, DC, DS, MC, VI.

SOME UNITS

【ASK】【SD】【🏃】【DATA PORT】/【✕】【🍽️】【🍽️】

TRAVEL INN   Phone: (804)745-7500   **24**
AAA SAVE   All Year   1P: $45-$60   2P: $50-$65   XP: $5   F12
🔷🔷 🔷🔷   Location: 0.3 mi e of jct SR 150 and US 60, exit 60E; off Chippenham Pkwy. 6511 Midlothian Tpke 23225.
Motel   Fax: 804/745-7590. **Facility:** 17 one-bedroom standard units. 2 stories (no elevator), exterior corridors.
Parking: on-site. **Amenities:** irons, hair dryers. **Business Services:** fax. **Cards:** AX, DC, DS, MC, VI.
**Special Amenities: early check-in/late check-out and preferred room (subject to availability with
advance reservations).**

【SD】【🍴】【VCR】【🏃】【DATA PORT】【🍽️】【🍽️】

WYNDHAM RICHMOND AIRPORT   *Book at aaa.com*   Phone: (804)226-4300   **18**
AAA SAVE   12/1-2/28   1P: $99-$109   2P: $99-$119   XP: $10   F17
🔷🔷 🔷🔷   3/1-11/30   1P: $89-$99   2P: $89-$109   XP: $10   F17
Small-scale Hotel   Location: I-64, exit 195, 0.5 mi s. 4700 S Laburnum Ave 23231. Fax: 804/226-6516. **Facility:** 155 units. 152 one-
bedroom standard units. 3 two-bedroom suites with whirlpools. 4 stories, interior corridors. *Bath:* combo or
shower only. **Parking:** on-site. **Terms:** cancellation fee imposed, small pets only ($50 fee). *Some:*
Amenities: video games, high-speed Internet (fee), dual phone lines, voice mail, irons, hair dryers. *Some:*
CD players. **Dining:** 6:30 am-11 pm, cocktails. **Pool(s):** heated indoor. **Leisure Activities:** whirlpool, exercise room. **Guest
Services:** sundries, valet laundry, area transportation-within 5 mi. **Business Services:** conference facilities, fax. **Cards:** AX,
CB, DC, DS, MC, VI.

SOME UNITS

【✈】【🛏️】【🍴】【🍷】【♿】【🐕】【🏃】【DATA PORT】【💻】/【✕】【VCR】【🍽️】【🍽️】/
      FEE   FEE   FEE   FEE

──────── **WHERE TO DINE** ────────

AKIDA JAPANESE RESTAURANT   Lunch: $9-$18   Dinner: $9-$18   Phone: 804-762-8878   **6**
🔷🔷 🔷🔷   Location: I-64, exit Parham Rd N, 1 mi w on W Broad St at jct with Tuckernuck; in Sassafras Square. 9039-3 W Broad
Japanese   St 23294. **Hours:** 11:30 am-2:30 & 5-10 pm, Sat from 5 pm. Closed: Sun. **Features:** Diners can slip into this
narrow spot and choose a wooden bench with a good view of the chefs at the sushi bar. Options range from
colorful bites of traditional, innovative sushi to tamer standbys, such as noodle soups and pork katsu.
Casual dress; cocktails. **Parking:** on-site. **Cards:** AX, MC, VI.

AZZURRO   Lunch: $9-$13   Dinner: $9-$28   Phone: 804/282-1509   **25**
🔷🔷🔷   Location: 6 mi w of downtown; Chippenham Pkwy/SR 150, exit Huguenot Rd, 1.8 mi ne; in River Road Center. 6221
Italian   River Rd 23229. **Hours:** 11:30 am-3 & 5:30-10 pm, Fri-11 pm, Sat 11:30 am-2:30 & 5:30-11 pm, Sun 5:30 pm-
9:30 pm. Closed major holidays; also for lunch Sun. **Reservations:** suggested. **Features:** Located in an
upscale strip mall, Azzurro has quickly become a trendy spot for fine Italian food in casual trattoria setting
enhanced by sunny mosaics. Unique homemade pasta, wood-fired pizza, veal and daily fresh fish. With seating by a roaring fire
in the winter or a garden patio in spring, it's right for all seasons. Casual dress; cocktails. **Parking:** on-site. **Cards:** AX, DC, DS,
MC, VI.

【♿】【🍷】【✕】

BAKER'S CRUST BREAD MARKET   Lunch: $5-$7   Dinner: $7-$18   Phone: 804/213-0800   **26**
🔷🔷 🔷🔷   Location: Just e of jct I-195; in International Shopping Center; in Carytown. 3553 W Cary St 23221. **Hours:** 8 am-10
American   pm, Fri & Sat-11 pm, Sun-9 pm. Closed: 11/24, 12/25. **Features:** First and foremost, this place is the home
of crusty bread loaves and sweet bakery treats. Lunch favorites include interesting sandwiches and daily
soup in edible bread bowl, while dinner offerings lean to more sophisticated fare, such as steak, seafood
and rotisserie fowl. Seating at the crepe bar in the rear is a special treat. Casual dress; cocktails. **Parking:** on-site. **Cards:** AX,
DS, MC, VI.

【✕】

BANGKOK CAFE   Lunch: $7-$12   Dinner: $8-$15   Phone: 804/330-9390   **33**
🔷   Location: US 60, 1.3 mi w of Powhite Pkwy (SR 76); in Pocono Green Shopping Center. 10445 Midlothian Tpke 23235.
Thai   **Hours:** 11 am-9:30 pm. Closed: 11/24, 12/25; also Sun. **Features:** This casual spot offers authentic Thai
cuisine, such as crispy whole fish with basil, pad Thai noodles, four curry varieties and vegetarian stir fry.
The desserts are unusual, using tropical fruits and sweet rice. Thai tea and coffee also are available. Casual
dress; beer & wine only. **Parking:** on-site. **Cards:** DC, DS, MC, VI.

【✕】

(See map and index starting on p. 828)

BINIGI'S CAFE & DELI **Lunch:** $4-$10 **Dinner:** $4-$10 **Phone:** 804/261-2224 ⑧
Peruvian
Location: I-95, exit 83B, just s on Parham Rd, then just e. 7424 Brook Rd 23227. **Hours:** 10 am-8:30 pm. Closed major holidays; also Sun. **Features:** The friendly family that operates this small spot serves up generations of Peruvian favorites such as crispy flat bread with dipping sauces, roasted chicken, chicarrones-slow cooked chunks of pork, and ceviche on the weekends. Casual dress. **Parking:** on-site. **Cards:** AX, MC, VI.

BUCKHEAD'S **Dinner:** $22-$41 **Phone:** 804/750-2000 ⑮
Steak House
Location: I-64, exit 181A (Parham Rd), 2.1 mi s; in Beverly Hills Shopping Center. 8510 Patterson Ave 23229. **Hours:** 5 pm-10 pm, Sun-9 pm. Closed major holidays. **Reservations:** suggested. **Features:** A dark, club-like setting—with rich wood paneling and wine bottles lining the walls—sets an upscale mood. The specialty here is prime aged beef and chops, although selected seafood specialties are offered nightly. The classic lobster bisque's rich stock simmers for days. The award-winning extensive wine book is accented at the dessert course by fine ports and single malts. Dressy casual; cocktails. **Parking:** on-site. **Cards:** AX, CB, DC, DS, MC, VI.

CACTUS CAFE **Lunch:** $5-$13 **Dinner:** $7-$13 **Phone:** 804/377-2166 ㉙
Mexican
Location: I-64, exit 195, 1.4 mi s. 5205 S Laburnum Ave 23231. **Hours:** 11:30 am-2:30 & 5-10 pm, Sat & Sun noon-9 pm. Closed major holidays. **Features:** This simple spot offers light and fresh California-style Mexican cuisine including burritos, fajitas, and more. Casual dress; cocktails. **Parking:** on-site. **Cards:** AX, DS, MC, VI.

THE CRAZY GREEK **Lunch:** $5-$12 **Dinner:** $5-$12 **Phone:** 804/355-3786 ⑲
Greek
Location: Jct W Broad St, just s. 1903 Staples Mill Rd 23230. **Hours:** 11 am-10 pm. Closed: 7/4, 11/24, 12/25. **Features:** The long-standing Richmond mainstay offers great, affordable Greek food in a family-friendly setting. Delicious favorites include souvlaki, moussaka, gyros and Greek pizza, as well as a smattering of Italian pasta dishes. Try the Greek spaghetti and baklava. Casual dress; cocktails. **Parking:** on-site.
Cards: AX, DC, DS, MC, VI.

DENA'S GRECIAN RESTAURANT **Lunch:** $3-$5 **Dinner:** $8-$12 **Phone:** 804/794-9551 ㉜
Greek
Location: Midlothian Tpke (US 60), just e of jct Huguenot Rd; in Towne Center Plaza; adjacent to Chesterfield Towne Center. 11374 Midlothian Tpke 23235. **Hours:** 11:30 am-2:30 & 5-9 pm, Fri & Sat-10 pm. Closed: Sun & Mon. **Features:** Robust flavors result when the restaurant mingles Greek and Italian flavors in its intricate dishes, such as the popular Greek spaghetti. The atmosphere is comfortable, and the prices great for the generous portions and great tastes served. Casual dress; cocktails. **Parking:** on-site. **Cards:** AX, DC, DS, MC, VI.

DUJOUR **Lunch:** $5-$9 **Dinner:** $14-$21 **Phone:** 804/285-1301 ㉔
American
Location: Jct W Libbie Ave, just w. 5806 Grove Ave 23226. **Hours:** 11:30 am-2:30 & 5:30-9 pm, Fri & Sat-10 pm, Sun-2:30 pm. **Features:** Creative, unlikely combinations and fresh ingredients come together to create mouthwatering dishes, vegetarian sandwiches, salad with fish, and chicken dinners. A friendly and upscale cafe, very cozy with close tables and sidewalk seating. Casual dress; cocktails. **Parking:** on-site.
Cards: AX, DS, MC, VI.

FILIBERTI'S **Dinner:** $13-$27 **Phone:** 804/423-5850 ㉛
Regional Seafood
Location: 1.5 mi w of jct Powhite Pkwy; adjacent to Chesterfield Towne Center. 11016 Midlothian Tpke 23235. **Hours:** 5 pm-10 pm. Closed major holidays; also Mon. **Reservations:** suggested, weekends. **Features:** Fresh local seafood with a Charleston flair is the specialty at the new modern spot. Among favorites are fried green tomatoes, crawfish etouffee, shrimp and grits and excellent crab cakes. Casual dress; cocktails. **Parking:** on-site. **Cards:** AX, MC, VI.

FRANCO'S RISTORANTE **Dinner:** $18-$26 **Phone:** 804/270-9124 ⑤
Regional Italian
Location: I-64, exit Parham Rd N, 1 mi w on W Broad St, jct of W Broad St and Tuckermuck; in West Broad Commons. 9031 W Broad St, Suite 1 23294. **Hours:** 5 pm-10 pm, Fri & Sat-10:30 pm. Closed major holidays; also Sun. **Reservations:** suggested. **Features:** Searching for excellent classic Italian cuisine served in either a formal dining room or a more casual cafe? You've come to the right place. This restaurant specializes in veal and seasonal menu specials. An extensive wine list is also available. Dressy casual; cocktails; entertainment. **Parking:** on-site. **Cards:** AX, CB, DC, DS, MC, VI.

FULL KEE RESTAURANT **Lunch:** $5-$14 **Dinner:** $5-$14 **Phone:** 804/673-2233 ⑬
Chinese
Location: Jct W Broad St, just s. 6400 Horsepen Rd 23226. **Hours:** 11 am-10:30 pm, Fri & Sat-11 pm. **Features:** Catering to a nearby Chinese population, the restaurant mingles Cantonese, Hunan, Szechuan and Mandarin cuisines on its often-exotic menu. Traditional favorites—such as lemon chicken and Peking duck—also are plentiful. A dim sum lunch is served daily. Casual dress; cocktails. **Parking:** on-site.
Cards: DC, MC, VI.

GRAFITI GRILLE **Lunch:** $7-$11 **Dinner:** $7-$20 **Phone:** 804/288-0633 ⑱
American
Location: Jct Patterson, 3 mi s; in Tuckahoe Shopping Center. 403-B Ridge Rd 23229. **Hours:** 11:30 am-2:30 & 5:30-9 pm, Sat from 5:30 pm; Sunday brunch 10:30 am-2:30 pm. Closed major holidays. **Reservations:** accepted. **Features:** A twist on the typical neighborhood grill, this spot in the 'burbs is bright and fun with humorous spray-painted artwork. The food is self-styled "California eclectic," with such seasonally changing specialties as veal meatloaf and blackberry-glazed tuna. Menu options are hearty in the winter and lighter in the summer. Sunday's jazz brunch is popular with locals. Casual dress; cocktails. **Parking:** on-site. **Cards:** AX, MC, VI.

(See map and index starting on p. 828)

GRAND DYNASTY RESTAURANT
▽▽▽
Chinese
Lunch: $5-$14   **Dinner:** $6-$14   **Phone:** 804/222-8545   [28]
Location: I-64, exit 195, 1.4 mi s on Laburnum Ave, jct Williamsburg Rd; in Laburnum Square Shopping Center. 4734 Finlay St 23231. **Hours:** 11:30 am-10 pm. Closed: 11/24, 12/25. **Features:** The restaurant has stayed away from the buffet formula that seems to overrun Chinese food in the states and sticks to offering freshly made Hunan and Szechuan specialties. Casual dress; cocktails. **Parking:** on-site. **Cards:** AX, DS, MC, VI.

GRAYWOLF GRILL
▽▽▽
Asian
Lunch: $7-$10   **Dinner:** $8-$13   **Phone:** 804/673-4110   [17]
Location: On W Broad St, just w of jct with Staple Mill Rd; in The Shops of Willow Lawn. 1601 Willow Lawn Dr, Suite 300 23230. **Hours:** 11:15 am-9 pm, Fri-10 pm, Sat noon-10 pm, Sun noon-9 pm. Closed: 11/24, 12/25. **Features:** The upbeat restaurant affords a modern American twist on traditional Mongolian barbecue. Choose your own meat, seafood, vegetables and sauce from the bar and then hand your own bowl over to the grill chef, who will cook it before your eyes. This is a fun way to try your own healthy creations. Casual dress; cocktails. **Parking:** on-site. **Cards:** AX, DC, MC, VI.

THE HILL CAFE
▽▽▽ ▽▽▽
American
Lunch: $6-$10   **Dinner:** $6-$20   **Phone:** 804/648-0360   [27]
Location: Just e at jct 28th St; in Church Hill Historic District. 2800 E Broad St 23223. **Hours:** 11:30 am-2 am, Sun from 10:30 am. Closed: 11/24, 12/24, 12/25. **Features:** Amid the restored row houses of historic Church Hill, the restaurant and bar is known for classic eats with a twist. Among choices are corn and crab chowder and the chicken salad BLT. Casual dress; cocktails. **Parking:** street. **Cards:** AX, DS, MC, VI.

INDIA HOUSE
▽▽▽
Indian
Lunch: $7-$13   **Dinner:** $9-$13   **Phone:** 804/355-8378   [23]
Location: Just n of jct Broad St. 2313 Westwood Ave 23230. **Hours:** 11:30 am-2:30 & 5:30-9:30 pm. Closed: Sun. **Features:** Tucked just south of a highway underpass, the cozy spot is painted in a mix of bright colors and festive patterns. The tandoor oven warms delicious breads, savory meats and spicy seafood dishes. The weekday lunch buffet is a great way to sample many dishes. Casual dress; beer & wine only. **Parking:** on-site. **Cards:** MC, VI.

LA PETITE FRANCE
AAA
▽▽▽ ▽
French
Lunch: $9-$14   **Dinner:** $19-$33   **Phone:** 804/353-8729   [16]
Location: I-64, exit Staple Mill Rd, just s to Thalbro Rd, then just e. 2108 Maywill St 23230. **Hours:** 11:30 am-2 & 5:30-10 pm, Sat from 5:30 pm. Closed major holidays; also Sun & Mon. **Reservations:** suggested, Fri & Sat. **Features:** Attentive, professional service is emphasized in the intimate, candlelit dining room, a sumptuous setting for fabulous French cuisine. A loyal local following patronizes the 30-year-old restaurant. For dessert, consider the fabulous strawberry souffle. Semi-formal attire; cocktails. **Parking:** on-site. **Cards:** AX, CB, DC, DS, MC, VI.

LA SIESTA MEXICAN RESTAURANT
▽▽▽ ▽▽▽
Mexican
Lunch: $4-$7   **Dinner:** $5-$12   **Phone:** 804/272-7333   [35]
Location: Midlothian Tpke (US 60), 1.5 mi w of jct Powhite Pkwy. 9900 Midlothian Tpke 23235. **Hours:** 11:30 am-10 pm, Fri & Sat-11 pm, Sun-9 pm. Closed major holidays; also Mon. **Features:** For more than 30 years, the Zajur family has been satisfying locals with family recipes such as zacatecanas (savory pork tortillas), and carne Tampiquena (tender, grilled and marinated steak). Casual dress; cocktails. **Parking:** on-site. **Cards:** AX, DS, MC, VI.

LITTLE SAIGON
▽▽▽ ▽▽▽
Vietnamese
Lunch: $4-$6   **Dinner:** $6-$15   **Phone:** 804/320-6098   [30]
Location: Jct Midlothian Tpke (US 60) and Robious Rd; in Robious Hall Shopping Center. 10012 Robious Rd 23235. **Hours:** 11 am-2:30 & 5-9:30 pm, Fri 9:30 am-10:30 pm, Sat 11 am-10:30 pm, Sun noon-8:30 pm. Closed: 7/4, 11/24, 12/25. **Features:** Enjoy an extensive selection of specialties, such as noodle soup, rice crepes, garden rolls and grilled dishes as well as many healthful choices showcasing fresh produce and seafood. The large, open dining room is crisp and sparsely decorated. Casual dress; cocktails. **Parking:** on-site. **Cards:** AX, DS, MC, VI.

MANILA! MANILA! CAFE & GRILLE
▽▽▽
Philippine
Lunch: $8-$19   **Dinner:** $8-$19   **Phone:** 804/346-9928   [4]
Location: I-64, exit Parham Rd N, 1 mi w on W Broad St at jct Tuckernuck; in West Broad Commons. 9047-1 W Broad St 23294. **Hours:** 11:30 am-2:30 & 5:30-9 pm, Fri-10 pm, Sat 5:30 pm-10 pm. Closed: Mon. **Features:** Diners can experience the taste of the Philippines in a semi-tropical setting. Savory stew, spicy empanadas, crisp lumpia and grilled fish lead the tasty delicacies. Casual dress; cocktails. **Parking:** on-site. **Cards:** AX, DS, MC, VI.

MELITO'S
▽▽▽ ▽▽▽
American
Lunch: $5-$8   **Dinner:** $10-$18   **Phone:** 804/285-1899   [12]
Location: Jct Ridge and Three Chopt Rd; in Westbury Shopping Center. 8815 Three Chopt Rd 23229. **Hours:** 11 am-midnight. Closed major holidays; also Sun. **Features:** Although the daily specials show more creativity, there's a good selection of tasty sandwiches and salad on the menu. This very popular neighborhood spot features homemade rolls, great soup and rich dessert. Grilled pork tenderloin is a specialty. Casual dress; cocktails. **Parking:** on-site. **Cards:** AX, MC, VI.

MEXICO RESTAURANT
▽▽▽
Mexican
Lunch: $4-$6   **Dinner:** $4-$12   **Phone:** 804/282-7357   [14]
Location: Jct W Broad St, just s. 6406 Horsepen Rd 23226. **Hours:** 11 am-2:30 & 5-10 pm, Sat & Sun noon-10 pm. **Features:** Affordable and consistent, the bright, cheery restaurant has an extensive menu of combination dinners and a la carte selections, with six varieties of fajitas. Colorful murals decorate the walls. Servers are quick with the chips, salsa and drink refills. Casual dress; cocktails. **Parking:** on-site. **Cards:** AX, DC, DS, MC, VI.

PASSAGE TO INDIA
▽▽▽
Ethnic
Lunch: $6-$10   **Dinner:** $13-$15   **Phone:** 804/745-5291   [36]
Location: US 60 and SR 150; US 60 E off Chippenham Pkwy. 6856 Midlothian Tpke 23225. **Hours:** 11:30 am-3 & 5-10 pm, Fri & Sat-10:30 pm, Sun 5 pm-10 pm. **Reservations:** accepted. **Features:** The menu comprises a full range of authentic classics—samosas, curries, pakoras, roasted meat and tandoori-baked dishes. Tabletop condiments spice up sides of basmati rice. Portion sizes are generous, and the naan bread is simply wonderful. Casual dress; cocktails. **Parking:** on-site. **Cards:** DS, MC, VI.

(See map and index starting on p. 828)

PASTA LUNA   **Lunch:** $8-$13   **Dinner:** $10-$20   **Phone:** 804/762-9029   ③
Italian
Location: Just w of jct Parham Rd; in Gold's Gym Plaza. 8902-D W Broad St 23294. **Hours:** 11:30 am-10 pm, Fri & Sat-11 pm, Sun 4 pm-9 pm. Closed: 12/25. **Reservations:** suggested. **Features:** Pasta, salad, antipasto and veal dishes greet dinners as they peruse the menu. Large portions, all served family-style, are excellent for sharing and sampling. Decor is classy and simple; the service is prompt, efficient and pleasant. Casual dress; cocktails. **Parking:** on-site. **Cards:** AX, CB, DC, DS, MC, VI.

PEKING RESTAURANT   **Lunch:** $6-$14   **Dinner:** $10-$14   **Phone:** 804/270-9898   ②
Chinese
Location: Just w of jct Parham Rd; in Gold's Gym Plaza. 8904-F W Broad St 23294. **Hours:** 11:30 am-2:15 & 4:45-9:30 pm, Fri & Sat from 4:45 pm, Sun 11:30 am-2 & 4:45-9:30 pm. Closed: 11/24. **Features:** The small chain is a local favorite for its wide selection of dishes, including such specialties as crispy duck, velvet shrimp and dry sauteed green beans. The atmosphere is refined. Casual dress. **Parking:** on-site. **Cards:** AX, MC, VI.

RUCHEE INDIAN RESTAURANT   **Lunch:** $6-$14   **Dinner:** $10-$14   **Phone:** 804/323-5999   ㉞
Indian
Location: 1.5 mi w of jct Powhite Pkwy; in Midlothian Green. 9930 Midlothian Tpke 23235. **Hours:** 11:30 am-2:30 & 5-9:30 pm, Fri & Sat-10 pm, Sun noon-3 & 5-9:30 pm. Closed major holidays; also Mon. **Features:** The restaurant occupies a charming setting accented by wood paneling and pale shades of pink. The food, including tandoori specialties, is a showcase for the fresh flavors of Northern and Southern Indian cuisine. Locals love the luncheon buffet. The spicy tastes are even better washed down with a cool mango lassi. Casual dress; beer & wine only. **Parking:** on-site. **Cards:** AX, DC, DS, MC, VI.

SAL FEDERICO'S ITALIAN RESTAURANT **Lunch:** $8-$12   **Dinner:** $12-$25   **Phone:** 804/358-9111   ⑳
Italian
Location: I-64, exit 185, just s of jct Broad St. 1808 Staples Mill Rd 23230. **Hours:** 11:30 am-2:30 & 5:30-9:30 pm, Sat 5:30 pm-10:30 pm. Closed: 11/24, 12/24, 12/25; also Sun. **Reservations:** suggested. **Features:** A longtime community staple, the popular eatery offers traditional Italian specialties, such as tender, tasty veal tips, a great garlicky marinara sauce and baked pasta dishes, as well as preparations of seafood, poultry and beef. Casual dress; cocktails. **Parking:** on-site. **Cards:** AX, DC, DS, MC, VI.

SHACKLEFORD'S RESTAURANT   **Lunch:** $5-$12   **Dinner:** $14-$25   **Phone:** 804/741-9900   ⑩
American
Location: I-64, exit 180A (Gaskins Rd S), 1 mi s to Ridgefield Pkwy, then 1.5 mi w; in Gleneagle Center. 10496 Ridgefield Pkwy 23233. **Hours:** 11 am-midnight. Closed major holidays. **Reservations:** accepted. **Features:** In addition to a raw bar, the popular, neighborhood restaurant focuses on regional seafood entrees, such as trout stuffed with seafood and spinach. Creativity is a big strength of the menu. A great selection of beer and microbrew is available. Casual dress; cocktails. **Parking:** on-site. **Cards:** AX, DS, MC, VI.

SUPER STARS GOURMET PIZZA   **Lunch:** $4-$10   **Dinner:** $4-$10   **Phone:** 804/673-3663   ㉑
Pizza
Location: Jct Libbie and Willow Lawn rds. 5700 Patterson Ave 23226. **Hours:** 11 am-9 pm. Closed: 7/4, 11/24, 12/25. **Features:** Locals love the quirky little pizza spot both for its sunny patio and "take and bake" pizzas. Gourmet toppings include pesto, barbecue chicken and the beloved "cheeseburger in paradise." Hot subs such as the veggie monster also are popular. Casual dress; beer only. **Parking:** street.

TANDOOR INDIAN RESTAURANT   *Menu on aaa.com*   **Lunch:** $8-$16   **Dinner:** $8-$16   **Phone:** 804/755-4400   ⑨
Indian
Location: I-64, exit 183C westbound; exit 183 eastbound, 2 mi w; in Olde Towne Square. 7801 W Broad St 23294. **Hours:** 11:30 am-2:30 & 5-10 pm, Sat & Sun noon-2:45 & 5-10 pm. Closed major holidays. **Reservations:** accepted. **Features:** The crisp, bright interior invites diners to relax and savor the deeply seasoned and sometimes spicy cuisine of India. The menu features extensive vegetarian selections, tandoori meats, vindaloos and easy-to-share appetizers, such as pakoras, samosas, parathas and other breads. Sample it all at the weekday lunch buffet. Casual dress; cocktails. **Parking:** on-site. **Cards:** AX, DS, MC, VI.

THAI DINER   **Lunch:** $6-$7   **Dinner:** $7-$10   **Phone:** 804/270-2699   ⑦
Thai
Location: Jct Parham Rd, just e; in Westland Shopping Center. 8059 W Broad St 23294. **Hours:** 11:30 am-3 & 5-10 pm, Sat noon-3 & 5-10 pm. Closed: Sun. **Features:** Authentic Thai food is served in a former ice cream shop (that's the reason for the big pink booths). Specialties include fish with basil, noodle soup and spicy dishes, but the menu itself is nearly the size of a book. Sundaes are still available. Casual dress; cocktails. **Parking:** on-site. **Cards:** AX, DS, MC, VI.

VIETNAM GARDEN   **Lunch:** $6-$7   **Dinner:** $6-$13   **Phone:** 804/262-6114   ⑪
Vietnamese
Location: Jct Glenside Dr and Staples Mill Rd, just w. 3991 Glenside Dr 23228. **Hours:** 11 am-10 pm, Fri-11 pm, Sat 5 pm-11 pm. Closed: 7/4, 11/24. **Reservations:** accepted. **Features:** Diners can sample Vietnamese fare amid soft lighting and a simple but soothing decor. Favorite menu choices include grilled shrimp on sugar cane, spicy seafood hot pot and barbecue pork on rice noodles. Flavors are spicy and fresh, with delicate flavorings such as cilantro, lemon grass and crunchy peanuts. Casual dress; cocktails. **Parking:** on-site. **Cards:** AX, DS, MC, VI.

YUM YUM GOOD   **Lunch:** $4-$6   **Dinner:** $5-$13   **Phone:** 804/673-9226   ㉒
Chinese
Location: Jct Willow Lawn Rd, just w. 5612 Patterson Ave 23226. **Hours:** 11 am-9:45 pm, Fri-10:45 pm, Sat noon-10:45 pm, Sun noon-9:45 pm. **Features:** The dining room functions as a simple, elegant setting. Menu choices include hearty portions of traditional favorites, with sauce that tend to be sweeter than average. Servers don't speak much English, but they're efficient and unflaggingly friendly. Casual dress; cocktails. **Parking:** on-site. **Cards:** AX, DS, MC, VI.

(See map and index starting on p. 828)

ZORBA'S
Lunch: $5-$14   Dinner: $9-$14   Phone: 804/270-6026   ①

Greek

DC, DS, MC, VI.

Location: Between Gaskins and Parham rds; in Tuckernuck Shopping Center. 9068 W Broad St 23294. **Hours:** 11 am-10 pm, Fri & Sat-11 pm. Closed major holidays. **Features:** The casual spot presents an everyday menu of standard Greek favorites, from pasticcio to spanakopita. Daily specials can veer more upscale, with options such as leg of lamb and fresh seafood. Casual dress; cocktails. **Parking:** on-site. **Cards:** AX, CB,

---

The following restaurant has not been evaluated by AAA but is listed for your information only.

SIDEWALK CAFE
Phone: 804/358-0645

[fyi]   Not evaluated. **Location:** Jct W Main and Rowland sts; in Historic Fan District. 2101 W Main St 23220. **Features:** Buffalo wings and Greek nachos are staples at the neighborhood bar, a favorite despite the often-rowdy crowds and loud music.

The Richmond Vicinity

ASHLAND pop. 6,619   (See map and index starting on p. 828)

——— WHERE TO STAY ———

ASHLAND INN

Small-scale Hotel

5/1-9/30	1P: $85-$160
3/1-4/30	1P: $70-$140
10/1-2/28	1P: $65-$140

Phone: (804)752-7777   35

Location: I-95, exit 92B, 0.5 mi w on SR 54. 101 Cottage Green Dr 23005. Fax: 804/798-0327. **Facility:** 126 units. 124 one-bedroom standard units. 2 one-bedroom suites with whirlpools. 2 stories (no elevator), exterior corridors. **Parking:** on-site. **Amenities:** irons, hair dryers. *Some:* high-speed Internet. **Pool(s):** outdoor. **Leisure Activities:** exercise room. **Guest Services:** coin laundry. **Business Services:** meeting rooms. **Cards:** AX, DC, DS, MC, VI.

SOME UNITS

DAYS INN ASHLAND   *Book at aaa.com*

Motel

| 3/1-9/30 | 1P: $70-$90 | 2P: $70-$90 |
| 10/1-2/28 | 1P: $50-$60 | 2P: $50-$60 |

Phone: (804)798-4262   37

Location: I-95, exit 92B, just w on SR 54. 806 England St 23005. Fax: 804/798-7009. **Facility:** 89 one-bedroom standard units. 2 stories (no elevator), exterior corridors. **Parking:** on-site. **Terms:** package plans, pets ($10 extra charge). **Amenities:** dual phone lines, hair dryers. **Pool(s):** outdoor. **Business Services:** fax. **Cards:** AX, CB, DC, DS, JC, MC, VI.

SOME UNITS

(See map and index starting on p. 828)

ECONO LODGE *Book at aaa.com* Phone: (804)798-9221 **32**

AAA SAVE

Motel

5/1-10/31 [CP]	1P: $49-$110	2P: $49-$110	XP: $10 F18
3/1-4/30 [CP]	1P: $42-$110	2P: $42-$110	XP: $10 F18
11/1-2/28 [CP]	1P: $42-$70	2P: $42-$70	XP: $10 F18

Location: I-95, exit 92, just w. 103 N Carter Rd 23005. Fax: 804/798-9221. **Facility:** 87 one-bedroom standard units. 2 stories (no elevator), exterior corridors. **Parking:** on-site. **Terms:** weekly rates available, package plans. **Amenities:** safes (fee). **Pool(s):** outdoor. **Business Services:** fax. **Cards:** AX, DC, DS, JC, MC, VI.
Special Amenities: free continental breakfast and free local telephone calls.

SOME UNITS

HAMPTON INN *Book at aaa.com* Phone: (804)752-8444 **39**

Small-scale Hotel

All Year   1P: $89-$129   2P: $89-$129
Location: I-95, exit 92B northbound; exit 92 southbound, 0.5 mi w on SR 54. 705 England St 23005. Fax: 804/752-8445. **Facility:** 74 units. 72 one-bedroom standard units, some with whirlpools. 2 one-bedroom suites ($129-$159) with whirlpools. 3 stories, interior corridors. *Bath:* combo or shower only. **Parking:** on-site. **Amenities:** dual phone lines, voice mail, irons, hair dryers. **Pool(s):** heated outdoor. **Leisure Activities:** exercise room. **Guest Services:** valet and coin laundry. **Business Services:** meeting rooms, business center. **Cards:** AX, CB, DC, DS, MC, VI.

SOME UNITS

HANOVER HOUSE MOTOR LODGE *Book at aaa.com* Phone: (804)550-2805 **40**

Motel

6/17-9/3	1P: $79	2P: $79	XP: $5 F12
3/1-6/16 & 9/4-12/31	1P: $55-$69	2P: $55-$69	XP: $5 F12
1/1-2/28	1P: $55	2P: $55	XP: $5 F12

Location: I-95, exit 86, 1 mi n of jct I-295. 10296 Sliding Hill Rd 23005. Fax: 804/550-2104. **Facility:** 93 one-bedroom standard units. 2 stories (no elevator), interior/exterior corridors. **Parking:** on-site. **Amenities:** irons, hair dryers. **Pool(s):** outdoor. **Guest Services:** coin laundry. **Business Services:** conference facilities. **Cards:** AX, CB, DC, DS, MC, VI.

SOME UNITS

THE HENRY CLAY INN Phone: (804)798-3100 **33**

Country Inn

All Year   1P: $90   2P: $90   XP: $15
Location: I-95, exit 92, 1.5 mi w on SR 54, then n. Located opposite the Amtrak station. 114 N Railroad Ave 23005. Fax: 804/752-7555. **Facility:** Built in the Georgian Revival style and painted yellow, the inn is modeled after a 1906 hotel that burned to the ground on this spot in 1946. Smoke free premises. 14 units. 12 one-bedroom standard units, some with whirlpools. 2 one-bedroom suites ($145-$165) with whirlpools. 2 stories (no elevator), interior/exterior corridors. **Parking:** on-site. **Terms:** office hours 7 am-7 pm, 7 day cancellation notice, pets (small dogs only, 1st floor units). **Amenities:** irons, hair dryers. **Business Services:** meeting rooms, fax. **Cards:** AX, MC, VI.

SOME UNITS

HOLIDAY INN EXPRESS HOTEL & SUITES *Book at aaa.com* Phone: (804)752-7889 **38**

Small-scale Hotel

All Year [BP]   1P: $79-$129   2P: $99-$129
Location: I-95, exit 92, just w. 107 S Carter Rd 23005. Fax: 804/752-7180. **Facility:** 115 units. 49 one-bedroom standard units, some with whirlpools. 66 one-bedroom suites ($99-$129). 3 stories, interior corridors. *Bath:* combo or shower only. **Parking:** on-site. **Amenities:** high-speed Internet, dual phone lines, voice mail, irons, hair dryers. **Pool(s):** heated indoor. **Leisure Activities:** whirlpool, exercise room. **Guest Services:** valet and coin laundry. **Business Services:** meeting rooms, business center. **Cards:** AX, DC, DS, MC, VI.

SOME UNITS

MICROTEL INN & SUITES *Book at aaa.com* Phone: (804)521-2377 **31**

Small-scale Hotel

4/1-9/30	1P: $69-$109	2P: $69-$109	XP: $5 F18
3/1-3/31 & 10/1-2/28	1P: $49-$89	2P: $49-$89	XP: $5 F18

Location: I-95, exit 92, just off SR 54 W. 107 N Carter Rd 23005. Fax: 804/521-2378. **Facility:** 64 one-bedroom standard units. 3 stories, interior corridors. *Bath:* combo or shower only. **Parking:** on-site. **Terms:** package plans. **Amenities:** voice mail, safes (fee). *Some:* dual phone lines. **Guest Services:** valet laundry. **Business Services:** fax. **Cards:** AX, DC, DS, MC, VI.

SOME UNITS

QUALITY INN & SUITES *Book at aaa.com* Phone: 804/798-4231 **36**

AAA SAVE

Small-scale Hotel

All Year   1P: $50-$100   2P: $50-$100   XP: $10 F17
Location: I-95, exit 92B, just w on SR 54. 810 England St 23005. Fax: 804/798-9074. **Facility:** 156 units. 136 one-bedroom standard units. 20 one-bedroom suites ($100-$150). 2 stories (no elevator), interior/exterior corridors. *Bath:* combo or shower only. **Parking:** on-site. **Terms:** cancellation fee imposed, pets ($15 extra charge). **Amenities:** dual phone lines, voice mail, safes (fee), irons, hair dryers. **Dining:** 6 am-9 & 5-10 pm, cocktails. **Pool(s):** outdoor, wading. **Leisure Activities:** exercise room. **Guest Services:** coin laundry. **Business Services:** meeting rooms, fax. **Cards:** AX, DC, DS, MC, VI. *(See color ad p 854)*

SOME UNITS

SLEEP INN & SUITES *Book at aaa.com* Phone: (704)752-2355 **34**

AAA SAVE

Small-scale Hotel

All Year [ECP]   1P: $64-$139   2P: $64-$139   XP: $5 F18
Location: I-95, exit 92B northbound; exit 92 southbound, 0.5 mi w on SR 54. 80 Cottage Green Rd 23005. Fax: 804/752-2855. **Facility:** 69 one-bedroom standard units, some with whirlpools. 3 stories, interior corridors. *Bath:* some combo or shower only. **Parking:** on-site. **Amenities:** high-speed Internet, dual phone lines, voice mail, irons, hair dryers. **Pool(s):** heated indoor. **Leisure Activities:** whirlpool, exercise room. **Guest Services:** valet and coin laundry. **Business Services:** meeting rooms, business center. **Cards:** AX, DC, DS, JC, MC, VI. **Special Amenities:** free continental breakfast and free newspaper.

SOME UNITS

(See map and index starting on p. 828)

──── WHERE TO DINE ────

ASHLAND COFFEE & TEA **Lunch:** $5-$12 **Dinner:** $5-$12 **Phone:** 804/798-1702 ④⓪
▼▼▼
American **Location:** Just w of railroad track, entrance on England St. 100 N Railroad Ave 23005. **Hours:** 7 am-8 pm, Thurs & Fri-11 pm, Sat 7:30 am-11 pm, Sun 8:30 am-2 pm. Closed major holidays. **Features:** In the heart of a quaint college town, the quirky coffeehouse serves overstuffed sandwiches, daily soups and a wide array of delicious coffee drinks. Live music often is scheduled for weekend evenings. Casual dress; beer & wine only; entertainment. **Parking:** on-site. **Cards:** AX, MC, VI.   ⊠

EL AZTECA **Lunch:** $5-$12 **Dinner:** $6-$17 **Phone:** 804/798-4652 ③⑨
▼▼▼
Mexican **Location:** I-95, exit 92B, 0.5 mi w on SR 54. 103 N Washington Hwy 23005. **Hours:** 11 am-10 pm, Fri-11 pm, Sat noon-11 pm, Sun noon-9 pm. Closed major holidays. **Features:** The restaurant prepares one of the widest varieties of Mexican cuisine around. In addition to standard favorites, the menu lists more adventurous offerings, including chicken in mole sauce—a rich and savory sauce derived from the cocoa bean. Entrees are fresh, delicious and served quickly. Casual dress; cocktails. **Parking:** on-site. **Cards:** AX, DS, MC, VI.   ▼ ⊠

HOMEMADES BY SUZANNE **Lunch:** $5-$8 **Phone:** 804/798-8331 ④①
▼▼▼
Regional American **Location:** I-95, exit 92, 1.5 mi w on SR 54, then just n. 102 N Railroad Ave 23005. **Hours:** 9 am-2 pm, Sat-3 pm. Closed major holidays; also Sun. **Features:** A great stop for lunch or picnic-packing, the eatery specializes in home-style American and Southern favorites, which are served cafeteria style. Boxed lunches, homemade bread and numerous fabulous desserts—cream puffs, pies, cakes and more—fill the menu. Casual dress. **Parking:** on-site. **Cards:** AX, CB, DC, DS, MC, VI.

THE IRONHORSE RESTAURANT **Lunch:** $8-$18 **Dinner:** $8-$30 **Phone:** 804/752-6410 ④②
▼▼ ▼▼
Regional American **Location:** I-95, exit 92, 1.5 mi w on SR 54 (S England St). 100 S Railroad Ave 23005. **Hours:** 11:30 am-2:30 & 5:30-9 pm, Fri & Sat-10 pm. Closed: for dinner Sun & Mon. **Reservations:** suggested. **Features:** The 1903 storefront retains many original architectural details, such as the pressed-tin ceiling. Picture windows overlook the railroad tracks, and the decor—including prominently displayed railroad collectibles—reflects the town's heritage. Monthly changing specialties use local market produce, seafood and certified Angus beef and reflect creative international and Southern influences. Casual dress; cocktails. **Parking:** street. **Cards:** AX, DC, DS, MC, VI.   ▼ ⊠

THE SMOKEY PIG **Lunch:** $4-$19 **Dinner:** $4-$19 **Phone:** 804/798-4590 ④③
▼▼
Barbecue **Location:** I-95, exit 92B, just s of jct SR 54 (England St) on US 1. 212 S Washington Hwy 23005. **Hours:** 11 am-9 pm, Sun from noon. Closed major holidays; also Mon. **Features:** As the name implies, this restaurant specializes in Southern barbecue ribs, chicken, beef and pork. Add a few of the traditional fixings like greens, sweet potatoes and hush puppies, and you've got a good, satisfying meal. Prime rib is served Saturday and Sunday. Casual dress; cocktails. **Parking:** on-site. **Cards:** MC, VI.   ⊠

CARMEL CHURCH

──── WHERE TO STAY ────

COMFORT INN & SUITES *Book at aaa.com* **Phone:** (804)448-1144
▼▼▼▼ All Year 1P: $55-$139
Small-scale Hotel **Location:** I-95, exit 104 (SR 207), just w. 24058 Welcome Way Dr 22546 (PO Box 1000, RUTHER GLEN). Fax: 804/448-1694. **Facility:** 64 one-bedroom standard units. 3 stories, interior corridors. *Bath:* combo or shower only. **Parking:** on-site. **Amenities:** dual phone lines, irons, hair dryers. **Pool(s):** heated indoor. **Leisure Activities:** limited exercise equipment. **Business Services:** meeting rooms, fax. **Cards:** AX, CB, DC, DS, JC, MC, VI.

SOME UNITS
(ASK) (SD) (▮▼) (⌖M) (⌖) (≈) (▼) (DATA PORT) / ⊠ (▮) (▭) (▯) /

RED ROOF INN *Book at aaa.com* **Phone:** (804)448-2828
▼▼ ▼▼ 4/1-9/15 1P: $59-$85 2P: $59-$85 XP: $5 F18
3/1-3/31 & 9/16-2/28 1P: $49-$69 2P: $49-$69 XP: $5 F18
Small-scale Hotel **Location:** I-95, exit 104 (SR 207), just w. 23500 Welcome Way Dr 22546 (PO Box 105, RUTHER GLEN). Fax: 804/448-4441. **Facility:** 134 units. 133 one-bedroom standard units. 1 one-bedroom suite ($159-$169). 2 stories (no elevator), interior corridors. *Bath:* combo or shower only. **Parking:** on-site. **Terms:** small pets only. **Pool(s):** outdoor. **Guest Services:** coin laundry. **Business Services:** meeting rooms, fax. **Cards:** AX, CB, DC, DS, MC, VI.

SOME UNITS
(ASK) (SD) (🐾) (▮▼) (⌖) (∅) (≈) (▼) (DATA PORT) / ⊠ (▮) (▭) /
FEE FEE

CHESTER pop. 17,890 (See map and index starting on p. 828)

──── WHERE TO STAY ────

AMERISUITES (CHESTER/RIVER'S BEND) *Book at aaa.com* **Phone:** (804)530-4600 ⑨⑤
(AAA) (SAVE) 3/1-9/30 1P: $129-$159 2P: $129-$159 XP: $10 F
▼▼▼▼ 10/1-11/30 1P: $109-$139 2P: $109-$139 XP: $10 F
12/1-2/28 1P: $99-$109 2P: $99-$109 XP: $10 F
Small-scale Hotel **Location:** I-295, exit 15B, just w; I-95, exit 61A 4.5 mi e; in River's Bend. 13148 Kingston Ave 23836. Fax: 804/530-0610. **Facility:** 80 one-bedroom standard units. 4 stories, interior corridors. *Bath:* combo or shower only. **Parking:** on-site. **Terms:** cancellation fee imposed. **Amenities:** video games, high-speed Internet, voice mail, irons, hair dryers. *Some:* dual phone lines. **Pool(s):** heated outdoor. **Leisure Activities:** golf privileges, exercise room. **Guest Services:** valet and coin laundry, area transportation-within 10 mi. **Business Services:** meeting rooms, fax. **Cards:** AX, DC, DS, JC, MC, VI. **Special Amenities:** free expanded continental breakfast and free newspaper.

SOME UNITS
(SD) (▮▼) (⌖) (≈) (▼) (DATA PORT) (▮) (▭) (▯) / (⊠) /

(See map and index starting on p. 828)

CLARION HOTEL   *Book at aaa.com*   Phone: (804)748-6321   **90**
AAA SAVE
3/1-9/30 — 1P: $59-$99 — 2P: $59-$99 — XP: $5 — F10
10/1-2/28 — 1P: $59-$79 — 2P: $59-$79 — XP: $5 — F10
Location: I-95, exit 61B, just e on jct SR 10. 2401 W Hundred Rd 23831. **Fax:** 804/796-9706. **Facility:** 165 one-
bedroom standard units. 2 stories (no elevator), interior corridors. **Parking:** on-site. **Terms:** cancellation fee
Small-scale Hotel   imposed. **Amenities:** video games, voice mail, irons, hair dryers. **Dining:** 7 am-midnight. **Pool(s):** outdoor,
wading. **Guest Services:** valet and coin laundry. **Business Services:** meeting rooms, business center.
Cards: AX, CB, DC, DS, MC, VI. **Special Amenities:** free local telephone calls and free newspaper.

SOME UNITS

COMFORT INN-RICHMOND/CHESTER   *Book at aaa.com*   Phone: (804)751-0000   **89**
AAA SAVE
All Year — 1P: $59-$119 — 2P: $59-$119
Location: I-95, exit 61A, just e on SR 10. 2100 W Hundred Rd 23836. **Fax:** 804/748-5581. **Facility:** 122 units. 112
one-bedroom standard units. 10 one-bedroom suites with whirlpools. 5 stories, interior corridors. *Bath:*
combo or shower only. **Parking:** on-site. **Terms:** small pets only. **Amenities:** voice mail, irons, hair dryers.
Small-scale Hotel   **Dining:** 4 pm-10 pm, wine/beer only. **Pool(s):** outdoor. **Leisure Activities:** exercise room. **Guest Services:**
valet and coin laundry. **Business Services:** meeting rooms, fax. **Cards:** AX, DC, DS, MC, VI.
Special Amenities: free expanded continental breakfast and free newspaper. *(See color ad below)*

SOME UNITS

COURTYARD BY MARRIOTT   *Book at aaa.com*   Phone: (804)414-1010   **92**
All Year — 1P: $85-$94 — 2P: $85-$94
Location: I-95, exit 61A; I-295, exit 15B, 4 mi n. 2001 W Hundred Rd 23836. **Fax:** 804/414-1011. **Facility:** 135
Small-scale Hotel   units. 124 one-bedroom standard units, some with whirlpools. 11 one-bedroom suites. 6 stories, interior
corridors. *Bath:* combo or shower only. **Parking:** on-site. **Terms:** [MAP] meal plan available.
Amenities: high-speed Internet, dual phone lines, voice mail, irons, hair dryers. **Pool(s):** heated indoor. **Leisure
Activities:** whirlpool, exercise room. **Guest Services:** sundries, valet and coin laundry. **Business Services:** meeting rooms,
fax. **Cards:** AX, DC, DS, MC, VI.

SOME UNITS
FEE

FAIRFIELD INN BY MARRIOTT   *Book at aaa.com*   Phone: 804/778-7500   **87**
All Year [ECP] — 1P: $59-$149 — 2P: $59-$149
Location: I-95, exit 61B, just w of jct SR 10. 12400 Redwater Creek Rd 23831. **Fax:** 804/778-4555. **Facility:** 115
Small-scale Hotel   one-bedroom standard units, some with whirlpools. 4 stories, interior corridors. *Bath:* combo or shower only.
Parking: on-site. **Amenities:** video games, voice mail, irons, hair dryers. **Pool(s):** heated indoor. **Leisure
Activities:** whirlpool, exercise room. **Guest Services:** valet laundry. **Business Services:** fax. **Cards:** AX, DC, DS, MC, VI.

SOME UNITS

HAMPTON INN   *Book at aaa.com*   Phone: (804)768-8888   **88**
AAA SAVE
All Year [ECP] — 1P: $79-$129
Location: I-95, exit 61A, jct SR 10. Located behind Comfort Inn. 12610 Chestnut Hill Rd 23836. **Fax:** 804/768-0521.
Facility: 66 units. 64 one-bedroom standard units. 2 one-bedroom suites ($99-$139) with whirlpools. 2
stories (no elevator), interior corridors. *Bath:* combo or shower only. **Parking:** on-site. **Terms:** 2 night
Small-scale Hotel   minimum stay - seasonal, 30 day cancellation notice. **Amenities:** high-speed Internet, voice mail, irons, hair
dryers. *Some:* safes (fee). **Leisure Activities:** exercise room. **Guest Services:** coin laundry. **Business
Services:** business center. **Cards:** AX, DC, DS, MC, VI. **Special Amenities: free expanded continental breakfast and free
newspaper.**

SOME UNITS

HOLIDAY INN EXPRESS   *Book at aaa.com*   Phone: (804)751-0123   **93**
All Year [BP] — 1P: $59-$69 — 2P: $69-$79
Location: I-95, exit 61A, just e. 1911 W Hundred Rd 23836. **Fax:** 804/768-2488. **Facility:** 95 one-bedroom
Small-scale Hotel   standard units. 4 stories, interior corridors. *Bath:* combo or shower only. **Parking:** on-site. **Amenities:** voice
mail, irons, hair dryers. **Leisure Activities:** exercise room. **Guest Services:** valet and coin laundry.
Business Services: meeting rooms, fax (fee). **Cards:** AX, CB, DC, DS, JC, MC, VI.

SOME UNITS

(See map and index starting on p. 828)

HOMEWOOD SUITES RICHMOND/CHESTER *Book at aaa.com* — Phone: (804)751-0010 — 94
All Year [BP] — 1P: $89-$99 — 2P: $99-$189
Small-scale Hotel — **Location:** I-95, exit 61A; I-295, exit 15B, 4 mi w. 12810 Old Stage Rd 23836. Fax: 804/751-0031. **Facility:** 118 units. 68 one-bedroom standard units with kitchens. 49 one- and 1 two-bedroom suites with kitchens, some with whirlpools. 7 stories, interior corridors. *Bath:* combo or shower only. **Parking:** on-site. **Amenities:** video library (fee), high-speed Internet, dual phone lines, voice mail, irons, hair dryers. **Pool(s):** heated indoor. **Leisure Activities:** whirlpool, exercise room, basketball. **Guest Services:** sundries, complimentary evening beverages: Mon-Thurs, valet and coin laundry. **Business Services:** meeting rooms, business center. **Cards:** AX, DC, DS, JC, MC, VI.

SOME UNITS
(ASK) (S♦) (¶↑) (♿M) (⌨) (≈) (✕) (VCR) (📷) (DATA PORT) (🛏) (🖥) (📽) / (✕) /

QUALITY INN & SUITES *Book at aaa.com* — Phone: (804)796-5200 — 91
(AAA) (SAVE) — 3/1-9/30 [ECP] — 1P: $79-$99 — 2P: $79-$99 — XP: $10 — F10
10/1-2/28 [ECP] — 1P: $69-$89 — 2P: $69-$89 — XP: $10 — F10
Small-scale Hotel — **Location:** I-95, exit 61A, just e on SR 10/W Hundred Rd. 12711 Old Stage Rd 23836. Fax: 804/796-3703. **Facility:** 70 one-bedroom standard units. 3 stories, interior corridors. *Bath:* combo or shower only. **Parking:** on-site. **Terms:** cancellation fee imposed, package plans. **Amenities:** high-speed Internet, voice mail, irons, hair dryers. *Some:* dual phone lines. **Pool(s):** heated indoor. **Leisure Activities:** exercise room. **Guest Services:** valet and coin laundry. **Business Services:** meeting rooms, fax. **Cards:** AX, CB, DC, DS, MC, VI. **Special Amenities:** free local telephone calls and free newspaper.

SOME UNITS
(S♦) (¶↑) (⌨) (≈) (📷) (DATA PORT) (🛏) (🖥) (📽) / (✕) /

SUPER 8 MOTEL *Book at aaa.com* — Phone: (804)748-0050 — 86
All Year — 1P: $54-$99 — 2P: $54-$99 — XP: $6 — F12
Motel — **Location:** I-95, exit 61B, just w. 2421 Southland Dr 23831. Fax: 804/751-9146. **Facility:** 44 one-bedroom standard units. 3 stories (no elevator), interior corridors. **Parking:** on-site. **Amenities:** hair dryers. **Business Services:** fax. **Cards:** AX, DC, DS, MC, VI.

SOME UNITS
(ASK) (S♦) (¶↑) (📷) (DATA PORT) (🛏) (🖥) / (✕) /

━━━━━━ **WHERE TO DINE** ━━━━━━

CENTRAL PARK DELI — **Lunch:** $5-$7 — **Dinner:** $5-$7 — Phone: 804/796-9660 — 75
Deli/Subs Sandwiches — **Location:** I-95, exit 61B, 1 mi w; in Breckenridge Shopping Center. 12744 Jefferson Davis Hwy 23831. **Hours:** 11 am-8 pm, Fri-9 pm, Sat-3 pm. Closed major holidays. **Features:** Regulars can't last a few days without a patty melt or corned beef sandwich from the casual spot. Also on offer are delicious daily soups, pickles, a glass case full of desserts and cookies and barbecue ribs in the evening. Casual dress; beer & wine only. **Parking:** on-site. **Cards:** AX, MC, VI.
(♿M) (✕)

CESARE'S RESTAURANT & PIZZERIA — **Lunch:** $6-$14 — **Dinner:** $6-$14 — Phone: 804/530-1047 — 77
Italian — **Location:** I-95, exit 61A, 2 mi e; in River's Bend Shopping Center. 13127 River's Bend Blvd 23831. **Hours:** 11 am-10 pm, Fri & Sat-11 pm, Sun noon-10 pm. Closed major holidays. **Features:** Diners can catch a glimpse of their pizza being made or choose from such daily specials as calzones, baked manicotti, vegetable-stuffed shells and Italian hoagies. The setting is casual, and the service friendly and attentive. Casual dress; beer & wine only. **Parking:** on-site. **Cards:** AX, DC, DS, MC, VI.
(✕)

DON PAPA GRANDE MEXICAN RESTAURANT — **Lunch:** $4-$13 — **Dinner:** $6-$13 — Phone: 804/796-7988 — 76
Mexican — **Location:** I-95, exit 61B, 1 mi w; in Breckenridge Shopping Center. 12806 Jefferson Davis Hwy 23831. **Hours:** 11 am-2:30 & 5-10 pm, Sun-9 pm. Closed major holidays. **Features:** Walls are painted with colorful, festive murals at the neighborhood spot. Patrons can order all the favorite Mexican combination plates, as well as more authentic specialties, such as tostadas de ceviche on weekends, chile Colorado and carne asada. Casual dress; cocktails. **Parking:** on-site. **Cards:** MC, VI.
(♿M) (✕)

JALAPENOS — **Lunch:** $5-$11 — **Dinner:** $7-$14 — Phone: 804/530-2787 — 79
Mexican — **Location:** I-295, exit 15B, just w; in River's Bend. 13130 Kingston Ave 23836. **Hours:** 11:30 am-10 pm, Fri-11 pm, Sun-9 pm. Closed: 7/4, 11/24, 12/25. **Features:** In addition to Mexican standards, the bright, cheerful spot serves some more creative dishes, such as marinated shrimp cocktail, tortilla soup and chile Colorado. Casual dress; cocktails. **Parking:** on-site. **Cards:** AX, DS, MC, VI.
(♿M) (✕)

NARITA JAPANESE RESTAURANT — **Lunch:** $6-$25 — **Dinner:** $7-$50 — Phone: 804/530-0013 — 78
Japanese — **Location:** I-95, exit 61A, 2 mi e; River's Bend Shopping Center. 13115 River's Bend Blvd 23836. **Hours:** 11 am-2 & 5-10 pm, Sat from 5 pm. Closed major holidays; also Sun. **Features:** In a cool, uncluttered setting, the restaurant serves fresh, colorful sushi, along with other specialties ranging from soups to teriyakis. Casual dress; beer & wine only. **Parking:** on-site. **Cards:** AX, DS, MC, VI.
(♿M) (✕)

PEKING RESTAURANT — **Lunch:** $5-$7 — **Dinner:** $7-$12 — Phone: 804/751-9898 — 74
Chinese — **Location:** I-95, exit 61B, 1 mi w; in Breckenridge Shopping Center. 12730 Jefferson Davis Hwy 23831. **Hours:** 11:30 am-2:15 & 4:30-9:30 pm, Fri & Sat-10:30 pm. Closed: 11/24. **Features:** You'll find all your favorites on the extensive menu, from lo mein to chicken imperial and everything in between. Chinese, Hunan, Mandarin and Szechuan cuisines are the highlights. A good choice is the hot and sour soup and the tasty Hunan chicken entree. Casual dress; cocktails. **Parking:** on-site. **Cards:** AX, MC, VI.
(✕)

CHESTERFIELD   (See map and index starting on p. 828)

──────── **WHERE TO STAY** ────────

COUNTRY INN & SUITES, RICHMOND I-95S
AAA SAVE
Book at aaa.com
Phone: (804)275-5900   **82**
All Year   1P: $59-$99   2P: $59-$99   XP: $6   F16
Location: I-95, exit 64, just w. 2401 Willis Rd 23237. Fax: 804/275-3092. **Facility:** 50 units. 37 one-bedroom standard units, some with whirlpools. 13 one-bedroom suites ($79-$125). 2 stories, interior corridors. **Parking:** on-site. **Terms:** 10 day cancellation notice, package plans. **Amenities:** dual phone lines, voice
Small-scale Hotel mail, irons, hair dryers. **Guest Services:** coin laundry. **Business Services:** fax. **Cards:** AX, CB, DC, DS, JC, MC, VI. **Special Amenities:** free newspaper and early check-in/late check-out.
(See color ad p 847)

SOME UNITS

ROYAL INN MOTEL
AAA SAVE
Phone: (804)276-4500   **80**
All Year   1P: $45-$50   2P: $50-$55   XP: $5   F18
Location: US 360, 4 mi e of SR 288 and 4 mi w of SR 150 (Chippenham Pkwy). 9801 Hull St Rd 23236.
Motel   Fax: 804/276-7800. **Facility:** 15 one-bedroom standard units. 1 story, exterior corridors. **Parking:** on-site. **Business Services:** fax. **Cards:** AX, CB, DC, MC, VI. **Special Amenities:** preferred room (subject to availability with advance reservations).

SOME UNITS

SLEEP INN
AAA SAVE
Book at aaa.com
Phone: (804)275-8800   **83**
3/1-9/15 [ECP]   1P: $59-$99   2P: $59-$99   XP: $10   F
9/16-2/28 [ECP]   1P: $49-$69   2P: $49-$69   XP: $10   F
Location: I-95, exit 64, just w. 2321 Willis Rd 23237. Fax: 804/275-0949. **Facility:** 51 one-bedroom standard units. 3 stories, interior corridors. *Bath:* combo or shower only. **Parking:** on-site. **Terms:** 10 day cancellation
Small-scale Hotel notice-fee imposed. **Amenities:** high-speed Internet (fee), voice mail, irons, hair dryers. **Business Services:** fax. **Cards:** AX, CB, DC, DS, JC, MC, VI. **Special Amenities:** free expanded continental breakfast and free newspaper.

SOME UNITS

SUPER 8 MOTEL
Book at aaa.com
Phone: (804)743-0770   **81**
All Year   1P: $59-$69   XP: $6   F18
Location: I-95, exit 64, just w. 9040 Pams Ave 23237 (9040 Pams Ave, RICHMOND). Fax: 804/521-2892.
Small-scale Hotel **Facility:** 50 one-bedroom standard units, some with whirlpools. 3 stories, interior corridors. *Bath:* combo or shower only. **Parking:** on-site. **Terms:** weekly rates available, package plans. **Amenities:** voice mail, irons, hair dryers. **Leisure Activities:** exercise room. **Guest Services:** coin laundry. **Business Services:** fax. **Cards:** AX, CB, DC, DS, MC, VI.

SOME UNITS

COLONIAL HEIGHTS pop. 16,897   (See map and index starting on p. 835)

──────── **WHERE TO STAY** ────────

COMFORT SUITES SOUTHPARK
AAA SAVE
Book at aaa.com
Phone: (804)520-8900   **18**
3/1-9/15 [ECP]   1P: $95-$139   2P: $95-$149   XP: $10   F18
9/16-2/28 [ECP]   1P: $85-$112   2P: $85-$122   XP: $10   F18
Location: I-95, exit 53, just n. Located adjacent to Southpark Mall. 931 South Ave 23834. Fax: 804/518-2001.
Facility: 92 one-bedroom standard units, some with whirlpools. 5 stories, interior corridors. *Bath:* combo or
Small-scale Hotel shower only. **Parking:** on-site. **Amenities:** high-speed Internet, dual phone lines, voice mail, safes (fee), irons, hair dryers. **Pool(s):** heated indoor. **Leisure Activities:** whirlpool. **Guest Services:** valet and coin laundry, area transportation-within 5 mi. **Business Services:** meeting rooms, business center. **Cards:** AX, CB, DC, DS, JC, MC, VI.

SOME UNITS

HILTON GARDEN INN RICHMOND SOUTH/SOUTHPARK
fyi
Phone: 804/520-0600
All Year   1P: $79-$179   2P: $89-$199   XP: $10   F18
Too new to rate, opening scheduled for September 2004. **Location:** I-95, exit 53. 800 Southpark Blvd 23834.
Small-scale Hotel Fax: 804/520-0676. **Amenities:** 155 units, coffeemakers, microwaves, refrigerators, pool. **Terms:** cancellation fee imposed. **Cards:** AX, DC, DS, MC, VI.

DOSWELL

──────── **WHERE TO STAY** ────────

BEST WESTERN-KINGS QUARTERS
AAA SAVE
Book at aaa.com
Phone: (804)876-3321
5/27-9/5   1P: $69-$169   2P: $69-$169   XP: $5   F17
3/1-5/26 & 9/6-10/29   1P: $34-$149   2P: $34-$149   XP: $5   F17
10/30-2/28   1P: $34-$69   2P: $34-$69   XP: $5   F17
Location: I-95, exit 98, just e on SR 30; at entrance to theme park. Located adjacent to Paramount King's Dominion.
Small-scale Hotel 16102 Theme Park Way 23047. Fax: 804/876-3182. **Facility:** 248 units. 247 one-bedroom standard units. 1 one-bedroom suite. 2 stories (no elevator), exterior corridors. *Bath:* combo or shower only. **Parking:** on-site.
Terms: 3 day cancellation notice-fee imposed, package plans, small pets only ($25 deposit). **Amenities:** safes (fee), irons, hair dryers. **Dining:** 24 hours, cocktails. **Pool(s):** outdoor. **Leisure Activities:** putting green, 2 lighted tennis courts, playground, shuffleboard, volleyball. *Fee:* game room. **Guest Services:** coin laundry, area transportation-theme park. **Business Services:** meeting rooms, fax. **Cards:** AX, CB, DC, DS, MC, VI.

SOME UNITS
FEE   FEE   FEE

GLEN ALLEN pop. 12,562   (See map and index starting on p. 828)

——— WHERE TO STAY ———

AMERISUITES (RICHMOND/INNSBROOK)   *Book at aaa.com*   Phone: (804)747-9644   **47**
AAA SAVE
▼▼▼▼
Small-scale Hotel
All Year   1P: $99-$159   2P: $99-$159   XP: $10   F
Location: I-64, exit 178B, 0.5 mi e to Dominion Blvd, then just n. Located in the Innsbrook Corporate Center. 4100 Cox Rd 23060. Fax: 804/346-9320. **Facility:** 126 one-bedroom standard units. 6 stories, interior corridors. **Parking:** on-site. **Terms:** small pets only. **Amenities:** voice mail, irons, hair dryers. *Some:* dual phone lines. **Pool(s):** outdoor. **Leisure Activities:** exercise room. **Guest Services:** valet and coin laundry, area transportation-Corporate Center. **Business Services:** meeting rooms, fax. **Cards:** AX, CB, DC, DS, JC, MC, VI. **Special Amenities:** free expanded continental breakfast and free newspaper. *(See color ad p 837)*

SOME UNITS
[icons] / X /

CANDLEWOOD SUITES RICHMOND-WEST   *Book at aaa.com*   Phone: (804)364-2000   **48**
▼▼▼▼
Small-scale Hotel
All Year   1P: $89-$109   2P: $89-$109
Location: I-64, exit 178, just w on W Broad St. 4120 Brookriver Dr 23060. Fax: 804/364-8701. **Facility:** 122 units. 98 one-bedroom standard units with kitchens. 24 one-bedroom suites ($109-$139) with kitchens. 3 stories, interior corridors. *Bath:* combo or shower only. **Parking:** on-site. **Terms:** office hours 7 am-11 pm, 7 day cancellation notice, pets ($150 fee). **Amenities:** video library, CD players, high-speed Internet, dual phone lines, voice mail, irons, hair dryers. **Leisure Activities:** exercise room. **Guest Services:** sundries, complimentary laundry. **Business Services:** fax. **Cards:** AX, DC, DS.

SOME UNITS
[icons]   FEE   / X /

COMFORT SUITES-INNSBROOK   *Book at aaa.com*   Phone: (804)217-9200   **51**
▼▼▼▼
Small-scale Hotel
All Year [BP]   1P: $69   2P: $99-$109
Location: I-64, exit 178B, just e on W Broad St to Cox Rd, then just n. 4051 Innslake Dr 23060. Fax: 804/217-9205. **Facility:** 125 units. 118 one-bedroom standard units. 7 one-bedroom suites ($159) with whirlpools. 5 stories, interior corridors. *Bath:* combo or shower only. **Parking:** on-site. **Amenities:** video games, high-speed Internet, dual phone lines, voice mail, irons, hair dryers. **Pool(s):** heated indoor. **Leisure Activities:** exercise room. **Guest Services:** valet and coin laundry, area transportation. **Business Services:** meeting rooms, business center. **Cards:** AX, CB, DC, DS, JC, MC, VI.

SOME UNITS
[icons] / X VCR /

COURTYARD BY MARRIOTT RICHMOND NORTHWEST   *Book at aaa.com*   Phone: (804)346-5427   **54**
▼▼▼▼
Small-scale Hotel
All Year   1P: $129-$139   2P: $129-$139
Location: I-64, exit 178B, 0.5 mi e, jct W Broad St and Westerre Pkwy. 3950 Westerre Pkwy 23233. Fax: 804/346-5429. **Facility:** 154 units. 146 one-bedroom standard units, some with whirlpools. 8 one-bedroom suites. 4 stories, interior corridors. *Bath:* combo or shower only. **Parking:** on-site. **Amenities:** dual phone lines, voice mail, irons, hair dryers. **Pool(s):** small heated indoor. **Leisure Activities:** whirlpool, exercise room. **Guest Services:** valet and coin laundry. **Business Services:** meeting rooms, fax. **Cards:** AX, DC, DS, MC, VI.

SOME UNITS
[icons] / X   FEE FEE /

HAMPTON INN-RICHMOND WEST   *Book at aaa.com*   Phone: (804)747-7777   **52**
▼▼▼▼
Small-scale Hotel
All Year   1P: $86-$112   XP: $7   F18
Location: I-64, exit 178B, just e, jct Cox Rd. Located in Innsbrook shopping and corporate complex. 10800 W Broad St 23060. Fax: 804/747-7069. **Facility:** 136 one-bedroom standard units. 5 stories, interior corridors. *Bath:* combo or shower only. **Parking:** on-site. **Amenities:** dual phone lines, voice mail, irons, hair dryers. **Pool(s):** outdoor. **Leisure Activities:** exercise room. **Guest Services:** valet laundry. **Business Services:** meeting rooms, fax. **Cards:** AX, DC, DS, MC, VI.

SOME UNITS
[icons] / X VCR /

HILTON GARDEN INN RICHMOND INNSBROOK   *Book at aaa.com*   Phone: 804/521-2900   **50**
▼▼▼▼
Small-scale Hotel
All Year   1P: $79-$159   2P: $79-$159   XP: $10   F
Location: I-64, exit 178B, just e on W Broad St, to Dominion Blvd, just n. Located in Innsbrook Corporate Center. 4050 Cox Rd 23060. Fax: 804/521-2901. **Facility:** 155 one-bedroom standard units, some with whirlpools. 6 stories, interior corridors. *Bath:* combo or shower only. **Parking:** on-site. **Terms:** cancellation fee imposed. **Amenities:** video games, high-speed Internet, dual phone lines, voice mail, irons, hair dryers. **Pool(s):** small heated indoor. **Leisure Activities:** whirlpool, exercise room. **Guest Services:** sundries, valet and coin laundry. **Business Services:** meeting rooms, business center. **Cards:** AX, CB, DC, DS, JC, MC, VI.

SOME UNITS
[icons] / X /

HOLIDAY INN EXPRESS   *Book at aaa.com*   Phone: (804)934-9300   **56**
▼▼▼▼
Small-scale Hotel
All Year [CP]   1P: $101   2P: $101   XP: $6   F18
Location: I-64, exit 180B, just n to Mayland Dr, then just w. 9933 Mayland Dr 23233. Fax: 804/934-0983. **Facility:** 113 one-bedroom standard units. 4 stories, interior corridors. *Bath:* combo or shower only. **Parking:** on-site. **Terms:** 3 day cancellation notice. **Amenities:** video games, high-speed Internet, dual phone lines, voice mail, irons, hair dryers. **Pool(s):** outdoor. **Guest Services:** valet and coin laundry. **Business Services:** meeting rooms, PC, fax. **Cards:** AX, CB, DC, DS, MC, VI.

SOME UNITS
[icons] / X /

(See map and index starting on p. 828)

HOMESTEAD STUDIO SUITES
HOTEL-RICHMOND/INNSBROOK   *Book at aaa.com*   Phone: (804)747-8898   53
All Year   1P: $54-$74   2P: $59-$79   XP: $5   F17
Location: I-64, exit 178B, just e on W Broad St, then just s on Cox Rd. 10961 W Broad St 23060. Fax: 804/747-8909.
Motel   **Facility:** 141 one-bedroom standard units with efficiencies. 2 stories (no elevator), exterior corridors. *Bath:* combo or shower only. **Parking:** on-site. **Terms:** office hours 6:30 am-10 pm, weekly rates available, small pets only ($75 fee, limit 1). **Amenities:** voice mail, irons. **Guest Services:** valet and coin laundry. **Business Services:** fax.
Cards: AX, CB, DC, DS, JC, MC, VI.

SOME UNITS
ASK SD 🐾 ▥ 🕁 📷 DATA PORT 🖥 📠 💻 / ✕ VCR
FEE   FEE

HOMEWOOD SUITES BY HILTON RICHMOND WEST
END-INNSBROOK   *Book at aaa.com*   Phone: (804)217-8000   49
All Year   1P: $109-$159   2P: $109-$159   XP: $10   F3
Location: I-64, exit 178B, just e on W Broad St to Cox Rd, then just n. 4100 Innslake Dr 23060. Fax: 804/747-1498.
Small-scale Hotel   **Facility:** 123 units. 116 one- and 7 two-bedroom suites with kitchens. 4 stories, interior corridors. *Bath:* combo or shower only. **Parking:** on-site. **Terms:** small pets only ($150 fee). **Amenities:** video library, video games, high-speed Internet, dual phone lines, voice mail, irons, hair dryers. *Some:* DVD players. **Pool(s):** outdoor. **Leisure Activities:** exercise room. **Guest Services:** sundries, valet and coin laundry, area transportation. **Business Services:** meeting rooms, business center. **Cards:** AX, DC, DS, MC, VI.

SOME UNITS
ASK SD 🐾 🕁 �&M ⚿ 🏊 VCR 📷 DATA PORT 🖥 📠 💻 / ✕ /
FEE

HOWARD JOHNSON EXPRESS INN   Phone: (804)261-0188   42
All Year   1P: $65-$150   2P: $67-$150   XP: $5   F17
Location: I-95, exit 83B, 0.5 mi w to Brook Rd, then just n. 8613 Brook Rd 23060. Fax: 804/261-7667. **Facility:** 36 one-bedroom standard units, some with whirlpools. 2 stories, interior corridors. **Parking:** on-site.
Small-scale Hotel   **Amenities:** voice mail, irons, hair dryers. **Cards:** AX, DS, MC, VI.

SOME UNITS
ASK SD �&M VCR 📷 DATA PORT 🖥 📠 💻 / ✕ /

RESIDENCE INN BY MARRIOTT   *Book at aaa.com*   Phone: (804)762-9852   55
All Year [BP]   1P: $129-$169   2P: $129-$169
Location: I-64, exit 180, n on Gaskins Rd to W Broad St. 3940 Westerre Pkwy 23233. Fax: 804/762-9865.
Small-scale Hotel   **Facility:** 104 units. 44 one-bedroom standard units with kitchens. 44 one- and 16 two-bedroom suites with kitchens. 4 stories, interior corridors. *Bath:* combo or shower only. **Parking:** on-site. **Terms:** pets ($100 fee).
Amenities: video games, dual phone lines, voice mail, irons, hair dryers. **Pool(s):** heated outdoor. **Leisure Activities:** whirlpool, lighted tennis court, exercise room, sports court. **Guest Services:** valet and coin laundry. **Business Services:** meeting rooms, fax. **Cards:** AX, CB, DC, DS, MC, VI.

SOME UNITS
ASK SD 🐾 🕁 �&M ⚿ 🏊 ✕ 📷 DATA PORT 🖥 📠 💻 / ✕ /
FEE

RICHMOND MARRIOTT WEST   *Book at aaa.com*   Phone: (804)965-9500   46
All Year   1P: $89-$300   2P: $89-$300
Location: I-64, exit 178B, 0.5 mi e to Dominion Blvd, then just n. Located in the Innsbrook Corporate Center. 4240 Dominion Blvd 23060. Fax: 804/965-5559. **Facility:** 242 units. 234 one-bedroom standard units. 8 one-bedroom suites. 6 stories, interior corridors. *Bath:* combo or shower only. **Parking:** on-site.
Small-scale Hotel   **Amenities:** video games, dual phone lines, voice mail, irons, hair dryers. **Pool(s):** heated indoor. **Leisure Activities:** whirlpool, exercise room. **Guest Services:** sundries, valet laundry. **Business Services:** conference facilities, business center. **Cards:** AX, CB, DC, DS, JC, MC, VI.

SOME UNITS
ASK SD 🕁 ⦆M ⚿ 🏊 ✕ 📷 DATA PORT 💻 / ✕ 🖥 📠 /

SPRINGHILL SUITES BY MARRIOTT   *Book at aaa.com*   Phone: (804)266-9403   44
(AAA) (SAVE)   All Year   1P: $105-$115   2P: $105-$115
Location: I-295, exit 43C, just n on US 1. Located near the Virginia Center Commons. 9701 Brook Rd 23059.
Fax: 804/266-6703. **Facility:** 136 one-bedroom standard units. 4 stories, interior corridors. *Bath:* combo or shower only. **Parking:** on-site. **Amenities:** video games, high-speed Internet, dual phone lines, voice mail,
Small-scale Hotel   irons, hair dryers. **Pool(s):** heated indoor. **Leisure Activities:** exercise room. **Guest Services:** valet and coin laundry. **Business Services:** meeting rooms, business center. **Cards:** AX, CB, DC, DS, JC, MC, VI.
Special Amenities: free expanded continental breakfast and free local telephone calls.

SOME UNITS
SD ⦆M ⚿ 🏊 📷 DATA PORT 🖥 📠 💻 / ✕ /

TOWNEPLACE SUITES BY MARRIOTT   *Book at aaa.com*   Phone: (804)747-5253   45
All Year   1P: $59-$89   2P: $59-$89
Location: I-64, exit 178B, just e on W Broad St to Cox Rd, then just n to Innslake Dr; in Innsbrook Corporate Center. 4231 Park Place Ct 23060. Fax: 804/747-5254. **Facility:** 95 units. 69 one-bedroom standard units with
Small-scale Hotel   kitchens. 4 one- and 22 two-bedroom suites with kitchens. 3 stories, interior corridors. *Bath:* combo or shower only. **Parking:** on-site. **Terms:** weekly rates available, pets ($100 extra charge). **Amenities:** high-speed Internet, voice mail, irons. **Pool(s):** outdoor. **Leisure Activities:** exercise room. **Guest Services:** valet and coin laundry. **Business Services:** meeting rooms, fax. **Cards:** AX, DC, DS, MC, VI.

SOME UNITS
ASK SD 🐾 ⦆M ⚿ 🏊 📷 DATA PORT 🖥 📠 💻 / ✕ /
FEE

(See map and index starting on p. 828)

VIRGINIA CROSSINGS RESORT *Book at aaa.com* Phone: (804)727-1400 **43**

(AAA) (SAVE) All Year 1P: $119-$179 XP: $10 F18
Location: I-295, exit 43C, just n on US 1, then 1 mi e. 1000 Virginia Center Pkwy 23059. Fax: 804/727-1690.
▽▽▽▽ ▽▽▽▽ **Facility:** Virginia's Colonial legacy sets the theme in this elegant hotel perched atop a hillside overlooking
the rolling fields of the resort's golf course. 183 units. 178 one-bedroom standard units. 5 one-bedroom
Large-scale Hotel suites, some with whirlpools. 5 stories, interior corridors. *Bath:* combo or shower only. **Parking:** on-site.
Terms: check-in 4 pm, cancellation fee imposed, package plans. **Amenities:** video games, high-speed
Internet (fee), dual phone lines, voice mail, irons, hair dryers. *Some:* DVD players (fee), CD players. **Dining:** 2 restaurants, 6:30
am-11 pm, Fri & Sat-midnight, also, The Glen Restaurant, see separate listing. **Pool(s):** heated outdoor. **Leisure
Activities:** whirlpool, driving range, racquetball court, jogging, exercise room, sports court, horseshoes, volleyball. *Fee:* golf-18
holes, massage. **Guest Services:** valet laundry, area transportation-within 5 mi. **Business Services:** conference facilities,
business center. **Cards:** AX, DC, DS, MC, VI. **Special Amenities:** free newspaper. *(See color ad p 839)*

SOME UNITS

[icons] FEE

━━━━━━ **WHERE TO DINE** ━━━━━━

BISTRO R Lunch: $5-$8 Dinner: $20-$26 Phone: 804/747-9484 **55**
▽▽▽▽ **Location:** I-64, exit 178B, 1.5 mi e; in Lexington Commons. 10190 W Broad St 23060. **Hours:** 11:30 am-2:30 &
5:30-9:30 pm, Fri-10 pm, Sat 5:30 pm-10 pm. Closed major holidays; also Sun. **Reservations:** suggested.
French **Features:** Attentive servers present such discriminating mostly French fare as escargots bourguignon,
braised lamb shank and veal blanketed in a sauce of caramelized shallots and white wine. The atmosphere
is casual cafe bistro, the service knowledgeable and sure. Semi-formal attire; cocktails. **Parking:** on-site. **Cards:** AX, DC, DS,
MC, VI.

GARLAND'S WAY Lunch: $6-$11 Dinner: $11-$20 Phone: 804/967-9060 **49**
▽▽▽▽ **Location:** I-295, exit 51A (Nuckols Rd), just n; in Town Center at Hickory. 11351 Nuckols Rd 23059. **Hours:** 11:30 am-
2 & 5:30 pm, Sat from 5:30 pm. Closed major holidays; also Sun. **Reservations:** suggested. **Features:** This
American modern spot offers something for everyone. The setting is casual as well as trendy and the ever-changing
menu is creative as well as accessible to all tastes offering everything from sandwiches and salads to grilled
seafood and steaks. Casual dress; cocktails. **Parking:** on-site. **Cards:** AX, DC, DS, MC, VI.

THE GLEN RESTAURANT Lunch: $13 Dinner: $16-$28 Phone: 804/727-1480 **50**
▽▽▽▽ **Location:** I-295, exit 43C, just n on US 1, then 1 mi e; in Virginia Crossings Resort. 1000 Virginia Center Pkwy 23059.
Hours: 6:30-10 am, 11:30-2 & 5:30-9:30 pm, Sat from 7 am, Sun 7 am-10 & 11:30-2 pm.
American **Reservations:** suggested. **Features:** Dine in Colonial elegance overlooking the rolling fields of the resort's
golf course while sampling the Chef's regional specialties ranging from crab cakes to venison; a
complimentary chef's bar of assorted cold appetizers is an extra treat for guests. Dressy casual; cocktails. **Parking:** on-site.
Cards: AX, CB, DC, DS, MC, VI.

THE GRAPEVINE II Lunch: $5-$10 Dinner: $9-$18 Phone: 804/440-9100 **56**
▽▽▽▽ **Location:** I-64, exit 178B, just e on Broad St, just s; in Granville Square. 11055 Three Chopt Rd 23233. **Hours:** 11:30
am-2:30 & 5-10 pm, Sat 5 pm-10:45 pm, Sun noon-9:45 pm. Closed major holidays. **Features:** Motifs of
Greek Grecian columns and grapevines deck the walls at the intimate spot. The owners serve a delightful array of
Greek and Italian specialties, from pizza to seafood to baked pasta dishes. Casual dress; cocktails.
Parking: on-site. **Cards:** AX, DS, MC, VI.

MAMA CUCINA Lunch: $7-$9 Dinner: $13-$17 Phone: 804/346-3350 **53**
▽▽▽▽ **Location:** I-64, exit 178B, 0.5 mi e to Dominion Blvd, then just n; in Innsbrook Shoppes. 4028-0 Cox Rd 23060.
Hours: 11 am-2:30 & 5-10 pm, Sat from 5 pm. Closed major holidays; also Sun. **Reservations:** suggested.
Italian **Features:** The warm, welcoming restaurant treats diners to heaping plates of freshly made pasta with
savory sauces, as well as numerous other Italian specialties. Casual dress; cocktails. **Parking:** on-site.
Cards: AX, MC, VI.

MEXICO RESTAURANT Lunch: $4-$11 Dinner: $7-$11 Phone: 804/290-0400 **54**
▽▽▽▽ **Location:** I-64, exit 178B, just e; in the Shoppes at Innsbrook. 4040-G Cox Rd 23060. **Hours:** noon-10 pm. Closed
major holidays. **Features:** The casual cafe setting is home to fine Mexican dishes, such as fajitas,
Mexican enchiladas and chiles rellenos. Guacamole is fresh and delicious, and mole poblano sauce is a special treat
mostly undiscovered by American diners. Casual dress; beer & wine only. **Parking:** on-site. **Cards:** AX, DC,
DS, MC, VI.

OSAKA SUSHI & STEAK Lunch: $8-$11 Dinner: $12-$20 Phone: 804/364-8800 **51**
▽▽▽▽ **Location:** Just w of jct I-64 and 295, on US 250; downtown Short Pump. 11674 W Broad St 23233. **Hours:** 11:30 am-
3 & 5-10 pm, Fri & Sat-10:30 pm, Sun noon-10 pm. **Features:** The decisions here are endless: Watch
Japanese teppanyaki chefs cook at hibachi grills; watch sushi chefs prepare fine, fresh fish delicacies; or grab a booth
and sample from teriyaki, gyoza dumplings, udon soup and more. Casual dress; cocktails. **Parking:** on-site.
Cards: AX, MC, VI.

SHORT PUMP GRILL Lunch: $9-$14 Dinner: $11-$27 Phone: 804/364-1004 **52**
▽▽▽▽ **Location:** Just w of jct I-64 and 295; in downtown Short Pump. 11530 W Broad St 23233. **Hours:** 11:30 am-10 pm,
Fri-11 pm, Sat 4:30 pm-11 pm, Sun 4:30 pm-9 pm. Closed: 12/25. **Reservations:** required. **Features:** The
American stylish spot fast became a favorite of local workers for its large portions of new American favorites. Among
choices are homemade potato chips with gorgonzola dip, sesame-seared tuna, shrimp BLTs and gourmet
macaroni and cheese. Casual dress; cocktails. **Parking:** on-site. **Cards:** AX, MC, VI.

GOOCHLAND

―――――― WHERE TO DINE ――――――

TANGLEWOOD ORDINARY COUNTRY
RESTAURANT   **Dinner:** $13   **Phone:** 804/556-3284

(AAA)
◆◆◆   **Location:** I-64, exit 173, 1 mi s to US 250, just w to SR 623, 5.2 mi s, then 9.5 mi w on SR 6. 2210 River Rd W 23102-
              2705. **Hours:** 5 pm-9 pm, Sun noon-8 pm; holiday hours vary. Closed: 12/25; also Mon-Wed.
Regional   **Reservations:** accepted. **Features:** Way out in the country, the homey log cabin is a quaint, charming place
American   in which to enjoy home-style Southern cooking. All-you-can-eat specials are served family style. Casual
              dress; cocktails. **Parking:** on-site.   ☒

HANOVER (See map and index starting on p. 828)

―――――― WHERE TO DINE ――――――

HOUNDSTOOTH CAFE   **Lunch:** $4-$9   **Dinner:** $4-$22   **Phone:** 804/537-5404   46
◆◆   **Location:** I-95, exit 92A, just US 54 and 301. 13271 Hanover Courthouse Rd 23069. **Hours:** 11 am-2 & 5-8
             pm, Fri & Sat 5 pm-9 pm. Closed: Sun & Mon. **Features:** This is a very popular country spot for succulent
Regional American Southern barbecue including ribs, pork, beef, and chicken as well as the freshest local seafood such as fried
             flounder and shrimp, famous crabcakes, and she-crab soup. Expect a wait. Casual dress; beer & wine only.
Parking: on-site. **Cards:** DC, MC, VI.   ☒

MANAKIN

―――――― WHERE TO DINE ――――――

THE FOX HEAD INN   **Dinner:** $58   **Phone:** 804/784-5126
◆◆◆ ◆◆◆   **Location:** I-64, exit 173, 1 mi s on SR 623, 1 mi w on US 250, then just s on SR 621. 1840 Manakin Rd 23103.
             Hours: 5:30 pm-9:30 pm, Fri & Sat-10 pm. Closed: 12/25; also Mon & Tues. **Reservations:** required.
French   **Features:** The hunt room atmosphere is intimate and romantic in this restored country farmhouse. What
             better then to savor superb French cuisine that showcases fresh Virginia products, often from the chef's
garden? The menu changes seasonally, and the wine list is extensive. Dressy casual; cocktails. **Parking:** on-site. **Cards:** AX,
DS, MC, VI.   Ⓣ ☒

MECHANICSVILLE pop. 30,464 (See map and index starting on p. 828)

―――――― WHERE TO STAY ――――――

HAMPTON INN   *Book at aaa.com*   **Phone:** (804)559-7001   60
◆◆◆   All Year [ECP]   1P: $89-$99   2P: $89-$99
             Location: I-295, exit 37A (US 360 E) to Bell Creek Rd, just n. 7433 Bell Creek Rd 23111. Fax: 804/559-0559.
Small-scale Hotel **Facility:** 80 one-bedroom standard units, some with whirlpools. 3 stories, interior corridors. *Bath:* combo or
             shower only. **Parking:** on-site. **Terms:** 3 day cancellation notice-fee imposed, weekly rates available.
Amenities: high-speed Internet, dual phone lines, voice mail, irons, hair dryers. **Pool(s):** small heated indoor. **Leisure
Activities:** exercise room. **Guest Services:** valet laundry. **Business Services:** meeting rooms, fax. **Cards:** AX, DC, DS,
MC, VI.   SOME UNITS

[ASK] [S⊘] [Ⓣ] [Ġ⌖] [⌀] [➔] [⊞] [DATA PORT] [⊟] [▭] [▱] / [☒] [VCR]
                                                                                         FEE

HOLIDAY INN
EXPRESS-RICHMOND-MECHANICSVILLE   *Book at aaa.com*   **Phone:** (804)559-0022   59
◆◆◆   All Year [BP]   1P: $59-$129   2P: $59-$129
             Location: I-295, exit 37A (US 360 E) to Bell Creek Rd, just n. 7441 Bell Creek Rd 23111. Fax: 804/559-6810.
Small-scale Hotel **Facility:** 105 units. 101 one-bedroom standard units. 4 one-bedroom suites ($105-$145). 5 stories, interior
             corridors. *Bath:* combo or shower only. **Parking:** on-site. **Amenities:** irons, hair dryers. **Pool(s):** outdoor.
Leisure Activities: exercise room. **Guest Services:** valet and coin laundry. **Business Services:** fax. **Cards:** AX, CB, DC, DS,
JC, MC, VI.   SOME UNITS

[ASK] [S⊘] [Ⓣ] [Ġ⌖] [⌖] [➔] [⊞] [DATA PORT] [▱] / [☒] [⊟] [▭] /

―――――― WHERE TO DINE ――――――

MEXICO RESTAURANT   **Lunch:** $5-$13   **Dinner:** $6-$13   **Phone:** 804/559-8126   60
◆◆   **Location:** I-295, exit 34A (US 360 E), just ne. 7162 Mechanicsville Tpke 23111. **Hours:** 11 am-10 pm, Fri-11 pm,
             Sat & Sun noon-10 pm. Closed major holidays; also 12/24. **Features:** The family-owned chain is a favorite
Mexican   of locals for reliable Mexican fare and a friendly atmosphere. Most opt for the expected combination dinners,
             but the more adventurous will be pleased by the delicious rendition of mole poblano sauce, a traditional
sauce made from cocoa beans. Casual dress; cocktails. **Parking:** on-site. **Cards:** AX, DC, DS, MC, VI.   Ⓣ ☒

PEKING RESTAURANT   **Lunch:** $5-$16   **Dinner:** $9-$16   **Phone:** 804/730-9898   59
◆◆◆ ◆◆   **Location:** I-295, exit 37A (US 360 E), 0.5 mi e. 7100 Mechanicsville Tpke 23111. **Hours:** 11:30 am-2:15 & 4:30-9:30
             pm, Sat from 4:30 pm, Sun 11:30 am-2:15 pm. Closed major holidays. **Features:** The small chain is a local
Chinese   favorite for its wide selection of dishes, including such specialties as crispy duck, velvet shrimp and dry
             sauteed green beans. The atmosphere is refined. Casual dress; cocktails. **Parking:** on-site. **Cards:** AX,
MC, VI.   [Ġ⌖] ☒

MIDLOTHIAN   (See map and index starting on p. 828)

────── **WHERE TO STAY** ──────

HAMPTON INN-RICHMOND-SOUTH WEST-HULL STREET   *Book at aaa.com*   **Phone: (804)675-0000**   **76**
▼▼▼▼▼   3/1-10/31 [ECP]   1P: $69-$89   2P: $69-$89
   11/1-2/28 [ECP]   1P: $59-$79   2P: $59-$79
Small-scale Hotel   **Location:** On Hull St Rd, 5 mi w of jct US 150. 3620 Price Club Blvd 23112. Fax: 804/675-7110. **Facility:** 68 one-bedroom standard units, some with whirlpools. 3 stories, interior corridors. *Bath:* combo or shower only. **Parking:** on-site. **Terms:** 2 night minimum stay - seasonal. **Amenities:** high-speed Internet, dual phone lines, voice mail, irons, hair dryers. **Pool(s):** heated indoor. **Leisure Activities:** exercise room. **Guest Services:** valet laundry. **Business Services:** meeting rooms, fax. **Cards:** AX, DC, DS, MC, VI.

SOME UNITS
(ASK) (S&D) (¶→) (&M) (≈) (❋) (DATA PORT) (■) (➤) (⬛) / (✕) /

HOLIDAY INN EXPRESS HOTEL & SUITES-BRANDERMILL   *Book at aaa.com*   **Phone: (804)744-7303**   **77**
▼▼▼▼▼   All Year [BP]   1P: $59-$89   2P: $89
   Location: SR 288, Chippenham Pkwy, just w on Hull Street Rd. 5030 W Village Green Dr 23112. Fax: 804/744-7304.
Small-scale Hotel   **Facility:** 96 one-bedroom standard units, some with whirlpools. 4 stories, interior corridors. *Bath:* combo or shower only. **Parking:** on-site. **Amenities:** high-speed Internet, dual phone lines, voice mail, irons, hair dryers. **Leisure Activities:** exercise room. **Guest Services:** valet and coin laundry. **Business Services:** meeting rooms, business center. **Cards:** AX, CB, DC, DS, JC, MC, VI.

SOME UNITS
(ASK) (S&D) (¶→) (&M) (&) (⊘) (❋) (DATA PORT) (■) (➤) (⬛) / (✕) /

SUPER 8 MOTEL   *Book at aaa.com*   **Phone: (804)276-3900**   **75**
(AAA) (SAVE)   All Year   1P: $49-$150   2P: $49-$150   XP: $5   F18
▼▼▼▼▼   **Location:** US 360, 4 mi e of US 288; 5 mi w of US 150 (Chippenham Pkwy). 10300 Hull St Rd 23112. Fax: 804/276-5718. **Facility:** 41 one-bedroom standard units, some with whirlpools. 2 stories (no elevator), interior corridors. **Parking:** on-site. **Amenities:** irons, hair dryers. **Business Services:** fax. **Cards:** AX, CB, Small-scale Hotel   DC, DS, MC, VI. **Special Amenities:** free continental breakfast and free local telephone calls.

SOME UNITS
(S&D) (&M) (VCR) (❋) (DATA PORT) / (✕) (■) (➤) /

────── **WHERE TO DINE** ──────

AL DENTE'S RESTAURANT   **Dinner:** $9-$20   **Phone:** 804/794-4444   **69**
▼▼▼   **Location:** On Midlothian Tpke; 1 mi w of jct Courthouse Rd; in the BP Shopping Plaza. 133 Brown's Way Rd 23113.
Italian   **Hours:** 5 pm-10 pm. Closed: 11/24, 12/25; also Sun. **Features:** Hidden at the back of a small shopping strip, the narrow, cozy spot glows a rosy, terra-cotta hue. The family's version of "fusione Gitano" is a blend of Sicilian recipes and modern flavors. Representative of dishes are sake in chile cream sauce, panko-crusted tuna and saffron shrimp. Also on the menu is more traditional fare, such as penne alla vodka and veal Marsala. Casual dress; cocktails. **Parking:** on-site. **Cards:** AX, MC, VI.

(&M)

BOTTEGA BISTRO   **Lunch:** $6-$10   **Dinner:** $9-$20   **Phone:** 804/379-9899   **67**
▼▼▼▼   **Location:** Jct Midlothian Tpke, 1.3 mi n; in The Shoppes at Bellgrade. 11400 W Huguenot Rd 23113. **Hours:** 11:30
American   am-10 pm, Fri & Sat-11 pm, Sun 5 pm-9 pm. Closed major holidays. **Reservations:** suggested. **Features:** A cozy gas-light lantern ambience envelops the eclectic, American-style bistro, which offers an appealing menu of innovative beef, pasta, salad, fish and veal preparations, as well as pizza made in a wood-burning oven. During nice weather, the iron tables lining the sidewalk are a popular seating option. Dressy casual; cocktails. **Parking:** on-site. **Cards:** AX, CB, DC, DS, MC, VI.

(Y)

NUCCIO'S TRATTORIA & PIZZA   **Lunch:** $5-$13   **Dinner:** $5-$16   **Phone:** 804/594-0040   **70**
▼▼ ▼▼   **Location:** 0.5 mi n of jct Powhite Pkwy; in Luck's Lane shopping center. 1108A Courthouse Rd 23236. **Hours:** 11 am-
Italian   10 pm, Fri & Sat-11 pm, Sun noon-10 pm. Closed: 3/27, 11/24, 12/25. **Features:** A suburban favorite, the restaurant presents a menu of such Italian-American favorites as veal dishes, New York- or Sicilian-style pizza, hoagies, seafood and numerous pasta specialties, including gnocchi with creamy pesto sauce. Casual dress; cocktails. **Parking:** on-site. **Cards:** AX, DS, MC, VI.

(&M) (✕)

RUTH'S CHRIS STEAK HOUSE   **Dinner:** $20-$34   **Phone:** 804/378-0600   **68**
▼▼▼▼   **Location:** 1.4 mi n of jct Midlothian Tpke; in Shoppes at Bellgrade Plantation. 11500 W Huguenot Rd 23113. **Hours:** 5
Steak House   pm-10 pm, Fri & Sat-11 pm, Sun 4 pm-9 pm. Closed: 1/1, 11/24, 12/25; also Super Bowl Sun. **Reservations:** suggested. **Features:** Restaurants in the chain are well-respected throughout the country for the finest steaks and chops served on sizzling platters. What makes this site unique is its location in a historic 1732 columned plantation home. The main dining room is a new addition, and patrons should enjoy a drink in the plank-floored parlor beside a roaring fire before dinner. Rich New Orleans-style desserts, such as creme brulee and bananas Foster, are house specialties. Dressy casual; cocktails; entertainment. **Parking:** on-site. **Cards:** AX, DC, DS, MC, VI.

(Y) (✕)

SAIGON GOURMET   **Lunch:** $5-$10   **Dinner:** $6-$14   **Phone:** 804/745-0199   **71**
▼▼▼   **Location:** 0.5 mi w of Courthouse Rd. 11033 Hull St Rd 23113. **Hours:** 11 am-3 & 4:30-9:30 pm, Fri-10:30 pm,
Vietnamese   Sat 11:30 am-10:30 pm, Sun 11:30 am-9 pm, Mon 5 pm-9:30 pm. **Features:** Tinted in soothing shades of green, the calming dining room is a great spot to sample the fresh, flavorful tastes of Vietnam. Favorites include grilled meats on rice noodles, pho noodle soups, rice paper rolls and peppery hot and sour soup. Casual dress. **Parking:** on-site. **Cards:** AX, DS, MC, VI.

(✕)

PROVIDENCE FORGE

———— **WHERE TO STAY** ————

JASMINE PLANTATION BED & BREAKFAST   **Phone:** (804)966-9836
▽▽▽▽ All Year   1P: $110-$140   2P: $120-$175   XP: $25   F12
Historic Bed **Location:** I-64, exit 214, 2.4 mi s on SR 155. 4500 N Courthouse Rd 23140. Fax: 804/966-5679. **Facility:** Antiques
& Breakfast and displays of Americana lend a nostalgic feel to this restored farmhouse, the oldest section of which dates
to 1750. Smoke free premises. 5 units. 4 one-bedroom standard units. 1 two-bedroom suite with whirlpool. 2
stories (no elevator), interior corridors. **Parking:** on-site. **Terms:** check-in 4 pm, age restrictions may apply,
10 day cancellation notice-fee imposed, package plans. **Amenities:** video library, hair dryers. *Some:* irons. **Leisure**
Activities: hiking trails. **Business Services:** fax. **Cards:** AX, MC, VI.

SOME UNITS
(ASK) (✕) (☎) / (W) (VCR) (DATA PORT) /

SANDSTON   (See map and index starting on p. 828)

———— **WHERE TO STAY** ————

COMFORT INN RICHMOND AIRPORT   *Book at aaa.com*   **Phone:** (804)226-1800   [68]
▽▽▽▽ 3/1-8/15   1P: $69   2P: $79   XP: $10
8/16-2/28   1P: $64-$69   2P: $64-$69   XP: $10
Small-scale Hotel **Location:** I-64, exit 197A (Sandston-RIC Airport), 0.3 mi s to Williamsburg Rd, then 1 mi w. 5240 Airport Square Ln
23150. Fax: 804/226-0958. **Facility:** 61 one-bedroom standard units. 2 stories (no elevator), interior
corridors. **Bath:** combo or shower only. **Parking:** on-site. **Amenities:** voice mail, irons, hair dryers. **Leisure Activities:** exercise
room. **Guest Services:** valet laundry. **Business Services:** fax. **Cards:** AX, CB, DC, DS, MC, VI.

SOME UNITS
(ASK) (SD) (⊣) (¶✦) (&M) (&) (▦) (DATA PORT) (🛏) (🖥) (📺) / (✕) /

COURTYARD BY MARRIOTT-RICHMOND AIRPORT   *Book at aaa.com*   **Phone:** (804)652-0500   [69]
(AAA) (SAVE) All Year   1P: $109-$199   2P: $109-$199   XP: $10   F18
Location: I-64, exit 197A (Sandston-RIC Airport), just s to Williamsburg Rd E, then 1 mi e. 5400 Williamsburg Rd
▽▽▽▽ 23150. Fax: 804/652-0527. **Facility:** 142 units. 136 one-bedroom standard units, some with whirlpools. 6
Small-scale Hotel one-bedroom suites ($129-$229). 3 stories, interior corridors. **Bath:** combo or shower only. **Parking:** on-site.
Terms: package plans. **Amenities:** video games, high-speed Internet, dual phone lines, voice mail, irons,
hair dryers. **Dining:** 6 am-10:30 & 5-9 pm, Fri-Sun 7-11 am, cocktails. **Pool(s):** small heated indoor.
Leisure Activities: whirlpool, exercise room. **Guest Services:** valet and coin laundry. **Business Services:** meeting rooms, PC,
fax. **Cards:** AX, CB, DC, DS, MC, VI. **Special Amenities:** free newspaper and early check-in/late check-out.

SOME UNITS
(SD) (⊣) (¶¶) (&M) (&) (▦) (🛏) (💺) (📺) (DATA PORT) (🖥) / (✕) (🛏) (🖥) /
FEE FEE

DOUBLETREE RICHMOND AIRPORT   *Book at aaa.com*   **Phone:** (804)226-6400   [72]
(AAA) (SAVE) All Year   1P: $69-$209   2P: $69-$209   XP: $10   F18
Location: I-64, exit 197 (Airport Dr), 1 mi s. 5501 Eubank Rd 23150. Fax: 804/226-1269. **Facility:** 160 units. 38
▽▽▽▽ one-bedroom standard units. 122 one-bedroom suites ($99-$229). 5 stories, interior corridors. **Parking:** on-
Small-scale Hotel site. **Terms:** cancellation fee imposed, [AP], [BP] & [CP] meal plans available, package plans.
Amenities: video games, dual phone lines, voice mail, safes (fee), irons, hair dryers. *Some:* high-speed
Internet. **Dining:** Wings, see separate listing. **Pool(s):** outdoor. **Leisure Activities:** whirlpool, exercise
room, volleyball. **Guest Services:** valet laundry, area transportation-within 5 mi. **Business Services:** conference facilities, fax.
Cards: AX, DC, DS, MC, VI. **Special Amenities:** free newspaper and free room upgrade (subject to availability with
advance reservations).

SOME UNITS
(✈) (¶¶) (▦) (🛏) (✕) (📺) (DATA PORT) (🖥) / (✕) (🛏) (🖥) /

HAMPTON INN-RICHMOND AIRPORT   *Book at aaa.com*   **Phone:** (804)222-8200   [67]
▽▽▽▽ All Year   1P: $89-$169   2P: $89-$169
Location: I-64, exit 197A (Sandston-RIC Airport), just s to Williamsburg Rd, then 1 mi w. 5300 Airport Square Ln 23150.
Small-scale Hotel Fax: 804/222-4915. **Facility:** 124 one-bedroom standard units. 4 stories, interior corridors. **Parking:** on-site.
Terms: 15 day cancellation notice-fee imposed. **Amenities:** video games, high-speed Internet, voice mail,
irons, hair dryers. *Some: Fee:* DVD players. **Pool(s):** outdoor. **Leisure Activities:** exercise room. **Guest Services:** valet
laundry. **Business Services:** meeting rooms, business center. **Cards:** AX, DC, DS, MC, VI.

SOME UNITS
(ASK) (SD) (⊣) (¶✦) (&M) (▦) (🛏) (📺) / (✕) (VCR) (🛏) (🖥) /
FEE FEE FEE

HOLIDAY INN-AIRPORT   *Book at aaa.com*   **Phone:** (804)222-6450   [71]
▽▽▽▽ All Year   1P: $79-$169   2P: $79-$169
Location: I-64, exit 195, 1.5 mi s to Williamsburg Rd, then just e. 5203 Williamsburg Rd 23150. Fax: 804/652-0492.
Small-scale Hotel **Facility:** 230 one-bedroom standard units. 3-6 stories, interior/exterior corridors. **Bath:** combo or shower
only. **Parking:** on-site. **Terms:** package plans, small pets only ($25 fee). **Amenities:** dual phone lines, voice
mail, irons, hair dryers. *Some:* safes. **Pool(s):** outdoor, wading. **Leisure Activities:** exercise room. **Guest Services:** valet and
coin laundry. **Business Services:** conference facilities, business center. **Cards:** AX, CB, DC, DS, MC, VI.

SOME UNITS
(ASK) (SD) (⊣) (🛏) (¶¶) (💺) (&) (▦) (🛏) (📺) (DATA PORT) (🖥) / (✕) (🛏) (🖥) /
FEE FEE FEE

HOMEWOOD SUITES RICHMOND AIRPORT   *Book at aaa.com*   **Phone:** (804)737-1600   [64]
▽▽▽▽ All Year [BP]   1P: $89-$119   2P: $99-$129
Location: I-64, exit 197A (Sandston-RIC Airport), just s. 5996 Audubon Dr 23231. Fax: 804/737-1666. **Facility:** 125
Small-scale Hotel units. 52 one-bedroom standard units with kitchens. 72 one- and 1 two-bedroom suites with kitchens, some
with whirlpools. 6 stories, interior corridors. **Bath:** combo or shower only. **Parking:** on-site. **Amenities:** video
library (fee), high-speed Internet, dual phone lines, voice mail, irons, hair dryers. **Pool(s):** heated indoor. **Leisure**
Activities: whirlpool, exercise room, sports court. **Guest Services:** sundries, complimentary evening beverages: Mon-Thurs,
valet and coin laundry, area transportation. **Business Services:** meeting rooms, business center. **Cards:** AX, CB, DC, DS,
MC, VI.

SOME UNITS
(ASK) (SD) (⊣) (&M) (&) (▦) (🛏) (✕) (VCR) (📺) (DATA PORT) (🛏) (🖥) (🖥) / (✕) /

(See map and index starting on p. 828)

MICROTEL INN & SUITES   *Book at aaa.com*

▼▼ Small-scale Hotel

Phone: (804)737-3322 63

All Year   1P: $59-$79

Location: I-64, exit 197A (Sandston-RIC Airport), just s. 6000 Audubon Dr 23150. Fax: 804/737-0807. **Facility:** 100 one-bedroom standard units. 3 stories, interior corridors. *Bath:* combo or shower only. **Parking:** on-site. **Terms:** cancellation fee imposed, weekly rates available, package plans, pets ($15 extra charge). **Amenities:** voice mail. **Leisure Activities:** limited exercise equipment. **Guest Services:** complimentary laundry. **Business Services:** meeting rooms, fax. **Cards:** AX, DC, DS, MC, VI.

SOME UNITS

FEE

MOTEL 6-RICHMOND AIRPORT #435   *Book at aaa.com*

▼ Motel

Phone: 804/222-7600 66

3/1-11/13	1P: $37-$47	2P: $43-$53	XP: $3 F17
11/14-2/28	1P: $34-$44	2P: $40-$50	XP: $3 F17

Location: I-64, exit 197A (Sandston-RIC Airport), just s to Williamsburg Rd, then just w. 5704 Williamsburg Rd 23150. Fax: 804/222-4153. **Facility:** 119 one-bedroom standard units. 2 stories (no elevator), exterior corridors. *Bath:* shower only. **Parking:** on-site. **Terms:** small pets only (must be attended). **Pool(s):** outdoor. **Cards:** AX, CB, DC, DS, MC, VI.

SOME UNITS

SUPER 8 MOTEL   *Book at aaa.com*

▼ Motel

Phone: (804)222-8008 70

All Year [CP]   1P: $52-$62   2P: $58-$68   XP: $10 D12

Location: I-64, exit 197A (Sandston-RIC Airport), 0.3 mi s to Williamsburg Rd, then 1 mi w. 5110 Williamsburg Rd 23231. Fax: 804/222-8207. **Facility:** 51 one-bedroom standard units. 3 stories (no elevator), interior corridors. **Parking:** on-site. **Terms:** weekly rates available. **Business Services:** fax (fee). **Cards:** AX, DC, DS, MC, VI.

SOME UNITS

WINGATE INN RICHMOND AIRPORT

▼▼▼ Small-scale Hotel

Phone: (804)222-1499 65

All Year   1P: $89   2P: $89

Location: I-64, exit 197A (Sandston-RIC Airport), just s to Audobon Dr, then just n. 491 International Centre Dr 23150. Fax: 804/222-1498. **Facility:** 100 one-bedroom standard units. 4 stories, interior corridors. *Bath:* combo or shower only. **Parking:** on-site. **Terms:** package plans, small pets only (in smoking units). **Amenities:** video games, high-speed Internet, dual phone lines, voice mail, safes, irons, hair dryers. **Pool(s):** heated indoor. **Leisure Activities:** whirlpool, exercise room. **Guest Services:** valet laundry. **Business Services:** meeting rooms, business center. **Cards:** AX, CB, DC, DS, JC, MC, VI.

SOME UNITS

FEE

——— **WHERE TO DINE** ———

MEXICO RESTAURANT

▼ Mexican

Lunch: $4-$7   **Dinner:** $4-$7   **Phone:** 804/226-2388 63

Location: I-64, exit 195, 1.5 mi s to Williamsburg Rd, then just e. 5213 Williamsburg Rd 23150. **Hours:** 11 am-10 pm, Fri-11 pm, Sat & Sun noon-10 pm. Closed major holidays. **Features:** Affordable and consistent, the bright, cheery restaurant has an extensive menu of combination dinners and a la carte selections, with six varieties of fajitas. Colorful murals decorate the walls. Servers are quick with the chips, salsa and drink refills. Casual dress; cocktails. **Parking:** on-site. **Cards:** AX, DC, DS, MC, VI.

WINGS

AAA ▼▼ American

Lunch: $5-$12   **Dinner:** $5-$24   **Phone:** 804/226-6400 64

Location: I-64, exit 197 (Airport Dr), 1 mi s; in Doubletree Richmond Airport. 5501 Eubank Rd 23150. **Hours:** 6 am-11 pm. **Reservations:** suggested. **Features:** The house specialties are endless: New York sirloin, chicken cordon bleu, seafood sampler, crabcakes and a variety of dessert. Glass and greenery prevail, lending to a contemporary ambience. The buffet breakfast and pasta bar are available Monday-Friday. Casual dress; cocktails. **Parking:** on-site. **Cards:** AX, DC, DS, MC, VI.

VARINA

——— **WHERE TO DINE** ———

——— *The following restaurant has not been evaluated by AAA but is listed for your information only.* ———

CHILLIN' & GRILLIN' SHACK

[fyi]

Phone: 804/795-4114

Not evaluated. **Location:** I-295, exit 22 (SR 5), 2 mi w. 2097 New Market Rd 23231. **Features:** The tiny roadside spot serves up Cajun specialties and tasty barbecue for those on the go.

This ends listings for the Richmond Vicinity.
The following page resumes the alphabetical listings of cities in Virginia.

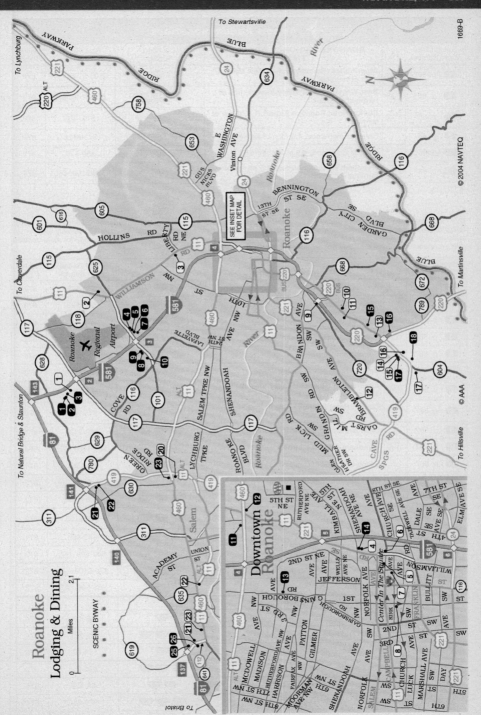

Roanoke
Lodging & Dining

Downtown
Roanoke

✈ Airport Accommodations

Spotter/Map Page Number	OA	ROANOKE REGIONAL-WOODRUM FIELD	Diamond Rating	Rate Range High Season	Listing Page
7 / p. 867	AAA	AmeriSuites (Roanoke/Valley View Mall), 1 mi s of terminal	◈◈◈	$109-$179 SAVE	870
6 / p. 867	AAA	Best Western Inn at Valley View, 1 mi s of terminal	◈◈◈	$59-$149 SAVE	870
8 / p. 867	AAA	Clarion Hotel Roanoke Airport, 1.5 mi sw of terminal	◈◈◈	$75 SAVE	870
3 / p. 867		Hampton Inn Airport, 1.5 mi n of terminal	◈◈◈	$73-$125	872
1 / p. 867		Holiday Inn-Airport, 1.5 mi n of terminal	◈◈◈	$59-$75	872
10 / p. 867	AAA	Wyndham Roanoke Airport, 1.5 mi sw of terminal	◈◈◈	$89-$109 SAVE	874

Roanoke

This index helps you "spot" where approved accommodations and restaurants are located on the corresponding detailed maps. Lodging rate ranges are for comparison only and show the property's high season; rates are per night, unless only weekly (W) rates are available. Restaurant rate range is for dinner, unless only lunch (L) is served. Turn to the listing page for more detailed rate information and consult display ads for special promotions.

Spotter/Map Page Number	OA	ROANOKE - Lodgings	Diamond Rating	Rate Range High Season	Listing Page
1 / p. 867		Holiday Inn-Airport	◈◈◈	$59-$75	872
2 / p. 867		Super 8 Motel	◈◈	$46-$68	873
3 / p. 867		Hampton Inn Airport	◈◈◈	$73-$125	872
4 / p. 867	AAA	MainStay Suites Roanoke Airport	◈◈◈	$74-$175 SAVE	872
5 / p. 867	AAA	Comfort Inn Airport - see color ad p 871	◈◈◈	$64-$150 SAVE	871
6 / p. 867	AAA	Best Western Inn at Valley View	◈◈◈	$59-$149 SAVE	870
7 / p. 867	AAA	AmeriSuites (Roanoke/Valley View Mall) - see color ad p 870	◈◈◈	$109-$179 SAVE	870
8 / p. 867	AAA	Clarion Hotel Roanoke Airport - see color ad p 288 & ad p 870	◈◈◈	$75 SAVE	870
9 / p. 867		Courtyard By Marriott Roanoke Airport	◈◈◈	$69-$139	871
10 / p. 867	AAA	Wyndham Roanoke Airport	◈◈◈	$89-$109 SAVE	874
11 / p. 867		Econo Lodge Civic Center	◈◈	$40-$64	871
12 / p. 867	AAA	Rodeway Inn-Civic Center	◈◈	$35-$100 SAVE	873
13 / p. 867		Holiday Inn Express	◈◈◈	$79-$139	872
14 / p. 867		The Hotel Roanoke & Conference Center, A Doubletree Hotel - see color ad p 873	◈◈◈	$89-$169	872
15 / p. 867		Colony House Motor Lodge	◈◈	$49-$69	871
16 / p. 867	AAA	Quality Inn/Tanglewood	◈◈◈	$49-$99 SAVE	873
17 / p. 867	AAA	Holiday Inn Hotel Tanglewood	◈◈◈	$79-$109 SAVE	872
18 / p. 867	AAA	Sleep Inn	◈◈	$35-$99 SAVE	873
		ROANOKE - Restaurants			
① / p. 867		El Toreo	◈	$6-$11	874
② / p. 867		Coach and Four	◈◈◈	$9-$21	874
③ / p. 867		New Yorker Delicatessen and Restaurant	◈	$4-$9	875
④ / p. 867		The Regency Room	◈◈◈	$20-$35	875
⑤ / p. 867		Nawab Indian Cuisine	◈◈	$8-$25	875
⑥ / p. 867		Arzu	◈◈◈	$10-$30	874

Spotter/Map Page Number	OA	ROANOKE - Restaurants (continued)	Diamond Rating	Rate Range High Season	Listing Page
7 / p. 867		Wertz's Restaurant	◈◈◈	$12-$25	875
8 / p. 867		Swagat Indian Cuisine	◈◈	$6-$18	875
9 / p. 867	AAA	**The Roanoker Restaurant**	◈	$5-$11	875
10 / p. 867		Stephen's	◈◈	$15-$25	875
11 / p. 867		The Library	◈◈◈	$20-$30	874
12 / p. 867		Luigi's	◈◈◈	$11-$27	874
13 / p. 867		Montano's International Gourmet	◈◈	$8-$18	875
14 / p. 867		Mac & Maggie's	◈◈	$7-$15	874
15 / p. 867		Carlos Brazilian International Cuisine	◈◈◈	$7-$28	874
16 / p. 867		Macado's	◈◈	$5-$12	874
17 / p. 867	AAA	**Szechuan Restaurant**	◈◈	$6-$14	875
		SALEM - Lodgings			
21 / p. 867	AAA	**Quality Inn Roanoke/Salem**	◈◈◈	$54-$83 [SAVE]	877
22 / p. 867	AAA	**Baymont Inn Roanoke-Salem**	◈◈◈	$64-$89 [SAVE]	876
23 / p. 867		Holiday Inn Express	◈◈◈	$71-$89	877
25 / p. 867	AAA	**Econo Lodge-Roanoke/Salem**	◈◈	$46-$91 [SAVE]	877
26 / p. 867	AAA	**Comfort Inn**	◈◈◈	$74-$99 [SAVE]	877
		SALEM - Restaurants			
20 / p. 867		Sake House	◈◈	$8-$20	878
21 / p. 867		El Rodeo	◈	$6-$11	877
22 / p. 867		Fast Freddy's	◈	$5-$15	878
23 / p. 867	AAA	**Mamma Maria's Italian Restaurant**	◈	$6-$20	878

ROANOKE pop. 94,911   (See map and index starting on p. 867)

─── WHERE TO STAY ───

AMERISUITES (ROANOKE/VALLEY VIEW MALL)   *Book at aaa.com*   **Phone: (540)366-4700**   **7**
AAA SAVE   All Year [ECP]   1P: $109-$179   2P: $109-$179   XP: $10   F18
▽▽▽▽   **Location:** I-581, exit 3E, just e, then just s via shopping center exit. 5040 Valley View Blvd 24012. Fax: 540/366-1157.
Facility: 128 one-bedroom standard units. 6 stories, interior corridors. *Bath:* combo or shower only.
Parking: on-site. **Terms:** pets (with prior approval). **Amenities:** high-speed Internet, voice mail, safes, irons,
Small-scale Hotel   hair dryers. **Pool(s):** heated indoor. **Leisure Activities:** exercise room. **Guest Services:** coin laundry.
Business Services: meeting rooms. **Cards:** AX, CB, DC, DS, JC, MC, VI. **Special Amenities:** free
expanded continental breakfast and free newspaper. *(See color ad below)*

SOME UNITS
[icons]

BEST WESTERN INN AT VALLEY VIEW   *Book at aaa.com*   **Phone: (540)362-2400**   **6**
AAA SAVE   All Year [ECP]   1P: $59-$149   2P: $59-$149   XP: $10   F15
▽▽▽▽   **Location:** I-581, exit 3E, just e, then just s via shopping center exit. 5050 Valley View Blvd 24012. Fax: 540/362-2400.
Facility: 85 one-bedroom standard units. 3 stories, interior corridors. *Bath:* combo or shower only. **Parking:**
on-site. **Terms:** small pets only ($20 fee). **Amenities:** high-speed Internet, irons, hair dryers. **Pool(s):**
Small-scale Hotel   heated indoor. **Guest Services:** valet laundry. **Business Services:** meeting rooms. **Cards:** AX, CB, DC,
DS, JC, MC, VI.

SOME UNITS
[icons]   FEE

CLARION HOTEL ROANOKE AIRPORT   *Book at aaa.com*   **Phone: (540)362-4500**   **8**
AAA SAVE   7/1-8/31   1P: $75   2P: $75   XP: $10   F18
▽▽▽▽   3/1-6/30 & 9/1-2/28   1P: $70   2P: $70   XP: $10   F18
Location: I-581, exit 3W, just w to Ordway Dr, then 0.6 mi n via service road. 3315 Ordway Dr 24017.
Small-scale Hotel   Fax: 540/362-4506. **Facility:** 154 one-bedroom standard units. 5 stories, interior corridors. *Bath:* combo or
shower only. **Parking:** on-site. **Terms:** check-in 4 pm, package plans, small pets only ($25 deposit).
Amenities: video games, high-speed Internet, voice mail, irons, hair dryers. **Pool(s):** heated indoor/outdoor.
Leisure Activities: whirlpool, 2 lighted tennis courts, exercise room, horseshoes, volleyball. **Guest Services:** valet and coin
laundry, area transportation-within 3 mi. **Business Services:** conference facilities. **Cards:** AX, CB, DC, DS, MC, VI.
(See color ad p 288 & ad below)

SOME UNITS
[icons]   FEE

(See map and index starting on p. 867)

COLONY HOUSE MOTOR LODGE
Phone: 540/345-0411 **15**
All Year 1P: $49-$60 2P: $57-$69 XP: $5 F13
Motel **Location:** I-581/US 220, exit Franklin Rd/Salam, 0.5 mi n on US 220 business route. 3560 Franklin Rd SW 24014. Fax: 540/345-1137. **Facility:** 69 one-bedroom standard units. 2 stories (no elevator), interior/exterior corridors. **Parking:** on-site. **Terms:** 7 day cancellation notice, weekly rates available. **Amenities:** *Some:* irons. **Pool(s):** outdoor. **Leisure Activities:** exercise room. **Guest Services:** coin laundry. **Business Services:** meeting rooms, business center. **Cards:** AX, CB, DC, DS, MC, VI.

SOME UNITS
ASK SD TI+ ➲ 🐾 DATA PORT / ✕ 🖥 🖨 🖳 /

COMFORT INN AIRPORT *Book at aaa.com*
Phone: (540)527-2020 **5**
All Year [ECP] 1P: $64-$150 XP: $10 F15
Location: I-81, exit 143 to I-581, exit 3, e to Hershberger Rd. 5070 Valley View Blvd 24012. Fax: 540/527-2040. **Facility:** 96 one-bedroom standard units. 3 stories, interior corridors. *Bath:* combo or shower only. **Parking:** on-site. **Terms:** weekly rates available. **Amenities:** high-speed Internet, voice mail, irons, hair dryers. **Pool(s):** outdoor. **Leisure Activities:** exercise room. **Guest Services:** coin laundry, area transportation-within 3 mi. **Business Services:** meeting rooms. **Cards:** AX, CB, DC, DS, JC, MC, VI.
Small-scale Hotel

(See color ad below)

SOME UNITS
SD ✈ 👨‍🦽 ➲ 📶 🎬 DATA PORT 🖥 / ✕ 🖨 🖳 /

COUNTRY INN & SUITES BY CARLSON *Book at aaa.com*
Phone: (540)366-5678
3/31-11/30 1P: $85-$145 2P: $85-$145 XP: $5 F18
3/1-3/30 & 12/1-2/28 1P: $81-$125 2P: $81-$125 XP: $5 F18
Location: I-81, exit 146, just se on SR 115. 7860 Plantation Rd 24019. Fax: 540/366-8214. **Facility:** 77 one-bedroom standard units, some with whirlpools. 2-3 stories, interior corridors. **Parking:** on-site. **Amenities:** high-speed Internet, voice mail, irons, hair dryers. **Pool(s):** indoor. **Leisure Activities:** whirlpool, exercise room. *Fee:* game room. **Guest Services:** coin laundry. **Business Services:** meeting rooms. **Cards:** AX, CB, DC, DS, MC, VI. **Special Amenities:** free expanded continental breakfast and free newspaper. *(See color ad p 847)*
Small-scale Hotel

SOME UNITS
SD TI+ 📀 🕹 ➲ ✕ 🎬 DATA PORT 🖥 / ✕ 🖨 🖳 /

COURTYARD BY MARRIOTT ROANOKE AIRPORT *Book at aaa.com*
Phone: (540)563-5002 **9**
All Year 1P: $69-$139
Location: I-581, exit 3W, just w to Ordway Dr. 3301 Ordway Dr 24017. Fax: 540/563-2177. **Facility:** 135 one-bedroom standard units, some with whirlpools. 4 stories, interior corridors. *Bath:* combo or shower only. **Parking:** on-site. **Amenities:** video games, high-speed Internet, voice mail, irons, hair dryers. **Pool(s):** heated indoor. **Leisure Activities:** whirlpool, exercise room. **Guest Services:** coin laundry, area transportation. **Business Services:** meeting rooms, business center. **Cards:** AX, DC, DS, MC, VI.
Small-scale Hotel

SOME UNITS
ASK ✈ TI ✕ 🍽 👨‍🦽 ➲ 🎬 DATA PORT 🖥 / ✕ 🖨 🖳 /

DAYS INN *Book at aaa.com*
Phone: (540)366-0341 **?**
All Year 1P: $49-$99 2P: $54-$104 XP: $5 F15
Location: I-81, exit 146, just e on SR 115. 8118 Plantation Rd 24019. Fax: 540/366-3935. **Facility:** 121 one-bedroom standard units, some with whirlpools. 2 stories (no elevator), interior/exterior corridors. **Parking:** on-site. **Terms:** package plans, small pets only ($15 extra charge). **Amenities:** video library (fee), hair dryers. **Pool(s):** outdoor. **Leisure Activities:** exercise room. **Guest Services:** valet laundry. **Business Services:** meeting rooms. **Cards:** AX, DC, DS, MC, VI.
Small-scale Hotel

SOME UNITS
ASK SD ✈ 🐾 🍽 ➲ 🎬 DATA PORT 🖨 🖳 🖥 / ✕ /
FEE

ECONO LODGE CIVIC CENTER *Book at aaa.com*
Phone: (540)343-2413 **11**
All Year 1P: $40-$60 2P: $44-$64 XP: $5 F18
Motel **Location:** I-581, exit 4E, just e on US 460. Located in a commercial area. 308 Orange Ave 24016. Fax: 540/343-2413. **Facility:** 46 one-bedroom standard units. 2 stories (no elevator), exterior corridors. **Parking:** on-site. **Cards:** AX, DS, MC, VI.

SOME UNITS
ASK SD TI+ 🎬 / ✕ 🖨 🖳 🖥 /

(See map and index starting on p. 867)

HAMPTON INN AIRPORT *Book at aaa.com*   Phone: (540)265-2600   **3**
▽▼▽▼▽   All Year   1P: $73-$125   2P: $81-$125
Small-scale Hotel   Location: I-581, exit 2S, just s on SR 117 (Peters Creek Rd), then just w. 6621 Thirlane Rd NW 24019. Fax: 540/366-2091. **Facility:** 79 one-bedroom standard units, some with whirlpools. 2 stories (no elevator), exterior corridors. *Bath:* combo or shower only. **Parking:** on-site. **Terms:** 2 night minimum stay - seasonal, 14 day cancellation notice-fee imposed, package plans. **Amenities:** voice mail, irons, hair dryers. **Pool(s):** outdoor. **Leisure Activities:** exercise room. **Guest Services:** coin laundry. **Business Services:** meeting rooms, business center. **Cards:** AX, CB, DC, DS, MC, VI.

SOME UNITS
(ASK) (S/D) (✈) (†1†) (⊘) (➞) (VCR) (✲) (DATA PORT) (🖬) (🖨) (▣) / (✕) /

HAMPTON INN ROANOKE/HOLLINS *Book at aaa.com*   Phone: (540)563-5656
▽▼▽▼▽   All Year   1P: $89-$120   2P: $90-$140
Small-scale Hotel   Location: I-81, exit 146, 0.3 mi e on SR 115. 7922 Plantation Rd 24019. Fax: 540/563-0700. **Facility:** 60 one-bedroom standard units, some with whirlpools. 3 stories, interior corridors. **Parking:** on-site. **Terms:** 10 day cancellation notice. **Amenities:** voice mail, irons, hair dryers. **Pool(s):** indoor. **Leisure Activities:** exercise room. **Guest Services:** coin laundry. **Business Services:** meeting rooms. **Cards:** AX, DC, DS, MC, VI.

SOME UNITS
(ASK) (S/D) (&) (⊘) (➞) (✲) (DATA PORT) (▣) / (✕) (🖬) (🖨)

HOLIDAY INN-AIRPORT *Book at aaa.com*   Phone: 540/366-8861   **1**
▽▼▽▼▽   All Year   1P: $59-$75   2P: $59-$75
Small-scale Hotel   Location: I-581, exit 2S, just s on SR 117 (Peters Creek Rd), then just w. 6626 Thirlane Rd 24019. Fax: 540/366-1637. **Facility:** 161 one-bedroom standard units. 2 stories (no elevator), exterior corridors. **Parking:** on-site. **Amenities:** video games, voice mail, irons, hair dryers. **Pool(s):** outdoor, wading. **Leisure Activities:** exercise room. **Guest Services:** coin laundry. **Business Services:** meeting rooms. **Cards:** AX, CB, DC, DS, JC, MC.

SOME UNITS
(ASK) (✈) (†1†) (Y) (⊘) (➞) (✲) (DATA PORT) (▣) / (✕) (🖬)
FEE

HOLIDAY INN EXPRESS *Book at aaa.com*   Phone: 540/982-0100   **13**
▽▼▽▼▽   All Year   1P: $79-$139   2P: $79-$139
Small-scale Hotel   Location: I-581, exit 4W, just w, then just s. 815 Gainsboro Rd 24016. Fax: 540/345-4551. **Facility:** 98 one-bedroom standard units, some with whirlpools. 3 stories, interior corridors. **Parking:** on-site. **Terms:** 7 day cancellation notice. **Amenities:** irons, hair dryers. **Pool(s):** outdoor. **Guest Services:** valet laundry. **Business Services:** business center. **Cards:** AX, DC, DS, MC, VI.

SOME UNITS
(ASK) (S/D) (➞) (†+†) (✲) (DATA PORT) (▣) / (✕) (🖬) (🖨)

HOLIDAY INN HOTEL TANGLEWOOD *Book at aaa.com*   Phone: (540)774-4400   **17**
(AAA) (SAVE)   All Year   1P: $79-$109
▽▼▽▼▽   Location: I-581, exit Franklin Rd/Salem, 0.8 mi n on SR 419. 4468 Starkey Rd 24014. Fax: 540/774-1195. **Facility:** 190 one-bedroom standard units, some with whirlpools. 5 stories, interior corridors. *Bath:* combo or
Small-scale Hotel   shower only. **Parking:** on-site. **Terms:** package plans. **Amenities:** voice mail, irons, hair dryers. **Dining:** 6:30 am-1:30 & 3-10 pm, cocktails. **Pool(s):** outdoor. **Leisure Activities:** exercise room. **Guest Services:** coin laundry, area transportation-within 5 mi. **Business Services:** conference facilities. **Cards:** AX, CB, DC, DS, JC, MC, VI. **Special Amenities:** free local telephone calls and free newspaper.

SOME UNITS
(S/D) (✈) (†1†) (Y) (&) (⊘) (➞) (✲) (DATA PORT) (🖬) (🖨) (▣) / (✕) /

**THE HOTEL ROANOKE & CONFERENCE CENTER, A
DOUBLETREE HOTEL** *Book at aaa.com*   Phone: (540)985-5900   **14**
▽▼▽▼▽   All Year   1P: $89-$169   2P: $89-$169   XP: $10   F18
Classic Historic   Location: I-581, exit 5 southbound; exit 4E northbound, 0.5 mi s on US 11/221/SR 16, then just w on Wells Ave. 110
Large-scale Hotel   Shenandoah Ave 24016. Fax: 540/853-8290. **Facility:** Grand historic elegance and a wide variety of room types characterize this long-standing property. 332 units. 331 one- and 1 two-bedroom standard units. 7 stories, interior corridors. *Bath:* combo or shower only. **Parking:** on-site (fee). **Terms:** check-in 4 pm, cancellation fee imposed. **Amenities:** video games, high-speed Internet, dual phone lines, voice mail, irons, hair dryers. **Dining:** The Regency Room, see separate listing. **Pool(s):** outdoor. **Leisure Activities:** whirlpool, exercise room. **Guest Services:** gift shop, valet laundry, area transportation. **Business Services:** conference facilities, business center. **Cards:** AX, CB, DC, DS, MC, VI. *(See color ad p 873)*

SOME UNITS
(ASK) (✈) (†1†) (Y) (🛗) (&) (⊘) (➞) (✲) (DATA PORT) (🖬) (🖨) (▣) / (✕) (VCR) (🖬) (🖨) /
FEE   FEE

MAINSTAY SUITES ROANOKE AIRPORT *Book at aaa.com*   Phone: (540)527-3030   **4**
(AAA) (SAVE)   All Year [ECP]   1P: $74-$160   2P: $79-$175   XP: $10   F15
▽▼▽▼▽   Location: I-581, exit 3E, just n. 5080 Valley View Blvd 24012. Fax: 540/527-3035. **Facility:** 77 one-bedroom standard units with kitchens. 4 stories, interior corridors. *Bath:* combo or shower only. **Parking:** on-site.
Small-scale Hotel   **Terms:** weekly rates available, small pets only ($25 fee). **Amenities:** high-speed Internet, voice mail, irons, hair dryers. **Leisure Activities:** putting green, exercise room. **Guest Services:** coin laundry. **Business Services:** meeting rooms, business center. **Cards:** AX, CB, DC, DS, JC, MC, VI. **Special Amenities:** free expanded continental breakfast and free local telephone calls.

SOME UNITS
(S/D) (✈) (🐾) (†1†) (✲) (DATA PORT) (🖬) (🖨) (▣) / (✕) /
FEE

(See map and index starting on p. 867)

QUALITY INN/TANGLEWOOD   *Book at aaa.com*   Phone: (540)989-4000 **16**

4/16-10/31	1P: $49-$79	2P: $49-$99	XP: $6	F18
1/1-2/28	1P: $45-$59	2P: $55-$65	XP: $6	F18
3/1-4/15 & 11/1-12/31	1P: $49-$59	2P: $49-$65	XP: $6	F18

Small-scale Hotel **Location:** I-581/US 220, exit Franklin Rd/Salem, just n on US 220 business route, then w on Frontage Rd. 3816 Franklin Rd SW 24014. **Fax:** 540/989-0250. **Facility:** 58 one-bedroom standard units. 2 stories (no elevator), exterior corridors. **Parking:** on-site. **Terms:** 7 day cancellation notice, [ECP] meal plan available. **Amenities:** irons, hair dryers. **Leisure Activities:** exercise room. **Guest Services:** coin laundry. **Business Services:** meeting rooms, business center. **Cards:** AX, DC, DS, MC, VI. **Special Amenities: free expanded continental breakfast and free local telephone calls.**

SOME UNITS

RODEWAY INN-CIVIC CENTER   *Book at aaa.com*   Phone: (540)981-9341 **12**

All Year [CP]	1P: $35-$75	2P: $38-$100	XP: $5	F18

Small-scale Hotel **Location:** I-581, exit 4E, jct US 400 and 11, just n. Truck parking on premises. 526 Orange Ave NE 24016. **Fax:** 540/345-8477. **Facility:** 102 one-bedroom standard units. 2 stories (no elevator), exterior corridors. **Parking:** on-site. **Terms:** small pets only ($10 fee). **Amenities:** safes. **Guest Services:** coin laundry. **Business Services:** meeting rooms. **Cards:** AX, DC, DS, MC, VI. **Special Amenities: free continental breakfast and free newspaper.**

SOME UNITS

FEE

SLEEP INN   *Book at aaa.com*   Phone: (540)772-1500 **18**

All Year [ECP]	1P: $35-$99	2P: $35-$99	XP: $10	F15

Small-scale Hotel **Location:** I-581/US 220, exit Franklin Rd/Salem, 0.7 mi n on SR 419. 4045 Electric Rd 24014. **Fax:** 540/772-1642. **Facility:** 92 one-bedroom standard units. 2-3 stories (no elevator), interior corridors. *Bath:* combo or shower only. **Parking:** on-site. **Terms:** package plans. **Amenities:** *Some:* irons, hair dryers. **Guest Services:** valet laundry. **Business Services:** meeting rooms. **Cards:** AX, CB, DC, DS, JC, MC, VI.

SOME UNITS

FEE

SUPER 8 MOTEL   *Book at aaa.com*   Phone: (540)563-8888 **2**

All Year	1P: $46-$64	2P: $50-$68	XP: $5	F

Small-scale Hotel **Location:** I-581, exit 25, s on SR 117 (Peters Creek Rd), then just w. 6616 Thirlane Rd 24019. **Fax:** 540/563-8888. **Facility:** 60 one-bedroom standard units. 2-3 stories (no elevator), interior corridors. **Parking:** on-site. **Terms:** pets ($10 deposit). **Amenities:** safes. **Cards:** AX, DC, DS, MC, VI.

SOME UNITS

FEE

(See map and index starting on p. 867)

WYNDHAM ROANOKE AIRPORT   *Book at aaa.com*   Phone: (540)563-9300   **10**

AAA SAVE	12/1-2/28	1P: $89-$99	2P: $89-$109	XP: $10	F17
	3/1-11/30	1P: $79-$89	2P: $79-$99	XP: $10	F17

Fax: 540/366-5846. **Location:** I-581, exit 3W, just w to Ordway Dr, then just n via service road. 2801 Hershberger Rd 24017. **Facility:** 320 one-bedroom standard units. 7-8 stories, interior corridors. **Parking:** on-site. **Terms:** cancellation fee imposed, small pets only ($25 extra charge). **Amenities:** video games, high-speed Internet, dual phone lines, voice mail, irons, hair dryers. *Some:* CD players. **Dining:** 6:30 am-2 & 5-10 pm, cocktails. **Pool(s):** outdoor, indoor. **Leisure Activities:** sauna, whirlpool, 2 lighted tennis courts, exercise room. **Guest Services:** valet laundry, airport transportation-Roanoke Regional-Woodrum Field Airport, area transportation-within 3 mi & Valley View Mall. **Business Services:** conference facilities, fax. **Cards:** AX, CB, DC, DS, MC, VI.

Large-scale Hotel

SOME UNITS

🛬 🐾 🍴 📷 🏊 ✕ 📷 DATA PORT 📺 / ✕ 📶 🍽 /
FEE

──── WHERE TO DINE ────

ARZU   Lunch: $8-$18   Dinner: $10-$30   Phone: 540/982-7160   **6**
American
Location: Center. 213 Williamson Rd SE 24011. **Hours:** 11 am-9 pm, Fri & Sat-10 pm, Sun noon-8 pm. Closed major holidays. **Features:** A combination of classic French and Turkish cuisine is served in an upscale atmosphere. Casual dress; cocktails. **Parking:** on-site. **Cards:** AX, DC, DS, MC, VI.
✕

CARLOS BRAZILIAN INTERNATIONAL CUISINE   Lunch: $7-$10   Dinner: $7-$28   Phone: 540/776-1117   **15**
Brazilian
Location: Corner of Church St; downtown; at Market Square. 4167 Electric Rd 24014. **Hours:** 11:30 am-2 & 5-9:30 pm, Fri-10 pm, Sat 5 pm-10 pm, Mon & Tues 5 pm-9:30 pm. Closed major holidays; also Sun. **Reservations:** suggested, for dinner. **Features:** Cuisine is prepared with an unusual flair, as evidenced by such selections as grilled chicken breast with a sweet sauce and fried bananas, fruit and steamed vegetables. The atmosphere is informal, and service is attentive and pleasant. Casual dress; cocktails. **Parking:** street. **Cards:** AX, MC, VI.
✕

COACH AND FOUR   Dinner: $9-$21   Phone: 540/362-4220   **2**
American
Location: I-81, exit 146, 1.5 mi e on SR 115, then right 1 mi. 5206 Williamson Rd 24012. **Hours:** 4 pm-10 pm, Fri & Sat-11 pm, Sun 11:30 am-10 pm. Closed: 11/24, 12/24, 12/25. **Features:** A favorite with the locals, the traditional restaurant is known for its exciting gourmet entrees. Patrons can mingle in the large lounge or enjoy quiet, elegant dining. Little extras, such as a single meatball with salad, enhance the overall experience. Casual dress. **Parking:** on-site. **Cards:** AX, DC, DS, MC, VI.
✕

EL TOREO   Lunch: $5-$9   Dinner: $6-$11   Phone: 540/265-9116   **1**
Mexican
Location: I-81, exit 146, just e. 6617 Therlane Rd 24019. **Hours:** 11 am-10 pm, Sat from noon, Sun noon-9 pm. Closed major holidays. **Features:** A lengthy list of Mexican favorites tempts patrons. Prompt, courteous service is the norm, as are ample portions. Casual dress; cocktails. **Parking:** on-site. **Cards:** AX, DS, MC, VI.
✕

HARBOR INN SEAFOOD RESTAURANT   Dinner: $8-$15   Phone: 540/563-0001
Seafood
Location: I-81, exit 146, 1 mi se on SR 115, then just s on US 11. 7416 Williamson Rd NE 24019. **Hours:** 4 pm-9 pm, Fri & Sat-10 pm, Sun 11 am-9 pm. Closed: 1/1, 11/24, 12/25; also Mon. **Features:** The restaurant is popular for its good selection of flavorful, affordably priced seafood selections. The atmosphere is welcoming to families. Landlubbers may choose from a handful of steak and chicken entrees. Portions are ample. Casual dress; beer & wine only. **Parking:** on-site. **Cards:** MC, VI.
✕

THE LIBRARY   Dinner: $20-$30   Phone: 540/985-0811   **11**
French
Location: I-581, exit US 220 (Franklin Rd/Salem), 1 mi n on US 220 business route; in Piccadilly Square Shopping Center. 3117 Franklin Rd SW 24014. **Hours:** 5:30 pm-close. Closed major holidays; also Sun & Mon. **Reservations:** suggested. **Features:** French cuisine is at the heart of the intimate restaurant's menu. A few walls with shelves of books help this place live up to its name. Attractive artwork and tables set with a candle and fresh flower in slim brass vase add to the sophistication. The dining room is nice for celebrating an anniversary or other special occasion. Dressy casual; cocktails. **Parking:** on-site. **Cards:** AX, CB, DC, DS, MC, VI.
✕

LUIGI'S   Dinner: $11-$27   Phone: 540/989-6277   **12**
Italian
Location: I-581, exit US 220 (Franklin Rd/Salem), 2.1 mi nw on SR 419, then 1 mi n. 3301 Brambleton Ave SW 24018. **Hours:** 4:30 pm-11 pm, Fri & Sat-midnight. Closed: 1/1, 11/24, 12/25. **Reservations:** suggested, weekends. **Features:** Luigi's offers authentic Italian gourmet specialties such as veal bella bola and steak-n-such. Intimate surroundings,wonderful background music and a knowledgeable friendly staff. Casual dress; cocktails. **Parking:** on-site. **Cards:** AX, DS, MC, VI.
🍸 ✕

MACADO'S   Lunch: $4-$8   Dinner: $5-$12   Phone: 540/776-9884   **16**
American
Location: I-581, exit US 220 (Franklin Rd/Salem), 0.4 mi n on SR 419; at Grand Pavillion Shopping Center. 4237 Electric Rd 24014. **Hours:** 8 am-12:30 am, Fri & Sat-1:30 am. Closed: 11/24, 12/25. **Features:** The loud, lively college hangout sports a lengthy menu of creatively prepared sandwiches and wraps. Among enjoyable choices are the grilled chicken wrap, stuffed with flavorful vegetables and melted provolone cheese, and French onion soup served in a cup. Casual dress; cocktails. **Parking:** on-site. **Cards:** AX, DC, MC, VI.
🍸 ✕

MAC & MAGGIE'S   Lunch: $5-$15   Dinner: $7-$15   Phone: 540/774-7427   **14**
American
Location: I-581, exit US 220 (Franklin Rd/Salem), 0.5 mi n on SR 419; at Tanglewood Shopping Mall. 4202 Electric Rd 24014. **Hours:** 11 am-2 am. Closed: 12/25. **Features:** Ribs rule, but there are a few steak and chicken entrees as well. The atmosphere at the Tanglewood Mall eatery is casual and relaxed, and service is prompt and good. Lighter fare is served until 2 am. Casual dress; cocktails. **Parking:** on-site. **Cards:** AX, DS, MC, VI.

(See map and index starting on p. 867)

MONTANO'S INTERNATIONAL GOURMET
Lunch: $7-$10   **Dinner:** $8-$18   **Phone:** 540/344-8960   ⑬

Continental

Location: I-581, exit US 220 (Franklin Rd/Salem), just n on US 220 business route; in Townside Festival Mall. 3733 Franklin Rd SW 24014. **Hours:** 10 am-10:30 pm. Closed: 1/1, 11/24, 12/25; also Sun. **Features:** Popular at lunch with the local business crowd, the extensive menu features soup, salad and sandwiches. House specials at the family-owned eatery include paella, surf and turf and some pasta dishes. The delicatessen serves quality meat and cheese. Casual dress; cocktails. **Parking:** on-site. **Cards:** AX, DS, MC, VI.

NAWAB INDIAN CUISINE
Lunch: $7-$17   **Dinner:** $8-$25   **Phone:** 540/345-5150   ⑤

Indian

Location: Center. 118 A Campbell Ave SE 24011. **Hours:** 11:30 am-2:30 & 5-10 pm, Sat from 5 pm. **Features:** The menu centers on fragrant, colorful and tasty Indian cuisine. Delicious traditional bread is baked in a tandoor oven. The lunch buffet changes daily. Casual dress; cocktails. **Parking:** on-site. **Cards:** AX, DS, MC, VI.

NEW YORKER DELICATESSEN AND RESTAURANT
Lunch: $4-$9   **Dinner:** $4-$9   **Phone:** 540/366-0935   ③

American

Location: I-581, exit 4E, just e, then 1 mi n. 2802 Williamson Rd 24012. **Hours:** 11 am-10 pm, Fri & Sat-11 pm. Closed: 11/24, 12/25; also Mon. **Features:** In operation here for more than 40 years, the delicatessen has the atmosphere of a big-city operation. Meat cases are visible from the entrance, and the many selections of shaven sandwich meats and knockwursts will get the appetite juices flowing. Lunch is busy, but the price is right. Casual dress; cocktails. **Parking:** on-site.

THE REGENCY ROOM
Lunch: $9-$13   **Dinner:** $20-$35   **Phone:** 540/853-8210   ④

American

Location: I-581, exit 5 southbound; exit 4E northbound, 0.5 mi s on US 11/221/SR 16, then just w on Wells Ave; in The Hotel Roanoke & Conference Center, A Doubletree Hotel. 110 Shenandoah Ave 24016. **Hours:** 6:30-10:30 am, 11:30-2 & 5-10 pm, Sun 7 am-9 pm. **Reservations:** suggested. **Features:** The circular, open dining room is considered a regional landmark. The historic lobby opens into the lovely dining room, where the charming staff tends to diners' needs. Dressy casual; cocktails; entertainment. **Parking:** on-site (fee) and valet. **Cards:** AX, CB, DC, DS, MC, VI. **Historic**

THE ROANOKER RESTAURANT
Lunch: $5-$7   **Dinner:** $5-$11   **Phone:** 540/344-7746   ⑨

American

Location: I-581, exit Colonial Ave, just sw. 2522 Colonial Ave SW 24015. **Hours:** 7 am-9 pm, Sun from 8 am. Closed: 12/25, 12/26; also Mon. **Features:** The long-established eatery is popular for its well-priced, homemade country cooking. Patrons would be hard-pressed not to find a tasty meal. Pork tenderloin is perfectly cooked and accompanied by country vegetables and sweet, moist corn sticks. Casual dress; cocktails. **Parking:** on-site. **Cards:** MC, VI.

STEPHEN'S
Dinner: $15-$25   **Phone:** 540/344-7203   ⑩

Regional American

Location: I-581, exit US 220 (Franklin Rd/Salem), 1.2 mi n on US 220 business route. 2926 Franklin Rd SW 24014. **Hours:** 5 pm-9 pm, Fri & Sat from 5:30 pm. Closed major holidays; also Sun. **Reservations:** suggested. **Features:** Tall ceilings and lots of wrought iron give the multilevel restaurant the feeling of south Louisiana. The chef's specialties, which emphasize seafood but also include lamb and duck, reflect the same influences. The atmosphere is relaxed and subdued. Casual dress; cocktails. **Parking:** on-site. **Cards:** AX, DC, DS, MC, VI.

SWAGAT INDIAN CUISINE
Lunch: $6-$12   **Dinner:** $6-$18   **Phone:** 540/342-4887   ⑧

Indian

Location: Between Church and Kirk aves; center. 303 First St 24011. **Hours:** 11:30 am-10 pm. Closed: 12/25. **Features:** Swagat Indian Cuisine has a huge menu, friendly wait staff and cozy and warm dining surroundings. Casual dress; cocktails. **Parking:** street. **Cards:** AX, CB, DC, DS, JC, MC, VI.

SZECHUAN RESTAURANT
Lunch: $5-$8   **Dinner:** $6-$14   **Phone:** 540/989-7947   ⑰

Chinese

Location: I-581, exit US 220 (Franklin Rd/Salem), 1 mi w on SR 419; in The Corners Shopping Center. 5207 Bernard Dr 24018. **Hours:** 11:30 am-10 pm, Fri & Sat-11 pm. Closed: 11/24, 12/25. **Features:** Excellent chicken, beef, seafood and vegetarian entrees are served in a family-friendly atmosphere. Artfully presented on a bed of lettuce, shrimp toast is more than tasty. Guests can sample a little bit of everything at the lunch buffet, available Sunday through Friday. Casual dress; cocktails. **Parking:** on-site. **Cards:** AX, DC, DS, MC, VI.

WERTZ'S RESTAURANT
Lunch: $9-$18   **Dinner:** $12-$25   **Phone:** 540/342-5133   ⑦

American

Location: I-581, exit 5, just s. 215 Market St 24011. **Hours:** 11 am-2:30 & 5:30-10 pm, Mon-2:30 pm. Closed: 1/1, 12/25; also Sun. **Features:** In the heart of downtown, the restaurant enjoys a strong local following for lunch and dinner. The huge wine list is something to savor. Casual dress; cocktails. **Parking:** street. **Cards:** AX.

WILDFLOUR AT HOLLINS
Lunch: $7-$12   **Dinner:** $7-$21   **Phone:** 540/362-1812

American

Location: I-81, exit 146, 0.6 mi e on SR 115, then 0.3 mi n. 7770 Williamson Rd 24019. **Hours:** 11 am-10 pm. Closed: 1/1, 12/25; also Sun. **Features:** Fresh food is prepared from family recipes. Servers are friendly, courteous and attentive. Casual dress; beer & wine only. **Parking:** on-site. **Cards:** AX, DS, MC, VI.

ROCKY MOUNT pop. 4,066

―――― WHERE TO STAY ――――

THE CLAIBORNE HOUSE B & B
Phone: 540/483-4616
▽▽▽▽ All Year 1P: $90-$130 2P: $90-$130
Historic Bed **Location:** Just w of Main St; in historic district. 185 Claiborne Ave 24151. Fax: 540/484-1504. **Facility:** Set in a
& Breakfast sleepy town halfway between the Blue Ridge Parkway and Smith Mountain Lake, this Victorian structure
was built by a local family in 1895. Smoke free premises. 5 one-bedroom standard units. 2 stories (no
elevator), interior corridors. **Bath:** combo or shower only. **Parking:** on-site. **Terms:** check-in 4 pm, 2 night
minimum stay - seasonal, age restrictions may apply, 7 day cancellation notice. **Guest Services:** gift shop. **Business Services:**
meeting rooms. **Cards:** AX, DC, DS, MC, VI.

(ASK) (X) (🐾) (☎)

COMFORT INN-ROCKY MOUNT *Book at aaa.com*
Phone: (540)489-4000
▽▽▽▽ All Year [ECP] 1P: $55-$100 2P: $60-$100 XP: $6 F18
Motel **Location:** 1.5 mi n on US 220 business route. 1730 N Main St 24151. Fax: 540/489-4000. **Facility:** 61 one-
bedroom standard units. 2 stories, interior corridors. **Parking:** on-site. **Amenities:** safes, irons, hair dryers.
Pool(s): outdoor. **Leisure Activities:** Fee: game room. **Guest Services:** coin laundry. **Business Services:**
meeting rooms. **Cards:** AX, CB, DC, DS, MC, VI.

SOME UNITS
(ASK) (S/D) (📶↑) (🛩) (☎) (DATA PORT) (🖥) / (X) (🛏) (📠) /

FRANKLIN MOTEL
Phone: (540)483-9962
(AAA) (SAVE) All Year 1P: $37-$60 2P: $45-$80 XP: $5 D12
▽▽ ▽▽ **Location:** 6.5 mi n on US 220. 20281 Virgil H Goode Hwy 24151. Fax: 540/483-9962. **Facility:** 22 one-bedroom
Motel standard units, some with whirlpools. 1 story, exterior corridors. **Parking:** on-site. **Terms:** package plans,
pets ($10 deposit, $20 extra charge). **Cards:** AX, DS, MC, VI.

SOME UNITS
(S/D) (🐾) (📶↑) (☎) / (X) (🛏) (📠) /
FEE FEE FEE

―――― WHERE TO DINE ――――

FISHERMAN'S GALLEY **Lunch:** $5-$10 **Dinner:** $6-$17 **Phone:** 540/483-3474
▽▽▽▽ **Location:** 2.1 mi n on US 220. 17890 Virgil H Goode Hwy 24151. **Hours:** 11 am-9 pm, Sat 3 pm-9:30 pm, Sun
Seafood noon-8 pm. Closed: 12/25; also Mon. **Features:** Fisherman's Galley is a family owned and operated
restaurant that is known far and wide for fresh seafood. Do not miss the hushpuppies. Casual dress;
cocktails. **Parking:** on-site. **Cards:** AX, CB, DC, DS, JC, MC, VI.

(🍽) (X)

IPPY'S UNCLE TOM'S RESTAURANT **Lunch:** $6-$12 **Dinner:** $13-$50 **Phone:** 540/489-5600
▽▽ ▽▽ **Location:** 1.8 mi n on US 220 business route. 1760 N Main St 24151. **Hours:** 11 am-2 & 5-9 pm, Thurs & Fri-10
American pm, Sat 5 pm-10 pm. Closed: 12/25; also Sun. **Features:** A unique name and plave that serves all the
classic American favorites from ribs to steaks and everything in between. Casual dress; cocktails. **Parking:**
on-site. **Cards:** AX, CB, DC, DS, JC, MC, VI.

(🍽) (X)

OLDE VIRGINIA BARBECUE **Lunch:** $5-$12 **Dinner:** $5-$15 **Phone:** 540/489-1788
▽▽ ▽▽ **Location:** 1.6 mi n on US 220 business route. 35 Meadowview Ave 24151. **Hours:** 11 am-9 pm. Closed: 11/24,
American 12/25. **Features:** A city tradition, the eatery satisfies diners with delicious, hickory wood-smoked beef and
pork, as well as succulent ribs. Casual dress; beer only. **Parking:** on-site. **Cards:** MC, VI.

(X)

ROUND HILL —See District Of Columbia p. 547.

SALEM pop. 24,747 (See map and index starting on p. 867)

―――― WHERE TO STAY ――――

BAYMONT INN ROANOKE-SALEM *Book at aaa.com*
Phone: (540)562-2717 (22)
(AAA) (SAVE) All Year 1P: $64-$79 2P: $69-$89 F18
▽▽▽▽▽ **Location:** I-81, exit 141, 0.5 mi se on SR 419. 140 Sheraton Dr 24153. Fax: 540/562-1690. **Facility:** 67 one-
bedroom standard units, some with whirlpools. 3 stories, interior corridors. **Bath:** combo or shower only.
Parking: on-site. **Terms:** package plans. **Amenities:** video games, voice mail, irons, hair dryers. **Pool(s):**
Small-scale Hotel small outdoor. **Leisure Activities:** exercise room. **Guest Services:** coin laundry. **Business Services:**
meeting rooms. **Cards:** AX, CB, DC, DS, MC, VI.

SOME UNITS
(S/D) (📶↑) (♿) (🛩) (☎) (DATA PORT) (🛏) (📠) (🖥) / (X) /
FEE FEE

BLUE JAY BUDGET HOST INN
Phone: 540/380-2080
(AAA) (SAVE) 3/1-11/15 1P: $35-$54 2P: $38-$80 XP: $5 F15
▽▽ 11/16-2/28 1P: $28-$45 2P: $32-$49 XP: $5 F15
Motel **Location:** I-81, exit 132, just e, then 0.3 mi n on US 11/460. 5399 W Main St 24153. Fax: 540/380-2080. **Facility:** 14
one-bedroom standard units. 1 story, exterior corridors. **Bath:** combo or shower only. **Parking:** on-site.
Terms: 3 day cancellation notice-fee imposed, weekly rates available, package plans, pets ($5 extra
charge, in designated units). **Pool(s):** outdoor. **Cards:** AX, DC, MC, VI. **Special Amenities:** free local
telephone calls and preferred room (subject to availability with advance reservations).

SOME UNITS
(S/D) (🐾) (📶↑) (🛩) / (X) (🛏) (📠) /
FEE

(See map and index starting on p. 867)

COMFORT INN
Book at aaa.com
Phone: (540)387-1600   26

3/1-12/31	1P: $74-$99	2P: $79-$99	XP: $5	F18
1/1-2/28	1P: $69-$79	2P: $69-$79	XP: $5	F18

Location: I-81, exit 137, 0.3 mi e on SR 112. 151 Wildwood Rd 24153. Fax: 540/387-9747. **Facility:** 50 one-bedroom standard units, some with whirlpools. 2 stories (no elevator), exterior corridors. **Parking:** on-site.
Small-scale Hotel   **Terms:** 7 day cancellation notice. **Amenities:** high-speed Internet, irons, hair dryers. **Pool(s):** small outdoor. **Cards:** AX, CB, DC, DS, JC, MC, VI. **Special Amenities:** free expanded continental breakfast and free local telephone calls.

SOME UNITS

COMFORT SUITES INN AT RIDGEWOOD FARM
Book at aaa.com
Phone: (540)375-4800

All Year [ECP]	1P: $55-$125	2P: $59-$130	XP: $10	F15

Location: I-81, exit 141, 4.7 mi s on SR 419, then just w. 2898 Keagy Rd 24153. Fax: 540/302-0097. **Facility:** 78 one-bedroom standard units, some with whirlpools. 3 stories, interior corridors. *Bath:* combo or shower only. **Parking:** on-site. **Terms:** pets ($35 fee). **Amenities:** high-speed Internet, voice mail, irons, hair dryers.
Small-scale Hotel   **Pool(s):** outdoor. **Leisure Activities:** whirlpool. **Guest Services:** coin laundry. **Business Services:** meeting rooms, business center. **Cards:** AX, CB, DC, DS, JC, MC, VI.

SOME UNITS
FEE

ECONO LODGE-ROANOKE/SALEM
Book at aaa.com
Phone: (540)389-0280   25

4/1-10/31	1P: $46-$86	2P: $51-$91	XP: $5	F18
3/1-3/31 & 11/1-2/28	1P: $39-$59	2P: $44-$64	XP: $5	F18

Location: I-81, exit 137, just e on SR 112. 301 Wildwood Rd 24153. Fax: 540/387-1553. **Facility:** 64 one-bedroom standard units. 1 story, exterior corridors. **Parking:** on-site. **Terms:** small pets only ($5 extra charge).
Motel   **Cards:** AX, DC, DS, MC, VI.

SOME UNITS
FEE

HAMPTON INN SALEM
Book at aaa.com
Phone: (540)776-6500

All Year	1P: $85-$99	2P: $95-$129

Location: I-81, exit 141, 4.6 mi s on SR 419. Located adjacent to hospital, connected by pedestrian walkway. 1886 Electric Rd 24153. Fax: 540/776-3069. **Facility:** 114 one-bedroom standard units, some with whirlpools. 6
Small-scale Hotel   stories, interior corridors. *Bath:* combo or shower only. **Parking:** on-site. **Terms:** 2 night minimum stay - seasonal and/or weekends, 7 day cancellation notice-fee imposed, [ECP] meal plan available. **Amenities:** high-speed Internet, dual phone lines, voice mail, irons, hair dryers. **Pool(s):** outdoor. **Leisure Activities:** exercise room. **Guest Services:** coin laundry. **Business Services:** meeting rooms, business center. **Cards:** AX, CB, DC, DS, MC, VI.

SOME UNITS

HOLIDAY INN EXPRESS
Book at aaa.com
Phone: (540)986-1000   23

3/17-11/15 [ECP]	1P: $71-$89	2P: $71-$89	XP: $7	F18
3/1-3/16 & 11/16-2/28 [ECP]	1P: $55-$71	2P: $55-$71	XP: $7	F18

Location: I-81, exit 141, 2 mi s on SR 419, then just w on US 460. Located across from a shopping center. 1535 E Main
Small-scale Hotel   St 24153. Fax: 540/986-0355. **Facility:** 70 one-bedroom standard units. 3 stories (no elevator), exterior corridors. **Parking:** on-site. **Amenities:** voice mail, irons, hair dryers. **Guest Services:** coin laundry. **Business Services:** meeting rooms, business center. **Cards:** AX, CB, DC, DS, MC, VI.

SOME UNITS
FEE

QUALITY INN ROANOKE/SALEM
Book at aaa.com
Phone: (540)562-1912   21

5/1-10/31	1P: $54-$77	2P: $60-$83	XP: $6	F18
3/1-4/30 & 11/1-12/31	1P: $50-$65	2P: $56-$71	XP: $6	F18
1/1-2/28	1P: $45-$60	2P: $51-$65	XP: $6	F18

Location: I-81, exit 141, 0.4 mi s on SR 419. Truck parking on premises. 179 Sheraton Dr 24153. Fax: 540/562-0507.
Small-scale Hotel   **Facility:** 120 one-bedroom standard units. 2 stories (no elevator), interior corridors. **Parking:** on-site. **Terms:** 7 day cancellation notice, [ECP] meal plan available, small pets only ($15 extra charge, in smoking units). **Amenities:** irons, hair dryers. **Pool(s):** outdoor. **Leisure Activities:** picnic tables, playground, exercise room. **Guest Services:** coin laundry. **Business Services:** meeting rooms, business center. **Cards:** AX, DC, DS, MC, VI. **Special Amenities:** free expanded continental breakfast and free local telephone calls.

SOME UNITS
FEE

------ WHERE TO DINE ------

CHIP & JO'S RESTAURANT
Lunch: $5-$10   **Dinner:** $5-$12   **Phone:** 540/387-9585

Location: I-81, exit 141, 4.1 mi s on SR 419. 315 8th St 24153. **Hours:** 6 am-8 pm, Sat 7 am-3 pm. Closed: 12/25; also Sun. **Features:** Chip & Jo's is a family operated eatery that serves breakfast all day. A wide variety menu of classic American cuisine. Casual dress. **Parking:** on-site. **Cards:** MC, VI.
American

EL RODEO
Lunch: $5-$9   **Dinner:** $6-$11   **Phone:** 540/387-4045   21

Location: I-81, exit 137, 0.3 mi e on SR 112. 260 Wildwood Rd 24153. **Hours:** 11 am-10 pm, Sat from noon, Sun noon-9 pm. Closed major holidays. **Features:** Traditional favorites are menu mainstays at the family eatery. The lengthy list of selections includes chips and salsa, chiles rellenos and hot and tasty beef enchiladas.
Mexican   Portions are large, and service is prompt and courteous. Casual dress; cocktails. **Parking:** on-site.
Cards: AX, DS, MC, VI.

(See map and index starting on p. 867)

FAST FREDDY'S
American

Lunch: $5-$11　　　Dinner: $5-$15　　　Phone: 540/389-5409 [22]
Location: I-81, exit 137, just e. 816 W Main St 24153. **Hours:** 11 am-10 pm. Closed major holidays.
Features: This place is a fast-food restaurant without the fast-food mentality. On the menu is a huge variety of dishes. Service is quick and friendly. Casual dress. **Parking:** on-site.

MAMMA MARIA'S ITALIAN RESTAURANT
Italian

Lunch: $6-$12　　　Dinner: $6-$20　　　Phone: 540/389-2848 [23]
Location: I-81, exit 137, just e. 2025 W Main St 24153. **Hours:** 11 am-10 pm. Closed: 1/1, 12/25; also Mon.
Features: A Southern Virginia favorite, the restaurant prepares a wide variety of pizza and pasta dishes. Service is friendly. Casual dress; cocktails. **Parking:** on-site. **Cards:** MC, VI.

SAKE HOUSE
Japanese

Lunch: $5-$8　　　Dinner: $8-$20　　　Phone: 540/986-1207 [20]
Location: I-81, exit 141, 2 mi s on SR 419, just w on US 460; in Lakeside Plaza. 141 Electric Rd 24153. **Hours:** 11:30 am-3 & 5-10 pm, Fri & Sat-10:30 pm, Sun 5 pm-9 pm. Closed major holidays; also Mon. **Features:** The menu centers on Japanese tempura, teriyaki and sushi preparations, highlights of which include miso soup to open and a lovely dessert of deep-fried sesame balls with sweet sesame paste to close. Tea room seating is available. Casual dress; cocktails. **Parking:** on-site. **Cards:** AX, MC, VI.

SZECHUAN RESTAURANT
Chinese
DC, DS, MC, VI.

Lunch: $6-$9　　　Dinner: $6-$10　　　Phone: 540/387-9869
Location: I-81, exit 141, 4.6 mi s on SR 419. 1923-G Electric Rd 24153. **Hours:** 11:30 am-10 pm, Fri & Sat-11 pm. Closed: 11/24, 12/25. **Features:** A wide range of traditional favorites is authentically prepared and served promptly. Among choices on the daily lunch buffet are General Tso's chicken, beef with broccoli, seafood, spare ribs, soup and Szechwan-style green beans. Casual dress; cocktails. **Parking:** on-site. **Cards:** AX,

SANDSTON —*See Richmond p. 865.*

SMITHFIELD —*See Hampton Roads Area p. 789.*

SOUTH BOSTON pop. 8,491

———— **WHERE TO STAY** ————

HOLIDAY INN-EXPRESS　*Book at aaa.com*
Small-scale Hotel

		Phone: (434)575-4000
All Year	1P: $90	2P: $90	XP: $6	F19

Location: Just e on US 58, from jct US 501. 1074 Bill Tuck Hwy 24592. Fax: 434/575-1600. **Facility:** 66 one-bedroom standard units, some with whirlpools. 2 stories (no elevator), interior corridors. *Bath:* combo or shower only. **Parking:** on-site. **Terms:** pets ($20 deposit). **Amenities:** high-speed Internet, dual phone lines, voice mail, irons, hair dryers. **Pool(s):** outdoor. **Leisure Activities:** exercise room. **Guest Services:** valet and coin laundry. **Business Services:** meeting rooms, business center. **Cards:** AX, CB, DC, DS, JC, MC, VI.

SOME UNITS

QUALITY INN HOWARD HOUSE　*Book at aaa.com*
Small-scale Hotel

		Phone: (434)572-4311
4/1-9/30	1P: $62-$119	2P: $72-$129	XP: $10	F18
3/1-3/31 & 10/1-2/28	1P: $52	2P: $62	XP: $10	F18

Location: Jct US 58, 501 and 360, 1 mi e on US 360. 2001 Seymour Dr 24592. Fax: 434/572-2740. **Facility:** 52 one-bedroom standard units. 2 stories (no elevator), exterior corridors. **Parking:** on-site. **Terms:** cancellation fee imposed, weekly rates available, [CP] meal plan available, small pets only ($10 extra charge). **Amenities:** irons, hair dryers. **Dining:** 5 pm-9 pm, cocktails. **Pool(s):** outdoor. **Guest Services:** valet laundry. **Business Services:** meeting rooms, fax. **Cards:** AX, DC, DS, JC, MC, VI.

SOME UNITS

SUPER 8 MOTEL　*Book at aaa.com*
Motel
MC, VI.

		Phone: (434)572-8868
All Year	1P: $49-$60	2P: $61-$75	XP: $6	F17

Location: Just e on US 58, from jct US 501. 1040 Bill Tuck Hwy 24592. Fax: 434/572-8868. **Facility:** 58 one-bedroom standard units. 2 stories (no elevator), interior corridors. **Parking:** on-site, winter plug-ins. **Terms:** [CP] meal plan available. **Amenities:** safes (fee). **Business Services:** fax. **Cards:** AX, DC, DS,

SOME UNITS

———— **WHERE TO DINE** ————

BISTRO 1888
American

Dinner: $11-$20　　　Phone: 434/572-1888
Location: Between Arch and Seymoure sts; downtown. 221 Main St 24592. **Hours:** 5 pm-10 pm. Closed major holidays; also Sun & Mon. **Reservations:** suggested, weekends. **Features:** The chic interior mixes urban cool with turn-of-the-20th-century charm at the refurbished downtown building. The menu shows sophistication and creativity with influences as wide-ranging as the Pacific Northwest, Asia, Europe and, of course, the South. Dressy casual; cocktails. **Parking:** street. **Cards:** AX, DS, MC, VI.

ERNIE'S RESTAURANT   **Lunch:** $4-$13   **Dinner:** $4-$13   **Phone:** 434/572-3423
Location: Jct US 58, 501 and 360, 1.5 mi e on US 501. 1010 John Randolph Blvd 24592. **Hours:** 11 am-9 pm.
Closed: 7/4; also Mon & 12/25-1/2. **Features:** Since 1958, the Green family has been serving Southside
Southern   locals and travelers such country-style favorites as Brunswick stew, biscuits, succotash, barbecue and fried
seafood on the weekends and more. Casual dress; cocktails. **Parking:** on-site. **Cards:** AX, CB, DC,
MC, VI.

SOUTH HILL pop. 4,403

———— WHERE TO STAY ————

COMFORT INN   *Book at aaa.com*   **Phone:** 434/447-2600
All Year   1P: $59-$79   2P: $59-$79   XP: $10   F
Location: I-85, exit 12B, just w. 918 E Atlantic St 23970. Fax: 434/447-2590. **Facility:** 50 one-bedroom standard
units. 2 stories (no elevator), exterior corridors. **Parking:** on-site, winter plug-ins. **Terms:** cancellation fee
imposed, weekly rates available, pets ($5 extra charge). **Amenities:** hair dryers. *Some:* high-speed Internet.
Small-scale Hotel   **Leisure Activities:** exercise room. **Guest Services:** coin laundry. **Business Services:** business center.
Cards: AX, CB, DC, DS, MC, VI. **Special Amenities: free continental breakfast and free local telephone
calls.** *(See color ad below)*

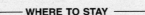

HAMPTON INN

(AAA) SAVE

Small-scale Hotel

Book at aaa.com

All Year | 1P: $75-$99 | 2P: $75-$99 | XP: $15 | F15

Phone: (434)447-4600

Location: I-85, exit 12A, just e on US 58. 200 Thompson Rd 23970 (Box 430). Fax: 434/447-2553. **Facility:** 55 units. 53 one-bedroom standard units, some with whirlpools. 2 one-bedroom suites ($100-$159) with whirlpools. 3 stories, interior corridors. *Bath:* combo or shower only. **Parking:** on-site, winter plug-ins. **Amenities:** high-speed Internet, voice mail, irons, hair dryers. **Pool(s):** outdoor. **Leisure Activities:** exercise room. **Guest Services:** valet and coin laundry. **Business Services:** meeting rooms, business center. **Cards:** AX, CB, DC, DS, MC, VI. *(See color ad p 879)*

SOME UNITS

HOLIDAY INN EXPRESS

Small-scale Hotel

5/1-9/30 | 1P: $75-$85 | 2P: $75-$85 | XP: $5
3/1-4/30 & 10/1-2/28 | 1P: $72 | 2P: $72 | XP: $5

Phone: 434/955-2777

Location: I-85, exit 12, just e on US 58. 101 Thompson Rd 23950. Fax: 434/955-2700. **Facility:** 55 one-bedroom standard units, some with whirlpools. 2 stories (no elevator), interior corridors. *Bath:* combo or shower only. **Parking:** on-site, winter plug-ins. **Amenities:** high-speed Internet, dual phone lines, voice mail, irons, hair dryers. **Pool(s):** outdoor. **Leisure Activities:** exercise room. **Guest Services:** valet laundry. **Business Services:** meeting rooms, fax. **Cards:** AX, CB, DC, DS, JC, MC, VI.

SOME UNITS

SUPER 8 MOTEL

Small-scale Hotel

Book at aaa.com

All Year [ECP] | 1P: $47-$85 | 2P: $53-$91 | XP: $6 | F12

Phone: (434)447-2313

Location: I-85, exit 12A, just n. 250 Thompson St 23950. Fax: 434/447-2313. **Facility:** 52 one-bedroom standard units, some with whirlpools. 3 stories, interior corridors. *Bath:* combo or shower only. **Parking:** on-site, winter plug-ins. **Terms:** package plans, pets ($10 deposit). **Amenities:** safes (fee). **Guest Services:** coin laundry. **Business Services:** meeting rooms. **Cards:** AX, DS, MC, VI.

SOME UNITS

------- **WHERE TO DINE** -------

KAHILL'S

American

Lunch: $5-$15 | Dinner: $5-$15 | **Phone: 434/447-6941**

Location: I-85, exit 15, just s; 2 mi n of downtown. 1799 N Mecklenburg Ave 23950. **Hours:** 7 am-10 pm. Closed: 11/24, 12/25. **Features:** Rustic dining room with wood pegged floors and log walls. Casual setting, entrees include pasta, regional seafood and steak. Also known for our Cowboy Chili breakfast. Casual dress; cocktails. **Parking:** on-site. **Cards:** AX, DS, MC, VI.

SPERRYVILLE

------- **WHERE TO DINE** -------

THORNTON RIVER GRILLE

American

Lunch: $6-$14 | Dinner: $10-$20 | **Phone: 540/987-8790**

Location: Just n on SR 522. 3710 SperryVille Pike 22740. **Hours:** 11 am-3 & 5-9 pm, Sun 10 am-3 pm. Closed: 1/1, 11/24, 12/25; also Mon. **Features:** Thornton River Grille offers all the classic American favorites as well as beef and seafood entrees and hometown friendly service. Casual dress; cocktails. **Parking:** on-site. **Cards:** AX, CB, DC, DS, JC, MC, VI.

SPRINGFIELD — *See District Of Columbia p. 548.*

STAFFORD

------- **WHERE TO STAY** -------

COMFORT INN

(AAA) SAVE

Small-scale Hotel

Book at aaa.com

4/1-10/31 | 1P: $89-$109 | 2P: $89-$109 | XP: $10 | F18
3/1-3/31 & 11/1-2/28 | 1P: $79-$99 | 2P: $79-$99 | XP: $10 | F18

Phone: (540)659-8999

Location: I-95, exit 143, w on Garrisonville Rd. 20 Salisbury Dr 22554. Fax: 540/659-8005. **Facility:** 83 one-bedroom standard units, some with whirlpools. 4 stories, interior corridors. *Bath:* combo or shower only. **Parking:** on-site. **Terms:** cancellation fee imposed, [ECP] meal plan available. **Amenities:** dual phone lines, voice mail, safes, irons, hair dryers. **Pool(s):** outdoor. **Leisure Activities:** whirlpool, exercise room. **Guest Services:** valet and coin laundry. **Business Services:** meeting rooms, business center. **Cards:** AX, CB, DC, DS, JC, MC, VI. **Special Amenities:** free continental breakfast and free local telephone calls.

SOME UNITS

COUNTRY INN BY CARLSON

(AAA) SAVE

Small-scale Hotel

Book at aaa.com

3/1-10/31 [ECP] | 1P: $79-$109 | 2P: $79-$109 | XP: $6 | F18
11/1-2/28 [ECP] | 1P: $64-$109 | 2P: $64-$109 | XP: $6 | F18

Phone: (540)659-4330

Location: I-95, exit 143B, just w. 153 Garrisonville Rd 22554. Fax: 540/659-3987. **Facility:** 58 one-bedroom standard units, some with whirlpools. 2 stories (no elevator), interior corridors. *Bath:* combo or shower only. **Parking:** on-site. **Terms:** cancellation fee imposed. **Amenities:** high-speed Internet, dual phone lines, voice mail, irons, hair dryers. **Leisure Activities:** exercise room. **Guest Services:** valet and coin laundry. **Business Services:** meeting rooms, fax. **Cards:** AX, CB, DC, DS, MC, VI. **Special Amenities:** free expanded continental breakfast and free local telephone calls. *(See color ad p 847)*

SOME UNITS

DAYS INN AQUIA-QUANTICO
Book at aaa.com

 SAVE

Small-scale Hotel

Phone: (540)659-0022

All Year [ECP]   1P: $73-$76   2P: $73-$89   XP: $5   F13
Location: I-95, exit 143A, jct US 1 and SR 610. Located adjacent to Aquia Town Center. 2868 Jefferson Davis Hwy 22554. **Fax:** 540/659-0212. **Facility:** 123 one-bedroom standard units. 2 stories (no elevator), exterior corridors. **Parking:** on-site. **Terms:** 7 day cancellation notice-fee imposed, pets ($6 extra charge, in smoking units). **Amenities:** hair dryers. *Some:* high-speed Internet, dual phone lines, voice mail. **Dining:** King Street Blues, see separate listing. **Pool(s):** outdoor. **Guest Services:** valet and coin laundry. **Business Services:** meeting rooms, fax (fee). **Cards:** AX, CB, DC, DS, JC, MC, VI. **Special Amenities:** free expanded continental breakfast and free room upgrade (subject to availability with advance reservations).

SOME UNITS

HAMPTON INN
Book at aaa.com

Small-scale Hotel

Phone: 540/657-0999

Property failed to provide current rates
Location: I-95, exit 143A, just n of jct Garrisonville Rd. 2925 Jefferson Davis Hwy 22554. **Fax:** 540/657-4711. **Facility:** 88 one-bedroom standard units, some with whirlpools. 4 stories, interior corridors. *Bath:* combo or shower only. **Parking:** on-site. **Amenities:** dual phone lines, voice mail, irons, hair dryers. **Pool(s):** outdoor. **Leisure Activities:** limited exercise equipment. **Guest Services:** valet laundry. **Business Services:** meeting rooms, fax.

SOME UNITS

HOLIDAY INN EXPRESS
Book at aaa.com

Small-scale Hotel

Phone: (540)657-5566

3/1-9/30   1P: $99-$119   2P: $99-$119   XP: $10   F18
10/1-2/28   1P: $99-$109   2P: $99-$109   XP: $10   F18
Location: I-95, exit 143B, just w. 28 Greenspring Dr 22554. **Fax:** 540/657-4840. **Facility:** 54 units. 50 one-bedroom standard units, some with whirlpools. 4 one-bedroom suites ($109-$149). 2 stories, interior corridors. *Bath:* combo or shower only. **Parking:** on-site. **Amenities:** dual phone lines, voice mail, irons, hair dryers. **Leisure Activities:** exercise room. **Guest Services:** valet laundry. **Business Services:** meeting rooms, fax (fee). **Cards:** AX, CB, DC, DS, MC, VI.

SOME UNITS

SUPER 8 MOTEL
Book at aaa.com

Motel

Phone: (540)659-9990

All Year   1P: $59-$79   2P: $69-$89   XP: $10   F8
Location: I-95, exit 143B, just w. 25 Wicomico Dr 22554. **Fax:** 540/659-9571. **Facility:** 27 one-bedroom standard units. 2 stories (no elevator), exterior corridors. **Parking:** on-site. **Terms:** cancellation fee imposed. **Business Services:** fax. **Cards:** AX, DC, DS, MC, VI.

SOME UNITS

WINGATE INN STAFFORD
Book at aaa.com

Small-scale Hotel

Phone: (540)659-3600

All Year [ECP]   1P: $85   2P: $85   XP: $10   F
Location: I-95, exit 143B, just w on Garrisonville Rd. 15 Salsibury Dr 22554. **Fax:** 540/659-8995. **Facility:** 99 one-bedroom standard units, some with whirlpools. 4 stories, interior corridors. *Bath:* combo or shower only. **Parking:** on-site. **Terms:** 7 day cancellation notice. **Amenities:** video games, high-speed Internet, dual phone lines, voice mail, safes, irons, hair dryers. **Pool(s):** heated indoor. **Leisure Activities:** exercise room. **Guest Services:** valet and coin laundry. **Business Services:** meeting rooms, business center. **Cards:** AX, CB, DC, DS, JC, MC, VI.

SOME UNITS

—— WHERE TO DINE ——

IMPERIAL GARDEN RESTAURANT

Chinese

Lunch: $4-$6   **Dinner:** $8-$19   **Phone:** 540/720-2200
Location: I-95, exit 143A, jct SR 610; in Aquia Town Center. 2848 Jefferson Davis Hwy, Suite 806 22554. **Hours:** 11:30 am-10 pm. Closed: 11/24, 12/25. **Features:** A stately grand piano sits in the center of the dining room, which has a more upscale feel than most restaurants of its type. Exceptional, well-presented entrees are offered with such special complements as enticing plates of flavorful hors d'oeuvres and a fine hot and sour soup. Casual dress; cocktails. **Parking:** on-site. **Cards:** AX, DC, DS, MC, VI.

KING STREET BLUES

American

Lunch: $7-$14   **Dinner:** $7-$14   **Phone:** 540/288-1100
Location: I-95, exit 143A, jct US 1 and SR 610; in Days Inn Aquia-Quantico. 2866 Jefferson Davis Hwy 22554. **Hours:** 11 am-10 pm, Fri & Sat-11 pm. Closed: 11/24, 12/25. **Features:** The atmosphere is joyful and exuberant with colorful papier mache figures popping out from all corners; the menu is lively as well with barbecue and ribs a specialty but a large list of other offerings as well from salads to macaroni bowls. Casual dress; cocktails. **Parking:** on-site. **Cards:** AX, DC, DS, MC, VI.

THE LOG CABIN

Seafood

Dinner: $14-$30   **Phone:** 540/659-5067
Location: I-95, exit 140, 1.5 mi e to US 1, then 1 mi s. 1749 Jefferson Davis Hwy 22554. **Hours:** 4 pm-10 pm. Closed major holidays. **Reservations:** suggested. **Features:** The natural bark log interior and brick fireplace contribute to the warm, cozy ambience of the rustic dining room. Steak, pasta and seafood choices, including many dishes with fresh Chesapeake blue crab and Maine lobster, make up an interesting, tempting menu. Casual dress; cocktails. **Parking:** on-site. **Cards:** AX, MC, VI.

SOUTHERN FLAVOR FISH & CHIPS

Seafood

Parking: on-site.

Lunch: $4-$14   **Dinner:** $4-$14   **Phone:** 540/288-8868
Location: I-95, exit 143, just s on US 1. 2608 Jefferson Davis Hwy, Suite 108 22554. **Hours:** noon-8 pm, Fri & Sat-9 pm. Closed major holidays; also Sun & Mon. **Features:** Fried fish and country-style vegetables—from collards to macaroni and cheese—are pleasing tastes at the bright, tidy spot. Among other offerings served in hearty portions are fried chicken and ribs. Locals frequent this place for take-home meals. Casual dress.

VINNY'S ITALIAN GRILL & PIZZERIA

Lunch: $5-$11 **Dinner:** $5-$11 **Phone:** 540/657-8400

▼◇▼◇▼◇▼

Italian

Location: I-95, exit 143B, 1.5 mi w; in Garrison Village Center. 397 Garrisonville Rd, Suite 105 22554. **Hours:** 11 am-10 pm, Fri & Sat-11 pm, Sun noon-10 pm. Closed major holidays; also 12/24. **Features:** Whether taking-out or eating-in, patrons can choose from many tasty options, including pasta and fish dishes, veal parmigiana and pizza—by the slice or by the pie. The dining room is cozy. Casual dress; beer & wine only. **Parking:** on-site. **Cards:** AX, DS, MC, VI.

✕

ZUM RHEINGARTEN RESTAURANT

Dinner: $17-$23 **Phone:** 703/221-4635

▼◇▼◇▼◇▼

German

Location: I-95, exit 150A southbound, 3 mi s on US 1; exit 143A northbound, 4.5 mi n on US 1. 3998 Jefferson Davis Hwy 22554. **Hours:** 5 pm-9 pm, Sun 4 pm-8 pm. Closed: 7/4, 12/24, 12/25; also Mon, Tues, 8/20-8/30 & Super Bowl Sun. **Reservations:** suggested, weekends. **Features:** The restaurant is housed in a quaint stone farmhouse whose stone terrace serves as a summer beer garden. Dining rooms center around a stone hearth and whimsical murals highlight some of the walls. The menu offers authentic dishes such as sauerbraten, Wiener schnitzel, bratwurst, and spatzle. Traditional side dishes include red cabbage, potato dumplings, and potato pancakes. Don't forget the traditional dessert of apple streudel and black forest cake. Dressy casual; cocktails. **Parking:** on-site. **Cards:** AX, DC, MC, VI.

✕

STANLEY pop. 1,326

——— WHERE TO STAY ———

MILTON HOUSE BED & BREAKFAST INN

All Year [BP] 1P: $85-$155 2P: $85-$155 **Phone:** (540)778-2495

▼◇▼◇▼◇▼

Historic Bed & Breakfast

Location: On US 340 business route; center. 113 W Main St 22851 (PO Box 366). **Facility:** In the Shenandoah Valley, this B&B offers mountain views in two directions; guest rooms and common areas mix urban and rural decor. 4 one-bedroom standard units, some with whirlpools. 2 stories (no elevator), interior/exterior corridors. *Bath:* combo or shower only. **Parking:** on-site. **Terms:** 2 night minimum stay - weekends, age restrictions may apply, 7 day cancellation notice-fee imposed, weekly rates available. **Amenities:** irons. *Some:* CD players, hair dryers. **Guest Services:** gift shop. **Business Services:** meeting rooms. **Cards:** AX, CB, DC, DS, MC, VI.

SOME UNITS

(ASK) (S/D) ✕ ☎ / (VCR) 🔲 🔲

STAUNTON pop. 23,853

——— WHERE TO STAY ———

ASHTON COUNTRY HOUSE

Phone: (540)885-7819

5/1-10/30 [BP] 1P: $80-$110 2P: $95-$140 XP: $20 F10

▼◇▼◇▼◇▼

Bed & Breakfast

Location: I-81, exit 220, 1 mi to SR 252 (Middlebrook Ave), then 0.3 mi n. Located in a quiet rural area. 1205 Middlebrook Ave 24401. Fax: 540/885-6029. **Facility:** This country mansion, dating from 1860, offers a porch swing and gardens as well as scenic mountain views. Smoke free premises. 6 one-bedroom standard units. 2 stories (no elevator), interior corridors. *Bath:* combo or shower only. **Parking:** on-site. **Terms:** open 5/1-10/30, check-in 4 pm, 2 night minimum stay - seasonal and/or weekends, 7 day cancellation notice, package plans. **Amenities:** video library. **Business Services:** meeting rooms. **Cards:** AX, DC, MC, VI.

SOME UNITS

(ASK) (S/D) 🛏 🛗 ✕ ☎ / (PV) (VCR)

THE BELLE GRAE INN AND RESTAURANT

Phone: (540)886-5151

All Year 2P: $109-$299 XP: $35

▼◇▼◇▼◇▼

Historic Country Inn

Location: Between N Madison and N Jefferson sts. 515 W Frederick St 24401-3333. Fax: 540/886-6641. **Facility:** Private baths adjoin all guest rooms at this comfortably restored Victorian mansion; set in an urban area, it is within walking distance of shops. Smoke free premises. 14 one-bedroom standard units, some with whirlpools. 2 stories (no elevator), interior/exterior corridors. *Bath:* combo or shower only. **Parking:** on-site. **Terms:** 2 night minimum stay - seasonal, age restrictions may apply, 3 day cancellation notice-fee imposed, weekly rates available, package plans, $10 service charge, no pets allowed (owner's dog on premises). **Amenities:** hair dryers. *Some:* irons. **Dining:** dining room, see separate listing. **Guest Services:** coin laundry. **Business Services:** meeting rooms. **Cards:** AX, DC, MC, VI.

SOME UNITS

(ASK) (S/D) 🍽 ✕ / (PV) ☎ 🔲 🖥 🔲

BEST WESTERN STAUNTON INN

Book at aaa.com

Phone: (540)885-1112

(AAA) (SAVE)

All Year [ECP] 1P: $59-$125 2P: $64-$130 XP: $10 F15

▼◇▼◇▼◇▼

Small-scale Hotel

Location: I-81, exit 222, just e on US 250. 92 Rowe Rd 24401. Fax: 540/885-0166. **Facility:** 80 one-bedroom standard units. 4 stories, interior corridors. **Parking:** on-site. **Terms:** small pets only. **Amenities:** irons, hair dryers. **Pool(s):** heated indoor. **Guest Services:** valet laundry. **Business Services:** meeting rooms. **Cards:** AX, CB, DC, DS, JC, MC, VI. **Special Amenities:** free expanded continental breakfast.

SOME UNITS

(S/D) 🛏 🍽 🌀 🛟 🎬 (DATA PORT) 🔲 / ✕ 🔲 🖥

COMFORT INN

Book at aaa.com

Phone: (540)886-5000

(AAA) (SAVE)

All Year [ECP] 1P: $69-$119 2P: $69-$119 XP: $10 F18

▼◇▼◇▼◇▼

Small-scale Hotel

Location: I-81, exit 222, just w on US 250. 1302 Richmond Ave 24401. Fax: 540/886-6643. **Facility:** 98 one-bedroom standard units, some with whirlpools. 5 stories, interior corridors. **Parking:** on-site. **Terms:** small pets only ($10 extra charge, in smoking units). **Amenities:** voice mail, safes, irons, hair dryers. **Pool(s):** outdoor. **Cards:** AX, CB, DC, DS, JC, MC, VI. **Special Amenities:** free expanded continental breakfast and free newspaper.

SOME UNITS

(S/D) 🛏 🍽 🌀 🛟 🎬 (DATA PORT) 🔲 🖥 🔲 / ✕ /

FEE

DAYS INN - BUSINESS PLACE

Book at aaa.com

Phone: (540)248-0888

(AAA) (SAVE)
◇◇◇◇ ◇◇

Small-scale Hotel

All Year   1P: $49-$90   2P: $49-$90

Location: I-81, exit 225, just w. 273-D Bells Ln 24401. Fax: 540/248-2736. **Facility:** 92 one-bedroom standard units. 2 stories (no elevator), exterior corridors. *Bath:* combo or shower only. **Parking:** on-site. **Terms:** weekly rates available, package plans, small pets only ($10 extra charge). **Amenities:** voice mail, irons, hair dryers. **Pool(s):** outdoor. **Leisure Activities:** exercise room. **Guest Services:** coin laundry. **Business Services:** meeting rooms. **Cards:** AX, CB, DC, DS, MC, VI. **Special Amenities:** free continental breakfast and free newspaper.

SOME UNITS

[icons] FEE

ECONO LODGE STAUNTON

Book at aaa.com

Phone: (540)885-5158

(AAA) (SAVE)
◇◇◇◇ ◇◇

Motel

10/1-10/31	1P: $62-$82	2P: $66-$86	XP: $4 F18
3/1-9/30 & 11/1-2/28	1P: $52-$79	2P: $56-$84	XP: $4 F18

Location: I-81, exit 222, 0.7 mi w on US 250. 1031 Richmond Ave 24401. Fax: 540/885-5281. **Facility:** 88 one-bedroom standard units. 2 stories (no elevator), interior/exterior corridors. **Parking:** on-site. **Terms:** [CP] meal plan available, small pets only ($10 fee). **Guest Services:** coin laundry. **Cards:** AX, CB, DC, DS, MC, VI. **Special Amenities:** free continental breakfast and free local telephone calls.

SOME UNITS

[icons] FEE

FREDERICK HOUSE

Phone: (540)885-4220

(AAA) (SAVE)
◇◇◇◇ ◇◇

Small-scale Hotel

10/1-2/28 [BP]	1P: $95-$165	2P: $95-$195	XP: $35
3/1-9/30 [BP]	1P: $85-$155	2P: $85-$175	XP: $35

Location: I-81, exit 222, New and Frederick sts; 2 mi w on US 250; downtown. 28 N New St 24401. Fax: 540/885-5180. **Facility:** Smoke free premises. 23 units. 19 one- and 4 two-bedroom standard units. 2-3 stories (no elevator), interior/exterior corridors. *Bath:* combo or shower only. **Parking:** on-site. **Terms:** package plans. **Guest Services:** valet laundry. **Business Services:** meeting rooms. **Cards:** AX, DC, DS, MC, VI. **Special Amenities:** free full breakfast and free local telephone calls.

SOME UNITS

[icons] / VCR

GUESTHOUSE INN

Book at aaa.com

Phone: (540)885-3117

◇◇◇ ◇◇

Motel

4/1-10/31	1P: $60-$110	2P: $60-$110	XP: $8 F18
3/1-3/31 & 11/1-2/28	1P: $52-$75	2P: $52-$75	XP: $8 F18

Location: I-81, exit 222, just e on US 250. Truck and camper parking. 42 Sangers Ln 24401. Fax: 540/885-5620. **Facility:** 88 one-bedroom standard units, some with whirlpools. 2 stories (no elevator), exterior corridors. *Bath:* combo or shower only. **Parking:** on-site. **Amenities:** *Some:* hair dryers. **Pool(s):** heated indoor. **Leisure Activities:** sauna, whirlpool, exercise room. **Guest Services:** valet laundry. **Cards:** AX, DS, MC, VI.

[icons]

HAMPTON INN

Book at aaa.com

Phone: (540)886-7000

(AAA) (SAVE)
◇◇◇◇ ◇◇

Small-scale Hotel

5/1-10/31 [BP]	1P: $89-$140	2P: $94-$140	
3/1-4/30 [BP]	1P: $84-$109	2P: $89-$109	
11/1-2/28 [BP]	1P: $79-$109	2P: $84-$109	

Location: I-81, exit 220, 0.6 mi w on US 11. 40 Payne Ln 24401. Fax: 540/886-7098. **Facility:** 76 one-bedroom standard units. 3 stories, interior corridors. *Bath:* combo or shower only. **Parking:** on-site. **Terms:** package plans. **Amenities:** voice mail, irons, hair dryers. **Pool(s):** outdoor. **Leisure Activities:** exercise room. **Guest Services:** valet laundry. **Business Services:** meeting rooms. **Cards:** AX, CB, DC, DS, JC, MC, VI. **Special Amenities:** free full breakfast and free local telephone calls.

SOME UNITS

[icons] FEE FEE FEE

HOLIDAY INN GOLF & CONFERENCE CENTER *Book at aaa.com*   Phone: (540)248-6020

(AAA) (SAVE)

All Year   1P: $64-$200   2P: $64-$200

▼▼▼▼

Location: I-81, exit 225, 0.3 mi w on SR 275 (Woodrow Wilson Pkwy). 152 Fairway Ln 24401 (PO Box 3209, 24402). **Fax:** 540/248-2902. **Facility:** 114 one-bedroom standard units. 6 stories, interior corridors. **Parking:** on-site. **Terms:** package plans, small pets only ($10 extra charge). **Amenities:** voice mail, irons, hair dryers.

Small-scale Hotel

Dining: Cafe on the Green, see separate listing. **Pool(s):** heated indoor. **Leisure Activities:** exercise room. **Fee:** golf & tennis privileges. **Guest Services:** valet laundry, airport transportation-Shenandoah Regional Airport, area transportation-Amtrak & bus station. **Business Services:** conference facilities. **Cards:** AX, CB, DC, DS, JC, MC, VI. **Special Amenities: free local telephone calls and free newspaper.** *(See ad p 883)*

SOME UNITS

(S)(D) (✈) FEE (¶)(Y)(⌁)(☂)(⊛) (□) / (✕) (📶) FEE

MICROTEL INN *Book at aaa.com*   Phone: (540)887-0200

(AAA) (SAVE)

3/1-11/30	1P: $54-$74	2P: $54-$74	XP: $10	F16
12/1-2/28	1P: $44-$69	2P: $44-$69	XP: $10	F16

▼▼ ▼▼

Location: I-81, exit 222, 0.4 mi w on US 250, then 0.3 mi s. 200 Frontier Dr 24401. Fax: 540/887-9676. **Facility:** 58 one-bedroom standard units. 2 stories, interior corridors. *Bath:* combo or shower only. **Parking:** on-site.

Small-scale Hotel

Terms: cancellation fee imposed. **Pool(s):** heated outdoor, wading. **Leisure Activities:** playground. **Guest Services:** coin laundry. **Business Services:** meeting rooms. **Cards:** AX, DC, DS, MC, VI. **Special Amenities: free continental breakfast and free local telephone calls.** *(See color ad below)*

SOME UNITS

(S)(D) (♿) (⌁)(☂)(⊛) (DATA PORT) / (✕) (🛢)(🖥) /

QUALITY INN-CONFERENCE CENTER *Book at aaa.com*   Phone: (540)248-5111

(AAA) (SAVE)

All Year   1P: $55-$95   2P: $55-$95   XP: $5   F17

▼▼▼▼

Location: I-81, exit 225, just e on SR 275 (Woodrow Wilson Pkwy). 96 Baker Ln 24401. Fax: 540/248-5111. **Facility:** 100 one-bedroom standard units. 2 stories (no elevator), exterior corridors. **Parking:** on-site.

Small-scale Hotel

Terms: pets ($6 extra charge, in designated units). **Amenities:** irons, hair dryers. **Pool(s):** outdoor. **Guest Services:** coin laundry. **Business Services:** meeting rooms. **Cards:** AX, DC, DS, MC, VI. **Special Amenities: free local telephone calls and free newspaper.**

SOME UNITS

(S)(D) (🐾) FEE (⌁)(☂)(⊛) (□) / (✕) (DATA PORT) (🛢) /

THE SAMPSON EAGON INN   Phone: (540)886-8200

▼▼▼▼

All Year [BP]   1P: $98-$130   2P: $115-$150   XP: $30

Bed & Breakfast

Location: I-81, exit 222; corner of N Coalter and E Beverley sts, just s of the Woodrow Wilson Birthplace; parking entry on N Coalter St; downtown. 238 E Beverley St 24401. **Facility:** Modern comforts mingle with antique furnishings at this restored 1840 home; breakfast is served on crystal and bone china. Smoke free premises. 5 one-bedroom standard units. 2 stories (no elevator), interior corridors. *Bath:* combo or shower only. **Parking:** on-site. **Terms:** 2 night minimum stay - weekends, age restrictions may apply, 7 day cancellation notice. **Amenities:** CD players, irons. **Cards:** AX, MC, VI.

SOME UNITS

(✕) (VCR) (DATA PORT) / (🛢) /

SLEEP INN   *Book at aaa.com*   Phone: (540)887-6500

(AAA) (SAVE)

All Year [ECP]   1P: $59-$128   2P: $64-$130   XP: $10   F15

Location: I-81, exit 222, just e on US 250. 222 Jefferson Hwy 24401. **Fax:** 540/885-8325. **Facility:** 87 one-bedroom standard units. 4 stories, interior corridors. *Bath:* combo or shower only. **Parking:** on-site. **Terms:** small pets only. **Amenities:** voice mail, hair dryers. *Some:* irons. **Leisure Activities:** pool privileges.

Small-scale Hotel   **Guest Services:** valet laundry. **Cards:** AX, CB, DC, DS, JC, MC, VI.

SOME UNITS

SUPER 8 MOTEL   *Book at aaa.com*   Phone: (540)886-2888

(AAA) (SAVE)

10/1-10/31	1P: $55-$89	2P: $65-$99	XP: $5 D10
3/1-9/30	1P: $48-$79	2P: $55-$89	XP: $5 D10
11/1-2/28	1P: $40-$65	2P: $45-$75	XP: $5 D10

Motel

Location: I-81, exit 222, 1.2 mi w on US 250. 1015 Richmond Rd 24401. **Fax:** 540/886-7432. **Facility:** 63 one-bedroom standard units. 2 stories (no elevator), interior corridors. *Bath:* combo or shower only. **Parking:** on-site. **Terms:** 3 day cancellation notice-fee imposed, package plans, small pets only ($10 extra charge). **Cards:** AX, CB, DC, DS, JC, MC, VI. **Special Amenities:** free continental breakfast and free local telephone calls.

SOME UNITS

FEE

THORNROSE HOUSE AT GYPSY HILL   Phone: (540)885-7026

All Year [BP]   1P: $65-$85   2P: $75-$95   XP: $20

Bed & Breakfast   **Location:** I-81, exit 222, 3.2 mi w via US 250 through downtown, then just s. Located adjacent to Gypsy Hill Park. 531 Thornrose Ave 24401. **Fax:** 540/885-6458. **Facility:** An acre of gardens surrounds this comfortable 1912 Georgian home; in the parlor is a "bottomless" cookie jar that is kept filled for guests. Smoke free premises. 5 one-bedroom standard units. 2 stories (no elevator), interior corridors. *Bath:* combo or shower only. **Parking:** on-site. **Terms:** 2 night minimum stay - seasonal and/or weekends, age restrictions may apply, 7 day cancellation notice. **Amenities:** *Some:* hair dryers. **Guest Services:** area transportation. **Business Services:** meeting rooms. **Cards:** AX, MC, VI.

———— WHERE TO DINE ————

THE BELLE GRAE INN & RESTAURANT   Dinner: $18-$38   Phone: 540/886-5151

Regional American   **Location:** Between N Madison and N Jefferson sts; in The Belle Grae Inn & Restaurant. 515 W Frederick St 24401-3333. **Hours:** 5:30 pm-9 pm. Closed: Mon & Tues; also Wed in winter. **Features:** Creaky wooden floors are expected in the historic inn, and so is the stylish fare. Picnic dinner baskets for two, $50, with wine are available on Monday. The premises are smoke-free. Casual dress; cocktails. **Parking:** on-site and valet. **Cards:** AX, MC, VI. **Historic**

BISMARK BEEF COMPANY   Dinner: $9-$20   Phone: 540/885-1390

American   **Location:** I-81, exit 222, just w. 1300 Churchville St 24401. **Hours:** 5 pm-10 pm. Closed: 11/24, 12/25; also Mon. **Reservations:** suggested, weekends. **Features:** Wonderful selections of choice cut steaks awaits at this restaurant. Friendly service and do not miss the filet mignon. Casual dress; cocktails. **Parking:** on-site. **Cards:** AX, MC, VI.

CAFE ON THE GREEN   Lunch: $4-$8   Dinner: $8-$18   Phone: 540/248-6020

American   **Location:** I-81, exit 225, 0.3 mi w on SR 275 (Woodrow Wilson Pkwy); in Holiday Inn Golf & Conference Center. 152 Fairway Ln 22401. **Hours:** 6:30 am-2 & 5-10 pm, Sat from 7 am. Closed: 12/25. **Features:** The "hen house," chicken salad in cantaloupe, is fresh and incorporates a generous array of four fruits. French onion soup is tasty and hot. Beef is the house specialty. Popular, too, is the golf course view, with some tables affording better views than others. Casual dress; cocktails. **Parking:** on-site. **Cards:** AX, CB, DC, DS, JC, MC, VI.

THE DEPOT GRILLE   Lunch: $6-$22   Dinner: $6-$22   Phone: 540/885-7332

American   **Location:** I-81, exit 222; downtown; in the Wharf Historic District; at train station. 42 Middlebrook Ave 24401. **Hours:** 11 am-11 pm. Closed: 11/24, 12/25. **Features:** The Depot Grille is set at a converted train station with wonderful ambience and a diverse menu. Casual dress; cocktails. **Parking:** on-site. **Cards:** AX, CB, DC, DS, JC, MC, VI.

THE DINING ROOM   Lunch: $12-$20   Dinner: $14-$31   Phone: 540/213-0606

American   **Location:** Augusta and Frederick sts; 2 mi w of US 250; downtown. 29 N Augusta St 24401. **Hours:** 11 am-2:30 & 4:30-10 pm. Closed: 12/25; also Sun. **Reservations:** suggested, weekends. **Features:** In historic old downtown, the dining area displays a cozy and elegant decor. Formally attired staff members present an upscale menu and wine list. Casual dress; cocktails. **Parking:** street. **Cards:** AX, CB, DC, DS, JC, MC, VI.

L'ITALIA RESTAURANT   Lunch: $6-$10   Dinner: $10-$21   Phone: 540/885-0102

Italian   **Location:** I-81, exit 222, just w. 23 E Beverly St 24401. **Hours:** 11 am-10 pm, Fri & Sat-11 pm, Sun-9 pm. Closed major holidays; also Mon. **Features:** Attractive paintings, plants and soft music set a relaxed mood in the cozy restaurant. Veal, pasta and seafood dishes as well as such specialties as chicken rolatini make up a thoughtful, pleasing menu. Servers are knowledgeable and professional. Casual dress; cocktails. **Parking:** street. **Cards:** AX, CB, DC, DS, MC, VI.

MILL STREET GRILL   Lunch: $7-$18   Dinner: $10-$20   Phone: 540/886-0656

American   **Location:** I-81, exit 222, just w. 1 Mill St 24401. **Hours:** 4 pm-10 pm, Fri & Sat-10:30 pm, Sun 11:30 am-10 pm. Closed: 11/24, 12/25. **Reservations:** suggested, weekends. **Features:** This restaurant is a contemporary environment with many American favorites. Do not miss the ribs. Casual dress; cocktails. **Parking:** on-site. **Cards:** AX, CB, DC, DS, JC, MC, VI.

MRS ROWE'S FAMILY RESTAURANT & BAKERY **Lunch:** $6-$10 **Dinner:** $6-$13 **Phone:** 540/886-1833
American
Cards: DS, MC, VI.
Location: I-81, exit 222, just e on US 250. Rowe Rd 24401. **Hours:** 7 am-9 pm, Sun-7 pm. Closed major holidays. **Features:** Reliable country specialties range from spoon bread to baked tomatoes to rich homemade pie. Family-owned and operated since 1947, the wonderful eatery—and Mrs. Rowe—are popular and with good reason. Peak hours can be busy. Casual dress; beer & wine only. **Parking:** on-site.

THE PULLMAN RESTAURANT **Lunch:** $5-$10 **Dinner:** $6-$20 **Phone:** 540/885-6612
American
Historic
Location: I-81, exit 222; downtown; in the Wharf Historic District; at train station. 36 Middlebrook Ave 24401. **Hours:** 11 am-11 pm, Sun-9 pm. Closed: 11/24, 12/25. **Features:** In the restored C&O Railroad Station, the restaurant welcomes diners back to the days of Victorian-style soda fountains and ice cream parlors. A daily changing menu is offered. Casual dress; cocktails. **Parking:** on-site. **Cards:** AX, CB, DC, DS, MC, VI.

SHORTY'S DINER **Lunch:** $5-$12 **Dinner:** $5-$15 **Phone:** 540/885-8861
American
Location: I-81, exit 222, 1.2 mi w on US 250. 1013 Richmond Ave 24401. **Hours:** 7 am-10 pm. Closed: 12/25. **Features:** Shorty's Diner offers wonderfully friendly service. A diverse American menu and a nostalgic setting. Casual dress. **Parking:** on-site. **Cards:** AX, CB, DC, DS, JC, MC, VI.

WRIGHT'S DAIRY-RITE FAMILY RESTAURANT **Lunch:** $5-$10 **Dinner:** $5-$12 **Phone:** 540/886-0435
American
Location: I-81, exit 222, 1.7 mi w on US 250, just s. 346 Greenville Ave 24401. **Hours:** 9 am-9 pm, Fri & Sat-11 pm. Closed: 1/1, 12/25. **Features:** The nostalgic restaurant has been family owned and operated since 1952 and offers exceedingly friendly service. Casual dress. **Parking:** on-site.

STEELES TAVERN

――――― **WHERE TO STAY** ―――――

STEELES TAVERN MANOR COUNTRY INN **Phone:** (540)377-6444
All Year [BP] 2P: $135-$220
Historic Bed & Breakfast
Location: I-81, exit 205, 1.5 mi e on SR 606, then just s. Rt 11, Box 39 24476. **Fax:** 540/377-5937. **Facility:** The landscaped grounds of this 1916 manor home are designed around a pond and a creek where tubing is popular; dinners are served upon prior request. Smoke free premises. 8 units. 5 one-bedroom standard units with whirlpools. 3 cabins ($185-$220) with whirlpools. 2 stories (no elevator); interior/exterior corridors. **Parking:** on-site. **Terms:** 2 night minimum stay - weekends, age restrictions may apply, 14 day cancellation notice-fee imposed, package plans. **Amenities:** video library, CD players, irons, hair dryers. **Pool(s):** outdoor. **Leisure Activities:** fishing, hiking trails, horseshoes. **Guest Services:** gift shop, complimentary evening beverages, valet laundry. **Business Services:** meeting rooms. **Cards:** DS, MC, VI.

SOME UNITS

STEPHENS CITY pop. 1,146

――――― **WHERE TO STAY** ―――――

COMFORT INN-STEPHENS CITY *Book at aaa.com* **Phone:** (540)869-6500

	1P: $65-$95	2P: $69-$99	XP: $5	F18
3/1-10/31				
11/1-2/28	1P: $65-$95	2P: $69	XP: $5	F18

Small-scale Hotel
Location: I-81, exit 307, just se. 167 Town Run Ln 22655. **Fax:** 540/869-2558. **Facility:** 60 one-bedroom standard units, some with whirlpools. 2 stories (no elevator); interior corridors. **Parking:** on-site. **Terms:** small pets only ($10 extra charge). **Amenities:** voice mail, irons, hair dryers. **Pool(s):** outdoor. **Guest Services:** valet laundry. **Cards:** AX, CB, DC, DS, JC, MC, VI. **Special Amenities:** free continental breakfast and free local telephone calls.

SOME UNITS
FEE

HOLIDAY INN EXPRESS *Book at aaa.com* **Phone:** (540)869-0909

	1P: $69-$85	2P: $69-$85	XP: $10	F18
5/1-10/31				
11/1-2/28	1P: $65-$79	2P: $65-$79	XP: $10	F18
3/1-4/30	1P: $62-$74	2P: $62-$74	XP: $10	F18

Small-scale Hotel
Location: I-81, exit 307, just se. 165 Town Run Ln 22655. **Fax:** 540/869-5499. **Facility:** 69 one-bedroom standard units, some with whirlpools. 3 stories, interior corridors. **Parking:** on-site. **Terms:** cancellation fee imposed. **Amenities:** voice mail, irons, hair dryers. **Pool(s):** outdoor. **Leisure Activities:** exercise room. **Guest Services:** coin laundry. **Business Services:** meeting rooms. **Cards:** AX, DC, DS, MC, VI.

SOME UNITS

――――― **WHERE TO DINE** ―――――

NEW TOWN TAVERN **Lunch:** $6-$15 **Dinner:** $8-$20 **Phone:** 540/868-0111
American
Location: I-81, exit 307, just se. 356 Fairfax Pike 22655. **Hours:** 11 am-1 am, Sun noon-11 pm. Closed major holidays. **Features:** The restaurant sets forth a winning combination of friendly service, a fun atmosphere and award-winning ribs that shouldn't be missed. The menu is lengthy. Casual dress; cocktails. **Parking:** on-site. **Cards:** AX, CB, DC, DS, MC, VI. **Historic**

STERLING —See District Of Columbia p. 550.

STONY CREEK pop. 202

------ **WHERE TO STAY** ------

HAMPTON INN-STONY CREEK
Book at aaa.com

Phone: (434)246-5500

(AAA) (SAVE)

All Year   1P: $79-$129   2P: $79-$129   XP: $10   F
Location: I-95, exit 33, just sw. 10476 Blue Star Hwy 23882. Fax: 434/246-5775. **Facility:** 70 one-bedroom standard units. 3 stories, interior corridors. *Bath:* combo or shower only. **Parking:** on-site. **Terms:** pets ($10 extra charge). **Amenities:** video games, high-speed Internet, voice mail, irons, hair dryers. **Pool(s):** outdoor.
Small-scale Hotel **Leisure Activities:** exercise room. **Guest Services:** coin laundry. **Business Services:** meeting rooms.
Cards: AX, DC, DS, JC, MC, VI. **Special Amenities: free expanded continental breakfast and free newspaper.**

SOME UNITS

SLEEP INN & SUITES   **Book at aaa.com**

Phone: (434)246-5100

(AAA) (SAVE)

All Year   1P: $60-$109   2P: $60-$109   XP: $10   F18
Location: I-95, exit 33, 0.3 mi s on SR 301. 11019 Blue Star Hwy 23882. Fax: 434/246-5115. **Facility:** 64 one-bedroom standard units. 3 stories, interior corridors. *Bath:* combo or shower only. **Parking:** on-site.
Small-scale Hotel **Terms:** pets ($10 extra charge). **Amenities:** high-speed Internet, dual phone lines, voice mail, irons, hair dryers. **Pool(s):** small heated indoor. **Leisure Activities:** exercise room. **Guest Services:** coin laundry.
Business Services: PC, fax. **Cards:** AX, DC, DS, MC, VI. **Special Amenities: free continental breakfast and free newspaper.**

SOME UNITS

ST. PAUL pop. 1,000

------ **WHERE TO DINE** ------

RUBY B'S HOMETOWN GRILL
Lunch: $7-$14   **Dinner:** $7-$18   Phone: 276/762-7701
Location: 0.5 mi n on US 58. 15535 Bull Run Rd 24283. **Hours:** 6:30 am-9 pm, Fri & Sat-10 pm. Closed major holidays. **Features:** The restaurant's name says it all. The "hometown grill" serves country cooking with a smile. Casual dress. **Parking:** on-site. **Cards:** MC, VI.

American

STRASBURG pop. 4,017

———— WHERE TO STAY ————

HOTEL STRASBURG   **Phone:** (540)465-9191

(AAA) (SAVE)   All Year   1P: $83-$105   2P: $83-$105   XP: $15   F
▼▼▼   **Location:** I-81, exit 298, 2.2 mi s on US 11, then just s. 213 Holliday St 22657. **Fax:** 540/465-4788. **Facility:** This
       service-oriented Victorian hotel offers scenic views, comfortable accommodations and easy access to
Historic   shops. 29 one-bedroom standard units, some with whirlpools. 3 stories (no elevator), interior corridors. *Bath:*
Country Inn   combo, shower or tub only. **Parking:** on-site. **Terms:** package plans, small pets only. **Amenities:** *Some:*
       hair dryers. **Dining:** restaurant, see separate listing. **Business Services:** meeting rooms. **Cards:** AX, CB,
       DC, DS, MC, VI. **Special Amenities:** free local telephone calls and preferred room (subject to
availability with advance reservations). *(See color ad below)*

                                                                        SOME UNITS

———— WHERE TO DINE ————

HOTEL STRASBURG RESTAURANT   **Lunch:** $6-$10   **Dinner:** $10-$22   **Phone:** 540/465-9191
▼▼▼   **Location:** I-81, exit 298, 2.2 mi s on US 11, just s; in Hotel Strasburg. 213 Holliday St 22657. **Hours:** 11:30 am-2:30
       & 5-9 pm, Fri & Sat 8-10:30 am, 11:30-2:30 & 5-10 pm, Sun 8-10:30 am, 11-2:30 & 3-9 pm.
Regional American   **Reservations:** suggested. **Features:** Victorian-period antiques and quaint decor set a casual, relaxed tone.
       The sophisticated menu focuses on pasta and veal specialties, such as sauteed veal scaloppine with diced
tomatoes, fresh mozzarella and wine sauce. The weekday lunch buffet is popular. The large lounge is perfect for pre-dinner
meetings or after-dinner drinks. Visitors should take a look at the inn. Casual dress; cocktails. **Parking:** on-site. **Cards:** AX, CB,
DC, DS, MC, VI. **Country Inn** *(See color ad below)*

SUFFOLK —See Hampton Roads Area p. 790.

SURRY pop. 262

──────── WHERE TO DINE ────────

THE SURREY HOUSE **Lunch:** $4-$18 **Dinner:** $4-$18 **Phone:** 757/294-3389
▼▼▼ ▼▼▼ **Location:** Just s jct SR 10 and 31. 11865 Rolfe Hwy 23883. **Hours:** 7:30 am-8 pm; to 9 am 4/1-9/30. Closed:
12/24-12/26; also 2nd week in Jan. **Reservations:** suggested. **Features:** Traditional Southern comfort
Regional American foods—fried chicken, country ham, fritters and turnip greens—taste as if Grandma made them. Servers in
long, country dresses and a dining room decorated in heavy wallpaper and dark wood reflect a quaint 1960s
Americana. Casual dress; beer & wine only. **Parking:** on-site. **Cards:** AX, MC, VI. ✖

TANGIER pop. 604

──────── WHERE TO STAY ────────

──────── *The following lodging was either not evaluated or did not* ────────
meet AAA rating requirements but is listed for your information only.

SHIRLEY'S BAY VIEW INN **Phone:** 757/891-2396
[fyi] Not evaluated. **Location:** West side of island. W Ridge Rd 23440 (Box 183). Facilities, services, and decor
characterize a basic property.

──────── WHERE TO DINE ────────

──────── *The following restaurant has not been evaluated by AAA* ────────
but is listed for your information only.

HILDA CROCKETT'S CHESAPEAKE HOUSE **Phone:** 757/891-2331
[fyi] Not evaluated. **Location:** 16243 Main Ridge Rd 23440. **Features:** This is the spot to stop for meals any
Southern grandmother would be proud to serve. All served family style at long tables, heaping platters of
crabcakes, clam fritters, baked ham, hot rolls, corn pudding, potato salad, and more.

TAPPAHANNOCK pop. 2,068

──────── WHERE TO STAY ────────

SUPER 8 MOTEL *Book at aaa.com* **Phone:** 804/443-3888
▼ All Year 1P: $50-$71 2P: $56-$76 XP: $6 F13
Motel **Location:** SR 17 and 360. 1800 Tappahannock Blvd 22560 (PO Box 1748). Fax: 804/443-3888. **Facility:** 43 one-
bedroom standard units. 2 stories (no elevator), interior corridors. **Parking:** on-site. **Terms:** pets ($6 fee).
Cards: AX, DC, DS, MC, VI.

SOME UNITS
(ASK) (S) (🛏) (📶) (🎥) / (✖) (🏢) (📷) /
FEE

──────── WHERE TO DINE ────────

LOWERY'S SEAFOOD RESTAURANT **Lunch:** $6-$25 **Dinner:** $8-$25 **Phone:** 804/443-4314
▼▼ ▼▼ **Location:** On US 17/360; center. 528 Church Ln 22560. **Hours:** 11 am-9 pm, Fri & Sat-9:30 pm; to 8:30 pm in
winter. Closed: 12/25. **Features:** Established in 1938, the family-run spot sits along the Rappahannock
Regional Seafood River. Regional fresh seafood, Southern-style vegetables, delightful corn muffins and such sinful desserts as
hot fudge cake and bread pudding make for a pleasing and satisfying menu. Casual dress; beer & wine
only. **Parking:** on-site. **Cards:** AX, DS, MC, VI. ✖

THORNBURG

──────── WHERE TO STAY ────────

HOLIDAY INN EXPRESS *Book at aaa.com* **Phone:** 540/582-1097
▼▼▼ 6/1-9/30 1P: $79-$169 2P: $79-$169 XP: $5 F13
3/1-5/31 & 10/1-2/28 1P: $49-$149 2P: $49-$149 XP: $5 F13
Small-scale Hotel **Location:** I-95, exit 118 (SR 606), just w. 6409 Dan Bell Ln 22565 (PO Box 559). Fax: 540/582-1097. **Facility:** 54
one-bedroom standard units, some with whirlpools. 2 stories (no elevator), exterior corridors. *Bath:* combo
or shower only. **Parking:** on-site. **Terms:** cancellation fee imposed, small pets only ($10 extra charge). **Amenities:** irons, hair
dryers. **Pool(s):** outdoor. **Business Services:** fax. **Cards:** AX, CB, DC, DS, MC, VI.

SOME UNITS
(ASK) (S) (🛏) (🔥M) (♿) (🔄) (🎥) (DATA PORT) (🏢) (📷) (📺) / (✖) /
FEE

TROUTVILLE pop. 432

──────── WHERE TO STAY ────────

COMFORT INN TROUTVILLE *Book at aaa.com* **Phone:** (540)992-5600
(AAA) (SAVE) All Year [ECP] 1P: $44-$99 XP: $10 F15
▼▼▼ ▼▼▼ **Location:** I-81, exit 150A, just s on US 11. 2545 Lee Hwy S 24175. Fax: 540/992-5600. **Facility:** 72 one-bedroom
standard units. 2 stories (no elevator), interior corridors. **Parking:** on-site. **Terms:** small pets only ($20 fee).
Amenities: irons, hair dryers. **Pool(s):** small outdoor. **Guest Services:** valet laundry. **Cards:** AX, CB, DC,
Small-scale Hotel DS, JC, MC, VI. *(See color ad p 871)*

SOME UNITS
(S) (🛏) (📶) (🔄) (🎥) (DATA PORT) (📺) / (✖) (🏢) (📷) /
FEE

DAYSTOP ROANOKE

Phone: (540)992-3100

(AAA) (SAVE)

Motel

All Year   1P: $51-$75   2P: $57-$75   XP: $6   F18
Location: I-81, exit 150, just e on US 220, jct US 11. Located at a busy truck stop. US 220 24175 (PO Box 305). Fax: 540/992-5069. **Facility:** 24 one-bedroom standard units. 2 stories (no elevator), exterior corridors. **Parking:** on-site. **Amenities:** hair dryers. **Guest Services:** gift shop, coin laundry. **Cards:** AX, CB, DS, MC, VI. **Special Amenities:** free local telephone calls.

SOME UNITS

HOLIDAY INN EXPRESS   *Book at aaa.com*

Phone: 540/966-4444

(AAA) (SAVE)

Small-scale Hotel

5/1-10/31 [ECP]	1P: $69-$84	2P: $79-$94	XP: $5 F
3/1-4/30 [ECP]	1P: $64-$79	2P: $69-$89	XP: $5 F
11/1-2/28 [ECP]	1P: $59-$79	2P: $64-$89	XP: $5 F

Location: I-81, exit 150A, just ne on US 11. 3139 Lee Hwy S 24175. Fax: 540/966-5798. **Facility:** 82 one-bedroom standard units, some with whirlpools. 2 stories (no elevator), interior/exterior corridors. *Bath:* combo or shower only. **Parking:** on-site. **Amenities:** dual phone lines, voice mail, irons, hair dryers. **Pool(s):** outdoor. **Leisure Activities:** whirlpool, exercise room. **Guest Services:** valet laundry. **Business Services:** meeting rooms. **Cards:** AX, CB, DC, DS, MC, VI. **Special Amenities:** free expanded continental breakfast and free local telephone calls.

SOME UNITS

TRAVELODGE ROANOKE NORTH   *Book at aaa.com*

Phone: (540)992-6700

(AAA) (SAVE)

Motel

3/1-10/31 [CP]	1P: $40-$85	2P: $40-$85	XP: $6 F12
11/1-2/28 [CP]	1P: $40-$65	2P: $40-$65	XP: $6 F12

Location: I-81, exit 150A, just e, then just s on US 11. Located adjacent to truck and camper parking. 2619 Lee Hwy S 24175. Fax: 540/992-3991. **Facility:** 108 one-bedroom standard units. 1 story, exterior corridors. **Parking:** on-site. **Terms:** weekly rates available, pets ($6 extra charge). **Pool(s):** outdoor. **Leisure Activities:** picnic area & barbecue grill, playground, horseshoes, volleyball. **Cards:** AX, CB, DC, DS, JC, MC, VI. **Special Amenities:** free continental breakfast and free local telephone calls.

SOME UNITS

FEE

------- **WHERE TO DINE** -------

COUNTRY PRIDE RESTAURANT

Lunch: $6-$12   **Dinner:** $6-$14   **Phone:** 540/992-3100

(AAA)

American

Location: I-81, exit 150A, just e on US 220, jct US 11; in Travel Centers of America. US 220 24175. **Hours:** 24 hours. **Features:** Diners get just what they would expect from the popular truck stop: fast service, cheerful servers and good food. The all-you-can-eat buffet is loaded with hot and cold fare. Chicken, chops, lasagna and sausage with peppers are favorites. Casual dress. **Parking:** on-site. **Cards:** AX, DC, DS, MC, VI.

THE GREENWOOD RESTAURANT

Lunch: $4-$8   **Dinner:** $4-$8   **Phone:** 540/992-3550

American

Location: I-81, exit 156, 0.5 mi e on SR 640, 1 mi s on US 11. 8176 Lee Hwy 24175. **Hours:** 7 am-8 pm, Fri & Sat-9 pm. Closed: 12/25. **Features:** The restaurant has been serving home-style cooking since 1952. Servers are friendly. Casual dress. **Parking:** on-site.

VARINA —*See Richmond p. 866.*

VERONA pop. 3,638

------- **WHERE TO STAY** -------

RAMADA LIMITED   *Book at aaa.com*

Phone: (540)248-8981

(AAA) (SAVE)

Small-scale Hotel

3/1-10/31	1P: $45-$125	2P: $45-$125	XP: $6 F12
11/1-2/28	1P: $35-$59	2P: $39-$69	XP: $6 F12

Location: I-81, exit 227, just w, then just n. 70 Lodge Ln 24482. Fax: 540/248-4312. **Facility:** 100 one-bedroom standard units. 2 stories (no elevator), exterior corridors. **Parking:** on-site. **Terms:** pets ($10 extra charge). **Amenities:** irons, hair dryers. **Pool(s):** outdoor. **Guest Services:** coin laundry. **Business Services:** meeting rooms. **Cards:** AX, DC, DS, MC, VI. **Special Amenities:** free expanded continental breakfast and early check-in/late check-out. *(See color ad p 884)*

SOME UNITS

FEE

VESUVIUS

------- **WHERE TO STAY** -------

SUGAR TREE INN

Phone: 540-377-2197

Historic
Country Inn

3/1-12/31   1P: $150-$185   2P: $150-$185
Location: SR 56, 3 mi e; 0.9 mi w of jct Blue Ridge Pkwy; very narrow, steep, one-lane winding mountain road; in George Washington National Forest. 145 Lodge Tr 24483 (PO Box 10, STEELES TAVERN, 24476). Fax: 540/377-9524. **Facility:** Using pioneer techniques and 125-year-old, hand-hewn logs, local craftsmen built the main lodge at this upscale property. 12 one-bedroom standard units, some with whirlpools. 2 stories (no elevator), interior/exterior corridors. *Bath:* combo or shower only. **Parking:** on-site. **Terms:** open 3/1-12/31, age restrictions may apply, 14 day cancellation notice-fee imposed. **Amenities:** CD players, hair dryers. **Leisure Activities:** whirlpool, hiking trails. **Cards:** MC, VI.

SOME UNITS

VIENNA —*See District Of Columbia p. 552.*

VIRGINIA BEACH —*See Hampton Roads Area p. 738.*

WAKEFIELD pop. 1,038

——— WHERE TO DINE ———

VIRGINIA DINER
◈
Regional American
MC, VI.

Lunch: $6-$15   **Dinner:** $6-$15   **Phone:** 757/899-3106
Location: SR 460; center. 322 W Main St 23888. **Hours:** 6 am-8 pm, Fri-Sun to 9 pm. Closed: 12/25.
Features: In the heart of Virginia's peanut country, the long-standing Southern diner is a regional favorite that started in 1929 in a renovated railroad car. Look for specialties such as peanut soup, country ham, Brunswick stew and Southern fried chicken. Casual dress; beer only. **Parking:** on-site. **Cards:** AX, DS,

WARM SPRINGS

——— WHERE TO STAY ———

THE INN AT GRISTMILL SQUARE   **Phone:** (540)839-2231
▽▽◈
Historic
Country Inn
cancellation notice. **Amenities:** irons, hair dryers. **Dining:** Waterwheel Restaurant, see separate listing. **Pool(s):** outdoor.
All Year   1P: $80-$150   2P: $90-$150
Location: US 220, 0.4 mi w on SR 619. Rt 645 Old Mill Rd 24484 (PO Box 359). Fax: 540/839-5770.
Facility: Centered around a gristmill dating from 1900, this pleasant cluster of historic buildings offers such rooms as the Singapore and the Silo. 20 one-bedroom standard units, some with efficiencies, kitchens and/or whirlpools. 2 stories (no elevator), interior/exterior corridors. **Parking:** on-site. **Terms:** 3 day
Leisure Activities: sauna, 3 tennis courts, exercise room. *Fee:* massage. **Guest Services:** gift shop. **Business Services:**
meeting rooms. **Cards:** MC, VI.

SOME UNITS

——— WHERE TO DINE ———

WATERWHEEL RESTAURANT   **Phone:** 540/839-2231
▽▽◈
American
walnuts, snap peas and red potatoes. Service is attentive and professional. Casual dress; cocktails. **Parking:** on-site.
Cards: DS, MC, VI. **Historic**
Dinner: $18-$25
Location: US 220, 0.4 mi w on SR 619; in The Inn at Gristmill Square. Old Mill Rd (Rt 645) 24484. **Hours:** 6 pm-9 pm, Fri & Sat-10 pm, Sun 11 am-2 & 6-9 pm; hours vary in winter. Closed: Tues 11/1-5/1.
Reservations: suggested. **Features:** Cozy, relaxed fine dining is the mode in the restored circa 1900 grist mill. Included in the good selection of specialties is mountain trout with cornmeal breading and black

WARRENTON pop. 6,670

——— WHERE TO STAY ———

BLACK HORSE INN   **Phone:** 540/349-4020
(AAA) (SAVE)
▽▽▽
Bed & Breakfast
walking trails, hiking trails. **Business Services:** meeting rooms. **Cards:** AX, MC, VI.
All Year [BP]   1P: $125-$295   2P: $125-$295   XP: $35   F3
Location: I-66, exit 43A, 1.2 mi e. 8393 Meetze Rd 20187. Fax: 540/349-4242. **Facility:** The inn, which carries an equine theme throughout its main house and grounds, offers named guest rooms and a gazebo where readers may retreat. 8 one-bedroom standard units, some with whirlpools. 2 stories (no elevator), interior/exterior corridors. **Parking:** on-site. **Terms:** check-in 4 pm, 14 day cancellation notice-fee imposed, weekly rates available. **Amenities:** video library. *Some:* CD players. **Leisure Activities:** lending library,

SOME UNITS

COMFORT INN   **Phone:** (540)349-8900
(AAA) (SAVE)
▽▽▽
Small-scale Hotel
Business Services: meeting rooms. **Cards:** AX, CB, DC, DS, JC, MC, VI. **Special Amenities:** free
expanded continental breakfast and free newspaper.
All Year [ECP]   1P: $69-$109   2P: $69-$109   XP: $6   F16
Location: 1.5 mi n on US 15/29, on service road. 7379 Comfort Inn Dr 20187. Fax: 540/347-5759. **Facility:** 97 one-bedroom standard units, some with whirlpools. 2 stories (no elevator), interior/exterior corridors. **Parking:** on-site. **Terms:** small pets only ($10 extra charge). **Amenities:** voice mail, irons, hair dryers. **Pool(s):** outdoor. **Leisure Activities:** picnic tables, grills, exercise room, basketball. **Guest Services:** coin laundry.

SOME UNITS
FEE

HAMPTON INN   *Book at aaa.com*   **Phone:** (540)349-4200
▽▽▽
Small-scale Hotel
voice mail, irons, hair dryers. **Pool(s):** outdoor. **Leisure Activities:** exercise room. **Guest Services:** coin laundry. **Cards:** AX,
CB, DC, DS, MC, VI.
All Year   1P: $89-$125   2P: $89-$125
Location: 1 mi n on US 29 business route and US 211. 501 Blackwell Rd 20186. Fax: 540/349-0061. **Facility:** 99 one-bedroom standard units. 2 stories (no elevator), exterior corridors. **Parking:** on-site. **Terms:** 2 night minimum stay - seasonal and/or weekends, small pets only. **Amenities:** video library, dual phone lines,

SOME UNITS

HOWARD JOHNSON INN-WARRENTON   *Book at aaa.com*   **Phone:** (540)347-4141
(AAA) (SAVE)
▽▽▽ ▽▽
Motel
All Year   1P: $70-$99   2P: $70-$110   XP: $10   F18
Location: US 17/29 business route, jct US 211 W. 6 Broadview Ave 20186. Fax: 540/347-5632. **Facility:** 79 one-bedroom standard units. 2 stories (no elevator), interior corridors. **Parking:** on-site. **Terms:** small pets only ($10 fee). **Amenities:** voice mail, irons, hair dryers. **Pool(s):** outdoor. **Guest Services:** coin laundry.
Cards: AX, DC, DS, MC, VI. **Special Amenities:** free local telephone calls and free newspaper.

SOME UNITS
FEE

─────── **WHERE TO DINE** ───────

THE DEPOT RESTAURANT   Phone: 540/347-1212
                    Location: US 29 business district to Main St, turn on S 3rd St, just 1 1/2 blks; in historic district. 65 S 3rd St 20186.
American   **Hours:** 5 pm-10 pm. Closed: 12/25; also Sun & Mon. **Reservations:** suggested. **Features:** In a distinctive
                    turn-of-the-20th-century train depot, the cozy restaurant appeals primarily to upscale professionals. Stylish
                    presentation adds to thoughtfully prepared Mediterranean creations. The wine list aptly complements the
choices. Service is attentive. Cocktails; entertainment. **Parking:** on-site. **Cards:** MC, VI. **Historic**

GRANPA GROOVEY'S   **Lunch:** $7-$15   **Dinner:** $8-$20   Phone: 540/347-5757
                    Location: US 17/29 business route, just w on US 211 W. 573 Frost Ave 20186. **Hours:** 11:30 am-10 pm, Sun noon-
American   8 pm. Closed: 1/1, 12/25. **Features:** The specialty is fresh, flavorful seafood, which is available in a large
                    variety. The dining room offers plenty of ambience. Casual dress; cocktails. **Parking:** on-site. **Cards:** AX,
                    CB, DC, DS, JC, MC, VI.

LEGEND'S RESTAURANT   **Lunch:** $6-$11   **Dinner:** $7-$20   Phone: 540/347-9401
                    Location: Corner of Lee and Pelham sts; in the historic district. 67 W Lee St 20186. **Hours:** 11 am-11 pm, Fri & Sat-
American   1 am, Sun 10 am-9 pm. Closed: 11/24, 12/25. **Features:** Photographs of American legends, such as James
                    Dean and Marilyn Monroe, decorate the restaurant's second floor. The menu focuses heavily on familiar fare
                    but also includes some twists. Among homemade desserts is the luscious mocha hazelnut chocolate torte.
The bi-level dining space has a large bar waiting area. Casual dress; cocktails. **Parking:** on-site. **Cards:** CB, DC, DS, MC, VI.

NAPOLEON'S RESTAURANT   **Lunch:** $7-$10   **Dinner:** $15-$25   Phone: 540/347-4300
                    Location: At Waterloo and Diagonal sts; in historic district. 67 Waterloo St 20186. **Hours:** 11 am-11 pm, Fri & Sat-
Continental   midnight, Sun 11 am-10 pm. Closed: 12/25. **Reservations:** suggested, weekends. **Features:** In an 1830
                    Greek Revival home in the historic district, the restaurant seats guests in formal and informal dining areas or
                    on the seasonal patio. Beautifully presented Continental cuisine exhibits a French flair. The atmosphere at
lunchtime is casual and bustling. Dessert selections are plentiful and tempting. Casual dress; cocktails. **Parking:** on-site.
Cards: AX, DS, MC, VI. **Historic**

WARSAW pop. 1,375

─────── **WHERE TO STAY** ───────

BEST WESTERN WARSAW   ***Book at aaa.com***   Phone: (804)333-1700
                         4/2-10/1   1P: $77-$90   2P: $77-$90   XP: $10   F17
                         10/2-2/28   1P: $77   2P: $77   XP: $10   F17
Small-scale Hotel   3/1-4/1   1P: $74   2P: $74   XP: $10   F17
                    Location: US 360, just w of town. 4522 Richmond Rd 22572 (PO Box 157). Fax: 804/333-1708. **Facility:** 38 units.
37 one-bedroom standard units. 1 one-bedroom suite ($115-$155). 2 stories, interior corridors. *Bath:* combo or shower only.
Parking: on-site. **Terms:** small pets only ($10 extra charge). **Amenities:** irons, hair dryers. **Pool(s):** outdoor. **Leisure
Activities:** limited exercise equipment. **Business Services:** fax. **Cards:** AX, DC, DS, MC, VI.

WASHINGTON pop. 183

─────── **WHERE TO STAY** ───────

FOSTER HARRIS HOUSE BED & BREAKFAST   Phone: (540)675-3757
                         10/1-10/31   2P: $150-$295   XP: $50
                         3/1-9/30 & 11/1-2/28   2P: $125-$275   XP: $50
Historic Bed   **Location:** 0.5 mi w on US 211 business route. Located in a quiet area. 189 Main St 22747 (PO Box 333).
& Breakfast   Fax: 540/675-1615. **Facility:** This turn-of-the-20th-century house is nestled in the foothills of the Blue Ridge
                    Mountains and offers good views and a perennial garden. Smoke free premises. 5 one-bedroom standard
units, some with whirlpools. 2 stories (no elevator), interior corridors. **Parking:** on-site. **Terms:** age restrictions may apply, 7 day
cancellation notice-fee imposed, package plans. **Business Services:** meeting rooms. **Cards:** AX, MC, VI.

THE HERITAGE HOUSE BED & BREAKFAST   Phone: (540)675-3207
                         All Year [BP]   1P: $150-$320   2P: $150-$320
                         Location: Just w on US 211 business route. 291 Main St 22747 (PO Box 427). Fax: 540/675-2004. **Facility:** Lace
                    and Amish are among the room themes at this quaint 1837 manor house, which offers a large parlor area,
                    scenic views and an inviting garden. Smoke free premises. 5 units. 4 one-bedroom standard units. 1 one-
Historic Bed   bedroom suite. 2 stories (no elevator), interior corridors. *Bath:* combo or shower only. **Parking:** on-site.
& Breakfast   **Terms:** age restrictions may apply, 7 day cancellation notice-fee imposed, package plans. **Business
                    Services:** meeting rooms. **Cards:** MC, VI. **Special Amenities:** free full breakfast and preferred room
(subject to availability with advance reservations).

THE INN AT LITTLE WASHINGTON   Phone: 540/675-3800
                         All Year   1P: $470-$715   2P: $470-$715   XP: $50   F3
                         Location: Intersection of Middle and Main sts. Business Rt US 211 22747 (PO Box 300). Fax: 540/675-3100.
                    Facility: European fabrics and antiques create a sumptuous ambience in this service-oriented inn's guest
Country Inn   units and public areas. Designated smoking area. 16 units. 13 one-bedroom standard units, some with
                    whirlpools. 1 one-bedroom suite. 1 vacation home and 1 cottage. 3 stories, interior corridors. *Bath:* combo
                    or shower only. **Parking:** on-site and valet. **Terms:** 14 day cancellation notice-fee imposed. **Amenities:** CD
players, safes, irons, hair dryers. *Some:* DVD players. **Dining:** picnic lunch available, dining room, see separate listing. **Leisure
Activities:** bicycles. *Fee:* massage. **Guest Services:** gift shop, complimentary evening beverages, valet laundry. **Business
Services:** meeting rooms, PC. **Cards:** MC, VI. **Special Amenities:** free continental breakfast and free local telephone
calls.

MIDDLETON INN

Phone: (540)675-2020

AAA SAVE
▼▼▼ ▼▼▼
Historic Bed
& Breakfast

All Year [BP]   1P: $225-$425   2P: $225-$525   XP: $50   F
Location: 0.5 mi w on US 211 business route. 176 Main St 22747 (PO Box 254). Fax: 540/675-1050. **Facility:** Afternoon tea and a greeting by friendly resident dogs await new arrivals to this Federal-style manor house fronted by a long, winding driveway. Smoke free premises. 5 units. 4 one-bedroom standard units. 1 cottage ($275-$525) with whirlpool. 2 stories (no elevator), interior/exterior corridors. *Bath:* combo or shower only. **Parking:** on-site. **Terms:** age restrictions may apply, 14 day cancellation notice-fee imposed, 10% service charge. **Amenities:** irons, hair dryers. *Some:* CD players. **Leisure Activities:** croquet, badminton. **Guest Services:** complimentary evening beverages, valet laundry. **Business Services:** meeting rooms. **Cards:** AX, MC, VI. **Special Amenities: free full breakfast and free newspaper.**

SOME UNITS
⊠ 🕾 DATA PORT / 🛏 🖭 🖵 /

WHERE TO DINE

THE INN AT LITTLE WASHINGTON
DINING ROOM

Dinner: $118-$158

Phone: 540/675-3800

AAA
▼▼▼ ▼▼▼
Regional
American

Location: Intersection of Middle and Main sts; in The Inn at Little Washington. Business Route US 211 22747. **Hours:** 6 pm-9:30 pm, Fri & Sat from 5:30 pm, Sun 4 pm-8:30 pm. Closed: Tues except 4/20-6/15 & 9/21-12/21. **Reservations:** required, 2-3 weeks advance. **Features:** Uncompromising cuisine with a prix-fixe menu representing the freshest of premium ingredients artfully prepared and presented is what makes this restaurant shine. The opulent atmosphere, world-class wine list and gracious staff are well orchestrated by chef/owner Patrick O'Connell. Don't miss the opportunity to tour the kitchen and the outside garden area. One of a kind. Cocktails. **Parking:** on-site and valet. **Cards:** MC, VI. **Country Inn**

🍽 ⊠

WAVERLY pop. 2,309

WHERE TO DINE

COWLINGS BARBEQUE

Lunch: $3-$11   **Dinner:** $3-$11   **Phone:** 804/834-3100

▼▼▼
Barbecue

Location: Just e of center on US 460. 7019 General Mahone Hwy 23890. **Hours:** 11 am-8 pm. Closed major holidays; also Tues. **Features:** For more than 20 years, lovers of North Carolina-style barbecue have traveled from far and wide to the simple spot for delicious pork barbecue, cornbread and homemade pies. Casual dress; beer only. **Parking:** on-site. **Cards:** MC, VI.

⊠

WAYNESBORO pop. 19,520

WHERE TO STAY

BELLE HEARTH BED & BREAKFAST

Phone: (540)943-1910

▼▼▼
Bed & Breakfast

All Year   1P: $95-$125   2P: $95-$125
Location: 0.3 mi s from Main St. 320 S Wayne Ave 22980. Fax: 540/942-2443. **Facility:** A gabled roof and heart-pine floors enhance the ambience at this 1909 Victorian home, where some units include gas fireplaces. 4 one-bedroom standard units. 2 stories (no elevator), interior corridors. *Bath:* combo or shower only. **Parking:** on-site. **Terms:** 2 night minimum stay - seasonal, age restrictions may apply, 10 day cancellation notice. **Pool(s):** outdoor. **Cards:** AX, MC, VI.

ASK 🏊 ⊠

COMFORT INN WAYNESBORO

Book at aaa.com

Phone: (540)932-3060

AAA SAVE
▼▼▼ ▼▼▼
Small-scale Hotel

5/1-10/31 [ECP]   1P: $89-$139   2P: $89-$139   XP: $5   F
3/1-4/30 & 11/1-2/28 [ECP]   1P: $79-$129   2P: $79-$129   XP: $5   F
Location: I-64, exit 94, 0.5 mi n on US 340, then just e. 15 Windigrove Dr 22980. Fax: 540/932-3060. **Facility:** 56 one-bedroom standard units, some with whirlpools. 3 stories, interior corridors. *Bath:* combo or shower only. **Parking:** on-site. **Amenities:** high-speed Internet, voice mail, irons, hair dryers. **Pool(s):** outdoor. **Leisure Activities:** limited exercise equipment. **Business Services:** meeting rooms. **Cards:** AX, DC, DS, MC, VI. **Special Amenities: free expanded continental breakfast and free newspaper.**

SOME UNITS
S/D 🍴 ♿ 🏊 🕾 DATA PORT 🛏 🖭 🖵 / ⊠ /

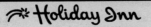

DAYS INN WAYNESBORO   *Book at aaa.com*

AAA [SAVE]
Motel

All Year [CP]   1P: $49-$89   2P: $49-$89   XP: $5   F17
Location: I-64, exit 94, 0.5 mi n on US 340. 2060 Rosser Ave 22980. Fax: 540/949-7586. **Facility:** 97 one-bedroom standard units. 2 stories (no elevator), exterior corridors. **Parking:** on-site. **Terms:** pets ($10 extra charge). **Amenities:** hair dryers. **Pool(s):** outdoor, wading. **Guest Services:** valet laundry. **Business Services:** meeting rooms. **Cards:** AX, CB, DC, DS, MC, VI. **Special Amenities:** free continental breakfast and free newspaper.

Phone: (540)943-1101

SOME UNITS

DELUXE BUDGET MOTEL

AAA [SAVE]
Motel

9/24-11/6   1P: $40-$55   2P: $45-$70   XP: $7   D12
3/1-9/23   1P: $40-$50   2P: $44-$58   XP: $7   D12
11/7-2/28   1P: $32-$38   2P: $35-$39   XP: $7   D12
Location: I-64, exit 94, 0.5 mi n on US 340, 1 mi w on Lew Dewitt Blvd, 0.8 mi e on US 250. 2112 W Main St 22980. Fax: 540/943-3393. **Facility:** 23 one-bedroom standard units. 1 story, exterior corridors. **Bath:** combo or shower only. **Parking:** on-site. **Terms:** 3 day cancellation notice-fee imposed. **Leisure Activities:** playground. **Cards:** AX, DC, DS, MC, VI. **Special Amenities:** free local telephone calls. *(See color ad p 893)*

Phone: (540)949-8253

SOME UNITS

HOLIDAY INN EXPRESS   *Book at aaa.com*

AAA [SAVE]
Small-scale Hotel

5/1-10/31   1P: $105-$161   2P: $105-$161
3/1-4/30 & 11/1-2/28   1P: $105-$131   2P: $105-$131
Location: I-64, exit 94, 0.5 mi n on US 340, then just e. 20 Windigrove Dr 22980. Fax: 540/932-7150. **Facility:** 80 one-bedroom standard units, some with whirlpools. 3 stories, interior corridors. **Bath:** combo or shower only. **Parking:** on-site. **Amenities:** voice mail, irons, hair dryers. **Pool(s):** heated indoor. **Leisure Activities:** sauna, whirlpool, exercise room. **Guest Services:** coin laundry. **Business Services:** meeting rooms, business center. **Cards:** AX, CB, DC, DS, JC, MC, VI. **Special Amenities:** free expanded continental breakfast and free newspaper. *(See color ad p 893)*

Phone: (540)932-7170

SOME UNITS

THE IRIS INN

Bed & Breakfast

5/1-10/31   1P: $100-$215   2P: $110-$225   XP: $20
3/1-4/30 & 11/1-2/28   1P: $90-$215   2P: $100-$200   XP: $20
Location: I-64, exit 96, just s on SR 624, just e. Located in a quiet rural area. 191 Chinquapin Dr 22980. Fax: 540/942-2093. **Facility:** Offering observation decks for taking in the view, this inn centers on a stunning great room featuring a cathedral ceiling and painted murals. Smoke free premises. 9 one-bedroom standard units, some with whirlpools. 2 stories (no elevator), interior/exterior corridors. **Bath:** combo or shower only. **Parking:** on-site. **Terms:** 2 night minimum stay - weekends, age restrictions may apply, 7 day cancellation notice-fee imposed. **Amenities:** hair dryers. *Some:* irons. **Leisure Activities:** whirlpools, exercise room. **Business Services:** meeting rooms. **Cards:** AX, DC, MC, VI.

Phone: 540/943-1991

SOME UNITS

QUALITY INN WAYNESBORO   *Book at aaa.com*

AAA [SAVE]
Small-scale Hotel

All Year   1P: $59-$79   2P: $79-$109   XP: $5   F12
Location: I-64, exit 96, 3 mi w on SR 624, jct US 250 and 340. 640 W Broad St 22980. Fax: 540/942-4785. **Facility:** 72 one-bedroom standard units. 2 stories (no elevator), interior/exterior corridors. **Parking:** on-site. **Terms:** weekly rates available, small pets only. **Amenities:** irons, hair dryers. **Pool(s):** outdoor, wading. **Guest Services:** valet laundry. **Cards:** AX, DC, DS, MC, VI. **Special Amenities:** free continental breakfast and free local telephone calls.

Phone: 540/942-1171

SOME UNITS

SUPER 8 MOTEL   *Book at aaa.com*

AAA [SAVE]
Small-scale Hotel

10/1-10/31   1P: $60-$115   2P: $66-$125   XP: $6   F18
5/1-9/30   1P: $54-$100   2P: $60-$110   XP: $6   F18
3/1-4/30 & 11/1-2/28   1P: $54-$80   2P: $60-$85   XP: $6   F18
Location: I-64, exit 94, n on US 340 to Lew DeWitt Blvd, then just w to Apple Tree Ln. 2045 Rosser Ave 22980. Fax: 540/943-3888. **Facility:** 48 one-bedroom standard units. 3 stories (no elevator), interior corridors. **Parking:** on-site. **Terms:** 3 day cancellation notice, small pets only ($5 extra charge). **Cards:** AX, DC, DS, MC, VI. **Special Amenities:** free continental breakfast and free local telephone calls.

Phone: 540/943-3888

SOME UNITS

----- WHERE TO DINE -----

SOUTH RIVER GRILL

AAA
American

Lunch: $6-$15   Dinner: $6-$21   Phone: 540/942-5567
Location: I-64, exit 94, 0.5 mi n on US 340, then just e. 23 Windigrove Ln 22980. **Hours:** 11 am-11 pm. Closed: 11/24, 12/24, 12/25. **Features:** The open-air, equestrian-themed restaurant offers many choices of classic American cuisine. Upscale design elements enhance the relaxed atmosphere. Seating is laid-back on the two porches and in the large lounge. Try the pork platter with homemade barbecue sauce. Casual dress; cocktails. **Parking:** on-site. **Cards:** AX, DS, MC, VI.

WEYERS CAVE pop. 1,225

——— WHERE TO STAY ———

THE INN AT KEEZLETOWN ROAD   Phone: 540/234-0644

All Year   1P: $90-$130   2P: $95-$145

Bed & Breakfast

Location: I-81, exit 235, 1 mi e, then just n. 1224 Keezletown Rd 24486. **Facility:** A home-style breakfast is served daily in a common dining area at this Victorian inn set in a small, quiet town. Smoke free premises. 4 one-bedroom standard units. 2 stories (no elevator), interior corridors. *Bath:* combo or shower only. **Parking:** on-site. **Terms:** 2 night minimum stay - seasonal, age restrictions may apply, 7 day cancellation notice-fee imposed, no pets allowed (owner's pets on premises). **Business Services:** meeting rooms. **Cards:** MC, VI.

WHITE HALL

——— WHERE TO STAY ———

THE INN AT SUGAR HOLLOW FARM   Phone: 434/823-7086

All Year   1P: $140-$195   2P: $140-$195   XP: $25   D18

Bed & Breakfast

Location: SR 614, 2.5 mi w of jct SR 810. Located in a secluded rural area. 6051 Sugar Hollow Rd 22905 (PO Box 5705, CHARLOTTESVILLE). Fax: 434/823-2002. **Facility:** A series of small bridges must be crossed to access this secluded property set back in the woods; a loft offers celestial views. Smoke free premises. 5 one-bedroom standard units, some with whirlpools. 2 stories (no elevator), interior corridors. *Bath:* combo or shower only. **Parking:** on-site. **Terms:** check-in 4 pm, 2 night minimum stay - weekends, age restrictions may apply, 14 day cancellation notice-fee imposed. **Amenities:** CD players. **Leisure Activities:** fishing, bicycles, hiking trails. **Guest Services:** complimentary laundry. **Business Services:** meeting rooms. **Cards:** AX, MC, VI.

WHITE POST

——— WHERE TO STAY ———

L'AUBERGE PROVENCALE FRENCH COUNTRY INN   Phone: (540)837-1375

3/1-1/1 & 1/28-2/28 [BP]   1P: $125-$275   2P: $150-$325   XP: $35

Historic
Country Inn

Location: US 340, 1 mi s of jct US 50 and 17. 13630 Lord Fairfax Hwy 22663 (PO Box 190). Fax: 540/837-2004. **Facility:** This inn in the heart of hunt and wine country reflects European influences in its furnishings and food service. Smoke free premises. 14 one-bedroom standard units, some with whirlpools. 2 stories (no elevator), interior/exterior corridors. *Bath:* combo or shower only. **Parking:** on-site. **Terms:** open 3/1-1/1 & 1/28-2/28, age restrictions may apply, 7 day cancellation notice. **Amenities:** hair dryers. **Dining:** dining room, see separate listing. **Guest Services:** valet laundry. **Business Services:** meeting rooms. **Cards:** AX, CB, DC, DS, MC, VI.

SOME UNITS

——— WHERE TO DINE ———

L'AUBERGE PROVENCALE   Dinner: $82   Phone: 540/837-1375

Regional French

Location: US 340, 1 mi s of jct US 50 and 17; in L'Auberge Provencale French Country Inn. 13630 Lord Fairfax Hwy 22663. **Hours:** 6 pm-10 pm, Sun 5 pm-9 pm. **Closed:** 12/25; also Mon, Tues & 1/1-1/21. **Reservations:** suggested. **Features:** Dinner is deliberately lengthy, as a five-course event evokes the traditions of Southern France. Chef/owner Alain Borel artfully presents "cuisine Provencal moderne" in the 1753 fieldstone home, which is appointed in lovely decor. Professional and knowledgeable service is notable. The atmosphere is soothing and relaxed. Guests can unwind in the large parlor room with pre-dining cocktails. Semi-formal attire; cocktails. **Parking:** on-site. **Cards:** AX, CB, DC, DS, MC, VI. **Historic**

WILLIAMSBURG —See Williamsburg, Jamestown & Yorktown p. 905.

Destination Williamsburg, Jamestown & Yorktown

*T*ime—whether you spend it in the past or the present—is on your side when you visit Virginia's Historic Triangle. In this compact heritage region you're only minutes from the next diversion of choice.

*S*hop for the old in Williamsburg's historic district or seek out the new in outlet malls. Take your golf clubs to the nearest course. Pack a picnic lunch and drive Colonial Parkway, end to end.

Windmill at Colonial Williamsburg. Windmills were a common feature of Colonial properties.

Golfing in Williamsburg. Aged-oaks and maples line the fairways of Williamsburg National Golf Club.

Williamsburg Area CVB

Yorktown Monument to Alliance and Victory. Overlooking the York River, the monument pays tribute to the lives lost during battle. (See listing page 302)

Williamsburg Area

To Charles City

Lightfoot

Central Williamsburg

Yorktown

See Vicinity map page 898

Glasshouse, Jamestown. Glassmaking in America is said to have begun in 17th-century Jamestown.

*P*laces included in this AAA Destination Area:

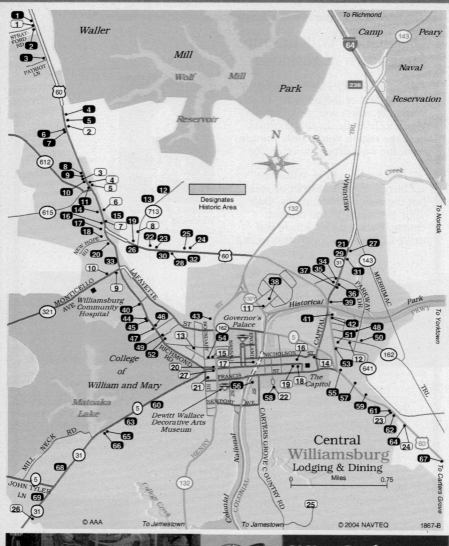

Central Williamsburg Lodging & Dining

© AAA   © 2004 NAVTEQ   1867-B

Central Williamsburg

This index helps you "spot" where approved accommodations and restaurants are located on the corresponding detailed maps. Lodging rate ranges are for comparison only and show the property's high season; rates are per night, unless only weekly (W) rates are available. Restaurant rate range is for dinner, unless only lunch (L) is served. Turn to the listing page for more detailed rate information and consult display ads for special promotions.

Spotter/Map Page Number	OA	CENTRAL WILLIAMSBURG - Lodgings	Diamond Rating	Rate Range High Season	Listing Page
❶ / p. 898	AAA	Days Inn & Suites/West-Colonial	◈◈	$69-$119 SAVE	922
❷ / p. 898	AAA	Ramada Inn & Suites	◈◈	$59-$109 SAVE	937
❸ / p. 898	AAA	Holiday Inn Patriot	◈◈	$89-$149 SAVE	929
❹ / p. 898	AAA	Captain John Smith Inn - see color ad p 904	◈◈	$39-$99 SAVE	917
❺ / p. 898	AAA	Comfort Inn Central - see color ad p 919	◈◈◈	$69-$139 SAVE	918
❻ / p. 898	AAA	Econo Lodge Central - see color ad p 925	◈◈	$55-$110 SAVE	924
❼ / p. 898		Hampton Inn & Suites - see color ad p 925	◈◈◈	$59-$149	927
❽ / p. 898		Residence Inn by Marriott Williamsburg	◈◈◈	$59-$359	939
❾ / p. 898		SpringHill Suites by Marriott	◈◈◈	$69-$169	939
❿ / p. 898	AAA	Hilton Garden Inn - see color ad p 928, inside front cover	◈◈◈	$79-$179 SAVE	927
⓫ / p. 898	AAA	Best Western Williamsburg Westpark Hotel	◈◈◈	$69-$109 SAVE	917
⓬ / p. 898		Fairfield Williamsburg Condo Rentals @ Governor's Green	◈◈◈	$199-$299	926
⓭ / p. 898		Fairfield Williamsburg Condo Rentals at Kingsgate	◈◈◈	$159-$249	926
⓮ / p. 898		Holiday Inn Express	◈◈◈	$129-$149	929
⓯ / p. 898	AAA	Embassy Suites - see color ad p 905	◈◈◈	$149-$209 SAVE	924
⓰ / p. 898		Comfort Inn & Suites	◈◈◈	$89-$199	918
⓱ / p. 898		Fairfield Inn & Suites by Marriott	fyi	$59-$139	924
⓲ / p. 898	AAA	Quality Suites Williamsburg - see color ad p 939	◈◈◈	$149-$199 SAVE	935
⓳ / p. 898	AAA	La Quinta Inn Williamsburg (Historic Area) - see color ad p 931	◈◈◈	$85-$135 SAVE	932
⓴ / p. 898		The Princess Anne	◈◈	$71-$108	933
㉑ / p. 898	AAA	Motel Rochambeau - see color ad p 942	◈	$38-$56 SAVE	933
㉒ / p. 898	AAA	Hampton Inn Williamsburg	◈◈◈	$49-$129 SAVE	927
㉓ / p. 898	AAA	Days Inn Historic Area - see color ad p 923	◈◈◈	$69-$99 SAVE	924
㉔ / p. 898	AAA	Ramada Inn 1776	◈◈◈	$79-$129 SAVE	937
㉕ / p. 898	AAA	Homewood Suites by Hilton - see color ad p 930	◈◈◈	$149-$359 SAVE	929
㉖ / p. 898	AAA	Sleep Inn-Historic - see color ad p 915	◈◈	$59-$119 SAVE	939
㉗ / p. 898	AAA	Country Hearth Inn & Suites Capitol Historic - see color ad p 904	◈◈	$69-$89 SAVE	918
㉘ / p. 898		The Hotel Williamsburg (Now Known as Quality Inn Historic Williamsburg) - see color ad p 929	◈◈◈	$99-$159	929
㉙ / p. 898	AAA	Colonel Waller Inn & Suites - see color ad p 917	◈◈	$59-$99 SAVE	918
㉚ / p. 898	AAA	Country Inn and Suites by Carlson - see color ad p 847, p 921	◈◈◈	$89-$159 SAVE	922
㉛ / p. 898	AAA	White Lion Motel - see color ad p 942	◈◈	$44-$66 SAVE	942
㉜ / p. 898	AAA	Comfort Inn King George Historic - see color ad p 920, inside front cover	◈◈◈	$99-$129 SAVE	918
㉝ / p. 898	AAA	Westgate Historic Williamsburg	◈◈◈	$89-$117 SAVE	942
㉞ / p. 898	AAA	Quality Inn Lord Paget - see color ad p 935	◈◈	$89-$119 SAVE	935

Spotter/Map Page Number	OA	CENTRAL WILLIAMSBURG - Lodgings (continued)	Diamond Rating	Rate Range High Season	Listing Page
35 / p. 898	AAA	Econo Lodge-Parkway Historic Area	◆◆	$55-$99 SAVE	924
36 / p. 898	AAA	TraveLodge-King William Inn - see color ad p 941	◆◆	$65-$235 SAVE	939
37 / p. 898	AAA	Red Roof Inn-Williamsburg - see color ad p 938	◆◆	$59-$99 SAVE	939
38 / p. 898		Woodlands Hotel & Suites - see color ad p 936	◆◆◆	$115-$195	943
39 / p. 898	AAA	Holiday Inn-Downtown & Holidome	◆◆◆	$129-$149 SAVE	929
40 / p. 898	AAA	Days Inn Colonial Downtown - see color ad p 922	◆◆	$85-$99 SAVE	922
41 / p. 898		Fox & Grape Bed & Breakfast	◆◆◆	$100-$140	926
42 / p. 898		Hite's Bed & Breakfast	◆◆◆	$95-$125	927
43 / p. 898		Governor's Inn - see color ad p 936	◆◆◆	$90-$115	926
44 / p. 898		A Boxwood Inn of Williamsburg	◆◆◆	$95-$195	914
45 / p. 898	AAA	A Primrose Cottage	◆◆◆	$95-$165 SAVE	914
46 / p. 898		Applewood Colonial Bed & Breakfast	◆◆◆	$100-$175	914
47 / p. 898	AAA	An American Inn-Williamsburg Manor	◆◆◆	$109-$169 SAVE	914
48 / p. 898	AAA	Econo Lodge Colonial - see color ad p 906	◆◆	$65-$95 SAVE	924
49 / p. 898	AAA	Colonial Capital Bed & Breakfast	◆◆◆	$128-$165 SAVE	918
50 / p. 898	AAA	Super 8 Motel-Historic - see color ad p 940	◆◆	$60-$85 SAVE	939
51 / p. 898	AAA	Quality Inn Colony - see color ad p 934	◆◆	$99-$149 SAVE	934
52 / p. 898	AAA	Williamsburg Hospitality House	◆◆◆	$69-$210 SAVE	942
53 / p. 898	AAA	Best Western Colonial Capitol Inn - see color ad p 916	◆◆	$89-$129 SAVE	914
54 / p. 898		The Fife and Drum Inn	◆◆◆	$155-$175	926
55 / p. 898	AAA	Best Western Patrick Henry Inn - see color ad p 916	◆◆◆	$109-$179 SAVE	916
56 / p. 898		Williamsburg Lodge - see color ad p 936	◆◆◆	$155-$275	942
57 / p. 898	AAA	Four Points by Sheraton Hotel & Suites Williamsburg Historic District - see color ad p 927	◆◆◆	$89-$169 SAVE	926
58 / p. 898		Williamsburg Inn - see color ad p 936	◆◆◆◆	$225-$775	942
59 / p. 898	AAA	Ramada Limited Historic Area - see color ad p 938	◆◆	$49-$119 SAVE	938
60 / p. 898	AAA	Cedars of Williamsburg Bed & Breakfast	◆◆◆	$120-$300 SAVE	917
61 / p. 898	AAA	Quarterpath Inn - see color ad p 935	◆◆	$69-$119 SAVE	935
62 / p. 898	AAA	Bassett Motel	◆	$49-$58 SAVE	914
63 / p. 898		Inn at 802	◆◆◆	$135-$160	932
64 / p. 898	AAA	Radisson Fort Magruder Hotel & Conference Center - see color ad p 937, p 932	◆◆◆	$99-$159 SAVE	937
65 / p. 898	AAA	Williamsburg Sampler Bed & Breakfast Inn	◆◆◆	$150-$180 SAVE	942
66 / p. 898		Legacy of Williamsburg Bed & Breakfast Inn	◆◆◆	$135-$175	932
67 / p. 898	AAA	Howard Johnson Hotel-Historic Area - see color ad p 931	◆◆◆	$89-$120 SAVE	931
68 / p. 898	AAA	Liberty Rose Bed & Breakfast	◆◆◆◆	$195-$275 SAVE	932
69 / p. 898		Colonial Gardens Bed & Breakfast	◆◆◆	$135-$175	918

Spotter/Map Page Number	OA	CENTRAL WILLIAMSBURG - Restaurants	Diamond Rating	Rate Range High Season	Listing Page
① / p. 898		Captain Georges Seafood Restaurant	◆◆	$19-$30	943
② / p. 898	AAA	**Fireside Steak Chophouse -** see color ad p 919	◆◆◆	$9-$24	944
③ / p. 898	AAA	**Seafare Restaurant -** see color ad p 920	◆◆◆	$13-$23	945
④ / p. 898	AAA	**Kyoto Japanese Steak & Seafood House**	◆◆	$10-$24	945
⑤ / p. 898	AAA	**Aberdeen Barn**	◆◆	$14-$42	943
⑥ / p. 898	AAA	**The Jefferson**	◆◆	$11-$20	945
⑦ / p. 898	AAA	**The Prime Rib House**	◆◆◆	$10-$20	945
⑧ / p. 898		Peking & Mongolian Grill	◆	$5-$10	945
⑨ / p. 898		Chez Trinh	◆	$7-$16	943
⑩ / p. 898		Nawab Indian Cuisine	◆◆	$8-$15	945
⑪ / p. 898		Huzzah!	◆◆	$7-$18	944
⑫ / p. 898		La Tolteca Mexican Restaurante	◆	$5-$10	945
⑬ / p. 898		A. Carroll's Martini Bar & Bistro	◆◆◆	$14-$25	943
⑭ / p. 898		Christiana Campbell's Tavern - see color ad p 303	◆◆	$25-$35	944
⑮ / p. 898		Aromas	◆	$5-$7	943
⑯ / p. 898		Shields Tavern - see color ad p 303	◆◆	$38	946
⑰ / p. 898		Chowning's Tavern - see color ad p 303	◆◆	$6-$8	943
⑱ / p. 898		King's Arms Tavern - see color ad p 303	◆◆	$28-$38	945
⑲ / p. 898		The Cheese Shop	◆	$5-$9	943
⑳ / p. 898	AAA	**The Trellis Restaurant**	◆◆◆	$16-$30	946
㉑ / p. 898	AAA	**Berret's Seafood Restaurant and Taphouse Grill**	◆◆◆	$18-$26	943
㉒ / p. 898		The Regency Dining Room	◆◆◆◆	$22-$37	945
㉓ / p. 898	AAA	**Yorkshire Steak & Seafood Restaurant -** see color ad p 944	◆◆◆	$15-$20	946
㉔ / p. 898	AAA	**Veranda Dining Room -** see color ad p 937	◆◆	$14-$19	946
㉕ / p. 898		Golden Horseshoe Gold Course Grill	◆◆	$8-$15(L)	944
㉖ / p. 898		Old Chickahominy House	◆◆	$3-$7(L)	945
㉗ / p. 898		Fat Canary	◆◆◆	$20-$28	944

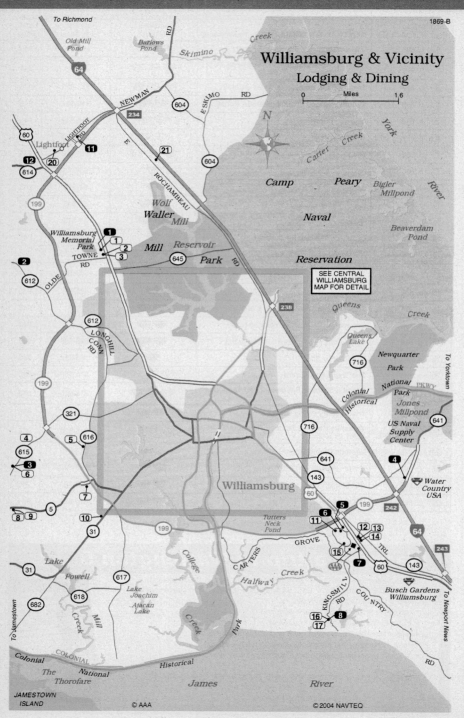

Williamsburg & Vicinity
Lodging & Dining

1869-B

Williamsburg and Vicinity

This index helps you "spot" where approved accommodations and restaurants are located on the corresponding detailed maps. Lodging rate ranges are for comparison only and show the property's high season; rates are per night, unless only weekly (W) rates are available. Restaurant rate range is for dinner, unless only lunch (L) is served. Turn to the listing page for more detailed rate information and consult display ads for special promotions.

Spotter/Map Page Number	OA	WILLIAMSBURG - Lodgings	Diamond Rating	Rate Range High Season	Listing Page
❶ / p. 902	AAA	Comfort Inn Outlet Center - see color ad p 906	▽▽▽	$69-$119 SAVE	905
❷ / p. 902	AAA	War Hill Inn Bed & Breakfast	▽▽▽	$85-$160 SAVE	912
❸ / p. 902		Sunterra Resorts Powhatan Plantation	▽▽▽	$140-$400	912
❹ / p. 902	AAA	Days Hotel Busch Gardens Area - see color ad p 907	▽▽▽	$79-$119 SAVE	905
❺ / p. 902	AAA	Quality Inn At Kingsmill - see color ad p 910	▽▽▽	$89-$129 SAVE	910
❻ / p. 902		Courtyard by Marriott	▽▽▽	$69-$189	905
❼ / p. 902		Marriott Hotel Williamsburg	▽▽▽	$159-$169	910
❽ / p. 902	AAA	Kingsmill Resort - see color ad p 909	▽▽▽▽	$219-$1069 SAVE	908
		WILLIAMSBURG - Restaurants			
① / p. 902		La Tolteca	▽	$6-$12	913
② / p. 902		Hayashi Japanese Restaurant	▽▽	$10-$19	913
③ / p. 902		Giuseppe's Italian Cafe	▽▽	$6-$18	913
④ / p. 902		Shackelford's II	▽▽	$7-$18	913
⑤ / p. 902		The Backfin Seafood Restaurant	▽▽	$7-$14	912
⑥ / p. 902		The Kitchen at Powhatan Plantation	▽▽	$21-$35	913
⑦ / p. 902		Florimonte's Fine Foods & Deli	▽	$5-$10	913
⑧ / p. 902		Cities Grille	▽▽	$9-$19	912
⑨ / p. 902		Soya Japanese Cuisine & Sushi Bar	▽▽	$8-$14	913
⑩ / p. 902		La Grande Tea Room	▽▽	$6-$10(L)	913
⑪ / p. 902		The Sportsman's Grille	▽▽	$7-$15	914
⑫ / p. 902		Doraldo Ristorante Italiano	▽▽	$5-$22	912
⑬ / p. 902		Le Yaca French Restaurant	▽▽▽	$20-$30	913
⑭ / p. 902		The Pottery Wine & Cheese Shop	▽	$3-$9(L)	913
⑮ / p. 902	AAA	The Whaling Company	▽▽	$13-$19	914
⑯ / p. 902		Eagles	▽▽▽	$20-$45	912
⑰ / p. 902		The Bray Dining Room	▽▽▽	$15-$40	912
		LIGHTFOOT - Lodgings			
⓫ / p. 902	AAA	Days Inn Colonial Resort - see color ad p 911	▽▽▽	$69-$109 SAVE	947
⓬ / p. 902	AAA	Ramada Inn - see color ad p 925	▽▽	$60-$110 SAVE	948
		LIGHTFOOT - Restaurants			
⑳ / p. 902		La Petite Tea Room	▽	$6-$13	948
㉑ / p. 902		Pierce's Bar-B-Que	▽	$3-$15	948

WILLIAMSBURG pop. 11,998   (See map and index starting on p. 902)

──────── WHERE TO STAY ────────

COMFORT INN OUTLET CENTER   *Book at aaa.com*   Phone: (757)565-1100   **1**

(AAA) (SAVE)	5/28-9/5	1P: $69-$119	2P: $69-$119	XP: $6	F18
	3/1-5/27	1P: $39-$119	2P: $39-$119	XP: $10	F18
▽▽◆◆▽▽	9/6-12/4	1P: $49-$99	2P: $49-$99	XP: $10	F18
	12/5-2/28	1P: $39-$69	2P: $39-$69	XP: $10	F18

Small-scale Hotel   **Location:** I-64, exit 234 (SR 199 E) to US 60, 1.5 mi e. Located adjacent to outlet shopping. 5611 Richmond Rd 23188. Fax: 757/565-1443. **Facility:** 80 one-bedroom standard units. 2 stories (no elevator), interior corridors. **Parking:** on-site. **Terms:** check-in 4 pm. **Amenities:** safes (fee), irons, hair dryers. **Dining:** 11 am-10 pm, cocktails. **Pool(s):** outdoor. **Guest Services:** valet and coin laundry. **Business Services:** meeting rooms, fax. **Cards:** AX, CB, DC, DS, JC, MC, VI. **Special Amenities:** free expanded continental breakfast and free local telephone calls. *(See color ad p 906)*

SOME UNITS
[icons] / FEE FEE /

COURTYARD BY MARRIOTT   *Book at aaa.com*   Phone: (757)221-0700   **6**

▽▽◆◆▽▽	All Year	1P: $69-$189	2P: $69-$189

Location: I-64, exit 242A, just e of jct SR 199 on US 60. Located in the Busch Corporate Center. 470 McLaws Cir
Small-scale Hotel   23185. Fax: 757/221-0741. **Facility:** 151 units. 139 one-bedroom standard units. 12 one-bedroom suites ($109-$209). 4 stories, interior corridors. *Bath:* combo or shower only. **Parking:** on-site. **Terms:** package plans. **Amenities:** high-speed Internet, voice mail, irons, hair dryers. **Pool(s):** heated indoor/outdoor. **Leisure Activities:** whirlpool, exercise room. **Guest Services:** sundries, valet and coin laundry. **Business Services:** meeting rooms, fax. **Cards:** AX, CB, DC, DS, JC, MC, VI.

SOME UNITS
[icons] / FEE /

DAYS HOTEL BUSCH GARDENS AREA   *Book at aaa.com*   Phone: 757-253-6444   **4**

(AAA) (SAVE)	6/10-9/4	1P: $79-$119	2P: $79-$119	XP: $10	F17
	3/1-6/9	1P: $49-$79	2P: $49-$79	XP: $10	F17
▽▽◆◆▽▽	9/5-12/31	1P: $47-$69	2P: $47-$69	XP: $10	F17
	1/1-2/28	1P: $39-$49	2P: $39-$49	XP: $10	F17

Small-scale Hotel   **Location:** I-64, exit 24B, just w on SR 199; facing Water Country. 201 Water Country Pkwy 23185. Fax: 757/253-1466. **Facility:** 210 one-bedroom standard units. 8 stories, interior corridors. **Parking:** on-site. **Terms:** [BP] & [MAP] meal plans available. **Amenities:** voice mail, safes (fee), irons, hair dryers. **Dining:** 6:30 am-1 & 5-9 pm, cocktails. **Pool(s):** outdoor. **Leisure Activities:** playground, volleyball. *Fee:* game room. **Guest Services:** valet and coin laundry. **Business Services:** meeting rooms, fax. **Cards:** AX, CB, DC, DS, JC, MC, VI. **Special Amenities:** free newspaper and free room upgrade (subject to availability with advance reservations). *(See color ad p 907)*

SOME UNITS
[icons] / FEE FEE /

WILLIAMSBURG'S ALL NEW DAYS HOTEL

You will immediately feel the difference of a Days Hotel. Our HIGH LEVEL of service and amenities are enhanced only by our great value.

❖ *A full service hotel*
❖ *Closest hotel to the entrance of Busch Gardens*
❖ *Located at Water Country USA*

IT IS IMPORTANT TO US THAT YOU ENJOY THE LATEST AMENITIES THAT WE HAVE TO OFFER:

outdoor pool, volleyball court, picnic area, playground, guest laundry, data port phones, irons/ironing boards, deluxe rooms, 25"cable TV, Wireless High Speed Internet Service and the award-winning Gazebo Restaurant & Grill.

www.williamsburgvacations.com

Managed by Carlton Group

201 Water Country Parkway • Williamsburg, VA • 1-800-635-5366

(See map and index starting on p. 902)

KINGSMILL RESORT *Book at aaa.com* Phone: (757)253-1703 🔳8

• (AAA) (SAVE)

| | 3/1-11/30 | 1P: $219-$1069 | 2P: $219-$1069 | XP: $20 | F18 |
| | 12/1-2/28 | 1P: $169-$669 | 2P: $169-$669 | XP: $20 | F18 |

🔻🔻🔻 🔻🔻🔻

Resort
Condominium

Location: I-64, exit 242A to US 60, 1 mi e, follow signs. 1010 Kingsmill Rd 23185. Fax: 757/253-3993. **Facility:** This sprawling resort on the banks of the James River offers extensive golf and tennis facilities, a full-service spa and full conference facilities. 407 units. 172 one-bedroom standard units. 225 one- and 10 two-bedroom suites with kitchens. 3 stories (no elevator), exterior corridors. *Bath:* combo or shower only. **Parking:** on-site. **Terms:** check-in 4 pm, 3 day cancellation notice-fee imposed, package plans. **Amenities:** dual phone lines, voice mail, safes, irons, hair dryers. *Fee:* video games, high-speed Internet. *Some:* DVD players (fee), CD players, fax. **Dining:** 3 restaurants, 6 am-midnight, cocktails, also, The Bray Dining Room, see separate listing, nightclub, entertainment. **Pool(s):** 2 outdoor, heated indoor, wading. **Leisure Activities:** saunas, whirlpools, marina, fishing, racquetball courts, recreation programs, hiking trails, jogging, playground, spa, sports court, basketball. *Fee:* golf-63 holes, 15 tennis courts (2 lighted), bicycles, game room. **Guest Services:** gift shop, valet laundry, area transportation-attractions & in resort, beauty salon. **Business Services:** conference facilities, business center. **Cards:** AX, DC, DS, MC, VI. Affiliated with A Preferred Hotel.

(See color ad p 909)

SOME UNITS

🍴 🍸 🛗 🌀 🏊 🕎 ✖️ 🎿 [DATA PORT] 🖥️ / ✖️ [VCR] 📶 📺 /
FEE

(See map and index starting on p. 902)

MARRIOTT HOTEL WILLIAMSBURG   *Book at aaa.com*   Phone: (757)220-2500   **7**

5/27-9/7	1P: $159-$169	2P: $159-$169
3/1-5/26 & 9/8-2/28	1P: $139-$149	2P: $139-$149

Large-scale Hotel **Location:** I-64, exit 242A, 0.5 mi e on SR 199 to US 60, just w of Busch Gardens. 50 Kingsmill Rd 23185. Fax: 757/253-0541. **Facility:** 295 units. 291 one-bedroom standard units. 4 one-bedroom suites ($189-$299). 6 stories, interior corridors. **Parking:** on-site. **Terms:** check-in 4 pm, [AP] meal plan available, package plans. **Amenities:** voice mail, irons, hair dryers. **Pool(s):** heated indoor/outdoor. **Leisure Activities:** saunas, whirlpool. **Fee:** 2 tennis courts, racquetball courts, game room. **Guest Services:** sundries, valet and coin laundry. **Business Services:** conference facilities, business center. **Cards:** AX, CB, DC, DS, JC, MC, VI.

SOME UNITS

QUALITY INN AT KINGSMILL   *Book at aaa.com*   Phone: (757)220-1100   **5**

6/11-9/6	1P: $89-$129	2P: $89-$129
3/1-6/10	1P: $49-$99	2P: $49-$99
9/7-10/31	1P: $49-$89	2P: $49-$89
11/1-2/28	1P: $49-$79	2P: $49-$79

Small-scale Hotel **Location:** I-64, exit 242A, just e of jct SR 199 to US 60 E. 480 McLaws Cir 23185. Fax: 757/564-0386. **Facility:** 111 one-bedroom standard units. 3 stories, interior corridors. **Parking:** on-site. **Amenities:** high-speed Internet, hair dryers. *Some:* safes, irons. **Pool(s):** heated indoor/outdoor. **Leisure Activities:** Fee: game room. **Guest Services:** valet laundry. **Business Services:** meeting rooms, business center. **Cards:** AX, DC, DS, MC, VI. **Special Amenities:** free expanded continental breakfast. *(See color ad below)*

SOME UNITS

SUNTERRA RESORTS GREENSPRINGS PLANTATION   *Book at aaa.com*   Phone: 757/253-1177

4/23-9/9 & 12/10-2/28	2P: $274-$361
9/10-12/9	2P: $228-$286
3/1-4/22	2P: $104-$256

Condominium **Location:** 3 mi w on SR 5 from jct SR 199, just n on Greensprings Plantation Dr. 3500 Ludwell Pkwy 23188. Fax: 757/253-8646. **Facility:** Spacious two-bedroom apartments with washer/dryers are featured in this wooded community. 282 two-bedroom suites with kitchens and whirlpools. 3 stories (no elevator), exterior corridors. **Parking:** on-site. **Terms:** office hours 7 am-10 pm, check-in 4 pm, 2-3 night minimum stay - seasonal, 21 day cancellation notice, weekly rates available. **Amenities:** voice mail, irons. *Fee:* video library, safes. **Pool(s):** outdoor, heated indoor, wading. **Leisure Activities:** whirlpools, 2 lighted tennis courts, recreation programs, playground, exercise room, sports court, basketball, horseshoes, shuffleboard, volleyball. *Fee:* golf-18 holes, miniature golf, bicycles. **Guest Services:** gift shop, complimentary laundry. **Business Services:** fax. **Cards:** AX, DS, MC, VI.

SOME UNITS

(See map and index starting on p. 902)

SUNTERRA RESORTS POWHATAN PLANTATION *Book at aaa.com* Phone: (757)220-1200 **3**

4/22-9/9	1P: $140-$400	2P: $140-$400
9/10-12/9	1P: $122-$295	2P: $122-$295
12/10-2/28	1P: $110-$273	2P: $110-$273
3/1-4/21	1P: $108-$249	2P: $108-$249

Resort Condominium **Location:** Jct SR 5, just n. 3601 Ironbound Rd 23188. Fax: 757/253-0987. **Facility:** Geese linger around ponds on the landscaped grounds of this restored 17th-century plantation; townhouse units include fireplaces. 819 units. 43 one- and 776 two-bedroom suites, some with efficiencies, kitchens and/or whirlpools. 2 stories (no elevator), exterior corridors. **Parking:** on-site. **Terms:** check-in 4 pm, 3 night minimum stay - seasonal and/or weekends, 21 day cancellation notice-fee imposed, weekly rates available. **Amenities:** video library (fee), voice mail, irons, hair dryers. **Dining:** The Kitchen at Powhatan Plantation, see separate listing. **Pool(s):** 3 outdoor, heated indoor, wading. **Leisure Activities:** sauna, whirlpool, fishing, 2 lighted tennis courts, racquetball courts, recreation programs, hiking trails, jogging, playground, exercise room, sports court, basketball, horseshoes, volleyball. *Fee:* miniature golf, bicycles, game room. **Guest Services:** gift shop, complimentary laundry. **Business Services:** meeting rooms, business center. **Cards:** AX, DC, MC, VI.

(ASK) (TI) (swim) (X) (VCR) (DATA PORT) (box) (box) (box)

WAR HILL INN BED & BREAKFAST Phone: 757/565-0248 **2**

(AAA) (SAVE) All Year [BP] 1P: $85-$160 2P: $85-$160 XP: $30 D16

Bed & Breakfast **Location:** I-64, exit 234, just e on SR 199, 1.4 mi nw. Located in a quiet rural area. 4560 Longhill Rd 23188-1533. Fax: 757/565-4550. **Facility:** A large working farm serves as a backdrop for this Colonial-style home featuring country furnishings in cottages; two rooms have gas fireplaces. Smoke free premises. 6 units. 4 one-bedroom standard units. 2 cottages ($160-$205) with whirlpools. 2 stories (no elevator), interior/exterior corridors. **Parking:** on-site. **Terms:** check-in 4 pm, 2 night minimum stay - seasonal and/or weekends, 14 day cancellation notice-fee imposed. **Amenities:** hair dryers. **Business Services:** fax. **Cards:** MC, VI. **Special Amenities:** free full breakfast and free local telephone calls.

SOME UNITS
(X) (Z) / (box) (box) (box) /

——— *The following lodging was either not evaluated or did not* ———
meet AAA rating requirements but is listed for your information only.

COLONIAL HOUSES & TAVERNS Phone: 757/565-8440

(fyi) Not evaluated. **Location:** In Colonial Willamsburg restored area; registration on Francis St. 136 E Francis St 23187. Facilities, services, and decor characterize a mid-range property.

——— **WHERE TO DINE** ———

THE BACKFIN SEAFOOD RESTAURANT Lunch: $4-$6 Dinner: $7-$14 Phone: 757/565-5430 **5**

Seafood **Location:** Jct Ironboard Rd, 0.6 mi s. 3701 Strawberry Plains Rd 23188. **Hours:** 11 am-3 & 4:30-9 pm, Fri & Sat-9:30 pm. Closed major holidays; also Sun. **Features:** Hand-painted murals of sea birds on the beach, tinted-wood walls and airy sails suspended from the ceiling set the casual restaurant apart from many other area seafood establishments. Diners can munch on healthy servings of fried or broiled oysters, scallops and shrimp and excellent crab cakes. Seating options include the dining room and new deck. Casual dress; cocktails. **Parking:** on-site. **Cards:** MC, VI.

(&M) (X)

THE BRAY DINING ROOM Lunch: $8-$20 Dinner: $15-$40 Phone: 757/253-3900 **17**

Continental **Location:** I-64, exit 242A to US 60, 1 mi e, follow signs; in Kingsmill Resort. 1010 Kingsmill Rd 23185. **Hours:** 6:30-10 am, 11:30-2 & 6-10 pm. **Reservations:** suggested, for dinner. **Features:** Classic dishes with modern, creative influences from Europe and the Chesapeake Bay region are served in contemporary surroundings in the Kingsmill Resort, overlooking the James River. Jackets are required during winter. Dressy casual; cocktails. **Parking:** on-site. **Cards:** AX, DC, DS, MC, VI.

(Y) (X)

CITIES GRILLE Lunch: $6-$9 Dinner: $9-$19 Phone: 757/564-3955 **8**

Regional American **Location:** Jct SR 5 and Ironbound Rd; in Governor's Green Shopping Center. 4511 C John Tyler Hwy 23185. **Hours:** 11:30 am-3 & 5-9 pm, Fri & Sat-10 pm, Sun noon-3 & 5-9 pm. Closed major holidays. **Reservations:** suggested. **Features:** This fun, neighborhood bistro revamps its menu seasonally to spotlight three to four American cities and their distinctive cuisines. Steak, seafood and pasta act as foundations. Standards that never leave the menu include Hawaiian salmon, grilled rack of lamb and seared catfish over succotash. Casual dress; cocktails. **Parking:** on-site. **Cards:** AX, DC, DS, MC, VI.

(X)

DORALDO RISTORANTE ITALIANO Lunch: $5-$13 Dinner: $5-$22 Phone: 757/220-0795 **12**

Italian **Location:** I-64, exit 242A to US 60, just e of SR 199; in Village Shoppes at Kingsmill, just w of Busch Gardens. 1915 Pocahontas Tr, Suite D2 23185. **Hours:** 11:30 am-2:30 & 5-9 pm, Sat from 5 pm. Closed major holidays; also Sun. **Features:** The casual, family restaurant has a menu of a wide variety of Italian favorites. Seating is cozy and intimate on the covered patio. For dessert, try cannoli or tartuffo. Casual dress; beer & wine only. **Parking:** on-site. **Cards:** AX, MC, VI.

(X)

EAGLES Lunch: $8-$20 Dinner: $20-$45 Phone: 757/253-3900 **16**

Steak House **Location:** I-64, exit 242A to US 60, 1 mi e, follow signs at Kingsmill Resort Golf Club. 1010 Kingsmill Rd 23185. **Hours:** 6 am-11 pm. **Reservations:** suggested, for dinner. **Features:** Steaks and chops are cold-smoked over beechwood chips straight from the Anheuser-Busch brewery, resulting in a distinctive flavor. The dining room overlooks the championship river golf course. Dressy casual; cocktails. **Parking:** on-site. **Cards:** AX, DC, DS, MC, VI.

(Y) (X)

(See map and index starting on p. 902)

FLORIMONTE'S FINE FOODS & DELI   Lunch: $5-$10   Dinner: $5-$10   Phone: 757/253-2266   (7)
Location: Jct SR 199 and 5; in Williamsburg Crossing. 5251 John Tyler Hwy 23185. **Hours:** 8 am-7 pm. Closed
major holidays; also Sun. **Features:** In the heart of Colonial Virginia, the New York-style delicatessen
prepares thin crust and Sicilian pizza, hot and cold sandwiches and daily hot specials. Refrigerated cases
Deli/Subs   display fabulous take-home meals, from fresh pasta and sauce, dressings and refined entrees to seafood
Sandwiches   and steak. Also offered are Italian pastries and desserts. Casual dress; beer & wine only. **Parking:** on-site.
Cards: MC, VI.

GIUSEPPE'S ITALIAN CAFE   Lunch: $6-$13   Dinner: $6-$18   Phone: 757/565-1977   (3)
Location: 3 mi w on US 60; in Ewell Station Shopping Center. 5601 Richmond Rd 23188. **Hours:** 11:30 am-2 & 5-9
pm, Fri & Sat-9:30 pm. Closed major holidays; also Sun. **Reservations:** accepted. **Features:** Well-
prepared, hearty offerings, including a lentil soup that was featured in Bon Appetit Magazine, make up a
Italian   varied, traditional menu with lots of interesting pasta and pizza. Photographs and prints decorate the walls
of the comfortable cafe. Casually dressed servers are friendly and prompt. Casual dress; cocktails. **Parking:** on-site.
Cards: AX, DS, MC, VI.

HAYASHI JAPANESE RESTAURANT   Lunch: $5-$11   Dinner: $10-$19   Phone: 757/253-0282   (2)
Location: 2 mi w on US 60; in Ewell Station Shopping Center. 5601 Richmond Rd 23185. **Hours:** 11:30 am-2:30 &
5-9:30 pm, Fri & Sat-10:30 pm. Closed: 1/1, 11/24, 12/25. **Reservations:** suggested. **Features:** Traditional
Japanese dishes such as teriyaki, tempura, gyoza dumplings and noodle soup are featured as well as a full
Japanese   sushi bar. The atmosphere is warm and contemporary, and noticeably nicely bereft of the standardized
decor. The service is friendly. Casual dress; cocktails. **Parking:** on-site. **Cards:** AX, DS, MC, VI.

THE KITCHEN AT POWHATAN PLANTATION   Dinner: $21-$35   Phone: 757/253-7893   (6)
Location: Jct SR 5, just n; in Sunterra Resorts Powhatan Plantation. 3601 Ironbound Rd 23188. **Hours:** 5:30 pm-10
pm. Closed: 12/25; also Mon. **Reservations:** suggested. **Features:** A Colonial atmosphere combines with a
cutting-edge contemporary menu that showcases regional food and farm-raised game. The innovative and
Regional American excellent menu, which changes frequently, includes a la carte, prix fixe and five-course tasting choices.
Dressy casual; cocktails. **Parking:** on-site. **Cards:** AX, DC, DS, MC, VI.

LA GRANDE TEA ROOM   Lunch: $6-$10   Phone: 757/229-4493   (10)
Location: On SR 5, just s of jct SR 199. 1325 Jamestown Rd 23185. **Hours:** 11 am-3 pm. Closed major holidays;
also Thurs-Sun. **Features:** Colonial antiques and blue and white china create a charming setting in which to
Specialty   enjoy a pot of fine tea, scones, sandwiches, and their famous savory chowders. Casual dress. **Parking:** on-
site. **Cards:** MC, VI.

LA TOLTECA   Lunch: $4-$7   Dinner: $6-$12   Phone: 757/253-2939   (1)
Location: I-64, exit 234 (SR 199 E) to US 60, 1.5 mi e. 5611 Richmond Rd 23185. **Hours:** 11 am-10 pm, Sat noon-
10:30 pm, Sun noon-9:30 pm. Closed major holidays. **Features:** The restaurant breaks out of the mold of
Mexican   other Mexican eateries with its daily buffets. Diners can make their own burritos, fajitas, nachos and more.
Casual dress; cocktails. **Parking:** on-site. **Cards:** AX, CB, DC, DS, JC, MC, VI.

LE YACA FRENCH RESTAURANT   Dinner: $20-$30   Phone: 757/220-3616   (13)
Location: US 60, just e of jct SR 199; in the Village Shops at Kingsmill. 1915 Pocahontas Tr 23185. **Hours:** 5:45 pm-
9:45 pm. Closed: 1/1, 12/25; also Sun. **Reservations:** suggested. **Features:** French country elegance
reigns as does a signature entree of leg of lamb prepared over an open hearth. Marquise au chocolate
French   dessert is delightful. Four prix fixe menus with ten entree selections are offered. Casual dress; cocktails.
Parking: on-site. **Cards:** AX, CB, DC, DS, MC, VI.

THE POTTERY WINE & CHEESE SHOP   Lunch: $3-$9   Phone: 757/229-6754   (14)
Location: I-64, exit 242A, just e of jct SR 199 on US 60; in Shoppes at Kingsmill. 1915 Pocahontas Tr 23185.
Hours: 9:30 am-6 pm, Sun noon-5 pm. Closed: 1/1, 11/24, 12/25. **Features:** Hearty sandwiches, daily
Gourmet Grocery soups, and gourmet desserts are tasty treats to enjoy either inside or at the sidewalk tables on a sunny day.
Casual dress; beer & wine only. **Parking:** on-site. **Cards:** AX, DS, MC, VI.

SHACKELFORD'S II   Dinner: $7-$18   Phone: 757/258-5559   (4)
Location: SR 199, exit Monticello Ave; in Monticello Marketplace. 4640-7 Monticello Ave 23188. **Hours:** 4 pm-11 pm,
Sun-10 pm. Closed major holidays. **Reservations:** accepted, except Tues. **Features:** The focus of the
inviting neighborhood bar and grill is on regional American cuisine, particularly seafood selections from
Regional American Chesapeake Bay and choices from the great raw bar. Among the more creative and original dishes are crab
and shrimp sofrito or pork loin attakas. Casual dress; cocktails. **Parking:** on-site. **Cards:** AX, DS, MC, VI.

SOYA JAPANESE CUISINE & SUSHI BAR   Lunch: $6-$9   Dinner: $8-$14   Phone: 757/229-1212   (9)
Location: Jct SR 5 and Ironbound Rd; in Governor's Green Shopping Center. 4511 John Tyler Hwy 23185.
Hours: 11:30 am-2 & 5-9:30 pm, Sat & Sun from 5 pm. **Features:** Difficult choices start when guests enter:
Sit at the sushi bar or at one of the hibachi tables to watch the chefs in action. The menu, heavy on sushi
Japanese   selections, also includes such tempting specialties as teriyaki, udon noodles and soya bento. Casual dress;
cocktails. **Parking:** on-site. **Cards:** AX, CB, DC, DS, JC, MC, VI.

(See map and index starting on p. 902)

THE SPORTSMAN'S GRILLE   **Lunch: $5-$7**   **Dinner: $7-$15**   **Phone:** 757/221-8002   ⑪

American   **Location:** I-64, exit 242A, just w on SR 199, then e on US 60; in Busch Corporate Center. 240 McLaws Cir, Suite 154 23185. **Hours:** 11 am-10 pm. Closed major holidays; also Sun. **Features:** More than your average sports bar, this restaurant has a neighborly feel. Try such specialties as chef's lasagna, burgers, nachos, pot roast sandwich, large salad and daily soup which watching kids sort through the fish tank of trading cards. Decoys and fish trophies hint at the real favorite sport around here. Casual dress; cocktails. **Parking:** on-site. **Cards:** AX, DC, DS, MC, VI.

THE WHALING COMPANY   **Dinner: $13-$19**   **Phone:** 757/229-0275   ⑮

Steak & Seafood   **Location:** I-64, exit 242A, just e of jct SR 199 and US 60. 494 McLaws Cir 23185. **Hours:** 4:30 pm-10 pm. Closed: 12/25. **Reservations:** suggested. **Features:** Divided into cozy rooms with wood and nautical accents, the large space is appropriately relaxed. Although delightful seafood specialties include tilapia Norfolk, seafood skillet and tuna peppercorn, the menu also has excellent hand-cut steaks and combination platters. Casual dress; cocktails. **Parking:** on-site. **Cards:** AX, CB, DC, DS, MC, VI.

CENTRAL WILLIAMSBURG   (See map and index starting on p. 898)

─── WHERE TO STAY ───

A BOXWOOD INN OF WILLIAMSBURG   **Phone:** 757/221-6607   ㊹

Bed & Breakfast   All Year [BP]   1P: $95-$195   2P: $95-$195   XP: $35
Location: Just w of Colonial Williamsburg restored area on US 60/Richmond Rd. Located in a residential area. 708 Richmond Rd 23185. Fax: 757/221-8150. **Facility:** This B&B is housed in a charming 1928 Dutch Colonial and features a spacious sunroom and rear porch overlooking picturesque perennial gardens. Smoke free premises. 4 one-bedroom standard units, some with whirlpools. 2 stories (no elevator), interior corridors. **Bath:** combo or shower only. **Parking:** on-site. **Terms:** age restrictions may apply, 14 day cancellation notice-fee imposed, package plans. **Amenities:** CD players, hair dryers. **Business Services:** fax. **Cards:** AX, MC, VI.

SOME UNITS
(ASK) (X) (DATA PORT) / (VCR) /

AN AMERICAN INN-WILLIAMSBURG MANOR   **Phone:** (757)220-8011   ㊷

Historic Bed & Breakfast   4/1-12/31   1P: $109-$169
3/1-3/31 & 1/1-2/28   1P: $99-$169
Location: US 60/Richmond Rd, just w of William and Mary College. Located in a residential area. 600 Richmond Rd 23185. Fax: 757/220-0245. **Facility:** Featuring hardwood floors and canopy beds, this stately brick Colonial Revival home dating from 1926 is just steps from the college. Smoke free premises. 5 one-bedroom standard units. 2 stories (no elevator), interior corridors. **Bath:** combo or shower only. **Parking:** on-site. **Terms:** check-in 4:30 pm, 2 night minimum stay - weekends, 21 day cancellation notice-fee imposed, package plans, $2 service charge. **Dining:** dinner available to guests by advanced reservation. **Business Services:** fax. **Cards:** AX, DS, MC, VI. **Special Amenities:** free expanded continental breakfast and free newspaper.

APPLEWOOD COLONIAL BED & BREAKFAST   **Phone:** (757)229-0205   ㊻

Bed & Breakfast   All Year   1P: $100-$175   2P: $110-$175   XP: $25   D
Location: US 60 W/Richmond Rd, just w of William and Mary College and Merchants Square. Located in a residential area. 605 Richmond Rd 23185. Fax: 757/229-9405. **Facility:** Flemish-bond brick fronts this Colonial-style home built in 1929 by restoration craftsmen; inside are finely detailed woodwork and queen canopy beds. Smoke free premises. 4 units. 3 one-bedroom standard units. 1 one-bedroom suite ($150-$175). 3 stories (no elevator), interior corridors. **Parking:** street. **Terms:** 2 night minimum stay - weekends, 14 day cancellation notice-fee imposed, package plans. **Amenities:** video library, CD players, irons, hair dryers. **Business Services:** fax. **Cards:** MC, VI.

(X) (VCR) (■)

A PRIMROSE COTTAGE   **Phone:** 757/229-6421   ㊺

Bed & Breakfast   All Year   1P: $95-$165   2P: $95-$165   XP: $25
Location: Just w of Colonial Williamsburg restored area on US 60/Richmond Rd. 706 Richmond Rd 23185. Fax: 757/259-0717. **Facility:** Overflowing gardens surround this cozy Cape Cod-style cottage decorated with German folk-art accents. Smoke free premises. 4 one-bedroom standard units, some with whirlpools. 2 stories, interior corridors. **Parking:** on-site. **Terms:** check-in 4 pm, 2 night minimum stay - seasonal and/or weekends, age restrictions may apply, 14 day cancellation notice, package plans. **Amenities:** Some: irons, hair dryers. **Business Services:** fax. **Cards:** MC, VI.

(X) (☎)

BASSETT MOTEL   **Phone:** 757/229-5175   ㊽

Motel   5/1-9/11   1P: $49-$54   2P: $55-$58   XP: $5   D5
3/1-4/30 & 9/12-1/3   1P: $34-$39   2P: $39-$44   XP: $5   D5
1/4-2/28   1P: $29-$34   2P: $34-$39   XP: $5   D5
Location: US 60, 0.5 mi se of jct SR 5 and 31. 800 York St 23185. Fax: 757/221-0936. **Facility:** 18 one-bedroom standard units. 1 story, exterior corridors. **Bath:** combo or shower only. **Parking:** on-site. **Terms:** 3 day cancellation notice-fee imposed, package plans, $2 service charge. **Cards:** MC, VI. **Special Amenities:** free local telephone calls and early check-in/late check-out.

SOME UNITS
(T→) (✳) (DATA PORT) (■) / (X) (▤) /
FEE

BEST WESTERN COLONIAL CAPITOL INN   _Book at aaa.com_   **Phone:** (757)253-1222   ㊼

Small-scale Hotel   6/17-9/4 [ECP]   1P: $89-$129   2P: $89-$129   XP: $5   F12
9/5-10/30 [ECP]   1P: $69-$119   2P: $69-$119   XP: $5   F12
3/18-6/16 [ECP]   1P: $59-$109   2P: $59-$109   XP: $5   F12
Location: Just n of jct US 60 and SR 5. 111 Penniman Rd 23187 (PO Box 3564, WILLIAMSBURG, 23187-3564). Fax: 757/229-9264. **Facility:** 85 one-bedroom standard units. 3 stories, interior corridors. **Bath:** combo or shower only. **Parking:** on-site. **Terms:** open 3/18-10/30, 3 day cancellation notice, package plans, small pets only ($10 extra charge). **Amenities:** safes, irons, hair dryers. **Pool(s):** outdoor, wading. **Leisure Activities:** playground. **Business Services:** fax. **Cards:** AX, CB, DC, DS, MC, VI. **Special Amenities:** free expanded continental breakfast and early check-in/late check-out. _(See color ad p 916)_

SOME UNITS
(SD) (▤) (T→) (ⓜ) (♿) (≈) (DATA PORT) (□) / (X) (▤) /
FEE   FEE   FEE

(See map and index starting on p. 898)

BEST WESTERN PATRICK HENRY INN   Phone: (757)229-9540   **55**

6/17-9/4 [ECP]	1P: $109-$179	2P: $109-$179	XP: $5	F12
9/5-12/31 [ECP]	1P: $89-$159	2P: $89-$159	XP: $5	F12
3/1-6/16 [ECP]	1P: $79-$139	2P: $79-$139	XP: $5	F12
1/1-2/28 [ECP]	1P: $59-$109	2P: $59-$109	XP: $5	F12

Small-scale Hotel **Location:** E on US 60 at jct SR 5 and 31; 1 blk from Colonial Williamsburg. 249 E York St NW 23187 (PO Drawer 3678, WILLIAMSBURG, 23187-3678). Fax: 757/220-1273. **Facility:** 301 units. 298 one-bedroom standard units, some with whirlpools. 3 one-bedroom suites with whirlpools. 4 stories, interior corridors. *Bath:* combo or shower only. **Parking:** on-site. **Terms:** 3 day cancellation notice, [MAP] meal plan available, package plans, pets ($15 fee). **Amenities:** high-speed Internet, voice mail, safes, irons, hair dryers. **Dining:** 7 am-10 pm, cocktails. **Pool(s):** heated outdoor. **Leisure Activities:** playground. **Guest Services:** valet and coin laundry. **Business Services:** conference facilities, fax. **Cards:** AX, CB, DC, DS, MC, VI. **Special Amenities:** early check-in/late check-out and free room upgrade (subject to availability with advance reservations). *(See color ad below)*

(See map and index starting on p. 898)

BEST WESTERN WILLIAMSBURG WESTPARK
HOTEL *Book at aaa.com*

		Phone: (757)229-1134	⑪
6/17-9/4 [ECP]	1P: $69-$109	2P: $69-$109	XP: $5	F17
3/1-6/16 [ECP]	1P: $49-$89	2P: $49-$89	XP: $5	F17
9/5-10/31 [ECP]	1P: $49-$79	2P: $49-$79	XP: $5	F17
11/1-2/28 [ECP]	1P: $39-$69	2P: $39-$69	XP: $5	F17

Small-scale Hotel **Location:** Jct US 60 (Richmond Rd) and SR 612 (Ironbound Rd). 1600 Richmond Rd 23185. Fax: 757/229-3215. **Facility:** 163 units. 159 one-bedroom standard units. 4 one-bedroom suites ($79-$139). 2-3 stories (no elevator), interior/exterior corridors. *Bath:* combo or shower only. **Parking:** on-site. **Terms:** cancellation fee imposed, package plans, small pets only ($10 extra charge). **Amenities:** irons, hair dryers. **Pool(s):** heated indoor. **Leisure Activities:** Fee: game room. **Guest Services:** valet and coin laundry. **Business Services:** meeting rooms, fax. **Cards:** AX, CB, DC, DS, MC, VI. **Special Amenities:** free expanded continental breakfast and free local telephone calls.

SOME UNITS

CAPTAIN JOHN SMITH INN *Book at aaa.com*

| | | Phone: (757)220-0710 | ④ |
| All Year | 1P: $39-$99 | 2P: $39-$99 | XP: $10 | F17 |

Motel   **Location:** US 60, 2 mi w of jct Bypass Rd. 2225 Richmond Rd 23185. Fax: 757/220-1166. **Facility:** 68 one-bedroom standard units. 2 stories, exterior corridors. **Parking:** on-site. **Terms:** office hours 7 am-11 pm, 2 night minimum stay - seasonal, weekly rates available, package plans. **Pool(s):** small outdoor. **Leisure Activities:** Fee: game room. **Business Services:** fax. **Cards:** AX, DC, DS, MC, VI. *(See color ad p 904)*

SOME UNITS

CEDARS OF WILLAMSBURG BED & BREAKFAST

| | | Phone: (757)229-3591 | ㊿ |
| All Year | 1P: $120-$300 | 2P: $120-$300 | XP: $15 | D10 |

Historic Bed & Breakfast   **Location:** SR 31 and 5 (Jamestown Rd). Located across from William and Mary College. 616 Jamestown Rd 23185. Fax: 757/229-0756. **Facility:** Colonial-style appointments decorate this brick Georgian home which is one of the town's longest-operating B&Bs. Smoke free premises. 9 units. 6 one- and 1 two-bedroom standard units. 2 one-bedroom suites. 3 stories (no elevator), interior/exterior corridors. *Bath:* combo or shower only. **Parking:** on-site. **Terms:** 2 night minimum stay - seasonal and/or weekends, 14 day cancellation notice-fee imposed, package plans. **Leisure Activities:** Fee: massage. **Cards:** MC, VI. **Special Amenities:** free full breakfast and free newspaper.

SOME UNITS

(See map and index starting on p. 898)

COLONEL WALLER INN & SUITES

Phone: (757)253-0999   [29]

(AAA) [SAVE]

6/16-9/3	1P: $59-$99	2P: $59-$99	XP: $6
3/1-6/15 & 9/4-10/31	1P: $27-$64	2P: $27-$64	XP: $6
11/1-2/28	1P: $27-$52	2P: $27-$52	XP: $6

Motel

Location: I-64, exit 238, 1.5 mi e on SR 143, then just w on SR 5 (Jamestown Rd). 917 Capitol Landing Rd 23185. Fax: 757/253-0276. **Facility:** 28 one-bedroom suites. 2 stories (no elevator), exterior corridors. **Parking:** on-site. **Terms:** 3 day cancellation notice. **Amenities:** irons, hair dryers. **Pool(s):** outdoor. **Guest Services:** coin laundry. **Business Services:** fax. **Cards:** AX, DS, MC, VI. *(See color ad p 917)*

SOME UNITS

COLONIAL CAPITAL BED & BREAKFAST

Phone: 757/229-0233   [49]

(AAA) [SAVE]

3/15-12/31 [BP]	1P: $128-$141	2P: $150-$165	XP: $30
3/1-3/14 & 1/1-2/28 [BP]	1P: $113-$124	2P: $132-$145	XP: $30

Historic Bed & Breakfast

Location: Just w of Colonial Williamsburg and William and Mary College. Located across from the stadium. 501 Richmond Rd 23185-3537. Fax: 757/253-7667. **Facility:** This 1926 Colonial Revival home offers gracious units furnished with canopy beds; a private third-floor suite includes a seating area. Designated smoking area. 5 units. 4 one-bedroom standard units. 1 one-bedroom suite ($160-$180). 2 stories (no elevator), interior corridors. *Bath:* combo or shower only. **Parking:** on-site. **Terms:** 2 night minimum stay - weekends, age restrictions may apply, 14 day cancellation notice, package plans. **Amenities:** video library, hair dryers. **Leisure Activities:** bicycles. **Business Services:** fax. **Cards:** AX, DS, MC, VI. **Special Amenities:** free local telephone calls and free newspaper.

COLONIAL GARDENS BED & BREAKFAST

Phone: (757)220-8087   [69]

All Year [BP]	2P: $135-$175	XP: $30

Bed & Breakfast

Location: Just ne of jct SR 5 and 31; jct SR 199. 1109 Jamestown Rd 23185. Fax: 757/253-1495. **Facility:** Original artwork and 18th- and 19th-century antiques decorate the large guest rooms at this Colonial-style home with wooded gardens. Smoke free premises. 4 units. 3 one-bedroom standard units. 1 one-bedroom suite. 2 stories, interior corridors. *Bath:* combo or shower only. **Parking:** on-site. **Terms:** check-in 4 pm, 2 night minimum stay - seasonal and/or weekends, age restrictions may apply, 14 day cancellation notice-fee imposed, package plans. **Amenities:** video library, hair dryers. **Business Services:** fax. **Cards:** DS, MC, VI.

COMFORT INN & SUITES   *Book at aaa.com*

Phone: (757)229-2981   [16]

5/20-9/4 [ECP]	1P: $89-$199	2P: $89-$199	XP: $10	F17
3/18-5/19 [ECP]	1P: $59-$159	2P: $59-$159	XP: $10	F17
3/1-3/17 & 9/5-2/28 [ECP]	1P: $49-$139	2P: $49-$139	XP: $10	F17

Small-scale Hotel

Location: 1.5 mi nw of Colonial Williamsburg on US 60; jct Richmond and Bypass rds. 1420 Richmond Rd 23185. Fax: 757/229-8179. **Facility:** 110 units. 89 one-bedroom standard units, some with whirlpools. 21 one-bedroom suites ($99-$199). 3 stories, interior/exterior corridors. **Parking:** on-site. **Terms:** package plans. **Amenities:** high-speed Internet, voice mail, safes, irons, hair dryers. **Pool(s):** outdoor. **Guest Services:** valet and coin laundry. **Business Services:** fax. **Cards:** AX, CB, DC, DS, MC, VI.

SOME UNITS

COMFORT INN CENTRAL   *Book at aaa.com*

Phone: (757)220-3888   [5]

(AAA) [SAVE]

6/17-9/5	1P: $69-$139	2P: $69-$139	XP: $7	F17
3/1-6/16	1P: $49-$119	2P: $49-$119	XP: $7	F17
9/6-2/28	1P: $39-$89	2P: $39-$89	XP: $7	F17

Small-scale Hotel **Location:** I-64, exit 234, 2 mi s to US 60, then 3 mi e. 2007 Richmond Rd 23185. Fax: 757/229-6329. **Facility:** 128 one-bedroom standard units, some with whirlpools. 5 stories, interior corridors. **Parking:** on-site. **Terms:** cancellation fee imposed, package plans. **Amenities:** dual phone lines, voice mail, irons, hair dryers. **Dining:** 2 restaurants, 6 am-2 & 4-11 pm, cocktails, also, Fireside Steak Chophouse, see separate listing. **Pool(s):** heated indoor. **Leisure Activities:** game room. **Guest Services:** valet laundry. **Business Services:** fax. **Cards:** AX, CB, DC, DS, JC, MC, VI. **Special Amenities:** free continental breakfast and free local telephone calls. *(See color ad p 919)*

SOME UNITS

COMFORT INN KING GEORGE HISTORIC   *Book at aaa.com*

Phone: (757)229-9230   [32]

(AAA) [SAVE]

6/10-9/4 [ECP]	1P: $99-$129	2P: $99-$129	XP: $10	F18
3/1-6/9 [ECP]	1P: $49-$99	2P: $49-$99	XP: $10	F18
9/5-12/31 [ECP]	1P: $49-$89	2P: $49-$89	XP: $10	F18
1/1-2/28 [ECP]	1P: $49-$69	2P: $49-$69	XP: $10	F18

Small-scale Hotel **Location:** US 60 Bypass, 0.5 mi w of jct SR 132. 706 Bypass Rd 23185. Fax: 757/253-1654. **Facility:** 157 one-bedroom standard units, some with whirlpools. 3-4 stories, interior/exterior corridors. **Parking:** on-site. **Terms:** cancellation fee imposed, package plans. **Amenities:** voice mail, irons, hair dryers. **Pool(s):** outdoor, heated indoor. **Leisure Activities:** sauna, whirlpool, limited exercise equipment. **Guest Services:** valet laundry. **Business Services:** meeting rooms, fax. **Cards:** AX, DC, DS, JC, MC, VI. **Special Amenities:** free expanded continental breakfast and free newspaper. *(See color ad p 920 & inside front cover)*

SOME UNITS

COUNTRY HEARTH INN & SUITES CAPITOL HISTORIC   *Book at aaa.com*

Phone: (757)229-5215   [27]

(AAA) [SAVE]

7/1-9/4	1P: $69-$89	2P: $69-$89	XP: $10	F17
3/1-6/30 & 9/5-2/28	1P: $39-$59	2P: $39-$59	XP: $10	F17

Motel

Location: I-64, exit 238, 1 mi e on SR 143, then just w on SR 5. 924 Capitol Landing Rd 23185. Fax: 757/220-3810. **Facility:** 58 units. 49 one-bedroom standard units. 9 one-bedroom suites ($59-$129) with kitchens. 2 stories (no elevator), exterior corridors. **Parking:** on-site. **Terms:** office hours 8 am-10 pm. **Amenities:** safes (fee), hair dryers. *Some:* irons. **Pool(s):** outdoor. **Guest Services:** coin laundry. **Business Services:** fax. **Cards:** AX, CB, DC, DS, JC, MC, VI. **Special Amenities:** free expanded continental breakfast and free local telephone calls. *(See color ad p 904)*

SOME UNITS

(See map and index starting on p. 898)

COUNTRY INN AND SUITES BY CARLSON   *Book at aaa.com*   Phone: (757)259-7990   30

AAA SAVE

11/1-2/28 [ECP]	1P: $89-$159	2P: $89-$159	XP: $10	F18
3/1-10/31 [ECP]	1P: $79-$159	2P: $79-$159	XP: $10	F18

Location: US 60 Bypass, just e of jct Richmond Rd; 0.7 mi w of jct SR 132. 400 Bypass Rd 23185.
Fax: 757/259-9510. **Facility:** 66 units. 50 one-bedroom standard units. 16 one-bedroom suites ($69-$259).

Small-scale Hotel   3 stories, interior corridors. *Bath:* combo or shower only. **Parking:** on-site. **Terms:** 2 night minimum stay - seasonal, cancellation fee imposed. **Amenities:** video library (fee), DVD players, high-speed Internet, voice mail, irons, hair dryers. *Some:* dual phone lines. **Pool(s):** heated indoor. **Leisure Activities:** whirlpool, exercise room. **Guest Services:** valet and coin laundry. **Business Services:** meeting rooms, fax. **Cards:** AX, DC, DS, MC, VI. **Special Amenities:** free expanded continental breakfast and free local telephone calls. *(See color ad p 847 & p 921)*

SOME UNITS

DAYS INN & SUITES/WEST-COLONIAL   *Book at aaa.com*   Phone: (757)565-2700   1

AAA SAVE

6/17-9/4 [BP]	1P: $69-$119	2P: $69-$119	XP: $10	F17
4/2-6/16 [BP]	1P: $69-$89	2P: $69-$89	XP: $10	F17
3/1-4/1 & 9/5-2/28 [BP]	1P: $49-$89	2P: $49-$89	XP: $10	F17

Location: I-64, exit 234, 1 mi s on SR 199, then 2 mi e on US 60. 5437 Richmond Rd 23188. Fax: 757/565-3700.

Motel   **Facility:** 122 one-bedroom standard units. 2 stories (no elevator), exterior corridors. **Parking:** on-site. **Terms:** package plans. **Amenities:** safes (fee), hair dryers. *Some:* irons. **Pool(s):** outdoor. **Leisure Activities:** playground. *Fee:* game room. **Business Services:** fax. **Cards:** AX, DS, MC, VI. **Special Amenities:** free full breakfast and free newspaper.

SOME UNITS

DAYS INN COLONIAL DOWNTOWN   *Book at aaa.com*   Phone: (757)229-5060   40

AAA SAVE

6/7-9/6	1P: $85-$99	2P: $85-$99	XP: $10	F15
3/1-6/6 & 9/7-12/31	1P: $45-$85	2P: $45-$85	XP: $10	F15
1/1-2/28	1P: $35-$49	2P: $35-$49	XP: $10	F15

Location: Just w of Colonial Williamsburg on US 60. 902 Richmond Rd 23185. Fax: 757/220-9153. **Facility:** 100

Small-scale Hotel   one-bedroom standard units. 2 stories (no elevator), exterior corridors. **Parking:** on-site. **Terms:** cancellation fee imposed, package plans, pets ($10 extra charge). **Amenities:** irons, hair dryers. **Pool(s):** outdoor. **Guest Services:** valet laundry. **Business Services:** meeting rooms, fax. **Cards:** AX, CB, DC, DS, MC, VI. **Special Amenities:** free expanded continental breakfast and free newspaper. *(See color ad below)*

SOME UNITS

(See map and index starting on p. 898)

DAYS INN HISTORIC AREA   *Book at aaa.com*   Phone: 757/253-1166   [23]

6/10-9/4 [CP]	1P: $69-$99	2P: $69-$99	XP: $10	F17
3/1-6/9 & 9/5-12/31 [CP]	1P: $47-$89	2P: $47-$89	XP: $10	F17
1/1-2/28 [CP]	1P: $33-$49	2P: $33-$49	XP: $10	F17

Small-scale Hotel **Location:** Jct Richmond Rd, 1 mi e on US 60 Bypass. 331 Bypass Rd 23185. Fax: 757/221-0637. **Facility:** 120 units. 117 one-bedroom standard units. 3 one-bedroom suites ($79-$189) with whirlpools. 4 stories, interior corridors. **Parking:** on-site. **Terms:** package plans. **Amenities:** voice mail, safes (fee), irons, hair dryers. **Pool(s):** heated outdoor. **Leisure Activities:** whirlpool, picnic area, volleyball. *Fee:* game room. **Guest Services:** valet laundry. **Business Services:** meeting rooms, fax. **Cards:** AX, CB, DC, DS, JC, MC, VI. **Special Amenities:** free newspaper and preferred room (subject to availability with advance reservations).** *(See color ad p 923)*

SOME UNITS

ECONO LODGE CENTRAL   *Book at aaa.com*   Phone: (757)229-6600   [6]

6/1-9/6 [CP]	1P: $55-$110	2P: $55-$110	XP: $5	F17
3/1-5/31 [CP]	1P: $45-$75	2P: $45-$75	XP: $5	F17
9/7-10/31 [CP]	1P: $45-$59	2P: $45-$59	XP: $5	F17
11/1-2/28 [CP]	1P: $35-$49	2P: $35-$49	XP: $5	F17

Motel **Location:** US 60, 2 mi w of jct W Bypass Rd. 1900 Richmond Rd 23185. Fax: 757/941-0107. **Facility:** 85 one-bedroom standard units. 2 stories (no elevator), exterior corridors. **Parking:** on-site. **Terms:** 7 day cancellation notice. **Amenities:** safes (fee). **Pool(s):** outdoor. **Business Services:** fax. **Cards:** AX, CB, DC, DS, JC, MC, VI. **Special Amenities:** free continental breakfast and free local telephone calls. *(See color ad p 925)*

SOME UNITS

ECONO LODGE COLONIAL   *Book at aaa.com*   Phone: (757)253-6450   [48]

5/27-9/5 [CP]	1P: $65-$75	2P: $85-$95	XP: $5	F16
4/11-5/26 [CP]	1P: $50-$55	2P: $55-$60	XP: $5	F16
9/6-2/28 [CP]	1P: $45-$55	2P: $55-$60	XP: $5	F16
3/1-4/10 [CP]	1P: $40-$45	2P: $45-$50	XP: $5	F16

Motel **Location:** Just n of 2nd St and Parkway Dr. 216 Parkway Dr 23185. Fax: 757/229-2888. **Facility:** 48 one-bedroom standard units, some with efficiencies (no utensils). 2 stories (no elevator), interior/exterior corridors. **Parking:** on-site. **Terms:** 2 night minimum stay - seasonal and/or weekends, 3 day cancellation notice, [CP] meal plan available. **Amenities:** hair dryers. **Pool(s):** outdoor. **Leisure Activities:** picnic area. **Business Services:** fax. **Cards:** AX, DS, MC, VI. *(See color ad p 906)*

SOME UNITS
FEE

ECONO LODGE-PARKWAY HISTORIC AREA   *Book at aaa.com*   Phone: (757)229-7564   [35]

6/16-9/5 [CP]	1P: $55-$70	2P: $55-$99	XP: $5	F18
3/16-6/15 [CP]	1P: $45-$55	2P: $50-$60	XP: $5	F18
9/6-2/28 [CP]	1P: $30-$40	2P: $35-$60	XP: $5	F18
3/1-3/15 [CP]	1P: $30-$40	2P: $35-$44	XP: $5	F18

Motel **Location:** I-64, exit 238 to SR 143 E, 2 mi to SR 5, then 1 blk. 442 Parkway Dr 23185. Fax: 757/229-0916. **Facility:** 48 one-bedroom standard units. 2 stories, exterior corridors. **Parking:** on-site. **Business Services:** fax. **Cards:** AX, CB, DC, DS, MC, VI. **Special Amenities:** free continental breakfast and free local telephone calls.

SOME UNITS
FEE FEE

EMBASSY SUITES   *Book at aaa.com*   Phone: (757)229-6800   [15]

6/17-9/3	1P: $149-$209	2P: $149-$209	XP: $15	F17
4/1-6/16	1P: $129-$189	2P: $129-$189	XP: $15	F17
9/4-2/28	1P: $89-$159	2P: $89-$159	XP: $15	F17
3/1-3/31	1P: $89-$129	2P: $89-$129	XP: $15	F17

Small-scale Hotel **Location:** US 60 (Bypass Rd), just w of jct Richmond Rd. Located adjacent to Kingsgate Shopping Center. 3006 Mooretown Rd 23185. Fax: 757/220-3486. **Facility:** 168 one-bedroom suites, some with whirlpools. 5 stories, interior corridors. **Parking:** on-site. **Terms:** check-in 4 pm, 3 day cancellation notice-fee imposed, package plans. **Amenities:** voice mail, irons, hair dryers. **Dining:** 6:30 am-10:30 & 5-10 pm, cocktails. **Pool(s):** heated indoor. **Leisure Activities:** whirlpool, exercise room. **Guest Services:** gift shop, complimentary evening beverages, valet and coin laundry. **Business Services:** meeting rooms, fax. **Cards:** AX, DC, DS, MC, VI. **Special Amenities:** free full breakfast and free newspaper. *(See color ad p 905)*

SOME UNITS

FAIRFIELD INN & SUITES BY MARRIOTT   Phone: (757)645-3600   [17]

[fyi] All Year   1P: $59-$139

Small-scale Hotel Under major renovation, scheduled to be completed September 2004. **Last rated:** ▼▼▼ **Location:** US 60, jct Richmond and Bypass rds. 1402 Richmond Rd 23185. Fax: 757/220-3527. **Facility:** 135 units. 125 one-bedroom standard units. 10 one-bedroom suites. 4 stories, interior corridors. **Parking:** on-site. **Terms:** check-in 4 pm, 3 night minimum stay - seasonal, package plans. **Amenities:** voice mail, irons. *Some:* hair dryers. **Pool(s):** outdoor, heated indoor. **Leisure Activities:** whirlpool, playground. **Guest Services:** valet laundry. **Business Services:** fax. **Cards:** AX, CB, DC, DS, JC, MC, VI.

SOME UNITS
FEE FEE

WILLIAMSBURG
3 Great Locations!

(See map and index starting on p. 898)

FAIRFIELD WILLIAMSBURG CONDO RENTALS AT KINGSGATE
Phone: (757)941-1159 🔟3️⃣

6/11-9/5	1P: $159-$249
9/6-12/31	1P: $159-$209
3/1-6/10	1P: $119-$209
1/1-2/28	1P: $119-$139

Condominium

Location: US 60 (Bypass Rd), just n on Waller Mill Rd. 619 Georgetown Crescent 23185 (725 Bypass Rd, WILLIAMSBURG). Fax: 757/220-3124. **Facility:** Kingsgate is a large time-share community spread over sprawling well-landscaped grounds. 600 units. 300 one- and 300 two-bedroom suites, some with efficiencies, kitchens and/or whirlpools. 2-3 stories (no elevator), exterior corridors. **Parking:** on-site. **Terms:** check-in 4 pm, 21 day cancellation notice-fee imposed, weekly rates available, package plans. **Amenities:** video library (fee), CD players, high-speed Internet, voice mail, safes, irons, hair dryers. **Pool(s):** 2 outdoor, heated indoor. **Leisure Activities:** sauna, whirlpool, miniature golf, 2 lighted tennis courts, recreation programs, playground, exercise room. *Fee:* massage, game room. **Guest Services:** complimentary laundry. **Business Services:** meeting rooms, fax. **Cards:** AX, DC, DS, MC, VI.

FAIRFIELD WILLIAMSBURG CONDO RENTALS GOVERNOR'S GREEN
Phone: (757)941-1159 🔟2️⃣

6/11-9/5	1P: $199-$299
9/6-12/31	1P: $179-$259
3/1-6/10	1P: $129-$259
1/1-2/28	1P: $129-$179

Condominium

Location: US 60 (Bypass Rd), just n to Willer Mill Rd, 0.5 mi n on Mooretown Rd. 300 Cameron Cir 23185 (725 Bypass Rd, WILLIAMSBURG). Fax: 757/220-3124. **Facility:** This large resort offers spacious and stylish apartments which are fully equipped and a large family activity center which includes a walk-in pool. 199 units. 14 one-, 91 two- and 94 three-bedroom suites with kitchens and whirlpools. 3 stories, exterior corridors. **Parking:** on-site. **Terms:** check-in 4 pm, 21 day cancellation notice-fee imposed, weekly rates available, package plans. **Amenities:** video library (fee), CD players, voice mail, safes, irons, hair dryers. *Some:* DVD players. **Pool(s):** 2 heated outdoor, heated indoor, wading. **Leisure Activities:** whirlpools, putting green, miniature golf, tennis court, recreation programs, playground, exercise room. *Fee:* massage, game room. **Guest Services:** complimentary laundry. **Business Services:** meeting rooms, PC, fax. **Cards:** AX, DC, DS, MC, VI.

THE FIFE AND DRUM INN *Book at aaa.com*
Phone: (757)345-1776 5️⃣4️⃣

All Year — 1P: $155-$175 — 2P: $155-$175 — XP: $20

Bed & Breakfast

Location: Between Henry and Boundary sts; center; at Merchants Square. Located on the second floor. 441 Prince George St 23185. Fax: 757/253-1675. **Facility:** Tucked away on the second floor of Merchants Square, this B&B features a stylish, modern interpretation of Colonial decor. Smoke free premises. 9 units. 7 one-bedroom standard units. 2 one-bedroom suites. 2 stories (no elevator), interior/exterior corridors. *Bath:* combo or shower only. **Parking:** no self-parking. **Terms:** 2 night minimum stay - weekends, 30 day cancellation notice-fee imposed, package plans. **Amenities:** video library, voice mail, hair dryers. **Guest Services:** gift shop. **Cards:** AX, DS, MC, VI.

FOUR POINTS BY SHERATON HOTEL & SUITES WILLIAMSBURG HISTORIC DISTRICT *Book at aaa.com*
Phone: (757)229-4100 5️⃣7️⃣

5/27-9/4	1P: $89-$169	2P: $89-$169	XP: $10	F18
3/1-5/26	1P: $59-$159	2P: $59-$159	XP: $10	F18
9/5-10/31	1P: $69-$129	2P: $69-$129	XP: $10	F18
11/1-2/28	1P: $59-$129	2P: $59-$129	XP: $10	F18

AAA SAVE — Small-scale Hotel

Location: US 60 E, 0.3 mi se of jct SR 5 and 31. 351 York St 23185. Fax: 757/229-0176. **Facility:** 199 units. 143 one-bedroom standard units. 56 two-bedroom suites ($99-$269) with kitchens. 4 stories, interior/exterior corridors. *Bath:* combo or shower only. **Parking:** on-site. **Terms:** 3 day cancellation notice-fee imposed, package plans, small pets only ($25 deposit). **Amenities:** video library, dual phone lines, voice mail, irons, hair dryers. *Some:* video games, safes. **Dining:** 6:30 am-10 pm, cocktails. **Pool(s):** heated indoor. **Leisure Activities:** whirlpool, picnic tables, playground, exercise room. **Guest Services:** valet and coin laundry. **Business Services:** conference facilities, fax. **Cards:** AX, CB, DC, DS, JC, MC, VI. **Special Amenities:** free local telephone calls and free newspaper. *(See color ad p 927)*

SOME UNITS

FOX & GRAPE BED & BREAKFAST
Phone: 757/229-6914 4️⃣1️⃣

All Year — 1P: $100-$140 — 2P: $100-$140 — XP: $15

Bed & Breakfast

Location: I-64, exit 238, s on SR 143 to SR 5, 0.8 mi w, then just n. Located in a residential area. 701 Monumental Ave 23185. **Facility:** The owners' own quilts, cross-stitch samplers, hand-carved walking sticks and decoys decorate this Colonial-style home with wraparound porch. Smoke free premises. 4 one-bedroom standard units. 2 stories (no elevator), interior corridors. **Parking:** on-site. **Terms:** 2 night minimum stay - seasonal and/or weekends, age restrictions may apply, 14 day cancellation notice. **Business Services:** fax. **Cards:** MC, VI.

GOVERNOR'S INN *Book at aaa.com*
Phone: (757)229-7940 4️⃣3️⃣

6/13-9/5	1P: $90-$115	2P: $90-$115	XP: $10	F
3/15-6/12 & 9/6-12/31	1P: $75-$105	2P: $75-$105	XP: $10	F

Small-scale Hotel

Location: SR 132, 0.5 mi s of jct US 60. 506 N Henry St 23185 (PO Box 1776, WILLIAMSBURG). Fax: 757/220-7019. **Facility:** 200 one-bedroom standard units. 3 stories, exterior corridors. **Parking:** on-site. **Terms:** open 3/15-12/31, office hours 6 am-11 pm, check-in 4 pm, 3 day cancellation notice-fee imposed, [MAP] meal plan available, package plans. **Amenities:** voice mail, irons, hair dryers. **Pool(s):** outdoor. **Guest Services:** valet laundry, area transportation. **Business Services:** fax. **Cards:** AX, DC, DS, MC, VI. *(See color ad p 936)*

SOME UNITS

(See map and index starting on p. 898)

HAMPTON INN & SUITES   *Book at aaa.com*   Phone: (757)229-4900   **7**

All Year   1P: $59-$149   2P: $59-$149

Location: On US 60, 2 mi w of jct W Bypass Rd. 1880 Richmond Rd 23185. Fax: 757/229-4800. **Facility:** 100

Small-scale Hotel   units. 76 one-bedroom standard units, some with whirlpools. 24 one-bedroom suites ($79-$199) with kitchens. 4 stories, interior corridors. *Bath:* combo or shower only. **Parking:** on-site. **Terms:** 2 night minimum stay - weekends, cancellation fee imposed. **Amenities:** voice mail, irons, hair dryers. *Some:* dual phone lines. **Pool(s):** heated indoor. **Leisure Activities:** exercise room. **Guest Services:** sundries, coin laundry. **Business Services:** fax. **Cards:** AX, DC, DS, MC, VI. *(See color ad p 925)*

SOME UNITS

(ASK) (S/D) (¶↑) (⅃M) (🖥) (🏊) (🎦) (DATA PORT) (💻) / (✕) (VCR) (📞) (🖨) /
FEE FEE FEE

HAMPTON INN WILLIAMSBURG   *Book at aaa.com*   Phone: (757)220-0880   **22**

AAA (SAVE)   All Year [BP]   1P: $49-$129   2P: $49-$129

Location: US 60 (Bypass Rd), just se of jct Richmond Rd. 201 Bypass Rd 23185. Fax: 757/229-7175. **Facility:** 121 one-bedroom standard units, some with whirlpools. 4 stories, interior corridors. **Parking:** on-site.

Small-scale Hotel   **Terms:** check-in 4 pm, 3 day cancellation notice-fee imposed. **Amenities:** voice mail, irons, hair dryers. **Pool(s):** heated indoor. **Leisure Activities:** whirlpool. **Guest Services:** valet laundry. **Business Services:** meeting rooms, fax. **Cards:** AX, CB, DC, DS, MC, VI. **Special Amenities:** free full breakfast and free local telephone calls.

SOME UNITS

(S/D) (¶↑) (⅃M) (🏊) (🎦) (DATA PORT) (💻) / (✕) (📞) (🖨) /
FEE FEE

HILTON GARDEN INN   *Book at aaa.com*   Phone: (757)253-9400   **10**

AAA (SAVE)   All Year   1P: $79-$179   2P: $79-$179   F18

Location: On US 60, w of jct Bypass Rd. 1624 Richmond Rd 23185. Fax: 757/253-8600. **Facility:** 119 one-bedroom standard units. 4 stories, interior corridors. *Bath:* shower only. **Parking:** on-site.

Small-scale Hotel   **Terms:** cancellation fee imposed, [BP] meal plan available, package plans. **Amenities:** video games, high-speed Internet, dual phone lines, voice mail, irons, hair dryers. **Dining:** 6:30-10:30 am. **Pool(s):** heated indoor. **Leisure Activities:** whirlpool, exercise room. **Guest Services:** sundries, valet and coin laundry. **Business Services:** meeting rooms, business center. **Cards:** AX, DC, DS, JC, MC, VI. **Special Amenities:** free newspaper. *(See color ad p 928 & inside front cover)*

SOME UNITS

(S/D) (¶↑) (🍸) (⅃M) (🖥) (📷) (🏊) (🎦) (DATA PORT) (📞) (🖨) (💻) / (✕) /

HITE'S BED & BREAKFAST   Phone: 757-229-4814   **42**

All Year [BP]   1P: $95-$125   2P: $95-$125   XP: $20   F6

Location: I-64, exit 238, s on SR 143 to SR 5, 0.8 mi w, then just n. Located in a residential area. 704 Monumental Ave

Bed & Breakfast   23185. **Facility:** A charming garden adds curb appeal to this Cape Cod-style B&B, which is furnished with collectibles and antiques. Smoke free premises. 2 one-bedroom standard units. 2 stories (no elevator), interior corridors. **Parking:** on-site. **Terms:** 14 day cancellation notice. **Amenities:** irons, hair dryers.

SOME UNITS

(✕) (💻) / (VCR) /

Expect more value at Hilton Garden Inn.® Whenever you travel to Virginia, the Hilton Garden Inn® Williamsburg is waiting to serve you. Along with 119 luxurious guest rooms and suites, we offer a fitness center, indoor pool, Pavilion Pantry® and breakfast café. We also provide valet & self-serve laundry facilities. We're just minutes from historic Williamsburg, Yorktown, Busch Gardens,® Jamestown, Water Country U.S.A.® and championship golf courses. We're also close to many major attractions, endless shopping and a wide variety of dining choices. To receive your special rate, just contact your AAA travel office, Hilton's private AAA number at **1-800-916-2221** or the hotel directly at toll free **877-609-9400**. Visit us online at **hiltongardeninn.com**.

1624 Richmond Road
Williamsburg, VA 23185
757-253-9400

(See map and index starting on p. 898)

HOLIDAY INN-DOWNTOWN & HOLIDOME — *Book at aaa.com* — Phone: (757)229-0200 — **39**

AAA SAVE

Small-scale Hotel

6/1-9/1	1P: $129-$149	2P: $129-$149
9/2-10/31	1P: $69-$129	2P: $69-$129
3/1-5/31 & 11/1-2/28	1P: $59-$119	2P: $59-$119

Location: SR 5, just e of jct US 60. 814 Capitol Landing Rd 23185. Fax: 757/220-1642. **Facility:** 137 units. 136 one-bedroom standard units. 1 one-bedroom suite. 3 stories, interior corridors. **Parking:** on-site. **Terms:** cancellation fee imposed, package plans. **Amenities:** voice mail, irons, hair dryers. **Dining:** 2 restaurants, 7 am-10 pm, cocktails. **Pool(s):** heated indoor. **Leisure Activities:** sauna, whirlpool, exercise room. **Guest Services:** valet and coin laundry. **Business Services:** conference facilities, fax. **Cards:** AX, CB, DC, DS, JC, MC, VI. **Special Amenities:** free newspaper.

SOME UNITS
FEE FEE

HOLIDAY INN EXPRESS — *Book at aaa.com* — Phone: (757)941-1057 — **14**

Small-scale Hotel

6/1-9/5	1P: $129-$149
4/1-5/31	1P: $89-$99
9/6-2/28	1P: $69-$79
3/1-3/31	1P: $69-$99

Location: On US 60, just w of jct Bypass Rd. 1452 Richmond Rd 23185. Fax: 757/941-1058. **Facility:** 93 one-bedroom standard units. 4 stories, interior corridors. *Bath:* combo or shower only. **Parking:** on-site. **Terms:** 2 night minimum stay - seasonal, 3 day cancellation notice-fee imposed, package plans. **Amenities:** high-speed Internet, voice mail, irons, hair dryers. **Pool(s):** heated indoor. **Leisure Activities:** exercise room. **Guest Services:** sundries, valet and coin laundry. **Business Services:** fax. **Cards:** AX, DC, DS, MC, VI.

SOME UNITS

HOLIDAY INN PATRIOT — *Book at aaa.com* — Phone: (757)565-2600 — **3**

AAA SAVE

Small-scale Hotel

6/3-9/5	1P: $89-$149	2P: $89-$149
3/1-6/2 & 9/6-2/28	1P: $69-$109	2P: $69-$109

Location: I-64, exit 234 (SR 199 E) to US 60, 2.5 mi e. 3032 Richmond Rd 23185. Fax: 757/564-9738. **Facility:** 160 one-bedroom standard units. 4 stories, interior corridors. **Parking:** on-site. **Terms:** check-in 4 pm, 3 day cancellation notice, package plans, small pets only ($10 extra charge). **Amenities:** high-speed Internet, dual phone lines, voice mail, irons, hair dryers. **Dining:** 7 am-10 & 5:30-10:30 pm, cocktails, entertainment. **Pool(s):** heated indoor/outdoor. **Leisure Activities:** whirlpool, playground, exercise room. *Fee:* golf privileges. **Guest Services:** valet laundry. **Business Services:** conference facilities, fax. **Cards:** AX, DC, DS, MC, VI. **Special Amenities:** free continental breakfast and free local telephone calls.

SOME UNITS
FEE   FEE FEE

HOMEWOOD SUITES BY HILTON — *Book at aaa.com* — Phone: (757)259-1199 — **25**

AAA SAVE

Small-scale Hotel

6/17-9/4 [BP]	1P: $149-$359	2P: $149-$359	XP: $12	F18
3/1-6/16 [BP]	1P: $99-$329	2P: $99-$329	XP: $12	F18
9/5-1/2 [BP]	1P: $89-$329	2P: $89-$329	XP: $12	F18
1/3-2/28 [BP]	1P: $69-$199	2P: $69-$199	XP: $12	F18

Location: US 60 Bypass, 0.5 mi w of jct SR 132. 601 Bypass Rd 23185. Fax: 757/259-1666. **Facility:** 61 units. 43 one- and 18 two-bedroom suites ($69-$359) with kitchens. 5 stories, interior corridors. **Parking:** on-site. **Terms:** check-in 4 pm, 2 night minimum stay - seasonal, 3 day cancellation notice-fee imposed, package plans. **Amenities:** video library, high-speed Internet, dual phone lines, voice mail, irons, hair dryers. **Pool(s):** heated indoor. **Leisure Activities:** exercise room. **Guest Services:** sundries, valet and coin laundry. **Business Services:** meeting rooms, fax. **Cards:** AX, CB, DC, DS, MC, VI. **Special Amenities:** free full breakfast and free newspaper. *(See color ad p 930)*

SOME UNITS

THE HOTEL WILLIAMSBURG (NOW KNOWN AS QUALITY INN HISTORIC WILLIAMSBURG — Phone: (757)220-2800 — **28**

Small-scale Hotel

6/10-9/5	1P: $99-$159	2P: $99-$159	XP: $10	F18
3/1-6/9	1P: $59-$119	2P: $59-$119	XP: $10	F18
9/6-2/28	1P: $49-$99	2P: $49-$99	XP: $10	F18

Location: US 60 Bypass, 0.5 mi w of jct SR 132. 600 Bypass Rd 23185. Fax: 757/220-8986. **Facility:** 141 one-bedroom standard units. 5 stories, interior corridors. *Bath:* combo or shower only. **Parking:** on-site. **Terms:** check-in 4 pm, cancellation fee imposed, package plans. **Amenities:** dual phone lines, voice mail, irons, hair dryers. **Pool(s):** outdoor. **Leisure Activities:** exercise room. **Guest Services:** valet and coin laundry. **Cards:** AX, DC, DS, MC, VI. *(See color ad below)*

SOME UNITS

Homewood Suites by Hilton® Williamsburg

601 Bypass Road • Williamsburg, VA 23185

(757) 259-1199

MAKE YOURSELF AT HOME.™

- Nestled in a peaceful wooded resort setting
- Champion golf courses nearby
- 2 miles to Colonial Williamsburg
- 1 mile to the College of William and Mary
- 1 to 3 miles to boutique and outlet shopping
- 3 miles to Busch Gardens and Water Country
- Meeting facilities
- Spacious 1 and 2 bedroom residential suites

*2 and 3 room suites
with private bedrooms*

- Featuring king and queen beds
- Suites accommodate up to 8 people
- Sofa sleepers and 2 or 3 TVs in each suite
- Iron and ironing board, video cassette player
- Fully equipped home-style kitchens
- Guest laundry room and valet service
- Exercise room and indoor heated pool
- Honeymoon whirlpool suites available
- Complimentary daily hot breakfast
- Complimentary evening Manager's Reception†
  (Monday - Thursday)
- Complimentary gas barbecues and picnic area

homewoodsuites.com
1-800-CALL-HOME®

(See map and index starting on p. 898)

HOWARD JOHNSON HOTEL-HISTORIC AREA   *Book at aaa.com*   Phone: (757)229-6900   67

5/27-9/4 [ECP]	1P: $89-$120	2P: $89-$120	XP: $15	F17
3/25-5/26 [ECP]	1P: $69-$99	2P: $69-$99	XP: $15	F17
9/5-2/28 [ECP]	1P: $59-$99	2P: $59-$99	XP: $15	F17
3/1-3/24 [ECP]	1P: $59-$79	2P: $59-$79	XP: $15	F17

Small-scale Hotel **Location:** I-64, exit 242 (SR 199), 0.5 mi w on US 60. 7135 Pocahontas Tr 23185. Fax: 757/220-3211. **Facility:** 98 units. 94 one- and 4 two-bedroom standard units. 5 stories, interior corridors. **Parking:** on-site. **Terms:** 2 night minimum stay - seasonal, package plans, $2 service charge. **Amenities:** video library, voice mail, irons, hair dryers. **Pool(s):** outdoor, wading. **Leisure Activities:** picnic area, exercise room. *Fee:* game room. **Guest Services:** valet and coin laundry. **Business Services:** meeting rooms, fax. **Cards:** AX, CB, DC, DS, MC, VI. **Special Amenities:** free expanded continental breakfast and early check-in/late check-out. *(See color ad below)*

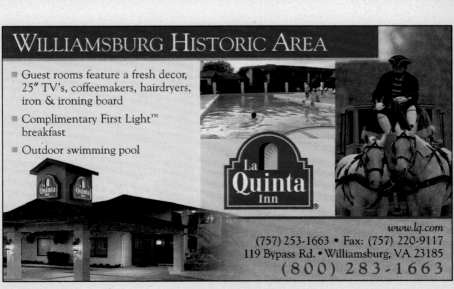

(See map and index starting on p. 898)

INN AT 802

Phone: (757)345-3316 [63]

▼▼✦▼▼ All Year [BP]   2P: $135-$160   XP: $20

Bed & Breakfast

Location: Just w of SR 199, 1 mi ne of SR 31 and 5. Located across from William & Mary College's Phi Beta Kappa Hall. 802 Jamestown Rd 23185. Fax: 757/221-9561. **Facility:** Comfort features at this brick Cape Cod include goose-down comforters with handmade covers and a sunroom overlooking the garden. Smoke free premises. 4 one-bedroom standard units. 2 stories, interior corridors. **Parking:** on-site. **Terms:** check-in 4 pm, 2 night minimum stay - weekends, age restrictions may apply, 7 day cancellation notice-fee imposed, package plans, 3% service charge, no pets allowed (owner's pet on premises). **Amenities:** DVD players, irons, hair dryers. **Guest Services:** complimentary evening beverages. **Business Services:** PC, fax. **Cards:** AX, DC, MC, VI.   ⊠ ☎

LA QUINTA INN WILLIAMSBURG (HISTORIC AREA)   *Book at aaa.com*

Phone: (757)253-1663 [19]

ⒶⒶⒶ [SAVE]   6/10-9/3 [ECP]   1P: $85-$135   2P: $85-$135
              3/1-6/9 [ECP]   1P: $65-$105   2P: $65-$105
▼▼▼▼ 9/4-2/28 [ECP]   1P: $45-$75   2P: $45-$75

Small-scale Hotel

Location: US 60 Bypass Rd, 0.3 mi e of Richmond Rd. 119 Bypass Rd 23185. Fax: 757/220-9117. **Facility:** 131 one-bedroom standard units. 2 stories (no elevator), exterior corridors. **Parking:** on-site. **Terms:** package plans, small pets only. **Amenities:** dual phone lines, voice mail, irons, hair dryers. **Pool(s):** outdoor. **Guest Services:** valet laundry. **Business Services:** meeting rooms, fax. **Cards:** AX, DC, DS, MC, VI. **Special Amenities:** free expanded continental breakfast and free local telephone calls. *(See color ad p 931)*

SOME UNITS

[icons] 🆓 🛏 🍴 🔊 📶 ♿ 🛁 [DATA PORT] 📺 / ⊠ 🔌 📷 /
FEE   FEE

LEGACY OF WILLIAMSBURG BED & BREAKFAST
INN

Phone: 757/220-0524 [66]

▼▼▼▼ All Year [BP]   1P: $135-$175   2P: $135-$175   XP: $25

Bed & Breakfast

Location: SR 31 and 5, just ne of jct SR 199. Located in a residential area bordering William and Mary College. 930 Jamestown Rd 23185-3917. Fax: 757/220-0524. **Facility:** This B&B, which offers three fireplace suites, evokes the style of the 18th-century with antique furnishings, reproduction fabrics and canopy beds. Smoke free premises. 4 units. 1 one-bedroom standard unit. 3 one-bedroom suites. 3 stories (no elevator), interior corridors. *Bath:* combo or shower only. **Parking:** on-site. **Terms:** 2 night minimum stay - weekends, age restrictions may apply, 14 day cancellation notice-fee imposed, package plans. **Amenities:** irons, hair dryers. **Business Services:** fax. **Cards:** MC, VI.

SOME UNITS

[ASK] 🆓 ⊠ / 🅿 /

LIBERTY ROSE BED & BREAKFAST

Phone: (757)253-1260 [68]

ⒶⒶⒶ [SAVE]   All Year [BP]   2P: $195-$275

▼▼▼▼ ▼▼▼▼

Historic Bed & Breakfast

Location: SR 31 and 5, just ne of jct SR 199. 1022 Jamestown Rd 23185. Fax: 757/253-8529. **Facility:** This charming Cape Cod home on a wooded hillside reflects English, French and Victorian influences in its richly romantic decor. Smoke free premises. 4 units. 3 one-bedroom standard units. 1 one-bedroom suite. 2 stories (no elevator), interior corridors. *Bath:* combo, shower or tub only. **Parking:** on-site. **Terms:** 2 night minimum stay - seasonal and/or weekends, age restrictions may apply, 18 day cancellation notice. **Amenities:** video library, irons, hair dryers. **Guest Services:** area transportation-Amtrak station. **Cards:** AX, MC, VI. **Special Amenities:** free full breakfast and free local telephone calls.

⊠ [VCR] 📷

(See map and index starting on p. 898)

MOTEL ROCHAMBEAU   **Phone:** (757)229-2851   21

6/17-8/18	1P: $38-$54	2P: $40-$56	XP: $5
3/1-6/16	1P: $28-$42	2P: $30-$44	XP: $4
8/19-10/31	1P: $26-$32	2P: $28-$36	XP: $4
11/1-2/28	1P: $24-$30	2P: $26-$32	XP: $4

Motel   **Location:** I-64, exit 238, 1 mi e on SR 143, then just w on SR 5. 929 Capitol Landing Rd 23185. **Fax:** 757/229-3156. **Facility:** 21 one-bedroom standard units. 1 story, exterior corridors. *Bath:* combo or shower only. **Parking:** on-site. **Terms:** office hours 8 am-midnight, cancellation fee imposed, package plans, pets ($10 deposit). **Leisure Activities:** pool privileges. **Business Services:** fax. **Cards:** AX, DS, MC, VI. *(See color ad p 942)*

SOME UNITS   (S) / (X)   FEE

THE PRINCESS ANNE   **Phone:** 757/229-2455   20

5/1-9/8	1P: $71-$98	2P: $81-$108	XP: $10 F17

Motel   **Location:** 1.5 mi nw of Colonial Williamsburg restored area. 1350 Richmond Rd 23185. **Fax:** 757/229-0122. **Facility:** 70 units. 69 one-bedroom standard units. 1 one-bedroom suite. 1 story, exterior corridors. *Bath:* combo or shower only. **Parking:** on-site. **Terms:** open 5/1-9/8. **Amenities:** video library, irons, hair dryers. **Pool(s):** outdoor. **Guest Services:** coin laundry. **Business Services:** fax. **Cards:** AX, DC, DS, MC, VI.   SOME UNITS

(ASK) (S) / (X)   FEE

Traveling can be so Suite.

Suites with living room, fully equipped kitchen, separate bedroom, full bath.

A new approach to business and leisure travel. On-premises parking, Chatfield's Restaurant and Lounge, indoor pool with sun patio, BBQ Pavilion, fitness room, guest laundry, and kids activities.

Located right off I-64, Exit 258B, just north on US 17. 5 min. from Newport News / Williamsburg Int'l. Airport. Just minutes from Williamsburg.

950 J. Clyde Morris Blvd, Newport News, VA
757- 599-4460 • 1-800-841-1112

POINT PLAZA
SUITES AND CONFERENCE HOTEL
www.pointplazasuites.com

A Beck Company Hotel

Busch Gardens / Williamsburg Family Package

- **2 Nights / 3 Days Lodging**
- **Busch Gardens (in season) or Colonial Williamsburg Tickets**
- **Deluxe Continental Breakfast**
- **Outdoor Pool / Fitness Center**

Located 10 Minutes East of Williamsburg adjacent to Fort Eustis, I-64, Exit 250A

800-223-0404

Use reservation code AAMI for special rates.

THE **MULBERRY INN**

16890 Warwick Blvd.
Newport News, VA
www.mulberryinnva.com

A Beck Company Hotel

(See map and index starting on p. 898)

QUALITY INN COLONY

Phone: (757)229-1855 **51**

	6/17-9/4 [ECP]	1P: $99-$149	2P: $99-$149	XP: $10	F18
	3/1-6/16 & 9/5-1/2 [ECP]	1P: $50-$99	2P: $50-$99	XP: $10	F18
	1/3-2/28 [ECP]	1P: $50-$90	2P: $50-$90	XP: $10	F18

Small-scale Hotel

Location: US 60 E and SR 5; jct SR 162. Page & 2nd sts 23187 (PO Box 3569, WILLIAMSBURG). **Fax:** 757/229-3470. **Facility:** 58 one-bedroom standard units, some with whirlpools. 1 story, exterior corridors. **Parking:** on-site. **Terms:** 2 night minimum stay - seasonal. **Amenities:** video library, irons, hair dryers. **Pool(s):** outdoor. **Guest Services:** valet laundry. **Business Services:** fax. **Cards:** AX, CB, DC, DS, MC, VI. **Special Amenities:** free expanded continental breakfast and free local telephone calls. *(See color ad below)*

SOME UNITS

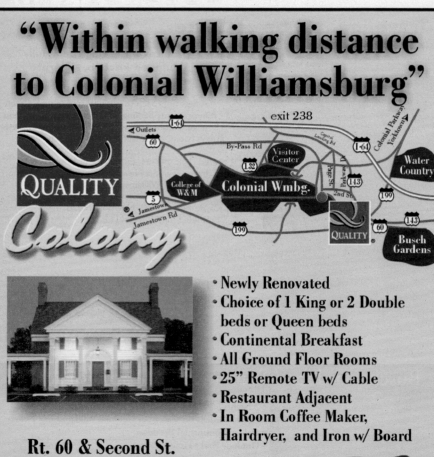

"Within walking distance to Colonial Williamsburg"

- Newly Renovated
- Choice of 1 King or 2 Double beds or Queen beds
- Continental Breakfast
- All Ground Floor Rooms
- 25" Remote TV w/ Cable
- Restaurant Adjacent
- In Room Coffee Maker, Hairdryer, and Iron w/ Board

Rt. 60 & Second St.
Williamsburg, VA 23185
(757) 229-1855

(See map and index starting on p. 898)

QUALITY INN LORD PAGET *Book at aaa.com*   Phone: (757)229-4444 **34**

5/28-9/6 [ECP]	1P: $89-$119	2P: $89-$119
9/7-12/31 [ECP]	1P: $59-$89	2P: $59-$89
3/1-5/27 [ECP]	1P: $59-$79	2P: $59-$79
1/1-2/28 [ECP]	1P: $49-$69	2P: $49-$69

Motel   **Location:** I-64, exit 238, 0.5 mi s to SR 5, then 0.5 mi s. 901 Capitol Landing Rd 23185. Fax: 757/220-9314. **Facility:** 94 units. 90 one-bedroom standard units. 4 one-bedroom suites ($99-$199). 2 stories (no elevator), exterior corridors. *Bath:* combo or shower only. **Parking:** on-site. **Terms:** 3 day cancellation notice, package plans. **Amenities:** video library, voice mail, irons. **Pool(s):** outdoor, wading. **Leisure Activities:** fishing, putting green. **Guest Services:** coin laundry. **Business Services:** fax. **Cards:** AX, CB, DC, DS, JC, MC, VI. *(See color ad below)*

SOME UNITS

QUALITY SUITES WILLIAMSBURG   *Book at aaa.com*   Phone: (757)220-9304 **18**

6/10-9/4 [BP]	1P: $149-$199	2P: $149-$199	XP: $15	F18
3/1-6/9 [BP]	1P: $89-$169	2P: $89-$169	XP: $15	F18
9/5-10/31 [BP]	1P: $109-$159	2P: $109-$159	XP: $15	F18

Small-scale Hotel **Location:** US 60, jct Bypass and Richmond rds. 1406 Richmond Rd 23185. Fax: 757/220-1823. **Facility:** 118 units. 6 one-bedroom standard units. 112 one-bedroom suites, some with whirlpools. 4 stories, interior corridors. *Bath:* combo or shower only. **Parking:** on-site. **Terms:** package plans. **Amenities:** video library, high-speed Internet, voice mail, safes, irons, hair dryers. *Some:* CD players. **Pool(s):** outdoor, heated indoor. **Leisure Activities:** exercise room. *Fee:* game room. **Guest Services:** valet and coin laundry. **Business Services:** fax. **Cards:** AX, DC, DS, JC, MC, VI. **Special Amenities:** free full breakfast and free local telephone calls. *(See color ad p 939)*

SOME UNITS

QUARTERPATH INN *Book at aaa.com*   Phone: (757)220-0960 **61**

6/10-9/6	1P: $69-$99	2P: $69-$119	XP: $10	F18
9/7-10/31	1P: $62-$89	2P: $82-$99	XP: $10	F18
3/1-6/9	1P: $52-$89	2P: $52-$89	XP: $10	F18
11/1-2/28	1P: $39-$69	2P: $39-$69	XP: $10	F18

Motel   **Location:** I-64, exit 242 (SR 199 W), 0.6 mi w to US 60 E, then just w. Located adjacent to a public park. 620 York St 23185. Fax: 757/220-1531. **Facility:** 130 one-bedroom standard units, some with whirlpools. 2 stories (no elevator), exterior corridors. **Parking:** on-site. **Terms:** 3 day cancellation notice-fee imposed, package plans, small pets only. **Pool(s):** outdoor. **Business Services:** meeting rooms, fax. **Cards:** AX, DC, DS, MC, VI. *(See color ad below)*

SOME UNITS

(See map and index starting on p. 898)

RADISSON FORT MAGRUDER HOTEL &
CONFERENCE CENTER *Book at aaa.com*   Phone: (757)220-2250 [64]

(AAA) [SAVE]

	6/16-9/7	1P: $99-$159	2P: $99-$159	XP: $10	F17
	9/8-10/31	1P: $79-$149	2P: $79-$149	XP: $10	F17
	3/1-6/15	1P: $79-$129	2P: $79-$129	XP: $10	F17
	11/1-2/28	1P: $69-$119	2P: $69-$119	XP: $10	F17

Small-scale Hotel **Location:** US 60, 0.8 mi e of jct SR 5 and 31. 6945 Pocahontas Tr 23185. **Fax:** 757/220-3215. **Facility:** 303 units. 290 one-bedroom standard units. 13 one-bedroom suites, some with whirlpools. 4 stories, interior corridors. *Bath:* combo or shower only. **Parking:** on-site. **Terms:** check-in 4 pm, package plans. **Amenities:** video games, voice mail, irons, hair dryers. **Dining:** Veranda Dining Room, see separate listing. **Pool(s):** outdoor, heated indoor, wading. **Leisure Activities:** saunas, whirlpool, 2 lighted tennis courts, exercise room, game room. **Guest Services:** gift shop, valet and coin laundry. **Business Services:** conference facilities, business center. **Cards:** AX, DC, DS, MC, VI.
(See color ad below & p 932)   SOME UNITS
[icons] / [icons] FEE FEE

RAMADA INN 1776 *Book at aaa.com*   Phone: (757)220-1776 [24]

(AAA) [SAVE]

| | 6/17-9/4 | 1P: $79-$129 | 2P: $79-$129 | XP: $10 | F18 |
| | 3/1-6/16 & 9/5-2/28 | 1P: $49-$99 | 2P: $49-$99 | XP: $10 | F18 |

Location: US 60 (Bypass Rd), 0.5 mi w of jct SR 132. 725 Bypass Rd 23185. **Fax:** 757/220-8961. **Facility:** 202 one-bedroom standard units. 2 stories (no elevator), interior corridors. **Parking:** on-site. **Terms:** check-in 4 Small-scale Hotel pm, [BP] meal plan available, package plans, small pets only. **Amenities:** voice mail, irons, hair dryers. **Dining:** 7 am-11 & 5-10 pm, cocktails. **Pool(s):** outdoor, wading. **Leisure Activities:** 2 tennis courts, playground, sports court, volleyball. *Fee:* game room. **Guest Services:** valet and coin laundry. **Business Services:** conference facilities, fax. **Cards:** AX, DC, DS, MC, VI. **Special Amenities:** free newspaper and early check-in/late check-out.
SOME UNITS
[icons] / [icons] FEE FEE

RAMADA INN & SUITES *Book at aaa.com*   Phone: (757)565-2000 [2]

(AAA) [SAVE]

	3/1-9/4 [BP]	1P: $59-$109	2P: $59-$109	XP: $10	F18
	9/5-11/13 [BP]	1P: $59-$89	2P: $59-$89	XP: $10	F18
	11/14-2/28 [BP]	1P: $59-$69	2P: $59-$69	XP: $10	F18

Small-scale Hotel **Location:** 3 mi w on US 60. 5351 Richmond Rd 23188. **Fax:** 757/565-4652. **Facility:** 162 units. 142 one- and 17 two-bedroom standard units. 3 one-bedroom suites ($99-$179), some with whirlpools. 3 stories, interior/exterior corridors. **Parking:** on-site. **Terms:** weekly rates available, package plans, small pets only ($10 extra charge). **Amenities:** voice mail, irons, hair dryers. **Dining:** 7 am-11 & 4:30-11 pm; Murder Mystery Dinner theater, cocktails, entertainment. **Pool(s):** outdoor. **Guest Services:** valet laundry. **Business Services:** meeting rooms, fax. **Cards:** AX, CB, DC, DS, JC, MC, VI. **Special Amenities:** free full breakfast and free newspaper.
SOME UNITS
[icons] / [icons] FEE FEE

(See map and index starting on p. 898)

RAMADA LIMITED HISTORIC AREA   *Book at aaa.com*   Phone: (757)220-3100   59

[AAA] [SAVE]   All Year [ECP]   1P: $49-$119   2P: $49-$119
[diamonds]   **Location:** I-64, exit 242A, 1 mi w to US 60, then 1.5 mi w. 505 York St 23185. Fax: 757/229-2447. **Facility:** 85 one-bedroom standard units. 3 stories, interior/exterior corridors. **Parking:** on-site. **Terms:** check-in 4 pm, 3 day cancellation notice-fee imposed. **Amenities:** voice mail, irons, hair dryers. **Pool(s):** heated indoor. **Leisure**
Small-scale Hotel   **Activities:** whirlpool. **Guest Services:** valet laundry. **Business Services:** fax. **Cards:** AX, CB, DC, DS, MC, VI. **Special Amenities:** free expanded continental breakfast and free local telephone calls.
(See color ad below)

SOME UNITS
[icons: 🅂🄳 🍴 🛗M 🏊 DATA PORT 📺 / ✕ /]

(See map and index starting on p. 898)

RED ROOF INN-WILLIAMSBURG   *Book at aaa.com*   Phone: 757/259-1948   **37**

AAA SAVE

6/1-9/10	1P: $59-$99	2P: $59-$99	XP: $5 F17
4/1-5/31	1P: $49-$79	2P: $49-$79	XP: $5 F17
3/1-3/31	1P: $39-$59	2P: $39-$59	XP: $5 F17
9/11-2/28	1P: $39-$49	2P: $39-$49	XP: $5 F17

Motel   **Location:** I-64, exit 238, 0.9 mi se on SR 143, then just w on SR 5. 824 Capitol Landing Rd 23185. Fax: 757/229-5344. **Facility:** 72 one-bedroom standard units. 2 stories (no elevator), exterior corridors. **Parking:** on-site. **Amenities:** safes (fee), hair dryers. **Pool(s):** outdoor. **Guest Services:** coin laundry. **Business Services:** fax. **Cards:** AX, CB, DC, DS, MC, VI. **Special Amenities: free continental breakfast and free local telephone calls.** *(See color ad p 938)*

SOME UNITS

RESIDENCE INN BY MARRIOTT WILLIAMSBURG   *Book at aaa.com*   Phone: 757/941-2000   **8**

All Year   1P: $59-$359   2P: $59-$359

Small-scale Hotel   **Location:** US 60, just w of jct Bypass Rd. 1648 Richmond Rd 23185. Fax: 757/941-2001. **Facility:** 108 units. 16 one-bedroom standard units with efficiencies. 68 one- and 24 two-bedroom suites, some with kitchens. 4 stories, interior corridors. *Bath:* combo or shower only. **Parking:** on-site. **Terms:** check-in 4 pm, 3 day cancellation notice-fee imposed, pets ($75 fee). **Amenities:** high-speed Internet, dual phone lines, voice mail, irons, hair dryers. **Pool(s):** heated outdoor. **Leisure Activities:** whirlpool, exercise room, sports court. **Guest Services:** valet and coin laundry. **Business Services:** fax. **Cards:** AX, DC, DS, MC, VI.

SOME UNITS
FEE

SLEEP INN-HISTORIC   *Book at aaa.com*   Phone: (757)259-1700   **26**

AAA SAVE

3/1-10/31 [ECP]	1P: $59-$119	2P: $59-$119	XP: $10 F18
11/1-2/28 [ECP]	1P: $39-$69	2P: $39-$69	XP: $10 F18

Small-scale Hotel   **Location:** US 60 (Bypass Rd), just e of jct Richmond Rd. 220 Bypass Rd 23185. Fax: 757/220-3075. **Facility:** 66 one-bedroom standard units, some with whirlpools. 3 stories, interior corridors. *Bath:* combo or shower only. **Parking:** on-site. **Terms:** 2 night minimum stay - seasonal and/or weekends, cancellation fee imposed. **Amenities:** video library (fee), high-speed Internet, voice mail, irons, hair dryers. *Some:* DVD players. **Pool(s):** heated indoor. **Leisure Activities:** exercise room. **Guest Services:** valet and coin laundry. **Business Services:** meeting rooms, fax. **Cards:** AX, DC, DS, MC, VI. **Special Amenities: free expanded continental breakfast and free local telephone calls.** *(See color ad p 915)*

SOME UNITS
FEE   FEE

SPRINGHILL SUITES BY MARRIOTT   *Book at aaa.com*   Phone: (757)941-3000   **9**

All Year [CP]   1P: $69-$159   2P: $69-$169

Small-scale Hotel   **Location:** US 60, just w of jct Bypass Rd. 1644 Richmond Rd 23185. Fax: 757/941-3001. **Facility:** 120 one-bedroom standard units. 4 stories, interior corridors. *Bath:* combo or shower only. **Parking:** on-site. **Terms:** check-in 4 pm. **Amenities:** high-speed Internet, dual phone lines, voice mail, irons, hair dryers. **Pool(s):** small heated indoor. **Leisure Activities:** whirlpool, exercise room. **Guest Services:** sundries, valet and coin laundry. **Business Services:** fax. **Cards:** AX, DC, DS, JC, MC, VI.

SOME UNITS

SUPER 8 MOTEL-HISTORIC   *Book at aaa.com*   Phone: (757)229-0500   **50**

AAA SAVE

6/17-9/4	1P: $60-$85	2P: $60-$85	XP: $5 F18
5/6-6/16	1P: $50-$65	2P: $50-$65	XP: $5 F18
3/1-5/5	1P: $38-$50	2P: $38-$50	XP: $5 F18
9/5-2/28	1P: $30-$45	2P: $30-$45	XP: $5 F18

Motel   **Location:** I-642, exit 242 (SR 199 W), 0.6 mi w on SR 199 to SR 143, 1.6 mi w to SR 162, then just w. 304 2nd St 23185. Fax: 757/229-0500. **Facility:** 107 one-bedroom standard units. 2 stories (no elevator), exterior corridors. **Parking:** on-site. **Amenities:** irons, hair dryers. **Pool(s):** outdoor. **Leisure Activities:** poolside grills, basketball, volleyball. **Guest Services:** coin laundry. **Business Services:** fax. **Cards:** AX, DC, DS, MC, VI. **Special Amenities: free continental breakfast and free room upgrade (subject to availability with advance reservations).** *(See color ad p 940)*

SOME UNITS

(See map and index starting on p. 898)

TRAVELODGE-KING WILLIAM INN   *Book at aaa.com*   Phone: (757)229-4933   **36**

6/16-9/5 [CP]	1P: $65-$235	2P: $65-$235	XP: $5	F17
9/6-10/31 [CP]	1P: $45-$55	2P: $45-$55	XP: $5	F17
3/1-6/15 [CP]	1P: $35-$55	2P: $35-$55	XP: $5	F17
11/1-2/28 [CP]	1P: $30-$45	2P: $30-$45	XP: $5	F17

Motel   **Location:** On SR 5 and 31, just e of jct US 60. 834 Capitol Landing Rd 23185. Fax: 757/229-9686. **Facility:** 108 one-bedroom standard units. 3 stories, exterior corridors. **Parking:** on-site. **Terms:** package plans. **Amenities:** safes (fee), irons, hair dryers. **Pool(s):** outdoor. **Guest Services:** coin laundry. **Business Services:** fax. **Cards:** AX, DS, MC, VI. **Special Amenities:** free continental breakfast and free local telephone calls. *(See color ad p 941)*

SOME UNITS

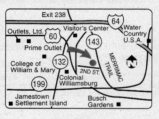

(See map and index starting on p. 898)

WESTGATE HISTORIC WILLIAMSBURG — *Book at aaa.com*   Phone: 757/229-6220   **33**

5/1-8/31	1P: $89-$107	2P: $99-$117	XP: $10 F17
3/1-4/30 & 9/1-10/31	1P: $62-$89	2P: $72-$99	XP: $10 F17
11/1-2/28	1P: $53-$89	2P: $63-$99	XP: $10 F17

Location: Just e of jct Richmond and Bypass rds. 1324 Richmond Rd 23185. Fax: 757/229-2774. **Facility:** 121 units. 82 one-bedroom standard units, some with whirlpools. 39 one-bedroom suites with kitchens and whirlpools. 3 stories, interior corridors. **Bath:** combo or shower only. **Parking:** on-site. **Terms:** 7 day cancellation notice-fee imposed. **Amenities:** dual phone lines, voice mail, hair dryers. *Some:* CD players, irons. *Fee:* DVD players, safes. **Pool(s):** outdoor, wading. **Leisure Activities:** whirlpool. *Fee:* kids club. **Business Services:** fax. **Cards:** AX, DC, DS, MC, VI.

Small-scale Hotel

WHITE LION MOTEL   Phone: (757)229-3931   **31**

6/17-8/18 [CP]	1P: $44-$60	2P: $46-$66	XP: $5
3/1-6/16 & 8/19-10/31 [CP]	1P: $32-$46	2P: $34-$48	XP: $5
11/1-2/28 [CP]	1P: $28-$34	2P: $30-$36	XP: $5

Location: I-64, exit 238, 1 mi e on SR 143, then just w on SR 5. 912 Capitol Landing Rd 23185. Fax: 757/229-3156. **Facility:** 37 units. 36 one-bedroom standard units, some with efficiencies (no utensils). 1 two-bedroom suite. 3 stories (no elevator), exterior corridors. **Bath:** combo or shower only. **Parking:** on-site. **Terms:** office hours 8 am-midnight, cancellation fee imposed, package plans. **Pool(s):** outdoor. **Business Services:** fax. **Cards:** AX, DS, MC, VI. **Special Amenities:** free continental breakfast. *(See color ad below)*

Motel

SOME UNITS

WILLIAMSBURG HOSPITALITY HOUSE — *Book at aaa.com*   Phone: (757)229-4020   **52**

All Year	1P: $69-$200	2P: $79-$210	XP: $10 F17

Location: Just w of restored area on US 60/Richmond Rd. Located across from William and Mary College Stadium. 415 Richmond Rd 23185. Fax: 757/220-1560. **Facility:** 295 units. 284 one-bedroom standard units. 11 one-bedroom suites ($250-$475). 4 stories, interior corridors. **Parking:** on-site. **Terms:** 3 day cancellation notice-fee imposed, package plans. **Amenities:** voice mail, irons, hair dryers. **Dining:** 2 restaurants, 6:30 am-11 & 11:30-10 pm, Sun from 7 am, cocktails. **Pool(s):** outdoor. **Leisure Activities:** exercise room. *Fee:* game room. **Guest Services:** gift shop, valet laundry. **Business Services:** conference facilities, fax. **Cards:** AX, DC, DS, MC, VI.

Small-scale Hotel

SOME UNITS

WILLIAMSBURG INN   Phone: (757)220-7978   **58**

4/1-12/31	1P: $225-$775	2P: $225-$775	XP: $15 F18
3/1-3/31	1P: $195-$675	2P: $195-$675	XP: $15 F18
1/1-2/28	1P: $175-$650	2P: $175-$650	XP: $15 F18

Location: In Colonial Williamsburg restored area. 136 E Francis St 23187 (PO Box 1776, WILLIAMSBURG). Fax: 757/220-7096. **Facility:** Constructed in 1936 in Regency-style. Decor reflects a bygone era; public rooms have warmth and charm. 40 units in Providence wing offer a more modern decor, some with balcony overlooking a fountain pond. 110 units. 102 one-bedroom standard units. 8 one-bedroom suites. 3 stories (no elevator), interior corridors. **Parking:** valet. **Terms:** check-in 4 pm, 3 night minimum stay - seasonal, 3 day cancellation notice-fee imposed, [MAP] meal plan available, package plans. **Amenities:** CD players, high-speed Internet (fee), dual phone lines, voice mail, safes, irons, hair dryers. *Some:* DVD players (fee), honor bars. **Dining:** The Regency Dining Room, see separate listing. **Pool(s):** outdoor, wading. **Leisure Activities:** recreation programs, exercise room. *Fee:* golf-45 holes, 8 tennis courts, bicycles, massage. **Guest Services:** gift shop, valet laundry, area transportation. **Business Services:** conference facilities, fax. **Cards:** AX, DC, DS, MC, VI. *(See color ad p 936)*

Classic Small-scale Hotel

SOME UNITS
FEE

WILLIAMSBURG LODGE — *Book at aaa.com*   Phone: (757)220-7976   **56**

4/1-12/31	1P: $155-$275	2P: $155-$275	XP: $15 F17
3/1-3/31 & 1/1-2/28	1P: $120-$250	2P: $120-$250	XP: $15 F17

Location: Just s of jct Francis St and restored area. 310 S England St 23187 (PO Box 1776, WILLIAMSBURG). Fax: 757/220-7799. **Facility:** 204 one-bedroom standard units. 4 stories, interior corridors. **Parking:** on-site. **Terms:** check-in 4 pm, 2 night minimum stay - seasonal, 3 day cancellation notice-fee imposed, [MAP] meal plan available, package plans. **Amenities:** voice mail, irons, hair dryers. **Pool(s):** outdoor, wading. **Leisure Activities:** jogging, exercise room. *Fee:* golf-45 holes, 8 tennis courts, bicycles. **Guest Services:** gift shop, valet and coin laundry, area transportation. **Business Services:** conference facilities, business center. **Cards:** AX, DC, DS, MC, VI. *(See color ad p 936)*

Small-scale Hotel

SOME UNITS

(See map and index starting on p. 898)

WILLIAMSBURG SAMPLER BED & BREAKFAST INN

Bed & Breakfast

Phone: 757/253-0398   65

All Year   2P: $150-$180   XP: $25

Location: Jct SR 199, 1 mi ne on SR 5; just w of William and Mary College. Located in a residential area. 922 Jamestown Rd 23185. Fax: 757/253-2669. **Facility:** Samplers, pewter pieces and an antique organ in the game room contribute to the rich decor of this B&B. 4 units. 2 one-bedroom standard units. 2 one-bedroom suites. 3 stories (no elevator), interior corridors. *Bath:* shower only. **Parking:** on-site. **Terms:** check-in 4 pm, 2 night minimum stay - weekends, age restrictions may apply, 14 day cancellation notice-fee imposed, [BP] meal plan available. **Amenities:** video library, irons, hair dryers. **Leisure Activities:** sauna, exercise room. **Business Services:** fax. **Cards:** MC, VI. **Special Amenities:** free full breakfast.

SOME UNITS

⊠ VCR DATA/PORT ☎ / 🖥 /

WOODLANDS HOTEL & SUITES   *Book at aaa.com*   Phone: (757)220-7960   38

Small-scale Hotel

	4/1-12/31	1P: $115-$195	2P: $115-$195	XP: $12	F18
	3/1-3/31	1P: $105-$155	2P: $105-$155	XP: $12	F18
	1/1-2/28	1P: $75-$135	2P: $75-$135	XP: $12	F18

Location: I-64, exit 238, s on SR 143 to SR 132. Located in Colonial Williamsburg Visitor Center Complex. 105 Visitor Center Dr 23185. Fax: 757/565-8942. **Facility:** 300 units. 204 one-bedroom standard units. 96 one-bedroom suites. 3 stories, interior corridors. *Bath:* combo or shower only. **Parking:** on-site. **Terms:** check-in 4 pm, 2 night minimum stay - seasonal, 3 day cancellation notice-fee imposed, package plans. **Amenities:** dual phone lines, voice mail, irons, hair dryers. *Some: Fee:* high-speed Internet. **Dining:** Huzzah!, see separate listing. **Pool(s):** outdoor. **Guest Services:** gift shop, valet and coin laundry, area transportation. **Business Services:** conference facilities, fax. **Cards:** AX, DC, MC, VI. *(See color ad p 936)*

SOME UNITS

🍽 ♿ 🚭 🏊 DATA/PORT / ⊠ 🖥 🗄 🖵 /
FEE   FEE   FEE

———— **WHERE TO DINE** ————

ABERDEEN BARN

Steak House

Dinner: $14-$42   Phone: 757/229-6661   5

Location: 1.8 mi nw on US 60, just w of jct Bypass Rd. 1601 Richmond Rd 23185. **Hours:** 5 pm-9:30 pm, Fri & Sat-10 pm. **Closed:** 11/24, 12/25; also 1/1-1/15. **Reservations:** suggested. **Features:** Known for its slow-roasted prime rib of beef, the rustic steakhouse features an open hearth grill, post-and-beam construction and simple barn decor. Fresh local seafood and mouthwatering desserts round out the menu. Casual dress; cocktails. **Parking:** on-site. **Cards:** AX, DS, MC, VI.

🍸 ⊠

A. CARROLL'S MARTINI BAR & BISTRO

American

Lunch: $6-$10   Dinner: $14-$25   Phone: 757/258-8882   13

Location: Just w of Merchants Square at jct Armistead. 601 Prince George St 23185. **Hours:** 11:30 am-2 & 5:30-9:30 pm, Fri-10:30 pm, Sat 5:30 pm-10:30 pm. Closed major holidays; also Sun. **Reservations:** suggested. **Features:** On the edge of the restored area, the stylish spot serves a mix of modern and traditional American dishes. Casual dress; cocktails. **Parking:** on-site. **Cards:** AX, DS, MC, VI.

🍸

AROMAS

Coffee/Espresso

Lunch: $5-$7   Dinner: $5-$7   Phone: 757/221-6676   15

Location: Between Henry and Boundary; at Merchants Square; center. 431 Prince George St 23185. **Hours:** 7 am-10 pm, Fri & Sat-11 pm, Sun 8 am-8 pm. **Closed:** 1/1, 11/24, 12/25. **Features:** Locals and students who patronize the cozy spot favor the gourmet coffee, desserts, sandwiches and daily soup specials. Casual dress; beer & wine only; entertainment. **Parking:** street. **Cards:** MC, VI.

⊠

BERRET'S SEAFOOD RESTAURANT AND TAPHOUSE GRILL

Seafood

Lunch: $7-$12   Dinner: $18-$26   Phone: 757/253-1847   21

Location: Jct SR 5; center; in Merchants Square. 199 S Boundary St 23185. **Hours:** 11:30 am-3:30 & 5:30-10 pm. Closed major holidays; also Mon 1/1-2/28. **Reservations:** suggested, for dinner. **Features:** Berret's is centrally located and offers contemporary fine dining with emphasis on fresh Chesapeake Bay seafood. The seasonal patio offers raw bar favorites — steamed seafood and sandwiches — in a very casual setting. Service is friendly and attentive. Casual dress; cocktails. **Parking:** on-site. **Cards:** AX, DS, MC, VI.

🍸 ⊠

CAPTAIN GEORGES SEAFOOD RESTAURANT

Seafood

Dinner: $19-$30   Phone: 757/565-2323   1

Location: 3 mi w on US 60. 5363 Richmond Rd 23188. **Hours:** 4:30 pm-10 pm, Sat from 4 pm, Sun from noon. **Closed:** 12/25. **Features:** You'll be in good company if you order the all-you-can-eat seafood buffet; almost everyone does. Plenty of fried, steamed, au gratin and stuffed seafood is available along with a humongous selection of salad and side dishes, bread and dessert. Casual dress; cocktails. **Parking:** on-site. **Cards:** AX, MC, VI.

⊠

THE CHEESE SHOP

Gourmet Grocery

Lunch: $5-$9   Dinner: $5-$9   Phone: 757/220-0298   19

Location: On Merchants Square; downtown. 410 Duke of Gloucester St 23185. **Hours:** 10 am-9 pm, Sun 11 am-6 pm. Closed major holidays. **Features:** The shop offers a wide range of specialty food products, Virginia delicacies, wines and sandwiches with house dressing. Casual dress; beer & wine only. **Parking:** no self-parking. **Cards:** AX, DS, MC, VI.

[AC] ⊠

CHEZ TRINH

Vietnamese

Lunch: $5-$7   Dinner: $7-$16   Phone: 757/253-1888   9

Location: On Lafayette Ave, just s of jct W Richmond Rd; in Williamsburg Shopping Center. 157 Monticello Ave 23185. **Hours:** 11:30 am-3 & 5-10 pm. Closed major holidays. **Features:** Vietnamese dishes and nightly specials— including excellent noodle soup and fresh, not fried, rice paper rolls—are presented in a casual setting within a local shopping center. The crowd comprises mostly locals and students. Casual dress; cocktails. **Parking:** on-site. **Cards:** MC, VI.

⊠

(See map and index starting on p. 898)

CHOWNING'S TAVERN
♦♦♦ American
Historic *(See color ad p 303)*

Lunch: $6-$8   **Dinner:** $6-$8   **Phone:** 757-229-2141   (17)
Location: In restored area. 109 E Duke of Gloucester St 23185. **Hours:** 11 am-10 pm; winter hours may vary. **Features:** The menu in the historic tavern and summer garden centers on lighter fare at lunchtime and from 9 p.m. to 1 a.m. Pub foods are served evenings, when an ale pub ambience prevails. Southern specialties range from chicken pot pie and crab soup to Sally Lunn bread. The service staff dons period costumes and performs Colonial entertainment. Casual dress; cocktails; entertainment. **Parking:** on-site. **Cards:** AX, DC, DS, MC, VI.

CHRISTIANA CAMPBELL'S TAVERN
♦♦♦ Seafood
Historic *(See color ad p 303)*

Dinner: $25-$35   **Phone:** 757-229-1000   (14)
Location: In restored area. 120 E Waller St 23185. **Hours:** 5 pm-9 pm. Closed: Sun; also Mon except in summer. **Reservations:** suggested. **Features:** The charming, Old World atmosphere is very popular in this 18th-century tavern, replete with roving balladeers, costumed wait staff and Southern seafood specialties, some diligently made from scratch using authentic 17th-century family recipes. Casual dress; cocktails; entertainment. **Parking:** on-site. **Cards:** AX, DS, MC, VI.

FAT CANARY
♦♦♦♦ Regional American

Dinner: $20-$28   **Phone:** 757-229-3333   (27)
Location: At Merchants Square. 410 Duke of Gloucester St 23185. **Hours:** 5 pm-10 pm. **Reservations:** required. **Features:** This stylish new spot overlooks historic Merchants Square but is all modern inside with crisp lines and creative gourmet fare which changes seasonally so as to offer the freshest regional ingredients. The South is heavy influence but one will find the chef has also drawn inspiration from around the world. An excellent complement of wines is offered. Dressy casual; cocktails. **Parking:** on-site. **Cards:** AX, DS, MC, VI.

FIRESIDE STEAK CHOPHOUSE
AAA
♦♦♦ Steak House

Dinner: $9-$24   **Phone:** 757-229-3310   (2)
Location: I-64, exit 234, 2 mi s to US 60, then 3 mi e; adjacent to Comfort Inn Central. 1995 Richmond Rd 23185. **Hours:** 4:30 pm-11 pm, Sun noon-10 pm. **Reservations:** suggested, weekends. **Features:** Prime rib, seafood and grilled, aged steak are house specialties at the casual, family-oriented restaurant. The owners' Greek heritage makes an appearance in a few dishes, such as the salad, appetizers and baklava for dessert. Casual dress; cocktails. **Parking:** on-site. **Cards:** AX, MC, VI. *(See color ad p 919)*

GOLDEN HORSESHOE GOLD COURSE GRILL
♦♦♦ American

Lunch: $8-$15   **Phone:** 757-229-1000   (25)
Location: Jct Francis St, just s. 401 S England St 23185. **Hours:** 11:30 am-3 pm. **Features:** On a sunny day, a table on the patio can't be beat. Guests can enjoy the view of the inn's golf course and duck pond while dining on juicy burgers, grilled panini sandwiches, daily pasta and entree specials and delicious, freshly made ice cream. Casual dress; cocktails. **Parking:** on-site. **Cards:** AX, DS, MC, VI.

(See map and index starting on p. 898)

HUZZAH!
American

Lunch: $7-$10   **Dinner:** $7-$18   **Phone:** 757/220-7960   ⑪
Location: I-64, exit 238, s on SR 143 to SR 132; in Woodlands Hotel & Suites. 113 Visitor Center Dr 23188. **Hours:** Open 4/15-12/31; 11:30 am-9 pm; hours may vary in winter. **Features:** A break from all things Colonial can be found at the casual visitor center eatery. Families enjoy snacking on turkey chili, burgers, Brunswick stew and other American favorites. Casual dress. **Parking:** on-site. **Cards:** AX, DC, DS, MC, VI.

THE JEFFERSON
Regional American

Dinner: $11-$20   **Phone:** 757/229-2296   ⑥
Location: On US 60 W (Richmond Rd), just w of jct Bypass Rd. 1453 Richmond Rd 23185. **Hours:** 4 pm-10 pm. Closed: 11/24, 12/24, 12/25. **Reservations:** suggested. **Features:** Family-owned and operated since 1956, the restaurant specializes in Southern favorites such as fried chicken, Smithfield ham and homemade Virginia peanut soup. Steak and seafood also are good choices as are a few Greek dishes that reflects the family's heritage. An English country decor sets a cozy, relaxed mood. Casual dress; cocktails. **Parking:** on-site. **Cards:** AX, CB, DC, MC, VI.   ⊠

KING'S ARMS TAVERN
American

Lunch: $9-$13   **Dinner:** $28-$38   **Phone:** 757/229-1000   ⑱
Location: In restored area. 416 E Duke of Gloucester St 23187. **Hours:** 11:30 am-2:30 & 5-9:30 pm; days vary seasonally. **Reservations:** suggested, for dinner. **Features:** This Colonial eatery was reconstructed on the site of the original King's Arms, opened in 1772. Servers don Colonial attire and roving balladeers entertain. Garden seating is offered, weather permitting. Lamb, game, meat and vegetable pies are served. Casual dress; cocktails; entertainment. **Parking:** on-site. **Cards:** AX, DS, MC, VI. **Historic** *(See color ad p 303)*   ⊠

**KYOTO JAPANESE STEAK &
SEAFOOD HOUSE**
Japanese

Dinner: $10-$24   **Phone:** 757/220-8888   ④
Location: 2 mi nw on US 60, just w of jct Bypass Rd. 1621 Richmond Rd 23185. **Hours:** 4 pm-10 pm. Closed: 1/1, 11/24, 12/25. **Reservations:** suggested. **Features:** Kyoto offers a fun and filling family-friendly dinner. In the front room, sit at the teppanyaki grill tables as Japanese chefs prepare steak and seafood specialties in an entertaining show. Or sit in the rear room and try traditional sushi specialties in artful arrangements. Casual dress; cocktails. **Parking:** on-site. **Cards:** AX, DC, DS, MC, VI.

LA TOLTECA MEXICAN RESTAURANTE
Mexican

Lunch: $4-$10   **Dinner:** $5-$10   **Phone:** 757/259-0598   ⑫
Location: Just e of jct with Page St (US 5 and 31). 135 Second St 23185. **Hours:** 11 am-10:30 pm, Sun noon-9:30 pm. Closed: 11/24, 12/24, 12/25. **Features:** Authentic Mexican cuisine, lunch specials and combination dinners are served in the festive atmosphere of La Tolteca. The menu is categorized with both a vegetarian section and glossary of terms for those less familiar with the cuisine and ingredients. Casual dress; cocktails. **Parking:** on-site. **Cards:** AX, DS, MC, VI.   ⬛Ⓜ ⊠

NAWAB INDIAN CUISINE
Indian

Lunch: $4-$8   **Dinner:** $8-$15   **Phone:** 757/565-3200   ⑩
Location: Just w of jct Monticello Shopping Center. 204 Monticello Ave 23185. **Hours:** 11:30 am-2:30 & 5-10 pm, Fri-10:30 pm, Sat noon-3 & 5-10:30 pm, Sun noon-3 & 5-10 pm. **Features:** An attractive dining room with rich fabric and murals complements a wide variety of choices, from vegetarian to seafood and lamb dishes. Tandoori grilled items, curry, clay oven-baked bread, great sampler platters and a weekday lunch buffet are featured. Casual dress; cocktails. **Parking:** on-site. **Cards:** AX, DS, MC, VI.   ⬛Ⓜ ⊠

OLD CHICKAHOMINY HOUSE
Regional American

Lunch: $3-$7   **Phone:** 757/229-4689   ㉖
Location: SR 31 (Jamestown Rd), just sw of jct SR 199. 1211 Jamestown Rd 23185. **Hours:** 8:30 am-10:30 & 11:30-2:30 pm. Closed major holidays. **Features:** The small menu offers traditional Southern favorites like country ham and biscuits, Brunswick stew and buttermilk pie in a restored 18th-century cottage. Even the dumplings will remind you, if you grew up lucky, of Grandma's cooking. Casual dress; beer & wine only. **Parking:** on-site. **Cards:** MC, VI.   ⊠

PEKING & MONGOLIAN GRILL
Chinese

Lunch: $5-$8   **Dinner:** $5-$10   **Phone:** 757/229-2288   ⑧
Location: US 60 Bypass Rd; in K-Mart Shopping Center. 120 J Waller Mill Rd 23185. **Hours:** 11:30 am-10 pm, Fri & Sat-11 pm. **Reservations:** suggested. **Features:** The decor is somewhat standard but the cuisine tastes are varied, from Cantonese and Hunan to Peking Szechuan and Shanghai. A new addition included a lengthy buffet and Mongolian grill where one chooses their favorite meat, seafood, vegetables and sauce that chefs prepare in front of them. Casual dress; cocktails. **Parking:** on-site. **Cards:** AX, DC, DS, MC, VI.   ⊠

THE PRIME RIB HOUSE
Steak & Seafood

Dinner: $10-$20   **Phone:** 757/229-6823   ⑦
Location: 1.5 mi nw on US 60. 1433 Richmond Rd 23185. **Hours:** 4:30 pm-10 pm, Fri & Sat-10:30 pm. Closed: 12/24. **Reservations:** suggested. **Features:** The menu features a selection of seafood, black Angus steak and Southwestern dishes, as well as some vegetarian entrees. Grilled salmon over black beans with the soup sampler is a pleasing choice. Casual dress; cocktails. **Parking:** on-site. **Cards:** AX, DC, DS, MC, VI.   Ⓨ ⊠

THE REGENCY DINING ROOM
Regional American

Lunch: $9-$20   **Dinner:** $22-$37   **Phone:** 757/220-7978   ㉒
Location: In Colonial Williamsburg restored area; in Williamsburg Inn. 136 E Francis St 23185. **Hours:** 7 am-10, noon-2 & 6-9 pm. **Reservations:** suggested, for dinner. **Features:** Sophisticated dishes are matched with choices from the lengthy wine list at the elegant dining room, which remains much the same as it was when first opened in 1938. Semi-formal attire; cocktails; entertainment. **Parking:** valet. **Cards:** AX, CB, DC, DS, MC, VI.   Ⓨ ⊠

(See map and index starting on p. 898)

SEAFARE RESTAURANT   Dinner: $13-$23   Phone: 757/229-0099   ③
AAA   **Location:** 2 mi nw on US 60. 1632 Richmond Rd 23185. **Hours:** 4 pm-11 pm, Sun noon-10 pm.
◇◇◇◇   **Reservations:** suggested. **Features:** Diners who crave Atlantic or Chesapeake Bay seafood and prime
         beef are likely to enjoy this casual, nautical spot. There are many seafood dishes from which to choose, in
Seafood addition to good bread and excellent homemade Caesar salad. Expect more formal service than is the
         norm. Casual dress; cocktails. **Parking:** on-site. **Cards:** AX, DS, MC, VI. *(See color ad p 920)*
                                                                                                    ✕

SHIELDS TAVERN   Lunch: $8-$10   Dinner: $38   Phone: 757/229-2141   ⑯
◇◇◇ ◇◇◇ **Location:** In restored area. 422 E Duke of Gloucester St 23185. **Hours:** 11:30 am-2:30 & 5-9:30 pm; winter hours
         may vary. **Reservations:** suggested. **Features:** Signature entrees are spit-roasted beef and fowl, and other
American items reminiscent of the cooking of the 1700s. This restored tavern and its authentic Colonial decor
         complement all of the tasty offerings. Garden service is available, weather permitting. Casual dress;
cocktails; entertainment. **Parking:** on-site. **Cards:** AX, DC, DS, MC, VI. **Historic** *(See color ad p 303)*
                                                                                                    ✕

THE TRELLIS RESTAURANT   *Menu on aaa.com*   Lunch: $7-$18   Dinner: $16-$30   Phone: 757/229-8610   ⑳
AAA   **Location:** In Merchants Square at Duke of Gloucester and Henry sts. 403 Duke of Gloucester St 23185. **Hours:** 11
◇◇◇◇◇◇   am-3:45 & 5-9:30 pm. Closed: 1/1, 11/24, 12/24, 12/25; also 12/31. **Reservations:** suggested.
         Features: The owner/chef, who boasts many best-selling cookbooks, conceives an imaginative, seasonally
Regional changing menu with innovative food preparations. Desserts are creative and decadent, such as his famous
American 'Death by Chocolate'. Each dining area, including the airy patio, has a different personality. Nationally
         renowned. Dressy casual; cocktails. **Parking:** on-site. **Cards:** AX, DC, DS, MC, VI.
                                                                                               🍸 ✕

VERANDA DINING ROOM   Lunch: $7-$14   Dinner: $14-$19   Phone: 757/220-2250   ㉔
AAA   **Location:** US 60, 0.8 mi e of jct SR 5 and 31; in Radisson Hotel Fort Magruder Hotel & Conference Center. 6945
◇◇◇ ◇◇◇ Pocahontas Tr 23187. **Hours:** 7 am-10 pm. **Features:** Patrons are attracted to the soup, salad and pasta bars
         that are part of the buffet lunch served weekdays overlooking the pool. The spacious main dining room
Regional supports an older crowd at breakfast, lunch and dinner. Casual dress; cocktails. **Parking:** on-site.
American **Cards:** AX, DC, DS, MC, VI. *(See color ad p 937)*
                                                                                         ♿M 🍸 ✕

YORKSHIRE STEAK & SEAFOOD
   RESTAURANT   Dinner: $15-$20   Phone: 757/229-9790   ㉓
AAA   **Location:** US 60 E, 0.5 mi se of jct SR 5 and 31. 700 York St 23185. **Hours:** 5 pm-10 pm. Closed: 12/25.
◇◇◇◇   **Reservations:** suggested. **Features:** A beautiful Colonial atmosphere, with two quiet, candlelit dining
         rooms, gives the comfortable, family-oriented restaurant its charm. Meat and seafood, such as the popular
         crabcakes, are always fresh. Mouthwatering pastries are prepared on the premises. Casual dress; cocktails.
Steak & Seafood **Parking:** on-site. **Cards:** AX, MC, VI. *(See color ad p 944)*
                                                                                                    ✕

CHARLES CITY

———— **WHERE TO STAY** ————

EDGEWOOD PLANTATION
◆◆◆◆◆
Historic Bed & Breakfast

All Year   2P: $148-$198   XP: $35   D12
Phone: (804)829-2962

Location: Jct SR 609, just e; on SR 5. 4800 John Tyler Memorial Hwy 23030. Fax: 804/829-2962. **Facility:** This 1849 Gothic Revival-style home on the site of what was once a working plantation features manicured grounds and tasteful decor. Smoke free premises. 7 units. 5 one-bedroom standard units, some with whirlpools. 2 one-bedroom suites ($268). 3 stories (no elevator), interior/exterior corridors. *Bath:* some shared or private, combo or shower only. **Parking:** on-site. **Terms:** age restrictions may apply, 15 day cancellation notice-fee imposed, package plans, no pets allowed (owner's cat on premises). **Amenities:** video library, hair dryers. *Some:* CD players, irons. **Pool(s):** outdoor. **Business Services:** fax. **Cards:** MC, VI.

SOME UNITS
(A$K) (S♦D) (⇌) (✕) (CTV) (VCR) (☎) / (🖥) (▦) /

NORTH BEND PLANTATION BED & BREAKFAST
◆◆◆
Historic Bed & Breakfast

All Year [BP]   1P: $115-$125   2P: $135-$175   XP: $40
Phone: (804)829-5176

Location: Jct SR 5 and 619, 1 mi s on SR 619. 12200 Weyanoke Rd 23030. **Facility:** On the grounds of this Bed and Breakfast are trenches said to have been used by soldiers in the Civil War; inside, many artifacts from that era are displayed. Smoke free premises. 4 units. 3 one- and 1 two-bedroom standard units. 2 stories (no elevator), interior corridors. *Bath:* combo or shower only. **Parking:** on-site. **Terms:** age restrictions may apply, 14 day cancellation notice-fee imposed, package plans. **Amenities:** video library, irons, hair dryers. **Pool(s):** outdoor. **Leisure Activities:** bicycles, hiking trails, horseshoes, volleyball. **Business Services:** fax. **Cards:** MC, VI.

SOME UNITS
(A$K) (S♦D) (⇌) (✕⃠) (✕) (CTV) (VCR) (🖥) / (DATA PORT) (☎) /

PINEY GROVE AT SOUTHALL'S PLANTATION-1790
◆◆◆◆
Historic Bed & Breakfast

All Year [BP]   1P: $130   2P: $130   XP: $15
Phone: (804)829-2480

Location: 1 mi e on SR 5, 8 mi n on SR 615. 16920 Southall Plantation Ln 23030 (PO Box 1359, WILLIAMSBURG, 23187). **Facility:** Flower beds peppered with perennials surround the meandering red-brick walkway at this plantation inn, which features numerous outbuildings. Smoke free premises. 5 units. 4 one-bedroom standard units. 1 two-bedroom suite ($170-$260). 2 stories (no elevator), interior corridors. **Parking:** on-site. **Terms:** check-in 4 pm, 30 day cancellation notice-fee imposed, package plans. **Amenities:** hair dryers. **Pool(s):** outdoor. **Leisure Activities:** hiking trails. **Business Services:** fax.

SOME UNITS
(⇌) (✕) (CTV) (☎) (🖥) (▦) / (🅟) /

———— **WHERE TO DINE** ————

INDIAN FIELDS TAVERN
◆◆◆
Regional American

Lunch: $7-$14   Dinner: $16-$26   **Phone: 804/829-5004**

Location: On SR 5. 9220 John Tyler Memorial Hwy 23030. **Hours:** 11 am-3:30 & 5-9 pm, Fri & Sat-10 pm. **Closed:** 1/1, 7/4, 12/25; also Mon 1/1-2/28. **Reservations:** suggested. **Features:** The menu features "new" Southern cuisine, with emphasis on regional specialties, and features ample portions. This charming restored farmhouse in the historic plantation region boasts quaint screened porches overlooking the gardens for seasonal dining. Casual dress; cocktails. **Parking:** on-site. **Cards:** AX, DS, MC, VI.

(✕)

LIGHTFOOT   (See map and index starting on p. 902)

———— **WHERE TO STAY** ————

DAYS INN COLONIAL RESORT   *Book at aaa.com*   **Phone: 757/220-0062**   **11**
(AAA) (SAVE)
◆◆◆

6/10-9/4 [CP]	1P: $69-$109		2P: $69-$109	XP: $10	F17
3/1-6/9 & 9/5-12/31 [CP]	1P: $47-$93		2P: $47-$93	XP: $10	F17
1/1-2/28 [CP]	1P: $39-$53		2P: $39-$53	XP: $10	F17

Small-scale Hotel

Location: I-64, exit 234 (SR 199 E), 0.5 mi s to International Pkwy. 720 Lightfoot Rd 23188 (720 Lightfoot Rd, WILLIAMSBURG). Fax: 757/941-2098. **Facility:** 120 units. 117 one-bedroom standard units. 3 one-bedroom suites ($89-$199), some with whirlpools. 5 stories, interior corridors. *Bath:* combo or shower only. **Parking:** on-site. **Terms:** package plans. **Amenities:** voice mail, safes (fee), hair dryers. **Pool(s):** heated indoor. **Leisure Activities:** whirlpool, exercise room. *Fee:* game room. **Guest Services:** valet and coin laundry. **Business Services:** meeting rooms, fax. **Cards:** AX, CB, DC, DS, JC, MC, VI. **Special Amenities:** free continental breakfast and free newspaper.
(See color ad p 911)

SOME UNITS
(S♦D) (⚙M) (▣) (⇌) (✕) (📷) (DATA PORT) / (✕) (🖥) (🖥) (▦) /
FEE FEE FEE

ECONO LODGE-POTTERY   *Book at aaa.com*   **Phone: (757)564-3341**
(AAA) (SAVE)
◆◆◆

5/27-9/4	1P: $59-$130		2P: $59-$130	XP: $10	F17
9/5-12/15	1P: $49-$130		2P: $49-$130	XP: $10	F17
3/1-5/26	1P: $39-$130		2P: $39-$130	XP: $10	F17
12/16-2/28	1P: $29-$79		2P: $29-$79	XP: $10	F17

Motel

Location: I-64, exit 231A, 1 mi s on SR 607, then 2.4 mi e on US 60. 7051 Richmond Rd 23188. Fax: 757/564-8668. **Facility:** 74 one-bedroom standard units. 2 stories (no elevator), exterior corridors. **Parking:** on-site. **Terms:** 2 night minimum stay - seasonal and/or weekends. **Pool(s):** outdoor. **Business Services:** fax. **Cards:** AX, CB, DC, DS, JC, MC, VI. **Special Amenities:** free continental breakfast and free local telephone calls.

SOME UNITS
(S♦D) (🍴) (⇌) / (✕) (🖥) (🖥) (▦) /
FEE FEE

GREAT WOLF LODGE   **Phone: 757/229-9700**
(fyi)
Small-scale Hotel

Under construction, scheduled to open March 2005. **Location:** I-64, exit 199. 559 E Rochambeau Dr 23188-2145 (559 E Rochambeau Dr, WILLIAMSBURG). Fax: 757/229-9780. **Planned Amenities:** coffeemakers, microwaves, refrigerators, pool. *(See color ad p 908)*

(See map and index starting on p. 902)

RAMADA INN   *Book at aaa.com*   Phone: (757)565-1111   **12**

🔺🔺 SAVE   6/11-9/10   1P: $60-$110   2P: $60-$110   XP: $10   F17
            3/1-6/10 & 9/11-10/31   1P: $40-$70   2P: $40-$70   XP: $10   F17
🔻🔻🔻🔻   11/1-2/28   1P: $40-$60   2P: $40-$60   XP: $10   F17
Small-scale Hotel **Location:** I-64, exit 234A, 1.7 mi s on SR 199, exit US 60, then just w. 6493 Richmond Rd 23188. Fax: 757/564-3033. **Facility:** 128 one-bedroom standard units. 2 stories (no elevator), exterior corridors. **Parking:** on-site. **Terms:** package plans. **Amenities:** safes (fee), irons. *Some:* hair dryers. **Pool(s):** outdoor. **Business Services:** fax. **Cards:** AX, DC, DS, MC, VI. **Special Amenities:** free continental breakfast and free local telephone calls.
(See color ad p 925)

SOME UNITS

[icons]

———— **WHERE TO DINE** ————

LA PETITE TEA ROOM   **Lunch:** $6-$13   **Dinner:** $6-$13   Phone: 757/565-3422   **20**

🔻   **Location:** I-64, exit 234A, s on SR 199, then just w; in the Williamsburg Antique Mall. 500 Lightfoot Rd 23188.
Specialty   **Hours:** 11 am-5:30 pm, Sun noon-5 pm, Mon 11:30 am-5:30 pm. **Features:** This tea room is super tiny, tucked in a corner of a busy antique mall, and the menu is small as well but full of flavor from the tea sandwiches, famous chowders, scones, and luscious desserts such as chocolate cream puffs. Casual dress. **Parking:** on-site.

[icon]

PIERCE'S BAR-B-QUE   **Lunch:** $3-$15   **Dinner:** $3-$15   Phone: 757/565-2955   **21**

🔻   **Location:** I-64, exit 238A westbound, just s to E Rochambeau Dr, 3 mi w; exit 234A eastbound, 1.2 mi s on US 199,
Barbecue   then 3 mi e on F-L37. 447 E Rochambeau Dr 23185. **Hours:** 7 am-9 pm, Fri & Sat-10 pm. Closed: 11/24, 12/25.
            Features: Nationally known and beloved for its sweet and tangy barbecue sauce—which is great on
chopped pork sandwiches, chicken and ribs—the restaurant also is a good spot for hushpuppies, catfish and Brunswick stew. Casual dress. **Parking:** on-site. **Cards:** MC, VI.

[icon]

YORKTOWN pop. 203   (See map and index starting on p. 707)

———— **WHERE TO STAY** ————

CANDLEWOOD SUITES-YORKTOWN   *Book at aaa.com*   Phone: (757)952-1120   **19**

🔻🔻🔻   4/1-10/31   1P: $99-$109   2P: $99-$109
            3/1-3/31 & 11/1-2/28   1P: $69-$99   2P: $69-$99
Small-scale Hotel **Location:** I-64, exit 256B, just n, then just e. 329 Commonwealth Dr 23693. Fax: 757/952-1121. **Facility:** 59 units. 47 one-bedroom standard units with kitchens. 12 one-bedroom suites with kitchens. 3 stories, interior corridors. *Bath:* combo or shower only. **Parking:** on-site. **Terms:** check-in 4 pm, pets ($75-$150 fee). **Amenities:** video library, DVD players, CD players, high-speed Internet (fee), dual phone lines, voice mail, irons, hair dryers. **Pool(s):** outdoor. **Leisure Activities:** exercise room. **Guest Services:** sundries, valet and coin laundry. **Business Services:** meeting rooms, fax. **Cards:** AX, DC, DS, MC, VI.

SOME UNITS

[icons] FEE

COURTYARD BY MARRIOTT   *Book at aaa.com*   Phone: 757/874-9000   **18**

🔻🔻🔻   3/1-9/30   1P: $129   2P: $129
            10/1-2/28   1P: $119   2P: $119
Small-scale Hotel **Location:** I-64, exit 256B, just n to Kiln Creek Pkwy. Located in a residential area. 105 Cybernetics Way 23693. Fax: 757/874-6200. **Facility:** 90 units. 87 one-bedroom standard units, some with whirlpools. 3 one-bedroom suites. 3 stories, interior corridors. *Bath:* combo or shower only. **Parking:** on-site. **Terms:** cancellation fee imposed, package plans. **Amenities:** high-speed Internet, voice mail, irons, hair dryers. **Pool(s):** small heated indoor. **Leisure Activities:** whirlpool, exercise room. **Guest Services:** sundries, valet and coin laundry. **Business Services:** meeting rooms, fax. **Cards:** AX, DC, DS, MC, VI.

SOME UNITS

[icons]

DUKE OF YORK MOTOR HOTEL   Phone: (757)898-3232

🔺🔺 SAVE   All Year   1P: $49-$145   2P: $49-$145
🔻🔻   **Location:** SR 238; downtown; on the waterfront. 508 Water St 23690 (PO Box 100). Fax: 757/898-5922. **Facility:** 57 one-bedroom standard units, some with whirlpools. 2-3 stories, interior/exterior corridors. *Bath:* combo or shower only. **Parking:** on-site. **Amenities:** hair dryers. **Dining:** 7:30 am-10:30 & 11-2 pm. **Pool(s):** outdoor.
Small-scale Hotel **Cards:** AX.

SOME UNITS

[icons] FEE FEE

TOWNEPLACE SUITES BY MARRIOTT   *Book at aaa.com*   Phone: 757/874-8884   **17**

🔺🔺 SAVE   All Year   1P: $125-$139
🔻🔻🔻   **Location:** I-64, exit 256B, e to Kiln Creek Pkwy. 200 Cybernetics Way 23693. Fax: 757/874-3089. **Facility:** 95 units. 68 one-bedroom standard units with kitchens. 4 one- and 23 two-bedroom suites with kitchens. 3 stories, interior corridors. *Bath:* combo or shower only. **Parking:** on-site. **Terms:** pets ($100 fee). **Amenities:** video
Small-scale Hotel games, high-speed Internet, voice mail, irons, hair dryers. **Pool(s):** heated outdoor. **Leisure Activities:** exercise room. **Guest Services:** valet and coin laundry. **Business Services:** PC, fax. **Cards:** AX, DC, MC, VI. **Special Amenities:** free continental breakfast and free local telephone calls.

SOME UNITS

[icons] FEE

(See map and index starting on p. 707)

YORKTOWN MOTOR LODGE   *Book at aaa.com*   Phone: (757)898-5451
⟨AAA⟩ ⟨SAVE⟩   4/1-9/5   1P: $59-$89   2P: $65-$99   XP: $7   F16
▽▽ ▽▽   3/1-3/31 & 9/6-2/28   1P: $55-$65   2P: $65-$79   XP: $7   F16
          Location: 3 mi s of York River bridge on US 17. 8829 George Washington Memorial Hwy 23692. Fax: 757/898-1766.
Motel   **Facility:** 42 one-bedroom standard units. 1 story, exterior corridors. **Parking:** on-site. **Terms:** office hours 7
          am-11 pm, 3 day cancellation notice-fee imposed, [CP] meal plan available. **Amenities:** irons, hair dryers.
          Pool(s): outdoor. **Business Services:** fax. **Cards:** AX, DS, MC, VI. **Special Amenities:** free continental
breakfast and free room upgrade (subject to availability with advance reservations).   SOME UNITS

[S/D] [≈] [🍴] [DATA PORT] [🛏] [📷] [💳] / [⊠] /

———— **WHERE TO DINE** ————

CARROT TREE KITCHEN AT THE COLE DIGGS
   HOUSE   **Lunch:** $5-$11   Phone: 757/246-9559
▽▽▽   **Location:** Jct Read St; in Colonial District. 411 Main St 23692. **Hours:** 8 am-5 pm, Fri & Sat-8 pm, Sun 10 am-5
         pm. Closed: 3/27, 11/24, 12/24, 12/25. **Features:** In the center of a Colonial village, the charming historic
Regional American cottage employs a staff that serves tasty lunch specialties made with a Southern flair. Examples include
         tomato basil soup, ham biscuits, hot crab dip and rich desserts, including, of course, the specialty carrot
cake. Casual dress; beer & wine only. **Parking:** street. **Cards:** AX, DS, MC, VI.
                                                                                        [⊠]

EMPRESS RESTAURANT   **Lunch:** $6-$11   **Dinner:** $6-$11   Phone: 757/875-5460   ⟨20⟩
▽▽▽   **Location:** I-64, exit 256B, just e. 5005 Victory Blvd 23606. **Hours:** 11 am-10 pm, Fri & Sat-11 pm. Closed: 11/24,
         12/25. **Features:** The bountiful lunch and dinner buffets line up a wide range of Chinese specialties and a
Chinese few Japanese and Korean ones as well. A la carte dishes also are available. Casual dress. **Parking:** on-site.
         Cards: AX, DC, DS, MC, VI.   [&M] [⊠]

THE GLASS PHEASANT ENGLISH TEA ROOM   **Lunch:** $5-$9   Phone: 757/595-9012   ⟨19⟩
▽▽ ▽▽   **Location:** I-64, exit 258B, 2 mi n on US 17; in Kiln Creek Shopping Center. 1215Q SR 17 23693. **Hours:** 11 am-2:30
         pm. Closed: Sat & Sun. **Features:** The tea room offers a menu of sandwiches, soup, salad and quiche in a
American setting of antiques and English china. **Parking:** on-site.
                                                                                   [&M] [🍴] [⊠]

SMOKIN' JOE'S BARBEQUE   **Lunch:** $6-$15   **Dinner:** $6-$15   Phone: 757/875-7774
▽▽▽   **Location:** On US 17, 2 mi n of SR 134. 5619 George Washington Memorial Hwy 23692. **Hours:** 11 am-8 pm, Fri &
         Sat-9 pm, Sun noon-4 pm. Closed: 11/24, 12/25. **Features:** The bright and clean roadside spot serves lots
Barbecue of tasty barbecue and country sides to hungry patrons. Pork and ribs are the specialty, but yummy chicken,
         wraps and salads are find a place on the menu. Casual dress. **Parking:** on-site. **Cards:** MC, VI. [&M] [⊠]

SPRING GARDEN   **Lunch:** $5-$7   **Dinner:** $6-$13   Phone: 757/599-0088   ⟨18⟩
▽▽▽   **Location:** I-64, exit 258B, 1 mi n on US 17; in Kiln Creek Center. 1215-X George Washington Memorial Hwy 23963.
         Hours: 11 am-9:30 pm, Fri-10 pm, Sat 4:30 pm-10 pm, Sun 4:30 pm-9 pm. Closed major holidays.
Chinese **Features:** Inside, the pleasant little spot has the feel of a greenhouse, with plenty of plants and cozy pink
         bistro curtains. The menu is all Chinese, from the fresh and tasty lunch buffet to seasonal dinner specialties
of Mandarin roast duck and soft-shell crabs. Casual dress. **Parking:** on-site. **Cards:** DS, MC, VI.
                                                                                              [⊠]

This ends listings for the Williamsburg, Jamestown & Yorktown.
The following page resumes the alphabetical listings of
cities in Virginia.

WILLIAMSVILLE

―――――― **WHERE TO STAY** ――――――

FORT LEWIS LODGE   Phone: (540)925-2314
▼◆◆◆▼   All Year   1P: $87-$150   2P: $87-$150   XP: $25   F14
Country Inn **Location:** 5.8 mi s on SR 678, just w on SR 625; from SR 39, just w on SR 625, 11 mi n. Located in rural area. SR 625
(River Rd) 24460 (HCR 3, Box 21A, MILLBORO). Fax: 540/925-2352. **Facility:** A friendly dog roams the grounds
of this mountain farm which houses guests in converted silo rooms, standard lodge rooms and two cabins.
Smoke free premises. 18 units. 15 one- and 3 two-bedroom standard units. 2-3 stories (no elevator), interior/exterior corridors.
Bath: combo or shower only. **Parking:** on-site. **Terms:** 2 night minimum stay - weekends, 7 day cancellation notice-fee
imposed, weekly rates available, package plans. **Amenities:** *Some:* hair dryers. **Leisure Activities:** whirlpool, canoeing, fishing,
basketball, volleyball. **Business Services:** meeting rooms. **Cards:** AX, MC, VI.
                                                                                        SOME UNITS
(A$K) (S⬢) (▮◀) (✕) (✕) (W) (☎) / (▯) (▭)

WINCHESTER pop. 23,585

―――――― **WHERE TO STAY** ――――――

BEST VALUE INN   *Book at aaa.com*   Phone: (540)662-2521
(AAA) (SAVE)   10/1-11/15   1P: $65-$80   2P: $75-$85   XP: $5   F12
▼◆◆▼   5/1-9/30   1P: $55-$75   2P: $62-$80   XP: $5   F12
            11/16-2/28   1P: $45-$60   2P: $50-$69   XP: $5   F12
            3/1-4/30   1P: $48-$62   2P: $55-$68   XP: $5   F12
Small-scale Hotel **Location:** I-81, exit 310, just w to US 11, then 2 mi n. 2649 Valley Ave 22601. Fax: 540/662-6683. **Facility:** 70 one-
bedroom standard units. 1-2 stories (no elevator), exterior corridors. **Parking:** on-site. **Amenities:** hair
dryers. *Some:* irons. **Pool(s):** outdoor. **Guest Services:** coin laundry. **Cards:** AX, DS, MC, VI. **Special Amenities:** free
continental breakfast.
                                                                                        SOME UNITS
(S⬢) (▮◀+) (⊃) (✦) (DATA PORT) (▭) / (✕) (▯) (▭) /

BEST WESTERN LEE-JACKSON MOTOR INN   *Book at aaa.com*   Phone: (540)662-4154
(AAA) (SAVE)   4/1-4/30   1P: $61-$66   2P: $66-$71   XP: $5   F12
▼◆◆◆▼   5/1-2/28   1P: $54-$66   2P: $59-$71   XP: $5   F12
            3/1-3/31   1P: $54-$59   2P: $59-$64   XP: $5   F12
            Location: I-81, exit 313B, just nw on US 50/522/17. 711 Millwood Ave 22601. Fax: 540/662-2618. **Facility:** 139
Small-scale Hotel one-bedroom standard units. 2 stories (no elevator), exterior corridors. **Parking:** on-site. **Terms:** small pets
only ($5 deposit). **Amenities:** high-speed Internet, voice mail, irons, hair dryers. **Dining:** 6 am-10 pm,
wine/beer only. **Pool(s):** outdoor. **Leisure Activities:** exercise room. **Guest Services:** coin laundry, airport transportation-
Winchester Regional Airport, area transportation-hospital. **Business Services:** conference facilities. **Cards:** AX, DC, DS, JC,
MC, VI. **Special Amenities:** free newspaper and early check-in/late check-out. *(See ad below)*
                                                                                        SOME UNITS
(S⬢) (✈) (🐾) (▮◀) (⊃) (✦) (DATA PORT) (▯) (▭) (▭) / (✕) /
                          FEE

COMFORT INN   *Book at aaa.com*   Phone: (540)667-8894
(AAA) (SAVE)   All Year [ECP]   1P: $62-$82   2P: $62-$82   XP: $5   F18
▼◆◆▼   **Location:** I-81, exit 317, just s on US 11. 1601 Martinsburg Pike 22603. Fax: 540/667-0823. **Facility:** 82 one-
bedroom standard units. 2 stories (no elevator), interior corridors. *Bath:* combo or shower only. **Parking:** on-
site. **Amenities:** voice mail, irons, hair dryers. **Pool(s):** outdoor. **Leisure Activities:** picnic and grill area,
Small-scale Hotel exercise room, horseshoes. **Guest Services:** coin laundry. **Business Services:** meeting rooms. **Cards:** AX,
CB, DC, DS, JC, MC, VI. **Special Amenities:** free expanded continental breakfast and free
newspaper.
                                                                                        SOME UNITS
(S⬢) (🐾) (⊃) (✕) (✦) (DATA PORT) (▭) / (✕) (▯) (▭) /

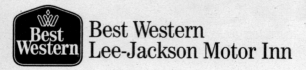

DAYS INN   *Book at aaa.com*   Phone: (540)667-1200

(AAA) [SAVE]

9/30-10/31	1P: $55-$75	2P: $55-$75	XP: $8	F17
4/1-9/29	1P: $55-$65	2P: $55-$65	XP: $8	F17
3/1-3/31 & 11/1-2/28	1P: $49-$54	2P: $49-$54	XP: $8	F17

Small-scale Hotel   **Location:** I-81, exit 310, just w, then 1.8 mi n on US 11. 2951 Valley Ave 22601. **Fax:** 540/667-7128. **Facility:** 66 one-bedroom standard units. 2 stories (no elevator), exterior corridors. **Parking:** on-site. **Terms:** small pets only ($8 extra charge). **Amenities:** hair dryers. **Dining:** 7 am-9 pm, Fri & Sat-10 pm, Sun-2 pm, cocktails. **Pool(s):** outdoor. **Guest Services:** valet laundry. **Business Services:** meeting rooms. **Cards:** AX, DC, DS, MC, VI. **Special Amenities:** free local telephone calls and free newspaper.

SOME UNITS

ECONO LODGE NORTH   *Book at aaa.com*   Phone: (540)662-4700

(AAA) [SAVE]

4/1-10/29	1P: $62-$67	2P: $67-$72	XP: $5	F17
3/1-3/31 & 10/30-2/28	1P: $57-$62	2P: $62-$67	XP: $5	F17

Small-scale Hotel   **Location:** I-81, exit 317, 0.3 mi sw on US 11. 1593 Martinsburg Pike 22603. **Fax:** 540/665-1762. **Facility:** 50 one-bedroom standard units. 2 stories (no elevator), interior corridors. **Parking:** on-site. **Leisure Activities:** pool privileges. **Guest Services:** valet laundry. **Cards:** AX, CB, DC, DS, MC, VI. **Special Amenities:** free continental breakfast and free local telephone calls.

SOME UNITS

HAMPTON INN NORTH   *Book at aaa.com*   Phone: (540)678-4000

5/2-11/1	1P: $89-$139	2P: $89-$139
3/1-5/1 & 11/2-2/28	1P: $79-$129	2P: $79-$129

Small-scale Hotel   **Location:** I-81, exit 315, just w. 1204 Berryville Ave 22601. **Fax:** 540/678-8277. **Facility:** 100 one-bedroom standard units, some with whirlpools. 4 stories, interior corridors. **Bath:** combo or shower only. **Parking:** on-site. **Amenities:** voice mail, irons, hair dryers. **Pool(s):** outdoor. **Leisure Activities:** exercise room. **Guest Services:** coin laundry. **Business Services:** meeting rooms, business center. **Cards:** AX, DC, DS, MC, VI.

SOME UNITS

HAMPTON INN WINCHESTER UNIVERSITY MALL   *Book at aaa.com*   Phone: (540)667-8011

All Year	1P: $89-$95	2P: $89-$95

Small-scale Hotel   **Location:** I-81, exit 313 northbound; exit 313B southbound, 0.5 mi nw on US 50/522/17. 1655 Apple Blossom Dr 22601. **Fax:** 540/667-8033. **Facility:** 101 one-bedroom standard units. 4 stories, interior corridors. **Parking:** on-site. **Terms:** cancellation fee imposed. **Amenities:** video games, voice mail, irons, hair dryers. **Pool(s):** outdoor. **Leisure Activities:** exercise room. **Guest Services:** valet laundry. **Business Services:** meeting rooms, business center. **Cards:** AX, DC, DS, MC, VI.

SOME UNITS

HOLIDAY INN EXPRESS & SUITES WINCHESTER   *Book at aaa.com*   Phone: (540)667-7050

All Year	1P: $79-$109	2P: $79-$109

Small-scale Hotel   **Location:** I-81, exit 317, 2.7 mi w on SR 37. 142 Fox Ridge Ln 22601. **Fax:** 540/667-7150. **Facility:** 81 one-bedroom standard units. 3 stories, interior corridors. **Bath:** combo or shower only. **Parking:** on-site. **Terms:** 3 day cancellation notice-fee imposed, package plans. **Amenities:** video games, high-speed Internet, voice mail, irons, hair dryers. **Pool(s):** heated indoor. **Leisure Activities:** whirlpool, exercise room. **Guest Services:** valet and coin laundry. **Business Services:** meeting rooms, business center. **Cards:** AX, CB, DC, DS, JC, MC, VI.

SOME UNITS

HOLIDAY INN WINCHESTER   Phone: (540)667-3300

(AAA) [SAVE]

All Year	1P: $69-$89	2P: $69-$89

Small-scale Hotel   **Location:** I-81, exit 313 northbound; exit 313A southbound, just se on US 50/17, at US 522. 1017 Millwood Pike 22602. **Fax:** 540/722-2730. **Facility:** 173 one-bedroom standard units. 2 stories (no elevator), interior/exterior corridors. **Parking:** on-site. **Amenities:** voice mail, irons, hair dryers. **Dining:** 6:30 am-1 & 5-9 pm, cocktails. **Pool(s):** outdoor. **Leisure Activities:** exercise room. **Guest Services:** valet laundry, airport transportation-Winchester Regional Airport, area transportation-within 5 mi. **Business Services:** meeting rooms. **Cards:** AX, CB, DC, DS, MC, VI. **Special Amenities:** free local telephone calls and free newspaper.

SOME UNITS

MOHAWK MOTEL   Phone: (540)667-1410

Motel

All Year	1P: $48-$53	2P: $48-$53	XP: $5	F

Location: I-81, exit 317, 3 mi s on SR 37, then 1.7 mi w on US 50. 2754 Northwestern Pike 22603. **Fax:** 540/667-7820. **Facility:** 11 one-bedroom standard units. 1 story, exterior corridors. **Bath:** combo or shower only. **Parking:** on-site. **Terms:** cancellation fee imposed, weekly rates available. **Cards:** MC, VI.

SOME UNITS

QUALITY INN EAST   *Book at aaa.com*   Phone: (540)667-2250

4/28-10/31	1P: $66-$73	2P: $66-$73	XP: $8	F18
3/1-4/27	1P: $58-$66	2P: $58-$66	XP: $7	F18
11/1-2/28	1P: $58-$66	2P: $58-$66	XP: $8	F18

Small-scale Hotel   **Location:** I-81, exit 313 northbound; exit 313B southbound, 0.5 mi nw on US 50/522/17. 603 Millwood Ave 22601. **Fax:** 540/667-0850. **Facility:** 96 one-bedroom standard units. 2 stories (no elevator), exterior corridors. **Parking:** on-site. **Terms:** pets ($7 extra charge). **Amenities:** Some: irons. **Pool(s):** outdoor, wading. **Leisure Activities:** exercise room. **Guest Services:** coin laundry. **Cards:** AX, CB, DC, DS, JC, MC, VI.

SOME UNITS

RED ROOF INN   *Book at aaa.com*   Phone: (540)667-5000
(AAA) [SAVE]
▼▼▼
| | 4/1-10/31 [ECP] | 1P: $65-$79 | 2P: $65-$79 | XP: $5 | F18 |
| | 3/1-3/31 & 11/1-2/28 [ECP] | 1P: $58-$72 | 2P: $58-$72 | XP: $5 | F18 |

Location: I-81, exit 313 northbound; exit 313A southbound, just se on US 50/17. 991 Millwood Pike 22602.
Small-scale Hotel Fax: 540/667-7108. **Facility:** 113 one-bedroom standard units. 2 stories (no elevator), exterior corridors. **Parking:** on-site. **Terms:** package plans, small pets only. **Amenities:** irons, hair dryers. **Guest Services:** coin laundry. **Business Services:** meeting rooms. **Cards:** AX, DC, DS, MC, VI. **Special Amenities:** free expanded continental breakfast and free newspaper.

SOME UNITS

ROYAL INN   Phone: (540)667-8881
(AAA) [SAVE]
▼
Motel
| | 3/1-10/31 | 1P: $39-$49 | 2P: $45-$54 | XP: $10 | F10 |
| | 11/1-2/28 | 1P: $35-$44 | 2P: $40-$48 | XP: $7 | F10 |

Location: I-81, exit 310, just w, then 1.9 mi n on US 11. 2930 Valley Ave 22601. Fax: 540/667-7410. **Facility:** 16 one-bedroom standard units. 1 story, exterior corridors. **Parking:** on-site. **Leisure Activities:** picnic area. **Cards:** AX, DS, MC, VI.

SOME UNITS

SLEEP INN & SUITES   *Book at aaa.com*   Phone: (540)667-7636
▼▼▼▼
	7/1-10/31	1P: $89-$139	2P: $89-$139
	11/1-2/28	1P: $79-$139	2P: $79-$139
	4/1-6/30	1P: $75-$139	2P: $75-$139
	3/1-3/31	1P: $69-$139	2P: $69-$139

Small-scale Hotel **Location:** I-81, exit 313, s on US 522, then left. 140 Costello Dr 22602. Fax: 540/667-5060. **Facility:** 72 one-bedroom standard units, some with whirlpools. 4 stories, interior corridors. *Bath:* combo or shower only. **Parking:** on-site. **Terms:** package plans. **Amenities:** voice mail, irons, hair dryers. *Some:* safes. **Pool(s):** heated indoor. **Leisure Activities:** exercise room. **Guest Services:** valet and coin laundry. **Business Services:** business center. **Cards:** AX, DC, DS, MC, VI.

SOME UNITS

SUPER 8 MOTEL   Phone: (540)665-4450
(AAA) [SAVE]
▼▼
| | 4/1-10/31 [CP] | 1P: $53-$60 | 2P: $53-$60 | XP: $5 | F15 |
| | 3/1-3/31 & 11/1-2/28 [CP] | 1P: $49-$55 | 2P: $49-$55 | XP: $5 | F15 |

Location: I-81, exit 313 northbound; exit 313A southbound, 0.3 mi se on US 50/17. 1077 Millwood Pike 22602. Fax: 540/665-4450. **Facility:** 62 one-bedroom standard units. 2 stories (no elevator), interior corridors. Small-scale Hotel **Parking:** on-site. **Terms:** package plans, small pets only ($7 extra charge). **Cards:** AX, CB, DC, DS, MC, VI. **Special Amenities:** free continental breakfast and free local telephone calls.

SOME UNITS

TOURIST CITY MOTEL   Phone: 540/662-9011
(AAA) [SAVE]
▼
Motel
	4/1-10/31	1P: $33-$37	2P: $38-$42	XP: $5	D14
	3/1-3/31	1P: $32-$36	2P: $37-$41	XP: $4	D14
	11/1-2/28	1P: $31-$35	2P: $37-$40	XP: $4	D14

Location: I-81, exit 313 northbound; exit 313B southbound, 1 mi nw on US 50/522. 214 Millwood Ave 22601. Fax: 540/662-0607. **Facility:** 11 one-bedroom standard units. 1 story, exterior corridors. *Bath:* shower only. **Parking:** on-site. **Terms:** 5 day cancellation notice, pets ($4 extra charge). **Cards:** AX, CB, DC, MC, VI. **Special Amenities:** free local telephone calls and preferred room (subject to availability with advance reservations).

SOME UNITS

TRAVELODGE OF WINCHESTER   *Book at aaa.com*   Phone: (540)665-0685
(AAA) [SAVE]
▼▼▼
| | All Year [ECP] | 1P: $76-$80 | 2P: $82-$85 | XP: $5 | F18 |

Location: I-81, exit 313 northbound; exit 313A southbound, just s on US 522. 160 Front Royal Pike 22602. Fax: 540/665-0689. **Facility:** 149 one-bedroom standard units, some with whirlpools. 3 stories, interior corridors. **Parking:** on-site. **Terms:** pets ($5 extra charge). **Amenities:** video library, voice mail, irons, hair Small-scale Hotel dryers. **Pool(s):** outdoor. **Guest Services:** coin laundry. **Business Services:** meeting rooms. **Cards:** AX, CB, DC, DS, JC, MC, VI. **Special Amenities:** free expanded continental breakfast and free local telephone calls.

SOME UNITS

WINGATE INN   *Book at aaa.com*   Phone: (540)678-4283
(AAA) [SAVE]
▼▼▼
| | 4/1-10/29 | 1P: $95-$115 | 2P: $95-$115 |
| | 3/1-3/31 & 10/30-2/28 | 1P: $95 | 2P: $95 |

Location: I-81, exit 313 northbound; 313B southbound, 0.6 mi nw, then just s. 150 Wingate Dr 22601. Fax: 540/662-4439. **Facility:** 84 one-bedroom standard units, some with whirlpools. 4 stories, interior corridors. *Bath:* combo or shower only. **Parking:** on-site. **Terms:** [BP] & [CP] meal plans available, package Small-scale Hotel plans. **Amenities:** high-speed Internet, voice mail, safes, irons, hair dryers. **Pool(s):** indoor. **Leisure Activities:** sauna, whirlpool, exercise room. **Guest Services:** coin laundry. **Business Services:** meeting rooms, business center. **Cards:** AX, DC, DS, MC, VI. **Special Amenities:** free continental breakfast and free local telephone calls.

SOME UNITS

────────── **WHERE TO DINE** ──────────

CAFE SOFIA   **Lunch:** $9-$10   **Dinner:** $20-$23   Phone: 540/667-2950
▼▼▼
Ethnic
Location: I-81, exit 310, just w to US 11, then 2.2 mi n. 2900 Valley Ave 22601. **Hours:** Open 3/1-6/30 & 9/1-2/28; noon-2 & 5-9 pm, Sat from 5 pm. Closed: Sun & Mon. **Reservations:** required, weekends. **Features:** Guests can drop in to the quaint, intimate restaurant to enjoy Bulgarian cuisine, such as the goulash, which is praised. The dining room brims with charming displays of imported handicrafts, dolls and assorted collectibles. Servers don traditional Bulgarian attire during dinner. Casual dress; cocktails. **Parking:** on-site. **Cards:** AX, CB, DC, DS, MC, VI.

CASTIGLIA'S

Italian

Lunch: $5-$11   **Dinner:** $7-$19   **Phone:** 540/722-6084

Location: I-81, exit 317, just w. 2100 S Pleasant Valley Rd 22601. **Hours:** 11 am-10 pm. Closed major holidays. **Features:** Castiglia's Italian Eatery offers delicious Italian Cuisine in a family friendly atmosphere. Outstanding bread selections. Casual dress; beer & wine only. **Parking:** on-site. **Cards:** MC, VI.

CORK STREET TAVERN   *Menu on aaa.com*

American

Lunch: $6-$13   **Dinner:** $10-$24   **Phone:** 540/667-3777

Location: Between Braddock and Loudoun sts; in historic district. 8 W Cork St 22601. **Hours:** 11 am-midnight, Sun noon-11 pm. Closed major holidays. **Features:** Flavorful specialties are served in a cozy tavern, with some areas dating to the 1830s. The atmosphere is casual and laid-back. Sandwiches, salads, seafood, steak and barbecue dishes grace the downtown eatery's varied menu. Be sure to ask for a brief history of the building while dining. Casual dress; cocktails. **Parking:** on-site. **Cards:** AX, DC, DS, MC, VI. **Historic**

PARGO'S

American

Lunch: $5-$16   **Dinner:** $9-$16   **Phone:** 540/678-8800

Location: I-81, exit 313 northbound; exit 313B southbound, 0.5 mi nw on US 50/522/17; in Apple Blossom Mall. 645 E Jubal Early Dr 22601. **Hours:** 11 am-11 pm, Fri & Sat-midnight, Sun 10:30 am-10 pm. Closed major holidays. **Features:** The local crowd loves the bustling eatery, as evidenced by the long lines that often wait for seating. The menu offers standard favorites, such as pasta and steak, in plentiful portions. The French dip sandwich and house salad are delicious. Casual dress; cocktails. **Parking:** on-site. **Cards:** AX, CB, DC, DS, MC, VI.

VENICE ITALIAN RESTAURANT

Italian

Lunch: $7-$14   **Dinner:** $8-$20   **Phone:** 540/722-0992

Location: 1 mi n on US 522, just e. 1490 N Frederick Pike 22601. **Hours:** 10:30 am-10 pm. Closed major holidays; also Sun. **Features:** Patrons don't need a gondola or even a passport to journey to Venice and enjoy the sights, sounds and cuisine of Italy. The restaurant offers a taste of it all in its decor, background music and great menu. Casual dress; cocktails. **Parking:** on-site. **Cards:** AX, CB, DC, DS, JC, MC, VI.

WINTERGREEN

——— WHERE TO STAY ———

WINTERGREEN RESORT INC   *Book at aaa.com*   **Phone:** (434)325-2200

Resort
Large-scale Hotel

	1P:	2P:
12/23-2/28	1P: $145-$232	2P: $145-$232
6/1-10/31	1P: $185-$218	2P: $185-$218
3/1-5/31	1P: $181-$211	2P: $181-$211
11/1-12/22	1P: $155-$180	2P: $155-$180

Location: SR 664, 4.5 mi w of jct SR 151. Located in a quiet area. (PO Box 706). Fax: 434/325-8003. **Facility:** Recreational activities for every age are offered at this all-season resort, which is perched atop a mountain and affords great views. 316 units. 158 one- and 98 two-bedroom standard units, some with kitchens. 60 three-bedroom suites with efficiencies. 2-4 stories, interior/exterior corridors. **Parking:** on-site. **Terms:** check-in 4 pm, 2 night minimum stay - seasonal, 14 day cancellation notice-fee imposed, [MAP] meal plan available, package plans, 6% service charge. **Amenities:** voice mail, irons. **Pool(s):** 3 heated outdoor, heated indoor, 3 wading. **Leisure Activities:** saunas, whirlpools, rental canoes, rental paddleboats, fishing, 21 tennis courts (3 indoor, 10 lighted), recreation programs, playground, spa. *Fee:* golf-45 holes, downhill skiing, bicycles, horseback riding. **Guest Services:** gift shop, coin laundry, area transportation (fee). **Business Services:** conference facilities, business center. **Cards:** AX, DS, MC, VI.

SOME UNITS

(ASK) (✈) FEE (♣♣) (♀) (♠) (🛶) (👥) (✕) (VCR) (📷) (DATA PORT) (🖥) (🖨) (🖳) / (✕) /

WOODBRIDGE —*See District Of Columbia p. 555.*

WOODSTOCK pop. 3,952

——— WHERE TO STAY ———

BUDGET HOST INN (SAVE)

Motel

Phone: 540/459-4086

All Year	1P: $40-$50	2P: $45-$52	XP: $5	F16

Location: I-81, exit 283, 0.8 mi se on SR 42, then 0.6 mi s on US 11. 1290 S Main St 22664. Fax: 540/459-4043. **Facility:** 43 one-bedroom standard units. 1-2 stories (no elevator), exterior corridors. **Parking:** on-site. **Terms:** weekly rates available. **Pool(s):** outdoor. **Leisure Activities:** picnic tables. **Guest Services:** coin laundry. **Cards:** AX, CB, DC, DS, MC, VI.

SOME UNITS

(S/D) (🐾) (🍴) (🛶) / (✕) (🖳)

COMFORT INN SHENANDOAH (SAVE)   *Book at aaa.com*

Small-scale Hotel

Phone: (540)459-7600

5/7-11/13 [ECP]	1P: $74-$95	2P: $79-$99	XP: $10	F19
3/1-5/6 & 11/14-2/28 [ECP]	1P: $69-$85	2P: $74-$90	XP: $10	F19

Location: I-81, exit 283, just e. 1011 Motel Dr 22664. Fax: 540/459-7601. **Facility:** 66 one-bedroom standard units, some with whirlpools. 3 stories, interior corridors. *Bath:* combo or shower only. **Parking:** on-site. **Terms:** small pets only. **Amenities:** irons, hair dryers. **Pool(s):** outdoor. **Leisure Activities:** exercise room. **Guest Services:** coin laundry. **Business Services:** meeting rooms. **Cards:** AX, CB, DC, DS, JC, MC, VI. **Special Amenities:** free expanded continental breakfast and free local telephone calls.

SOME UNITS

(S/D) (🐾) (♿) (🛶) (📷) (🖳) / (✕) (VCR) (🖳) (🖨) /

THE INN AT NARROW PASSAGE

◆◆◆◆◆◆ ◇ All Year [BP]   1P: $95-$110   2P: $120-$165   XP: $20   D16

Bed & Breakfast   **Location:** I-81, exit 283, just e to US 11, 1.7 mi s to SR 672, then just e. Located in a rural area. 30 Chapman Landing Rd 22664 (PO Box 608). Fax: 540/459-8001. **Facility:** Handmade furnishings, queen-size beds and some rooms with fireplaces reflect a Colonial-style ambience at this 1740 inn. Smoke free premises. 12 one-bedroom standard units. 2 stories (no elevator), interior/exterior corridors. *Bath:* combo or shower only. **Parking:** on-site. **Terms:** 2 night minimum stay - seasonal and/or weekends, 3 day cancellation notice. **Amenities:** hair dryers. *Some:* irons. **Leisure Activities:** canoeing, fishing, hiking trails, horseshoes. *Fee:* horseback riding. **Guest Services:** complimentary evening beverages. **Business Services:** meeting rooms. **Cards:** MC, VI.

Phone: (540)459-8000

SOME UNITS
(ASK) ⊠ ☒ / 🅿 🔟 🛗 /

RAMADA INN

(AAA) (SAVE)   *Book at aaa.com*

◆◆◆◆ ◆◆◆◆   5/1-11/7   1P: $69-$99   2P: $69-$99   XP: $8   F18
   3/1-4/30 & 11/8-2/28   1P: $59-$79   2P: $59-$79   XP: $8   F18

Small-scale Hotel   **Location:** I-81, exit 283, just e on SR 42. 1130 Motel Dr 22664. Fax: 540/459-8219. **Facility:** 123 one-bedroom standard units, some with efficiencies. 3 stories, interior corridors. **Parking:** on-site. **Terms:** small pets only ($10 extra charge). **Amenities:** voice mail, irons, hair dryers. **Dining:** 6:30 am-2:30 & 5-9 pm, cocktails. **Pool(s):** outdoor. **Leisure Activities:** exercise room. **Guest Services:** coin laundry. **Business Services:** meeting rooms. **Cards:** AX, CB, DC, DS, JC, MC. **Special Amenities:** free local telephone calls and early check-in/late check-out.

Phone: (540)459-5000

SOME UNITS
🆂🅳 🛏 🍽 🍸 🏊 👷 [DATA PORT] 💻 / ☒ 🛗 /
FEE

———— WHERE TO DINE ————

CHAPPALINO'S   **Lunch:** $6-$10   **Dinner:** $6-$15   Phone: 540/459-7332

◆◆   **Location:** I-81, exit 283, just e. 121 S Main St 22664. **Hours:** 11 am-11 pm, Fri & Sat-midnight, Sun-10 pm.

Italian   **Features:** Patrons can unwind in the casual, fun atmosphere and choose from a wide variety of Italian specialties. Don't pass up the chance to sample the "doughboys.". Casual dress; beer only. **Parking:** street. **Cards:** MC, VI.

☒

PAISANO'S   **Lunch:** $6-$12   **Dinner:** $8-$21   Phone: 540/459-8756

◆◆ ◆◆   **Location:** I-81, exit 283, just w. 483 W Reservoir Rd 22664. **Hours:** 10:30 am-10 pm. Closed: 1/1, 12/25.

Italian   **Features:** Paisano's offers a relaxing atmosphere with authentic Italian Cuisine. You'll make friends quickly at this restaurant and don't miss the bruscette. Casual dress; beer & wine only. **Parking:** on-site. **Cards:** AX, CB, DC, DS, JC, MC, VI.

🍸 ☒

SPRING HOUSE TAVERN   **Lunch:** $5-$15   **Dinner:** $8-$20   Phone: 540/459-4755

◆◆ ◆◆   **Location:** I-81, exit 283, just e. 325 S Main St 22664. **Hours:** 11 am-midnight, Sun noon-10 pm. Closed major

American   holidays. **Features:** Plenty of choices line the relaxed restaurant's menu of American cuisine. The staff is friendly and the atmosphere nice. Casual dress; cocktails. **Parking:** on-site. **Cards:** AX, CB, DC, DS, JC, MC, VI. **Historic**

🍸 ☒

WOOLWINE

———— WHERE TO STAY ————

THE MOUNTAIN ROSE INN

◆◆◆ ◇ All Year [BP]   2P: $125-$150   XP: $25

Historic Bed & Breakfast   **Location:** SR 8, 1.8 mi e on SR 40; Blue Ridge Pkwy, Milepost 165.2, 6.5 mi s on SR 8, 1.8 mi e on SR 40. Located in a quiet area. 1787 Charity Hwy 24185. Fax: 276/930-2165. **Facility:** Originally a distillery, this 1901 Victorian inn set in a mountain meadow has cozy rooms appointed with antiques and warmed by fireplaces. Smoke free premises. 5 one-bedroom standard units. 2 stories (no elevator), interior corridors. *Bath:* shower only. **Parking:** on-site. **Terms:** 2 night minimum stay - weekends, age restrictions may apply, 7 day cancellation notice-fee imposed, package plans, no pets allowed (owner's pets on premises). **Amenities:** irons, hair dryers. **Pool(s):** outdoor. **Leisure Activities:** fishing, hiking trails. **Business Services:** meeting rooms. **Cards:** DS, MC, VI.

Phone: (276)930-1057

SOME UNITS
🏊 ☒ 👷 / 🔟 🛗 /

WYTHEVILLE pop. 7,804

———— WHERE TO STAY ————

BEST WESTERN WYTHEVILLE INN

(AAA) (SAVE)   *Book at aaa.com*

   5/1-10/31 [ECP]   1P: $60-$155   2P: $60-$155   XP: $6   F17
◆◆◆ ◇   3/1-4/30 [ECP]   1P: $50-$155   2P: $50-$155   XP: $6   F17
   11/1-2/28 [ECP]   1P: $50-$120   2P: $50-$120   XP: $6   F17

Small-scale Hotel   **Location:** I-77, exit 41, just e. 355 Nye Rd 24382. Fax: 276/228-4223. **Facility:** 100 one-bedroom standard units, some with whirlpools. 2 stories (no elevator), interior corridors. **Parking:** on-site. **Terms:** 3 day cancellation notice, pets ($6 extra charge). **Amenities:** voice mail, safes, irons, hair dryers. **Pool(s):** outdoor. **Business Services:** meeting rooms. **Cards:** AX, CB, DC, DS, JC, MC, VI. **Special Amenities:** free expanded continental breakfast and free local telephone calls.

Phone: (276)228-7300

SOME UNITS
🆂🅳 🛏 🍽 🏊 👷 [DATA PORT] 💻 / ☒ 🛗 🖼 /
FEE

BUDGET HOST INN/INTERSTATE INN

◆◆   *Book at aaa.com*

   4/1-10/31   1P: $32-$40   2P: $45-$150   XP: $5   F18
   3/1-3/31   1P: $31-$39   2P: $39-$45   XP: $5   F18
Motel   11/1-2/28   1P: $29-$32   2P: $32-$39   XP: $5   F18

   Location: I-77/81, exit 73, just w. 705 Chapman Rd 24382. Fax: 276/228-2433. **Facility:** 42 one-bedroom standard units. 2 stories (no elevator), exterior corridors. **Parking:** on-site. **Terms:** weekly rates available, package plans, small pets only ($5 extra charge). **Amenities:** voice mail. **Cards:** AX, DC, DS, MC, VI.

Phone: (276)228-8618

SOME UNITS
(ASK) 🆂🅳 🛏 👷 [DATA PORT] / ☒ 🛗 🖼 /
FEE

COMFORT INN
AAA SAVE
◆◆◆ ◆◆
Small-scale Hotel

Book at aaa.com
All Year   1P: $59-$130   2P: $69-$130   XP: $5   F18
Location: I-81, exit 70, just w. 315 Holston Rd 24382 (PO Box 567). **Fax:** 276/228-4092. **Facility:** 80 one-bedroom standard units. 2 stories (no elevator), interior corridors. **Parking:** on-site. **Amenities:** hair dryers. *Some:* irons. **Pool(s):** outdoor. **Cards:** AX, DC, DS, MC, VI. **Special Amenities:** free full breakfast and free local telephone calls.
Phone: (276)228-4488
SOME UNITS
🅂🄳 🍴 🏊 🎥 DATA PORT 💻 / ✕ /

DAYS INN
◆◆◆ ◆◆
Small-scale Hotel

Book at aaa.com
5/27-10/31 [ECP]   1P: $50-$60   2P: $60-$70   XP: $5   F17
3/1-5/26 & 11/1-12/31 [ECP]   1P: $45-$55   2P: $55-$65   XP: $5   F17
1/1-2/28 [ECP]   1P: $40-$50   2P: $50-$60   XP: $5   F17
Location: I-81, exit 73, just w. 150 Malin Dr 24382. **Fax:** 276/228-6301. **Facility:** 118 one-bedroom standard units. 2-3 stories (no elevator), exterior corridors. **Parking:** on-site. **Terms:** pets ($5 extra charge). **Amenities:** hair dryers. **Cards:** AX, CB, DC, DS, MC, VI.
Phone: (276)228-5500
SOME UNITS
ASK 🅂🄳 🐾 🍴 🉐 🎥 DATA PORT / ✕ /
FEE

ECONO LODGE
AAA SAVE
◆◆◆
Motel

Book at aaa.com
All Year [CP]   1P: $34-$95   2P: $39-$115   XP: $5   F18
Location: I-81, exit 73, 0.8 mi w. 1160 E Main St 24382. **Fax:** 276/223-0696. **Facility:** 72 one-bedroom standard units. 2 stories (no elevator), exterior corridors. **Parking:** on-site. **Terms:** small pets only ($10 fee). **Amenities:** safes. **Cards:** AX, DC, DS, MC, VI. **Special Amenities:** free continental breakfast.
Phone: (276)228-5517
SOME UNITS
🅂🄳 🐾 🍴 🉐 💻 / ✕ 🍴 🖨 /
FEE

HAMPTON INN
◆◆◆◆
Small-scale Hotel

Book at aaa.com
All Year   1P: $70-$175   2P: $70-$175
Location: I-77, exit 41, just w. 950 Peppers Ferry Rd 24382. **Fax:** 276/228-4123. **Facility:** 68 one-bedroom standard units, some with whirlpools. 3 stories, interior corridors. *Bath:* combo or shower only. **Parking:** on-site. **Amenities:** voice mail, irons, hair dryers. **Pool(s):** outdoor. **Guest Services:** valet laundry. **Business Services:** meeting rooms. **Cards:** AX, CB, DC, DS, MC, VI. *(See color ad below)*
Phone: (276)228-6090
SOME UNITS
ASK 🅂🄳 🍴 🄼 🉐 🏊 🎥 DATA PORT 💻 / ✕ 🍴 🖨 /

HOLIDAY INN
◆◆ ◆◆
Small-scale Hotel

Book at aaa.com
6/1-10/31   1P: $85-$105
3/1-5/31   1P: $80-$90
11/1-2/28   1P: $75-$88
Location: I-81, exit 73, just w. 1800 E Main St 24382 (PO Box 697). **Fax:** 276/228-5417. **Facility:** 199 one-bedroom standard units. 2-4 stories, interior/exterior corridors. *Bath:* combo or shower only. **Parking:** on-site. **Amenities:** irons, hair dryers. **Pool(s):** outdoor, wading. **Guest Services:** valet laundry. **Business Services:** meeting rooms. **Cards:** AX, CB, DC, DS, MC, VI.
Phone: (276)228-5483
SOME UNITS
ASK 🅂🄳 🐾 🍴 🍸 🉐 🉐 🏊 🎥 DATA PORT 💻 / ✕ 🍴 🖨 /

QUALITY INN & SUITES
AAA SAVE
◆◆◆ ◆◆
Small-scale Hotel

Book at aaa.com
All Year [ECP]   1P: $45-$175   2P: $50-$175   XP: $5   F18
Location: I-77/81, exit 73, just e. 2015 E Main St 24382. **Fax:** 276/228-2615. **Facility:** 61 one-bedroom standard units, some with whirlpools. 4 stories, interior corridors. *Bath:* combo or shower only. **Parking:** on-site. **Amenities:** irons, hair dryers. **Pool(s):** indoor. **Leisure Activities:** whirlpool. **Guest Services:** coin laundry. **Cards:** AX, CB, DC, DS, JC, MC, VI. **Special Amenities:** free expanded continental breakfast and free local telephone calls.
Phone: (276)228-4241
SOME UNITS
🅂🄳 🍴 🉐 🉐 🏊 🎥 DATA PORT 💻 / ✕ 🍴 🖨 /

RAMADA INN
AAA SAVE
◇◇ ◇◇
Small-scale Hotel

Book at aaa.com

Phone: (276)228-6000

3/1-10/31	1P: $59-$109	2P: $69-$119	XP: $10	F17
11/1-2/28	1P: $49-$89	2P: $59-$99	XP: $10	F17

Location: I-77, exit 41, just e. 955 Peppers Ferry Rd 24382. Fax: 276/228-6009. **Facility:** 154 one-bedroom standard units. 2 stories (no elevator), exterior corridors. **Parking:** on-site. **Amenities:** voice mail, irons, hair dryers. **Dining:** 6:30 am-9 pm, Fri & Sat-10 pm, cocktails. **Pool(s):** outdoor. **Guest Services:** coin laundry. **Business Services:** meeting rooms. **Cards:** AX, CB, DC, DS, MC, VI. **Special Amenities: free newspaper.**

SOME UNITS

RED CARPET INN
AAA SAVE
◇◇ ◇◇
Motel

Book at aaa.com

Phone: (276)228-5525

3/1-10/31	1P: $45-$120	2P: $65-$130	XP: $7	D12
11/1-2/28	1P: $40-$60	2P: $45-$65	XP: $7	D12

Location: I-77/81, exit 73, just w. 280 Lithia Rd 24382. Fax: 276/228-5010. **Facility:** 34 one-bedroom standard units. 2 stories (no elevator), exterior corridors. **Parking:** on-site. **Terms:** pets ($6-$10 extra charge). **Amenities:** hair dryers. **Cards:** AX, DC, MC, VI. **Special Amenities: free continental breakfast and free local telephone calls.**

SOME UNITS

SLEEP INN
AAA SAVE
◇◇ ◇◇
Small-scale Hotel

Book at aaa.com

Phone: (276)625-0667

5/26-9/6 [ECP]	1P: $55-$125	2P: $65-$125	XP: $7	F17
3/1-5/25 & 9/7-10/31 [ECP]	1P: $55-$85	2P: $65-$95	XP: $7	F17
11/1-2/28 [ECP]	1P: $55-$65	2P: $65-$65	XP: $7	F17

Location: I-77, exit 41, just e. 135 Nye Cir 24382. Fax: 276/625-0463. **Facility:** 73 one-bedroom standard units. 3 stories, interior corridors. *Bath:* some combo or shower only. **Parking:** on-site. **Amenities:** *Some:* irons, hair dryers. **Leisure Activities:** exercise room. **Cards:** AX, CB, DC, DS, JC, MC, VI. **Special Amenities: free expanded continental breakfast and free newspaper.**

SOME UNITS

SUPER 8 MOTEL
◇◇
Small-scale Hotel

Phone: 276/228-6620

3/1-10/31	1P: $54-$62	2P: $59-$67	XP: $5	F17
11/1-2/28	1P: $48-$54	2P: $53-$59	XP: $5	F17

Location: I-77, exit 41, just e. 130 Nye Cir 24382. Fax: 276/228-2600. **Facility:** 92 one-bedroom standard units. 2 stories (no elevator), exterior corridors. **Parking:** on-site. **Terms:** weekly rates available, package plans, small pets only ($10 extra charge, with prior approval). **Cards:** AX, CB, DC, DS, MC, VI.

SOME UNITS

TRAVELODGE
◇◇
Motel

Phone: 276/228-3188

All Year	1P: $65-$120	2P: $65-$120	XP: $6	F16

Location: I-77/81, exit 73, on US 11. 140 Lithia Rd 24382 (PO Box 552). Fax: 276/228-6458. **Facility:** 64 one-bedroom standard units. 1-2 stories (no elevator), interior/exterior corridors. **Parking:** on-site. **Terms:** pets ($5 extra charge). **Cards:** AX, DS, MC, VI.

SOME UNITS

——— **WHERE TO DINE** ———

1776 LOG HOUSE
◇◇◇
American

Lunch: $7-$12   **Dinner:** $9-$23   Phone: 276/228-4139

Location: I-77/81, exit 73, 2.1 mi e. 520 E Main St 24382. **Hours:** 11 am-3 & 4-10 pm. Closed: 1/1, 12/25; also Sun. **Features:** Enjoy a trip back in time to the beginning of our great nation at this restaurant. Fine dining with a history. Casual dress; cocktails. **Parking:** on-site. **Cards:** AX, CB, DC, MC, VI.

OCEAN BAY RESTAURANT
◇◇
American

Lunch: $5-$12   **Dinner:** $6-$19   Phone: 276/228-5300

Location: I-77/81, exit 73, just e. 1505 E Main St 24382. **Hours:** 1 pm-10 pm, Sun 11:30 am-9 pm. Closed: 11/24, 12/25; also Mon. **Features:** Welcoming to families, the restaurant serves seafood, steaks and spaghetti. Friendly servers contribute to the casual, comfortable atmosphere. Easy access from the interstate makes it a good stop for travelers. Good food is reasonably priced. Casual dress; cocktails. **Parking:** on-site. **Cards:** AX, CB, DC, DS, JC, MC, VI.

PEKING RESTAURANT
AAA
◇◇ ◇◇
Chinese

Lunch: $5-$6   **Dinner:** $8-$11   Phone: 276/228-5515

Location: I-77/81, exit 73, just e. 105 Malin Dr 24382. **Hours:** 11 am-9:30 pm, Sat-10 pm. Closed: 11/24, 12/25. **Reservations:** suggested, weekends. **Features:** Atop a small hill immediately off the busy interstate, the restaurant occupies a brick structure with large, round windows and a pagoda-type green roof. Canadians and Northerners who frequent the interstate often stop in for tasty food. The traditional theme employs lots of dragons and splashes of red. Cocktails. **Parking:** on-site. **Cards:** AX, DS, MC, VI.

SMOKEY'S BAR-B-Q
◇◇
Barbecue

Dinner: $7-$19   Phone: 276/228-6622

Location: I-81, exit 70, just w; behind Comfort Inn. 255 Holston Rd 24382. **Hours:** 4 pm-10 pm. Closed: 1/1, 11/24, 12/25; also Sun & Mon. **Features:** The fun and casual restaurant cheekily boasts that it will serve no swine before it's time. Expect a limited menu. Casual dress; cocktails. **Parking:** on-site. **Cards:** AX, DC, DS, MC, VI.

WOHLFAHRT HAUS DINNER THEATRE
◇◇◇
American

Lunch: $35-$38   **Dinner:** $35-$38   Phone: 276/223-0891

Location: I-77/81, exit 73, just e. 170 Malin Dr 24382. **Hours:** 6 pm seating, Sun 1 pm seating. Closed: 1/1, 11/24, 12/25; also Mon-Wed. **Features:** America's musicals in the mountains. This restaurant offers great cuisine combined with live theater. Cocktails. **Parking:** on-site. **Cards:** AX, MC, VI.

YORKTOWN —*See Williamsburg, Jamestown & Yorktown p. 948.*

West Virginia

Audra State Park, near
Belington
© Michael P. Gadomski

ANSTED pop. 1,576

———— WHERE TO STAY ————

HAWKS NEST LODGE
Phone: 304/658-5212

4/1-10/31	1P: $75	2P: $75	XP: $6 F12
11/1-2/28	1P: $55-$59	2P: $55-$59	XP: $6 F12
3/1-3/31	1P: $51-$55	2P: $51-$55	XP: $6 F12

Small-scale Hotel **Location:** 1.7 mi w. Located in Hawks Nest State Park. US 60 25812 (PO Box 857). Fax: 304/658-4549. **Facility:** 31 one-bedroom standard units. 2-4 stories, interior/exterior corridors. **Parking:** on-site. **Terms:** 15% service charge. **Amenities:** *Some:* irons, hair dryers. **Pool(s):** outdoor. **Leisure Activities:** tennis court, hiking trails, playground, horseshoes, volleyball. **Guest Services:** gift shop. **Business Services:** meeting rooms. **Cards:** AX, CB, DC, DS, MC, VI.

SOME UNITS

BARBOURSVILLE pop. 3,183

———— WHERE TO STAY ————

BEST WESTERN HUNTINGTON MALL INN *Book at aaa.com*
Phone: (304)736-9772

All Year [ECP]   1P: $69-$79   2P: $69-$79   XP: $10   F17

Small-scale Hotel **Location:** I-64, exit 20A eastbound; exit 20 westbound, 0.3 mi s. 3441 US 60 E 25504. Fax: 304/736-4386. **Facility:** 130 one-bedroom standard units. 2 stories (no elevator), interior corridors. *Bath:* combo or shower only. **Parking:** on-site. **Terms:** package plans. **Amenities:** irons, hair dryers. **Pool(s):** outdoor. **Leisure Activities:** exercise room. **Business Services:** meeting rooms. **Cards:** AX, CB, DC, DS, MC, VI.

SOME UNITS

COMFORT INN BY CHOICE HOTELS *Book at aaa.com*
Phone: (304)733-2122

All Year   1P: $65-$85   2P: $70-$90   XP: $5   F18

Small-scale Hotel **Location:** I-64, exit 20, 0.4 mi n. Located at a shopping mall. 249 Mall Rd 25504. Fax: 304/733-2122. **Facility:** 58 one-bedroom standard units. 3 stories, interior corridors. *Bath:* combo or shower only. **Parking:** on-site. **Terms:** pets ($20 fee). **Amenities:** irons, hair dryers. **Pool(s):** heated indoor. **Leisure Activities:** whirlpool. **Guest Services:** valet laundry. **Business Services:** meeting rooms. **Cards:** AX, DC, DS, MC, VI.

SOME UNITS
FEE

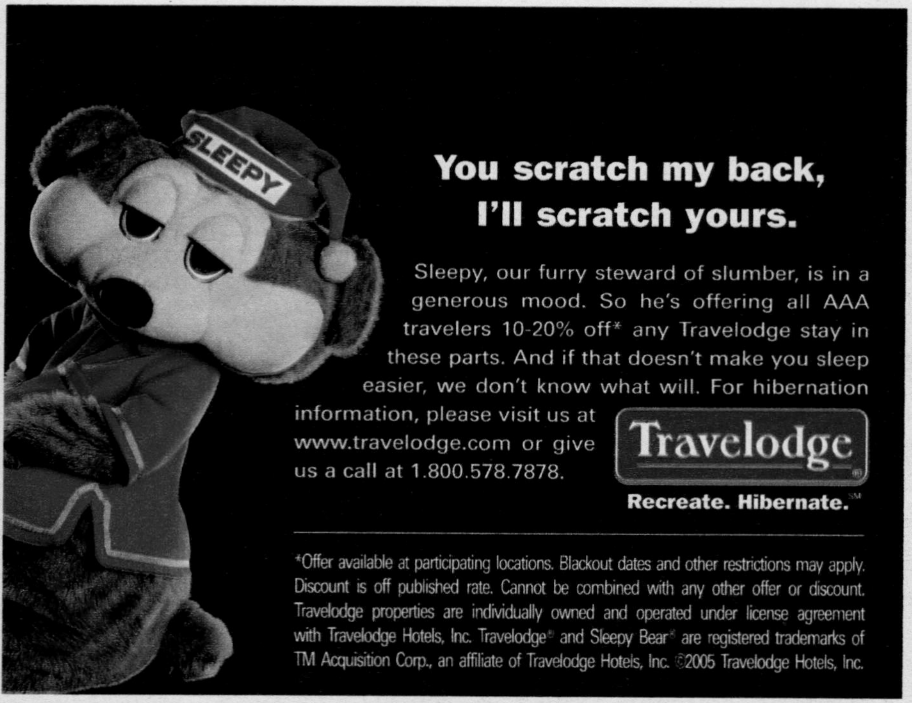

HAMPTON INN HUNTINGTON/BARBOURSVILLE   *Book at aaa.com*   **Phone:** 304/733-5300
▼▼▼▼   6/1-9/30 [ECP]   1P: $80-$95   2P: $85-$100
         3/1-5/31 & 10/1-2/28 [ECP]   1P: $75-$90   2P: $80-$95
Small-scale Hotel   **Location:** I-64, exit 20, just s. 1 Cracker Barrel Dr 25504. **Fax:** 304/733-3700. **Facility:** 90 one-bedroom standard units, some with whirlpools. 5 stories, interior corridors. *Bath:* combo or shower only. **Parking:** on-site. **Terms:** cancellation fee imposed. **Amenities:** voice mail, irons, hair dryers. **Pool(s):** outdoor. **Leisure Activities:** exercise room. **Guest Services:** coin laundry. **Business Services:** meeting rooms. **Cards:** AX, CB, DC, DS, MC, VI.

SOME UNITS

(ASK) (S/D) (🛏) (💺) (DATA PORT) (💻) / (✕) (🛢) (📠) /

———— **WHERE TO DINE** ————

TASCALI'S   **Lunch:** $6-$12   **Dinner:** $9-$18   **Phone:** 304/736-0504
▼▼ ▼▼   **Location:** I-64, exit 15, just e. 5505 Rt 60 E 25504. **Hours:** 11 am-9 pm, Fri & Sat-10 pm. Closed major holidays.
      Features: A West Virginia tradition for many years, the restaurant prepares wonderful, homespun choices.
Italian   The staff is friendly. Casual dress; cocktails. **Parking:** on-site. **Cards:** AX, CB, DC, DS, JC, MC, VI.

(Y) (✕)

BEAVER pop. 1,378

———— **WHERE TO STAY** ————

SLEEP INN   *Book at aaa.com*   **Phone:** (304)255-4222
▼▼▼ ▼▼▼   All Year   1P: $60-$75   2P: $75-$99   XP: $5   F18
      Location: I-64, exit 125B eastbound; exit 125 westbound, 0.4 mi n. 1124 Airport Rd 25813 (PO Box 250).
Small-scale Hotel   **Fax:** 304/255-4222. **Facility:** 104 one-bedroom standard units. 2 stories (no elevator), interior corridors. *Bath:* combo or shower only. **Parking:** on-site, winter plug-ins. **Terms:** 30 day cancellation notice-fee imposed, package plans. **Amenities:** video library, safes, irons, hair dryers. **Business Services:** meeting rooms. **Cards:** AX, CB, DC, DS, JC, MC, VI.

SOME UNITS

(ASK) (S/D) (🐾) (🍽) (💺) (DATA PORT) (💻) / (✕) (VCR) (🛢) (📠) /
               FEE   FEE   FEE

———— **WHERE TO DINE** ————

PADRINO'S   **Lunch:** $6-$12   **Dinner:** $6-$15   **Phone:** 304/255-7755
▼▼▼ ▼▼▼   **Location:** I-64, exit 125B eastbound; exit 125 westbound, 1.8 mi s. 167 Beaver Plaza 25813. **Hours:** 10:30 am-10
      pm. Closed major holidays; also Sun. **Features:** Real Italian food is prepared and served in a comfortable,
Italian   family-friendly setting. Casual dress; beer & wine only. **Parking:** on-site. **Cards:** MC, VI.

(✕)

BECKLEY pop. 17,254

———— **WHERE TO STAY** ————

BEST WESTERN FOUR SEASONS INN   *Book at aaa.com*   **Phone:** (304)252-0671
(AAA) (SAVE)   3/1-10/31   1P: $59-$99   2P: $64-$104   XP: $5   F17
      11/1-2/28   1P: $54-$79   2P: $59-$84   XP: $5   F17
▼▼ ▼▼   **Location:** I-64/77, exit 44, just e on SR 3. 1939 Harper Rd 25801. **Fax:** 304/252-3951. **Facility:** 80 one-bedroom standard units. 2 stories (no elevator), interior/exterior corridors. **Parking:** on-site. **Terms:** cancellation fee
Small-scale Hotel   imposed, [CP] meal plan available, small pets only ($5 extra charge). **Amenities:** irons, hair dryers. **Leisure Activities:** whirlpool. **Cards:** AX, CB, DC, DS, JC, MC, VI. **Special Amenities:** free continental breakfast and free local telephone calls.

SOME UNITS

(S/D) (🛏) (🍽) (💺) (DATA PORT) (💻) / (✕) /
         FEE

COMFORT INN   *Book at aaa.com*   **Phone:** (304)255-2161
▼▼▼ ▼▼▼   All Year [ECP]   1P: $55-$110   2P: $55-$110
      Location: I-64/77, exit 44, 0.3 mi e on SR 3. 1909 Harper Rd 25801. **Fax:** 304/255-2161. **Facility:** 130 one-
Small-scale Hotel   bedroom standard units. 2-3 stories, interior/exterior corridors. **Parking:** on-site. **Terms:** small pets only.
      Amenities: safes, irons, hair dryers. **Leisure Activities:** exercise room. **Guest Services:** coin laundry.
Business Services: meeting rooms. **Cards:** AX, DC, DS, MC, VI.

SOME UNITS

(ASK) (S/D) (🛏) (🍽) (🐾) (💺) (DATA PORT) (🛢) (📠) (💻) / (✕) /

COUNTRY INN & SUITES BY CARLSON   *Book at aaa.com*   **Phone:** (304)252-5100
(AAA) (SAVE)   6/1-10/31 [ECP]   1P: $90-$160   2P: $90-$160   XP: $8   F18
      3/1-5/31 & 11/1-2/28 [ECP]   1P: $83-$145   2P: $83-$145   XP: $8   F18
▼▼▼ ▼▼▼   **Location:** I-64/77, exit 44, just w on SR 3. 2120 Harper Rd 25801. **Fax:** 304/252-3135. **Facility:** 157 one-bedroom standard units, some with whirlpools. 3 stories, interior corridors. *Bath:* combo or shower only. **Parking:** on-
Small-scale Hotel   site. **Terms:** package plans, small pets only ($25 fee, in smoking units). **Amenities:** video games, dual phone lines, voice mail, irons, hair dryers. **Pool(s):** heated indoor/outdoor. **Leisure Activities:** whirlpools, exercise room. *Fee:* game room. **Guest Services:** coin laundry. **Business Services:** conference facilities. **Cards:** AX, DC, DS, MC, VI. **Special Amenities:** free expanded continental breakfast and free newspaper. *(See color ad p 965 & p 960)*

SOME UNITS

(S/D) (🛏) (🍽) (♿M) (💺) (🐾) (✕) (💺) (DATA PORT) (💻) / (✕) (🛢) (📠) /
       FEE

COURTYARD BY MARRIOTT *Book at aaa.com* **Phone:** 304/252-9800
All Year 1P: $80-$127 2P: $80-$127
▼▼▼▼ **Location:** I-64/77, exit 44, just e. 124 Hylton Ln 25801. **Fax:** 304/252-9808. **Facility:** 106 one-bedroom standard
Small-scale Hotel units, some with whirlpools. 4 stories, interior corridors. *Bath:* combo or shower only. **Parking:** on-site.
Terms: cancellation fee imposed. **Amenities:** high-speed Internet, voice mail, irons, hair dryers. **Pool(s):**
indoor. **Leisure Activities:** whirlpool, exercise room. **Guest Services:** coin laundry. **Business Services:** meeting rooms.
Cards: AX, DS, MC, VI.

SOME UNITS
(ASK) (SD) (&) (≈) (✱) (DATA PORT) (▯) / (✕) (▮) (▭) /

DAYS INN *Book at aaa.com* **Phone:** (304)255-5291
All Year 1P: $50-$100 2P: $50-$100
▼▼▼▼ **Location:** I-64/77, exit 44, just w, then 0.4 mi s. 300 Harper Rd 25801. **Fax:** 304/252-1105. **Facility:** 120 one-
Small-scale Hotel bedroom standard units. 2 stories (no elevator), interior corridors. **Parking:** on-site. **Amenities:** safes, irons,
hair dryers. **Pool(s):** outdoor. **Business Services:** meeting rooms. **Cards:** AX, CB, DC, DS, JC, MC, VI.

SOME UNITS
(ASK) (SD) (▥) (≈) (✱) (DATA PORT) (▮) (▭) (▯) / (✕) /

FAIRFIELD INN *Book at aaa.com* **Phone:** 304/252-8661
All Year 1P: $68-$71 2P: $68-$71
▼▼▼ **Location:** I-64/77, exit 44, just e. 125 Hylton Ln 25801. **Fax:** 304/252-6026. **Facility:** 90 one-bedroom standard
Small-scale Hotel units. 5 stories, interior corridors. *Bath:* combo or shower only. **Parking:** on-site. **Amenities:** high-speed
MC, VI. Internet, voice mail, irons, hair dryers. **Pool(s):** outdoor. **Leisure Activities:** whirlpool. **Cards:** AX, DC, DS,

SOME UNITS
(ASK) (SD) (&) (≈) (✱) (DATA PORT) / (✕) (▮) (▭) /

HAMPTON INN *Book at aaa.com* **Phone:** (304)252-2121
5/28-10/31 1P: $86-$99 2P: $90-$99
▼▼▼▼ 3/1-5/27 1P: $82-$99 2P: $90-$99
Small-scale Hotel 11/1-2/28 1P: $80-$90 2P: $80-$90
Location: I-64/77, exit 44, just w on SR 3. 110 Harper Park Dr 25801. **Fax:** 304/255-6238. **Facility:** 108 one-
bedroom standard units. 5 stories, interior corridors. **Parking:** on-site. **Amenities:** voice mail, irons, hair dryers. **Pool(s):**
outdoor. **Guest Services:** valet laundry. **Business Services:** meeting rooms. **Cards:** AX, DC, DS, MC, VI.
(See color ad below)

SOME UNITS
(ASK) (SD) (▥) (≈) (✱) (DATA PORT) (▯) / (✕) /

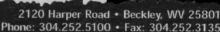

HOWARD JOHNSON EXPRESS INN *Book at aaa.com*   **Phone:** (304)255-5900

All Year   1P: $70-$105   2P: $70-$110   XP: $5   F12

Location: I-64/77, exit 44, 0.4 mi e on SR 3. 1907 Harper Rd 25801. **Fax:** 304/255-6003. **Facility:** 50 one-bedroom standard units, some with whirlpools. 2 stories (no elevator), interior corridors. **Parking:** on-site. **Terms:** pets ($15 extra charge). **Amenities:** high-speed Internet, irons, hair dryers. **Pool(s):** small outdoor. **Cards:** AX, DC, DS, MC, VI. **Special Amenities: free continental breakfast and free local telephone calls.**

Small-scale Hotel

SOME UNITS

MICROTEL INN   *Book at aaa.com*   **Phone:** (304)256-2000

All Year   1P: $49-$89   2P: $49-$89

Location: I-64/77, exit 44. 2130 Harper Rd 25801. **Fax:** 304/256-2098. **Facility:** 75 one-bedroom standard units. 3 stories, interior corridors. *Bath:* combo or shower only. **Parking:** on-site. **Terms:** small pets only (in smoking units). **Pool(s):** indoor. **Leisure Activities:** whirlpool. **Guest Services:** coin laundry. **Cards:** AX, CB, DC, DS, MC, VI.

Small-scale Hotel

SOME UNITS

PARK INN & SUITES   *Book at aaa.com*   **Phone:** (304)255-9091

6/1-10/31   1P: $59-$79   2P: $69-$89

3/1-5/31 & 11/1-2/28   1P: $49-$59   2P: $49-$59

Location: I-64/77, exit 44, just w on SR 3. 134 Harper Park Dr 25801. **Fax:** 304/255-6533. **Facility:** 55 one-bedroom standard units, some with whirlpools. 3 stories, interior corridors. **Parking:** on-site. **Terms:** small pets only ($10 deposit). **Amenities:** voice mail, irons, hair dryers. **Pool(s):** outdoor. **Guest Services:** valet laundry. **Cards:** AX, DC, DS, MC, VI. *(See color ad p 965)*

Small-scale Hotel

SOME UNITS

QUALITY INN OF BECKLEY   *Book at aaa.com*   **Phone:** (304)255-1511

6/1-10/31 [BP]   1P: $99   2P: $99   XP: $5   F18

3/1-5/31 & 11/1-2/28 [BP]   1P: $79   2P: $79   XP: $5   F18

Location: I-64/77, exit 44, 0.3 mi e on SR 3. 1924 Harper Rd 25801. **Fax:** 304/256-0526. **Facility:** 103 one-bedroom standard units, some with whirlpools. 3 stories (no elevator), interior corridors. **Parking:** on-site. **Amenities:** voice mail, irons, hair dryers. **Dining:** 6 am-2 & 5-10 pm, cocktails. **Pool(s):** heated outdoor. **Leisure Activities:** exercise room. **Guest Services:** coin laundry. **Business Services:** meeting rooms. **Cards:** AX, CB, DC, DS, MC, VI. **Special Amenities: free full breakfast and free local telephone calls.**

Small-scale Hotel

(See color ad below)

SOME UNITS

—— WHERE TO DINE ——

THE CHAR   **Dinner:** $9-$38   **Phone:** 304/253-1760

American

Location: I-64/77, exit 44, 0.3 mi w on SR 3, then 0.5 mi n on Dry Hill Rd. 100 Char Dr 25801. **Hours:** Open 3/1-12/31 & 2/1-2/28; 5:30 pm-10 pm. Closed major holidays; also Sun. **Features:** The country setting is bathed in a rich green and burgundy color scheme with wildlife art on the walls. Known for quality steaks, seafood and Italian specialties, the restaurant boasts brascioli—a beef filet with bread crumbs and cheese—as its specialty. The atmosphere, enhanced by soothing background music, and service are great. Casual dress; cocktails. **Parking:** on-site. **Cards:** AX, DC, MC, VI.

PASQUALE MIRA'S ITALIAN RESTAURANT   **Lunch:** $5-$8   **Dinner:** $7-$20   **Phone:** 304/255-5253

Italian

Location: I-64/77, exit 44, just w, then 0.3 mi s. 224 Harper Park Dr 25801. **Hours:** 11 am-10 pm. Closed: 11/24, 12/25. **Reservations:** suggested, weekends. **Features:** Excellent specialties, including veal and seafood dishes, are offered in two dining rooms—one casual and one more formal—and on the patio. Family owned since 1960, the restaurant prepares fare with a welcomed homemade flavor. Don't miss the aquarium. Casual dress; cocktails. **Parking:** on-site. **Cards:** AX, DS, MC, VI.

YOUNG CHOW'S
Chinese

Lunch: $6-$10   Dinner: $8-$20   Phone: 304/253-2469

Location: I-64/77, exit 44, just e on SR 3, then 0.7 mi n. 219 Pikeview Dr 25801. **Hours:** 11 am-10 pm. Closed major holidays. **Features:** The restaurant has wonderful cuisine and a lovely setting in which to dine. The atmosphere begins with the shrub-lined walkway up to the entrance and is rounded out by artwork on display inside. Casual dress; cocktails. **Parking:** on-site. **Cards:** AX, DC, MC, VI.

BENWOOD pop. 1,585

─── **WHERE TO DINE** ───

UNDO'S FAMILY RISTORANTE
Italian

Lunch: $7-$15   Dinner: $10-$22   Phone: 304/233-0560

Location: SR 2, exit 4th St, just sw. 753 Main St 26031. **Hours:** 11:30 am-10 pm, Fri & Sat-11 pm. Closed: 1/1, 12/25; also Mon. **Features:** Italian and American specialties are served in the family-oriented restaurant. Casual dress; cocktails. **Parking:** on-site. **Cards:** AX, DC, DS, MC, VI.

BERKELEY SPRINGS pop. 663

─── **WHERE TO DINE** ───

MARIA'S GARDEN & INN
Italian

Lunch: $5-$13   Dinner: $8-$15   Phone: 304/258-2021

Location: Just w of US 522. 42 Independence St 25411. **Hours:** 10 am-8 pm, Fri-Sun 8 am-9 pm. Closed: 11/24, 12/25; also Wed. **Reservations:** suggested, weekends. **Features:** Religious-themed artwork, an attractive garden room and a setting at the foot of the mountains give the restaurant a peaceful, serene ambience. Traditional dishes are well-prepared, well-presented and flavorful. Servers are knowledgeable and pleasant. Casual dress; beer & wine only. **Parking:** on-site. **Cards:** AX, DS, MC, VI.

BLUEFIELD pop. 11,451

─── **WHERE TO STAY** ───

DIAN-LEE HOUSE BED & BREAKFAST
Bed & Breakfast

Phone: 304/327-6370

All Year [BP]   1P: $65-$70   2P: $75-$100   XP: $10   F3

Location: I-77, exit 1, 1 mi w on SR 52, 4 mi nw on SR 460 to Washington St exit, then just n. 2109 Jefferson St 24701. Fax: 304/327-6410. **Facility:** Built in 1900, the Dian-Lee House offers large parlor rooms, swings on the porch and a quiet and quaint setting. 6 one-bedroom standard units. 3 stories (no elevator), interior/exterior corridors. **Parking:** on-site. **Terms:** weekly rates available. **Amenities:** *Some:* irons, hair dryers. **Guest Services:** valet laundry. **Business Services:** meeting rooms. **Cards:** AX, CB, DC, DS, MC, VI.
Special Amenities: free full breakfast and free local telephone calls. *(See color ad p 329)*

SOME UNITS

EAST RIVER MOUNTAIN INN
Small-scale Hotel

Phone: (304)325-5421

All Year   1P: $56   2P: $62   XP: $5   F18

Location: I-77, exit 1, 3.8 mi nw via US 52/460, then 0.7 mi n on US 52. 3175 E Cumberland Rd 24701. Fax: 304/325-6045. **Facility:** 98 one-bedroom standard units. 2 stories (no elevator), exterior corridors. **Parking:** on-site. **Terms:** 3 day cancellation notice, small pets only ($20 extra charge). **Amenities:** irons, hair dryers. **Pool(s):** heated indoor. **Leisure Activities:** saunas, whirlpool, exercise room, game room. **Guest Services:** valet laundry. **Business Services:** meeting rooms. **Cards:** AX, CB, DC, DS, MC, VI.

SOME UNITS

ECONO LODGE   *Book at aaa.com*
Motel

Phone: (304)327-8171

All Year [CP]   1P: $37-$90   2P: $44-$135   XP: $5   F18

Location: I-77, exit 1, 3.8 mi nw via US 52/460, then 0.4 mi n on US 52. Located adjacent to truck parking. 3400 Cumberland Rd 24701. Fax: 304/324-4259. **Facility:** 47 one-bedroom standard units. 2 stories (no elevator), exterior corridors. **Parking:** on-site. **Terms:** small pets only ($10 extra charge). **Amenities:** safes, hair dryers. **Cards:** AX, DC, DS, MC, VI. **Special Amenities: free continental breakfast.**

SOME UNITS

HOLIDAY INN-ON THE HILL *Book at aaa.com*   Phone: (304)325-6170

(AAA) (SAVE)   6/1-8/31   1P: $90-$99   2P: $90-$99   XP: $10   F18
                     3/1-5/31 & 9/1-2/28   1P: $81-$89   2P: $81-$89   XP: $10   F18
                     Location: I-77, exit 1, 3.8 mi nw via US 52/460. 3350 Big Laurel Hwy 24701. Fax: 304/323-2451. **Facility:** 120 one-
                     bedroom standard units. 2 stories (no elevator), interior corridors. *Bath:* combo or shower only. **Parking:** on-
Small-scale Hotel   site. **Terms:** [AP] meal plan available. **Amenities:** safes (fee), irons, hair dryers. **Dining:** 2 restaurants, 6
                     am-2 & 5-10 pm, cocktails. **Pool(s):** heated outdoor. **Leisure Activities:** exercise room. **Guest Services:**
valet laundry. **Business Services:** conference facilities. **Cards:** AX, DC, DS, JC, MC, VI. **Special Amenities: free local
telephone calls.** *(See ad p 962)*

SOME UNITS

BOWDEN

———— **WHERE TO DINE** ————

THE RIVER CAR RESTAURANT   Lunch: $7-$12   Dinner: $10-$27   Phone: 304/636-4001

(AAA)   **Location:** SR 33, just n. 9 Faulkner Rd 26254. **Hours:** 11 am-10 pm. Closed: 12/25; also Mon.
                   Reservations: suggested, weekends. **Features:** In a majestic setting along the river, the restaurant offers
                   fine dining in the distinctive setting of a rail car. The views are great, as is the menu. Casual dress;
American   cocktails. **Parking:** on-site. **Cards:** AX, CB, DC, DS, JC, MC, VI.

BRADLEY pop. 2,371

———— **WHERE TO STAY** ————

RAMADA INN OF BECKLEY *Book at aaa.com*   Phone: (304)877-6455

(AAA) (SAVE)   All Year   1P: $45-$74   2P: $50-$79   XP: $5   F18
                   Location: I-64/77, exit 48, 1 mi ne on US 19. 127 Ontario Dr 25880 (127 Ontario Dr, MOUNT HOPE).
                   Fax: 304/877-2501. **Facility:** 119 one-bedroom standard units. 2 stories (no elevator), interior corridors.
Motel   **Parking:** on-site. **Amenities:** voice mail, irons, hair dryers. **Pool(s):** outdoor. **Guest Services:** valet laundry.
                   Business Services: meeting rooms. **Cards:** AX, DC, DS, MC, VI. **Special Amenities: free continental
                   breakfast and free local telephone calls.**

SOME UNITS

BRIDGEPORT pop. 7,306

———— **WHERE TO STAY** ————

DAYS INN & SUITES CLARKSBURG *Book at aaa.com*   Phone: (304)842-7371

                   All Year   1P: $67-$199   2P: $67-$199   XP: $3   F12
                   Location: I-79, exit 119, just e. Located in a busy commercial area. 112 Tolley Dr 26330. Fax: 304/842-3904.
Small-scale Hotel **Facility:** 98 one-bedroom standard units, some with kitchens and/or whirlpools. 2 stories (no elevator),
                   interior corridors. *Bath:* combo or shower only. **Parking:** on-site. **Amenities:** safes, hair dryers. *Some:* irons.
Pool(s): heated indoor. **Guest Services:** valet laundry. **Business Services:** meeting rooms, business center. **Cards:** AX, DC,
DS, MC, VI.

SOME UNITS

HOLIDAY INN CLARKSBURG-BRIDGEPORT *Book at aaa.com*   Phone: (304)842-5411

(AAA) (SAVE)   4/3-11/9   1P: $72-$85
                   3/1-4/2 & 11/10-2/28   1P: $62-$75
                   Location: I-79, exit 119, just e on US 50. Located in a busy commercial area. 100 Lodgeville Rd 26330.
                   Fax: 304/842-2707. **Facility:** 159 one-bedroom standard units. 2 stories (no elevator), interior corridors.
Small-scale Hotel *Bath:* combo or shower only. **Parking:** on-site. **Terms:** package plans, small pets only. **Amenities:** video
                   games, voice mail, irons, hair dryers. **Dining:** 6 am-2 & 5-10 pm, Sat & Sun from 7 am, cocktails. **Pool(s):**
outdoor. **Guest Services:** valet laundry. **Business Services:** meeting rooms. **Cards:** AX, CB, DC, DS, JC, MC.

SOME UNITS

FEE   FEE   FEE

KNIGHTS INN-CLARKSBURG *Book at aaa.com*   Phone: (304)842-7115

                   All Year [CP]   1P: $52-$85   2P: $56-$85   XP: $3   F18
                   Location: I-79, exit 119, 0.3 mi e on US 50. Located in a commercial area. 1235 W Main St 26330.
Motel   Fax: 304/842-7258. **Facility:** 116 one-bedroom standard units. 1 story, exterior corridors. **Parking:** on-site.
                   Terms: weekly rates available. **Pool(s):** outdoor. **Guest Services:** coin laundry. **Business Services:**
meeting rooms. **Cards:** AX, DC, MC, VI.

SOME UNITS

SLEEP INN *Book at aaa.com*   Phone: (304)842-1919

                   All Year   1P: $65-$75   2P: $65-$75
                   Location: I-79, exit 119, just e on US 50. Located in an industrial area. 115 Tolley Dr 26330. Fax: 304/842-9524.
                   Facility: 73 one-bedroom standard units. 2 stories (no elevator), interior corridors. *Bath:* combo or shower
Small-scale Hotel only. **Parking:** on-site. **Terms:** small pets only. **Amenities:** voice mail, irons, hair dryers. **Guest Services:**
coin laundry. **Business Services:** meeting rooms. **Cards:** AX, CB, DC, DS, JC, MC, VI.

SOME UNITS

BUCKHANNON pop. 5,725

———— WHERE TO STAY ————

DEER PARK COUNTRY INN
Phone: (304)472-8400

[AAA] [SAVE]
All Year 1P: $110-$265 2P: $110-$265 XP: $40 D8
Location: 3.6 mi e on US 33, exit SR 151, 0.6 mi e, then 1.3 mi sw. Heavener Grove Rd 26201 (PO Box 817). Fax: 304/472-5363. **Facility:** A two-level porch with rocking chairs provides outdoor lounging space at this tree-shaded inn; reading materials are provided. Designated smoking area. 6 one-bedroom standard units. 2 stories (no elevator), interior/exterior corridors. *Bath:* combo or shower only. **Parking:** on-site. **Terms:** age restrictions may apply, 7 day cancellation notice-fee imposed, weekly rates available, [BP] meal plan available, package plans. **Amenities:** video library, hair dryers. *Some:* DVD players. **Dining:** dining room, see separate listing. **Leisure Activities:** fishing, recreation programs, lawn games. **Business Services:** meeting rooms. **Cards:** AX, DS, MC, VI. **Special Amenities:** free full breakfast and early check-in/late check-out.

Historic Bed & Breakfast

SOME UNITS

[🍴] [⊗] [✕] [DATA PORT] / [VCR] /

HAMPTON INN *Book at aaa.com*
Phone: (304)473-0900
All Year 1P: $62-$79 2P: $65-$82
Location: I-79, exit 99, 9 mi e on US 33. 1 Commerce Blvd 26201. Fax: 304/473-1108. **Facility:** 62 one-bedroom standard units, some with whirlpools. 3 stories, interior corridors. *Bath:* combo or shower only. **Parking:** on-site. **Amenities:** high-speed Internet, voice mail, irons, hair dryers. **Pool(s):** heated indoor. **Leisure Activities:** exercise room. **Guest Services:** valet laundry. **Business Services:** meeting rooms. **Cards:** AX, CB, DC, DS, JC, MC, VI.

Small-scale Hotel

SOME UNITS

[ASK] [S🐕] [♿] [⊿] [📷] [DATA PORT] [💻] / [✕] [🛏] [🖥] /

———— WHERE TO DINE ————

DEER PARK COUNTRY INN & RESTAURANT
Dinner: $18-$30
Phone: 304/472-8400
Location: 3.6 mi e on US 33, exit SR 151, 0.6 mi e, then 1.3 mi sw; in Deer Park Country Inn. Heavener Grove Rd 26201. **Hours:** 5 pm-9 pm, Fri & Sat-10 pm. **Features:** Enhanced by cottage gardens and beautiful views, the dining rooms reflect American country elegance. Cocktails. **Parking:** on-site. **Cards:** AX, DS, MC, VI.

American

[🍴] [⊗]

CEREDO pop. 1,675

———— WHERE TO DINE ————

ROCCO'S RISTORANTE
Dinner: $11-$30
Phone: 304/453-3000

[AAA]
Location: I-64, exit 1, 0.7 mi nw on SR 75, 1.1 mi e on US 60, then just n. 252 Main St 25507. **Hours:** 5 pm-10 pm, Fri & Sat-10:30 pm. Closed major holidays. **Features:** Popular with the locals, the romantic, candlelit restaurant makes its own pasta and specialty sauces. Hand-painted walls reflect casual scenes of Italy. Well-sized portions are attractively garnished and nicely flavored. Service is friendly and attentive. Casual dress; cocktails. **Parking:** on-site. **Cards:** AX, DS, MC, VI.

Italian

[⊗]

CHAPMANVILLE pop. 1,211

———— WHERE TO STAY ————

BEST WESTERN LOGAN INN *Book at aaa.com*
Phone: (304)831-2345
3/18-9/30 [CP] 1P: $94-$104 2P: $94-$104 XP: $5 F
3/1-3/17 & 10/1-2/28 [CP] 1P: $74-$94 2P: $74-$94 XP: $5 F
Location: 0.2 mi s on US 119. 2 Central Ave 25508. Fax: 304/831-2368. **Facility:** 60 one-bedroom standard units, some with whirlpools. 3 stories, interior corridors. *Bath:* combo or shower only. **Parking:** on-site. **Amenities:** high-speed Internet, voice mail, safes, irons, hair dryers. **Pool(s):** heated indoor. **Leisure Activities:** exercise room. **Guest Services:** coin laundry. **Business Services:** meeting rooms. **Cards:** AX, DC, MC, VI.

Small-scale Hotel

SOME UNITS

[ASK] [S🐕] [⊿] [📷] [DATA PORT] [💻] / [✕] [🛏] [🖥] /

CHARLESTON pop. 53,421—*See also SOUTH CHARLESTON.*

———— WHERE TO STAY ————

BUDGET HOST INN
Phone: 304/925-2592
3/1-10/31 1P: $37-$47 2P: $43-$65 XP: $5 F14
11/1-2/28 1P: $32-$38 2P: $38-$48 XP: $5 F14
Location: I-64/77, exit 96. 3313 Kanawha Blvd E 25306. Fax: 304/925-9086. **Facility:** 26 one-bedroom standard units. 1 story, exterior corridors. **Parking:** on-site. **Amenities:** hair dryers. **Cards:** AX, DS, MC, VI. **Special Amenities:** free local telephone calls and early check-in/late check-out.

[AAA] [SAVE]

Motel

SOME UNITS

[S🐕] [🍴↑] [VCR] [📷] / [✕] [🛏] /

CHARLESTON COMFORT SUITES *Book at aaa.com*
Phone: (304)925-1171
3/1-10/31 1P: $89-$150 2P: $89-$150 XP: $10 F18
11/1-2/28 1P: $84-$139 2P: $84-$139 XP: $10 F18
Location: I-77, exit 95, just s on SR 61. 107 Alex Ln 25304. Fax: 304/925-2252. **Facility:** 67 one-bedroom standard units, some with whirlpools. 3 stories, interior corridors. *Bath:* combo or shower only. **Parking:** on-site. **Terms:** package plans, small pets only ($10 extra charge). **Amenities:** high-speed Internet, voice mail, safes (fee), irons, hair dryers. **Pool(s):** heated indoor. **Leisure Activities:** whirlpool, exercise room. **Guest Services:** coin laundry. **Business Services:** meeting rooms. **Cards:** AX, DC, DS, MC, VI.

Small-scale Hotel

SOME UNITS

[ASK] [S🐕] [🛏] [⊿] [📷] [DATA PORT] [🛏] [🖥] [💻] / [✕] /
FEE

CHARLESTON MARRIOTT TOWN CENTER HOTEL   *Book at aaa.com*   Phone: (304)345-6500
▼▽▼▽▼▽   All Year   1P: $89-$149
Large-scale Hotel   **Location:** I-64, exit 58C; downtown. Located opposite Charleston Civic Center. 200 Lee St E 25301. Fax: 304/353-3722. **Facility:** 352 one-bedroom standard units. 16 stories, interior corridors. **Parking:** on-site (fee). **Terms:** check-in 4 pm, package plans. **Amenities:** high-speed Internet, voice mail, irons, hair dryers. **Dining:** Tarragon, see separate listing. **Pool(s):** heated indoor. **Leisure Activities:** saunas, whirlpool, exercise room. **Guest Services:** gift shop, coin laundry, tanning facility. **Business Services:** conference facilities, business center. **Cards:** AX, CB, DC, DS, JC, MC, VI.

SOME UNITS

(ASK) 🏧 🍴 🍽 🅿 🔜 ✕ 🐾 📠 💻 / ✕ 🔒 🖥 /

COUNTRY INN & SUITES BY CARLSON   *Book at aaa.com*   Phone: (304)925-4300
▼▽▼▽▼▽   3/1-10/31   1P: $89-$119   2P: $89-$119   XP: $10   F18
          11/1-2/28   1P: $84-$109   2P: $84-$109   XP: $10   F18
Small-scale Hotel   **Location:** I-77, exit 95, just s on SR 61. 105 Alex Ln 25304. Fax: 304/925-1500. **Facility:** 64 one-bedroom standard units. 3 stories, interior corridors. *Bath:* combo or shower only. **Parking:** on-site. **Terms:** small pets only. **Amenities:** high-speed Internet, voice mail, irons, hair dryers. **Pool(s):** heated indoor. **Leisure Activities:** whirlpool, exercise room. **Guest Services:** coin laundry. **Business Services:** meeting rooms. **Cards:** AX, CB, DC, DS, JC, MC, VI. *(See color ad below)*

SOME UNITS

(ASK) 🆓 🐾 🔜 🐾 📠 🔒 🖥 💻 / ✕ /

DAYS INN CHARLESTON EAST *Book at aaa.com* **Phone:** (304)925-1010

▽▼▽▼ All Year [ECP] 1P: $49-$52 2P: $57-$63 XP: $5

Motel **Location:** I-77, exit 95, just s on SR 61. 6400 MacCorkle Ave 25304. Fax: 304/925-1364. **Facility:** 147 one-bedroom standard units, some with whirlpools. 3 stories, interior corridors. *Bath:* combo or shower only. **Parking:** on-site. **Terms:** weekly rates available, package plans, small pets only. **Amenities:** irons, hair dryers. **Pool(s):** outdoor. **Leisure Activities:** exercise room. **Guest Services:** coin laundry. **Business Services:** meeting rooms. **Cards:** AX, CB, DC, DS, MC, VI.

SOME UNITS
(ASK) 🛏 🍽+ 🦽 🏊 📹 DATA PORT 🔒 🖥 / ✕ 📶 /

EMBASSY SUITES HOTEL *Book at aaa.com* **Phone:** (304)347-8700

(AAA) (SAVE) All Year 1P: $109-$209 2P: $109-$209 XP: $5 F18

▽▼▽▼ **Location:** I-64, exit 58C; center. 300 Court St 25301. Fax: 304/347-8737. **Facility:** 252 one-bedroom standard units, some with whirlpools. 9 stories, interior corridors. *Bath:* combo or shower only. **Parking:** on-site. **Terms:** cancellation fee imposed, [BP] meal plan available. **Amenities:** video games, high-speed Internet, Large-scale Hotel dual phone lines, voice mail, irons, hair dryers. **Dining:** 11 am-11 pm, cocktails. **Pool(s):** heated indoor. **Leisure Activities:** sauna, whirlpool. **Guest Services:** gift shop, valet and coin laundry. **Business Services:** meeting rooms, business center. **Cards:** AX, CB, DC, DS, MC, VI. **Special Amenities:** free full breakfast and free newspaper. *(See color ad below)*

SOME UNITS
🍽 🍷 🦽 🏊 📶 📹 DATA PORT 🔒 🖥 / ✕ /

FAIRFIELD INN *Book at aaa.com* **Phone:** (304)343-4661

▽▼▽▼ All Year [ECP] 1P: $59-$79 XP: $6 F18

Small-scale Hotel **Location:** I-64/77, exit 100, 0.5 mi w. 1000 Washington St 25301. Fax: 304/343-6269. **Facility:** 136 one-bedroom standard units. 9 stories, interior corridors. *Bath:* combo or shower only. **Parking:** on-site. **Terms:** cancellation fee imposed. **Amenities:** voice mail, irons, hair dryers. **Pool(s):** heated outdoor. **Leisure Activities:** whirlpool, exercise room. **Guest Services:** coin laundry. **Cards:** AX, CB, DC, DS, JC, MC, VI.

SOME UNITS
(ASK) (S🅳) 🏊 📹 DATA PORT / ✕ /

HAMPTON INN SOUTHRIDGE *Book at aaa.com* **Phone:** 304/746-4646

▽▼▽▼ All Year 1P: $84-$140 2P: $89-$140 XP: $5 F18

Small-scale Hotel **Location:** I-64, exit 58A, 4 mi s on US 119. Located adjacent to a shopping center. 1 Preferred Pl 25309. Fax: 304/746-4665. **Facility:** 104 one-bedroom standard units, some with whirlpools. 6 stories, interior corridors. *Bath:* combo or shower only. **Parking:** on-site. **Terms:** package plans. **Amenities:** high-speed Internet, voice mail, irons, hair dryers. **Pool(s):** heated indoor. **Leisure Activities:** whirlpool, playground, exercise room, basketball. **Guest Services:** coin laundry. **Business Services:** meeting rooms, business center. **Cards:** AX, DC, DS, MC, VI.

SOME UNITS
(ASK) (S🅳) ✈ 🛏 🐾 🏊 ✕ 📹 DATA PORT 🖥 / ✕ 🔒 📶 /

HOLIDAY INN DOWNTOWN CHARLESTON HOUSE *Book at aaa.com* **Phone:** (304)344-4092

▽▼▽▼ All Year 1P: $71-$119

Large-scale Hotel **Location:** I-64, exit 58B eastbound; exit 58C westbound, Virginia St to corner of Laidley and Kanawha Blvd; I-64/77, exit 97, 4.5 mi w on US 60 (Kanawha Blvd); downtown. 600 Kanawha Blvd E 25301. Fax: 304/345-4847. **Facility:** 256 one-bedroom standard units. 12 stories, interior corridors. *Bath:* combo or shower only. **Parking:** on-site (fee). **Terms:** cancellation fee imposed, [AP] meal plan available, package plans. **Amenities:** voice mail, irons, hair dryers. **Pool(s):** outdoor. **Leisure Activities:** exercise room. **Guest Services:** valet laundry, area transportation. **Business Services:** conference facilities, business center. **Cards:** AX, CB, DC, DS, JC, MC, VI.

SOME UNITS
(ASK) (S🅳) ✈ 🍽 🍷 🦽 🐾 🏊 📹 DATA PORT 🖥 / ✕ 🔒 📶 /

HOLIDAY INN EXPRESS CIVIC CENTER *Book at aaa.com* **Phone:** (304)345-0600

▽▼▽▼ 3/1-3/31 [ECP] 1P: $89-$139 2P: $89-$139

4/1-2/28 [ECP] 1P: $89-$129 2P: $89-$129

Small-scale Hotel **Location:** I-64, exit 58B eastbound; exit 58C westbound, just s; downtown. 100 Civic Center Dr 25301. Fax: 304/343-1322. **Facility:** 196 one-bedroom standard units. 6 stories, interior corridors. *Bath:* combo or shower only. **Parking:** on-site. **Terms:** small pets only (in smoking units). **Amenities:** video games, dual phone lines, voice mail, irons, hair dryers. **Leisure Activities:** exercise room. **Guest Services:** coin laundry. **Business Services:** meeting rooms. **Cards:** AX, CB, DC, DS, JC, MC, VI.

SOME UNITS
(ASK) (S🅳) ✈ 🛏 🦽 📹 DATA PORT 🖥 / ✕ /

KNIGHTS INN-CHARLESTON EAST *Book at aaa.com* Phone: (304)925-0451

7/4-8/31	1P: $48-$53	2P: $53-$58	XP: $5	F17
5/17-7/3	1P: $43-$48	2P: $48-$53	XP: $5	F17
3/1-5/16	1P: $41-$46	2P: $46-$51	XP: $5	F17
9/1-2/28	1P: $39-$45	2P: $45-$50	XP: $5	F17

Motel **Location:** I-77, exit 95, just s on SR 61. 6401 MacCorkle Ave SE 25304. Fax: 304/925-4703. **Facility:** 133 one-bedroom standard units, some with kitchens and/or whirlpools. 1 story, exterior corridors. **Parking:** on-site. **Terms:** 3 day cancellation notice, small pets only ($15 extra charge). **Pool(s):** outdoor. **Guest Services:** coin laundry. **Business Services:** meeting rooms. **Cards:** AX, DC, DS, MC, VI. **Special Amenities:** free continental breakfast and free local telephone calls.

SOME UNITS

RED ROOF INN-KANAWHA CITY *Book at aaa.com* Phone: (304)925-6953

9/5-2/28	1P: $42-$48	2P: $47-$53	XP: $5	F18
3/1-5/15	1P: $40-$48	2P: $45-$53	XP: $5	F18
5/16-9/4	1P: $45-$50	2P: $50	XP: $5	F18

Motel **Location:** I-77, exit 95, just s on SR 61. 6305 SE MacCorkle Ave 25304. Fax: 304/925-8111. **Facility:** 108 one-bedroom standard units. 2 stories (no elevator), exterior corridors. *Bath:* combo or shower only. **Parking:** on-site. **Terms:** small pets only. **Amenities:** video games, voice mail. **Guest Services:** valet laundry. **Cards:** AX, CB, DC, DS, MC, VI.

SOME UNITS

SLEEP INN *Book at aaa.com* Phone: (304)345-5111

All Year	1P: $67-$120	2P: $67-$120	XP: $5	F18

Small-scale Hotel **Location:** I-79, exit 1, just e. 2772 Pennsylvania Ave 25302. Fax: 304/344-5150. **Facility:** 81 one-bedroom standard units. 3 stories, interior corridors. *Bath:* combo or shower only. **Parking:** on-site. **Amenities:** hair dryers. *Some:* high-speed Internet, irons. **Leisure Activities:** exercise room. **Guest Services:** valet and coin laundry. **Business Services:** meeting rooms. **Cards:** AX, CB, DC, DS, JC, MC, VI.

SOME UNITS

SUPER 8 MOTEL *Book at aaa.com* Phone: (304)345-9779

All Year	1P: $38-$60	XP: $6	F

Small-scale Hotel **Location:** I-64/77, exit 100, 0.3 mi w. 1010 Washington St E 25301. Fax: 304/345-6120. **Facility:** 160 one-bedroom standard units. 9 stories, interior corridors. *Bath:* combo or shower only. **Parking:** on-site. **Terms:** cancellation fee imposed. **Pool(s):** outdoor. **Guest Services:** valet laundry. **Cards:** AX, CB, DC, DS, JC, MC, VI.

SOME UNITS

------ **WHERE TO DINE** ------

CHESTERFIELD HOUSE **Lunch:** $6-$10 **Dinner:** $9-$20 Phone: 304/345-5071

Continental **Location:** Just s of MacCorkle Ave SE; at 31st St and Chesterfield Ave SE. 3112 Chesterfield Ave SE 25304. **Hours:** 11 am-2 & 4:30-10 pm, Fri-11 pm, Sat 5 pm-11 pm. Closed major holidays; also Sun. **Reservations:** suggested, weekends. **Features:** The somewhat clubby atmosphere is popular with the business crowd, as are the prime rib, seafood, rack of lamb, homemade soups and desserts. The nice salad bar lines up a variety of dressings, and homemade bananas Foster is well worth a try. The wine list is extensive. The restaurant has been locally owned and operated for almost 20 years. Casual dress; cocktails. **Parking:** on-site. **Cards:** AX, CB, DC, DS, MC, VI.

THE CHOP HOUSE **Dinner:** $20-$40 Phone: 304/344-3954

American **Location:** I-64, exit 58C; center of downtown. 1003 Charleston Town Center 25389. **Hours:** 5 pm-10 pm. Closed major holidays. **Reservations:** suggested, weekends. **Features:** An elegant restaurant with upscale surroundings, a fine wine list and superb menu. Formally attired wait staff help in selections. Casual dress; cocktails. **Parking:** on-site (fee) and street. **Cards:** AX, CB, DC, DS, JC, MC, VI.

FIFTH QUARTER STEAK HOUSE **Lunch:** $6-$9 **Dinner:** $10-$18 Phone: 304/345-3933

Steak & Seafood **Location:** Jct Quarrier and Clendenin sts; adjacent to Civic Center. 201 Clendenin St 25301. **Hours:** 11 am-10 pm, Fri & Sat-11 pm. Closed: 12/24, 12/25. **Features:** Prime rib is the big seller at the rustic steakhouse, decorated in an attractive Early American motif. Fish and fowl dishes, such as chicken Monterey, also are on the menu. The restaurant's casual atmosphere makes it a popular place with families. Casual dress; cocktails. **Parking:** on-site. **Cards:** AX, CB, DC, DS, MC, VI.

HARDING'S FAMILY RESTAURANT **Lunch:** $5-$12 **Dinner:** $5-$16 Phone: 304/344-5044

American **Location:** I-79, exit 1, just e. 2772 Pennslyvania Ave 25302. **Hours:** 6 am-11 pm, Sun from 7 am. Closed: 12/25. **Features:** The restaurant's laid-back atmosphere is welcoming to families. The menu offers breakfast, lunch and dinner selections. Casual dress. **Parking:** on-site. **Cards:** AX, CB, DC, DS, JC, MC, VI.

THE RIVERSIDE ANCHOR **Lunch:** $5-$15 **Dinner:** $5-$18 Phone: 304/925-9902

American **Location:** I-64/77, exit 96, just sw. 3315 Kanawha Blvd E 25306. **Hours:** 11 am-11 pm, Sun 5 pm-10 pm, Mon 11 am-10 pm. Closed: 3/27, 11/24, 12/25. **Features:** Serving the Kanawha Valley since 1936, the restaurant affords wonderful river views. The food is great, and service is friendly. Casual dress; beer only. **Parking:** on-site. **Cards:** AX, DS, MC, VI.

TARRAGON

AAA

▽▽▽ ▽▽▽

Continental

Dinner: $17-$33 **Phone:** 304/353-3636
Location: I-64, exit 58C; downtown; in Charleston Marriott Town Center Hotel. 200 Lee St E 25301. **Hours:** 5:30 pm-11 pm. Closed major holidays; also Sun. **Reservations:** suggested. **Features:** Guests who unwind in the upscale hotel dining room can peruse a lengthy menu that includes some unexpected specialty items, such as ostrich. Many choices include stylish tableside preparation, particularly the flambe. Service is attentive. Semi-formal attire; cocktails. **Parking:** on-site. **Cards:** AX, DC, DS, JC, MC, VI.

TIDEWATER GRILL

▽▽▽ ▽▽▽

American

Lunch: $7-$14 **Dinner:** $8-$21 **Phone:** 304/345-2620
Location: I-64, exit 58C; center of downtown. 1060 Charleston Town Center 25389. **Hours:** 11 am-10 pm, Fri & Sat-11 pm, Sun noon-9 pm. Closed: 12/25. **Features:** This restaurant is fun and casual, has an exciting contemporary menu and is close to all the action at the Town Center. Casual dress; cocktails. **Parking:** street. **Cards:** AX, CB, DC, DS, JC, MC, VI.

The following restaurants have not been evaluated by AAA but are listed for your information only.

CHEF DAN'S

fyi

touch of class.

Phone: 304/344-2433
Not evaluated. **Location:** I-64/77, exit 100, 0.8 mi w. 222 Leon Sullivan Way 25301. **Features:** Chef Dan's is where the possibilities are. Fusion type menu from hot dogs to lobster. Family friendly atmosphere with a

FAZIO'S

fyi

Phone: 304/344-3071
Not evaluated. **Location:** I-64, exit 58C, just s. 1008 Bullitt St 25301. **Features:** A Charleston landmark and mainstay since 1934. Delicious Italian fare, a casual atmosphere and worth every "penne".

CHARLES TOWN pop. 2,907

--- **WHERE TO STAY** ---

COTTONWOOD INN

▽▽▽

Historic Bed
& Breakfast

All Year 1P: $75-$110 2P: $85-$120 XP: $10 **Phone:** (304)725-3371
Location: Jct US 340 and SR 9 E, 1.3 mi e on SR 9, 3.1 mi s on CR 25 (Kabletown Rd), then 0.3 mi w. Located in a quiet rural area. 199 Mill Ln 25414. Fax: 304/728-4763. **Facility:** Nestled in the farmlands of the Shenandoah Valley, the inn is decorated with quilts and Colonial-style furnishings and offers a tempting breakfast. Smoke free premises. 7 one-bedroom standard units. 3 stories (no elevator), interior/exterior corridors. *Bath:* combo, shower or tub only. **Parking:** on-site. **Terms:** age restrictions may apply, 3 day cancellation notice. **Leisure Activities:** recreation programs. **Cards:** AX, DC, MC, VI.

WASHINGTON HOUSE INN BED & BREAKFAST

AAA SAVE

▽▽▽

Historic Bed
& Breakfast

1P: $99-$150 2P: $99-$175 XP: $25 **Phone:** (304)725-7923
All Year
Location: SR 115, just e of jct Washington St. 216 S George St 25414. Fax: 304/728-5150. **Facility:** Fireplaces, antique furnishings and carved oak mantels grace this turn-of-the-20th-century Victorian inn tucked in the Blue Ridge Mountains. Smoke free premises. 7 one-bedroom standard units. 3 stories (no elevator), interior corridors. *Bath:* shower only. **Parking:** on-site. **Terms:** 2 night minimum stay - sesaonal, age restrictions may apply, 5 day cancellation notice, weekly rates available, package plans, no pets allowed (owner's dog on premises). **Amenities:** hair dryers. **Guest Services:** complimentary evening beverages; valet laundry. **Cards:** AX, DS, MC, VI. **Special Amenities: free full breakfast and preferred room (subject to availability with advance reservations).**

--- **WHERE TO DINE** ---

AVANTI RISTORANTE

▽▽▽

Italian

Lunch: $5-$12 **Dinner:** $5-$18 **Phone:** 304/728-8880
Location: SR 9, just e. 119 E Washington St 25414. **Hours:** 11:30 am-9:30 pm, Fri & Sat-10:30 pm, Sun noon-9:30 pm. Closed: 12/25. **Features:** The restaurant offers patrons an escape from the mundane. Splashed in large murals, the dining room nurtures an inviting atmosphere. The friendly wait staff serves great Italian cuisine. Casual dress; cocktails. **Parking:** on-site. **Cards:** AX, CB, DC, DS, JC, MC, VI.

CHESTER pop. 2,592

--- **WHERE TO STAY** ---

MOUNTAINEER RACETRACK & GAMING RESORT

▽▽▽

Large-scale Hotel

5/1-12/31	1P: $90-$225	2P: $90-$225	XP: $10
1/1-2/28	1P: $75-$225	2P: $75-$225	XP: $10
3/1-4/30	1P: $75-$209	2P: $75-$209	XP: $10

Phone: (304)387-8000

Location: On SR 2, 6 mi s. Route 2 26034 (PO Box 358). Fax: 304/387-8001. **Facility:** With horse racing, a casino, concert events, a grand spa and gift shopping, this river-view property provides a plethora of diversions. 359 one-bedroom standard units, some with whirlpools. 2-6 stories, interior/exterior corridors. *Bath:* combo or shower only. **Parking:** on-site and valet. **Terms:** check-in 4 pm. **Amenities:** irons. *Some:* safes, honor bars, hair dryers. **Pool(s):** 2 outdoor, heated indoor, wading. **Leisure Activities:** whirlpools, steamrooms, 2 lighted tennis courts, exercise room, spa, basketball, volleyball. *Fee:* golf-18 holes. **Guest Services:** gift shop, valet laundry, area transportation. **Business Services:** conference facilities, business center. **Cards:** AX, DC, DS, MC, VI.

SOME UNITS

CLARKSBURG pop. 16,743

———— **WHERE TO DINE** ————

MINARD'S SPAGHETTI INN   **Lunch:** $8-$13   **Dinner:** $8-$14   **Phone:** 304/623-1711

♦♦ ♦♦   **Location:** I-79, exit 119, 2 mi w on US 50, exit Joyce St, just n, then just e. 813 E Pike St 26301. **Hours:** 11 am-10
Italian   pm, Fri & Sat-11 pm. Closed major holidays. **Reservations:** accepted. **Features:** The fare consists of
      popular homemade pasta, especially the spaghetti dishes, specially baked Italian bread and beef
      cacciatore. Some American cuisine also is served in the homey, family-oriented atmosphere. The service
staff is friendly and prompt. Casual dress; cocktails. **Parking:** on-site. **Cards:** AX, DS, MC, VI.   ⊠

CROSS LANES pop. 10,353

———— **WHERE TO STAY** ————

COMFORT INN WEST CHARLESTON   *Book at aaa.com*   **Phone:** (304)776-8070

Ⓐ SAVE   All Year   1P: $69-$89   2P: $69-$89
♦♦ ♦♦   **Location:** I-64, exit 47, just s. 102 Racer Dr 25313. **Fax:** 304/776-6460. **Facility:** 112 one-bedroom standard
Small-scale Hotel units, some with kitchens. 2 stories (no elevator), interior corridors. *Bath:* combo or shower only. **Parking:**
      on-site. **Terms:** 2 night minimum stay - seasonal, cancellation fee imposed, package plans, small pets only
      ($10 extra charge, in designated units). **Amenities:** video games, voice mail, irons, hair dryers. **Pool(s):**
      heated outdoor. **Leisure Activities:** whirlpool, exercise room. **Guest Services:** valet laundry, area
transportation-dog track. **Business Services:** meeting rooms, business center. **Cards:** AX, CB, DC, DS, JC, MC, VI.
Special Amenities: free continental breakfast and free local telephone calls.   SOME UNITS

FEE

DANIELS pop. 1,846

--------- WHERE TO STAY ---------

GLADE SPRINGS HOTEL AND CONFERENCE RESORT   *Book at aaa.com*

Phone: (304)763-2000

3/15-12/23	1P: $99-$239	2P: $109-$249	XP: $10 F
12/24-2/28	1P: $109-$225	2P: $119-$235	XP: $10 F
3/1-3/14	1P: $99-$215	2P: $109-$225	XP: $10 F

Resort
Small-scale Hotel

Location: I-64, exit 125, 1.5 mi w on SR 307, then 2.8 mi w on US 19. 200 Lake Dr 25832. **Fax:** 304/763-3398. **Facility:** On extensive grounds featuring many ponds and trails, the property also offers recreational facilities. 134 units. 118 one- and 12 two-bedroom standard units, some with kitchens. 4 three-bedroom suites ($250-$339). 2 stories (no elevator), exterior corridors. **Parking:** on-site. **Terms:** 2 night minimum stay - seasonal, 7 day cancellation notice, package plans, 10% service charge. **Amenities:** voice mail, honor bars, irons, hair dryers. **Dining:** Glade's Grill & Bar, see separate listing. **Pool(s):** outdoor. **Leisure Activities:** saunas, whirlpools, steamrooms, canoeing, paddleboats, 8 tennis courts (3 indoor), racquetball court, recreation programs, hiking trails, jogging, playground, basketball, horseshoes, volleyball. *Fee:* fishing, golf-36 holes, bicycles, horseback riding, massage. **Guest Services:** valet laundry, area transportation-within 10 mi. **Business Services:** conference facilities, business center. **Cards:** AX, DC, DS, MC, VI. *(See color ad below)*

SOME UNITS

--------- WHERE TO DINE ---------

GLADE'S GRILL & BAR

Dinner: $14-$22

Phone: 304/763-3033

American

Location: I-64, exit 125, 1.5 mi w on SR 307, then 2.8 mi w on US 19; in Glade Springs Hotel and Conference Resort. 200 Lake Dr 25832. **Hours:** 5:30 pm-9 pm. **Features:** Fantastic artwork and table settings enhance the atmosphere at the fine-dining establishment. Large picture windows afford wonderful woodland and golf views. The highly trained staff will assist with wine and food selections. Casual dress; cocktails. **Parking:** on-site. **Cards:** AX, DC, DS, MC, VI.

DAVIS pop. 624

——— WHERE TO STAY ———

CANAAN VALLEY RESORT & CONFERENCE CENTER

Phone: 304/866-4121

3/1-3/5 & 12/25-2/28	1P: $95-$122	2P: $102-$129	XP: $7	F12
3/6-10/15	1P: $61-$92	2P: $67-$99	XP: $7	F12
10/16-12/24	1P: $61-$67	2P: $68-$74	XP: $7	F12

Resort
Large-scale Hotel

Location: On SR 32, 10 mi s; 2 mi w off SR 32, follow signs. Located in Canaan Valley State Park. SR 32 26260 (HC 70 Box 330). Fax: 304/866-2172. **Facility:** This resort set within the state park offers several recreation options including golf, tennis, hiking, skiing and deer-watching. 273 units. 250 one-bedroom standard units, some with kitchens. 23 cabins. 2 stories (no elevator), exterior corridors. **Parking:** on-site. **Terms:** check-in 4 pm, 2 night minimum stay - seasonal and/or weekends, 7 day cancellation notice-fee imposed, package plans. **Amenities:** irons. *Some:* high-speed Internet, hair dryers. **Dining:** 7 am-10 pm, cocktails, also, Aspen Dining Room, see separate listing. **Pool(s):** heated outdoor, heated indoor. **Leisure Activities:** saunas, whirlpool, fishing, scenic lift, recreation programs, playground, exercise room, basketball, horseshoes, volleyball. *Fee:* golf-18 holes, miniature golf, 5 lighted tennis courts, downhill & cross country skiing, ice skating, hay rides, bicycles, game room. **Guest Services:** gift shop, coin laundry. **Business Services:** conference facilities, fax. **Cards:** AX, DS, MC, VI. *(See color ad below)*

SOME UNITS

DEERFIELD VILLAGE RESORT-CANAAN VALLEY

Phone: 304/866-4698

All Year

2P: $140-$275

Condominium

Location: 7 mi s on SR 32. Cortland Ln 26260 (HC 70, Box 152). Fax: 304/866-4015. **Facility:** Luxuriously furnished villas, all with fireplaces and washer/dryers, are in a great mountain setting offering many recreational opportunities. 98 units. 5 one- and 26 two-bedroom standard units with kitchens and whirlpools. 67 three-bedroom suites with kitchens and whirlpools. 1-2 stories (no elevator), exterior corridors. *Bath:* combo or shower only. **Parking:** on-site. **Terms:** 2 night minimum stay, cancellation fee imposed, $5 service charge, pets ($50 extra charge). **Amenities:** CD players, irons, hair dryers. **Dining:** 2 restaurants, 11 am-10 pm, Sat & Sun 8 am-9 pm, cocktails, also, Deerfield Village Restaurant, see separate listing. **Pool(s):** heated outdoor. **Leisure Activities:** fishing, tennis court, ski rental, snowboarding, hiking trails, playground, basketball, horseshoes, volleyball. *Fee:* miniature golf, bicycles. **Guest Services:** gift shop, complimentary laundry, area transportation-state park. **Business Services:** meeting rooms, PC, fax. **Cards:** AX, DC, DS, MC, VI. **Special Amenities:** early check-in/late check-out and preferred room **(subject to availability with advance reservations).**

SOME UNITS

FEE

——— WHERE TO DINE ———

ASPEN DINING ROOM

Lunch: $9-$16   **Dinner:** $14-$28   **Phone:** 304/866-4121

American

Location: On SR 32, 10 mi s; 2 mi w off SR 32, follow signs; in Canaan Valley Resort & Conference Center. SR 32 26260. **Hours:** 8 am-9 pm. **Features:** This restaurant affords stunning views of the mountains, nature and golf course. A huge fireplace sits in the center of the dining area. On the menu are classic American favorites. Casual dress; cocktails. **Parking:** on-site. **Cards:** AX, CB, DC, DS, JC, MC, VI.

DEERFIELD VILLAGE RESTAURANT

Dinner: $10-$26   **Phone:** 304/866-4559

American

Location: 7 mi s on SR 32; in Deerfield Village Resort-Canaan Valley. Cortland Rd 26260. **Hours:** 5 pm-9 pm, Fri & Sat-10 pm. Closed: 12/25. **Features:** The restaurant is a wonderful setting for a meal. Views of the Canaan Valley, which often include deer, are beautiful. The comfortable spot has a lodge feel. Casual dress; cocktails. **Parking:** on-site. **Cards:** AX, DC, DS, MC, VI.

DUNBAR pop. 8,154

———— WHERE TO STAY ————

DUNBAR SUPER 8 MOTEL   *Book at aaa.com*   **Phone:** (304)768-6888
▽▽▽   All Year   1P: $50-$55   2P: $56-$61   XP: $5   F18
Small-scale Hotel **Location:** I-64, exit 53, just w. 911 Dunbar Ave 25064. Fax: 304/768-6888. **Facility:** 62 one-bedroom standard units. 3 stories (no elevator), interior corridors. **Parking:** on-site. **Terms:** 10 day cancellation notice. **Amenities:** safes. **Guest Services:** coin laundry. **Cards:** AX, DC, DS, MC, VI.

SOME UNITS
(ASK) (S/D) [ ] [DATA PORT] / [X] [ ] [ ] /

TRAVELODGE DUNBAR   *Book at aaa.com*   **Phone:** (304)768-1000
(AAA) (SAVE)   All Year   1P: $49   2P: $54   XP: $5
▽▽▽▽   **Location:** I-64, exit 53, just sw. 1007 Dunbar Ave 25064. Fax: 304/768-2705. **Facility:** 133 one-bedroom
Motel   standard units, some with whirlpools. 3-4 stories, interior corridors. **Parking:** on-site. **Amenities:** voice mail, irons, hair dryers. **Leisure Activities:** exercise room. **Guest Services:** coin laundry. **Business Services:** meeting rooms. **Cards:** AX, CB, DC, DS, MC, VI. **Special Amenities:** free continental breakfast and free newspaper.

SOME UNITS
(S/D) [ ] [ ] [DATA PORT] [ ] / [X] [ ] [ ] [ ] /

EDRAY

———— WHERE TO STAY ————

MARLINTON MOTOR INN   **Phone:** 304/799-4711
(AAA) (SAVE)   All Year   1P: $49-$69   2P: $59-$86   XP: $7   F12
▽▽▽ ▽▽▽   **Location:** Center. US 219 N 24954 (HC 69, PO Box 47, MARLINTON). Fax: 304/799-7402. **Facility:** 69 one-
Motel   bedroom standard units, some with whirlpools. 2 stories (no elevator), exterior corridors. **Parking:** on-site. **Terms:** 3 day cancellation notice-fee imposed, [AP] meal plan available, package plans. **Dining:** 5 pm-9 pm, wine/beer only. **Pool(s):** outdoor. **Guest Services:** gift shop. **Business Services:** meeting rooms. **Cards:** AX, DC, DS, MC, VI. **Special Amenities:** free local telephone calls and early check-in/late
check-out.

SOME UNITS
(S/D) [ ] [ ] [ ] [ ] / [X] [ ] [ ] [ ] /

ELKINS pop. 7,032

———— WHERE TO STAY ————

BEST COUNTRY INN & SUITES   **Phone:** (304)636-7711
(AAA) (SAVE)   9/22-10/9   1P: $73-$120   2P: $80-$120   XP: $10   F12
▽▽▽▽ ▽▽▽▽   5/18-9/21   1P: $56-$65   2P: $63-$70   XP: $10   F12
Motel   3/1-5/17 & 10/10-2/28   1P: $51-$60   2P: $58-$65   XP: $10   F12
Location: 0.9 mi s of SR 219. Route 219/250 S 26241 (PO Box 1879). Fax: 304/636-5419. **Facility:** 68 one-bedroom standard units, some with whirlpools. 2 stories (no elevator), interior/exterior corridors. **Parking:** on-site. **Terms:** 3 day cancellation notice, small pets only ($5 extra charge). **Amenities:** hair dryers.
Cards: AX, DC, DS, MC, VI. **Special Amenities:** free continental breakfast and free local telephone calls.

SOME UNITS
(S/D) [ ] [ ] [ ] / [X] [ ] [ ] /
FEE

CHEAT RIVER LODGE & INN   **Phone:** 304/636-2301
(AAA) (SAVE)   All Year   1P: $68-$83   2P: $68-$83   XP: $10   F5
▽▽▽▽   **Location:** 4.8 mi e on US 33, then 1.5 mi ne. Rt 1, Box 115, Faulkner Rd 26241. Fax: 304/636-8019. **Facility:** This
Cabin   property offers wonderful river views with a serene setting; a gift shop, eatery and recreational opportunities are all on site. 15 units. 7 one-bedroom standard units. 8 cabins ($171-$196) with whirlpools. 1 story, exterior corridors. **Parking:** on-site. **Terms:** 2 night minimum stay - weekends, 30 day cancellation notice-fee imposed, weekly rates available, package plans, small pets only ($10 extra charge). **Dining:** 4 pm-10 pm, cocktails. **Leisure Activities:** fishing, bicycles, hiking trails. **Guest Services:** gift shop. **Cards:** MC, VI.

SOME UNITS
[ ] [ ] [ ] [X] [X] [ ] [ ] [ ] / [ ] [ ] [ ] /
FEE

ECONO LODGE   *Book at aaa.com*   **Phone:** (304)636-5311
▽▽▽ ▽▽▽   All Year   1P: $48-$80   2P: $53-$85   XP: $5   F19
Motel   **Location:** 1 mi e. US 33 E 26241. Fax: 304/636-5311. **Facility:** 72 one-bedroom standard units, some with whirlpools. 1-2 stories (no elevator), interior/exterior corridors. **Parking:** on-site. **Terms:** check-in 4 pm, pets ($5 extra charge). **Pool(s):** heated indoor. **Leisure Activities:** whirlpool. **Guest Services:** coin laundry.
Business Services: meeting rooms. **Cards:** AX, DC, DS, MC, VI.

SOME UNITS
(ASK) (S/D) [ ] [ ] [DATA PORT] / [X] [ ] [ ] /
FEE

ELKINS DAYS INN   *Book at aaa.com*   **Phone:** (304)637-4667
▽▽▽ ▽▽▽   All Year   1P: $70-$105   2P: $70-$105   XP: $5   F12
Small-scale Hotel **Location:** 1 mi w on US 33/250/SR 92; downtown; in an office building. 1200 Harrison Ave 26241. Fax: 304/636-8948. **Facility:** 46 one-bedroom standard units, some with whirlpools. 4 stories, interior corridors. *Bath:* combo or shower only. **Parking:** on-site. **Terms:** pets ($5 extra charge). **Amenities:** hair dryers. *Some:* irons. **Guest Services:** coin laundry. **Business Services:** meeting rooms. **Cards:** AX, CB, DC, DS, MC, VI.

SOME UNITS
(ASK) (S/D) [ ] [ ] [ ] [ ] [ ] [ ] [DATA PORT] / [X] [ ] [ ] /
FEE   FEE

ELKINS SUPER 8 MOTEL   *Book at aaa.com*
▼▼▼
Small-scale Hotel

All Year   1P: $49-$59   2P: $55-$65   XP: $6   F12

Phone: (304)636-6500

Location: 0.8 mi s on SR 219. 350 Beverly Pike 26241. Fax: 304/636-6500. **Facility:** 44 one-bedroom standard units. 2 stories (no elevator), interior corridors. **Parking:** on-site. **Terms:** [CP] meal plan available. **Amenities:** safes. **Cards:** AX, CB, DC, DS, MC, VI.

SOME UNITS

[A$K] [S/D] [🛏] [📷] [DATA PORT] / [✕] [🔒] [📺] /

——— WHERE TO DINE ———

CHEAT RIVER INN
AAA
▼▼▼
American

Dinner: $14-$26   **Phone:** 304/636-6265

Location: 4.8 mi e on US 33, 1.5 mi ne on Faulkner Rd. Rt 1, Box 115, Faulkner Rd 26241. **Hours:** 5 pm-9 pm, Fri & Sat-10 pm. Closed: Tues 11/1-5/31 & Mon. **Reservations:** suggested, weekends. **Features:** The comfortable and exquisite setting is on the banks of the Cheat River. A balanced menu and knowledgeable staff can be expected. Casual dress; cocktails. **Parking:** on-site. **Cards:** CB, DS, MC, VI.

[🍽] [✕]

ELKVIEW pop. 1,182

——— WHERE TO STAY ———

COUNTRY INN & SUITES BY CARLSON   *Book at aaa.com*
▼▼▼
Small-scale Hotel

All Year   1P: $75-$150   2P: $75-$150   XP: $6   F18

Phone: (304)965-9200

Location: I-79, exit 9, just e. 101 Crossings Shopping Center 25071. Fax: 304/965-9201. **Facility:** 90 one-bedroom standard units, some with whirlpools. 5 stories, interior corridors. **Bath:** combo or shower only. **Parking:** on-site. **Amenities:** high-speed Internet, voice mail, irons, hair dryers. **Pool(s):** heated outdoor. **Leisure Activities:** whirlpool, exercise room. **Guest Services:** valet laundry. **Business Services:** meeting rooms. **Cards:** AX, DC, DS, MC, VI. *(See color ad p 965)*

SOME UNITS

[A$K] [♿] [🛏] [📷] [DATA PORT] [💻] / [✕] [🔒] [📺] /

FAIRMONT pop. 19,097

——— WHERE TO STAY ———

COMFORT INN & SUITES   *Book at aaa.com*
AAA [SAVE]
▼▼▼
Motel

All Year   1P: $49-$125

Phone: (304)367-1370

Location: I-79, exit 133, just w. 1185 Airport Rd 26554. Fax: 304/367-1806. **Facility:** 82 one-bedroom standard units, some with whirlpools. 2 stories (no elevator), interior corridors. **Parking:** on-site. **Amenities:** irons, hair dryers. **Pool(s):** outdoor. **Leisure Activities:** exercise room. **Guest Services:** coin laundry. **Business Services:** meeting rooms. **Cards:** AX, DC, DS, JC, MC, VI. **Special Amenities:** free continental breakfast and free local telephone calls.

SOME UNITS

[S/D] [🍴] [🛏] [📷] [DATA PORT] [💻] / [✕] [VCR] [🔒] [📺] /

COUNTRY CLUB MOTOR LODGE
AAA [SAVE]
▼▼
Motel

5/1-10/31   1P: $32-$42   2P: $32-$42   XP: $5   F16
3/1-4/30 & 11/1-2/28   1P: $32-$38   2P: $32-$38   XP: $5   F16

Phone: (304)366-4141

Location: I-79, exit 132, 3 mi n on US 250, then 1 mi w on Country Club Rd. Located at a busy high-traffic intersection. 1499 Locust Ave 26554. Fax: 304/367-1882. **Facility:** 30 one-bedroom standard units. 2 stories (no elevator), exterior corridors. **Parking:** on-site. **Cards:** AX, DS, MC, VI. **Special Amenities:** free local telephone calls and early check-in/late check-out.

SOME UNITS

[🍴] [♿] / [✕] [🔒] [📺] /
FEE

DAYS INN   *Book at aaa.com*
AAA [SAVE]
▼▼ ▼▼
Small-scale Hotel

5/1-10/31 [CP]   1P: $60-$65   2P: $65-$70   XP: $7   F18
3/1-4/30 & 11/1-2/28 [CP]   1P: $49-$55   2P: $53-$59   XP: $7   F18

Phone: (304)366-5995

Location: I-79, exit 132, just se on US 250, then just s. Located in an industrial area. 228 Middletown Rd 26554. Fax: 304/366-6092. **Facility:** 41 one-bedroom standard units. 2 stories (no elevator), exterior corridors. **Parking:** on-site. **Terms:** 14 day cancellation notice, pets ($10 extra charge). **Amenities:** hair dryers. **Cards:** AX, DC, DS, MC, VI. **Special Amenities:** free continental breakfast and free newspaper.

(See color ad p 635)

SOME UNITS

[S/D] [🛏] [♿] [📷] [DATA PORT] [💻] / [✕] [🔒] [📺] /
FEE

HOLIDAY INN FAIRMONT   *Book at aaa.com*
AAA [SAVE]
▼▼ ▼▼
Small-scale Hotel

4/3-11/19   1P: $79-$99   2P: $79-$99
3/1-4/2 & 11/20-2/28   1P: $59-$79   2P: $59-$79

Phone: (304)366-5500

Location: I-79, exit 137, just e. 930 E Grafton Rd 26554. Fax: 304/363-3975. **Facility:** 106 one-bedroom standard units. 2 stories (no elevator), interior corridors. **Bath:** combo or shower only. **Parking:** on-site. **Terms:** package plans, small pets only (in smoking units). **Amenities:** video games, voice mail, irons, hair dryers. **Dining:** 6 am-10 & 5-10 pm, cocktails. **Pool(s):** outdoor. **Guest Services:** valet laundry. **Business Services:** meeting rooms. **Cards:** AX, CB, DC, DS, JC, MC, VI.

SOME UNITS

[S/D] [🛏] [🍴] [🍽] [♿M] [♿] [📽] [🛏] [📷] [DATA PORT] [💻] / [✕] [🔒] [📺] /

RED ROOF INN   *Book at aaa.com*
▼▼▼
Motel

5/11-8/6   1P: $42-$57   2P: $45-$60   XP: $3   F18
3/1-5/10 & 8/7-2/28   1P: $40-$57   2P: $43-$60   XP: $3   F18

Phone: (304)366-6800

Location: I-79, exit 132, 0.3 mi s on US 250, just w, then just s. 50 Middletown Rd 26554. Fax: 304/366-6812. **Facility:** 108 one-bedroom standard units. 2 stories (no elevator), exterior corridors. **Parking:** on-site. **Terms:** small pets only (with prior approval). **Cards:** AX, CB, DC, DS, MC, VI.

SOME UNITS

[🛏] [🍴] [🔲] [📷] [DATA PORT] / [✕] /

SUPER 8 MOTEL   *Book at aaa.com*   **Phone: (304)363-1488**

▽▽▽ ▽▽▽   All Year [CP]   1P: $51-$73   2P: $57-$79   XP: $6   F17
Motel   **Location:** I-79, exit 133, just e. 2208 Pleasant Valley Rd 26554. **Fax:** 304/363-1488. **Facility:** 54 one-bedroom standard units, some with whirlpools. 2 stories (no elevator), interior corridors. **Parking:** on-site. **Terms:** small pets only (with prior approval). **Amenities:** irons. **Business Services:** meeting rooms.
Cards: AX, CB, DC, DS, MC, VI.

SOME UNITS

[ASK] [S/D] [🐾] [🍴+] [📷] [DATA PORT] [🛏] [🖥] / [✕] /

——— **WHERE TO DINE** ———

DJ'S 50'S & 60'S DINER   **Lunch:** $6-$10   **Dinner:** $6-$10   **Phone:** 304/366-8110
▽▽▽   **Location:** I-79, exit 133, just n. 1181 Airport Rd 26554. **Hours:** 7 am-10 pm, Fri & Sat-midnight. Closed: 12/25.
American   **Features:** Decorated in a 1950s and '60s style, the retro diner prepares tried-and-true American favorites. Casual dress. **Parking:** on-site. **Cards:** AX, DS, MC, VI.

[✕]

MURIALE'S RESTAURANT   **Lunch:** $7-$16   **Dinner:** $7-$16   **Phone:** 304/363-3190
▽▽ ▽▽   **Location:** I-79, exit 132, 1.5 mi n on US 250. 1742 Fairmont Ave Ext 26554. **Hours:** 11 am-9 pm, Fri & Sat-10 pm,
Italian   Sun-8 pm. Closed: 3/27, 7/4, 12/25. **Features:** On the Tiger River, the casual restaurant makes its own excellent pasta and sauce. Photographs of Italian singers decorate the walls of the indoor dining area, the outdoor deck is laid-back and bright, and the large lounge is the newest area in which to unwind. Private inlet rooms also are available. Save room for Italian rum cake. Casual dress; cocktails. **Parking:** on-site. **Cards:** AX, DC, DS, MC, VI.

[✕]

POKY DOT   **Lunch:** $4-$8   **Dinner:** $8-$12   **Phone:** 304/366-3271
▽▽   **Location:** I-79, exit 132, 3.3 mi n on US 250. 1111 Fairmont Ave 26554. **Hours:** 7 am-11 pm, Fri & Sat-midnight.
American   Closed: 1/1, 11/24, 12/25. **Features:** An area tradition, the restaurant blends '50s nostalgia and quick, but tasty, meals. The friendly atmosphere is welcoming to families. Casual dress. **Parking:** on-site. **Cards:** DS, MC, VI.

[✕]

THE SIMMERING POT FAMILY RESTAURANT   **Dinner:** $7-$18   **Phone:** 304/366-5500
▽▽ ▽▽   **Location:** I-79, exit 137, just e. 930 E Grafton Rd 26554. **Hours:** 6 am-10 & 5-10 pm. **Features:** This restaurant
American   is boiling over with classic American favorites, friendly service and a home-spun cozy family friendly atmosphere. Casual dress; cocktails. **Parking:** on-site. **Cards:** AX, CB, DC, DS, JC, MC, VI.

[🍸] [✕]

VELTRI'S STEAK & PASTA   **Dinner:** $6-$13   **Phone:** 304/366-2114
▽▽ ▽▽   **Location:** I-79, exit 137, just w on US 250, 1.2 mi s. 110 Merchant St 26554. **Hours:** 4 pm-10 pm. Closed major
American   holidays; also Mon. **Features:** A local favorite with loads of atmosphere and tradition, the restaurant appeals to a wide selection of patrons who want to experience good food. Casual dress; cocktails. **Parking:** on-site.
Cards: MC, VI.

[✕]

FALLING WATERS

——— **WHERE TO STAY** ———

HOLIDAY INN EXPRESS MARTINSBURG NORTH   *Book at aaa.com*   **Phone:** 304/274-6100
▽▽▽ ▽▽   4/1-10/31   1P: $79   2P: $79   XP: $6   F
3/1-3/31 & 11/1-2/28   1P: $69   2P: $69   XP: $6   F
Small-scale Hotel   **Location:** I-81, exit 20, just w. 1220 TJ Jackson Dr 25419. **Fax:** 304/274-0575. **Facility:** 71 one-bedroom standard units. 3 stories, interior corridors. *Bath:* combo or shower only. **Parking:** on-site. **Terms:** 5 day cancellation notice. **Amenities:** voice mail, irons, hair dryers. **Pool(s):** outdoor. **Guest Services:** coin laundry. **Cards:** AX, DC, JC, MC, VI.

SOME UNITS

[ASK] [S/D] [&] [🏊] [📷] [DATA PORT] [🖥] / [✕] /

FLATWOODS pop. 348

——— **WHERE TO STAY** ———

DAYS INN SUTTON/FLATWOODS   *Book at aaa.com*   **Phone:** (304)765-5055
▽▽ ▽▽   6/1-11/30   1P: $75-$80   2P: $80-$85   XP: $5   F
3/1-5/31   1P: $69-$75   2P: $75-$80   XP: $5   F
12/1-2/28   1P: $64-$69   2P: $69-$74   XP: $5   F
Small-scale Hotel   **Location:** I-79, exit 67, just e. 2000 Sutton Ln 26601. **Fax:** 304/765-2067. **Facility:** 200 one-bedroom standard units, some with whirlpools. 5 stories, interior corridors. **Parking:** on-site. **Terms:** 14 day cancellation notice, package plans. **Amenities:** irons, hair dryers. **Pool(s):** outdoor, heated indoor. **Leisure Activities:** sauna, exercise room. **Guest Services:** gift shop. **Business Services:** conference facilities. **Cards:** AX, CB, DC, DS, MC, VI.

SOME UNITS

[ASK] [S/D] [🍴] [🍸] [🌀] [🏊] [📷] [DATA PORT] [🖥] / [✕] [VCR] [🛏] [🖥] /

FROST

——— **WHERE TO STAY** ———

THE INN AT MOUNTAIN QUEST   **Phone:** (304)799-7267
▽▽▽ ▽▽   All Year [BP]   1P: $85-$130   2P: $95-$140   XP: $10   D17
Country Inn   **Location:** On SR 92, 0.4 mi n. Rt 92 Frost 24954 (Box 109, MARLINTON). **Fax:** 304/799-0861. **Facility:** The Inn at Mountain Quest offers an observation tower, a large and award-winning library and many ways to enjoy nature. 12 one-bedroom standard units. 2-3 stories (no elevator), exterior corridors. **Parking:** on-site.
Terms: 7 day cancellation notice-fee imposed, [AP] & [CP] meal plans available, package plans. **Amenities:** irons, hair dryers. **Leisure Activities:** whirlpool, fishing, hiking trails, exercise room, basketball. **Guest Services:** complimentary laundry. **Business Services:** conference facilities, business center. **Cards:** MC, VI.

[ASK] [S/D] [🐾] [🍴] [🍸] [✕] [✕] [DATA PORT]

GLEN DALE pop. 1,552

─────── WHERE TO STAY ───────

BONNIE DWAINE BED & BREAKFAST
▼▼▼▼▼
Bed & Breakfast

All Year   1P: $69-$115   2P: $79-$125   XP: $10   F6
Phone: (304)845-7250
Location: I-470, exit 1, 7 mi s on SR 2. 505 Wheeling Ave 26038. Fax: 304/845-7256. **Facility:** Breakfast is served by candlelight at this renovated Victorian home located 7 miles south of Wheeling. Smoke free premises. 5 one-bedroom standard units with whirlpools. 3 stories (no elevator), interior corridors. **Parking:** on-site. **Terms:** cancellation fee imposed, weekly rates available, package plans. **Amenities:** hair dryers. *Some:* irons. **Guest Services:** complimentary laundry. **Cards:** AX, CB, DC, DS, JC, MC, VI.

SOME UNITS
(ASK) (S•D) (†|•) (X) (VCR) (DATA PORT) / (🛏) (📺) /

GLENVILLE pop. 1,544

─────── WHERE TO STAY ───────

BEST WESTERN GLENVILLE INN
(AAA) (SAVE)
▼▼▼▼▼
Small-scale Hotel

All Year   1P: $69-$99   2P: $69-$99   XP: $10   F17
Phone: (304)462-5511
Location: 1.5 mi e on SR 5. Rt 76, Box 25 26351 (PO Box 397). Fax: 304/462-0235. **Facility:** 60 one-bedroom standard units, some with whirlpools. 3 stories, interior corridors. *Bath:* combo or shower only. **Parking:** on-site. **Terms:** 7 night minimum stay - seasonal and/or weekends, package plans. **Amenities:** voice mail, irons, hair dryers. **Leisure Activities:** sauna, exercise room. **Guest Services:** coin laundry. **Business Services:** meeting rooms. **Cards:** AX, CB, DC, DS, MC, VI. **Special Amenities:** free continental breakfast and free local telephone calls.

SOME UNITS
(S•D) (&) (📺) (DATA PORT) (🖥) / (X) (🛏) (📺) /

HARPERS FERRY pop. 307

─────── WHERE TO STAY ───────

COMFORT INN
(AAA) (SAVE)
▼▼▼▼▼
Small-scale Hotel

Book at aaa.com
4/1-12/31 [ECP]   1P: $65-$125   2P: $70-$125   XP: $6   F18
1/1-2/28 [ECP]   1P: $70-$80   2P: $75-$90   XP: $6   F18
3/1-3/31 [ECP]   1P: $60-$70   2P: $65-$70   XP: $6   F18
Phone: (304)535-6391
Location: On US 340, just e. Rt 340 & Union St 25425 (PO Box 980). Fax: 304/535-6395. **Facility:** 50 one-bedroom standard units. 2 stories (no elevator), interior corridors. *Bath:* combo or shower only. **Parking:** on-site. **Terms:** 2 night minimum stay - seasonal, cancellation fee imposed. **Amenities:** video library (fee), voice mail, irons, hair dryers. **Guest Services:** valet laundry. **Cards:** AX, CB, DC, DS, JC, MC, VI.

SOME UNITS
(S•D) (DATA PORT) (🛏) (🖥) (📺) / (X) (VCR) /
FEE

QUALITY INN & CONFERENCE CENTER
▼▼▼▼▼
Small-scale Hotel

Book at aaa.com
6/2-2/28 [CP]   1P: $89-$158   2P: $89-$158   XP: $10   F18
3/1-6/1 [CP]   1P: $70-$99   2P: $70-$99   XP: $10   F18
Phone: (304)535-6302
Location: 0.2 mi w on US 340. 4328 William L Wilson Frwy 25425. Fax: 304/535-6313. **Facility:** 100 one-bedroom standard units, some with whirlpools. 2-3 stories, interior corridors. *Bath:* combo or shower only. **Parking:** on-site. **Terms:** cancellation fee imposed, [AP], [BP] & [CP] meal plans available, package plans. **Amenities:** voice mail, irons, hair dryers. **Pool(s):** heated indoor. **Leisure Activities:** 2 tennis courts, exercise room, game room. *Fee:* miniature golf. **Guest Services:** coin laundry. **Business Services:** conference facilities. **Cards:** AX, DC, DS, JC, MC, VI.

SOME UNITS
(ASK) (S•D) (🛏) (†|) (🍽) (&) (⇌) (X) (📺) (DATA PORT) (🖥) / (X) (🛏) (📺) /

THE ANVIL RESTAURANT *Menu on aaa.com* **Lunch:** $5-$12 **Dinner:** $11-$23 **Phone:** 304/535-2582
American
Location: Washington St and Old Furnace Rd; center. 1270 Washington St 25425. **Hours:** 11 am-9 pm. Closed: 11/24, 12/25; also Mon & Tues. **Reservations:** suggested, Fri-Sun. **Features:** Steak, chicken, veal and seafood, including the specialty crab cakes, share menu space with several dessert offerings and a nice selection of children's dishes. The surroundings are rustic—with fireplaces, brick walls and soft lighting—and the atmosphere casual. Casual dress; cocktails. **Parking:** on-site. **Cards:** AX, DC, MC, VI.

HICO

------- WHERE TO STAY -------

COUNTRY ROAD CABINS **Phone:** 304/658-5266
Cabin
All Year 2P: $125-$245 XP: $20 F11
Location: SR 19 to US 60 (Midland Tr), just w. Sunday Rd 25884 (PO Box 44). Fax: 304/658-5817. **Facility:** Located close to two national recreation areas that offer activities ranging from golf to whitewater rafting to skiing. 16 cabins with whirlpools. 1-3 stories, exterior corridors. *Bath:* combo or shower only. **Parking:** on-site. **Terms:** 2 night minimum stay, 30 day cancellation notice-fee imposed, weekly rates available. **Leisure Activities:** volleyball. **Business Services:** meeting rooms. **Cards:** AX, DC, DS, MC, VI.
(See color ad p 329)

HUNTINGTON pop. 51,475

------- WHERE TO STAY -------

DAYS INN *Book at aaa.com* **Phone:** (304)733-4477
Small-scale Hotel
5/28-9/15 [ECP] 1P: $59-$85 2P: $74-$85 XP: $5 F18
3/1-5/27 & 9/16-2/28 [ECP] 1P: $49-$85 2P: $58-$85 XP: $5 F18
Location: I-64, exit 15, just s. 5196 US Rt 60 25705. Fax: 304/733-4493. **Facility:** 153 one-bedroom standard units, some with whirlpools. 2 stories (no elevator), exterior corridors. **Parking:** on-site. **Terms:** weekly rates available. **Amenities:** irons, hair dryers. **Pool(s):** outdoor. **Guest Services:** coin laundry. **Business Services:** meeting rooms. **Cards:** AX, DC, DS, MC, VI.
SOME UNITS

HOLIDAY INN HOTEL & SUITES *Book at aaa.com* **Phone:** (304)523-8880
Small-scale Hotel
All Year 1P: $79-$109
Location: I-64, exit 11, 3 mi n on SR 10, then 0.9 mi w; downtown. 800 3rd Ave 25701. Fax: 304/525-0372. **Facility:** 135 one-bedroom standard units, some with whirlpools. 5 stories, interior corridors. *Bath:* combo or shower only. **Parking:** on-site. **Terms:** cancellation fee imposed. **Amenities:** high-speed Internet, voice mail, irons, hair dryers. **Pool(s):** heated indoor. **Leisure Activities:** exercise room. **Guest Services:** coin laundry. **Business Services:** meeting rooms, business center. **Cards:** AX, CB, DC, DS, JC, MC, VI.
SOME UNITS

RADISSON HOTEL HUNTINGTON *Book at aaa.com* **Phone:** (304)525-1001
Small-scale Hotel
All Year 1P: $71 2P: $81 XP: $10 F18
Location: I-64, exit 11, 3 mi n on SR 10, then 0.7 mi w; downtown. 1001 3rd Ave 25701. Fax: 304/525-1048. **Facility:** 202 one-bedroom standard units, some with whirlpools. 11 stories, interior corridors. **Parking:** on-site. **Terms:** 14 day cancellation notice-fee imposed. **Amenities:** video games, high-speed Internet, voice mail, irons, hair dryers. **Dining:** 2 restaurants, 6:30 am-10 pm, cocktails. **Pool(s):** heated outdoor. **Leisure Activities:** saunas, steamrooms. **Guest Services:** valet laundry, area transportation-within 10 mi. *Fee:* tanning facility. **Business Services:** conference facilities. **Cards:** AX, CB, DC, DS, MC, VI. **Special Amenities:** early check-in/late check-out. *(See color ad p 965)*
SOME UNITS
FEE

RAMADA LIMITED AND CONFERENCE CENTER *Book at aaa.com* **Phone:** (304)523-4242
Small-scale Hotel
All Year 1P: $70-$80 2P: $70-$80 XP: $5 F18
Location: I-64, exit 11, just n. 3094 16th Street Rd 25701. Fax: 304/523-8369. **Facility:** 68 one-bedroom standard units, some with whirlpools. 3 stories, interior corridors. *Bath:* combo or shower only. **Parking:** on-site. **Amenities:** voice mail, irons, hair dryers. **Pool(s):** heated indoor. **Leisure Activities:** whirlpool, exercise room. **Guest Services:** coin laundry. **Business Services:** conference facilities, business center. **Cards:** AX, CB, DC, DS, MC, VI.
SOME UNITS

RED ROOF INN *Book at aaa.com* **Phone:** (304)733-3737
Small-scale Hotel
5/2-7/2 1P: $45-$60 2P: $50-$65 XP: $5 F18
7/3-8/27 1P: $45-$55 2P: $50-$60 XP: $5 F18
3/1-5/1 & 8/28-2/28 1P: $40-$50 2P: $45-$55 XP: $5 F18
Location: I-64, exit 15, just s. 5190 US Rt 60 E 25705. Fax: 304/733-3786. **Facility:** 108 one-bedroom standard units. 2 stories (no elevator), exterior corridors. **Parking:** on-site. **Terms:** small pets only. **Amenities:** video games, voice mail. **Guest Services:** valet laundry. **Cards:** AX, CB, DC, DS, MC, VI.
SOME UNITS
FEE FEE

SUPER 8 MOTEL *Book at aaa.com* **Phone:** (304)525-1410
Small-scale Hotel
All Year 1P: $70-$80 2P: $70-$80 XP: $5 F18
Location: I-64, exit 11, just n. 3090 16th Street Rd 25701. Fax: 304/781-8223. **Facility:** 78 one-bedroom standard units, some with whirlpools. 3 stories, interior corridors. *Bath:* combo or shower only. **Parking:** on-site. **Amenities:** irons, hair dryers. **Pool(s):** heated indoor. **Leisure Activities:** whirlpool, exercise room. **Guest Services:** coin laundry. **Business Services:** meeting rooms. **Cards:** AX, DC, DS, MC, VI.
SOME UNITS

——— WHERE TO DINE ———

THE MARSHALL HALL OF FAME CAFE   **Lunch:** $6-$12   **Dinner:** $6-$17   **Phone:** 304/697-9800
♦♦♦
American
Location: I-64, exit 11, 3 mi n on SR 10, then 0.9 mi w; downtown. 857 3rd Ave 25701. **Hours:** 11 am-11 pm.
Closed: 1/1, 12/25. **Features:** The charming cafe appeals to nearly everyone, not just fans of the
Thundering Herd. A wide variety of classic American favorites and friendly service abound. Casual dress;
cocktails. **Parking:** on-site. **Cards:** AX, CB, DC, DS, JC, MC, VI.

REBELS & REDCOATS TAVERN   **Lunch:** $9-$18   **Dinner:** $10-$20   **Phone:** 304/523-8829
♦♦♦
American
Location: I-64, exit 6, just n on US 52, then 1.1 mi e on Madison Ave. 412 7th Ave W 25704. **Hours:** 11 am-11 pm.
Closed major holidays; also Sun. **Reservations:** suggested. **Features:** Contributing to the Colonial decor
are dark wood accents and stained-glass windows. Well-prepared entrees include veal, steak, seafood and
pasta. The wine cellar is extensive. Guests who eat a hearty meal can work it off at the adjacent bowling
alley. Dressy casual; cocktails. **Parking:** on-site. **Cards:** AX, DC, DS, MC, VI.

——— *The following restaurants have not been evaluated by AAA* ———
but are listed for your information only.

BUDDY'S   **Phone:** 304/522-9869
[fyi]
Not evaluated. **Location:** I-64, exit 11, 3 mi n on SR 10, then 0.8 mi w; downtown. 1537 3rd Ave 25701.
Features: Big screen televisions, open porch seating when weather permits, trivia games and an All-
American cuisine menu awaits at Buddy's.

HERITAGE VILLAGE   **Phone:** 304/523-6373
[fyi]
Not evaluated. **Location:** I-64, exit 11, 3 mi n on SR 10, then 0.6 mi w; downtown. 15 Heritage Village 25701.
Features: The converted B & O Station from circa 1887 is the modern setting for Heritage Station. A
Huntington dining landmark with distinguished service.

JIM'S RESTAURANT   **Phone:** 304/969-9788
[fyi]
Not evaluated. **Location:** I-64, exut 11, 3 mi n on SR 10, then 0.4 mi w; downtown. 920 54th Ave 25701.
Features: Homemade pies and award winning spaghetti are just two of the cuisine choices you'll find at the
family owned and operated Jim's Restaurant.

SAVANNAH'S   **Phone:** 304/529-0919
[fyi]
Not evaluated. **Location:** I-64, exit 11, 3 mi n on SR 10, then 0.4 mi w; downtown. 1208 6th Ave 25701.
Features: Savannah's offers Southern charm and elegance along with gourmet cuisine and an exquisite
wine and martini bar.

HURRICANE pop. 5,222

——— WHERE TO STAY ———

HOLIDAY INN EXPRESS   *Book at aaa.com*   **Phone:** (304)757-7177
♦♦♦
Small-scale Hotel
4/2-10/1 [CP]	1P: $80-$125
3/1-4/1 [CP]	1P: $70-$110
10/2-2/28 [CP]	1P: $65-$110
Location: I-64, exit 39, just n. 4218 SR 34 25526. Fax: 304/757-5005. **Facility:** 68 one-bedroom standard units,
some with whirlpools. 3 stories, interior corridors. *Bath:* combo or shower only. **Parking:** on-site. **Amenities:** high-speed
Internet, voice mail, irons, hair dryers. **Pool(s):** indoor. **Leisure Activities:** whirlpool, exercise room. **Guest Services:** coin
laundry. **Business Services:** meeting rooms. **Cards:** AX, CB, DC, DS, JC, MC, VI.
SOME UNITS

RED ROOF INN   *Book at aaa.com*   **Phone:** (304)757-6392
♦♦
Motel
3/1-3/26 & 10/23-2/28	1P: $40-$50	2P: $45-$55	XP: $5 F18
3/27-10/22	1P: $40-$51	2P: $45-$51	XP: $5 F18
Location: I-64, exit 39, just n on SR 34, then just e. Located behind Liberty Square Shopping Center. 500 Putnam
Village Dr 25526. Fax: 304/757-6734. **Facility:** 79 one-bedroom standard units. 2 stories (no elevator),
exterior corridors. *Bath:* combo or shower only. **Parking:** on-site. **Terms:** small pets only. **Amenities:** video games, voice mail.
Guest Services: coin laundry. **Cards:** AX, CB, DC, DS, MC, VI.
SOME UNITS
FEE FEE

SUPER 8 MOTEL-HURRICANE   *Book at aaa.com*   **Phone:** 304/562-3346
♦♦
Motel
All Year   1P: $50   2P: $50   XP: $5   F18
Location: I-64, exit 34, just s. 419 Hurricane Creek Rd 25526. Fax: 304/562-7408. **Facility:** 144 one-bedroom
standard units, some with whirlpools. 2 stories (no elevator), exterior corridors. *Bath:* combo or shower only.
Parking: on-site. **Terms:** small pets only ($10 extra charge). **Pool(s):** outdoor. **Guest Services:** coin
laundry. **Business Services:** meeting rooms. **Cards:** AX, DC, DS, MC, VI.
SOME UNITS
FEE

JANE LEW pop. 406

——— WHERE TO STAY ———

WILDERNESS PLANTATION INN   **Phone:** 304/884-7806
[AAA] [SAVE]
♦♦
Small-scale Hotel
All Year   1P: $49-$69   2P: $60-$70   XP: $7   F18
Location: I-79, exit 105, just e, then 0.3 mi s. Rt 7 Berlin Rd 26378 (PO Drawer 1278). Fax: 304/884-7670.
Facility: 39 one-bedroom standard units, some with whirlpools. 2 stories (no elevator), exterior corridors.
Parking: on-site. **Terms:** cancellation fee imposed, pets ($6 extra charge). **Amenities:** video library.
Pool(s): heated outdoor. **Leisure Activities:** volleyball. **Guest Services:** gift shop, area transportation
(fee). *Fee:* tanning facility. **Cards:** AX, DC, MC, VI.
SOME UNITS
FEE   FEE

KEARNEYSVILLE

——— WHERE TO STAY ———

COMFORT SUITES *Book at aaa.com*   Phone: (304)263-8888

5/27-9/5 [ECP]		1P: $75-$85	2P: $75-$85	XP: $5	F18
3/1-1/5/26 & 9/6-2/28 [ECP]		1P: $65-$80	2P: $65-$80	XP: $5	F18

Location: I-81, exit 12, 1.1 mi e on SR 45, then 4.5 mi e. Rt 9 E (Short Rd) 25401 (PO Box 6010, MARTINSBURG, 25402). Fax: 304/263-1540. **Facility:** 76 one-bedroom standard units, some with whirlpools. 2-3 stories (no
Small-scale Hotel elevator), interior corridors. *Bath:* combo or shower only. **Parking:** on-site. **Terms:** check-in 4 pm, cancellation fee imposed. **Amenities:** high-speed Internet, dual phone lines, voice mail, irons, hair dryers.
Pool(s): outdoor. **Leisure Activities:** exercise room. **Guest Services:** coin laundry. **Business Services:** meeting rooms.
Cards: AX, DC, DS, MC, VI.

SOME UNITS

KEYSER pop. 5,303

——— WHERE TO STAY ———

KEYSER INN   Phone: 304/788-0913

All Year		1P: $54-$61	2P: $58-$65	XP: $5	F17

Location: On US 220, 2.3 mi s. Located next to Wal-Mart. Rt 220 S 26726 (PO Box 160). Fax: 304/788-6219.
Facility: 44 one-bedroom standard units, some with whirlpools. 2 stories (no elevator), interior corridors.
Parking: on-site. **Terms:** check-in 4 pm, package plans. **Amenities:** irons, hair dryers. **Cards:** AX, DC, DS,
Small-scale Hotel MC, VI.

SOME UNITS

FEE

LEWISBURG pop. 3,624

——— WHERE TO STAY ———

BRIER INN   Phone: (304)645-7722

4/1-10/31 [CP]		1P: $59-$75	2P: $64-$80	XP: $5	F13
3/1-3/31 & 11/1-2/28 [CP]		1P: $54-$71	2P: $59-$76	XP: $5	F13

Location: I-64, exit 169, just s on US 219. Truck parking on site. 540 N Jefferson St 24901. Fax: 304/645-7865.
Facility: 162 one-bedroom standard units, some with whirlpools. 2 stories (no elevator), exterior corridors.
Small-scale Hotel *Bath:* combo or shower only. **Parking:** on-site. **Terms:** [MAP] meal plan available, small pets only ($10 extra charge, in designated units). **Amenities:** video library (fee), voice mail, irons, hair dryers. *Some:* honor bars.
Dining: 11 am-10 pm, cocktails. **Pool(s):** outdoor. **Guest Services:** valet laundry, airport transportation-Greenbrier Valley Airport. **Business Services:** conference facilities. **Cards:** AX, DC, DS, MC, VI. **Special Amenities:** free continental breakfast and preferred room (subject to availability with advance reservations).

SOME UNITS

FEE   FEE

DAYS INN *Book at aaa.com*   Phone: (304)645-2345

5/1-10/31 [CP]		1P: $55-$125	2P: $65-$150	XP: $10	D13
11/1-2/28 [CP]		1P: $55-$75	2P: $55-$90	XP: $7	D13
3/1-4/30 [CP]		1P: $55-$65	2P: $55-$90	XP: $6	D13

Location: I-64, exit 169, 0.3 mi n on US 219. 635 N Jefferson St 24901. Fax: 304/645-5501. **Facility:** 26 one-
Small-scale Hotel bedroom standard units. 1 story, exterior corridors. **Parking:** on-site. **Terms:** 3 day cancellation notice-fee imposed, small pets only ($10 extra charge). **Amenities:** hair dryers. **Leisure Activities:** basketball.
Cards: AX, DC, DS, MC, VI. **Special Amenities:** free continental breakfast and free local telephone calls.

SOME UNITS

FEE

GENERAL LEWIS INN   Phone: (304)645-2600

All Year		1P: $95-$145	2P: $95-$145	XP: $10

Location: I-64, exit 169, 1.4 mi s on US 219, then just e on US 60. 301 E Washington St 24901. Fax: 304/645-2601.
Facility: Pioneer tools and memorabilia are displayed in the inn's 1834 original building and its 1928
addition; an extensive garden surrounds both structures. Smoke free premises. 25 units. 23 one- and 2 two-
Country Inn bedroom standard units. 2 stories (no elevator), interior corridors. **Parking:** on-site. **Terms:** 10 day cancellation notice-fee imposed, package plans. **Amenities:** high-speed Internet, hair dryers. **Dining:** dining
room, see separate listing. **Cards:** AX, DS, MC, VI. **Special Amenities:** free local telephone calls.

RODEWAY INN *Book at aaa.com*   Phone: (304)645-7070

6/1-8/31 [CP]		1P: $40-$100	2P: $40-$100
3/1-5/31 & 9/1-2/28 [CP]		1P: $30-$70	2P: $30-$70

Location: I-64, exit 169, 3.1 mi s on US 219, then just e. 107 W Fair St 24901. Fax: 304/645-3383. **Facility:** 31
one-bedroom standard units. 2 stories (no elevator), exterior corridors. **Parking:** on-site. **Terms:** pets ($10
Motel fee). **Leisure Activities:** whirlpool. **Guest Services:** coin laundry. **Cards:** AX, CB, DC, DS, MC, VI.

SOME UNITS

FEE

SUPER 8 MOTEL *Book at aaa.com*   Phone: 304/647-3188

All Year		1P: $51-$61	2P: $57-$67	XP: $6	F12

Location: I-64, exit 169, just s on US 219. 550 N Jefferson St 24901. Fax: 304/647-3188. **Facility:** 54 one-
Small-scale Hotel bedroom standard units. 2 stories (no elevator), interior corridors. **Parking:** on-site. **Terms:** 30 day cancellation notice, small pets only ($10 deposit). **Amenities:** safes. **Cards:** AX, CB, DC, DS, MC, VI.

SOME UNITS

FEE   FEE FEE

─────── **WHERE TO DINE** ───────

FOOD & FRIENDS

American

Lunch: $5-$9   Dinner: $9-$20   **Phone: 304/645-4548**
Location: I-64, exit 169, 1.4 mi s on US 219, then just w on US 60. 213 W Washington St 24901. **Hours:** 11 am-9 pm. Closed major holidays; also Sun. **Reservations:** suggested, weekend evening. **Features:** Busily decorated with lots of memorabilia on the walls, the relaxed downtown restaurant builds its menu around steaks and seafood. Many dining areas derive their atmosphere from enhanced lighting and piped-in jazz music. A difficult-to-resist counter case of chocolates and bonbons tempts at the checkout. Casual dress; cocktails. **Parking:** street. **Cards:** AX, DC, DS, MC, VI.

THE GENERAL LEWIS INN DINING ROOM
American

Lunch: $6-$10   Dinner: $11-$23   **Phone: 304/645-2600**
Location: I-64, exit 169, 1.4 mi s on US 219, then just e on US 60; in General Lewis Inn. 301 E Washington St 24901. **Hours:** 7-11 am, 11:30-2 & 6-9 pm, Sun 7:30 am-11 & noon-9 pm. Closed: for lunch 12/25. **Reservations:** required, for dinner. **Features:** Not only can guests sample the restaurant's tasty entrees and homemade soup, bread and cobbler, they also can tour the inn and gardens, listed on the National Register of Historic Places; relax in a front-porch rocking chair; or view the scenic garden pond. Many antiques furnish the dining room and waiting area. Casual dress; cocktails. **Parking:** on-site. **Cards:** AX, DS, MC, VI. **Historic**

MARTINSBURG pop. 14,972

─────── **WHERE TO STAY** ───────

COMFORT INN AIKENS CENTER   *Book at aaa.com*   **Phone: (304)263-6200**
Small-scale Hotel
| All Year [ECP] | 1P: $69-$125 | 2P: $69-$125 | XP: $6 | F12 |
Location: I-81, exit 16E, 0.5 mi e on SR 9. 1872 Edwin Miller Blvd 25401. **Fax:** 304/267-0995. **Facility:** 109 one-bedroom standard units, some with whirlpools. 4 stories, interior corridors. **Parking:** on-site. **Amenities:** video games, voice mail, irons, hair dryers. **Pool(s):** outdoor. **Leisure Activities:** exercise room. **Fee:** game room. **Guest Services:** gift shop, coin laundry. **Business Services:** meeting rooms. **Cards:** AX, DC, DS, MC, VI.
SOME UNITS

DAYS INN MARTINSBURG   *Book at aaa.com*   **Phone: 304/263-1800**
Small-scale Hotel
| 4/1-10/31 | 1P: $69 | 2P: $69 | XP: $6 | F |
| 3/1-3/31 & 11/1-2/28 | 1P: $59 | 2P: $59 | XP: $6 | F |
Location: I-81, exit 13, just e on W King St (CR 15). 209 Viking Way 25401. **Fax:** 304/263-1384. **Facility:** 62 one-bedroom standard units. 3 stories, interior/exterior corridors. **Parking:** on-site. **Amenities:** hair dryers. **Leisure Activities:** exercise room. **Guest Services:** coin laundry. **Cards:** AX, DC, DS, JC, MC, VI.
SOME UNITS

ECONO LODGE   *Book at aaa.com*   **Phone: (304)274-2181**
Motel
| All Year | 1P: $53-$61 | 2P: $60-$63 | XP: $4 | F18 |
Location: I-81, exit 20, just e. 5595 Hammonds Mill Rd 25401. **Fax:** 304/274-6989. **Facility:** 48 one-bedroom standard units. 2 stories (no elevator), interior/exterior corridors. **Parking:** on-site. **Terms:** [CP] meal plan available. **Cards:** AX, CB, DC, MC, VI.
SOME UNITS

ECONOMY INN   **Phone: 304/267-2994**
Motel
| All Year | 1P: $38-$50 | 2P: $42-$60 | XP: $5 | F |
Location: I-81, exit 12, 0.3 mi e on SR 45, then 0.3 mi s. 1616 Winchester Ave (US 11 S) 25401. **Fax:** 304/267-2282. **Facility:** 22 one-bedroom standard units. 1 story, exterior corridors. **Parking:** on-site. **Terms:** cancellation fee imposed, small pets only ($5 extra charge). **Pool(s):** outdoor. **Leisure Activities:** picnic area. **Cards:** AX, DC, MC, VI. **Special Amenities:** free local telephone calls.
SOME UNITS
FEE

HAMPTON INN   *Book at aaa.com*   **Phone: (304)267-2900**
Small-scale Hotel
| All Year | 1P: $89-$109 | 2P: $89-$109 | | |
Location: I-81, exit 12, just e on SR 45, then just n. 975 Foxcroft Ave 25401. **Fax:** 304/262-4365. **Facility:** 99 one-bedroom standard units, some with whirlpools. 5 stories, interior corridors. **Bath:** combo or shower only. **Parking:** on-site. **Terms:** pets (in designated units). **Amenities:** video games, high-speed Internet, voice mail, irons, hair dryers. **Pool(s):** outdoor. **Guest Services:** coin laundry. **Cards:** AX, DC, DS, MC, VI.
SOME UNITS
FEE

HOLIDAY INN MARTINSBURG   *Book at aaa.com*   **Phone: (304)267-5500**
Small-scale Hotel
| All Year | 1P: $89-$99 | 2P: $89-$99 | | |
Location: I-81, exit 13, just e on W King St (CR 15). 301 Foxcroft Ave 25401. **Fax:** 304/264-9157. **Facility:** 120 one-bedroom standard units. 5 stories, interior corridors. **Bath:** combo or shower only. **Parking:** on-site. **Terms:** package plans. **Amenities:** video games, high-speed Internet, voice mail, irons, hair dryers. **Pool(s):** indoor/outdoor. **Leisure Activities:** saunas, whirlpool, 4 lighted tennis courts, horseshoes, volleyball. **Guest Services:** coin laundry. **Business Services:** meeting rooms. **Cards:** AX, CB, DC, DS, JC, MC, VI.
SOME UNITS

KNIGHTS INN-MARTINSBURG   *Book at aaa.com*   Phone: (304)267-2211

(AAA) (SAVE)

◇◇◇

Motel

All Year   1P: $47-$65   2P: $57-$75   XP: $5   F17
Location: I-81, exit 16E, 0.4 mi e on SR 9. 1997 Edwin Miller Blvd 25401. Fax: 304/267-9606. **Facility:** 59 one-bedroom standard units. 1 story, exterior corridors. **Parking:** on-site. **Terms:** pets ($5 extra charge, in designated units). **Amenities:** video library, irons, hair dryers. **Cards:** AX, DC, DS, MC, VI. **Special Amenities: free local telephone calls.**

[icons] SOME UNITS

QUALITY INN OF MARTINSBURG   *Book at aaa.com*   Phone: (304)263-8811

(AAA) (SAVE)

◇◇◇◇

Motel

5/1-10/31 [ECP]   1P: $79-$99   2P: $89-$109   XP: $10   F16
3/1-4/30 [ECP]   1P: $69-$99   2P: $79-$109   XP: $10   F16
11/1-2/28 [ECP]   1P: $59-$89   2P: $69-$99   XP: $10   F16
Location: I-81, exit 16E, just e. 94 McMillan Ct 25401. Fax: 304/263-0538. **Facility:** 115 one-bedroom standard units. 1-2 stories (no elevator), interior/exterior corridors. *Bath:* combo or shower only. **Parking:** on-site. **Terms:** 7 day cancellation notice, pets ($15 extra charge). **Amenities:** irons, hair dryers. **Pool(s):** indoor. **Leisure Activities:** whirlpool, exercise room, shuffleboard. *Fee:* game room. **Guest Services:** coin laundry. **Business Services:** meeting rooms. **Cards:** AX, DC, DS, MC, VI. **Special Amenities: free expanded continental breakfast and free local telephone calls.**

[icons] SOME UNITS

RELAX INN   Phone: (304)263-0831

(AAA) (SAVE)

◇◇

Motel

3/1-10/31   1P: $32-$59   2P: $34-$59   XP: $5   D8
11/1-2/28   1P: $30-$59   2P: $32-$59   XP: $5   D8
Location: I-81, exit 12, 0.3 mi e on SR 45, then just n. 1022 Winchester Ave (US 11 N) 25401. Fax: 304/264-4326. **Facility:** 16 one-bedroom standard units. 1 story, exterior corridors. *Bath:* combo or shower only. **Parking:** on-site. **Terms:** 3 day cancellation notice-fee imposed, small pets only ($5 extra charge, in designated units). **Pool(s):** outdoor. **Cards:** AX, DC, MC, VI. **Special Amenities: free local telephone calls and early check-in/late check-out.**

[icons] SOME UNITS

SCOTTISH INNS   *Book at aaa.com*   Phone: 304/267-2935

(AAA) (SAVE)

◇◇

Motel

All Year   1P: $35-$55   2P: $40-$59   XP: $5   F18
Location: I-81, exit 12, 0.3 mi e on SR 45, then just n. 1024 Winchester Ave (US 11 N) 25401. Fax: 304/267-1543. **Facility:** 18 one-bedroom standard units. 1 story, exterior corridors. **Parking:** on-site. **Terms:** small pets only ($5 extra charge). **Amenities:** *Some:* irons, hair dryers. **Pool(s):** outdoor. **Leisure Activities:** basketball. **Cards:** AX, DC, DS, MC, VI. **Special Amenities: free local telephone calls and early check-in/late check-out.**

[icons] SOME UNITS

———— WHERE TO DINE ————

TOSCANA, AN ITALIAN BISTRO   Lunch: $7-$14   Dinner: $10-$21   Phone: 304/260-9099

◇◇ ◇◇

Italian

Location: I-81, exit 13, 2.8 mi e. 301 W King St 25401. **Hours:** 11 am-2 & 5:30-9 pm, Sat from 5:30 pm. Closed major holidays; also Sun. **Features:** A quaint Italian Bistro located in the downtown area of Martinsburg. Cozy atmosphere and do not miss the bread and virgin olive oil. Casual dress; cocktails. **Parking:** street. **Cards:** AX, CB, DC, DS, JC, MC, VI.

[icons]

MEADOW BRIDGE pop. 321

———— WHERE TO STAY ————

DAWSON INN   Phone: 304/392-6661

◇◇ ◇◇

Small-scale Hotel

All Year   1P: $55-$65   2P: $59-$69
Location: I-64, exit 150, just s. 2625 Lawn Rd 25976. Fax: 304/392-6689. **Facility:** 24 one-bedroom standard units. 2 stories (no elevator), interior corridors. **Parking:** on-site. **Amenities:** hair dryers. **Cards:** AX, CB, DC, DS, MC, VI.

[icons] SOME UNITS

MINERALWELLS pop. 1,860

———— WHERE TO STAY ————

AMERIHOST INN PARKERSBURG SOUTH AT I-77   *Book at aaa.com*   Phone: (304)489-3111

(AAA) (SAVE)

◇◇◇◇

Small-scale Hotel

All Year   1P: $60-$120   2P: $65-$120
Location: I-77, exit 170, just w. 201 Hospitality Ln 26150. Fax: 304/489-3444. **Facility:** 61 one-bedroom standard units, some with whirlpools. 2 stories (no elevator), interior corridors. *Bath:* combo or shower only. **Parking:** on-site. **Terms:** weekly rates available, [CP] meal plan available, package plans. **Amenities:** voice mail, safes (fee), irons, hair dryers. **Pool(s):** heated indoor. **Leisure Activities:** whirlpool, exercise room. **Guest Services:** valet and coin laundry. **Business Services:** meeting rooms. **Cards:** AX, DC, DS, MC, VI. **Special Amenities: free expanded continental breakfast and free newspaper.**

[icons] SOME UNITS

COMFORT SUITES   *Book at aaa.com*   **Phone:** (304)489-9600
▼▼▼▼   All Year   1P: $77-$150   2P: $77-$150   XP: $6   F18
Location: I-77, exit 170, 0.3 mi se. I-77 & SR 14 26150 (PO Box 400). Fax: 304/489-1896. **Facility:** 114 one-
Small-scale Hotel   bedroom standard units, some with efficiencies and/or whirlpools. 3 stories, interior/exterior corridors.
Parking: on-site. **Terms:** check-in 4 pm, [BP] meal plan available, package plans. **Amenities:** video library,
voice mail, irons, hair dryers. **Pool(s):** heated indoor/outdoor. **Leisure Activities:** sauna, whirlpool, exercise room. **Guest
Services:** complimentary evening beverages: Mon-Thurs, coin laundry. **Business Services:** meeting rooms. **Cards:** AX, CB,
DC, DS, JC, MC, VI.
SOME UNITS
ASK SÒ ✈ 🍽 📷 🦢 ✕ VCR 📷 DATA/PORT 📶 🖨 💳 / ✕ /

HAMPTON INN-PARKERSBURG   *Book at aaa.com*   **Phone:** (304)489-2900
▼▼▼▼   All Year   1P: $72-$85   2P: $77-$90
Location: I-77, exit 170, just e on SR 14. Rt 4, Box 1 26150. Fax: 304/489-2920. **Facility:** 68 one-bedroom
Small-scale Hotel   standard units. 3 stories, interior corridors. *Bath:* combo or shower only. **Parking:** on-site.
Terms: cancellation fee imposed. **Amenities:** voice mail, irons, hair dryers. **Pool(s):** outdoor. **Leisure
Activities:** exercise room. **Guest Services:** valet and coin laundry. **Business Services:** meeting rooms. **Cards:** AX, DC, DS,
MC, VI.
SOME UNITS
ASK SÒ 🍽↑ 🔧 🦢 📷 DATA/PORT 📶 / ✕ 📶 🖨 /
FEE FEE

MICROTEL INN   *Book at aaa.com*   **Phone:** (304)489-3892
▼▼   4/1-10/31 [CP]   1P: $52-$61   2P: $57-$61   XP: $5   F16
11/1-12/31 [CP]   1P: $42-$45   2P: $50-$55   XP: $5   F16
Small-scale Hotel   3/1-3/31 & 1/1-2/28 [CP]   1P: $43-$50   2P: $47-$51   XP: $5   F16
Location: I-77, exit 170, just w. 104 Nickolette Rd 26150. Fax: 304/489-9193. **Facility:** 54 one-bedroom standard
units. 2 stories (no elevator), interior corridors. *Bath:* combo or shower only. **Parking:** on-site. **Terms:** small pets only ($10 extra
charge). **Amenities:** high-speed Internet. **Guest Services:** coin laundry. **Cards:** MC, VI.
SOME UNITS
ASK SÒ 🐾 🔧 📷 DATA/PORT / ✕ 📶 🖨 /
FEE

MOOREFIELD pop. 2,375

———— **WHERE TO STAY** ————

SOUTH BRANCH INN   **Phone:** 304-538-2033
▼▼▼▼   All Year   1P: $70-$80   2P: $77-$90   XP: $7   F12
Location: On US 220/SR 28, 1.3 mi n. 1500 US 220 N 26836. Fax: 304/538-2036. **Facility:** 100 one-bedroom
Small-scale Hotel   standard units, some with whirlpools. 2 stories (no elevator), interior corridors. *Bath:* combo or shower only.
Parking: on-site. **Terms:** check-in 4 pm. **Amenities:** hair dryers. **Leisure Activities:** exercise room. **Guest
Services:** coin laundry. **Business Services:** meeting rooms. **Cards:** AX, DC, DS, MC, VI.
SOME UNITS
ASK 🍽↑ 🔧M 🔧 📷 📷 DATA/PORT / ✕ VCR 📶 🖨 /
FEE

———— **WHERE TO DINE** ————

**THE 1853 RESTAURANT AT
MCMECHEN HOUSE INN**   **Lunch:** $8-$18   **Dinner:** $10-$21   **Phone:** 304-530-1853
AAA   **Location:** 0.5 mi n on US 220. 109 N Main St 26836. **Hours:** 11 am-9 pm, Sun 2 pm. Closed: 12/25; also Mon.
▼▼▼▼   **Features:** In an old downtown building, the restaurant nurtures great ambience and offers nice views. The
upscale menu shows a wide variety. Casual dress; beer only. **Parking:** on-site. **Cards:** MC, VI.   ✕
American

ANNEE'S COTTAGE RESTAURANT   **Lunch:** $5-$12   **Dinner:** $5-$21   **Phone:** 304-530-2727
▼▼ ▼▼   **Location:** 1.1 mi n on US 220/SR 28. 614 N Main St 26836. **Hours:** 11 am-2 & 5-8 pm, Fri-9 pm, Sat 4 pm-9 pm,
Sun 11 am-8 pm. Closed: 12/25; also Mon. **Reservations:** suggested. **Features:** A wonderful place to
American   escape, the restaurant invites guests to unwind with varied selections of flavorful food. Servers are
outgoing. Casual dress; beer & wine only. **Parking:** on-site. **Cards:** AX, MC, VI.   ✕

THE HARVEST GRILL   **Lunch:** $5-$10   **Dinner:** $6-$12   **Phone:** 304-530-2259
▼▼ ▼▼   **Location:** 0.9 mi n on US 220. 139 N Main St 26836. **Hours:** 11 am-9 pm. Closed: 12/25; also Sun.
Features: The grill serves a bounty of classic American favorites, from wings to burgers to pizza to salads.
American   Casual dress; beer only. **Parking:** on-site. **Cards:** AX, CB, DC, DS, JC, MC, VI.

MORGANTOWN pop. 26,809—See also STAR CITY.

—— WHERE TO STAY ——

COMFORT INN-MORGANTOWN　　*Book at aaa.com*　　　　　　　　　　Phone: (304)296-9364
(AAA) [SAVE]　All Year [ECP]　　1P: $55-$125　　2P: $55-$125　　XP: $6　　　　　　F18
▽▽▽▽▽　**Location:** I-68, exit 1, 0.3 mi n on US 119. 225 Comfort Inn Dr 26508. Fax: 304/296-0469. **Facility:** 80 one-bedroom standard units, some with whirlpools. 2 stories (no elevator), interior corridors. **Parking:** on-site.
Small-scale Hotel　**Terms:** small pets only. **Amenities:** safes (fee), irons, hair dryers. **Dining:** 11 am-9:30 pm, cocktails. **Pool(s):** outdoor. **Leisure Activities:** whirlpool, exercise room. **Guest Services:** valet laundry. **Business Services:** meeting rooms. Cards: AX, CB, DC, DS, MC, VI.

SOME UNITS

🆂🆔 🐾 🍽 🍸 ⬜ ⋗ 🎥 📠 💻 / ✖ 🗄 🖼 /

EURO-SUITES HOTEL　　*Book at aaa.com*　　　　　　　　　　　Phone: (304)598-1000
(AAA) [SAVE]　All Year [ECP]　　1P: $89-$165　　2P: $99-$199　　XP: $10　　　　F18
▽▽▽▽▽　**Location:** I-79, exit 155, 2 mi s on US 19, then 1 mi e on SR 705. 501 Chestnut Ridge Rd 26505. Fax: 304/599-2736. **Facility:** 79 one-bedroom standard units. 5 stories, interior corridors. *Bath:* combo or shower only. **Parking:** on-site. **Terms:** 2 night minimum stay - seasonal and/or weekends, weekly rates available, package plans.
Small-scale Hotel　**Amenities:** high-speed Internet, voice mail, irons, hair dryers. **Guest Services:** valet laundry, area transportation-hospital. **Business Services:** meeting rooms, business center. Cards: AX, CB, DC, DS, MC, VI. **Special Amenities:** free expanded continental breakfast and free newspaper.

SOME UNITS

🆂🆔 ⊞ 🍽 🍸 ⬜ ⋗ 🎥 📠 🗄 🖼 💻 / ✖ VCR /
FEE

FRIENDS INN　　　　　　　　　　　　　　　　　　　　　　　Phone: (304)599-4850
(AAA) [SAVE]　All Year　　1P: $45-$65　　2P: $65-$75　　XP: $5　　　　　　　D12
▽▽▽　**Location:** I-79, exit 155, s on US 19 to SR 705, then e on University Ave. Located adjacent to University Health Center. 452 Country Club Rd 26505. Fax: 304/599-4866. **Facility:** 54 one-bedroom standard units. 2 stories (no
Motel　elevator), exterior corridors. *Bath:* combo or shower only. **Terms:** cancellation fee imposed, weekly rates available, small pets only ($5 extra charge). **Amenities:** hair dryers. *Some:* irons. Cards: AX, DC, DS, MC, VI. **Special Amenities:** free local telephone calls and free newspaper.

SOME UNITS

🆂🆔 🐾 ⚒ 🎥 📠 🗄 🖼 / ✖ 💻 /
FEE

HAMPTON INN　　*Book at aaa.com*　　　　　　　　　　　　　Phone: 304/599-1200
(AAA) [SAVE]　All Year　　1P: $66-$70　　2P: $77-$80
▽▽▽　**Location:** I-79, exit 155, 2 mi s on US 19, then 0.7 mi e on SR 705. 1053 Van Voorhis Rd 26505. Fax: 304/598-7331. **Facility:** 107 one-bedroom standard units. 5 stories, interior corridors. *Bath:* combo or shower only.
Small-scale Hotel　**Parking:** on-site. **Amenities:** voice mail, irons, hair dryers. **Guest Services:** valet laundry. **Business Services:** meeting rooms, business center. Cards: AX, DC, DS, MC, VI. **Special Amenities:** free expanded continental breakfast and free local telephone calls. *(See color ad below)*

SOME UNITS

🆂🆔 ⊞ ⚒M ⚒ ⬜ ⋗ 🎥 📠 💻 / ✖ 🗄 🖼 /
FEE

HISTORIC CLARION HOTEL MORGAN　　*Book at aaa.com*　　　Phone: (304)292-8200
▽▽▽　All Year [ECP]　　1P: $95-$150　　2P: $95-$150　　XP: $5　　　　F18
Location: Center. 127 High St 26505. Fax: 888/241-7944. **Facility:** 76 one-bedroom standard units, some with
Small-scale Hotel　whirlpools. 7 stories, interior corridors. **Parking:** on-site. **Terms:** 7 day cancellation notice, package plans. **Amenities:** high-speed Internet, voice mail, safes, irons, hair dryers. **Leisure Activities:** exercise room.
Guest Services: valet laundry, area transportation. **Business Services:** meeting rooms, business center. Cards: AX, DC, DS, JC, MC, VI.

SOME UNITS

[ASK] 🆂🆔 ⊞ 🍽 🍸 🎥 📠 🗄 🖼 💻 / ✖ /

HOLIDAY INN EXPRESS　　*Book at aaa.com*　　　　　　　　Phone: (304)291-2600
▽▽▽　All Year　　1P: $70-$95　　2P: $70-$95
Location: I-68, exit 7, just n. 605 Venture Dr 26508. Fax: 304/291-3553. **Facility:** 68 one-bedroom standard
Small-scale Hotel　units, some with whirlpools. 3 stories, interior corridors. *Bath:* combo or shower only. **Parking:** on-site. **Terms:** cancellation fee imposed. **Amenities:** dual phone lines, voice mail, irons, hair dryers. **Pool(s):** heated indoor. **Leisure Activities:** whirlpool, exercise room. **Guest Services:** valet laundry. **Business Services:** meeting rooms, business center. Cards: AX, DC, DS, MC, VI.

SOME UNITS

[ASK] 🆂🆔 ⚒ ⋗ 🎥 📠 🗄 🖼 💻 / ✖ /

LAKEVIEW GOLF RESORT & SPA

AAA SAVE

Book at aaa.com

Phone: (304)594-1111

4/1-11/1	1P: $99-$159	2P: $99-$159	XP: $10 F18
11/2-2/28	1P: $79-$109	2P: $79-$109	XP: $10 F18
3/1-3/31	1P: $69-$79	2P: $69-$99	XP: $10 F18

Resort
Small-scale Hotel

Location: I-68, exit 10, 1 mi s, follow signs. 1 Lakeview Dr 26508. Fax: 304/594-9472. **Facility:** Near West Virginia University, the resort offers recreational activities, an on-site restaurant and grounds that overlook a lake and golf course. 187 one-bedroom standard units, some with whirlpools. 2-3 stories, interior corridors. *Bath:* combo or shower only. **Parking:** on-site. **Terms:** 2 night minimum stay - weekends, 14 day cancellation notice-fee imposed, weekly rates available, package plans. **Amenities:** voice mail, safes, irons, hair dryers. **Dining:** 6:30 am-10 pm, cocktails, also, Reflections On The Lake, see separate listing. **Pool(s):** 2 outdoor, 2 indoor. **Leisure Activities:** saunas, whirlpools, rental boats, fishing, basketball, volleyball. *Fee:* golf-36 holes, golf instruction, 2 lighted indoor tennis courts, racquetball courts, aerobic instruction, indoor rock climbing, bicycles, massage. **Guest Services:** valet laundry. **Business Services:** conference facilities. **Cards:** AX, DC, DS, MC, VI. **Special Amenities: free newspaper and free room upgrade (subject to availability with advance reservations).**

SOME UNITS

(SD) ✈ ❤¶ ▼ ⬇ ✎ ⇆ ♿ ✕ ❖ DATA PORT ▭ / ✕ ❸ ▭ / FEE

MORGANTOWN ECONO LODGE

AAA SAVE

Book at aaa.com

Phone: (304)296-8774

All Year	1P: $58-$68	2P: $58-$68	XP: $10 F18

Motel

Location: I-79, exit 152, 0.4 mi e on US 19. Located adjacent to shopping plaza. 15 Commerce Dr 26502. Fax: 304/296-8774. **Facility:** 81 one-bedroom standard units. 2 stories (no elevator), interior corridors. **Parking:** on-site. **Terms:** weekly rates available. **Guest Services:** valet laundry. **Cards:** AX, DC, DS, MC, VI. **Special Amenities: free local telephone calls.**

SOME UNITS

(SD) ❤¶▸ DATA PORT / ✕ VCR ❸ ▭ ▭ / FEE

RADISSON HOTEL AT WATERFRONT PLACE

▼▼▼

Book at aaa.com

Phone: (304)296-1700

All Year	1P: $99-$149	XP: $10 F13

Large-scale Hotel

Location: I-68, exit 1, just n. 2 Waterfront Pl 26501. Fax: 304/296-1726. **Facility:** 206 one-bedroom standard units. 11 stories, interior corridors. *Bath:* combo or shower only. **Parking:** on-site and valet. **Terms:** package plans. **Amenities:** video games, high-speed Internet, dual phone lines, voice mail, irons, hair dryers. **Dining:** The Regatta Bar & Grille, see separate listing. **Pool(s):** indoor. **Leisure Activities:** whirlpool, exercise room. *Fee:* massage. **Guest Services:** sundries, valet laundry, area transportation. **Business Services:** conference facilities, business center. **Cards:** AX, DC, DS, JC, MC, VI. *(See color ad p 965 & below)*

SOME UNITS

(ASK) (SD) ¶¶ ▼ ⬇ ⇆ ✕ ❖ DATA PORT ▭ / ✕ ❸ ▭ /

RAMADA INN AND CONFERENCE CENTER

AAA SAVE

Book at aaa.com

Phone: (304)296-3431

6/1-2/28	1P: $65-$105	2P: $70-$110	XP: $10 F17
3/1-5/31	1P: $65-$95	2P: $70-$100	XP: $10 F17

Small-scale Hotel

Location: I-68, exit 1, 0.3 mi n. 20 Scott Ave 26508. Fax: 304/296-8841. **Facility:** 149 one-bedroom standard units. 4 stories, interior corridors. **Parking:** on-site. **Terms:** package plans. **Amenities:** voice mail, safes (fee), irons, hair dryers. **Dining:** 6 am-1:30 & 5-10 pm, cocktails. **Pool(s):** heated outdoor. **Leisure Activities:** exercise room, horseshoes, volleyball. **Guest Services:** gift shop, valet and coin laundry, airport transportation-Morgantown Airport, area transportation-bus station. **Business Services:** meeting rooms. **Cards:** AX, DC, DS, MC, VI. **Special Amenities: free full breakfast and free room upgrade (subject to availability with advance reservations).**

SOME UNITS

✈ 🛏 ¶¶ ▼ ⇆ ✕ ❖ DATA PORT ▭ / ✕ ❸ ▭ / FEE FEE

───── WHERE TO DINE ─────

ASIAN GARDEN RESTAURANT

▼▼▼

Lunch: $5-$7　　**Dinner:** $5-$15　　**Phone:** 304-599-1888

Chinese

Location: I-79, exit 155, 1.3 mi s on US 19, just e on Boyers Ave, then 1 mi s; in Sellaro Plaza. 3109-D University Ave 26505. **Hours:** 11 am-2 & 4:30-9:30 pm, Fri-10 pm, Sat 4:30 pm-10 pm. Closed major holidays; also Sun. **Reservations:** suggested, weekends. **Features:** The laid-back restaurant serves such flavorful dishes as phai pepper chicken and stir-fried scallops with snow peas, shiitake mushrooms, carrots, broccoli and bamboo shoots in a garlic brown sauce. The lengthy menu also offers Thai and Malaysian cuisine. The relaxed dining area displays Asian artwork and collectibles. Casual dress; beer & wine only. **Parking:** on-site. **Cards:** AX, DC, DS, MC, VI.　✕

FLYING FISH AND CO.
Lunch: $5-$12   **Dinner:** $5-$12   **Phone:** 304/225-3474

Seafood

Location: I-79, exit 155, 2 mi s on US 19, then 0.8 mi e on SR 705. 1111 Van Voorhis Rd 26505. **Hours:** 11 am-8 pm. Closed: Sun. **Features:** This restaurant has a wonderful, casual atmosphere and incredibly fresh seafood. Casual dress; beer only. **Parking:** on-site. **Cards:** AX, DC, DS, MC, VI.

THE GLASSHOUSE GRILLE
Lunch: $8-$10   **Dinner:** $12-$22   **Phone:** 304/296-8460

American

Location: I-79, exit 155, 3.5 mi e on US 19/SR 7; in the Seneca Center. 709 Beechurst Ave 26505. **Hours:** 11 am-2 & 5-9 pm. Closed major holidays; also Sun. **Reservations:** suggested. **Features:** The relaxed restaurant entices diners interested in fine dining in a cozy, candlelit setting. On the varied menu are fresh seafood, chargrilled steaks and a generous array of homemade fare: soups, sauces, dressing and desserts. The wine list has received awards. Casual dress; cocktails. **Parking:** on-site. **Cards:** AX, DC, DS, MC, VI.

PARGO'S RESTAURANT
Lunch: $7-$14   **Dinner:** $7-$18   **Phone:** 304/598-0700

American

Location: I-79, exit 155, 2 mi s on US 19/SR 7, then 0.3 mi e on SR 705. 334 Patteson Dr 26505. **Hours:** 11 am-10:30 pm, Fri & Sat-11:30 pm. Closed: 11/24, 12/25. **Features:** A lengthy menu of crowd-pleasing favorites is presented in the casual, fun and lively eatery. Guests are treated to such dishes as spicy Thai-style chicken soup and grilled chicken with cilantro and lemon. Friendly servers are attentive and prompt. The atmosphere is good for lunch or dinner, and visitors find this a good place to go before or after the game. Casual dress; cocktails. **Parking:** on-site. **Cards:** AX, DC, DS, MC, VI.

PEKING HOUSE
Lunch: $4-$12   **Dinner:** $7-$14   **Phone:** 304/598-3333

Chinese

Location: I-79, exit 155, 2 mi s on US 19, then 0.9 mi e on SR 705. 1125 Van Voorhis Rd 26505. **Hours:** 11:30 am-2 & 4:30-9:30 pm. **Features:** You can enjoy all your Chinese favorites in a warm Oriental atmosphere that is a Morgantown staple for meals. Casual dress; cocktails. **Parking:** on-site. **Cards:** AX, CB, DC, DS, JC, MC, VI.

PRIME THYME
Lunch: $6-$12   **Dinner:** $8-$20   **Phone:** 304/292-9190

American

Location: I-68, exit 1, 0.3 min on US 119. 226 Comfort Inn Dr 26508. **Hours:** 11 am-10 pm. Closed: Mon. **Features:** Prime Thyme has all the classic American favorites. No need to just go at prime time, they are opne for lunch also. Friendly wait staff abound. Casual dress; cocktails. **Parking:** on-site. **Cards:** AX, CB, DC, DS, JC, MC, VI.

REFLECTIONS ON THE LAKE
Dinner: $15-$27   **Phone:** 304/594-1111

American

Location: I-68, exit 10, 1 mi s, follow signs; in Lakeview Golf Resort & Spa. 1 Lakeview Dr 26505. **Hours:** 5 pm-10 pm, Sun also 11 am-2 pm. **Reservations:** suggested. **Features:** The atmosphere is comfortable inside the large, elegant dining room, which occupies Lakeview Resort and Conference Center. Beautiful lake views share the spotlight with diversified menu options, particularly the well-prepared, cooked-to-order prime rib. Casual dress; cocktails. **Parking:** on-site. **Cards:** AX, DC, DS, MC, VI.

THE REGATTA BAR & GRILLE
Lunch: $8-$16   **Dinner:** $10-$24   **Phone:** 304/284-9850

American

Location: I-68, exit 1, just n; in Radisson Hotel at Waterfront Place. 2 Waterfront Pl 26501. **Hours:** 11 am-10 pm. **Features:** The riverside restaurant affords wonderful views. The dining room carries out a regatta and nautical theme. On the menu are all the American classics. Casual dress; cocktails. **Parking:** on-site and valet. **Cards:** AX, CB, DC, DS, JC, MC, VI.

NEW MARTINSVILLE pop. 5,984

——— WHERE TO STAY ———

AMERIHOST INN-NEW MARTINSVILLE
Book at aaa.com   **Phone:** (304)455-6100

Small-scale Hotel

All Year   1P: $79   2P: $79   XP: $6   F18
Location: 1.5 mi n on SR 2, 0.3 mi n of bridge. 166 N SR 2 26155. Fax: 304/455-6160. **Facility:** 60 one-bedroom standard units, some with whirlpools. 2 stories (no elevator), interior corridors. *Bath:* combo or shower only. **Parking:** on-site. **Amenities:** voice mail, safes (fee), irons, hair dryers. **Pool(s):** heated indoor. **Leisure Activities:** whirlpool. **Guest Services:** valet laundry. **Cards:** AX, CB, DC, DS, JC, MC, VI. **Special Amenities:** free expanded continental breakfast and free local telephone calls.

NITRO pop. 6,824

——— WHERE TO STAY ———

ECONO LODGE
Book at aaa.com   **Phone:** (304)755-8341

Motel

All Year   1P: $56-$66   2P: $56-$66   XP: $5   D17
Location: I-64, exit 45, 0.8 mi e on SR 25. 4115 1st Ave 25143. Fax: 304/755-2933. **Facility:** 42 one-bedroom standard units. 2-3 stories (no elevator), exterior corridors. **Parking:** on-site. **Terms:** weekly rates available, small pets only ($10 extra charge). **Amenities:** irons, hair dryers. **Business Services:** meeting rooms. **Cards:** AX, CB, DC, DS, MC, VI. **Special Amenities:** free local telephone calls and early check-in/late check-out.

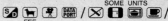

OAK HILL pop. 7,589

------ **WHERE TO STAY** ------

HOLIDAY INN
Book at aaa.com
All Year
Phone: (304)465-0571
1P: $99-$109   2P: $99-$109
Location: US 19, exit Oyler Ave, just w. 340 Oyler Ave 25901. Fax: 304/465-3700. **Facility:** 119 one-bedroom
Small-scale Hotel   standard units. 3 stories, interior corridors. **Parking:** on-site. **Terms:** cancellation fee imposed.
Amenities: safes, irons, hair dryers. **Pool(s):** heated indoor. **Leisure Activities:** whirlpool. **Guest Services:**
coin laundry. **Business Services:** conference facilities. **Cards:** AX, CB, DC, DS, MC, VI. *(See ad below)*

SOME UNITS

(A$K) (S/D) (⎁⎁) (Y) (&M) (⇌) (🛏) (🎦) (DATA PORT) (💻) / (⊠) (📠) (🖨) /

PARKERSBURG pop. 33,099

------ **WHERE TO STAY** ------

AMERIHOST INN PARKERSBURG NORTH AT PMC
CENTER   **Book at aaa.com**
(AAA) (SAVE)   All Year
Phone: (304)424-5300
1P: $84-$175   2P: $88-$200   XP: $6   F18
Location: 2.4 mi n on SR 14, via SR 14 and 68; 0.9 mi n of Memorial Bridge. 401 37th St 26101. Fax: 304/422-0312.
Facility: 78 one-bedroom standard units, some with whirlpools. 2 stories (no elevator), interior corridors.
Bath: combo or shower only. **Parking:** on-site. **Terms:** [ECP] meal plan available. **Amenities:** voice mail,
Small-scale Hotel   safes (fee), irons, hair dryers. **Pool(s):** heated indoor. **Leisure Activities:** whirlpool, board games. **Guest
Services:** valet laundry. **Business Services:** meeting rooms. **Cards:** AX, CB, DC, DS, JC, MC, VI.
Special Amenities: free expanded continental breakfast and free newspaper.

SOME UNITS

(S/D) (⎁⎁⁺) (&M) (⇌) (🛏) (🎦) (DATA PORT) (💻) / (⊠) (📠) (🖨) /
FEE   FEE

EXPRESSWAY MOTOR INN
Phone: (304)485-1851
(AAA) (SAVE)   All Year [CP]
1P: $38-$45   2P: $45-$56   XP: $5   F12
Location: I-77, exit 179, 0.4 mi sw on SR 68. 6333 Emerson Ave 26101. Fax: 304/485-4978. **Facility:** 46 one-
Motel   bedroom standard units, some with whirlpools. 2 stories (no elevator), exterior corridors. **Parking:** on-site.
Terms: weekly rates available, package plans, small pets only ($3 extra charge). **Cards:** AX, DS, MC, VI.
Special Amenities: free continental breakfast and free local telephone calls.

SOME UNITS

(S/D) (🛏) (🎦) / (⊠) (📠) (🖨) (💻) /
FEE

HOLIDAY INN PARKERSBURG   **Book at aaa.com**
All Year
Phone: (304)485-6200
1P: $100   2P: $100
Location: I-77, exit 176, just e. 225 Holiday Hills Dr 26104. Fax: 304/485-6261. **Facility:** 149 one-bedroom
Small-scale Hotel   standard units, some with efficiencies. 2 stories (no elevator), interior corridors. **Parking:** on-site.
Terms: cancellation fee imposed, package plans. **Amenities:** video games, irons, hair dryers. **Pool(s):**
heated indoor. **Leisure Activities:** saunas, whirlpool, exercise room. **Guest Services:** valet and coin laundry. **Business
Services:** meeting rooms. **Cards:** AX, CB, DC, DS, MC, VI.

SOME UNITS

(A$K) (S/D) (⎁⎁) (Y) (⇌) (⊠) (🎦) (DATA PORT) (💻) / (⊠) (📠) (🖨) /

KNIGHTS INN
Phone: 304/420-2420
3/1-10/1   1P: $45-$100   2P: $50-$100   XP: $5   F17
10/2-2/28   1P: $40-$80   2P: $45-$80   XP: $5   F17
Motel   **Location:** I-77, exit 176, just w. 3604 1/2 7th St 26104. Fax: 304/420-2427. **Facility:** 51 one-bedroom standard
units, some with whirlpools. 1 story, exterior corridors. **Parking:** on-site. **Terms:** weekly rates available.
Business Services: meeting rooms. **Cards:** AX, CB, DC, DS, MC, VI.

SOME UNITS

(A$K) (S/D) (⎁⎁⁺) (🎦) / (⊠) (🖨) /
FEE

RED ROOF INN *Book at aaa.com* Phone: (304)485-1741

5/16-8/21	1P: $47-$58	2P: $52-$63	XP: $5 F17
8/22-2/28	1P: $45-$58	2P: $50-$63	XP: $5 F17
3/1-5/15	1P: $42-$58	2P: $48-$63	XP: $5 F17

Motel

Location: I-77, exit 176, just w on US 50. 3714 E 7th St 26104. Fax: 304/485-1746. **Facility:** 106 one-bedroom standard units. 2 stories (no elevator), exterior corridors. **Parking:** on-site. **Terms:** weekly rates available, package plans, small pets only. **Amenities:** video games, voice mail. *Some:* irons, hair dryers. **Leisure Activities:** exercise room. **Guest Services:** coin laundry. **Business Services:** meeting rooms. **Cards:** AX, DC, DS, MC, VI.

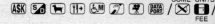

——— WHERE TO DINE ———

J. P. HENRY'S Dinner: $6-$20 Phone: 304/485-9390

American

Location: I-77, exit 179, 2.4 mi sw on SR 86. 5106 Emerson Ave 26101. **Hours:** 4 pm-11 pm, Sat & Sun from 1 pm. Closed: 12/25. **Features:** At this restaurant they do all the work, so you can have all the fun. Friendly service and a very diverse menu. Casual dress; cocktails. **Parking:** on-site. **Cards:** AX, CB, DC, DS, JC, MC, VI.

MOUNTAINEER FAMILY RESTAURANT Lunch: $4-$10 Dinner: $6-$12 Phone: 304/422-0101

American

Location: I-77, exit 176, just w. 4006 7th St 26101. **Hours:** 24 hours. Closed: 12/25. **Features:** With the restaurant being open 24 hours a day, it gives the guest great freedom to come and dine anytime, and that is their motto: Mountaineers are always free. Casual dress. **Parking:** on-site. **Cards:** AX, CB, DC, DS, MC, VI.

PETERSBURG pop. 2,423

——— WHERE TO STAY ———

HERMITAGE MOTOR INN Phone: (304)257-1711

All Year [CP] 1P: $53-$55 2P: $59-$61 XP: $6 F12

Small-scale Hotel

Location: 0.3 mi n on US 220/SR 28/55. 203 Virginia Ave 26847 (PO Box 1077). Fax: 304/257-4330. **Facility:** 38 one-bedroom standard units. 2 stories (no elevator), interior/exterior corridors. *Bath:* combo or shower only. **Parking:** on-site. **Terms:** weekly rates available. **Dining:** Hermitage Inn Restaurant, see separate listing. **Pool(s):** outdoor. **Leisure Activities:** whirlpool. **Guest Services:** gift shop. **Business Services:** meeting rooms. **Cards:** AX, CB, DC, DS, MC, VI.

HOMESTEAD INN AND MOTEL Phone: (304)257-1049

All Year 1P: $45-$52 2P: $55-$58 XP: $5 F6

Motel

Location: On SR 55 and 28, 1.5 mi w. Located in a rural area. SR 28/55 26847 (HC 59, Box 146). Fax: 304/257-9564. **Facility:** 12 one-bedroom standard units. 2 stories (no elevator), exterior corridors. **Parking:** on-site. **Terms:** weekly rates available. **Guest Services:** gift shop. **Cards:** AX, CB, DC, DS, MC, VI.

——— WHERE TO DINE ———

HERMITAGE INN RESTAURANT Lunch: $5-$12 Dinner: $7-$19 Phone: 304/257-4800

American

Location: 0.3 mi n on US 220/SR 28/55; in Hermitage Motor Inn. 203 Virginia Ave 26847. **Hours:** 11 am-9 pm, Sat from 4 pm, Sun 11 am-2 pm. Closed: 12/25. **Features:** Homespun goodness, country cooking and friendly service await patrons of the restaurant. Casual dress. **Parking:** on-site. **Cards:** AX, CB, DC, DS, JC, MC, VI.

PHILIPPI pop. 2,870

——— WHERE TO STAY ———

PHILIPPI LODGING Phone: (304)457-5888

All Year 1P: $45-$58 2P: $53-$64 XP: $5 F

Motel

Location: 2.5 mi s on US 250. Rt 4, Box 155 26416. Fax: 304/457-5888. **Facility:** 39 one-bedroom standard units, some with whirlpools. 2 stories (no elevator), interior corridors. **Parking:** on-site. **Terms:** small pets only. **Cards:** AX, DC, DS, MC, VI.

——— WHERE TO DINE ———

PHILIPPI INN RESTAURANT Lunch: $5-$12 Dinner: $6-$17 Phone: 304/457-1733

American

Location: On US 250, 2.5 mi s. Rt 250 S 26416. **Hours:** 6 am-8 pm, Fri & Sat-9 pm, Sun 7 am-8 pm. Closed: 11/24, 12/25. **Features:** This restaurant thrives on home cooking, a huge menu selection and a friendly, welcoming staff. Casual dress. **Parking:** on-site. **Cards:** MC, VI.

PRINCETON pop. 6,347

——— WHERE TO STAY ———

COMFORT INN-PRINCETON   *Book at aaa.com*   **Phone:** (304)487-6101
▼▼▼▼   All Year [ECP]   1P: $70-$75   2P: $75-$80   XP: $6   F18
Location: I-77, exit 9, 0.3 mi w on US 460. Ambrose Ln & US 460 24740 (Rt 4, Box 222). **Fax:** 304/425-7002.
Small-scale Hotel   **Facility:** 51 one-bedroom standard units, some with whirlpools. 2 stories (no elevator), interior corridors.
Parking: on-site. **Amenities:** safes, irons, hair dryers. **Leisure Activities:** whirlpool. **Guest Services:** valet
laundry. **Cards:** AX, CB, DC, DS, MC, VI.

SOME UNITS
(A$K) (S/D) (¶↑) (⌂) (☆) (DATA PORT) (▭) / (✕) (📷) (🖥) /

DAYS INN   *Book at aaa.com*   **Phone:** (304)425-8100
AAA (SAVE)   All Year   1P: $48-$63   2P: $53-$78   XP: $5   F17
▼▼▼▼   **Location:** I-77, exit 9, 0.3 mi w on US 460, just s on Ambrose Ln, then just e. Graveled truck and camper parking on
site. 347 Meadowfield Ln 24740. **Fax:** 304/487-1734. **Facility:** 122 one-bedroom standard units. 2 stories (no
Small-scale Hotel   elevator), exterior corridors. **Parking:** on-site. **Terms:** 3 night minimum stay - seasonal, 3 day cancellation
notice, pets ($5 extra charge). **Amenities:** voice mail, hair dryers. *Some:* irons. **Pool(s):** indoor. **Leisure
Activities:** whirlpool. **Guest Services:** coin laundry. **Business Services:** meeting rooms. **Cards:** AX, CB,
DC, DS, JC, MC, VI. **Special Amenities:** free expanded continental breakfast and free local telephone calls.

SOME UNITS
(S/D) (🐾) (¶↑) (⌂) (🛏) (☆) (DATA PORT) (▭) / (✕) (🖥) (🖥) /
FEE   FEE

HAMPTON INN   *Book at aaa.com*   **Phone:** 304/431-2580
▼▼▼▼   All Year [ECP]   1P: $86-$94   2P: $91-$99
Location: I-77, exit 9, 0.3 mi w on US 460, just s on Ambrose Ln, then just e. 277 Meadowfield Ln 24740.
Small-scale Hotel   **Fax:** 304/431-2366. **Facility:** 112 one-bedroom standard units. 5 stories, interior corridors. *Bath:* combo or
shower only. **Parking:** on-site. **Amenities:** irons, hair dryers. **Pool(s):** heated indoor. **Leisure
Activities:** whirlpool, exercise room. **Guest Services:** valet laundry. **Business Services:** meeting rooms. **Cards:** AX, DC, DS,
MC, VI.

SOME UNITS
(A$K) (S/D) (¶↑) (🛏) (⌂) (🛏) (☆) (DATA PORT) (▭) / (✕) /

SLEEP INN   *Book at aaa.com*   **Phone:** (304)431-2800
▼▼ ▼▼   All Year [ECP]   1P: $55-$125   2P: $60-$150
Location: I-77, exit 9, just w on US 460, then just n via service road. 1015 Oakvale Rd 24740 (PO Box 5625).
Small-scale Hotel   **Fax:** 304/425-7693. **Facility:** 81 one-bedroom standard units. 3 stories, interior corridors. *Bath:* combo or
shower only. **Parking:** on-site. **Terms:** small pets only. **Amenities:** safes, irons, hair dryers. **Pool(s):** heated
indoor. **Leisure Activities:** whirlpool. **Guest Services:** valet laundry. **Business Services:** meeting rooms. **Cards:** AX, CB, DC,
DS, MC, VI.

SOME UNITS
(A$K) (S/D) (🐾) (🛏) (⌂) (🛏) (☆) (DATA PORT) (▭) / (✕) (🖥) (🖥) /

RIPLEY pop. 3,263

——— WHERE TO STAY ———

**BEST WESTERN MCCOYS INN & CONFERENCE
CENTER**   *Book at aaa.com*   **Phone:** 304/372-9122
AAA (SAVE)   All Year [ECP]   1P: $69-$89   2P: $69-$89
Location: I-77, exit 138, just e. 701 W Main St 25271. **Fax:** 304/372-4400. **Facility:** 123 one-bedroom standard
▼▼▼▼   units. 2 stories (no elevator), interior/exterior corridors. **Parking:** on-site. **Terms:** package plans, small pets
only (in kennel). **Amenities:** irons, hair dryers. **Dining:** 5 pm-10 pm, cocktails. **Pool(s):** heated outdoor.
Small-scale Hotel   **Business Services:** conference facilities, administrative services. **Cards:** AX, CB, DC, DS, MC, VI.
Special Amenities: free expanded continental breakfast and free local telephone calls.

SOME UNITS
(S/D) (🐾) (¶↑) (⌂) (🛏) (📠) (☆) (DATA PORT) (▭) / (✕) (VCR) (🖥) /
FEE

HOLIDAY INN EXPRESS   *Book at aaa.com*   **Phone:** 304/372-5000
AAA (SAVE)   All Year [BP]   1P: $79-$89   2P: $79-$89
▼▼▼▼   **Location:** I-77, exit 138, just w on SR 33, then 0.3 mi n. 1 Hospitality Dr 25271. **Fax:** 304/372-5600. **Facility:** 65
one-bedroom standard units, some with whirlpools. 2 stories (no elevator), interior/exterior corridors. *Bath:*
combo or shower only. **Parking:** on-site. **Amenities:** high-speed Internet, dual phone lines, voice mail,
Small-scale Hotel   irons, hair dryers. **Leisure Activities:** exercise room. **Guest Services:** valet laundry. **Business Services:**
meeting rooms. **Cards:** AX, CB, DC, DS, MC, VI. **Special Amenities:** free full breakfast and free local
telephone calls.

SOME UNITS
(S/D) (¶↑) (🛏) (⌂) (☆) (DATA PORT) (▭) / (✕) (🖥) (🖥) /

RIPLEY SUPER 8 MOTEL   **Phone:** (304)372-8880
▼▼▼   All Year   1P: $48-$54   2P: $60-$70   XP: $6   F12
Location: I-77, exit 138, just e on SR 33. 102 Duke Dr 25271. **Fax:** 304/372-8880. **Facility:** 44 one-bedroom
Motel   standard units. 2 stories (no elevator), interior corridors. **Parking:** on-site. **Terms:** package plans, small pets
only. **Cards:** AX, CB, DC, DS, MC, VI.

SOME UNITS
(A$K) (S/D) (🐾) (¶↑) (⌂) (☆) (DATA PORT) (▭) / (✕) (🖥) (▭) /

——— WHERE TO DINE ———

FRATELLO'S   **Lunch:** $6-$15   **Dinner:** $6-$20   **Phone:** 304/373-0070
▼▼▼   **Location:** I-77, exit 132, just ne. 1825 Rt 21 S & I-77 25271. **Hours:** 10:30 am-9 pm, Fri & Sat-10 pm, Sun noon-
9 pm. Closed: 1/1, 11/24, 12/25. **Features:** The diverse menu lists award-winning pasta dishes and other
Italian   Italian favorites. Families appreciate the pleasant atmosphere. Homemade ice cream is a delicious meal-
ender. Casual dress; cocktails. **Parking:** on-site. **Cards:** MC, VI.

(✕)

RIPPON

———— WHERE TO DINE ————

JOHN'S FAMILY RESTAURANT　　　**Lunch:** $5-$12　　　**Dinner:** $7-$18　　　**Phone:** 304/725-4348
◆◆◆ ◆◆◆　　**Location:** Center. Rt 340 25441. **Hours:** 7 am-9:30 pm. Closed: 1/1, 3/27, 12/25; also Sun. **Features:** This
　　　　　　restaurant has a family atmosphere, home cooking and friendly people. Casual dress. **Parking:** on-site.
American　　**Cards:** MC, VI.
　　　⊠

ROANOKE

———— WHERE TO STAY ————

STONEWALL RESORT　　*Book at aaa.com*　　　　　　　　　　　　　　　　　　　　**Phone:** (304)269-7400
ⒶⒶⒶ ⓈⒶⓋⒺ　　All Year　　　　　　　　1P: $99-$159　　　2P: $99-$159　　　XP: $20　　　　F18
◆◆◆ ◆◆◆◆　　**Location:** I-79, exit 91, just e. 940 Resort Dr 26337. Fax: 304/269-4358. **Facility:** This property is close to nature
　　　　　　　but far from ordinary. Nestled in the mountains, this resort brings guests close to nature with a retreatlike
Resort　　　ambience enhanced by many dining and recreational choices. 208 units. 198 one-bedroom standard units,
Large-scale Hotel　some with whirlpools. 10 cottages ($250-$450). 3 stories, interior/exterior corridors. *Bath:* combo or shower
　　　　　only. **Parking:** on-site. **Terms:** check-in 4 pm, $8 service charge. **Amenities:** high-speed Internet, voice
mail, irons, hair dryers. *Some:* CD players. **Dining:** 6:30 am-11 pm, cocktails, also, Stillwaters Restaurant,
see separate listing. **Pool(s):** heated indoor/outdoor. **Leisure Activities:** saunas, whirlpools, steamrooms, boating, marina,
waterskiing, fishing, excursion tour boat, recreation programs, badminton, bocci, croquet, bicycles, hiking trails, playground,
exercise room, spa, basketball, horseshoes, volleyball. *Fee:* canoes, paddleboats, golf-18 holes, 3 lighted tennis courts, game
room. **Guest Services:** valet laundry, area transportation-within 10 mi. **Business Services:** conference facilities. **Cards:** AX,
DC, DS, MC, VI. **Special Amenities:** free local telephone calls and free newspaper. *(See color ad p 326)*

　　　　　　　　　　　　　　　　　　　　　　　　　　　　　　　　　　SOME UNITS
　　　　　　　　⊗ ⊗ ⊗ ⊗ ⊗ ⊗ ⊗ ⊗ / ⊗ ⊗ ⊗ /

———— WHERE TO DINE ————

STILLWATERS RESTAURANT　　　**Lunch:** $8-$18　　　**Dinner:** $12-$26　　　**Phone:** 304/269-7400
◆◆◆ ◆◆◆◆　**Location:** I-79, exit 91, just e; in Stonewall Resort. 940 Resort Dr 26447. **Hours:** 7 am-11 pm. **Features:** As the
　　　　　　name implies, the restaurant nurtures a tranquil setting. Lakeside seating is a seasonal option. Casual
American　　dress; cocktails. **Parking:** on-site. **Cards:** AX, CB, DC, DS, JC, MC, VI.
　　　　　　　　　　　　　　　　　　　　　　　　　　　　　　　　　　　　　　⊗ ⊠

ROMNEY pop. 1,940

———— WHERE TO STAY ————

HAMPSHIRE HOUSE 1884　　　　　　　　　　　　　　　　　　　　　　　**Phone:** (304)822-7171
◆◆◆ ◆◆◆　All Year [BP]　　　　　　　　　　　　　2P: $80-$100　　　　XP: $15
　　　　　　Location: Just ne of jct US 50 and SR 28; center. 165 N Grafton St 26757. Fax: 304/822-7582. **Facility:** An old-
Historic Bed　time music box in the front room plays period tunes at this restored 1880s-era inn located in West Virginia's
& Breakfast　oldest hamlet. Designated smoking area. 6 one-bedroom standard units. 2 stories (no elevator), interior
　　　　　corridors. *Bath:* combo or shower only. **Parking:** on-site. **Terms:** 3 day cancellation notice.
Amenities: video library. **Leisure Activities:** bicycles. **Business Services:** meeting rooms. **Cards:** AX, DC, DS, MC, VI.

　　　　　　　　　　　　　　　　　　　　　　　　　SOME UNITS
　　　　　　　　⊗ ⊗ ⊗ ⊗ / ⊗ ⊗ ⊗ ⊗ ⊗ /

———— WHERE TO DINE ————

MARIO'S ITALIAN CUISINE　　　**Lunch:** $6-$12　　　**Dinner:** $6-$18　　　**Phone:** 304/822-7776
◆◆◆ ◆◆◆　**Location:** Just s. 33 S High St 26757. **Hours:** 11 am-9 pm. Closed: 12/25; also Mon. **Features:** The fun and
　　　　　　casual hometown place prepares many homemade pasta and desserts with care. Casual dress; beer only.
Italian　　**Parking:** street. **Cards:** AX, CB, DC, DS, JC, MC, VI.
　　⊠

ST. ALBANS pop. 11,567

———— WHERE TO STAY ————

SMILEY'S MOTEL　　　　　　　　　　　　　　　　　　　　　　　　　　**Phone:** (304)766-6231
ⒶⒶⒶ ⓈⒶⓋⒺ　　All Year　　　　　　　　1P: $50-$60　　　2P: $50-$60　　　XP: $10　　　　F16
◆　　　　　**Location:** I-64, exit 54, 3.2 mi w on US 60. Located in a commercial area. 6210 MacCorkle Ave SW 25177.
　　　　　　Fax: 304/768-4938. **Facility:** 135 one-bedroom standard units, some with whirlpools. 2 stories (no elevator),
Small-scale Hotel　exterior corridors. **Parking:** on-site. **Terms:** 30 day cancellation notice, weekly rates available, package
　　　　　plans. **Amenities:** *Some:* hair dryers. **Dining:** 6 am-2 & 5-10 pm, cocktails. **Pool(s):** outdoor. **Leisure
Activities:** racquetball courts, picnic area on river with barbecue grills. **Guest Services:** coin laundry.
Business Services: meeting rooms. **Cards:** AX, DC, MC, VI. **Special Amenities:** free local telephone calls and free
newspaper.

　　　　　　　　　　　　　　　　　　　　　　　　　　　SOME UNITS
　　　　　　　⊗ ⊗ ⊗ ⊗ ⊗ ⊗ / ⊗ ⊗ ⊗ ⊗ /

SHEPHERDSTOWN pop. 803

------ **WHERE TO STAY** ------

BAVARIAN INN

Phone: (304)876-2551

(AAA) [SAVE]

| | 9/1-11/15 | 1P: $105-$300 | 2P: $105-$300 | XP: $10 | F |
| | 3/1-8/31 & 11/16-2/28 | 1P: $95-$285 | 2P: $95-$285 | XP: $10 | F |

▼▽▼▽▼▽ **Location:** 0.3 mi n on SR 480 at south end of Potomac River Bridge. 164 Shepherd Grade Rd 25443.
Fax: 304/876-9355. **Facility:** A gazebo and walkways add appeal to the gardens around this Alpine-style
Small-scale Hotel complex's chalets, all of which offer good views of the Potomac River. 72 one-bedroom standard units. 3-4
stories, interior/exterior corridors. **Parking:** on-site. **Terms:** cancellation fee imposed, package plans.
Amenities: CD players, high-speed Internet, voice mail, irons, hair dryers. *Some:* DVD players. **Dining:** restaurant, see
separate listing. **Pool(s):** outdoor. **Leisure Activities:** putting green, lighted tennis court, exercise room. *Fee:* golf & tennis
privileges, bicycles. **Guest Services:** gift shop, valet laundry. **Business Services:** meeting rooms. **Cards:** AX, DC, DS,
MC, VI. *(See color ad p 975)*

SOME UNITS

[⊓] [Y] [&M] [🖉] [⊇] [✕] [✕] [📹] [DATA PORT] [💻] / [VCR] [📠] /

CLARION HOTEL & CONFERENCE CENTER   *Book at aaa.com*

Phone: (304)876-7000

(AAA) [SAVE]

| | 5/1-10/31 | 1P: $109-$129 | 2P: $109-$129 | XP: $10 | F18 |
| | 3/1-4/30 & 11/1-2/28 | 1P: $84-$104 | 2P: $84-$104 | XP: $10 | F18 |

▼▽▼▽ **Location:** Just s on SR 480; center. 233 Lowe Dr 25443. Fax: 304/876-8454. **Facility:** 168 one-bedroom
standard units, some with whirlpools. 4 stories, interior corridors. *Bath:* combo or shower only. **Parking:** on-
Small-scale Hotel site. **Terms:** check-in 4 pm, cancellation fee imposed, package plans. **Amenities:** high-speed Internet,
voice mail, irons, hair dryers. **Dining:** 6:30 am-2 & 5-10 pm. **Pool(s):** outdoor. **Leisure Activities:** saunas,
whirlpool, aerobic instruction, indoor walking & running track, hiking trails, exercise room, basketball, volleyball. *Fee:* golf &
tennis privileges. **Guest Services:** coin laundry, area transportation-within 5 mi. **Business Services:** conference facilities,
business center. **Cards:** AX, DC, DS, MC, VI.

SOME UNITS

[S/D] [✈] [⊓] [Y] [&M] [⊇] [🖉] [⊇] [✕] [📹] [DATA PORT] [💻] / [✕] [📠] [📺] /
FEE   FEE FEE

DAYS INN

Phone: (304)876-3160

(AAA) [SAVE]

| | All Year | 1P: $94-$117 | 2P: $94-$117 | XP: $10 | D17 |

▼▽▼▽ **Location:** Just w on SR 45; center. 70 Maddex Square Dr 25443. Fax: 304/876-3161. **Facility:** 51 one-bedroom
standard units. 3 stories, interior corridors. *Bath:* combo or shower only. **Parking:** on-site.
Terms: cancellation fee imposed. **Amenities:** voice mail, hair dryers. **Business Services:** meeting rooms.
Small-scale Hotel **Cards:** AX, DC, DS, MC, VI. **Special Amenities:** free continental breakfast and free newspaper.

SOME UNITS

[S/D] [⊇] [DATA PORT] [💻] / [✕] [📠] [📺] /

------ **WHERE TO DINE** ------

BAVARIAN INN

Lunch: $7-$15   Dinner: $17-$32   Phone: 304/876-2551

(AAA)

▼▽▼▽ **Location:** 0.3 mi n on SR 480 at south end of Potomac River Bridge; in Bavarian Inn. 164 Shepherd Grade Rd 25443.
Hours: 7-10:30 am, 11:30-2:30 & 5-10 pm, Sat 7-10:30 am, 11:30-2:30 & 4-10 pm, Sun 7 am-10:30 & noon-
Continental 9 pm. **Reservations:** suggested. **Features:** German and American cuisine is served in a 1930s gray stone
residence surrounded by well-manicured grounds. Wiener schnitzel is notably flavorful, and the well-
presented torte is tasty and light. Service is courteous and prompt. Dressy casual; cocktails. **Parking:** on-
site. **Cards:** AX, CB, DC, DS, MC, VI. **Country Inn** *(See color ad p 975)*   [Y] [✕]

THE YELLOW BRICK BANK RESTAURANT

Lunch: $6-$12   Dinner: $14-$25   Phone: 304/876-2208

▼▽▼ **Location:** Just e on German St; center. 201 German St 25443. **Hours:** 11 am-9 pm. Closed: 11/24, 12/25.
Features: Set in an old bank with a bright new atmosphere, the restaurant has a wide variety on the menu
American and friendly service. Casual dress; cocktails. **Parking:** street. **Cards:** CB, DC, MC, VI.   [Y] [✕]

SNOWSHOE

------ **WHERE TO STAY** ------

INN AT SNOWSHOE

Phone: (304)572-6520

(AAA) [SAVE]

| | 3/1-4/8 & 11/16-2/28 | 1P: $89-$229 | | | |
| | 4/9-11/15 | 1P: $89-$149 | | | |

▼▽▼▽ **Location:** 0.5 mi e on SR 66, from US 219 jct, follow signs. SR 66 26209 (PO Box 10). Fax: 304/572-6537.
Facility: Recreational opportunities abound at this sprawling complex where visitors can ski, golf, watch
Resort wildlife or stroll to nearby shops. 149 one-bedroom standard units, some with whirlpools. 2 stories, interior
Small-scale Hotel corridors. **Parking:** on-site. **Terms:** check-in 5 pm, 21 day cancellation notice, package plans.
Amenities: voice mail, irons, hair dryers. **Dining:** 6:30 am-11 & 5:30-10 pm, cocktails. **Pool(s):** heated
indoor. **Leisure Activities:** whirlpools, exercise room, horseshoes, volleyball, game room. *Fee:* ski equipment, bicycles,
horseback riding. **Guest Services:** gift shop, coin laundry. **Business Services:** meeting rooms. **Cards:** AX, DC, DS, MC, VI.

SOME UNITS

[S/D] [⊓] [Y] [🖉] [⊇] [✕] [📹] [DATA PORT] / [✕] [📠] [📺] [💻] /

------ **WHERE TO DINE** ------

RED FOX RESTAURANT

Dinner: $18-$36   Phone: 304/572-1111

▼▽▼▽ **Location:** Jct US 219/55 and SR 66, 0.6 mi e on SR 66, 6 mi n on CR 9/3 (Snowshoe Rd). 1 Whistlepunk Village
26209. **Hours:** Open 3/1-3/31 & 6/1-2/28; 5:30 pm-10 pm; to 9:30 pm 6/1-10/15. Closed: 11/1-11/30; Mon &
Continental Tues 5/30-10/15. **Reservations:** suggested. **Features:** Beautiful mountain views enhance the upscale,
intimate atmosphere. An excellent wine list accompanies tempting preparations of poultry, seafood, steak
and even some wild game. A professional, well-attired staff provides service. Casual dress; cocktails. **Parking:** on-site.
Cards: AX, DS, MC, VI.   [Y] [✕]

SOUTH CHARLESTON pop. 13,390—*See also CHARLESTON.*

——— WHERE TO STAY ———

HOLIDAY INN EXPRESS HOTEL & SUITES   *Book at aaa.com*   Phone: (304)746-4748
▼▼▼▼▼   All Year   1P: $79-$149   2P: $79-$149   XP: $10   F17
Small-scale Hotel   Location: I-64, exit 58A, 3.5 mi s. 95 RHL Blvd 25309. Fax: 304/746-4749. Facility: 84 one-bedroom standard units, some with whirlpools. 5 stories, interior corridors. *Bath:* combo or shower only. Parking: on-site. Terms: cancellation fee imposed, [ECP] meal plan available. Amenities: high-speed Internet, dual phone lines, voice mail, irons, hair dryers. Pool(s): heated indoor. Leisure Activities: whirlpool, exercise room. Guest Services: valet and coin laundry. Business Services: meeting rooms, business center. Cards: AX, CB, DC, DS, JC, MC, VI.

SOME UNITS
(ASK) (S⌀) (†↑) (&) (⇌) (※) (DATA PORT) (⊟) (⊞) (⊑) / (✕) /

MICROTEL INN   *Book at aaa.com*   Phone: (304)744-4900
▼▼▼▼   3/1-10/31   1P: $47-$59   2P: $47-$59   XP: $5   F18
          11/1-2/28   1P: $42-$54   2P: $42-$54   XP: $5   F18
Small-scale Hotel   Location: I-64, exit 56, just ne. Located in an industrial area. 600 2nd Ave 25303. Fax: 304/744-6300. Facility: 102 one-bedroom standard units. 3 stories, interior corridors. *Bath:* combo or shower only. Parking: on-site. Terms: weekly rates available, package plans. Amenities: video games, safes. Guest Services: valet laundry. Cards: AX, DC, DS, MC, VI.

SOME UNITS
(ASK) (S⌀) (&) (†↑) (※) (DATA PORT) / (✕) (⊟) (⊞) /
FEE   FEE

RAMADA PLAZA HOTEL CHARLESTON   *Book at aaa.com*   Phone: (304)744-4641
▼▼▼▼   All Year [BP]   1P: $85-$94   2P: $85-$94   XP: $10   F18
Small-scale Hotel   Location: I-64, exit 56, just nw. Located in an industrial area. 400 2nd Ave 25303. Fax: 304/744-4525. Facility: 173 one-bedroom standard units, some with whirlpools. 6 stories, interior corridors. Parking: on-site. Terms: [MAP] meal plan available, pets ($10 extra charge). Amenities: video games, dual phone lines, voice mail, irons, hair dryers. Pool(s): heated indoor. Leisure Activities: whirlpool, exercise room. Guest Services: valet laundry. Business Services: conference facilities, business center. Cards: AX, DC, DS, MC, VI. *(See color ad below)*

SOME UNITS
(ASK) (S⌀) (✈) (🛏) (†↑) (🍸) (👂) (⇌) (※) (DATA PORT) (⊑) / (✕) (⊟) (⊞) /
FEE

WINGATE INN-CHARLESTON   *Book at aaa.com*   Phone: (304)744-4444
▼▼▼▼   All Year [ECP]   1P: $97-$140   2P: $97-$140   XP: $10   F18
Small-scale Hotel   Location: I-64, exit 56, just nw. Located in an industrial area. 402 2nd Ave 25303. Fax: 304/744-4343. Facility: 94 one-bedroom standard units, some with whirlpools. 6 stories, interior corridors. *Bath:* combo or shower only. Parking: on-site. Terms: 14 day cancellation notice. Amenities: video games, high-speed Internet, voice mail, safes, irons, hair dryers. Leisure Activities: whirlpool, exercise room. Guest Services: coin laundry, area transportation. Business Services: meeting rooms, business center. Cards: AX, DC, DS, MC, VI.

SOME UNITS
(ASK) (S⌀) (✈) (†↑) (&) (※) (DATA PORT) (⊟) (⊞) (⊑) / (✕) /

——— WHERE TO DINE ———

TANG'S   Lunch: $6-$14   Dinner: $6-$18   Phone: 304/746-9588
▼▼   Location: I-64, exit 58A, 3.9 mi s on US 119. 2478 Mountaineer Blvd 25309. Hours: 11 am-10:30 pm.
Chinese   Features: Guests can sample Chinese favorites in a lively atmosphere decorated with Oriental appointments. Servers are friendly. Casual dress; cocktails. Parking: on-site. Cards: AX, DS, MC, VI.

(🍸) (✕)

STAR CITY pop. 1,366—*See also MORGANTOWN.*

———— WHERE TO STAY ————

ECONO LODGE-COLISEUM   *Book at aaa.com*   Phone: 304/599-8181

(AAA) (SAVE)

All Year   1P: $59-$66   2P: $59-$66
Location: I-79, exit 155, 1.4 mi s on US 119/SR 7. 3506 Monongahela Blvd 26505. Fax: 304/599-8186. **Facility:** 70 one-bedroom standard units, some with whirlpools. 2 stories (no elevator), exterior corridors. *Bath:* combo or shower only. **Parking:** on-site. **Terms:** small pets only (with prior approval). **Cards:** AX, DC, MC, VI.

Small-scale Hotel **Special Amenities: free continental breakfast and free local telephone calls.**

SOME UNITS

HOLIDAY INN MORGANTOWN   *Book at aaa.com*   Phone: (304)599-1680

(AAA) (SAVE)

4/3-10/31   1P: $72-$129   2P: $72-$129
3/1-4/2 & 11/1-2/28   1P: $63-$73   2P: $63-$73
Location: I-79, exit 155, 1.7 mi s on US 119/SR 7. 1400 Saratoga Ave 26505. Fax: 304/598-0989. **Facility:** 146 one-bedroom standard units. 2-4 stories (no elevator), exterior corridors. *Bath:* combo or shower only.

Small-scale Hotel **Parking:** on-site. **Terms:** cancellation fee imposed, package plans, small pets only. **Amenities:** voice mail, irons, hair dryers. **Dining:** 6 am-10 & 5-10 pm, Sat & Sun 7 am-11 & 5-10 pm, cocktails. **Pool(s):** outdoor. **Guest Services:** valet laundry, area transportation-hospital. **Business Services:** conference facilities. **Cards:** AX, DC, DS, MC, VI.

SOME UNITS

SUMMERSVILLE pop. 3,294

———— WHERE TO STAY ————

BEST WESTERN SUMMERSVILLE LAKE MOTOR LODGE   *Book at aaa.com*   Phone: (304)872-6900

(AAA) (SAVE)

5/1-10/31   1P: $60-$66   2P: $66-$80   XP: $7   F12
3/1-4/30 & 11/1-2/28   1P: $50-$60   2P: $60-$70   XP: $7   F12
Location: US 19 and Broad St; 0.6 mi s of jct SR 39. Located in busy industrial area. 1203 S Broad St 26651. Fax: 304/872-6908. **Facility:** 58 one-bedroom standard units. 3 stories, exterior corridors. **Parking:** on-site.

Small-scale Hotel **Terms:** small pets only ($7 fee). **Amenities:** irons, hair dryers. **Guest Services:** coin laundry. **Cards:** AX, CB, DC, DS, MC, VI. **Special Amenities: free continental breakfast and free local telephone calls.**

SOME UNITS

COMFORT INN   *Book at aaa.com*   Phone: (304)872-6500

(AAA) (SAVE)

4/1-10/31 [CP]   1P: $70-$150   2P: $70-$150   XP: $7   F18
3/1-3/31 & 11/1-2/28 [CP]   1P: $65-$135   2P: $65-$135   XP: $7   F18
Location: US 19, 1.9 mi n of jct SR 39. 903 Industrial Dr N 26651. Fax: 304/872-3090. **Facility:** 99 one-bedroom standard units, some with whirlpools. 2 stories (no elevator), interior corridors. *Bath:* combo or shower only.

Small-scale Hotel **Parking:** on-site. **Terms:** 30 day cancellation notice-fee imposed, small pets only ($5 extra charge, in smoking units). **Amenities:** irons, hair dryers. **Pool(s):** heated outdoor, wading. **Leisure Activities:** sauna, racquetball courts, recreation programs, exercise room. **Guest Services:** coin laundry. **Business Services:** meeting rooms. **Cards:** AX, DC, DS, MC, VI. **Special Amenities: free continental breakfast and free local telephone calls.**

SOME UNITS

COUNTRY INN & SUITES   *Book at aaa.com*   Phone: (304)872-0555

(AAA) (SAVE)

All Year   1P: $62-$119
Location: US 19, just w. 106 Merchants Walk 26651. Fax: 304/872-9585. **Facility:** 106 one-bedroom standard units, some with whirlpools. 4 stories, interior corridors. *Bath:* combo or shower only. **Parking:** on-site. **Amenities:** irons, hair dryers. **Pool(s):** outdoor. **Leisure Activities:** whirlpool, exercise room. **Guest**

Small-scale Hotel **Services:** valet laundry. **Business Services:** meeting rooms. **Cards:** AX, DC, DS, MC, VI.

(See color ad p 965)

SOME UNITS

HAMPTON INN   *Book at aaa.com*   Phone: 304/872-7100

5/22-10/17   1P: $67-$77   2P: $72-$81
3/1-5/21 & 10/18-2/28   1P: $59-$64   2P: $64-$69
Small-scale Hotel **Location:** Just s on SR 41 from US 19. 5400 Webster Rd 26651. Fax: 304/872-7101. **Facility:** 76 one-bedroom standard units. 3 stories, interior corridors. *Bath:* combo or shower only. **Parking:** on-site. **Terms:** [ECP] meal plan available. **Amenities:** high-speed Internet, voice mail, irons, hair dryers. *Some:* DVD players. **Pool(s):** outdoor. **Leisure Activities:** playground, exercise room, horseshoes. **Business Services:** meeting rooms. **Cards:** AX, DC, DS, MC, VI.

SOME UNITS

SLEEP INN OF SUMMERSVILLE   *Book at aaa.com*   Phone: (304)872-4500

(AAA) (SAVE)

4/2-11/1 [CP]   1P: $55-$95   2P: $60-$100   XP: $7   F18
11/2-2/28 [CP]   1P: $50-$80   2P: $55-$85   XP: $7   F18
3/1-4/1 [CP]   1P: $45-$75   2P: $50-$80   XP: $7   F18
Location: US 19, 1.7 mi n of jct SR 39. Located at Northside Plaza. 701 Professional Park Dr 26651.
Small-scale Hotel Fax: 304/872-0288. **Facility:** 97 one-bedroom standard units. 2 stories (no elevator), interior corridors. *Bath:* combo or shower only. **Parking:** on-site. **Terms:** 30 day cancellation notice-fee imposed, small pets only ($5 extra charge, in smoking units). **Amenities:** *Some:* irons, hair dryers. **Pool(s):** heated outdoor. **Leisure Activities:** horseshoes, volleyball. **Guest Services:** coin laundry. **Business Services:** meeting rooms. **Cards:** AX, DC, DS, MC, VI. **Special Amenities: free continental breakfast and free local telephone calls.** SOME UNITS

SUPER 8 MOTEL-SUMMERSVILLE   *Book at aaa.com*   **Phone:** (304)872-4888
All Year   1P: $49-$58   2P: $54-$64   XP: $6   F
Location: US 19, just n. 306 Merchants Walk 26651. Fax: 304/872-4888. **Facility:** 56 one-bedroom standard
Small-scale Hotel   units. 3 stories (no elevator), interior corridors. **Parking:** on-site. **Terms:** cancellation fee imposed.
Amenities: safes. **Guest Services:** coin laundry. **Cards:** AX, CB, DC, DS, JC, MC, VI.

SOME UNITS

──────── WHERE TO DINE ────────

CORNERSTONE CAFE   **Dinner:** $12-$24   **Phone:** 304/872-8180
Location: Center. 800 Main St 26651. **Hours:** Open 3/1-12/31 & 2/1-2/28; 5 pm-9 pm, Fri & Sat-10 pm. Closed:
11/24, 12/25; also Sun. **Features:** The cafe sits in an old bank, with the vault still in view and a wonderful
collection of rooms and ambience. Patrons can stop in for lunch or dinner. Casual dress; cocktails. **Parking:**
American   on-site. **Cards:** AX, MC, VI.

TEAYS

──────── WHERE TO STAY ────────

DAYS INN TEAYS   *Book at aaa.com*   **Phone:** (304)729-3006
3/1-11/1   1P: $46-$50   2P: $50-$65   XP: $4   D17
11/2-2/28   1P: $42-$46   2P: $46-$60   XP: $4   D17
Motel   **Location:** I-64, exit 39, just n on SR 34, then just e. Located behind Liberty Square Shopping Center. Putnam Village Dr
25569 (PO Box 316). Fax: 304/729-3020. **Facility:** 89 one-bedroom standard units. 1 story, exterior corridors.
Bath: combo or shower only. **Parking:** on-site. **Amenities:** hair dryers. **Pool(s):** outdoor. **Business
Services:** meeting rooms. **Cards:** AX, DC, DS, MC, VI. **Special Amenities: free continental breakfast
and free local telephone calls.**

SOME UNITS

TRIADELPHIA pop. 817

──────── WHERE TO STAY ────────

HOLIDAY INN EXPRESS WHEELING EAST   *Book at aaa.com*   **Phone:** (304)547-1380
All Year [ECP]   1P: $69-$129   2P: $69-$129   XP: $10   F18
Location: I-70, exit 11. (RR 1, Box 258). Fax: 304/547-9270. **Facility:** 115 one-bedroom standard units. 2
stories (no elevator), interior corridors. *Bath:* combo or shower only. **Parking:** on-site. **Terms:** small pets
only ($10 extra charge). **Amenities:** high-speed Internet, voice mail, irons, hair dryers. **Pool(s):** outdoor.
Leisure Activities: exercise room. **Guest Services:** valet and coin laundry. **Business Services:** meeting
Small-scale Hotel   rooms, business center. **Cards:** AX, CB, DC, DS, JC, MC, VI. **Special Amenities: free expanded
continental breakfast.** *(See color ad p 993)*

SOME UNITS
FEE

WEIRTON pop. 20,411

──────── WHERE TO STAY ────────

AMERIHOST INN & SUITES WEIRTON   **Phone:** 304/723-0050
All Year   1P: $99   2P: $99   XP: $6   F18
[fyi]   Too new to rate. **Location:** US 22, exit 4. 1 AmeriHost Dr 26062. Fax: 304/723-6303. **Amenities:** 79 units,
Small-scale Hotel   coffeemakers, microwaves, refrigerators, pool. **Cards:** AX, CB, DC, DS, MC, VI.

HOLIDAY INN   *Book at aaa.com*   **Phone:** (304)723-5522
4/15-10/15   1P: $109-$159   2P: $109-$159   XP: $10   F18
3/1-4/14   1P: $99-$149   2P: $109-$159   XP: $10   F18
10/16-2/28   1P: $99-$149   2P: $99-$149   XP: $10   F18
Small-scale Hotel   **Location:** 4.5 mi e on US 22, exit Three Springs Dr. 350 Three Springs Dr 26062. Fax: 304/723-1608. **Facility:** 118
units. 114 one-bedroom standard units, some with whirlpools. 4 one-bedroom suites ($139-$159). 5 stories, interior corridors.
Bath: combo or shower only. **Parking:** on-site. **Terms:** cancellation fee imposed, [BP] & [MAP] meal
plans, pets ($50 extra charge, in designated units). **Amenities:** video games, high-speed Internet, voice mail, irons, hair dryers.
Pool(s): outdoor. **Leisure Activities:** exercise room, horseshoes, volleyball. **Guest Services:** coin laundry. **Business
Services:** meeting rooms. **Cards:** AX, DC, DS, MC, VI.

SOME UNITS
FEE

──────── WHERE TO DINE ────────

MARIO'S ITALIAN RESTAURANT   **Lunch:** $6-$12   **Dinner:** $6-$16   **Phone:** 304/748-1179
Location: 2.5 mi e on US 22. 3810 Main St 26062. **Hours:** 11 am-9 pm, Fri & Sat-10 pm, Sun noon-9 pm.
Closed major holidays. **Features:** Open since 1970, the restaurant is known for homemade spaghetti,
Italian   gnocchi, chicken and steak. The wait staff is welcoming and efficient. Casual dress; beer & wine only.
Parking: on-site. **Cards:** MC, VI.

WESTON pop. 4,317

—— WHERE TO STAY ——

COMFORT INN

Book at aaa.com
Phone: (304)269-7000
All Year   2P: $59-$109
Location: I-79, exit 99, just e. 2906 US 33 E 26452 (PO Box 666). Fax: 304/269-7001. **Facility:** 70 one-bedroom standard units, some with whirlpools. 2 stories (no elevator), exterior corridors. *Bath:* combo or shower only. **Parking:** on-site. **Terms:** pets ($10 extra charge, in designated units). **Amenities:** voice mail, irons, hair dryers. **Pool(s):** heated outdoor. **Business Services:** meeting rooms. **Cards:** AX, DC, DS, MC, VI.

Small-scale Hotel

SOME UNITS

INGEBERG ACRES B&B
All Year [BP]   1P: $50-$60   2P: $60-$80   XP: $10   F6
Location: I-79, exit 105, 4.8 mi s on SR 19, 4 mi s on Jackson's Mill Rd, 1.5 mi w on Valley Chapel Rd, then 1 mi s on Millstone Rd. 712 Left Millstone Rd 26452. Fax: 304/269-2834. **Facility:** 5 units. 4 one-bedroom standard units, some with kitchens. 1 cottage ($70-$80). 2 stories (no elevator), interior/exterior corridors. *Bath:* combo or shower only. **Parking:** on-site. **Terms:** no pets allowed (owner's pets on premises). **Amenities:** video library, hair dryers. **Pool(s):** outdoor.

Bed & Breakfast

SOME UNITS

WESTON SUPER 8 MOTEL   **Book at aaa.com**   **Phone:** (304)269-1086
All Year   1P: $50-$60   2P: $56-$66
Location: I-79, exit 99, just e. 100 Market Place Mall, Suite 12 26452. Fax: 304/269-1086. **Facility:** 62 one-bedroom standard units. 2 stories (no elevator), interior corridors. *Bath:* combo or shower only. **Parking:** on-site. **Amenities:** safes. **Guest Services:** coin laundry. **Cards:** AX, CB, DC, DS, MC, VI.

Small-scale Hotel

SOME UNITS

WHEELING pop. 31,419

—— WHERE TO STAY ——

HAMPTON INN   **Book at aaa.com**   **Phone:** 304/233-0440
5/29-12/31 [ECP]   1P: $94-$109   2P: $99-$114
4/3-5/28 [ECP]   1P: $91-$106   2P: $96-$111
1/1-2/28 [ECP]   1P: $94-$104   2P: $99-$104
3/1-4/2 [ECP]   1P: $89-$99   2P: $94-$104
Small-scale Hotel
Location: I-70, exit 2A (SR 88 N), just e on US 40. 795 National Rd 26003. Fax: 304/233-2198. **Facility:** 104 one-bedroom standard units. 5 stories, interior corridors. **Parking:** on-site. **Terms:** 2 night minimum stay - seasonal, cancellation fee imposed. **Amenities:** high-speed Internet, dual phone lines, voice mail, irons, hair dryers. **Guest Services:** valet laundry. **Business Services:** meeting rooms. **Cards:** AX, CB, DC, DS, MC, VI.

SOME UNITS

OGLEBAY RESORT   **Phone:** (304)243-4000
9/6-12/31 [BP]   1P: $99-$750   2P: $99-$750   XP: $15   D12
5/2-9/5 [BP]   1P: $99-$750   2P: $99-$750   XP: $20   D12
3/1-5/1 & 1/1-2/28 [BP]   1P: $89-$750   2P: $89-$750   XP: $15   D12
Resort
Small-scale Hotel
Location: I-70, exit 2A (SR 88 N), 4 mi s. Rt 88 N 26003. Fax: 304/243-4070. **Facility:** In addition to great views of the mountains, the lodge offers recreational activities for a range of travelers from families to singles. 212 one-bedroom standard units. 3 stories, interior/exterior corridors. *Bath:* combo or shower only. **Parking:** on-site. **Terms:** 2 night minimum stay - weekends, 10 day cancellation notice-fee imposed, package plans. **Amenities:** high-speed Internet, voice mail. *Some:* safes, irons, hair dryers. **Pool(s):** heated outdoor, heated indoor, wading. **Leisure Activities:** sauna, whirlpool, paddleboats, boat dock, fishing, hiking trails, playground, exercise room, basketball, horseshoes, volleyball. *Fee:* golf-36 holes, miniature golf, 9 lighted tennis courts, massage, game room. **Guest Services:** gift shop, coin laundry. **Business Services:** conference facilities. **Cards:** AX, DS, MC, VI.

SOME UNITS

RAMADA PLAZA CITY CENTER HOTEL *Book at aaa.com* Phone: (304)232-0300

11/1-12/31	1P: $90	2P: $110	XP: $5	F12
3/1-10/31 & 1/1-2/28	1P: $84	2P: $90	XP: $5	F12

Small-scale Hotel

Location: I-70, exit 1B, 16th St to Market and 12th sts; downtown. 1200 Market St 26003. Fax: 304/233-1653. **Facility:** 170 units. 169 one-bedroom standard units. 1 one-bedroom suite ($110-$175). 7 stories, interior corridors. **Parking:** on-site. **Terms:** 2 night minimum stay - seasonal and/or weekends, 30 day cancellation notice. **Amenities:** high-speed Internet, voice mail. *Some:* irons, hair dryers. **Dining:** 7 am-7 pm, Fri & Sat-11 pm, cocktails. **Guest Services:** coin laundry. **Business Services:** conference facilities, PC. **Cards:** AX, DC, DS, MC, VI. **Special Amenities:** early check-in/late check-out and free room upgrade (subject to availability with advance reservations).

—— WHERE TO DINE ——

ABBEY'S RESTAURANT **Lunch:** $5-$12 **Dinner:** $5-$22 Phone: 304/233-0729

American

Location: I-70, exit 0, just n. 145 Zane St 26003. **Hours:** 11 am-11 pm. Closed major holidays. **Features:** This restaurant is known locally for its steak, seafood, chicken and ribs. Friendly servers do what they can to ensure no one leaves a stranger. Casual dress; cocktails. **Parking:** on-site. **Cards:** AX, DC, MC, VI.

BELLA VIA RESTAURANT **Lunch:** $5-$14 **Dinner:** $6-$20 Phone: 304/242-8181

Italian

Location: I-70, exit 5, just n. 1 Burkham Ct 26003. **Hours:** 11 am-10 pm, Sat from 4 pm. Closed major holidays. **Reservations:** suggested, weekends. **Features:** An Old World atmosphere prevails in the relaxed restaurant, which serves homemade Italian and American dishes. Servers are outgoing. Casual dress; cocktails. **Parking:** on-site. **Cards:** AX, CB, DC, DS, JC, MC, VI.

ENZIO'S BRICK OVEN PIZZA & PASTA **Lunch:** $6-$12 **Dinner:** $6-$20 Phone: 304/242-3694

Italian

Location: I-70, exit 2, just e. 2053 National Rd 26003. **Hours:** 11 am-10 pm. Closed: 12/25. **Features:** Diners find great food, fun and a family atmosphere at the restaurant. A family tradition, this place serves homemade pizza and pasta. Casual dress; cocktails. **Parking:** on-site. **Cards:** AX, CB, DC, DS, JC, MC, VI.

FIGARETTI'S **Lunch:** $7-$16 **Dinner:** $7-$21 Phone: 304/243-5685

Italian

Location: I-70, exit 2D, just w. 1035 Mt. DeChantal Rd 26003. **Hours:** 11 am-10 pm. Closed: 12/25. **Reservations:** suggested, weekends. **Features:** The family-owned-and-operated restaurant has been part of the city landscape since 1948. Homemade pasta dishes and salads make up the menu. Casual dress; cocktails. **Parking:** on-site. **Cards:** AX, CB, DC, DS, JC, MC, VI.

RIVER CITY ALE WORKS **Lunch:** $7-$10 **Dinner:** $7-$17 Phone: 304/233-4555

American

Location: Corner of Main and 14th St; downtown. 1400 Main St 26003. **Hours:** 11 am-10 pm, Fri & Sat-midnight. Closed: 12/25; also Sun. **Features:** In historic downtown's Wheeling Artisan Center, the spacious and sunny atrium restaurant prepares varied dishes, most notably the Thai peanut wings appetizer, homemade gnocchi entree and pizza. Service is prompt. Organic micro-brewed beer is available. Casual dress; cocktails. **Parking:** street. **Cards:** AX, DC, DS, MC, VI.

STRATFORD SPRINGS RESTAURANT **Lunch:** $7-$11 **Dinner:** $16-$25 Phone: 304/233-5100

American

Location: I-70, exit 2A (SR 88 N), 0.5 mi e on US 40, then 1.5 mi n on SR 88. 100 Kensington Dr 26003. **Hours:** 11:30 am-2 & 5-10 pm, Sun-8:30 pm. Closed: 1/1, 12/24, 12/25. **Reservations:** suggested. **Features:** Built in 1906 and listed on the National Register of Historic Places, the historic inn, nestled on 30 acres of rolling hills near Oglebay Park, is an elegant place for fine dining. Menu selections include well-prepared dishes of chicken, steak, seafood and lamb. Don't skip the dessert tray. Dressy casual; cocktails. **Parking:** on-site. **Cards:** AX, DC, MC, VI. **Historic**

TJ'S SPORTS GARDEN RESTAURANT **Lunch:** $7-$14 **Dinner:** $7-$14 Phone: 304/232-9555

American

Location: I-70, exit 2A, just n. 808 National Rd 26003. **Hours:** 11 am-1 am. Closed: 12/25. **Features:** Geared toward families, the restaurant has a sporty feel, with pool tables and game rooms. Casual dress; cocktails. **Parking:** on-site. **Cards:** AX, DS, MC, VI.

WHITE SULPHUR SPRINGS pop. 2,315

──────── WHERE TO STAY ────────

THE GREENBRIER *Book at aaa.com* **Phone:** (304)536-1110

4/1-10/31 [MAP]	1P: $542-$634	2P: $592-$684	XP: $185	F17
3/1-3/31 [MAP]	1P: $286-$363	2P: $492-$530	XP: $185	F17
11/1-1/2 [MAP]	1P: $270-$363	2P: $474-$530	XP: $185	F17
1/3-2/28 [MAP]	1P: $281-$342	2P: $492-$518	XP: $185	F17

Classic Historic
Large-scale Hotel
Location: I-64, exit 181 westbound, 1.8 mi w on US 60; exit 175 eastbound, just n, then 3.2 mi e on US 60. 300 W Main St 24986. Fax: 304/536-7854. **Facility:** The grand resort's flamboyant interior design, which spans a range of eras, employs vibrant colors and striking patterns. 803 units. 562 one-bedroom standard units. 241 cottages ($632-$4104), some with whirlpools. 1-6 stories, interior/exterior corridors. **Parking:** on-site and valet. **Terms:** check-in 4 pm, 15 day cancellation notice-fee imposed, package plans, $28 service charge. **Amenities:** video games, CD players, dual phone lines, voice mail, safes, honor bars, irons, hair dryers. *Some:* DVD players (fee). **Dining:** 5 restaurants, 6 am-10 pm, cocktails, nightclub, entertainment. **Pool(s):** heated outdoor, heated indoor, wading. **Leisure Activities:** steamrooms, recreation programs, rental bicycles, hiking trails, jogging, playground, spa, horseshoes, shuffleboard. *Fee:* saunas, canoes, fishing, sulphur baths, mineral water spa, kayaking, white-water rafting, golf-54 holes, Golf Digest Academy, 10 tennis courts (5 indoor, 5 lighted), Falconry Academy, hunting preserve, Land Rover Driving School, billiards, bowling, carriage ride, horse drawn sleighs, cooking classes, croquet, hot air ballooning, movie theater, horseback riding, trap & skeet shooting & sporting clay course, game room. **Guest Services:** gift shop, complimentary evening beverages, valet laundry, airport transportation (fee)- Greenbrier Valley Airport, area transportation. **Business Services:** conference facilities, business center. **Cards:** AX, DC, DS, MC, VI. **Special Amenities:** free full breakfast and free local telephone calls. *(See color ad below)*

SOME UNITS
⊬ ❙❙ 24☎ ⅄ 🔒 ⅏M 🚭 📄 🏊 🛅 ✕ 📹 DATA PORT / ✕ VCR 🔋 🛏 💻 /
FEE

WILLIAMSON pop. 3,414

――――― WHERE TO STAY ―――――

SYCAMORE INN
▼▼▼ ▼▼▼
Small-scale Hotel

Phone: 304/235-3656

All Year
1P: $64-$79
Location: US 52 and 119, Main St and 2nd Ave; downtown. 201 W 2nd Ave 25661 (PO Box 1348). Fax: 304/235-4609. **Facility:** 64 one-bedroom standard units. 3 stories, interior corridors. **Parking:** on-site. **Amenities:** voice mail. **Guest Services:** valet laundry. **Business Services:** meeting rooms. **Cards:** AX, DC, DS, MC, VI.

SOME UNITS
ASK S/D ❘❘ Y 🐾 DATA PORT / ✕ 🛏 💻 /

WILLIAMSTOWN pop. 2,996

――――― WHERE TO STAY ―――――

DAYS INN
AAA SAVE
▼▼▼ ▼▼▼
Small-scale Hotel

Book at aaa.com

Phone: (304)375-3730

3/1-10/31	1P: $52-$80	2P: $60-$90	XP: $10 D17
11/1-2/28	1P: $45-$70	2P: $50-$80	XP: $10 D17

Location: I-77, exit 185, just w on SR 31. 1339 Highland Ave 26187 (Rt 1, Box 39). Fax: 304/375-4761. **Facility:** 110 one-bedroom standard units. 2 stories (no elevator), interior corridors. **Parking:** on-site. **Terms:** 7 day cancellation notice, [ECP] meal plan available. **Amenities:** hair dryers. *Some:* irons. **Pool(s):** outdoor. **Leisure Activities:** horseshoes. **Guest Services:** coin laundry. **Business Services:** meeting rooms. **Cards:** AX, DC, DS, MC, VI. **Special Amenities:** free expanded continental breakfast and free newspaper.

SOME UNITS
S/D ❘❘↑ 🏊 🐾 DATA PORT 💻 / ✕ 🛏 💻 /
FEE FEE

――――― WHERE TO DINE ―――――

DA VINCI'S
▼▼▼ ▼▼▼
Italian

Lunch: $6-$13　　　**Dinner:** $7-$18　　　**Phone:** 304/375-3633
Location: I-77, exit 185, 1.4 mi w on SR 14. 215 Highland Ave 26187. **Hours:** 11 am-10 pm, Fri & Sat-11 pm. Closed: 3/27, 11/24, 12/24, 12/25; also Mon. **Features:** Homemade dessert and the unusual spaghetti Mona Lisa—baked capellini topped with meat sauce, green peppers, mushrooms, pepperoni and cheese— are wonderful offerings at the cheerful restaurant. The four dining rooms are inviting, and the atmosphere is great with large, inviting booths, good background music and warm greeting and seating. The chef prepares weekly specials; a variety including duck and lamb. Casual dress; cocktails. **Parking:** on-site. **Cards:** AX, DS, MC, VI.

Y ✕

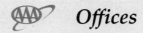 *Offices*

Cities with main offices are listed in **BOLD TYPE** and toll-free member service numbers in *ITALIC TYPE*.
All are closed Saturdays, Sundays and holidays unless otherwise indicated.

The type of service provided is designated below the name of the city where the office is located:

✛ Auto travel services, including books/maps, marked maps and on-demand Triptik maps
● Auto travel services, including books/maps, marked maps, but no on-demand Triptik maps
■ Provides books/maps only. No marked maps or on-demand Triptik maps available
▲ Travel agency services

NATIONAL OFFICE: 1000 AAA DRIVE, HEATHROW, FLORIDA 32746-5063, (407) 444-7000

DELAWARE

DOVER—AAA MID-ATLANTIC, 55 GREENTREE DR RT 8, 19904. MON-FRI 9-6, SAT 9-3. (302) 674-8020.✛▲

NEWARK—AAA MID-ATLANTIC, 875 AAA BLVD, 19713. MON-FRI 9-7, SAT 9-3. (302) 368-4500.✛▲

WILMINGTON—AAA MID-ATLANTIC, 4107 CONCORD PIKE, 19803. MON-FRI 9-5, THU 9-8, SAT 9-3. (302) 479-0144.▲

DISTRICT OF COLUMBIA

WASHINGTON—AAA MID-ATLANTIC, 701-15TH ST NW 1ST FLOOR, 20005. MON-FRI 9-5:30. (202) 331-3000.✛▲

MARYLAND

ARNOLD—AAA MID-ATLANTIC, 1450 RITCHIE HWY #110, 21012. MON-FRI 9-5, THU 9-7, SAT 9-3. (410) 757-7400.✛▲

BEL AIR—AAA MID-ATLANTIC, 520 BALTIMORE PIKE, 21014. MON-FRI 9-5, THU 9-8, SAT 9-3. (410) 838-5121.✛▲

COLUMBIA—AAA MID-ATLANTIC, 10840 LITTLE PATUXENT PKY, 21044. MON-FRI 9-5, THU 9-8, SAT 9-3. (410) 997-5611.✛▲

FREDERICK—AAA MID-ATLANTIC, 1305 W 7TH ST, 21702. MON-FRI 9-5, THU 9-8, SAT 9-3. (301) 663-4161.✛▲

HAGERSTOWN—AAA MID-ATLANTIC, 1079 MARYLAND AVE, 21740. MON-FRI 9-5. (301) 739-6920.✛▲

LARGO—AAA MID-ATLANTIC, 10412 CAMPUS WAY S, 20774. MON-FRI 9-6, SAT 9-3. (301) 345-7701.✛▲

LUTHERVILLE—AAA MID-ATLANTIC, 1306 BELLONA AVE, 21093. MON-FRI 9-5, THU 9-8, SAT 9-3. (410) 821-1458.✛▲

MONTGOMERY VILLAGE—AAA MID-ATLANTIC, 19200 MONTGOMERY VLG AVE, 20886. MON-FRI 9-6, SAT 9-3. (301) 921-4250.✛▲

SALISBURY—AAA MID-ATLANTIC, 8245F DICKERSON LN, 21804. MON-FRI 9-5, SAT 9-3. (410) 860-2885, *(800) 492-0282.*✛▲

WESTMINSTER—AAA MID-ATLANTIC, 1030 BALTIMORE BLVD #140, 21157. MON-FRI 9-5, THU 9-8, SAT 9-3. (410) 848-8500.✛▲

WHEATON—AAA MID-ATLANTIC, 2730 UNIVERSITY BLVD W, 20902. MON-FRI 9-6, SAT 9-3. (301) 946-5200.✛▲

VIRGINIA

ALEXANDRIA—AAA MID-ATLANTIC, 801 N FAIRFAX ST, 22314. MON-FRI 9-6, SAT 9-3. (703) 549-1080.✛▲

CHARLOTTESVILLE—AAA MID-ATLANTIC, 1820 RIO HILL CTR, 22901. MON-FRI 9-5, SAT 9-3. (434) 974-1426.✛▲

CHESAPEAKE—AAA OF TIDEWATER VIRGINIA, 111 KEMPSVILLE RD, 23320. MON-FRI 8:30-5:30, SAT 8:30-12:30. (757) 547-9741, *(800) 258-1730.*●▲

COLONIAL HEIGHTS—AAA MID-ATLANTIC, 707 SOUTHPARK BLVD #7, 23834. MON-FRI 9-5, SAT 9-3. (804) 520-7388.✛▲

FAIRFAX—AAA MID-ATLANTIC, 4100 MONUMENT CORNER DR, 22030. MON-FRI 9-6, SAT 9-3. (703) 222-4200.✛▲

FOREST—AAA MID-ATLANTIC, 18013 FOREST RD STE A, 24551. MON-FRI 9-5, SAT 9-3. (434) 385-0091.✛▲

FREDERICKSBURG—AAA MID-ATLANTIC, 1171 CENTRAL PARK BL #100, 22401. MON-FRI 9-5, SAT 9-3. (540) 785-0282.✛▲

HAMPTON—AAA OF TIDEWATER VIRGINIA, 305 MARTHA LEE DR, 23666. MON-FRI 8:30-5:30, SAT 8:30-12:30. (757) 826-1061, *(800) 258-1730.*✛▲

MIDLOTHIAN—AAA MID-ATLANTIC, 6661 LAKE HARBOUR DR #8B, 23112. MON-FRI 9-5, SAT 9-3. (804) 639-2015.▲

NEWPORT NEWS—AAA OF TIDEWATER VIRGINIA, 733 J CLYDE MORRIS BLVD, 23601. MON-FRI 8:30-5:30, SAT 8:30-12:30. (757) 246-4746, *(800) 258-1730.*✛▲

NORFOLK—AAA OF TIDEWATER VIRGINIA, 141 W VIRGINIA BEACH BLVD, 23510. MON-FRI 8:30-5:30, SAT 8:30-12:30. (757) 622-5634.✛▲

NORTON—AAA BLUE GRASS/KENTUCKY, 613 PARK AVE NW, 24273. MON-FRI 8:30-5. (276) 679-5160.✛▲

PORTSMOUTH—AAA OF TIDEWATER VIRGINIA, 3521 WESTERN BRANCH BLVD, 23707. MON-FRI 8:30-5:30, SAT 8:30-12:30. (757) 397-5941, *(800) 258-1730.*✛▲

RICHMOND—AAA MID-ATLANTIC, 1201 MALL DR, 23235. MON-FRI 9-5, SAT 9-3. (804) 379-4487.✛▲

RICHMOND—AAA MID-ATLANTIC, 5001 W BROAD ST #1000, 23230. MON-FRI 9-5, SAT 9-3. (804) 285-8912.✛▲

ROANOKE—AAA MID-ATLANTIC, 707 5TH ST NE, 24016. MON-FRI 9-5, SAT 9-3. (540) 344-0943.✛▲

VIENNA—AAA MID-ATLANTIC, 8300 OLD COURTHOUSE RD, 22182. MON-FRI 9-6, SAT 9-3. (703) 790-2600.✛▲

VIRGINIA BEACH—**AAA OF TIDEWATER VIRGINIA**, 5366 VIRGINIA BEACH BLVD, 23462. MON-FRI 8:30-5:30, SAT 8:30-12:30. (757) 233-3800, *(800) 258-1730.*✛▲

VIRGINIA BEACH—AAA OF TIDEWATER VIRGINIA, 296 KINGS GRANT RD, 23452. MON-FRI 8:30-5:30, SAT 8:30-12:30. (757) 340-7271, *(800) 258-1730.*✛▲

WILLIAMSBURG—AAA OF TIDEWATER VIRGINIA, 260 MCLAWS CIR, 23185. MON-FRI 8:30-5:30, SAT 8:30-12:30. (757) 564-7711, *(800) 258-1730.*✛▲

WEST VIRGINIA

BECKLEY—AAA ALLIED GROUP INC, 1004 N EISENHOWER DR, 25801. MON-FRI 9-5:30. (304) 255-4147.✛▲

BLUEFIELD—AAA BLUE GRASS/KENTUCKY, 622 COMMERCE ST, 24701. MON-FRI 8:30-5. (304) 327-8187.✛▲

BRIDGEPORT—AAA EAST CENTRAL, 169 BARNETT RUN RD, 26330. MON-FRI 9-5:30. (304) 842-2221.✛▲

CHARLESTON—AAA ALLIED GROUP INC, 3920 MACCORKLE AVE SE, 25304. MON-FRI 9-5:30, SAT 9-1. (304) 925-6681.✛▲

HUNTINGTON—AAA EAST CENTRAL, 1126 SIXTH AVE, 25701. MON-FRI 9-5. (304) 523-6423.✛▲

MARTINSBURG—AAA EAST CENTRAL, 135 N QUEEN ST, 25401. MON-FRI 9-5. (304) 263-4619.✛▲

MORGANTOWN—AAA EAST CENTRAL, 6520 MALL RD, 26501. MON-FRI 10-6, SAT 10-2. (304) 983-6480.✛▲

VIENNA—AAA EAST CENTRAL, 1107 NINTH ST STE K, 26105. MON-FRI 9-5:30. (304) 295-9715.✛▲

WEIRTON—AAA EAST CENTRAL, 3126 WEST ST, 26062. MON-FRI 9-5, SAT 9-12. (304) 748-1616.✛▲

WHEELING—AAA EAST CENTRAL, 846 NATIONAL RD, 26003. MON-FRI 8:30-5:30. (304) 233-1810.✛▲

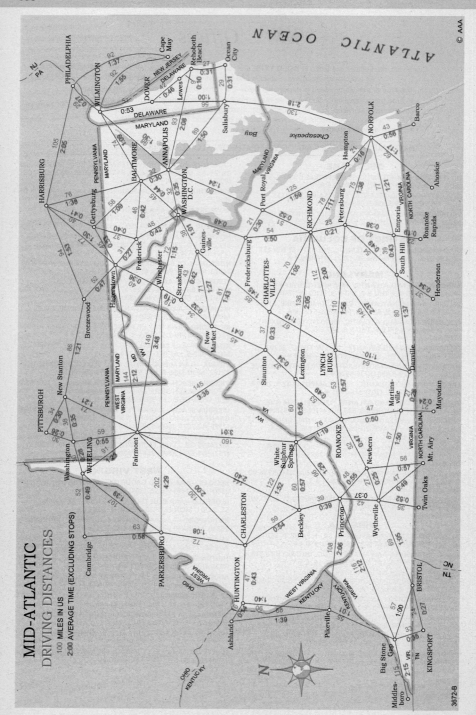

MID-ATLANTIC
DRIVING DISTANCES
100 MILES IN US
2:00 AVERAGE TIME (EXCLUDING STOPS)

© AAA

3672-B

GOLDEN PASSPORTS

Golden Passports, available in three types, offer benefits and significant savings to individuals who plan to visit federal recreation sites.

The Golden Eagle Passport, available for a **$65** annual fee, is valid for entrance only to all federal recreation areas that have an entrance fee. Sites include those operated by the National Forest Service, National Park Service, Bureau of Land Management and the U.S. Fish and Wildlife Service. The passport admits all occupants of a private vehicle at locations where entrance is on a per vehicle basis. At locations where a per person fee is charged, the pass covers the pass holder, spouse, parents and children.

Citizens or permanent residents of the United States who are 62 and older can obtain *Golden Age Passports* for a one-time **$10** fee. Proof of age is required.

Golden Access Passports are free to citizens or permanent residents of the United States (regardless of age) who are medically blind or permanently disabled. Medical documention is required.

Both *Golden Age and Golden Access Passports* cover entrance fees for the holder and accompanying private party to all national parks and sites managed by the U.S. Fish and Wildlife Service, the U.S. Forest Service and the Bureau of Land Management, plus a 50% discount on federal recreation use fees. When a per person fee is imposed, the pass covers the pass holder, spouse and children. Apply in person at a federally operated area where an entrance fee is charged.

NATIONAL PARKS PASS

The *National Parks Pass*, valid for 1 year from its first use in a park, allows unlimited admissions to all U.S. national parks. The **$50** pass covers all occupants of a private vehicle at parks where the entrance fee is per vehicle. At parks with individual entry fees, the pass covers the pass holder, spouse, parents and children.

As a result of a partnership with the National Park Foundation, AAA members may purchase the pass for **$48**, either through AAA's internet site (www.aaa.com) or by visiting a participating AAA office. Members may also phone the National Park Foundation at **(888) 467-2757** or purchase the pass online at www.nationalparks.org. Non-members may purchase the pass through participating AAA offices for the full **$50** price or online at www.nationalparks.org.

For an upgrade fee of **$15**, a Golden Eagle Hologram sticker can be added to a *National Parks Pass*. The hologram covers entrance fees not just at national parks, but at any federal recreation area that has an admission fee. Valid for the duration of the *National Parks Pass* to which it is affixed, the Golden Eagle hologram is available at National Park Service, Fish and Wildlife Service and Bureau of Land Management fee stations.

Bed & Breakfast Lodgings Index

Some bed and breakfasts listed below might have historical significance. Those properties are also referenced in the Historical index. The indication that continental [CP] or full breakfast [BP] is included in the room rate reflects whether a property is a Bed-and-Breakfast facility.

Country Inns Index

Some of the following country inns can also be considered as bed-and-breakfast operations. The indication that continental [CP] or full breakfast [BP] is included in the room rate reflects whether a property is a Bed-and-Breakfast facility.

Historical Lodgings & Restaurants Index

Some of the following historical lodgings can also be considered as bed-and-breakfast operations. The indication that continental [CP] or full breakfast [BP] is included in the room rate reflects whether a property is a Bed-and-Breakfast facility.

Resorts Index

Many establishments are located in resort areas; however, the following places have extensive on-premises recreational facilities:

Points of Interest Index

Index Legend

NB.	national battlefield	NR.	national river
NBP.	national battlefield park	NS.	national seashore
NC.	national cemetery	NWR.	national wildlife refuge
NF.	national forest	PHP.	provincial historic(al) park
NHM.	national historic(al) monument	PHS.	provincial historic(al) site
NHP.	national historic(al) park	PP.	provincial park
NHS.	national historic(al) site	SF.	state forest
NL.	national lakeshore	SHM.	state historic(al) monument
NME.	national memorial	SHP.	state historic(al) park
NMO.	national monument	SHS.	state historic(al) site
NMP.	national military park	SME.	state memorial
NP.	national park	SP.	state park
NRA.	national recreation area	SRA.	state recreation area

▽ GEM: Points of Interest Offering a *Great Experience for Members*®

[SAVE] *Attraction Admission Discount Index*

Comprehensive City Index

Here is an alphabetical list of all cities appearing in this TourBook® guide. Cities are presented by state/province. Page numbers under the POI column indicate where points of interest text begins. Page numbers under the L&R column indicate where lodging and restaurant listings begin.

COMPREHENSIVE CITY INDEX (CONT'D)

COMPREHENSIVE CITY INDEX (CONT'D)

Going
to the city?

**Visiting
the country?**

Stay in the
same hotel.

Whatever road you choose, you'll find a Howard Johnson at the end of it. From high rises in the heart of the city, to quaint rooms conveniently located 30 minutes outside of nowhere. So whether it's business or pleasure, point your compass to the one destination sure to please everyone: Howard Johnson. And before you hit the road, check out our "Best Rate or it's Free" Guarantee*, as well as our TripRewards® program. **trip**rewards

Go anywhere. Stay here.™